MW00773018

CONTRACTS

CONTRACTS

Cases and Materials

Third Edition

FRIEDRICH KESSLER

Sterling Professor of Law, Emeritus
Yale University Law School

GRANT GILMORE

Late Sterling Professor of Law
Yale University Law School

ANTHONY T. KRONMAN

Edward J. Phelps Professor of Law
Yale University Law School

 ASPEN LAW & BUSINESS
Aspen Publishers, Inc.

Library of Congress Catalog Card No. 84-81752

ISBN 0-7355-1286-8

Fourteenth Printing

Published by Aspen Law & Business
Formerly published by Little, Brown & Company

Printed in the United States of America

SUMMARY OF CONTENTS

Contents	ix
Preface	xxix
Acknowledgments	xxxi
Table of Abbreviated References	xxxv

Introduction: Contract as a Principle of Order	1

Chapter 1. From Status to Contract and Beyond	**19**

Chapter 2. The Basic Ideals of an Individualistic Law of Contracts and Their Erosion	**55**

Chapter 3. The Bargain	**111**
Section 1. The Contract as a Promissory Transaction	111
Section 2. The Tripartite Distinction of Contracts — The Implied Contract	141
Section 3. Indefinite Contracts	179
Section 4. The Duty to Bargain in Good Faith	201
Section 5. The Assent and Some of Its Mysteries	238
Section 6. Standard Form Contracts — The Battle of the Forms and Contracts of Adhesion	257
Section 7. The Bargain Theory of Contracts and the Reliance Principle	279
Section 8. Firm Offers and the Bargain Principle	315
Section 9. Consideration and the Contract by Correspondence	348
Section 10. Unilateral vs. Bilateral Contracts — Manufactured Difficulties	370
Section 11. Requirement Contracts and Mutuality	418
Section 12. "Instinct with an Obligation"	450
Section 13. The Gratuitous Noncommercial Promise	470
Section 14. Moral Consideration	510

Chapter 4. Fairness of the Bargain and Equality: The Idea of Justice in Exchange	**553**
Section 1. Bargaining and Economic Liberty	553
Section 2. Consumer Protection: Unconscionability and Beyond	583

Section 3.   Freedom of Contract in the Field of Private
             Insurance   625
Section 4.   Franchises and the New Feudalism   634
Section 5.   The Classical Struggle Between Creditor and
             Debtor: Readjustment of a Going Business Deal
             and Discharge   650

Chapter 5.   Formalism in Our Law of Contracts   705
Section 1.   The Peppercorn Theory of Consideration   706
Section 2.   The Seal and the Written Obligation   721

**Chapter 6.   More About Formalism: The Statute
             of Frauds   753**
Section 1.   Introductory Note   753
Section 2.   The Transactions Affected   757
Section 3.   Compliance with the Statute   783
Section 4.   Counterrules: Estoppel and Restitution   801

Chapter 7.   The Parol Evidence Rule   821
Section 1.   Introductory Note   821
Section 2.   The Circle of Interpretation   827

**Chapter 8.   Reality and Illusion (Herein of the
             Doctrines of Mistake, Impossibility, and
             Frustration)   861**
Section 1.   Introductory Note   861
Section 2.   The Unruliness of Words   866
Section 3.   "The Value of a Thing Is Just Exactly What
             'Twill Bring"   886
Section 4.   The Vanishing Synthesis (England)   910
Section 5.   The Vanishing Synthesis (United States)   936

**Chapter 9.   Protection of the Exchange Relationship
             (Herein of the Theory of Conditions)   973**
Section 1.   Introductory Note   973
Section 2.   The Basic Themes: Some History by Way of
             Background   976
Section 3.   The Sale of Goods: A Case Study in the
             Implication of Conditions   990
Section 4.   The Problem of Forfeiture   1021

Chapter 10. Remedies   1061
Section 1.   Introduction   1061
Section 2.   Specific Performance and the Right to Break a
             Contract   1069

Section 3.   Money Damages: The Limits of Compensation   1108
Section 4.   Freedom of Contract and the Judicial
              Prerogative: The Power of the Parties to
              Control Remedy and Risk   1202
Section 5.   The Burdens of Innocence: Anticipatory
              Repudiation and the Duty to Mitigate Damages   1269

Chapter 11.   Third Party Beneficiaries   1329
Section 1.   Introductory Note   1329
Section 2.   The Origins: Cross-Currents of Doctrine   1333
Section 3.   The Search for Doctrinal Clarity   1361
Section 4.   Government Contracts and Citizen
              Beneficiaries   1384
Section 5.   The Problem of Defenses, Modifications, and
              Rescission   1418

Chapter 12.   Assignment: The Liquidity of
Contractual Obligations   1441
Section 1.   Introductory Note   1441
Section 2.   Intangible Claims and Their Transferability   1444
Section 3.   The Present Assignability of Future Claims   1477
Section 4.   Assignment of Rights vs. Delegation of Duties   1500
Section 5.   The Problem of Defenses, Modifications, and
              Rescission   1520
Section 6.   Priorities   1547

Table of Cases   1559
Index   1571

CONTENTS

Preface   xxix
Acknowledgments   xxxi
Table of Abbreviated References   xxxv

Introduction: Contract as a Principle of Order   1

Chapter 1.   From Status to Contract and Beyond   19

             Maine, Ancient Law   19
             Adam Smith, Lectures on Justice, Policy,
                Revenue and Arms   20
          A. Background   22
          B. The Emancipation and Evolution of the
                Substantive Law of Contract   38
          C. Codifications and Restatements   50

Chapter 2.   The Basic Ideals of an Individualistic Law
             of Contracts and Their Erosion   55

             Hurley v. Eddingfield   56
             Note   56
             Great Atlantic & Pacific Tea Co. v. Cream of
                Wheat Co.   58
             United States v. Colgate Co.   59
             Note   59
             Poughkeepsie Buying Service, Inc. v.
                Poughkeepsie Newspapers, Inc.   64
             Note   66
             Continental Forest Products v. Chandler
                Supply Co.   67
             Note   73
             Watteau v. Fenwick   74
             Note   76
             Noble v. Williams   76

Note   77
Davis & Co. v. Morgan   77
Note   79
Schwartzreich v. Bauman-Basch, Inc.   79
Note   83
Wood v. Boynton   84
Note   87
Sherwood v. Walker   88
Note   88
Laidlaw v. Organ   89
Note   91
Swinton v. Whitinsville Savings Bank   93
Note   94
Blair v. National Security Insurance Co.   96
Note   96
Sternaman v. Metropolitan Life Ins. Co.   96
Note   97
School Trustees of Trenton v. Bennett   99
Note   104
O. W. Holmes, The Common Law   105
Note   105
Hadley v. Baxendale   106
Note   109

Chapter 3.   The Bargain   **111**

   Section 1.   The Contract as a Promissory Transaction   111
                Restatement of Contracts Second §1   111
                Note   111
                Restatement of Contracts Second §2   111
                Note   112
                *Restatement of Contracts Second §§3, 17, 18,
                22, 23, 24*   112
                Uniform Commercial Code §1-201   113
                Balfour v. Balfour   116
                Note   119
                Davis v. General Foods Corp.   121
                Note   123
                The Mabley & Carew Co. v. Borden   124
                Note   127
                Armstrong v. M'Ghee   128
                Note   129
                Anderson v. Backlund   129
                Note   130
                Sullivan v. O'Connor   131

Contents

	Note	137
	Shaheen v. Knight	*137*
	Note	140
Section 2.	The Tripartite Distinction of Contracts — The Implied Contract	141
	Young and Ashburnham's Case	*146*
	Note	146
	Hertzog v. Hertzog	*147*
	Note	152
	Barnet's Estate	*152*
	Cropsey v. Sweeney	153
	Shaw v. Shaw	*154*
	Note	155
	Hewitt v. Hewitt	*155*
	Note	162
	Cotnam v. Wisdom	*163*
	Note	167
	Sommers v. Putnam Board of Education	*168*
	Note	171
	Upton-on-Severn Rural District Council v. Powell	*171*
	Note	173
	Vickery v. Ritchie	*173*
	Note	175
	Michigan Central R.R. v. State	*175*
	Martin v. Campanaro	178
	Note	179
Section 3.	Indefinite Contracts	179
	Young and Ashburnham's Case	*183*
	Lefkowitz v. Great Minneapolis Surplus Store, Inc.	*183*
	Note	186
	Jenkins Towel Service, Inc. v. Fidelity-Philadelphia Trust Co.	*186*
	Note	190
	Moulton v. Kershaw	*190*
	Fairmount Glass Works v. Crunden-Martin Woodenware Co.	*193*
	Note	196
	Channel Master Corp. v. Aluminum Ltd. Sales	*196*
	Note	200
Section 4.	The Duty to Bargain in Good Faith	201
	Hill v. Waxberg	*203*
	Note	207
	Heyer Products v. United States	207

Note   208
Goodman v. Dicker   209
Note   211
Chrysler Corp. v. Quimby   211
Note   212
Collins Radio Co.   212
Note   215
*The Sun Printing and Publishing Assn. v.
  Remington Paper and Power Co., Inc.*   216
Note   222
Hoffman v. Red Owl Stores   223
Note   224
Wheeler v. White   225
Borg-Warner Corp. v. Anchor Coupling Co.   226
Note   236
Itek Corp. v. Chicago Aerial Industries, Inc.   236
Note   238
Section 5.   The Assent and Some of Its Mysteries   238
Prescott v. Jones   238
Note   241
*National Union Fire Insurance Co. v. Joseph
  Ehrlich*   241
Austin v. Burge   242
Note   244
Cole-McIntyre-Norfleet Co. v. Holloway   244
Note   247
Langellier v. Schaefer   247
Note   250
Butler v. Foley   250
Note   252
United States v. Braunstein   253
Note   257
Section 6.   Standard Form Contracts — The Battle of the
              Forms and Contracts of Adhesion   257
              Kessler, Contracts of Adhesion — Some
              Thoughts about Freedom of Contract   257
  A. The Battle of the Forms   258
      Roth-Lith, Ltd. v. F. P. Bartlett & Co.   260
      Note   264
      Air Products & Chem., Inc. v. Fairbanks
        Morse, Inc.   265
      Note   272
  B. Contracts of Adhesion   272
      Woodburn v. Northwestern Bell Telephone Co.   276
      Note   278

Section 7. The Bargain Theory of Contracts and the
            Reliance Principle   279
            Siegel v. Spear & Co.   285
            Note   287
            *Lusk-Harbison-Jones, Inc., v. Universal Credit
               Co.*   289
            Fisher v. Jackson   291
            Note   294
            *Underwood Typewriter Co. v. Century Realty
               Co.*   294
            Note   298
            Capital Savings & Loan Assn. v. Przybylowicz   299
            Note   302
            Chapman v. Bomann   303
            Note   307
            Feinberg v. Pfeiffer Co.   308
            Note   314
Section 8. Firm Offers and the Bargain Principle   315
            Dickinson v. Dodds   316
            Note   319
            Jordan v. Dobbins   320
            Note   322
            James Baird Co. v. Gimbel Bros.   323
            Note   326
            Drennan v. Star Paving Co.   326
            *Loranger Construction Co. v. E. F.
               Hauserman Co.*   331
            *Southern California Acoustics v. C. V. Holder,
               Inc.*   335
            Note   340
            *Elsinore Union Elementary School District v.
               Kastorff*   341
Section 9. Consideration and the Contract by
            Correspondence   348
            Cushing v. Thomson   349
            Note   352
            Lewis v. Browning   353
            Note   353
            Rhode Island Tool Co. v. United States   354
            Note   357
            *Palo Alto Town & Country Village v. BBTC
               Company*   357
            Note   363
            C. Langdell, Summary of the Law of
               Contracts   364

Llewellyn, Our Case-Law of Contract: Offer
    and Acceptance   364
Postal Telegraph-Cable Co. v. Willis   365
Note   367
Caldwell v. Cline   368
Note   370

Section 10. Unilateral vs. Bilateral Contracts —
             Manufactured Difficulties   370
Carlill v. Carbolic Smoke Ball Co.   373
Taft v. Hyatt   377
Note   380
Strong v. Sheffield   381
Note   382
Hay v. Fortier   383
Note   385
Davis v. Jacoby   385
Note   391
Crook v. Cowan   391
Note   400
Bishop v. Eaton   400
Note   404
White v. Corlies   405
Note   407
Los Angeles Traction Co. v. Wilshire   407
Note   409
Petterson v. Pattberg   410
Whittier, The Restatement of Contracts and
    Mutual Assent   410
Note on Real Estate Brokerage Agreements   411
Baumgartner v. Meek   412
Note   417

Section 11. Requirement Contracts and Mutuality   418
Great Northern Ry. v. Witham   420
Note   422
Westesen v. Olathe State Bank   422
Note   424
Swindell & Co. v. First National Bank   424
Note   426
*Lima Locomotive & Machine Co. v. National
    Steel Castings Co.*   427
Eastern Air Lines Inc. v. Gulf Oil Corp.   428
*Utah International, Inc. v. Colorado-Ute Elec.
    Assn. Inc.*   437
*Schlegel Manufacturing Co. v. Cooper's Glue
    Factory*   446
Note   450

Section 12. "Instinct with an Obligation" 450
    Wood v. Lucy, Lady Duff-Gordon 451
    Note 453
    Hammond v. C.I.T. Financial Corp. 453
    Note 456
    Sylvan Crest Sand & Gravel Co. v. United States 457
    Note 460
    Carlton v. Smith 461
    Note 463
    Reinert v. Lawson 463
    Note 464
    Bernstein v. W. B. Manufacturing Co. 465
    Note 467
    Gurfein v. Werbelovsky 467
    Note 470
Section 13. The Gratuitous Noncommercial Promise 470
    1 Williston on Contracts §112 472
    Note 473
    Kirksey v. Kirksey 473
    Note 474
    Forward v. Armstead 475
    Note 476
    Seavey v. Drake 476
    Note 478
    Roberts-Horsfield v. Gedicks 478
    Note 480
    Devecmon v. Shaw 480
    Note 481
    Hamer v. Sidway 483
    Note 490
    Ricketts v. Scothorn 491
    Note 494
    De Cicco v. Schweizer 494
    Note 500
    Allegheny College v. National Chautauqua County Bank of Jamestown 501
    Note 508
Section 14. Moral Consideration 510
    Gillingham v. Brown 512
    Note 517
    Lampleigh v. Brathwait 518
    Note 518
    Eastwood v. Kenyon 519
    Note 522
    Mills v. Wyman 523

Note   526
C._____ v. W._____   527
Note   532
Perreault v. Hall   532
Note   535
In re Schoenkerman's Estate   535
Note   537
Elbinger v. Capitol & Teutonia Co.   537
Note   539
Webb v. McGowin (Alabama Court of Appeals)   539
Webb v. McGowin (Alabama Supreme Court)   543
Note   544
Medberry v. Olcovich   544
Note   547
Lawrence v. Oglesby   547
New York General Obligations Law §5-1105   549
Note   550
California Civil Code (1872) §1606   550
Note   550
Georgia Code Annotated §20-303   550
Restatement of Contracts Second §86   551

Chapter 4.   Fairness of the Bargain and Equality: The
             Idea of Justice in Exchange   553

Section 1.   Bargaining and Economic Liberty   553
             Cohen, The Basis of Contract   553
             Note, The Peppercorn Theory of
               Consideration and the Doctrine of Fair
               Exchange in Contract Law   553
             Haigh v. Brooks   564
             Cook v. Wright   566
             Note   569
             Jackson v. Seymour   569
             Note   571
             Marks v. Gates   571
             Note   574
             Embola v. Tuppela   574
             United States v. Bethlehem Steel Corp.   576
             Note   583
Section 2.   Consumer Protection: Unconscionability and
             Beyond   583
             American Home Improvement Co. v. MacIver   589

	Note	592
	Williams v. Walker-Thomas Furniture Co.	596
	Note	600
	Patterson v. Walker-Thomas Furniture Co.	603
	Note	607
	Jones v. Star Credit Corp.	607
	Note	610
	Kugler v. Romain	611
	Note	623
Section 3.	Freedom of Contract in the Field of Private Insurance	625
Section 4.	Franchises and the New Feudalism	634
Section 5.	The Classical Struggle Between Creditor and Debtor: Readjustment of a Going Business Deal and Discharge	650
	Stilk v. Myrick	651
	Note	652
	Lingenfelder v. The Wainwright Brewing Co.	652
	Note	655
	Goebel v. Linn	655
	Note	657
	Austin Instrument Inc. v. Loral Corp.	657
	Note	662
	Schwartzreich v. Bauman-Basch, Inc.	663
	Central London Property Trust, Ltd. v. High Trees House, Ltd.	663
	Note	664
	Skinner v. Tober Foreign Motors Inc.	665
	Note	667
	Foakes v. Beer	668
	Note	672
	Hackley v. Headley	674
	Note	678
	Mitchell v. C. C. Sanitation	679
	Fitts v. Panhandle & S. F. R.	679
	Note	680
	Ricketts v. Pennsylvania R.R.	681
	Consolidated Edison Co. v. Arroll	681
	Note	684
	Hudson v. Yonkers Fruit Co., Inc.	685
	Petterson v. Pattberg	689
	Note	693
	Goldbard v. Empire State Mutual Life Insurance Co.	694
	Note	700

| | *Boshart v. Gardner* | 701 |
| | Note | 703 |

Chapter 5. Formalism in Our Law of Contracts   **705**

	Cohen, The Basis of Contract	705
	Fuller, Consideration and Form	706
	Note	706
Section 1.	The Peppercorn Theory of Consideration	706
	Sir Anthony Sturlyn v. Albany	706
	Whitney v. Stearns	707
	W. H. Page, The Law of Contracts	707
	Thomas v. Thomas	707
	Note	710
	Fischer v. Union Trust Co.	710
	Note	713
	Murphy, Thompson & Co. v. Reed	713
	Note	716
	Real Estate Co. of Pittsburgh v. Rudolph	716
	Note	718
	Marsh v. Lott	718
	Note	719
	Wheat v. Morse	720
Section 2.	The Seal and the Written Obligation	721
	J. Ames, Lectures on Legal History	723
	Warren v. Lynch	725
	Note	727
	Krell v. Codman	728
	Goulet v. Goulet	730
	Aller v. Aller	731
	Note	735
	Schnell v. Nell	737
	Note	739
	Cochran v. Taylor	739
	Note	744
	Pillans and Rose v. Van Mierop and Hopkins	744
	Note	750
	Uniform Written Obligations Act	751
	Note	751

Chapter 6. More About Formalism: The Statute of Frauds   **753**

| Section 1. | Introductory Note | 753 |
| | *An Act for Prevention of Frauds and Perjuries,* St. 29 Car. II, C.3. | 753 |

Section 2. The Transactions Affected   757
            Lawrence v. Anderson   757
            Note   759
            Eastwood v. Kenyon   760
            Note   760
            Taylor v. Lee   761
            Note   762
            Witschard v. A. Brody & Sons, Inc.   763
            Note   764
            Colpitts v. L. C. Fisher Co.   765
            Note   768
            Bader v. Hiscox   770
            Note   773
            Doyle v. Dixon   773
            Note   774
            Harvey v. J. P. Morgan & Co.   775
            Note   777
            Montuori v. Bailen   777
            Note   779
            Uniform Commercial Code §2-201   780
            Note   780
            Amsinck v. American Insurance Co.   781
            Note   782
Section 3. Compliance with the Statute   783
            Crabtree v. Elizabeth Arden Sales
               Corp.   783
            Note   788
            Hughes v. Payne   789
            Note   792
            Baldridge v. Centgraf   793
            Note   794
            Ablett v. Sencer   795
            Note   796
            Cash v. Clark   797
            Note   797
            Harry Rubin Sons, Inc. v. Consolidated Pipe
               Co. of America, Inc.   798
            Note   801
Section 4. Counterrules: Estoppel and Restitution   801
            Imperator Realty Co., Inc. v. Tull   801
            Note   807
            Boone v. Coe   808
            Note   813
            Alaska Airlines, Inc. v. Stephenson   814
            Note   817

Chapter 7. The Parol Evidence Rule   821

Section 1. Introductory Note   821
            Corbin, The Parol Evidence Rule   825
            Note   827
Section 2. The Circle of Interpretation   827
            Thompson v. Libby   827
            Note   831
            Pym v. Campbell   831
            Crawford v. France   832
            Note   835
            Mitchill v. Lath   837
            Note   841
            Uniform Commercial Code §2-202   842
            Note   842
            Danann Realty Corp. v. Harris   843
            Note   847
            Hurst v. Lake Co., Inc.   849
            Note   851
            Zell v. American Seating Co.   852
            American Seating Co. v. Zell   859

Chapter 8. Reality and Illusion (Herein of the Doctrines of Mistake, Impossibility, and Frustration)   861

Section 1. Introductory Note   861
Section 2. The Unruliness of Words   866
            Hotchkiss v. National City Bank of New York   866
            1 Williston on Contracts §95   866
            Ricketts v. Pennsylvania R.R. (Frank, J.,
              concurring)   867
            Note   868
            Raffles v. Wichelhaus   869
            Note   870
            Miller v. Stanich   875
            Note   880
            Ricketts v. Pennsylvania R.R.   883
            Note   886
Section 3. "The Value of a Thing Is Just Exactly What
            'Twill Bring"   886
            Wood v. Boynton   886
            Sherwood v. Walker   887
            Note   891

	McRae v. Commonwealth Disposals Commission	898
	Note	909
Section 4.	The Vanishing Synthesis (England)	910
	Paradine v. Jane	911
	Note	912
	Savile v. Savile	914
	Note	916
	Hall v. Wright	916
	Note	918
	Taylor v. Caldwell	920
	Note	924
	Krell v. Henry	926
	Note	930
	Chandler v. Webster	931
	Note	932
	Fibrosa Spolka Akcyjna v. Fairbairn Lawson Combe Barbour, Ltd.	932
	Law Reform (Frustrated Contracts) Act, 1943	934
	Note	935
Section 5.	The Vanishing Synthesis (United States)	936
	School Trustees of Trenton v. Bennett	936
	Note	936
	Butterfield v. Byron	937
	Note	942
	Canadian Industrial Alcohol Co. v. Dunbar Molasses Co.	944
	Note	946
	Lloyd v. Murphy	948
	Note	954
	American Trading & Production Corp. v. Shell International Marine Ltd.	955
	Note	960
	Note on the Restatements of Contracts and the Uniform Commercial Code	964

Chapter 9. Protection of the Exchange Relationship (Herein of the Theory of Conditions)   973

Section 1.	Introductory Note	973
Section 2.	The Basic Themes: Some History by Way of Background	976
	Nichols v. Raynbred	976

		Pordage v. Cole	976
		Note	977
		Kingston v. Preston	979
		Note	980
		Boone v. Eyre	981
		Note	981
		Note on the Historical Development of the Law of Conditions	982
	Section 3.	The Sale of Goods: A Case Study in the Implication of Conditions	990
		Norrington v. Wright	990
		Note	1000
		Note on the Uniform Commercial Code and the Perfect Tender Rule	1005
		Miron v. Yonkers Raceway, Inc.	1007
		Note	1013
		Maurice O'Meara Co. v. National Park Bank of New York	1014
		Note	1019
		O. W. Holmes, The Path of the Law	1020
	Section 4.	The Problem of Forfeiture	1021
		Britton v. Turner	1021
		Note	1028
		Smith v. Brady	1029
		Note	1037
		Avery v. Wilson	1038
		Clark v. West	1039
		Jacob & Youngs, Inc. v. Kent	1042
		Note	1048
		Lawrence v. Miller	1054
		Amtorg Trading Corp. v. Miehle Printing Press & Manufacturing Co.	1055
		Note	1057

Chapter 10. Remedies   1061

	Section 1.	Introduction	1061
		Acme Mills & Elevator Co. v. Johnson	1061
		O. W. Holmes, The Common Law	1064
		E. A. Harriman, The Law of Contracts	1065
	Section 2.	Specific Performance and the Right to Break a Contract	1069
		Lumley v. Wagner	1075

	Note	1078
	Stokes v. Moore	*1079*
	Note	1084
	City Stores Co. v. Ammerman	1089
	Note	1091
	Campbell Soup Co. v. Wentz	*1097*
	Uniform Commercial Code §2-716	*1101*
	Note	1101
	Grossfeld, Money Sanctions for Breach of Contract in a Communist Economy	1106
Section 3.	Money Damages: The Limits of Compensation	1108
	Sedgwick, On the Measure of Damages	1108
	Freund v. Washington Square Press	*1113*
	Note	1116
	Jacob & Youngs, Inc. v. Kent	*1119*
	Peevyhouse v. Garland Coal & Mining Co.	*1119*
	Note	1127
	Gainsford v. Carroll	*1129*
	Note	1130
	Uniform Commercial Code §§2-706, 2-708, 2-710, 2-712, 2-713, 2-715	*1132*
	Panhandle Agri-Service Inc. v. Becker	*1134*
	Note	1137
	Hadley v. Baxendale	*1138*
	Note	1138
	Danzig, Hadley v. Baxendale: A Study in the Industrialization of the Law	*1140*
	Globe Refining Co. v. Landa Cotton Oil Co.	*1144*
	Note	1149
	Kerr S.S. Co., Inc. v. Radio Corporation of America	*1152*
	Note	1156
	The Heron II (Kaufos v. C. Czarnikow, Ltd.)	*1157*
	Note	1164
	Neri v. Retail Marine Corp.	*1165*
	Note	1170
	Fuller and Perdue, The Reliance Interest in Contract Damages	*1172*
	United States v. Behan	*1174*
	Note	1177
	Kehoe v. Rutherford	*1179*
	Philadelphia v. Tripple	*1182*
	Note	1186

Security Stove & Mfg. Co. v. American Ry.
   Express Co.   1188
Note   1196
L. Albert & Son v. Armstrong Rubber Co.   1197
Note   1201

Section 4. Freedom of Contract and the Judicial
Prerogative: The Power of the Parties to
Control Remedy and Risk   1202
Nute v. Hamilton Mutual Insurance Co.   1203
Note   1208
Garrity v. Lyle Stuart, Inc.   1212
Note   1221
Kemble v. Farren   1223
McCarthy v. Tally   1225
Note   1231
Klar v. H. & M. Parcel Room, Inc.   1237
Note   1239
Uniform Commercial Code §§2-718, 2-719   1239
Note   1240
Henningsen v. Bloomfield Motors, Inc.   1243
Note   1253
Uniform Commercial Code §2-316   1256
Note   1257
Fair v. Negley   1257
Note   1265

Section 5. The Burdens of Innocence: Anticipatory
Repudiation and the Duty to Mitigate
Damages   1269
Daniels v. Newton   1270
Note   1278
Roehm v. Horst   1279
Note   1287
Phelps v. Herro   1291
Note   1298
Missouri Furnace Co. v. Cochran   1301
Note   1305
Uniform Commercial Code §§2-610, 2-611   1307
Note   1308
Oloffson v. Coomer   1308
Note   1312
Clark v. Marsiglia   1313
Note   1314
Mount Pleasant Stable Co. v. Steinberg   1316
Jameson v. Board of Education   1317
Note   1321

Louise Caroline Nursing Home, Inc. v. Dix
    Construction Co.   1324
    Note   1328

Chapter 11. Third Party Beneficiaries   1329

Section 1.   Introductory Note   1329
Section 2.   The Origins: Cross-Currents of Doctrine   1333
              Lawrence v. Fox   1333
              Note   1340
              Vrooman v. Turner   1346
              Note   1350
              Seaver v. Ransom   1356
              Note   1361
Section 3.   The Search for Doctrinal Clarity   1361
              Socony-Vacuum Oil Co., Inc. v. Continental
                  Casualty Co.   1364
              Note   1370
              Lucas v. Hamm   1371
              Note   1375
              Isbrandtsen Co., Inc. v. Local 1291 of
                  International Longshoremen's Assn.   1380
              Note   1383
Section 4.   Government Contracts and Citizen
              Beneficiaries   1384
              H. R. Moch Co., Inc. v. Rensselaer Water Co. 1386
              Note   1390
              Martinez v. Socoma Companies, Inc.   1391
              Note   1403
              Holbrook v. Pitt   1405
              Note   1414
              Waters, The Property in the Promise: A Study
                  of the Third Party Beneficiary Rule   1416
Section 5.   The Problem of Defenses, Modifications, and
              Rescission   1418
              Ford v. Mutual Life Insurance Company of
                  New York   1420
              Copeland v. Beard   1421
              Note on The Restatement of Contracts and
                  the Problem of Rescission   1424
              Note   1427
              Rouse v. United States   1428
              Note   1429

Lewis v. Benedict Coal Corp.   1431
Note   1437

Chapter 12. Assignment: The Liquidity of Contractual Obligations   1441

Section 1.   Introductory Note   1441
             1 G. Gilmore, Security Interests in Personal
               Property §7.3   1441
Section 2.   Intangible Claims and Their Transferability   1444
             Muller v. Pondir   1444
             Note   1449
             Shiro v. Drew   1452
             Note   1456
             In re Dodge-Freedman Poultry Co.   1458
             Note   1464
             Sillman v. Twentieth Century-Fox Film Corp.   1466
             Note   1475
Section 3.   The Present Assignability of Future Claims   1477
             Rockmore v. Lehman   1477
             Note   1483
             In re City of New York v. Bedford Bar & Grill,
               Inc.   1485
             Note   1492
             Speelman v. Pascal   1492
             Note   1496
Section 4.   Assignment of Rights vs. Delegation of Duties 1500
             Langel v. Betz   1500
             Note   1503
             Boston Ice Co. v. Potter   1504
             Note   1507
             British Waggon Co. v. Lea & Co.   1507
             Arkansas Valley Smelting Co. v. Belden
               Mining Co.   1511
             Note   1515
             Uniform Commercial Code §2-210   1519
             Note   1520
Section 5.   The Problem of Defenses, Modifications, and
               Rescission   1520
             Cuban Atlantic Sugar Sales Corp. v. The
               Marine Midland Trust Co. of New York   1520
             Note   1525
             Restatement of Contracts Second §336   1527
             Uniform Commercial Code §9-318   1527

Note	1528
Commercial Credit Corp. v. Orange County Machine Works	1529
Note	1533
Homer v. Shaw	1538
Note	1539
Babson v. Village of Ulysses	1541
Note	1545
Section 6. Priorities	1547
A. The Common Law Rules	1547
Dearle v. Hall	1547
Note	1550
State Factors Corp. v. Sales Factors Corp.	1550
Note	1552
Restatement of Contracts Second §342	1553
Note	1553
B. The *Klauder* Case and the End of the Common Law Priority Rules	1554
2 G. Gilmore, Security Interests in Personal Property §25.7	1554
Note	1556
C. Priorities under Article 9 of the Uniform Commercial Code	1556
Table of Cases	**1559**
Index	**1571**

PREFACE

In this revision, we have attempted to preserve the spirit and general outlook of the previous edition, while making those changes we felt were necessary to bring the casebook up-to-date with developments in the law of contracts over the past fifteen years. We have also made a number of changes in the organization of the book to improve its coverage of certain topics inadequately treated in the second edition, and to clarify the relationship between the subjects covered. Among the more important changes are these: the elimination of Part II, which dealt principally with insurance contracts and franchise agreements, and the incorporation of this material, in much abbreviated form, in earlier sections; a significant expansion of the material dealing with the law of consumer protection and the doctrine of unconscionability; a reorganization, and expansion, of the chapter on remedies, drawing together a number of topics (including the duty to mitigate damages and the doctrine of anticipatory repudiation) previously treated elsewhere in the book; the consolidation of the chapters on mistake and impossibility; and a thorough revision of the chapter dealing with the history of contract law, which takes account of the most recent work in the field. Footnotes to the principal cases have in many instances been eliminated, entirely or in part, and those that remain have been renumbered for the reader's convenience.

This book is intended to provide the beginning law student with a comprehensive grounding in all the main doctrinal branches of contract law, while at the same time emphasizing the many connections between our modern law of contracts and the larger social reality that it reflects and has helped to shape. We have sought to put the law of contracts in a historical and jurisprudential perspective that will not only help the student to a deeper understanding of its structure and inner tensions, but suggest, as well, the subject's intellectual richness and endless fascination. All of the social and political problems that today, at the end of the twentieth century, seem most absorbing, are reflected in the law of contracts; many, indeed, begin there. From even the most technical doctrinal question, lines of inquiry lead off to the farthest horizon. We have tried to convey a sense of the spaciousness of our subject, of its vast potential as an instrument of freedom and control.

Grant Gilmore died shortly after beginning work on this third edition of the casebook, and Anthony Kronman joined Friedrich Kessler in the preparation of the text. Grant was our colleague, teacher, and friend, and we shall miss him. When we imagine all he might have done, and the many satisfactions he might still have had, it pleases both of us to think that among them would have been his pleasure at seeing this revision of the casebook, to which he contributed so much, completed and in print. It is to the memory of Grant Gilmore that we dedicate this book.

ACKNOWLEDGMENTS

Professor Kessler wishes to express his gratitude to Roy Geiger, Esquire, of the University of California-Berkeley Law School Class of 1979 (now associated with Irell & Manella, Los Angeles), for giving the benefit of his solid learning and creative imagination, with unfailing generosity of spirit. Professor Kessler is equally grateful to Miss Ingrid Radkey, librarian at the University of California, who not only typed most of the manuscript but also made valuable suggestions for its improvement. Thanks are also due to his colleagues at Boalt Hall, Berkeley, Thomas Jorde, Edward Rubin, and Lawrence Sullivan.

Professor Kronman wishes to acknowledge Robert Adelson, Yale Law School Class of 1985, Raymond Thek, Class of 1986, and Henry Weissman, Class of 1987, for the helpful assistance they rendered in the preparation of this edition. We are also grateful to Diane Hart and Margaret Chisholm for the help they have given us in preparing the manuscript for publication, and to Edward Bander for his work on the index. To Karen Jones of the Little, Brown editorial staff we owe a special debt; with her unfailing judgment and good-humored encouragement Karen has guided us through the shoals that always make the final approach to publication so formidable.

We thank the authors and copyright holders of the following works for permitting their inclusion in this book:

American Law Institute, Restatement of the Law of Contracts §§90, 133, 142, 143, 147, 178, 288, 346, 357, 454, 455, 459, 468, 512. Copyright © 1932 by the American Law Institute. Reprinted with the permission of the American Law Institute.

American Law Institute, Restatement (Second) of the Law of Contracts, §§1, 21A, 30, 40, 45, 62, 63, 71, 86, 90, 112, 116, 131, 139, 180, 211, 216, 253, 281, 285, 286, 294, 302, 311, 313, 315, 321, 326(1), 328, 330, 348, 377, 388, 467, and Introductory Notes to Chs. 11, 14, and Copyright © 1981 by the American Law Institute. Reprinted with the permission of the American Law Institute.

American Law Institute, Restatement (Second) of the Law of Contracts (Tent. Draft No. 9, 1974), §292. Copyright © 1974 by the American Law Institute. Reprinted with the permission of the American Law Institute.

American Law Institute, Restatement (Second) of the Law of Contracts (Tent. Draft No. 14, 1979), §292. Copyright © 1979 by the American

Law Institute. Reprinted with the permission of the American Law Institute.

American Law Institute, Restatement of Restitution, §12. Copyright © 1937 by the American Law Institute. Reprinted with the permission of the American Law Institute.

American Law Institute, Restatement (Second) of Torts, §402A. Copyright © 1965 by the American Law Institute. Reprinted with the permission of the American Law Institute.

Ames, James Barr, Lectures on Legal History 98-99, 104-106 (Harvard University Press, 1913). Reprinted with permission of James B. Ames.

Berman, Excuse for Non-performance in the Light of Contract Practices in International Trade, 63 Colum. L. Rev. 1413, 1417 (1963). Copyright © 1963 by the Directors of the Columbia Law Review Association, Inc. All rights reserved. This article originally appeared at 63 Colum. L. Rev. 1413 (1963). Reprinted by permission.

Cohen, The Basis of Contract, 46 Harv. L. Rev. 553, 581-583, 1105 (1933). Copyright © 1933 by the Harvard Law Review Association. Reprinted with permission.

Corbin, A., Corbin on Contracts, §§3, 19, 302, 403, 535, 541, 543, 544, 573, 579, 582, 1145, 1171, 1322, 1432 (1950-1964) (West Publishing Company, publishers). Copyright © Yale University (Corbin on Contracts (1950-1964)). Reprinted with permission.

Corbin, The Parol Evidence Rule, 53 Yale L.J. 603 (1944). Reprinted by permission of The Yale Law Journal Company and Fred B. Rothman & Company from The Yale Law Journal, Vol. 53, pp. 609-610, 622-624.

Danzig, R., The Capability Problem in Contract Law 121-123 (Foundation Press 1978). Reprinted with permission.

Danzig, Hadley v. Baxendale: A Study in the Industrialization of the Law, 4 J. Legal Stud. 249, 257-259, 267-274 (1975). Published by the University of Chicago. Copyright © 1975 by the University of Chicago. All rights reserved. Reprinted with permission.

Eisenberg, The Bargain Principle and Its Limits, 95 Harv. L. Rev. 741, 798-799 (1982). Copyright © 1982 by the Harvard Law Review Association. Reprinted with permission.

Fuller, Consideration and Form, 41 Colum. L. Rev. 799-800 (1941). Reprinted with permission of the Lon Fuller Trust.

Fuller & Perdue, The Reliance Interest in Contract Damages (pt. 1), 46 Yale L.J. 52 (1936). Reprinted by permission of The Yale Law Journal Company and Fred B. Rothman & Company from The Yale Law Journal, Vol. 46, pp. 53-57.

Goetz & Scott, Enforcing Promises — An Examination of the Basis of Contract, 89 Yale L.J. 1261 (1980). Reprinted by permission of The Yale Law Journal Company and Fred B. Rothman & Company from The Yale Law Journal, Vol. 89, pp. 1307-1308.

Grossfeld, Money Sanctions for Breach of Contract in a Communist Economy, 72 Yale L.J. 1326 (1963). Reprinted by permission of The Yale Law Journal Company and Fred B. Rothman & Company from The Yale Law Journal, Vol. 72, pp. 1330-1332, 1334, 1336.

Holmes, O. W., The Common Law 5, 177, 230, 234-237, 242 (M. Howe ed. 1963). Reprinted with permission of Harvard University Press, publisher.

Jackson, Anticipatory Repudiation and the Temporal Element of Contract Law, 31 Stan. L. Rev. 83-86 (1978). Copyright © 1978 by the Board of Trustees of the Leland Stanford Junior University. Reprinted material originally appeared in the Stanford Law Review, Volume 31, at pages 83-86. Reprinted with permission.

Keeton, Fraud, Concealment and Non-disclosure. Published originally in 15 Texas L. Rev. 32 (1936). Copyright © 1936 by the Texas Law Review. Reprinted by permission.

Kronman, Specific Performance, 45 U. Chi. L. Rev. 371-373, 358-362. Reprinted with permission.

Llewellyn, Our Case Law of Contract: Offer and Acceptance (pts. 1 & 2), 48 Yale L.J. 1, 779 (1938-1939). Reprinted by permission of The Yale Law Journal Company and Fred B. Rothman & Company from The Yale Law Journal, Vol. 48, pp. 32, 779, 785-786, 795.

Page, The Power of the Contracting Parties to Alter a Contract for Rendering Performance to a Third Party, 12 Wis. L. Rev. 141 (1936-1937). Copyright © 1936 by the University of Wisconsin. Reprinted materials originally appeared in the Wisconsin Law Review, Vol. 12, pp. 183-184. Reprinted with permission.

Pollock, F., Principles of Contract 21 (13th ed. 1950). Reprinted with permission of Sweet & Maxwell Ltd., publisher.

Pollock, F., & Maitland, F., The History of English Law, Vol. 2, pp. 210, 232-233, 423 (1968). Reprinted with permission of Cambridge University Press, publisher.

Reich, The New Property, 73 Yale L.J. 733 (1964). Reprinted by permission of The Yale Law Journal Company and Fred B. Rothman & Company from The Yale Law Journal, Vol. 73, pp. 733, 770, 785, 787.

Schwartz, The Case for Specific Performance, 89 Yale L.J. 271 (1979). Reprinted by permission of The Yale Law Journal Company and Fred B. Rothman & Company from The Yale Law Journal, Vol. 89, pp. 274-277.

Waters, The Property in the Promise, 98 Harv. L. Rev. 1109, 1123-1127, 1192-1198, 1199 (1985) (footnotes omitted). Copyright © 1985 by the Harvard Law Review Association. Reprinted with permission.

Williston, S., Williston on Contracts (Jaeger 3d ed. 1957-1970 & Supplements) §§3, 95, 112. Reprinted with permission of Lawyers Cooperative Publishing Co., publisher.

Williston, Repudiation of Contracts, 14 Harv. L. Rev. 317, 421, 438-439
    (1901). Copyright © 1901 by the Harvard Law Review Association.
    Reprinted with permission.
Young, Half Measures, 81 Colum. L. Rev. 19, 24 (1981). Copyright ©
    1981 by the Directors of the Columbia Law Review Association, Inc.
    All rights reserved. This article originally appeared at 81 Colum. L.
    Rev. 19 (1981). Reprinted by permission.

TABLE OF ABBREVIATED REFERENCES

Full Citation	Abbreviated Reference
Atiyah, P., The Rise and Fall of Freedom of Contract (1979)	Atiyah
Baker, J. H., Introduction to English Legal History (2d ed. 1979)	Baker
Baker, The Dark Age of English Legal History, in Legal History Studies 1 (D. Jankins ed. 1972)	Baker, Dark Age
Baker, Introduction to Spelman's Reports, 94 Selden Society 263 (1978)	Baker, Introduction
Baker, New Light on Slade's Case (pts. 1 & 2), 29 Cambridge L.J. 51, 213 (1971)	Baker, Slade's Case
Blackstone, W., Commentaries on the Laws of England (facsimile of first edition, 1765-1769) (U. Chicago 1979)	Blackstone, Commentaries
Corbin, A. L., Corbin on Contracts (1950-1964 & Supp.)	Corbin
Fifoot, C. H. S., History and Sources of the Common Law: Tort and Contract (1949)	Fifoot
Horwitz, M. J., The Transformation of American Law, 1780-1860 (1977)	Horwitz
Milsom, S. F. C., Historical Foundations of the Common Law (2d ed. 1981)	Milsom
Pollock, F. & Maitland, F., The History of English Law (S. F. C. Milsom ed. 1968)	Pollock & Maitland
Restatement of the Law of Contracts	Restatement First

Full Citation	*Abbreviated Reference*
Restatement of the Law of Contracts Second	Restatement Second
Simpson, A. W., A History of the Common Law of Contract: The Rise of the Action of Assumpsit (1975)	Simpson
Simpson, Historical Introduction to Cheshire & Fifoot's Law of Contracts (Furmston 9th ed. 1976)	Simpson, Historical Introduction
Williston, S., Williston on Contracts (Jaeger 3d ed. 1957-1970)	Williston

CONTRACTS

INTRODUCTION

Contract as a Principle
of Order*

There are, according to Hume, three fundamental laws of nature which are necessary for the preservation of society:

> [T]hat of stability of possession, of its transference by consent and of the performance of promises. . . . [T]hough it is possible for men to maintain a small uncultivated society without government, it is impossible that they should maintain a society of any kind without justice, and subservience to those fundamental laws. . . .[1]

Most of us take contract for granted. Together with family and property, contract is one of the basic institutions of our social fabric. Price bargains, wage bargains, and rent bargains, to use the classification of Commons, belong to our daily experience. Indeed, contract is a principle of order of such universal usefulness that even a socialist economy cannot dispense with it.[2]

A profitable approach to the law of contract, and perhaps to law in general, is to view legal doctrine, rules, principles, and standards as re-

---

* Compare L. Fuller, The Principles of Order, in The Problems of Jurisprudence 693 (1949).

1. 2 D. Hume, A Treatise on Human Nature, Book III: of Morals, ch. 6, at 293, 306 (T. H. Greene & T. H. Grose eds. 1890). Although Hume's Treatise contains an elaborate analysis of the nature of promises and a refutation of the contractarian theory of Hobbes and Locke, a general theory of contract is missing. There are, however, many references to contract as an institution. In another passage of his Treatise (at 258), Hume explains what he means by "fundamental laws of human nature": "Tho' the rules of justice be *artificial*, they are not *arbitrary*. Nor is the expression improper to call them *Laws of Nature*; if by natural we understand what is common to any species, or even if we confine it to mean what is inseparable from the species."

2. For the role of contract in a socialist society, see K. Grzybowski, Soviet Legal Institutions 85 (1967); H. Berman, Justice in the U.S.S.R. 108, 114-117, and *passim* (rev. ed. 1963); W. Friedmann, Legal Theory 377-378 (5th ed. 1967); Berman, Commercial Contracts in Soviet Law, 35 Calif. L. Rev. 191 (1947); Grossfeld, Money Sanctions for Breach of Contract in a Communist Economy, 72 Yale L.J. 1326 (1963); Markevitz, Civil Law in East Germany — Its Development and Relation to Soviet History and Ideology, 78 Yale L.J. 1, 20 (1968); Loeber, Plan and Contract Performance in Soviet Law, 1964 U. Ill. L.F. 128; Hsias, The Role of Economic Contract in Communist China, 53 Calif. L. Rev. 1029 (1965).

1

flecting the value system of the culture in which the legal system is embedded.[3] In our modern society, a tension exists between those values favoring individual freedom and those favoring social control.[4] Whatever the merits of the claim that a society without tension is conceivable (and desirable),[5] in our society we encounter every day the tension beween individual freedom and social control in debates over government regulation of the economy, abortion, use of marijuana and laetrile, sexual practices between consenting adults, gun control, the rights of criminal defendants, busing, affirmative action, and the teaching of evolution. The list is virtually endless. Small wonder, then, that modern contract law reproduces this same tension within itself, drawing much of its drama and vitality from our divided commitment to individual freedom and social control.

The law of contracts comprises many different doctrinal elements and encompasses exchange relationships of limitless variety. If these relationships were arranged along a continuum, we would find at one end transactions based on free bargain and genuine agreement, or at least on promises voluntarily given. Here, the dominant theme is respect for the autonomy of the parties and noninterference in the arrangements they have made for themselves, provided all the ground rules laid down to insure the smooth working of the system have been observed. Social control is at a minimum. As we proceed along the continuum, the freedom of the parties increasingly is limited by a system of judicial and legislative control designed to protect the community interest. And finally, at the opposite end of the scale, we find the so-called compulsory and adhesive contracts, the first type entered into under an enforceable

3. The distinction between rules, principles, and standards is discussed in R. Dworkin, Taking Rights Seriously, 22-28, 71-80 (1979); 1 F. A. Hayek, Law, Legislation, and Liberty 115 et seq. (1973). See also T. Parson's discussion of the role of residual categories in his Structure of Social Action, 16 et seq. (1949).

4. This conflict is reflected in the two main theories of contractual liability. One, the will theory, emphasizes the autonomy of the individual. The other, the objective theory, bases contractual liability on the social consequences of promise-making, or, as Hume put it, on the fact that "[p]romises are human inventions founded on the necessity and interests of society." Hume, *supra* note 1, at 287. The former view has found powerful support in Kantian ethics, which in recent years has experienced renewed interest if not a philosophical revival, e.g., J. Rawls, A Theory of Justice (1971). See further W. Sandell, Liberalism and the Limits of Justice (1982); 1 F. A. Hayek, Law, Legislation and Liberty (1973); M. Gregor, Laws of Freedom (1962).

Kennedy, Form and Substance in Private Law Adjudication, 89 Harv. L. Rev. 1685 (1976), has pointed out that the conflict between individual freedom and social control is played out even in the choice of forms of legal regulation, specifically in the choice between narrowly defined rules and broad-based standards.

5. The possibility and desirability of a social system without tension is discussed in S. Freud, Civilization and Its Discontents (1946) and in his correspondence with Einstein written in 1932, Why War?, 22 The Complete Psychoanalytical Works of Sigmund Freud 203 (Standard ed. 1964). Kant's emphasis on the creative force of "ungesellige Geselligkeit" is still valid. Idee zu einer allgemeinen Geschichte in Weltbürgerlicher Absicht, 7(1) Sämtliche Werke 321 (K. Rosenkrantz & F. Schubert eds. 1838); so is the saying attributed to a pre-Socratic philosopher: "Strife is the father of all things."

duty to serve the public and the second unilaterally dictated by the stronger to the weaker party in need of goods or services. In recent years, there has undoubtedly been a shift all along this vast continuum in the direction of greater social control, a phenomenon reflecting the socialization of modern law in general.[6] But the idea of private autonomy remains influential in wide areas of contract law and even where it is no longer dominant, its appeal can still be heard, albeit often only as a distant echo.

To better understand the main tenets of modern contract law, and its distinctive tendencies, it will be helpful to recall the outlines of what has been called the "classical" theory of contractual obligation. Classical contract theory starts from the belief that the individual is the best judge of his own welfare and of the means of securing it,[7] and is inspired by the hope that given a "suitable system of general rules and institutions there will arise spontaneous relationships also deserving the term 'order' but which are self-sustaining and within the limits prescribed by the rules need no detailed and specific regulation."[8] To achieve such order, according to the proponents of the classical theory, all that is required besides a system of general rules is "a free market guaranteeing and guiding the division of labor through a system of incentives it provides to the interest of the individual producers."[9] Within this framework, contract provides the legal machinery required by an economic system that relies on free exchange rather than tradition, custom, or command.[10]

6. 3 R. Pound, Jurisprudence 429 et seq. (1959).
7. F. Knight, Freedom and Reform 54 (1946):

[A]ccording to the liberal view, a greater total *achievement* of ends, actually desired and pursued, and in that sense a greater realization of "good" will result from a general application of the principle of freedom with the limitation of mutual consent, than from the application of any other general rule.

(Emphasis added.)
8. Lord Robbins, Political Economy Past and Present 5-9 (1976).
9. T. Sowell, Classical Economics Reconsidered, ch. 1 (1974). Adam Smith, Wealth of Nations 13 (Cannan ed. 1937):

This division of labor, from which so many advantages are derived, is not originally the effect of any human wisdom which foresees and intends the general opulence to which it gives occasion. It is the necessary, though very slow and gradual, consequence of a certain propensity in human nature which has in view no such extensive utility: the propensity to truck, barter and exchange one thing for another.

On Adam Smith, see Viner, Adam Smith and Laissez-faire, 33 J. Pol. Economy 198, 208, 214 et seq., Coase, The Wealth of Nations, 15 Economic Inquiry 309 (1977); see further, A. Marshall, Principles of Economics, ch. 8 (8th ed. 1920); see also P. Stein, Legal Evolution 29 et seq. (1980). On early economic theory in this country, see the symposium in the supplement issue to the J. Econ. Hist. 1943; 1 W. Grampp, Economic Liberalism: The Beginnings 48-97 (1965); P. Stein, Adam Smith's Jurisprudence, 64 Cornell L.Q. 621 (1964).
10. Llewellyn, What Price Contract? — An Essay in Perspective, 40 Yale L.J. 704, 717 (1931). It goes without saying that there is a cost to using the "price [contract] mechanism." At a certain point, therefore, it may become advantageous to supersede the contract mechanism "by forming an organisation [a firm] and allowing some authority (an "entrepreneur") to direct the resources. . . ." Coase, The Nature of the Firm, 4 Economica (N.S.) 385, 392 (1937).

The triumph of capitalism during the eighteenth and nineteenth centuries, with its spectacular increase in the productivity of labor, was possible only because of a constant refinement of the division of labor. This development in turn presupposed that enterprisers could depend on a continuous flow of goods and services exchanged in a free market. And to be able to exploit the factors of production in the most efficient way, enterprisers had (and still have) to be able to bargain for goods and services to be delivered in the future and to rely on promises for future delivery. Thus, it became one of the main functions of our law of contracts to keep this flow running smoothly, making certain that bargains would be kept and that legitimate expectations created by contractual promises would be honored. "The foundation of contract," in the language of Adam Smith, "is the reasonable expectation, which the person who promises raises in the person to whom he binds himself; of which the satisfaction may be extorted by force."[11] In this sense, contract liability is promissory liability. In an industrial and commercial society, whose wealth, as Pound said, is largely made up of promises, the interest of society as a whole demands protection of the interest of the individual promisee.

Contract, to be useful to the business enterpriser within the setting of a free-enterprise economy, must be a tool of almost unlimited pliability. To accomplish this end, the legal system has to reduce the ceremony necessary to vouch for the deliberate nature of a contractual transaction to the indispensable minimum; it has to give freedom of contract as to form. Furthermore, since the law must keep pace with the constant widening of the market without being able to anticipate the content of an infinite number of transactions into which members of the community may need to enter, parties must be given freedom as to the content of their contractual arrangements as well. Contract, then, in the sense of a system of free contract, enhances the mobility of factors of production in the interest of the enterpriser who wishes to utilize them in the most efficient way and to be able to experiment rationally with new methods of satisfying wants. For that matter, such a system is required by every member of the community who seeks to achieve rationality of conduct in the adaptation of means to ends, and who does not want to adhere passively to the compulsory uniformity of behavior imposed by tradition and custom. Thus, its emergence has greatly increased the area and the potentialities of rational conduct.[12]

Within the framework of a free-enterprise system the esential prerequisite of contractual liability is volition, that is, consent freely given, and not coercion or status.[13] Contract, in this view, is the "meeting place of

11. Lectures on Justice, Police, Revenue and Arms 7 (Cannan ed. 1896).
12. For a discussion of the significance of rationality for modern capitalism, see p. 8, note 31 *infra*.
13. Freedom of contract thus means that, subject to narrow limits, the law, in the field of contracts, has delegated legislation to the contracting parties. As far as the parties are

the ideas of agreement and obligation."[14] As a matter of historical fact, the rise of free and informal contract within western civilization reflected the erosion of a status-organized society; contract became, at an ever-increasing rate, a tool of change and of growing self-determination and self-assertion. Self-determination during the nineteenth century was regarded as the goal towards which society progressed; the movement of progressive societies, in the words of Sir Henry Maine, is a movement from status to contract, Ancient Law, *infra* p. 19. "It is through contract that man attains freedom. Although it appears to be the subordination of one man's will to another, the former gains more than he loses."[15] Contract, in this view, is the principle of order par excellence and the only legitimate means of social integration in a free society. Translated into legal language this means that in a progressive society all law is ultimately based on contract.[16] And since contract as a social phenomenon is the result of a "coincidence of free choices" on the part of the members of the community, merging their egoistical and altruistic tendencies, a contractual society safeguards its own stability. Contract is an instrument of peace in society. It reconciles freedom with order, particularly since, as we have been told, with increasing rationality man becomes less rather than more egoistic (see Marshall, *supra* note 9).

The high hopes with regard to the potentialities inherent in the contractual mechanism found admirable expression in Henry Sidgwick's Elements of Politics 82 (1879):

> In a summary view of the civil order of society, as constituted in accordance with the individualistic ideal, performance of contract presents itself as the chief *positive* element, protection of life and property being the chief *negative* element. Withdraw contract — suppose that no one can count upon the fulfillment of any engagement — and the members of a human community are atoms that cannot effectively combine; the complex cooperation and division of employments that are the essential characteristics of modern industry cannot be introduced among such beings. Suppose contracts freely made and effectively sanctioned, and the most elaborate

---

concerned, the law of contracts is of their own making; society merely lends its machinery of enforcement to the party injured by the breach. To be sure, society, in order to accommodate the members of the business community, has placed at their disposal a great variety of typical transactions whose consequences are regulated in advance; it has thus "supplied the shortsightedness of individuals, by doing for them what they would have done for themselves, if their imagination had anticipated the march of nature." J. Bentham, A General View of a Complete Code of Laws, in 3 Works 191 (J. Bowring ed. 1843). Bentham's statement does not do justice to the significance of statutory provisions. They often reflect existing patterns of behavior. But these statutory provisions come into operation only in the absence of an agreement to the contrary.

14. W. Watt, The Theory of Contract in Its Social Light 2 (1897).

15. W. G. Miller, Lectures in the Philosophy of Law 216 (1884).

16. See 1 Parsons, The Law of Contracts 3 (1855). For the Marxist critique of this aspect of "bourgeois" law, its commodity exchange conception, see Pashukanis, The General Theory of Law and Marxism, reprinted in 5 Twentieth Century Legal Philosophy Series (Soviet Legal Philosophy) 111-225 (1951).

social organisation becomes possible, at least in a society of such human beings as the individualistic theory contemplates — gifted with mature reason, and governed by enlightened self-interest. Of such beings it is *prima facie* plausible to say that, when once their respective relations to the surrounding material world have been determined so as to prevent mutual encroachment and secure to each the fruits of his industry, the remainder of their positive mutual rights and obligations ought to depend entirely on that coincidence of their free choices, which we call contract. Thoroughgoing individualists would even include the rights corresponding to governmental services, and the obligations to render services to Government, which we shall have to consider later: only in this latter case the contract is tacit.

Thus, a system of free contract did not recommend itself solely for reasons of sheer expediency and utilitarianism; it was deeply rooted in the moral sentiments of the period in which it found strongest expression. The dominant current of belief inspiring nineteenth-century industrial society — an open society of "removable inequalities," to use Burke's phrase — was the deep-felt conviction that individual and cooperative action should be left unrestrained in family, church, and market, and that such a system of laissez-faire would protect the freedom and dignity of the individual and secure the greatest possible measure of social justice.[17] The representatives of this school of thought were firmly convinced, to state it somewhat roughly, of the existence of a natural law according to which, at least in the long run, the individual serving his own interest was also serving the interest of the community.[18] Profits, under this system, could be earned only by supplying desired commodities, and freedom of competition would prevent profits from rising unduly. The play of the market, if left to itself, would therefore maximize net satisfactions and establish the ideal conditions for the distribution of wealth. Justice within this context has a very definite meaning.[19] It means freedom of property and of contract, of profit making and of trade. A social system based on freedom of enterprise and competition sees to it that the private autonomy of contracting parties is kept within bounds and works for the benefit of society as a whole.

It is hardly surprising that contract played a significant role in the evolution of free enterprise capitalism in this country, in England,[20] and for that matter, in western continental Europe.[21] In America, the law of

17. S. Fine, Laissez-Faire and the General Welfare State, A Study of Conflict in American Thought, 1865-1901 (1982).

18. Adam Smith, Wealth of Nations 423 (Cannan ed. 1937): "By pursuing his own interest the individual member of society promotes that of the society more effectively than when he really intends to promote it." For a more guarded expression of this idea, see F. Knight, Freedom and Reform 45, 54 (1947).

19. Hamilton, Competition in 2 Encyc. Soc. Sci. 141, 142 (1930).

20. See Atiyah.

21. The discussion that follows will be confined to American law and literature.

contracts underwent an extraordinary process of expansion and refinement in the first three-quarters of the nineteenth century.[22] During this formative period, when the country was still, for the most part, an elemental and unexplored vastness, the "hands-off" attitude of classical contract law facilitated what J. W. Hurst has called a "release of creative human energy."[23] With the constant widening of the market, exchange transactions became more numerous and complex, and the principle of freedom of contract established itself as a paramount postulate of public policy.[24] Though the expression itself did not acquire wide currency until later,[25] its underlying philosophy was already implicit in the case law of the early nineteenth century (if not before), and its influence was felt in every branch of our developing law of contracts. The idea of freedom of contract found expression, for example, in the general opposition to compulsory contracts of every sort (*infra* p. 55), in the rise and short-lived triumph of the will theory of obligation (*infra* p. 114), in the rejection of older, equitable approaches to the problems of consideration and contract damages (*infra* p. 558), in the rule of caveat emptor (*infra* pp. 7 and 9) and, finally, in the nearly universal acceptance of the axiom that courts do not make contracts for the parties (*infra* p. 141).

Of course, it was often said that fraud, misrepresentation, and duress must be ruled out by the courts in the exercise of their function of making sure that the "rules of the game" are adhered to. But these categories were narrowly defined (at least by the nineteenth-century common law)[26] due to the strong belief in the policing force of the market. It was taken for granted that oppressive bargains could be avoided by careful shopping around. Contracting parties were expected to look out for their own interest and their own protection. "Let the bargainer beware" was (and to some extent still is) the ordinary rule of contract.[27] It is not the function

22. G. Gilmore, The Ages of American Law (1977).

23. Law and the Conditions of Freedom in the Nineteenth Century United States 6 (1956). For English law, see Atiyah, ch. 13. See also Gilmore, *supra* note 22, at 1-41 (1977); Horwitz at 145, 154-155, reviewed by Genovese, 91 Harv. L. Rev. 727 (1978).

24. 2 M. Weber, Economy and Society 889-892, 668-681 (G. Roth & C. Wittich eds. 1978). For the origins of freedom of contract in England in terms of the administrative structure of the court system, see Francis, The Structure of Judicial Administration and the Development of Contract Law in Seventeenth Century England, 83 Colum. L. Rev. 35, 134, 135 (1983).

25. Printing and Numerical Registering Co. v. Sampson, 19 L.R.-Eq. 462, 465 (1875). The philosophy powerfully expressed in the opinion had a retarding influence on the evolution of the doctrine of public policy. On Sir George Jessel, see 16 W. Holdsworth, A History of English Law 121 (1966). The opinion is quoted in Diamond Match Co. v. Raber, 106 N.Y. 473, 482 (1887).

26. Dawson, Economic Duress — An Essay in Perspective, 45 Mich. L. Rev. 253 (1947).

27. In sales law, the principle found its most striking expression in the maxim of caveat emptor (let the purchaser take care of its own interests): the seller is not liable even for a latent defect, unless the buyer has requested an express warranty. 1 Parsons on Contracts 461 (3d ed. 1857); 12 Williston §1497 (1970); Seixas v. Wood, 2 Cai. R. 48 (N.Y. 1804); see, however, 2 J. Kent, Commentaries 479 (2d ed. 1832); Smith v. Hughes, 6 L.R.-Q.B. 597, 607 (1871).

of courts to strike down improvident bargains. Courts have only to interpret contracts made by the parties. They do not make them. Within this
framework contract justice is commutative and not distributive justice.[28]
This attitude is in keeping with liberal social and moral philosophy according to which it pertains to the dignity of man to lead his own life as a
reasonable person and to accept responsibility for his own mistakes. If the
diligent is not to be deprived of the fruits of his own superior skill and
knowledge acquired by legitimate means, the law cannot afford to go to
the "romantic length of giving indemnity against the consequences of
indolence and folly, or a careless indifference to the ordinary and accessible means of information."[29] Sir George Jessel, one of the great defenders
of freedom of contract remarked,

> [I]f there is one thing more than another which public policy requires, it is
> that men of full age and competent understanding shall have the utmost
> liberty of contracting, and that their contracts entered into freely and vol-
> untarily shall be held sacred and shall be enforced by Courts of Justice.[30]

These pronouncements, however, are representative only of the main
current of thought that shaped our law of contracts in its formative period. Anglo-American law never became the perfect mirror image of free
enterprise capitalism, but always retained a measure of independence
from the underlying market relations it was helping to rationalize, a characteristic that neo-Marxist writers describe as its "relative autonomy."[31]

28. F. A. Hayek, Constitution of Liberty 232, 464 (1960).
29. 2 J. Kent, Commentaries *485 (O. W. Holmes 12th ed. 1873); Bolden, Voluntary
Assumption of Risk, 20 Harv. L. Rev. 14, 22 (1906):

> While the common law makes no pretence of being a social reformer and does not
> profess to reduce all persons to an absolutely equal position by eliminating all natural
> advantages, but rather, recognizing society as it is, considers social inequalities as the
> natural inevitable tactical advantages of those lucky enough to possess them, it does
> prohibit their misuse while permitting their use within fair limits.

30. See note 25 *supra*. "Freely and voluntarily" should not be underemphasized.
31. See, e.g., Tushnet, A Marxist Interpretation of American Law, 1 Marxist Perspectives, Spring 1978. Neo-Marxists often refer in this connection to Max Weber's discussion of
the role played by civil and common law in the evolution of capitalism. In describing the
formal qualities of law, Max Weber has this to say about the differences between contemporary civil and Anglo-American law:

> The differences between continental and common law methods of legal thought
> have been produced mostly by factors which are respectively connected with the
> internal structure and the modes of existence of the legal profession as well as by
> factors related to differences in political development. The economic elements, how-
> ever, have been determinative only in connection with these elements. What we are
> concerned with here is the fact that, once everything is said and done about these
> differences in historical developments, modern capitalism prospers equally and man-
> ifests essentially identical economic traits under legal systems containing rules and
> institutions which considerably differ from each other at least from the judicial point
> of view.

See Weber, *supra* note 24, at 889. For an interpretation of Weber's sociology of law, see A.
Kronman, Max Weber (1983); Trubek, Max Weber and the Rise of Capitalism, 1972 Wis. L.
Rev. 129; for the "symbiotic" relationship between law and economy, see Francis, *supra*
note 24, at 131-136.

Interestingly, however, the independence or autonomy of contract law did not significantly impede the evolution of the free enterprise system, which seems, for the most part, to have developed in accordance with an inner law or logic of its own.[32] To be sure, in this country, the legal profession (in alliance with commercial and industrial interests) succeeded in removing many anti-commercial doctrines that had survived as irrational vestiges from the colonial period.[33] But even where they identified themselves with more traditional and conservative views, lawyers and judges could do little to slow the expansion of the market and its antifraternal ethic, though they did succeed in establishing a few important counterweights to the principle of contractual autonomy and in this way helped to establish a balance between the claims of freedom and order.[34]

Pound is entirely correct when he states that "there has never been in our law any such freedom [of contract] as they [i.e., the advocates of doctrinaire liberalism] postulate."[35] Thus, common law courts have never hesitated to deny enforcement, for reasons of public policy, to contracts contemplating a crime, a tort, or an immoral act. Nor have they hesitated, to take another example, to strike down contracts in restraint of trade.[36] Furthermore, courts became increasingly aware of the presuppositions underlying the doctrine of caveat emptor, and began around the middle of the last century to enlarge the responsibility of the seller for the quality of his goods in favor of the buyer who does not trade face to face with his neighbor for merchandise there to be seen. So-called implied warranties were added to express warranties to make sure that goods bought were of fair merchantable quality, or fit for the buyer's purpose provided he had relied on the seller's judgment for the determination of quality.[37]

Turning to equity, this branch of law has for centuries given relief against contractual penalties and forfeitures. For example, equity granted the mortgagor a right to redeem his property, even if he had failed to so stipulate, and did not permit him to bargain away in advance his "equity

32. Although the common law never achieved the formal rationality ascribed by Max Weber to the legal system of continental western Europe, it achieved a high degree of predictability as the result of built-in "steadying forces," brilliantly described by Karl Llewellyn in The Common Law Tradition 17 et seq. (1960), and by F. A. Hayek in 1 Law, Legislation and Liberty 115 et seq. (1973). Although Professor Hayek apparently was unfamiliar with Llewellyn's analysis, his ideas run strikingly parallel to those of Llewellyn and to Levin Goldschmidt's conviction that situational logic is ultimately guiding in all decisions (cited by Llewellyn at 122).

33. On the evolution of our own legal system, see L. Friedman, Contract Law in America, a Social and Economic Case Study (1965); 2 P. Miller, The Life of the Mind in America from the Revolution to the Civil War: The Legal Mentality (1969); Gilmore, *supra* note 22; Horwitz. For the role of the judge, see further E. Levi, Introduction to Legal Reasoning (1948).

34. Genovese, *supra* note 23, at 727, 729 (1978).

35. Pound, Liberty of Contract, 18 Yale L.J. 454, 482 (1909). Even Sir George Jessel's famous formula leaves a wide berth for different, and perhaps restrictive, interpretations.

36. Williston, Freedom of Contract, 6 Cornell L.Q. 365, 373 (1921); pp. 93-96 *infra*.

37. K. Llewellyn, Cases and Materials on the Law of Sales, 268 et seq. (1930).

of redemption."[38] Equity also interfered with contracts in order to protect the interests of weak, necessitous, and unfortunate persons.[39] These doctrines were too firmly established to be dislodged by the spirit of laissez-faire.[40]

In the eighteenth century, there was a tendency, at least in this country, toward a more equitable conception of contractual obligation, a conception that emphasized, among other things, a substantive theory of consideration which allowed courts to scrutinize the fairness of a bargain by using an objective theory of commodity value. This view of the matter was, as we know, short-lived, and a subjective theory of value soon emerged to replace it (*infra* p. 558). As a result, the consideration doctrine was forced to pay tribute to the great principle of freedom of contract and the adequacy of the quid pro quo was (in theory at least) left to free bargaining (Ch. 5 *infra*). But courts quickly came to realize the usefulness of the consideration requirement as an instrument of social control, and in the subsequent elaboration of this requirement many of the equitable ideas that had been so widely accepted in the previous century enjoyed a second (if somewhat disguised) existence. Throughout the nineteenth century, the doctrine of consideration was used to implement and enlarge notions of public policy that a judicial commitment to the philosophy of laissez-faire[41] made impossible to promote more directly.

The tendency to control contractual freedom received support from growing movements of protest and reform which, toward the end of the nineteenth century, began everywhere to share political and social power and to influence the formation of social policy. These movements gained strength during the great depressions of the late nineteenth century, fueled by the vigorous public reaction against railroad amalgamations and the pioneer trusts, child labor, unregulated working conditions, social insecurity, and other evils of contemporary industrial society. Experience in dealing with these problems strengthened doubts as to the universal validity of the belief in the success of unregulated individualism. Society, in granting freedom of contract, does not guarantee that all members of the community will be able to utilize it to the same extent. The use that can actually be made of contract depends on the system governing the distribution of property: to the extent that the law sanctions an unequal distribution of property, freedom of contract inevitably be-

---

38. On this development, see G. Gilmore, Security Interests in Personal Property §43.2 (1965).

39. Pound, *supra* note 35, at 482; United States v. Bethlehem Steel, 315 U.S. 289, 312 (1942), *infra* p. 576; on the attitude of English courts of equity in the eighteenth century, see Atiyah.

40. Williston, Freedom of Contract, 6 Cornell L.Q. 365, 373 (1921). On the decline of equity, see Stone, The Decline of Equity, 5 Colum. L. Rev. 20 (1905); Hanbury, The Field of Modern Equity, 45 L.Q. Rev. 12 (1920); see, however, Baker at 79-82, 89-99.

41. See p. 558 *infra*.

comes a one-sided privilege. Society, by guaranteeing that it will not interfere with the exercise of power by contract, enables the enterpriser to legislate by contract in a substantially authoritarian manner without using the appearance of authoritarian forms. According to a theory that has gained wide popular appeal, many an industrial empire has strengthened its power by employing contract as a weapon of industrial warfare.[42]

Only slowly did American courts recognize the dangers inherent in the inequality of bargaining power. Convinced of the justice of the system of property,[43] upon which the justice of freedom of contract rests, they believed that the existence of large industrial empires served the interest of society as a whole. Only the fittest deserved to survive, and the failure of many enterprises to survive the competitive struggle simply indicated that their services did not sufficiently benefit society as a whole. Antitrust laws, designed to promote freedom of competition, were in some famous cases interpreted in ways favorable to the power of industrial combina-

---

42. As always when dealing with opinion, the student should be alert to the possibility that the countercurrent supporting social control by state action draws its psychological strength from attitudes and convictions that may not have accurately reflected the objective facts of economic and social life. See Sharp, The Limits of Law, 61 Ethics 270, 276-279 (1951); Promises, Mistake and Reciprocity, 19 U. Chi. L. Rev. 286, 294-296 (1952).

43. The following excerpt from a lecture of the late President Hadley of Yale, delivered at the University of Berlin in 1908, contains a provocative formulation of the significance of the system of property. Discussing "The Constitutional Position of Property in America," he said:

> When it is said, as it commonly is, that the fundamental division of powers in the modern State is into legislative, executive and judicial, the student of American institutions may fairly note an exception. The fundamental division of powers in the Constitution of the United States is between voters on the one hand and property owners on the other. The forces of democracy on one side, divided between the executive and the legislature, are set over against the forces of property on the other side, with the judiciary as arbiter between them: the Constitution itself not only forbidding the legislature and executive to trench upon the rights of property, but compelling the judiciary to define and uphold those rights in a manner provided by the Constitution itself.
>
> This theory of American politics has not often been stated. But it has been universally acted upon. One reason why it has not been more frequently stated is that it has been acted upon so universally that no American of earlier generations ever thought it necessary to state it. It has had the most fundamental and far-reaching effects upon the policy of the country. To mention but one thing among many, it has allowed the experiment of universal suffrage to be tried under conditions essentially different from those which led to its ruin in Athens or in Rome. The voter was omnipotent — within a limited area. He could make what laws he pleased, as long as those laws did not trench upon property right. He could elect what officers he pleased, as long as those officers did not try to do certain duties confided by the Constitution to the property holders. Democracy was complete as far as it went, but constitutionally it was bound to stop short of social democracy. I will not go so far as to say that the set of limitations on the political power of the majority in favor of the political power of the property owner has been a necessary element in the success of universal suffrage in the United States. I will say unhesitatingly that it has been a decisive factor in determining the political character of the nation and the actual development of its industries and institutions.

64 Independent 837 (1908).

tions. State statutes attempting to protect the weaker contracting party against abuses of freedom of contract by fixing minimum wages and maximum hours in employment and by attempting to outlaw discrimination against union members by means of yellow dog contracts did not fare any better at the hands of American courts. The climate of opinion prevailing at the end of the last century and well into this one is strikingly illustrated by the celebrated cases of Lochner v. New York, 198 U.S. 45 (1904), Adair v. United States, 208 U.S. 161 (1907), and Coppage v. Kansas, 236 U.S. 1 (1914). Declaring such statutes unconstitutional under the due process clause of the fourteenth amendment, these decisions elevated liberty of contract to the status of a fundamental property right. Pitney, J., speaking for the majority of the court in Coppage v. Kansas, which declared an anti-yellow dog statute unconstitutional, formulated the then-prevailing philosophy of Social Darwinism.

> . . . No doubt, wherever the right of private property exists, there must and will be inequalities of fortune; and thus it naturally happens that parties negotiating about a contract are not equally unhampered by circumstances. This applies to all contracts, and not merely to that between employer and employee. Indeed a little reflection will show that wherever the right of private property and the right of free contract co-exist, each party when contracting is inevitably more or less influenced by the question whether he has much property, or little, or none; for the contract is made to the very end that each may gain something that he needs or desires more urgently than that which he proposes to give in exchange. And, since it is self-evident that, unless all things are held in common, some persons must have more property than others, it is from the nature of things impossible to uphold freedom of contract and the right of private property without at the same time recognizing as legitimate those inequalities of fortune that are the necessary result of the exercise of those rights. But the Fourteenth Amendment, in declaring that a State shall not "deprive any person of life, liberty or property without due process of law," gives to each of these an equal sanction; it recognizes "liberty" and "property" as co-existent human rights, and debars the States from any unwarranted interference with either.[44]

It is significant that the opposing viewpoint had already found expression ten years earlier in the dissenting opinion of Mr. Justice Holmes in Lochner v. New York. (The majority had declared unconstitutional a

---

44. 236 U.S. 1, 17 (1914). As late as 1936 a New York act fixing a minimum wage for women was held invalid in Morehead v. New York ex rel. Tipaldo, 298 U.S. 587 (1936). The whole doctrine was abandoned a year later. West Coast Hotel v. Parrish, 300 U.S. 379 (1937). Consult also Phelps Dodge Corp. v. NLRB, 313 U.S. 177 (1941). An attempt on the part of labor unions to have anti-closed-shop statutes declared invalid because they interfered with freedom of contract was unsuccessful. Lincoln Federal Labor Union v. Northwestern Iron Metal Co., 335 U.S. 525 (1949).

New York statute imposing maximum hours for work in bakeries.) In the words of Mr. Justice Holmes:

> The case is decided upon an economic theory which a large part of the country does not entertain. If it were a question whether I agreed with that theory, I should desire to study it further and long before making up my mind. But I do not conceive that to be my duty, because I strongly believe that my agreement or disagreement has nothing to do with the right of a majority to embody their opinions in law. It is settled by various decisions of this court that state constitutions and state laws may regulate life in many ways which we as legislators might think as injudicious or if you like as tyrannical as this, and which equally with this interfere with the liberty to contract. Sunday laws and usury laws are ancient examples. A more modern one is the prohibition of lotteries. The liberty of the citizen to do as he likes so long as he does not interfere with the liberty of others to do the same, which has been a shibboleth for some well-known writers, is interfered with by school laws, by the Post Office, by every state or municipal institution which takes his money for purposes thought desirable, whether he likes it or not. The Fourteenth Amendment does not enact Mr. Herbert Spencer's Social Statics.[45]

It was several decades before the spirit of Holmes' *Lochner* dissent, with its recognition that freedom must sometimes be limited in the interest of its own preservation, began to have an appreciable influence on the law of contracts. As Aaron Director observed,

> There may once have been substantial merit in the notion that the free-market system would steadily gain in strength if only it were freed of widespread state interference. By 1934 it became evident that a combination of a hands-off policy, which permitted the proliferation of monopoly power, and promiscuous political interference, which strengthened such power, threatened "disintegration and collapse" of the economic organisation. And only the "wisest measures by the state" could restore and maintain a free-market system.[46]

Very gradually the conviction took hold that political democracy is not sufficient by itself to secure the meaningful liberty men rightly desire. To overcome the deep sense of frustration felt by many, and to establish the material conditions needed to give existing legal freedoms something more than paper worth, political democracy (many argued) had to be

45. 198 U.S. 45, 75 (1904). Consult also Muller v. Oregon, 208 U.S. 412 (1908), and the dissenting opinions in Morehead v. New York ex rel. Tipaldo, 298 U.S. 587 (1936).
46. Aaron Director's Prefatory Note to H. Simons, Economic Policy for a Free Society *vi* (1948). A school of thought, influenced by both Simons and Director, has emerged in recent years that advocates the testing of contract doctrines in terms of economic efficiency and wealth maximization. See R. Posner, Economic Analysis of Law (2d ed. 1977); A. Kronman & R. Posner, The Economics of Contract Law (1979). The views of Simons and the Chicago School are not identical.

supplemented by economic and social democracy.[47] In the course of this debate, the rhetoric of freedom of contract was drowned out by the rhetoric of freedom *from* contract, and equality of opportunity.[48]

Social control of contractual association, which began as a counter-current in the early days of laissez-faire libertarianism, has finally swelled into a main current of thought. One consequence of this development has been the breakdown of the classical conception of contract law as a unitary body of legal doctrine and the emergence (typically through legislative enactment) of whole branches of specialized law, and even specialized tribunals, associated with particular contracts. Labor law now regulates a substantial number of contracts between employer and employee.[49] Securities law regulates the purchase and sale of corporate securities. Public utilities must make contracts with persons in their service areas on terms set by a governmental body.[50] Special consumer legislation abounds, many insurance contracts are standardized by statute in whole or in part,[51] and government contracts, which play an increasingly important role in our economy, have peculiar characteristics of their own.[52] It has been said that special law has increased to such an extent that the general law of contract now covers only a small portion of the actual contracts made.[53] And even within this restricted field, the law is said to have little practical effect, since businessmen are inclined to view contracts as flexible commitments and to avoid litigation whenever possible.[54]

47. This is taken from Kessler, Natural Law, Justice and Democracy — Some Reflections about Law and Justice, 19 Tul. L. Rev. 32, 59-60 (1944). On the changing meaning of democracy, see C. B. Macpherson, The Life and Times of Liberal Democracy (1977). See also Kronman, Contract Law and Distributive Justice, 89 Yale L.J. 472 (1980).

48. The phrase "freedom from contract" is taken from Patterson, An Apology for Consideration, 58 Colum. L. Rev. 929, 949 (1958). See also W. Friedmann, Law in a Changing Society 90 et seq. (1959).

49. On American labor law see further Summers, Collective Agreements and the Law of Contracts, 78 Yale L.J. 525 (1968); p. 16 *infra*.

50. Restatement of Torts §763. For a discussion of the economic issues, see J. Bain, Industrial Organization 542 (1959).

51. On consumer legislation, see Ch. 4, §2; on insurance, see Ch. 4, §3.

52. Government contracts are based on forms provided in advance, which are submitted to contractors for competitive bidding; typically, they contain stringent clauses to protect the government against unjust claims, clauses that may not stand up under judicial scrutiny in litigation. In the adjustment of claims, administrative boards often have the final say on questions of fact. The government has a higher duty than the ordinary party to a contract to disclose facts affecting the decision of the other party. Finally, government contracts are subject to renegotiation to prevent undue profits. This note is conspicuously indebted to Patterson, The Interpretation and Construction of Contracts, 64 Colum. L. Rev. 833, 862 (1964); see further, Government Contracts, 29 Law and Contemp. Prob. 1-646 (1964); F. Kessler & M. Sharp, Contracts: Cases and Materials 274-276 (1953); Ch. 11, §4.

53. L. Friedman, Contract Law in America 20-24 (1965).

54. Macaulay, Non-Contractual Relations in Business: A Preliminary Study, 28 Am. Soc. Rev. 55 (1963); Macaulay, The Use and Non-Use of Contracts in the Manufacturing Industry, 9 Practical Lawyer, No. 7, 13-27 (1963).

It should not be overlooked that the law of contract is always in the background, and

Today, therefore, the individual member of the community continuously finds himself involved in contractual relations, the contents of which are predetermined for him by statute, public authority, or group action.[55] The terms and conditions under which he obtains his supply of electricity and gas will in all likelihood be regulated by a public utility commission. So will his fare, should he use a public conveyance going to work. The rent he will have to pay may be fixed by governmental authority. The price of his food will depend partly on the government's farm support program and not solely on the interplay of supply and demand in a free market. Many of the goods he uses in daily consumption will have prices that reflect suggested list prices.[56] The wages he earns, or must pay, may also have been fixed for him beforehand. And if he is a businessman, he must take care not to violate the antitrust laws which, during the last half century, have grown steadily in importance, transforming the business environment.

This picture of our world has led many to the conclusion that the idea of contract has undergone a dramatic change. Some view contract as an anachronistic concept, anticipating its merger with the general law of obligations,[57] or argue that Maine's famous formula has to be qualified if not reversed.[58] Closely connected with this criticism is the idea that more attention should be given to the difference between discrete (transactional) exchanges and continuing relations, since many of the terms of the latter type of transaction must be left open for further negotiation.[59] It has also been suggested that the modern law of contracts can be more meaningfully explained in terms of a tripartite distinction between benefit-based, detriment-based, and promise-based obligations.[60] Most chal-

---

doubtless businessmen act on many occasions with this in mind. The decision to sue will depend on many factors, including: whether the goods are "stock goods" or to be manufactured; whether the non-breaching party has suffered damages; whether the non-breaching party expects future dealings with the breaching party; in the case of relations between a large enterprise and a small supplier or distributor, whether the large enterprise feels that permitting the supplier or distributor to breach with impunity will encourage its other suppliers or distributors to rebel in a like manner.

55. Eastwood & Wortley, Administrative Law and Teaching of the Law of Contracts, 1938 J. Soc. Public Teachers of Law 23, 29; P. Atiyah, An Introduction to the Law of Contract, Ch. 1 (3d ed. 1981); W. Anson, Principles of the Law of Contracts 3-4 (Guest 25th ed. 1979).

56. Price fixing agreements would be illegal per se under Dr. Miles Medical Co. v. John D. Park & Sons Co., 220 U.S. 373 (1911), Continental T.V. Inc. v. GTE Sylvania, 433 U.S. 36 (1977), Monsanto Co. v. Spray-Rite Service Corp., 104 S. Ct. 1464, 79 L. Ed. 2d 775 (1984). See also pp. 59 et seq. *infra.*

57. G. Gilmore, The Death of Contract (1974).

58. Rehbinder, Status, Contract, and Welfare State, 23 Stan. L. Rev. 941 (1971); Hunter, An Essay on Contract and Status: Race, Marriage and the Meretricious Spouse, 64 Va. L. Rev. 1039 (1978).

59. Macneil, The Many Futures of Contracts, 47 S. Cal. L. Rev. 691 (1974); Goetz & Scott, Principles of Relational Contracts, 67 Va. L. Rev. 1089 (1981).

60. Atiyah at 5.

lenging is the controversial suggestion to merge law with economics.[61] No less challenging are the ideas developed by the Critical Legal Studies movement (*infra* p. 64).

These observations doubtless have some validity. Today, few judges (and fewer legislatures) feel enthusiasm, or even respect, for the elegant simplicities of the classical law of contracts. On the contrary, the carefully delimited classical defenses of mistake, fraud, and duress — the only defenses allowable in a strict libertarian regime — seem continually on the verge of further expansion and have recently been supplemented by a revitalized, and potentially far-reaching concept of unconscionability.[62] Social policy arguments are frequently advanced to strike down obnoxious clauses. Caveat emptor is a mere shadow of its former self. The rules of the contracting game have been softened, and bargainers are expected to act in good faith toward one another.[63] The old model of arm's length dealing is in retreat, along with the notion that a contractual relation is one of "limited commitment."[64] In their place, the confidential relation — the relation of fiduciary trust — has emerged or is emerging as the new model for both bargaining and contract performance in a large number of cases.[65]

Despite all this, however, the classical theory of contract reflects a set of values that continue to enjoy wide acceptance in our society. Most special legislation leaves considerable freedom to the parties to arrange their affairs as they wish. Labor law, for example, while imposing a duty to bargain in good faith, does not require that the parties come to terms.[66] Disclosure statutes, such as those found in the consumer field, may require that the provisions of the contract be set out clearly, but mandate very few terms. The federal government in recent years has shown a marked reluctance to impose mandatory wage and price controls, even in times of high inflation. Faith in market forces, or perhaps a lack of faith in governmental controls, is widespread and growing. Despite paternalistic arguments for directly regulating the consuming habits of the poor, con-

61. See Posner, Some Uses and Abuses of Economics in Law, 46 U. Chi. L. Rev. 281 (1979), and the Comment by Michelman, id. at 307; see further Leff, Economic Analysis of Law: Some Realism about Nominalism, 64 Va. L. Rev. 451 (1974).

62. See p. 561 *infra*.

63. Kessler & Fine, Culpa in Contrahendo, Bargaining in Good Faith and Freedom of Contract: A Comparative Study, 77 Harv. L. Rev. 401 (1964).

64. The phrase is taken from Selznick, The Ethos of American Law, included in The Americans: 1976, at 221 (I. Kristol & P. Weaver eds. 1976).

65. See Ch. 3, §4 *infra*.

66. Cox, The Duty to Bargain in Good Faith, 71 Harv. L. Rev. 1401 (1958); Duvin, The Duty to Bargain: Law in Search of Policy, 64 Colum. L. Rev. 248 (1964); Fleming, The Obligation to Bargain in Good Faith, 47 Va. L. Rev. 988 (1961); Wellington, Freedom of Contract and the Collective Bargaining Agreement, 112 U. Pa. L. Rev. 467 (1964); H. Wellington, Labor and the Legal Process 49-125 (1968); Summers, Collective Agreements and the Law of Contracts, 78 Yale L.J. 525 (1969); Weiler, Striking a New Balance: Freedom of Contract and the Prospects for Union Representation, 98 Harv. L. Rev. 311 (1984); see further Note, *infra* p. 63.

sumer legislation has not gone so far.[67] Self-reliance, it would seem, is still a valued concept in late twentieth-century America, and even those who argue that we are turning back to status after a brief flirtation with contract recognize that the roles that define a person's rights and responsibilities are not ascribed to one at birth, but are assumed more or less freely, and just as freely given up. Finally, the planning element of contract, so important in the field of business, has in recent years become increasingly important in the domain of interpersonal relations, such as marriage and cohabitation, where traditionally the contractual freedom of the individual was restricted or nonexistent.[68] As freedom of contract wanes in one area, it waxes in another, and the overall result is a world that may well be more free than its nineteenth-century counterpart (though it is certainly free in different ways).

Any society that sees value in individual autonomy must have a strong commitment to contract and to contract values. For those who think contract is dead, Selznick provides the following balanced view of the role of contract in contemporary society.

> The idea of contract is not wholly suited to modern experience; it does not help the law to grasp the realities of an administered society. Voluntarism is eroded when standardized "contracts of adhesion" leave little or no room for negotiation and when "private governments" largely determine the conditions of participation in economic life. The contract model presumes a world of independent, roughly equal actors who enter relationships of limited duration and limited commitment. A world of large-scale organizations, with their clients and constituencies, is forced into that mold only at the cost of significant distortion.
>
> Nevertheless, contract remains a pervasive and powerful instrument of facilitative law. Its premises have sometimes required reconstruction to account for stubborn realities, as when a new type of "collective" contract was evolved to make sense of labor relations. But the appeal of contract as a general idea has not yet waned significantly. In part this is so because contract, being firmly embedded in common-law experience, casts a benign light of legitimacy over rules and relationships elaborated in its name and applied to new contexts. Furthermore, the law of contracts since the nineteenth century has embodied values of freedom, equality, self-government, and legal competence. Contract preserves the integrity of the parties and upholds the principle of authority founded in consent.[69]

---

67. See 15 U.S.C.A. §§1691 et seq. (West 1982).

68. See Hunter, *supra* note 58.

69. Selznick, *supra* note 64, at 221. The persistence of contract values in our society is reinforced by the emergence of the school of thought that stresses the economic efficiency of classical contract doctrines and thereby the wisdom of laissez-faire economics. See Hayek, *supra* note 32.

CHAPTER 1

From Status to Contract
and Beyond

SIR HENRY MAINE, ANCIENT LAW 163-165 (1864): "The movement of the progressive societies has been uniform in one respect. Through all its course it has been distinguished by the gradual dissolution of family dependency, and the growth of individual obligation in its place. The Individual is steadily substituted for the Family, as the unit of which civil laws take account. The advance has been accomplished at varying rates of celerity, and there are societies not absolutely stationary in which the collapse of the ancient organisation can only be perceived by careful study of the phenomena they present. But, whatever its pace, the change has not been subject to reaction or recoil, and apparent retardations will be found to have been occasioned through the absorption of archaic ideas and customs from some entirely foreign source. Nor is it difficult to see what is the tie between man and man which replaces by degrees those forms of reciprocity in rights and duties which have their origin in the Family. It is Contract. Starting, as from one terminus of history, from a condition of society in which all the relations of Persons are summed up in the relations of Family, we seem to have steadily moved towards a phase of social order in which all these relations arise from the free agreement of Individuals. In Western Europe the progress achieved in this direction has been considerable.

"The word Status may be usefully employed to construct a formula expressing the law of progress thus indicated, which, whatever be its value, seems to be me to be sufficiently ascertained. All the forms of Status taken notice of in the Law of Persons were derived from, and to some extent are still coloured by, the powers and privileges anciently residing in the Family. If then we employ Status, agreeably with the usage of the best writers, to signify these personal conditions only, and avoid applying the term to such conditions as are the immediate or remote result of agreement, we may say that the movement of the progressive societies has hitherto been a movement *from Status to Contract*."[1]

---

1. This does not mean that Maine underestimated the role of contract in feudal society (see 323).

The master who taught us that "the movement of the progressive societies has

ADAM SMITH, LECTURES ON JUSTICE, POLICY, REVENUE
AND ARMS 131 (Cannan ed. 1896): "Breach of contract is naturally the
slightest of all injuries, because we naturally depend more on what we
possess than what is in the hands of others. A man robbed of five pounds
thinks himself much more injured than if he had lost five pounds by a
contract. Accordingly in rude ages crimes of all kinds, except those that
disturb the public peace, are slightly punished, and society is far advanced before a contract can sustain action or the breach of it be redressed. The causes of this were the little importance of contracts in
those times, and the uncertainty of language."

We all repeatedly make contracts; they are a routine part of our lives. It
is not always appreciated, however, that the perfection of the system of
contract law, as we know it today, has been accomplished only during the
last few centuries. To be sure, the term "contract" appeared early in the
common law, but it had, in the beginning, a rather restricted meaning,
including within its scope only a few of the transactions that we now
would not hesitate to classify as contracts.[2] Indeed, it was not until the
end of the eighteenth century that the term came to acquire its modern
connotation with its emphasis on the promissory basis of the contractual
branch of civil liability.[3] And, well into the next century, the law of

---

hitherto been a movement from Status to Contract," was quick to add that feudal
society was governed by the contract. There is no paradox here. In the really feudal
centuries men could do by a contract, by the formal contract of vassalage or com-
mendation, many things that can not be done now-a-days. They could contract to
stand by each other in warfare "against all men who can live and die"; they could (as
Domesday Book says) "go with their land" to any lord whom they pleased; they could
make the relation between king and subject look like the outcome of agreement; the
law of contract threatened to swallow up all public law. Those were the golden days
of "free," if "formal," contract. The idea that men can fix their rights and duties by
agreement is in its early days an unruly, anarchical idea. If there is to be any law at
all, contract must be taught to know its place.

2 Pollock & Maitland at 232-233.
    For an evaluation and criticism of Maine's thesis, see Pollock's Notes L and R to the 1930
edition (190-193, 386-388); Isaacs, The Standardizing of Contracts, 27 Yale L.J. 34, 47 (1917)
(Describing the development of status law, i.e., the standardizing of an increasing number
of contractual relationships in which society has an interest. Status law in many instances
increases "social enfranchisement," i.e., freedom in a positive sense. See further, Rehbinder, Status, Contract and the Welfare State, 23 Stan. L. Rev. 941 (1947); Macneil, The
Many Futures of Contract, 47 S. Cal. L. Rev. 691 (1974); on Maine, see further P. Stein,
Legal Evolution, ch. 5 (1980).
    2. Jackson, The Scope of the Term "Contract," 53 L.Q. Rev. 525 (1937). Medieval
lawyers, like their Roman counterparts, had no comprehensive theory of contracts and for
the same reason: the substantive law of contract was shaped in a formulary system. Simpson
at 185-196. For a modern view of just when a general law or theory of contract came into
being, see Simpson, Innovation in Nineteenth Century Contract Law, 91 L.Q. Rev. 247,
250 et seq. (1975). For a different view, at least in connection with this country, see G.
Gilmore, The Death of Contract 5 et seq. (1974).
    3. For the modern definition of contract, see 1 Corbin §3 (1963); Restatement Second
§1; U.C.C. §1-201(11); pp. 2 et seq. *supra* and Ch. 3, §1.

contracts was still not fully prepared to cope with such important matters as the contract by correspondence,[4] and the formulation of precise rules for the measure of damages.[5] Even Adam Smith's contemporary, Blackstone, whose Commentaries were first published in 1765, thought, we are told, so little of the importance of contract that he covered it in little more than forty pages.[6]

Since the days of Blackstone, the law of contract has been gradually improved to meet the needs of modern society. Yet the idea of contract is still influenced by the principle of reciprocity, a notion that can be traced back to the early period of the common law and that has stayed with us ever since in the form of the consideration doctrine.[7] "Contract," according to its famous definition in Termes de la Ley, a widely used text first published in 1527, "is a bargain or covenant between two parties where one thing is given for another which is called quid pro quo."[8] To be sure, our notions of reciprocity have become quite sophisticated as the needs of society have required a broader and more liberal enforcement of promises, and "exceptions" to the consideration requirement have been introduced by case law to protect reasonable expectations. In addition, resort has increasingly been had to legislation broadening promissory liability.[9] And yet, even if we take into account all of these changes, Anglo-American law has not yet caught up with its great rival, the civil law, in making promises generally enforceable (although it is coming closer).

"Group persistencies" (to use Pareto's term), so characteristic of the evolution of the common law,[10] have prevented the legal profession from completely remodelling the law of contracts to meet modern needs.

4. Cooke v. Oxley, 3 Durnford & East 653, 3 T.R. 653, 100 Eng. Rep. 785 (1790). The law of offer and acceptance goes back only to the nineteenth century. The common law borrowed this doctrine, along with many other doctrines, from civilian writers. Simpson, *supra* note 2, at 247, 258 et seq.

5. C. T. McCormick, Law of Damages 24 et seq. (1935). The rules relating to damages have also been traced to the civilians. Simpson, *supra* note 2, at 273 et seq. (1975).

6. 2 Blackstone, Commentaries 422-470 (1766). This is not quite accurate. 3 Blackstone, ch. 9, which is entitled Injuries to Personal Property, discusses contracts in §§202-223. Also, as Atiyah reminds us, at 215, the discussion of the Law of Persons in the first volume contains much material that we would now classify under the heading of contract.

See further Horwitz at 162-163, 170-171. Kennedy, The Structure of Blackstone's Commentaries, 28 Buff. L. Rev. 205, 231 (1979).

7. Indeed reciprocity, a universal principle of social action, can be seen at work in primitive exchange transactions in the form of gifts. Reciprocity, we are told by anthropologists and sociologists, is at the core of exchange and survives in the modern consensual contract. Gouldner, The Norm of Reciprocity, 25 Am. Soc. Rev. 171 (1960); Blau, Interaction Social Exchange, 7 Int. Enc. Soc. Sci. 452 (1968). On the bargain theory of consideration, see pp. 279 et seq. *infra*.

8. The quotation is taken from Jackson, *supra* note 2, at 525-527. In the Mirror of Justices, contract is defined as "a discourse (purparlance) between persons that something that is not done shall be done." 7 Selden Society 73 (Whitaker & Maitland eds. 1895).

9. See Ch. 5, §2.

10. For a description of the English judicial process in Weberian terms see Marsh, Principle and Discretion in the Judicial Process, 68 L.Q. Rev. 226 (1952).

Thus, only a study of the past can enable us to understand adequately the present law of contracts and its deficiencies.

A. Background

The early development of what we now call contracts (or torts, for that matter) took place not in the King's courts at Westminster, but (leaving aside the Courts Christian)[11] in local courts: county, borough, and manor courts, courts of the fair and of staple.[12] The law developed by these courts provided for the protection of such transactions as sales, loans, bailments, and suretyship. Much of this law was "unsophisticated" customary law; however, some courts, particularly those of the great cities of London, Bristol, and York, developed a highly flexible commercial law (law merchant), a matter of no small consequence since England all through the Middle Ages was an important commercial country. The law developed by the courts of London, in particular, may have significantly influenced the law of the royal courts in medieval and Tudor times.[13]

> The story of the growth of the common law in contract and elsewhere is the story of the expansion of the common law jurisdiction at the expense of other jurisdictions and the consequent development — whether by invention or reception — of a common law with which to regulate the newly acquired business.[14]

In the twelfth century the royal courts had already acquired jurisdiction over criminal and property law but had hardly begun to handle contracts. Glanvil, to whom tradition has attributed a treatise, "On the Law and Customs of the Kingdom of England" (c.1188), informs us that the royal courts could not be troubled with a breach of "private conventions" (ch. X-8). Yet, in building up a system of feudal law, the royal

11. The role of the ecclesiastical courts in the enforcement of private agreements should not be underestimated. Helmholz, Assumpsit and *Fidei Laesio*, 91 L.Q. Rev. 406 (1975); 2 Pollock & Maitland at 200-203.

12. Fifoot, ch. 13 (1949). R. Henry, Contracts in the Local Courts of Medieval England (1926); J. J. Dawson, The History of Lay Judges, 178-186 (1960). On law merchant and the merchant's court, see F. R. Sanborn, Origins of the Early English Maritime and Commercial Law (1930); R. Speidel, R. Summers & J. White, Commercial and Consumer Law 647-648 (2d ed. 1974); Baker, The Law Merchant and the Common Law Before 1700, 38 Cambridge L.J. 295 (1979).

13. Milsom at 343 and *passim*.

14. Simpson, Historical Introduction, at 2. The essay by Francis, The Structure of Judicial Administration and the Development of Contract Law in Seventeenth Century England, 83 Colum. L. Rev. 35 (1983), is an attempt to go beyond "doctrinal legal history" traditionally used and "to link law to the dynamics of common law administration." (See p. 29 *infra*.) Simpson at 1-16 and L. Fuller & M. Eisenberg, Basic Contract Law, at 40-47 (4th ed. 1981) contain admirable overviews of the evolution of contract law.

courts inevitably had to protect many rights that would now arise out of contract but that then arose out of more permanent relationships, which we might call proprietary.[15] To quote Maitland, "the feeble law of contract [was] supplemented by a generous liberality in the creation of incorporeal things."[16]

In the interest of a smooth administration, the techniques of dispensing royal justice became standardized in a formulary system. Royal justice was set in motion by "writs,"[17] obtained for a fee from the Chancellor's office, that received the plaintiff's complaint and authorized the courts to take his case. Gradually, common forms were established and the writs themselves became, according to Fitzherbert, the "'fundamentals' on which the whole law depends."[18] The process of standardization of writs resulted in a rigid and formal system of justice, which could only develop through judicial fictions and evasions and what Baker calls "jurisdictional shifts," the spread of one form of action to remedy the deficiencies of others.[19] Small wonder that the evolution of the law of contract was not an unbroken line of principle, for if the logic of the writs had been meticulously followed, the "development," in the words of Milsom, "would have been impossible."[20]

In choosing the form of action with which to proceed in the royal courts, a plaintiff had to consider, with respect to each writ, the nature of the judicial process available, the remedy that could be obtained, the mode of proof called for, and the factual and formal requirements of the particular writ. Some forms of action were clearly more advantageous than others to a plaintiff in any or all of these respects. The evolution of the substantive law of contracts therefore has to be explored in terms of adjective law: the slow but steady extension of the forms of action most procedurally advantageous to the enforcement of private agreements.[21]

---

15. Milsom's Introduction to Pollock & Maitland at *lii*. See also 1 W. H. Page, The Law of Contracts 11 (1920):

> In place of contracts for work and labor of the modern law, we find land held by tenure of rendering services for the overlord. At a time at which interest could not be recovered, the favorite means by which a landowner borrowed money was by granting a lease for years at a nominal rent in consideration of present payment of money. . . . Contracts for support in money or in kind were treated as grants or realty and this theory was extended even to cases in which no charge was made upon any corporeal realty to secure payment.

16. The quotation is taken from Milsom's introduction to Pollock & Maitland at *liii*.
17. For a description of the writs, see F. Maitland, Forms of Action at Common Law (1909, repr. 1962).
18. Baker at 52, citing the Preface to De Natura Brevium (c.1530); see also id. at 49.
19. Baker at 263.
20. Milsom at 249.
21. 2 Pollock & Maitland at 568. "The subsequent development of forms will consist almost entirely of modifications of a single action, namely, Trespass, until at length it and its progeny — Ejectment, Case, Assumpsit, Trover — will have ousted neary all the older actions." Id. at 564.

Covenant. Of the two older writs, debt and covenant, debt is the more ancient.[22] Covenant, however, as Milsom has said, represents "an elementary legal idea . . . familiar to the modern mind." To the medieval lawyer the word covenant (Latin, *conventio*) meant agreement.[23] The writ of covenant, which became available in the royal courts "as a matter of course" in the thirteenth century,[24] held out the promise of a form of action applicable to all contracts. But the destiny of covenant lay in a different direction. By the late thirteenth or early fourteenth century the common law courts had imposed on the writ of covenant the requirement of a sealed instrument (a specialty) as evidence of the agreement.[25] "Simple" (informal) contracts were thus eliminated from the scope of the writ, the enforcement of such contracts being left to the local courts.[26] This shift in jurisdiction reduced the influx of cases from the local to the royal courts.[27]

The writ of covenant was rarely used except in apprenticeship litigation.[28] Its unpopularity, however, cannot be attributed entirely to the requirement of a seal. Drawing up a specialty and affixing a seal was no "great chore,"[29] and, as we shall see, sealed instruments were very common, especially among the commercial classes. More probably, the demise of the writ of covenant was due to the fact that it had certain disadvantages when compared with debt, the next writ to be discussed: after 1352 the rigorous process of arrest or outlawry was available in debt but not in covenant.[30] Another explanation is that the remedy given by covenant was inadequate. Originally, the remedy may have been specific performance.[31] Eventually, however, a plaintiff suing in covenant could only recover damages for the wrong or tort of nonperformance. But damages for nonperformance were insufficient in many cases, since the plaintiff might not recover for consequential losses caused by the nonperformance. Thus, the losses occasioned by poor or tardy performance might not be compensated.[32] For example, a defendant whose failure to

22. Simpson at 9.
23. Milsom at 246.
24. Simpson at 9.
25. Simpson at 10-11. This made all the more sense since the parties could not testify. As a result the word "covenant" eventually lost its meaning as "agreement"; indeed the very idea that an agreement could be the basis of an action got lost. Covenant came to mean a formal executory contract under seal. Milsom at 248-249.
26. Provided the claim was for less than 40 shillings, a sizable sum before the decline in the purchasing power of money resulting from the influx of silver from the New World. Milsom at 60, 240, 241; Beckerman, The Forty Shilling Jurisdictional Limit in Medieval English Personal Actions, Legal History Studies 110 (D. Jenkins ed. 1972). See further p. 29 *infra*.
27. Milsom at 65; see also id. at 244-246; Baker at 265, 266; Simpson at 10-13.
28. Milsom at 251-252.
29. Simpson at 90.
30. Milsom at 252.
31. Simpson at 13-14.
32. Milsom at 252, 326-328; Baker, Introduction at 264 et. seq.

fulfill his promise to strengthen a river wall caused the plaintiff's land to be flooded and his crop to be lost had only to strengthen the wall to avoid liability in covenant.[33] The sealed instruments used by the commercial classes avoided this problem of inadequate damages by providing for substantial liquidated damages in case of nonperformance.[34] These instruments, known as bonds, were actionable in debt; they will be discussed in more detail in the next section.

Debt. The royal courts did not leave the enforcement of all informal contracts to the local courts for very long. As early as the twelfth century, the common law courts recognized the writ of debt, which could be used to enforce "real" contracts, in the terminology of the civilians. The writ of debt was originally used, for example, by a lender to recover money lent, by a buyer to recover specific goods or fungible goods from stock, by a seller to recover the purchase price of goods sold, etc. Later the writ of detinue came to be distinguished from the writ of debt, the latter being restricted to recovery of specific goods (or their value[35]), the former being used to recover a fixed sum in the remaining instances mentioned above and others. Tradition has it that detinue was based on property, on an owning, debt on a duty or an owing.[36] In the language of the controversial theory of Barbour, debt and detinue illustrate the distinction between obligation and property.[37]

The action of debt was not limited to informal contracts. "As anything that we should call contract was not of its essence . . . it could be used whenever a fixed sum, a sum certain, was due from one man to another."[38] There was, to use the traditional classification, debt on the record, debt on an obligation (when the creditor produced a deed or bond), and debt sur contract (when a creditor sued for a fixed sum owed under an informal agreement).[39]

According to Ames, "[a] simple contract debt, as well as a debt by specialty, was originally conceived of, not as a contract, in the modern sense, that is, as a promise, but as a grant."[40] Although the medieval

33. The example is taken from Milsom at 252.
34. See also Simpson at 117 for the procedural advantages of debt sur obligation over covenant.
35. For a discussion of the splitting of the composite writ of debt-detinue, see Fifoot at 217.
36. Baker at 267, 2 Pollock & Maitland at 206.
37. W. T. Barbour, The History of Contract in Early English Equity 26-28 (1914). See Simpson at 75 for a criticism.
38. 2 Pollock & Maitland at 210.
39. See Jackson, The Scope of the Term "Contract," 53 L.Q. Rev. 525 (1937). The word "contract" was intimately connected with the action of debt until after Slade's Case (discussed *infra* p. 32), while the scope of the action of debt was wider than what we now call contract. A penalty imposed by statute, for instance, could be recovered in debt. Lawyers in describing this phenomenon frequently spoke of contracts-in-law. Id. at 529. See also 2 Pollock & Maitland at 204.
40. J. B. Ames, Lectures on Legal History and Miscellaneous Legal Essays 150 (1913); Simpson at 79-80.

lawyers did not emphasize the consensual nature of the debts actionable
by the writ of debt, they were aware that in many cases a debt arising out
of an informal contract or a debt by specialty was the result of a voluntary
agreement. The relationship between "contract," which gave rise to a
writ of debt, and "covenant," which was the medieval word for agreement, was not lost on the legal profession of this period.[41]

The most striking example of the consensual nature of debt comes in
the field of sales. A seller could sue in debt not only if he delivered the
goods, but also if he was willing to deliver. For the seller, the contract had
the effect of passing property in the goods sold to the buyer.[42] The buyer
was in a different position. Unless there was an express agreement for
credit, the buyer could not bring an action of debt (in the case of fungible
goods) or detinue (in the case of specific goods) until he paid or tendered
payment. The seller could withdraw from the contract until such time.
The interesting aspect of this rule respecting buyers is that it was rationalized on the basis of the intent of the parties.[43]

Whatever the consensual aspects of the writ of debt may have been,
promise was not of its essence. If, for example, a debtor defaulted in an
installment, and therefore broke his promise to pay in a timely manner,
the creditor generally had no recourse by the action of debt to recover the
installment. He had to wait in most cases until the last installment fell due
and then sue for the entire debt. The breach of promise to pay on time
was later redressed by the action of assumpsit.[44] The contractual debt
itself was not considered to be based on promise. Debt lay to enforce an
obligation or duty of payment arising out of a transaction *re*.[45] Thus, the
remedy afforded by an action of debt was recuperative in nature. A successful plaintiff received the amount owed, plus damages for wrongful
detention.[46]

41. Simpson at 188.
42. Milsom, Sale of Goods in the Fifteenth Century, 77 L.Q. Rev. 257, 282-284 (1961);
Simpson at 161-164; Stoljar, A History of Contract at Common Law 27 (1975) (maintains
that bargain and sale remained a real contract until the advent of assumpsit); Francis, *supra*
note 14, at 79-80.
43. Simpson at 164-169; see also Barton, Review of Simpson, 27 Toronto L. Rev. 373,
375 (1977), referring to the "eccentric" view of Brian, C.J. in Y.B. Pasch. 17 Edw. IV, f. 1,
pl. 2 (1478), and Y.B. Hil. 18 Edw. IV, f. 21, pl. 1 (1479), that property passed to the buyer
immediately on sale even when credit was not given, a view that passed into the law of sales
in the nineteenth century. See Blackburn, Contract on Sale 196 (1845).
44. Simpson at 66-68.
45. Baker at 267.
46. The measure of damages in debt is a matter of controversy. Frowicke, C.J.C.P., in
Orwell v. Mortoft, Y.B. Mich. 20 Henry VII, f. 8, pl. 18, Keilway 69, 72 (1505), argued that a
plaintiff buyer could only receive back his down payment in an action of debt against a
defaulting seller. See Stoljar, *supra* note 42, at 40-41 (1975). Cases do exist, however, where
the plaintiff suing in debt obtained substantial damages for wrongful detention. See Wolf v.
Meggs, Cro. Eliz. 545, 78 Eng. Rep. 70 (Q.B. 1597); McGovern, The Enforcement of
Informal Contracts in the Later Middle Ages, 59 Calif. L. Rev. 1145, 1161 (1971); 2 Pollock
& Maitland at 215.

The recuperative nature of the remedy in debt may help to explain the statement frequently found in the old case law that debt sur contract presupposed a quid pro quo.[47] The requirement of a quid pro quo is the basis for the theory advanced by Ames and others that debt presupposed a half-performed bargain, and that medieval law recognized only two types of contracts: sealed and real (unilateral, half-performed) contracts.[48] Simpson has pointed out, however, that quid pro quo did not mean that one party had to perform his side of the agreement for the contract to be binding. As we have seen in the case of sales, wholly executory contracts were binding and actionable. In those cases, the quid pro quo meant simply that a reciprocity of exchange was required, a reciprocity that could be satisfied where a debtor-buyer had a reciprocal remedy against a creditor-seller for the goods sold but not yet delivered.[49]

In most cases, a defendant in an action of debt sur contract could elect compurgation, or wager of law, as the mode of trial. The defendant, along with eleven others (or however many the court might designate), would swear that he owed or detained nothing.[50] This mode of trial, viewed today as having distinct advantages over jury trial for the debtor, may have enjoyed more popularity with creditors than one might expect.[51] Be that as it may, a prudent creditor rarely had to take the risk of a debtor successfully waging his law. Wager of law was unavailable if the plaintiff was able to introduce a sealed instrument or if the obligation had become a debt of recognizance. To be on the safe side, a creditor either insisted on a bond under seal containing a defeasance clause making the bond null and void when the debtor performed (in which case the creditor sued in debt, but, to use the traditional classification, on the "obligation"); or he refused to make an advance until a judgment (by default) against the prospective debtor had been obtained or a recognizance had been recorded on the plea rolls, often with the covenant that the sheriff could levy execution in case of default. A mercantile creditor could also have his claim recorded on a roll kept by the mayor of each important town, and could obtain speedy execution.[52]

In transactions of financial importance, the business community and its lawyers hit upon a most ingenious device to cope with the slow development of contract law, and to avoid wager of law and the arbitrariness of

47. Mervyn v. Lyds, Dyer 90A, 73 Eng. Rep. 195 (1553); "quid pro quo is necessary to every contract." See Simpson at 193-194.
48. See generally Ames, *supra* note 40, Lecture VIII (1913), and Fifoot, ch. 10.
49. Simpson at 194-195; Baker, Review of Atiyah, 43 Cambridge L.J. 467, 468 (1980). On the development of "pure" executory contracts in assumpsit, see Baker, id., at 467, 468; note 123 *infra*; Simpson at 459 et seq.
50. Simpson at 137 et seq.
51. T. F. T. Plucknett, A Concise History of the Common Law 116, 647 (5th ed. 1956); Simpson at 139-140.
52. Plucknett, *supra* note 51, at 391; Thorne, Tudor Social Transformation and Social Change, 26 N.Y.U. L. Rev. 10, 19-20 (1951); Simpson at 140-144.

damage awards by juries. If the parties wanted to enter into what we now call a bilateral contract, they set up their agreement indirectly by the exchange of bonds: two independent unilateral contracts were used. A seller of land that had been sold at one hundred pounds, for instance, deliverd to the buyer a bond promising two hundred pounds in case of default. The buyer in turn delivered a bond for double the purchase price. These bonds contained defeasance clauses, typically written on the back; the bond became void on performance of the terms of the contract laid down in the sealed indenture.[53]

Any kind of agreement (for example, large family settlements) could be cast in this mold. Penal bonds were quite popular even though the argument that the penal sum was excessive was unavailable, as was the defense of usury.[54] Contests about the performance of the conditions in the indenture, by contrast, went to the jury.[55]

These conditional bonds, which were the means of doing large scale business, were in use for a long time in both England and this country, and they involved some of the most important transactions coming before the central courts.[56] Their importance began to wane in the seventeenth century, however, when equity and common law courts began to show an increasing willingness to give relief against excessive bonds, a movement that culminated in the distinction between penalties and liquidated damages.[57]

Like covenant, debt never succeeded in becoming the principal means of enforcing contracts. It could not, because of its shortcomings with respect to informal contracts. Quid pro quo was rather narrowly defined, pleading rules were most complex, recoverable damages were apparently inadequate, debt did not lie against a debtor's executor, and the defendant in most cases was entitled to wage his law. Prudence dictated the use of formalities, but promisees were not always prescient or educated enough to avail themselves of the necessary forms, nor were formalities always convenient.

Assumpsit. Debt and detinue covered a very considerable area of informal contract law, the sale of goods, bailments and loans of money. Covenant was appropriate for the residue of promises. However, the development of these "personal actions" was stunted by formal requirements, technical rules, inadequate remedies, and antiquated modes of

53. Milsom at 250-251; 2 Pollock & Maitland 213 et seq.; Simpson at 90-112.
54. Simpson at 113-117. On usury see generally J. T. Noonan, The Scholastic Analysis of Usury (1957); R. Tawney, Religion and the Rise of Capitalism (1926); R. Tawney's Introduction to T. Wilson, A Discourse upon Usury (1925); B. Nelson, The Idea of Usury (1949).
55. Simpson at 101. The law of conditions was developed in connection with conditional bonds. See Kingston v. Preston, *infra* p. 979.
56. Simpson at 88; Baker at 270.
57. Simpson at 118-125; Baker at 271. For the American experience, see Horwitz at 167-170.

trial.[58] Covenant, as we have seen, could not be used in suits at common law on informal agreements or on formal promises to do something; e.g., promises to build a house or to convey land were unprotected.[59] As a result, it became increasingly frequent for there to be "just claims" for which no remedy was available.[60]

So long as local courts adequately handled most contractual obligations, the need for an expanded royal jurisdiction was hardly felt. But the local courts were reluctant or unable to change their archaic procedures to accommodate the changing needs of society.[61] Furthermore, the drop in the value of currency due to inflation meant that more and more informal contracts fell within the jurisdiction of the royal courts,[62] all the more since the extensive role played by ecclesiastical tribunals in disputes over breach of faith had begun to decline, and by 1550 had disappeared completely.[63]

In the fifteenth century, the Chancellor began to intervene to fill the gaps left by debt and covenant. Equity granted specific performance on parol contracts and even entertained actions on the ground that at common law the defendant could wage his law.[64] During the reign of Henry VIII it came to be said that "a man shall have remedy in the Chancery for covenants made without specialty if the party have sufficient witnesses to prove the covenants."[65] This liberal attitude of the Chancellor toward contracts could not remain unnoticed; it doubtless gave encouragement to the common law courts to "remedy the defects of their own system."[66] This was all the more necessary since there was a phenomenal increase in the amount of litigation in the course of the sixteenth century due to the rise in population, the growth of industry and, according to the controversial theory of Coke, the increase of wealth by lay persons resulting from the dissolution of monasteries.[67]

One of the many problems facing the legal system was how to reform

58. Simpson, Introduction at 3.
59. Baker, 2 Spelman's Reports, 94 Selden Society 51-53 (1978).
60. Milsom at 342-343.
61. Simpson, Introduction at 3, 4.
62. Baker, *supra* note 59.
63. Id.
64. Helmholz, *supra* note 11, at 426-428.
65. Baker at 272-273. Simpson, Historical Introduction, at 4. For details of the theory of contracts developed by Chancery, see Barbour, *supra* note 37, ch. 4. The competition of Chancery is alluded to in Y.B. Mich. 21 Hen. VII, f. 41, pl. 66 (1506).
66. According to the thesis developed by Francis (*supra* note 14), the judiciary and the legal profession had a substantial interest, pecuniary and otherwise, in preserving the existing structure of adjudication. To do this, the caselaw capacity of the court system had to be maximized. An administrative structure emerged that conserved judicial energy by permitting delegation of function and at the same time facilitated tight judicial control over the delegated task. This "controlled delegation system" strongly influenced the development of procedural and substantive contract law, e.g., the form of pleading, the law of evidence, the roles of judge and jury, the law of conditions and of substantial performance, and the law of damages.
67. Francis, *supra* note 14, at 41 et seq. See further Milsom at 60-81.

the writ system, i.e., how to construct another writ to do the work of the
writs of debt and covenant (without being too conspicuous about it, for
by the reign of Henry VIII the rule against double remedies had become a
settled rule of law).[68] The form of action chosen to accomplish this task
was trespass on the case,[69] and (to anticipate the future) by the sixteenth
century a species of case, assumpsit, had acquired "its own identity" and
was well on its way to supporting a law of consensual contract.[70]

Assumpsit and Covenant. In the fourteenth century a plaintiff bringing an action of trespass on the case against a defendant for doing badly
what he had undertaken to do, i.e., for misfeasance, would face the argument that he was using the wrong writ. "This sounds in covenant." But
the plaintiff could not sue in covenant if he lacked a sealed instrument.
Nor would a person in his position be likely to have formalized his agreement with the defendant. He might be a patient suing his surgeon for
maiming his hand, a customer suing his smith for incompetently shoeing
his horse, thereby causing its death, or a bailor suing a ferryman for
overloading the ferry, causing it to sink and the plaintiff's goods to be
lost.[71] Even if the plaintiff could have brought an action of covenant, "[i]t
would have been useless to order [the defendant] to keep his covenant."[72]
The damage was done, and the plaintiff had been wronged.

In the course of the fourteenth century, the royal courts began to
reject the defendant's argument that actions for negligent misfeasance of
this sort should be brought in covenant and not case. At the time it was
not asked whether the basis of the defendant's liability was negligence or
breach of contract; it would be several centuries before the law would
draw the distinction between tort and contract. It can be said, however,
that the undertaking, the assumpsit, played an important (if not decisive)
role in actions on the case for misfeasance.[73]

If a carpenter undertook to build a house and did nothing, no action
would lie without a sealed instrument. This was decided in 1400,[74] the

    68. Baker, Introduction at 76-77.
    69. Trespass (Latin, *transgressio*) meant wrong, and trespass on the case gave a plaintiff
damages as compensation for the wrong done to him. The development of trespass on the
case in the fourteenth century, which represented a relaxation of a jurisdictional boundary
that barred royal courts from entertaining suit for wrongs other than those alleging force
and arms (*vi et armis*) or a breach of the king's peace (*contra pacem regis*), need not detain
us here. For details of the controversial origins of the action on the case, see Milsom at 244
et seq.; Plucknett, Case and the Statute of Westminster II, 31 Calif. L. Rev. 778 (1931);
Holdsworth, Note, 47 L.Q. Rev. 334 (1931); Landon, The Action on the Case and the Statute
of Westminster II, 52 L.Q. Rev. 68 (1936); Dix, The Origins of the Action of Trespass on the
Case, 46 Yale L.J. 1142 (1937); A. K. Kiralfy, The Action on the Case (1951); Baker at 58-59.
    70. Simpson at 199, 273, 274.
    71. See Simpson at 203-204.
    72. Baker at 274. On the limitations to the remedy in covenant, see p. 24 *supra*.
    73. Simpson at 207.
    74. Watton v. Brinth, Y.B. Mich. 2 Hen. IV, f. 3, pl. 9; Fifoot at 91.

courts drawing a distinction between misfeasance and nonfeasance. "A mere failure to perform cannot be anything but a matter of covenant."[75] The distinction was often difficult to make, and lawyers attempted to devise artful ways of getting around it; at times, courts would simply characterize a nonfeasance as a misfeasance.

Early on, plaintiffs successfully brought actions of assumpsit for non-feasance against innkeepers and others who by virtue of their calling were required by the common law or custom to contract with the public.[76] In other cases a plaintiff might allege that he had been deceived by the defendant's promise. The allegation of deceit, borrowed from the law of warranty developed in the mercantile courts, was first successfully used in cases against attorneys who had taken fees from both sides, or revealed counsel to adversaries. These were also public offenses. An action of assumpsit in which deceit was alleged was also held proper in a case against a counsellor who had agreed to try to procure a piece of land for his client, but who instead bought it himself and sold it to a third party.[77] A vendor was then held liable in assumpsit for conveying land to a third party, land which had been promised to the plaintiff and for which he had prepaid.[78] The allegation of deceit, which apparently meant that the promisee was deceived and not necessarily that the promisor was deceitful, became increasingly popular in the sixteenth century.

The distinction between misfeasance and nonfeasance was finally abandoned in the sixteenth century with the case of Pickering v. Thoroughgood (1533).[79] This "momentous development" posed problems, however. *Pickering* itself was a case of a buyer suing a seller in case for failure to deliver malt that had already partially been paid for. The problem posed by this and other cases was that, in theory at least, the plaintiff already had an action against the defendant in debt sur contract. As we have mentioned, there was a rule against double remedies. A second problem, posed by all nonfeasance cases, was in drawing a line between enforceable and unenforceable promises. Without the "doctrine of non-

75. Milsom, Reason in the Development of the Common Law, 81 L.Q. Rev. 496, 507 et seq. (1965).

76. In Y.B. 21 Hen. VI, f. 55, pl. 12 (1443), a judge observes:

If I'm riding on the highway and I come to a village in which a smith lives, who has sufficient stuff to shoe my horse, if my horse has lost a shoe and I request him to shoe him at proper time, and I offer him sufficient for his labor, and he refuses, and if my horse is lost for want of shoes, and by his default, I say that in that event, I will have trespass on the case.

See also Baker, *supra* note 59, at 262 et seq.

77. Somerton's Case, Y.B. Hil. 11 Hen. VI, f. 18, pl. 10 (1433). See Simpson at 253, Baker at 278-279.

78. Doige's Case, Y.B. Trin. 20 Hen. VI, f. 34, pl. 4 (1442), 51 Selden Society 97 (Hemmant); Simpson at 255 et seq.

79. Spelman's Reports, 93 Selden Society 4, 5 (1977); 94 Selden Society 247; also given in Simpson at 608.

feasance," the potential existed for the enforcement of any promise or undertaking. The first problem was eventually resolved in Slade's Case.[80] The second problem was answered with the development of the doctrine of consideration.[81]

Assumpsit and Debt. The story of assumpsit's encroachment on the domain of debt is long, complex, and controversial. Its details need not detain us here; a few observations must suffice.[82]

If a debtor promised to pay off an existing debt, a creditor might argue that assumpsit should lie on the basis of the promise. The creditor's case would be enhanced if, relying on the promise, he delayed in suing for the debt, or was otherwise injured. Of the two great royal courts, King's Bench and Common Pleas, King's Bench for various reasons permitted a creditor to bring assumpsit to collect a debt, and was not particularly concerned about the promise made by the debtor, so long as the debt was proved. Common Pleas, a more conservative court with a larger interest in the preservation of the writ of debt,[83] insisted on proof of the promise, and insisted as well that the promise be supported by some consideration other than the debt itself. This conflict between the two courts came to a head in Slade's Case,[84] where it was decided that the King's Bench view should prevail.

In Slade's Case, plaintiff brought an action on the case in King's Bench for the purchase price of wheat and rye that he had sold the defendant at the defendant's special instance and request. According to the pleadings, the defendant then and there promised to pay sixteen pounds. The defendant disputed not the money owed but the availability of assumpsit. The jury found that the sale had taken place, but "there was no [other][85] promise or undertaking other than the said bargain." The purpose of the special verdict was probably to determine whether case could lie on a contract (debt) in the absence of an express promise to pay. This issue was argued for over five years by the best lawyers of the day, among them

80. 76 Eng. Rep. 1072, 4 Co. Rep. 91a, Yelv. 20; Moo. K.B. 433 (K.B. 1602).
81. On consideration and nonfeasance, see Baker at 279 et seq.; Simpson at 271-272. On consideration in general, see p. 37 *infra* and the introduction to Ch. 3, §7.
82. For more details, consult Baker, Slade's Case; Simpson at 289 et seq.; Baker at 282 et seq.; Baker, Introduction at 275 et seq.; Baker, Dark Age at 1.
83. The popular explanation for the reluctance of Common Pleas was jealousy of its monopoly over debt cases. Although Common Pleas in theory had a monopoly over cases in debt, in practice King's Bench could entertain such suits by means of a fiction involving the Bill of Middlesex. Moreover, Common Pleas itself had a general jurisdiction permitting it to entertain assumpsit actions. Thus, Common Pleas would benefit by an expansion of assumpsit. The modern explanation for the position taken by Common Pleas is that judges of that court were simply more conservative in outlook. See Simpson at 294.
84. 4 Co. Rep. 91b, 76 Eng. Rep. 1074; Yelv. 21, 80 Eng. Rep. 439, Moo. K.B. 433, 29 Eng. Rep. 677. For a discussion of Slade's Case and its background, see Baker, Slade's Case; Baker, Introduction at 275; Baker, Dark Age at 4; Simpson at 292 et seq.; Milsom at 339-353.
85. We have borrowed the insertion from Milsom at 303.

Francis Bacon for the defendant and Edward Coke for the plaintiff. According to Coke, the problem was considered by "all the judges of England" in the Exchequer Chamber and eventually the King's Bench view triumphed.[86]

After Slade's Case, the term "contract" lost its intimate connection with debt.[87] The availability of assumpsit in place of debt marked the end of wager of law for all practical purposes,[88] the action of assumpsit being tried before a jury. Although the demise of wager of law might seem to be a step forward from the modern point of view, it should be kept in mind that jury trial in the sixteenth century was a much cruder means of determining truth than it is today. The problem of perjured oath helpers was now replaced by the problem of perjured jurors, or of jurors who had a far greater freedom in deciding cases than they have today.[89] Slade's Case has therefore been cited as a contributing factor in the passage of the Statute of Frauds in 1677, which required a writing for transactions having large consequences for the parties.[90]

Another possible advantage of assumpsit was that, in contrast to debt, special damages caused by nonpayment were recoverable, e.g., losses caused by a rise in the market and other losses suffered by plaintiff in his business.[91] Whatever the availability might have been, before or even during the sixteenth century, of damages in debt for losses due to nonpayment, a frequent argument in favor of the action of assumpsit was that it allowed recovery of such damages.[92] Indeed, in theory at least, a plaintiff suing in assumpsit could only obtain damages;[93] the action was not for the recovery of debt, though Slade's Case decided that the "whole debt" should also be awarded in addition to damages, so that an action in assumpsit would bar a later action in debt.[94] Slade himself recovered sixteen pounds damages, which just happened to be equal to the debt owed.[95]

Whatever the mysteries surrounding the genesis, historical soundness, and meaning of Slade's Case,[96] one thing is certain: after it, debt sur contract became obsolete and assumpsit (case) became almost the sole

---

86. The Exchequer Chamber referred to here was not the newly created statutory court, but the older, informal Exchequer Chamber consisting of common law judges. Baker, Slade's Case at 225.

87. See note 39 *supra*.

88. Wager of law was not abolished until 1832.

89. Baker, Slade's Case at 230; Simpson at 298-299.

90. Stoljar, *supra* note 42, at 85.

91. On the controversy surrounding the measure of damages in debt, see note 46 *supra*.

92. See the argument of Frowicke, C.J.C.P., in Orwell v. Mortoft, Y.B. Mich. 20 Hen. VII, f. 8, pl. 18, Keilway 69, 72 (1505).

93. Milsom at 353.

94. 76 Eng. Rep. 1072, 1074, 4 Co. Rep. 91a, 92b, Yelv. 15, Moo K.B. 433 (K.B. 1602).

95. Baker, Slade's Case at 221 n. 45 (1971). Slade had asked for forty pounds. Kiralfy, *supra* note 69, at 228-229.

96. Consult the sources cited in note 82 *supra*.

remedy for contracts by parol that did not involve a bailment.[97] In this sense Slade's Case marks a break with the past and, according to some authors, the beginning of the modern law of contracts.[98]

Elaboration of Assumpsit: The Common Counts. However important a step Slade's Case was towards the unification of contract law, the process was not complete. Assumpsit had come to be divided into two classes: special and indebitatus assumpsit. The distinction between the two was in the manner in which they were pleaded; in indebtitatus assumpsit the plaintiff merely alleged a debt in a certain sum and a promise to pay, while in special assumpsit all the detail of the underlying transaction had to be set out specifically.[99] Both types of assumpsit could be used in place of the action of debt after Slade's Case, though special assumpsit harbored many technical traps for the careless pleader and indebitatus assumpsit was frequently attacked as invalid.[100] However, because of the opposition to general indebitatus assumpsit, and in order to avoid the pitfalls of faulty pleading in special assumpsit, the legal profession after Slade's Case revived the indebitatus count, but with a new twist.[101] Since after Slade's Case there were still a few transactions that could only be enforced by the action of debt,[102] the cautious pleader would not simply plead that the defendant was indebted to the plaintiff; he had to impress upon the court that the debt arose out of a simple contract and not out of a transaction within the exclusive jurisdiction of debt.[103] So, to be on the safe side, lawyers adopted the practice of pleading that the defendant was indebted for the price of goods sold and delivered, for money lent, for work and services performed, etc.[104] These became the so-called common counts, embodying and standardizing everyday transactions that could be enforced by assumpsit. The use of the common counts had its disadvantages for the defendant, however, particularly since the various counts could be and were combined in the pleadings so that the defen-

97. On bailment, see Simpson at 299.
98. Baker at 287.
99. A plea in special assumpsit had to set out all the facts necessary to explain the intention of the parties and the nature of the transaction, plaintiff's performance of all he was bound to perform, defendant's nonperformance or breach of contract and plaintiff's damages. Even the Latin had to be impeccable (Gardner v. Fulford, 83 Eng. Rep. 369, 1 Lev. 204 (1688)). See generally, Simpson at 301-307.
100. Simpson at 308.
101. Milsom at 354; Baker, Slade's Case at 214; Luecke, Slade's Case and the Origin of the Common Counts (pt. 3), 82 L.Q. Rev. 81, 91 (1965); Simpson at 309-313.
102. For example, an action to recover rent, or by specialty, or by record. See Simpson at 299-300.
103. Luecke, *supra* note 101.
104. H. J. Stephen, A Treatise on the Principles of Pleading in Civil Actions 312 (1824). E. Bullen & M. Leake, Precedents of Pleadings 35 (3d ed. 1868), contains a specimen and a list. It is now assumed that Slade's Case did not deal with indebitatus assumpsit. See Simpson, The Place of Slade's Case in the History of Contract, 74 L.Q. Rev. 381, 384 (1958), and his change of mind in his book, Simpson at 305 n.2.

dant could not know until trial what evidence was needed to contest the plaintiff's allegations.[105] Still, the common counts survived until the pleading reforms of the nineteenth century.[106]

Implied Contracts. Indebitatus assumpsit proved to be a highly flexible device for enforcing obligations. A central feature of that form of action, and one that accounts for its flexibility, was the implied promise. When indebitatus assumpsit was brought in lieu of debt, the promise, though alleged, did not have to be proved. The idea of an implied promise permitted the expansion of indebitatus assumpsit into areas where the implied promise could only be a fiction. In the eighteenth century, the areas covered by indebitatus assumpsit had expanded so far that Lord Mansfield in Moses v. Macferlan, 2 Burr. 1005 (1760), could make the assertion that an action of indebitatus assumpsit would lie "whenever natural justice and equity required a defendant to return money."[107]

Debt could only be brought to recover a sum certain. There were, however, situations in which parties had failed to fix the amount due. A victualer may have supplied food or a servant services without coming to an agreement beforehand about payment. Since debt was unavailable to recover a reasonable payment,[108] indebitatus assumpsit, it was thought, was also unavailable.[109] The plaintiff did, however, have an action in assumpsit on a quantum meruit or quantum valebat. Thus began the evolution of the implied (in fact) contract, as contrasted with the express contract.[110] It may be that quantum meruit and quantum valebat grew up in connection with claims by those who were bound by law to provide services, e.g., the common carrier or innkeeper.[111] Be that as it may, sometime after the seventeenth century it came to be held that indebitatus assumpsit lay on a quantum meruit or quantum valebat.[112]

Indebitatus assumpsit eventually came to be used to enforce other obligations that were not strictly contractual at all. This category of civil liability in modern terminology is called quasi contract, an anglicization of the Roman category of obligation *quasi ex contractu.* Quasi contracts are contracts implied in law, and unlike contracts implied in fact, which are genuine contracts that differ from express contracts only in that the promise is circumstantially proved, quasi contracts are not contracts at all.

Instances of what we now call quasi-contractual liability were known

105. The Baker's Case of Gray's Inn v. Occould, 78 Eng. Rep. 113, Godbolt 186 (C.P. 1612); Luecke, *supra* note 101, at 92.
106. Fifoot at 370.
107. Simpson, Historical Introduction at 11.
108. Young and Ashburnham's Case, 3 Leon. 161, 74 Eng. Rep. 606 (1587); p. 146 *infra.*
109. Simpson at 497.
110. Simpson at 496-499.
111. The Six Carpenters' Case, 8 Co. Rep. 146, 77 Eng. Rep. 695 (1610).
112. Simpson at 499.

to the common law (and to equity) long before the advent of indebitatus
assumpsit. Where, for instance, a bailiff had failed to account for rents
collected, or a person had neglected to remit the proceeds of goods sold
for the account of another or had failed to pay over money received from
a third person for another's use, the injured party was accorded protection by the "cumbersome" action of account.[113] Gradually the action of
account was replaced by the action of debt in cases where the plaintiff
could allege and prove a sum certain due him. After Slade's Case, indebitatus assumpsit naturally expanded to cover these areas of arguably nonconsensual liability. Under the name of the action for money had and
received, indebitatus assumpsit became available for the recovery of
money paid or received by mistake or because of improper conduct or on
a consideration that had failed.[114] By an expansion of the action of quantum meruit (*valebat*), indebitatus assumpsit could be used for the recovery of the value of goods or services rendered to a party guilty of breach of
contract or under the mistaken assumption that there was a contract.[115]

In the nineteenth century, treatise writers on the common law came to
realize, under the influence of civilian writers, that indebitatus assumpsit
included more than contractual obligations[116] and that a court, when
allowing recovery under an implied-in-law contract, was merely pretend-
ing "that there was a contract because it thought there ought to be recovery."[117] The English courts, however, failed to pick up on this suggestion

113. Fifoot at 365 et seq.; Simpson at 499 et seq.
114. Simpson at 494-495; Fifoot at 364 et seq.
115. In the last mentioned illustration, recovery was regarded as sufficiently similar to
the action of quantum meruit (quantum valebat), available for the enforcement of an
implied-in-fact contract to merit the same label. As a result the term quantum meruit
acquired a double meaning and covered both contractual and quasi-contractual recovery.
P. Winfield, The Province of the Law of Tort 157 et seq. (1931); Martin v. Campanaro, p.
178 *infra*.
This triumph of indebitatus assumpsit did not mean, however, that special assumpsit
had become superfluous; it was still indispensable for the enforcement of contracts executory on either side and for the recovery of damages. S. Warren, Introduction to Law Studies
486 et seq. (2d ed. 1845).
116. Indebitatus assumpsit traditionally required the allegation of a promise to pay at
plaintiff's request. The promise would be purely fictitious in the case of an implied-in-law
contract. Nonetheless, liability in quasi-contract was rationalized as contract liability. 3
Blackstone, Commentaries 155 et seq. (1768).
117. I. Stone, Legal Systems and Lawyers' Reasonings 260 (1964) contains an interesting
discussion of the technique of "circuitous reference" involved here. The nature of quasi-
contractual liability was clearly understood by Lord Mansfield, who, in the celebrated case
of Moses v. Macferlan, 2 Burr. 1005 (1760), attempted to develop its general theory within
the framework of the action for money had and received "if the defendant be under an
obligation, from the ties of natural justice to refund, the law implies a debt, and gives this
action indebitatus assumpsit, founded in the equity of the plaintiff's case, as it were upon a
contract ('quasi ex contractu,' as the Roman Law expresses it)." For the fate of this attempt,
see Lord Wright, Sinclair v. Brougham, 6 Cambridge. L.J. 305 (1938); J. Dawson, Unjust
Enrichment 10 (1951). According to Lord Justice Scrutton, "the whole history of this
particular form of action has been what I may call a history of well-meaning sloppiness of
thought." Holt v. Markham, [1923] 1 K.B. 504, 513. In this country the Restatement of the
Law of Restitution, prepared by the American Law Institute, has undertaken to replace the

to acknowledge the difference between implied-in-fact and implied-in-law contracts.[118] It was not until 1937 that Lord Wright in Brooks Wharf and Bull Wharf Ltd. v. Goodman Bros., 1 K.B. 54, introduced to the case law the textbook learning of the nineteenth century, although there is evidence that the textbook learning was tacitly recognized in many nineteenth-century cases.[119]

Consideration. When at common law assumpsit came to be used to enforce informal parol promises problems arose. No legal system can afford to enforce "any old promise," as Corbin put it. Different legal systems have developed different techniques for separating the sheep from the goats; yet however different the techniques used by various legal systems to accomplish this end, they can all be traced back to a "common stock of ideas prevailing in medieval Western Europe," and in particular to the idea of reciprocity,[120] a concept that has influenced the development of the law not only in central Europe, but also in England.

In England, the consideration doctrine was gradually developed to set limits to the enforcement of promises. Its early history is still controversial and so is its genealogy. The question has often been asked whether it is an "indigenous product" or the adaptation of notions coming from civil, canon and natural law fitted into the framework of the writ system. Simpson, for example, relates the early beginnings of consideration to the law of uses of land and through it to the canon and civil law. Simpson, chs. IV-VII; Simpson, Historical Introduction at 89; Milsom at 356-360. This controversy, however, need not detain us.

Roughly speaking, it is sufficient to point out that English law took the course of protecting the promisor against the consequences of unguarded utterances made without consideration, i.e. deliberation. Strangeborough v. Warner, 4 Leon. 3 (1589). If, on the other hand, the promisor had begun to perform his promise, for instance to repair a roof but had abandoned the job in midstream, the courts did not find the problem of recovery insuperable. Tort (trespass) and later contract (assumpsit) were expanded to protect the promisee who had lost his cattle due to defendant's misfeasance. But the problem became really serious if the defendant had done nothing at all. "Not doing is no trespass." Milsom, [1954] Cambridge L.J. 105. But this solution became intolerable, and violated

---

"vague jurisprudence" of unjustifiable enrichment by a detailed enumeration of the typical fact situations in which the remedy is available; its provisions should be consulted in addition to the pertinent sections of the Restatement of Contracts. A Restatement Second of Restitution is now in preparation.

118. Atiyah at 482. In this country the courts were quicker to pick up on the distinction. See Hertzog v. Hertzog, *infra* p. 147, which is referred to in 2 Kent, Commentaries 450 n.1 (Holmes 12th ed. 1873) (no clear-cut distinction is drawn in earlier editions).

119. Atiyah at 482 et seq.

120. Barton, Early History of Consideration, 85 L.Q. Rev. 372, 390 (1969); Baker, Introduction at 257 et seq.

the sense of common decency and fairness, particularly if the promisor
had received full or partial payment or other recompense. The changing
attitude of the case law in favor of liability can be traced back as far as a
remark of Fineaux, C.J., referred to by Frowicke, C.J.C.P., in Orwell v.
Mortoft, *supra* note 46.

When the common law inherited a large part of the business of the
local courts, it was only natural for it to take over the idea of reciprocity
used by the local courts in deciding contract cases.[121] Furthermore, the
common law courts could not remain unaware of the existence of a link
between the notion of consideration and the idea of a quid pro quo used
in explaining and justifying the liability of the borrower to his lender in
debt. The borderline between these ideas was, for a while at least, rather
fluid, as some of the misfeasance cases which use quid pro quo indicate.[122]

Gradually the various strands of liability came together and found an
untidy alliance in the technical meaning of consideration, defined as a
detriment to the promisee or a benefit to the promisor. Stone v. Wythipol, Cro. Eliz. 126, 1 Leon. 113, Owen 94 (1588): "Every consideration
that doth charge the defendant in an assumpsit must be to the benefit of
the defendant or charge to the plaintiff and no case can be put out of this.
rule." This was all the more natural since there is hardly a situation where
a benefit to the promisor is not at the same time a detriment to the
promisee (though the reverse is not necessarily true). (Manwood v. Burston, 2 Leon. 203 (1587). Simpson suggests a "more helpful way of looking
at the decisions" and urges us "to distinguish between detriment consideration, benefit consideration and meritorious consideration as three different categories." Simpson at 489.

Consideration aided the emergence and recognition of "pure" executory bilateral contracts. Strangeborough v. Warner (1589) — a promise
against a promise will maintain an action on the case — reflects existing
case law.[123] It was the task of succeeding generations to amplify and refine
the consideration doctrine.

B. The Emancipation and Evolution of the
Substantive Law of Contract

As J. H. Baker has observed, Slade's Case, decided in 1604, marked
"the final stage in the unification of the law of contract through the action
of assumpsit."[124] But this does not mean that the modern concept of
contract with all its constituent elements had arrived. The development

121. Milsom, *supra* note 58, at 323.
122. Barton, *supra* note 120, at 374.
123. Barton, *supra* note 120, at 390; Baker, Introduction at 292 et seq.
124. Baker at 187.

of a unified theory integrating the strands contained in the various writs of assumpsit was retarded for some time by the intricacies and complexities of the writ system; the classical law of contract is really the child of the late eighteenth and nineteenth centuries.

Since the principles of the common law developed around the forms of action it is not surprising that the law of procedure and the famous treatises on pleading enjoyed such great prestige.[125] During the golden age of pleading — the nineteenth century — pleading became an art in its own right. Its rules were regarded as logically derived from accepted principles and hence as inevitable, and the view was widely held that "any radical change would inflict damage not only on the law of pleading but on the common law as a whole."[126]

To be sure, Lord Mansfield informs us that the "substantial rules of pleading were formed on a strong sense and soundest and closest logic."[127] Unfortunately, however, quite a few rules did not live up to these high expectations, but rather shielded the unscrupulous pleader so that many a good case was lost and a bad one won before it came to trial.[128] Pleading, in Maitland's words, had become "the most exact if not the most occult of the sciences." This affected the emerging substantive law, which was, in Maine's words "secreted in the interstices of procedure." In an action of assumpsit for breach of an informal promise, the forms of pleading "had been settled," according to the prevailing view, in the sixteenth and seventeenth centuries and remained unchanged until the nineteenth.[129] Because of the technical pleading requirements peculiar to assumpsit, the inference was drawn, early on, that in an executory contract the exchanged promises were dependent in the making but independent in the performance stage, unless the parties had expressly agreed otherwise, with the result that the exchange relationship remained unprotected. Thus, the buyer of the cow in Nichols v. Raynbred[130] had to pay for the undelivered cow and then bring his own separate action. The transition from promise to contract occurred very slowly indeed.[131]

125. H. J. Stephen, A Treatise on the Law of Pleading in Civil Action (1824). It appeared in innumerable editions in England and here. See further E. Bullen & M. Leake, Precedents of Pleading (3d ed. 1868).

126. Holdsworth, The New Rules of Pleading at the Hilary Term, 1 Cambridge L.J. 261, 282 (1925), quoting Bryant v. Herbert, 3 C.P.D. at 390 (1878) per Bramwell, L.J.

127. Robinson v. Raley, 1 Burr. 361, 319, 94 Eng. Rep. 330 (1757); Bristow v. Wright, 2 Doug. 665, 99 Eng. Rep. 421 (1781).

128. G. Radcliffe & G. Cross, The English Legal System, 181 (G. Hand & J. J. Bentley eds. 1977). As late at 1830 there were seventy variations from which plaintiff had to choose and each writ had its own prerequisites. Use of the wrong writ was fatal and forced plaintiff to begin all over again, so long as no verdict had been reached. In the latter case, the suit was lost forever. Fifoot at 151.

129. Baker, From Sanctity of Contract to Reasonable Expectations?, 32 Current Legal Probs. 17, 20 (1979).

130. P. 976 infra.

131. Contrast Nichols v. Raynbred, infra p. 976, with Pordage v. Cole, infra p. 976; Kingston v. Preston, infra p. 979; Morton v. Lamb, infra p. 983. Francis, supra note 14.

Another formidable roadblock to the development of a substantive law of contract was the dominant role of the jury in a lawsuit. The line of demarcation between the domains of court and jury, law and fact, was to begin with not clearly drawn. So long as this state of affairs persisted, a "mechanism" for the development of contract law was lacking.[132] "What was a contract and what not was a question of fact."[133] As late as 1847, the determination of the measure of damages in a contract action was still a jury matter.[134] Not until 1854, when Hadley v. Baxendale was decided, did a *law* of damages begin to take shape.[135]

This state of affairs was highly detrimental to the commercial community, which needed clear-cut rules of law. England had become the foremost commercial nation of the western world. New forms of commercial transactions had to be dealt with. The terms and risks involved were of greater complexity than those associated with the land-based transactions of an earlier period.[136] An ordinary jury was not up to the task of dealing with these new fact situations. Small wonder that in the eighteenth century enlightened members of the profession reacted favorably not only to demands for ridding the legal system of inequities, uncertainties and delays, but also to the demand to bring order into the chaos by creating a coherent system of substantive law.[137] Living in a rational and cosmopolitan age, they became convinced that the law could be mastered only by going back to fundamental principles (frequently called axioms or maxims)[138] and not by the "crude pragmatism" of Rolle's and others' Abridg-

132. Baker, *supra* note 129, at 20.

133. Baker at 291. To give an illustration: If, for instance, in an action of assumpsit the defendant pleaded the general issue, i.e. denied plaintiff's allegation in toto, the only question of substantive law for the court to decide was the question of consideration; all the other prerequisites of contract were within the domain of the jury and its inscrutable verdict. Baker, *supra* note 129, at 20.

This state of affairs illustrates the importance of a special verdict, agreed upon by the parties. See Baker, Slade's Case, *supra* note 82. The special verdict was unrivalled as a vehicle for legal development. Milsom at 77.

134. Black v. Baxendale, 1 Ex. 410, 154 Eng. Rep. 174 (1847).

135. 9 Ex. 341, 156 Eng. Rep. 145 (1854).

136. Francis, *supra* note 14, at 121.

137. John Stuart Mill on Bentham & Coleridge, at 76 (F. R. Leavis ed. 1962):

The law came to be like the costume of a full-grown man who had never put off the clothes made for him when he first went to school. Band after band had burst, and, as the rent widened, then, without removing anything except what might drop off of itself, the hole was darned, or patches of fresh law were brought from the nearest shop and stuck on.

138. P. Stein, Regulae Juris 153-159 (1966). A venerable tradition was thereby revived, a tradition going back at least as far as Fortescue's De Laudibus Legum Angliae (1st ed. c.1470). Fortescue, following the approach of Scholastic Aristotelianism, attempted to penetrate to first principles. However we may feel about the success of his approach, the search for and insistence on principles (maxims) has been with us ever since, though maxims often were trivialized (particularly by Coke; the treatment by Bacon is far superior in this respect). This has affected our theories of the judicial process and bears upon the question whether law consists only of rules or includes principles as well as standards. See R. Dworkin, Taking Rights Seriously 14-80 (1977) (especially pp. 22-28). For a penetrating account of the judicial process, see E. Levi, An Introduction to Legal Reasoning (1949); Levi points out that legal analysis uses neither induction nor deduction, but reasoning by analogy.

ments, which arranged their materials according to the forms of action, sometimes presented simply in alphabetical order.

The professional elite in search of a system sought guidance in the Digest, in the civilian literature on natural law and jurisprudence, and in writings on commercial and admiralty law.[139] Unsurprisingly, these ideas had a strong influence on Lord Mansfield, who once declared: "The Law of England would be a strange science if it were [based] on precedents alone. Precedents serve only to illustrate principles."[140]

Going beyond Lord Holt,[141] Lord Mansfield had the courage to break with the dominant role of the jury in commercial cases. In remaking the laws of shipping, insurance and commerce, a thorough familiarity with the customs and practices existing in the world of trade and commerce was, he felt, indispensable. To bring the necessary information to his court, he dared to change the role of the jury drastically. He sought the advice of "knowledgeable" and "substantial" merchants who, informed of the issue in litigation, gave him the information on commercial practices needed to assure protection of good faith dealing between honest merchants.[142] The role of "Lord Mansfield's jury" was advisory only. His court, when sitting in banc, was the final arbiter as to whether a given practice, carefully written down in his famous notebooks,[143] deserved to become part of the law of merchants and thereby of the common law. Furthermore, Mansfield's technique of interpretation was guided by his conviction that it was the intention of the parties and not the accidental features of the particular forms of action which determined the scope of the contract.[144] Mansfield also succeeded in streamlining the practice of procedure so as to enable his court to give speedy justice,[145] but he failed in his effort to merge law and equity (this had to wait for another hundred years).[146] Moreover, his success in rationalizing the doctrine of consider-

---

139. 1 W. Paley, Principles of Moral and Political Philosophy 15-20 (1825); T. H. Plucknett, A Concise History of the Common Law 299, 300 (5th ed. 1955); Atiyah at 345 et seq.

140. Robinson v. Raley, *supra* note 127, at 319, 94 Eng. Rep. at 331. But he adds by way of qualification: ". . . and so appear, when well understood and explained; though by being misunderstood and misapplied, they are often made use of as instruments of Chicane." See further Bristow v. Wright, *supra* note 127. On Lord Mansfield, see C. H. S. Fifoot, Lord Mansfield (1936); 7 W. Holdsworth, History of English Law 44-45 (1926).

141. Lord Holt consulted goldsmiths about their usages, Ford v. Hopkins, 1 Salk. 283, 91 Eng. Rep. 250 (1750). But he saw no need for making promissory notes negotiable, Clerk v. Martin, 2 Ld. Raym. 757, Eng. Rep. 1 (1702). A statute, 34 Anne, ch. 8 (1703), had to be passed to remedy the situation.

142. Lord Birkenhead, Fourteen English Judges 186 (1926); Atiyah at 115-116.

143. Howard, Lord Mansfield's Notebooks, 93 L.Q. Rev. 438 (1976).

144. Fifoot, *supra* note 140, at 18.

145. Id. at 52-81.

146. A summary of his point of view is given in 3 Blackstone at 429 et seq. On the fusion of law and equity, see the Judicature Acts of 1873 at 175, briefly discussed in Baker at 46-48, 97-99. For the evolution of the American law of civil procedure, see C. Hepburn, The Historical Development of Code Pleading in American and England (1897); R. Richard Millar, Civil Procedure of the Trial Court in Historical Perspective (1952); L. Friedman, A History of American Law, 49-51, 126-134, 340-347 (1973).

ation by making a commercial promise in writing as binding as a promise under seal was short-lived;[147] again he was ahead of his time.[148]

The impact of Lord Mansfield's innovations was eloquently praised by Buller, J. in his valedictory address shortly before Lord Mansfield's retirement.[149]

> Within the last thirty years the commercial law of this country has taken a very different turn from what it did before. We find in Snee v. Prescot [1 Atkyns 245] that Lord Hardwicke himself was proceeding with great caution, not establishing any general principle, but decreeing on all the circumstances of the case put together. Before that period we find that in Courts of Law all the evidence in mercantile cases was thrown together; they were left generally to a jury and they produced no established principle. From that time we all know the great study has been to find some certain general principles, which shall be known to all mankind, not only to rule the particular case then under consideration, but to serve as a guide for the future. Most of us have heard these principles stated, reasoned upon, enlarged and explained, till we have been lost in admiration at the strength and stretch of the human understanding. And I should be very sorry to find myself under a necessity of differing from any case on this subject which has been decided by Lord Mansfield, who may be truly said to be the founder of the commercial law of this country.

Of course, Mansfield had his detractors as well.[150]

Attempts to give a general account of English law in terms of its guiding principles were repeated time and time again. Blackstone's Commentaries on the Laws of England (1765-1769), preceded by an Analysis of the Laws of England (1765), is the most outstanding example.[151] Blackstone

---

147. Pillans & Rose v. Van Mierop & Hopkins, 8 Burr. 1663, 97 Eng. Rep. 1035 (K.B. 1765), *infra* p. 744. The opinion of Wilmot, J. shows that it was not impossible to find a consideration.

Lord Mansfield's heretical view on consideration was overturned in Rann v. Hughes, 7 T.R. 350 note, 101 Eng. Rep. 1014 note (1778).

148. For the modern law, see Ch. 3, §7 and p. 752 *infra*.

149. Lickbarrow v. Mason, 2 T.R. 63, 100 Eng. Rep. 35, 40 (1787).

150. 12 W. Holdsworth, History of English Law 464, 560 (1926). Mansfield was viciously attacked by the anonymous Junius for his leanings toward Roman law. Even Dean Ames of Harvard reportedly could not resist the temptation of calling Mansfield a fraud in front of the law school class on account of his attempt to merge law and equity. See A. Sutherland, Law at Harvard 188 (1967). These criticisms contrast with Lord Birkenhead's high praise: "Coke captured the law merchant for the common law. Holt retained it; Mansfield formally incorporated it into our system." Birkenhead, *supra* note 142, at 186. See Baker, The Law Merchant and the Common Law Before 1700, 38 Cambridge L.J. 295 (1979).

151. In his analysis he mentions some of his predecessors: A. Finch, Law or a Discourse Thereof (1613) (originally in French); T. Wood, An Institute of the Laws of England (1720). He has high praise for M. Hale, An Analysis of the Civil Part of the Law (1713), to whom he acknowledges a great debt (Preface vii-viii). Coke is mentioned with only faint praise. The difficulties Blackstone encountered are illustrated by the frustrations Hale and Wood met in attempting to arrange their materials.

was a contemporary and admirer of Lord Mansfield and his work shows Mansfield's influence, particularly in later editions.

Vinerian Professor of English law at Oxford, Blackstone set himself the formidable task of doing for the common law what had already been done for the civil law by the civilians, and to a large degree he succeeded. Inspired by the great philosophers of the Enlightenment[152] (whom he used but did not always follow)[153] Blackstone set out to cover the whole law of England, both public and private — an undertaking that had not been attempted since the days of Bracton.

The Commentaries — intended to justify and preserve the social order that the Revolution had established — open with praise for the English system of protecting life, liberty, and private property. "To Blackstone the common law was the most fitting and ingenious means for fulfilling the law of nature."[154] Intended as an elementary text addressed to beginning students[155] and to the educated public, the Commentaries are written in an agreeable, often eloquent style that is easy to follow since it is not burdened with an embarrassing richness of detail. (Intricate parts of the law of inheritance and of property are often omitted or glossed over.)

The Commentaries came at the right moment and satisfied a need for bringing the multilayered common law into a rational system of substantive rules. Blackstone transformed law, the "dreariest of all sciences," into a respectable subject matter worthy of being taught at the university. Moreover, the Commentaries did not offend the Establishment by advocating radical reforms.[156] "The eighteenth century," as seen by Black-

---

152. 2 H. Grotius, The Rights of War and Peace (De Jure Belli ac Pacis), chs. XI-XII (F. W. Kelsey ed. 1964) (1st ed. 1625); 3 S. Pufendorf, Of the Law of Nature and Nations (De Jure Naturae et Gentium), ch. IV, §3, and chs. V, VI, IX (1720); E. Vattel, The Law of Nations, or Principles of the Law of Nature (1760); J. Domat, The Civil Law in Its Natural Order: Together with the Publick Law (2d ed. 1737); and J. J. Burlamaqui, Principes de Droit Naturel (1748).

It is not possible to reconcile Blackstone's positivism and his natural law theory. See Finnis, Blackstone's Theoretical Intentions, 12 Nat. Law Forum 163-187 (1967). We owe this reference to Doolittle, Sir William Blackstone and The Laws of England: A Biographical Approach, 3 Oxford J. of Legal Studies 89, 108 (1980).

153. Examples are given in B. Gagnebin, Burlamaqui et le Droit Natural 270 (1944). Burlamaqui was a professor at the University of Geneva; his work appeared in translation shortly after its publication (1748). Burlamaqui's writing influenced the teaching of natural law at Cambridge. The work of Vattel (who also taught at Geneva) was cited for more than a hundred years by the U.S. Supreme Court, 2 J. B. Scott, Law, the State and the International Community 264 (1939). Vattel also influenced Kent's Commentaries (1826).

154. 2 M. Howe, Justice Olive W. Holmes, The Proving Years 1870-1882, 141 (1963).

155. This was Mansfield's evaluation. For a recent discussion of Blackstone, see Milsom, The Nature of Blackstone's Achievements, 1 Oxford J. of Legal Studies 7 (1981). G. Jones, The Sovereignty of the Law: Selections from Blackstone's Commentaries on the Laws of England (1873), contains, in its Introduction, an admirable discussion of Blackstone. See also D. Boorstin, The Mysterious Science of Law (1941); Kennedy, The Structure of Blackstone's Commentaries, 28 Buffalo L. Rev. 205 (1979).

156. This does not mean that he was against reforming à tout prix. He strongly advocated, for instance, reforms of the penal law, Holdsworth, Some Aspects of Blackstone and his Commentaries, [1932] Cambridge L.J. 273, 274.

stone, "was stable and felt itself stable."[157] The French Revolution and
the Napoleonic wars were still decades away, and the Industrial Revolution had just begun.

This introduction will not undertake to discuss the Commentaries as a
whole, nor to examine their deficiencies, which have often been commented upon,[158] but will focus on Blackstone's contribution to the law of
contracts. The treatment of contracts in the Commentaries has "vexed"
modern commentators, according to Milsom. Inspired by Hale's system
(*supra* p. 42), the four books of the Commentaries distinguish between
Rights of Persons (Book I), Rights of Things (Book II), Private Wrongs,
including the organization of courts and the formulary system (Book III),
and Public Wrongs (Book IV). The first book deals with constitutional
law, the second with the law of property. Book III deals with civil procedure and the court system, Book IV with criminal law and procedure.

Chapter 30 of Book II, devoted to the Rights of Things, contains a
discussion of contract as a means of acquiring property. "A contract,
which usually conveys an interest merely in action, is thus defined: 'an
agreement, upon sufficient consideration, to do or not to do a particular
thing'" (at 442). The passage continues: "From which definition there
arise three points to be contemplated in all contracts; 1. the *agreement*: 2.
the *consideration*: and 3. the *thing* to be done or omitted, or the different
species of contracts" (at 442). Express and implied executory and executed contracts are distinguished (at 443). Express contracts are those in
which the terms of an agreement are openly uttered and avowed at the
time of the making. Implied are such as reason and justice dictate, and
which therefore the law presumes that every man undertakes to perform
(at 443). This is followed by the observation (at 446) that the most usual
contracts whereby the right of a chattel may be acquired are "1. That of
sale or *exchange*. 2. That of *bailment*. 3. That of *hiring* and *borrowing*. 4.
That of *debt*[!]." The discussion of consideration is not of particular interest.

In the third book, Blackstone returns to the distinction between express and implied (implied-in-law) contracts. These are divided into two
groups. The first includes judgment debts, forfeitures and statutory penalties (ch. 9, at 158-160); the discussion of this group is most interesting,
for its shows Blackstone's indebtedness to natural law theory. According
to Blackstone, these types of contracts "are necessarily implied by the
fundamental constitution of government, to which every man is a contracting party" (at 158). With regard to sentences and assessments, he
continues: "it is part of the original contract, entered into by all mankind
who partakes the benefits of society, to submit in all points to the munici-

157. Taken from G. M. Young, Victorian England, Portrait of an Age 47 (1953), describing the spirit of the period.
158. H. Lévy-Ullmann, The English Legal Tradition 148 (1935) (translated by M. Mitchell, revised and edited by F. M. Goadly, with a Foreword by Holdsworth).

pal constitutions and local ordinances of the state of which each individual is a member" (at 158).

The second group is made up of obligations "by natural reason and the just construction of law." These extend to "all presumptive undertakings or *assumpsits*; which though never perhaps actually made, yet constantly arise from this general implication and intendment of the courts of judicature, that every man has engaged to perform what his duty or justice requires" (at 161). This group includes the common counts, the action for money had and received, and the action of account.

This last class of contracts, implied by reason and construction of law, "arises upon this supposition, that everyone who undertakes any office, employment, trust, or duty, contracts with those who employ or entrust him, to perform it with integrity, diligence, and skill" (at 163). Nowhere, in all of this, is a clear distinction made between contracts implied in fact and those implied in law. (Hertzog v. Hertzog, *infra* p. 147).

The contract of employment is not mentioned in Books II and III.[159] It appears instead in Book I, which is devoted to what Blackstone calls the Rights of Persons. In addition to public relations between magistrates and citizens, Book I deals with private relationships: master and servant, husband and wife, parent and child, guardian and ward.

Blackstone's abbreviated treatment of contracts has often been commented upon.[160] Only a small fraction of the Commentaries is devoted to contracts, which suggests that Blackstone did indeed feel more at home in the field of land law than in the law of commerce. Still, there are many passages in the Commentaries that clearly show that Blackstone was aware of the commercial character of the England of his day. Thus, he quotes a foreign author who had said: "The English people know better than any other people on earth how to value at the same time these great advantages, religion, liberty and Commerce." Moreover, there are repeated references in the Commentaries to "this commercial age" and to the great change in property brought about by the expansion of trade.[161] To be sure, Blackstone does not mention freedom of contract and he failed to anticipate that in the next century contract would come to be viewed as the principal form of social organization. But this lack of vision does not mean that the Commentaries represent only the typical eighteenth-century view that contract law is an adjunct of the law of property.[162]

Blackstone has been called the Gaius of English law. Others surpassed

159. Kahn-Freund, Blackstone's Neglected Child: The Contract of Employment, 93 L.Q. Rev. 508-528 (1977).

160. Atiyah at 102, 215.

161. According to Doolittle, *supra* note 152, at 103, Blackstone's contemporaries did not regard him as an academic, but as "a man of business." He was quite successful in managing the financial affairs of All Souls College as well as his own.

162. See Horwitz at 162, 163.

him in depth and originality,[163] but he had a rare gift of synthesis and made a unique contribution to the broad development of English law. To be sure, Bentham — who next to Austin[164] was Blackstone's severest critic — faulted Blackstone for his quietistic conservationism and his uncritical admiration of the legal system as he presented it. But even Bentham had to admit that "first of all institutional writers, [he] taught jursprudence to speak the language of the scholar and the gentleman."[165]

Though the Commentaries never achieved the reputation enjoyed by the work of Coke, they were a huge financial success.[166] "Working editions," as Milsom calls them, appeared in England until the Judicature Act. Updated and modernized versions by Sergeant H. J. Stephen have been appearing until recently and have by now reached to more than twenty editions.[167]

The success of the Commentaries in the United States was enormous.[168] More than 2,000 copies went across the Atlantic before the Declaration of Independence; nine editions were published during Blackstone's lifetime. The Commentaries proved to be one of the dominant factors in the development of American law and its institutions, and after the Declaration of Independence their influence helped to prevent the reception of French law. The settlers of the West, who often lacked adequate libraries, were helped by the Commentaries to secure a modicum of order and to build new states out of the acquired territories. James Kent and John Marshall owed their learning and vocation, as they acknowledged, to Blackstone. Edition after edition, as well as condensations of the book, appeared,[169] and were used as teaching tools in universities and law schools — at Harvard, judging by the catalogue, as late as 1850 and at other schools, including Yale, much longer.[170]

Blackstone's success encouraged a new type of legal literature. Treatises appeared on various legal topics, many dealing with the law of contracts.[171] Apart from the medieval work of Christopher St. Germain,

163. Grotius' Treatment of Contracts is far superior.

164. J. Bentham, in A Fragment of Government (1881), says of the Commentaries that "they are a superficial defense of an oligarchic constitution and inequitable laws." See Cross, Blackstone v. Bentham, 92 L.Q. Rev. 516 (1976). For Austin's critique see Dicey, Blackstone's Commentaries, 4 Cambridge L.J. 286, 287-288 (1932).

165. J. Bentham, A Commentary on the Commentaries and A Fragment of Government 413 (J. H. Burns & H. L. A. Hart eds. 1977). In Baker's view, Bentham failed to realize that "Blackstone was both a final survey of the old common law and the first textbook of a new legal era." Baker at 166.

166. 2 D.N.B. 595, 597.

167. But the title page no longer states that it is based on Blackstone, and it is no longer called New Commentaries.

168. L. Friedman, A History of American Law 16, 88 and *passim* (1975).

169. Id.

170. Yale used W. Robinson's version, "more than one hundred years out of date," according to Corbin. See Kessler, Arthur Corbin, 78 Yale L.J. 517 (1969).

171. They are listed in Simpson, The Rise and Fall of the Legal Treatise: Legal Principles and the Forms of Legal Literature, 48 U. Chi. L. Rev. 632, 651 (1981).

Doctor and Student (1530, 1532)[172] few English writers had attempted to speculate about the general principles of contract law until John Joseph Powell published his two-volume Essay Upon the Law of Contracts and Agreements in 1785.[173] Powell's work, and the treatises of English and American[174] writers that were to follow, possessed, in the words of Simpson, an abstract and speculative character evolved outside the courtroom, a feature lacking in the legal literature of an earlier period.[175]

The common law literature of the nineteenth century drew heavily from civilian writers. Speculative writing on contract and other branches of law had a long tradition on the continent. The works of Grotius, Pufendorf, Domat, Vattel and Burlamaqui, and later of Pothier and Savigny,[176] were available to English and American lawyers and all influenced Anglo-American thinking about law and jurisprudence.

By far the most influential of the continental writers was the French jurist Robert Pothier, whose Treatise on Obligations was published in the United States in 1802 and in England, in the popular Evans translation with elaborate Notes, in 1806.[177]

The influence of these writers on the common law cannot be overstated. English courts, sitting in banc on complex questions of law (a practice introduced by Lord Mansfield in commercial cases), made good use of the information on foreign law presented by the lawyers in their briefs, and frequently filled the gaps in the existing law to create a workable law of contracts.[178]

Gradually, the classical law of contracts took shape. Its emergence was reinforced by the teachings of the classical economists with their emphasis on individualism, freedom of trade and of contract. Economics was taught at the university as part of Moral Science and most if not all

172. 91 Selden Society (T. Plucknett & L. Barton eds. 1974).

173. American editions appeared in 1809 and 1823. Powell's treatise was preceded by Sir William Jones' famous essay on Bailments (1781). Jones, insisting that law was a science, treated his subject matter in an analytical (emphasizing the first principles of natural reason), historical (comparative law) and synthetic fashion. He aimed at the discovery of axioms flowing from natural reason, good morals and good conscience. "[I]f law *be* a *science*, and really deserve so sublime a name," he claims, "it must be founded on principle; . . . but if it be *merely* an unconnected series of decrees and ordinances, its use may remain, though its dignity be lessened, and He will become the greatest lawyer who has the strongest habitual or artificial memory" (at 123-124). Jones was the first author to call attention to the French jurist Pothier.

174. See *supra* note 171.

175. Simpson, *supra* note 2, at 252; J. C. Perkins published a fourth edition of Chitty's Practical Treatise on the Law of Contracts, with appendices, in 1839.

176. See note 146 *supra* on Grotius, Pufendorf, Domat, Vattel, and Burlamaqui; R. Pothier, Treatise on Obligations (1802, 1806); and Savigny, 3 System des Heutigen Roemischen Rechts (1840). The translation of Savigny dates to 1860 and was published in Madras.

177. On the high regard in which he was held, see Cox v. Troy, 5 B. & H. 474, 481, 106 Eng. Rep. 1266 (1822); see also Foster v. Wheeler, 36 Ch. D. 695, 698 (1887).

178. Hadley v. Baxendale, 9 Ex. 341, 156 Eng. Rep. 145 (1854); *infra* p. 106 (damages); Offord v. Davis, 12 C.B. (N.S.) 748 (formation of contract); Taylor v. Caldwell, 3 B. & S. 826, 122 Eng. Rep. 309 (K.B. 1863); Smith v. Hughes, L.R. 6 at B597 (1871) (mistake); Phillips v. Brooks [1919] 2 K.B. 243.

Victorian judges who had no legal but a broad liberal education were familiar with the works of Hume, Smith, Locke, Ricardo, the two Mills, and the "Philosophical Radicals."[179]

The new, classical law of contracts found expression in a series of treatises which began to appear towards the end of the eighteenth century. Only a few works will be mentioned.[180] William Paley's Principles of Moral and Political Philosophy (1785) contains an impressive discussion of the fundamental principles of contract law, missing in earlier treatments. Chitty's Practical Treatise on the Law of Contracts, enormously successful from the beginning, shows the spirit of the new age in its second edition, and Leake's Elements of Contracts (1867) states in its preface that there had existed previously no English work with the exclusive object of presenting contracts in a general and abstract form apart from its specific applications. Leake's most significant contribution to contract doctrine is the clear distinction between express and implied-in-fact contracts and constructive (implied-in-law) contracts, a third category of civil liability covering cases of unjust enrichment. These treatises had their counterpart in the United States in the works of Kent, the two Storys, Parsons, and Sedgwick.

Simpson summarizes the result of the work as follows:

> This survey of doctrinal innovation in contract law is perhaps unflattering to the common law tradition — indigenous, judge-made law; the new ideas are largely plagiarized from the civil law, and it is to the rise of the treatise that we must attribute the change in the character and structure of basic contract law, rather than to judicial originality.

Simpson, Innovation in Nineteenth Century Contract Law, 91 L.Q. Rev. 247, 277 (1975).

In the latter half of the nineteenth century, the influence of these systematic treatise writers began to wane and was replaced for a time by the historical school centered in Germany. Maitland described Savigny, the founder of the historical school, as "the herald of the evolution, the man who substitutes development for manufacture, organism for mechanism, natural laws for Natural Law, the man who is nervously afraid that a code should impede the beautiful process of natural growth."[181] Unsur-

179. Pollock, A Plea for Historical Interpretation, 9 L.Q. Rev. 163 (1923). English judges from Parke to MacNaughten had no legal education:

> There was none to have. Until 1852, where the Common Law Procedure Act furnished at once the need and the opportunity for judges to think in terms of principles there was no serious study of law at the universities and the old professional training in the Inns of Court where they dined had long disappeared.

C. H. S. Fifoot, Judge and Jurist in the Reign of Victoria 21 (1959).
180. Simpson, supra note 2, at 248.
181. Introduction to O. Gierke, Political Theories of The Middle Age at xv (1900). We owe the reference to C. H. S. Fifoot, Judge and Jurist in the Reign of Victoria (1959).

prisingly, text writers in the next generation, like Pollock and Anson, were strongly influenced by Savigny.[182] The chief representative of the historical school in England was Sir Henry Maine (1822-1888)[183] who, unlike Savigny, believed in stages of evolution bringing the law into harmony with society.[184]

Beginning in the middle of the nineteenth century, the effort to construct a comprehensive theory embracing the whole law of contracts was resumed and gained increasing momentum. Building upon the works of Powell, Chitty, Leake, W. W. Story, Kent, and Parsons,[185] their successors sought to construct a closed and unitary system that would articulate the fundamental principles on which the legal system is based. A formalistic approach using high-level abstractions became the fashion. Thus, for example, in the first two editions of Pollock's Principles, the essential components of contract are said to be agreement and obligation, agreement being the outcome of two consenting minds or wills. Later editions of Pollock moved towards an objective theory of contracts stressing its historical basis and the element of good faith reliance rather than the artificial equations of will and intentions.[186] Langdell, whom tradition has credited with being the originator of the case method of teaching, also emphasized the consensual nature of contract as contrasted with tort liability, and developed an elaborately formalistic system of contract principles. Arguments of public policy had little, if any, bearing on Langdell's analytical constructs. To make his analytical approach work, Langdell had to severely limit the number of cases he included; cases which did not fit into his preconceived system were disregarded as "useless."[187] Williston's "magisterial" treatise, which brought a great deal of order into the chaos of existing case law, was the high point of the formalist period, and the First Restatement of Contracts, for which Williston was the Chief Reporter, followed the lines of his famous text.[188]

The Langdell-Williston scheme was eminently successful and responded to deeply felt needs for rationality and certainty. Inevitably,

182. F. Pollock, Treatise on the General Principles of Contract Law Concerning the Validity of Agreements in the Law of England (1876). W. Anson, Principles of the English Law of Contract (1879). Anson's book is a good deal less sophisticated than Pollock's, which may explain its popularity. He had no wish to "oppress and dishearten" the students. 1 Oxford Studies at 269. Anson's book had many editions, the latest one by A. Guest (1979). One of the many American editions was edited by Corbin with American notes. The preface to the fifth edition sets out the purpose of the work and contains a critique of Leake as well as of Pollock.

183. See squib, *supra* p. 19.

184. For the theories of legal evolution beginning with the natural law tradition and ending with the aftermath of "Ancient Law," see P. Stein, Legal Evolution, The Story of an Idea (1980).

185. See p. 47 *supra*.

186. *Supra* note 182 and p. 115 *infra*.

187. Preface to the first edition of Cases on Contracts, reprinted in Cases on Contracts at *viii* (2d ed. 1879).

188. Corbin served as a special adviser and Reporter on Remedies.

however, its impressive edifice began to crumble. Unruly case law, rejected by Langdell and Williston and reflecting a polytheism of values, clamored for recognition. It became evident that the "clear ideas" that had led the two to believe that "whatever seemed to be confused does not exist" did not work.[189] Holmes, Corbin, and the Legal Realists (led by Llewellyn) launched an all-out "attack on the citadel."[190] Holmes, who wrote The Common Law with the intention of freeing his generation from the past,[191] tells us on the first page of his book that the life of law has not been logic but experience;[192] law, in Holmes' view, is not a closed system of syllogistic reasoning: "The felt necessities of the time, the prevalent moral and political theories, intuitions of public policy, avowed or unconscious, even the prejudices which judges share with their fellowmen, have had a good deal more to do than the syllogism in determining the rules by which men should be governed. . . ."[193] According to Corbin, all generalizations should be regarded as tentative working rules, continually to be tested and reexamined in light of the sources from which they are drawn: the customs, business practices, and opinions of society, and the prevailing morals of the time and place.[194] This reexamination is all the more necessary since, "for every question worth calling a problem, at least two contradictory solutions and propositions can be found in past decisions."[195] Corbin, and his disciple Llewellyn, constantly emphasized the significance of the facts of a particular case, the relative economic positions of the parties and the nature and purpose of their transaction. This new and non-formalistic conception of contract law was to have a considerable influence on the courts, and to play an important role in the drafting of both the Second Restatement of Contracts and the Uniform Commercial Code.

C. Codifications and Restatements

In the creation of the law of contracts the courts have played a decisive role both here and in England. Our federal system of government

189. This citation is taken from J. S. Mill's famous essay on Bentham, reproduced in Dissertations and Discussions at 378 (1868). Essays on Politics and Culture by John Stuart Mill, 85, 103 (G. Himmelfarb ed. 1962).
190. The expression is from the title of William Prosser's article on products liability, The Assault upon the Citadel (Strict Liability and the Consumer), 69 Yale L.J. 1099 (1960).
191. Law In Science and Science In Law, in Collected Legal Papers 210, 225 (1920).
192. O. W. Holmes, The Common Law 1 (1881).
193. Ibid. To quote a modern author, it is "neither logical demonstration, nor inductive generalization, nor the comprehension of certain evident truths." J. Esser, Grundsatz and Norm 183, 184 (1956). See also J. Stone, Legal Systems and Lawyer's Reasoning 322 (1964).
194. Corbin §331.
195. Ibid.

granted almost complete control over private law to the states. Since the state legislatures failed to play a major role in developing a body of private law, the job remained for the courts.[196] However powerful the forces working toward uniformity, the ideal of a "general law" of contracts was never fully realized, and each jurisdiction remained free to develop its own case law.[197]

So long as commerce remained largely local, this state of affairs did not present a serious problem. But with the growth of commerce into an interstate activity, local differences of law began to impair the usefulness of contract as a planning device. To make matters worse, "the mass of law," as Story observed even in 1820, was accumulating with inordinate rapidity.[198] Inevitably, conflicting decisions appeared even within the same jurisdiction. As a result, uniformity and predictability — the twin goals of any legal system — were seriously jeopardized.

It is understandable, therefore, that a movement was begun to eliminate the defects of uncertainty and complexity. The first attempts to harmonize conflicting decisional law took place in commercially significant fields, such as negotiable instruments and sales. With legislative help, sensible common law rules were distinguished from less sensible ones and the good rules given statutory form. In this country, the National Conference of Commissioners on Uniform State Laws drafted model statutes for adoption by state legislatures. This approach succeeded only in part. The Uniform Sales Act, for instance, was never adopted in every state, and the uniform laws did not even cover such subjects as contracts, agency, torts or trusts. In the effort to achieve uniformity, another organization took the lead, using a different technique. The American Law Institute, a private organization of judges, practitioners, and law teachers, set itself the task of "restating" the law in a substantial number of fields so that a judge, lawyer or law teacher could "go to one source, find what the law in point [is] and with confidence state it to be so."[199] The various Restatements are systems of generalizations

196. The provisions of the Civil Code drafted in the nineteenth century by David Dudley Field form an exception. Its contract provisions (sometimes in amended form) were enacted in California, Georgia, Montana, the Dakotas, and Idaho. Harrison, The First Half-Century of the California Civil Code, 10 Calif. L. Rev. 185 (1922). Contract law in Louisiana is based on the French Code Civil. See in general G. Gilmore, The Ages of American Law 27, 119 n.113 (1977).
197. On case law and common law, see Llewellyn, Our Case Law of Contract: Offer and Acceptance (pt. 1), 48 Yale L.J. 1-9 (1938).
198. J. Story, Progress of Jurisprudence, in Miscellaneous Writings 237-238 (1852).
199. Goodrich, The Story of the American Law Institute, 1951 Wash. U.L.Q. 283, 286. According to Williston, the Restatement endeavors "to restate the law, as it is, not as new law." 3 A.L.I. Proceedings 159 (1925). Even the famous §90, qualifying the bargain theory (see Ch. 3, §7), is based on existing decisional law. The final draft of the Restatement First was approved in 1932.

drawn from the welter of individual decisions. In form they consist of
"concise rules analogous to those in a carefully drawn statute,"[200] accompanied by comments and illustrations. Although they have only persuasive authority, it was hoped that the influence of the Restatements would
be "greater than that . . . accorded to any legal treatise, more nearly on a
par with that accorded to the decisions of the courts."[201] No doubt, the
impact of the Restatements has been substantial: this is certainly true for
the Restatement of the Law of Contracts.

Once reform movements got underway, they did not stop with these
attempts. Shortly before 1940, the American Law Institute and the Commissioners on Uniform State Laws joined forces and began a campaign to
modernize the whole of commercial law by codification.[202] The Uniform
Commercial Code (U.C.C.) was the result. The Code has been adopted
in all states but Louisiana (which has not adopted Article 2), and substantially affects the general law of contracts. To be sure, the Code does not
displace all principles of law and equity,[203] but in contrast to the Uniform
Sales Act, it does state rules governing significant aspects of the law of
contracts, such as offer and acceptance, consideration, and unconscionability, which are not always in harmony with traditional contract
rules.[204] To bring the general law of contracts into line with the provisions
of the U.C.C., a revision of the Restatement, the Restatement Second,
was begun in 1952 and published in 1981. Although its "black-letter" law
occasionally departs from the provisions of the U.C.C., the technique
used in the Second Restatement is a vast improvement on that employed
in its predecessor. It is forward-looking[205] and contains more open-ended
provisions; the comments are a good deal more elaborate, and decisional
law is always given to illustrate its general rules. Still, one may wonder
whether it is the "vocation" of our time (Savigny) of transition to under-

200. Williston, The Restatement of Contracts, 18 A.B.A.J. 775, 777 (1932).

201. Goodrich, *supra* note 199, at 283, 286.

202. On codification, its goals and disadvantages, see Pound, Sources and Forms of Law
(pt. 3), 22 Notre Dame Law. 1, 46, 61 (1946); Patterson, The Codification of Commercial
Law in the Light of Jurisprudence, 1 N.Y. Law Rev. Commission Report 50 (1950); Gilmore,
Legal Realism: Its Cause and Cure, 70 Yale L.J. 1037, 1042 (1961); Hawkland, Uniform
Commercial "Code" Methodology, 1962 U. Ill. L.F. 291; Diamond, Codification of the Law
of Contracts, 31 Modern L. Rev. 361 (1968); consult also the materials collected in J.
Honnold, The Life of the Law, ch. 3 (1964).

203. U.C.C. §1-103 provides as follows:

Supplementary General Principles of Law Applicable
Unless displaced by the particular provisions of this Act, the principles of law and
equity, including the law merchant and the law relative to capacity to contract,
principal and agent, estoppel, fraud, misrepresentation, duress, coercion, mistake,
bankruptcy, or other validating or invalidating cause shall supplement its provisions.

204. Note, 105 U. Pa. L. Rev. 836 (1957).

205. Wechsler, Restatements and Legal Change: Problems of Policy in the Restatement
Work of the American law Institute, 13 St. Louis U.L.J. 185 (1968).

take an enterprise like the Restatement, as parts of contract law continue to spin off in a kind of centrifugal process and are made the subject of special legislation, while at the same time the remaining core is reinvigorated by new ideas[206] and changing standards of behavior.[207]

206. A survey of the ferment prevailing in today's legal scholarship is to be found in C. Fried, Contract as Promise 1-6 (1981) and in Barnett, Contract Scholarship and the Emergence of Legal Philosophy, A Review of Farnsworth's Contracts, 97 Harv. L. Rev. 1123 (1984); On the Law and Economics movement with its emphasis on efficiency (wealth maximization), see the Symposium, "Change in the Common Law: Legal and Economic Perspectives," 9 J. Legal Stud. (1980), continued in Symposium on Efficiency as Legal Concern, 8 Hofstra L. Rev. 485 (1980). This Symposium contains a challenging reply to the Law and Economics movement by scholars defending the legitimacy of normative discourse in Law. See further A. Kronman & R. Posner, The Economics of Contract Law (1979), an anthology with running commentary. On the Critical Legal Studies movement, see the bibliography attached to the article by Duncan Kennedy and Karl E. Klare in 94 Yale L.J. 461, 464-490 (1985). See also Forbach's review of The Politics of Law (D. Kairys ed. 1982), 92 Yale L.J. 1041 (1983); p. 64 infra. For the most thorough discussion of the philosophical premises of the Critical Legal Studies approach, see Unger, The Critical Legal Studies Movement, 96 Harv. L. Rev. 561 (1983). An interesting collection of symposium articles on the movement, some more sympathetic than others, may be found in 36 Stan. L. Rev. 1-674 (1984). See further R. Unger, Knowledge and Politics (1975).

207. Gordley, European Codes and American Restatements, 81 Colum. L. Rev. 140 (1981).

CHAPTER 2

The Basic Ideals of an
Individualist Law of Contracts
and Their Erosion

This chapter is designed to give the reader an overview of many of the main doctrines of classical contract law. As we have said, classical theory was distinguished by the emphasis it placed on individual freedom both in the creation and the design of contractual relationships. Two fundamental principles underlie freedom of contract: (1) There can be no contracts by compulsion, i.e., one cannot be forced into a contract against one's will, and (2) the parties to a contract are free to give it whatever content they wish.

Within the classical law itself there was always a counter-principle favoring social control, which should not be overlooked. The consideration requirement came to be used by courts to police certain types of contracts. Although courts were reluctant to look into the adequacy of consideration, cases like Davis & Co. v. Morgan, *infra* p. 77, show how counter-principles could be devised to do just that. Manipulation of narrowly drawn rules of mistake could also result in a relaxing of the principle of self-reliance (compare Wood v. Boynton, *infra* p. 84, with Sherwood v. Walker, *infra* p. 887). But these are exceptions, and the dominant liberal ethic of individualism can be seen working with undiminished vigor in the doctrine of caveat emptor, as illustrated by Swinton v. Whitinsville Savings Bank, *infra* p. 93, and in the nineteenth-century judicial attitude toward fraud and nondisclosure, exemplified by Laidlaw v. Organ, *infra* p. 89.

In some instances only the techniques used for social control of private contract-making have changed. In other cases, the fundamental ideals of liberal individualism have come under attack. The Notes following the cases provide a glimpse at the modern trend away from freedom of contract.

HURLEY v. EDDINGFIELD

156 Ind. 416, 59 N.E. 1058 (1901)

BAKER, J. Appellant sued appellee for $10,000 damages for wrongfully causing the death of his intestate. The court sustained appellee's demurrer to the complaint; and the ruling is assigned as error.

The material facts alleged may be summarized thus: At and for years before decedent's death appellee was a practicing physician at Mace in Montgomery county, duly licensed under the laws of the State. He held himself out to the public as a general practitioner of medicine. He had been decedent's family physician. Decedent became dangerously ill and sent for appellee. The messenger informed appellee of decedent's violent sickness, tendered him his fees for his services, and stated to him that no other physician was procurable in time and that decedent relied on him for attention. No other physician was procurable in time to be of any use, and decedent did rely on appellee for medical assistance. Without any reason whatever, appellee refused to render aid to decedent. No other patients were requiring appellee's immediate service, and he could have gone to the relief of decedent if he had been willing to do so. Death ensued, without decedent's fault, and wholly from appellee's wrongful act.

The alleged wrongful act was appellee's refusal to enter into a contract of employment. Counsel do not contend that, before the enactment of the law regulating the practice of medicine, physicians were bound to render professional service to every one who applied. Wharton on Neg., §731. The act regulating the practice of medicine provides for a board of examiners, standards of qualifications, examinations, licenses to those found qualified, and penalties for practicing without license. Acts 1897, p. 255; Acts 1899, p. 247. The act is a preventive, not a compulsive, measure. In obtaining the State's license (permission) to practice medicine, the State does not require, and the licensee does not engage, that he will practice at all or on other terms than he may choose to accept. Counsel's analogies, drawn from the obligations to the public on the part of innkeepers, common carriers, and the like, are beside the mark.

Judgment affirmed.

NOTE

1. The principle set forth in the opinion has retained its vitality over the years. L. S. Ayres & Co. v. Hicks, 220 Ind. 86, 40 N.E.2d 334 (1942); Harper v. Baptist Medical Center-Princeton, 341 So. 2d 133 (Ala. 1976); Lyons v. Grether, 218 Va. 630, 239 S.E.2d 103 (1977); 61 Am. Jur. 2d, Physicians, Surgeons, and Other Healers, §14, p. 159. But it is also generally recognized that

when a physician or surgeon takes charge of a case and is employed to
attend a patient, unless the terms of employment otherwise limit the service, or notice be given that he will not undertake, or cannot afford, the
subsequent treatment, his employment, as well as the relation of physician
and patient, continues until ended by the mutual consent of the parties, or
revoked by the dismissal of the physician or surgeon, or until his services
are no longer needed. And he must exercise, at his peril, reasonable care
and judgment in determining when his attendance may properly and safely
be discontinued.

Nash v. Royster, 189 N.C. 408, 413, 127 S.E. 356, 359 (1925). Whether a
physician-patient relationship exists is a question of fact. Compare Lyons
v. Grether, *supra*, and Harper v. Baptist Medical Center-Princeton,
supra. Paradoxically, a physician who is summoned by a bystander to
render services to an unconscious person injured in a road accident is
entitled to compensation from the estate, even if the patient dies without
ever regaining consciousness. Cotnam v. Wisdom, *infra* p. 163.

Does the *Hurley* case still reflect our moral sentiments? More than a
hundred years ago Bentham argued for imposing a duty to aid backed up
by criminal sanctions.

Every man is bound to assist those who have need of assistance if he can do
it without exposing himself to sensible inconvenience. This obligation is
stronger, in proportion as the danger is the greater for the one and the
trouble of preserving him the less for the other. . . . [T]he crime would be
greater if he refrained from acting not simply from idleness, but from
malice or some pecuniary interest.

J. Bentham, Introduction to the Principles of Morals and Legislation, in 1
Works 164 (J. Bowring ed. 1843). See Weinrib, The Case for a Duty to
Rescue, 90 Yale L.J. 247 (1980). Is the recent suggestion that social goods
should be distributed according to their "internal goal" (in the case of
physicians' services, the prevention and cure of physical suffering) helpful in deciding the doctor's case? See B. Williams, The Idea of Equality,
in 2 Philosophy, Politics and Society 121-122 (P. Laslett & W. Runciman
eds. 1962). Should a doctor bear the costs of the desired allocation just
because he happens to have the requisite skill? "[I]s he less entitled to
pursue his own goals, within the special circumstances of practicing medicine, than anybody else?" R. Nozick, Anarchy, State, and Utopia 234
(1974). Should society be able to compel a physician to render aid, on the
grounds that its licensing statutes give the physician the benefit of an
artificial monopoly? See generally A. Kronman & R. Posner, The Economics of Contract Law 264-265 (1979).

Assume that a court, inspired by a concern for distributive justice,
decides to impose liability on the doctor. How should liability be confined
to prevent runaway social engineering? Would a rule be workable that

imposed a duty to give aid, unless the physician had a legitimate reason for refusing? Should a statute be passed that imposes on a physician the duty to give aid in an emergency? Should such a statute be passed only in a jurisdiction that has a good Samaritan law? For examples of good Samaritan laws, see Cal. Bus. & Prof. Code §2144 (West 1959), §2725.5 (West 1963); Conn. Gen. Stat. Ann. §52-557b (1983). On the duty to aid imposed by admiralty law, see G. Gilmore & C. Black, The Law of Admiralty §8-4 (2d ed. 1975). See 1964 Wis. L. Rev. 494; 51 Calif. L. Rev. 816 (1963).

2. In the modern urban setting, the hospital emergency ward has relieved the individual physician from many of the burdens of rendering individual emergency care. Should a hospital with an emergency ward be held liable for refusing to treat an emergency patient? Some courts, though not all, have so held. See the policy discussion in Mercy Medical Center of Oshkosh, Inc. v. Winnebago County, 58 Wis. 2d 260, 206 N.E.2d 198, 200-201 (1973). See also Powers, Hospital Emergency Service and the Open Door, 66 Mich. L. Rev. 1455 (1968); Annot., 35 A.L.R.3d 841 (1971).

On the constitutional and public policy aspects of a private hospital's refusal to allow its facilities to be used for elective abortions, see Doe v. Bridgeton Hospital Assn., 71 N.J. 478, 366 A.2d 641 (1976); Annot., 42 A.L.R. Fed. 463, 526 et seq. (1979). Receipt by a private hospital of federal funding may also have an effect on its freedom to deny members of the public use of its facilities, even if they are unable to pay. See Hill-Burton Act, 42 U.S.C. §§291 et seq.; Annot., 11 A.L.R. Fed. 683 (1972) (discussing whether there is a private right of action under the Hill-Burton Act).

3. In recent years, freedom of contract has been severely limited in an effort to prevent discrimination in employment, housing, and public accommodation. Could a private physician/dentist today refuse to treat a patient because of race? See Rice v. Rinaldo, 67 Ohio Abs. 183, 119 N.E.2d 657 (1951).

On legislation controlling discrimination in the credit market, see p. 603 *infra*. Discussion on the pertinent legislation and case law in other fields lies outside the scope of this casebook.

4. Consult Wyman, The Inherent Limitation of the Public Service Duty to Particular Classes, 23 Harv. L. Rev. 339 (1910); Lenhoff, The Scope of Compulsory Contracts Proper, 43 Colum. L. Rev. 586 (1943). For the attitude of the common law with regard to the duty to render aid in an emergency, see Bohlen, The Moral Duty to Aid Others as a Basis of Tort Liability, 56 U. Pa. L. Rev. 217 (1908); 52 Colum. L. Rev. 631 (1952). For the compensation of the rescuer, see Dawson, The Altruistic Intermeddler, 74 Harv. L. Rev. 817, 1073 (1961).

GREAT ATLANTIC & PACIFIC TEA CO. v. CREAM OF WHEAT CO., 227 F. 46 (2d Cir. 1915). Lacombe, J.: "We had supposed that it was elementary law that a trader could buy from whom he pleased and sell to whom he pleased, and that his selection of seller and buyer was wholly his own concern. 'It is a part of a man's civil rights that he be at liberty to refuse business relations with any person whomsoever, whether the refusal rests upon reason, or is the result of whim, caprice, prejudice, or malice.' Cooley on Torts, p. 278. See, also, our own opinion in Greater New York Film Co. v. Biograph Co., 203 Fed. 39, 121 C.C.A. 375.

"Before the Sherman Act it was the law that a trader might reject the offer of a proposing buyer, for any reason that appealed to him; it might be because he did not like the other's business methods, or because he had some personal difference with him, political, racial, or social. That was purely his own affair, with which nobody else had any concern. Neither the Sherman Act, nor any decision of the Supreme Court construing the same, nor the Clayton Act, has changed the law in this particular. We have not yet reached the stage where the selection of a trader's customers is made for him by the government."

UNITED STATES v. COLGATE & CO., 250 U.S. 300, 307 (1919): "The purpose of the Sherman Act is to prohibit monopolies, contracts and combinations which probably would unduly interfere with the free exercise of their rights by those engaged, or who wish to engage, in trade and commerce—in a word to preserve the right of freedom to trade. In the absence of any purpose to create or maintain a monopoly, the act does not restrict the long recognized right of trader or manufacturer engaged in an entirely private business, freely to exercise his own independent discretion as to parties with whom he will deal. And of course, he may announce in advance the circumstances under which he will refuse to sell. 'The trader or manufacturer, on the other hand, carries on an entirely private business, and can sell to whom he pleases.' United States v. Trans-Missouri Freight Association, 166 U.S. 290, 320. 'A retail dealer has the unquestioned right to stop dealing with a wholesaler for reasons sufficient to himself, and may do so because he thinks such dealer is acting unfairly in trying to undermine his trade.'"

NOTE

1. As the excerpts from the two preceding cases dealing with the validity of resale price-maintenance agreements show, a system committed to liberty of trade and competition requires close scrutiny of contract as an instrument of commercial and industrial organization. Freedom of contract cannot be used as a means to bring about unreasonable restraint of trade. Small wonder that freedom of contract has been subjected to extensive limitation through the antitrust laws, particularly the Sherman[1]

1. 26 Stat. 209 (1890).

and Clayton Acts.[2] These statutes, enacted to protect the competitive framework of the market, deal with horizontal restraints of trade (e.g., cartels aimed at price fixing or market allocation), as well as vertical integration (the combination of various phases of the production and distribution process before the goods reach the ultimate consumer). To be sure, integration by contract (both backwards and forwards), restricting the freedom of the distributor by means of resale price setting, tie-ins,[3] the allocation of territories, and other exclusive arrangements, is not the only means of integration. But contract integration has one advantage over ownership integration that is of particular importance: it enhances flexibility and thereby affords protection against the movement of the business cycle.[4]

Since the antitrust laws are exceedingly vague, they amount in effect to a legislative command to the judiciary to develop a common law of antitrust; as a result, in the antitrust field judicial lawmaking has become of paramount importance. Excellent illustrations are furnished by the excerpts from the *Cream of Wheat* and *Colgate* cases (whose implications are still felt today, though less broadly and more remotely than before).[5]

Both cases deal with one aspect of freedom of contract: the refusal to deal. Given unlimited scope, the refusal to deal is a means of controlling the distribution process and of enforcing resale price-maintenance agreements. The law has not gone so far as to take away the privilege of a single

2. 38 Stat. 731 (1914).

3. They are made illegal under the Clayton Act. Clayton Act §3, 38 Stat. 731 (1914), 15 U.S.C. 14 (1958); Standard Oil Co. of New Jersey v. United States, 221 U.S. 1 (1910). For a criticism of the treatment of tie-ins, see Bowman, Tying Arrangements and the Leverage Problem, 67 Yale L.J. 19 (1957); see pp. 61-63 *infra*.

4. For the most eloquent defense of the Sherman Act, see Black, J., in Northern Pacific Railway Co. v. United States, 356 U.S. 1, 4-5 (1958):

> The Sherman Act was designed to be a comprehensive charter of economic liberty aimed at preserving free and unfettered competition as the rule of trade. It rests on the premise that the unrestrained interaction of competitive forces will yield the best allocation of our economic resources, the lowest prices, the highest quality and the greatest material progress, while at the same time providing an environment conducive to the preservation of our democratic political and social institutions. But even were that premise open to question, the policy unequivocally laid down by the Act is competition. And to this end it prohibits, "Every contract, combination . . . or conspiracy, in restraint of trade or commerce among the several States." Although this prohibition is literally all-encompassing, the courts have construed it as precluding only those contracts or combinations which "unreasonably" restrain competition. Standard Oil Co. of New Jersey v. United States, 221 U.S. 1, 31.

5. For an early analysis of the *Cream of Wheat* case, see Slichter, The Cream of Wheat Case, 31 Pol. Sci. Q. 392 (1916). On the erosion of the *Colgate* doctrine, see in general Levi, The Parke, Davis-Colgate Doctrine: The Ban on Resale Price Maintenance, 1960 Sup. Ct. Rev. 258; Turner, The Definition of Agreement under the Sherman Act: Conscious Parallelism and Refusals to Deal, 75 Harv. L. Rev. 655, 684-695 (1961). But see P. Areeda & D. Turner, Antitrust Law (1978); Fulda, Individual Refusals to Deal: When Does Single-Firm Conduct Become Vertical Restraint?, 30 Law & Contemp. Prob. 590 (1965); L. Sullivan, Antitrust §139 (1977). See also the discussion of franchising in Chapter 4, Section 4.

trader to deal with whom he pleases, but it has expanded its control over what may be termed "joint action." Even here the protection accorded to the injured party is still imperfect under present antitrust laws.[6] A single trader, on the other hand, is free to deal with whom he pleases, absent any purpose to create or maintain a monopoly. And it would seem that he is free to announce in advance (unilaterally) the conditions under which he will refuse to deal with those who fail to abide by his wishes and thus, for example, is free to terminate a recalcitrant dealer who is unwilling to accede to a scheme in restraint of trade. So long as he acts unilaterally, he is safe, but once he enlists the help of others in the scheme of distribution, his privilege is forfeited; see, for example, United States v. Parke, Davis & Co., 362 U.S. 29 (1960).

This book is not the place to deal with the economics of vertical integration or to evaluate the relevant statute and case law. It must be sufficient to sketch a few highlights and to point out that the field is a highly controversial one. Congress and the courts have vacillated when dealing with the legitimacy of vertical integration. This is not surprising since the relevant antitrust statutes reflect different and somewhat inconsistent legislative purposes and, as a result, internal tensions exist within the antitrust structure. To make matters worse, a tension also exists between the "per se" and "rule of reason" yardsticks employed to determine the existence of an antitrust violation. A rule of reason standard requires the court to assay the economic consequences of business behavior and to ban only behavior that is "unreasonable" in purpose or effect. The application of this standard necessitates a comprehensive and costly economic analysis, a task for which courts may be most ill-suited (Standard Oil Co. v. United States, 337 U.S. 293, 310 (1949)). Therefore, a catalogue of per se offenses has emerged. Within this category the courts are relieved of the necessity of a comprehensive economic analysis, since "the practice facially appears to be one that would almost always tend to restrict competition. . . ." (Broadcast Music, Inc. v. CBS, 441 U.S. 1, 19-20 (1979)). Unfortunately, "there is often no bright line separating per se from rule of reason analysis. Per se rules may require considerable inquiry into market conditions before the evidence certifies a presumption of anticompetitive effect. For example, while the Court has spoken of a per se rule against tying arrangements, it has also recognized that tying may have procompetitive justifications that make it inappropriate to condemn without considerable market analysis." See Jefferson Parish Hosp. Dist. 2 v. Hyde, — U.S. — , 104 S. Ct. 155 (1984). Inquiry into market conditions is also necessary to determine the pro- or anti-competitive effects of exclusive dealings.

---

6. Nelson Radio & Supply Co. v. Motorola, Inc., 200 F.2d 911 (5th Cir. 1952), *cert. denied*, 345 U.S. 925 (1953); Kessler & Stern, Competition, Contract, and Vertical Integration, 69 Yale L.J. 1, 83-91, 115-116 (1959); Stern, A Proposed Uniform State Antitrust Law: Text and Commentary on a Draft Statute, 39 Tex. L. Rev. 717, 731, 747-751 (1961).

As early as 1911, the Supreme Court was confronted with the problem of resale price maintenance in the celebrated case of Dr. Miles Medical Co. v. John D. Park and Sons, Co., 220 U.S. 373 (1911). The Court treated the scheme as an illegal restraint on alienation on the grounds that the seller sought to maintain prices after he had parted with the article. The scheme was declared illegal per se, and thus the public was given the benefit of price competition in the market subsequent to the first sale. Congress stepped in to overturn the decision, making resale price maintenance legal, but subsequent legislation restored the per se rule of the *Dr. Miles* case. Consumer Goods Pricing Act of 1975, 89 Stat. 801.

Non-price restraints are treated differently. With regard to these there is a growing tendency to advocate a hands-off policy on the grounds of efficiency. This attitude is reflected in Continental TV, Inc. v. GTE Sylvania, Inc., 433 U.S. 36 (1971). Although the Court explicitly said that it was not changing the per se rule in vertical price fixing, there has been an increasing tendency in the legal literature to question whether price and territory restraints can logically be treated differently under the per se rule. See, e.g., Posner, The Chicago School of Antitrust Analysis, 127 U. Pa. L. Rev. 925, 936 (1979), and the amicus brief of the Department of Justice in Monsanto Co. v. Spray-Rite Service Co., 104 S. Ct. 1464 (1984) (where the Court in that case sidestepped the issue). See further Nelson, Comments on a Paper by Posner, 127 U. Pa. L. Rev. 949 (1970); Williamson, Assessing Vertical Market Restrictions: Antitrust Ramifications of the Transaction Cost Approach, 127 U. Pa. L. Rev. 953 (1979); United States Department of Justice Vertical Restraints Guidelines, Jan. 23, 1985. The testimony of L. A. Sullivan before the Subcommittee on Monopolies and Commercial Law of the Committee on the Judiciary is highly critical, 16 Antitrust Law and Economics Review 11 (1984); see further L. A. Sullivan, Antitrust, Ch. 5 (1977) and Comanor, Vertical Price Fixing, Vertical Market Restraints, and the New Antitrust Policy, 98 Harv. L. Rev. 949 (1985) (critical); Bork, The Rule of Reason and the Per Se Concept: Price Fixing and Market Division (pt. 2), 75 Yale L.J. 373 (1966); Kramer, The Supreme Court and Tying Arrangements: Antitrust as History, 69 Minn. L. Rev. 1013 (1985). See further Chapter 4, Section 4 on dealer franchises.

2. A statutory approach to the refusal-to-deal problem has been suggested by Vernon Mund in a report prepared for the Senate Small Business Committee (Sen. Doc. No. 32, 85th Cong., 1st Sess. (1957)). The report proposed legislation "requiring producers of standard products who hold themselves out as dealing with the public, and who control a substantial percentage of the output in their area of practical shipment, to sell to all comers offering to meet the terms of sale" (pp. 92, 102). His proposal was not unlike a section of the original Clayton Bill which passed the House in 1914 but was deleted by the Senate Committee before the

passage of the Act. The excised section imposed a duty upon owners and transporters of hydroelectric energy, coal, oil, gas, and other minerals to sell to all responsible persons (H.R. 15657, 63d Cong., 2d Sess. §3 (1914)). The Senate felt such a statute "would practically compel owners of the products named to sell to anyone or else decline to do so at the peril of incurring heavy penalties, [and] would project us into a field of legislation at once untried, complicated, and dangerous" (S. Rep. No. 698, 63d Cong., 2d Sess. (1914)).

3. The economic plight of workers laid off by plant shutdowns and relocations is not a new problem, but until recently it has been regarded as an unavoidable consequence of the market system. Traditionally, a belief in the mobility of both capital and labor supported the view that employers should be free to close or relocate when an operation became unprofitable due to obsolescence, increased transportation costs, or for other reasons. Over the last decades, however, the plight of workers, along with their families and communities, has become a matter of increasing national concern, and the traditional wisdom of leaving the problem of dislocation to free market decisionmaking has become problematical. It is not surprising that we observe a tendency, in recent years, to bring the problem of dislocation to courts and legislatures.

As yet, efforts to prevent shutdowns through the application of labor law, antitrust legislation, and the common law have for the most part been unsuccessful. In particular, attempts to expand the duty imposed by labor legislation to bargain in good faith to include a duty on the part of management to bargain with the employees' representative about plant-closing decisions have come to naught: an employer, it has been held, has an almost absolute right to terminate the business for economic reasons. First National Maintenance Corporation v. NLRB, 452 U.S. 666 (1981).

Common law principles have proven equally unhelpful from the worker's point of view. For example, one federal court quite recently refused to make a contract out of assurances by local managers and public relations experts that the plant would remain open if the joint efforts of management and the union were successful in making the plant profitable. Accepting the management's accounting procedures, the court found that this "condition precedent" had not been met. Also unsuccessful was the argument, advanced in the same case, for the imposition of a duty to sell the plant to community interests, based on a "new concept of community property." Attempts to get financing apparently failed, thus foreclosing the possibility left open by the court that the workers might pursue an antitrust remedy based on the contention that management was anxious to prevent the emergence of a competitor. Local 1330, United Steel Workers of America v. United States Steel Corp., 631 F.2d 1264 (6th Cir. 1980). (See further Abbington v. Dayton Malleable, Inc., 561 F. Supp. 1290 (S.D. Ohio 1983).)

While the court in the *United Steel Workers* case could not have reached any other result under traditional doctrine, the decision has led the author of a recent article to advocate the extension of contract principles in recognition of the social dimension of contract law. Freedom of contract, he argues, "in the utopian vision requires a social order in which people possess the practical ability to connect with each other to find meaning in their lives through common endeavor, a freedom that denies the life and death power of distant corporate managers over workers and their town." The analysis and reform of contract law, this author asserts, should be the next step on the agenda of critical legal theory. Feinman, Critical Approaches to Contract Law, 30 U.C.L.A.L. Rev. 829, at 857 et seq. (1983). Feinman is associated with the Critical Legal Studies movement, a somewhat amorphous group of legal scholars and law reformers that is broadly concerned with the relationship between legal rules and institutions and the prerequisites for a "more humane, egalitarian and democratic society." Kennedy & Klare, A Bibliography of Critical Legal Studies, 94 Yale L.J. 460 (1984). Some members of the group have been influenced by legal realism and others by contemporary social theory (especially the work of those in the Neo-Marxist "Frankfurt School"). On the movement, see The Politics of Law: A Progressive Critique (D. Kairys ed. 1982); Symposium in 36 Stan. L. Rev. 1-674 (1984); Unger, The Critical Legal Studies Movement, 96 Harv. L. Rev. 561 (1982).

Despite these setbacks, there are continuing efforts to persuade plant owners to sell, and even to impose upon them a *duty* to sell to unions or to other community interests, plants regarded as obsolete. These efforts have so far succeeded only with regard to the transfer of ownership of the Wireton steel mill. See the recent article in the New York Times of Jan. 30, 1985, at 7, entitled "Pittsburgh Area Rallies to Save Blast Furnace."

Efforts to obtain help by legislation on the federal level have as yet yielded no positive results, although a substantial number of bills have been introduced. On the state level, similar efforts have also been largely unsuccessful. Only in three states, Maine, South Carolina, and Wisconsin, have legislatures acted favorably. See Barton, Common Law and Its Substitutes: The Allocation of Social Problems to Alternative Decisional Institutions, 63 N.C.L. Rev. 518, 525-526 (1985). See in general Aarons, Plant Closings: American and Comparative Perspectives, 59 Chi. Kent L. Rev. 941 (1983); MacNeil, Plant Closings and Workers' Rights, 14 Ottawa L. Rev. 122 (1982).

POUGHKEEPSIE BUYING SERVICE, INC. v. POUGHKEEPSIE NEWSPAPERS, INC.
205 Misc. 982, 131 N.Y.S.2d 515 (Sup. Ct. 1954)

EAGER, J. This is a motion to dismiss the complaint herein upon the ground that it fails to state facts sufficient to constitute a cause of action.

The action is by a merchant, who alleges he conducts two retail stores in the city of Poughkeepsie, N.Y., and is brought against a publisher of a Poughkeepsie daily newspaper. The complaint alleges that the newspaper published by the defendant is the only general daily newspaper in Poughkeepsie and is known as the "Poughkeepsie New Yorker," and that, by reason of its large circulation and high reputation, it is "the dominant advertising medium in the entire area of its publication." It is further alleged that the defendant refuses, because of the persuasion and coercion of local merchants in competition with plaintiff, to publish advertising of the plaintiff in the defendant's newspaper and that, as a result, the plaintiff's business has been seriously reduced and such refusal has caused and will continue to cause irreparable damage to plaintiff's business. Further alleging that plaintiff has no adequate remedy at law, injunctive relief is demanded, namely, judgment directing the defendant to accept and publish plaintiff's advertising on payment of the usual charges of the defendant.

To dispose of the motion, the court must decide whether a newspaper publisher may be required to publish proper advertising matter upon the tender of the usual charge therefor or whether such publisher is free to contract and deal with whom he pleases. There are no New York decisions in point. The holding of courts in other States is summarized in a note in volume 87 of American Law Reports at page 979 as follows: — "With the exception of one case, Uhlman v. Sherman (1919) 22 Ohio N.P.N.S. 225, 31 Ohio Dec. N.P. 54, it has been uniformly held in the few cases which have considered the question that the business of publishing a newspaper is a strictly private enterprise, as distinguished from a business affected with a public interest, and that its publisher is under no legal obligation to sell advertising to all who may apply for it."

The plaintiff contends that this court should reject the majority view and adopt the resoning laid down by the Ohio decision of Uhlman v. Sherman (*supra*). It was there held that the newspaper business was clothed with a public interest and that a corporation owning and publishing a newspaper was in the class of a quasi-public corporation bound to treat all advertisers fairly and without discrimination. It was further there specifically held that a newspaper publisher, having advertising space to sell, had no right to discriminate against a local merchant, who, in his application for advertising, complies with the law and all reasonable rules of the publisher, and tenders the regular and ordinary fee charged therefor by the paper. Courts in other State have, however, expressly refused to follow this Ohio decision. (See Shuck v. Carroll Daily Herald, 247 N.W. 813 [Iowa], 87 A.L.R. 975, Matter of Louis Wohl, Inc., 50 F.2d 254, 256, and Friedenberg v. Times Pub. Co., 170 La. 3.)

This court has also reached the conclusion that the rationale of said Ohio decision is not to be followed in this State in that it is contrary to general and fundamental doctrine laid down in our decisional law. For

instance, we find decisions here, though not in point, in which it has
been generally held that the publication and distribution of newspapers is
a private business and that newspaper publishers lawfully conducting
their business have the right to determine the policy they will pursue
therein and the persons with whom they will deal. (Lepler v. Palmer, 150
Misc. 546; Collins v. American News Co., 34 Misc. 260, 263, *affd.* 69 App.
Div. 639.) And it is said to be "the well-settled law of this State that the
refusal to maintain trade relations with any individual is an inherent right
which every person may exercise lawfully, for reasons he deems sufficient
or for no reasons whatever, and it is immaterial whether such refusal is
based upon reason or is the result of mere caprice, prejudice or malice. It
is a part of the liberty of action which the Constitutions, State and Federal, guarantee to the citizen." (Locker v. American Tobacco Co., 121
App. Div. 443, 451-452, *affd.* 195 N.Y. 565.) There are limitations to this
inherent right, but such limitations must be found either in firmly established common-law principles or in statutory regulations enacted pursuant to the police power for the public good. It has been ably pointed out
that there was no rule at common law, similar to the rules applicable to
common carriers and inns, whereby a newspaper was forbidden to discriminate between customers. (See Shuck v. Carroll Daily Herald, *supra.*) And there are no pertinent statutory regulations in this State. It may
be that the Legislature has the right to reasonably regulate the newspaper
business but the fact that it has not seen fit to do so does not confer power
upon the courts to impose rules for the conduct of such business.

This court holds, therefore, that, in this State, the newspaper business
is in the nature of a private enterprise and that, in the absence of valid
statutory regulation to the contrary, the publishers of a newspaper have
the general right either to publish or reject a commercial advertisement
tendered to them. Their reasons for rejecting a proposed advertisement
are immaterial, assuming, of course, there are absent factual allegations
connecting them with a duly pleaded fraudulent conspiracy or with fur-
thering an unlawful monopoly. There are no such allegations in this case.

The complaint is dismissed. Submit order on notice.

NOTE

Consult Developments in the Law, Competitive Torts, 77 Harv. L.
Rev. 888, 925-932 (1964); J. J. Gordon, Inc. v. Worcester Telegram Publishing Co., 343 Mass. 142, 177 N.E.2d 586 (1961), discussed in 3 B.C.
Ind. & Com L. Rev. 522 (1962); Approved Personnel, Inc. v. Tribune Co.,
177 So. 2d 704, 18 A.L.R.3d 1277 (Fla. Dist. Ct. App. 1965). For the
impact of the antitrust laws, see further Lorain Journal Co. v. United
States, 342 U.S. 143 (1951); Times-Picayune Publishing Co. v. United
States, 345 U.S. 594 (1953). On first amendment problems and the different treatment of electronic and print media, consult Barron, Freedom of

the Press for Whom? (1974); Lange, The Role of the Access Doctrine in the Regulation of the Mass Media: A Critical Review and Assessment, 52 N.C.L. Rev. 1 (1973). See also Chicago Joint Board, Amalgamated Clothing Workers v. Chicago Tribune, 435 F.2d 470 (7th Cir. 1970), *cert. denied*, 402 U.S. 973 (1971).

CONTINENTAL FOREST PRODUCTS, INC. v. CHANDLER SUPPLY CO.
95 Idaho 739, 518 P.2d 1201 (1974)

BAKES, Justice.

Continental Forest Products, Inc., the plaintiff-respondent, is an Oregon corporate lumber broker. As plaintiff, it instituted this action against Chandler Supply Company, also a corporation, the defendant-appellant, seeking recovery of $10,231.45, plus interest, for two carloads of plywood allegedly sold defendant in the summer of 1969. Following trial without a jury, the court entered findings of fact and conclusions of law in favor of the plaintiff (hereinafter referred to as Continental), and entered judgment in conformity with its findings and conclusions. The defendant-appellant (hereinafter referred to as Chandler) appeals from this judgment and from the order of the trial court denying its objections to the findings of fact, conclusions of law and judgment of the court.

The appellant Chandler is a wholesale lumber distributor at Boise and has done business, both buying and selling of lumber products, with a company known as North America Millwork, Inc., of Tacoma, Washington. On June 26, 1969, Larry Williams, an employee of Chandler, phoned North America Millwork, Inc., for quotations on plywood prices, advising North America it was in the market for a carload of $\frac{1}{2}$ inch plywood and a carload of $\frac{5}{8}$ inch plywood. Williams spoke with Ed Barker, an employee of North America, giving him the necessary data. Later on the same day, Barker advised Williams of the quoted prices for plywood, and Williams ordered the two carloads of plywood from North America Millwork, giving Barker the Chandler purchase order numbers 3246 and 3247.

On the same day, Williams prepared two separate Chandler purchase orders covering the two carloads of plywood fixing the delivery date as two weeks or sooner, f.o.b. mill, with the quoted prices. These two purchase orders, one numbered 3246 and the other numbered 3247, were mailed by Chandler to North America Millwork on the same day.

This was Chandler's first order for plywood from North America Millwork, although it had transacted a considerable volume of other lumber business with North America Millwork between December, 1968, and July, 1969. In prior transactions when Chandler had purchased from North America, North America had sent its own written acknowledgments of Chandler's purchase orders placed with it and later had submitted invoices upon shipments being made. In the instance, North America neither confirmed nor rejected the June 26, 1969, Chandler purchase orders by written acknowledgment nor did it send its invoices to Chandler.

However, on July 2, 1969, Chandler received two acknowledgments of the order for plywood from Continental, both dated June 27, 1969, one for a carload of $\frac{1}{2}$ inch plywood, and the other for a carload of $\frac{5}{8}$ inch plywood. The specifications, prices and terms for the plywood as recited in the acknowledgments were substantially the same as the orders placed by Chandler with North America on June 26. The acknowledgments also referred to the Chandler purchase order 3246 and 3247 which had been sent to North America Millwork. It is not entirely clear how Continental received Chandler's orders sent to North America. Apparently Ed Barker left his employment with North America and commenced brokering for Continental and gave the order to Continental.

On July 7, 1969, the Monday following the Fourth of July holiday, Earl Chandler, the president of appellant company, in his own handwriting, wrote on each duplicate copy of the acknowledgments of orders received from Continental, "Purchased from North America Millwork. Earl Chandler 7-7-69" and directed that they be mailed to Continental. Earl Chandler testified that in writing this notation he assumed that Continental was making the shipments for North America. Mrs. Hebein, Earl Chandler's secretary, testified that she mailed these copies of the acknowledgments of orders, addressed to Continental, by regular mail. Witnesses for Continental testified that even though they searched through their files for these copies of the acknowledgments, they could not be found. Chandler kept copies of these acknowledgments with his handwritten note on them, and they were introduced into evidence.

Chandler received the first carload of plywood on July 24, 1969, and received an invoice from Continental for this carload. The second carload of plywood arrived August 6, 1969, and the invoice from Continental arrived on August 15. Chandler took delivery of both of these carloads, and at no time offered to return the plywood.

The terms of the orders provided for a 2% discount if paid for within five days after arrival of the invoice. On August 11, 1969, Chandler made a check for $3,636.36 payable to both Continental and North America Millwork and returned it to North America Millwork in payment of these two carloads of plywood. In calculating the amount of the payment, Chandler first deducted the 2% discount for the two carloads of plywood and also deducted a $6,212.95 trade debt owing from North America to Chandler.[7]

---

7. During the summer of 1969 North America Millwork began experiencing financial difficulties. Eventually, in December, 1969, North America Millwork made a common law assignment of assets to its creditors in an effort to liquidate its trade obligations. Through a letter of July 17, 1969, North America Millwork advised Chandler of its financial problems. At this time there was a balance due from North America to Chandler on other transactions in the amount of $6,212.95.

North America returned Chandler's check and denied that Chandler owed it money for the shipment of plywood. Chandler sent the payment to North America a second time, but it was again returned. Through a series of letters and telephone calls Chandler attempted to induce North America to accept payment. During this time, Ed Barker (who was then acting as an independent lumber broker, having left employment with North America on June 30, 1969), sent a letter to Williams (employee of Chandler) indicating that Continental was the actual supplier of the plywood. Chandler's attempt to pay North America failed, and Chandler refused to tender payment to Continental without deducting North America's trade debt.

Not having received payment for the two carloads, Continental brought this action for the quoted price of the plywood plus interest. Continental subsequently filed its supplemental complaint alleging a second claim against Chandler on the theory of unjust enrichment on the part of Chandler and seeking as damages $10,231.45

Appellant Chandler answered the complaint and supplemental complaint, denying that it owed Continental any money or that Continental had sold it any goods. Chandler alleged that it had a contract only with North America to whom it had tendered payment. Following trial to the court on the issues framed by the pleadings, the trial court rendered its memorandum opinion in favor of Continental. Pursuant to I.R.C.P. Rule 52, Chandler moved for reconsideration of the memorandum opinion and proposed findings, which motion the court denied. Thereafter findings of fact, conclusions of law and judgment for $11,559,93 were entered, to which appellant objected. The district court denied these objections, and this appeal was taken.

Appellant first assigned as error the trial court's failure to find that Continental's claim was subject to Chandler's right of set off against North America.

In the trial court's memorandum opinion, rendered on May 26, 1971, the court discussed the relationship between Continental and Chandler and found that "the very least we have was an implied agreement or quasi contract."

Basically the courts have recognized three types of contractual arrangements. Restatement of Contracts, §5, comment *a*, at p. 7 (1932); 3 Corbin on Contracts, §562 at p. 283 (1960). First is the express contract wherein the parties expressly agree regarding a transaction. Alexander v. O'Neil, 77 Ariz. 316, 267 P.2d 730 (1954). Secondly, there is the implied in fact contract wherein there is no express agreement but the conduct of the parties implies an agreement from which an obligation in contract exists. Clements v. Jungert, 90 Idaho 143, 408 P.2d 810 (1965). The third category is called an implied in law contract, or quasi contract. However, a contract implied in law is not a contract at all, but an obligation imposed by law for the purpose of bringing about justice and equity without reference to the intent or the agreement of the parties and, in some cases, in spite of an agreement between the parties. Hixon v. Allphin, 76 Idaho 327, 281 P.2d 1042 (1955); McShane v. Quillin, 47 Idaho 542, 277 P.2d 554 (1929); 3 Corbin on Contracts, §561, at p. 276 (1960). It is a non-contractual obligation that is to be treated procedurally *as if* it were a contract, and is often referred to as quasi contract, unjust enrichment, implied in law contract or restitution. In discussing a quasi contract or an action founded on unjust enrichment, the California Supreme Court stated in Ward v. Taggart, 51 Cal. 2d 736, 336 P.2d 534 (1959):

> The promise is purely fictitious and unintentional, originally implied to circumvent rigid common-law pleading. It was invoked not to deny a remedy, but to create one "for the purpose of bringing about justice without reference to the intention of the parties." 1 Williston, Contracts (rev. ed.) p. 9; . . ."

336 P.2d at 538. Similarly, in Roberts v. Roberts, 64 Wyo. 433, 196 P.2d 361 (1948), the court stated at p. 367:

> This brings us to the question as to an implied or quasi-contract pleaded in the second cause of action. Black's Law Dictionary defines it thus: "A quasi-contract is what was formerly known as the contract implied in law; it has no reference to the intentions or expressions of the parties. The obligation is imposed despite and frequently in frustration of their intention."

196 P.2d at 367. *See also*, Trollope v. Koerner, 106 Ariz. 164, 470 P.2d 91 (1970), and 1 Williston on Contracts (3d Ed.), §3A at p. 13 (1957).

In this case it is clear that there is neither an express nor an implied in fact contract since there was an express rejection by Chandler of any intention to enter into a contract with Continental as evidenced by the notation made on the acknowledgments and Chandler's subsequent attempts to pay North America Millwork for the carloads of plywood. However, we agree with the trial court that under the peculiar circumstances of this case, the third type of contract, implied in law or quasi contract, exists obligating Chandler to pay for the materials which he received. However, the problem which arises is determining the amount of recovery to which Continental is entitled.

As the essence of a contract implied in law lies in the fact that the defendant has received a benefit which it would be inequitable for him to retain, it necessarily follows that the measure of recovery in a quasi-contractual action is not the actual amount of the enrichment, but the amount of the enrichment which, as between the two parties it would be unjust for one party to retain. Hixon v. Allphin, *supra*; 66 Am. Jur. 2d, Restitution and Implied Contracts, at p. 946 (1973); Meehan v. Cheltenham, 410 Pa. 446, 189 A.2d 593 (1963); Farmers National Bank of Bloomsburg v. Albertson, 203 Pa. Super. 205, 199 A.2d 486 (Pa. 1964). In the instant case we feel that the enrichment which Chandler "unjustly received" was the value of the plywood shipped less the trade set off which Chandler had against North America Millwork and which he would have been entitled to take had the transaction been completed the way Chandler had intended and attempted to complete it. Chandler had a right to deal exclusively with North America and use his trade set off as part of the purchase price. Chandler should not be deprived of this set off in view of the way that Continental became involved in this transaction.

The foregoing conclusions necessarily follow as a matter of law from the salient facts found in the record. Those facts are that Chandler had placed the orders initially with North America Millwork, knowing that he had a trade set off; that the North America Millwork employee Ed Barker left his employment with North America Millwork and apparently took the Chandler orders with him, and that the orders subsequently wound up in the Continental organization; that Continental, without notifying Chandler that Barker had terminated his employment with North America and was now brokering for Continental, mailed its acknowledgments of the two orders which Chandler had placed with North America Millwork, referring to them by Chandler purchase order numbers which were sent to North America Millwork; that Chandler wrote on those acknowledgments that he had purchased the plywood from North America Millwork and mailed the acknowledgments back to Continental; and that Chandler attempted to make payment for the plywood to North America Millwork. If any party was responsible for the situation present in this case, it was Continental. Although it is not entirely clear from the record, it would appear that Barker breached the fiduciary duty which he owed to his employer North America Millwork by taking the Chandler purchase orders to Continental. Continental then, wittingly or unwittingly, took advantage of that breach of a fiduciary relationship and filled the orders, apparently without inquiry concerning the status of North America Millwork, the existence of a trade debt, the situation behind Barker's taking the purchase orders to Continental, or notifying Chandler that it was attempting to take over the North America transactions. Under these circumstances we feel that it would not be unjust to require Chandler to pay only that amount which he would have had to pay to North America had the transaction gone the way Chandler had intended and attempted to have it go.

Since the resolution of the quasi-contractual issue is dispositive in this case it is unnecessary to become embroiled in a discussion of the presumption of receipt of a letter duly mailed versus the weight to be given to testimony on non-receipt, as did the trial court in deciding the case and as did the parties on appeal.

Judgment should be entered for Continental against Chandler in the amount of the principal claim less the amount of the North America Millwork trade debt which Chandler had. The matter should be remanded to the trial court to make the necessary computations including adjustments for interest on account.

Judgment reversed and remanded. Costs awarded to appellant.

Donaldson and McQuade, JJ., concur; Shepard, C.J., concurs in result.

McFADDEN, Justice (dissenting).

It is my conclusion that the judgment of the trial court should be affirmed, and I dissent from that portion of the majority opinion which after determining that Chandler was obligated to pay for the plywood it received, then proceeds to grant an offset to Chandler for an alleged debt owed to it by North America Millwork.

The basic reason for this dissent is that the majority opinion in effect grants to Chandler an offset for a trade debt allegedly due Chandler from North America, who is never a party to this action, nor in privity with Continental. Stringent requirements are established for a court to recognize an offset. See, Brown v. Porter, 42 Idaho 295, 245 P. 398 (1926), which considered the provisions governing the right to a setoff, C.S. §§6694-6697 (I.C. §§5-612 to 5-615). See I.R.C.P. 13(a) and 13(b). In Petersen v. Lyders, 139 Cal. App. 303, 33 P.2d 1030, 1031 (1934), cert. den. 294 U.S. 716, 55 S. Ct. 514, 79 L. Ed. 1249, reh. den. 294 U.S. 734, 55 S. Ct. 635, 79 L. Ed. 1262, the Supreme Court of California considered statutes governing the right to setoff which were identical to Idaho's:

> It is elementary that a set-off may not be invoked unless the parties and the debts are mutual and that the doctrine of mutuality requires that the debts be due to and from the same persons in the same capacity.

Later in Advance Ind. Fin. Co. v. Western Equities, Inc., 173 Cal. App. 2d 420, 343 P.2d 408 (1959), the California Supreme Court again emphasized the necessity of mutuality in setoff cases in the following language:

> A counterclaim or a setoff is defined as a cause of action in favor of the defendant on which he might have sued the plaintiff in a separate action and, in the case of a counterclaim, might have obtained affirmative relief. . . . A claim based on an equitable right may be set up as a counterclaim against a claim based on a legal right. While the doctrine of setoff, as distinguished from statutory counterclaim, is eminently an equitable one, the equitable right is founded on the idea that mutual existing indebtedness, arising out of contracts between parties to the record, creates payment of both demands so far as they equal each other. The two demands must be mutual.

(Citations omitted.) 343 P.2d at 412. See also, Cruzan v. Franklin Stores Corp., 72 N.M. 42, 380 P.2d 190 (N.M. 1963); Sarkeys v. Marlow, 205 Okl. 15, 235 P.2d 676 (1951); A. S. & R. Co. v. Swisshelm Gold Silver Co., 63 Ariz. 204, 160 P.2d 757 (Ariz. 1945).

In this case there is no record of mutuality. The alleged debt is owing from North America to Chandler, Continental has not been shown to have been connected with North America by agency, contract, or assignment, and the trial court did not find any such relationship between Continental and North America.

The majority opinion reaches its final conclusion on the basis that Chandler was going to be unjustly enriched if it was allowed to retain the plywood shipped by Continental without paying somebody. By some process the opinion places fault on the part of Continental, and then states "Under these circumstances we feel that it would not be unjust to require Chandler to pay only that amount which he would have had to pay to North America had the transaction gone the way Chandler had intended and attempted to have it go." This conclusion is then followed by a refusal of the majority opinion to consider what in my opinion is one of the crucial points of the case, i.e., whether Continental ever received the copies of the acknowledgment of orders on which Earl Chandler had written "Purchased from North America Millwork. Earl Chandler 7-7-69."

The majority opinion in faulting Continental for its activities in effect holds the trial court erred when it specifically found "the return acknowledgment with the notation by Mr. Earl Chandler was not received by Continental Forest Products." At trial both parties contested this issue and appellant assigned the issue as an error on appeal. In such cases, when there is testimony by the addressee denying receipt of the mailed instrument, an issue of fact is presented for resolution by the trier of facts. American Surety Co. v. Black, 54 Idaho 1, 27 P.2d 972 (1933); IX Wigmore (3d ed.) §2519; Bell, Handbook of Evidence (1972), p. 239. The trial court sat as a trier of the facts and its function was to weigh the evidence and judge the credibility of the witnesses. A conflict in the evidence as to the receipt of the acknowledgments was presented, and in light of competent, substantial, although conflicting evidence, the trial court's findings in this regard should have been considered and upheld. Ivie v. Peck, 94 Idaho 625, 495 P.2d 1110 (1972).

There are numerous other points wherein I disagree with the majority opinion, particularly in regard to what it claims the trial court found. Extended discussion of these would be futile in a dissent and would unduly lengthen it.

NOTE

1. Compare Boston Ice Co. v. Potter, 123 Mass. 28 (1877), *infra* p. 1504. For more on *Boston Ice Co.*, see the notes following that case, and also Costigan, The Doctrine of Boston Ice Co. v. Potter, 7 Colum. L. Rev. 32 (1907).

2. The *Boston Ice Co.* case was cited with mild approval by Cardozo in Kelly Asphalt Block Co. v. Barber Asphalt Paving Co., 211 N.Y. 68, 105 N.E. 88 (1914), a suit by an undisclosed principal-buyer against the seller for breach of warranty. For the treatment of the undisclosed principal, see the following case.

WATTEAU v. FENWICK
[1893] 1 Q.B. 346 (1892)

Appeal from the decision of the county court judge of Middlesborough.

From the evidence it appeared that one Humble had carried on business at a beer-house called the Victoria Hotel, at Stockton-on-Tees, which business he had transferred to the defendants, a firm of brewers, some years before the present action. After the transfer of the business, Humble remained as defendants' manager; but the license was always taken out in Humble's name, and his name was painted over the door. Under the terms of the agreement made between Humble and the defendants, the former had no authority to buy any goods for the business except bottled ales and mineral waters; all other goods required were to be supplied by the defendants themselves. The action was brought to recover the price of goods delivered at the Victoria Hotel over some years, for which it was admitted that the plaintiff gave credit to Humble only: they consisted of cigars, bovril, and other articles. The learned judge allowed the claim for the cigars and bovril only, and gave judgment for the plaintiff for 22*l*. 12*s*. 6*d*. The defendants appealed.

Finlay, Q.C. (Scott Fox, with him), for the defendants. The decision of the county court judge was wrong. The liability of a principal for the acts of his agent, done contrary to his secret instructions, depends upon his holding him out as his agent — that is, upon the agent being clothed with an apparent authority to act for his principal. Where, therefore, a man carries on business in his own name through a manager, he holds out his own credit, and would be liable for goods supplied even where the manager exceeded his authority. But where, as in the present case, there is no holding out by the principal, but the business is carried on in the agent's name and the goods are supplied on his credit, a person wishing to go behind the agent and make the principal liable must shew an agency in fact.

[Lord Coleridge, C.J. Cannot you, in such a case, sue the undisclosed principal on discovering him?]

Only where the act done by the agent is within the scope of his agency; not where there has been an excess of authority. Where any one has been held out by the principal as his agent, there is a contract with the principal by estoppel, however much the agent may have exceeded his authority; where there has been no holding out, proof must be given of an agency in fact in order to make the principal liable. . . .

WILLS, J. The plaintiff sues the defendants for the price of cigars supplied to the Victoria Hotel, Stockton-upon-Tees. The house was kept, not by the defendants, but by a person named Humble, whose name was over the door. The plaintiff gave credit to Humble, and to him alone, and had never heard of the defendants. The business, however, was really the defendants', and they had put Humble into it to manage it for them, and had forbidden him to buy cigars on credit. The cigars, however, were such as would usually be supplied to and dealt in at such an establishment. The learned county court judge held that the defendants were liable. I am of opinion that he was right.

There seems to be less of direct authority on the subject than one would expect. But I think that the Lord Chief Justice during the argument laid down the correct principle, viz., once it is established that the defendant was the real principal, the ordinary doctrine as to principal and agent applies — that the principal is liable for all the acts of the agent which are within the authority usually confided to an agent of that character, notwithstanding limitations, as between the principal and the agent, put upon that authority. It is said that it is only so where there has been a holding out of authority — which cannot be said of a case where the person supplying the goods knew nothing of the existence of a principal. But I do not think so. Otherwise, in every case of undisclosed principal, or at least in every case where the fact of there being a principal was undisclosed, the secret limitation of authority would prevail and defeat the action of the person dealing with the agent and then discovering that he was an agent and had a principal.

But in the case of a dormant partner it is clear law that no limitation of authority as between the dormant and active partner will avail the dormant partner as to things within the ordinary authority of a partner. The law of partnership is, on such a question, nothing but a branch of the general law of principal and agent, and it appears to me to be undisputed and conclusive on the point now under discussion.

The principle laid down by the Lord Chief Justice, and acted upon by the learned county court judge, appears to be identical with that enunciated in the judgments of Cockburn, C.J., and Mellor, J., in Edmunds v. Bushell, Law Rep. 1 Q.B. 97, the circumstances of which case, though not identical with those of the present, come very near to them. There was no holding out, as the plaintiff knew nothing of the defendant. I appreciate the distinction drawn by Mr. Finlay in his argument, but the principle laid down in the judgments referred to, if correct, abundantly covers the present case. I cannot find that any doubt has ever been expressed that it is correct, and I think it is right, and that very mischievous consequences would often result if that principle were not upheld.

In my opinion this appeal ought to be dismissed with costs.
Appeal dismissed.

NOTE

For a criticism of the undisclosed principal doctrine, see Ames, Undisclosed Principal — Rights and Liabilities, 18 Yale L.J. 443 (1909); Pollock, 3 L.Q. Rev. 358, 359 (1887):

> The plain truth ought never to be forgotten that the whole law as to the rights and liabilities of an undisclosed principal is inconsistent with the elementary doctrines of the law of contract. The right of one person to sue another on a contract not really made with the person suing is unknown to every other legal system except that of England and America. It rests originally on a sort of common law equity, and originates in the feeling that a principal who had got the advantage of a purchase ought to pay for it if the agent to whom the seller really trusted was not able to do so. Whether it was not from the first a mistake to suppose that the rights of a principal must of necessity be correlative to his liabilities is a question of some speculative interest. It is still more doubtful whether it be not inadvisable to extend by a process of judicial logic analogous rights which ought rather to be lessened than increased.

For a defense, see W. Seavey, Studies in Agency 87 (1949); Müller-Freienfels, The Undisclosed Principal, 16 Modern L. Rev. 299 (1953), and see also his Comparative Aspects of Undisclosed Agency, 18 Modern L. Rev. 33 (1955). See, in general, S. Stoljar, The Law of Agency, ch. 10 (1961).

NOBLE v. WILLIAMS
150 Ky. 439, 150 S.W. 507 (1912)

Winn, J. According to the allegations of the petition, the appellants, the plaintiffs, were hired to teach the public school in Jackson, Ky., for the fall term of 1908. The school board failed to pay rent for the schoolhouse, to buy the coal, to furnish the seats, crayons, blackboards, and the like, incident and necessary to the conduct of the school. Plaintiffs allege that they, in order to conduct the school, were obliged to and did pay the rent and buy these supplies. They allege no request by the school board that they should do so, nor any promise by the board to reimburse them. They sought to recover, nevertheless, against the appellee board for these expenditures. The circuit court sustained a demurrer to their petition, and they appeal.

The circuit court was right. The teachers, in contracting and paying these obligations, were volunteers. No man, entirely of his own volition, can make another his debtor. The school board could have been required by mandamus, at the suit of any proper party, to furnish a place for the conduct of the school. The teachers had no right to supply it themselves, and then recover the rent. They had their teaching contract; and if the board made it impossible for them to teach, by failing to furnish a place for conducting the school, they had their right of action on their contract, subject to the customary principles involved in such cases. They adopted neither of these courses, but instead voluntarily paid an obligation which was not theirs.

Judgment affirmed.

NOTE

Contrast Sommers v. Putnam Board of Education, *infra* p. 168. For a case denying recovery in restitution to a concerned citizen who made payment on a contract for a piano in order to "save it for the school," see Grand Isle v. McGowan, 88 Vt. 140, 92 A. 6 (1914).

DAVIS & CO. v. MORGAN
117 Ga. 504, 43 S.E. 732 (1903)

LAMAR, J. Davis & Co. employed Morgan for one year at $40 per month. After the contract had been in force for some time, Morgan received an offer of $65 per month from a company in Florida, and mentioned the fact to Davis, saying that of course he would not go without consent. Davis insists that he then said, if Morgan would stay out the balance of the term, and work satisfactorily, he would give him $120 at the end of the year. Morgan says that Davis stated, "I will add $10 a month from the time you began, and owe you $120 when your time is up." Davis & Co. discharged Morgan two or three weeks before the end of the term, because the latter had gone to Florida for several days without their consent. Morgan insists that he told Davis that he was going, and the latter made no objection. He claimed that he was discharged without proper cause, and brought suit for the extra compensation promised. The jury found a verdict in his favor, and, the court having refused to grant a new trial, Davis & Co. excepted.

If the promise contemplated that Davis & Co. were to pay Morgan $10 per month for that part of the year which had already passed, and as to which there had been a settlement, it was manifestly nudum pactum; for a past transaction, the obligation of which has been fully satisfied, will not sustain a new promise. Gay v. Mott, 43 Ga. 254. And the result is practically the same whether Morgan or Davis was correct in the statement of the conversation. Both proved a promise to give more than was due, and to pay extra for what one was already legally bound to perform. The employer, therefore, received no consideration for his promise to give the additional money at the end of the year. Morgan had agreed to work for 12 months at the price promised, and if during the term he had agreed to receive less, the employer would still have been liable to pay him the full $40 per month. On the other hand, the employer could not be forced to pay more than the contract price. He got no more services than he had already contracted to receive, and according to an almost unbroken line of decisions the agreement to give more than was due was a nudum pactum, and void, as having no consideration to support the promise. The case is something like that of Bush v. Rawlins, 89 Ga. 117, 14 S.E. 886, where the landlord agreed to give the tenant certain property if he would pay his rent promptly; and it was held that such a promise was a gratuity, and void, as without consideration to support it. And see Tatum v. Morgan, 108 Ga. 336, 33 S.E. 940 (2); Civ. Code 1895, §3735. It is also within the principle of Stilk v. Myrick, 2 Campb. 317, 170 Eng. Reprint, 1168, where Lord Ellenborough held that an agreement to pay seamen extra for what they were bound by their articles to do was void. And so in Bartlett v. Wyman, 14 Johns. 260, a similar ruling was made in a case where a master agreed to give more wages if the seamen would not abandon the ship. See, also, Ayres v. Chicago, R.I. & P. Ry. Co., 52 Iowa 478, 3 N.W. 522. There are cases holding that a new promise is binding where one of the parties to a contract refuses to perform, and, to save a loss, the innocent party agrees to pay more than the original contract price, if the actor will perform as originally agreed. Goebel v. Linn, 47 Mich. 489, 11 N.W. 284, 41 Am. Rep. 723. But even if that line of cases should not be disregarded as tending to encourage a breach of contract, they do not affect the rights of Morgan here, because he does not bring himself within their ruling. Had there been a rescission or formal cancellation (Vanderbilt v. Schreyer, 91 N.Y. 402) of the old contract by mutual consent, and if a new contract with new terms had been made, or if there had been any change in the hours, services, or character of work, or other consideration to support the promise to pay the increased wages it would have been enforceable. But, as it was, Morgan proved that Davis promised to pay more for the performance of the old contract than he had originally agreed. Such a promise was not binding. . . .

When one receives a naked promise, and such promise is broken, he is no worse off than he was. He gave nothing for it, he has lost nothing by it, and on its breach he has suffered no damage cognizable by the courts. No benefit accrued to him who made the promise, nor did any injury flow to him who received it. Such promises are not made within the scope of transactions intended to confer rights enforceable at law. They are lightly made, dictated by generosity, courtesy, or impulse, often by ruinous prodigality. To enforce them by a judgment in favor of those who gave nothing therefore would often bring such imperfect obligations into competition with the absolute duties to wife and children, or into competition with debts for property actually received, and make the law an instrument by which a man could be forced to be generous before he was just. . . .

Judgment reversed.

NOTE

In evaluating the decision of Davis & Co. v. Morgan, two questions should be asked. Did both parties regard the defendant's promise as gratuitous? And even assuming that the parties understood the promise for additional compensation to be gratuitous, are the policy reasons advanced by the court self-evidently sound, absent fraud, duress, or other forms of unconscionability? See Chapter 4, Section 5. See further U.C.C. §2-209, discussed *infra* p. 667. Do not overlook Comment 2, which subjects modifications to the test of good faith, U.C.C. §§1-203, 2-103. When is a promise gratuitous?

For a discussion of the consideration doctrine, see pp. 279 et seq. *infra.* Contrast *Davis & Co.* with Schwartzreich v. Bauman-Basch, Inc., which follows.

SCHWARTZREICH v. BAUMAN-BASCH, INC.
231 N.Y. 196, 131 N.E. 887 (1921)

CRANE, J. On the 31st day of August, 1917, the plaintiff entered into the following employment agreement with the defendant: . . .

Agreement entered into this 31st day of August, 1917, by and between Bauman-Basch, Inc., a domestic corporation, party of the first part, and Louis Schwartzreich, of the borough of Bronx, city of New York, party of the second part, witnesseth:

The party of the first part does hereby employ the party of the second part, and the party of second part agrees to enter the services of the party of the first part as a designer of coats and wraps.

The employment herein shall commence on the 22d day of November, 1917, and shall continue for twelve months thereafter. The party of the second part shall receive a salary of ninety ($90.00) per week, payable weekly.

The party of the second part shall devote his entire time and attention to the business of the party of the first part, and shall use his best energies and endeavors in the furtherance of its business.

In witness thereof, the party of the first part has caused its seal to be affixed hereto and these presents to be signed, and the party of the second part has hereunto set his hand and seal the day and year first above written.

Bauman-Basch, Inc.,

S. BAUMAN.

LOUIS SCHWARTZREICH.

In presence of:

In October the plaintiff was offered more money by another concern. Mr. Bauman, an officer of the Bauman-Basch, Inc., says that in that month he heard that the plaintiff was going to leave and thereupon had with him the following conversation:

A. I called him in the office, and I asked him, "Is that true that you want to leave us?" and he said "Yes," and I said, "Mr. Schwartzreich, how can you do that; you are under contract with us?" He said, "Somebody offered me more money." . . . I said, "How much do they offer you?" He said, "They offered him $115 a week." . . . I said, "I cannot get a designer now, and, in view of the fact that I have to send my sample line out on the road, I will give you a hundred dollars a week rather than to let you go." He said, "If you will give me $100, I will stay."

Thereupon Mr. Bauman dictated to his stenographer a new contract, dated October 17, 1917, and in the exact words of the first contract and running for the same period, the salary being $100 a week, which contract was duly executed by the parties and witnessed. Duplicate originals were kept by the plaintiff and defendant.

Simultaneously with the signing of this new contract, the plaintiff's copy of the old contract was either given to or left with Mr. Bauman. He testifies that the plaintiff gave him the paper but that he did not take it from him. The signatures to the old contract plaintiff tore off at the time according to Mr. Bauman.

The plaintiff's version as to the execution of the new contract is as follows:

A. I told Mr. Bauman that I have an offer from Scheer & Mayer of $110 a week, and I said to him, "Do you advise me as a friendly matter — will you advise me as a friendly matter what to do; you see I have a contract with you, and I should not accept the offer of $110 a week, and I ask you, as a matter of friendship, do you advise me to take it or not." At the minute he did not say anything, but the day afterwards he came to me in and he said, "I will give you $100 a week, and I want you to stay with me." I said, "All right, I will accept it; it is very nice of you that you do that, and I appreciate it very much."

The plaintiff says that on the 17th of October, when the new contract was signed, he gave his copy of the old contract back to Mr. Bauman, who said: "You do not want this contract any more because the new one takes its place."

The plaintiff remained in the defendant's employ until the following December when he was discharged. He brought this action under the contract of October 17th for his damages.

The defense, insisted upon through all the courts, is that there was no consideration for the new contract as the plaintiff was already bound under his agreement of August 31, 1917, to do the same work for the same period at $90 a week.

The trial justice submitted to the jury the question whether there was a cancellation of the old contract and charged as follows:

> If you find that the $90 contract was prior to or at the time of the execution of the $100 contract canceled and revoked by the parties by their mutual consent, then it is your duty to find that there was a consideration for the making of the contract in suit, viz., the $100 contract, and, in that event, the plaintiff would be entitled to your verdict for such damages as you may find resulted proximately, naturally, and necessarily in consequence of the plaintiff's discharge prior to the termination of the contract period of which I shall speak later on.

Defendant's counsel thereupon excepted to the portion of the charge in which the court permitted the jury to find that the prior contract may have been canceled simultaneously with the execution of the other agreement. Again the court said:

"The test question is whether by word or by act, either prior to or at the time of the signing of the $100 contract, these parties mutually agreed that the old contract from that instant should be null and void."

The jury having rendered a verdict for the plaintiff, the trial justice set it aside and dismissed the complaint on the ground that there was not sufficient evidence that the first contract was canceled to warrant the jury's findings.

The above quotations from the record show that a question of fact was presented and that the evidence most favorable for the plaintiff would sustain a finding that the first contract was destroyed, canceled, or abrogated by the consent of both parties.

The Appellate Term was right in reversing this ruling. Instead of granting a new trial, however, it reinstated the verdict of the jury and the judgment for the plaintiff. The question remains, therefore, whether the charge of the court, as above given, was a correct statement of the law or whether on all the evidence in the plaintiff's favor a cause of action was made out.

Can a contract of employment be set aside or terminated by the parties to it and a new one made or substituted in its place? If so, is it competent to end the one and make the other at the same time?

It has been repeatedly held that a promise made to induce a party to do that which he is already bound by contract to perform is without consideration. But the cases in this state, while enforcing this rule, also recognize that a contract may be canceled by mutual consent and a new one made. Thus Vanderbilt v. Schreyer, 91 N.Y. 392, 402, held that it was no consideration for a guaranty that a party promise to do only that which he was before legally bound to perform. This court stated, however:

> It would doubtless be competent for parties to cancel an existing contract and make a new one to complete the same work at a different rate of compensation, but it seems that it would be essential to its validity that there should be a valid cancellation of the original contract. Such was the case of Lattimore v. Harsen, 14 Johns. 330.

In Cosgray v. New England Piano Co., 10 App. Div. 351, 353, 41 N.Y.S. 886, 888, it was decided that where the plaintiff had bound himself to work for a year at $30 a week, there was no consideration for a promise thereafter made by the defendant that he should notwithstanding receive $1,800 a year. Here it will be noticed there was no termination of the first agreement which gave occasion for Bartlett, J., to say in the opinion:

"The case might be different if the parties had, by word of mouth, agreed wholly to abrogate and do away with a pre-existing written contract in regard to service and compensation, and had substituted for it another agreement."

Any charge in an existing contract, such as a modification of the rate of compensation, or a supplemental agreement, must have a new consideration to support it. In such a case the contract is continued, not ended. Where, however, an existing contract is terminated by consent of both parties and a new one executed in its place and stead, we have a different situation and the mutual promises are again a consideration. Very little difference may appear in a mere change of compensation in an existing and continuing contract and a termination of one contract and the making of a new one for the same time and work, but at an increased compensation. There is, however, a marked difference in principle. Where the new contract gives any new privilege or advantage to the promisee, a consideration has been recognized, though in the main it is the same contract. Triangle Waist Co., Inc. v. Todd, 223 N.Y. 27, 119 N.E. 85.

If this which we are now holding were not the rule, parties having once made a contract would be prevented from changing it no matter how willing and desirous they might be to do so, unless the terms conferred an additional benefit to the promisee.

All concede that an agreement may be rescinded by mutual consent and a new agreement made thereafter on any terms to which the parties may assent. Prof. Williston, in his work on Contracts, says (volume 1, §130a):

"A rescission followed shortly afterwards by a new agreement in regard to the same subject-matter would create the legal obligations provided in the subsequent agreement."

The same effect follows in our judgment from a new contract entered into at the same time the old one is destroyed and rescinded by mutual consent. The determining factor is the rescission by consent. Provided this is the express and acted upon intention, the time of the rescission, whether a moment before or at the same time as the making of the new contract, is unimportant. . . .

There is no reason that we can see why the parties to a contract may not come together and agree to cancel and rescind an existing contract, making a new one in its place. We are also of the opinion that reason and authority support the conclusion that both transactions can take place at the same time.

For the reasons here stated, the charge of the trial court was correct, and the judgments of the Appellate Division and the Appellate Term should be affirmed, with costs.

Chase, J. dissents.

Judgments affirmed.

NOTE

1. For the decision of the lower court, see A. Corbin, Cases on the Law of Contracts 294 (3d ed. 1947). For a general discussion, see Williston, Consideration in Bilateral Contracts, 27 Harv. L. Rev. 503, 514 et seq.; 1A Corbin §186; N.Y. Law Revision Commission, Report Recommendations and Studies 172 et seq. (1936); DeKoven, Modification of a Contract in New York: Criteria for Enforcement, 35 U. Chi. L. Rev. 173 (1967).

2. Posner, in Gratuitous Promises in Economics and Law, 6 J. Leg. Stud., 411, 424 (1977), defends the principal case on the following grounds:

Because the higher price [offered by a third party] is a genuine opportunity cost of continued compliance with the contract, the promisor should be allowed to terminate subject only to his obligation to make good the promisee's loss from the breach, and hence he should be allowed to negotiate with the promisee over a modification that will compensate the promisor for the lost opportunity.

Do you agree with this interpretation? Has Posner overlooked the fact that the defendant Bauman-Basch may have been a victim of compulsion, despite the promisee's ostentatious civility? Even if there was an interval between "tearing up" the old contract and making the new one, isn't the issue of compulsion the central one in the case? See Sistrom v. Anderson, 51 Cal. App. 2d 213, 124 P.2d 372 (D.C. App. 1942). Consult Restatement Second §74, Comment *b*; U.C.C. §2-209, Comment 2.

WOOD v. BOYNTON
64 Wis. 265, 25 N.W. 42 (1885)

TAYLOR, J. This action was brought in the circuit court for Milwaukee county to recover the possession of an uncut diamond of the alleged value of $1,000. The case was tried in the circuit court and, after hearing all the evidence in the case, the learned circuit judge directed the jury to find a verdict for the defendants. The plaintiff excepted to such instruction, and, after a verdict was rendered for the defendants, moved for a new trial upon the minutes of the judge. The motion was denied, and the plaintiff duly excepted, and, after judgment was entered in favor of the defendants, appealed to this court.

The defendants are partners in the jewelry business. On the trial it appeared that on and before the 28th of December, 1883, the plaintiff was the owner of and in the possession of a small stone of the nature and value of which she was ignorant; that on that day she sold it to one of the defendants for the sum of one dollar. Afterwards it was ascertained that the stone was a rough diamond, and of the value of about $700. After learning this fact the plaintiff tendered the defendants the one dollar, and ten cents as interest, and demanded a return of the stone to her. The defendants refused to deliver it, and therefore she commenced this action.

The plaintiff testified to the circumstances attending the sale of the stone to Mr. Samuel B. Boynton, as follows:

> The first time Boynton saw that stone he was talking about buying the topaz, or whatever it is, in September or October. I went into his store to get a little pin mended, and I had it in a small box, — the pin, — a small ear-ring; . . . this stone, and a broken sleeve-button were in the box. Mr. Boynton turned to give me a check for my pin. I thought I would ask him what the stone was, and I took it out of the box and asked him to please tell me what that was. He took it in his hand and seemed some time looking at it. I told him I had been told it was a topaz and he said it might be. He says, "I would buy this; would you sell it?" I told him I did not know but what I would. What would it be worth? And he said he did not know; he would give me a dollar and keep it as a specimen, and I told him I would not sell it; and it was certainly pretty to look at. He asked me where I found it, and I told him in Eagle. He asked about how far out, and I said right in the village, and I went out. Afterwards, and about the 28th of December, I needed money pretty badly, and thought every dollar would help, and I took it back to Mr. Boynton and told him I had brought back the topaz, and he says,

"Well, yes; what did I offer you for it?" and I says, "One dollar," and he stepped to the change drawer and gave me the dollar, and I went out.

In another part of her testimony she says:

Before I sold the stone I had no knowledge whatever that it was a diamond. I told him that I had been advised that it was probably a topaz, and he said probably it was. The stone was about the size of a canary bird's egg, nearly the shape of an egg, — worn pointed at one end; it was nearly straw color, — a little darker.

She also testified that before this action was commenced she tendered the defendants $1.10, and demanded the return of the stone, which they refused. This is substantially all the evidence of what took place at and before the sale to the defendants, as testified to by the plaintiff herself. She produced no other witness on that point.

The evidence on the part of the defendant is not very different from the version given by the plaintiff, and certainly is not more favorable to the plaintiff. Mr. Samuel B. Boynton, the defendant to whom the stone was sold, testified that at the time he bought this stone, he had never seen an uncut diamond; had seen cut diamonds, but they are quite different from the uncut ones; "he had no idea this was a diamond, and it never entered his brain at the time." Considerable evidence was given as to what took place after the sale and purchase, but that evidence has very little if any bearing upon the main point in the case.

This evidence clearly shows that the plaintiff sold the stone in question to the defendants, and delivered it to them in December, 1883, for a consideration of one dollar. The title to the stone passed by the sale and delivery to the defendants. How has that title been divested and again vested in the plaintiff? The contention of the learned counsel for the appellant is that the title became vested in the plaintiff by the tender to the Boyntons of the purchase money, with interest, and a demand of a return of the stone to her. Unless such tender and demand revested the title in the appellant, she cannot maintain her action.

The only question in the case is whether there was anything in the sale which entitled the vendor (the appellant) to rescind the sale and so revest the title in her. The only reasons we know of for rescinding a sale and revesting the title in the vendor so that he may maintain an action at law for the recovery of the possession against his vendee are (1) that the vendee was guilty of some fraud in procuring a sale to be made to him; (2) that there was a mistake made by the vendor in delivering an article which was not the article sold, — a mistake in fact as to the identity of the thing sold with the thing delivered upon the sale. This last is not in reality a rescission of the sale made, as the thing delivered was not the thing sold, and no title ever passed to the vendee by such delivery.

In this case, upon the plaintiff's own evidence, there can be no just ground for alleging that she was induced to make the sale she did by any fraud or unfair dealings on the part of Mr. Boynton. Both were entirely ignorant at the time of the character of the stone and of its intrinsic value. Mr. Boynton was not an expert in uncut diamonds, and had made no examination of the stone, except to take it in his hand and look at it before he made the offer of one dollar, which was refused at the time, and afterwards accepted without any comment or further examination made by Mr. Boynton. The appellant had the stone in her possession for a long time, and it appears from her own statement that she made some inquiry as to its nature and qualities. If she chose to sell it without further investigation as to its intrinsic value to a person who was guilty of no fraud or unfairness which induced her to sell it for a small sum, she cannot repudiate the sale because it is afterwards ascertained that she made a bad bargain. Kennedy v. Panama, etc., Mail Co. L.R. 2 Q.B. 580.

There is no pretense of any mistake as to the identity of the thing sold. It was produced by the plaintiff and exhibited to the vendor before the sale was made, and the thing sold was delivered to the vendee when the purchase price was paid. Kennedy v. Panama, etc., Mail Co., L.R. 2 Q.B. 587; Street v. Blay, 2 Barn. & Adol. 456; Gompertz v. Bartlett, 2 El. & Bl. 849; Gurney v. Womersly, 4 El. & Bl. 133; Ship's Case, 2 De G., J. & S. 544. Suppose the appellant had produced the stone, and said she had been told that it was a diamond, and she believed it was, but had no knowledge herself as to its character or value, and Mr. Boynton had given her $500 for it, could he have rescinded the sale if it had turned out to be a topaz or any other stone of very small value? Could Mr. Boynton have rescinded the sale on the ground of mistake? Clearly not, nor could he rescind it on the ground that there had been a breach of warranty, because there was no warranty, nor could he rescind it on the ground of fraud, unless he could show that she falsely declared that she had been told it was a diamond, or, if she had been told, still she knew it was not a diamond. See Street v. Blay, *supra.*

It is urged, with a good deal of earnestness, on the part of the counsel for the appellant that, because it has turned out that the stone was immensely more valuable than the parties at the time of the sale supposed it was, such fact alone is a ground for the rescission of the sale, and that fact was evidence of fraud on the part of the vendee. Whether inadequacy of price is to be received as evidence of fraud, even in a suit in equity to avoid a sale, depends upon the facts known to the parties at the time the sale is made.

When this sale was made the value of the thing sold was open to the investigation of both parties, neither knew its intrinsic value, and, so far as the evidence in this case shows, both supposed that the price paid was adequate. How can fraud be predicated upon such a sale, even though after-investigation showed that the intrinsic value of the thing sold was hundreds of times greater than the price paid? It certainly shows no such fraud as would authorize the vendor to rescind the contract and bring an action at law to recover the possession of the thing sold. Whether the fact would have any influence in an action in equity to avoid the sale we need not consider. See Stettheimer v. Killip, 75 N.Y. 287; Etting v. Bank of U.S., 11 Wheat. 59.

We can find nothing in the evidence from which it could be justly inferred that Mr. Boynton, at the time he offered the plaintiff one dollar for the stone, had any knowledge of the real value of the stone, or that he entertained even a belief that the stone was a diamond. It cannot, therefore, be said that there was a suppression of knowledge on the part of the defendant as to the value of the stone which a court of equity might seize upon to avoid the sale. The following cases show that, in the absence of fraud or warranty, the value of the property sold, as compared with the price paid, is no ground for a rescission of the sale. Wheat v. Cross, 31 Md. 99; Lambert v. Heath, 15 Mees. & W. 487; Bryant v. Pember, 45 Vt. 487; Kuelkamp v. Hidding, 31 Wis. 503, 511.

However unfortunate the plaintiff may have been in selling this valuable stone for a mere nominal sum, she has failed entirely to make out a case either of fraud or mistake in the sale such as will entitle her to a rescission of such sale so as to recover the property sold in an action at law.

By the Court. — The judgment of the circuit court is affirmed.

NOTE

1. "'Pure' contract doctrine is blind to details of subject matter and persons. It does not ask who buys and who sells, and what is bought and sold. . . . Contract law is abstraction — what is left in the law relating to agreement when particularities of person and subject-matter are removed." L. Friedman, Contract Law in America 20 (1965).

2. The new Restatement seems to take the position that the risk of mistake was properly placed on Mrs. Wood. See Restatement Second §§151, 154, Illus. 3 and Reporter's note thereto. See also Rabin, A Proposed Black-Letter Rule Concerning Mistaken Assumptions in Bargain Transactions, 45 Tex. L. Rev. 1273, 1293 (1967).

3. How should a court decide on whom to place the risk, in the absence of an express allocation by the contracting parties? Kronman says that the risk should be placed on the better information-gatherer in order to reduce "the transaction costs of the contracting process." Kronman, Mistake, Disclosure, Information and the Law of Contracts, 7 J. Legal Stud. 1 (1978). Was Wood or Boynton the better information gatherer? Consult Ohio Co. v. Rosmeier, 32 Ohio App. 2d 116, 288 N.E.2d 326 (1972); Thomas v. Caldwell, 27 Utah 2d 423, 497 P.2d 31 (1972). Restatement Second §154(c).

A different view is expressed in 2 G. Palmer, Restitution §12.17, p. 666

(1978): "While the court denied restitution to the seller, it seems likely that such relief would now be granted because of manifest enrichment of the buyer." Was defendant in the principal case "unjustly enriched," or was his enrichment "just" because Mrs. Wood assumed the risk that the stone was more valuable than the two parties had originally thought?

Should "unjust enrichment" be the principal criterion for setting aside a contract based on mistake? Is this idea more helpful than the distinction drawn by the *Wood* court between the identity of the subject matter and its intrinsic value? See Comment *a* to §154 of Restatement Second, describing distinctions of the latter sort as "artificial and specious." See also 2 G. Palmer, Restitution §12.17, p. 666 (1978), who notes that courts inclined to grant relief often say that the mistake is one of identity, while those not so inclined usually consider the mistake to be of a less fundamental nature. For an illustration of this process, see Sherwood v. Walker, *infra* p. 887, and compare Backus v. Maclaury, 278 A.D. 504, 106 N.Y.S.2d 401 (1951).

4. Suppose Mr. Boynton had permitted Mrs. Wood to keep the stone until January 2, and before handing it over, she discovered its value. In a suit by the jeweller against her, same result? Consult Sherwood v. Walker, *infra* p. 887.

Suppose plaintiff had entered the store and offered the stone for $1.00 without haggling and the defendant, ignorant of the value of the stone, had accepted the offer, or suppose both parties had regarded the stone as a very pretty piece of glass and agreed on a sales price of $.25. Can the plaintiff now rescind?

Under the doctrine of *laesio enormis*, supposedly developed by late Roman law and quite influential during the Middle Ages, a seller could rescind a contract for the sale of land, if the price received was less than one-half of the reasonable price; the buyer, however, could validate the contract by agreeing to pay the full price. See p. 555 *infra* for more on the doctrine.

SHERWOOD v. WALKER
66 Mich. 568, 333 N.W. 919 (1887)

For a report of the case, see p. 887 *infra*.

NOTE

Consult 13 Williston §§1569, 1570, 1570A (1970); 1 W. H. Page, The Law of Contracts §§379, 384 (1920); 2 J. N. Pomeroy, Equity Jurisprudence §927 (4th ed. 1918); Thayer, Unilateral Mistake and Unjust Enrichment as a Ground for the Avoidance of Legal Transactions, in Harvard Legal Essays 467, 480, 494 (R. Pound ed. 1934).

Do not overlook the fact that the ultimate decision as to whether there was a mutual mistake was left to the jury.

If the statement of facts given by the dissenting judge is correct, and the plaintiff prospective buyer did not share the defendant seller's belief concerning the sterility of the cow, was the plaintiff under a duty to warn the defendant that the defendant might be mistaken?

Suppose the plaintiff was not a gentleman farmer but a butcher who really bought the cow for its meat value. What result?

LAIDLAW v. ORGAN
15 U.S. (2 Wheat.) 178 (1817)

[Error to the District Court for the District of Louisiana. The plaintiff (defendant in error), Organ, filed suit against Laidlaw & Co., commission merchants in the city of New Orleans, to recover possession of 111 hogsheads of tobacco, alleged to have been wrongfully taken by defendants from plaintiff's possession. Plaintiff introduced in evidence a written memorandum, dated February 18, 1815, reciting that he had bought the 111 hogsheads from Laidlaw & Co. for $7,544.69. The defendant sellers in denying liability relied upon fraud in the inception of the contract of sale. They claimed that plaintiff buyer had learnt of the peace treaty of Ghent ending the war of 1812 and the end of the British blockade of New Orleans before the seller had such information. Plaintiff, according to the defendant, when calling upon the seller to complete the purchase which had been under negotiation, was asked by the seller (plaintiff in error) if there was any news which was calculated to enhance the price or value of the tobacco. The plaintiff having remained silent, the purchase was then and there made at a depressed price and the bill of parcels annexed to the plaintiff's petition was delivered to the plaintiff. There was no evidence that the plaintiff had asserted or suggested anything calculated to impose upon the seller with respect to the news of the peace and to induce him to think or imply that it did not exist. The seller when applied to on the next day for an invoice of the tobacco did not then object to the sale but promised to deliver the invoice to the plaintiff in the course of the day. The seller delivered the tobacco to the buyer after the news of the treaty had become public. He subsequently took possession of the tobacco, the value of which had risen from 30 to 50 per cent. In a suit by the buyer (defendant in error) to recover the tobacco, the court instructed the jury to find for the plaintiff and the jury returned a verdict accordingly.]

C.J. Ingersoll, for the plaintiffs in error. The first question is, whether the sale, under the circumstances of the case, was a valid sale; whether fraud, which vitiates every contract, must be proved, by the communication of positive misinformation, or by withholding information when asked. Suppression of material circumstances, within the knowledge of the vendee, and not accessible to the vendor, is equivalent to fraud, and vitiates the contract. Pothier, in discussing this subject, adopts the distinction of the forum of conscience, and the forum of law; but he admits that *fides est servanda*. The parties treated on an unequal footing, as the one party had received intelligence of the peace of Ghent, at the time of the contract, and the other had not. This news was unexpected, even at Washington, much more at New Orleans, the recent scene of the most sanguinary operations of the war. In answer to the question, whether there was any news calculated to enhance the price of the article, the vendee was silent. This reserve, when such a question was asked, was equivalent to a false answer, and as much calculated to deceive as the communication of the most fabulous intelligence. Though the plaintiffs in error, after they heard the news of peace, still went on, in ignorance of their legal rights, to complete the contract, equity will protect them. . . .

Key, contrà. . . . The only real question in the cause is, whether the sale was invalid, because the vendee did not communicate information which he received precisely as the vendor might have got it, had he been equally diligent or equally fortunate? And, surely, on this question, there can be no doubt. Even if the vendor had been entitled to the disclosure, he waived it, by not insisting on an answer to his question; and the silence of the vendee might as well have been interpreted into an affirmative as a negative answer. But, on principle, he was not bound to disclose. Even admitting that his conduct was unlawful, in foro conscientiae, does that prove that it was so, in the civil forum? Human laws are imperfect in this respect, and the sphere of morality is more extensive than the limits of civil jurisdiction. The maxim of caveat emptor could never have crept into the law, if the province of ethics had been co-extensive with it. There was, in the present case, no circumvention or manoeuvre practised by the vendee, unless rising earlier in the morning, and obtaining, by superior diligence and alertness, that intelligence by which the price of commodities was regulated, be such. It is a romantic equality that is contended for on the other side. Parties never can be precisely equal in knowledge, either of facts or of the inferences from such facts, and both must concur, in order to satisfy the rule contended for. The absence of all authority in England and the United States, both great commercial countries, speaks volumes against the reasonableness and practicability of such a rule.

C.J. Ingersoll, in reply. Though the record may not show that anything tending to mislead, by positive assertion, was said by the vendee, in answer to the question proposed by [the seller's representative], yet it is a case of manoeuvre; of mental reservation; of circumvention. The information was monopolized by the messengers from the British fleet, and not imparted to the public at large, until it was too late for the vendor to save himself. The rule of law and of ethics is the same. It is not a romantic, but a practical and legal rule of equality and good faith, that is proposed to be applied. . . .

MARSHALL, CH. J. delivered the opinion of the court: The question in this case is, whether the intelligence of extrinsic circumstances, which might influence the price of the commodity, and which was exclusively within the knowledge of the vendee, ought to have been communicated by him to the vendor. The court is of opinion that he was not bound to communicate it. It would be difficult to circumscribe the contrary doctrine within proper limits, where the means of intelligence are equally accessible to both parties. But at the same time, each party must take care not to say or do anything tending to impose upon the other. The court thinks that the absolute instruction of the judge was erroneous, and that the question whether any imposition was practiced by the vendee upon the vendor ought to have been submitted to the jury. For these reasons the judgment must be reversed, and the cause remanded to the District Court of Louisiana, with directions to award a venire facias de novo.

Venire de novo awarded.

NOTE

1. 12 Williston §1497; 2 Kent, Commentaries 485 (12th ed. 1873); Smith v. Hughes, L.R. 6 Q.B. 597 (1871); Bell v. Lever Brothers, [1932] A.C. 161, 227, *infra* p. 896.

How would the case be decided today? Consult Restatement Second §161, Comment *d*. Did the defendant not act in an exceedingly unbusinesslike fashion in disregarding the plaintiff's silence?

2. For an analysis contemporary to the decision, see G. Verplanck, Essay on the Doctrine of Contracts (1826). Verplanck, an outspoken critic of the just price theory, would have required disclosure of "material facts concerning the terms or the subject of the contract, which necessarily and of course enter into all calculations of price among those whose demand and supply, and estimation of value, fix the market price of similar things." According to Verplanck, the concealment of such facts is unfair and a breach of confidence. On the issue of unfairness, compare the following passage from Keeton, Fraud — Concealment and Non-Disclosure, 15 Texas L. Rev. 1, 32-33 (1936):

> [T]he case of Laidlaw v. Organ has received a storm of criticism, but it seems that the buyer in that case acted in the way in which buyers generally would be expected to act. If those facts were given to a normal person, as an abstract question, he would probably say that the buyer's conduct was unethical; on the other hand, if the same individual were given the opportunity that the buyer had in Laidlaw v. Organ, he would do precisely the

same thing. In this connection it would seem that the conception of negligence as the care of the ordinary prudent man would be of benefit. It has been said that the standard man in his conduct on the question of negligence evaluates interests in accordance with the sentiment of the community. Why not employ the standard man in this connection? This would be, not the ordinary man's views as to the ethical quality of the silence, but what the man of ordinary moral sensibilities would have done; would he have disclosed the information or would he have remained silent? This is not the same as saying that when a person is negligent he cannot recover, because the circumstances may be such that however negligent the uninformed person might be, the ordinary ethical man would disclose the information. Of course, the opportunity which the uninformed person might have to ascertain the fact not disclosed is a factor of importance since a person would seem to be entitled to reap some benefit if he is more diligent and careful or has a wider experience. Society requires or should require of a person a judgment on moral questions which represents the sentiment of the community, and the fictitious standard man is set up with that judgment. Under this standard, it would seem that the question in a particular case as to whether the non-disclosure under the circumstances would be fraudulent, would be a mixed question of law and fact.

Dean Keeton's article contains a most valuable discussion of factors to be considered in determining the extent of the duty to disclose. According to Dean Prosser, "the law appears to be working toward the ultimate conclusion that full disclosure of all material facts must be made whenever elementary fair conduct demands it." Handbook of the Law of Torts 698 (4th ed. 1971). Prosser's book contains an interesting policy discussion regarding the different treatment accorded the injured party by contract and tort law (at 698). See further Keeton, Rights of Disappointed Purchasers, 32 Texas L. Rev. 1 (1953).

3. Kronman, in Mistake, Disclosure, Information and the Law of Contracts, 7 J. Legal Stud. 1 (1978), offers another approach to the problem. According to Kronman, "allocative efficiency is promoted by getting information of changed circumstances to the market as quickly as possible." The information in question, however, does not arrive of its own accord; individuals supply it. To promote efficiency, judicial rules should encourage the gathering and provision of information. This requires that deliberate search be rewarded, or at least compensated as a cost. The casual acquisition of information, on the other hand, need not be protected, as a disclosure requirement for casually-acquired information would have little or no effect on the production of socially useful information. One may have doubts, of course, about the ability of courts to discriminate between the deliberate and chance acquisition of information. Kronman feels that the courts should make a blanket rule for different classes of cases, depending on "whether the kind of information involved is (on the whole) more likely to be generated by chance or by

deliberate searching" (at 17-18). Using this analysis, how should a case like *Laidlaw* be decided?

SWINTON v. WHITINSVILLE SAVINGS BANK
311 Mass. 677, 42 N.E.2d 808 (1942)

Tort. Writ in the Superior Court dated November 10, 1941.

A demurrer to the declaration was sustained by Swift, J. The plaintiff appealed. . . .

QUA, J. The declaration alleges that on or about September 12, 1938, the defendant sold the plaintiff a house in Newton to be occupied by the plaintiff and his family as a dwelling, that at the time of the sale the house "was infested with termites, an insect that is most dangerous and destructive to buildings"; that the defendant knew the house was so infested; that the plaintiff could not readily observe this condition upon inspection; that, "knowing the internal destruction that these insects were creating in said house," the defendant falsely and fraudulently concealed from the plaintiff its true condition; that the plaintiff at the time of his purchase had no knowledge of the termites, exercised due care thereafter, and learned of them about August 30, 1940; and that, because of the destruction that was being done and the dangerous condition that was being created by the termites, the plaintiff was put to great expense for repairs and for the installation of termite control in order to prevent the loss and destruction of said house.

There is no allegation of any false statement or representation, or of the uttering of a half truth which may be tantamount to a falsehood. There is no intimation that the defendant by any means prevented the plaintiff from acquiring information as to the condition of the house. There is nothing to show any fiduciary relation between the parties, or that the plaintiff stood in a position of confidence toward or dependence upon the defendant. So far as appears the parties made a business deal at arm's length. The charge is concealment and nothing more; and it is concealment in the simple sense of mere failure to reveal, with nothing to show any peculiar duty to speak. The characterization of the concealment as false and fraudulent of course adds nothing in the absence of further allegations of fact. Province Securities Corp. v. Maryland Casualty Co., 269 Mass. 75, 92.

If this defendant is liable on this declaration every seller is liable who fails to disclose any nonapparent defect known to him in the subject of the sale which materially reduces its value and which the buyer fails to discover. Similarly it would seem that every buyer would be liable who fails to disclose any nonapparent virtue known to him in the subject of the purchase which materially enhances its value and of which the seller is ignorant. See Goodwin v. Agassiz, 283 Mass. 358. The law has not yet, we believe, reached the point of imposing upon the frailties of human nature a standard so idealistic as this. That the particular case here stated by the plaintiff possesses a certain appeal to the moral sense is scarcely to be denied. Probably the reason is to be found in the facts that the infestation of buildings by termites has not been common in Massachusetts and constitutes a concealed risk against which buyers are off their guard. But the law cannot provide special rules for termites and can hardly attempt to determine liability according to the varying probabilities of the existence and discovery of different possible defects in the subjects of trade. The rule of nonliability for bare nondisclosure has been stated and followed by this court in Matthews v. Bliss, 22 Pick. 48, 52, 53, Potts v. Chapin, 133 Mass. 276, Van Houten v. Morse, 162 Mass. 414, Phinney v. Friedman, 224 Mass. 531, 533, Windram Manuf. Co. v. Boston Blacking Co., 239 Mass. 123, 126, Wellington v. Rugg, 243 Mass. 30, 35, 36, and Brockton Olympia Realty Co. v. Lee, 266 Mass. 550, 561. It is adopted in the American Law Institute's Restatement of Torts, §551. See Williston on Contracts (Rev. ed.) §§1497, 1498, 1499.

The order sustaining the demurrer is affirmed, and judgment is to be entered for the defendant. Keljikian v. Star Brewing Co. 303 Mass. 53, 55-63.

So ordered.

NOTE

The case represents a striking example of the caveat emptor principle: let the purchaser take care of his own interest. This principle found its most powerful expression in nineteenth century sales law. A seller, for instance, was not responsible for any defects of the chattel sold, absent fraud or express warranty of quality.

> . . . The common law does not oblige a seller to disclose all that he knows which lessens the value of the property he would sell. He may be silent, and be safe; but if he be more than silent, if by acts, and certainly if by words, he leads the buyer astray, inducing him to suppose that he buys with warranty, or otherwise preventing his examination or inquiry, this becomes a fraud of which the law will take cognizance. The distinction seems to be, — and it is grounded upon the apparent necessity of leaving men to take some care of themselves in their business transactions, — the seller may let the buyer cheat himself ad libitum, but must not actively assist him in cheating himself.[8]

The principle was regarded as eminently fair since the buyer could protect himself by an express warranty of quality. Its opposite, namely the

8. 1 Parsons on Contracts 486 (3d ed. 1857).

rule that every sales contract implies a warranty of quality, we were told, would cause an immense amount of litigation and would accord protection to a buyer against "the consequences of his own neglect of duty."[9]

However powerful the sentiments in favor of caveat emptor, the emergence of so-called implied warranties became inevitable with the advent of mass production of goods which were no longer there to be seen and traded face to face by neighbors: sales law had to make sure that goods bought were of fair merchantable quality and even fit for the buyer's "particular purpose," provided the seller at the time of contracting had "reason to know" the purpose for which the goods were required and the buyer was relying on the seller's "skill or judgment to select or furnish suitable goods."[10] As a result of this development, the doctrine of caveat emptor, a New Jersey court has asserted, "is very nearly abolished" so far as personal property is concerned. Levy v. C. Young Construction Co., 46 N.J. Super. 293, 296, 134 A.2d 717, 719 (App. Div. 1957), *aff'd on other grounds*, 26 N.J. 330, 139 A.2d 738 (1958).

The rule set forth in the *Swinton* case has been rejected by many jurisdictions. Obde v. Schlemeyer, 56 Wash. 2d 449, 353 P.2d 672 (1960); Cohen v. Blessing, 259 S.C. 40, 192 S.E.2d 204 (1972). In both *Obde* and *Cohen*, the courts based their decisions not on an implied warranty but on the assertion that it is a fraud for a seller to fail to disclose a known defect that cannot be discovered by means of a reasonable examination, whether or not the buyer asked specific questions regarding the possibility of its existence. See Restatement of Torts Second §551, Comment on clause (e); Restatement Second §161, Illus. 5. In Hughes v. Strusser, 68 Wash. 2d 707, 415 P.2d 89 (1966), the Supreme Court of Washington declared that a seller could not be held liable for a defect unknown to him. Recently, however, warranties have been implied in the sale of residential housing when the seller is a builder, or is in the business of selling real estate, other than as a broker. See, e.g., Humber v. Morton, 426 S.W.2d 554, 25 A.L.R.3d 372 (Tex. 1968); Uniform Land Transactions Act §2-309. Federal and state legislation, requiring extensive disclosure, has also been enacted to regulate the sale of subdivided property. See, e.g., Interstate Land Sales Full Disclosure Act, 15 U.S.C. §§170 et seq. (1968); Uniform Land Sales Practices Act. In the field of real estate leases, especially those involving residential apartments, many courts and legislatures have imposed on landlords an implied warranty of habitability. Green v. Superior Court, 10 Cal. 3d 616, 517 P.2d 1168, 111 Cal. Rptr. 704 (1974); Uniform Residential Landlord and Tenant Act §2-104.

---

9. Id. at 485.
10. This is the language used in U.C.C. §2-315. For the gradual evolution of warranties of quality, see Llewellyn, On Warranty of Quality, and Society, 36 Colum. L. Rev. 697 (1930); Id., On Warranty of Quality, and Society (pt. 2), 37 Colum. L. Rev. 341 (1937); Prosser, The Implied Warranty of Merchantable Quality, 27 Minn. L. Rev. 117 (1943). On the warranty of merchantability, see U.C.C. §2-314.

For more on the warranty of habitability, and the issue of its disclaimability, see Fair v. Negley, *infra* p. 1257, and the Note following that case.

BLAIR v. NATIONAL SECURITY INSURANCE CO., 126 F.2d 955 (3d Cir. 1942), Clark, J.: ". . . It may be some reflection of the business ethics fostered by a system of individual competition that the parties to a contract are permitted to deal at arm's length. I can buy my neighbor's land for a song, although I know and he doesn't that it is oil bearing. That isn't dishonest, it is 'smart business' and the just reward of my superior individualism. In some instances the law, at any rate, gagged a bit; if competitive conditions do not prevail, for instance, as in cases of fiduciary relationships or if the rule discourages competition altogether."

NOTE

For the duty to disclose material facts in so-called good faith contracts (e.g., insurance and suretyship contracts) and confidential fiduciary relations, see 5 Williston §1499 (Rev. ed. 1937) (giving instances where silence may be fraudulent). See further A.B.C. Packard, Inc. v. General Motors Corp., 275 F.2d 63 (9th Cir. 1960); J. Dawson, W. Harvey, & S. Henderson, Cases and Comment on Contracts 175-176 (4th ed. 1982); Jackson v. Seymour, *infra* p. 569. See further Letch Gold Mines Ltd. v. Texas Gulf Sulphur, 1 Ont. Rep. 469, 492-493 (1969).

For the duty to correct an assertion that later turns out to be inaccurate, see Stipcich v. Metropolitan Life Insurance Co., 277 U.S. 311 (1928) (serious health deterioration after application for life insurance).

STERNAMAN v. METROPOLITAN LIFE INS. CO., 170 N.Y. 13, 62 N.E. 763 (1902), Vann, J.: "The power to contract is not unlimited. While, as a general rule, there is the utmost freedom of action in this regard, some restrictions are placed upon the right by legislation, by public policy, and by the nature of things. Parties cannot make a binding contract in violation of law or of public policy. They cannot in the same instrument agree that a thing exists, and that it does not exist, or provided that one is the agent of the other, and at the same time, and with reference to the same subject, that there is no relation of agency between them. They cannot bind themselves by agreeing that a loan in fact void for usury is not usurious, or that a copartnership which actually exists between them does not exist. They cannot by agreement change the laws of nature or of logic, or create relations, physical, legal, or moral, which cannot be created. In other words, they cannot accomplish the impossible by contract."

NOTE

Restatement Second, unlike its predecessor,[11] does not characterize certain bargains as illegal, but speaks instead of a promise or term as being unenforceable on grounds of public policy. "A promise or other term of an agreement is unenforceable on grounds of public policy if legislation provides that it is unenforceable or if the interest in its enforcement is clearly outweighed in the circumstances by a public policy against the enforcement of such terms." Restatement Second §178. Subsections 2 and 3 list various general considerations of public policy to be weighed in favor of and against enforcement in particular cases.

To be sure, it has occasionally been said by English courts that they are no longer free to enlarge the heads of public policy.[12] But the existing heads are sufficiently vague to leave room for judicial discretion. To mention only a few illustrations: contracts in restraint of trade, usurious and unconscionable bargains, contracts adversely affecting the administration of justice, bargains in violation of public or fiduciary duty or to defraud or injure third parties have all been denied enforcement for reasons of public policy.

Public policy has a positive as well as a negative meaning. In one sense, every legal doctrine is the expression of public policy; it is at the basis of all legal development.[13] In another sense, public policy is invoked as a limiting factor, enabling courts to strike down bargains regarded as inimical to the common good. The two sides of public policy are illustrated by a paradox: considerations of public policy have led to the demand that liberty of contract be respected; on the other hand, liberty of contract has had to be limited in the interest of its own preservation, and this, too, has been done in the name of public policy.[14]

Public policy is not a static but a dynamic concept. It varies with the needs of society and is used to adjust the legal system to its current needs. To complicate matters still further, in the name of public policy conflicting social demands have frequently been pressed upon a court. Small wonder that courts in the past, aware of the emotive nature of the term, have often been reluctant to invoke it or to rationalize results in terms of public policy. It is, an English judge informs us, "a very unruly horse, and

---

11. Restatement First §512.

12. Janson v. Drifontein Consolidated Mines, Ltd., [1902] A.C. 484, 491.

13. Holmes, The Common Law 35, 36 (1881):

Every important principle which is developed by litigation is in fact and at bottom the result of more or less definitely understood views of public policy; most generally, to be sure, under our practice and traditions, the unconscious result of instinctive preferences and inarticulate convictions, but none the less traceable to views of public policy in the last analysis.

14. Williams, Language and the Law, 62 L.Q. Rev. 387, 399 (1946).

when once you get astride it you will never know where it will carry you. It may lead you from the sound law. It is never argued at all but when other points fail."[15] But today it is no longer true to say with Holmes that considerations of public policy are those "which judges most rarely mention and always with an apology" (The Common Law 35 (1881)). Still, it should not be forgotten that courts often apply notions of public policy under the guise of other doctrines. The consideration doctrine, for instance, has been used to filter out transactions that courts are agreed should remain unenforceable. On the other hand, the same concept has responded to changing notions of public policy favoring expansion of promissory liability and this has meant a loosening of the doctrine of consideration.

Attempts to work out the effect of illegality have caused considerable difficulties. Generally speaking, courts have taken the attitude that no legal remedy is available to either party to an illegal bargain. The parties are left where they find themselves. This attitude has found its classic expression in a famous statement of Lord Mansfield in the case of Holman v. Johnson, 1 Cowper 341 (1775):

> . . . The principle of public policy is this: *Ex dolo malo non oritur actio.* No court will lend its aid to a man who founds his cause of action upon an immoral or an illegal act. If, from the plaintiff's own stating or otherwise, the cause of action appears to arise *ex turpi causa* or the transgression of a positive law of this country, there the court says he has no right to be assisted. It is upon this ground the court goes; not for the sake of the defendant, but because they will not lend their aid to such a plaintiff. So if the plaintiff and defendant were to change sides, and the defendant was to bring his action against the plaintiff, the latter would then have the advantage of it; for where both are equally in fault, *potior est conditio defendentis.*

But considerations of fairness and of common sense have required the courts to graft exceptions upon this general rule. They have protected, for instance, a party who is justifiably ignorant of the facts which led to illegality or of minor statutory regulations involving illegality. See Restatement Second §180. See also Restatement Second §§181-184.

See, in general, Winfield, Public Policy in English Law, 42 Harv. L. Rev. 76 (1928); Gellhorn, Contract and Public Policy, 35 Colum. L. Rev. 679 (1935); R. Wright, Public Policy in Legal Essays and Addresses 66 (1939); D. Lloyd, Public Policy (1953); 6A Corbin, Part VIII.

15. Richardson v. Mellish, 2 Bing. 229, 252, 130 Eng. Rep. 294, 303 (1824).

SCHOOL TRUSTEES OF TRENTON v.
BENNETT

27 N.J.L. 513 (1859)

This was an action of assumpsit, brought against Bennett and Carlisle, as guarantors for Evernham and Hill. In the fall of 1856, the plaintiffs made a contract with Evernham and Hill to build and complete a school-house, and find all materials therefor, according to specifications annexed to the contract; the building to be located on a lot owned by the plaintiffs, and designated in the contract. Bennett and Carlisle guarantied the fulfilment of this contract on the part of Evernham and Hill. When the building was partially erected, it was blown down by a gale of wind. The contractors rebuilt it, and when nearly completed, the house again fell down, and the contractors, alleging that the second fall was occasioned by latent defects in the soil, refused to rebuild it.

The contract price was $2610, of which $2200 was to be paid in instalments, as follows: $300 when the first floor of joists was on; $300 when the second floor of joists was on; $1000 when the building was enclosed; $400 when the plastering was done; $200 when the building was completed, except the rough-casting, and the balance to be paid when the whole was finished. When the building fell down the second time, instalments to the amount of $1600 had been paid to the contractors. To recover the damages which the plaintiffs had sustained by reason of the nonfulfilment of the contract on the part of the contractors, this suit was brought against the guarantors.

The cause was tried at the Mercer circuit, at April term, 1858. On the trial, the plaintiffs, having proved the amount paid to the contractors, and that they had failed to complete the building according to contract, rested their case.

The defendants then opened their case, and offered to prove — that the plaintiffs procured the plan and specifications for the building to be made under the advice of builders or architects employed by them, and purchased the lot of land whereon the building was to be erected, and designated the particular location of the building, and the precise elevation of said building and its first floor, and that the contractors and defendants were not consulted about either the plan, specifications, lot purchased, particular location, or elevation; that the plaintiffs advertised for proposals to erect said building according to said plan and specifications, and that the contractors were the lowest bidders therefor, and proceeded to erect said building, and did erect the same in strict accordance with said specifications, and that as each portion of the building was completed, the completion of which was a condition precedent to the payment of an instalment of the contract price, such completion was reported to the plaintiffs by the plaintiffs' agents; that all the work of the said contractors was done, in strict accordance with the plans and specifications, in a workmanlike manner and of proper materials, and that they exercised all proper care over said building while in course of erection; that after the second floor of joists were laid on said building, and the instalment due therefor was paid, a violent gale of wind arose suddenly, without any of the usual premonitory signs of a storm, and prostrated the said building; that the said contractors thereupon again proceeded to, and did erect said building of proper materials, and in a good workmanlike manner, in strict accordance with the said plans and specifications, until said building was enclosed, and the plastering near completed; that as each portion of said building was so again completed, its completion was reported to the plaintiffs by their agents, and the instalment of one thousand dollars was paid; that when the building was thus enclosed, and nearly plastered, it fell, solely on account of the soil on which it stood having become soft and miry, and unable to support the weight of said building; that at the time the foundation walls were laid, the said soil appeared to be in all respects suitable for the support of such building; that said soil was at that time so hard as to be penetrated with difficulty by the pick-axe, and that its defects were latent; that said soil became soft and miry in the spring of the year, either by reason of the rising of the springs, or from other natural causes wholly beyond the control of said contractors; that by the uniform custom of the trade, the phrase "with a cellar under the building to be eight feet deep," is a trade phrase, meaning that the height of the foundation wall is to be of the depth of the cellar, measuring from the bottom of the cellar to the joists of the first floor.

The counsel of the plaintiffs moved to overrule said evidence so offered by said defendants, upon the ground, that if all the facts offered to be proved were proved, they would constitute no legal defence to said action. The court overruled said defence, and, under the direction of the court, a verdict was taken for the plaintiffs for the amount of the instalments paid the contractors, with interest subject to the opinion of the court; and to the end that it might be decided whether the said verdict was properly rendered, it was directed that the case be certified to the Supreme Court, for its opinion upon the following points.

1. Were all or either of the facts offered to be proved on the part of the defendants competent evidence; if proved, would they constitute a valid legal defence to the action of said plaintiffs.

2. Should the damage occasioned by the destruction of the part of said building first erected, by the aforesaid gale of wind, be borne by the plaintiffs or the defendants. . . .

The opinion of the court was delivered by WHELPLEY, J. This case presents the naked question, whether, where a builder has agreed, by a contract under seal, with the owner of a lot of land "to build, erect, and complete a building upon the lot for a certain entire price, but payable in arbitrary instalments, fixed without regard to the value of the work done, and the house before its completion falls down, solely by reason of a latent defect in the soil, and not on account of faulty construction, the loss falls upon the builder or the owner of the land."

The case comes before the court, upon a certificate from the Mercer circuit, for the advisory opinion of this court.

The covenant of Evernham and Hill was to build, erect, and complete the school-house upon the lot in question for the sum of $2610; the whole price was to be paid for the whole building; the division of that sum into instalments, payable at certain stages of the work, was not intended to sever the entirety of the contract, and make the payment of the instalments payment for such parts of the work as might be done when they were payable: this division was made, not to apportion the price to the different parts of the work, but to suit the wants of the contractor, and aid him in the completion of the work; the consideration of the covenant to complete the building was the whole price, and not the mere balance that might remain after the payment of the instalments: it cannot be pretended that the contractor, after payment of a part of the instalments, might refuse to go on and complete the building, and yet retain that part of the price he had received. Haslack v. Mayers, 2 Dutcher 284.

No rule of law is more firmly established by a long train of decisions than this, that where a party, by his own *contract*, creates a duty or charge upon himself, he is bound to make it good if he may, notwithstanding any accident by inevitable necessity, because he might have provided against it by his contract; therefore if a lessee covenant to repair a house, though it be burned by lightning, or thrown down by enemies, yet he is bound to repair it. Paradine v. Jayne, Alleyn 26; Walton v. Waterhouse, 2 Wm. S. Saunders 422, a, note 2; Brecknock Company v. Pritchard, 6 Term Rep. 750. This case was an action upon a covenant to build a bridge, and keep it in repair: the defendant pleaded that the bridge was carried away by the act of God, by a great and extraordinary flood, although well built and in good repair. The plea was held bad on demurrer.

To the same effect are Bullock v. Dommit, 6 Term Rep. 650; Phillips v. Stevens, 16 Mass. 238; Dyer 33, a. And there is no relief in equity. Gates v. Green, 4 Paige 355; Holtzapffell v. Baker, 18 Ves. 115. Chancellor Walworth, in Gates v. Green, in denying relief in equity against a covenant to pay rent after the destruction of the demised premises, admits the rule to be against natural law, and not to be found in the law of other countries where the civil law prevails; yet says, it is firmly established, notwithstanding the struggles of some of the early English chancellors against it.

In Beebe v. Johnson, 19 Wend. 500, it was held, by Nelson, C.J., delivering the opinion of the court, that the defendant was not excused from performing his covenant to perfect, in England, a patent granted in this country, so as to insure to the plaintiff the exclusive right of vending the patented article in the Canadas, because the power of granting such an exclusive privilege appertained not to the mother country, but to the provinces, and was never granted, except to subjects of Great Britain and residents of the provinces; and the plaintiff and defendant were both American citizens.

The court said, if the covenant be within the range of possibility, however absurd or improbable the idea of execution may be, it will be upheld, as where one covenants it shall rain to-morrow, or that the pope shall be at Westminster on a certain day. To bring the case within the rule of dispensation, it must appear that the thing to be done cannot by any means be accomplished; for if it be only improbable, or out of the power of the obligor, it is not deemed in law impossible. 3 Comyn's Dig. 93. If a party enter into an absolute contract, without any qualification or exception, and receives from the party with whom he contracts the consideration of such engagement, he must abide by the contract, and either do the act or pay the damages: *his liability arises from his own direct and positive undertaking.*

In Lord v. Wheeler, 1 Gray 282, where a workman had agreed to repair a building for an entire sum, and after the owner had moved in, it was burned up before the repairs were completed, it was held, that where one person agrees to expend labor upon a specific subject, the property of another, as to shoe his horse, or slate his dwelling-house, if the horse dies, or the dwelling-house is destroyed by fire, before the work is done, the performance of the contract becomes impossible, and *with the principal perishes the incident.* The case was clearly distinguished from the ordinary contract of one to erect a building upon the lands of another, performing the labor and supplying the materials therefor; where, if before the building is completed or accepted, it is destroyed by fire or other casualty, the loss falls upon the builder, he must rebuild. *The thing may be done, and he has contracted to do it.* 19 Pick. 275, Nichols v. Adams; Brumby v. Smith, 3 Ala. 123; 2 Parsons on Con. 184; 1 Chit. on Con. 568.

No matter how harsh and apparently unjust in its operation the rule may occasionally be, it cannot be denied that it has its foundations in good sense and inflexible honesty. He that agrees to do an act should *do it,* unless absolutely impossible. He should provide against contingencies in his contract. Where one of two innocent persons must sustain a loss, the law casts it upon him who has agreed to sustain it, or rather the law leaves it where the agreement of the parties has put it; the law will not insert, for the benefit of one of the parties, by construction, an exception which the parties have not, either by design or neglect, inserted in their engagement. If a party, for a sufficient consideration, agrees to erect and complete a building upon a particular spot, and find all the materials, and do all the labor, he must erect and complete it, because he has agreed so to do. No matter what the expense, he must provide such a substruction as will sustain the building upon that spot, until it is complete and delivered to the owner. If he agrees to erect a house upon a spot where it cannot be done without driving piles, he must drive them, because he has agreed to do everything necessary to erect and complete the building. If the difficulties are apparent on the surface, he must overcome them. If they are not, but become apparent by excavation or the sinking of the building, the rule is the same. He must overcome them, and erect the building, simply because he has agreed to do so — to do everything necessary for that purpose.

The cases make no distinction between accidents that could be foreseen when the contract was entered into, and those that could not have been foreseen. Between accidents by the fault of the contractor, and those where he is without fault, they all rest upon the simple principle — such *is* the agreement, clear and unqualified, and it *must* be performed, no matter what the cost, if performance be not absolutely impossible.

The case of a bailment of an article — *locatio operis faciendi* — is not analogous to the case before the court; there, if the article intrusted to the workman is lost without his fault, the owner sustains the loss; not because he is *the owner*, but because the contract of bailment is well defined by the law; there is no *express* agreement to return the article to the owner in a finished state; but the agreement is an implied agreement, a duty imposed by the law upon a bailee, because the chattel has been bailed to him, to use his best endeavors to protect the bailment from injury. Parsons states the obligation of the workman to be, to do the work in a proper manner, to employ the materials furnished in the right way. These obligations grow out of the act of bailment; they are its legal consequences, and the law declares them to be so, not because the parties have actually so stipulated, but because they are equitable and fair; and in the absence of express agreement such will be implied.

The case of Menetone v. Athawes, 3 Burr. 1592, was relied upon by defendants' counsel to show, that when the failure to perform the contract was not the fault of the contractor he can recover. It was the bailment of a ship, to be repaired while in the shipwright's dock, for the use of which the owner paid £5. The vessel was burned when the repairs were nearly completed; the action was for these repairs. It was like the case of Lord v. Wheeler, before cited. The right to recover was put upon the ground, that the plaintiff was not answerable for the accident, which happened without his default, unless there had been a special undertaking; that this liability did not grow out of the law of bailments.

The cases of Trippe v. Armitage, 4 Mees. & Wels. 689; Woods v. Russell, 5 B. & Ald. 942; Clarks v. Spence, 4 Ad. & Ellis 448, have no application; they are all cases arising under the bankrupt laws, involving the question when, under the circumstances of each case, the property in an incomplete chattel in process of manufacture passed out of the bankrupt, so as not to belong to his assignees. They are inapplicable, because the rights of the parties to this suit do not turn upon the question, whether the property in an incomplete building is in the owner of the land or the builder, or whether the owner would derive a partial benefit from partial performance, but upon what was the express contract between the parties. The question, upon whom the loss is to fall, occasioned by an inevitable accident, is not to be settled by determining what is equitable, what is right, or by the application of the maxim, *res perit domino*, or by any nice philosophical disquisitions whether the owner or the builder shall bear the loss. These considerations — this maxim — have their full application in cases where the rights of the parties have not been fixed by contract, but are to be settled by the law upon facts of the case; where resort is to be had to an implied contract, to a legal obligation raised by the law out of the natural equities of the case, in the absence of an express agreement.

Neither the destruction of the incomplete building by a sudden tornado, nor its falling by reason of a latent softness of the soil which rendered the foundation insecure, *necessarily* prevented the performance of the contract to build, erect, and complete this building for the specified price; it can still be done, for aught that was opened to the jury as a defence, and overruled by the court.

The whole defence was properly overruled, because it did not show the performance of the covenant impossible, or any lawful excuse for nonperformance of the contract.

I am also of opinion that the damage occasioned by the destruction of the building by the gale of wind must be borne by the defendants, for the reasons before given, and that the Circuit Court be advised accordingly.

NOTE

Could defendant have protected himself by an appropriate clause? Draft such a clause. Contrast Stees v. Leonard, 20 Minn. 494 (1874); Kurland v. United Pacific Insurance Co., 251 Cal. App. 2d 112, 59 Cal. Rptr. 258 (1967). See further the Notes on pp. 936-937 *infra*, and compare Butterfield v. Byron, reprinted *infra* p. 937.

If, as some economic theorists contend, the central issue in cases like *Bennett* is which of the parties is the more efficient risk-bearer, how should a judge go about making such a determination? Does it help to ask who is the cheaper insurer, or who is in the best position to prevent the occurrence of the feared event (or at least reduce its likelihood)? See R. Posner, Economic Analysis of Law 74-79 (1977); Posner & Rosenfield, Impossibility and Related Doctrines in Contract Law: An Economic Analysis, 6 J. Legal Stud. 83 (1977). Is it perhaps simpler to establish a rule of law, however arbitrary or harsh, that fixes the risk of an unforeseen occurrence (whether or not preventable) so that the parties will know in advance who should purchase insurance? See G. Gilmore, The Death of Contract 77-79 (1974). Is this view of the matter inconsistent with the economic approach?

HOLMES, THE COMMON LAW 301 (1881): ". . . The only universal consequence of a legally binding promise is, that the law makes the promisor pay damages if the promised event does not come to pass. In every case it leaves him free from interference until the time for fulfilment has gone by, and therefore free to break his contract if he chooses."

NOTE

One of the stated objectives of Holmes' approach was the advantage of "freeing the subject from the superfluous theory that a contract is a qualified subjection of one will to another, a kind of limited slavery" (The Common Law 300). But, as Cohen correctly observed, the theory fails to attain this objective, "[f]or the paying of damages does not flow from the promisor's willingness, but is the effect of the law's lending its machinery to the promisee." Cohen, The Basis of Contract, 46 Harv. L. Rev. 553, 583 (1933). Holmes' view reflects his skepticism with regard to the distinction between "primary rights and duties and consequences or sanctioning rights." 1 Holmes-Pollock Letters 20 (M. Howe ed. 1941). On the need for distinguishing between primary and secondary legal rights, see 1A Corbin §182 (1963); J. W. Salmond, Jurisprudence 124 (G. Williams 11th ed. 1957); Pollock, in 1 Holmes-Pollock Letters 80, 2 id. at 201. See further Cook, The Utility of Jurisprudence in the Solution of Legal Problems, in 5 Lectures on Legal Topics 337, 346 (Association of the Bar of the City of New York, 1928). For Holmes' analysis of contract as a device of risk distribution, see Chapter 9, Section 1. Consult further, in addition to the Cohen article, Buckland, The Nature of Contractual Obligation, 8 Camb. L.J. 247 (1944); W. W. Buckland, Some Reflections on Jurisprudence 96 (1945); 2 M. Howe, Justice Oliver Wendell Holmes 233 (1963).

In a fairly recent English case, the question was raised whether an executor was under a duty to repudiate a contract if paying damages instead of performing would be beneficial to the estate. The argument was put thus: "there is nothing immoral in breaking a contract, and if an executor can benefit the estate by committing an actionable wrong and paying damages therefore, so that the person wronged really suffered nothing in the end, it is his duty to do so." This doctrine was rejected by the Privy Council in Ahmed Angullia Bin Hadjee Mohamed Salleh Angullia v. Estate and Trust Agencies (1927) Ltd., [1938] A.C. 624, 107 L.J.P.C. 71. In the case the executor, instead of breaking the contract entered into by the deceased with a building contractor, had permitted the latter to complete the contract and had performed himself. The question, therefore, in Hohfeldian language, was whether the executor, who unquestionably had a power vis-a-vis the building contractor to change a primary obligation into a secondary one by breaking the contract, was under a duty vis-a-vis the estate to exercise the power. The court, though recognizing that the executor is under a duty to the estate to come to a friendly arrangement with the other contracting party beneficial to the estate should the opportunity present itself, correctly decided that he is under no duty to commit a wrongful act, i.e., a breach of contract. The decision in favor of the executor makes eminent good sense, otherwise his duties would be far too onerous, 55 L.Q. Rev. 1 (1939). On the distinction between rights and duties on the one hand and powers and liabilities on the other, see W. N. Hohfeld, Fundamental Legal Conceptions as Applied in Judicial Reasoning (1923); Corbin, Legal Analysis and Terminology, 29 Yale L.J. 163 (1919); Cook, *supra*, at 346-351; J. Stone, Legal Systems and Lawyers' Reasonings 137 (1964). For the so-called right to break a contract, see further Chapter 10, Section 2. For an economist's reinterpretation of the Holmesian view, see R. Posner, Economic Analysis of Law 88 et seq. (1977). For a strong defense of the usefulness of specific performance, see Schwartz, The Case for Specific Performance, 89 Yale L.J. 271 (1979).

HADLEY v. BAXENDALE
9 Ex. 341, 156 Eng. Rep. 145 (1854)

At the trial before Crompton, J., at the last Gloucester Assizes, it appeared that the plaintiffs carried on an extensive business as millers at Gloucester; and that, on the 11th of May, their mill was stopped by a breakage of the crank shaft by which the mill was worked. The steam-engine was manufactured by Messrs. Joyce & Co., the engineers, at Greenwich, and it became necessary to send the shaft as a pattern for a new one to Greenwich. The fracture was discovered on the 12th, and on the 13th the plaintiffs sent one of their servants to the office of the defendants, who are the well-known carriers trading under the name of Pickford & Co., for the purpose of having the shaft carried to Greenwich. The plaintiffs' servant told the clerk that the mill was stopped, and that the shaft must be sent immediately; and in answer to the inquiry when the shaft would be taken, the answer was, that if it was sent up by twelve o'clock any day, it would be delivered at Greenwich the following day. On the following day the shaft was taken by the defendants, before noon, for the purpose of being conveyed to Greenwich, and the sum of 2*l*. 4*s*. was paid for its carriage for the whole distance; at the same time the defendants' clerk was told that a special entry, if required, should be made to hasten its delivery. The delivery of the shaft at Greenwich was delayed by some neglect; and the consequence was, that the plaintiffs did not receive the new shaft for several days after they would otherwise have done, and the working of their mill was thereby delayed, and they thereby lost the profits they would otherwise have received.

On the part of the defendants, it was objected that these damages were too remote, and that the defendants were not liable with respect to them. The learned Judge left the case generally to the jury, who found a verdict with 25*l*. damages beyond the amount paid into Court.

Whateley, in last Michaelmas Term, obtained a rule nisi for a new trial, on the ground of misdirection. . . .

ALDERSON, B. — We think that there ought to be a new trial in this case; but, in so doing, we deem it to be expedient and necessary to state explicitly the rule which the Judge, at the next trial, ought, in our opinion, to direct the jury to be governed by when they estimate the damages.

It is, indeed, of the last importance that we should do this; for, if the jury are left without any definite rule to guide them, it will in such cases as these, manifestly lead to the greatest injustice. The Courts have done this on several occasions; and, in Blake v. Midland Railway Company, 21 L.J., Q.B., 237, the Court granted a new trial on this very ground, that the rule had not been definitely laid down to the jury by the learned Judge at Nisi Prius.

"There are certain established rules," this Court says, in Alder v. Keighley, 15 M. & W. 117, "according to which the jury ought to find." And the Court, in that case, adds: "and here there is a clear rule, that the amount which would have been received if the contract had been kept, is the measure of damages if the contract is broken."

Now we think the proper rule in such a case as the present is this: — Where two parties have made a contract which one of them has broken, the damages which the other party ought to receive in respect of such breach of contract should be such as may fairly and reasonably be considered either arising naturally, i.e., according to the usual course of things, from such breach of contract itself, or such as may reasonably be supposed to have been in the contemplation of both parties, at the time they made the contract, as the probable result of the breach of it. Now, if the special circumstances under which the contract was actually made were communicated by the plaintiffs to the defendants, and thus known to both parties, the damages resulting from the breach of such a contract, which they would reasonably contemplate, would be the amount of injury which would ordinarily follow from a breach of contract under these special circumstances so known and communicated. But, on the other hand, if these special circumstances were wholly unknown to the party breaking the contract, he, at the most, could only be supposed to have had in his contemplation the amount of injury which would arise generally, and in the great multitude of cases not affected by any special circumstances, from such a breach of contract. For, had the special circumstances been known, the parties might have specially provided for the breach of contract by special terms as to the damages in that case; and of this advantage it would be very unjust to deprive them. Now the above principles are those by which we think the jury ought to be guided in estimating the damages arising out of any breach of contract. It is said, that other cases, such as breaches of contract in the non-payment of money, or in the not making a good title to land, are to be treated as exceptions from this, and as governed by a conventional rule. But as, in such cases, both parties must be supposed to be cognizant of that well-known rule, these cases may, we think, be more properly classed under the rule above enunciated as to cases under known special circumstances, because there both parties may reasonably be presumed to contemplate the estimation of the amount of damages according to the conventional rule. Now, in the present case, if we are to apply the principles above laid down, we find that the only circumstances here communicated by the plaintiffs to the defendants at the time the contract was made, were, that the article to be carried was the broken shaft of a mill, and that the plaintiffs were the millers of that mill. But how do these circumstances show reasonably that the profits of the mill must be stopped by an unreasonable delay in the delivery of the broken shaft by the carrier to the third person? Suppose the plaintiffs had another shaft in their possession put up or putting up at the time, and that they only wished to send back the broken shaft to the engineer who made it; it is clear that this would be quite consistent with the above circumstances, and yet the unreasonable delay in the delivery would have no effect upon the intermediate profits of the mill. Or, again, suppose that, at the time of the delivery to the carrier, the machinery of the mill had been in other respects defective, then, also, the same results would follow. Here it is true that the shaft was actually sent back to serve as a model for a new one, and that the want of a new one was the only cause of the stoppage of the mill, and that the loss of profits really arose from not sending down the new shaft in proper time, and that this arose from the delay in delivering the broken one to serve as a model. But it is obvious that, in the great multitude of cases of millers sending off broken shafts to third persons by a carrier under ordinary circumstances, such consequences would not, in all probability, have occurred; and these special circumstances were here never communicated by the plaintiffs to the defendants. It follows, therefore, that the loss of profits here cannot reasonably be considered such a consequence of the breach of contract as could have been fairly and reasonably contemplated by both the parties when they made this contract. For such loss would neither have flowed naturally from the breach of this contract in the great multitude of such cases occurring under ordinary circumstances, nor were the special circumstances, which, perhaps, would have made it a reasonable and natural consequence of such breach of contract, communicated to or known by the defendants. The judge ought, therefore, to have told the jury that, upon the facts then before them, they ought not to take the loss of profits into consideration at all in estimating the damages. There must therefore be a new trial in this case.

Rule absolute.

NOTE

"[A]s the contract is by mutual consent, the parties themselves expressly or by implication, fix the rule by which damages are to be measured." Holmes, J., in Globe Refining Co. v. Landa Cotton Oil Co., 190 U.S. 540, 543 (1903), infra p. 1144.

The rule of Hadley v. Baxendale

> . . . by subjecting all contract claims to a test of foreseeability by the contract breaker of the loss at the time of the making of the contract, diminishes the risk of business enterprise, and the result harmonized well with the free-trade economic philosophy of the Victorian era during which our law of contracts became systematized.

C. T. McCormick, Law of Damages 566-567 (1935). For an excellent discussion of the rules in Hadley v. Baxendale, consult *The Heron II* and Victoria Laundry v. Newman Industries, pp. 1157 and 1164 *infra*.

> The scope of damage for breach of contract is much narrower than the "proximate consequence" rule which prevails in actions to recover for a tort. If we may assume that the defaulting promisor is usually an *entrepreneur*, a businessman who has undertaken a risky enterprise, the law here manifests a policy to encourage the *entrepreneur* by reducing the extent of his risk below that amount of damage which, it might be plausibly argued, the promisee has actually been caused to suffer.

Patterson, The Apportionment of Business Risks Through Legal Devices, 24 Colum. L. Rev. 335, 342 (1924). For a further discussion of the measure of damages in tort and contract, see 5 Corbin §1019. See, in general, Chapter 10.

In Hadley v. Baxendale: A Study in the Industrialization of the Law, 4 J. Legal Stud. 249 (1975), Professor Danzig offers some fascinating insights into the circumstances surrounding the case and suggests a variety of reasons for the rule, some turning on contemporary deficiencies in the substantive law and others on administrative needs of the judiciary. He further points out that however sensible the rule was for business enterprises in nineteenth-century England, "a survey of the most recent American cases brings home the fact that as the economy has become more diverse and complex, the rule has become less viable." Id. at 280. An extract from the Danzig article is reproduced *infra* p. 1140.

Despite criticism of the rule, Restatement Second §365 carries it forward, as does U.C.C. §2-715(2)(a), albeit in a modified form.

CHAPTER 3

The Bargain

Section 1. Contract as a Promissory Transaction

RESTATEMENT OF CONTRACTS SECOND

§1. CONTRACT DEFINED

A contract is a promise or a set of promises for the breach of which the law gives a remedy, or the performance of which the law in some way recognizes as a duty.

NOTE

1. 1 Corbin §3 (1963):

> A study of its common usage will show that the term 'contract' has been made to denote three different kinds of things in various combinations: (1) the series of operative acts of the parties expressing their assent, or some part of these acts; (2) a physical document executed by the parties as an operative fact in itself and as lasting evidence of their having performed other necessary acts expressing their intentions; (3) the legal relations resulting from the operative acts of the parties, always including the relation of right in one party and duty in the other.

See also Llewellyn, What Price Contract?, 40 Yale L.J. 704, 708 (1931).

Which of the three meanings has been adopted by the Restatement? For a comparison of the scope of contract as defined by the Restatement with the constitutional meaning of contract, see Patterson, The Restatement of the Law of Contract, 33 Colum. L. Rev. 397, 410 (1933).

RESTATEMENT OF CONTRACTS SECOND

§2. PROMISE . . .

(1) A promise is a manifestation of intention to act or refrain from acting in a specified way, so made as to justify a promisee in understanding that a commitment has been made.

111

NOTE

According to the Restatement, contractual liability is promissory liability. Promise, on this view, is the centerpiece of contractual obligation. "We do not have promises because we have a law of contracts; we have a law of contracts because we have promises." H. Havighurst, The Nature of Private Contract 10 (1961). The act of promising has attracted much philosophical attention. See C. Fried, Contract as Promise (1981) and P. Atiyah, Promises, Morals and the Law (1981). For a criticism of the explanation of contractual liability in terms of promises as too narrow, see I. Macneil, The New Social Contract 4 et seq.; see also P. Atiyah, The Rise and Fall of Freedom of Contract (1979), and G. Gilmore, The Death of Contract (1974); Kronman, A New Champion for the Will Theory (Review of C. Fried, Contract as Promise), 91 Yale L.J. 404 (1981).

RESTATEMENT OF CONTRACTS SECOND

§3. AGREEMENT DEFINED; BARGAIN DEFINED

An Agreement is a manifestation of mutual assent on the part of two or more persons. A bargain is an agreement to exchange promises or to exchange a promise for a performance or to exchange performances.

§17. REQUIREMENT OF A BARGAIN

(1) Except as stated in Subsection (2), the formation of a contract requires a bargain in which there is a manifestation of mutual assent to the exchange and a consideration. . . .

§18. MANIFESTATION OF MUTUAL ASSENT

Manifestation of mutual assent to an exchange requires that each party either make a promise or begin or render a performance.

§22. MODE OF ASSENT: OFFER AND ACCEPTANCE

(1) The manifestation of mutual assent to an exchange ordinarily takes the form of an offer or proposal by one party followed by an acceptance by the other party or parties.

(2) A manifestation of mutual assent may be made even though neither offer nor acceptance can be identified and even though the moment of formation cannot be determined.

§23.   NECESSITY THAT MANIFESTATIONS HAVE REFERENCE TO EACH OTHER

It is essential to a bargain that each party manifest assent with reference to the manifestation of the other.

§24.   OFFER DEFINED

An offer is the manifestation of willingness to enter into a bargain, so made as to justify another person in understanding that his assent to that bargain is invited and will conclude it.

UNIFORM COMMERCIAL CODE

§1-201.   GENERAL DEFINITIONS

(11)   "Contract" means the total obligation in law which results from the parties' agreement as affected by this Act and any other applicable rules of law. (Compare "Agreement.")

(3)   "Agreed" or "Agreement" means the bargain in fact as found in the language of the parties or in the course of dealing or usage of trade or course of performance or by implication from other circumstances. (Compare "Contract.")

A general theory of contract was unknown in the Anglo-American legal tradition until sometime in the late eighteenth or early nineteenth century.[1] Theorizing before then centered around the various forms of action — debt, covenant, and assumpsit.[2] When Anglo-American lawyers finally came to the realization "that a theory of contract had a place not only in political and moral philosophy but in jurisprudence as well,"[3] they turned to civil law writers "for a scientific and rational analysis of contract."[4] As late as 1887, an English judge observed that the definitions

---

1. P. Atiyah, An Introduction to the Law of Contracts 2 (2d ed. 1977); Simpson, Innovation in Nineteenth Century Contract Law, 91 L.Q. Rev. 247, 250 (1975); E. A. Harriman, The Law of Contracts §645 (2d ed. 1901).

2. There existed a considerable number of Abridgments with a wealth of contractual material more or less classified, such as William Sheppard's Action on the Case for Deeds (1683). But even catergories that we regard as central to the law of contracts were not regarded as worthy of analysis. In Simpson's words, the question "What is a promise?" was left to the jury. Simpson, *supra* note 1, at 252.

3. M. Howe, Oliver Wendell Holmes, The Proving Years 223 (1963).

4. Harriman, *supra* note 1.

of contract in the textbooks were all founded on that of Pothier,[5] who defined a contract as "an agreement by which two parties reciprocally promise and engage, or one of them singly promises and engages to the other to give some particular thing, or to do or abstain from doing some particular act."[6]

Continental influence went beyond Pothier and the French Civil Code. A generation of text writers, including Anson, Pollock, and Holland,[7] drew heavily from the German writer Savigny, and thus indirectly from Kant. Through these writers the will theory of contract was introduced to Anglo-American jurisprudence. Contract, according to Savigny, is a union of two or more persons in an accordant expression of will with the object of determining their legal relations.[8] The will theory holds that "[t]he will of the parties is something inherently worthy of respect. Hence, the first essential of a contract is the agreement of wills, or the meeting of minds."[9] According to this view, the salient characteristic of contract is the creation of a right not to a thing but to another person's future conduct,[10] and the law recognizes such rights not only to protect the promisee but also to insure the dignity of the promisor by permitting him to exercise greater control over himself and his affairs. "By allowing one to bind oneself effectively so that what is promised for the future can be counted among the present possessions of the promisee,"[11] the institution of promising enables a person to enlarge the scope of his will.

The will theory has left a deep impression on our law of contracts. For example, unwillingness to probe too deeply into the fairness of an agreement has often been rationalized in terms of the will theory: if individual dignity is to have any meaning at all, each person must be deemed capable of caring for himself, and exculpatory rules dealing with capacity, fraud, duress, and mistake must therefore be narrowly construed.

Toward the end of the nineteenth century, the will theory lost much of its appeal in this country and in England, perhaps because of its foreign origin, but also because the security of transactions was threatened by

---

5. Foster v. Wheeler, 36 Ch. D. 695, 698 (1887). Parke, B., in his argument with counsel for plaintiff in Hadley v. Baxendale, *supra* p. 106, referred to the sensible rule on damages of the French Civil Code §1149-1151, introducing the foreseeability test. Best, J., remarked in Cox v. Troy, 5 B. & Ald. 474, 480, 106 Eng. Rep. 1264 (1822), that Pothier is the "highest authority that can be had, next to a decision of a Court of Justice in this country."

6. Treatise on Obligations or Contracts, Pt. I, ch. 1, §1, Art. 1 (Evans trans. 1806).

7. The first edition of Pollock's Treatise on the General Principles Concerning the Validity of Agreements in the Law of England appeared in 1875, the first edition of Anson's Principles of the English Law of Contract in 1879, and the first edition of Holland's work in 1880.

8. 3 System des Heutigen Römischen Rechts 309.

9. Cohen, The Basis of Contract, 46 Harv. L. Rev. 553, 575 (1933).

10. Pollock, Principles of Contract, Preface to 4th ed., at ix (Wald, 2d Am. ed., 1885).

11. Fried, Review of Atiyah, The Rise and Fall of Freedom of Contract, 93 Harv. L. Rev. 1858, 1862 (1980), paraphasing Kant, Metaphysical Elements of Justice 248 (J. Ladd ed. 1965). See also C. Fried, Contract as Promise (1981).

what were perceived to be the "subjective" elements of the theory. Pollock, who drew heavily, if not literally, on Savigny in the first chapter of the first two editions of his book on contracts, had apparently experienced a change of heart by the third edition, which stresses the historical basis of English contract law and the impact of the forms of action, and emphasizes the element of reliance rather than "the artificial equation of wills or intentions."[12] According to the more historically minded Pollock of the third edition, "he who has given a promise is bound to him who accepts it not merely because he has expressed a certain intention but because he has so expressed himself as to entitle the other party to rely on his action in a certain way."[13] With the decline of the will theory and the rise in importance of the concept of reliance, a more objective approach to the theory of contractual obligation became firmly established. Manifestation of intent, and not intent itself, now provided the ground for the enforcement of contracts. The objective theory was ardently supported by Holmes, Langdell, and Williston. In the language of Holmes, "the whole doctrine of contracts is formal and external."[14] As Corbin pointed out, however, "the law of contract cannot be explained by either of these theories standing alone."[15] So long as consent and freedom of choice remain basic social values that are reflected in our law of contracts, the will theory will continue to have appeal and influence.

The basis of promissory or contractual obligation is currently a subject of much controversy. It has been argued that promise-based liability, with its emphasis on the traditional liberal value of free choice, is anachronistic. Atiyah, for example, asserts that liability based on benefit or detrimental reliance is more in keeping with contemporary values.[16] As Atiyah points out, liability based on benefit and reliance is more consistent with a "paternalist social philosophy, and a redistributive economic system,"[17] than was the classical will theory with its exclusive emphasis on promissory liability.

It has also been argued that promise is losing its importance as a guiding principle because exchange increasingly occurs in the context of long-term relations between mutually dependent parties who share only certain broadly defined goals, rather than in the context of brief, episodic transactions with specific and relatively well-articulated ends. According

12. F. Pollock, Principles of Contract 1 (9th ed. 1921). Lord Cairns in Crundy v. Lindsay, 3 A.C. 459, 465 (1873), still emphasized that contracts were based on a "meeting of minds."

13. Pollock, *supra* note 12, at 1.

14. Holmes, The Common Law 230 (M. Howe ed. 1963). The passage just quoted was added by Howe on the basis of Holmes' marginal notes in his own copy. See also Learned Hand, J., in Hotchkiss v. National City Bank of New York, 200 F. 287, 293 (S.D.N.Y. 1911), *aff'd*, 201 F. 664 (2d Cir. 1912), *aff'd*, 231 U.S. 50 (1913).

15. 1 Corbin §106 (1960 & Supp. 1984).

16. Atiyah at 6-7, 778-779 (1979).

17. Id. at 6-7

to this view, the expectations of the parties must be measured less by what is said or written at any particular moment in time, than by the ongoing requirements of the particular relationships.[18]

These latter views, of course, are not universally held. A number of writers view recent developments in the law of contracts as marking a regrettable movement away from a system of commutative to one of distributive justice.[19] In the work of these writers, the principles of promise and free choice continue to operate with undiminished vigor.

BALFOUR v. BALFOUR
L.R. 2 K.B. 571 (C.A. 1919)

The plaintiff sued the defendant (her husband) for money which she claimed to be due in respect to an agreed allowance of £30 a month. The alleged agreement was entered into under the following circumstances. The parties were married in August, 1900. The husband, a civil engineer, had a post under the Government of Ceylon as Director of Irrigation, and after the marriage he and his wife went to Ceylon, and lived there together until the year 1915, except that in 1906 they paid a short visit to this country, and in 1908 the wife came to England in order to undergo an operation, after which she returned to Ceylon. In November, 1915, she came to this country with her husband, who was on leave. They remained in England until August, 1916, when the husband's leave was up and he had to return. The wife however on the doctor's advice remained in England. On August 8, 1916, the husband being about to sail, the alleged parol agreement sued upon was made. The plaintiff, as appeared from the judge's note, gave the following evidence of what took place: "In August, 1916, defendant's leave was up. I was suffering from rheumatic arthritis. The doctor advised my staying in England for some months, not to go out till November 4. On August 8 my husband sailed. He gave me a cheque from 8th to 31st for £24, and promised to give me £30 per month until I returned." Later on she said: "My husband and I wrote the figures together on August 8; £34 shown. Afterwards he said £30." In cross-examination she said that they had not agreed to live apart until subsequent differences arose between them, and that the agreement of August, 1916, was one which might be made by a couple in amity. Her husband in consultation with her assessed her needs, and said he would send £30 per month for her maintenance. She further said that she understood that the defendant would be returning to England in a few

18. Macneil, The Many Futures of Contract, 47 S. Cal. L. Rev. 691, 807 et seq. (1974).
19. See, for example, Epstein, Unconscionability: A Critical Reappraisal, 18 J. Law & Econ. 293 (1975); R. Posner, Economic Analysis of Law, ch. 4 (2d ed. 1977); Fried, *supra* note 11.

months, but that he afterwards wrote to her suggesting that they had better remain apart. In March, 1918, she commenced proceeding for restitution of conjugal rights, and on July 30 she obtained a decree nisi. On December 16, 1918, she obtained an order for alimony.

Sargant J. held that the husband was under an obligation to support his wife, and the parties had contracted that the extent of that obligation should be defined in terms of so much a month. The consent of the wife to that arrangement was a sufficient consideration to constitute a contract which could be sued upon.

He accordingly gave judgment for the plaintiff.

The husband appealed. . . .

ATKIN, L.J. The defence to this action on the alleged contract is that the defendant, the husband, entered into no contract with his wife, and for the determination of that it is necessary to remember that there are agreements between parties which do not result in contracts within the meaning of that term in our law. The ordinary example is where two parties agree to take a walk together, or where there is an offer and an acceptance of hospitality. Nobody would suggest in ordinary circumstances that those agreements result in what we know as a contract, and one of the most usual forms of agreement which does not constitute a contract appears to me to be the arrangements which are made between husband and wife. It is quite common, and it is the natural and inevitable result of the relationship of husband and wife, that the two spouses should make arrangements between themselves — agreements such as are in dispute in this action — agreements for allowances, by which the husband agrees that he will pay to his wife a certain sum of money, per week, or per month, or per year, to cover either her own expenses or the necessary expenses of the household and of the children of the marriage, and in which the wife promises either expressly or impliedly to apply the allowance for the purpose for which it is given. To my mind those agreements, or many of them, do not result in contracts at all, and they do not result in contracts even though there may be what as between other parties would constitute consideration for the agreement. The consideration, as we know, may consist either in some right, interest, profit or benefit accruing to one party, or some forbearance, detriment, loss of responsibility given, suffered or undertaken by the other. That is a well-known definition, and it constantly happens, I think, that such arrangements made between husband and wife are arrangements in which there are mutual promises, or in which there is consideration in form within the definition that I have mentioned. Nevertheless they are not contracts, and they are not contracts because the parties did not intend that they should be attended by legal consequences.

To my mind it would be the worst possible example to hold that agreements such as this resulted in legal obligations which could be enforced in the Courts. It would mean this, that when the husband makes his wife a promise to give her an allowance of 30s. or £2 a week, whatever he can afford to give her, for the maintenance of the household and children, and she promises so to apply it, not only could she sue him for his failure in any week to supply the allowance, but he could sue her for non-performance of the obligation, express or implied, which she had undertaken upon her part. All I can say is that the small Courts of this country would have to be multiplied one hundred-fold if these arrangements were held to result in legal obligations. They are not sued upon, not because the parties are reluctant to enforce their legal rights when the agreement is broken, but because the parties, in the inception of the arrangement, never intended that they should be sued upon. Agreements such as these are outside the realm of contracts altogether. The common law does not regulate the form of agreements between spouses. Their promises are not sealed with seals and sealing wax. The consideration that really obtains for them is that natural love and affection which counts for so little in these cold Courts. The terms may be repudiated, varied or renewed as performance proceeds or as disagreements develop, and the principles of the common law as to exoneration and discharge and accord and satisfaction are such as find no place in the domestic code. The parties themselves are advocates, judges, Courts, sheriff's officer and reporter. In respect of these promises each house is a domain into which the King's writ does not seek to run, and to which his officers do not seek to be admitted.

The only question in this case is whether or not this promise was of such a class or not. For the reasons given by my brethren it appears to me to be plainly established that the promise here was not intended by either party to be attended by legal consequences. I think the onus was upon the plaintiff, and the plaintiff has not established any contract. The parties were living together, the wife intending to return. The suggestion is that the husband bound himself to pay £30 a month under all circumstances, and she bound herself to be satisfied with that sum under all circumstances, and although she was in ill-health and alone in this country, that out of that sum she undertook to defray the whole of the medical expenses that might fall upon her, whatever might be the development of her illness, and in whatever expenses it might involve her. To my mind neither party contemplated such a result. I think that the parol evidence upon which the case turns does not establish a contract. I think that the letters do not evidence such a contract or amplify the oral evidence which was given by the wife, which is not in dispute. For these reasons I think the judgment of the Court below was wrong and that this appeal should be allowed.

Appeal allowed.

[The concurring opinions of Warrington, L.J., and Duke, L.J., have been omitted.]

NOTE

Consult Kahn-Freund, Inconsistencies and Injustices in the Law of Husband and Wife, 15 Mod. L. Rev. 133, 138 (1952); Unger, Intent to Create Legal Relations, Mutuality and Consideration, 19 Mod. L. Rev. 96 (1956), discussing Simpkins v. Pays, [1955] 3 All E.R. 10. The case of Jones v. Patavatton, [1969] 1 W.L.R. 328 (C.A.), makes clear that the result in *Balfour* is based on a presumption of fact and not a conclusion of law. See 85 L.Q. Rev. 314-317 (1969); Pettit v. Pettit, [1969] 2 W.L.R. 966. For a better understanding of the decision, the distinction between community and society may be helpful. See 16 Int. Encyc. of Soc. Sciences 98, s.v. Toennies (1968).

On the requirement of an intent to contract, see 1 Williston §21 (1958):

> . . . The . . . statement of Savigny which has been popularized . . . by Sir Frederick Pollock and others, that not only mental assent to a promise in fact, but an intent to form a legal relation is a requisite for the formation of contracts, . . . cannot be accepted. Such a repetition of the opinion of an influential Civil-law jurist shows the danger of assuming that a sound principle in that law may be successfully transplanted. Nowhere is there greater danger in attempting such a transfer than in the law governing the formation of contracts. In a system of law which makes no requirement of consideration, it may well be desirable to limit enforceable promises to those where a legal bond was contemplated, but in a system of law which does not enforce promises unless some benefit to the promisor or detriment to the promisee has been asked and given, there is no propriety in such a limitation. The only proof of its existence will be the production of cases holding that, though consideration was asked and given for a promise, it is, nevertheless, not enforceable because a legal relation was not contemplated. On the contrary, the assertion is ventured that the common law does not require any positive intention to create a legal obligation as an element of contract. Conversely, though both parties may think they have made a contract, they may not have done so. The views of parties to an agreement as to what are the requirements of a contract, as to what mutual assent means, or consideration, or what contracts are enforceable without a writing, and what are not, are wholly immaterial. They are as immaterial as the views of an individual as to what constitutes a tort. In regard to both torts and contracts, the law, not the parties, fixes the requirements of a legal obligation.

See further, Restatement Second §21.

Of course, even in business matters the parties are free to state their unwillingness to be legally bound. Businessmen may, for example, enter into "gentlemen's agreements" or use "honourable pledge clauses." Rose

& Frank Co. v. J. R. Crompton & Bros., [1972] 2 K.B. 261 (C.A.);[20] Restatement Second §21, Illus. 4, citing *Rose & Frank Co.* Lack of intent to be legally bound can also be implied from the subject matter of the agreement. There is an inevitable grey area, however, since the parties sometimes use ambiguous language and even the lack of indication of their intention may be inconclusive. On letters of intent in underwriting transactions, see 1 L. Loss, Securities Regulation 163-171 (2d ed. 1961); E. A. Farnsworth, Contracts 116-117 (1982).

In England, a well-known case, decided in 1969, held collective bargaining agreements to be unenforceable. Ford Motor Co., Ltd. v. Amalgamated Union of Engineering and Foundry Workers, [1969] 2 All E.R. 201, at 396.[21] This is all the more remarkable since the collective contract involved in the litigation in the *Ford Motor* case, unlike many such agreements, did not contain a clause expressly stating that it was not intended to be legally enforceable (a so-called TINALEA clause: "This is not a legally enforceable agreement"). The Industrial Relations Act, 1971, §34, laid down a presumption that the parties to a written collective agreement intend to be legally bound, unless the agreement includes a TINALEA clause. The presumption was reversed, however, by the Trade Union and Labor Relations Act, 1974, §18. Under our law, collective bargaining agreements are enforceable. Labor Management Relations Act, 29 U.S.C.A. §301 (West 1975 & Supp. 1985).

According to Restatement Second §21, Comment *c,* "contracts within the family present more of family law than of the law of contracts." This statement is amplified in §190, which emphasizes that an agreement changing some essential incident of the marital relationship in a way detrimental to the public interest in the relationship is unenforceable on grounds of public policy. Comment *a* to §190 states:

> Many terms of the relationship are seen as largely fixed by the state and beyond the power of the parties to modify. Two reasons support this view. One is that there is a public interest in the relationship, and particularly in such matters as support and child custody, that makes it inappropriate to subject it to modification by the parties. Another is that the courts lack workable standards and are not an appropriate forum for the types of contract disputes that would arise if such promises were enforceable.

The second reason is illustrated by Miller v. Miller, 78 Iowa 177, 35 N.W. 464, 42 N.W. 641 (1887).

Unquestionably, there has been an intrusion of contract law into the

20. In the Rose & Frank Co. case, plaintiff was successful in the House of Lords on his claim for the specific orders accepted by defendants before they terminated the agreement, despite the presence of an honourable pledge clause; the transaction was regarded as separate and independent of the clause. [1925] A. C. 445, 455.

21. The case is discussed by Selvyn, Collective Agreements and the Law, 32 Mod. L. Rev. 377 (1969).

field of domestic relations in recent years, as the discussion that follows indicates. Property settlement agreements made as part of a reconciliation have been upheld in Hoyt v. Hoyt, 213 Tenn. 117, 372 S.W.2d 300 (1963), and Holsomback v. Caldwell, 218 Ga. 393, 128 S.E.2d 47 (1962). In *Hoyt*, the couple was already involved in divorce proceedings; in *Holsomback*, the administrator of the wife's estate was suing the administrator of the husband's estate.

The case that comes closest to upholding a contract requiring payment for a wife's services is Department of Human Resources v. Williams, 130 Ga. App. 149, 202 S.E.2d 504 (1973). In the *Williams* case, the couple sought to recover welfare payments for the wife's services to her incapacitated husband, and the court found consideration for the husband's agreement in the extraordinary nature of the services rendered by the wife. For a discussion of the case, see Hunter, An Essay on Contract and Status: Race, Marriage and the Meretricious Spouse, 65 Va. L. Rev. 1039, 1072 et seq. (1978).

On the enforcement of interspousal contracts, and on recent proposals for marriage contracts that alter the standard legal relations between spouses, see Note, 29 N.Y.U. L. Rev. 1161 (1974); Weitzman, Legal Regulation of Marriage: Tradition and Change, 62 Calif. L. Rev. 1169 (1974) (which contains excerpts from various alternative marriage contracts at pp. 1278-1288); McDowell, Contracts in the Family, 45 B.U.L. Rev. 43 (1965). See also Note, 79 Harv. L. Rev. 1650 (1966); Restatement Second §190. On cohabitation agreements, see Hewitt v. Hewitt and the Note following it in Section 2, *infra* p. 155.

DAVIS v. GENERAL FOODS CORP.
21 F. Supp. 445 (S.D.N.Y. 1937)

CLANCY, District Judge. This is a motion brought pursuant to rule 112 of the Rules of Civil Practice for judgment on the pleadings dismissing the complaint on the ground that it does not state facts sufficient to constitute a cause of action.

The complaint alleges that the plaintiff and the defendant entered into an agreement whereby the plaintiff, at the special instance and request of the defendant, revealed to the defendant the plaintiff's new idea and recipe for the making and sale of fruit flavors to be used in the household for the making of ice cream and that the defendant agreed to pay to the plaintiff a reasonable compensation for the disclosing of the said idea and recipe if the defendant should thereafter use the same in its business. The complaint further alleges that the plaintiff duly performed all the terms and conditions of the said agreement on her part to be performed, but that, although the defendant used the idea and recipe in its business, it has failed and refused to pay the plaintiff any compensation.

In her bill of particulars, which may properly be considered on this motion (Dineen v. May, 149 App. Div. 469, 134 N.Y.S. 7), the plaintiff stated that the agreement was contained in a letter addressed to an officer of the defendant to the effect that the plaintiff had an idea for a new food product and for the form of merchandizing thereof by the defendant and the following letter received in reply from the defendant:

General Foods Corporation
Postum Building, 250 Park Avenue
New York

LEWIS W. WATERS
Vice President

February 13th, 1934

Miss Beatrice Davis,
172 West 79th St.,
New York, N. Y.

Dear Miss Davis:

This will acknowledge your letter of February 10th addressed to Mr. E. F. Hutton.

We shall be glad to examine your idea for a new food product, but only with the understanding that the use to be made of it by us, and the compensation, if any, to be paid therefor, are matters resting solely in our discretion.

Very truly yours,
[Signed] LEWIS W. WATERS
Vice President.

LWW/s

This letter is so indefinite as to terms that it cannot give rise to a binding obligation. As is stated by Williston in section 43 of his Revised Edition on the Law of Contracts, 1939: "One of the commonest kind of promises too indefinite for legal enforcement is where the promisor retains an unlimited right to decide later the nature or extent of his performance. This unlimited choice in effect destroys the promise and makes it merely illusory." Chiapparelli v. Baker, Kellogg & Co., 252 N.Y. 192, 169 N.E. 274; section 32, Restatement Law of Contracts.

However, the plaintiff urges that this does not prevent her recovering upon quantum meruit and relies on the principle set forth in Varney v. Ditmars, 217 N.Y. 223, 111 N.E. 822, Ann. Cas. 1916 B, 758; United Press v. New York Press Co., 164 N.Y. 406, 58 N.E. 527, 53 L.R.A. 288; and Canet v. Smith, 173 App. Div. 241, 159 N.Y.S. 593, to the effect that, where a party has performed in reliance upon an alleged contract, the terms of which are too vague and indefinite for enforcement, the law will presume a promise to pay reasonable value and will permit proof thereof to be given under an allegation in the complaint of an express contract. Assuming that the complaint contains sufficient averments to enable the plaintiff to recover the value of the recipe without reference to the allegations of the agreement (see Sussdorff v. Schmidt, 55 N.Y. 319 and Blair Engineering Co. v. Page Steel & Wire Co., 3 Cir., 288 F. 622), I am of the opinion that the facts as alleged in the complaint, supplemented by the bill of particulars, are inconsistent with the existence of a contract implied in fact and do not give rise to a quasi contract or obligation implied in law. See Miller v. Schloss, 218 N.Y. 400, 113 N.E. 337.

Woodward, in section 65 of his work on Quasi Contracts, states that, where the form or character of the promise leads to the conclusion that the plaintiff did not rely upon it as a contractual obligation but trusted the fairness and liberality of the defendant, there is not only no contract but no misreliance upon a supposed contract, and subsequently no legal obligation whatever.

This is my construction of the defendant's understanding "that the use to be made of it (the recipe) by us, the compensation, if any, to be paid therefor, are matters resting solely in our discretion." Webster's New International Dictionary, Second Edition, defines "discretion" when used in the sense of "at one's discretion" as meaning "at will; according to one's judgment or pleasure." As employed in the context of the defendant's letter when viewed in the light of the facts disclosed by the pleadings the word "discretion" must receive this interpretation. Woodward, supra, quotes the case of Taylor v. Brewer, 1 Maule & S. 290, also reported in 105 English Reports 108, where the plaintiff was promised that "such remuneration be made as shall be deemed right." Lord Ellenborough, C.J., was of the opinion that this "was an engagement accepted by the bankrupt on no definite terms, but only in confidence that if his labour deserved anything he should be recompensed for it by the defendants. This was throwing himself upon the mercy of those with whom he contracted." The opinion of Bayley, J., was that "it was to be in the breast of the committee whether he was to have anything, and if anything, then how much." This is one of the leading English cases on the subject and was followed in Roberts v. Smith, 4 Hurl. & N. 315, reported in 157 English Reports 861. Also see McDonald v. Acker, Merrall & Condit Co., 192 App. Div. 123, 182 N.Y.S. 607, and other cases collected in 92 A.L.R. 1391.

Accordingly, I am obliged to grant the defendant's motion and to hold that the plaintiff in disclosing her recipe relied upon the good faith and sense of fairness of the defendant corporation to recompense her for the value of the recipe.

NOTE

Has the court correctly interpreted the clause used by the defendant? What was its function? Compare Osborn v. Boeing Airplane Company,

309 F.2d 99 (9th Cir. 1962). Consult 31 Cornell L.Q. 382 (1946); 16 U. Chi. L. Rev. 323 (1949).

An employee at will — one who may be discharged for good, bad, or no cause at all — is in a position analogous to that of Miss Davis, in that he must rely on the "fairness and liberality" of the employer for his continued employment. In recent years courts have limited the employer's discretionary power to terminate employees at will, most frequently by invoking the "public policy exception" to protect employees who have been discharged for especially objectionable reasons. For an argument in favor of expanding this exception, see Note, Protecting Employees at Will Against Wrongful Discharge: The Public Policy Exception, 96 Harv. L. Rev. 1931 (1983).

THE MABLEY & CAREW CO. v. BORDEN
129 Ohio St. 375, 195 N.E. 697 (1935)

Ida C. Borden brought an action in the Court of Common Pleas of Hamilton county against the Mabley & Carew Company, alleging in her petition that Anna Work, her sister, now deceased, was and had been for some years an employee of such company and that it promised and agreed in writing to pay to such person as was designated by Anna Work on the back of a certificate issued to her a sum equal to the wages received by her from the company for the year next preceding the date of her death. The plaintiff in error further alleges that she is the person designated on the back of the certificate; that Anna Work continued in the employ of the company until the date of her death; that her wages for the year preceding were $780, and she prays judgment for this amount with interest from the date of the death of Anna Work.

The Mabley & Carew Company in effect denies these allegations and states affirmatively that if the certificate was issued as claimed, it was issued voluntarily and gratuitously and without consideration, and was issued to Anna Work and accepted by her with the express understanding that it carried no legal obligation.

A reply was filed, denying the affirmative allegations of this answer. The case came on for trial in the Court of Common Pleas and at the conclusion of the plaintiff's evidence the trial court sustained a notion directing a verdict for the Mabley & Carew Company.

Motion for new trial was overruled, judgment was entered and error was prosecuted to the Court of Appeals of Hamilton county, which court reversed, set aside and held for naught the judgment of the Court of Common Pleas. The Court of Appeals, finding that its decision was in conflict with the decision in the case of Black v. W. S. Tyler Co., 12 Ohio App., 27, certified the case to this court for review and final determination.

The following is a copy of the certificate upon which the action was predicated:

No. 378

The Mabley & Carew Co.

To Mrs. Anna Work.

In appreciation of the duration and faithful character of your services heretofore rendered as an employee of this Company, there will be paid in the event of your death, if still an employee of this Company, (except under those circumstances which would give rise to an obligation on the State of Ohio under any Workmen's Compensation Act to reimburse your Estate for your death,) to the party or parties designated by you on the back of this certificate a sum equal to the wages you have received from this Company for the year next preceding the day of your death, but in no event to exceed the sum of Two Thousand Dollars.

The issue and delivery of this certificate is understood to be purely voluntary and gratuitous on the part of this Company and is accepted with the express understanding that it carries no legal obligation whatsoever or assurance or promise of future employment, and may be withdrawn or discontinued at any time by this Company.

The Mabley & Carew Co.

ADOLPH C. WEISS, *Secy.*

Cincinnati, Ohio, Dec. 24, 1919.

Endorsement.

Date, _____

The Mabley & Carew Co.

Gentlemen: — It is my desire that you make all benefits payable under this Certificate to the following and in the proportions here indicated:

Name	Relation to Beneficiary	Address	Proportion
Mrs. Ida Borden	Sister		

Signature _____

STEPHENSON, J. It is contended by the Mabley & Carew Company that there is no proof of the designation of Ida C. Borden as beneficiary under the certificate in question.

The name appears on the back of the certificate and, while it is typewritten, it is certainly a sufficient designation, taken in connection with the fact that Anna Work had it in her possession until her death.

There is just one question in this case, and that is the consideration for the issuance of this certificate. It is true that Anna Work could not maintain an action on this certificate in her lifetime, as no right of action existed in her favor, but that fact did not prevent it from being enforceable, after her death, in the hands of Ida C. Borden.

This certificate was not a pure gratuity on the part of the Mabley & Carew Company, as there was a provision in the certificate to the effect that the payment would not be made in the event of death unless Anna Work was still an employee of the company. This was an inducement to Anna Work to continue in the employ of the company. This is not the only consideration, as it is expressed at the outset that the company appreciates the duration and faithful character of the services of the employee theretofore rendered. The employee, by virtue of the insurance of the certificate, had a right to expect that the person nominated by her would in the event of her death receive the amount designated by the certificate. This was certainly an incentive to remain in the service of the company.

It is not a tenable proposition that, because Anna Work had no enforceable right during her life, her beneficiary could take no more than she had. We think the learned Court of Appeals was right in holding that Anna Work, by continuing in the service of the company until her death, created a binding obligation upon the company to pay to her designated beneficiary the sum mentioned in the certificate.

It is stated in the certificate: "The issue and delivery of this certificate is understood to be purely voluntary and gratuitous on the part of this Company." That was a part of the contract so far as Anna Work was concerned. She had no right that she could possibly assert, as she had to die before the right would ripen in anyone.

The case of Zwolanek v. Baker Mfg. Co., 150 Wis., 517, 137 N.W., 769, 44 L.R.A. (N.S.), 1214, Ann. Cas., 1914A, 793, pronounces the law relative to certificates of this character in its true light as we see it. The court there said, at page 521 of the opinion:

> While the practice initiated by the defendant is beneficial to its employees, it is not difficult to see wherein it is also beneficial to the employer. It tends to induce employees to remain continuously in the employ of the same master and to render efficient services so as to minimize the possibility of discharge. It also tends to relieve the employer of the annoyance of hiring and breaking in new men to take the place of those who might otherwise voluntarily quit, and to insure a full working force at times when jobs are plentiful and labor is scarce.

True, Anna Work by reason of this certificate was under no obligation to continue in the service of the Mabley & Carew Company if she did not see fit so to do; neither was the company, by reason of the certificate, obligated to give her continuous or definite employment. But neither of these facts in any wise affected the right of the beneficiary, so far as Anna Work was concerned after this contract was executed.

We find no case exactly on all fours with the one before us; but we do find a number of cases that support the finding made by the Court of Appeals herein. The subject is well digested and thoroughly discussed in an annotation in 28 A.L.R., beginning at page 331.

It is a well known proposition of law that a contract should be given that construction that will uphold it and preserve to the parties thereto their rights if the same can be done without doing violence to language. We find no trouble in upholding this contract.

The judgment of the Court of Appeals is hereby affirmed.

Judgment affirmed.

Weygandt, C.J., Williams, Jones, Matthias, Day and Zimmerman, JJ. concur.

NOTE

Note, 34 Mich. L. Rev. 129, 129 (1935):

It is generally accepted that, where it is apparent that there was no intention to contract, there can be no contract. The court has apparently overlooked this fundamental principle in the instant case, as it has not squarely faced the problem of whether the parties intended a contract, but has rather based its decision upon a question of consideration.

Note, 49 Harv. L. Rev. 148, 149 (1935):

Even if the employee could not reasonably regard the qualified promise as an offer, however, it is not impossible to uphold the result. The certificate is apparently designed to induce the employee to remain with the company. If she did so, relying upon what she considered a mere chance of performance of the promise, there would be neither a unilateral contract nor an injustice; but if in so acting she regarded performance of the promise as highly probable, it would seem unjust not to enforce the promise. If the company designedly induced a definite and substantial act by its promissory representation, it should be estopped to deny liability on the promise. . . ; see Restatement Contracts [First] §90. The fact that in the instant case the induced act was of benefit to the promisor adds to the justice of the result. . . . Although the instant decision maybe incompatible with orthodox contract theory, it would seem to evidence a tendency to avoid unconscionable results by the application of more flexible principles.

The promissory estoppel argument was rejected in a case involving a similar issue. Spooner v. Reserve Life Insurance Co., 47 Wash. 2d 246, 287 P.2d 735, 737 (1955) (promise to pay annual bonus to a departing employee). See also Employment Retirement Income Security Act, 29 U.S.C.A. §§1053-1054.

ARMSTRONG v. M'GHEE

Addison 261 (Westmoreland County Ct., Pa. 1795)

Armstrong appearing disgusted with a valuable horse, that, after a hard ride, seemed jaded and lame, offered him for sale to several persons, for a trifle, and to M'Ghee, for £5. M'Ghee agreed, and by Armstrong's direction, took the horse home to his stable. Both lived in Greensburgh, and were on terms of intimacy. At the time, some supposed Armstrong in jest. He said so himself afterwards, and demanded the horse back, as supposing M'Ghee understood him to have been in jest. However, M'Ghee chose to keep the horse; and Armstrong brought a replevin for him. M'Ghee claimed property, and retained the horse. During the suit, the horse died, having been very hard ridden, in a hot day, and drunk cold water.

Brackenridge and Young, for the plaintiff. A contract must have an agreement of the mind, understood by both parties. Inadequacy of price, known to the other party, is a ground to set aside a contract. So is imposition, as selling a horse for a barley corn for the first nail, in his shoes, and so in a duplicate ratio for every other. A contract to be carried into effect, must be fair, reasonable, and free from circumvention.

Purviance and H. Ross, for the defendant.

President. A contract may be made by any signs, which shew an agreement of mind, though they be neither words nor writing: if there be understanding, it may be made between two men deaf and dumb.

There is a difference between carrying into effect an incomplete contract, and annulling a complete one. When a court of Chancery is called on for its aid, to carry into effect an incomplete contract, they will, before they give that aid which the complainant requires, compel him to do equity. If Armstrong had been overreached, and the contract incomplete, perhaps a court of equity would not carry this contract into effect.

Here is a complete contract; and the question is not, whether it shall be carried into effect, for that has been done already; but whether it shall be annulled, and the parties brought back to where they were, before it was made. Did both parties understand it as a binding contract? Though Armstrong did not, and though M'Ghee knew that he did not; if he gave no signs to Armstrong, that he did not understand it as a binding contract; why did Armstrong trust him? And if he trusted him, why should he come here now, to save himself from the consequences of such gross folly? Is it for wanton and idle purposes, like this, that you and we sit here? It is one thing, whether M'Ghee has acted ungenerously, unneighbourly, and unhandsomely; and another thing, whether he has acted illegally, so as to raise no obligation, or vest no right. This contract, as far as signs and all the formal parts of a contract can go, is complete: and, if there be no fraud, I do not see how it can be annulled. If M'Ghee gave Armstrong ground to believe, that he considered this contract, which to all appearance is a complete one, as a mere sham or jest, conveying no right; he must take it as he then gave signs that he understood it, and remain a mere trustee to Armstrong, and bound to deliver up the horse when required. In this case he never had any right: the horse continued to be the property of Armstrong: and so you will now say.

As to damages, it is proper to consider what the one party lost, and what the other gained.

The jury after sitting for the remaining part of the day, and the whole of the succeeding night, were sent for into court next day, and not having then agreed on a verdict, they were discharged by consent.

At next term this cause was tried again; and a verdict was found for the plaintiff for £8 damages.

NOTE

Consult Keller v. Holderman, 11 Mich. 248 (1863); Higgins v. Lessig, 49 Ill. App. 459 (1893).

ANDERSON v. BACKLUND
159 Minn. 423, 199 N.W. 90 (1924)

WILSON, C.J. This is an action to recover on a promissory note. Plaintiff's cause of action is not in controversy. The defendant alleged a counterclaim. Defendant was a tenant on a 640-acre farm owned by plaintiff and a written lease defined the terms of this tenancy. He alleges, however, that, in the month of June, the parties made a further oral agreement, for the purpose of more securely assuring plaintiff that he would receive certain cash rent accruing in prior years, wherein defendant agreed to buy 100 head of cattle and bring upon the farm and consume good pasture thereon and that plaintiff agreed to provide, keep and maintain on the farm a well, watering equipment and water ample and sufficient for the needs of such 100 head of cattle as well as for 67 head of cattle then owned and kept on the farm by defendant; and that, relying upon such agreement and being induced thereby, defendant purchased and placed on the farm 107 head of cattle. That plaintiff violated his agreement; that the water supply failed, and because thereof all the 174 head of cattle became wasted, thin and depreciated in value and defendant was damaged in the sum of $2,500.

The court directed a verdict for the plaintiff for the amount claimed in the complaint, and from an order denying defendant's motion for a new trial he has appealed.

Our first inquiry is as to whether the oral contract as alleged by defendant is in fact established by the proofs. The only evidence in support of this allegation is the testimony of the defendant, John Backlund, which is as follows:

> Well, Mr. Anderson drove on the place, come there the same as always, and asked how everything was and how we got along. I told him it began to look pretty blue for me, two years kind of light crop I said and it looked to me I can't make both ends meet, and Mr. Anderson said, "Well now John" — I remember the words — "Why don't you get some more cattle on here and make good use of all that grass and make some money." Well, I says, "Some of my neighbors tells me if I stock up too heavy in the pasture and there be a 'short spell' I will be short of water and I will be up against it and that is the reason I am waiting for you." Well he said "Never mind the water, John, I will see there will be plenty of water because it never failed in Minnesota yet" and I say "all right, I got it all arranged to get all the cattle I want from Long & Hanson in Sioux City, all I have to do is to go to the phone and call them up and the cattle be here in two or three days." And he said all right. And then furthermore Anderson always told me "I am good for my word."

If this constitutes a contract, what were the terms? How was he to provide water? Was he to drill a well? If so, when? What was the significance of the words, "because it never failed in Minnesota yet"? This rather characterized the talk more as visiting or advice than a contract, and we are forced to the conclusion that the parties did not make a contract. There is a lack of mutual assent to the same proposition, and the language is entirely too indefinite and general as to the usual elements of a contract. Contracts must be certain in terms and not so indefinite and illusory as to make it impossible to say just what is promised. The proof in this respect is insufficient. Because of such insufficiency the counter-claim falls, and the learned trial court was right in directing a verdict.

It becomes unnecessary to discuss the assignment of error relating to the rulings of the court in excluding testimony offered in support of the measure of damages.

Order affirmed.

NOTE

Has not the court overlooked the fact that defendant was aware that plaintiff took definitive action in reliance on the defendant's encouraging advice? Doesn't this dispose of the court's argument that defendant's language was indefinite? See also Holmes, The Common Law 298 et seq.

(1881); Gardner, An Inquiry into the Principles of the Law of Contracts, 46 Harv. L. Rev. 1, 4 (1932); Restatement Second §2.

SULLIVAN v. O'CONNOR
363 Mass. 579, 296 N.E.2d 183 (1973)

KAPLAN, J. The plaintiff patient secured a jury verdict of $13,500 against the defendant surgeon for breach of contract in respect to an operation upon the plaintiff's nose. The substituted consolidated bill of exceptions presents questions about the correctness of the judge's instructions on the issue of damages.

The declaration was in two counts. In the first count, the plaintiff alleged that she, as patient, entered into a contract with the defendant, a surgeon, wherein the defendant promised to perform plastic surgery on her nose and thereby to enhance her beauty and improve her appearance; that he performed the surgery but failed to achieve the promised result; rather the result of the surgery was to disfigure and deform her nose, to cause her pain in body and mind, and to subject her to other damage and expense. The second count, based on the same transaction, was in the conventional form for malpractice, charging that the defendant had been guilty of negligence in performing the surgery. Answering, the defendant entered a general denial.

On the plaintiff's demand, the case was tried by jury. At the close of the evidence, the judge put to the jury, as special questions, the issues of liability under the two counts, and instructed them accordingly. The jury returned a verdict for the plaintiff on the contract count, and for the defendant on the negligence count. The judge then instructed the jury on the issue of damages.

As background to the instructions and the parties' exceptions, we mention certain facts as the jury could find them. The plaintiff was a professional entertainer, and this was known to the defendant. The agreement was as alleged in the declaration. More particularly, judging from exhibits, the plaintiff's nose had been straight, but long and prominent; the defendant undertook by two operations to reduce its prominence and somewhat to shorten it, thus making it more pleasing in relation to the plaintiff's other features. Actually the plaintiff was obliged to undergo three operations, and her appearance was worsened. Her nose now had a concave line to about the midpoint, at which it became bulbous; viewed frontally, the nose from bridge to midpoint was flattened and broadened, and the two sides of the tip had lost symmetry. This configuration evidently could not be improved by further surgery. The plaintiff did not demonstrate, however, that her change of appearance had resulted in loss of employment. Payments by the plaintiff covering the defendant's fee and hospital expenses were stipulated at $622.65.

The judge instructed the jury, first, that the plaintiff was entitled to recover her out-of-pocket expenses incident to the operations. Second, she could recover the damages flowing directly, naturally, proximately, and foreseeably from the defendant's breach of promise. These would comprehend damages for any disfigurement of the plaintiff's nose — that is, any change of appearance for the worse — including the effects of the consciousness of such disfigurement on the plaintiff's mind, and in this connection the jury should consider the nature of the plaintiff's profession. Also consequent upon the defendant's breach, and compensable, were the pain and suffering involved in the third operation, but not in the first two. As there was no proof that any loss of earnings by the plaintiff resulted from the breach, that element should not enter into the calculation of damages.

By his exceptions the defendant contends that the judge erred in allowing the jury to take into account anything but the plaintiff's out-of-pocket expenses (presumably at the stipulated amount). The defendant excepted to the judge's refusal of his request for a general charge to that effect, and, more specifically, to the judge's refusal of a charge that the plaintiff could not recover for pain and suffering connected with the third operation or for impairment of the plaintiff's appearance and associated mental distress. . . .

We conclude that the defendant's exceptions should be overruled.

It has been suggested on occasion that agreements between patients and physicians by which the physician undertakes to effect a cure or to bring about a given result should be declared unenforceable on grounds of public policy. See Guilmet v. Campell, 385 Mich. 57, 76 (dissenting opinion). But there are many decisions recognizing and enforcing such contracts, see annotation, 43 A.L.R.3d 1221, 1225, 1229-1233, and the law of Massachusetts has treated them as valid, although we have had no decision meeting head on the contention that they should be denied legal sanction. Small v. Howard, 128 Mass. 131. Gabrunas v. Miniter, 289 Mass. 20. Forman v. Wolfson, 327 Mass. 341. These causes of action are, however, considered a little suspect, and thus we find courts straining sometimes to read the pleadings as sounding only in tort for negligence, and not in contract for breach of promise, despite sedulous efforts by the pleaders to pursue the latter theory. See Gault v. Sideman, 42 Ill. App. 2d 96; annotation, *supra* at 1225, 1238-1244.

It is not hard to see why the courts should be unenthusiastic or skeptical about the contract theory. Considering the uncertainties of medical science and the variations in the physical and psychological conditions of individual patients, doctors can seldom in good faith promise specific results. Therefore it is unlikely that physicians of even average integrity will in fact make such promises. Statements of opinion by the physician with some optimistic coloring are a different thing, and may indeed have therapeutic value. But patients may transform such statements into firm promises in their own minds, especially when they have been disappointed in the event, and testify in that sense to sympathetic juries.[22] If actions for breach of promise can be readily maintained, doctors, so it is said, will be frightened into practising "defensive medicine." On the other hand, if these actions were outlawed, leaving only the possibility of suits for malpractice, there is fear that the public might be exposed to the enticements of charlatans, and confidence in the profession might ultimately be shaken. See Miller, The Contractual Liability of Physicians and Surgeons, 1953 Wash. L.Q. 413, 416-423. The law has taken the middle of the road position of allowing actions based on alleged contract, but insisting on clear proof. Instructions to the jury may well stress this requirement and point to tests of truth, such as the complexity or difficulty of an operation as bearing on the probability that a given result was promised. See annotation, 43 A.L.R.3d 1225, 1225-1227.

If an action on the basis of contract is allowed, we have next the question of the measure of damages to be applied where liability is found. Some cases have taken the simple view that the promise by the physician is to be treated like an ordinary commercial promise, and accordingly that the successful plaintiff is entitled to a standard measure of recovery for breach of contract — "compensatory" ("expectancy") damages, an amount intended to put the plaintiff in the position he would be in if the contract had been performed, or, presumably, at the plaintiff's election, "restitution" damages, an amount corresponding to any benefit conferred by the plaintiff upon the defendant in the performance of the contract disrupted by the defendant's breach. See Restatement: Contracts §329 and comment a, §§347, 384 (1). Thus in Hawkins v. McGee, 84 N.H. 114, the defendant doctor was taken to have promised the plaintiff to convert his damaged hand by means of an operation into a good or perfect hand, but the doctor so operated as to damage the hand still futher. The court, following the usual expectancy formula, would have asked the jury to estimate and award to the plaintiff the difference between the value of a good or perfect hand, as promised, and the value of the hand after the operation. (The same formula would apply, although the dollars result would be less, if the operation had neither worsened nor improved the condition of the hand.) If the plaintiff had not yet paid the doctor his fee, that amount would be deducted from the recovery. There could be no recovery for the pain and suffering of the operation, since that detriment would have been incurred even if the operation had been successful; one can say that this detriment was not "caused" by the breach. But where the plaintiff by reason of the operation was put to more pain than he would

___

22. Judicial skepticism about whether a promise was in fact made derives also from the possibility that the truth has been tortured to give the plaintiff the advantage of the longer period of limitations sometimes available for actions on contract as distinguished from those in tort or for malpractice. See Lillich, The Malpractice Statute of Limitations in New York and Other Jurisdictions, 47 Cornell L. Q. 339; annotation, 80 A.L.R. 2d 368.

have had to endure, had the doctor performed as promised, he should be compensated for that difference as a proper part of his expectancy recovery. It may be noted that on an alternative count for malpractice the plaintiff in the *Hawkins* case had been nonsuited; but on ordinary principles this could not affect the contract claim, for it is hardly a defence to a breach of contract that the promisor acted innocently and without negligence. The New Hampshire court further refined the *Hawkins* analysis in McQuaid v. Michou, 85 N.H. 299, all in the direction of treating the patient-physician cases on the ordinary footing of expectancy. . . .

Other cases, including a number in New York, without distinctly repudiating the *Hawkins* type of analysis, have indicated that a different and generally more lenient measure of damages is to be applied in patient-physician actions based on breach of alleged special agreements to effect a cure, attain a stated result, or employ a given medical method. This measure is expressed in somewhat variant ways, but the substance is that the plaintiff is to recover any expenditures made by him and for other detriment (usually not specifically described in the opinions) following proximately and foreseeably upon the defendant's failure to carry out his promise. Robins v. Finestone, 308 N. Y. 543, 546. . . .

This, be it noted, is not a "restitution" measure, for it is not limited to restoration of the benefit conferred on the defendant (the fee paid) but includes other expenditures, for example, amounts paid for medicine and nurses; so also it would seem according to its logic to take in damages for any worsening of the plaintiff's condition due to the breach. Nor is it an "expectancy" measure, for it does not appear to contemplate recovery of the whole difference in value between the condition as promised and the condition actually resulting from the treatment. Rather the tendency of the formulation is to put the plaintiff back in the position he occupied just before the parties entered upon the agreement, to compensate him for the detriments he suffered in reliance upon the agreement. This kind of intermediate pattern of recovery for breach of contract is discussed in the suggestive article by Fuller and Perdue, The Reliance Interest in Contract Damages, 46 Yale L.J. 52, 373, where the authors show that, although not attaining the currency of the standard measures, a "reliance" measure has for special reasons been applied by the courts in a variety of settings, including noncommercial settings. See 46 Yale L.J. at 396-401.

For breach of the patient-physician agreements under consideration, a recovery limited to restitution seems plainly too meager, if the agreements are to be enforced at all. On the other hand, an expectancy recovery may well be excessive. The factors, already mentioned, which have made the cause of action somewhat suspect, also suggest moderation as to the breadth of the recovery that should be permitted. Where, as in the case at bar and in a number of the reported cases, the doctor has been absolved of negligence by the trier, an expectancy measure may be thought harsh. We should recall here that the fee paid by the patient to the doctor for the alleged promise would usually be quite disproportionate to the putative expectancy recovery. To attempt, moreover, to put a value on the condition that would or might have resulted, had the treatment succeeded as promised, may sometimes put an exceptional strain on the imagination of the fact finder. As a general consideration, Fuller and Perdue argue that the reasons for granting damages for broken promises to the extent of the expectancy are at their strongest when the promises are made in a business context, when they have to do with the production or distribution of goods or the allocation of functions in the market place; they become weaker as the context shifts from a commercial to a noncommerical field. 46 Yale L.J. at 60-63.

There is much to be said, then, for applying a reliance measure to the present facts, and we have only to add that our cases are not unreceptive to the use of that formula in special situations. We have, however, had no previous occasion to apply it to patient-physician cases.[23]

The question of recovery on a reliance basis for pain and suffering or mental distress requires further attention. We find expressions in the decisions that pain and suffering (or the like) are simply not compensable in actions for breach of contract. The defendant seemingly espouses this proposition in the present case. True, if the buyer under a contract for the purchase of a lot of merchandise, in suing for the seller's breach, should claim damages for mental anguish caused by his disappointment in the transaction, he would not succeed; he would be told, perhaps, that the asserted psychological injury was not fairly foreseeable by the defendant as a probable consequence of the breach of such a business con-

23. In Mt. Pleasant Stable Co. v. Steinberg, 238 Mass. 567, the plaintiff company agreed to supply teams of horses at agreed rates as required from day to day by the defendant for his business. To prepare itself to fulfil the contract and in reliance on it, the plaintiff bought two "Cliest" horses at a certain price. When the defendant repudiated the contract, the plaintiff sold the horses at a loss and in its action for breach claimed the loss as an element of damages. The court properly held that the plaintiff was not entitled to this item as it was also claiming (and recovering) its lost profits (expectancy) on the contract as a whole. Cf. Noble v. Ames Mfg. Co., 112 Mass. 492. (The loss on sale of the horses is analogous to the pain and suffering for which the patient would be disallowed a recovery in Hawkins v. McGee, 84 N.H. 114, because he was claiming and recovering expectancy damages.) The court in the Mt. Pleasant case referred, however, to Pond v. Harris, 113 Mass. 114, as a contrasting situation where the expectancy could not be fairly determined. There the defendant had wrongfully revoked an agreement to arbitrate a dispute with the plaintiff (this was before such agreements were made specifically enforceable). In an action for the breach, the plaintiff was held entitled to recover for his preparations for the arbitration which had been rendered useless and a waste, including the plaintiff's time and trouble and his expenditures for counsel and witness. The context apparently was commercial but reliance elements were held compensable when there was no fair way of estimating an expectancy. See, generally, annotation, 17 A.L.R.2d 1300. A noncommercial example is Smith v. Sherman, 4 Cush. 408, 413-414, suggesting that a conventional recovery for breach of promise of marriage included a recompense for various efforts and expenditures by the plaintiff preparatory to the promised wedding. See Garfield & Proctor Coal Co. v. Pennsylvania Coal & Coke Co., 199 Mass. 22, 43; Narragansett Amusement Co. v. Riverside Park Amusement Co., 260 Mass. 265, 279-281. Cf. Johnson v. Arnold, 2 Cush. 46, 47; Greany v. McCormick, 273 Mass. 250, 253. But cf. Irwin v. Worcester Paper Box Co., 246 Mass. 453.

tract. See Restatement: Contracts, §341 and comment *a*. But there is no general rule barring such items of damage in actions for breach of contract. It is all a question of the subject matter and background of the contract, and when the contract calls for an operation on the person of the plaintiff, psychological as well as physical injury may be expected to figure somewhere in the recovery, depending on the particular circumstances. The point is explained in Stewart v. Rudner, 349 Mich. 459, 469. Cf. Frewen v. Page, 238 Mass. 499; McClean v. University Club, 327 Mass. 68. Again, it is said in a few of the New York cases, concerned with the classification of actions for statute of limitations purposes, that the absence of allegations demanding recovery for pain and suffering is characteristic of a contract claim by a patient against a physician, that such allegations rather belong in a claim for malpractice. See Robins v. Finestone, 308 N.Y. 543, 547; Budoff v. Kessler, 2 App. Div. 2d (N.Y.) 760. These remarks seem unduly sweeping. Suffering or distress resulting from the breach going beyond that which was envisaged by the treatment as agreed, should be compensable on the same ground as the worsening of the patient's conditions because of the breach. Indeed it can be argued that the very suffering or distress "contracted for" — that which would have been incurred if the treatment achieved the promised result — should also be compensable on the theory underlying the New York cases. For that suffering is "wasted" if the treatment fails. Otherwise stated, compensation for this waste is arguably required in order to complete the restoration of the status quo ante.[24]

In the light of the foregoing discussion, all the defendant's exceptions fail: the plaintiff was not confined to the recovery of her out-of-pocket expenditures; she was entitled to recover also for the worsening of her condition,[25] and for the pain and suffering and mental distress involved in

---

24. Recovery on a reliance basis for breach of the physician's promise tends to equate with the usual recovery for malpractice, since the latter also looks in general to restoration of the condition before the injury. But this is not paradoxical, especially when it is noted that the origins of contract lie in tort. See Farnsworth, The Past of Promise: An Historical Introduction to Contract, 69 Col. L. Rev. 576, 594-596; Breitel, J. in Stella Flour & Feed Corp. v. National City Bank, 285 App. Div. (N.Y.) 182, 189 (dissenting opinion). A few cases have considered possible recovery for breach by a physician of a promise to sterilize a patient, resulting in birth of a child to the patient and spouse. If such an action is held maintainable, the reliance and expectancy measures would, we think, tend to equate, because the promised condition was preservation of the family status quo. See Custodia v. Bauer, 251 Cal. App. 2d 303; Jackson v. Anderson, 230 So. 2d 503 (Fla. App.). Cf. Troppi v. Scarf, 31 Mich. App. 240. But cf. Ball v. Mudge, 64 Wash. 2d 247; Doerr v. Villate, 74 Ill. App. 2d 332; Shaheen v. Knight, 11 D. & C. 2d (Pa.) 41. See also annotation, 27 A.L.R.3d 906.

It would, however, be a mistake to think in terms of strict "formulas." For example, a jurisdiction which would apply a reliance measure to the present facts might impose a more severe damage sanction for the wilful use by the physician of a method of operation that he undertook not to employ.

25. That condition involves a mental element and appraisal of it properly called for consideration of the fact that the plaintiff was an entertainer. Cf. McQuaid v. Michou, 85 N.H. 299, 303-304 (discussion of continuing condition resulting from physician's breach.)

the third operation. These items were compensable on either an expectancy or a reliance view. We might have been required to elect between the two views if the pain and suffering connected with the first two operations contemplated by the agreement, or the whole difference in value between the present and the promised conditions, were being claimed as elements of damage. But the plaintiff waives her possible claim to the former element, and to so much of the latter as represents the difference in value between the promised condition and the condition before the operations.

Plaintiff's exceptions waived.

Defendant's exceptions overruled.

NOTE

Danzig and Kidwell conducted interviews with the parties, their lawyers, four of the jurors, and the trial judge in the principal case. These interviews and other background materials are collected in R. Danzig, The Capability Problem in Contract Law 15 et seq. (1978). Do you think that Dr. O'Connor's malpractice insurance covered the judgment against him? Do you think the jury considered this question? See id. at 21, 23. As it turned out, Dr. O'Connor's insurer decided not to disclaim liability. Id. at 18. This was not the case in Hawkins v. McGee, 84 N.H. 114, 146 A. 641 (1929), discussed *supra* p. 133. See McGee v. United States Fidelity Guaranty Co., 53 F.2d 953 (1st Cir. 1931).

Some jurisdictions permit lawsuits against doctors for breach of warranty to effect a cure but impose the virtually insurmountable requirement of proof of separate consideration for the warranty. See Coleman v. Garrison, 349 A.2d 8 (Del. 1975). Several states have passed legislation in recent years requiring that warranties to effect a cure be in writing to be actionable. See, e.g., Ind. Stat. Ann. §16-9.5-1-4 (Burns 1983); Pa. Stat. Ann. tit. 40, §1301.606 (Purdon 1985 Supp.); La. Rev. Stat. Ann. §40:1299.41C (West 1977); Fla. Stat. Ann. §725.01 (1985 Supp.); Mich. Comp. Laws Ann. §566.132(g) (West 1974 Supp.).

SHAHEEN v. KNIGHT

11 Pa. D. & C.2d (1957)

WILLIAMS, P.J., March 15, 1957. — Plaintiff, Robert M. Shaheen, is suing defendant physician because of an operation. He alleges defendant contracted to make him sterile. According to the complaint, the operation occurred on September 16, 1954, and a "blessed event" occurred on February 11, 1956, when plaintiff's wife, Doris, was delivered of a fifth child as a result of marital relations continued after the operation.

Plaintiff in his complaint does not allege any negligence by defendant. The suit is based on contract.

Plaintiff does not claim that the operation was necessary because of his wife's health. He claims that in order to support his family in comfort and educate it, it is necessary to limit the size of his family, and that he would be emotionally unable to limit his family's size by reason or will power alone, or by abstention.

Plaintiff claims damages as follows:

> That the Plaintiff, as a result, despite his love and affection for his fifth (5th) child, as he would for any other child, now has the additional expenses of supporting, educating and maintaining said child, and that such expense will continue until the maturity of said child, none of which expense would have been incurred, had the Defendant, Dr. John E. Knight, fulfilled the contract and undertaking entered into by him, or fulfilled the representation made by him.

Defendant has filed preliminary objections to the complaint, alleging:

> 1. An alleged contract to sterilize a man whose wife may have a child without any hazard to her life is void as against public policy and public morals.
> 2. Under Pennsylvania law there is no "warranty of cure" by a physician.
> 3. That the complaint charges no lack of skill, malpractice, or negligence in any respect in the performance of the operation, a vasectomy, but merely seeks to recover upon the ground that the operation did not achieve the purpose sought and the results allegedly promised.
> 4. That while the complaint is said to be in assumpsit, it appears to be grounded on deceit, that is that the defendant made a statement, misrepresenting material facts, known to be false or made in ignorance or reckless disregard of its truth, with an intent to induce the plaintiff to act in reliance thereon, and the plaintiff, believing it to be true, did act thereon to his damage. If this be true the plaintiff has made no allegation of fraudulent intent on defendant's part, or any of the elements of deceit.
> 5. The duty of a physician or surgeon to bring skill and care to the amelioration of the condition of his patient does not arise from contract but has its foundation in public considerations which are inseparable from the nature and exercise of his calling; it is predicated by the law on the relation which exists between physician and patient, which is the result of a consensual transaction.
> 6. That the plaintiff has suffered no damage but "has been blessed with the fatherhood of another child."

We are of the opinion that a contract to sterilize a man is not void as against public policy and public morals. It was so held in Christensen v. Thornby, 192 Minn. 123, 255 N.W. 620. Also see 93 A.L.R. 570. It is argued, however, that in the Christensen case the operation was for a man whose wife could not have a child without hazard to her life, whereas in the instant case claimant has contracted for sterilization because he cannot afford children.

It is only when a given policy is so obviously for or against the public health, safety, morals or welfare that there is a virtual unanimity of opinion in regard to it, that a court may constitute itself the voice of the community in declaring such policy void: Mamlin v. Genoe, 340 Pa. 320. It has been said: "There must be a positive, well-defined, universal public sentiment, deeply integrated in the customs and beliefs of the people and in their conviction of what is just and right and in the interests of the public weal."

It is the faith of some that sterilization is morally wrong whether to keep wife from having children or for any other reason. Many people have no moral compunctions against sterilization. Others are against sterilization, except when a man's life is in danger, when a person is low mentally, when a person is an habitual criminal. There is no virtual unanimity of opinion regarding sterilization. The Superior Court, in Wilson v. Wilson, 126 Pa. Superior Ct. 423, ruled that the incapacity to procreate is not independent ground for divorce where it appears that the party complained against is capable of natural and complete copulation. This case so held whether or not there was natural or artificial creation of sterility. It would appear that an exception would have been made had there been recognized any public policy against sterilization.

Defendant argues that there is no "warranty of cure" by physician in Pennsylvania. He also argues that the duty of a physician or surgeon does not arise from contract and suggests that it is against public policy for such a contract to be upheld.

It is true that there is no implied "warranty of cure" in Pennsylvania: McCandless v. McWha, 22 Pa. 261. An action against a physician for malpractice can only be sustained by proof of his negligence: Nixon v. Pfahler, 279 Pa. 377. The surgeon's duty and obligation is to employ only such reasonable skill and diligence as is ordinarily exercised in the profession.

A doctor and his patient, however, are at liberty to contract for a particular result. If that result be not attained, the patient has a cause of action for breach of contract. The cause of action is entirely separate from malpractice, even though both may arise out of the same transaction. The two causes of action are dissimilar as to theory, proof and damages recoverable. Negligence is the basis of malpractice, while the action in contract is based upon a failure to perform a special agreement: Colvin v. Smith, 92 N.Y.S.2d 794; Budorf v. Kessler, 137 N.Y.S.2d 696, Manning v. 1234 Corporation, 19 N.Y.S.2d 323; Lewis v. Dunbar and Sullivan Dredging Co., 36 N.Y.S.2d 897. Damages in a contract action between doctor and patient are restricted in some jurisdictions.

In the instant case plaintiff is suing, according to his claim, under a special contract in which defendant agreed to make him "immediately and permanently sterile and guaranteed the results thereof." Defendant's "warranty of cure" argument therefore does not apply to this case.

We see little merit in defendant's argument that the action seems to be grounded on deceit and that therefore we should dismiss the complaint.

Defendant argues, however, and pleads, that plaintiff has suffered no damage. We agree with defendant. The only damages asked are the expenses of rearing and educating the unwanted child. We are of the opinion that to allow damages for the normal birth of a normal child is foreign to the universal public sentiment of the people.

Many consider the sole purpose of marriage a union for having children.

As Chief Justice Gibson said in Matchin v. Matchin, 6 Pa. 332:

> The great end of matrimony is not the comfort and convenience of the immediate parties, though these are necessarily embarked in it; but the procreation of a progeny having a legal title to maintenance by the father; and the reciprocal taking for better, for worse, for richer, for poorer, in sickness and in health, to love and cherish till death, are important, but only modal conditions of the contract, and no more than ancillary to the principal purpose of it. The civil rights created by them may be forfeited by the misconduct of either party; but though the forfeiture can be incurred, so far as the parties themselves are concerned, only by a responsible agent, it follows not that those rights must not give way without it to public policy, and the paramount purpose of the marriage — the procreation and protection of legitimate children, the institution of families, and the creation of natural relations among mankind; from which proceed all the civilization, virtue, and happiness to be found in the world.

To allow damages in a suit such as this would mean that the physician would have to pay for the fun, joy and affection which plaintiff Shaheen will have in the rearing and educating of this, defendant's fifth child. Many people would be willing to support this child were they given the right of custody and adoption, but according to plaintiff's statement, plaintiff does not want such. He wants to have the child and wants the doctor to support it. In our opinion to allow such damages would be against public policy.

Order

And now, March 15, 1957, it is ordered and decreed that plaintiff's action be dismissed, costs on plaintiff.

NOTE

The case is noted in 19 U. Pitt. L. Rev. 802 (1958). On the issue of whether damages are recoverable for birth of an unwanted child, con-

sider the following from Troppi v. Scarf, 31 Mich. App. 240, 253, 187
N.W.2d 511, 517 (1971):

> Contraceptives are used to prevent the birth of healthy children. To say
> that for reasons of public policy contraceptive failure can result in no
> damage as a matter of law ignores the fact that tens of millions of persons
> use contraceptives daily to avoid the very result which the defendant would
> have us say is always a benefit, never a detriment. Those tens of millions of
> persons, by their conduct, express the sense of the community.

See also Custodio v. Bauer, 251 Cal. App. 2d 303, 59 Cal. Rptr. 463, 27
A.L.R.3d 884 (1967); Comment, Liability for Failure of Birth Control
Methods, 76 Colum. L. Rev. 1187 (1976).

Section 2.   The Tripartite Distinction of Contracts

"Not everything is contractual in a contract."
Durkheim

The tripartite distinction between express, implied-in-fact, and implied-
in-law contracts (frequently called constructive or quasi contracts) has
become a commonplace. In terms of this analysis, express and implied-
in-fact contracts are genuine contracts; the source of obligation in either
case is the intention of the parties. Implied-in-law contracts, by contrast,
are fictions of law adopted to enforce legal duties by actions of contract
where no proper contract exists, either express or implied; they are imposed for the purpose of bringing about justice without reference to the
intention of the parties. S. M. Leake, Elements of the Law of Contracts
38 (1867); 1 Williston §3A (Jaeger 3d ed. 1957). Furthermore, courts do
not make contracts for the parties; they only carry out the parties' intentions. Sceva v. True, 53 N.H. 627 (1873); 3 Corbin §541 (1960). These
famous, plausible, and innocent-looking statements raise a host of troublesome questions that deserve careful examination in the light of the
case material which follows in this and the succeeding section. A few
guideposts are in order.

Tradition has it that the distinction between express and implied-in-
fact contracts "is not one of legal effect but in the way in which mutual
assent is manifested." 1 Williston §3 (1957). A contract implied in fact, we
are told, "must rest upon the intent of the parties; it requires an agreement, a meeting of the minds, an intent to promise and be bound; it does
not differ from an express contract, except that it is circumstantially
proved." Prosser, Delay in Acting on an Application for Insurance, 3 U.

Chi. L. Rev. 39, 49 (1935). On this view, the implied-in-fact (implied from the facts) contract is not an interesting phenomenon at all. The most serious drawback of this approach lies in obscuring the institutional aspects of contract. The techniques developed in dealing with implied-in-fact contracts help us to a better understanding of the social structure of contract in general. Confronted with the issue of whether or not to imply a contract, courts must find objective criteria for determining the intention of the parties in the light of the circumstances surrounding the transaction. Courts that want to avoid the arbitrariness of "random behavior," so as not to disappoint the reasonable expectations of litigants and in order to make future decisions predictable, have to look, whenever possible, to the facts of general business experience and understanding. And their experience with implied contracts has helped courts to realize that the task of interpreting and enforcing an express contract is not fundamentally different. "The meaning to be given to . . . all . . . modes of expression is found by a process of implication and inference. In this sense, all contracts are implied contracts." 1 Corbin §§18, 19 (1963); 3 id. §562 (1960).[26] Even an express contract, in the language of Durkheim, "is not sufficient unto itself, but is possible only thanks to a regulation which is originally social."[27] The language used by the contracting parties, therefore, cannot be divorced from the "environment" in which they have conducted negotiations.

> The normal contract is not an isolated act, but an incident in the conduct of business or in the framework of some more general relation. . . . It will frequently be set against the background of usage, familiar to all who engage in similar negotiations and which may be supposed to govern the language of a particular agreement.

Cheshire & Fifoot's Law of Contracts 121 (Furmston 9th ed. 1976). Thus, "a contract includes not only the promises set forth in express words, but, in addition, all such implied provisions as are indispensable to effectuate the intentions of the parties and as arise from the language of the contract and the circumstances under which it was made." New York Casualty Co. v. Sinclair Refining Co., 108 F.2d 65, 69 (10th Cir. 1939).

Finally, it should not be forgotten that contract is an institution that receives its ultimate sanction from organized society. Since a court's power to enforce a contract carries with it the power to interpret, the legal concept of contract has come to include "not merely the agreement itself, but the entire body of law guarding its interpretation and enforcement so that official control becomes an integral part of the contract itself." J. M.

---

26. Thus, for example the meaning of the word "offer" must be determined in the light of the business context within which it is used; likewise, the meaning of the word "quotation" cannot be known out of context. See pp. 190 et seq. *infra*.

27. Division of Labor, as paraphrased in Parsons, Structure of Social Action 311 (1949).

Clark, Social Control of Business 100 (2d ed. 1939); Home Building and Loan Association v. Blaisdell, 290 U.S. 398 (1934).

The role that courts play in carrying out the intention of the parties is in some measure obscured by the fact that the courts habitually speak of "interpretation" even though their task of determining the fate of an agreement has led them far beyond a mere determination of the meaning of the symbols of expression used by the contracting parties.[28]

Unfortunately, many courts have adopted the notion that the security of transactions — which is of vital importance — can only be achieved by a literal interpretation of a contractual document, a misconception that sometimes does violence to the understanding and expectations of the parties. These courts have been guided by a false sense of security. Their rule-oriented system would work only if the business community conformed in practice to the formal rules of contract laid down by abstract theory.[29] But the business community is not so obliging.[30]

To be sure, the preservation of the fiction that it is merely carrying out the intention of the parties has enabled many a court to achieve socially desirable results that could not have been attained had the court been conscious of and explicit about its own processes. But it is also true that the use of the symbol "interpretation" has frequently prevented a court from clearly articulating the policy bases of its decision, with the result that the decision's actual rationale in many instances cannot be adequately explored. On the desirability of the distinction between "interpretation" and "construction," consult 3 Corbin §§534, 561 (1960); Patterson, The Interpretation and Construction of Contracts, 64 Colum. L. Rev. 833-838; see further Chapters 7 and 8.

To remedy the resulting confusion, the U.C.C. (inspired by the writings of Corbin) has attempted to bring contract doctrine closer to reality and to create a more reliable yardstick for determining the security of transactions. The approach adopted in the Code is based upon a study of the contractual context of commercial transactions and attempts to provide "a statutory framework responsive to that context."[31] The result is

---

28. Interpretation of a promise or agreement or a term therof is the ascertainment of its meaning. Restatement Second §200. Chapter 9 of Restatement Second, on the scope of contractual obligations, contains detailed signposts for interpretation: Topic 1 is on the meaning of contractual obligations; Topic 2 is on considerations of fairness and public policy; Topic 3 deals with the adaptation of a writing; Topic 4 is on usage; Topic 5 covers conditions and similar events.
   See, in general, Williams, Language and the Law (pt. 4), 61 L.Q. Rev. 384, 400-406 (1945); Farnsworth, "Meaning" in the Law of Contracts, 76 Yale L.J. 938 (1967); Id., Disputes Over Omissions in Contracts, 64 Colum. L. Rev. 860 (1968).
   29. Kirst, Usage of Trade and Course of Dealing: Subversion of the U.C.C. Theory, 1977 Ill. L. Forum 811.
   30. Macaulay, The Use or Non-Use of Contracts in the Manufacturing Industry, 9 Pract. Law. 13, 16 (November 1963); Macneil, The Many Futures of Contract, 47 S. Cal. L. Rev. 691, 744-745 (1974); E. Farnsworth, Contracts, 190 et seq. (1982).
   31. Kirst, *supra* note 29. Lewie, The Interpretation of Contracts in New York under the Uniform Commercial Code, 10 N.Y.L. Forum 350, 354-355 (1946).

§1-205(3), which states: "A course of dealing between parties and any usage of trade in the vocation or trade in which they are engaged or of which they are or should be aware give particular meaning to and supplement or qualify terms of an agreement." Subsections 1 and 2 define "course of dealing" and "usage of trade."[32] The new Restatement has parallel and more elaborate provisions in §§219-223, 202, and 203.[33]

Subsection 4 deals with a possible conflict between express terms, course of dealing, and usage of trade. It provides a system of priorities and states:

> The express terms of an agreement and an applicable course of dealing or usage of trade shall be construed wherever reasonable as consistent with each other; but when such construction is unreasonable express terms control both course of dealing and usage of trade and course of dealing controls usage of trade.[34]

Unfortunately, Subsection 4 of U.C.C. §1-205 has led to a host of difficulties as a result of misinterpretation. It has been interpreted by a number of decisions as a rule of evidence,[35] with evidence as to a usage of trade that is in conflict with an express term contained in a writing being held inadmissible. Thus, when a franchise contract provided for a three-year term, automatically renewable for successive three-year periods unless terminated by 90 days' notice, evidence of a trade usage to the effect that termination can only be exercised for cause has been held inadmissible.[36] Columbia Nitrogen Corp. v. Royster Co.[37] represents the opposite extreme, holding that evidence of course of dealing and usage of trade was admissible under the Code's parol evidence rule, §2-202.

We have met the constructive or implied-in-law contract when we discussed Noble v. Williams.[38] The court in that case, it will be remembered, denied recovery to the schoolteachers on the grounds that "no man, entirely of his own volition, can make another his debtor." The school teachers were, in the language of the law, officious intermeddlers. And yet the law can ill afford to deny the remedy of restitution when a person has received a benefit and the retention of the benefit is regarded as inequitable. In accordance with other legal systems, our law, there-

---

32. "Usage of trade" has replaced custom, which is only mentioned in §1-102. A course of performance is relegated to §2-208.

33. In addition, the intentions (expectations) of the parties may be inferred from a course of performance and from preliminary negotiations, subject, however, to the limitations of the parol evidence rule. Restatement Second §§201, 202, 214. On the parol evidence rule, see Ch. 7. For discussion of indefinite contracts, see §3.

34. Restatement Second §203(b).

35. Kirst, *supra* note 29, at 817.

36. Division of Triple T Service, Inc. v. Mobil Oil Corp., 60 Misc. 2d 720, 304 N.Y.S.2d 191 (1969), *aff'd mem.*, 34 A.D.2d 618, 311 N.Y.S.2d 961 (1970).

37. 451 F.2d 3 (4th Cir. 1971).

38. *Supra* p. 76.

fore, permits a debtor, for instance, who mistakenly overpays his debt to recover his overpayment. More generally, a person who performs in the mistaken belief that he is under a contractual duty to perform is entitled to compensation. Similarly, our law permits a person who had made a down payment in expectation of a counterperformance to recover his down payment if the counterperformance is not forthcoming. Restatement Second §§344, 345, 373. In sum, our legal system has not limited civil liability to the categories of contract and tort; to prevent unjust enrichment it has added a third category which since the days of the Romans has been referred to as quasi contract (this label is historically understandable since the form of action used for quasi contractual recovery was general assumpsit).

Once the category of quasi contract had been invented, problems arose as to its limitations. If it is unduly extended, private autonomy, as was correctly observed in Noble v. Williams, will suffer erosion.

To be sure,

> "considerations of equity and morality play a large part in the process of finding a promise by inference of fact as well as in constructing a quasi contract without any such inference at all. The exact terms of the promise that is "implied" must frequently be determined by what equity and morality appear to require after the parties have come into conflict."

1 Corbin §19 (1963). In the interest of good faith and fair dealing and to balance the equities between two contracting parties, courts are frequently asked to "imply a condition" in a contract. Consult Parev Products v. Rokeach, 124 F.2d 147 (2d Cir. 1941). Furthermore, there are many situations where the measure of recovery is the same under a genuine contract and under a constructive contract. If, for instance, the parties to a sales contract that was intended to be binding have deliberately left the price term open, the buyer is liable for the reasonable price at the time of delivery (U.C.C. §2-305). Ordinarily, the recipient owes the same amount in making restitution for unjust enrichment where a person delivers goods or renders services under the mistaken impression that he is performing a contract. Restatement of Restitution §107, Comment b.

Despite these points of contact between genuine and constructive contracts, the distinction between an action for breach of contract and an action for restitution is not to be ignored. A person seeking recovery for a breach of contract is entitled to recover not merely an amount commensurate with the extent of unjust enrichment, but is entitled to the benefit of his bargain, i.e., the value of the promised performance. The measure of restitution, on the other hand, may exceed the extent of unjust enrichment only where the recipient of an unjust benefit is more at fault than the claimant, Restatement of Restitution §107, Comment b; see also §§151-155; see further Chapter 10, Section 3 on damage remedies.

(Courts not infrequently have had considerable difficulty in keeping the two categories of implied contract apart.)

The difference between damages and restitution is highlighted in the treatment of losing contracts. In a losing contract, the party injured by the breach is, of course, not entitled to expectation damages but he is entitled to restitution. The amount or restitution, measured in terms of the benefit conveyed, may give the injured party a greater amount in restitution than he would have recovered in damages. Restatement Second §373, Comment d (a theory that is controversial). This rule, however, is limited under §373(a) if the injured party has performed all of his duties and no performance by the other party remains except the payment of a definite sum of money. In this situation, the injured party is barred from recovering as restitution a greater sum than the price. Comment d. See further Chapter 10 Section 3.

Bibliography: Costigan, Implied-In-Fact Contracts and Mutual Assent, 33 Harv. L. Rev. 376 (1920); 3A Corbin chs. 24, 25 (1960). The law of quasi contract is dealt with at length in the four-volume work of Palmer, Law of Restitution (1978). See also Dawson, Restitution or Damages?, 20 Ohio St. L.J. 175 (1959); Palmer, The Contract Price as Limit on Restitution for Defendant's Breach, 20 Ohio St. L.J. 264 (1959); Sullivan, The Concept of Benefit in Quasi-Contract, 64 Geo. L.J. 1 (1975); Posner, Gratuitous Promises in Economics and Law, 6 J. Legal Stud. 411 (1977); R. Goff & G. Jones, The Law of Restitution (1966).

YOUNG AND ASHBURNHAM'S CASE
3 Leon. 161, 74 Eng. Rep. 606 (C.P. 1587)

In an Action of Debt brought by the Administrators of Young against Ashburnham; The Defendant pleaded, Nihil debet: And the Enquest was taken by default. And upon the Evidence given for the Plaintiff, the Case appeared to be this, That the said Young was an Innholder in a great Town in the County of Sussex where Sessions used to be holden; And that the Defendant was a Gentleman of Quality in the Country there; And he, in going to the Sessions, used to lodge in the house of said Young, and there took his lodging and his diet for himself, his servants, and horses: Upon which, the Debt in demand grew: but the said Young was not at any price in certain with the Defendant, nor was there ever any agreement made betwixt them for the same. It was said by Anderson, Chief Justice, That upon that matter, an Action of Debt did not lie. And therefore afterwards, the Jury gave a Verdict for the Defendant.

NOTE

For the technical requirements of the action of debt, see Simpson at 497. "In the course of the seventeenth century there developed a tenuous

chain of authority in favour of allowing debt to lie on a *quantum meruit.*"
Id. at 498. For the history of implied contracts, see Simpson, ch. 8, and p.
35 *supra.*

HERTZOG v. HERTZOG
29 Pa. St. 465 (1857)

Error to the Common Pleas of Fayette County.

This suit was brought by John Hertzog to recover from the estate of his
father compensation for services rendered the latter in his lifetime, and
for money lent. The plaintiff was twenty-one years of age about the year
1825, but continued to reside with his father, who was a farmer, and to
labour for him on the farm, except one year that he was absent in Virginia, until 1842, when the plaintiff married and took his wife to his
father's, where they continued for some time as he had done before. His
father then put him on another farm which he owned, and some time
afterwards the father and his wife moved into the same house with John,
and continued to reside there until death in 1849.

The testimony of Adam Stamm and Daniel Roderick was relied on to
prove a contract or agreement on the part of George Hertzog to pay for
the services of plaintiff.

Adam Stamm, affirmed:

John laboured for his father; all worked together. The old man got the
proceeds. I know the money from the grain went to pay for the farm — the
old man said so. John's services worth $12 per month; the wife's worth $1
per week, besides attending to her own family.

I heard the old man say he would pay John for the labour he had done.

Daniel Roderick, sworn:

John Hertzog requested him to see his father about paying him for his
work, which he had done and was doing, and stated that he had frequently
spoken to the old man, his father, about it, and he had still put him off; he
agreed to see him, and thinks it was in June, 1849. Coming from Duncan's
Furnace, he spoke to the old man about paying John for his work. He said
he intended to make John safe. John spoke to me in the spring of 1848: the
old man died in August, 1849, I think.

The plaintiff also proved the services rendered by himself and by his
wife, and by the declarations of the intestate that he had received from
the plaintiff $500, money that belonged to the latter's wife, at the time of
purchasing a farm in 1847. The court, after the defendant's points were
presented, permitted the plaintiff to add to his declaration a count on a
quantum meruit.

The defendant pleaded the statute of limitations, and presented the
following points:

1. The court are respectfully requested to charge the jury that where a son, after he arrives at the age of twenty-one years, and continues to live with and work for his father, without any special contract, he cannot "recover for wages or services rendered, from the estate of his deceased parent, unless upon clear and unequivocal proof, leaving no doubt that the relation between the parties was not the ordinary one of parent and child, but master and servant."

2. That according to the plaintiff's own showing the $500 claimed by him belonged to the wife of the plaintiff, and, since the Act of 1848, is her separate property, and cannot be recovered in this suit, the same having been instituted in the name of the husband alone.

3. The plaintiff cannot recover in this action on a quantum meruit, there being no such count in the plaintiff's narr.

The court below (Gilmore, P.J.) answered these points as follows:

"1. We answer this in affirmative: it was so ruled in Candor's Appeal, 5 W. & S. 515. If the plaintiff was working for his father, without a mutual understanding between them that he was to be paid for his labour, he cannot recover wages.

"The jury must be satisfied from the evidence that it was understood between him and his father that he was to be compensated, not by the way of gift or legacy, but by the payment of wages." Here the court referred to the evidence of Adam Stamm and Daniel Roderick, and said, "From this evidence, if you believe it, you may infer such an agreement."

"2. If the jury are satisfied from the evidence that the $500 was in the possession of plaintiff's wife in 1847, and that the defendant (decedent) then received it from her, this would be considered the possession of the same by the husband, and plaintiff could sue without joining his wife.

"3. The court permit the declaration to be amended so as to embrace this point."

The jury found a verdict for the plaintiff of $2203.97; and the court entered judgment thereon.

The defendant sued out a writ of error, and assigned the answers of the court below for error.

The opinion of the court was delivered by LOWRIE, J. —

> Express contracts are, where the terms of the agreement are openly uttered and avowed at the time of the making: as, to deliver an ox or ten loads of timber, or to pay a stated price for certain goods. Implied are such as reason and justice dictate: and which, therefore, the law presumes that every many undertakes to perform. As, if I employ a person to do any business for me, or perform any work, the law implies that I undertook and contracted to pay him as much as his labour deserves. If I take up wares of a tradesman without any agreement of price, the law concludes that I contracted to pay their real value.

This is the language of Blackstone, 2 Comm. 433, and it is open to some criticism. There is some looseness of thought in supposing that reason and justice ever dictate any contracts between parties, or impose such upon them. All true contracts grow out of the intentions of the parties to transactions, and are dictated only by their mutual and accordant wills. When this intention is expressed, we call the contract an express one. When it is not expressed, it may be inferred, implied, or presumed, from circumstances as really existing, and then the contract, thus ascertained, is called an implied one. The instances given by Blackstone are an illustration of this.

But it appears in another place, 3 Comm. 159-166, that Blackstone introduces this thought about reason and justice dictating contracts, in order to embrace, under his definition of an implied contract, another large class of relations, which involve no intention to contract at all, though they may be treated as if they did. Thus, whenever, not our variant notions of reason and justice, but the common sense and common justice of the country, and therefore the common law or statute law imposed upon any one a duty, irrespective of contract, and allow it to be enforced by a contract remedy, he calls this a case of implied contract. Thus out of torts grows the duty of compensation, and in many cases the tort may be waived, and the action brought in assumpsit.

It is quite apparent, therefore, that radically different relations are classified under the same term, and this must often give rise to indistinctness of thought. And this was not at all necessary; for we have another well-authorized technical term exactly adapted to the office of making the true distinction. The latter class are merely *constructive* contracts, while the former are truly implied ones. In one case the contract is mere fiction, a form imposed in order to adapt the case to a given remedy; in the other it is a fact legitimately inferred. In one, the intention is disregarded; in the other, it is ascertained and enforced. In one, the duty defines the contract; in the other, the contract defines the duty.

We have, therefore, in law three classes of relations called contracts.

1. Constructive contracts, which are fictions of law adapted to enforce legal duties by actions of contract, where no proper contract exists, express or implied.

2. Implied contracts, which arise under circumstances which, according to the ordinary course of dealing and the common understanding of men, show a mutual intention to contract.

3. Express contracts, already sufficiently distinguished.

In the present case there is no pretence of a constructive contract, but only of a proper one, either express or implied. And it is scarcely insisted that the law would imply one in such a case as this; yet we may present the principle of the case the more clearly, by showing why it is not one of implied contract.

The law ordinarily presumes or implies a contract whenever this is necessary to account for other relations found to have existed between the parties.

Thus if a man is found to have done work for another, and there appears no known relation between them that accounts for such service, the law presumes a contract of hiring. But if a man's house takes fire, the law does not presume or imply a contract to pay his neighbours for their services in saving his property. The common principles of human conduct mark self-interest as the motive of action in the one case, and kindness in the other; and therefore, by common custom, compensation is mutually counted on in one case, and in the other not.

On the same principle the law presumes that the exclusive possession of land by a stranger to the title is adverse, unless there be some family or other relation that may account for it. And such a possession by one tenant in common is not presumed adverse to his co-tenants, because it is, prima facie, accounted for by the relation. And so of possession of land by a son of the owner. And in Magaw's Case, Latch 168, where an heir was in a foreign land at the time of a descent cast upon him, and his younger brother entered, he was presumed to have entered for the benefit of the heir. And one who enters as a tenant of the owner is not presumed to hold adversely even after his term has expired. In all such cases, if there is a relation adequate to account for the possession, the law accounts for it by that relation, unless the contrary be proved. A party who relies upon a contract must prove its existence; and this he does not do by merely proving a set of circumstances that can be accounted for by another relation appearing to exist between the parties.

Mr. Justice Rogers is entitled to the gratitude of the public for having, in several cases, demonstrated the force of this principle in interpreting transactions between parents and children: 3 Penn. R. 365, 3 Rawle 249; 5 W. & S. 375, 513; and he has been faithfully followed in many other cases: 8 Watts 366; 8 State R. 213; 9 Id. 262; 12 Id. 175; 14 Id. 201; 19 Id. 251, 366; 25 Id. 308; 26 Id. 372, 383.

Every induction, inference, implication, or presumption in reasoning of any kind, is a logical conclusion derived from, and demanded by, certain data or ascertained circumstances. If such circumstances demand the conclusion of a contract to account for them, a contract is proved; if not, not. If we find, as ascertained circumstances, that a stranger has been in the employment of another, we immediately infer a contract of hiring, because the principles of individuality and self-interest, common to human nature, and therefore the customs of society, require this inference.

But if we find a son in the employment of his father, we do not infer a contract of hiring, because the principle of family affection is sufficient to account for the family association, and does not demand the inference of a contract. And besides this, the position of a son in a family is always esteemed better than that of a hired servant, and it is very rare for sons remaining in their father's family even after they arrive at age, to become mere hired servants. If they do not go to work or business on their own account, it is generally because they perceive no sufficient inducement to sever the family bond, and very often because they lack the energy and independence necessary for such a course; and very seldom because their father desires to use them as hired servants. Customarily no charges are made for boarding and clothing and pocket-money on one side, or for work on the other; but all is placed to the account of filial and parental duty and relationship.

Judging from the somewhat discordant testimony in the present case, this son remained in the employment of his father until he was about forty years old; for we take no account of his temporary absence. While living with his father, in 1842, he got married, and brought his wife to live with him in the house of his parents. Afterwards his father placed him on another farm of the father, and very soon followed him there, and they all lived together until the father's death in 1849. The farm was the father's, and it was managed by him and in his name, and the son worked on it under him. No accounts were kept between them, and the presumption is that the son and his family obtained their entire living from the father while they were residing with him.

Does the law, under the circumstances, presume that the parties mutually intended to be bound, as by contract, for the service and compensation of the son and his wife? It is not pretended that it does. But it is insisted that there are other circumstances besides these which, taken together, are evidence of an express contract for compensation in some form, and we are to examine this.

In this court it is insisted that the contract was that the farm should be worked for the joint benefit of the father and son, and that the profits were to be divided; but there is not a shadow of evidence of this. And moreover it is quite apparent that it was wages only that was claimed before the jury for the services of the son and his wife, and all the evidence and the charge point only in that direction. There was no kind of evidence of the annual products.

Have we then any evidence of an express contract of the father to pay his son for his work or that of his wife? We concede that, in a case of this kind, an express contract may be proved by indirect or circumstantial evidence. If the parties kept accounts between them, these might show it. Or it might be sufficient to show that money was periodically paid to the son as wages; or, if there be no creditors to object, that a settlement for wages was had, and a balance agreed upon. But there is nothing of the sort here.

The court told the jury that a contract of hiring might be inferred from the evidence of Stamm and Roderick. Yet these witnesses add nothing to the facts already recited, except that the father told them, shortly before his death, that he intended to pay his son for his work. This is no making of a contract or admission of one; but rather the contrary. It admits that the son deserved some reward from his father, but not that he had a contract for any.

And when the son asked Roderick to see the father about paying him
for his work, he did not pretend that there was any contract, but only that
he had often spoken to his father about getting pay, and had always been
put off. All this makes it very apparent that it was a contract that was
wanted, and not at all that one already existed; and the court was in error
in saying it might be inferred, from such talk, that there was a contract of
any kind between the parties.

The difficulty in trying causes of this kind often arises from juries
supposing that, because they have the decision of the cause, therefore
they may decide according to general principles of honesty and fairness,
without reference to the law of the case. But this is a despotic power, and
is lodged with no portion of this government.

Their verdict may, in fact, declare what is honest between the parties,
and yet it may be a mere usurpation of power, and thus be an effort to
correct one evil by a greater one. Citizens have a right to form connex-
ions on their own terms and to be judged accordingly. When parties claim
by contract, the contract proved must be the rule by which their rights
are to be decided. To judge them by any other rule is to interfere with the
liberty of the citizen.

It is claimed that the son lent $500 of his wife's money to his father.
The evidence of the fact and of its date is something indistinct. Perhaps it
was when the farm was bought. If the money was lent by her husband, or
both, before the law of 1848 relating to married women, we think he
might sue for it without joining his wife.

Judgment reversed and a new trial awarded.

NOTE

For the aftermath, see Hertzog v. Hertzog's Administrator, 34 Pa. 418
(1859). See also Havighurst, Services in the Home — A Study of Contract Concepts in Domestic Relations, 41 Yale L.J. 386 (1932).

In many states, plaintiffs in cases of this kind confront another obstacle: the so-called dead man's statute. In general, this type of statutory
provision bars one suing an administrator or executor from testifying
about any fact occurring prior to the decedent's death. See N.Y. Civ.
Prac. Act & Rules §4519; Sheldon v. Thornburg, 153 Iowa 622, 133 N.W.
1076 (1912). California has abolished this rule. Cal. Evid. Code §1261.

BARNET'S ESTATE
320 Pa. 408, 182 A. 699 (1936)

Opinion by Mr. Chief Justice KEPHART, January 31, 1936: The appeal
concerns a widow's claim against the estate of her deceased husband for

$31,000, the total salary which she alleges her husband contracted to pay her as general manager of his concessions at Willow Grove Park for the years 1917 to 1921. Claimant took against her husband's will and, there being no children, she received one-half of the estate; she also had the benefit of a life insurance policy for $15,000, and of a certain property placed in the name of herself and her husband as tenants by the entirety, which is valued at $25,000. This claim would take the remainder of his estate.

A husband, if he sees fit, may employ his wife and contract to pay her a stipulated salary, but generally her services are rendered without expectation of specific reward. Her compensation is the increase in the husband's property and, through that, the improvement of their mutual well-being. The policy of the law requires that one seeking to recover for services rendered a decedent, with whom there is a close family relationship, must show an express agreement in terms clear and unequivocal. See Goodheart's Est., 278 Pa. 381, 382. No claim therefore can here be based on a quantum meruit. To show an express contract, various witnesses testified to certain oral declarations of the decedent, but none of them stated with any degree of certainty the time, place or manner of contracting, or that decedent's declarations were made in the claimant's presence. Moreover, the court below did not place reliance on the testimony tending to show decedent regarded his wife as a paid employee.

The written evidence showed an extract from a letter in which decedent stated his wife was in business with him. This gave no support to the claim that the services were rendered under contract. The claimant's federal income tax return for the year 1921, prepared by *decedent*, was offered in evidence, and it showed a payment of salary for that year. The auditing judge stated: "If the 1921 salary *is* still due and owing, as claimed, why should both claimant and decedent declare that claimant had received that sum in 1921?" The probable explanation is decedent's difficulties with the government over his income tax, but this writing did not aid the theory of an express contract.

The court below found there was no positive and direct proof such as is necessary to maintain an action against a decedent's estate (see Gross's Est., 248 Pa. 73, 75, and authorities cited therein), and we are not confronted with sufficient proof to disturb that finding.

Decree affirmed at appellant's cost.

CROPSEY v. SWEENEY, 27 Barb. 310 (N.Y. 1858). James Ridgeway and Catharine Dob were married in 1812 and separated in 1815. In 1821 James married plaintiff and in that same year Catharine sued him for divorce on the ground of adultery. A decree of divorce was issued in 1822. In 1825 James and plaintiff again solemnized their marriage. James died in 1847. Unknown to plaintiff, and perhaps to James, neither the marriage in 1821 nor that in 1825 was valid: under New York law at that time, if a divorce was granted on the ground of adultery, the spouse guilty of adultery could not remarry during the lifetime of his or her former spouse. See Cropsey v. Ogden, 1 Kern. 288. Catharine was still alive in 1825. Plaintiff sued James' administrator for the value of services rendered to James during their life together. The court denied plaintiff any relief, refusing to imply a contract:

"[T]he law will not presume that work or labor performed *as a servant or laborer* was voluntary, and performed without any view to compensation; but the law cannot presume that the domestic and household work and services of a wife for a husband are performed with the view to pay as a servant or laborer.

"The law would do injustice to the plaintiff herself, by implying a promise to pay for these services; and respect for the plaintiff herself, as well as for the law, compels us to infer and hold, that these services were performed not as a servant, with a view to pay, but from higher and holier motives; and that therefore her complaint does not constitute any cause of action."

SHAW v. SHAW
2 Q.B. 429 (C.A. 1954)

[In 1937, Percy Shaw, a farmer, met the plaintiff, a widow, and later in that year proposed marriage to her, describing himself as a widower. She accepted him and on December 10, 1938 they went through a form of marriage at the Cannok Registry Office. For fourteen years, Percy Shaw and the plaintiff lived as husband and wife at Cannok during which time the plaintiff advanced to Shaw about £250 to buy stock, to assist him in acquiring land and to pay for agricultural machinery. In 1952, Shaw died intestate. After Shaw's death, the plaintiff became aware for the first time that she had not been legally married to him (his legal wife died in 1950) and she brought an action against the administrators, a son and daughter of the deceased, claiming damage for breach of a promise of marriage by the deceased. The lower court gave judgment for the defendants holding that the alleged promise to marry was unenforceable being contrary to public policy since at the time of the promise Shaw had a wife living. The plaintiff successfully appealed.]

DENNING, L.J. Every man who proposes marriage to a woman impliedly warrants that he is in a position to marry her, and that he is not himself a married man; and he reaffirms that warranty when he afterwards goes through a form of marriage with her — whether in church or in a registry office. To take the familiar words of the banns of marriage, he warrants that there is no "cause or just impediment" why he should not marry her. Every day of their married life he continues the warranty; he warrants that their marriage was valid and that there was no impediment to it.

In a present case the law imports that Percy Shaw gave such a warranty to the plaintiff. On the faith of it, she went through a form of marriage with him, she lived with him as his wife for 14 years, she put her money into the farm and did all the work of a farmer's wife, and when he died she followed his coffin to the grave as his widow. His estate was worth £1,500 or more, which she had helped to make; and yet the administrators now turn round and say that she was never his wife because he was already married, and that his real wife did not die until 1950. In my judgment Shaw broke his warranty at every point. He broke it when he proposed marriage; he broke it when he married the plaintiff; and he broke it throughout their married life. The breach continued all the time. The most important breach of all was at the moment of his death, because when he died she was not his widow, as she thought she was. She was in law a stranger. That is the breach for which, in my judgment, damages can be recovered.

But what is the proper measure of damages? If she had been his widow when he died intestate, as she thought she was, she would have received the widow's £1,000 and life interest in half of the remainder of the estate. Those are the direct damages which she has suffered by this breach of warranty, and which, in my judgment, she is entitled to recover. It is said that an implied warranty is not alleged in the pleadings, but all the material facts are alleged, and in these days, so long as those facts are alleged, that is sufficient for the court to proceed to judgment without putting any particular legal label upon the cause of action. . . . ,

[The concurring opinions of Singleton, L.J. and Morris, L.J. have been omitted.]

NOTE

For a discussion of the case, see 70 L.Q. Rev. 445 (1954). Consult In re Fox's Estate, 178 Wis. 369, 190 N.W. 90 (1922); Estate of Vargas, 36 Cal. App. 3d 714, 111 Cal. Rptr. 779, 81 A.L.R.3d 1 (1974), Comment, 20 Wash. & Lee L. Rev. 91 (1963).

The cause of action in *Shaw* has apparently been abolished by section 1 of the Law Reform (Miscellaneous Provisions) Act of 1970. See G. H. Treitel, The Law of Contract 326-327 (5th ed. 1979). A person in Mrs. Shaw's position is now protected by section 6 of the aforementioned act. See 33 Mod. L. Rev. 534, 538-539 (1970).

HEWITT v. HEWITT

62 Ill. App. 3d 861, 380 N.E.2d 454 (1974)

Mr. Justice TRAPP delivered the opinion of the court:

Plaintiff appeals from the order of the trial court dismissing her complaint which prayed that the court grant to her a just, fair share of the property, earnings, and profits of the defendant, order a proper provision for support and maintenance of plaintiff and their minor children, or, in the alternative, divide the joint tenancy property of the parties and impress a trust on other property acquired through the joint efforts of plaintiff and defendant.

[The trial court found that the Hewitts had never been married, and that there was no common law marriage that the court might recognize. Defendant admitted paternity of the three minor children.]

The order on appeal was directed to an amended count which contained the following allegations: That prior to June 1960, the parties were residents of Illinois attending Grinell College in Iowa, that plaintiff became pregnant, and that on or about such date the defendant told plaintiff that they were husband and wife and that they would thereafter live together as such; that no formal marriage ceremony was necessary and that defendant stated that he would thereafter share his life, future earnings, and property with plaintiff; that the parties immediately announced their marriage to their respective parents, thereafter lived together as husband and wife and that in reliance upon defendant's representations she devoted her entire efforts to assisting in the completion of defendant's professional education and the establishing of his successful practice of pedodontia; that such professional education was assisted financially by the parents of plaintiff; that plaintiff assisted defendant in the practice of his profession by virtue of her special skills and that although plaintiff was given a payroll check for such services the monies were placed in the family funds and used for family purposes. It is further alleged that defendant is a successful professional man with an income of $80,000 per year who has acquired property both in joint tenancy and as separate property, and that the assistance and encouragement and industry of the plaintiff were directed to the acquiring of such property and professional pecuniary advancement of defendant.

It is alleged that plaintiff furnished defendant with every assistance that a wife and mother could give, including social activities designed to enhance defendant's social and professional reputation. Plaintiff further alleges that for 17 years defendant represented to her and to all the world that they were husband and wife and that she has relied upon such representations to her detriment, and that she should be entitled to equal division of the property whether in joint tenancy or in the sole name of defendant.

It is alleged that the court should enforce the implied contract evidenced by the conduct of the parties; that plaintiff relied upon defendant's representation that they were partners within the family relationship; and that defendant knowing that the alleged marriage was not legal nevertheless continued to assure plaintiff that she was his wife and continued to hold himself out as husband of the plaintiff to secure the benefits to be gained through the services, devotion, thrift, and industry of plaintiff invested in the family relationship so that the property of the defendant should be impressed with a trust to protect plaintiff from the frauds and deception of the defendant.

The order of the trial court on appeal found that the law and public policy of the State requires the claims of plaintiff to be based upon a valid legal marriage; that there was no such legal marriage shown by the facts alleged; and that the allegations failed to state a cause of action recognized in Illinois upon a theory of implied contract, joint venture, or partnership. The order does not expressly speak to the allegation of an express oral contract, but we will presume that the ruling would be the same.

In argument, defendant has referred to plaintiff as a meretricious spouse living in a meretricious relationship. The adjective should be examined in its precise meaning, i.e., "Of, pertaining to, befitting or of a character of a harlot" (Shorter Oxford English Dictionary (1934)), or, "Of or relating to a prostitute" (Webster's New Collegiate Dictionary (1973)). Neither is it correct to refer to plaintiff as a concubine which is defined as "1: a woman living in a *socially recognized* state of concubinage . . . MISTRESS." (Emphasis supplied.) Webster's New Collegiate Dictionary (1973).

The well-pleaded facts contradict the terms in showing that the parties lived, and for a time, enjoyed a most conventional, respectable and ordinary family life. The single flaw is that for reasons not explained, the parties failed to procure a license, a ceremony, and a registration of a marriage. Upon the present pleading nothing discloses a scandal, an affront to family living or society, or anything other than that the parties were known as husband and wife. We refuse to weigh defendant's claim in the context of such epithets.

All parties agreed that no court of review in Illinois has examined claims arising under comparable circumstances. See cases collected in Annot., 31 A.L.R. 2d 1255 (1953), and its supplements.

Defendant argues that plaintiff's claims must be defeated upon the grounds of public policy in that all rights must rest upon a valid marriage contract within the provisions of the Illinois Marriage and Dissolution of Marriage Act, effective October 1, 1977. Section 102 of that Act (Ill. Rev. Stat. 1977, ch. 40, par. 102) states that:

[I]ts underlying purposes . . . are to:
    (1)   provide adequate procedures for the solemnization and registration of marriage;
    (2)   strengthen and preserve the integrity of marriage and safeguard family relationships; . . .

The provisions of the Act do not undertake to prohibit cohabitation without such solemnization of marriage. Its section 201 provides:

A marriage between a man and a woman licensed, solemnized and registered as provided in this Act is valid in this State.

Upon the facts pleaded, plaintiff has for more than 15 years lived within the legitimate boundaries of a marriage and family relationship of a most conventional sort. The record does not suggest that the parties' relationship came within the proscription of prohibited marriages. Ill. Rev. Stat. 1977, ch. 40, par. 212.

[The court at this point held that the public policy embodied in Illinois criminal statutes proscribing adultery and fornication did not bar relief in this case, where "the family relationship was conventional without an open flouting of accepted standards."]

Plaintiff has alleged that she was induced and persuaded to live and cohabit with the defendant as an adult by reason of his assurances that a marriage ceremony was not required, and the representations and promises that they would live as husband and wife sharing the benefits resulting from his professional career which she aided through procuring financial assistance, as well as her role and services as companion, housewife and mother. The practical question is whether she should be denied all claims by reason of the absence of a marriage ceremony.

Plaintiff urges that this court adopt the rationale of the Supreme Court of California stated in its well-publicized opinion, Marvin v. Marvin (1976), 18 Cal. 3d 660, 557 P.2d 106, 134 Cal. Rptr. 815. Under the name Michelle Marvin that plaintiff alleged that she had lived with defendant for seven years without a marriage ceremony under an express oral contract that they would share equally in any property accumulated by their efforts while living together; that they should be known as husband and wife; that defendant would provide for plaintiff's needs for life and that plaintiff would forego her career to devote her time to defendant as a companion, homemaker and cook, and that she had so performed her duties until defendant forced her to leave. Plaintiff prayed a declaratory judgment to determine her contract and property rights and the declaration of a constructive trust in one-half of the property accumulated while the parties lived together. Of the cases examined, Marvin includes facts most clearly comparable to those present here, although Marvin was known to be married to another during the first three years of the relationship with Michelle.

The trial court entered a judgment for defendant upon the pleadings without assigning reasons.

As here, Marvin argued that the character of their relationship was immoral and violated public policy. While no courts of review in Illinois have considered such relationship, California courts had examined a number of instances concerning agreements to share accumulated property by unmarried persons cohabitating together. Reviewing such cases, the court said:

Although the past decisions hover over the issue in the somewhat wispy form of the figures of a Chagall painting, we can abstract from those decisions a clear and simple rule. The fact that a man and woman live together without marriage, and engage in a sexual relationship, does not in itself invalidate agreements between them relating to their earnings, property, or expenses. Neither is such an agreement invalid merely because the parties may have contemplated the creation or continuation of a nonmarital relationship when they entered into it. Agreements between nonmarital partners fail only to the extent that they rest upon a consideration of meretricious sexual services. Thus the rule asserted by defendant, that a contract fails if it is "involved in" or made "in contemplation" of a nonmarital relationship, cannot be reconciled with the decisions.

18 Cal. 3d 660, 670, 557 P.2d 106, 113, 134 Cal. Rptr. 815, 822.
The court continued:

The principle that a contract between nonmarital partners will be enforced unless expressly and inseparably based upon an illicit consideration of sexual services not only represents the distillation of the decisional law, but also offers a far more precise and workable standard than that advocated by defendant.

18 Cal. 3d 660, 672, 557 P.2d 106, 114, 134 Cal. Rptr. 815, 823.
The court said that the authorities demonstrate:

. . . that a contract between nonmarital partners, even if expressly made in contemplation of a common living arrangement, is invalid only if sexual acts form an inseparable part of the consideration for the agreement. In sum, a court will not enforce a contract for the pooling of property and earnings if it is explicitly and inseparably based upon services as a paramour. . . .

18 Cal. 3d 660, 672, 557 P.2d 106, 114, 134 Cal. Rptr. 815, 823.
The court concluded:

So long as the agreement does not rest upon illicit meretricious consideration, the parties may order their economic affairs as they choose, and no policy precludes the courts from enforcing such agreements.

18 Cal. 3d 660, 674, 557 P.2d 106, 116, 134 Cal. Rptr. 815, 825.
Defendant argues that plaintiff has engaged in improper conduct, and in effect, should be punished by denial of relief. This argument may be answered as in *Marvin:*

Indeed, to the extent that denial of relief "punished" one partner, it necessarily rewards the other by permitting him to retain a disproportionate amount of the property. Concepts of "guilt" thus cannot justify an unequal division of property between two equally "guilty" persons.

(18 Cal. 3d 660, 682, 557 P.2d 106, 121, 134 Cal. Rptr. 815, 830.)
He also argues that any claim of plaintiff to equity should be barred by the
doctrine of "unclean hands." However, as stated in West v. Knowles
(1957), 50 Wash. 2d 311, 316, 311 P.2d 689, 692-93:

> Under such circumstances [the dissolution of a nonmarital relationship],
> this court and the courts of other jurisdictions have, in effect, sometimes
> said, "We will wash our hands of such disputes. The parties should and
> must be left to their own devices, just where they find themselves." To me,
> such pronouncements seem overly fastidious and a bit fatuous. They are
> unrealistic and, among other things, ignore the fact that an unannounced
> (but nevertheless effective and binding) rule of law is inherent in any such
> terminal statements by a court of law.
>
> The unannounced but inherent rule is simply that a party who has title,
> or in some instances who is in possession, will enjoy the rights of ownership
> of the property concerned. The rule often operates to the great advantage
> of the cunning and the shrewd, who wind up with possession of the prop-
> erty, or title to it in their names, at the end of a so-called meretricious
> relationship. So, although the courts proclaim that they will have nothing
> to do with such matters, the proclamation in itself establishes, as to the
> parties involved, an effective and binding rule of law which tends to operate
> purely by accident or perhaps by reason of the cunning, anticipatory de-
> signs of just one of the parties.

Here, plaintiff prays relief not only under allegations of an express oral
contract, but also seeks recovery upon allegations supporting implied
contract, equitable relief upon allegations of misrepresentation, and as
constructive trust. Upon determination that plaintiff states a cause of
action upon an express oral contract we observe no reasons of public
policy to conclude that other forms of relief framed upon appropriate
allegations of fact and proved before the trier of fact should not be available to plaintiff.

In *Marvin*, the court unanimously determined that the plaintiff's complaint stated a cause of action upon an express contract. The court continued, with one dissent expressing belief that it was unnecessary, to
examine in *dicta* those other forms of relief which might be available to
plaintiff and upon consideration of the existing authorities in that State
said:

> But, although parties to a nonmarital relationship obviously cannot have
> based any expectations upon the belief that they were married, other ex-
> pectations and equitable considerations remain. The parties may well ex-
> pect that property will be divided in accord with the parties' own tacit
> understanding and that in the absence of such understanding the courts
> will fairly apportion property accumulated through mutual effort. We need
> not treat nonmarital partners as putatively married persons in order to
> apply principles of implied contract, or extend equitable remedies; we need
> to treat them only as we do any other unmarried person.

(18 Cal. 3d 660, 682, 557 P.2d 106, 121, 134 Cal. Rptr. 815, 830.)
And continued:

> We conclude that the judicial barriers that may stand in the way of a policy based upon the fulfillment of the reasonable expectations of the parties to a nonmarital relationship should be removed. As we have explained, the courts now hold that express agreements will be enforced unless they rest on an unlawful meretricious consideration. We add that in the absence of an express agreement, the courts may look to a variety of other remedies in order to protect the parties' lawful expectations.
>
> The courts may inquire into the conduct of the parties to determine whether that conduct demonstrates an implied contract or implied agreement of partnership or joint venture (see *Estate of Thornton* (1972) 81 Wash. 2d 72, 499 P.2d 864), or some other tacit understanding between the parties. The courts may, when appropriate, employ principles of constructive trust (see Omer v. Omer (1974), 11 Wash. App. 386, 523 P.2d 957) or resulting trust (see Hyman v. Hyman (Tex. Civ. App. 1954) 275 S.W.2d 149). Finally, a nonmarital partner may recover in quantum meruit for the reasonable value of household services rendered less the reasonable value of support received if he can show that he rendered services with the expectation of monetary reward.

18 Cal. 3d 660, 684, 557 P.2d 106, 122-23, 134 Cal. Rptr. 815, 831-32.

We conclude that the reasoning followed in *Marvin* is particularly persuasive upon the allegations here pleaded wherein plaintiff has alleged facts which demonstrate a stable family relationship extending over a long period of time.

It would be superficial to conclude that by this determination this court has revived or restored a form of common law marriage now forbidden by statute. It is apparent that the matters to be alleged and the facts to be proved here are substantially, if not enormously, different.

The value of a stable marriage remains unchallenged and is not denigrated by this opinion. It is not realistic to conclude that this determination will "discourage" marriage for the rule for which defendant contends can only encourage a partner with obvious income-producing ability to avoid marriage and to retain all earnings which he may acquire. One cannot earnestly advocate such a policy.

It has been documented that:

> The 1970 census figures indicate that today perhaps eight times as many couples are living together without being married as cohabited ten years ago.

Comment, In re Cary: A Judicial Recognition of Illicit Cohabitation, 25 Hastings L.J. 1226 (1974).

It has been concluded that reasons for such way of life include the economic forces of loss of pension or welfare rights and the impact of income taxes, as well as personal reasons. While the court cannot now predict what the evidence will prove, the courts should be prepared to deal realistically and fairly with the problems which exist in the life of the day.

We conclude that upon the record it neither can be said that plaintiff participated in a meretricious relationship nor that her conduct so affronted public policy that she should be denied any and all relief.

The judgment of the trial court is reversed and the cause remanded for further proceedings not inconsistent with the views expressed.

Reversed and remanded.

NOTE

The case law treatment of cohabitation agreements between nonmarried couples is best illustrated by the well-known case of Marvin v. Marvin, 18 Cal. 3d 660, 557 P.2d 106, 134 Cal. Rptr. 815 (1976), discussed and relied upon in Hewitt v. Hewitt. The court in *Marvin* held that plaintiff, who had pleaded an express oral agreement that she and defendant would combine their efforts and earnings and would share equally any and all property accumulated as a result, had stated a prima facie case.

> [W]e base our opinion on the principle that adults who voluntarily live together and engage in sexual relations are nonetheless as competent as any other persons to contract respecting their earnings and property rights. . . . So long as the agreement does not rest upon illicit meretricious consideration, that parties may order their economic affairs as they choose, and no policy precludes the courts from enforcing such agreements.

Id. at 674, 557 P.2d at 116, 134 Cal. Rptr. at 825. In footnotes, the court suggested that the abandoned cohabitant might also be able to recover on the theory of an implied contract based on all the surrounding circumstances, and be entitled to quasi-contractual and equitable relief (see footnotes 25 and 26).

The trial itself was rather anticlimactic: sitting without a jury, the court found that plaintiff's allegation of an agreement was unsubstantiated and denied her claim for support and maintenance. The trial court's order to the defendant to pay plaintiff a substantial sum to be used by her primarily for economic rehabilitation was overturned by the Court of Appeals:

> [T]he special findings in support of the challenged rehabilitative award merely established plaintiff's need therefor and defendant's ability to respond to that need. This is not enough. The award, being nonconsensual in nature, must be supported by some recognized underlying obligation in law or in equity. A court of equity admittedly has broad powers, but it may not create totally new substantive rights under the guise of doing equity.

Marvin v. Marvin, 122 Cal. App. 3d 871, 876, 176 Cal. Rptr. 552 (1981). A petition for rehearing before the California Supreme Court was denied. The case has been widely commented on but there are conflicting opinions as to its soundness. See E. Farnsworth, Contracts 346-347 (1982). Hunter, An Essay on Contract and Status: Race, Marriage and the Meretricious Spouse, 64 Va. L. Rev. 1039, 1067 (1978); Kay & Amyx, Marvin v. Marvin: Preserving the Options, 65 Calif. L. Rev. 937 (1977); Bruch, Property Rights of De Facto Spouses Including Thoughts on the Value of Homemakers' Services, 10 Fam. L.Q. 101 (1976).

For an extended discussion of the *Marvin* and *Hewitt* cases from a Critical Legal Studies perspective that makes use of the French philosopher and literary critic Jacques Derrida, see Dalton, An Essay in the Deconstruction of Contract Doctrine, 94 Yale L.J. 997, 1095-1113 (1985).

COTNAM v. WISDOM
83 Ark. 601, 104 S.W. 164 (1907)

F. L. Wisdom and George C. Abel presented a claim against the estate of A. M. Harrison, deceased, of which T. T. Cotnam is administrator, for $2,000 on account of surgical attention to the deceased, who was killed by being thrown from a street car.

The probate court allowed the account in the sum of $400, and the administrator appealed to the circuit court.

The evidence showed that deceased received fatal injuries in a street car wreck; that while he was unconscious some person summoned Dr. Wisdom to attend him; that Dr. Wisdom called in Dr. Abel, an experienced surgeon, to assist him; that they found that the patient was suffering from a fracture of the temporal and parietal bones, and that it was necessary to perform the operation of trephining; that the patient lived only a short time after the operation, and never recovered consciousness.

Dr. Abel testified, over defendant's objection, that the charge of $2,000 was based on the result of inquiry as to the financial condition of deceased's estate. It was further proved, over defendant's objection that deceased was a bachelor, and that his estate, which amounted to about $18,500, including $10,000 of insurance, would go to collateral heirs.

Various physicians testified as to the customary fees of doctors in similar cases, and fixed the amount at various sums ranging from $100 to $2,000. There was also evidence that the ability of the patient to pay is usually taken into consideration by surgeons in fixing their fee.

At the plaintiff's request the court charged the jury as follows:

1. If you find from the evidence that plaintiffs rendered professional services as physicians and surgeons to the deceased, A. M. Harrison, in a sudden emergency following the deceased's injury in a street car wreck, in

an endeavor to save his life, then you are instructed that plaintiffs are entitled to recover from the estate of the said A. M. Harrison such sum as you may find from the evidence is a reasonable compensation for the services rendered.

2. The character and importance of the operation, the responsibility resting upon the surgeon performing the operation, his experience and professional training, and the ability to pay of the person operated upon, are elements to be considered by you in determining what is a reasonable charge for the services performed by plaintiffs in the particular case.

In his opening statement to the jury, counsel for claimants stated that "Harrison was worth $8,000, and had insurance, and his estate was left to collateral heirs, that is, to nephews and nieces." Counsel for defendant objected to such argument, but the court overruled the objection; and the defendant saved his exceptions.

Verdict for $650 was returned in plaintiff's favor. Defendant has appealed. . . .

Hill, C.J. 1. . . . The first question is as to the correctness of this instruction. As indicated therein, the facts are that Mr. Harrison, appellant's intestate, was thrown from a street car, receiving serious injuries which rendered him unconscious, and while in that condition the appellees were notified of the accident and summoned to his assistance by some spectator, and performed a difficult operation in an effort to save his life, but they were unsuccessful, and he died without regaining consciousness. The appellant says:

Harrison was never conscious after his head struck the pavement. He did not and could not, expressly or impliedly, assent to the action of the appellees. He was without knowledge or will power. However merciful or benevolent may have been the intention of the appellees, a new rule of law, of contract by implication of law, will have to be established by this court in order to sustain the recovery.

Appellant is right in saying that the recovery must be sustained by a contract by implication of law, but is not right in saying that it is a new rule of law, for such contracts are almost as old as the English system of jurisprudence. They are usually called "implied contracts;" more properly, they should be called quasi-contracts or constructive contracts. See 1 Page on Contracts, §14; also 2 Page on Contracts, §771.

The following excerpts from Sceva v. True, 53 N.H. 627, are peculiarly applicable here:

We regard it as well settled by the cases referred to in the briefs of counsel, many of which have been commented on at length by Mr. Shirley for the defendant, that an insane person, an idiot, or a person utterly bereft of all sense and reason by the sudden stroke of an accident or disease, may be held liable, in assumpsit, for necessaries furnished to him in good faith while in that unfortunate and helpless condition. And the reasons upon which this rests are too broad, as well as too sensible and humane, to be overborne by any deductions which a refined logic may make from the circumstances that in such cases there can be no contract or promise in fact — no meeting of the minds of the parties. The cases put it on the ground of an implied contract; and by this is not meant, as the defendant's counsel seems to suppose, an actual contract — that is, an actual meeting of the minds of the parties, an actual, mutual understanding, to be inferred from language, acts and circumstances by the jury — but a contract and promise, said to be implied by the law, where, in point of fact, there was no contract, no mutual understanding, and so no promise. The defendant's counsel says it is usurpation for the court to hold, as a matter of law, that there is a contract and a promise when all the evidence in the case shows that there was not a contract, nor the semblance of one. It is doubtless a legal fiction, invented and used for the sake of the remedy. If it was originally usurpation, certainly it has now become very inveterate, and firmly fixed in the body of the law. . . .

In its practical application, [the law of implied contracts] sustains recovery for physicians and nurses who render services for infants, insane persons and drunkards. 2 Page on Contracts, §§867, 897, and 906. And services rendered by physicians to persons unconscious or helpless by reason of injury or sickness are in the same situation as those rendered to persons incapable of contracting, such as the classes above described. Raoul v. Newman, 59 Ga. 408; Meyer v. K. of P., 64 L.R.A. 839.

The court was therefore right in giving the instruction in question.

2. The defendant sought to require the plaintiff to prove, in addition to the value of the services, the benefit, if any, derived by the deceased from the operation, and alleges error in the court refusing to place this burden upon the physicians. The same question was considered in Ladd v. Witte, 116 Wis. 35, where the court said:

That is not at all the test. So that a surgical operation be conceived and performed with due skill and care, the price to be paid therefor does not depend upon the result. The event so generally lies with the forces of nature that all intelligent men know and understand that the surgeon is not responsible therefor. In absence of express agreement, the surgeon, who brings to such a service due skill and care earns the reasonable and customary price therefor, whether the outcome be beneficial to the patient or the reverse.

3. The court permitted to go to the jury the fact that Mr. Harrison was a bachelor, and that his estate would go to his collateral relatives, and also permitted proof to be made of the value of the estate, which amounted to about $18,500, including $10,000 from accident and life insurance policies.

There is a conflict in the authorities as to whether it is proper to prove the value of the estate of a person for whom medical services were rendered, or the financial condition of the person receiving such services. In Robinson v. Campbell, 47 Ia. 625, it was said: "There is no more reason why this charge should be enhanced on account of the ability of the defendants to pay than that the merchant should charge them more for a yard of cloth, or the druggist for filling a prescription, or a laborer for a day's work." On the other hand, see Haley's Succession, 50 La. Ann. 840; and Lange v. Kearney, 4 N.Y. Supp. 14, which was affirmed by the Court of Appeals, 127 N.Y. 676, holding that the financial condition of the patient may be considered.

Whatever may be the true principle governing this matter in contracts, the court is of the opinion that the financial condition of a patient cannot be considered where there is no contract and recovery is sustained on a legal fiction which raises a contract in order to afford a remedy which the justice of the case requires.

In Morrissett v. Wood, 123 Ala. 384, the court said:

> The trial court erred in admitting testimony as to the value of the patient's estate, against the objection of the defendant. The inquiry was as to the value of the professional services rendered by the plaintiff to the defendant's testator, and, as the case was presented below, the amount or value of the latter's estate could shed no legitimate light upon this issue nor aid in its elucidation. The cure or amelioration of disease is as important to a poor man as it is to a rich one, and, prima facie at least, the services rendered the one are of the same value as the same services rendered to the other. If there was a recognized usage obtaining in the premises here involved to graduate professional charges with reference to the financial condition of the person for whom such services are rendered, which had been so long established and so universally acted upon as to have ripened into a custom of such character that it might be considered that these services were rendered and accepted in contemplation of it, there is no hint of it in the evidence.

There was evidence in this case proving that it was customary for physicians to graduate their charges by the ability of the patient to pay, and hence, in regard to that element, this case differs from the Alabama case. But the value of the Alabama decision is the reason given which may admit such evidence, viz., because the custom would render the financial condition of the patient a factor to be contemplated by both parties when the services were rendered and accepted. The same thought, differently expressed, is found in Lange v. Kearney, 4 N.Y. Supp. 14.

This could not apply to a physician called in an emergency by some bystander to attend a stricken man whom he never saw or heard of before; and certainly the unconscious patient could not, in fact or in law, be held to have contemplated what charges the physician might properly bring against him. In order to admit such testimony, it must be assumed that the surgeon and patient each had in contemplation that the means of the patient would be one factor in determining the amount of the charge for the services rendered. While the law may admit such evidence as throwing light upon the contract and indicating what was really in contemplation when it was made, yet a different question is presented when there is no contract to be ascertained or construed, but mere fiction of law creating a contract where none existed in order that there might be a remedy for a right. This fiction merely requires a reasonable compensation for the services rendered. The services are the same, be the patient prince or pauper, and for them the surgeon is entitled to fair compensation for his time, service and skill. It was, therefore, error to admit this evidence and to instruct the jury in the 2nd instruction that in determining what was a reasonable charge they could consider the "ability to pay of the person operated upon."

It was improper to let it go to the jury that Mr. Harrison was a bachelor, and that his estate was left to nieces and nephews. This was relevant to no issue in the case, and its effect might well have been prejudicial. While this verdict is no higher than some of the evidence would justify, yet it is much higher than some of the other evidence would justify, and hence it is impossible to say that this was a harmless error.

Judgment is reversed and cause remanded.

Justices Battle and Wood concur in sustaining the recovery and in holding that it was error to permit the jury to consider the fact that his estate would go to collateral heirs, but they do not concur in holding that it was error to admit evidence of the value of the estate and instructing that it might be considered in fixing the charge.

NOTE

Reread Hurley v. Eddingfield, *supra* p. 56. Do you see an inconsistency between that case and the holding in Cotnam v. Wisdom?

On the determination of the amount of recovery, contrast Schoenberg v. Rose, 145 N.Y.S. 831 (1914); see also A. Kronman & R. Posner, The Economics of Contract Law 59-61 (1979). Assume that plaintiff was summoned by the daughter of the deceased who told the plaintiff, "I want my father taken care of and given the best care you can give him." Will the daughter be liable? Assume that she added: "I will pay for the charges." If the doctor sent his bill to the estate, and the administrator of the estate refused to pay, could the doctor collect from the daughter? See Lawrence v. Anderson, 108 Vt. 176, 184 A. 689 (1936), reprinted *infra* p. 757.

A rich man who did not disclose his wealth was erroneously admitted to a hospital as a charity patient. No arrangement was made regarding the cost of a necessary operation and the attendant physicians, mistaking the patient for a pauper, did not expect to charge. Are they entitled to compensation for the reasonable value of their services after discovering the true financial condition of their patient? Matter of Agnew, 132 Misc. 466, 811, 230 N.Y.S. 519, 231 N.Y.S. 4 (1928). See further In re Crisan Estate, 362 Mich. 569, 107 N.W.2d 907 (1961).

SOMMERS v. PUTNAM BOARD
OF EDUCATION

113 Ohio St. 177, 148 N.E. 682 (1925)

[The plaintiff, a resident taxpayer of Riley Township, Putnam County, Ohio, was the father of four children of compulsory school age, all of whom were under the age of eighteen and were eligible for admission to high school work under the laws of Ohio. The plaintiff and his four children resided four-and-a-half miles from the nearest high school maintained by the Township Board of Education of Riley Township, in the village of Pandora, Putnam County, Ohio. Plaintiff unsuccessfully requested the Township Board and the Putnam County Board of Education, the defendants, either to furnish high school work within four miles of his residence or to furnish transportation for his four children to and from the high school of Pandora or to furnish and provide board and lodging for his children in Pandora. As a result of the refusal of his request, the plaintiff transported his children to and from high school at his own expense from September 1922 to May 1923 and then presented his itemized bill for such services in the sum of $397 and requested the defendant, the Township Board of Education, to pay the same. When the bill was rejected, the plaintiff sued both defendants. A demurrer to his petition was sustained, final judgment was entered for the defendants and this judgment was affirmed by the Court of Appeals. Plaintiff brings error.]

ALLEN, J. . . . [In State ex rel. Masters v. Beamer, 109 Ohio St. 133, 141 N.E. 851], this court held that it was the mandatory duty of the local board of education, or, in case of the failure of the local board to perform its duties, the mandatory duty of the county board of education, either to provide work in high school branches at some school within 4 miles of the plaintiff's residence, or to have such branches made accessible as to the plaintiff's children by transportation to, or board and lodging within, 4 miles of the school wherein such high school branches are offered. That case, therefore, while holding that the several duties enumerated were optional with the local and with the county board of education, held specifically that it was mandatory upon the local board, and, in case of its default, upon the county board of education, to perform one or the other of these duties.

In the instant case the record shows that both the local board of education and the county board of education have refused to perform any one of the several optional duties resting upon them. The record discloses that the district in question did not provide high school work in high school branches within 4 miles of the residence of the plaintiff. The duty of providing such high school work is enjoined upon the local board by Section 7764-1, General Code. Since the local board has failed to provide these high school branches, the same duty, or the duty of making such high school work accessible to children of compulsory school age, is imposed upon the county board of education under Section 7610-1, General Code. . . .

Plaintiff in error concedes that there is no contractual relationship existing between the school boards and the plaintiff in error, but contends that, under the familiar rule of quasi contracts, this action lies for money expended in transporting his 4 minor children to a high school outside of the 4-mile limit. With this contention we are in accord. The parent has discharged the obligation first of the local school board and next of the county school board. Moreover, this duty was imposed upon the board partly for the parent's benefit, as well as for the benefit of the children and of the public. As the performance of that duty by another is a benefit to the school boards, when he performed the duty the parent conferred a benefit upon the school boards. For this benefit the school board ought in justice to pay, and hence the intervener, that is, the parent who performed the duty, is entitled to compensation therefor.

An act of beneficial intervention in the discharge of another's legal obligation, which results in a quasi contractual obligation, must contain the following elements: The obligation must be of such a nature that actual and prompt performance thereof is of grave public concern; the person upon whom the obligation rests must have failed or refused with knowledge of the facts to perform the obligation; or it must reasonably appear that it is impossible to perform it; and the person who intervenes must, under the circumstances, be not a mere intermeddler but a proper person to perform the duty. Woodward, Law of Quasi Contracts, p. 310; Forsyth v. Ganson, 5 Wend. (N.Y.), 558, 21 Am. Dec., 241; Rundell v. Bentley, 53 Hun. (N.Y.), 272, 6 N.Y.S., 609.

It is plain that the actual performance of this duty of making high school branches accessible to children is a matter of grave public concern. It is of the utmost importance that the coming race receive school training. The moral sense of the community requires that this obligation be actually performed, and the school boards, upon whom the obligation rested, failed to perform the duty.

Passing to the question of the appropriateness of the intervention of the parent, the father was surely the proper person to perform the obligation. It is his obligation to see that his children attend school, and the fact that the transportation has not been supplied cannot be pleaded as an excuse for his failure to send such children to school, or as an excuse for the failure of the children to attend school. Section 7731-4, General Code (109 Ohio Laws, p. 290).

The performance of this legal obligation was a benefit to the school boards because it saved them from the necessity of performing the duty themselves. Hence the retention of the benefit was inequitable, although there was no contract between the parties. It would be unjust to permit those who failed to perform a duty which was a matter of such public concern to retain the benefit bestowed upon them by the plaintiff in error.

It is urged that, inasmuch as this court held in the *Masters* case, *supra*, that an action in mandamus lay upon the failure of the local board and of the county board to perform the duty of making high school branches accessible to children of school age, an action does not lie herein to collect reimbursement for the money expended by the relator in transporting his children to the high school. No authority has been cited upon this proposition, but the defendant in error contends that, since the right of mandamus was granted in the *Masters* case, necessarily no action for money exists herein.

This specific question was reserved for decision in the *Masters* case. However, the plaintiff in error here is in quite a different position from the plaintiff in the *Masters* case. In the *Masters* case the parent was endeavoring to make a school board perform its duty. In this case the plaintiff in error has proceeded to perform the duty enjoined by statute upon the school boards. He, therefore, through no fault of his own, has been placed in a position where it would be futile to resort to mandamus. Under these circumstances the defendants in error cannot be heard to say that, because mandamus would have lain if the father had not transported his children, an action for money will not now lie.

The defendants in error seem to consider that an action for money is an extraordinary action which does not lie if an action for mandamus could be brought under the circumstances of the *Masters* case. In other words, because mandamus is an extraordinary writ, the defendants in error apparently maintain that an action for money is an extraordinary remedy — surely a novel contention. Defendants in error, however, lose sight of the fact that, when the parent has actually transported his children, he can, of course, bring no action for mandamus to compel the school board to do the thing which he has done after their default. The fact that, at a little different stage in the proceedings, mandamus would lie is no answer to the argument of the plaintiff here that, when he has expended money, time, and effort in performing a duty enjoined by statute upon the boards, he is entitled to receive a money reimbursement.

The demurrer will be overruled, and the judgment of the lower courts reversed.

Judgment reversed.

NOTE

Contrast Noble v. Williams, *supra* p. 76.

UPTON-ON-SEVERN RURAL DISTRICT
COUNCIL v. POWELL
1 All E.R. 220 (C.A. 1942)

Appeal by the defendant from an order of His Honour, Judge Roope Reeve, K.C., the Great Malvern County Court, dated Oct. 13, 1941. The facts are fully set out in the judgment of Lord Greene, M.R.

Vick, K.C.: In the circumstances of the present case, the judge was quite wrong in inferring that any contract has been entered into. There is no evidence of animus contrahendi in anybody at all. The fire brigade went intending to render a gratuitous service. It was only when it was discovered that the fire was in another area that it was decided that a charge should be made. The police officer to whom the appellant telephoned was under a public duty to inform the fire brigade. He was not acting as the agent of the appellant.

Counsel for the respondents was not called upon.

LORD GREENE, M.R.: The appellant lives at Strensham, and in Nov., 1939 a fire broke out in his Dutch barn; he thereupon telephoned to the police inspector at the Upton police office and told him that there was a fire and asked for the fire brigade to be sent. The police inspector telephoned a garage near to the fire station at Upton, which itself had no telephone, the Upton brigade was informed and immediately went to the fire, where it remained for a long time engaged in putting it out. It so happens that, although the appellant's farm is in the Upton police district, it is not in the Upton fire district. It is in the Pershore fire district, and the appellant was entitled to have the services of the Pershore fire brigade without payment. The Upton fire brigade, on the other hand, was entitled to go to a fire outside its area and, if it did so, quite apart from its statutory rights, it could make a contract that it would be entitled to repayment of its expenses.

The sole question here is whether or not any contract was made by which the Upton fire brigade rendered services on an implied promise to pay for them made by or on behalf of the appellant. It appears that some 6 hours after the arrival of the Upton fire brigade, the officer of the Pershore brigade arrived on the scene, but without his brigade; he pointed out to the Upton officer that it was a Pershore fire, and not an Upton fire, but the Upton fire brigade continued rendering services until the next day when the Pershore fire brigade arrived and took over. In the view that I take in this case, what happened in relation to the arrival of the Pershore officer and his conversation with the Upton officer and the subsequent arrival of the Pershore fire brigade has nothing whatever to do with the issue which we have to decide. The county court judge held that the appellant when he rang up the police inspector, asked for the "fire brigade" to be sent. He also held that the inspector summoned the local Upton fire brigade, which was perfectly natural, and that he took the order as being one for the fire brigade with which he was connected. It appears that neither the appellant, nor the police officer, nor the Upton fire brigade, until it was so informed by the Pershore officer, knew that the appellant's farm was, in fact, not in the Upton area, but was in the Pershore area. The county court judge then goes on to find that the inspector passed on the order and sent his fire brigade, and that was the fire brigade, I have no doubt, which the appellant expected. The county court judge said:

> The defendant did not know that if he sent for the Pershore fire brigade what advantage he would have obtained. In my view, there is no escape from the legal liability the defendant has incurred. I think he gave the order for the fire brigade he wanted, and he got it.

Now those findings are attacked, because it is said that, as the defendant did not know what fire brigade area he was in, what he really wanted was to get the fire brigade of his area, whatever it might be. It does not seem to me that there is any justification for attacking the finding of the judge on that basis. What the defendant wanted was somebody to put out his fire, and put it out as quickly as possible, and in ringing up the Upton police he must have intended that the inspector at Upton would get the Upton fire brigade; that is the brigade which he would naturally ask for when he rang up Upton. Even apart from that, it seems to me quite sufficient if the Upton inspector reasonably so construed the request made to him, and, indeed, I do not see what other construction the inspector could have put upon that request. It follows, therefore, that on any view the appellant must be treated as having asked for the Upton fire brigade. That request having been made to the Upton fire brigade by a person who was asking for its services, does it prevent there being a contractual relationship merely because the Upton fire brigade, which responds to that request and renders the services, thinks, at the time it starts out and for a considerable time afterwards, that the farm in question is in its area, as the officer in charge appears to have thought? In my opinion, that can make no difference. The real truth of the matter is that the appellant wanted the services of Upton; he asked for the services of Upton — that is the request he made — and Upton, in response to that request, provided those services. He cannot afterwards turn round and say: "Although I wanted Upton, although I did not concern myself when I asked for Upton as to whether I was entitled to get free services, or whether I would have to pay for them, nevertheless, when it turns out that Upton can demand payment, I am not going to pay them, because

Upton were under the erroneous impression that they were rendering gratuitous services in their own area." That, it seems to me, would be quite wrong on principle. In my opinion, the county court judge's finding cannot be assailed and the appeal must be dismissed with costs.

NOTE

1. For comments on the case, see 6 Mod. L. Rev. 157 (1943); 58 L.Q. Rev. 296 (1942); 20 Can. B. Rev. 557 (1942); 3 Corbin §§561, 597 (1960). See also Kessler, Some Thoughts on the Evolution of the German Law of Contracts — A Comparative Study, Pt. 1, 22 U.C.L.A.L. Rev. 1066, 1073-1074 (1975).

2. Did defendant intend to pay? Did plaintiff expect to be paid? If there is a contract, has it not been "created by life"?

3. Should the court not have rationalized recovery, if any, in terms of quasi contract? Was Powell unjustly enriched? Consult the *Cotnam* case, *supra* p. 163; 3 Corbin §561 (1960). Is plaintiff entitled to recovery under the Restatmeent of Restitution? Consult §117. Would not the best solution be to let Upton recover from Pershore? But can this be accomplished? Under the reasoning of the *Sommers* case, *supra* p. 168? Consult further Restatement of Restitution §§43, 54, 115; McClary v. Michigan R.R., 102 Mich. 312, 60 N.W. 695 (1894); Johnson v. Boston & Maine R.R., 69 Vt. 521, 38 A. 267 (1897). For an economic justification of the rule, see A. Kronman & R. Posner, The Economics of Contract Law 60-61 (1979).

4. Assume that the fire in Powell's barn was extinguished during Powell's absence by a neighbor at considerable expense. Is the neighbor entitled to compensation? The answer given in Bartholomew v. Jackson, 2 Johnson 28 (N.Y. 1822) is in the negative: if a man humanely bestows his labor and even risks his life in voluntarily preserving his neighbor's house from destruction by fire, the law considers the service rendered gratuitous and therefore no ground for compensation. Is this still true in light of Restatement of Restitution §117?

VICKERY v. RITCHIE
202 Mass. 247, 88 N.E. 835 (1909)

Contract for a balance of $10,467.16 alleged to be due for the erection of a Turkish bath house upon land of the defendant on Carver Street in Boston, with a count upon an alleged contract in writing and another count upon an account annexed. Writ dated January 9, 1904.

In the Superior Court the case was referred to Clarence H. Cooper, Esquire, as auditor. He filed a report containing the findings which are stated in the opinion. The case afterwards was tried before Pierce, J. The defendant introduced no evidence. At the close of the plaintiff's evidence the judge ruled that the plaintiff could not recover, and ordered a verdict for the defendant. The plaintiff alleged exceptions.

KNOWLTON, C.J. This is an action to recover a balance of $10,467.16, alleged to be due to the plaintiff as a contractor, for the construction of a Turkish bath house on land of the defendant. The parties signed duplicate contracts in writing, covering the work. At the time when the plaintiff signed both copies of the contract the defendant's signature was attached, and the contract price therein named was $33,721. When the defendant signed them the contract price stated in each was $23,200. Until the building was completed the plaintiff held a contract under which he was to receive the larger sum, while the defendant held a contract for the same work, under which he was to pay only the smaller sum. This resulted from the fraud of the architect who drew the contracts, and did all the business and made all the payments for the defendant. The contracts were on typewritten sheets, and it is supposed that the architect accomplished the fraud by changing the sheets on which the price was written, before the signing by the plaintiff, and before the delivery to the defendant. The parties did not discover the discrepancy between the two writings until after the building was substantially completed. Each of them acted honestly and in good faith, trusting the statements of the architect. The architect was indicted, but he left the Commonwealth and escaped punishment.

The auditor found that the market value of the labor and materials furnished by the plaintiff, not including the customary charge for the supervision of the work, was $33,499.30, and that their total cost to the plaintiff was $32,950.96. He found that the land and building have cost the defendant much more than their market value. The findings indicate that it was bad judgment on the part of the defendant to build such a structure upon the lot, and that the increase in the market value of the real estate, by reason of that which the plaintiff put upon it, is only $22,000. The failure of the parties to discover the difference between their copies of the contract was caused by the frequently repeated fraudulent representations of the architect to each of them.

The plaintiff and the defendant were mistaken in supposing that they had made a binding contract for the construction of this building. Their minds never met in any agreement about the price. The labor and materials were furnished at the defendant's request and for the defendant's benefit. From this alone the law would imply a contract on the part of the defendant to pay for them. The fact that the parties supposed the price was fixed by a contract, when in fact there was no contract, does not prevent this implication, but leaves it as a natural result of their relations. Both parties understood and agreed that the work should be paid for, and both parties thought that they had agreed upon a price. Their mutual mistake in this particular left them with no express contract by which

their rights and liabilities could be determined. The law implies an obligation to pay for what has been done and furnished under such circumstances, and the defendant, upon whose property the work was done, has
no right to say that it is not to be paid for. The doctrine is not applicable
to work upon real estate alone. The rule would be the same if the work
and materials were used in the repair of a carriage, or of any other article
of personal property, under a supposed contract with the owner, if,
through a mutual mistake as to the supposed agreement upon the price,
the contract became unenforceable. [The discussion of several cases is
omitted.]

If the law implies an agreement to pay, how much is to be paid? There
is but one answer. The fair value of that which was furnished. No other
rule can be applied. Under certain conditions the price fixed by the
contract might control in such cases. In this case there was no price fixed.
[The discussion of several cases is omitted.]

The right of recovery depends upon the plaintiff's having furnished
property or labor, under circumstances which entitle him to be paid for
it, not upon the ultimate benefit to the property of the owner at whose
request it was furnished.

It follows that the plaintiff is entitled to recover the fair value of his
labor and materials.

Exceptions sustained.

NOTE

For an argument that the contract in *Vickery* was an implied-in-fact
contract, see Costigan, Implied-In-Fact Contracts and Mutual Assent, 33
Harv. L. Rev. 376, 386 (1920). In Vickery v. Ritchie, 207 Mass. 318, 93
N.E. 578, 579 (1911), the Massachusetts Supreme Judicial Court refused
to enforce a liquidated damages clause favorable to defendant on the
ground that the supposed contract containing the clause "never took
effect between the parties." Does this mean that its earlier decision was
based on the view that the contract between the parties was one implied
in law?

See 12 Williston §1485 at 315 (1970); Restatement of Restitution §§40,
155; Seavey, Embezzlement by Agent of Two Principals: Contribution, 64
Harv. L. Rev. 431, 435 (1951).

MICHIGAN CENTRAL R.R. v. STATE
85 Ind. App. 557, 155 N.E. 50 (1927)

Action by the Michigan Central Railroad Company against the State
of Indiana. From a judgment for the plaintiff in an unsatisfactory
amount, the plaintiff appeals. Affirmed. By the court in banc.

REMY, J. — On June 10, 1920, and pursuant to §2 of the Appropriation Act of 1919 (Acts 1919 p. 196), the State of Indiana, through its Joint Purchasing Committee, contracted for a year's supply of coal for the Indiana State Prison, a penal institution located at Michigan City, the contract price for the coal being $3.40 per ton, delivered. On October 22, 1920, while the contract was in force, appellant railway company, a carrier of interstate commerce, had in its possession for interstate transportation a carload of coal of the same kind and quality as that contracted for by the state, which coal, by mutual mistake of the carrier and agents of the state, was delivered to the Indiana State Prison and there consumed. This carload of coal at the time and place of its delivery was of the market value of $6.85 per ton. Upon learning of the misdelivery of the coal and its consumption, appellant paid to the consignee of the coal the market value thereof, and demanded of the state that it be reimbursed for the amount so paid. With this demand the state refused to comply. Whereupon appellant commenced this action against the state to recover the market value of the coal. Edward J. Fogarty, Warden of the Indiana State Prison, was joined as a party defendant. In its complaint, appellant specifically waived any action in tort which it may have had. The cause was submitted to the court upon an agreed statement of facts, the substance of which is as above set forth. The court found against the state, but limited recovery to $3.40 per ton, the price of the year's supply of coal as contracted for by the Joint Purchasing Committee, the judgment was so rendered.

Claiming that the amount of the recovery should have been $6.85 per ton, the market value of the coal, and was therefore too small, the railroad company prosecutes this appeal. The state not having assigned cross-errors, the only question for determination by this court is whether, under the facts stipulated, the measure of recovery is the market value of the coal at the time and place of the misdelivery; or, as held by the trial court, the price at which the Joint Purchasing Committee had purchased the year's supply. A decision of the question will require a consideration of the nature and character of the action.

The facts in this case are unusual, as is the legal proceeding. By reason of a mistake of fact, the state received the coal from the carrier, and before the mistake was discovered, the coal had been consumed. Recognizing its liability for the conversion of the coal, the carrier paid to the consignee the market value thereof, and by this action seeks indemnity from the state. That a carrier may recover for a consignment of goods delivered to the wrong person by mistake, in an action against the person who received and retained the goods, is not questioned by appellees, nor can it be (Hudson River, etc., R. Co. v. Lounsberry [1857], 25 Barb. [N.Y.] 597; Johnson v. Gulf, etc., R. Co. [1903], 82 Miss. 452, 34 So. 357; Brown v. Hogson [1811], 4 Taunt. [Eng.] 188; Coles v. Bulman [1848], 6 C.B. [Eng.] 184; Hutchinson, Carriers [3d ed.] §863); nor do appellees question the right of appellants to sue the state in an action of this character. That such an action against the state may be maintained, see, State v. Mutual Life Ins. Co. (1910), 175 Ind. 59, 74, 93 N.E. 213, 42 L.R.A. (N.S.) 256. The state's obligation which forms the basis of this action is what is termed quasi contractual. Though frequently referred to by the courts as equitable in character, it is a legal obligation on the part of the obligor to make restitution in value, that is, to pay the equivalent of the benefit received and unjustly enjoyed. Woodward, Law of Quasi Contracts, §3; Quasi-Contractual Obligations, 21 Yale Law J. 533; Grossbier v. Chicago, etc., R. Co. (1921), 173 Wis. 503, 181 N.W. 746.

The legal obligation of the state in this action is to pay to appellant a sum equal to the benefit to the state which resulted from the misdelivery. The benefit is not fixed by any agreement, for there had been no agreement by the state as to this carload of coal; and since this is not an action in tort, the rules governing the measure of damages in actions ex delicto are not controlling. In actions to enforce quasi-contractual obligations, the general rule is that the measure of recovery is the value of the benefit received by the defendant (Bowen v. Detroit Union Railway [1920], 212 Mich. 432, 180 N.W. 495; Moore v. Richardson [1902], 68 N.J. Law 305, 53 Atl. 1032); but it cannot be said that to this rule there are no exceptions. If, for example, the carrier has settled with the owner of a consignment of goods which had been misdelivered, the settlement being for a sum less than the market value, it would not be contended that the carrier could recover the market value in an action against the person who had received the goods. It is unnecessary, however, to discuss the exceptions to the general rule.

Quasi-contractual obligations usually arise between the parties to illegal or unenforceable contracts. This action is between the parties whose mutual mistake resulted in the conversion of the coal. One of the parties to the conversion, having made restitution to the owner of the property converted, is seeking indemnity from the other. See Keener, Quasi-Contracts 396; Woodward, Law of Quasi-Contracts §259. Furthermore, the defendant in the action is the State of Indiana against which an action in tort could not have been maintained. Acts 1889 p. 265, §1550 Burns 1926. The obligation forming the basis of the action is essentially an obligation to restore a benefit received by the defendant, and not to compensate the plaintiff for damages sustained. The obligation rests upon the principle that the defendant — the state in this case — cannot be allowed, in equity and good conscience, to keep what it has obtained. But affirmatively, the state must restore what in good conscience it cannot retain. The state having contracted, in the way provided by the statute, for a year's supply of coal for its penal institution, at the price of $3.40 per ton, the state's representatives could not, by their mistake in receiving from a common carrier coal of a like quality, but which had been sold and consigned to another, obligate the state to pay the carrier for the coal a price in excess of the state's contract price, the carrier having been a party to the mistake. It would be contrary to sound public policy to require the state to pay more for coal delivered and received by mistake than it would be required to pay under a contract resulting from competitive bids. We hold that the measure of recovery is the state's contract price, and not the market value of the coal at the time and place of the misdelivery.

Affirmed.

MARTIN v. CAMPANARO, 156 F.2d 127 (2d Cir. 1946). Plaintiffs, among them Campanaro, had been working for the Suburban Bus Company under a series of collective contracts effective for one year, from 1937 to 1944. Prior to the expiration of the last of the contracts the employees' union, Amalgamated, notified the employer that the old contract should be revised. Negotiations continued for almost a year after the contract had expired; the employees continued to work at the old pay scale. When bargaining broke down the dispute was referred to the War Labor Board which finally entered an order recommending a pay increase retroactive to the day when the last contract had expired. Martin, the trustee in bankruptcy of the bus company which had become bankrupt before the issuance of the order of the War Labor Board, refused to comply with the order. Thereupon the employees who had been discharged in the meantime brought a group action to recover the increase in wages as recommended. The District court held that the claimants were not entitled to extra compensation since the order of the Board was not enforceable against the bus company. It found that the implied-in-fact contract created by the conduct of the parties contained the same terms as the old contract. The Court of Appeals reversed. Although affirming the ruling of the lower court as to the effect of the board order, it held the implied-in-fact contract to have called for payment measured by the reasonable value of the services rendered. It therefore ordered a new hearing to determine the value of these services. In the course of his opinion Frank, J. made the following observations: ". . . A contract implied in fact derives from the 'presumed' intention of the parties as indicated by their conduct. When an agreement expires by its terms, if, without more, the parties continue to perform as theretofore, an implication arises that they have mutually assented to a new contract containing the same provisions as the old. . . ." But such implication is inappropriate here since the union was seeking higher wages.

Judge Frank added a lengthy footnote (n.5), which is worth reprinting in part:

"This conclusion might be stated thus: The claimants are entitled to recover on a quantum meruit basis. But 'quantum meruit' is ambiguous; it may mean (1) that there is a contract 'implied in fact' to pay the reasonable value of the services, or (2) that, to prevent unjust enrichment, the claimant may recover on a quasi-contract (an 'as if' contract) for that reasonable value. It has been suggested that the latter is a rule-of-thumb measure of damages adopted in quasi contract cases where the actual unjust enrichment or benefit to the defendant is too difficult to prove; see Costigan, Implied-in-Fact Contracts, (1920) 33 Harv. Law Rev. 376, 387.

"The confusion involved in the use of the old phrase "implied contracts' to label both those 'implied in fact' and those 'implied in law' (now called 'quasi contracts') has not been entirely obliterated. Nor is it easy to eradicate. Thus it is said that a quasi contract is 'imposed by law . . . irrespective of, and sometimes in violation of, . . . intention' and therefore not a 'true' contract, while a 'true' contract (including a contract 'implied in fact') arises from 'intent'. Williston, §3; Woodward, The Law of Quasi Contracts (1913) §4. But, where the courts apply the 'objective' (i.e., behavioristic) test, they hold that a 'true' contract exists despite the actual ('subjective') contrary intent of the parties; Williston, §21; Restatement, Contracts §§70, 71, 503; Hotchkiss v. National City Bank, D.C., 200 F. 287, 293; cf. Ricketts v. Pennsylvania R. Co., 153 F.2d 757, 760, 761, 762, C.C.A.2d. In such cases, it might be said that a 'true' contract, paradoxically, is but a kind of quasi-contract — an 'as if' contract — since it is 'imposed by law irrespective of, and . . . in violation of, intent.' In such cases, the courts, when a certain kind of conduct occurs, create an unintended legal 'relation' (or 'status') fully as much as if the intent to create it had been present."

NOTE

Consult the excerpts from Judge Frank's opinion in Ricketts v. Pennsylvania R.R., *infra* p. 867.

Section 3.   Indefinite Contracts

"It is a commonplace of the law," Williston informs us, "that mutual assent is necessary for the formation of contracts, at least unless they are under seal." Mutual Assent in the Formation of Contracts, 14 Ill. L. Rev. 85, 85 (1919). There is no contract without assent. But once the objective manifestations of assent are present, their author is bound, even if he did not read the contract or understand the meaning of its terms. Cf. Restatement Second §26. Otherwise, to paraphrase Holmes, no rational theory of contract can be constructed. And, to paraphrase Corbin, since a court cannot enforce an agreement without knowing what the agreement is, its terms must be certain or at least susceptible of being made certain. 1 Corbin §95 (1963 & Supp. 1984). An agreement, therefore, by the parties "to enter into negotiations, and agree upon the terms of a contract, if they can, cannot be made the basis of a cause of action." Shepard v. Carpenter, 54 Minn. 153, 156, 55 N.W. 906, 906 (1893). In their search for an agreement, the courts habitually use an offer and acceptance approach. This assumes that every contract can be analyzed into offer and acceptance. On this view, an agreement is said to be made when one party accepts an offer made by the other party. Restatement Second §§22, 23. The first step is to determine the addressee of the offer and to find out whether he communicated an acceptance that matches the offer. Within the framework of this analysis, it is quite important to determine whether the person who took the initiative "really" made an offer or merely invited the other party to make an offer, so that what looks like an acceptance is in reality an offer which itself needs an acceptance. Restatement Second §§24, 26, 33, 50. It is the purpose of this and several other sections to test the range of these statements.

Anxious not to incur the reproach of being a destroyer of bargains, modern contract law has abandoned the idea advanced during the last century that a contract presupposes a meeting of minds in full and final agreement, a consensus of mind. All that is required is the mutual manifestation of assent. The law, furthermore, permits the parties to keep the arrangement flexible[39] and takes into account that businessmen often "record the most important agreements in crude and summary fashion." Hillas & Co. v. Arcos, Ltd., 147 L.T.R. (n.s.) 503, 514 (H.L. 1932). In consummating a contract, parties frequently do not make express provision for all its essential terms. Without stating so explicitly, they often expect that the express terms of their contract are to be supplemented by terms based on the "surrounding circumstances." This is particularly true in fields that are governed by trade custom and usage. In general, courts have been well aware of this way of doing business and, on the whole, they have successfully carried out the intention of the parties with the help of the device of "interpretation." Upon being satisfied that an agreement was intended or that one party justifiably relied on the deal and the other party ought to have known that he would so rely, the courts have been ready to supply missing terms and to give concrete meaning to indefinite terms, provided (it is often said), that objective criteria for establishing terms are available in the agreement itself, or that such terms can be inferred from a prior or subsequent course of dealing, or accepted business practices. To be sure, the mere fact that the parties thought they had a contract is not enough to turn an agreement utterly lacking in definiteness into a contract, but before courts are ready to strike down a bargain, "indefiniteness must reach the point where construction becomes futile." Cohen & Sons, Inc. v. Lurie Woolen Co., 232 N.Y. 112, 114, 133 N.E. 370, 371 (1921).

---

39. On flexible pricing, see U.C.C. §2-305, *infra* p. 182.

Before courts take this step, however, and abandon hope of discovering the intentions of the parties, they frequently resort to using the "hypothetical intentions" of the parties, if this technique of filling gaps and preserving the contract can be reconciled with notions of fairness and justice. This is particularly true for long-term contracts where the parties have failed to foresee the contingency and therefore did not provide for it. In the language of L. Hand, J., "[a]s courts become increasingly sure of themselves, interpretation more and more involves imaginative projection of the express purpose upon situations for which the parties did not provide and which they did not have in mind."[40]

The attitude of modern law was anticipated if not reflected in a passage written by Corbin more than fifty years ago:

> The legal relations consequent upon offer and acceptance are not wholly dependent, even upon the reasonable meaning of the words and acts of the parties. The law determines these relations in the light of subsequent circumstances, these often being totally unforeseen by the parties. In such cases it is sometimes said that the law will create that relation which the parties would have intended had they foreseen. The fact is, however, that the decision will depend upon the notions of the court as to policy, welfare, justice, right and wrong, such notions often being inarticulate and subconscious.[41]

Both the Uniform Commercial Code and the Restatement Second have attempted to consolidate the gains made by progressive case law towards flexibility and fairness. See U.C.C. §§1-201(3), 1-205, 2-204, 2-207, 2-208, 2-305. For parallel and more elaborate provisions of the Restatement Second, see §§22, 33, 34, 202, 204, 205, 221, 362.

The attitude with regard to the offer and acceptance paradigm is reflected in U.C.C. §2-204, which reads as follows:

(1)   A contract for sale of goods may be made in any manner sufficient to show agreement, including conduct by both parties which recognizes the existence of such a contract.

(2)   An agreement sufficient to constitute a contract for sale may be found even though the movement of its making is undetermined.

(3)   Even though one or more terms are left open a contract for sale does not fail for indefiniteness if the parties have intended to make a con-

---

40. But, the sentence immediately following ends on a note of caution. "Out of the rivers of ink that have been spilled upon that subject I know nothing that has emerged which enlightens us beyond the caution that departure from the text — necessary as it is — must always be made with circumspection." L. Hand dissenting in L. N. P. Jackson & Co. v. Royal Norwegian Government, 177 F.2d 694, 702 (2d Cir. 1949). See further the discussion in E. Farnsworth, Contracts 7, 16 (1982) (In long-term contracts, unforeseeability is endemic).

41. Corbin, Offer and Acceptance, and Some of the Resulting Legal Relations, 26 Yale L.J. 169, 206 (1917); Atiyah, Contract and Fair Exchange, 35 U. Toronto L.J. (1985).

tract and there is a reasonably certain basis for giving an appropriate remedy.[42]

Subsection 3 has found further elaboration in U.C.C. §2-305, dealing with open-price terms.[43]

Section 204 of the Restatement Second contains a parallel provision. It provides that when the parties to a bargain sufficiently defined to be a contract have not agreed with respect to a term that is essential to a determination of their rights and duties, the court will supply a term that is reasonable in the circumstances. See further §§33, 34, which deal with the requirement of certainty.[44]

For a criticism of U.C.C. §2-204(3), see Williston, The Law of Sales in the Proposed Uniform Commercial Code, 63 Harv. L. Rev. 561, 576 (1950), advocating that the rule should be limited to the omission of "minor" terms: "If the parties choose to leave important terms open and nevertheless 'intend a contract,' I think their only reliance should be on business honor." This position has been rejected in Pennsylvania Co. v. Wilmington Trust Co., 39 Del. Ch. 453, 166 A.2d 63 (1960); aff'd, 40 Del. Ch. 140, 172 A.2d 63 (1961), a bill for specific performance by plaintiff-buyer against the trustee-seller of corporate stock. Motions of both parties for summary judgment were denied by the chancellor since the submitted writings did not clearly show intention to contract. The decision was affirmed by the higher court. Since both courts indicated that

42. See Restatement Second §§22, 23, 33, 34, 362. The requirement of certainty laid down in §33 "may be affected by the dispute which arises and by the remedy sought" as Comment 6 points out. Section 34 deals with certainty and choice of terms and effect of performance or reliance.

43. Section 2-305 reads as follows:

(1) The parties if they so intend can conclude a contract for sale even though the price is not settled. In such a case the price is a reasonable price at the time for delivery if
  (a) nothing is said as to price; or
  (b) the price is left to be agreed by the parties and they fail to agree; or
  (c) The price is to be fixed in terms of some agreed market or other standard as set or recorded by a third person or agency and it is not so set or recorded.
(2) A price to be fixed by the seller or by the buyer means a price for him to fix in good faith.
(3) When a price left to be fixed otherwise than by agreement of the parties fails to be fixed through fault of one party the other may at his option treat the contract as cancelled or himself fix a reasonable price.
(4) Where, however, the parties intend not to be bound unless the price be fixed or agreed and it is not fixed or agreed there is no contract. In such a case the buyer must return any goods already received or if unable so to do must pay their reasonable value at the time of delivery and the seller must return any portion of the price paid on account.

44. For the rationale behind the U.C.C. rule, see E. Farnsworth, Contracts 202-204 (1982). Should it be extended by analogy? To a renewal option in a lease? Consult Joseph Martin, Inc. Delicatessen v. Schumacher, 52 Misc. 2d 105, 436 N.Y.S.2d 247, 417 N.E.2d 541 (1982)

the question of intention was a triable fact, the defendant settled with the plaintiff. But the defendant was later held liable to the beneficiaries of the trust for the amount of the settlement. Wilmington Trust Co. v. Coulter, 40 Del. Ch. 548, 260 A.2d 441 (1964). We owe this reference to Knapp, Enforcing a Contract to Bargain, 44 N.Y.U. L. Rev. 673, 718 n.159 (1969). U.C.C. §2-204 and its comment were the basis of the decision in the *Pennsylvania Co.* case. The comment to subsection (3) is worth reading:

> Subsection (3) states the principle as to "open terms" underlying later sections of the Article. If the parties intend to enter into a binding agreement, this subsection recognizes that agreement is valid in law, despite missing terms, if there is any reasonably certain basis for granting a remedy. The test is not certainty as to what the parties were to do nor as to the exact amount of damages due the plaintiff. Nor is the fact that one or more terms are left to be agreed upon enough of itself to defeat an otherwise adequate agreement. Rather, commercial standards on the point of "indefiniteness" are intended to be applied, this Act making provision elsewhere for missing terms needed for performance, open price, remedies and the like.

Furthermore, an agreement of the parties to reduce their formal understanding to a writing does not necessarily mean that until this has been done either party can back out with impunity. The writing envisaged may, according to the intention of the parties as interpreted, constitute a mere memorial whose absence will not prevent the formation of a contract. Restatement Second §27. Llewellyn, Our Case-Law of Contracts (pt. 1), Offer and Acceptance, 48 Yale L.J. 1, 30-40 (1938).

YOUNG AND ASHBURNHAM'S CASE
3 Leon. 161, 74 Eng. Rep. 606 (C.P. 1587)

For a report of the case, see p. 146 *supra*.

LEFKOWITZ v. GREAT MINNEAPOLIS SURPLUS STORE, INC.
251 Minn. 188, 86 N.W.2d 689 (1957)

MURPHY, Justice. — This is an appeal from an order of the Municipal Court of Minneapolis denying the motion of the defendant for amended findings of fact, or, in the alternative, for a new trial. The order for judgment awarded the plaintiff the sum of $138.50 as damages for breach of contract.

This case grows out of the alleged refusal of the defendant to sell to the plaintiff a certain fur piece which it had offered for sale in a newspaper advertisement. It appears from the record that on April 6, 1956, the defendant published the following advertisement in a Minneapolis newspaper:

SATURDAY 9 A. M. SHARP
3 BRAND NEW
FUR COATS
Worth to $100.00
First Come
First Served
$1
EACH

On April 13, the defendant again published an advertisement in the same newspaper as follows:

SATURDAY 9 A. M.
2 BRAND NEW PASTEL
MINK 3-SKIN SCARFS
Selling for $89.50
Out they go
Saturday. Each $1.00
1 BLACK LAPIN STOLE
Beautiful,
worth $139.50 $1.00
FIRST COME
FIRST SERVED

The record supports the findings of the court that on each of the Saturdays following the publication of the above-described ads the plaintiff was the first to present himself at the appropriate counter in the defendant's store and on each occasion demanded the coat and the stole so advertised and indicated his readiness to pay the sale price of $1. On both occasions, the defendant refused to sell the merchandise to the plaintiff, stating on the first occasion that by a "house rule" the offer was intended for women only and sales would not be made to men, and on the second visit that plaintiff knew defendant's house rules.

The trial court properly disallowed plaintiff's claim for the value of the fur coats since the value of these articles was speculative and uncertain. The only evidence of value was the advertisement itself to the effect that the coats were "Worth to $100.00," how much less being speculative especially in view of the price for which they were offered for sale. With reference to the offer of the defendant on April 13, 1956, to sell the "1

Black Lapin Stole . . . worth $139.50 . . ." the trial court held that the value of this article was established and granted judgment in favor of the plaintiff for that amount less the $1 quoted purchase price.

The defendant contends that a newspaper advertisement offering items of merchandise for sale at a named price is a "unilateral offer" which may be withdrawn without notice. . . .

The defendant relies principally on Craft v. Elder & Johnston Co. [34 Ohio L.A. 603, 38 N.E.2d 416]. In that case, the court discussed the legal effect of an advertisement offering for sale, as a one-day special, an electric sewing machine at a named price. The view was expressed that the advertisement was (34 Ohio L.A. 605, 38 N.E.[2d] 417) "not an offer made to any specific person but was made to the public generally. Thereby it would be properly designated as a unilateral offer and not being supported by any consideration could be withdrawn at will and without notice." It is true that such an offer may be withdrawn before acceptance. Since all offers are by their nature unilateral because they are necessarily made by one party or on one side in the negotiation of a contract, the distinction made in that decision between a unilateral offer and a unilateral contract is not clear. On the facts before us we are concerned with whether the advertisement constituted an offer, and, if so, whether the plaintiff's conduct constituted an acceptance.

There are numerous authorities which hold that a particular advertisement in a newspaper or circular letter relating to a sale of articles may be construed by the court as constituting an offer, acceptance of which would complete a contract. [Citations.]

The test of whether a binding obligation may originate in advertisements addressed to the general public is "whether the facts show that some performance was promised in positive terms in return for something requested." 1 Williston, Contracts (Rev. ed.) §27.

The authorities above cited emphasize that, where the offer is clear, definite, and explicit, and leaves nothing open for negotiation, it constitutes an offer, acceptance of which will complete the contract. . . .

Whether in any individual instance a newspaper advertisement is an offer rather than an invitation to make an offer depends on the legal intention of the parties and the surrounding circumstances. Annotation, 157 A.L.R. 744, 751; 77 C.J.S., Sales, §25b; 17 C.J.S., Contracts, §389. We are of the view on the facts before us that the offer by the defendant of the sale of the Lapin fur was clear, definite, and explicit, and left nothing open for negotiation. The plaintiff having successfully managed to be the first one to appear at the seller's place of business to be served, as requested by the advertisement, and having offered the stated purchase price of the article, he was entitled to performance on the part of the defendant. We think the trial court was correct in holding that there was in the conduct of the parties a sufficient mutuality of obligation to constitute a contract of sale.

The defendant contends that the offer was modified by a "house rule" to the effect that only women were qualified to receive the bargains advertised. The advertisement contained no such restriction. This objection may be disposed of briefly by stating that, while an advertiser has the right at any time before acceptance to modify his offer, he does not have the right, after acceptance, to impose new or arbitrary conditions not contained in the published offer. Payne v. Lautz Bros. & Co., 166 N.Y.S. 844, 848; Mooney v. Daily News Co., 116 Minn. 212, 133 N.W. 573, 37 L.R.A. (N.S.) 183.

Affirmed.

NOTE

Consult 56 Mich. L. Rev. 1016. On bait advertising, see 69 Yale L.J. 830 (1960); see further New York General Business Law ch. 22-A.

A sees in the display window of a shop an article marked $5. When he asks for it, the shopkeeper realizes that the wrong price tag has been affixed and that the article should have been marked $15. He refuses to sell the article for $5. Is he bound? No, according to Professor Winfield, commenting on the South African case of Crawley v. Rex, [1909] Transvaal L.R. 1005. Some Aspects of Offer and Acceptance, 55 L.Q. Rev. 499, 516-518 (1939): "a shop is a place for bargaining and not for compulsory sales." See further, Pharmaceutical Society of Great Britain v. Boots Cash Chemists (Southern) Ltd., [1953] 1 Q.B. 401; Kahn, Some Mysteries of Offer and Acceptance, 72 S.A.L.J. 246, 251 (1955).

A newspaper invites its readers to submit letters on matters of public interest to its letters-to-the-editor column. A reader sends in a signed letter on a campaign issue, giving his address. Is the paper in breach of contract if it refuses to publish it? Wall v. World Pub. Co., 263 P.2d 1010 (Okla. 1953).

On sales by auction, see U.C.C. §2-328.

JENKINS TOWEL SERVICE, INC. v. FIDELITY-PHILADELPHIA TRUST CO.

400 Pa. 98, 161 A.2d 334 (1960)

[The Trust Company, after many unsuccessful attempts to sell a piece of real estate owned as trustee, on June 18, 1959 circulated a letter in which it requested interested parties to submit sealed bids for the property. The letter provided that on June 24, 1959 the bids were to be opened and that an agreement of sale would be tendered "to the highest acceptable bidder whose offer is in excess of $92,000." The Trust Company reserved to itself the right to "approve or disapprove of any or all offers, or to withdraw the properties from the market." It also emphasized its fiduciary duty to recommend "the most advantageous offer." Plaintiff submitted a bid of $95,600 meeting all the terms of the letter. The only other bid was a bid by the Esso Standard Oil Corporation for the same amount conditioned however on a change in zoning and subject to approval by its home office in New York. When the Trust Company refused to effect an agreement of sale with plaintiff, preferring Esso to plaintiff, the latter sued for specific performance. The Court of Common Pleas dismissed the bill and plaintiff appealed.]

BELL, J. . . . The rights of the parties depend upon the proper construction of Fidelity's letter of June 18, 1959. Plaintiff claims the letter was an offer, which it unconditionally accepted. Defendants claim that the letter was merely "preliminary negotiations" and "an invitation to bid."

Fidelity's letter of June 18 is ambiguous and therefore it must be interpreted most strongly against the Fidelity, which drew it: Betterman v. American Stores Co., 367 Pa. 193, 80 A.2d 66. [Quotations from the case and several others are omitted.]

Plaintiff's sealed bid of $95,600 was unequivocal, unconditional, and in full compliance with all the terms and conditions set forth by the Fidelity in its letter-offer dated June 18, 1959. On the other hand the bid of Esso Standard Oil Company was conditional and qualified. Esso's bid was not an acceptance of the offer made by Fidelity; on the contrary it was a rejection of this offer and a counter-offer. Restatement, Contracts, §60, and particularly comment a; §27, Illustration 3. It is clear that plaintiff was the only party which accepted the Fidelity's offer.

If, as defendants contend, Fidelity's letter of June 18 was merely an invitation to prospective purchasers who had been negotiating unsuccessfully for several years to submit a higher bid or offer which it could accept or reject in its sole and arbitrary discretion, why did Fidelity ask for "sealed bids" from all interested parties on or before June 24, 1959, and further state "at that time the bids will be opened and an *Agreement of Sale tendered* to the highest acceptable bidder, provided the offer is in excess of $92,000 cash, free and clear of all brokerage commissions," and then specify in detail the other provisions which were to be incorporated in the agreement of sale? On its face, and especially in the light of the prior negotiations, the surrounding circumstances and the objects which the parties apparently had in view, the contention of defendants that this was merely an invitation to bid, which Fidelity could reject in its unfettered discretion, is unreasonable.

In an attempt to support Fidelity's construction and position, defendants have overlooked not only the law as to the interpretation of a contract which must be considered in its entirety, but also the most important provision, viz. that after the bids are opened it will tender to

the highest acceptable bidder[45] an agreement of sale, the details of which
are set forth in Fidelity's letter of June 18.

Defendants rely upon the statement in Fidelity's letter that it was
acting as fiduciary and was "obligated to recommend the offer which it
believed most advantageous to its estate." This contention is devoid of
merit. Plaintiff unconditionally and unqualifiedly accepted all the terms
and conditions of Fidelity's offer, and no other party did; and there was
no higher or more advantageous offer. Defendants also rely upon the
following sentence — "The Trustees, of course, reserve the right to approve or disapprove of any and all offers, or to withdraw the properties
from the market." This sentence standing alone is what creates a possible
ambiguity. This sentence must be interpreted, we repeat, by considering
the surrounding circumstances, the objects Fidelity apparently had in
view, and the contract in its entirety, and if there is any ambiguity which
is reasonably susceptible of two interpretations, the ambiguity must be
resolved against the Fidelity which drew the letter-offer. So interpreted,
we believe the sentence means that Fidelity can withdraw the properties
from the market at any time before the opening of the sealed bids, and
can approve or disapprove any offer which does not *fully* comply with all
the conditions set forth by the Fidelity, or which complies but adds unsatisfactory terms. . . .

We are convinced that the letter of Fidelity Trust Company dated June
18, 1959, was an offer of the properties in question by Fidelity, subject to
the terms and conditions therein set forth and that the offer was duly and
unconditionally accepted by plaintiff alone. The Court below therefore
erred in sustaining the defendants' preliminary objections and in dismissing plaintiff's amended bill of complaint. If the defendants are unable to
controvert the facts set forth in the amended complaint, the plaintiff
should be awarded specific performance of the contract.

Decree reversed with a procedendo at the cost of the trust estate of
which Fidelity-Philadelphia Trust Company is trustee or co-trustee.

Dissenting Opinion by Mr. Justice BENJAMIN R. JONES: The crux of my
disagreement with the majority of this Court lies in the interpretation of
the letter of June 18, 1959 from Fidelity to Jenkins. The majority construes this letter as a firm *offer* on the part of Fidelity to sell this real estate
to the highest bidder, whereas I construe this letter as an *invitation for an
offer* to be submitted to purchase this real estate.

Fidelity held title to this property as a fiduciary: such fact, known to
Jenkins, required that in the disposal of such property Fidelity exercise a
high degree of care: Herbert Estate, 356 Pa. 107, 110, 51 A.2d 753. In
recognition of its fiduciary duty, Fidelity warned Jenkins that, as a fiduci-

45. There is no contention that plaintiff was not acceptable.

ary, it was "obligated to *recommend* the offer which it believes most advantageous to its Estate." (Emphasis added).

Four different times the letter employs the words "offer" or "offers" to describe that which Jenkins is to submit. The letter requests the addressee to "forward your highest offer"; it states that all "*offers*" were to be made on a cash basis: it directs that a check should accompany the offer "in the amount of at least 10% of the *offer*"; lastly, Fidelity reserved the right to approve or disapprove of "any or all *offers*."

The majority bases its interpretation of the letter as an "offer" on two facets of its language: first, the letter asks for "sealed bids" and, second, the letter state that "at that time [June 24, 1959] the bids will be opened and an Agreement of Sale tendered". A "sealed bid" is simply an "offer" of a "bid" submitted in such form that its contents are concealed until the time of opening, a cautionary measure which insures to bidders an equality of treatment at the hands of the person who invites such offers or bids. The mere fact that a "bid" is sealed does not determine whether the bid is an "offer" or "an acceptance of an offer." The employment of the word "sealed" adds no magic to the situation.

Had the letter stated an "Agreement of Sale [will be] tendered to the highest bidder" the majority view *might* be supportable, but the majority overlooks an all-important word in the phrase actually employed, i.e., the word "acceptable." An Agreement of Sale was not to be tendered to "the *highest* bidder," but to "the *highest acceptable* bidder." The word "acceptable" certainly and clearly modifies the word "highest" and reveals a clear intent on the part of Fidelity that an agreement of sale will be tendered to the highest bidder *only if such bidder is "acceptable."* This phrase does support not the majority, but my view that *Fidelity* reserved the right of rejection of any bid that was not *acceptable* to it.

Finally, Fidelity's letter expressly states: "The Trustees, of course, reserve the right to approve or disapprove of any or all offers, or to withdraw the properties from the market." The majority states that this "sentence means that Fidelity can withdraw the properties from the market at any time before the opening of the sealed bids, and can approve or disapprove any offer which does not *fully* comply with all the conditions set forth by Fidelity, or which complies but adds unsatisfactory terms." Such a construction is absolutely unjustified under the clear language employed by Fidelity. If a bid did not *fully* comply with the terms of the letter, or, if it complied, but added any terms, whether satisfactory or unsatisfactory, such a bid, even if called an "acceptance," would not constitute an acceptance to any offer contained in the letter. As to the interpretation by the majority that Fidelity's right to withdraw ceased at the time the sealed bids were opened, such a construction rewrites the language of the letter and imposes on Fidelity's part a condition judge-created and not Fidelity intended and expressed.

If the English language ever was effectively employed to express a fiduciary's reservation of the right to reject any and all bids it appears in this letter. Fundamental concepts inherent in the law of contracts should not be lightly cast aside for the sake of expediency in the determination of a particular case. Instead of construing this letter as *written* the majority, under the guise of a supposed ambiguity of language, now undertakes to rewrite the letter and to create a contract where no contract exists.

I, accordingly, dissent.

NOTE

Besides the Trust Co., defendants included Esso and an agent of Esso. In addition to specific performance, plaintiff prayed for an injunction restraining the defendants from seeking a change in the zoning to permit the erection of a gasoline station.

MOULTON v. KERSHAW
59 Wis. 316, 18 N.W. 172 (1884)

[The defendants, dealers in salt in the city of Milwaukee, including salt of the Michigan Salt Association wrote to the plaintiff, also a dealer in salt in the city of La Crosse, the following letter:

Dear Sir: In consequence of a rupture in the salt trade, we are authorized to offer Michigan fine salt, in full car-load lots of eighty to ninety-five bbls., delivered at your city, at 85c. per bbl., to be shipped per C. & N.W.R.R. Co. only. At this price it is a bargain, as the price in general remains unchanged. Shall be pleased to receive your order.

Plaintiff immediately wired as follows: "Your letter of yesterday received and noted. You may ship me two thousand (2,000) barrels Michigan fine salt, as offered in your letter. Answer."

Defendants on the receipt of telegram withdrew the offer and failed to ship the salt. The defendants interposed a general demurrer to plaintiff's suit for damages. The Circuit Court overruled the demurrer and the defendants appealed.]

TAYLOR, J. The only question presented is whether the appellants' letter, and the telegram sent by the respondent in reply thereto, constitute a contract for the sale of 2,000 barrels of Michigan fine salt by the appellants to the respondent at the price named in such letter.

We are very clear that no contract was perfected by the order telegraphed by the respondent in answer to appellants' letter. The learned counsel for the respondent clearly appreciated the necessity of putting a construction upon the letter which is not apparent on its face, and in their complaint have interpreted the letter to mean that the appellants by said letter made an express offer to sell the respondent, on the terms stated, such reasonable amount of salt as he might order, and as the appellants might reasonably expect him to order, in response thereto. If in order to entitle the plaintiff to recover in this action it is necessary to prove these allegations then it seems clear to us that the writings between the parties do not show the contract. It is not insisted by the learned counsel for the respondent that any recovery can be had unless a proper construction of the letter and telegram constitute a binding contract between the parties. The alleged contract being for the sale and delivery of personal property of a value exceeding $50, is void by the statute of frauds, unless in writing. Sec. 2308. R.S. 1878.

The counsel for the respondent claims that the letter of appellants is an offer to sell to the respondent, on the terms mentioned, any reasonable quantity of Michigan fine salt that he might see fit to order, not less than one car-load. On the other hand, the counsel for the appellants claim that the letter is not an offer to sell any specific quantity of salt, but simply a letter such as a business man would send out to customers or those with whom he desired to trade, soliciting their patronage. To give the letter of appellants the construction claimed for it by the learned counsel for the respondent, would introduce such an element of uncertainty into the contract as would necessarily render its enforcement a matter of difficulty, and in every case the jury trying the case would be called upon to determine whether the quantity ordered was such as the appellants might reasonably expect from the party. This question would necessarily involve an inquiry into the nature and extent of the business of the person to whom the letter was addressed, as well as to the extent of the business of the appellants. So that it would be a question of fact for the jury in each case to determine whether there was a binding contract between the parties. And this question would not in any way depend upon the language used in the written contract, but upon proofs to be made outside of the writings. As the only communications between the parties, upon which a contract can be predicated, are the letter and the reply of the respondent, we must look to them, and nothing else, in order to determine whether there was a contract in fact. We are not at liberty to help out the written contract, if there be one, by adding by parol evidence additional facts to help out the writing so as to make out a contract not expressed therein. If the letter of the appellant is an offer to sell salt to the respondent on the terms stated, then it must be held to be an offer to sell any quantity at the option of the respondent not less than one car-load. The difficulty and injustice of construing the letter into such an offer is so apparent that the learned counsel for the respondent do not insist upon it, and consequently insist that it ought to be construed as an offer to sell such quantity as the appellants, from their knowledge of the business of the respondents might reasonably expect him to order.

Rather than introduce such an element of uncertainty into the contract, we deem it much more reasonable to construe the letter as a simple notice to those dealing in salt that the appellants were in a condition to supply that article for the prices named, and requested the person to whom it was addressed to deal with them. This case is one where it is eminently proper to heed the injunction of Justice Foster in the opinion in Lyman v. Robinson, 14 Allen, 254: "That care should always be taken not to construe as an agreement letters which the parties intended only as preliminary negotiations."

We do not wish to be understood as holding that a party may not be bound by an offer to sell personal property, where the amount or quantity is left to be fixed by the person to whom the offer is made, when the offer is accepted and the amount or quantity fixed before the offer is withdrawn. We simply hold that the letter of the appellants in this case was not such an offer. If the letter had said to the respondent we will sell you all the Michigan fine salt you will order, at the price and on the terms named, then it is undoubtedly the law that the appellants would have been bound to deliver any reasonable amount the respondent might have ordered, possibly any amount, or make good their default in damages. The case cited by the counsel decided by the California supreme court (Keller v. Ybarru, 3 Cal., 147) was an offer of this kind with an additional limitation. The defendant in that case had a crop growing grapes, and he offered to pick from the vines and deliver to the plaintiff, at defendant's vineyard, so many grapes then growing in said vineyard as the plaintiff should wish to take during the present year at ten cents per pound on delivery. The plaintiff, within the time and before the offer was withdrawn, notified the defendant that he wished to take 1,900 pounds of his grapes on the terms stated. The court held there was a contract to deliver the 1,900 pounds. In this case the fixing of the quantity was left to the person to whom the offer was made, but the amount which the defendant offered, beyond which he could not be bound, was also fixed by the amount of grapes he might have in his vineyard in that year. The case is quite different in its facts from the case at the bar.

The cases cited by the learned counsel for the appellant, (Beaupre v. P. & A. Tel. Co., 21 Minn., 155, and Kinghorne v. Montreal Tel. Co., U.C., 18 Q.B. 60), are nearer in their main facts to the case at bar, and in both it was held there was no contract. We, however, place our opinion upon the language of the letter of the appellants, and hold that it cannot be fairly construed into an offer to sell to the respondent any quantity of salt he might order, nor any reasonable amount he might see fit to order. The language is not such as a business man would use in making an offer to sell to an individual a definite amount of property. The word "sell" is not used. They say, "we are authorized to offer Michigan fine salt," etc., and volunteer an opinion that at the terms stated it is a bargain. They do not say, we offer to sell to you. They use general language proper to be addressed generally to those who were interested in the salt trade. It is clearly in the nature of an advertisement or business circular, to attract the attention of those interested in that business to the fact that good bargains in salt could be had by applying to them, and not as an offer by which they were to be bound, if accepted, for any amount the persons to whom it was addressed might see fit to order. We think the complaint fails to show any contract between the parties, and the demurrer should have been sustained.

By the Court. — The order of the circuit court is reversed, and the cause remanded for further proceedings according to law.

FAIRMOUNT GLASS WORKS v. CRUNDEN-MARTIN WOODENWARE CO.

106 Ky. 659, 51 S.W. 196 (Ky. Ct. App. 1899)

HOBSON, J. On April 20, 1895, appellee wrote appellant the following letter:

St. Louis, Mo., April 20, 1895. Gentlemen: Please advise us the lowest price you can make us on our order for ten car loads of Mason green jars, complete, with caps, packed one dozen in case, either delivered here, or f.o.b. cars your place, as you prefer. State terms and cash discount. Very truly, Crunden-Martin W.W. Co.

To this letter appellant answered as follows:

Fairmount, Ind., April 23, 1895. Crunden-Martin Wooden Ware Co., St. Louis, Mo. — Gentlemen: Replying to your favor of April 20th, we quote you Mason fruit jars, complete, in one-dozen boxes, delivered in East St. Louis, Ill.: Pints, $4.50; quarts, $5.00; half gallons, $6.50 per gross, for immediate acceptance, and shipment not later than May 15, 1895; sixty days' acceptance, or 2 off, cash in ten days. Your truly, Fairmount Glass Works.

Please note that we make all quotations and contracts subject to the contingencies of agencies or transportation, delays or accidents beyond our control.

For reply thereto, appellee sent the following telegram on April 24, 1895:

Fairmount Glass Works, Fairmount, Ind.: Your letter twenty-third received. Enter order ten car loads as per your quotation. Specifications mailed. Crunden-Martin W.W. Co.

In response to this telegram, appellant sent the following:

Fairmount, Ind., April 24, 1895. Crunden-Martin W.W. Co., St. Louis, Mo.: Impossible to book your order. Output all sold. See letter. Fairmount Glass Works.

Appellee insists that, by its telegram sent in answer to the letter of April 23d, the contract was closed for the purchase of ten car loads of Mason fruit jars. Appellant insists that the contract was not closed by this telegram, and that it had the right to decline to fill the order at the time it sent its telegram of April 24th. This is the chief question in the case. The court below gave judgment in favor of appellee, and appellant has appealed, earnestly insisting that the judgment is erroneous.

We are referred to a number of authorities holding that a quotation of prices is not an offer to sell, in the sense that a completed contract will arise out of the giving of an order for merchandise in accordance with the proposed terms. There are a number of cases holding that the transaction is not completed until the order so made is accepted. 7 Am. & Eng. Enc. Law (2d Ed.), p. 138; Smith v. Gowdy, 8 Allen, 566; Beaupre v. P. & N.A. Telegraph Co., 21 Minn., 155.

But each case must turn largely upon the language there used. In this case we think there was more than a quotation of prices, although appellant's letter uses the word "quote" in stating the prices given. The true meaning of the correspondence must be determined by reading it as a whole. Appellee's letter of April 20th, which began the transaction, did not ask for a quotation of prices. It reads: "Please advise us the lowest price you can make us on our order for ten car loads of Mason green jars . . . State terms and cash discount." From this appellant could not fail to understand that appellee wanted to know at what price it would sell it ten car loads of these jars; so when, in answer, it wrote: "We quote you Mason fruit jars . . . pints $4.50, quarts $5.00, half gallons $6.50 per gross, for immediate acceptance; . . . 2 off, cash in ten days," — it must be deemed as intending to give appellee the information it had asked for. We can hardly understand what was meant by the words "for immediate acceptance," unless the latter was intended as a proposition to sell at these prices if accepted immediately. In construing every contract, the aim of the court is to arrive at the intention of the parties. In none of the cases to which we have been referred on behalf of appellant was there on the face of the correspondence any such expression of intention to make an offer to sell on the terms indicated.

. . . The expression in appellant's letter, "for immediate acceptance," taken in connection with appellee's letter [asking], in effect, at what price it would sell it the goods, is, it seems to us, much stronger evidence of a present offer, which, when accepted immediately closed the contract. Appellee's letter was plainly an inquiry for the price and terms on which appellant would sell it the goods, and appellant's answer to it was not a quotation of prices, but a definite offer to sell on the terms indicated, and could not be withdrawn after the terms had been accepted.

It will be observed that the telegram of acceptance refers to the specifications mailed. These specifications were contained in the following letter:

> St. Louis, Mo., April 24, 1895. Fairmount Glass Works Co., Fairmount, Ind. — Gentlemen: We received your letter of 23d this morning, and telegraphed you in reply as follows. "Your letter 23d received. Enter order ten car loads as per your quotation. Specifications mailed," — which we now confirm. We have accordingly entered this contract on our books for the ten cars Mason green jars, complete, with caps and rubbers, one dozen in case, delivered to us in East St. Louis, at $4.50 per gross for pint, $5.00 for quart, $6.50 for one-half gallon. Terms, sixty days' acceptance, or 2 per cent. for cash in ten days, to be shipped not later than May 15, 1895. The jars and caps to be strictly first quality goods. You may ship the first car to us here assorted: Five gross pint, fifty-five gross quart, forty gross one-half gallon. Specifications for the remaining nine cars we will send later. Crunden-Martin W.W. Co.

It is insisted for appellant that this was not an acceptance of the offer as made; that the stipulation, "The jars and caps to be strictly first-quality goods," was not in their offer; and that, it not having been accepted as made, appellant is not bound. But it will be observed that appellant declined to furnish the goods before it got this letter, and in the correspondence with appellee it nowhere complained of these words as an addition to the contract. Quite a number of other letters passed, in which the refusal to deliver these goods was placed on other grounds, none of which have been sustained by the evidence. Appellee offers proof tending to show that these words, in the trade in which parties were engaged, conveyed the same meaning as the words used in appellant's letter, and were only a different form of expressing the same idea. Appellant's conduct would seem to confirm this evidence.

Appellant also insists that the contract was indefinite, because the quantity of each size of the jars was not fixed, that ten car loads is too indefinite a specification of the quantity sold, and that appellee had no right to accept the goods to be delivered on different days.

The proofs shows that "ten car loads" is an expression used in the trade as equivalent to 1,000 gross, 100 gross being regarded a car load. The offer to sell the different sizes at different prices gave the purchaser the right to name the quantity of each size, and, the offer being to ship not later than May 15th, the buyer had the right to fix the time of delivery at any time before that. Sousely v. Burns' Adm'r, 10 Bush, 87; Williamson's Heirs v. Johnston's Heirs, 4 T.B. Mon., 253; Wheeler v. N.B. Railroad Co., 115 U.S., 34 [5 S. Ct., 1061, 1160].

The petition, if defective, was cured by the judgment, which is fully sustained by the evidence.

Judgment affirmed.

NOTE

Read Wilhelm Lubricating Co. v. Battrud, 197 Minn. 626, 268 N.W. 634, 106 A.L.R. 1279 (1936). How would both cases be decided under U.C.C. §§2-204(3), 2-311? See further Patterson, Analysis of Uniform Commercial Code 268-279, N.Y.L. Revision Commission, Leg. Doc. No. 65(c), 329-330 (1955); Comment, 23 U. Chi. L. Rev. 499 (1956).

CHANNEL MASTER CORP. v. ALUMINUM LTD. SALES
4 N.Y.2d 403, 151 N.E.2d 833 (1958)

Appeal, by permission of the Appellate Division of the Supreme Court in the third judicial department, from an order of said court, entered December 27, 1957, which (1) reversed an order and judgment of the Supreme Court at Special Term (Leonard J. Supple, J.), entered in Ulster County, granting a motion by defendant to dismiss the complaint, and (2) denied the motion. The following questions were certified:

"1. Does the first cause of action in the amended complaint state facts sufficient to constitute a cause of action?

"2. Does the second cause of action in the amended complaint state facts sufficient to constitute a cause of action?"

FULD, J. On this appeal, here on questions certified by the Appellate Division, we are called upon to determine the sufficiency of a complaint in a tort action for damages based on fraud and deceit.

The plaintiff, a manufacturer and processor of aluminum, requires for its business a dependable supply of aluminum ingot in large quantity. The defendant is engaged in the business of selling that metal. The amended complaint states two causes of action.

In the first cause of action, the plaintiff alleges that in April, 1954, the defendant represented that

> its available and uncommitted supplies and productive capacity of alumi-
> num ingot, then existing, were such as rendered it then capable of selling to
> the plaintiff 400,000 pounds per month and that it had entered into no
> binding commitments with other customers which could in the future
> reduce such available and uncommitted supplies and productive capacity.

The complaint then recites that such representations were made "with the intention and knowledge that plaintiff should rely thereon and in order to induce the plaintiff to refrain from entering into commitments with other suppliers and to purchase the greater part of its requirements from the defendant," that the plaintiff acted in reliance on the representations and that they were false and known by the defendant to be so. In truth and in fact, the complaint further asserts, the defendant had previously entered into long-term contracts with other customers which committed all of the defendant's supplies and productive capacity for many years to come. By reason of the defendant's fraudulent misrepresentations and the plaintiff's reliance thereon, the complaint continues, the plaintiff refrained from securing commitments for future supplies from others and was thereby injured in its business.

In the second cause of action, the plaintiff alleges that the defendant represented that it was its intention to make available to the plaintiff 400,000 pounds of aluminum ingot a month for a period of five years; that such representation was false and known by the defendant to be false; that it was the defendant's intention to sell to the plaintiff only such aluminum as might from time to time become available in the event that other customers to whom the defendant had given binding commitments should choose to forego the supplies committed to them and that the plaintiff relied on that representation to its injury.

The defendant moved to dismiss the complaint, urging the insufficiency of both causes of action, under rule 106 of the Rules of Civil Practice, and the inadequacy of the second cause, under rule 107, on the ground that it "is predicated on an alleged oral promise unenforceable under the . . . Statute of Frauds." The court at Special Term denied the motion insofar as it was based on the statute of frauds, for the reason that "no agreement or contract is alleged," but granted the defendant's motion to strike both causes of action for insufficiency. On appeal, the Appellate Division unanimously reversed and denied the motion to dismiss.

To maintain an action based on fraudulent representations, whether it be for the rescission of a contract or, as here, in tort for damages, it is sufficient to show that the defendant knowingly uttered a falsehood intending to deprive the plaintiff of a benefit and that the plaintiff was thereby deceived and damaged. (See Brackett v. Griswold, 112 N.Y. 454, 467; Hadcock v. Osmer, 153 N.Y. 604, 608; Rice v. Manley, 66 N.Y. 82, 84; 3 Restatement, Torts §525, p. 59; 1 Harper & James on The Law of Torts [1956], §7.1, pp. 527-528; Prosser on Torts [2d ed., 1955], §86, p. 523.) The essential constituents of the action are fixed as representation of a material existing fact, falsity, *scienter*, deception and injury. (See Sabo v. Delman, 3 N.Y.2d 155, 159-160; Deyo v. Hudson, 225 N.Y. 602, 612; Ochs v. Woods, 221 N.Y. 335, 338; Urtz v. New York Cent. & H.R.R.R. Co., 202 N.Y. 170, 173.) Accordingly, one "who fraudulently makes a misrepresentation of . . . intention . . . for the purpose of inducing another to act or refrain from action in reliance thereon in a business transaction" is liable for the harm caused by the other's justifiable reliance upon the misrepresentation. (3 Restatement, Torts, §525, p. 59.)

As examination of the complaint demonstrates, it contains all the necessary elements of a good cause of action, including statements of existing fact, as opposed to expressions of future expectation. The representations allegedly made, that the defendant had "available and uncommitted supplies and productive capacity of aluminum ingot" sufficient to render it then capable of selling to the plaintiff 400,000 pounds a month and that it had entered into no binding commitments which could in the future reduce such available and uncommitted supplies and productive capacity and that it was its intention to make available and to sell to the plaintiff the number of pounds specified for a period of five years, related to the defendant's present intention. A person's intent, his state of mind, it has long been recognized, is capable of ascertainment and a statement of present intention is deemed a statement of a material existing fact, sufficient to support a fraud action. (See Sabo v. Delman, 3 N.Y.2d 155, 160, *supra*; Deyo v. Hudson, 225 N.Y. 602, 612, *supra*; Ritzwoller v. Lurie, 225 N.Y. 464, 468; Adams v. Gillig, 199 N.Y. 314, 319-322; 3 Restatement, Torts, §530, pp. 69-71; 1 Harper & James, op. cit., §7.10, pp. 570-573; Prosser, op. cit., §90, pp. 563-564.) Here, just as in Sabo v. Delman (3 N.Y.2d, at p. 160) and in the *Ritzwoller* case (225 N.Y., at p. 468),

> the allegations in the complaint describe a case where a defendant has fraudulently and positively as with personal knowledge stated that something was to be done when he knew all the time it was not to be done and that his representations were false. It is not a case of prophecy and prediction of something which it is merely hoped or expected will occur in the future, but a specific affirmation of an arrangement under which something is to occur, when the party making the affirmation knows perfectly well that no such thing is to occur. Such statements and representations when false are actionable.

The defendant also argues that the action cannot be founded on any promise which falls within the statute of frauds. Although there is considerable doubt that the questions certified pose that defense for our consideration, we shall assume that the second question could be so construed.

The present action is in tort, not contract, depending not upon agreement between the parties, but rather upon deliberate misrepresentation of fact, relied on by the plaintiff to his detriment. In other words, the "legal relations" binding the parties are created by the utterance of a falsehood "with a fraudulent intent" and by reliance thereon (Deyo v. Hudson, 225 N.Y. 602, 612, *supra*) and the cause of action is entirely "independent of contractual relations between the parties." (1 Harper & James, op. cit., p. 527.) As we wrote in Sabo v. Delman (3 N.Y.2d 155,

159, *supra*), "it is well to bear in mind that the complaint before us neither asserts a breach of contract nor attempts to enforce any promise made by defendants." If the proof of a promise or contract, void under the statute of frauds, is essential to maintain the action, there may be no recovery, but, on the other hand, one who fraudulently misrepresents himself as intending to perform an agreement is subject to liability *in tort* whether the agreement is enforcible or not. (3 Restatement, Torts, §525, p. 59 et seq.; §530, Comment *b*, p. 70.) The policy of the statute of frauds is "not directed at cases of dishonesty in making" a promise (Prosser, op. cit., p. 565); never intended as an instrument to immunize fraudulent conduct, the statute may not be so employed.

It is not inappropriate to say, as we did in the *Sabo* case (3 N.Y.2d, at p. 162), that whether the plaintiff will be able to establish the allegations of its complaint is "necessarily reserved for trial. We decide only that the complaint before us states a cause of action."

The order appealed from should be affirmed, with costs, and the questions certified answered in the affirmative.

BURKE, J. (dissenting). The amended complaint should be dismissed because the misrepresentations alleged relate only to future expectations.

No doubt a remedy in tort would be available to the plaintiff if the fraudulent promissory representations dealt with matters completely under the control of the defendant and implemented existing contractual obligations (Sabo v. Delman, 3 N.Y.2d 155; A. S. Rampell, Inc., v. Hyster Co., 3 N.Y.2d 369). It does not follow that there would be also a remedy where the representations are nothing more than a recital of the defendant's predictions or statements of expectations (Adams v. Clark, 239 N.Y. 403, 410). The amendment of the original complaint by the incorporation of the words "then existing"; "then capable of selling"; "that it had entered into no binding commitments with other customers" and "the period of scarcity which followed" has not cured the defects inherent in the original complaint. When the amended complaint is read as a whole and compared with the original complaint, it is clearly evident that the alleged representations relate to an unknown, uncertain and indefinite future period, not to an existing fact. These allegations do not treat at a particular time with the state of mind of a person in possession of all information whose expressed intentions as to the future can readily be effectuated, but with unpredictable problems of the logistics of supply and demand of not only finished products but also raw materials in a huge industry beset by many varieties of weather, of labor relations, of customers' demands and of government needs. The alleged representations under such circumstances could neither be affirmation of events which, when made, defendant knew would not occur nor assertions of present facts susceptible of knowledge. Any reliance on the alleged representations, therefore, was unjustifiable as plaintiff knew perfectly well that the representations of necessity were speculative. Such representations will not support an action for fraud. We do not say that an allegation of a promise made with the present intention to break it would not be actionable. Cases such as Deyo v. Hudson (225 N.Y. 602) and Adams v. Clark (*supra*) are cited to uphold this doctrine. But here the defendant made no promise and the plaintiff parted with nothing.

As we regard them, the alleged representations do not reflect a statement of present intention which could be judged a statement of an existing fact which may be the basis for a fraud action.

Therefore, the order appealed from should be reversed and the amended complaint should be dismissed.

Chief Judge Conway and Judges Desmond and Froessel concur with Judge Fuld; Judge Burke dissents in an opinion in which Judges Dye and Van Voorhis concur.

Order affirmed, etc.

NOTE

1. Llewellyn criticizes both the majority and the dissent in the *Channel Master* case with uncharacteristic vehemence:

> The court finds allegations of fact and reliance sufficient to make a case in fraud, finds the cause to be entirely independent of contractual relations, and finds the statute of frauds to be inapposite in law and, on the basis of an inconclusive passage from Prosser, in policy. The three-judge dissent this time accepts, seemingly, each of these doctrinal premises; it attacks solely the application: the representations were not of facts susceptible of knowledge. For such a court, on such an issue, this is truly extraordinary. The situation is one in which the torts theorists (Restatement, Harper and James, Prosser, all gathered and cited) have launched as unconsidered a jamboree as ever has been suggested in the books: in the instant "application" of the idea, word-of-mouth negotiations for a contract which have led to no acceptance, which need not have led even to an offer, and which would in an action on an actually completed contract be incapable of submission to the jury for lack of a signed writing — these become admissible in the teeth of the statute against frauds and perjuries, admissible, moreover, in such fashion as to allow damages of a range and extent which would be dubious of procurement in any action based on an agreement fully closed, formally authenticated, and unambiguously relied on. All of this by virtue of merely adjusting the pleadings and the evidence to run down an alley which is rather easier to travel with persuasiveness than is the alley of contract-closing — and one in which any perjury or mistake is harder to pinpoint for pillory. For these are not the type of "conversations" which (like a true-blue offer or acceptance for a five-year deal) are hard to believe in unless "confirmed" in writing on the same day; instead, they run loose, without confirmation, or exactness, or top limit, or any other check-

up. And these adventures into space are undertaken on the policy say-so not of thoughtful commercial scholars who are for instance somewhat bothered about a bit of untoward tightness and overtechnicality in the contract rules of damages, or about an unwise and unbusinesslike precisionism in requiring a mere "note or memorandum" under the Statute of Frauds to recite accurately every agreed term. No, these adventures are undertaken instead on somewhat loose general language about misrepresentation put out by scholars whose delight is to see the law of torts inherit the earth. Extraordinary indeed; and happily most uncharacteristic.

Llewellyn, The Common Law Tradition 473 (1960).

Hill, Damages for Innocent Misrepresentation, 73 Colum. L. Rev. 679, 715 (1973), defends the *Channel Master* court's treatment of the Statute of Frauds and points out that "[t]he issue is one on which the courts are divided."

2. Suppose that after lengthy bickering about the sale of a generator, the parties have come to an agreement as to its price. But the terms of payment have not been agreed upon. The seller wants 10 percent of the purchase price, 50 percent on delivery, and the balance on acceptance. The buyer in response tells the seller that he generally pays 9 percent on the tenth of the month following delivery and the balance on final acceptance. The seller, who claims that he does not recall the buyer's response, fails to deliver. Is this a situation covered by U.C.C. §2-204(3), dealing with "open terms"? If this is the case, would §§2-305, 3-310 apply? The hypothetical was suggested by Southwest Engineering Co. v. Martin Tractor Co., 205 Kan. 684, 473 P.2d 18 (1970), applying §§2-204(3) and 3-310(a). Does that situation involve an assent, or a failure to agree? See further C & J Fertilizer, Inc. v. Allied Mutual Insurance Co., 227 N.W.2d 169, 172, 176 (Iowa 1975).

Section 4.   The Duty to Bargain in Good Faith

Occasionally the thesis has been advanced that once parties have entered into negotiations for a contract, neither can break off arbitrarily without compensating the other for his reliance damages. The case law and literature, on the whole, however, have displayed the good sense to reject this idea. If the utility of contract as an instrument of self-government is not to be seriously weakened, parties must be free to break off preliminary negotiations without being held to an accounting.

Tradition has it that absent fraud, misrepresentation, concealment, and duress, parties negotiating for a contract are dealing at arm's length and are under no duty to act in good faith toward each other.

Bargaining in good faith is dealt with neither by the Uniform Commercial Code (§1-203), nor by the Restatement Second (§205). Both "codifications" deal only with good faith in performance.

By contrast, the National Labor Relations Act §8(d)[46] imposes on both parties a duty to bargain in good faith. But this means only that the parties have to meet at regular times and confer in good faith. This obligation does not compel either party to agree to a proposal or require the making of a concession. (H. Wellington, Labor and the Legal Process, 52-53 (1968)).[47] The National Labor Relations Board is empowered to promulgate orders enforceable in the courts to implement §8, but although it may order a party to cease and desist from refusing to bargain, it may not order the party to include a particular term in the agreement. H. K. Porter Co. v. N.L.R.B., 397 U.S. 99 (1970).

Until fairly recently, it has been argued that a good faith principle like that embodied in the National Labor Relations Act ought not to be carried over into the formative stage of contracts,[48] except in fiduciary and confidential relationships. A majority of courts have taken and still take the view that a contract to make a contract, or an agreement to agree, is not binding,[49] thus allowing each party to abandon negotiation with impunity. But it should not be overlooked that this privilege presupposes that the parties have not yet come to an agreement. Consequently, the further negotiations have progressed, the more unsafe it is to withdraw. The Uniform Commercial Code and the progressive case law endorsed by the Restatement Second, as we saw in the previous section, long ago abandoned the idea that a contract presupposes a consensus ad idem.[50]

The materials that follow, too important to be ignored and often in conflict, show a tendency to tamper with tradition and to recognize good faith duties, even if the contract in the traditional sense never came into existence. The courts are willing to grant damages when the party claiming lack of agreement has invited or encouraged the other's reliance so that non-enforcement would leave the relying party in a disadvantageous position. Some courts have gone even further, developing in appropriate

---

46. 61 Stat. 142 (1947), 29 U.S.C. §158(d)(1958).

47. For the meaning of the term "good faith" see N.L.R.B. v. Insurance Agents' Int'l Union, 361 U.S. 477 (1960); Cox, The Duty to Bargain in Good Faith, 71 Harv. L. Rev. 1401 (1958).

48. United States v. Braunstein, 75 F. Supp. 137 (S.D.N.Y. 1947), *appeal dismissed*, 168 F.2d 749 (2d Cir. 1948); Ruebsamen v. Maddocks, 340 A.2d 31 (Maine 1975); A.B.C. Packard, Inc. v. General Motors Corp., 275 F.2d 63, 69 & n.6 (9th Cir. 1960); Woodmont, Inc. v. Daniels, 274 F.2d 132, 137-138 (10th Cir. 1959).

49. Ansorge v. Kane, 244 N.Y. 395, 155 N.E. 683 (1927); 1 Corbin §29 (1963) discusses the problem in a good deal more guarded way: a contemplated writing, for instance, might not be the final step in the consummation of an agreement, but a "mere" memorial of the agreement already reached. See further Shepard v. Carpenter, 54 Minn. 153, 55 N.W. 906 (1893); Lord Wright in Hillas v. Argos, 147 L.T. 503 (1902).

50. U.C.C. §§2-204(3), 2-305(1). The distinction, for instance, between an understanding that the price should be reasonable and an agreement to negotiate in a reasonable way to reach such a price can become quite fluid. A good deal may depend on the remedy sought.

cases what has been called a "contract to bargain."[51] This happens when the parties have committed themselves in good faith to complete the contract. In this situation neither party may "arbitrarily" back out of the deal. One may do so only if a fair and honest understanding cannot be reached, but not merely because an outsider has offered better terms. There is thus a gray area between a completed bargain and no contract at all. Of course, it may be exceedingly difficult to shape the appropriate remedy in such a case. Unlike most of the cases in this chapter, where the injured party must be satisfied with either restitution or reliance damages, a few cases, like *Borg-Warner, infra* p. 226, confront the difficult question of specifically enforcing terms calling for future negotiations, or alternatively, of awarding damages with an allowance for the failure of such negotiations.

HILL v. WAXBERG
237 F.2d 936 (9th Cir. 1956)

HALBERT, District Judge.

The appellee, Waxberg, brought this action in the District Court for the Territory of Alaska to recover the reasonable value of his services and the expenditures made by him in connection with a proposed building contract which was never consummated. The action was originally instituted against R. P. Hill and Mary Hill, his wife, but it was, by stipulation, dismissed as to Mrs. Hill, so we are not concerned with her on this appeal. The jury returned a verdict in favor of Waxberg for the sum of $11,167.46. Appellant attacks the judgment entered on this verdict as excessive, and at the same time asserts that the trial court incorrectly instructed the jury.

In December of 1949 appellant, R. P. Hill, summoned Waxberg, a contractor, to assist him in making preparations for the construction of a building on Hill's lot in the city of Fairbanks. It was decided between the parties that the only method of financing the transaction was to secure a commitment from the F.H.A. From the time of their first meeting, it was the understanding of the parties that if the financing could be arranged through the F.H.A. as contemplated, Waxberg would be awarded the building contract.

Pursuant to this plan, Waxberg made several trips to Seattle at the request of Hill to confer with the architects; hired a third party to secure a drill log on the property; surveyed the property; and was generally instrumental in providing the requisite data consisting of plans and cost figures

---

51. Knapp, Enforcing the Contract to Bargain, 44 N.Y.U. L. Rev. 673 (1969); Summers, "Good Faith" in General Contract Law and the Sales Provisions of the Uniform Commercial Code, 54 Va. L. Rev. 195 (1968); Kessler & Fine, Culpa in Contrahendo, Bargaining in Good Faith, and Freedom of Contract: A Comparative Study, 77 Harv. L. Rev. 401 (1964).

for the consideration of the F.H.A. Waxberg expected to be compensated for those expenditures out of the profits derived from the contemplated contract.

In February, 1950, the F.H.A. issued the commitment, under §608 of the Federal Housing Authority Act, 12 U.S.C.A. §1743, which, in essence, insured a loan up to 90% of the estimated cost figure. With the commitment secured as contemplated, the parties entered into negotiations for the building contract. There is considerable conflict in the testimony over what actually transpired at these negotiations, with each party claiming that it was the unconscionable demands of the other that ultimately caused the termination of their relationship.

Hill finally entered into a building contract with another contractor and caused the original commitment to be amended to conform thereto. The evidence shows that Waxberg's plans, ideas and efforts were of some value and assistance to Hill in his endeavors.

The trial court's instructions to the jury confined the factual issues to the question of whether Waxberg [the plaintiff] was the party on whom blame for the failure to enter into the contemplated construction contract could be placed. Thus, the jury was told that it must find for Waxberg, if it found that Hill [the defendant] was at fault, or if both, or neither were at fault. The trial court concluded that the evidence undisputedly established the existence of an agreement between the parties that Waxberg would be awarded the contract.

On the question of damages the court gave the following instruction:

> If you find in favor of the plaintiff you will return a verdict in favor of the plaintiff for the value of the benefit which the defendant received as a result of the plaintiff's services and expenditures.

It is the propriety of this instruction, together with the alleged excessiveness of the verdict returned thereunder, which appellant attacks by this appeal. Appellant also asserts that the requisite elements for quasi-contractual recovery were not established by the evidence.

This Court is of the opinion that the District Judge's finding that there was no issue as to the existence of the elements necessary to ground an action based on an implied contract was supported by the evidence. Certain general principles of law are so immutably fixed in the continuum of Anglo-American jurisprudence that the endless citation of authority is scarcely needed to support them. That something in the nature of an implied contract results where one renders services at the request of another with the expectation of pay therefor, and in the process confers a benefit on the other, is such a principle.[52] It makes no difference whether

52. Restatement of Contracts, §90; Restatement of Restitution, §107(2); Costigan, Implied in Fact Contracts, 33 Harvard Law Rev. (1920) 376; Note, 44 Harvard Law Rev. 623; 12 Am. Jur. 502.

the pay expected is in the form of an immediate cash payment, or in the form of profits to be derived from a contract, the consummation of which would or should be anticipated by reasonable men, and it follows *a fortiori* that such a rule obtains where the contract is in fact contemplated by *both* parties.[53] That a benefit was conferred in this case is also beyond question, when it is borne in mind that the commitment which the appellant secured as a result of the efforts of the appellee was virtually irreplaceable and in no event could a substitute have been provided for it without considerable additional expense as well as a drastic alteration of terms.[54]

Unfortunately neither the District Court nor counsel during the course of the proceedings attempted to categorize the action as one based on an "implied in fact" contract or an "implied in law" contract. Although the distinction may be somewhat doctrinaire, the application of certain formalized distinctions is necessary in order to arrive at the proper measure of damages.

An "implied in fact" contract is essentially based on the intentions of the parties. It arises where the court finds from the surrounding facts and circumstances that the parties intended to make a contract but failed to articulate their promises and the court merely implies what it feels the parties really intended. It would follow then that the general contract theory of compensatory damages should be applied. Thus, if the court can in fact imply a contract for services, the compensation therefor is measured by the going contract rate.

An "implied in law" contract, on the other hand, is a fiction of the law which is based on the maxim that one who is unjustly enriched at the expense of another is required to make restitution to the other. The intentions of the parties have little or no influence on the determination of the proper measure of damages. In the absence of fraud or other tortious conduct on the part of the person enriched, restitution is properly limited to the value of the benefit which was acquired.[55]

The distinction is based on sound reason, too, for where a contract is all but articulated, the expectations of the parties are very nearly mutually understood, and the Court has merely to protect those expectations

53. Western Asphalt Co. v. Valle, 1946, 25 Wash. 2d 428, 171 P.2d 159, noted in 22 Washington Law Rev. 139 (1947); see also Restatement of Restitution, §57, illustration 7.

54. The cash value of the commitment was placed at $4,800. After February of 1950, the appellant, Hill, would have been unable to secure a commitment under §608 of the Federal Housing Authority Act since Congress had withdrawn its availability to territorial applicants. Instead, Hill would have had as his only recourse to attempt to secure a commitment under §207 of the Act, 12 U.S.C.A. §1713, which, *inter alia*, would have required Hill to issue controlling interest in the proposed building to the Housing Authority. It goes without saying that without the original commitment, Hill would have found himself in the precise position which he has asserted he was trying to avoid, namely, the presence of someone else with a controlling interest in his project thereby diminishing his already slim equity.

55. Martin v. Campanaro, 2 Cir., 1946, 156 F.2d 127, at page 130, note 5; 44 Harvard Law Rev. 623 (1931); Restatement of Restitution, §107, comment *b*, §155 (1).

as men in the ordinary course of business affairs would expect them to be protected, whereas in a situation where one has acquired benefits, without fraud and in a non-tortious manner, with expectations so totally lacking in such mutuality that no contract in fact can be implied, the party benefited should not be required to reimburse the other party on the basis of such party's losses and expenditures, but rather on a basis limited to the benefits, which the benefited party has actually acquired.[56]

The facts in this case are such that a reasonable man might be persuaded that the elements of either theory could be satisfied, but since counsel has declined to choose between them, we are not prepared to make the choice for him. Seemingly the trial court was faced with the same dilemma, and chose to resolve it by first deciding that an agreement in fact had been reached by the parties. Unfortunately, however, it followed this decision by giving an instruction on the issue of damages couched in terms of unjust enrichment. It appears that the jury was in a like manner confused, because it returned a verdict which apparently included not only the value of the benefit conferred on Hill, but also the full measure of the value of Waxberg's services and expenditures as they were given in the evidence. The instructions should have been drawn so as to avoid a commingling of the theory of damages in "implied in fact" contracts and the theory of damages in "implied in law" contracts, and if, as would appear to have been the intention of the trial court, the instructions were to be based on an "implied in law" contract growing out of the unjust enrichment of Hill, then the instructions should have identified with precision exactly what the limits of the recovery could be.[57]

[6] We have given this case careful consideration, and notwithstanding what we have said above, we feel constrained to observe that in view of the record in the case, and what appeared to us to be the attitude of counsel at the time of the hearing before us, the ends of justice would best be served if the judgment were, by agreement of the parties, reduced to the sum of $5,896.88 (the asserted reasonable value of plaintiff's services for 43 days, plus his claimed expenses of $1,596.88).

It will, therefore, be our order that if the parties will agree that the amount of the judgment be reduced to the sum of $5,896.88 within forty days from the date on which this order is filed, that the judgment thus modified shall be affirmed, but in the event the parties are unwilling to agree to such a reduced judgment within the time prescribed, then the judgment shall be reversed and the cause then will be remanded for further proceedings not inconsistent with this opinion.

56. Note [55] *supra*.
57. The value of the benefit conferred in the form of the commitment was fixed at $4,800. This should be the outward limit of damages unless it can be shown that the defendant appropriated any of the plaintiff's plans, suggestions, or ideas in connection with the building as it was ultimately constructed.

NOTE

Contrast Cronin v. National Shawmut Bank, 306 Mass. 202, 27 N.E.2d 717 (1940). See further Restatement of Restitution Second §2 (Tent. Draft No. 1, 1983).

HEYER PRODUCTS CO. v. UNITED STATES, 135 Ct. Cl. 63, 140 F. Supp. 409 (1956). The Army's Ordnance Tank Automotive Center (OTAC) requested bids for the manufacture of a quantity of low-voltage circuit testers. The plaintiff alleged in a complaint against the United States that the Center had rejected the plaintiff's bid in "bad faith," having decided to retaliate against the plaintiff for testifying against the contracting agency at a senate hearing. The plaintiff claimed in addition to his expenses in preparing the bid ($7,000), a sum of $38,000 to compensate him for his lost profits. The court denied the Government's motion to dismiss.

"The advertisement for bids was, of course, a request for offers to supply the things the Ordnance Department wanted. It could accept or reject an offer as it pleased, and no contract resulted until an offer was accepted. Hence, an unsuccessful bidder cannot recover the profit he would have made out of the contract, because he had no contract.

"But this is not to say that he may not recover the expense to which he was put in preparing his bid.

"It was an implied condition of the request for offers that each of them would be honestly considered, and that that offer which in the honest opinion of the contracting officer was most advantageous to the Government would be accepted. No person would have bid at all if he had known that 'the cards were stacked against him.' No bidder would have put out $7,000 in preparing its bid, as plaintiff says it did, if it had known the Ordnance Department had already determined to give the contract to the Weidenhoff Company. It would not have put in a bid unless it thought it was to be honestly considered. It had a right to think it would be. The Ordnance Department impliedly promised plaintiff it would be. This is what induced it to spend its money to prepare its bid. . . .

"The facts in United States v. Purcell Envelope Co., 249 U.S. 313, 39 S. Ct. 300, 301, 63 L. Ed. 620, differ from the facts in this case in that in that case plaintiff's bid was accepted. But after acceptance the head of the department refused to execute the written contract. Plaintiff sued and the Government defended on the ground that discretion rested in the department head to choose with whom it would contract, and that it had chosen not to contract with plaintiff, and, hence, plaintiff had no legal capacity to sue.

"The court held that a contract resulted from the offer and acceptance and that the subsequent signing of a written contract was not required.

"The facts in the two cases are, therefore, different, but in the course

of its opinion the Supreme Court used this language, which is applicable
to the present case:

> "There must be a point of time at which discretion is exhausted. The
> procedure for the advertising for bids for supplies . . . to the government
> would else be a mockery — a procedure, we may say, that is not permissive
> but required. . . . By it the government is given the benefit of the competi-
> tion of the market and each bidder is given the chance of a bargain. It is a
> provision, therefore, in the interest of both government and bidder, neces-
> sarily giving rights to both and placing obligations on both. And it is not out
> of place to say that the government should be animated by a justice as
> anxious to consider the rights of the bidder as to insist upon its own.

> "The cases we cited in the beginning of this opinion hold that acts
requiring advertising and letting to the lowest responsible bidder confer
no right on the bidder to secure the contract, whether or not he is the
lowest responsible bidder, and, hence, he may not recover his loss of
anticipated profits. We do not understand the Supreme Court in the
Purcell Envelope case, *supra*, to have intended to hold to the contrary,
but it did definitely recognize that the bidder had certain rights, and that
the Government was under an obligation to respect those rights.
> "Among these rights is the right to have his bid honestly considered.
The Government is under the obligation to honestly consider it and not
to wantonly disregard it. If this obligation is breached and plaintiff is put
to needless expense in preparing its bid, it is entitled to recover such
expenses."

Two judges dissented from the majority opinion: Judge Madden would
have read the Armed Services Procurement Act of 1947 (41 U.S.C.A.
§151(b)) as affording plaintiff the right to recover any damages he may
have suffered. Judge Laramore, however, regarded the action as one
sounding in tort (since it was founded on fraud) and therefore outside the
original jurisdiction of the Court of Claims.

NOTE

At the subsequent trial the plaintiff was unable to prove the bad faith
alleged. 147 Ct. Cl. 256, 177 F. Supp. 251 (1959). In fact, few *Heyer*-type
plaintiffs have succeeded in claims of the kind the majority in that case
put forward. For examples of such failures, see, e.g., Robert F. Simmons
& Associates v. United States, 360 F.2d 962 (Ct. Cl. 1966); Edelman v.
F.H.A., 251 F. Supp. 715 (E.D.N.Y. 1966). See, in general, Summers,
"Good Faith" in General Contract Law and the Sales Provisions of the
Uniform Commercial Code, 54 Va. L. Rev. 195, 221 (1968). See further

Keco Industries Inc. v. United States, 428 F.2d 1233 (Ct. Cl. 1970) and
the cases discussed in Grossbaum, Procedural Fairness in Public Contracts: The Procurement Regulations, 57 Va. L. Rev. 171, 240 et seq.
(1971).

Recovery of preparation costs was allowed in Armstrong & Armstrong
v. United States, 514 F.2d 402 (9th Cir. 1975); McCurly Corp. v. United
States, 490 F.2d 633 (Ct. Cl. 1974). Swinerton & Walberg Co. v. City of
Inglewood, 40 Cal. App. 3d 98, 114 Cal. Rptr. 834 (1974), is an example of
a state court decision holding for a *Heyer*-type plaintiff. The court in that
case relied on an implied contract or promise that was held enforceable
by virtue of Section 90 of the Restatement Second, and on the decision in
Drennan v. Star Paving Co., *infra* p. 326. Note that the court in *Swinerton* (and possibly the court in *Heyer Products*, see Grossbaum, *supra*, at
p. 241) had to rely on contract theory to avoid jurisdictional limitations
and limitations on governmental liability for tort. In cases involving private auctions, where such limitations are not present, a plaintiff may sue
for fraud or deceit instead. See Block v. Tobin, 45 Cal. App. 3d 214, 119
Cal. Rptr. 288 (1975), where the plaintiffs, bidders at a privately held sale
under a deed of trust, alleged that the defendants had held a mock auction and sought damages for deceit. The damages were limited by the
court to the amount plaintiffs had expended in preparing their bid, but
the court left open the possibility that the defendants might be held liable
for punitive damages as well.

GOODMAN v. DICKER
169 F.2d 684 (D.C. Cir. 1948)

PROCTOR, Associate Justice. This appeal is from a judgment of the
District Court in a suit by appellees for breach of contract.

Appellants are local distributors for Emerson Radio and Phonograph
Corporation in the District of Columbia. Appellees, with the knowledge
and encouragement of appellants, applied for a "dealer franchise" to sell
Emerson's products. The trial court found that appellants by their representations and conduct induced appellees to incur expenses in preparing
to do business under the franchise, including employment of salesmen
and solicitation of orders for radios. Among other things, appellants represented that the application had been accepted; that the franchise would
be granted, and that appellees would receive an initial delivery of thirty to
forty radios. Yet, no radios were delivered, and notice was finally given
that the franchise would not be granted.

The case was tried without a jury. The court held that a contract had
not been proven but that appellants were estopped from denying the
same by reason of their statements and conduct upon which appellees

relied to their detriment. Judgment was entered for $1500, covering cash outlays of $1150 and loss of $350, anticipated profits on sale of thirty radios.

The main contention of appellants is that no liability would have arisen under the dealer franchise had it been granted because, as understood by appellees, it would have been terminable at will and would have imposed no duty upon the manufacturer to sell or appellees to buy any fixed number of radios. From this it is argued that the franchise agreement would not have been enforceable (except as to acts performed thereunder) and cancellation by the manufacturer would have created no liability for expenses incurred by the dealer in preparing to do business. Further, it is argued that as the dealer franchise would have been unenforceable for failure of the manufacturer to supply radios appellants would not be liable to fulfill their assurance that radios would be supplied.

We think these contentions miss the real point of this case. We are not concerned directly with the terms of the franchise. We are dealing with a promise by appellants that a franchise would be granted and radios supplied, on the faith of which appellees with the knowledge and encouragement of appellants incurred expenses in making preparations to do business. Under these circumstances we think that appellants cannot now advance any defense inconsistent with their assurance that the franchise would be granted. Justice and fair dealing require that one who acts to his detriment on the faith of conduct of the kind revealed here should be protected by estopping the party who has brought about the situation from alleging anything in opposition to the natural consequences of his own course of conduct. Dair v. United States, 1872, 16 Wall. 1, 4, 21 L. Ed. 491. In Dickerson v. Colgrove, 100 U.S. 578, 580, 25 L. Ed. 618, the Supreme Court, in speaking of equitable estoppel, said:

> The law upon the subject is well settled. The vital principle is that he who by his language or conduct leads another to do what he would not otherwise have done, shall not subject such person to loss or injury by disappointing the expectations upon which he acted. Such a change of position is sternly forbidden. . . . This remedy is always so applied as to promote the ends of justice.

See also Casey v. Galli, 94 U.S. 673, 680, 24 L. Ed. 168; Arizona v. Copper Queen Mining Co., 233 U.S. 87, 95, 34 S. Ct. 546, 58 L. Ed. 863.

In our opinion the trial court was correct in holding defendants liable for moneys which appellees expended in preparing to do business under the promised dealer franchise. These items aggregated $1150. We think, though, the court erred in adding the item of $350 for loss of profits on radios promised under an initial order. The true measure of damage is the

loss sustained by expenditures made in reliance upon the assurance of a dealer franchise. As thus modified, the judgment is
   Affirmed.

NOTE

   The case is noted in 97 U. Pa. L. Rev. 731 (1949). See also 1 Corbin §205 (1963).
   In Prince v. Miller Brewing Co., 434 S.W.2d 232 (Tex. App. 1968) the court refused to follow *Goodman* or to apply §90 in a case where the franchise agreement in issue granted the franchisor unlimited discretion to terminate. See further the note to Chrysler v. Quimby.

CHRYSLER CORP. v. QUIMBY, 51 Del. 264, 144 A.2d 123, 885 (1958). Randall was the President and active executive of Randall Motors, Inc., a Chrysler dealer in Washington, D.C., operating since 1944 under a franchise terminable by Chrysler on 90 days' notice. Quimby, a lawyer and long-standing friend, was a director and secretary of Randall Motors, owning ten shares of the corporation. On Randall's death Quimby told Neely, Chrysler's regional manager, that he wanted to see Randall Motors continue with the business. Neely reported to Chrysler that Quimby was making an effort to obtain the business for himself, and that he (Neely) could under no circumstances recommend that Quimby succeed Randall. On his recommendation, a 90-day notice of termination was given in accordance with the dealer agreement. Neely indicated to Quimby that this was largely a matter of form and that the franchise would be continued if Quimby would purchase the interest of Randall's widow and the rest of the stock from the other stockholders and transfer a 51 percent interest to a qualified person named by Chrysler. Quimby bought the stock of the widow for $38,000 and Randall Motors acquired the shares of the other shareholders so that Quimby became sole stockholder. He was however unable to perform the other condition because the transfer of 51 percent of the stock was prevented by Chrysler's failure to name the transferee. Chrysler gave the franchise to another dealer, thereby greatly reducing the value of the assets of the corporation and of the corporate stock acquired by the plaintiff in reliance on Neely's promise. Quimby sued Chrysler in his own name and as assignee of the corporation.
   Assuming that Neely's motives for his assurances to Quimby were to obtain a fair price for the stock for Mrs. Randall, to whom Chrysler felt a moral obligation, is Quimby entitled to recover? If your answer is affirmative, would you decide the issue differently if Neely had not made his recommendation against Quimby succeeding Randall? Assuming, on the

actual facts of the case, that plaintiff is entitled to recovery, what should
be the measure of his damages?

NOTE

For a parallel case, see Guilbert v. Phillips Petroleum Co., 503 F.2d
587 (6th Cir. 1974). See also Restatement Second §90, Illus. 8 & 9. According to the Restatement, the recovery of expectation damages in
Chrysler was justified since the defendant had acted willfully, whereas in
Goodman the defendant had acted inadvertently. For another explanation see Wheeler v. White, *infra* p. 225.

Is not the true reason for denying expectation damages in *Goodman*
that such damages would amount to a double recovery? Remember that
plaintiffs did not ask for net but for gross profits (out of which their
expenses should have been paid). Suppose plaintiffs could have sold three
hundred radios at a profit of $10 each. Could they recover $3,000 and
ignore their expenses?

COLLINS RADIO CO.
21 Comp. Gen. 605 (B-21873 (1941))

[The Collins Radio Company was the only bidder on a United States
Government proposal for furnishing high frequency radio transmitters.
The Government represented by the Civil Aeronautics Administration
advised Collins by "letter of intent" (dated August 14, 1941) that its bid
was "conditionally accepted subject to the execution of a formal contract
by the Civil Aeronautics Administration." Collins signed the contract,
gave a performance bond, and was issued a preference rating certificate
enabling it to obtain materials. Subsequently, but before the Government signed the contract, its needs changed and it inquires as to whether
it is bound to reimburse the bidder for expenses incurred toward the
manufacture of the transmitters.

The decision of the Comptroller General in reply to a letter dated
November 13, 1941, from the Secretary of Commerce follows in part]:
    . . . It appears further that the contractor executed and returned the
formal contract and performance bond forms, which were transmitted to
it with the letter of August 14, 1941, but, for the reasons stated in your
letter of November 13, 1941, supra, it was decided by the Government
that the radio transmitters were not required; and, accordingly, the formal contract was not executed by the Civil Aeronautics Administration.
Moreover, by telegram dated September 19, 1941, the Civil Aeronautics
Administration notified the contractor that due to a change in Government requirements, the transmitters covered by proposal No. 1109 would

not be needed, and that the formal contract which had been submitted by the contractor would not be accepted by the Government. By telegram of September 23, 1941, and letter of the same date, the contractor protested the refusal of the Civil Aeronautics Administration to execute the formal contract, contending, in substance, that the letter of August 14, 1941, constituted an expression of intent on the part of the Government to purchase the radio transmitters, and, therefore, that a binding agreement was formed which the Government had no right to refuse to carry out. Also, the contractor urged that by the issuance of preference-rating certificate No. VG-89775, the Government represented that a valid contract for the purchase of the radio transmitters existed. Therefore, the contractor contended that in reliance on the letter of August 14, 1941, and the preference-rating certificate of August 28, 1941, it had a right to proceed with the manufacture of the radio transmitters even though the formal contract had not been executed by the Civil Aeronautics Administration.

The rule appears to be established that, generally, the acceptance of a contractor's offer or proposal by an authorized contracting officer of the Government results in the formation of a valid and binding contract between the parties even though it may be contemplated at the time that the negotiations between the parties are to be incorporated subsequently into a formal written agreement. See Garfielde v. United States, 93 U.S. 242; United States v. New York and Porto Rico Steamship Company, 239 U.S. 88; United States v. Purcell Envelope Company, 249 U.S. 313; American Smelting and Refining Company v. United States, 259 U.S. 75; Waters v. United States, 75 Ct. Cls. 126, and 18 Comp. Gen. 54. However, it is equally well settled that in such event the acceptance of the contractor's offer by the Government must be clear and unconditional; and it also must appear that both parties intended to make a binding agreement at the time of the acceptance of the contractor's bid. See Rocky Brook Mills Company v. United States, 70 Ct. Cls. 646; United States v. P. J. Carlin Construction Company, et al. (C.C.A.2d), 224 Fed. 859; Elkhorn-Hazard Coal Company, et al. v. Kentucky River Coal Corporation (C.C.A. 6th), 20 F.(2d) 67, 70.

In passing on the question as to whether parties to a contract, who reach an agreement by negotiating, are bound from the time an agreement as to terms is reached, or whether a binding agreement is not formed until the terms of the negotiations are reduced to a formal contract and signed by the parties, the court, in the case of Elkhorn-Hazard Coal Company, et al. v. Kentucky River Coal Corporation, supra, stated, at page 70, as follows:

> . . . Whether a contract results from an exchange of definite communications, when a formal contract is intended later to be prepared and executed, is a question which has received much consideration. *Whether*

one so results is mainly a question of intention. The law is well stated in
Mississippi & Dominion Steamship Co. v. Swift, 86 Me. 248, 29 A. 1063, 41
Am. St. Rep. 545, 553, as follows:

> "If the party sought to be charged intended to close a contract prior to the
> formal signing of a written draft, or if he signified such an intention to
> the other party, he will be bound by the contract actually made, though
> the signing of the written draft be omitted. *If, on the other hand, such party
> neither had nor signified such an intention to close the contract until it was
> fully expressed in a written instrument and attested by signatures, then he will
> not be bound until the signatures are affixed.* The expression of the idea may
> be attempted in other words: If the written draft is viewed by the parties merely
> as a convenient memorial, or record of their previous contract, its absence
> does not affect the binding force of the contract; if, however, it is viewed as the
> consummation of the negotiations; there is no contract until the written draft
> is finally signed. . . ." [Italics supplied.]

Considering the facts in the present case in the light of the above
principles, it appears that while the contractor was notified by an officer
of the Civil Aeronautics Administration, in the letter of August 14, 1941
. . . that award had been made to it under invitation No. 1109, it cannot
be said that the letter, in itself, was a clear and unconditional acceptance
of the contractor's bid so as to bind the Government in the matter from
the date of the issuance of said letter. On the contrary, the letter of
August 14, 1941, expressly advised the contractor that "Your bid on Proposal No. 1109 . . . is conditionally accepted subject to the execution of a
formal contract by the Civil Aeronautics Administration." In other
words, the letter of August 14, 1941, expressly negatived any intent of the
Government to be bound in the transaction by the issuance thereof and
definitely put the contractor on notice that there would be no binding
agreement between the parties until a formal contract had been executed
by the Civil Aeronautics Administration. Hence, it appears that the letter
of August 14, 1941, was not an unconditional acceptance of the contractor's bid nor can it be considered as evidencing an intention on the part of
the Civil Aeronautics Administration to enter into a binding agreement at
that time to purchase the radio transmitters from the contractor.

Furthermore, it cannot be said that by the issuance of preference
rating certificate No. VG-89775 on August 28, 1941, the Government
considered that a binding contract to purchase the radio transmitters had
been made between the parties as a result of the issuance of the letter of
August 14, 1941. No reference was made in said certificate to any existing
contract between the parties, and, in the space provided in the preference
rating certificate for the insertion of the applicable contract, it was expressly stipulated that the only agreement between the parties was proposal No. 1109 and the letter of August 14, 1941, which is specifically
referred to as "Letter of Intent." Therefore, the preference rating certificate shows clearly that, while at the time of its issuance the Government
had intended to enter into a contract for the radio transmitters, the Civil

Aeronautics Administration considered that the contract had not been consummated.

Accordingly, I have to advise that neither the issuance of the letter of August 14, 1941, nor of the preference rating certificate of August 28, 1941, resulted in the formation of a binding contract between the parties and, therefore, since no valid contract exists, there is no authority for entering into any agreement to reimburse the contractor for any work which may have been performed by it in connection with the matter. See Rocky Brook Mills Company v. United States, supra. . . .

NOTE

1. Compare Briggs & Turivas v. United States, 83 Ct. Cl. 664 (1936), *cert. denied*, 302 U.S. 690 (1937).

2. Mississippi & Dominion Steamship Co. v. Swift, quoted in the opinion, contains (at 259) a most helpful discussion of the circumstances to be considered in determining the intention of the parties:

> In determining which view is entertained in any particular case, several circumstances may be helpful, as: whether the contract is of that class which are usually found to be in writing; whether it is of such nature as to need a formal writing for its full expression; whether it has few or many details; whether the amount involved is large or small; whether it is a common or unusual contract; whether the negotiations themselves indicate that a written draft is contemplated as the final conclusion of the negotiations. If a written draft is proposed, suggested or referred to, during the negotiations, it is some evidence that the parties intended it to be the final closing of the contract.

See further Llewellyn, Our Case Law of Contract, Offer and Acceptance, I, 48 Yale L.J. 1, 14 n.29 (1938); Massee v. Gibbs, 169 Minn. 100, 210 N.W. 872 (1926); Schwartz v. Greenberg, 304 N.Y. 250, 107 N.E.2d 65 (1952); Ryan v. Schott, 109 Ohio App. 317, 159 N.E.2d 907 (1959).

3. The predicament that confronted the supplier in the *Collins Radio* case was dealt with during World War II by so-called Letters of Intent issued by the government. The Letter of Intent used by the Navy Department, Bureau of Supplies and Accounts (5 February 1942) contained the following pertinent provisions:

> The Secretary of the Navy finds that in the interest of National Defense it is necessary that production be not delayed awaiting the placing of the aforesaid order. You are hereby authorized to purchase such materials as are necessary for the production of the airplanes and spare parts and to proceed with the production thereof in anticipation of the placing of the order, subject to the receipt by the Purchasing Officer of notification of the

items to be purchased and the estimated maximum prices and confirmation by the Purchasing Officer of authorization to proceed with such purchases.

You will agree in connection with the purchase of such material as aforesaid that you will comply with all laws pertaining or relating to the purchase of such material. All applicable contract clauses required by Federal Law to be incorporated in contracts for articles of the kind herein contracted for are hereby incorporated herein by reference. Your attention is invited to the National Defense clause included in present classified contracts.

In the event that the order for the airplanes and spare parts is not placed with you prior to 1 April 1942, the Government will, upon demand made prior to 1 May 1942, reimburse you for the cost incurred by you and will assume your obligation for any commitment which you have made in this connection. Upon payment and assumption by the Government, title to such material, including rights under commitments assumed, will vest in the Government.

For the modern Letter of Intent (letter contract), see 41 C.F.R. §1-3.408 (as of July, 1984).

THE SUN PRINTING AND PUBLISHING ASS'N v. REMINGTON PAPER AND POWER CO., INC.
235 N.Y. 338, 139 N.E. 470 (1923)

Appeal, by permission, from an order of the Appellate Division of the Supreme Court in the first judicial department, entered April 24, 1922, which reversed an order of Special Term denying a motion by plaintiff for judgment on the pleadings and granted said motion.

The following question was certified: "Does the complaint state facts sufficient to constitute a cause of action?"

CARDOZO, J. Plaintiff agreed to buy and defendant to sell 1,000 tons of paper per month during the months of September, 1919, to December, 1920, inclusive, 16,000 tons in all. Sizes and quality were adequately described. Payment was to be made on the 20th of each month for all paper shipped the previous month. The price for shipments in September, 1919, was to be $3.73¾ per 100 pounds, and for shipments in October, November and December, 1919, $4 per 100 pounds. "For the balance of the period of this agreement the price of the paper and length of terms for which such price shall apply shall be agreed upon by and between the parties hereto fifteen days prior to the expiration of each period for which the price and length of term thereof have been previously agreed upon, said price in no event to be higher than the contract price for newsprint charged by the Canadian Export Paper Company to the large consumers, the seller to receive the benefit of any differentials in freight rates."

Between September, 1919, and December of that year, inclusive, shipments were made and paid for as required by the contract. The time then arrived when there was to be an agreement upon a new price and upon the term of its duration. The defendant in advance of that time gave notice that the contract was imperfect, and disclaimed for the future an obligation to deliver. Upon this, the plaintiff took the ground that the price was to be ascertained by resort to an established standard. It made demand that during each month of 1920 the defendant deliver 1,000 tons of paper at the contract price for newsprint charged by the Canadian Export Paper Company to the large consumers, the defendant to receive the benefit of any differentials in freight rates. The demand was renewed month by month till the expiration of the year. This action has been brought to recover the ensuing damage.

Seller and buyer left two subjects to be settled in the middle of December and at unstated intervals thereafter. One was the price to be paid. The other was the length of time during which such price was to govern. Agreement as to the one was insufficient without agreement as to the other. If price and nothing more had been left open for adjustment, there might be force in the contention that the buyer would be viewed, in the light of later provisions, as the holder of an option (Cohen & Sons v. Lurie Woolen Co., 232 N.Y. 112). This would mean that in default of an agreement for a lower price, the plaintiff would have the privilege of calling for delivery in accordance with a price established as a maximum. The price to be agreed upon might be less, but could not be more than "the contract price for newsprint charged by the Canadian Export Paper Company to the large consumers." The difficulty is, however, that ascertainment of this price does not dispense with the necessity for agreement in respect of the term during which the price is to apply. Agreement upon a maximum payable this month or to-day is not the same as an agreement that it shall continue to be payable next month or to-morrow. Seller and buyer understood that the price to be fixed in December for a term to be agreed upon, would not be more than the price then charged by the Canadian Export Paper Company to the large consumers. They did not understand that if during the term so established the price charged by the Canadian Export Paper Company was changed, the price payable to the seller would fluctuate accordingly. This was conceded by plaintiff's counsel on the argument before us. The seller was to receive no more during the running of the prescribed term, though the Canadian maximum was raised. The buyer was to pay no less during that term, though the maximum was lowered. In brief, the standard was to be applied at the beginning of the successive terms, but once applied was to be maintained until the term should have expired. While the term was unknown, the contract was inchoate.

The argument is made that there was no need of an agreement as to time unless the price to be paid was lower than the maximum. We find no evidence of this intention in the language of the contract. The result would then be that the defendant would never know where it stood. The plaintiff was under no duty to accept the Canadian standard. It does not assert that it was. What it asserts is that the contract amounted to the concession of an option. Without an agreement as to time, however, there would be not one option, but a dozen. The Canadian price to-day might be less than the Canadian price to-morrow. Election by the buyer to proceed with performance at the price prevailing in one month would not bind it to proceed at the price prevailing in another. Successive options to be exercised every month would thus be read into the contract. Nothing in the wording discloses the intention of the seller to place itself to that extent at the mercy of the buyer. Even if, however, we were to interpolate the restriction that the option, if exercised at all, must be exercised only once, and for the entire quantity permitted, the difficulty would not be ended. Market prices in 1920 happened to rise. The importance of the time element becomes apparent when we ask ourselves what the seller's position would be if they had happened to fall. Without an agreement as to time, the maximum would be lowered from one shipment to another with every reduction of the standard. With such an agreement, on the other hand, there would be stability and certainty. The parties attempted to guard against the contingency of failing to come together as to price. They did not guard against the contingency of failing to come together as to time. Very likely they thought the latter contingency so remote that it could safely be disregarded. In any event, whether through design or through inadvertence, they left the gap unfilled. The result was nothing more than "an agreement to agree" (St. Regis Paper Co. v. Hubbs & Hastings Paper Co., 235 N.Y. 30, 36). Defendant "exercised its legal right" when it insisted that there was need of something more (St. Regis Paper Co. v. Hubbs & Hastings Paper Co., supra; 1 Williston Contracts, §45). The right is not affected by our appraisal of the motive (Mayer v. McCreery, 119 N.Y. 434, 440).

We are told that the defendant was under a duty, in default of an agreement, to accept a term that would be reasonable in view of the nature of the transaction and the practice of the business. To hold it to such a standard is to make the contract over. The defendant reserved the privilege of doing its business in its own way, and did not undertake to conform to the practice and beliefs of others (United Press v. N.Y. Press Co., 164 N.Y. 406, 413). We are told again that there was a duty, in default of other agreement, to act as if the successive terms were to expire every month. The contract says they are to expire at such intervals as the agreement may prescribe. There is need, it is true, of no high degree of ingenuity to show how the parties, with little change of language, could have framed a form of contract to which obligation would attach. The difficulty is that they framed another. We are not at liberty to revise while professing to construe.

We do not ignore the allegation of the complaint that the contract price charged by the Canadian Export Paper Company to the large consumers "constituted a definite and well defined standard of price that was readily ascertainable." The suggestion is made by members of the court that the price so charged may have been known to be one established for the year, so that fluctuation would be impossible. If that was its character, the complaint should so allege. The writing signed by the parties calls for an agreement as to time. The complaint concedes that no such agreement has been made. The result, prima facie, is the failure of the contract. In that situation, the pleader has the burden of setting forth the extrinsic circumstances, if there are any, that make agreement unimportant. There is significance, moreover, in the attitude of counsel. No point is made in brief or in argument that the Canadian price, when once established, is constant through the year. On the contrary, there is at least a tacit assumption that it varies with the market. The buyer acted on the same assumption when it renewed the demand from month to month, making tender of performance at the prices then prevailing. If we misconceive the course of dealing, the plaintiff by amendment of its pleading can correct our misconception. The complaint as it comes before us leaves no escape from the conclusion that agreement in respect of time is as essential to a completed contract as agreement in respect of price. The agreement was not reached, and the defendant is not bound.

The question is not here whether the defendant would have failed in the fulfilment of its duty by an arbitrary refusal to reach any agreement as to time after notice from the plaintiff that it might make division of the terms in any way it pleased. No such notice was given so far as the complaint discloses. The action is not based upon a refusal to treat with the defendant and attempt to arrive at an agreement. Whether any such theory of liability would be tenable we need not now inquire. Even if the plaintiff might have stood upon the defendant's denial of obligation as amounting to such a refusal, it did not elect to do so. Instead, it gave its own construction to the contract, fixed for itself the length of the successive terms, and thereby coupled its demand with a condition which there was no duty to accept (Rubber Trading Co. v. Manhattan R. Mfg. Co., 221 N.Y. 120; 3 Williston Contracts, §1334). We find no allegation of readiness and offer to proceed on any other basis. The condition being untenable, the failure to comply with it cannot give a cause of action.

The order of the Appellate Division should be reversed and that of the Special Term affirmed, with costs in the Appellate Division and in this court, and the question certified answered in the negative.

CRANE, J. (dissenting). I cannot take the view of this contract that has been adopted by the majority. The parties to this transaction beyond question thought they were making a contract for the purchase and sale of 16,000 tons rolls news print. The contract was upon a form used by the defendant in its business, and we must suppose that it was intended to be what it states to be, and not a trick or device to defraud merchants. It begins by saying that in consideration of the mutual covenants and agreements herein set forth the Remington Paper and Power Company, Incorporated, of Watertown, state of New York, hereinafter called the seller, agrees to sell and hereby does sell and the Sun Printing and Publishing Association of New York city, state of New York, hereinafter called the purchaser, agrees to buy and pay for and hereby does buy the following paper, 16,000 tons rolls news print. The sizes are then given. Shipment is to be at the rate of 1,000 tons per month to December, 1920, inclusive. There are details under the headings consignee, specifications, price and delivery, terms, miscellaneous, cores, claims, contingencies, cancellations.

Under the head of miscellaneous comes the following:

> The price agreed upon between the parties hereto, for all papers shipped during the month of September, 1919, shall be $3.73\frac{3}{4}$ per hundred pounds gross weight of rolls on board cars at mills.
>
> The price agreed upon between the parties hereto for all shipments made during the months of October, November and December, 1919, shall be $4.00 per hundred pounds gross weight of rolls on board cars at mills.
>
> For the balance of the period of this agreement the price of the paper and length of terms for which such price shall apply shall be agreed upon by and between the parties hereto fifteen days prior to the expiration of each period for which the price and length of term thereof has been previously agreed upon, said price in no event to be higher than the contract price for newsprint charged by the Canadian Export Paper Company to the large consumers, the seller to receive the benefit of any differentials in freight rates.
>
> It is understood and agreed by the parties hereto that the tonnage specified herein is for use in the printing and publication of the various editions of the Daily and Sunday New York Sun, and any variation from this will be considered a breach of contract.

After the deliveries for September, October, November and December, 1919, the defendant refused to fix any price for the deliveries during the subsequent months, and refused to deliver any more paper. It has taken the position that this document was no contract, that it meant nothing, that it was formally executed for the purpose of permitting the defendant to furnish paper or not, as it pleased.

Surely these parties must have had in mind that some binding agreement was made for the sale and delivery of 16,000 tons rolls of paper, and that the instrument contained all the elements necessary to make a binding contract. It is a strain upon reason to imagine the paper house, the Remington Paper and Power Company, Incorporated, and the Sun Printing and Publishing Association, formally executing a contract drawn up upon the defendant's prepared form which was useless and amounted to nothing. We must, at least, start the examination of this agreement by believing that these intelligent parties intended to make a binding contract. If this be so, the court should spell out a binding contract, if it be possible.

I not only think it possible, but think the paper itself clearly states a contract recognized under all the rules at law. It is said that the one essential element of price is lacking; that the provision above quoted is an agreement to agree to a price, and that the defendant had the privilege of agreeing or not, as it pleased; that if it failed to agree to a price there was no standard by which to measure the amount the plaintiff would have to pay. The contract does state, however, just this very thing. Fifteen days before the first of January, 1920, the parties were to agree upon the price of the paper to be delivered thereafter, and the length of the period for which such price should apply. However, the price to be fixed was not "to be higher than the contract price for newsprint charged by the Canadian Export Paper Company to large consumers." Here surely was something definite. The 15th day of December arrived. The defendant refused to deliver. At that time there was a price for newsprint charged by the Canadian Export Paper Company. If the plaintiff offered to pay this price, which was the highest price the defendant could demand, the defendant was bound to deliver. This seems to be very clear.

But while all agree that the price on the 15th day of December could be fixed, the further objection is made that the period during which that price should continue was not agreed upon. There are many answers to this.

We have reason to believe that the parties supposed they were making a binding contract; that they had fixed the terms by which one was required to take and the other to deliver; that the Canadian Export Paper Company price was to be the highest that could be charged in any event. These things being so, the court should be very reluctant to permit a defendant to avoid its contract. (Wakeman v. Wheeler & Wilson Mfg. Co., 101 N.Y. 205.)

On the 15th of the month, the time when the price was to be fixed for subsequent deliveries, there was a price charged by the Canadian Export Paper Company to large consumers. As the defendant failed to agree upon a price, made no attempt to agree upon a price and deliberately broke its contract, it could readily be held to deliver the rest of the paper, a thousand rolls a month, at this Canadian price. There is nothing in the complaint which indicates that this is a fluctuating price, or that the price of paper as it was on December 15th was not the same for the remaining twelve months.

Or we can deal with this contract, month by month. The deliveries were to be made 1,000 tons per month. On December 15th 1,000 tons could have been demanded. The price charged by the Canadian Export

Paper Company on the 15th of each month on and after December 15th, 1919, would be the price for the thousand ton delivery for that month.

Or again, the word as used in the miscellaneous provision quoted is not "price," but "contract price" — "in no event to be higher than the contract price." Contract implies a term or period and if the evidence should show that the Canadian contract price was for a certain period of weeks or months, then this period could be applied to the contract in question.

Failing any other alternative, the law should do here what it has done in so many other cases, apply the rule of reason and compel parties to contract in the light of fair dealing. It could hold this defendant to deliver its paper as it agreed to do, and take for a price the Canadian Export Paper Company contract price for a period which is reasonable under all the circumstances and conditions as applied in the paper trade.

To let this defendant escape from its formal obligations when any one of these rulings as applied to this contract would give a practical and just result is to give the sanction of law to a deliberate breach. (Wood v. Duff-Gordon, 222 N.Y. 88; Moran v. Standard Oil Co., 211 N.Y. 187; United States Rubber Co. v. Silverstein, 229 N.Y. 168.)

For these reasons I am for the affirmance of the courts below.

Hiscock, Ch. J., Pound, McLaughlin and Andrews, JJ., concur with Cardozo, J.; Crane J., reads dissenting opinion with which Hogan, J., concurs.

Order reversed, etc.

NOTE

The plaintiff subsequently amended his complaint in accordance with Cardozo's suggestions. It was dismissed at Special Term. No appeal was taken because of a settlement. Shientag, The Opinions and Writings of Judge Benjamin N. Cardozo, 30 Colum. L. Rev. 597, 629 (1930).

In his Growth of the Law 110-111 (1924), a series of lectures given a short while later, Cardozo defended his position as follows:

Here was a case where advantage had been taken of the strict letter of a contract to avoid an onerous engagement. Not inconceivably a sensitive conscience would have rejected such an outlet of escape. We thought this immaterial. The court subordinated the equity of a particular situation to the overmastering need of certainty in the transactions of commercial life. The end to be attained in the development of the law of contract is the supremacy, not of some hypothetical, imaginary will, apart from external manifestations, but of will outwardly revealed in the spoken or the written word. The loss to business would in the long run be greater than the gain if judges were clothed with power to revise as well as to interpret. Perhaps, with a higher conception of business and its needs, the time will come when even revision will be permitted if it is revision in consonance with established standards of fair dealing, but the time is not yet. In this department of activity, the current axiology still places stability and certainty in the forefront of the virtues. "The field is one where the law should hold fast to fundamental conceptions of contract and of duty, and follow them with loyalty to logical conclusions." [Imperator Realty Co. v. Tull, 228 N.Y. 447, 455.]

In a footnote, Cardozo makes the following qualification: "Of course, a different result may be reached if the omitted term is of subsidiary importance (1 Williston, Contracts §48), but ordinarily the price to be paid, if reserved for subsequent agreement, is to be ranked as fundamental." In contrast to the Court of Appeals, the Appellate Division had treated the arrangement as an enforceable option and held that the contract was no longer indefinite as to the price as soon as the buyer agreed to pay the maximum provided in the contract. For a further discussion of the case, see Notes, 23 Colum. L. Rev. 783 (1923); 27 Colum. L. Rev. 708 at 711, n.11 (1927); Corbin, Mr. Justice Cardozo and the Law of Contracts, 39 Colum. L. Rev. 56, 58 (1939); 52 Harv. L. Rev. 408, 410 (1939); 48 Yale L.J. 426, 428 (1939). The Wood v. Duff-Gordon case is reprinted *infra* p. 451.

What does the reference to arbitrary refusal mean?

Suppose the contract had contained the following clause: "If any disputes or differences shall arise on the subject matter or construction of this agreement the same shall be submitted to arbitration." Same result? Foley v. Classique Coaches, Ltd., [1934] 2 K.B. 1 (C.A.). See Note, 44 Yale L.J. 684 (1935).

HOFFMAN v. RED OWL STORES, INC., 26 Wis. 2d 683, 133 N.W.2d 267 (1965). Hoffman and his wife, the plaintiffs, owned and operated a bakery in Wautoma, Wisconsin. Wanting to expand his operations, Hoffman contacted the District Manager of Red Owl Stores to inquire about obtaining a franchise. Hoffman mentioned that $18,000 was all the capital he had to invest, and was repeatedly assured that this was enough. On the recommendation of the manager, Hoffman bought the inventory and fixtures of a small local grocery store to gain experience. The store made a profit, but Hoffman sold it within three months on the insistence of the manager, who promised that Red Owl would find him a larger store in another city. The manager then advised Hoffman to spend $1000 on an option on a piece of land costing $6000 in Chilton, where the future store would be. After spending $1000 for the option, Hoffman, again on the advice of the manager, sold his bakery business and the bakery building, which he and his wife owned. Hoffman rented a house in Chilton on the assurance that "everything would be set" after the sale of the bakery. He never moved to Chilton, however, Red Owl having advised him to get experience at a Red Owl store in Neenah. The family moved to Neenah, but Hoffman never got the job.

Having done all this on the advice of the District Manager, Hoffman was informed that he would have to invest $34,000, not $18,000. Negotiations were abandoned when the parties were unable to agree on the terms of the financing agreement.

The Hoffmans sued Red Owl to recover the losses incurred in reliance on defendant's representations and assurances.

The court, relying on §90, upheld a damage award to plaintiffs for losses on the sale of the bakery, the rental and moving expenses, and the down payment on the Chilton property. The court also sustained an order for a new trial on the issue of damages incurred in the sale of the grocery store fixtures and inventory, since the damages awarded by the jury were not sustained by the evidence. On this latter issue, the court followed the trial court in ruling that damages for the sale of the grocery store be "limited to the difference between the sales price received and the fair market value of the assets sold, giving consideration to any goodwill attaching thereto by reason of the transfer of a going business." The court rejected the plaintiff's contention that the damages should include loss of profits. When the plaintiffs sold the store they were concerned about the loss of large profits during the ensuing summer months (profits that the buyer of the store subsequently realized). After noting that this was not a breach of contract action, the court said that "[w]here damages are awarded in promissory estoppel instead of specifically enforcing the promisor's promise, they should be only such as in the opinion of the court are necessary to prevent injustice. . . . At the time Hoffman bought the equipment and inventory of the [grocery store] he did so in order to gain experience in the grocery store business. . . . Thus Hoffman made this purchase more or less as a temporary experiment. Justice does not require that the damages awarded him, because of selling those assets at the behest of defendants, should exceed any actual loss sustained measured by the difference between the sales price and the fair market value." The court, however, did point out that evidence of past profits would be admissible to aid in determining the fair market value of the assets in question.

NOTE

1. The promises and assurances made by the defendant in *Hoffman* were not "so comprehensive in scope as to meet the requirements of an offer that would ripen into a contract if accepted by the promisee." 26 Wis. 2d at 698, 133 N.W.2d at 275. But as the court pointed out, §90 does not require an offer.

Rather the conditions imposed are:

(1)   Was the promise one which the promisor should reasonably expect to induce action or forbearance of a definite and substantial character on the part of the promisee?

(2)   Did the promise induce such action or forbearance?

(3)   Can injustice be avoided only by enforcement of the promise?

Id. at 698, 133 N.W.2d at 275.

The *Hoffman* court went on to point out that "it would be a mistake to regard an action grounded on promissory estoppel as the equivalent of a breach of contract action."

2. If promissory estoppel is not an action for breach of contract, what is it? Promissory estoppel has been called "a peculiarly equitable doctrine." Henderson, Promissory Estoppel and Traditional Contract Doctrine, 78 Yale L.J. 343, 379-380 (1969). From this, the California Supreme Court, misreading Henderson and over the strong dissent of Newman, J., drew the inference that there could be no right to a jury trial in an action based on promissory estoppel. C & K Engineering Contractors v. Amber Steel Co., 23 Cal. 3d 1, 587 P.2d 1136, 151 Cal. Rptr. 323 (1978). The *Hoffman* court did not go so far. Of the three issues set forth above, the first two were left to the jury.

3. If promissory estoppel is not based on contract, how should the jurisdictional and government liability questions noted in connection with *Heyer Products, supra* p. 207, be resolved when a plaintiff bases his claim on Section 90? Note that under both Restatements an action based on Section 90 is an action for breach of contract. See §1. Which statute of limitations should apply in promissory estoppel actions? See Huhtala v. Travelers Ins. Co., 401 Mich. 118, 257 N.W.2d 640 (1977).

4. *Goodman, Chrysler,* and *Hoffman* have all been explained in terms of bad faith. Although the bad faith in *Chrysler* was clear, it was more subtle in *Goodman* and *Hoffman*. In the latter cases, bad faith has been found in the failure promptly to withdraw a "rash promise" and post-promise assurances about future performance. Goetz & Scott, Enforcing Promises: An Examination of the Basis of Contract, 89 Yale L.J. 1261, 1319-1320 (1890). Is the use of promissory estoppel in this context filling a gap left by the tort law of fraud and deceit? Can a connection be made between the bad faith in these three cases and the bad faith doctrine in the insurance cases described in Chapter 4, Section 3? See Holmes, Is There Life After Gilmore's Death of Contract? — Inductions from a Study of Commercial Good Faith in First-Party Insurance Contracts, 65 Cornell L. Rev. 330, 369-370 (1980).

WHEELER v. WHITE, 398 S.W.2d 93 (Tex. 1965): Wheeler owned certain property in Port Arthur, Texas on which he wished to construct a commercial building or shopping center. He and White entered into a written loan agreement which provided that White would obtain the money necessary for the construction work from some third party, or provide it himself. Wheeler agreed, in return, to repay the loan in fifteen monthly installments at an interest rate of "not more than six (6%) per cent per annum"; he also promised to pay White a commission fee for obtaining the loan as well as a percentage share of "all rentals received from any tenants procured by White. . . ."

After the contract had been signed, White urged Wheeler to proceed with the destruction of several buildings already on the property in order to make room for the new construction, telling Wheeler that if he (White) could not obtain loan funds from anyone else, he would supply them himself. After the buildings (which had a reasonable market value of $58,500 and a rental value of $400 per month) had been destroyed, White informed Wheeler that there would be no loan. Wheeler made an unsuccessful effort to obtain funds elsewhere, and then sued White for breach of contract, arguing in the alternative that White was liable on a theory of promissory estoppel. The trial court dismissed both causes of action. On appeal, the Texas Supreme Court agreed that the contract "did not contain essential elements to its enforceability" in that it failed to specify the amount of the monthly installments Wheeler was to pay as well as the exact rate of interest. The court also concluded, however, that Wheeler's alternative plea of promissory estoppel did state a good cause of action, and remanded the case for trial. In its opinion, the Texas court relied heavily on the holding in Goodman v. Dicker, *supra* page 209, particularly with respect to the problem of calculating whatever damages Wheeler might subsequently recover. Do you think the two cases are in fact similar? In which is the plaintiff's case more compelling? Suppose that Wheeler wins the trial; how exactly should his damages be measured?

BORG-WARNER CORP. v. ANCHOR COUPLING CO.
16 Ill. 2d 234, 156 N.E.2d 513, 930 (1959)

KLINGBIEL, Justice.

This action was brought by Borg-Warner Corporation for specific performance or, in the alternative, money damages, on an alleged contract between plaintiff and Anchor Coupling Co. and its chief officers, Charles L. Conroy and Walter Fritsch. The amended complaint was dismissed on the ground that plaintiff had failed to allege a completed contract capable of specific performance or a cause of action for damages.

This appeal was transferred to this court from the Appellate Court, Second District, for the reason that a freehold is involved, certain real property being among the assets of defendant which were the subject of the alleged contract.

Since the propriety of the lower court's dismissal of the case depends solely on the sufficiency of plaintiff's amended complaint, it is necessary to set forth the facts as alleged in said complaint in some detail.

["Anchor Coupling Company is an Illinois corporation having its principal office in Libertyville, Illinois. The founders of the Company were Charles Conroy and Walter Fritsch. In 1956 Conroy and Fritsch owned approximately ninety percent of Anchor's outstanding stock. Early in that year they entered into negotiations for the sale of Anchor's assets to Borg-Warner. On February 20 Borg-Warner wrote Anchor setting forth a proposed agreement which gave Borg-Warner a sixty-day option to purchase Anchor's assets."[58]

On February 29 Anchor replied, expressing its unwillingness to enter into a formal option, but a readiness to sell the assets of the corporation for $4,025,000. Anchor's letter stated "You may consider this as a letter of intent authorizing you to make the survey that you deem necessary to make your offer a firm and binding one; and we assure you of our full cooperation in making it." the letter also contained, however, the following requirements (among others) for any offer made by Borg-Warner: "(a) That suitable assurances are given for the retention of the lower level executive personnel; (b) That mutually satisfactory arrangements are made for the continued employment of Charles L. Conroy." — EDS.]

Plaintiff thereafter inquired of defendants whether their letter of February 29 was correctly understood by plaintiff as a firm offer which would not be revoked during the period stated in said letter [Fifty days from February 29, 1956] (which period was later extended to April 26, 1956) and which plaintiff could accept within said period so as to create a binding contract of sale, and whether plaintiff could make its survey of Anchor's business operations in reliance thereon. In response thereto, defendants Conroy and Fritsch, by their agent, assured plaintiff that plaintiff had "in effect an option"; that said letter was "in legal effect . . . an offer by us [defendants] to enter into a contract with those four very minor things [referring to paragraphs (a) through (d) of defendants' letter of February 29] still to be agreed on"; that the further agreements referred to were not intended to prevent said offer from being a complete offer capable of acceptance but were minor details which, upon the acceptance of said offer, the parties would be obligated to work out in good faith in a reasonable manner, and that if plaintiff within fifty days made an offer in conformity with said letter, defendants would be obligated, subject only to the conditions that the acceptance be delivered within the time limited and that the investigation be conducted in secrecy, to accept such offer.

On March 14, 1956, plaintiff wrote a letter to Conroy, Fritsch and Anchor saying, "You indicate that our offer on the basis outlined will be

---

58. Taken from *Anchor Coupling Co. v. United States*, 427 F.2d 429 (7th Cir. 1970).

accepted if made within fifty days from this date" and asking that the fifty days time be extended to April 26 and that the purchase price be adjusted to $4,024,000. This letter was initialed by Conroy and Fritsch and returned to plaintiff.

Finally, on April 26, 1956, plaintiff wrote to defendants saying that plaintiff had decided to proceed in the acquisition of Anchor's assets. This letter read in part:

> Please consider this our formal offer, therefore, to enter into an agreement in accordance with our letters to you of March 14th, and February 20th and your letter to us of February 29th. Our letter to you of March 14th, the terms of which were accepted by you indicates that this offer will be accepted by you if mailed on April 26th.

Plaintiff alleges that at this point a completed contract came into existence. Plaintiff also alleges that in various subsequent conversations defendants represented and agreed that there was a complete contract between plaintiff and defendants until on August 1, 1956, defendant Conroy raised objections to the performance of said contract, and on September 27, 1956, refused to perform said contract.

Defendant Fritsch filed an answer admitting the allegations of plaintiff's complaint and stating that "he did believe that he did enter into a contract and agreement, that the same was fair, open and truly performed on its part by the plaintiff, and this defendant does again reiterate his willingness to perform the same for and on behalf of the shares of stock owned by him and by his son, John Fritsch." Defendants Conroy and Anchor filed motions to dismiss plaintiff's amended complaint.

On these facts, the trial court dismissed the amended complaint on the ground that it appeared on the face of the pleadings that the parties had failed to agree on material terms of the proposed contract, viz.: (a) The failure to agree on the retention of lower level executive personnel, and (b) failure to make mutually satisfactory arrangements for the continued employment of Conroy.[59] Further, the court held that there was no ambiguity in the written correspondence between the parties and therefore the Statute of Frauds and the parol evidence rule barred consideration of any parol evidence pleaded by plaintiff.

First, let us analyze the correspondence between the parties in terms of the contract rules of offer and acceptance. Plaintiff's letter of February

---

59. Anchor Coupling v. United States, 427 F.2d 429 (7th Cir. 1970) gives us a clearer picture of why negotiations broke off. At some point

> it became apparent that Borg-Warner intended upon consummation of the sale to reduce the salaries and responsibilities of certain executives, and that some of the executives intended to seek employment elsewhere. As a result Conroy, over the opposition of Fritsch, decided to terminate the negotiations and to resist, by litigation if necessary, Borg-Warner's efforts to acquire Anchor's assets.

Id. at 430. — EDS.

20, setting forth the detailed option agreement, was an offer by plaintiff. This offer was not accepted by defendants, but instead, defendants Conroy and Fritsch wrote a letter to plaintiff stating that they would be willing to sell the assets of Anchor in accordance with certain paragraphs of plaintiff's February 20th letter, that plaintiff could consider this a "letter of intent," and that if plaintiff should make a firm offer within fifty days, defendants would enter into a contract with them on the basis of the enumerated paragraphs of the February 20 letter, with the exceptions: (a), (b), (c) and (d). This letter varied the terms of plaintiff's offer and thus constituted a counteroffer. Snow v. Schulman, 352 Ill. 63, 71, 185 N.E. 262. Although it spoke in terms of plaintiff making an offer, it must be viewed as an offer itself, asking that plaintiff's acceptance be worded as an offer. This is clear from the fact that defendants referred to plaintiff's offer as a "firm and binding" one. The only way it could be firm and binding would be that it legally constituted an acceptance. As requested, plaintiff accepted by submitting a "formal offer" on April 26.

Was this acceptance sufficient to create a contract at this point or, as defendants contend, did exceptions (a) and (b) prevent the formation of a contract? The answer depends on what the parties intended. (1 Corbin on Contracts, 1st ed. 1950, p. 69.) Were defendants asking that contracts of employment between plaintiff and the lower level executive personnel and between plaintiff and Conroy actually had to be agreed to as to conditions precedent to the existence of the contract? Or, were defendants merely asking that plaintiff, by a general acceptance, give assurance as to the retention of lower executive personnel and agree that mutually satisfactory arrangements would be made for the employment of Conroy?

In this regard, we find the offer in the February 29 letter to be ambiguous. Thus this case falls within the well-recognized exception to the parol evidence rule that if the terms and provisions of a contract are ambiguous, or if the writings are capable of more than one construction, parol evidence is admissible to explain and ascertain what the parties intended. Street v. Chicago Wharfing & Storage Co., 157 Ill. 605, 41 N.E. 1108; 32 C.J.S. Evidence §959. This applies to contracts within the Statute of Frauds as well as to any other contract. Plaintiff is not seeking to add terms to the writings by parol, but is merely trying to explain what the parties intended by the written words. The trial court was in error in holding that the parol evidence pleaded by plaintiff could not be considered.

The question then is whether the written correspondence, together with the facts pleaded explaining the terms of the written communications, taken in its most favorable aspect, disclose a contract. We believe the following factors, if proved, are sufficient to support a finding that a completed contract came into existence at the time plaintiff submitted its formal offer on April 26. In so holding, it is impossible to place great reliance on other cases except insofar as they state general principles of law. Contract cases, particularly, must each turn on their own particular facts. As said by Professor Corbin, "A transaction is complete when the parties mean it to be complete. It is a mere matter of interpretation of their expressions to each other, a question of fact." 1 Corbin on Contracts, 1st ed. 1950, p. 69.

Both plaintiff and defendant Fritsch intended that a general acceptance by plaintiff was all that was necessary for a contract to come into existence. Fritsch has so admitted by his answer stating that he believes there was a binding contract. Although we do not believe this admission is determinative of the case, it is extremely significant as tending to show that the parties so intended.

The fact that plaintiff spent large sums of money in conducting a survey of Anchor's business certainly tends to indicate that it believed a mere acceptance of defendants' offer would be sufficient to form a contract. If plaintiff had believed that employment contracts had first to be agreed upon, one would seriously question whether it would expend such large sums without attempting to negotiate such contracts. Furthermore, plaintiff was not unreasonable in its belief. Defendants' letter of February 29 was sprinkled with "assurances" to induce plaintiff to expend substantial money in making a survey. It referred to plaintiff's right to make a "firm and binding" offer and defendants' offer to "enter into a contract with you." Such language warranted a reasonable belief on the part of plaintiff that a contract would be completed by its acceptance of the offer.

Defendants themselves quote Professor Corbin as saying: "Even though one of the parties may believe that the negotiations have been concluded, all items agreed upon, and the contract closed, there is still not contract *unless he is reasonable in his belief and the other party ought to have known that he would so believe.*" (1 Corbin on Contracts, sec. 29, 1st ed. 1950, p. 66.) (Emphasis supplied.) We are of the opinion that plaintiff was reasonable in its belief and that defendants, knowing of plaintiff's large expenditures, "ought to have known that (plaintiff) would so believe" that its acceptance of defendants' terms would create a contract.

Another important factor is the allegation that plaintiff specifically inquired whether defendants' February 29 letter was intended as a firm offer which plaintiff could accept within fifty days so as to create a binding contract. In response, defendants, by their agent, assured plaintiff that it had "in effect an option" and that exceptions (a) through (d) were not intended to prevent said offer from being a complete offer capable of acceptance but were minor details which, upon the acceptance of said offer, the parties would be obligated to work out in good faith in a reasonable manner. Such facts clearly support plaintiff's contention that the parties intended that all that was necessary to complete the contract was plaintiff's general acceptance of defendants' terms.

Plaintiff further alleges that subsequent to its acceptance of April 26, defendants, by their actions and conversations, represented that there was a completed contract between the parties.

If, as the above evidence indicates, the parties intended that a general acceptance by plaintiff would complete the contract, the fact that the employment contracts of Conroy and other executive personnel were left for future agreement does not preclude the existence of an enforceable contract. See Welsh v. Jakstas, 401 Ill. 288, 297, 82 N.E.2d 53, 58, where this court said:

> The option, when accepted, resulted in a present contract for the sale of real estate. The provisions of the option agreement then constituted the contract of sale and stated in clear and unambiguous language, the price, terms and conditions of the sale. *A contract is not rendered void because the parties thereto contract or agree to contract concerning additional matters.*

(Emphasis supplied.)

We are of the opinion that on the allegations of the complaint, the trier of fact could find that there was a binding contract of sale in the instant case. Plaintiff therefore was entitled to a trial on the question of the existence of the contract. Where it is necessary to have recourse to parol evidence to determine the meaning of language used in letters or telegrams which are relied upon as evidencing a contract, the question as to the factual meaning of such language is for the jury if opposite conclusions may be drawn. Brown v. M'Gran, 14 Pet. 479, 493, 39 U.S. 479, 10 L. Ed. 550.

If, upon a trial, it is found that there was a binding contract, we see nothing to prevent the specific performance of that contract. Defendants' argument that the contract is not specifically enforceable because it did not purport to bind defendant corporation is without merit. Whether Anchor was bound or not is not controlling since plaintiff is seeking a decree requiring Conroy and Fritsch (who owns 93 per cent of the stock) personally to carry out the steps necessary to cause Anchor to transfer its assets. In Schmidt v. J. F. Schmidt Bros. Co., 272 Ill. 340, 111 N.E. 1025, 1027, where a similar argument was made, this court said:

> While the agreement of the parties to sell the property of the corporation was not sufficient to transfer the legal title to such property, their contract, upon sufficient consideration, to do any lawful act was binding. While the sale of the tools for $1,000 did not transfer the title to them, this fact does not relieve John F. Schmidt from the obligation of his contract. He agreed to wind up the corporation in a lawful manner within three months, to pay all accounts and bills of the corporation, and not to use its name for any new work. It was within his power to do or not to do these things. There was nothing unlawful in his agreement and the contract is one which a court of equity will enforce.

Neither do we think the contract was too indefinite to be capable of specific enforcement. The only thing left for future agreement was the employment contract of Conroy. Under the terms of the offer and acceptance, the parties have agreed that Conroy is to be employed under "mutually satisfactory arrangements." A mutually satisfactory arrangement is a reasonable arrangement.

> The phrase "mutual satisfaction" means reasonable satisfaction. . . . Assuming that mutual satisfaction is equivalent to satisfaction to each party independently, that mutual satisfaction necessarily would have to be reasonable satisfaction. . . . The burden we have here is to find out whether the parties have reserved the right to be arbitrary or whether they have such right for a reasonable satisfaction controlling upon both contracting parties. We think that we should construe "mutual satisfaction" as reasonable satisfaction and thus uphold the contract.

Bondy v. Harvey, 2 Cir., 1933, 62 F.2d 521, 524, *cert. denied* 289 U.S. 740, 53 S. Ct. 659, 77 L. Ed. 1487. A promise to render performance satisfactory to a reasonable man is not too indefinite. (3 Williston, Contracts, section 675A.) Cases relied on by defendants in which promises were held too indefinite for enforcement because the contract reserved a unilateral right to satisfaction by one party are not in point here where the contract provides that the arrangement will be mutually satisfactory. If the parties cannot agree, proof of Conroy's present terms of employment, of the prevailing rates of compensation and other terms of employment of persons in a similar standing in similar businesses, and of established prior practices at Anchor, would enable a court or jury to fix reasonable terms of employment. Thus the contract, if established, is capable of specific performance.

For the aforesaid reasons, the decree is reversed and the cause is remanded to the trial court with directions to overrule defendants' motions to dismiss and to order defendants to answer.

Reversed and remanded, with directions.

SCHAEFER, Justice (dissenting).

It seems to me that when a large corporation is purchasing a smaller one, the fate of the employees of the selling corporation will naturally be a matter of concern to its management. It was a matter of concern here, expressed in the exception taken with respect to the "lower level executive personnel." I do not find that agreement was ever reached as to that matter. Nor was agreement ever reached as to the employment and compensation of Conroy by the purchasing corporation. For these reasons I think that no contract existed and that the judgment of the trial court should be affirmed.

BRISTOW, Justice (dissenting).

I must respectfully dissent from the majority opinion in this case. I disagree with the premises set out in the opinion and the conclusions of law based thereon. . . .

Pleaded as a part of plaintiff's amended complaint is Borg-Warner's letter under date of July 12, 1956, addressed to Conroy, which letter is not alluded to in the majority opinion. Although this letter is a self-serving declaration, it is interesting to note that (1) it shows that negotiation was being carried on to reach agreement as to exceptions (a) and (b); and (2) that *agreement on these open required terms had not yet been reached.* For example, as to exception (b), Conroy's employment, it says "if any question remains in your mind, I am sure it can be answered." As to exception (a), retention of lower level executives, it says: "although there are two or three questionable cases, you felt no unsurmountable problems remained as to the lower level executive personnel. We . . . believe we can mutually develop a fair basis for their continuing employment. . . . As to two or three salaries where you felt some further consideration should be given, I told you that we were open-minded and would be glad to go into this with you further." Most certainly this letter does not establish a completed agreement on April 26, 1956, but just the contrary.

In analyzing this correspondence, the court concludes that Conroy and Fritsch's letter of February 29 was a counteroffer, because it "varied the terms of plaintiff's offer" of February 20. [156 N.E.2d 516.] This infers plaintiff's proposal to purchase an option was, in fact, an offer to purchase Anchor's assets, which it plainly was not. The proposal to purchase an option was explicitly rejected by Conroy and Fritsch.

Then the court reasons that Conroy and Fritsch's letter of February 29 is to be construed as an offer in and of itself. This reasoning is based on the use of the phrase "firm and binding" offer in the paragraph wherein the controlling stockholders authorize plaintiff to make the survey, without which plaintiff would not consider making an offer to purchase Anchor's assets. This letter, in my opinion, is not an offer nor a counteroffer but merely an invitation to plaintiff to make an offer. The paragraph wherein the phrase is used, "firm and binding" offer, is clear and explicit, and this phrase is employed merely to differentiate the offer invited from the plaintiff — one to purchase the assets — from plaintiff's previous offer to purchase an option. Indeed, in the only paragraph of the letter of February 29 expressing contractual intent, the offer invited from plaintiff was expressed as "a firm offer," — "you are assured that should you make a firm offer within 50 days . . . we are willing to enter into a contract with you."

I can find nothing in the letter of February 29 from Conroy and Fritsch to warrant the statement in the majority opinion that this letter is ambiguous. Most of the text of this letter is set out in the opinion. In it, Conroy and Fritsch spell out the terms on which they are willing to contract. There can be no question but that this letter is the starting point of the alleged contract, because the option proposal made by the letter of February 20 was categorically rejected, thus putting an end to it. The only purposes the letter of February 20 here serve are as a background circumstance and to supply certain terms that were from it incorporated into Conroy and Fritsch's letter of February 29.

The record here is explicit that Conroy and Fritsch would contract only if: "(a) That suitable assurances are given for the retention of the lower level executive personnel; (b) that mutually satisfactory arrangements are made for the continued employment of Charles L. Conroy." There is no ambiguity in these explicit requirements. It is patent on this record that the parties have never agreed on these two conditions. The only "ambiguity" or uncertainty that can arise is in the determination of these requirements in the absence of mutual agreement by the parties themselves.

The majority opinion lifts a quote from plaintiff's letter of March 14, "'You indicate that our offer on the basis outlined will be accepted if made within fifty days from this date.'" The most that can be said about this letter is that it asks for an extension of time to April 26 and that the purchase price be adjusted to $4,024,000, which clarifications were accepted by Conroy and Fritsch when they initialed this letter as requested. . . .

In reaching their decision the majority have said "it is impossible to place great reliance on other cases except insofar as they state general principles of law." [156 N.E.2d 517.] This expression can serve to bewilder those who look to the reviewing courts to establish precedent. Unless we, ourselves, are guided by precedent how else can we arrive at our decisions? And unless we establish precedents in given factual situations, how else can the trial judge and lawyer, or the scrivener, find guidance in the accomplishment of their daily tasks?

Contrary to what the majority says, there is a mass of precedent governing the factual situation presented here, compelling the conclusion that no contract was formed. For example, omitted from the majority's quotation from Prof. Corbin (1 Corbin on Contracts, 1st ed., 1950, sec. 29, p. 66) is this statement:

> Communications that include mutual expressions of agreement may fail to consummate a contract for the reason that they are not complete, some essential terms not having been included. Frequently agreements are arrived at piecemeal, different terms and items being discussed and agreed upon separately. As long as the parties know that there is an essential term not yet agreed on, there is no contract; the preliminary agreements on specific items are mere preliminary negotiation building up the terms of the final offer that may or may not be made.

And in Whitelaw v. Brady, 3 Ill. 2d 583, 590, 121 N.E.2d 785, 790, we said: "It is not unusual, however, for negotiations for a contract on any subject matter to be a series of proposals and counterproposals each narrowing the differences between the parties on certain matters and leaving open others for future determination." A similar statement appears in Upsal Street Realty Co. v. Rubin, 326 Pa. 327, 192 A. 481, 483:

> It is not unusual for persons to agree to negotiate with the view of entering into contractual relations and to reach an accord *at once* as to certain major items of the proposed contract and then later find that on other details they cannot agree. In such a case no contract results.

Prof. Corbin says further (1 Corbin on Contracts, sec. 22, p. 54):

> In the process of negotiation a party may use words that standing alone would normally be understood to be words of "contract," at the same time limiting them in such a way as to say that a subsequent expression of assent on his part is required. In such case the expression is neither an operative offer nor an operative acceptance; it is preliminary negotiation. Thus, a written proposal stating many terms may be made "subject to agreement" on another specified matter; or it may be said: "I reserve final determination for tomorrow." Words such as these will in nearly all cases be held to show that an operative assent has not satisfactorily been given.

See, too, 1 Corbin on Contracts, sec. 24, p. 58. Like expressions appear in Williston (1 Willison on Contracts, Rev. ed., sec. 45, p. 131) and the Restatement (Restatement of the Law of Contracts, chap. 3, sec. 25, pp. 31, 32). There are numberless cases involving facts similar to those involved here, holding that no contract was formed. . . .

It is well established that the province of a court in a specific performance suit is to enforce a contract as made by the parties and not to make a contract for them and then to enforce the contract thus made. White v. Lang, 401 Ill. 219, 81 N.E.2d 897; Morris v. Goldthorp, 390 Ill. 186, 60 N.E.2d 857; and Shaver v. Wickwire, 335 Ill. 46, 166 N.E. 458. As a basis for specific performance there must be not only a binding contract but said contract must be complete in itself without the necessity for further negotiations or agreement. Young v. Kowske, 402 Ill. 114, 83 N.E.2d 500; Peiffer v. Newcomer, 326 Ill. 189, 157 N.E. 240; and Westphal v. Buenger, 324 Ill. 77, 154 N.E. 426. . . .

The admitted facts in the present case establish that there was the necessity for further negotiations or agreement including, among other things, terms of personal employment. It is my opinion that the majority opinion in this case reaches a result contrary to long established principles of law.

NOTE

As things turned out, the case was settled at the beginning of the trial. The defendants agreed to pay Borg-Warner $1,000,000: the individual defendants paid $400,000 and Anchor Coupling Co. paid $600,000. See Anchor Coupling Co. v. United States, 427 F.2d 429 (7th Cir. 1970), disallowing Anchor's attempt to have the $600,000 corporate payment treated as an ordinary business expenditure for income tax purposes.

In commenting on *Borg-Warner*, Knapp, Enforcing the Contract to Bargain, 44 N.Y.U. L. Rev. 673, 715 (1969), remarks: "A better case can hardly be imagined to demonstrate the dilemma caused by the common law for the judges concerned, both with justice and with well structured reasoning."

ITEK CORP. v. CHICAGO AERIAL INDUSTRIES, INC.
248 A.2d 625 (Del. 1968)

[After several months of negotiations, Itek and defendant (hereinafter CAI) signed a lengthy "letter of intent" on January 15, 1965 containing the following provision:

> 2. Itek and CAI shall make every reasonable effort to agree upon and have prepared as quickly as possible a contract providing for the foregoing purchase by Itek and sale by CAI, subject to the approval of CAI stockholders, embodying the above terms and such other terms and conditions as the parties shall agree upon. If the parties fail to agree upon and execute such a contract they shall be under no further obligation to one another.

On February 23, 1965 CAI requested that Itek agree to three new conditions, and Itek complied on February 26, 1965. In the meantime CAI and Bourns, Inc., which had expressed an earlier interest in purchasing CAI, renewed negotiations. Bourns offered CAI a higher price, and on March 2, 1965 CAI told Itek that "it was terminating the transaction as a result of unforeseen circumstances and the failure of the parties to reach agreement." Itek sued CAI, alleging that the "letter of intent" was a binding contract. The trial court granted CAI's motion for summary judgment; the Delaware Supreme Court reversed, deciding the case on Illinois law.]

Under Illinois law, the question of whether an enforceable contract comes into being during the preliminary stages of negotiations, or whether its binding effect must await a formal agreement, depends on the intention of the parties. El Reno Wholesale Grocery Co. v. Stocking, 293 Ill. 494, 127 N.E. 642. In making that determination, the fact that some matters are left for future agreement among the parties does not necessarily preclude the finding that a binding agreement was entered into during the preliminary stages. Borg-Warner Corporation v. Anchor Coupling Co., 16 Ill.2d 234, 156 N.E.2d 513, 930.

In making that determination, the trier of fact, of necessity, must look at the circumstances surrounding the negotiations and the actions of the principals at the time and subsequently. Borg-Warner Corporation v. Anchor Coupling Co., *supra*. From all of these, the intention of the parties to be bound or not to be bound must be ascertained.

The trial judge, however, reached his decision solely because of the last sentence of paragraph 2 of the January 15, 1965 letter to the effect that the failure to execute a formal contract absolved the parties from "further obligation." We think, however, that it was error to separate the last sentence from the rest of paragraph 2. All its provisions must be read and considered together. If this is done, then it is apparent that the parties obligated themselves to "make every reasonable effort" to agree upon a formal contract, and only if such effort failed were they absolved from "further obligation" for having "failed" to agree upon and execute a formal contract. We think these provisions of the January 15 letter obligated each side to attempt in good faith to reach final and formal agreement.

We think the first issue to be resolved in this case is the existence or nonexistence on January 15, 1965 of an enforceable agreement. If there was none, then obviously Itek's case falls. Under Illinois law, this decision is to be reached after consideration of the surrounding circumstances and what the parties intended and believed to have been the result. This does not violate the parol evidence rule since that rule comes into play only after the existence of a contract has been determined. 3 Corbin on Contracts, §577.

We have examined the record before us and are of the opinion that there is evidence which, if accepted by the trier of fact, would support the conclusion that on January 15, 1965 both Itek and CAI intended to be bound, the former to purchase and the latter to sell all the assets of CAI. There is also evidence which, if accepted by the trier of fact, would support the conclusion that subsequently, in order to permit its stockholders to accept a higher offer, CAI willfully failed to negotiate in good faith and to make "every reasonable effort" to agree upon a formal contract, as it was required to do. We do not say that the evidence requires these conclusions, particularly since they are contested by CAI, but we think the evidence would permit these conclusions.

There were, then, issues of material fact unresolved which make the disposition of the case against CAI on summary judgment inappropriate. CAI has failed to demonstrate to a reasonable certitude that there is no issue of fact which, if resolved in favor of Itek, would have held CAI liable. Therefore, summary judgment for CAI was improvidently

granted. Allied Auto Sales, Inc. v. President, Directors and Company of
Farmers Bank, Del., 216 A.2d 666. . . .

The judgment below in favor of CAI will be reversed, and the judgment below in favor of the individual defendants will be affirmed.

NOTE

Itek ultimately lost at trial. See Itek Corp. v. Chicago Aerial Industries,
Inc., 274 A.2d 141 (Del. 1971), which discusses the types of evidence
admissible to show whether the parties intended to enter into a binding
agreement.

Section 5.   The Assent and Some of Its Mysteries

The case law that follows will explore an area of "assent" that has presented courts with considerable difficulties.

It is hornbook law everywhere that silence of itself does not constitute
assent. *Qui tacet consentire non videtur* makes eminently good sense so
long as we believe in contract as an instrument of self-government. The
great principle of freedom of contract would suffer seriously if the offeror
could compel the offeree to take positive action lest he be bound by an
offer against his intentions. There is, in theory, therefore, no duty to
reject an offer *expressis verbis*. But everywhere the rule that silence does
not constitute assent has been qualified. Where, for instance, the offeree
has appropriated the benefits of an offer without being justified in assuming a donative intent on the offeror's part, it is obviously fair to imply
assent and a promise to compensate. The real challenge to freedom of
contract is to be found in the growing recognition of a precontractual
duty to speak in situations where no benefit was conveyed.[60]

PRESCOTT v. JONES
69 N.H. 305, 41 A. 352 (1898)

Assumpsit. The declaration alleged, in substance, that the defendants,
as insurance agents, had insured the plaintiff's buildings in the Manchester Fire Insurance Company until February 1, 1897; that on January 23,
1897, they notified him that they would renew the policy and insure his

---

60. The duty to take positive action will be taken up again when we deal with insurance
contracts in Ch. 4, §3.

buildings for a further term of one year from February 1, 1897, in the sum of $500, unless notified to the contrary by him; that he, relying on the promise to insure unless notified to the contrary, and believing, as he had a right to believe, that the buildings would be insured by the defendants for one year from February 1, 1897, gave no notice to them to insure or not to insure; that they did not insure the buildings as they had agreed and did not notify him of their intention not to do so; that the buildings were destroyed by fire March 1, 1897, without fault on the plaintiff's part. The defendants demurred.

BLODGETT, J. While an offer will not mature into a complete and effectual contract until it is acceded to by the party to whom it is made and notice thereof, either actual or constructive, given to the maker (Abbott v. Shepard, 48 N.H. 14, 17; Perry v. Insurance Co., 67 N.H. 291, 294, 295), it must be conceded to be within the power of the maker to prescribe a particular form or mode of acceptance; and the defendants having designated in their offer what they would recognize as notice of its acceptance, namely, failure of the plaintiff to notify them to the contrary, they may properly be held to have waived the necessity of formally communicating to them the fact of its acceptance by him.

But this did not render acceptance on his part any less necessary than it would have been if no particular form of acceptance had been prescribed, for it is well settled that "a party cannot, by the wording of his offer, turn the absence of communication of acceptance into an acceptance, and compel the recipient of his offer to refuse it at the peril of being held to have accepted it." Clark Cont. 31, 32. "A person is under no obligation to do or say anything concerning a proposition which he does not choose to accept. There must be actual acceptance or there is no contract." More v. Insurance Co., 130 N.Y. 537, 547. And to constitute acceptance, "there must be words, written or spoken, or some other overt act." Bish. Cont., s. 329, and authorities cited.

If, therefore, the defendants might and did make their offer in such a way as to dispense with the communication of its acceptance to them in a formal and direct manner, they did not and could not so frame it as to render the plaintiff liable as having accepted it merely because he did not communicate his intention not to accept it. And if the plaintiff was not bound by the offer until he accepted it, the defendants could not be, because "it takes two to make a bargain," and as contracts rest on mutual promises, both parties are bound, or neither is bound.

The inquiry as to the defendants' liability for the non-performance of their offer thus becomes restricted to the question, Did the plaintiff accept the offer, so that it became by his action clothed with legal consideration and perfected with the requisite condition of mutuality? As, in morals, one who creates an expectation in another by a gratuitous promise is doubtless bound to make the expectation good, it is perhaps to be regretted that, upon the facts before us, we are constrained to answer the questions in the negative. While a gratuitous undertaking is binding in honor, it does not create a legal responsibility. Whether wisely or equitably or not, the law requires a consideration for those promises which it will enforce; and as the plaintiff paid no premium for the policy which the defendants proposed to issue, nor bound himself to pay any, there was no legal consideration for their promise, and the law will not enforce it.

Then, again, there was no mutuality between the parties. All the plaintiff did was merely to determine in his own mind that he would accept the offer — for there was nothing whatever to indicate it by way of speech or other appropriate act. Plainly, this did not create any rights in his favor as against the defendants. From the very nature of a contract this must be so; and it therefore seems superfluous to add that the universal doctrine is that an uncommunicated mental determination cannot create a binding contract.

Nor is there any estoppel against the defendants, on the ground that the plaintiff relied upon their letter and believed they would insure his buildings as therein stated.

The letter was a representation only of a present intention or purpose on their part.

> It was not a statement of a fact or state of things actually existing, or past and executed, on which a party might reasonably rely as fixed and certain, and by which he might properly be guided in his conduct. . . . The intent of a party, however positive or fixed, concerning his future action, is necessarily uncertain as to its fulfillment, and must depend on contingencies and be subject to be changed and modified by subsequent events and circumstances. . . . On a representation concerning such a matter no person would have a right to rely, or to regulate his action in relation to any subject in which his interest was involved as upon a fixed, certain, and definite fact or state of things, permanent in its nature and not liable to change. . . . The doctrine of estoppel . . . on the ground that it is contrary to a previous statement of a party does not apply to such a representation. The reason on which the doctrine rests is, that it would operate as a fraud if a party was allowed to aver and prove a fact to be contrary to that which he had previously stated to another for the purpose of inducing him to act and to alter his condition, to his prejudice, on the faith of such previous statement. But the reason wholly fails when the representation relates only to a present intention or purpose of a party, because, being in its nature uncertain and liable to change, it could not properly form a basis or inducement upon which a party could reasonably adopt any fixed and permanent course of action.

Langdon v. Doud, 10 Allen 433, 436, 437; Jackson v. Allen, 120 Mass. 64, 79; Jorden v. Money, 5 H.L. Cas. 185.

"An estoppel cannot arise from a promise as to future action with respect to a right to be acquired upon an agreement not yet made." Insurance Co. v. Mowry, 96 U.S. 544, 547. "The doctrine has no place for application when the statement relates to rights depending upon contracts yet to be made, to which the person complaining is to be a party. He has it in his power in such cases to guard in advance against any consequences of a subsequent change of intention by the person with whom he is dealing." Ib. 548. . . .

To sum it up in a few words, the case presented is, in its legal aspects, one of a party seeking to reap where he had not sown, and to gather where he had not scattered.

Demurrer sustained.

NOTE

Same decision today under §69 of Restatement Second? Is the distinction between promissory estoppel and estoppel in pais still adhered to? See the discussion in Feinberg v. Pfeiffer Co., *infra* p. 308.

The holder of a fire policy that has just expired claims that under a local custom fire policies are automatically renewed unless cancelled by either party. Relevant? City Mortgage & Discount Company v. Palatine Insurance Company, 226 Ala. 179, 145 So. 490 (1933); Restatement Second §§219-223.

NATIONAL UNION FIRE INSURANCE CO. v. JOSEPH EHRLICH
122 Misc. 682, 203 N.Y.S. 434 (App. T., 1st Dept. 1924)

Appeal by plaintiff from a judgment of the Municipal Court of the City of New York, borough of Manhattan, first district, dismissing the plaintiff's complaint after trial by the court without a jury.

PROSKAUER, J. A broker had for some time procured fire insurance policies for defendant. One such expired on December 22, 1921, and on that day the broker sent to defendant a renewal policy issued by plaintiff and a bill for the premium. Defendant retained the policy and bill for two months and then, in response to demand for payment, rejected the policy. This action is for premium accrued prior to the rejection and plaintiff appeals from dismissal of the complaint.

In 1 Williston on Contracts (p. 169) it is said:

Generally speaking an offeree has a right to make no reply to offers. . . . But the relations between the parties may have been such as to have justified the offeror in expecting a reply. . . . When property is sent to another though not ordered but under such circumstances that the latter knows that payment is expected, the silent acceptance of the property is in effect an assent to the offer of sale implied by the sending of the property.

This principle has been applied to the identical facts here presented.

In Joyce on Insurance (Vol. 1 [2d ed.]), it is stated: "The receipt and retention by assured of a renewal policy creates a binding contract," citing Peever Mercantile Co. v. State Mut. Fire Assoc., 23 So. Dak. 1.

The situation is analogous with that of a subscriber to a periodical, who, by accepting the periodical after the expiration of his subscription, impliedly engages to pay. See cases cited in 1 Williston Cont. 169, n.89.

The broker here was not a mere interloper. The previous relations justified him and the plaintiff in assuming that defendant's retention of the policy implied acceptance. If a fire had occurred under these circumstances plaintiff would not have been heard to say that defendant had not accepted the insurance and defendant should pay the premium for the time he unreasonably retained the policy.

Judgment reversed and new trial ordered, with thirty dollars cost to appellant and abide the event.

Guy, J., concurs; Burr, J., dissents.

BURR, J. (dissenting). There was a question of fact here. The plaintiff's evidence was insufficient to support its claim. Complaint was properly dismissed.

Judgment reversed.

AUSTIN v. BURGE
156 Mo. App. 286, 137 S.W. 618 (1911)

Action by O. D. Austin v. Charles Burge. From a judgment for defendant, plaintiff appeals. Reversed and remanded.

ELLISON, J. — This action was brought on an account for the subscription price of a newspaper. The judgment in the trial court was for the defendant.

It appears that plaintiff was publisher of a newspaper in Butler, Mo., and that defendant's father-in-law subscribed for the paper, to be sent to defendant for two years, and that the father-in-law paid for it that time. It was then continued to be sent to defendant, through the mail, for several years more. On two occasions defendant paid a bill presented for the subscription price, but each time directed it to be stopped. Plaintiff denies the order to stop; but for the purpose of the case we shall assume that defendant is correct. He testified that notwithstanding the order to stop it, it was continued to be sent to him and he continued to receive and read it, until finally he removed to another state.

We have not been cited to a case in this state involving the liability of a person who, though not having subscribed for a newspaper, continues to accept it by receiving it through the mail. There are, however, certain well understood principles in the law of contracts that ought to solve the question. It is certain that one cannot be forced into contractual relations with another and that therefore he cannot, against his will, be made the debtor of a newspaper publisher. But it is equally certain that he may cause contractual relations to arise by necessary implication from his conduct. The law in respect to contractual indebtedness for a newspaper is not different from that relation to other things which have not been made the subject of an express agreement. Thus, one may not have ordered supplies for his table, or other household necessities, yet if he continues to receive and use them, under circumstances where he had no right to suppose they were a gratuity, he will be held to have agreed, by implication, to pay their value. In this case defendant admits that notwithstanding he ordered the paper discontinued at the time when he paid a bill for it, yet plaintiff continued to send it and he continued to take it from the postoffice to his home. This was an acceptance and use of the property, and there being no pretense that a gratuity was intended, an obligation arose to pay for it.

A case quite applicable to the facts here involved arose in Fogg v. Atheneum, 44 N.H. 115. There the "Independent Democrat" newspaper was forwarded weekly by mail to the defendant from May 1, 1847, to May 1, 1849, when a bill was presented which defendant objected to paying on the ground of not having subscribed. Payment was, however, finally made and directions given to discontinue. The paper changed ownership and the order to stop it was not known to the new proprietors for a year; but after being notified of the order, they nevertheless continued to send it to defendant until 1860, a period of eleven years, and defendant continued to receive it through the postoffice. Payment was several times demanded during this time, but refused on the ground that there was no subscription. The court said that:

> During this period of time the defendants were occasionally requested, by the plaintiff's agent, to pay their bill. The answer was, by the defendants, we are not subscribers to your newspaper. But the evidence is, the defendants used, or kept the plaintiff's . . . newspapers, and never offered to return a number, as they reasonably might have done, if they would have avoided the liability to pay for them. Nor did they ever decline to take the newspapers from the postoffice.

The defendant was held to have accepted the papers and to have become liable for the subscription price by implication of law. . . .

The preparation and publication of a newspaper involves much mental and physical labor, as well as an outlay of money. One who accepts the paper by continuously taking it from the postoffice, receives a benefit and pleasure arising from such labor and expenditure as fully as if he had appropriated any other product of another's labor, and by such act he must be held liable for the subscription price.

On the defendant's own evidence plaintiff should have recovered. The judgment will therefore be reversed and the cause remanded. All concur.

NOTE

Neb. Rev. Stat. §63-101 (1958):

> No person in this state shall be compelled to pay for any newspaper, magazine or other publication which shall be mailed or sent to him without his having subscribed for or ordered it, or which shall be mailed or sent to him after the time of his subscription or order therefor has expired, notwithstanding that he may have received it.

Would defendant be liable under this statute?

California Civil Code §§1584.5-1584.6 (West 1982) are far more extensive, applying to all unsolicited goods, wares, or merchandise.

COLE-McINTYRE-NORFLEET CO.
v. HOLLOWAY
141 Tenn. 679, 214 S.W. 817 (1919)

Mr. Chief Justice LANSDEN delivered the opinion of the Court. This case presents a question of law, which so far as we are advised, has not been decided by this court in its exact phases. March 26, 1917, a traveling salesman of plaintiff in error solicited and received from defendant in error, at his country store in Shelby County, Tenn., an order for certain goods, which he was authorized to sell. Among these goods were fifty barrels of meal. The meal was to be ordered out by defendant by the 31st day of July, and afterwards five cents per barrel per month was to be charged him for storage.

After the order was given, the defendant heard nothing from it until the 26th of May, 1917, when he was in the place of business of plaintiff in error and told it to begin shipment of the meal on his contract. He was informed by plaintiff in error that it did not accept the order of March 26, and for that reason the defendant had no contract for meal.

The defendant in error never received confirmation or rejection from plaintiff in error, or other refusal to fill the order. The same traveling salesman of plaintiff in error called on defendant as often as once each week, and this order was not mentioned to defendant, either by him or by his principals, in any way. Between the day of the order and the 26th of May, the day of its alleged rejection, prices on all of the articles in the contract greatly advanced. All of the goods advanced about fifty per cent. in value.

Some jobbers at Memphis received orders from their drummers, and filled the orders or notified the purchaser that the orders were rejected; but this method was not followed by plaintiff in error.

The contract provided that it was not binding until accepted by the seller at its office in Memphis, and that the salesman had no authority to sign the contract for either the seller or buyer. It was further stipulated that the order should not be subject to countermand.

It will be observed that plaintiff in error was silent upon both the acceptance and rejection of the contract. It sent forth its salesman to solicit this and other orders. The defendant in error did not have the right to countermand orders and the contract was closed, if and when it was accepted by plaintiff in error. The proof that some jobbers in Memphis uniformly filled such orders unless the purchaser was notified to the contrary is of no value because it does not amount to a custom.

The case, therefore, must be decided upon its facts. The circuit court and the court of civil appeals were both of opinion that the contract was completed because of the lapse of time before plaintiff in error rejected it. The time intervening between the giving of the order by defendant and its alleged repudiation by plaintiff in error was about sixty days. Weekly opportunities were afforded the salesman of plaintiff in error to notify the defendant in error of the rejection of the contract, and, of course, daily occasions were afforded plaintiff in error to notify him by mail or wire. The defendant believed the contract was in force on the 26th of May, because he directed plaintiff in error to begin shipment of the meal on that day. Such shipments were to have been completed by July 31st, or defendant to pay storage charges. From this evidence the circuit court found as an inference of fact that plaintiff in error had not acted within a reasonable time, and therefore its silence would be construed as an acceptance of the contract. The question of whether the delay of plaintiff in error was reasonable or unreasonable was one of fact, and the circuit court was justified from the evidence in finding that the delay was unreasonable. Hence the case, as it comes to us, is whether delay upon the part of plaintiff in error for an unreasonable time in notifying the defendant in error of its action upon the contract is an acceptance of its terms.

We think such delay was unreasonable, and effected an acceptance of the contract. It should not be forgotten that this is not the case of an agent exceeding his authority, or acting without authority. Even in such cases the principal must accept or reject the benefits of the contract promptly and within a reasonable time. Williams v. Storm, 6 Cold., 207.

Plaintiff's agent in this case was authorized to do precisely that which he did do, both as to time and substance. The only thing which was left open by the contract was the acceptance or rejection of its terms by plaintiff in error. It will not do to say that a seller of goods like these could wait indefinitely to decide whether or not he will accept the offer of the proposed buyer. This was all done in the usual course of business, and the articles embraced with the contract were consumable in the use, and some of them would become unfitted for the market within a short time.

It is undoubtedly true that an offer to buy or sell is not binding until its acceptance is communicated to the other party. The acceptance, however, of such an offer may be communicated by the other party either by a formal acceptance, or acts amounting to an acceptance. Delay in communicating action as to the acceptance may amount to an acceptance itself. When the subject of a contract, either in its nature or by virtue or conditions of the market, will become unmarketable by delay, delay in notifying the other party of his decision will amount to an acceptance by the offerer. Otherwise, the offerer could place his goods upon the market, and solicit orders, and yet hold the other party to the contract, while he reserves time to himself to see if the contract will be profitable.

Writ denied.

RESPONSE TO PETITION TO REHEAR

An earnest petition to rehear has been filed, and we have re-examined the question with great care. The petition quotes the text of 13 Corpus Juris. p. 276 as follows:

> An offer made to another, either orally or in writing, cannot be turned into an agreement because the person to whom it is made or sent makes no reply, even though the offer states that silence will be taken as consent, for the offerer cannot prescribe conditions of rejection, so as to turn silence on the part of the offeree into acceptance.

And further: "In like manner mere delay in accepting or rejecting an offer cannot make an agreement."

It is also said that diligent search reveals only one case holding in accord with the court's decision of this case, and that case is Blue Grass Cordage Co. v. Luthy, 98 Ky., 583, 33 S.W., 835, and it is said this case was overruled by the later case of L.A. Becker Co. v. Alvey, 86 S.W., 974, 27 Ky. Law. Rep., 832. We have examined both of these cases, and we do not think either is authority on the question at issue. In the first case the contract was admittedly executed, and the suit was for damages for its breach. The second case does not refer to the first, and is upon another branch of contracts. The quotation from Corpus Juris contemplates the case of an original offer, unaccompanied by other circumstances, and does not apply to this case, where the parties had been dealing with each other before the contract, and were dealing in due course at the time.

It is a general principle of the law of contracts that, while an assent to an offer is requisite to the formation of an agreement, yet such assent is a condition of the mind, and may be either express or evidenced by circumstances from which the assent may be inferred. Hartford et al. v. Jackson, 24 Conn., 514, 63 Am. Dec., 177; 6 Ruling Case Law, 605; 13 Corpus Juris, 276; 9 Cyc., 258. And see the cases cited in the notes of these authorities. They all agree that acceptance of an offer may be inferred from silence. This is only where the circumstances surrounding the parties afford a basis from which an inference may be drawn from silence. There must be the right and the duty to speak, before the failure to do so can prevent a person from afterwards setting up the truth. We think it is the duty of a wholesale merchant, who sends out his drummers to solicit orders for perishable articles, and articles consumable in the use, to notify his customers within a reasonable time that the orders are not accepted; and if he fails to do so, and the proof shows that he had ample opportunity, silence for an unreasonable length of time will amount to an acceptance, if the offerer is relying upon him for the goods.

The petition to rehear is denied.

NOTE

1. What is the legal significance of the clause that the order should not be subject to countermand?

2. Was it not just as easy for the plaintiff to make inquiries as it was for the defendant to reject the offer?

3. Suppose on the 20th of May the price of meal had suddenly dropped below the contract price, and the defendant now confirmed the order or shipped without confirmation. Would the plaintiff be bound?

4. How would the case be decided under §69 of the Restatement Second? For a criticism of the case, see Corbin, When Silence Gives Consent, 29 Yale L.J. 441 (1920); see also Laufer, Silence as Acceptance: A Critique, 7 Duke B.A.J. 87 (1939).

5. What are the functions of confirmation clauses?

6. Suppose defendant had only noted an approval on the purchase order. Is there a contract? Restatement Second §56.

LANGELLIER v. SCHAEFER
36 Minn. 361 (1887)

Plaintiff brought this action in the district court for Ramsey county for specific performance of an alleged agreement by defendant to convey certain real estate to plaintiff. The defendant in his answer denied the making of any contract or that any negotiations were had between the parties except by means of certain letters which are set out in full. To this answer the plaintiff demurred, and by stipulation the issue of law thus raised was referred to A. S. Hall, Esq., for hearing and determination.

The demurrer was sustained by the referee, and the defendant appealed. The letters pleaded in the answer are as follows:

St. Paul. Minn., April 8, 1886

To Anthony Schaefer, Rushmore, Minn. — Dear Sir: I own lot 4, block 5, West St. Paul proper, and I understand you own lot 3, same block. I am anxious to have Custer street graded, and would like to know if you are willing to join in a petition asking for that improvement? I would also ask what is your price for lot 3, and on what terms you will sell it? If you don't want to sell it, what will you give me for lot 4? A prompt reply will greatly oblige me.

Yours truly,
A. L. LANGELLIER,
No. 37 Irvine Park, St. Paul, Minn.

Rushmore, Nobles Co., Minn., April 10, 1886.

A. L. Langellier, Esq. — Dear Sir: Your favor of eighth inst. received and noted. Do not think I would care to have the improvement made at present; but I am in need of money and would sell lot three for $800, cash. I refused $900 last year. I don't want lot 4. I am about to borrow some money on lot 3, so, if you want to buy, please let me know at once.

Yours truly,
A. SCHAEFER

St. Paul, Minn., April 13, 1886.

To Anthony Schaefer, Rushmore, Minn. — Dear Sir: Your offer to sell me lot 3, block 5, West St. Paul Prper, is accepted, although I am afraid I am paying $100 to $200 too much for it; but I am very anxious to have Custer Street graded at once, and this lot now gives me enough property there to influence the board to have the work done. As the street is now 7 feet below grade, I am afraid the expense of grading will be very heavy, and I should prefer to buy your lot on time, if you would sell it that way; but if you prefer not, then please execute the inclosed deed before a competent notary public, and send it to the Bank of Minnesota, St. Paul, with instructions to Herman Scheffer, assistant cashier of the bank, to collect the amount due you, and deliver deed. I will pay their charges if there are any. You will send with the deed an abstract of title, to be continued to date, or, if you have not one, please order one. Please instruct the bank to give me the necessary time to examine title, etc., after abstract is ready. I shall, however, take up the deed with as little delay as possible. It is usual to give one or two weeks. In case you would just as willingly take say $300 down, and balance on or before one year, with 10 per cent. interest, I would rather have it so; but please send papers at once in any case, as I am anxious to apply for the grading while the contracts are being let. If you prefer to send the deed to any one else, it does not matter much to me, only that I don't want anything to do with any *real-estate agent*. Please send it to the Minnesota Bank, if possible, as that is the most convenient for me.

A. L. LANGELLIER,
37 Irvine Park.

MITCHELL, J. These letters will not constitute a completed agreement for the sale and conveyance of this real estate, unless there is upon the face of the correspondence a clear accession on both sides to one and the same set of terms. Lanz v. McLaughlin, 14 Minn. 55, (72); Hamlin v. Wistar, 31 Minn. 418, (18 N.W. Rep. 145.) An offer of a bargain by one person to another imposes no obligation upon the former, unless it is accepted by the latter according to the terms on which the offer was made. Any qualification of or departure from those terms invalidates the offer, unless the same is agreed to by the party who made it. Where the negotiations are by letters, they will constitute no agreement unless the answer to the offer is a simple acceptance, without the introduction of any new term. 1 Sugden, v. & P. *132, 133; Eliason v. Henshaw, 4 Wheat. 225.

In this case the plaintiff resided in St. Paul, and the defendant at Rushmore, Nobles county, Minnesota. The letter of April 10th, written by the latter to the former, was an offer to sell the property for $800 *cash*. If, in his answer, the plaintiff had confined himself to a simple acceptance of this offer, there would have been a completed agreement, by the terms of which, in order to place the defendant in default, the plaintiff would have been required to tender the money to defendant personally at his residence at Rushmore. But by his letter of acceptance plaintiff introduces a qualification to and a departure from the terms of the offer by fixing a different place (St. Paul) for the delivery of the deed and the payment of the money. It is true, plaintiff commences this letter by saying that he accepts the offer, but the whole letter must be read together to get at its meaning. He immediately proceeds to state the terms and conditions on which he accepts. We cannot assent to the proposition that all of this part of the letter is to be construed, not as attaching conditions to plaintiff's acceptance, but as mere suggestions. Some parts of the letter doubtless are merely suggestive, but that directing the deed to be sent to St. Paul to some one who would deliver it, and receive the purchase-money for defendant, was clearly intended to indicate what plaintiff *required* of defendant, and it was none the less mandatory because it was prefaced by the polite phrase of correspondence, "please." That this is the construction put upon the matter by plaintiff himself is evident from his complaint. He nowhere alleges a tender of the purchase-money to defendant personally. In substance, all that he alleges is a refusal by defendant to execute the deed; and a readiness on his own part to pay. There having been no unconditional acceptance of defendant's offer, there never was any completed agreement between the parties. Maynard v. Tabor, 53 Me. 511; Northwestern Iron Co. v. Meade, 21 Wis. 474. Order reversed.

NOTE

1. On December 1, A gives B an option to buy his home for $10,000, the option to be open for three months. B "accepts," stating that he is going to give $10,000 in three installments. A does not reply. A few days later B offers to pay in two installments. Again no reply. A week later B offers to pay cash upon receipt of the deed. Is A bound? Consult Restatement Second §37.

2. For an ingenious deviation from standard offer and acceptance doctrine to protect an applicant for insurance, see Stonsz v. Equitable Life Assur. Soc., 324 Pa. 97, 187 A. 403 (1936), where the issue concerned a discrepancy between the policy and the original application.

BUTLER v. FOLEY
211 Mich. 668, 179 N.W.34 (1920)

BROOKE, J. This is an action for damages arising out of an alleged breach of contract to deliver certain stock. The contract is based upon three telegrams, as follows: [Some irrelevant notations are omitted.]

(Exhibit B)

September 19th, 1916

Received 3 P.M.
J. William Foley
Wyandotte, Mich.

We bid hundred fifty-two firm immediate acceptance fifty By-Products. Wire confirmation.

A. E. BUTLER & Co.

(Exhibit C)

1916, Sept. 20, P.M. 12:33
Sibley, Mich., 1020 A

A. E. Butler & Co.
La Salle St., Chicago, Ill.

Your bid one five two bi-products accepted on forty-four shares.

J. W. FOLEY

(Exhibit D)

September 20th, 1916 12:55

J. William Foley,
Sibley, Mich.

We confirm purchase forty-four By-Products hundred fifty-two. Please ship stock today. Draft attached.

A. E. Butler & Co.

Defendant failed to deliver the stock mentioned in the last two telegrams and plaintiff, having made sale of the stock, was obliged to purchase the same in the open market at a cost of $792 in excess of the price mentioned in the contract. A jury trial resulted in a verdict in plaintiff's favor for $885.39. A motion was thereafter made by defendant for judgment notwithstanding the verdict, which was denied. . . .

Defendant's entire contention as shown by the correspondence was based upon his claim that Exhibit C (his telegram of September 20, 1916) should have contained the word "subject," making the message read as follows:

"Your bid one hundred fifty-two By-Products accepted on forty-four shares, *subject*."

Defendant offered in evidence his office copy of the telegram (which contained the word "subject.") which was excluded, the court saying,

"I ruled that the telegram, Exhibit C here, cannot be varied; that cannot be varied by testimony of Mr. Foley and any claimed copy of something in his files."

It is undisputed that Exhibit C was received by plaintiff without the word "subject" and the evidence of the sending operator is to the effect that the message was transmitted by him exactly as received. But whether the message was erroneously or correctly sent is, as between the parties to this action, in our opinion, unimportant, for reasons hereinafter stated.

It is the contention of the defendant that the plaintiff, having chosen the telegraph company as a means of communication, and having asked an answer by telegraph, constituted that company its agent and that therefore, any error in transmission of defendant's reply (Exhibit C) should be chargeable to plaintiff. We are of the opinion that the authorities are clear that "the offerer takes the risk as to the effectiveness of communication if the acceptance is made in the manner either expressly or impliedly indicated by him." [Citations omitted.]

The difficulty with defendant's contention is that Exhibit C does not constitute an acceptance of plaintiff's offer, Exhibit B. It was, in fact, a counter-proposition, and, as such, under the authorities, it operated as a rejection of the original offer. 1 Mechem on Sales, §229; 1 Elliott on Contracts, §41; 9 Cyc., p. 290; Johnson v. Surety Co., 187 Mich. 467. By refusing to accept plaintiff's proposition for the sale of 50 shares and making the counter-offer to sell 44 shares, defendant became the offerer and, under the authorities above cited, constituted the telegraph company his agent; and, therefore, if any error occurred in the transmission of the message, his remedy would be against the telegraph company and not against the plaintiff.

It is claimed by defendant that plaintiff's Exhibit D is not an unqualified acceptance of defendant's offer (Exhibit C) by reason of the addition of the words "Please ship stock today. Draft attached." With this contention we are unable to agree. The offer contained in Exhibit C was accepted without qualification in Exhibit D and the added words are simply precatory and do not affect the binding character of the contract. 13 C.J., p. 283, §86; Marshall v. Jamison, 42 U.C.Q.B. 115; 1 Elliott on Contracts, §39; Purrington v. Grimm, 83 Vt. 466 (76 Atl. 158).

It is further defendant's contention that it was plaintiff's duty to pay for the stock and take delivery at Sibley, Michigan; and that not having performed this duty, he is in default and cannot recover. It is doubtless true, as contended by defendant, that he would have had a right to insist on payment at the place of sale under the provisions of Act No. 100, Pub. Acts 1913, §42 (3 Comp. Laws 1915, §11873). But defendant made no such suggestion to plaintiff at the time the controversy arose. The correspondence clearly demonstrates that he rested his alleged right to refuse delivery solely upon the ground that the telegraph company had erroneously failed to include the word "subject" in his offer. . . .

We find no reversible error in the record, and the judgment is affirmed.

NOTE

1. What does the omitted word "subject" mean? See Neer v. Lang, 252 F. 575 (2d Cir. 1918).

Did not the defendant suggest a typical way of doing business? Did plaintiff's proposal entail any extra risk for defendant?

2. Is it sound policy to say that the telegraph company was Foley's agent? Consult Whittier, The Restatement of Contracts and Mutual Assent, 17 Calif. L. Rev. 441, 447-448 (1929); 1 Corbin §105 (1963); Western Union Telegraph Co. v. Cowin & Co., 20 F.2d 103 (8th Cir. 1927). Consult also the cases in Note 3.

3. Assuming the defendant to be bound, has he a claim against the telegraph company? Ayer v. Western Union Tel. Co., 79 Me. 493, 10 A. 485 (1887). Does defendant have to litigate his liability to Butler first before proceeding against the telegraph company? Holtz v. Western Union Telegraph Co., 294 Mass. 543, 3 N.E.2d 180 (1936). Suppose Foley was not bound, has Butler a claim against the telegraph company? Webbe v. Western Union Telegraph Co., 169 Ill. 610, 48 N.E. 670 (1897).

For the prevailing standard clauses classifying messages and the corresponding limitations on recovery, and also the impact of federal legislation, dealing with interstate messages, on state law declaring limitation clauses void as against public policy, see 10 Williston §1134 (1967).

UNITED STATES v. BRAUNSTEIN
75 F. Supp. 137 (S.D.N.Y. 1947)

MEDINA, District Judge. The United States has brought suit for breach of a contract whereby defendants, it is said, agreed to buy from it 9599 twenty-five pound boxes of raisins unfit for human consumption which could be converted into alcohol. The parties have stipulated that an interchange of telegrams, hereinafter referred to, constitutes the contract, if there was one, that furnishes the foundation for the suit. Defendant Sidney Braunstein asserts this interchange of telegrams did not create a contract, and moves for summary judgment.

On July 21, 1945 the Commodity Credit Corporation, an instrumentality of the United States, issued Announcement AWS-11 which invited bids for the purchase of the off-condition raisins in question and laid down requirements to which all bids must conform. Thus, all bids were required to state that they were subject to the terms and conditions of that announcement and to designate what bonded distillery the raisins would be shipped to, should the bidder be successful. The announcement also required that the raisins be paid for by check within ten days from the date of the telegram accepting the bid.

The interchange of telegrams began on August 3, 1945, when the defendant Pearl Distilling Co. sent the following telegram to David Ludlum of the Washington office of the Commodity Credit Corporation:

> David Ludlum, Contracting and Adjustment Div Sales Branch Office of Supply U.S. Dep of Agriculture
>
> Offer ten cents per pound for 9599 boxes of raisins located Cleveland Ohio
>
> PEARL DISTILLING CO.

This telegram lacked the required reference to Announcement AWS-11 and did not designate the distillery for shipment. On receiving the telegram, David Ludlum telegraphed the Pearl Distilling Co. referring to Announcement AWS-11 and asking for shipping information. Pearl Distilling Co. supplied this information by a telegram of August 7, 1945 and inquired about shipping costs.

The Commodity Credit Corporation's telegram of August 9, 1945 is the crux of this whole interchange. It reads:

Pearl Distilling Company
377-91 East 163rd Street
New York, New York

Subject terms announcement AWS 11 CCC accepts your August 3 offer
to purchase and August 7 wire giving shipping instructions for 9599 boxes
raisins at 10 cents per box plus freight and 3 per cent tax from Cleveland
Ohio to New Brunswick, New Jersey, at 45 cents per cwt.

Forward certified check in the amount of $2,138.92. Contract AW-S (F)
31752

Commodity Credit Corporation DAVID S LUDLUM

Pearl Distilling Co. had offered ten cents a pound. The telegram of
August 9th specified a price of ten cents a box. The total price of
$2,138.92 appears to have been calculated on the basis of ten cents a box,
although the method of calculation is not entirely clear. Since a box
contained twenty-five pounds, the price was off by something like twenty-
three thousand dollars. It was the Commodity Credit Corporation's intention to accept the offer of ten cents a pound, but one of its employees
had made a mistake in preparing the telegram of August 9th and in
calculating the price.

When the defendants received this telegram, they did nothing and no
check was sent to the Commodity Credit Corporation. Ten days later,
when the time for receipt of the check had expired, the Commodity
Credit Corporation looked into the matter, discovered its error, and sent
this telegram:

Aug 20 PM 4:28

Pearl Distilling Co
377-91 East 163 St

Reourtel August 9 contract AW-S (F) -31752 covering sale of raisins
should read at 10 cents per pound instead 10 cents per box also certified
check should be in the amount of $25,176.52 instead of $2,138.92. Please
confirm

DAVID S LUDLUM
Commodity Credit Corporation

Again the defendants did nothing, and so matters stood for two
months. The raisins, of course, had not been shipped to the defendants.
Then, on October 19, 1945, the Commodity Credit Corporation notified
the defendants that if they failed to pay for the raisins by October 25, the
raisins would be sold and the defendants held for any loss. The defendants did not pay, the raisins were sold at a loss, and the United States
brought suit for breach of contract.

There is a contract if the telegram of August 9 was an acceptance of
the offer of August 3. If there can be an issue of fact as to whether the

telegram of August 9 was an acceptance, this motion for summary judgment must be denied. To put it another way, does the mistaken substitution of "ten cents per box" for "ten cents per pound" coupled with a calculation of the total price based on the wrong figure defeat, as a matter of law, what was intended as an acceptance?

The basic principles of law involved here are simple. To create a contract, an acceptance must be "unequivocal," Restatement, Contracts §58 (1932), "positive and unambiguous," 1 Williston, Contracts §72, Rev. Ed. 1936, and "must comply exactly with the requirements of the offer." Restatement, Contracts §59 (1932); Iselin v. United States, 271 U.S. 136, 46 S. Ct. 458, 70 L. Ed. 872 (1926). A reply to an offer that fails to comply with these requirements is a rejection. 1 Williston, Contracts §73, Rev. Ed. 1936.

Certainly no reasonable man could say that on its face the telegram of August 9 met these requirements. The mention of a price foreign to the negotiation renders the effect of the telegram uncertain and ambiguous. Furthermore, the mere use of the word "accept" does not automatically make a communication an acceptance. Candland v. Olroyd, 62 Utah 605, 248 P. 1101 (1926).

The government, however, insists that the defendants knew perfectly well what the telegram of August 9 meant; that, in spite of a clerical error, it was an acceptance; for no reasonable man could think that the government was in effect rejecting an offer of ten cents a pound and making what amounted to a counter-offer of ten cents for a twenty-five pound box. The argument comes to this: that a reasonable man would disregard the error and see behind the intention that, but for a surface obscurity, was perfectly clear.

There is limited merit to this contention. The law would not allow the defendants to treat the telegram of August 9 as a counter-offer which their acceptance could turn into a contract seriously disadvantageous to the government, since there was obviously something dubious about it. "An offeree may not snap up an offer that is on its face too good to be true." 1 Williston, Contracts §94, Rev. Ed. 1936. It is a justifiable conclusion that the defendants did not think the telegram was a counter-offer, but that they knew the Commodity Credit Corporation's intention varied from what the words of the telegram expressed. This conclusion, however, does not help the government. "If either party knows that the other does not intend what his words or other acts express, this knowledge prevents such words or other acts from being operative as an offer or acceptance." Restatement, Contracts §71 (c) (1932).

The government next urges that the court may interpret the telegrams in the interest of justice so as to make a contract out of them, citing 3 Williston, Contracts §§603, 605, 616, 618-620, 628, 629, Rev. Ed. 1936. There it is shown that courts have disregarded clerical errors or particular words, and have supplied and interposed words in their attempt to give

writings a construction which would not render them void or meaningless. This court is urged to interpret the telegram of August 9 into an
acceptance on the basis of such authority.

It is true that there is much room for interpretation once the parties
are inside the framework of a contract, but it seems that there is less in
the field of offer and acceptance. Greater precision of expression may be
required, and less help from the court given, when the parties are merely
at the threshold of a contract. If a court should undertake to resolve
ambiguities in the negotiations between parties, disregard clerical errors,
and rearrange words, leaving out some and putting in others, it is hard to
see where the line of demarcation could be drawn and the general effect
would inevitably be a condition of chaos and uncertainty.

But the courts have refrained from reforming offers and acceptances.
Thus, in the classic case of Harvey v. Facey, [1893] A.C. 552 (P.C.), it
would have taken but little interpretation to construe as an offer the
defendant's telegram, "Lowest price for Bumper Hall Pen £900," which
was a reply to plaintiff's telegram, "Will you sell us Bumper Hall Pen?
Telegraph lowest cash price." But the Judicial Committee of the Privy
Council ruled otherwise.

In 1 Williston, Contracts §72, Rev. Ed. 1936, are cited several examples of communications held to be insufficient as acceptances. They too
would have needed but slight interpretation to come up to the legal standard, but again the courts were reluctant to interpret parties into a contractual status. Indeed, this very reluctance may have been one of the
causes for the development of the doctrine of quasi-contract. And it
seems significant that the fictions indulged in that branch of the law were
made only in instances of clearly defined unjust enrichment. There is
nothing of that kind here.

It may be rigorous to disregard a purported acceptance because of a
clerical error, but if there is any fault, it lies with the Commodity Credit
Corporation. "Since one who speaks or writes, can, by exactness of expression, more easily prevent mistakes in meaning, than one with whom
he is dealing, doubts arising from ambiguity of language are resolved
against the former in favor of the latter." Restatement, Contracts §236,
comment d (1932).

A decision for defendants will not interfere with commercial dealings
by requiring formality in offer and acceptance. It will merely mean that if
a purported acceptance repeats the terms of the offer, the acceptor takes
the risk of his own clerical error in repetition.

The government made a point in passing, without pressing it, that the
telegram of August 3 in which the Commodity Credit Corporation asked
the defendants for shipping instructions was itself an acceptance, since
only the successful bidder would be asked for these instructions. This
telegram, however, was insufficiently unequivocal to be an acceptance.
Restatement, Contracts §58 (1932).

At the request of the government, and to avoid any possible misconception of the attendant facts and circumstances, an opportunity was afforded for the filing of supplemental affidavits, which were finally forthcoming. They add nothing of any relevance to the sole issue of offer and acceptance, which by the stipulation of the parties depends upon the telegrams above referred to.

Motion granted. Complaints dismissed.

NOTE

The government's appeal was dismissed in 168 F.2d 749 (2d Cir. 1948).

Can an offer be accepted only after it has been communicated to the offeree? Suppose after protracted dickering back and forth as to a term in a sales contract, both buyer and seller make identical proposals in letters which cross each other. Is there a contract? See Asinof v. Freudenthal, 195 A.D. 79, 186 N.Y. Supp. 383 (1st Dept. 1921).

Can one earn the compensation promised in an offer for a reward by giving the requested information without knowing about the offer? Consult 1 Corbin §60 (1963).

Section 6.   Standard Form Contracts — The Battle of the Forms and Contracts of Adhesion

KESSLER, CONTRACTS OF ADHESION — SOME THOUGHTS ABOUT FREEDOM OF CONTRACT, 43 Colum. L. Rev. 629, 631-632 (1943): "The development of large scale enterprise with its mass production and mass distribution made a new type of contract inevitable — the standardized mass contract. A standardized contract, once its contents have been reformulated by a business firm, is used in every bargain dealing with the same product or service. The individuality of the parties which so frequently gave color to the old type of contract has disappeared. The stereotyped contract of today reflects the impersonality of the market. It has reached its greatest perfection in the different types of contracts used on the various exchanges. Once the usefulness of these contracts was discovered and perfected in the transportation, insurance, and banking business, their use spread into all other fields of large scale enterprise, into international as well as national trade, and into labor relations. . . . Uniformity of terms of contracts typically recurring in a business enterprise is an important factor in the exact calculation of risks. Risks which are difficult to calculate can be excluded altogether. Unforeseeable contingencies affecting performance, such as strikes, fire, and transportation difficulties can be taken care of. The standard clauses in insurance policies are the most striking illustrations of successful attempts on the part of business enterprises to select and control risks assumed under a contract. The insurance business probably deserves credit also for having first realized the full importance of the so-called 'judicial risk', the danger that a court or jury may be swayed by 'irrational factors' to decide against a powerful defendant. Ingenious clauses have been the result. Once their practical utility was proven, they were made use of in other lines of business. It is highly probable that the desire to avoid juridical risks has been a motivating factor in the widespread use of repair clauses in many industries limiting the common law remedies of the buyer for breach of an implied warranty of quality and particularly excluding his right to claim (consequential) damages. The same is true for arbitration clauses, both in national and in international trade. Standardized contracts have thus become an important means of excluding or controlling the 'irrational factor' in litigation. In this respect they are a true reflection of the spirit of our time with its hostility to irrational factors in the judicial process."[61]

However useful they may be in tailoring the general law of contracts to the individual needs of the lines of business in which they are used,[62] standard form contracts present particular problems from the perspective of classical contract theory. One of the difficulties they have created has been described as the Battle of the Forms; a second arises from the tendency of standardized contracts to become take-it-or-leave-it propositions — contracts of adhesion — in the hands of an enterprise with strong bargaining power. Each problem poses a serious challenge to the classical conception of the role of consent in contractual exchange. We shall take up these two problems in turn.

A. The Battle of the Forms[63]

Classical contract theory asserted that the terms of offer and acceptance must match. In real life it happens all too frequently that both parties use their own standard forms, which are in conflict. When the

61. For brilliant accounts of standardized contracts see K. Llewellyn, *The Common Law Tradition* 362 (1960); Macaulay, Non-contractual Relations in Business: A Preliminary Study, 28 Am. Soc. Rev. 55, 57-60 (1963); Prausnitz, The Standardization of Commercial Contracts in English and Continental Law (1937).
62. "'The general law' is much too general. It needs tailoring to trades and to lines of trading." Llewellyn, Review of Prausnitz, 52 Harv. L. Rev. 700, 701 (1939).
63. L. Fuller & M. Eisenberg, Basic Contract Law 616 (4th ed. 1981); Baird & Weisberg, Rules, Standards and the Battle of the Forms: A Reassessment of Section 207, 68 Va. L. Rev. 1217 (1982).

classical conception of offer and acceptance is applied to this recurrent situation, problems arise and the legal status of many a deal may be called into question. This is a most undesirable result since businessmen, in the belief that a deal is on, frequently ignore discrepancies between offer and acceptance or settle them in the course of performance.[64] So long as both parties feel the contract is to their mutual advantage, no problem arises. But if one of the parties finds the contract unduly burdensome, he may be tempted to fall back on the common law rules of offer and acceptance in order to escape liability, even if the reason for denying the existence of a contract has nothing to do with the defective manifestation of assent. Poel v. Brunswick-Balke-Collender Co.,[65] involving a sale of rubber, furnishes an excellent example. The "acceptance" of the defendant buyer asked for a confirmation that the plaintiff seller neglected to give. Nothing happened for many months, during which time the price of rubber rose. When the price suddenly dropped, the buyer used the mirror-image or matching doctrine to successfully deny the existence of a contract.

To remedy this situation, trade associations have undertaken to work out standard forms that attempt to be "fair and acceptable" to both contracting parties. An ever-increasing number of such forms have appeared.[66] To give a few examples: the American Institute of Architects has prepared forms covering many aspects of the building industry.[67] (These forms contain arbitration clauses that have frequently been the source of problems.[68]) A joint committee of the National Coal Association and the National Association of Purchasing Agents developed the Standard Coal Contract for use in the sale of such commodities as coal, fuel, oil, scrap iron, and steel.[69] Finally, a substantial number of trade associations representing the principals in the "grey goods" trade (unfinished cloth coming from the loom) formulated the Worth Street Rules. The Rules define trade terms and customs, contain technical specifica-

64. Matter of Doughboy Indus., Inc. (Pantasote Co.) 17 App. Div. 2d 216, 233 N.Y.2d 488 (1962); Dorton v. Collins & Aikman Corp., 453 F.2d 1161 (6th Cir. 1972).

65. 216 N.Y. 310, 110 N.E. 619 (1915). Pound, J., dissenting; *rearg. denied,* 260 N.Y. 771, 111 N.E. 1998 (1916).

66. For the lawmaking of private organizations, see 62 Harv. L. Rev. 1346 (1949).

A detailed discussion of government contracts and their standardization lies outside the scope of this casebook. See Miller, Government Contracts and Social Control: A Preliminary Inquiry, 41 Va. L. Rev. 27 (1955). For the interpretation of the standard "changed conditions" and termination clauses contained in government contracts, see Jefferson Construction Co. v. United States, 392 F.2d 1006 (Ct. Cl. 1968), *cert. denied,* 393 U.S. 842 (1968); G. L. Christian & Associates v. United States, 312 F.2d 418 (Ct. Cl. 1963), *reh. denied,* 320 F.2d 345 (1963), *cert. denied,* 375 U.S. 954 (1963). For further information on the treatment of government contracts, see p. 14 *supra.*

67. Johnstone & Hopson, Lawyers and Their Work 335-340 (1967); J. Sweet, Legal Aspects of Architecture and Engineering 919 (2d ed. 1977); McCormick, Representing the Owner in Contracting with the Architect and Contractor, 8 Forum 435 (1973).

68. See generally Sweet, *supra* note 67, at 563 et seq. Architect approval clauses are also a source of conflict. City of Midland v. Waller, 430 S.W.2d 473 (Tex. 1968), and Note following Jacob & Youngs, Inc. v. Kent, *infra* p. 1042.

69. See Fuller & Eisenberg, *supra* note 63, at 617, 908-909.

tions of quality and tolerances, provide rules for arbitration, and have a standard Salesnote.[70]

But the trend towards uniformity has been only partially successful. The decision of the Supreme Court in Paramount Famous Players Corp v. United States, 282 U.S. 30 (1930), may have had a retarding influence. In that case, an agreement among motion picture distributors who controlled 60 percent of the industry not to deal with exhibitors who did not sign a standard exhibition contract containing an arbitration clause was held to violate §1 of the Sherman Act.[71]

To remedy the situation once and for all, the Uniform Commercial Code has introduced several sections designed to eliminate the "shortcomings" of the classical mirror-image rule, to bring contract law into line with the expectations of those dealing with merchants,[72] and to honor the belief of parties that a deal is on. Sections 1-201(10), 1-205, 2-204, 2-206, 2-209, 2-316. The interpretation of §2-207 has been, as we shall see, particularly troublesome.[73]

ROTO-LITH, LTD. v. F. P. BARTLETT & CO.
297 F.2d 497 (1st Cir. 1962)

ALDRICH, Circuit Judge. Plaintiff-appellant Roto-Lith, Ltd., is a New York corporation engaged inter alia in manufacturing, or "converting," cellophane bags for packaging vegetables. Defendant-appellee is a Massachusetts corporation which makes emulsion for us as a cellophane adhesive. This is a field of some difficulty, and various emulsions are employed, depending upon the intended purpose of the bags. In May and October 1959 plaintiff purchased emulsion from the defendant. Subsequent bags produced with this emulsion failed to adhere, and this action was instituted in the district court for the District of Massachusetts. At the conclusion of the evidence the court directed a verdict for the defendant.[74] This appeal followed.

Defendant asks us to review the October transaction first because of certain special considerations applicable to the May order. The defense

70. Id. at 908-909. On the effect of the incorporation clause on outsiders, see Level Export Corp. v. Wolz, Eakin and Co., 365 N.Y. 82, 111 N.E.2d 218 (1953).
71. Fuller & Eisenberg, supra note 63, at 617, 531, 849.
72. E.g., U.C.C. §2-316 (dealing with exclusion or modification of warranties): the language excluding or modifying the implied warranty of merchantability must use the word merchantability or in case of a writing must be conspicuous. For the meaning of "conspicuous" see U.C.C. §1-201(10). The subsection is however qualified by subsection (3). Some statutes describe the size of type used in certain contracts or the use of plain language. See, e.g., N.Y. Gen. Oblig. Law §5-702 (McKinney's Supp. 1984); Mass. Gen. Laws Ann. ch. 175, §2B (West Supp. 1985) (prescribing readability); Wis. Stat. Ann. §422.303(2) (West 1974).
73. For the European counterpart of §2-207, see Uniform Law for the Formation of Contracts for the International Law of Sales of Goods, Art. 7.
74. Also involved was a counter-claim, but this requires no separate discussion.

in each instance, however, is primarily the same, namely, defendant contends that the sales contract expressly negatived any warranties.[75] We will deal first with the October order.

On October 23, 1959, plaintiff in New York, mailed a written order to defendant in Massachusetts for a drum of "N-132-C" emulsion, stating "End use: wet pack spinach bags." Defendant on October 26 prepared simultaneously an acknowledgment and an invoice. The printed forms were exactly the same, except that one was headed "Acknowledgment" and the other "Invoice," and the former contemplated insertion of the proposed, and the latter of the actual, shipment date. Defendant testified that in accordance with its regular practice the acknowledgment was prepared and mailed the same day. The plaintiff's principal liability witness testified that he did not know whether this acknowledgment "was received, or what happened to it." On this state of the evidence there is an unrebutted presumption of receipt. Johnston v. Cassidy, 1932, 279 Mass. 593, 181 N.E. 748; cf. Tobin v. Taintor, 1918, 229 Mass. 174, 118 N.E. 247. The goods were shipped to New York on October 27. On the evidence it must be found that the acknowledgment was received at least no later than the goods. The invoice was received presumably a day or two after the goods.

The acknowledgment and the invoice bore in conspicuous type on their face the following legend, "All goods sold without warranties, express or implied, and subject to the terms on reverse side." In somewhat smaller, but still conspicuous, type there were printed on the back certain terms of sale, of which the following are relevant:

> 1. Due to the variable conditions under which these goods may be transported, stored, handled, or used, Seller hereby expressly excludes any and all warranties, guaranties, or representations whatsoever. Buyer assumes risk for results obtained from use of these goods, whether used alone or in combination with other products. Seller's liability hereunder shall be limited to the replacement of any goods that materially differ from the Seller's sample order on the basis of which the order for such goods was made.
>
> 7. This acknowledgment contains all of the terms of this purchase and sale. No one except a duly authorized officer of Seller may execute or modify contracts. Payment may be made only at the offices of the Seller. *If these terms are not acceptable, Buyer must so notify Seller at once.* [Ital. suppl.]

It is conceded that plaintiff did not protest defendant's attempt so to limit its liability, and in due course paid for the emulsion and used it. It is also conceded that adequate notice was given of breach of warranty, if

---

75. The defendant also contends that the warranties, if any there might have been, were not broken. This is a question of fact with which we are not concerned.

there were warranties. The only issue which we will consider is whether all warranties were excluded by defendant's acknowledgment.[76]

The first question is what law the Massachusetts court would look to in order to determine the terms of the contract. Under Massachusetts law this is the place where the last material act occurs. Autographic Register Co. v. Philip Hano Co., 1 Cir., 1952, 198 F.2d 208; Milliken v. Pratt, 1878, 125 Mass. 374. Under the Uniform Commercial Code, Mass. Gen. Laws Ann. (1958) ch. 106, §2-206, mailing the acknowledgment would clearly have completed the contract in Massachusetts by acceptance had the acknowledgment not sought to introduce new terms. Section 2-207 provides:

> (1) A definite and seasonable expression of acceptance or a written confirmation which is sent within a reasonable time operates as an acceptance even though it states terms additional to or different from those offered or agreed upon, unless acceptance is expressly made conditional on assent to the additional or different terms.
> (2) The additional terms are to be construed as proposals for addition to the contract. Between merchants such terms become part of the contract unless:
> (a)   the offer expressly limits acceptance to the terms of the offer;
> (b)   they materially alter it; or
> (c)   notification of objection to them has already been given or is given within a reasonable time after notice of them is received.

Plaintiff exaggerates the freedom which this section affords an offeror to ignore a reply from an offeree that does not in terms coincide with the original offer. According to plaintiff defendant's condition that there should be no warranties constituted a proposal which "materially altered" the agreement. As to this we concur. See Uniform Commercial Code comment to this section, Mass. Gen. Laws annotation, *supra*, paragraph 4. Plaintiff goes on to say that by virtue of the statute the acknowledgment effected a completed agreement without this condition, and that as a further proposal the condition never became part of the agreement because plaintiff did not express assent. We agree that section 2-207 changed the existing law, but not to this extent. Its purpose was to modify the strict principle that a response not precisely in accordance with the offer was a rejection and a counteroffer. Kehlor Flour Mills Co. v. Linden, 1918, 230 Mass. 119, 123, 119 N.E. 698; Sacco-Lowell Shops v. Clinton Mills Co., 1 Cir., 1921, 277 F. 349. Now, within stated limits, a response that does not in all respects correspond with the offer constitutes an acceptance of the offer, and a counteroffer only as to the differences. If plaintiff's contention is correct that a reply to an offer stating

76. Defendant also relies upon the terms of the invoice in view of the fact that it was admittedly received before plaintiff used the goods. Whether an invoice not received until after the goods can modify the contract raises some possible matters which we do not reach.

additional conditions unilaterally burdensome upon the offeror is a binding acceptance of the original offer plus simply a proposal for the additional conditions, the statute would lead to an absurdity. Obviously no offeror will subsequently assent to such conditions.

The statute is not too happily drafted. Perhaps it would be wiser in all cases for an offeree to say in so many words, "I will not accept your offer until you assent to the following: . . ." But businessmen cannot be expected to act by rubric. It would be unrealistic to suppose that when an offeree replies setting out conditions that would be burdensome only to the offeror he intended to make an unconditional acceptance of the original offer, leaving it simply to the offeror's good nature whether he would assume the additional restrictions. To give the statute a practical construction we must hold that a response which states a condition materially altering the obligation solely to the disadvantage of the offeror is an "acceptance . . . expressly . . . conditional on assent to the additional . . . terms."

Plaintiff accepted the goods with knowledge of the conditions specified in the acknowledgment. It became bound.[77] Garst v. Harris, 1900, 177 Mass. 72, 58 N.E. 174; Doerr v. Woolsey, 1889, 5 N.Y.S. 447 (Com. Pl. Gen. Term); cf. Joseph v. Atlantic Basin Iron Works, Inc., Sup., 1954, 132 N.Y.S.2d 671, *aff'd* Sup., 143 N.Y.S.2d 601 (App. Div.). Whether the contract was made in Massachusetts or New York, there has been no suggestion that either jurisdiction will not give effect to an appropriate disclaimer of warranties. See Mass. Gen. Laws Ann. c. 106, §2-316; New York Personal Property Law, McKinney's Consol. Laws, c. 41, §252. This disposes of the October order.

With respect to the May order a different situation obtains. Here plaintiff ordered a quantity of "N-136-F," which was defendant's code number for a dry-bag emulsion. The order stated as the end use a wet bag. Accordingly, defendant knew, by its own announced standards, that the emulsion ordered was of necessity unfit for the disclosed purpose. In this bald situation plaintiff urges that the defendant cannot be permitted to specify that it made no implied warranty of fitness.

We do not reach this question. In the court below, when plainly asked to state its opposition to the direction of a verdict, plaintiff did not advance the arguments it now makes, and in no way called the court's attention to any distinction between the May and the October orders. An appellant is not normally permitted to have the benefit of a new theory on appeal. It is true that this is not an absolute prohibition. The court in its discretion may relax the rule in exceptional cases in order to prevent a clear miscarriage of justice. Hormel v. Helvering, 1941, 312 U.S. 552, 61

---

77. It does not follow that if the acknowledgment had miscarried plaintiff's receipt of the goods would have completed a contract which did not include the terms of the acknowledgment. We are not faced with the question of how the statute may affect the common law under such circumstances.

S. Ct. 719, 85 L. Ed. 1037; Bergeron v. Mansour, 1 Cir., 1945, 152 F.2d 27, 32; Palo Blanco Fruit Co. v. Palo Alto Orchards Co., 1 Cir., 1952, 195 F.2d 90. Plaintiff's point, however, is by no means clear-cut. Financially the consequences are not large. Plaintiff was represented by competent counsel, and has had an eight-day trial. We do not think the case one for making an exception to the salutary rule that a party is normally entitled to but one "day" in court.

No question remains as to the counterclaim.

Judgment will be entered affirming the judgment of the District Court.

NOTE

Section 2-207 attempts to abolish the traditional "Last Shot" doctrine favoring the seller. *Roto-Lith*, misreading §2-207, appears to reaffirm the traditional view. Has §2-207 accomplished its goal? See J. White & R. Summers, Handbook of the Law under the Uniform Commercial Code 24-39 (2d ed. 1980). For a criticism of the codifiers' attempt to replace the formal rules of offer and acceptance, with their channeling function, with open standards, see Baird & Weisberg, *supra* note 63. The *Roto-Lith* decision has found a rather unfavorable press. See, e.g., Notes and Comments, 111 U. Pa. L. Rev. 132 (1962); 57 Nw. U.L. Rev. 477 (1962); 76 Harv. L. Rev 1481 (1963); 30 U. Chi. L. Rev. 540 (1963); C. Itoh & Co., Inc. v. Jordan Int'l Co., 552 F.2d 1228 (7th Cir. 1977). But it has also had its defenders. Construction Aggregates Corp. v. Hewitt-Robins, Inc., 404 F.2d 505, 509 (7th Cir. 1969) (dictum); Comment, A Look at a Strict Construction of Section 2-207 of the Uniform Commercial Code from the Seller's Point of View, *or* What's So Bad about *Roto-Lith?*, 8 Akron L. Rev. 111 (1974); Murray, Intention over Terms, 37 Fordham L. Rev. 317, 335 (1969).

Two questions should be distinguished in analyzing the decision: Is the reading of U.C.C. §2-207 technically accurate? Have other sections of the Code not been overlooked? Subsection (3)? It reads as follows:

> (3) Conduct by both parties which recognizes the existence of a contract is sufficient to establish a contract. In such case the terms of the particular contract consist of those terms on which the writings of the parties agree, together with any supplementary terms incorporated under any other provisions of this Act.

Does §2-207(2), read literally, cover *Roto-Lith?* Did plaintiff's acceptance contain an "additional" or a "different" term? Consult Dusenberg, General Provisions, Sales, Bulk Transfers, and Documents of Title, 29 Bus. Law. 1243, 1249-1250 (1974).

Suppose that the buyer's purchase order expressly stipulates against arbitration should a dispute arise, and the seller's acceptance on the other hand provides for arbitration. Do the two clauses knock each other out? See White & Summers, *supra*, at 27. Suppose seller's acceptance in *Roto-Lith* contains an arbitration clause to which the buyer did not object, and suppose further that the clause is regarded as material. Does it bind the buyer? Consult Matter of Doughboy Indus., Inc. (Pantasote Co.) 17 A.D.2d 216, 233 N.Y.2d 488 (1962).

Assuming that the seller's acknowledgment and invoice are received after consumption of the goods, what result? Celanese Corporation of America v. John Clark Indus. Inc., 214 F.2d 551 (5th Cir. 1954).

However poorly drafted §2-207 is, it clearly does set some limits: an offer to sell at $1,000 cannot be "accepted" by an expression of willingness to buy at $700.

For a suggested reform of §2-207, see Barron & Dunfee, Two Decades of 2-207: Review, Reflection and Revision, 24 Clev. St. L. Rev. 171 (1975).

AIR PRODUCTS & CHEM., INC. v. FAIRBANKS MORSE, INC.
58 Wis. 2d 193, 206 N.W.2d 414 (1973)

Actions commenced by Plaintiff-Respondent, Air Products and Chemicals, Inc. (hereinafter, "Air Products") and Air Products' insurer, Intervener-Respondent, The Hartford Steam Boiler Inspection and Insurance Co., (hereinafter, "Hartford") against Defendant-Appellant, Fairbanks Morse, Inc., (hereinafter, "Fairbanks") alleging various causes of action sounding in negligence, strict liability, breach of implied warranties of merchantability and fitness for particular purposes and breach of contract.

The facts upon which this case is based are gathered from the very extensive pleadings filed by all parties.

Air Products is a Delaware corporation with its principal business and engineering offices in Allentown, Pennsylvania. It is engaged in the business of producing industrial gas and other products, operating plants throughout the United States. Air Products designs, engineers and constructs its own industrial gas plants and for such plants purchases component parts from a large number of suppliers located throughout the United States. All of Air Products' engineering and design personnel and all of its personnel engaged in the specification and purchase of components for all of its plants are located at its offices in Allentown, Pennsylvania.

Fairbanks is a Delaware corporation with its principal offices in New York, New York. It, too, has manufacturing plants in several states and has a factory in Beloit, Wisconsin which manufactured the electric motors which are the subject of this action.

Hartford is a Connecticut corporation with its principal office in Hartford, Connecticut. Its involvement in this action arises from payments it has made to Air Products pursuant to a contract of insurance, which payments reimbursed Air Products for some of the alleged damages sustained.

The subject matter of this action is approximately ten large electric motors ranging in horsepower from 800 to 17,000 which Air Products purchased from Fairbanks in 1964. Air Products and Hartford allege that six of these motors failed to perform satisfactorily causing them to sustain substantial damages.

In or about March or early April, 1964, Fairbanks received from Air Products detailed specifications for the 800, 5,000, 6,000 and 11,000 horsepower motors which are described in plaintiff's complaint, as well as a group of other motors and was invited to submit its proposal to Air Products for the manufacture and sale of such motors. In late March and April, 1964, Fairbanks' sales agent whose offices were in Philadelphia, submitted proposals on Fairbanks' behalf in response to Air Products' invitation for quotations. On or about April 15, 1964 at a conference, Fairbanks' representatives were told by Air Products' agents that its proposal had been accepted and that Air Products would purchase the 11,000 and 6,000 horsepower motors and a second 6,000 horsepower motor pursuant to Fairbanks' quotations as they had been clarified and revised in the conference. On April 21, 1964, Air Products issued its purchase order confirming its verbal order of April 15, 1964. On April 30, 1964, Fairbanks returned an executed copy of Air Products' purchase order together with Fairbanks' acknowledgment of order form.

In or about July or August of 1964, a similar procedure was followed which culminated in Air Products purchasing another group of motors including the 17,000 horsepower motor in suit.

In October, a similar procedure was followed when Air Products exercised the option that had been previously granted to it in April to purchase 5,000 and 800 horsepower motors, as well as the second 6,000 horsepower motor. The option was confirmed by the issuance of purchase orders which were acknowledged by Fairbanks.

All of the motors were manufactured at Fairbanks' plant in Beloit, Wisconsin. The 11,000 and two 6,000 horsepower motors were shipped to Air Products' plant in Michoud, Louisiana on, respectively, March 20, April 13, and May 29, 1965. The 5,000 and 800 horsepower motors were shipped to Air Products' plant in Delaware City, Delaware in July, 1965. The 17,000 horsepower motor was shipped to Air Products' plant in Sparrow's Point, New Jersey in September, 1965. Each of the motors' function was to drive large compressors. The motors were not coupled to the compressors and tested in Beloit but were coupled to their respective compressors at the various plants to where they were shipped.

Air Products commenced its action against Fairbanks on May 8, 1969.

Hartford commenced its action against Fairbanks December 1, 1970. Air Products' complaints set forth forty-three causes of action. Hartford's complaint is of similar import. . . .

As an affirmative defense (Eighth Affirmative Defense) to all of Air Products' causes of action, and as an affirmative defense (Fifth Affirmative Defense) to all of Hartford's causes of action, Fairbanks set up a provision contained in its "Acknowledgments of Order" which were sent by Fairbanks to Air Products, along with an executed purchase order on each of the motors and which it is alleged, limits the liability of Fairbanks to Air Products. To each of these affirmative defenses, both Hartford and Air Products demurred. The trial court overruled their demurrers. From the order overruling their demurrers, Air Products and Hartford have appealed. . . .

HANLEY, Justice.

Four issues are presented on this appeal:

1. Is the four-year Pennsylvania Statute of Limitations a defense to any or all of Air Products' or Hartford's causes of action;

2. Can a contract which states that liquidated damages "shall be in addition to any and all other remedies of buyer" be interpreted to mean that liquidated damages is the buyer's sole and exclusive remedy;

3. Under Pennsylvania law can limitation of liability provisions contained in the seller's "acknowledgments of order" become terms in the contracts of sale when the buyer's purchase orders contained no such terms and the buyer never expressly agreed to such terms;

4. Under Pennsylvania law, is the tort doctrine of strict liability applicable to either economic losses caused by unreasonably defective products or products which are unreasonably dangerous to themselves which in fact injure themselves and cause economic losses?

[Only the court's discussion of the third issue is included here.]

LIMITATIONS OF LIABILITY PROVISIONS IN
FAIRBANKS ACKNOWLEDGMENTS

As an affirmative defense to all the causes of action pleaded by both Air Products and Hartford, Fairbanks set up a provision contained in its "acknowledgments of order" which were sent by Fairbanks to Air Products with Air Products' purchase order which it had executed. The "acknowledgment of order" from Fairbanks to Air Products has the following language printed in reasonably boldface type at the bottom:

"WE THANK YOU FOR YOUR ORDER AS COPIED HEREON, WHICH WILL RECEIVE PROMPT ATTENTION AND SHALL BE GOVERNED BY THE PROVISIONS ON THE REVERSE SIDE HEREOF UNLESS YOU NOTIFY US TO THE CONTRARY WITHIN 10 DAYS OR BEFORE SHIPMENT WHICH-EVER IS EARLIER. BEFORE ACCEPTING GOODS FROM TRANSPORTATION COMPANY SEE THAT

EACH ARTICLE IS IN GOOD CONDITION. IF SHORTAGE OR DAMAGE IS APPARENT REFUSE
SHIPMENT UNLESS AGENT NOTES DEFECT ON TRANSPORTATION BILL. ACCEPTANCE OF
SHIPMENT WITHOUT COMPLYING WITH SUCH CONDITIONS IS AT YOUR OWN RISK.
"THIS IS NOT AN INVOICE. AN INVOICE FOR THIS MATERIAL WILL BE SENT YOU WITHIN A
FEW DAYS.
                              "ACKNOWLEDGMENT OF ORDER"

On the reverse side of the "acknowledgment of order" there are
printed six separate provisions which are appropriately numbered and at
the very beginning it is stated that:

> The following provisions form part of the order acknowledged and ac-
> cepted on the face hereof, as express agreements between Fairbanks,
> Morse & Co. ("Company") and the Buyer governing the terms and condi-
> tions of the sale, subject to modification only in writing signed by the local
> manager or an executive officer of the Company:

Provision #6 which is the subject of the dispute between the parties
provides that:

> 6. — The Company nowise assumes any responsibility or liability with
> respect to use, purpose, or suitability, and shall not be liable for damages of
> any character, whether direct or consequential, for defect, delay, or other-
> wise, its sole liability and obligation being confined to the replacement in
> the manner aforesaid of defectively manufactured guaranteed parts failing
> within the time stated.

Fairbanks contends that provision #6 contained on the reverse side of
their "acknowledgment of order" became part of the contract between it
and Air Products while Air Products contends that its right to rely on the
implied warranty of merchantability (U.C.C. 2-314) fitness for particular
purposes (U.C.C. 2-315) and consequential damages (U.C.C. 2-714) has
in no way been limited by provision #6, since it never was assented to by
it, and, therefore, never became part of the contract. Both parties are in
agreement that sec. 2-207, of the Uniform Commercial Code (12A Pennsylvania Statutes Ann. sec. 2-207) is the appropriate standard by which
their rights must be determined. . . .

In reaching its conclusion that the demurrers of Air Products and
Hartford to this affirmative defense should be overruled, the trial court
summarized its reasoning as follows:

> It is therefore my conclusion that since these parties were merchants
> when they dealt with each other in the formation of this contract and since
> a contract actually came into existence by seasonable acceptance, that
> acceptance taking place by both the execution of the purchase order and
> the execution and delivery of the acknowledgment of order, simultaneous
> acts, and since the original offer to purchase contained no terms or provi-

sions pertaining to the limitation of damages as pleaded in the eighth affirmative defense, that therefore these were completely new and additional proposed terms and, as between merchants, became binding as between the parties and, therefore, if proven, they could constitute a defense to some of plaintiff's claims.

In reaching the above conclusion, apparently the trial court did not consider subsection (2)(b) of Sec. 2-207.

One commentator has aptly stated the threshold questions involved in subsection (1):

> The second situation covered by this clause concerns confirmatory memoranda which follow an agreement. "Confirmation" connotes that the parties reached an agreement before exchange of the forms in question. The purpose of Code drafters here must have been to make clear that confirmations need not mirror each other in order to find contract. Simply stated then, under this first clause of section 2-207(1), it is reasonable to assume that the parties have a deal, then there is a contract even though terms of the writings exchanged do not match.
>
> All of the language following the comma in subsection (1) simply preserves for the offeree his right to make a counter-offer if he does so expressly. This phrase cannot possibly affect the deal between parties that have reached an agreement and then exchanged confirmations. In that situation it is too late for a counter-offer and subsection (2) must be applied to determine what becomes of the non-matching terms of the confirmations. Thus, under subsection (1), there are two instances in which a contract may not have been formed. First, if the offeror could not reasonably treat the response of the offeree as an acceptance there is no contract. Second, if the offeree's acceptance is made expressly conditional on the offeror's assent to variant provisions, the offeree has made a counter-offer. However, under section 2-207(3) either situation may result in contract formation by subsequent conduct of the parties.[78]

Because the reverse side of Fairbanks' Acknowledgment of Order states that the provisions contained there ". . . form part of the order acknowledged and accepted on the face hereof . . ." it would seem that Air Products could have "reasonably" assumed that the parties "had a deal."

Since there is no express provision in the purchase orders making assent to different or additional terms conditioned upon Air Products' assent to them, the second requirement of coming under U.C.C. 2-207 is also met.

Once having satisfied the requirements of subsection (1), any additional matter must fall in subsection (2).

---

78. Section 2-207 of the Uniform Commercial Code — New Rules for the "Battle of the Forms" (1971), 32 U. of Pitt. L. Rev. 209, 210.

The major impact of sec. 2-207 is that it altered the common law rule which precluded an acceptance from creating a contract if it in any way varied any term of the offer. Subsection (1) expressly provides that there may be a legally binding contract even if the acceptance contains terms "different from" or "additional to" the terms of the offer.

At this point a contract does in fact exist between the parties under (1). Subsection (2) must now be resorted to to see which of the "variant" terms will actually become part of the contract.

At this juncture, Air Products and Hartford argue that 2-207(2) only applies to "additional terms" while Fairbanks' limitation of liability provisions were "different." To this extent they contend terms are "additional" if they concern a subject matter that is not covered in the offer and "different" if the subject matter, although covered in the offer, was covered in a variant way. Hartford and Air Products' argument seems to expressly contradict Official U.C.C. Comment #3 which unequivocally starts "Whether or not *additional or different* terms will become part of the agreement depends upon the provisions of subsection (2)." (Emphasis added). One commentator has noted that:

> On its face, subsection (2) seems only to apply to additional and not conflicting terms, and at least one court has interpreted the language this way. However, this is an unnecessarily limited construction and, as Comment 3 to the section points out, subsection (2) should apply to both additional and different provisions. [32 U. Pitt. L. Rev. at 211.]

The case referred to is American Parts Co., Inc. v. American Arbitration Association (1967), 8 Mich. App. 156, 154 N.W.2d 5, where in explicitly limiting the application of (2) to additional terms the court said of the policy behind 2-207:

> The policy of section 2-207 is that the parties should be able to enforce their agreement, whatever it is, despite discrepancies between the oral agreement and the confirmation (or between an offer and acceptance) *if enforcement can be granted without requiring either party to be bound to a material term to which he has not agreed.* (Emphasis added) [154 N.W.2d at p. 12.]

The implication seems clear. A party cannot be expected to have assented to a "different" term.

The thrust of the "additional-different" dichotomy as averred for by Air Products and Hartford is that their offer as effectuated by a purchase order includes not only those terms which are expressly stated therein, but also those which are implied by law (e.g. warranty and damage) that will become a part of the contract formed by the seller's acceptance of the offer. Therefore, Fairbanks' limitation of liability terms are different since they are at variance with the implied warranty and damage terms in Air

Products' offer. Fairbanks contends that because sec. 2-714(3) provides that "in a proper case" consequential damages may be recovered by an injured buyer they are clearly not impelled in all contracts. Comment #4 to sec. 2-714 refers to the comment for sec. 2-715. It is there stated in comment #3 to sec. 2-715 that:

> In the *absence of excuse under the section on merchant's excuse by failure of presupposed conditions*, the seller is liable for consequential damages in all cases where he had reason to know of the buyer's general or particular requirements at the time of contracting. (Emphasis added)

We think Fairbanks was aware of the particular needs of Air Products. A reading of section 2-714 and 2-715 indicates that a potential recovery for consequential loss is implicit in the contract.

Air Products and Hartford next contend that if the added terms of the "acknowledgment of order" were "additional" terms they still do not become part of the contract because the prerequisite to their becoming a part of the contract which are contained in subsection (2) were not satisfied. Section 2-207(2) required that:

> The additional terms are to be construed as proposals for addition to the contract. Between merchants such terms become part of the contract unless:
> (a) the offer expressly limits acceptance to the terms of the offer;
> (b) they materially alter it; or
> (c) notification of objection to them has already been given or is given within a reasonable time after notice of them is received.

The language employed by Air Products in its "terms and conditions" was not express enough to bring into play the provisions of either subsection 2-207(a) or (c). The ultimate question to be determined, therefore, is whether the disclaimer contained in Fairbanks' "acknowledgment of order" materially altered the agreement between the parties pursuant to sec. 2-207(2)(b). If they materially alter what would otherwise be firmed by the acceptance of an offer, they will not become terms unless the buyer expressly agrees thereto. "If, however, they are terms which would not so change the bargain they will be incorporated unless notice of objection to them has already been given or is given within a reasonable time." Comment #3 to sec. 2-207.

Hartford and Air Products contend that the eradication of a multi-million dollar damage exposure is per se material. Fairbanks bases its argument on the ground that consequential damages may not be recovered except in "special circumstances" or in a "proper case." (2-714(2), (3).) As already stated, these "special circumstances" would seem by Comment #3 to sec. 2-715 to be referring to situations which concern instances where the seller did not have reason to know of buyer's general or particular requirements at the time of contracting. "Consequential damages resulting from the seller's breach include (a) any loss resulting from general or particular requirements and needs of which the seller at the time of contracting had reason to know and which could not reasonably be prevented by cover or otherwise; . . ." U.C.C. sec. 2-715(2)(a).

While the comment #4 clearly indicates that a disclaimer of an implied warranty of merchantability is material, there is no good reason to hold that a disclaimer that has the effect of eliminating millions of dollars in damages should become a part of a contract by operation of law.

We conclude that the disclaimer for consequential loss was sufficiently material to require express conversation between the parties over its inclusion or exclusion in the contract. It follows that the order overruling the demurrers of Air Products and Hartford must be reversed. . . .

NOTE

See Macaulay, Contract Law and Contract Research (pt. 2), 20 J. Legal Ed. 460, 463 (1968); Macaulay, The Use and Non-use of Contracts in the Manufacturing Industry, 9 Pract. Law. No. 7, 13 (1963).

B. Contracts of Adhesion

Standard form contracts offered on a take-it-or-leave-it basis by a party with considerable bargaining power present another facet of the assent problem. Assuming that the weaker party needs the goods or services in question and is unable to shop around for better terms or is unfamiliar with the terms offered, there is a genuine danger of overreaching.[79] Are we still in the field of contract with its traditional emphasis on assent?

Karl Llewellyn, who thought deeply about this situation, suggests an ingenious answer to the assent problem. He first points out that most adhesion contracts contain certain terms that are subject to dicker as well as boiler-plate clauses that the author of the contract typically has put into every form and is unwilling to bargain over.[80] Llewellyn then offers this rather simple solution to the assent problem:

The answer, I suggest, is this: Instead of thinking about "assent" to boiler-plate clauses, we can recognize that so far as concerns the specific, there is no assent at all. What has in fact been assented to, specifically, are the few dickered terms, and the broad type of the transaction, and but one thing more. That one thing more is a blanket assent (not a specific assent) to any not unreasonable or indecent terms the seller may have on his form, which

79. Restatement Second §211, Comment c.
80. The quantity, quality, and price may be open to dicker.

do not alter or eviscerate the reasonable meaning of the dickered terms. The fine print which has not been read has no business to cut under the reasonable meaning of those dickered terms which constitute the dominant and only real expression of agreement, but much of it commonly belongs in. . . .

. . . There has been an arm's-length deal, with dickered terms. There has been accompanying that basic deal another which, if not on any fiduciary basis, at least involves a plain expression of confidence, asked and accepted, with a corresponding limit on the powers granted: the boiler-plate is assented to en bloc, "sight, unseen," on the implicit assumption and to the full extent that (1) it does not alter or impair the fair meaning of the dickered terms when read alone, and (2) that its terms are neither in the particular nor in the net manifestly unreasonable and unfair. Such is the reality, and I see nothing in the way of a court's operating on that basis, to truly effectuate the only intention which can in reason be worked out as common to the two parties, granted good faith. And if the boiler-plate party is not playing in good faith, there is law enough to bar that fact from benefiting it. We had a hundred years of sales law in which any sales transaction with explicit words resulted in two several contracts for the one consideration: that of sale, and the collateral one of warranty. The idea is applicable here, for better reason: any contract with boiler-plate results in *two* several contracts: the *dickered* deal, and the collateral one of *supplementary* boiler-plate.

Rooted in sense, history, and simplicity, it is an answer which could occur to anyone.[81]

Llewellyn's solution appears to be reflected in §211 of the new Restatement ("Standardized Agreements"), which reads as follows:

(1)   Except as stated in Subsection (3), where a party to an agreement signs or otherwise manifests assent to a writing and has reason to believe that like writings are regularly used to embody terms of agreements of the same type, he adopts the writing as an integrated agreement with respect to the terms included in the writing.

(2)   Such a writing is interpreted wherever reasonable as treating alike all those similarly situated, without regard to their knowledge or understanding of the standard terms of the writing.

(3)   Where the other party has reason to believe that the party manifesting such assent would not do so if he knew that the writing contained a particular term, the term is not part of the agreement.

According to the commentary that accompanies this section, customers who sign or otherwise agree to a standard form contract trust "to the good faith of the party using the form and to the tacit representation that like terms are being accepted regularly by others similarly situated.

81. Llewellyn, *supra* note 61, at 370-371 (footnote omitted).

But they understand that they are assenting to the terms not read or not understood, subject to such limitations as the law may impose."[82]

Section 211(2) is rather intriguing. It seems to say that a standardized contract is to be interpreted so as to effectuate the reasonable expectations of the average member of the public who accepts it. This reading of subsection 2 also protects those who are sophisticated enough to understand its "true" meaning.[83]

Subsection 3 affords protection against unfair terms; in addition, standard terms are subject to interpretation *contra proferentem*,[84] and must satisfy the requirements of good faith and conscionability.[85]

Professor Slawson has examined the relationship between the democratic lawmaking process and contractual self-government in the context of the standard form contract. Standard Form Contracts and Democratic Control of Lawmaking Power, 84 Harv. L. Rev. 529 (1971).

Professor Slawson begins with the traditional idea that contracts represent a form of private lawmaking and that the legitimacy of this process is derived from the agreement of the parties, much as the legitimacy of statutory laws is derived from their being enacted by a democratically elected legislature. He then points out that just as not all of what we call public law has democratic origins (e.g. administrative regulations), not all of what we call contract can be traced to the agreement of the parties. The standard form contract and the adhesion contract, which Slawson distinguishes, pose problems of nonconsensual private lawmaking.

In most consumer transactions the standard form contract is not a contract at all (at 544). It is generally not read, and if read, it is not understood, and this is something both parties know and expect (at 540-543). In a transaction involving a standard form, the true contract is based on the manifested consent of both parties (at 543). According to this view, the manifestation of consent is like a statute and the standard forms resemble rules or regulations promulgated by administrative agencies in accordance with a statute. The issuer of the standard form is to be viewed as having been delegated power by the consumer to draft rules governing their contractual relationship (at 533). These rules are to be reviewed by the courts in much the same way as rules of administrative

82. Restatement Second §211, Comment *b*. For a statement of the so-called duty to read, see 1 Williston at pp. 97-99. It is based on the rationale that the offeree has led the offeror to believe that the offeree has a sense of the terms of the offer. For extensive discussion of the rule and its many exceptions, see Calamari, Duty to Read — A Changing Concept, 43 Fordham L. Rev. 341 (1974); Macauley, Private Legislation and the Duty to Read — Business Run by IBM Machine, the Law of Contracts and Credit Cards, 19 Vanderbilt L. Rev. 1051 (1966). On the requirement of conspicuousness, see p. 260, n.72 *supra*. See further the *Woodburn* case, *infra* p. 276.

83. Restatement Second §211, Comment *e*; Keeton, Insurance Law Rights at Variance with Policy Provisions, 83 Harv. L. Rev. 961, 974-977 (1970).

84. Restatement Second §211, Comment *c*, and §206.

85. Id., Comment *c*, and §§205 and 208.

agencies, and must conform to the contract of the parties as well as to other principles (at 544).

Because "[i]n most instances the contract is either unwritten or provides no significant guidance for determining the enforceability of non-contractual standard forms which accompany it" (at 545), Professor Slawson proposes that the bundle of promises that make up the standard form be treated as though they constituted a tangible good.[86] Complex standard forms, like complex goods, would come with an implied warranty of fitness for the intended purposes of the consumer, since, in most instances, an issuer knows these purposes. On this view, the issuer of a standard form should be held to an implied promise that the form contains only what the recipient would reasonably expect it to contain (at 547).

As for adhesion contracts, Professor Slawson points out that not all standard contracts are adhesive and not all adhesive contracts are standardized (at 549). A person may be said to enter into an adhesion contract when he has no real choice as to one or all of the terms of the contract. This lack of choice deprives the adhesion contract or adhesive term of its contractual nature. Still, the contract or term may be enforced if it complies with "standards in the public interest" (at 556). Such standards will include the reasonable expectations of the buyer, but since the buyer's expectations may themselves be "shaped adhesively," conformity with the buyer's expectations will not necessarily be enough (at 559). The standards in question must take into account the "purposes of the industry and its products or services," and "[a] court would have to ask . . . what would a reasonable buyer under the circumstances have chosen to buy had he the range of choice which the industry-imposed adhesion had denied him" (at 560).

Professor Slawson makes an appeal for the development of general principles, capable of being applied to all standard form and adhesion contracts. He is critical of the use of unconscionability, which focuses on individual fact situations and yields results applicable only to particular cases, as a doctrinal tool for dealing with problems involving mass transactions. Unconscionability, in Slawson's view, should be limited to those cases where a party has actually consented to a harsh or shocking term (at 564).

Professor Rakoff, in an ambitious article, argues that contracts of adhesion should be presumptively unenforceable. Contracts of Adhesion: An Essay in Reconstruction, 96 Harv. L. Rev. 1174 (1983). Explicitly rejecting public law and monopoly power analyses, Rakoff views contracts of adhesion as part of the relationship between institutionalized

---

86. For a similar characterization of the consumer transaction phenomenon see Leff, Contract as a Thing, 19 Am. L. Rev. 131, 144 (1970). See further Kessler, Contracts of Adhesion — Some Thoughts about Freedom of Contract, 43 Colum. L. Rev. 629, 641 (1943).

firms and their customers. Institutionalized firms use contracts of adhesion to standardize market transactions and promote internal efficiency and hierarchy; these internal pressures prevent firms from responding to customer attempts to bargain over terms or shop between firms. In his analysis, the question of whether to enforce contracts of adhesion ultimately raises the issue of how to allocate power and freedom between commercial organizations and individuals.

Finding the authoritarian imposition of standardized terms unjustified, Rakoff would have courts reject "invisible" terms (i.e., those for which the usual adherent would neither bargain nor shop) and replace them with terms drawn from "background law," which the courts would formulate. Drafters of contracts of adhesion could attempt to show that invisible terms should be enforced, but terms that terrorized adherents, only served to preserve organizational structure, or deviated from usual commercial practice would be unenforceable.

Professor Rakoff insists that the use of a background law would not burden the courts, but his discussion of the sources and formulation of this law is vague. Without easy recourse to background law, his legal proposals would be difficult to apply. Under his analysis courts act to redress an authoritarian imbalance between firm and adherent. The proper balance, however, is not stated, and his own alternative, background law, must itself be formulated in light of what the proper balance should be.

Many of the cases in Chapter 4 illustrate the attempts made by courts to deal with the complex problems posed by adhesion contracts.

WOODBURN v. NORTHWESTERN BELL TELEPHONE CO.
275 N.W.2d 403 (Iowa 1979)

HARRIS, J.   B. T. Woodburn (plaintiff), a physician, was omitted from a professional listing in the yellow pages of defendant's 1971 directory. When he brought this suit for what he claims were the resulting damages, the Northwestern Bell Telephone Company (defendant) interposed two special defenses by way of express limitations of damages. One was based on a provision in defendant's tariff, on file with the Iowa commerce commission. The second defense was based on a provision printed on the reverse side of a form for placing the listing. Ruling on defendant's application for adjudication of law points, the trial court held in favor of both defenses. Thereafter the parties stipulated to the amounts of damages, computed on the basis of the adjudication of the two defenses.

Final judgment was entered for the limited damages. Plaintiff brought this appeal separately challenging the adjudication that the two provisions both effectively limited the amount plaintiff could recover. We affirm the trial court's determination that the tariff constituted a valid limitation of recoverable damages. We affirm in part and reverse in part the trial court's determination as to the contractual limitation.

As a part of business phone service, defendant provides, without extra charge, a white-page listing and a yellow-page listing in its telephone book. For an additional fee the patron can contract for special listings in the yellow pages.

Plaintiff's professional practice is in Des Moines where he specializes in plastic surgery and surgery of the hand. In connection with the relocation of his offices in August of 1971, plaintiff telephoned defendant and requested a change in his directory listing. Plaintiff wished to have his new professional address and phone number listed both in small type and bold type in the yellow pages. Defendant agreed to make the change. On October 7, 1971, plaintiff again telephoned to confirm the change of listing. Thereafter a copy of the listing contract was sent to him. Defendant failed to make the listing as agreed to.

Other facts are unclear due to the summary nature of the trial proceeding. There is no contention that plaintiff knew of an Iowa commerce commission tariff limitation which provides as follows:

> The telephone company's liability arising from errors in or omissions of directory listings shall be limited to and satisfied by an amount not exceeding one-half of the amount of the fixed charges for the service affected for the period from the date of issuance of the directory in which the mistake occurred to the date of issuance of a new directory containing the proper listing.

Plaintiff contends he was also unaware of the limitation of liability on the reverse of the form contract, as follows:

> If the telephone company shall omit said advertisement or any additional advertising from any issue of its directory, in whole or in part, or shall make errors therein, its liability therefor shall in no event exceed the amount of the charges for the advertising which was omitted or in which the error occurred in such directory issue.

Plaintiff contends he neither saw nor signed defendant's contract form prior to making the agreement. The agreement offered in evidence appears to have been signed November 3, 1971, by someone claiming to represent plaintiff.

[The discussion of the trial court's adjudication limiting liability in accordance with the tariff is omitted.]

II

There remains plaintiff's claim for damages because of defendant's failure to provide the separate, bold-face listing in the yellow pages. Defendant interposes, not the tariff, but the contractual provision to limit this claim.

Plaintiff insists the contractual limitation of liability is also contrary to public policy. The trial court disagreed and so do we. Courts generally enforce clauses which limit to a stated amount the liability of telephone companies on account of errors or omissions in directory listings. See Annot., 92 A.L.R.2d 917, 935-945. We find nothing contrary to public policy in such a provision.

We therefore agree with the trial court that defendant could properly limit its liability as to nonutility business. But the trial court did not stop with this ruling. It went on to hold that the only question remaining in the suit was damages as limited by the tariff and contract.

The trial court seems to have found, as a matter of law, that the parties were bound by the contract terms. This was in spite of plaintiff's contention that the clause was contrary to the reasonable expectations of the parties. Plaintiff asserted: ". . . At no time when the listing requests were made did Woodburn see the exculpatory language on the reverse side of the standard form nor was he advised of it orally. . . ."

The effect of the trial court's decree was to foreclose any consideration of plaintiff's assertion that the contract lacked mutuality of assent. But we have said: "Usually as an essential prerequisite to the formation of an informal contract there must be an agreement; a mutual manifestation of assent *to the stated terms.* The agreement is ordinarily reached by a process of offer and acceptance. [Authorities.]" (Emphasis added.) . . .

Plaintiff should not have been deprived of the opportunity to present his version of the facts as to assent. . . .

Upon remand plaintiff should be accorded an opportunity to make whatever showing he can in support of his claim that there was no mutuality of assent. If mutuality of assent is established, so that the contractual provision is applicable, it would, as hereinbefore explained, limit defendant's liability. But if there was no mutuality of assent the contractual provision would not limit plaintiff's recovery.

The case is accordingly affirmed in part, reversed in part, and remanded for further proceedings in conformance herewith.

NOTE

How would the case be decided under §211 of the Restatement Second?

Section 7.   The Bargain Theory of Contract and the Reliance Principle

The consideration doctrine, regarded by many as the centerpiece of contract law, has produced a vast literature and intense controversy. Its origins are still shrouded in mystery,[87] and its functions, of which there are many,[88] are ill-defined. Because the history of the doctrine has many layers, those who have attempted to study it from the perspective of their own age have often been misled into taking a narrower view of its meaning than the historical record would warrant.

The best way to approach the problem is to begin with the most basic feature of consideration doctrine: the notion of reciprocity that underlies the classical theory of contract as bargain. The notions of exchange, bargain, and reciprocity have had a long association with consideration. Reciprocity was "a principle of contemporary morality, 'part of the common stock of ideas of medieval Europe,'"[89] and it would have been extraordinary if a paid-for promise was not held binding.[90] The intuitive appeal of the bargain idea was not lost on the judges and lawyers of the fourteenth and fifteenth centuries, a fact that may help to explain the ease with which executory bilateral contracts came to be recognized.[91]

But the idea of a reciprocal bargain was not the only one that lay behind the emerging doctrine of consideration. A second principle, associated with "promises and statements, rather than bargains," emphasized the element of reliance and asserted that "if a man make a promise or a statement, and another relies on the promise or statement, the other is liable for the loss."[92] The two principles of bargain and reliance were often confused and the relation between them remained unclear until the

87. Simpson, Historical Introduction at 8-9; Simpson, ch. 4 (with further literature); Baker, Introduction at 285-290; J. L. Barton, The Early History of Consideration, 85 L.Q. Rev. 372 (1969).

88. 1A Corbin §204, at 489 (1963): the doctrine of consideration is many doctrines. Corbin's thesis (Recent Developments in the Law of Contracts, 50 Harv. L. Rev. 449, 454 (1937)) — that the courts determine whether a sound and sufficient reason exists for the enforcement of the promise and "cheerfully" call the reason found a "sufficient consideration" — is no longer as heretical as it was when his article first appeared. See, e.g., P. Atiyah, Consideration in Contract: A Fundamental Restatement 11 (1971).

89. Baker, Introduction at 294.

90. Simpson at 326. The remarks of Milsom at 311 help round out the picture:

. . . [I]f the promise was enforceable because of some overall morality in the circumstances, that may still have been the residue of the almost proprietary notion the *quid pro quo*, to the extent that the idea of the common law of contracts has its ultimate basis in bargain rather than in promise may reflect history.

See also the second edition at 357-358.

91. See Strangeborough v. Warner, discussed *supra* p. 38, and its discussion in Simpson at 461.

92. Baker, Introduction at 296-297.

sixteenth century, when an uneasy alliance was established by the definition of consideration as either a benefit to the promisor or a detriment to
the promisee.[93] After this, the main task was to determine which benefits
and detriments would in fact constitute a valid consideration, and the
common law system of adjudication made it inevitable that this process of
definition was carried out in a more or less ad hoc fashion.[94]

Holmes, recognizing that the doctrine of consideration, in its historically evolved form, lacked logic and consistency, sought to give it greater
rigor by emphasizing the element of bargain. In his well-known discussion of the problem, Holmes narrowed the meaning of the bargain idea
by insisting that promise and consideration must each purport to be the
motive for the other.[95] The Holmes formula can be interpreted to mean,
in the words of Professor Dawson, that both parties must agree "that each
was induced to promise or to act by the promise or the act of the other."
On this view, the doctrine of consideration requires that the parties
"agree not only on what was to be exchanged, but also on why; this would
mean that the way — the inducement — for each must be disclosed and
agreed to by the other."[96]

Holmes' rather stringent interpretation of the consideration doctrine
was rejected by both Restatements, which define consideration in
broader terms.[97] Even under this broader approach, however, a question
remained as to whether the principle of detrimental reliance could be
completely absorbed by the bargain theory. If a court is confronted with a
claim for damages based on A's reliance on B's promise, can B defend on
the grounds that his promise was in no way motivated by a desire that A
take the particular action he took (that A's reliance was in no sense the

---

93. "Every consideration that doth charge the defendant in an assumpsit must be to the
detriment of the defendant or charge to the plaintiff, and no case can be put out of this
rule." Stone v. Wythipol, Cro. Eliz. 126, 1 Leon. 113, Owen 94 (1588). The narrow approach laid down by Lord Coke was not shared by Barton Manwood, who, in arguing his
own case in Manwood v. Burston, 2 Leon. 3 (1587), broadened the scope of consideration:

> There are three manner of considerations upon which an assumpsit may be
> grounded: 1. a debt of precedent; 2. where he to whom such a promise is made is
> damnified by doing any thing or spends his return at the instance of the promiser,
> although no benefit cometh to the promiser, as I agree with a surgeon to cure a poor
> man (who is a stranger unto me) of a sore, who doth it accordingly, he shall have an
> action; 3. or there is a present consideration.

On the conflicting interpretation of the passage, see 8 Holdsworth, History of English Law 7;
Fifoot at 40.

94. "The life of the law has not been logic; it has been experience." O. W. Holmes, The
Common Law 5 (M. Howe ed. 1963). To paraphrase Simpson, the bargain theory of consideration would have been adopted had the sixteenth-century lawyers been consistent. Simpson at 432-433.

95. Holmes, *supra* note 94, at 293-294.

96. J. P. Dawson, Gifts and Promises 203-204 (1980). Holmes' formula, whatever its
interpretation, is one of many expressions of the individualistic spirit animating his great
book. For a challenging criticism of the Holmesian approach, see G. Gilmore, The Death of
Contract 18 (1974).

97. Sections 75 and 71, respectively; see Corbin, *supra* note 88, at 453.

"price" of B's promise)? It is one thing to say that courts will grant relief for detrimental reliance on a promise. It is something quite different to say that the only kind of reliance for which relief will be granted is reliance that in one way or another has been bargained for by the promisor. Bargained-for consideration may be a sufficient cause for enforcing a promise. It is not a necessary one. This insight has found expression in §90 of both Restatements; under §90, promises not bargained for but reasonably relied upon are enforceable without assent or consideration.[98] Section 90 of the Restatement First stated that

> A promise which the promisor should reasonably expect to induce action or forbearance of a definite and substantial character on the part of the promisee and which does induce such action or forbearance is binding if injustice can be avoided only by enforcement of the promise.

In the Restatement Second, the language of §90 was changed as follows:

> A promise which the promisor should reasonably expect to induce action or forbearance on the part of the promisee or a third person and which does induce such action or forbearance is binding if injustice can be avoided only by enforcement of the promise. The remedy granted for breach may be limited as justice requires.[99]

The reasons for the change are explained in the Reporter's Notes. Though Corbin objected to it,[100] the term used to describe a cause of action under §90 is "promissory estoppel." The end result of this development is that the law of contractual liability is today a two-track system, one track resting on the notion of bargain and the other on the "vaguely delictual"[101] idea that an act of reasonable reliance can create liability for a subsequent loss.

98. It makes good sense that the Restatement does not treat §90 in the chapter on consideration. Corbin, Recent Developments in the Law of Contracts, 50 Harv. L. Rev. 449, 453-457 (1957). The contrary thesis, advanced in preceding editions of this casebook, has been abandoned.

99. At common law, prior to the nineteenth century, all promises were, in a manner of speaking, enforced only to the extent required by justice. Juries at the time had wide discretion in awarding damages and could tailor relief according to the requirements of justice in each particular case. Today, liability under §90 may in many cases be a weaker form of liability than the protection afforded the promisee's expectancy in a regular contract action, an idea already expressed in 2 F. Hutcheson, System of Morals 5-6, as quoted in P. Stein, Legal Evolution (1980). We owe this reference to Professor Jan Vetter, University of California, Berkeley.

100. 1A Corbin §204 (1963). For the distinction between promissory and equitable estoppel (misrepresentation of fact relied upon by the other party), see Mazer v. Jackson Ins. Agency, 340 So. 2d 770 (Ala. 1976).

101. Atiyah at 185-186. The "weakness of the reasonable expectation principle" is emphasized by Baker, From Sanctity of Contract to Reasonable Expectation?, 32 Current Legal Problems 17, 25 et seq. (1979); see further Knapp, Reliance in the Revised Restatement: The Proliferation of Promissory Estoppel, 81 Colum. L. Rev. 52 (1980); Feinman, Promissory Estoppel and Judicial Method, 97 Harv. L. Rev. 678 (1984).

The history of consideration doctrine has in large part been determined by the effort to reconcile individual responsibility with protection of the expectations raised by reposing trust and confidence in the words of the promisor. The bargain theory proved insufficiently flexible to achieve such a reconciliation, and the doctrine of promissory estoppel helped to keep the system open by accommodating a new (and more generous) attitude towards reliance that began to take shape in the late nineteenth century. In the words of Atiyah:

> In a period of greater stability, greater regularity of law, and greater predictability of behaviour of the courts and of businessmen, reliance became more natural and more justifiable. The concept was in a sense pulling itself up by its own bootstraps. As people grew to rely on others so they grew to think it justifiable to do so; and as they found it more justifiable to do so, they expected the law to protect them when their confidence turned out to have been misplaced.[102]

Since there is a fundamental difference between the ideas underlying the bargain theory of consideration, on the one hand, and the doctrine of promissory estoppel, on the other, a problem arises as to how to distinguish these two kinds of liability (a problem that is compounded by calling them both "contractual"). Innumerable attempts to draw the line have left the issue still in doubt and as a result, both branches of liability have come under attack, the former for its narrowness of focus, the latter for its expansiveness and the potential it creates for exuberant social engineering. This is illustrated by the tendency in some jurisdictions to be satisfied with an implied promise (rather than an express promise) based on surrounding circumstances and to extend the protection given to reasonable expectations.[103]

Small wonder that a reform movement has set in. The first serious attack on the doctrine was contained in a famous article by Lord Wright entitled, "Ought the Doctrine of Consideration to be Abolished from the Common Law?"[104] In his words: "a scientific or logical theory of contract would . . . take as the test of contractual intention the answer to the overriding question whether there was a deliberate and serious intention free from illegality, immorality, mistake, fraud, or duress to make a binding contract." In this view, consideration ceases to be a condition of the contract and becomes merely a piece of evidence.

The Sixth Interim Report of the English Law Revision Commission (1937) attempted to follow a middle course. "In very many cases the doctrine of consideration is a mere technicality which is irreconcilable

---

102. Atiyah at 186-189.
103. The controversial and conflicting case law is discussed in Feinman, Promissory Estoppel and Judicial Method, 97 Harv. L. Rev. 678 (1984).
104. 49 Harv. L. Rev. 1225 (1936).

either with business expedience or common sense." Nevertheless, the Commission regarded as unwise the recommendation to abolish the doctrine "root and branch. . . . It is so deeply imbedded in our law that any measure which now proposed to do away with it altogether would almost certainly arouse suspicion and hostility." Consequently, the Report limited its suggestions for reform to certain areas where application of the doctrine caused hardship and inconvenience (12 et. seq.).[105]

In this country the reform movement also took a less radical approach,[106] seeking primarily to eliminate the historical excrescences with which the doctrine of consideration had become overburdened. Modification and discharge, for example, were taken out from under the domination of consideration doctrine. Firm offers received similar treatment, and an expansion in our notions of duress and unconscionability helped to take pressure off the doctrine of consideration in other areas as well.

A question remains whether, stripped of these unnatural growths, the consideration doctrine is still needed.[107] The defenders of the doctrine point out that in addition to its evidentiary role, it has a cautionary function (serving to guard the promisor against ill-considered action), a deterrent function (discouraging transactions of doubtful utility), and finally, a channeling function (helping to distinguish one particular type of transaction from other types and from tentative or exploratory expressions of intent).[108] No legal system, they emphasize, has seen fit to enforce all promises indiscriminately without some safeguard for the promisor. To be sure, the civil law has no consideration doctrine. (The doctrine of *causa*, whatever its early connection with consideration, is not its equivalent). But the absence of a consideration requirement in civilian systems does not entail unqualified enforcement of all informal gratuitous promises. In German law, for example, a gratuitous promise has to be made in a most solemn form to be enforceable (Civil Code §518).

Still the bargain theory, pruned of its outgrowths, has an important precautionary function. We cannot simply say that a bilateral contract becomes binding by offer and acceptance whether or not there is consideration; a gift promise, for example, cannot be turned into a bilateral contract merely by the offeree's promise to accept. It can even be

105. For a summary of the report and a criticism, see G. H. Treitel, The Law of Contracts 104-106 (5th ed. 1979).

106. In 1937, a statute abolishing the consideration doctrine was passed by the New York legislature, but vetoed by Governor Lehman "upon urgent representation from bench, bar and business organizations that the great commercial fabric of the Empire State was unprepared for so radical a change without opportunity for study and discussion." Thompson, Some Current and Political Impacts on the Law of Contracts, 26 Cornell L.Q. 4 n.7 (1940).

107. Some of these reforms have not taken place throughout the country, but the tendency to abolish the excrescences is unmistakable. For an admirable discussion of the problems, see Patterson, An Apology for Consideration, 58 Colum. L. Rev. 929 (1955). Dawson, *supra* note 96, at ch. IV.

108. Fuller, Consideration and Form, 41 Colum. L. Rev. 799 (1941); Restatement Second §72, Comments *a-d*.

doubted whether it makes good sense to make a gift promise binding if couched in the form of a simulated bargain.[109]

In these and other ways, the influence of the bargain idea can still be felt. It is an old idea and one firmly rooted in our moral intuitions. Suitably trimmed, and balanced by the reliance principle, it is likely to remain an enduring feature of our law of contracts.[110]

This introduction would be incomplete if it failed to note the close connection between the principles of bargain and reliance and the system of remedies available for their protection. A most challenging study of the interrelationship has recently been undertaken by Eisenberg, The Bargain Principle and Its Limits, 95 Harv. L. Rev. 741 (1982). Part of the conclusion of his article is worth quoting:

> The proposition that promises made as part of a bargain ought to be enforced is relatively straightforward; the real question is to what extent.
>
> The traditional answer to this question is embodied in the paradigmatic bargain principle, namely, that damages for the unexcused breach of a bargain promise should invariably be measured by the value that the promised performance would have had to the plaintiff, regardless of the value for which the defendant's promise was exchanged.
>
> This principle, which in the typical case is supported by considerations of both fairness and efficiency, finds its fullest justification in the exemplary case of a half-completed bargain made in a perfectly competitive market. Bargains made in other kinds of markets are not intrinsically suspect. Nevertheless, that a market is less than perfectly competitive does set the stage for transactions in which the bargain principle loses much or all of its force, because it is supported by neither fairness nor efficiency. For example, a market that involves a monopoly sets the stage for the exploitation of distress; a market in which transactions are complex and differentiated rather than simple and homogeneous sets the stage for the exploitation of transactional incapacity; a market in which actors do not simply take a price established by a general market and are susceptible to transient economic irrationality sets the stage for unfair persuasion; a market that involves imperfect price-information sets the stage for the exploitation of price-ignorance.
>
> Until recently, courts have tended either to apply the bargain principle to cases raising such problems, despite the difficulties this application presents, or to deal with these difficulties in covert and unsystematic ways. Over the past thirty years, however, a new paradigmatic principle — unconscionability — has emerged. This principle explains and justifies the limits that should be placed upon the bargain principle on the basis of the quality of a bargain.

95 Harv. L. Rev. at 798-799.

109. Restatement Second §71, Illus. 5; E. Farnsworth, Contracts 66 et seq. (1982).
110. Note, 39 N.Y.U. L. Rev. 816, 829 et seq. (1964); Comment, 37 U. Chi. L. Rev. 559, 572 et seq. (1970).

SIEGEL v. SPEAR & CO.

234 N.Y. 479, 138 N.E. 414 (1923)

CRANE, J. The plaintiff commenced this action in the City Court of the city of New York to recover his loss sustained by failure of the defendants to insure his household furniture stored in its storehouse. The action is based upon an alleged agreement to insure made with the defendant's creditman. So far the plaintiff has been successful, the Appellate Division, however, certifying that in its opinion there is a question of law involved which should be reviewed by this court.

In August of 1917 and January of 1918 the plaintiff purchased of the defendant certain household furniture for the sum of $909.25 and took it to his apartment in New York City. He gave back to the defendant two chattel mortgages, which provided for monthly payments of the purchase price, and also that the furniture should not be removed from the plaintiff's residence without the written consent of the mortgagee.

By May of 1918 the plaintiff had paid in all $295. In that month, desiring to move from the city for the summer months and give up his apartment, the plaintiff went to the defendant's place of business in New York City to see about storing his furniture until his return. It was arranged with the defendant's creditman, McGrath, that the plaintiff should send his furniture by his own truck to the defendant's storehouse, and that the defendant would keep it for him free of charge. It is claimed that McGrath, at the time of making these arrangements, also promised and agreed to insure the furniture for the plaintiff's benefit. The furniture had not been insured by the plaintiff at any time. The conversation is given by Mr. Siegel as follows:

> At that time he said, "You had better transfer your insurance policy over to our warehouse." I said: "I haven't any insurance. I never thought of taking it out, as I never had time to take it out." But I said: "Before the furniture comes down I will have my insurance man, who insures my life, have the furniture insured and transferred over to your place." He said: "That won't be necessary to get that from him; I will do it for you; it will be a good deal cheaper; I handle lots of insurance; when you get the next bill — you can send a check for that with the next installment."

The furniture was sent to the defendant's storehouse about the 15th of May, and about the 15th of the following June was destroyed by fire. No insurance had been placed upon it.

Upon these facts the plaintiff has recovered the amount of his loss. The defendant raises at least two objections to this result. It claims, *first*, that there was no consideration for the alleged agreement made with McGrath to insure the furniture, and, *second*, that McGrath had no authority to make any such contract even if he did.

We are inclined to think that if the contract were made — and we must assume it was as there is evidence to sustain the findings of the jury to this effect — there was in the nature of the case a consideration sufficient to sustain the promise. It is, of course, a fact that the defendant undertook to store the plaintiff's property without any compensation. The fact that it had a chattel mortgage upon the property did not affect its relationship as a bailee without pay. Under these circumstances it was not liable for the destruction of the goods by fire unless due to its gross neglect. Van Zile on Bailments and Carriers, §93; First Nat. Bank of Lyons v. Ocean Nat. Bank, 60 N.Y. 278, 19 Am. Rep. 181. There is no such element in this case.

But if in connection with taking the goods McGrath also voluntarily undertook to procure insurance for the plaintiff's benefit, the promise was part of the whole transaction and was linked up with the gratuitous bailment. The bailee, if such a contract were within McGrath's agency, was then under as much of an obligation to procure insurance as he was to take care of the goods.

When McGrath stated that he would insure the furniture it was still in the plaintiff's possession. It was after his statements and promises that the plaintiff sent the furniture to the storehouse. The defendant or McGrath entered upon the execution of the trust. It is in this particular that this case differs from Thorne v. Deas, 4 Johns. 84, 99, so much relied upon by the defendant. In that case A. and B. were joint owners of a vessel. A. voluntarily undertook to get the vessel insured but neglected to do so. The vessel having been lost at sea, it was held that no action would lie against A. for the non-performance of his promise, although B. had relied upon that promise to his loss. It was said that there was no consideration for the promise. In that case there was the mere naked promise of A. that he would insure the vessel. B. parted with nothing to A. He gave up possession of none of his property to A., nor of any interest in his vessel. The case would have been decided differently, no doubt, if he had. As Chancellor Kent said in referring to the earlier cases: "There was no dispute or doubt but that an action upon the case lay for a misfeasance, in the breach of a trust undertaken voluntarily." . . .

In the case of Rutgers v. Lucet, 2 Johns. Cas. 92, 95, the law on this point was stated to be as follows:

> A mere agreement to undertake a trust, in futuro, without compensation, it is true, is not obligatory; but when once undertaken, and the trust actually *entered upon*, the bailee is bound to perform it, according to the terms of his agreement. The confidence placed in him, and his undertaking to execute the trust, raise a sufficient consideration; a contrary doctrine would tend to injure and deceive his employer, who might be unwilling to consent to the bailment on any other terms.

In Hammond v. Hussey, 51 N.H. 40, 50 (12 Am. Rep. 41), the court, quoting Professor Parsons, says:

"If a person makes a gratuitous promise, and then enters upon the performance of it, he is held to a full execution of all he has undertaken."

Where one had gratuitously undertaken to carry the money of a bailor to a certain place and deliver it to another and after receiving the money the bailee gave it to a neighbor who undertook to make delivery and lost it, it was held that the bailee had violated his trust in handling the money, that he was guilty of gross negligence in not fulfilling the terms of the bailment. Colyar v. Taylor, 41 Tenn. (1 Cold.) 372; Van Zile on Bailments and Carriers, §98; Davis v. Gay, 141 Mass. 531, 534, 6 N.E. 549; Isham v. Post, 141 N.Y. 100, 106, 35 N.E. 1084, 23 L.R.A. 90, 38 Am. St. Rep. 766; Glanzer v. Shepard, 233 N.Y. 236, 135 N.E. 275; 6 Ruling Case Law, p. 656, §67.

From this aspect of the case we think there was a consideration for the agreement to insure. This renders it unnecessary to determine whether the plaintiff, in refraining from insuring through his own agent at the suggestion of McGrath surrendered any right which would furnish a consideration for McGrath's promise.

I find that Thorne v. Deas, *supra*, has been seldom cited upon this question of consideration, and whether or not we would feel bound to follow it to-day must be left open until the question comes properly before us.

As to McGrath's authority to act in this matter, we do not find the point raised by any sufficient exception.

For the reasons here stated, the judgment must be affirmed, with costs.

NOTE

1. See Shattuck, Gratuitous Promises — A New Writ?, 35 Mich. L. Rev. 908 (1937); Seavey, Reliance on Gratuitous Promises and Other Conduct, 64 Harv. L. Rev. 913 (1951).

Could plaintiff's lawyer have avoided the risk of losing his client's case on the consideration issue by bringing a tort action? Consult Colonial Savings Assn. v. Taylor, 544 S.W.2d 116 (Tex. 1976) and Restatement of Torts Second §323 (1965).

2. In Hazlett v. First Federal Savings & Loan Ass'n, 14 Wash. 2d 124, 127 P.2d 273 (1942), the court considered the application of §90 and observed that every illustration following that section deals with a promise inducing affirmative action on the part of the promisee. "Surely, forbearance was not intended to include the mere passive failure of the promisee to procure elsewhere, or by other means, the service as the

thing promised. If so it would be difficult to imagine a promise which would not be supported by some sort of 'forebearance' consideration." Id. at 131, 127 P.2d at 277. Do you agree? Is the same not true of affirmative action taken in reliance? Goetz & Scott, Enforcing Promises: An Examination of the Basis of Contract, 89 Yale L.J. 1261, 1267-1270, 1291 (1980).

3. Early cases draw a sharp distinction between misfeasance and nonfeasance in determining the liability of a gratuitous promisor. Comfort v. McCorkle, 149 Misc. 826, 268 N.Y.S. 192 (1933); Wilkinson v. Coverdale, 1 Esp. 73, 170 E.R. 284 (1793); Thorne v. Deas, 4 Johns. 84 (N.Y. 1809), discussed in Seavey, Reliance upon Gratuitous Promises and Other Conduct, 64 Harv. L. Rev. 913 (1951). See also Cardozo's opinion in Barile v. Wright, 256 N.Y. 1, noted in 26 Ill. L. Rev. 916 (1932). The Restatement of Torts Second §323 expresses no opinion as to whether nonfeasance of a gratuitous promise is sufficient to impose liability. The Restatement of Agency Second §378 does not distinguish between misfeasance and nonfeasance. The Comments to that section suggest, however, that a gratuitous agent may be liable either in tort or for breach of contract under §90. See Comments a and e.

For a case that holds a gratuitous promisor liable for nonfeasance, see Spiegel v. Metropolitan Life Ins. Co., 6 N.Y.2d 91, 188 N.Y.S.2d 486 (1959). See also the Lusk-Harbison-Jones case that follows.

4. In Dufton v. Mechanicks National Bank, 95 N.H. 299, 62 A.2d 715 (1948), noted in 62 Harv. L. Rev. 1069 (1949), the court held a promisor liable for failure to procure insurance by implying a promise on the part of the promisee to pay the premium. By implying a promise, the court created a bilateral contract and thereby avoided the problems associated with gratuitous promises.

5. The enforcement of gratuitous promises to obtain insurance has been explained on the grounds that the promisee would have attained similar insurance from someone else if the promise had not been made. "In this case, the opportunity cost of acceptance of a promisor's representations that designated property would be insured or safeguarded is equal to the entire loss if the risk materializes after the promise is broken." Goetz & Scott, Enforcing Promises: An Examination of the Basis of Contract, 89 Yale L.J. 1261, 1318 (1980). Judicial reluctance to impose liability in such cases is probably attributable to great disparity between the amount of the promisee's reliance loss and the value of the promise. Id. at 1317 n.158. Note that the Restatement of Agency Second §378 imposes a duty of care on a gratuitous agent when the gratuitous promise "causes the [promisee] to refrain from having such acts done by other available means," and the duty of care ceases if the promisor gives notice that he will not perform "while other means are available." See Seavey, Reliance Upon Gratuitous Promises or Other Conduct, 64 Harv. L. Rev. 913 (1951). If the promisee could not have paid the premium at the time the promise was made, could he still recover? See East Providence Credit

Union v. Geremia, 103 R.I. 597, 239 A.2d 725 (1968) (the court relied on §90, but also found consideration for the promise).

6. Should the amount of the premium be deducted from the award to the promisee? See Eisenberg, Donative Promises, 47 U. Chi. L. Rev. 1, 30 (1979):

> A final problem is the treatment of benefits received under a relied-upon donative promise. If the benefits are financial or tangible, and damages are measured by reliance, the amount of the benefits should normally be deducted from the recovery. For example, suppose A makes a donative promise to buy on B's behalf fire insurance covering B's goods, B accordingly forbears from insuring the goods himself, A does not buy the policy, and the goods are destroyed by fire. If the goods had been insured, the premium would have been $50 and the insurance company would have paid $2000 to make good B's loss. B's damages against A should be, not $2000, but $1950, his net proceeds had he insured the goods himself.

LUSK-HARBISON-JONES, INC. v. UNIVERSAL CREDIT CO.
164 Miss. 693, 145 So. 623 (1933)

Action by the Universal Credit Company against Lusk-Harbison-Jones, Inc. Judgment for plaintiff, and defendant appeals. Reversed and remanded.

GRIFFITH, J., delivered the opinion of the court. During the years herein mentioned, appellant was the authorized agent for Ford automobiles at Leland and adjacent territory. Appellee is a dealer in automobile paper; that is to say, it advances the cash to the local distributors of automobiles on the conditional sales contracts and notes of the purchasers evidencing deferred installment payments. It would appear from the record that appellee is a subsidiary of the Ford company. In any event, it works in close connection with that company and its local distributors. In 1929 three, and in 1930, two, sales contracts were purchased by appellee from appellant. Under these contracts appellant guaranteed the payment of the full amount of the installments. At different times during the latter part of 1930, default in the installment payments were made by the purchasers under each of the five conditional sales contracts, and, by authority of the terms thereof, the five automobiles were repossessed.

There was no available market for these repossessed cars, and it was deemed to be to the best interest of both the parties hereto that appellant should repair and recondition the cars and hold them in its possession until the times might improve and a more favorable market condition might be found for resale. The cars were therefore allowed by appellee to be repaired and reconditioned by appellant and thereupon to remain in appellant's possession, but appellant was required to execute and did execute a written agreement for each of the five repossessed cars confirming the fact that the title was and remained in appellee, and that appellant had taken and would hold the automobiles for appellee, but at appellant's "sole risk as to all loss or injury." Nothing was said in the said written agreement about insurance.

In October, 1931, while still in appellant's possession, the five automobiles were destroyed by a nonnegligent fire. Appellant had no insurance on the five cars, and it is the claim of appellee that it had none. Appellee thereupon sued appellant for the balance due on the five vehicles, and recovered judgment.

Effective on January 1, 1931, appellee had issued to Ford distributors what is termed Confidential Pamphlet B. In this pamphlet there is contained the following paragraph:

> Dealer Protection on Repossessed Cars: In cases where a car is repossessed by the dealer and/or UCC, insurance protection for the dealer's interest will continue in force from the date of physical possession until the account is liquidated, after which the dealer should provide such coverage as he may require.

After this pamphlet came out, the matter of insurance was the subject of interviews between appellant and the authorized representatives of appellee, and on each occasion, when discussed, appellant was advised by these agents of appellee that appellant should not carry or attempt to carry any insurance on these repossessed cars; that appellee would carry the insurance and that this was one of the purposes of pamphlet B to announce. The proof of these statements, representations, and advice to appellant by the agents of appellee was received without any objection by appellee, nor was any intimation advanced that these agents were not authorized in the premises.

Appellee contends that the representation or statements of its agents, as above mentioned, are of no force here for three asserted reasons: First, that pamphlet B did not apply to sales and sales contracts upon which defaults had occurred or where the repossession had taken place prior to January 1, 1931; and, second, that the statements and representations of appellee's agents that appellant should not take insurance and that appellee was carrying and would continue to carry insurance on the repossessed cars here involved are not to be allowed to be effective, because this would modify by oral evidence the previous written agreement between the parties that appellant would hold the cars at appellant's "sole risk as to all loss or injury"; and, third, that such a modification would be without any consideration to support it.

As to appellee's first contention, pamphlet B is not clear and free from doubt upon an examination of its entire contents that it refers only to sales and sales contracts made on and after January 1, 1931. But, if otherwise, that question is absorbed in what is said in respect to the second contention, as to what second contention we have only to apply the rule, well settled generally and in this state, that a subsequent oral agreement to modify a prior written contract is valid and proof thereof does not violate the parol evidence rule, especially where the subsequent agreement is acted upon. 3 Jones on Evidence (2 Ed.), section 1500 et seq., and authorities there cited. Moreover, we have already called attention to the fact that the written agreement relied on by appellee makes no mention of insurance.

Upon the third point that no consideration is shown for the alleged agreement that appellee would carry the insurance, we bottom our conclusion upon the fact that appellant acted upon the statements made by appellee that the latter had the insurance and would continue to carry it; a very reasonable course on the part of appellant and about which if appellant had acted otherwise there might have arisen the question of unauthorized double concurrent insurance on the same property, and upon well-recognized principle applicable to such a situation, which has been summarized in A.L.I. Restatement of the Law of Contracts, vol. 1, p. 110, as follows: "A promise which the promisor should reasonably expect to induce action or forbearance of a definite and substantial character on the part of the promisee and which does induce such action and forbearance is binding if injustice can be avoided only by the enforcement of the promise." We are mindful that the principle just stated is one to be applied with caution and only when the facts are well within it; but here the parties had each an insurable interest in the property, and the evidence in the record is not only to the effect that appellee's agents after January 1, 1931, represented that appellee had the insurance, but the statements and representations made were equivalent to a promise to continue that insurance in force; and the promisee having reasonably relied thereon, the promise can only be enforced by casting the loss on the promisor, if, in fact, the promisor contrary to the promise carried no insurance.

Reversed and remanded.

FISHER v. JACKSON

142 Conn. 734, 118 A.2d 316 (Sup. Ct. Err. 1955)

Action to recover damages for breach of an employment contract, brought to the Superior Court in New Haven County and tried to the jury before Devlin, J.; verdict and judgment for the plaintiff and appeal by the defendant. Error; judgment directed.

WYNNE, J. The plaintiff instituted this action to recover damages for the breach of an oral agreement of employment. The defendant has appealed from the judgment rendered upon a plaintiff's verdict. The questions presented are whether the court was in error in denying the defendant's motion to set the verdict aside on the ground that it is not supported on the issue of liability, and in denying the defendant's motion for judgment notwithstanding the verdict.

The substituted complaint alleged that the defendant, through his authorized agent, induced the plaintiff to give up his employment with a firm of bakers, where he was making $50 per week, and to enter upon employment as a reporter, for $40 per week, under an oral contract that the employment would be for the life of the plaintiff or until he was physically disabled for work, with a yearly increase in salary of $5 per week. The defendant's contention is that there was no evidence that the parties had agreed upon such a contract. The defendant's claim is that the job under discussion was a permanent one rather than for a definite term and was terminable at will by either party.

In the absence of a consideration in addition to the rendering of services incident to the employment, an agreement for a permanent employment is no more than an indefinite general hiring, terminable at the will of either party without liability to the other. Carter v. Bartek, 142 Conn. 448, 450, 114 A.2d 923, and cases there cited.

The plaintiff was hired by the defendant's managing editor in January, 1944, and went to work as a reporter for the New Haven Register, a newspaper owned by the defendant. He was discharged on or about January 7, 1949. The contract between the parties began with a notice which was put in a trade magazine by the defendant, just prior to the admitted hiring of the plaintiff. That advertisement set forth that a "permanent position" as a reporter awaited an "all-around male newsman with experience on several beats and educational background that [would stand] up in a University city." The plaintiff wrote a letter in response to the advertisement and as a result was interviewed by the defendant's managing editor for about ten minutes and was thereafter hired. Whether or not the plaintiff was an "all-around newsman" with experience on several beats and with an educational background, however nebulous, that would stand up in a university city nowhere appears. The managing editor, who was the only other party to the interview, was deceased at the time of the trial. The plaintiff, in his letter seeking an interview, had written that he was looking for a connection which, "in the event my services are satisfactory, will prove permanent." So it must be quite apparent that the significant thought expressed was in his mind during his brief interview with the defendant's managing editor. It seems clear to us that the negotiations amounted to nothing more than the hiring of a reporter for a job which was permanent in the sense that it was not a mere temporary place. The hiring was indefinite as to time and terminable by either party at his will.

There is no occasion to discuss at length the claim advanced by the plaintiff that special consideration moved to the defendant because the plaintiff gave up his job with the bakery firm. The plaintiff did no more than give up other activities and interests in order to enter into the service of the defendant. The mere giving up of a job by one who decides to accept a contract for alleged life employment is but an incident necessary on his part to place himself in a position to accept and perform the contract; it is not consideration for a contract of life employment. Chesapeake & Potomac Telephone Co. v. Murray, 198 Md. 526, 533, 84 A.2d 870; Minter v. Tootle, Campbell Dry Goods Co., 187 Mo. App. 16, 28, 173 S.W. 4; Adolph v. Cookware Co., 283 Mich. 561, 568, 278 N.W. 687.

The plaintiff argues that he suffered a detriment by giving up his job. To constitute sufficient consideration for a promise, an act or promise not only must be a detriment to the promisee but must be bargained for and given in exchange for the promise. Lynas v. Maxwell Farms, 279 Mich. 684, 688, 273 N.W. 315; Edwards v. Kentucky Utilities Co., 286 Ky. 341, 346, 150 S.W.2d 916; Heideman v. Tall's Travel Shops, Inc., 192 Wash. 513, 516, 73 P.2d 1323; Restatement, 1 Contracts §75. In the present case, the plaintiff's giving up of his job at the bakery was not something for which the defendant bargained in exchange for his promise of permanent employment. Nowhere in the plaintiff's testimony does it appear that the defendant's agent even suggested that the plaintiff give up the job he had with the bakery firm, much less that the agent induced him to do so. It would thus appear that there was not even a semblance of a claim that the giving up of the plaintiff's job was consideration for any promise that may have been made by the defendant's agent.

Practice Book, §234, provides that a trial court under certain circumstances can direct a judgment notwithstanding the verdict or order a new trial. We are faced with the question in the present case whether the court erred in not adopting one or the other of these alternatives. Under the rule, action upon a motion for judgment notwithstanding the verdict is, in part, postponed action upon a motion for a direct verdict. Accordingly, the first test to be applied to a court's action upon a motion for judgment notwithstanding the verdict is the determination whether a direction of the verdict in favor of the defendant would have been proper. On the evidence in the present case, there was no basis for a verdict in favor of the plaintiff.

Inasmuch as the contract of employment which was proved would not in any event warrant a judgment in favor of the plaintiff, even though the case were retried, the court should have directed judgment for the defendant notwithstanding the verdict. Robinson v. Southern New England Telephone Co., 140 Conn. 414, 421, 101 A.2d 491.

There is error, the judgment is set aside and the case is remanded with direction to render judgment for the defendant notwithstanding the verdict.

In this opinion the other judges concurred.

NOTE

Compare Millsap v. National Funding Corp., 57 Cal. App. 2d 772, 776, 135 P.2d 407 (1943):

> Where the prospective employee clearly states to his prospective employer, as in the case before us, that he will not give up his present employment unless the prospective employer will agree to give him permanent employment and the prospective employer expressly agrees to those terms, it seems clear that the prospective employee (to paraphrase the language of section 1605 Civil Code) in giving up his present employment suffers a prejudice as an inducement to the promisor for his promise of permanent employment. "It is not necessary to the existence of a good consideration that a benefit should be conferred upon the promisor. It is enough that a 'prejudice be suffered or agreed to be suffered' by the promisee." (6 Cal. Jur. 171.)

On the other hand, in Forrer v. Sears Roebuck & Co., 36 Wis. 2d 388, 153 N.W.2d 587 (1967), where the plaintiff alleged that he gave up his farming operation at a loss on the strength of the defendant's promise to provide him with permanent employment, the court held that although it "would not hesitate to apply the doctrine of promissory estoppel under these facts if justice required it . . . [j]ustice . . . does not require the invocation of the doctrine, for the promise of the defendant was kept, and this court is not required, therefore, to enforce it." Id. at 392, 153 N.W.2d at 589. The court went on to point out that the presumption that a contract for permanent employment is terminable at will is based on public policy grounds, and laid down the rule that "a permanent employment contract is terminable at will unless there is additional consideration in the form of an economic or financial benefit to the employer. A mere detriment to the employee is not enough." Id. at 394, 153 N.W.2d at 590.

UNDERWOOD TYPEWRITER CO. v. CENTURY REALTY CO.

220 Mo. 522, 119 S.W. 400 (1909)

LAMM, J. This case is here from the St. Louis Court of Appeals on the dissent of Judge Bland. 118 Mo. App. 197, 94 S.W. 787. The majority opinion of that court reversed the judgment of the circuit court sustaining a demurrer to the petition, and remanded the case to be tried on its merits. We think the majority opinion is soundly reasoned on both principle and precedent. It should be read in connection with this; for we shall not restate its reasoning, but rest content with adopting it, only supplying a sufficient statement here to make this opinion intelligible, and adding some observation of our own.

The statement: Plaintiff was tenant of defendant in possession under a written lease for a five-year term beginning on the 1st day of February, 1901, and ending on the last day of January, 1906. The lease provided, inter alia, the plaintiff could not assign or underlet without the written consent of defendant indorsed on it. Thereafter plaintiff and defendant entered into a written agreement to the effect that defendant would give its written assent to an assignment of the lease to an acceptable tenant. The petition pleads the lease, the provision against assigning or subletting, and the subsequent written agreement to give consent in writing to an acceptable tenant and then states, in substance, that plaintiff, in reliance on said written agreement, with the knowledge of defendant, expended a large amount of time and labor in securing an acceptable and satisfactory tenant and did secure such tenant, but that, notwithstanding that fact, defendant refused and still refuses to consent to the assignment of said lease and to permit said tenant to enter into the possession of said premises, though often requested to do so; that by reason of defendant's refusal to consent to said assignment of said lease plaintiff was and is prevented by defendant from securing such tenant at a large advance over the rent reserved by defendant under said lease, to its damage in the sum of $4,500. Wherefore, etc.

The circuit court sustained a general demurrer to the petition. Thereat plaintiff stood on its petition and, refusing to plead over, judgment went on the demurrer. From that judgment plaintiff appealed to the court of appeals with the result indicated.

When the case came here it was assigned to Division 1, and there argued and submitted. That division was evenly divided, and the cause came into Banc. So much by way of statement.

The observations: True, the typewriter company was not bound to do anything under the written agreement. True, it was executory only, and may be called in a sense a nude pact *as born*. True, defendant realty company could at no time have sued the typewriter company on that agreement for failure to perform. Why *should* it sue? It already had a tenant in the person of the typewriter company. It wanted no other. But mutuality, in its essence, is but a *phase*, strictly speaking, of the consideration that will support a contract. It is not the only phase. If mutuality, in a broad sense, was held to be an essential element in every valid contract, to the extent that both contracting parties could sue on it, there could be no such a thing as a valid unilateral or option contract, or a contract evidenced by a subscription paper, or a contract to enforce a reward offer, or a guaranty, or in many other instances readily put in ordinary business affairs. The contract sued on in this case was made for the benefit of the typewriter company. It could furnish an acceptable tenant to defendant to take its place, or let it alone. In that respect it does not differ from many contracts, the breach of which is actionable at the option of the promisee.

Being in writing, and signed by the party to be charged, it was not obnoxious to the Statute of Frauds. Being fully performed by the promisee, it was no longer a nude pact, but became clothed with a consideration executed on request. That performance on the strength of the offer made, having been accomplished at an outlay of time and labor on the part of the offeree or promisee, with defendant's knowledge as alleged in the petition, makes it enforceable against the offerer or promisor so long as both parties were capable of contracting and their contract be not vitiated by fraud or as against good morals or public policy.

We take it as good doctrine worthy of all acceptance that it is the primary duty of courts to enforce contracts, not to abrogate them. A contract (such as this) between two parties not in fiduciary relation, but dealing at arm's length, free from taint of fraud, duress, or other form of overreaching or oppression, when performed by the promisee, comes into a court of justice entitled to every fair presumption of validity. Such a contract bespeaks, in the first instance, judicial diligence and astuteness to support the act of the party by the act and art of the law. To that extent, at least, those fine rules of personal honor obtaining between man and man, requiring one to keep his word with another, accord with the rules of law. . . .

In a learned note to American Cotton Oil Co. v. Kirk, 15 C.C.A. 543, Mr. Clark, author of Clark on Contracts, in speaking to the point says:

> Again, contracts may be formed by the offer of a promise for an act and acceptance by performing the act, as where a man requests another to perform services for him, and the latter does so. The request is an offer of a promise to pay for the services, and performance of the services is an acceptance of the offer. This is described as consideration executed upon request. Here, also, the act of one party forms the consideration which supports the promise of the other. In these two cases one of the parties, in the formation of the contract, does all that he can be required to do, and there remains an outstanding obligation on the other side only. The contract is unilateral. It is obvious that in these cases the question of mutuality of obligation or contract cannot arise. The question is whether the act is such as to supply a consideration for the promise of the other party.

To illustrate, if Roe writes Doe: "If you loan Lowe your Jersey cow, I will see she is returned in good order." And, if Doe (relying) loan her to Lowe and she is not returned in good order, is Roe not liable to Doe?

If Box write Cox: "If you find my lost horses, Bucephalus and Rosinante, I will release the debt of $50 you owe me." And if Cox (relying) find and return Bucephalus and Rosinante, is his debt not paid to Box?

If Smith agree in writing with Jehu that he will pay him $100 if he drive from Jefferson City to Kansas City and return in four days, and Jehu presently (relying) drives it in four days, is not Smith liable?

If John agree in writing with Gambrinus that if the latter will not drink beer for a year, he will pay him a sum certain, and if Gambrinus (relying) drink no beer for that year, is not John bound?

Yet in each of these cases neither Doe, Cox, Jehu nor Gambrinus was bound to do anything. In each of them there was no consideration other than acceptance by actual performance on request. In the last two and the first no benefit accrued to Roe, Smith, or John. But in each of them there was a consideration (i.e., performance) moving from the promisee in the form of labor done and inconvenience and detriment suffered. . . .

The upshot of it all is the conclusion that the petition was good and the demurrer bad. Hence, the judgment of the circuit court should be reversed, and the cause remanded to be tried on its merits. It is so ordered.

Gantt, Fox, and Graves, JJ., concur. Woodson, J., dissents in an opinion filed, in which Valliant, C.J., and Burgess, J., concur.

Woodson, J. (dissenting). . . . In the case at bar the promise of respondent to permit appellant to assign the lease was unilateral, and was without consideration of any kind to support it. The appellant never at any time, even down to the time of bringing this suit, agreed to find or furnish respondent a suitable tenant; and if appellant had at any time, or even now should withdraw its tender of such tenant, clearly the respondent would have no cause of action against the former of said refusal or withdrawal, for the obvious reason that it never agreed to do so. According to the allegations of the petition, the appellant was under no legal or moral obligation to find for respondent a suitable tenant for the occupancy of the floor space in question.

For the purpose of illustration, let us suppose a farmer should enter a shoe store and ask the proprietor thereof if he would take a cord of hickory wood for a certain designated pair of shoes, and in reply thereto the proprietor should say, "Yes"; and without more the former should turn and walk from the store without agreeing to take the shoes or to furnish the wood, and he should then return home and chop a cord of hickory wood, load it upon his wagon, haul it to town, drive up to the store, and say to the proprietor that he had chopped the wood, hauled it in for him, and demand the shoes in consideration of and in payment for the wood; and in reply thereto suppose the merchant had said to the farmer that he was sorry, but he could not deliver the shoes to him, for the reason that he had sold them during the time which had elapsed between the first conversation and the time when the wood was hauled to town and tendered to the merchant — could it be seriously contended that the farmer would have a cause of action against the merchant for breach of contract for his failure to deliver the shoes? I think not, for the reason the farmer never agreed to take the shoes, or to cut, haul, and deliver the wood in exchange for them. Such a contract, if it may be so called, would clearly be unilateral in character, and the subsequent tender of the wood would not change the agreement into a bilateral contract. The tender of the wood could not perform the twofold office of furnishing a consideration for the contract, and at the same time constitute an agreement to accept the shoes, which had never been done before. And the same is true as regards the case at bar. The finding of a suitable tenant could not perform the twofold function of furnishing a consideration to support the promise of the Century Realty Company to agree to subletting the floor space to such tenant, and at the same time constitute an agreement on the part of the typewriter company to furnish such tenant, which confessedly, it has never done down to this date in any mode or manner whatsoever.

The principle announced in the majority opinion is too far-reaching and startling in its effect. Under that holding no merchant or property owner could safely answer a question as to what he would take for a certain article or piece of property, for, if he should do so, he would be liable at any time within the period prescribed by the statute of frauds [sic] to be called upon to deliver the property to the party who asked the question, and be subjected to an action for damages for breach of contract for failure to deliver the property, if for any reason he should see proper to decline to deliver it, even though he had disposed of it in the meantime. . . .

I am, therefore, of the opinion that the action of the trial court in sustaining the demurrer to the petition was proper, and that the judgment of the St. Louis Court of Appeals reversing the judgment of the circuit court is erroneous.

Valliant, C.J., and Burgess, J., concur.

NOTE

1. Consult Raedeke v. Gibraltar Savings & Loan Assn., 10 Cal. 3d 665, 517 P.2d 1157, 111 Cal. Rptr. 693 (1974).

2. Fisher and Brill are partners and together operate a flower shop. Fisher decides to withdraw from the business and set up a shop of his own in a nearby town. The landlord who owns the flower shop in which Fisher and Brill are currently doing business (Fried) agrees to release Fisher from any remaining obligations under the lease, and states that he will be "perfectly satisfied" if Brill assumes sole responsibility for it. Fisher pays Fried nothing for his release. Subsequently, after Fisher has moved away and Brill has defaulted on his rent payments, Fried recovers judgment against both Fisher and Brill for breach of contract. Fisher appeals from

the judgment, invoking Section 90 of the Restatement. Result? See Fried v. Fisher, 328 Pa. St. 497, 196 A. 39, 115 A.L.R. 147 (1938). Suppose that Fisher has been hugely successful in his new business. Should this affect the outcome?

CAPITAL SAVINGS & LOAN ASSN.
v. PRZYBYLOWICZ
83 Mich. App. 404, 268 N.W.2d 662 (1978)

D. E. HOLBROOK, Jr., Presiding Judge.

In this case we must make the difficult choice of allocating a loss between an innocent party and a party who made an innocent mistake.

There is no dispute about the basic facts. Defendants approached the plaintiff savings and loan institution about obtaining a residential mortgage loan of $34,500. Plaintiff's representative told defendants that to repay a twenty-five year mortgage loan at a 9% interest rate the monthly payment would be $251.76. This same combination of figures appears in the mortgage loan application, the mortgage commitment letter and in the mortgage note itself. The figures in the loan application were undoubtedly dictated by plaintiff's representative and the other two documents were prepared by plaintiff.

Stated quite simply, the problem is that this combination of figures is hopelessly inconsistent — payments of $251.76 per month for 300 months will not pay off a $34,500 loan at a 9% interest rate. Defendants sold their former home and entered into a building agreement for a new home. When the first mortgage payment was due, plaintiff discovered the inconsistency and demanded that defendants execute a new note and pay the amount, $289.53 per month, which plaintiff claims should have been used in the first place. When defendants refused plaintiff's demands, plaintiff filed suit.

The complaint requested a declaratory judgment and a reformation of the contract on the grounds of mutual mistake. Defendants answered, claiming the mistake was unilateral on the part of the plaintiff and that plaintiff was engaging in fraud and deception by demanding a higher monthly payment than agreed. Defendants contend they relied on plaintiff's calculations and representations that 300 payments of $251.76 would pay off a $34,500 loan at a 9% rate and that plaintiff is estopped from demanding any greater monthly amount. In order to correct the inconsistent figures, defendants requested the interest rate be reformed so that 300 monthly payments of $251.76 would discharge their $34,500 obligation.

In a written opinion the trial judge agreed with defendants.

> This is a proceeding which is equitable in nature and the Court feels that the burden must be placed on the party responsible for the error, and

whose superior position of knowledge and control requires it to assume
resulting hardship or economic loss, since it is too late to undo the transaction.

This Court is of the opinion that the mortgage obligation should be
reformed to provide an interest rate which will satisfy the loan obligation,
within the specified twenty-five (25) years at the specified payment of Two
Hundred Fifty One and 76/100 ($251.76) Dollars.

An order of declaratory judgment was entered consistent with the judge's
opinion. We agree with the trial court.

This Court reviews equity cases *de novo*, but does not reverse or modify unless convinced it would have reached a different result had it occupied the position of the trial court. Mazur v. Blendea, 74 Mich. App. 467,
469, 253 N.W.2d 801 (1977); Ford v. Howard, 59 Mich. App. 548, 552, 229
N.W.2d 841 (1975).

A court of equity may reform a contract where there is clear evidence
of a mutual mistake, Ross v. Damm, 271 Mich. 474, 481, 260 N.W. 750
(1935); Kidder v. Collum, 61 Mich. App. 281, 283, 232 N.W.2d 384 (1975),
or in other appropriate circumstances, Najor v. Wayne National Life Ins.
Co., 23 Mich. App. 260, 178 N.W.2d 504 (1970), *lv. den.*, 383 Mich. 802
(1970).

> "A written instrument may be reformed where it fails to express the
> intentions of the parties thereto as the result of accident, inadvertence,
> mistake. . . ."

23 Mich. App. at 272, 178 N.W.2d at 511.

It is clear the inconsistent terms in the mortgage note cannot be reconciled and that at least one term must be reformed. Unfortunately there is
no perfect solution. Either the defendants will be required to pay almost
$40 a month more than they anticipated and for which they budgeted or
the plaintiff will be forced to absorb a loss due to a lowered interest rate
(approximately $7\frac{3}{8}$% rather than 9%).

The combination of a number of equitable considerations leads us to
conclude that the interest rate, rather than the monthly payment, should
be reformed. As noted above plaintiff's representative told defendants
what the terms would be and defendants applied for a mortgage loan on
the basis of those terms. Plaintiff prepared the mortgage commitment
letter and the mortgage note which essentially confirmed the inconsistent
figures. Defendants were led to believe that payments of $251.76 per
month would satisfy their loan obligation.

Calculations of the proper monthly payments to satisfy a long term
debt at a specified interest rate are quite difficult to make and indeed
plaintiff admits it resorts to tables to determine payment amounts. Plaintiff is in the business of lending money and engages in such mortgage
transactions all the time. As a matter of course plaintiff calculates interest

rates and determines payment schedules. Defendant Richard Przybylo-
wicz, according to the loan application, has an eleventh grade education
and is employed as a surface grinder at a tool and die shop. We find a
helpful analogy in the case of Hetchler v. American Life Ins. Co., 266
Mich. 608, 254 N.W. 221 (1934), in which an insurance company made
some erroneous calculations of the date of coverage under a policy and
advised the insured by letter that he was to be covered through a certain
date. The insured died before that date and, discovering its error, the
insurance company refused to pay the beneficiaries. In concluding the
insurance company was estopped from denying liability on the policy,
the Court said:

> The fact that the representations of the company here relied upon were
> not made fraudulently, but were due solely to a mistake in computation,
> does not operate to prevent the raising of an estoppel. It is commonly held
> that, although the party making the representations was ignorant or mis-
> taken as to the real facts, if he was in such a position that he ought to have
> known them, ignorance or mistake will not prevent an estoppel. [Citations
> omitted.] In the instant case defendant had all the facts and figures before it
> from the time of the first letter to the insured until his death, almost six
> years later. Under the circumstances the error was the result of defendant's
> own negligence, and knowledge of the real facts must be imputed to the
> company.
>
> It cannot be said that the insured was negligent in not discovering the
> error, or that he was charged with knowledge as to the time when his policy
> could expire. He had a right to rely on defendant's statements in the two
> letters written to him by the company. It is well-nigh impossible for the
> ordinary layman to understand the intricacies of actuarial accounting. The
> insurance company itself even deemed it necessary to have its figures
> checked by a university professor. The alleged mistake is not a palpable one
> that could be easily discovered.

Hetchler, supra, at 613-614, 254 N.W. at 223.

The calculation of the proper monthly payment on a long term debt is
also quite complicated and the plaintiff's error was not one easily discoverable by defendants. Defendants justifiably relied on plaintiff's expertise
in setting a payment schedule and on plaintiff's repeated representations
that $251.76 a month would repay the loan.

While plaintiff argues the parties contemplated a 9% interest rate and
that therefore the interest rate should control the monthly payment figure, we believe the ordinary consumer applying for a mortgage loan
is more concerned with a monthly payment which will fit within the
purchaser's budget. A consumer has no control over the mysterious fluctuations in interest rates but he or she can decide whether a monthly
payment is or is not affordable. Defendants contemplated a contract
which would require them to pay $251.76 a month.

We address several of plaintiff's arguments. Plaintiff argues vigorously that a court is without power to make a new contract never contemplated by the parties. All the cases cited by plaintiff, however, militate just as strongly against plaintiff's prayer for reformation of the monthly payment — to an amount never contemplated by defendants. Plaintiff next argues that the "scrivener's mistake" doctrine allows a court of equity to correct human error. In order for this doctrine to apply the scrivener must be acting for *both* parties. Miles v. Shreve, 179 Mich. 671, 679, 146 N.W. 374 (1914). Since the mistake was one made by plaintiff's employee, the "scrivener's mistake" doctrine is not available to plaintiff. Finally plaintiff relies on Drysdale v. Marheine, 240 Mich. 529, 215 N.W. 329 (1927), which allowed reformation of an option based on an error in mathematical computation. We find this case distinguishable on the grounds that the error involved was so glaring — requiring one party to pay $150,000 rather than $38,890 — that there was no question that there was a simple copying mistake. The instant case is much more like *Hetchler, supra,* where the erroneous calculation was not obvious and not easily checked by a layman.

Balancing the equities on each side leads us to conclude the interest rate on the mortgage note should be reformed so that the defendants will discharge their obligation by making 300 monthly payments of $251.76. Recognizing the potential for fraud in cases where a party deliberately conceals an error from the other contracting party, we narrowly confine our holding to the combination of factors in this case.

Finally, plaintiff contends its motion to amend its complaint to add a count for recision was improperly denied by the trial court. In general, leave to amend is to be freely given when justice so requires, GCR 1963, 118. In plaintiff's motion for rehearing the trial judge stated that basically he had made a decision on the merits since there was really no factual dispute. Recision would have been an appropriate and actually a preferred remedy had defendants not sold their former home and entered into a building agreement for their new home. Since there was no way to restore defendants to their prior position, recision was not an available option and the trial judge did not abuse his discretion in denying plaintiff's motion for leave to amend.

Affirmed.

NOTE

Equitable estoppel or estoppel in pais has frequently been asserted in insurance litigation. Hetchler v. American Life Ins. Co., discussed in the principal case, is illustrative. In most cases, the doctrine has been used to prevent the insurer from insisting on conditions that result in forfeiture. For example, suppose that A, who has suffered a fire loss, has a fire policy that calls for proof of loss within 60 days. On the third day after the loss, A asks for an extension of 10 days in order to go on a trip. His request is granted. The insurance company would likely be estopped from insisting on the condition of proof of loss within 60 days after the 60 days has run. But suppose the company remains silent and A allows the 60 days to expire, relying on the extension. Is the company bound? Suppose that one day after the 60-day period has expired A, who has not previously asked the company for an extension, files proof of loss and a duly authorized agent of the company informs A that he should forget about the delay — is the company bound to pay?

Most courts refuse to apply equitable estoppel when the insured is attempting to expand coverage that was not provided for or was excluded in the contract. Ahnapee & Western Ry. Co. v. Challoner, 34 Wis. 2d 134, 148 N.W.2d 646 (1967). At least one court, however, has imposed liability on an insurance company for representing to the insured that he was covered under his policy, when in fact he was not. See Travelers Indemnity Co. v. Holman, 330 F.2d 142 (5th Cir. 1964), where the court, while acknowledging that equitable estoppel did not apply, held that the facts of the case "exactly fit the mold of §90."

CHAPMAN v. BOMANN
381 A.2d 1123 (Me. 1978)

WERNICK, Justice.

On September 13, 1974 John W. Chapman, Jr., his wife Margaret Chapman and Chapman-Hall Realty, as plaintiffs, brought a civil action in the Superior Court (Lincoln County) against George A. Bomann, III as defendant. Plaintiffs sought specific performance, or alternatively damages for breach, of a contract allegedly made between plaintiffs and defendant for the sale and purchase of real property in New Harbor, Maine, owned by defendant and his wife Betsy as joint tenants and used by them as a summer residence. Defendant's answer included the affirmative defense that the agreement plaintiffs were seeking to enforce was unenforceable for failure to meet particular requirements of the Maine Statute of Frauds, 33 M.R.S.A. §51(4).

Ruling on a motion by defendant asking that summary judgment be awarded in his favor, the presiding Justice on May 27, 1975, ordered entry of summary judgment for the defendant. Plaintiffs John and Margaret Chapman have appealed from this judgment.

We sustain the appeal.

On June 8, 1974 plaintiffs signed a document, not yet signed by defendant, the contents of which set forth an agreement that, through Chapman-Hall Realty, defendant Bomann would sell and plaintiffs would purchase the Bomann summer residence at New Harbor.

The presiding Justice ordered summary judgment for defendant on the rationale that since defendant had never signed the above-described document, the agreement contained in it was unenforceable for failure to comply with the writing requirement of the Maine Statute of Frauds. 33 M.R.S.A. §51(4).

The presiding Justice had before him for consideration facts stated in sworn answers to interrogatories and in various affidavits submitted in connection with the motion for summary judgment.

The affidavit of Joan E. Simonds, a Chapman-Hall Realty broker, disclosed that plaintiffs rejected an initial offer made by defendant and defendant then submitted a counter-proposal for a sale and purchase agreement. Plaintiffs accepted it and signed the document setting forth the agreement. Thereafter, on June 14, 1974, Chapman-Hall Realty received from plaintiff John Chapman a check for $4,000.00 which, as added to an earlier down payment of $500.00, completed a 10% down payment to be deposited in an escrow account for the benefit of defendant. On the same day that the plaintiffs signed the document containing defendant's proposal for a purchase-sale contract the document was returned to the office of Chapman-Hall Realty. It was then forwarded to the defendant to be signed on his part.

On July 2, 1974 another person associated with Chapman-Hall Realty arranged for Joan Simonds to communicate with defendant regarding the document already signed by plaintiffs and forwarded to defendant for signature. This was done because plaintiffs had arranged, and were scheduled that same day to complete, a refinancing of their home in Massachusetts in anticipation of their purchase of defendant's summer residence in New Harbor. Joan Simonds reached defendant's wife by telephone and explained these circumstances to her and the consequent need for confirmation that the Bomanns would sign the document which had been forwarded for signature. Defendant's wife told Joan Simonds that she and her husband would sign the contract and return it to the office of Chapman-Hall Realty the following Saturday. Joan Simonds then called plaintiff Margaret Chapman and told her exactly what defendant's wife had said. The Chapmans then refinanced their Massachusetts house that same day.

Defendant filed an affidavit stating that he had not signed the purchase-sale document and had not signed either a note·or memorandum as to it, and he had never received any portion of the purchase price and, further, plaintiffs never took possession of the premises or made any repairs to them. Defendant's affidavit also said that defendant lacked authority to bind his wife to a contract for the sale of their summer residence and that defendant had no knowledge that plaintiffs were refinancing their home on the basis of any oral negotiations.

A separate affidavit of defendant's wife stated that she had not authorized defendant to make an agreement to sell the Bomann residence in New Harbor.

To avoid applicability of the Statute of Frauds to the document signed by them and which they seek to enforce against defendant plaintiffs invoke the equitable principles of estoppel in pais and part performance.

While we conclude that plaintiffs' appeal must be sustained, we reach this decision on grounds other than those asserted by plaintiffs. We find it unnecessary to reach the question whether in the instant circumstances the document signed by plaintiffs, but not signed by defendant, should *as such* be *directly* enforceable as a contract binding on defendant, despite applicability of the Statute of Frauds. Rather, as more fully explained hereinafter, we decide this case by holding that the doctrine of promissory estoppel (as distinguished from estoppel in pais) applies here, to raise genuine issues of material fact concerning (1) whether the *separate ancillary promise* made by defendant's wife, as attributable also to defendant, that she and her husband would sign, and return, the document signed by plaintiffs became a contract binding on defendant, and (2) whether, further, with the promise of defendant's wife being deemed a promise binding on defendant's wife and also defendant, defendant should be barred from asserting the Statute of Frauds to deny its enforceability.

I

[The court adopted the doctrine of promissory estoppel set forth in §90 of the Restatement Second.]

With the law of Maine thus declared, it is apparent that the circumstances set forth in the record raise several genuine issues of fact material to the question whether the promise made by Betsy Bomann should be attributable to her husband, and if so, whether that promise should be held binding by virtue of promissory estoppel.

The affidavit of Joan Simonds discloses sufficient information warranting factual conclusions that when Betsy Bomann made her promise that she and defendant would sign and return the document forwarded to them, she should reasonably have expected that her promise would induce plaintiffs to act in reliance on it. Betsy Bomann gave the promise in direct response to what she had been told was an inquiry being specially made because plaintiffs were about to undertake a substantial financial commitment to refinance their Massachusetts home in connection with their undertaking to purchase the Bomanns' summer residence. The "substantial financial commitment" language appearing in the affidavit also indicates a genuine factual issue concerning whether plaintiffs had suffered harm or detriment by relying on the promise.

Despite the conclusory statement in defendant's affidavit concerning his wife's lack of authority to act on his behalf, the record reveals a genuine issue of fact on this question. The document containing the sale-purchase agreement identifies not only defendant but also his wife as a "seller." In his sworn answer to interrogatories John C. Chapman, President of Chapman-Hall Realty, stated that defendant had suggested various changes to be made in the drafting of the document setting forth defendant's counter-proposal for a sale-purchase agreement with the plaintiffs. These circumstances would warrant a finding that by participating in the drafting of the document defendant knew its contents, and the designation of defendant's wife as well as defendant as a "seller" was a holding out by defendant that defendant and his wife were acting together in selling their summer residence and, therefore, defendant's wife was authorized to act for defendant in relation to the sale.

II

The question remaining to be discussed, then, is whether, in addition to making Betsy Bomann's separate ancillary promise binding as a contract capable of being attributed to defendant, promissory estoppel will bar defendant from asserting the Statute of Frauds to deny enforceability of that otherwise binding promise. . . . Although some authorities hold to the contrary, many others agree . . . that on principles of equity (among which estoppel would be included) a defendant may be barred from asserting the policy of the Statute of Frauds to deny enforceability to a separate, ancillary oral promise, otherwise binding, to sign as a writing an agreement which, lacking such signature, the Statute of Frauds in terms renders unenforceable.

This limitation upon the penumbral policy applicability of the Statute of Frauds is conceived to be a particularized application of the general equitable principle that since it is the purpose of the Statute of Frauds to prevent fraud, that Statute cannot be permitted to be itself an instrument of fraud. Cf. Dehahn v. Innes, Me., 356 A.2d 711 (1976); Gosselin v. Better Homes, Inc., Me., 256 A.2d 629 (1969). . . .

This principle . . . we now reaffirm as the law of Maine. . . .

In the present situation the affidavits sufficiently indicate that the defendant's wife, as a joint tenant with defendant of the realty at issue, was told (1) plaintiffs were about to make a substantial change in their financial position in connection with the already existing oral agreement for the sale and purchase of the land, (2) before plaintiffs did this, they wanted to know whether defendant would sign the document which plaintiffs had already signed. Fully aware of what plaintiffs were seeking, defendant's wife gave exactly the confirmation being sought, promising that she and her husband would sign the purchase and sale agreement as a writing and return it to the real estate broker involved in the transaction.

These circumstances give rise to genuine issues of material fact concerning whether defendant's wife, by conduct attributable also to defendant, actually intended or reasonably should have expected that the promise made would induce plaintiffs to make a substantial change in their financial position, a change which plaintiffs in fact made in reliance upon their justifiable belief that the absence of a writing was not to be a matter of concern. In sum, the totality of the circumstances depicted in the record precipitate general factual issues material to whether it would be grossly unjust and, therefore, tantamount to a fraud on the plaintiffs to allow defendant to assert the Statute of Frauds, by invoking the penumbral policy (rather than the actual terms) of the Statute, to bar enforceability of the separate ancillary promise for the making of a sufficient writing.

If, after the requisite evidentiary hearing, it is found that on promissory estoppel grounds defendant is barred from asserting the Statute of Frauds to deny specific enforcement of the binding separate ancillary promise of defendant's wife, as attributable also to defendant, the Court, as an incident of the present proceeding, could order defendant to sign the document which plaintiffs had already signed. By defendant's compliance with that order, the Statute of Frauds would be rendered inapplicable to the principal sale-purchase agreement between defendant and plaintiffs, and plaintiffs would be in position to continue seeking enforcement of it as alleged in their complaint. See 21 Turtle Creek Square, Ltd. v. New York State Teachers' Retirement System, supra; see also enlightening discussion in Annot. 56 A.L.R.3d 1037, 1058-1064.[111]

The entry is:

Appeal sustained; judgment for defendant set aside; remanded to the Superior Court for further proceedings consistent with the opinion herein.

NOTE

For the use of estoppel in avoiding the requirements of the Statute of Frauds, see Chapter 6, Section 4. See also Henderson, Promissory Estoppel and Traditional Contract Doctrine, 78 Yale L.J. 343, 381-383 (1969).

Is a court order compelling defendants to sign the contract justifiable? If the doctrine of promissory estoppel is designed to protect the plaintiffs'

111. We previously emphasized in delineating the precise scope of our decision herein that we do not reach, or intimate opinion on, the question whether promissory estoppel would enable plaintiffs *directly* to enforce the oral sale-purchase agreement *as such*, notwithstanding that the Statute of Frauds applies in terms to that agreement. . . .

reliance interest only, shouldn't their remedy be limited to damages? The plaintiffs presumably still have the money they borrowed, which they could pay back early; if so, their loss will be limited to interest and points already paid and a prepayment penalty, if any.

FEINBERG v. PFEIFFER CO.
322 S.W.2d 163 (Mo. Ct. App. 1959)

Action on alleged contract by defendant to pay plaintiff a specified monthly amount upon her retirement from defendant's employ. The Circuit Court, City of St. Louis, rendered judgment for plaintiff, and defendant appealed.

DOERNER, Commissioner. This is a suit brought in the Circuit Court of the City of St. Louis by plaintiff, a former employee of the defendant corporation, on an alleged contract whereby defendant agreed to pay plaintiff the sum of $200 per month for life upon her retirement. A jury being waived, the case was tried by the court alone. Judgment below was for plaintiff for $5,100, the amount of the pension claimed to be due as of the date of the trial together with interest thereon, and defendant duly appealed.

The parties are in substantial agreement on the essential facts. Plaintiff began working for the defendant, a manufacturer of pharmaceuticals, in 1910, when she was but 17 years of age. By 1947 she had attained the position of bookkeeper, office manager, and assistant treasurer of the defendant, and owned 70 shares of its stock out of a total of 6,503 shares issued and outstanding. Twenty shares had been given to her by the defendant or its then president, she had purchased 20, and the remaining 30 she had acquired by a stock split or stock dividend. Over the years she received substantial dividends on the stock she owned, as did all of the other stockholders. Also, in addition to her salary, plaintiff from 1937 to 1949, inclusive, received each year a bonus varying in amount from $300 in the beginning to $2,000 in the later years.

On December 27, 1947, the annual meeting of the defendant's Board of Directors was held at the Company's offices in St. Louis, presided over by Max Lippman, its then president and largest individual stockholder. The other directors present were George L. Marcus, Sidney Harris, Sol Flammer, and Walter Weinstock, who, with Max Lippman, owned 5,007 of the 6,503 shares then issued and outstanding. At that meeting the Board of Directors adopted the following resolution, which, because it is the crux of the case, we quote in full:

The Chairman thereupon pointed out that the Assistant Treasurer, Mrs. Anna Sacks Feinberg, has given the corporation many years of long and faithful service. Not only has she served the corporation devotedly, but with exceptional ability and skill. The President pointed out that although all of the officers and directors sincerely hoped and desired that Mrs. Feinberg would continue in her present position for as long as she felt able, nevertheless, in view of the length of service which she has contributed provision should be made to afford her retirement privileges and benefits which should become a firm obligation of the corporation to be available to her whenever she should see fit to retire from active duty, however many years in the future such retirement may become effective. It was, accordingly, proposed that Mrs. Feinberg's salary which is presently $350.00 per month, be increased to $400.00 per month, and that Mrs. Feinberg would be given the privilege of retiring from active duty at any time she may elect to see fit so to do upon a retirement pay of $200.00 per month for life, with the distinct understanding that the retirement plan is merely being adopted at the present time in order to afford Mrs. Feinberg security for the future and in the hope that her active services will continue with the corporation for many years to come. After due discussion and consideration, and upon motion duly made and seconded, it was —

Resolved, that the salary of Anna Sacks Feinberg be increased from $350.00 to $400.00 per month and that she be afforded the privilege of retiring from active duty in the corporation at any time she may elect to see fit so to do upon retirement pay of $200.00 per month, for the remainder of her life.

At the request of Mr. Lippman his sons-in-law, Messrs. Harris and Flammer, called upon the plaintiff at her apartment on the same day to advise her of the passage of the resolution. Plaintiff testified on cross-examination that she had no prior information that such a pension plan was contemplated, that it came as a surprise to her, and that she would have continued in her employment whether or not such a resolution had been adopted. It is clear from the evidence that there was no contract, oral or written, as to plaintiff's length of employment, and that she was free to quit, and the defendant to discharge her, at any time.

Plaintiff did continue to work for the defendant through June 30, 1949, on which date she retired. In accordance with the foregoing resolution, the defendant began paying her the sum of $200 on the first of each month. Mr. Lippman died on November 18, 1949, and was succeeded as president of the company by his widow. Because of an illness, she retired from that office and was succeeded in October, 1953, by her son-in-law, Sidney M. Harris. Mr. Harris testified that while Mrs. Lippman had been president she signed the monthly pension check paid plaintiff, but fussed about doing so, and considered the payments as gifts. After his election, he stated, a new accounting firm employed by the defendant questioned the validity of the payments to plaintiff on several occasions, and in the Spring of 1956, upon its recommendation, he consulted the Company's then attorney, Mr. Ralph Kalish. Harris testified that both Ernst and Ernst, the accounting firm, and Kalish told him there was no need of giving plaintiff the money. He also stated that he had concurred in the view that the payments to plaintiff were mere gratuities rather than amounts due under a contractual obligation, and that following his discussion with the Company's attorney plaintiff was sent a check for $100 on April 1, 1956. Plaintiff declined to accept the reduced amount, and this action followed. Additional facts will be referred to later in this opinion. . . .

Appellant's next complaint is that there was insufficient evidence to support the court's findings that plaintiff would not have quit defendant's employ had she not known and relied upon the promise of defendant to pay her $200 a month for life, and the finding that, from her voluntary retirement until April 1, 1956, plaintiff relied upon the continued receipt of the pension installments. The trial court so found, and, in our opinion, justifiably so. Plaintiff testified, and was corroborated by Harris, defendant's witness, that knowledge of the passage of the resolution was communicated to her on December 27, 1947, the very day it was adopted. She was told at that time by Harris and Flammer, she stated, that she could take the pension as of that day, if she wished. She testified further that she continued to work for another year and a half, through June 30, 1949; that at that time her health was good and she could have continued to work, but that after working for almost forty years she thought she would take a rest. Her testimony continued:

Q. Now, what was the reason — I'm sorry. Did you then quit the employment of the company after you — after this year and a half?
A. Yes.
Q. What was the reason that you left?
A. Well, I thought almost forty years, it was a long time and I thought I would take a little rest.
Q. Yes.
A. And with the pension and what earnings my husband had, we figured we could get along.
Q. Did you rely upon this pension?
A. We certainly did.
Q. Being paid?
A. Very much so. We relied upon it because I was positive that I was going to get it as long as I lived.
Q. Would you have left the employment of the company at that time had it not been for this pension?
A. No.
Mr. Allen: Just a minute, I object to that as calling for a conclusion and conjecture on the part of this witness.
The Court: It will be overruled.
Q. (Mr. Agatstein continuing): Go ahead, now. The question is whether you would have quit the employment of the company at that time had you not relied upon this pension plan?
A. No, I wouldn't.

> Q. You would not have. Did you ever seek employment while this pen-
>   sion was being paid to you —
> A. (interrupting): No.
> Q. Wait a minute, at any time prior — at any other place?
> A. No, sir.
> Q. Were you able to hold any other employment during that time?
> A. Yes, I think so.
> Q. Was your health good?
> A. My health was good.

It is obvious from the foregoing that there was ample evidence to
support the findings of fact made by the court below.

We come, then, to the basic issue in the case. While otherwise defined
in defendant's third and fourth assignments of error, it is thus succinctly
stated in the argument in its brief: ". . . whether plaintiff has proved that
she has a right to recover from defendant based upon a legally binding
contractual obligation to pay her $200 per month for life."

It is defendant's contention, in essence, that the resolution adopted by
its Board of Directors was a mere promise to make a gift, and that no
contract resulted either thereby, or when plaintiff retired, because there
was no consideration given or paid by the plaintiff. It urges that a promise
to make a gift is not binding unless supported by a legal consideration;
that the only apparent consideration for the adoption of the foregoing
resolution was the "many years of long and faithful service" expressed
therein; and that past services are not a valid consideration for a promise.
Defendant argues further that there is nothing in the resolution which
made its effectiveness conditional upon plaintiff's continued employment, that she was not under contract to work for any length of time but
was free to quit whenever she wished, and that she had no contractual
right to her position and could have been discharged at any time.

Plaintiff conceded that a promise based upon past services would be
without consideration, but contends that there were two other elements
which supplied the required element: First, the continuation by plaintiff
in the employ of the defendant for the period from December 27, 1947,
the date when the resolution was adopted, until the date of her retirement on June 30, 1949. And, second, her change of position, i.e., her
retirement, and the abandonment by her of her opportunity to continue
in gainful employment, made in reliance on defendant's promise to pay
her $200 per month for life.

We must agree with the defendant that the evidence does not support
the first of these contentions. There is no language in the resolution
predicating plaintiff's right to a pension upon her continued employment. She was not required to work for the defendant for any period of
time as a condition to gaining such retirement benefits. She was told that
she could quit the day upon which the resolution was adopted, as she
herself testified, and it is clear from her own testimony that she made no

promise or agreement to continue in the employ of the defendant in return for its promise to pay her a pension. Hence there was lacking that mutuality of obligation which is essential to the validity of a contract. . . .

But as to the second of these contentions we must agree with plaintiff. By the terms of the resolution defendant promised to pay plaintiff the sum of $200 a month upon her retirement. Consideration for a promise has been defined in the Restatement of the Law of Contracts, Section 75, as:

> (1)   Consideration for a promise is (a) an act other than a promise, or (b) a forbearance, or (c) the creation, modification or destruction of a legal relation, or (d) a return promise, bargained for and given in exchange for the promise.

As the parties agree, the consideration sufficient to support a contract may be either a benefit to the promisor or a loss or detriment to the promisee. . . .

Section 90 of the Restatement of the Law of Contracts states that: "A promise which the promisor should reasonably expect to induce action or forbearance of a definite and substantial character on the part of the promisee and which does induce such action or forbearance is binding if injustice can be avoided only by enforcement of the promise." This doctrine has been described as that of "promissory estoppel," as distinguished from that of equitable estoppel or estoppel in pais, the reason for the differentiation being stated as follows:

> It is generally true that one who has led another to act in reasonable reliance on his representations of fact cannot afterwards in litigation between the two deny the truth of the representations, and some courts have sought to apply this principle to the formation of contracts, where, relying on a gratuitous promise, the promisee has suffered detriment. It is to be noticed, however, that such a case does not come within the ordinary definition of estoppel. If there is any representation of an existing fact, it is only that the promisor at the time of making the promise intends to fulfill it. As to such intention there is usually no misrepresentation and if there is, it is not that which has injured the promisee. In other words, he relies on a promise and not on a misstatement of fact; and the term "promissory" estoppel or something equivalent should be used to make the distinction.

Williston on Contracts, Rev. Ed., Sec. 139, Vol. 1.

In speaking of this doctrine, Judge Learned Hand said in Porter v. Commissioner of Internal Revenue, 2 Cir., 60 F.2d 673, 675, that ". . . 'promissory estoppel' is now a recognized species of consideration."

As pointed out by our Supreme Court in In re Jamison's Estate, Mo., 202 S.W.2d 879, 887, it is stated in the Missouri Annotations to the Restatement under Section 90 that:

"'There is a variance between the doctrine underlying this section and the theoretical justifications that have been advanced for the Missouri decisions.'"

That variance, as the authors of the Annotations point out, is that:

> This §90, when applied with §85, means that the promise described is a contract without any consideration. In Missouri the same practical result is reached without in theory abandoning the doctrine of consideration. In Missouri three theories have been advanced as ground for the decisions. (1) *Theory of act for promise.* The induced "action or forbearance" is the consideration for the promise. Underwood Typewriter Co. v. Century Realty Co. (1909) 220 Mo. 522, 119 S.W. 400, 25 L.R.A., N.S., 1173. See §76. (2) *Theory of promissory estoppel.* The induced "action of forbearance" works on estoppel against the promisor. (Citing School District of Kansas City v. Sheidley (1897) 138 Mo. 672, 40 S.W. 656 [37 L.R.A. 406]). . . . (3) *Theory of bilateral contract.* When the induced "action or forbearance" is begun, a promise to complete is implied, and we have an enforceable bilateral contract, the implied promise to complete being the consideration for the original promise.

(Citing cases.)

Was there such an act on the part of plaintiff, in reliance upon the promise contained in the resolution, as will estop the defendant, and therefore create an enforceable contract under the doctrine of promissory estoppel? We think there was. One of the illustrations cited under Section 90 of the Restatement is: "2. A promises B to pay him an annuity during B's life. B thereupon resigns a profitable employment, as A expected that he might. B receives the annuity for some years, in the meantime becoming disqualified from again obtaining good employment. A's promise is binding." This illustration is objected to by defendant as not being applicable to the case at hand. The reason advanced by it is that in the illustration B became "disqualified" from obtaining other employment *before* A discontinued the payments, whereas in this case the plaintiff did not discover that she had cancer and thereby became unemployable until *after* the defendant had discontinued the payments of $200 per month. We think the distinction is immaterial. The only reason for the reference in the illustration to the disqualification of A is in connection with that part of Section 90 regarding the prevention of injustice. The injustice would occur regardless of when the disability occurred. Would defendant contend that the contract would be enforceable if the plaintiff's illness had been discovered on March 31, 1956, the day before it discontinued the payment of the $200 a month, but not if it occurred on April 2nd, the day after? Furthermore, there are more ways to become disqualified for work, or unemployable, than as the result if illness. At the time she retired plaintiff was 57 years of age. At the time the payments were discontinued she was over 63 years of age. It is a matter of common knowledge that it is virtually impossible for a woman of that age to find satisfactory employment, much less a position comparable to that which plaintiff enjoyed at the time of her retirement.

The fact of the matter is that plaintiff's subsequent illness was not the "action or forbearance" which was induced by the promise contained in the resolution. As the trial court correctly decided, such action on plaintiff's part was her retirement from a lucrative position in reliance upon defendant's promise to pay her an annuity or pension.

The Commissioner therefore recommends, for the reasons stated, that the judgment be affirmed.

PER CURIAM. The foregoing opinion by Doerner, C., is adopted as the opinion of the court. The judgment is, accordingly, affirmed.

NOTE

1. Consult 45 Iowa L. Rev. 656 (1960); 56 Colum. L. Rev. 251, 263-268 (1956); 23 U. Chi. L. Rev. 96 (1956); 70 Colum. L. Rev. 909, 920 (1970). See also Employee Retirement Income Security Act (ERISA) 514(a), 20 U.S.C.A. §1144(a).

2. In July 1930 an employer sent to a number of employees the following letter:

> Confirming our conversation of today, it is necessary with conditions as they are throughout the petroleum industry, to effect substantial economies throughout the plant operation. This necessitates the reducing of the working force to a minimum necessary to maintain operation. In view of your many years of faithful service, the management is desirous of shielding you as far as possible from the effect of reduced plant operation and has, therefore, placed you upon a retirement list which has just been established for this purpose.
>
> Effective August 1, 1930, you will be carried on our payroll at a rate of $ — per month. You will be relieved of all duties except that of reporting to Mr. T. E. Sullivan at the main office for the purpose of picking up your semi-monthly checks. Your group insurance will be maintained on the same basis as at present, unless you desire to have it cancelled. [Signed by the vice-president.]

Payments were regularly made until June 1, 1931 when the employees were told that the arrangement was terminated. Consideration? Plowman v. Indian Refining Co., 20 F. Supp. 1 (D.C. Ill. 1937).

Section 8.   Firm Offers and the Bargain Principle

According to classical contract theory, during preliminary negotiations each party can, as a rule, break off with impunity, and a party who in anticipation of a forthcoming contract incurs preparation expenses or turns down another deal cannot hold the withdrawing party to an accounting. He acts at his own risk. As we saw in Section 4, however, this doctrine has in recent years been somewhat modified by the introduction of a duty to bargain in good faith.[112]

Contract law everywhere has been confronted with the problem whether it should take the same attitude when negotiations have ripened into an offer. Should an offeree be entitled to rely on an offer or should the offeror be free to revoke so long as the other party has not committed himself by an acceptance? It is also possible to take a middle ground. While the "mere" (naked) offer cannot be relied upon, a firm offer, i.e., an offer coupled with a promise to keep it open for a period of time, might be treated differently.

The material that follows shows the impact of the consideration doctrine on the binding effect of offers and the gradual relaxation of its stranglehold. Under the bargain theory of consideration, a "naked" offer, including a firm offer, can be revoked with impunity until accepted, just like any other gratuitous promise, unless it is given under seal (provided the so-called common law effect of the seal has been preserved).[113] Gradually courts have come to realize that there is a vast difference between gift promises in the narrow sense of the word (i.e., promises with the motivation of conferring a gift) and offers, particularly firm offers. Although not "immediately directed toward accomplishing an exchange [they] are necessary preliminary steps towards exchanges." Fuller, Consideration and Form, 41 Colum. L. Rev. 799, 818 (1941). Small wonder that there has been some tendency to invoke promissory estoppel to protect the offeree. Restatement Second §87(2). See the *Loranger* case, *infra* p. 331. To give the offeree added protection, legislation has changed the common law by providing for the binding effect of firm offers if given in writing, e.g., U.C.C. §2-205.[114] This innovation is of particular importance in the many jurisdictions where the common law effect of a seal has been abolished.[115] The formalities required by U.C.C. §2-205 form an interesting contrast to the prerequisites of liability under §87(1)(a) of the Restatement Second.[116]

112. See p. 201 *supra*.
113. See p. 736 *infra*.
114. U.C.C. §2-205 applies only to offers by merchants; its requirements deserve careful study. See also New York General Obligations Law §5-1109.
115. See p. 736 *infra*.
116. See also Restatement Second §89B (Tent. Draft No. 2, 1965).

Understandably, the first target of the reform movement was the firm offer. But it was not long before the attack was broadened and the question raised whether reliance on an offer ought not to be protected so long as it was foreseeable by the offeror. We no longer share Langdell's conviction that an irrevocable offer is a "legal impossibility." Law of Contracts §78 (2d ed. 1880); see Restatement Second §87(2).

DICKINSON v. DODDS
2 Ch. D. 463 (C.A. 1876)

On Wednesday, the 10th of June, 1874, the Defendant John Dodds signed and delivered to the Plaintiff, George Dickinson, a memorandum, of which the material part was as follows:

> I hereby agree to sell to Mr. George Dickinson the whole of the dwelling-houses, garden ground, stabling, and outbuildings thereto belonging, situate at Croft, belonging to me, for the sum of £800. As witness my hand this tenth day of June, 1874.
>
> £800   (Signed) JOHN DODDS.
>
> P.S. — This offer to be left over until Friday, 9 o'clock, A.M. J.D. (the twelfth), 12th June, 1874.[117]
>
>   (Signed) J. DODDS.

. . . In the afternoon of the Thursday the Plaintiff was informed by a Mr. Berry that Dodds had been offering or agreeing to sell the property to Thomas Allan, the other Defendant. Thereupon the Plaintiff, at about half-past seven in the evening, went to the house of Mrs. Burgess, the mother-in-law of Dodds, where he was then staying, and left with her a formal acceptance in writing of the offer to sell the property. According to the evidence of Mrs. Burgess this document never in fact reached Dodds, she having forgotten to give it to him.

On the following (Friday) morning, at about seven o'clock, Berry, who was acting as agent for Dickinson, found Dodds at the Darlington railway station, and handed to him a duplicate of the acceptance by Dickinson, and explained to Dodds its purport. He replied that it was too late, as he had sold the property. A few minutes later Dickinson himself found Dodds entering a railway carriage, and handed him another duplicate of the notice of acceptance, but Dodds declined to receive it, saying, "You are too late. I have sold the property."

117. Could Dodds, intending to keep the property, prevent timely acceptance by being unavailable till the 13th? Absent timely revocation, could Dickinson still accept on that day? 1 Corbin §35. — EDS.

It appeared that on the day before, Thursday, the 11th of June, Dodds had signed a formal contract for the sale of the property to the Defendant Allan for £800, and had received from him a deposit of £40.

The bill in this suit prayed that the Defendant Dodds might be decreed specifically to perform the contract of the 10th of June, 1874; that he might be restrained from conveying the property to Allan; that Allan might be restrained from taking any such conveyance; that, if any such conveyance had been or should be made, Allan might be declared a trustee of the property for, and might be directed to convey the property to, the Plaintiff; and for damages.

The cause came on for hearing before Vice-Chancellor Bacon on the 25th of January, 1876.

[BACON, V.C., decreed specific performance, holding that Dodds could withdraw only by giving notice to Dickinson and that owing to the relation back of the acceptance to the date of the agreement, the property in equity was the property of plaintiff and Dodds had nothing to sell to Allan.]

From this decision both the defendants appeal. . . .

MELLISH, L.J. . . . The first question is, whether this document of the 10th of June, 1874, which was signed by Dodds, was an agreement to sell, or only an offer to sell, the property therein mentioned to Dickinson; and I am clearly of opinion that it was only an offer, although it is in the first part of it, independently of the postcript, worded as an agreement. I apprehend that, until acceptance, so that both parties are bound, even though an instrument is so worded as to express that both parties agreed, it is in point of law only an offer, and until both parties are bound, neither party is bound. It is not necessary that both parties should be bound within the Statute of Frauds, for, if one party makes an offer in writing, and the other accepts it verbally, that will be sufficient to bind the person who has signed the written document. But, if there be no agreement, either verbally or in writing, then, until acceptance, it is in point of law an offer only, although worded as if it were an agreement. But it is hardly necessary to resort to that doctrine in the present case, because the postscript calls it an offer, and says, "This offer to be left over until Friday, 9 o'clock A.M." Well, then, this being only an offer, the law says — and it is a perfectly clear rule of law — that, although it is said that the offer is to be left open until Friday morning at 9 o'clock, that did not bind Dodds. He was not in point of law bound to hold the offer over until 9 o'clock on Friday morning. He was not so bound either in law or in equity. Well, that being so, when on the next day he made an agreement with Allan to sell the property to him, I am not aware of any ground on which it can be said that that contract with Allan was not as good and binding a contract as ever was made. Assuming Allan to have known (there is some dispute about it, and Allan does not admit that he knew of it, but I will assume that he did) that Dodds had made the offer to

Dickinson, and had given him till Friday morning at 9 o'clock to accept it, still in point of law that could not prevent Allan from making a more favourable offer than Dickinson, and entering at once into a binding agreement with Dodds.

Then Dickinson is informed by Berry that the property has been sold by Dodds to Allan. Berry does not tell us from whom he heard it, but says that he did hear it, that he knew it, and that he informed Dickinson of it. Now, stopping there, the question which arises is this — If an offer has been made for the sale of property, and before that offer is accepted, the person who has made the offer enters into a binding agreement to sell the property to somebody else, and the person to whom the offer was first made receives notice in some way that the property has been sold to another person, can he after that make a binding contract by the acceptance of the offer? I am of opinion that he cannot. The law may be right or wrong in saying that a person who has given to another a certain time within which to accept an offer is not bound by his promise to give that time; but, if he is not bound by that promise, and may still sell the property to some one else, and if it be the law that, in order to make a contract, the two minds must be in agreement at some one time, that is, at the time of the acceptance, how is it possible that when the person to whom the offer has been made knows that the person who has made the offer has sold the property to someone else, and that, in fact, he has not remained in the same mind to sell it to him, he can be at liberty to accept the offer and thereby make a binding contract? It seems to me that would be simply absurd. If a man makes an offer to sell a particular horse in his stable, and says, "I will give you until the day after to-morrow to accept the offer," and the next day goes and sells the horse to somebody else, and receives the purchase-money from him, can the person to whom the offer was originally made then come and say, "I accept," so as to make a binding contract, and so as to be entitled to recover damages for the non-delivery of the horse? If the rule of law is that a mere offer to sell property, which can be withdrawn at any time, and which is made dependent on the acceptance of the person to whom it is made, is a mere nudum pactum, how is it possible that the person to whom the offer has been made can by acceptance make a binding contract after he knows that the person who has made the offer has sold the property to some one else? It is admitted law that, if a man who makes an offer dies, the offer cannot be accepted after he is dead, and parting with the property has very much the same effect as the death of the owner, for it makes the performance of the offer impossible. I am clearly of opinion that, just as when a man who has made an offer dies before it is accepted it is impossible that it can then be accepted, so when once the person to whom the offer was made knows that the property has been sold to some one else, it is too late for him to accept the offer, and on that ground I am clearly of opinion that there was no binding contract for the sale of this property by Dodds to Dickinson, and even if there had been, it seems to me that the sale of the property to Allan was first in point of time. However, it is not necessary to consider, if there had been two binding contracts, which of them would be entitled to priority in equity, because there is no binding contract between Dodds and Dickinson.

BAGGALLAY, J.A. I entirely concur in the judgments which have been pronounced.

JAMES, L.J. The bill will be dismissed with costs.

[The concurring opinion of James, L.J. has been omitted.]

NOTE

1. Professor Winfield, in criticizing the decision as unsound, makes the following point in Pollock's Principles of Contract 21 (13th ed. 1950):

> A [Dodds] stated in his offer the exact price of the house. That was the consideration on his side. Why should the law insist that he was entitled to extra consideration for allowing the offeree a certain time within which he could accept? Presumably he might have taken that very factor into account in fixing the sum that constituted the price, i.e., he may have fixed it rather higher than he would have done if no time had been specified.

See also State of New York, Law Revision Commission 57 (2d Annual Report, 1936). Suppose Dodds before acceding to the postscript had raised the price to £805. Different result? Is not the increased chance of an acceptance on the part of the offeree or the likelihood of reliance by the offeree sufficient consideration? For an interesting explanation of Dickinson v. Dodds in terms of the philosophy of contracts of the time, see J. Dawson, W. Harvey & S. Henderson, Cases and Comment on Contracts 335, 336 (4th ed. 1982). Consult Maughs v. Porter, 157 Va. 415, 161 S.E. 242 (1931); Boston & Maine R.R. v. Bartlett, 57 Mass. (3 Cush.) 224 (1849). Was it of any significance that the postscript contained the word "over" instead of "open"? Is either word free from ambiguity? See The New York Statute on Irrevocable Offers, 43 Colum. L. Rev. 487, 488-490 (1943); 46 Mich. L. Rev. 58, 60 (1947).

2. Suppose plaintiff, relying on the offer, had spent £5 to have the title searched. Should he be entitled to get specific performance, or at least to get a refund? Bard v. Kent, 19 Cal. 2d 449, 122 P.2d 8, 139 A.L.R. 1032 (1942).

3. Was it irrelevant that the defendant's promise was in writing?

4. Has the "naked" promise to keep an offer open for a certain period any legal significance? Suppose on Thursday plaintiff had offered £750

and the defendant had remained silent. Could plaintiff still accept on Friday, assuming that the property had not been sold in the meantime? Restatement Second §39. Assume that the defendant replied, "Must insist on £800"; can plaintiff accept? Consult Livingstone v. Evans, [1954] 4 D.L.R. (Alta. Sup. Ct.).

5. Suppose Dodds had sold the property but without plaintiff's knowledge. Same result? Threlkeld v. Inglett, 289 Ill. 90, 124 N.E. 368 (1919). Is it relevant whether Berry was authorized by Dodds to convey the information, and whether Dickinson could regard the information as reliable? Restatement second §43.

6. Why did the notice of acceptance left by plaintiff with Mrs. Burgess not complete the contract? Restatement Second §68.

7. The rule in Dickinson v. Dodds has been one of the main targets of the critics of the consideration doctrine. "It may . . . be ordinary business understanding that an offer for a bargain is revocable until the bargain is made, and to that extent, our common law is sound. To say, however, that a firm offer will not be given effect according to its terms, is something quite different." Sharp, Promissory Liability (pt. 1), 7 U. Chi. L. Rev. 10 (1939). The Sixth Interim Report of the English Law Revision Commission (1937) has expressed itself (p. 22) in favor of making the firm offer irrevocable even if orally made, provided it contains a definite time limit. Statutory changes enacted in New York since 1941 require a writing to dispense with consideration. See p. 549 *infra*. For the English law, see G. H. Treitel, The Law of Contract 99-100 (5th ed. 1974). In the case of international sales of goods, the rule has been expressly abolished by legislation. ULFIS Art. 5(2). See Farnsworth, Mutuality of Obligation in Contract Law, 3 Dayton L. Rev. 271 (1978).

JORDAN v. DOBBINS
122 Mass. 168 (1877)

Contract upon the following guaranty:

> For value received, the receipt whereof is hereby acknowledged, the undersigned does hereby guaranty to Jordan, Marsh & Co. the prompt payment by George E. Moore to Jordan, Marsh & Co., at maturity, of all sums of money and debts which he may hereafter owe Jordan, Marsh & Co. for merchandise, which they may from time to time sell to him, whether such debts be on book account, by note, draft or otherwise, and also any and all renewals of any such debt. The undersigned shall not be compelled to pay on this guaranty a sum exceeding $1000, but this guaranty shall be a continuing guaranty, and apply to and be available to said Jordan, Marsh & Co., for all sales of merchandise they may make to said George E. Moore until written notice shall have been given by the undersigned to said Jordan, Marsh & Co. and received by them, that it shall not apply to future

purchases. Notice of the acceptance of this guaranty and of sales under the same, and demand upon said George E. Moore for payment, and notice of me of nonpayment, is hereby waived. In witness whereof I, the undersigned, have hereunto set my hand and seal this twenty-eighth day of February, A.D. 1873. William Dobbins. (Seal.)

Annexed to the declaration was an account of goods sold to Moore.

The case was submitted to the Superior Court, and, after judgment for the plaintiffs, to this court, on appeal, on an agreed statement of facts in substance as follows:

The plaintiffs are partners under the firm name of Jordan, Marsh & Co., and the defendant is the duly appointed administratrix of the estate of William Dobbins.

William Dobbins, on February 28, 1873, executed and delivered to the plaintiffs the above written contract of guaranty. The plaintiffs thereafter, relying on this contract, sold to said Moore the goods mentioned in the account annexed to the declaration, at the times and for the prices given in said account, all of the goods having been sold and delivered to Moore between January 16 and May 28, 1874. All the amounts claimed were due from Moore, and payment was duly demanded of him and of the defendant before the date of the writ. Other goods had been sold by the plaintiffs to Moore between the date of the guaranty and the first date mentioned in the account, but these had been paid for.

William Dobbins died on August 6, 1873, and the defendant was appointed administratrix of his estate on September 2, 1873. The plaintiffs had no notice of his death until after the last of the goods mentioned in the account had been sold to Moore.

If upon these facts the defendant was liable, judgment was to be entered for the plaintiffs for the amount claimed; otherwise, judgment for the defendant.

MORTON, J. An agreement to guarantee the payment by another of goods to be sold in the future, not founded upon any present consideration passing to the guarantor, is a contract of a peculiar character. Until it is acted upon, it imposes no obligation and creates no liability of the guarantor. After it is acted upon, the sale of the goods upon the credit of the guaranty is the only consideration for the conditional promise of the guarantor to pay for them.

The agreement which the guarantor makes with the person receiving the guaranty is not that I now become liable to you for anything, but that if you sell goods to a third person, I will then become liable to pay for them if such third person does not. It is of the nature of an authority to sell goods upon the credit of the guarantor, rather than of a contract which cannot be rescinded except by mutual consent. Thus such a guaranty is revocable by the guarantor at any time before it is acted upon.

In Offord v. Davies, 12 C.B. (N.S.) 748, the guaranty was of the due payment for the space of twelve months of bills to be discounted, and the court held that the guarantor might revoke it any time within the twelve months, and the plaintiff could not recover for bills discounted after such revocation. The ground of the decision was that the defendant's promise by itself created no obligation, but was in the nature of a proposal which might be revoked at any time before it was acted on.

Such being the nature of a guaranty, we are of opinion that the death of the guarantor operates as a revocation of it, and that the person holding it cannot recover against his executor or administrator for goods sold after the death. Death terminates the power of the deceased to act, and revokes any authority or license he may have given, if it has not been executed or acted upon. His estate is held upon any contract upon which a liability exists at the time of his death, although it may depend upon future contingencies. But it is not held for a liability which is created after his death, by the exercise of a power or authority which he might at any time revoke.

Applying these principles to the case at bar, it follows that the defendant is entitled to judgment. The guaranty is carefully drawn, but it is in its nature nothing more than a simple guaranty for a proposed sale of goods. The provision, that it shall continue until written notice is given by the guarantor that it shall not apply to future purchases, affects the mode in which the guarantor might exercise his right to revoke it, but it cannot prevent its revocation by his death. The fact that the instrument is under seal cannot change its nature or construction. No liability existed under it against the guarantor at the time of his death, but the goods for which the plaintiffs seek to recover were all sold afterwards.

We are not impressed by the plaintiff's argument that it is inequitable to throw the loss upon them. It is no hardship to require traders, whose business it is to deal in goods, to exercise diligence so far as to ascertain whether a person upon whose credit they are selling is living. . . .

Judgment for the defendant.

NOTE

See Oliphant, The Duration and Termination of an Offer, 18 Mich. L. Rev. 201, 209 (1920); Parks, Indirect Revocation and Termination by Death of Offers, 19 Mich. L. Rev. 152, 158 (1920); Corbin, The Restatement of the Common Law by the American Law Institute, 15 Iowa L. Rev. 19, 36 (1929).

How would the outcome of the case have been affected by the following clause?:

This agreement shall be enforceable by and against the respective administrators, executors, successors and assigns of the parties hereto, and

the death of the guarantors shall not terminate the liability of such guarantors under this agreement, except by the giving of notice of termination of
this agreement by the representatives of such deceased in the manner
hereinbefore provided with respect to the termination of this agreement.

Would it be helpful if in addition the document recited the receipt of $1
paid cash in hand? Consult American Chain Co. v. Arrow Grip Mfg. Co.,
134 Misc. 321, 235 N.Y.S. 228 (1929).

In United States ex rel. Wilhelm v. Chain, 300 U.S. 31 (1937), a bond
with defendant as surety was given by a national bank pursuant to the
bankruptcy laws to induce the appointment of the bank as a designated
depositor of bankruptcy funds. The bond named the United States as
obligee and was conditioned on the faithful discharge and performance
by the bank of all duties pertaining to it as depository. The plaintiff
trustee in bankruptcy deposited funds after the death of the surety, and
the bank collapsed. Is the surety's estate or the government liable?
The bond contained no provision limiting the surety's obligation to his
lifetime.

JAMES BAIRD CO. v. GIMBEL BROS.
64 F.2d 344 (2d Cir. 1933)

L. HAND, Circuit Judge. The plaintiff sued the defendant for breach of
a contract to deliver linoleum under a contract of sale; the defendant
denied the making of the contract; the parties tried the case to the judge
under a written stipulation and he directed judgment for the defendant.
The facts as found, bearing on the making of the contract, the only issue
necessary to discuss, were as follows: The defendant, a New York merchant, knew that the Department of Highways in Pennsylvania had asked
for bids for the construction of a public building. It sent an employee to
the office of a contractor in Philadelphia, who had possession of the
specifications, and the employee there computed the amount of the linoleum which would be required on the job, underestimating the total
yardage by about one-half the proper amount. In ignorance of this mistake, on December twenty-fourth the defendant sent to some twenty or
thirty contractors, likely to bid on the job, an offer to supply all linoleum
required by the specifications at two different lump sums, depending
upon the quality used. These offers concluded as follows: "If successful in
being awarded this contract, it will be absolutely guaranteed, . . . and
. . . we are offering these prices for reasonable" (sic), "prompt acceptance after the general contract has been awarded." The plaintiff, a contractor in Washington, got one of these on the twenty-eighth, and on the
same day the defendant learned its mistake and telegraphed all the contractors to whom it had sent the offer, that it withdrew it and would
substitute a new one at about double the amount of the old. This with-

drawal reached the plaintiff at Washington on the afternoon of the same day but not until after it had put in a bid at Harrisburg at a lump sum, based as to linoleum upon the prices quoted by the defendant. The public authorities accepted the plaintiff's bid on December thirtieth, the defendant having meanwhile written a letter of confirmation of its withdrawal, received on the thirty-first. The plaintiff formally accepted the offer on January second, and, as the defendant persisted in declining to recognize the existence of a contract, sued it for damages on a breach.

Unless there are circumstances to take it out of the ordinary doctrine, since the offer was withdrawn before it was accepted, the acceptance was too late. Restatement of Contracts, §35. To meet this the plaintiff argues as follows: It was a reasonable implication from the defendant's offer that it should be irrevocable in case the plaintiff acted upon it, that is to say, used the prices quoted in making its bid, thus putting itself in a position from which it could not withdraw without great loss. While it might have withdrawn its bid after receiving the revocation, the time had passed to submit another, and as the item of linoleum was a very trifling part of the cost of the whole building, it would have been an unreasonable hardship to expect it to lose the contract on that account, and probably forfeit its deposit. While it is true that the plaintiff might in advance have secured a contract conditional upon the success of its bid, this was not what the defendant suggested. It understood that the contractors would use its offer in their bids, and would thus in fact commit themselves to supplying the lineoleum at the proposed prices. The inevitable implication from all this was that when the contractors acted upon it, they accepted the offer and promised to pay for the linoleum, in case their bid were accepted.

It was of course possible for the parties to make such a contract, and the question is merely as to what they mean; that is, what is to be imputed to the words they used. Whatever plausibility there is in the argument, is in the fact that the defendant must have known the predicament in which the contractors would be put if it withdrew its offer after the bids went in. However, it seems entirely clear that the contractors did not suppose that they accepted the offer merely by putting in their bids. If, for example, the successful one had repudiated the contract with the public authorities after it had been awarded to him, certainly the defendant could not have sued him for a breach. If he had become bankrupt, the defendant could not prove against his estate. It seems plain therefore that there was no contract between them. And if there be any doubt as to this, the language of the offer sets it at rest. The phrase, "if successful in being awarded this contract," is scarcely met by the mere use of the prices in the bids. Surely such a use was not an "award" of the contract to the defendant. Again, the phrase, "we are offering these prices for . . . prompt acceptance after the general contract has been awarded," looks to the usual communication of an acceptance, and precludes the idea that the use of the offer in the bidding shall be the equivalent. It may indeed be argued that this last language contemplated no more than an early notice that the offer had been accepted, the actual acceptance being the bid, but that would wrench its natural meaning too far, especially in the light of the preceding phrase. The contractors had a ready escape from their difficulty by insisting upon a contract before they used the figures; and in commercial transactions it does not in the end promote justice to seek strained interpretations in aid of those who do not protect themselves.

But the plaintiff says that even though no bilateral contract was made, the defendant should be held under the doctrine of "promissory estoppel." This is to be chiefly found in those cases where persons subscribe to a venture, usually charitable, and are held to their promises after it has been completed. It has been applied much more broadly, however, and has now been generalized in section 90, of the Restatement of Contracts. We may arguendo accept it as it there reads, for it does not apply to the case at bar. Offers are ordinarily made in exchange for a consideration, either a counter-promise or some other act which the promisor wishes to secure. In such cases they propose bargains; they presuppose that each promise or performance is an inducement to the other. Wisconsin, etc., Ry. v. Powers, 191 U.S. 379, 386, 387, 24 S. Ct. 107, 48 L. Ed. 229; Banning Co. v. California, 240 U.S. 142, 152, 153, 36 S. Ct. 338, 60 L. Ed. 569. But a man may make a promise without expecting an equivalent; a donative promise, conditional or absolute. The common law provided for such by sealed instruments, and it is unfortunate that these are no longer generally available. The doctrine of "promissory estoppel" is to avoid the harsh results of allowing the promisor in such a case to repudiate, when the promisee has acted in reliance upon the promise. Siegel v. Spear & Co., 234 N.Y. 479, 138 N.E. 414, 26 A.L.R. 1205. Cf. Allegheny College v. National Bank, 246 N.Y. 369, 159 N.E. 173, 57 L.R.A. 980. But an offer for an exchange is not meant to become a promise until a consideration has been received, either a counter-promise or whatever else is stipulated. To extend it would be to hold the offeror regardless of the stipulated condition of his offer. In the case at bar the defendant offered to deliver the linoleum in exchange for the plaintiff's acceptance, not for its bid, which was a màtter of indifference to it. That offer could become a promise to deliver only when the equivalent was received; that is, when the plaintiff promised to take and pay for it. There is no room in such a situation for the doctrine of "promissory estoppel."

Nor can the offer be regarded as of an option, giving the plaintiff the right seasonably to accept the linoleum at the quoted prices if its bid was accepted, but not binding it to take and pay, if it could get a better bargain elsewhere. There is not the least reason to suppose that the defendant meant to subject itself to such a one-sided obligation. True, if so construed, the doctrine of "promissory estoppel" might apply, the plaintiff having acted in reliance upon it, though, so far as we have found, the decisions are otherwise. Ganss v. Guffey Petroleum Co., 125 A.D. 760,

110 N.Y.S. 176; Comstock v. North, 88 Miss. 754, 41 So. 374. As to that, however, we need not declare ourselves.

Judgment affirmed.

NOTE

Should the mistaken bid case be handled by manipulating the consideration doctrine? The case is noted in 28 Ill. L. Rev. 419 (1933); 20 Va. L. Rev. 214 (1933).

An interesting case study of the problems in the building industry is Schultz, The Firm Offer Puzzle: A Study of Practices in the Construction Industry, 19 U. Chi. L. Rev. 237 (1952), discussing the Indiana construction industry; for a more recent discussion of the Virginia construction industry, see Note, Another Look at Construction Building Contracts and Formation, 53 Va. L. Rev. 1270 (1967). See further, Recent Cases, 62 Harv. L. Rev. 693 (1949); Sharp, Promises, Mistake and Reciprocity, 19 U. Chi. L. Rev. 286 (1952); Keys, Consideration Reconsidered — The Problems of the Withdrawn Bid, 10 Stan. L. Rev. 441 (1958); Note, 39 N.Y.U. L. Rev. 816 (1964); 37 U. Chi. L. Rev. 798 (1968); J. Dawson, W. Harvey & S. Henderson, Cases and Comment on Contracts 352 (4th ed. 1982).

Williams v. Favret, 161 F. 822 (5th Cir. 1947), discussed in the Schultz article, involved a suit by a subcontractor (sub) against a general contractor (general). The quotation of the sub solicited by the general contained the following clause: "If our estimate used, wire us collect prior to June 6 or else same is withdrawn." General sent the following wire back: "June 6 we used your bid." After being awarded the contract, general gave the contract to another sub. Is the quotation an offer? Is the wire of June 6 an acceptance? See 1 Corbin §24, n.11 (1963).

For a discussion of the revocability of offers submitted to municipal corporations under statutory competitive bidding, see 47 Mich. L. Rev. 1220 (1949), discussing Conduit & Foundation Corporation v. Atlantic City, 2 N.J. Super. 433, 64 A.2d 382 (1949). See further, 1 Corbin §46 (1963). For the firm-bid rule in contracts with the federal government, see, e.g., Refining Associates, Inc. v. United States, 109 F.Supp. 259 (1953), noted in 66 Harv. L. Rev. 1312 (1953).

DRENNAN v. STAR PAVING CO.
51 Cal. 2d 409, 333 P.2d 757 (1958)

TRAYNOR, J. — Defendant appeals from a judgment for plaintiff in an action to recover damages caused by defendant's refusal to perform certain paving work according to a bid it submitted to plaintiff.

On July 28, 1955, plaintiff, a licensed general contractor, was preparing a bid on the "Monte Vista School Job" in the Lancaster school district. Bids had to be submitted before 8 p. m. Plaintiff testified that it was customary in that area for general contractors to receive the bids of subcontractors by telephone on the day set for bidding and to rely on them in computing their own bids. Thus on that day plaintiff's secretary, Mrs. Johnson, received by telephone between 50 and 75 subcontractors' bids for various parts of the school job. As each bid came in, she wrote it on a special form, which she brought into plaintiff's office. He then posted it on a master cost sheet setting forth the names and bids of all subcontractors. His own bid had to include the names of subcontractors who were to perform one-half of one per cent or more of the construction work, and he had also to provide a bidder's bond of 10 per cent of his total bid of $317,385 as a guarantee that he would enter the contract if awarded the work.

Later in the afternoon, Mrs. Johnson had a telephone conversation with Kenneth R. Hoon, an estimator for defendant. He gave his name and telephone number and stated that he was bidding for defendant for the paving work at the Monte Vista School according to plans and specifications and that his bid was $7,131.60. At Mrs. Johnson's request he repeated his bid. Plaintiff listened to the bid over an extension telephone in his office and posted it on the master sheet after receiving the bid form from Mrs. Johnson. Defendant's was the lowest bid for the paving. Plaintiff computed his own bid accordingly and submitted it with the name of defendant as the subcontractor for the paving. When the bids were opened on July 28th, plaintiff's proved to be the lowest, and he was awarded the contract.

On his way to Los Angeles the next morning plaintiff stopped at defendant's office. The first person he met was defendant's construction engineer, Mr. Oppenheimer. Plaintiff testified:

> I introduced myself and he immediately told me that they had made a mistake in their bid to me the night before, they couldn't do it for the price they had bid, and I told him I would expect him to carry through with their original bid because I had used it in compiling my bid and the job was being awarded them. And I would have to go and do the job according to my bid and I would expect them to do the same.

Defendant refused to do the paving work for less than $15,000. Plaintiff testified that he "got figures from other people" and after trying for several months to get as low a bid as possible engaged L & H Paving Company, a firm in Lancaster, to do the work for $10,948.60.

The trial court found on substantial evidence that defendant made a definite offer to do the paving on the Monte Vista job according to the plans and specifications for $7,131.60, and that plaintiff relied on defendant's bid in computing his own bid for the school job and naming defendant therein as the subcontractor for the paving work. Accordingly, it entered judgment for plaintiff in the amount of $3,817 (the difference between defendant's bid and the cost of the paving to plaintiff) plus costs.

Defendant contends that there was no enforceable contract between the parties on the ground that it made a revocable offer and revoked it before plaintiff communicated his acceptance to defendant.

There is no evidence that defendant offered to make its bid irrevocable in exchange for plaintiff's use of its figures in computing his bid. Nor is there evidence that would warrant interpreting plaintiff's use of defendant's bid as the acceptance thereof, binding plaintiff, on condition he received the main contract, to award the subcontract to defendant. In sum, there was neither an option supported by consideration nor a bilateral contract binding on both parties.

Plaintiff contends, however, that he relied to his detriment on defendant's offer and that defendant must therefore answer in damages for its refusal to perform. Thus the question is squarely presented: Did plaintiff's reliance make defendant's offer irrevocable?

Section 90 of the Restatement of Contracts states: "A promise which the promisor should reasonably expect to induce action or forbearance of a definite and substantial character on the part of the promisee and which does induce such action or forbearance is binding if injustice can be avoided only by enforcement of the promise." This rule applies in this state. [Citations.]

Defendant's offer constituted a promise to perform on such conditions as were stated expressly or by implication therein or annexed thereto by operation of law. (See 1 Williston, Contracts [3d ed.], §24A, p. 56, §61, p. 196.) Defendant had reason to expect that if its bid proved the lowest it would be used by plaintiff. It induced "action . . . of a definite and substantial character on the part of the promisee."

Had defendant's bid expressly stated or clearly implied that it was revocable at any time before acceptance we would treat it accordingly. It was silent on revocation, however, and we must therefore determine whether there are conditions to the right of revocation imposed by law or reasonably inferable in fact. In the analogous problem of an offer for a unilateral contract, the theory is now obsolete that the offer is revocable at any time before complete performance. Thus section 45 of the Restatement of Contracts provides:

> If an offer for a unilateral contract is made, and part of the consideration requested in the offer is given or tendered by the offeree in response thereto, the offeror is bound by contract, the duty of immediate performance of which is conditional on the full consideration being given or tendered within the time stated in the offer, or, if no time is stated therein, within a reasonable time.

In explanation, comment *b* states that the

> main offer includes as a subsidiary promise, necessarily implied, that if part
> of the requested performance is given, the offeror will not revoke his offer,
> and that if tender is made it will be accepted. Part performance or tender
> may thus furnish consideration for the subsidiary promise. Moreover,
> merely acting in justifiable reliance on an offer may in some cases serve as
> sufficient reason for making a promise binding (see §90).

Whether implied in fact or law, the subsidiary promise serves to preclude the injustice that would result if the offer could be revoked after the
offeree had acted in detrimental reliance thereon. Reasonable reliance
resulting in a foreseeable prejudicial change in position affords a compelling basis also for implying a subsidiary promise not to revoke an offer for
a bilateral contract.

The absence of consideration is not fatal to the enforcement of such a
promise. It is true that in the case of unilateral contracts the Restatement
finds consideration for the implied subsidiary promise in the part performance of the bargained-for exchange, but its reference to section 90
makes clear that consideration for such a promise is not always necessary.
The very purpose of section 90 is to make a promise binding even though
there was no consideration "in the sense of something that is bargained
for and given in exchange." (See 1 Corbin, Contracts 634 et seq.) Reasonable reliance serves to hold the offeror in lieu of the consideration ordinarily required to make the offer binding. In a case involving similar facts
the Supreme Court of South Dakota stated that

> we believe that reason and justice demand that the doctrine [of section 90]
> be applied to the present facts. We cannot believe that by accepting this
> doctrine as controlling in the state of facts before us we will abolish the
> requirement of a consideration in contract cases, in any different sense
> than an ordinary estoppel abolishes some legal requirement in its applica-
> tion. We are of the opinion, therefore, that the defendants in executing the
> agreement [which was not supported by consideration] made a promise
> which they should have reasonably expected would induce the plaintiff to
> submit a bid based thereon to the Government, that such promise did
> induce this action, and that injustice can be avoided only by enforcement
> of the promise.

(Northwestern Engineering Co. v. Ellerman, 69 S.D. 397, 408 [10
N.W.2d 879]; see also Robert Gordon, Inc. v. Ingersoll-Rand Co., 117
F.2d 654, 661; cf. James Baird Co. v. Gimbel Bros., 64 F.2d 344.)

When plaintiff used defendant's offer in computing his own bid, he
bound himself to perform in reliance on defendant's terms. Though defendant did not bargain for this use of its bid neither did defendant make
it idly, indifferent to whether it would be used or not. On the contrary it is

reasonable to suppose that defendant submitted its bid to obtain the subcontract. It was bound to realize the substantial possibility that its bid would be the lowest, and that it would be included by plaintiff in his bid. It was to its own interest that the contractor be awarded the general contract; the lower the subcontract bid, the lower the general contractor's bid was likely to be and the greater its chance of acceptance and hence the greater defendant's chance of getting the paving subcontract. Defendant had reason not only to expect plaintiff to rely on its bid but to want him to. Clearly defendant had a stake in plaintiff's reliance on its bid. Given this interest and the fact that plaintiff is bound by his own bid, it is only fair that plaintiff should have at least an opportunity to accept defendant's bid after the general contract has been awarded to him.

It bears noting that a general contractor is not free to delay acceptance after he has been awarded the general contract in the hope of getting a better price. Nor can he reopen bargaining with the subcontractor and at the same time claim a continuing right to accept the original offer. (See R. J. Daum Const. Co. v. Child, 122 Utah 194 [247 P.2d 817, 823].) In the present case plaintiff promptly informed defendant that plaintiff was being awarded the job and that subcontract was awarded to defendant.

Defendant contends, however, that its bid was the result of mistake and that it was therefore entitled to revoke it. It relies on the rescission cases of M. F. Kemper Const. Co. v. City of Los Angeles, 37 Cal. 2d 696 [235 P.2d 7], and Brunzell Const. Co. v. G. J. Weisbrod, Inc., 134 Cal. App. 2d 278 [285 P.2d 989]. (See also Lemoge Electric v. San Mateo County, 46 Cal. 2d 659, 662 [297 P.2d 638].) In those cases, however, the bidder's mistake was known or should have been to the offeree, and the offeree could be placed in status quo. Of course, if plaintiff had reason to believe that defendant's bid was in error, he could not justifiably rely on it, and section 90 would afford no basis for enforcing it. (Robert Gordon, Inc. v. Ingersoll-Rand Co., 117 F.2d 654, 660.) Plaintiff, however, had no reason to know that defendant had made a mistake in submitting its bid, since there was usually a variance of 160 per cent between the highest and lowest bids for paving in the desert around Lancaster. He committed himself to performing the main contract in reliance on defendant's figures. Under these circumstances defendant's mistake, far from relieving it of its obligation, constitutes an additional reason for enforcing it, for it misled plaintiff as to the cost of doing the paving. Even had it been clearly understood that defendant's offer was revocable until accepted, it would not necessarily follow that defendant had no duty to exercise reasonable care in preparing its bid. It presented its bid with knowledge of the substantial possibility that it would be used by plaintiff; it could foresee the harm that would ensue from an erroneous underestimate of the cost. Moreover, it was motivated by its own business interest. Whether or not these considerations alone would justify recovery for negligence had the case been tried on that theory (see Biakanja v. Irving, 49 Cal. 2d 647, 650

[320 P.2d 16]), they are persuasive that defendant's mistake should not defeat recovery under the rule of section 90 of the Restatement of Contracts.

As between the subcontractor who made the bid and the general contractor who reasonably relied on it, the loss resulting from the mistake should fall on the party who caused it.

Leo F. Piazza Paving Co. v. Bebek & Brkich, 141 Cal. App. 2d 226 [296 P.2d 368], and Bard v. Kent, 19 Cal. 2d 499 [122 P.2d 8, 139], are not to the contrary. In the *Piazza* case the court sustained a finding that defendants intended, not to make a firm bid, but only to give the plaintiff "some kind of an idea to use" in making its bid; there was evidence that the defendants had told plaintiff they were unsure of the significance of the specifications. There was thus no offer, promise, or representation on which the defendants should reasonably have expected the plaintiff to rely. The *Bard* case held that an option not supported by consideration was revoked by the death of the optioner. The issue of recovery under the rule of section 90 was not pleaded at the trial, and it does not appear that the offeree's reliance was "of a definite and substantial character" so that injustice could be avoided "only by the enforcement of the promise."

There is no merit in defendant's contention that plaintiff failed to state a cause of action, on the ground that the complaint failed to allege that plaintiff attempted to mitigate the damages or that they could not have been mitigated. Plaintiff alleged that after defendant's default, "plaintiff had to procure the services of the L & H Co. to perform said asphaltic paving for the sum of $10,948.60." Plaintiff's uncontradicted evidence showed that he spent several months trying to get bids from other subcontractors and that he took the lowest bid. Clearly he acted reasonably to mitigate damages. In any event any uncertainty in plaintiff's allegation as to damages could have been raised by special demurrer. (Code Civ. Proc., §430, subd. 9.) It was not so raised and was therefore waived. (Code Civ. Proc., §434.)

The judgment is affirmed.

LORANGER CONSTRUCTION CORP.
v. E. F. HAUSERMAN CO.
376 Mass. 757, 384 N.E.2d 176 (1978)

BRAUCHER, Justice.

The plaintiff, a contractor, was preparing its bid for construction at the Cape Cod Community College. It received an "estimate" of $15,900 for movable steel partitions from the defendant, and used the estimate in preparing the bid it submitted. The construction contract was awarded to the plaintiff, the defendant refused to perform in accordance with its estimate, and the plaintiff engaged another company to supply and install the partitions for $23,000. The Appeals Court upheld an award of damages to the plaintiff, we allowed the defendant's petition for further appellate review, and we affirm the judgment for the plaintiff.

The action was filed in 1970. Demurrers to the declaration and to an amended declaration were sustained, and leave to file a second amended declaration was then denied, the judge "being of opinion there is no cause of action." The Appeals Court held that count 1 of the amended declaration did set out a cause of action, and reversed the order denying leave to amend. 1 Mass. App. 801, 294 N.E.2d 453 (1973). Thereafter the plaintiff filed an amended declaration containing four counts, the case was tried to a jury in October, 1974, and a verdict was returned for the plaintiff in the amount of $7,100. The Appeals Court held that the plaintiff was "foreclosed from recovery on any traditional contract theory," but could "recover on the theory of promissory estoppel, a basis for recovery not previously explicitly accepted in the courts of this Commonwealth." 6 Mass. App. 152, 154, 374 N.E.2d 306, 308 (1978). The defendant argues that "the adoption of this new theory of law is procedurally unfair, unwarranted by the facts in the case, and contrary to the statutory policy of the Commonwealth."

We summarize the evidence most favorable to the plaintiff. On May 20, 1968, the plaintiff was preparing its bid to become general contractor on the construction project. The specifications called for movable metal partitions from the defendant or one of two other suppliers, "or equal." About fifteen days earlier, a sales engineer employed by the defendant had prepared a "quotation" or "estimate" of $15,900 for supplying and installing the partitions. The figure was based on information received from the architect's office, and the engineer knew that the general contractor would submit a bid based on such estimates from subcontractors. The estimate was given to the plaintiff by telephone on May 20, 1968; it was also given to other general contractors. The engineer waited until shortly before bids were due on the general contract to prevent the general contractor from shopping for a lower price from other subcontractors. The plaintiff received no other quotations on the partitions, and used the defendant's quotation in preparing the bid on the general contract, submitted the same day.

The general contract was awarded to the plaintiff on June 21 or 26, 1968. Some time in August or September, the plaintiff informed the defendant that it was getting ready to award the partition contract and asked whether it had the defendant's lowest price. Thereafter, on September 12, 1968, the plaintiff sent the defendant an unsigned subcontract form based on the $15,900 figure. The defendant rejected the subcontract, and the plaintiff engaged another company to supply and install the partitions for $23,000. The partition work was not scheduled to begin until the summer of 1969; in fact, work began in the summer of 1970, and the last payment for it was made in 1972.

At the close of the plaintiff's evidence, it waived counts 2, 3 and 4 of the declaration. The defendant rested and moved for a directed verdict. The motion was denied. After verdict, the defendant moved for judgment notwithstanding the verdict, and that motion was denied. The questions argued to us relate to the question whether the evidence made a case for the jury.

1. *The offer or promise.* The defendant argues that the "quotation" or "estimate" made by its sales engineer was not an offer or promise, but merely an invitation to further negotiations, citing Cannavino & Shea, Inc. v. Water Works Supply Corp., 361 Mass. 363, 366, 280 N.E.2d 147 (1972). But the *Cannavino* case involved the circulation of a price list without specification of quantity. Here there was more; the defendant was to do a portion of the work called for by the plans and specifications. Of course, it was possible for the sales engineer to invite negotiations or offers. See Kuzmeskus v. Pickup Motor Co., 330 Mass. 490, 492-494, 115 N.E.2d 461 (1953). But it was also possible for him to make a commitment. His employer stated in answer to interrogatories that it was "unable to determine whether or not an employee of the defendant spoke with any of the plaintiff's employees on or about May 20, 1968," and the only direct evidence of the estimate was the testimony of the engineer. We think the jury were warranted in resolving ambiguities in his testimony against the defendant, and in finding that the estimate, in the circumstances, was an offer or promise. See Jaybe Constr. Co. v. Beco, Inc., 3 Conn. Cir. Ct. 406, 410-411, 216 A.2d 208 (1965).

2. *Reliance on the promise.* It seems clear enough, as the Appeals Court held, that the evidence made a case for the jury on the basis of the plaintiff's reliance on the defendant's promise. "An offer which the offeror should reasonably expect to induce action or forebearance of a substantial character on the part of the offeree before acceptance and which does induce such action or forebearance is binding as an option contract to the extent necessary to avoid injustice." Restatement (Second) of Contracts §89B(2) and Illustration 6 (Tent. Drafts Nos. 1-7, 1973). This doctrine is not so novel as the defendant contends. In addition to the authorities cited by the Appeals Court, see Cannavino & Shea, Inc. v. Water Works Supply Corp., 361 Mass. 363, 365-366, 280 N.E.2d 147 (1972); Crane Co. v. Park Constr. Co., 356 Mass. 13, 17, 247 N.E.2d 591 (1969). When a promise is enforceable in whole or in part by virtue of reliance, it is a "contract," and it is enforceable pursuant to a "traditional contract theory" antedating the modern doctrine of consideration. See Sullivan v. O'Connor, 363 Mass. 579, 588 n.6, 296 N.E.2d 183 (1973); Restatement (Second) of Contracts §90, Comment *a* (Tent. Drafts Nos. 1-7, 1973). We do not use the expression "promissory estoppel," since it tends to confusion rather than clarity.

3. *Procedural unfairness.* The defendant contends that the decision of the Appeals Court, resting on "the new theory of promissory estoppel,"

departed from the pleadings and from the theory on which the case was
tried. So far as the pleadings are concerned, count 1 of the declaration
alleged an exchange of promise for promise and also the submission of a
bid by the plaintiff in reliance on the agreement between the parties. If
either allegation was sustained by proof, the other could be treated as
surplusage. The pleadings could have been amended to conform to the
evidence, even after judgment; failure so to amend does not affect the
result of the trial. Mass. R. Civ. P. 15(b), 365 Mass. 761 (1974). Janke
Constr. Co. v. Vulcan Materials Co., 527 F.2d 772, 776 (7th Cir. 1976).
Schafer v. Fraser, 206 Or. 446, 481, 290 P.2d 190 (1955). See Babler v.
Roelli, 39 Wis. 2d 566, 572-573, 159 N.W.2d 694 (1968). The record does
not disclose any authorization by the judge for the pleadings to go to the
jury. See Rule 7 of the Superior Court (1974).

In view of the defendant's claim of procedural unfairness, we requested and received a transcript of the judge's charge to the jury. The
defendant does not assert any error with respect to the charge, and did
not include the charge in its record appendix. We do not treat the charge
as the "law of the case." See Commonwealth v. Krasner, 360 Mass. 848,
849, 274 N.E.2d 347 (1971), and cases cited. But we find that the case was
presented to the jury on the basis of offer, acceptance and consideration;
there was no reference in the charge to reliance on a promise. We therefore cannot attribute to the jury a finding that the offer or promise of the
defendant induced action "of a substantial character" on the part of the
plaintiff. We consider the case on the basis on which it was submitted to
the jury. See Dalton v. Post Publishing Co., 328 Mass. 595, 598-599, 105
N.E.2d 385 (1952).

Pursuant to the charge and on the evidence before them, the jury
might have found that the defendant's offer was accepted in any one of
three ways. First, there might have been an exchange of promises in the
plaintiff's telephone conversation with the defendant's engineer, before
the plaintiff's bid was submitted. Second, the offer might have been
accepted by the doing of an act, using the defendant's estimate in submitting the plaintiff's bid. Acceptance in this way might be complete without
notification to the offeror. Bishop v. Eaton, 161 Mass. 496, 499, 37 N.E.
665 (1894). See Restatement (Second) of Contracts §56(1), (2)(c) (Tent.
Drafts Nos. 1-7, 1973). Finally, the offer might have remained outstanding, unrevoked, until September, 1968, or it might have been renewed or
extended when the plaintiff asked whether it had the defendant's lowest
price; in either case it might have been accepted when the plaintiff sent
the defendant a subcontract form on September 12. The evidence warranted the jury in finding that the defendant invited acceptance in any
one of the three modes, and in finding that the plaintiff's promise or act
furnished consideration to make the defendant's promise binding.

"In the typical bargain, the consideration and the promise bear a reciprocal relation of motive or inducement: the consideration induces the
making of the promise and the promise induces the furnishing of the

consideration." Restatement (Second) of Contracts §75, Comment *b* (Tent. Drafts Nos. 1-7, 1973). In the present case, the jury could infer that the defendant's engineer intended to induce the plaintiff's promise or action in the hope that the defendant would benefit, and thus that his offer or promise was induced by the hoped-for acceptance. Even more clearly, the jury could find that the plaintiff's promise or action was induced by the defendant's offer or promise. Such findings would warrant the conclusion that there was a "typical bargain," supported by consideration. See Air Conditioning Co. of Hawaii v. Richards Constr. Co., 200 F. Supp. 167, 170-171 (D. Haw. 1961), *aff'd on other grounds*, 318 F.2d 410, 412-413 (9th Cir. 1963). Indeed, review of the cases suggests that many decisions based on reliance might have been based on bargain. See Henderson, Promissory Estoppel and Traditional Contract Doctrine, 78 Yale L.J. 343, 368-371 (1969). Once consideration and bargain are found, there is no need to apply §90 of the Restatement, dealing with the legal effect of reliance in the absence of consideration.

4. *Statutory policy.* The defendant did not argue any question of statutory policy to the Appeals Court. It argues to us that the decision of the Appeals Court is contrary to the policy of G.L. c. 149, §§44A-44L, regulating bidding on contracts for the construction of public works. The argument seems to relate primarily to subcontract bids described in §44C. Such bids must be listed in the general contractor's bid under §44F, and must be filed with the awarding authority under §44H. The defendant was not in any of the trades to which those provisions apply. In any event, the argument relates only to the reliance doctrine on which the Appeals Court based its decision. We decide on a different basis.

5. *Other issues.* Several other matters argued by the defendant to the Appeals Court are discussed in the opinion of that court: unreasonable delay by the plaintiff in notifying the defendant that it was to be the subcontractor, "bid shopping" by the plaintiff, and application of the statute of frauds, G.L. c. 106, §2-201, and c. 259, §1, Fifth. The defendant has not emphasized these matters in its argument to us. The Appeals Court held that they did not bar recovery based on reliance, and they have no more force to bar recovery based on bargain plus reliance. We therefore do not consider them.

Judgment of the Superior Court Department affirmed.

SOUTHERN CALIFORNIA ACOUSTICS CO. v. C. V. HOLDER, INC.

79 Cal. Rptr. 319 (Sup. Ct. In Bank, 1969)

Traynor, Chief Justice. Plaintiff appeals from a judgment of dismissal entered after a demurrer to its second amended complaint was sustained without leave to amend.

Plaintiff alleged that it is a licensed specialty subcontractor. On November 24, 1965, it submitted by telephone to defendant C. V. Holder, Inc., a general contractor, a subcontract bid in the amount of $83,400 for the furnishing and installation of acoustical tile on a public construction job. Later that day Holder submitted a bid for the prime contract to codefendant Los Angeles Unified School District. As required by law, Holder listed the subcontractors who would perform work on the project of a value in excess of one-half of one percent of the total bid. [Cal. Gov't Code §4104.] Holder listed plaintiff as the acoustical tile subcontractor. Holder was subsequently awarded the prime contract for construction of the facility and executed a written contract with the school district on December 9, 1965. A local trade newspaper widely circulated among subcontractors reported that Holder had been awarded the contract and included in its report the names of the subcontractors listed in Holder's bid. Plaintiff read the report and, acting on the assumption that its bid had been accepted, refrained from bidding on other construction jobs in order to remain within its bonding limits.

Sometime between December 27, 1965, and January 10, 1966, Holder requested permission from the school district to substitute another subcontractor for plaintiff, apparently on the ground that plaintiff had been inadvertently listed in the bid in place of the intended subcontractor. The school district consented, and the substitution was made. Plaintiff then sought a writ of mandamus to compel the school district to rescind its consent to the change in subcontractors. The trial court sustained the district's demurrer and thereafter dismissed the proceeding. Plaintiff did not appeal. Plaintiff then brought this action for damages against Holder and the school district.

Plaintiff contends that the trial court erred in sustaining the demurrer on the ground that the facts alleged in its complaint would support recovery of damages for breach of contract, breach of a statutory duty, and for negligence. We conclude that plaintiff has stated a cause of action for breach of a statutory duty.

There was no contract between plaintiff and Holder, for Holder did not accept plaintiff's offer. Silence in the face of an offer is not an acceptance, unless there is a relationship between the parties or a previous course of dealing pursuant to which silence would be understood as acceptance. (See Wood v. League of the Cross (1931) 114 Cal. App. 474, 479-481, 300 P. 57; Wood v. Gunther (1949) 89 Cal. App. 2d 718, 730-731, 201 P.2d 874; 1 Williston on Contracts (3d ed.) 1957 §§91-91A; 1 Witkin, Summary of Cal. Law (7th ed. 1960) Contracts, §60, pp. 65-67.) No such relationship or course of dealing is alleged. Nor did Holder accept the bid by using it in presenting its own bid. In the absence of an agreement to the contrary, listing of the subcontractor in the prime bid is not an implied acceptance of the subcontractor's bid by the general contractor. (Klose v. Sequoia Union High School Dist. (1953) 118 Cal. App. 2d 636,

641, 258 P.2d 515; Norcross v. Winters (1962) 209 Cal. App. 2d 207, 217, 25 Cal. Rptr. 821. See Williams v. Favret, 5 Cir. (1947) 161 F.2d 822; 1 Corbin on Contracts (1963) §24 and fn. 11 at pp. 72-73). The listing by the general contractor of the subcontractors he intends to retain is in response to statutory command (Gov. Code, §4104) and cannot reasonably be construed as an expression of acceptance. (Cf. Western Concrete Structures Co. v. James I. Barnes Constr. Co. (1962) 206 Cal. App. 2d, 1, 13, 23 Cal. Rptr. 506; Klose v. Sequoia Union High School Dist., *supra*, 118 Cal. App. 2d 636, 641, 258 P.2d 515.)

Plaintiff contends, however, that its reliance on Holder's use of its bid and Holder's failure to reject its offer promptly after Holder's bid was accepted constitute acceptance of plaintiff's bid by operation of law under the doctrine of promissory estoppel. Section 90 of the Restatement of Contracts states: "A promise which the promisor should reasonably expect to induce action or forbearance of a definite and substantial character on the part of the promisee and which does induce such action or forbearance is binding if injustice can be avoided only by enforcement of the promise." The rule applies in this state. (Drennan v. Star Paving Co. (1958) 51 Cal. 2d 409, 413, 333 P.2d 757). Before it can be invoked, however, there must be a promise that was relied upon. (Bard v. Kent (1942) 19 Cal. 2d 449, 453, 122 P.2d 8, 139 A.L.R. 1032; Hilltop Properties v. State of California (1965) 233 Cal. App. 2d 349, 364, 43 Cal. Rptr. 605; 1A Corbin on Contracts (1963) §200, p. 218).

In *Drennan*, we held that implicit in the subcontractor's bid was a subsidiary promise to keep his bid open for a reasonable time after award of the prime contract to give the general contractor an opportunity to accept the offer on which he relied in computing the prime bid. The subsidiary promise was implied "to preclude the injustice that would result if the offer could be revoked after the offeree had acted in detrimental reliance thereon." (51 Cal. 2d at p. 414, 333 P.2d at p. 760.)

Plaintiff urges us to find an analogous subsidiary promise not to reject its bid in this case, but it fails to allege facts showing the existence of any promise by Holder to it upon which it detrimentally relied. Plaintiff did not rely on any promise by Holder, but only on the listing of subcontractors required by section 4104 of the Government Code and on the statutory restriction on Holder's right to change its listed subcontractors without the consent of the school district. (Gov. Code, §4107.) Holder neither accepted plaintiff's offer, nor made any promise or offer to plaintiff intended to "induce action or forbearance of a definite and substantial character. . . ."

Plaintiff contends, however, that the Subletting and Subcontracting Fair Practices Act confers rights on listed subcontractors that arise when the prime contract is awarded and that these rights may be enforced by an action for damages. Before that act was adopted in 1963, it was settled that the Government Code sections governing subcontracting, which the

338 3. The Bargain

act superseded, conferred no rights on subcontractors. (Klose v. Sequoia Union High School Dist., *supra*, 118 Cal. App. 2d 636, 641, 258 P.2d 515.) *Klose* was a proceeding in mandate brought by a taxpayer against the awarding authority to compel the latter to assess a penalty against a prime contractor. The prime contractor had changed subcontractors with the consent of the awarding authority on the ground that the original listing had been the result of error. The plaintiff contended that under the language of then Government Code section 4104, subdivision (d) an awarding authority had no legal power to consent to the change on the ground stated and that the substitution was therefore in violation of the statute. Such a violation would render the prime contractor liable for penalties provided for by then section 4106. (Now §4110.)

The court denied relief on the ground that the language of subdivision (d) of section 4104 that authorized the substitution of another for a subcontractor who failed to execute a written contract did not limit the awarding authority's discretion to consent to the substitution of subcontractors in other situations. In so concluding the court listed a series of situations in which substitutions not provided for by subdivision (d) would be necessary to the efficient execution of a public project. The court also concluded that the purpose of the listing and substitution sections was not to grant rights to listed subcontractors, but to provide an opportunity to the awarding authority to investigate and approve the initial subcontractors and any proposed substitutions.

The amendments made by the 1963 Subletting and Subcontracting Fair Practices Act stated the purposes of the statute in a preamble (§4101) and completely revised the section dealing with substitution of subcontractors, renumbering it section 4107. The purpose of the amended statute is not limited, as *Klose* had concluded with respect to the prior statute, to providing the awarding authority with an opportunity to approve substitute subcontractors. Its purpose is also to protect the public and subcontractors from the evils attendant upon the practices of bid shopping and bid peddling subsequent to the award of the prime contract for a public facility.[118] Thus section 4107 now clearly limits the right of

118. Bid shopping is the use of the low bid already received by the general contractor to pressure other subcontractors into submitting even lower bids. Bid peddling, conversely, is an attempt by a subcontractor to undercut known bids already submitted to the general contractor in order to procure the job. (See Schueller, Bid Depositories (1960) 58 Mich. L. Rev. 497, 498, fn. 6; Note (1967) 53 Va. L. Rev, 1720, 1724.) The statute is designed to prevent only bid shopping and peddling that takes place after the award of the prime contract. The underlying reasons are clear. Subsequent to the award of the prime contract at a set price, the prime contractor may seek to drive down his own cost, and concomitantly increase his profit, by soliciting bids lower than those used in computing his prime bid. When successful this practice places a profit squeeze on subcontractors, impairing their incentive and ability to perform to their best, and possibly precipitating bankruptcy in a weak subcontracting firm. (See Gov. Code, §4101; Note, *supra*, 53 Va. L. Rev. 1720, 1724; Ring Constr. Corp. (1947) 8 T.C. 1070, 1076.) Bid peddling and shopping prior to the award of the prime contract foster the same evils, but at least have the effect of passing the reduced costs on to the public in the form of lower prime contract bids.

the prime contractor to make substitutions and the discretion of the awarding authority to consent to substitutions to those situations listed in subdivision (a), all of which are keyed to the unwillingness or inability of the listed subcontractor properly to perform.[119] Unless a listed subcontractor "becomes insolvent or fails or refuses to perform a written contract for the work or fails or refuses to meet the bond requirements of the prime contractor," the prime contractor may not substitute another subcontractor for the listed subcontractor and the awarding authority may not consent to such a substitution until the contract is presented to the listed subcontractor and he, after having had a reasonable opportunity to do so, fails or refuses to execute the written contract. Accordingly, under the facts as pleaded in this case, Holder had no right to substitute another subcontractor in place of plaintiff, and the school district had no right to consent to that substitution.

Since the purpose of the statute is to protect both the public and subcontractors from the evils of the proscribed unfair bid peddling and bid shopping (Gov. Code, §§4100, 4101), we hold that it confers the right on the listed subcontractor to perform the subcontract unless statutory grounds for a valid substitution exist. Moreover, that right may be enforced by an action for damages against the prime contractor to recover the benefit of the bargain the listed subcontractor would have realized had he not wrongfully been deprived of the subcontract. (See Bermite Power Co. v. Franchise Tax Board (1952) 38 Cal. 2d 700, 703, 242 P.2d 9; Paxton v. Paxton (1907) 150 Cal. 667, 670, 89 P. 1083; Civ. Code, §3523.) Accordingly, plaintiff has stated a cause of action against defendant Holder for breach of section 4107.

The question remains whether plaintiff has stated a cause of action against the school district. Since there is no statutory provision for the recovery of damages against a public entity for its consenting to a substitution of subcontractors in violation of section 4107, the school district is not liable for such violation. (Gov. Code, §815.) Plaintiff contends, however, that it was a third-party beneficiary of the contract between Holder and the school district and that therefore it may recover against the school district for breach of contract. (See Gov. Code, §814.) There is no merit in this contention. Plaintiff was listed in response to statutory command and not because the contracting parties' purpose was expressly to benefit it. Accordingly, plaintiff was at most an incidental beneficiary and therefore cannot recover as a third-party beneficiary of the contract between Holder and the school district. (Civ Code, §1559; West v. Guy F. Atkinson Constr. Co. (1967) 251 Cal. App. 2d 296, 302, 59 Cal. Rptr. 286;

---

119. It is significant that the amended statute allows for substitution of subcontractors in all those situations listed by the court in *Klose* as necessary to efficient construction of public facilities. . . . Accordingly, there is no basis for construing the present statute, as the court in *Klose* felt compelled to construe subdivision (a) of former section 4104, to confer "plenary power of substitution on the awarding authority." (118 Cal. App. at p. 639, 258 P.2d at p. 517.)

Southern California Gas Co. v. ABC Construction Co. (1962) 204 Cal.
App. 2d 747, 751-752, 22 Cal. Rptr. 540.)

The judgment of dismissal as to defendant school district is affirmed.
The judgment of dismissal as to defendant Holder is reversed with directions to the trial court to overrule the demurrer as to defendant Holder
and allow it to answer.

McCombs, Peters, Tobriner, Mosk, Burke and Sullivan, JJ., concur.

NOTE

1. The *Robert Gordon* case mentioned in Drennan v. Star Paving Co.
has found an excellent discussion in 9 U. Chi. L. Rev. 153 (1941). See also
20 Texas L. Rev. 478 (1942). For a further amendment of the provision of
the Government Code see §§4107, 4110, 41075.

2. The role of bid depositories is described in Oakland-Alameda
County Builders' Exchange v. F. P. Lathrop Constr. Co., 4 Cal. 3d 354,
482 P.2d 226, 93 Cal. Rptr. 602 (1971).

> Bid depositories are creations of the construction industry, generally
> established by construction trades subcontractors to control the process of
> submitting subbids to general contractors who are bidding on large con-
> struction jobs. The operation of a typical bid depository is succinctly de-
> scribed by a commentator as follows:
>
>> A "locked box" procedure is the most common method of depository opera-
>> tion. Subcontractors wishing to bid to one or more general contractors on a
>> certain job submit bids in sealed envelopes to the depository. An envelope
>> containing a bid addressed to each general contractor to whom the subcon-
>> tractor wishes to bid is placed in the "locked box," and another envelope
>> containing a copy of that bid is addressed to the depository itself and similarly
>> deposited in the box or another secure receptacle. There will be a cut-off
>> point, typically 4 hours or so before the prime bid opening time (*i.e.*, the time
>> by which all bids must be submitted to the owner or awarding authority), and
>> after that cut-off point (or depository closing time) is reached, no more bids
>> may be received, and none received may be amended or withdrawn.
>>
>> Promptly at the depository closing time, the locked box is opened, and the
>> envelopes contained therein are dispensed to the general contractors to whom
>> addressed. Each general contractor then prepares his own bid to the owner or
>> awarding authority based upon subbids received and his estimates of his own
>> work costs.
>
> (Orrick, Trade Associations Are Boycott-Prone — Bid Depositories As A
> Case Study (1968) 19 Hastings L.J. 505, 520.)
>
> The "locked box" operation is said to serve several salutary purposes. It
> permits orderly preparation of bids and estimates by providing a reasonable
> time for computations, and thereby reduces error. Also, it tends to prevent
> "bid piracy" which occurs when one subcontractor is able to avoid the
> expense of preparing his own bid by using the bid submitted by another
> subcontractor as a starting vehicle. Most importantly, it inhibits practices

known variously as "bid shopping," "bid peddling," and "bid chiseling." These pejorative expressions appear to be used interchangeably to describe (1) the practice of a general contractor who, before the award of the prime contract, discloses to interested subcontractors the current low subbids on certain subcontracts in an effort to obtain lower subbids, (2) the identical practice of a general contractor engaged in after he has been awarded the prime contract, and (3) the practice of a subcontractor who determines the currently low subbid on a subcontract and then submits a lower bid to the general contractor in return for assurance from the general that the sub will receive the subcontract if the general is the successful prime bidder. (Id. at pp. 520-521; Schueller, Bid Depositories (1960) 58 Mich. L. Rev. 497, 498 and fn. 6, 499-500.)[120]

Id. at 356-357, 482 P.2d at 227, 93 Cal. Rptr. at 603 (1971).

3. For the relationship of subcontractors to general contractors see J. Sweet, Legal Aspects of Architecture, Engineering, and the Construction Process §32.01 et seq. (3d ed. 1985).

4. For the use of standardized terms in the construction industry see, in general, Johnstone & Hopson, Lawyers and Their Work 335, 340 (1967); Sweet, *supra* Note 3, at ch. 18. In the field of federal procurement contracts, see the Federal Procurement Regulations and the Armed Services Procurement Regulations (ASPR).

ELSINORE UNION ELEMENTARY SCHOOL DISTRICT v. KASTORFF

54 Cal 2d. 380, 353 P.2d 713, 6 Cal. Rptr. 1 (1960)

SCHAUER, J. — Defendants who are a building contractor and his surety, appeal from an adverse judgment in this action by plaintiff school district to recover damages allegedly resulting when defendant Kastorff, the contractor, refused to execute a building contract pursuant to his previously submitted bid to make certain additions to plaintiff's school buildings. We have concluded that because of an honest clerical error in the bid and defendant's subsequent prompt rescission he was not obliged to execute the contract, and that the judgment should therefore be reversed.

Pursuant to plaintiff's call for bids, defendant Kastorff secured a copy of the plans and specifications of the proposed additions to plaintiff's

120. Some authorities draw precise distinctions among the several expressions. "Bid chiseling" is limited to the practice of a general contractor who solicits lower subbids after he has been awarded the prime contract. "Bid shopping" is used to refer to such solicitation by general contractors before the award of the prime contract. And "bid peddling" applies to the conduct of a subcontractor. (See People v. Inland Bid Depository (1965) 233 Cal. App. 2d 851, 863-864, 44 Cal. Rptr. 206; Comment (1970) 18 U.C.L.A. L. Rev. 389, 394.)

school buildings and proceeded to prepare a bid to be submitted by the deadline hour of 8 p. m., August 12, 1952, at Elsinore, California. Kastorff testified that in preparing his bid he employed work sheets upon which he entered bids of various subcontractors for such portions of the work as they were to do, and that to reach the final total of his own bid for the work he carried into the right hand column of the work sheets the amounts of the respective sub bids which he intended to accept and then added those amounts to the cost of the work which he would do himself rather than through a subcontractor; that there is "a custom among subcontractors, in bidding on jobs such as this, to delay giving . . . their bids until the very last moment"; that the first sub bid for plumbing was in the amount of $9,285 and he had received it "the afternoon of the bid opening," but later that afternoon when "the time was drawing close for me to get my bids together and get over to Elsinore" (from his home in San Juan Capistrano) he received a $6,500 bid for the plumbing. Erroneously thinking he had entered the $9,285 plumbing bid in his total column and had included that sum in his total bid and realizing that the second plumbing bid was nearly $3,000 less than the first, Kastorff then deducted $3,000 from the total amount of his bid and entered the resulting total of $89,994 on the bid form as his bid for the school construction. Thus the total included no allowance whatsoever for the plumbing work.

Kastorff then proceeded to Elsinore and deposited his bid with plaintiff. When the bids were opened shortly after 8 p. m. that evening, it was discovered that of the five bids submitted that of Kastorff was some $11,306 less than the next lowest bid. The school superintendent and the four school board members present thereupon asked Kastorff whether he was sure his figures were correct, Kastorff stepped out into the hall to check with the person who had assisted in doing the clerical work on the bid, and a few minutes later returned and stated that the figures were correct. He testified that he did not have his work sheets or other papers with him to check against at the time. The board thereupon, on August 12, 1952, voted to award Kastorff the contract.

The next morning Kastorff checked his work sheets and promptly discovered his error. He immediately drove to the Los Angeles office of the firm of architects which had prepared the plans and specifications for plaintiff, and there saw Mr. Rendon. Mr. Rendon testified that Kastorff

> had his maps and estimate work-sheets of the project, and indicated to me that he had failed to carry across the amount of dollars for the plumbing work. It was on the sheet, but not in the total sheet. We examined that evidence, and in our opinion we felt that he had made a clerical error in compiling his bill. . . . In other words, he had put down a figure, but didn't carry it out to the "total" column when he totaled his column to make up his bid. . . . He exhibited . . . at that time . . . his work-sheets from which he had made up his bid.

That same morning (August 13) Rendon telephoned the school superintendent and informed him of the error and of its nature and that Kastorff asked to be released from his bid. On August 14 Kastorff wrote a letter to the school board explaining his error and again requesting that he be permitted to withdraw his bid. On August 15, after receiving Kastorff's letter, the board held a special meeting and voted not to grant his request. Thereafter, on August 28, *written notification* was given to Kastorff of award of the contract to him.[121] Subsequently plaintiff submitted to Kastorff a contract to be signed in accordance with his bid, and on September 8, 1952, Kastorff returned the contract to plaintiff with a letter again explaining his error and asked the board to reconsider his request for withdrawal of his bid.

Plaintiff thereafter received additional bids to do the subject construction; let the contract to the lowest bidder, in the amount of $102,900; and brought this action seeking to recover from Kastorff the $12,906 difference between that amount and the amount Kastorff had bid.[122] Recovery of $4,499.60 is also sought against Kastorff's surety under the terms of the bond posted with his bid.

Defendants in their answer to the complaint pleaded, among other things, that Kastorff had made an honest error in compiling his bid; that "he thought he was bidding, and intended to bid, $9500.00 more, making a total of $99,494.00 as his bid"; that upon discovering his error he had promptly notified plaintiff and rescinded the $89,994 bid. The trial court found that it was true that Kastorff made up a bid sheet, which was introduced in evidence; that the subcontractor's bids thereupon indicated were those received by Kastorff; that he "had 16 subcontracting bids to ascertain from 31 which were submitted"; and that Kastorff had neglected to carry over from the left hand column on the bid sheet to the right hand column on the sheet a portion of the plumbing (and heating) subcontractor's bid. Despite the uncontradicted evidence related hereinabove, including that of plaintiff's architect and of its school superintendent, both of whom testified as plaintiff's witnesses, the court further found, however, that

> it is not true that the right hand column of figures was totaled for the purpose of arriving at the total bid to be submitted by E. J. Kastorff. . . . It cannot be ascertained from the evidence for what purpose the total of the right hand column of figures on the bid sheet was used nor can it be

121. On the bid form, provided by plaintiff, the bidder agreed "that if he is notified of the acceptance of the proposal within forty-five (45) days from the time set for the opening of bids, he will execute and deliver to you within five (5) days after having received *written notification* a contract as called for in the 'Notice to Contractors.'" (Italics added.)

122. Plaintiff's original published call for bids contained the following statement: "No Bidder may withdraw his bid for a period of forty-five (45) days after the date set for the opening thereof." Whether upon Kastorff's rescission for good cause prior to expiration of the 45 day period plaintiff could have accepted the next lowest bid is not an issue before us.

ascertained from the evidence for what purpose the three bid sheets were
used in arriving at the total bid.

And although finding that "on or about August 15, 1952," plaintiff received Kastorff's letter of August 14 explaining that he "made an error of
omitting from my bid the item of Plumbing," the court also found that

> It is not true that plaintiff knew at any time that defendant Kastorff's bid
> was intended to be other than $89,994.00. . . . It is not true that the
> plaintiff knew at the time it requested the execution of the contract by
> defendant Kastorff that he had withdrawn his bid because of an honest
> error in the compilation thereof. It is not true that plaintiff had notice of an
> error in the compilation of the bid by defendant Kastorff and tried never-
> theless to take advantage of defendant Kastorff by forcing him to enter a
> contract on the basis of a bid he had withdrawn. . . . It is not true that it
> would be either inequitable or unjust to require defendant Kastorff to per-
> form the contract awarded to him for the sum of $89,994.00, and it is not
> true that he actually intended to bid for said work the sum of $99,494.00.[123]

Judgment was given for plaintiff in the amounts sought, and this appeal
by defendants followed.

In reliance upon M. F. Kemper Const. Co. v. City of Los Angeles
(1951), 37 Cal. 2d 696 [235 P.2d 7], and Lemoge Electric v. County of San
Mateo (1956), 46 Cal. 2d 659, 662, 664 [1a, 1b, 2, 3] [297 P.2d 638],
defendants urge that where, as defendants claim is the situation here, a
contractor makes a clerical error in computing a bid on a public work he
is entitled to rescind.

In the *Kemper* case one item on a work sheet in the amount of
$301,769 was inadvertently omitted by the contractor from the final tabu-
lation sheet and was overlooked in computing the total amount of a bid to
do certain construction work for the defendant city. The error was caused
by the fact that the men preparing the bid were exhausted after working
long hours under pressure. When the bids were opened it was found that
plaintiff's bid was $780,305, and the next lowest bid was $1,049,592. Plaintiff discovered its error several hours later and immediately notified a
member of defendant's board of public works of its mistake in omitting
one item while preparing the final accumulation of figures for its bid. Two
days later it explained its mistake to the board and withdrew its bid. A few
days later it submitted to the board evidence which showed the uninten-

---

123. Other findings are that Kastorff

in the company of his wife and another couple left San Juan Capistrano for Elsinore
. . . at 6:00 P.M. on August 12, 1952, a distance of 34 miles by way of California State
Highway . . . Kastorff had ample time and opportunity after receiving his last subcontractor's bid to extend the figures on his bid sheet from one column to the other,
to check and recheck his bid sheet figures and to take his papers to Elsinore and to
check them there prior to close of receipt of bids at 8:00 P.M.

tional omission of the $301,769 item. The board nevertheless passed a resolution accepting plaintiff's erroneous bid of $780,305, and plaintiff refused to enter into a written contract at that figure. The board then awarded the contract to the next lowest bidder, the city demanded forfeit- ure of plaintiff's bid bond, and plaintiff brought action to cancel its bid and obtain discharge of the bond. The trial court found that the bid had been submitted as the result of an excusable and honest mistake of a material and fundamental character, that plaintiff company had not been negligent in preparing the proposal, that it had acted promptly to notify the board of the mistake and to rescind the bid, and that the board had accepted the bid with knowledge of the error. The court further found and concluded that it would be unconscionable to require the company to perform for the amount of the bid, that no intervening rights had accrued, and that the city had suffered no damage or prejudice.

On appeal by the city this court affirmed, stating the following applica- ble rules (pp. 700-703 of 37 Cal. 2d):

> [1] Once opened and declared, the company's bid was in the nature of an irrevocable option, a contract right of which the city could not be deprived without its consent unless the requirements for rescission were satisfied. . . . [2] . . . the city had actual notice of the error in the esti- mates before it attempted to accept the bid, and knowledge by one party that the other is acting under mistake is treated as equivalent to mutual mistake for purposes of rescission. . . . [3] Relief from mistaken bids is consistently allowed where one party knows or has reason to know of the other's error and the requirements for rescission are fulfilled. . . .
>
> [4] Rescission may be had for mistake of fact if the mistake is material to the contract and was not the result of neglect of a legal duty, if enforcement of the contract as made would be unconscionable, and if the other party can be placed in statu quo. . . . In addition, the party seeking relief must give prompt notice of his election to rescind and must restore or offer to restore to the other party everything of value which he has received under the contract.
>
> [5] Omission of the $301,769 item from the company's bid was, of course, a material mistake. . . . [E]ven if we assume that the error was due to some carelessness, it does not follow that the company is without rem- edy. Civil Code section 1577, which defines mistake of fact for which relief may be allowed, describes it as one not caused by "the neglect of a legal duty" on the part of the person making the mistake. [6] It has been recog- nized numerous times that not all carelessness constitutes a "neglect of legal duty" within the meaning of the section. . . . On facts very similar to those in the present case, courts of other jurisdictions have stated that there was no culpable negligence and have granted relief from erroneous bids. . . . [7] The type of error here involved is one which will sometimes occur in the conduct of reasonable and cautious businessmen, and, under all the circumstances, we cannot say as a matter of law that it constituted a neglect of legal duty such as would bar the right to equitable relief.

[8] The evidence clearly supports the conclusion that it would be unconscionable to hold the company to its bid at the mistaken figure. The city had knowledge before the bid was accepted that the company had made a clerical error which resulted in the omission of an item amounting to nearly one third of the amount intended to be bid, and, under all the circumstances, it appears that it would be unjust and unfair to permit the city to take advantage of the company's mistake. [9, 10] There is no reason for denying relief on the ground that the city cannot be restored to status quo. It had ample time in which to award the contract without readvertising, the contract was actually awarded to the next lowest bidder, and the city will not be heard to complain that it cannot be placed in statu quo because it will not have the benefit of an inequitable bargain. . . . [11] Finally, the company gave notice promptly upon discovering the facts entitling it to rescind, and no offer of restoration was necessary because it had received nothing of value which it could restore. . . . We are satisfied that all the requirements for rescission have been met.

In the *Lemoge* case (Lemoge Electric v. County of San Mateo (1956), *supra*, 46 Cal. 2d 659, 662, 664 [1a, 1b, 2, 3]), the facts were similar to those in Kemper, except that plaintiff Lemoge did not attempt to rescind but instead, after discovering and informing defendant of inadvertent clerical error in the bid, entered into a formal contract with defendant on the terms specified in the erroneous bid, performed the required work, and then sued for reformation. Although this court affirmed the trial court's determination that plaintiff was not, under the circumstances, entitled to have the contract reformed, we also reaffirmed the rule that

Once opened and declared, plaintiff's bid was in the nature of an irrevocable option, a contract right of which defendant could not be deprived without its consent unless the requirements for rescission were satisfied. . . . Plaintiff then had the right to rescind, and it could have done so without incurring any liability on its bond.

(See also Brunzell Const. Co. v. G. J. Weisbrod, Inc. (1955), 134 Cal. App. 2d 278, 286-287 [1, 2] [285 P.2d 989]; Klose v. Sequoia Union High School Dist. (1953), 118 Cal. App. 2d 636, 641-642 [5] [258 P.2d 515].)

The rules stated in the *Kemper* and *Lemoge* cases would appear to entitle defendant to relief here, were it not for the findings of the trial court adverse to defendant. However, certain of such findings are clearly not supported by the evidence and others are immaterial to the point at issue. The finding that it is not true that the right hand column of figures on the bid sheet was totaled for the purpose of arriving at the total bid, and that it cannot be ascertained from the evidence for what purpose either the bid sheets or the right hand column total thereon were used in arriving at the total bid, is without evidentiary support in the face of the work sheets which were introduced in evidence and of the uncontradicted testimony not alone of defendant Kastorff, but also of plaintiff's own architect and witness Rendon, explaining the purpose of the work sheets and the nature of the error which had been made. We have examined such sheets, and they plainly show the entry of the sums of $9,285 and of $6,500 in the left hand columns as the two plumbing sub bids which were received by defendant, and the omission from the right hand totals column of any sum whatever for plumbing.

The same is true of the finding that although "on or about August 15" plaintiff received Kastorff's letter of August 14 explaining the error in his bid, it was not true that plaintiff knew at any time that the bid was intended to be other than as submitted. Again, it was shown by the testimony of plaintiff's architect, its school superintendent, and one of its school board members, all produced as plaintiff's witnesses, that the board was informed of the error and despite such information voted at its special meeting of August 15 not to grant defendant's request to withdraw his bid.

Further, we are persuaded that the trial court's view, as expressed in the finding set forth in the margin, that "Kastorff had ample time and opportunity after receiving his last subcontractor's bid" to complete and check his final bid, does not convict Kastorff of that "neglect of legal duty" which would preclude his being relieved from the inadvertent clerical error of omitting from his bid the cost of the plumbing. (See Civ. Code, §1577; M. F. Kemper Const. Co. v. City of Los Angeles (1951), *supra*, 37 Cal. 2d 696, 702 [6].) Neither should he be denied relief from an unfair, inequitable, and unintended bargain simply because, in response to inquiry from the board when his bid was discovered to be much the lowest submitted, he informed the board, after checking with his clerical assistant, that the bid was correct. He did not have his work sheets present to inspect at that time, he did thereafter inspect them at what would appear to have been the earliest practicable moment, and thereupon promptly notified plaintiff and rescinded his bid. Further, as shown in the margin, Kastorff's bid agreement, as provided by plaintiff's own bid form, was to execute a formal written contract only after receiving written notification of acceptance of his bid, and such notice was not given to him until some two weeks following his rescission.

If the situations of the parties were reversed and plaintiff and Kastorff had even executed a formal written contract (by contrast with the preliminary bid offer and acceptance) calling for a fixed sum payment to Kastorff large enough to include a reasonable charge for plumbing but inadvertently through the *district's* clerical error omitting a mutually intended provision requiring Kastorff to furnish and install plumbing, we have no doubt but that the district would demand and expect reformation or rescission. In the case before us the district expected Kastorff to furnish and install plumbing; surely it must also have understood that he intended to, and that his bid did, include a charge for such plumbing. The omission of any such charge was as unexpected by the board as it was unintended by Kastorff. Under the circumstances the "bargain" for which the board presses (which action we, of course, assume to be impelled by advice of counsel and a strict concept of official duty) appears too sharp for law and equity to sustain.

Plaintiff suggests that in any event the amount of the plumbing bid omitted from the total was immaterial. The bid as submitted was in the sum of $89,994, and whether the sum for the omitted plumbing was $6,500 or $9,285 (the two sub bids), the omission of such a sum is plainly material to the total. In *Lemoge* (Lemoge Electric v. County of San Mateo (1956), *supra*, 46 Cal. 2d 659, 661-662) the error which it was declared would have entitled plaintiff to rescind was the listing of the cost of certain materials as $104.52, rather than $10,452, in a total bid of $172,421. Thus the percentage of error here was larger than in Lemoge, and was plainly material.

The judgment is reversed.

Gibson, C.J., Traynor, J., McComb, J., Peters, J., White, J., and Dooling, J., concurred.

Section 9.   Consideration and the Contract by Correspondence

Courts have little trouble holding the parties to a contract so long as the offer is accepted in the presence of the offeror.[124] But in the typical modern case of contract by correspondence, special difficulties may arise. In such situations, agreement cannot be reached in a matter of minutes, and communications are necessarily delayed by the normal processes of the postal or telegraph system. Contracts by correspondence therefore present a problem not raised in the face-to-face exchange: the problem of determining at what stage in the exchange of correspondence a contract is formed and the parties are bound.

The Anglo-American and civil law systems have developed varying solutions, which may be summarized as follows: the parties to a contract are bound 1) by the mere posting of the acceptance; 2) by the simple delivery of the letter of acceptance, whether or not the offeror actually reads it; 3) when the offeror receives the acceptance, but the binding effect of the contract relates back to the moment the acceptance was dispatched; 4) at the moment the offeror has been informed of the acceptance.

---

124. Consult Akers v. J. B. Sedberry, Inc., 39 Tenn. App. 633, 286 S.W.2d 617 (1955); Caldwell v. E. F. Spears & Sons, 186 Ky. 64, 216 S.W. 83 (1919).

The issue of when the parties to a contract by correspondence are bound raises several subsidiary issues that cannot be dealt with by simply applying one of the above solutions across the board to all fact situations. An offeror may send a revocation of his offer before he receives the acceptance, but either before or after the acceptance is sent. When is the revocation effective? Again, the solutions developed vary. An offeree may attempt to withdraw his acceptance, or may attempt to accept after posting a rejection. Is the offeree bound by the acceptance, or can he withdraw? When is the rejection effective, and when the acceptance? If the acceptance is effective on posting, should this rule apply even if the acceptance is lost or delayed? If an offer calls for acceptance within a certain number of days, should the acceptance be effective on posting or receipt or at some other time? What difference should it make that the offer is in the form of an option?

For an analysis of the answers that various legal systems have given to these questions, see Nussbaum, Comparative Aspects of the Anglo-American Offer-and-Acceptance Doctrine, 36 Colum. L. Rev. 920 (1936); Corman, Formation of Contracts for the Sale of Goods, 42 Wash. L. Rev. 347, 394 et seq. (1967); Riegert, The West German Civil Code, Its Origin and Its Contract Provisions, 45 Tul. L. Rev. 48, 97-99 (1970). On the Anglo-American solution, see Llewellyn, Our Case Law of Contract: Offer and Acceptance, 48 Yale L.J. 1, 779 (1938-1939); Winfield, Some Aspects of Offer and Acceptance, 55 L.Q. Rev. 499 (1939); Macneil, Time of Acceptance: Too Many Problems for a Single Rule, 112 U. Pa. L. Rev. 947 (1964).

Modern forms of rapid communication aggravate the problem of determining when a contract is formed, a relevant issue in jurisdictional, procedural, and conflict-of-law disputes. These latter problems will not be discussed here. For two distinct solutions see Linn v. Employers Reinsurance Corp., 392 Pa. 58, 139 A.2d 638 (1958), and Entores Ltd. v. Miles Far East Corp., 2 Q.B. 327, 3 W.L.R. 48, 2 All E.R. 493 (1955).

CUSHING v. THOMSON.

118 N.H. 292, 386 A.2d 805 (1978), *mem. op.*,
118 N.H. 308, 386 A.2d 807 (1978)

PER CURIAM.

This is a bill in equity brought by five members of an antinuclear protest group called the Portsmouth Area Clamshell Alliance against Governor Meldrim Thomson, Jr., and John Blatsos, adjutant general of the State of New Hampshire. The bill seeks specific performance of a contract allegedly entered into by the parties for the use of the New Hampshire National Guard armory in Portsmouth. Plaintiffs alternatively allege that both the first amendment and the equal protection clause of the fourteenth amendment of the United States Constitution require the defendants to permit the plaintiff's use of the armory.

A hearing was held before the superior court on April 21, 1978, at which the parties presented pleadings, exhibits, memoranda, representations of counsel, and oral argument. The court ruled that a binding contract existed, granted the plaintiff's specific performance, and enjoined the defendants from any and all acts that would impede performance. The court denied plaintiffs' request for attorneys' fees without prejudice to future proceedings. Both parties excepted to portions of the court's order, and King, J., reserved and transferred all questions of law raised by these exceptions. The case was expedited and orally argued in this court on April 25, 1978.

On or about March 30, 1978, the adjutant general's office received an application from plaintiff Cushing for the use of the Portsmouth armory to hold a dance on the evening of April 29, 1978. On March 31 the adjutant general mailed a signed contract offer agreeing to rent the armory to the Portsmouth Clamshell Alliance for the evening of April 29. The agreement required acceptance by the renter affixing his signature to the accompanying copy of the agreement and returning the same to the adjutant general within five days after its receipt. On Monday, April 3, plaintiff Cushing received the contract offer and signed it on behalf of the Portsmouth Clamshell Allliance. At 6:30 on the evening of Tuesday, April 4, Mr. Cushing received a telephone call from the adjutant general advising him that the Governor had ordered withdrawal of the rental offer, and accordingly the offer was being withdrawn. During that conversation Mr. Cushing stated that he had already signed the contract. A written confirmation of the withdrawal was sent by the adjutant general to the plaintiffs on April 5. On April 6 defendants received by mail the signed contract dated April 3, postmarked April 5.

[1] The first issue presented is whether the trial court erred in determining that a binding contract existed. Neither party challenges the applicable law.

> To establish a contract of this character . . . there must be . . . an offer and an acceptance thereof in accordance with its terms. . . . [W]hen the parties to such a contract are at a distance from one another and the offer is sent by mail . . . the reply accepting the offer may be sent through the same medium, and the contract will be complete when the acceptance is mailed . . . properly addressed to the party making the offer and beyond the acceptor's control.

Busher v. Insurance Co., 72 N.H. 551, 552, 58 A. 41 (1904). Withdrawal of the offer is ineffectual once the offer has been accepted by posting in the mail. Abbott v. Shepard, 48 N.H. 14, 16 (1868).

The defendants argue, however, that there is no evidence to sustain a finding that plaintiff Cushing had accepted the adjutant general's offer before it was withdrawn. Such a finding is necessarily implied in the court's ruling that there was a binding contract. *See* Tibbetts v. Tibbetts, 109 N.H. 239, 240-41, 248 A.2d 75, 76-77 (1968); Rosenblum v. Judson Eng'r Corp., 99 N.H. 267, 271, 109 A.2d 558, 561 (1954). The implied finding must stand if there is any evidence to support it. Milne v. Burlington Homes, Inc., 117 N.H. [813], 379 A.2d 1251, 1252 (1977); New Bradford Co. v. Meunier, 117 N.H. [774], 378 A.2d 748, 750 (1977).

Plaintiffs introduced the sworn affidavit of Mr. Cushing in which he stated that on April 3, he executed the contract and placed it in the outbox for mailing. Moreover plaintiffs' counsel represented to the court that it was customary office practice for outgoing letters to be picked up from the outbox daily and put in the U.S. mail. No testimony was submitted in this informal hearing, and the basis for the court's order appears to be in part counsels' representations, a procedure which was not objected to by the parties. Rosenblum v. Judson Eng'n Corp., 99 N.H. at 270-71, 109 A.2d at 561 (1951). Spain v. Company, 94 N.H. 400, 401, 54 A.2d 364, 364-65 (1947). Thus the representation that it was customary office procedure for the letters to be sent out the same day that they are placed in the office outbox, together with the affidavit, supported the implied finding that the completed contract was mailed before the attempted revocation. Stanton v. Mills, 94 N.H. 92, 95, 47 A.2d 112, 114 (1946).

Because there is evidence to support it, this court cannot say as a matter of law that the trial court's finding that there was a binding contract is clearly erroneous, and therefore it must stand. Chute v. Chute, 117 N.H. [676], 377 A.2d 890 (1977); Vittum v. N.H. Ins. Co., 117 N.H. [1], 369 A.2d 184, 186 (1977).

The granting of the equitable relief of specific performance and injunction is within the sound discretion of the trial court. Chute v. Chute, *supra*; see Cornwell v. Cornwell, 116 N.H. 205, 210, 356 A.2d 683, 686 (1976). On the record before us we cannot say that the court abused its discretion.

In deciding the legal issues of contract law in this case, we, of course, are not passing on the aims or activities of the Clamshell Alliance.

In view of the result reached, we need not consider other issues raised.

Decree affirmed; exceptions overruled.

Douglas, J., as an officer in the National Guard, did not sit.

MEMORANDUM OPINION

Following our opinion in this case dated April 27, 1978, defendants petitioned the superior court to modify the contract for rental of the Portsmouth armory by requiring that plaintiffs file a bond in the amount of $10,000 to cover any damage that may be caused during the rental.

After hearing, the petition was denied by King, J. this date. Defendants asked for and received an expedited appeal in this court. After hearing

without a record and based only on oral argument we cannot say that the
superior court was in error.

Exception overruled.

Douglas, J., did not sit.

NOTE

1. The *Cushing* case reflects the common law rule that an acceptance
is effective on dispatch, the so-called mailbox rule. This rule was first laid
down in Adams v. Lindsell, 1 Barn. & Ald. 681, 106 Eng. Rep. 250 (K.B.
1818). The defendants offered by letter to sell plaintiffs "eight hundred
tods of wether fleeces." Plaintiffs accepted by letter. While plaintiffs' letter was in transit, however, the defendants sold the fleeces to a third
party. Plaintiffs sued, and the court held in their favor reasoning that if
no binding contract could come into being until plaintiffs' answer were
received by defendants,

> no contract could ever be completed by post. For if the defendants were
> not bound by their offer when accepted by the plaintiffs till the answer was
> received, then the plaintiffs ought not to be bound till after they had re-
> ceived the notification that the defendants had received their answer and
> assented to it. And so it might go on ad infinitum. The defendants must be
> considered in law as making, during every instant of the time their letter
> was traveling, the same identical offer to the plaintiffs; and then the con-
> tract is completed by the acceptance of it by the latter.

A striking aspect of the case is that defendants never informed the
plaintiffs that their offer was revoked. The court was apparently influenced by Cooke v. Oxley, 3 T.R. 653, 100 Eng. Rep. 785 (K.B. 1790).

Is the reasoning of the court in Adams v. Lindsell persuasive? See 1
Williston §81 (1958); Cook, Williston on Contracts, 33 Ill. L. Rev. 497, 511
et seq. (1939). For a discussion of the different theories behind the mailbox rule, see Rhode Island Tool Co. v. United States, *infra* p. 354, and
the Note following that case. What roles do the consideration doctrine
and the classical principle that an offer is revocable until accepted play in
Adams v. Lindsell? See Corman, Formation of Contracts for the Sale of
Goods, 42 Wash. L. Rev. 347, 394-395 (1967).

2. In McCulloch v. Eagle Insurance Co., 18 Mass. (1 Pick.) 278
(1822), the Massachusetts Supreme Judicial Court, apparently ignorant
of Adams v. Lindsell, adopted the view that an acceptance is effective
only on receipt. This case is considered to have been overruled by Brauer
v. Shaw, 168 Mass. 198, 46 N.E. 617 (1897). See also McTernan v. Le-
Tendre, 4 Mass. App. 502, 351 N.E.2d 566 (1976).

3. If a person mails a letter of acceptance to insure his property against
loss by fire, and a destructive fire occurs while the letter is in transit,

under the prevailing view the insurance company is liable. See Tayloe v. Merchant's Fire Insurance Co., 50 U.S. (9 How.) 390 (1850). The same result will be reached in those jurisdictions where an acceptance is only effective when received if the date for determining liability under the contract relates back to the time when the acceptance was dispatched. See Swiss General Obligations Law Art. 1, §1.

4. While an acceptance, under the common law rule, is effective on posting, a revocation of the offer is generally held to be effective only on receipt. See the leading case of Byrne & Co. v. Leon Van Tienhoven & Co., 5 C.P.D. 344 (1880). Thus, even if an offeror sends a revocation before an offeree sends his acceptance, the offeror is nevertheless bound so long as the offeree receives the revocation after he has sent his acceptance. The principal case illustrates what happens when an offeror's revocation is sent and received after the offeree's acceptance is sent.

In some states, there are statutory provisions making the offeror's revocation effective on posting. See, e.g., Cal. Civ. Code §§1583 & 1587. To what extent is the rationale behind the mailbox rule as stated in Comment *a* of Restatement Second §63, reprinted p. 357 *infra*, undermined by this rule? Consult Watters v. Lincoln, 29 S.D. 98, 135 N.W. 712 (1912).

LEWIS v. BROWNING 130 Mass. 173, 175-176 (1881): Gray, C.J.: "In M'Culloch v. Eagle Ins. Co. 1 Pick. 278, this court held that a contract made by mutual letters was not complete until the letter accepting the offer had been received by the person making the offer; and the correctness of the decision is maintained, upon an able and elaborate discussion of reasons and authorities, in Langdell on Contracts (2d ed.) 989-996. In England, New York and New Jersey, and in the Supreme Court of the United States, the opposite view has prevailed, and the contract has been deemed to be completed as soon as the letter of acceptance has been put into the post-office duly addressed. . . .

"But this case does not require a consideration of the general question; for, in any view, the person making the offer may always, if he chooses, make the formation of the contract which he proposes dependent upon the actual communication to himself of the acceptance. . . ."

NOTE

A stipulation that the actual communication of the acceptance will be necessary to consummate a contract may be inserted for the benefit of the offeree also, as applications for life insurance policies, which are offers, illustrate. Such applications typically provide, among other things, that the policy will not take effect unless and until the policy has been delivered to the applicant. Patterson, The Delivery of a Life Insurance Policy, 33 Harv. L. Rev. 198 (1919). In a great number of jurisdictions

such clauses have been honored in the name of freedom of contract. Id.
at 221. There are, however, cases protecting the applicant despite the
delivery clause, with the help of a constructive delivery doctrine when the
policy has been delivered or even mailed to the local agent for unconditional delivery. See Jackson v. N.Y. Life Insurance Co., 7 F.2d 31 (9th
Cir. 1925); Republic Nat. Life Insurance Co. v. Merkley, 59 Ariz. 125, 124
P.2d 313 (1942); Patterson, Essentials of Insurance Law §19 (2d ed. 1957).
Can the applicant revoke his offer until he has accepted the policy? See
Wheelock v. Clark, 21 Wyo. 300, 131 P. 35 (1913).

RHODE ISLAND TOOL CO. v. UNITED STATES

128 F. Supp. 417 (Ct. Cl. 1955)

[Plaintiff sues for the recovery of $1,640.60 on the ground that it made
a mistake in figuring its bid for the furnishing of certain bolts. It also
alleges that it withdrew its bid before it received notice of award.

On September 10, 1948, in response to an invitation to bid, plaintiff
submitted a bid for fifteen lots of bolts to the Navy Department. In
making his calculations, plaintiff had failed to notice that the department
had changed the specifications on three lots from stud to more expensive
machine bolts. Notice of the award was made to plaintiff on October 4th.
On the same day, before the acceptance was received but presumably
after it was mailed, plaintiff notified the department of his error and
expressed his desire to restore the bid. This request was rejected, plaintiff
performed and brought suit for the value of the goods delivered.]

JONES, Chief Judge. The sales manager of the plaintiff who prepared its
bid failed to notice the change in the description of the bolts from stud to
machine on the third page and calculated plaintiff's bid on the basis of
stud bolts. The machine bolts were a more expensive type of bolt. . . .

A rather well-established rule of law seems to be that after bids have
been opened the bidder cannot withdraw his bid unless he can prove that
the desire to withdraw is due solely to an honest mistake and that no fraud
is involved. United States v. Lipman, D.C., 122 F. Supp. 284, 287; Alta
Electric and Mechanical Co., Inc., v. United States, 90 Ct. Cl. 466;
Leitman v. United States, 60 F. Supp. 218, 104 Ct. Cl. 324; Nason Coal
Co. v. United States, 64 Ct. Cl. 526; Moffett, Hodgkins & Clarke Co. v.
City of Rochester, 178 U.S. 373, 20 S. Ct. 957, 44 L. Ed. 1108. The case of
Refining Associates, Inc., v. United States, 124 Ct. Cl. 115, cited by both
parties and emphasized by the defendant, is inapplicable to the facts of
this case. No mistake was found to exist in that case. In fact, in that case
the court recognized that on many occasions it has granted relief to
plaintiffs seeking to withdraw or modify a bid after the date of the open-

ing. It cites and discusses several such cases and distinguishes them from that particular case. In the instant case the plaintiff on account of its mistake had a right to withdraw its bid, provided a binding contract had not yet been made.

The question is whether, in all the circumstances of this case, the depositing of the notice of award in the mail constitutes a binding contract from which plaintiff cannot escape, notwithstanding the mistake was brought to the attention of the contracting officials before the notice of award was received.

We believe that when the record is considered as a whole in the light of modern authorities, there was no binding contract, since plaintiff withdrew its bid before the acceptance became effective.

Under the old post office regulations when a letter was deposited in the mail the sender lost all control of it. It was irrevocably on its way. After its deposit in the mail the post office became, in effect, the agent of the addressee. Naturally the authorities held that the acceptance in any contract became final when it was deposited in the post office, since the sender had lost control of the letter at that time. That was the final act in consummating the agreement.

But some years ago the United States Postal authorities completely changed the regulation, [permitting the sender to retrieve a letter from the mail]. . . .[125]

When this new regulation became effective, the entire picture was changed. The sender now does not lose control of the letter the moment it is deposited in the post office, but retains the right to control up to the time of delivery. The acceptance, therefore, is not final until the letter reaches destination, since the sender has the absolute right of withdrawal from the post office, and even the right to have the postmaster at the delivery point return the letter at any time before actual delivery.

We have so held. Dick v. United States, 82 F. Supp. 326, 113 Ct. Cl. 94, and authorities therein cited. . . .

Does any one believe that if the mistake had been the other way, that is, if the machine bolts had been listed first and the stud bolts as later items, and that through oversight the defendant had mailed an acceptance for too high a price and the same day had wired withdrawing and cancelling the acceptance before it left the sending post office the defendant would nevertheless have been held to an excessive price? Or again, if after mailing such an acceptance the defendant, discovering its mistake, had gone to the sending post office and withdrawn the letter, the plaintiff on hearing of it, could have enforced an excessive contract on the ground that the acceptance actually had been posted and became final and enforceable, notwithstanding its withdrawal and nondelivery?

125. This change took place in 1885, not as the court states in 1948. — EDS.

We cannot conceive of such an unjust enforcement. No, under the new regulation, the Post Office Department becomes, in effect, the agency of the sender until actual delivery.

We are living in a time of change. The theories of yesterday, proved by practice today, give way to the improvements of tomorrow.

To apply an outmoded formula is not only unjust, it runs counter to the whole stream of human experience. It is like insisting on an oxcart as the official means of transportation in the age of the automobile. The cart served a useful purpose in its day, but is now a museum piece.

The old rule was established before Morse invented the telegraph as a means of communication. Commerce must have a breaking point upon which it may rely for the completion of a contract. At that time no faster mode of communication was known. But in the light of the faster means of communication the Post Office Department wisely changed the rule. The reason for the old rule had disappeared. This does not change any principle, it simply changes the practice to suit the changed conditions, but leaves unchanged the principle of finality, which is just as definite as ever, though transferred to a different point by the new regulation.

This change seems to have been recognized by the Government officials who prepared the Invitation for bids. The offer by the defendant stated that when the award was "received" by the bidder it would "thereupon" become a binding contract. This it would seem clinches the correctness of our interpretation.

The interpretation reaches the ends of justice for all parties. It preserves the definite time at which acceptance becomes final and does so in full accord with the changed regulation.

Manifestly, a mistake was made. The defendant is not injured by permitting its correction. It only forbids defendant's unjust enrichment by preventing its taking technical advantage of an evident mistake.

Plaintiff is allowed to recover its actual losses, if any, in furnishing the machine bolts, limited, however, to the difference between its bid and that of the next lowest bidder on these particular items, that amount being not a yardstick, but a ceiling on any losses it may be able to prove; or, in the alternative, the reasonable value of the items furnished, subject to the same limitation.

The case is remanded to a commissioner of this court for the purpose of hearing evidence as to such losses, if any, or as to the reasonable value of the items furnished.

It is so ordered.

Laramore and Littleton, Judges, concur.

WHITAKER, Judge (dissenting). I think a binding contract was made in this case. I shall state my reason for this opinion very briefly. The invitation for bids asked the bidders to state the time the bid would remain in effect. The bidder stated it would remain in effect 20 days. This was a binding agreement. The bid could not be withdrawn within that time in the absence of fraud or mistake, but the mistake must have been mutual. The plaintiff admits this in its brief. A mutual mistake would invalidate plaintiff's agreement to hold his bid open for 20 days, but a unilateral mistake will not.

There were wide variations in the bids on the several items covered by the invitation. In the circumstances there was nothing to put the contracting offer on notice that the plaintiff had made a mistake.

For these reasons I dissent.

Madden, Judge, concurs in the foregoing dissent.

NOTE

See Comment, 8 Stan. L. Rev. 279 (1956). Has the reason for the mailbox rule "disappeared," as the court says? The Restatement Second gives the following rationale for the rule (§63, Comment *a*):

> It is often said that an offeror who makes an offer by mail makes the post office his agent to receive the acceptance, or that the mailing of a letter of acceptance puts it irrevocably out of the offeree's control. Under United States postal regulations, however, the sender of a letter has long had the power to stop delivery and reclaim the letter. A better explanation of the rule that the acceptance takes effect on dispatch is that the offeree needs a dependable basis for his decision whether to accept. In many legal systems such a basis is provided by a general rule that an offer is irrevocable unless it provides otherwise. The common law provides such a basis through the rule that a revocation of an offer is ineffective if received after an acceptance has been properly dispatched.

For a discussion of the reasons behind the mailbox rule, see Morrison v. Thoelke, 155 So. 2d 889 (Fla. Dist. Ct. App. 1963).

What is the significance of the irrevocability of the bid (the offer) in the principal case? See Comment *f* to §63. Assuming plaintiff is deserving of protection, can this be done without tampering with the mailbox rule? Consult Restatement Second §153 and §63 Comment *c*; 3 Corbin §609 (1960). For an extension of the rules laid down in Dick v. United States, 82 F. Supp. 326 (Ct. Cl. 1949), discussed *infra* p. 367, and *Rhode Island Tool* to a non-mistake situation, see Pacific Alaska Contractors Inc. v. United States, 157 F. Supp. 844 (Ct. Cl. 1958).

PALO ALTO TOWN & COUNTRY VILLAGE, INC. v. BBTC COMPANY
11 Cal. 3d 494, 521 P.2d 1097, 113 Cal. Rptr. 705 (1974)

SULLIVAN, J. — The sole issue confronting us in this case is whether, absent any provisions in the option contract to the contrary, a written notice by the optionee of his exercise of an option is effective upon its deposit in the mail or only upon its receipt by the optioner. As we explain *infra*, we have concluded that pursuant to sections 1582 and 1583 of the Civil Code,[126] the exercise of the option is effective upon mailing. We therefore affirm the judgment.

The facts of the case are briefly these. By written lease dated November 20, 1964, plaintiff leased to defendant, for the operation of a restaurant and bar, certain premises in a shopping center in San Jose for a five-year term commencing on January 1, 1965, and ending on December 31, 1969. The lease granted defendant two successive options to extend the term for a period of five years on each option. According to the options contained in paragraph 45 of the lease the "Lessee may, by giving not less than six months prior notice in writing to the Lessor, extend this lease for an additional five years" under specified terms and conditions, and after such extension "may extend this lease for a further five-year period . . . by giving Lessor not less than six months notice in writing prior to the end of the tenth year of the term of this lease."

On June 5, 1969, and more than six months prior to the end of the term of the lease, defendant prepared and signed a letter to plaintiff notifying the latter that it was exercising its option to extend the lease and deposited the same in the mail in a stamped envelope addressed to plaintiff. Defendant continued with its usual operation of the bar and restaurant and made various improvements on the premises in anticipation of the extended term of the lease. On February 13, 1970, a month and a half after the end of the initial term and eight and a half months after defendant's letter exercising the option, plaintiff notified defendant that the lease had expired for want of renewal and demanded surrender of the premises by March 31, 1970. Plaintiff claimed that it had never received defendant's letter. Defendant, on the other hand, claimed that it had properly exercised its option and refused to vacate.

Plaintiff thereupon commenced the present action for declaratory relief seeking a determination of its rights and duties under the lease and a declaration as to whether defendant properly exercised its option and whether the lease terminated on December 31, 1969. Defendant filed an answer and cross-complaint, essentially alleging that it had by written notice to plaintiff exercised its option to extend the term and that in addition thereto, defendant's use, possession, improvement of and continued operations on the premises were such that plaintiff knew, or should have known, that defendant intended to extend its tenancy. . . .

The trial court found and concluded that defendant on June 5, 1969, prepared, signed and mailed, properly stamped and adequately addressed, a letter to plaintiff unconditionally exercising its first renewal

126. Hereafter, unless otherwise indicated, all section references are to the Civil Code.

option in the lease; that defendant exercised the option, properly and validly in all respects; and that defendant at all material times was rightfully in possession of the premises under the lease. Judgment was entered accordingly. This appeal followed.

It is well settled that when the provisions of an option contract prescribe the particular manner in which the option is to be exercised, they must be strictly followed. (Flickinger v. Heck (1921) 187 Cal. 111, 114 [200 P. 1045]; Callisch v. Farnham (1948) 83 Cal. App. 2d 427, 430 [188 P.2d 775]; see generally 1 Witkin, Summary of Cal. Law (8th ed. 1973) p. 127.) However, when the option contract merely suggests, but does not positively require, a particular manner of communicating the exercise of the option, another means of communication is not precluded. (Estate of Crossman (1964) 231 Cal. App. 2d 370, 372 [41 Cal. Rptr. 800].)

Accordingly, we must first ascertain if the lease requires that the exercise of the option be communicated to the lessor in a particular manner. An examination of that document discloses that paragraph 45 requires that notice of the exercise of the option be given "in writing" but the lease does not prescribe any particular manner of communicating such written notice to the lessor. . . .

[The court concluded that "since the lease does not prescribe the manner of communicating the exercise of the option of the optionor, 'any reasonable and usual mode may be adopted' (§1582)" and that communication by mail was a reasonable mode. It also concluded that the term "giving notice" in the option agreement did not necessarily mean that the notice had to be received by the optionor.]

We turn to the crucial issue in the case. Was defendant's exercise of its option to extend the lease effective upon its deposit in the mail of its written notice of acceptance or only upon the actual receipt of such notice by plaintiff?

The so-called "effective upon posting" rule[127] was codified in California in 1872 as section 1583 of the Civil Code: "WHEN COMMUNICATION DEEMED COMPLETE. Consent is deemed to be fully communicated between the parties as soon as the party accepting a proposal has put his acceptance in the course of transmission to the proposer, in conformity to the last section." Although the question as to whether the exercise of an option is effective at the time written acceptance is deposited in the mail has never been squarely presented to this court, we have declared and a number of Courts of Appeal have held that option contracts are subject to the provisions of sections 1582 and 1583 and that an option is effectively exercised

127. "It is well established that an acceptance of an offer to enter into a bilateral contract is effective and deemed communicated as soon as deposited in the regular course of mail if the offer was made by mail, or if the circumstances are such that an acceptance by mail would be authorized." (State of California v. Agostini (1956) 139 Cal. App. 2d 909, 915 [294 P.2d 769]; Ivey v. Kern County Land Co. (1896) 115 Cal. 196, 200-201 [46 P. 926].)

when written acceptance is deposited in the mail. (Dawson v. Goff (1954) 43 Cal. 2d 310, 316 [273 P.2d 1];[128] Estate of Crossman, *supra*, 231 Cal. App. 2d 370, 373-374; State of California v. Agostini (1956) 139 Cal. App. 2d 909, 915 [294 P.2d 769]; Morello v. Growers Grape Prod. Assn. (1947) 82 Cal. App. 2d 365, 370-371 [186 P.2d 463]; Canty v. Brown (1909) 11 Cal. App. 487, 491 [105 P. 428]; 1 Witkin, Summary of Cal. Law 8th ed. 1973) §130, p. 127.) We today reaffirm our observations in *Dawson* and hold that sections 1582 and 1583 apply to irrevocable options as well as to revocable offers and that absent any provisions in the option contract to the contrary, by virtue of section 1583 the exercise of an option becomes effective at the time written notice of acceptance is deposited in the mail.

Plaintiff, however, points out that the majority rule in other jurisdictions is that notice of exercise of an option is effective only upon receipt. Our attention is directed to Dynamics Corporation of America v. United States, supra, 389 F.2d 424, 431, where the court stated: "Turning now to the general rule governing exercise of an option, it is well settled that notice to exercise an option is effective only upon receipt." An additional example is presented in Cities Service Oil Co. v. National Shawmut Bank (1961) 342 Mass. 108 [172 N.E.2d 104], where the Supreme Court of Massachusetts declared: "It is at least the majority rule that notice to exercise an option is effective only upon its receipt by the party to be notified unless the parties otherwise agreed." (*Id.* at p. 105, fn. 1, see cases therein cited.) Finally it is noted that Professor Corbin supports such a rule:

> If in an option contract the duty of the promisor is conditional on 'notice within 30 days', does this mean notice received or notice properly mailed? It is believed that in the absence of an expression of contrary intention, it should be held that the notice must be received. . . . The rule that an acceptance by post is operative on mailing was itself subjected to severe criticism; and, even though it may now be regarded as settled, it should not be extended to notice of acceptance in already binding option contracts.

(1A Corbin on Contracts (1963 ed.) §264, p. 521, fn. omitted; accord, Rest. 2d Contracts [§63, Comment *f*].)

Arguing that section 1583 is inapplicable to option contracts since an option, properly analyzed, is not a "proposal" as used in the section and that we are free of any restraint of stare decisis, plaintiff urges us to apply the above so-called majority rule. We decline to do so. As we have explained, the "effective on posting" rule rests solidly on California statu-

---

128. In *Dawson* we decided the sole issue of venue on the basis of the option contract itself. But assuming that it was not a binding contract, we went on to comment as to when the contract to which the option related was made. Although not actually necessary for our decision, we declared that sections 1582 and 1583 "have been held applicable to acceptance or exercise of an option by an optionee under an option contract as well as to a revocable offer. [Citations.]" (43 Cal. 2d at p. 316.)

tory and decisional law. An analysis of the legal theory of option contracts to the end of determining whether an optionee is a "party accepting a proposal" and whether the exercise of the option is an "acceptance" from which "[c]onsent is deemed to be fully communicated" (§1583; and see §§1550, 1565, 1580 and 1581), satisfies us that our decision in this respect is a sound one.

An option, as a matter of legal theory, is considered to have a dual nature: on the one hand it is an irrevocable offer, which upon acceptance ripens into a bilateral contract, and on the other hand, it is a unilateral contract which binds the optionor to perform an underlying agreement upon the optionee's performance of a condition precedent. Professor Corbin explains the option as follows:

> [The option] is a binding unilateral contract, since it is a promise exchanged for a sufficient cash consideration. It is also commonly called an offer. . . . This usage is not at all objectionable, if we realize that an offered promise may also be a binding promise. It certainly creates a power in B to be exercised . . . by giving notice of consent. . . . And on the giving of such notice within the time limit, the legal result is almost identical with that of the acceptance of an ordinary revocable offer. . . . It is a "binding" promise, because a consideration was paid for it; it is an "offer," because it invites a second and different exchange of equivalents. . . . O's [optionor's] promise is from the very beginning a binding contract, his duty to convey being conditional on notice by B within the stated time. The sending of such a notice by B is not merely the acceptance of an offer; it is also the performance of a condition precedent to O's duty of immediate performance.

(1A Corbin on Contracts (1963 ed.) §264, pp. 508-509, fn. omitted.)

This court in its exhaustive analysis of an option in Warner Bros. Pictures v. Brodel, *supra*, 31 Cal. 2d 766, 772-773, explicitly recognized the dual aspect of an option, referring to it sometimes as an irrevocable offer which is completed by the acceptance of the optionee and sometimes as a binding contractual promise to perform the underlying contract subject to the condition precedent of acceptance by the optionee. Which aspect of an option is emphasized depends upon which party's duties are under consideration. From the point of view of the optionor's duty it is binding upon the making of the option contract.

> [T]he optionor has irrevocably promised upon the exercise of the option to perform the contract or make the conveyance upon the terms specified in his binding offer. . . . The creation of the final contract requires no promise or other action by the optionor, for the contract is completed by the acceptance of the irrevocable offer of the optionor by the optionee. "The contract has already been made, as far as the optionor is concerned, but is subject to conditions which are removed by the acceptance." (Seeburg v. El Royale Corp. [1942] 54 Cal. App. 2d 1, 4. . . .)

(Warner Bros. Pictures v. Brodel, *supra*, 31 Cal. 2d 766, 772-773; Dawson v. Goff, *supra*, 43 Cal. 2d 310, 316-318; Caras v. Parker (1957) 149 Cal. App. 2d 621, 626-627 [309 P.2d 104].)

However, the optionee has no duty until, and unless, he accepts the irrevocable offer proposed to him by the optionor. As we observed in Warner Bros. Pictures v. Brodel, supra, 31 Cal. 2d 766, 772,

> In an option contract the optionor stipulates that for a specified or reasonable period he waives the right to revoke the offer. [Citations.] Such a contract is clearly different from the contract to which the irrevocable offer of the optionor relates, for the optionee by parting with special consideration for the binding promise of the optionor refrains from binding himself with regard to the contract or conveyance to which the option relates. . . .
> "A contract conferring an option to purchase is . . . an irrevocable and continuing offer to sell, and conveys no interest in land to the optionee, but vests in him only a right in personam to buy at his election."

Thus it has been held in California that an option to purchase real property "is by no means a sale of property, but is the sale of a right to purchase" (Hicks v. Christeson (1917) 174 Cal. 712, 716 [164 P. 395]) and on acceptance the option becomes a contract of sale binding on both parties. (Smith v. Post (1914) 167 Cal. 69, 74 [138 P. 705]; Rheingans v. Smith (1911) 161 Cal. 362, 367 [119 P. 494].)

Therefore from the viewpoint of the optionor, an option is a binding contract subject to the performance of a condition precedent by the optionee. From the viewpoint of the optionee, an option is an irrevocable offer which the optionee can convert into a binding bilateral contract by acceptance of the offer. Where the issue presented in a case focused upon the optionor's obligation, the former analysis prevailed, so that in *Dawson* it was held that, as to the optionor, the contract was made upon the signing of the option contract and therefore venue in a suit to enforce the option lay where the option contract was made and not where the option was exercised. However, where the issue focused upon the optionee's action the latter analysis prevailed, as in *Crossman* where the court held that acceptance of an option was effective upon posting pursuant to section 1583.

Viewing the exercise of an option as an acceptance of an irrevocable offer, or in other words from the optionee's viewpoint under the preceding analysis, we think it is clear that the notice of the exercise of an option falls within the language of section 1583. The optionee is a "party accepting a proposal," namely the irrevocable offer; the notice of exercise is an "acceptance" of that offer and signifies the optionee's "consent" to be bound according to the terms of the bilateral contract created by the acceptance.

As plaintiff points out, it is true that if the exercise of the option is viewed as the performance of a condition precedent to the optionor's existent contractual duty, or in other words from the optionor's viewpoint under the preceding analysis, the language of section 1583 is not so apt, since a contractual duty is not a "proposal," and performance is not a "consent." Indeed Professor Corbin chooses to emphasize the theoretical possibility of viewing the notice of the exercise of an option in this aspect so as to thwart the extension of the "effective upon posting" rule, which he views with disfavor.[129]

In California, however, the "effective upon posting" rule has received legislative sanction and is the declared policy of this state. We must effectuate this policy in all cases reasonably included within the scope and language of the statute promoting this policy. As previously explained, when the notice of exercise of the option is viewed as an acceptance of an irrevocable offer, such notice is clearly covered by section 1583.

To recapitulate, we hold first, that since pursuant to section 1582 the lease prescribed no condition concerning the communication to the optionor of the exercise of the option except that the notice be in writing, notice of acceptance by ordinary mail was a reasonable mode of communication; and second, that pursuant to section 1583 defendant's exercise of the option became effective when notice of acceptance was deposited in the mail.

The judgment is affirmed.

Wright, C.J., McComb, J., Tobriner, J., Mosk, J., Burke, J., and Clark, J., concurred.

NOTE

1. As the court points out, the Restatement Second §63, Comment f is in accord with Corbin's view that the mailbox rule should not be extended to options. The Restatement's position rests on the belief that where an offer is irrevocable the offeree already has a dependable basis for his decision whether to accept. See Comments a, reprinted supra p. 357, and f to §63. See also Salinen v. Frankson, 309 Minn. 438, 245 N.W.2d 839, 87 A.L.R.3d 800 (1976).

2. To what extent was the court swayed by the fact that the optionee had made improvements in the premises and continued to operate the bar and restaurant during the period after the notice to exercise the option was sent? Could the court have followed the majority rule and still

129. "It is believed that, in the absence of an expression of contrary intention, it should be held that the notice must be received. As above explained, the notice is in one aspect a notice of acceptance of an offer; but in another aspect it is a condition of the promisor's already existing contractual duty. . . . The rule that an acceptance by post is operative on mailing was itself subjected to severe criticism; and, even though it may now be regarded as settled, it should not be extended to notice of acceptance in already binding option contracts." (1A Corbin on Contracts (1963 ed.) §264, p. 521, fn. omitted.)

afforded the optionee relief? See Note, 63 Calif. L. Rev. 11, 126 (1965) and Sy Jack Realty Co. v. Pergament Syosset Corp., 27 N.Y.2d 449, 318 N.Y.S.2d 720, 267 N.E.2d 462 (1971).

3. In the principal case, the optionee's letter, though sent on time, was never received by the optionor. The general rule with respect to acceptances is that they are effective on dispatch even though they are lost or delayed in the course of transit. The leading case announcing this rule is Household Fire & Carriage Acc. Ins. Co. v. Grant, 4 Ex. D. 216 (1879). See also Restatement Second §56 and §63 Comment b; 37 Mich. L. Rev. 655 (1939). Do you agree with the rule?

C. LANGDELL, SUMMARY OF THE LAW OF CONTRACTS 20-21 (2d ed. 1880): "It has been claimed that the purposes of substantial justice, and the interests of contracting parties as understood by themselves, will be best served by holding that the contract is complete the moment the letter of acceptance is mailed; and cases have been put to show that the contrary view would produce not only unjust but absurd results. The true answer to this argument is, that it is irrelevant; but, assuming it to be relevant, it may be turned against those who use it without losing any of its strength. The only cases of real hardship are where there is a miscarriage of the letter of acceptance, and in those cases a hardship to one of the parties is inevitable. Adopting one view, the hardship consists in making one liable on a contract which he is ignorant of having made; adopting the other view, it consists of depriving one of the benefit of a contract which he supposes he has made. Between these two evils the choice would seem to be clear: the former is positive, the latter merely negative; the former imposes a liability to which no limit can be placed, the latter leaves everything in statu quo. As to making provision for the contingency of the miscarriage of a letter, this is easy for the person who sends it, while it is practically impossible for the person to whom it is sent."

LLEWELLYN, OUR CASE-LAW OF CONTRACT: OFFER AND ACCEPTANCE (pt. 2), 48 Yale L.J. 779, 795 (1939): "As between hardship on the offeror which is really tough, and hardship on the offeree which would be even tougher,[130] the vital reason for throwing the hardship of an

130. For regarding the hardship of an opposing rule as even tougher on the offeree there are two good reasons. In the first place, the ingrained usage of business is to answer letters which look toward deals, but the usage is not so clear about acknowledging letters which close deals. The absence of an answer to a letter of offer is much more certain to lead to inquiry than is the absence of an answer to a letter of acceptance, so that the party bitten by the mischance has under our rule a greater likelihood of being aware of uncertainty and of speedily discovering his difficulty. This goes to the hazards of communication. In the second place, and regarding the time of closing, the risk of the market shifting against the offeror, unbalanced by the chance of gain if it shifts in his favor, rests under our law on the offeror during one transmission period plus time for answer — subject to effective telegraphic or telephone communication. He wants the deal; he takes that risk. But to fail to

odd delayed or lost letter upon the offeror remains this: the offeree is already relying, with the best reason in the world, on the deal being on; the offeror is only holding things open; and, in view of the efficiency of communication facilities, we can protect the offeree in *all* these deals at the price of hardship on offerors in very few of them."

POSTAL TELEGRAPH-CABLE CO. v. WILLIS
93 Miss. 540, 47 So. 380 (1908)

Action by Floyd Willis against the Postal Telegraph Company. From a judgment for plaintiff, defendant appeals.

MAYES, J., delivered the opinion of the court. Floyd Willis was engaged in buying and selling cotton in the city of Jackson, Miss. On the 5th day of December, 1906, he sent a telegram to Knight, Yancey & Co., of Mobile, Ala., submitting to them an offer to sell certain cotton which he then owned. The message was duly transmitted by the telegraph company to Mobile and duly delivered. On receipt of the telegram Knight, Yancey & Co. wired Willis, accepting the offer. This message of acceptance by them was duly delivered to the telegraph company at Mobile, and by it sent to Willis, at Jackson, and received at the Jackson office at 1:05 p.m. At 2 o'clock of the same day this message of acceptance had not been delivered to Willis although his office was within a short distance of the telegraph office. About 2 o'clock, and while this message lay undelivered in the Jackson office, Morrow, agent and manager of the firm of Knight, Yancey & Co., of Mobile, called Willis over the phone, and according to Mr. Willis' own statement asked him (Willis) if he had received the acceptance of his offer; that is, the acceptance he sent by telegraph. Willis replied to him over the phone that he had not. Whereupon Morrow said he was very glad of it, and would then withdraw his acceptance, to which Willis assented. Willis, up to this time, had not received the telegram of acceptance from the telegraph office, and went immediately to the telegraph office, called for the telegram, and the same was delivered to him. The same cotton was subsequently sold about 10 o'clock at night to the same parties, at a loss of some $218 to Willis, and the object of this suit is to hold the telegraph company liable for the loss

close the deal as against the offeree until the letter of agreement arrives is to extend that unbalanced risk of the market without observable reason. We have seen that it will be rough on the offeree if he is not permitted to rely on having obligated the offeror; but it will be even rougher on the offeror if he is obligated whereas the offeree, at the offeree's option, is not — *when there is no reason for the inequality.* It is not a question of principle that both must be bound, or neither; it is a question of principle that there must be a *good reason* for "binding" one while leaving the other free. This is why the cases suggesting power in the offeree of effective recapture or telegraphic annulment of his letter of acceptance are to be viewed as unwise in their possible application to deals of mutual obligation; and as untrustworthy as well. Of course the offeree's counsel can offer a rule of thumb; try it and see; it can't be worse than letting the letter go through. That is no case-law rule for judges.

thus sustained by Willis. There was a verdict in the court below in favor of the plaintiff, from a judgment on which the telegraph company appeals.

It is settled law and seems to be conceded on both sides, that under ordinary circumstances the acceptance of Willis' offer was complete when the telegram of acceptance of the proposition made was delivered by Knight, Yancey & Co. to the telegraph company in Mobile, and that the agreement then and there became a binding contract according to the express terms contained in the telegram from Willis. The main contention of appellee is that, while this is ordinarily true, yet in this particular instance the contract was not a binding contract, for the reason that, according to the custom prevailing among men engaged in the cotton business, the acceptance of the offer did not become binding until the actual delivery of the telegram by the telegraph company into the hands of Willis. It is claimed on the part of appellee that this is a general custom or usage prevailing among those engaged in the cotton trade, recognized by and acted under by them, and for this reason there was no contract until actual delivery to Willis, and, because there was no contract, the loss to the plaintiff was occasioned directly by the negligence of the telegraph company in failing to properly deliver the message. On the other hand, it is claimed by the telegraph company that there was a binding contract at the time when this telegram was delivered in Mobile, and that any action taken by Mr. Willis occasioning loss to him was caused by his own act in releasing Knight, Yancey & Co. from a valid contract; that they cannot be held responsible for it, because no loss occurred by reason of their negligence. According to Willis' own testimony, he was advised of the fact that there had been a telegram of acceptance before the order was cancelled over the telephone.

The contract made by the parties by virtue of these telegrams is clear, unambiguous, and valid, unless the so-called usage or custom can be invoked to relieve the parties from the legal effect of their acts. There is no such uncertainty about this contract as makes it necessary, because of indeterminate terms, to resort to custom or usage in order to understand exactly what was meant; but the contract is express in its terms, unambiguous, and became binding on the parties when the telegram of acceptance was delivered to the telegraph company in Mobile. It would be in the highest degree impolitic, and be the cause of introducing interminable confusion into contracts, if, when the terms of a contract are express, clear, and valid under the law, its legal effect could be controlled by some local or trade custom. Our court has long since been committed to this wise doctrine. Shackleford v. N.O., J. & Great Northern Ry., 37 Miss. 202. In the case of Hopper v. Sage, 112 N.Y. 530, 20 N.E. 350, 8 Am. St. Rep. 771, citing many authorities, the court says:

> Usage and custom cannot be proved to contravene a rule of law, or to alter
> or contradict the express or implied terms of a contract free from ambigu-

ity, or to make the legal rights or liabilities of the parties to a contract other than they are by the terms thereof. When the terms of a contract are clear, unambiguous, and valid, they must prevail, and no evidence of custom can be permitted to change them.

In the case of Shackleford v. New Orleans, Jackson & Great Northern Railroad Company, 37 Miss. 202, the court has said:

> These usages, many judges are of the opinion, should be sparingly adopted by the courts as rules of law, as they are often founded on mere mistake, or on the want of enlarged and comprehensive views of the full bearings of principles. Their true office is to interpret the otherwise indeterminate intentions of parties, and to ascertain the nature and extent of the contracts, arising, not from express stipulations, but from mere implications and presumptions and acts of a doubtful and equivocal character, and to fix and explain the meaning of words and expressions of doubtful or various senses. On this principle the usage or habit or trade, or conduct of an individual, which is known to the person who deals with him, may be given in evidence to prove what was the contract between them.

2 Greenleaf's Ev. §251, and note 5. And the court further says that, where a custom or usage is resorted to, such customs must be certain, uniform, reasonable, and not contrary to law. To the same effect is 2 Page on Contracts, p. 928: "The true and appropriate office of a usage or custom is to interpret the otherwise indeterminate intention of parties, and to ascertain the nature and extent of their contracts, arising, not from express stipulations, but from mere implications, assumptions, and acts of a doubtful or equivocal character."

Where the contract is definite and certain, the obligations of a party, by reason of the contract, became fixed by law by the terms of the contract which they have entered into, and, where there is nothing uncertain left in the contract, usage or custom has no place. There are many instances in which a contract may be explained and controlled by a custom prevailing among men engaged in a certain line of business, but this is not one of them. We think the court below erred in refusing to exclude all evidence in reference to the damages arising out of the failure of appellant to deliver the telegram.

For this reason, the case is reversed and remanded.

Reversed.

NOTE

In Dick v. United States, 82 F. Supp 326 (Ct. Cl. 1949), the court indicated, but did not actually hold, that a revocation that overtakes a previously sent acceptance will be effective. It rested its decision on the same grounds used in *Rhode Island Tool, supra* p. 354, namely, that changes in postal department regulations have undercut the rationale for the rule that an acceptance is effective on dispatch. The case is discussed in 34 Cornell L.Q. 632 (1949); 62 Harv. L. Rev. 1231 (1949); 44 Ill. L. Rev. 394 (1949); 25 Ind. L.J. 202 (1950); 34 Minn. L. Rev. 140 (1950); 17 U. Chi. L. Rev. 375 (1950); 59 Yale L.J. 374 (1950). See also the concurring opinion of Judge Collins in G. C. Casebolt Co. v. United States, 421 F.2d 710 (Ct. Cl. 1970).

Is it not true that the rule laid down in *Dick* lends itself to easy abuse? The offeree, having received an offer by mail, accepts immediately. The market shows signs of favorable movement. Under the *Dick* rule, the acceptor can watch the market while the acceptance is in transit: should the market develop unfavorably, he will do nothing; if it becomes favorable, he can telegraph a rejection that will protect him if it arrives before the acceptance. See Macneil, Time of Acceptance: Too Many Problems for a Single Rule, 112 U. Pa. L. Rev. 947, 952-962 (1964); Restatement Second §63 Comment *c*; Morrison v. Thoelke, 155 So. 2d 889 (Fla. Dist. Ct. App. 1963).

Suppose the offeree has mailed an acceptance, and also a rejection (containing no mention of the acceptance), which arrives first: The offeror, relying on the rejection, makes a second contract with a third party. A) He sells at a large profit, the market having risen. B) He sells at a large loss, due to a drop in the market. Is the offeror liable to the offeree in situation A? Is the offeree liable in situation B? See Comment *c* to Restatement Second §63, and §40, which reads as follows:

> Time when Rejection or Counter-Offer Terminates the
> Power of Acceptance
>
> Rejection or counter-offer by mail or telegram does not terminate the power of acceptance until received by the offeror, but limits the power so that a letter or telegram of acceptance started after the sending of an otherwise effective rejection or counter-offer is only a counter-offer unless the acceptance is received by the offeror before he receives the rejection or counter-offer.

CALDWELL v. CLINE
109 W. Va. 553, 156 S.E. 55 (1930)

LIVELY, President: In this chancery suit for the specific performance of a contract for the sale and exchange of real estate, the chancellor sustained a demurrer to plaintiff's bill of complaint and dismissed the bill. Plaintiff appeals.

According to the allegations contained in the bill, W. D. Cline, residing at Valls Creek, McDowell County, West Virginia, owner of a tract of land on Indian Creek, McDowell County, addressed a letter, dated January 29, 1929, to W. H. Caldwell, at Peterstown, Monroe County, West

Virginia in which Cline proposed to pay to Caldwell the sum of $6,000.00 cash and to deed to Caldwell his land on Indian Creek in exchange for Caldwell's land known as the McKinsey farm. The letter further provided that Cline "will give you (Caldwell) eight days in which" to accept or reject the offer. Caldwell received the letter at Peterstown on February 2, 1929. On February 8, 1929, the offeree wired Cline as follows: "Land deal is made. Prepare deed to me. See letter." The telegram reached Cline on February 9, 1929. Upon Cline's refusal to carry out the terms of the alleged agreement, plaintiff instituted this suit for specific performance, the titles to the farm remaining unchanged. . . .

Defendant's main contention is that the offer was not accepted within the time limit specified in the offer, and counsel for defendant, in his brief, states the law to be as "the time for acceptance runs from the date of the offer and not from the date of its delivery." The subject of contract by mail began with the English case of Kennedy v. Lee, 3 Meriv., and was followed a few years later by Adams v. Lindsell, 1. B. & Ald. 681 (1818), and courts have had no hesitation in recognizing the validity of simple contracts thus made. . . . The court, adjudging that a contract had been made upon the posting of the acceptance, stated "that defendants must be considered in law as making, during every instant of the time their letter was traveling, the same identical offer to the plaintiffs." Taken literally, it would follow that an offer was made at the instant the letter is mailed. That the quoted statement from Adams v. Lindsell lends difficulty is recognized and criticized by an eminent writer, who finds "the truth of the matter" stated thus in Bennett v. Cosgriff, 38 L.T. Rep. (N.S.) 177: "A letter is a continuing offer or order, or statement by the sender which takes effect in the place where the person to whom it is sent receives it." Williston, Contracts, Vol. 1, p. 50; and other courts and text writers have recognized the rule that where a person uses the post to make an offer, the offer is not made when it is posted but when it is received. . . . The reason for such a rule is clear. When contracting parties are present, words spoken by one party must strike the ear of the other before there can be mutual assent. So inter absentes, letters, which perform the office of words, must come to the knowledge of the party to whom they are addressed before they are accorded legal existence.

> The distinction between contracts inter presentes and those inter absentes has no metaphysical existence, for even inter presentes some appreciable time must elapse between the offer on the one hand and the acceptance on the other. As the parties withdraw from each other this time increases, and when they are so far apart that they are obliged to resort to writing to communicate their thoughts to each other, it is none the less true of the communications made by this medium, than of those made by means of spoken words, that in law they are allowed no existence until they reach the intelligence of the person to whom they are addressed.

1 Amer. Law. Rev. 434, 456.

As in other contracts, to consummate a contract for the sale of land, there must be mutual assent (27 R.C.L. 323) and where the proposal to sell stipulates a limited time for acceptance, it is essential, to constitute a valid contract, that the acceptance be communicated to the proposer within the time limited. Dyer v. Duffy, 30 W. Va. 148.

The letter, proposing that Cline "will give you eight days" to accept or reject the offer, is, without more, conclusive of the offerer's intention; and, the unconditional acceptance having been received by Cline within the specified time limit, the result was a concurrence of the minds of the contracting parties upon the subject matter of their negotiations; in other words, a consummated contract (Iron Works v. Construction Co., 86 W. Va. 173), and one which equity may enforce. Hastings v. Montgomery, 95 W. Va. 734.

The contention of defendant, relied upon as a third ground in his demurrer, that acceptance could be made only by letter is without merit, since the offer did not provide the means of communication. Lucas v. Telegraph Co., 109 N.W. (Iowa) 191.

Being of the opinion that the allegations contained in the bill were sufficient, we reverse the decree of the lower court and reinstate plaintiff's bill of complaint.

Reversed; bill reinstated; cause remanded.

NOTE

For a discussion of the case, see 79 U. Pa. L. Rev. 637 (1931); 17 Va. L. Rev. 503 (1931). On silence in response to a delayed acceptance, see 1 Corbin §74 (1963).

If A sends an offer by mail to B dated August 13 and states that the offer must be accepted within five days, should A be bound if the acceptance is sent within five days but arrives August 19? See Falconer v. Mazess, 403 Pa. 165, 168 A.2d 558 (1961).

Section 10.   Unilateral vs. Bilateral Contracts — Manufactured Difficulties

The common law, as the Sixth Interim Report of the English Law Revision Committee 23 (1937) informs us,

> traditionally divides parol contracts into two classes, the bilateral contract of a promise for a promise, and the unilateral contract of a promise for an act. In the case of bilateral contracts one promise is held to be consideration for the other, the agreement, therefore, becoming effective at the moment when the promises are exchanged. In the case of a unilateral

contract, however, the promise does not become binding until the act has been completely performed. A promisor may therefore withdraw his promise at any time before completion of the act, even though he knows that the promisee has already entered upon the performance and has nearly completed it.

Not so long ago, the practical wisdom of "the great dichotomy," ingeniously elaborated and defended by Langdell in his Summary of the Law of Contracts 248 (2d ed. 1880) and by Williston, 1 Williston §13, was accepted as if grounded in the nature of things, and its application was not regarded as difficult, at least in theory. Its implications, however harsh in an individual case, were treated as just, since the division purported to be in keeping with the intentions of the offeror, "the master of the bargain." In terms of this analysis, the doing of the act constitutes acceptance, the bargained-for consideration, and the offeree's performance.

The case material that follows serves to show the powerful influence of the famous distinction and its gradual erosion. Some courts have not hesitated to apply the distinction literally even where performance of the requested act would require considerable time and effort, and have permitted the offeror to revoke his offer as long as he had not received the whole consideration. These courts regarded the offeree as adequately protected by a recovery in quantum meruit. Other courts, however, have found the rigid application of the division, when applied to actual life situations and not to the hypothetical case of the climbing of a flag-pole, difficult to reconcile with their sense of justice. Small wonder that they did not regret the discovery that the line of demarcation between the two institutions is often blurred; nor did they hesitate to tamper with the whole doctrine, even at the risk of an over-correction. The Restatement of Contracts, reflecting modern case law, has narrowed the gap between unilateral and bilateral contracts. See §§31, 45, 56, 63.

The reform movement received a powerful impetus by the attack on the famous distinction in Llewellyn's article, On Our Case-Law of Contract: Offer and Acceptance, 48 Yale L.J. 1, 779 (1938-1939), which makes the argument that "the great dichotomy," based on the erroneous assumption that businessmen always bargain in terms of acts or of promises, fails to correspond to the notions of businessmen as to when "a deal is on." His observations are worth quoting.

   . . . The great dichotomy in the orthodox doctrine of Offer and Acceptance is that between bilateral and unilateral contract.[131] But there have

131. The argument is that the classical bilateral-unilateral distinction dies as it approaches fact either of life or of case decision. I put forward as a major piece of evidence the prominence which that distinction has in the table of contents of 1 Williston and Thompson, [Contracts (1936)], and the lack of correspondence of the text, and much more of the notes, to the suggestions in the table of contents. The Restatement shows the distinction only in the background, coloring much, but not explicitly, as a fundamental cleavage.

been signs over thirty years or more of difficulty with it and its implications. Perhaps it is time to recanvass the *life-situation* with which it has to deal. And so to recanvass the cases which its office is to reflect and to guide.

This will not be easy doing. The rules of Offer and Acceptance have been worked over; they have been written over; they have been shaped and rubbed smooth with pumice, they wear the deep rich polish of a thousand class rooms; they have a grip on the vision and indeed on the affections held by no other rules "of law," real or pseudo. For it was Offer and Acceptance which first led each of us out of laydom into The Law. Puzzled, befogged, adrift in the strange words and technique of cases, with only our sane feeling of what was decent for a compass, we felt the warm sun suddenly, we knew that we were arriving, we knew we too could "think like a lawyer." That was when we learned to down seasickness as A revoked when B was almost up the flag-pole. Within the first October, we had achieved a technical glee in justifying judgment then for A; and succulent memory lingers, of the way our dumber brethren were pilloried as Laymen still. This is therefore no area of "rules" to be disturbed. It is an area where we *want* no disturbance, and will brook none. It is the Rabbit-Hole down which we fell into the Law, and to him who has gone down it, no queer phenomenon is strange; he has been magicked; the logic of Wonderland we then entered makes mere discrepant decision negligible. And it is not only hard, it is obnoxious, for any of us who have gone through that experience to even conceive of Offer and Acceptance as perhaps in need of re-examination.

(Id. at 32)

The impact of this criticism is reflected in the Uniform Commercial Code and the Restatement of Contracts. U.C.C. §2-206, "Offer and Acceptance in Formation of Contract," reads as follows:

> (1)   Unless otherwise unambiguously indicated by the language or circumstances
>   (a)   an offer to make a contract shall be construed as inviting acceptance in any manner and by any medium reasonable in circumstances;
>   (b)   an order or other offer to buy goods for prompt or current shipment shall be construed as inviting acceptance either by a prompt promise to ship or by the prompt or current shipment of conforming or non-conforming goods, but such a shipment of non-conforming goods does not constitute an acceptance if the seller seasonably notifies the buyer that the shipment is offered only as an accommodation to the buyer.
> (2)   Where the beginning of a requested performance is a reasonable mode of acceptance an offeror who is not notified of acceptance within a reasonable time may treat the offer as having lapsed before acceptance.

The Restatement Second has followed this trend by deleting §12 of the original Restatement which defined unilateral and bilateral contracts. These terms are no longer used because of doubts as to the utility of the distinction (Reporter's note to §12).[132] While §31 of the original Restatement laid down a presumption that an offer invites a bilateral contract, §32 of the Restatement Second favors a different interpretation. It reads:

Invitation of Promise or Performance

In case of doubt an offer is interpreted as inviting the offeree to accept either by promising to perform what the offer requests or by rendering the performance, as the offeree chooses.[133]

This does not mean, however, that the Restatement Second has ignored the fact that a promise is often binding on the promisor even though the promisee is not bound by any corresponding obligation. This is strikingly illustrated by the rule laid down in §45.[134] Consult Braucher, Offer and Acceptance in The Second Restatement, 74 Yale L.J. 302 (1964).

CARLILL v. CARBOLIC SMOKE BALL CO.

[1893] 1 Q.B. 256 (C.A. 1892)

Appeal from a decision of Hawkins, J. [1892] 2 Q.B. 484.

The defendants, who were the proprietors and vendors of a medical preparation called "The Carbolic Smoke Ball," inserted in the Pall Mall

---

132. Restatement Second §12, Reporter's Note (Tent. Draft No. 1, 1964):

As defined in the original Restatement, "unilateral contract" included three quite different types of transaction: (1) the promise which does not contemplate a bargain, such as the promise under seal to make a gift, (2) certain option contracts, such as the option under seal (see §§24A, 45), and (3) the bargain completed on one side, such as the loan which is to be repaid. This grouping of unlike transactions was productive of confusion.

133. See also §30. It reads:

Form of Acceptance Invited

(1) An offer may invite or require acceptance to be made by an affirmative answer in words, or by performing or refraining from performing a specified act, or may empower the offeree to make a selection of terms in this acceptance.

(2) Unless otherwise indicated by the language or the circumstances, an offer invites acceptance in any manner and by any medium reasonable in the circumstances.

[See also §55].

134. It reads:

Option Contract Created by Part Performance or Tender

(1) Where an offer invites an offeree to accept by rendering a performance and does not invite a promissory acceptance, an option contract is created when the offeree begins the invited performance or tenders part of it.

(2) The offeror's duty of performance under any option contract so created is conditional on completion or tender of the invited performance in accordance with the terms of the offer.

Consult also, §25; §87, supra p. 315.

Gazette of November 13, 1891, and in other newspapers, the following advertisement:

> £100 reward will be paid by the Carbolic Smoke Ball Company to any person who contracts the increasing epidemic influenza, colds, or any disease caused by taking cold, after having used the ball three times daily for two weeks according to the printed directions supplied with each ball. £1000 is deposited with the Alliance Bank, Regent Street shewing our sincerity in the matter.
>
> During the last epidemic of influenza many thousand carbolic smoke balls were sold as preventives against this disease, and in no ascertained case was the disease contracted by those using the carbolic smoke ball.
>
> One carbolic smoke ball will last a family several months, making it the cheapest remedy in the world at the price, 10s., post free. The ball can be refilled at a cost of 5s. Address, Carbolic Smoke Ball Company, 27 Princes Street, Hanover Square, London.

The plaintiff, a lady, on the faith of this advertisement, bought one of the balls at a chemist's and used it as directed, three times a day, from November 20, 1891, to January 17, 1892, when she was attacked by influenza. Hawkins, J., held that she was entitled to recover the £100. The defendants appealed.

LINDLEY, L.J. . . . We must first consider whether this was intended to be a promise at all, or whether it was a mere puff which meant nothing. Was it a mere puff? My answer to that question is "No," and I base my answer upon this passage: "£1000 is deposited with the Alliance Bank, shewing our sincerity in the matter." Now, for what was that money deposited or that statement made except to negative the suggestion that this was a mere puff and meant nothing at all? The deposit is called in aid by the advertiser as a proof of his sincerity in the matter — that is, the sincerity of his promise to pay this £100 in the event which he has specified. I say this for the purpose of giving point to the observation that we are not inferring a promise; there is the promise, as plain as words can make it.

Then it is contended that it is not binding. In the first place, it is said that it is not made with anybody in particular. Now that point is common to the words of this advertisement and to the words of all other advertisements offering rewards. They are offers to anybody who performs the conditions named in the advertisement, and anybody who does perform the conditions accepts the offer. In point of law this advertisement is an offer to pay £100 to anybody who will perform these conditions, and the performance of the conditions, is the acceptance of the offer. That rests upon a string of authorities, the earliest of which is Williams v. Carwardine, 4 Barn. & Adol. 621, which has been followed by many other decisions upon advertisements offering rewards.

But then it is said, "Supposing that the performance of the conditions is an acceptance of the offer, that acceptance ought to have been notified." Unquestionably, as a general proposition, when an offer is made, it is necessary in order to make a binding contract, not only that it should be accepted, but that the acceptance should be notified. But is that so in cases of this kind? I apprehend that they are an exception to that rule, or, if not an exception, they are open to the observation that the notification of the acceptance need not precede the performance. This offer is a continuing offer. It was never revoked, and if notice of acceptance is required — which I doubt very much, for I rather think the true view is that which was expressed and explained by Lord Blackburn in the case of Brogden v. Railway Co., 2 App. Cas. 666, 691, — if notice of acceptance is required, the person who makes the offer gets the notice of acceptance contemporaneously with his notice of the performance of the condition. If he gets notice of the acceptance before his offer is revoked, that in principle is all you want. I, however, think that the true view, in a case of this kind, is that the person who makes the offer shows by his language and from the nature of the transaction that he does not expect and does not require notice of the acceptance apart from notice of the performance. . . .

I come now to the last point which I think requires attention: that is, the consideration. It has been argued that this is nudum pactum — that there is no consideration. We must apply to that argument the usual legal tests. Let us see whether there is no advantage to the defendants. It is said that the use of the ball is no advantage to them, and that what benefits them is the sale; and the case is put that a lot of these balls might be stolen, and that it would be no advantage to the defendants if the thief or other people used them. The answer to that, I think, is as follows: It is quite obvious that in view of the advertisers a use by the public of their remedy, if they can only get the public to have confidence enough to use it, will react and produce a sale which is directly beneficial to them. Therefore, the advertisers get out of the use an advantage which is enough to constitute a consideration.

But there is another view. Does not the person who acts upon this advertisement and accepts the offer put himself to some inconvenience at the request of the defendants? Is it nothing to use this ball three times daily for two weeks according to the directions at the request of the advertiser? Is that to go for nothing? It appears to me that there is a distinct inconvenience, not to say a detriment, to any person who so uses the smoke ball. I am of opinion, therefore, that there is ample consideration for the promise. . . .

BOWEN, L.J. . . . Then it was said that there was no notification of the acceptance of the contract. One cannot doubt that, as an ordinary rule of law, an acceptance of an offer made ought to be notified to the person who makes the offer, in order that the two minds may come together. Unless this is done, the two minds may be apart, and there is not that consensus which is necessary according to the English law — I say nothing about the laws of other countries — to make a contract. But there is this clear gloss to be made upon that doctrine, that as notification of acceptance is required for the benefit of the person who makes the offer, the person who makes the offer may dispense with notice to himself if he thinks it desirable to do so, and I suppose there can be no doubt that where a person in an offer made by him to another person, expressly or impliedly intimates a particular mode of acceptance as sufficient to make the bargain binding, it is only necessary for the other person to whom such offer is made to follow the indicated method of acceptance; and if the person making the offer, expressly or impliedly intimates in his offer that it will be sufficient to act on the proposal without communicating acceptance of it to himself, performance of the condition is a sufficient acceptance without notification.

That seems to me to be the principle which lies at the bottom of the acceptance cases, of which two instances are the well-known judgment of Mellish, L. J., in Harris's Case, L.R. 7 Ch. 587, and the very instructive judgment of Lord Blackburn in Brogden v. Railway Co., 2 App. Cas. 666, 691, in which he appears to me to take exactly the line I have indicated.

Now, if that is the law, how are we to find out whether the person who makes the offer does intimate that notification of acceptance will not be necessary in order to constitute a binding bargain? In many cases you look to the offer itself. In many cases you extract from the character of the transaction that notification is not required, and in the advertisement cases it seems to me to follow as an inference to be drawn from the transaction itself that a person is not to notify his acceptance of the offer before he performs the condition, but that if he performs the condition notification is dispensed with. It seems to me that from the point of view of common sense no other idea could be entertained. If I advertise to the world that my dog is lost, and that anybody who brings the dog to a particular place will be paid some money, are all the police or other persons whose business it is to find lost dogs to be expected to sit down and write a note saying that they have accepted my proposal? Why, of course, they at once look after the dog, and as soon as they find the dog they have performed the condition. The essence of the transaction is that the dog should be found, and it is not necessary under such circumstances, as it seems to me, that in order to make the contract binding there should be any notification of acceptance. It follows from the nature of the thing that the performance of the condition is sufficient acceptance without the notification of it, and a person who makes an offer in an advertisement of that kind makes an offer which must be read by the light of that common sense reflection. He does, therefore, in his offer impliedly indicate that he does not require notification of the acceptance of the offer.

Appeal dismissed.

TAFT v. HYATT
105 Kan. 35, 180 P. 213 (1919)

Suit by B. L. Taft and others against William S. Hyatt and others in nature of interpleader to determine the right to a reward. From a decree for defendant named, the remaining defendants appeal. Reversed and remanded, with directions.

PORTER, J. The controversy is between rival claimants for a reward offered for the apprehension of a criminal. The suit is an equitable one instituted by the persons who offered the reward, and who alleged that they were threatened with litigation by different parties claiming it, that some one or more of the defendants are entitled to the money, which the plaintiffs brought into court, and asked the defendants be required to set up their respective claims.

On May 16, 1917, it became known in the city of Parsons that Agnes Smith, the Wife of Dr. Asa Smith, had been assaulted, and that a negro physician by the name of Robert E. Smith was suspected of the crime. (The victim of the assault died, and Robert E. Smith was charged with and convicted of murder in the first degree. The judgment was affirmed. State v. Smith, 103 Kan. 148, 174 P. 551.)

The plaintiffs are Dr. Asa Smith, husband of the murdered woman, and certain individuals who are members of the A.H.T.A. They caused to be published and circulated an offer of $750 reward "for the arrest or information that will lead to" the arrest of the accused.

As to the claims of the defendant Wm. S. Hyatt, the findings of fact are, in substance, these: Hyatt is an attorney at law with an office in the city of Parsons. Another attorney notified him that R. E. Smith desired to see him, and told him where Smith could be found. During the afternoon of May 17, 1917, Hyatt went to the hiding place of the accused in the city of Parsons in compliance with the directions that had been given him, and there found Smith. The two talked together for an hour or more, but were unable to reach an agreement as to the employment of Hyatt to defend Smith. There is a finding that the relation of attorney and client never existed between them at any time, and that Hyatt came away without being employed. Shortly before he went to see Smith, Hyatt learned that the reward had been offered, and after returning from his interview, he went to the office of the county attorney and told him where Smith could be found, and an arrangement was made to have the deputy sheriff go to the place for the purpose of arresting Smith. The deputy sheriff was called, and with Hyatt drove to the place where Smith had been left by Hyatt earlier in the afternoon, when they discovered that Smith was not there, but had been taken away by the other defendants. The court further found that Hyatt gave the first information to the proper officers which would lead to the arrest of Smith after the offer of the reward had been made, and that the information was given more than an hour previous to the time Smith was removed by the other defendants from the house where he had been hiding, and that Hyatt's purpose in giving the information to the county attorney and the deputy sheriff was to obtain the reward offered by the plaintiffs; that the fact that Smith was not arrested from the information given by Hyatt was due to no fault or neglect of Hyatt. As a conclusion of law the court held that Hyatt was entitled to the reward.

The findings with reference to the other claimants are that Clarence Glass and Charles C. Edwards went to Thomas A. Murry, the chief of police of the city of Parsons, shortly after 6 o'clock on the afternoon of May 17, 1917, and requested Murry to go in a closed cab to a certain place in the city and take charge of Smith and deliver him to the jail at Oswego. Murry complied with the request, and went to the place directed, where he found the accused, together with the defendants Glass, Edwards, Tyson, Cook, and Ransom. All of them got into the cab with the chief of police, and the party went to Oswego where Smith was delivered to the sheriff of Labette county. Before leaving Parsons, and just as the party got into the cab with the chief of police, the latter told the accused to consider himself under arrest and informed him of the intention to deliver him at the county jail at Oswego. The evidence shows that the defendants who secured the services of the chief of police in taking the accused to Oswego were all members of the lodge of Colored Masons, to which the accused belonged. The court finds that Smith expressed to them his fears of mob violence, and it was agreed that he would give himself into their custody, and they agreed to protect him; that none of these defendants had heard of the offer of reward at the time they called Murry, the chief of police, to their assistance. Murry testified that he had heard of the reward before he arrested Smith, and that the reason he placed him under arrest and took him to Oswego was partly to earn the reward and partly to protect Smith from mob violence. The court finds that it was the duty of Murry, as chief of police, to make arrest of fugitives from justice, that at the time of receiving Smith into custody Murry was not armed with a warrant or other process for the arrest, and that Smith had not committed any offense within the view of the chief of police.

The court found in favor of Hyatt and against the other defendants. The costs were directed to be paid out of the fund, and the balance of the $750 was ordered paid to Hyatt. The other defendants bring the case here for review. . . .

It is urged that it would be unconscionable to permit an attorney, under such circumstances, to avail himself of an offer of reward; that to do so would sanction conduct highly unprofessional in an attorney, and would permit him to obtain from one who occupies the position of a prospective client information which he uses to the other's prejudice and to gain a pecuniary benefit to himself. Without passing upon the question of the propriety of the conduct of an attorney in attempting to obtain a pecuniary advantage to the prejudice of an accused person under such circumstances, we think that Hyatt is not entitled to recover, because, from his own statement and the undisputed facts in evidence, his efforts to secure the apprehension of the accused were unavailing. The information which he gave to the officers did not result, even remotely, in bringing about the apprehension of the accused. The court finds that the information Hyatt gave would lead to the arrest of the guilty person if it had been acted upon promptly, and the fact that it did not bring about the result was through no fault of Hyatt's. But this finding does not help Hyatt's case. It may have been that the officers to whom he confided his information were too slow. Whatever the reason, before any action was taken by them which resulted in apprehending the accused, the latter was on his way to the county jail in the custody of another officer, having, with the aid of his friends, surrendered himself. So far as the apprehension of the guilty person was concerned, Hyatt might as well have kept his information to himself.

The defendants who admit that they had not heard of the offer or the reward until after the accused had been surrendered to the sheriff at Oswego are not entitled to recover. A private offer of reward for the apprehension of a fugitive from justice or of a person suspected or charged with an offense stands, as a general rule, upon a different footing from a statutory offer, or one made by virtue of a statute. 34 Cyc. 1752, 1753, and cases cited in notes. The offer of a private individual is a mere proposal, which, when accepted, becomes a contract. Until it is accepted by some person who upon the strength of the offer takes some steps to earn the reward, there is no contract. Van Vlissingen v. Manning, 105 Ill. App. 255. There must be a meeting of the minds of the parties — on the one side, of the person who makes the offer; on the other, of the person who performs the service. Where a claimant for the reward was not aware that it had been offered until after he had performed his services, there has been no meeting of minds which would constitute a contract. Besides, the undisputed facts with respect to those defendants who called the chief of police to assist them in taking the accused to Oswego are that these claimants were simply assisting the accused in surrendering himself. Their testimony is that what they did was for the purpose of protecting him from mob violence. They had never heard of the reward, and, of course, are not entitled to any part of it.

Thomas A. Murry cannot recover, because, as chief of police of the city of Parsons, it was his duty to make an arrest of fugitives from justice or persons charged with or suspected of crimes. The fact that he was not armed with a warrant or other process for the arrest of the accused is immaterial, because there was reasonable ground for believing that Smith had committed the particular offense charged against him, and his subsequent conviction established his actual guilt. . . .

It had been repeatedly held that public policy does not permit an officer to claim a reward for merely doing his duty. . . .

Inasmuch as none of the defendants are entitled to recover any part of the reward, we think it would be a harsh rule to say that the plaintiffs are estopped from claiming it because of the admissions in their petition. In our view of the matter, justice requires that the trial court be directed to render judgment against all of the defendants, and that the plaintiffs, after paying the cost of the proceeding, be entitled to the return of the money. . . .

The judgment is reversed, and the cause remanded, with directions to carry this order into effect. All the Justices concurring.

NOTE

1. For an interesting discussion of the *Carlill* case, and of the self-inflicted predicament of the court in superimposing offer and acceptance analysis on unilateral contracts, see Simpson, Innovation in Nineteenth Century Contract Law, 91 L.Q. Rev. 237, 258, especially 262 (1975).

2. Consult Hall v. Bean, 582 S.W.2d 263 (Tex. Civ. App. 1979); Alexander v. Russo, 1 Kan. App. 2d 546, 571 P.2d 350 (1977). The role that the unilateral contract doctrine plays in reward cases can be defended on economic grounds.

> Because the potential finders of lost property will often be numerous and unidentified, there is no feasible way in which the owner could negotiate with each of them for the return of his property. The unilateral-contract approach enables voluntary transacting without actual negotiations with potential transactors. . . . Since the unilateral-contract doctrine enables the parties in the lost-property situation in effect to write their own contract, the law need not intervene and write a contract for them prescribing the finder's reward.

A. Kronman & R. Posner, The Economics of Contract Law 58 (1979).

In some states, a finder can obtain a fixed reward whether or not the owner has offered one. See, e.g., Flood v. City National Bank of Clinton, 218 Iowa 898, 253 N.W. 509 (1934). If state law requires that a finder turn over lost property to the rightful owner, should the finder be able to recover a reward? Is there consideration for the owner's promise to pay a reward? If he is behaving in an economically rational manner, "the owner of the property, knowing of the law and gauging its effect, will adjust the reward according to his perception of its effectiveness. If he still offers a positive reward, this suggests that the resources devoted to enforcing the law are insufficient to induce the optimal level of finding." A. Kronman & R. Posner, The Economics of Contract Law 59 (1979). Would this argument be applicable to the sheriff in the principal case?

STRONG v. SHEFFIELD
144 N.Y. 392, 39 N.E. 330 (1895)

ANDREWS, C.J. The contract between a maker or endorser of a promissory note and the payee forms no exception to the general rule that a promise, not supported by a consideration, is nudum pactum. The law governing commercial paper which precludes an inquiry into the consideration as against bona fide holders for value before maturity, has no application where the suit is between the original parties to the instrument. It is undisputed that the demand note upon which the action was brought was made by the husband of the defendant and endorsed by her at his request and delivered to the plaintiff, the payee, as security for an antecedent debt owing by the husband to the plaintiff. The debt of the husband was past due at the time, and the only consideration for the wife's endorsement, which is or can be claimed, is that as part of the transaction there was an agreement by the plaintiff when the note was given to forbear the collection of the debt, or a request for forbearance, which was followed by forbearance for a period of about two years subsequent to the giving of the note. There is no doubt that an agreement by the creditor to forbear the collection of a debt presently due is a good consideration for an absolute or conditional promise of a third person to pay the debt, or for any obligation he may assume in respect thereto. Nor is it essential that the creditor should bind himself at the time to forbear collection or to give time. If he is requested by his debtor to extend the time, and a third person undertakes in consideration of forbearance being given to become liable as surety or otherwise, and the creditor does in fact forbear in reliance upon the undertaking, although he enters into no enforcible agreement to do so, his acquiescence in the request, and an actual forbearance in consequence thereof for a reasonable time, furnishes a good consideration for the collateral undertaking. In other words, a request followed by performance is sufficient, and mutual promises at the time are not essential, unless it was the understanding that the promisor was not to be bound, except on condition that the other party entered into an immediate and reciprocal obligation to do the thing requested. Morton v. Burn, 7 A. & E. 19; Wilby v. Elgee, L.R., 10 C.P. 497; King v. Upton, 4 Greenl. (Me.) 387, 16 Am. Dec. 266; Leake on Con., p. 54; Am. Lead. Cas. Vol. 2, p. 96 et seq. and cases cited. The general rule is clearly, and in the main accurately, stated in the note to Forth v.

Stanton (1 Saund. 210, note b). The learned reporter says: "And in all cases of forbearance to sue, such forbearance must be either absolute or for a definite time, or for a reasonable time; forbearance for a little, or for some time, is not sufficient." The only qualification to be made is that in the absence of a specified time a reasonable time is held to be intended. Oldershaw v. King, 2 H. & N. 517; Calkins v. Chandler, 36 Mich. 320, 24 Am. Rep. 593. The note in question did not in law extend the payment of the debt. It was payable on demand, and although being payable with interest it was in form consistent with an intention that payment should not be immediately demanded, yet there was nothing on its face to prevent an immediate suit on the note against the maker or to recover the original debt. Merritt v. Todd, 23 N.Y. 28, 80 Am. Dec. 243; Shutts v. Fingar, 100 N.Y. 539, 3 N.E. 588, 53 Am. Rep. 231.

In the present case the agreement made is not left to inference, nor was it a case of request to forbear, followed by forbearance, in pursuance of the request, without any promise on the part of the creditor at the time. The plaintiff testified that there was an express agreement on his part to the effect that he would not pay the note away, nor put it in any bank for collection, but (using the words of the plaintiff) "I will hold it until such time as I want my money, I will make a demand on you for it." And again: "No, I will keep it until such time as I want it." Upon this alleged agreement the defendant endorsed the note. It would have been no violation of the plaintiff's promise if, immediately on receiving the note, he had commenced suit upon it. Such a suit would have been an assertion that he wanted the money and would have fulfilled the condition of forbearance. The debtor and the defendant, when they became parties to the note, may have had the hope or expectation that forbearance would follow, and there was forbearance in fact. But there was no agreement to forbear for a fixed time or for a reasonable time, but an agreement to forbear for such time as the plaintiff should elect. The consideration is to be tested by the agreement, and not by what was done under it. It was a case of mutual promises, and so intended. We think the evidence failed to disclose any consideration for the defendant's endorsement, and that the trial Court erred in refusing so to rule.

The order of the General Term reversing the judgment should be affirmed, and judgment absolute directed for the defendant on the stipulation with costs in all courts.

Ordered accordingly.

NOTE

Consult Restatement Second §2. Why wasn't the plaintiff's express promise "that he would not pay the note away, nor put it in any bank for collection," good consideration?

Has the rule of the case been altered by the Uniform Commercial Code? See U.C.C. §§3-408, 3-303(b), and 3-415. See also First National City Bank v. Valentia, 61 Misc. 2d 554, 306 N.Y.S.2d 227 (1970), *reargument denied*, 62 Misc. 2d 719, 309 N.Y.S.2d 563 (1970).

The appellate record reveals that plaintiff Strong was Mrs. Sheffield's uncle, and that Mrs. Sheffield had her own successful business and was reluctant to endorse the note because she feared her credit might be impaired. See E. A. Farnsworth & W. F. Young, Cases and Materials on Contracts 72 note a (3d ed. 1980).

HAY v. FORTIER

116 Me. 455, 102 A. 294 (1917)

Action by George G. Hay against Mary A. Fortier. Case reserved. Judgment for plaintiff.

KING, J. The case made by the agreed statement is this: The defendant became a surety on a 15-day bond given by one Henry H. Sawyer to the plaintiff. The conditions of the bond were not complied with, and the defendant was notified of her liability under the bond and requested to make payment thereof. On February 4, 1915, the defendant's attorney wrote the attorney of the plaintiff as follows:

> I have seen Mrs. Fortier, who says it will be a great hardship to pay this entire amount at the present time as the other signers are worthless. She suggests . . . that she will pay you $100 next week, if the papers are regular, and settle the balance by payments, the whole bill to be paid before your April term of court. . . .

To that the plaintiff, through his attorney, replied sending copies of the papers and saying:

"I am willing to accept $100 on account, providing you send same to me immediately and the balance on or before the first Tuesday of April. . . ."

The defendant paid the $100 forthwith, but no more. The plaintiff waited till long after the first Tuesday of April, and on June 1, 1915, brought an action of debt on the bond against the principal and all the sureties. Mrs. Fortier answered to that action at the return term thereof, and at a subsequent term, on November 3, 1915, by agreement, that action was "discontinued without costs and without prejudice," the counsel of the respective parties signing the docket entry to that effect. Why that action was thus discontinued does not appear in this case. On the following day, November 4, 1915, this action was brought against Mrs. Fortier, based upon a breach of her alleged special promise to pay the balance due under the bond before the April term of court, as stated in the correspondence referred to. The declaration is not made a part of the case, but the parties stipulate that it "is in due form." The defense is that the alleged promise on which the action is based was without a legal consideration and is therefore nonenforceable.

We think the agreed statement justifies the conclusion, that the defendant promised to pay at once $100, and the balance due under the bond before the April term of court, provided the plaintiff would forbear action on the bond, and that the plaintiff on his part, in consideration of such part payment at once, and the promise to pay the balance on or before the time specified, agreed to forbear, and did in fact forbear, action on the bond until after the time specified. And a promise to forbear and give time for the payment of a debt followed by actual forbearance for the time specified or for a reasonable time when no definite time is named, is certainly a sufficient consideration for a promise to pay the debt. Moore v. Kenney, 83 Me. 80, 90, 21 A. 749, 23 Am. St. Rep. 753.

On the other hand, it is obvious that the defendant by her special promise did not agree to do anything that she was not then legally bound to do. Her liability under the bond was then due and payable. She might then have been required to pay it all forthwith. And it is a well-recognized principle that the payment, or promise of payment, of money which is then due and payable by virtue of an existing valid contract of the promisor, is not in contemplation of law a sufficient consideration for any new contract. Wescott v. Mitchell, 95 Me. 377, 383, 50 A. 21; Dunn v. Collins, 70 Me. 230; Wimer v. Worth Township Poor Overseers, 104 Pa. 317; Mathewson v. Strafford Bank, 45 N.H. 104; Parmelee v. Thompson, 45 N.Y. 58, 6 Am. Rep. 33; Bedford's Ex'r v. Chandler, 81 Vt. 270, 273, 69 A. 874, 17 L.R.A., N.S., 1239, 130 Am. St. Rep. 1057; 6 R.C.L. 664. The defendant therefore contends that the plaintiff's promise to forbear action on the bond was without a legal consideration and not binding on him; in other words, that he could have brought action on the bond immediately after the part payment was made, in total disregard of his promise to wait until the April term of court. We think that contention is sound, and well supported by authorities. In Warren v. Hodge, 121 Mass. 106, the court said:

> It is too well settled to require discussion or reference to authorities that an agreement to forbear to sue upon a debt already due and payable, for no other consideration than a payment of a part of the debt, is without legal consideration, and cannot be availed of by the debtor, either by way of contract or of estoppel.

But it does not follow, as the defendant claims, that this action against her is not maintainable, simply because the plaintiff's promise to forbear action on the bond could not have been enforced against him during the specified period of forbearance.

If a contract, although not originally binding for want of mutuality, is nevertheless executed by the party not originally bound, so that the party asserting the invalidity of the contract has actually received the benefit contracted for, the latter will be estopped from refusing performance on his part on the ground that the contract was not originally binding on the other, who has performed.

6 R.C.L. 690.

Granting that the parties, through the correspondence referred to, entered into a bilateral contract, and that there was want of mutuality in that contract because the plaintiff was not bound to perform his part of it, nevertheless, he did fully perform the contract on his part, and the defendant received the full benefit contracted for. Having enjoyed the forbearance of the plaintiff from bringing action against her on the bond for the full period agreed upon, the defendant is now estopped from refusing performance on her part on the ground that the contract was not originally binding on the plaintiff, who did, nevertheless, perform it and she received the benefit thereof.

It is therefore the opinion of the court that this action is maintainable, and that the plaintiff is entitled to judgment against the defendant for $175.60 and costs, with interest from the date of the writ.

So ordered.

NOTE

Consult Restatement Second §75, Illus. 4, and Ward v. Goodrich, 34 Colo. 369, 82 P. 701 (1905)

DAVIS v. JACOBY
1 Cal. 2d 370, 34 P.2d 1026 (1934)

THE COURT. Plaintiffs appeal from a judgment refusing to grant specific performance of an alleged contract to make a will. The facts are not in dispute and are as follows:

The plaintiff Caro M. Davis was the niece of Blanche Whitehead, who was married to Rupert Whitehead. Prior to her marriage in 1913 to her coplaintiff Frank M. Davis, Caro lived for a considerable time at the home of the Whiteheads, in Piedmont, California. The Whiteheads were childless and extremely fond of Caro. The record is replete with uncontradicted testimony of the close and loving relationship that existed between Caro and her aunt and uncle. During the period that Caro lived with the Whiteheads, she was treated as and often referred to by the Whiteheads as their daughter. In 1913, when Caro was married to Frank

Davis, the marriage was arranged at the Whitehead home and a reception held there. After the marriage Mr. and Mrs. Davis went to Mr. Davis' home in Canada, where they have resided ever since. . . .

By the year 1930 Mrs. Whitehead had become seriously ill. She had suffered several strokes and her mind was failing. . . . On March 30, 1931, Mr. Whitehead wrote a long letter to Mr. Davis, in which he explained in detail the condition of Mrs. Whitehead's health and also referred to his own health. He pointed out that he had lost a considerable portion of his cash assets but still owned considerable realty, that he needed some one to help him with his wife and some friend he could trust to help him with his business affairs and suggested that perhaps Mr. Davis might come to California. He then pointed out that all his property was community property; that under his will all the property was to go to Mrs. Whitehead; that he believed that under Mrs. Whitehead's will practically everything was to go to Caro. Mr. Whitehead again wrote to Mr. Davis under date of April 9, 1931, pointing out how badly he needed some one he could trust to assist him, and giving it as his belief that if properly handled he could still save about $150,000. He then stated: "Having you [Mr. Davis] here to depend on and to help me regain my mind and courage would be a big thing." Three days later, on April 12, 1931, Mr. Whitehead again wrote, addressing his letter to "Dear Frank and Caro," and in this letter made the definite offer, which offer it is claimed was accepted and is the basis of this action. In this letter he first pointed out that Blanche, his wife, was in a private hospital and that "she cannot last much longer . . . my affairs are not as bad as I supposed at first. Cutting everything down I figure $150,000 can be saved from the wreck." He then enumerated the values placed upon his various properties and then continued:

> My trouble was caused by my friends taking advantage of my illness and my position to skin me.
>
> Now if Frank could come out here and be with me, and look after my affairs, we could easily save the balance I mention, provided I don't get into another panic and do some more foolish things.
>
> The next attack will be my end, I am 65 and my health has been bad for years, so, the Drs. don't give me much longer to live. So if you can come, Caro will inherit everything and you will make our lives happier and see Blanche is provided for to the end.
>
> My eyesight has gone back on me, I cant read only for a few lines at a time. I am at the house alone with Stanley [the chauffeur] who does everything for me and is a fine fellow. Now, what I want is some one who will take charge of my affairs and see I don't lose any more. Frank can do it, if he will and cut out the booze.
>
> Will you let me hear from you as soon as possible, I know it will be a sacrifice but times are still bad and likely to be, so by settling down you can help me and Blanche and gain in the end. If I had you here my mind would get better and my courage return, and we could work things out.

This letter was received by Mr. Davis at his office in Windsor, Canada, about 9:30 A.M. April 14, 1931. After reading the letter to Mrs. Davis over the telephone, and after getting her belief that they must go to California, Mr. Davis immediately wrote Mr. Whitehead a letter, which, after reading it to his wife, he sent by air mail. This letter was lost, but there is no doubt that it was sent by Davis and received by Whitehead; in fact, the trial court expressly so found. Mr. Davis testified in substance as to the contents of this letter. After acknowledging receipt of the letter of April 12, 1931, Mr. Davis unequivocally stated that he and Mrs. Davis accepted the proposition of Mr. Whitehead and both would leave Windsor to go to him on April 25. This letter of acceptance also contained the information that the reason they could not leave prior to April 25 was that Mr. Davis had to appear in court on April 22 as one of the executors of his mother's estate. The testimony is uncontradicted and ample to support the trial court's finding that this letter was sent by Davis and received by Whitehead. In fact, under date of April 15, 1931, Mr. Whitehead again wrote to Mr. Davis and stated:

> Your letter by air mail received this A.M. Now, I am wondering if I have put you to unnecessary trouble and expense, if you are making any money don't leave it, as things are bad here. . . . You know your business and I don't and I am half crazy in the bargain but, I don't want to hurt you or Caro.
>
> Then on the other hand if I could get some one to trust and keep me straight I can save a good deal, about what I told you in my former letter."

This letter was received by Mr. Davis on April 17, 1931, and the same day Mr. Davis telegraphed to Mr. Whitehead: "Cheer up — we will soon be there, we will wire you from the train."

Between April 14, 1931, the date the letter of acceptance was sent by Mr. Davis, and April 22, Mr. Davis was engaged in closing out his business affairs, and Mrs. Davis in closing up their home and in making other arrangements to leave. On April 22, 1931, Mr. Whitehead committed suicide. Mr. and Mrs. Davis were immediately notified and they at once came to California. From almost the moment of her arrival Mrs. Davis devoted herself to the care and comfort of her aunt and gave her aunt constant attention and care until Mrs. Whitehead's death on May 30, 1931. On this point the trial court found:

> From the time of their arrival in Piedmont, Caro M. Davis administered in every way to the comforts of Blanche Whitehead and saw that she was cared for and provided for down to the time of the death of Blanche Whitehead on May 30, 1931; during said time Caro M. Davis nursed Blanche Whitehead, cared for her and administered to her wants as a natural daughter would have done toward and for her mother. . . .

After the death of Mrs. Whitehead, for the first time it was discovered that the information contained in Mr. Whitehead's letter of March 30, 1931, in reference to the contents of his and Mrs. Whitehead's will was incorrect. By a duly witnessed will dated February 28, 1931, Mr. Whitehead, after making several specific bequests, had bequeathed all of the balance of his estate to his wife for life, and upon her death to respondents Geoff Doubble and Rupert Ross Whitehead, his nephews. Neither appellant was mentioned in his will. It was also discovered that Mrs. Whitehead by a will dated December 17, 1927, had devised all of her estate to her husband. The evidence is clear and uncontradicted that the relationship existing between Whitehead and his two nephews, respondents herein, was not nearly as close and confidential as that existing between Whitehead and appellants.

After the discovery of the manner in which the property had been devised was made, this action was commenced upon the theory that Rupert Whitehead had assumed a contractual obligation to make a will whereby "Caro Davis would inherit everything"; that he had failed to do so; that plaintiffs had fully performed their part of the contract; that damages being insufficient, *quasi* specific performance should be granted in order to remedy the alleged wrong, upon the equitable principle that equity regards that done which ought to have been done. The requested relief is that the beneficiaries under the will of Rupert Whitehead, respondents herein, be declared to be involuntary trustees for plaintiffs of Whitehead's estate.

It should also be added that the evidence shows that as a result of Frank Davis leaving his business in Canada he forfeited not only all insurance business he might have written if he had remained, but also forfeited all renewal commissions earned on past business. According to his testimony this loss was over $8,000. . . .

The theory of the trial court and of respondents on this appeal is that the letter of April 12 was an offer to contract, but that such offer could only be accepted by performance and could not be accepted by a promise to perform, and that said offer was revoked by the death of Mr. Whitehead before performance. In other words, it is contended that the offer was an offer to enter into a unilateral contract, and that the purported acceptance of April 14 was of no legal effect.

The distinction between unilateral and bilateral contracts is well settled in the law. It is well stated in section 12 of the American Institute's Restatement of the Law of Contracts as follows: "A unilateral contract is one in which no promisor receives a promise as consideration for his promise. A bilateral contract is one in which there are mutual promises between two parties to the contract; each party being both a promisor and a promisee." This definition is in accord with the law of California. Chrisman v. So. Cal. Edison Co., 83 Cal. App. 249, 256 Pac. 618.

In the case of unilateral contracts no notice of acceptance by performance is required. Section 1584 of the Civil Code provides: "Performance of the conditions of a proposal . . . is an acceptance of the proposal." (See Cuthill v. Peabody, 19 Cal. App. 304, 125 Pac. 926; Los Angeles Traction Co. v. Wilshire, 135 Cal. 654, 67 Pac. 1086.)

Although the legal distinction between unilateral and bilateral contracts is thus well settled, the difficulty in any particular case is to determine whether the particular offer is one to enter into a bilateral or unilateral contract. Some cases are quite clear cut. Thus an offer to sell which is accepted is clearly a bilateral contract, while an offer of a reward is a clear-cut offer of a unilateral contract which cannot be accepted by a promise to perform, but only by performance. Berthiaume v. Doe, 22 Cal. App. 78, 133 Pac. 515. Between these two extremes is a vague field where the particular contract may be unilateral or bilateral depending upon the intent of the offer and the facts and circumstances of each case. The offer to contract involved in this case falls within this category. By the provisions of the Restatement of the Law of Contracts it is expressly provided that there is a *presumption* that the offer is to enter into a bilateral contract. Section 31 provides:

> In case of doubt it is presumed that an offer invites the formation of a bilateral contract by an acceptance amounting in effect to a promise by the offeree to perform what the offer requests, rather than the formation of one or more unilateral contracts by actual performance on the part of the offeree.

Professor Williston, in his Treatise on Contracts, volume 1, section 60, also takes the position that a presumption in favor of bilateral contracts exists.

In the comment following section 31 of the Restatement the reason for such presumption is stated as follows: "It is not always easy to determine whether an offerer requests an act or a promise to do the act. As a bilateral contract immediately and fully protects both parties, the interpretation is favored that a bilateral contract is proposed."

While the California cases have never expressly held that a presumption in favor of bilateral contracts exists, the cases clearly indicate a tendency to treat offers as offers of bilateral rather than of unilateral contracts. Roth v. Moeller, 185 Cal. 415, 197 Pac. 62; Boehm v. Spreckels, 183 Cal. 239, 191 Pac. 5; see, also, Wood v. Lucy, Lady Duff-Gordon, 222 N.Y. 88, 118 N.E. 214.

Keeping these principles in mind, we are of the opinion that the offer of April 12 was an offer to enter into a bilateral as distinguished from a unilateral contract. Respondents argue that Mr. Whitehead had the right as offerer to designate his offer as either unilateral or bilateral. That is undoubtedly the law. It is then argued that from all the facts and circumstances it must be implied that what Whitehead wanted was performance and not a mere promise to perform. We think this is a non sequitur, in fact the surrounding circumstances lead to just the opposite conclusion. These parties were not dealing at arm's length. Not only were they related, but a very close and intimate friendship existed between them. The record indisputably demonstrates that Mr. Whitehead had confidence in Mr. and Mrs. Davis, in fact that he had lost all confidence in every one else. The record amply shows that by an accumulation of occurrences Mr. Whitehead had become desperate, and that what he wanted was the promise of appellants that he could look to them for assistance. He knew from his past relationship with appellants that if they gave their promise to perform he could rely upon them. The correspondence between them indicates how desperately he desired this assurance. Under these circumstances he wrote his offer of April 12, above quoted, in which he stated, after disclosing his desperate mental and physical condition, and after setting forth the terms of his offer: *"Will you let me hear from you as soon as possible* — I know it will be a sacrifice but times are still bad and likely to be, so by settling down you can help me and Blanche and gain in the end." By thus specifically requesting an immediate reply Whitehead expressly indicated the nature of the acceptance desired by him, namely, appellants' promise that they would come to California and do the things requested by him. This promise was immediately sent by appellants upon receipt of the offer, and was received by Whitehead. It is elementary that when an offer has indicated the mode and means of acceptance, an acceptance in accordance with that mode or means is binding on the offerer.

Another factor which indicates that Whitehead must have contemplated a bilateral rather than a unilateral contract, is that the contract required Mr. and Mrs. Davis to perform services until the death of both Mr. and Mrs. Whitehead. It is obvious that if Mr. Whitehead died first some of these services were to be performed after his death, so that he would have to rely on the promise of appellants to perform these services. It is also of some evidentiary force that Whitehead received the letter of acceptance and acquiesced in that means of acceptance. . . .

For the foregoing reasons we are of the opinion that the offer of April 12, 1931, was an offer to enter into a bilateral contract which was accepted by the letter of April 14, 1931. Subsequently appellants fully performed their part of the contract. Under such circumstances it is well settled that damages are insufficient and specific performance will be granted. Wolf v. Donahue, 206 Cal. 213, 273 Pac. 547. Since the consideration has been fully rendered by appellants the question as to mutuality of remedy becomes of no importance. 6 Cal. Jur. sec. 140.

Respondents also contend the complaint definitely binds appellants to the theory of a unilateral contract. This contention is without merit. The complaint expressly alleges the parties entered into a contract. It is true that the complaint also alleged that the contract became effective by performance. However, this is an action in equity. Respondents were not misled. No objection was made to the testimony offered to show the acceptance of April 14. A fair reading of the record clearly indicates the case was tried by the parties on the theory that the sole question was whether there was a contract — unilateral or bilateral.

For the foregoing reasons the judgment appealed from is reversed. Rehearing denied.

NOTE

This case is noted in 23 Calif. L. Rev. 213 (1935). See Restatement Second §32, *supra* p. 373, and U.C.C. §2-206(1), *supra* p. 372.

CROOK v. COWAN
64 N.C. 627, 743 (1870)

Assumpsit, tried before Russell, J., at December Special Term, 1867, of New Hanover.

The action was brought to recover the price of two carpets, the transaction in regard to which is presented in the following correspondence:

Robeson, N.C., Dec. 10th, 1866.

Walter Crook, Jr., Esq., Baltimore:

Sir: — General R. of Wilmington, has kindly furnished me your name, and recommends your house.

I want similar carpets for two rooms, good three ply carpet, medium color, small figures. I would prefer no white in them. Description of rooms: No. 1, 14 feet 6 inches by 16 feet 3 inches square; No. 2, 14 feet 2 inches by 16 feet 3 inches square. For jambs of chimney, four (4) pieces, one breadth, each piece (5, 8 in.) five feet eight inches long.

I want good durable carpets, and wish you to have them made up. You can forward them to my address at Wilmington, N.C. per Express, C.O.D., or else, advise me of the cost, and I will remit while you are having them made up. Number each as per description.

Yours respectfully,
D. S. COWAN

This letter was received by the plaintiff upon the 14th of December.

The defendant, receiving no reply, sent the following telegraphic dispatch:

Wilmington, N.C., Dec. 26th, 1866.
(Received at Baltimore, December 26th:)
To Walter Crook, Jr., Baltimore Street:

Have you received an order for carpets? If so, do you intend sending them?

D. S. Cowan

The next communication was the following:

Baltimore, Jan. 16th, 1867.
Mr. D. S. Cowan, Wilmington, N.C.:

Dear Sir: I have the pleasure to notify you that we have this day received advice from Adams' Express Company that the carpets ordered by you through letter dated December 10th, 1866, are at their office in Wilmington on hand, their notification having, up to date, received no reply. Be good enough to respond. The goods were shipped you December 21st, 1866.

Yours, etc.
Walter Crook, Jr.

Robeson, N.C., Jan. 18th, 1867.
Walter Crook, Jr., Baltimore, Md.:

Dear Sir: I was somewhat surprised on yesterday at receiving a notification of the fact that a roll of carpeting was in the Express office for me. I declined to receive it, and cannot let it go back to you, without a word of explanation in justification of myself.

It was on or about the 10th December, 1866, that I wrote you ordering carpets. I received no acknowledgment of my letter, and was in doubt whether it ever reached you. On the 26th of December, I dispatched you a telegram from Wilmington to the following effect, to wit:

Walter Crook, Jr., Baltimore Street, Baltimore:
Have you received an order for carpets? If so, do you intend sending them?

(Signed) D. S. Cowan

The above copy I got from the original on file in telegraph office in Wilmington on yesterday. I called at telegraph office frequently from 26th Dec. to 2nd Jan. 1867, seeking a reply, but received none. Concluding that my letter had miscarried, and consequently you did not understand the dispatch, I bought carpets in Wilmington and had them made up. Agreeable to the above facts, I cannot think I am morally bound to take the carpets. Should you think differently, I will be pleased to hear from you.

Yours very respectfully,
D. S. Cowan.

Some other letters passed between the parties, presenting their respective views of the controversy, but they are not material here.

It was further in evidence that by general custom, known to all who had any dealings with the Express Company, the letters C.O.D. marked upon goods, means that such Company is not to deliver the goods without payment of the bill for the purchase money which accompanies them; and that the carpets sent to the defendant were so marked.

The counsel for the defendant requested the Court to instruct the jury:

1. That there was no *contract*;

2. That, if there was a contract, the failure of the plaintiff to reply to the original order of the defendant, and to his dispatch of December 26th, 1866, authorized the latter to believe that the order would not be complied with, and that, so, the defendant was discharged.

The Court declined to give either instruction.

Verdict for the plaintiff, etc. Appeal by the defendant.

READE, J. If one writes to another, who has not offered his property for sale, proposing to buy, the letter is of course nothing but an offer, and is of no force until the other answers and accepts the offer; then the contract is made. But if one holds his property out for sale, naming the terms, and another accepts the terms, the contract is complete; or, if one bids at an auction, and the hammer falls, the contract is complete; or, if one advertises, offering a reward for something to be done, as soon as the thing is done the contract is complete, and the reward is due. So, in our case, the plaintiff held himself out as a carpet manufacturer and vender, and offered his carpets for sale, and invited purchases; and when the defendant sent him the unconditional order for carpets, that was an acceptance of his offer, and the bargain was struck, and the moment that the carpets were delivered to the Express, the agent designated by the defendant to receive and transport them and collect the bill, the delivery was made, and the property passed to the defendant. But, if that were not so, our case is stronger than that. Consider the case as if the first offer was made by the defendant to the plaintiff. The defendant, knowing that the plaintiff was a carpet vender, sent him an unconditional order for carpets, specifying the Express as the agent to receive and transport them, and to collect the bill, and the order was filled to the letter. Thereby, the offer was accepted, the property in the carpets passed to the defendant, and he became liable for the price, as for goods sold and delivered. The order was an offer, the filling the order was an acceptance; and an *offer* and an *acceptance* is the common definition of a contract.

The defence is put upon this ground: the defendant's letter to plaintiff was only an offer, there was no contract until the plaintiff accepted it and notified the defendant; and the notice ought to have been by mail, within a reasonable time.

The plaintiff says, that he did assent immediately upon the receipt of the order, and forwarded the carpets as soon as he could have them made up, which was within a reasonable time — seven days, and that this was all he had to do. The point of divergence between the plaintiff and the defendant is, that the defendant says, the plaintiff ought to have notified him by mail that he had accepted the offer, and forwarded the goods; that merely filling the order, although in the exact terms thereof, was not an acceptance, without notice. The propriety of giving notice by mail, must depend a good deal upon the circumstances of each particular case; — as, if the order requires it, or, if the order is not sufficiently specific, and leaves something further to be arranged, or, if considerable time must pass in the manufacture of the article, or, if the route or means of transportation is not known, or the voyage long and dangerous, and the like. But if an offer and an acceptance — an unconditional and specific order, and an exact fulfillment, as in this case, does not complete the contract, how would it be possible to complete a contract by mail? A sends an unconditional order to B, and, instead of B's filling the order, he writes back that he accepts the order and will fill it, but in the meantime, A may have changed his mind, and lest he has, he must write back to B and so on, for ever. Adams v. Lindsell, 1 B. & Ald. 681, is the leading English case, illustrating, and repudiating, this circumlocution; and that case has been followed ever since both in England and America, as is said in 1 Parsons on Contracts, note p, page 483. In that case, it was said, speaking of the above rule,

> If it were not so, no contract could ever be completed by post. For if the defendant was not bound by his offer, when accepted by the plaintiff, until the answer was received, then the plaintiff ought not to be bound until after he had received the notification that the defendant had received his answer and assented to it. And so it might go on ad infinitum.

We admit that the rule, that filling an order completes the contract, is confined to unconditional and specific orders. And, if the purchaser thinks proper, he can make his order as guarded as he pleases. He may say, "I want such goods — can you furnish them? If so, at what price, and within what time? Inform me by return mail. I will pay if the goods arrive safe, — otherwise not," — and the like. Then he will not be liable unless the terms are strictly complied with.

In the case before us, the order was unconditional and specific, and was complied with to the letter. The defendant did not ask the plaintiff to inform him whether he would fill the order. He had no doubt about it. It was the plaintiff's business to fill such orders, and the defendant had confidence in him. So far from requiring the plaintiff to notify him by mail, he impliedly informed him that he need not do so: Send the goods by Express, C.O.D., without more say; and send the bill by Express for collection; or, if you are afraid to trust me, then, and in that case only, you may write to me and I will send the money, before you ship the goods, — is substantially, what the defendant said in his order to the plaintiff. There was no use in informing the defendant by mail of the shipment of the goods, because the Express is as speedy as the mail; and there is certainly no magic in sending by mail. And sending the goods is the best notification.

The defendant also complains that the plaintiff did not answer his telegram. The answer is, that neither the mail nor the telegraph had been designated as the means of communication, but the Express. And it was the defendant's misfortune, if not his fault, to go elsewhere than to the place designated for information. His duty ended when he delivered the goods to the agent designated by the defendant, the Express, with the bill for the price to collect. The goods were at their destination — the Express office — when the defendant sent his telegram. He did not go to the Express office at all, and offers no explanation why he did not, but left the plaintiff to infer, as he seems to have done, that his purpose was to avoid the contract.

RODMAN, J. (dissenting). The question in this case is whether what took place between the plaintiff and defendant amounted to a complete contract of sale, or to a binding contract by the defendant to accept and pay for the goods, so as to enable the plaintiff to recover the price.

The letter of the defendant of December 10th, was merely an offer to purchase the goods named: it is called an *order;* but an order on a merchant or manufacturer for a specified article — that is, a request to sell the article to the writer — *can be* nothing but an offer to purchase. It does not bind the proposed vendor, until it is assented to by him; nor can it bind the proposed vendee until the vendor himself becomes bound; a contract which binds only one of the parties, (except in certain special cases, as where one of the parties is an infant, etc.,) is an impossibility.

"A mere affirmation or proposition is not enough," "There must be a request on one side, and an assent on the other:" 1 Pars. Cont. 475, Chit. Cont. 9-15. "A contract includes a concurrence of intentions in two parties, one of whom promises something to the other, who, on his part, accepts such promise. A pollicitation is a promise not yet accepted by the person to whom it is made:" 1 Pothier Obl., 4.

" 'It takes two to make a bargain,' is a maxim of law, the soundness of which strikes the good sense of every one, so that it has become a common saying." Pearson, J. in Spruill v. Trader, 5 Jon. 41.

It is unnecessary to attempt to enforce so familiar a principle by illustration; but the decision of this case depends on bearing it in mind, and fairly applying it. The assent must be given in a reasonable time. If the proposition be by letter, the assent must be given by letter, by the first post on the next day, unless farther time be allowed by the proposition: 1 Pars. Cont. 483, note; Dunlop v. Higgins, 1 H.L. Cases, 381; Mizell v. Burnett, 4 Jon. 249; Meynell v. Surtees, 31, E.L. & E., 475.

The point of the case is, was the proposition of the defendant assented to by the plaintiff, so as to convert it from a mere offer into a binding contract?

First, to put away what is not material: The letter from plaintiff to defendant, of 16th January 1867, was not such an assent, because it was not intended as such, and was not given in reasonable time, even if we admit that the defendant's original offer was kept open by his telegram of 26th December, for a reasonable time thereafter: Mizzell v. Burnett, and Dunlop v. Higgins, *ubi sup.*

So that the question becomes at last, whether the delivery of the goods to the carrier on the 21st of December was such an assent. In considering this, it must be borne in mind, that the defendant never received any notice other than this, either that the plaintiff assented to his proposition to purchase and would send the goods accordingly, or that he had complied with it by a delivery to the carrier, or any reply to his telegram of the 26th of December, inquiring if the plaintiff intended to send the goods.

The proposition, that the mere delivery of goods to the carrier on the 21st of December was equivalent to an assent communicated to the plaintiff in a reasonable time, and completed the contract, so as to vest the property in the defendant, or to bind him to accept and pay for the goods, can only be maintained on one of two grounds:

1. That a compliance with the terms of a proposition to purchase goods that require to be manufactured, or in some way prepared for use, and which preparation must occupy a time more or less considerable, but greater than what would be a reasonable one within which to give an assent to the proposition, is a sufficient assent, or will suffice in lieu of such assent; or,

2. That the carrier was the agent of the defendant to manifest such assent, and did manifest it, by receiving the goods.

As to the first ground, which seems principally relied on: When goods are sent in compliance with an order, and are accepted by the vendee, of course no question as to his liability for the price can arise. If they are sent immediately upon the receipt of the order, or within what would be a reasonable time for giving an assent thereafter, and a bill of lading or equivalent document is sent to the vendee, as is usually the case, or if he is informed of the arrival of the goods at their destination; that also is sufficient notice of the vendor's assent. Notice of the assent in due time is indispensable, but it is not material how or through whom it is given. It is only when there is a delay in the transmission, beyond what would be deemed a reasonable time for the vendor's assent, either from a difficulty in collecting or preparing the goods, or from any other cause, that the question whether a compliance with the proposition is equivalent to or dispenses with the vendor's assent, is likely to arise. In such a case I hold that mere compliance by preparing and sending the goods within what, considering the time necessary for the preparation, is a reasonable time *for that purpose*, but within what is an unreasonable time for the communication of the vendor's assent, is insufficient, and that the proposition to purchase must be assented to in a reasonable time, and notice of the assent given to the proposed vendee. It is from not noticing the distinction between cases in which a delay does or does not occur, that any difficulty in the decision of this case can arise, and attention to it will reconcile and explain every case in which it is held that a delivery to a carrier vests the property in the consignee, a doctrine which, properly understood, is incontestable. If the proposition were true, it would form so wide and important an exception to the general and admitted rule, requiring a personal communication of assent to a proposing purchaser, that, as such, it could scarcely have escaped prominent notice by the able writers on the law of contracts with whose works the profession is familiar. Yet no such exception is found, and no case has been cited, and we may suppose none can be found, in which, in a case substantially like this, an assent like that which it is contended is sufficient in this case, has been so held. The contrary is expressly stated in 1 Pars. Cont. p. 475, note c, citing the cases of Johnson v. Fessler, 7 Watts 48, and Ball v. Newton, 7 Cush. 599.

There are many cases in which it has been held that upon an offer to guaranty, a compliance with the offer is not sufficient; notice must also be given to the proposing guarantor that his terms are accepted: 1 Pars. Cont. 478, note h, McIver v. Richardson, 1 M. & S. 557; Mozley v. Tinker, 1 M.G.&R. 692; Cope v. Albinson, 16 E.L. & E. 470; Shewell v. Knox, 1 Dev. 404, 2 Pars. Cont. 13. These cases are strictly analogous. The same principle must necessarily apply to an offer to purchase goods, as to an offer to make any other contract.

In the case of an order for goods, such as in this case, where a certain time, more or less considerable, must be consumed in obtaining or manufacturing them, so that there is a delay in complying with the order, it would be unreasonable to hold that the party making the offer to purchase, was to remain ignorant during all such time, whatever its duration may be, whether or not the vendor has assented to his offer; and to remain bound while the other was loose; and finally to receive no other notice that his letter had been received and his offer assented to, than such as may be implied from a delivery of the goods to a common carrier. Instead of being only for a carpet, which, as it happened, required only ten or eleven days to be prepared for use, the offer might have been for a steam-engine, or other elaborate article which would require months in its fabrication; or, it might have been for an article of fluctuating value, which, if the rule contended for, were established, the vendor might legally send or not, according to his interest. The value or the character of the goods cannot change the principle of law requiring an assent to the proposal. To hold otherwise will be, in my opinion, to violate a recognized principle of universal commercial law, to encourage negligence and a wanton disregard of settled commercial usage; and to introduce a perplexing and injurious uncertainty into a very important class of commercial dealings.

But it is said, it was the duty of the Express Company to have given notice to the defendant of the arrival of the goods. This may be conceded. But the question would still remain, whether such notice would have been a sufficient and legal assent by the plaintiff. I think it would not have been, because not in reasonable time *for that purpose.* Moreover, if the Express Company neglected its duty in this respect, to whom is it liable? To the owner of the goods, certainly; but the question of ownership is the one in controversy, and it is a begging of the question, to assume that the defendant could recover of the Company for such omission.

Again, it is said, it was the duty of the defendant to have called at the Express office in Wilmington, where he would have heard of the arrival of the goods. But how could this duty be thrown on the defendant, until he had received an answer to his letter to the plaintiff? Was it not more convenient for the plaintiff to answer that letter, than for the defendant and all others similarly situated, to call daily at the Express office, for an indefinite time, inquiring for goods which they had received no notice would be sent? Is this the common usage in the great commercial cities? If it is, it could scarcely fail to be well known to us from the inconvenience it would occasion. How long was the defendant to continue calling? I think these questions cannot be answered without displaying the erroneous conception on which the argument for the plaintiff is found.

Again, it is said, the plaintiff is a dealer in carpets, and offered to all the world to sell them; and that the letter of the defendant, therefore, instead of being an offer to purchase, was, in fact, an assent to the plaintiff's offer to sell. This principle, it is true, applies to a class of cases in which a public officer, or a private individual, offers a certain reward to any one who will capture an offender. In such cases, the terms are fixed and certain, and the doing the act for which the reward is offered, before the offer is revoked, and notice that it has been done, suffices. But those cases are sui generis, and a well known exception to the general rule, which arises out of the impossibility of giving a previous assent to the offer. When was such a principle ever applied to the case of a merchant or manufacturer? Is such an one so notoriously bound to manufacture and send his goods to every one who will send him an order, C.O.D., that the person sending such an order, has no occasion to look for a reply to his letter, but may confidently go to the Express office to get them in a reasonable time for their manufacture after the receipt of his order in due course? How can he know how long it will take to manufacture the goods, or that the merchant will trust him to pay on delivery? The goods may be spoiled in the course of manufacture for the use of all others. The merchant or manufacturer may be out of the particular goods, or he may have to quit business, or there may be many other reasons to prevent a compliance. There is no proof that the plaintiff in this case offered his goods for sale, otherwise than as merchants and manufacturers in general do; and it will probably take the mercantile community somewhat by surprise, to discover that the consequences of a general advertisement are such as are supposed.

As to the second ground: All the reasons which support the necessity for an assent to an offer to purchase, imply that the notice of the assent must be to the proposed purchaser in person, or to some agent appointed by him *for that purpose.* Did the defendant appoint the Express Company his agent for that purpose? The defendant in fact never made the carrier his agent for any purpose, even to receive the goods — *he offered to do so;* — but to say that this offer, unaccepted by the plaintiff, was a complete and effective contract for that purpose, is to beg the very question we are discussing, and to confound all distinction between an offer to contract, and a completed contract.

But, waiving that point, it seems clear that the defendant never made, or intended to make, the carrier his agent to receive notice of the acceptance by the plaintiff, of his offer to purchase. Brown (Action, 200) takes the distinction thus:

> *Where the sale is complete,* so that the vendee is bound at all events to receive the goods, or, if he do not, is liable to an action by the vendor for the price, a delivery by the vendor to the carrier, is, in law, a delivery to the vendee. . . . But where the sale is not complete (as in the case of a sale of goods above the value of £10., where the provisions of the Statute of Frauds have not been complied with,) a delivery to a carrier not named by the vendee, is not sufficient, as there must be an acceptance by the vendee, (within the meaning of the Statute,) as well as a delivery by the vendor. And an acceptance by a carrier not named by the vendee, is not an acceptance by him.

He says that the question in a case where the carrier was named by the vendee had not been decided, but in a note he intimates the opinion that such naming would make no difference. Certainly the mere offer to authorize the carrier to receive the goods in this case, cannot be construed to confer on the carrier, the additional power of completing the sale. The naming the carrier simply as carrier, can confer on him no power beyond that of carrying the defendant's goods. Whether or not any particular goods were the defendant's must depend on the proof of the contract between him and the plaintiff, and is independent of any act of the carrier.

It being thus shown that the defendant by naming the carrier gave him no authority to contract for him, or to receive the plaintiff's assent to his offer; did any such authority result simply from his employment and duty as a public carrier? If such be the power of a public carrier, and such the result of a mere delivery of goods to him, why has it ever become a general, if not universal, usage, for a consignor to take from the carrier a bill of lading, receipt, or equivalent document, and to forward it to the consignee? If the carrier is so far the agent of the consignee, that a delivery to the carrier must be presumed to be known eo instanti to the assignee [consignee], such a custom would for most of its purposes be unnecessary, and could never have grown up. That it is a usual, and ordinarily an indispensable duty of a consignor on a shipment by sea, is too notorious to need, or to find, support from decisions. It is also usual on a shipment by river or canal: 1 Pars. Ship. and Ad. 180; Dows v. Green, 16 Barb. 72; Bryans v. Nix, 4 M. & W. 775. Such a document is the symbol of property: without it, in general, upon a shipment, the property does not pass to the consignee, and certainly a consignor who omitted to take and forward it, would be liable to the consignee for all damages which might result. That the same rule applies on land, we have high authority. . . .

If the necessity for this custom were not proved by its existence, many reasons might be assigned for it. Without some document of title, (bill of lading, receipt or correspondence, Bryans v. Nix, *ubi sup.*) the consignee might have a difficulty in obtaining possession of the goods; he might want to insure them during their transit, or to sell, or to borrow money on them. The rule must be the same whether the goods be a carpet, or many bales of cotton. Neither can it make any difference whether the voyage be a short one, as from Baltimore to Wilmington, or a comparatively long one, as from San Francisco to New York; or whether it be wholly by land or water, or partly by both. The rules of law are founded on deeper principles than to be affected by such accidents as the nature of the highway, or the vehicle.

PER CURIAM. Affirmed.

NOTE

Do §§62 (*infra* p. 407) and 54 of the Restatement Second help us to solve the problems presented in the principal case? Suppose it would take a letter of acceptance three days to arrive. Does the shipment of goods that needs five days for arrival complete the contract?

For a criticism of §62, previously §63 of the First Restatement, see Goble, Is Performance Always as Desirable as a Promise to Perform?, 22 Ill. L. Rev. 789 (1928).

How would the case be decided under U.C.C. §2-206, *supra* p. 372?

BISHOP v. EATON
161 Mass. 496, 37 N.E. 665 (1894)

Contract, on a guaranty. Writ dated February 2, 1892. Trial in the Superior Court without a jury, before Braley, J., who found the following facts.

The plaintiff in 1886 was a resident of Sycamore in the State of Illinois, and was to some extent connected in business with Harry H. Eaton, a brother of the defendant. In December, 1886, the defendant in a letter to the plaintiff said, "If Harry needs more money, let him have it, or assist him to get it, and I will see that it is paid."

On January 7, 1887, Harry Eaton gave his promissory note for two hundred dollars to one Stark, payable in one year. The plaintiff signed the note as surety, relying on the letter of the defendant, and looked to the defendant solely for reimbursement, if called upon to pay the note. Shortly afterward the plaintiff wrote to the defendant a letter stating that the note had been given and its amount, and deposited the letter in the mail at Sycamore, postage prepaid, and properly addressed to the defendant at his home in Nova Scotia. The letter, according to the testimony of the defendant, was never received by him. At the maturity of the note that time for its payment was extended for a year, but whether with the knowledge or consent of the defendant was in dispute. In August, 1889, in an interview between them, the plaintiff asked the defendant to take up the note still outstanding, and pay it, to which the defendant replied: "Try to get Harry to pay it. If he don't, I will. It shall not cost you anything."

On October 1, 1891, the plaintiff paid the note, and thereafter made no effort to collect it from Harry Eaton, the maker. The defendant testified that he had no notice of the payment of the note by the plaintiff until December 22, 1891.

The defendant requested the judge to rule: 1. The letter of the defendant constituted in law no more than an offer to guaranty. 2. The defendant did not become bound by a contract of guaranty unless it appeared from a preponderance of the evidence that, within a reasonable time after his offer was accepted and acted upon, he had notice of such acceptance, and the giving of credit thereon. 3. The mere deposit in the mail of a letter accepting an offer of guaranty which has been made by mail, such letter being properly stamped and addressed to the party making the offer, and mailed within a reasonable time after the acceptance, does not in law constitute such notice to the latter as thereupon to bind him. 4. The defendant did not become bound by a contract of guaranty, if at all, unless he actually received such letter of acceptance. 5. A delay for two years and a half after accepting and acting upon an offer of guaranty to give notice to the person making the offer is an unreasonable delay. 6. If within a reasonable time after the plaintiff's acceptance and action upon the offer of guaranty, the defendant had notice thereof, then the obligation by which he became bound was not an original promise, but an undertaking collateral to the debt of the maker of the note and within the statute of frauds, and was in substance a promise or obligation that if the plaintiff as surety upon the note was obliged to pay it at maturity through the default of the maker, and if further the plaintiff, after due notice to the defendant of the default, used due diligence in attempting to collect from the maker the sum so paid, and gave due notice to the defendant of his failure so to collect, then the defendant would repay the plaintiff what he had paid out. 7. If for a year and a half after the maturity of the note and the default of payment by the maker, the defendant had no notice of the default, he was discharged from his contract unless he subsequently waived his rights arising from the plaintiff's laches. 8. The extension of time for the payment of the note given at its maturity without the knowledge or consent of the defendant discharged him from his contract unless subsequently with a full knowledge of the facts he assented to and ratified the same. 9. The conversation between the parties in August, 1889, was too equivocal to constitute a ratification of a prior contract, or a waiver of the defendant's rights arising from the laches of the plaintiff. 10. After paying the note the plaintiff did not use due diligence in trying first to collect from the maker the amount he had paid on the note, and hence he cannot recover in this action. 11. After payment of the note the plaintiff did not within a reasonable time notify the defendant of the payment by him, and the default of the maker, and so the plaintiff cannot recover in this action.

The judge declined so to rule, and ruled, as matter of law upon the findings of fact, that the plaintiff was entitled to recover, and ordered judgment for him; and the defendant alleged exceptions.

KNOWLTON, J. The first question in this case is whether the contract proved by the plaintiff is an original and independent contract or a guaranty. The judge found that the plaintiff signed the note relying upon the letter, "and looked to the defendant solely for reimbursement if called upon to pay the note." The promise contained in the letter was in these words: "If Harry needs more money, let him have it, or assist him to get it, and I will see that it is paid." On a reasonable interpretation of this promise, the plaintiff was authorized to adopt the first alternative, and let Harry have the money in such a way that a liability of Harry to him would be created, and to look to the defendant for payment if Harry failed to pay the debt at maturity; or he might adopt the second alternative and assist him to get money from some one else in such a way as to create a debt from Harry to the person furnishing the money, and, if Harry failed to pay, might look to the defendant to relieve him from the liability. The words fairly imply that Harry was to be primarily liable for the debt, either to the plaintiff or to such other person as should furnish the money, and that the defendant was to guarantee the payment of it. We are therefore of opinion, that, if the plaintiff relied solely upon the defendant, he was authorized by the letter to rely upon him only as a guarantor.

The defendant requested many rulings in regard to the law applicable to contracts of guaranty, most of which it becomes necessary to consider. The language relied on was an offer to guarantee, which the plaintiff might or might not accept. Without acceptance of it there was no contract, because the offer was conditional and there was no consideration for the promise. But this was not a proposition which was to become a contract only upon the giving of a promise for the promise, and it was not necessary that the plaintiff should accept it in words, or promise to do anything before acting upon it. It was an offer which was to become effective as a contract upon the doing of the act referred to. It was an offer to be bound in consideration of an act to be done, and in such a case the doing of the act constitutes the acceptance of the offer and furnishes the consideration. Ordinarily there is no occasion to notify the offerer of the acceptance of such an offer, for the doing of the act is a sufficient acceptance, and the promisor knows that he is bound when he sees that action has been taken on the faith of his offer. But if the act is of such a kind that knowledge of it will not quickly come to the promisor, the promisee is bound to give him notice of his acceptance within a reasonable time after doing that which constitutes the acceptance. In such a case it is implied in the offer that, to complete the contract, notice shall be given with due diligence, so that the promisor may know that a contract has been made. But where the promise is in consideration of an act to be done, it becomes binding upon the doing of the act so far that the promisee cannot be affected by a subsequent withdrawal of it, if within a reasonable time afterward he notifies the promisor. In accordance with these principles, it has been held in cases like the present, where the guarantor would not know of himself, from the nature of the transaction, whether the offer has been accepted or not, that he is not bound without notice of the acceptance, seasonably given after the performance which constitutes the consideration. Babcock v. Byrant, 12 Pick. 133. Whiting v. Stacy, 15 Gray, 270. Schlessinger v. Dickinson, 5 Allen, 47.

In the present case the plaintiff seasonably mailed a letter to the defendant, informing him of what he had done in compliance with the defendant's request, but the defendant testified that he never received it, and there is no finding that it ever reached him. The judge ruled, as matter of law, that upon the facts found, the plaintiff was entitled to recover, and the question is thus presented whether the defendant was bound by the acceptance when the letter was properly mailed, although he never received it.

When an offer of guaranty of this kind is made, the implication is that notice of the act which constitutes an acceptance of it shall be given in a reasonable way. What kind of a notice is required depends upon the nature of the transaction, the situation of the parties, and the inferences fairly to be drawn from their previous dealings, if any, in regard to the matter. If they are so situated that communication by letter is naturally to be expected, then the deposit of a letter in the mail is all that is necessary. If that is done which is fairly to be contemplated from their relations to the subject matter and from their course of dealing, the rights of the parties are fixed, and a failure actually to receive the notice will not affect the obligation of the guarantor.

The plaintiff in the case now before us resided in Illinois, and the defendant in Nova Scotia. The offer was made by letter, and the defendant must have contemplated that information in regard to the plaintiff's acceptance or rejection of it would be by letter. It would be a harsh rule which would subject the plaintiff to the risk of the defendant's failure to receive the letter giving notice of his action on the faith of the offer. We are of opinion that the plaintiff, after assisting Harry to get the money, did all that he was required to do when he seasonably sent the defendant the letter by mail informing him of what had been done.

How far such considerations are applicable to the case of an ordinary contract made by letter, about which some of the early decisions are conflicting, we need not now consider.

The plaintiff was not called upon under his contract to attempt to collect the money from the maker of the note, and it is no defence that he did not promptly notify the defendant of the maker's default, at least in the absence of evidence that the defendant was injured by the delay. This rule in cases like the present was established in Massachusetts in Vinal v. Richardson, 13 Allen, 521, after much consideration, and it is well founded in principle and strongly supported by authority.

We find one error in the rulings which requires us to grant a new trial. It appears from the bill of exceptions that when the note became due the time for the payment of it was extended without the consent of the defendant. The defendant is thereby discharged from his liability, unless he subsequently assented to the extension and ratified it. Chace v. Brooks, 5 Cush. 43. Carkin v. Savory, 14 Gray, 528. The court should therefore have ruled substantially in accordance with the defendant's eighth request, instead of finding for the plaintiff, as matter of law, on the facts reported. Whether the judge would have found a ratification on the evidence if he had considered it, we have no means of knowing.

Exceptions sustained.

NOTE

In John Deere Co. v. Babcock, 89 Wis. 2d 672, 278 N.W.2d 885, 886 (1979) the court noted that it had

> consistently adhered to the proposition that notice of acceptance is required unless there are special circumstances excusing it, in contrast to the Restatement rule that it is necessary only when the guarantor did not reasonably know of the extension of credit. Restatement of Security, sec. 86 (1941); Restatement [First] of Contracts, sec. 56 (1932).

See 1 Corbin §68 (1963) for a discussion of the principal case. See also Miller v. Walter, 165 Mont. 96, 527 P.2d 240 (1974).

WHITE v. CORLIES
46 N.Y. 467 (1871)

Appeal from First Judicial District.

The action was for an alleged breach of contract.

The plaintiff was a builder with his place of business in Fortieth street, New York City.

The defendants were merchants at 32 Dey street.

In September, 1865, the defendants furnished the plaintiff with specifications, for fitting up a suit of offices at 57 Broadway, and requested him to make an estimate of the cost of doing the work.

On September 28th the plaintiff left his estimate with the defendants, and they were to consider upon it, and inform the plaintiff of their conclusions.

On the same day the defendants made a change in their specifications and sent a copy of the same, so changed, to the plaintiff, for his assent under his estimate which he assented to by signing the same and returning it to the defendants.

On the day following the defendants' bookkeeper wrote the plaintiff the following note:

> New York, September 29th. Upon an agreement to finish the fitting up of offices 57 Broadway in two weeks from date you can begin at once. The writer will call again, probably between five and six this p.m. W. H. R., for J. W. Corlies & Co., 32 Dey street.

No reply to this note was ever made by the plaintiff; and on the next day the same was countermanded by a second note from the defendants.

Immediately on receipt of the note of September 29th, and before the countermand was forwarded, the plaintiff commenced a performance by the purchase of lumber and beginning work thereon.

And after receiving the countermand, the plaintiff brought this action for damages for a breach of contract.

The court charged the jury as follows:

> From the contents of this note which the plaintiff received, was it his duty to go down to Dey street (meaning to give notice of assent) before commencing the work. In my opinion it was not. He had a right to act upon this note and commence the job, and that was a binding contract between the parties.

To this defendants excepted.

FOLGER. J. We do not think that the jury found, or that the testimony shows that there was any agreement between the parties before the written communication of the defendants of September 29 was received by the plaintiff. This note did not make an agreement. It was a proposition, and must have been accepted by the plaintiff before either party was bound in contract to the other. The only overt action which is claimed by the plaintiff as indicating on his part an acceptance of the offer, was the purchase of the stuff necessary for the work, and commencing work as we understand the testimony, upon that stuff.

We understand the rule to be that where an offer is made by one party to another when they are not together, the acceptance of it by that other must be manifested by some appropriate act. It does not need that the acceptance shall come to the knowledge of the one making the offer before he shall be bound. But though the manifestation need not be brought to his knowledge before he becomes bound, he is not bound if that manifestation is not put in a proper way to be the usual course of events, in some reasonable time communicated to him. Thus a letter received by mail containing a proposal may be answered by letter by mail containing the acceptance. And in general as soon as the answering letter is mailed, the contract is concluded. Though one party does not know of the acceptance, the manifestation thereof is put in the proper way of reaching him.

In the case in hand the plaintiff determined to accept. But a mental determination not indicated by speech, or put in course of indication by act to the other party, is not an acceptance which will bind the other. Nor does an act which in itself is no indication of an acceptance, become such because accompanied by an unevinced mental determination. Where the act uninterpreted by concurrent evidence of the mental purpose accompanying it is as well referable to one state of facts as another, it is no indication to the other party of an acceptance, and does not operate to hold him to his offer.

Conceding that the testimony shows that the plaintiff did resolve to accept this offer, he did no act which indicated an acceptance of it to the defendants. He, a carpenter and builder, purchased stuff for the work. But it was stuff as fit for any other like work. He began work upon the stuff, but as he would have done for any other like work. There was nothing in his thought formed but not uttered, or in his acts that indicated or set in motion an indication to the defendants of his acceptance of their offer, or which could necessarily result therein.

But the charge of the learned judge was fairly to be understood by the jury as laying down the rule to them, that the plaintiff need not indicate to the defendants his acceptance of their offer; and that the purchase of stuff and working on it after receiving the note, made a binding contract between the parties. In this we think the learned judge fell into error.

The judgment appealed from must be reversed and a new trial ordered, with costs to abide the event of the action. All concur, but Allen, J., not voting.

Judgment reversed, and new trial ordered.

NOTE

For further details taken from the appellate record, see E. A. Farnsworth & W. Young, Cases and Materials on Contracts 202 note a (3d ed. 1980).

Suppose the plaintiff had already loaded the materials on a wagon when defendant's second note arrived. Same result? See Ever-Tite Roofing Corp. v. Green, 83 So. 2d 449 (La. App. 1955).

Restatement Second §62 reads as follows:

> Effect of Performance by Offeree Where Offer Invites Either
> Performance or Promise
> (1) Where an offer invites an offeree to choose between acceptance by promise and acceptance by performance, the beginning of the invited performance or a tender of part of it is an acceptance by performance.
> (2) Such an acceptance operates as a promise to render complete performance.

Consult U.C.C. §2-206, Comment 2.

LOS ANGELES TRACTION CO. v. WILSHIRE
135 Cal. 654, 67 P. 1086 (1902)

GRAY, C. — The action is based on a written instrument, signed by appellants, and reading as follows: —

$2,000   Los Angeles, Cal., July 19th, 1895.

> Thirty days after the completion of the double-track street railway of the Los Angeles Traction Company to the intersection of Seventh and Hoover Streets, for value received, I promise to pay to the order of the Los Angeles Traction Company, the sum of two thousand (2,000) dollars, negotiable and payable at Citizens' Bank, with interest at the rate of eight percent per annum, payable after maturity. I further promise and agree to pay a reasonable attorney's fee if suit should be instituted for the collection of this note.

The above instrument was placed in the hands of the Citizens' Bank, together with a duly signed written escrow agreement, as follows: —

> To the Citizens' Bank, Los Angeles, Cal.: Herewith is handed you by the undersigned the following named notes, to be held in escrow upon the terms and conditions herein stated: You are requested to hold said notes in escrow until the completion of the line of railroad of the Los Angeles Traction Company, now being constructed in the city of Los Angeles westerly on Eighth Street to the vicinity of West Lake Park; thence by a route to be selected by said company westward on Seventh Street, and by one or more streets to the intersection of Hoover Street with Sixth Street bounding the south side of the West End University Addition to Los Angeles;

thence west on said Sixth Street to Commonwealth Avenue; thence north on Commonwealth Avenue to First Street; thence west on First Street to Virgil Avenue. Upon completion and operation of the same with electric power you are instructed to deliver said notes to said Los Angeles Traction Company. In case a franchise for such streetcar line to said Hoover Street is not obtained by said Traction Company within . . . months from date hereof, then, in that event, said notes shall be returned to their respective markers upon demand to be cancelled. Said notes are made by the following named persons and in the sums set opposite their names.

Then follow the names of the parties giving the notes, including the names of these appellants, who also signed the said agreement.

The findings show that, on the faith of the foregoing instruments, and other instruments of like character executed by other parties, who, like defendants, were the owners of property that would be made valuable by the construction of the proposed road, the plaintiff, in November, 1895, less than four months from the execution of said instrument, bid and paid to the city of Los Angeles $1,505 for a franchise to construct the road over the part of the course agreed upon and within the city limits. Before the 28th of April, 1896, the plaintiff commenced work upon said railway, but said work was not performed with the intention of prosecuting the construction of said railway continuously and with diligence to completion, and the plaintiff did not so commence work upon said railway with said purpose until after the first day of July, 1897. On July 1, 1897, defendants served upon plaintiff a written notice to the effect that they did not recognize any liability on account of the foregoing written contracts, for the reason that the road had not been completed within the time agreed upon. Soon after the service of this notice, the plaintiff actively engaged in the construction of the road and completed it, and commenced operating the same to the intersection of Seventh and Hoover streets, as provided for in said instruments, before the expiration of the year 1897. Thereafter, and on May 17th, 1898, plaintiff completed its railway to First and Virgil Streets. Upon these facts plaintiff had judgment for two thousand dollars, besides interest and attorney's fees. Defendants appeal from this judgment and from an order denying them a new trial. . . .

The contract at the date of its making was unilateral, a mere offer that, if subsequently accepted and acted upon by the other party to it, would ripen into a binding, enforceable obligation. When the respondent purchased and paid upwards of fifteen hundred dollars for a franchise, it had acted upon the contract; and it would be manifestly unjust thereafter to permit the offer that had been made to be withdrawn. The promised consideration had then been partly performed, and the contract had taken on a bilateral character, and if appellant thereafter thought he discovered a ground for rescinding the contract, it was, as it always is, a necessary condition to the rescission that the other party should be made whole as to what he had parted with on the strength of the contract. The notice of withdrawal from the contract was ineffectual, therefore, for several reasons. In the first place, it was based on a wrong theory; the reason given for it was that the road was not constructed within the agreed time, when, as was determined subsequently by the court, there was no time agreed upon. Again, it came too late, after the obligations of the parties had become fixed. . . .

[The judgment of the trial court was affirmed by the Commissioners; and their judgment was affirmed by the Supreme Court.]

NOTE

1. Is the case now covered by §45 of the Restatement First[135]? By §90, reprinted *supra* p. 281? Was plaintiff under a duty to complete the street railway? Consult Pollock, Book Review, 28 L.Q. Rev. 100, 101 (1912). See also Goble, Is Performance Always as Desirable as a Promise to Perform?, 22 Ill. L. Rev. 789 (1928). Is §62 of the Restatement Second, *supra* p. 407, applicable? Can you imagine a situation in which the traction company, under the court's theory, would be liable in damages to Wilshire?

2. A, in a well-known hypothetical case, says to B, "You have never kept your promise in the past, but if you plow my acre I shall give you $80 and if you complete the job before Thanksgiving I shall give you a bonus of $20." Can B abandon the half-completed job with impunity? Is he entitled to any compensation? B has just done half of the job when A revokes. The value of B's work is $40. Is B entitled to $40, $50, or $60, or can he complete the work and demand $100? Should not the offeree be given the full benefit of the bargain only if he is under a duty to complete the job? See Fuller & Perdue, Reliance Interest in Contract Damages (pt. 2), 46 Yale L.J. 373, 410-413 (1937). Consult further Hays, Formal Contracts and Consideration: A Legislative Program, 41 Colum. L. Rev. 849 at 860 (1941).

Suppose B has spent $5 to have his plow repaired; has A's promise become irrevocable by virtue of this fact? Does Restatement §45 control? Section 90?

3. In Bickerstaff v. Gregston, 604 P.2d 382 (Okla. Ct. App. 1979), the court declined to apply §90 where the promise explicitly called for an act, and the act was not completed by the plaintiff-promisee.

---

135. It reads as follows:

Revocation of Offer for Unilateral Contract; Effect of Part Performance
or Tender

   If an offer for a unilateral contract is made, and part of the consideration requested in the offer is given or tendered by the offeree in response thereto, the offeror is bound by a contract, the duty of immediate performance of which is conditional on the full consideration being given or tendered within the time stated in the offer, or, if no time is stated therein, within a reasonable time.

For the text of the same section in the Restatement Second, see p. 373 *supra*.

PETTERSON v. PATTBERG
248 N.Y. 86, 161 N.E. 428 (1928)

For a report of the case, see p. 689 *infra*.

WHITTIER, THE RESTATEMENT OF CONTRACTS AND MU-
TUAL ASSENT, 17 Calif. L. Rev. 441, 450 (1929). In his criticism of §45
of the Restatement of Contracts, the author has this to say (citations are
omitted):

"The writer prefers Professor McGovney's solution of this problem.
[McGovney, Irrevocable Offers, 27 Harv. L. Rev. 644 (1914).] He says
that in such a case there is an offer implied in fact not to withdraw the
main offer after the offeree has started to perform which collateral offer
becomes a binding unilateral contract when performance is started. This
suggestion has been criticized on the ground that the collateral offer is a
pure fiction. But is this so? In many cases of contracts implied in fact
there is no conscious mental image of the promise made. A orders a roast
from the meat market. He impliedly promises to pay the price therefor.
But does he think with every such order, 'Now I am binding myself to pay
the price?' Probably not. If A promises to pay John ten dollars if he swims
a stream, does he not impliedly agree that if John starts on time he will
give him a fair chance to finish before withdrawing the offer? Is this
implication any more of a fiction than that made effective in the case of
the order for meat? Furthermore, this view indicates the reason why an
offer to a real estate agent to pay him a commission for selling property
may be withdrawn before he obtains a willing and responsible buyer. Due
to custom, there is no promise not to revoke such an offer. An offer of a
reward for the apprehension of a criminal may be withdrawn after some
steps have been taken. There again by common understanding there is
no implied promise to keep the offer open. True, the law may perhaps be
explained on the ground that the steps taken are preparation rather than
performance. But if an *exclusive* agency to sell land is given to a realtor
there is an implied promise not to revoke and expenditures in attempting
to sell are sufficient as consideration to make it binding. The courts have
reached results here which cannot be arrived at by applying the rule of
Section 45. But they may be justified by considering the fair implication
of each situation, custom included. The McGovney view, then, seems
much nearer to the law than the hard and fast rule of the Restatement,
namely, that in every case part performance or tender makes the contract
complete. In the cases where such a collateral promise is fairly implied
the remedy on it would be much the same as that on the contract which is
made according to the Restatement. Space forbids a discussion of possible differences.

"Finally, the making of offers irrevocable as a short cut to specific
performance seems unnecessary and unsound. It is unusual to allow

specific performance at law. This is more than specific performance; it makes a breach of the contract to keep the offer open impossible. If the above discussion is correct, all the really desirable results which would flow from treating some offers as irrevocable may be obtained without this departure from the general principles of law."

Note on Real Estate Brokerage Agreements

A real estate brokerage agreement has traditionally been treated as an offer to enter a unilateral contract. Under this view, the seller can revoke the offer at any time prior to the broker's "acceptance" by performance.[136] The seller can revoke by withdrawing the property from the market or by selling it himself or through another broker. If the seller revokes, the broker's time and effort will be for naught.

An obvious limitation on the seller's right to revoke is that the revocation must not be for the purpose of depriving the broker of his commission. Goodman v. Marcol, 261 N.Y. 188, 184 N.E. 755 (1933). In the absence of a bad faith revocation, how else might a broker be protected? Could he invoke the authority of Restatement Second §45? Devices have been developed to insure that brokers receive their commissions. The open or general listing, perhaps the most common form of brokerage agreement, has all the pitfalls mentioned above. To this type of arrangement have been added the exclusive agency agreement and the exclusive right to sell. An exclusive agency agreement deprives the seller of the right to sell through another broker during the term of the agency, but the seller may sell the property on his own. The exclusive right to sell deprives the seller of the right to sell on his own or through another broker during the term the brokerage contract is in effect.

Several questions arise with respect to these exclusive listings. If the seller breaches the agreement by selling himself or through another broker, is the broker entitled to his commission even though he has been unable to find a purchaser ready, willing and able to buy? The answer may depend on whether the broker has expended time and effort in procuring a purchaser. Should it? How much time and effort is sufficient to bind the seller? Should not the broker be limited to recovery for time and effort spent, instead of the agreed commission? These are nice questions, and the answers given by the courts have not always been consistent.

---

136. A recurring issue in the case law concerns the time at which the broker may be said to have completed his performance. Has the broker performed his end of the bargain when he has obtained a willing and able purchaser? When a contract is signed? When the sale is complete? Many brokerage agreements specify when the broker has performed; but such provisions give rise to problems of their own, of the sort dealt with in Ellsworth Dobbs, Inc. v. Johnson, discussed *infra* p. 417.

A further problem arises with regard to exclusive listings when the seller withdraws the property from the market because he has changed his mind about selling it. Circumstances may have changed; the seller may not have to move to that new job out of state after all. Should he nevertheless have to pay the broker's commission if he decides not to sell? On the one hand, the seller is expected to pay the broker out of the proceeds of the sale. If there is no sale, the seller may not have the money for the commission. On the other hand, the broker may have spent considerable time and effort searching for a purchaser. He may even have found one. These cases pose serious difficulties for the courts, and as might be expected the solutions are not uniform.

A trend can be detected in the brokerage commission cases. In former years, judicial solicitude for the broker resulted in a less rigorous application of the unilateral contract doctrine. Exclusive listings were frequently cast in the form of a bilateral contract, with the broker promising to use his best efforts to obtain a purchaser, and the courts showed a willingness to award the broker his commission when the seller breached. Even brokers with open listings were sometimes given their commissions with the help of §45 of the Restatement. But the brokerage business has become a big business. Standard forms are now used, which are prepared by brokers and their attorneys. The assertion that the "offeror is the master of the bargain" is simply not applicable to the average brokerage agreement. Courts are now cutting back on some of the protection given to brokers, in the interest of protecting the reasonable expectations of the people with whom they deal. This is not to say that courts are reviving the unilateral contract doctrine in the brokerage field. The distinction between unilateral and bilateral contracts is not much help in solving the problems posed by these agreements. Rather, courts are looking more closely at the relationship between the seller and broker, at their relative bargaining power and sophistication, and at the bona fides of their actions.

Space permits only a brief look at brokerage agreements and the problems surrounding them. A single case has been selected, which illustrates only a few of the problems mentioned and only one court's solution. Some of the other problems and their judicial treatment will be dealt with in the Note following the case.

BAUMGARTNER v. MEEK
126 Cal. App. 2d 505, 272 P.2d 552 (Cal. Dist. Ct. App. 1954)

Appeal from a judgment of the Superior Court of Napa County. Raymond J. Sherwin, Judge, pro term. Affirmed.

Action for broker's commission. Judgment for plaintiff affirmed.

PAULSEN, J. pro tem. — This is an appeal from a judgment of $15,000 and interest upon the verdict of a jury in an action to recover upon a real estate brokerage listing. The document signed by the parties conformed to the California Real Estate Association standard form and so far as material to this appeal reads as follows:

> In consideration of the services of W. B. Griffiths Company, hereinafter called broker, I hereby list with said broker, exclusively and irrevocably, for the period of time beginning January 8, 1951 and ending March 1, 1951, the property situated in the Berryessa Valley, County of Napa, California, described as follows, to-wit: [Description] and I hereby grant said broker the exclusive and irrevocable right to sell said property within said time for Three Hundred Thousand — 00/100 ($300,000.00) Dollars. . . .
>
> I hereby agree to pay said broker as commission five (5%) per centum of the selling price should, during the time set forth herein, said property be sold by said broker or by me or by another broker or through some other source or whether said property be withdrawn from sale, transferred, conveyed or leased without approval of said broker.
>
> Dated January 8, 1951
>
> (Signed) N. T. M<small>EEK</small>
F<small>LORA</small> E. M<small>EEK</small>

> ┌─────────────────────────────┐
> │ Contract extended to   │
> │   Dec. 1/51   │
> │ (*Signed*) N. T. M<small>EEK</small>   │
> │   F<small>LORA</small> E. M<small>EEK</small>   │
> └─────────────────────────────┘

> In consideration of the foregoing listing and authorization the undersigned broker agrees to use diligence in procuring a purchaser:
>
> W. B. G<small>RIFFITHS</small> C<small>OMPANY</small>
(Signed) By E<small>DITH</small> R. B<small>AUMGARTNER</small>
Broker

It will be noted that the contract was originally made in January, 1951, and ran to March 1, 1951. There was evidence to the effect that after March 1st, at appellant's request, respondent continued her attempts to find a buyer, and that in September of that year she obtained an offer of $200,000 which was refused by appellants. They asked her to try to find a buyer who would pay more, and respondent then insisted upon again having an exclusive authorization. A new contract was executed, but this was later superseded by the extension of the original agreement as shown above.

On November 8, 1951, respondent called appellant N. T. Meek in San Jose and advised him she had a prospective purchaser of $250,000 and discussed the possibility of a sale at that price. The following morning N. T. Meek called respondent and told her he would have to take the ranch off the market. There is a dispute regarding the rest of the conversation at that time. Respondent testified that when N. T. Meek told her he was taking the property off the market, she said, "But, Tom, how about my authorization; I still have until the 1st of December and you know I have done a great deal of work on this and I have spent a great deal of money and I have interested people; I am going to be in a most embarrassing position with my people." Appellant N. T. Meek testified that "Edith said that she thought she ought to be recompensed for what she was out for advertising. I asked her how much it was; she said 'About $480.00,' and I told her I would pay her. It was okay with her to take it off the market."

Appellant N. T. Meek then wrote respondent, under date of November 9, 1951, advising her that he was taking his ranch off the market.

In December, 1951, respondent filed an action to recover from appellants the sum of $15,000. Her first cause of action alleged she was entitled to that sum because of the withdrawal of the property from sale and the second cause of action alleged that she was entitled to that sum because defendants, without her approval, had sold the property to other purchasers. This second cause of action was subsequently dismissed and the cause proceeded to trial upon the first count alone.

There can be no doubt but that respondent, in accordance with her written statement that she would in consideration of the listing use diligence in procuring a purchaser, did expend considerable sums of money advertising the property, taking photographs of it, gathering data for use in promoting the sale and listing it with other brokers. Supportive of this is the testimony of appellant N. T. Meek concerning the phone conversation in which he offered to pay her $480 to recompense her for her expenditures in efforts to sell the property. It cannot be doubted either that respondent actively continued her efforts to obtain a satisfactory sale up to the time when she was advised by appellants through the letter of N. T. Meek that they had taken the property off the market. This happened within the terms stipulated by the writings executed by the parties.

Appellants first contend that respondent could not recover a commission without pleading and proving that she had procured a purchaser ready, able and willing to pay the price at which appellants had authorized her to sell. In support of this they cite Merkeley v. Fisk, 179 Cal. 748 [178 P. 945]. The case is not in point. In that case the plaintiff's claim was based upon allegations of performance by the broker who claimed that he had made a sale. A demurrer to his complaint was sustained and it was held on appeal that the pleading was insufficient because it did not contain allegations that the purchaser procured by the broker was one that was able, ready and willing to buy.

Appellants next argue that the contract was unilateral and without consideration. Basically, a brokerage listing is an offer of a unilateral contract, the act requested being the procuring by the broker of a purchaser ready, able and willing to buy upon the terms stated in the offer.

Conformable to the settled rules governing offers of unilateral contracts such a listing, which we might term a general listing, is held to be revocable at the will of the owner in good faith at any time before performance, regardless of the efforts expended by the broker. Furthermore, such a listing leaves the owner free to list with other brokers, to sell the property through his own efforts, to withdraw the property from the market, or otherwise to revoke his offer. Latterly, however, and particularly in California, there has developed a concept of irrevocability which brokers have generally sought to implement by written provisions placing restrictions upon the freedom of the owner under a general listing. These stipulations take the form of a stated term within which the broker might accept the offer of unilateral contract by performing the required act, or of a so-called exclusive agency, doing away with the right of the owner to deal through other brokers, or of an exclusive right to sell, precluding the owner himself from selling and the like. In view of the nature of the basic transaction between the owner and the broker, that is, a listing which is no more than an offer of a unilateral contract to be accepted only by a performance of the requested act, these additional stipulations were challenged in many courts as not resulting in any contract in fact between the parties (e.g. see Bartlett v. Keith, 325 Mass. 265 [90 N.E.2d 308]; 37 Iowa L. Rev. 350, 354). But in many states, and in this state, courts have accepted such written listings as resulting in contractual relations. Though the basic offer to pay a commission for the procuring of a purchaser ready, able and willing to buy can still be accepted only by performance, nevertheless it has been held that these restrictive stipulations bind the owner and subject him to liability if he refuses to abide by them. These holdings are sometimes based on the idea that the restrictive clauses constitute subsidiary promises resting upon the consideration that the broker agrees to and does expend time and effort to bring about a sale. Thus we find in Restatement of Contracts, section 45:

> If an offer for a unilateral contract is made and part of the consideration requested in the offer is given or tendered by the offeree in response thereto, the offeror is bound by a contract, the duty of immediate performance of which is conditional on the full consideration being given or tendered within the time stated in the offer. . . .

It is unnecessary to attempt to follow the reasoning given in the many opinions of courts dealing with this subject. We think that in California the rule has been too long declared and too often enforced to leave the matter open. This position of our courts is well set out in Kimmel v. Skelly, 130 Cal. 555.

Appellants next insist that the "attempted withdrawal of the land from sale was ineffectual since the authorization to sell was exclusive and irrevocable." To this effect they cite Sill v. Ceschi, 167 Cal. 698 [140 P.

949], where it is held that where the brokerage contract is for a definite term it cannot be revoked within the term if the broker has expended money and effort in seeking a purchaser.

It appears to be appellants' view that because they had no legal right to withdraw the property from sale, respondent therefore had the legal right to continue her efforts to find a purchaser and was required to do so before she could recover. As stated in Rucker v. Hall, [105 Cal. 425, 38 P. 962] the withdrawal "placed it out of her power to complete" a sale. If appellants' contentions in this respect are correct the respondent would have been required to spend additional money and time trying to find a buyer who could not have viewed the property without permission of the owner. Respondent would also have been required, in order to interest such a buyer at all, to misrepresent her position in the matter, or, what is equally as bad, to persuade a prospective buyer to enter into an agreement which she knew would not be honored by the seller, and all this for the sole purpose of placing herself in a position to collect a commission and not with the hope of making a sale. The law does not demand such absurdities or sanction such questionable practices.

Finally, it is contended that the promise to pay if the owner withdrew the property from sale during the term must be considered either as a penalty or as a liquidated damage provision and in either view void as a matter of law. As we have noted, provisions in brokerage contracts similar to those contained in this contract have been approved and enforced by our courts in such cases as Kimmel v. Skelly and cases therein cited. (See also Walter v. Libby, 72 Cal. App. 2d 138 [164 P.2d 21], Fleming v. Dolfin, 214 Cal. 269, 271 [4 P.2d 776, 78 A.L.R. 585], and Mills v. Hunter, 103 Cal. App. 2d 352 [229 P.2d 456].) We think this contention cannot be sustained in view of the contrary holdings in the cases referred to. The distinction between an action for breach of the promise by the owner not to revoke or deal through others or sell himself during the stipulated term, wherein damages are sought for such breach, and a contractual provision whereby, in consideration of the services of the broker to be and being rendered, the owner directly promises that if he sells through others or by himself or revokes he will pay a sum certain, is made clear in the cited cases, particularly in the quotations we have taken from the opinion in Kimmel v. Skelley. The action is for money owed, an action in debt (Maze v. Gordon, [96 Cal. 61, 30 P. 962]), and the only breach involved is the failure to pay the promised sum. Plaintiff in such cases seeks to recover actual damages, not liquidated damages. The code provisions, therefore, concerning penalties and concerning stipulated damages are not applicable. It is not for this court at this stage to defend or attack the rationale of these decisions upon this subject. Brokerage contracts have been formulated for many years in reliance upon them. These contracts in their language are so plain that the intent of the parties to bind themselves, just as these decisions have declared they are bound in such instances, cannot be disregarded. As we have indicated, the whole question of the relationships between owner and broker in respect of this type of transaction is one wherein there has been much conflict in decisions. Our courts have ruled in the way indicated by us and we think the rule of the cases in which they have done so ought not now to be disturbed. Although these decisions have not specifically discussed the challenge here made to the contractual provisions upon which respondent relies, it can hardly be said that they have been rendered without consideration of such attacks, for, as we have seen, the contentions were advanced in the brief in at least one, and that the principal one, of the cases cited.

The judgment appealed from is affirmed.

Van Dyke, P.J., and Schottky, J., concurred.

NOTE

The decision in *Baumgartner* was upheld by the California Supreme Court in Blank v. Borden, 11 Cal. 3d 963, 524 P.2d 127, 115 Cal. Rptr. 31 (1974), against the argument that the withdrawal-from-sale clause in the brokerage contract constituted an unenforceable penalty. The Oregon Supreme Court took the opposite view in Wright v. Schutt Construction Co., 262 Or. 619, 500 P.2d 1045, 69 A.L.R. 3d 1260 (1972). On the distinction between penalties and liquidated damages, see Chapter 10, Section 4. Even if the withdrawal-from-sale clause is found to be an invalid penalty, the broker is entitled to recover actual damages. What might those damages be? If the withdrawal-from-sale clause is a penalty, what about the clauses in the brokerage agreement that call for payment of the commission when the seller sells himself or through another broker? Are they not penalties as well?

Another troublesome clause common to brokerage agreements is the one that says the brokerage commission is earned when the seller and buyer sign their contract. In the leading case of Ellsworth Dobbs Inc. v. Johnson, 50 N.J. 528, 236 A.2d 843 (1967), the New Jersey Supreme Court, per Francis, J., held that the commission is earned only if the deal goes through, unless the seller's improper conduct prevented the sale. The broker does, however, have an action against the defaulting purchaser for the commission. The court went on to hold, on grounds of public policy, that the parties to a brokerage contract cannot alter this rule "whenever there is substantial inequality of bargaining power, position or advantage between the broker and the other party involved." Id. at 555, 236 A.2d at 857. A number of courts have followed the *Ellsworth Dobbs* decision. See, e.g., Setser v. Commonwealth, Inc., 256 Or. 11, 470 P.2d 142 (1970). For a discussion of the *Ellsworth Dobbs* case see Note, 25 Rutgers L. Rev. 83 (1968).

If, as the court in *Baumgartner* says, the exclusive listing agreement forms a contractual relation between broker and seller, could the seller sue the broker for breach of contract? On what grounds? What are the broker's obligations under the contract?

Section 11.   Requirement Contracts and Mutuality

While it has seldom been doubted that a sale on approval (or a sale or return, for that matter) is a binding contract before the buyer has expressed his approval (U.C.C. §2-326), contracts that give one of the parties an option as to quantity (as contrasted with quality) have had an uphill fight for recognition.[137] The early Minnesota case of Bailey v. Austrian, 19 Minn. 535 (Gil. 465) (1873), illustrates the predicament of the buyer. Plaintiffs offered evidence that defendant had promised to supply and plaintiffs promised to buy at specified prices all the pig-iron they might want in their foundry during a stated period. A quantity of pig-iron was furnished,[138] but before the contract had expired defendant stopped requested deliveries. In holding that the evidence offered was properly excluded because if admitted it would not have established a contract between the parties, the court had this to say:[139]

> Upon the foregoing state of facts the engagement of plaintiffs was to purchase all of said pig-iron which they might want in their said business during the time specified; but they do not engage to *want* any quantity whatever. They do not even engage to continue their business. If they see fit to discontinue it on the very day on which the supposed agreement is entered into, they are at entire liberty to do so at their own option, and, whatever might have been defendant's expectation, he is without remedy. In other words, there is no absolute engagement on plaintiffs' part to "want," and of course no absolute engagement to *purchase* any iron of defendant.
>
> Without such absolute engagement on plaintiffs' part, there is "no absolute mutuality of engagement," so that defendant "has the right at once to hold" plaintiffs "to a positive agreement." . . .
>
> To be a sufficient consideration it is necessary that plaintiffs' promise be a benefit to defendant or an injury to plaintiffs. 1 Parsons, Cont. 431. But so long as . . . plaintiffs are not bound to do anything whatever by virtue of their promise, the promise cannot be such benefit or injury.

137. Recognition of such contracts in an early Tennessee case, Cherry v. Smith, 22 Tenn. (3 Hum.) 19 (1822), was rather short-lived.
138. This fact is mentioned only in the Gilfillan report.
139. The paragraph closely follows Lavery, The Doctrine of Bailey v. Austrian, 10 Minn. L. Rev. 584 (1926).

Business necessity, however, dictated enforceability of requirement as well as output contracts, i.e., contracts where the quantity sold is measured by either the requirements of the buyer or the output of the seller, (U.C.C. §2-306). The advantages of these types of contract become obvious when we contrast them with contracts providing for fixed quantity terms.[140] In the latter type of contract the seller is assured that a certain portion of its output is taken care of and the buyer is assured of its supply. But the risk of having surplus goods on hand is not taken care of. Depending on business developments it may fall on either party. Requirement and output contracts, on the other hand, aim at the allocation of this risk. Requirement contracts assure the buyer of supply,

> may afford protection against rises in price, enable long term planning on the basis of known costs and obviate the expense and risk of storage in the quantity necessary for a commodity having a fluctuating demand. From the seller's point of view, requirement contracts may make possible the substantial reduction of selling expenses, give protection against price fluctuations, and — of particular advantage to a newcomer to the field to whom it is important to know what capital expenditures are justified — offer the possibility of a predictable market.

Standard Oil Company of California v. United States, 337 U.S. 293, 306-307 (1949).[141] In output contracts the situation is reversed. While in a requirement contract the risk of nondisposal because of a drop in the buyer's business as well as the risk of filling increasing needs is on the seller, these risks have to be borne by the buyer in an output contract. The risk of marketing put on the buyer is often paid for by a price concession, which the seller can afford because his selling costs are diminished. Maximum and minimum contracts partially limit the risks involved in these types of contract; so do flexible prices. A more detailed discussion of the economic role of such arrangements may be found in Havighurst & Berman, Requirement and Output Contracts, 27 Ill. L. Rev. 1 (1927). See also K. Llewellyn, Cases and Materials on the Law of Sales 452 (1930); Patterson, Illusory Promises and Promisor's Options, 6 Iowa L. Bull. 129, 209 (1921); Corbin, The Effect of Options on Consideration, 34 Yale L.J. 571, 579-583 (1925); Note, Requirement and Output Contracts Under the Uniform Commercial Code, 102 U. Pa. L. Rev. 654 (1954); Note, Requirement Contracts: Problems of Drafting and Construction, 78 Harv. L. Rev. 1212 (1965). On the treatment of requirement contracts in the

---

140. On the disadvantages (costs) of having contracts with fixed terms see Coase, The Nature of the Firm, 4 Economica (n.s.) 386 (1937).

141. For the impact of the antitrust laws on requirement contracts, see further United States v. Richfield Oil Corp., 99 F. Supp. 280 (S.D. Cal. 1951), aff'd per curiam, 343 U.S. 292 (1952); Tampa Electric Co. v. Nashville Coal Co., 365 U.S. 320 (1961).

British Commonwealth see Howard, Requirements and the Output Contracts, 2 U. Tasmania L. Rev. 446 (1967).

GREAT NORTHERN RY. v. WITHAM
L.R. 9 C.P. 16 (1873)

. . . The cause was tried before Brett, J., at the sittings at Westminster after the last term. The facts were as follows: In October, 1871, the plaintiffs advertised for tenders for the supply of goods (amongst other things iron) to be delivered at their station at Doncaster, according to a certain specification. The defendant sent in a tender, as follows:

I, the undersigned, hereby undertake to supply the Great Northern Railway Company, for twelve months from the 1st of November 1871, to 31st of October 1872, with such quantities of each or any of the several articles named in the attached specification as the company's storekeeper may order from time to time, at the price set opposite each article respectively, and agree to abide by the conditions stated on the other side.

[Signed] SAMUEL WITHAM.

The company's officer wrote in reply, as follows:

Mr. S. Witham:

Sir: I am instructed to inform you that my directors have accepted your tender, dated, etc., to supply this company at Doncaster station any quantity they may order during the period ending October 31st, 1872, of the descriptions of iron mentioned on the enclosed list, at the prices specified therein. The terms of the contract must be strictly adhered to. Requesting an acknowledgment of the receipt of this letter,

[Signed] S. FITCH, *Assistant Secretary*.

To this the defendant replied:

I beg to own receipt of your favor of 20th instant, accepting my tender for bars, for which I am obliged. Your specifications shall receive my best attention.

S. WITHAM.

Several orders for iron were given by the company, which were from time to time duly executed by the defendant; but ultimately the defendant refused to supply any more, whereupon this action was brought.

A verdict having been found for the plaintiffs,

Digby Seymour, Q.C., moved to enter a nonsuit. . . .

KEATING, J. In this case Mr. Digby Seymour moved to enter a nonsuit. The circumstances were these: The Great Northern Railway Company advertised for tenders for the supply of stores. The defendant made a tender in these words: "I hereby undertake to supply the Great Northern Railway Company, for twelve months, from etc. to etc., with such quantities of each or any of the several articles named in the attached specifications as the company's store-keeper may order from time to time, at the price set opposite each article respectively," etc. Some orders were given by the company, which were duly executed. But the order now in question was not executed; the defendant seeking to excuse himself from the performance of his agreement, because it was unilateral, the company not being bound to give the order. The ground upon which it was put by Mr. Seymour was that there was no consideration for the defendant's promise to supply the goods; in other words, that, inasmuch as there was no obligation on the company to give an order, there was no consideration moving from the company, and therefore no obligation on the defendant to supply the goods. The case mainly relied on in support of that contention was Burton v. Great Northern Railway Co. [9 Ex. 507; 23 L.J. (Ex.) 184]. But that is not an authority in the defendant's favor. It was the converse case. The Court there held that no action would lie against the company for not giving an order. If before the order was given the defendant had given notice to the company that he would not perform the agreement, it might be that he would have been justified in so doing. But here the company had given the order, and had consequently done something which amounted to a consideration for the defendant's promise. I see no ground for doubting that the verdict for the plaintiffs ought to stand.

BRETT, J. The company advertised for tenders for the supply of stores, such as they might think fit to order, for one year. The defendant made a tender offering to supply them for that period at certain fixed prices; and the company accepted his tender. If there were no other objection, the contract between the parties would be found in the tender and the letter accepting it. This action is brought for the defendant's refusal to deliver goods ordered by the company; and the objection to the plaintiffs' right to recover is, that the contract is unilateral. I do not, however, understand what objection that is to a contract. Many contracts are obnoxious to the same complaint. If I say to another, "If you will go to York, I will give you £100," that is in a certain sense a unilateral contract. He has not promised to go to York. But if he goes, it cannot be doubted that he will be entitled to receive the £100. His going to York at my request is a sufficient consideration for my promise. So, if one says to another, "If you will give me an order for iron, or other goods, I will supply it as a given price"; if the order is given, there is a complete contract which the seller is bound to perform. There is in such a case ample consideration for the promise. So, here, the company having given the defendant an order at his request, his

acceptance of the order would bind them. If any authority could have
been found to sustain Mr. Seymour's contention, I should have considered that a rule ought to be granted. But none has been cited. Burton v.
Great Northern Railway Co. [9 Ex. 507; 23 L.J. (Ex.) 184] is not at all to
the purpose. This is matter of every day's practice; and I think it would be
wrong to countenance the notion that a man who tenders for the supply
of goods in this way is not bound to deliver them when an order is given. I
agree that this judgment does not decide the question whether the defendant might have absolved himself from the further performance of the
contract by giving notice. . . .

Rule refused.

NOTE

What obligation did plaintiff incur by "accepting" the tender? Consult
Percival, Ltd. v. L.C.C. Asylums and Mental Deficiency Committee, 87
L.J. 677 (K.B. 1918); Cheshire & Fifoot's Law of Contract 41 (Furmston
10th ed. 1981). The system used by Great Northern in dealing with its
suppliers has its counterpart in the so called "blanket orders" used in
some parts of the American automobile industry. For an illuminating
description and discussion of their legal implications, see Macaulay, The
Standardized Contract of United States Automobile Manufacturers, 7
Int'l Ency. of Comp. Law, ch. 3 (1973).

Did the letter of acceptance bind plaintiff to give any order? Taken
together with defendant's reply, was not a one-year supply contract consummated? Suppose the case had come up under U.C.C. §2-205. Had
plaintiff acquired an option committing defendant to comply with purchase orders made during the year? Did not plaintiff's acceptance letter
imply a promise not to buy from somebody else during the twelve-month
period?

WESTESEN v. OLATHE STATE BANK
71 Colo. 102, 204 P. 329 (1922)

TELLER, J. The plaintiff in error sued the defendant in error for damages for a breach of a contract by which the bank agreed to loan plaintiff
money for a trip to California. A general demurrer to the complaint was
sustained, upon the ground that the contract was unilateral, and void for
want of mutuality, there being, the court held, no obligation on the part
of the plaintiff to borrow any money from the bank. Plaintiff elected to
stand upon his complaint, the action was dismissed, and the cause is now
here on error. . . .

The complaint alleges that the plaintiff explained to the vice president of the banking company that he —

> . . . was about to take a trip of vacation to California, and would require a credit of $5,000 for use on such trip, and then and thereupon defendant, through the said vice president, caused plaintiff to execute his five promissory notes of $1,000 each to defendant, and plaintiff did execute said notes to the defendant, and in consideration thereof defendant promised and agreed that plaintiff should have a credit of $5,000 with said bank, against which plaintiff could check at his convenience; that said notes would be held by defendant, and whenever his account, by reason of checking thereon in accordance with said agreement, should be overdrawn, that said notes would be severally deposited, and credited to plaintiff's account, less the usual discount thereon; and plaintiff then and there explained to defendant, and defendant knew, the purpose of said trip to California, and that the obtaining of said credit was for the trip of plaintiff and his wife to California for a vacation, and that plaintiff did not and would not have the funds for said trip and vacation, except through said credit.

It is further alleged that plaintiff, after arriving in California, drew a check on said bank, which was dishonored.

It is to be observed that the complaint alleges that the execution and delivery of the promissory notes to the bank upon the condition and for the purpose stated, was the consideration upon which the bank was to give plaintiff a credit of $5,000. Unquestionably such delivery was a sufficient consideration for that contract, even if there were nothing else, because the plaintiff thereby put himself in a worse position, and because he did something he was not bound to do.

The complaint is good under another line of authorities, which hold that an agreement on the one part to sell, and upon the other part to buy, all the goods, or articles, that the purchaser may *require* during a stated term, is a valid contract. This, of course, is confined to those cases in which there is good ground for believing that some goods at least will be required.

Construing the complaint as an entirety, it is clear that the bank agreed that if the plaintiff would borrow of it the money which he would require on his proposed trip and gave to the bank his notes, it would advance him money through his checking account, as required by him; in short, the bank agreed to loan plaintiff the money *required* for the trip. The moment that a check by the plaintiff called for more money than he had on deposit, the bank had the right to take one of the notes, and make it a binding obligation upon the plaintiff. It is immaterial that the exact sum he might require was not fixed. The contract was made with that fact in view. The bank, being in the business of lending money, in effect, proposed that if the plaintiff would borrow from it what he needed for the purpose stated, it would loan it to him as called for. The delivery of the notes was an acceptance of the proposition, and completed the contract. The fact that he might shorten his trip, and so borrow less money, is not material, because that, too, was a contingency which must have been recognized by the bank. That might be of some moment upon the question of the advisability of making the contract, but it does not affect its validity. Since the contract was made, the question whether or not the bank got much or little profit out of it is beside the mark. The complaint stated a cause of action and the court erred in sustaining the demurrer.

The judgment is therefore reversed, and the cause remanded for further proceedings in accordance with the view herein expressed.

Denison and Whiteford, JJ., concur.

NOTE

The subsequent history of the litigation is rather interesting. Plaintiff, whose checks drawn on defendant bank in payment of two automobiles had been dishonored, claimed $1,200 actual and $5,000 exemplary damages. On the ground that plaintiff and his wife spent almost 6 weeks in California before returning home, thus getting some benefit out of their expenditure of railroad fare and other expenses, the trial court instructed the jury that they should not consider any sum expended by plaintiff on his vacation except an item of $10, which he had paid for the examination of one of the automobiles purchased. The jury returned a verdict for the plaintiff in accordance with this instruction. Deeming the relief insufficient, plaintiff brought error and again the judgment was reversed and remanded, 75 Colo. 340, 225 P. 837 (1924). The Supreme Court held that the instruction that allowed but $10 as damages was in conflict with another instruction which told the jury that any damage allowed should be such as might reasonably have been contemplated by the parties at the time of making the contract for the loan. At the second trial the jury returned a verdict assessing damages for loss of expenses at $700 and for humiliation and suffering at $1,000. The trial court set aside the item of damages for mental suffering. Again the Supreme Court reversed and remanded with instructions to enter judgment upon the verdict in its entirety, 78 Colo. 217, 240 P. 689 (1925). See U.C.C. §4-402.

SWINDELL & CO. v. FIRST NATIONAL BANK
121 Ga. 714, 49 S.E. 673 (1905)

EVANS, J. The First National Bank brought a suit against E. Swindell & Co., a partnership, to recover the amount due on certain promissory notes executed by that firm. The defendant filed a plea of recoupment alleging, in brief, that the partnership was engaged in the manufacture of lumber and required a large amount of money with which to conduct its business; that the partnership entered into a contract with the bank, whereby it was to advance to the firm $20,000, as called for from time to time, in order that it might carry on its business successfully, the firm being induced by the bank to sever its financial relations with another banking institution and to get its advances from the plaintiff bank; that the bank did advance the money for which the notes sued on were given, but later, without cause or excuse, committed a breach of the contract, by refusing to advance any further sums of money to the partnership, and that by reason of such breach the firm had been unable to profitably conduct its business and had been damaged in the sum of ten thousand dollars. On the trial of the case the defendant admitted the execution of the notes and assumed the burden of proof. Evidence was introduced to the effect that an arrangement had been made with the bank, whereby it was to advance money to the partnership to enable it to carry on its milling operations; but it affirmatively appeared from the testimony of the member of the firm who made this arrangement with the bank and upon whose testimony the defendant wholly relied as establishing the making of the alleged contract, that the partnership was "to take $20,000 if necessary to run [its] business," but not otherwise, and "more, if necessary to the amount of $30,000," it being optional with the firm whether it would "take the $20,000 or not." The plaintiff denied entering into any such contract, and introduced evidence tending to show that it had merely advanced money to the defendant partnership on particular occasions, in the same way as it had done to other customers, relying on Swindell & Co. to reimburse it when remittances for shipments of lumber were received by that firm. The jury returned a verdict in favor of the plaintiff, and the defendant filed a motion for a new trial, therein complaining of various rulings and charges of the court. To the overruling of this motion the defendant excepts.

An essential requisite of a contract dependent on mutual promises for a consideration is that the obligations imposed should be reciprocal. One promise must need be the complement of the other. The performance of the promise or agreement to perform by one party enjoins a duty on the opposite party to execute his reciprocal obligation. If the contract be such that performance by one of the parties of his promise does not confer the right to demand the correlative obligation from the other, it is lacking in mutuality. The contract between the bank and the plaintiff in error, as averred on the plea of recoupment, was mutual and binding. By its terms the bank agreed to loan, within the lumber season, twenty thousand dollars, and the plaintiff in error agreed to borrow that sum. However, when the plaintiff in error undertook at the trial to establish the contract set out in this plea, the testimony offered failed in a vital particular. The member of the firm who claimed to have made the contract with the bank was the only witness offered to prove it. This witness testified that the bank agreed to loan $20,000 to his firm, but his firm was not to borrow the money unless its business necessities required it. In the course of his testimony he said: "We were to take $20,000 if necessary to run our business; we were not to take it if not necessary; more, if necessary, to the amount of $30,000. It was with us whether we were to take the $20,000 or not." The contention of the plaintiff in error, as proved by this witness, might be elaborated after this manner: We are not bound to borrow any money unless we need it, but the bank must keep in reserve the necessary funds to meet the demands of our business, up to the amount of $20,000; if we do not happen to need it, we are under no obligation to borrow, and the bank cannot expect any remuneration for maintaining a state of readiness to meet possible sudden demands for money; yet, if the demand is made and the money is not loaned, the bank is liable to us in damages for a failure to make the exacted loan. A contract of this kind is manifestly unilateral, without consideration, and incapable of enforcement. McCaw Manufacturing Co. v. Felder, 115 Ga. 408, and authorities cited.

The execution of the notes sued on having been admitted, the plaintiff was entitled to recover, unless the plea of recoupment was sustained by evidence. As pointed out in the preceding division of this opinion, the evidence discloses that this plea was in fact based upon the violation of a unilateral contract. This amounted to no defense at all; therefore the verdict was demanded by the evidence, and the court with propriety might well have directed a verdict for the plaintiff for the full amount sued for. Instead of so doing, the trial judge submitted certain issues of fact to the jury, and error is assigned upon certain portions of his charge. Exception is also taken to various rulings in admitting or excluding evidence relating to a breach of this unilateral contract. Inasmuch, however, as the verdict was demanded, any possible errors committed by the court in charging the jury, or in ruling upon the admissibility of evidence touching the alleged breach of such contract, afford no cause for ordering a new trial. Peoples Bank v. Smith, 114 Ga. 185.

Judgment affirmed.

NOTE

For a criticism of the case, see 5 Corbin §1078 (1964). Did not plaintiff bank make a continuing offer to lend that became irrevocable upon defendant's change of position? Assuming that the plaintiff made such an offer, would it have to continue making loans by discounting the defendant's notes even though the defendant had become a poor credit risk? If plaintiff bank can refuse to lend on the basis of its belief that the borrower's conditions have changed, has it promised anything at all? Why didn't the transfer of funds to defendant bank create a binding option?

For a discussion of the mechanics of borrowing from a commercial bank and the meaning of what is usually called a "line of credit," see H. V. Prochnow & R. Foulke, Practical Bank Credit 292-296 (1963). Lines of credit are to be distinguished from loan commitments for a fee, which have become "a fact of financial life." See *In re* Four Seasons Nursing Centers of America, Inc. 483 F.2d 599 (1973): the lender, as a rule, is entitled to the full fee, even though the borrower, for one reason or another, does not draw on the committed funds.

Farabee-Treadville Co. v. Bank & Trust Co., 135 Tenn. 208, 186 S.W. 92 (1916), is an interesting case, allowing recovery of foreseeable damages (lost profits) for breach of a loan agreement since the promised funds were not procurable elsewhere. See further National Bank of Cleburne v. M. M. Potman Roller Mill, 265 S.W. 1024 (Tex. Com. App. 1924); again, damages were limited to the plaintiff's foreseeable loss of profits.

LIMA LOCOMOTIVE & MACHINE CO. v. NATIONAL STEEL CASTINGS CO.
155 F. 77 (6th Cir. 1907)

Action upon account for goods sold and delivered, and cross-action for damages for breach of contract. Jury waived. The trial judge made a finding of facts and a general finding for the plaintiff for the full amount of the account and against the defendant upon its cross-petition.

On April 10, 1902, the National Steel Castings Company made in writing the following proposition to the Lima Locomotive & Machine Company:

> Gentlemen: We make the following proposition for furnishing all your requirements in steel castings for the remainder of the present year at the prices mentioned below, f.o.b. cars at Montpelier, the terms to be thirty days net. You agree to furnish us on or before the 15th of each month the tonnage that you wish to order during the following month. We agree to fill your orders as specified to the amount of this tonnage, and to make such deliveries as you require.

Then followed a schedule of steel castings and prices per pound. This was accepted in writing by indorsing thereon, at the foot of the proposition, "Accepted April 10, 1902," and duly signed by the Lima Company. This contract the defendant set out in its cross-petition and averred: First, that the castings for which the plaintiff had sued were ordered and supplied under this contract; second, that the plaintiff had failed and refused, though requested, to supply it with other castings necessary to meet the requirements of its business, and that defendant in consequence had been obliged to contract for same with other founders and had paid for the castings so procured $5,498.24 over and above the contract price with plaintiff.

The defenses to the cross-petition were: First, that the contract was void for want of mutuality. . . .

LURTON, Circuit Judge, delivered the opinion of the court. We find ourselves unable to agree with the learned circuit judge in respect to the nonmutuality of the contract by which the plaintiff agreed to supply all of the "requirements" of the defendant's business for the remainder of the year 1902. The defendant was engaged in an established manufacturing business which required a large amount of steel castings. This was well known to the plaintiff, and the proposition made and accepted was made with reference to the "requirements" of that well-established business. The plaintiffs were not proposing to make castings beyond the current requirements of that business, and would not have been obligated to supply castings not required in the usual course of that business. By the acceptance of the plaintiff's proposal, the defendant was obligated to take from the plaintiff all castings which their business should require. The contract, if capable of two equally reasonable interpretations, should be given that interpretation which will tend to support it and thus carry out the presumed intent of both parties. The second and third paragraphs must be read in the light of the first. Thus read, there is no ground for doubting that the words the "tonnage you wish to order," and "such deliveries as you may require," have reference to the established "requirements" of the business for the following "month," and the deliveries of the tonnage thus estimated. The contract falls under and is governed by the case of Loudenback Fertilizer Co. v. Tennessee Phosphate Co., 121 Fed. 298, 58 C.C.A. 220, 61 L.R.A. 402, where the contract was to sell to a manufacturer of fertilizer "its entire consumption of phosphate rock" for a term of five years. In that case we held that the contract was mutual, and the buyer under obligation to take its entire requirement of phosphate rock from the seller. Concerning the definiteness of such a contract, we said:

> A contract to buy all that one shall require for one's own use in a particular manufacturing business is a very different thing from a promise to buy all that one may desire, or all that one may order. The promise to take all that one can consume would be broken by buying from another, and it is this obligation to take the entire supply of an established business which saves the mutual character of the promise. . . .

Judgment reversed.

EASTERN AIR LINES, INC. v. GULF OIL CORP.

415 F. Supp. 429 (S.D. Fla. 1975)

JAMES LAWRENCE KING, District Judge.
Eastern Air Lines, Inc., hereafter Eastern, and Gulf Oil Corporation,

hereafter Gulf, have enjoyed a mutually advantageous business relationship involving the sale and purchase of aviation fuel for several decades.

This controversy involves the threatened disruption of that historic relationship and the attempt, by Eastern, to enforce the most recent contract between the parties. On March 8, 1974 the correspondence and telex communications between the corporate entities culminated in a demand by Gulf that Eastern must meet its demand for a price increase or Gulf would shut off Eastern's supply of jet fuel within fifteen days.

Eastern responded by filing its complaint with this court, alleging that Gulf had breached its contract and requesting preliminary and permanent mandatory injunctions requiring Gulf to perform the contract in accordance with its terms. By agreement of the parties, a preliminary injunction preserving the status quo was entered on March 20, 1974, requiring Gulf to perform its contract and directing Eastern to pay in accordance with the contract terms, pending final disposition of the case.

Gulf answered Eastern's complaint, alleging that the contract was not a binding requirements contract, was void for want of mutuality, and, furthermore, was "commercially impracticable" within the meaning of Uniform Commercial Code §2-615; Fla. Stat. §§672.614 and 672.615.

The extraordinarily able advocacy by the experienced lawyers for both parties produced testimony at the trial from internationally respected experts who described in depth economic events that have, in recent months, profoundly affected the lives of every American.

THE CONTRACT

On June 27, 1972, an agreement was signed by the parties which, as amended, was to provide the basis upon which Gulf was to furnish jet fuel to Eastern at certain specific cities in the Eastern system. Said agreement supplemented an existing contract between Gulf and Eastern which, on June 27, 1972, had approximately one year remaining prior to its expiration.

The contract is Gulf's standard form aviation fuel contract and is identical in all material particulars with the first contract for jet fuel, dated 1959, between Eastern and Gulf and, indeed, with aviation fuel contracts antedating the jet age. It is similar to contracts in general use in the aviation fuel trade. The contract was drafted by Gulf after substantial arm's length negotiation between the parties. Gulf approached Eastern more than a year before the expiration of the then-existing contracts between Gulf and Eastern, seeking to preserve its historic relationship with Eastern. Following several months of negotiation, the contract, consolidating and extending the terms of several existing contracts, was executed by the parties in June, 1972, to expire January 31, 1977.

The parties agreed that this contract, as its predecessor, should provide a reference to reflect changes in the price of the raw material from which jet fuel is processed, i.e., crude oil, in direct proportion to the cost per gallon of jet fuel.

Both parties regarded the instant agreement as favorable, Eastern, in part, because it offered immediate savings in projected escalations under the existing agreement through reduced base prices at the contract cities; while Gulf found a long term outlet for a capacity of jet fuel coming on stream from a newly completed refinery, as well as a means to relate anticipated increased cost of raw material (crude oil) directly to the price of the refined product sold. The previous Eastern/Gulf contracts contained a price index clause which operated to pass on to Eastern only one-half of any increase in the price of crude oil. Both parties knew at the time of contract negotiations that increases in crude oil prices would be expected, were "a way of life," and intended that those increases be borne by Eastern in a direct proportional relationship of crude oil cost per barrel to jet fuel cost per gallon.

Accordingly, the parties selected an indicator (West Texas Sour); a crude which is bought and sold in large volume and was thus a reliable indicator of the market value of crude oil. From June 27, 1972 to the fall of 1973, there were in effect various forms of U.S. government imposed price controls which at once controlled the price of crude oil generally, West Texas Sour specifically, and hence the price of jet fuel. As the government authorized increased prices of crude those increases were in turn reflected in the cost of jet fuel. Eastern has paid a per gallon increase under the contract from 11 cents to 15 cents (or some 40%).

The indicator selected by the parties was "the average of the posted prices for West Texas sour crude, 30.0-30.9 gravity of Gulf Oil Corporation, Shell Oil Company, and Pan American Petroleum Corporation." The posting of crude prices under the contract "shall be as listed for these companies in Platts Oilgram Service — Crude Oil Supplement . . . ."

"Posting" has long been a practice in the oil industry. It involves the physical placement at a public location of a price bulletin reflecting the current price at which an oil company will pay for a given barrel of a specific type of crude oil. Those posted price bulletins historically have, in addition to being displayed publicly, been mailed to those persons evincing interest therein, including sellers of crude oil, customers whose price of product may be based thereon, and, among others, Platts Oilgram, publishers of a periodical of interest to those related to the oil industry.

In recent years, the United States has become increasingly dependent upon foreign crude oil, particularly from the "OPEC" nations most of which are in the Middle East. OPEC was formed in 1970 for the avowed purpose of raising oil prices, and has become an increasingly cohesive and potent organization as its member nations have steadily enhanced their equity positions and their control over their oil production facilities. Nationalization of crude oil resources and shutdowns of production and distribution have become a way of life for oil companies operating in OPEC nations, particularly in the volatile Middle East. The closing of the Suez Canal and the concomitant interruption of the flow of Mid-East oil during the 1967 "Six-Day War," and Libya's nationalization of its oil industry during the same period, are only some of the more dramatic examples of a trend that began years ago. By 1969 "the handwriting was on the wall" in the words of Gulf's foreign oil expert witness, Mr. Blackledge.

During 1970 domestic United States oil production "peaked;" since then it has declined while the percentage of imported crude oil has been steadily increasing. Unlike domestic crude oil, which has been subject to price control since August 15, 1971, foreign crude oil has never been subject to price control by the United States Government. Foreign crude oil prices, uncontrolled by the Federal Government, were generally lower than domestic crude oil prices in 1971 and 1972; during 1973 foreign prices "crossed" domestic prices; by late 1973 foreign prices were generally several dollars per barrel higher than controlled domestic prices. It was during late 1973 that the Mid-East exploded in another war, accompanied by an embargo (at least officially) by the Arab oil-producing nations against the United States and certain of its allies. World prices for oil and oil products increased.

Mindful of that situation and for various other reasons concerning the nation's economy, the United States government began a series of controls affecting the oil industry culminating, in the fall of 1973, with the implementation of price controls known as "two-tier." In practice "two-tier" can be described as follows: taking as the bench mark the number of barrels produced from a given well in May of 1972, that number of barrels is deemed "old" oil. The price of "old" oil then is frozen by the government at a fixed level. To the extent that the productivity of a given well can be increased over the May, 1972, production, that increased production is deemed "new" oil. For each barrel of "new" oil produced, the government authorized the release from price controls of an equivalent number of barrels from those theretofore designated "old" oil. For example, from a well which in May of 1972, produced 100 barrels of oil; all of the production of that well would, since the imposition of "two-tier" in August of 1973, be "old" oil. Increased productivity to 150 barrels would result in 50 barrels of "new" oil and 50 barrels of "released" oil; with the result that 100 barrels of the 150 barrels produced from the well would be uncontrolled by the "two-tier" pricing system, while the 50 remaining barrels of "old" would remain government price controlled.

The implementation of "two-tier" was completely without precedent in the history of government price control action. Its impact, however, was nominal, until the imposition of an embargo upon the exportation of crude oil by certain Arab countries in October, 1973. Those countries deemed sympathetic to Israel were embargoed from receiving oil from the Arab oil producing countries. The United States was among the principal countries affected by that embargo, with the result that it experienced an immediate "energy crisis."

Following closely after the embargo, OPEC (Oil Producing Export Countries) unilaterally increased the price of their crude to the world market some 400% between September, 1973, and January 15, 1974. Since the United States domestic production was at capacity, it was dependent upon foreign crude to meet its requirements. New and released oil (uncontrolled) soon reached parity with the price of foreign crude, moving from approximately $5 to $11 a barrel from September, 1974 to January 15, 1975.

Since imposition of "two-tier," the price of "old oil" has remained fixed by government action, with the oil companies resorting to postings reflecting prices they will pay for the new and released oil, not subject to government controls. Those prices, known as "premiums," are the subject of supplemental bulletins which are likewise posted by the oil companies and furnished to interested parties, including Platts Oilgram.

Platts, since the institution of "two-tier" has not published the posted prices of any of the premiums offered by the oil companies in the United States, including those of Gulf Oil Corporation, Shell Oil Company and Pan American Petroleum, the companies designated in the agreement. The information which has appeared in Platts since the implementation of "two-tier" with respect to the price of West Texas Sour crude oil has been the price of "old" oil subject to government control.

Under the court's restraining order, entered in this cause by agreement of the parties, Eastern has been paying for jet fuel from Gulf on the basis of the price of "old" West Texas Sour crude oil as fixed by government price control action, i.e., $5 a barrel. Approximately 40 gallons of finished jet fuel product can be refined from a barrel of crude.

Against this factual background we turn to a consideration of the legal issues.

I. THE "REQUIREMENTS" CONTRACT

Gulf has taken the position in this case that the contract between it and Eastern is not a valid document in that it lacks mutuality of obligation; it is vague and indefinite; and that it renders Gulf subject to Eastern's whims respecting the volume of jet fuel Gulf would be required to deliver to the purchaser Eastern.

The contract talks in terms of fuel "requirements." The parties have interpreted this provision to mean that any aviation fuel purchased by Eastern at one of the cities covered by the contract, must be bought from

Gulf. Conversely, Gulf must make the necessary arrangements to supply Eastern's reasonable good faith demands at those same locations. This is the construction the parties themselves have placed on the contract and it has governed their conduct over many years and several contracts.

In early cases, requirements contracts were found invalid for want of the requisite definiteness, or on the grounds of lack of mutuality. Many such cases are collected and annotated at 14 A.L.R. 1300.

As reflected in the foregoing annotation, there developed rather quickly in the law the view that a requirements contract could be binding where the purchaser had an operating business. The "lack of mutuality" and "indefiniteness" were resolved since the court could determine the volume of goods provided for under the contract by reference to objective evidence of the volume of goods required to operate the specified business. Therefore, well prior to the adoption of the Uniform Commercial Code, case law generally held requirements contracts binding. See 26 A.L.R.2d 1099, 1139.

The Uniform Commercial Code, adopted in Florida in 1965, specifically approves requirements contracts in F.S. 672.306 (U.C.C. §2-306(1)).

> (1) A term which measures the quantity by the output of the seller or the requirements of the buyer means such actual output or requirements as may occur in good faith, except that no quantity unreasonably disproportionate to any stated estimate or in the absence of a stated estimate to any normal or otherwise comparable prior output or requirements may be tendered or demanded.

The Uniform Commercial Code Official Comment interprets §2-306(1) as follows:

> 2. Under this Article, a contract for output or requirements is not too indefinite since it is held to mean the actual good faith output or requirements of the particular party. Nor does such a contract lack mutuality of obligation since, under this section, the party who will determine quantity is required to operate his plant or conduct his business in good faith and according to commercial standards of fair dealing in the trade so that his output or requirements will approximate a reasonably foreseeable figure. Reasonable elasticity in the requirements is expressly envisaged by this section and good faith variations from prior requirements are permitted even when the variation may be such as to result in discontinuance. A shutdown by a requirements buyer for lack of orders might be permissible when a shut-down merely to curtail losses would not. The essential test is whether the party is acting in good faith. Similarly, a sudden expansion of the plant by which requirements are to be measured would not be included within the scope of the contract as made but normal expansion undertaken in good faith would be within the scope of this section. One of the factors in an expansion situation would be whether the market price has risen greatly in a case in which the requirements contract contained a fixed price. Rea-

sonable variation of an extreme sort is exemplified in Southwest Natural
Gas Co. v. Oklahoma Portland Cement Co., 102 F.2d 630 (C.C.A. 10,
1939).

Some of the prior Gulf-Eastern contracts have included the estimated
fuel requirements for some cities covered by the contract while others
have none. The particular contract contains an estimate for Gainesville,
Florida requirement.

The parties have consistently over the years relied upon each other to
act in good faith in the purchase and sale of the required quantities of
aviation fuel specified in the contract. During the course of the contract,
various estimates have been exchanged from time to time, and, since the
advent of the petroleum allocations programs, discussions of estimated
requirements have been on a monthly (or more frequent) basis.

The court concludes that the document is a binding and enforceable
requirements contract.

II. BREACH OF CONTRACT

Gulf suggests that Eastern violated the contract between the parties by
manipulating its requirements through a practice known as "fuel freighting" in the airline industry. Requirements can vary from city to city
depending on whether or not it is economically profitable to freight fuel.
This fuel freighting practice in accordance with price could affect lifting
from Gulf stations by either raising such liftings or lowering them. If the
price was higher at a Gulf station, the practice could have reduced liftings
there by lifting fuel in excess of its actual operating requirements at a
prior station, and thereby not loading fuel at the succeeding high price
Gulf station. Similarly where the Gulf station was comparatively cheaper,
an aircraft might load more heavily at the Gulf station and not load at
other succeeding non-Gulf stations.

The court however, finds that Eastern's performance under the contract does not constitute a breach of its agreement with Gulf and is
consistent with good faith and established commercial practices as required by U.C.C. §2-306.

"Good Faith" means "honesty in fact in the conduct or transaction
concerned" U.C.C. §1-201(19). Between merchants, "good faith" means
"honesty in fact and the observance of reasonable commercial standards
of fair dealing in the trade"; U.C.C. §2-103(1)(b) and Official Comment 2
of U.C.C. §2-306. The relevant commercial practices are "courses of
performance," "courses of dealing" and "usages of trade."

Throughout the history of commercial aviation, including 30 years of
dealing between Gulf and Eastern, airlines' liftings of fuel by nature have
been subject to substantial daily, weekly, monthly and seasonal varia-

tions, as they are affected by weather, schedule changes, size of aircraft, aircraft load, local airport conditions, ground time, availability of fueling facilities, whether the flight is on time or late, passenger convenience, economy and efficiency of operation, fuel taxes, into-plane fuel service charges, fuel price, and, ultimately, the judgment of the flight captain as to how much fuel he wants to take.

All these factors are, and for years have been, known to oil companies, including Gulf, and taken into account by them in their fuel contracts. Gulf's witnesses at trial pointed to certain examples of numerically large "swings" in monthly liftings by Eastern at various Gulf stations. Gulf never complained of this practice and apparently accepted it as normal procedure. Some of the "swings" were explained by the fueling of a single aircraft for one flight, or by the addition of one schedule in mid-month. The evidence establishes that Eastern, on one occasion, requested 500,000 additional gallons for one month at one station, without protest from Gulf, and that Eastern increased its requirements at another station more than 50 percent year to year, from less than 2,000,000 to more than 3,000,000 gallons, again, without Gulf objection.

The court concludes that fuel freighting is an established industry practice, inherent in the nature of the business. The evidence clearly demonstrated that the practice has long been part of the established courses of performance and dealing between Eastern and Gulf. As the practice of "freighting" or "tankering" has gone on unchanged and unchallenged for many years accepted as a fact of life by Gulf without complaint, the court is reminded of Official Comment 1 to U.C.C. §2-208:

> The parties themselves know best what they have meant by their words of agreement and their action under that agreement is the best indication of what that meaning was.

From a practical point of view, "freighting" opportunities are very few, according to the uncontradicted testimony, as the airline must perform its schedules in consideration of operating realities. There is no suggestion here that Eastern is operating at certain Gulf stations but taking no fuel at all. The very reason Eastern initially desired a fuel contract was because the airline planned to take on fuel, and had to have an assured source of supply.

If a customer's demands under a requirements contract become excessive, U.C.C. §2-306 protects the seller and, in the appropriate case, would allow him to refuse to deliver unreasonable amounts demanded (but without eliminating his basic contract obligation); similarly, in an appropriate case, if a customer repeatedly had no requirements at all, the seller might be excused from performance if the buyer suddenly and without warning should descend upon him and demand his entire inventory, but the court is not called upon to decide those cases here.

Rather, the case here is one where the established courses of performance and dealing between the parties, the established usages of the
trade, and the basic contract itself all show that the matter complained of
for the first time by Gulf after commencement of this litigation are the
fundamental given ingredients of the aviation fuel trade to which the
parties have accommodated themselves successfully and without dispute
over the years.

> The practical interpretation given to their contracts by the parties to
> them while they are engaged in their performance, and before any contro-
> versy has arisen concerning them, is one of the best indications of their true
> intent, and courts that adopt and enforce such a construction are not likely
> to commit serious error.

Manhattan Life Ins. Co. of New York v. Wright, 126 F. 82, 87 (8th Cir.
1903). Accord, Spindler v. Kushner, 284 So. 2d 481, 484 (Fla. App. 1973).
  The court concludes that Eastern has not violated the contract.

III.   COMMERCIAL IMPRACTICABILITY

[The court found that Gulf had not discharged its burden of proof in
attempting to establish that the contract was commercially impracticable,
and held that both the rise in foreign oil prices and the "two-tier" system
of price control were foreseeable at the time the contract was made. On
commercial impracticability, see Chapter 8 *infra*. The court's opinion on
this matter is fascinating and gives a glimpse into the workings of a major
oil company. It is recommended reading.]

IV.   REMEDY

Having found and concluded that the contract is a valid one, should be
enforced, and that no defenses have been established against it, there
remains for consideration the proper remedy.
  The Uniform Commercial Code provides that in an appropriate case
specific performance may be decreed. This case is a particularly appropriate one for specific performance. The parties have been operating for
more than a year pursuant to a preliminary injunction requiring specific
performance of the contract and Gulf has stipulated that it is able to
perform. Gulf presently supplies Eastern with 100,000,000 gallons of fuel
annually or 10 percent of Eastern's total requirements. If Gulf ceases to
supply this fuel, the result will be chaos and irreparable damage.
  Under the U.C.C. a more liberal test in determining entitlement to
specific performance has been established than the test one must meet

for classic equitable relief. U.C.C. §2-716(1); Kaiser Trading Co. v. Associated Metals & Minerals Corp., 321 F. Supp. 923, 932 (N.D. Cal. 1970), *appeal dismissed per curiam*, 443 F.2d 1364 (9th Cir. 1971).

It has previously been found and concluded that Eastern is entitled to Gulf's fuel at the prices agreed upon in the contract. In the circumstances, a decree of specific performance becomes the ordinary and natural relief rather than the extraordinary one. The parties are before the court, the issues are squarely framed, they have been clearly resolved in Eastern's favor, and it would be a vain, useless and potentially harmful exercise to declare that Eastern has a valid contract, but leave the parties to their own devices. Accordingly, the preliminary injunction heretofore entered is made a permanent injunction and the order of this court herein.

UTAH INTERNATIONAL INC. v. COLORADO-UTE ELECTRIC ASSN., INC.
425 F. Supp. 1093 (D. Colo. 1976)

MEMORANDUM OPINION AND ORDER

ARRAJ, District Judge.

Plaintiff Utah International, a mining company with international operations, brings this declaratory judgment action against Colorado-Ute Electric Association, Inc., Platte River Power Authority, Tri-State Generation and Transmission Association, and Salt River Project Agriculture Improvement and Power District, all wholesalers of electric power and energy. Plaintiff seeks a declaration of its rights and duties as a party to a contract for the sale of coal, and defendants have counter-claimed for the specific performance of that contract.

The contract in question is a thirty five year requirements contract containing a maximum sales obligation and minimum purchase obligation. Plaintiff as seller claims that defendants have breached the contract by building electric generating units with generating capacities larger than specified in the sales contract. As a result of such construction, plaintiff contends that it will be required to provide more coal than was anticipated by this requirements contract and that its contractual obligations thereunder should, therefore, be terminated. Trial was to the Court and this Opinion shall constitute the findings of facts and conclusions of law in conformance with Fed. R. Civ. P. 52(a).

In 1969, the four defendants, along with Public Service Company of Colorado, Intermountain Consumers Power Association, and Arizona Public Service formed the Western Colorado Resource Study to consider the possibility of constructing coal-fired electric generating units near Craig, Colorado. This project later became known as the Yampa Project.

These original participants appointed a Steering Committee to be in over-all charge of the project, the membership consisting of senior executives of each defendant and representatives of the United States Bureau of Reclamation. This committee in turn created a task force system to carry out specific study assignments.

On April 13, 1970 the participants commenced negotiations with plaintiff for the supply of fuel for the Yampa Project and sent to plaintiff, and to other prospective suppliers an invitation to submit proposals for the mining and delivery of coal fuel. The amount of coal contemplated as necessary to fuel the project was at that time undetermined but the participants provided coal consumption estimates for the different unit alternatives then being considered. In response, plaintiff proposed a pricing schedule based on calculations made from the estimated coal consumption figures provided by defendants in their invitation.

In December of 1970, defendant Salt River, as the participant in charge of the initial purchase negotiations for the project's turbine-generators, obtained a quotation from General Electric for two 450,000 kilowatt generators. In March of the following year, Salt River and General Electric executed a letter of intent for these generators with the stipulation that the size of the units could subsequently be changed.

By early 1971 Public Service Company of Colorado, Intermountain Consumers Power Association, and Arizona Public Service Company had withdrawn from the Western Colorado Resource Study leaving the defendants as the remaining participants. As a result of that withdrawal the participants began re-evaluating their projected consumer power demands and their plans regarding the size of the generating units to be constructed. By December of 1971 they had decided that two units, each rated at 350,000 kilowatts net, would be capable of providing the generating capacity necessary to meet their re-evaluated projections.

In choosing the machine to meet their needs, defendants operated under certain assumptions generally accepted by the electrical generating industry. The first and most important assumption is that a generating unit of the type being installed at Craig will not operate at 100% capacity but rather at approximately 75% capacity over an extended period, such as the thirty five year term of this contract. The reason for this is that all such machines require regularly scheduled maintenance periods and also periods of unanticipated maintenance during which it is necessary to shut down the machines.

Once the unit size was chosen, the parties then calculated the amount of coal that such units would burn over thirty five years. This process was a joint effort between representatives of the defendants and representatives of the plaintiff. Both parties used the net figure 350,000 kilowatts as a starting point in estimating the probable coal consumption and then communicated their calculations to the other party for verification. Gradually, through this process, the estimates became refined, and both parties as of May of 1972 understood that there would be constructed two generators of approximately 350,000 kilowatt net capacity each, which machines would operate at an average capacity factor of about 75% and would burn approximately 76 million tons of coal over the life of the contract. It was additionally understood that the generating units would operate at almost 90% capacity during the first ten years of the contract and then steadily decline in capacity during the balance of the term of the contract. The parties expected some variance from these predicted capacity factors and these predictions for coal consumption but there was no suggestion that it was expected by either party that the variance would be substantial.

It is clear that the generating unit size and the coal consumption calculations derived from the customary operation of such units were important to plaintiff during the negotiations of this contract. Plaintiff relied on the calculations in conducting its feasibility study, developing a pricing schedule, and designing its mine. Defendants were aware that plaintiff was so utilizing these figures. It is noted that defendants' expert witness testified to the effect that it is a common procedure in the negotiation of such a fuel contract for the public utility or other buyer of coal to calculate the amount of coal expected to be burned and then to communicate such calculations to the coal miner.

Negotiations between defendants and plaintiff were completed by February 3, 1973 and the contract in question was signed April 6, 1973. The contract provides that plaintiff's obligation is to supply the coal requirements for two generating units, each with a capacity of about 350,000 kilowatts net. Plaintiff's sales obligation, however, is not to exceed the mining and delivery of coal sufficient to produce 1830 trillion Btu's over the thirty five year life of the contract. Defendants' purchase obligation is to pay for a yearly quantity of coal, regardless of whether they order that amount. This quantity is a negotiated figure based on a calculation of 85% of the expected coal consumption of the machines. Between these maximum and minimum limits, the contract provides that the actual requirements of the units is to be determinative of the amount of coal ordered and delivered.

It is noted that shortly after the execution of the contract, coal prices began to rise dramatically, due in part to the Arab oil embargo in September of 1973. Prior to that time the price of coal had reflected only a slight upward trend.

Presumably these negotiations and the resulting contract would not have reached this court had the defendants not made two significant decisions in February of 1973 and prior to the execution of the contract. One decision was to build units with a net capacity of 410,000 kilowatts each instead of the 350,000 net capacity specified in the contract. The other decision was to refrain from communicating to plaintiff any information regarding this increase — at least until some undetermined future date.

Defendants recognized that such an increase in unit capacity, if communicated to plaintiff when the decisions were made, might adversely affect the then status of the contract negotiations. The fuel contract was signed by the parties before the increased size of the units was revealed and at the time of trial, defendants had completed a substantial portion of the construction of these larger sized units.

Plaintiff and defendants draw different conclusions from these facts. Plaintiff contends that the size of the units to be constructed, and "about 350,000 kilowatts" net size described in the contract, was the essential condition of the contract and that defendants abrogated the entire contract by building units of a size larger than that described. Defendants on the other hand, contend that neither the size of the units nor the calculations of estimated coal consumption were essential to this contract and that they should not have been relied upon by plaintiff in its pricing and in its mine design. Defendants assert rather that the maximum and minimum amounts contained in the contract define the obligations of the plaintiff and that construction of units larger than those described in the contract was not, therefore, in breach of the contract. Neither view accurately reflects the evidence nor the controlling law.

I

Both parties to this litigation recognize that the contract in question is a requirements contract. As such, it requires that plaintiff provide and defendants purchase the fuel necessary to operate the generating units described in the contract. It is not, however, a pure requirements contract, but one modified by the maximum seller's obligation and the minimum buyer's obligation. It is necessary to this litigation to understand the legal significance of these modifications.

From my reading of the contract, it is clear that one of the effects of the minimum purchase obligation is that plaintiff mine company may at all times require that the defendant utility companies take or pay for the contractual minimum amount of coal regardless of the actual fuel requirements of the generating units. Testimony at trial disclosed that the parties to the contract likewise understand the contract to impose such an obligation on the buyer. There is no suggestion that the defendant purchasers can avoid this obligation, for example, by shutting down their plant or by limiting its operation, even if such a decision is motivated by sound business management.

Such a purchase obligation is a protective provision for the seller and as such eliminates some of the risks for seller which normally attend the type of requirements contract containing no such minimum purchase obligation. Expert testimony at trial indicated that this type of minimum purchase obligation is becoming a more common feature in coal sales agreements such as the one here in dispute.

Since defendants are thus obligated to purchase a minimum amount of coal, regardless of the actual generating requirements of the units specified in the contract, it follows, in my view, that defendants have the concomitant right to demand delivery of that minimum amount regardless of their actual fuel requirements. The few cases that have dealt with such requirements contracts, all containing similar minimum purchase obligations, have almost unanimously reasoned as we have and have held that the absolute *obligation* to buy a minimum amount necessarily implies the absolute *right* to buy that amount, and that buyer, in demanding delivery of its minimum purchase obligation need not be motivated by the business requirements envisioned by the contract but may, in fact, utilize the commodity completely apart from the operation of the business specified in the contract. See Magnolia Petroleum Co. v. Farmersville Independent Gin Co., 243 S.W. 568 (Tex. Civ. App. 1922); Corsicana Compress Co. v. Magnolia Petroleum Co., 253 S.W. 559 (Tex. Civ. App. 1923); and Diamond Alkali Co. v. Aetna Explosives Co., 264 Pa. 304, 107 A. 711 (1919).

In contrast to the minimum purchase obligation in this contract, the purchase of coal in excess of the contractual minimum is controlled by and dependent upon the actual requirements of the defendants and may be demanded pursuant to those requirements up to the maximum sales limit contained in the contract. More specifically, it is my reading of the contract that it does not give the defendants the right to demand delivery of the contract maximum unless that demand is justified as being required for the actual operation of the two 350,000 kilowatt net machines specified in the contract.

The nature of the negotiations leading up to the execution of this contract is consistent with such an interpretation. All parties recognized that the anticipated unit size was crucial in estimating probable coal consumption and that such estimates were significant to all parties in developing their bargaining positions. Such negotiations would have been meaningless if the parties had not contemplated that the fuel requirements of the generating units would define the purchase and sale obligations above the minimum.

Indeed, since plaintiff and defendants both characterize the contract as a requirements contract it would seem that neither would disagree with this construction of the contract. Both parties have cited the case of M. W. Kellogg Co. v. Standard Steel Fabricating Co., 189 F.2d 629 (10th Cir. 1951) for the proposition that in a requirements contract, the project itself, and the material required to finish that project becomes "the essence of the contract. . . ." 189 F.2d at 631. Nevertheless, the defendants assert that they have an absolute right to the maximum amount of coal specified in the contract regardless of their actual requirements. Such an assertion is simply not consistent with defendants' own characterization of the contract as being a requirements contract.

Careful consideration has been given to *Diamond Alkali Co., supra,* cited by defendants for the proposition that a buyer in a requirements contract can demand the maximum purchase amount of the contract whether or not it was required in its business. In that case, the contract provided that the seller was obligated to furnish soda ash at a fixed price to the extent of "buyer's entire requirements" within certain maximum and minimum sales limits. The price of soda ash apparently rose and the buyer took advantage of the low contractual price by purchasing in excess of its business requirements and reselling on the open market. The court stated that such transactions did not violate the parties' contract and did not obligate the purchaser to account to the seller for his resale profits. This holding, however, is no more logically consistent than is the position of the defendants in the instant case, in that it also fails to reconcile its conclusion with the fact that the contract was a requirements contract and was so characterized by that court. The opinion does state that the contract was vague as to what purchase requirements were anticipated by the parties to the contract since the nature of the buyer's business could not be detected from the contractual terms. Therefore, the court in *Diamond Alkali Co.* might have viewed the obligations differently had the anticipated purchase requirements been more specifically described in that contract as they are so described in the contract at issue in the instant case.

At any rate, the weight of authority is contrary to this case and to defendants' position. The court in Staver Carriage Co. v. Park Steel Co., 104 F. 200 (7th Cir. 1900) held that any deliveries above the minimum limit in a requirements contract could be demanded only to the extent of the actual business requirements of the purchaser, as those business requirements were contemplated by the parties to the contract. Likewise in *Magnolia Petroleum Co., supra,* the court held that all deliveries in excess of the contractual minimum must be justified by the business requirements of the purchaser.

Finally, in National Home Products Co. Inc. v. Union Carbide and Carbon Corp., 281 App. Div. 604, 121 N.Y.S.2d 130 (1953), *aff.* 306 N.Y. 638, 116 N.E.2d 245 (1953) the court held that minimum and maximum limits in a requirements contract do not transform such a contract into a contract for the sale of a definite quantity. Instead, the court held that such a contract is still a requirements contract obligating the seller to provide the materials necessary to meet the buyer's operational necessities in the business specified by the contract. Unless the contract were given such an interpretation, the court felt that "the 'requirements' provisions of the contracts would seem to be mere surplusage and meaning-less." 121 N.Y.S.2d at 132.[142]

It is, therefore, my view that the proper construction of the contract here in question is one that acknowledges the buyer's absolute obligation and its concomitant absolute right to purchase the contract minimum. Additionally, purchases in excess of the minimum limit but less than the maximum must be provided by seller only insofar as they are required by buyer's business operations, as those operations are described in the contract.

We now turn to the question of whether defendants have altered such rights and duties under this contract by departing from the terms of the contract with their construction of generators larger than those specified in the contract.

II

Plaintiff contends that the defendants have abrogated this contract by building generator units substantially larger than anticipated by the parties and larger than specified in the contract. We turn to Colorado law regarding rescission in evaluating this claim.

Under Colorado law, a breach of a contract will not terminate a contract and relieve the other party of its duties thereunder unless that breach is a major breach going to the essential condition of the contract. Gulick v. A. Robert Strawn & Associates, 477 P.2d 489 (Colo. App. 1970). Furthermore, the party seeking rescission must show that the injury caused by the breach is irreparable and that more than a mere variance of the contract terms is involved. Kole v. Parker Yale Development Company, 536 P.2d 848 (Colo. App. 1975); Briggs v. Robinson, 82 Colo. 1, 256 P. 639 (1927).

Colorado law is clear in its requirement that a court exercise caution in terminating a contract. It is widely held, and Colorado is no exception, that forfeitures pursuant to a forfeiture provision in a contract are not looked upon with favor and will be avoided if possible. Moorman Manufacturing Co. v. Rivera, 155 Colo. 413, 395 P.2d 4 (1964). Gulick, supra, points out that declaring a contract terminated because of a breach in performance is tantamount to declaring such a forfeiture and, therefore, the same caution exercised in declaring a forfeiture was held to be required in terminating a contract. This court has likewise recognized this

142. This is the only case we have found that also holds that the minimum purchase limit in a requirements contract can not be demanded unless it is likewise necessary for the actual business operations of the purchaser. I do not agree with this interpretation of the minimum purchase obligation for the reasons discussed *supra*. It is also noted that this aspect of the court's opinion has been criticized unfavorably. *See* 54 Colum. L. Rev. 296 (1954).

policy of avoiding contractual forfeitures, United Buckingham Freight
Lines v. Riss & Company, 241 F. Supp. 861 (D. Colo. 1965), and concludes as the court did in *Gulick* that terminating a contract upon breach
of that contract and in the absence of a forfeiture provision should *a
fortiori* be avoided if possible.

I recognize that Colorado law generally requires a court to rescind the
whole contract and not to affirm or disaffirm the contract in part. Kelley
v. Silver State Savings and Loan Ass'n, 534 P.2d 326 (Colo. App. 1975);
Tomkins v. Tomkins, 78 Colo. 574, 243 P. 632 (1926); Walker v. MacMillan, 62 Colo. 136, 160 P. 1062 (1916). The Colorado courts, however,
have not addressed the question of the partial cancellation of a contract
containing separate and divisible obligations. Since that issue is presented
by this dispute this court must attempt to predict how a Colorado court
would rule if faced with the question of the partial rescission of such a
contract. Two facts lead me to believe that Colorado would grant the
partial rescission of a divisible contract if the equities require it.

First, the Colorado Supreme Court has held that a court of equity,
when declaring the rights and duties under a contract, "should make
such adjustment of the case as the facts pleaded and proved will justify."
Cahill v. Readon, 85 Colo. 9, 15, 273 P. 653, 656 (1928). Such a holding
thereby acknowledges that the court in an equitable action must have the
necessary flexibility to make a disposition consistent with whatever the
equitable requirements of the case may be.

Second, the law from jurisdictions outside Colorado clearly allows the
partial rescission of a divisible contract if justice so requires. *See* for
example Reina v. Erassarrett, 90 Cal. App. 2d 418, 203 P.2d 72 (1949);
Mitzel v. Schatz, 175 N.W.2d 659 (N.D. Sup. Ct. 1970); Thompson v.
Williams, 246 S.W.2d 506 (Tex. Civ. App. 1952). See also annotation at
148 A.L.R. 417 (1944). I therefore conclude that the partial rescission of a
divisible contract would not be inconsistent with Colorado law if such
were required for an equitable resolution of a contractual conflict.

In applying the above discussed legal principles to the contract here in
question, I find that the contract is divisible in the obligations it imposes
on the parties. As pointed out in the previous section, the contract contains an absolute minimum purchase obligation and a requirements
purchase obligation for purchases in excess of the minimum. These obligations operate independently of each other and impose obligations of
significantly different natures.

I further conclude that the Colorado law governing the possible
grounds for rescission justifies the cancelling of only a portion of this
contract and that the equities of this case demands such partial rescission. The minimum purchase obligation in this contract, as an absolute
obligation, is not influenced by defendants' fuel requirements and is,
therefore, equally unaffected by the unit size chosen by defendants. It
follows, therefore, that the generating capacities of the units were not a

major factor in either establishing this obligation or in negotiating the particular extent of the obligation. Therefore, even though defendants have breached this contract by constructing larger generating units than specified in the contract, that breach does not go to the essential condition of the contract's minimum purchase obligation. Therefore, under Colorado's stringent rules governing the termination of a contract, defendants' breach does not justify cancelling that portion of the contract.

This breach of performance by defendants, however, does go to the heart of the requirements purchase obligation for amounts of coal in excess of the minimum. As this court concluded above, defendants are entitled to receive coal in amounts in excess of their minimum purchase obligation only if that coal is required by the operation of the generating units specified in the contract. Therefore, in construing this portion of the contract it becomes apparent that the size of the coal consuming units is the essential element in determining the parties' rights and duties thereunder. The contract specified that the generating units would have net capacities of about 350,000 kilowatts each. Defendants, however, are building units with capacities of 410,000 kilowatts net. This increase in size will result in the consumption of an amount of coal substantially in excess of the amount contemplated by plaintiff and in excess of the coal consumption calculations prepared and relied on by both parties during the negotiation of the contract. Defendants should not be allowed to take advantage of this breach, particularly in view of the continuing dramatic rise in the price of coal; this breach is of such a nature as to require rescission of that portion of the contract. Certainly the breach is more than a mere variance of the contractual terms and in it threatens to do irreparable damage to plaintiff. See *Briggs* and *Kole, supra.*

Defendants, however, point to the rule of law allowing the purchaser in a requirements contract to modify his business operations after the contract is signed and cite Southwest Natural Gas Co. v. Oklahoma Portland C. Co., 102 F.2d 630 (10th Cir. 1939) as authority for that rule. Defendants' reliance on that case is misplaced and entirely inappropriate.

In the case at bar, the purchaser's business requirements specified in the contract were modified prior to the execution of the contract and without notifying plaintiff. In *Southwest*, the improvements made in the business operation of the purchaser were made subsequently to the execution of the contract and were the type of improvements that seller should have anticipated would occur over the life of that contract.

The court in *Southwest* also pointed out that the changes made in purchaser's business were not precluded by the terms of the contract. Defendants in the instant case, however, have made a modification prohibited by the terms of the contract in that the contract specifically stipulates the size of the generating units that were to be built.

Additionally, *Southwest* emphasizes that the modifications were made in good faith and were necessary for the continued efficiency of the purchaser's plant. Defendants in this action have failed to meet the burden of establishing that their changing the size of the consuming generating units was in good faith. In fact, the evidence strongly suggests to the contrary.

As noted above, this court is aware of the caution that must be exercised in terminating any contractual obligation. The case at bar, however, clearly presents a situation where such an equitable remedy is the only appropriate remedy. A party to a contract may not unilaterally alter the obligations of any of the parties to that contract. Defendants, however, have attempted to increase plaintiff's sales obligation under the requirements portion of this contract by altering their business operations in such a manner as to constitute a material breach of that portion of the contract. Rescission, therefore, is an appropriate remedy. As pointed out, however, the breach does not affect that portion of the contract containing the defendants' minimum purchase obligation and as such, prohibits the termination of that obligation. It is therefore,

ORDERED that

1) Plaintiff must yearly sell to defendants, if defendants so demand, that amount of fuel specified in the "Table for the Minimum Annual Payments" contained in Section 8 of the Craig Station Fuel Agreement, a portion of which is attached hereto as Appendix A.

2) Defendants may purchase, regardless of their operational requirements, that amount of fuel specified in that same Table for Minimum Annual Payments contained in Section 8 of the Craig Station Fuel Agreement.

3) Defendants must make the minimum yearly payments pursuant to the provisions of Section 8 of the Craig Station Fuel Agreement regardless of whether defendants actually receive any coal during that year.

4) Plaintiff is not obligated to furnish to defendants any coal in excess of the above prescribed amounts unless pursuant to a new or supplemental agreement between the plaintiff and defendants.

5) All other provisions of the Craig Station Fuel Agreement, including but not limited to those provisions regarding price, delivery schedules, arbitration, the term of the contract and emergency storage shall remain binding on plaintiff and defendants except insofar as they are modified by this order.

[Appendix A has been omitted.]

SCHLEGEL MANUFACTURING CO. v. COOPER'S GLUE FACTORY

231 N.Y. 459, 132 N.E. 148 (Ct. App. 1921)

Appeal from a judgment of the Appellate Division of the Supreme Court in the first judicial department, entered Dec. 27, 1919, affirming a judgment in favor of plaintiff entered upon a decision of the court at a Trial Term without a jury.

McLAUGHLIN, J. Action to recover damages for alleged breach of contract. The complaint alleged that on or about December 9, 1915, the parties entered into a written agreement by which the defendant agreed to sell and deliver to the plaintiff, and the plaintiff agreed to purchase from the defendant, all its "requirements" of special BB glue for the year 1916, at the price of nine cents per pound. It also alleged the terms of payment, the manner in which the glue was to be packed, the place of delivery, the neglect and refusal of defendant to make certain deliveries, the damages sustained, for which judgment was demanded. The answer put in issue the material allegations of the complaint. At the trial a jury was waived and the trial proceeded before the trial justice. At its conclusion he rendered a decision awarding the plaintiff a substantial amount [$6,431.28]. Judgment was entered upon the decision, from which an appeal was taken to the Appellate Division, first department, where the same was affirmed, two of the justices dissenting. The appeal to this court followed.

I am of the opinion that judgment appealed from should be reversed, upon the ground that the alleged contract, for the breach of which a recovery was had, was invalid since it lacked mutuality. It consisted solely of a letter written by defendant to plaintiff, the material part of which is as follows:

> Gentlemen — We are instructed by our Mr. Von Schuckmann to enter your contract for your requirements of "Special BB" glue for the year 1916, price to be 9¢ per lb., terms 2% 20th to 30th of month following purchase. Deliveries, to be made to you as per your orders during the year and quality same as heretofore. Glue to be packed in 500 lb. or 350 lb. barrels and 100 lb. kegs, and your special Label to be carefully pasted on top, bottom and side of each barrel or keg. . . .
>
> Peter Cooper's Glue Factory,
W. D. DONALDSON,
Sales Manager.

At the bottom of the letter the president of the plaintiff wrote: "Accepted, Oscar Schlegel Manufacturing Company," and returned it to the defendant.

The plaintiff, at the time, was engaged in no manufacturing business in which glue was used or required, nor was it then under contract to deliver glue to any third parties at a fixed price or otherwise. It was simply a jobber, selling, among other things, glue to such customers as might be obtained by sending out salesmen to solicit orders therefor. The contract was invalid since a consideration was lacking. Mutual promises or obligations of parties to a contract, either express or necessarily implied, may furnish the requisite consideration. The defect in the alleged contract here under consideration is that it contains no express consideration, nor are there any mutual promises of the parties to it from which such consideration can be fairly inferred. The plaintiff, it will be observed, did not agree to do or refrain from doing anything. It was not obligated to sell a pound of defendant's glue or to make any effort in that direction. It did not agree not to sell other glue in competition with defendant's. The only obligation assumed by it was to pay nine cents a pound for such glue as it might order. Whether it should order any at all rested entirely with it. If it did not order any glue, then nothing was to be paid. The agreement was not under seal, and, therefore, fell within the rule that a promise not under seal made by one party, with none by the other, is void. Unless both parties to a contract are bound, so that either can sue the other for a breach, neither is bound. (Grossman v. Schenker, 206 N.Y. 466; Levin v. Dietz, 194 N.Y. 376; Chicago & Gt. E. Ry. Co. v. Dane, 43 N.Y. 240; Hurd v. Gill, 45 N.Y. 341; Commercial Wood & Cement Co. v. Northampton Portland Cement Co., 115 App. Div. 388; Jackson v. Alpha Portland Cement Co., 122 App. Div. 345; Crane v. Crane & Co., 105 Fed. Rep. 869; Williston on Contracts, sec. 104.) Had the plaintiff neglected or refused to order any glue during the year 1916, defendant could not have maintained an action to recover damages against it, because there would have been no breach of the contract. In order to recover damages, a breach had to be shown, and this could not have been established by a mere failure on the part of the plaintiff to order glue, since it had not promised to give such orders.

There are certain contracts in which mutual promises are implied: Thus, where the purchaser, to the knowledge of the seller, has entered into a contract for the resale of the article purchased (Shipman v. Straitsville Central Mining Co., 158 U.S. 356); where the purchaser contracts for his requirements of an article necessary to be used in the business carried on by him (Wells v. Alexandre, 130 N.Y. 642); or for all the cans needed in a canning factory (Dailey Co. v. Clark Can Co., 128 Mich. 591); all the lubricating oil for party's own use (Manhattan Oil Co. v. Richardson Lubricating Co., 113 Fed. Rep. 923); all the coal needed for a foundry during a specified time (Minnesota Lumber Co. v. Whitebreast Coal Co., 160 Ill. 85); all the iron required during a certain period in a furnace (National Furnace Co. v. Keystone Mfg. Co., 110 Ill. 427); and all the ice required in a hotel during a certain season (G. N. Railway Co. v. Witham, L.R. 9 C.P. 16). In cases of this character, while the quantity of the article contracted to be sold is indefinite, nevertheless there is a certain standard mentioned in the agreement by which such quantity can be determined by an approximately accurate forecast. In the contract here under consideration there is no standard mentioned by which the quantity of glue to be furnished can be determined with any approximate degree of accuracy.

The view above expressed is not in conflict with the authorities cited by the respondent. Thus, in N.Y.C. Iron Works Co. v. U.S. Radiator Co. (174 N.Y. 331), principally relied upon and cited in the prevailing opinion at the Appellate Division, "the defendant bound the plaintiff to deal exclusively in goods to be ordered from it under the contract, and to enlarge and develop the market for the defendant's wares so far as possible."

In Fuller & Co. v. Schrenk (58 App. Div. 222; affd., 171 N.Y. 671) the contract provided: "It is hereby agreed that in consideration of W. P. Fuller & Co. buying *all* their supply of German Mirror Plates from the United Bavarian Looking Glass Works, for a period of six months from this date, the said United Bavarian Looking Glass Works" agrees to sell certain mirrors at specified prices. [The discussion of Wood v. Duff-Gordon, 222 N.Y. 88, *infra* p. 451, is omitted.]

In Ehrenworth v. Stuhmer & Co. (229 N.Y. 210) defendant and its predecessor were desirous of obtaining a market for a particular kind of bread which it manufactured. In order to accomplish this purpose it was agreed that plaintiff should purchase and defendant sell *all* the bread of the kind specified which plaintiff required in a certain locality and pay therefor a price specified in the agreement. The plaintiff also agreed he would not sell any other bread of that kind on that route during the life of the contract, which was to continue so long as the parties remained in business. This contract, it will be noticed, specified the articles to be sold, the price to be paid, the quantity to be furnished, and the term of the contract, during which time plaintiff agreed not to sell any other bread of the kind named in that territory.

In the instant case, as we have already seen, there was no obligation on the part of the plaintiff to sell any of the defendant's glue, to make any effort towards bringing about such sale, or not to sell other glues in competition with it. There is not in the letter a single obligation from which it can fairly be inferred that the plaintiff was to do or refrain from doing anything whatever.

The price of glue having risen during the year 1916 from nine to twenty-four cents per pound, it is quite obvious why orders for glue increased correspondingly. Had the price dropped below nine cents it may fairly be inferred such orders would not have been given. In that case, if the interpretation put upon the agreement be the correct one, plaintiff would not have been liable to the defendant for damages for a breach, since he had not agreed to sell any glue.

The judgments of the Appellate Division[143] and trial court should be reversed and the complaint dismissed, with costs in all courts.

Hiscock, Ch. J., Hogan, Pound, Crane and Andrews, JJ., concur; Chase, J., deceased.

Judgments reversed, etc.

143. 189 A.D. 843, 179 N.Y.S. 271 (1919). — EDS.

NOTE

1. In the five years preceding the contract in litigation, plaintiff's orders had never exceeded 35,000 pounds per year. During the 1916 contract period, plaintiff ordered about 170,000 and received 65,000 pounds. Plaintiff tried to fill his 1917 requirement and defendant never repudiated the orders; in fact, defendant's representative promised repeatedly as late as December 1916 that he would ship. 189 A.D. 843, at 846, 179 N.Y.S. 273, at 280. Does the decision amount to saying that jobber's requirement contracts are unenforceable? In the Appellate Division decision, Page. J., in his dissenting opinion had this to say: "The facts in this case show conclusively in my opinion that the plaintiff was not acting in good faith but was using the contract speculatively and not as contemplated by the parties." 189 A.D. 849, 855. Was the promise of defendant's representative not binding?

Why was not the defendant's promise a continuing offer which in turn was accepted?

2. The defendant, a wholesale ice company, agreed to sell to plaintiff coal company 100 tons of ice at a stated price, and plaintiff agreed to purchase all the ice used by it up to 100 tons. Payments were to be made daily and the agreement was to continue for one year. Unknown to defendant, plaintiff at the time of the agreement was not in the ice business and had no use for ice. Two months after the contract was entered into, plaintiff made its first demand for ice to be delivered to a former customer of defendant, who had bought ice until his supply was stopped for failure of payment. Upon defendant's refusal to deliver, plaintiff sued for damages. Held, for defendant. Plaintiff

> impliedly represented that it was either in the ice business or would be in the ice business with a market for ice in May or June and would require ice daily not to exceed one hundred (100) tons. It was in no such business and made no bona fide demand for any ice under this contract. In other words, it had no need for ice.

Nassau Supply Company, Inc. v. Ice Service Co., 252 N.Y. 277, 169 N.E. 383 (1929), discussed in 43 Harv. L. Rev. 828 (1930). Comment 2 to U.C.C. §2-306, reprinted *supra* pp. 433-434, requires careful reading.

Section 12. "Instinct with an Obligation"

We have discussed the obligation of good faith on several occasions thus far. We have seen how this obligation has crept into precontractual negotiations, and we have also encountered it in our discussion of requirements and brokerage contracts as well as franchise agreements. In Chapter 4, we shall once again meet the obligation of good faith in connection with insurance contracts.

This section continues the exploration of the notion of good faith in relation to another group of cases. These cases all involve ongoing contractual relations in which one of the two parties appears to be left with a wide discretion about what he must do under the contract. A question is often raised as to whether the scope of discretion is so wide as to render the contract void for want of mutuality. In an effort to safeguard the expectations of those who have entered into a contract, the courts have increasingly imposed a limitation of good faith on the exercise of discretion. In some cases, such a limitation has had the effect of providing a counterpromise where one appeared to be lacking. In other cases, the limitation has entailed a reinterpretation of broadly worded clauses that give one of the parties the right to cancel or make his own obligation conditioned on his satisfaction with the other party's performance. In still other cases, the assertion of a lack of mutuality has been met by judicial manipulation of the consideration doctrine.

WOOD v. LUCY, LADY DUFF-GORDON
222 N.Y. 88, 118 N.E. 214 (1917)

Cardozo, J. The defendant styles herself "a creator of fashions." Her favor helps a sale. Manufacturers of dresses, millinery, and like articles are glad to pay for a certificate of her approval. The things which she designs, fabrics, parasols, and what not, have a new value in the public mind when issued in her name. She employed the plaintiff to help her to turn this vogue into money. He was to have the exclusive right, subject always to her approval, to place her indorsements on the designs of others. He was also to have the exclusive right to place her own designs on sale, or to license others to market them. In return she was to have one-half of "all profits and revenues" derived from any contracts he might make. The exclusive right was to last at least one year from April 1, 1915, and thereafter from year to year unless terminated by notice of 90 days. The plaintiff says that he kept the contract on his part, and that the defendant broke it. She placed her indorsement on fabrics, dresses, and millinery without his knowledge, and withheld the profits. He sues her for the damages, and the case comes here on demurrer.

The agreement of employment is signed by both parties. It has a wealth of recitals. The defendant insists, however, that it lacks the elements of a contract. She says that the plaintiff does not bind himself to anything. It is true that he does not promise in so many words that he will use reasonable efforts to place the defendant's indorsements and market her designs. We think, however, that such a promise is fairly to be implied. The law has outgrown its primitive stage of formalism when the precise word was the sovereign talisman, and every slip was fatal. It takes a broader view to-day. A promise may be lacking, and yet the whole writing may be "instinct with an obligation," imperfectly expressed (Scott, J., in McCall Co. v. Wright, 133 App. Div. 62, 117 N.Y.S. 775; Moran v. Standard Oil Co., 211 N.Y. 187, 198, 105 N.E. 217). If that is so, there is a contract.

The implication of a promise here finds support in many circumstances. The defendant gave an exclusive privilege. She was to have no right for at least a year to place her own indorsements or market her own designs except through the agency of the plaintiff. The acceptance of the exclusive agency was an assumption of its duties. . . . We are not to suppose that one party was to be placed at the mercy of the other. . . . Many other terms of the agreement point the same way. We are told at the outset by way of recital that:

"The said Otis F. Wood possesses a business organization adapted to the placing of such indorsements as the said Lucy, Duff-Gordon, has approved."

The implication is that the plaintiff's business organization will be used for the purpose for which it is adapted. But the terms of the defendant's compensation are even more significant. Her sole compensation for the grant of an exclusive agency is to be one-half of all the profits resulting from the plaintiff's efforts. Unless he gave his efforts, she could never get anything. Without an implied promise, the transaction cannot have such business "efficacy, as both parties must have intended that at all events it should have." Bowen, L.J., in The Moorcock, 14 P.D. 64, 68. But the contract does not stop there. The plaintiff goes on to promise that he will account monthly for all moneys received by him, and that he will take out all such patents and copyrights and trade-marks as may in his judgment be necessary to protect the rights and articles affected by the agreement. It is true, of course, as the Appellate Division has said, that if he was under no duty to try to market designs or to place certificates of indorsement, his promise to account for profits or take out copyrights would be valueless. But in determining the intention of the parties the promise has a value. It helps to enforce the conclusion that the plaintiff had some duties. His promise to pay the defendant one-half of the profits and revenues resulting from the exclusive agency and to render accounts monthly was a promise to use reasonable efforts to bring profits and revenues into existence. For this conclusion the authorities are ample. [Citations omitted.]

The judgment of the Appellate Division should be reversed, and the order of the Special Term affirmed, with costs in the Appellate Division and in this court.

Cuddeback, McLaughlin, and Andrews, JJ., concur. Hiscock, C.J., and Chase and Crane, JJ., dissent.

Judgment reversed, etc.

NOTE

Suppose defendant has reason to be dissatisfied with plaintiff's performance of his duties under the exclusive agency arrangement. What remedies are at her disposal? Damages?

U.C.C. §2-306(2): "A lawful agreement by either the seller or the buyer for exclusive dealing in the kind of goods concerned imposes unless otherwise agreed an obligation by the seller to use best efforts to supply the goods and by the buyer to use best efforts to promote their sale."

Consult Comment 5 and U.C.C. §2-609.

HAMMOND v. C.I.T. FINANCIAL CORP.
203 F.2d 705 (2d Cir. 1953)

AUGUSTUS N. HAND, Circuit Judge. This action was brought by Paul Hammond, a citizen of the State of New York, H. Donald Harvey, a citizen of the State of Connecticut, and Carter M. Braxton, a citizen of the State of New York, copartners doing business under the firm name of The Hammond, Harvey, Braxton Company, against the C.I.T. Financial Corporation, organized under the laws of the State of Delaware, for breach of a contract giving Braxton (hereafter sometimes referred to as the plaintiff) the exclusive right to sell defendant's wholly owned subsidiary corporation, known as the Holtzer-Cabot Division. Federal jurisdiction was invoked because of diversity of citizenship, the amount in controversy exceeding $3,000.

The facts as found by the district court sitting without a jury may be summarized as follows:

In January 1948 the defendant decided to sell its wholly owned subsidiary, Holtzer-Cabot. On January 27, the defendant's vice-president Urquhart approached Braxton with a view to enlisting his services in finding a buyer. The plaintiff was given the exclusive right to negotiate the sale of the Holtzer-Cabot assets. All inquiries were to be referred to him by the defendant, and all negotiations were to be conducted by him. His fee was to be five per cent of the first two million dollars of the sales price with lesser percentages upon amounts received in excess of that sum, but the plaintiff agreed to discuss an adjustment of his fixed commission in the event of "unusual circumstances" attending the sale. The defendant was given the right to terminate the contract at any time it was dissatisfied with the plaintiff's efforts. The parties decided that no written contract was necessary. The plaintiff, who was engaged in the business of acting as broker in the sales of going concerns, prepared a prospectus which he sent to prospective buyers and in some instances where interest was manifested, he exhibited the plant to the prospect.

On April 13, 1948, Braxton brought a prospective buyer to Urquhart's office. Some interest was indicated on the part of this prospect but no offer was made. Following this interview Braxton was informed by Urquhart that an inquiry had been made on behalf of Redmond Company and that if the company showed any interest, it would be turned over to Braxton. On April 21 the latter was told by Urquhart that an offer of $1,000,000 had been made for the plant and inventory by this prospect and that this offer was the subject of pending negotiations. Braxton said that his late participation in the negotiations which had been initiated by the defendant's president would be futile. The plaintiff was also informed that his position was not affected in any way, but a decrease in his compensation was discussed. Urquhart agreed to consider any offer from the prospect previously introduced by Braxton.

On May 12 the defendant closed the sale of the Holtzer-Cabot plant and inventory to Redmond Company without Braxton's knowledge or intervention; the contract was executed on May 28. The price was $1,165,743.39, of which $65,743.39 was represented by promissory notes. On May 17 Braxton had sent an offer from still another prospect. Later on that day he was told by Urquhart that the contract of sale was being prepared; Braxton's commission was discussed on the theory that "unusual circumstances" had developed when the defendant had consummated the sale itself and a low price had been received. At the trial the price was admitted to be the best then obtainable and to represent the true market value. A compromise commission was rejected by the plaintiff. The plaintiff's brief indicates that a counter proposal for arbitration of the controversy was rejected by the defendant.

The district court further found that except for the eventual buyer all leads were referred to the plaintiff by the defendant; that the defendant never terminated its contract with the plaintiff; and that the plaintiff would have been at least equally successful in negotiating the sale. A judgment of five per cent of the sales price was awarded, with interest from May 28, 1948, for breach of the contract giving plaintiff the exclusive right to sell the property in question.

The defendant's first contention is that the district court erred in finding that the defendant had given the plaintiff an "exclusive right to sell," while agreeing not to sell the property itself. The essentially factual question as to the parties' intention was resolved by the district court in favor of the plaintiff and we think it cannot be said to have been "clearly erroneous." In view of the defendant's agreement to refer all leads to the plaintiff this construction was a reasonable one. See Gaillard Realty Co. v. Rogers Wire Works, Inc., 1st Dep't., 215 App. Div. 326, 213 N.Y.S. 616. The defendant's explanation of the reason for this part of the contract is unconvincing. Moreover, if there was any ambiguity in the agreement, consideration of the parties' own conduct in construing it as entitling plaintiff to his commission (although defendant asserted that the rate must be reduced because of "unusual circumstances") would lead to the same result. See New York Central R. Co. v. New York & Harlem R.

Co., 185 Misc. 420, 425-426, 56 N.Y.S.2d 712, *affirmed* 297 N.Y. 820, 78 N.E.2d 612; cf. Brainard v. New York Central R. Co., 242 N.Y. 125, 133, 151 N.E. 152, 45 A.L.R. 751. The defendant argues that its conduct was not an admission of the existence of a legal obligation to pay a commission, but the trial court's findings do not appear to us to be "clearly erroneous." Further, we agree with the district court that the plaintiff's disinclination to participate in the negotiations already started by the defendant was not conduct inconsistent with his "exclusive right to sell" since he could have been of no particular assistance at that stage and the contract had already been breached by the failure to refer.

The defendant's next contention is that the agreement was terminable at will, and was terminated by the sale even without notice to the plaintiff. Reliance is placed primarily on the Restatement of Agency, §449(c). This section, however, relates to unilateral contracts of employment. The district court found that a valid bilateral contract had been formed, citing Wood v. Lucy Duff-Gordon, 222 N.Y. 88, 118 N.E. 214. Cf. Restatement of Contracts, §31. We think that Braxton's promise to work intensively, since a speedy sale was desired, and to handle the matter with the utmost discretion may fairly be implied. In return defendant promised that plaintiff was to handle the sale on an exclusive basis and that all leads would be referred to him. Nor was the contract terminable at will because it was indefinite as to time; a reasonable duration may be implied. Moreover, the district court found on sufficient evidence that the contract was only terminable if the defendant in good faith became dissatisfied with the plaintiff's efforts, and in view of the desire for speed such dissatisfaction would naturally arise before too long a period had elapsed. The defendant further argues that a reasonable time had elapsed without a sale being made by the plaintiff and that it had ample grounds for dissatisfaction. However that may be, the trial court found that there was no termination, nor does the defendant contend that it ever gave any notice of termination. Since the contract was not terminable at will, the sale after the defendant breached the contract by its failure to refer can hardly be considered a termination. Cf. Sibbald v. Bethlehem Iron Co., 83 N.Y. 378, 384. We see no merit in the contention that the arrangement was so far modified as to put Braxton on a non-exclusive basis in so far as Redmond Company was concerned. He went no further than being willing to follow out his agreement to discuss a reduction in his commission because of the "special circumstances" asserted by the defendant.

The defendant also argues that the failure of the lower court to find whether or not there were "unusual circumstances" requires a reversal. It was found that the parties agreed that "in the event of 'unusual circumstances' attending the sale he [plaintiff] would discuss an adjustment of the fixed commission." The defendant contends that this construction, giving it only the right which it would have in any event of "discussing" a reduction, is unrealistic, since the defendant sought protection against unforeseen circumstances and must have intended something more. However, if as the defendant contends there was an agreement to renegotiate the commission, the existence of "unusual circumstances" would leave the defendant with no enforceable legal obligation but with an agreement to agree. Thus the finding that the parties intended only that a discussion in good faith would ensue in the event of "unusual circumstances" is not without a reasonable foundation and we do not think that it was "clearly erroneous." Cf. Cohen & Sons, Inc. v. M. Lurie Woolen Co., 232 N.Y. 112, 114, 133 N.E. 370. The failure to find whether there were in fact "unusual circumstances" within the contemplation of the parties is not reversible error, since even if they were present, plaintiff carried out whatever obligation he had to discuss a reduction, rejecting the defendant's offer of $20,000 but suggesting arbitration.

We also think that the district court was right in awarding the plaintiff five per cent of the consideration of the sale as damages for breach of the contract. Gaillard Realty Co. v. Rogers Wire Works, Inc., 1st Dep't., 215 App. Div. 326, 213 N.Y.S. 616; Cf. Slattery v. Cothran, 4th Dep't., 210 App. Div. 581, 206 N.Y.S. 576. The contract was breached by the defendant's failure to refer Redmond to the plaintiff. Since the district court found that the plaintiff would have been as successful in negotiating with Redmond as was the defendant, the damages consist of the loss sustained when Redmond was not referred to the plaintiff, i.e., five per cent of the sales price. Chevrolet Motor Co. v. McCullough Motor Co., 9 Cir., 6 F.2d 212, relied on by the defendant is not in point since the contract there could be cancelled on five days' notice; here the contract was not terminable on notice at any time, but only if the defendant was dissatisfied with the plaintiff's efforts, and it was not so terminated prior to the breach which gave rise to the damages.

The plaintiff appeals from the failure to award damages based on the right to sell Holtzer-Cabot's accounts receivable. They were initially among the assets which were the subject of the exclusive arrangement between the defendant and the plaintiff. But they were not included in the assets sold by the defendant to Redmond Company; the defendant collected them itself. We fail to understand how the defendant's breach caused the plaintiff any loss as to the assets which were never sold. We find no obligation on the defendant's part to include these assets in the sale, and hence the failure to refer caused the plaintiff no loss. Further, there is no proof that Braxton could have sold the accounts receivable together with the other assets had Redmond Company been referred to him.

Accordingly, the judgment is affirmed.

NOTE

Recall the discussion of brokerage cases in Section 10.

SYLVAN CREST SAND & GRAVEL CO. v. UNITED STATES

150 F.2d 642 (2d Cir. 1945)

Appeal from the District Court of the United States for the District of Connecticut.

Action by the Sylvan Crest Sand & Gravel Company, a legal corporation of the Town of Trumbull, County of Fairfield, and State of Connecticut, against the United States for breach of four alleged contracts to purchase trap rock from plaintiff. From a summary judgment for the government, plaintiff appeals.

SWAN, Circuit Judge. This is an action for damages for breach of four alleged contracts under each of which the plaintiff was to deliver trap rock to an airport project "as required" and in accordance with delivery instructions to be given by the defendant. The breach alleged was the defendant's refusal to request or accept delivery within a reasonable time after the date of the contracts, thereby depriving the plaintiff of profits it would have made in the amount of $10,000. The action was commenced in the District Court, federal jurisdiction resting on 28 U.S.C.A. §41(20). Upon the pleadings, consisting of complaint, answer and reply, the defendant moved to dismiss the action for failure of the complaint to state a claim or, in the alternative, to grant summary judgment for the defendant on the ground that no genuine issue exists as to any material fact. The contracts in suit were introduced as exhibits at the hearing on the motion. Summary judgment for the defendant was granted on the theory that the defendant's reservation of an unrestricted power of cancellation caused the alleged contracts to be wholly illusory as binding obligations. The plaintiff has appealed.

The plaintiff owned and operated a trap rock quarry in Trumbull, Conn. Through the Treasury Department, acting by its State Procurement Office in Connecticut, the United States invited bids on trap rock needed for the Mollison Airport, Bridgeport, Conn. The plaintiff submitted four bids for different sized screenings of trap rock and each bid was accepted by the Assistant State Procurement officer on June 29, 1937. The four documents are substantially alike and it will suffice to describe one of them. It is a printed government form, with the blank spaces filled in in typewriting, consisting of a single sheet bearing the heading:

Invitation, Bid, and Acceptance
(Short Form Contract)

Below the heading, under the subheadings, follow in order the "Invitation," the "bid," and the "Acceptance by the Government." The Invitation, signed by a State Procurement Officer, states that "Sealed bids in triplicate, subject to the conditions on the reverse hereof, will be received at this office . . . for furnishing supplies . . . for delivery at WP 2752 —

Mollison Airport, Bridgeport, Ct." Then come typed provisions which, so far as material, are as follows:

> Item No. 1. ½″ Trap Rock to pass the following screening test . . . approx. 4000 tons, unit price $2.00 amount $8000. To be delivered to project as required. Delivery to start immediately. Communicate with W. J. Scott. Supt. W.P.A. Branch Office, 147 Canon Street, Bridgeport, Ct., for definite delivery instructions. Cancellation by the Procurement Division may be effected at any time.

The Bid, signed by the plaintiff, provides that

> In compliance with the above invitation for bids, and subject to all of the conditions thereof, the undersigned offers, and agrees, if this bid be accepted . . . to furnish any or all of the items upon which prices are quoted, at the prices set opposite each item, delivered at the point(s) as specified, . . .

The Acceptance, besides its date and the signature of an Assistant State Procurement Officer, contains only the words "Accepted as to items numbered 1." The printing on the reverse side of the sheet under the heading "Conditions" and "Instructions to Contracting Officers" clearly indicates that the parties supposed they were entering into an enforcible contract. For example, Condition 3 states that "in case of default of the contractor" the government may procure the articles from other sources and hold the contractor liable for any excess in cost; and Condition 4 provides that "if the contractor refuses or fails to make deliveries . . . within the time specified . . . the Government may by written notice terminate the right of the contractor to proceed with deliveries. . . ." The Instructions to Contracting Officers also presupposes the making of a valid contract; No. 2 reads:

"Although this form meets the requirements of a formal contract (R.S. 3744), if the execution of a formal contract with bond is contemplated, U.S. Standard Forms 31 and 32 should be used."

No one can read the document as a whole without concluding that the parties intended a contract to result from the Bid and the Government's Acceptance. If the United States did not so intend, it certainly set a skilful trap for unwary bidders. No such purpose should be attributed to the government. See United States v. Purcell Envelope Co., 249 U.S. 313, 318, 38 S. Ct. 300, 63 L. Ed. 620. In construing the document the presumption should be indulged that both parties were acting in good faith.

Although the Acceptance contains no promissory words, it is conceded that a promise by the defendant to pay the stated price for rock delivered is to be implied.[144] Since no precise time for delivery was speci-

---

144. The answer alleges that certain deliveries were made, all of which were duly paid for by the United States, and the reply admitted this.

fied, the implication is that delivery within a reasonable time was contemplated. Allegheny Valley Brick Co. v. C. W. Raymond Co., 2 Cir., 219 F. 477, 480; Frankfurt-Barnett v. William Prym Co., 2 Cir., 237 F. 21, 25. This is corroborated by the express provision that the rock was "to be delivered to the project as required. Delivery to start immediately." There is also to be implied a promise to give delivery instructions; nothing in the language of the contracts indicates that performance by the plaintiff was to be conditional upon the exercise of the defendant's discretion in giving such instructions. A more reasonable interpretation is that the defendant was placed under an obligation to give instructions for delivery from time to time when trap rock was required at the project. Such were the duties of the defendant, unless the cancellation clause precludes such a construction of the document.

Beyond question the plaintiff made a promise to deliver rock at a stated price; and if the United States were suing for its breach the question would be whether the "acceptance" by the United States operated as a sufficient consideration to make the plaintiff's promise binding. Since the United States is the defendant the question is whether it made any promise that has been broken. Its "acceptance" should be interpreted as a reasonable business man would have understood it. Surely it would not have been understood thus: "We accept your offer and bind you to your promise to deliver, but we do not promise either to take the rock or pay the price." The reservation of a power to effect cancellation at any time meant something different from this. We believe that the reasonable interpretation of the document is as follows: "We accept your offer to deliver within a reasonable time, and we promise to take the rock and pay the price unless we give you notice of cancellation within a reasonable time." Only on such an interpretation is the United States justified in expecting the plaintiff to prepare for performance and to remain ready and willing to deliver. Even so, the bidder is taking a great risk and the United States has an advantage. It is not "good faith" for the United States to insist upon more than this. It is certain that the United States intended to bind the bidder to a "contract," and that the bidder thought that the "acceptance" of his bid made a "contract." A reasonable interpretation of the language used gives effect to their mutual intention. Consequently we cannot accept the contention that the defendant's power of cancellation was unrestricted and could be exercised merely by failure to give delivery orders. The words "cancellation may be effected at any time" imply affirmative action, namely, the giving of notice of intent to cancel. The defendant itself so construed the clause by giving notice of cancellation on June 11, 1939, as alleged in its answer. While the phrase "at any time" should be liberally construed, it means much less than "forever." If taken literally, it would mean that after the defendant had given instructions for delivery and the plaintiff had tendered delivery in accordance therewith, or even after delivery had actually been made, the defendant could refuse to accept and when sued for the price give notice of cancellation of the contract. Such an interpretation would be not only unjust and unreasonable, but would make nugatory the entire contract, contrary to the intention of the parties, if it be assumed that the United States was acting in good faith in accepting the plaintiff's bid. The words should be so construed as to support the contract and not render illusory the promises of both parties. This can be accomplished by interpolating the word "reasonable," as is often done with respect to indefinite time clauses. See Starkweather v. Gleason, 221 Mass. 552, 109 N.E. 635. Hence the agreement obligated the defendant to give delivery instructions or notice of cancellation within a reasonable time after the date of its "acceptance." This constituted consideration for the plaintiff's promise to deliver in accordance with delivery instructions, and made the agreement a valid contract.

It must be conceded that the cases dealing with agreements in which one party has reserved to himself an option to cancel are not entirely harmonious. Where the option is completely unrestricted some courts say that the party having the option has promised nothing and the contract is void for lack of mutuality. Miami Coca-Cola Bottling Co. v. Orange Crush Co., 5 Cir., 296 F. 693; Oakland Motor Car Co. v. Indiana Automobile Co., 7 Cir., 201 F. 499. These cases have been criticized by competent text writers and the latter case cited by this court "with distinct lack of warmth," as Judge Clark noted in Bushwick-Decatur Motors v. Ford Motor Co., 2 Cir., 116 F.2d 675, 678. But where, as in the case at bar, the option to cancel "does not wholly defeat consideration," the agreement is not nudum pactum. Corbin, The Effect of Options on Consideration, 34 Yale L.J. 571, 585; see Hunt v. Stimson, 6 Cir., 23 F.2d 447; Gurfein v. Werbelovsky, 97 Conn. 703, 118 A. 32. A promise is not made illusory by the fact that the promisor has an option between two alternatives, if each alternative would be sufficient consideration if it alone were bargained for. A.L.I. Contracts, §79. As we have construed the agreement the United States promised by implication to take and pay for the trap rock or give notice of cancellation within a reasonable time. The alternative of giving notice was not difficult of performance, but it was a sufficient consideration to support the contract.

The judgment is reversed and the cause remanded for trial.

NOTE

Consult U.C.C. §2-309. Illustration 5 to Restatement Second §205 is based on the principal case.

CARLTON v. SMITH

285 Ill. App. 380, 2 N.E.2d 116 (1936)

Mr. Presiding Justice EDWARDS delivered the opinion of the court. On July 25, 1928, appellants brought suit in the circuit court of Jackson county to recover from appellee damages claimed to be resultant from a failure of the latter to perform a contract entered into between said parties for the sale of a laundry business in the city of West Frankfort. A demurrer to the declaration being sustained, appellants took leave to file additional counts thereto, which same was done, and such counts designated as five to eleven inclusive. Appellee demurred to the additional counts and the court held with him. Appellants refused to plead further and judgment was entered against them in bar of the action and for costs, from which judgment this appeal has been perfected.

The clause of the contract of sale, which forms the basis of this suit, and upon which each count is based, reads: "Parties hereto agree that this agreement is subject to the procurement of a satisfactory lease between second party and owner of building wherein business is now located." Appellee being the one designated as "second party."

Counts six, eight and nine, after reciting such clause, further aver that at the time and prior to the execution of the written contract, the parties thereto verbally agreed with each other that if the appellee could secure from the owner of the building in which the business was being conducted, a lease, such as was in effect between the owner and appellants, that he (the appellee) would be satisfied therewith. Appellee contends that to permit such to be pleaded and proven would be to vary the terms of the written agreement.

It will be observed that the terms of the clause in question are unambiguous, clear and easy of understanding. Where such is true, the primary rule that all antecedent negotiations are merged into the written agreement, as the final repository of the intentions and understandings of the parties, is controlling, and the contract may not be varied or explained by showing a contrary parol agreement. Schweickhardt v. Chessen, 329 Ill. 637; Robinson v. Yetter, 238 Ill. 320. We think the demurrer to these counts was properly sustained.

Count number ten sets out the written contract, including said clause, but does not aver a compliance therewith, that appellee either procured such a lease as was satisfactory to him, or that he wilfully and purposely refused to do so. We think such a condition precedent to appellants' right of recovery, and that same should have been so alleged.

The rule of law is that where a right of action depends upon the performance of an antecedent condition, the pleader must aver that such has been met, or a legal excuse for its nonfulfillment. Meyers v. Phillips, 72 Ill. 460; Mumaw v. Western & Southern Life Ins. Co., 97 Ohio St. 1,

119 N.E. 132; 13 Corpus Juris, p. 724, sec. 847. The count failed to allege this necessary element, hence was obnoxious to the demurrer.

In counts five and seven it was charged that the owner of the building tendered to appellee a lease, which was satisfactory to the latter, but that appellee, however, capriciously and to avoid the terms of the contract, and to evade his obligations thereunder, refused to accept such lease. It is the position of appellee that the averment is merely the statement of a conclusion, and that facts should be pleaded from which such inference might be drawn.

Whether a lease, satisfactory to appellee, was in fact tendered to him by the owner of the building, was an ultimate fact, the existence of which was essential to appellants' right of recovery. The rule appears to be that it is competent for the pleader to allege ultimate facts, notwithstanding that they to an extent represent conclusions. [Citations.]

The averent of such ultimate fact is necessarily a conclusion drawn from intermediate and evidential facts, and we are of opinion that appellants could not differently have charged the fact unless they had pleaded the evidential matters from which the deduction was made, which would have been repugnant to the fundamental rule that evidence should not be pleaded. Zimmerman v. Willard, 114 Ill. 364. We do not think the objection thus argued is tenable, and are of opinion that the demurrer to these counts should have been overruled.

The eleventh count charged that appellee, notwithstanding his contract obligation so to do, did not endeavor or attempt in any way to obtain from the owner of the building in which the laundry was then located a satisfactory lease therefor.

The enforcement of the contract was by its terms dependent upon "the procurement of a satisfactory lease between second party and owner of the building wherein business is now located." This clearly contemplated that there should be some effort on the part of appellee to procure from the landlord a lease which was satisfactory to him. If he could, without good reason, refrain from doing so, then the agreement, at his whim, could be rendered nugatory and the execution of the contract an idle and meaningless ceremony. We cannot ascribe to the parties, as evidenced by the language of the contract, such an intent; on the contrary, it is our conclusion that they purposed that appellee should, in good faith, attempt to secure from the landlord a lease which was satisfactory to him, and failing in the endeavor, should be excused from the performance of his contract.

The court charges that appellee did not attempt to secure such a lease, and if he, without good reason, did not, it amounted to a failure on his part to perform the obligations of the contract. We think the count is sufficient and that the court erred in sustaining the demurrer thereto.

The judgment is reversed and the cause is remanded, with directions to overrule the demurrer to the fifth, seventh and eleventh additional counts of the declaration.

Reversed and remanded with directions.

NOTE

Compare Paul v. Rosen, 3 Ill. App. 2d 423, 122 N.E.2d 603 (1954).

REINERT v. LAWSON
113 S.W.2d 293 (Tex. Civ. App. 1938)

Suit by Otto Reinert against W. P. Lawson for defendant's alleged breach of a contract to purchase a gin plant. Judgment of dismissal upon plaintiff's declining to amend after the court sustained defendant's general demurrer, and plaintiff appeals.

GALLAGHER, Chief Justice. Appellant, Otto Reinert, sued appellee, W. P. Lawson, for damages for the alleged breach of a contract by the terms of which appellant agreed to sell to appellee, and he agreed to purchase from appellant, a certain gin plant in the city of Hamilton. Appellant copied said contract in his petition. It contained a provision for the payment of a forfeit or liquidated damages by either party who refused to consummate the same. Appellant alleged that appellee declined to consummate said contract and that he had stopped payment on the check put up by him as a forfeit or liquidated damages.

The following stipulation was indorsed on said contract: "This contract is signed with the understanding that said W. P. Lawson and wife are not obligated hereunder in the event the deal between them and the Hamilton National Bank is not closed." The authenticity of said indorsement was not questioned. Appellant alleged that the deal between appellee and said bank referred to in said stipulation was a then existing agreement between appellee and said bank for the purchase by him of a certain farm from it; that the consideration had been agreed upon; that it had agreed to furnish a merchantable title to said farm; that it tendered to him a merchantable title thereto and asked him to pay the agreed consideration; that he refused to do so and thereby breached his contract with said bank.

Appellant pleaded special damages alleged to have been sustained by him on account of appellee's failure to comply with his contract to convey said gin plant to him, and asked for judgment therefor and also for judgment for said liquidated damages. The court sustained appellee's general demurrer to appellant's petition, and upon his declining to amend, dismissed the suit.

Appellant contends that his petition states a cause of action. Such contention is based on the theory that the stipulation indorsed on the contract as above recited was ineffective if appellee could have closed his deal with the bank and did not do so. The parties to a contract may agree that it shall not become effective or binding until or unless some specified condition is performed or occurs, in which case there is no binding contract until such condition has been complied with. 10 Tex. Jur. p. 52, §29, and authorities there cited. Such a stipulation is called a "condition precedent." 10 Tex. Jur. p. 343, §197, and authorities there cited. When a promise is subject to a condition precedent, there is no liability or obligation on the promisor and there can be no breach of the contract by him until and unless such condition or contingency is performed or occurs. 10 Tex. Jur. p. 396, §225, and authorities cited; Ferguson v. Mansfield, 114 Tex. 112, 263 S.W. 894, 900, par. 4; First Methodist Episcopal Church v. Soden, 131 Wash. 228, 229 P. 534, 536, par. 3. The stipulation under consideration, by its express terms, made the closing of appellee's deal with the bank a prerequisite to the existence of any obligation on the part of appellee to perform his contract with appellant. It, therefore, contains the essential elements of a condition precedent. The pending deal between appellee and the bank had no direct connection with the contract between the parties hereto. It was an uncertain thing, which might or might not occur. Making the closing thereof a condition precedent to liability on said contract did not imply any promise on the part of appellee or impose any duty on him to close such deal if he could. 5 Page on Contracts, p. 4516, §2576, and authorities cited; Supplement thereto, vol. 2, p. 1813, §2576, and authorities cited; 1 Restatement Law of Contracts, p. 366 et seq., §257.

The rule is otherwise with reference to covenants embraced in a contract sued upon. A covenant, as distinguished from a condition precedent, is an agreement of one of the parties to a contract to act or forbear to act in a certain specified way, and in a proper case, such agreement may be implied. If the party who has thus agreed to act or forebear to act breaks his covenant and the covenant is a part of an enforceable contract, legal liability arises upon such breach. 5 Page on Contracts, p. 4516 et seq., §§2576 and 2577; 12 Tex. Jur. p. 11, par. 7. The cases cited by appellant belong to this class.

Since the deal between appellee and the bank was never closed, the contract between appellant and appellee never became effective and was wholly insufficient to support an action for damages.

The judgment of the trial court is affirmed.

NOTE

Consult Restatement Second §225, Illus. 8.

BERNSTEIN v. W. B. MANUFACTURING CO.

238 Mass. 589, 131 N.E. 200 (1921)

Contract for breach of an alleged contract to purchase boys' wash suits from the plaintiffs doing business under the name and style, the Gotham Novelty Co. Writ dated March 15, 1919.

In the Superior Court the action was tried before Morton, J. The order relied on by the plaintiffs was as follows:

Date 7/3/18

The Gotham Novelty Co.,
37 West 26th Street, New York
Order given by the W. & B. Mfg. Co.,
of 65 Essex   Boston, Mass.
Ship by Fall River   Delivery about Jan. 15
Terms Net 60   Salesman Henry Sturz

All orders accepted to be delivered to the best of our ability, but will under no circumstances hold ourselves liable for failure to deliver any portion of orders taken, sometimes caused by circumstances over which we have no control.

This order is given and accepted subject to a limit of credit and determination at any time by us.

174 doz. Boys' wash suits   at $16.50 a dozen
5 sets of samples at once.

The case previously was before this court upon a contention by the defendant that the phrase in the contract "All orders accepted to be delivered to the best of our ability, but will under no circumstances hold ourselves liable for failure to deliver any portion of orders taken, sometimes caused by circumstances over which we have no control," destroyed the mutuality of the agreement and made it unenforceable. In a decision reported in 235 Mass. 425, this court held that that contention of the defendant could not be sustained.

Other material evidence is described in the opinion. At the close of the evidence the defendant moved that a verdict be ordered in its favor. The motion was denied. The jury found for the plaintiffs in the sum of $1,171.83; and the defendant alleged exceptions. . . .

PIERCE, J. This is an action to recover damages for the alleged breach of a contract, which the plaintiffs claim resulted from an order that the defendant admits it placed with the plaintiffs for the delivery of certain goods.

The order so given called for the sale and delivery of one hundred and seventy-four dozen boys' wash suits, and five sets of samples thereof at $16.50 a dozen. The admitted facts and evidence show that the plaintiffs delivered to the defendant on August 20, 1918, the five sets of samples called for by the order, and that it was paid therefor by the defendant in September, 1918. The evidence also shows that the plaintiffs on December 15, 1918, shipped to the defendant seventy-two dozen wash suits; that they delivered in the shipping room of the defendant; that the defendant "opened them up" and immediately notified the plaintiffs that it would not accept the goods. A memorandum of the order was made by the representative of the plaintiffs on a printed order blank of the plaintiffs. It was not signed by the defendant, and it contained the following printed clause: "This order is given and accepted subject to a limit of credit and determination at any time by us." At the close of the evidence the defendant excepted to the refusal of the judge to direct a verdict for the defendant.

Because of the clause above quoted the defendant contends that the agreement was invalid in its inception for want of mutuality of obligation; and rests its defence upon the accepted legal maxim that in a bilateral agreement both of the mutual promises must be binding or neither will be, for if one of the promises is for any reason invalid the other has no consideration and so they both fall. Bernstein v. W. B. Manuf. Co. 235 Mass. 425, 427. The plaintiffs admit the legal force of the rule invoked by the defendant, and reply thereto that the clause does not have the effect of reserving to the plaintiffs the right to determine the contract (which otherwise resulted from the placing and acceptance of the order) but is obviously only referable to a determination of "the limit of credit." Giving to the clause a fair construction, we think the right of "determination" was intended to embrace the "order" as well as "the limit of credit."

The plaintiffs next contend that the delivery and acceptance of five sample suits were such partial performance by the plaintiffs as afforded a sufficient consideration for the defendant's promises, even though there was no obligation to support the contract at its inception. We do not think the agreement, which was void in its inception for want of mutuality, became an agreement which was supported by a sufficient consideration upon the delivery and acceptance of part of the goods called for in the order of the defendant, because the plaintiffs were not thereby precluded from exercising their reserved option. They were not bound to fill the balance of the order unless they chose to do so, and the defendant gained thereby no additional contractual right against the plaintiffs. Richardson v. Hardwick, 106 U.S. 252, 255. Bernstein v. W. B. Manuf. Co., *supra*, and cases cited.

It becomes unnecessary to consider the defence of the statute of frauds. It results that the motion to direct a verdict for the defendant should have been granted, that the exceptions must be sustained, and that judgment be now entered for the defendant. G.L. c. 231, §122.

So ordered.

NOTE

Under the Uniform Sales Act which controlled the transaction, an unpaid seller in possession of the goods was entitled to convert a credit into a cash sale if the buyer became insolvent (§§54, 1(c)). But the seller in order to enjoy this protection had to establish that the buyer had "ceased to pay his debts in the ordinary course of business or cannot pay his debts as they mature" (§76(3)). This scheme of statutory protection frequently turned out to be inadequate. A seller, for instance, who had reason to doubt the financial stability of his buyer did run a considerable risk because it might turn out that the buyer was not insolvent in the technical sense. Understandably, therefore, sellers have tried to better their position with the help of contractual provisions. Clauses have appeared which entitle the seller to demand cash whenever he has reason to believe the buyer to be insolvent. Other clauses go further and do not even qualify the power of the seller to demand cash. For a discussion of the Worth Street Rules which govern the grey goods trade see L. Fuller & M. Eisenberg, Basic Contract Law 192-193, 770-771 (1972).

Given this background, the clause in the principal case, however poorly phrased, might well have been given the interpretation advanced by the seller (1 Corbin §146 n.49 (1963)). The court's lack of daring is all the more interesting since, on the previous appeal in the same case, it had no difficulty saving the contract by denying that the exculpation clause gave the seller an unrestricted power to cancel delivery (235 Mass. 425, 126 N.E. 796 (1920)).

For the protection of the seller under the U.C.C., consult §§2-702, 1-201(23), 1-208, 2-609. Is the clause involved in the *Bernstein* case still needed?

GURFEIN v. WERBELOVSKY
97 Conn. 703, 118 A. 32 (1922)

Action to recover damages for breach of a written agreement to sell to the plaintiff a lot of glass, brought to the Superior Court in Fairfield County where a demurrer to the complaint was sustained (Maltbie, J.) and judgment was afterward rendered for the defendant (Haines, J.), from which the plaintiff appealed. Error and cause remanded.

The complaint alleges that on October 20th, 1919, the defendant made a contract with the plaintiff, doing business under the name of the Bridgeport Glass Company, in the form following. —

October 29, 1919.

Bridgeport Glass Co.,
          Bdgpt. Conn.

Gentlemen: We have this day accepted and entered your order for 5 cases
of plate glass, the following:

	1 case	60″	wide
Widths	1 ″	70″	″
	2 ″	80″	″
	1 ″	90″	″

in the following brackets 25 to 50 square feet at .98 cents per sq. ft. and
50/100 at One dollar per sq. ft. F.O.B. N.Y. City.
     The above cases are to be shipped within 3 months from date. You have
the option to cancel the above order before shipment.

> Yours truly,
> J. H. WERBELOVSKY'S SON,
> By Joseph Rosenblum.

The complaint further avers that the plaintiff frequently demanded
delivery of the goods, but the defendant refused to ship the same though
more than three months has elapsed; and damages based on an increase
in the market price over the contract price are demanded.
     Defendant demurred to the complaint on the following grounds: "1.
Because it appears from said instrument, Exhibit A, that the same was of
the nature of an option, and that said option was without consideration
and was, therefore, void and of no effect. 2. Because it appears from said
instrument Exhibit A that the same was of the nature of an option, but it
does not appear that the same was ever properly exercised. 3. Because it
appears that said instrument by reason of the uncertainty of the terms
and the lack of mutuality in the obligations it purports to create, is unenforceable as a contract, and is wholly invalid, void and of no effect." . . .
     BEACH, J. The writing sued on is in the form of a letter from the
defendant to the plaintiff accepting an antecedent proposal to buy five
cases of glass on terms set forth in the acceptance. The final sentence of
the letter is as follows: "You have the option to cancel the above order
before shipment." It is this phrase which gives rise to the claim that the
contract is void for want of mutuality. The defendant's acceptance appears to be unconditional, and the objection is that the plaintiff in making
his proposal reserved the right to cancel it at will. If that is so, the demurrer must be sustained. "To agree to do something and reserve the right to
cancel the agreement at will is no agreement at all." Ellis v. Dodge Bros.,
237 Fed. Rep. 860, 867.
     It might be said at the outset that the objection begs the entire ques-
tion, for it is not clear that the "above order" as originally made contains

any reservation at all, but as the case has been briefed and argued on the assumption that the buyer's privilege of cancellation at any time before shipment is one of the terms of the contract, we proceed to treat it as such and to enquire whether on that understanding an enforcible contract ever came into existence; that is, whether the seller ever had any right, the exercise of which the buyer could not prevent or nullify, to compel the buyer to take the goods and pay for them. If so, there was a promise for a promise, and the contract is valid in law; for the question before us is not whether the contract is mutual in the sense in which that adjective is used to influence the discretion of a court of equity in decreeing specific performance, but whether the seller's promise to sell was with or without a consideration sufficient in law to support it. Of course, the right to enforce the buyer's promise to buy is such a consideration, and if that right existed, even for the shortest space of time, it is enough to bring the contract into existence.

On the face of this contract the buyer must exercise his option "before shipment," otherwise he is bound to take and pay for the goods. No time of shipment is specified otherwise than the words "to be shipped within three months." Hence the seller had a right to ship at any time within the three months, and shipment made before receiving notice of cancellation would put an end to the buyer's option. The seller's right of shipment accrued at the moment the contract was formed, and as he might have shipped at the same time that he accepted, there was one clear opportunity to enforce the entire contract, which the buyer could not have prevented or nullified by any attempted exercise of his option. This is all that is necessary to constitute a legal consideration and to bring the contract into existence. If the defendant voluntarily limited his absolute opportunity of enforcing the contract to the shortest possible time, the contract may have been improvident, but it was not void for want of consideration.

Whether it is so improvident that an equitable defense on that ground ought to prevail, is a question of fact which cannot be raised by demurrer. It should, however, be said that, in addition to the one clear opportunity to enforce the contract already pointed out, the defendant has had a continuing right to enforce it during its entire term; for it appears from the complaint not only that the plaintiff never attempted to exercise his option, but that he repeatedly demanded performance. In this connection it is important that the contract is framed on the theory that it remains enforcible by either party unless and until the plaintiff brings home notice of cancellation before shipment.

Referring to the authorities cited, it is of course undoubted that a contract for the sale of goods in which one party retains an unconditional option of cancellation is no contract at all, for the reason that no mutual obligation ever arises. Rehm-Zeiher Co. v. Walker Co., 156 Ky. 6, 160 S.W. 777, cited on the defendant's brief, and American Agricultural

Chemical Co. v. Kennedy, 103 Va. 171, 48 S.E. 868, cited in the note to 13 Corpus Juris, 337, are cases of this kind.

In Nicolls v. Wetmore, 174 Iowa, 132, 156 N.W. 319; Velie Motor Co. v. Kopmeier Motor Car Co., 194 Fed. Rep. 324, and Ellis v. Dodge Bros., 237 Fed. Rep. 860, the contracts in suit presented a double aspect. Regarded as contracts for the purchase and sale of motorcars, they were held void for the want of any promise by the maker to sell, and regarded as executory contracts of agency, they were held to be terminable at the option of either party. This was correct, because the agency was not expressed to continue for a definite time or for the accomplishment of a stated purpose. Willcox & Gibbs Sewing Machine Co. v. Ewing, 141 U.S. 627, 12 Sup. Ct. 94.

There is error, the judgment is set aside and the cause remanded for further proceedings according to law.

In this opinion the other judges concurred.

NOTE

For the principal and the preceding cases, consult Restatement Second §77; Patterson, Illusory Promises and Promisor's Options, 6 Iowa L. Bull. 179, 209 (1921); 1 Corbin §§162, 163 (1963); Corbin, The Effect of Options on Consideration, 34 Yale L.J. 571 (1925).

Section 13. The Gratuitous Noncommercial Promise

Common and civil law are agreed that gifts, i.e., transactions with the intention of gratuitously enriching another, present special problems. "We live in a world in which self interest is the measure of our actions."[145] "It is not from the benevolence of the butcher, the brewer or the baker," to quote Adam Smith, "that we expect our dinner, but from their regard to their own interest. We address ourselves not to their humanity but to their self-love, and never talk to them of our necessities but of their advantages." Wealth of Nations 24 (Modern Library ed. 1937).

In such a system a high value is assigned to exchange transactions. Society must protect these transactions to safeguard the existing division of labor. Ballantine, Mutuality and Consideration, 28 Harv. L. Rev. 121,

145. 3 G. Ripert & J. Boulanger, Traité Elementaire de Droit Civil de Planiol 1021-1022 (3d ed. 1951), translated in A. T. Von Mehren & J. Gordley, The Civil Law System 791-792 (1977).

134 (1914). Gifts fall into another human sphere, the realm of altruistic activities, and have sometimes been called "sterile" transactions on the grounds that they do not tend to promote an increase in public wealth.[146] But it has been pointed out in reply that a gift must make the donor happier (or else he would refrain from making it) and therefore necessarily increase the total happiness or utility of the parties, just as an exchange transaction does.[147] In addition, "gifts have a wealth-redistribution effect, and taken as a class probably redistribute wealth to persons who have more utility for money than the donors. . . ."[148]

An exhaustive list of reasons for the traditional reluctance to enforce gift promises is not possible. A few examples may suffice. Such promises are often made impulsively and with little reflection. The ingratitude of the donee may later cause the donor to regret his promise, as may a change in the donor's circumstances. There is also a risk that the donor was the victim of fraud or undue influence. The administrative cost of determining the existence of an informal gift promise may be great, and the possibilities of error substantial. It has also been pointed out that extrajudicial sanctions, as well as the solicitude of the donor for the donee's interests, diminish the likelihood that the gift promise will be broken for no reason, thus making judicial intervention less necessary.[149] Finally, it has been argued that legal enforcement either would decrease the quantity of donative promises, or would have little effect on the accuracy and reliability of such promises. In the former instance, the donee would, it is argued, prefer to bear the risk that the donor might break his promise. In the latter instance, legal intervention would be unlikely to discourage rash promises that induce injurious reliance since social factors frequently work against the promisor's placing too many restrictions on his promise in the first place.[150]

It is not surprising that everywhere gifts have been singled out for special treatment. Freedom of contract has often been restricted. Some legal systems limit the amount of property that can be given away; others have introduced formalities to safeguard deliberation and to avoid evidentiary problems. In this connection a distinction is often made between executed and executory transactions. Frequently, the duties owed by the donor to the donee are limited when compared to the duties imposed on parties to an exchange. The adage "you must not look a gift horse in the mouth" has in varying degrees appealed to many legal systems. In a sale, for instance, the buyer is protected under our law if the goods sold turn out to be defective, irrespective of his fault. The liability to a donee by

146. C. Bufnoir, Propriété et Contrat 487 (2d ed. 1924), translated in Eisenberg, Donative Promises, 47 U. Chi. L. Rev. 1, 4 (1979).
147. Posner, Gratuitous Promises in Economics and Law, 6 J. Legal Stud. 411 (1977).
148. Eisenberg, *supra* note 146, at 4.
149. Eisenberg, *supra* note 146, at 2-7.
150. Goetz & Scott, Enforcing Promises: An Examination of the Basis of Contract, 89 Yale L.J. 1261, 1304-1305 (1980).

contrast is more limited. He has to resort to tort (negligence) law for protection. Marsh, The Liability of the Gratuitous Transferor: A Comparative Study, 66 L.Q. Rev. 39 (1950). In the civil law, the donor is generally permitted to reclaim the donation or to defeat a gift promise if he has become impoverished without his fault, and he can revoke the donation for reasons of gross ingratitude on the part of the donee.

By distinguishing between executed gifts and gift promises, the common law has attempted to protect the interests of the maker of a gift promise with the help of the consideration doctrine. One of the doctrine's functions is to make gift promises unenforceable or, more accurately, to safeguard deliberation by channeling such promises into formalities that are meant to impress the maker with the seriousness of the transaction.

One final point is worth noting. Because of the consideration doctrine, the common law historically has had a wider conception of gift promises than that of the civil law: in the common law view, all promises not supported by consideration are treated as gift promises.[151] A firm offer made without consideration, for instance, is a gratuitous promise. This section deals only with gift promises in the narrow sense, i.e., promises made with the intention of conferring a gift. Promises made in a commercial context, but unsupported by consideration, have already been treated in Section 7.

On §90 of the Restatements, see Shattuck, Gratuitous Promises — A New Writ?, 35 Mich. L. Rev. 903 (1937); Boyer, Promissory Estoppel: Requirements and Limitations of the Doctrine, 98 U. Pa. L. Rev. 459 (1950); Boyer, Promissory Estoppel: Principle from Precedents, 50 Mich. L. Rev. 639, 678 (1952); Henderson, Promissory Estoppel and Traditional Contract Doctrine, 78 Yale L.J. 343 (1969); Eisenberg, Donative Promises, 47 U. Chi. L. Rev. 1 (1979); Goetz & Scott, Enforcing Promises: An Examination of the Basis of Contract, 89 Yale L.J. 1261, 1305 et seq. (1980).

1 WILLISTON ON CONTRACTS §112, p. 445 (3d ed. 1957): "If a benevolent man says to a tramp: 'If you go around the corner to the clothing shop there, you may purchase an overcoat on my credit,' no reasonable person would understand that the short walk was requested as the consideration for the promise, but that in the event of the tramp going to the shop the promisor would make him a gift. Yet the walk to the shop is in its nature capable of being consideration. It is a legal detriment to the tramp to make the walk, and the only reason why the walk is not consideration is because on a reasonable construction it must be held that the walk was not requested as the price of the promise, but was merely a condition of a

---

151. This approach is discussed and criticized in connection with promises for benefits received in Henderson, Promises Grounded in the Past: The Idea of Unjust Enrichment and the Law of Contracts, 57 Va. L. Rev. 1115, 1156 et seq. (1971).

gratuitous promise. It is often difficult to determine whether words of condition in a promise indicate a request for consideration or state a mere condition in a gratuitous promise. An aid, though not a conclusive test, in determining which construction of the promise is more reasonable is an inquiry whether the happening of the condition will be a benefit to the promisor. If so, it is a fair inference that the happening was requested as a consideration. On the other hand, if, as in the case of the tramp stated above, the happening of the condition will be not only of no benefit to the promisor but is obviously merely for the purpose of enabling the promisee to receive a gift, the happening of the event on which the promise is conditional, though brought about by the promisee in reliance on the promise, will not properly be construed as consideration. In case of doubt where the promisee has incurred a detriment on the faith of the promise, courts will naturally be loath to regard the promise as a mere gratuity and the detriment incurred as merely a condition. But in some cases it is so clear that a conditional gift was intended that even though the promisee has incurred detriment, the promise has been held unenforceable."

NOTE

For an early expression of similar sentiments, see Erwin & Williams v. Erwin, 25 Ala. 236 (1854).

What is the exact fact situation Williston has in mind? Could the benefactor revoke after the overcoat has been handed over to the tramp? Suppose the tramp had to walk two miles to get to the store, same result? Under §90? Consult the example of the trip to York used in Great Northern Ry. v. Witham, *supra* p. 420; 1A Corbin §200 (1963).

KIRKSEY v. KIRKSEY
8 Ala. 131 (1845)

Assumpsit by the defendant, against the plaintiff in error. The question is presented in this court, upon a case agreed, which shows the following facts:

The plaintiff was the wife of defendant's brother, but had for some time been a widow, and had several children. In 1840, the plaintiff resided on public land, under a contract of lease, she had held over, and was comfortably settled, and would have attempted to secure the land she lived on. The defendant resided in Talladega county, some sixty or seventy miles off. On the 10th October, 1840, he wrote to her the following letter:

> Dear sister Antillico — Much to my mortification, I heard, that brother Henry was dead, and one of his children. I know that your situation is one

of grief and difficulty. You had a bad chance before, but a great deal worse now. I should like to come and see you, but cannot with convenience at present. . . . I do not know whether you have a preference on the place you live on or not. If you had, I would advise you to obtain your preference, and sell the land and quit the country, as I understand it is very unhealthy, and I know society is very bad. If you will come down and see me, I will let you have a place to raise your family, and I have more open land than I can tend; and on account of your situation, and that of your family, I feel like I want you and the children to do well.

Within a month or two after the receipt of this letter, the plaintiff abandoned her possession, without disposing of it, and removed with her family, to the residence of the defendant, who put her in comfortable houses and gave her land to cultivate for two years, at the end of which time he notified her to remove, and put her in a house not comfortable, in the woods, which he afterwards required her to leave.

A verdict being found for the plaintiff, for two hundred dollars, the above facts were agreed, and if they will sustain the action, the judgment is to be affirmed, otherwise it is to be reversed.

ORMOND, J. The inclination of my mind, is, that the loss and inconvenience which the plaintiff sustained in breaking up and moving to the defendant's, a distance of sixty miles, is a sufficient consideration to support the promise, to furnish her with a house, and land to cultivate, until she could raise her family. My brothers, however, think that the promise on the part of the defendant was a mere gratuity, and that an action will not lie for its breach.

The judgment of the Court below must therefore be reversed, pursuant to the agreement of the parties.

NOTE

Consult 1A Corbin §§203, 205 (1963); Richards v. Richards, 46 Pa. 78, 82 (1863):

Assurances of assistance accompanying kind advice are never intended as contracts. And conformance to advice is never intended to stand as a legal consideration for the kind assurances that accompany the advice, though it is a motive for their fulfillment. It would be exceedingly hurtful to the freedom of social intercourse to create even a suspicion in the public mind, that those kind offers of advice and assistance, which take place among friends and kindred, could be converted into contracts which the law would enforce.

"It would cut up the doctrine of consideration by the roots if a promisee could make a gratuitous promise binding by subsequently acting in reliance on it." Holmes, J. in Commonwealth v. Scituate Savings Bank, 137 Mass. 301, 302 (1883).

How is the line to be drawn between an unenforceable conditional gift promise and an offer for an exchange? Recall Williston's discussion at p. 472 *supra*. In the principal case, was not the action of the promisee desired and intentionally induced by the promisor? Would the defendant be liable today? Consult the Restatement Second §90.

If the defendant were held liable under §90, what would be the measure of plaintiff's damages? Eisenberg makes the following observations on this point:

> Antillico's financial costs were probably very small. Her nonfinancial costs, however, were probably substantial, consisting not only of the emotional and physical travail of the journey to Kirksey's farm, but also the loss of an opportunity to remain in a settled existence rather than twice resettling. It would be hard not to let her recover for those costs, yet it would be very difficult to measure those costs directly in an objective manner. One solution would be to throw the issue to the factfinder for intuitive measurement, as in personal injury cases. In those cases, however, the transaction typically is not consensual, and, partly for that reason, no objective financial measure is at hand. In contrast, where a donative promise has been relied upon, it is the promise that causes the resulting cost, and the promise can frequently provide an objective financial measure of that cost. For example, in Kirksey v. Kirksey, we know that the promise was sufficient to induce Antillico to relocate; we do not know if a lesser promise would have been sufficient. Rather than attempting to measure Antillico's costs intuitively, it seems preferable to measure them objectively, although indirectly, by using her financial expectation (the rental value of a place on Kirksey's farm) as a surrogate measure of her costs.

Eisenberg, Donative Promises, 47 U. Chi. L. Rev. 1, 28 (1979).

Would Antillico have moved if her expected financial gain did not exceed the anticipated cost of the move? Is it just to award damages based on expected gain, assuming such gain normally exceeds anticipated cost?

FORWARD v. ARMSTEAD, 12 Ala. 124 (1847): The plaintiff's father promised him a plantation in order to induce plaintiff to move with his family from North Carolina to Alabama. Plaintiff did move, and made improvements on the Alabama land. The father died without deeding the land to plaintiff, and plaintiff sued the father's executors in equity to have title placed in his name. The court, following *Kirksey*, held for the executors, and made the following observations, which are strikingly reminiscent of the bargain theory of consideration.

"It will be seen that the promise by the father to give his son the plantation and slaves, is stated in the bill as a contract, of which the consideration is asserted to be the breaking up in North Carolina, and the expense and trouble of removing to Alabama. The proof, if it can be said to sustain the allegations of the bill even as to the form of a contract, has not the slightest effect in proving the substance of one. It is entirely evident that there was no subject or thing to be contracted for. The son was not bargaining for the plantation and slaves, nor was the father contracting for the son's removal. In other words, the slaves and plantation were not to be paid as the consideration for the removal, nor was the removal the cause which induced the promise to make the gift. . . .

"It seems to us that the expense incurred in a removal under such inducements, does not furnish the test whether the engagement is to be considered a contract, instead of a gratuity, because expense, or at least trouble, which is equivalent to it, must always be incurred; but as we have before indicated, the test is, whether the thing is to be paid in consideration of the removal, instead of being given from motives of benevolence, kindness, or natural affection."

NOTE

The court in *Forward* also apparently denied recovery for the value of improvements made by the plaintiff. "[I]t was his own folly to improve lands which he knew in point of law to belong to another, and when the uncertainty with regard to the title, could be determined at once by asking for a conveyance." 12 Ala. at 128. Compare Evans v. Pattle, 19 Ala. 398 (1851), and the following two cases.

Does *Forward* substantiate Holmes' claim regarding the historical validity of the bargain theory? Compare Crosbie v. M'Doual, 13 Ves. Jun. 149, 33 E.R. 241 (1806), an equity case in which the Chancellor, Lord Erskine, held that by entering into a contract to purchase a house on the strength of the donor's promise to make the payments, the donee had given "consideration in the law" sufficient to support the donor's promise. See R. Pound, Consideration in Equity, Wigmore Celebration Essays (1919).

SEAVEY v. DRAKE
62 N.H. 393 (1882)

Bill in Equity, for specific performance of a parol agreement of land. At the hearing the plaintiff offered to prove that he was the only child of Shadrach Seavey, the defendants' testate, who died in 1880. In January, 1860, the testator, owning a tract of land, and wishing to assist the plaintiff, went upon the land with him and gave him a portion of it, which the plaintiff then accepted and took possession of. The plaintiff had a note against his father upon which there was due about $200, which he then or subsequently gave up to him. Subsequently his father gave him an additional strip of land adjoining the other tract. Ever since the gifts, the plaintiff has occupied and still occupies the land, and has paid all taxes upon it. He has expended $3,000 in the erection of a dwelling-house, barn, and stable, and in other improvements upon the premises. Some of the lumber for the house was given him by his father, who helped him do some of the labor upon the house.

The defendants moved to dismiss the bill because no cause for equitable relief was stated, and because the parol contract, which is sought to be enforced, was without consideration, and is executory. The bill alleges a gift of the land to the plaintiff and a promise to give him a deed for it. The defendants also demurred, and answered denying the material allegations of the bill.

If the bill can be sustained on proof of these facts, or if not on these facts, but would be with the additional proof of a consideration for the promise, there is to be a further hearing, the plaintiff having leave to amend his bill. If on proof of these facts, with or without proof of consideration, the bill cannot be sustained, it is to be dismissed.

SMITH, J. The bill alleges a promise by the defendants' testator to give the plaintiff a deed. The plaintiff offered to prove that the deceased gave him the land, and that he thereupon entered into possession and made valuable improvements. We assume that the plaintiff in his offer meant that he was induced by the gift of the land to enter into possession and make large expenditures in permanent improvements upon it. The evidence offered is admissible. Specific performance of a parol contract to convey land is decreed in favor of the vendee who has performed his part of the contract, when a failure or refusal to convey would operate as a fraud upon him. [Citations.] The statute of frauds (G.L., c. 220, s. 14) provides that "No action shall be maintained upon a contract for the sale of land, unless the agreement upon which it is brought, or some memorandum thereof, is in writing, and signed by the party to be charged, or by some person by him thereto authorized in writing." Equity, however, lends its aid, when there has been part performance, to remove the bar of the statute, upon the ground that it is a fraud for the vendor to insist upon the absence of a written instrument, when he has permitted the contract to be partly executed.

It is not material in this case to know whether the promissory note given up by the plaintiff was or was not intended as payment or part payment for the land, for equity protects a parol gift of land equally with a parol agreement to sell it, if accompanied by possession, and the donee has made valuable improvements upon the property induced by the promise to give it. [Citations.] There is no important distinction in this respect between a promise to give and a promise to sell. The expenditure in money or labor in the improvement of the land induced by the donor's promise to give the land to the party making the expenditure, constitutes, in equity, a consideration for the promise, and the promise will be enforced. Crosbie v. M'Doual, 13 Ves. 148; Freeman v. Freeman, 43 N.Y. 34, 39; 3 Par. Cont. 359.

Case discharged.

Allen and Clark, JJ., did not sit: the others concurred.

NOTE

3 Parsons, The Law of Contracts 359 (9th ed. 1904); Pound, Consideration in Equity, 13 Ill. L. Rev. 667, 671 (1919); J. Dawson & W. Harvey, Contracts and Contract Remedies 605-608 (1959).

Suppose specific performance is denied because plaintiff failed to establish an oral gift promise by clear and unequivocable proof. Is he entitled to compensation for the value of the improvements? Consult Kaufman v. Miller, 214 Ill. App. 213 (1919). For the applicability of the part performance doctrine in actions at law for damages, see Goodwin v. Gillingham, 10 Wash. 2d 656, 117 P.2d 959 (1941).

ROBERTS-HORSFIELD v. GEDICKS
94 N.J. Eq. 82, 118 A. 275 (Ch. 1922)

BACKES, V.C. The object of this suit is to enforce a gift of land. The facts are these: When Mrs. Horsfield was a little girl of nine, at the death of her mother, she went to live with her aunt and uncle, who raised and educated her, and after she married she and her husband lived with them until 1912. The aunt was the wife of the defendant Albert C. Gedicks, and is now deceased. Prior to 1909 the two couples lived together in Brooklyn. In that year they moved to the outskirts of Plainfield, where Mr. and Mrs. Gedicks bought a tract of land, title to which they held by the entirety, and erected a home purposely large enough to accommodate the two families. By this time the Horsfield family had additions. The separation in 1912 was because either the Horsfield children annoyed Mrs. Gedicks, who was then ill, as Mr. Gedicks says, or, as Mr. and Mrs. Horsfield assert, Mr. Gedicks' conduct sometimes created an atmosphere in which they did not care to rear their children. The cause is unimportant. They were thereafter on friendly and intimate terms until the aunt died in 1916, and with Mr. Gedicks until he married his present wife, the other defendant. When the Gedickses learned that the Horsfields were looking about for a house they remonstrated, saying, in substance, to use the language of Mrs. Horsfield:

Why we wouldn't think of having you move away from us. We have all this land here. We will give you that corner there for yourself, and aunty

said she would help build a house for me — contribute towards it; because
she had her own money from the sale of this property that she had sold in
Brooklyn.

The house was built on a piece of the tract, the boundaries of which
were well defined, the aunt furnishing the money, $1,800, and when it
was finished the Horsfields moved in and remained in undisturbed possession until recently, when the present Mrs. Gedicks, to whom the land
had been conveyed by her husband, began an action of ejectment.
Thereupon this bill was filed to restrain the suit and to compel a conveyance of the land which had been promised. The Horsfields had contributed some little towards the original construction of the house, and later
on made improvements at an outlay of five to six hundred dollars. I have
not the least doubt that Mr. and Mrs. Gedicks intended to and promised
to give the house and lot to Mrs. Horsfield — to convey it. Even the
defendant Gedicks' testimony indicates that that had been his attitude. A
feeble effort was made to establish a contract, the alleged consideration
being propinquity, and, in consequence, the comfort of the society of the
Horsfields by the continued intimacy with them and the pleasures derived
from close touch with their children. These things were undoubtedly the
inducements for the gift, but they fall far short of a legal consideration to
sustain a contract. The transaction was a gift pure and simple, and, under
the circumstances above shown, is enforceable in equity. A parol gift of
land is invalid, but when the gift is accompanied by possession, and the
donee has been induced by the promise of the gift to make valuable
improvements of a permanent nature, equity will enforce it. The principle is well settled; the doctrine is stated in 20 Cyc. 1200, and 12 Rul. C.L.
938, where many of the cases supporting it are cited. Proof of a parol gift
of land must be clear and unequivocal. Bevington v. Bevington, 9 L.R.A.
(N.S.), where the meaning of this rule is explained and the cases are
collected. The instant case comes within the doctrine. The Horsfields, at
their own expense, made some improvements, as already indicated, and
if this were the extent of Mrs. Horsfield's claim, she could be relieved by
compensation. But I think her equities go further, and to support them
she is entitled to the benefit of the aunt's expenditures. Combined they
represent the improvement, which is both substantial and permanent.
The money laid out by the aunt in the original construction was in fact a
gift to her niece. She intended it to be so, and it was none the less a gift
that she paid it directly to the contractor instead of handing it first to Mrs.
Horsfield and by her paid over. The entire improvement must be regarded as having been made by Mrs. Horsfield. Mr. Gedicks knew of his
wife's donative purpose in furnishing the money and he realized that the
improvement was not made other than in reliance upon the gift, and he
ought not to be permitted to profit by the mere accident of his survivor-
ship. Mrs. Gedicks II is not an innocent purchaser for value and is

chargeable with notice of the complainants' right. She, perhaps, did not know all the circumstances attending the gift, but the open and notorious possession by the complainants put her on notice and reasonable inquiry would have disclosed the truth.

I will advise a decree ordering a conveyance of the land by the description established at the trial, and suggest that the bill be amended describing the land to a certainty, and a prayer to conform to the decree.

NOTE

Affirmed, 96 N.J. Eq. 384, 124 A. 925 (Ct. Err. & App. 1924). How would the case be decided under §90 of the Restatement Second?

DEVECMON v. SHAW
69 Md. 199, 14 A. 464 (1888)

BRYAN, J. John Semmes Devecmon brought suit against the executors of John S. Combs, deceased. He declared on the common counts, and also filed a bill of particulars. After judgment by default, a jury was sworn to assess the damages sustained by the plaintiff. The evidence consisted of certain accounts taken from the books of the deceased, and testimony that the plaintiff was a nephew of the deceased, and lived for several years in his family, and was in his service as clerk for several years. The plaintiff then made an offer of testimony which is thus stated in the bill of exceptions:

> That the plaintiff took a trip to Europe in 1878, and that said trip was taken by said plaintiff, and the money spent on said trip was spent by the said plaintiff, at the instance and request of said Combs, and upon a promise from him that he would reimburse and repay to the plaintiff all money expended by him in said trip; and that the trip was so taken, and the money so expended, by the said plaintiff, but that the said trip had no connection with the business of said Combs; and that said Combs spoke to the witness of his conduct, in being thus willing to pay his nephew's expenses, as liberal and generous on his part.

On objection the court refused to permit the evidence to be given, and the plaintiff excepted.

It might very well be, and probably was the case, that the plaintiff would not have taken a trip to Europe at his own expense. But, whether this be so or not, the testimony would have tended to show that the plaintiff incurred expense at the instance and request of the deceased, and upon an express promise by him that he would repay the money spent. It was a burden incurred at the request of the other party, and was certainly a sufficient consideration for a promise to pay. Great injury might be done by inducing persons to make expenditures beyond their means, on express promise of repayment, if the law were otherwise. It is an entirely different case from a promise to make another a present, or render him a gratuitous service. It is nothing to the purpose that the plaintiff was benefited by the expenditure of his own money. He was induced by this promise to spend it in this way, instead of some other mode. If it is not fulfilled, the expenditure will have been procured by a false pretense.

As the plaintiff, on the theory of this evidence, had fulfilled his part of the contract, and nothing remained to be done but the payment of the money by the defendant, there could be a recovery in indebitatus assumpsit, and it was not necessary to declare on the special contract. The fifth count in the declaration is for "money paid by the plaintiff for the defendants' testator in his life-time, at his request." In the bill of particulars we find this item:

> To cash contributed by me, J. Semmes Devecmon, out of my own money, to defray my expenses to Europe and return, the said John S. Combs, now deceased, having promised me in 1878 "that, if I would contribute part of my own money towards the trip, he would give me a part of his, and would make up to me my part," and the amount below named is my contribution, as follows. . . .

It seems to us that this statement is a sufficient description of a cause of action covered by the general terms of the fifth count. The evidence ought to have been admitted. . . .

Judgment reversed, and new trial ordered.

NOTE

Was a trip to Europe bargained for and given in exchange for the promise of the uncle, or did the uncle make a gratuitous conditional promise? Or, finally, did the trip to Europe amount to an act of foreseeable substantial reliance?

Suppose the uncle promises to pay plaintiff $3,000 for a two-week European trip. After plaintiff has been in Europe for two days, his uncle calls him and says that he is going to reimburse him only for what the plaintiff has already spent. Plaintiff returns immediately, having spent only $1,000. How much should plaintiff recover? Suppose plaintiff gets only one two-week vacation a year and had his uncle not made the promise, would have gone camping with friends. What recovery? See Eisenberg, Donative Promises, 47 U. Chi. L. Rev. 1, 27, 29 (1979).

Llewellyn, Our Case-Law of Contract: Offer and Acceptance (pt. 2), 48 Yale L.J. 779, 785-786 (1939):

> . . . Whatever facts provide in the way of suggestion of norm should thus flow in all cases from the business cases. Or so one might lightly think. So to think would however be to overlook, at least for the family cases, the fact that judges have an experience with family matters which is earlier and more intimate than any understanding of business. And the business cases prove not to be wholly adequate guides to the family cases.[152] A fortiori the family cases are not adequate guides to the business cases.[153] Until the two have been studied, each group by itself, synthesis must wait. What is already indicated is that it is not safe to reason about business cases from cases in which an uncle became interested in having his nephew see Europe, go to Yale, abstain from nicotine, or christen his infant heir 'Alvardus Torrington III.' And it may even be urged that safe conclusions as to business cases of the more ordinary variety cannot be derived from what courts or scholars rule about the idiosyncratic desires of one A to see one B climb a fifty-foot greased flagpole or push a peanut across the Brooklyn Bridge. This paper will not even reason from such cases as that of a book collector who is favored as a Christmas present with all but one of the volumes for which he has offered a peculiar price. It is not suggested that a court in solving such problems might not be seeking to apply a principle applicable equally in business cases; nor is it suggested that the solution reached for such problems by a court might not have repercussions in business cases. The position taken is this: The influence of the facts relative to the influence of the normally applicable rule increases roughly with the square of the peculiarity of the facts. Therefore the decision of a case really peculiar on its facts is never a safe guide to the decision of normal cases *which have not yet been* decided under its rule. *But* if a peculiar case is decided in true accordance with a rule *in use* in normal cases, that is excellent indication of the living power of that normal rule; it has overcome even tough and troublesome facts."[154]

---

152. Compare Havighurst, Services in the Home — A Study of Contract Concepts in Domestic Relations, 41 Yale L.J. 386 (1932); Shattuck, Gratuitous Promises — A New Writ? 35 Mich. L. Rev. 908 (1937). The law of voidable preferences would no less reward study from this angle.

153. Would a careful counsellor advise a business client in a business transaction to rely on De Cicco v. Schweizer, 221 N.Y. 431, 117 N.E. 807 (1917), or Thomas v. Thomas, 2 Q.B. 851 (1842), or Devecmon v. Shaw, 69 Md. 199, 14 Atl. 464 (1888), or Orr v. Orr, 181 Ill. App. 148 (1913)? Of course there are business cases which no careful counsellor would rely on, and those mentioned ought not to be relied on in counselling even about family matters. But the unreliable business cases are not thick as daisies; and the family cases mentioned would give an *advocate* in a family case a pretty solid footing. But a counsellor wants an utterly solid footing.

154. In a word, rules and principles announced in or concerning caselaw must be regarded as containing an ad hoc element; only the test reveals whether and how far the phrasing bears weight.

HAMER v. SIDWAY

124 N.Y. 538, 27 N.E. 256 (1891)

Appeal from order of the General Term of the Supreme Court in the fourth judicial department, made July 1, 1890, which reversed a judgment in favor of plaintiff entered upon a decision of the court on trial at Special Term and granted a new trial.

This action was brought upon an alleged contract.

The plaintiff presented a claim to the executor of William E. Story, Sr., for $5,000 and interest from the 6th day of February, 1875. She acquired it through several mesne assignments from William E. Story, 2d. The claim being rejected by the executor, this action was brought. It appears that William E. Story, Sr., was the uncle of William E. Story, 2d; that at the celebration of the golden wedding of Samuel Story and wife, father and mother of William E. Story, Sr., on the 20th day of March, 1869, in the presence of the family and invited guests he promised his nephew that if he would refrain from drinking, using tobacco, swearing and playing cards or billiards for money until he became twenty-one years of age he would pay him a sum of $5,000. The nephew assented thereto and fully performed the conditions inducing the promise. When the nephew arrived at the age of twenty-one years and on the 31st day of January, 1875, he wrote to his uncle informing him that he had performed his part of the agreement and had thereby become entitled to the sum of $5,000. The uncle received the letter and a few days later and on the sixth of February, he wrote and mailed to his nephew the following letter:

Buffalo, Feb. 6, 1875.

W. E. Story, Jr.:

Dear Nephew — Your letter of the 31st ult. came to hand all right, saying that you had lived up to the promise made to me several years ago. I have no doubt but you have, for which you shall have five thousand dollars as I promised you. I had the money in the bank the day you was 21 years old that I intend for you, and you shall have the money certain. Now, Willie I do not intend to interfere with this money in any way till I think you are capable of taking care of it and the sooner that times comes the better it will please me. I would hate very much to have you start out in some adventure that you thought all right and lose this money in one year. The first five thousand dollars that I got together cost me a heap of hard work. You would hardly believe me when I tell you that to obtain this I shoved a jackplane many a day, butchered three or four years, then came to this city, and after three months' perseverence I obtained a situation in a grocery store. I opened this store early, closed late, slept in the fourth story of the building in a room 30 by 40 feet and not a human being in the building but myself. All this I done to live as cheap as I could to save something. I don't want you to take up with this kind of fare. I was here in the cholera season

'49 and '52 and the deaths averaged 80 to 125 daily and plenty of smallpox. I wanted to go home, but Mr. Fisk, the gentleman I was working for, told me if I left then, after it got healthy he probably would not want me. I stayed. All the money I have saved I know just how I got it. It did not come to me in any mysterious way, and the reason I speak of this is that money got in this way stops longer with a fellow that gets it with hard knocks than it does when he finds it. Willie, you are 21 and you have many a thing to learn yet. This money you have earned much easier than I did besides acquiring good habits at the same time and you are quite welcome to the money; hope you will make good use of it. I was ten long years getting this together after I was your age. Now, hoping this will be satisfactory, I stop. One thing more. Twenty-one years ago I bought you 15 sheep. These sheep were put out to double every four years. I kept track of them the first eight years; I have not heard much about them since. Your father and grandfather promised me that they would look after them till you were of age. Have they done so? I hope they have. By this time you have between five and six hundred sheep, worth a nice little income this spring. Willie, I have said much more than I expected to; hope you can make out what I have written. To-day is the seventeenth day that I have not been out of my room, and have had the doctor as many days. Am a little better to-day; think I will get out next week. You need not mention to father, as he always worries about small matters.

Truly Yours,
W. E. STORY.

P.S. — You can consider this money on interest.

The nephew received the letter and thereafter consented that the money should remain with his uncle in accordance with the terms and conditions of the letters. The uncle died on the 29th day of January, 1887, without having paid over to his nephew any portion of the said $5,000 and interest.

PARKER, J. The question which provoked the most discussion by counsel on this appeal, and which lies at the foundation of plaintiff's asserted right of recovery, is whether by virtue of a contract defendant's testator William E. Story became indebted to his nephew William E. Story, 2d, on his twenty-first birthday in the sum of five thousand dollars. The trial court found as a fact that "on the 20th day of March, 1869, . . . William E. Story agreed to and with William E. Story, 2d, that if he would refrain from drinking liquor, using tobacco, swearing, and playing cards or billiards for money until he should become 21 years of age then he, the said William E. Story, would at that time pay him, the said William E. Story, 2d, the sum of $5,000 for such refraining, to which the said William E. Story, 2d, agreed," and that he "in all things fully performed his part of said agreement."

The defendant contends that the contract was without consideration to support it, and, therefore, invalid. He asserts that the promisee by refraining from the use of liquor and tobacco was not harmed but benefited; that that which he did was best for him to do independently of his uncle's promise, and insists that it follows that unless the promisor was benefited, the contract was without consideration. A contention, which if well founded, would seem to leave open for controversy in many cases whether that which the promisee did or omitted to do was, in fact, of such benefit to him as to leave no consideration to support the enforcement of the promisor's agreement. Such a rule could not be tolerated, and is without foundation in the law. The Exchequer Chamber, in 1875, defined consideration as follows: "A valuable consideration in the sense of the law may consist either in some right, interest, profit or benefit accruing to the one party, or some forbearance, detriment, loss or responsibility given, suffered or undertaken by the other." Courts

> will not ask whether the thing which forms the consideration does in fact benefit the promisor (*sic*) or a third party, or is of any substantial value to anyone. It is enough that something is promised, done, forborne or suffered by the party to whom the promise is made as consideration for the promise made to him.

(Anson's Prin. of Con. 63.)

"In general a waiver of any legal right at the request of another party is a sufficient consideration for a promise." (Parsons on Contracts, 444.)

"Any damage, or suspension, or forbearance of a right will be sufficient to sustain a promise." (Kent, vol. 2, 465, 12th ed.)

Pollock, in his work on contracts, page 166, after citing the definition given by the Exchequer Chamber already quoted, says:

> The second branch of this judicial description is really the most important one. Consideration means not so much that one party is profiting as that the other abandons some legal right in the present or limits his legal freedom of action in the future as an inducement for the promise of the first.

Now, applying this rule to the facts before us, the promisee used tobacco, occasionally liquor, and he had a legal right to do so. That right he abandoned for a period of years upon the strength of the promise of the testator that for such forbearance he would give him $5,000. We need not speculate on the effort which may have been required to give up the use of those stimulants. It is sufficient that he restricted his lawful freedom of action within certain prescribed limits upon the faith of his uncle's agreement, and now having fully performed the conditions imposed, it is of no moment whether such performance actually proved a benefit to the promisor, and the court will not inquire into it, but were it a proper subject of inquiry, we see nothing in this record that would permit a determination that the uncle was benefited in a legal sense. Few cases have been found which may be said to be precisely in point, but such as have been support the position we have taken.

In Shadwell v. Shadwell (9 C.B.[N.S.] 159), an uncle wrote to his nephew as follows:

> My Dear Lancey — I am so glad to hear of your intended marriage with Ellen Nicholl, and as I promised to assist you at starting, I am happy to tell you that I will pay to you 150 pounds yearly during my life and until your annual income derived from your profession of a chancery barrister shall amount to 600 guineas, of which your own admission will be the only evidence that I shall require.
>
> Your affectionate uncle,
CHARLES SHADWELL.

It was held that the promise was binding and made upon good consideration.

In Lakota v. Newton, an unreported case in the Superior Court of Worcester, Mass., the complaint averred defendant's promise that "if you (meaning plaintiff) will leave off drinking for a year I will give you $100," plaintiff's assent thereto, performance of the condition by him, and demanded judgment therefor. Defendant demurred on the ground, among others, that the plaintiff's declaration did not allege a valid and sufficient consideration for the agreement of the defendant. The demurrer was overruled.

In Talbott v. Stemmons (a Kentucky case not yet reported), the step-grandmother of the plaintiff made with him the following agreement: "I do promise and bind myself to give my grandson, Albert R. Talbott, $500 at my death, if he will never take another chew of tobacco or smoke another cigar during my life from this date up to my death, and if he breaks this pledge he is to refund double the amount to his mother." The executor of Mrs. Stemmons demurred to the complaint on the ground that the agreement was not based on a sufficient consideration. The demurrer was sustained and an appeal taken therefrom to the Court of Appeals, where the decision of the court below was reversed. In the opinion of the court it is said that

> the right to use and enjoy the use of tobacco was a right that belonged to the plaintiff and not forbidden by law. The abandonment of its use may have saved him money or contributed to his health, nevertheless, the surrender of that right caused the promise, and having the right to contract with reference to the subject-matter, the abandonment of the use was a sufficient consideration to uphold the promise.

Abstinence from the use of intoxicating liquors was held to furnish a good consideration for a promissory note in Lindell v. Rokes (60 Mo. 249).

The cases cited by the defendant on this question are not in point. In Mallory v. Gillett (21 N.Y. 412); Belknap v. Bender (75 id. 446), and Berry

v. Brown (107 id. 659), the promise was in contravention of that provision
of the Statute of Frauds, which declares void all promises to answer for
the debts of third persons unless reduced to writing. In Beaumont v.
Reeve (Shirley's L.C. 6), and Porterfield v. Butler (47 Miss. 165), the
question was whether a moral obligation furnishes sufficient consideration to uphold a subsequent express promise. In Duvoll v. Wilson (9
Barb. 487), and In re Wilber v. Warren (104 N.Y. 192), the proposition
involved was whether an executory covenant against incumbrances in a
deed given in consideration of natural love and affection could be enforced. In Vanderbilt v. Schreyer (91 N.Y. 392), the plaintiff contracted
with defendant to build a house, agreeing to accept in part payment
therefor a specific bond and mortgage. Afterwards he refused to finish his
contract unless the defendant would guarantee its payment, which was
done. It was held that the guarantee could not be enforced for want of
consideration. For in building the house the plaintiff only did that which
he had contracted to do. And in Robinson v. Jewett (116 N.Y. 40), the
court simply held that "The performance of an act which the party is
under a legal obligation to perform cannot constitute a consideration for
a new contract." It will be observed that the agreement which we have
been considering was within the condemnation of the Statute of Frauds,
because not to be performed within a year, and not in writing. But this
defense the promisor could waive, and his letter and oral statements
subsequent to the date of final performance on the part of the promisee
must be held to amount to a wavier. Were it otherwise, the statute could
not now be invoked in aid of the defendant. It does not appear on the face
of the complaint that the agreement is one prohibited by the Statute of
Frauds, and, therefore, such defense could not be made available unless
set up in the answer. (Porter v. Wormser, 94 N.Y. 431, 450.) This was not
done.

In further consideration of the questions presented, then, it must be
deemed established for the purposes of this appeal, that on the 31st day of
January, 1875, defendant's testator was indebted to William E. Story, 2d,
in the sum of $5,000, and if this action were founded on that contract it
would be barred by the Statute of Limitations which has been pleaded,
but on that date the nephew wrote to his uncle as follows:

> Dear Uncle — I am now 21 years old to-day, and I am now my own
> boss, and I believe, according to agreement, that there is due me $5,000. I
> have lived up to the contract to the letter in every sense of the word.

A few days later, and on February sixth, the uncle replied, and, so far
as it is material to this controversy, the reply is as follows:

> Dear Nephew — Your letter of the 31st ult. came to hand all right
> saying that you had lived up to the promise made to me several years ago. I

have no doubt but you have, for which you shall have $5,000 as I promised you. I had the money in the bank the day you was 21 years old that I intended for you, and you shall have the money certain. Now, Willie, I don't intend to interfere with this money in any way until I think you are capable of taking care of it, and the sooner that time comes the better it will please me. I would hate very much to have you start out in some adventure that you thought all right and lose this money in one year. . . . This money you have earned much easier than I did, besides acquiring good habits at the same time, and you are quite welcome to the money. Hope you will make good use of it. . . .

W. E. STORY.

P.S. — You can consider this money on interest.

The trial court found as a fact that "said letter was received by said William E. Story, 2d, who thereafter consented that said money should remain with the said William E. Story in accordance with the terms and conditions of said letter." And further,

That afterwards, on the first day of March, 1877, with the knowledge and consent of his said uncle, he duly sold, transferred and assigned all his right, title and interest in and to said sum of $5,000 to his wife Libbie H. Story, who thereafter duly sold, transferred and assigned the same to the plaintiff in this action.

We must now consider the effect of the letter, and the nephew's assent thereto. Were the relations of the parties thereafter that of debtor and creditor simply, or that of trustee and cestui que trust? If the former, then this action is not maintainable, because barred by lapse of time. If the latter, the result must be otherwise. No particular expressions are necessary to create a trust. Any language clearly showing the settler's intention is sufficient if the property and disposition of it are definitely stated. (Lewin on Trusts, 55.)

A person in the legal possession of money or property ackowledging a trust with the assent of the cestui que trust, becomes from that time a trustee if the acknowledgment be founded on a valuable consideration. His antecedent relation to the subject, whatever it may have been, no longer controls. (2 Story's Eq. §972.) If before a declaration of trust a party be a mere debtor, a subsequent agreement recognizing the fund as already in his hands and stipulating for its investment on the creditor's account will have the effect to create a trust. (Day v. Roth, 18 N.Y. 448.)

It is essential that the letter interpreted in the light of surrounding circumstances must show an intention on the part of the uncle to become a trustee before he will be held to have become such; but in an effort to ascertain the construction which should be given to it, we are also to observe the rule that the language of the promisor is to be interpreted in the sense in which he had reason to suppose it was understood by the promisee. (White v. Hoyt, 73 N.Y. 505, 511.) At the time the uncle wrote the letter he was indebted to his nephew in the sum of $5,000, and payment had been requested. The uncle recognizing the indebtedness, wrote the nephew that he would keep the money until he deemed him capable of taking care of it. He did not say "I will pay you at some other time," or use language that would indicate that the relation of debtor and creditor would continue. On the contrary, his language indicated that he had set apart the money the nephew had "earned" for him so that when he should be capable of taking care of it he should receive it with interest. He said: "I had the money in the bank the day you were 21 years old that I intended for you and you shall have the money certain." That he had set apart the money is further evidenced by the next sentence: "Now, Willie, I don't intend to interfere with this money in any way until I think you are capable of taking care of it." Certainly, the uncle must have intended that his nephew should understand that the promise not "to interfere with this money" referred to the money in the bank which he declared was not only there when the nephew became 21 years old, but was intended for him. True, he did not use the word "trust," or state that the money was deposited in the name of William E. Story, 2d, or in his own name in trust for him, but the language used must have been intended to assure the nephew that his money had been set apart for him, to be kept without interference until he should be capable of taking care of it, for the uncle said in substance and in effect:

> This money you have earned much easier than I did . . . you are quite welcome to. I had it in the bank the day you were 21 years old and don't intend to interfere with it in any way until I think you are capable of taking care of it and the sooner that time comes the better it will please me.

In this declaration there is not lacking a single element necessary for the creation of a valid trust, and to that declaration the nephew assented.

The learned judge who wrote the opinion of the General Term, seems to have taken the view that the trust was executed during the life-time of defendant's testator by payment to the nephew, but as it does not appear from the order that the judgment was reversed on the facts, we must assume the facts to be as found by the trial court, and those facts support its judgment.

The order appealed from should be reversed and the judgment of the Special Term affirmed, with costs payable out of the estate.

All concur.

Order reversed and judgment of Special Term affirmed.

NOTE

Additional interesting facts, which tend to show that the uncle fulfilled the promise prior to his death, are provided in the trial court opinion. See Hamer v. Sidway, 64 N.Y. Sup. Ct. (57 Hun.) 229, 11 N.Y.S. 182 (1890).

Suppose an uncle promises to give his nephew, who has just entered college, $5,000 should the nephew make Phi Beta Kappa. Is this promise binding under Hamer v. Sidway? Consult further Restatement Second §24, Illus. 2.

Suppose an uncle who is told by his nephew that he needs a car says, "Well, I will give you $2,000." The nephew then buys a car for $950. Is the uncle bound to pay? How much? Assume the uncle makes the same promise, but without having first been informed by the nephew that he wants to buy a car. Relying on the promise, the nephew buys a car for $950. Same result? Would the result under §90 of the Restatement First be different from that under §90 of the Restatement Second? Consult Eisenberg, Donative Promises, 47 U. Chi. L. Rev. 1, 20-26 (1979), and Appendix, 4 A.L.I. Proc. 88 et seq. (1926). See further Fuller & Perdue, The Reliance Interest in Contract Damages, 46 Yale L.J. 52, 64, 401 (1936-1937); 2A Corbin §205 (1963).

Suppose the uncle in the above example promises to buy his nephew a new car. If the nephew goes out and buys a stereo instead with the money he would otherwise have spent on a car, does he have an action against his uncle if the uncle refuses to pay? Under §90? A creditor who promised to accept less from his debtor than the amount of the debt was at common law not bound by his promise for want of consideration. See pp. 668 et seq. *infra*. Could a debtor argue that his change in consumption or spending is sufficient detrimental reliance to estop the creditor from claiming the full amount? In Baggs v. Anderson, 528 P.2d 141, 144 (Utah 1974), the court said that the requirement of detrimental reliance "is not satisfied by the mere fact that the [promisee] indulged in the pleasant and euphoric assumption that he would not have to meet his obligations and that he bought a more expensive apartment." Consider also the following from Goetz & Scott, Enforcing Promises: An Examination of the Basis of Contract, 89 Yale L.J. 1261, 1302 (1980):

> In fact . . . detrimental reliance is likely to occur even if no visible evidence of it exists. Between the date of the [gratuitous] promise and that of the repudiation, [the promisee] will have modified his consumption habits in adjustment to his suddenly increased expected wealth. If this expectation is disappointed, [the promisee's] excessive consumption will have produced a permanent net loss in welfare; this loss is his reliance injury. Courts rarely acknowledge the existence of such uncompensated reliance when they refuse to enforce gratuitous promises. The absence of bargained-for consideration triggers instead a presumption of nonenforcement.

Recall Williston's tramp case, *supra* p. 472. Reconsider it in the light of the following statement:

> If A promises to buy a house for his nephew, that is nothing; but if A promises to buy a house for his nephew, and requests the nephew to enter into a contract of purchase in the nephew's own name and the nephew does so, the law implies a promise on the part of A to reimburse the nephew any part of the purchase-money which he may be called up to pay. Skidmore v. Bradford, L.R. 8 Eq. 134.

Young Men's Christian Association v. Estill, 140 Ga. 291, 296, 78 S.E. 1075, 1077 (1913).

For the requirement of consideration in declarations of trust, see 1 Scott on Trusts, §§12.4, 28 (1956); Hebrew University Association v. Nye, 148 Conn. 223, 169 A.2d 641 (1961) (dealing with prerequisites).

RICKETTS v. SCOTHORN
57 Neb. 51, 77 N.W. 365 (1898)

SULLIVAN J. In the district court of Lancaster county the plaintiff Katie Scothorn recovered judgment against the defendant Andrew D. Ricketts, as executor of the last will and testament of John C. Ricketts, deceased. The action was based upon a promissory note, of which the following is a copy:

> May the first, 1891. I promise to pay to Katie Scothorn on demand, $2,000, to be at 6 per cent annum.
>
> J. C. Ricketts.

In the petition the plaintiff alleges that the consideration for the execution of the note was that she should surrender her employment as bookkeeper for Mayer Bros. and cease to work for a living. She also alleges that the note was given to induce her to abandon her occupation, and that, relying on it, and on the annual interest, as a means of support, she gave up the employment in which she was then engaged. These allegations of the petition are denied by the executor. The material facts are undisputed. They are as follows: John C. Ricketts, the maker of the note, was the grandfather of the plaintiff. Early in May — presumably on the day the note bears date, — he called on her at the store where she was working. What transpired between them is thus described by Mr. Flodene, one of the plaintiff's witnesses:

> A.   Well, the old gentleman came in there one morning about 9 o'clock — probably a little before or a little after, but early in the morning, —

and he unbuttoned his vest and took out a piece of paper in the shape of a note; that is the way it looked to me; and he says to Miss Scothorn, "I have fixed out something that you have not got to work any more." He says, "None of my grandchildren work and you don't have to."

Q. Where was she?

A. She took the piece of paper and kissed him; and kissed the old gentleman and commenced to cry.

It seems Miss Scothorn immediately notified her employer of her intention to quit work and that she did soon after abandon her occupation. The mother of the plaintiff was a witness and testified that she had a conversation with her father, Mr. Ricketts, shortly after the note was executed in which he informed her that he had given the note to the plaintiff to enable her to quit work; that none of his grandchildren worked and he did not think she ought to. For something more than a year the plaintiff was without an occupation; but in September, 1892, with the consent of her grandfather, and by his assistance, she secured a position as bookkeeper with Messrs. Funke & Ogden. On June 8, 1894, Mr. Ricketts died. He had paid one year's interest on the note, and a short time before his death expressed regret that he had not been able to pay the balance. In the summer or fall of 1892 he stated to his daughter, Mrs. Scothorn, that if he could sell his farm in Ohio he would pay the note out of the proceeds. He at no time repudiated the obligation. We quite agree with counsel for the defendant that upon this evidence there was nothing to submit to the jury, and that a verdict should have been directed peremptorily for one of the parties. The testimony of Flodene and Mrs. Scothorn, taken together, conclusively establishes the fact that the note was not given in consideration of the plaintiff pursuing, or agreeing to pursue, any particular line of conduct. There was no promise on the part of the plaintiff to do or refrain from doing anything. Her right to the money promised in the note was not made to depend upon an abandonment of her employment with Mayer Bros. and future abstention from like service. Mr. Ricketts made no condition, requirement, or request. He exacted no quid pro quo. He gave the note as a gratuity and looked for nothing in return. So far as the evidence discloses, it was his purpose to place the plaintiff in a position of independence where she could work or remain idle as she might choose. The abandonment by Miss Scothorn of her position as bookkeeper was altogether voluntary. It was not an act done in fulfillment of any contract obligation assumed when she accepted the note. The instrument in suit being given without any valuable consideration, was nothing more than a promise to make a gift in the future of the sum of money therein named. Ordinarily, such promises are not enforceable even when put in the form of a promissory note. (Kirkpatrick v. Taylor, 43 Ill. 207; Phelps v. Phelps, 28 Barb. [N.Y.] 121; Johnston v. Griest, 85 Ind. 503; Fink v. Cox, 18 Johns. [N.Y.] 145.) But it has often been held that an action on a note given to a church, college, or other like institution, upon the faith of which money has been expended or obligations incurred, could not be successfully defended on the ground of a want of consideration. (Barnes v. Perine, 12 N.Y. 18; Philomath College v. Hartless, 6 Ore. 158; Thompson v. Mercer County, 40 Ill. 379; Irwin v. Lombard University, 56 O. St. 9.) In this class of cases the note in suit is nearly always spoken of as a gift or donation, but the decision is generally put on the ground that the expenditure of money or assumption of liability by the donee, on the faith or the promise, constitutes a valuable and sufficient consideration. It seems to us that the true reason is the preclusion of the defendant, under the doctrine of estoppel, to deny the consideration. Such seems to be the view of the matter taken by the supreme court of Iowa in the case of Simpson Centenary College v. Tuttle, 71 Ia. 596, where Rothrock, J., speaking for the court, said:

> Where a note, however, is based on a promise to give for the support of the objects referred to, it may still be open to this defense [want of consideration], unless it shall appear that the donee has, prior to any revocation, entered into engagements or made expenditures based on such promise, so that he must suffer loss or injury if the note is not paid. This is based on the equitable principle that, after allowing the donee to incur obligations on the faith that the note would be paid, the donor would be estopped from pleading want of consideration.

And in the case of Reimensnyder v. Gans, 110 Pa. St. 17, 2 Atl. Rep. 425, which was an action on a note given as a donation to a charitable object, the court said: "The fact is that, as we may see from the case of Ryerss v. Trustees, 33 Pa. St. 114, a contract of the kind here involved is enforceable rather by way of estoppel than on the ground of consideration in the original undertaking." It has been held that a note given in expectation of the payee performing certain services, but without any contract binding him to serve, will not support an action. (Hulse v. Hulse, 84 Eng. Com. Law 709.) But when the payee changes his position to his disadvantage, in reliance on the promise, a right of action does arise. (McClure v. Wilson, 43 Ill. 356; Trustees v. Garvey, 53 Ill. 401.)

Under the circumstances of this case is there an equitable estoppel which ought to preclude the defendant from alleging that the note in controversy is lacking in one of the essential elements of a valid contract? We think there is. An estoppel in pais is defined to be "a right rising from acts, admissions, or conduct which have induced a change of position in accordance with the real or apparent intention of the party against whom they are alleged." Mr. Pomeroy has formulated the following definition:

> Equitable estoppel is the effect of the voluntary conduct of a party whereby he is absolutely precluded, both at law and in equity, from asserting rights which might perhaps have otherwise existed, either of property, or con-

tract, or of remedy, as against another person who in good faith relied upon such conduct, and has been led thereby to change his position for the worse, and who on his part acquires some corresponding right either of property, of contract, or of remedy.

(2 Pomeroy, Equity Jurisprudence 804.)

According to the undisputed proof, as shown by the record before us, the plaintiff was a working girl, holding a position in which she earned a salary of $10 per week. Her grandfather, desiring to put her in a position of independence, gave her the note, accompanying it with the remark that his other grandchildren did not work, and that she would not be obliged to work any longer. In effect he suggested that she might abandon her employment and rely in the future upon the bounty which he promised. He, doubtless, desired that she should give up her occupation, but whether he did or not, it is entirely certain that he contemplated such action on her part as a reasonable and probable consequence of his gift. Having intentionally influenced the plaintiff to alter her position for the worse on the faith of the note being paid when due, it would be grossly inequitable to permit the maker, or his executor, to resist payment on the ground that the promise was given without consideration. The petition charges the elements of an equitable estoppel, and the evidence conclusively establishes them. If errors intervened at the trial they could not have been prejudicial. A verdict for the defendant would be unwarranted. The judgment is right and is

Affirmed.

NOTE

See *In re* Estate of Bucci, 488 P.2d 216 (Colo. App. 1971) (not selected for official publication).

Did the grandfather's use of a promissory note serve any of the functions of legal formality — evidentiary, cautionary, or channeling? On formalism in contract law, see Chapters 5 and 6.

Was the principal case a case of equitable estoppel, as the court held, or one of promissory estoppel?

DE CICCO v. SCHWEIZER
221 N.Y. 431, 117 N.E. 807 (1917)

Appeal from a judgment of the Appellate Division of the Supreme Court in the first judicial department, entered February 2, 1915, modifying and affirming as modified a judgment in favor of plaintiff entered upon a verdict directed by the court.

The nature of the action and the facts, so far as material, are stated in the opinion. . . .

CARDOZO, J. On January 16, 1902, "articles of agreement" were executed by the defendant Joseph Schweizer, his wife Ernestine, and Count Oberto Gulinelli. The agreement is in Italian. We quote from a translation the part essential to the decision of this controversy:

> Whereas, Miss Blanche Josephine Schweizer, daughter of said Mr. Joseph Schweizer and of said Mrs. Ernestine Teresa Schweizer, is now affianced to and is to be married to the above said Count Oberto Giacomo Giovanni Francesco Maria Gulinelli, now, in consideration of all that is herein set forth the said Mr. Joseph Schweizer promises and expressly agrees by the present contract to pay annually to his said daughter Blanche, during his own life and to send her, during her lifetime, the sum of Two Thousand Five Hundred dollars, or the equivalent of said sum in Francs, the first payment of said amount to be made on the 20th day of January, 1902.

Later articles provide that "for the same reason heretofore set forth," Mr. Schweizer will not change the provision made in his will for the benefit of his daughter and her issue, if any. The yearly payments in the event of his death are to be continued by his wife.

On January 20, 1902, the marriage occurred. On the same day, the defendant made the first payment to his daughter. He continued the payments annually till 1912. This action is brought to recover the installment of that year. The plaintiff holds an assignment executed by the daughter, in which her husband joined. The question is whether there is any consideration for the promised annuity.

That marriage may be a sufficient consideration is not disputed. The argument for the defendant is, however, that Count Gulinelli was already affianced to Miss Schweizer and that the marriage was merely the fulfillment of an existing legal duty. For this reason, it is insisted, consideration was lacking. The argument leads us to the discussion of a vexed problem of the law which has been debated by courts and writers with much subtlety of reasoning and little harmony of results. There is general acceptance of the proposition that where A is under a contract with B, a promise made by one to the other to induce performance is void. The trouble comes when the promise to induce performance is made by C, a stranger. Distinctions are then drawn between bilateral and unilateral contracts; between a promise by C in return for a new promise by A, and a promise by C in return for performance by A. Some jurists hold that there is consideration in both classes of cases (Ames, Two Theories of Consideration, 12 Harvard Law Review, 515; 13 id. 29, 35; Langdell, Mutual Promises as a Consideration, 14 id. 496; Leake, Contracts, p. 622). Others hold that there is consideration where the promise is made for a new promise, but not where it is made for performance (Beale,

Notes on Consideration, 17 Harvard Law Review, 71; 2 Street, Foundations of Legal Liability, pp. 114, 116; Pollock, Contracts [8th ed.], 199;
Pollock, Afterthoughts on Consideration, 17 Law Quarterly Review, 415;
7 Halsbury, Laws of England, Contracts, p. 385; Abbot v. Doane, 163
Mass. 433). Others hold that there is no consideration in either class of
cases (Williston, Successive Promises of the Same Performance, 8 Harvard Law Review, 27, 34; Consideration in Bilateral Contracts, 27 id. 503,
521; Anson on Contracts [11th ed.], p. 92).

The storm-centre about which this controversy has raged is the case of
Shadwell v. Shadwell (9 C.B. [N.S.] 159; 99 E.C.L. 158) which arose out
of a situation similar in many features to the one before us. Nearly everything that has been written on the subject has been a commentary on that
decision. There an uncle promised to pay his nephew after marriage an
annuity of £150. At the time of the promise the nephew was already
engaged. The case was heard before Erle, Ch. J., and Keating and Byles,
JJ. The first two judges held the promise to be enforcible. Byles, J.,
dissented. His view was that the nephew, being already affianced, had
incurred no detriment upon the faith of the promise, and hence that
consideration was lacking. Neither of the two opinions in Shadwell v.
Shadwell can rule the case at bar. There are elements of difference in the
two cases, which raise new problems. But the earlier case, with the literature which it has engendered, gives us a point of departure and a method
of approach.

The courts of this state are committed to the view that a promise by A
to B to induce him not to *break* his contract with C is void (Arend v.
Smith, 151 N.Y. 502; Vanderbilt v. Schreyer, 91 N.Y. 392; Seybolt v.
N.Y., L.E. & W. R.R. Co., 95 N.Y. 562; Robinson v. Jewett, 116 N.Y.
40). If that is the true nature of this promise, there was no consideration.
We have never held, however, that a like infirmity attaches to a promise
by A, not merely to B, but to B and C jointly, to induce them not to
rescind or *modify* a contract which they are free to abandon. To determine whether that is in substance the promise before us, there is need of
closer analysis.

The defendant's contract, if it be one, is not bilateral. It is unilateral
(Miller v. McKenzie, 95 N.Y. 575). The consideration exacted is not a
promise, but an act. The Count did not promise anything. In effect the
defendant said to him: If you and my daughter marry, I will pay her an
annuity for life. Until marriage occurred, the defendant was not bound.
It would not have been enough that the Count remained willing to
marry. The plain import of the contract is that his bride also should be
willing, and that marriage should follow. The promise was intended to
affect the conduct, not of one only, but of both. This becomes the more
evident when we recall that though the promise ran to the Count, it was
intended for the benefit of the daughter (Durnherr v. Rau, 135 N.Y. 219).
When it came to her knowledge, she had the right to adopt and enforce it

(Gifford v. Corrigan, 117 N.Y. 257; Buchanan v. Tilden, 158 N.Y. 109; Lawrence v. Fox, 20 N.Y. 268). In doing so, she made herself a party to the contract (Gifford v. Corrigan, *supra*). If the contract had been bilateral, her position might have been different. Since, however, it was unilateral, the consideration being performance (Miller v. McKenzie, *supra*), action on the faith of it put her in the same position as if she had been in form the promisee. That she learned of the promise before the marriage is a legitimate inference from the relation of the parties and from other attendant circumstances. The writing was signed by her parents; it was delivered to her intended husband; it was made four days before the marriage; it called for a payment on the day of the marriage; and on that day payment was made, and made to her. From all these circumstances, we may infer that at the time of the marriage the promise was known to the bride as well as the husband, and that both acted upon the faith of it.

The situation, therefore, is the same in substance as if the promise had run to husband and wife alike, and had been intended to induce performance by both. They were free by common consent to terminate their engagement or to postpone the marriage. If they forbore from exercising that right and assumed the responsibilities of marriage in reliance on the defendant's promise, he may not now retract it. The distinction between a promise by A to B to induce him not to break his contract with C, and a like promise to induce him not to join with C in a voluntary rescission, is not a new one. It has been suggested in cases where the new promise ran to B solely, and not to B and C jointly (Pollock, Contracts (8th ed.), p. 199; Williston, 8 Harv. L. Rev. 36). The criticism has been made that in such circumstances there ought to be some evidence that C was ready to withdraw (Williston, *supra*, at pp. 36, 37). Whether that is true of contracts to marry is not certain. Many elements foreign to the ordinary business contract enter into such engagements. It does not seem a far-fetched assumption in such cases that one will release where the other has repented. We shall assume, however, that the criticism is valid where the promise is intended as an inducement to only one of the two parties to the contract. It may then be sheer speculation to say that the other party could have been persuaded to rescind. But where the promise is held out as an inducement to both parties alike, there are new and different implications. One does not commonly apply pressure to coerce the will and action of those who are anxious to proceed. The attempt to sway their conduct by new inducements is an implied admission that both may waver; that one equally with the other must be strengthened and persuaded; and that rescission or at least delay is something to be averted, and something, therefore, within the range of not unreasonable expectation. If pressure, applied to both, and holding both to their course, is not the purpose of the promise, it is at least the natural tendency and the probable result.

The defendant knew that a man and woman were assuming the responsibilities of wedlock in the belief that adequate provision had been made for the woman and for future offspring. He offered this inducement to both while they were free to retract or to delay. That they neither retracted nor delayed is certain. It is not to be expected that they should lay bare all the motives and promptings, some avowed and conscious, others perhaps half-conscious and inarticulate, which swayed their conduct. It is enough that the natural consequence of the defendant's promise was to induce them to put the thought of rescission or delay aside. From that moment, there was no longer a real alternative. There was no longer what philosophers call a "living" option. This in itself permits the inference of detriment (Smith v. Chadwick, 9 App. Cas. 187, 196; Smith v. Land & House Corp. 28 Ch. D. 7, 16; Voorhis v. Olmstead, 66 N.Y. 113, 118; Fottler v. Moseley, 179 Mass. 295).

> If it is proved that the defendants with a view to induce the plaintiff to enter into a contract made a statement to the plaintiff of such a nature as would be likely to induce a person to enter into the contract, it is a fair inference of fact that he was induced to do so by the statement

(Blackburn, L.J., in Smith v. Chadwick, *supra*). The same inference follows, not so inevitably, but still legitimately, where the statement is made to induce the preservation of a contract. It will not do to divert the minds of others from a given line of conduct, and then to urge that because of the diversion the opportunity has gone by to say how their minds would otherwise have acted. If the tendency of the promise is to induce them to persevere, reliance and detriment may be inferred from the mere fact of performance. The springs of conduct are subtle and varied. One who meddles with them must not insist upon too nice a measure of proof that the spring which he released was effective to the exclusion of all others.

One other line of argument must be considered. The suggestion is made that the defendant's promise was not made *animo contrahendi*. It was not designed, we are told, to sway the conduct of any one; it was merely the offer of a gift which found its *motive* in the engagement of the daughter to the Count. Undoubtedly, the prospective marriage is not to be deemed a consideration for the promise "unless the parties have dealt with it on that footing" (Holmes, Common Law, p. 292; Fire Ins. Assn. v. Wickham, 141 U.S. 564, 579). "Nothing is consideration that is not regarded as such by both parties" (Philpot v. Gruninger, 14 Wall. 570, 577; Fire Ins. Assn. v. Wickham, *supra*). But here the very formality of the agreement suggests a purpose to affect the legal relations of the signers. One does not commonly pledge one's self to generosity in the language of a covenant. That the parties believed there was a consideration is certain. The document recites the engagement and the coming marriage. It states that these are the "consideration" for the promise. The failure to marry would have made the promise ineffective. In these circumstances we cannot say that the promise was not intended to control the conduct of those whom it was designed to benefit. Certainly we cannot draw that inference as one of law. Both sides moved for the direction of a verdict, and the trial judge became by consent the trier of the facts. If conflicting inferences were possible, he chose those favorable to the plaintiff.

The conclusion to which we are thus led is reinforced by those considerations of public policy which cluster about contracts that touch the marriage relation. The law favors marriage settlements, and seeks to uphold them. It puts them for many purposes in a class by themselves (Phalen v. U.S. Trust Co., 186 N.Y. 178, 181). It has enforced them at times where consideration, if present at all, has been dependent upon doubtful inference (McNutt v. McNutt, 116 Ind. 545; Appleby v. Appleby, 100 Minn. 408). It strains, if need be, to the uttermost the interpretation of equivocal words and conduct in the effort to hold men to the honorable fulfillment of engagements designed to influence in their deepest relations the lives of others.

The judgment should be affirmed with costs.

CRANE, J. (concurring.) I concur for affirmance and agree with what Judge Cardozo has said about the law of consideration, but I prefer other reasons for my conclusions in this case.

Marriage settlements are usually made between husband and wife; but marriage settlements by third parties have been recognized by law. (Schouler's Dom. Rel. [5th ed.] sec. 178; Phalen v. U.S. Trust Co., 186 N.Y. 178.) The policy of the law to uphold and enforce such contracts is applicable to both classes.

Count Gulinelli and the defendant's daughter being engaged, the defendant, through his lawyer, prepared and executed the agreement in question on the 16th day of January, 1902, and handed it to his prospective son-in-law on the 18th of January, 1902. Two days thereafter Gulinelli and the defendant's daughter were married. This formal document reads in part as follows:

> Whereas, Miss Blanche Josephine Schweizer, daughter of said Mr. Joseph Schweizer and of said Mrs. Ernestine Teresa Schweizer, is now affianced to and is to be married to the above said Count Oberto Giacomo Giovanni Francesco Maria Gulinelli.

Now, in consideration of all that is herein set forth the said Mr. Joseph Schweizer promises and expressly agrees by the present contract to pay annually to his said daughter Blanche, during his own life and to send her, during her lifetime, the sum of Two Thousand Five Hundred dollars, or the equivalent of said sum in Francs, the first payment of said amount to be made on the 20th day of January, 1902.

The only reasonable inference to be drawn from these facts is that this agreement was a marriage settlement made by the father upon his daughter in view of the impending marriage and to take effect upon the marriage. The marriage having taken place, the settlement became binding.

In the *Phalen* Case (*supra*) it was said by this court: "The strict legal definition of consideration need not here be discussed, since marriage settlements have always been regarded as exceptions to the general rule upon this question." (p. 186.)

If, however, consideration were necessary for this marriage settlement, the marriage was that consideration.

The parties were not bound by the recitals in the instrument, but could show, by surrounding circumstances and by natural inferences, the actual consideration. (10 Ruling Case Law, 1042; Barker v. Bradley, 42 N.Y. 316, 320; Wheeler v. Billings, 38 N.Y. 263, 264; Arnot v. Erie Railway Co., 67 N.Y. 315, 321; Ferris v. Hard, 135 N.Y. 354, 363; Sturmdorf v. Saunders, 117 App. Div. 762; *affd.*, 190 N.Y. 555.)

This case is similar to Coverdale v. Eastwood (L.R. 15 Eq. 121); Laver v. Fielder (32 Beav. 1); Keays v. Gilmore (Irish Rep. 8 Eq. 290); Bold v. Hutchinson (20 Beav. 250), and Ayliffe v. Tracy (2 P. Wms. 65).

Romilly's words in Laver v. Fielder (*supra*) are pertinent here.

> It is of great importance that all persons should understand, that when a man makes a solemn engagement upon an important occasion, such as the marriage of his daughter, he is bound by the promise he then makes. If he induce a person to act upon a particular promise, with a particular view, which affects the interest in life of his own children and of the persons who become united to them, this Court will not permit him afterwards to forego his own words, and say that he was not bound by what he then promised.

The trial court to whom all the facts were submitted was justified in finding that this agreement was a marriage settlement by a father upon his daughter and that it influenced the parties, at least in part, to marry *at the time* they did and was, therefore, a legal agreement.

Hiscock, Ch. J., Cuddeback, Pound and Andrews, JJ., concur with Cardozo, J., and Crane, J., concurs in opinion; Collin, J., not voting.

Judgment affirmed.

NOTE

The requirement of consideration, as applied to promises given on account of marriage, has had an interesting history. According to Simpson, such promises were held to be supported by consideration very early on, and "it is probably to the attempt to explain marriage in terms of benefit to the promisor in Sharrington v. Strotten (1566) [Plowden 298] that we owe the formulation of the doctrine of consideration (or rather one half of it) in terms of benefit to the promisor." Simpson at 421.

A rather different approach became influential in later law. On this second view, marriage was deemed good consideration in the eyes of the law "because nature instils into man a desire to look after his blood, and so marriage as good consideration is not an example of a wider principle about benefit, but instead an example of a wider principle which recognizes natural love and affection as good consideration." Ibid.

Are Cardozo's observations regarding the form of the promise in *De Cicco* equally applicable to Devecmon v. Shaw, *supra* p. 480?

On the treatment of promises on account of marriage under the Restatement Second, see §90(2).

ALLEGHENY COLLEGE v. NATIONAL CHAUTAUQUA COUNTY BANK OF JAMESTOWN

246 N.Y. 369, 156 N.E. 173 (1927)

Appeal, by permission, from a judgment of the Appellate Division of the Supreme Court in the fourth judicial department, entered April 13, 1927, unanimously affirming a judgment in favor of defendant entered upon a dismissal of the complaint by the court on trial at an Equity Term.

CARDOZO, Ch. J. The plaintiff, Allegheny College, is an institution of liberal learning at Meadville, Pennsylvania. In June 1921, a "drive" was in progress to secure for it an additional endowment of $1,250,000. An appeal to contribute to this fund was made to Mary Yates Johnston of Jamestown, New York. In response thereto, she signed and delivered on June 15, 1921, the following writing:

Estate Pledge,
Allegheny College Second Century Endowment
Jamestown, N.Y., June 15, 1921.

In consideration of my interest in Christian Education, and in consideration of others subscribing, I hereby subscribe and will pay to the order of the Treasurer of Allegheny College, Meadville, Pennsylvania, the sum of Five Thousand Dollars; $5,000.

This obligation shall become due thirty days after my death, and I hereby instruct my Executor, or Administrator, to pay the same out of my estate. This pledge shall bear interest at the rate of . . . per cent per annum, payable annually, from . . . till paid. The proceeds of this obligation shall be added to the Endowment of said Institution, or expended in accordance with instructions on reverse side of this pledge.

Name	MARY YATES JOHNSTON,
Address	36 East 6th Street,
	Jamestown, N.Y.
Dayton E. McClain	Witness
T. R. Courtis	Witness
to authentic signature	

On the reverse side of the writing is the following indorsement:

> In loving memory this gift shall be known as the Mary Yates Johnston
> Memorial Fund, the proceeds from which shall be used to educate students
> preparing for the Ministry, either in the United States or in the Foreign
> Field.
>   This pledge shall be valid only on the condition that the provisions of my
> Will, now extant, shall be first met.
>
>   MARY YATES JOHNSTON.

This subscription was not payable by its terms until thirty days after the
death of the promisor. The sum of $1,000 was paid, however, upon ac-
count in December, 1923, while the promisor was alive. The college set
the money aside to be held as a scholarship fund for the benefit of students preparing for the ministry. Later, in July, 1924, the promisor gave
notice to the college that she repudiated the promise. Upon the expiration of thirty days following her death, this action was brought against the
executor of her will to recover the unpaid balance.

The law of charitable subscriptions has been a prolific source of controversy in this State and elsewhere. We have held that a promise of that
order is unenforcible like any other if made without consideration (Hamilton College v. Stewart, 1 N.Y. 581; Presb. Church v. Cooper, 112 N.Y.
517; 32nd St. Bap. Church v. Cornell, 117 N.Y. 601). On the other hand,
though professing to apply to such subscriptions the general law of contract, we have found consideration present where the general law of
contract, at least as then declared, would have said that it was absent
(Barnes v. Perine, 12 N.Y. 18; Presb. Soc. v. Beach, 74 N.Y. 72; Keuka
College v. Ray, 167 N.Y. 96; cf. Eastern States League v. Vail, 97 Vt. 495,
508, and cases cited; Y.M.C.A. v. Estill, 140 Ga. 291; Amherst Academy
v. Cowls, 6 Pick. 427; Ladies Collegiate Inst. v. French, 16 Gray, 196;
Martin v. Meles, 179 Mass. 114; Robinson v. Nutt, 185 Mass. 345; U. of
Pa. v. Coxe, 277 Penn. St. 512; Williston, Contracts, §116.)

A classic form of statement identifies consideration with detriment to
the promisee sustained by virtue of the promise (Hamer v. Sidway, 124
N.Y. 538; Anson, Contracts (Corbin's ed.), p. 116; 8 Holdsworth, History
of English Law, 10.) So compendious a formula is little more than a half
truth. There is need of many a supplementary gloss before the outline
can be so filled in as to depict the classic doctrine. "The promise and the
consideration must purport to be the motive each for the other, in whole
or at least in part. It is not enough that the promise induces the detriment
or that the detriment induces the promise if the other half is wanting"
(Wis. & Mich. Ry. Co. v. Powers, 191 U.S. 379, 386; McGovern v. City of
N.Y., 234 N.Y. 377, 389; Walton Water Co. v. Village of Walton, 238
N.Y. 46, 51; 1 Williston, Contracts, §139; Langdell, Summary of the law
of Contracts, pp. 82-88). If A promises B to make him a gift, consideration

may be lacking, though B has renounced other opportunities for betterment in the faith that the promise will be kept.

The half truths of one generation tend at times to perpetuate themselves in the law as the whole truths of another, when constant repetition
brings it about that qualifications, taken once for granted, are disregarded
or forgotten. The doctrine of consideration has not escaped the common
lot. As far back as 1881, Judge Holmes in his lectures on the Common
Law (p. 292), separated the detriment which is merely a consequence of
the promise from the detriment which is in truth the motive or inducement, and yet added that the courts "have gone far in obliterating this
distinction." The tendency toward effacement has not lessened with the
years. On the contrary, there has grown up of recent days a doctrine that
a substitute for consideration or an exception to its ordinary requirements
can be found in what is styled "a promissory estoppel" (Williston, Contracts, §§139, 116). Whether the exception has made its way in this State
to such an extent as to permit us to say that the general law of consideration has been modified accordingly, we do not now attempt to say. Cases
such as Siegel v. Spear & Co. (234 N.Y. 479) and DeCicco v. Schweizer
(221 N.Y. 431) may be signposts on the road. Certain, at least, it is that we
have adopted the doctrine of promissory estoppel as the equivalent of
consideration in connection with our law of charitable subscriptions. So
long as those decisions stand, the question is not merely whether the
enforcement of a charitable subscription can be squared with the doctrine of consideration in all its ancient rigor. The question may also be
whether it can be squared with the doctrine of promissory estoppel.

We have said that the cases in this State have recognized this exception, if exception it is thought to be. Thus, in Barnes v. Perine (12 N.Y.
18) the subscription was made without request, express or implied, that
the church do anything on the faith of it. Later, the church did incur
expense to the knowledge of the promisor, and in the reasonable belief
that the promise would be kept. We held the promise binding, though
consideration there was none except upon the theory of a promissory
estoppel. In Presbyterian Society v. Beach (74 N.Y. 72) a situation substantially the same became the basis for a like ruling. So in Roberts v.
Cobb (103 N.Y. 600) and Keuka College v. Ray (167 N.Y. 96) the moulds
of consideration as fixed by the old doctrine were subjected to a like
expansion. Very likely, conceptions of public policy have shaped, more
or less subconsciously, the rulings thus made. Judges have been affected
by the thought that "defenses of that character" are "breaches of faith
toward the public, and especially toward those engaged in the same enterprise, and an unwarrantable disappointment of the reasonable expectations of those interested" (W. F. Allen, J., in Barnes v. Perine, *supra*, page
24; and cf. Eastern States League v. Vail, 97 Vt. 495, 505, and cases there
cited). The result speaks for itself irrespective of the motive. Decisions
which have stood so long and which are supported by so many consider-

ations of public policy and reason, will not be overruled to save the
symmetry of a concept which itself came into our law, not so much from
any reasoned conviction of its justice, as from historical accidents of
practice and procedure (8 Holdsworth, History of English Law, 7 et seq.).
The concept survives as one of the distinctive features of our legal system. We have no thought to suggest that it is obsolete or on the way to be
abandoned. As in the case of other concepts, however, the pressure of
exceptions has led to irregularities of form.

It is in this background of precedent that we are to view the problem
now before us. The background helps to an understanding of the implications inherent in subscription and acceptance. This is so though we may
find in the end that without recourse to the innovation of promissory
estoppel the transaction can be fitted within the mould of consideration
as established by tradition.

The promisor wished to have a memorial to perpetuate her name. She
imposed a condition that the "gift" should "be known as the Mary Yates
Johnston Memorial Fund." The moment that the college accepted $1,000
as a payment on account, there was an assumption of a duty to do
whatever acts were customary or reasonably necessary to maintain the
memorial fairly and justly in the spirit of its creation. The college could
not accept the money, and hold itself free thereafter from personal responsibility to give effect to the condition (Dinan v. Coneys, 143 N.Y.
544, 547; Brown v. Knapp, 79 N.Y. 136; Gridley v. Gridley, 24 N.Y. 130;
Grossman v. Schenker, 206 N.Y. 466, 469; 1 Williston, Contracts, §§90,
370). More is involved in the receipt of such a fund than a mere acceptance of money to be held to a corporate use (cf. Martin v. Meles, 179
Mass. 114, citing Johnson v. Otterbein University, 41 Ohio St. 527, 531,
and Presb. Church v. Cooper, 112 N.Y. 517). The purpose of the founder
would be unfairly thwarted or at least inadequately served if the college
failed to communicate to the world, or in any event to applicants for the
scholarship, the title of the memorial. By implication it undertook, when
it accepted a portion of the "gift," that in its circulars of information and
in other customary ways, when making announcement of this scholarship, it would couple with the announcement the name of the donor.
The donor was not at liberty to gain the benefit of such an undertaking
upon the payment of a part and disappoint the expectation that there
would be payment of the residue. If the college had stated after receiving
$1,000 upon account of the subscription that it would apply the money to
the prescribed use, but that in its circulars of information and when
responding to prospective applicants it would deal with the fund as an
anonymous donation, there is little doubt that the subscriber would have
been at liberty to treat this statement as the repudiation of a duty impliedly assumed, a repudiation justifying a refusal to make payments in
the future. Obligation in such circumstances is correlative and mutual. A
case much in point is N.H. Hospital v. Wright (95 N.J.L. 462, 464), where

a subscription for the maintenance of a bed in a hospital was held to be enforcible by virtue of an implied promise by the hospital that the bed should be maintained in the name of the subscriber (cf. Bd. of Foreign Missions v. Smith, 209 Penn. St. 361). A parallel situation might arise upon the endowment of a chair or a fellowship in a university by the aid of annual payments with the condition that it should commemorate the name of the founder or that of a member of his family. The university would fail to live up to the fair meaning of its promise if it were to publish in its circulars of information and elsewhere the existence of a chair or a fellowship in the prescribed subject, and omit the benefactor's name. A duty to act in ways beneficial to the promisor and beyond the application of the fund to the mere uses of the trust would be cast upon the promisee by the acceptance of the money. We do not need to measure the extent either of benefit to the promisor or of detriment to the promisee implicit in this duty. "If a person chooses to make an extravagant promise for an inadequate consideration it is his own affair" (8 Holdsworth, History of English Law, p. 17). It was long ago said that "when a thing is to be done by the plaintiff, be it never so small, this is a sufficient consideration to ground an action" (Sturlyn v. Albany, 1587, Cro. Eliz. 67, quoted by Holdsworth, *supra*; cf. Walton Water Co. v. Village of Walton, 238 N.Y. 46, 51). The longing for posthumous remembrance is an emotion not so weak as to justify us in saying that its gratification is a negligible good.

   We think the duty assumed by the plaintiff to perpetuate the name of the founder of the memorial is sufficient in itself to give validity to the subscription within the rules that define consideration for a promise of that order. When the promisee subjected itself to such a duty at the implied request of the promisor, the result was the creation of a bilateral agreement (Williston, Contracts, §§60-a, 68, 90, 370; Brown v. Knapp, *supra*; Grossman v. Schenker, *supra*; Williams College v. Danforth, 12 Pick. 541, 544; Ladies' Collegiate Inst. v. French, 16 Gray, 196, 200). There was a promise on the one side and on the other a return promise, made, it is true, by implication, but expressing an obligation that had been exacted as a condition of the payment. A bilateral agreement may exist though one of the mutual promises be a promise "implied in fact," an inference from conduct as opposed to an inference from words (Williston, Contracts, §§90, 22-a; Pettibone v. Moore, 75 Hun, 461, 464). We think the fair inference to be drawn from the acceptance of a payment on account of the subscription is a promise by the college to do what may be necessary on its part to make the scholarship effective. The plan conceived by the subscriber will be mutilated and distorted unless the sum to be accepted is adequate to the end in view. Moreover, the time to affix her name to the memorial will not arrive until the entire fund has been collected. The college may thus thwart the purpose of the payment on account if at liberty to reject a tender of the residue. It is no answer to say that a duty would then arise to make restitution of the money. If such a duty be imposed, the only reason for its existence must be that there is then a failure of "consideration." To say that there is a failure of consideration is to concede that consideration has been promised since otherwise it could not fail. No doubt there are times and situations in which limitations laid upon a promisee in connection with the use of what is paid by a subscriber lack the quality of a consideration, and are to be classed merely as conditions (Williston, Contracts, §112; Page, Contracts, §523).

> It is often difficult to determine whether words of condition in a promise indicate a request for consideration or state a mere condition in a gratuitous promise. An aid, though not a conclusive test in determining which construction of the promise is more reasonable is an inquiry whether the happening of the condition will be a benefit to the promisor. If so, it is a fair inference that the happening was requested as a consideration

(Williston, *supra*, §112). Such must be the meaning of this transaction unless we are prepared to hold that the college may keep the payment on account, and thereafter nullify the scholarship which is to preserve the memory of the subscriber. The fair implication to be gathered from the whole transaction is assent to the condition and the assumption of a duty to go forward with performance (DeWolf Co. v. Harvey, 161 Wis. 535; Pullman Co. v. Meyer, 195 Ala. 397, 401; Braniff v. Baier, 101 Kan. 117; cf. Corbin, Offer & Acceptance, 26 Yale L.J. 169, 177, 193; McGovney, Irrevocable Offers, 27 Harv. L.R. 644; Sir Frederick Pollock, 28 L.Q.R. 100, 101). The subscriber does not say: I hand you $1,000, and you may make up your mind later, after my death, whether you will undertake to commemorate my name. What she says in effect is this: I hand you $1,000, and if you are unwilling to commemorate me, the time to speak is now.

The conclusion thus reached makes it needless to consider whether, aside from the feature of a memorial, a promissory estoppel may result from the assumption of a duty to apply the fund, so far as already paid, to special purpose not mandatory under the provisions of the college charter (the support and education of students preparing for the ministry), an assumption induced by the belief that other payments sufficient in amount to make the scholarship effective would be added to the fund thereafter upon the death of the subscriber (Ladies Collegiate Inst. v. French, 16 Gray, 196; Barnes v. Perine, 12 N.Y. 18, and cases there cited).

The judgment of the Appellate Division and that of the Trial Term should be reversed, and judgment ordered for the plaintiff as prayed for in the complaint, with costs in all courts.

KELLOGG, J. (dissenting). The Chief Judge finds in the expression "In loving memory this gift shall be known as the Mary Yates Johnston Memorial Fund" an offer on the part of Mary Yates Johnston to contract with Allegheny College. The expression makes no such appeal to me. Allegheny College was not requested to perform any act through which the sum offered might bear the title by which the offeror states that it shall be known. The sum offered was termed a "gift" by the offeror. Consequently, I can see no reason why we should strain ourselves to make it, not a gift, but a trade. Moreover, since the donor specified that the gift was made "In consideration of my interest in Christian education, and in consideration of others subscribing," considerations not adequate in law, I can see no excuse for asserting that it was otherwise made in consideration of an act or promise on the part of the donee, constituting a sufficient quid pro quo to convert the gift into a contract obligation. To me the words used merely expressed an expectation or wish on the part of the donor and failed to exact the return of an adequate consideration. But if an offer indeed was present, then clearly it was an offer to enter into a unilateral contract. The offeror was to be bound provided the offeree performed such acts as might be necessary to make the gift offered become known under the proposed name. This is evidently the thought of the Chief Judge, for he says: "She imposed a condition that the 'gift' should be known as the Mary Yates Johnston Memorial Fund." In other words, she proposed to exchange her offer of a donation in return for acts to be performed. Even so there was never any acceptance of the offer and, therefore, no contract, for the acts requested have never been performed. The gift has never been made known as demanded. Indeed, the requested acts, under the very terms of the assumed offer, could never have been performed at a time to convert the offer into a promise. This is so for the reason that the donation was not to take effect until after the death of the donor, and by her death her offer was withdrawn. (Williston on Contracts, sec. 62.) Clearly, although a promise of the college to make the gift known, as requested, may be implied, that promise was not the acceptance of an offer which gave rise to a contract. The donor stipulated for acts, not promises.

> In order to make a bargain it is necessary that the acceptor shall give in return for the offer or the promise exactly the consideration which the offeror requests. If an act is requested, that very act and no other must be given. If a promise is requested, that promise must be made absolutely and unqualifiedly.

(Williston on Contracts, sec 73.)

> It does not follow that an offer becomes a promise because it is accepted; it may be, and frequently is, conditional, and then it does not become a promise until the conditions are satisfied; and in case of offers for a consideration, the performance of the consideration is always deemed a condition.

(Langdell, Summary of the Law of Contracts, sec. 4). It seems clear to me
that there was here no offer, no acceptance of an offer, and no contract.
Neither do I agree with the Chief Judge that this court "found consideration present where the general law of contract, at least as then declared,
would have said that it was absent" in the cases of Barnes v. Perine (12
N.Y. 18), Presbyterian Society v. Beach (74 N.Y. 72) and Keuka College
v. Ray (167 N.Y. 96). In the *Keuka College* case an offer to contract, in
consideration of the performance of certain acts by the offeree, was converted into a promise by the actual performance of those acts. This form
of contract has been known to the law from time immemorial (Langdell,
sec. 46) and for at least a century longer than the other type, a bilateral
contract. (Williston, sec. 13.) It may be that the basis of the decisions in
Barnes v. Perine and Presbyterian Society v. Beach (*supra*) was the same
as in the *Keuka College* case. (See Presbyterian Church of Albany v.
Cooper, 112 N.Y. 517.) However, even if the basis of the decisions be a
so-called "promissory estoppel," nevertheless they initiated no new doctrine. A so-called "promissory estoppel," although not so termed, was
held sufficient by Lord Mansfield and his fellow judges as far back as the
year 1765. (Pillans v. Van Mierop, 3 Burr. 1663.) Such a doctrine may be
an anomaly; it is not a novelty. Therefore, I can see no ground for the
suggestion that the ancient rule which makes consideration necessary to
the formation of every contract is in danger of effacement through any
decisions of this court. To me that is a cause for gratulation rather than
regret. However, the discussion may be beside the mark, for I do not
understand that the holding about to be made in this case is other than a
holding that consideration was given to convert the offer into a promise.
With that result I cannot agree and, accordingly, must dissent.

Pound, Crane, Lehman and O'Brien, JJ., concur with Cardozo, Ch.
J.; Kellogg, J. dissents in opinion, in which Andrews, J., concurs.

Judgment accordingly.

NOTE

Suppose no payment had been made by Mary Yates Johnson before
her death. Recovery?

Suppose the benefactor suffers a serious financial setback before payment. Is she still liable? Consult Hamson, The Reform of Consideration,
54 L.Q. Rev. 233 at 244 (1938).

In Goetz & Scott, Enforcing Promises, An Examination of the Basis of
Contract, 89 Yale L.J. 1261, 1307, 1308 (1980), the authors observe: "The
frequent argument that the societal interest in eleemosynary activities
explains the distinctive legal treatment of charitable promises is not convincing. The social benefit from promise-making would be similarly impaired if enforcement led to restraints on future charitable promises."

Compare Salsbury v. Northwestern Bell Tel. Co., 221 N.W.2d 609 (Iowa 1974). Goetz and Scott go on to explain why, in their view, courts are more prone to enforce charitable subscriptions than intrafamilial gift promises.

> First, self-sanctions are probably less effective in the charitable than in the intrafamilial setting, because extra-legal sanctions are often limited to the goodwill value of the promisor's word. Second, in the extrafamilial context, promisors are not as disabled by social considerations from making qualitative precautionary adjustments [i.e., conditioning their promises on the occurrence or non-occurrence of future events]. Thus, in general, enforcement may induce cost-effective precautionary adjustments that increase the net beneficial reliance on charitable promises. Excessively costly self-protection by promisees may be reduced both because qualitative precautions improve the information concerning future regret contingencies and because legally imposed reassurance improves the promise's overall reliability.

89 Yale L.J. at 1308.

For a discussion of the principal case and the one preceding, see Corbin, Mr. Justice Cardozo and the Law of Contracts, 39 Colum. L. Rev. 56, 60, 52 Harv. L. Rev. 408, 412, 48 Yale L.J. 426, 430 (1939).

The *Allegheny College* case is not referred to in the many illustrations that accompany §90 of the Restatement Second. Why?

For a discussion of the various theories employed to make charitable subscriptions binding, and of the problems of public policy that such arrangements involve, see In re Stack's Estate, 164 Minn. 57, 204 N.W. 546 (1925); Danby v. Osteopathic Hosp. Assn. of Delaware, 34 Del. Ch. 427, 434-435, 104 A.2d 903 (1954). See further Note, 24 Ind. L.J. 412 (1949). For the English law, see Sixth Interim Report of the English Law Revision Committee n.25 (1937); see further Restatement Second §90, Comments *b* and *f*.

For the treatment of subscriptions for business purposes, see 1 Williston §117 (1957).

Professor Leon Lipson, in an article analyzing the "literary/rhetorical features" of Justice Cardozo's opinion, describes the way in which Cardozo oscillates back and forth between his argument based on consideration and his argument based on promissory estoppel:

> . . . Judge Cardozo goes from consideration to promissory estoppel to consideration to duty-&-obligation to promise to consideration to promissory estoppel to victory for Allegheny College. Whenever his argument emphasizing consideration runs thin, he moves on to promissory estoppel; whenever his hints in favor of promissory estoppel approach the edge of becoming a committed ground of decision, he veers off in the direction of the doctrine of consideration. Arguments that oscillate in this way, repeatedly promoting each other by the alternation, call to mind [the logician

Richard] Whately's simile of "the optical illusion effected by that ingenious
and philosophical toy called the Thaumatrope: in which two objects are
painted on opposite sides of a card, — for instance, a man and a horse,
[or] — a bird and a cage"; the card is fitted into a frame with a handle, and
the two objects are, "by a sort of rapid whirl [of the handle], presented to
the mind as combined in one picture — the man *on* the horse's back, the
bird *in* the cage."

Now what were the objects painted on the opposite sides of Judge Cardozo's Thaumatrope? His trouble was that on the consideration side he had
a solid rule but shaky facts; on the promissory-estoppel side he had a shaky
rule but (potentially) solid facts. He twirled the Thaumatrope in order to
give the impression that he had solid facts fitting a solid rule. Some lawyers
think that what emerges instead is a picture of a bird on the horse's back.

Lipson, The Allegheny College Case, 23 Yale L. Rep. 8 (Spring, 1977).

Suppose Benefactor signs and delivers to his favorite hospital a pledge
agreement that states: "To aid and assist the hospital in its humanitarian
work and in consideration of the hospital's continuing to perform that
work in the future as it has done in the past, I promise to pay $5,000 in
equal installments over the next five years." After paying the first installment, Benefactor notifies the hospital that he intends to make no further
payments. Hospital sues to recover the unpaid amount, alleging that it
has continued to perform its humanitarian work without interruption.
Under the holding of the *Allegheny College* case, as you understand it,
has the hospital stated a cause of action? Under §90 of the Restatement,
First or Second? See I. & I. Holding Corp. v. Gainsburg, 276 N.Y. 427, 12
N.E.2d 532 (1938).

For a commentary on the *Gainsburg* case, see Recent Decisions, 39
Colum. L. Rev. 283 (1939). See further Matter of Field, 11 Misc. 2d 427,
172 N.Y.S.2d 740 (1958); Hirsch v. Hirsch, 32 Ohio App. 2d 200, 289
N.E.2d 386 (1972); Mount Sinai Hospital, Inc. v. Jordan, 290 So. 2d 484
(Fla. 1974).

Section 14.   Moral Consideration

Where a man is under a legal or equitable obligation to pay, the law implies
a promise, though none was ever actually made. A fortiori, a legal or
equitable duty is a sufficient consideration for an actual promise. Where a
man is under a moral obligation, which no Court of Law or Equity can
inforce, and promises, the honesty and rectitude of the thing is a consideration. As if a man promises to pay a just debt, the recovery of which is
barred by the Statute of Limitations: or if a man, after he comes of age,
promises to pay a meritorious debt contracted during his minority, but not

for necessaries; or if a bankrupt, in affluent circumstances after his certificate, promises to pay the whole of his debts; or if a man promise to perform a secret trust, or a trust void for want of writing, by the Statute of Frauds.

Hawkes v. Saunders, 1 Cowper 289, 290, 98 Eng. Rep. 1091 (1782).

This statement, in which the doctrine of moral consideration has found its most challenging articulation, illustrates the attitude of Lord Mansfield and his fellow judges toward consideration. They were ready to cut the historical connection between consideration and the action of assumpsit and came close, it has been claimed, to identifying consideration with moral obligation. Holdsworth, The Modern History of the Doctrine of Consideration, 2 B.U.L. Rev. 87, 174 at 186 (1922). Lord Mansfield was unwilling to confine the application of the doctrine to the instances enumerated in the excerpt given above. In Hawkes v. Saunders, for instance, the promise of an executrix to pay a pecuniary legacy "in consideration of assets" was held enforceable.

Towards the middle of the nineteenth century, if not earlier, a reaction set in which found its culmination in Eastwood v. Kenyon, *infra* p. 519. In refutation of the doctrine, it was claimed that recognition of moral consideration as sufficient consideration "would annihilate the necessity for any consideration at all, in as much as the mere fact of giving a promise creates a moral obligation to perform it." Still the doctrine did not die. It survived, and not only in cases involving infant contracts, debts barred by the statute of limitations, and discharged bankrupts. Courts in this country have found the doctrine a useful tool to "escape from more hardened and definitely worded rules of law. By making a direct appeal to the mores of the time, [the doctrine] permits an easy and satisfying evolution of the law of promises by judicial action." 1A Corbin §230 (1963). To be more specific, in many cases the doctrine has been used to overcome the rule, anchored in bargain theory, that a past consideration is no consideration at all — a rule often regarded as socially undesirable, particularly where the subsequent promise was meant to assure compensation for past benefits. Even without resorting to the moral consideration doctrine, courts occasionally have seen their way clear to enforcing a promise of payment in recognition of long and faithful service by "inferring" consideration. Patterson, An Apology for Consideration, 58 Colum. L. Rev. 929, 954 (1958), citing Griffin v. Louisville Trust Co., 312 Ky. 145, 226 S.W.2d 786 (1950). In a number of states, efforts have been made to deal with past and moral consideration with the help of legislation (see pp. 549-550 *infra*). Judicial interpretation of such legislation, however, has not always been very friendly. See Henderson, Promises Grounded in the Past: The Idea of Unjust Enrichment and the Law of Contracts, 57 Va. L. Rev. 1115, 1128 et seq. (1971).

A word should be said about §86 of the Restatement Second, reprinted at p. 551 *infra*. That section dispenses with the term "moral obligation," which has been criticized for diverting judicial attention from the enrichment factor in many moral obligation cases (Henderson, *supra*, at 1126), and instead links the promise to compensate for a benefit received to the idea of unjust enrichment. Recent commentators have also pointed out that in many cases of a promise to pay for past benefits, there is an element of detrimental reliance on the part of the promisee as well. See, e.g., Perrault v. Hall, *infra* p. 532. For a useful discussion of these matters, see Henderson, *supra*, and Goetz & Scott, Enforcing Promises: An Examination of the Basis of Contract, 89 Yale L.J. 1261, 1310-1312 (1980).

GILLINGHAM v. BROWN
178 Mass. 417, 60 N.E. 122 (1901)

HAMMOND, J. This is an action upon a demand note dated October 22, 1872. At the trial, the plaintiff, in order to meet the defence of the statute of limitations, proved that the defendant delivered to the agent of the plaintiff in April, 1898, $5; and the chief question was whether this money was delivered in part payment of the note, and, if so, whether under the circumstances it had the effect of making the defendant liable to pay the remainder of the note at once, or only by instalments.

The plaintiff's evidence tended to show that in February, 1898, the defendant orally agreed to pay the note in monthly instalments of $10 each, the first instalment to be paid on the first of the following month; that, the defendant failing to pay as promised, the plaintiff's sister as agent called upon the defendant and demanded payment "of the ten dollars," or a payment "on account of the note"; that the defendant said he could not pay $10, but would pay her $5, and did so, and the payment was indorsed on the note.

The defendant admitted giving the agent the $5, but testified that "it was an act of charity" and that it was done "to get rid of her," and that in giving it he stated that it was not on account of the note; and he denied that he ever agreed to pay in monthly instalments.

In this state of the evidence the defendant asked the court to rule that if the jury should find that the defendant agreed to pay the note only in instalments of $10 per month, and that the payment of the $5 was given and taken in pursuance thereof, the plaintiff could only recover the instalments due to the date of the writ. The court declined so to rule, and instructed the jury in substance that if the defendant made this payment on account of the note their verdict should be for the plaintiff for the amount of the note and interest from the date of the demand after deducting the payments indorsed on the note. To the refusal as above requested and to the ruling given the defendant excepted. The jury found for the plaintiff in the sum of $1,049.40.

The verdict shows that the jury found that the $5 was paid by the defendant on account of the note and not as an act of charity as he contended. But it does not settle the question whether it was paid in pursuance of an agreement to pay in instalments, or upon the note generally without reference to that agreement; and since the evidence would warrant a finding either way on that question, it is plain that if it was material it should have been submitted to the jury.

The St. 21 Jac. I. c. 16, in which first appears a limitation as to the time of bringing personal actions, and upon which are modelled the various statutes of limitations in the United States, expressly provides that all such actions should be brought within the times therein prescribed; and it makes no mention of the effect of a new promise, acknowledgment or part payment. In every form of action but that of assumpsit, the construction has been in unison with the express words of the statute, but, as to that action, the statute has had varied experience in running the gauntlet of judicial exposition. There was early read into it a provision that in an action of assumpsit a promise of payment within six years prior to the action would avoid the statute, but that a confession, or simple acknowledgment by the debtor that he owed the debt would not be sufficient. Dockson v. Thomson, 2 Show. 126. At a later period, however, it was held that an acknowledgment was evidence from which a jury might properly find a new promise to pay. Heyling v. Hastings, 1 Ld. Raym. 421; S.C. Comyns, 54. Still later, Lord Mansfield said in Quantock v. England, Burr. 2628, that the statute did not destroy the debt, but only took away the remedy; and that if the debt be older than the time limited for bringing the action the debtor may waive this advantage, and in honesty he ought not to defend by such a plea, "and the slightest word of acknowledgment will take it out of the statute." In Tanner v. Smart, 6 B. & C. 603, however, the pendulum swung the other way, and Lord Tenterden, C.J., after saying that there were undoubtedly authorities to the effect that the statute is founded on a presumption of payment, that whatever repels that presumption is an answer to the statute, that any acknowledgment which repels that presumption is in legal effect a promise to pay the debt, and that, though such acknowledgment is accompanied with only a conditional promise or even a refusal to pay, the law considers the condition or refusal void, and the acknowledgment itself an unconditional answer to the statute, proceeds in an able opinion to say in substance that these cases are unsatisfactory and in conflict with some others, and that the true doctrine is that an acknowledgment can be an answer to the statute only upon the ground that it is an evidence of a new promise, and that, while, upon a general acknowledgment, where nothing is said to prevent it, a general promise to pay may and ought to be implied, yet, where a debtor guards his acknowledgment and accompanies it with a declaration to prevent any such implication, a promise to pay could not be raised by implication. This is a leading case in England on this subject.

In this country, it has very generally been held that the statute of limitations is a wise and beneficial law, not designed merely to raise a presumption of payment of a just debt from lapse of time, but to afford security against stale demands after the true state of things may have been forgotten, or may be incapable of explanation by reason of the loss of evidence, that if a new express promise be set up in answer to the statute, its terms ought to be clearly proved, and that, if there be no express promise, but a promise is to be raised in law from the acknowledgment of the debtor, such an acknowledgment ought to contain an unqualified admission of a previous subsisting debt for which the party is liable and which he is willing to pay. It follows that if the acknowledgment be accompanied by circumstances, or words, which repel the idea of an intention to pay, no promise can be implied. Bell v. Morrison, 1 Pet. 351, 7 L. ed. 175; Jones v. Moore, 5 Binn. 573. Berghaus v. Calhoun, 6 Watts, 219. Sands v. Gelston, 15 Johns. 511. Danforth v. Culver, 11 Johns. 146. Purdy v. Austin, 3 Wend. 187. In this last case the court says that the statute is one of repose and should be maintained as such; that, while the unqualified and unconditional acknowledgment of a debt is adjudged in law to imply a promise to pay, the acknowledgment of the original justice of the claim without recognizing its present existence is not sufficient; and that anything going to negative a promise or intention to pay must be regarded as qualifying the language used.

This doctrine was approved by this court in the leading case of Bangs v. Hall, 2 Pick. 368, in which Putman, J., after a review of the authorities, says: "On the whole, we are satisfied that there must be an unqualified acknowledgment not only that the debt was just originally, but it continues to be so, . . . or that there has been a conditional promise which has been performed, as is before explained."

To answer the statute there must be a promise express or implied from an acknowledgment of the debt as a present existing debt. If the promise whether express or implied be conditional, it must be shown that the conditions have been fulfilled. Cambridge v. Hobart, 10 Pick. 232. Sigourney v. Drury, 14 Pick. 38. Krebs v. Olmstead, 137 Mass. 504.

While the original debt is the cause of action, Ilsley v. Jewett, 3 Met. 439, the liability of the debtor is determined not by the terms of the old but by those of the new promise. As stated by Vice Chancellor Wigram in Phillips v. Phillips, 3 Hare, 281, 300,

The new promise, and not the old debt, is the measure of the creditor's right. . . . If the debtor promises to pay the old debt when he is able, or by instalments, or in two years, or out of a particular fund, the creditor can claim nothing more than the promise gives him.

Custy v. Donlan, 159 Mass. 245. Boynton v. Moulton, 159 Mass. 248.

Pub. Stat. chap. 197, sec. 15, provides that no acknowledgment or promise shall be evidence of a new or continuing contract to take the case out of the operation of the statute, unless contained in some writing signed by the debtor, and in sec. 16, that nothing in this provision shall be taken to alter, take away or lessen the effect of a part payment of principal or interest; and it may be contended that the effect of these two sections is to exclude all parol evidence whatever bearing upon an acknowledgment or new promise by part payment or otherwise, whether the creditor be attempting to avail himself of it for attack or the debtor for defense. But that does not seem to us to be the result. The language is that the provision of the fifteenth section shall not be taken to alter, take away or lessen the effect of part payment. But what was the effect of part payment before this statute requiring the promise or acknowledgment to be in writing? Its effect depended upon the circumstances. If a debtor made a part payment as such, it was considered as an acknowledgment that the whole debt was due, otherwise, it could not be a part payment; and so it stood upon the same footing as any other unconditional acknowledgment, and from it the law, in the absence of anything to the contrary, implied a promise to pay the whole. It has no validity to answer the statute except as an acknowledgment of the debt. In the language of Tindal, C.J., in Clark v. Hooper, 10 Bing. 480, in the mind of the party paying such a payment must be "a direct acknowledgment and admission of the debt, and is the same thing in effect as if he had written a letter to a third person that he still owed the sum in question."

But suppose a debtor says to his creditor

> I acknowledge the debt to be just, that it never has been paid, and that I have no defence except the statute of limitations. I am willing to pay and I do hereby pay to you one half of the debt, but I do not intend to waive the statute as to the rest. On the contrary I insist on my defence as to that, and I never will pay any more.

Can it be said that from such a part payment, accompanied by such a distinct affirmation of the debtor's intention not to pay more but to insist upon his defence under the statute, the law would have implied a promise to pay the remaining half?

Again, suppose a debtor says to his creditor

> Your claim against me is just, it never has been paid, and my only defence to it is the statute of limitations. I am not able to pay it now, but I will pay it when and as fast as I am able, but I will not pay in any other way, and I insist upon my defence under the statute except so far as I now waive it. I am able to pay and I do now pay you ten dollars with this understanding.

Can it be said that from such a part payment the law would have implied a promise to pay the debt according to its original terms?

To come a little more closely to what the jury might have found the facts to be in this case, suppose the debtor agrees to pay in instalments and in no other way, and clearly declares his intention to pay in no other way, and then makes a payment in compliance with the new promise. Can it be said that from such a part payment the law would have implied a promise to pay the debt in any other way? Such an interpretation of the words and act of the debtor would be inconsistent with the understanding of both parties, and would be unreasonable and unjust.

Such a partial payment as that named in either of the three cases above supposed must be construed as a conditional and not an absolute waiver. The waiver must be taken as it is, absolute if absolute, conditional if conditional. And on principle that must be so, whether it be found in a verbal promise or in a payment. There is no ground for a satisfactory distinction between a waiver by word and a waiver by an act. Each is evidence of a new promise and operative only as such; and while the cause of action is the old promise, the measure of the liability is determined by the new one.

Now it is expressly declared in Pub. Stat. chap. 197, sec. 16, that the provisions of the preceding section shall not be taken to alter, take away or lessen the effect of a part payment. There can be no doubt that prior to the passage of the law contained in sec. 15, a partial payment made in pursuance of an agreement to pay by instalments did not have the effect of making the debtor liable in any way. To say that the provisions of sec. 15 do have that effect is to alter the effect of such a part payment, and so is inconsistent with sec. 16. The law with respect to part payment is to remain as before, and the language accompanying the payment is admissible to show the intent with which the payment is made, just as it was admissible before, and that is so whether or not it contains a promise to pay upon which the creditor could have maintained an action prior to the requirement that it should be in writing.

In the case at a bar there was evidence tending to show that the defendant had orally agreed to pay in monthly instalments of $10 each, and if such an agreement had been in writing it could have been enforced according to its terms, but the right of the creditor as against a plea of the statute would have been measured by this new promise; and, even if the debtor had failed to pay, the creditor could recover only the instalment due under the terms of the agreement; and that would be so even if the defendant had made several of the payments. The creditor could take the money under the terms which the debtor had prescribed, and upon no other.

And by the reason of the thing the same principle must apply where the payment is made upon an agreement which, not being in writing, could not be enforced. If this $5 was paid in part performance of his agreement to pay by instalments, then it cannot be inferred that he intended to recognize the existence of the old debt as an actual subsisting obligation in any other way. The nature of the act is to be determined by the intention of the debtor as shown by the act, his words, and the circumstances accompanying and explaining it. Taylor v. Foster, 32

Mass. 30. Roscoe v. Hale, 7 Gray 274. See also 13 Am. & Eng. Ency. of Law, 750 et seq., for a good collection of the cases.

While in this case the evidence is conflicting, we think it would warrant a finding that the only express promise made by the defendant was to pay in monthly instalments of $10 each, and that he paid the $5 solely under that agreement. If that was so, then no other promise can be inferred from this payment and the instruction requested should have been given.

Exception sustained.

NOTE

For the various purposes of statutes of limitations, see Developments in the Law, Statutes of Limitations, 63 Harv. L. Rev. 1177, 1185 (1950). For the origins and scope of the rule that a new promise, acknowledgment, or part payment revives the indebtedness, and the nature of the creditor's cause of action, see 1 Williston §§160, 186-188, 196 (1958); 1A Corbin §214 (1963); Restatement Second §82, Comments b and c.

Following Lord Tenterden's Act, a statute passed in 1829 (9 Geo. 4, c. 14), most states, in the interest of certainty, require a new promise or acknowledgement to be in writing and signed by, or on behalf of, the promisor. An exception to the writing requirement is typically provided for in the case of part payment or the giving of a negotiable instrument or collateral security. Furthermore, a new promise supported by contemporaneous consideration need not be in writing, Cafritz v. Koslow, 167 F.2d 749 (D.C. Cir. 1948). The exact language of the English act has not been copied and there are many individual variations. On the meaning of the much litigated requirement that the acknowledgement must be definite and unqualified, see 1A Corbin §216 (1963).

Should an insolvent debtor be permitted to waive the statute of limitations? For a discussion of the question in terms of public policy, consult Central Hanover Bank and Trust Co. v. United Traction Co., 95 F.2d 50 (2d Cir. 1938).

Debts Discharged in Bankruptcy. Prior to the enactment of the Bankruptcy Reform Act of 1978, a promise to pay a debt discharged in bankruptcy was generally held enforceable. See Restatement of Contracts §83. The 1978 Act placed numerous restrictions on the enforceability of such promises. An agreement to affirm a discharged debt may be rescinded within thirty days, and in the case of a consumer debt, the agreement must be approved by the bankruptcy court as, among other things, "not imposing an undue hardship on the debtor or dependent of the debtor" and as being "in the best interest of the debtor." The bankruptcy court must also inform a debtor wishing to make a reaffirmation agreement of the consequences of doing so and tell him that such an agreement is not required under either the Bankruptcy Act or nonbankruptcy law. 11 U.S.C §524. What are the reasons for this change in the law?

A discharge by composition agreement outside bankruptcy, or any other discharge by voluntary act of the creditor, did not leave the moral obligation intact at common law. Warren v. Whitney, 24 Me. 561 (1845).

LAMPLEIGH v. BRATHWAIT
Hobart 105, 80 Eng. Rep. 255 (C.P. 1615)

Anthony Lampleigh brought an Assumpsit against Thomas Brathwait and declared, that whereas the Defendant had Feloniously slain one Patrick Mahume, the Defendant after the said Felony done, instantly required the Plaintiff to labour, and do his endeavour to obtain his Pardon from the King: Whereupon the Plaintiff upon the same Request did, by all the means he could and many Days Labour, do his Endeavor to obtain the King's pardon for the said Felony, viz. in Riding and Journeying at his own Charges from London to Roiston, when the King was there, and to London back, and so to and from Newmarket, to obtain pardon for the Defendant for the said Felony. Afterwards, scil. &c. in Consideration of the Premises, the said Defendant did Promise the said Plaintiff to give him 100 pounds, and that he had not etc. to his Damage 120 pounds.

To this the Defendant pleaded non Assumpsit, and found for the Plaintiff damage one Hundred Pounds. It was said in Arrest of Judgment, that the Consideration was passed.

But the chief Objection was, that it doth not appear, that he did any Thing towards the obtaining of the Pardon, but Riding up and down, and nothing done when he came there. And of this Opinion was my Brother [Warburton] but my self and the other two Judges were of Opinion for the Plaintiff, and so he had Judgment.

First, it was agreed, that a meer Voluntary Courtesie will not have a Consideration to uphold an Assumpsit. But if that Courtesie were moved by a Suit or Request of the Party that gives the Assumpsit, it will bind, for the Promise, though it follows, yet it is not naked, but couples it self with the Suit before, and the Merits of the Party procured by that Suit, which is the Difference. . . .

NOTE

Consult Kennedy v. Broun (1863) 13 C.B. (n.s.) 677, 740; 143 Eng. Rep. 268; A. Corbin, Cases on Contracts 326 (3d ed. 1947); Fifoot at 405; Notes, 16 Minn. L. Rev. 808 (1932), 7 U. Chi. L. Rev. 124 (1939); Corbin, Recent Developments in Contracts, 50 Harv. L. Rev. 449, 454 (1937).

The previous request rationale was ingeniously used in the following fact situation: A business house in urgent need of funds drew a time bill of exchange on defendant, another business house. Defendant held no funds of the drawer; indeed, the first house was rather deeply indebted to the second. The bill was discounted to plaintiff the day it was drawn. Having made a loan to the first business house, plaintiff then procured the defendant's acceptance of the bill, which made the defendant the principal obligor on the bill. Although the court had little trouble finding consideration for defendant's assumption of liability in plaintiff's forbearance to sue, it added: "When a man borrows money and draws on his friend, who accepts, it should be intended that the acceptor authorized him originally to borrow on the terms that he would accept, which is equivalent to a request of the loan on the part of the acceptor." Commercial Bank of Lake Erie v. Norton & Fox, 1 Hill 501 (N.Y. 1841).

EASTWOOD v. KENYON
11 Ad. & E. 438, 113 Eng. Rep. 482 (Q.B. 1840)

Lord Denman, C.J. . . . The second point arose in arrest of judgment — namely, whether the declaration showed a sufficient consideration for the promise. It stated, in effect, that the plaintiff was executor under the will of the father of the defendant's wife, who had died intestate as to his real estate, leaving the defendant's wife, an infant, his only child; that the plaintiff had voluntarily expended his money for the improvement of the real estate, while the defendant's wife was sole and a minor; and that, to reimburse himself, he had borrowed money of Blackburn, to whom he had given his promissory note; that the defendant's wife, while sole, had received the benefit, and, after she came of age, assented and promised to pay the note, and did pay a year's interest; that after the marriage the plaintiff's accounts were shown to the defendant, who assented to them, and it appeared that there was due to the plaintiff a sum equal to the amount of the note to Blackburn; that the defendant in right of his wife had received all the benefit, and, in consideration of the premises, promised to pay and discharge the amount of the note to Blackburn.

Upon motion in arrest of judgment this promise must be taken to have been proved, and to have been an express promise, as indeed it must of necessity have been, for no such implied promise in law was ever heard of. It was then argued for the plaintiff that the declaration disclosed a sufficient moral consideration to support the promise.

Most of the older cases on this subject are collected in a learned note to the case of Wennal v. Adney [3 Bosanquet & Puller 249], and the conclusion there arrived at seems to be in general,

> that an express promise can only revive a precedent good consideration, which might have been enforced at law through the medium of an implied

promise, had it not been suspended by some positive rule of law; but can give no original cause of action, if the obligation, on which it is founded, never could have been enforced at law, though not barred by any legal maxim or statute provision.

Instances are given of voidable contracts, as those of infants ratified by an express promise after age, and distinguished from void contracts, as of married women, not capable of ratification by them when widows; Lloyd v. Lee [1 Stra. 94]; debts of bankrupts revived by subsequent promise after certificate, and similar cases. Since that time some cases have occurred upon this subject, which required to be more particularly examined. Barnes v. Hedley [2 Taunt. 184] decided that a promise to repay a sum of money, with legal interest, which sum had originally been lent on usurious terms, but, in taking the account of which, all usurious items had been by agreement struck out, was binding. Lee v. Muggeridge [5 Taunt. 36] upheld an assumpsit by a widow that her executors should pay a bond given by her while a feme covert to secure money then advanced to a third person at her request. On the latter occasion the language of Mansfield, C.J., and of the whole Court of Common Pleas, is very large, and hardly susceptible of any limitation. It is conformable to the expressions used by the Judges of this Court in Cooper v. Martin [4 East, 76] where a stepfather was permitted to recover from the son of his wife, after he had attained his full age, upon a declaration for necessaries furnished to him while an infant, for which, after his full age, he promised to pay. It is remarkable that in none of these there was any allusion made to the learned note in 3 Bosanquet & Puller above referred to, and which has been very generally thought to contain a correct statement of the law. The case of Barnes v. Hedley is fully consistent with the doctrine in that note laid down. Cooper v. Martin also, when fully examined, will be found not to be inconsistent with it. This last case appears to have occupied the attention of the Court much more in respect of the supposed statutable liability of a stepfather, which was denied by the Court, and in respect of what a court of equity would hold as to a stepfather's liability, and rather to have assumed the point before us. It should, however, be observed that Lord Ellenborough in giving his judgment says: "The plaintiff having done an act beneficial for the defendant in his infancy, it is good consideration for the defendant's promise after he came of age. In such a case the law will imply a request, and the fact of the promise has been found by the jury"; and undoubtedly the action would have lain against the defendant while an infant, inasmuch as it was for necessaries furnished at his request, in regard to which the law raises an implied promise. The case of Lee v. Muggeridge must, however, be allowed to be decidedly at variance with the doctrine in the note alluded to, and is a decision of great authority. It should, however, be observed that in that case there was an actual request of the defendant during coverture, though not one binding in law; but the ground of decision there taken was

also equally applicable to Littlefield v. Shee [2 B. & Ad. 811], tried by
Gaselee, J., at N.P., when that learned judge held, notwithstanding, that
"the defendant having been a married woman when the goods were supplied, her husband was originally liable, and there was no consideration
for the promises declared upon." After time taken for deliberation this
Court refused even a rule to show cause why the nonsuit should not be
set aside. Lee v. Muggeridge was cited on the motion, and was sought to
be distinguished by Lord Tenterden, because there the circumstances
raising the consideration were set out truly upon the record; but in Littlefield v. Shee the declaration stated the consideration to be that the plaintiff had supplied the defendant with goods at her request, which the
plaintiff failed in proving, inasmuch as it appeared that the goods were in
point of law supplied to the defendant's husband, and not to her. But
Lord Tenterden added that the doctrine that a moral obligation is a
sufficient consideration for a subsequent promise is one which should be
received with some limitation. The sentence, in truth amounts to a dissent from the authority of Lee v. Muggeridge, where the doctrine is
wholly unqualified.

The eminent counsel who argued for the plaintiff in Lee v. Muggeridge spoke of Lord Mansfield as having considered the rule of nudum
pactum as too narrow, and maintained that all promises deliberately
made ought to be held binding. I do not find this language ascribed to
him by any reporter, and do not know whether we are to receive it as a
traditional report, or as a deduction from what he does appear to have
laid down. If the latter, the note to Wennal v. Adney shows the deduction
to be erroneous. If the former, Lord Tenterden and this Court declared
that they could not adopt it in Littlefield v. Shee. Indeed the doctrine
would annihilate the necessity for any consideration at all, inasmuch as
the mere fact of giving a promise creates a moral obligation to perform it.

The enforcement of such promises by law, however plausibly reconciled by the desire to effect all conscientious engagements, might be
attended with mischievous consequences to society; one of which would
be the frequent preference of voluntary undertakings to claims for just
debts. Suits would thereby be multiplied, and voluntary undertakings
would also be multiplied, to the prejudice of real creditors. The tempta-
tions of executors would be much increased by the prevalence of such a
doctrine, and the faithful discharge of their duty be rendered more difficult.

Taking, then, the promise of the defendant, as stated on this record, to
have been an express promise, we find that the consideration for it was
past and executed long before, and yet it is not laid to have been at the
request of the defendant, nor even of his wife while sole (though if it had,
the case of Mitchinson v. Hewson [7 T.R. 348] shows that it would not
have been sufficient), and the declaration really discloses nothing but a
benefit voluntarily conferred by the plaintiff and received by the defendant, with an express promise by the defendant to pay money.

If the subsequent assent of the defendant could have amounted to a *ratihabitio*, the declaration should have stated the money to have been expended at his request, and the ratification should have been relied on as matter of evidence; but this was obviously impossible, because the defendant was in no way connected with the property or with the plaintiff, when the money was expended. If the ratification of the wife while sole were relied on, then a debt from her would have been shown, and the defendant could not have been charged in his own right without some further consideration, as of forbearance after marriage, or something of that sort; and then another point would have arisen upon the Statute of Frauds which did not arise as it was, but which might in that case have been available under the plea of non assumpsit.

In holding this declaration bad because it states no consideration but a past benefit not conferred at the request of the defendant, we conceive that we are justified by the old common law of England.

Lampleigh v. Brathwait [Hob. 105] is selected by Smith [1 Sm. L.C. 67] as the leading case on this subject, which was there fully discussed, though not necessary to the decision. Hobart, C.J., lays it down that

> a mere voluntary courtesy will not have a consideration to uphold an assumpsit. But if that courtesy were moved by a suit or request of the party that gives the assumpsit, it will bind; for the promise, though it follows, yet it is not naked, but couples itself with the suit before, and the merits of the party procured by that suit; which is the difference.

a difference brought fully out by Hunt v. Bate [Dyer, 272a], there cited from Dyer, where a promise to indemnify the plaintiff against the consequences of having bailed the defendant's servant, which the plaintiff had done without request of the defendant, was held to be made without consideration; but a promise to pay £20 to plaintiff, who had married defendant's cousin, but at defendant's special instance, was held binding.

The distinction is noted, and was acted upon, in Townsend v. Hunt [Cro. Car. 408], and indeed in numerous old books; while the principle of moral obligation does not make its appearance till the days of Lord Mansfield, and then under circumstances not inconsistent with this ancient doctrine when properly explained.

Upon the whole, we are of opinion that the rule must be made absolute to arrest the judgment.

Rule to enter verdict for defendant, discharged.

Rule to arrest judgment absolute.

NOTE

The soundness of the remark of Lord Denman that the doctrine of moral consideration "would annihilate the necessity for any consideration . . ." was criticized in Muir v. Kane, 55 Wash. 131, 137, 104 P. 153, 154 (1909). The court called it "more specious than sound for it entirely ignores the distinction between a promise to pay money which the promisor is under moral obligation to pay and a promise to pay money which the promisor is under no obligation, either legal or moral, to pay."

For discussions of the case in its historical context, and for some reasons for the decision, see Atiyah at 491-493; Simpson, Innovation in Nineteenth Century Contract Law, 91 L.Q. Rev. 247 (1975).

If Sarah Suttcliffe, the minor promisor in *Eastwood*, had been liable in quasi contract for the benefits conveyed, her subsequent promise to pay would have been binding. Her husband was at common law liable for his wife's antenuptial debts[155] and his express promise would have been binding.

Under the Infants' Relief Act, enacted in England in 1874, contracts made by infants are no longer capable of ratification. The application of the statute presupposes that ratification was necessary for the enforcement of the contract made by the infant. Liability for necessaries supplied, for instance, is not affected by the statute. In this country, no comparable statute exists; a few states, however, require a promise of the former infant to be in writing and signed, e.g., N.J. Stat. Ann. §25:1-6.

MILLS v. WYMAN

3 Pick. 207 (Mass. 1825)

This was an action of assumpsit brought to recover a compensation for the board, nursing, &c., of Levi Wyman, son of the defendant, from the 5th to the 20th of February 1821. The plaintiff then lived at Hartford, in Connectict; the defendant, at Shrewsbury, in this county. Levi Wyman, at the time when the services were rendered, was about 25 years of age, and had long ceased to be a member of his father's family. He was on his return from a voyage at sea, and being suddenly taken sick at Hartford, and being poor and in distress, was relieved by the plaintiff in the manner and to the extent above stated. On the 24th of February, after all the expenses had been incurred, the defendant wrote a letter to the plaintiff, promising to pay him such expenses. There was no consideration for this promise, except what grew out of the relation which subsisted between Levi Wyman and the defendant, and Howe, J., before whom the cause was tried in the Court of Common Pleas, thinking this not sufficient to support the action, directed a nonsuit. To this direction the plaintiff filed exceptions. . . .

PARKER, C.J. General rules of law established for the protection and security of honest and fair-minded men, who may inconsiderately make

155. 1 Blackstone, Commentaries 443 (1765).

promises without any equivalent, will sometimes screen men of a different character from engagements which they are bound in foro conscientiae to perform. This is a defect inherent in all human systems of legislation. The rule that a mere verbal promise, without any consideration, cannot be enforced by action, is universal in its application, and cannot be departed from to suit particular cases in which a refusal to perform such a promise may be disgraceful.

The promise declared on in this case appears to have been made without any legal consideration. The kindness and services towards the sick son of the defendant were not bestowed at his request. The son was in no respect under the care of the defendant. He was twenty-five years old, and had long left his father's family. On his return from a foreign country, he fell sick among strangers, and the plaintiff acted the part of the good Samaritan, giving him shelter and comfort until he died. The defendant, his father, on being informed of this event, influenced by a transient feeling of gratitude, promises in writing to pay the plaintiff for the expenses he had incurred. But he has determined to break this promise, and is willing to have his case appear on record as a strong example of particular injustice sometimes necessarily resulting from the operation of general rules.

It is said a moral obligation is a sufficient consideration to support an express promise; and some authorities lay down the rule thus broadly; but upon examination of the cases we are satisfied that the universality of the rule cannot be supported, and that there must have been some pre-existing obligation which has become inoperative by positive law, to form a basis for an effective promise. The cases of debts barred by the statute of limitations, of debts incurred by infants, of debts of bankrupts, are generally put for illustration of the rule. Express promises founded on such pre-existing equitable obligations may be inforced; there is a good consideration for them; they merely remove an impediment created by law to the recovery of debts honestly due, but which public policy protects the debtors from being compelled to pay. In all these cases there was originally a quid pro quo; and according to the principles of natural justice the party receiving ought to pay; but the legislature has said he shall not be coerced; then comes the promise to pay the debt that is barred, the promise of the man to pay the debt of the infant, of the discharged bankrupt to restore to his creditor what by law he had lost. In all these cases there is a moral obligation founded upon an antecedent valuable consideration. These promises therefore have a sound legal basis. They are not promises to pay something for nothing; not naked pacts; but the voluntary revival or creation of obligation which before existed in natural law, but which had been dispensed with, not for the benefit of the party obliged solely, but principally for the public convenience. If moral obligation, in its fullest sense, is a good substratum for an express promise, it is not easy to perceive why it is not equally good to support an implied promise. What a man ought to do, generally he ought to be made to do, whether he promise or refuse. But the law of society has left most of such obligations to the *interior* forum, as the tribunal of conscience has been aptly called. Is there not a moral obligation upon every son who has become affluent by means of the education and advantages bestowed upon him by his father, to relieve that father from pecuniary embarrassment, to promote his comfort and happiness, and even to share with him his riches, if thereby he will be made happy? And yet such a son may, with impunity, leave such a father in any degree of penury above that which will expose the community in which he dwells, to the danger of being obliged to preserve him from absolute want. Is not a wealthy father under strong moral obligation to advance the interest of an obedient, well disposed son, to furnish him with the means of acquiring and maintaining a becoming rank in life, to rescue him from the horrors of debt incurred by misfortune? Yet the law will uphold him in any degree of parsimony, short of that which would reduce his son to the necessity of seeking public charity.

Without doubt there are great interests of society which justify withholding the coercive arm of the law from these duties of imperfect obligation, as they are called; imperfect, not because they are less binding upon the conscience than those which are called perfect, but because the wisdom of the social law does not impose sanctions upon them.

A deliberate promise, in writing, made freely and without any mistake, one which may lead the party to whom it is made into contracts and expenses, cannot be broken without a violation of moral duty. But if there was nothing paid or promised for it, the law, perhaps wisely, leaves the execution of it to the conscience of him who makes it. It is only when the party making the promise gains something, or he to whom it is made loses something, that the law gives the promise validity. And in the case of the promise of the adult to pay the debt of the infant, of the debtor discharged by the statute of limitations or bankruptcy, the principle is preserved by looking back to the origin of the transaction, where an equivalent is to be found. An exact equivalent is not required by the law; for there being a consideration, the parties are left to estimate its value; though here the courts of equity will step in to relieve from gross inadequacy between the consideration and the promise.

These principles are deduced from the general current of decided cases upon the subject, as well as from the known maxims of the common law. The general position, that moral obligation is a sufficient consideration for an express promise, is to be limited in its application, to cases where at some time or other a good or valuable consideration has existed.

A legal obligation is always a sufficient consideration to support either an express or an implied promise; such as an infant's debt for necessaries, or a father's promise to pay for the support and education of his minor children. But when the child shall have attained to manhood, and shall have become his own agent in the world's business, the debts he incurs, whatever may be their nature, create no obligation upon the father; and it seems to follow, that his promise founded upon such a debt has no legally binding force.

The cases of instruments under seal and certain mercantile contracts, in which consideration need not be proved, do not contradict the principles above suggested. The first import a consideration in themselves, and the second belong to a branch of the mercantile law, which has found it necessary to disregard the point of consideration in respect to instruments negotiable in their nature and essential to the interest of commerce.

Instead of citing a multiplicity of cases to support the positions I have taken, I will only refer to a very able review of all the cases in the note in 3 Bos. & Pul. 249. The opinions of the judges had been variant for a long course of years upon this subject, but there seems to be no case in which it was nakedly decided, that a promise to pay the debt of a son of full age, not living with his father, though the debt were incurred by sickness which ended in the death of the son, without a previous request by the father proved or presumed, could be enforced by action.

It has been attempted to show a legal obligation on the part of the defendant by virtue of our statute, which compels lineal kindred in the ascending or descending line to support such of their poor relations as are likely to become chargeable to the town where they have their settlement. But it is a sufficient answer to this position, that such legal obligation does not exist except in the very cases provided for in the statute, and never until the party charged has been adjudged to be of sufficient ability thereto. We do not know from the report any of the facts which are necessary to create such an obligation. Whether the deceased had a legal settlement in this commonwealth at the time of his death, whether he was likely to become chargeable had he lived, whether the defendant was of sufficient ablity, are essential facts to be adjudicated by the court to which is given jurisdiction on this subject. The legal liability does not arise until these facts have all been ascertained by judgment, after hearing the party intended to be charged.

For the foregoing reasons we are all of the opinion that the non-suit directed by the Court of Common Pleas was right, and that judgment be entered thereon for costs for the defendant.

NOTE

Would a promise on the part of Levi Wyman to pay Mills $30 have been binding? Consult Restatement of Restitution §116; 1 Williston §§144-146 (1958); Corbin, Cases on Contracts 326, 327 (1947). See also R.

Pound, Law and Morals 37-38 (1926). Would such a promise be binding today? Restatement Second §86, *infra* p. 551, and Comments *d* and *e*.

C_____ v. W_____
480 S.W.2d 474 (Tex. Ct. Civ. App. 1972)

ELLIS, Chief Justice.

This is an appeal from a judgment decreeing the enforcement of a child support agreement entered into by the child's natural father and mother who have never been married to each other. The validity of such contract is challenged by the father-appellant on the ground of the lack of consideration.

Reversed and rendered.

The child's mother, herein referred to as appellee, along with her attorneys, as plaintiffs, brought suit against the father-appellant for an alleged breach of two contracts between the appellant and appellee. The first of the two contracts, designated as "Agreement For Child Support," purported to obligate the father-appellant for the support of R_____ A. C_____, the natural child of appellant and mother-appellee who were never married to each other. The support agreement set out that the appellant was to pay to the appellee the sum of $125 each month "until such child reaches the age of eighteen years, or becomes married, whichever occurs first." The evidence shows that appellant had paid the total sum of $1,375 under such agreement. The plaintiffs' petition alleged that the last payment on the support agreement was made in May of 1966, and appellant was sued for sixty defaulted payments of $125 each, making the total sum of $7,500 claimed to be due thereunder as of May 10, 1971. The second contract, designated as "Settlement Agreement," dated May 13, 1966, was predicated upon a previous claim asserted by the appellee against the appellant that dealt wholly with matters other than child support, whereunder the appellant agreed to pay appellee and her attorneys the monthly sum of $300 on the 15th day of each month thereafter until a total sum of $18,000 had been paid. The plaintiffs alleged that appellant had made only two such payments, the total sum of $600, and sued appellant under the "Settlement Agreement" for the total sum of $17,400, plus interest from August 15, 1966.

The appellant answered the plaintiffs' pleading by general denial and the defense of failure or want of consideration. The trial was to the court without a jury. Judgment was entered for the plaintiffs and recited separate amounts of recovery with respect to each of the two contracts. As to the "Settlement Agreement," recovery was awarded under the judgment in separate specified sums for the appellee and her attorneys, respectively, while the recovery under the "Agreement For Child Support" was awarded to the appellee alone. The award under the judgment as to the "Settlement Agreement" is not questioned in this appeal. It is from the judgment rendered against him on the "Agreement For Child Support" that the appellant has perfected this appeal.

The record discloses that the facts are undisputed. The appellant and appellee, natural father and mother, respectively, of the above mentioned minor child, signed and swore to the above designated "Agreement For Child Support" before a notary public. Those provisions of the respective agreements which are deemed pertinent to the determination of the questions raised in this appeal shall be paraphrased and/or quoted in part. In substance, the child support agreement recites that the appellant acknowledged and represented that the minor child, who was born to the appellee, "is my child, and I am therefore, and in consideration thereof, entering into the following support agreement." In addition to the monthly payments of $125 each, the appellant agreed to pay all reasonable expenses for the child's medical care, and to carry at all times a hospitalization policy upon such child. Also, appellant agreed to take out a non-cancellable policy of decreasing term insurance on his life for a term of eighteen years with the child named as beneficiary. The mother-appellee agreed that this contract shall be the basis of "all child support obligations of" [appellant], "the father of my said child." We find nothing in the record which would require the court to take judicial notice of or apply the laws of any state other than those of the State of Texas.

Upon appellant's request, the court made and entered findings of fact and conclusions of law; however, the court refused to comply with appellant's request to make a finding as to specific consideration for the agreement. In its Conclusions of Law, the court found, among other matters, that (1) the "Agreement For Child Support" constituted an enforceable contract between appellant and appellee; (2) the appellee "is the sole owner of the contractual rights contained within that contract and for enforcement of which this lawsuit is brought"; and (3) appellant had breached the contract entitled "Agreement For Child Support" by his failure to make all of the required monthly payments up to the date specified in the plaintiff's pleadings.

In appellant's points of error, he contends (1) that the court erred in failing to render judgment for appellant on the "Agreement For Child Support" because the agreement was supported by no consideration as a matter of law, and (2) alternatively, in the event absence of consideration is not established as a matter of law, the court erred in failing to make, after due request, a finding as to specific consideration to support the agreement. The appellee joined issue with appellant's assignments of error by submitting three reply points.

In support of this first point of error, appellant urges that the agreement was supported by no consideration as a matter of law because, under such agreement, the appellant received no benefit and the appellee suffered no detriment. Appellant insisted that, absent consideration, he had no obligation to support an illegitimate child. The appellee objects to the appellant's reference to the child as an illegitimate child and insists that the well-known presumption in favor of legitimacy should prevail until the party raising the issue of illegitimacy has discharged his burden of controverting such presumption with sufficient and competent evidence. According to Webster's Third New International Dictionary, the word "illegitimate" is an adjective meaning "born of parents not married to each other." It is well established that legitimacy of children necessarily depends on the marriage of their parents, but in the absence of such marriage the children are illegitimate. 8 Tex. Jur. 2d Bastardy §8, at p. 525. During cross examination by appellant's counsel the mother-appellee gave the uncontroverted testimony that she was never married to the appellant, the acknowledged natural father of the child. By virtue of this evidence, the presumption of legitimacy no longer continued, and, in the absence of any further evidence on the matter, under the state of the record we conclude that the child in question would be deemed as illegitimate.

We note in appellee's brief that the possibility was mentioned that two persons may discover that there was a relationship between them which one or both of the parties believed to be in the nature of a common law marriage, but fell short of that status and was instead merely a putative relationship, and thus, the two persons would never have been married to each other. In this connection, appellee has cited various cases holding that children born of a putative relationship should nevertheless be legitimate as to both parents. In general, the cited cases dealt with situations in which there was some evidence of circumstances and/or conduct on the part of one or both of the parents of the child partaking of the nature of a common law marriage relationship. The record contains no such evidence in the instant case, and it is our opinion that the cited cases and rule relied upon are inapplicable here. When the presumption of the status of legitimacy no longer prevailed by reason of appellee's uncontroverted testimony, and in the absence of any further evidence to alter such status, we do not agree that we can with propriety speculate that some sort of relationship existed between the parents which could be construed to effectively re-establish the presumption of legitimacy.

It is well established that at common law the father is under no legal obligation for the support and maintenance of his illegitimate child. Home of the Holy Infancy v. Kaska, 397 S.W.2d 208 (Tex. Sup. 1965); Lane v. Phillips, 69 Tex. 240, 6 S.W. 610 (1887); Beaver v. State, 96 Tex. Cr. R. 179, 256 S.W. 929 (1923); and G_____ v. P_____, 466 S.W.2d 41 (Tex. Civ. App. — San Antonio 1971, *writ ref'd n.r.e.*). Also, it is the majority view of the courts that, absent legislation on the subject, the father of an illegitimate child cannot be required to support his child. 30 A.L.R. Anno. Illegitimate — Duty to Support, 1069, 10 Am. Jur. 2d,

Bastards §68; 10 C.J.S. Bastards §18. There is no Texas statute requiring the natural father to support and maintain his illegitimate child. The Texas courts, have uniformly held that a father is not under a common law or statutory duty to support his illegitimate child. See G_____ v. P_____, *supra,* and cases cited therein.

With respect to the particular basis upon which a father's liability to the mother of an illegitimate child may be grounded, we note the following language set out in 8 Tex. Jur. 2d Bastardy §13, Duty to Support, at p. 530:

> Texas has no statutory bastardy proceeding so common to many of the states. The father might be liable to the mother, for special damage, in a proper case, as for breach of promise . . . , but this is the mother's action and not the child's. *It is not "support."* (emphasis added)

It is thus recognized that, although a father may be held liable for "special damages," a different rule may be applicable as to an alleged obligation for child support. Further, we deem it significant that the two contracts involved in the suit from which this appeal arises were each entered into for different purposes and are treated separately in all essential respects. The "Agreement For Child Support" is confined to the subject of support of the child, and the subsequent contract designated as "Settlement Agreement" deals strictly with subjects other than child support, including an asserted claim by the appellee for an "alleged breach of promise of marriage." Also, under the "Settlement Agreement," the appellee expressly releases all claims and causes of action against the appellant, specifically providing that the *only* remedy appellee shall have for breach of the "Settlement Agreement" is to enforce the payment of the specific sum recited as the consideration therefor. The agreement further provides that the "Settlement Agreement" in no way affects, alters or in any manner changes the obligations of the appellant to make the child support payments set forth in the parties' previous "Agreement For Child Support," and that appellee's remedies under the support agreement "are in no manner controlled or affected by this release and settlement." Thus, the two contracts are completely segregated, one not being dependent upon the other for any purpose. Also, it is noted that the court made separate findings and entered separate and unrelated awards in its judgment with respect to each of the two contracts, one dealing with appellee's claims on matters other than support and the other dealing with wholly support. The appellant here is challenging only that part of the judgment dealing with the support contract on the grounds that he is not legally obligated for the support and therefore recovery under the contract is unenforceable.

It is well settled that there can be no recovery under a contract unless it is supported by adequate consideration, which requires that there be either a benefit to the promisor or a detriment to the promisee. Under the established law in Texas, prior to the execution of the agreement for child support, there existed no legal obligation for the father to support his illegitimate child. Also, prior to the execution of the agreement, the mother had custody of the child, and she was the one burdened with the legal obligation to support it. After the appellant had executed the agreement, he had only promised to do something that was not his legal obligation. Additionally, since the agreement to support ran to the mother, it was merely a promise to do something that she, and not the appellant, was legally bound to do. Thus, the appellant gained no legal benefit by virtue of the agreement. Further, under Texas law, after the appellee executed the agreement, she suffered no detriment, for by this contract she assumed no greater legal obligation than she already had, i.e., that which is associated with the mere support and maintenance of the child. Even the recitation in the agreement to the effect that the contract would be the basis of all child support obligations of the appellant did not change her status with respect to her expectations for child support, for, in the light of the authorities above cited, she had no legal right to expect or obtain *any* support from the appellant. Thus, when she made such agreement, she gave up no right and thereby suffered no detriment. In a legal sense, the appellant gained nothing and the appellee lost nothing in the transaction.

It has been generally held that in the absence of any statutory obligations on the father to support his illegitimate child, his express promise to the child's mother, who is legally bound to support it, to pay for the maintenance of the child, resting alone on his natural affection for the child and his moral obligation to support it, is a promise which the law cannot enforce for want of legal consideration. See 30 A.L.R., *supra*, and Illegitimate Child-Support Agreement, 20 A.L.R. 3d 500 (1968). Further, in Texas, a moral obligation is not regarded as sufficient consideration for support of a contract. McBride v. McBride, 256 S.W. 2d 250 (Tex. Civ. App. — Austin 1953, *no writ*). Also, see 13 Tex. Jur. 2d Moral Obligation §68.

Appellee takes the position that the contract, which is the basis of the suit, contained within its terms an acknowledgment of consideration by the appellant and that he is estopped from contradicting such assertion and statement. Under the theory of estoppel by contract relied upon by appellee, a person is estopped to deny the truth of the matters agreed upon as consideration for the execution of the contract. This contract recites what the appellant's consideration is — "That I . . . do acknowledge that" [the named child] born to [appellee] "is my child and *I am therefore, and in consideration thereof,* entering into the following agreement. . . ." (emphasis added). Under the theory of "estoppel by contract" a party to the contract is estopped to deny the truth of the facts as stated in the contract. The appellant does not seek to deny the facts

recited. These undenied facts relative to the consideration are not sufficient consideration in law to support his promise, for they, in effect,
obligate him to support his illegitimate child which he is not legally obligated to do. In effect, the recited consideration is a recognition of his
moral obligation which in law is insufficient to support the contract.
Thus, we find no merit in appellee's contention that estoppel by contract
is applicable in the instant case.

By reason of the absence of a Texas statute imposing the legal obligation upon the father to support his illegitimate child, the continued uniform recognition of the long established rule of the common law, and the
recent consideration by our Supreme Court in Home of the Holy Infancy
v. Kaska, *supra*, regarding the standing of the father of an illegitimate
child and its positive pronouncement that the father is not under a common law or statutory duty to support his illegitimate child, we must hold
that the "Agreement For Child Support" is unenforceable by reason of
absence of consideration as a matter of law. This conclusion renders
unnecessary our consideration of appellant's other point of error. As to
whether a recognized moral duty of a father to support his illegitimate
child should be converted into a legal one whereby the courts can compel
its performance is a proper subject for legislative consideration.

The judgment of the trial court is reversed and here rendered that
appellee take nothing by her suit on the child support agreement.

NOTE

Would the analysis of Medberry v. Olcovich, *infra* p. 544, and §90 have
helped the mother in this case?

PERREAULT v. HALL
94 N.H. 191, 49 A.2d 812 (1946)

Assumpsit on an express contract for the continuation of services as
forelady in a manufacturing enterprise with an agreement not to marry.
The two counts of the plaintiff's declaration are substantially the same,
although one is designated "in a plea of the case" and the other, as "based
upon contract." The defendants' testator, Archer H. Fownes, purchased
a paper box factory in Rochester in 1912, in which the plaintiff had been
employed since 1895. She continued as an employee and in about four
years became forelady in charge of all the girl workers, which position she
held until her retirement, agreed to by both Mr. Fownes and herself, in
May of 1937. The plaintiff alleged, in substance, that on or about July,
1929, and at other times the testator promised her that he would pay her
well and enough so that she would be assured of a good living for the rest

of her life, if she would remain with him as business assistant and adviser, give her full attention to said business by not becoming married and make no statements or claims against him relating to past happenings. It is alleged further that she agreed to do as requested. The declaration also states that in February, 1937, the testator wrote her acknowledging that she had worked as agreed and had never married as requested. On May 7, 1937, Mr. Fownes gave the plaintiff the following writing:

Fownes Manufacturing Co.
Manufacturers of
Paper Boxes
Rochester, New Hampshire
May 7th 37

In consideration of forty years of continuous service, twenty in charge of my box mfg. business, I agree to pay to Sadie Pearault of Rochester, twenty dollars ($20) per week as long as she lives, or until some other agreement is agreed on, the same to be given as a pension for continuous service. In case of my death the pension is to continue as long as there is sufficient income from my estate to take care of it. If a settlement for a single amount at one payment is made this document is to be returned and destroyed.

If at any time this document is made public for any reason, except for the purpose of collection, or if at any time the beneficiary should make statements against the moral character of the signer of this document then it becomes null and void. If Miss Pearault should marry this contract ends one year after her marriage.

Signed Archer H. Fownes.

Mr. Fownes paid the plaintiff $20 a week from May 7, 1937, to the time of his death in July, 1943.

A motion to dismiss filed by the defendants was denied by the Court subject to their exception. All questions of law raised by said motion were reserved and transferred in advance of trial by Leahy, J. . . . .

JOHNSTON, J. The defendants argue that the plaintiff alleges inconsistent claims in her two counts. It is unnecessary to decide whether such a matter of abatement can be raised by a motion to dismiss. The counts are wrongly designated but may be amended. The first does not describe a tort action and is not a plea of the case. Each is based upon an express promise and accordingly is a count in special assumpsit. They are brought for the same cause of action. A cause of action may be described in different counts that vary in allegations of facts. Hitchock v. Munger, 15 N.H. 97, 102. This is true even of counts in contract and tort based on a single cause of action. Crawford v. Parsons, 63 N.H. 438, 443.

It is not quite clear from the declaration just what were the promises of the plaintiff, if a bilateral contract is established, or the acts to be performed by her, if a unilateral contract is proven. However, no defense on the ground of indefiniteness of consideration can be made in view of the testator's positive admission in February, 1937, that the plaintiff had complied with his requests. "If, however, the side of the agreement which was originally too vague for enforcement becomes definite by entire or partial performance, the other side of the agreement (or a divisible part thereof, corresponding to the performance received), though originally unenforceable, becomes binding." 1 Williston, Contracts (Rev. ed.), s. 49, p. 139.

Recovery cannot be based on the writing of May 7, 1937, for it recites nothing to be given by the plaintiff in exchange for or in reliance upon the promises of said document. "Accordingly, something which has been given before the promise was made and therefore, without reference to it, cannot, properly speaking, be legal consideration." 1 Williston, Contracts (Rev. ed.), s. 142, p. 508. Wilson v. Edmonds, 24 N.H. 517, 546. If no agreement concerning the subject matter of the declaration in this case that is legally binding upon the parties was reached before May 7, 1937, then the defendants are entitled to a directed verdict. The writing of said date signed by the testator and accepted by the plaintiff is evidence of what the parties may have agreed to earlier either bilaterally or unilaterally. It is not a discharge or release of any earlier agreement since it is incomplete and not a binding contract. 17 C.J.S. 887; Connell v. Company, 88 N.H. 316.

It is impossible to say without the evidence of the facts whether the allegation "make no statements or claims against him relating to past happenings" is a statement of forbearance that is in and of itself alone sufficient consideration for a contract. No opinion is given concerning this in advance of trial.

The motion to dismiss raises the point whether the contract sued upon is not void because it is in restraint of marriage and so against public policy. All agreements against marriage are not illegal. A contract for personal services that contains a provision in restraint of marriage is incidental thereto is valid if the provision is reasonable. "The modern law regards bargains and conditions in restraint of marriage as only prima facie illegal and will accord them validity if the restraint is shown to be reasonable under the circumstances. For example, reasonable contracts involving the performance of services which are inconsistent with matrimony have been upheld." 6 Williston, Contracts (Rev. ed.), s. 1741, p. 4926. Restatement, Contracts, s. 581; 122 A.L.R. 19, 127; Gleason v. Mann, 312 Mass. 420; Fletcher v. Osborn, 282 Ill. 143; King v. King, 63 Ohio St. 363.

The term "reasonable" in the above statements of a valid agreement in restraint of marriage means that the provisions against marriage should be limited to the requirements of the main object of the contract. In the present case the provision that the plaintiff should not marry and so perhaps interrupt or put an end to the service of employment, should be limited to the term of employment, not last for the plaintiff's life. In Gleason v. Mann, *supra*, it was held that if the plaintiff's promise meant that she was never to marry unless she married the defendant, it would impose a general restraint upon marriage that would be void, and that under such circumstances she could not recover.

The stipulation of the writing of May 7, 1937, "if Miss Pearault should marry this contract ends one year after of marriage," if it should be found to be a provision of a contract between the parties, is not in restraint of marriage. It contemplates merely the termination of the pension from Mr. Fownes one year after marriage, which ordinarily would provide at least an equivalent support. Lewis v. Johnson, 212 Mo. App. 19.

The exception of the defendants is overruled.

Case discharged.

All concurred.

NOTE

Suppose Mr. Fownes had promised plaintiff the pension in order to make up for inadequate wages and the document had contained a clause to this effect. Recovery? Consult and contrast Megines v. McChesney, 179 Iowa 563, 160 N.W. 50 (1917); Griffin v. Louisville Trust Co., 213 Ky. 145, 226 S.W.2d 786 (1950). Would there be recovery under Restatement Second §86, *infra* p. 551? Consider the following observation: "Benefit beyond an agreed contractual valuation is surely to be found in satisfactory and uninterrupted service of long tenure. Besides, the very fact of promise after performance tends to verify an actual receipt of value." Henderson, Promises Grounded in the Past: The Idea of Unjust Enrichment and the Law of Contracts, 57 Va. L. Rev. 1115, 1176 (1971).

In re SCHOENKERMAN'S ESTATE
236 Wis. 311, 294 N.W. 810 (1940)

FOWLER, J. Goldie Sucher and Ethel Sucher filed claims against the estate of Ben S. Schoenkerman, deceased. The claimants were mother-in-law and sister-in-law, respectively, of the decedent. Both claims are for services rendered to the decedent during a series of years in caring for the decedent's home and children. After continuance of the service for ten years the decedent executed and delivered to the mother-in-law his promissory note for $500 and to the sister-in-law his like note for $1,500. The claimants in their claims applied the amount of the notes upon the aggregates claimed, and demanded judgment for the difference. The mother-in-law's claim aggregated $500 and the sister-in-law's $4,610. The court allowed judgments for the amounts of the notes, but disallowed anything in excess of these sums.

The wife of the deceased died in May, 1928. She was a daughter of the one claimant and sister of the other. At the time of the death the claimants were maintaining a home in Chicago. The mother kept the house, and the daughter was employed outside at $15 per week. The decedent had two children, a son thirteen years old and a daughter seventeen years old. At the solicitation of the decedent the mother and daughter broke up their home in Chicago, and went to Milwaukee there to take care of the decedent's home and the children and continued to do so until a short time before the death of the decedent, who died May 18, 1939. The notes were executed May 14, 1938, and were payable in eight months from date. In maintaining the decedent's home, the mother did the cooking for the family and the daughter did the entire purchasing for the maintenance of the home and of the clothing for the children. She took entire charge of the household and of caring for the children and did everything of that nature that the wife and mother could have done had she lived. The appellant contends that the mother and daughter lived as members of the family, and that their relations to the decedent were such that the services were gratuitous, and intent to make compensation for them will not be presumed, but express agreement to pay therefor must be proved in order to warrant compensation. This may be conceded. An express agreement was not proved. The trial court so found, and held that there was no legal obligation to pay for the services rendered except as was covered by the notes, but that the notes were valid. The court did not state the basis of his holding that the notes were valid, but if such basis appears his ruling must be sustained.

The crucial question in this case is whether there was consideration for the notes other than natural love and affection. If the sole consideration was the latter then there can be no recovery. Estate of Smith, 226 Wis. 556, 560, 277 N.W. 141. However, the *Smith* Case recognizes the rule that a moral obligation will operate as consideration for an executory promise "whenever the promisor has originally received value, material pecuniary benefit, under circumstances giving rise to a moral obligation on his part to pay for that which he has received." To this rule the opinion in the *Smith* Case cites Park Falls State Bank v. Fordyce, 206 Wis. 628, 238 N.W. 516; Elbinger v. Capitol & Teutonia Co. 208 Wis. 163, 242 N.W. 568; Onsrud v. Paulsen, 219 Wis. 1, 261 N.W. 541. In the *Elbinger* Case, *supra*, the rule is stated as above quoted. The rule above stated was also applied in Estate of Hatten, 233 Wis. 199, 218, 288 N.W. 278, wherein the *Elbinger* and *Park Falls State Bank* Cases, *supra*, are cited in support.

The appellant contends that as in this case the claimants were relatives of the deceased living in his family there was no legal obligation on the part of the deceased to pay for the services rendered, and that a legal obligation must have existed in order to render the moral-obligation rule applicable. If it be true under the circumstances of this case the presumption arises that the services were gratuitous, a fact we need not and therefore do not decide, it does not follow that there must have been a legal obligation to compensate in order to constitute a moral obligation a good consideration. It is said of the *Park Falls State Bank* Case, *supra,* in the *Elbinger* Case, *supra,* p. 165:

> We there repudiated, as too narrow, the principle obtaining in some jurisdictions that in order for a moral consideration to be sufficient to support an executory promise there must have been a pre-existing legal obligation to do the thing promised, which, for some reason, as the statute of limitations, discharge in bankruptcy, or the like, is unenforceable.

In the instant case the decedent was manifestly under a moral obligation to pay the claimants in addition to what they had received for their ten years of service to him. In executing and delivering the notes to them he plainly recognized that obligation, and from any point of view it afforded more than ample consideration for the notes. The notes were negotiable instruments. They recite that they were executed for "value received." There is a presumption that they were given for a consideration. As a moral obligation existed to pay for the great excess of value of the services received by the decedent over the value of the board and lodging received from the decedent by the claimants, that moral obligation will be presumed to be the consideration for the notes. The notes therefore became a legal obligation, as distinguished from a mere unexecuted promise to make a gift of money.

By the Court. — The order of the county court is affirmed.

NOTE

Assume that the note had been "far in excess" of the real value of the benefits conveyed. Liability? In re Hatten's Estate, 233 Wis. 199, 288 N.W. 278 (1940). See further Earl v. Peck, 60 N.Y. 596 (1876); Cal. Civ. Code §1606, *infra* p. 550; Restatement Second §86, *infra* p. 551. In connection with the "disproportion principle" set forth in §86(2)(b), see Goetz & Scott, Enforcing Promises: An Examination of the Basis of Contract, 89 Yale L.J. 1261, 1312 n.133 (1980).

ELBINGER v. CAPITOL & TEUTONIA CO.
208 Wis. 163, 242 N.W. 568 (1932)

OWEN, J. The plaintiff is a licensed real-estate broker. Pursuant to an oral understanding between the defendant Capitol & Teutonia Company, the plaintiff, Karl Elbinger, and his associate, Herbert Baer, said Elbinger and Baer negotiated a lease of certain premises owned by the defendant. These services were not rendered pursuant to a written contract, as required by sec. 240.10, Stats., and it is conceded that an action by the brokers could not have been maintained to recover the value of the brokerage services. However, after the transaction was consummated, the defendant voluntarily settled with the brokers, paying them $200 in cash and giving to each of them its promissory note in the sum of $146. This action is brought to recover on the promissory note given by the defendant to the plaintiff, and the defense is that there was no consideration for the note and it is void. The contention is that as the brokers could not have recovered on their original contract because it was not in writing as required by the provisions of sec. 240.10, the voluntary promise to pay, made after the services were performed, is without any consideration and unenforceable.

The plaintiff contends that he rendered valuable services to the defendant of which it enjoyed the benefit, and that, while he could not have recovered on the original contract because declared void by statute, nevertheless the fact that he rendered services of value to the defendant, which services were not against public policy, in a transaction not involving moral turpitude, a moral obligation arose on the part of the defendant to pay therefor, which obligation constituted a good consideration for the subsequent and independent promise of the defendant to pay. We recently had under consideration the question of what constitutes a good consideration to support a contract in Park Falls State Bank v. Fordyce, 206 Wis. 628, 238 N.W. 516. We there repudiated, as too narrow, the principle obtaining in some jurisdictions that in order for a moral consideration to be sufficient to support an executory promise there must have been a pre-existing legal obligation to do the thing promised, which, for some reason, as the statute of limitations, discharge in bankruptcy, or the like, is unenforceable. We there said that "one ought, in morals, to make return for things of value not intended as a gift that he has accepted, and he ought in morals to do what he knowingly and advisedly gave one acting for his benefit and to his own hurt to understand he would do." We there held that whenever the promisor has originally received value, material pecuniary benefit, under circumstances giving rise to a moral obligation on his part to pay for that which he has received, it is a sufficient consideration to support a promise on his part to pay therefor. The mere fact that a statute enacted for the benefit of the promisor prevents legal liability on his part does not deprive him of the power by a subsequent promise to assume a legal obligation to do that which an honest man should do where no moral turpitude is involved in the transaction.

Sec. 240.10, Stats., was enacted to curb the tendency of real-estate brokers to impose upon their clients and to prevent frauds and perjuries of which such transactions seemed to afford a prolific source. If a real-estate broker would recover his commission upon his original contract, the contract must be in compliance with sec. 240.10. However, that section has accomplished its purpose when it relieves the owner of legal liability under a contract resting in parol. When the contract is completed, when the services of which the owner has received the benefit have been performed, he is at liberty to say how much he will pay the broker for those services. He may pay him therefor in cash and, when he does so, such payment may not be recovered by him. He may settle with his promissory note, and when he does so at a time when he is dealing at arms' length, at a time when he knows what he has received, the moral consideration resting upon him to pay for that which he has received is a sufficient consideration to support his promise to pay. This is all in accordance with the law as laid down by this court in Park Falls State Bank v. Fordyce, *supra*. It is also in accordance with many decisions from other jurisdictions involving identical transactions under a similar statute. Bagaeff v. Prokopik, 212 Mich. 265, 180 N.W. 427; Mohr v. Rickgauer, 82 Neb. 398, 117 N.W. 950; Muir v. Kane, 55 Wash. 131, 104 Pac. 153; Coulter v. Howard, 203 Cal. 17, 262 Pac. 751. These cases all hold that the promise of an owner made after the services have been rendered is sufficient to constitute a legal obligation on his part to pay the broker for his services even though the original contract was not in accordance with the statute and did not give rise to a legal enforceable obligation on the part of the owner. Bagnole v. Madden, 76 N.J.L. 255, 69 Atl. 967, is the only case called to our attention to the contrary.

By the Court. — Judgment affirmed.

NOTE

Consult Muir v. Kane, 55 Wash. 131, 105 P. 153 (1909); Homefinders v. Lawrence, 80 Idaho 543, 335 P.2d 893 (1959). On the role of formality in establishing liability for a promise for benefit received, see Henderson, Promises Grounded in the Past: The Idea of Unjust Enrichment and the Law of Contracts, 57 Va. L. Rev. 1115, 1159 et seq. (1971).

WEBB v. McGOWIN

27 Ala. App. 82, 168 So. 196 (1935)

Appeal from Circuit Court, Butler County; A. E. Gamble, Judge.

Action by Joe Webb against N. Floyd McGowin and Joseph F. McGowin, as executors of the estate of J. Greeley McGowin, deceased. From a judgment of nonsuit, plaintiff appeals. . . .

BRICKEN, Presiding Judge. This action is in assumpsit. The complaint as originally filed was amended. The demurrers to the complaint as

amended were sustained, and because of this adverse ruling by the court
the plaintiff took a nonsuit, and the assignment of errors on this appeal
are predicated upon said action or ruling of the court.

A fair statement of the case presenting the questions for decision is set
out in appellant's brief, which we adopt.

On the 3d day of August, 1925, appellant while in the employ of the W.
T. Smith Lumber Company, a corporation, and acting within the scope of
his employment, was engaged in clearing the upper floor of mill No. 2 of
the company. While so engaged he was in the act of dropping a pine block
from the upper floor of the mill to the ground below; this being the usual
and ordinary way of clearing the floor, and it being the duty of the plaintiff
in the course of his employment to so drop it. The block weighed about 75
pounds.

As appellant was in the act of dropping the block to the ground below,
he was on the edge of the upper floor of the mill. As he started to turn the
block loose so that it would drop to the ground, he saw J. Greeley McGowin, testator of the defendants, on the ground below and directly under
where the block would have fallen had appellant turned it loose. Had he
turned it loose it would have struck McGowin with such force as to have
caused him serious bodily harm or death. Appellant could have remained
safely on the upper floor of the mill by turning the block loose and allowing
it to drop, but had he done this the block would have fallen on McGowin
and caused him serious injuries or death. The only safe and reasonable way
to prevent this was for appellant to hold to the block and divert its direction
in falling from the place where McGowin was standing and the only safe
way to divert it so as to prevent its coming into contact with McGowin was
for appellant to fall with it to the ground below. Appellant did this, and by
holding to the block and falling with it to the ground below, he diverted the
course of its fall in such way that McGowin was not injured. In thus
preventing the injuries to McGowin appellant himself received serious
bodily injuries, resulting in his right leg being broken, the heel of his right
foot torn off and his right arm broken. He was badly crippled for life and
rendered unable to do physical or mental labor.

On September 1, 1925, in consideration of appellant having prevented
him from sustaining death or serious bodily harm and in consideration of
the injuries appellant had received, McGowin agreed with him to care for
and maintain him for the remainder of appellant's life at the rate of $15
every two weeks from the time he sustained his injuries to and during the
remainder of appellant's life; it being agreed that McGowin would pay this
sum to appellant for his maintenance. Under the agreement McGowin
paid or caused to be paid to appellant the sum so agreed on up until
McGowin's death on January 1, 1934. After his death the payments were
continued to and including January 27, 1934, at which time they were
discontinued. Thereupon plaintiff brought suit to recover the unpaid installments accruing up to the time of the bringing of the suit. . . .

In other words, the complaint as amended averred in substance: (1)
That on August 3, 1925, appellant saved J. Greeley McGowin, appellee's

testator, from death or grievous bodily harm; (2) that in doing so appellant sustained bodily injury crippling him for life; (3) that in consideration of the services rendered and the injuries received by appellant, McGowin agreed to care for him the remainder of appellant's life, the amount to be paid being $15 every two weeks; (4) that McGowin complied with this agreement until he died on January 1, 1934, and the payments were kept up to January 27, 1934, after which they were discontinued.

The action was for the unpaid installments accruing after January 27, 1934, to the time of the suit.

The principal grounds of demurrer to the original and amended complaint are: (1) It states no cause of action; (2) its averments show the contract was without consideration; (3) it fails to allege that McGowin had, at or before the services were rendered, agreed to pay appellant for them; (4) the contract declared on is void under the statute of frauds.

1. The averments of the complaint show that appellant saved McGowin from death or grievous bodily harm. This was a material benefit to him of infinitely more value than any financial aid he could have received. Receiving this benefit, McGowin became morally bound to compensate appellant for the services rendered. Recognizing his moral obligation, he expressly agreed to pay appellant as alleged in the complaint and complied with this agreement up to the time of his death; a period of more than 8 years.

Had McGowin been accidentally poisoned and a physician, without his knowledge or request, had administered an antidote, thus saving his life, a subsequent promise by McGowin to pay the physician would have been valid. Likewise, McGowin's agreement is disclosed by the complaint to compensate appellant for saving him from death or grievous bodily injury is valid and enforceable.

Where the promisee cares for, improves, and preserves the property of the promisor, though done without his request, it is sufficient consideration for the promisor's subsequent agreement to pay for the service, because of the material benefit received. [Citations.]

In Boothe v. Fitzpatrick, 36 Vt. 681, the court held that a promise by defendant to pay for the past keeping of a bull which had escaped from defendant's premises and had been cared for by plaintiff was valid, although there was no previous request, because the subsequent promise obviated that objection; it being equivalent to a previous request. On the same principle, had the promisee saved the promisor's life or his body from grievous harm, his subsequent promise to pay for the services rendered would have been valid. Such service would have been far more material than caring for his bull. Any holding that saving a man from death or grievous bodily harm is not a material benefit sufficient to uphold a subsequent promise to pay for the service, necessarily rests on the assumption that saving life and preservation of the body from harm have only a sentimental value. The converse of this is true. Life and preservation of the body have material, pecuniary values, measurable in dollars and cents. Because of this, physicians practice their profession charging for services rendered in saving life and curing the body of its ills, and surgeons perform operations. The same is true as to the law of negligence, authorizing the assessment of damages in personal injury cases based upon the extent of the injuries, earnings, and life expectancies of those injured.

In the business of life insurance, the value of a man's life is measured in dollars and cents according to his expectancy, the soundness of his body, and his ability to pay premiums. The same is true as to health and accident insurance.

It follows that if, as alleged in the complaint, appellant saved J. Greeley McGowin from death or grievous bodily harm, and McGowin subsequently agreed to pay him for the service rendered, it became a valid and enforceable contract.

2. It is well-settled that a moral obligation is a sufficient consideration to support a subsequent promise to pay where the promisor has received a material benefit, although there was no original duty or liability resting on the promisor. [Citations.] In the case of State ex rel. Bayer v. Funk, [105 Or. 134, 199 P. 592, 209 P. 113], the court held that a moral obligation is a sufficient consideration to support an executory promise where the promisor has received an actual pecuniary or material benefit for which he subsequently expressly promised to pay.

The case at bar is clearly distinguishable from that class of cases where the consideration is a mere moral obligation or conscientious duty unconnected with receipt by promisor of benefits of a material or pecuniary nature. Park Falls State Bank v. Fordyce, [206 Wis. 628, 238 N.W. 516]. Here the promisor received a material benefit constituting a valid consideration for his promise.

3. Some authorities hold that, for a moral obligation to support a subsequent promise to pay, there must have existed a prior legal or equitable obligation, which for some reason had become unenforceable, but for which the promisor was still morally bound. This rule, however, is subject to qualification in those cases where the promisor, having received a material benefit from the promisee, is morally bound to compensate him for the services rendered and in consideration of this obligation promises to pay. In such cases the subsequent promise to pay is an affirmance or ratification of the services rendered carrying with it the presumption that a previous request for the services was made. [Citations.]

Under the decisions above cited, McGowin's express promise to pay appellant for the services rendered was an affirmation or ratification of what appellant had done raising the presumption that the services had been rendered at McGowin's request.

4. The averments of the complaint show that in saving McGowin from death or grievous bodily harm, appellant was crippled for life. This

was part of the consideration of the contract declared on. McGowin was benefited. Appellant was injured. Benefit to the promisor or injury to the promisee is a sufficient legal consideration for the promisor's agreement to pay. Fisher v. Bartlett, 8 Greenl. (Me.) 122, 22 Am. Dec. 225; State ex rel. Bayer v. Funk, *supra.*

5. Under the averments of the complaint the services rendered by appellant were not gratuitous. The agreements of McGowin to pay and the acceptance of payment by appellant conclusively shows the contrary.

6. The contract declared on was not void under the statute of frauds (Code 1923, §8034). The demurrer on the ground was not well taken. 25 R.C.L. 456, 457 and 470, §49.

The cases of Shaw v. Boyd, 1 Stew. & P. 83, and Duncan v. Hall, 9 Ala. 128, are not in conflict with the principles here announced. In those cases the lands were owned by the United States at the time the alleged improvements were made, for which subsequent purchasers from the government agreed to pay. These subsequent purchasers were not the owners of the lands at the time the improvements were made. Consequently, they could not have been made for their benefit.

From what has been said, we are of the opinion that the court below erred in the ruling complained of; that is to say, in sustaining the demurrer, and for this error the case is reversed and remanded.

Reversed and remanded.

SAMFORD, Judge (concurring).

The questions involved in this case are not free from doubt, and perhaps the strict letter of the rule, as stated by judges, though not always in accord, would bar a recovery by plaintiff, but following the principle announced by Chief Justice Marshall in Hoffman v. Porter, Fed. Cas. No. 6,577, 2 Brock. 156, 159, where he says, "I do not think that law ought to be separated from justice, where it is at most doubtful," I concur in the conclusions reached by the court.

WEBB v. McGOWIN

232 Ala. 374, 168 So. 199 (1936)

FOSTER, Justice. . . .

The opinion of the Court of Appeals here under consideration recognizes and applies the distinction between a supposed moral obligation of the promisor, based upon some refined sense of ethical duty, without material benefit to him, and one in which such a benefit did in fact occur. We agree with that court that if the benefit be material and substantial, and was to the person of the promisor rather than to his estate, it is within the class of material benefits which he has the privilege of recognizing and compensating either by an executed payment or an executed promise to pay. The cases are cited in that opinion. The reason is emphasized when the compensation is not only for the benefits which the promisor received, but also for the injuries either to property or person of the promisee by reason of the service rendered.

Writ [of certiorari] denied.

NOTE

The case is noted in 31 Ill. L. Rev. 390 (1936). Contrast Harrington v. Taylor, 225 N.C. 690, 36 S.E.2d 227 (1945). Would J. Greeley McGowin have under an obligation to Webb in the absence of any subsequent promise on McGowin's part? Consult Restatement of Restitution §116.

After noting that one of the reasons for refusing to enforce unilateral (gift) promises is evidentiary, i.e., that it often is difficult in such cases to determine whether in fact a promise was made, Posner argues that "the presence of altruistic motivation makes the promise a more plausible one — i.e., one less likely to be a figment of the promisee's imagination — than in the standard unilateral promise case. Stated otherwise, the legal-error costs of enforcing the promise are lower in the rescue case." Posner, Gratuitous Promises in Economics and Law, 6 J. Legal Stud. 411, 419 (1977). Posner goes on to defend the decision in the principal case on this ground. Ibid. On the basis of this reasoning, if Webb had been killed in the fall, would a promise to his widow to pay her a small annuity be binding? Consider Pershall v. Elliott, 249 N.Y. 183, 163 N.E. 554 (1928) (a non-rescue case).

MEDBERRY v. OLCOVICH
15 Cal. App. 2d 263, 59 P.2d 551 (1936)

WHITE, J., pro tem. This appeal is prosecuted from a judgment entered against plaintiffs and in favor of defendants. The action was one for damages for personal injuries sustained by the minor plaintiff, who was a guest in an automobile which was overturned near the intersection of Norton Avenue and Fourth Street, in the city of Los Angeles, shortly after 7 o'clock on the evening of September 27, 1933. Plaintiff C. J. Medberry, Jr., was joined as plaintiff in the capacity of guardian ad litem and also individually. Named as defendants are the owner and driver of the guest car, John Olcovich, a minor and his parents, Emil Olcovich and Dorothy Olcovich, who had signed his application for a driver's license.

The complaint herein contains three causes of action. . . . The third cause of action is in contract, and is predicated upon a promise of the defendant Emil Olcovich to pay the hospital and surgical expenses for the injuries sutained by John Raymond Medberry. . . .

Appellants' attack upon the court's findings and judgment as to count three of the complaint presents a more serious question. The trial court found as facts that plaintiff C. J. Medberry, Jr., father of the minor plaintiff, John Raymond Medberry, necessarily incurred expenses in the sum of $1,058 for medical and surgical attention to said minor plaintiff; that said sum was the reasonable value of such services; that defendant Emil Olcovich had agreed to pay the reasonable medical and surgical expenses, and that in reliance upon said promise the father of said minor plaintiff incurred such expenses. The finding that such promise was made by defendant Emil Olcovich and that the father of the minor plaintiff relied thereon is supported by testimony in the record given by plaintiff C. J. Medberry, Jr., and corroborated by the witness C. E. Brooks. The father of the minor plaintiff testified:

> He said that he was very sorry that the accident happened and got up to go, and as he got to the door, he said, "Now, Mr. Medberry, we are sorry that this thing happened, but you have whatever done is necessary to get the boy fixed up, and I will stand any reasonable expense." And I thanked him, and said that was nice, "I appreciate that"; that I thought the doctor knew my financial condition; and I would see to it that they were made as low as could be and I would have those things done for the boy; and he replied, "Well, you have the boy taken good care of and send me the bills."

It also appears from the record that subsequent to this conversation, and at the time the minor plaintiff was about to be dismissed from the hospital, plaintiff C. J. Medberry, Jr., had a conversation with defendant Emil Olcovich in which the former advised Mr. Olcovich that his financial condition was such that he did not have money to pay the hospital bill, amounting to approximately $60. The following morning defendant Emil Olcovich brought to the father of the minor plaintiff $60, which was used to pay the hospital bill. On another subsequent occasion, defendant Emil Olcovich, pursuant to his promise, paid to plaintiff, C. J. Medberry, Jr., $75.

But the trial court further found as a fact that said promise on the part of defendant Emil Olcovich was without "good consideration"; by reason of which defendant Emil Olcovich was not liable thereunder.

Appellants contend that the findings of fact as to lack of consideration for the promise of defendant Emil Olcovich to pay the reasonable value of medical and surgical expenses necessarily incurred by plaintiff C. J. Medberry, Jr., in an effort to cure his minor son, are contrary to law and without support in the evidence. We find ourselves in accord with this view of appellants. It is true that the defendant Emil Olcovich was in no way legally responsible for the injuries received by the minor plaintiff herein, and he might therefore have refused to assist or care for the minor plaintiff in any way; but the minor plaintiff had been injured while riding in an automobile driven by defendant Emil Olcovich's son, by reason of which the former expressed his sympathy for said minor plaintiff and his anxiety that the minor plaintiff should have good care. He was also aware of the fact that the minor plaintiff needed attention and care which, by reason of inadequate financial ability, the father of said minor plaintiff was unable to procure for the boy. Coupled with this is the fact that on two separate occasions the defendant Emil Olcovich, in conformity with his promise, made payments to the minor plaintiff's father, in the sum of $135. Under such circumstances, it seems to us there was some moral obligation resting on the defendant Emil Olcovich, predicated on his promise, to furnish to the minor plaintiff such assistance and care as were necessary to relieve the latter's suffering. This obligation is shown by the evidence to have been recognized from the start, was partially executed by him, and in our opinion should be held to constitute a sufficient consideration for the legal obligation resting thereon. The defendant Emil Olcovich ought not now, therefore, after the services have been rendered and the expenses incurred in reliance upon his promise, and after he has made partial payments pursuant to his promise, be permitted to repudiate it, and deny all liability thereunder. This line of reasoning has been followed by the courts in numerous instances as for example, in Scott v. Monte Cristo Oil etc. Co., 15 Cal. App. 453 [115 Pac. 64]; Fraser v. San Francisco Bridge Co., 103 Cal. 79, 84 [36 Pac. 1037]; Scott v. Superior Sunset Oil Co., 144 Cal. 140 [77 Pac. 817]. In our opinion, therefore, the appellants were entitled to judgment for the $1,058 which the court found to be the reasonable value of the medical and surgical expenses, less the $135 paid by defendant Emil Olcovich on account thereof. . . .

For the foregoing reasons, the judgment is affirmed as to respondents John Olcovich and Dorothy Olcovich. As to the respondent Emil Olcovich the judgment is reversed, with directions to the court below to enter judgment in favor of appellants and against respondent Emil Olcovich in the sum of $923; the parties to bear their respective costs on appeal.

York, Acting P.J., and Doran, J., concurred.

A petition by respondents to have the cause heard in the Supreme Court, after judgment in the District Court of Appeal, was denied by the Supreme Court on September 4, 1936, and the following opinion then rendered thereon:

THE COURT. The petition for a hearing in this court is denied on the ground that the judgment of the District Court of Appeal is proper even though it may be assumed to be based upon the conclusion, among others, that the agreement was sufficiently supported by a moral obligation. The plaintiffs suffered prejudice by reason of the expenses incurred by them on the promise of the defendant Emil Olcovich. Under such circumstances a sufficient legal consideration for the promise was present. (§§1605, 1606, Civ. Code.)

NOTE

On the relation between reliance theory and promises grounded in the past, see Henderson, Promises Gounded in the Past: The Idea of Unjust Enrichment and the Law of Contracts, 57 Va. L. Rev. 1115, 1181-1182 (1971); Goetz & Scott, Enforcing Promises: An Examination of the Basis of Contract, 89 Yale L.J. 1261, 1311-1312 (1980).

LAWRENCE v. OGLESBY
178 Ill. 122, 52 N.E. 945 (1899)

Appeal from the Appellate Court for the Third District; — heard in that court on appeal from the Circuit Court of Logan county; the Hon. George W. Herdman, Judge, presiding.

Mr. Justice PHILLIPS delivered the opinion of the court: Appellant, a brother of appellee, was, with the latter, a legatee under the will of Alexander Lawrence, who had by his will devised to appellant property of the value of about $25,000, subject to a charge in favor of another brother, amounting to about $3500. By the will a life estate in land of about the value of $7000 was devised to appellee, with remainder to her children who attained the age of twenty-one. In his lifetime Alexander Lawrence promised his daughter, the appellee, to build on the land so devised to her a house of the value of $1500. On or about June 29, 1896, Alexander Lawrence received a serious injury, which caused his death about five weeks thereafter. Within two hours after receiving the injury he asked to be left alone with Mrs. Turner, his sister-in-law, and the appellant. Mrs. Turner tesifies:

> He asked all to go away except Arthur and myself. He said to me, "I want you to hear what I am going to say"; then, "I have made my will"; then to Arthur, "I want you to pay Georgia $1500 not mentioned in my will." He asked Arthur if he heard that. He bowed his head and said he did. He says, "You hear that Frank?" I said, "Yes; sir." He said to Arthur again. "You will do that, Arthur?" and Arthur said that he would. This was an hour or two after the injury. My given name is Frances. I am called Frank in the family.

A part of this conversation was overheard by the appellee.

The appellant admits the conversation was had as testified to by Mrs. Turner, but claims that subsequently to that time, — about two or three weeks afterwards, — he had another conversation with his father, which he details, and which, as shown by the abstract, was as follows: "Now, you may state, Mr. Lawrence, what was said in that conversation." To this question plaintiff objected; the court overruled the objection and plaintiff excepted, and the witness answered:

> My best recollection is that father broached the subject in regard to this $1500, and I asked him; I says: "As I haven't the money," I says, "do I have to mortgage the land or do I have to borrow the money to pay this?" He says, "No, sir," he says, "as you get the money off of the farm you pay it to them." I says, "I will." My sister came in there when I told my father that I would, and I told her in just a little bit afterwards what it was that I had agreed to do. I agreed to pay the $1500. I don't know that my father said anything more, only just what I have told. I have not at any time since coming into possession of those lands under my father's will been able to raise the $1500 for my sister without encumbering the property.

The appellee brought an action at law to recover the $1500, and filed a declaration containing the common counts and a special count. The plaintiff recovered in the trial court, and on appeal to the Appellate Court for the Third District that judgment was affirmed. . . .

Appellant insists that no consideration existed for the promise, and that the same is a nullity, as attempting to enforce a parol trust in opposition to the terms of a will; that no spoken words can revoke or annul a will or a verbal agreement change any testamentary terms; that there is no remedy by an action at law, even conceding the facts, but that resort must be had to a court of equity. The evidence is clear the father stated he had made a will, and desired his son, the appellant, to pay appellee $1500. Prior to the time of his injury he had promised appellee he would expend that amount for her benefit. He recognized that compliance with this promise was a duty and an obligation on his part. In the shadow of death he remembered it and desired his promise should be carried out. His will was merely ambulatory, and could be changed by him. He knew he had a right to do this and the son knew it. With this knowledge he retained his sister-in-law and the son near him, and said: "I have made a will. I want you, Arthur, to pay Georgia $1500. Will you do it?" He recognized a moral obligation as existing in consequence of his promise to his daughter. "When a man is under a moral obligation which no court of equity can enforce, and promises, the honesty and rectitude of the thing is a consideration." (Hawks v. Saunders, Cowp. 290.) Recognizing that obligation, and exacting a promise from his son to carry out that promise, the promise of the son has for its consideration the honesty and rectitude of the duty of compliance. Promises of this character have frequently been recognized as enforceable and as founded on a sufficient consideration. [Citations.]

To hold the son could not be required to comply with such promise, as not being based on a sufficient consideration, would be to disregard the fact that the will was merely ambulatory and could be changed by the testator so long as he was of sound and disposing mind, and that he must have known that fact, and would be, in effect, to aid the appellant in the preparation of a fraud on appellee. Gilpatrick v. Glidden, 81 Me. 137; Drakeford v. Wilks, [3 Atk. 539]; Russell v. Jacobson, [10 Hare 204].

It is not a change of testamentary terms by a verbal agreement nor a revocation of a will by spoken words; neither is it an attempt to engraft a parol trust in opposition to the terms of a will. The will remained as it was written. It was not changed because of the promise; neither can it be doubted that had the promise not been made it would not have remained as written. There was here a full and sufficient consideration for the promise. That promise was for the benefit of appellee. Where a contract is entered into by one with another for the benefit of a third person, which third person may maintain an action in his own name for a breach thereof. Such is the well recognized rule, and one not an open question in this State. [Citations.] In the enforcement of such right on such a promise resort may be had to a court of law. It is not necessary to resort to chancery. The common count for money had and received for the use of another is an equitable form of common law pleading, and of itself is sufficient on which to authorize the admission of this evidence and sustain a recovery. Eggleston v. Buck, 24 Ill. 262.

The judgment of the Appellate Court for the Third District is affirmed. Judgment affirmed.

Statutory Provisions. After reviewing the case law under the following statutes, Henderson observes that "[t]he interplay between these various statutory efforts and the common law system of case analysis serves to point up the general failure of contract to establish a set of distinctions capable of dealing with promises which reach into the past." Henderson, Promises Grounded in the Past: The Idea of Unjust Enrichment and the Law of Contracts, 57 Va. L. Rev. 1115, 1133 (1971).

NEW YORK GENERAL OBLIGATIONS LAW

§5-1105. WRITTEN PROMISE EXPRESSING PAST CONSIDERATION

A promise in writing and signed by the promisor or by his agent shall not be denied effect as a valid contractual obligation on the ground that consideration for the promise is past or executed, if the consideration is expressed in the writing and is proved to have been given or performed and would be a valid consideration but for the time when it was given or performed.

NOTE

See N.Y.L. Revision Commission, Leg. Doc. No. 65, 395-396 (1941); Patterson, An Apology for Consideration, 58 Colum. L. Rev. 929, 954-956 (1958).

CALIFORNIA CIVIL CODE (1872)

§1606. GOOD CONSIDERATION; LEGAL OR MORAL OBLIGATION.
HOW FAR LEGAL OR MORAL OBLIGATION IS A
GOOD CONSIDERATION

An existing legal obligation resting upon the promisor, or a moral obligation originating in some benefit conferred upon the promisor, or prejudice suffered by the promisee, is also a good consideration for a promise, to an extent corresponding with the extent of the obligation, but no further or otherwise.

NOTE

Keys, Cause and Consideration in California, A Re-Appraisal, 47 Calif. L. Rev. 74 (1959); see Medberry v. Olcovich, *supra* p. 544; In re McConnell's Estate, 6 Cal. 2d 493, 58 P.2d 639 (1936); Herbert v. Lankershim, 9 Cal. 2d 409, 71 P.2d 220 (1937). Consult also §1605 of the California Civil Code.

GEORGIA CODE ANNOTATED

§20-303. GOOD AND VALUABLE CONSIDERATIONS; DEFINITIONS

Considerations are distinguished into good and valuable. A good consideration is such as is founded on natural duty and affection, or on a strong moral obligation. A valuable consideration is founded on money, or something convertible into money, or having a value in money, except marriage, which is a valuable consideration.

RESTATEMENT OF CONTRACTS SECOND

§86.   PROMISE FOR BENEFIT RECEIVED

(1)   A promise made in recognition of a benefit previously received by the promisor from the promisee is binding to the extent necessary to prevent injustice.

(2)   A promise is not binding under Subsection (1)

(a)   if the promisee conferred the benefit as a gift or for other reasons the promisor has not been unjustly enriched; or

(b)   to the extent that its value is disproportionate to the benefit.

CHAPTER 4

Fairness of the Bargain and Equality: The Idea of Justice in Exchange

Section 1. Bargaining and Economic Liberty

COHEN, THE BASIS OF CONTRACT, 46 Harv. L. Rev. 553, 581, 582 (1933): "While a legal theory must not ignore common sense, it must also go beyond it. For common sense, while generally sound at its core, is almost always vague and inadequate. Common sentiment, for instance, demands an equivalent. But what things are equivalent? It is easy to answer this in regard to goods or services that have a standard market value. But how shall we measure things that are dissimilar in nature, or in a market where monopolistic or other factors prevent a fair or just price? Modern law therefore professes to abandon the effort of more primitive systems to enforce material fairness within the contract. The parties to the contract must themselves determine what is fair. Thereby, however, the law loses a good deal of support in the moral sense of the community.

"Though legal historians like Ames are right in insisting that the common-law doctrine of consideration did not originate in the law's insistence on equivalence in every contract, the latter idea cannot be eliminated altogether. It colors the prevailing language as to consideration, and especially the doctrine that in a bilateral contract each promise is consideration for the other. If a bare promise is of no legal validity, how can it be of any profit to the promisee or of any detriment to the promisor? Clearly, two things that are valueless cannot become of value by being exchanged for the other. The real reason for the sanctioning of certain exchanges of promises is that thereby certain transactions can be legally protected, and when we desire to achieve this result we try to construe the transaction as an exchange of promises."

NOTE, THE PEPPERCORN THEORY OF CONSIDERATION AND THE DOCTRINE OF FAIR EXCHANGE IN CONTRACT LAW, 35 Colum. L. Rev. 1090, 1090-1091 (1935): "Pervading the complex field of fine-spun theories of consideration are two inconsistent ideas. On the one hand, consideration is said to be only a form; on the other, it assures a fair exchange. In substantiation of the first view and in virtually absolute negation of the second stands the age-old formula that mere inadequacy of consideration is never a bar to enforcement of a contract. Although frequently subject to evasion this general formula has gone virtually unchallenged by the courts and has met with only occasional criticism by the writers.

"Justification for this purported refusal to supervise the ethics of the market place is sought in doctrines of laissez-faire. Aside from the somewhat anachronistic character of the argument in a period of rising recognition of the social interest in 'private business,' it is clear that there has been constant judicial delimitation, in the law of fraud and duress, of the permissible pressures to be used in the bargaining process. In general, the freedom from regulation postulated by laissez-faire adherents is demonstrably non-existent and virtually inconceivable. Bargaining power exists only because of government protection of the property rights bargained, and is properly subject to government control. Undaunted, the courts urge that their inability to compare values justifies the inadequacy rule. While the complexity of the exchange process renders a precise standard utopian, the total inability is belied in practice. Enforcement has been denied to contracts involving unfair disparity. Even more refined comparison is attempted by those jurisdictions which recognize 'inadequacy' as a bar to specific performance but will decree cancellation only for 'gross inadequacy.' Valid logical or practical opposition to judicial enforcement of fair exchange has thus not been offered. Further, however, the weight of the mass of pronouncements supporting the rule that inadequacy is immaterial is substantially weakened by an examination of the cases."

The issue of whether the validity of a contract requires an equivalence of exchange values, though dormant in most legal systems for some time, has experienced a revival of sorts in the last few decades.[1] The questions

1. For modern treatment of this issue, see generally Hale, Coercion and Distribution in a Supposedly Noncoercive State, 38 Pol. Sci. Rev. 470-479 (1923); Dalzell, Duress by Economic Pressure, 20 N.C.L. Rev. 237 (1942); Hale, Bargaining, Duress, and Economic Liberty, 43 Colum. L. Rev. 603 (1943); Dawson, Economic Duress — An Essay in Perspective, 45 Mich. L. Rev. 253 (1947); R. Hale, Freedom Through Law, chs. 2 & 7 (1952); the review by F. H. Knight in 39 Va. L. Rev. 871 (1953) is worth reading; Leff, Unconscionability and the Code: The Emperor's New Clause, 115 U. Pa. L. Rev. 485, 528-541 (1967); Ellinghaus, In Defense of Unconscionability, 78 Yale L.J. 757 (1969); Goldberg, Institutional Change and the Quasi-Invisible Hand, 17 J. Law & Econ. 461 (1974); Epstein, Unconscionability: A Critical Reappraisal, 18 J. Law & Econ. 293 (1975); Trebilcock, The Doctrine of Inequality of Bargaining Power, 26 U. Toronto L.J. 359 (1976); discussing Macaulay v. Schroeder Publishing Co. Ltd.; Posner, Gratuitous Promises in Economics and Law, 6 J. Legal Studies 411 (1977); Schwartz, A Reexamination of Non-Substantive Unconscionability, 63 Va. L. Rev. 1053 (1977); Kronman, Contract Law and Distributive Justice, 89 Yale L.J. 472 (1980).

that beset us now were already known to Roman law, which offered conflicting answers. According to a famous passage in the Corpus Juris that reflects the individualism of classical Roman law, the parties to a sales contract were by nature permitted to outwit one another.[2] There was no remedy for gross unfairness unaccompanied by fraud, and duress was given a rather restricted meaning.

In the postclassical period, an imperial rescript imposed a limitation on freedom of contract, introducing with regard to sales of land the famous *laesio enormis* principle: the seller of land could rescind the contract, if the purchase price was less than half the "true value" of the property. But the buyer was permitted to avoid rescission by paying the "true value." The authority of this provision is highly controversial. Be that as it may, due to the growing influence of the precepts of "Christian morality," it found its way into the Corpus Juris by "interpolation."[3]

The doctrine of *laesio enormis* greatly appealed to the scholars and jurists (glossators and postglossators) of the Middle Ages, since it fit comfortably into their notions of a divine world plan. A theory of the just price emerged which in the hands of St. Thomas showed the strong influence of Aristotelean ethics. The details of this theory will be omitted, as they are admirably presented elsewhere.[4] It is sufficient to point out that while the theory of a just price was constantly broadened, neither canonists nor civilians arrived at a unified theory. In fact, the theory underwent considerable changes. Of particular interest are those variations that resorted to a labor theory of value or that asserted that a just price was most likely to be reached under freedom of contract, on the grounds that the mere fact a bargain had been struck showed that both parties were satisfied (a notion that has its modern counterparts).[5]

The attitude of the Enlightenment is typically represented by Grotius and Pufendorf.[6] Influenced by Thomistic and Aristotelean philosophy, Grotius insisted that a contract required for its validity substantive equivalence *(equalitas)*; "*ne plus exigitur quam par est.*" This idea was further elaborated by Pufendorf, and it found expression in various civilian codifications that had been influenced by the philosophy of the Enlighten-

2. Code 4, 44, 2.

3. Dawson, Economic Duress and Fair Exchange in French and German Law, 11 Tul. L. Rev. 345, 365 (1937); Holstein, Vices of Consent in the Law of Contracts, 13 Tul. L. Rev. 560, 569 (1939).

4. W. J. Ashley, An Introduction to English Economic History and Theory 126 (1920); R. H. Tawney, Religion and the Rise of Capitalism 52 et seq. (1922); 1 M. Weber, Economy and Society 578, 583, 589, 2 id. 1198 (G. Roth & C. Wittich eds. 1978); A. T. von Mehren & J. Gordley, The Civil Law System 822, 988 (1977); Gordley, Equality in Exchange, 69 Calif. L. Rev. 1387 (1981).

5. See, e.g., M. Wolf, Rechtsgeschäftliche Entscheidungsfreiheit und vertraglicher Interessenausgleich (1971).

6. 2 H. Grotius, De Jure Belli ac Pacis, ch. XI, (F. W. Kelsey trans. 1964). The leading authority on the medieval attitude is F. Endemann, Studien zur romanistisch-kanonistischen Wirtschaftslehre (1879). On Grotius and Pufendorf, see F. Wieacker, Privatrechtsgeschichte der Neuzeit 295 et seq. (2d ed. 1967); von Mehren & Gordley, *supra* note 4, at 33-36, 822-833, 986-988, 997-1004, and *passim*.

ment. The provisions introducing a ration of two-to-one as a measure of unfairness can be traced back to an author of the fifteenth century.

With the development of capitalism and its quite different ethos, a countermovement became inevitable. Restrictions of the *laesio enormis* principle began in France, although the Code Civil still reserved it for land transactions.[7] In Germany, by contrast, the reaction came more slowly. The principle of *laesio enormis* was first abolished for commercial transactions by the Allgemeine deutsche Handelsgesetzbuch.[8] The Gemeine Recht[9] preserved it until the enactment of the Bürgerliches Gesetzbuch (BGB) in 1900.[10] The draftsmen of the BGB regarded the principle as artificial, useless, and in conflict with the basic conceptions of a competitive economy.[11] Still, when the draft was submitted to the Reichstag (diet) for enactment, an amendment was added making a contract *contra bonos mores* illegal (§138(1)). In addition, §138(2) makes illegal and void any transaction "whereby one person through exploitation of another's distressed situation, inexperience, lack of judgmental ability or gross weakness of will causes economic advantages to be given or promised to himself or to a third party, which economic advantages exceed the value of the counterperformance to such an extent as to be, under the circumstances, strikingly disproportionate."[12]

As a result, although *laesio enormis* has disappeared, its "core idea," as Dawson termed it, has been preserved in §138(2) in the form of a timid revival of the medieval usury prohibition, aimed not only at the moneylender but also at other exploiters. Subsection 138(2) combines objective and subjective criteria. Objectively, there must be a glaring discrepancy between the reciprocal duties or values exchanged. Subjectively, the exploitation of the victim in favor of the exploiter or third party must have been made possible by the victim's "distressed situation, inexperience, lack of judgmental ability or gross weakness of will." The victim's lack of financial means is insufficient to establish a claim under §138(2), but if there has been exploitation of the sort the subsection proscribes, it is

7. C. Civ. art. 1674 introduces a 7-to-12 ratio. For recent extensions of the doctrine by statutory fiat, see von Mehren & Gordley, *supra* note 4, at 926.

8. ADHGB artt. 249, 252; 1 H. Thöl, Das Handelsrecht 252 (5th ed. 1875). The Federation of German States meeting in the Paulskirche had no legislative power but succeeded by negotiation among its member states in enacting a uniform law of bills of exchange and later on, a commercial code. With the unification of Germany these became federal law.

9. The Gemeine Recht, which was uncodified, prevailed in large parts of Germany. It was strongly influenced by the evolving Roman law tradition, which culminated in the Pandektenschule. It was to a considerable extent *Professorenrecht*. See von Mehren & Gordley, *supra* note 4, at 11, 162-172.

10. Thöl, *supra* note 8, at 252; Dawson, *supra* note 3, at 367.

11. 2 Motive zu dem Entwurfe eines bürgerlichen Gesetzbuchs 322 (1888).

12. This version was brought about by an amendment in 1976, Bundesgesetzblatt I 2034, 2036 (Art. 3). We have followed the Gordley translation, *supra* note 4, at 1667; for the earlier version, which stresses "necessity, thoughtlessness or inexperience," see Dawson, Unconscionable Coercion: The German View, 89 Harv. L. Rev. 1041 (1976); see also J. Dawson, W. Harvey & S. Henderson, Cases and Comment on Contracts, 537, 538 (4th ed. 1982).

irrelevant whether the victim or the exploiter has taken the initiative. The applicability of §138(2) does presuppose, however, that the exploiter is aware of the situation or is wilfully shutting his eyes and has the intention to exploit. (Even in the absence of subjective intent, the transaction may be void under §138(1).) A related and significant change in the law of contracts has been brought about by the increased readiness of courts to resort to two other sections of the BGB — §§157 and 242 — so as to be able to apply the principle of good faith and fair dealing at the interpretation and performance stages of the contract.[13] As one insightful author has observed, §242 has become the central provision in the entire German law of contracts.[14] Resort to §242 has the great advantage of enabling a court to declare invalid only the obnoxious term and to leave the rest of the contract intact (§139).[15]

An increasing number of commentators, dissatisfied with the justification of the binding force of contractual promises in terms of the principle of private autonomy,[16] have claimed that the idea of "rightness" is "immanent" in the notion of contract. Private autonomy and immanent rightness, it has been claimed, are not in opposition, but "in dialectical correlation." The term rightness has not been clearly defined: expediency, security of transactions and, according to the latest version of the theory, respect for the individual and his informed choice all have to be considered. These elements, admittedly, may come into conflict with one another. Since the theory is most complex, only its latest version will be given. Under this theory, all that is required is that the parties be given an opportunity to arrive at a just result.[17]

The just price theory, particularly in its more arithmetical versions was, we are told, uncongenial to the common law of contracts "when it moved out from under the shadow of the penal bond."[18] According to tradition dating back to medieval times, the fairness of the bargain was not subject to judicial inquiry. This thesis does not seem to have been questioned in the case law or legal literature, which proclaimed that the adequacy of consideration would not be scrutinized. As Sheppard informs us, "the value and proportion of . . . consideration is not consider-

---

13. A. Lüderitz, Auslegung von Rechtsgeschäften: Vergleichende Untersuchungen anglo-amerikanischen und deutschen Rechts (1966).

14. F. Wieacker, Zur rechtstheoretischen Präzisierung des §242 BGB (Recht und Staat. Nos. 192-193, (1956); critical, Esser, §242 und die Privatautonomie, 56 J.Z. 555 (1956).

15. Sandrock, Subjektive und objektive Gestaltungskräfte bei der Teilnichtigkeit von Rechtsgeschäften, 159 Archiv für die civilisistische Praxis [AcP] 461 (1960-1961).

16. The paragraph is largely based on a summary of the theories in Kessler, Some Thoughts on the Evolution of the German Law of Contract, 22 U.C.L.A. L. Rev. 1066, 1075 (1975). Footnotes 60-64 of the article contain references to some of the relevant literature. Since the style of the originator of the idea is quite complicated, a misunderstanding is quite possible. One thing is certain, however: no revival of the just price theory is intended.

17. Wolf, *supra* note 5.

18. Dawson, *supra* note 1, at 276.

able; for the penny is just as much obliging in a promise as £100."[19] "But," he adds significantly, "there it is probable the jury will give damage according to the loss." Sheppard's qualification was forgotten when the jury lost its equitable powers.[20] The tradition that equivalence of value is not required, provided there has been no abuse of bargaining power, became the rule.[21] But this does not tell the full story of the fate of the just price doctrine. To begin with, in the Middle Ages the price and quality of many commodities sold in the local market were fixed by local authority.[22] Furthermore, as Sheppard's statement suggests, the fairness doctrine may have had an indirect effect on the law of contracts, coming in through the back door, so to speak (e.g., through jury control of damages). Moreover, adequacy of consideration became relevant when the two values exchanged were capable of exact measurement. Richard v. Bartlett, 1 Leon. 19, 74 Eng. Rep. 17 (1583). Thus, to some degree, equivalence was always taken into account. Also, at the end of the eighteenth and the beginning of the nineteenth centuries, a substantive (in contrast to a formal) theory of consideration that safeguarded the fairness of the bargain may have enjoyed some appeal for a short period of time, particularly in this country.[23] Finally, the common law developed in sales contracts a sound price doctrine, i.e., the rule that a sound price carries with it a warranty of sound merchandise. Although this doctrine, too, enjoyed only a short life, its eventual demise did not mean the total

19. W. Sheppard, Action on the Case 18, 22 (1622); Sturlyn v. Albany, Cro. Eliz. 67, 78 Eng. Rep. 327 (Q.B. 1587), infra p. 706. For a discussion of the case see A. Corbin, Cases on Contracts 209 (3d ed. 1947); Hitchcock v. Coker, 6 Ad. & E. 438, 457, 112 Eng. Rep. 167, 175 (Ex. 1837); Buckner v. McIlroy, 31 Ark. 631 634 (1877); Hardesty v. Smith, 3 Ind. 39, 41-43 (1851).

20. This occurred at the close of the eighteenth century.

21. The two Restatements deal with the adequacy of consideration in §§81 and 84(a) of Restatement First and §§79(b) and 87(1)(a) of the Restatement Second. The provisions in the two Restatements are by no means identical, however. The principle of equivalence has received greater emphasis in the Restatement Second. While the Restatement First regarded a consideration of trivial value — a merely nominal or "peppercorn" consideration — as sufficient, under the Restatement Second a trivially small consideration may be insufficient if it is part and parcel of a simulated bargain, a sham transaction that is not a bargain in fact (§79, Comment d). An exception is made for transactions that are a mixture of bargain and gift (§79, Comment c). Comment d cites with approval Schnell v. Nell, infra p. 737, and the highly problematical case of Newman and Snell's State Bank v. Hunter, 243 Mich. 331, 220 N.W. 665 (1928), which 1 Corbin §127, n.76 (1963) criticizes, conceding, however, that the court may have applied "widow's law." Comment d qualifies the attack upon the "peppercorn" rule by admitting that the endangered promise may be binding after all under §90. Section 87(1)(a) preserves the effectiveness of the peppercorn in a written option contract, if the contract proposes an exchange on fair terms within a reasonable time.

22. Hamilton, The Ancient Maxim of Caveat Emptor, 40 Yale L.J. 1133 (1931); Viness, Caveat Emptor Versus Caveat Venditor, 7 Md. L. Rev. 177 (1943); Simpson at 446. For discussion of the peppercorn theory of consideration, see pp. 706 et seq. infra.

23. The evolution of the just price theory is brilliantly described in Horwitz, ch. 6 ("The Triumph of Contract"), at 160 et seq. (1977), and more cautiously and convincingly in Simpson, The Horwitz Theory and the History of Contracts, 46 U. Chi. L. Rev. 532 (1979).

victory of caveat emptor: the buyer in a sale by description was, and still is, protected by a warranty of merchantability.[24]

With the decline of direct market controls and increasing limitation of the power of juries to assess damages, existing supports for the idea that an enforceable bargain must be substantively fair were swept away. This process was encouraged by the commercial community, whose needs were better served by a formalistic doctrine of consideration, and reflected the constant widening of the market and the moral temper of the times.[25]

It is hardly surprising that during this period continental writers, particularly Pothier, who anchored the validity of a contract in the voluntary agreement of the parties and not in notions of fairness, exercised considerable appeal.[26] Pothier's treatise on obligation with its highly systematic approach must have filled a need, for the book was translated at least six times, the first translation appearing in 1806.[27]

And yet, although in the latter half of the nineteenth century and the early part of this one, the common law increasingly emphasized freedom of contract, it never totally abandoned its efforts to control the bargaining process as well as the contents of the bargain. To be sure, unlike equity, which will be dealt with shortly, the common law did not develop an outright unconscionability doctrine.[28] But, to quote Corbin, "[t]here is sufficient flexibility in the concepts of fraud, duress, misrepresentation, and undue influence . . . to enable the courts to avoid enforcement of a bargain that is shown to be unconscionable by reason of gross inadequacy of consideration accompanied by other relevant factors."[29] Corbin in this connection emphasizes the mores and business practices of the time and place. He might have mentioned in his catalogue of protective devices the overexpansions and manipulation of the consideration doctrine, the concept of mistake, and notions of public policy. Not surprisingly, duress and fraud experienced a gradual expansion.[30]

24. Simpson, *supra* note 23, at 500 et seq.; Kessler, The Protection of the Consumer Under Modern Sales Law (pt. 1), 74 Yale L.J. 262, 266 (1964). Warranties by description are no longer implied warranties; they have become express warranties under U.C.C. §2-313(1)(b). See also Comment 4 to U.C.C. §2-313.

25. Simpson, *supra* note 23, at 533. 1 J. Powell, Essay upon the Law of Contracts and Agreements, chs. V, VI, and *passim* (1790); G. Verplanck, An Essay on the Doctrine of Contracts, ch. 166 and *passim* (1825); W. Story, a Treatise on the Law of Contracts (1844).

26. Simpson, *supra* note 23, at 590.

27. Simpson, *supra* note 23, at 533. The American translation by W. Evans, entitled A Treatise on the Law of Obligation or Contracts (1806), became quite famous.

28. See, however, Schnell v. Nell, 17 Ind. 29 (1861), *infra* p. 737; Williams v. Walker-Thomas Furniture Co., 350 F.2d 445, 18 A.L.R. 3d 1297 (D.C. Cir. 1965), *infra* p. 572; Scott v. United States, 79 U.S. (12 Wall.) 443, 445 (1870): "If a contract be unreasonable and unconscionable, but not void for fraud, a court of law will give to the party who sues for its breach damages, not according to its letter, but only such as he is equitably entitled to." The court cites in this connection Hume v. United States, 132 U.S. 408 (1889), and other cases.

29. 1 Corbin §128 (1963); 5 Corbin §1174 (1969).

30. Note, 45 Iowa L. Rev. 843, 861-866 (1960).

Equity was a good deal less squeamish. With the help of their discretionary powers, equity courts developed the unconscionability doctrine, issued temporary injunctions, denied specific performance, and protected the mortgagor's equity of redemption and the rights of the expectant heir. Equity introduced the compensatory principle, mitigated the harshness of penal bonds, canceled unconscionable transactions, enjoined lawsuits in appropriate cases, and took into account the abuse of confidential relationships.[31] Even in the cases of "mere" inadequacy of price, specific performance was occasionally denied, leaving the plaintiff with his remedy at law.[32] Lord Eldon wanted to protect the victim of sharp dealing only when the price was so inadequate as to shock the conscience and amounted in itself to conclusive and decisive evidence of fraud,[33] but some courts of equity were prepared to go further.[34]

The result was, and still is, a dual system of law.[35] In order to overcome this dualism, common law courts were forced to make inventive, and sometimes covert, use of the doctrinal techniques at their disposal. Fraud, for example, was extended to constructive fraud, the gap between fraud and material misrepresentation (even if innocent) was narrowed, and duress, after a timid beginning, was extended to business compulsion.[36] In situations which do not fall easily under the category of duress,

31. Dawson, *supra* note 1, at 253, 276; J. Pomeroy, Specific Performance, 40, ch. 8 (2d ed. 1897); 1 J. Story, Commentaries on Equity Jurisprudence 138(1)(9th ed. 1866); J. Murray, On Contracts (2d ed. 1974). For a collection of authorities see Leff, Unconscionability and the Code: The Emperor's New Clause, 115 U. Pa. L. Rev. 485, 528-541 (1967).

32. Seymour v. Delancey, 6 Johnson's Ch. 278 (N.Y. 1824). Chancellor Kent, in denying specific performance, was, however, willing to remand the plaintiff to the common law courts to let the jury decide what was equitable. The higher court reversed Kent by the narrowest of margins; see 3 Cowen 445, 502 (N.Y. 1824), and the dissent of Chief Justice Savage, who also would have remanded plaintiff to his remedy at law. Equity courts left an executed contract intact unless there was actual or constructive fraud. See further Marks v. Gates, *infra* p. 571. Cal. Civ. Code §3391(1) makes adequacy of consideration a prerequisite for granting specific performance. See further, the interesting case of McKinnon v. Benedict, 38 Wis. 2d 607, 157 N.W.2d 665 (1968), denying a temporary injunction to enforce the terms of an obnoxious contract to the extent that plaintiff had suffered minimal harm.

33. Coles v. Trecothick, (1804) 9 Ves. 234, 246, 32 Eng. Rep. 592 (1804).

34. For an interesting case in which the buyer sought specific performance and the seller cancellation (both were unsuccessful), see Day v. Newman, 2 Cox Ch. 77, 30 Eng. Rep. 36 (1786). For the so-called equitable clean-up doctrine, see *infra* p. 574.

35. Newman, The Renaissance of Good Faith in Contracting in Anglo-American Law, 54 Cornell L. Rev. 553 (1969); U.C.C. §1-103. See further Gordley, *supra* note 4, Atiyah, Contract and Fair Exchange, 35 U. Toronto L.J. 1 (1985).

36. No attempt will be made in this book to deal in extenso with fraud, misrepresentation, or undue influence, or with failure to disclose. Innocent material misrepresentation has the same effect as fraud in rendering a contract or discharge voidable. Restatement Second §164.

If the misrepresentation affects the essential character of essential terms, the contract may be void (§163). Broad duties of disclosure are imposed in fiduciary and confidential relationships such as insurance and suretyship contracts. Nondisclosure is dealt with in Restatement Second §161.

On the tort aspect of misrepresentation and the measure of damages (as contrasted with rescission), see W. Prosser, Torts 700-714 (4th ed. 1971); Hill, Damages for Innocent Misrepresentation, 73 Colum. L. Rev. 679 (1973); Hill, Breach of Contract as a Tort, 74 Colum. L. Rev. 40 (1974). Common law rules thought to be inadequate have been replaced by statu-

courts resorted to the doctrine of undue influence, and, in general, made room for interpretation by finding ambiguities where none existed (the interpretation of insurance policies is an excellent example).[37]

The Uniform Commercial Code provided its draftsmen with an opportunity to create a unified system of control enabling courts to use the concept of unconscionability in an overt, rather than covert, fashion. Covert tools, Llewellyn observed, are not reliable tools. "Practically all" of today's judges, Corbin reminds us, are "chancellors as well as judges," and thus cannot "fail to be influenced by equitable doctrines in the granting of remedies that are available."[38] Section 2-302 was the result.

According to Llewellyn (who drafted it), U.C.C. §2-302 is "probably one of the Code's most valuable sections."[39] It reads as follows:

§2-302. Unconscionable Contract or Clause

(1) If the court as a matter of law finds the contract or any clause of the contract to have been unconscionable at the time it was made, the court may refuse to enforce the contract, or it may enforce the remainder of the contract without the unconscionable clause, or it may so limit the application of any unconscionable clause as to avoid any unconscionable result.

(2) When it is claimed or appears to the court that the contract or any clause thereof may be unconscionable, the parties shall be afforded a reasonable opportunity to present evidence as to its commercial setting, purpose and effect to aid the court in making the determination.[40]

Understandably, the literature on §2-302 is voluminous.[41] The section does not define unconscionability, and its draftsmanship has often been

---

tory disclosure requirements on both federal and state levels. J. D. Calamari & J. M. Perillo, The Law of Contracts 288 (2d ed. 1977) lists the federal statutes. See further subsection 3 of this chapter.

37. Llewellyn, Review of Prausnitz's The Standardization of Commercial Contracts in English and Continental Law, 52 Harv. L. Rev. 700 (1939); Patterson, The Interpretation and Construction of a Contract, 64 Colum. L. Rev. 833 (1964).

38. See in this connection 1 Corbin §128 (1963). The equity concept of unconscionability, it has been maintained, has not been adopted by the U.C.C. The concept is broader, according to Murray, (On Contracts 78 (1974)), who gives a narrow reading to U.C.C. §2-302; contrast Leff, supra note 31, at 528-541.

39. 1954 N.Y. Hearings at 121. See, however, his skepticism with regard to the desirability of a statutory approach in The Common Law Tradition at 370 (1960).

California and North Carolina initially omitted the section. See Special Report of California Bar Committee on Commercial Code, 37 Cal. St. B.J. 135 (1962). The section was later incorporated in Cal. Civ. Code §1670.05 and N.C. Gen. Stat. §25-2-302.

40. Section 2-302, which has to be read in the light of §1-103, has its counterpart in Restatement Second §208, which uses many consumer cases for illustrations. The history of §2-302 is detailed in Leff, supra note 31, at 485. The section covers the sale of goods under oral as well as standardized written contracts. See In re Matter of Elkins-Dell Manufacturing Co., 253 F. Supp. 864 (E.D. Pa. 1966). For the role of the parties in assisting the court, see Speidel, Unconscionability, Assent, and Consumer Protection, 31 U. Pitt. L. Rev. 359, at 369 et seq. (1970).

41. A list of the literature is given in the Reporter's Note to §2-208 of the Restatement Second. See further Epstein, Unconscionability: A Critical Reappraisal, 18 J.L. & Econ. 293, 293-294 (1975), and Kronman, Contract Law and Distributive Justice, 89 Yale L.J. 472 (1980) (with copious references).

criticized.[42] Leff, one of the severest and most frequently cited critics of the provision, has called it "unintelligible" and without "reality referrents." In his view, §2-302 amounts to an "emotionally satisfying incantation," which shows that "it is easy to say nothing with words." A distinction between procedural and substantive unconscionability has to be made, but was not, he claims, sufficiently appreciated by the draftsmen of §2-302 to avoid its "amorphous unintelligibility" or to save the section's "finally irrelevant" accompanying Comments.[43] According to Leff, the crucial term in §2-302 has been defined "in terms of itself"; in a later article, he complains about the expensiveness and ineffectiveness of fighting the many abuses of consumer transactions on a case-by-case basis and expresses his preference for statutory regulation.[44] Similar criticism has been voiced in J. White & R. Summers, Handbook of the Law under the Uniform Commercial Code 451 (1977).

The idea that §2-302 is intended to achieve social (distributive) justice has also often been attacked.[45] But §2-302 cannot be read as promoting social justice. Comment 1 makes that reasonably clear:

> This section is intended to make it possible for the courts to police explicitly against the contracts or clauses which they find to be unconscionable. In the past such policing has been accomplished by adverse construction of language, by manipulation of the rules of offer and acceptance or by determinations that the clause is contrary to public policy or to the dominant purpose of the contract. This section is intended to allow the court to pass directly on the unconscionability of the contract or particular clause therein and to make a conclusion of law as to its unconscionability. The basic test is whether, in the light of the general commercial background and the commercial needs of the particular trade or case, the clauses involved are so one-sided as to be unconscionable under the circumstances existing at the time of the making of the contract. Subsection (2) makes it clear that it is proper for the court to hear evidence upon these questions. The principle is one of the prevention of oppression and unfair surprise (Cf. Campbell Soup Co. v. Wentz, 172 F.2d 80, 3d Cir. 1948) and not of disturbance of allocation of risks because of superior bargaining power. . . .

The guarded reference to Campbell Soup Co. v. Wentz (reprinted *infra* p. 1097) is somewhat puzzling: does it indicate a willingness to leave the door open for substantial (commutative) justice in situations where

---

42. See, e.g., Murray, Unconscionability: Unconscionability, 31 Pitt. L. Rev. 1 (1969).

43. See Leff, *supra* note 31.

44. Leff, Unconscionability and the Crowd — Consumers and the Common Law Tradition, 31 U. Pitt. L. Rev. 349, 356-357 (1970).

45. 2 F. A. Hayek, Law, Legislation and Liberty: The Mirage of Social Justice, ch. 9 (1976).

there is an overall imbalance, or does it simply indicate that *Campbell* is an equity case?[46]

In contrast to Leff's view, other scholars believe that the draftsmen wisely refrained from defining unconscionability, since such a definition could never encompass all situations. Ellinghaus, one of the strongest defenders of §2-302, maintains that the definition of unconscionability is "as impossible as it is undesirable."[47] The notion should function as a "standard" as opposed to a "rule," "principle," or "conception." Like other "residual" categories such as "reasonableness," "good faith," and "due care," the doctrine of unconscionability is "essential to the well-being of any system and serves to counteract its inherent tendency to become logically closed."[48] Ellinghaus believes, further, that §2-302 should be read as mainly directed at the prevention of "substantive" unconscionability, since defects in the bargaining process have already been taken care of by the common law, even if only covertly.[49]

Be that as it may, Restatement Second §208 explicitly deals with an "overall imbalance" (to use Leff's phrase) in the contract as a whole. Comment *c* to §208 reads:

> Inadequacy of consideration does not of itself invalidate a bargain, but gross disparity in the values exchanged may be an important factor in a determination that a contract is unconscionable and may be sufficient ground, without more, for denying specific performance. See §§79, 364. Such a disparity may also corroborate indications of defects in the bargaining process, or may affect the remedy to be granted when there is a violation of a more specific rule. Theoretically it is possible for a contract to be oppressive taken as a whole, even though there is no weakness in the bargaining process and no single term which is in itself unconscionable. Ordinarily, however, an unconscionable contract involves other factors as well as overall imbalance.

Indeed, it has been argued that the doctrine, carefully applied, does not destroy, but rather strengthens freedom of contract, since it forces the

46. The *Campbell* case is discussed in Note, Grower-Canner Agreements: An Abuse of Mass Standardized Contracts, 58 Yale L.J. 1161 (1949). Braucher, The Unconscionable Contract or Term, 31 U. Pitt. L. Rev. 337, 340 (1969), asserts that the contract at issue "written on the manufacturer's standard form was obviously drawn to protect the manufacturer's interest and not the farmer's; it contained numerous provisions to protect the manufacturer against various contigencies but contained none giving analogous protection to the farmer."

When the manufacturer redrafted the contract and the farmers still refused to deliver, the contract was specifically enforced. 111 F. Supp. 211 (E.D. Pa. 1952); see reprint, *infra* p. 1097.

47. Ellinghaus, In Defense of Unconscionability, 78 Yale L.J. 757 (1969).

48. Id. at 759. This view is shared by J. White & R. Summers, Handbook of the Law Under the Uniform Commercial Code 151 (2d ed. 1980).

49. See Ellinghaus, *supra* note 47, at 763, 773.

parties to codetermine the terms of their relationship, thus enhancing its overall stability.[50]

Furthermore, although Leff's distinction between procedural and substantive unconscionability has been widely accepted, there is a growing tendency to doubt that a clear line between the two notions can be drawn.[51] Still the problem remains as to whether there can be substantive unconscionability per se. Price unconscionability as such furnishes an example.[52]

The materials that follow show the ingenuity, and the occasional carelessness, with which courts have used the tools of the common law to achieve a measure of fairness in exchange, and document the steady expansion of U.C.C. §2-302. Section 2 covers some aspects of consumer protection, both judicial and statutory. Here again, we will see the influence of earlier case law and of §2-302. The field of consumer protection has grown so large that only a small portion of it can be covered here. For more complete coverage, the student must look to the separate courses on the subject that have become a standard part of the law school curriculum.

HAIGH v. BROOKS

10 Adol. & El. 309, 113 Eng. Rep. 119 (Q.B. 1839, Ex. 1840)

[The following written guarantee was in the possession of the plaintiffs:

Manchester, February 4, 1837.

Messrs. Haigh and Franceys:

Gentlemen: In consideration of your being in advance to Messrs. John Lees & Sons in the sum of £10,000 for the purchase of cotton, I do hereby give you my guarantee for that amount (say, £10,000) on their behalf.

JOHN BROOKS.

In assumpsit, the plaintiffs now allege that at the defendant's request they surrendered this document to the defendant in return for his promise that he would see paid at maturity three bills of exchange for some £9,666, payable three months after date, accepted and to be paid by John Lees and Sons; that the bills became due and have not been paid.

The defendant pleaded that the written guarantee surrendered to him was void and of no value for the reason that it was a promise to pay the debt of another to wit: John Lees and Sons, and so was within the provisions of the statute of frauds, and that the writing did not express the

50. See Spanogle, Analyzing Unconscionability Problems, 117 U. Pa. L. Rev. 931 (1969).
51. Ibid.
52. See the consumer cases in Section 2.

consideration for which the promise was made, as the said statute requires.

To this plea the plaintiff demurred, assigning for cause,

> that it is admitted by the plea that the memorandum, the giving up of which was the consideration of the guarantee in the said declaration mentioned, was actually given up to the said defendant by the said plaintiffs, and the consideration was therefore executed by the said defendant [plaintiffs], and that, even if the original memorandum was not binding in point of law, the giving up was a sufficient consideration for the promise in the declaration mentioned.

Joinder.

The judgment of the Court of Queen's Bench was rendered by[53]

LORD DENMAN, C.J. This action was brought upon an assumpsit to see certain acceptances paid, in consideration of the plaintiffs giving up a guarantee of £10,000, due from the acceptor to the plaintiffs. Plea, that the guarantee was for the debt of another, and that there was no writing wherein the consideration appeared, signed by the defendant, and so the giving it up was no good consideration for the promise. Demurrer, stating for cause that the plea is bad, because the consideration was executed, whether the guarantee were binding in law or not. The form of the guarantee was set out in the plea. "In consideration of your being in advance to Messrs. John Lees and Sons, in the sum of £10,000, for the purchase of cotton, I do hereby give you my guarantee for that amount (say £10,000), on their behalf. John Brooks."

It was argued for the defendant, that this guarantee is of no force, because the fact of the plaintiffs being already in advance to Lees could form no consideration for the defendant's promise to guarantee to the plaintiffs the payment of Lees' acceptances. In the first place, this is by no means clear. That "being in advance" must necessarily mean to assert that he was in advance of the time of giving the guarantee, in an assertion open to argument. It may, possibly, have been intended as prospective. If the phrase had been "in consideration of your becoming in advance," or, "on condition of your being in advance," such would have been the clear import. As it is, nobody can doubt that the defendant took a great interest in the affairs of Messrs. Lees, or believe that the plaintiffs had not come under the advance mentioned at the defendant's request. Here is then sufficient doubt to make it worth the defendant's while to possess himself of the guarantee; and, if that be so, we have no concern with the adequacy or inadequacy of the price paid or promised for it.

But we are by no means prepared to say that any circumstances short of the imputation of fraud in fact, could entitle us to hold that a party was

---

53. This statement was taken from A. Corbin, Cases on Contracts 213 (3d ed. 1947) — EDS.

not bound by a promise made upon any consideration which could be valuable; while of its being so the promise by which it was obtained from the holder of it must always afford some proof.

Here, whether or not the guarantee could have been available within the doctrine of Wain v. Warlters, 5 East, 10, the plaintiffs were induced by the defendant's promise to part with something which they might have kept, and the defendant obtained what he desired by means of that promise. Both being free and able to judge for themselves, how can the defendant be justified in breaking this promise, by discovering afterwards that the thing in consideration of which he gave it did not possess that value which he supposed to belong to it? It cannot be ascertained that that value was what he most regarded. He may have had other objects and motives; and of their weight he was the only judge. We therefore, think the plea bad: and the demurrer must prevail.

Judgment for the plaintiffs. . . .

From this judgment a writ of error was argued in the Exchequer Chamber before Lord Abinger, C.B., Bosanquet, Coltman, and Maule, JJ., and Alderson and Rolfe, BB. Speaking for this court, LORD ABINGER said:

It is the opinion of all the Court that there was in the guarantee an ambiguity that might be explained by evidence, so as to make it a valid contract, and therefore this was a sufficient consideration for the promise declared upon.

It is also the opinion of all the Court, with the exception of my Brother Maule, who entertained some doubt on the question, that the words both of the declaration and the plea import that the paper on which the guarantee was written was given up, and that the actual surrender of the possession of the paper to the defendant was a sufficient consideration without reference to its contents.

Judgment affirmed.

COOK v. WRIGHT
1 Best & Smith 559, 121 Eng. Rep. 822 (Q.B. 1861)

BLACKBURN, J. In this case it appeared on the trial that the defendant was agent for a Mrs. Bennett, who was non-resident owner of houses in a district subject to a local Act. Works had been done in the adjoining street by the Commissioners for executing the Act, the expenses of which, under the provisions of their Act, they charged on the owners of the adjoining houses. Notice had been given to the defendant, as if he had himself been owner of the houses, calling on him to pay the proportion chargeable in respect of them. He attended at a Board meeting of the Commissioners, and objected both to the amount and nature of the charge, and also stated that he was not the owner of the houses, and that

Mrs. Bennett was. He was told that, if he did not pay, he would be treated as one Goble had been. It appeared that Goble had refused to pay a sum charged against him as owner of some houses, and the Commissioners had taken legal proceedings against him, and he had then submitted and paid, with costs. In the result it was agreed between the Commissioners and the defendant that the amount charged upon him should be reduced, and that time should be given to pay it in three instalments; he gave three promissory notes for the three instalments; the first was duly honored; the others were not, and were the subject of the present action. At the trial it appeared that the defendant was not in fact owner of the houses. As agent for the owner he was not personally liable under the Act. In point of law, therefore, the Commissioners were not entitled to claim the money from him; but no case of deceit was alleged against them. It must be taken that the Commissioners honestly believed that the defendant was personally liable, and really intended to take legal proceedings against him, as they had done against Goble. The defendant, according to his own evidence, never believed that he was liable in law, but signed the notes in order to avoid being sued as Goble was. Under these circumstances the substantial question reserved (irrespective of the form of the plea) was whether there was any consideration for the notes. We are of opinion that there was.

There is no doubt that a bill or note given in consideration of what is supposed to be a debt is without consideration if it appears that there was a mistake in fact as to the existence of the debt, Bell v. Gardiner [4 M. & Gr. 11]; and, according to the cases of Southall v. Rigg and Forman v. Wright [11 C.B. 481], the law is the same if the bill or note is given in consequence of a mistake of law as to the existence of the debt. But here there was no mistake on the part of the defendant either of law or fact. What he did was not merely the making an erroneous account stated, or promising to pay a debt for which he mistakenly believed himself liable. It appeared on the evidence that he believed himself not to be liable; but he knew that the plaintiffs thought him liable, and would sue him if he did not pay, and in order to avoid the expense and trouble of legal proceedings against himself he agreed to a compromise; and the question is, whether a person who has given a note as a compromise of a claim honestly made on him, and which but for that compromise would have been at once brought to a legal decision, can resist the payment of the note on the ground that the original claim thus compromised might have been successfully resisted.

If the suit had been actually commenced, the point would have been concluded by authority. In Longridge v. Dorville [5 B. & A. 117], it was held that the compromise of a suit instituted to try a doubtful question of law was a sufficient consideration for a promise. In Atlee v. Blackhouse [3 M. & W. 633], where the plaintiff's goods had been seized by the excise, and he had afterwards entered into an agreement with the Commissioners of Excise that all proceedings should be terminated, the goods delivered up to the plaintiff, and a sum of money paid by him to the Commissioners, Parke, B., rests his judgment, p. 650, on the ground that this agreement of compromise honestly made was for consideration, and binding. In Cooper v. Parker [15 Com. B. 822], the Court of Exchequer Chamber held that the withdrawal of an untrue defense of infancy in a suit, with payment of costs, was a sufficient consideration for a promise to accept a smaller sum in satisfaction of a larger.

In these cases, however, litigation had been actually commenced; and it was argued before us that this made a difference in point of law, and that though, where a plaintiff has actually issued a writ against a defendant, a compromise honestly made is binding, yet the same compromise, if made before the writ actually issues, though the litigation is impending, is void. Edwards v. Baugh [11 M. & W. 641], was relied upon as an authority for this proposition. But in that case Lord Abinger expressly bases his judgment (pp. 645, 646) on the assumption that the declaration did not, either expressly or impliedly, show that a reasonable doubt existed between the parties. It may be doubtful whether the declaration in that case ought not to have been construed as disclosing a compromise of a real bona fide claim, but it does not appear to have been so construed by the Court. We agree that unless there was a reasonable claim on the one side, which it was bona fide intended to pursue, there would be no ground for a compromise; but we cannot agree that (except as a test of the reality of the claim in fact) the issuing of a writ is essential to the validity of the compromise. The position of the parties must necessarily be altered in every case of compromise, so that, if the question is afterwards opened up, they cannot be replaced as they were before the compromise. The plaintiff may be in a less favorable position for renewing his litigation, he must be at an additional trouble and expense in again getting up his case, and he may no longer be able to produce the evidence which would have proved it originally. Besides, though he may not in point of law be bound to refrain from enforcing his rights against third persons during the continuance of the compromise, to which they are not parties, yet practically the effect of the compromise must be to prevent his doing so. For instance, in the present case, there can be no doubt that the practical effect of the compromise must have been to induce the Commissioners to refrain from taking proceedings against Mrs. Bennett, the real owner of the houses, while the notes given by the defendant, her agent, were running; though the compromise might have afforded no ground of defense had such proceedings been resorted to. It is this detriment to the party consenting to a compromise arising from the necessary alteration in his position which, in our opinion, forms the real consideration for the promise, and not the technical and almost illusory consideration arising from the extra costs of litigation. The real consideration therefore depends, not on the actual commencement of a suit, but on the reality of the claim made and the bona fides of the compromise.

In the present case we think that there was sufficient consideration for the notes in the compromise made as it was.

The rules to enter a verdict for the plaintiff must be made absolute. Rule absolute.

NOTE

Assuming that there had been no reduction of the claim, same result? Has Mr. Wright a remedy against Mrs. Bennett? Is she still liable to the district for the unpaid assessment? See, in general, Dawson, Duress Through Civil Litigation (pts. 1 & 2), 45 Mich. L. Rev. 571, 679 (1947).

JACKSON v. SEYMOUR, 193 Va. 735, 71 S.E.2d 181 (1952). The trial court found the facts in the case to be as follows:

"Since 1931 Mrs. Jackson had been the owner of a farm of 166 acres in Brunswick county which adjoined lands owned by her brother, Benjamin J. Seymour, the defendant. After the death of her husband (the date of which is not shown in the record) Mrs. Jackson sought and obtained the assistance of her brother, who is a successful farmer and business man, in renting the farm for her. He rented the tillable portions of the farm, collected the rents, and made settlements with her which she never questioned. Up to the time of the transaction with which we are concerned they were devoted to each other and she had, as she says, "the utmost confidence in him.""

"In 1946 Tazewell Wilkins approached Seymour about the purchase of a tract of Seymour's land containing 30.46 acres for a pasture. He also wanted to buy the adjoining tract of 31 acres, which was a part of the land owned by Mrs. Jackson. Seymour told Wilkins that while he was willing to take $275 for his (Seymour's) land, he did not own the 31-acre tract and suggested that Wilkins see Mrs. Jackson about buying it. While Seymour also conveyed this information to Mrs. Jackson the record discloses no negotiations between Wilkins and Mrs. Jackson for the purchase of her land.

"In February, 1947, Mrs. Jackson approached her brother, saying that she was in need of funds and was anxious to sell the 31-acre tract in which Wilkins had shown interest. Seymour did not want to buy the property, but because of his sister's need for money he agreed to purchase it at $275, which was the price which had been mentioned in his negotiations with Wilkins. The brother was then unaware that there was valuable timber on the land and contemplated using it for a pasture. Seymour gave his sister a check for $275 and she signed a receipt therefor. On the next

day Mrs. Jackson executed and delivered a deed conveying the property
to her brother. The deed was prepared by a local attorney at Seymour's
request and expense.

"A short while after Seymour had acquired the property it came to his
attention that some trees had been cut from the tract. Upon investigation
he discovered for the first time that there was valuable timber on the land.

"The evidence does not disclose the exact quantity and value of this
timber. It shows that in 1948 Seymour cut from the land which he had
purchased from his sister and from adjoining lands owned by him,
148,055 feet of lumber and that the greater portion of this came from the
Jackson tract. This timber had a stumpage value of approximately $20 per
1,000 feet."

In reversing the trial court and holding that the plaintiff was entitled to
equitable relief on a theory of constructive fraud, the Supreme Court of
Appeals had this to say:

"The undisputed evidence shows that shortly after the defendant had
acquired this tract of land from his sister for the sum of $275, he cut and
marketed therefrom timber valued at approximately ten times what he
had paid for the property. A mere statement of the matter shows the gross
and shocking inadequacy of the price paid.

"This is not the ordinary case in which the parties dealt at arm's length
and the shrewd trader was entitled to the fruits of his bargain. The parties
were brother and sister. He was a successful business man and she a
widow in need of money and forced by circumstances, according to the
defendant's own testimony, to sell a part of the lands which she had
inherited. Because of their friendly and intimate relations she entrusted
to him and he assumed the management and renting of a portion of this
very land. He engaged tenants for such of the land as could be cultivated
and collected the rents. She accepted his settlements without question.

"Moreover, it is undisputed that neither of the parties knew of the
timber on the land and we have from the defendant's own lips the admission that as it turned out "afterwards" he had paid a grossly inadequate
price for the property and that he would not have bought it from her for
the small amount paid if he had then known of the true situation. . . .

"In addition to the gross inadequacy of consideration we have the
confidential relation of the parties, the pecuniary distress of the vendor,
and the mutual mistake of the parties as to the subject matter of the
contract. Unquestionably, we think, to permit the transaction to stand
would result in constructive fraud upon the rights of the plaintiff. Hence,
she is entilted to relief in equity. . . .

"We are, therefore, of opinion that the lower court should have entered a decree granting the plaintiff's prayer for a rescission of the conveyance and restoring the parties to the status quo in so far as practicable.
By way of incidental relief the plaintiff is entitled to recover of the defendant the fair stumpage value of the timber removed by the latter from the

land, with interest from the date of such removal, and the fair rental value of the property during the time the defendant was in possession. The defendant is entitled to a return of the purchase price paid by him, with interest from the date that the plaintiff offered to rescind the transaction, and taxes paid by him on the land since the date of the conveyance, with interest."

NOTE

Do you agree with the court's conclusion? What remedy is appropriate in a case of this sort? See Dawson, Economic Duress — An Essay in Perspective, 45 Mich. L. Rev. 253, 272-282 (1947); J. Story, Commentaries on Equity Jurisprudence §§244, 246 (8th ed. 1861). For the distinction between confidential and fiduciary relationships, see J. Dawson, W. Harvey & S. Henderson, Contracts: Cases and Commentaries 175-176 (4th ed. 1985).

MARKS v. GATES
154 F. 481 (9th Cir. 1907)

On April 27, 1903, the appellant and the appellee William C. Gates, entered into an agreement at San Francisco, Cal., as follows:

> This agreement made and entered into this 27th day of April, 1903, by and between William C. Gates, of Seattle, state of Washington, the party of the first part, and Isaac L. Marks, of the city and county of San Francisco, state of California, the party of the second part, witnesseth:
> That the said William C. Gates, for and in consideration of one dollar (1) to him in hand paid, the receipt whereof is hereby acknowledged, does hereby agree to and with the said party of the second part that he will convey to said party of the second part a twenty (20) per centum interest in any and all property which said Gates shall acquire, either by location, purchase or otherwise, in the Territory of Alaska.
> In witness whereof the said parties hereto have hereunto set their hands and seals the day and year first above written.

To enforce the specific performance of this contract, the appellant brought a suit alleging that the real consideration of the agreement was the cancellation of a prior indebtedness of $11,225 due to him from Gates, and the payment by the appellant to Gates of the further sum of $1,000 in cash; that in pursuance of said agreement Gates went to Alaska, and thereafter and prior to June 20, 1905, the date of the commencement of the suit, acquired there, by location, purchase, and otherwise, various properties, including certain specified mining claims in the Fairbanks mining district of Alaska, the value of which is more than $750,000. The appellee, Gates, demurred to the complaint on the ground that it did not state facts sufficient to constitute a cause of action. The demurrer was sustained on the ground that the contract set forth in the complaint is so unjust and inequitable as not to entitle the appellant to relief.

GILBERT, Circuit Judge, after stating the case as above, delivered the opinion of the court.

The enforcement of a contract by a decree for its specific performance rests in the sound discretion of the court — a judicial discretion to be exercised in accordance with established principles of equity. A contract may be valid in law and not subject to cancellation in equity, and yet the terms thereof, the attendant circumstances, and in some cases the subsequent events, may be such as to require the court to deny its specific performance. In Pomeroy, §400, it is said:

> He who seeks equity must do equity. The doctrine, thus applied, means that the party asking the aid of the court must stand in conscientious relations towards his adversary; that the transaction from which his claim arises must be fair and just, and that the relief itself must not be harsh and oppressive upon the defendant. . . .

. . . In Pope Manufacturing Co. v. Gormully, 144 U.S. 224-236, 12 S. Ct. 632, 637, 36 L. Ed. 414, Mr. Justice Brown said:

> To stay the arm of a court of equity from enforcing a contract, it is by no means necessary to prove that it is invalid; from time immemorial it has been the recognized duty of such courts to exercise a discretion, to refuse their aid in the enforcement of unconscionable, oppressive, or inquitous contracts, and to turn the party claiming the benefit of such contract over to a court of law.

The contract in the present case had, at the time when it was made, no reference to any property then owned by the contracting parties, or even to property then in existence. It did not obligate the appellee, Gates, ever to go to Alaska or to acquire property there. It bound him during his lifetime to transfer to the appellant a one-fifth interest in all property of every description that he might acquire in Alaska by whatever means, whether by location, purchase, devise, gift, or inheritance — property of which neither party could know even approximately the value. It was a bargain made in the dark. The complaint is silent as to the means whereby the property therein described was obtained by Gates. It alleges that its value is more than $750,000. For aught that appears in the complaint to the contrary, the appellee, Gates, purchased this property and paid therefor its full value. The appellant, for the payment of $1,000 in cash and the cancellation of a debt of $11,225, which may or may not have been valid or collectible, now comes into a court of equity and asks

the court to decree that the appellee, Gates, transfer to him property of
the value of more than $150,000. If he now has the right to such relief, it
follows that he may hereafter sustain suits to acquire a like interest in all
property of every nature and description which Gates may at any time
obtain in Alaska, and that such right will end only with the life of Gates.
Courts of equity have often decreed specific performance where the consideration was inadequate, and it may be said in general that mere inadequacy of consideration is not of itself ground for withholding specific
performance unless it is so gross as to render the contract unconscionable. But where the consideration is so grossly inadequate as it is in the
present case, and the contract is made without any knowledge at the time
of its making on the part of either of the parties thereto of the nature of
the property to be affected thereby, or of its value, no equitable principle
is violated if specific performance is denied, and the parties are left to
their legal remedies, if any they have. In King v. Hamilton, *supra* [4
Peters 311], specific performance of a contract for the sale of a patented
grant of land within the Virginia Military District was denied in a case
where the patent specified, and the parties understood, that the grant
contained 1,533⅓ acres, and it subsequently appeared from a survey that
it contained 876 acres in excess of that quantity. In Day v. Newman, 10
Ves. Jr. 300, Lord Alvanley refused to enforce the specific performance of
an agreement for the sale for £20,000 of an estate worth only £10,000.
There was no actual fraud in the case, but the inadequacy was so great
that the court would not enforce it. In Earl of Chesterfield v. Jansen, 2
Ves. Sr. 125, Lord Hardwicke declared unconscionable a contract
whereby an expectant heir, in consideration of £5,000 obligated himself
to pay £10,000 out of his grandmother's estate if he survived her, but was
to pay nothing if she survived him. In Mississippi & Missouri R.R. Co. v.
Cromwell, 91 U.S. 643, 23 L. Ed. 367, Mr. Justice Bradley said:

> He comes into court with a very bad grace when he asks to use its extraordi-
> nary power to put him in possession of $30,000 worth of stock for which he
> paid only $50. The court is not bound to shut its eyes to the evident
> character of the transaction. It will never lend its aid to carry out an
> unconscionable bargain, but will leave the party to his remedy at law.

The facts presented in the complaint are not such as to entitle the
court to retain the case for the assessment of such damages as the appellant may have sustained for breach of the contract. A court of equity will
not grant pecuniary compensation in lieu of specific performance unless
the case presented is one for equitable interposition such as would entitle
the plaintiff to performance but for intervening facts, such as the destruction of the property, the conveyance of the same to an innocent third
person, or the refusal of the vendor's wife to join in a conveyance. Cooley
v. Lobdell, 153 N.Y. 596, 47 N.E. 783; Matthews v. Matthews, 133 N.Y.

679, 31 N.E. 519; Bourget v. Monroe, 58 Mich. 573, 25 N.W. 514; East-
man v. Reid, 101 Ala. 320, 13 South. 46; Milkman v. Ordway, 106 Mass.
232.

The decree of the court below is affirmed.

NOTE

Suppose plaintiff now brings an action at law for damages, will he be
able to recover $150,000? Does the case stand for the proposition that
there is no doctrine of unconscionability in the common law?

The last paragraph of the opinion rejects the so-called "clean-up" principle; the court refuses to retain jurisdiction for the final disposition of the
case. There is considerable case law contra, e.g., Gabrielson v. Hogan,
298 F. 722 (8th Cir. 1924). In the damage action, the defendant has, of
course, the greatest interest to play down the value of the property, to
reduce the quantum of damages. Consult, in general, Levin, Equitable
Clean-up of the Jury, 100 U. Pa. L. Rev. 320 (1951); Frank & Endicott,
Defenses in Equity and "Legal Rights," 14 La. L. Rev. 380 (1954);
Spanogle, Analyzing Unconscionability Problems, 117 U. Pa. L. Rev. 931
(1969); J. Dawson, W. Harvey & S. Henderson, Cases and Comment on
Contracts 695-697 (4th ed. 1982).

Will the plaintiff at least be able to recover $12,225? Under what
theory?

EMBOLA v. TUPPELA
127 Wash. 285, 220 P. 789 (1923)

PEMBERTON, J. John Tuppela joined the gold seekers' rush to Alaska,
and after remaining there a number of years prospecting, was adjudged
insane, and committed to an asylum in Portland, Oregon. Upon his
release, after a confinement of about four years, he found that his mining
properties in Alaska had been sold by his guardian. In May of 1918,
Tuppela, destitute and without work, met respondent at Astoria, Oregon.
They had been close friends for a period of about 30 years. Respondent
advanced money for his support, and in September brought him to Seattle to the home of Herman Lindstrom, a brother-in-law of respondent.
Tuppela had requested a number of people to advance money for an
undertaking to recover his mining property in Alaska, but found no one
who was willing to do so. The estimated value of this mining property was
about $500,000. In the month of September Tuppela made the following
statement to respondent:

"You have already let me have $270. If you will give me $50 more so I
can go to Alaska and get my property back, I will pay you ten thousand
dollars when I win my property."

Respondent accepted this offer, and immediately advanced the sum of $50. In January, 1921, after extended litigation, Tuppela recovered his property. Tuppela, remembering his agreement with respondent, requested Mr. Cobb, his trustee, to pay the full amount, and upon his refusal so to do this action was instituted to collect the same.

The answer of the appellant denies the contract, and alleges that, if it were made, it is unconscionable, not supported by adequate consideration, procured through fraud, and is usurious. The appellant also alleges that the amount advanced did not exceed $100, and he has paid $150 into the registry of the court for the benefit of respondent.

The court found in favor of the respondent, and from the judgment entered this appeal is taken.

It is contended by appellant that the amount advanced is a loan, and therefore usurious, and that the sum of $300 is not an adequate consideration to support a promise to repay $10,000. It is the contention of respondent that the money advanced was not a loan, but an investment; that the transaction was in the nature of a grubstake contract, which has been upheld by this court. Raymond v. Johnson, 17 Wash. 232, 49 Pac. 492, 61 Am. St. Rep. 908; Ranahan v. Gibbons, 23 Wash. 255, 62 Pac. 773; Mack v. Mack, 39 Wash. 190, 81 Pac. 707; Mattocks v. Great Northern R. Co., 94 Wash. 44, 162 Pac. 19.

This is not a case wherein respondent advanced money to carry on prospecting. The money was advanced to enable appellant to recover his mining property. Appellant had already been advised by an attorney that he could not recover this property. The risk of losing the money advanced was as great in this case as if the same had been advanced under a grubstake contract. Where the principal sum advanced is to be repaid only on some contingency that may never take place, the sum so advanced is considered an investment, and not a loan, and the transaction is not usurious. "To constitute usury it is essential that the principal sum loaned shall be repayable at all events and not put in hazard absolutely. If it is payable only on some contingency then the transaction is not usurious. . . ." 27 R.C.L. §21, p. 220. The fact that the money advanced was not to be returned until appellant won his property, a contingency at that time unlikely to occur, supports the finding that the consideration was not inadequate.

To the contention that the contract was procured through fraud the testimony shows that appellant voluntarily offered to pay the $10,000, and at the time was of sound and disposing mind, and considered that the contract was to his advantage.

The trial court having found that there was no fraud and that the contract was not unconscionable, we should uphold these findings unless the evidence preponderates against them. Thompson v. Seattle Park Co., 94 Wash. 539, 162 Pac. 994; Austin v. Union Lumber Co., 95 Wash. 608, 164 Pac. 245; Mottinger v. Reagan, 96 Wash. 49, 164 Pac. 595; Hayes v.

Hayes, 96 Wash. 125, 164 Pac. 740. We are satisfied that the evidence
supports the findings.

The judgment is affirmed.

UNITED STATES v. BETHLEHEM
STEEL CORP.
315 U.S. 289 (1942)

[In the early part of 1918 after protracted negotiations a series of contracts was entered into between the United States Shipping Board Fleet
Corporation and the Bethlehem Shipbuilding Corporation, a subsidiary
of Bethlehem Steel. Efforts on the part of the Fleet Corporation to obtain
a lump sum contract was unsuccessful. Bethlehem insisted on cost-plus-
fixed-fee contracts which also included bonus-for-saving clauses amounting to 50 percent of the difference between actual and estimated costs. To
accelerate production and to avoid the responsibility for commandeering
the plant, the negotiators for the Fleet Corporation finally acquiesced.
Under the terms of the contract, Bethlehem was entitled in addition to
the total costs of building the ships (about $91 million) a fixed fee of $11
million and a bonus for saving, amounting to $13 million since the esti-
mated costs greatly exceed actual costs.

The Government paid Bethlehem in addition to the actual costs, the
fixed fees and about $8 million by way of bonus but refused to pay the
balance amounting to $5 million. It brought a suit in equity for an ac-
counting and for a refund of amounts paid in excess of a just and reasonable compensation, claiming fraud and economic duress. Bethlehem in
return brought a damage suit for breach of contract.

Consolidating the cases, the Federal District Court, strictly interpreted
the contract, upheld the Master's report granting Bethlehem full recovery. On certiorari to the Circuit Court of Appeals which had affirmed the
decision of the lower court, the Supreme Court affirmed. Neither fraud
nor duress was shown according to the majority speaking through Mr.
Justice Black. Twenty-two percent profit on the contract was not such an
exorbitant amount as to shock the conscience of the Court. It was much
less than many other war contracts.

The dissenting opinion of Mr. Justice Frankfurter holding Bethlehem
guilty of economic duress is reprinted only in part.] . . .

The Master expressly found that it was essential that Bethlehem undertake to build the vessels provided for in the contracts, and that, since
the Government needed Bethlehem's organization, it had no satisfactory
alternative. It had to make the contracts on Bethlehem's terms or not at
all. He concluded, nevertheless, that since "the Fleet Corporation made
the contracts with open eyes, although resenting the commercial attitude
of Bethlehem and condemning Bethlehem for demanding its 'pound of

flesh','" the contracts were enforceable by Bethlehem in the absence of any proof of fraud.

The District Court concurred in the proposition that the absence of fraud made the contracts invulnerable. But its conclusion is contradicted by its findings:

> The managers for the contractor adopted the famous Rob Roy distinction who admitted he was a robber but proudly proclaimed that he was no thief. The contractor boldly and openly fixed the figures in the estimated cost so high as to give them the promise of large bonus profits. The managers for the Fleet Corporation knew that the estimate was high and why it was made high and so protested it. The reply of the contractor's managers was, "We will take the contract with this promise of bonus profits incorporated in it but not otherwise. You take or leave it." Whatever wrong there was in this may have been the wrong in a daylight robbery but there was no element of deception in it.

23 F. Supp. 676, 679.

Similarly, the affirmance of the Circuit Court of Appeals appears to have been based upon the assumption that the Government's failure to show fraud was fatal:

> It is of course obvious that these negotiations took place in time of war when the need of the Government for ships was extremely urgent and the necessity of reaching an agreement with Bethlehem, therefore, vital. It is equally clear that Bethlehem insisted upon assuring itself a margin of profit which in view of the necessities of the Government was so large as to indicate an attitude of commercial greed but little diluted with patriotic feeling. There is no doubt that this attitude on the part of Bethlehem was deeply resented by the Government representatives but the latter were faced with the alternative of either agreeing to Bethlehem's terms or taking possession of its shipyards and having the Government itself construct the vessels. We think the record clearly indicates that the Government representatives felt that the latter course could not have accomplished the shipbuilding program with the speed which was essential. It was Bethlehem's existing shipbuilding organization that was necessary to insure success to the program of the Fleet Corporation. Consequently the Government representatives, feeling as they did that Bethlehem's organization was necessary to their program, were obliged to accept the terms offered by Bethlehem. This they did with full knowledge, as we have said, that the estimated cost figures included in the contracts did not represent close approximations but were so prepared as to assure to Bethlehem substantial additional profits by way of the bonus for savings. It follows that while Bethlehem may be condemned for having taken advantage of the Nation's necessities to secure inordinate profits it cannot be charged with having misrepresented the facts to the Government's representatives.

113 F.2d 301, 305-06.

Thus, not less than six times did the Circuit Court of Appeals declare that the unconscionable terms of this contract were forced upon the Government by the dire necessities of national self-preservation. Nevertheless the Court found itself impotent to resist the demand that the courts themselves become the means of realizing these "inordinate profits." But law does not subject courts to such impotence. Courts need not be the agents of a wrong that offends their conscience if they heed the commands of law.

In England prior to 1285 (Statute of Westminster II, 13 Edw. I, c. 50) suitors were frequently "obliged to depart from the Chancery without getting writs, because there are none which will exactly fit their cases, although these cases fall within admitted principles." Maitland, Forms of Action at Common Law, Lect. IV (1936 ed.) p. 51. Today it is held that because the circumstances of this case cannot be fitted into a neatly carved pigeonhole in the law of contracts, "daylight robbery," exploitation of the "necessities" of the country at war, must be consummated by this Court. It is said that familiar principles would be outraged if Bethlehem were denied recovery on these contracts. But is there any principle which is more familiar or more firmly embedded in the history of Anglo-American law than the basic doctrine that the courts will not permit themselves to be used as instruments of inequity and injustice? Does any principle in our law have more universal application than the doctrine that courts will not enforce transactions in which the relative positions of the parties are such that one has unconscionably taken advantage of the necessities of the other?

These principles are not foreign to the law of contracts. Fraud and physical duress are not the only grounds upon which courts refuse to enforce contracts. The law is not so primitive that it sanctions every injustice except brute force and downright fraud. More specifically, the courts generally refuse to lend themselves to the enforcement of a "bargain" in which one party has unjustly taken advantage of the economic necessities of the other. "And there is great reason and justice in this rule, for necessitous men are not, truly speaking, free men, but, to answer a present exigency, will submit to any terms that the crafty may impose upon them." Vernon v. Bethell, 2 Eden 110, 113. So wrote Lord Chancellor Northington in 1761.

The fact that the representatives of the Government entered into the contracts "with their eyes wide open" does not mean thay they were not acting under compulsion. "It always is for the interest of a party under duress to choose the lesser of two evils. But the fact that a choice was made according to interest does not exclude duress. It is the characteristic of duress properly so called." Holmes, J., in Union Pacific R. Co. v. Public Service Comm'n, 248 U.S. 67, 70. In that case a state unconstitutionally exacted a fee for a certificate of authority to issue railroad bonds. A railroad which had paid the fee and obtained a certificate, rather than run the risk of subsequent invalidation of its bonds and imposition of serious penalties, was held to have been coerced into making the payments. In Swift Company v. U.S., 111 U.S. 22, 29, the taxpayer's only alternatives were "to submit to an illegal exaction, or discontinue its business." The payment of the tax in these circumstances was held to be under duress. See also Ward v. Love County, 253 U.S. 17, 23. The courts generally regard the dilemma of the taxpayer who must either pay the taxes or incur serious business losses as a species of duress. E.g., Morgan v. Palmer, 2 Barn. & C. 729; Ripley v. Gelston, 9 Johns. 201; Scottish U. & N. Ins. Co. v. Herriott, 109 Iowa 606, 80 N.W. 665; see Notes, 64 A.L.R. 9, 84 A.L.R. 294.

Underlying all these cases is the law's recognition of a basic psychological truth. In Atkinson v. Denby, 7 Hurlst. & N. 934, 936, Cockburn, C.J., said that "where the one person can dictate, and the other has no alternative but to submit, it is coercion." See also Abbott, C.J., in Morgan v. Palmer, 2 Barn. & C. 729, 735: "But if one party has the power of saying to the other, 'that which you require shall not be done except upon the conditions which I choose to impose,' no person can contend that they stand upon anything like an equal footing." And these were decisions in days when law was supposed to be much more rigid and more respectful of forms than we now ordinarily deem just.

The fundamental principle of law that the courts will not enforce a bargain where one party has unconscionably taken advantage of the necessities and distress of the other has found expression in an almost infinite variety of cases. See Lonergan v. Buford, 148 U.S. 581, 589-91; Snyder v. Rosenbaum, 215 U.S. 261, 265-66. Perhaps the most familiar is the situation of the mortgagor who under the pressure of financial distress conveys his equity of redemption to the mortgagee. The courts will scrutinize the transaction very carefully, Villa v. Rodriguez, 12 Wall. 323, 339, and if it appears that the mortgagee has taken unfair advantage of the other's position, the conveyance will not be enforced. Compare Vernon v. Bethell, 2 Eden 110; Close v. Phipps, 7 M. & G. 586; Richardson v. Barrick, 16 Iowa 407.

Similarly, an heir or remainderman who is compelled by financial circumstances to sell his expectancy for a song may recover it if the vendee has unduly exploited the other's distress. Wood v. Abrey, 3 Maddock's Chan. 216, 219 (where the Vice-Chancellor, Sir John Leach, said: "If a man who meets his purchaser on equal terms, negligently sells his estate at an under value, he has no title to relief in equity. But a Court of Equity will inquire whether the parties really did meet on equal terms; and if it be found that the vendor was in distressed circumstances, and that advantage was taken of that distress, it will avoid the contract."); Underhill v. Horwood, 10 Ves. Jr. 209; M'Kinney v. Pinckard, 29 Va. 149; Butler v. Duncan, 47 Mich. 94, 10 N.W. 123; Brown v. Hall, 14 R.I. 249. In Administrators of Hough v. Hunt, 2 Ohio 495, 502, a person heavily in debt, in order to obtain a further loan with which to meet debts falling due, agreed to buy land at more than double its value. The court found that the lender had unjustly taken advantage of the borrower's necessities and therefore rescinded the contract: "The rule in chancery is well established. When a person is incumbered with debts, and that fact is known to a person with whom he contracts, who avails himself of it to exact an unconscionable bargain, equity will relieve upon account of the advantage and hardship." This was written in 1826. To the same effect are Vyne v. Glenn, 41 Mich. 112, and Bither v. Packard, 115 Maine 306, 98 A. 929.

Another class of cases in which this principle has been applied arises where a customer of a gas or electric company pays charges which he asserts he is not obligated to pay, rather than have his service disconnected. Payments made in such circumstances are regarded as coerced. See Boston v. Edison Electric Illuminating Co., 242 Mass. 305, 310, 136 N.E. 113; Westlake & Button v. St. Louis, 77 Mo. 47; Note, 34 A.L.R. 185.

Cobb v. Charter, 32 Conn. 358, illustrates another type of controversy in which the courts have given effect to the historic principle of duress which is now seemingly rejected as an innovation. The defendant there had possession of a chest of tools belonging to the plaintiff, a mechanic. He refused to give up the chest, which the plaintiff needed in order to ply his trade, unless the latter would pay a bill for which he denied responsibility. The plaintiff's payment of the bill in these circumstances was held to have been made under duress. Accord: Lonergan v. Buford, 148 U.S. 581, 589-91; Fenwick Shipping Co. v. Clarke Bros., 133 Ga. 43, 65 S.E. 140; Stenton v. Jerome, 54 N.Y. 480; Harmony v. Bingham, 12 N.Y. 99.

In Stiefler v. McCullough, 97 Ind. App. 123, 174 N.E. 823, a merchant who had to obtain a loan in order to remain in business agreed to pay the president of a bank an exorbitant sum in consideration for his services in procuring a loan. The court refused to enforce this agreement as unconscionable. Similarly, in Niedermeyer v. Curators of State University, 61 Mo. App. 654, a student paid tuition fees which he regarded as excessive, and which he did not believe he was required to pay under his contract with the university, only because he feared expulsion for non-payment. This payment was held to have been made under duress and hence recoverable. Cf. Baldwin v. Sullivan Timber Co., 20 N.Y. Supp. 496; Kelly v. Caplice, 23 Kan. 474.

Strikingly analogous to the case at bar are the decisions that a salvor who takes advantage of the helplessness of the ship in distress to drive an unconscionable bargain will not be aided by the courts in his attempts to enforce the bargain. Post v. Jones, 19 How. 150, 160; The Tornado, 109 U.S. 110, 117; The Elfrida, 172 U.S. 186, 193-94. In Post v. Jones, supra, it was said that the courts "will not tolerate the doctrine that a salvor can take the advantage of his situation, and avail himself of the calamities of others to drive a bargain; nor will they permit the performance of a public duty to be turned into a traffic of profit." These cases are not unlike the familiar example of the drowning man who agrees to pay an exorbitant sum to a rescuer who would otherwise permit him to drown. No court would enforce a contract made under such circumstances.

To deny the existence of duress in a Government contract by ironic reference to the feebleness of the United States as against the overpowering strength of a single private corporation is an indulgence of rhetoric in disregard of fact. The United States with all its might and majesty never makes a contract. To speak of a contract by the United States is to employ an abstraction. Contracts are made not by 130 million Americans but by some official on their behalf. Because the national interest is represented not by the power of the nation but by an individual professing to exercise authority of vast consequence to the nation, action by Government officials is often not binding against the Government in situations where private parties would be bound. The contracts here were not made by an abstraction known as the United States or by the millions of its citizens. For all practical purposes, the arrangement was entered into by two persons, Bowles and Radford. And it was entered into by them against their better judgment because they had only Hobson's choice — which is no choice. They had no choice in view of the circumstances which subordinated them and by which they were governed, namely, that ships were needed, and needed quickly, and Bethlehem was needed to construct them quickly. The legal alternative — that the Government take over Bethlehem — was not an actual alternative, and Bethlehem knew this as well as the representatives of the Government.

The suggestion is made that Bethlehem's profits under these contracts were not exceptional when compared with the profits made under similar contracts, and that the enormous profits claimed by Bethlehem under these contracts cannot be regarded as supporting the inference that Bethlehem took advantage of the Government's distress. But the only contracts before us are those involved in this litigation. There is nothing in this record which enables us to say that although these contracts are unconscionable, all contracts made by the Government during the same period were no less unconscionable. And even if this were so, it would be no argument that this Court should give its sanction to these contracts by making itself the instrument for realizing the unconscionable profits. What little light the record does cast upon contemporary contracts gives no justification for regarding these contracts as typical. The policy of Charles M. Schwab, Director General of the Fleet Corporation, was to make contracts providing for a maximum profit of 10%, out of which all federal taxes would have to be paid. See Letter of Oct. 2, 1918, to Edward N. Hurley, Chairman of the Shipping Board, relating to contracts with the American Shipbuilding Company.

If we are to go outside the record, the evidence is confusing and unreliable. It must be borne in mind that Bethlehem took no risk of loss,

582 4. Fairness of the Bargain and Equality

that under the contracts it was protected from the risks of rising costs of labor, materials, transportation, etc., that under the contracts it was not required to make any capital expenditures, that the Government agreed to advance all sums that should be necessary for the performance of the contracts. It is idle to compare the profits made by Bethlehem under these contracts with profits made by industrial concerns of various types under different types of contracts. Such figures are statistical quicksand unless we are told also that in each case the contractor was not required to make any capital investment, that he was insured against normal business risks, and that he was guaranteed a profit, regardless of any change in circumstances. . . .

Mr. Justice Holmes has said that "Men must turn square corners when they deal with the Government." Rock Island, A. & L. R. Co. v. United States, 254 U.S. 141, 143. His admonition has particular relevance when this Court is called upon to enforce agreements made with the Government at war for the production of supplies essential to the prosecution of the war. During wartime the bargaining position of Government contracting officers is inherently weak, no matter how conscientious they may be. If they are to deal on equal terms with private contractors, particularly where the subject matter of contracts is so intricate and so specialized as the building of ships, they must have available to them not only detailed information but also the time within which to study the data and the freedom to exercise a real choice. In the last war, at least, this was not generally true. See Sen. Rep. No. 944, 74th Cong., 1st Sess., pt. 4, p. 30. It is not difficult in these days to appreciate the position of negotiators for the Government in time of war and to realize how much the pressures of war deprive them of equality of bargaining power in situations where bargaining with private contractors is the only practicable means of securing necessary war supplies. Because the Government is in such a dependent position, and because those who deal with it on a cost-plus arrangement, or some similar basis, are assured of a profit, it is wholly consistent with practicalities and makes no unduly idealistic demand for the law to judge the arrangement of such wartime contractors by standards not unlike those by which a fiduciary's conduct is judged. Those upon whom the Nation is dependent for its supplies in the defense of its life would hardly wish to be judged by lower standards.

The modes are vast and varied by which the Nation obtains its war supplies. What will best supply war needs in amplest measure in the quickest time and least wastefully — whether by private letting and, if so, under what restrictions and safeguards; under what circumstances the Government should do its own supplying either by taking over old plants or building new ones or a combination of the two; to what extent and through what means peacetime habits and traditions may be displaced and disregarded — these are questions of policy for the wisdom and responsibility of the Congress and the Executive. The very limited scope of inquiry to which a litigation on a particular transaction is confined is hardly the basis for judgment on such far-flung issues. If the history of this Court permits one generalization above all others, it is the unwisdom of entering the domain of policy outside the very narrow legal limits presented by the record of a particular litigation. Such intrusion into the executive and legislative domains is not conducive to the just disposition of the immediate controversy. We are much less likely to go wrong if we do not depart from the well-grooved path of judicial competence.

This Court should not permit Bethlehem to recover these unconscionable profits, and thereby "make the court the instrument of this injustice." Thomas v. Brownville, Ft. K. & P. R. Co., 109 U.S. 522, 526.

[The concurring opinion of Mr. Justice Murphy and the opinion of Mr. Justice Douglas have been omitted, as have the footnotes.]

NOTE

The case is noted in 51 Yale L.J. 855 (1942); 26 Minn. L. Rev. 898 (1942); 21 Texas L. Rev. 56 (1942); Hale, Bargaining, Duress, and Economic Liberty, 43 Colum. L. Rev. 603, 621 (1943); F. Kessler & M. Sharp, Contracts 274-276 (1953); Braucher, Fixed Prices and Price Reduction in Defense Contracts, 53 Colum. L. Rev. 936 (1953). Contrast the philosophy expressed in President Eisenhower's veto message concerning a bill attempting to compensate a contractor who had entered into a fixed-price contract and who had suffered unavoidable loss. It is reprinted in H. Shepherd & B. Sher, Law in Society, An Introduction to Freedom of Contract 275-276 (1960), together with an editorial in The Wall Street Journal of August 22, 1958, approving the position taken by President Eisenhower.

On government contracts in general, see 29 Law & Contemp. Prob. (1964).

Section 2.   Consumer Protection: Unconscionability and Beyond

Classical contract law presupposes a world of self-reliant, self-interested individuals. After informing themselves about the character and quality of the goods they wish to buy and the legal relations they desire to enter into, they dicker in a competitive market, where the resulting agreements leave each person with something just a bit more valuable than what he gave up (or so he hopes). The market, the process of give and take, the threat constantly lurking in the background that business will be taken elsewhere, guarantee that agreements will be fair, and exchanges equivalent. In this world, government, and more specifically the courts, should play a limited role in policing agreements, using only the narrowly defined doctrines of misrepresentation, duress, undue influence, incompetence, and mistake.[54]

However descriptive this view may be of some past period, it is an inaccurate picture of the world of the modern consumer,[55] or so the consumer advocates would contend. Dickering is almost a forgotten art among consumers, who confront daily the impersonal world of standardized goods and standard form contracts. This is not to say that standardization is evil, or that dickering should be revived. Consumers have benefited enormously from standardization of both goods and contracts. Standard form contracts save sellers of goods and services substantial amounts in transaction costs, and these savings are passed on to the consumer in the form of lower prices. Moreover, even though consumers no longer have the opportunity to bargain over the terms of their agreements, they still have a choice: they can always shop around for a better deal, assuming, of course, that the market for what they are seeking is competitive.[56]

Still, the goods consumers buy and the contracts they enter into have become increasingly complex over the years. In many cases they have become so complex that the cost to the consumer of acquiring sufficient information and understanding about them to make an informed choice is simply prohibitive. As one commentator has put it, "Given the limited

54. See Leff, Contract as a Thing, 19 Am. U.L. Rev. 131, 137-141 (1970).

In discussing American law of the early nineteenth century, Professor Lawrence Friedman points out that "American commercial law, on paper, had a certain Adam Smith severity, a certain flavor of the rugged individual." L. Friedman, A History of American Law 233 (1973). In accord is the recent work by Horwitz at 160 et seq. See also McFarland v. Newman, 9 Watts 55 (Pa. 1839); Hardesty v. Smith, 3 Ind. 39, 41-43 (1851). Nineteenth-century English attitudes were similar. See generally Atiyah.

55. "Consumer" is generally defined in legislation according to the primary purpose for which a person enters into a transaction to obtain goods or services. If he enters a transaction to obtain goods or services for personal, family, or household purposes, he is a consumer of those goods or services. See Consumer Credit Protection Act, 15 U.S.C.A. §1602(h); Uniform Consumer Credit Code (U.C.C.C.) §1.301(11-13)(1974). For some of the definitional problems posed by the elusive concept of consumer, see Commercial Credit Equipment Co. v. Carter, 83 Wash. 136, 516 P.2d 767 (1973).

In the United Kingdom, consumer contracts are regulated by the Fair Trading Act 1973, supplemented by the Unfair Contract Terms Act 1977. For a list of consumer protection legislation in other countries, see Berg, The Israeli Standard Contracts Law 1964: Judicial Controls of Standard Form Contracts, 28 Int'l & Comp. L.Q. 560, 560 n.5 (1979).

56. See Schwartz, A Re-examination of Non-substantive Unconscionability, 63 Va. L. Rev. 1053, 1064-1071 (1977); Schwartz & Wilde, Intervening in Markets on the Basis of Imperfect Information: A Legal and Economic Analysis, 127 U. Pa. L. Rev. 630 (1979).

innate ability to make accurate price/quality comparisons, extensive search, evaluation, self-education, or purchased expertise may be necessary to generate even modest marginal returns and would be an economically irrational investment on the part of a consumer."[57] To make matters worse, the "natural" laws of the competitive marketplace often fail to provide the consumer with the needed information and understanding to assist him in choosing.[58]

We are told by consumer advocates that in a showdown between the uninformed and bewildered consumer and the business-wise merchant and manufacturer, the consumer needs protection, more protection than the natural forces of a free, competitive market and traditional contract law can give. They point to the sharp and deceptive practices of high pressure salesmen who take advantage of the meek and ignorant; to the detailed printed form contracts written in technical language, often unreadable and even more often unread, which fail to convey meaningful information about what the consumer is getting and what he is giving up; and to the formidable obstacles placed in the path of the consumer who is seeking to redress a wrong: the costs of litigation, high attorney's fees and the relatively small amount of money at stake. And the poor suffer most. The poor are the most vulnerable to sharp tactics. Frequently lacking in education, they have the greatest difficulty in using whatever information is available to them to make an intelligent choice.[59] They are the most likely to default as defendants, and they are the least able to afford legal services as plaintiffs. Finally, whatever loss they do suffer, however small, is acutely felt.

Small wonder, in this era of the Consumer Movement, that consumers have become the object of an ever-increasing array of legislation and of an increasingly solicitous judiciary. They have also become the wards of a multitude of administrative agencies at both the state and national levels. These attempts at shielding consumers from the tactics of the unscrupulous and, indeed, from their own folly, have not been without their critics, however. A chorus of critics of the consumer protection movement has been growing in recent years, stridently attacking even those who would argue for legislative and judicial attempts to protect the poor on the ground that the net economic effect of such protection has

57. Trebilcock, *supra* note 1, at 372. See Leff, Contract as a Thing, 19 Am. U.L. Rev. 131 (1970); Leff, The Pontiac Prospectus, 2 Loyola Consumer L.J. 25 (1974); Slawson, Mass Contracts: Lawful Fraud in California, 48 S. Cal. L. Rev. 1 (1974). Very simply put, the thrust of these articles is that the concept of contract in the consumer context should be limited to the terms that are bargained over. The remainder of the documents now conventionally called contracts should be treated by courts and legislatures as "things," and therefore subject to regulation.

58. R. Posner, Economic Analysis of Law 82 (2d ed. 1977).

59. See D. Caplovitz, The Poor Pay More 18-19 (1963) (but see also his preface to the 1967 edition); W. Magnuson & J. Carper, The Dark Side of the Marketplace (1968).

been more harmful than helpful. These critics argue for minor adjustments in traditional contract doctrines while defending the salutary effects of the policing function of the market.[60]

Whatever the merits of the arguments on both sides of the consumer protection debate, it is the intent of this section to give the student a brief introduction to some of the protections consumers now enjoy.

The legislative and judicial answers to consumer problems are as numerous and varied as the problems themselves. The quality and safety of consumer goods are regulated.[61] Statutory provisions and administrative rulings outlaw specific practices, require disclosure of important information in an understandable form, and dictate which contract terms are permissible, which are necessary, and which are prohibited. Governmental agencies are authorized to bring suits to enjoin illegal practices and to obtain damages on behalf of injured consumers. Minimum damages are recoverable under many statutes, as are attorney's fees and court costs. And there is the class action, a formidable consumer weapon. Finally, consumer debtors are protected from the depredations of overanxious debt collectors by both federal and state legislation.

Three broad developments have aided consumers in recent years. The United States Supreme Court and many state courts have erected procedural safeguards around creditors' remedies in the name of due process of law. The Federal Trade Commission and comparable state agencies have outlawed unfair or deceptive trade practices, proscribed certain terms and required others in consumer contracts. And finally, consumers have benefited from an expansion in the concept of unconscionability.[62]

Prior to the onslaught of special consumer legislation, the unconscionability provision of the U.C.C. (§2-302) was an important source of consumer protection.[63] The courts used this provision to safeguard consumers from the sharp practices and harsh terms of sellers. The draftsmen of state consumer legislation, realizing the importance of unconscionability as an instrument of consumer protection, included unconscionability provisions in their codes and acts. These provisions were, on the whole, more detailed than the one found in the U.C.C. In addition to a broad definition of unconscionability, many pieces of consumer legislation include a list of factors to be considered in determining whether a particular contract or term is unconscionable. The following is

60. See Schwartz, *supra* note 56; Epstein, Unconscionability: A Critical Re-Appraisal, 18 J.L. & Econ. 293 (1975).

61. This aspect of consumer protection, although important and often controversial, will not be discussed, nor will the consumer protection aspects of trade regulation, such as licensing statutes and antitrust laws. For a general discussion of both of these matters see Reich, Toward a New Consumer Protection, 128 U. Pa. L. Rev. 1 (1979).

62. See U.C.C.C. §5.108, *infra*.

63. The U.C.C., imbued with the spirit of freedom of contract, does not generally distinguish between consumers and others, except in Article 9. Stiff opposition thwarted a plan to treat consumers differently. G. Gilmore, Security Interests in Personal Property, 1093 (1965).

a portion of the unconscionability provision of one such piece of consumer legislation, the Uniform Consumer Credit Code (U.C.C.C.) (1974):[64]

Section 5.108   [Unconscionability; Inducement by
Unconscionable Conduct; Unconscionable Debt Collection]

(1) With respect to a transaction that is, gives rise to, or leads the debtor to believe will give rise to, a consumer credit transaction, if the court as a matter of law finds:

(a) the agreement or transaction to have been unconscionable at the time it was made, or to have been induced by unconscionable conduct, the court may refuse to enforce the agreement; or

(b) any term or part of the agreement or transaction to have been unconscionable at the time it was made, the court may refuse to enforce the agreement, enforce the remainder of the agreement without the unconscionable term or part, or so limit the application of any unconscionable term or part as to avoid any unconscionable result.

(2) With respect to a consumer credit transaction, if the court as a matter of law finds that a person has engaged in, is engaging in, or is likely to engage in unconscionable conduct in collecting a debt arising from that transaction, the court may grant an injunction and award the consumer any actual damages he has sustained.

(3) If it is claimed or appears to the court that the agreement or transaction or any term or part thereof may be unconscionable, or that a person has engaged in, is engaging in, or is likely to engage in unconscionable conduct in collecting a debt, the parties shall be afforded a reasonable opportunity to present evidence as to the setting, purpose, and effect of the agreement or transaction or term or part thereof, or of the conduct, to aid the court in making the determination.

(4) In applying subsection (1), consideration shall be given to each of the following factors, among others, as applicable:

(a) belief by the seller, lessor, or lender at the time a transaction is entered into that there is no reasonable probability of payment in full of the obligation by the consumer or debtor;

(b) in the case of a consumer credit sale or consumer lease, knowledge by the seller or lessor at the time of the sale or lease of the inability of the consumer to receive substantial benefits from the property or services sold or leased;

(c) in the case of a consumer credit sale or consumer lease, gross disparity between the price of the property or services sold or leased and the value of the property or services measured by the price at which similar property or services are readily obtainable in credit transactions by like consumers;

(d) the fact that the creditor contracted for or received separate charges for insurance with respect to a consumer credit sale or consumer

---

64. For a discussion of the U.C.C.C. and its history, see p. 595 *infra*.

loan with the effect of making the sale or loan, considered as a whole, unconscionable; and

(e) the fact that the seller, lessor, or lender has knowingly taken advantage of the inability of the consumer or debtor reasonably to protect his interests by reason of physical or mental infirmities, ignorance, illiteracy, inability to understand the language of the agreement, or similar factors.

(5) In applying subsection (2), consideration shall be given to each of the following factors, among others, as applicable:

(a) using or threatening to use force, violence, or criminal prosecution against the consumer or members of his family;

(b) communicating with the consumer or a member of his family at frequent intervals or at unusual hours or under other circumstances so that it is a reasonable inference that the primary purpose of the communication was to harass the consumer;

(c) using fraudulent, deceptive, or misleading representations such as a communication which simulates legal process or which gives the appearance of being authorized, issued, or approved by a government, governmental agency, or attorney at law when it is not, or threatening or attempting to enforce a right with knowledge or reason to know that the right does not exist;

(d) causing or threatening to cause injury to the consumer's reputation or economic status by disclosing information affecting the consumer's reputation for credit-worthiness with knowledge or reason to know that the information is false; communicating with the consumer's employer before obtaining a final judgment against the consumer, except as permitted by statute or to verify the consumer's employment; disclosing to a person, with knowledge or reason to know that the person does not have a legitimate business need for the information, or in any way prohibited by statute, information affecting the consumer's credit or other reputation; or disclosing information concerning the existence of a debt known to be disputed by the consumer without disclosing that fact; and

(e) engaging in conduct with knowledge that like conduct has been restrained or enjoined by a court in a civil action by the Administrator against any person pursuant to the provisions on injunctions against fraudulent or unconscionable agreements or conduct (Section 6.111).

(6) If in an action in which unconscionability is claimed the court finds unconscionability pursuant to subsection (1) or (2), the court shall award reasonable fees to the attorney for the consumer or debtor. If the court does not find unconscionability and the consumer or debtor claiming unconscionability has brought or maintained an action he knew to be groundless, the court shall award reasonable fees to the attorney for the party against whom the claim is made. In determining attorney's fees, the amount of the recovery on behalf of the consumer is not controlling.

(7) The remedies of this section are in addition to remedies otherwise available for the same conduct under law other than this Act, but double recovery of actual damages may not be had.

(8) For the purpose of this section, a charge or practice expressly permitted by this Act is not in itself unconscionable.

The cases that follow illustrate the application of unconscionability in the consumer field. Consumer legislation and administrative regulations have endeavored to remedy specific abuses that contributed to the findings of unconscionability in many of these cases. These responses to consumer problems will be discussed in detail in the Notes following the cases.

AMERICAN HOME IMPROVEMENT CO.
v. MacIVER
105 N.H. 435, 201 A.2d 886 (1964)

This is an agreed case submitted on exhibits and certain stipulated facts. The plaintiff seeks to recover damages for breach by the defendants of an alleged agreement for home improvements. The agreement (Exhibit No. 1) was signed by the defendants April 4, 1963 and it provided that the plaintiff would "furnish and install 14 combination windows and 1 door" and "flintcoat" the side walls of the defendants' property at a cost of $1,759. At the same time the defendants signed an application for financing to a finance corporation (Exhibit No. 2). This application also contained a blank note and a blank power of attorney to the finance corporation which were undated and were signed by the defendants. The application stated the total amount due, the number of months that payments were to be made (60) and the monthly payment but did not state the rate of interest. The defendants received a copy of exhibit 2 on April 4, 1963.

"At some time after April 7, 1963, the defendants received notice of approval of the application for financing . . . Exhibit A." This exhibit stated that the application for credit in the net amount of $1,759 had been approved and that the monthly payments would be $42.81 for 60 months "including principal, interest and life and disability insurance."

It is further agreed that on or about April 9, 1963 the defendants notified the plaintiff to cease work on the defendants' premises, and plaintiff complied. By April 9, 1963, the plaintiff had done a negligible amount of work on the premises but had already paid a sales commission of Eight Hundred Dollars ($800.00) in reliance upon the contract. It is agreed that the plaintiff did not willfully violate any provision of RSA 399-B.

The defendants moved to dismiss on the ground that the action could not be maintained because the plaintiff failed to comply with the provisions of RSA 399-B (supp); Laws 1961, 245:7 which requires disclosure of finance charges to the borrower by the lender. The Court (Grimes, J.) reserved and transferred without ruling questions of law arising out of the defendant's motion to dismiss.

KENISON, Chief Justice.

RSA 399-B:2 (supp) as enacted by laws 1961, 245:7 provides as follows:

Statement Required

Any person engaged in the business of extending credit shall furnish to each person to whom such credit is extended, concurrently with the consummation of the transaction or agreement to extend credit, a clear statement in writing setting forth the finance charges, expressed in dollars, rate of interest, or monthly rate of charge, or a combination thereof, to be borne by such person in connection with such extension of credit as originally scheduled.

Credit is defined broadly in the act and includes any ". . . contract of sale of property or services, either for present or future delivery, under which part or all of the price is payable subsequent to the making of such sale or contract. . . ." RSA 399-B:1 I (supp). The definition of finance charges ". . . includes charges such as interest, fees, service charges, discounts, and other charges associated with the extension of credit." RSA 399-B:1 II.

The first question is whether credit was extended to the defendants in compliance with the statute. The application for financing (Exhibit No. 2) and the approval of the financing (Exhibit A) informed the defendants of the monthly payments, the time credit was extended (60 months) and the total amount of the credit extended but neither of them informed the defendants the rate of interest, or the amount of interest or other charges or fees they were paying. This is not even a token compliance with the statute which requires ". . . a clear statement in writing setting forth the finance charges, expressed in dollars, rate of interest, or monthly rate of charge or a combination thereof . . . ." RSA 399-B:2 (supp). The obvious purpose of the statute was to place the burden on the lender to inform the borrower in writing of the finance charges he was to pay. This burden was not met in this case. Annot. 116 A.L.R. 1363. Disclosure statutes are designed to inform the uninformed and this includes many average individuals who have neither the capability nor the strength to calculate the cost of the credit that has been extended to them. Economic Institutions and Value Survey: The Consumer in the Market Place — A Survey of the Law of Informed Buying, 38 Notre Dame Lawyer 555, 582-588 (1963); Ford Motor Co. v. F.T.C., 6 Cir., 120 F.2d 175, 182 (6th Cir. 1941). RSA 339-B:3 (supp) provides that "[n]o person shall extend credit in contravention of this chapter." We conclude that the extension of credit to the defendants was in violation of the disclosure statute.

The parties have agreed that the plaintiff did not willfully violate the disclosure statute and this eliminates any consideration of RSA 399-B:4

(supp) which provides a criminal penalty of a fine of not more than five hundred dollars or imprisonment not more than sixty days, or both. This brings us to the second question whether the agreement is "void so as to prevent the plaintiff from recovering for its breach."

"At first thought it is sometimes supposed that an illegal bargain is necessarily void of legal effect, and that an 'illegal contract' is self-contradictory. How can the illegal be also legal? The matter is not so simple." 6 A Corbin, Contracts, s. 1373 (1962). The law is not always black or white and it is in the flexibility of the gray areas that justice can be done by a consideration of the type of illegality, the statutory purpose and the circumstances of the particular case. "It is commonly said that illegal bargains are void. This statement, however, is clearly not strictly accurate." 5 Williston, Contracts (Rev. ed. 1937) s. 1630. The same thought is well summarized in 6 A Corbin, Contracts, s. 1512 (1962): "It has often been said that an agreement for the doing of that which is forbidden by statute is itself illegal and necessarily unenforceable. This is an unsafe generalization, although most such agreements are unenforceable." This section was cited in the recent case of William Coltin & Co. v. Manchester Savings Bank, 105 N.H. 254, 197 A.2d 208, holding unenforceable a contract for a broker's commission for the sale of real estate without a license in violation of a statute.

In examining the exhibits and agreed facts in this case we find that to settle the principal debt of $1,759 the defendants signed instruments obligating them to pay $42.81 for 60 months, making a total payment of $2,568.60, or an increase of $809.60 over the contract price. In reliance upon the total payment the defendants were to make, the plaintiff pay a sales commission of $800. Counsel suggests that the goods and services to be furnished the defendants thus had a value of only $959, for which they would pay an additional $1,609.60 computed as follows:

Value of goods and services		$ 959.00
Commission	800.00 ⎱	
Interest and carrying charges	809.60 ⎰	1,609.60
Total payment		$2,568.60

In the circumstances of the present case we conclude that the purpose of the disclosure statute will be implemented by denying recovery to the plaintiff on its contract and granting the defendants' motion to dismiss. Burque v. Brodeur, 85 N.H. 310, 158 A. 127; Park, Board of Aviation Trustees v. Manchester, 96 N.H. 331, 76 A.2d 514; Albertson & Co. v. Shenton, 78 N.H. 216, 98 A. 516.

There is another and independent reason why the recovery should be barred in the present case because the transaction was unconscionable. "The courts have often avoided the enforcement of unconscionable provisions in long printed standardized contracts, in part by the process of 'interpretation' against the parties using them, and in part by the method used by Lord Nelson at Copenhagen." 1 Corbin, Contracts, s. 128 (1963). Without using either of these methods reliance can be placed upon the Uniform Commercial Code (U.C.C. 2-302 (1)). See RSA 382-A:2-302(1) which reads as follows:

> If the court as a matter of law finds the contract or any clause of the contract to have been unconscionable at the time it was made the court may refuse to enforce the contract, or it may enforce the remainder of the contract without the unconscionable clause, or it may so limit the application of any unconscionable clause as to avoid any unconscionable result.

Inasmuch as the defendants have received little or nothing of value and under the transaction they entered into they were paying $1,609 for goods and services valued at far less, the contract should not be enforced because of its unconscionable features. This is not a new thought or a new rule in this jurisdiction. See Morrill v. Bank, 90 N.H. 358, 365, 9 A.2d 519, 525; "It has long been the law in this state that contracts may be declared void because unconscionable and oppressive. . . ."

The defendants' motion to dismiss should be granted. In view of the result reached it is unnecessary to consider any other questions and the order is

Remanded.

All concurred.

NOTE

The portion of the case invoking U.C.C. §2-302 may be regarded as dictum, since the court had already found that the New Hampshire disclosure statute had been violated.[65] On the other hand, who violated the statute, the plaintiff or the finance company? The statute imposes the duty to disclose on "the person extending credit," which in this case appears to have been the finance company. The court may have felt either that the purpose of the statute — to inform consumers of the cost of a loan — would be thwarted if plaintiff could collect on the underlying contract, or that plaintiff should be charged with the obligation of the finance company because of the close relationship that each may have had with the other. We do not know.

One problem that used to confront consumers involving the dealings of sellers and finance companies has been effectively eliminated by a 1976

---

65. Professor Leff criticizes the *MacIver* court for its failure to analyze the problems surrounding price unconscionability and for its willingness simply to equate "too expensive" with "unconscionable." Leff, *supra* note 31, at 548 et seq. (1967).

Federal Trade Commission regulation.[66] 16 C.F.R. §§433 et seq. In the past, a seller extending credit to a consumer might include in the printed form contract a provision that the consumer waives all defenses against an assignee, or he might even be able to convince the consumer to sign a negotiable instrument, thereby cutting off most of the consumer's defenses vis-à-vis a holder in due course of that instrument. The FTC regulation enables the consumer obtaining goods or services or credit to assert against assignees and holders in due course all defenses he would have had against the seller. For a leading case illustrating how the courts use to deal with this practice, see Unico v. Owen, 50 N.J. 101, 232 A.2d 405 (1967).[67]

Today, the credit card has in many cases replaced the installment sales contract as a means of financing consumer purchases. State legislatures have found it meet, therefore, to preserve against the credit card issuer the claims and defenses that the consumer has against the seller of goods or services, although only to the extent of the price paid by the consumer. See, e.g., Cal. Civ. Code §1747.90.

Consumer credit transactions have become the object of a large amount of legislative and administrative regulation at both the state and national levels. In the past, the states were almost exclusively responsible for this regulation. To insure that only reputable persons engaged in the business of loaning money to consumers, licensing statutes were passed. Interest rates were controlled by usury statutes, but early on courts developed the time-price doctrine, which exempted those who sold goods on credit from these statutes.[68] Retail installment sales acts were then passed to regulate the charges that a seller could demand for extending credit in connection with a sale, the so-called time-price differential. Then there was the problem of loan sharking: bad credit risks, usually the poor, could not obtain loans from legitimate sources because interest rates fixed by usury laws were too low, and so small loan laws were passed to permit these persons to borrow from legitimate sources.[69]

---

66. For a discussion of the Federal Trade Commission, see p. 623 *infra*.

67. U.C.C. §9-206 preserves the effects of judicial decisions and legislation that protect consumers from waiver of defense clauses. See U.C.C.C. (1974) §§3.404 and 3.307, and Wisconsin Consumer Act §422.407 (both acts discussed *infra* p. 601) for examples of state legislative approaches to the problem of negotiable consumer paper and waiver of defense clauses. For a review of the holder in due course doctrine in the consumer field, see Rohner, Holder in Due Course in Consumer Transactions: Requiem, Revival, or Reformation, 60 Cornell L. Rev. 503 (1975). The FTC regulation preserving claims and defenses (16 C.F.R. §433.2) applies only to the sale or lease of goods or services.

68. Usury, not illegal at common law, was made illegal by statute in some states for some loans, in other states for all loans, and in still other states for only specified types of lenders. For a definition of usury, see Restatement First §§527-537. For some of the difficulties that must be faced in drawing a line between a sale under the time-price doctrine and a loan, see Lee v. Household Finance Corp., 263 A.2d 635 (D.C. Ct. App. 1970).

69. For further details about early state efforts at consumer protection see Curran, Legislative Controls as a Response to Consumer Credit Problems, 8 B.C. Ind. & Comm. L. Rev. 409 (1967); McEwen, Economic Issues in State Regulation of Consumer Credit, 8 B.C. Ind. & Comm. L. Rev. 387 (1967).

The federal government entered the scene in 1966 with the passage of the Consumer Credit Protection Act (CCPA).[70] Title I of the CCPA, the Truth-in-Lending Act (TILA), is administered by the Federal Reserve Board, which has issued detailed regulations interpreting the Act. In addition, TILA itself has been revised by Congress several times, the most recent and extensive revision being the Truth in Lending Simplification and Reform Act of 1980.[71] The object of TILA is to enable the consumer to make an informed choice about credit by requiring disclosure of the cost of financing (finance charge) expressed in terms of an annual percentage rate and, in the case of closed end credit and straight loans,[72] in dollars and cents. "Finance charge" is broadly defined to cover interest, service charges, fees, and a variety of other credit-related costs.[73] The TILA gives consumers a limited right to rescind credit transactions in which a security interest in the consumer's residence "is or will be retained or acquired."[74] For a highly readable discussion of TILA, see D. Epstein & S. Nickles, Consumer Law in a Nutshell 79-207 (1981).

If the TILA had been applicable to the *MacIver* case, plaintiff and finance company would both have been required to comply with the Act's disclosure provisions. 12 C.F.R. §226.2[75] and §226.6(d). Would the commission charged be disclosable as part of the finance charge, thereby increasing the annual percentage rate, or as part of the amount financed? See 12 C.F.R. §226.4. Would defendant have had a right to rescind under TILA? Although defendant did not give plaintiff a security interest in his residence, plaintiff would have had a lien against the residence for material and labor by virtue of New Hampshire's mechanic's lien law. N.H. Rev. Stat. Ann. §499. TILA would therefore have given defendant a right to rescind the transaction within three days of its consummation. U.S.C. §1635 and 12 C.F.R. §226.23. The three-day limit would not have applied, however, if the plaintiff had failed to disclose to defendant his right to rescind. Before 1974, a consumer who had not been informed of his right to rescission could rescind at any time or until disclosure was made. In 1974 Congress provided that the right to rescind be cut off after three years. See 15 U.S.C. §1635(f).

The TILA sets no limitations on the amount of the finance charge,

70. 15 U.S.C. §§1601 et seq. See also Regulation Z, 12 C.F.R. §§226 et seq.
71. Incorporated in 15 U.S.C. §§1601 et seq.
72. "Closed end credit" sales and "straight loans" are to be distinguished from open end credit sales and loans. For a definition of the latter see 12 C.F.R. §226.2(a). An example of the closed end credit sale is the typical installment sales contract. A loan from a finance company to buy a car would be an example of a straight loan. An example of an open end credit sale is a purchase made with a department store credit card. Purchases made with national credit cards, such as Visa and Mastercard, involve open end loans.
73. 12 C.F.R. §226.4.
74. 15 U.S.C. §1635, as amended in 1974 and 1980; Comment, The Right of Rescission and the Home Improvement Industry, 37 Albany L. Rev. 247 (1973).
75. Federal preemption of state usury laws in certain cases has been made necessary recently by the rapid rise in interest rates. See Pub. L. 96-161.

although the Act and the Board's Regulation Z do prescribe what is included in the finance charge, and how the annual percentage rate and other charges are to be calculated. Rate regulation is left up to the states.[76] The systems of rate regulation vary from state to state, with many states having a patchwork of rate limitations applicable to different types of creditors and borrowers. This chaos and complexity, largely due to the legislative habit of meeting a problem as it arises, prompted the commissioners on Uniform State Laws to promulgate the U.C.C.C. in 1968. The U.C.C.C. provides a rate structure for loans, including credit card loans, and for credit sales, including revolving charge accounts. The U.C.C.C. also has numerous other provisions, which will be discussed in subsequent Notes.

The U.C.C.C. received a great deal of criticism from both consumer groups and the credit industry. The Consumer Law Center of Boston College School of Law went so far as to propose two rival pieces of consumer legislation, the National Consumer Act (NCA), promulgated in 1971, and the Model Consumer Credit Act (MCCA), promulgated in 1973. Neither of these acts has been enacted by any state, although the Wisconsin Consumer Act (Wis. Stat. Ann. §§421 et seq. (West 1974)), one of the most consumer-oriented pieces of legislation in the country, is a synthesis of the U.C.C.C. and the National Consumer Act. In 1974, the U.C.C.C. was thoroughly revised, principally because so few states had adopted the original version. The 1974 version has enjoyed no greater success, however.

Finally, it should be pointed out that not everyone agrees about the effectiveness of disclosure statutes. These statutes have been criticized as middle class solutions to a lower-class problem.[77] Many would argue that even if the consumer bothers to read what has been disclosed, contractual terms that statutes like TILA prescribe and the subtle distinctions between these terms are far too complex for even the moderately well-educated person to understand. Still, disclosure statutes in the consumer field are popular among legislators. For example, the Magnuson-Moss Consumer Warranty Act, enacted by Congress in 1975, is basically a disclosure statute that attempts to make uniform the descriptive titles of warranties on consumer products.[78]

---

76. Jordan & Warren, A Proposed Uniform Code for Consumer Credit, 8 B.C. Ind. & Comm. L. Rev. 441, 449 (1967).

77. A study published in 1971 reveals that frequently even consumers who are good credit risks not only fail to read or understand credit agreements, but do not bother to shop around for better terms. White & Munger, Consumer Sensitivity to Interest Rates: An Empirical Study of New Car Buyers and Auto Loans, 69 Mich. L. Rev. 1207 (1971). See also, Kripke, Gesture and Reality in Consumer Credit Reform, 44 N.Y.U. L. Rev. 1 (1969). Empirical evidence supports the view that TILA has not significantly changed this situation. See Brandt & Day, Information Disclosure and Consumer Behavior: An Empirical Evaluation of Truth in Lending, 7 U. Mich. J.L. Ref. 297 (1974); T. Durkin & G. Ellichausen, the 1977 Consumer Credit Survey (Federal Reserve Board 1977).

78. 15 U.S.C. §§2301 et seq. (Supp. 1979), discussed *infra* p. 624.

WILLIAMS v. WALKER-THOMAS
FURNITURE CO.

121 U.S. App. D.C. 315, 350 F.2d 445, 18 A.L.R.3d 1297
(D.C. Cir. 1965)

J. Skelly Wright, Circuit Judge: Appellee, Walker-Thomas Furniture Company, operates a retail furniture store in the District of Columbia. During the period from 1957 to 1962 each appellant in these cases purchased a number of household items from Walker-Thomas, for which payment was to be made in installments. The terms of each purchase were contained in a printed form contract which set forth the value of the purchased item and purported to lease the item to appellant for a stipulated monthly rent payment. The contract then provided, in substance, that title would remain in Walker-Thomas until the total of all the monthly payments made equaled the stated value of the item, at which time appellants could take title. In the event of a default in the payment of any monthly installment, Walker-Thomas could repossess the item.

The contract further provided that

> the amount of each periodical installment payment to be made by [purchaser] to the Company under this present lease shall be inclusive of and not in addition to the amount of each installment payment to be made by [purchaser] under such prior leases, bills or accounts; *and all payments now and hereafter made by [purchaser] shall be credited pro rata on all outstanding leases, bills and accounts* due the Company by [purchaser] at the time each such payment is made.

(Emphasis added.) The effect of this rather obscure provision was to keep a balance due on every item purchased until the balance due on all items, whenever purchased, was liquidated. As a result, the debt incurred at the time of purchase of each item was secured by the right to repossess all the items previously purchased by the same purchaser, and each new item purchased automatically became subject to a security interest arising out of the previous dealings.

On May 12, 1962, appellant Thorne purchased an item described as a Daveno, three tables, and two lamps, having total stated value of $391.10. Shortly thereafter, he defaulted on his monthly payments and appellee sought to replevy all the items purchased since the first transaction in 1958. Similarly, on April 17, 1962, appellant Williams bought a stereo set of stated value of $514.95.[79] She too defaulted shortly thereafter, and appellee sought to replevy all the items purchased since December, 1957. The Court of General Sessions granted judgment for appellee. The Dis-

---

79. At the time of this purchase her account showed a balance of $164 still owing from her prior purchases. The total of all the purchases made over the years in question came to $1,800. The total payments amounted to $1,400.

trict of Columbia Court of Appeals affirmed, and we granted appellants' motion for leave to appeal to this court.

Appellants' principal contention, rejected by both the trial and the appellate courts below, is that these contracts, or at least some of them, are unconscionable and, hence, not enforceable. In its opinion in Williams v. Walker-Thomas Furniture Company, 198 A.2d 914, 916 (1964), the District of Columbia Court of Appeals explained its rejection of this contention as follows:

> Appellant's second argument presents a more serious question. The record reveals that prior to the last purchase appellant had reduced the balance in her account to $164. The last purchase, a stereo set, raised the balance due to $678. Significantly, at the time of this and the preceding purchases, appellee was aware of appellant's financial position. The reverse side of the stereo contract listed the name of appellant's social worker and her $218 monthly stipend from the government. Nevertheless, with full knowledge that appellant had to feed, clothe and support both herself and seven children on this amount, appellee sold her a $514 stereo set.
>
> We cannot condemn too strongly appellee's conduct. It raises serious questions of sharp practice and irresponsible business dealings. A review of the legislation in the District of Columbia affecting retail sales and the pertinent decisions of the highest court in this jurisdiction disclose, however, no ground upon which this court can declare the contracts in question contrary to public policy. We note that were the Maryland Retail Installment Sales Act, Art. 83 §§128-153, or its equivalent, in force in the District of Columbia, we could grant appellant appropriate relief. We think Congress should consider corrective legislation to protect the public from such exploitive contracts as were utilized in the case at bar.

We do not agree that the court lacked the power to refuse enforcement to contracts found to be unconscionable. In other jurisdictions, it has been held as a matter of common law that unconscionable contracts are not enforceable.[80] While no decision of this court so holding has been found, the notion that an unconscionable bargain should not be given full enforcement is by no means novel. In Scott v. United States, 79 U.S. (12 Wall.) 443, 445, 20 L. Ed. 438 (1870), the Supreme Court stated:

> . . . If a contract be unreasonable and unconscionable, but not void for fraud, a court of law will give to the party who sues for its breach damages, not according to its letter, but only such as he is equitably entitled to. . . .[81]

80. Campbell Soup Co. v. Wentz, 3 Cir., 172 F.2d 80 (1948); Indianapolis Morris Plan Corporation v. Sparks, 132 Ind. App. 145, 172 N.E.2d 899 (1961); Henningsen v. Bloomfield Motors, Inc., 32 N.J. 358, 161 A.2d 69, 84-96, 75 A.L.R.2d 1 (1960). Cf. 1 Corbin §128 (1963).

81. See Luing v. Peterson, 143 Minn. 6, 172 N.W. 692 (1919); Greer v. Tweed, N.Y.C.P., 13 Abb. Pr., N.S., 427 (1872); Schnell v. Nell, 17 Ind. 29 (1861); and see generally the discussion of the English authorities in Hume v. United States, 132 U.S. 406, 10 S. Ct. 134, 33 L. Ed. 393 (1889).

Since we have never adopted or rejected such a rule,[82] the question here presented is actually one of first impression.

Congress has recently enacted the Uniform Commercial Code, which specifically provides that the court may refuse to enforce a contract which it finds to be unconscionable at the time it was made. 28 D.C. Code §2-302 (Supp. IV 1965). The enactment of this section, which occurred subsequent to the contracts here in suit, does not mean that the common law of the District of Columbia was otherwise at the time of enactment, nor does it preclude the court from adopting a similar rule in the exercise of its powers to develop the common law for the District of Columbia. In fact, in view of the absence of prior authority on the point, we consider the congressional adoption of §2-302 persuasive authority for following the rationale of the cases from which the section is explicitly derived.[83] Accordingly, we hold that where the element of unconscionability is present at the time a contract is made, the contract should not be enforced.

Unconscionability has generally been recognized to include an absence of meaningful choice on the part of one of the parties together with contract terms which are unreasonably favorable to the other party.[84] Whether a meaningful choice is present in a particular case can only be determined by consideration of all the circumstances surrounding the transaction. In many cases the meaningfulness of the choice is negated by a gross inequality of bargaining power.[85] The manner in which the

82. While some of the statements in the court's opinion in District of Columbia v. Harlan & Hollingsworth Co., 30 App. D.C. 270 (1908), may appear to reject the rule, in reaching its decision upholding the liquidated damages clause in that case the court considered the circumstances existing at the time the contract was made, see 30 App. D.C. at 279, and applied the usual rule on liquidated damages. See 5 Corbin §§1054-1075 (1964); Note, 72 Yale L.J. 723, 746-755 (1963). Compare Jaeger v. O'Donoghue, 57 App. D.C. 191, 18 F.2d 1013 (1927).

83. See Comment, §2-302, Uniform Commercial Code (1962). Compare Note, 45 Va. L. Rev. 583, 590 (1959), where it is predicted that the rule of §2-302 will be followed by analogy in cases which involve contracts not specifically covered by the section. Cf. 1 State of New York Law Revision Commission, Report and Record of Hearings on the Uniform Commercial Code 108-110 (1954) (remarks of Professor Llewellyn).

84. See Henningsen v. Bloomfield Motors, Inc., supra [note 80]; Campbell Soup Co. v. Wentz, supra [note 80].

85. See Henningsen v. Bloomfield Motors, Inc., supra [note 80], 161 A.2d at 86, and authorities there cited. Inquiry into the relative bargaining power of the two parties is not an inquiry wholly divorced from the general question of unconscionability, since a one-sided bargain is itself evidence of the inequality of the bargaining parties. This fact was vaguely recognized in the common law doctrine of intrinsic fraud, that is, fraud which can be presumed from the grossly unfair nature of the terms of the contract. See the oft-quoted statement of Lord Hardwicke in Earl of Chesterfield v. Janssen, 28 Eng. Rep. 82, 100 (1751):

". . . [Fraud] may be apparent from the intrinsic nature and subject of the bargain itself; such as no man in his senses and not under delusion would make. . . ."

And cf. Hume v. United States, supra [note 81], 132 U.S. at 413, 10 S. Ct. at 137, where the Court characterized the English cases as "cases in which one party took advantage of the other's ignorance of arithmetic to impose upon him, and the fraud was apparent from the face of the contracts." See also Greer v. Tweed, supra [note 81].

contract was entered is also relevant to this consideration. Did each party to the contract, considering his obvious education or lack of it, have a reasonable opportunity to understand the terms of the contract, or were the important terms hidden in a maze of fine print and minimized by deceptive sales practices? Ordinarily, one who signs an agreement without full knowledge of its terms might be held to assume the risk that he has entered a one-sided bargain.[86] But when a party of little bargaining power, and hence little real choice, signs a commercially unreasonable contract with little or no knowledge of its terms, it is hardly likely that his consent, or even an objective manifestation of his consent, was ever given to all the terms. In such a case the usual rule that the terms of the agreement are not to be questioned[87] should be abandoned and the court should consider whether the terms of the contract are so unfair that enforcement should be withheld.[88]

In determining reasonableness or fairness, the primary concern must be with the terms of the contract considered in light of the circumstances existing when the contract was made. The test is not simple, nor can it be mechanically applied. The terms are to be considered "in the light of the general commercial background and the commercial needs of the particular trade or case."[89] Corbin suggests the test as being whether the terms are "so extreme as to appear unconscionable according to the mores and business practices of the time and place." 1 Corbin, op. cit. *supra* [note 80].[90] We think this formulation correctly states the test to be applied in those cases where no meaningful choice was exercised upon entering the contract.

Because the trial court and the appellate court did not feel that enforcement could be refused, no findings were made on the possible un-

---

86. See Restatement, Contracts §70 (1932); Note, 63 Harv. L. Rev. 494 (1950). See also Daley v. People's Building, Loan & Savings Ass'n, 178 Mass. 13, 59 N.E. 452, 453 (1901), in which Mr. Justice Holmes, while sitting on the Supreme Judicial Court of Massachusetts, made this observation:

> . . . Courts are less and less disposed to interfere with parties making such contracts as they choose, so long as they interfere with no one's welfare but their own. . . . It will be understood that we are speaking of parties standing in an equal position where neither has any oppressive advantage of power. . . .

87. This rule has never been without exception. In cases invoking merely the transfer of unequal amounts of the same commodity, the courts have held the bargain unenforceable for the reason that "in such a case, it is clear, that the law cannot indulge in the presumption of equivalence between the consideration and the promise." 1 Williston, Contracts §115 (3d ed. 1957).

88. See the general discussion of "Boiler-Plate Agreements" in Llewellyn, The Common Law Tradition 362-371 (1960).

89. Comment, Uniform Commercial Code §2-307.

90. See Henningsen v. Bloomfield Motors, Inc., *supra* [note 80]; Mandel v. Liebman, 303 N.Y. 88, 100 N.E.2d 149 (1951). The traditional test as stated in Greer v. Tweed, *supra* [note 81], 13 Abb. Pr., N.S., at 429, is "such as no man in his senses and not under delusion would make on the one hand, and as no honest or fair man would accept, on the other."

conscionablity of the contracts in these cases. Since the record is not
sufficient for our deciding the issue as a matter of law, the cases must be
remanded to the trial court for further proceedings.

So ordered.

DANAHER, Circuit Judge (dissenting): The District of Columbia Court
of Appeals obviously was as unhappy about the situation here presented
as any of us can possibly be. Its opinion in the *Williams* case, quoted in
the majority text, concludes: "We think Congress should consider corrective legislation to protect the public from such exploitive contracts as
were utilized in the case at bar."

My view is thus summed up by an able court which made no finding
that there had actually been sharp practice. Rather the appellant seems to
have known precisely where she stood.

There are many aspects of public policy here involved. What is a
luxury to some may seem an outright necessity to others. Is public oversight to be required of the expenditure of relief funds? A washing machine, e.g., in the hands of a relief client might become a fruitful source
of income. Many relief clients may well need credit, and certain business
establishments will take long chances on the sale of items, expecting their
pricing policies will afford a degree of protection commensurate with the
risk. Perhaps a remedy when necessary will be found within the provisions of the "Loan Shark" law, D.C. Code §§26-601 et seq. (1961).

I mention such matters only to emphasize the desirability of a cautious
approach to any such problem, particularly since the law for so long has
allowed parties such great latitude in making their own contracts. I dare
say there must annually be thousands upon thousands of installment
credit transactions in this jurisdiction, and one can only speculate as to
the effect the decision in these cases will have. I join the District of
Columbia Court of Appeals in its disposition of the issues.

NOTE

Mrs. Williams was represented by the Legal Assistance Office of the
Bar Association. Her lawyers were willing to allow repossession of the
stereo, but plaintiff insisted on repossessing all the items. By far the best
discussion of the case is in Skilton & Halstead, Protection of the Installment Buyer of Goods under the UCC, 65 Mich. L. Rev. 1465 (1967).

The lower court gives us a few more facts. Williams v. Walker-Thomas
Furniture, 198 A.2d 914 (D.C. Dist. Ct. App. 1964). Some of the items
were bought in door-to-door sales. Frequently the defendants signed the
documents "in blank" (the court's phrase, apparently meaning that blank
spaces were left for plaintiffs to fill in later), and the add-on clauses were
in extremely fine print, not to mention "obscure" language. Mrs. Williams had made payments of $1,400 on a total debt of $1,800 over the

years. Under the add-on clause, each payment was applied proportionately to the outstanding balance on each item so that Mrs. Williams still owed $.25 out of $54.67 on the first item and $.03 out of $13.21 on another item. There were no finance charges.[91]

Why did Judge Wright reverse the lower court? Was it because of the obnoxious add-on clause? See Illustration 5 of Restatement Second §208. Professor Leff, an ardent critic of the decision, argues that "it does seem a bit much to find 'so extreme as to appear unconscionable according to the mores and business practices of the time and place' an add-on clause in the District of Columbia which is used and statutorily permitted almost every place else. . . ." Leff, Unconscionability and the Code — The Emperor's New Clause, 115 U. Pa. L. Rev. 485, 554 (1967). Leff points out that add-on clauses were permitted by 36 of the 37 states having retail installment sales statutes, but he fails to mention that there are three different types of add-on clauses, two of which are less severe than the one used by Walker-Thomas. See Spanogle, Analyzing Unconscionability Problems, 117 U. Pa. L. Rev. 931, 961 n.151 (1969).

One major objection to the type of add-on clause used in the *Williams* case is that it gives the secured party, the seller, a continuous security interest in property which, under most if not all state statutes, would be exempt from execution by creditors otherwise unsecured. See Leff, *supra*. On the other hand, Professor Epstein defends this type of add-on clause as commercially sound. He argues that since consumer goods rapidly depreciate in value, the merchant selling on credit needs the added measure of protection of additional security to guard against the risk that the buyer will not be able to pay and the items most recently sold will not be of sufficient value to cover the remaining payments and the costs of collection. Epstein, Unconscionability, a Critical Reappraisal, 18 J.L. & Econ. 293, 307 (1975).

The two versions of the U.C.C.C., the NCA, the MCCA, and the Wisconsin Consumer Act all prohibit the use of the type of add-on clause found in the *Williams* case. These acts require that "payments be applied to the payment of debts arising from the sales first made." U.C.C.C. §3.303. In addition, these acts severely limit the right of a creditor to obtain judgment against the debtor for the amount by which the balance owing plus the costs incurred for collection exceeds the value of the collateral. The U.C.C.C. (1974), for example, in general limits the creditor's recovery to the collateral, if the price or amount loaned is less than $1,750. U.C.C.C. §5.103. Compare U.C.C. §9-504(2), which generally

91. Although the TILA requires disclosure only in transactions in which "a finance charge is or may be imposed," the Federal Reserve Board has issued regulations requiring certain disclosures when the credit transaction is payable in more than four installments, whether or not a finance charge is imposed. The board apparently believes that merchants who sell on payment terms of multiple installments are actually charging for credit even though no charge is separately stated. The charge for credit is in the inflated price. The Supreme Court upheld the Board practice in Mourning v. Family Publication Service Inc., 411 U.S. 356 (1973).

permits deficiency judgments. If the creditor chooses not to resort to the collateral, and proceeds directly to obtaining a personal judgment against the debtor, the U.C.C.C. prohibits him from taking possession of or levying execution on the collateral. U.C.C.C. §5.103 and comments 1 and 3. The consumer also has the right to cure a default under U.C.C.C. (1974) §5.110 and §5.111 and the right to redeem the collateral under U.C.C. §9-506.

The creditor may resort to self-help repossession, but only if doing so does not result in a breach of peace. U.C.C. §9-503. Sale of collateral by this method may be subject to constitutional limitations (see e.g., Adams v. Department of Motor Vehicles, 11 Cal. 3d 146, 520 P.2d 961, 113 Cal. Rptr. 145 (1974)), but self-help repossession has generally withstood constitutional attack on the ground that there is no state action. See Adams v. Southern Calif. First Natl. Bank, 492 F.2d 324 (9th Cir. 1974). On the other hand, if the creditor should have to resort to the courts for a writ of replevin to repossess collateral, due process requires that the debtor be afforded certain procedural safeguards. Fuentes v. Shevin, 407 U.S. 67 (1972); Mitchell v. W. T. Grant, 416 U.S. 600 (1974).

Three further notes on consumer protection in the field of creditors' remedies, which is covered more extensively in other courses: the U.C.C.C. (1974) and other consumer protection acts limit the kinds of property of the consumer in which a seller or lender may take a security interest. See, e.g., U.C.C.C. (1974) §3.301. Title III of the CCPA places limitations on the amount of a consumer's wages that is subject to garnishment, and prohibits the discharge of an employee whose wages have been garnished. State consumer statutes have similar provisions. See, e.g., U.C.C.C. (1974) §5.105 and §5.106. Finally, debt collection practices are now regulated by both federal and state law since the enactment of Title VIII of the CCPA in 1978, the Fair Debt Collection Practices Act. 15 U.S.C.A. §1692 et seq.

Professor Leff's contention that the add-on clause could not itself be unconscionable because it is permitted by many states raises several interesting questions about U.C.C. §2-302. Although *Williams* was a pre-Code case, the court was guided by U.C.C. §2-302 in its application of the common law. Does this mean that unconscionability as defined by the Code applies to cases not covered by the U.C.C.? The Restatement Second has adopted an unconscionability section similar to U.C.C. §2-302, and applicable to all types of contracts.[92] Many courts have also applied unconscionability to non-Code transactions.[93] Second, does §2-302 apply to cases covered by parts of the Code other than Article 2, the Article on Sales? Third, does §2-302 apply to other sections within Article 2, although neither the sections nor their comments specifically refer to unconscionability or §2-302? Fourth, does §2-302 apply to a warranty

92. Restatement Second §208.
93. See, e.g., Albert Merril School v. Godoy, 357 N.Y.S.2d 378 (1974).

disclaimer that fully complies with the disclosure provisions of U.C.C. §2-314 and §2-315? Finally, what is the relationship between §2-302 "unconscionability" and the "unconscionability" referred to in other sections, such as §2-719? For a general discussion of all these questions see S. Deutch, Unfair Contracts (1977).

If Leff is correct that the presence of the add-on clause in *Williams* is insufficient to justify the court's decision, what other reason is there for the reversal of the trial court? Can the reversal be justified on the grounds that Walker-Thomas took advantage of its superior bargaining position to impose the add-on clause on one who had no meaningful choice but to accept? Comment 1 to U.C.C. §2-302 should be considered in this context. It says: "The principle [of unconscionability] is one of the prevention of oppression and unfair surprise . . . and not of disturbance of allocation of risks because of superior bargaining power." Was Mrs. Williams unfairly surprised because she did not know of the clause and did not understand its significance? If she had known of and assented to the add-on clause, would it still have been unconscionable had the items been available elsewhere without the clause? See Speidel, Unconscionability, Assent and Consumer Protection, 31 U. Pitt. L. Rev. 159 (1969).

Is the true ground of the decision that Walker-Thomas sold a "luxury item," a stereo, to a welfare recipient, whose status was well known to the plaintiff? Apart from the fact that a stereo is not a necessity, does it matter that Mrs. Williams was on welfare with seven children? See U.C.C.C. (1974) §5.108(4)(a), reprinted *supra* p. 587 and Comment 4. Consider the following provision of the Equal Credit Opportunity Act, Title VII of the CCPA, 15 U.S.C. §1691(a)(2): "It shall be unlawful for any creditor to discriminate against any applicant, with respect to any aspect of a credit transaction . . . (2) because all or part of the applicant's income derives from any public assistance program." Consider also the arguments of Professor Schwartz in A Reexamination of Nonsubstantive Unconscionability, 63 Va. L. Rev. 1053 (1977): the poor are hurt more than helped by judicial and legislative prohibitions of seemingly unfair contract clauses. There is no evidence that the poor, or consumers in general, are as unsophisticated and irrational in economic decision-making as many consumer advocates might think. Businessmen in relatively strong bargaining positions are not necessarily unresponsive to consumer needs, nor are courts and legislators necessarily more responsive.

PATTERSON v. WALKER-THOMAS FURNITURE CO.

277 A.2d 111 (D.C. 1971)

KELLY, Associate Judge.

According to an agreed statement of proceedings and evidence the appellant, Mrs. Bernice Patterson, bought merchandise from appellee in three separate transactions during 1968. In January she bought an 18-inch Emerson portable television, with stand, for $295.95, signing an installment contract which obligated her to pay appellee $20 a month on account. In March she bought a five-piece dinette set for $119.95, increasing her monthly payments to $24. In July she purchased a set of wedding rings for $159.95 and the payments rose to $25 per month. The total price for all the goods, including sales tax, was $597.25. Mrs. Patterson defaulted in her payments after she had paid a total of $248.40 toward the agreed purchase price.

Appellant answered[94] Walker-Thomas' action to recover the unpaid balance on the contracts by claiming, in pertinent part,[95] that she had paid an amount in excess of the fair value of the goods received and that the goods themselves were so grossly overpriced as to render the contract terms unconscionable and the contracts unenforceable under the Uniform Commercial Code as enacted in the District of Columbia.

Objections to interrogatories addressed to appellee in an effort to establish her defense that the goods were in fact grossly overpriced were sutained, the court ruling in part that the information sought was outside the scope of discovery "because the defense of unconscionability based on price is not recognized in this jurisdiction." It ruled further "that certain information sought was readily obtainable to defendant by resort to the contracts admittedly in her possession and that certain of the interrogatories amounted to 'harassment of the business community'."

Appellant persisted in her efforts to present the defense of unconscionability by issuing a subpoena *duces tecum* for the production of appellee's records, and, alleging indigency, by moving for the appointment of a special master or expert witness to establish the value of the goods, the price Walker-Thomas paid for them, and their condition (whether new or secondhand) when she purchased them. The pretrial judge quashed the subpoena *duces tecum* on the ground that appellant was precluded from obtaining the same information by means of the subpoena that she had been denied through the use of interrogatories. The motion to appoint a special master or expert witness was also denied.

A trial judge subsequently held that the prior rulings of the motions judge and the pretrial judge established the law of the case. Inasmuch as appellant's then sole defense was that the goods were grossly overpriced and no proof on this issue was presented, the court entered judgment for appellee.[96] We affirm.

94. Originally, appellant filed a pro se answer stating she was behind in her payments because of illness and that Walker-Thomas had refused to accept a partial payment on account. She was later allowed to file an amended answer.
95. A second affirmative defense, that the contract had been reformed by setting new terms of payment, was not pursued. Nor does appellant complain of the court's action in striking her counterclaim for damages.
96. The agreed statement of proceedings and evidence says (R. 79, 80) that

[d]efendant [appellant], not present in Court, proferred [sic] testimony through counsel and over objection of plaintiff [appellee] that in January 1968 defendant had

Suggested guidelines for deciding whether or not a contract is unconscionable appear in Williams v. Walker-Thomas Furniture Co., 121 U.S.
App. D.C. 315, 319-320, 350 F.2d 445, 449-450, 18 A.L.R.3d 1297, 1301-
1303 (1965), as follows:[97]

[The court quoted from the text of *Williams* appearing on p. 599
supra. — EDS.]

Later, citing *Williams* in another context, this court said that "two
elements are required to exist to prove unconscionability; i.e., 'an absence of meaningful choice on the part of one of the parties together with
contract terms which are *unreasonably favorable to the other party*.'" Diamond Housing Corp. v. Robinson, D.C. App., 257 A.2d 492, 493 (1969).
(Emphasis in the original.)

On the basis of these authorities we conclude that in a proper case
gross overpricing may be raised in defense as an element of unconscionability.[98] Under the test outlined in *Williams* price is necessarily an element to be examined when determining whether a contract is reasonable.
The Corbin test mentioned in the opinion specifically deals with the
"terms" of the contract and certainly the price one pays for an item is one
of the more important terms of any contract. We emphasize, however,
that price as an unreasonable contract term is only one of the elements
which underpin proof of unconscionability. Specifically, therefore, in
the instant case the reasonableness of the contracts is not to be gauged
by an examination of the price stipulation alone or any other term of
the contract without parallel consideration being given to whether
or not appellant exercised a meaningful choice in entering into the
contracts.

We conclude also that because excessive price-value may comprise
one element of unconscionability, discovery techniques may be employed to garner information relevant to that issue for purposes of

---

bad credit at Montgomery Ward, the store at which she previously made her household purchases; defendant did not have credit lines established at any other retail
store; defendant met a salesman of Walker-Thomas who, understanding defendant's
credit situation, encouraged her to go to plaintiff's store and represented to defendant that credit would be available to her at Walker-Thomas; and relying on this
representation defendant went to plaintiff's store, was extended credit and executed
the first of the series of three contracts upon which plaintiff sues.

The proffered testimony, of course, is not evidence in this case. An offer of proof is made
when testimony to be given by a witness in court is, upon objection, excluded by the court.
It is not made through counsel when the witness is not present to testify. *See generally* 88
C.J.S. Trial §73 (1955).

97. Although *Williams* was decided on principles of common law, it is upon these
principles that §28:2-302 is based.

98. Other courts have said that in certain circumstances excessive price might constitute
an unreasonable contractual provision within §28:2-302. *See* Toker v. Perl, 103 N.J. Super.
500, 247 A.2d 701 (1968); Central Budget Corp. v. Sanchez, 53 Misc. 2d 620, 279 N.Y.S.2d
391 (1967); State by Lefkowitz v. ITM, Inc., 52 Misc. 2d 39, 275 N.Y.S.2d 303 (1966);
American Home Improvement, Inc. v. MacIver, 105 N.H. 435, 201 A.2d 886, 889, 14
A.L.R.3d 324, 328-329 (1964).

defense. By statute, upon a claim of unconscionability, the court determines as a matter of law whether a contract or any clause thereof is unconscionable *only* after the parties have been given a reasonable opportunity to present evidence as to its commercial setting, purpose and effect. Certainly, therefore, interrogatories may be used to develop evidence of the commercial setting, purpose and effect of a contract at the time it was made in order to assure an effective presentation of the defense at an evidentiary hearing.

In our judgment, however, appellant here was not erroneously precluded from developing evidence through the use of interrogatories by the ruling of the trial court. Having said that under proper circumstances excessive price may be a component of the defense of unconscionability and that discovery techniques may be used to develop that defense, we are nevertheless of the opinion that a sufficient factual predicate for the defense must be alleged before wholesale discovery is allowed. An unsupported conclusory allegation in the answer that a contract is unenforceable as unconscionable is not enough. Sufficient facts surrounding the "commercial setting, purpose and effect" of a contract at the time it was made should be alleged so that the court may form a judgment as to the existence of a valid claim of unconscionability and the extent to which discovery of evidence to support that claim should be allowed.

Admittedly, appellant neither alleged nor attempted to prove the existence of any fraud, duress or coercion when she entered into the instant contracts. Her verified complaint alleges only that the goods she purchased and still retains were grossly overpriced and that she has already paid appellee a sum in excess of their fair value. These are conclusions without factual support. It cannot be said that the goods were grossly overpriced merely from an examination of the prices which appear on the face of the contracts. No other term of the contract is alleged to be unconscionable, nor is an absence of meaningful choice claimed.[99] We hold that the two elements of which unconscionability is comprised; namely, an absence of meaningful choice and contract terms unreasonably favorable to the other party, must be particularized in some detail before a merchant is required to divulge his pricing policies through interrogatories or through the production of records in court.[100] An answer, such as the one here, asserting the affirmative defense of unconscionability only on the basis of a stated conclusion that the price is excessive is insufficient.

Accordingly, the judgment of the trial court is
Affirmed.

---

99. The proffered testimony at trial is the first mention of any purported facts surrounding these transactions.

100. The same reasoning applies to a request for appointment of a master or expert witness.

NOTE

See Zuckman, Walker-Thomas Strikes Back: Comment on the Pleading and the Proof of Price Unconscionability, 30 Fed. Bar J. 308 (1972).

To overcome the obstacles placed in the way of the consumer by U.C.C. §2-302(2), Professor Speidel has advanced the ingenious theory (reminiscent of the *laesio enormis* doctrine) that the buyer should be permitted to make out a prima facie case of unconscionability by showing a 2-to-1 disparity between the price charged a consumer and the price prevailing in the same market. Speidel, *supra* p. 561, at 372-374.

It should not be overlooked that the "huge profits" of a seller may reflect the high-risk nature of his operation. Compare FTC, Economic Report on Installment Credit and Retail Sales Practices of District of Columbia Retailers (1968) with Note, Is the High Mark-up in Low Income Areas Unconscionable?, 16 How. L.J. 406, 423-425 (1971). Should the law dry up credit sources by imposing low interest ceilings on consumer loans and consumer credit sales? A note in 4 Golden Gate L. Rev. 299 (1977) advocates publicly subsidized consumer loans to help the poor. See also the comments of a director of a legal aid office in Proceedings of the ABA National Institute on Consumer Credit, 33 Bus. Lawyer 945, 1037 (1978). One of the aims of the Federal Equal Credit Opportunity Act, 15 U.S.C.A. §§1691 et seq., is to make reputable credit sources more readily accessible to the low income consumer. Has U.C.C.C. §5.108, *supra* p. 587, solved the problem of price unconscionability? See in general J. White & R. Summers, *supra* note 48.

JONES v. STAR CREDIT CORP.
59 Misc. 2d 189, 298 N.Y.S.2d 264 (1969)

Sol M. Wachtler, Justice.

On August 31, 1965 the plaintiffs, who are welfare recipients, agreed to purchase a home freezer unit for $900 as the result of a visit from a salesman representing Your Shop At Home Service, Inc. With the addition of the time credit charges, credit life insurance, credit property insurance, and sales tax, the purchase price totalled $1,234.80. Thus far the plaintiffs have paid $619.88 toward their purchase. The defendant claims that with various added credit charges paid for an extension of time there is a balance of $819.81 still due from the plaintiffs. The uncontroverted proof at the trial established that the freezer unit, when purchased, had a maximum retail value of approximately $300. The question is whether this transaction and the resulting contract could be considered unconscionable within the meaning of Section 2-302 of the Uniform Commercial Code [the text of §2-302 is omitted — Eds.]

There was a time when the shield of "caveat emptor" would protect the most unscrupulous in the marketplace — a time when the law, in granting parties unbridled latitude to make their own contracts, allowed exploitive and callous practices which shocked the conscience of both legislative bodies and the courts.

The effort to eliminate these practices has continued to pose a difficult problem. On the one hand it is necessary to recognize the importance of preserving the integrity of agreements and the fundamental right of parties to deal, trade, bargain, and contract. On the other hand there is the concern for the uneducated and often illiterate individual who is the victim of gross inequality of bargaining power, usually the poorest members of the community.

Concern for the protection of these consumers against overreaching by the small but hardy breed of merchants who would prey on them is not novel. The dangers of inequality of bargaining power were vaguely recognized in the early English common law when Lord Hardwicke wrote of a fraud, which "may be apparent from the intrinsic nature and subject to the bargain itself; such as no man in his senses and not under delusion would make." The English authorities on this subject were discussed in Hume v. United States, 132 U.S. 406, 441, 10 S. Ct. 134, 136, 33 L. Ed. 393 (1889) where the United States Supreme Court characterized (p. 413, 10 S. Ct. p. 137) these as "cases in which one party took advantage of the other's ignorance of arithmetic to impose upon him, and the fraud was apparent from the face of the contracts."

The law is beginning to fight back against those who once took advantage of the poor and illiterate without risk of either exposure or interference. From the common law doctrine of intrinsic fraud we have, over the years, developed common and statutory law which tells not only the buyer but also the seller to beware. This body of laws recognizes the importance of a free enterprise system but at the same time will provide the legal armor to protect and safeguard the prospective victim from the harshness of an unconscionable contract.

Section 2-302 of the Uniform Commercial Code enacts the moral sense of the community into the law of commercial transactions. It authorizes the court to find, as a matter of law, that a contract or a clause of a contract was "unconscionable at the time it was made," and upon so finding the court may refuse to enforce the contract, excise the objectionable clause or limit the application of the clause to avoid an unconscionable result. "The principle," states the Official Comment to this section, "is one of the prevention of oppression and unfair surprise." It permits a court to accomplish directly what heretofore was often accomplished by construction of language, manipulations of fluid rules of contract law and determinations based upon a presumed public policy.

There is no reason to doubt, moreover, that this section is intended to encompass the price term of an agreement. In addition to the fact that it has already been so applied (State by Lefkowitz v. ITM, Inc., 52 Misc. 2d

39, 275 N.Y.S.2d 303; Frostifresh Corp. v. Reynoso, 52 Misc. 2d 26, 274 N.Y.S.2d 757, *revd.* 54 Misc. 2d 119, 281 N.Y.S.2d 964; American Home Improvement, Inc. v. MacIver, 105 N.H. 435, 201 A.2d 886, 14 A.L.R.3d 324), the statutory language itself makes it clear that not only a clause of the contract, but the contract in toto, may be found unconscionable as a matter of law. Indeed, no other provision of an agreement more intimately touches upon the question of unconscionability than does the term regarding price.

Fraud, in the instant case, is not present; nor is it necessary under the statute. The question which presents itself is whether or not, under the circumstances of this case, the sale of a freezer unit having a retail value of $300 for $900 ($1,439.69 including credit charges and $18 sales tax) is unconscionable as a matter of law. The court believes it is.

Concededly, deciding the issue is substantially easier than explaining it. No doubt, the mathematical disparity between $300, which presumably includes a reasonable profit margin, and $900, which is exorbitant on its face, carries the greatest weight. Credit charges alone exceed by more than $100 the retail value of the freezer. These alone, may be sufficient to sustain the decision. Yet, a caveat is warranted lest we reduce the import of Section 2-302 solely to a mathematical ratio formula. It may, at times, be that; yet it may also be much more. The very limited financial resources of the purchaser, known to the sellers at the time of the sale, is entitled to weight in the balance. Indeed, the value disparity itself leads inevitably to the felt conclusion that knowing advantage was taken of the plaintiffs. In addition, the meaningfulness of choice essential to the making of a contract, can be negated by a gross inequality of bargaining power. (Williams v. Walker-Thomas Furniture Co., 121 U.S. App. D.C. 315, 350 F.2d 445.)

There is no question about the necessity and even the desirability of instalment sales and the extension of credit. Indeed, there are many, including welfare recipients, who would be deprived of even the most basic conveniences without the use of these devices. Similarly, the retail merchant selling on instalment or extending credit is expected to establish a pricing factor which will afford a degree of protection commensurate with the risk of selling to those who might be default prone. However, neither of these accepted premises can clothe the sale of this freezer with respectability.

Support for the court's conclusion will be found in a number of other cases already decided. In American Home Improvement, Inc. v. MacIver, *supra,* the Supreme Court of New Hampshire held that a contract to install windows, a door and paint, for the price of $2,568.60, of which $809.60 constituted interest and carrying charges and $800. was a salesman's commission was unconscionable as a matter of law. In State by Lefkowitz v. ITM, Inc., *supra,* a deceptive and fraudulent scheme was involved, but standing alone, the court held that the sale of a vacuum cleaner, among other things, costing the defendant $140 and sold by it for $749 cash or $920.52 on time purchase was unconscionable as a matter of law. Finally, in Frostifresh Corp. v. Reynoso, *supra*, the sale of a refrigerator costing the seller $348 for $900 plus credit charges of $245.88 was unconscionable as a matter of law.

One final point remains. The defendant argues that the contract of June 15, 1966, upon which this suit is based, constitutes a financing agreement and not a sales contract. To support its position, it points to the typed words "Refinance of Freezer A/C #6766 and Food A/C #56788" on the agreement and to a letter signed by the plaintiffs requesting refinance of the same items. The request for "refinancing" is typed on the defendant's letterhead. The quoted refinance statement is typed on a form agreement entitled "Star Credit Corporation — Retail Instalment Contract." It is signed by the defendant as "seller" and by the purchasers as "buyer." Above the signature of the buyers, they acknowledge "receipt of an executed copy of this RETAIL INSTALMENT CONTRACT" (capitalization in original). The June 15, 1966 contract by defendant is on exactly the same form as the original contract of August 31, 1965. The original, too, is entitled "Star Credit Corporation — Retail Instalment Contract." It is signed, however, by "Your Shop At Home Service, Inc." Printed beneath the signatures is the legend "Duplicate for Star." In substance and effect, the agreement of June 25, 1966 constitutes a novation and replacement of the earlier agreement. It is, in all respects, as it reads, a Retail Instalment Contract.

Having already paid more than $600 toward the purchase of this $300 freezer unit, it is apparent that the defendant has already been amply compensated. In accordance with the statute, the application of the payment provision should be limited to amounts already paid by the plaintiffs and the contract be reformed and amended by changing the payments called for therein to equal the amount of payment actually so paid by the plaintiffs.

NOTE

The principal case appears to hold that excessive price itself makes the sale unconscionable, even though fraud, inadequate disclosure and other deceptive practices (procedural unconscionability) are absent. Is it important that the defendants were on welfare and that this was a home solicitation sale? Is the court implying that the defendants were uneducated or illiterate?

Since the price term by itself is typically the result of bargaining, it has generally been assumed that however high, this provision in the contract is not covered by §2-302, which aims at the prevention of unfair surprise and oppression. Patterson, 1 N.Y. Law Revn. Commission. Study of the Uniform Commercial Code 63 (Legisl. Doc. 65) (1955). Professor

Spanogle, however, favors a result-oriented approach, and would consider severely harsh terms (including the price term) unconscionable
without procedural abuses. Spanogle, *supra* p. 601, at 952. See also Note,
33 U. Pitt. L. Rev. 589 (1962). Could excessive price be analyzed as
overall imbalance?

Jones, like *MacIver*, *Williams*, and the following case, involved a home
solicitation sale. In the middle of the 1960s many legislatures began to
recognize that this type of sale is uniquely susceptible to abuse. States
began to enact home solicitation sales acts, which provided the consumer
with the right to cancel or rescind a deal within a limited period of time
after it was consummated. The U.C.C.C., for example, provides for a
three day "cooling-off period" in the case of door-to-door solicitations of
consumer credit sales.[101] The NCA took a more radical approach, applying the cooling-off period not only to home solicitations of consumer
credit sales, but to all consumer sales transactions, whether door-to-door
or at the merchant's place of business, and requiring that the consumer,
in the case of a home solicitation sale, confirm the sale within three days
in order to make it effective.[102] The MCCA follows the NCA only in the
latter regard.[103] In 1973, the FTC made it an unfair or deceptive trade
practice to fail to give a consumer notice at the time of a home solicitation sale (credit or otherwise) that he has a right to cancel within three
days. 16 C.F.R. §429.1 (1973). For further details, see Metzger &
Wollkoff, Fulfilling a Promise: Extending a Cooling-off Period to Retail
Sales in General, 58 Minn. L. Rev. 753 (1974).

KUGLER v. ROMAIN
58 N.J. 522, 279 A.2d 640 (1971)

FRANCIS, J.

Acting under the Consumer Fraud Act, N.J.S.A. 56:8-1 et seq., the
Attorney General instituted this action in the Superior Court, Chancery
Division, against defendant Richard Romain individually and trading as
Educational Services Co. Injunctive and other affirmative relief was
sought based on charges that in connection with the house-to-house sale
of certain so-called educational books defendant had engaged in business
practices which violated Section 2 of the Act, N.J.S.A. 56:8-2. Section 2
provides in pertinent part as follows:

> The act, use or employment by any person of any deception, fraud, false
> pretense, false promise, misrepresentation, or the knowing concealment,

---

101. U.C.C.C. (1968) §3.501 & §3.502; (1974) §3.305 & §3.307. For a criticism of the
U.C.C.C. and its short cooling-off period, see Schrag, On Her Majesty's Secret Service:
Protecting the Consumer in New York, 80 Yale L.J. 1529, 1563-1564 (1971).
   102. NCA §2.501, §§2.504-2.505.
   103. MCAA §§2.701-2.703.

suppression, or omission of any material fact with intent that others rely upon such concealment, suppression or omission, in connection with the sale . . . of any merchandise, or with the subsequent performance of such person as aforesaid, whether or not any person has in fact been misled, deceived or damaged thereby, is declared to be an unlawful practice. . . .

The specific authorization for this proceeding appears in N.J.S.A. 56:8-8:

> Whenever it shall appear to the Attorney General that a person has engaged in, is engaging in or is about to engage in any practice declared to be unlawful by this act he may seek and obtain in an action in the Superior Court an injunction prohibiting such person from continuing such practices or engaging therein or doing any acts in furtherance thereof. . . . The court may make such orders or judgments as may be necessary to prevent the use or employment by a person of any prohibited practices, or which may be necessary to restore to any person in interest any moneys or property, real or personal which may have been acquired by means of any practice herein declared to be unlawful.

The Attorney General prayed for (1) injunctive relief barring the specific practices allegedly violative of N.J.S.A. 56:8-2; (2) a declaration that the price of the books printed in the form of contract was a transgression of the statute either because it constituted a fraud within the express terms of N.J.S.A. 56:8-2 or because it was unconscionable under the Uniform Commercial Code, N.J.S.A. 12A:2-302 which he argued is implicitly included within N.J.S.A. 56:8-2; (3) restoration and remedial orders for all persons who were induced to execute such purchase contracts; (4) rescission of all contracts with purchasers listed on a schedule attached to the complaint; (5) imposition of civil penalties against defendant, as provided in the Act, N.J.S.A. 56:8-13, 14; and (6) an order restraining defendant from doing business in New Jersey until he registered his trade name as required by N.J.S.A. 56:1-2.

The relief sought was not limited to the 24 customers whose names were set out in the schedule referred to. The complaint asked for

> (3) An order enjoining defendant from enforcing or collecting in any manner those obligations arising out of the contracts entered into with those consumers set forth in Schedule A and *those consumers similarly situated.*
>
> (4) An order rescinding any and all obligations arising out of the purported contracts entered into by those consumers set forth in the attached schedule and *those consumers similarly situated.* (Emphasis added.)

After a plenary hearing, the trial court found that defendant violated N.J.S.A. 56:8-2 by using deceptive and fraudulent practices to induce the 24 customers named in the schedule to execute contracts for the purchase of an "educational package" of books and related materials. Accordingly, a judgment was entered in favor of the Attorney General granting certain specified injunctive, restorative and remedial relief which will be discussed more fully hereafter. Kugler v. Romain, 110 N.J. Super. 470, 266 A.2d 144 (Ch. Div. 1970). Believing that the relief granted was not as extensive as the circumstances warranted, the Attorney General appealed from the trial court's judgment. Defendant cross-appealed but abandoned his appeal before argument and limited his participation to a defense of the portions of the judgment attacked by the Attorney General. We certified the cause on our own motion before the appeal was heard in the Appellate Division.

The trial court's reported opinion contains a substantial outline of facts and findings thereon, as well as a comprehensive discussion of the legal issues involved, with most of which we are in agreement. However, since we have concluded that full effectuation of the statute, N.J.S.A. 56:8-1 et seq., and of the remedies intended to be made available thereby to the merchandise-consuming public requires more extensive remedial application, it is necessary to set forth some factual background relating to defendant's business practices and methods of operation.

Defendant, a resident and member of the bar of the State of New York, was engaged in the installment sale of so-called educational books and related materials in New York and New Jersey. He operated under the trade name Educational Services Company from an office in New York City. The trade name was not registered in New Jersey as required by N.J.S.A. 56:1-2 as a condition to doing business here.

Sales solicitations were made exclusively through house-to-house canvass by defendant's employees. No advance appointments were made. The solicitors simply descended upon a selected section of a municipality and undertook by house-to-house calls to sell a package of books which was described in large type on the contract presented to the prospective customers as "A Complete Ten Year Educational program." It was also indicated thereon that the package was the product of the "Junior Institute," and nearby was the plea "Give your child its chance." In engaging his sales personnel, defendant sought persons who were "sales oriented" and extroverted. They were trained by defendant and his sales manager. The sales force fluctuated in number depending upon the season; the number was greater in the summer, reaching 30-35 persons. Defendant's "crew leader" transported them by car to the New Jersey area to be covered.

The geographical areas to be the subject of sales solicitation were primarily the urban centers of Newark, Paterson, Elizabeth and Rahway. They were chosen by defendant who was familiar with them and the class of people to be sought out by his sales force. Within these target areas, the sales solicitations were consciously directed toward minority group consumers and consumers of limited education and economic means. Persons with incomes of less than $5000 a year were favored; some buyers were welfare recipients. Sales among these people were thought to be "easier." Although the canvassing was door-to-door, ordinances in the municipalities involved in this case which required licensing or registration were ignored.

Defendant's educational package consisted of the following books and materials:

1. Questions Children Ask (1 Vol.)
2. Child Horizons (4 Vols.)
3. New Achievement Library (5 Vols.)
4. High School Subjects Self-Taught (4 Vols.)
5. Science Library (1 Vol.)
6. Play-Way French and Spanish Records (2 45 r.p.m. Records)
7. Tell Time Flash Card Set.

Additionally a "bonus" volume — a Negro History, a World Atlas or a Bible — was offered either along with the original package or after completion of payment.

The printed contract form marked "Retail Installment Obligation," which was presented to the customer for signature, consisted of a single sheet covered with printed matter on both sides. The cash and time sale prices were printed on the face of the contract, the former at $249.50, and the latter at $279.95, less a $9 down payment which was obtained whenever possible. Apparently no one paid the cash price. Also printed on the face in small print was the statement: "This order is not subject to cancellation and set is not returnable."

On the reverse side under "Conditions" appeared certain payment acceleration and waiver of defenses clauses, including waiver of all exemptions and right to jury trial. It is noted also that on the face of the form in large print appears "Credit Life Insurance at no additional charge" and "Property Insurance Certificate at no additional charge." Moreover, in the sales price computation column, which likewise appears on the face of the contract, "Credit Life Insurance" and "Property Insurance" are listed again with the notation "No Add. Chg." But on the reverse side under "Conditions," it is noted in small type that the insurance is not provided unless a charge is made for it in the price computation column "on the face hereof."

The trial court found that the wholesale price for the basic package, including the bonus items, was $35 to $40. Thus the cash sale price was six or seven times the wholesale price. Defendant's sales personnel were paid on a commission basis, ranging from $16.50 to $33 per sale; the amount paid depended upon whether (1) he secured the $9 down payment; (2) he obtained the customer's home telephone number; (3) the customer was not self-employed; and (4) the customer had been employed for at least 1½ years. In most cases the commission averaged

$16.50. The crew leader also worked on a commission basis and additionally received an over-ride commission of $5 on every approved order of a member of his crew.

The Attorney General offered uncontradicted expert evidence that in view of industry-wide practices the maximum retail price which should have been charged for the entire package was approximately $108-$110. In the witness's opinion, the price charged by defendant was about two and one-half times the retail maximum, and he said that it was exorbitant. The trial court found that the price was exorbitant but held that such exorbitance per se did not constitute a fraud under N.J.S.A. 56:8-2. In its view, proof of deceptive practices was required in addition to the excessive price before a consumer's contract could be vitiated under the statute.

In deciding whether defendant, contrary to the statute, used any deception, fraud, false pretense, or misrepresentation, or whether he concealed, suppressed or omitted any material fact in connection with the sales to book purchasers, the price charged the consumer is only one element to be considered. If the price is grossly excessive in relation to the seller's costs, and if in addition the goods sold have little or no value to the consumer for the purpose for which he was persuaded to buy them and which the seller pretended they would serve, the price paid by the consumer takes on even more serious characteristics of imposition. Here the Attorney General offered persuasive evidence that the books had little or no educational value for the children in the age group and socio-economic position the defendant represented would be benefited by them.

The testimony showed that as to the New Achievement Library, three of the five volumes dealing with Nature, Science and Civilization, represented "very poor, watered-down articles which cover the . . . areas very superficially." They were of "extremely little use" or value as a means of raising the educational level of the children they were supposed to help. Another volume entitled "Getting Acquainted with Your Opportunities in Education" was extremely poor both in quality and content. Although the volume required a tenth grade reading level, it contained articles which the witness characterized as obsolete at the time it was being sold and irrelevant to 98% of its intended readers. "Child Horizons," consisting of four volumes and designed for children 6 to 10 years of age, was said to have no relevance to children whose unfortunate socio-economic conditions did not make them susceptible to the concepts and ideas reflected therein. It was, according to the expert, like giving calculus to a person who had never studied simple algebra. As to "High School Self Taught," the four volumes were useless not merely for members of a minority group but for basic education for any individual. They might have some value for refreshment purposes for a person who has been through high school, "but for one to self teach, it is just impossible." Similar comments were made about other books in the package. Taken as a whole, the witness said that, in his judgment, the books "will serve no purpose in improving the intellectual level of these children, arousing their intellectual curiosity and compensating for the deficient intellectual climate in which they are being raised." Defendant offered no contradictory proof on this subject.

The Attorney General produced 24 consumers who testified concerning their own experiences with defendant's sales personnel which led to the execution of the printed form purchase contracts. In no case was there any real explanation of the obligation being assumed upon signing the contract. Many buyers, relying on the representations of defendant's agents, did not read the form being signed. Even if they had read it, it is implicit in the trial court's finding that either they were incapable of comprehending its real import or they believed that, whatever it said, the real bargain they were making was the one outlined to them by defendant's sales representatives. These 24 consumers also described defendant's contract enforcement and collection practices. In each case the trial court found that "[t]he proofs abundantly support the finding that deceptive and fraudulent practices prohibited by N.J.S.A. 56:8-2 have been perpetrated by the defendant's sales representatives upon each of the 24 customers who testified. 110 N.J. Super. at 478, 266 A.2d at 148." As already noted, defendant does not dispute that finding on this appeal.

For purposes of this opinion it is sufficient to set forth generally the nature of the misrepresentations and deceptions practiced by defendant's solicitors:

1. Statements that defendant's employee was selling books under a special federal grant;

2. Statements that the books were being sold for "Head Start," for a school, for the Newark Board of Education, for the school system, for a high school, or for a named school which did not exist:

3. Statements that the total contract price was $49.50, payable by the accumulation of 10¢ per day to meet the monthly payments, that the price was $115, $160, $199 or "pennies a day," $25, $75, 48¢ per week, etc., or that the package was free for experimental or demonstration purposes;

4. Statements that the contract was cancellable at the option of the consumer (where the consumer wanted to review the contract with her husband) followed by institution of suit to collect upon the contract:

5. Statements that the contract was not effective until receipt of the deposit, followed by litigation of the contract to collect even though no deposit was ever paid;

6. Institution of suit to collect against a non-signatory spouse following misrepresentative statements;

7. Statements that purchase of the package would lead to a high school equivalency diploma.

In a comprehensive opinion, the trial court resolved all factual issues in favor of the Attorney General. Its consequent judgment

(1) enjoined defendant from continuing or engaging in any fraud or deception as defined in N.J.S.A. 56:8-2 and particularly from engaging in any of the deceptive practices or misrepresentations hereinabove outlined;

(2) ordered that defendant enter cancellations of all judgments arising out of the sales contracts involved in the case which were docketed against any of the consumers or their spouses who testified at this trial;

(3) ordered defendant to restore to the testifying customers all moneys they paid him pursuant to default judgments entered against them; upon receiving payment, such persons were directed to return to defendant whatever books and materials they had received under the contracts which they still had in their possession; it was provided also that their inability to make complete return of the books, etc. would not bar their right to recovery of the sums they paid under the default judgments;

(4) enjoined defendant from instituting any action seeking a money recovery under the sales contract against any of the 24 consumers who had testified in the case;

(5) recited that since the 24 contracts involved in the action were obtained through practices violative of N.J.S.A. 56:8-2 a penalty of $100 in each instance or $2400 would be imposed upon defendant under N.J.S.A. 56:8-13.

However, the trial court declined certain additional relief sought, hence this appeal. More particularly, although it was declared that all of the 24 contracts discussed in the proofs were procured in violation of the statute, restoration of moneys paid by some victims though their attorneys in settlement of defendant's claims against them was denied. But more important, it was held that although the contract price for the "educational package" was exorbitant it did not constitute a fraud per se under the statute. Further, and of crucial importance to the Attorney General's position as representative of the public and of the Office of Consumer Protection, N.J.S.A. 52:17B-5.6, 5.7, the court held that the unconscionability of a contract or clause thereof within the meaning of the Uniform Commercial Code, N.J.S.A. 12A:2-302, and the remedy provided therefor by that section, are matters of private concern and cannot be asserted by the Attorney General under the consumer fraud statute here involved, N.J.S.A. 56:8-8. See N.J.S.A. 52:17A-4(h), 52:17B-5.7. Therefore it declared that the unconscionability section of the Code was neither relevant nor available to the Attorney General in the action either as it related to the 24 named consumers or to other consumers similarly situated for whom relief was sought. That view resulted in the rejection of the Attorney General's contention that the contract, being unconscionable within Section 2-302 of the Code, was also violative of Section 2 of the Consumer Fraud Act, and therefore for that reason

alone should be adjudged illegal, not only in the 24 specific cases covered
by the proof, but also in behalf of all others similarly situated, i.e., those
consumers who had executed the same contract for the same so-called
educational package at the same price. We find ourselves in agreement
with the Attorney General's contention that his claims for broader affirmative relief should be recognized. Denial of such relief would be unfortunate not only in this case, but it would operate as a serious impairment to
the deterrent effect of the sanctions which we believe underlies the Consumer Fraud Act.

I

In resolving the problems presented, first attention must be given to the
authority and status of the Attorney General to institute an action in
consumer fraud cases seeking affirmative relief not only for the benefit of
specifically named consumers but also for a large number of unnamed
consumers similarly situated who wish to be represented and to benefit by
the judgment entered therein. Obviously a just resolution can be reached
only through a sensitive awareness of the climate of our time as it has
been influenced by legislative and judicial measures affecting the buyer-
seller relationship in the marketing of consumer goods. There can be no
doubt that, in today's society, sale of consumer goods, especially on an
installment credit basis, has become a matter of ever-increasing state and
national anxiety. In recent years New Jersey lawmakers have become
deeply concerned with suppression of commercial deception in consumer transactions. See General Investment Corp. v. Angelini, 58 N.J.
396, 278 A.2d 193 (1971); Unico v. Owen, 50 N.J. 101, 232 A.2d 405 (1967);
Henningsen v. Bloomfield Motors, Inc., 32 N.J. 358, 388-391, 161 A.2d 69
(1960). The Consumer Fraud Act invoked here, N.J.S.A. 56:8-1 et seq., is
only one example of the concern. To it may be added the Retail Installment Sales Act, N.J.S.A. 17:16C-1 et seq., the Home Repair Financing
Act, N.J.S.A. 17:16C-62 et seq. See General Investment Corp. v. Angelini, supra.

The courts, recognizing the current trends in consumer protection
legislation, have realized that with such measures, as well as with utilization of the common law concepts of fraud and unconscionability, they
can assume an active role in strengthening the consumer's limited market
leverage. As this Court said in Ellsworth Dobbs, Inc. v. Johnson, 50 N.J.
528, 236 A.2d 843 (1967):

> Courts and legislatures have grown increasingly sensitive to imposition,
> conscious or otherwise, on members of the public by persons with whom

they deal, who through experience, specialization, licensure, economic strength or position, or membership in associations created for their mutual benefit and education, have acquired such expertise or monopolistic or practical control in the business transactions involved as to give them an undue advantage. 50 N.J. at 553, 236 A.2d at 856.

. . . The existing statutes in our State, and particularly N.J.S.A. 56:8-1 et seq. and 12A:2-302, reveal that the Legislature did not limit its consideration or treatment of the need for consumer protection to the creation of private remedies between the individual buyers and seller. Obviously it recognized that the deception, misrepresentation and unconscionable practices engaged in by professional sellers seeking mass distribution of many types of consumer goods frequently produce an adverse effect on large segments of disadvantaged and poorly educated people, who are wholly devoid of expertise and least able to understand or to cope with the "sales oriented," "extroverted" and unethical solicitors bent on capitalizing upon their weakness, and who therefore most need protection against predatory practices. As we see the statutes cited, as well as the act establishing the Office of Consumer Protection, N.J.S.A. 52:17B-5.6, it seems plain that the lawmakers accepted the premise that the market bargaining process does not protect ordinary consumers from serious damage in a large number of transactions. Obviusly, giving the consumer rights and remedies which he must assert individually in the courts would provide little therapy for the overall public aspect of the problem. It has been said that "[o]ne cannot think of a more expensive and frustrating course than to seek to regulate goods or 'contract' quality through repeated lawsuits against inventive 'wrongdoers.'" Leff, "Unconscionability and the Crowd — Consumers and The Common Law Tradition," 31 U. Pitt. L. Rev. 349, 356 (1970). As Professor Leff suggests, mass consumer transactions growing out of unequal bargaining power and unfair practices should not be handled on a case-by-case basis. The emphasis must be upon public rather than private remedies, and the natural remedial step is government intervention. Id. 351.

. . . In our judgment the statutes referred to above in their total impact, when considered in connection with the Attorney General's general statutory and common law authority to act in matters affecting the public welfare (N.J.S.A. 52:17A-4(h); O'Regan v. Schermerhorn, 25 N.J. Misc. 1, 9, 50 A.2d 10 (Sup. Ct. 1946)), require the conclusion that he has authority to bring action in the public interest under N.J.S.A. 56:8-8 either on behalf of specifically named buyers who have been imposed upon contrary to Section 2 thereof, or in the nature of a class action on behalf of all similarly situated buyers. Although the procedural aspects of such a suit need not be passed upon at this time, guidance may be found in R. 4:32-1, 2 and 3 which relate generally to class actions. . . .

II

Since we are satisfied that the public welfare would be sufficiently adversely affected by a consumer goods seller's engagement in practices condemned by N.J.S.A. 56:8-2 to justify a remedial action by the Attorney General in behalf of consumers who constitute an ascertainable class of victims with a sufficient community of interest, we turn to his right to the specific relief denied below. Quite obviously the Attorney General recognized that a class action is not maintainable if the right of each individual claimant to relief depended upon a separate set of facts applicable only to him. . . .

The Attorney General's claim was that there was one illegal aspect of the sales contract which was common to every transaction, namely the fixed price. This price for the package of books and materials, which the testimony showed was about two and a half times a reasonable price in the relevant market, was found by the trial court to be exorbitant. As we have already noted, the Attorney General pointed out that in addition to being excessive in relation to defendant's cost, the books had very little and in some cases no value for the purpose for which the consumers were persuaded to buy them. Consequently he urged that under the circumstances the price was unconscionable under Section 2-302 of the Uniform Commercial Code and, as such, was within the proscription of Section 2 of the Consumer Fraud Act. More particularly, he contends that on the uncontradicted and common facts of each transaction, the unconscionable price must be equated with the deception, fraud, false pretense, misrepresentation or knowing material omission condemned by Section 2. If the contention is sound, then it should follow that every consumer who executed the form agreement for the educational package described above at the price fixed by defendant ought to be considered similarly situated, and the Attorney General would therefore be entitled to a judgment invalidating the contract for the entire class of such consumers.

As already noted, however, the trial court declined to hold that the price per se constituted a violation of Section 2 in the absence of some concomitant deceptive practice perpetrated by the seller. The opinion pointed out that the word "unconscionable" did not appear in Section 2 and consequently should not be considered as included therein. 110 N.J. Super. at 482, 266 A.2d 144. Further the court declared that even though enforcement of an unconscionable contract may be denied under Section 2-302 of the Code, the remedy provided thereby is "strictly a matter of private concern" and cannot be asserted or relied upon by the Attorney General in a suit allegedly brought for protection of the consuming public. 110 N.J. Super. at 481, 266 A.2d 144.

Unconscionability is not defined in Section 2-302 of the Uniform Commercial Code, and we agree that it is not mentioned by name in

Section 2 of the Consumer Fraud Act. It is an amorphous concept obviously designed to establish a broad business ethic. The framers of the Code naturally expected the courts to interpret it liberally so as to effectuate the public purpose, and to pour content into it on a case-by-case basis. In that way a substantial measure of predictability will be achieved and professional sellers of consumer goods as well as draftsmen of contracts for their sale to ordinary consumers will become aware of the abuses the courts have declared unacceptable and will avoid them. The intent of the clause is not to erase the doctrine of freedom of contract, but to make realistic the assumption of the law that the agreement has resulted from real bargaining between parties who had freedom of choice and understanding and ability to negotiate in a meaningful fashion. Viewed in that sense, freedom to contract survives, but marketers of consumer goods are brought to an awareness that the restraint of unconscionability is always hovering over their operations and that courts will employ it to balance the interests of the consumer public and those of the sellers.

The standard of conduct contemplated by the unconscionability clause is good faith, honesty in fact and observance of fair dealing. The need for application of the standard is most acute when the professional seller is seeking the trade of those most subject to exploitation — the uneducated, the inexperienced and the people of low incomes. In such a context, a material departure from the standard puts a badge of fraud on the transaction and here the concept of fraud and unconscionability are interchangeable. Thus we believe that in consumer goods transactions such as those involved in this case, unconscionability must be equated with the concepts of deception, fraud, false pretense, misrepresentation, concealment and the like, which are stamped unlawful under N.J.S.A. 56:8-2. We do not consider that absence of the word "unconscionable" from the statute detracts in any substantial degree from the force of this conclusion. That view is aided and strengthened by the plain inference that the Legislature intended to broaden the scope of responsibility for unfair business practices by stating in Section 2 that the use of any of the described practices is unlawful "whether or not any person [the consumer] has in fact been misled, deceived or damaged thereby."

We have no doubt that an exorbitant price ostensibly agreed to by a purchaser of the type involved in this case — but in reality unilaterally fixed by the seller and not open to negotiation — constitutes an unconscionable bargain from which such a purchaser should be relieved under Section 2. If, therefore, in this case the price charged for the educational package is so exorbitant as to be unconscionable, Section 2 makes it unnecessary to decide whether the Attorney General could maintain a class action for all similarly affected consumers based solely upon violation of Section 2-302, the unconscionability clause of the Uniform Commercial Code. Adequate and proper relief for all consumers victimized by an unconscionable price may be obtained by the Attorney General through Section 2 of the Consumer Fraud Act under which his action was brought here.

Sale at an exorbitant price especially in the market described by the evidence in this case raises a strong inference of imposition. Here the facts reveal that the seller's price was not only roughly two and one half times a reasonable market price, assuming functional adequacy of the book package for the represented purpose, but they indicate also that most of the package was actually practically worthless for that purpose. Such price-value clearly constitutes unconscionability and renders Section 2 available to the Attorney General in a class-type remedial action for the benefit of all similarly situated consumers. The statement to the Consumer Fraud Act, N.J.S.A. 56:8-1 et seq., supports this view. It said:

> The purpose of this bill is to permit the Attorney General to combat the increasingly widespread practice of defrauding the consumer. The authority conferred will provide effective machinery to investigate and prohibit deceptive and fraudulent advertising and selling practices which have caused extensive damage to the public.

In other jurisdictions exorbitant prices for consumer goods sold in a marketing milieu similar to our case have been declared unconscionable. In State by Lefkowitz v. ITM, Inc., *supra*, 275 N.Y.S.2d 303, the seller marketed broilers, vacuum cleaners and color television sets using various types of deceptive sales practices. Among other things it appeared that the sales prices to the consumers for the various items ranged from two to six times the costs to the seller. The proof showed also that defendant represented that the goods were not obtainable elsewhere at its prices. But they were available and at much lower prices. The court said it was clear that "these excessively high prices constituted 'unconscionable contractual provisions' within the meaning of section 63, subsection 12 of the Executive Law," N.Y. Executive Law §63(12) (McKinney, 1970-71 Supp.), and further that even if the prices were not unconscionable per se, "they were unconscionable within the context of this case" under Section 2-302 of the Uniform Commercial Code.

[The court here discusses several decisions, including *Jones, MacIver,* and *Williams.*]

As set forth above, we are satisfied that the price for the book package was unconscionable in relation to defendant's cost and the value to the consumers and was therefore a fraud within the contemplation of N.J.S.A. 56:8-2. Further, for the reasons stated we are convinced that a view that such price unconscionability gives rise only to a private remedy is an unreasonable limitation on the aim and scope of the Consumer Fraud Act, N.J.S.A. 56:8-1 et seq. The public purpose to be served thereby (and we see the legislative emphasis as being more on public than on private remedies) can be accomplished effectively only by recognizing the authority of the Attorney General to intervene in behalf of all consumers similarly affected by the broadly described fraudulent sales tactics of merchandise sellers.

More specifically here, since the price unconscionability rendered the sales contract invalid as to all consumers who executed it, the Attorney General was entitled to a judgment so holding as to the entire class of such persons. Accordingly, the trial court's order must be modified to the end that such a judgment may be entered. The mechanics of effectuating the judgment with respect to the individuals comprising the class and of accomplishing the necessary restorative relief required by N.J.S.A. 56:8-8 are left to the trial court.

As modified the judgment is affirmed and the cause is remanded for further proceedings consistent with this opinion.

For affirmance as modified: Chief Justice Weintraub and Justices Jacobs, Francis, Proctor, Hall, Schettino and Mountain — 7.

For reversal: None.

NOTE

The New Jersey Attorney General is empowered by §56.8-4 of the Consumer Fraud Act to "promulgate such rules and regulations . . . which shall have the force of law" in order to "accomplish the objectives and to carry out the duties prescribed by this act." Could the Attorney General make rules defining unconscionable conduct? The U.C.C.C. (1974) and the Uniform Consumer Sales Practices Act (discussed *infra*) both deny the administrator authority to promulgate rules defining the amorphous concept of unconscionability. U.C.C.C. §6.104(e) and UCSPA §6(b). A contrary view is taken by the NCA (§6.109), the MCCA (§9.103 and §8.104) and the Wisconsin Consumer Act (§426.808). If a governmental agency were permitted to define unconscionable conduct, would it be possible (or wise) for the agency to adopt a simple mathematical ratio for price unconscionability, or to declare per se unconscionable such clauses as the add-on clause used in *Williams*? How would a rule characterizing certain terms or contracts as per se unconscionable affect the requirement that the court consider evidence of commercial setting, purpose, and effect?

Both federal and state agencies are involved in promulgating and enforcing administrative regulations and in bringing actions to curb sharp business practices. At the federal level numerous agencies are charged with protecting the consumer. The most important of these is probably the FTC, which owes its existence to the FTC Act of 1914. 15 U.S.C. §§41 et seq. In its original form, the FTC Act, more particularly §5, did not give the FTC authority to protect consumers. In 1938, Congress amended the Act to give the FTC power to protect consumers by declaring "unfair or deceptive acts or practices in commerce" unlawful. The Act was further amended in 1975 by the Federal Trade Commission Improvement Act (Magnuson-Moss Act). The Magnuson-Moss Act has two titles. Title I, the Warranty Act, imposes uniform standards for written warranties on consumer goods and standardizes the description of consumer warranties. If a warranty is given, it must, with a few exceptions, be described as either "full" or "limited." Title II broadens the jurisdiction of the FTC by giving it the power to regulate intrastate trade that affects interstate commerce, gives the FTC authority to define deceptive acts or practices, and broadens the types of relief available against such practices. See Note, 53 Tex. L. Rev. 831 (1975). On the Warranty Act, see C. Reitz, Consumer Protection Under the Magnuson-Moss Warranty Act (1978). On the FTC, see further L. Feldman, Consumer Protection, Problems and Prospects 65-73 (1976). The FTC alone has the right to bring an action under the FTC Act. There is no private right of action.

At the state level there is an array of legislation creating consumer protection agencies or authorizing the attorney general of a state to enforce consumer protection legislation. The Commissioners on Uniform State Laws have drafted two uniform acts in this field. The Uniform Deceptive Trade Practices Act (UDTPA, 1966), like the FTC Act, is directed at both deceptive or unfair trade practices and unfair competition. The Uniform Consumer Sales Practices Act (UCSPA) has a narrower focus, being directed only at consumer protection. The UCSPA follows the UDTPA closely, but it provides for a greater arsenal of weapons, including class actions. The UCSPA, however, has been adopted in only two states to date, Ohio and Utah. A well-received model act is the Model Unfair Trade Practices and Consumer Protection Law. This model law, recommended by the Council on State Governments, has three alternative forms. The text of the law is in 1970 Suggested State Legislation 141 (1970). For further details, including a discussion of the so-called Printer's Ink statutes, which are directed at deceptive advertising and provide criminal sanctions, see D. A. Rice, Consumer Transactions 220 et seq. (1975). See also S. Deutch, Unfair Contracts 204 et seq. (1977).

Protection of consumers by a public agency is limited in effectiveness.[104] The budgets of these agencies are frequently small, especially when compared with the number of businesses and transactions to be regulated. On the other hand, consumer transactions generally involve trivial sums. Both the injured consumer and the legal profession have

104. S. Deutch, Unfair Contracts (1977). R. Posner, Economic Analysis of Law, ch. 13 (2d ed. 1977). (The concept of "market failure" needs to be balanced against a concept of "government failure," e.g., the complexity of mandated disclosure provisions required by federal and state statutes.)

little incentive to prosecute or defend a lawsuit for such insignificant amounts. To remedy this situation and to make private suits a more effective device for controlling business conduct, consumer legislation often provides for class actions, minimum statutory penalties, attorney's fees, and court costs. In addition, some legislation permits private individuals to seek injunctive relief and even to obtain punitive damages. Perhaps the most liberal of all pieces of consumer legislation enacted to date in this regard, and one that should be consulted by those interested in the field, is the Wisconsin Consumer Act.

Class actions in federal courts are governed by Rule 23 of the Federal Rules of Civil Procedure. Their usefulness, however, was restricted by Eisen v. Carlisle, 470 U.S. 156 (1974). The availability of class actions in state courts depends on state law.

Most consumer legislation provides for class actions. The class may be represented by private individuals or by a public official, such as the attorney general. Frequently a statute will provide that a public official has the right to intervene in a private class action. The consumer class action can be an awesome and sometimes frightful weapon. Many statutes permit consumers to recover penalties unrelated both to actual loss and to the egregiousness of the violation. If these penalties were multiplied by the number of members of the class, potential damage awards would be staggering. See, e.g., Ratner v. Chemical Bank N.Y. Trust Co., 54 F.R.D. 412 (1972). To avoid this result, consumer legislation often provides either that statutory penalties are not recoverable in class actions or that recoveries in general are limited. The U.C.C.C. (1974) permits recovery only of actual damages in class actions. §5.201(1) and Comment 2. The TILA, which also permits class actions, was amended in 1975 to limit the amount recoverable in such actions to the lesser of $500,000 or 1% of the creditor's net worth.

Section 3.   Freedom of Contract in the Field of Private Insurance

There are numerous older cases, and some recent ones as well, informing us that an insurance policy is no different from any other contract.[105] "[T]he insurance company is entitled to have its contract enforced by the courts as written."[106] No other result is possible, it has been said, if the

---

105. This section is adapted from Kessler, Forces Shaping the Insurance Contract, a paper delivered at the Chicago Conference on Insurance (Conference Series No. 14, 1954). The field of insurance law is so large that many of its aspects have had to be omitted.

106. Drilling v. New York Life Ins. Co., 234 N.Y. 243, 137 N.E. 314 (1922); Swentusky v. Prudential Ins. Co., 116 Conn. 526, 165 A.68 (1933).

fundamental principle of the security of transactions is to be preserved. A court, on this view, may not strike out or change any part of the policy so as to vary or contradict a statement in the original agreement; its function is limited to the interpretation of, and only of, the policy's ambiguous terms.[107] Having signed the application and having retained the policy based on the application, the policyholder (and for that matter, the beneficiary) is bound by the statements and terms that it contains.[108] "After all," as Holmes said, "no rational theory of contracts can be made that does not hold the assured to know the contents of the instrument to which he seeks to hold the other party."[109]

Yet, despite the repeated assertion of such views, a growing body of case law too large to be ignored strains to distinguish the insurance policy from ordinary run-of-the-mill contracts and to treat the former as standing in a class by itself.[110]

The time has long passed when the ordinary insurance policy could be characterized as the result of individual haggling. Once insurance became a mass industry, the drafting of a policy became a one-sided affair. The standard policy emerged, drafted by the individual insurer or by the industry as a whole, acting in cooperative fashion, as in the case of motor vehicle insurance.

Today, the choice of a policyholder is about as restricted as the choice of a car buyer. An applicant for insurance is offered a limited number of policy forms and must accept one of these if he desires insurance with a given company.[111] In this way, standardization saves transactions costs — a benefit for both parties. From the industry's point of view, standardization (uniformity) is an advantage because it makes possible the calculation of risks and therefore provides the statistical basis for its efficient distribution. Risks that are difficult to calculate can be excluded altogether or insured only at an increased price. To the policyholder, uniformity means reduced costs and equal treatment. In addition it means standard wording, which increases the chance the policyholder will understand the contract: the greater the ignorance of the policyholder, the more he is protected by standardization, which approximates his normal needs. To this extent, the sophisticated purchaser of insurance, who

107. Morgan v. State Farm Life Ins. Co., 240 Ore. 113, 400 P.2d 223 (1965) (4/3 decision).

108. Russo v. Metropolitan Life Ins. Co., 125 Conn. 132, 3 A.2d 844 (1930).

109. Lumber Underwriters of New York v. Rife, 237 U.S. 605 (1915).

110. Pfister v. Missouri State Life Ins., 87 Kan. 97, 102, 116 P. 245, 247 (1911); Woodruff, Selection of Cases on the Law of Insurance, Preface at iv, v (2d ed. 1914); Schultz, The Special Nature of Insurance Contracts: A Few Suggestions for Further Study, 15 Law & Contemp. Prob. 376 (1950).

111. Individualization and flexibility are provided by permitting endorsements ("riders"). The New York fire policy, enacted by statutory fiat and adopted in almost every state of the union, permits a variety of endorsements, so long as they are not "inconsistent" with the basic form. E. Patterson, Essentials of Insurance Law 34-35 (2d ed. 1957).

understands the policy, may have little advantage over his less experienced peer.[112]

The insurance policy is the prototype of a standardized mass contract. Once its usefulness was proven in the field of marine insurance, it spread quickly from industry to industry. And yet, the standardized mass contract, despite its unquestionable advantages, has frequently been a tool for overreaching, because of the unequal bargaining power of the majority of contracting parties. However important it is for the insurance industry to be able to select and control the risk incurred, the history of insurance furnishes many illustrations of the abuse of freedom of contract.

The evolution of warranty law from its early beginnings in marine insurance is a case in point. Dissatisfied with the existing law of misrepresentation and concealment, marine insurers invented an additional device for the selection and control of risks: in their policies they included clauses (labeled "warranties") that made the existence of facts affecting the risk a condition of the insurer's liability.[113] These warranties, typically based on information coming from the insured or his agent, were rigidly enforced, and any deviation from the true state of affairs, however trivial or immaterial to the risk and however innocent, was, according to a famous decision by Lord Mansfield, fatal to recovery.[114]

The insurance industry knew a good thing when it saw one. When new types of insurance, such as fire or life insurance, became popular, the industry, particularly in this country, made the fullest use of freedom of contract to impose on the policyholder strict warranty law and to constantly increase the number of exceptions to coverage, which were often couched in obscure language.[115] "Machine made" warranties came into existence. Some life insurance applications contained close to one hundred questions, including the most trivial matters concerning the health of the applicant or his close relatives, which the applicant would almost

112. R. Keeton, Insurance Law (Basic Text) 68-69 (1971); Restatement Second §211(2).

113. Patterson, *supra* note 111, at 308; id., Warranties in Insurance Law, 34 Colum. L. Rev. 595 (1934). A "warranty" relates to facts potentially affecting a particular risk, in contrast to "coverage" clauses, which identify the risks that fall outside the scope of coverage, and "exceptions," which exclude liability for an insured event that is caused in certain ways. Patterson's definition has been adopted by the New York Legislature. The insurance law of many states has failed to define the term *warranty*, though using it quite freely. For a criticism of Patterson, see Keeton, *supra* note 112, at 388; see also W. Young, Cases and Materials on the Law of Insurance 209 (1971).

114. De Hahn v. Hartley, 1 T.R. 343, 90 Eng. Rep. 1130 (1740); Park, Insurance 339 (1769). Park's classic makes it clear that one of the functions of warranty clauses was to exclude the so-called juridical risk. See further Vance, The History of the Development of Warranty in Insurance, 20 Yale L.J. 523 (1913).

115. Wilson v. Assurance Co., 90 Vt. 105, 108, 96 A. 340, 342 (1915). On the "readability" of insurance policies, particularly automobile policies, see Harding, The Standard Automobile Insurance Policy: A Study of Its Readability, 34 J. Risk & Ins. 39 (1967). See further Insurance Co. of N. A. v. Electronic Co., 67 Cal. 2d 679, 433 P.2d 174 (1967).

certainly be unable to answer correctly.[116] Many a policyholder or beneficiary came to grief after making payments for years. The owners of fire policies often did not fare any better.[117]

A backlash became inevitable. In time, the marketing of insurance was regulated and the terms of insurance transactions were controlled by legislation, administrative action,[118] and judicial decision.

The first attempts at statutory regulation were rather feeble and inefficient, in part because the judicial branch, constrained by traditional contract theory, felt, on the whole, that it lacked authority to tamper with the terms of the insurance contract. Gradually, however, the principle of freedom of contract was hemmed in by restrictions. To protect the insured, ambiguities were discovered by the courts (where none existed) in order to make room for interpretations that protected the legitimate expectations of the policyholder. Warranties were narrowly construed,[119] and the doctrines of waiver and estoppel were used with increasing frequency,[120] often with conflicting results. It is no wonder that the law of insurance fell into a state of deplorable uncertainty. Since insurance

116. Moulor v. American Life Ins. Co., 111 U.S. 335 (1884); Globe Mutual Life Ins. Assn. v. Wagner 138 Ill. 133, 58 N.E. 970 (1900).

117. For the evolution of insurance in this country see Horwitz at 226.

118. Regulation by legislation has the disadvantage of inflexibility. On the purpose of regulation, see S. Kimball, The Purpose of Insurance Regulation: A Preliminary Inquiry in the Theory of Insurance Law, 45 Minn. L. Rev. 471 (1961); Legislative and Judicial Control of the Terms of Insurance Contracts: A Comparative Study of American and European Practice, 39 Ind. L.J. 675 (1964); Administrative Control of the Terms of Insurance Contracts: A Comparative Study, 40 Ind. L.J. 143 (1965).

Control by administrative agencies has its considerable advantages, provided the commission is well staffed and financed, but this is often not the case.

The New York Insurance Department, headed by an Insurance Commissioner, is an outstanding exception. The New York Insurance Commissioner has broad power of control, for instance, the power with regard to certain policies to disapprove a form "if it contains provisions which encourage misrepresentation or are unjust, unfair, unequitable, misleading, deceptive, or contrary to law or to the public policy of the state." (Insurance Law §141).

The following discussion does not deal with the regulations aiming at the solvency of insurers or the regulation of premiums in the interest of fairness. As to these aspects, see Keeton, supra note 112, at 554 et seq.

Although the insurance business is interstate commerce (U.S. Const. art. I, §8, cl. 3; United States v. Southeastern Underwriters Assn., 332 U.S. 53 (1944)) and therefore subject to federal control, the McCarran-Ferguson Act, 15 U.S.C.A. §1011-1015 (West 1976), conceded to state governments the regulation of insurance business to the extent that it is not explicitly regulated by federal law. Federal antitrust laws, however, are applicable. (15 U.S.C.A. §1012.) In addition, a 1982 law provided that even if the business of insurance is regulated by state law, it will not be immunized if it constitutes an agreement or act of boycott, coercion or intimidation, 15 U.S.C. §§1011-1013 (1982). See Kintner, Bauer & Allen, Application of the Antitrust Laws to the Activities of Insurance Companies: Heavier Risks, Expanded Coverage and Greater Liability, 63 N.C.L. Rev. 431 (1985).

119. Moulor v. American Life Ins. Co., supra note 116.

120. Patterson, supra note 111, at 493. See Morris, Waiver and Estoppel in Insurance Policy Litigation, 105 U. Pa. L. Rev. 925 (1957). See further F. Kessler & G. Gilmore, Contracts 860-863 (2d ed. 1970).

policies did not fit into the conventional pattern of contract law with its individualistic presuppositions (the common law of offer and acceptance, the doctrines of agency, the canons of interpretation, and the parol evidence rule, to mention only a few), the latter were "in various instances badly warped, if not broken, in order that insurance law could accommodate itself to the actuality of fact."[121]

The cases leave very little doubt that insurance law is a field where, to use the language of Max Weber, "antiformalist tendencies" were, and still are, at work.[122] The "peculiar legal aspect" of insurance law cannot be sufficiently explained by its aleatory element, but is due, in large measure, to the solicitude that courts have shown for the insured.[123] Although only a few courts have said that an insurance contract is one of the utmost good faith,[124] a high standard of fair dealing has been imposed in a number of significant respects. Courts have imposed a duty to warn, to explain,[125] and to communicate information in the formation and performance stages[126] (a reaction against misrepresentation on the part of the insurer or his agent),[127] as well as a duty to make good faith efforts to defend and to settle, on pain of being subject to excess liability, e.g., recovery beyond the policy limits.[128] These duties are "matched" by du-

---

121. Woodruff, *supra* note 110. According to Slawson, most insurance policies are not contracts at all but exercises of private lawmaking power. To the extent that they are not contracts, he argues they should be governed by principles derived from administrative law. See Slawson, Standard Form Contracts and Democratic Control of Lawmaking Power, 84 Harv. L. Rev. 529 (1971). For a suggestion to apply the implied warranty of sales law to insurance policies, see Comment, 35 Yale L.J. 203, 207-208 (1925); State Security Life Ins. Co. v. Kintner, 243 Ind. 331, 185 N.E. 2d 572 (1926) (dissenting opinion). See further 7 Williston §900 (Jaeger 3d ed. 1963).

122. Max Weber, Economy and Society (G. Roth & C. Wittich eds. 1978):

> New demands for a "social law" to be based upon such emotionally colored ethical postulates as "justice" or "human dignity," and directed against the very dominance of a mere business morality, have arisen with the emergence of the modern class problem. They are advocated not only by labor and other interested groups but also by legal ideologists. By these demands legal formalism itself has been challenged.

(The translation is by Max Rheinstein; a footnote has been omitted.)

123. E. Patterson, Essentials of Insurance Law 62 (2d ed. 1957).

124. Bowler v. Fidelity & Casualty Co., 53 N.J. 313, 250 A.2d 580 (1969); Keeton, Ancillary Rights of the Insured, 13 Vand. L. Rev. 844 (1960); Comment, The Emerging Fiduciary Obligation and Strict Liability in Insurance Law, 14 Cal. W.L. Rev. 358 (1978).

The requirement of utmost good faith originated in English marine insurance law (British Marine Insurance Act of 1906 §18(1)) and was applied to lapses of nondisclosure on the part of the insured. It is still applied in England in marine as well as nonmarine insurance. E. G. Horne v. Poland, [1932] 2 K.B. 384; Hasson, The Doctrine of Uberrima Fides in Insurance Law — A Critical Evaluation, 33 Mod. L. Rev. 615 (1969). The powerful opinion of Taft, J. in Penn Mutual Life Ins. Co. v. Mechanics Savings Bank & Trust Co., 72 F. 413 (1896), may have led to the demise of the rule in this country in life and fire insurance cases.

125. Holz Rubber Co., Inc. v. American Star Ins. Co., 14 Cal. 3d 45, 533 P.2d 1015, 120 Cal. Rptr. 415 (1975). See further note 156 *infra*.

126. Bowler v. Fidelity & Casualty Co., *supra* note 124.

127. 136 A.L.R. 5 (1942).

128. Crisci v. Security Insurance Co., 58 Cal. Rptr. 13 (1967).

ties on the part of the insured to cooperate,[129] and to make available vital information — duties, however, which have been softened by the downgrading of warranties[130] and incontestability clauses,[131] as well as by liberal use of the doctrines of estoppel, waiver, and laches.[132]

To improve the lot of the policyholder still further, and to bring about a rational system protecting reasonable expectations, renewed efforts were made at legislative and administrative reform. In the field of fire insurance, regulation largely took the form of legislative fiat,[133] which reduced warranties, coverage limitations, and exceptions to a minimum.[134] The techniques used for controlling life insurance and related policies have been quite different; here, all that is typically required is that the policy contain certain provisions to protect the minimum expectations of the policyholder.[135] In many states, strict warranty law has been abolished *in toto*, with warranties sometimes being converted into mere representations.[136] As a result, so long as there is no fraud or concealment, the untruth of a statement by the applicant for insurance is fatal to recovery only if material to the risk.[137] The criteria of materiality, however, are not uniform and in many states the law can be evaded by rephrasing warranties so as to make them into coverage provisions.[138]

Outside the field of motor vehicle insurance and worker's compensa-

129. MFA Mutual Ins. Co. v. Sailors, 180 Neb. 201, 141 N.W.2d 846 (1966); Puppkes v. Sailors, 183 Neb. 784, 164 N.W.2d 441 (1909); Billington v. Interim Ins. Exchange of Southern California, 71 Cal. 2d 728, 456 P.2d 982 (1969). The duty, according to Keeton, *supra* note 124, exists even in the absence of a policy provision. It is fatal to coverage only if prejudicial to the insurance carrier (a jury question). The insurer, on his part, has the duty to elicit information. Noncooperation presents, of course, a danger to the victim. On the duty to notify see Young, *supra* note 113, at 609f.

130. See *infra*.

131. Keeton, *supra* note 112, at 322. The clause has often been extended beyond life to disability and accident insurance.

132. Morris, Waiver and Estoppel in Insurance Policy Litigation, 105 U. Pa. L. Rev. 925 (1957).

133. Patterson, *supra* note 111, at 33, 141, 256.

134. See, in general, New York Standard Fire Policy, lines 1-37.

135. The "incontestable" clause may serve as an illustration.

136. See, e.g., Illinois Insurance Code, §154. Most states have left the old and rigid law intact in marine insurance. For an exception, see Mass. Gen. Laws, ch. 175, §186. See further Wilburn Boat Co. v. Fireman's Ins. Fund, 388 U.S. 320 (1955), which applies state and not federal admiralty law. For the subsequent history of the case see Keeton, *supra* note 112, at 322.

137. W. Vance, Handbook of the Law of Insurance 417 (Anderson 3d ed. 1951). Roughly speaking, the materiality test imposed by many statutes means either that the insurer, if correctly informed, would have denied coverage or would have charged higher premiums (or according to some case law, would have made further inquiries). Other statutes have a "contribute to the loss" test of materiality. Both types of statute apply in an all or nothing manner. By contrast, New Hampshire is the only state whose statute provides for proportionate reduction of recovery across the board. Elsewhere, this principle is generally applied only to misstatement of age and, in most states, to changes of occupation under an accident or health insurance policy (e.g., N.Y. Insurance Law §155(1)(d) and §164(E)(1)).

138. Metropolitan Life Insurance Co. v. Conway, 151 N.Y. 449, 169 N.E. 942 (1913). New York has tried to close the gap by restricting the number of coverage clauses, permitting some and excluding others.

tion, only a few states have gone so far as to impose on insurance companies a duty to insure acceptable risks.[139] And interim insurance, usually provided in the form of "binders" protecting the applicant in the interval between application and issuance of a policy, has, unfortunately, escaped regulation, with the result that binders are often worded in such a way as to enable the insurer to play fast and loose with the applicant.[140]

The various improvements in insurance regulation, however useful and important, have not dispensed with the need for regulation by creative judicial decision, particularly since many of the statutes in question are poorly drafted.[141] This is particularly true since insurance policies cannot avoid the use of technical terms with which the majority of policyholders are likely to be unfamiliar. Ambiguities are inescapable. The insured buys a product with a deplorable lack of understanding of what he is getting.[142] The technical language of the policy has created an atmosphere in which most policyholders are forced to rely on the skill, honesty, and fairness of their broker and his interpretation of the terms. It is only natural that prior to the issuance of an insurance policy, the insurer or his agent will be most anxious to please.

> In this atmosphere of selling, "roseate with promises," it can hardly be expected that agents will call attention to defects or dangers lurking behind technical language. Rather, the insurer focuses attention on the small cost, the value of his services, and the insured's duty to his family and his creditors. . . . If anything is said about collection in case of loss, it is the most glowing account of the record of full and prompt payment.[143]

Small wonder that the individual policyholder is seldom able to determine the value of the policy. To make matters worse, the policy is presented to the buyer as a packaged product and he does not ordinarily gain access to it until he receives it in the mail. The applicant for life insurance, for instance, does not usually see the policy terms until he has signed the application and sent in the first premium, and the company has approved the application and executed and issued the policy, a proce-

---

139. Patterson, The Delivery of a Life Insurance Policy, 33 Harv. L. Rev. 198, 222 (1919). For the problem of the unwarranted insured in the fields of workman's compensation insurance and motor vehicle insurance under state funds or assigned risk plans, see Keeton, *supra* note 112, at 581-583.

140. For the various forms of binders see Comment, 44 Yale L.J. 1223 (1935), 63 Yale L.J. 523 (1954); Keeton, *supra* note 112, at 41-45. For their control, see Gaunt v. John Hancock Mutual Life Insurance Co., 169 F.2d 599, *cert. denied*, 333 U.S. 849 (1947). See, however, the "Guidelines" issued by the New York Insurance Department; Young, *supra* note 113, at 471. According to the Department, approval types of binders are generally not acceptable.

141. Patterson, *supra* note 111, at 8.

142. Keeton, *supra* note 112, at 350 et seq.

143. Hutcheson, Law and Fact in Insurance Cases, 1944 A.B.A. Insurance Law Proceedings 6, 12.

dure that may take weeks.[144] This delay substantially enhances the policy-holder's disinclination to read the policy carefully, or even to read it at all, a fact of which insurance companies are well aware.

However indispensable judicial creativity is in compensating for poor statutory drafting and gaps in the law, residues of irrationality inevitably remain in a field as emotionally charged as that of insurance.[145] The impact of the jury system is a case in point. Juries, which have the power to decide disputed questions of fact, have often been allowed to bring in general verdicts in insurance cases.[146] Although such a verdict, to quote Patterson,

> is not supposed to decide issues of law but only issues of fact, it frequently does decide the entire merits of the controversy, both legal and factual, against the insurer. This jury control of insurance, while it often results in mistaken generosity to unworthy claimants, serves as a check upon the dilatory or technical defenses that some insurers will raise.[147]

The expectation principle has assumed a paramount role in an increasing number of cases. All too often the courts have failed to heed Llewellyn's warning that chaos lies in broad words of generalization, and salvation in the close study of facts.[148] Even at the risk of disregarding Llewellyn's advice, however, a few generalizations can safely be made. The chief weapon of courts willing to protect expectations "at variance with policy provisions"[149] (besides the traditional tools of waiver and estoppel) has been the technique of finding ambiguities in the policy, even where none exist.[150] In this way, courts have been able to interpret insurance policies against their draftsmen by choosing from among the variant reasonable meanings of a term the one which is most favorable to the insured.[151] Ambiguity has frequently been assessed from the point of view of the average policyholder, and not from the point of view of an experi-

144. To protect the applicant against "negligent delay," tort law has often been invoked. See, e.g., Duffie v. Bankers' Life Assn. of Des Moines, Iowa, 160 Iowa 19, 139 N.W. 1087 (1913); Kessler, Contracts of Adhesion, Some Thoughts about Freedom of Contract, 43 Colum. L. Rev. 629 (1943); Note, 40 Colum. L. Rev. 1007 (1940).

145. Slawson, Mass Contracts: Lawful Fraud in California, 48 S. Cal. L. Rev. 1 (1974).

146. On general verdicts see Skidmore v. Baltimore & O. R. Co., 167 F.2d 54 (2d Cir. 1948).

147. Patterson, *supra* note 111, at 7. The magnitude of the juridical risk attributable to the power of the jury is dramatically illustrated by a recent case, Neal v. Farmers Ins. Exchange, 21 Cal. 3d 910, 148 Cal. Rptr. 389, 502 P.2d 980 (1978).

148. Llewellyn, What Price Contract?, 40 Yale L.J. 704, 751 (1931).

149. Keeton, *supra* note 112, at ch. 6. It has also appeared in 83 Harv. L. Rev. 961, 1281 (1970).

150. Keeton, *supra* note 112, at 356. For a glaring illustration of the interpretation technique, see the opinion of Bird, C.J., in Searle v. All-State Life Insurance Co., 212 Cal. Rptr. 1308 (1985), dealing with "sane or insane" suicide clauses.

151. Restatement Second §206.

enced underwriter.[152] Further, ambiguity may be found to exist if the marketing techniques of the company make it impossible for the policyholder to obtain notice of an exclusion. Air trip insurance furnishes a striking illustration: although not covered by express provision in the policy, passengers on non-scheduled airlines have received protection because the vending machines did not make the exclusion clearly visible.[153]

A few courts have ventured beyond the older method of finding (or inventing) ambiguities,[154] and have sought to protect "insurance law rights at variance with policy provisions" by relying on arguments of public policy or on the doctrine of unconscionability, particularly when enforcing the terms of the policy would negate the very essence of the insurance contract.[155] Other courts have imposed on the insured a duty to inform the applicant of a limitation of coverage, or a duty to disclose its own knowledge of the reach of a policy provision under existing case law.[156]

These decisions are indicative of the extent to which, as Justice Tobriner has pointed out, courts today derive the reasonable expectations of

152. Gaunt v. John Hancock Mutual Life Ins. Co., 169 F.2d 599, *cert. denied*, 333 U.S. 849 (1947). The attitude of the courts stands in marked contrast to that attributed to the

> professionals who write and review insurance contracts. . . . [T]hese men — form committee members and the like — disregarding the preachments of judges, do not as a rule address themselves to the understanding of the common man. They seem to regard themselves as lawgivers: "primarily our policies are drafted for the courts not the layman, that is to say, not the policyholders."

Young, *supra* note 113, at 79, quoting Foster, Humpty Dumpty, 1961 Ins. Couns. J. 130, 131-132 (a member of the Joint Form Committee representing Casualty Underwriters.)

153. Lachs v. Fidelity and Casualty Co., 306 N.Y. 357, 118 N.E. 555 (1954); Steven v. Fidelity and Casualty Co. of New York, 58 Cal. 2d 862, 377 P.2d 284, 27 Cal. Rptr. 172 (1963).

154. Gray v. Zurich Ins. Co., 65 Cal. 2d 263, 419 P.2d 108, 54 Cal. Rptr. 104 (166). A liability policy imposed a duty on the insurer to defend a lawsuit against a policyholder, except in cases of intentional acts. The policyholder had struck another car whose owner seemed to threaten him. He claimed the action was in self-defense, and that he had therefore not acted intentionally. Held, the insurer must defend policyholder in a suit that seeks recovery within the potential coverage of the policy. See the critical Note, 14 U.C.L.A. L. Rev. 1328 (1967). See further Prudential Ins. Co. v. Lumme, 83 Nev. 146, 425 P.2d 346 (1967). See also Kamarick, Opening the Gate: The *Steven* Case and the Doctrine of Reasonable Expectations, 29 Hastings L.J. 153 et seq. (1977-1978); Tobriner & Grodin, The Individual and the Public Service Enterprise in the New Industrial State, 55 Calif. L. Rev. 1247, 1272-1278 (1967); Meyer, Contracts of Adhesion and the Doctrine of Fundamental Breach, 15 Va. L. Rev. 1178, 1188 (1964); Keeton, Insurance Law Rights at Variance with Policy Provisions, 83 Harv. L. Rev. 961, 968 (1970).

155. Prudential Ins. Co. v. Lumme, 83 Nev. 146, 425 P.2d 346 (1967). As Professor Keeton points out, many of the cases that purport to interpret unambiguous policy terms are best explained as denying enforcement to unconscionably harsh provisions. Keeton, *supra* note 112, at 360.

156. Logan v. John Hancock Mutual Life Insurance Co., 41 Cal. App. 3d 988, 116 Cal. Rptr. 528 (1974); Bowler v. Fidelity and Casualty Co., 53 N.J. 313, 327, 250 A.2d 285 (1966); contra, Mutual of Omaha Insurance Co. v. Russell, 402 F.2d 339 (10th Cir. 1968), *cert. denied*, 394 U.S. 973 (1969).

the parties to a contract of insurance from their relationship, as well as from the consensual transaction itself.[157] This should not be understood as a denial of the contractual nature of the insurance contract. But although such contracts are entered voluntarily the range of obligations they create is defined in part by the role of insurance companies in our industrial society.[158] To this extent, the evolution of American case law may be an illustration of the thesis developed by Zweigert and Kötz that freedom of contract has found a limitation in the demands for contractual justice.[159]

Section 4.   Franchises and the New Feudalism

During the last decades, franchising has experienced a phenomenal growth in the United States.[160] Despite considerable differences in detail among the various types of franchises used in different lines of business, franchising can roughly be described as the system of vertical contractual integration of the distribution of goods and services.[161] It enables the franchisor to reach the consumer with the help of authorized intermediaries and at the same time to exercise the control deemed necessary to achieve an effective distribution system. More often than not, the franchisee is identified as a "member of the franchisor's family."[162]

The franchised dealer is a businessman who is neither an employee of the franchisor nor an independent retailer who (ideally, at least) is free to

157. Tobriner & Grodin, *supra* note 154, at 1247, 1272-1278; Kamarick, *supra* note 154; Restatement Second §§211 & Comment *f*, 206, 208.

158. Isaacs, The Standardization of Contracts, 27 Yale L.J. 34, 47-48 (1917); Tobriner & Grodin, *supra* note 154. Some courts and text writers have attempted to strengthen their discussion by labeling insurance policies contracts to adhesion. According to Keeton, *supra* note 112, at 360, insurance contracts are contracts of adhesion since most insurance policy provisions are still drafted by insurers and supervision is, on the whole, relatively inefficient. The weakness of this argument becomes apparent when we realize that no air traveler, for example, has to take out expensive air trip insurance; the same is true for many other kinds of insurance policies as well. For the loss ratio in air travel insurance, see Young, *supra* note 113, at 48-58. See in general Patterson, The Interpretation and Construction of Contracts, 64 Colum. L. Rev. 833, 855 et seq. (1964).

159. 2 K. Zweigert & H. Kötz, An Introduction to Comparative Law 9 (T. Weir trans. 1977).

160. The Franchising Sourcebook (J. McCall ed. 1970); D. Thompson, Franchise Operations and the Antitrust (1971); E. McGuire, Franchised Distribution (The Conference Board, 1971).

161. Preston & Schramm, Dual Distribution and its Impact on Marketing Organization, 8 Calif. Mgmt. Rev. 59, 61 (1965).

162. Bushwick-Decatur Motors, Inc. v. Ford Motor Co., 116 F.2d 675, 678 (2d Cir. 1940): " 'Once a Ford dealer, always a Ford dealer'; . . . by the dealership contract the plaintiff had become a member of the great Ford family. . . ."

"In virtually all the cases . . . the franchise activity represents the major, if not the sole business of the franchisor." Thompson, *supra* note 160, at 6.

choose his own supplies. This arrangement dispenses with the need for the supplier to combine production and distribution under one ownership, something that many manufacturers may be unable to afford financially.[163]

Franchising is found in all phases of the process of distributing goods or services, or both.[164] It may link manufacturer and wholesaler, wholesaler and retailer, or cooperatives and their members. Franchisor and franchisee, ideally, have one goal in common: the protection and development of the commodities carrying the trademark or brand name of the franchisor.[165] In this sense the trademark or trade name is the cornerstone of the franchise system.[166]

Given the great variety of franchise types, it is not surprising that the term "franchise" has been used rather indiscriminately in the business world and in statutory definitions,[167] and that all attempts at a uniform system of regulation seem doomed to failure.[168]

There appears to be agreement in the legal literature that the franchise is a contract sui generis. It is neither a sales nor a pure agency contract, and it is more than a mere license.[169] Franchising, according to a widely held view, is an institution that has introduced a new type of enterprise. The franchise method of operation, in the words of an often cited opinion, "has the advantage, from the standpoint of our American system of competitive enterprise economy, of enabling numerous groups of individuals with small amounts of capital to become enterpreneurs. If our economy had not developed that system of operation, these individuals would have turned out to be merely employees."[170]

Under the franchise system, the distribution of the product is limited

---

163. See, e.g., the arguments of counsel for appellant in White Motor Co. v. United States, 372 U.S. 253, 258 (1963), in defense of territorial and customer restriction clauses. Chrysler has used upstream integration less than its competitors. Ownership integration, however, has been growing in recent years. Thompson, *supra* note 160, at 40.

164. Thompson, *supra* note 160, at 17 et seq. Trademark licensing franchise systems, which have to be distinguished from products franchise systems, will not be discussed in this section. For discussion, see Thompson, *supra* note 160, at 12-17. Examples include restaurants, such as Howard Johnson's, and motels, such as the Holiday Inn. This type of franchise is included in the broad definition of franchises contained in the proposed Franchise Distribution Act of 1967, S. 2507, 90th Cong., 1st Sess. §3(a).

165. Thompson, *supra* note 160, at 17. On the importance of the Lanham Act (15 U.S.C. 1051-1157) for quality control, see Treece, Trademark Licensing and Vertical Restraints in Franchising Agreements, 116 U. Pa. L. Rev. 435 (1968).

166. See the franchise definitions in Bohling, Franchise Termination under the Sherman Act: Populism and Relational Power, 53 Tex. L. Rev. 1180 n.2 (1975).

167. The definitions of franchise used by the Senate Select Committee on Small Business have constantly been expanded.

168. See *infra* p. 603.

169. Note, 74 Colum. L. Rev. 1487, 1488 (1974).

170. Susser v. Carvel Corp., 206 F. Supp. 636, 640 (S.D.N.Y. 1962), *aff'd*, 332 F.2d 505 (2d Cir. 1964), *cert. dismissed*, 381 U.S. 125 (1965). See further Douglas, J., dissenting in Standard Oil Co. v. United States, 337 U.S. 293, 319, 321 (1949); Atlantic Refining Co. v. F.T.C., 33 F.2d 394, 400 (7th Cir. 1964), *aff'd*, 381 U.S. 357 (1965), *infra* p. 647; Wilson, An Emerging Enforcement Policy for Franchising, 15 N.Y.L.F. 1 (1969).

to chosen retailers in each community. In return for a franchise fee, or a commission on gross sales, or the obligation to buy equipment or supplies from the parent company (or a combination of all of these features), they are entitled to hold themselves out as authorized dealers, using the brand name or trademark of the manufacturer along with their own name in advertising, signs, or displays.[171]

The unique advantage of franchising for the manufacturer lies in the considerable amount of control he gains over the process of distribution without exposing himself to the burden and responsibility of an agency relationship.[172] Ideally, the dealers are carefully chosen from among those of proven ability. Selected dealers, experience has shown, tend to be more aggressive in cultivating the market and servicing the product. They are generally cooperative in carrying out the manufacturer's program of selling. And the franchises of dealers who do not prove their worth can be eliminated by cancellation or nonrenewal. Manufacturers may require satisfactory sales performance, provide for exclusive dealing and tying (often justified to achieve quality control), or require territorial and customer restrictions and suggested list prices if not resale price maintenance. Some of these restrictions (such as exclusive dealing and territorial and customer restriction, location clauses, areas of primary responsibility and profit "pass over" agreements) have the function of limiting intra- as contrasted with interbrand competition.[173]

In return, the franchise dealer receives from the manufacturer added capacity to build and maintain a strong retail organization. Restriction of outlets tends to protect the dealer's inventory and planned investment. Moreover, the nature of the relationship fosters mutual dependence and the dealer can expect the manufacturer to assist him in effective merchandising. The dealer also obtains increased prestige through affiliation within a large organization, frequently of national scope.

Finally, the consumer, we are told, gets better service under the franchise system and is assured that the retailer carries a complete stock of the manufactured products.

But however great these advantages, the franchise system is not free from shortcomings and frictions. The manufacturer may suffer because the dealer, sheltered by the restriction of outlets, does not make a maximum effort. The uncooperative dealer may lose his franchise and, to the extent that it is built around a popular trademark or brand name, his

171. H. Kursh, The Franchise Boom 14 (1962), as quoted by Thompson, *supra* note 160, at 6.

172. The text of this and the three paragraphs that follow are taken from Kessler & Brenner, Automobile Dealer Franchises: Vertical Integration by Contract, 66 Yale L.J. 1135, 1136 (1957).

173. Thompson, *supra* note 160, at 43 et seq. ABA Antitrust Section, Vertical Restrictions Limiting Intrabrand Competition 3-4, 20-25 (Monograph No. 2, 1977); P. Areeda, Antitrust Analysis 498-665 (2d ed. 1974). In automobile distribution many of these restrictions have been considerably revised; see, e.g., the 1985 Chevrolet Franchise, Article 2.

business. And because of a lack of outlet competition, consumers may pay unreasonably high prices or be at the mercy of a dealer whose services are inadequate. Small wonder that some of the mechanisms of control used by the manufacturer, typically laid down in a written document, were (and still are) a constant source of complaint on the part of dealers and their organizations, particularly in the field of automobile and gasoline distribution. But it would be a mistake to assume that dealers on the whole are opposed to any and all restrictions imposed by their franchise agreements. Experience has taught us that many restrictions on competition require for their success the cooperation of the dealer.[174]

It is inherent in some of these control mechanisms that they restrain competition and thus present serious antitrust problems, particularly if one agrees with Justice Black that the preservation of competition is a fundamental goal of antitrust policy.[175] As a result, conflicts between the interests of the franchisor and the franchisee and the public have become inevitable and the courts have not always been up to the task of striking a balance between them.

The field of franchises is so wide that it cannot be covered in toto. The discussion in this section, therefore, will concentrate primarily on automobile and secondarily on gasoline retailing, both of which have experienced phenomenal growth and produced very detailed franchise contracts.

In automobile franchising[176] the modern franchise enables a powerful manufacturer to wield great "vertical power" over retail operations. The

174. United States v. General Motors Corp., 384 U.S. 127 (1966), gives a good illustration; also Ford Motor Co. v. Webster Auto Sales, Inc., 361 F.2d 874 (1st Cir. 1966). See further the attitude of the dealers toward Fair Trade Laws.

175. Northern Pacific Railway Co. v. United States 356 U.S. 1, 4 (1957):

The Sherman Act was designed to be a comprehensive charter of economic liberty aimed at preserving free and unfettered competition as the rule of trade. It rests on the premise that the unrestrained interaction of competition will yield the best allocation of our economic resources, the lowest prices, the highest quality and the greatest material progress, while at the same time providing an environment conducive to the preservation of our democratic political and social institutions. But even if the premise is open to question, the policy unequivocally laid down by the Sherman Act is competition.

176. The best and most comprehensive description of automobile franchising is to be found in S. Macaulay, Law and Balance of Power, the Automobile Manufacturers and Their Dealers (1966) (hereinafter called Macaulay). See also id., The Standard Contracts of United States Automobile Manufacturers, Int'l Enc. of Comp. Law, ch. 3, at 18 et seq. (1973) [hereinafter called Macaulay II]; J. Palamountain, The Politics of Distribution, ch. 5 (1955). J. Dawson, W. Harvey & S. Henderson, Cases and Comment on Contracts 249-254 (4th ed. 1982), have given us an admirable summary which is indispensable reading; see also Weiss, Comment, The Automobile Dealers Franchise, 48 Cornell L.Q. 71 (1963); Kessler & Brenner, supra note 172; Kessler & Stern, Competition, Contract and Vertical Integration, 69 Yale L.J. 103-114 (1959). (The interpretation of The Dealers' Day in Court Act offered here, infra p. 641, is not identical with the one offered in this last article. See id. at 105 n.475 (1959)). See further B. Pashigian, The Distribution of Automobiles, An Economic Analysis of the Franchise System (1961).

franchise is embodied in a detailed standardized contract presented by the manufacturer to the dealer. The master contract is frequently accompanied by printed addenda concerning such matters as capital requirements and succession. Foremost among his duties is the duty to give "adequate sales performance" (adequate representation) and to give satisfactory service to owners in his territory. In the beginning the test of adequate performance was the manufacturer's "satisfaction"; objective criteria were introduced later.[177] In addition, there are clauses dealing with operating requirements. Under this heading fall provisions prescribing and defining satisfactory location of the dealer's place of business, and regulating sales and service facilities, parts, accessories, used car sales, advertising, and sales personnel. Furthermore, the dealer, in the interest of establishing production schedules and evaluating current market trends, has to submit every month a "three months' estimate of requirements" and a "ten day report showing retail sales of both new and used cars made during that period, new and used car stocks, and unfilled orders on hand at the end of said period." The high degree of standardization is best illustrated by the "entire agreement" clause. Patterned after provisions frequently found in insurance policies, the modern franchise states that it supersedes all prior agreements, that it constitutes the "entire agreement of the parties," and that only certain executives of the manufacturer, usually the vice president or sales manager, have authority to alter the written contract.

The terms of the franchise contract, however elaborate, do not give a complete picture of the dealership as an institution. "[They] do not show that 'priceless ingredient' of prime importance — namely, the manner in which the contract is administered."[178] The policies and practices of the manufacturer may be made relevant with the help of skillfully drafted clauses in the franchise agreement. But often the dealer must comply simply because of the economic power of the manufacturer. A prospective dealer, to be sure, is free to accept or reject a dealer franchise. Once he has committed his capital and entered the business, however, the power of the manufacturer comes into operation. The dealer must, on pain of cancellation or non-renewal, accede to the demands which the manufacturer, in the interest of market penetration, deems necessary and reasonable.

The duties of the dealer are backed up by a powerful sanction: the power of cancellation or nonrenewal of the franchise. Early automobile franchise contracts reflected the seasonal fluctuation in demand for the product. Franchises typically provided for termination at the end of a

177. Macaulay, *supra* note 176, at 83.
178. F.T.C. Report on Motor Vehicle Industry 139 (1939). See Hearings Before the Subcomm. on Antitrust and Monopoly of the Senate Comm. of the Judiciary, 89th Cong., 1st Sess., pt. 1 at 69, 164 (1965); 7 Hearings Before the Subcomm. on Antitrust and Monopoly of the Senate Comm. on the Judiciary, 84th Cong., 1st Sess. 3194 (1955).

model year. In addition, the manufacturer could cancel for cause. The growing financial strength of manufacturers was reflected by changes in duration clauses; the contract, though often providing for automatic extension if not canceled, terminated or superseded by a new agreement — thus giving the semblance of a permanent arrangement — could be terminated by either party on short notice, even without cause. The manufacturer alone profited from such clauses; for the dealer who had to protect his investment, the power to terminate was usually empty.

Over the protests of its dealers, General Motors in 1944 returned to a one-year franchise that could be terminated for cause. This modification may have been motivated by a desire to escape regulatory provisions enacted by state legislatures prohibiting the manufacturer from canceling "unfairly and without regard to the equities." Whatever its origin, the change enabled the manufacturer to accomplish by nonrenewal what it had been able to do before by cancellation, without fear of court intervention. Under this type of contract, General Motors has hardly ever needed to invoke the cancellation for cause provisions.[179]

By way of compensation, the dealer in the past was given a protected territory, safe against the raids of outsiders, originally including even the manufacturer. Gradually, the latter reserved for itself the qualified right to sell directly within the dealer's territory and insisted on the right to appoint other dealers within that territory. The resulting nonexclusive dealership was, however, still protected against raiding by outsiders, cross-selling, and bootlegging. Cross-selling refers to selling to residents of another franchised dealer's territory. Bootlegging means selling to another nonfranchised dealer for resale. The benefits of a protected territory were lost altogether for the dealer in the late '40s and early '50s.[180]

The law on automobile dealer franchises, dating from the early history of the industry, dramatically reveals unending attempts by dealers to break the vertical power of the manufacturer, exercised through the franchise terms. These efforts have been only partially successful. This is by and large true of attempts to stop burdensome practices, particularly "wrongful" terminations, with the help of the common law of contracts. Courts respecting the principle of freedom of contract have been unwilling to tamper with termination clauses, or to impose a duty to renew a franchise.[181]

By contrast, the impact of the antitrust laws on the terms of franchises, if not on merchandising practices, has been considerable. Many restric-

179. Macaulay, *supra* note 176, at 82.
180. Note, Restricted Channels of Distribution Under the Sherman Act, 75 Harv. L. Rev. 795 (1962); Note, Restrictive Distribution Arrangements After the Schwinn Case, 53 Cornell L.Q. 514 (1968).
181. Bushwick-Decatur Motors, Inc. v. Ford Motor Co., 116 F.2d 675 (2d Cir. 1940). For the challenging suggestion to better the lot of the dealer with the help of notions of good faith and unconscionability, see Gellhorn, Limitations on Contract Termination Rights — Franchise Cancellations, 1967 Duke L.J. 465.

tive clauses were regarded as inimical to competition and have disappeared as the result of antitrust decisions[182] or because of advice from the Department of Justice. This was true for clauses favoring the dealer, such as territory security provisions that prohibit cross-selling[183] and bootlegging, as well as clauses favoring the manufacturer, such as provisions on exclusive representation, tying arrangements,[184] and customer restrictions. Thus, the dealer had to pay a price for his greater freedom; also it must not be overlooked that the manufacturer has been able to maintain dealer "loyalty" in exchange for granting dealers some of the benefits of exclusive representation as well as the use of complimentary products and services without express franchise provision. Convenience, and the risk of non-renewal, have powerfully reinforced dealer loyalty. In vain, dealers have attempted to overcome the strong position of the manufacturer in this regard with the help of private antitrust suits. Repeated attempts of canceled or nonrenewed dealers to show that cancellation or nonrenewal was due to their refusal to abide by clauses aimed at the restriction of competition have been unsuccessful. The dealer had to be satisfied to be an incidental beneficiary of government intervention against restrictive arrangements that unlawfully foreclose the market, but such intervention against specific cancellations or instances of nonrenewal has not occurred in the context of a private antitrust suit.[185]

To sum up, the dealers did not succeed in achieving one of their main goals: protection against "arbitrary" termination or nonrenewal, provided the manufacturer stayed within the terms of the franchise. Nor did the dealers succeed in obtaining "territorial security." The franchisor was, and still is, permitted to restrict the dealer's territory according to changes in market conditions and to unilaterally appoint other dealers. A weak manufacturer was even permitted to terminate one of his dealers and to give a binding, exclusive franchise to a remaining dealer, provided market dominance was not an issue and close substitutes were readily available.[186] Exclusive dealing clauses are no longer found in automobile fran-

---

182. Franchising Sourcebook (J. McCord ed. 1970); Commercial Law and Practice, Sourcebook Series No. 2, 456-457 (Practicing Law Institute).

183. See generally Franchising Sourcebook, *supra* note 182.

184. See United States Department of Justice, Vertical Restraint Guidelines, Section 2.5 (1985). Pass-over arrangements require a dealer to compensate other dealers for sales made in their territory. All these arrangements are presumably cost saving and therefore pro-competitive devices, and consequently subject to a rule of reason approach. See Continental TV, Inc. v. GTE Sylvania, 433 U.S. 36 (1977), discussed *supra* p. 62. Tying arrangements are illegal only if the seller has market power in the tying product, the tying and tied products are separate, and there is a substantial adverse affect on the market of the tied product. Jefferson Parish Hospital District Co. #2 v. Hyde, 104 S. Ct. 155 (1984).

185. The leading case of Nelson Radio & Supply Co. v. Motorola, Inc., 200 F.2d 911 (5th Cir. 1952), *cert. denied*, 345 U.S. 925 (1953), has formed a formidable obstacle. See, however, Emich Motors Corporation v. General Motors Corporation, 181 F.2d 70 (7th Cir. 1950); the case was apparently settled out of court.

186. Packard Motor Car Co. v. Webster Motor Car Co., 243 F.2d 418 (D.C. Cir. 1956), *cert. denied*, 358 U.S. 822 (1957).

chises.[187] The industry can afford to live with nonexclusive franchises by insisting on clauses requiring market penetration and sales quotas, or clauses that commit the franchisee to concentrate his efforts in a specific geographic territory for which he is primarily responsible.[188] These requirements, the violation of which may lead to cancellation or nonrenewal, have been a constant source of complaints.

While admitting that the manufacturer should have the power to weed out inefficient dealers and replace them with efficient ones, dealers and their organizations have challenged the power of the manufacturer to summarily terminate franchises, even though the terms of the franchise permit the manufacturer to do so. Similarly, they have complained that there is no duty to renew the franchise after its expiration date and to take into account the "equities of the dealer," i.e., his investment and good will. As a result it was claimed (and not without justification), that many efficient dealers suffered heavy losses on their investments.[189]

Since the dealers and their organizations felt that neither common law nor antitrust law afforded enough protection, they turned for help to the legislatures, both federal and state.

On the federal level, a 1956 statute, The Automobile Dealers' Day in Court Act,[190] provided damages for losses sustained by a dealer through the failure of a manufacturer to act "in good faith" in performing, termi-

---

187. The interesting Note, Restricted Channels of Distribution under the Sherman Act, 795 Harv. L. Rev. (1962), does not deal with one type of exclusive representation: the prohibition of so-called dual lining, the privilege of the dealer to deal with automobiles produced by different companies. This type of exclusiveness has been dropped. An example is afforded by the Autocenter in San Francisco whose owner has consolidated five franchises. "Dual lining" has the advantage for the dealer to alleviate his dependency on one manufacturer. See in general N.Y. Times, April 15, 1985, Business Day, at 21-31.

188. Primary responsibility clauses are described in United States v. General Motors Corp., 384 U.S. 127 (1966). The case gives a specimen. Their legality was upheld in Continental T.V., Inc., v. GTE Sylvania, Inc., 433 U.S. 36 (1977). For the economic justification, see R. Posner, Antitrust 564 (1974). "Profit pass-over" arrangements were introduced to protect the dealer from inroads into "his" territory. Their legality is discussed in Justice Brennan's concurring opinion in White Motor Car Co. v. United States, 372 U.S. 253 (1963).

189. The number of dealerships has fallen from about 45,000 in the 1950s to about 25,000 in the 1980s. The survivors are larger and stronger. They have grown in size and density. No attempt is made to predict the future of automobile dealer franchises, but we can expect rather substantial changes in the foreseeable future due to manufacturers' attempts to cut distribution costs. The attempt of Porsche, the West German manufacturer, to convert its dealerships into simple sales agents, with delivery to them to be made from company-owned Porsche centers, was successfully fought by the dealers. But we can expect the new franchise available to dealers of the Saturn car (produced by a separate company owned by General Motors) to be streamlined in the interest of cost reduction. Furthermore, the new franchise available to Merkur dealerships gives the Ford Motor Company a greater amount of leeway than the traditional Ford franchises. See the N.Y. Times article, *supra* note 187.

190. 15 U.S.C.A. 1221. For the history of the act, see Macaulay, *supra* note 176, and for the impact of the Hearings on franchising reform, see Macaulay II, *supra* note 176, at 3-36, n.51.

nating, or not renewing the dealer's franchise.[191] The history of the act is quite interesting. As introduced in the Senate, good faith was defined so as to impose upon the manufacturer, its officers, employees, and agents a duty:

> To act in a fair, equitable and non-arbitrary manner so as to guarantee the dealer freedom from coercion, in order to preserve and to protect all the equities of the automobile dealer which are inherent in the nature of the relationship between the automobile dealer and automobile manufacturer.[192]

As passed by the Senate, the bill defined good faith to include the action of both parties. But only the dealer was given a cause of action for breach of the duty to act in good faith. The manufacturer was limited to using lack of good faith as a defensive weapon in suits brought by the dealer.[193]

As finally passed, the bill incorporates further amendments introduced in the House of Representatives. The most important changes were an antitrust savings clause and a rewording of the good faith provision.

> The term "good faith" shall mean the duty of each party to any franchise, and all officers, employees or agents thereof, to act in a fair and equitable manner toward each other so as to guarantee the one party freedom from coercion or intimidation from the other party; Provided, That recommendation, endorsement, exposition, persuasion, urging, or argument shall not be deemed to constitute a lack of good faith.[194]

Thus, coercion or intimidation was made an essential element of bad faith. Given this narrow interpretation, a manufacturer is not prevented from terminating a franchise at will or not renewing a franchise after the expiration date so long as he stays within the terms of the franchise,

---

191. As to the "hybrid" nature of the damage action, see Dawson, Harvey & Henderson, *supra* note 176, at 300, citing American Motors Sales Corp. v. Semke, 384 F.2d 192 (10th Cir. 1967). As the authors point out, citing Hanly v. Chrysler Motor Corporation, 433 F.2d 708 (10th Cir. 1970), the statute of limitations controlling actions for breach of contract does not apply, but rather "a shorter period for wrongs unconnected with contract" (at 300 n.4).

Although The Automobile Dealers' Day in Court Act does not mention injunctions, they have played an increasing role in helping dealers secure the continuation of their franchises. Temporary injunctions have been used to protect dealers during the length of the trial. Semmes Motor Co. v. Ford Motor Co., 429 F.2d 1197, 1297 (2d Cir. 1970). See in general Note, 74 Yale L.J. 454 (1964). On the expansion of the remedies of the dealer beyond the existing antitrust laws, see Kessler & Stern, *supra* note 176, at 107.

192. S. 3879, 84th Cong., 2d Sess. §3 (1956).

193. Id. §2.

194. Milos v. Ford Motor Company, 317 F.2d 712 (3d Cir. 1963); Dawson & Harvey, *supra* note 176, at 300.

absent any finding of coercion or intimidation.[195] "A franchise," as one court observed, "is not a marriage for life . . . no protection should extend longer than the termination made in good faith."[196] Under this narrow interpretation, a goodly number of courts were persuaded to permit a franchisor to terminate a dealer for failure to meet his commitments, including stringent requirements as to adequate representation.[197]

In recent years, decisions favoring the dealer have been on the increase.[198] Still, these victories have been considered by the dealers themselves to be rather meager,[199] especially since the dealers' grievance boards, established by the manufacturers, are generally thought to be ineffective. Franchise revisions, conceded by the manufacturers under pressure, have likewise often been regarded as inadequate.[200]

Numerous attempts have been made to improve the dealers' position by introducing into Congress additional legislation providing for fairness of termination or nonrenewal and protecting the "equities of the dealer." But until now these bills, applicable to dealerships in general, have been unsuccessful.[201] One reason for their lack of success is the fact that they use a broad definition of franchise and fail to discriminate among various types of franchises.[202] The latest attempt at improving the lot of the dealer

195. Garvin v. American Motors Sales Corporation, 318 F.2d 518 (3d Cir. 1963); Victory Motors of Savannah, Inc. v. Chrysler Motors Corp., 357 F.2d 429 (5th Cir. 1966); Kotula v. Ford Motor Co., 338 F.2d 732 (8th Cir. 1964), *cert. denied*, 380 U.S. 979 (1964); Sink v. Ford Motor Co., 549 F. Supp. 245 (E.D. Mich, S.D. 1982); Howard v. Chrysler Motor Corp., 705 F.2d 1285 (10th Cir. 1983); Kizzier Chevrolet v. G.M., 705 F.2d 323 (8th Cir. 1983). See further Ed Houser Enterprises, Inc. v. General Motors Corp., 595 F.2d 366 (4th Cir. 1979); Autohaus Brugger, Inc. v. Saab Motors, Inc., 567 F.2d 901 (9th Cir. 1978).

196. Bateman v. Ford Motor Co., 302 F.2d 63, 66-67 (3d Cir. 1962) the dealer nevertheless succeeded in obtaining a preliminary injunction.

197. For the difficulties courts are confronted with when dealing with this issue, see Dawson, Harvey, & Henderson, *supra* note 176. For the limitation of the privilege to terminate for not giving adequate representation see the cases in the following footnote.

For a criticism of the narrow conception of coercion see Macaulay, in Hearings before the Subcomm. on Antitrust and Monopoly of the Comm. on the Judiciary, United States Senate, 90th Cong., 1st Sess. (1967). For a broader interpretation of coercion see Kessler & Stern, Competition, Contract and Vertical Integration, 69 Yale L.J. 105-109 (1959): coercion is always present if the manufacturer forces the dealer to engage in activities that violate the antitrust laws. This interpretation was followed in Autowest, Inc. v. Peugeot, Inc., 434 F.2d 556, 561 (2d Cir. 1970).

198. Rea v. Ford Motor Co., 497 F.2d 577 (3d Cir. 1974). See further Madsen v. Chrysler Motors Corp., 261 F. Supp. 488 (1966) (dismissed as moot by the Circuit Court of Appeals in 375 F.2d 773 (1967)); Swartz v. Chrysler Motor Corp., 297 F. Supp. 834 (D.N.J. 1969) (temporary injunction); Mt. Lebanon Motors Co. v. Chrysler Corp., 283 F. Supp. 453 (W.D. Pa. 1968) (failure to meet MSR (Minimum Sales Responsibility) arbitrarily applied to plaintiff but not to other dealers); Jay Edwards, Inc. v. New England Toyota, 708 F.2d 814 (1st Cir. 1983), *cert. denied*, 104 S. Ct. 241 (1983); see further 54 A.L.R.3d 324 (1974).

199. Von Kalinowski, Antitrust Laws and Trade Regulation §65.03[2] (1972); Freed, a Study of Dealers' Suits under The Automobile Dealers' Day in Court Act, 41 U. Det. L.J. 245 (1964).

200. See Macaulay, *supra* note 176, at 73.

201. Zeidman, The View from Capitol Hill, in The Franchising Sourcebook 214-246 (J. McCord ed. 1970).

202. Id. at 235.

is H.R. 298, 98th Cong, 1st Sess. (1983), which again does not distinguish among franchises of different sorts.[203] But this failure to enact a "good cause" act does not mean that dealers have been completely unsuccessful on the federal level. In 1979, the Federal Trade Commission established minimum standards of disclosure applicable to all franchises and business offerings.[204]

On the state level, the dealers have been more successful. As a matter of fact, state legislation antedated federal legislation. Early on, dealers succeeded in persuading many state legislatures to enact statutes that permitted the franchisor to terminate only for "good cause."[205] In addition, they succeeded in introducing grievance procedures that provided for the cancellation of the license of any franchisor who acted unfairly. "Baby" F.T.C. acts using the Federal Trade Commission Act as a model to prevent unfair methods of competition and unfair or deceptive trade practices have also become quite common.[206]

Of particular interest is the Massachusetts Fair Dealing Act of 1971, substantially amended in 1977 (M.G.L.A., ch. 93B, implemented by ch. 93A and patterned after the F.T.C. Act). According to the proud statement of its author, it has introduced a "bill of rights for dealers" and expresses the idea that a franchise is not a contractual arrangement but a status: "Such a relationship . . . is made akin to a marriage, contractual in its inception, but otherwise subject to tenure on the ground of public policy."[207]

To further its goal, the statute prohibits "any action which is arbitrary, in bad faith, or unconscionable and which causes damage to any of such parties or to the public." The statute contains a lengthy catalog of activities that constitute violations.[208] Among these provisions, §4(3)(e) is of particular interest. It contains a prohibition against cancellation or termination of the franchise or selling agreement without good cause and without giving notice within a specific period; it prohibits a refusal to

---

203. Another recent attempt is H.R. 5416, which is reprinted in H. Brown, Franchising — Realities and Remedies 428-436 (2d ed. 1978). No attempt will be made to predict the future of franchising as a result of changes in the structure of the economic system. For a report on the decline of the number of dealerships, see 102 Fortune 54 (August 25, 1980).

204. Disclosure Requirements and Prohibitions Concerning Franchising and Business Opportunity Ventures, 16 C.F.R. 436; Comment, 40 Ohio St. L.J. 387 (1979). To strengthen its requirements Uniform Offering Circulars have been introduced on the state level. The Illinois specimen is printed in Brown, supra note 203, in Appendix B.

205. Macaulay II, supra note 176, at 3-36. Brown, supra note 203, at 199 et seq. Some of these statutes apply to franchises in general. See further Note, 33 Vand. L. Rev. 385, 403 (1980), which discusses the constitutional problems involved. As of 1980, only three states had no laws regarding termination, cancellation, and nonrenewal of franchises and dealerships: Alabama, Oregon, and Wyoming. Eaton, State Regulation of Franchise and Dealership Termination: An Overview, 49 Antitrust L.J. 1331 (1980).

206. Brown, supra note 203, at 183.

207. Brown, A Bill of Rights for Auto Dealers, 12 B.C. Ind. & Comm. L. Rev. 757 at 799 (1971).

208. See §4.

extend the franchise after the expiration date without good cause and without giving notice; it prohibits an offer to renew which contains terms and provisions that substantially change the sales and service obligations or capital requirements of the dealer arbitrarily and without good cause and without giving notice within a stated period. These provisions override any term or provision contained in a franchise or selling agreement. "Either party within the notice period may petition the superior court, which is provided with guidelines, to pass on the justification for cancellation, nonrenewal, or change of condition. The petition shall be entitled to a speedy trial."[209] Of special interest is a provision against granting to another dealership, arbitrarily and without notice, the right to conduct its business within the relevant market of an existing franchise.[210]

The constitutionality of the statute has been upheld.[211] As a result of these and similar statutes, dealers have succeeded in creating a new feudalism which gives them fiefdoms from which they can be dislodged by their overlords only with difficulty.

A discussion of gasoline dealer franchises will help to illustrate the evolution of the law of franchising.[212] The petroleum industry has the largest number of franchises, with 139,000 in 1983 — almost a third of the total. Although this is a decline from the 1970 figure of 222,000 (56% of all franchises), it remains true that more than 99% of gasoline service station sales are made through franchises.[213]

Instead of selling gasoline and petroleum products directly, the petroleum companies use numerous and conveniently located service stations run by "independent businessmen."[214] Although the term "franchise" is rarely used, the arrangement is in substance a franchise. Typically, there are two documents in standard form which together constitute the basis of the distributor relationship.[215] One is a distributor contract between the dealer and the company in which the dealer promises to buy the

209. Section 4(3)(e)(3).
210. Section 4(3)(1).
211. Tober Foreign Motors v. Reiher Oldsmobile, 376 Mass. 313, 381 N.E.2d 908 (1978). Several recent cases have declared state statutes resembling the Massachusetts statute to be unconstitutional on grounds that they unduly burden interstate commerce: American Motors Sales Corp. v. Division of Motor Vehicles of Virginia, 445 F. Supp. 902 (E.D. Va. 1978); General GMC Trucks v. General Motors Corp., 239 Georgia 373, 237 S.E.2d 194, *cert. denied* 434 U.S. 996 (1977). The *Tober* court distinguished the statutes at issue in these cases from the Massachusetts statute by pointing out that they required a blanket, rather than multifactored analysis (381 N.E.2d at 914). Under the Massachusetts statute, for example, one of the factors for analysis by the court is "whether the establishment of an additional franchise would increase competition and therefore be in the public interest." Section 4(3)(1)(viii).
212. In the following discussion of gasoline franchises we have made free use of teaching materials that Professor Stewart Macaulay has been kind enough to provide.
213. U.S. Bureau of the Census, Statistical Abstract of the United States, 1984, at 803-806 (10th ed. 1983). Jordan, Unconscionability at the Gas Station, 62 Minn. L. Rev. 813, 817 (1978); Comment, 4 U.S.F.L. Rev. 65 (1969); Note, 25 S.D.L. Rev. 69 (1980).
214. Thompson, *supra* note 160, at 21-22, giving the reason for the development.
215. Jordan, *supra* note 213.

franchisor's products — gas, oil, tires, batteries, and accessories (TBA) — in return for the use of the trademark. The other document deals with the property rights to the premises on which the station is located. Today, this typically takes the form of a lease, the distributor leasing the property from the oil company which has bought the land and erected the station; the equipment is also leased from the oil company or is given as a free loan.[216] Both agreements typically run from one to three years and provide for renewal, unless cancelled. But the clauses establishing the time schedules for the required notice of cancellation are not synchronized and typically favor the franchisor (the oil company producer), who in addition often has the power to cancel on short notice for cause determined at his own discretion.[217] The threat of eviction contributes to the insecurity of the gasoline dealer, who often regards his station as a means of selling automotive services (repair and maintenance) which he and not the oil company provides. The latter by contrast is interested in selling gasoline products.[218]

The precariousness of the dealer's position worsens once the dealer has contributed his capital and time to building up the franchise. The degree of independent business judgment allowed the dealer is further threatened, though not as much as in the past, by clauses concerning the exclusiveness of the arrangement, the price to be charged for gasoline, the possibility of cutting the price in a price war, and the extent to which the dealer must stock the oil company's brand of oil, tires, and accessories.[219] Of particular importance is the right of the distributor to terminate the franchise on short notice so as to convert the station into a company-owned entity, a partial self-service station, a car wash, or an auto diagnostic shop, or to shut it down altogether.

In protecting the "independence" of the dealer, the antitrust laws have played and continue to play a significant role. Exclusive dealings were

216. The controversial issue of the availability of specific performance based on options to buy often granted to oil companies many years before and exercised much later during times of inflation, will not be discussed. This kind of distributorship belongs largely to the past when the distributor typically owned the premises. Some of these options are still outstanding; today, however, a number of courts would recognize the inflation factor and deny specific performance.

217. In the past, the reciprocal rights of the parties to a gasoline franchise agreement were rarely worked out with the degree of care given to automobile dealer franchises. Often the distribution agreement was (and still is) supplemented by informal understanding and trade custom concerning duration and other terms. On the effect of the parol evidence rule in this regard see Division of Triple T Service Inc. v. Mobil Oil Corp., 60 Misc. 2d 720, 304 N.Y.S.2d 191 (S. Ct. Westchester Co. 1969), aff'd without opinion, 34 A.D.2d 618, 311 N.Y.S.2d 961 (2d Dept. 1970). In the last paragraph of its lengthy opinion, the court, although sympathetic to the plight of successful dealers who had been canceled, took the position that it could not mitigate the harshness of the express contractual provisions by invoking the requirement of good faith termination, but expressed the hope that the opinion would give impetus to remedial legislation. See further notes 227 and 228 infra.

218. This conflict of interest is emphasized by Jordan, supra note 213, at 817.

219. Cf. Blanton v. Mobil Oil Corp., 721 F.2d 1207 (9th Cir. 1983).

seriously curtailed by the often misunderstood *Standard Stations* case,[220] which controlled the use of requirement contracts by the major oil companies to foreclose (collectively but not conclusively) a substantial part of the market to competitors. In the wake of the *Standard Stations* case, vertical retail price maintenance backed up by the threat of cancellation came under attack. A consent decree was entered into by the Pacific Coast producers which barred them from coercing dealers in order to maintain a price maintenance scheme. Still, the decree left the producers free to persuade dealers to sell at indicated prices.[221] It also left the oil producers free not to renew the franchises of their dealers.

Today, retail price maintenance, even if introduced unilaterally, is no longer protected by the Colgate Doctrine[222] if it is accompanied by a threat of termination or nonrenewal.[223] It runs afoul of the antitrust laws, and their application cannot be evaded by camouflaging the transaction as a consignment.[224]

The prohibition against tie-ins was extended by the so-called TBA Commission Plan cases, with the help of §5 of the Federal Trade Commission Act.[225] The "cease and desist" order of the F.T.C., designed to insure that dealers could not be coerced into pushing the brand of a third party tire manufacturer who was willing to pay a commission to the oil company, was upheld in a number of cases. The last of these, F.T.C. v. Texaco, even extended the category of coercion to include "inherent" coercion due to the dominant position of the producer and the activities of salesmen of the tire and gas companies.[226]

Until recently the antitrust laws did not accord protection against the cancellation or nonrenewal of franchise agreements regarded as unfair

220. 337 U.S. 293 (1949), discussed in Kessler & Stern, *supra* note 176, at 24 et seq. As to the misinterpretation by Frankfurter, J., of his own opinion, see F.T.C. v. Motor Picture Advertising Service Co., 344 U.S. 392 (1953); see Kessler & Stern, *supra*, at 51 et seq.

221. See United States v. Standard Oil Co. of California, Trade Reg. Rep. (1959 Trade Cas.) §69399 at XI-XII (S.D. Cal. June 19, 1959).

222. United States v. Colgate & Co., 250 U.S. 300 (1919), *supra* p. 59.

223. Sahm v. V-1 Oil Co., 402 F.2d 69 (10th Cir. 1968). The written one-year lease had a thirty-day termination clause. It was accompanied by an oral agreement providing for the consignment of gasoline to be retailed at prices set by the defendant. Plaintiff's profits were variable and depended in amount upon the retail price level set by the defendant. The two agreements constituted one agreement in the court's view, an agreement it held illegal under the Sherman Act.

224. Simpson v. Union Oil, 377 U.S. 13 (1963).

225. Atlantic Refining Co. v. F.T.C., 381 U.S. 357 (1965); Shell Oil Co. v. F.T.C., 360 F.2d 470, *cert. denied*, 385 U.S. 1002 (1967). As Wisdom, J., wrote in *Shell*, "a man operating a gas station is bound to be overawed by the great corporation that is his superior, his banker, and his landlord." Id. at 487.

226. F.T.C. v. Texaco, Inc., 393 U.S. 223 (1968); the sales commission system was regarded as inherently coercive, and despite absence of the kind of overtly coercive acts shown in *Atlantic*, *supra* note 225, Shell was found to have exerted its dominant economic power over the dealer. Of particular interest is the concurring opinion of Justice Harlan, which abandons the position he had taken in his dissent in the *Atlantic* case. See in general L. Sullivan, Antitrust 468 (1977).

(absent bad faith) and it was therefore only natural for dealers to shift the basis of their attacks. Early attempts to prevent domination of the dealer-lease contract by invoking the unconscionability provision of the Uniform Commercial Code (§2-302) were unsuccessful. The New York courts took the position that the franchise was not a sale of goods transaction and refused to treat the two documents as an integrated contract.[227] Other courts took the opposite view and treated the distribution arrangement as an integrated document, with the result that U.C.C. §2-302 was held applicable.[228]

Gasoline dealers and their associations next turned to state legislatures for help and succeeded in persuading a number of them to pass "good faith (good cause)" legislation severely restricting the franchisor's right of discretionary renewal. Most of these statutes are careful not to extend their domain to existing franchises, but several of the cases already mentioned, though controversial, have given these statutes retroactive effect by treating franchises as a fiduciary relationship that overrides short termination clauses or failures to renew.[229]

In 1978, Congress enacted the Petroleum Marketing and Practice Act, 15 U.S.C §§2801 et seq., which sets out the circumstances under which a service station franchise may be terminated or not renewed. The grounds for nonrenewal (i.e., failure to renew an existing franchise that has expired) and termination are treated separately, although a franchisor may fail to renew on any of the grounds for which he may terminate a franchise. The right to terminate is more circumscribed.

When a franchise comes up for renewal, the Act provides for negotia-

227. Division of Triple T Service, Inc. v. Mobil Oil Corp., *supra* note 217; Mobil Oil Co. v. Rubenfeld, 339 N.Y.S.2d 623 (Civ. Ct. N.Y.C. 1972). The opinion was reversed in 48 A.D.2d 428, 370 N.Y.S.2d 943 (2d Dept. 1975).

228. See Ashland Oil Co., Inc. v. Donahue, 223 S.E.2d 433 (W. Va. 1976); Shell Oil Co. v. Marinello, 63 N.J. 402, 307 A.2d 598 (1973), *cert. denied*, 415 U.S. 920 (1974). In *Marinello*, the provision to give Shell the absolute right to terminate on 10 days' notice was regarded as void because it violated public policy. Furthermore, as the court said,

> public policy requires that there be read into the existing lease and dealer agreement, and all future lease and dealer agreements which may be negotiated in good faith between the parties, the restriction that Shell not have the unilateral right to terminate, cancel or fail to renew the franchise, including the lease, in absence of a showing the Marinello has failed to substantially perform his cause. . . .

The *Marinello* case has received a considerable amount of criticism; see Note, Franchise Termination and Refusal to Renew: The Lanham Act and Preemption of State Regulation, 60 Iowa L. Rev. 122, 128-131 (1974); Jordan, *supra* note 213, at 826. The decision has the support of Arnott v. Athenium Oil Co., 609 F.2d 873, at 881 (8th Cir. 1979), which treats the dealer franchise as a fiduciary relationship. Ironically, a subsequent action in which a brother of the Marinello mentioned above sought retention of his own service station as well as treble damages from Shell for violation of the antitrust law, was unsuccessful in a federal district court (this decision was vacated by the court of appeals in 511 F.2d 853 (3d Cir. 1975).

229. See note 228 *supra*.

tion of new terms and conditions. The franchisor, however, is obligated to exercise good faith in negotiating the new franchise, and may not insist upon changes for the purpose of preventing renewal of the franchise relation.[230] 15 U.S.C. §2802(b)(3). A franchisor may terminate an existing franchise on several grounds, among them "[a] failure by the franchisee to comply with any provision of the franchise, which provision is both reasonable and of material significance to the franchise relationship. . . ." 15 U.S.C. §2802(b)(2)(A). The act has elaborate provisions for giving the franchisee advance notice of any defaults, and in many cases allows the franchisee a period of time to remedy past failures.[231]

The Act covers not only future franchises, but franchises existing at the effective date of its enactment. However, existing franchises are treated differently from future franchises in one important respect: when an existing franchise is terminated, the subsection on renewal and not the subsection on termination applies. In other words, a franchisor has the opportunity to renegotiate an existing franchise terminated after the effective date of the Act for reasons other than those set out in the subsection on termination. Congress felt that "[d]irect application of the provisions of the title, respecting termination of a franchise, to franchises entered into prior to the date of enactment [ought to be] avoided due to unanswered questions regarding the constitutionality of such a direct approach." 1978 U.S. Code Cong. & Administrative News 890.

---

230. Although the negotiations must be in good faith, a decision not to renew does not have to be based on a reasonable business judgment, nor does the franchisor have the responsibility to exhaust all possibilities to keep a franchise going. Brach v. Amoco, 677 F.2d 1213 (7th Cir. 1982). The franchisor may, for example, change a full-service station to a pump-only station. Baldauf v. Amoco, 700 F.2d 326 (6th Cir. 1983). Or the franchisor may impose additional requirements, for example, that the franchisee devote himself full-time to the operation of the franchise. Davy Enterprises Inc. v. Crown Central Petroleum Corp., 529 F. Supp. 1291 (D.C. Md. 1982).

If the franchisor is leasing the land from a third party, he is not required to negotiate with the franchisee before failing to renew the lease, although the franchisor must notify the franchisee "prior to the commencement of the term of the then existing franchise" that the lease might expire and not be renewed. Hifai v. Shell Oil Co., 180 N.J. Super. 399, 434 A.2d 1151 (1981); Veracka v. Shell Oil Co., 655 F.2d 445 (1st Cir. 1981). This requirement applies even where the lease is automatically renewed unless the franchisor takes affirmative action. See Finch, Judicial Interpretation of the Petroleum Marketing Practices Act: Strict Construction of Remedial Legislation, 37 Bus. Lawyer 141 (1981).

231. The PMPA requires 90-day notice for termination of a franchise resulting from the franchisee's failure to "exert good faith efforts to carry out the provision of the franchise." U.S.C.A. 2802(b)(2)(B). There is an exception for cases where such notice would be unreasonable. U.S.C.A. 2804(b)(1). This may prove to be the weak link in the franchisee's armor. At least one court has held that the provision in question refers only to "circumstances created by an outside agency, such as condemnation of the marketing premises." Escobar v. Mobil Oil Corp., 522 F. Supp. 593, 600 (D. Conn. 1981), rev'd on other grounds, 678 F.2d 398 (2d Cir. 1982) (per curiam). This view has since been rejected by the Second Circuit, in a case holding that it is reasonable to give short notice of termination for a failure to carry out some terms of the franchise itself. Wisser Co., Inc. v. Mobil Oil Corp., 730 F.2d 54 (2d Cir. 1984) (misbranding of gasoline).

Section 5. The Classical Struggle between Creditor and Debtor: Readjustment of a Going Business Deal and Discharge

It has often been observed that consideration is not one doctrine but many doctrines serving different purposes. The concept of consideration has often been manipulated in order to police the fairness of the contract process. Frequently, this has occurred in a rather mechanical way. To give one example, courts have frequently invoked the dogma that the performance of, or promise to perform, an already existing duty should not be treated as a sufficient consideration, instead of recognizing that the issue of fairness in such situations is best solved with the help of categories like duress, unconscionability, or public policy. In practically none of the court opinions in such cases "is there found a discussion for the reason for the rule and the policy on which it can be based."[232] "As a result, more appropriate doctrines were slow in coming."[233] The materials that follow may serve as illustrations. They also show how easy it is for an unscrupulous debtor to avoid the obstacles imposed by the doctrine of consideration. Without going as far as Lord Denning,[234] who claimed that performance of a preexisting duty is always good consideration, we can safely assert that it will often be the case that the demand of one of the contracting parties for an increase in his compensation is perfectly reasonable — if, for instance, during performance he has run into severe difficulties that were unanticipated by either party.[235] The problems in-

---

232. 1A Corbin §183. For a striking illustration of how courts can get entangled in the drapery of their own words, see McDevitt v. Stokes, 174 Ky. 515, 192 S.W. 681 (1917). Plaintiff, a jockey, was engaged to drive B's horse in the celebrated Kentucky Futurity Race in Lexington. The defendant, who owned the dam of B's horse, promised plaintiff a bonus of $1,000, should plaintiff win the race — which would entitle the defendant to a prize. Plaintiff, having won the race, sued for the unpaid balance of $800. According to the court defendant's promise was unsupported by consideration since plaintiff was already under a duty to make his best effort. This made it unnecessary to decide the public policy question. The Restatement Second has brought about a change in this regard. But Illustration 12 to §73 adds that B may have been entitled to the bonus, citing Restatement of Agency Second §§313, 338. The fallacy of the court's reasoning is exposed by W. W. Cook, The Utility of Jurisprudence with Solution of Legal Problems, in 5 Lectures on Legal Topics 337, 345 (1923-1924). On the policy reasons behind the preexisting legal obligation rule, see 1A Corbin on §§171, 172; Llewellyn, Common-Law Reform of Consideration: Are There Measures?, 41 Colum. L. Rev. 863, 867 (1941); Patterson, An Apology for Consideration, 58 Colum. L. Rev. 929, 936-938 (1958). Recall De Cicco v. Schweizer, supra p. 494.

233. Sharp, Pacta Sunt Servanda, 41 Colum. L. Rev. 783, 796 (1941); Kessler, Review of 1 Corbin, On Contracts, 61 Yale L.J. 1092, 1102 (1952).

234. Ward v. Byham, [1956] 1 W.L.R. 496, 498; Williams v. Williams, [1957] 1 W.L.R. 148, 151.

235. The problem of modification is of particular significance in long-term relations. See Macneil, Contracts: Adjustment of Long-Term Economic Relations under Classical, Neoclassical, and Relational Contract Law, 72 Nw. U.L. Rev. 854 (1978); Speidel, Court Imposed Price Adjustments Under Long-Term Supply Contracts, 76 Nw. U.L. Rev. 369 (1981).

volved in these situations can be more helpfully analyzed by asking whether one of the parties has taken unfair advantage of the other, than by speculating about the adequacy or inadequacy of the consideration each has received in exchange. Modern case and statutory law appears to be moving in this direction, albeit slowly.[236] Similar problems arise in the area of discharge. Since the impediment of a preexisting legal duty is of major importance to both modification and discharge (e.g., Foakes v. Beer[237]), these two topics will be discussed together.

STILK v. MYRICK

2 Camp. 317, 170 Eng. Rep. 1168 (K.B. 1809)

This was an action for seaman's wages, on a voyage from London to the Baltic and back.

By the ship's articles, executed before the commencement of the voyage, the plaintiff was to be paid at the rate of £5 a month; and the principal question in the cause was, whether he was entitled to a higher rate of wages. In the course of the voyage two of the seamen deserted, and the captain, having in vain attempted to supply their places at Cronstadt, there entered into an agreement with the rest of the crew that they should have the wages of the two who had deserted equally divided among them if he could not procure two other hands at Gottenburgh. This was found impossible and the ship was worked back to London by the plaintiff and eight more of the original crew with whom the agreement had been made at Cronstadt. . . .

LORD ELLENBOROUGH. I think Harris v. Watson [Peake, 72] was rightly decided; but I doubt whether the ground of public policy, upon which Lord Kenyon is stated to have proceeded, be the true principle on which the decision is to be supported. Here, I say, the agreement is void for want of consideration. There was no consideration for the ulterior pay promised to the mariners who remained with the ship. Before they sailed from London they had undertaken to do all they could under all the emergencies of the voyage. They had sold all their services till the voyage should be completed. If they had been at liberty to quit the vessel at Cronstadt, the case would have been quite different; or if the captain had

---

236. U.C.C. §§1-107, 1-201(19), 1-203, 2-103(1)(b), 2-209(1), 2-305, 2-306(1), 2-311(1), 2-323(a)&(b), 2-328(4), 2-403(1), 2-506(2), 2-603(3), 2-615(a), 2-702(3), 2-706(1), 2-712(1); Farnsworth, Good Faith Performance and Commercial Reasonableness under the Uniform Commercial Code, 30 U. Chi. L. Rev. 666 (1963); Summers, Good Faith in General Contract Law and the Sales Prohibitions of the Uniform Commercial Code, 54 Va. L. Rev. 195 (1968). For a skeptical view, see Powell, Good Faith in Contracts, 9 Current Legal Problems 16, 25 (1956); Hillman, Policing Contract Modifications under the U.C.C.: Good Faith and the Doctrine of Economic Duress, 64 Iowa L. Rev. 849 (1979). For other statutory materials, see pp. 549-551 *supra*; Restatement Second §89 Comment *c*.

237. See p. 668 *infra*.

capriciously discharged the two men who were wanting, the others might not have been compelled to take the whole duty upon themselves, and their agreeing to do so might have been a sufficient consideration for the promise of an advance of wages. But the desertion of a part of the crew is to be considered an emergency of the voyage as much as their death, and those who remain are bound by the terms of their original contract to exert themselves to the utmost to bring the ship in safety to her destined port. Therefore, without looking to the policy of this agreement, I think it is void for want of consideration, and that the plaintiff can only recover at the rate of £5 a month.

Verdict accordingly.

NOTE

Only the report in Campbell mentions consideration. The opinion in Espinasse (6 Esp. 129, 170 Eng. Rep. 851), which is often overlooked, turns on issues of public policy. Harris v. Carter, 3 E. & B. 559, 118 Eng. Rep. 1251 (1854), gives both reasons.

Suppose that the shortage of hands had been so great as to make the continuation of the voyage unsafe. Would the decision have been the same? Hartley v. Ponsonby, 7 E. & B. 872, 119 Eng. Rep. 1471 (1857); see further Liston v. S.S. Carpathian [owners], [1915] 2 K.B. 42; Restatement Second §73.

For a challenging discussion of the case see G. Gilmore, The Death of Contract 21-28, 115 n.57; on Harris v. Watson, id. at 25-28.

Consult Alaska Packers Assn. v. Domenico, 117 F. 99 (9th Cir. 1902), which is highly critical of Goebel v. Linn, *infra* p. 655.

LINGENFELDER v. THE WAINWRIGHT BREWING CO.

103 Mo. 578, 15 S.W. 844 (1890)

This was an action by Philipp J. Lingenfelder and Leo Rasieur, executors of Edmund Jungenfeld, against the Wainwright Brewing Company upon a contract for services as an architect.

GANTT, P.J. . . . The referee found that Jungenfeld, the plaintiffs' testator, was not entitled to the commission of five per cent on the cost of the refrigerator plant. He found that Jungenfeld's employment as architect was to design plans and make drawings and specifications for certain brewery buildings for the Wainwright Brewing Company and superintend their construction to completion for a commission of five per cent on the cost of the buildings. He found further that Jungenfeld's contract did not include the refrigerator plant, that was to be constructed in these buildings. He further found, and the evidence does not seem to admit of a doubt as to the propriety of his finding, that this refrigerator plant was ordered not only without Mr. Jungenfeld's assistance, but against his wishes. He was in no way connected with its erection.

> Mr. Jungenfeld was president of the Empire Refrigerator Company and largely interested therein. . . . The De La Vergne Ice Machine Company was a competitor in business. . . . Against Mr. Jungenfeld's wishes Mr. Wainwright awarded the contract for the refrigerating plant to the De La Vergne Company. . . . The brewery was at that time in process of erection and most of the plans were made. When Mr. Jungenfeld heard that the contract was awarded he took his plans, called off his superintendent on the ground, and notified Mr. Wainwright that he would have nothing more to do with the brewery. The defendant was in great haste to have its new brewery completed for divers reasons. It would be hard to find an architect in Mr. Jungenfeld's place and the making of new plans and arrangements when another architect was found would involve much loss of time. *Under these circumstances* Mr. Wainwright promised to give Jungenfeld five per cent on the cost of the De La Vergne ice machine if he would resume work. Jungenfeld accepted and fulfilled the duties of superintending architect till the completion of the brewery.
>
> As I understand the facts and as I accordingly formally find defendant promised Jungenfeld a bonus to resume work and complete the *original* contract under the *original* terms.
>
> I accordingly submit that in my view defendant's promise to pay Jungenfeld five per cent on the cost of the refrigerating plant *was without consideration, and recommend that the claim be not allowed.*

The referee also finds "that Mr. Jungenfeld never claimed that defendant had broken the contract or intended to do so, or that any of his legal rights had been violated."

The learned circuit judge, upon this state of facts, held that the defendant was liable on his promise of Wainwright to pay the additional five per cent on the refrigerator plant. The point was duly saved, and from the decision this appeal is taken.

Was there any consideration for the promise of Wainwright to pay Jungenfeld five per cent on the refrigerator plant? If there was not, plaintiff cannot recover the $3,449.75, the amount of that commission. The report of the referee, and the evidence upon which it is based, alike show that Jungenfeld's claim to this extra compensation is based upon Wainwright's promise to pay him this sum to induce him, Jungenfeld, to complete his original contract under its original terms.

It is urged upon us by respondents that this was a new contract. New in what? Jungenfeld was bound by his contract to design and supervise this building. Under the new promise he was not to do anything more or anything different. What benefit was to accrue to Wainwright? He was to receive the same service from Jungenfeld under the new that Jungenfeld was bound to render under the original contract. What loss, trouble or inconvenience could result to Jungenfeld that he had not already assumed? No amount of metaphysical reasoning can change the plain fact that Jungenfeld took advantage of Wainwright's necessities, and extorted the promise of five per cent on the refrigerator plant, as the condition of his complying with his contract already entered into. Nor had he even the flimsy pretext that Wainwright had violated any of the conditions of the contract on his part.

Jungenfeld himself put it upon the simple proposition, that "if he, as an architect, put up the brewery, and another company put up the refrigerating machinery, it would be a detriment to the Empire Refrigerating Company" of which Jungenfeld was president. To permit plaintiff to recover under such circumstances, would be to offer a premium upon bad faith, and invite men to violate their most sacred contracts, that they may profit by their own wrong.

"That a promise to pay a man for doing that which he is already under contract to do is without consideration," is conceded by respondents. The rule has been so long imbedded in the common law and decisions of the highest courts of the various states that nothing but the most cogent reasons ought to shake it. . . .

But "it is carrying coals to New Castle" to add authorities on a proposition so universally accepted and so inherently just and right in itself. The learned counsel for respondents do not controvert the general proposition. Their contention is, and the circuit court agreed with them, that, when Jungenfeld declined to go further on his contract, the defendant then had the right to sue for damages, and not having elected to sue Jungenfeld, but having acceded to his demand for the additional compensation, defendant cannot now be heard to say his promise is without consideration. While it is true Jungenfeld became liable in damages for the obvious breach of his contract, we do not think it follows that defendant is estopped from showing its promise was made without consideration.

It is true that as eminent a jurist as Judge Cooley, in Goebel v. Linn, 47 Mich. 489, held that an ice company which had agreed to furnish a brewery with all the ice they might need for their business from November 8, 1879, until January 1, 1881, at $1.75 per ton, and afterwards in May, 1880, declined to deliver any more ice unless the brewery would give it $3 per ton, could recover on a promissory note given for the increased price. Profound as is our respect for the distinguished judge who delivered that opinion, we are still of the opinion that his decision is not in accord with the almost universally accepted doctrine and is not convincing, and certainly so much of the opinion as holds that the payment by a debtor of a part of his debt then due would constitute a defense to a suit for the remainder is not the law of this state, nor do we think of any other where the common law prevails. . . .

What we hold is that, when a party merely does what he has already obligated himself to do, he cannot demand an additional compensation therefor, and, although by taking advantage of the necessities of his adversary, he obtains a promise for more, the law will regard it as nudum pactum, and will not lend its process to aid in the wrong. . . .

[Judgment reversed.]

NOTE

Suppose Wainwright had made a down payment. Could he get it back? Consult Restatement of Restitution §70; Astley v. Reynolds, 2 Strange 915, 93 Eng. Rep. 999 (1722).

GOEBEL v. LINN
47 Mich. 489, 11 N.W. 284 (1882)

[Defendants were large brewers and had a contract with an ice company to supply them with ice during the season of 1880 at one dollar and seventy-five cents a ton, or two dollars if the crop was short. The contract was made in November, 1879. The following winter was so mild that the ice crop was a failure. In May the defendants were notified by the ice company that no more ice would be furnished them under the contract. Defendants had then on hand a considerable amount of beer that would be spoiled without ice, and under stress of the circumstances they made a new arrangement with the ice company, and agreed to pay three dollars and a half per ton for the ice. From that time defendants paid three dollars and a half per ton for the ice as it was delivered to them. Notes were given for the ice at this rate from time to time, and, with the exception of one note which was given in October, paid as they fell due. The plaintiff sued on the unpaid note and the defendant claimed a set-off of the sums paid by them for ice in excess of two dollars a ton. In holding for the plaintiff, Judge COOLEY had this to say:]

It is very manifest that there is no ground for saying that the note in suit was given without consideration. It was given for ice which was furnished by the payee to the defendants; which was owned by the payee and bought by the defendants, and for which defendants concede their liability to make payment. What the defendants dispute is, the justice of compelling them to pay the sum stipulated in the note when according to their previous contract they ought to have received the ice for a sum much smaller. The defence, therefore, is not that the consideration has failed, but that a note for a sum greater than the contract price has been extorted under circumstances amounting to duress.

It is to be observed of these circumstances that if we confine our attention to the very time when the arrangement for an increased price was made the defendants make out a very plausible case. They had then a very considerable stock of beer on hand, and the case they make is one in which they must have ice at any cost, or they must fail in business. If the ice company had the ability to perform their contract, but took advantage of the circumstances to extort a higher price from the necessities of the defendants, its conduct was reprehensible, and it would perhaps have been in the interest of good morals if defendants had temporarily submitted to the loss and brought suit against the ice company on their contract. No one disputes that at their option they might have taken that course, and that the ice company would have been responsible for all damages legally attributable to the breach of its contract.

But the defendants did not elect to take that course. They chose for reasons which they must have deemed sufficient at the time to submit to the company's demand and pay the increased price rather than rely upon their strict rights under the existing contract. What these reasons were is not explained to us except as above shown. It is obvious that there might be reasons that would go beyond the immediate injury to the business. Suppose, for example, the defendants had satisfied themselves that the ice company under the very extraordinary circumstances of the entire failure of the local crop of ice must be ruined if their existing contracts were to be insisted upon, and must be utterly unable to respond in damages; it is plain that then, whether they chose to rely upon their contract or not, it could have been of little or no value to them. Unexpected and extraordinary circumstances had rendered the contract worthless; and they must either make a new arrangement, or, in insisting on holding the ice company to the existing contract, they would ruin the ice company and thereby at the same time ruin themselves. It would be very strange if under such a condition of things the existing contract, which unexpected events had rendered of no value, could stand in the way of a new arrangement, and constitute a bar to any new contract which should provide for a price that would enable both parties to save their interests.

We do not know that the condition of things was as supposed, but that it may have been is plain enough. What is certain is, that the parties immediately concerned and who knew all the facts, joined in making a new arrangement out of which the note in suit has grown. The case of Moore v. Detroit Locomotive Works 14 Mich. 266, where a similar case was fully considered, is ample authority for supporting the new arrangement.

If unfair advantage was taken of defendants, whereby they were forced into a contract against their interests, it is very remarkable that they submitted to abide by it as they did for nearly eight months without in the meantime taking any steps for their protection. Whatever compulsion there was in the case was to be found in the danger of their business in consequence of the threat made at the beginning of May to cut off the supply of ice; but the force of the threat would be broken the moment they could make arrangements for a supply elsewhere; and there is no showing that such a supply was unattainable. The force of the threat was therefore temporary; and the defendants, as soon as they were able to supply their needs elsewhere, might have been in position to act independently, and to deal with the ice company as freely as they might with any other party who declined to keep his engagements. On any view, therefore, which we may take of the law, the defence must fail.

But if our attention were to be restricted to the very day when notice was given that ice would no longer be supplied at the contract price, we could not agree that the case was one of duress. It is not shown to be a case even of a hard bargain; and the price charged was probably not too much under the circumstances. But for the pre-existing contract the one now questioned would probably have been fair enough, and if made with any other party would not have been complained of. The duress is therefore to be found in the refusal to keep the previous engagements. How far this falls short of legal duress was so recently considered by us in Hackley & McGordon v. Headley 45 Mich. 569, that further discussion now would serve no valuable purpose. . . .

NOTE

Posner, Gratuitous Promises in Economics and Law, 6 J. Legal Studies 411 (1977), contains an interesting discussion of *Goebel, Alaska Packers* (*supra* p. 652), and *Schwartzreich* (*supra* p. 79). Is Posner's analysis convincing? For a criticism of the principal case, see Dalzell, Duress by Economic Pressure, 20 N.C.L. Rev. 237 (1942).

AUSTIN INSTRUMENT, INC. v. LORAL CORP.
29 N.Y.2d 124, 272 N.E.2d 533, 324 N.Y.S.2d 22 (1971)

FULD, Chief Judge.

The defendant, Loral Corporation, seeks to recover payment for goods delivered under a contract which it had with the plaintiff Austin Instrument, Inc., on the ground that the evidence establishes, as a matter of law, that it was forced to agree to an increase in price on the items in question under circumstances amounting to economic duress.

In July of 1965, Loral was awarded a $6,000,000 contract by the Navy for the production of radar sets. The contract contained a schedule of deliveries, a liquidated damages clause applying to late deliveries and a cancellation clause in case of default by Loral. The latter thereupon solicited bids for some 40 precision gear components needed to produce the radar sets, and awarded Austin a subcontract to supply 23 such parts. That party commenced delivery in early 1966.

In May, 1966, Loral was awarded a second Navy contract for the production of more radar sets and again went about soliciting bids. Austin bid on all 40 gear components but, on July 15, a representative from Loral informed Austin's president, Mr. Krauss, that his company would be awarded the subcontract only for those items on which it was low bidder. The Austin officer refused to accept an order for less than all 40 of the gear parts and on the next day he told Loral that Austin would cease deliveries of the parts due under the existing subcontract unless Loral consented to substantial increases in the prices provided for by that agreement — both retroactively for parts already delivered and prospectively on those not yet shipped — and placed with Austin the order for all 40 parts needed under Loral's second Navy contract. Shortly thereafter, Austin did, indeed, stop delivery. After contacting 10 manufacturers of precision gears and finding none who could produce the parts in time to meet its commitments to the Navy, Loral acceded to Austin's demands; in a letter dated July 22, Loral wrote to Austin that

> We have feverishly surveyed other sources of supply and find that because of the prevailing military exigencies, were they to start from scratch as would have to be the case, they could not even remotely begin to deliver on time to meet the delivery requirements established by the Government. . . . Accordingly, we are left with no choice or alternative but to meet your conditions.

Loral thereupon consented to the price increases insisted upon by Austin under the first subcontract and the latter was awarded a second subcontract making it the supplier of all 40 gear parts for Loral's second contract with the Navy. Although Austin was granted until September to resume deliveries, Loral did, in fact, receive parts in August and was able to produce the radar sets in time to meet its commitments to the Navy on both contracts. After Austin's last delivery under the second subcontract in July, 1967, Loral notified it of its intention to seek recovery of the price increases.

On September 15, 1967, Austin instituted this action against Loral to recover an amount in excess of $17,750 which was still due on the second subcontract. On the same day, Loral commenced an action against Austin claiming damages of some $22,250 — the aggregate of the price increases under the first subcontract — on the ground of economic duress. The two actions were consolidated and, following a trial, Austin was awarded the sum it requested and Loral's complaint against Austin was dismissed on the ground that it was not shown that "it could not have obtained the items in question from other sources in time to meet its commitment to the Navy under the first contract." A closely divided

Appellate Division affirmed (35 A.D.2d 387, 316 N.Y.S.2d 528, 532). There was no material disagreement concerning the facts; as Justice Steuer stated in the course of his dissent below, "[t]he facts are virtually undisputed, nor is there any serious question of law. The difficulty lies in the application of the law to these facts." (35 A.D.2d 392, 316 N.Y.S.2d 534.)

The applicable law is clear and, indeed, is not disputed by the parties. A contract is voidable on the ground of duress when it is established that the party making the claim was forced to agree to it by means of a wrongful threat precluding the exercise of his free will. (See Allstate Med. Labs., Inc. v. Blaivas, 20 N.Y.2d 654, 282 N.Y.S.2d 268, 229 N.E.2d 50; Kazaras v. Manufacturers Trust Co., 4 N.Y.2d 930, 175 N.Y.S.2d 172, 151 N.E.2d 356; Adams v. Irving Nat. Bank, 116 N.Y. 606, 611, 23 N.E. 7, 9; see, also, 13 Williston, Contracts [3d ed., 1970], §1603, p. 658.) The existence of economic duress or business compulsion is demonstrated by proof that "immediate possession of needful goods is threatened" (Mercury Mach. Importing Corp. v. City of New York, 3 N.Y.2d 418, 425, 165 N.Y.S.2d 517, 520, 144 N.E.2d 400) or, more particularly, in cases such as the one before us, by proof that one party to a contract has threatened to breach the agreement by withholding goods unless the other party agrees to some further demand. (See, e.g., Du Pont de Nemours & Co., v. J. I. Hass Co., 303 N.Y. 785, 103 N.E.2d 896; Gallagher Switchboard Corp. v. Heckler Elec. Co., 36 Misc. 2d 225, 232 N.Y.S.2d 590; see, also, 13 Williston, Contracts [3d ed., 1970], §1617, p. 705.) However, a mere threat by one party to breach the contract by not delivering the required items, though wrongful, does not in itself constitute economic duress. It must also appear that the threatened party could not obtain the goods from another source of supply and that the ordinary remedy of an action for breach of contract would not be adequate.

We find without any support in the record the conclusion reached by the courts below that Loral failed to establish that it was the victim of economic duress. On the contrary, the evidence makes out a classic case, as a matter of law, of such duress.

It is manifest that Austin's threat — to stop deliveries unless the prices were increased — deprived Loral of its free will. As bearing on this, Loral's relationship with the Government is most significant. As mentioned above, its contract called for staggered monthly deliveries of the radar sets, with clauses calling for liquidated damages and possible cancellation on default. Because of its production schedule, Loral was, in July, 1966, concerned with meeting its delivery requirements in September, October and November, and it was for the sets to be delivered in those months that the withheld gears were needed. Loral had to plan ahead, and the substantial liquidated damages for which it would be liable, plus the threat of default, were genuine possibilities. Moreover, Loral did a substantial portion of its business with the Government, and it feared that a failure to deliver as agreed upon would jeopardize its chances for future contracts. These genuine concerns do not merit the label "'self-imposed, undisclosed and subjective'" which the Appellate Division majority placed upon them. It was perfectly reasonable for Loral, or any other party similarly placed, to consider itself in an emergency duress situation.

Austin, however, claims that the fact that Loral extended its time to resume deliveries until September negates its alleged dire need for the parts. A Loral official testified on this point that Austin's president told him he could deliver some parts in August and that the extension of deliveries was a formality. In any event, the parts necessary for production of the radar sets to be delivered in September were delivered to Loral on September 1, and the parts needed for the October schedule were delivered in late August and early September. Even so, Loral had to "work . . . around the clock" to meet its commitments. Considering that the best offer Loral received from the other vendors it contacted was commencement of delivery sometime in October, which, as the record shows, would have made it late in its deliveries to the Navy in both September and October, Loral's claim that it had no choice but to accede to Austin's demands is conclusively demonstrated.

We find unconvincing Austin's contention that Loral, in order to meet its burden, should have contacted the Government and asked for an extension of its delivery dates so as to enable it to purchase the parts from another vendor. Aside from the consideration that Loral was anxious to perform well in the Government's eyes, it could not be sure when it would obtain enough parts from a substitute vendor to meet its commitments. The only promise which it received from the companies it contacted was for *commencement* of deliveries, not full supply, and, with vendor delay common in this field, it would have been nearly impossible to know the length of the extension it should request. It must be remembered that Loral was producing a needed item of military hardware. Moreover, there is authority for Loral's position that nonperformance by a subcontractor is not an excuse for default in the main contract. (See, e.g., McBride & Wachtel, Government Contracts, §35.10, [11].) In light of all this, Loral's claim should not be held insufficiently supported because it did not request an extension from the Government.

Loral, as indicated above, also had the burden of demonstrating that it could not obtain the parts elsewhere within a reasonable time, and there can be no doubt that it met this burden. The 10 manufacturers whom Loral contacted comprised its entire list of "approved vendors" for precision gears, and none was able to commence delivery soon enough. As Loral was producing a highly sophisticated item of military machinery requiring parts made to the strictest engineering standards, it would be unreasonable to hold that Loral should have gone to other vendors, with whom it was either unfamiliar or dissatisfied, to procure the needed parts.

As Justice Steuer noted in his dissent, Loral "contacted all the manufacturers whom it believed capable of making these parts" (35 A.D.2d at p. 393, 316 N.Y.S.2d at p. 534), and this was all the law requires.

It is hardly necessary to add that Loral's normal legal remedy of accepting Austin's breach of the contract and then suing for damages would have been inadequate under the circumstances, as Loral would still have had to obtain the gears elsewhere with all the concomitant consequences mentioned above. In other words, Loral actually had no choice, when the prices were raised by Austin, except to take the gears at the "coerced" prices and then sue to get the excess back.

Austin's final argument is that Loral even if it did enter into the contract under duress, lost any rights it had to a refund of money by waiting until July, 1967, long after the termination date of the contract, to disaffirm it. It is true that one who would recover moneys allegedly paid under duress must act promptly to make his claim known. (See Oregon Pacific R.R. Co. v. Forrest, 128 N.Y. 83, 93, 28 N.E. 137, 139; Port Chester Elec. Constr. Corp. v. Hastings Terraces, 284 App. Div. 966, 967, 134 N.Y.S.2d 656, 658.) In this case, Loral delayed making its demand for a refund until three days after Austin's last delivery on the second subcontract. Loral's reason — for waiting until that time — is that it feared another stoppage of deliveries which would again put it in an untenable situation. Considering Austin's conduct in the past, this was perfectly reasonable, as the possibility of an application by Austin of further business compulsion still existed until all of the parts were delivered.

In sum, the record before us demonstrates that Loral agreed to the price increases in consequence of the economic duress employed by Austin. Accordingly, the matter should be remanded to the trial court for a computation of its damages.

The order appealed from should be modified, with costs, by reversing so much thereof as affirms the dismissal of defendant Loral Corporation's claim and, except as so modified, affirmed.

BERGAN, Judge (dissenting).

Whether acts charged as constituting economic duress produce or do not produce the damaging effect attributed to them is normally a routine type of factual issue.

Here the fact question was resolved against Loral both by the Special Term and by the affirmance at the Appellate Division. It should not be open for different resolution here.

In summarizing the Special Term's decision and its own, the Appellate Division decided that "the conclusion that Loral acted deliberately and voluntarily, without being under immediate pressure of incurring severe business reverses, precludes a recovery on the theory of economic duress" (35 A.D.2d 387, 391, 316 N.Y.S.2d 528, 532).

When the testimony of the witnesses who actually took part in the negotiations for the two disputing parties is examined, sharp conflicts of fact emerge. Under Austin's version the request for a renegotiation of the existing contract was based on Austin's contention that Loral had failed to carry out an understanding as to the items to be furnished under that contract and this way the source of dissatisfaction which led both to a revision of the existing agreement and to entering into a new one.

This is not necessarily and as a matter of law to be held economic duress. On this appeal it is needful to look at the facts resolved in favor of Austin most favorably to that party. Austin's version of events was that a threat was not made but rather a request to accommodate the closing of its plant for a customary vacation period in accordance with the general understanding of the parties.

Moreover, critical to the issue of economic duress was the availability of alternative suppliers to the purchaser Loral. The demonstration is replete in the direct testimony of Austin's witnesses and on cross-examination of Loral's principal and purchasing agent that the availability of practical alternatives was a highly controverted issue of fact. On that issue of fact the explicit findings made by the Special Referee were affirmed by the Appellate Division. Nor is the issue of fact made the less so by assertion that the facts are undisputed and that only the application of equally undisputed rules of law is involved.

Austin asserted and Loral admitted on cross-examination that there were many suppliers listed in a trade registry but that Loral chose to rely only on those who had in the past come to them for orders and with whom they were familiar. It was, therefore, at least a fair issue of fact whether under the circumstances such conduct was reasonable and made what might otherwise have been a commercially understandable renegotiation an exercise of duress.

The order should be affirmed.

Burke, Scileppi and Gibson, JJ., concur with Fuld, C.J.

Bergan, J., dissents and votes to affirm in a separate opinion in which Breitel and Jasen, JJ., concur.

Ordered accordingly.

NOTE

1. For the difference between duress and undue influence see Odorizzi v. Bloomfield School District, 246 Cal. App. 2d 123, 54 Cal. Rptr. 533 (1966); Note, 22 Baylor L. Rev. 572 (1970). See further Restatement Second §§175, 177.

2. In Watkins & Son v. Carrig, 91 N.H. 459, 21 A.2d 591 (1941), the New Hampshire Supreme Court observed:

[I]n common understanding there is, importantly, a wide divergence between a bare promise and a promise in adjustment of a contractual promise already outstanding. A promise with no supporting consideration would upset well and long established human interrelations if the law did not treat it as a vain thing. But parties to a valid contract generally understand that it is subject to any mutual action they may take in its performance. Changes to meet changes in circumstances and conditions should be valid if the law is to carry out its function and service by rules conformable with reasonable practices and understandings in matters of business and commerce.

In applying this policy, the court enforced the claim of a contractor who had undertaken to excavate a cellar for a stated price. After discovering that the excavation would be a good deal more costly due to the unanticipated presence of solid rock, the parties agreed on a vastly higher price. To overcome the preexisting legal duty rule, which would otherwise have been an obstacle to recovery, the court invoked the notion of a gift.

> Conceding that the plaintiff did no more than the contract called for, yet it was presented with a discharge from its duty, as an element of the transaction by application of the law of gift. . . . The gift here was not of the promise to pay more, but of release of the plaintiff's duty to work for less. . . . Conceding that the plaintiff threatened to break its contract because it found the contract to be improvident, yet the defendant yielded to the threat without protest, excusing the plaintiff, and making a new arrangement. Not insisting on his rights, but relinquishing them, fairly he should be held to the new arrangement. . . .

Whatever one may think of the reasoning in the decision, the case has found acceptance in the Restatement Second §89 (Illus. 1).

3. King v. Duluth, Massabe & Northern Ry., 61 Minn. 482, 63 N.W. 1105 (1895), another suit on a modified contract, is not without interest. In *King*, the builder of a railway ran into difficulty due to weather conditions. This was not considered enough to support the railroad's promise of additional compensation, although the court conceded that an occurrence sufficient to excuse on grounds of impossibility was not required. The difficulty in question (hardening of the soil in a particularly severe winter) was foreseeable by plaintiff. But the defendant, by changing the railroad line and by its own defaults, had caused a delay in the work. For this reason, the court found for the plaintiff on the second count of his complaint.

SWARTZREICH v. BAUMAN-BASCH, INC.
231 N.Y. 196, 131 N.E. 887 (1921)

For a report of the case, see p. 79 *supra*.

CENTRAL LONDON PROPERTY TRUST, LTD. v. HIGH TREES HOUSE, LTD., [1947] K.B. 130. The facts as stated in the headnote were as follows: "By a lease under seal dated September 24, 1937, the plaintiff company let to the defendant company (a subsidiary of the plaintiffs) a block of flats for a term of ninety-nine years from September 29, 1937, at a ground rent of 2,500*l.* a year. In the early part of 1940, owing to war conditions then prevailing, only a few of the flats in the block were let to tenants and it became apparent that the defendants would be unable to pay the rent reserved by the lease out of the rents of the flats. Discussions took place between the directors of the two companies, which were closely connected, and, as a result, on January 3, 1940, a letter was written by the plaintiffs to the defendants confirming that the ground rent of the premises would be reduced from 2,500*l.* to 1,250*l.* as from the beginning of the term. The defendants thereafter paid the reduced rent. By the beginning of 1945 all the flats were let but the defendants continued to pay only the reduced rent. In September, 1945, the plaintiffs wrote to the defendants claiming that rent was payable at the rate of 2,500*l.* a year and, subsequently, in order to determine the legal position, they initiated friendly proceedings in which they claimed the difference between rent at the rates of 2,500*l.* and 1,250*l.* for the quarters ending September 29 and December 25, 1945. By their defence the defendants pleaded that the agreement for the reduction of the ground rent operated during the whole term of the lease and, as alternative, that the plaintiffs were estopped from demanding rent at the higher rate or had waived their right to do so down to the date of their letter of September 21, 1945."

Denning, J. upheld their claim on the ground that the agreement to accept the lower rent was only meant to cover wartime conditions. But by way of dictum he maintained that the plaintiffs could not have sued for the arrears accrued during the suspensory period covered by the agreement, citing Hughes v. Metropolitan Ry., 2 App. 499 (1877). He emphasized that although the plaintiffs could not have been sued in damages for breach of their promise to accept the lower rent, given the fusion of law and equity, they were nevertheless estopped to act inconsistently with their promise. In this sense they were estopped.

NOTE

Denning's opinion contains an interesting attempt to reconcile his decision with Foakes v. Beer, *infra* p. 668, and a strong criticism of that case. For a reformulation of the estoppel doctrine by Lord Denning, see Combe v. Combe, [1951] 2 K.B. 215, 220. See further Woodhouse A.C. Israel Cocoa Ltd., S.A. v. Nigerian Produce Marketing Co., Ltd., [1972] A.C. 741, 758; [1972] 2 All E.R. 271, 281. See also G. Treitel, The Law of Contract 84 et seq. (2d ed. 1975).

For the American counterpart of the *High Trees* case see Restatement Second §89, Illustration 7. See further Liebreich v. State Bank and Trust

Co., 100 S.W.2d 152 (Tex. Civ. App. 1936), 50 Harv. L. Rev. 1937. Contra Levine v. Blumenthal, 117 N.J.L. 23, 186 A. 457 (1936). For the privilege of retraction, see Atlantic Fish Co. v. Dollar S.S. Line, 205 Cal. 65, 269 P. 926 (1928). Section 89 goes beyond §84 of the Restatement Second. Modification is not limited to immaterial terms (§89, Comment *a*). The "original terms can be reinstated for the future by reasonable notification received by the promisee unless reinstatement would be unjust in view of a change of position on his part" (§89, Comment *d*).

To avoid the roadblock created by the preexisting legal duty rule, courts have sometimes imported the old consideration into the new contract. See Jacobs v. J. C. Penney Co., 170 F.2d 501 (7th Cir. 1948).

SKINNER v. TOBER FOREIGN MOTORS, INC.
345 Mass. 429, 187 N.E.2d 669 (1963)

SPALDING, J. In this suit the plaintiffs seek equitable replevin of an airplane alleged to belong to them and to be detained against their right by the defendant; in the alternative, damages were sought.

A master, to whom the case was referred, found the following facts: The plaintiffs at all times here material were residents of Connecticut. The defendant is a Massachusetts corporation and its principal place of business at the time of the transactions under consideration was at Springfield in this Commonwealth. On October 3, 1959, the plaintiffs purchased an airplane from the defendant. Negotiations for the purchase were carried on in Springfield and all of the instruments in connection with the transaction were executed there. These instruments included a bill of sale, an instalment contract, and an instalment note. . . .

The instruments executed by the parties provided for payments of $200 per month over a period of twenty-four months with a payment of $353.34 on the twenty-fifth month. Prior to the due date of the first payment the airplane developed engine trouble. This necessitated either the rebuilding of the engine or the installation of a new one at a cost of $1,400. After discussion between the plaintiffs and officers of the defendant, the plaintiffs decided that a new engine should be installed. But the necessity of replacing the engine so soon after the purchase of the plane imposed a financial burden on the plaintiffs which they would be unable to bear. Accordingly, they "offered to return the unrepaired plane to the . . . [defendant] without charge in exchange for a cancellation of all agreements." In order to alleviate the plaintiffs' burdens, and rather than accept the return of the plane, the defendant, through its officers, agreed that for the first year of the instalment contract the payments were to be $100 per month. The plaintiffs agreed to this arrangement and the new engine was installed. This agreement, which was made late in October, 1959, was oral. The defendant derived no benefit from this agreement other than the facts that the plane was not returned and the payments hereinafter mentioned were made.

Following the making of this agreement the plaintiffs, beginning in November, 1959, and continuing through May, 1960, made payments of $100 each month. Throughout this period the plane was kept in Connecticut.

In March of 1960 the defendant's president told the plaintiffs that thereafter the monthly payments would have to be increased to $200 or "he would have to take action." The plaintiffs did not agree to this proposal and, after another discussion with the defendant's president, made the April and May payments of $100 each.

On May 26, 1960, the defendant's president, accompanied by two deputy sheriffs of Connecticut and another man, went to the Windham Airport at Willimantic, Connecticut, took possession of the plane, and flew it to an airport in this Commonwealth. No demand for full payment was ever made. If the oral modification was controlling the plaintiffs were not in default in their payments.[238] After repossessing the plane, the defendant sold it for $4,400. The master concluded that, subject to the determination of certain questions of law by the court, the damages sustained by the plaintiffs were $2,280, plus interest. This amount was arrived at by deducting from the value of the plane ($6,200) the unpaid balance ($3,920) of the purchase price. From a final decree awarding the plaintiffs damages in the amount found by the master, together with interest, the defendant appeals.

The master reported several questions of law for the court's determination, but we need not deal with all of them; those discussed below are decisive of the case. . . .

The defendant argues that the oral modification is unenforceable and invalid because of the statute of frauds and because it was not supported by consideration. The short answer to the first point is that the defence of the statute of frauds is not available to the defendant, for it was not pleaded. Watkins v. Briggs, 314 Mass. 282, 284. Abalan v. Abalan, 329 Mass. 182, 183, and cases cited. We do not, therefore, reach the question whether the transactions would be taken out of the statute by reason of delivery and acceptance of the goods, or by part payment. See §2-201(3)(c). As to the oral modification not being supported by consideration the answer may be found in §2-209(1) which provides that an

238. We lay to one side the fact that, although the contract called for the making of the monthly payment on the fifteenth of each month, they were in fact made between the fifteenth and the eighteenth. But the defendant never protested, and continued to accept payments on that basis as long as the contract remained in force. The defendant makes no point of this tardiness in its brief. Also of no importance is the fact that for a brief period (seven days) the plaintiffs failed to carry the insurance on the plane which the contract called for. This breach likewise is not relied on by the defendant. Moreover, there were findings that would amply justify the conclusion that the defendant waived these breaches.

"agreement modifying a contract within this Article needs no consideration to be binding."

If the oral modification to the written contract was valid and binding — and we hold that it was — the defendant had no right to take possesion of the plane. The defendant makes no contention to the contrary. Rather it seeks to justify what it did on the basis that the oral modification was invalid. It follows that the final decree is affirmed and the plaintiffs are to have costs of this appeal.

So ordered.

NOTE

The interpretation of §2-209 of the U.C.C., which is the counterpart of Restatement Second §89, has raised many questions. The two sections have a common purpose, i.e., to permit modification of a contract without consideration, thus avoiding the preexisting legal duty rule. The new agreement must, however, be made in good faith and for legitimate business reasons.[239]

In contrast to §89 of the Restatement Second, §2-209 of the U.C.C. allows the parties to prohibit oral modification or rescission. To prevent fictitious waivers, it provides for a "private" statute of frauds, requiring that the modification or rescission be in writing.[240] If a written modification is presented by a merchant to a nonmerchant (i.e., a consumer) it must be separately signed by the latter (§2-209).

U.C.C. §2-209(3) makes the "public" statute of frauds (Chapter 6) applicable to modification agreements. This raises the interesting question whether an oral reduction of the price from $500 to $400 in a sales contract is binding. Should §2-209(3) be read to apply to all contracts originally subject to the statute of frauds, the oral modification would be unenforceable. This position was taken in Asco Mining Co. v. Gross Mining Co., 3 U.C.C. Rep. Serv. 273 (PLP 1965).

Section 2-209(4) dilutes §2-209(2) by making it possible to treat an attempt at modification or rescission (i.e., an oral modification) as a waiver, which can, however, be retracted "unless the retraction would be unjust in view of a material change of position in reliance on the waiver." See Rennie & Laughlin, Inc. v. Chrysler Corp., 242 F.2d 208 (9th Cir. 1957).

---

239. Restatement Second §89, Comment 2, requires the modification to be "fair and equitable in view of circumstances not anticipated by the parties when the contract was made." See, however, Comment b. The U.C.C. has no such qualification, but as Comment 2 observes, modification "must meet the test of good faith imposed by the act" (U.C.C. §1-203).

240. State statutes not infrequently require the modification to be in writing; see, e.g., New York General Obligations Law §5-1103, infra p. 673.

Modification need not be *expressis verbis*, but can also take the form of a course of conduct. If, for instance, the seller ignores a covering letter sent by the buyer setting a definite time for performance and then ships the goods, which the buyer accepts, the buyer may be held bound despite the fact that the shipment came later than was requested in the covering letter. Gateway Co., Inc. v. Charlotte Theatres, Inc., 297 F.2d 483 (1st Cir., 1961).[241]

FOAKES v. BEER
9 App. Cas. 605 (1884)

Appeal from an order of the Court of Appeal.

On August 11th, 1875, the respondent recovered judgment against the appellant for £2,077 17s. 2d. for debt and £13 1s. 10d. for costs. On December 21st, 1876, a memorandum of agreement was made and signed by the appellant and respondent in the following terms:

> Whereas the said John Weston Foakes is indebted to the said Julia Beer, and she has obtained a judgment in her Majesty's High Court of Justice, Exchequer Division, for the sum of £2,090 19s. And whereas the said John Weston Foakes has requested the said Julia Beer to give him time in which to pay such judgment, which she has agreed to do on the following conditions. Now this agreement witnesseth that in consideration of the said John Weston Foakes paying to the said Julia Beer on the signing of this agreement the sum of £500, the receipt whereof she doth hereby acknowledge in part satisfaction of the said judgment debt of £2,090 19s., and on condition of his paying to her or her executors, administrators, assigns or nominee the sum of £150 on July 1st and January 1st or within one calendar month after each of the said days respectively in every year until the whole of the said sum of £2,090 19s. shall have been fully paid and satisfied, the first of such payments to be made on July 1st next, then she the said Julia Beer hereby undertakes and agrees that she, her executors, administrators or assigns, will not take any proceedings whatever on the said judgment.

The respondent having in June, 1882, taken out a summons for leave to proceed on the judgment, an issue was directed to be tried between the respondent as plaintiff and the appellant as defendant whether any and what amount was on July 1st, 1882, due upon the judgment.

At the trial of the issue before Cave, J., it was proved that the whole sum of £2,090 19s. had been paid by instalments, but the respondent claimed interest. The jury under his Lordship's direction found that the appellant had paid all the sums which by the agreement of December

241. U.C.C. §2-201(2).

21st, 1876, he undertook to pay and within the times therein specified. Cave, J., was of opinion that whether the judgment was satisfied or not, the respondent was, by reason of the agreement, not entitled to issue execution for any sum on the judgment.

The Queen's Bench Division (Watkin Williams and Mathew, JJ.) discharged an order for a new trial on the ground of misdirection.

The Court of Appeal (Brett, M.R., Lindley, and Fry, L.JJ.) reversed that decision and entered judgment for the respondent for the interest due, with costs. . . .

LORD BLACKBURN. My Lords, the first question raised is as to what was the true construction of the memorandum of agreement made on December 21st, 1876. What was it that the parties by that writing agreed to?

The appellants contend that they meant that on payment down of £500, and payment within a month after July 1st and January 1st in each ensuing year of £150, until the sum of £2,090 19s. was paid, the judgment for that sum and interest should be satisfied, for an agreement to take no proceedings on the judgment is equivalent to treating it as satisfied. This construction of the memorandum requires that after the tenth payment of £150 there should be a further payment of £90 19s. made within the next six months. This is the construction which all three Courts below have put upon the memorandum.

The respondent contends that the true construction of the memorandum was that time was to be given on those conditions for five years, the judgment being on default of any one payment enforceable for whatever was still unpaid, with interest from the date the judgment was signed, but that the interest was not intended to be forgiven at all. If this is the true construction of the agreement the judgment appealed against is right and should be affirmed, whether the reason on which the Court of Appeal founded its judgment was right or not. I am, however, of opinion that the Courts below, who on this point were unanimous, put the true construction on the memorandum. I do not think the question free from difficulty. It would have been easy to have expressed, in unmistakable words, that on payment down of £500, and punctual payment at the rate of £300 a year till £2,090 19s. was paid, the judgment should not be enforced either for principal or interest; or language might have been used which should equally clearly have expressed that, though time was to be given, interest was to be paid in addition to the instalments. The words actually used are such that I think it is quite possible that the two parties put a different construction on the words at the time; but I think the words "till the said sum of £2,090 19s. shall have been fully paid and satisfied" cannot be construed as meaning "till that sum, with interest from the day judgment was signed, shall have been fully paid and satisfied," nor can the promise "not to take any proceedings whatever on the judgment" be cut down to meaning any proceedings except those necessary to enforce payment of interest.

I think, therefore, that it is necessary to consider the ground on which the Court of Appeal did base their judgment, and to say whether the agreement can be enforced. I construe it as accepting and taking £500 in satisfaction of the whole £2,090 19s., subject to the condition that unless the balance of the principal debt was paid by the instalments, the whole might be enforced with interest. If, instead of £500 in money, it had been a horse valued at £500 or a promissory note for £500, the authorities are that it would have been a good satisfaction, but it is said to be otherwise as it was money.

This is a question, I think, of difficulty.

In Coke, Littleton, 212b, Lord Coke says:

> Where the condition is for payment of £20, the obligor or feoffor cannot at the time appointed pay a lesser sum in satisfaction of the whole, because it is apparent that a lesser sum of money cannot be a satisfaction of a greater. . . . If the obligor or feoffor pay a lesser sum either before the day or at another place than is limited by the condition, and the obligee or feoffee receiveth it, this is a good satisfaction.

For this he cites Pinnel's Case [5 Rep. 117a.]. That was an action on a bond for £16, conditioned for the payment of £8 10s. on November 11th, 1600. Plea that defendant, at plaintiff's request, before the said day, to wit, on October 1st, paid to the plaintiff £5 2s. 2d., which the plaintiff accepted in full satisfaction of the £8 10s. The plaintiff had judgment for the insufficient pleading. But though this was so, Lord Coke reports that it was resolved by the whole Court of Common Pleas

> that payment of a lesser sum on the day in satisfaction of a greater cannot be any satisfaction for the whole, because it appears to the judges that by no possibility a lesser sum can be a satisfaction to the plaintiff for a greater sum; but the gift of a horse, hawk, or robe, etc., in satisfaction is good, for it shall be intended that a horse, hawk, or robe, etc., might be more beneficial to the plaintiff than the money, in respect of some circumstance, or otherwise the plaintiff would not have accepted of it in satisfaction. But when the whole sum is due, by no intendment the acceptance of parcel can be a satisfaction to the plaintiff; but in the case at bar it was resolved that the payment and acceptance of parcel before the day in satisfaction of the whole would be a good satisfaction in regard of circumstance of time; for peradventure parcel of it before the day would be more beneficial to him than the whole at the day, and the value of the satisfaction is not material; so if I am bound in £20 to pay you £10 at Westminster, and you request me to pay you £5 at the day at York, and you will accept it in full satisfaction for the whole £10, it is a good satisfaction for the whole, for the expenses to pay it at York is sufficient satisfaction.

There are two things here resolved. First, that where a matter paid and accepted in satisfaction of a debt certain might by any possibility be more beneficial to the creditor than his debt, the Court will not inquire into the adequacy of the consideration. If the creditor, without any fraud, accepted it in satisfaction when it was not a sufficient satisfaction it was his own fault. And that payment before the day might be more beneficial, and consequently that the plea was in substance good, and this must have been decided in the case.

There is a second point stated to have been resolved — viz.: "That payment of a lesser sum on the day cannot be any satisfaction of the whole, because it appears to the judges that by no possibility a lesser sum can be a satisfaction to the plaintiff for a greater sum." This was certainly not necessary for the decision of the case; but though the resolution of the Court of Common Pleas was only a dictum, it seems to me clear that Lord Coke deliberately adopted the dictum, and the great weight of his authority makes it necessary to be cautious before saying that what he deliberately adopted as law was a mistake. . . .

For instance, in Sibree v. Tripp [15 M. & W. 33, 37], Parke, B., says: "It is clear if the claim be a liquidated and ascertained sum, payment of part cannot be satisfaction of the whole, although it may under certain circumstances, be evidence of a gift of the remainder." And Alderson, B., in the same case says:

> It is undoubtedly true that payment of a portion of a liquidated demand, in the same manner as the whole liquidated demand which ought to be paid, is payment only in part, because it is not one bargain, but two — viz., payment of part, and an agreement without consideration to give up the residue. The Courts might very well have held the contrary, and have left the matter to the agreement of the parties, but undoubtedly the law is so settled.

After such strong expressions of opinion, I doubt much whether any judge sitting in a Court of the first instance would be justified in treating the question as open. But as this has very seldom, if at all, been the ground of the decision even in a Court of the first instance, and certainly never been the ground of a decision in the Court of Exchequer Chamber, still less in this House, I did think it open in your Lordships' House to reconsider this question. And, notwithstanding the very high authority of Lord Coke, I think it is not the fact that to accept prompt payment of a part only of a liquidated demand, can never be more beneficial than to insist on payment of the whole. And if it be not the fact, it cannot be apparent to the judges.

[Lord Blackburn here reviewed the cases since Pinnel's Case, finding that on the whole they supported Lord Coke's dictum.] And I think that their expressions justify Mr. John William Smith in laying it down as he does in his note to Cumber v. Wane, in the second edition of his Leading Cases, that a liquidated and undisputed money demand, of which the day of payment is passed (not founded upon a bill of exchange or promissory note), cannot even with the consent of the creditor be discharged by mere payment by the debtor of a smaller amount in money in the same manner as he was bound to pay the whole.

I am inclined to think that this was settled in a Court of the first instance. I think, however, that it was originally a mistake.

What principally weighs with me in thinking that Lord Coke made a mistake of fact is my conviction that all men of business, whether merchants or tradesmen, do every day recognize and act on the ground that prompt payment of a part of their demand may be more beneficial to them than it would be to insist on their rights and enforce payment of the whole. Even where the debtor is perfectly solvent, and sure to pay at last, this often is so. Where the credit of the debtor is doubtful it must be more so. I had persuaded myself that there was no such long-continued action on this dictum as to render it improper in this House to reconsider the question. I had written my reasons for so thinking; but as they were not satisfactory to the other noble and learned Lords who heard the case, I do not now repeat them nor persist in them.

I assent to the judgment proposed, though it is not that which I had originally thought proper.

[The concurring opinions of the Earl of Selborne, L.C. and of Lord Watson and Lord Fitzgerald have been omitted.]

Order appealed from affirmed, and appeal dismissed with costs.

NOTE

The Lord Chancellor in his opinion emphasized that nothing was done by Mrs. Beer "on the receipt of the last payment, which could be tantamount to an acquittance, if the agreement did not previously bind her." What is the meaning of this observation? Would, for instance, a simple statement (not under seal) in which Mrs. Beer acknowledged that she had been paid in full have been sufficient? Having signed the agreement could Mrs. Beer disregard it immediately and proceed on the judgment?

For a discussion of the case see 1A Corbin §175; 5A Corbin §§1247, 1281; 1 Williston §120.

The application of the preexisting legal duty rule in Foakes v. Beer makes sense only when we take into account that Mrs. Beer merely made a promise not to "take any proceeding whatever." This promise was not regarded as self-executory. The rule of Foakes v. Beer has proven quite unpopular; it has been riddled with exceptions invented by common law courts,[242] and a considerable number of states have abolished the rule by statute, e.g., Cal. Civil Code §1524 (writing required) and Mich. Comp. Laws §566.1 (substantially identical with the New York statute discussed below). Massachusetts provides for modification by sealed instrument and declares that an instrument reciting that it is a sealed instrument will be treated as such; see Mass. Gen. Laws c.4 §9A.

The New York statutory counterparts to U.C.C. §2-209 are N.Y. Gen. Obl. Law §§5-1103, 15-301, and 15-303. But there are differences between the U.C.C. and the New York provisions. Section 5-1103 applies not only to modification but also to discharge, and a writing is required in both situations. For an interesting interpretation of §15-301, dispensing with the requirement of a writing for the modification of a land contract on the basis of estoppel and partial performance, see Rose v. Spa Realty Assn., 42 N.Y.2d 338, 397 N.Y.S. 922, 366 N.E.2d 1279 (1977).

In a few states, the rule of Foakes v. Beer has been abolished by court decision. The leading case contra is Frye v. Hubbell, 74 N.H. 358, 68 A. 325 (1907).

Patterson, An Apology for Consideration, 58 Colum. L. Rev. 929, 937 (1958):

> It would be better, I submit, in the long run to drop the rule as to a preexisting contractual duty and decide the grounds for avoidance of each second bargain on its facts, i.e., the reference to coercion, deception or lack of good faith in cases where a special relation between the parties imposes such an obligation.

See further, Lord Wright, Ought the Doctrine of Consideration to Be Abolished from the Common Law?, 49 Harv. L. Rev. 1225, 1229 (1936).

In Gray v. Barton, 55 N.Y. 68, 14 Am. Rep. 181 (1873), the plaintiff sued to recover the balance of an account allegedly owed him. Some time before, the plaintiff had agreed to "give" the defendant back the entire debt. To ensure that the gift would be lawful, the plaintiff suggested that the defendant give him a dollar in return, which the defendant did. The plaintiff then gave the defendant a receipt that read "Received of William Barton one dollar, in full, to balance all book accounts, up to date, of whatever name and nature." When the plaintiff subsequently sued to recover the unpaid portion of the account, the defendant set up the gift as a defense. In holding for the defendant, the court maintained that the

---

242. An illustration is afforded by Brown Shoe Co. v. Beall, 107 S.W.2d 456 (Tex. Civ. App. 1937). The case involved a composition agreement between several creditors and their common debtor. The agreement was accompanied by a transfer of the debtor's assets to a trustee who paid the plaintiff's reduced debt by a check marked "paid in full" and cashed by the plaintiff without protest. Consult Note, 97 U. Pa. L. Rev. 99 (1948). For the various theories in favor of the validity of composition agreements, see Massey v. Del-Valley Corp., 46 N.J. Super. 400, 134 A.2d 801 (1957), discussed in 6 Corbin §1283 (1962).

plaintiff had been free, as a matter of law, to make a gift of the defendant's debt if he wished, and concluded that the only legal issue in the case was whether the plaintiff/donor's transfer of the property in question had been effective. In the court's view, the receipt given by the plaintiff worked as effective a delivery of the debt as was possible under the circumstances.

Does the court's conclusion in Gray v. Barton suggest an easy way around the strictures of Foakes v. Beer? Does the dollar given by the defendant strengthen or weaken his position?

For an interesting application of the Gray v. Barton rule in a reduction of rent case, see McKenzie v. Harrison, 120 N.Y. 260 (1880). How would Gray v. Barton be decided in a jurisdiction that has abolished the common law effect of the seal without providing the substitute of a writing as, for instance, New York has? Consult E. A. Farnsworth, Contracts 291 (1982). See further U.C.C. §§3-408, 3-605.

Is the case still good law in New York in the light of General Obligations Law §5-1103 or §15-303, or under the Model Written Obligations Act, which is still in force in Pennsylvania (33 Purdon's Statutes Ann. §6-8)? On pitfalls created by the Pennsylvania statute, consult Fedun v. Mike's Cafe, Inc., 204 Pa. Super. 356, 204 A.2d 776 (1964), aff'd, 419 Pa. 607, 213 A.2d 638 (1965).

HACKLEY v. HEADLEY
45 Mich. 569, 8 N.W. 511 (1881)

Assumpsit. Defendant brings error. Reversed. . . .

Cooley, J.   Headley sued Hackley & McGordon to recover compensation for cutting, hauling and delivering in the Muskegon river a quantity of logs. The performance of the labor was not disputed, but the parties were not agreed as to the construction of the contract in some important particulars, and the amount to which Headley was entitled depended largely upon the determination of these differences. The defendants also claimed to have had a full and complete settlement with Headley, and produced his receipt in evidence thereof. Headley admitted the receipt, but insisted that it was given by him under duress, and the verdict which he obtained in the circuit court was in accordance with his claim. . . .

The question of duress on the part of Hackley & McGordon, in obtaining the discharge, remains. The paper reads as follows:

Muskegon, Mich., August 3, 1875.

Received from Hackley & McGordon their note for four thousand dollars, payable in thirty days, at First National Bank, Grand Rapids, which is

in full for all claims of every kind and nature which I have against said
Hackley & McGordon.

Witness: THOMAS HUME.   JOHN HEADLEY.

Headley's account of the circumstances under which this receipt was
given is in substance as follows: On August 3, 1875, he went to Muskegon,
the place of business of Hackley & McGordon, from his home in Kent
county, for the purpose of collecting the balance which he claimed was
due him under the contract. The amount he claimed was upwards of
$6200, estimating the logs by the Scribner scale. He had an interview with
Hackley in the morning, who insisted that the estimate should be according to the Doyle scale, and who also claimed that he had made payments
to others amounting to some $1400 which Headley should allow. Headley
did not admit these payments, and denied his liability for them if they had
been made. Hackley told Headley to come in again in the afternoon, and
when he did so Hackley said to him: "My figures show there is 4260 and
odd dollars in round numbers your due, and I will just give you $4000. I
will give you our note for $4000." To this Headley replied: "I cannot take
that; it is not right, and you know it. There is over $2000 besides that
belongs to me, and you know it." Hackley replied: "That is the best I will
do with you." Headley said: "I cannot take that, Mr. Hackley," and Hackley replied, "You do the next best thing you are a mind to. You can sue
me if you please." Headley then said: "I cannot afford to sue you, because
I have got to have the money, and I cannot wait for it. If I fail to get the
money to-day, I shall probably be ruined financially, because I have made
no other arrangement to get the money only on this particular matter."
Finally he took the note and gave the receipt, because at the time he
could do nothing better, and in the belief that he would be financially
ruined unless he had immediately the money that was offered him, or
paper by means of which the money might be obtained.

If this statement is correct, the defendants not only took a most unjust
advantage of Headley, but they obtained a receipt which, to the extent
that it assumed to discharge anything not honestly in dispute between
the parties, and known by them to be owing to Headley beyond the sum
received, was without consideration and ineffectual. But was it a receipt
obtained by duress? That is the question which the record presents. The
circuit judge was of opinion that if the jury believed the statement of
Headley they would be justified in finding that duress existed; basing his
opinion largely upon the opinion of this Court in Vyne v. Glenn 41 Mich.
112.

Duress exists when one by the unlawful act of another is induced to
make a contract or perform some act under circumstances which deprive
him of the exercise of free will. It is commonly said to be of either the
person or the goods of the party. Duress of the person is either by imprisonment, or by threats, or by an exhibition of force which apparently

cannot be resisted. It is not intended that duress of the person existed in this case; it is if anything duress of goods, or at least of that nature, and properly enough classed with duress of goods. Duress of goods may exist when one is compelled to submit to an illegal exaction in order to obtain them from one who has them in possession but refuses to surrender them unless the exaction is submitted to.

The leading case involving duress of goods is Astley v. Reynolds 2 Strange, 915. The plaintiff had pledged goods for £20, and when he offered to redeem them, the pawnbroker refused to surrender them unless he was paid £10 for interest. The plaintiff submitted to the exaction, but was held entitled to recover back all that had been unlawfully demanded and taken. This, say the court,

> is a payment by compulsion: the plaintiff might have such an immediate want of his goods that an action of trover would not do his business: where the rule volenti non fit injuria is applied, it must be when the party had his freedom of exercising his will, which this man had not: we must take it he paid the money relying on his legal remedy to get it back again.

The principle of this case was approved in Smith v. Bromley Doug. 696, and also in Ashmole v. Wainwright 2 Q.B. 837. The latter was a suit to recover back excessive charges paid to common carriers who refused until payment was made to deliver the goods for the carriage of which the charges were made. There has never been any doubt but recovery could be had under such circumstances. Harmony v. Bingham 12 N.Y. 99. The case is like it of one having securities in his hands which he refuses to surrender until illegal commissions are paid. Scholey v. Mumford 60 N.Y. 498. So if illegal tolls are demanded, for passing a raft of lumber, and the owner pays them to liberate his raft, he may recover back what he pays. Chase v. Dwinal 7 Me. 134. Other cases in support of the same principle are Shaw v. Woodcock 7 B. & C. 73; Nelson v. Suddarth 1 H. & Munf. 350; White v. Heylman 34 Penn. St. 142; Sasportas v. Jennings 1 Bay, 470; Collins v. Westbury 2 Bay, 211; Crawford v. Cato 22 Ga. 594. So one may recover back money which he pays to release his goods from an attachment which is sued out with knowledge on the part of the plaintiff that he has no cause of action. Chandler v. Sanger 114 Mass. 364. See Spaids v. Barrett 57 Ill. 289. Nor is the principle confined to payments made to recover goods: it applies equally well when money is extorted as a condition to the exercise by the party of any other legal right; for example when a corporation refuses to suffer a lawful transfer of stock till the exaction is submitted to: Bates v. Insurance Co. 3 Johns. Cas. 238; or a creditor withholds his certificate from a bankrupt. Smith v. Bromley Doug. 696. And the mere threat to employ colorable legal authority to compel payment of an unfounded claim is such duress as will support an action to recover back what is paid under it. Beckwith v. Frisbie 32 Vt.

559; Adams v. Reeves 68 N.C. 134; Briggs v. Lewiston 29 Me. 472; Grim v. School District 57 Penn. St. 433; First Nat. Bank v. Watkins 21 Mich. 483.

But where the party threatens nothing which he has not a legal right to perform, there is no duress. Skeate v. Beale 11 Ad. & El. 983; Preston v. Boston 12 Pick. 14. When therefore a judgment creditor threatens to levy his execution on the debtor's goods, and under fear of the levy the debtor executes and delivers a note for the amount, with sureties, the note cannot be avoided for duress. Wilcox v. Howland 23 Pick. 167. Many other cases might be cited, but it is wholly unnecessary. We have examined all to which our attention has been directed, and none are more favorable to the plaintiff's case than those above referred to. Some of them are much less so; notably Atlee v. Backhouse 3 M. & W. 633; Hall v. Schultz 4 Johns. 240; Silliman v. United States 101 U.S. 465.

In what did the alleged duress consist in the present case? Merely in this: that the debtors refused to pay on demand a debt already due, though the plaintiff was in great need of the money and might be financially ruined in case he failed to obtain it. It is not pretended that Hackley & McGordon had done anything to bring Headley to the condition which made this money so important to him at this very time, or that they were in any manner responsible for his pecuniary embarrassment except as they failed to pay this demand. The duress, then, is to be found exclusively in their failure to meet promptly their pecuniary obligation. But this, according to the plaintiff's claim, would have constituted no duress whatever if he had not happened to be in pecuniary straits; and the validity of negotiations, according to this claim, must be determined, not by the defendants' conduct, but by the plaintiff's necessities. The same contract which would be valid if made with a man easy in his circumstances, becomes invalid when the contracting party is pressed with the necessity of immediately meeting his bank paper. But this would be a most dangerous, as well as a most unequal doctrine; and if accepted, no one could well know when he would be safe in dealing on the ordinary terms of negotiation with a party who professed to be in great need.

The case of Vyne v. Glenn 41 Mich. 112, differs essentially from this. There was not a simple withholding of moneys in that case. The decision was made upon facts found by referees who reported that the settlement upon which the defendant relied was made at Chicago, which was a long distance from plaintiff's home and place of business; that the defendant forced the plaintiff into the settlement against his will, by taking advantage of his pecuniary necessities, by informing plaintiff that he had taken steps to stop the payment of money due to the plaintiff from other parties, and that he had stopped the payment of a part of such moneys; that defendant knew the necessities and financial embarrassments in which the plaintiff was involved, and knew that if he failed to get the money so due to him he would be ruined financially; that plaintiff consented to such settlement only in order to get the money due to him, as aforesaid, and the payment of which was stopped by defendant, and which he must have to save him from financial ruin. The report, therefore, showed the same financial embarrassment and the same great need of money which is claimed existed in this case, and the same withholding of moneys lawfully due, but it showed over and above all that an unlawful interference by defendant between the plaintiff and other debtors, by means of which he had stopped the payment to plaintiff of sums due to him from such other debtors. It was this keeping of other moneys from the plaintiff's hands, and not the refusal by defendant to pay his own debt, which was the ruling fact in that case, and which was equivalent, in our opinion, to duress of goods.

These views render a reversal of the judgment necessary, and the case will be remanded for a new trial with costs to the plaintiffs in error.

The other Justices concurred.

NOTE

The *Hackley* case was relied upon by Judge Cooley in holding that no duress existed in Goebel v. Linn, *supra* p. 655. But when the *Hackley* case came up again in 1883, a verdict for the plaintiff, based on a finding that the defense to his claim was not asserted in good faith, was upheld and the release was declared invalid for lack of consideration, 50 Mich. 43, 14 N.W. 693.

The technique used by the Michigan court in coping with the *Hackley* situation, typical as it was, raises a serious problem. Its shortcomings have become apparent in situations where the debtor was careful enough to obtain a release under seal in a jurisdiction which has retained the common-law effect on the seal. This is strikingly illustrated by two Illinois cases.

In Woodbury v. United States Casualty Co., 284 Ill. 227, 120 N.E. 8 (1918), Woodbury, who carried large amounts of accident insurance, had an accident with his rifle in Oregon which resulted in the amputation of his leg. While still suffering from the effects of this ordeal, and after threats from an insurance adjuster that the powerful insurance companies would force him into bankruptcy and possibly imprisonment, Woodbury was induced to accept part of what was due him under the policies. He executed a release to the companies which contained the inscription "LS" after his name. In an action upon the policies for the balance, the Supreme Court held that Oregon, not Illinois law was applicable and that it was not shown that in the former state the symbol "LS" was effective as a seal. The Court however returned the case to the Appellate Court for a finding as to whether the companies' partial surrender of their alleged defenses was consideration for plaintiff's release, on the ground of a "real" or "bona fide" dispute about their liability.

In Jackson v. Security Mutual Life Insurance Co., 233 Ill. 161, 84 N.E. 198 (1908), plaintiff released for $2,500 a claim for $10,000 as beneficiary under her deceased husband's insurance policy. Subsequently, plaintiff brought an action on the policies. Because the release was under seal the court refused to inquire into the question of consideration. Plaintiff was not permitted to show that the insurance company's denial of liability was a sham and that she was induced to give the release by untrue representations that her husband's application for insurance contained false statements. Such facts could be shown only in a suit in equity for reformation or rescission. The fact that she was told to take the $2,500 or get nothing was irrelevant.

Although many states no longer sanction the seal, the same problem can arise today in those jurisdictions which have given a release in writing the same effect as a release under seal, e.g., N.Y. Gen. Obligations Law §5-1103, *supra* p. 673; Patterson, An Apology for Consideration, 58 Colum. L. Rev. 929, 937 (1950).

MITCHELL v. C. C. SANITATION CO., 430 S.W.2d 933 (Tex Civ. App. 1968): While working for his employer, Mitchell was injured in an accident caused by defendant's employee. Defendant's insurer refused to pay the claims of Mitchell's employer unless both Mitchell and the employer signed releases. His employer told Mitchell, an employee at will, that he would lose his job if he did not sign the release. Defendant and his insurer knew of the pressure being put on Mitchell and consented to it, though neither had contact with him. Mitchell received only $62.12 for his release. He subsequently brought an action for $40,000 in damages for pain and suffering, future doctor bills, and loss of earning capacity. The court held that there was a triable issue of fact as to whether Mitchell's release had been obtained by duress, even though he could have been fired by his employer for any reason.

FITTS v. PANHANDLE & S. F. RY.
222 S.W. 158 (Tex. Comm. App. 1920)

McCLENDON, J.   C. I. Fitts, the plaintiff, recovered judgment against the Panhandle & Santa Fe Railway Company, defendant, for the loss of his eye, alleged to have been caused by the actionable negligence of defendant. Among other defenses to the suit, defendant pleaded a release in full, the recited consideration whereof being: "An order on the treasurer of said company for $1, the receipt of which is hereby acknowledged," and "the promise of said company to employ me for one day as trucker at the usual rate of pay, the execution thereof being conclusive evidence that said company has made me such promise." Plaintiff alleged the invalidity of said release upon several grounds, one of which was that it was without consideration. Upon the trial, the plaintiff having testified that he never received the $1 recited in the release, the court declined to admit the release in evidence. The Court of Civil Appeals reversed and remanded the cause, holding this ruling to be erroneous. 188 S.W. 528. Writ of error was granted by the Committee of Judges, in the view that the Court of Civil Appeals committed error in this holding.

The full review and discussion by the Court of Civil Appeals of the authorities upon the question at issue renders unnecessary any extended observations thereupon. The release in question is identical in its language with that in the case of Quebe v. Railway, 98 Tex. 6, 81 S.W. 20, 66 L.R.A. 734, 4 Ann. Cas. 545, except as to the subject-matter dealt with. The cases are practically on all fours in every particular, except than in the *Quebe Case* the $1 was paid, whereas in the case at bar it was not paid. In the *Quebe Case* the Supreme Court, speaking through Judge Williams, says:

"The consideration was a valuable and legal one, though small. Considering the fact that the matter settled was regarded by both parties as involving no large amount, it cannot be said the smallness of the consideration, by itself, furnishes grounds for disregarding the release."

The distinguishing element in the two cases is the failure in the instant case to pay the dollar. We have the views of the Supreme Court upon the question thus presented, expressed in the following language:

> Since the recited consideration of $1 in the release in this case was not paid, it is our opinion that the release was wholly without consideration. It seems to us that a mere promise to re-employ for one day, paying for the work done for that one day no more than the ordinary or customary rate of wages, conferred, in practical effect, no benefit upon the plaintiff, and the railway company thereby suffered no detriment, since inevitably it was to receive the day's work for the re-employment.

We conclude that the judgment of the Court of Civil Appeals should be reversed, and that of the district court affirmed.

Phillips, C.J. We approve the judgment recommended in this case.

NOTE

For the impact of the Federal Employers' Liability Act on the validity of settlements, see Callen v. Pennsylvania Railroad Co., 332 U.S. 625, 68 S. Ct. 296, 92 L. Ed. 242 (1948); Rankin v. New York, New Haven & Hartford R.R., 338 Mass. 178, 154 N.E.2d 613 (1958).

RICKETTS v. PENNSYLVANIA R.R.

153 F.2d 757 (2d Cir. 1946)

For a report of the case, see p. 883 *infra*.

CONSOLIDATED EDISON CO. v. ARROLL

66 Misc. 2d 816, 322 N.Y.S.2d 420 (N.Y. Civ. Ct. 1971)

Milton SANDERS, Judge.

This is an action by Consolidated Edison Company of New York, Inc., ("Con Edison,") to recover a balance alleged to be due from defendant on five electric bills for the summer periods of 1968, 1969, and 1970. Defendant disputed the amounts of these bills on the basis that they exceeded past bills for comparable periods, including the summer of 1967, by too great an amount to have any validity. He questioned the accuracy of the meter and/or the readings taken, as well as Con Edison's statements as to the amount of electricity consumed. After a considerable amount of correspondence had taken place between the parties, defendant sent a letter on December 6, 1969 to the attention of the president of Con Edison, with carbon copies to the company at their local office and to the post office box designated for the payment of bills. The letter stated again defendant's disagreement with the amounts of the first three bills, and advised that he had arbitrarily picked the sum of $35.00 as the proper amount due on each bill, as that sum reflected his past experience, and stated further that he was sending three checks for $35.00 each to the office designated for collection. Each check would bear the legend:

> This check is in full payment and satisfaction of the bill of Consolidated Edison Company of New York, Inc., to Mark Arroll, Account Number 26-2726-0191-002 for the period of _____ to _____ and negotiation of this check consitutes release of any bills or claims of Consolidated Edison Company of New York, Inc., sometimes known as Con Edison, against Mark Arroll.

The letter went on to state that it is the law that the cashing or mere retention of the checks beyond a reasonable length of time constitutes an accord and satisfaction. On September 25, 1970, defendant took the same action with respect to the remaining two bills in dispute, sending a similar letter to the president of the company, and carbon copies to the same offices. Con Edison subsequently replied to defendant's letters, but it merely re-stated in its replies that the meter and the readings thereof had been found to be accurate, and that the electricity billed for had actually been consumed. The letters made no mention of and completely ignored the paragraphs advising about the checks. Five checks in the amount of $35.00 each were mailed by defendant to the address designated by Con Edison for the payment of bills. Each check bore the legend previously stated on the back thereof. On the face of each check the words "paid in full" were written, together with an identification of the bill to which it related, the defendant's account number, and a reference to the letter of either December 6, 1969 or September 25, 1970. All five checks were received and deposited and Con Edison has retained the proceeds thereof. Con Edison now seeks the difference between the payments received and the full amounts of the bills rendered. The customer's defense is accord and satisfaction.

After considering all of the competent and credible evidence presented, I am satisfied that the meter and the readings taken thereof by Con Edison were accurate, and that the electricity billed for was actually consumed, since defendant failed to submit any evidence to the contrary. I find, therefore, that the disputed bills reflected the proper charges for defendant's use of electricity. We are concerned, however, with whether or not the defense of accord and satisfaction has been established in the light of the facts and circumstances described.

The law is well settled that where an amount due is in dispute, and the debtor sends a check for less than the amount claimed, and clearly expresses his intention that the check has been sent as payment in full, and not on account or in part payment, the cashing or retention of the check by the creditor is deemed an acceptance by the creditor of the conditions stated, and operates as an accord and satisfaction of the claim (Fuller v. Kemp, 138 N.Y. 231, 33 N.E. 1034; Nassoiy v. Tomlinson, 148 N.Y. 326, 42 N.E. 715; Schuttinger v. Woodruff, 259 N.Y. 212, 181 N.E. 361; Carlton Credit Corp. v. Atlantic Refining Co., 12 A.D.2d 613, 208 N.Y.S.2d 622, aff'd 10 N.Y.2d 723, 219 N.Y.S.2d 269, 176 N.E.2d 837). Con Edison's contention that there was no bona fide dispute as to the amount due has no merit. As the Court stated in Schuttinger v. Woodruff, *supra*, in order for the rule to apply,

> the debtor must honestly hold the opinion either that he owes nothing or that he is bound only to the extent of paying less than his adversary seeks to exact. . . . The dispute need not rest upon factors arising from sound reasons. The debtor may be wrong in his contention. That he honestly believes in the correctness of his position is enough.

(See also Simons v. Supreme Council American Legion of Honor, 178 N.Y. 263, 70 N.E. 776). It is evident, and I so find, from the testimony and the documents and correspondence offered in evidence, that the defendant honestly and in good faith believed that he owed less than the amount Con Edison claimed. Under the circumstances it cannot be said that a bona fide dispute did not exist.

In view of the existence of an honest dispute as to the amount of electricity consumed, a settlement by way of accord and satisfaction would not violate Sections 65(2) or 66(12) of the Public Service Law, which prohibit the electric company from granting preferences to customers.

This brings us to the question as to whether the retention of the proceeds of the checks by Con Edison bound the company to an accord and satisfaction. Evidence was presented by Con Edison that the address designated for mailing payment of bills was a post office box from which all payments were picked up directly by employees of the bank in which the company maintained its account. The company argues that the nature and volume of its operations does not allow for an examination by bank employees of each and every check it receives for language written thereon which could bind it to an accord and satisfaction. What Con Edison is really saying is that because it conducts such a large operation, it should be exempted from the application of well settled principles of law which would bind individuals and all smaller business organizations. I cannot accept this conclusion. To permit Con Edison to follow one set of rules while everyone else is following another would cast an intolerable burden on the orderly functioning of the community. The fact remains that Con Edison accepted the benefits of defendant's checks. Con Edison cannot, by arranging for someone else to accept payment of bills for its own convenience, avoid the consequences of the law.

It should be noted that even if Con Edison had written to defendant and expressly rejected the condition that the checks were to be accepted as full payment, the depositing and retention of the proceeds of the checks would nevertheless operate as an accord and satisfaction. As the court stated in Carlton Credit Corp. v. Atlantic Refining Co., *supra*,

> The plaintiff could not accept the payment and reject the condition (citations omitted). It was fully aware of the attempt to satisfy the amount claimed with a lesser payment but despite that it accepted the check with the condition imposed. True, it is stated that there was no intention to accept the check in full satisfaction and protest was registered. However, such protest is unavailing.

(See also Rosenblatt v. Birnbaum, 16 N.Y.2d 212, 264 N.Y.S.2d 521, 212 N.E.2d 37). It is not the creditor's intent that controls. "What is said is overridden by what is done, and assent is imputed as an inference of law" (Cardozo, Ch. J., in Hudson v. Yonkers Fruit Co., 258 N.Y. 168, 179 N.E. 373).

There is no question that Con Edison was given sufficient notification that the checks were to be considered as payment in full. Defendant's letters to Con Edison's president clearly indicated defendant's intent. In

Carlton Credit Corp. v. Atlantic Refining Co., *supra*, a case quite similar to this one, it was said that:

> The acceptance and negotiation by the plaintiff of the defendant's check constituted an accord and satisfaction. The covering letter to which the check was annexed, itemizing in detail the deductions claimed, makes it clear that the payment made was conditioned upon its acceptance as payment in full for the larger amount claimed by the plaintiff to be due it from the defendant.

The affirmative defense of accord and satisfaction is sustained. Judgment for defendant.

NOTE

The court based its outrageous decision on Fuller v. Kemp, which has come in for severe criticism. L. Hand, J., in Matlack Coal & Iron Corp. v. New York Quebracho Extract Co., 30 F.2d 275 (2d Cir. 1929), regarded it as doubtful whether Fuller v. Kemp "is still good law in New York," referring to Eames Vacuum Brake Co. v. Prosser, 157 N.Y. 289, 51 N.E. 986 (1898). The latter case, in discussing Fuller v. Kemp and Nassoiy v. Tomlinson, 148 N.Y. 326, 42 N.E. 715 (1896), which followed *Fuller*, stated: "In these cases the doctrine of accord and satisfaction was carried to the extreme limit, and it is not our purpose to further extend the rule."

For the "law" on accounts stated, see Restatement Second §282; 6 Corbin, ch. 72. Not infrequently, courts have labeled an executory accord an account stated or a substituted contract to avoid the rule that no action lies on an executory accord. See 6 Corbin §1271; *infra* p. 689.

The 1950 version of the U.C.C. contained in §3-702(3) the following provision:

> Where a check or similar payment instrument provides that it is in full satisfaction of an obligation, the payee satisfies the underlying obligation by negotiating the instrument or obtaining its payment unless he establishes that the original obligor has taken unconscionable advantage in the circumstances or unless it is the drawer who has initiated collection on behalf of the payee.

For the present law see U.C.C. §1-207, critically discussed in Hawkland, The Effect of U.C.C. §1-207 on the Doctrine of Accord and Satisfaction by Conditional Check, 74 Comm. L.J. 329 (1969).

In Metropolitan Life Insurance Co. v. Richter, 173 Okla. 489, 49 P.2d 94 (1935), the defendant insurance company was not permitted to treat the cashing of a check given in full payment as an accord and satisfaction, on the grounds that it had failed to notify the claimant of ambiguities in his claim and had resorted to the interpretation most favorable to itself.

For Cardozo's attempt to control the harshness of New York case law, see the *Hudson* case, which follows.

Was there a way for Consolidated Edison to protect itself? Both the common law and the Code distinguish between liquidated and nonliquidated claims. A check given for a lesser amount than a liquidated claim can be cashed with impunity. The distinction between liquidated and nonliquidated claims is, however, wavering and blurred since an otherwise liquidated claim may become unliquidated by virtue of a bona fide dispute. See 6 Corbin §§1287-1290; Code §2-408, Comment 2. U.C.C. §1-207 enables the creditor of an unliquidated claim to preserve his rights by cashing a check for a smaller amount under protest. This device, however, was obviously not available to plaintiff, a huge enterprise with thousands of customers.

A court has another way to protect the creditor — by finding the contractual requisites of an accord lacking. See Bailee Lumber Co. v. Kincaid Carolina Corp., 4 N.C. App. 342, 167 S.E.2d 85 (1969). See, in general, Hawkland, The Effect of U.C.C. §1-207 on the Doctrine of Accord and Satisfaction by Conditional Check, 74 Comm. L.J. 329 (1969). Can a debtor protect himself against the creditor's abuse of the privilege of cashing under protest?

HUDSON v. YONKERS FRUIT CO., INC.
258 N.Y. 168, 179 N.E. 373 (1932)

Action by George C. Hudson against the Yonkers Fruit Company, Incorporated. From a judgment of the Appellate Division (233 App. Div. 884, 250 N.Y.S. 991) reversing a judgment in favor of the plaintiff, and directing judgment for the defendant dismissing the complaint, plaintiff appeals.

Judgment of Appellate Division reversed, and that of Trial Term affirmed.

CARDOZO, C.J. Plaintiff, then the owner and in possession of a quantity of apples, requested the defendant to procure a purchaser. This the defendant did, and collected the price. The plaintiff says that the service was to be rendered without charge; a friendly accommodation. The defendant says that there was an express agreement for the payment of a commission at the rate of ten per cent.

The defendant, after collecting the proceeds of the sales, sent a statement of the account to the plaintiff, in which items amounting in their total to $1,017.60, ten per cent. of the price, were deducted for commissions. With this statement there was sent a check for $3,184.50, the balance then due if the deduction was correct. The plaintiff kept the check, but made protest at once that the deduction was erroneous. In an action to recover the amount withheld, the jury returned a verdict in favor of the plaintiff, thereby finding that the defendant's service was to be gratuitous. The Appellate Division reversed and dismissed the complaint, holding that the acceptance by the plaintiff of the balance conceded to be his was an accord and satisfaction.

We discover nothing in the record to give support to that conclusion.

The defendant had in its custody money belonging to the plaintiff; collection made by the defendant upon a sale of the plaintiff's apples. It had no lien upon the money, for it had not acted as a factor intrusted with possession. At most it had a counterclaim for the recovery of a commission at the rate of ten per cent. What remained after the deduction of that commission was due to the plaintiff absolutely and at all events. In taking it, he was not taking anything belonging to the defendant. He was taking his own money, his in any event, whether the deduction of a commission was proper or erroneous. The defendant was more than a debtor. It was an agent holding in its possession the money of its principal, and guilty of a tort if it kept them for itself. Baker v. New York Nat. Exchange Bank, 100 N.Y. 31, 2 N.E. 452, 53 Am. Rep. 150.

Two forms of accord and satisfaction of unliquidated claims are to be discovered in the books. One is where there is a true assent to the acceptance of a payment in compromise of a dispute, or in extinguishment of a liability uncertain in amount. 1 Williston on Contracts, sec. 135; 3 Id. sec. 1851; Am. L. Inst., Restatement of Contracts, draft No. 9, sec. 36-A; Fuller v. Kemp, 138 N.Y. 231, 237, 33 N.E. 1034, 20 L.R.A. 785; Wahl v. Barnum, 116 N.Y. 87, 22 N.E. 280, 5 L.R.A. 623. The other is where the tender of the payment has been coupled with a condition whereby the use of the money will be wrongful if the condition is ignored. Protest will then be unavailing if the money is retained. What is said is overridden by what is done, and assent is imputed as an inference of law. 3 Williston on Contracts, secs. 1855, 1856; Am. L. Inst., Restatement of Contracts, draft No. 9, sec. 38-A.

Accord and satisfaction falling within the first of these classes, there plainly was not upon the facts of the case at hand. There had been no dispute between the parties and there was no assent by the creditor, but prompt and emphatic protest. There was not even any compromise. The amount deducted in the accounting did not involve an abatement by the defendant of anything, large or small, from the maximum commission due for its services, if it was entitled to anything. It kept the full commission of ten per cent. due according to its witness by force of an express agreement. . . . A compromise may result where something is abated from a demand which exists, if it exists at all, for a liquidated sum. A compromise may result where a demand, previously unliquidated, is fixed at a given figure, for the right is thus surrendered to make the figure higher. None of these elements of detriment is present in the case at hand. The defendant did not abate a dollar from a liquidated claim. It did not surrender the opportunity to add to the amount of an unliquidated claim. The conclusion is inescapable that there was no genuine assent to an accord and satisfaction, and that the debt was not discharged unless the situation is one in which the law imputes assent, irrespective of the state of mind accompanying the receipt.

The question then is whether the acceptance of the check without approval of the deduction is to be viewed as the breach of a condition lawfully imposed. A debtor paying his own money may couple the payment with such conditions as he pleases. Nassoiy v. Tomlinson, 148 N.Y. 326, 331, 42 N.E. 715, 716, 51 Am. St. Rep. 695; 3 Williston, *supra*, sec. 1854. The mere fact that he is a debtor does not deprive him of that privilege. If he has the title to the money, he may pick and choose among his creditors, or, refusing to pay any one until coerced by legal process, may keep the money for himself. From this the rule has grown up in connection with the satisfaction of unliquidated demands that one who sends a check to another upon a condition explicitly declared, that the demand shall be extinguished or the check sent back unused, may hold the creditor to the condition, however embarrassing the choice. Nassoiy v. Tomlinson, *supra*; Am. L. Inst., Contracts, sec. 38-A. "Always the manner of the tender and of the payment shall be directed by him that maketh the tender or payment, and not by him that accepteth it." Pinnel's Case, 5 Coke 117, quoted in Nassoiy v. Tomlinson, *supra*. The use of the check in violation of the condition would be an act of conversion. What is said or written by the creditor may be a refusal to assent. The law imputes to him an assent on the basis of his acts. Williston, *supra*; Restatement, Am. L. Inst., *supra*.

In the case at hand, the condition was not lawfully imposed, if we assume provisionally that it was imposed at all. The defendant was not merely a debtor, paying its own money, which it would have been free to retain or to disburse according to its pleasure. It was an agent, a fiduciary, accounting for money belonging to its principal. No matter whether the deduction of a commission was proper or improper, the balance represented by the check was due in any event. The law will not suffer an agent to withold moneys collected for a principal's account by the pressure of a threat that no part of the moneys will be remitted to the owner without the approval of deductions beneficial to the agent. Such conduct is a flagrant abuse of the opportunities and powers of a fiduciary position. Britton v. Ferrin, 171 N.Y. 235, 63 N.E. 954; Morris v. Windsor Trust Co., 213 N.Y. 27, 106 N.E. 753, Ann. Cas. 1916C, 972. We do not need to determine whether a condition would be lawful if the tender by the agent were to involve some abatement of deductions that might otherwise be his. Sufficient for the decision of this case is the ruling that the condition is unlawful when what is paid is no more than must certainly be due. A payment so made is not within Nassoiy v. Tomlinson, and other cases of that type. There, as the court was careful to point out (page 331 of 148 N.Y., 42 N.E. 715, 716), "the money tendered belonged to them [i.e., to the makers of the tender], and they had the right to say on what condition it should be received." The payment in this case is within the doctrine of such cases as Mance v. Hossington, 205 N.Y. 33, 36, 98 N.E. 203, and Eames Vacuum Brake Co. v. Prosser, 157 N.Y. 289, 51 N.E. 986. What was paid had no connection with what was disputed and reserved. "The payment of an admitted liability is not a payment of or consideration for, an alleged accord and satisfaction of another and independent alleged liability." Mance v. Hossington, *supra*; cf. Hettrick Mfg. Co. v. Barish, *supra*, at page 684 of 120 Misc. Rep., 199 N.Y.S. 755, 766, and cases there cited. The doctrine of accord and satisfaction by force of an assent that is merely constructive or imputed assumes as its foundation stone the existence of a condition lawfully imposed. The rationale of the doctrine fails if submission to the alternative would be submission to a crime. A principal does not put himself in the wrong way by repudiating a condition where the agent by withholding payment would be guilty of embezzlement.

Another difficulty confronts the defendant if all the objections thus far considered are overcome. The difficulty remains that nothing in the form of the account rendered or in the accompanying check amounts to the imposition of a condition that the check must be rejected if any item of the account is thereafter to be questioned by the creditor. All that the account does is to enumerate the debits and the credits (among which are items of commission), and strike a balance. The creditor is not informed that the deductions claimed by the debtor, the accounting agent, will be deemed to be finally approved by the acceptance of the check. He is not informed that the tender is in settlement of a dispute, for none had yet arisen. He is informed of nothing more than the readiness of his debtor to account to him for money admittedly his own, without the suggestion of a purpose to foreclose controversy as to the deductions if any are disputed. An accord and satisfaction is not so easily established. Eames Vacuum Brake Co. v. Prosser, 157 N.Y. 289, 51 N.E. 986; Komp v. Raymond, 175 N.Y. 102, 67 N.E. 113; Gaston & Co. v. Storch, 253 N.Y. 68, 71, 170 N.E. 496. "The debtor must make it clear that it is taken in full payment." 3 Williston on Contracts, sec. 1856, p. 3181; Gaston & Co. v. Storch, *supra*; Rose v. American Paper Co., 83 N.J.L. 707, 85 A. 354. An accord and satisfaction results only where the act of the creditor in "taking the check would be tortious except on the assumption of a taking in full satisfaction." Williston, *supra*; Lovekin v. Fairbanks, Morse & Co., 282 Pa. 100, 103, 127 A. 450. Surely no one would urge that, upon any showing here made, the acceptance by this principal of his own money, owing from his agent whether the deductions stand or fall, would constitute a tort, except on the assumption that the deductions were approved and would never be assailed.

The trial judge did not err in holding that the burden of proof was on the defendant to establish its right to the allowance of a commission. The plaintiff made out a prima facie case when he showed a sum of money in the possession of his agent; the proceeds of the sale that had been made for his account. If the defendant was at liberty to retain a portion of such fund as compensation for its service, the right to make such a deduction was to be enforced through the medium of a counterclaim. There was no lien upon the fund, for the defendant in this transaction was not intrusted with possession, and was not acting as a factor. At the end of the whole case, whatever may have been the inferences to be drawn at intermediate stages from the uncontradicted evidence of a service rendered at request, the defendant was under the burden of satisfying the triers of the facts that the service was not gratuitous, but was to be rendered for a price. 1 Williston on Contracts, sec. 36.

The judgment of the Appellate Division should be reversed and that of the Trial Term affirmed, with costs in the Appellate Division and in this court.

Judgment accordingly.

PETTERSON v. PATTBERG

248 N.Y. 86, 161 N.E. 428 (1928)

Appeal from a judgment of the Appellate Division of the Supreme Court in the second judicial department, entered November 18, 1927, affirming a judgment in favor of plaintiff entered upon a verdict directed by the court. . . .

KELLOGG, J. The evidence given upon the trial sanctions the following statement of facts: John Petterson, of whose last will and testament the plaintiff is the executrix, was the owner of a parcel of real estate in Brooklyn, known as 5301 Sixth avenue. The defendant was the owner of a bond executed by Petterson, which was secured by a third mortgage upon the parcel. On April 4, 1924, there remained unpaid upon the principal the sum of $5,450. This amount was payable in installments of $250 on April 25, 1924, and upon a like monthly date every three months thereafter. Thus the bond and mortgage had more than five years to run before the entire sum became due. Under date of the 4th of April, 1924, the defendant wrote Petterson as follows:

> I hereby agree to accept cash for the mortgage which I hold against premises 5301 6th Ave., Brooklyn, N.Y. It is understood and agreed as a consideration I will allow you $780 providing said mortgage is paid on or before May 31, 1924, and the regular quarterly payment due April 25, 1924, is paid when due.

On April 25, 1924, Petterson paid the defendant the installment of principal due on that date. Subsequently, on a day in the latter part of

May, 1924, Petterson presented himself at the defendant's home, and
knocked at the door. The defendant demanded the name of his caller.
Petterson replied: "It is Petterson. I have come to pay off the mortgage."
The defendant answered that he had sold the mortgage. Petterson stated
that he would like to talk with the defendant, so the defendant partly
opened the door. Thereupon Petterson exhibited the cash, and said he
was ready to pay off the mortgage according to the agreement. The
defendant refused to take the money. Prior to this conversation Petterson
had made a contract to sell the land to a third person free and clear of the
mortgage to the defendant. Meanwhile, also, the defendant had sold the
bond and mortgage to a third party. It, therefore, became necessary for
Petterson to pay to such person the full amount of the bond and mortgage. It is claimed that he thereby sustained a loss of $780, the sum which
the defendant agreed to allow upon the bond and mortgage, if payment in
full of principal, less than sum, was made on or before May 31st, 1924.
The plaintiff has had a recovery for the sum thus claimed, with interest.

Clearly the defendant's letter proposed to Petterson the making of a
unilateral contract, the gift of a promise in exchange for the performance
of an act. The thing conditionally promised by the defendant was the
reduction of the mortgage debt. The act requested to be done, in consideration of the offered promise, was payment in full of the reduced principal of the debt prior to the due date thereof. "If an act is requested, that
very act, and no other, must be given." Williston on Contracts §73. "In
case of offers for a consideration, the performance of the consideration is
always deemed a condition." Langdell's Summary of the Law of Contracts, §4. It is elementary that any offer to enter into a unilateral contract
may be withdrawn before the act requested to be done has been performed. Williston on Contracts, §60; Langdell's Summary, §4; Offord v.
Davis, 12 C.B. (N.S.) 748. A bidder at a sheriff's sale may revoke his bid at
any time before the property is struck down to him. Fisher v. Seltzer, 23
Penn. St. 308, 62 Am. Dec. 335. The offer of a reward in consideration of
an act to be performed is revocable before the very act requested has been
done. Shuey v. United States, 92 U.S. 73, 23 L. Ed. 697; Biggers v. Owen,
79 Ga. 658, 5 S.E. 193; Fitch v. Snedaker, 38 N.Y. 248, 97 Am. Dec. 791.
So, also, an offer to pay a broker commissions upon a sale of land for the
offeror, is revocable at any time before the land is sold, although prior to
revocation the broker performs services in an effort to effectuate a sale.
Stensgaard v. Smith, 43 Minn. 11, 44 N.W. 669, 19 Am. St. Rep. 205;
Smith v. Cauthen, 98 Miss. 746, 54 So. 844.

An interesting question arises when, as here, the offeree approaches
the offeror with the intention of proffering performance and, before actual tender is made, the offer is withdrawn. Of such a case Williston says:
"The offeror may see the approach of the offeree and know that an
acceptance is contemplated. If the offeror can say 'I revoke' before the
offeree accepts, however brief the interval of time between the two acts,

there is no escape from the conclusion that the offer is terminated."
Williston on Contracts, §60b. In this instance Petterson, standing at the
door of the defendant's house, stated to the defendant that he had come
to pay off the mortgage. Before a tender of the necessary money had been
made the defendant informed Petterson that he had sold the mortgage.
That was a definite notice to Petterson that the defendant could not
perform his offered promise and that a tender to the defendant, who was
no longer the creditor, would be ineffective to satisfy the debt.

> An offer to sell property may be withdrawn before acceptance without any
> formal notice to the person to whom the offer is made. It is sufficient if that
> person has actual knowledge that the person who made the offer has done
> some act inconsistent with the continuance of the offer, such as selling the
> property to a third person.

Dickinson v. Dodds, 2 Ch. Div. 463, headnote. To the same effect is
Coleman v. Applegarth, 68 Md. 21, 11 A. 284, 6 Am. St. Rep. 417. Thus,
it clearly appears that the defendant's offer was withdrawn before its
acceptance had been tendered. It is unnecessary to determine, therefore,
what the legal situation might have been had tender been made before
withdrawal. It is the individual view of the writer that the same result
would follow. This would be so, for the act requested to be performed was
the completed act of payment, a thing incapable of performance, unless
assented to by the person to be paid. Williston on Contracts §60b. Clearly
an offering party has the right to name the precise act performance of
which would convert his offer into a binding promise. Whatever the act
may be until it is performed the offer must be revocable. However, the
supposed case is not before us for decision. We think that in this particular instance the offer of the defendant was withdrawn before it became a
binding promise, and, therefore, that no contract was ever made for the
breach of which the plaintiff may claim damages.

The judgment of the Appellate Division and that of the Trial Term
should be reversed, and the complaint dismissed, with costs in all courts.

LEHMAN, J. (dissenting). The defendant's letter to Petterson constituted a promise on his part to accept payment at a discount of the mortgage he held, provided the mortgage is paid on or before May 31, 1924.
Doubtless by the terms of the promise itself, the defendant made payment of the mortgage by the plaintiff, before the stipulated time, a condition precedent to performance by the defendant of his promise to accept
payment at a discount. If the condition precedent has not been performed, it is because the defendant made performance impossible by
refusing to accept payment, when the plaintiff came with an offer of
immediate performance. "It is a principle of fundamental justice that if a
promisor is himself the cause of the failure of performance either of an

obligation due him or of a condition upon which his own liability depends, he cannot take advantage of the failure." Williston on Contracts §677. The question in this case is not whether payment of the mortgage is a condition precedent to the performance of a promise made by the defendant, but, rather, whether at the time the defendant refused the offer of payment, he had assumed any binding obligation, even though subject to condition.

The promise made by the defendant lacked consideration at the time it was made. Nevertheless the promise was not made as a gift or mere gratuity to the plaintiff. It was made for the purpose of obtaining from the defendant something which the plaintiff desired. It constituted an offer which was to become binding whenever the plaintiff should give, in return for the defendant's promise, exactly the consideration which the defendant requested.

Here the defendant requested no counter promise from the plaintiff. The consideration requested by the defendant for his promise to accept payment was, I agree, some act to be performed by the plaintiff. Until the act requested was performed, the defendant might undoubtedly revoke his offer. Our problem is to determine from the words of the letter, read in the light of surrounding circumstances, what act the defendant requested as consideration for his promise.

The defendant undoubtedly made his offer as an inducement to the plaintiff to "pay" the mortgage before it was due. Therefore, it is said, that "the act requested to be performed was the completed act of payment, a thing incapable of performance, unless assented to by the person to be paid." In unmistakable terms the defendant agreed to accept payment, yet we are told that the defendant intended, and the plaintiff should have understood, that the act requested by the defendant, as consideration for his promise to accept payment, included performance by the defendant himself of the very promise for which the act was to be consideration. The defendant's promise was to become binding only when fully performed; and part of the consideration to be furnished by the plaintiff for the defendant's promise was to be the performance of that promise by the defendant. So construed, the defendant's promise or offer, though intended to induce action by the plaintiff, is but a snare and delusion. The plaintiff could not reasonably suppose that the defendant was asking him to procure the performance by the defendant of the very act which the defendant promised to do, yet we are told that even after the plaintiff had done all else which the defendant requested, the defendant's promise was still not binding because the defendant chose not to perform.

I cannot believe that a result so extraordinary could have been intended when the defendant wrote the letter. "The thought behind the phrase proclaims itself misread when the outcome of the reading is injustice or absurdity." See opinion of Cardozo, C.J., in Surace v. Danna, 248 N.Y. 18, 161 N.E. 315. If the defendant intended to induce payment by the plaintiff and yet reserve the right to refuse payment when offered he should have used a phrase better calculated to express his meaning than the words: "I agree to accept." A promise to accept payment, by its very terms, must necessarily become binding, if at all, not later than when a present offer to pay is made.

I recognize that in this case only an offer of payment, and not a formal tender of payment, was made before the defendant withdrew his offer to accept payment. Even the plaintiff's part in the act of payment was then not technically complete. Even so, under a fair construction of the words of the letter I think the plaintiff had done the act which the defendant requested as consideration for his promise. The plaintiff offered to pay, with present intention and ability to make that payment. A formal tender is seldom made in business transactions, except to lay the foundation for subsequent assertion in a court of justice of rights which spring from refusal of the tender. If the defendant acted in good faith in making his offer to accept payment, he could not well have intended to draw a distinction in the act requested of the plaintiff in return, between an offer which unless refused would ripen into completed payment, and a formal tender. Certainly the defendant could not have accepted or intended that the plaintiff would make a formal tender of payment without first stating that he had come to make payment. We should not read into the language of the defendant's offer a meaning which would prevent enforcement of the defendant's promise after it had been accepted by the plaintiff in the very way which the defendant must have intended it should be accepted, if he acted in good faith.

The judgment should be affirmed.

Cardozo, Ch. J., and Pound, Crane, and O'Brien, JJ., concur with Kellogg, J. Lehman, J., dissents in opinion, in which Andrews, J., concurs.

Judgments reversed, etc.

NOTE

1. The case has been widely noted; 29 Colum. L. Rev. 199 (1929); 33 id. 463 (1933); 17 Calif. L. Rev. 153 (1929). The Note in 14 Cornell L.Q. 81 (footnote 18) (1928) contains an interesting piece of additional information:

> Other facts in the case [of Petterson v. Pattberg], not appearing in the opinion, may have influenced the court. The record of the trial (folios 95-97) reveals that the defendant was prevented from testifying as to a letter, sent to the plaintiff's testator, revoking the offer because such testimony was inadmissible under §347 of the Civil Practice Act, which excludes the testimony of one of the interested parties, to a transaction, where the other

is dead and so unable to contradict the evidence. The record (folio 59) also seems to suggest that the mortgagor knew of the previous sale of the mortgage, since he brought $4,000 in cash with him, and was accompanied by his wife and a notary public as witnesses: anticipation of the defendant's refusal by seeking to get evidence on which to base this action seems to be a plausible explanation. There was no actual proof of knowledge of the defendant's inability to carry out his offer but the situation was suspicious.

Does this throw any light on the decision? On the nature of the judicial process?

2. Taking the decision at its face value, the majority opinion strikingly illustrates the powerful force of the "flagpole" doctrine. But could not the court have reached the opposite result without sacrificing the distinction between unilateral and bilateral contracts? Can an offeror still revoke until acceptance even though he knows that the offeree has the honest intention and ability to accept (pay)? Suppose Petterson had mailed a postal money order or a check certified by the Chase National Bank for the amount of his debt to defendant. Would he have been protected from the moment of mailing? See Flowers' Case, Noy 67 (1600).

3. Same decision today under §§45 or 90 of the Restatement Second, or in New York under Gen. Obligations Law §15-503? On tender as a discharge, see 5A Corbin §§1233-1235 (1964). Is §15-503 needed in the light of §5-1103, discussed *supra* p. 673?

GOLDBARD v. EMPIRE STATE MUTUAL LIFE INSURANCE CO.

171 N.Y.S.2d 194, 5 A.D.2d 230 (1958)

BREITEL, Justice. Plaintiff appeals from a determination of the Appellate Term modifying a judgment rendered in his favor against defendant after trial without a jury in the Municipal Court. The Appellate Term modification, one justice dissenting, reduced plaintiff's recovery from $2,800 to $800. That court granted leave for plaintiff to appeal to this Court.

Plaintiff is the insured under an accident and health insurance policy providing monthly indemnity; defendant is the insurer. There were a number of legal and factual issues passed upon by the trial court in a thoughtful and considered opinion. With one exception the Appellate Term affirmed these findings and conclusions of the trial court. It is with that exception alone that discussion is necessary. The other issues have been considered, but it is not necessary to discuss them, since this Court is in agreement, to that extent, with both the trial court and the Appellate Term.

The issue which divided the Appellate Term is whether plaintiff-insured settled and compromised his claims against defendant-insurer prior to suit, with finality, and, as a consequence, is limited in recovery to the settlement figure of $800. The trial court found that insured was not so limited, but a majority of the Appellate Term disagreed.

It is concluded that the settlement negotiations between insured and insurer did not constitute either a substituted agreement or an enforceable executory accord; and, that therefore, insured is not prevented from pursuing his original claim. Hence, the order of the Appellate Term should, in effect, be reversed and the judgment of the Municipal Court reinstated, except that the latter judgment should be modified by reduction to the sum of $2,600 based on the concession of insured as to when liability under the policy commenced.

Insured is a barber by trade. Before his illness he ran his own one-man shop. In December, 1951 insurer issued its annually renewable policy to insured, who maintained his payment of premiums as required by the policy. In 1955 insured filed claims based upon a fungus hand infection from which he was suffering and which he asserted totally disabled him from engaging in his occupation. If true, he was entitled to monthly indemnity at fixed amounts under the policy. There then ensued a sequence of events in which some payments, vouchered as final, were offered by insurer, which insured refused to accept, believing they were less than that to which he was entitled. Insurer had misgivings concerning the nature of insured's illness and the extent of its disabling character. The parties remained in genuine dispute. In the early fall of 1955 insured made complaint to the State Insurance Department, and this triggered the occurrence upon which the main issue on this appeal is based.

While the disputants were before the department representative, insurer offered to settle the claims for $800, conditioned on a surrender of the policy, with consequent termination of its renewability. Insured, concededly, refused. He was willing to accept the $800, but not to surrender the renewable policy. However, later that day insured telephoned the department representative and asked him to advise insurer that he would accept the $800, without requiring that the policy be renewed. The department representative relayed the call. Insurer thereupon wrote insured a letter asking him to call at the office with his policy for surrender and advising, in effect, that he would then be paid the $800 upon signing a release. Insured ignored the letter, and in due time started this action.

Insurer contends that on the facts related there was a "settlement and compromise" which limits insured's right of recovery. Insured, on the other hand, contends that there was no more involved than a new offer by insurer, not accepted by insured, or, at best, an executory accord which is unenforceable for lack of a writing as required by section 33-a of the Personal Property Law.

There is no magic to the words "settlement" or "compromise" in deciding whether a disputed claim has been discharged with such finality that no action may be brought upon it, but only upon the later agreement. As a matter of fact, the words are used interchangeably to describe either a subsequent agreement which discharges an earlier agreement, that is, a substituted or superseding agreement (Morehouse v. Second Nat'l Bank, 98 N.Y. 503), or an executory accord which does not (Larscy v. T. Hogan & Sons, 239 N.Y. 298, 146 N.E. 430). Consequently, one does not advance the solution of any problem in this area by attaching either label, or presuming to conclude the discussion by making an initial determination that a negotiation has or has not achieved a "settlement" or a "compromise." (6 Corbin, Contracts, §1268.)

The question always is whether the subsequent agreement, whatever it may be, and in whatever form it may be, is, as a matter of intention, expressed or implied, a superseder of, or substitution for, the old agreement or dispute; or whether it is merely an agreement to accept performance, in futuro, as future satisfaction of the old agreement or dispute. The literature on the subject is voluminous. Restatement, Contracts, §§417-419; 6 Williston, Contracts, Rev. ed., §1838, et seq., but esp., §§1841, 1846, 1847; 6 Corbin, Contracts, supra, §1268, et seq., esp. §1293, at pp. 148-149; 1937 Report N.Y. Law Rev. Comm., p. 210 et seq.; e.g., Yonkers Fur Dressing Co. v. Royal Ins. Co., 247 N.Y. 435, 446, 160 N.E. 778, 781; Moers v. Moers, 229 N.Y. 294, 128 N.E. 202, 14 A.L.R. 225; Kromer v. Heim, 75 N.Y. 574; Atterbury v. James F. Walsh Paper Corp., 261 App. Div. 529, 26 N.Y.S.2d 43, affirmed 286 N.Y. 578, 35 N.E.2d 928; Ostrander v. Ostrander, 199 App. Div. 437, 191 N.Y.S. 470. There is, then, no simple rule to be applied, as a matter of law, to determine in all given situations whether the subsequent agreement extinguishes the old.

Nevertheless, there are principles which occasionally assist in the determination of the question of intention where settlement negotiations have consummated in an agreement. The Restatement has described these as giving rise to presumptions. (See, Restatement, Contracts, supra, §419, comment a). The New York Law Revision Commission takes the same view (1937 Report, supra, p. 213). This Court recently followed a similar analysis (Blair & Co. v. Otto V., 5 A.D.2d 276, 171 N.Y.S.2d 203).

There has arisen, however, a certain class of cases which have given color to the view that some settlements, are, as a matter of law, superseding or substituted agreements discharging the old obligations, without involving the determination of intention. Nothing said, or held, in those cases, however, warrants such a conclusion. In each there were circumstances pointed to, at least impliedly, as grounding the findings of intention to supersede the old agreement with the new. See, e.g., Langlois v. Langlois, 5 A.D.2d 75, 169 N.Y.S.2d 170; cf. Matter of Shaver's Estate, 282 App. Div. 816, 122 N.Y.S.2d 578; Moers v. Moers, supra, 229 N.Y. 294, 128 N.E. 202, supra; Ostrander v. Ostrander, supra, 199 App. Div. 437, 191 N.Y.S. 470. The persistent principle to be applied is that of determination of the intention of the parties, as objectively manifested (Reilly v. Barrett, 220 N.Y. 170, 115 N.E. 453; Matter of Campbell's

Estate, 256 App. Div. 693, 11 N.Y.S.2d 503, *affirmed* 281 N.Y. 685, 23 N.E.2d 17; Atterbury v. James F. Walsh Paper Corp., *supra*, 261 App. Div. 529, 26 N.Y.S.2d 43, *affirmed* 286 N.Y. 578, 35 N.E.2d 928, *supra*).

Sometimes, of course, the matter of intention may be determined from documents exclusively, in which event the conclusion may be drawn, as a matter of law, by the court (e.g., Moers v. Moers, supra, 229 N.Y. 294, 301, 128 N.E. 202, 204). At other times, the determination of intention will depend upon conversation, surrounding circumstances, or extrinsic proof, in addition to documentation, if any exist, in which event the issue is one of fact, for the trier of the facts, be it court or jury (e.g., Katz v. Bernstein, 236 App. Div. 456, 260 N.Y.S. 13; 6 Corbin, Contracts, *supra*, §1293, at pp. 148-9).

The complex of facts — conversations, circumstances and documents, if there be any — presents the basis for making inferences. Both experience and logic suggest that some recurring factors are more indicative of intention than others. These have given rise to what have been earlier described as presumptions. So it is that the courts hasten to find an intention to have a substituted or superseding agreement discharging the old where the settlement has resulted in formalized papers with unequivocal language (as in Blair v. Otto V., *supra*), or in formalized or deliberate proceedings in court during the pendency of an action (see, Langlois v. Langlois, *supra*, and the cases cited therein). These, of course, are not the only relevant recurring factors, or the only bases for presumptions; nor would it be true to suggest that the search for evidentiary inferences has not been influenced by various policy considerations. See, Restatement, Contracts, *supra*, §§418, 419, incl. comments; 6 Williston, Contracts, Rev. ed., *supra*, §1847; 6 Corbin, Contracts, *supra*, §§1268, 1271, 1293.

When, however, it is concluded that the settlement negotiations have resulted in no more than in an agreement to accept a future performance, albeit a promise presently made, in future satisfaction of the old obligations — in this state especially — another principle of law intervenes. In New York, an executory accord not fully performed was, prior to the enactment of section 33-a of the Personal Property Law, unenforceable. It was not even available as a defense. This was the rule at common law. 1937 Report, N.Y. Law Rev. Comm., *supra*, pp. 211-217; Restatement, Contracts, *supra*, §417, N.Y. annotations. Since the enactment of section 33-a an executory accord may be enforced, provided it is in writing and signed by the party to be held. If it remain unperformed, the promisee may elect to sue on the accord or the original obligation.

On this analysis, one does not reach the requirements for a writing provided in section 33-a, unless one has first found that the subsequent agreement is not one that supersedes or substitutes for the old one, and, therefore, extinguishes it. Such a subsequent agreement need not be in writing, unless, of course, a writing is required by some independent statute, such as a statute of frauds. But, if it is determined that the intention of the parties, expressed by their conduct or words, is that the subsequent agreement was designed to do no more than result in agreement that a future performance, albeit of a promise presently made, would be accepted as future satisfaction of the old obligations, then section 33-a comes into play and the subsequent agreement is unenforceable unless it is in writing and signed.[243]

Applying these principles to the facts in this case, the question is whether there was a substituted agreement, an executory accord, or no contract at all.

In the first place, we have a series of distinctly informal conversations with bargaining give and take. At no time are the bargainers, and the intermediary, agreeing on one occasion and in one place as to what the settlement should be. Instead, there was a triangular operation, the purportedly final terms of which were never expressed in the presence of all. Secondly, at no point do the conversations and communications converge on the precise terms, time or place for consummation. These were the facts that impelled the trial court to find no contract at all.

Thirdly, and crucially, there is nothing in the record which would support an inference that insured ever intended, let alone agreed, to accept only a promise of $800 to be paid in the future (as distinguished from an actual payment here and now) as a present discharge and satisfaction of the insurer's obligations.

Taking the three enumerated elements outlined above, they do not suggest the finality, the deliberateness, or the occasional formalization with which one associates substituted agreements and the specific intention to discharge pre-existing obligations. They do not attain the considered resolution of the entire dispute between the parties that moved the court in Moers v. Moers, *supra*, 229 N.Y. 294, 128 N.E. 202, or in Langlois v. Langlois, *supra*, 5 A.D.2d 75, 169 N.Y.S.2d 170, to find a superseding agreement. Indeed, they fall far short of the circumstances which the court held insufficient to infer a superseding agreement in cases like Atterbury v. James F. Walsh Paper Corp., *supra*, 261 App. Div. 529, 26 N.Y.S.2d 43, *affirmed* 286 N.Y. 578, 35 N.E.2d 928.

Generally, it is assumed that one does not surrender an existing obligation for a promise to perform in the future (Moers v. Moers, *supra*, 229

---

243. Rationalists have been disturbed by the distinction in enforceability between a substituted contract and an executory accord, and, more recently, by the requirement for a writing in order to enforce an executory accord and the absence of such a requirement for a substituted agreement. The reasons are historical, and the demarcation remains clear. 1937 Report, N.Y. Law Rev. Comm., *supra*; 6 Williston, Contracts, *supra*, Rev. ed. §1838, et seq.; 6 Corbin, Contracts, *supra*, §1271; Langlois v. Langlois, *supra*, 5 A.D.2d 75, 169 N.Y.S.2d 170. The distinction, perhaps, can be supported, today, by the differences in deliberateness and extent of negotiation that may be expected to occur before the conclusion of an executory accord and a substituted agreement. This case may be illustrative of occasion for the distinction.

N.Y. 294, 300, 128 N.E. 202, 203; see 6 Williston, Contracts, Rev. ed., *supra* §1847, where it was said: "it is not a probable inference that a creditor intends merely an exchange of his present cause of action for another. It is generally more reasonable to suppose that he bound himself to surrender his old rights only when the new contract of accord was performed"; 6 Corbin, Contracts, *supra* §§1268, 1271, 1293). The Restatement would seem to have taken a somewhat more advanced position (Restatement, Contracts, *supra*, §419[244]), but it is explicitly stated to be merely a guide for interpretation in case of doubt. So treated it is akin to a canon of construction, rather than a presumption that a court is bound to follow in the absence of proof to the contrary. Considering the inchoate and staccato negotiations that ensued in this case, culminating in a relayed telephone call, there is no warrant for inferring the making of a superseding agreement which thereby discharged insured's claims and his renewable policy.

Assuming then, although the trial court found to the contrary, that there was a contract, the factors present in this case, whether subsumed under some rule of interpretation or examined on an ad hoc basis, suggest that if any settlement was reached it was not a superseding or substituted agreement but at best only an executory accord. (Actually there is still another possibility applicable to this case, but it is not one urged here: the conversations which took place may have never achieved the finality of concluding a settlement. All negotiations in which parties verbally, and especially, if orally, concur on a settlement are not necessarily intended, instanter, to be binding. Just as often, in quite informal settings, the parties do no more than agree to agree, and consummation awaits some degree of implementation. This, of course, is also merely a matter of intention. 17 C.J.S. Contracts §49; cf. Sanders v. Pottlitzer, Bros. Fruit Co., 144 N.Y. 209, 39 N.E. 75, 29 L.R.A. 431.

And, of course, on the principles earlier discussed, if all that resulted from the telephone conversations and the letter written by insurer was an executory accord, it was not cognizable under New York law for lack of a writing as required by section 33-a of the Personal Property Law.

Accordingly, the determination of the Appellate Term modifying the judgment rendered in favor of plaintiff against defendant in the Municipal Court by reducing the recovery from $2,800 to $800 should be modified, on the law and on the facts, to reinstate the judgment of the Municipal Court, except as modified, in accordance with the concession

---

244. "Where a contract is made for the satisfaction of a pre-existing contractual duty, or duty to make compensation, the interpretation is assumed in case of doubt, if the pre-existing duty is an undisputed duty either to make compensation or to pay a liquidated sum of money, that only performance of the subsequent contract shall discharge the pre-existing duty; but if the pre-existing duty is of another kind, that the subsequent contract shall immediately discharge the pre-existing duty, and be substituted for it."

For applications of this rule in New York, see Restatement, N.Y. Annotations, to this section. See also 6 Corbin, Contracts, *supra*, §1271.

of plaintiff, by reduction to the sum of $2,600, together with costs and disbursements of this appeal to plaintiff-appellant.

Determination of Appellate Term unanimously modified on the law and on the facts to reinstate the judgment of the Municipal Court, except as modified, in accordance with the concession of plaintiff, by reduction to the sum of $2,600, together with costs and disbursements of this appeal to plaintiff-appellant. Settle order.

NOTE

6 Corbin §§1268, 1271, 1273.

As the opinion indicates, until the enactment of Personal Property Law §33a, New York followed the rule of the common law that an executory accord was unenforceable by action, and could not be used as a defense. To avoid the rule, courts not infrequently have turned the unenforceable executory accord into an enforceable substitute contract. The *Moers* case, mentioned in the opinion, is an illustration. For a recent discussion and defense of the common law rule, see Havighurst, Reflections on the Executory Accord, in Perspectives of Law, in Essays for A. W. Scott 190 (1964); see further Shepherd, The Executory Accord, 26 Ill. L. Rev. 22 (1931).

New York Personal Property Law §33a is now General Obligations Law §15-501. It reads as follows:

1. Executory accord as used in this section means an agreement embodying a promise express or implied to accept at some future time a stipulated performance in satisfaction or discharge in whole or in part of any present claim, cause of action, contract, obligation, or lease, or any mortgage or other security interest in personal or real property, and a promise express or implied to render such performance in satisfaction or in discharge of such claim, cause of action, contract, obligation, lease, mortgage or security interest.

2. An executory accord shall not be denied effect as a defense or as the basis of an action or counterclaim by reason of the fact that the satisfaction or discharge of the claim, cause of action, contract, obligation, lease, mortgage or other security interest which is the subject of the accord was to occur at a time after the making of the accord, provided the promise of the party against whom it is sought to enforce the accord is in writing and signed by such party or by his agent. . . .

3. If an executory accord is not performed according to its terms by one party, the other party shall be entitled either to assert his rights under the claim, cause of action, contract, obligation, lease, mortgage or other security interest which is the subject of the accord, or to assert his right under the accord.

BOSHART v. GARDNER

190 Ark. 104, 77 S.W.2d 642 (1935)

Appeal from Howard Chancery Court; P. P. Bacon, Chancellor; modified and affirmed.

JOHNSON, Chief Justice. On December 1, 1919, appellees Gardner and wife, executed and delivered to the Conservative Loan Company their note for the sum of $1,500 and interest, and to secure the due payment thereof executed a real estate mortgage upon certain lands situated in Howard county, Arkansas. Thereafter, the note and mortgage securing same, in regular course of business, were transferred and assigned to appellant Boshart. Subsequently in 1929 a renewal agreement was effected between the mortgagors and the holder and owner of said mortgage and note whereby the maturity of the debt was extended until 1931 and subsequent years. Neither the principal sum nor the interest thereon was paid by appellees at maturity, as provided in the renewal agreement. On May 8, 1933, appellant submitted to appellees, by letter, a proposition of settlement of the debt as follows:

Mr. Joe B. Gardner,

Dear Sir: I am sending Mr. E. L. Carter the mortgage note which I hold on your place, and in order to get this settled up I will take fifty per cent of the face of the mortgage if you can get a Federal loan and pay it up, or from some other source. Please let me know what you wish to do. Trusting you will find it convenient to do this, I am,

Sincerely yours,
L. H. BOSHART.

And on May 17, 1933, appellees wrote appellant the following letter in response to his proposition of settlement:

Center Point, Ark. 5-17-33

L. H. Boshart, Esq., Lowville, N.Y.

Dear Sir: Your very kind letter of recent date has been received and contents noted. In answer will state that I thank you for the kind offer to discount my paper fifty per cent for the cash. I intend trying for a Federal loan at once. Do not see why I should not be successful in securing a loan unless the laws of Ark. regarding deficiency judgments should preclude my getting a loan. If the Supreme Court which is soon to pass on the act passed by the Legislature of 1933 forbidding deficiency judgments in foreclosure suits does not declare the act invalid, then in that event, the Gov. will call a special session of the Legislature to repeal the act. In any event I intend to make a great effort to meet your generous offer. I will advise you.

Yours truly,
JOE B. GARDNER.

On July 5, 1933, appellant instituted this action in foreclosure, and a receiver was prayed and appointed thereby putting at an end the negotiations heretofore adverted to. Appellees answered appellant's complaint in foreclosure by asserting the novation of the contract as heretofore stated and, upon trial of the cause, the chancellor found the facts to be as contended by appellees, and directed that appellant was only entitled to judgment against appellees for the sum of 50 per cent of the debt and interest and denying any recovery for taxes paid. It was further decreed that if this sum be not paid by July 1, 1933, the mortgaged lands should be sold in satisfaction thereof, and from this decree comes this appeal.

The testimony introduced in said cause is not in material conflict and may be summarized as follows: That immediately after the correspondence heretofore referred to appellees made oral application to the local Federal agency for a loan sufficient to pay the amount submitted by appellant, but that due to local conditions over which neither appellant nor appellee had control the loan was not finally approved until the early part of 1934. Appellees expended a substantial sum of money in prosecuting the application for this loan before the Federal agency. A redemption certificate was introduced by appellant showing that he had expended $19.12 for past-due taxes against the mortgaged lands prior to the decree.

Appellant's first contention is that appellee's letter of May 17, 1933, was not an acceptance of his proposition of May 8, 1933, but we cannot agree with this contention. The fair interpretation of this correspondence is that appellant offered to accept 50 per cent of the face value of the mortgage, if paid in cash within a reasonable time thereafter, and that appellees accepted this proposition as outlined in appellant's letter. It is perfectly apparent that appellant knew that appellees had no ready funds when the offer was made; therefore, he suggested the course for appellees to pursue in procuring the money to pay the debt. This correspondence constituted an enforceable contract between the parties subject only to due performance by appellees within a reasonable time. Furthermore, this record reflects that appellant on July 5, 1933, instituted this foreclosure proceeding against appellees thereby repudiating his offer of May 8, 1933, without giving appellees any notice or opportunity to pay the debt as theretofore agreed upon by the parties and this action of appellant was amply sufficient to excuse appellees from further immediate negotiations in procuring a loan as contemplated by the parties.

Appellant next contends that, although his offer of settlement was accepted by appellees, such contract is not an enforceable contract because not supported by a sufficient consideration. The authorities are in accord on the proposition that contracts of novation are not different from other contracts and need be supported only by a good and sufficient consideration, and even a loss or an inconvenience to the promisee may suffice. 20 R.C.L. 367. Moreover, the testimony shows, and the chancellor so found, that appellees, relying upon said contract of novation, expended a substantial sum of money in prosecuting his [sic] application for a loan in compliance with appellant's suggestions. Therefore, it would be inequitable to permit appellant to repudiate his offer of settlement when appellee is now ready for consummation.

It follows therefore that the chancellor was correct in determining that there was a valid contract of novation between the parties to this action, and his decree in this behalf must be affirmed. The chancellor was in error, however, in refusing to allow appellant judgment for the taxes paid by him on the mortgaged lands. The decree will be modified so as to allow appellant judgment for $19.12 additional for taxes paid.

The chancellor was also in error in treating appellant's offer and appellee's acceptance thereof as a consummated novation. The offer and acceptance should be treated as executory and continuing for such reasonable length of time as may afford appellees a reasonable opportunity of procuring a loan and paying the debt.

If appellees will pay into the registry of this court within sixty days from this date 50 per cent of the mortgage debt and interest as decreed by the chancellor, plus $19.12 taxes, the decree will be affirmed; otherwise the cause must be reversed, and remanded with directions to enter a decree in favor of appellant for the full amount of his debt, interest and taxes paid.

NOTE

Consult Bank of Fairbanks v. Kay, 17 Alaska 23, 227 F.2d 566 (9th Cir. 1956); 6 Corbin §1273 (1962).

CHAPTER 5

Formalism in our Law
of Contracts

"[C]onsideration is as much a form as a seal,"
Holmes, J. in Krell v. Codman,
154 Mass. 454, 456, 28 N.E. 578 (1891).

COHEN, THE BASIS OF CONTRACT, 46 Harv. L. Rev. 553, 582-583 (1933): "Consideration is in effect a formality, like an oath, the affixing of a seal, or a stipulation in court. . . .

"The recognition of the formal character of consideration may help us to appreciate the historical myopia of those who speak of seal as 'importing' consideration. Promises under seal were binding (because of the formality) long before the doctrine of consideration was ever heard of. The history of forms and ceremonies in the law of contract offers an illuminating chapter in human psychology or anthropology. We are apt to dismiss the early Roman ceremonies of mancipatio, nexum, and sponsio, the Anglo-Saxon wed and borh, or the Frankish ceremonies of arramitio, wadiatio, and of the festuca, as peculiar to primitive society. But reflection shows that our modern practices of shaking hands to close a bargain, signing papers, and protesting a note are, like the taking of an oath on assuming office, not only designed to make evidence secure, but are in large part also expressions of the fundamental human need for formality and ceremony, to make sharp distinctions where otherwise lines of demarcation would not be so clearly apprehended.

"Ceremonies are the channels that the stream of social life creates by its ceaseless flow through the sands of human circumstance. Psychologically, they are habits; socially, they are customary ways of doing things; and ethically, they have what Jellinek has called the normative power of the actual, that is, they control what we do by creating a standard of respectability or a pattern to which we feel bound to conform. The daily obedience to the act of the government, which is the basis of all political and legal institutions, is thus largely a matter of conformity to established ritual or form of behavior. For the most part, we obey the law or the policeman as a matter of course, without deliberation. The customs of

705

other people seem to us strange and we try to explain them as ceremonies symbolic of things that are familiar or seem useful to us. But many of our own customs can appear to an outsider as equally non-rational rituals that we follow from habit. We may justify them as the sacred vessels through which we obtain the substance of life's goods. But the maintenance of old forms may also be an end in itself to all those to whom change from the familiar is abhorrent."

FULLER, CONSIDERATION AND FORM, 41 Colum. L. Rev. 799, 799-800 (1941): "That consideration may have both a 'formal' and a 'substantive' aspect is apparent when we reflect on the reasons which have been advanced why promises without consideration are not enforced. It has been said that consideration is 'for the sake of evidence' and is intended to remove the hazards of mistaken or perjured testimony which would attend the enforcement of promises for which nothing is given in exchange. Again, it is said that enforcement is denied gratuitious promises because such promises are often made impulsively and without proper deliberation. In both these cases the objection relates, not to the content and effect of the promise, but to the manner in which it is made. Objections of this sort, which touch the form rather than the content of the agreement, will be removed if the making of the promise is attended by some formality or ceremony, as by being under seal. On the other hand, it has been said that the enforcement of gratuitious promises is not an object of sufficient importance to our social and economic order to justify the expenditure of time and energy necessary to accomplish it. Here the objection is one of 'substance' since it touches the significance of the promise made and not merely the circumstances surrounding the making of it."

NOTE

For a brilliant account of the advantages and disadvantages of legal formalities, see 2 von Jhering, Geist des Roemischen Rechts 480-482 (Siebente Aufl. 1923), translated in L. Fuller & M. Eisenberg, Basic Contract Law 116 (3d ed. 1972).

Section 1.   The Peppercorn Theory of Consideration

SIR ANTHONY STURLYN v. ALBANY, Cro. Eliz. 67, 78 Eng. Rep. 327 (1587): ". . . when a thing is to be done by the plaintiff, be it never so small, this is a sufficient consideration to ground an action. . . ." For further references on the case, see p. 558 *supra*.

WHITNEY v. STEARNS, 16 Me. 394, 397 (1839): "A cent or a peppercorn, in legal estimation, would constitute consideration."

1 W. H. PAGE, THE LAW OF CONTRACTS §646 (1920): "The doctrine of nominal consideration should have no place in our law. If we are to insist upon a consideration to support an executory promise, it must at least be a genuine and substantial consideration. If we are ready to dispense with the necessity of consideration, a higher morality than that at present demanded by our law might require the performance of every promise which is made fairly and deliberately, and upon the performance of which the promisee has relied in good faith. To permit the nominal consideration, especially in jurisdictions where the recital of consideration is conclusive, is to reduce the doctrine of consideration to a requirement of form, and not of substance; a form as empty as the seal, but lacking its historic dignity, and yet to demand that form before the law will compel the performance of the most deliberate promise."

THOMAS v. THOMAS
2 Q.B. 851, 114 Eng. Rep. 330 (1842)

Assumpsit. The declaration stated an agreement between plaintiff and defendant that the defendant should, when thereto required by the plaintiff, by all necessary deeds, conveyances, assignments, or other assurances, grants, etc., or otherwise, assure a certain dwelling house and premises, in the county of Glamorgan, unto plaintiff for her life. . . .

At the trial, before Coltman, J., at the Glamorganshire Lent Assizes, 1841, it appeared that John Thomas, the deceased husband of the plaintiff, at the time of his death, in 1837, was possessed of a row of seven dwelling houses in Merthyr Tidvil, in one of which, being the dwelling house in question, he was himself residing; and that by his will he appointed his brother Samuel Thomas (since deceased) and the defendant executors thereof, to take possession of all his houses, etc., subject to certain payments in the will mentioned, among which were certain charges in money for the benefit of the plaintiff. In the evening before the day of his death he expressed orally a wish to make some further provision for his wife; and on the following morning he declared orally, in the presence of two witnesses, that it was his will that his wife should have either the house in which he lived and all that it contained, or an additional sum of £100 instead thereof.

This declaration being shortly afterward brought to the knowledge of Samuel Thomas and the defendant, the executors and residuary legatees, they consented to carry the intentions of the testator so expressed into effect; and, after the lapse of a few days, they and the plaintiff executed the agreement declared upon; which, after stating the parties, and briefly reciting the will, proceeded as follows:

"And, whereas the said testator, shortly before his death, declared, in the presence of several witnesses, that he was desirous his said wife should have and enjoy during her life, or so long as she should continue his widow, all and singular the dwelling house," etc., "or £100 out of his personal estate," in addition to the respective legacies and bequests given her in and by his said will;

> but such declaration and desire was not reduced to writing in the lifetime of the said John Thomas and read over to him; but the said Samuel Thomas and Benjamin Thomas are fully convinced and satisfied that such was the desire of the said testator, and are willing and desirous that such intention should be carried into full effect: now these presents witness, and it is hereby agreed and declared by and between the parties, that, in consideration of such desire and of the premises,

the executors would convey the dwelling house etc. to the plaintiff and her assigns during her life, or for so long a time as she should continue a widow and unmarried:

> provided nevertheless, and it is hereby further agreed and declared, that the said Eleanor Thomas, and her assigns, shall and will, at all times during which she shall have possession of the said dwelling house, etc., pay to the said Samuel Thomas and Benjamin Thomas, their executors, etc., the sum of £1 yearly toward the ground rent payable in respect of the said dwelling house and other premises thereto adjoining, and shall and will keep the said dwelling house and premises in good and tenantable repair;

with other provisions not affecting the questions in this case.

The plaintiff was left in possession of the dwelling house and premises for some time; but the defendant, after the death of his coexecutor, refused to execute a conveyance tendered to him for execution pursuant to the agreement, and, shortly before the trial, brought an ejectment, under which he turned the plaintiff out of possession. It was objected for the defendant that, a part of the consideration proved being omitted in the declaration, there was a fatal variance. The learned judge overruled the objection, reserving leave to move to enter a nonsuit. Ultimately a verdict was found for the plaintiff on all the issues; and, in Easter Term last, a rule nisi was obtained pursuant to the leave reserved. . . .

E. V. Williams [for the defendant, argued that this was "a mere gift cum onere," and that the only consideration was "the testator's expressed wish"].

What is meant by the consideration for a promise, but the cause or induce-ment for making it? Plowden, commenting on Sharington v. Strotton [Plowd. 309], says (page 309), "Note: That by the civil law nudum pactum is defined thus, *Nudum pactum est ubi nulla subest causa praeter conven-tionem; sed ubi subest causa, fit obligatio, et parit actionem.*" In Chitty on Contracts [(3d ed., 1841) 28] the following passage is cited from the Code Civil: "*L'obligation sans cause, ou sur une fausse cause, ou sur une cause illicite, ne peut avoir aucun effet.*" The rent and repairs cannot be said to have been the cause or motive which induced the executors to make this agreement. . . . The proviso merely causes the donee to take the gift charged with the burthen of paying the rent and keeping the premises in repair; and she cannot turn these conditions into a consideration. . . .

LORD DENMAN, C.J. There is nothing in this case but a great deal of ingenuity, and a little wilful blindness to the actual terms of the instru-ment itself. There is nothing whatever to show that the ground rent was payable to a superior landlord; and the stipulation for the payment of it is not a mere proviso, but an express agreement. (His Lordship here read the proviso.) This is in terms an express agreement, and shows a sufficient legal consideration quite independent of the moral feeling which dis-posed the executors to enter into such a contract. Mr. Williams' defini-tion of consideration is too large: the word causa in the passage referred to means one which confers what the law considers a benefit on the party. Then the obligation to repair is one which might impose charges heavier than the value of the life estate.

PATTESON, J. It would be giving to causa too large a construction if we were to adopt the view urged for the defendant: it would be confounding consideration with motive. Motive is not the same thing with consider-ation. Consideration means something which is of some value in the eye of the law, moving from the plaintiff; it may be some benefit to the [defendant], or some detriment to the [plaintiff]; but at all events it must be moving from the plaintiff. Now that which is suggested as the consid-eration here, a pious respect for the wishes of the testator, does not in any way move from the plaintiff; it moves from the testator; therefore, legally speaking, it forms no part of the consideration. Then it is said that, if that be so, there is no consideration at all, it is a mere voluntary gift; but when we look at the agreement we find that this is not a mere proviso that the donee shall take the gift with the burthens; but it is an express agreement to pay what seems to be a fresh apportionment of a ground rent, and which is made payable not to a superior landlord but to the executors. So that this rent is clearly not something incident to the assignment of the house; for in that case, instead of being payable to the executors, it would have been payable to the landlord. Then as to the repairs: these houses may very possibly be held under a lease containing covenants to repair; but we know nothing about it: for anything that appears, the liability to repair is first created by this instrument. The proviso certainly struck me at first as Mr. Williams put it, that the rent and repairs were merely attached to the gift by the donors; and, had the instrument been executed by the donors only, there might have been some ground for that construction; but the fact is not so. Then it is suggested that this would be held to be a mere voluntary conveyance as against a subsequent purchaser for value: possibly that might be so: but suppose it would: the plaintiff contracts to take it, and does take it, whatever it is, for better for worse: perhaps a bona fide purchase for a valuable consideration might override it; but that cannot be helped.

COLERIDGE, J. The concessions made in the course of the argument have, in fact, disposed of the case. It is conceded that mere motive need not be stated: and we are not obliged to look for the legal consideration in any particular part of the instrument, merely because the consideration is usually stated in some particular part: *ut res magis valeat*, we may look to any part. In this instrument, in the part where it is usual to state the consideration, nothing certainly is expressed but a wish to fulfil the intentions of the testator: but in another part we find an express agreement to pay an annual sum for a particular purpose; and also a distinct agreement to repair. If these had occurred in the first part of the instrument, it could hardly have been argued that the declaration was not well drawn: and supported by the evidence. As to the suggestion of this being a voluntary conveyance, my impression is that this payment of £1 annually is more than a good consideration: it is a valuable consideration: it is clearly a thing newly created, and not part of the old ground rent.

Rule discharged.

NOTE

Consult Schnell v. Nell, *infra* p. 737. Contrast Restatement First §75 with statement of Patteson, J.

How is the transaction in the *Thomas* case to be characterized? Does it support the so-called peppercorn theory of consideration or does it merely tell us that in determining sufficiency, consideration and motive have to be distinguished? Consult 1 W. H. Page, The Law of Contracts §644 (1920). See further Restatement First §84(a) and Illustration 1; Restatement Second §81.

FISCHER v. UNION TRUST CO.
138 Mich. 612, 101 N.W. 852 (1904)

Proceedings by Bertha Fischer against the Union Trust Company, administrator of the estate of William F. Fischer, deceased. Judgment for plaintiff, and defendant brings error. Reversed.

On December 21, 1895. William Fischer, Sr., conveyed by warranty deed certain property in the city of Detroit to the claimant, Bertha Fischer, his daughter, who had been incompetent for a number of years, and so remains, and is at present at the retreat for the insane at Dearborn. The deed was a warranty deed, in the usual form, with a covenant against all incumbrances, excepting two mortgages, which the grantor "agrees to pay when the same become due." The land described in the deed comprised the homestead where the father and daughter lived, and the adjoining lot, with the house thereon. Mr. Fischer, after signing and acknowledging it, handed it to claimant, saying, "Here is a deed of the Jefferson and Larned street property." He said it was a "nice Christmas present." She took it and read it. One of her brothers gave her a dollar, which she gave to her father, who took it. She then handed the deed to her brother Alexander, and asked him to take care of it. He put it in his safe, and did not record it until June 30, 1902, about a year after the grantor's death, and six and one-half years after its date. The reason given by the son for not recording is that there were unpaid taxes, in consequence of which, under the statute, it could not be recorded.

After the delivery of the deed, both grantor and grantee continued to live together on part of the property so conveyed. Mr. Fischer continued until his death to manage and control it, and to receive rents therefrom, just as he had done before the giving of the deed. During that time he took care of his daughter the same as before. At the time of the execution of the deed, the grantor was considered by his sons to be worth about $50,000. He had no debts except the two mortgages, one of $3,000 and the other of $5,000. If he was then worth that amount, the larger part of it was in some way disposed of in his lifetime. The $3,000 mortgage was foreclosed for nonpayment, and satisfied out of part of the property conveyed. The claim at bar is based upon this appropriation of her property to pay the mortgage.

GRANT, J. (after stating the facts). The facts and circumstances of the delivery of the deed are not in dispute. Counsel differ only in the conclusion to be drawn from them. We think that the conceded facts show a delivery. After the deed was signed and acknowledged, the grantor made manual delivery of it to the grantee. She took it and handed it to her brother, evidently to be kept by him for her. The grantor reserved no control over it, and retained no right to withdraw or cancel it. He never attempted to. Under those circumstances the delivery was complete.

The meritorious question in the case is: Was the claimant in position to enforce the executory contract in the deed against her father while living, and to enforce it against his estate now that he is dead, or to recover damages at law for nonperformance? To say that the one dollar was the real, or such valuable consideration as would of itself sustain a deed of land worth several thousand dollars, is not in accord with reason or common sense. The passing of the dollar by the brother to his sister, and by her to her father, was treated rather as a joke than as any actual consideration. The real and only consideration for the deed and the agreement, therein contained, to pay the mortgages, was the grantor's love and affection for his unfortunate daughter, and his parental desire to provide for her support after he was dead. The consideration was meritorious, but is not sufficient to compel the performance of a purely executory contract. The deed was a gift, and the gift was consummated by its execution and delivery. The title to the land, subject to the mortgages, passes as against all except the grantor's creditors. The gift was expressly made subject to the mortgages, and coupled with it was a promise to pay them. This promise has no additional force because it is contained in the deed. It has no other or greater force than would a promise by him to pay mortgages upon her own land, or to pay her $8,000 in money, or his promise to her evidenced by a promissory note for a like amount, and given for the same purpose and the same consideration.

> The doctrine of meritorious consideration originates in the distinction between the three classes of consideration on which promises may be based, viz., valuable consideration, the performance of a moral duty, and mere voluntary bounty. The first of these classes alone entitles the promisee to enforce his claim against an unwilling promisor; the third is for all legal purposes a mere nullity until actual performance of the promise.
>
> The second, or intermediate class, is termed the meritorious, and is confined to the three duties of charity, of payment of creditors, and of maintaining a wife and children; and under this last head are included provisions made for persons, not being children of the party promising, but in relation to whom he has manifested in intention to stand in loco parentis in reference to the parental duty of making provision for a child.
>
> Considerations of this imperfect class are not distinguished at law from mere voluntary bounty, but are to a modified extent recognized in equity. And the doctrine with respect to them is that, although a promise made without a valuable consideration cannot be enforced against the promisor, or against any one in whose favor he has altered his intention, yet if an intended gift on meritorious consideration be imperfectly executed, and if the intention remains unaltered at the death of the donor, there is an equity to enforce it, in favor of his intention, against persons claiming by operation of law without an equally meritorious claim.

Adams' Eq. (8th Ed.) 97. . . .

A gift of personalty can be consummated only by an unconditional delivery of the thing. A gift of realty can be consummated only by the execution and delivery of a deed. If either is incumbered, the donor gives only what he had to give. He cannot give the interest of a third party in the property. However clear may be the intention of the donor to pay the incumbrances and thus give the entire property, he can accomplish this only by actually paying them. Neither his promise without a valuable consideration, nor his intentions as evidenced by such promise, is of any avail to the donee.

Other interesting questions are raised, but they become immaterial in view of the conclusion we have reached.

Judgment is reversed, and new trial ordered. The other Justices concurred.

NOTE

On meritorious consideration, see J. Dawson & W. Harvey, Contracts and Contract Remedies 560-561 (1959); 1 Williston §110 (3d ed. 1957).

MURPHY, THOMPSON & CO. v. REED
125 Ky. 585, 101 S.W. 964 (1907)

Appeal from Ohio Circuit Court. Judgment for defendants. Plaintiffs appeal. Reversed. . . .

Opinion of the court by Chief Justice O'REAR — Reversing. These cases involve a common principle of law, viz., the binding force, of an option to sell real estate. The options describe the land, and recite a consideration of $1 paid. They obligate the owners of the soil to convey the coal in the land by general warranty deed to the optionee within a specified future period, on notice by the optionee to the owners of the acceptance of the option and the payment of $5 per acre cash. During the life of the options the optionee did accept their terms, notified the owners thereof, and tendered the contract price recited in the options. The owners having refused to accept the money or to convey the lands, these actions were brought by the optionees to have a specific execution of the contracts. Demurrers were sustained to the petitions on the ground that the contracts were unilateral, lacking in mutuality, and unenforceable, and the petitions were dismissed.

It is generally said that one essential of every executory contract is mutuality of obligation and remedy. That there must be mutuality of obligation, by which is meant an undertaking on one side and a consideration upon the other, is true always. But it is not true always that there must be a mutuality of remedy. One example is, a contract for a sufficient consideration between an adult and an infant may be enforced against the adult, although he might not enforce it against the infant. And there are others. An option to sell is a standing offer to sell to the person and upon the terms named in the option, and an agreement to keep the proposition open for acceptance for the time stated. If its terms are fair, and have been understandably entered into, there appears no reason why it should not be enforced, if accepted and offered to be complied with by the payment of the consideration within the time stipulated. If the same proposition had been made by the owner for immediate acceptance, and it had been immediately accepted, there would be no doubt that it was binding upon the offeror. The only difference between the one imagined and the contracts in suit is, instead of an offer for immediate acceptance, there is one left open for acceptance for a certain period, within which it is accepted. The option is said to contain two contracts, as it were: One, the contract to sell the land, which is the main contract, and which is uncompleted till accepted; and the other, the agreement to give the optionee a certain time within which to exercise his option of accepting and becoming bound upon the first contract, which is a completed contract. Each must have a consideration to support it. The consideration for the main contracts in this case is the price per acre stipulated to be paid upon the execution of the deeds. When the contract was accepted by the optionee, he became bound for the payment of the purchase price, and by tendering it complied fully with the element of mutual obligation upon his part.

The consideration for the agreement to give the optionee the definite time within which to exercise his choice, called the "option," is in these cases, the $1 recited. It might have been more, or an entirely different consideration. Though there are authorities holding a consideration of $1 as sufficient to uphold such an agreement, we are not disposed to go so far. Such consideration is so flagrantly disproportionate to the value of the privilege in these cases — the options extending over a year — that it is merely nominal. It is not substantial, and the parties could not have regarded it as in any sense an equivalent of the privilege which was being contracted for. While upon demurrer the courts will be slow to say that a recited consideration is no consideration, if it has any appearance of having been regarded by the parties as the agreed value of the thing contracted for, where the stated consideration is so manifestly inadequate and disproportionate to the value of the thing being sold (the privilege of option) as to represent no value, or only a nominal value, it will be construed on demurrer, as a matter of law, as not having a consideration at all. If there is doubt about the matter, then the question of its value or adequacy is a defense to be pleaded. An option, to be binding upon the owner, in the sense that it is irrevocable upon him during the period for which it was given, must be upon a valuable and sufficient consideration. It may consist in money paid or to be paid for it, or in property, services, or counter benefits accruing to the owner, or disadvantage incurred by the optionee. In short, it may be such consideration as will support any other sort of contract. In this view of the matter, the options in these cases were not supported by sufficient consideration to have bound the owners not to withdraw them during the term for which they were given. They could have been withdrawn before acceptance, without liability to the givers of the options. But, as they were not withdrawn, they constituted, instead of binding options, voluntary offers to sell, which like any other valid offer, were, when accepted, binding upon the person making them. The statute of frauds is not involved in these cases. Tyler v. Ontzs, 93 Ky. 331, 14 Ky. Law Rep. 321, 20 S.W. 256.

This conclusion is reached after a careful consideration of the cases heretofore in this court and of the state of authorities elsewhere. The great weight of authority, and what seems to us to be the right of the matter, is in favor of upholding and enforcing such contracts. While formerly there was a marked difference of opinions as to the validity of pure options, there seems to have been but little divergence among the courts as to the enforcibility of such options when connected with leases. However, this court in its early history took the contrary view in Boucher v. Vanbuskirk, 2 A. K. Marshall (Ky.) 345. But in the later case of Bank of Louisville v. Baumeister, 87 Ky. 12, 9 Ky. Law Rep. 845, 7 S.W. 170, and Bacon v. Ky. Cent. Ry. Co., 95 Ky. 373, 16 Ky. Law Rep. 77, 25 S.W. 747, the principle of the *Boucher-Vanbuskirk* case was repudiated. The real underlying principle of the case where the option is given as part of a lease, and is enforced, is that it was based upon a sufficient valuable consideration. Therefore any other sufficient valuable consideration ought to support an option contract to sell. In Litz v. Goosling, 93 Ky. 185, 14 Ky. Law Rep. 91, 19 S.W. 527, 21 L.R.A. 127, the option in suit was substantially the same as those now under consideration. It does not appear that the court considered the effect of an acceptance of the option during its term and before its withdrawal by the owner of the land. The court said:

> If the contract for an option to purchase real estate at a certain price within a certain time be based upon a sufficient consideration, which may consist, of course, either in an advantage moving to the one party, or a disadvantage to the other, then it is enforceable; but where a mere naked option, destitute of consideration, is given to one, it is not enforceable, because there is no mutuality of right and remedy.

Nor do we say now that such an option is enforceable as to the terms of the option (independent of the terms of the contract to sell the land); that is to say, the owner could not be compelled to keep the option open for acceptance for its full term, and that is the only contract embraced in the option, strictly speaking. The other contract, the one to buy the land, is yet to be consummated, and is not a contract at all until it is accepted within the time and terms stated in the agreement. What was said in Litz v. Goosling, *supra*, as to the binding validity of the option without consideration, is adhered to; but, if it should be deducible from the opinion that it was also intended to hold that the optionee could acquire no right in the contract by accepting it during its terms and before notice of its withdrawal, then we disavow the principle, and to that extent the case will no longer be regarded as authority.

The judgment in each case is reversed, and each cause is remanded, with directions to overrule the demurrers and for proceedings not inconsistent herewith.

NOTE

1 A Corbin §§262-263 (1963).

REAL ESTATE CO. OF PITTSBURGH
v. RUDOLPH
301 Pa. 502, 153 A. 438 (1930)

Suit by the Real Estate Company of Pittsburgh, for the use of B. Epstein, against J. A. Rudolph. On exceptions to a decree nisi in favor of plaintiff, court in banc decreed dismissal of the bill, and plaintiff appeals.
Reversed and remanded with directions.
Simpson, J. Defendant executed and delivered to the legal plaintiff an option as follows:

April 18th, 1928.

Real Estate Company of Pittsburgh,
Wood and Fourth
Pittsburgh, Pennsylvania

Gentlemen:

In consideration of One ($1.00) Dollar in hand paid, I hereby give you the option to purchase my property situate 1628 Penn Ave., at the price of $15000.00. This option to expire at 12 o'clock noon, April 24th, 1928.

If this option is accepted by you and transaction closed, I agree to pay you a commission of 3 per cent on the sale price. It is understood that the property is free and clear of encumbrances excepting a mortgage in the amount of $6,000.00.

Very truly yours,
J. A. Rudolph.

The next day, and before he was formally notified of the acceptance of the option, defendant informed plaintiffs that he would not sell the property because his wife would not join in the conveyance. They were willing, however, to accept a title without the joinder of the wife, as, of course, they had the right to do (Corson v. Mulvany, 49 Pa. 88, 88 Am. Dec. 485; Medoff v. Vandersaal, 271 Pa. 169, 116 A. 525); but he persisted in his revocation, and refused even to discuss the matter with them, whereupon they filed the present bill in equity for specific performance. The learned president judge of the court below, who sat as chancellor, found all the disputed facts in favor of plaintiffs, and reported a decree nisi awarding specific performance, the deed to be executed by defendant alone, without the joinder of his wife. On exceptions filed, the court in banc decreed a dismissal of the bill, solely because the one dollar, specified in the option as having been paid, had not in fact been paid, and hence the optioner was well within his right in revoking it before acceptance. This raises the only point to be considered by us on plaintiffs' appeal from the decree. It must be admitted that the authorities elsewhere are not harmonious, but in our judgment the final decree is wrong.

It is of course true that, if an option has no actual or legal consideration to support it, it may be revoked by the optioner at any time prior to acceptance. Defendant's answer does not aver a lack of consideration, however, and hence neither the fact nor effect of a want of it should have been considered by the court below. Moreover, this option has a legal consideration to support it. In Lawrence v. McCalmont, 2 How. (43 U.S.) 426, 452, 11 L. Ed. 326, it is said in an opinion by Mr. Justice Story:

> The second [defense] is, that the payment of the one dollar is merely nominal and not sufficient to sustain the guarantee, if it had been received; and it is urged that it was not received. As to this last point, we feel no difficulty. The guarantor acknowledged the receipt of the one dollar, and is now estopped to deny it. If she has not received it, she would now be entitled to recover it. A valuable consideration, however small or nominal, if given or stipulated for in good faith, is, in the absence of fraud, sufficient to support an action on any parol contract; and this is equally true as to contracts of guarantee as to other contracts. A stipulation in consideration of one dollar is just as effectual and valuable a consideration as a larger sum stipulated for or paid. . . . But, independently of all authority, we should arrive at the same conclusion. The receipt of the one dollar is acknowledged; no fraud is pretended or shown; and the consideration, if standing alone in a bona fide transaction would sustain the present suit.

That case is apposite here, since the traditional statement in the option of the "$1 in hand paid" can only mean that appellant acknowledges the receipt of that sum. . . .

There is no pretense here that defendants' signature to the agreement was obtained by any inducement other than as expressed in it, or that anything was added to or omitted from it by fraud, accident or mistake. Consequently it must be construed just as it is written, and every clause must be given its plain meaning. McHenry Lumber Co. v. Second National Bank of Wilkes-Barre, 281 Pa. 52, 126 A. 189. The insertion of the words, "In consideration of One Dollar in hand paid," could have had no other purpose than to state a consideration, which was necessary to make the agreement effective during the term of the option. To ignore them would be, therefore, to eliminate from the agreement words *intentionally* put in it, in order to reach a conclusion which their insertion was *intended* to render impossible. This is never permitted. Irvin v. Irvin, 142 Pa. 271, 21 A. 816; Union Storage Co. v. Speck, 194 Pa. 126, 133, 45 A. 48.

Moreover, it is quite possible, when taken in conjunction with a finding of the chancellor that defendant knew the agreement was sought because of a hoped-for resale to a third party, that its true interpretation is that defendant gave to the legal plaintiff an option until "12 o'clock noon, April 24th, 1928," to find a purchaser for the property at $15,000, and said to him, "if this option is accepted by you and transaction closed, I agree to give you a commission of three per cent on the sale price." No other construction satisfactorily explains why the vendor agreed to pay the vendee for buying the property, instead of merely stating that the sales price is to be $14,550. If that construction is correct, then the agreement contemplated services to be rendered by plaintiff to defendant forthwith, which the former impliedly agreed to render, and hence an additional valuable consideration appears.

The decree of the court below is reversed, at the cost of appellee, and the record is remitted that the decree nisi may be entered as the decree of the court.

NOTE

Consult 79 U. Pa. L. Rev. 1139 (1931).

Suppose the $1 payable for an option is tendered but not accepted, the offeror saying: "Never mind, I do not need the dollar." Is the offeror bound? George v. Schuman, 202 Mich. 241, 168 N.W. 486 (1918). Is offeree protected by estoppel or by the parol evidence rule?

At the time the *Rudolph* case was decided, though not mentioned in the opinion, Pennsylvania had on its books the Uniform Written Obligations Act, which provided that "a written release or promise, hereafter made, and signed by the person releasing or promising, shall not be invalid or unenforceable for lack of consideration, if the writing also contains an additional express statement, in any form of language, that the signer intends to be legally bound." Would the plaintiff have been protected under this act?

MARSH v. LOTT, 8 Cal. App. 384, 97 P. 163 (1908). The California Civil Code (§3391) provides that specific performance cannot be enforced against a party to a contract "if he has not received an adequate consideration for the contract" (1), or "if it is not, as to him, just and reasonable" (2). The meaning of these provisions was tested in the *Marsh* case. The defendant on February 25, 1905 in writing had given plaintiff an option to buy his land "for the sum of $100,000, payable $30,000 cash, balance on or before four (4) years, $4\frac{1}{2}\%$ net." The instrument acknowledged the receipt of 25 cents "in hand paid" and provided the option would expire on June 2 with privilege of 30 days extension. Plaintiff on June 1st in writing exercised his option to extend and on June 2 defendant, also in writing, revoked the option. On June 29 plaintiff in writing exercised the option and tendered the sum of $30,000 in gold coin and demanded performance. When defendant refused to convey, plaintiff sued for specific performance. It was denied by the trial court because "the sum of 25¢ paid for the option was an inadequate and insufficient consideration for the same, and that the option contract was not just and reasonable to defendant, and no adequate consideration was paid to [defendant] for it."

On appeal the interpretation of §3391(1) was held erroneous: payment of 25 cents was adequate, sufficient consideration for the option to buy for $100,000. "From the very nature of the case, no standard exists whereby to determine the adequate value of an option to purchase specific real estate. The land has a market value susceptible of ascertainment, but the value of an option upon a piece of real estate might, and oftentimes does, depend upon proposed or possible improvements in the particular vicinity. To illustrate: If A, having information that the erection of a gigantic department store is contemplated in a certain locality, wishes an option for a specific time to purchase property owned by B in the vicinity of such proposed improvement, and takes the option on B's property at the full market price at the time, must he pay a greater sum therefor because of his knowledge and the fact of B's ignorance of the proposed improvement? It is not possible that B, upon learning of the proposed improvement, can, in the absence of facts constituting fraud, etc., revoke or rescind the option upon the claim that he sold and transferred the right specified therein for an inadequate consideration. In our judgment, any money consideration, however small, paid and received for an option to purchase property at its adequate value is binding upon the seller thereof for the time specified therein, and is irrevocable for want of its adequacy."

Revocation, therefore, was ineffective. Nevertheless, the judgment of the lower court was affirmed because subsection 2 afforded protection to the defendant. "If the payment or tender of the $30,000 was full performance on his part, it necessarily follows that, under this view of the contract, all that defendant would have as evidence of her claim to the deferred payment of $70,000, not payable until the expiration of four years, would be the contract unsigned by anyone charged with the payment thereof and without any security therefor."

The trial court was therefore correct in holding that the contract as to the defendant was not just and reasonable.

NOTE

Consult Restatement Second §83, and discussion on p. 517 *supra*. On the various forms of options and the availability of specific performance, see 1A Corbin §262.

WHEAT v. MORSE

197 Cal. App. 203, 17 Cal. Rptr. 226 (1961)

CONLEY, Presiding Justice.

This is an appeal from a decree of specific performance of a written option executed by Ethel Upson Lee, who died prior to its exercise, in favor of Andy Wheat. The real property involved consists of approximately three hundred acres in Tulare County near the City of Corcoran.

Appellant urges three grounds for reversal, claiming (1) that the option itself was void in that it never was consented to by the decedent; (2) that there was a lack of adequate consideration for the option as such (appellant conceding, however, that the consideration for the purchase of the land — $75 per acre — is to be considered as technically adequate for the purpose of the appeal); (3) that there was undue influence exercised by the respondent because of the "grossly inadequate consideration" coupled with (a) a breach of confidential relationship and (b) a weak mental and physical condition of the decedent.

The facts, stated most strongly in favor of the respondent where there was a conflict of evidence, (Clark v. Redlich, 147 Cal. App. 2d 500, 504 [305 P.2d 239]) are as follows: Ethel Upson Lee, a widow, acquired ownership of the land by will from a stranger. Not desiring to operate the property herself, she leased it to respondent, an experienced farmer in the same territory. At the same time she gave respondent an oral option to purchase the land at $75 per acre, and on February 10, 1948, this option was reduced to writing; by its terms it was to expire on February 1, 1955. On April 11, 1952, decedent and respondent entered into a second crop share lease for a period of ten years.

One June 1, 1953, decedent executed the exclusive option here in question for a period of eleven years and eight months; the recited consideration was the sum of $1, which was in fact paid. At that time the decedent was a 69 year old widow suffering, as found by the court, from ". . . illness which included difficulty with her vision." When the document was executed, as found by the court on substantial evidence, ". . . she was mentally alert and in all respects fully competent to read, understand and execute the instrument in writing and option. . . ." She had come to Corcoran alone from Sacramento County to discuss the existing situation with Mr. Wheat. The parties went together to a real estate office where at their request the typewritten document was prepared; it followed practically word for word the form of the previous option which had been executed by Mrs. Lee; she read the instrument and understood it and signed it freely and voluntarily; and her health appeared at that time to three competent witnesses to be good.

On August 18, 1955, the decedent signed, served on the respondent and recorded an attempted rescission and withdrawal of the option. This purported rescission was found by the trial court to be ". . . wholly ineffectual for any purpose. . . ."

Mrs. Lee died on October 24, 1955, and the option was exercised on January 29, 1957.

The trial court found in favor of plaintiff and respondent on all issues, and a decree of specific performance followed. The record supports the findings in every respect. Appellant relies strongly upon Herbert v. Lankershim, 9 Cal. 2d 409 [71 P.2d 220]. But that case does not change the general rule that if findings are supported by substantial evidence an appellate court cannot reassess the weight of conflicting evidence or presume to pass upon the credibility of witnesses. [Citations.]

In Herbert v. Lankershim, *supra*, 9 Cal. 2d 409, 476 [71 P.2d 220, 253] the Supreme Court stated after a minute and painstaking analysis of the entire record that ". . . it is a very serious question whether, as a matter of law, the evidence adduced by the plaintiff is sufficiently substantial to support the judgment," and that errors of the trial court, which in other circumstances might conceivably be considered insufficient to reverse (Art. VI, §4½ of the Constitution), should be deemed sufficient in the light of the doubtful proof to constitute a miscarriage of justice. The Lankershim opinion, supra, 9 Cal. 2d at p. 471 [71 P.2d at p. 251] reasserts the ". . . often applied rule that an appellate court will not interfere with the judgment entered by a fact-finding body when there exists a substantial conflict in the evidence."

The contention made by appellant that there was a lack of consent on the part of decedent to the execution of the option is based upon the line of authorities which hold that a signed release is void and of no effect if there was actually no assent to the instrument by the party sought to be held (Tyner v. Axt, 113 Cal. App. 408, 412 [298 P. 537]; Wetzstein v. Thomasson, 34 Cal. App. 2d 554, 559 [93 P.2d 1028]; and Smith v. Occidental Steamship Co., 99 Cal. 462, 471 [34 P. 84].) It is elementary that if there is no actual assent to a signed writing, the alleged release, or contract, never becomes effective. But in this case the trial court found on substantial evidence that at the time of the execution of the document the decedent was fully competent to read, understand and execute the instrument, that she did read and understand it and that there was no fraud involved. Appellant's contention is thus without merit.

The uncontradicted evidence shows that the sum of $1, the consideration alleged in the option, was in fact paid. But appellant urges that "[I]t is time that our appellate courts take another long, hard and exhaustive look into the problem of the adequacy of nominal money consideration to support a long term option." The law, however, is firmly fixed that "[A]n option given for a consideration, however small, is irrevocable and cannot be terminated, without the consent of the other party during the time named in the option." (Stough v. Hanson, 46 Cal. App. 2d 504, 506 [116 P.2d 77].) [Citations.] We would be legislating if we were to change a rule of law so clearly established.

Defendant suggests that the court did not make findings on the issue of undue influence. He relies for his pleading of undue influence upon the allegations contained in defendant's "Separate, Distinct Answer and Affirmative Defense"; the words "undue influence" are not used in the pleading, but the facts which he claims constitute undue influence are alleged, and they unquestionably constitute what counsel relies upon as a statement of that defense; undoubtedly, the pretrial conference order stating undue influence as one of the issues is based upon the same pleading. The trial court specifically found that all of these allegations of fact were untrue except where affirmatively found to the contrary, and further determined that

> it is not true that said Ethel Upson Lee executed or delivered said instrument in writing and option to said plaintiff as the result of any fraud on the part of said plaintiff or as the result of any mistake on the part of said Ethel Upson Lee; and that it is not true that said plaintiff was guilty of any fraud whatsoever in connection with the execution and delivery to him of said instrument in writing and option.

Inasmuch as the court on substantial evidence found that the factual allegations contained in the separate defense which is relied on by defendant as a pleading of undue influence were untrue, it is clear that the trial court has in fact found against any claim of undue influence, and it further appears that such finding is based upon substantial evidence.

The affirmative defense in the answer contains the allegation:

> That decedent knew plaintiff and plaintiff's wife for some period of time prior to June 1953; that she believed plaintiff to be an honest and trustworthy person and had confidence in his truthfulness and integrity.

The record, fairly considered, does not show that a confidential relationship existed between the parties. No doubt, the decedent enjoyed a general friendship with the lessee and his wife through the many years of doing business at arm's length with him; she doubtless also had confidence in his honesty and integrity in the same sense that people dealing with each other for many years as lessor and lessee usually do; she had visited with the respondent and his wife, though at infrequent intervals, and received normal social kindnesses on her visits, but the record is wholly insufficient to establish confidential relationship or any undue influence on the part of the respondent. In Williams v. Williams, 163 Cal. App. 2d 144, 147 [329 P.2d 70, 73], the court quotes with approval the following statement from Webb v. Saunders, 79 Cal. App. 2d 863, 871 [181 P.2d 43]:

> "Undue influence has been defined to be that kind of influence or supremacy of one mind over another by which that other is prevented from acting according to his own wish or judgment, and whereby the will of the

person is overborne and he is induced to do or forbear to do an act which he would not do, or would do, if left to act freely."

The court legitimately found on the evidence that there was no fraud or undue influence.

We find no error in the record.

The judgment is affirmed.

Brown, J., concurs.

Stone, J., being disqualified, did not participate.

Appellant's petition for a hearing by the Supreme Court was denied January 17, 1962.

Section 2.   The Seal and the Written Obligation

J. AMES, LECTURES ON LEGAL HISTORY 98-99, 104-106 (1913): "When the Germans became familiar with Roman civilization it was natural to put the terms of the agreement into a written document, which was passed to the creditor along with the wadia; and in time the wadia itself was omitted. This document, adding the requirement of a seal to make it formal, is the English covenant.

"The earliest covenants we find in the books seem to touch the land. The earliest instance of a covenant not relating to land is of the time of Edward III. The earliest covenants were regarded as grants, and suit could not be brought on the covenant itself. So a covenant to stand seised was a grant, and executed itself. The same is true of a covenant for the payment of money; it was a grant of the money, and executed itself. For failure to pay the money, debt would lie. Afterwards an action of covenant was allowed, so that to-day there is an option.

"A seal was always essential. It was considered, formerly, of much greater importance than now. Glanvill says that if the defendant admits that a seal upon the instrument is his seal, but denies the execution of the instrument, he is, nevertheless, bound, for he must set it down to his own carelessness that he could not keep his seal. The case supposed would arise where the seal had been lost or stolen. There is a case to this effect in the time of John. The doctrine was somewhat qualified by the time of Bracton. He seems to think that a covenantor would not be liable unless it was by his negligence that the matter occurred, as by leaving the seal in the possession of his bailiff or his wife. In the time of Edward I. is a case on the same principle, being a petition to the King that a certain seal that had been lost should no longer have validity. In Riley's Memorial of London it is said that public cry was made that A. had lost his seal and that he would no longer be bound by the same. Riley also gives an account of making a new seal for the city of London, and it is stated, as if it was important, that the old seal was broken with due formality. Of course this doctrine has left no trace in modern times. For centuries a covenantor has not generally used a distinctive seal; any kind of impression has been sufficient. . . .

"It has been often said that a seal imports a consideration, as if a consideration were as essential in contracts by specialty as it is in the case of parol promises. But it is hardly necessary to point out the fallacy of this view. It is now generally agreed that the specialty obligation, like the Roman stipulatio, owes its validity to the mere fact of its formal execution. The true nature of a specialty as a formal contract was clearly stated by Bracton: 'Per scripturam vero obligatur quis, ut si quis scripserit alicui se debere, sive pecunia numerata sit sive non, obligatur ex scriptura, nec habebit exceptionem pecuniae non numeratae contra scripturam, quia scripsit se debere.'

"Bracton's statement is confirmed by a decision about a century later. The action was debt upon a covenant to pay £100 to the plaintiff upon the latter's marrying the defendant's daughter. it was objected that this being a debt upon a covenant touching marriage was within the jurisdiction of the spiritual court. But the common-law judges, while conceding the exclusive jurisdiction of the spiritual court if the promise had been by parol, gave judgment for the plaintiff, because this action was founded wholly upon the deed. In another case it is said: 'In debt upon a contract the plaintiff shall show in his count for what consideration (cause) the defendant became his debtor. Otherwise in debt upon a specialty (obligation), for the specialty is the contract in itself.'

"The specialty being the contract itself, the loss or destruction of the instrument would logically mean the loss of all the obligee's rights against the obligor. And such was the law. 'If one loses his obligation, he loses his duty.' 'Where the action is upon a specialty, if the specialty is lost, the whole action is lost.' The injustice of allowing the obligor to profit at the expense of the obligee by the mere accident of the loss of the obligation is obvious. But this ethical consideration was irrelevant in a court of common law. It did finally prevail in Chancery, which, in the seventeenth century, upon the obligee's affidavit of the loss or destruction of the instrument, compelled the obligor to perform his moral duty. A century later the common-law judges, not to be outdone by the chancellors, decided, by an act of judicial legislation, that if profert of a specialty was impossible by reason of its loss or destruction, the plaintiff might recover, nevertheless, upon secondary evidence of its contents.

"The difference between the ethical attitude of equity and the unmoral (not immoral) attitude of the common law in dealing with specialty contracts appears most conspicuously in the treatment of defenses founded upon the conduct of the obligee. As the obligee, who could not produce the specialty, was powerless at common law against an obligor, who unconscionably refused to fulfil his promise, so the obligor who had formally executed the instrument was, at common law, helpless against an obligee who had the specialty, no matter how reprehensible his conduct in seeking to enforce it. On the other hand, as equity enabled the owner of a lost obligation to enforce it against an unjust obligor, so also would the Chancellor furnish the obligor with a defense by enjoining the action of the obligee, whenever it was plainly unjust for him to insist upon his strict legal right."

WARREN v. LYNCH
5 Johns. 239 (N.Y. 1810)

This was an action of assumpsit brought by the plaintiff, as the first endorser of a promissory note, against the defendant as maker. The note was as follows:

Petersburg, Va., August 27, 1807.

Four months after date I promise to pay Hopkins Robertson or order, the sum of $719.12½ cents, witness my hand and seal. Payable in New York.

THOMAS LYNCH. [L. S.]

The flourish and initials L. S. at the end of the maker's name constituted what was called his seal. The defendant pleaded non assumpsit, with notice of special matter to be given in evidence at the trial. . . .

On this evidence the judge was of opinion that the plaintiff was entitled to recover, and under his direction the jury found a verdict for the plaintiff for the amount of the note with interest.

KENT, Ch. J. . . . 1. The note was given in Virginia, and by the laws of that State it was a sealed instrument or deed. But it was made payable in New York, and according to a well-settled rule, it is to be tested and governed by the law of this State. Thompson v. Ketcham, 4 Johns. 285. Independent then of the written agreement of the parties (and on the operation of which some doubt might possibly arise), this paper must be taken to be a promissory note, without seal, as contradistinguished from a specialty. We have never adopted the usage prevailing in Virginia and in some other States, of substituting a scrawl for a seal; and what was said by Mr. Justice Livingston, in the case of Meredith v. Hinsdale, 2 Caines, 362, in favor of such a substitute, was his own opinion and not that of the court. A seal, according to Lord Coke (3 Inst. 169), is wax with an impression. *Sigillum est cera impressa, quia cera sine impressione non est sigillum.*

A scrawl with a pen is not a seal, and deserves no notice. The law has not indeed declared of what precise materials the wax shall consist; and

whether it be a wafer or any other paste or matter sufficiently tenacious to
adhere and receive an impression, is perhaps not material. But the scrawl
has no one property of a seal. *Multum abludit imago.* To adopt it as such
would be at once to ablish the immemorial distinction between writings
sealed and writings not sealed. Forms will frequently, and especially
when they are consecrated by time and usage, become substance. The
calling a paper a deed will not make it one if it want the requisite formalities. "Notwithstanding," says Perkins (§129), "that words obligatory are
written on parchment or paper, and the obligor delivereth the same as his
deed, yet if it be not sealed, at the time of the delivery, it is but an escrow,
though the name of the obligor be subscribed." I am aware that ingenious
criticism may be indulged at the expense of this and of many of our legal
usages, but we ought to require evidence of some positive and serious
public inconvenience before we, at one stroke, annihilate so well-established and venerable a practice as the use of seals in the authentication of
deeds. The object in requiring seals, as I humbly presume, was misappre-
hended both by President Pendleton and by Mr. Justice Livingston. It
was not, as they seem to suppose, because the seal helped to designate the
party who affixed it to his name. *Ista ratio nullius pretii* (says Vinnius, in
Inst. 2, 10, 5) *nam et alieno annulo signare licet.* Seals were never introduced or tolerated in any code of law, because of any family impression
or image or initials which they might contain. One person might always
use another's seal, both in the English and in the Roman law.[1] The policy
of the rule consists in giving ceremony and solemnity to the execution of
important instruments, by means of which the attention of the parties is
more certainly and effectually fixed and frauds less likely to be practised
upon the unwary. President Pendleton, in the case of Jones and Temple
v. Logwood, 1 Wash. (Va.) 42, which was cited upon the argument, said
that he did not know of any adjudged case that determines that a seal
must necessarily be something impressed on wax; and he seemed to think
that there was nothing but Lord Coke's opinion to govern the question.
He certainly could not have examined this point with his usual diligence.
The ancient authorities are explicit, that a seal does, in legal contemplation, mean an impression upon wax. "It is not requisite," according to
Perkins (§134), "that there be for every grantor who is named in the deed
a several piece of wax, for one piece of wax may serve for all the grantors

---

1. In accord: Ball v. Dunsterville, 4 T.R. 313, 100 E.R. 1038 (1791), one partner attached
a seal for both in the other's presence. And where the instrument purports in its own terms
to be under the hands and seals of the parties, they will all be presumed to have adopted the
single seal appearing thereon. See Restatement, Contracts, §§97-99.

Nota. that it was held by all the Justices that where the obligation upon which suit
was brought read, *In cujus rei testim' sigillum apposui,* the deed is good even though
the word *meum* is omitted, because if the deed is delivered it is a good deed, whether
the seal is his own seal or the seal of another.

Y.B. 21 Edw. IV, 81, 30.

if every one put his seal upon the same piece of wax." And Brooke (tit. Faits, 30 and 17) uses the same language. In Lightfoot and Butler's Case, which was in the Exchequer, 29 Eliz. (2 Leon. 21) the Barons were equally explicit as to the essence of a seal, though they did not all concur upon the point, as stated in Perkins. One of them said that twenty men may seal with one seal upon one piece of wax only, and that should serve for them all, if they all laid their hands upon the seal; but the other two Barons held that though they might all seal a deed with one seal, yet it must be upon several pieces of wax. Indeed this point, that the seal was an impression upon wax, seems to be necessarily assumed and taken for granted in several other passages which might be cited from Perkins and Brooke, and also in Mr. Selden's Notes to Fortescue (De Laud. p. 72); and the nature of a seal is no more a matter of doubt in the old English law than it is that a deed must be written upon paper or parchment, and not upon wood or stone. Nor has the common law ever been altered in Westminster Hall upon this subject, for in the late case of Adam v. Keer, 1 Bos. & Puller, 360, it was made a question whether a bond executed in Jamaica, with a scrawl of the pen, according to the custom of that island, should operate as such in England, even upon the strength of that usage.

The civil law understood the distinction and solemnity of seals as well as the common law of England. Testaments were required not only to be subscribed, but to be sealed by the witnesses. *Subscriptione testium, et ex edicto praetoris, signacula testamentis imponerentur* (Inst. 2, 10, 3). The Romans generally used a ring, but the seal was valid in law, if made with one's own or another's ring; and, according to Heineccius (Elementa juris civilis secundum ord., Inst. 497), with any other instrument which would make an impression, and this, he says is the law to this day throughout Germany. And let me add that we have the highest and purest classical authority for Lord Coke's definition of a seal, *Quid si in ejusmodi cera centum sigilla hoc annulo impressero?* (Cicero. Academ. Quæst. Lucul. 4, 26.). . . .

Rule refused.

NOTE

In New York the strict formality of the common law was relaxed by an 1892 statute that provided:

> The private seal of a person, other than a corporation, to any instrument or writing shall consist of a wafer, wax or other similar adhesive substance affixed thereto, or of paper or other similar substance affixed thereto, by mucilage or other adhesive substance, or of the word "seal," or the letters "L.S.," opposite the signature.

(Ch. 677, §13.) In other states the common law rule suffered even greater
erosion either by statutory fiat or case law: a recital of sealing, a scrawl of
the pen (a scroll), for instance, was, as the opinion indicates, not uniformly frowned upon. Indeed, in the liberalization of the form of the seal,
the scroll still plays a rather significant role in states in which a seal is still
recognized (see Note, *infra* p. 736.) The statutory modifications of the
form of the seal are, however, by no means uniform. Some statutes, for
instance, require an express recital that the document is a sealed instrument if no wax or wafer is used. E.g., Mass. Gen. Laws Ann. ch. 4, §9A
(1958). Other statutes recognize substitute devices such as the word
"seal," the letters "L.S." or a scroll only if they are intended to represent a
seal, but permit extrinsic evidence to show intent.

KRELL v. CODMAN
154 Mass. 454 (1891)

HOLMES, J. This is an action on a voluntary covenant in an indenture
under seal, executed by the defendant's testatrix in England, that her
executors, within six months after her death, should pay to the plaintiffs,
upon certain trusts, the sum of £2,500, with interest at four per cent from
the day of her death.

It is agreed that by the law of England such a covenant constitutes a
debt of the covenantor legally chargeable upon his or her estate, ranking
after debts for value, but before legacies. But it is contended by the
defendant that a similar instrument executed here would be void. The
testatrix died domiciled in Massachusetts, and the only question is
whether the covenant can be enforced here. If a similar covenant made
here would be enforced in our courts, the plaintiffs are entitled to recover, and in the view which we take on that question it is needless to
examine with nicety how far the case is to be governed by the English law
as to domestic covenants, and how far by that of Massachusetts.

In our opinion, such a covenant as the present is not contrary to the
policy of our laws, and could be enforced here if made in this State. If it
were a contract upon valuable consideration, there is no doubt it would
be binding. Parker v. Coburn, 10 Allen, 82. We presume that, in the
absence of fraud, oppression, or unconscionableness, the courts would
not inquire into the amount of such consideration. Paris v. Stone, 14
Pick. 198, 207. This being so, consideration is as much a form as a seal. It
would be anomalous to say that a covenant in all other respects unquestionably valid and binding (Comstock v. Son, *ante*, 389, and Mather v.
Corliss, 103 Mass. 568, 571) was void as contravening the policy of our
statute of wills, but that a parol contract to do the same thing in consideration of a bushel of wheat was good. So, again, until lately an oral con-

tract founded on a sufficient consideration to make a certain provision by will for a particular person was valid. Wellington v. Apthorp, 145 Mass. 69. Now, by statute, no agreement of that sort shall be binding unless such agreement is in writing, signed by the party whose executor is sought to be charged, or by an authorized agent. St. 1888, c. 372. Again, it would be going a good way to say by construction that a covenant did not satisfy this statute.

The truth is, that the policy of the law requiring three witnesses to a will has little application to a contract. A will is an ambulatory instrument, the contents of which are not necessarily communicated to any one before the testator's death. It is this fact which makes witnesses peculiarly necessary to establish that the document offered for probate was executed by the testator as a final disposition of his property. But a contract which is put into the hands of the adverse party, and from which the contractor cannot withdraw, stands differently. See Perry v. Cross, 132 Mass. 454, 456, 457. The moment it is admitted that some contracts which are to be performed after the testator's death are valid without three witnesses, a distinction based on the presence or absence of a valuable consideration becomes impossible with reference to the objection which we are considering. A formal instrument like the present, drawn up by lawyers and executed in the most solemn form known to the law, is less likely to be a vehicle for fraud than a parol contract based on a technical detriment to the promisee. Of course, we are not now speaking of the rank of such contracts inter sese. Stone v. Gerrish, 1 Allen, 175, cited by the defendant, contains some ambiguous expressions, but was decided on the ground that the instrument did not purport to be and was not a contract. Cover v. Stem, 67 Md. 449, was to like effect. The present instrument indisputably is a contract. It was drawn in English form by English lawyers, and must be construed by English law. So construed, it created a debt on a contingency from the covenantor herself, which if she had gone into bankruptcy would have been provable against her. Ex parte Tindal, 8 Bing. 402; S.C. 1 D. & Ch. 291, and Mont. 375, 462. Robson, Bankruptcy, (5th ed.) 274. The cases of Parish v. Stone, 14 Pick. 198, and Warren v. Durfee, 126 Mass. 338, were actions on promissory notes, and were decided on the ground of a total or partial want of consideration.

There is no question here of any attempt to evade or defeat rights of third persons, which would have been paramount had the covenantor left the sum in question as a legacy by will. There is no ground for suggesting an intent to evade the provisions of our law regulating the execution of last wills, — if such intent could be material when an otherwise binding contract was made. See Stone v. Hackett, 12 Gray, 227, 232, 233. There was simply an intent to make a more binding and irrevocable provision than a legacy could be, and we see no reason why it should not succeed.

Judgment for the plaintiffs.

GOULET v. GOULET
105 N.H. 51, 192 A.2d 626 (1963)

Action for personal injuries brought by Marie L. Goulet against her husband William Goulet, both being domiciled in the State of Maine, for injuries resulting from an automobile accident in New Hampshire. The plaintiff signed in Maine a covenant not to sue the defendant. He moved to dismiss the case on the ground

> That the plaintiff, Marie L. Goulet, for consideration on April 2, 1954, executed a covenant not to sue her husband, William Goulet, and agreed to execute a full release of any and all claims and demands against her husband, William Goulet, as a result of an automobile accident which occurred in said Raymond, on March 21, 1954.

The Court, after a hearing at which it received evidence, denied the motion in the following terms: "Motion denied. The Court finds that there was no consideration for the Covenant not to sue." The defendant excepted to this denial and also to the Court's failure to grant certain findings of fact and rulings of law.

Further facts appear in the opinion.

Transferred by Sullivan, J. . . .

BLANDIN, J. The first issue before us is whether the effect of the covenant not to sue the defendant, which was signed by the plaintiff, is governed by the laws of Maine or New Hampshire. The material portions of the instrument read as follows:

> In consideration of the payment of one dollar ($1.00) receipt of which is hereby acknowledged, the undersigned hereby expressly covenants and agrees not to [sue] or to proceed after the date of the execution hereof with any suit or proceeding of any kind against William Goulet, either severally or jointly with any other person, on account of injuries claimed to have been sustained by me on March 21, 1954 at Raymond, N.H. and that undersigned will execute a full release of all claims and demands against my husband Wm. Goulet growing out of said alleged accident on demand.
>
> Dated April 2, 1954.
> Marie L. Goulet (Seal)

While the accident from which these proceedings arose happened in New Hampshire, the covenant was signed in Maine by a party domiciled there. As we interpret its terms they are inclusive to the end that the plaintiff wife agreed not to sue her defendant husband on account of the accident anywhere or at any time. In these circumstances and in the absence of any reasonably clear indication of the parties' intention that the laws of any other jurisdiction should control, we believe that the validity and effect of the instrument is to be governed by the law of the place where it was signed and where both parties were domiciled. Hinchey v. Surety Company, 99 N.H. 373, 377; Restatement, Conflict of Laws, ss. 332, 335. We therefore hold that the law of the state of Maine is controlling.

The defendant bases his defense on the sole proposition that the plaintiff "for consideration" executed this covenant not to sue him and further agreed to sign a full release of all claims and demands against him. Although the Court found that no consideration was given for the covenant not to sue, yet under the law of Maine a seal implies a consideration and the want of it cannot be averred against an instrument under seal. Tucker v. Smith, 4 Me. 415, 419; Wing v. Chase, 35 Me. 260; see Shaw v. Philbrick, 129 Me. 259. The case of Goodwin v. Amusement Company, 129 Maine 36, also states that neither the absence nor the failure of consideration avails to overcome the binding legal effect of a seal. Id., 42. No Maine cases have been called to our attention which indicate any departure from this established rule.

What we have said renders unnecessary consideration of other issues and the order is

Exception sustained.

All concurred.

ALLER v. ALLER

40 N.J.L. 446 (1878)

On rule to show cause why a new trial should not be granted on verdict for the plaintiff in Hunterdon county Circuit Court.

The action was brought on the following instrument, viz.:

> One day after date, I promise to pay my daughter, Angeline H. Aller, the sum of three hundred and twelve dollars and sixty-one cents, for value received, with lawful interest from date, without defalcation or discount, as witness my hand and seal this fourth day of September, one thousand eight hundred and seventy-three. $312.61. This note is given in lieu of one-half of the balance due the estate of Mary A. Aller, deceased, for a note given for one thousand dollars to said deceased by me.
>
> PETER H. ALLER [L.S.]
> Witnesses present, John J. Smith, John F. Grandin.

Both subscribing witnesses were examined at the trial, and it appeared that there was a note for $1000, dated May 1st, 1858, given by said Peter H. Aller to Mary Ann Aller, upon which there were endorsements of payments — April 1st, 1863, $50; April 1st, 1866, $46; April 1st, 1867, $278.78.

Mary Ann Aller, the wife, died, and on the day after her burial, Peter H. Aller told his daughter, the plaintiff, to get the note, which he said was among her mother's papers. She brought it, read the note; he said there was more money endorsed on it than he thought; requested the witness John F. Grandin to add up the endorsements and subtract them from the principal, to divide the balance by two, and draw a note to each of her daughters, Leonora and Angelina, for one-half. After they were drawn by the witness, Peter H. Aller said: "Now here, girls, is a nice present for you," and gave them the notes. Angelina was directed to put the old note back among her mother's papers. Grandin was afterwards appointed administrator of Mary A. Aller, and as such, he says, he destroyed the old note. . . .

The opinion of the court was delivered by SCUDDER, J. Whether the note for $1000 could have been enforced in equity as evidence of an indebtedness by the husband to the wife during her life, is immaterial, for after her death he was entitled, as husband of his deceased wife, to administer on her estate, and receive any balance due on the note, after deducting legal charges, under the statute of distribution. The daughters could have no legal or equitable claim on this note against their father after their mother's decease. The giving of these two sealed promises in writing to them by their father was therefore a voluntary act on his part. That it was just and meritorious to divide the amount represented by the original note between these only two surviving children of the wife, if it was her separate property, and keep it from going into the general distribution of the husband's estate among his other children, is evident, and such appears to have been his purpose.

The question now is, whether that intention was legally and conclusively manifested, so that it cannot now be resisted.

This depends on the legal construction and effect of the instrument which was given by the father to his daughter.

It has been treated by the counsel of the defendant in his argument, as a promissory note, and the payment was resisted at the trial on the ground that it was a gift. Being a gift inter vivos, and without any legal consideration, it was claimed that the action could not be maintained. But the instrument is not a promissory note, having the properties of negotiable paper by the law merchant; nor is it a simple contract, with all the latitude of inquiry into the consideration allowable in such a case; but it is in form and legal construction a deed under seal. It says in the body of the writing "as witness my hand and seal," and a seal is added to the name of Peter H. Aller. It is not therefore an open promise for the payment of money, which is said to be the primary requisite of a bill or promissory note, but it is closed or sealed, whereby it loses its character as a commercial instrument and becomes a specialty governed by the rules affecting common law securities. 1 Daniell's Neg. Inst., §§1, 31, 34.

It is not at this time necessary to state the distinction between this writing and corporation bonds and other securities which have been held to have the properties of negotiable paper by commercial usage. This is merely an individual promise "to pay my daughter, Angeline H. Aller, the sum of $312.61, for value received," &c. It is not even transferable in form, and there is no intention shown upon its face to make it other than it is clearly expressed to be, a sealed promise to pay money to a certain person or a debt in law under seal. How then will it be affected by the evidence which was offered to show that it was a mere voluntary promise, without legal consideration, or, as it was claimed, a gift unexecuted?

Our statute concerning evidence (Rev., p. 380, §16,) which enacts that in any action upon an instrument in writing, under seal, the defendant in such action may plead and set up as a defence therein fraud in the consideration, is not applicable for here there is no fraud shown.

But it is said that the act of April 6th, 1875, (Rev., p. 387, §52), opens it to the defence of want of sufficient consideration, as if it were a simple contract, and, that being shown, the contract becomes inoperative.

The statute reads — "that in every action upon a sealed instrument, or where a set-off is founded on a sealed instrument, the seal thereof shall be only presumptive evidence of a sufficient consideration, which may be rebutted, as if such instrument was not sealed," &c.

Suppose the presumption that the seal carries with it, that there is a sufficient consideration, is rebutted, and overcome by evidence showing there was no such consideration, the question still remains, whether an instrument under seal, without sufficient consideration, is not a good promise, and enforceable at law. It is manifest that here the parties intended and understood that there should be no consideration. The old man said: "Now here, girls, is a nice present for each of you," and so it was received by them. The mischief which the above quoted law was designed to remedy, was that where the parties intended there should be a consideration, they were prevented by the common law from showing none, if the contract was under seal. But it would be going too far to say that the statute was intended to abrogate all voluntary contracts, and to abolish all distinction between specialties and simple contracts.

It will not do to hold that every conveyance of land, or of chattels, is void by showing that no sufficient consideration passed when creditors are not affected. Nor can it be shown by authority that an executory contract, entered into intentionally and deliberately, and attested in solemn form by a seal, cannot be enforced. Both by the civil and the common law, persons were guarded against haste and imprudence in entering into voluntary agreements. The distinction between "nudum pactum" and "pactum vestitum," by the civil law, was in the formality of execution and not in the fact that in one case there was a consideration, and in the other none, though the former term, as adopted in the common law, has the signification of a contract without consideration. The latter was enforced without reference to the consideration, because of the formality of its ratification. 1 Parsons on Cont. (6th ed.) *427.

The opinion of Justice Wilmot, in Pillans v. Van Mierop, 3 Burr. 1663, is instructive on this point.

The early case of Sharington v. Strotton, Plow. 308, gives the same cause for the adoption of the sealing and delivery of a deed. It says, among other things,

> because words are oftentimes spoken by men unadvisedly and without deliberation, the law has provided that a contract by words shall not bind without consideration. And the reason is, because it is by words which pass from men lightly and inconsiderately, but where the agreement is by deed there is more time for deliberation, &c. So that there is great deliberation used in the making of deeds, for which reason they are received as a *lien* final to the party, and are adjudged to bind the party without examining upon what cause or consideration they were made. And therefore in the case put in 17 Ed. IV., if I by deed promise to give you £20 to make your sale de novo, here you shall have an action of debt upon the deed, and the consideration is not examinable, for in the deed there is sufficient consideration, viz., the will of the party that made the deed.

It would seem by this old law, that in case of a deed the saying might be applied, *stat pro ratione voluntas*.

In Smith on Contracts, the learned author, after stating the strictness of the rules of law, that there must be a consideration to support a simple contract to guard persons against the consequences of their own imprudence, says: "The law does not absolutely prohibit them from contracting a gratuitous obligation, for they may, if they will, do so by deed."

This subject of the derivation of terms and formalities from the civil law, and of the rule adopted in the common law, is fully described in Fonb. Eq. 335, note a. The author concludes by saying:

> If, however, an agreement be evidenced, by bond or other instrument, under seal, it would certainly be seriously mischievous to allow its consideration to be disputed, the common law not having pointed out any other means by which an agreement can be more solemnly authenticated. Every deed, therefore, in itself imports a consideration, though it be only the will of the maker, and therefore shall never be said to be nudum pactum.

See, also, 1 Chitty on Cont. (11th ed.) 6; Morly v. Boothby, 3 Bing. 107; Rann v. Hughes, 7 T.R. 350, note a.

These statements of the law have been thus particularly given in the words of others, because the significance of writings under seal, and their importance in our common law system, seem in danger of being overlooked in some of our later legislation. If a party has fully and absolutely expressed his intention in a writing sealed and delivered, with the most solemn sanction known to our law, what should prevent its execution where there is no fraud or illegality? But because deeds have been used to cover fraud and illegality in the consideration, and just defences have been often shut out by the conclusive character of the formality of sealing, we have enacted in our state the two recent statutes above quoted. The one allows fraud in the consideration of instruments under seal to be set up as defence, the other takes away the conclusive evidence of a sufficient consideration heretofore accorded to a sealed writing, and makes it only presumptive evidence. This does not reach the case of a voluntary agreement, where there was no consideration, and none intended by the parties. The statute establishes a new rule of evidence, by which the consideration of sealed instruments may be shown, but does not take from them the effect of establishing a contract expressing the intention of the parties, made with the most solemn authentication, which is not shown to be fraudulent or illegal. It could not have been in the mind of the legislature to make it impossible for parties to enter into such promises; and without a clear expression of the legislative will, not only as to the admissibility, but the effect of such evidence, such construction should not be given to this law. Even if it should be held that a consideration is required to uphold a deed, yet it might still be implied where its purpose is not within the mischief which the statute was intended to remedy. It was certainly not the intention of the legislature to abolish all distinction between simple contracts and specialties, for in the last clause of the section they say that all instruments executed with a scroll, or other device by way of scroll, shall be deemed sealed instruments. It is evident that they were to be continued with their former legal effect, except so far as they might be controlled by evidence affecting their intended consideration.

If the statute be anything more than a change of the rules of evidence which existed at the time the contract was made, and in effect makes a valuable consideration necessary, where such requisite to its validity did not exist at that time, then the law would be void in this case, because it would impair the obligation of a prior contract. This cannot be done. Cooley on Const. Lim. 288, and notes.

The rule for a new trial should be discharged.

NOTE

"The case has often been cited but never with disapproval," United & Globe Rubber Mfg. Co. v. Conard, 80 N.J.L. 286, 78 A. 203 (1910); 1A Corbin §254 (1963); but see 1 Williston §218 (3d ed. 1957), referring to N.J. Stat. Ann. §2A:82-3.

While a considerable number of states have retained the common law effect of the seal, e.g., Mass. Ann. Laws ch. 4, §9A, others have abolished it outright, e.g., N.Y. Gen. Constr. Law §44a (1961), replacing C.P.A. §342.[2] A third group of states has taken a middle course: statutes similar to the one involved in the *Aller* case have been passed declaring that a seal shall be only presumptive evidence of a sufficient consideration, e.g., Mich. Stat. Ann. §27A: 21-39. In some states this "demotion" of the seal applies only to "executory instruments" leaving the validity of releases under seal intact, e.g., Wis. Stat. §328.27 (1951). In a considerable number of states the presumption of consideration has been extended to all written instruments, Cal. Civ. Code §1614-1615, 1629. A few states have even upgraded written promises making them binding without consideration, Miss. Code Ann. tit. 2, c. 6, §§260-262; N.M. Stat. §§20-2-3, 20-2-9 (1953), see Note, *infra* p. 727. For a tabulation of the statutory material and a reference to the applicable statutes of limitations, see 1 Williston §219A (3d ed. 1957); Restatement Second §§122-130. For the attitude of the Uniform Commercial Code, see U.C.C. §2-203.

The drafting of the statutes often leaves something to be desired. Statutes abolishing the seal are not always clear whether they aim at liberalizing the form required for transfers of land only,[3] or whether they mean to abolish the common law effect of the seal with regard to promises also. For a narrow interpretation of Ill. Rev. Stat. §153D (1957), see Ward, Effect of Act "Abolishing" the Seal, U. Ill. L. Forum 113 (1954). See further Holbrook, The Status of the Common Law Seal Doctrine in Utah, 3 Utah L. Rev. 73 (1952), discussing the meaning of the Utah Statute (Utah Rev. Stat. §104-48-4 (1933)), which reads "It shall not be necessary to use private seals on any instrument in writing in this state."

The policy reasons for abolishing the common law effect of the seal are succinctly set out in the 1941 Report of the N.Y. Law Revision Commission at 359:

> There are several objections to the use of the seal as such a device. The seal has degenerated into an L.S. or other scrawl which, in modern practice, is frequently a printed L.S. upon a printed form. To the average man it conveys no meaning, and frequently the parties to instruments upon which it appears have no idea of its legal effects.[4] Moreover, under the

2. The statutory attempt has not always been successful, e.g., Monro v. National Sun & Co., 47 Wash. 488, 92 P. 280 (1907).

3. Sometimes the abolition clearly applies only to conveyances affecting real property, Colo. Rev. Stat. §§118-1-18 (1963).

4. "In our day, when the perfunctory initials 'L.S.' have replaced the heraldic devices, the law is conscious of its own absurdity when it preserves the rubric of a vanished era. Judges have made worthy, if shamefaced, efforts, while giving lip service to the rule, to riddle it with exceptions and by distinctions reduce it to a shadow. A recent case suggests that timidity, and not reverence, has postponed the hour of dissolution. The law will have cause for gratitude to the deliverer who will strike the fatal blow." B. Cardozo, The Nature of the Judicial Process 155 (1921).

present law, the character of an instrument which bears the magic letters, but which contains no recital of sealing, is left uncertain as to whether it is sealed, depending upon parol evidence of intent to be later adduced (Transbel Investment Co. v. Venetos, 279 N.Y. 207 (1938)). It would seem, therefore, that if a method of making promises binding without consideration is desirable, some method should be devised which more clearly than the seal brings to the attention of the promisor what he is doing, and which fixes the character of the instrument as of the time of its execution.

SCHNELL v. NELL

17 Ind. 29 (1861)

PERKINS, J. Action by J. B. Nell against Zacharias Schnell, upon the following instrument:

This agreement, entered into this 13th day of February, 1856, between Zach. Schnell, of Indianapolis, Marion county, State of Indiana, as party of the first part, and J. B. Nell, of the same place, Wendelin Lorenz, of Stilesville, Hendricks County, State of Indiana, and Donata Lorenz, of Frickinger, Grand Duchy of Baden, Germany, as parties of the second part, witnesseth: The said Zacharias Schnell agrees as follows: Whereas his wife, Theresa Schnell, now deceased, has made a last will and testament in which, among other provisions, it was ordained that every one of the above named second parties, should receive the sum of $200; and whereas the said provisions of the will must remain a nullity, for the reason that no property, real or personal, was in the possession of the said Theresa Schnell, deceased, in her own name, at the time of her death, and all property held by Zacharias and Theresa Schnell jointly, therefore reverts to her husband; and whereas the said Theresa Schnell has also been a dutiful and loving wife to the said Zach. Schnell, and has materially aided him in the acquisition of all property, real and personal, now possessed by him; for, and in consideration of all this, and the love and respect he bears to his wife; and, furthermore, in consideration of one cent, received by him of the second parties, he, the said Zach. Schnell, agrees to pay the above named sums of money to the parties of the second part, to wit: $200 to the said J. B. Nell; $200 to the said Wendelin Lorenz; and $200 to the said Donata Lorenz, in the following installments, viz., $200 in one year from the date of these presents; $200 in two years; and $200 in three years; to be divided between the parties in equal portions of $66⅔ each year, or as they may agree, till each one has received his full sum of $200.

And the said parties of the second part, for, and in consideration of this, agree to pay the above-named sum of money [one cent], and to deliver up to said Schnell, and abstain from collecting any real or supposed claims upon him or his estate, arising from the said last will and testament of the said Theresa Schnell, deceased.

In witness whereof, the said parties have, on this 13th day of February, 1856, set hereunto their hands and seals. Zacharias Schnell. [Seal]. J. B. Nell [Seal]. Wen. Lorenz [Seal].

The complaint contained no averment of a consideration for the instrument, outside of those expressed in it; and did not aver that the one cent agreed to be paid, had been paid or tendered.

A demurrer to the complaint was overruled.

The defendant answered, that the instrument sued on was given for no consideration whatever.

He further answered, that it was given for no consideration, because his said wife, Theresa, at the time she made the will mentioned and at the time of her death, owned, neither separately, nor jointly with her husband, or any one else (except so far as the law gave her an interest in her husband's property), any property, real or personal, etc.

The will is copied into the record, but need not be into this opinion.

The Court sustained a demurrer to these answers, evidently on the ground that they were regarded as contradicting the instrument sued on, which particularly set out the considerations upon which it was executed. But the instrument is latently ambiguous on this point. See Ind. Dig., p. 110.

The case turned below, and must turn here, upon the question whether the instrument sued on does express a consideration sufficient to give it legal obligation, as against Zacharias Schnell. It specified three distinct considerations for his promise to pay $600:

(1) A promise, on the part of the plaintiffs, to pay him one cent.

(2) The love and affection he bore his deceased wife, and the fact that she had done her part, as his wife, in the acquisition of property.

(3) The fact that she had expressed her desire, in the form of an inoperative will, that the persons named therein should have the sums of money specified.

The consideration of one cent will not support the promise of Schnell. It is true, that as a general proposition, inadequacy of consideration will not vitiate an agreement. Baker v. Roberts, 14 Ind. 552. But this doctrine does not apply to a mere exchange of sums of money, of coin, whose value is exactly fixed, but to the exchange of something of, in itself, indeterminate value, for money, or, perhaps, for some other thing of indeterminate value. In this case, had the one cent mentioned, been some particular one cent, a family piece, or ancient, remarkable coin, possessing an indeterminate value, extrinsic from its simple money value, a different view might be taken. As it is, the mere promise to pay six hundred dollars for one cent, even had the portion of that cent due from the plaintiff been tendered, is an unconscionable contract, void, at first blush, upon its face, if it be regarded as an earnest one. Hardesty v. Smith, 3 Ind. 39. The consideration of one cent is, plainly, in this case, merely nominal, and intended to be so. As the will and testament of Schnell's wife imposed no legal obligation upon him to discharge her bequests out of his property, and as she had none of her own, his promise to discharge them was not legally binding upon him, on that ground. A moral consideration, only, will not support a promise. Ind. Dig., p. 13. And for the same reason, a valid consideration for his promise cannot be found in the fact of a compromise of a disputed claim; for where such claim is legally groundless, a promise upon a compromise of it, or of a suit upon it, is not legally binding. Spahr v. Hollingshead, 8 Blackf. 415. There was no mistake of law or fact in this case, as the agreement admits the will inoperative and void. The promise was simply one to make a gift. The past services of his wife, and the love and affection he had borne her, are objectionable as legal considerations for Schnell's promise, on two grounds: (1) They are past considerations. Ind. Dig., p. 13. (2) The fact that Schnell loved his wife, and that she had been industrious, constituted no consideration for his promise to pay J. B. Nell, and the Lorenzes, a sum of money. Whether, if his wife, in her lifetime, had made a bargain with Schnell, that, in consideration of his promising to pay, after her death, to the persons named, a sum of money, she would be industrious, and worthy of his affection, such a promise would have been valid and consistent with public policy, we need not decide. Nor is the fact that Schnell now venerates the memory of his deceased wife, a legal consideration for a promise to pay any third person money.

The instrument sued on, interpreted in the light of the facts alleged in the second paragraph of the answer, will not support an action. The demurrer to the answer should have been overruled. See Stevenson v. Druley, 4 Ind. 519.

PER CURIAM. — The judgment is reversed, with costs.

Cause remanded &c.

NOTE

For the arguments of counsel and the background of the case, see L. Fuller, Basic Contract Law 347 (1947). Is it of any relevance whether the one cent was paid or only promised?

COCHRAN v. TAYLOR
273 N.Y. 172, 7 N.E.2d 89 (Ct. App. 1937)

Appeal from a judgment of the Appellate Division of the Supreme Court in the fourth judicial department, entered May 27, 1936, affirming a judgment in favor of defendant entered upon a decision of the court on trial without a jury. (See 156 Misc. Rep. 750.)

RIPPEY, J. On October 20, 1934, an agreement in writing and under seal was executed in duplicate, duly acknowledged and delivered by and between defendant and one William B. Chenault, whereby the former gave to Chenault an option to buy certain real and personal property located in Allegany County, New York, for $115,000 at any time within

120 days thereafter upon terms and conditions therein specified, and agreed to sell and convey the same to Chenault on condition that Chenault should, within such period of time, give her written notice of his intention to buy. On November 13, 1934, defendant notified Chenault that she revoked, rescinded and withdrew the offer to sell on the ground, as she asserted, that the contract was without consideration and was obtained from her through duress, fraud and undue influence. Chenault assigned all of his interest in the agreement to plaintiff on December 21, 1934, and on January 11, 1935, the latter served the required notice of his election to buy. Complying with the provisions of the agreement, plaintiff demanded delivery within thirty days of abstracts of title and of a suitable instrument of conveyance. Upon refusal of defendant to perform, this action for specific performance was brought.

The answer put in issue the material allegations of the complaint. Additionally, defendant set up, as defenses, (1) that the agreement was only an offer to sell, was without consideration and was revoked and withdrawn before acceptance and prior to the time of assignment to plaintiff who took the assignment with knowledge of the withdrawal and revocation, (2) that the option was not assignable and plaintiff acquired no interest by the instrument, and (3) that defendant's signature to the instrument and its delivery by her were obtained through imposition, fraud and undue influence. A counterclaim was interposed for damages arising out of the recording of the instruments which, it was asserted, prevented defendant from disposing of her property and from enjoying the full use and benefit thereof, all of which was put in issue by the reply.

The trial court found that there was no valid acceptance or tender of performance by plaintiff or by Chenault and sustained the first two defenses mentioned. No finding or decision was made on the material question of fact as to whether the execution and delivery of the instrument were procured, as defendant asserts, by plaintiff or by Chenault or by both through imposition, undue influence or fraud. The trial court specifically stated in his opinion that he limited his decision to holding that the option was nudum pactum, that defendant had a right to withdraw, revoke and cancel it and that, since the option by its terms involved the extension of credit to Chenault, it was not assignable to plaintiff or, in any event, enforceable by plaintiff without a tender of a bond executed by Chenault. Judgment was entered dismissing the complaint, with costs. The Appellate Division in the fourth department affirmed by a divided court upon the findings of fact as made by the trial court. The judgment appealed from cannot be sustained unless it can be held, as matter of law, that the option was without consideration, was not assignable and was not accepted according to its terms.

It is the rule that an offer or an option, not under seal, or given for a consideration, may be revoked at any time before acceptance (1 Williston on the Law of Contracts [Rev. ed., 1936], §55; Petterson v. Pattberg, 248

N.Y. 86, 88; Boston & Maine R.R. v. Bartlett, 3 Cush. [Mass.] 224.) That rule has no application here. In the instant case the agreement was *under seal* and the receipt of a consideration was acknowledged and confessed. In the body of the instrument the parties recited that they attached their seals, thereby establishing their intention concerning the sealing of the instrument, and, at the end, added the seal in the form required by section 44 of the General Construction Law (Cons. Laws, ch. 22). It cannot be successfully argued that the agreement was not a sealed instrument carrying with it all the force and implications attributable to an instrument so executed. The cases of Matter of Pirie (198 N.Y. 209) and Empire Trust Co. v. Heinze (242 N.Y. 475) hold nothing to the contrary. In the *Pirie* case the seal was present but an expression of intent to make the instrument one under seal was lacking. In the *Heinze* case the intention was expressed but the seal was lacking.

Prior to the time the law required consideration to support a contract, the seal was used conclusively to establish the authenticity and binding effect of the instrument to which it was attached. (1 Williston on the Law of Contracts [Rev. ed., 1936], §§109, 217.) The use and binding effect of the seal dates back to at least 2900 B.C. (Report of Law Revision Commission, Legislative Document, [1936] No. 65, p. 235.) Williston points out (§217) that long before the action of assumpsit was developed, a promise under seal but without consideration was binding and that it was binding by its own force by the common law (§109). It is agreed upon substantially universal authority that a statement of consideration in a sealed instrument is unnecessary. (Thomason v. Bescher, 176 N.C. 622; 2 A.L.R. note, p. 631.) It is also frequently stated by the courts that a sealed instrument carries with it a presumption that it is given for a valid consideration without the necessity of a recital of the consideration therein and that the party signing and sealing is estopped to assert lack of consideration. (Fuller v. Artman, 69 Hun 546; Petrie v. Barckley, 47 N.Y. 653; Torry v. Black, 58 N.Y. 185; Stiebel v. Grosberg, 202 N.Y. 266; McMillan v. Ames, 33 Minn. 257; Watkins v. Robertson, 105 Va. 269; Weaver v. Burr, 31 W. Va. 736.) Williston asserts that though it has been expressed that a sealed instrument "imported" a consideration, "however expressed the law has always been clear that apart from changes made by statute, a sealed promise, whether absolute or in the form of an offer, is binding without consideration." (§217). He adds that while there are cases where equity will not enforce a voluntary covenant, an option is not one of them. Throughout the centuries, the rule as to the binding effect of the seal has been founded in reason and based on necessity. Today, in the face of the tremendous number of business transactions open to investigation by the courts, reason continues to dictate and necessity to require more forcefully than before that a party to a sealed instrument should be estopped to assert want of consideration. (1 Williston on the Law of Contracts [Rev. ed., 1936], §219.)

The first statute in this State in any manner affecting the common law rule as to the conclusive character of the seal was the act of 1828 (2 R.S. [1st ed.], p. 406, pt. 3, ch. 7, tit. 3, §77) which provided that the seal should be only *"presumptive evidence of a sufficient consideration,* which may be rebutted in the same manner; and to the same extent, as if such instrument were not sealed." That act remained in effect until amended by chapter 448 of the Laws of 1876 (Code of Remedial Justice, §840) to read, "A seal upon an executory instrument is only presumptive evidence of a sufficient consideration, which may be rebutted, as if the instrument was not sealed." In chapter 416 of the Laws of 1877 (Code Civ. Proc. §840) the words "hereafter executed" were inserted after the first word "instrument." In that form the statute remained until 1920, when the words "hereafter executed" were stricken out and the statute, thus amended, continued to September 1, 1935. These statutory changes in the common law refer only to the question of *"sufficient consideration,"* and as to the sufficiency of the consideration, the seal, it is declared, shall be only presumptive evidence. The memorandum opinion in Baird v. Baird (145 N.Y. 659, 665), where it was said, among other things, that under section 840 of the Code of Civil Procedure "it is now open to the maker of such an instrument to allege and prove the absence of any consideration in fact as a defense," did not receive the approval of a majority of this court. The question of sufficiency of consideration has always been open to inquiry and the statute is merely declaratory of the common law, but the "consideration implied by the seal cannot be impeached for the purpose of invalidating the instrument or destroying its character as a specialty." (McMillan v. Ames, *supra*; Fuller v. Artman, *supra*.) Whether the intent and effect of chapter 708 of the Laws of 1935 (in effect September 1, 1935) was to destroy the conclusive effect of the seal on a written instrument, we are not here called upon to determine. The instrument in suit was executed and delivered prior to the time that act went into effect.

The instrument in suit recited a consideration of one dollar which the defendant "acknowledged and confessed" she had received. Oral evidence was admitted, over plaintiff's objection and exception, to the effect that neither the one dollar nor any other sum was paid by Chenault to defendant. It was upon this testimony that the court found and concluded that the instrument was without consideration, a mere offer, and revocable at any time before acceptance. Such evidence did not warrant the facts found nor the conclusion drawn. (Lawrence v. McCalmont, 2 How. [U.S.] 426.) Sometimes equity will inquire into the real consideration for the purpose of applying equitable principles on questions of enforcement arising in actions for specific performance. Equity will not refuse, however, to decree specific performance solely on the ground of inadequacy of consideration. (Pomeroy on Equity Jurisprudence [4th ed.], vols. 2 and 5, §§926, 2212.) There must be other grounds. But parol evidence is inadmissible to question or contradict the recited consideration in the sealed instrument for the purpose of showing that it was void for lack of consideration and thus to defeat it. (Fuller v. Artman, *supra*; McMillan v. Ames, *supra*; M'Crea v. Purmort, 16 Wend. 460; Grout v. Townsend, 2 Den. 336; Ruppert v. Singhi, 243 N.Y. 156, 159; Jamestown Business College Assn. v. Allen, 172 N.Y. 291; Poe v. Ulrey, 233 Ill. 56.) In Lawrence v. McCalmont (2 How. 426, at p. 452) Mr. Justice Story said:

> The second [defense] is, that the payment of the one dollar is merely nominal and not sufficient to sustain the guarantee, if it had been received; and it is urged that it was not received. As to this last point, we feel no difficulty. The guarantor acknowleged the receipt of the one dollar, *and is now estopped to deny it.* If she has not received it, she would now be entitled to recover it. A valuable consideration, however small or nominal, if given or stipulated for in good faith, is, in the absence of fraud, sufficient to support an action on any parol contract; and this is equally true as to contracts of guarantee as to other contracts. A stipulation in consideration of one dollar is just as effectual and valuable a consideration as a larger sum stipulated for or paid.

It is unnecessary to discuss or decide whether an option to purchase mineral rights and the like carries with it an interest in the land itself. It is sufficient here to say that the option in suit carries with it a presently existing contract right as valuable as the property promised to be conveyed and partakes of the incident of assignability. The option was not necessarily personal in its character. It did not involve the integrity or skill of Chenault, nor was it possible to say, as found by the trial court, that, in executing and delivering the agreement, defendant relied on the credit of Chenault. Assignment was not barred by any express terms contained in the instrument and it was not forbidden by statute or public policy. It was, under the general rule prevailing in this State as to assignability of property rights, assignable by Chenault. (Devlin v. Mayor etc., 63 N.Y. 8; Rosenthal Paper Co. v. National Folding Box & Paper Co., 226 N.Y. 313, 325.) Aside from the above, the parties asserted in the instrument that "this agreement is binding upon the respective parties, personal representatives, heirs, and assigns," and its assignability, within the clear and expressed intent of the parties, was thereby established.

Plaintiff accepted the offer in due form within the time required. For reasons that are clear, defendant could not decline to acknowledge that the acceptance was sufficient. [The plaintiff's tender of cash was held to eliminate an objection to his right to specific performance.]

The written option, being under seal and founded upon a valid consideration, could not be withdrawn, revoked or rescinded at will by defendant within the time within which she agreed that Chenault and his assigns might accept. (Fuller v. Artman, *supra*; Thomason v. Bescher, 176 N.C. 622; 2 A.L.R. note, p. 631, 6 R.C.L. [Contracts] §26.) It was a unilateral contract to convey, subject only to one express condition. (Heller v. Pope, 250 N.Y. 132.) When Chenault's assignee gave written notice within the time specified that he elected to buy, the condition was fulfilled and the unilateral option was thereby converted into a bilateral contract. (Heller v. Pope, *supra*; Thomason v. Bescher, *supra*.) The contract was reasonably certain in its terms, its subject-matter, its purposes and its parties. By acceptance, it became mutual in its obligations and its remedies. Upon the defendant's refusal to perform, the contract was enforceable by the assignee in an action for specific performance, in the absence of any available and satisfactorily established defense or counterclaim of an equitable character existing against the assignee or against Chenault before notice to defendant of the assignment. (Trustees of Hamilton College v. Roberts, 223 N.Y. 56; 4 Pomeroy on Equity Jurisprudence [4th ed.], §1405; 2 Williston on The Law of Contracts [Rev. ed., 1936], §415. Cf. State Bank v. Central Mercantile Bank, 248 N.Y. 428, 434-436.)

The judgment of the Appellate Division and that of the Trial Term should be reversed and a new trial granted, with costs to the appellant to abide the event.

Crane, Ch. J., Lehman, O'Brien, Hubbs and Loughran, JJ., concur; Finch, J., taking no part.

Judgments reversed, etc.

NOTE

Is the case still good law in New York in the light of Gen. Constr. Law §44a (1961)? Consult further Lloyd, Consideration and the Seal in New York — An Unsatisfactory Legislative Program, 46 Colum. L. Rev. 1 (1946); N.Y. Law Revision Commission, Report, Recommendations and Studies 65-80, 287-373 (1936); Report, Recommendations and Studies 345-414 (1941).

The willingness of some equity courts to "look behind the seal" even in option cases is illustrated by Corbett v. Cronkhite, 239 Ill. 9, 87 N.E. 874 (1909); Woodall v. Prevatt, 45 N.C. 199 (1853). The prevailing view is contra and represented by Thomason v. Besher, 176 N.C. 622, 97 S.E. 654 (1918). See in general Pound, Consideration in Equity, 13 Ill. L. Rev. 667 (1919).

PILLANS AND ROSE v. VAN MIEROP AND HOPKINS
3 Burr. 1663, 97 Eng. Rep. 1035 (K.B. 1765)

On Friday 25th of January last, Mr. Attorney General Norton, on behalf of the plaintiffs, moved for a new trial. He moved it as upon a verdict against evidence: the substance of which evidence was as follows.

One White, a merchant in Ireland, desired to draw upon the plaintiffs, who were merchants at Rotterdam in Holland, for £800 payable to one Clifford; and proposed to give them credit upon a good house in London, for their reimbursement; or any other method of reimbursement.

The plaintiffs, in answer, desired a confirmed credit upon a house of rank in London; as the condition of their accepting the bill. White names the house of the defendants, as this house of rank; and offers credit upon them. Whereupon the plaintiffs honoured the draught, and paid the money; and then wrote to the defendants Van Mierop and Hopkins, merchants in London, (to whom White also wrote, about the same time,) desiring to know "whether they would accept such bills as they, the plaintiffs, should in about a month's time draw upon the said Van Mierop's and Hopkins' house here in London, for £800 upon the credit of White:" and they, having received their assent, accordingly drew upon the defendants. In the interim White failed before their draught came to hand, or was even drawn: and the defendants gave notice of it to the plaintiffs, and forbid their drawing upon them. Which they, nevertheless, did: and therefore the defendants refused to pay their bills. . . .

LORD MANSFIELD — This is a matter of great consequence to trade and commerce, in every light.

If there was any kind of fraud in this transaction, the collusion and mala fides would have vacated the contract. But from these letters, it seems to me clear, that there was none. The first proposal from White, was "to reimburse the plaintiffs by a remittance, or by credit on the house of Van Mierop": this was the alternative he proposed. The plaintiffs chose the latter. Both the plaintiffs and White wrote to Van Mierop and company. They answered "that they would honour the plaintiffs' draughts." So that the defendants assent to the proposal made by White, and ratify it. And it does not seem at all, that the plaintiffs then doubted of White's sufficiency, or meant to conceal any thing from the defendants.

If there be no fraud, it is a mere question of law. The law of merchants and the law of the land, is the same: A witness can not be admitted, to prove the law of merchants. We must consider it as a point of law. A nudum pactum does not exist, in the usage and law of merchants.

I take it, that the ancient notion about the want of consideration was for the sake of evidence only: for when it is reduced into writing, as in covenants, specialties, bonds &c. there was no objection to the want of consideration. And the statute of frauds proceeded upon the same principle.

In commercial cases amongst merchants, the want of consideration is not an objection.

This is just the same thing as if White had drawn on Van Mierop and Hopkins, payable to the plaintiffs: it had been nothing to the plaintiffs, whether Van Mierop and Co. had effects of White's in their hands, or not; if they had accepted his bill. And this amounts to the same thing; —

"I will give the bill due honour," is, in effect, accepting it. If a man agrees that he will do the formal part, the law looks upon it (in the case of an acceptance of a bill) as if actually done. This is an engagement "to accept the bill, if there was a necessity to accept it; and to pay it, when due:" and they could not afterwards retract. It would be very destructive to trade, and to trust in commercial dealing, if they could. There was nothing of nudum pactum mentioned to the jury, nor was it, I dare say, at all in their idea or contemplation.

I think the point of law is with the plaintiffs.

Mr. Justice WILMOT — The question is, "whether this action can be supported, upon the breach of this agreement."

I can find none of those cases that go upon its being nudum pactum, that are in writing; they are all, upon parol.

I have traced this matter of the nudum pactum; and it is very curious.

He then explained the principle of an agreement being looked upon as a nudum pactum; and how the notion of a nudum pactum first came into our law. He said, it was echoed from the civil law: — "Ex nudo pacto non oritur actio." Vinnius gives the reason, in lib. 3, tit. De Obligationibus, 4to edition, 596. If by stipulation, (and a fortiori, if by writing),[5] it was good without consideration. There was no radical defect in the contract, for want of consideration. But it was made requisite, in order to put people upon attention and reflection, and to prevent obscurity and uncertainty: and in that view, either writing or certain formalities were required. Idem, on Justinian, 4to edit. 614.

Therefore it was intended as a guard against rash inconsiderate declarations: but if an undertaking was entered into upon deliberation and reflection, it had activity; and such promises were binding. Both Grotius and Puffendorff, hold them obligatory by the law of nations. Grot. lib. 2, c. 11, De Promissis. Puffend. lib. 3, c. 5. They are morally good; and only require ascertainment. Therefore there is no reason to extend the principle, or carry it further.

There would have been no doubt upon the present case, according to the Roman law; because here is both stipulation (in the express Roman form) and writing.

Bracton (who wrote[6] temp. Hen. 3) is the first of our lawyers that mention this. His writings interweave a great many things out of the Roman law. In his third book, cap. 1, De Actionibus, he distinguishes between naked and cloathed contracts. He says that "obligatio est mater actionis"; and that it may arise ex contractu, multis modis; sicut ex conventione, &c. sicut sunt pacta, coventa, quae nuda sunt aliquando, aliquando vestita, &c. &c.

5. This was denied by Baron Eyre in Cam Scac. Nov. 27, 1776; and so it was by all except the Ch. Bar.
6. Sub ultima tempora Regis H. 3.

Our own lawyers have adopted exactly the same idea as the Roman law.[7] Plowden, 308 b. in the case of Sheryngton and Pledal v. Strotton and Others, mentions it: and no one contradicted it. He lays down the distinction between contracts or agreements in words (which are more base,) and contracts or agreements in writing, (which are more high,) and puts the distinction upon the want of deliberation in the former case, and the full exercise of it in the latter. His words are the marrow of what the Roman lawyers had said. "Words pass from men lightly": but where the agreement is made by deed, there is more stay: &c. &c. For, first, there is &c. &c. And, thirdly, he delivers the writing as his deed.

> The delivery of the deed is a ceremony in law, signifying fully his good will that the thing in the deed should pass from him who made the deed, to the other. And therefore a deed, which must necessarily be made upon great thought and deliberation, shall bind without regard to the consideration.

The voidness of the consideration is the same, in reality, in both cases: the reason of adopting the rule was the same, in both cases; though there is a difference in the ceremonies required by each law. But no inefficacy arises merely from the naked promise.

Therefore, if it stood only upon the naked promise, its being, in this case, reduced into writing, is a sufficient guard against surprize; and therefore the rule of nudum pactum does not apply in the present case.

I cannot find, that a nudum pactum evidenced by writing has been ever holden bad: and I should think it good; though, where it is merely verbal, it is bad; yet I give no opinion for its being good, always, when in writing.[8]

Many of the old cases are strange and absurd: so also are some of the modern ones; particularly, that of Hayes v. Warren.[9]

It is now settled, "that where the act is done at the request of the person promising, it will be a sufficient foundation to graft the promise upon."

In another instance, the strictness has been relaxed: as for instance, burying[10] a son; or curing[11] a son; the considerations were both past, and yet holden good. It has been melting down into common sense, of late times.

However, I do here see a consideration. If it be a departure from any

---

7. This probably was Plowden's own argument. I suppose, he was himself that apprentice of the Middle Temple who argued for the defendants.

8. This was denied by the Judges and three Barons in the Exchequer Chamber, Nov. 27th, 1776.

9. V. 2 Sir J. S. 933. I have a very full note of this case. The reason of the reversal of the judgment was, "that it did not appear by the declaration, to be either for the benefit, or at the request of the defendant."

10. Church and Church's case; cited in Sir T. Raym. 260.

11. V. 2 Leon. 111.

right, it will be sufficient to grant a verbal promise upon. Now here, White, living in Ireland, writes to the plaintiffs "to honour his draught for £800[12] payable ten weeks after." The plaintiffs agree to it, on condition that they be made safe at all events. White offers good credit on a house in London; and draws: the plaintiffs accept his draught. Then White writes to them, "to draw on Van Mierop and Hopkins": to whom the plaintiffs write, "to inquire if they will honour their draught": they engage "that they will." The transaction has prevented, stopt, and disabled the plaintiffs from calling upon White, for the performance of his engagement. For, White's engagement is complied with: so that the plaintiffs could not call upon him for this security. I do not speak of the money; for, that was not payable till after two usances and a half. But the plaintiffs were prevented from calling upon White for a performance of his engagement "to give them credit on a good house in London, for reimbursement": so that here is a good consideration. The law does not weigh the quantum of the consideration. The suspension of the plaintiff's right "to call upon White for a compliance with his engagement" is sufficient to support an action; even if it be a suspension of the right, for a day only, or for ever so little a time.

But to consider this as a commercial case. All nations ought to have their laws conformable to each other, in such cases. *Fides servanda est; simplicitas juris gentium praevaleat. Hodierni* mores are such, that the old notion about the nudum pactum is not strictly observed, as a rule.

On a question of this nature, "whether by the law of nations, such as engagement as this shall bind — "; the law is to judge.

The true reason why the acceptance of a bill of exchange shall bind, is not on account of the acceptor's having or being supposed to have effects in hand; but for the convenience of trade and commerce. Fides est servanda. An acceptance for the honor of the drawer, shall bind the acceptor: so shall a verbal acceptance. And whether this be an actual acceptance, or an agreement to accept, it ought equally to bind. An agreement to accept a bill "to be drawn in future" would (as it seems to me) by connection and relation, bind on account of the antecedent relation. And I see no difference between its being before or after the bill was drawn. Here was an agreement sufficient to bind the defendants to pay the bill: agreeing "to honour it," is agreeing to pay it.

I see no sort of fraud. It rather seems as if the defendants had effects of White's in their hands. And it does not appear to me, that the defendants would have honoured the plaintiff's draughts, even though they had known that it was future credit.

But whether the plaintiffs or the defendants had effects of White's in their hands, or not; we must determine on the general doctrine.

And I am of opinion, that there ought to be a new trial.

12. For, between Ireland and Holland, each usance is one month.

Mr. Justice YATES was of the same opinion. He said it was a case of great consequence to commerce; and therefore he would give both his opinion and his reasons.

The arguments on the side of the defendants terminate in its being a nudum pactum, and therefore void.

This depends upon two questions.

1st question — "Whether this be a promise without a consideration";

2d question — If it is, then "whether this promise shall be binding, of itself, without any consideration."

First — The draught drawn by White on the plaintiffs, payable to Clifford, is no part of the consideration of the undertaking by the defendants. The draught payable to Clifford is never mentioned to the defendants. They are asked "whether they will answer a draught from the plaintiffs upon them": they answer "they will honour such a draught on them."

Whether the defendants had or had not effects of White's in their hands, is immaterial.

Any[13] damage to another, or suspension or forebearance of his right, is a foundation for an undertaking, and will make it binding; though no actual benefit accrues to the party undertaking.

Now here, the promise and undertaking of the defendants did occasion a possibility of loss to the plaintiffs. It is plain that the plaintiffs would not rely on White's assurance only: but wrote to the defendants, to know if they would accept their draughts. The credit of the plaintiffs might have been hurt, by the refusal of the defendant's to accept White's bills. They were or might have been prevented from resorting to him, or getting further security from him. It comes within the cases of promises, where the debtee forbears suing the original debtor.

Second question — Whether, by the law of merchants, this contract is not binding on the defendants; though it was without consideration.

The acceptance of a bill of exchange is an obligation to pay it: the end of their institution, their currency, requires that it should be so. On this principle, bills of exchange are considered, and are declared upon as special contracts; though, legally, they are only simple contracts: the declaration sets forth the bill and acceptance specifically: and that thereby the defendants, by the custom of merchants, became liable to pay it. . . .

Therefore, upon the whole circumstances of this transaction, 1st, there is a consideration: and 2dly, if there was none; yet, in this commercial case, the defendants would be bound.

Mr. Justice ASTON — I am of opinion "that there ought to be a new trial."

13. V. Coggs v. Bernard, 2 Ld. Raym. 919. [See also 2 Hen. Bl. 315. 4 East, 461.—EDS.]

If there be such a custom of merchants as has been alledged, it may be found by a jury: but it is the Court, not the jury, who are to determine the law.

This must be considered as a commercial transaction and is a plain case. The defendants have undertaken to honour the "plaintiffs' draught." Therefore they are bound to pay it.

This cannot be called a nudum pactum. The answer returned by the defendants is an admission of "having effects of White's in their hands," if that were necessary. And after this promise "to accept" (which is an implied acceptance) they might have applied any thing of White's that they had in their hands, to this engagement; even though White had drawn other bills upon them in the interim. The defendants voluntarily engaged to the plaintiffs; and they could not recede from their engagement.

As to its being a nudum pactum (which matter has been already so well explained) — if there be a turpitude or illegality in the consideration of a note, it will make it void, and may be given in evidence: but here nothing of that kind appears, nor any thing like fraud in the plaintiffs. Here was full notice of all the facts; a clear apprehension of them by the defendants; a question put to them, "whether they would accept"; and their answer, "that they would."

Upon the whole he concurred, "that an action will lay for the plaintiffs against them: and that the plaintiffs ought to recover."

By the Court, unanimously,

The rule "to set aside the verdict, and for a new trial," was made absolute.

NOTE

Lord Mansfield's victory over the consideration doctrine was rather short-lived. Rann v. Hughes, 7 T.R. 350 n., 101 Eng. Rep. 1014 n. (1778):

It is undoubtedly true that every man is by the law of nature, bound to fulfil his engagements. It is equally true that the law of this country supplies no means, nor affords any remedy, to compel the performance of an agreement made without sufficient consideration. . . . . All contracts are, by the laws of England, distinguished into agreements by specialty, and agreements by parol; nor is there any such third class as some of the counsel have endeavoured to maintain, as contracts in writing. If they be merely written and not specialities, they are parol, and a consideration must be proved.

Despite this setback, Justice Yates' treatment of the consideration doctrine should not be overlooked. His opinion contains the seeds of a possible expansion of consideration which would include not only actual reliance (forbearance) on the part of the promisee but also the likelihood or risk of reliance. Outside commercial cases, however, the potentialities inherent in this approach have been developed hardly at all. Occasionally, it is true, courts have shown a tendency to regard the consideration doctrine as satisfied where facts show the likelihood of reliance but do not permit proof of actual reliance. See, e.g., Lawrence v. Oglesby, 178 Ill. 122, 52 N.E. 945 (1899), discussed in Note, 7 U. Chi. L. Rev. 124, 133 (1939). But the significance of this and similar cases should not be exaggerated. The reluctance of the courts to apply a risk of reliance doctrine is strikingly illustrated by their treatment of firm offers. Under a risk of reliance doctrine, the enforcement of a firm offer would present no doctrinal difficulty.

Even in a field as significant commercially as negotiable instruments, the courts have not developed an explicit doctrine of risk of reliance. The most one can say is that in some cases, actual reliance is defined so liberally that it is hardly to be distinguished from a mere risk of reliance. But while risk of reliance has received little explicit development, it is implicit in the doctrine of "value" in negotiable instruments. Under this doctrine, a person who has taken an instrument in payment of, or as collateral security for, an antecedent debt is regarded as a bona fide purchaser of the instrument for value, and is protected, among other things, from defenses available against his predecessors, irrespective of whether he has given consideration. The reason for this protection is that taking an instrument in payment of, or as security for, an antecedent debt entails a risk of reliance on his part. Uniform Commercial Code §§3-302, 3-303; Swift v. Tyson, 16 Pet. 1 (U.S. 1842). For an explanation of the place of value in the world of negotiable instruments, and its function as a corrective of the consideration doctrine, consult Note, 7 U. Chi. L. Rev. 124 (1939). See also Steffen, Cases on Commercial and Investment Paper 707, 708 (3d ed. 1964); Fuller, Consideration and Form, 41 Colum. L. Rev. 799, 812 (1941). The Uniform Commercial Code has abolished the consideration doctrine with regard to letters of credit, U.C.C. §5-105.

UNIFORM WRITTEN OBLIGATIONS ACT

§1.   A written release or promise hereafter made and signed by the person releasing or promising shall not be invalid or unenforceable for lack of consideration, if the writing also contains an additional express statement, in any form of language, that the signer intends to be legally bound.

NOTE

1. This Act was adopted only in Pennsylvania, 33 Pa. Stat. §§6-8 (1936), Pa. Stat. Ann. tit. 33, §6.

A few states have enacted statutes to the effect that a written promise, like a sealed instrument at common law, is binding without consideration, see Miss. Code Ann. tit. 2, c. 6 §§260-262 (1942); N.M. Stat. §20-2-8, 20-2-9. In a considerable number of states, a written instrument is presumptive evidence of consideration. New York, having abolished the common law effect of the seal and recognizing the need for a substitute, has singled out certain clearly defined business situations in which a writing dispenses with the need for consideration. See, e.g., N.Y. Gen. Obligations Law §5-1103 (written agreement for modification or discharge), *supra* p. 673; §5-1105 (written promise expressing past consideration), *supra* p. 549; §5-1107 (written assignment); §5-1109 (written irrevocable offer), *supra* p. 316; §15-303 (release in writing without consideration or seal); §15-501 (executory accord), *supra* p. 701.

2. Several years before he died, William Dargie gave Etta Patterson a note that stated, "For value received I hereby instruct the administrator of my estate to pay to Miss Etta Patterson . . . the sum of Fifty Thousand Dollars, within one year from the date of my death — or two years at the least. . . ." The administrator subsequently refused to pay, maintaining that the note was testamentary in character, evidencing only Dargie's intention to make a post-mortem gift. Miss Patterson challenged this view, arguing that the note created a *debitum in praesenti*, a contractually binding obligation that came into existence during Dargie's lifetime, although it was to be discharged only after his death. To be contractually binding, of course, Dargie's promise had to be supported by consideration. In the court's judgment, Dargie's own statement that he had received something of value from the plaintiff, "not as a gift or as payment of any obligation to him," was sufficient to raise an implied contract in her favor, a contract that Dargie's written note merely made explicit and conditioned in various ways. See Patterson v. Chapman, 179 Cal. 203, 176 P. 37, 2 A.L.R. 1467 (1918). Doesn't the court in the *Patterson* case in effect treat Dargie's recitation of value received as the full legal equivalent of a seal? Do you think this, on the whole, a wise decision?

CHAPTER 6

More About Formalism: The Statute of Frauds

Section 1. Introductory Note

AN ACT FOR PREVENTION OF FRAUDS AND PERJURIES

St. 29 Car. II, Ch. 3 (1677)

. . . §IV.   And be it further enacted by the authority aforesaid, that from and after the said four and twentieth day of June no action shall be brought (1) whereby to charge any executor or administrator upon any special promise to answer damages out of his own estate; (2) or whereby to charge the defendant upon any special promise to answer for the debt, default, or miscarriages of another person; (3) or to charge any person upon any agreement made upon consideration of marriage; (4) or upon any contract or sale of lands, tenements, or hereditaments, or any interest in or concerning them; (5) or upon any agreement that is not to be performed within the space of one year from the making thereof; (6) unless the agreement upon which such action shall be brought, or some memorandum or note thereof, shall be in writing and signed by the party to be charged therewith, or some other person thereunto by him lawfully authorized. . . .

§XVII.   And be it further enacted by the authority aforesaid, That from and after the said four and twentieth day of June no contract for the sale of any goods, wares, merchandizes, for the price of ten pounds sterling or upwards, shall be allowed to be good, except the buyer shall accept part of the goods so sold, and actually receive the same, or give something in earnest to bind the bargain, or in part payment, or that some note or memorandum in writing of the said bargain be made and signed by the parties to be charged by such contract, or their agents thereunto lawfully authorized.

The Statute of Frauds was enacted by Parliament in 1677, seventy-five years after the Court of Exchequer Chamber rendered its opinion in the

celebrated lawsuit known as Slade's Case.[1] With its declaration that
"every contract executory imports in itself an assumpsit," Slade's Case
marked a final stage in "the evolution of the action of assumpsit for
breach of promise, and its victory over the action of debt *sur contract*."[2]
After Slade's Case, a disappointed promisee suing to enforce an informal
agreement could always bring his action in assumpsit rather than in debt.
This was of tremendous advantage to plaintiffs: in assumpsit, disputed
issues of fact were resolved by jury trial, whereas in debt the ancient (and
from a plaintiff's point of view irrational) method of compurgation continued to be employed.[3] But if the availability of jury trial was a boon to
plaintiffs, defendants tended to view it less favorably. In the seventeenth
century, the jury was still in a state of transition — it was no longer a
body of neighbors familiar with the parties and the facts of the dispute,
and not yet a panel of disinterested strangers composing a *tabula rasa* on
which the law of evidence would permit only certain facts to be in-
scribed.[4] The lack of a developed law of evidence, the absence of satisfactory methods for controlling jury verdicts, and the rule barring testimony
by the parties to a lawsuit (or others interested in the case) put defendants
at a disadvantage and exposed them to considerable risks.

> If the medieval common law, with its restrictive attitude to parole agree-
> ments, and its use of compurgation, had been excessively biased in favor of
> defendants, it was at least arguable that seventeenth century law had come
> to be excessively biased in favor of plaintiffs. And in evaluating the law of
> the time, it must be borne in mind that contemporaries were, by modern
> standards, extremely litigious, so that opportunities to bring groundless
> suits were likely to be taken.[5]

The Statute of Frauds sought to reduce such opportunity by requiring
written evidence for a variety of important transactions, including six
different classes of contracts (enumerated in sections four and sixteen of
the original statute).[6] Without written evidence, the Statute declared, no
action could be brought to enforce a contract falling within any of these
six categories.
    The Statute has been a source of litigation from the day of its enact-
ment. Most of the interpretive issues raised by the Statute fall into one of
two broad groups. The first concerns the Statute's scope or coverage:
which contracts are within the Statute and therefore unenforceable un-

1. 4 Co. Rep. 91a, Velverton 21, Moore K.B. 433, 667 (1602).
2. Simpson at 599.
3. Milsom at 353-354.
4. See T. F. T. Plucknett, A Precise History of the Common Law (5th ed. 1956) 127-138.
5. Simpson at 599.
6. In addition to these six classes of contracts, the Statute also required certain conveyances to be in writing; the conveyancing provision of the Statute may well have been
regarded by contemporaries as its most important one.

less in writing, and which may be enforced despite their informality? For example, if Smith agrees to work for Jones for a period of two years, their contract is clearly within the Statute. Does it follow that an oral agreement rescinding a written contract of employment for the same period of time is also unenforceable? And when the debt for which a surety or guarantor agrees to "answer" has been contracted for the surety's own benefit, is it still the debt "of another person" within the meaning of the so-called suretyship provision of the Statute of Frauds? These and a number of other questions regarding the Statute's coverage are the subject matter of the cases collected in the second section of this chapter.

The second major focus of concern in the case law that has grown around the Statute relates to the problem of compliance. The Statute speaks of a "memorandum or note" signed by "the party to be charged." Can a series of writings be pieced together to satisfy this requirement? May parol evidence be introduced for the purpose of reforming a writing in order to satisfy the Statute of Frauds? The third section of the chapter deals with these and similar problems.

The original English Statute of Frauds has been copied, in whole or in part, in nearly all American jurisdictions; in those few states where it has not been enacted by statute it has been incorporated into the common law by judicial decision (with the single exception of Louisiana).[7] Though varying in their precise language, these American copies for the most part carry forward the provisions of the original, often supplementing it by adding other classes of agreements to the six specified in the English statute. In addition, many states have adopted a hodgepodge of more particularized writing requirements, covering, for example, a promise to pay a debt discharged in bankruptcy or incurred while the promisor was a child.[8] And in every state except Louisiana, the Uniform Commercial Code imposes several additional writing requirements of its own, including one based on the sale of goods provision in the original Statute of Frauds.[9]

In 1954, Parliament repealed the Statute of Frauds except for those provisions dealing with suretyship agreements and contracts for the sale of land.[10] Although scholars and judges in this country have also expressed dissatisfaction with the Statute, the result has been a movement for reform rather than repeal, as the elaborate treatment of the Statute in the Second Restatement of Contracts demonstrates. It would be fair to

7. 1 Uniform Laws Annotated III, 146-149, U.C.C. §2-201; 8 L.S.A. Civil Code Art. 2277-2278 (1952).

8. See, e.g., 43 Mass. Gen. Laws Ann. c. 259, §3; 10 N.C. Gen. Stat. §22-4; 3 Va. Code §11-2.01 (promise to pay a debt discharged in bankruptcy); 5 Miss. Code Ann. §15-3-1; 3 Va. Code §11-8 (promise to pay a debt incurred while an infant).

9. U.C.C. §2-201; see also §§8-319 (investment securities), 9-203 (security agreement between debtor and secured party), and 1-206 ("Statute of Frauds for kinds of property not otherwise covered").

10. Law Reform (Enforcement of Contracts) Act, 2 & 3 Eliz. 2, ch. 34.

say, however, that both here and in England the Statute has often met
with a chilly reception in the courts and has been narrowly construed.
Modern critics have frequently declared the Statute to be an anachro-
nism whose usefulness as a method for preventing the deception of juries
has been negated by changes in the law of evidence, and whose provisions today more often tend to be a cause of fraud than a guard against it.
Corbin's attitude in this respect is typical:

> . . . The purpose of the statute of frauds is to prevent the enforcement of
> alleged promises that never were made; it is not, and never has been, to
> justify contractors in repudiating promises that were in fact made. The
> writer's study of the cases, above referred to, has fully convinced him as
> follows: 1. that belief in the certainty and uniformity in the application of
> any presently existing statute of frauds is a magnificent illusion; 2. that our
> existing judicial system is so much superior to that of 1677 that fraudulent
> and perjured assertions of a contract are far less likely to be successful; 3.
> that from the very first, the requirement of a signed writing has been at
> odds with the established habits of men, a habit of reliance upon the spoken
> word in increasing millions of cases; 4. that when the courts enforce
> detailed formal requirements they foster dishonest repudiation without pre-
> venting fraud; 5. that in innumerable cases the courts have invented de-
> vices by which to "take a case out of the statute"; 6. that the decisions do
> not justify some of the rules laid down in the Restatement of Contracts to
> which the present writer assented some 20 years ago.[11]

Why, then, after more than three centuries, is the Statute still with us?
Some have attempted to explain the Statute's longevity on the grounds
that it performs a cautionary and channelling function, as well as an
evidentiary one. Like other formalities, it is argued, the Statute of Frauds
continues to have value as a stimulus to reflection and a convenient
method for the easy resolution of disputes arising out of certain especially
important transactions.[12] In addition, as Llewellyn suggests, the endur-
ance of the Statute may in part be attributable to the growth of literacy
and the bureaucratization of commercial enterprise.

> That statute is an amazing product. In it de Leon might have found his
> secret of perpetual youth. After two centuries and a half the statute stands,
> in essence better adapted to our needs than when it first was passed. By
> 1676 literacy (which need imply no great consistency in spelling) may well
> have been expected in England of such classes as would be concerned in
> the transactions covered by the statute's terms. Certainly, however, we had

---

11. The Uniform Commercial Code — Sales; Should It Be Enacted?, 59 Yale L.J. 821,
829 (1950); Stephen & Pollock, Section Seventeen of the Statute of Frauds, 1 L.Q. Rev. 1, 5-
7 (1885): ". . . I can only recommend that it should be thrown out of the window — that
the 17th Section should be repealed, and the cases upon it be consigned to oblivion."
    12. For the various functions of legal formalities, see Fuller, Consideration and Form,
41 Colum. L. Rev. 799, 800-803 (1941).

our period here in which that would hardly hold — we counted our men of affairs, in plenty, who signed by mark. But schooling has done its work. The idea, which must in good part derive from the statute, that contracts at large will do well to be in writing, is fairly well abroad in the land. "His word is as good as his bond" contains a biting innuendo preaching caution. Meantime the modern developments of business — large units, requiring internal written records if files are to be kept straight, and officers informed, and departments coordinated, and the work of shifting personnel kept track of; the practice of confirming oral deals in writing, the use of typewriters, of forms — all these confirm the policy of the statute; all these reduce the price in disappointments exacted for its benefits.[13]

Along with the doctrine of consideration and the rules of offer and acceptance, the Statute of Frauds has been challenged in recent years by those who place protection of the reliance interest above a strict adherence to form. The doctrine of promissory estoppel is the banner under which the proponents of this anti-formalistic view have gathered and here, as in other areas of contract law, promissory estoppel continues to make headway. Whether this development points to the eventual demise of the Statute is impossible to say. In any legal world we can imagine, however, it is likely that the Statute will continue to play a useful disciplining role.

Section 2.   The Transactions Affected

LAWRENCE v. ANDERSON
108 Vt. 176, 184 A. 689 (1936)

Action of contract by physician to recover for services rendered. Declaration on common counts with specifications. Plea, general issue. Trial by jury in Chittenden municipal court, Aaron H. Grout, Municipal Judge, presiding. At conclusion of plaintiff's case defendant's motion for a directed verdict was granted. The plaintiff excepted. The opinion states the case. Affirmed.

POWERS, C.J. Answering an emergency call from an unknown source, the plaintiff, a licensed physician, administered to John Anderson, who had suffered severe injuries in an automobile accident, somewhere on the "Williston Road" outside of the city of Burlington. This was on October 1, 1933. When the plaintiff arrived at the scene of the accident, he found there the defendant, a daughter of the injured man; and when he had introduced himself to her, she directed him, as he testified, to "do

---

13. Llewellyn, What Price Contract? — An Essay in Perspective, 40 Yale L.J. 704, 707 (1931). See also note 12 in the Introduction.

everything you can under the sun to see this man is taken care of."
Thereupon, the plaintiff called an ambulance, in which Anderson was
taken to a hospital where the plaintiff treated him until the next morning,
when he was discharged by the defendant after she had conferred with
her father about it. The patient died from the effects of the injuries a few
days later. The plaintiff made his charges for his services to Mr. Anderson, and sent bills to his estate. He engaged a Burlington lawyer to proceed against the estate, for the collection of his charges, and some effort
in that direction was made, but nothing came of it. About a year after the
accident, the plaintiff began sending bills to Anderson's widow, but nothing came from that. Finally, about a year and a half after the accident,
this suit was brought. It was returnable to the Chittenden municipal
court, and there tried to a jury. At the close of the plaintiff's evidence, on
motion therefor, a verdict was ordered for the defendant. The plaintiff
excepted.

It is apparent that the facts above stated, standing alone, did not make
a case for the jury; and if nothing more had been shown, the judgment
would have to be affirmed. For it fully appears that the defendant's relations with her father were such that she was not liable for the plaintiff's
services unless she became so by reason of what she said or did. The rule
is fully established that one who merely calls a physician to render services to another is not liable therefor in the absence of an express agreement, unless he is legally bound to furnish such service, or it is a fair
inference from the evidence that it was the intention of both parties that
he should pay for it. The services here sued for were not, so far as the
above recited facts show, beneficial in a legal sense to the defendant and
she would not be liable therefore. Smith v. Watson, 14 Vt. 332, 337.

But in addition to what has been recited, one Charles Brown, who was
at the scene of the accident when the plaintiff arrived there, testified that
in his presence the defendant said to the plaintiff, "I want my father taken
care of, and give him the best care you can give him, and what the
charges are . . . I will pay for it."

Ordinarily, this statement might make an entirely different case for the
plaintiff. It shows that the defendant not only requested the services, but
also that she made a direct promise to pay the plaintiff. Such a promise is
not collateral or secondary, but primary and original. It comes within the
law as laid down in Pocket v. Almon, 90 Vt. 10, 96 Atl. 421, and Enos v.
Owens Slate Co., 104 Vt. 329, 160 Atl. 185. To such a contract the
Statute of Frauds does not apply, for the simple reason that it is not a
promise to pay the debt of another, but is a promise to pay the debt of the
promisor — one that he makes his own by force of his engagement.

But before he can apply this rule to the case in hand we must consider
the effect of the plaintiff's conduct.

When the defendant made the promise that Brown testified to, the
plaintiff was at liberty to accept it and to rely upon it. But he was not

obliged to do so. He could, if he chose, treat Anderson on his own credit. But could not hold both Anderson and the defendant. If he gave the credit to Anderson, he could not hold the defendant, though she had tendered an engagement direct in form. The plaintiff could not turn the defendant's sole obligation into a joint obligation without her concurrence. If he gave any credit to Anderson he elected to accept the defendant's engagement as collateral to that of Anderson. Of course it is only where the promise sued on is primary and direct that this question we are now discussing arises. 27 C.J. p. 42. But in such cases, the extension of any credit to the third party involved requires a written promise on the part of the promisor. Blodgett v. Lowell, 33 Vt. 174, 175, 176.

As we have seen, it appears here that the plaintiff made his original charges against Anderson. Such a fact is not always conclusive evidence of the person who is to be regarded as the original debtor. It is subject to explanation, to be sure, Greene v. Burton & Sowles, 59 Vt. 423, 425, 10 Atl. 575, but to rebut the inference arising from the fact that the charges were so made, the proof must be of a strong character. Hardman v. Bradley, 85 Ill. 162. As we said in Enos v. Owens Co., 104 Vt. 329, 335, 160 Atl. 185, the quality of a defendant's promise may usually be found by ascertaining whether the third person continues to be liable after the defendant's oral promise is made. In that case, it did not appear that the original charges for the services rendered by the plaintiff were made against the third person; and the plaintiff explained why he attempted to collect his pay from such person. Here no explanation is made or attempted. No reason is given why these charges were made against Anderson. So it must be taken that it was because the plaintiff considered him responsible therefor. Lomax v. McKinney, 61 Ind. 374; Langdon v. Richardson, 58 Ia. 610, 12 N.W. 622. Having given credit to Anderson, the plaintiff cannot collect from the defendant. There being no error in the ruling on the motion for a verdict, there is no occasion to consider the other exceptions argued.

Judgment affirmed.

NOTE

1. Though the preamble to the original Statute of Frauds stated that it was intended to prevent "many fraudulent practices which are commonly endeavored to be upheld by perjury and subornation of perjury," it would seem that several of its provisions, including the one at issue in Lawrence v. Anderson, were also meant to perform what Lon Fuller called a "cautionary" function. Consideration and Form, 41 Colum. L. Rev. 799 (1941). The additional time and effort required to formalize a promise by putting it in writing help to focus the attention of the promisor on the magnitude of the commitment he is assuming, and give him an opportu-

nity to withdraw if he wishes. The need for such protection, it may be argued, is greatest where the promise is motivated by generosity rather than self-interest. Does this help to explain the so-called main purpose exception to the suretyship provision of the Statute covering "any special promise to answer for the debt, default or miscarriages of another person"? See Colpitts v. L. C. Fisher Co., *infra* p. 765.

2. According to Judge Powers, the physician in Lawrence v. Anderson could have treated the victim "on his own credit." Did Anderson himself agree to pay the good doctor for his services? Compare Cotnam v. Wisdom, *supra* p. 163. In determining whether the daughter's promise was "original" or "secondary," Judge Powers attaches significance to the fact that the plaintiff considered Anderson, rather than his daughter, responsible for the debt. Is it the plaintiff's beliefs that matter? Or the daughter's?

EASTWOOD v. KENYON
11 Ad. & E. 438, 113 Eng. Rep. 482 (Q.B. 1840)

LORD DENMAN, C.J. The first point in this case arose on the fourth section of the Statute of Frauds, viz., whether the promise of the defendant was to "answer for the debt, default, or miscarriage of another person." Upon the hearing we decided, in conformity with the case of Buttemere v. Hayes, 5 M. & W. 456, that this defence might be set up under the plea of non assumpsit.

The facts were that the plaintiff was liable to a Mr. Blackburn on a promissory note; and the defendant, for a consideration, which may for the purpose of the argument be taken to have been sufficient, promised the plaintiff to pay and discharge the note to Blackburn. If the promise had been made to Blackburn, doubtless the statute would have applied: it would then have been strictly a promise to answer for the debt of another; and the argument on the part of the defendant is, that it is not less the debt of another, because the promise is made to that other, viz., the debtor, and not to the creditor, the statute not having in terms stated to whom the promise, contemplated by it, is to be made. But upon consideration we are of opinion that the statute applies only to promises made to the person to whom another is answerable. We are not aware of any case in which the point has arisen, or in which any attempt has been made to put that construction upon the statute which is now sought to be established, and which we think not to be the true one. . . .

NOTE

1. In accord, Restatement Second §112, Comment *d*. See also L. Simpson, Handbook on the Law of Suretyship §34 (1950) (explaining the

rationale in Eastwood v. Kenyon and similar cases). For the suretyship provision of the Statute to apply, both the promisor and the promisee must stand in a specific legal relationship to the third party — the "other" — for whose benefit the promise is made; the former must be a surety and the latter a creditor or obligee. To illustrate:

> S obtains goods from C on this oral promise: "Charge them to D, and if he does not pay for them, I will." S has no authority to charge the goods to D, and makes no promise to pay for them. S's promise is not within the suretyship provision of the Statute of Frauds, since D is under no duty, and hence is not a principal obligor.

Restatement Second §112, Illustrations. Suppose that A promises B he will pay B's debt to C. A's promise may be enforced by B even though it is not in writing. Can it also be enforced by C? On what theory?

2. The part of the opinion in Eastwood v. Kenyon dealing with past consideration is to be found at p. 519 *supra*.

TAYLOR v. LEE
187 N.C. 393, 121 S.E. 659 (1924)

Appeal by defendant, H. F. Lee, from Grady, J., at September Term, 1923, of Duplin. Civil action tried upon the following issues:

> 1. Did the defendant H. F. Lee promise and agree to become bound to the plaintiffs for supplies furnished to B. D. Parker during the year 1920, as alleged in the complaint?   A. Yes.
> 2. If so, in what amount is the defendant Lee indebted to the plaintiffs by reason of said contract?   A. $1,552.60 and interest.
> 3. In what amount is the defendant Parker indebted to the plaintiffs for supplies furnished him during the year 1920?   A. $1,552.60 and interest.

From a judgment of $1,552.60, rendered jointly and severally against the two defendants, the defendant H. F. Lee appeals.

STACY, J. Appellant's chief exception, as stressed on the argument and in his brief, is the one addressed to the refusal of the court to grant his motion for judgment as of nonsuit, made first at the close of plaintiffs' evidence and renewed at the close of all the evidence, and based upon the ground that appellant's special promise to plaintiff, which was not in writing, was to answer for the debt, default or miscarriage of his codefendant Parker, and was therefore void under the statute of frauds. C.S., 987.

It was in evidence that the defendants, Lee and Parker, landlord and tenant respectively, went to the plaintiffs' store and made arrangements with them whereby the plaintiffs were to furnish the defendant Parker with certain supplies during the year 1920. Plaintiffs understood that Lee was to be responsible for whatever Parker bought. He said to the plaintiffs: "Mr. Parker will be on our land this year and you sell him anything he wants and I will see it paid." Almost this identical language was held in Whitehurst v. Padgett, 157 N.C., 424, to be sufficient to warrant a finding that the promise was an original one and not within the statute of frauds, if made at the time or before the debt was created, upon sufficient consideration, and credit was given thereon solely to the promisor or to both promisors as principals, or if the promise were based upon a new consideration of benefit or harm passing between the promisor and the creditor, or if the promise were for the benefit of the promisor and he had a personal, immediate and pecuniary interest in the transaction in which a third party was the original obligor. See Peele v. Powell, 156 N.C., 553, and cases there cited.

In the instant case there was no exception to the charge, and we think the case was properly submitted to the jury. The verdict as rendered was warranted by the evidence.

No error.

NOTE

1. Isaacs, The Economic Advantages and Disadvantages of the Various Methods of Selling Goods on Credit, 2 Cornell L.Q. 199, 202-203 (1923):

> To the business man the fine distinctions between guaranty and suretyship rendered necessary in part by the Statute of Frauds are mere ghosts of the past. The living facts are these: That A who does not seem to be a sufficiently good risk has a friend who is willing to be responsible for him. Now this friend may either
>
> (a) buy the goods on his own account and stipulate that they shall be delivered to A, or,
>
> (b) this friend may agree that the goods should be charged jointly to A and himself, or,
>
> (c) the friend may stipulate that though the goods are to be charged to A and delivered to him, under certain conditions, for example, if A cannot be made to pay or if A simply does not pay, the friend will be liable, or,
>
> (d) the friend may avail himself of that shorthand system of writing contracts provided by the Negotiable Instruments Law and appear as maker, acceptor, drawer or endorser.
>
> That the consequences of becoming responsible in one of these forms should be so different from the consequences of becoming responsible in any other is a matter quite as surprising to the man of business as are the conditions in the workings out of insolvency in the cases of corporation and partnership.

For an explanation of the "fine distinctions between guaranty and suretyship," see Simpson, Suretyship §14 (1950).

2. In Taylor v. Lee, the defendants were held to be "jointly and severally" liable for the supplies which the plaintiff had provided. At common law, a distinction was drawn between "joint" and "joint and several" duties, and there are older cases holding that promises creating duties of the former sort are excluded from the Statute of Frauds on the grounds that a true joint promise "is original as to both [parties]," Gibbs v. Blanchard, 15 Mich. 292 (1867). The meaning of the distinction, and its procedural implications, are discussed in 4 Corbin §§925-926. The significance of the distinction is today much reduced as many states have passed statutes, or adopted procedural reforms, converting joint duties to joint and several ones. Where the distinction survives, however, it continues to be of relevance in determining the applicability of the Statute of Frauds. See Restatement Second §113(b).

3. The "sale of goods" provision in the original Statute of Frauds applied only to transactions in which the price of the goods was "ten pounds sterling or upwards." The other provisions of the Statute applied regardless of the value of the promise in question. What explains this disparity in treatment? Would it have been more sensible to require that *all* promises above a certain value — not merely those singled out by the Statute — be in writing to be enforceable?

WITSCHARD v. A. BRODY & SONS, INC.
257 N.Y. 97, 177 N.E. 385 (1931)

KELLOGG, J. The defendant Edwin S. Buckley entered into a contract with the defendant A. Brody & Sons, Inc., to perform certain work on the premises of the latter, in making excavations, building walls, and laying concrete floorings. Buckley, for necessary lumber supplied to the job, became indebted in a substantial sum to the defendant Westbury Lumber Company, Inc. More lumber was required to complete the job, but the Westbury Company refused to make further deliveries. Mr. Ben Brody, of the Brody firm, said to officers of the Westbury Company that if they "continued to deliver the balance of materials needed on that job he would guarantee payment of what had already been delivered, and what was to be delivered in the future." The Westbury Company thereupon resumed deliveries to Buckley. Their bill against Buckley never having been paid, the Westbury Company seeks in this action to recover the amount of the bill from the Brody company upon the promise made by that company, through Ben Brody, to guarantee the Buckley account. We think that the promise, made orally, was not enforceable under the Statute of Frauds, since it was "a special promise to answer for the debt, default or miscarriage or another person," Personal Property Law (Consol. Laws, c. 41) §31, subd. 2.

The fact that the Westbury Company, in continuing its deliveries to Buckley, at the request of the Brody company, supplied a consideration for the latter's promise is not sufficient to make the statute inoperative. A promise to guarantee the account of another, like every promise, requires the support of a consideration paid or promised, in order that an enforceable contract may have been formed. To say that the payment of a consideration removes an oral contract of guarantee from the application of the statute is to say that the statute can never operate, for there is no such thing as a contract without consideration. Williston on Contracts, §472. Prof. Williston says: "The true test of the validity of a new oral promise should be: Is the new promisor a surety?" Id. §475. If, as between the promisor and the original debtor, the promisor is bound to pay, the debt is his own and not within the statute. "Contrariwise if as between them the original debtor still ought to pay, the debt cannot be the promisor's own and he is undertaking to answer for the debt of another." Id. We find the same view expressed in Mallory v. Gillett, 21 N.Y. 412, 415, and Richardson Press v. Albright, 224 N.Y. 497, 502, 121 N.E. 362, 364, 8 A.L.R. 1195. In the former, Comstock, C.J., said that "the inquiry under that statute is, whether there be a debtor and a surety"; in the latter, Pound, J., said that the promise is original "only when the party sought to be charged clearly becomes, within the intention of the parties, a principal debtor primarily liable." In this instance, the language of the promisor unmistakably indicates its intention to become a surety, for the very promise relied upon is that it "would guarantee payment." We have no doubt that the oral promise was within the statute, and unenforceable.

The judgment in favor of respondent, Cloyd Davis against A. Brody & Sons, Inc., should be affirmed; and the judgment in favor of the respondent Westbury Lumber Company, Inc., against the appellant A. Brody & Sons, Inc., should be reserved, with costs to the appellant A. Brody & Sons, Inc., against the respondent Westbury Lumber Company, Inc.

Cardozo, C.J., and Pound, Crane, Lehman, O'Brien, and Hubbs, JJ., concur.

Judgment accordingly.

NOTE

In attempting to decide whether a promise is "original" (and therefore outside the Statute) or "collateral" (and hence within it), which should be given greater weight — the understanding the promisor had with the principal debtor, or the promisee's beliefs regarding their relationship? According to the Restatement Second, for the suretyship provision of the Statute to apply, "the obligee-promisee must know or have reason to know of the suretyship relation, either from the terms of his contract with the principal or with the surety or from extrinsic facts." §112, Comment d. Is *Witschard* consistent with the Restatement approach?

COLPITTS v. L. C. FISHER CO.
289 Mass. 232, 193 N.E. 833 (1935)

Bill in equity, filed in the Superior Court with a writ in trustee process dated December 8, 1932.

The suit was heard by Keating, J. Material findings by the judge are stated in the opinion. By his order there was entered a decree in favor of the plaintiffs against the defendant L. C. Fisher Co., Inc., and dismissing the bill as against the other defendants. That defendant appealed. . . .

LUMMUS, J. On March 21, 1932, the plaintiffs were employees of the defendant L. C. Fisher Company, and held its notes for money lent to it. Its indebtedness upon notes was about equal to its indebtedness for merchandise. On that day, that corporation decided to make an assignment for the benefit of its creditors, and its officers with a creditor named Bova decided to form a new corporation to be called L. C. Fisher Co., Inc., to succeed to the business. All the stockholders of the new corporation agreed orally with the plaintiffs on that day that if the plaintiffs would not enforce their claims against the old corporation, but would let its assets be used to satisfy the merchandise creditors, the new corporation would continue to employ the plaintiffs and would pay the notes given them by the old corporation. The judge found that this arrangement conferred a benefit on the new corporation. The assignee for the benefit of creditors sold all the assets of the old corporation to Bova for $3,000, which was used to pay dividends to the merchandise creditors, and then Bova turned the assets over to the new corporation for a consideration. The plaintiffs forbore to enforce their claims against the old corporation, and continued in the employ of the new corporation until they were discharged, but their notes have not been paid.

This bill was brought to require the new corporation, L. C. Fisher Co., Inc., to pay the notes. The final decree dismissed the bill as against the other defendants, but established liability against the new corporation, which appealed to this court. . . .

If we assume in favor of the plaintiffs, without so deciding, that a later adoption or remaking of the contract by the new corporation could be found [citations], the question remains whether recovery against the new corporation would not be precluded by the statute of frauds.

The new corporation sets up that any promise made by it was a "special promise to answer for the debt, default or misdoings of another," upon which G.L. (Ter. Ed.) c. 259, §1, provides that "No action shall be brought" in the absence of written contract or memorandum. This statute applies only to a promise made to the creditor (Hawes v. Murphy, 191 Mass. 469, 472, and cases cited), whereby the promisor purports to add his liability to a continuing liability on the part of a principal debtor. Williston, Contracts, §§466, 469, 475. If liability on the part of another never existed [citations], or is extinguished by a novation [citations], the promise is "original" and not within the statute. In the present case, the liability of the old corporation was not extinguished, but continued.

The question is, whether the case falls within a class of cases in which the essence of the transaction is a purchase of property or rights, or the obtaining of some other benefit, by the promisor from the promisee, and the payment of the continuing debt of a third person in accordance with the promise is merely incidental and not the real object of the transaction. The leading case is Williams v. Leper, 3 Burr. 1866, and the leading cases in Massachusetts are Nelson v. Boynton, 3 Met. 396, and Curtis v. Brown, 5 Cush. 488. The later case of Harburg India Rubber Comb Co. v. Martin, [1902] 1 K.B. 778, is illuminating. The reasoning is not unlike that by which a contract to manufacture goods especially for the buyer is deemed not to be a contract for the sale of goods, although incidentally a transfer of title must result. Goddard v. Binney, 115 Mass. 450. M. K. Smith Corp. v. Ellis, 257 Mass. 269, 271.

Obviously, the mere existence of consideration for the oral promise does not bring a case within this class. Consideration is required by general principles of contract, and the statute of frauds would add nothing to the law if the statute should be satisfied as soon as consideration is shown. Nelson v. Boynton, 3 Met. 396, 399, 400. Crowley v. Whittemore, 255 Mass. 99, 103. Even consideration which is not only a detriment to the promisee but also a benefit to the promisor, is not enough to take a case out of the statute. Curtis v. Brown, 5 Cush. 488, 492. Furbish v. Goodnow, 98 Mass. 296. Ames v. Foster, 106 Mass. 400. Richardson v. Robbins, 124 Mass. 105. A promise by an owner (Gill v. Herrick, 111 Mass. 501; Collins v. Abrams, 276 Mass. 106; Witschard v. A. Brody & Sons, Inc., 257 N.Y. 97) or a mortgagee (Ribock v. Canner, 218 Mass. 5) of land, to pay a contractor what another owes him if he will finish the building according to his contract, has been held within the statute, although the owner or mortgagee obtains a benefit. Williston, Contracts, §481, "A promise, upon which the statute of frauds declares that no action shall be maintained, cannot be made effectual by estoppel, merely because it has been acted upon by the promisee and not performed by the promisor." Brightman v. Hicks, 108 Mass. 246, 248.

The rule established in the class of cases under discussion has often been stated as limited to cases in which the transaction "is in the nature of a purchase of property or of a property right." Carleton v. Floyd, Rounds & Co. 192 Mass. 204, 206. In Ames v. Foster, 106 Mass. 400, 403, Morton, J., said,

We think the authorities in this state have gone no further than to decide that a case is not within the statute, where, upon the whole transaction, the fair inference is, that the leading object or purpose and the effect of the transaction was the purchase or acquisition by the promisor from the promisee of some property, lien or benefit which he did not before possess, but which enured to him by reason of his promise, so that the debt for which he is liable may fairly be deemed to be a debt of his own, contracted in such purchase or acquisition.

The statements in Dexter v. Blanchard, 11 Allen, 365, 367, Wills v. Brown, 118 Mass. 137, 138, and Crowley v. Whittemore, 255 Mass. 99, 103, are to the same effect. In Paul v. Wilbur, 189 Mass. 48, 52, P. Berry & Sons, Inc. v. Central Trust Co., 247 Mass. 241, 245, and Washington & Devonshire Realty Co. Inc. v. Freedman, 263 Mass. 554, 560, the rule was stated in an abbreviated and possibly broader form, to the effect that the statute does not apply "where the promisor receives something from the promisee for his own benefit"; but that statement does not mean that any consideration running directly from the promisee to the promisor is enough unless the obtaining of such consideration was the real object of of the contract. In Harburg India Rubber Comb Co. v. Martin, [1902] 1 K.B. 778, 786, Vaughan Williams, L.J., said,

In each of those cases [applying this rule] there was in truth a main contract — a larger contract — and the obligation to pay the debt of another was merely an incident of the larger contract. As I understand those cases, it is not a question of motive — it is a question of object. You must find what it was that the parties were in fact dealing about. What was the subject-matter of the contract? If the subject-matter of the contract was the purchase of property — the relief of property from a liability, the getting rid of incumbrances, the securing greater diligence in the performance of the duty of a factor, or the introduction of business into a stockbroker's office — in all those cases there was a larger matter which was the object of the contract. That being the object of the contract, the mere fact that as an incident to it — not as the immediate object, but indirectly — the debt of another to a third person will be paid, does not bring the case within the section.

See also Am. Law Inst. Restatement: Contracts, §184, excluding from the statute cases where the consideration for the promise to pay the debt of another "is in fact or apparently desired by the promisor mainly for his own pecuniary or business advantage, rather than in order to benefit the third person."

This court has never stated the rule more broadly than in the foregoing quotations from its own decided cases. In Alger v. Scoville, 1 Gray, 391, and P. Berry & Sons, Inc. v. Central Trust Co., 247 Mass. 241, the consideration was a transfer of stock from the promisee to the promisor or his nominee. In Paul v. Wilbur, 189 Mass. 48, 52, a lawyer turned over legal documents, drawn for a client, upon the promise of his assignee to pay for the legal services. In Washington & Devonshire Realty Co. Inc. v. Freedman, 263 Mass. 554, a landlord accepted a corporation as tenant upon its promise to pay back rent owed by its predecessor. In Manning v. Anthony, 208 Mass. 399, and Kahn v. Waldman, 283 Mass. 391, a mortgagee forbore to foreclose upon the promise of the purchaser of the equity of redemption to pay the mortgage. In other cases, the holder of a lien forbore to enforce it upon the promise of the owner of the property to pay the debt. [Citations.]

In the present case, the continuance of the plaintiffs in the employ of the new corporation was not part of the consideration for its promise, but rather a benefit to the plaintiffs in addition to the promise. The plaintiffs never became parties to, or entitled to benefits under, the assignment for the benefit of creditors, so far as appears. They held no lien, and surrendered nothing to the new corporation. The direct beneficiaries of their forbearance were the old corporation and its creditors. Only indirectly was the new corporation aided. Under these circumstances the case does not fall under the rule which we have discussed. The promise is unenforceable under the statute of frauds. [Citations.]

Final decree reversed.

Bill dismissed with costs.

NOTE

1. Restatement Second §116, Comment *a*, reads:

> Where the surety-promisor's main purpose is his own pecuniary or business advantage, the gratuitous or sentimental element present in suretyship is eliminated, the likelihood of disproportion in the values exchanged between promisor and promisee is reduced, and the commercial context commonly provides evidentiary safeguards. Thus there is less need for cautionary or evidentiary formality than in other cases of suretyship.

Assuming this is the rationale for the "main purpose" rule, was the principal case correctly decided? In its opinion, the court states that the new corporation was "only indirectly" benefitted by the plaintiffs' forbearance. How was it benefitted at all?

2. *A* holds a mortgage on *B*'s property, and is threatening to foreclose. *C*, a junior mortgagee, makes an oral promise to *A* to pay the debt that *B* owes to *A*. *C* later reneges, and *A* sues to enforce his promise. Result? See Kahn v. Waldman, 283 Mass. 391, 186 N.E. 587 (1933).

3. In applying the "main purpose" rule, "it is often easy to see that a surety derives some economic advantage from making his promise, but it is nevertheless difficult to decide whether that advantage was his main purpose in making it." E. A. Farnsworth, Contracts §6.3 (1982). This difficulty has produced some striking inconsistencies in the rule's application. Thus, for example, the rule has been held to apply where the owners of mineral rights on adjacent land promised to pay an oil drilling company to resume work on their neighbor's property, Abraham v. H. V. Middleton, Inc., 279 F.2d 107 (10th Cir. 1960), but has been held inapplicable where the surety-promisor was also a director and minority shareholder of the principal debtor, Burlington Industries v. Foil, 284 N.C. 740, 202 S.E.2d 591 (1974).

4. According to the court in *Colpitts*, had the agreement between the plaintiffs and the new corporation been a "novation," the corporation's promise would have been enforceable, on the theory that a novation extinguishes the liability of the principal debtor (here, the old company) and hence constitutes an original undertaking not within the suretyship provision of the Statute of Frauds. In accord, Restatement Second §115. Is this a sensible exception, or one that elevates form above substance? Suppose that novations were covered by the Statute of Frauds. What risk would this pose for the promisee? For a general discussion of novations, see 6 Corbin §§1293, 1297.

5. In a novation, one contractual relationship is extinguished and another substituted for it. Suppose that the parties to a contract (itself within the Statute of Frauds) agree to terminate their relationship entirely. Can their attempted rescission be enforced if it is not in writing? In ABC Outdoor Advertisement, Inc. v. Dolhun's Marine, Inc., 38 Wis. 2d 457, 157 N.W.2d 680 (1967), the plaintiff sought to enforce a written contract for the construction and maintenance of an outdoor advertising display. The defendant was to pay for the advertising at a stated monthly rate for a minimum of two years. After ten months, however, the parties orally agreed to cancel the contract (the defendant having decided to go out of the boating business). After a careful review of the authorities, the court concluded that the rescission was not itself within the Statute of Frauds and that the original contract was no longer enforceable. Does it make sense to subject the undoing of a contractual relationship to fewer formalities than its creation? Suppose the contract had contained a clause that stated, "this contract cannot be modified except by a writing signed by the party against whom enforcement of the modification is sought." This is sometimes called a "private" Statute of Frauds. Would such a provision be effective? Apparently not, at least at common law. See E. A. Farnsworth, Contracts §7.6 (1982). The draftsmen of the Uniform Commercial Code took a different view, however. See U.C.C. §2-209(2).

An exception to the rule that an oral recission is not within the Statute of Frauds has sometimes been made "where property is involved as well as contract," 2 Corbin §302. Suppose that *A* sells an automobile to *B* for $1,000. *B* pays the money and drives the car home. He and *A* then orally agree to rescind their contract. Since title or "property" in the car has passed to *B*, rescission entails a reconveyance to *A* and hence comes within the "sale of goods" provision of the Statute. See Padgham v. Wilson Music Co., 3 Wis. 2d 363, 88 N.W.2d 679 (1958). For a similar interpretation of the land contract provision, see McCulloch v. Tapp, 2 Ohio Dec. Reprint 678 (1863).

6. The section of the Statute covering promises by executors or administrators would seem to have the same rationale as the suretyship provision, and has been subjected to the same judicially created limitations. Mackie v. Dwyer, 205 Mass. 472. 91 N.E. 893 (1910), is illustrative. The plaintiff sought to recover $1,000 which she claimed the defendant had orally promised to pay her "if she would not contest the will of their father, of which he was appointed executor by the testator." The defendant denied liability on the grounds that his promise was within the provision of the Statute of Frauds which declares that "no action shall be brought . . . to charge any executor or administrator upon any special promise to answer damages out of his own estate." The court held for the plaintiff, on the grounds that the defendant's promise, being for his own benefit, "was an original and not a collateral undertaking on his part," and hence did not come within the Statute.

BADER v. HISCOX
188 Iowa 986, 174 N.W. 565 (1919)

Action at law, to recover damages for an alleged violation of contract. There was a directed verdict and judgment for defendant, and the plaintiff appeals. — Reversed.

WEAVER, J. — This action was begun on September 13, 1918. The petition alleges that, in the year 1891, when plaintiff was about 17 years of age, she was seduced by one Eugene Hiscox, son of the defendant herein, and, as a result of her association with the said Eugene, she became pregnant, and gave birth to a daughter in September, 1892; that, shortly before the birth of the child, plaintiff brought action against the said Eugene Hiscox in the district court of Cherokee County, to recover damages for her seduction and for breach of promise of marriage, and also instituted criminal proceedings against him in the courts of that county, to punish him for said offense.

Plaintiff further alleges that, soon after the institution of said proceedings, civil and criminal, the defendant, father of Eugene Hiscox, came to her and offered that, if she would marry Eugene, and dismiss the proceedings against him, civil and criminal, he, defendant, would convey to the plaintiff a certain designated 40 acres of land in Cherokee County;

that plaintiff accepted said offer, and did then and there dismiss her action for damages, and, by marrying the accused, caused the criminal proceedings against him to be abated; but the defendant neglected and refused, and still neglects and refuses, to perform his agreement to convey to her the land.

. . . We shall . . . confine our discussion to the question whether proof of the alleged contract is so affected by the statute of frauds as to preclude plaintiff's right to a recovery.

The provision of the statute referred to is that:

"Except when otherwise specially provided, no evidence . . . is competent, unless it be in writing and signed by the party to be charged," of certain specified contracts, among which are: "(2) Those made in consideration of marriage; (3) those wherein one person promises to answer for the debt, default or miscarriage of another . . . ; (4) those for the creation or transfer of any interest in lands, except leases for a term not exceeding one year." Code Section 4625.

By the next section, Code Section 4626, it is provided that the provisions of the fourth subdivision of Section 4625, above quoted, relating to lands, shall not apply when any part of the purchase price has been paid, "or when there is any other circumstance which, by the law heretofore in force, would have taken the case out of the statute of frauds."

It may be conceded, for the purposes of this case, that, if the promise upon which plaintiff relies, and for breach of which she asks damages, is within the statute of frauds, as being a promise in consideration of marriage, then the fact that she did enter into the marriage is not performance or part performance, bringing it within the exception provided for in Code Section 4626, — though there is very respectable authority to the contrary: English v. Richards Co., 109 Ga. 635; Browne on Statute of Frauds, Section 459; Nowack v. Berger, 133 Mo. 24; Larsen v. Johnson, 78 Wis. 300.

We have, then, to inquire whether the alleged promise in this case was within the statute, as having been made in consideration of marriage. In our judgment, this question must be answered in the negative. In the first place, let us recall that our statute of frauds does not make a contract which is within its terms either unlawful or void, and in this respect it differs from the statute of frauds in some other jurisdictions. The sole effect of the statute as we have it is to deny to the promisee the right to establish such contract or promise by parol proof. It follows, we think, that, if a promise be made upon a lawful and sufficient consideration, which is not within the statute, and may be established by parol testimony, the promisor cannot evade liability thereon because there was another or additional consideration, proof of which is excluded by the statute. But we think it clear that the promise in this case was not made in consideration of marriage. The thing for which the defendant was bargaining was not the marriage of his son, but the release of his son from liability to a judgment for damages in the plaintiff's civil suit, and to obtain a dismissal of the criminal prosecution against him. The marriage was a mere incident, and not the end to be attained or purpose to be accomplished, and to that end, defendant was willing to make a marriage settlement upon the plaintiff, for the protection of herself and of the child born, or to be born, of her relations with the accused. . . .

Now, plaintiff had the right to settle or dismiss her suit for damages, and to consent to the dismissal of the criminal prosecution. The defendant had the right to purchase immunity for his son, in the civil case, on the best terms he could obtain, and he could lawfully bind himself to make provision for the support of plaintiff or her child, in consideration of the release by her of his son from criminal liability for her seduction. Armstrong v. Lester, 43 Iowa 159; Wright v. Wright, 114 Iowa 748. To be sure, the only way plaintiff could effectually dismiss the criminal proceedings was by marriage with her alleged seducer; but here again is demonstrated the fact that the marriage was only an incident to the thing contracted for, the release of the accused from further liability, civil and criminal, for the wrong with which he was charged. Plaintiff has performed her part of the agreement; she has dismissed her action for damages, and by her act has secured the discharge of the defendant's son from criminal liability; and there is no apparent reason why defendant should not be held to performance on his part.

There is another aspect of the question we have discussed which, though possibly not quite pertinent to the case as made by the plea, is not without bearing upon the principles we affirm in this decision. The purpose and intent of the statute of frauds is to prevent fraud, and the courts will, so far as possible, refuse to permit it to be made the shield for fraud. Discussing the subject, the Massachusetts court says of precedents applying to this rule:

> The cases most frequently referred to are those arising out of agreements for marriage settlements. In such cases, the marriage, although not regarded as a part performance of the agreement for a marriage settlement, is such an irretrievable change of situation that, if procured by artifice, upon the faith that the settlement had been, or the assurance that it would be, executed, the other party is held to make good the agreement, and not permitted to defeat it by pleading the statute.

Glass v. Hulbert, 102 Mass. 24, 39.

See, also, Peek v. Peek, 77 Cal. 106; Green v. Green, 34 Kan. 740; 4 Pomeroy's Eq. (3d Ed.), Section 1409.

The further suggestion by appellee, that the alleged promise of the defendant is within the statute of frauds, as being an engagement or promise to answer for the debt, default, or miscarriage of another, is not sound. The defendant did not undertake to answer for the debt or default of his son. The promise, if made at all, was his own individual undertaking, and this is none the less true because his son enjoyed the benefit, in whole or in part, of the performance of the agreement on part of the plaintiff. The obligation assumed by him was primary, and upon his own credit. Nor can the promise be avoided on the theory that it was the transfer of title or interest in real estate, for plaintiff's evidence sufficiently shows full performance on her part. . . .

A new trial is, therefore, awarded.

The judgment below is — Reversed.

NOTE

To induce A to marry him, B orally promises to convey a piece of property to A, whereupon A orally promises to marry B. Which of the promises is covered by the Statute of Frauds? See Restatement Second §124. Recall De Cicco v. Schweizer, *supra* p. 494. Would the father's promise in *De Cicco* have been enforceable if it had been oral? Suppose he had made his promise to the bridegroom's father and had specified that performance of the promise was conditional upon the marriage of their children. Would the Statute of Frauds apply? See Costigan, Has There Been Judicial Legislation in the Interpretation and Application of the "Upon Consideration of Marriage" and Other Contract Clauses of the Statute of Frauds?, 14 Ill. L. Rev. 1 (1919).

DOYLE v. DIXON
97 Mass. 208 (1867)

[Contract for a breach of an agreement by the defendant as part of the sale of his grocery business at Chicopee.

The defendant requested the judge to rule that the plaintiff could not recover upon an oral agreement not to go into the grocery business in Chicopee within five years, because such agreement was not to be performed within one year from the making thereof and was within the statute of frauds; but the judge ruled the contrary. The defendant alleged exceptions.]

GRAY, J. It is well settled that an oral agreement which according to the expression and contemplation of the parties may or may not be fully performed within a year is not within that clause of the statute of frauds, which requires and "agreement not to be performed within one year from the making thereof" to be in writing in order to maintain an action. An agreement therefore which will be completely performed according to its terms and intention if either party should die within the year is not within the statute. Thus in Peters v. Westborough, 19 Pick. 364, it was held that an agreement to support a child until a certain age at which the child would not arrive for several years was not within the statute, because it depended upon the contingency of the child's life, and, if the child should die within one year, would be fully performed. On the other hand, if the agreement cannot be completely performed within a year, the fact that it may be terminated, or further performance excused or rendered impossible, by the death of the promisee or of another person within a year, is not sufficient to take it out of statute. It was therefore held in Hill v. Hooper, 1 Gray, 131, that an agreement to employ a boy for five years and to pay his father certain sums at stated periods during that time was within the statute; for although by the death of the boy the services which were the consideration of the promise would cease, and the promise therefore be determined, it would certainly not be completely performed. So if the death of the promisor within the year would merely prevent full performance of the agreement, it is within the statute; but if his death would leave the agreement completely performed and its purpose fully caried out, it is not. It has accordingly been repeatedly held by this court that an agreement not hereafter to carry on a certain business at a partic- ular place was not within the statute, because, being only a personal engagement to forbear doing certain acts, not stipulating for anything beyond the promisor's life, and imposing no duties upon his legal repre- sentatives, it would be fully performed if he died within the year. Lyon v. King, 11 Met., 411. Worthy v. Jones, 11 Gray, 168. An agreement not to engage in a certain kind of business at a particular place for a specified number of years is within the same principle; for whether a man agrees not to do a thing for his life, or never to do it, or only not to do it for a certain number of years, it is in either form an agreement by which he does not promise that anything shall be done after his death, and the performance of which is therefore completed with his life. An agreement to do a thing for a certain time may perhaps bind the promisor's represen- tatives, and at any rate is not performed if he dies within that time. But a mere agreement that he will himself refrain from doing a certain thing is fully performed if he keeps it so long as he is capable of doing or re- fraining. The agreement of the defendant not to go into business again at Chicopee for five years was therefore not within the statute of frauds. . . .

NOTE

1. E.A. Farnsworth, Contracts §6.4 (1982), comments on the one-year provision as follows (footnotes have been omitted):

> Although the one-year provision has been repealed in England, it is law in virtually all of the American states. But of all the provisions of the statute, it is the most difficult to rationalize.

If the one-year provision is based on the tendency of memory to fail and of evidence to go stale with the passage of time, it is ill-contrived, because the one-year period does not run from the making of the contract to the proof of the making, but from the making of the contract to the completion of performance. If an oral contract that cannot be performed within a year is broken the day after its making, the provision applies though the terms of the contract are fresh in the minds of the parties. But if an oral contract that can be performed within a year is broken and suit is not brought until nearly six years (the usual statute of limitations for contract actions) after the breach, the provision does not apply, even though the terms of the contract are no longer fresh in the minds of the parties.

If the one-year provision is an attempt to separate significant contracts of long duration, for which writings should be required, from less significant contracts of short duration, for which writings are unnecessary, it is equally ill-contrived because the one-year period does not run from the commencement of performance to the completion of performance, but from the making of the contract to the completion of performance. If an oral contract to work for one day, 13 months from now, is broken, the provision applies, even though the duration of performance is only one day. But if an oral contract to work for a year beginning today is broken, the provision does not apply, even though the duration of performance is a full year.

2. Suppose that A and B enter an oral contract that by its terms provides that either party may terminate the agreement within a year of its making. Is the contract within the Statute of Frauds? See Blue Valley Creamery Co. v. Consolidated Prods. Co., 81 F.2d 182 (8th Cir. 1936). What is the meaning of the distinction Judge Gray draws in *Doyle* between excuse and performance? A promise to *refrain* from doing a certain thing for a specified period of time is equivalent to a promise to refrain for the period in question or for the remainder of the promisor's life, whichever is shorter. A promise to *do* a thing for a certain time cannot be construed in a similar fashion (unless, of course, the parties have explicitly indicated that this is what they meant).

3. A orally offers to pay B, his employee, a $1,000 bonus if he will continue to work for A for two years. Supposing B does so, can he collect his bonus? See Hartung v. Billmeier, 243 Minn. 148, 66 N.W.2d 784 (1954).

HARVEY v. J. P. MORGAN & CO.

166 Misc. 455, 2 N.Y.S.2d 520 (Munic. Ct. N.Y. 1937)

Action on oral contract for payment of life pension by Marie Harvey against J. P. Morgan & Co. based on plaintiff's claim for personal injuries suffered while employed by defendant. On motion of both plaintiff and defendant for directed verdict.

Judgment for plaintiff.

PETTE, J. Plaintiff herein sues on an alleged oral contract, which is based upon a claim against the defendant for personal injuries sustained by her while in its employ. The accident occurred in the latter part of January, 1928, when a filing cabinet drawer fell, injuring her foot. The plaintiff received medical treatment for some time from the doctors employed by J. P. Morgan & Co. Plaintiff received her regular compensation during this period. Subsequently, the plaintiff alleges a conversation took place on or about January 2, 1929, with Dr. H. T. Lee, and that said Dr. Lee stated that the defendant had decided to offer her a pension. Following this conversation, plaintiff testified that she spoke to E. E. Thomas, the personnel manager in the defendant's office, and that he reaffirmed the conversation with Dr. Lee with respect to the alleged pension, which she claims was for life. She further testified that she thereupon thanked Mr. Junius Morgan, a partner in the defendant company, for his generosity, who made no reference whatever to the lack of authority of the defendant's agent or employee to act in its behalf. . . .

The alleged defense of the statute of frauds interposed herein is without merit. Personal Property Law, §31, subd. 1, provides:

> Every agreement, promise or undertaking is void, unless it or some note or memorandum thereof be in writing, and subscribed by the party to be charged therewith, or by his lawful agent, if such agreement, promise or undertaking:
> 1. By its terms is not to be performed within one year from the making thereof or the performance of which is not to be completed before the end of a lifetime.

In the leading case of the Rochester Folding Box Company v. Browne, 55 App. Div. 444, 66 N.Y.S. 867, *affirmed*, 179 N.Y. 542, 71 N.E. 1139, it was held that a parol agreement which does not, by its terms, extend for any definite time, is not void under the statute of frauds. The test of enforcibility under this statute is directed to the time of performance and not to the time of the incurring of the obligation under which performance is to be made (McCabe v. Green, Executor of Estate of Constable, 18 App. Div. 625, 45 N.Y.S. 723); if full performance such as the parties intended could possibly, at the time of the making of the contract, be completed within a year, no matter how unlikely or improbable that might be, the alleged contract was not within the statutory ban. Blake v. Voight, 134 N.Y. 69, 31 N.E. 256, 30 Am. St. Rep. 622; Warren Chemical & Mfg. Co. v. Holbrook, 118 N.Y. 586, 23 N.E. 908, 16 Am. St. Rep. 788.

An agreement made to pay X a sum of money for life, payments *to commence within a year* from the date when the contract is made, is considered to be one capable of being fully performed within a year and therefore not within the statute of frauds. Pronchlet v. Compagnie Generale Transatlantique, N.Y.L.J., Jan. 5, 1933, at page 69, *affirmed*

239 App. Div. 817, 263 N.Y.S. 982; Dresser v. Dresser, 35 Barb. 573; Kent v. Kent, 62 N.Y. 560, 20 Am. Rep. 502. On the other hand, an agreement made to pay X a sum of money for life, under which payments are not to commence till *more than a year from the date* of the contract's making, is within the statute and void. See Williston, Contracts, 1924, §496; Anson on Contracts, Corbin's Ed., §100; Wahl v. Barnum, 116 N.Y. 87, 22 N.E. 280, 5 L.R.A. 623; Fredenburg v. Fredenburg, 159 Misc. 525, 288 N.Y.S. 377. . . .

NOTE

The decision was reversed on the ground that the defendant's promise lacked consideration. 25 N.Y.S.2d 636 (App. Term 1938), *aff'd without opinion*, 260 A.D. 873, 23 N.Y.S.2d 844 (1940). Contrast the treatment of the consideration issue in Webb v. McGowin, *supra* p. 539. Personal Property Law §31(1) has become General Obligations Law §5-701(1). Whose lifetime did the draftsmen of the New York statute have in mind — the promisor's or the promisee's? See Meltzer v. Koenigsberg, 302 N.Y. 525, 99 N.E.2d 679 (1951).

MONTUORI v. BAILEN
290 Mass. 72, 194 N.E. 714 (1935)

LUMMUS, Justice.

The evidence tended to show the following facts. The plaintiff had bought land and buildings subject to a first mortgage for $36,000 and a second mortgage, held by the defendant, for $29,000. There was a breach of the second mortgage in that taxes for the previous year were unpaid, when the plaintiff's agent and the defendant's attorney talked about the matter on February 26, 1929. Both had full authority. The attorney said in substance that so long as the rents should be accounted for at his office, the defendant would not take possession nor foreclose. The attorney drew a written agreement whereby

> in consideration of the waiver of the taking of possession of said premises the [plaintiff] hereby agrees with the [defendant] that she will account to the [defendant] for all rents promptly as when collected and that the failure so to do shall be deemed conclusively an unlawful withholding of said rentals.

This was signed by the plaintiff's agent, under the words "witness my hand and seal," and she paid $200 towards the interest, as a part of the transaction. Later, about March 1, 1929, the defendant, discussing that agreement with the plaintiff's agent, said, "you fix the house better, more improvements, and spend a little money, and the rest of the money left on the rents you bring to the office of [the attorney;] and I will not foreclose you." The defendant later specified the repairs and improvements that he wished made. The plaintiff made them, to the defendant's knowledge, at a cost of $2,500, and also accounted fully to the attorney for all the rents.

Notwithstanding all this, the defendant took possession to foreclose his mortgage on May 15, 1929, and caused the property to be sold to his daughter at a foreclosure sale under a power in the mortgage on June 1, 1929.

The declaration contains two counts in contract. The jury returned a verdict for the plaintiff on each count in the same amount, $1,980.77. The counts are not stated to be for the same cause of action, but obviously both arise out of the same transaction. No question is raised as to the pleadings, or the taking of the verdicts. The only exception is to the refusal of the judge to direct a verdict for the defendant.

It could be found that the written instrument was not the complete agreement between the parties, but only part of it. . . . Consideration for the agreement could be found in the performance by the plaintiff of its terms, and that distinguishes this case from McCarthy v. Simon, 247 Mass. 514, 142 N.E. 806, and Sandler v. Green (Mass.) 192 N.E. 39. In Zwicker v. Gardner, 213 Mass. 95, 99 N.E. 949, 42 L.R.A. (N.S.) 1160, and Rosenberg v. Drooker, 229 Mass. 205, 118 N.E. 302, permitting the mortgagee to buy without competition at the foreclosure sale, was held sufficient consideration for his oral promise to pay money to the mortgagor.

The important question is, whether the agreement was unenforceable, in the absence of a writing signed by the defendant, because it was "a contract for the sale of lands, tenements or hereditaments or of any interest in or concerning them," within the statute of frauds, G. L. (Ter. Ed.) c. 259, §1, subd. 4, which is set up in the answer.

We assume that the defendant's mortgage, as is usual, gave him no right to possession until default. G. L. (Ter. Ed.) c. 183, §26. But there was a default. He was entitled to take immediate possession by an open and peaceable entry on the mortgaged premises. By continuing that peaceable possession for three years, the mortgage would be effectively foreclosed. G. L. (Ter. Ed.) c. 244 §§1, 2. Fletcher v. Gary, 103 Mass. 475; Fitchburg Co-operative Bank v. Normandin, 236 Mass. 332, 128 N.E. 415.

A contract whereby one is merely licensed to use real estate, conveys no interest in land, and is not within the statute. White v. Maynard, 111 Mass. 250, 15 Am. Rep. 28: Johnson v. Wilkinson, 139 Mass. 3, 29 N.E. 62, 52 Am. Rep. 698. On the other hand, a contract by a mortgagee to relinquish his interest in the land in favor of another, is within the statute. Parker v. Barker, 2 Metc. 423, 431, 432; Hunt v. Maynard, 6 Pick.

489. The present case concerns neither the mere use of land, nor the entire title of the mortgagee in it, but concerns the right of possession after breach, which is one of the incidents of that title. The oral agreement of the defendant not to foreclose involved an agreement not to take and retain the possession which is one of the customary means of effecting a foreclosure. If the agreement to surrender that right to take and retain possession is within the statute of frauds, the whole agreement is unenforceable, in the absence of a writing signed by the defendant. McMullen v. Riley, 6 Gray, 500; Hurley v. Donovan, 182 Mass. 64, 64 N.E. 685; Eaton v. Simcovitz, 239 Mass. 569, 132 N.E. 355.

The right to possession of land is an interest in it, and a contract to surrender possession or to forbear for a time to exercise a right to take and retain possession, is within the statute of frauds. Browne, Stat. of Frauds (5th Ed.) §231; Norton v. Webb, 35 Me. 218, 220. This was decided in Colman v. Packard, 16 Mass. 39, which was approved in Wales v. Mellen, 1 Gray, 512, although a contrary result on similar facts was reached in the latter case on a different ground. The contract upon which this action is brought is unenforceable under the statute of frauds.

[In the remainder of its opinion, omitted here, the court concluded that the doctrine of part performance was of no help to the plaintiff since the doctrine is recognized only in equity.]

NOTE

1. Although he thought Judge Lummus' reasoning "not illogical," Corbin considered Montuori v. Bailen "a very meticulous" application of the land contract provision of the Statute of Frauds, and concluded that the defendant's promise should have created an equitable estoppel against foreclosure.

> Such a promise is in part an extension of time. The mortgagee's right of entry and possession after default is an interest in the land that was created by the mortgage deed; but originally it was conditional upon default, and is made unconditional when the default occurs. The new oral agreement merely causes that interest to revert to its original conditional form, a result that certainly can be attained without a deed of conveyance.

2 Corbin §403, n.81.

2. Generally speaking, what is considered an "interest in land" for Statute of Frauds purposes will be determined by the local law of real property. It may therefore make a difference whether property law classifies a particular interest as a "license" (in which case it falls outside the Statute) or an "easement" (in which case a contract for its sale must be in writing to be enforceable). See Restatement Second §127. In many states, short-term leases are explicitly exempted from the writing requirement of

the Statute of Frauds. See, e.g., Cal. Civ. Code §1624(4) (West 1985); N.Y. Gen. Oblig. Law §5-703 (Consol. 1977).

3. For more on the part performance doctrine, see Baldridge v. Centgraf, *infra* p. 793.

UNIFORM COMMERCIAL CODE

§2-201. FORMAL REQUIREMENTS: STATUTE OF FRAUDS

(1) Except as otherwise provided in this section a contract for the sale of goods for the price of $500 or more is not enforceable by way of action or defense unless there is some writing sufficient to indicate that a contract for sale has been made (between the parties and signed by the party against whom enforcement is sought) or by his authorized agent or broker. A writing is not insufficient because it omits or incorrectly states a term agreed upon but the contract is not enforceable under this paragraph beyond the quantity of goods shown in such writing.

(2) Between merchants if within a reasonable time a writing in confirmation of the contract and sufficient against the sender is received and the party receiving it has reason to know its contents, it satisfies the requirements of subsection (1) against such party unless written notice of objection to its contents is given within ten days after it is received.

(3) A contract which does not satisfy the requirements of subsection (1) but which is valid in other respects is enforceable

(a) if the goods are to be specially manufactured for the buyer and are not suitable for sale to others in the ordinary course of the seller's business and the seller, before notice of repudiation is received and under circumstances which reasonably indicate that the goods are for the buyer, has made either a substantial beginning of their manufacture or commitments for their procurement; or

(b) if the party against whom enforcement is sought admits in his pleading or otherwise in court that a contract for sale was made; or

(c) with respect to goods for which payment has been made and accepted or which have been received and accepted (Section 2-606).

NOTE

1. Consult also §§8-319 (contracts for the sale of investment securities), 1-206 (other intangibles), and 9-203 (security agreements). A contract for services is not within §2-201 (though it may, of course, be

covered by some other Statute of Frauds provision). But what if the contract is a "mixed" one, calling for the provision of both goods and services? In National Historic Shrines Foundation v. Dali, 4 U.C.C. Rep. 71 (N.Y. Sup. Ct. 1967), the plaintiff sued Salvador Dali to enforce an oral agreement that the artist had allegedly made to appear on a television program, paint a picture of the Statute of Liberty before the cameras, and present the completed painting to the plaintiff at the end of the program "for its charitable purposes." The value of such a painting, according to Dali, would have been $25,000. Dali asserted that the contract, which he denied making, was in any case one for the sale of goods of the value of $500 or more and hence subject to the writing requirement of §2-201. The court disagreed, choosing to view Dali's agreement as one "for rendition of services." Is this a sensible result? Under the circumstances, mightn't the cautionary function of the Statute of Frauds have justified a more relaxed reading of §2-201? For an evaluation of §2-201 as an instrument of fraud prevention, see J. White & R. Summers, Handbook of the Law Under the Uniform Commercial Code §2-8 (1980).

2. Section 1-206 states that a contract for the sale of personal property not covered by any of the Code's other, more specific Statute of Frauds provisions "is not enforceable by way of action or defense beyond five thousand dollars in amount or value of remedy" unless the contract is in writing. This approach — which limits the extent to which an oral contract may be enforced without altogether denying its validity — appears to have been entertained, but finally rejected, by the draftsmen of the original English Statute of Frauds. See Hening, The Original Drafts of the Statute of Frauds and Their Authors, 61 U. Pa. L. Rev. 283, 285 (1913).

AMSINCK v. AMERICAN INSURANCE CO.
129 Mass. 185 (1880)

Three actions of contract upon policies of marine insurance. At the trial in this court, before Morton, J., the jury returned a verdict for the plaintiffs; the case was reported for the consideration of the full court, and appears in the opinion.

ENDICOTT, J. Upon the facts reported, the court is of opinion that Machado had an insurable interest in the vessel at the time the policies attached, even if we assume that they took effect on July 5, 1876, the day of their date. On that day, the plaintiffs, as agents for Machado, made an oral agreement in New York with the owners of the vessel for her purchase for the sum of $11,000, payable on delivery of a proper bill of sale; and, having previously ascertained that the defendants would insure her, they gave directions to have the insurance closed. The policies were written on that day; the precise time of their delivery does not appear.

The oral contract to purchase was reduced to writing and signed by the plaintiffs and the owners on July 7; and a portion of the purchase money was paid on that day. Possession was taken by Machado, the balance due was paid, and a bill of sale was duly executed to a third person in trust for Machado, who was a foreigner.

It is conceded by the defendants that Machado was the only person whose interest was insured, as appears by the declarations and the policies. But they contend that he had no insurable interest on July 5, for at that time he had only an oral contract for the purchase of the vessel; and that such a contract, being within the statute of frauds, and incapable of being enforced, gives no insurable interest.

But the oral contract to purchase was not void or illegal by reason of the statute of frauds. Indeed, the statute presupposes an existing lawful contract; it affects the remedy only as between the parties, and not the validity of the contract itself; and where the contract has actually been performed, even as between the parties themselves, it stands unaffected by the statute. It is therefore to be "treated as a valid subsisting contract when it comes in question between other parties for purposes other than a recovery upon it." Townsend v. Hargraves, 118 Mass. 325, 336. Cahill v. Bigelow, 18 Pick. 369. Beal v. Brown, 13 Allen, 114. Norton v. Simonds, 124 Mass. 19. See also Stone v. Dennison, 13 Pick. 1. Machado has under his oral agreement an interest in the vessel, and would have suffered a loss by her injury or destruction. Eastern Railroad v. Relief Ins. Co. 98 Mass. 420. This interest he could have assigned for a valuable consideration, and, if he had assigned it, all the rights afterwards perfected in him would have enured to the benefit of his assignee. Norton v. Simonds, *ubi supra*. The case of Stockdale v. Dunlop, 6 M. & W. 224, relied upon by the defendants, does not sustain their position, for reasons which are stated in Townsend v. Hargraves, *ubi supra*. . . .

As we decide that Machado had an insurable interest in the ship when the policies attached, and that it was open to the defendants to show that there was unreasonable delay at Bangor, the cases must stand for trial upon the questions of delay at New York and at Bangor.

Verdicts set aside.

NOTE

1. In accord, Commercial Union Ins. Co. v. Padrick Chevrolet Co., 196 So. 2d 235 (Fla. Dist. Ct. App.), *cert. denied*, 201 So. 2d 556 (1967). For a discussion of the problem of insurable interest, see Vance, Law of Insurance §§28-34 (3d ed. 1951). According to the court in *Amsinck*, the Statute of Frauds "affects the remedy only as between the parties and not the validity of the contract itself." One of the principal themes of Corbin's treatise is the impossibility of distinguishing right from remedy; it is not

surprising, therefore, that he criticises the inexactness of the language used in *Amsinck* (though approving the result). See 2 Corbin §279 n.41.

2. *A* and *B* make a contract, unenforceable because not in writing, which *C* then tortiously induces *A* to break. Can *C* interpose the Statute of Frauds as a defense in a suit by *B*? Consult Restatement Second §144.

Section 3.   Compliance with the Statute

CRABTREE v. ELIZABETH ARDEN
SALES CORP.

305 N.Y. 48, 110 N.E.2d 551 (1953)

Appeal from a judgment of the Appellate Division of the Supreme Court in the first judicial department, entered April 23, 1952, affirming, by a divided court, a judgment of the Supreme Court in favor of plaintiff, entered in New York County upon a decision of the court at a Trial Term (Rabin, J.), without a jury.

FULD, J. In September of 1947, Nate Crabtree entered into preliminary negotiations with Elizabeth Arden Sales Corporation, manufacturers and sellers of cosmetics, looking toward his employment as sales manager. Interviewed on September 26th, by Robert P. Johns, executive vice-president and general manager of the corporation, who had apprised him of the possible opening, Crabtree requested a three-year contract at $25,000 a year. Explaining that he would be giving up a secure well-paying job to take a position in an entirely new field of endeavor — which he believed would take him some years to master — he insisted upon an agreement for a definite term. And he repeated his desire for a contract for three years to Miss Elizabeth Arden, the corporation's president. When Miss Arden finally indicated that she was prepared to offer a two-year contract, based on an annual salary of $20,000 for the first six months, $25,000 for the second six months and $30,000 for the second year, plus expenses of $5,000 a year for each of those years, Crabtree replied that that offer was "interesting." Miss Arden thereupon had her personal secretary make this memorandum on a telephone order blank that happened to be at hand:

Employment Agreement with	
Nate Crabtree	Date Sept 26-1947
At 681 — 5th Ave	6: PM
Begin	20000.
6 months	25000.
6 "	30000.

> 5000. — per year
>   Expense money
>   [2 years to make good]
>   Arrangement with
>   Mr Crabtree
>   By Miss Arden
>   Present Miss Arden
>   Mr John
>   Mr Crabtree
>   Miss OLeary

A few days later, Crabtree 'phoned Mr. Johns and telegraphed Miss Arden; he accepted the "invitation to join the Arden organization", and Miss Arden wired back her "welcome". When he reported for work, a "pay-roll change" card was made up and initialed by Mr. Johns, and then forwarded to the payroll department. Reciting that it was prepared on September 30, 1947, and was to be effective as of October 22d, it specified the names of the parties, Crabtree's "Job Classification" and, in addition, contained the notation that "This employee is to be paid as follows:

First six months of employment	$20,000. per annum
Next six months of employment	25,000. " "
After one year of employment	30,000. " "

Approved by RPJ [initialed]"

After six months of employment, Crabtree received the scheduled increase from $20,000 to $25,000, but the further specified increase at the end of the year was not paid. Both Mr. Johns and the comptroller of the corporation, Mr. Carstens, told Crabtree that they would attempt to straighten out the matter with Miss Arden, and, with that in mind, the comptroller prepared another "pay-roll change" card, to which his signature is appended, noting that there was to be a "Salary increase" from $25,000 to $30,000 a year, "per contractual arrangements with Miss Arden". The latter, however, refused to approve the increase and, after further fruitless discussion, plaintiff left defendant's employ and commenced this action for breach of contract.

At the ensuing trial, defendant denied the existence of any agreement to employ plaintiff for two years, and further contended that, even if one had been made, the statute of frauds barred its enforcement. The trial court found against defendant on both issues and awarded plaintiff damages of about $14,000, and the Appellate Division, two justices dissenting, affirmed. Since the contract relied upon was not to be performed within a year, the primary question for decision is whether there was a memorandum of its terms, subscribed by defendant, to satisfy the statute of frauds (Personal Property Law, §31).

Each of the two payroll cards — the one initialed by defendant's general manager, the other signed by its comptroller — unquestionably constitutes a memorandum under the statute. That they were not prepared or signed with the intention of evidencing the contract, or that they came into existence subsequent to its execution, is of no consequence (see Marks v. Cowdin, 226 N.Y. 138, 145; Spiegel v. Lowenstein, 162 App. Div. 443, 448-449; see, also, Restatement, Contracts, §§209, 210, 214); it is enough, to meet the statute's demands, that they were signed with intent to authenticate the information contained therein and that such information does evidence the terms of the contract. (See Marks v. Cowdin, *supra*, 226 N.Y. 138; Bayles v. Strong, 185 N.Y. 582, *affg.* 104 App. Div. 153; Spiegel v. Lowenstein, *supra*, 162 App. Div. 443, 448; see, also, 2 Corbin on Contracts [1951], pp. 732-733, 763-764; 2 Williston on Contracts [Rev. ed., 1936], pp. 1682-1683.) Those two writings contain all of the essential terms of the contract — the parties to it, the position that plaintiff was to assume, the salary that he was to receive — except that relating to the duration of plaintiff's employment. Accordingly, we must consider whether that item, the length of the contract, may be supplied by reference to the earlier unsigned office memorandum, and, if so, whether its notation, "2 years to make good," sufficiently designates a period of employment.

The statute of frauds does not require the "memorandum . . . to be in one document. It may be pieced together out of separate writings, connected with one another either expressly or by the internal evidence of subject matter and occasion." (Marks v. Cowdin, *supra*, 226 N.Y. 138, 145; see, also, 2 Williston, op. cit., p. 1671; Restatement, Contracts, §208, subd. [a].) Where each of the separate writings has been subscribed by the party to be charged, little if any difficulty is encountered. (See, e.g., Marks v. Cowdin, *supra*, 226 N.Y. 138, 144-145.) Where, however, some writings have been signed, and others have not — as in the case before us — there is basic disagreement as to what constitutes a sufficient connection permitting the unsigned papers to be considered as part of the statutory memorandum. The courts of some jurisdictions insist that there be a reference, of varying degrees of specificity, in the signed writing to that unsigned, and, if there is no such reference, they refuse to permit consideration of the latter in determining whether the memorandum satisfies the statute. (See, e.g., Osborn v. Phelps, 19 Conn. 63; Hewitt Grain & Provision Co. v. Spear, 222 Mich. 608.) That conclusion is based upon a construction of the statute which requires that the connection between the writings and defendant's acknowledgment of the one not subscribed, appear from examination of the papers alone, without the aid of parol evidence. The other position — which has gained increasing support over the years — is that a sufficient connection between the papers is established simply by a reference in them to the same subject matter or transaction. (See, e.g., Frost v. Alward, 176 Cal. 691; Lerned v.

Wannemacher, 91 Mass. 412.) The statute is not pressed "to the extreme of a literal and rigid logic" (Marks v. Cowdin, *supra*, 226 N.Y. 138, 144), and oral testimony is admitted to show the connection between the documents and to establish the acquiescence, of the party to be charged, to the contents of the one unsigned. (See Beckwith v. Talbot, 95 U.S. 289; Oliver v. Hunting, 44 Ch. D. 205, 208-209; see, also, 2 Corbin, op. cit., §§512-518; cf. Restatement, Contracts, §208, subd. [b], par. [iii].)

The view last expressed impresses us as the more sound, and, indeed — although several of our cases appear to have gone the other way (see, e.g., Newbery v. Wall, 65 N.Y. 484; Wilson v. Lewiston Mill Co., 150 N.Y. 314) — this court has on a number of occasions approved the rule, and we now definitively adopt it, permitting the signed and unsigned writings to be read together, provided that they clearly refer to the same subject matter or transaction. (See, e.g., Peabody v. Speyers, 56 N.Y. 230; Raubitschek v. Blank, 80 N.Y. 478; Peck v. Vandemark, 99 N.Y. 29; Coe v. Tough, 116 N.Y. 273; Delaware Mills v. Carpenter Bros., 235 N.Y. 537, *affg.* 200 App. Div. 324.)

The language of the statute — "Every agreement . . . is void, unless . . . some note or memorandum thereof be in writing, and subscribed by the party to be charged" (Personal Property Law, §31) — does not impose the requirement that the signed acknowledgment of the contract must appear from the writings alone, unaided by oral testimony. The danger of fraud and perjury, generally attendant upon the admission of parol evidence, is at a minimum in a case such as this. None of the terms of the contract are supplied by parol. All of them must be set out in the various writings presented to the court, and at least one writing, the one establishing a contractual relationship between the parties, must bear the signature of the party to be charged, while the unsigned document must on its face refer to the same transaction as that set forth in the one that was signed. Parol evidence — to portray the circumstances surrounding the making of the memorandum — serves only to connect the separate documents and to show that there was assent, by the party to be charged, to the contents of the one unsigned. If that testimony does not convincingly connect the papers, or does not show assent to the unsigned paper, it is within the province of the judge to conclude, as a matter of law, that the statute has not been satisfied. True, the possibility still remains that, by fraud or perjury, an agreement never in fact made may occasionally be enforced under the subject matter or transaction test. It is better to run that risk, though, than to deny enforcement to all agreements, merely because the signed document made no specific mention of the unsigned writing. As the United States Supreme Court declared, in sanctioning the admission of parol evidence to establish the connection between the signed and unsigned writings.

There may be cases in which it would be a violation of reason and common sense to ignore a reference which derives its significance from such [parol] proof. If there is ground for any doubt in the matter, the general rule should be enforced. But where there is no ground for doubt, its enforcement would aid, instead of discouraging fraud.

(Beckwith v. Talbot, *supra*, 95 U.S. 289, 292; see, also, Raubitschek v. Blank, *supra*, 80 N.Y. 478; Freeland v. Ritz, 154 Mass. 257, 259; Gall v. Brashier, 169 F.2d 704, 708-709; 2 Corbin, op. cit., §512, and cases there cited.)

Turning to the writings in the case before us — the unsigned office memo, the payroll change form initialed by the general manager Johns, and the paper signed by the comptroller Carstens — it is apparent, and most patently, that all three refer on their face to the same transaction. The parties, the position to be filled by plaintiff, the salary to be paid him, are all identically set forth; it is hardly possible that such detailed information could refer to another or a different agreement. Even more, the card signed by Carstens notes that it was prepared for the purpose of a "Salary increase per contractual arrangements with Miss Arden." That certainly constitutes a reference of sorts to a more comprehensive "arrangement," and parol is permissible to furnish the explanation.

The corroborative evidence of defendant's assent to the contents of the unsigned office memorandum is also convincing. Prepared by defendant's agent, Miss Arden's personal secretary, there is little likelihood that that paper was fraudulently manufactured or that defendant had not assented to its contents. Furthermore, the evidence as to the conduct of the parties at the time it was prepared persuasively demonstrates defendant's assent to its terms. Under such circumstances, the courts below were fully justified in finding that the three papers constituted the "memorandum" of their agreement within the meaning of the statute.

Nor can there be any doubt that the memorandum contains all of the essential terms of the contract. (See N. E. D. Holding Co. v. McKinley, 246 N.Y. 40; Friedman & Co. v. Newman, 255 N.Y. 340.) Only one term, the length of the employment, is in dispute. The September 26th office memorandum contains the notation, "2 years to make good." What purpose, other than to denote the length of the contract term, such a notation could have, is hard to imagine. Without it, the employment would be at will (see Martin v. New York Life Ins. Co., 148 N.Y. 117, 121), and its inclusion may not be treated as meaningless or purposeless. Quite obviously, as the courts below decided, the phrase signifies that the parties agreed to a term, a certain and definite term, of two years, after which, if plaintiff did not "make good," he would be subject to discharge. And examination of other parts of the memorandum supports that construction. Throughout the writings, a scale of wages, increasing plaintiff's salary periodically, is set out; that type of arrangement is hardly consistent with the hypothesis that the employment was meant to be at will. The most that may be argued from defendant's standpoint is that "2 years to make good," is a cryptic and ambiguous statement. But, in such a case, parol evidence is admissible to explain its meaning. (See Martocci v. Greater New York Brewery, 301 N.Y. 57, 63; Marks v. Cowdin, *supra*, 226 N.Y. 138, 143-144; 2 Williston, op. cit., §576; 2 Corbin, op. cit., §527.) Having in mind the relations of the parties, the course of the negotiations and plaintiff's insistence upon security of employment, the purpose of the phrase — or so the trier of the facts was warranted in finding — was to grant plaintiff the tenure he desired.

The judgment should be affirmed, with costs.

Loughran, Ch. J., Lewis, Conway, Desmond, Dye and Froessel, JJ., concur.

Judgment affirmed.

NOTE

1. The approach taken in the principal case has not been followed everywhere. See Hoffman v. S.V. Co., 102 Idaho 187, 628 P.2d 218 (1981). Is there a self-contradiction in relying on parol evidence to piece together a composite writing capable of satisfying the Statute of Frauds?

2. It is generally said that in order to satisfy the Statute of Frauds, a writing (or set of writings) must state "with reasonable certainty the essential terms of the unperformed promises in the contract," Restatement Second §131. But why should this be so, as long as there is written evidence that the defendant made a binding promise to the other party (however vague or incomplete the terms of his promise might be)? Those who believe that the principal function of the Statute of Frauds is a cautionary one are more likely to question the need for an "essential terms" requirement.

3. In Schmoll Fils & Co. v. Wheeler, 242 Mass. 464, 136 N.E. 164 (1922), the plaintiff sued to recover damages for the defendant's refusal to accept and pay for a large quantity of horse hides the defendant had allegedly agreed to purchase. The plaintiff, a Chicago dealer, delivered the hides to a carrier for shipment on May 17 or 18. On May 20, he wrote the defendant in Boston, notifying him that the goods had been shipped and enclosing an itemized invoice stating the price and other terms of shipment. On May 22, the defendant replied, acknowledging receipt of the plaintiff's letter, but declining to accept the goods on the grounds that they had not been shipped promptly. There was some further correspondence between the parties, culminating in a letter from the defendant on June 2 reiterating his refusal to accept the hides "as they were not shipped promptly" and could therefore not be used. The plaintiff maintained that as the parties had not specified a particular delivery date in their contract, he was obligated only to make delivery within a reasonable time, which he of course claimed to have done. The defendant asked the trial judge to rule that the contract was within the Statute of Frauds and hence unen-

forceable since there was no note or memorandum of the agreement that he had signed. The requested ruling was refused. In upholding the trial judge's decision, the Massachusetts Supreme Judicial Court had this to say:

> It could be found that when [his letter of June 2] was written, signed and posted by the defendant, he had received the letter of May 20 and the invoice enclosed in that letter, and there can be no question of his full knowledge of the terms of the contract. The letter indeed says, "the butts were not shipped promptly," and the judge well could find that the invoice stated the contract as agreed upon by the parties. Hawkins v. Chace, 19 Pick. 502. The defendant raised no question that he was not responsible because he had not executed any contract in writing, and he did not repudiate the contract; but only claimed that it was unenforceable because of the delay. It seems clear, or at least it could be so found, that the defendant did not object to the contract as claimed by the plaintiff, but attempted to rescind because of alleged inexcusable delay in performance. The [defendant's] letter of June 2 is unintelligible unless read with the previous letters. The judge could say in view of all the correspondence ending in the [plaintiff's] letter of June 1 that there was a contract which the defendant had recognized, and that it was of no consequence that he did not specifically say, "that the letter you sent refers correctly to its terms." If the defendant had denied that he had ever made a contract, or that the plaintiff's statement of it was incorrect, no sufficient memorandum would have been shown. Cooper v. Smith, 15 East, 103. Thirkell v. Cambi, [1919] 2 K.B. 590. If however, the correspondence is read as a single instrument in the light of all the circumstances . . . the case at bar comes within the doctrine of George Lawley & Sons Corp. v. Buff, 230 Mass. 21, that the defendant's written recognition of the contract and its terms, as found by the judge, was sufficient.

Id. at 470, 136 N.E. at 165.

4. Suppose that A and B make an oral contract for the sale of Blackacre. B (the buyer) then writes A, "I repudiate our agreement which, because it was oral, was not binding upon me in any case." Does B's letter satisfy the Statute of Frauds? See Restatement Second §133, Illus. 4.

HUGHES v. PAYNE
22 S.D. 293, 117 N.W. 363 (1908)

CORSON, J. This is an appeal by the plaintiff from an order of the circuit court sustaining a demurrer to the complaint. The action was instituted by the plaintiff to reform a contract and for the specific performance of the same when so reformed.

It is alleged in the complaint:

That on the 5th day of April, 1906, the plaintiff purchased of the defendant, and the defendant agreed to sell and convey to the plaintiff by a good and sufficient warranty deed, the S. E. ¼ of section 30, in town 124 N., range 79 W., in Walworth county, state of South Dakota, for the sum of $12 per acre, which price was mutually agreed on by plaintiff and defendant, and at said time and in pursuance of said agreement the said plaintiff paid to said defendant on the purchase price for said real estate the sum of $300, and the balance of said purchase price was to be paid when defendant delivered to plaintiff a deed conveying said real estate to plaintiff, which deed defendant promised to execute as soon as he could go to Selby to have the same prepared, and would deliver the same to plaintiff within a week from said 5th day of April, 1906. That at said time said defendant made, signed, and delivered to said plaintiff a receipt in writing, which receipt is in the words and figures as follows: "Java, S.D., April 5th, 1906. Received of E. C. Hughes three hundred dollars ($300.00), in part payment on S. E. quarter section 30, R. 124-79 in Walworth county, S. Dak. W. H. Payne." And plaintiff alleges that through mistake, oversight, and inadvertence the purchase price for said real estate was omitted from said receipt, and also through mistake, oversight and inadvertence said receipt fails to state when deed was to be delivered and the balance of said purchase price paid, and plaintiff demands judgment that said receipt be reformed so as to express the whole transaction as aforesaid alleged. And plaintiff further alleges that ever since said contract was entered into he has been ready, willing, and able to pay the balance of said purchase price to said defendant, and offered to pay said defendant the balance of said purchase price, and ever since said contract was made said defendant has refused to execute and deliver, said deed, to the damage of said plaintiff in the sum of $1,000. That plaintiff offers to bring into court the balance of the purchase price for said real estate. Wherefore plaintiff prays judgment that said receipt be reformed to cover the whole transaction as aforesaid alleged, that he have judgement for specific performance of said contract as reformed, and that defendant be compelled to convey said real estate to the plaintiff, upon plaintiff bringing into court the balance of said purchase price, and for such other and further relief in the premises as shall be just and equitable and for the costs and disbursements of this action.

The demurrer was interposed upon the ground that the facts stated in the complaint do not constitute a cause of action against the defendant.

It is contended by the appellant that, as the facts stated in the complaint were admitted for the purpose of the demurrer, the plaintiff was entitled to have the contract reformed to correspond with the agreement made between the parties, and to have the same specifically enforced when so reformed. It is contended by the respondent that the contract is void under the statute of frauds, as such contracts are specifically required by statute to be in writing. Sections 1238, 1311, Rev. Civ. Code.

It may be conceded that the alleged contract without being reformed is insufficient to constitute a contract under the statute that will be specifically enforced, but it seems to be well settled that, when a mistake is made in a contract by the omission therefrom of certain terms of the same, it may be reformed, and, when so reformed, enforced specifically by a court of equity, and such mistake in the contract may be proved by oral evidence. 1 Story's Eq. Juris. (12th Ed.) §166; Pomeroy on Specific Performance, §261; Chambers v. Roseland, 21 S.D. 298, 112 N.W. 148; Keisselbrack v. Livingstone, 4 Johns. Ch. (N.Y.) 148; Keim v. Lindley, 30 Atl. 1087; Murphy v. Rooney, 45 Cal. 78; Murray v. Dake, 46 Cal. 645. In the latter case the learned Supreme Court of California held that the general rule that parol testimony is inadmissible to contradict, add to, or vary a written instrument does not exclude parol testimony of fraud or mistake in the execution of the contract, when a reformation of the instrument is sought. For this purpose, the testimony is always admissible, and the only question is whether it establishes such fraud or mistake as will induce a court of equity to interfere and correct the writing. Mr. Pomeroy in the section above cited says: "The doctrine is well settled in the United States that, where the mistake or fraud is such as admits the equitable remedy or reformation, parol evidence may be resorted to by the plaintiff seeking to enforce it, as well as by the defendant seeking to defeat a specific performance." It appears from the allegations of the complaint that on the 5th day of April, 1906, the plaintiff purchased of the defendant, and the defendant agreed to sell and convey to the plaintiff by good and sufficient deed, a quarter section of land described in the complaint for the agreed price of $12 per acre, $300 of which was paid in cash on that day, and the balance was to be paid on the delivery of the deed within one week from the said 5th day of April. It further appears that said respondent signed the written memorandum or receipt set forth in the complaint by which the receipt of $300 is acknowledged in part payment of the land in controversy, but the price for which the land was to be sold, and the time and manner of making the payment of the balance was not specified therein, and the plaintiff alleges that "through mistake, oversight, and inadvertence the purchase price of said real estate, was omitted from said receipt and also through mistake, oversight and inadvertence said receipt fails to state when said deed was to be delivered and the balance of said purchase price paid." And the appellant demands judgment that said receipt be reformed so as to express the whole transaction as aforesaid, and that the judgment may be entered by the court for specific performance of the contract as so reformed. We are of the opinion that, under the facts alleged, the appellant shows himself entitled to a reformation of the contract and specific enforcement of the same as reformed. While the contract or receipt is exceedingly meager, it contains sufficient to show that the respondent on the day specified agreed to sell to the plaintiff the quarter section of land described in the contract, and that he received $300 on account of said contract. It clearly appears from this receipt who was the party selling and the party purchasing the land and the description of the land contracted to be sold.

There seems to be a clerical error in the description of the land in the use of the letter "R" before "124-79 in Walworth county," when the letter "T" was probably intended. No reference is made to this error in the complaint, and it is not discussed in appellant's brief, but is referred to in the brief of respondent. In view of the fact that it is clearly a clerical error, we do not deem it necessary to further consider it in this opinion. Under the rules established by courts of equity, therefore, it was competent for the court to reform the instrument in such manner as to include the price to be paid and the time and manner of payment, if it should be satisfied that the amount of the purchase price and the time and manner of payment were omitted by mistake or inadvertence.

Of course, the views herein expressed are based entirely upon the assumption that the facts stated in the complaint are true, and so clearly and definitely established as to satisfy the court that the appellant is entitled to have the contract reformed in accordance with the allegations of the complaint.

Taking the view of the complaint, we are of the opinion that the circuit court was in error in sustaining the demurrer, and the order sustaining the same is reversed.

Fuller, J., dissents.

NOTE

In accord, Restatement Second §156. Would the result have been the same if the parties had intended the writing in question to be a completely integrated agreement (that is, a complete and exclusive statement of the terms of their contract)? See Calhoun v. Downs, 211 Cal. 766, 297 P. 548 (1931). Counsel for the defendant in Hughes v. Payne argued that to allow the reformation, on the basis of parol proof, of a writing that does not otherwise comply with the Statute of Frauds "would at once introduce all the mischief which the Statute was intended to prevent." Do you agree? For a general discussion of the problem, see Palmer, Reformation and the Statute of Frauds, 65 Mich. L. Rev. 421 (1967). The approach adopted in *Hughes* represents what the draftsmen of the Restatement Second call the "modern" (and presumably more enlightened) view; its wisdom, however, has not always been recognized. Indeed, §509 of the Restatement First stated that reformation of a writing within the Statute of Frauds ought to be allowed only in cases of part performance. For an example of a case in which reformation was denied on the grounds that it would give the writing in question "an evidentiary force which in its actual form it did not have" by conferring validity on an oral contract that was otherwise unenforceable given the absence of a written memorandum accurately reflecting the term of the agreement, see Friedman & Co. v. Newman, 255 N.Y. 340, 174 N.E. 703 (1931).

BALDRIDGE v. CENTGRAF

82 Kan. 240, 108 P. 83 (1910)

MASON, J.: D. M. Baldridge brought ejectment against Leopold Cent-graf, who defended on the ground of an oral contract for the purchase of the property, rendered enforceable by having been partly performed. The court found in favor of the defendant and rendered a judgment for the specific performance of the contract, from which the plaintiff appeals.

The evidence showed an oral agreement between the parties for the sale of the property, which included an unoccupied dwelling house. The buyer deposited his check for the purchase price with a third person, mutually agreed upon, to be delivered in exchange for a deed. According to his testimony (which, although contradicted, must be accepted as true in view of the finding of the trial court), he then said that he wanted to move in and the owner told him either that he would or that he could. He did move in, but on the same day received from the owner a writing notifying him to vacate the premises and asserting that he was merely a trespasser thereon. The owner followed up the notice with a proceeding under the forcible entry and detainer article, but, upon the defendant's claiming title, abandoned that for the present action.

Although by putting up his check the defendant did all that was in-cumbent upon him in that regard, the deposit did not amount to a payment. No money changed hands; the plaintiff received none, the defendant parted with none, and there was therefore none to be repaid in order to restore the parties to their original position. No showing was made that the defendant had improved the property or otherwise in-curred expenses or placed himself at a disadvantage in any respect in reliance upon the contract. The case therefore presents the question, which this court has not heretofore been required to decide, whether in and of itself the fact that a proposed buyer has taken possession of real estate with the consent of the owner, upon the faith of an oral agreement for its purchase, so far avoids the effect of the statute of frauds as to justify a decree for the specific performance of the contract. The opinion in Edwards v. Fry, 9 Kan. 417, 423, includes the statement that delivery of possession will take a case out of the statute of frauds, but there the possession was in fact accompanied by the making of permanent improvements, and that circumstance was treated as a determining factor. . . .

The mere payment of money is not such part performance as upon this principle to take a contract out of the statute of frauds, because the recipient can be compelled to restore it. (26 A. & E. Encycl. of L. 54; 29 A. & E. Encycl. of L. 838; 20 Cyc. 297, 298; Baldwin v. Squier, 31 Kan. 283, 284). The verbal agreement is not the basis of an action for that purpose, but evidence of its terms is often necessary to establish the implied contract upon which recovery is sought.

In an action to recover upon an implied promise to pay for partial performance of a contract within the statute of frauds, the contract is admissible in evidence, not as being binding and conclusive as to the amount of recovery, but merely as a circumstance to be considered in estimating the value of what has been done.

(29 A. & E. Encycl. of L. 842).

The ground upon which a court, notwithstanding the statute of frauds, may compel the complete performance of an oral contract for the sale of real estate, which has been partly performed, is that such a decree may be necessary in order to avoid injustice toward one who in reliance upon the agreement has so altered his position that he can not otherwise be afforded adequate relief. His mere entry into possession with the consent of the owner does not in and of itself meet this condition. It does not make him a trespasser in fact, and a decree of specific performance is not necessary to protect him from liability as such. Nor does it in and of itself place him at any disadvantage or involve him in any loss. True, whenever he has made permanent improvements upon the property the courts are ready to order a conveyance, even although it might be possible to provide compensation in damages. A sufficient reason for this is that alterations in the artificial features of real estate are so largely a matter of individual taste that the loss to their designer in being deprived of their benefit might not be adequately measured either by the increased value of the property or by his expenditures in making them. And whenever possession is taken under such circumstances that its relinquishment involves a disadvantage, apart from the mere loss of the benefits of the bargain, a case may be presented for equitable relief, dependent upon the special circumstances. Nothing having been shown here beyond the bare fact of possession, we think the court erred in finding for the defendant. . . .

The judgment is reversed and a new trial ordered.

NOTE

1. See Restatement Second §129, Illus. 1. Is the part performance doctrine based upon the view that actions are an evidentiary substitute for words — even written words — or on a desire to protect the reliance interest of the performing party? See §129, Comment B.

2. A orally promises his son, B, that he will make B a gift of Blackacre if B relinquishes a note he holds against A. B enters into possession of the property and lives there for twenty years, constructing a dwelling on the land and paying the real estate taxes. After A's death, B brings an action against the executor of A's estate to compel specific performance of A's oral promise to convey. Result? See Seavey v. Drake, *supra* p. 476.

3. The parties in Phelan v. Carey, 222 Minn. 1, 23 N.W.2d 10 (1946), had made an oral contract for the sale of the plaintiffs' home at an agreed-upon price of $2,500. After giving the plaintiffs a $500 check as a down-payment, the defendant apparently had second thoughts and stopped payment on the check before it was presented. In the plaintiffs' suit to enforce the check, the defendant argued that no consideration had been given for it since the vendors' oral promise to convey was unenforceable. The court rejected this defense, concluding that there was consideration for the check so long as the plaintiffs remained "ready, willing, and able to perform" their end of the bargain. Does this result defeat the purpose of the Statute of Frauds? Can it be reconciled with Baldridge v. Centgraf? What do you imagine the defendant in Phelan v. Carey did after he lost the lawsuit?

ABLETT v. SENCER, 130 Misc. 416, 224 N.Y.S. 251 (N.Y. City Ct. 1927): Plaintiff and defendant made an oral agreement for the sale of a quantity of light bulbs for the sum of $550. On the same day, the defendant gave the plaintiff a check for the full purchase price of the goods and the plaintiff gave him, in return, a receipted bill. Afterwards, the defendant stopped payment on his check and refused to complete the transaction. The plaintiff brought an action on the check and the defendant responded by claiming that his agreement with the plaintiff was unenforceable because of the statute of frauds. The plaintiff took the view that "the defendant's check, although subsequently dishonored, constituted a payment of the purchase price within the meaning of the statute, thus dispensing with the necessity of a writing." Judge Shientag held for the plaintiff and in the course of a learned opinion had this to say:

". . . The intention of the [original Statute of Frauds] obviously was, as summed up by the Earl of Halsbury, L.C., in Norton v. Davison (L.R. [1899] Q.B. 401), 'that mere words of mouth should not be sufficient to establish a contract for the sale of goods exceeding the prescribed value, but that something besides should be necessary for that purpose.' (P. 404) So the statute in the original form provided in substance that no contract for the sale of goods of the value of ten pounds sterling or upwards should be allowed to be good unless some note or memorandum in writing of the bargain be made and signed by the parties to be charged therewith (in New York the party to be charged) or their duly authorized agents. The requirement of a writing was dispensed with if certain acts were performed, viz., (1) if the buyer shall accept and actually receive a part of the goods sold; or (2) if the buyer shall give something in earnest to bind the bargain or in part payment. . . .

> The giving of earnest, and the part payment of the price, are two facts independent of the bargain, capable of proof by parol, and the framers of the Statute of Frauds said in effect that either of them, if proven in addition

to parol proof of the contract itself, is a sufficient safeguard against fraud
and perjury to render the contract good without a writing.

"(Benj. Sales [6th ed.], 255.) To-day the giving of earnest and part payment is practically synonymous. Some overt act is what the framers
wanted in addition to words of mouth. . . . What is meant by the term
'payment' as used in the statute? 'Payment is not a technical term,' says
Mr. Justice Maule in Maillard v. Duke of Argyle (6 M. & G. 40); 'it has
been imported into law proceedings from the exchange, and not from law
treatises.' (See Turney v. Dodwell, [1854] 3 E. & B. 136).

> A check, such as the one in question, is a negotiable instrument. It is a
> thing of value. It may be the subject of larceny. Checks are in common use,
> and pass from hand to hand. It is the usual and ordinary way of transacting
> business of any magnitude, and courts take judicial notice of such custom.

"(Rohrback v. Hammill, 162 Iowa, 131.) In Gould v. Town of Oneonta
(71 N.Y. 298, 307) the court said: 'Cash payment of such large sums is
usually made by check. In such a case, the check may be regarded as the
representative of the money.' Since that case was decided it has become
the practice in the commercial world to make substantially all payments,
large or small, by check. A check bearing the date on which it is issued is
regarded in a different light from a promissory note. It is the commonly
accepted method of payment in the business world to-day, and has largely
supplanted the use of currency as a medium for barter and exchange.
The giving of such a check is an overt act more easily proved and less
susceptible to misconstruction or perjury than the payment of a sum in
currency. (33 Harvard L. Rev. 870.) It is objected that a draft or check of a
debtor is only conditional payment and not satisfaction of the debt for
which it is given in the absence of some agreement to the contrary. That,
it is submitted, has nothing to do with the application of the Statute of
Frauds. The statute is not concerned with the legal effect of the payment;
it says nothing about the payment being in satisfaction, wholly or in part,
of the vendor's claim. The purpose of the statute is fully satisfied by the
physical delivery of the instrument, the overt act indicating that there was
a bargain between the parties. . . ."

NOTE

1. Why wasn't the "receipted bill" that the plaintiff sent to the defendant a memorandum of the contract sufficient to satisfy the Statute of
Frauds? What would be its legal effect under the U.C.C.? See §2-201(2).
Apparently, the defendant in Ablett v. Sencer neither denied having
made a contract nor disputed its terms. Under these circumstances,
should he have been allowed to raise the Statute of Frauds as a defense?

2. In Helen Whiting, Inc. v. Trojan Textile Corp., 307 N.Y. 360, 121 N.E.2d 367 (1954), the seller sought to enforce an oral contract for the sale of several thousand yards of cloth. The buyer had received three five-yard pieces, and the court held this to be a part performance sufficient to take the contract out of the Statute of Frauds and make it enforceable in its entirety. How would the case be decided under the U.C.C.? See §2-201, Comment 2. Suppose a buyer orally agrees to purchase an expensive automobile and makes a downpayment of $500 toward a purchase price of $15,000. If the seller reneges, can the buyer enforce the contract? See Sedmak v. Charlie's Chevrolet, 622 S.W.2d 694 (Mo. Ct. App. 1981).

CASH v. CLARK, 61 Mo. App. 636 (1895): "Defendant, by verbal contract, purchased a large lot of corn of the plaintiff, at sixty cents per bushel, to be delivered at a designated shipping point, on a line of railway. Defendant refused to take the corn. Plaintiff then brought an action on the contract, and thereupon subpoenaed defendant as a witness before the proper officer and took his deposition, which was duly signed by defendant, in which defendant, in response to inquiries from plaintiff, stated the terms of the verbal contract. Plaintiff then dismissed his suit and again instituted it (being the present action), in which he relies on the deposition aforesaid as being the memorandum in writing required by the statute of frauds. . . .

"Plaintiff's contention is that . . . the deposition of the party to be charged is a sufficient memorandum. With the qualification that it be a voluntary deposition, we concede the proposition. For it must be remembered that the statute was not enacted for the purpose of permitting a person to avoid a contract. The object was not to grant a privilege to a person to refuse to perform what he has agreed to perform. It was not enacted with a view of furnishing a shield to the dishonest, though, as an incident, it sometimes has that effect, by reason of the generality of its application. It was enacted to prevent fraud and perjury, thereby preventing fraudulent claims to be enforced against innocent parties by perjury. . . ."

NOTE

1. If a defendant's admission, in deposition or on cross-examination, is sufficient to take an oral contract out of the Statute of Frauds, it would seem, as the opinion in Cash v. Clark suggests, that he must choose between perjuring himself and abandoning the Statute as a defense. Is it unfair, or unwise, to put the defendant to such a choice? How would Cash v. Clark be decided under U.C.C. §2-201(3)(b)? In enacting the Code, the California Legislature deleted subsection 3(b) entirely. The California comments to the Code indicate that the deletion was moti-

vated by a belief that 3(b) would only encourage perjured denials. See Cal. Com. Code §2201 (1964), and A Special Report by the California State Bar Committee on the Commercial Code, 37 Cal. St. B.J. 141, 142 (1962).

HARRY RUBIN & SONS, INC. v. CONSOLIDATED PIPE CO. OF AMERICA, INC.

396 Pa. 506, 153 A.2d 472 (1959)

Opinion by Mr. Justice BENJAMIN R. JONES. This is an appeal from the action of the Court of Common Pleas No. 1 of Philadelphia County, which sustained, in part, the appellees'[14] preliminary objections to the appellants'[15] complaint in assumpsit.

Rubin-Arandell, in their complaint, alleged that on three different dates — August 22nd, 25th, and 28th, 1958 — they entered into three separate oral agreements, all for the sale of goods in excess of $500, with one Carl Pearl, an officer and agent of Consolidated-Lustro, for the purchase of plastic hoops and materials for use in assembling plastic hoops, and that Consolidated-Lustro failed to deliver a substantial portion of the hoops and material as required by the terms of the oral agreements. The court below, passing upon Consolidated-Lustro's preliminary objections, held that two of the alleged oral agreements violated the statute of frauds provision of the Uniform Commercial Code[16] and were unenforceable. Rubin-Arandell contend that certain memoranda[17] (attached as exhibits to the complaint) were sufficient to take both oral agreements out of the statute of frauds. Rubin-Arandell also contend that the court below erred in rejecting their claim for damages for loss of good will because of their inability to supply their customers with plastic hoops by reason of Consolidated-Lustro's breach of the agreements.

The statute of frauds provision of the Uniform Commercial Code, *supra*, states: [See §2-201 at p. 780 *supra*].

As between merchants, the present statute of frauds provision (i.e. under §2-201(2), *supra*) significantly changes the former law by obviating

___

14. Consolidated Pipe Company of America, Inc., Lustro Plastic Tile Company, Inc. and Lustro Tile Products Company, Inc. (herein termed Consolidated-Lustro) are the appellees.

15. Harry Rubin & Sons, Inc. and Leonard Rubin and Robert Rubin, t/a Arandell Products Company (herein termed Rubin-Arandell) are the appellants.

16. Act of April 6, 1953, P.L. 3, §2-201, 12A P.S. §2-201.

17.   Purchase Order

Lustro Plastic Tile Company	No. 2859
General Office & Warehouse	
1066 Home Avenue	
AKRON 10, OHIO	
POrtage 2-8801	

the necessity of having a memorandum signed by the party sought to be charged. The present statutory requirements are: (1) that, within a reasonable time, there be a writing in confirmation of the oral contract; (2) that the writing be sufficient to bind the sender; (3) that such writing be received; (4) that no reply thereto has been made although the recipient had reason to know of its contents. Section 2-201 (2) penalizes a party who fails to "answer a written confirmation of contract within ten days" of the receipt of the writing by depriving such party of the defense of the statute of frauds.[18]

The memoranda upon which Rubin-Arandell rely consist of the purchase order on the Lustro form signed by Rubin stating the quantity ordered as 30,000 hoops with a description, the size and the price of the hoops listed and the letter of August 25th from Rubin to Consolidated requesting the entry of a similar order for an additional 60,000 hoops at a fixed price: "As per our phone conversation of today." This letter closes

Ordered From
   Consolidated Pipe Co.

                              Date

                              Ship to

Ship when   Route Via   FOB

      Quantity   Number   Description   Price
      30,000   Hoopes Te-Vee   36½¢
                                 Red, Green, Blue
                                 as per sample
                                 From Lengths 8'-10"
                                 to 9'-3"   So they
                                 can nest

                                 Lustro Plastic Tile Co.
                         By /s/ Harry Rubin & Sons Inc.
                                 Leonard R. Rubin, V. Pres.

Consolidated Pipe Co.   August 25, 1958
1066 Homes Ave.
Akron, Ohio
Att: Mr. Carl Pearl

Dear Carl,

   As per our phone conversation of today kindly enter our order for the following:
      60,000 Tee-Vee Hoops made of rigid polyethylene tubing from
      lengths of 8'10" to 9'2"; material to weigh 15 feet per lb., colors red,
      green and yellow packed 2 Dozen per carton
                              39¢ each
   It is our understanding that these will be produced upon comp[l]etion of the present order for 30,000 hoops.

                              Very truly yours,
                              Harry Rubin & Sons, Inc.
                              /s/ Leonard R. Rubin, Vice-pres.

18. Comment to §2-201, 12A PS p. 87.

with the significant sentence that: "It is our understanding that these [the second order for 60,000 hoops] will be produced upon completion of the present order for 30,000 hoops."

Consolidated-Lustro's objection to the memoranda in question is that by employment of the word "order" rather than "contract" or "agreement," the validity of such memoranda depended upon acceptance thereof by Consolidated-Lustro and could not be "in confirmation of the contract[s]" as required by §2-201(2). We believe, however, that the letter of August 25th sufficiently complies with §2-201(2) to remove both oral contracts from the statute of frauds. The word "order" as employed in this letter obviously contemplated a binding agreement, at least, on the part of the sender, and in all reason, should have been interpreted in that manner by the recipient. The sender in stating that "It is our understanding that these will be produced upon completion of the present order for 30,000 hoops," was referring to the initial order as an accomplished fact, not as an offer depending upon acceptance for its validity. Any doubt that may exist as to the sender's use of the word "order" is clearly dispelled by its use in the communication confirming a third contract.[19] This letter of August 28th, 1958, states: "Pursuant to our phone conversation of yesterday, *you may enter our order* for the following [number, description and price]. . . . *This order is to be entered* based upon our phone conversation, in which you *agreed* to ship us your entire production of this Hoop material at the above price. . . ." (Emphasis supplied) The letter of August 25th was a sufficient confirmation in writing of the two alleged oral contracts, and, in the absence of a denial or rejection on the part of the recipient within ten days, satisfied the requirements of §2-201(2) of the Uniform Commercial Code.

Under the statute of frauds as revised in the Code "All that is required is that the writing afford a basis for believing that the offered oral evidence rests on a real transaction."[20] Its object is the elimination of certain formalistic requirements adherence to which often resulted in injustice, rather than the prevention of fraud. The present memoranda fulfill the requirement of affording a belief that the oral contracts rested on a real transaction and the court below erred in holding otherwise. Nor are Consolidated-Lustro harmed by such a determination since Rubin-Arandell must still sustain the burden of persuading the trier of fact that the contracts were in fact made orally prior to the written confirmation.[21] . . .

[The court's discussion of the measure of damages has been omitted.]

19. As to this alleged oral contract, the court below held Consolidated-Lustro's defense of the statute of frauds provision was without merit.

20. See: "Uniform Commercial Code Comment" under "Purpose of Changes 1", 12A PS §2-210.

21. Appellees also argue that parties not named in the communications cannot be bound. Oral testimony to establish that the addressee of the letter was an agent of the unnamed appellees is admissible and does not violate the Statute of Frauds. See: Penn Discount Corp. v. Sharp, 125 Pa. Superior Ct. 171, 189 A. 749.

NOTE

In Southwest Engineering Co. v. Martin Tractor Co., 205 Kan. 684, 473 P.2d 18 (1970), the plaintiff-buyer alleged that representatives of the two companies had reached an agreement for the sale of a generator (together with various accessories), which the seller later refused to honor. At the conclusion of their negotiations, the seller had given the buyer a piece of paper, on which the name of the seller was printed, listing the price of the generator and various other pieces of equipment. The Kansas Supreme Court concluded that this price list was a sufficient memorandum within the meaning of U.C.C. §2-201 and affirmed judgment in favor of the buyer. A student note in the Harvard Law Review criticized the court's reasoning:

> The memorandum before the court — on its face nothing more than a price list — was proof not of agreement, but, at most, only of negotiations. By the court's reasoning, a memorandum reading, "One generator, signed, Seller" would similarly be sustained. To hold that such "agreements" satisfy the requirement of a writing implies that the memorandum need merely plant the seed of agreement in the mind in the court: extrinsic evidence may then be used to determine the meaning and sufficiency of the writing. If pursued, the court's interpretation would allow the simple exchange of a price list or similar evidence of negotiation, which occurs in virtually every transaction for the sale of goods, to satisfy the statute. While the facts of Southwest Engineering would seem to induce sympathy for the court's position, it is the very possibility of a manufactured statement of favorable facts that the statute is designed to preclude. The expansive view of the Kansas Supreme Court would seem to substantially weaken this protection and effectively read the Statute of Frauds out of the Uniform Commercial Code except in very rare cases.

84 Harv. L. Rev. 1737, 1738-1739 (1971).

Section 4.   Counterrules: Estoppel and Restitution

IMPERATOR REALTY CO., INC. v. TULL
228 N.Y. 447, 127 N.E. 263 (1920)

Action by the Imperator Realty Company against Samuel P. Tull. From a judgment of the Appellate Division, First Department (179 App. Div. 761, 167 N.Y.S. 210), reversing on questions of fact and law a judgment of the Trial Term in favor of plaintiff, and dismissing the complaint, plaintiff appeals. Reversed, and judgment of the Trial Term affirmed.

CHASE, J. The parties to this action entered into a written contract under seal for the exchange of pieces of real property in the city of New

York. On the day fixed therein for carrying out the contract and making
the conveyances, the defendant deliberately defaulted. The action was
brought to cover damages alleged to have been sustained by the plaintiff.

At the trial the jury determined all of the issues in favor of the plaintiff
and rendered a verdict for it. The defendant appealed from the judgment
entered upon such verdict, and the Appellate Division reversed the judgment and dismissed the complaint. Imperator Realty Co., Inc., v. Tull,
179 App. Div. 761, 167 N.Y. Supp. 210. [Plaintiff appealed.]

One of the provisions of the contract is:

> All notes or notices of violations of law or municipal ordinances, orders,
> or requirements noted in or issued by any department of the city of New
> York against or affecting the premises at the date hereof, shall be complied
> with by the seller and the premises shall be conveyed free of the same.

There were several notices of violations of law or municipal ordinances, orders, or requirements noted in or issued by a department of the
city of New York against or affecting the premises to be conveyed by the
plaintiff at the date of the contract which, although aggregating an
amount that is comparatively very small, were not satisfied or discharged
on the day when the property was to be conveyed. The plaintiff sought to
avoid the failure to procure the discharge of such violations by an alleged
modification of the contract pursuant to a conversation between the
president of the plaintiff and the defendant in which it is claimed that
there were reciprocal promises. The president of the plaintiff testified that
after the making of the contract, and on the same day thereof, it was
agreed between the parties to the contract that either party in place of
satisfying any of the so-called violations that might be filed against the
pieces of real property therein mentioned might deposit with the New
York Title Insurance Company a sufficient amount of cash to pay and
discharge the same. There is evidence in the record to show that the
plaintiff was able and willing on the day and at the time and place for
closing the contract to carry out the same therein provided except that he
could not convey the property to be transferred by him free from such
violations, and there is also evidence that he was able and willing to
deposit a sufficient amount of cash to comply with and free the property
from the violations as required by such oral agreement between the parties. . . .

It is claimed by the defendant that the contract with the plaintiff was in
writing under seal and could not be changed as claimed by an oral agreement so as to be binding upon either party to it. The contract was also
within the provisions of section 259 of the Real Property Law (Consol.
Laws, c. 50), and it was therefore necessary that it should be in writing as
stated in the statute.

Where a contract is reduced to writing and appears to include the entire agreement of the parties and to be free from fraud, the rule is quite universal that oral evidence will not be received of conversations or transactions leading up to the making of a contract or in connection with the execution thereof for the purpose of varying, modifying, reducing or extending the terms thereof. Lese v. Lamprecht, 196 N.Y. 32, 89 N.E. 365; Eighmie v. Taylor, 98 N.Y. 288.

After the execution of a written contract including one within the statute the parties may, of course, reconsider the subject-matter thereof and decide to modify or rescind it. The oral agreement found in this case was made after the execution of the written contract. It is not the right to make a new and independent contract to modify a prior unperformed written contract that we are considering, but the effect, if any, of an oral contract upon a contract under seal or required by the statute to be in writing. We must assume in this case that the oral contract as claimed by the plaintiff, to accept a deposit in cash in place of the payment of outstanding violations, was actually made upon a sufficient consideration. The jury has so found. . . .

The oral contract in the case before us modified the written contract simply as to the manner of charging the plaintiff with the amount required to satisfy the violations. Such oral contract if carried out in good faith made unnecessary the haste otherwise required to make the slight changes to comply with the notices which constitute the incumbrances or so-called violations.

The defendant by his mutual oral contract with the plaintiff is estopped from now claiming that the plaintiff who relied thereon was in default on the due day of the written contract because of its omission to then have the property free of the violations. He should not be allowed to take advantage of an omission induced by his unrevoked consent. Thomson v. Poor, [147 N.Y. 402, 42 N.E. 13]; Arnot v. Union Salt Co., [186 N.Y. 501, 79 N.E. 719]; Swain v. Seamens, 76 U.S. (9 Wall.) 254, 19 L. Ed. 554; Brede v. Rosedale Terrace Co., 216 N.Y. 246, 110 N.E. 430.

Parol evidence of the waiver constituting an estoppel as against the defendant under the circumstances was not error. Penn. Steel Co. v. Title Guarantee & Trust Co., 193 N.Y. 37, 85 N.E. 820. We do not think that the objections made by the defendant to the admission of evidence were upon a consideration of the whole record of sufficient consequence to have materially affected the jury or to require further consideration in this opinion.

The judgment of the Appellate Division should be reversed, and that of the Trial Term affirmed, with costs in the Appellate Division and in this court.

CARDOZO, J. (concurring in result). The statute says that a contract for the sale of real property "is void unless the contract, or some note or memorandum thereof, expressing the consideration, is in writing, subscribed by the . . . grantor, or by his lawfully authorized agent." Real Property Law (Consol. Laws, c. 50) §259 (statute of frauds). In this instance, each party was a grantor, for the sale was an exchange. I think it is the law that, where contracts are subject to the statute, changes are governed by the same requirements of form as original provisions. Hill v. Blake, 97 N.Y. 216; Clark v. Fey, 121 N.Y. 470, 476, 24 N.E. 703. Abrogated by word of mouth such a contract may be (Blanchard v. Trim, 38 N.Y. 225), but its obligation may not be varied by spoken words of promise while it continues undissolved. [Citations omitted.] A recent decision of the House of Lords reviews the English precedents, and declares the rule anew. Morris v. Baron & Co., 1918, A.C. 1, 19, 20, 31. Oral promises are ineffective to make the contract, or any part of it, in the beginning. Wright v. Weeks, 25 N.Y. 153; Marks v. Cowdin, 226 N.Y. 138, 123 N.E. 139. Oral promises must also be ineffective to vary it thereafter. Hill v. Blake, *supra.* Grant and consideration alike must find expression in a writing. Real Prop. Law, §259; Consol. Laws, c. 50.

Some courts have drawn a distinction between the formation of the contract and the regulation of performance. Cummings v. Arnold, 3 Metc. 486, 37 Ame. Dec. 155; Stearns v. Hall, 9 Cush. 31; Whittier v. Dana, 10 Allen, 326; Hastings v. Lovejoy, 140 Mass. 261, 2 N.E. 776, 54 Am. Rep. 462; Wood on Statute of Frauds, p. 758. The distinction has been rejected in many jurisdictions. See cases cited *supra;* also, L.R.A. 1917B, 141 note. It has never been accepted by this court, and the question of its validity has been declared an open one. Thomson v. Poor, 147 N.Y. 402, 408, 42 N.E. 13, characterizing as dicta the statements in Blanchard v. Trim, *supra.* I think we should reject it now. The cases which maintain it hold that oral promises in such circumstances constitute an accord, and that an accord, though executory, constitutes a bar if there is a tender of performance. Cummings v. Arnold; Whittier v. Dana, *supra.* There seems little basis for such a distinction in this state where the rule is settled that an accord is not a bar unless received in satisfaction. Reilly v. Barrett, 220 N.Y. 170, 115 N.E. 453; Morehouse v. Second Nat. Bank of Oswego, 98 N.Y. 503, 509; cf. Ladd v. King, 1 R.I. 224, 51 Am. Dec. 624; Pollock on Contracts (3d Am. Ed.) p. 822. But there is another objection, more fundamental and far-reaching. I do not know where the line of division is to be drawn between variations of the substance and variations of the method of fulfillment. I think it is inadequate to say that oral changes are effective if they are slight and ineffective if they are important. Such tests are too vague to supply a scientific basis of distinction. "Every part of the contract in regard to which the parties are stipulating must be taken to be material." Per Parke, B., Marshall v. Lynn, 6 M. & W. 116, 117; 1 Williston on Contracts, §594. The field is one where the law should hold fast to fundamental conceptions of contract and of duty, and follow them with loyalty to logical conclusions.

The problem, thus approached, gains, I think, a new simplicity. A contract is the sum of its component terms. Any variation of the parts is a variation of the whole. The requirement that there shall be a writing extends to one term as to another. There can therefore be no contractual obligation when the requirement is not followed. This is not equivalent to saying that what is ineffective to create an obligation must be ineffective to discharge one. Duties imposed by law irrespective of contract may regulate the relations of parties after they have entered into a contract. There may be procurement or encouragement of a departure from literal performance which will forbid the assertion the the departure was a wrong. That principle will be found the solvent of many cases of apparent hardship. There may be an election which will preclude a forefeiture. There may be an acceptance of substituted performance, or an accord and satisfaction. McCreery v. Day, 119 N.Y. 1, 9, 23 N.E. 198, 6 L.R.A. 503, 16 Am. St. Rep. 793; Swain v. Seamens, *supra*; Long v. Hartwell, *supra*; Ladd v. King, *supra*. What there may not be, when the subject-matter is the sale of the land, is an executory agreement, partly written and partly oral, to which, by force of the agreement and nothing else, the law will attach the attribute of contractual obligation.

The contract, therefore, stood unchanged. The defendant might have retracted his oral promise an hour after making it, and the plaintiff would have been helpless. He might have retracted a week before closing, and, if a reasonable time remained within which to remove the violations, the plaintiff would still have been helpless. Retraction even at the very hour of the closing might not have been too late if coupled with the offer of an extension which would neutralize the consequences of persuasion and reliance. Arnot v. Union Salt Co., 186 N.Y. 501, 79 N.E. 719; Brede v. Rosedale Terrace Co., 216 N.Y. 246, 110 N.E. 430. The difficulty with the defendant's position is that he did none of these things. He had notified the plaintiff in substance that there was no need of haste in removing the violations, and that title would be accepted on deposit of adequate security for their removal in the future. He never revoked that notice. He gave no warning of a change of mind. He did not even attend the closing. He abandoned the contract, treated it as at an end, held himself absolved from all liability thereunder, because the plaintiff had acted in reliance on a consent which, even in the act of abandonment, he made no effort to recall.

I do not think we are driven by any requirement of the statute of frauds to sustain as lawful and effective this precipitate rescission, this attempt by an ex post facto revocation, after closing day and come and gone, to put the plaintiff in the wrong. "He who prevents a thing from being done may not avail himself of the nonperformance, which he has, himself, occasioned, for the law says to him, in effect: 'This is your own act, and, therefore, you are not damnified.'" Dolan v. Rodgers, 149 N.Y. 489, 491,

44 N.E. 167, quoting West v. Blakeway, 2 M. & Gr. 751. The principle is fundamental and unquestioned. U.S. v. Peck, 102 U.S. 64, 26 L. Ed. 46; Gallagher v. Nichols, 60 N.Y. 438; Risley v. Smith, 64 N.Y. 576, 582; Gen. El. Co. v. Nat. Contracting Co., 178 N.Y. 369, 375, 70 N.E. 928; Mackay v. Dick, 6 App. Cas. 251; New Zealand Shipping Co. v. Societe des Aletiers, etc., 1919 A.C. 1, 5. Sometimes the resulting disability has been characterized as an estoppel, sometimes as a waiver. Gallagher v. Nichols; Gen. El. Co. v. Nat. Constr. Co.; Thomson v. Poor, *supra*. We need not go into the question of the accuracy of the description. Ewart on Estoppel, pp. 15, 70; Ewart on Waiver Distributed, pp. 23, 143, 264. The truth is that we are facing a principle more nearly ultimate than either waiver or estoppel, one with roots in the yet larger principle that no one shall be permitted to found any claim upon his own inequity or take advantage of his own wrong. Riggs v. Palmer, 115 N.Y. 506, 22 N.E. 188, 5 L.R.A. 340, 12 Am. St. Rep. 819. The statute of frauds was not intended to offer an asylum of escape from that fundamental principle of justice. An opposite precedent is found in Thomson v. Poor, 147 N.Y. 402, 42 N.E. 13. In deciding that case, we put aside the question whether a contract within the statute of frauds could be changed by spoken words. We held that there was disability, or, as we styled it, estoppel, to take advantage of an omission induced by an unrevoked consent. Cf. Swain v. Seamens, *supra*, 9 Wall. at page 274, 19 L. Ed. 554; Arnot v. Union Salt Co., *supra*; Brede v. Rosedale Terrace Co., *supra*; 1 Williston on Contracts §595. A like principle is recognized even in the English courts, which have gone as far as those of any jurisdiction in the strict enforcement of the statute. They hold in effect that, until consent is acted on, either party may change his mind. After it has been acted on, it stands as an excuse for nonperformance. Hickman v. Haynes, L.R. 10 C.P. 598, 605; Ogle v. Lord Vane, 2 Q.B. 275; 3 I.B. 272; Cuff v. Penn, 1 Maule & S. 21; Morris v. Baron & Co., 1918 A.C. 1, at page 31. The defendant by his conduct has brought himself within the ambit of this principle. His words did not create a new bilateral contract. They lacked the written form prescribed by statute. They did not create a unilateral contract. Aside from the same defect in form, they did not purport to offer a promise for an act. They did, however, constitute the continuing expression of a state of mind, a readiness, a desire, persisting until revoked. A seller who agrees to change the wall paper of a room ought not to lose his contract if he fails to make the change through reliance on the statement of the buyer that new paper is unnecessary, and that the old is satisfactory. The buyer may change his mind again and revert to his agreement. He may not summarily rescind because of the breach which he encouraged. That is what the defendant tried to do. When he stayed away from the closing and acted upon an election to treat the contract as rescinded, he put himself in the wrong.

I concur in the conclusion that the judgment must be reversed.

Hiscock, C.J., concurs with Chase, J.

Cardozo, J., concurs in opinion in which Pound and Andrews, JJ., also concur.

Collin and Crane, JJ., dissent.

Judgment reversed, etc.

NOTE

1. In his concurrence, Cardozo describes the issue in *Imperator Realty* as "one where the law should hold fast to fundamental conceptions of contract and of duty, and follow them with loyalty to logical conclusions." In another context, Cardozo expressed his disapproval of "those who think more of symmetry and logic in the development of legal rules than of practical adaptation to the attainment of a just result," and after acknowledging that "something . . . may be said on the score of consistency and certainty," declared that "the courts have balanced such considerations against those of equity and fairness, and found the latter to be the weightier." Jacob & Youngs, Inc. v. Kent, *infra* p. 1042. Can these statements be reconciled? Does the relative importance of certainty vary from one branch of contract law to another? Which of Cardozo's jurisprudential dicta best explains his concurrence in the *Imperator Realty* case?

2. The rule in the principal case is codified in Restatement Second §150. Suppose the parties had orally agreed to rescind their earlier contract. Would the rescission be enforceable in the absence of reliance by either party? See Restatement Second §148. How do you explain the apparent disparity between these two sections?

3. A husband, upon divorcing his wife, agreed to pay her $900 each month for ten years or until she remarried. Ten months later she informed him that she had an offer of remarriage, but did not intend to accept it unless he would continue all or a part of her settlement payments. He thereupon promised to set up a trust fund naming her and himself as equal beneficiaries, to deposit $100 each week, and to share the profits from the fund with her. When she asked if she would need a lawyer and if the agreement should be put on paper, the ex-husband, a lawyer himself, told her that counsel was unnecessary and that he would confirm their agreement in a later letter. She remarried; he deposited less than $200 into a bank account for her benefit and never confirmed his oral promise in writing.

The Supreme Court of Illinois, in Loeb v. Gendel, 23 Ill. 2d 502, 179 N.E.2d 7 (1961), held that the wife's failure to have the agreement put in writing was induced by her ex-husband's intentionally misleading advice, and concluded that he was estopped from asserting the Statute of Frauds as a defense.

> With trust and confidence in her former husband, and in reliance upon his assurance that the agreement was valid and enforceable, she became re-married, thus relieving defendant of the obligation to make further payments under the divorce decree. If, contrary to his representations, he can now interpose the statute of frauds and thereby render the agreement void and unenforceable, the effect will be the accomplishment of a virtual fraud. This we cannot condone.

23 Ill. 2d at 505-506, 179 N.E.2d at 9.

BOONE v. COE
153 Ky. 233, 154 S.W. 900 (1913)

CLAY, J. Plaintiffs, W. H. Boone and J. T. Coe, brought this action against defendant, J. F. Coe, to recover certain damages alleged to have resulted from defendant's breach of a parol contract of lease for one year to commence at a future date. It appears from the petition that the defendant was the owner of a large and valuable farm in Ford County, Texas. Plaintiffs were farmers, and were living with their families in Monroe County, Kentucky. In the fall of 1909, defendant made a verbal contract with plaintiffs whereby he rented to them his farm in Texas for a period of twelve months, to commence from the date of plaintiffs' arrival at defendant's farm. Defendant agreed that if plaintiffs would leave their said home and businesses in Kentucky, and with their families, horses and wagons, move to defendant's farm in Texas, and take charge of, manage and cultivate same in wheat, corn and cotton for the twelve months following plaintiffs' arrival at said farm, the defendant would have a dwelling completed on said farm and ready for occupancy upon their arrival, which dwelling plaintiffs would occupy as a residence during the period of said tenancy. Defendant also agreed that he would furnish necessary material at a convenient place on said farm out of which to erect a good and commodious stock and grain barn, to be used by plaintiffs. The petition further alleges that plaintiffs were to cultivate certain portions of the farm and were to receive certain portions of the crops raised, and that plaintiffs, in conformity with their said agreement, did move from Kentucky to the farm in Texas, and carried with them their families, wagons, and horses and camping outfit, and in going to Texas they traveled for a period of 55 days. It is also charged that defendant broke his contract, in that he failed to have ready and completed on the farm a dwelling house in which plaintiffs and their families could move, and also failed to furnish the necessary material for the erection of a suitable barn; that on December 6th, defendant refused to permit plaintiffs to occupy the house and premises, and failed and refused to permit them to cultivate the land or any part thereof; that on the. . . . day of December, 1909, they started for their home in Kentucky, and arrived there after traveling for a period of four days. It is charged that plaintiffs and their teams in making the trip to Texas was reasonably worth $8 per day for a period of 55 days, or the sum of $440; that the loss of time to them and their teams during the period they remained in Texas was $8 a day for 22 days or $176; that they paid out in actual cash for transportation for themselves, families and teams from Texas to Kentucky, the sum of $211.80; that the loss of time to them and their teams in making the last named trip was reasonably worth the sum of $100; that in abandoning and giving up their homes and businesses in Kentucky, they had been damaged in the sum of $150, making a total damage of $1,387.80, for which judgment was asked. Defendant's demurrer to the petition was sustained and the petition dismissed. Plaintiffs appeal.

Under the rule in force in this State, the statute of frauds relates to the remedy or mode of procedure, and not to the validity of the contract. Though the land is located in Texas, the parol contract of lease was made here, and here it is sought to enforce it. If unenforceable under our statute, it cannot be enforced here. Kleeman & Co. v. Collins, 9 Bush, 460. If the statute requires the contract to be in writing, and the petition does not allege it to be in writing, defense may be presented by demurrer. Bull v. McCrea, 8 B. Mon., 423; Smith v. Fah, 15 B. Mon., 446; Smith v. Theobold, 86 Ky., 141.

The statute of frauds, section 470, sub-sections 6 and 7, Kentucky Statutes, provides as follows:

> No action shall be brought to charge any person:
> 6. Upon any contract for the sale of real estate, or any lease thereof, for longer term than one year; nor
> 7. Upon any agreement which is not to be performed within one year from the making thereof, unless the promise, contract, agreement, representation, assurance, or ratification, or some memorandum or note thereof, be in writing, and signed by the party to be charged therewith, or by his authorized agent; but the consideration need not be expressed in the writing; it may be proved when necessary, or disproved by parol or other evidence.

A parol lease of land for one year, to commence at a future date, is within the statute. Greenwood v. Strother, 91 Ky., 482

The question sharply presented is: May plaintiffs recover for expenses incurred and time lost on the faith of a contract that is unenforceable under the statute of frauds?

In the case of Hurley v. Woodsides, 21 Ky. L. Rep., 1073, Woodsides made a parol lease with Hurley for 25 acres of timber land for a period of five years. Under the contract Hurley was to clear five acres of the land in the winter of 1897 and 1898, ten acres in the winter of 1898 and 1899, and ten acres in the winter of 1899 and 1900, and was to have free use of the land so cleared up for three years thereafter. Woodsides agreed to erect a dwelling house, smoke house, kitchen and stable on the leased premises for Hurley's occupancy, and was to furnish a team of oxen with which to break up the land as soon as it was cleared. He was also to remove the logs lying upon the land at the time of the lease and to erect a tobacco barn for Hurley's use. Moreover, it was a part of the agreement that the contract was to be put in writing. Relying upon Woodsides' promise to do so, Hurley moved his personal effects into an old house located upon the land, which he was to occupy until the new house was finished, and gave up the premises previously occupied by him. After such removal, Woodsides denied that he had agreed to furnish cattle to break up the land or to remove the logs or to erect a tobacco barn, and refused to sign a contract embracing these stipulations. Alleging that as a result of Woodsides' failure to carry out the contract, he had been damaged in the sum of $100, the cost of removing his effects; $50 for time lost in hunting up another place; $200 in prospective profits which he would have realized by reason of his bargain, and $300 by reason of having been induced to surrender the premises formerly occupied by him. Hurley brought suit against Woodsides to recover the aforesaid item of damages, aggregating the sum of $650. The trial sustained a demurrer to the petition, and the petition was dismissed. On appeal here judgment was affirmed. After setting out the statute of frauds, the court said:

> Under this provision of the statute the alleged verbal contract was not binding or enforceable upon the parties thereto for the reason that it was a contract for the lease of real estate for a longer term that one year from the making thereof; and as the contract itself was not enforceable between the parties, no action for damages for refusing to execute it or to reduce it to writing can be maintained, as "it would leave but little, if anything, of the statute of frauds to hold that a party might be mulcted in damages for refusing to execute in writing a verbal agreement, which, unless in writing is invalid under the statute of frauds." (Chase v. Frits, 132 Mass., 361; Lawrence v. Chase, 54 Mo., 196.)

In the case of Bromley, et al. v. Broyles, 58 S.W., 984, it was held that a tenant with a parol agreement for a lease for another year, which was within the statute of frauds, could not recover as damages for breach of the contract the loss sustained by him in making preparations for raising a crop.

In the case of King v. Cheatham, 31 Ky. L. Rep., 1176, King sued upon a writing signed by himself alone, in which he bound himself to buy from Cheatham certain trees standing on her land, to be served in the future. It appears that he cut some 263 trees from the land before he was ousted.

He asked damages for his labor and profit. There was a judgment below for defendant. On appeal the judgment was affirmed. In discussing the validity of the contract, and the right of plaintiff to recover damages thereon, the court said:

> The statute merely withholds a right of action upon them as against the party who has not signed them. The prohibition of the statute must reach the spirit of its purpose. As a suit to recover damages for the breach of such a contract would be an indirect enforcement, such actions are held to be within the inhibition of the statute. [Citations.] Nor does part performance of the party signing affect the matter. [Citations.]
>
> Although a recovery of purchase money paid on such contract may be recovered if the party not bound refused to execute it, that is not in any sense an action upon the contract, but is for money had and received for which the consideration has failed, and for which the law implies a promise to repay. But nothing was paid by appellant as consideration on this contract.

The same doctrine is applied in the case of Greenwood v. Strother, *supra*.

Indeed, it is the general rule that damages cannot be recovered for violation of a contract within the statute of frauds. [Citations.]

To this general rule there are certain well recognized exceptions. Thus, in Speers v. Sewell, 4 Bush, 239; Myles v. Myles, 6 Bush, 237; Usher v. Flood, 83 Ky., 552; Thomas v. Feese, 21 Ky. L. Rep., 206; 51 S.W., 150; Story v. Story, 61 S.W., 279, 22 Ky. L. Rep., 1731; Doty v. Doty, 118 Ky., 204, 80 S.W. 803, 26 Ky. L. Rep., 63, 2 L.R.A. (n.s), 713; and a number of other cases, it has been held that where services have been rendered during the life of another, on the promise that the person rendering the service should receive at the death of the person served a legacy, and the contract so made is within the statute of frauds, a reasonable compensation may be recovered for the services actually rendered. It has also been held that the vendee of land under a parol contract is entitled to recover any portion of the purchase money he may have paid, and is also entitled to compensation for improvements. [Citations.]

Under a contract for personal services within the statute, an action may be maintained on a quantum meruit. Kleeman v. Collins, 9 Bush, 460; Myers v. Korb, 21 Ky. L. Rep., 163, S.W., 1108. The doctrine of these cases proceeds upon the theory that the defendant has actually received some benefits from the acts of part performance, and the law, therefore, implied a promise to pay. In 29 Am. & Eng. Encyc., 836, the rule is thus stated:

> Although part performance by one of the parties to a contract within the statute of frauds will not, at law, entitle such party to recover upon the contract itself, he may nevertheless recover for money paid by him, or

property delivered, or services rendered in accordance with and upon the faith of the contract. The law will raise an implied promise on the part of the other party to pay for what has been done in the way of part performance. But this right of recovery is not absolute. The plaintiff is entitled to compensation only under such circumstances as would warrant a recovery in case there was no express contract, and hence it must appear that the defendant has actually received or will receive some benefit from the acts of part performance. It is immaterial that the plaintiff may have suffered a loss because he is unable to enforce his contract.

In Brown on Statute of Frauds, section 118-a, the rule is announced in the following language.

The rule that, where one person pays money or performs services for another upon a contract void under the statute of frauds, he may recover the money upon account for money paid, or recover for the services upon a quantum meruit, applies only to cases where the defendant has received and holds the money paid for the benefit of the services rendered. It does not apply to cases of money paid by the plaintiff to a third person in execution of a verbal contract between the plaintiff and defendant, such as by the statute of frauds must be in writing.

[Supporting citations have been deleted.]

In the case under consideration, the plaintiffs merely sustained a loss. Defendant received no benefit. Had he received a benefit, the law would imply an obligation to pay therefor. Having received no benefit, no obligation to pay is implied. The statute says that the contract of defendant made with plaintiffs is unenforceable. Defendant, therefore, had the legal right to decline to carry it out. To require him to pay plaintiffs for losses and expenses incurred on the faith of the contract without any benefit accruing to him would, in effect, uphold a contract upon which the statute expressly declares no action shall be brought. The statute was enacted for the purpose of preventing frauds and perjuries. That it is a valuable statute is shown by the fact that similar statutes are in force in practically all, if not all, of the states of the union. Being a valuable statute, the purpose of the law-makers in its enactment should not be defeated by permitting recoveries in cases to which its provisions were intended to apply.

The contrary rule was announced by this court in the case of McDaniel v. Hutchinson, 136 Ky., 412. There the plaintiff lived in the State of Illinois. The defendant owned a farm in Mercer County, Kentucky. The defendant agreed with plaintiff that if plaintiff and his family would come to Kentucky and live with defendant, the defendant would furnish the plaintiff with a home during defendant's life, and upon his death, would give plaintiff his farm. It was held that although the contract was within the statute of frauds, plaintiff could recover his reasonable expenses in moving to Kentucky, and reasonable compensation for loss sustained in giving up his business elsewhere. Upon reconsideration of the question involved, we conclude that the doctrine announced in that case is not in accord with the weight of authority, and should be no longer adhered to. It is therefore overruled.

Judgment affirmed.

NOTE

In Kearns v. Andree, 107 Conn. 181, 139 A. 695, (1928), the facts of the case, as stated in Judge Maltbie's opinion, were these:

The plaintiff was the owner of a lot of land at the corner of Prospect and Edwards streets in the town of East Hartford, on which stood a dwellinghouse then in the process of construction but practically finished. In the rear of the land upon which this house stood, he owned other land upon which another house was located. He and the defendant entered into an oral contract whereby, as it is stated in the finding, "the defendant agreed to purchase the house and lot at the corner of Prospect and Edwards streets at a price of $8,500, it being agreed the defendant should assume a first mortgage of $4,500, a bank mortgage, and pay $4,000 in cash." This mortgage was not then in existence but the plaintiff promised to obtain it, there being no agreement, however, as to the identity of the mortgagee or as to its terms.

The defendant thereafter became dissatisfied with his purchase, but finally agreed to stand by the bargain, if certain alterations were made in the house, if it was finished in a certain way, and if certain trees standing upon the lot were cut down. The plaintiff proceded to make the changes and finish the house as desired by the defendant, and to cut down the trees, and he also secured a bank mortgage upon the premises in the sum of $4,500. The defendant, however, refused to complete the purchase. The way in which the house had been finished at the defendant's request made the premises less salable, but the plaintiff finally secured a purchaser for the price of $8,250, after, to meet this purchaser's desires, he had repainted the house a different color and repapered certain rooms. The plaintiff brings this action to recover the expenses to which he was put in order to finish the house to meet the defendant's wishes, and thereafter, to adapt it to the desires of the purchaser, and also to recover the difference between the price agreed to be paid by the defendant and that for which the house was finally sold.

107 Conn. at 182-183, 139 A. at 696. What, if anything, should the plaintiff recover? His lost profits? The expenses incurred in adapting the house to the defendant's wishes? The additional expenses incurred in preparing the house for the person who eventually bought it? Judge Maltbie concluded that only the second of these three items was recoverable

as a matter of law, and remanded the case for a new trial. Is this result consistent with Boone v. Coe?

ALASKA AIRLINES, INC. v. STEPHENSON
217 F.2d 295 (9th Cir. 1954)

CHAMBERS, Circuit Judge.

Arthur W. Stephenson, plaintiff-appellee, is the discharged general manager of Alaska Airlines, Inc., a company organized under the laws of the Territory of Alaska. The company was defendant in the trial court and is appellant herein. The case falls entirely on the territorial side of the district court in Alaska, i.e., no federal questions are presented and we take it that diversity of citizenship did not exist.

Stephenson seems to have had through the years a varied career in the airlines. One day he is a pilot. The next day he is an executive. In September, 1950, he was a pilot regularly employed by Western Airlines. At Western he had certain rights to continued employment. But he could take a leave of absence therefrom for a period of not to exceed six months without prejudice to his rights of continued employment with Western.

Alaska Airlines, Inc., herein called Alaska, Inc., in 1950 was a small airline operating in the Territory of Alaska. It was living from day to day in the hope of obtaining a certificate to operate from the states, probably from Seattle, Washington, to Alaska. When that day should come, it was to be a big airline.

The financial headquarters of the company, at least, was in the City of New York. There R. W. Marshall, chairman of the board, had his office.

Stephenson went to New York on September 15, 1950, at the request of an aviation consultant company to be interviewed by Marshall. Then and there Stephenson was employed as general manager. He took leave of absence from Western and rather promptly commenced his duties. He eventually in mid-winter moved his family to Anchorage, Alaska, from Redondo Beach, California. In the winter of 1950-1951, with Stephenson's six months' leave with Western about to expire, he was in and out of New York pressing for a written contract of definite duration and of substantial length. He had one drawn up and conferred not only with Marshall but with the company's lawyer. He could not get it signed. The company wasn't signing any contracts, we take it, until it found out whether it was to have its certificate. Later on we shall advert to some of the discussions.

The certificate apparently was granted in May, 1951. It seems strange that with the granting of the certificate there followed no negotiations or steps to put the agreement in writing, if Alaska, Inc., had agreed to do so. But we do get the impression that by this time Stephenson had lost favor with the company. It appears that he was relieved of his duties about

September 1, 1951, and was continued on the payroll until October 15, 1951.

Then Stephenson filed suit against Alaska, Inc., setting up two causes of action. The first claim is for salary beyond the time he was carried on the payroll. The second is for moneys he claimed due on his expense account and for salary admittedly due except for an offset claimed by Alaska, Inc. The evidence is in sharp conflict. If the jury had accepted Alaska, Inc.'s, testimony, it would have found Stephenson owed it money. On the claim for salary, it seems to us that Alaska, Inc., on the evidence, would have to concede that Stephenson sustained his burden of proof for $11,050 in unpaid salary awarded him by the jury. Of course, it does not concede the point.

But what of the statute of frauds and a contract clearly not to be performed fully within one year? Alaska, Inc., relied on the statute of frauds. We have a contract made in New York to be performed entirely or almost entirely in Alaska. Does New York law apply, or does the law of the Territory of Alaska apply. And what of the promissory estoppel.[22]

At the outset, one well may wonder if the courts from the beginning had vigorously enforced the statute of frauds from its first adoption in England, wouldn't we have less injustice? If people were brought up in the tradition that certain contracts inescapably had to be in writing, wouldn't those affected thereby get their contracts into writing and on the whole, wouldn't the public be better off?

But we have to take the law as we find it. For generations, in hard cases, the courts have been making exceptions to "do justice," granting relief here, calling a halt there. The result is that one with difficulty can predict the result in a given state and the situation becomes more confounded when the query arises as to whose (what state's) law we should apply.

Stephenson's version of his employment may be summed up as follows:

1. When he was hired by Marshall the agreement was that he would go to work at $1,300 a month and that they would get together in six weeks to three months and work out a long-range agreement; that he was to have a raise when the certificate of convenience and necessity was granted for Alaska, Inc., to fly to and from the states.

2. Negotiations were had for the "contract" about January 6, 1951, in New York, with Marshall. At that time about all that was agreed definitely was that Stephenson should take his family with him to the Territory of Alaska. This he did. Then, about March 15, 1951, Stephenson, his leave

---

22. The term promissory estoppel generally is considered to be properly applied when the existence of "promissory estoppel" is used as a substitute for consideration in the law of contracts to create a binding contract. However, the term, correctly or not, is found in many cases where courts are making exceptions to prevent manifest injustice in statute of frauds cases. 3 Stanford Law Review 281.

with Western about to expire, was in New York at the company office, pressing Marshall for the contract. He made clear to Marshall that because of this contingency the employment had to be made definite and formalized. (The testimony wobbles, but the jury could have found that on March 16 or 17 Marshall orally hired Stephenson for a period of two years at a salary of $1,300 per month, with the further understanding that on the granting of the certificate Stephenson was to have an increase in salary and a written contract.) Thereupon Stephenson let his right to return to Western expire.

[The court then considered the conflict of laws question and concluded that the Alaskan Statute of Frauds was applicable in the present case.]

Turning to the Alaska statute, what is it? Where did it come from? What history does it have behind it?

It would appear that it went to Alaska from Oregon. Oregon may have taken it form Iowa or New York. We find nothing in the decisions made by the Alaska courts (or by this court) or in Oregon prior to Alaska's adoption of the statute that will help us.

Section 90 of the Restatement of the Law of Contracts provides as follows:

> Promise Reasonably Inducing Definite and Substantial Action
> A promise which the promisor should reasonably expect to induce action or forbearance of a definite and substantial character on the part of the promisee which does induce such action or forbearance is binding if injustice can be avoided only by enforcement of the promise.

The foregoing section, not mentioning promissory estoppel, is addressed not to the statute of frauds but to promissory estoppel as a substitute for consideration. However, when one considers the part Samuel Williston took in the formulation of the Restatement of Contracts and then examines Section 178, Comment f.,[23] one must conclude that there was an intention to carry promissory estoppel (or call it what you will) into the statute of frauds if the additional factor of a promise to reduce the contract to writing is present. Williston on Contracts, 1936 Ed., Sec. 533A.

The circumstances of Stephenson's relinquishing his rights with Western and the promise to make a written contract on the future condition, we think, meets the test of the Restatement.

---

23. ["Though there has been no satisfaction of the Statute, an estoppel may preclude objection on that ground in the same way that objection to the non-existence of other facts essential for the establishment of a right or a defense may be precluded. A misrepresentation that there has been such satisfaction if substantial action is taken in reliance on the representation precludes proof by the party who made the representation that it was false; and a promise to made a memorandum, if similarly relied on, may give rise to an effective promissory estoppel if the statute would otherwise operate to defraud." — EDS.]

Parenthetically, we observe that California courts probably would reach the same result. Seymour v. Oelrichs, 156 Cal. 782, 106 P. 88. True it is that under earlier decisions where one gave up job A to take job B on an oral promise of long time employment on job B, no exception to the statute of frauds was made. But we believe with the growth of tenure rights and fringe benefits on a given job, the pendulum was swung the other way and that Seymour v. Oelrichs, *supra*, will generally be followed throughout the country.[24]

Further, it occurs to us that the Restatement of Contracts, Section 178, Comment *f.*, has come up with a very good compromise in the confusion of decisions under the statute of frauds which leaves some vitality to the statute, yet gives a workable rule in making exceptions. . . .

Defendant complains that the record shows plaintiff failed to mitigate his damages. Of course, the plaintiff did have a duty to mitigate his damage, and his excuses for failing to seek other employment are rather flimsy. But we take it, on the issue of failure to mitigate damages, the burden of proof rested upon the defendant. After carefully considering the evidence on the subject we think that a jury question was presented as to whether plaintiff should be charged with failure to mitigate.

Alaska, Inc., also complains that it was clearly entitled to an offset or to deduct from the plaintiff's claim for wages admittedly due by Alaska, Inc., payments made by plaintiff on purchase contract for a house in Anchorage, Alaska. The contract provided that in the event Stephenson did not complete the purchase of the house the payments should be considered as rent. We have considered the evidence which appellee argues entitled the question of reimbursement for home payments to go to the jury. We think plaintiff's evidence on this point was little more than that it was his opinion he was entitled to be repaid for the installments paid on his real estate contract. And for all that the record shows, Stephenson's equity in the place may have increased beyond the amount he paid. These payments being $2,000, the verdict on the second cause of action should be reduced in that amount.

The judgment on plaintiff's first claim in the amount of $11,050 is affirmed. The judgment for $2,695.20 on the second claim is to be modified by the trial court's reducing it to the extent of $2,000 to $695.20.

NOTE

1. In support of his claim that "California courts probably would reach the same result," Judge Chambers cites Monarcho v. Lo Greco, 35 Cal.

24. See Fibreboard Products, Inc. v. Townsend, 9 Cir., 202 F.2d 180, following Monarcho v. Lo Greco, 35 Cal. 2d 621, 220 P.2d 737.

2d 621, 220 P.2d 737 (1950). The plaintiff in *Monarcho* lived with his mother and stepfather, who promised him that if he remained on their farm, he would receive the property when they died. The plaintiff did in fact remain, giving up other opportunities and working the farm for twenty years until his stepfather's death. It was then discovered that the stepfather, in breach of his earlier oral promise to the plaintiff, had willed his half of the property to his own grandson. The California Supreme Court upheld the plaintiff's claim to the property over the objection that his stepfather's promise was unenforceable because not in writing. In his opinion, Justice Traynor stressed two factors, the plaintiff's reliance on the promise (which raised an estoppel to plead the Statute of Frauds as a defense) and the benefit conferred by the plaintiff on the promisor and his devisees (which would constitute an unjust enrichment if the promise were held unenforceable under the Statute). Traynor also explicitly rejected the older view "that an estoppel to plead the statute of frauds can only arise where there have been representations with respect to the requirements of the statute indicating that a writing is not necessary or will be executed or that the statute will not be relied upon as a defense." Id. at 625, 220 P.2d at 740. In reality, Traynor concluded, "it is not the representation that the contract will be put in writing or that the statute will not be invoked, but the promise that the contract will be performed that a party relies upon when he changes his position because of it." Id. at 626, 220 P.2d at 741.

Does Monarcho v. Lo Greco support the result in *Alaska Airlines*, as Judge Chambers suggests? In the *Alaska Airlines* case, the airline company apparently had promised to put its contract with the plaintiff in writing. In the absence of a promise to do so, would the plaintiff's reliance have been sufficient to take the contract out of the Statute of Frauds?

Suppose the plaintiff in *Monarcho* had declared, upon cross-examination, that he would have stayed on the farm and taken care of his mother and stepfather even if they had not promised to give him the property when they died. What result? See Klockner v. Green, 54 N.J. 230, 254 A.2d 782 (1969).

2. Restatement Second §139(1) provides:

> A promise which the promisor should reasonably expect to induce action or forbearance on the part of the promisee or a third person and which does induce the action or forbearance is enforceable notwithstanding the Statute of Frauds if injustice can be avoided only by enforcement of the promise. The remedy granted for breach is to be limited as justice requires.

Nothing in §139, or its accompanying commentary, limits application of the section to cases where nonenforcement would result in unjust enrichment to the promisor, nor is there any requirement that the promise relied upon have included a promise to reduce the agreement to writing. In effect, §139 codifies the "progressive" features of Monarcho v. Lo Greco but eliminates its more traditional, and qualifying, emphasis on unjust enrichment. For a generally favorable discussion of §139, see Knapp, Reliance in the Revised *Restatement*: The Proliferation of Promissory Estoppel, 81 Colum. L. Rev. 52, 67-71 (1981). The judicial reaction to §139 has been a mixed one; contrast Farmland Service Coop., Inc. v. Klein, 196 Neb. 538, 244 N.W.2d 86 (1976), with Warder & Lee Elevator, Inc. v. Britten, 274 N.W.2d 339 (Iowa 1979).

3. If A relies on an unenforceable oral promise by B, but confers no benefit on B, how should A's damages be measured? Should A be compensated only for his out-of-pocket expenses or for the loss of a favorable bargain? See Restatement Second §139(2)(a). How does Restatement Second §90(1) deal with this problem? If reliance on the part of the promisee is held to be a sufficient justification for enforcing a contract according to its terms, even when the contract is within the Statute of Frauds, what is left of the protection the Statute is meant to provide? The increased willingness of courts (encouraged by scholars) to protect the reliance interest of disappointed promisees seems everywhere to have had anti-formalistic consequences. (The doctrine of consideration, it has often been said, is as much a formality as the Statute of Frauds.) What have we gained — and lost — in the process? Does the growth of statutory regulation in the consumer field represent a contrary tendency — the reestablishment of a significant measure of formality in at least one branch of contract law? Or is it better understood as an expression of the same intensified concern with fair dealing and fiduciary care that is reflected in the rise of promissory estoppel to a position of ubiquitous importance?

CHAPTER 7

The Parol Evidence Rule

"No rules can determine their own application."
Wittgenstein

Section 1.   Introductory Note

When two people make a contract, they create new law for themselves,
new rights and duties that supplement or modify whatever entitlements
they already possess. The law of contracts facilitates this process and may
therefore aptly be described as an instrument of decentralized lawmaking.[1] There are, of course, limits to the lawmaking powers that private
parties enjoy. A rule of criminal law, for example, cannot be displaced by
private agreement and many of the nonconsensual duties deriving from
the law of torts are similarly immune to contractual alteration.[2] Moreover, even if the subject matter of an agreement is perfectly innocent, the
courts may refuse to enforce it if its terms are too one-sided or the agreement was reached by a route that is procedurally tainted through fraud,
duress, or "unfair surprise".[3] In these respects, as well, the parties' power
of self-rule is limited. Within these constraints, however, contracting
parties enjoy a legislative preeminence: the rules they must follow are
fixed by the terms of their own agreement and it is to the agreement that a
court will look in deciding whether each has given or done all he should.
This idea is sometimes expressed by saying "that the parties must be
content to perform and to receive performance in accordance with their
own agreement,"[4] and that the courts will not make a contract for them.

But even if an agreement is acknowledged to fall within the limits of
permissible private lawmaking, its scope and the meaning of its terms may

1. Max Weber, On Law in Economy and Society 89 (M. Rheinstein & E. Shils trans.
1954).
2. For a discussion of when a promisor may and may not disclaim responsibility for
losses resulting from his own negligence, see 6A Corbin §1472.
3. See pp. 554-564 *supra*.
4. 3 Corbin §541.

be uncertain. It may be unclear what the parties have agreed to, and where this is the case, even the least interventionist court must resolve a preliminary issue of interpretation before it can enforce the agreement according to its terms.

The need for interpretation can arise in many different ways. For example, the parties may have failed to address, or to even consider, a contingency whose occurrence has dramatically altered their original expectations. In cases of this sort, we speak of a "gap" in the contract, and the question the court must answer is, how shall the gap be filled? There are two possible responses: the court can either supply a term to fill the gap or do nothing, choosing instead to leave any losses where they may already have fallen. The first solution clearly requires an interpretive elaboration of the parties' bargain, typically through the implication of a risk-allocating term the court believes the parties themselves would have accepted had they addressed the matter at hand. Though less obviously, the second solution also represents an interpretation of the parties' agreement for it too is based upon a particular construction (or reconstruction) of their probable intent — why, after all, should losses that may have fallen in a wholly arbitrary way be allowed to remain where they are unless it is assumed this is what the parties would have wanted had they thought about the problem before it arose? These and related issues are explored more fully in Chapter 8, which deals with the gap-filling doctrines of mistake and impossibility.

Gaps are not, however, the only reason an agreement may require interpretation. What the parties have said, as well as what they have left unsaid, can be a source of confusion and controversy requiring an interpretive resolution. If, for example, the parties have included an ambiguous term in their agreement it may be necessary for the court to decide which of the term's several meanings to adopt. Statements and promises made in the course of negotiations but not explicitly included in the parties' final agreement constitute another fertile source of ambiguity. When are prior statements and promises to be deemed an integral part of the bargain and when should we assume that the parties meant to deny them legal effect through a calculated act of silence or exclusion? A number of interpretive rules have been devised to help answer this question; often described collectively as *the* parol evidence rule, they are the subject of the present chapter.

We may begin with a black-letter statement of the rule itself:

> When two parties have made a contract and have expressed it in a writing to which they have both assented as the complete and accurate integration of that contract, evidence, whether parol or otherwise, of antecedent understandings and negotiations will not be admitted for the purpose of varying or contradicting the writing.[5]

_____
5. 3 Corbin §573.

The definition is Corbin's and if it seems uncomplicated, we should re-member that it is followed by more than two hundred pages of dense commentary. Each clause of the rule shines, deceptively, from innumer-able glosses. Indeed, even its name is a deception for the parol evidence rule is not, properly speaking, a rule of evidence at all, nor is its applica-tion limited to parol (as distinct from written) agreements.

The rationale for the parol evidence rule was stated, with Elizabethan eloquence, in the Countess of Rutland Case, 5 Co. 26a, 77 Eng. Rep. 89 (1604). "[I]t would be inconvenient," declared Chief Justice Popham,

> that matters in writing made by advice and on consideration, and which finally import the certain truth of the agreement of the parties should be controlled by averment of the parties to be proved by the uncertain testi-mony of slippery memory. And it would be dangerous to purchasers and farmers, and all others in such cases, if such averments against matter in writing should be admitted.

Since the days of Chief Justice Popham, if not earlier, the parol evi-dence rule has been defended as a device to preserve the security of transactions. Its policy goal has found its most forceful articulation in a well-known Minnesota case.[6] The defendants, when sued on a written instrument guaranteeing the payment of "any and all sums of money" requested by a milling company in which they were interested, pleaded an oral agreement limiting their liability. Since, in the court's view, the instrument was the "final expression of the contractual assent of the parties," it could not be varied or contradicted by parol evidence of pre-ceding or contemporaneous agreement. Absent fraud or mistake, the court declared, the negotiations preceding the written contract were not its concern.

> Were it otherwise, written contracts would be enforced not according to the plain effect of their language, but pursuant to the story of their negotia-tions as told by the litigant having at the time being the greater power of persuading the trier of fact. So far as contracts are concerned, the rule of law would give way to the mere notions of man as to who should win law suits. [Without the parol evidence rule] there would be no assurance of the enforceability of a written contract. If such assurance were removed today from our law, general disaster would result because of the consequent destruction of confidence, for the tremendous but closely adjusted machin-ery of modern business cannot function at all without confidence in the enforceability of contracts.[7]

In justification of its conclusion that the instrument sued on was the final and complete integration of the understanding of the parties, the

6. Cargill Commn. Co. v. Swartwood, 159 Minn. 1, 198 N.W. 536 (1924).
7. Id. at 6, 7, 198 N.W. at 538.

court in the *Cargill* case invoked the doctrine, often repeated, that
the test of completeness of a written contract is the document itself: if the
document "appears to be complete, that ends the inquiry and parol evidence is inadmissible to prove first the fact, and then the purport, of the
alleged omission."[8] The court conceded, however, that incompleteness
need not "appear on the face of the document from mere inspection" and
added a significant qualification: "it is enough that the omission appear
when the court, aided if necessary, and *only if necessary*, by extrinsic
evidence, comes to apply the contract to the designated subject matter."[9]

The modern history of the parol evidence rule has been marked by a
growing appreciation of the consequences of this last observation and its
implications for our view not only of the rule but of contract interpretation in general. The parol evidence rule bars the proof of prior agreements where the parties have embodied their contract in a writing that is
meant to be a complete and accurate statement of its terms. Application
of the rule in any particular case clearly requires, therefore, a preliminary
judgment concerning the parties' intentions with regard to the writing
itself: did they mean it to be an exclusive source of contractual liability or
something less than this, a partial statement of the terms of their agreement requiring supplementation from other sources? To determine what
the writing means, or meant, to the parties, it must be viewed against the
background of their attitudes and expectations, and while the writing
serves an important evidentiary function in the reconstruction of this
background, it cannot provide its own interpretive framework (any more
than a literary text can criticize itself). An object is never the same as a
person's attitude toward it, though the object may provide evidence as to
what that attitude is and help to make it interpretively accessible to us. No
matter how complete and authoritative it appears to be, a written agreement is only a sign pointing to something it is not and logically can never
be — the matrix of intentions in which it has its own place and meaning.
It is from the standpoint of this invisible web of expectations that we must
always take our bearings in attempting to determine what agreement the
parties have made. A writing cannot provide the standpoint from which
its own meaning may be assessed, and the skills of draftsmanship are as
useless in this regard as speed in the effort to jump over one's shadow.

But to say that a writing can never be more than evidence of the
parties' intentions is not to say that all writings should be treated equally:
some provide better evidence of the parties' intentions than others do,
and should be given greater weight in the court's interpretive delibera-
tions. Where it seems obvious from an inspection of the writing that the
parties did in fact assent to it as an integrated statement of their agreement, it may seem like a metaphysical quibble to insist that a writing can

8. Id. at 8, 198 N.W. at 538.
9. Id at 9, 198 N.W. at 539.

only have greater or lesser evidentiary weight and can never be self-validating. But quibbles of this sort, though of seemingly little practical consequence, can help us to a deeper philosophical understanding of the law and to a more realistic appraisal of its rules. Corbin's discussion of the parol evidence rule is exemplary in both respects.

CORBIN, THE PAROL EVIDENCE RULE

53 Yale L.J. 603, 609-610, 622-624 (1944)

STATUTE OF FRAUDS COMPARED WITH THE "PAROL EVIDENCE RULE"

The Statute of Frauds and the "parol evidence rule" have sometimes both been applied in a single case. To promote clear thinking and correct decision, they should be compared and contrasted. They appear to have a similar purpose, at least when we regard the latter rule as in truth a rule of admissibility. That purpose is the prevention of successful fraud and perjury. Under both Statute and rule, this purpose is only haltingly attained; and if attained at all, it is at the expense and to the injury of many honest contractors. Both the Statute and the rule may have caused more litigation than they have prevented. Both may have done more harm than good. Both have been convenient hooks on which a judge can support a decision actually reached on other grounds. Both are attempts to determine justice and the truth by a mechanistic device and thus evidence a distrust of the capacity of courts and juries to weigh human credibility. And, in order to prevent the infliction of gross injustice on honest men, the courts have been forced to make numerous exceptions and fine distinctions in connection with both Statute and rule, with such resulting complexity and inconsistency that a reasoned statement of their operation requires volumes instead of pages and the case must be rare in which a plausible argument can not be made for deciding either way.

So much for the apparent similarities of the Statute of Frauds and the "parol evidence rule." These similarities are found in their social aims. But in the means that they employ and in their juristic effects, they are very different. The Statute makes certain oral contracts unenforceable by action, if not evidenced by a signed memorandum; the "parol evidence rule" protects a completely integrated writing from being varied and contradicted by parol. The Statute does not exclude any parol evidence, such evidence always being admissible to show that the writing does not correctly represent the agreement actually made; the "parol evidence rule," as commonly stated, purports to exclude such evidence. The Statute does not require that the written memorandum shall be an "integration" of the agreement, although such an integration satisfies its requirements; the "parol evidence rule" does not purport to have any operation at all unless such an integration exists. The Statute, when strictly applied, may prevent the enforcement of a contract that the parties in fact made; the application of the "parol evidence rule" results in the enforcement of a contract that the parties did not make, if in fact the written document was not agreed upon as a final and complete integration of terms.

The Statute stipulates a requirement for enforceability which the party to be charged may at any time supply (without knowledge or consent of the other party), recognizes oral agreements as operative for many purposes, and is in no respect a rule as to discharge of contracts; the "parol evidence rule," in its only true operation, is a rule of discharge, a discharge of previous understandings by mutual agreement, a discharge the nullification of which requires the assent of both parties. . . .

PAROL EVIDENCE ADMISSIBLE FOR PURPOSES OF INTERPRETATION

No parol evidence that is offered can be said to vary or contradict a writing until by process of interpretation the meaning of the writing is determined. The "parol evidence rule" is not, and does not purport to be, a rule of interpretation or a rule as to the admission of evidence for the purpose of interpretation. Even if a written document has been assented to as the complete and accurate integration of the terms of a contract, it must still be interpreted and all those factors that are of assistance in this process may be proved by oral testimony.

It is true that the language of some agreements has been believed to be so plain and clear that the court needs no assistance in interpretation. Even in these case, however, the courts seem to have had the aid of parol evidence of surrounding circumstances. The meaning to be discovered and applied is that which each party had reason to know would be given to the words by the other party. Antecedent and surrounding factors that throw light upon this question may be proved by any kind of relevant evidence.

The more bizarre and unusual an asserted interpretation is, the more convincing must be the testimony that supports it. At what point the court should cease listening to testimony that white is black and that a dollar is fifty cents is a matter for sound judicial discretion and common sense. Even these things may be true for some purposes. As long as the court is aware that there may be doubt and ambiguity and uncertainty in the meaning and application of agreed language, it will welcome testimony as to antecedent agreements, communications, and other factors that may help to decide the issue. Such testimony does not vary or contradict the written words; it determines that which cannot afterwards be varied or contradicted.

Mr. Justice Holmes once gave us the dictum that

> you cannot prove a mere private convention between the two parties to give language a different meaning from its common one. It would open too great risks if evidence were admissible to show that when they said five hundred feet they agreed it should mean one hundred inches, or that Bunker Hill Monument should signify the Old South Church.

It is believed, however, that the great judge was in error. The risks which he says would be "too great" are in fact being borne; they are not so great as he feared. We must remember that a person asserting that "five hundred feet" was used to mean "one hundred inches" bears the heavy risk of not being able to persuade the court and jury that it is true. . . .

NOTE

1. The Holmes dictum is to be found in Goode v. Riley, 153 Mass. 585, 586, 28 N.E. 228 (1891). Does Corbin's view seem to you, on the whole, preferable to Holmes'? Corbin stresses the costs of formalism; has he given sufficient weight to its benefits? For a general discussion of the advantages and disadvantages of formalism, and its philosophical implications, see Kennedy, Legal Formality, 2 J. Leg. Stud. 351 (1973).

2. "The truth is that whatever virtue and strength lies in the argument for the antique rule leads not to a fixed rule of law, but only to a general maxim of prudent discussion," 9 Wigmore on Evidence §2462 (3d. ed 1940). According to Learned Hand, J., "we must recognize, not only that there is a critical breaking point, as it were, beyond which no language can be forced, but that in approaching that limit the strain increases." Eustis Mining Co. v. Beer, Sondheimer & Co., 239 F. 976, 982 (S.D.N.Y. 1917). Do you agree? See, in general, Patterson, The Interpretation and Construction of Contracts, 64 Colum. L. Rev. 833, 838 (1964); Young, Equivocation in the Making of Agreements, 64 Colum. L. Rev. 619 (1964); Farnsworth, "Meaning" in the Law of Contracts, 76 Yale L.J. 939 (1967); Sweet, Contract Making and Parol Evidence: Diagnosis and Treatment of a Sick Rule, 53 Cornell L.Q. 1036 (1968).

Section 2.   The Circle of Interpretation

THOMPSON v. LIBBY

34 Minn. 374, 26 N.W. 1 (1885)

MITCHELL, J. The plaintiff being the owner of a quantity of logs marked "H. C. A.," cut in the winters of 1882 and 1883, and lying in the Mississippi river, or on its banks, above Minneapolis, defendant and the plaintiff, through his agent, D. S. Mooers, having fully agreed on the terms of a sale and purchase of the logs referred to, executed the following written agreement:

Agreement
Hastings, Minn., June 1, 1883.

I have this day sold to R. C. Libby, of Hastings, Minn., all my logs marked "H. C. A.," cut in the winters of 1882 and 1883, for ten dollars a thousand feet, boom scale at Minneapolis, Minnesota. Payments cash as fast as scale bills are produced.

[Signed]
J. H. Thompson,
Per D. S. Mooers.
R. C. Libby.

This action having been brought for the purchase-money, the defendant — having pleaded a warranty of the quality of the logs, alleged to have been made at the time of the sale, and a breach of it — offered on the trial oral testimony to prove the warranty, which was admitted, over the objection of plaintiff that it was incompetent to prove a verbal warranty, the contract of sale being in writing. This raises the only point in the case.

No ground was laid for the reformation of the written contract, and any charge of fraud on part of plaintiff or his agent in making the sale was on the trial expressly disclaimed. No rule is more familiar than that "parol contemporaneous evidence is inadmissible to contradict or vary the terms of a valid written instrument," and yet none has given rise to more misapprehension as to its application. It is a rule founded on the obvious inconvenience and injustice that would result if matters in writing, made with consideration and deliberation, and intended to embody the entire agreement of the parties, were liable to be controlled by what Lord Coke expressly calls "the uncertain testimony of slippery memory." Hence, where the parties have deliberately put their engagements into writing in such terms as to import a legal obligation, without any uncertainty as to the object or extent of such engagement, it is conclusively presumed that the whole engagement of the parties, and the manner and extent of their undertaking, was reduced to writing. 1 Greenl. Ev. §275. Of course, the rule presupposes that the parties intended to have the terms of their complete agreement embraced in the writing, and hence it does not apply where the writing is incomplete on its face and does not purport to contain the whole agreement, as in the case of mere bills of parcels, and the like.

But in what manner shall it be ascertained whether the parties intended to express the whole of their agreement in writing? It is sometimes
loosely stated that where the whole contract be not reduced to writing,
parol evidence may be admitted to prove the part omitted. But to allow a
party to lay the foundation for such parol evidence by oral testimony that
only part of the agreement was reduced to writing, and then prove by
parol the part omitted, would be to work in a circle, and to permit the
very evil which the rule was designed to prevent. The only criterion of the
completeness of the written contract as a full expression of the agreement
of the parties is the writing itself. If it imports on its face to be a complete
expression of the whole agreement, — that is, contains such language as
imports a complete legal obligation, — it is to be presumed that the parties have introduced into it every material item and term; and parol
evidence cannot be admitted to add another term to the agreement, although the writing contains nothing on the particular one to which the
parol evidence is directed. The rule forbids to add by parol where the
writing is silent, as well as to vary where it speaks, — 2 Phil. Evidence,
(Cow. & H. Notes,) 669; Naumberg v. Young, 44 N.J. Law, 331; Hei v.
Heller, 53 Wis. 415, — and the law controlling the operation of a written
contract becomes a part of it, and cannot be varied by parol any more
than what is written. 2 Phil. Ev. (Cow. & H. Notes,) 668; La Farge v.
Rickert, 5 Wend. 187; Creery v. Holly, 14 Wend. 26; Stone v. Harmon, 31
Minn. 512.

The written agreement in the case at bar, as it appears on its face, in
connection with the law controlling its construction and operation, purports to be a complete expression of the whole agreement of the parties as
to the sale and purchase of these logs, solemnly executed by both parties.
There is nothing on its face (and this is a question of law for the court) to
indicate that it is a mere informal and incomplete memorandum. Parol
evidence of extrinsic facts and circumstances would, if necessary, be
admissible, as it always is, to apply the contract to its subject-matter, or in
order to a more perfect understanding of its language. But in that case
such evidence is used, not to contradict or vary the written instrument,
but to aid, uphold, and enforce it as it stands. The language of this
contract "imports a legal obligation, without any uncertainty as to its
object or the extent of the engagement," and therefore "it must be conclusively presumed that the whole engagement of the parties, and the
manner and extent of the undertaking, was reduced to writing." No new
term, forming a mere incident to or part of the contract of sale, can be
added by parol.

That in case of a sale of personal property a warranty of its quality is an
item and term of the contract of sale, and not a separate and independent
collateral contract, and therefore cannot be added to the written agreement by oral testimony, has been distinctly held by this court, in accor-

dance, not only with the great weight of authority, but also, as we believe, with the soundest principles. Jones v. Alley, 17 Minn. 269, (292).

We are referred to Healy v. Young, 21 Minn. 389, as overruling this. This is an entire misapprehension of the point decided in the latter case. In Healy v. Young the claim of defendant was that for a certain consideration plaintiff agreed *verbally* to release a certain debt, and also to convey certain personal property; and that, in *part-performance* of this prior verbal agreement, he executed a bill of sale of the property. What was decided was that the execution in writing of the bill of sale in part-performance of this verbal agreement did not preclude defendant from proving by parol the prior agreement. The parties had not put their original agreement in writing, and the bill of sale executed in part-performance in no way superseded it. Moreover, the promise to release the debt was a *distinct* collateral matter from that covered by the bill of sale, and in that view of the case it was immaterial whether the oral agreement preceded or was contemporaneous with the bill of sale.

In opposition to the doctrine of Jones v. Alley, we are referred to a few cases which seem to hold that parol evidence of a warranty is admissible on the ground that a warranty is collateral to the contract of sale, and that the rule does not exclude parol evidence of matters collateral to the subject of the written agreement. It seems to us that this is based upon a misapprehension as to the sense in which the term "collateral" is used in the rule invoked. There are a great many matters that, in a general sense, may be considered collateral to the contract; for example, in the case of leases, covenants for repairs, improvements, payment of taxes, etc., are, in a sense, collateral to a demise of the premises. But parol evidence of these would not be admissible to add to the terms of a written lease. So, in a sense, a warranty is collateral to a contract sale, for the title would pass without a warranty. It is also collateral in the sense that its breach is no ground for a rescission of the contract by the vendor, but that he must resort to his action on the warranty for damages. But, when made, a warranty is a part of the contract of sale. The common sense of men would say, and correctly so, that when, on a sale of personal property, a warranty is given, it is one of the terms of the sale, and not a separate and independent contract. To justify the admission of a parol promise by one of the parties to a written contract, on the ground that it is collateral, the promise must relate to a subject distinct from that to which the writing relates. Dutton v. Gerrish, 9 Cush. 89; Naumberg v. Young, *supra*; 2 Taylor, Ev. §1038. See Lindley v. Lacey, 34 Law J., C.P., 7.

We have carefully examined all the cases cited in the quite exhaustive brief of counsel for defendant, and find but very few that are at all in conflict with the views already expressed, and these few do not commend themselves to our judgment. Our conclusion therefore is that the court erred in admitting parol evidence of a warranty, and therefore the order refusing a new trial must be reversed.

NOTE

1. According to Judge Mitchell, "[t]he only criterion of the completeness of the written contract as a full expression of the agreement of the
parties is the writing itself." What exactly does he mean by this? Do you
agree? Professor Corbin defended the opposite view:

> [A] writing cannot prove its own completeness and accuracy. Even though
> it contains an express statement to that effect, the assent of the parties
> thereto must still be proved. Proof of its completeness and accuracy, dis-
> charging all antecedent agreements, must be made in large part by the oral
> testimony of parties and other witnesses. The very testimony that the "parol
> evidence rule" is supposed to exclude is frequently, if not always, necessary
> before the court can determine that the parties have agreed upon the
> writing as a complete and accurate statement of terms. The evidence that
> the rule seems to exclude must sometimes be heard and weighed before it
> can be excluded by the rule.

3 Corbin §582. Doesn't this take us in the circle Judge Mitchell warns
against? How do you suppose Professor Corbin would have replied to the
charge that his view of the parol evidence rule permits "the very evil
which the rule was designed to prevent"?

2. Suppose the case had come up under the Uniform Commercial
Code, and the buyer claimed the logs were not merchantable (U.C.C.
§2-314). Would the parol evidence rule bar the introduction of evidence
to support this claim? Consult the rules for disclaiming warranty liability
under the Code (§2-316). Judge Mitchell assumes that a writing can purport "on its face to be a complete expression of the whole agreement"
even though it is silent as to certain issues (such as the seller's warranty
obligation). When is the silence of a writing consistent with its being a
complete expression of the contract, and when is silence evidence of
incompleteness? Is this a question that can be answered by an inspection
of the writing alone?

3. Whether a writing constitutes a complete expression of the agreement depends, presumably, upon the intentions of the parties: did they
mean it to be a complete expression, or something less? Determining the
intent of the parties is usually thought to raise a question of fact. Despite
this, the application of the parol evidence rule has often been characterized as a question of law. What are the reasons for doing so? Is this a
solution to the problem of circularity noted above? See 3 Corbin §595; 9
Wigmore on Evidence §2430 (3d ed. 1940). Does the parol evidence rule,
like the Statute of Frauds, reflect a distrust of juries? See Meyers v.
Selznick Co., 373 F.2d 218 (2d Cir. 1966) (Friendly, J.); Zell v. American
Seating Co., *infra* p. 852.

PYM v. CAMPBELL, 6 El. & Bl. 370, 119 Eng. Rep. 903 (1856). In a suit
for breach of a written contract to buy an invention, plaintiff produced a

written document purporting to be such a contract, duly signed by the parties. The defendant offered evidence that although negotiations had gone so far that the price had been agreed upon, the defendant was bound to make the purchase only if two engineers, one of them Abernethie, approved. At a later meeting, Abernethie not being present, the writing put in evidence was signed with the understanding that if Abernethie approved of the invention it should be the agreement. Defendant offered evidence that Abernethie did not approve. The trial court, Lord Campbell, C.J. permitted the evidence to be introduced and instructed the jury that, if they were satisfied that, before the paper was signed, it was agreed amongst them all that it should not operate as an agreement until Abernethie approved of the invention, they should find for the defendant on the pleas denying the agreement. Verdict for the defendants.

A rule was obtained for the new trial on the ground of misdirection:

". . . ERLE, J. — I think that this rule ought to be discharged. The point made is that this is a written agreement, absolute on the face of it, and that evidence was admitted to show it was conditional: and if that had been so it would have been wrong. But I am of opinion that the evidence showed that in fact there was never any agreement at all. The production of a paper purporting to be an agreement by a party, with his signature attached, affords a strong presumption that it is his written agreement; and, if in fact he did sign the paper *animo contrahendi*, the terms contained in it are conclusive, and cannot be varied by parol evidence: but in the present case the defence begins one step earlier: the parties met and expressly stated to each other that, though for convenience they would then sign the memorandum of the terms, yet they were not to sign it as an agreement until Abernethie was consulted. I grant the risk that such a defence may be set up without ground; and I agree that a jury should therefore always look on such a defence with suspicion: but, if it be proved that in fact the paper was signed with the express intention that it should not be an agreement, the other party cannot fix it as an agreement upon those so signing. The distinction in point of law is that evidence to vary the terms of an agreement in writing is not admissible, but evidence to show that there is not an agreement at all is admissible. . . ."

CRAWFORD v. FRANCE

219 Cal. 439, 27 P.2d 645 (1933)

THOMPSON, J. This action was brought by an architect for a fee claimed to be due him under the terms of a written contract for professional services in connection with the construction of a hotel building. Judgment was rendered for the defendant and the plaintiff has appealed.

More specifically, the contract for the plaintiff's services provided:

(1) That the Architect is to design a hotel building suitable for the needs of the Owner; is to furnish all necessary preliminary sketches and estimates of cost; is to furnish complete working drawings, specifications and details necessary for the construction of such a hotel building.

(2) The Architect is to supervise all of the work committed to his control. The Architect is to carry all of the necessary administrative work required in the proper keeping of accounts, the issuance of certificates of payment and such superintendence of the work as is hereinafter mentioned.

(3) The Architect is to keep an inspector acceptable to the Owner on the work during the pouring of concrete or the erection of masonry construction. The cost of such an inspector is to be paid by the Architect.

(4) The Owner agrees that the Architect is to be paid for his services, the sum equal to six per cent of the cost of the work exclusive of the cost of the land, installments as follows: $\frac{1}{5}$ of the total fee based upon the estimated cost, on acceptance of preliminary drawings and estimates of cost; on completion of working drawings exclusive of details, a sum sufficient to bring the total payments to $\frac{3}{5}$ of the total fee based on the estimated cost or upon the lowest reputable bids for construction; the balance, $\frac{2}{5}$, to be in installments as the work progresses.

There was a fifth paragraph which required the owner to pay for surveys and borings and to make prompt statements of his requirements and decisions relating to the conduct of the work.

The plaintiff prepared plans and specifications for a thirty-room hotel which the defendant admits were satisfactory to him. Thereafter bids for its construction were sought and the lowest bid received was something over $61,000. The defendant thereupon abandoned the project because of the excessive cost of construction and refused to pay the plaintiff on the theory that he had failed to perform his part of the contract in the preparation of plans suitable to the needs of the defendant. This action was commenced on the written contract for the sum of $1963.50, $\frac{3}{5}$ of the total fee based upon the lowest bid submitted, in accordance with the provisions of paragraph (4) of the contract.

The defendant's answer contained a general denial and, in addition thereto, affirmative allegations of the oral agreement of the plaintiff to prepare plans and specifications for a hotel building which would not cost over $45,000; that the plaintiff failed to design a hotel building "suitable to the needs of the owner" since one of the defendant's known needs was that the cost of construction should not exceed $45,000; and, predicating it upon these same facts, fraud in inducing the defendant to enter into the written contract.

At the trial defendant abandoned the defense of fraud "because proof constituting the elements of fraud was lacking," but the defendant was allowed by the trial court to introduce parol evidence of the prior conversation, conduct and acts of the parties for the purpose of proving the parol agreement as to the cost of the building. It is the appellant's contention that this evidence was inadmissible except to substantiate the third affirmative defense of fraud, and that, after this defense had been abandoned, it could not properly be considered by either the court or the jury with respect to any of the remaining issues. It is urged as error that the trial court allowed the defendant to add by parol an *"entirely new, distinct and independent clause"* to the written contract. It is also urged that the defendant's failure to make an affirmative showing and ask for the reformation of the contract on the ground of mistake precluded the introduction of any evidence in support of the omitted clause of the contract.

The appellant further complains of numerous instructions, refusals to give instructions and changes made by the trial court in instructions offered by the plaintiff, which resulted in the jury's being told that they might find that plaintiff and defendant had orally agreed that the plans and specifications were to be prepared for a building, the cost of construction of which was not to exceed $45,000, and, if they further found that the plaintiff had failed to furnish such plans and specifications, the defendant would not be bound to accept the plans and that unless he did accept or make use of them he would not be liable for the plaintiff's services. One such instruction was as follows:

> If you find that the plaintiff agreed to design a building so that the cost thereof should not exceed $45,000, there is the implied agreement that the architect cannot recover unless he performs his contract in this respect, and it is not necessary in order to produce this result that the parties should expressly agree that the architect should receive no pay in the event that he failed to perform this part of the agreement.

The one question to be determined upon this appeal is whether it was proper to permit defendant to show the oral agreement limiting the cost of construction. Its solution depends upon whether the case can be said to come within one of the recognized exceptions to the parol evidence rule upon which the appellant relies. Although a contract has been reduced to writing by the parties, parol evidence is admissible to show fraud, accident or mistake, to show the omitted portion of the contract where the writing is incomplete on its face, and to clear up an ambiguity or uncertainty. (Ayers v. Southern Pac. R.R. Co., 173 Cal. 74, 81 [159 Pac. 144, L.R.A. 1917F, 949]; and see note, 70 A.L.R. 752, collecting cases.)

This evidence was offered to complete the written contract by adding a term which was obviously omitted and with which the appellant admittedly had not complied. The written contract was entirely silent as to cost of construction, the only subject which it covered with any degree of thoroughness being the architect's fees and the manner of their payment, which fees, however, could not be determined until the estimated cost was ascertained.

> It has long been the rule that when parties have not incorporated into an instrument all of the terms of their contract evidence is admissible to prove the existence of a separate oral agreement as to any manner on which the document is silent and which is not inconsistent with its terms. . . .

(Buckner v. Leon & Co., 204 Cal. 225, 227 [267 Pac. 693].) Where it appears upon the face of the writing that it is incomplete, parol evidence may be received for the purpose of supplying the missing matter. "If the writing does not show upon its face it was intended to express the whole agreement between the parties, parol evidence is admissible to show other conditions or explain latent ambiguities.". . .

In addition it is to be noted that there exists an uncertainty upon the face of the contract. In paragraph (1) it is provided that "the Architect is to design a hotel building suitable for the needs of the Owner." Those needs are in no way described in the written contract. Obviously there must have been some discussion and agreement as to the size, type and style of the building to be planned and erected, and the cost of construction must almost necessarily have been inseparably connected with any discussion of such questions. This is such an uncertainty as may be cleared up by parol evidence as to the nature and character of the building which, within the contemplation and understanding of the parties at the time of the execution of the written contract, would be "suitable for the needs of the Owner." That its cost was a material factor seems to me to admit of no doubt. . . . We consequently conclude that there was no error in the admission by the trial court of the testimony complained of and that such evidence was relevant to the issue of the appellant's performance.

Appellant's contention that the respondent should have sought affirmative relief through reformation of the contract for mutual mistake is beside the point, since it was never urged that the written contract was not in accordance with the real agreement of the parties, but rather that the whole of the agreement was not reduced to writing.

The judgment is affirmed.

NOTE

1. Parol evidence is always admissible to clarify an ambiguity that appears from an inspection of the writing itself. A more difficult question arises when one of the parties seeks to demonstrate, by means of parol

evidence, the existence of an ambiguity that would not otherwise be obvious — a "latent" ambiguity, as it is sometimes called. Should parol be admissible for this purpose? If you believe there are certain words or expressions that cannot possibly have more than one meaning, you will oppose the admission of parol to show their latent ambiguity. Professor Corbin was a tireless champion of the opposite view. "It is true," he said,

> that when a judge reads the words of a contract he may jump to the instant and confident opinion that they have but one reasonable meaning and that he knows what it is. A greater familiarity with dictionaries and the usages of words, a better understanding of the uncertainties of language, and a comparative study of more cases in the field of interpretation, will make one beware of holding such an opinion so recklessly arrived at.

3 Corbin §535. Corbin concluded that parol evidence should never be excluded for purposes of interpretation, but stressed that "[t]he more bizarre and unusual an asserted interpretation is, the more convincing must be the testimony that supports it." Id. at §579. Compare Learned Hand's celebrated dictum in Eustis Mining Co. v. Beer, Sondheimer & Co., 239 F.2d 976, 982 (S.D.N.Y. 1917), quoted *supra* p. 827. Are the views of Professor Corbin and Judge Hand significantly different?

2. What is the difference between varying a term, adding to it, and interpreting its meaning? How are these distinctions treated under the Uniform Commercial Code? See §2-202, *infra* p. 842. Compare the similar (though not identical) treatment of these issues in §§215 and 216 of the Restatement of Contracts Second. §216 is especially interesting. It provides, among other things, that "evidence of a consistent additional term is admissible to supplement an integrated agreement unless the court finds that the agreement was completely integrated," and states that a writing is not completely integrated if it omits "a consistent additional agreed term" that "in the circumstances might naturally be omitted from the writing." For a helpful guide to this labyrinthine section of the Restatement, consult Murray, The Parol Evidence Process and Standardized Agreements Under the Restatement (Second) of Contracts, 123 U. Pa. L. Rev. 1342 (1975). As to when circumstances show that a particular term "might naturally be omitted from the writing," the following case, Mitchill v. Lath, is instructive.

3. A and B enter a loan agreement, the terms of which are set forth in what appears to be an integrated writing. A, the creditor, sues B for default and B asserts the parties had an oral understanding that the loan would be forgiven upon the occurence of certain contingencies, one of which has come to pass. Does the rationale of Pym v. Campbell apply here as well? See Conn Organ Corp. v. Walt Whitman Music Studies, 67 A.D.2d 995, 413 N.Y.S.2d 725 (1979); Restatement Second §217, Comment *b*. Should it make any difference whether the oral agreement is

characterized as a condition precedent or a condition subsequent? For the meaning of this distinction, see p. 983 *infra*.

MITCHILL v. LATH

247 N.Y. 377, 160 N.E. 646 (1928)

Appeal, by permission, from a judgment of the Appellate Division of the Supreme Court in the second judicial department entered May 27, 1927, unanimously affirming a judgment in favor of plaintiff entered upon a decision of the court on trial at Special Term in an action to compel specific performance of an alleged contract to remove an ice house.

ANDREWS, J. In the fall of 1923 the Laths owned a farm. This they wished to sell. Across the road, on land belonging to Lieutenant-Governor Lunn, they had an ice house which they might remove. Mrs. Mitchill looked over the land with a view to its purchase. She found the ice house objectionable. Thereupon "the defendants orally promised and agreed, for and in consideration of the purchase of their farm by the plaintiff, to remove the said ice house in the spring of 1924." Relying upon this promise, she made a written contract to buy the property for $8,400, for cash and a mortgage and containing various provisions usual in such papers. Later receiving a deed, she entered into possession and has spent considerable sums in improving the property for use as a summer residence. The defendants have not fulfilled their promise as to the ice house and do not intend to do so. We are not dealing, however, with their moral delinquencies. The question before us is whether their oral agreement may be enforced in a court of equity.

This requires a discussion of the parol evidence rule — a rule of law which defines the limits of the contract to be construed. (Glackin v. Bennett, 226 Mass. 316.) It is more than a rule of evidence and oral testimony even if admitted will not control the written contract (O'Malley v. Grady, 222 Mass. 202), unless admitted without objection. (Brady v. Nally, 151 N.Y. 258.) It applies, however, to attempts to modify such a contract by parol. It does not affect a parol collateral contract distinct from and independent of the written agreement. It is, at times, troublesome to draw the line. Williston, in his work on Contracts (sec. 637) points out the difficulty. "Two entirely distinct contracts," he says,

> each for a separate consideration may be made at the same time and will be distinct legally. Where, however, one agreement is entered into wholly or partly in consideration of the simultaneous agreement to enter into another, the transactions are necessarily bound together, . . . Then if one of the agreements is oral and the other is written, the problem arises whether the bond is sufficiently close to prevent proof of the oral agreement.

That is the situation here. It is claimed that the defendants are called upon to do more than is required by their written contract in connection with the sale as to which it deals.

The principle may be clear, but it can be given effect by no mechanical rule. As so often happens, it is a matter of degree, for as Professor Williston also says where a contract contains several promises on each side it is not difficult to put any one of them in the form of a collateral agreement. If this were enough written contracts might always be modified by parol. Not form, but substance is the test.

In applying this test the policy of our courts is to be considered. We have believed that the purpose behind the rule was a wise one not easily to be abandoned. Notwithstanding injustice here and there, on the whole it works for good. Old precedents and principles are not to be lightly cast aside unless it is certain that they are an obstruction under present conditions. New York has been less open to arguments that would modify this particular rule, than some jurisdictions elsewhere. Thus in Eighmie v. Taylor (98 N.Y. 288) it was held that a parol warranty might not be shown although no warranties were contained in the writing.

Under our decisions before such an oral agreement as the present is received to vary the written contract at least three conditions must exist, (1) the agreement must in form be a collateral one; (2) it must not contradict express or implied provisions of the written contract; (3) it must be one that parties would not ordinarily be expected to embody in the writing; or put in another way, an inspection of the written contract, read in the light of surrounding circumstances must not indicate that the writing appears "to contain the engagements of the parties, and to define the object and measure the extent of such engagement." Or again, it must not be so clearly connected with the principal transaction as to be part and parcel of it.

The respondent does not satisfy the third of these requirements. It may be, not the second. We have a written contract for the purchase and sale of land. The buyer is to pay $8,400 in the way described. She is also to pay her portion of any rents, interest on mortgages, insurance premiums and water meter charges. She may have a survey made of the premises. On their part the sellers are to give a full covenant deed of the premises as described, or as they may be described by the surveyor if the survey is had, executed and acknowledged at their own expense; they sell the personal property on the farm and represent they own it; they agree that all amounts paid them on the contract and the expense of examining the title shall be a lien on the property; they assume the risk of loss or damage by fire until the deed is delivered; and they agree to pay the broker his commissions. Are they to do more? Or is such a claim inconsistent with these precise provisions? It could not be shown that the plaintiff was to pay $500 additional. Is it also implied that the defendants are not to do anything unexpressed in the writing?

That we need not decide. At least, however, an inspection of this contract shows a full and complete agreement, setting forth in detail the obligations of each party. On reading it one would conclude that the reciprocal obligations of the parties were fully detailed. Nor would his opinion alter if he knew the surrounding circumstances. The presence of the ice house, even the knowledge that Mrs. Mitchill thought it objectionable would not lead to the belief that a separate agreement existed with regard to it. Were such an agreement made it would seem most natural that the inquirer should find it in the contract. Collateral in form it is found to be, but it is so closely related to the subject dealt with in the written agreement — so closely that we hold it may not be proved.

Where the line between the competent and the incompetent is narrow the citation of authorities is of slight use. Each represents the judgment of the court on the precise facts before it. How closely bound to the contract is the supposed collateral agreement is the decisive factor in each case. But reference may be made to Johnson v. Oppenheim (55 N.Y. 280, 292); Thomas v. Scutt (127 N.Y. 133); Eighmie v. Taylor (98 N.Y. 288); Stowell v. Greenwich Ins. Co. (163 N.Y. 298); Newburger v. American Surety Co. (242 N.Y. 134); Love v. Hamel (59 App. Div. 360); Daly v. Piza (105 App. Div. 496); Seitz v Brewers Refrigerating Co. (141 U.S. 510); American Locomotive Co. v. Nat. Grocery Co. (226 Mass. 314); Doyle v. Dixon (12 Allen, 576). Of these citations, Johnson v. Oppenheim and the two in the Appellate Division relate to collateral contracts said to have been the inducing cause of the main contract. They refer to leases. A similar case is Wilson v. Deen (74 N.Y. 531). All hold that an oral stipulation, said to have been the inducing cause for the subsequent execution of the lease itself, concerning some act to be done by the landlord, or some condition as to the leased premises, might not be shown. In principle they are not unlike the case before us. Attention should be called also to Taylor v. Hopper (62 N.Y. 649), where it is assumed that evidence of a parol agreement to remove a barn, which was an inducement to the sale of lots, was improper.

We do not ignore the fact that authorities may be found that would seem to support the contention of the appellant. Such are Erskine v. Adeane (L.R. 8 Ch. App. 756) and Morgan v. Griffith (L.R. 6 Exch. 70), where although there was a written lease a collateral agreement of the landlord to reduce the game was admitted. In this State Wilson v. Deen might lead to the contrary result. Neither are they approved in New Jersey (Naumberg v. Young, 15 Vroom, 331.) Nor in view of later cases in this court can Batterman v. Pierce (3 Hill, 171) be considered an authority. A line of cases in Massachusetts, of which Durkin v. Cobleigh (156 Mass. 108) is an example, have to do with collateral contracts made before a deed is given. But the fixed form of a deed makes it inappropriate to insert collateral agreements, however closely connected with the sale. This may be cause for an exception. Here we deal with the contract on the basis of which the deed to Mrs. Mitchill was given subsequently, and we confine ourselves to the question whether its terms may be modified. [The Court limited and distinguished Chapin v. Dobson, 78 N.Y. 74 (1879), where an oral warranty was permitted to be shown in a case of a written agreement for a sale of chattels.]

It is argued that what we have said is not applicable to the case as presented. The collateral agreement was made with the plaintiff. The contract of sale was with her husband and no assignment of it from him appears. Yet the deed was given to her. It is evident that here was a transaction in which she was the principal from beginning to end. We must treat the contract as if in form, as it was in fact, made by her.

Our conclusion is that the judgment of the Appellate Division and that of the Special Term should be reversed and the complaint dismissed, with costs in all courts.

LEHMAN, J. (dissenting). . . . [T]he question we must decide is whether or not, *assuming* an agreement was made for the removal of an unsightly ice house from one parcel of land as an inducement for the purchase of another parcel, the parties would ordinarily or naturally be expected to embody the agreement for the removal of the ice house from one parcel in the written agreement to convey the other parcel. Exclusion of proof of the oral agreement on the ground that it varies the contract embodied in the writing may be based only upon a finding or presumption that the written contract was intended to cover the oral negotiations for the removal of the ice house which lead up to the contract of purchase and sale. To determine what the writing was intended to cover

> the document alone will not suffice. What it was intended to cover cannot be known till we know what there was to cover. The question being whether certain subjects of negotiation were intended to be covered, we must compare the writing and the negotiations before we can determine whether they were in fact covered.

(Wigmore on Evidence [2d ed.], section 2430.)

The subject-matter of the written contract was the conveyance of land. The contract was so complete on its face that the conclusion is inevitable that the parties intended to embody in the writing all the negotiations covering at least the conveyance. The promise by the defendants to remove the ice house from other land was not connected with their obligation to convey, except that one agreement would not have been made unless the other was also made. The plaintiff's assertion of a parol agreement by the defendants to remove the ice house was completely established by the great weight of evidence. It must prevail unless that agreement was part of the agreement to convey and the entire agreement was embodied in the writing.

The fact that in this case the parol agreement is established by the overwhelming weight of evidence is, of course, not a factor which may be considered in determining the competency or legal effect of the evidence. Hardship in the particular case would not justify the court in disregarding or emasculating the general rule. It merely accentuates the outlines of our problem. The assumption that the parol agreement was made is no longer obscured by any doubts. The problem then is clearly whether the parties are presumed to have intended to render that parol agreement legally ineffective and non-existent by failure to embody it in the writing. Though we are driven to say that nothing in the written contract which fixed the terms and conditions of the stipulated conveyance suggests the existence of any further parol agreement, an inspection of the contract, though it is complete on its face in regard to the subject of the convey-ance, does not, I think, show that it was intended to embody negotiations or agreements, if any, in regard to a matter so loosely bound to the conveyance as the removal of an ice house from land not conveyed.

The rule of integration undoubtedly frequently prevents the assertion of fraudulent claims. Parties who take the precaution of embodying their oral agreements in a writing should be protected against the assertion that other terms of the same agreement were not integrated in the writing. The limits of the integration are determined by the writing, read in the light of the surrounding circumstances. A written contract, however complete, yet covers only a limited field. I do not think that in the written contract for the conveyance of land here under consideration we can find an intention to cover a field so broad as to include prior agreements, if any such were made, to do other acts on other property after the stipu-lated conveyance was made.

In each case where such a problem is presented, varying factors enter into its solution. Citation of authority in this or other jurisdictions is useless, at least without minute analysis of the facts. The analysis I have made of the decisions in this State leads me to the view that the decision of the courts below is in accordance with our own authorities and should be affirmed.

Cardozo, Ch. J., Pound, Kellogg and O'Brien, JJ., concur with An-drews, J.; Lehman, J., dissents in opinion in which Crane, J., concurs.

Judgment accordingly.

NOTE

1. Grantor and his wife convey property to the sister of the grantor and her husband. The deed of conveyance contains a clause "reserving unto the grantors herein" a ten-year option to repurchase the property on certain stated conditions. When the grantor becomes bankrupt, his trustee in bankruptcy attempts to exercise the option for the benefit of the

grantor's creditors. The grantees object, claiming that the parties to the original transaction wanted to keep the property in their family; since the option was intended to be personal, the grantees argue, it cannot be enforced by the grantor's trustee. Should parol evidence be admitted to show that the parties had such an understanding? Consult Masterson v. Sine, 68 Cal. 2d 222, 436 P.2d 561, 65 Cal. Rptr. 545 (1968). Judge Traynor's opinion contains an especially elegant statement of the policies underlying the parol evidence rule.

2. Photographs of the controversial ice house and the main residence may be found in J. Dawson, W. Harvey & S. Henderson, Cases and Comment on Contracts 427, 430 (4th ed. 1982).

UNIFORM COMMERCIAL CODE

§2-202. FINAL WRITTEN EXPRESSION: PAROL OR EXTRINSIC EVIDENCE

Terms with respect to which the confirmatory memoranda of the parties agree or which are otherwise set forth in a writing intended by the parties as a final expression of their agreement with respect to such terms as are included therein may not be contradicted by evidence of any prior agreement or of a contemporaneous oral agreement but may be explained or supplemented

(a) by course of dealing or usage of trade (Section 1-205) or by course of performance (Section 2-208); and

(b) by evidence of consistent additional terms unless the court finds the writing to have been intended also as a complete and exclusive statement of the terms agreed upon.

NOTE

1. Comment 3 to §2-202 states: "If the additional terms are such, that if agreed upon, they would certainly have been included in the document in the view of the court, then evidence of their alleged making must be kept from the trier in fact."

For a discussion of the problems that §2-202 presents from a draftsman's point of view, see Note, Contract Draftsmanship Under Article Two of the Uniform Commercial Code, 112 U. Pa. L. Rev. 564 (1964). The parol evidence rule applies only to prior and contemporaneous agreements; proof of subsequent agreements, even those that modify a completely integrated writing, is not barred by the rule. An oral modification may be unenforceable, however, if it does not comply with the

Statute of Frauds or if the parties have provided that all modifications must be in writing; see §2-209(2) and (3).

2. In Columbia Nitrogen Corp. v. Royster Co., 451 F.2d 3 (4th Cir. 1971), a seller of fertilizer and fertilizer ingredients sued to recover damages resulting from the buyer's alleged breach of a contract to purchase phosphate. The contract provided that the buyer was to purchase a minimum of 31,000 tons of phosphate per year for three years, at a stated price (subject to an escalation clause dependent upon production costs). Following execution of the contract, the market price of phosphate dropped sharply. The parties negotiated a limited price reduction; despite this, the buyer agreed to accept only a fraction of the minimum tonnage specified in the contract. At trial, the buyer offered to prove a trade usage in the fertilizer industry according to which express price and quantity terms are treated as "mere projections to be adjusted according to market forces." Id. at 7. The court concluded that the buyer's evidence was not inconsistent with the express terms of the contract and could therefore be admitted, under §2-202, for purposes of interpretive clarification. "The contract is silent about adjusting prices and quantities to reflect a declining market. It neither permits nor prohibits adjustment, and this neutrality provides a fitting occasion for recourse to usage of trade and prior dealing to supplement the contract and explain its terms." Id. at 9-10. The contract also contained an integration clause stating that it expressed "all the terms and conditions of the agreement." Id. at 10. For a spirited criticism of the *Columbia Nitrogen* case, see Kirst, Usage of Trade and Course of Dealing: Subversion of the UCC Theory, 1977 U. Ill. L. Forum 811.

DANANN REALTY CORP. v. HARRIS
5 N.Y.2d 317, 157 N.E.2d 597 (1959)

[The plaintiff's contract for the purchase of a lease on business property contained the following disclaimer clause:

> The Purchaser has examined the premises agreed to be sold and is familiar with the physical condition thereof. The Seller has not made and does not make any representations as to the physical condition, rents, leases, expenses, operation or any other matter or thing affecting or related to the aforesaid premises, except as is herein specifically set forth, and the Purchaser hereby expressly acknowledges that no such representations have been made, and the Purchaser further acknowledges that it has inspected the premises and agrees to take the premises "as is". . . neither party relying upon any statement or representation, not embodied in this contract. . . .

Alleging that he was induced to enter into the contract because of defendant's fraudulent oral misrepresentations as to the operating expenses and the profits, plaintiff affirming the contract, seeks damages for fraud.

The Court of Appeals, Burke, J. speaking for a majority of six, though accepting as true plaintiff's statement that in the case of negotiations defendants were guilty of the oral misrepresentations, dismissed the complaint (thereby reinstating the Special Term) holding that the disclaimer being specific and not a vague and general merger clause barred as a matter of law any allegation or showing of justifiable reliance.]

BURKE, J. . . . . In this case, of course, the plaintiff made a representation in the contract that it was not relying on specific representations not embodied in the contract, while, it now asserts, it was in fact relying on such oral representations. Plaintiff admits then that it is guilty of deliberately misrepresenting to the seller its true intention. To condone this fraud would place the purchaser in a favored position. (Cf. Riggs v. Palmer, 115 N.Y. 506, 511, 512.) This is particularly so, where, as here, the purchaser confirms the contract, but seeks damages. If the plaintiff has made a bad bargain he cannot avoid it in this manner.

If the language here used is not sufficient to estop a party from claiming that he entered the contract because of fraudulent representations, then no language can accomplish that purpose. To hold otherwise would be to say that it is impossible for two businessmen dealing at arm's length to agree that the buyer is not buying in reliance on any representations of the seller as to a particular fact.

Accordingly, the order of the Appellate Division should be reversed and that of Special Term reinstated, without costs. The question certified should be answered in the negative.

FULD, J. (dissenting). If a party has actually induced another to enter into a contract by means of fraud — and so the complaint before us alleges — I conceive that language may not be devised to shield him from the consequences of such fraud. The law does not temporize with trickery or duplicity, and this court, after having weighed the advantages of certainty in contractual relations against the harm and injustice which result from fraud, long ago unequivocally declared that

> a party who has perpetrated a fraud upon his neighbor may [not] . . . contract with him in the very instrument by means of which it was perpetrated, for immunity against its consequence, close his mouth from complaining of it and bind him never to seek redress. Public policy and morality are both ignored if such an agreement can be given effect in a court of justice. The maxim that fraud vitiates every transaction would no longer be the rule but the exception.

(Bridger v. Goldsmith, 143 N.Y. 424, 428). It was a concern for similar considerations of policy which persuaded Massachusetts to repudiate the contrary rule which it had initially espoused. "The same public policy that in general sanctions the avoidance of a promise obtained by deceit," wrote that state's Supreme Judicial Court in Bates v. Southgate (308 Mass. 170, 182),

> strikes down all attempts to circumvent that policy by means of contractual devices. In the realm of fact it is entirely possible for a party knowingly to agree that no representations have been made to him, while at the same time believing and relying upon representations which in fact have been made and in fact are false but for which he would not have made the agreement. To deny this possibility is to ignore the frequent instances in everyday experience where parties accept . . . and act upon agreements containing . . . exculpatory clauses in one form or another, but where they do so, nevertheless, in reliance upon the honesty of supposed friends, the plausible and disarming statements of salesmen, or the customary course of business. To refuse relief would result in opening the door to a multitude of frauds and in thwarting the general policy of the law.

It is impossible, on either principle or reasoning, to distinguish the present case from the many others which this court has decided. (See, e.g., Bridger v. Goldsmith, 143 N.Y. 424, 428, *supra*, Jackson v. State of New York, 210 App. Div. 115, *affd.* 241 N.Y 563; Ernst Iron Works v. Duralith Corp., 270 N.Y. 165, 169; Angerosa v. White Co., 248 App. Div. 425, 431, *affd.* 275 N.Y. 524; Sabo v. Delman, 3 N.Y.2d 155, 162; Crowell-Collier Pub. Co. v. Josefowitz, 5 N.Y.2d 998, also decided today.) As far back as 1894, we decided, in the *Bridger* case (143 N.Y. 424, *supra*), that the plaintiff was not prevented from bringing an action for fraud, based on oral misrepresentations, even though the written contract provided that it was "understood and agreed" that the defendant seller had not made, ". . . for the purpose of inducing the sale . . . or the making of this agreement . . . any statements or representations . . . other than" the single one therein set forth (pp. 426-427). And, just today, we are holding, in the *Crowell-Collier Publishing* case, that the plaintiffs were not barred from suing the defendants for fraud in inducing them to make the contract, despite its recital that

". . . This Agreement constitutes the entire understanding between the parties, [and] was not induced by any representations . . . not herein contained."

In addition, in Jackson v. State of New York (210 App. Div. 115, *affd.* 241 N.Y. 563, *supra*), the contract provided that

> the contractor (plaintiff's predecessor in interest) agreed that he had satisfied himself by his own investigation regarding all the conditions of the work to be done and that his conclusion to enter into the contract was based solely upon such investigation and not upon any information or data imparted by the State.

It was held that even this explicit disavowal of reliance did not bar the plaintiff from recovery. In answering the argument that the provision prevented proof either of misrepresentation by the defendant or reliance on the part of the plaintiff, the Appellate Division, in an opinion approved by this court, wrote:

> A party to a contract cannot, by misrepresentation of a material fact, induce the other party to the contract to enter into it to his damage and then protect himself from the legal effect of such misrepresentation by inserting in the contract a clause to the effect that he is not to be held liable for the misrepresentation which induced the other party to enter into the contract. The effect of misrepresentation and fraud cannot be thus easily avoided. (pp. 119-120)

Although the clause in the contract before us may be differently worded from those in the agreements involved in the other cases decided in this court, it undoubtedly reflects the same thought and meaning, and the reasoning and the principles which the court deemed controlling in those cases are likewise controlling in this one. Their application, it seems plain to me, compels the conclusion that the complaint herein should be sustained and the plaintiff accorded a trial of its allegations.

It is said, however, that the provision in this contract differs from those heretofore considered in that it embodies a specific and deliberate exclusion of a particular subject. The quick answer is that the clause now before us is not of such a sort. On the contrary, instead of being limited, it is all-embracing, encompassing every representation that a seller could possibly make about the property being sold and, instead of representing a special term of a bargain, is essentially "boiler plate." (See Contract of Sale, Standard N.Y.B.T.U. Form 8041; Bicks, Contracts for the Sale of Realty [1956 ed.], pp. 79-80, 94-95.) The more elaborate verbiage in the present contract cannot disguise the fact that the language which is said to immunize the defendants from their own fraud is no more specific than the general merger clause in Sabo v. Delman (3 N.Y.2d 155, *supra*) and far less specific than the provision dealt with in the *Jackson* case (210 App. Div. 115, *affd.* 241 N.Y. 563, *supra*) or in *Crowell-Collier*.

In any event, though, I cannot believe that the outcome of a case such as this, in which the defendant is charged with fraud, should turn on the particular language employed in the contract. As Judge Augustus Hand, writing for the Federal Court of Appeals, observed,

> the ingenuity of draftsmen is sure to keep pace with the demands of wrong-doers, and if a deliberate fraud may be shielded by a clause in a contract that the writing contains every representation made by way of inducement, or that utterances shown to be untrue were not an inducement to the agreement,

a fraudulent seller would have a simple method of obtaining immunity for his misconduct. (Arnold v. National Aniline & Chem. Co., 20 F.2d 364, 369.) . . .

Contrary to the intimation in the court's opinion (p. 323), the nonreliance clause cannot possibly operate as an estoppel against the plaintiff. Essentially equitable in nature, the principle of estoppel is to be invoked to prevent fraud and injustice, not to further them. The statement that the representations in question were not made was, according to the complaint, false to the defendant's knowledge. Surely, the perpetrator of a fraud cannot close the lips of his victim and deny him the right to state the facts as they actually exist. Indeed, the contention that a person, such as the defendant herein, could urge an estoppel was considered and emphatically disposed of in Bridger v. Goldsmith with this statement:

> The question now is whether [the no-representation noninducement clause] can be given the effect claimed for it by the learned counsel for the defendant, to preclude the plaintiff from alleging fraud in the sale and pursuing in the courts the remedies which the law gives in such cases. *It cannot operate by way of estoppel for the obvious reason that the statements were false to the defendant's knowledge.* He may, indeed, have relied upon its force and efficacy to protect him from the consequences of his own fraud, but he certainly could not have relied upon the truth of any statement in it. A mere device of the guilty party to a contract intended to shield himself from the results of his own fraud, practiced upon the other party, cannot well be elevated to the dignity and importance of an equitable estoppel.

(143 N.Y. 424, 427-428, emphasis supplied; see, also, Angerosa v. White Co., 248 App. Div. 425, 433-434, *affd.* 275 N.Y. 524, *supra*).

The rule heretofore applied by this court presents no obstacle to honest business dealings, and dishonest transactions ought not to receive judicial protection. The clause in the contract before us may lend support to the defense and render the plaintiff's task of establishing its claim more difficult, but it should not be held to bar institution of an action for fraud. Whether the defendants made the statements attributed to them and, if they did, whether the plaintiff relied upon them, whether, in other words, the defendants were guilty of fraud, are questions of fact not capable of determination on the pleadings alone. The plaintiff is entitled to its day in court.

Chief Judge Conway and Judges Desmond, Dye, Froessel and Van Voorhis concur with Judge Burke; Judge Fuld dissents in a separate opinion.

Order reversed, etc.

NOTE

1. The *Danann* case is criticized in Recent Decisions, 59 Colum. L. Rev. 525 (1959); Note, 45 Cornell L.Q. 360 (1960). Compare Crowell-

Collier Pub. Co. v. Josefowitz, 9 Misc. 2d 613, 170 N.Y.S.2d 373 (Sup. Ct. 1957), *aff'd mem.*, 5 A.D.2d 987, 173 N.Y.S.2d 992 (1958), *aff'd mem.*, 5 N.Y.2d 998, 157 N.E.2d 730, 184 N.Y.S.2d 859 (1959).

2. Suppose the plaintiff had sought to rescind the contract. Same result? When a person makes a contract, he does so on the basis of many different assumptions about the world, himself, and his contractual partner. Any of these assumptions may prove false; each, therefore, entails some risk. The law permits the parties to allocate certain of these risks in whatever way they wish. Should the risk that one has been deliberately defrauded by the other party be freely allocable in this way? Can the disclaimer at issue in the *Danann* case be viewed as an attempt to shift the risk of fraud from the seller to the buyer? Is Judge Fuld denying that this is what the parties intended or is he asserting that the right to sue for fraud is inalienable?

3. A promises in writing to deliver Blackacre to his daughter, B. The writing is integrated and states that the property is being conveyed in consideration of $1,000, receipt of which is acknowledged. May A prove that he has not received the money and that his transfer of the property was intended to be a gift? See Restatement Second §218, Illus. 3.

4. In International Milling Co. v. Hachmeister, Inc., 380 Pa. 407, 110 A.2d 186 (1955), the plaintiff sold a number of carloads of flour to defendant under standard form contracts, used in the milling and baking industries and approved by the Millers' National Federation and the American Bakers' Association, the final provision being, "This Contract constitutes the complete agreement between the parties hereto; and cannot be changed in any manner except in writing subscribed by Buyer and Seller or their duly authorized officers." The standard form carried no specification as to the purity of the flour. The buyer objected to this omission before signing the contract and insisted that the written specifications prescribed by the American Institute of Baking for flour intended for human consumption should be incorporated in the contract. The seller refused to make any change in the standard form since "these milling contracts . . . are uniform all over the country and they didn't want to violate the normal contract." He agreed, however, to take care of the matter by letter. Thereupon, the buyer gave his written order for flour, dated September 11, stating that the flour must be guaranteed to comply with the specifications. On that day the seller accepted the buyer's order by telegram. The following day, the seller forwarded the printed contract form, containing none of these specifications; but he also sent the letter he had promised assuring delivery of the flour in accordance with the specifications. The buyer executed the contract form, and subsequently executed four other similar forms for additional orders. After accepting some of the flour, the buyer rejected several carloads because the flour did not meet the purity specifications. The seller sued for damages and the trial court directed a verdict for the seller holding that the

evidence as to the qualification of the standard contract was inadmissible by reason of the parol evidence rule; the court en banc denied a motion for a new trial. The buyer appealed. What result? Professor Corbin's comments on the case are instructive; see 3 Corbin §582.

HURST v. LAKE & CO., INC., 141 Ore. 306, 16 P.2d 627 (1932): Plaintiff and defendant made a contract for the sale of horse meat scraps. According to the terms of the contract, if any of the scraps tested at less than "50% protein," the buyer was to receive a discount of $5.00 per ton. Roughly 170 tons of the scraps delivered by the seller contained less than 50 percent protein; of these 170 tons, 140 contained between 49.53 and 49.96 percent protein. The buyer took a $5.00 discount on the entire 170 tons, contrary to the seller's claim that he was entitled to do so on 30 tons only. When the buyer refused to pay the balance allegedly due, the seller brought an action against him. In his complaint the seller alleged "[t]hat at the time the written contract heretofore referred to for the sale of horse meat scraps was entered into on or about the 20th day of March, 1930, both plaintiff and defendant then were, and for some time prior thereto had been, engaged in the business of buying and selling horse meat scraps; that at the time said contract was entered into there was a custom and usage of trade in said business well known to both plaintiff and defendant as to the meaning of the terms 'minimum 50 per cent protein' and 'less than 50 per cent protein' used in the agreement between plaintiff and defendant. That by virtue of said custom so prevailing in said business of buying and selling horse meat scraps it was well known and understood among all members of the trade, including both plaintiff and defendant, that the terms 'minimum 50 per cent protein' and 'less than 50 per cent protein' when used in a contract for the sale of horse meat scraps with reference to a test of its protein content, meant that a protein content of not less than 49.5 per cent was equal to and the same as a content of 50 per cent protein."

The trial court granted the buyer's motion for judgment on the pleadings, but the Oregon Supreme Court reversed. In his opinion, Judge Rossman had this to say:

"The flexibility of or multiplicity in the meaning of words is the principal source of difficulty in the interpretation of language. Words are the conduits by which thoughts are communicated, yet scarcely any of them have such a fixed and single meaning that they are incapable of denoting more than one thought. In addition to the multiplicity in meaning of words set forth in the dictionaries there are the meanings imparted to them by trade customs, local uses, dialects, telegraphic codes, etc. One meaning crowds a word full of significance, while another almost empties the utterance of any import. The various groups above indicated are constantly amplifying our language; in fact, they are developing what may be called languages of their own. Thus one is justified in saying that the language of the dictionaries is not the only language spoken in America. For instance, the word, "thousand" as commonly used has a very specific meaning; it denotes ten hundreds or fifty scores, but the language of the various trades and localities has assigned to it meanings quite different from that just mentioned. Thus in the bricklaying trade a contract which fixes the bricklayer's compensation at "$5.25 a thousand" does not contemplate that he need lay actually one thousand bricks in order to earn $5.25 but that he should build a wall of a certain size: Brunold v. Glasser, 25 Misc. 285 (52 N.Y.S. 1021); Walker v. Syms, 118 Mich. 183 (76 N.W. 320). In the lumber industry a contract requiring the delivery of 4,000 shingles will be fulfilled by the delivery of only 2,500 when it appears that by trade custom two packs of a certain size are regarded as 1,000 shingles and that, hence, the delivery of eight packs fulfills the contract, even though they contain only 2,500 shingles by actual count: Soutier v. Kellerman, 18 Mo. 509. And where the custom of locality considers 100 dozen as constituting a thousand, one who has 19,200 rabbits upon a warren under an agreement for their sale at the price of 60 pounds for each thousand rabbits will be paid for only 16,000 rabbits: Smith v. Wilson, 3 Barn. & Adol. 728. Numerous other instances could be readily cited showing the manner in which the meaning of words has contracted, expanded or otherwise altered by local usage, trade custom, dialect influence, code agreement, etc. In fact, it is no novelty to find legislative enactments preceded by glossaries or brief dictionaries defining the meaning of the words employed in the act. Technical treaties dealing with aeronautics, the radio, engineering, etc., generally contain similar glossaries defining the meaning of many of the words employed by the craft. A glance at these glossaries readily shows that the different sciences and trades, in addition to coining words of their own, appropriate common words and assign to them new meanings. Thus it must be evident that one cannot understand accurately the language of such sciences and trades without knowing the peculiar meaning attached to the words which they use. It is said that a court in construing the language of the parties must put itself into the shoes of the parties. That alone would not suffice; it must also adopt their vernacular. . . .

"The defendant cites numerous cases in many of which the courts held that when a contract is expressed in language which is not ambiguous upon its face the court will receive no evidence of usage but will place upon the words of the parties their common meaning; in other words, in those decisions the courts ran the words of the parties through a judicial sieve whose meshes were incapable of retaining anything but the common meaning of the words, and which permitted the meaning which the parties had placed upon them to run away as waste material. Surely those courts did not believe that words are always used in their orthodox sense. The rulings must have been persuaded by other considerations. The rule which rejects evidence of custom has the advantage of simplicity; it protects the writing from attack by some occasional individual who will seek to employ perjured testimony in proof of alleged custom; and if one can believe that the parol evidence rule is violated when common meaning is rejected in favor of special meaning, then the above rule serves the purpose of the parol evidence rule. Without setting forth the manner in which we came to our conclusion, we state that none of these reasons appeals to us as sufficient to exclude evidence of custom and assign to the words their common meaning only, even though the instrument is non-ambiguous upon its face. . . .

". . . We believe that it is safe to assume, in the absence of evidence to the contrary, that when tradesmen employ trade terms they attach to them their trade significance. If, when they write their trade terms into their contracts, they mean to strip the terms of their special significance and demote them to their common import, it would seem reasonable to believe that they would so state in their agreement. Otherwise, they would refrain from using the trade term and express themselves in other language. We quote from Nicol v. Pittsvein Coal Co., 269 Fed. 968:

> "Indeed, when tradesmen say or write anything, they are perhaps without present thought on the subject, writing on top of a mass of habits or usages which they take as a matter of course. So (with Professor Williston) we think that anyone contracting with knowledge of a usage will naturally say nothing about the matter unless desirous of excluding its operation; if he does wish to exclude he will say so in express terms. Williston, Contracts, §653.

"Nothing in the contract repels the meaning assigned by the trade to the two above terms unless the terms themselves reject it. But if these terms repel the meaning which usage has attached to them, then every trade term would deny its own meaning. We reject this contention as being without merit. . . ."

NOTE

1. Compare Hartford Mining Co. v. Cambria Mining Co., 80 Mich. 491, 45 N.W. 351 (1890); Rasmussen v. New York Life Insurance Co., 267 N.Y. 129, 195 N.E. 821 (1935). Even " 'white' may be interpreted as black, where by trade usage 'white selvage' meant a selvage that was relatively dark, Mitchell v. Henry, 15 Ch. D. 181 (1880), reversing Sir George Jessel who declared that 'nobody could convince *him* that black was white'." 3 Corbin §544, n.96. See also Restatement Second §220.

2. Suppose the buyer in the *Hurst* case had been a newcomer to the horse meat business. Same result? See Heggblade-Marquleas-Tenneco, Inc. v. Sunshine Biscuit, Inc., 59 Cal. App. 3d 948, 131 Cal. Rptr. 183

(1976). If ignorance of a trade custom does not bar its use as an interpretive aid, newcomers will have an incentive to master the relevant commercial practices as quickly as possible; if ignorance *is* a bar, those who
deal with newcomers will have an incentive to make sure that important
trade customs are understood by both parties. Which approach seems
preferable?

3. "Think of the tools in a tool-box: there is a hammer, pliers, a saw, a
screw-driver, a rule, a glue-pot, glue, nails and screws. — The functions
of words are as diverse as the functions of these objects. (And in both
cases there are similarities.)

"Of course, what confuses us is the uniform appearance of words
when we hear them spoken or meet them in script and print. For their
application is not presented to us so clearly. Especially when we are doing
philosophy!" L. Wittgenstein, Philosophical Investigations, §11 (G. Ans-
combe, trans. 1958).

ZELL v. AMERICAN SEATING CO.
138 F.2d 641 (2d Cir. 1943)

Action by Lucian T. Zell against the American Seating Company, a
New Jersey corporation, for commission alleged to have been earned in
obtaining contracts for defendant. From a summary judgment dismissing
the complaint, 50 F. Supp. 543, the plaintiff appeals.

Reversed and remanded.

Before L. Hand, Swan, and Frank, Circuit Judges.

FRANK, Circuit Judge. On defendant's motion for summary judgment,
the trial court, after considering the pleadings and affidavits, entered
judgment dismissing the action. From that judgment, plaintiff appeals.

On a motion for summary judgment, where the facts are in dispute, a
judgment can properly be entered against the plaintiff only if, on the
undisputed facts, he has no valid claim; if, then, any fact asserted by the
plaintiff is contradicted by the defendant, the facts as stated by the plaintiff must, on such a motion, be taken as true. Accordingly for the purpose
of our decision here, we take the facts as follows:

Plaintiff, by a letter addressed to defendant company dated October
17, 1941, offered to make efforts to procure for defendant contracts for
manufacturing products for national defense or war purposes, in consideration of defendant's agreement to pay him $1,000 per month for a three
months' period if he were unsuccessful in his efforts, but, if he were
successful, to pay him a further sum in an amount not to be less than 3%
nor more than 8% of the "purchase price of said contracts." On October
31, 1941, at a meeting in Grand Rapids, Michigan, between plaintiff and
defendant's President, the latter, on behalf of his company, orally made
an agreement with plaintiff substantially on the terms set forth in plain-

tiff's letter, one of the terms being that mentioned in plaintiff's letter as to commissions; it was orally agreed that the exact amount within the two percentages was to be later determined by the parties. After this agreement was made, the parties executed, in Grand Rapids, a written instrument dated October 31, 1941, appearing on its face to embody a complete agreement between them; but that writing omitted the provision of their agreement that plaintiff, if successful, was to receive a bonus varying from three to eight per cent; instead, there was inserted in the writing a clause that the $1,000 per month "will be full compensation, but the company may, if it desires, pay you something in the nature of a bonus." However, at the time when they executed this writing, the parties orally agreed that the previous oral agreement was still their actual contract, that the writing was deliberately erroneous with respect to plaintiff's commissions, and that the misstatement in that writing was made solely in order to "avoid any possible stigma which might result" from putting such a provision "in writing," the defendant's President stating that "his fears were based upon the criticism of contingent fee contracts." Nothing in the record discloses whose criticism the defendant feared; but plaintiff, in his brief, says that defendant was apprehensive because adverse comments had been made in Congress of such contingent-fee arrangements in connection with war contracts. The parties subsequently executed further writings extending, for two three-month periods, their "agreement under date of October 31, 1941." Through plaintiff's efforts and expenditures of large sums for traveling expenses, defendant, within this extended period, procured contracts between it and companies supplying aircraft to the government for war purposes, the aggregate purchase price named in said contracts being $5,950,000. The defendant has refused to pay the plaintiff commissions thereon in the agreed amount (i.e., not less than three per-cent) but has paid him merely $8,950 (at the rate of $1,000 a month) and has offered him, by way of settlement, an additional sum of $9,000 which he has refused to accept as full payment.

Defendant argues that the summary judgment was proper on the ground that, under the parol evidence rule, the court could not properly consider as relevant anything except the writing of October 31, 1941, which appears on its face to set forth a complete and unambiguous agreement between the parties. If defendant on this point is in error, then, if the plaintiff at a trial proves the facts as alleged by him, and no other defenses are successfully interposed, he will be entitled to a sum equal to 3% of $5,950,000.

Were the parol evidence rule a rule of evidence, we could decide this question without reference to state court decisions. But the federal courts have held, in line with what has become the customary doctrine in most states, that it is a rule of substantive law, i.e., the extrinsic proof is excluded because no claim or defense can be founded upon it. The acid test of whether the rule is substantive or procedural would seem to be whether, if extrinsic evidence is received without objection, it can be regarded as material and made the basis of the court's decision; if it can, then, presumably the rule is like the hearsay rule. But in Higgs v. De Maziroff, 263 N.Y. 473, 189 N.E. 555, 92 A.L.R. 807, the court said that if extrinsic evidence is thus received and if the attention of the trial court is not otherwise called to the parol evidence rule, that evidence becomes relevant and that no complaint because of the reception of that evidence can be raised on appeal. It might therefore be argued that, in New York, the parol evidence rule is procedural, with the consequence that, although the contract was made in Michigan, the New York parol evidence decisions would govern. But the court, in Higgs v. De Maziroff, explicitly stated that the rule creates a substantive defense and, in effect, held that, like many other substantive defenses, it is "waived" if not properly raised in the trial court; in other words, "waivability" is not a unique quality of procedural errors. The substantive character of the rule, although perhaps shadowy, still exists in New York. It seems clear then that, for purposes of conflict of laws, New York would consider that rule as not procedural. Consequently, we must here apply the law of Michigan.

It is not surprising that confusion results from a rule called "the parol evidence rule" which is not a rule of evidence, which relates to extrinsic proof whether written or parol, and which has been said to be virtually no rule at all. As Thayer said of it, "Few things are darker than this, or fuller of subtle difficulties." The rule is often loosely and confusingly stated as if, once the evidence establishes that the parties executed a writing containing what appears to be a complete and unambiguous agreement, then no evidence may be received of previous or contemporaneous oral understandings which contradict or vary its terms. But, under the parol evidence rule correctly stated, such a writing does not acquire that dominating position if it has been proved by extrinsic evidence that the parties did not intend it to be an exclusive authoritative memorial of their agreement. If they did intend it to occupy that position, their secret mutual intentions as to the terms of the contract or its meaning are usually irrelevant, so that parties who exchange promises may be bound, at least "at law" as distinguished from "equity," in a way which neither intended, since their so-called "objective" intent governs. When, however, they have previously agreed that their written promises are not to bind them, that agreement controls and no legal obligations flow from the writing. It has been held virtually everywhere, when the question has arisen that (certainly in the absence of any fraudulent or illegal purpose) a purported written agreement, which the parties designed as a mere sham, lacks legal efficacy, and that extrinsic parol or other writing evidence will always be received on that issue. So the highest court of Michigan has several times held. It has gone further: In Woodard v. Walker, 192 Mich. 188, 158 N.W. 846, that court specifically enforced against the seller an oral agreement for the sale of land which had been followed by a sham written agreement, for sale of the same land at a higher price, intended to deceive the seller's children who were jealous of the buyer.

We need not here consider where third persons have relied on the delusive agreement to their detriment or cases in other jurisdictions (we find none in Michigan) where the mutual purpose of the deception was fraudulent or illegal. For the instant case involves no such elements. As noted above, the pleadings and affidavits are silent as to the matter of whom the parties here intended to mislead, and we cannot infer a fraudulent or illegal purpose. Even the explanation contained in plaintiff's brief discloses no fraud or illegality: No law existed rendering illegal the commission provision of the oral agreement which the parties here omitted from the sham writing; while it may be undesirable that citizens should prepare documents so contrived as to spoil the scent of legislators bent on proposing new legislation, yet such conduct is surely not unlawful and does not deserve judicial castigation as immoral or fraudulent; the courts should not erect standards of morality so far above the customary. Woodard v. Walker leaves no doubt that the Michigan courts would hold the parol evidence rule inapplicable to the facts as we have interpreted them.

Candor compels the admission that, were we enthusiastic devotees of that rule, we might so construe the record as to bring this case within the rule's scope; we could dwell on the fact that plaintiff, in his complaint, states that the acceptance of his offer "was partly oral and partly contained" in the October 31 writing, and could then hold that, as that writing unambiguously covers the item of commissions, the plaintiff is trying to use extrinsic evidence to "contradict" the writing. But the plaintiff's affidavit, if accepted as true and liberally construed, makes it plain that the parties deliberately intended the October 31 writing to be a misleading, untrue, statement of their real agreement.

We thus construe the record because we do not share defendant's belief that the rule is so beneficent, so promotive of the administration of justice, and so necessary to business stability, that it should be given the widest possible application. The truth is that the rule does but little to achieve the ends it supposedly serves. Although seldom mentioned in modern decisions, the most important motive for perpetuation of the rule is distrust of juries, fear that they cannot adequately cope with, or will be unfairly prejudiced by, conflicting "parol" testimony. If the rule were frankly recognized as primarily a device to control juries, its shortcomings would become obvious, since it is not true that the execution by the parties of an unambiguous writing, "facially complete," bars extrinsic proof. The courts admit such "parol" testimony (other than the parties' statements of what they meant by the writing) for a variety of purposes: to show "all the operative usages" and "all the surrounding circumstances prior to and contemporaneous with the making" of a writing; to show an agreed oral condition, nowhere referred to in the writing, that the writing was not to be binding until some third person approved; to show that a deed, absolute on its face, is but a mortgage. These and numerous other exceptions have removed most of that insulation of the jury from "oral" testimony which the rule is said to provide.

The rule, then, does relatively little to deserve its much advertised virtue of reducing the dangers of successful fraudulent recoveries and defenses brought about through perjury. The rule is too small a hook to catch such a leviathan. Moreover, if at times it does prevent a person from winning, by lying witnesses, a lawsuit which he should lose, it also, at times, by shutting out the true facts, unjustly aids other persons to win lawsuits they should and would lose, were the suppressed evidence known to the courts. Exclusionary rules, which frequently result in injustice, have always been defended — as was the rule, now fortunately extinct, excluding testimony of the parties to an action — with the danger-of-perjury argument. Perjury, of course, is pernicious and doubtless much of it is used in our courts daily with unfortunate success. The problem of avoiding its efficacious use should be met head on. Were it consistently met in an indirect manner — in accordance with the viewpoint of the adulators of the parol evidence rule — by wiping out substantive rights provable only through oral testimony, we would have wholesale destruction of familiar causes of action such as, for instance, suits for personal injury and for enforcement of wholly oral agreements.

The parol evidence rule is lauded as an important aid in the judicial quest for "objectivity," a quest which aims to avoid that problem the solution of which was judicially said in the latter part of the fifteenth century to be beyond even the powers of Satan — the discovery of the inner thoughts of man. The policy of stern refusal to consider subjective intention, prevalent in the centralized common law courts of that period, later gave way; in the latter part of the 18th and the early part of the 19th century, the recession from that policy went far, and there was much talk of the "meeting of the minds" in the formation of contracts, or giving effect to the actual "will" of the contracting parties. The obstacles to learning the actual intention have, more recently, induced a partial reversion to the older view. Today a court generally restricts its attention to the outward behavior of the parties: the meaning of their acts is not what either party or both parties intended but the meaning which a "reasonable man" puts on those acts; the expression of mutual assent, not the assent itself, is usually the essential element. We now speak of "externality," insisting on judicial consideration of only those manifestations of intention which are public ("open to the scrutiny and knowledge of the community") and not private ("secreted in the heart" of a person). This objective approach is of great value, for a legal system can be more effectively administered if legal rights and obligations ordinarily attach only to overt conduct. Moreover, to call the standard "objective" and candidly confess that the actual intention is not the guiding factor serves desirably to high-light the fact that much of the "law of contracts" has nothing whatever to do with what the parties contemplated but consists of rules — founded on considerations of public policy — by which the courts impose on the contracting parties obligations of which the parties were often unaware; this "objective" perspective discloses that the voluntary act of entering into a contract creates a jural "relation" or "status" much in the same way as does being married or holding a public office.

But we should not demand too much of this concept of "objectivity"; like all useful concepts it becomes a thought-muddler if its limitations are disregarded. We can largely rid ourselves of concern with the subjective reactions of the parties; when, however, we test their public behavior by inquiring how it appears to the "reasonable man," we must recognize, unless we wish to fool ourselves, that although one area of subjectivity has been conquered, another remains unsubdued. For instance, under the parol evidence rule, the standard of interpretation of a written contract is usually "the meaning that would be attached to" it "by a *reasonably intelligent person* acquainted with all operative usages and knowing all the circumstances prior to, and contemporaneous with, the making" of the contract, "other than oral statements by the parties of what they intended it to mean." We say that "the objective viewpoint of a third person is used." But where do we find that "objective" third person? We ask judges or juries to discover that "objective viewpoint" — through their own subjective processes. Being but human, their beliefs cannot be objectified, in the sense of being standardized. Doubtless, there is some moderate approximation to objectivity, that is, to uniformity of beliefs, among judges — men with substantially similar training — although less than is sometimes supposed. But no one can seriously maintain that such uniformity exists among the multitude of jurymen, men with the greatest conceivable variety of training and background. When juries try cases, objectivity is largely a mirage; most of the objectivity inheres in the words of the "reasonable man" standard which the judges, often futilely, admonish juries to apply to the evidence. Certain aspects of subjectivity common to all men seem to have been successfully eliminated in the field of science through the "relativity theory" — which might better be called the "anti-relativity" or "absolute" theory. But equal success has not attended the anti-relativity or objective theory in the legal field. Perhaps nine-tenths of legal uncertainty is caused by uncertainty as to what courts will find, on conflicting evidence, to be the facts of cases. Early in the history of our legal institutions, litigants strongly objected to a determination of the facts by mere fallible human beings. A man, they felt, ought to be allowed to demonstrate the facts "by supernatural means, by some such process as the ordeal or the judicial combat; God may be for him, though his neighbors be against him." We have accepted the "rational" method of trial based on evidence but the longing persists for some means of counter-acting the fallibility of the triers of the facts. Mechanical devices, like the parol evidence rule, are symptoms of that longing, a longing particularly strong when juries participate in trials. But a mechanical device like the parol evidence rule cannot satisfy that longing, especially because the injustice of applying the rule rigidly has led to its being riddled with exceptions.

Those exceptions have, too, played havoc with the contention that business stability depends upon that rule, that, as one court put it "the tremendous but closely adjusted machinery of modern business cannot function at all without" the assurance afforded by the rule and that, "if such assurance were removed today from our law, general disaster would result. . . ." We are asked to believe that the rule enables businessmen, advised by their lawyers, to rely with indispensable confidence on written contracts unimpeachable by oral testimony. In fact, seldom can a conscientious lawyer advise his client, about to sign an agreement, that, should the client become involved in litigation relating to that agreement, one of the many exceptions to the rule will not permit the introduction of uncertainty-producing oral testimony. As Corbin says, "That rule has so many exceptions that only with difficulty can it be correctly stated in the form of a rule." One need but thumb the pages of Wigmore, Williston, or the Restatement of Contracts to see how illusory is the certainty that the rule supplies. "Collateral parol agreements contradicting a writing are inadmissible," runs the rule as ordinarily stated; but in the application of that standard there exists, as Williston notes, "no final test which can be applied with unvarying regularity." Wigmore more bluntly says that only vague generalizations are possible, since the application of the rule,

> resting as it does on the parties' intent, can properly be made only after a comparison of the kind of transaction, the terms of the document, and the circumstances of the parties. . . . Such is the complexity of circumstances and the variety of documentary phraseology, and so minute the indicia of intent, that one ruling can seldom be controlling authority or even of utility for a subsequent one.

The recognized exceptions to the rule demonstrate strikingly that business can endure even when oral testimony competes with written instruments. If business stability has not been ruined by the deed-mortgage exception, or because juries may hear witnesses narrate oral understandings that written contracts were not to be operative except on the performance of extrinsic conditions, it is unlikely that commercial disaster would follow even if legislatures abolished the rule in its entirety.

In sum, a rule so leaky cannot fairly be described as a stout container of legal certainty. John Chipman Gray, a seasoned practical lawyer, expressed grave doubts concerning the reliance of businessmen on legal precedents generally. If they rely on the parol evidence rule in particular, they will often be duped. It has been seriously questioned whether in fact they do so to any considerable extent. We see no good reason why we should strain to interpret the record facts here to bring them within such a rule.

Reversed and remanded.

AMERICAN SEATING CO. v. ZELL

322 U.S. 709, 64 S. Ct. 1053, 88 L. Ed. 1552 (1944)

May 8, 1944. PER CURIAM. In this case two members of the Court think that the judgment of the Circuit Court of Appeals should be affirmed. Seven are of opinion that the judgment should be reversed and the judgment of the District Court affirmed — four because proof of the contract alleged in respondent's affidavits on the motion for summary judgment is precluded by the applicable state parol evidence rule, and three because the contract is contrary to public policy and void, see Tool Company v. Norris, 2 Wall., 45, 54, 17 L. Ed. 868; Hazelton v. Sheckells, 202 U.S. 71, 79, 26 S. Ct. 567, 568, 50 L. Ed. 939, 6 Ann. Cas. 217; Executive Order No. 9001, Tit. II, par. 5, 6 Fed. Reg. 6788, 50 U.S.C.A. Appendix §611 note; War Department Procurement Regulations, 10 Code Fed. Reg. (Cum. Supp.) sec. 81.1181. The judgment of the Circuit Court of Appeals is reversed.

CHAPTER 8

Reality and Illusion (Herein of the Doctrines of Mistake, Impossibility, and Frustration)

Section 1. Introductory Note

Any contract reflects an infinite series of assumptions made by the contracting parties about the nature of the real world. A contract that contemplates future performance reflects not only assumptions as to the state of the real world now but predictions as to what that state will be next week or next month or next year. Only an infinitesimal fraction of these assumptions ever comes to the conscious attention of the parties; as with an iceberg, the great bulk of the contractual construct lies beneath the surface. This self-evident proposition remains true even if the contractual agreement is memorialized by a carefully drawn writing, even if the writing is drafted by the most gun-shy of lawyers. For every contingency that can be identified and dealt with, a hundred others will escape detection. And, as any experienced contract draftsman knows, specificity soon becomes a self-defeating game.

The assumptions or predictions on which the contract rests will often prove to be false. The private world of the contract does not correspond with the objective universe. What was assumed to be possible was in fact impossible. What had been expected to happen did not happen. What did happen was unexpected. By the time the truth has been revealed, one of the parties, or both of them, may have incurred costs, in preparation for performance of the contract or in reliance on its being performed, which will represent a dead loss if it is not performed. The case will frequently be that, in the light of the revealed facts, performance of the contract (or the payment of damages in lieu of performance) will represent an unanticipated benefit to one of the parties at the cost of an equally unanticipated loss to the other. In such a situation the party to whose advantage the situation has turned will naturally insist on performance or damages. The disadvantaged party will plead that he would never have entered into the contract if he had known the truth, that he is in no way at fault, and that he should be discharged from his obligation.

Traditional legal analysis has sharply distinguished between mistaken assumptions as to the state of things that, in truth or fact, obtained at the time the parties entered into their contract and mistaken predictions as to the future course of events. The two situations do seem intuitively distinguishable. Statements about whether it is raining here and now are, we feel, quite different from statements about whether it will rain tomorrow, even though we may assume that tomorrow's weather is entirely determined by today's conditions and that, under a perfected science of meteorology, the predictive statement about tomorrow would have the same qualities as the descriptive statement about today. In the absence of such knowledge, however, the felt difference between description and prediction — between present and future — will continue to afflict us, even though, on reflection, we may agree that the difference is less important than it seems or, indeed, no difference at all.

As our legal categories evolved, mistaken assumptions about the present (the time reference being to the moment of contracting) have been dealt with under the rubric Mistake. Mistaken predictions about the future have been dealt with under the rubrics Impossibility (during the nineteenth century) and Frustration (during this century). The law of Mistake and the law of Impossibility (or Frustration) have been thought of as being distinct and unrelated branches of the law of Contracts: they have been discussed in different chapters of treatise and Restatement, without benefit of cross-reference or cross-fertilization. Until recently, there have been few suggestions in the literature, scholarly or judicial, that the question whether A should get relief under the doctrine of Mistake is, in many or all respects, the same as the question whether A should get relief under the doctrine of Impossibility (or Frustration). (For one such suggestion, see the opinion by Lord Atkin in Bell v. Lever Brothers, Ltd., *infra* p. 896.)

The cases categorized as Mistake cases have mostly involved contracts that called for an exchange of values at the time the contract was entered into or shortly thereafter; the cases categorized as Impossibility (or Frustration) cases have mostly involved contracts that called for an exchange at some time in the future or for performance by one party over a considerable period of time. Since the dividing line between what is present (or almost so) and what is future is not a clear one, there are many cases in which substantially similar or identical fact situations have been analyzed by one court under Mistake theory and by another court (or even by the same court at a different time) under Impossibility (or Frustration) theory. Since the two theories march to quite different drums and may lead to different results on identical facts, the confusion and overlap are, evidently, jurisprudential misfortunes.

The law of mistake, in all its intricacy, was a nineteenth-century creation. During the period when the courts, with remarkable speed, were elaborating what appeared to be a comprehensive theory of mistake, they had little to say about the effect of dramatic changes of circumstance except to reiterate the propositions that contractual liability is absolute and that the "general rule" is that even actual impossibility of performance is no excuse. (If you cannot do whatever it is you have promised to do, you can always pay damages for not having done it.) The focus of litigation was, however, on the mistake cases and in that area the developing rules seemed well designed progressively to narrow the range within which mistake could be successfully pleaded to avoid liability.

Shortly after the turn of the century, both English and American courts began to analyze the problem of excuse from liability because of changed circumstances in terms of "frustration" of purpose of the contract instead of in terms of "impossibility" of performance. It is entirely unclear why this terminological shift took place but that it did take place is undisputed. Thus the development of frustration theory has been a twentieth-century improvisation which has led to a progressive broadening of the range within which excuse from liability will be decreed. Most commentators, noting the increasingly liberal attitude toward excuse under frustration theory, have also noted (usually in separate chapters) that the beautifully organized network of nineteenth-century mistake rules (which operated to deny relief to mistaken contracting parties) has itself been in course of breakdown for a long time. At all events one of the things our speculations must account for is that the law of frustration was being put together at roughly the same time that the law of mistake was being taken apart.

It may be that the growing commercial importance of long-term contractual arrangements in this century throws some light on what has been going on. Arguably, to a nineteenth-century judge the paradigmatic transaction reflected in the rules of contract law was the short-term contract that called for an immediate (or almost immediate) exchange of values. If the contract term is a few days or a few weeks, it is easy (and may be tempting) to conclude that people ought to know what they are about and should not easily be excused from the consequences of their mistakes. If, however, we shift paradigms and start thinking about contract terms that run over years, our conclusions will shift too. We all know from painful experience how much can (and will) go wrong in the long run. The argument for excusing the long-term contractor from the consequences of his mistaken predictions becomes attractive, even compelling. And once we have got that far, it is not difficult, by a sort of backlash, to start rethinking our earlier (perhaps over-simplified) ideas about short-term contracts.

The assimilation of Mistake and Impossibility has been further hastened by a twentieth-century tendency to view the doctrinal nuances of each from the common perspective of accident law and to see both as responses to the more general problem of risk-allocation. A contract is a way of making the future less risky. If, for example, I contract to purchase wheat from my neighbor at a stated price, he obtains an assured market for his goods, I acquire a guaranteed source of supply, and we are both protected against price fluctuations that work to our disadvantage. Through our contract we become, in effect, reciprocal insurers. But no contract can make the future entirely risk-free. Even if we ignore the most obvious dangers (that one of the parties will simply refuse to perform, or leave to start life over in another jurisdiction, or become insolvent) there is always some risk that the parties' expectations may be upset by what Charles Fried has called a "contractual accident,"[1] just as my plans for a pleasant walk may be frustrated by the automobile that unexpectedly comes around the corner. In every contract, some contingencies are anticipated and planned for; others are not. But unexpected things happen and there is no way of avoiding the unpleasant fact that their cost must be borne by one or the other (or both) of the parties, just as the cost of an automobile accident must be borne by either the driver or the pedestrian or both (social insurance, which spreads the cost among the members of some larger group, being yet another alternative). In this respect, a contractual accident is like any other, except that it happens to occur in the context of a contractual relation. But since the contract itself provides no guidance as to who should bear the costs of such an accident, a court faced with the task of rendering a judgment one way or the other must of necessity look beyond the parties' own agreement to the general principles of accident law, that is, to the law of torts. In a real sense, the problems of Mistake and Impossibility are not problems of contract law at all. The questions they raise and the solutions they call forth are more naturally framed in the language of tort law, and it makes little difference, from this perspective, whether the accident that wrecks the contract happens to occur after the parties have begun to perform, or is discovered to have existed at the time the contract was made. In either case, if we view the problem from the standpoint of accident law, we are likely to conclude that the costs of the mishap should be borne by the party that was best able to prevent it or insure against it or bring the possibility of its occurrence to the attention of the other party or do whatever else might be thought relevant in deciding how the costs of any accident, including a contractual accident, should be allocated.

Restatement Second follows tradition in devoting separate chapters to Mistake (Chapter 12) and to the twin doctrines of Impossibility (renamed Impracticability) and Frustration (Chapter 11). It would be unfair to say, however, that the two chapters proceed with no relationship or connection whatsoever. Excuse under the Mistake chapter depends on one or both parties having been mistaken at the time the contract was entered

---

1. C. Fried, Contract as Promise: A Theory of Contractual Obligation (1981).

into "as to a basic assumption on which the contract was made" (§294, When Mistake of Both Parties Makes a Contract Voidable; cf. §295, When Mistake of One Party Makes a Contract Voidable). Excuse under the Impracticability and Frustration chapter depends on the same criterion: "the occurrence of an event the non-occurrence of which was a basic assumption on which the contract was made" (§281, Discharge by Supervening Impracticability; §285, Discharge by Supervening Frustration; cf. §286, Existing Impracticability or Frustration). (The "basic assumption" phrase, which appears in all the sections cited, is taken from U.C.C. §2-615, discussed *infra* p. 967.) The Commentary to both chapters might be taken by an unsympathetic observer to suggest that the draftsmen were uneasily aware that, compelled by history, they were attempting to maintain in a state of artificial separation doctrines and concepts that for the past hundred years have been tending to merge and fuse and become one. Achieving the separation would have been simpler if the Mistake chapter had been restricted (as it is) to mistaken assumptions about the state of things that existed at the time the contract was made and the Impracticability and Frustration chapter had been restricted (as it is not) to events occurring thereafter. But §286 on Existing Impracticability and Frustration makes that approach impossible, or at least impracticable. As the commentary to §286 rather despairingly observes, "In many of the cases that come under this section, relief based on the rules relating to mistake . . . will also be appropriate." The Introductory Note to the Mistake chapter cheerfully acknowledges the overlap with §286, but goes on bravely to argue that there is a difference still, suggesting a distinction between "void" (§286) and merely "voidable" contracts.

The Restatement Second draftsmen were quite aware of the fact that twentieth-century excuse theory has largely undone nineteenth-century absolute liability theory. The Reporter's Note to the Introductory Note to the Mistake chapter lists a series of sections in which Restatement Second has adopted a rule more "liberal" than the rule adopted in Restatement First, in accord with "the current trend of judicial decisions." The Introductory Note to the Impracticability and Frustration chapter comments: "In recent years courts have shown increasing liberality in discharging obligors on the basis of such extraordinary circumstances." As a way of coping with a body of law conceived to be in a state of rapid change, the draftsmen elected to leave the Restatement Second "flexible" by the use of "imprecise language." The Introductory Note to the Mistake chapter, following its references to "flexibility" and "imprecision," goes on to say: "In addition, §300 makes it clear that if these rules will not suffice to do substantial justice, it is within the discretion of the court to supply an omitted term. . . . Compare §292, which makes this clear in cases of impracticability and frustration." Thus the courts are invited to do "substantial justice," no matter what Restatement Second may say. As Hamlet

remarked: "Use every man after his desert, and who should 'scape whip-
ping?"

Section 2. The Unruliness of Words

Humpty Dumpty remarked in the course of his conversation with Alice:
"When *I* use a word, it means just what I choose it to mean — neither
more nor less." Few of us can hope to match the great grammarian. We
say Plato when we mean Aristotle, as the late Alfred North Whitehead is
reported to have done throughout a course in Greek philosophy. We use
a word that means one thing to us, only to find out that it has quite a
different meaning to those hearing or reading it. The possibilities for
confusion (and fraud) are endless. The following materials illustrate some
of the problems into which we are led by our own propensity for error
compounded by the inescapable ambiguity of language. The suggestion
was made in the preceding section that the law of mistake was a nineteenth-century creation. The nineteenth century was not, of course, all
of a piece. We shall begin with a brief look at a celebrated nineteenth-
century controversy between the proponents of a subjective ("meeting of
the minds") theory of contract and the proponents of what came to be
called the objective theory.

HOTCHKISS v. NATIONAL CITY BANK OF NEW YORK, 200 F. 287,
293 (S.D.N.Y. 1911), *aff'd*, 201 F. 664 (2d Cir. 1912), 231 U.S. 50 (1913).
LEARNED HAND, J.: "A contract has, strictly speaking, nothing to do with
the personal, or individual, intent of the parties. A contract is an obligation attached by the mere force of law to certain acts of the parties,
usually words, which ordinarily accompany and represent a known intent. If, however, it were proved by twenty bishops that either party,
when he used the words, intended something else than the usual meaning which the law imposes upon them, he would still be held, unless there
were some mutual mistake, or something else of the sort. Of course, if it
appear by other words, or acts, of the parties, that they attribute a peculiar meaning to such words as they use in the contract, that meaning will
prevail, but only by virtue of the other words, and not because of their
unexpressed intent."

1 WILLISTON ON CONTRACTS §95: "It is often said broadly that if
the parties do not understand the same thing, there is no contract. But
. . . it is clear that so broad a statement cannot be justified. It is even
conceivable that a contract may be formed which is in accordance with
the intention of neither party. If a written contract is entered into, the

meaning and effect of the contract depends on the interpretation given the written language by the court. The court will give the language its natural and appropriate meaning; and, if the words are unambiguous, will not even admit evidence of what the parties may have thought the meaning to be."

FRANK, J., concurring in RICKETTS v. PENNSYLVANIA R.R., 153 F.2d 757, 760-762, 766-767 (2d Cir. 1946): "In the early days of this century a struggle went on between the respective proponents of two theories of contracts, (a) the 'actual intent' theory — or 'meeting of the minds' or 'will' theory — and (b) the so-called 'objective' theory. Without doubt, the first theory had been carried too far: Once a contract has been validly made, the courts attach legal consequences to the relation created by the contract, consequences of which the parties usually never dreamed — as, for instance, where situations arise which the parties had not contemplated. As to such matters, the 'actual intent' theory induced much fictional discourse which imputed to the parties intentions they plainly did not have.

"But the objectivists also went too far. They tried (1) to treat virtually all the varieties of contractual arrangements in the same way, and (2), as to all contracts in all their phases, to exclude, as legally irrelevant, consideration of the actual intention of the parties or either of them, as distinguished from the outward manifestation of that intention. The objectivists transferred from the field of torts that stubborn anti-subjectivist, the 'reasonable man'; so that, in part at least, advocacy of the 'objective' standard in contracts appears to have represented a desire for legal symmetry, legal uniformity, a desire seemingly prompted by aesthetic impulses. Whether (thanks to the 'subjectivity' of the jurymen's reactions and other factors) the objectivists' formula, in its practical workings, could yield much actual objectivity, certainty, and uniformity may well be doubted. At any rate, the sponsors of complete 'objectivity' in contracts largely won out in the wider generalizations of the Restatement of Contracts and in some judicial pronouncements.

"Influenced by their passion for excessive simplicity and uniformity, many objectivists have failed to give adequate special consideration to releases of claims for personal injuries, and especially to such releases by employees to their employers. Williston, the leader of the objectivists, insists that, as to all contracts, without differentiation, the objective theory is essential because 'founded upon the fundamental principle of the security of business transactions.' . . .

"Two approaches have been suggested which diverge from that of Williston and the Restatement but which perhaps come closer to the realities of business experience. (1) The first utilizes the concept of an 'assumption of risk': The parties to a contract, it is said, are presumed to undertake the risk that the facts upon the basis of which they entered into the contract might, within a certain margin, prove to be non-existent; accordingly, one who is mistaken about any such fact should not, absent a deliberate assumption by him of that risk, be held for more than the actual expenses caused by his conduct. Otherwise, the other party will receive a windfall to which he is not entitled. (2) The second suggestion runs thus: Business is conducted on the assumption that men who bargain are fully informed as to all vital facts about the transactions in which they engage; a contract based upon a mistake as to any such fact as would have deterred either of the parties from making it, had he known that fact, should therefore be set aside in order to prevent unjust enrichment to him who made the mistake; the other party, on this suggestion also, is entitled to no more than his actual expenses. Each of those suggestions may result in unfairness, if the other party reasonably believing that he has made a binding contract, has lost the benefit of other specific bargains available at that time but no longer open to him. But any such possibility of unfairness will seldom, if ever, exist in the case of a release of liability for personal injury whatever the nature of the mistake (i.e., whether it fits into one or the other of Williston's categories).

"In short, the *'security of business transactions' does not require a uniform answer to the question when and to what extent the non-negligent use of words should give rise to rights in one who has reasonably relied on them. That the answer should be favorable to the relier when the words are used in certain kinds of contracts, does not mean that it should also be when they are used in a release of a claim for personal injury; and there may be still further reasons for an unfavorable answer when the claim is by an employee against his employer.*"

NOTE

1. Judge Learned Hand's majority opinion in the *Ricketts* case is reprinted *infra* p. 883.

2. Illustration 2 to §71 (Undisclosed Understanding of Offeror or Offeree, When Material) of the Restatement First puts the following hypothetical case:

> A says to B, "I offer to sell you my horse for $100." B, knowing that A intends to offer to sell his cow, not his horse for that price, and that the use of the word "horse" is a slip of the tongue, replies, "I accept." There is no contract for the sale of either the horse or the cow.

In Restatement Second, the material covered in §71 of the original Restatement appears in §21A (Effect of Misunderstanding). Illustration 5 to §21A is as follows:

A says to B, "I offer to sell you my horse for $100." B, knowing that A intends to offer to sell his cow for that price, not his horse, and that the word "horse" is a slip of the tongue, replies, "I accept." There is a contract for the sale of the cow and not of the horse.

3. Does the shift between the two Restatements in the solution proposed for the absurd horse-cow hypothetical seem to signify a changing attitude toward the controversy between subjectivists and objectivists?

RAFFLES v. WICHELHAUS

2 Hurl. & C. 906, 159 Eng. Rep. 375 (Ex. 1864)

Declaration. For that it was agreed between the plaintiff and the defendants, to wit, at Liverpool, that the plaintiff should sell to the defendants, and the defendants buy of the plaintiff, certain goods, to wit, 125 bales of Surat cotton, guaranteed middling fair merchant's Dhollorah, to arrive ex Peerless from Bombay; and that the cotton should be taken from the quay, and that the defendants would pay the plaintiff for the same at a certain rate, to wit, at the rate of 17¼ d. per pound, within a certain time then agreed upon after the arrival of the said goods in England. Averments: that the said goods did arrive by the said ship from Bombay in England, to wit, at Liverpool, and the plaintiff was then and there ready and willing and offered to deliver the said goods to the defendants, etc. Breach: that the defendants refused to accept the said goods or pay the plaintiff for them.

Plea. That the said ship mentioned in the said agreement was meant and intended by the defendant to be the ship called the Peerless, which sailed from Bombay, to wit, in October; and that the plaintiff was not ready and willing and did not offer to deliver to the defendants any bales of cotton which arrived by the last-mentioned ship, but instead thereof was only ready and willing, and offered to deliver to the defendants 125 bales of Surat cotton which arrived by another and different ship, which was also called the Peerless, and which sailed from Bombay, to wit, in December.

Demurrer, and joinder therein.

Milward, in support of the demurrer. The contract was for the sale of a number of bales of cotton of a particular description, which the plaintiff was ready to deliver. It is immaterial by what ship the cotton was to arrive, so that it was a ship called the Peerless. The words "to arrive ex Peerless," only mean that if the vessel is lost on the voyage, the contract is to be at an end. [Pollock, C.B. It would be a question for the jury whether both parties meant the same ship called the Peerless.] That would be so if the contract was for the sale of a ship called the Peerless; but it is for the sale of cotton on board a ship of that name. [Pollock, C.B. The defendant only bought that cotton which was to arrive by a particular ship. It may as well be said, that if there is a contract for the purchase of certain goods in warehouse A., that is satisfied by the delivery of goods of the same description in warehouse B.] In that case there would be goods in both warehouses; here it does not appear that the plaintiff had any goods on board the other Peerless. [Martin, B. It is imposing on the defendant a contract different from that which he entered into. Pollock, C.B. It is like a contract for the purchase of wine coming from a particular estate in France or Spain, where there are two estates of that name.] The defendant has no right to contradict by parol evidence, a written contract good upon the face of it. He does not impute misrepresentation or fraud, but only says that he fancied the ship was a different one. Intention is of no avail, unless stated at the time of the contract. [Pollock, C.B. One vessel sailed in October and the other in December.] The time of sailing is no part of the contract.

Mellish (Cohen with him), in support of the plea. There is nothing on the face of the contract to show that any particular ship called the Peerless was meant; but the moment it appears that two ships called the Peerless were about to sail from Bombay there is a latent ambiguity, and parol evidence may be given for the purpose of showing that the defendant meant one Peerless and the plaintiff another. That being so, there was no *consensus ad idem*, and therefore no binding contract. He was then stopped by the Court.

PER CURIAM. There must be judgment for the defendants.

Judgment for the defendants.

NOTE

1. Kyle v. Kavanagh, 103 Mass. 356 (1869), involved a contract for the sale of land located on "Prospect Street" in Waltham. In the seller's action for the price, the buyer pleaded that there were two "Prospect Streets" in Waltham; the seller had offered to convey land located on the other Prospect Street. In affirming a judgment for the defendant-buyer the Court approved the instructions that the trial judge had given the jury. These were that

> if the defendant was negotiating for one thing and the plaintiff was selling another thing, and their minds did not agree as to the subject matter of the sale, there would be no contract by which the defendant would be bound, though there was no fraud on the part of the plaintiff.

Id. at 357. That, said Morton, J., was "in accordance with the elementary principles of the law of contracts." Id. at 359-360. Holmes, in the course of his discussion of Raffles v. Wichelhaus (see Note 4, *infra*), after giving the citation to *Raffles*, added: "Cf. Kyle v. Kavanagh, 103 Mass. 356, 357." The "Cf." reference presumably meant that Holmes thought that *Raffles* and *Kyle* were "like" cases. Do you agree?

2. Mellish, as counsel in the principal case, argued that no contract had been formed because there had been no meeting of the minds. Subsequently, as a judge of the Court of Appeal, he had occasion to consider the problem of the revocability of offers in Dickinson v. Dodds, L.R. 2 Ch. D. 463 (1876). For his views on the relevance of the "meeting of the minds" theory in that context, see his opinion in the *Dickinson* case, reprinted *supra* p. 316.

3. Section 2-322 of the Uniform Commercial Code deals with the meaning to be given a contract term which provides for "delivery of goods 'ex-ship.'" Comment 2 to §2-322 is as follows: "Delivery need not be made from any particular vessel under a clause calling for delivery 'ex-ship,' even though a vessel on which shipment is to be made originally is named in the contract, unless the agreement by appropriate language restricts the clause to delivery from a named vessel."

The Code Comment might be read to support Milward's argument that it was "immaterial by what ship the cotton was to arrive," no objection having been made by the defendant to either the time or the method of delivery. Such support, of course, came a hundred years too late to do Milward and his client any good.

In technical language, Milward's argument might be put this way: the promise to ship the cotton by a particular ship named Peerless was merely an independent covenant and not a true condition of the contract. The author of the Code Comment evidently took the same position. On the distinction between covenants and conditions (or between independent and dependent promises), see the Introductory Note to Chapter 9.

Does the court's decision seem to rest, implicitly, on the assumption that the name of the carrying vessel was a true condition and not merely a covenant? Suppose the court had agreed with Milward that it was "immaterial by what ship the cotton was arrive." Would that change the result if it still appeared that the parties were mistaken as to which Peerless was meant?

4. Holmes, in his lecture on void and voidable contracts in The Common Law (M. Howe ed. 1963), offered what might be called an objectivist explanation of the principal case. After stating the facts, he continued (at 242):

> It is commonly said that such a contract is void, because of mutual mistake as to the subject-matter, and because therefore the parties did not consent to the same thing. But this way of putting it seems to me misleading. The law has nothing to do with the actual state of the parties' minds. In contract, as elsewhere, it must go by externals, and judge parties by their conduct. If there had been but one "Peerless," and the defendant had said

"Peerless" by mistake, meaning "Peri," he would have been bound. The true ground of the decision was not that each party meant a different thing from the other, as is implied by the explanation which has been mentioned, but that each said a different thing. The plaintiff offered one thing, the defendant expressed his assent to another.

5. Friendly, J., found himself confronted with what may have been a *Raffles*-type situation in Frigaliment Importing Co., Ltd. v. B.N.S. International Sales Corp., 190 F. Supp. 116 (S.D.N.Y. 1960). The contract called for the shipment from New York to Switzerland of 75,000 pounds of 2½-3 pound "chickens" at 33 cents per pound, FAS New York. (By agreement of the parties, the case was decided on the assumption that New York law governed.) The New York seller procured and shipped 75,000 pounds of "stewing chickens," the New York market price being 30 cents per pound. The Swiss buyer, having accepted and presumably paid for the shipment, brought an action for breach of warranty on the ground that "chickens" meant "broilers." The New York market price for broilers at the relevant time had been 37 cents per pound. Thus the seller stood to make a profit of not more than 3 cents per pound on the stewing chickens and would have incurred a loss of at least 4 cents a pound on broilers. Judge Friendly concluded that both parties had acted in good faith — that is, the seller, honestly and reasonably, had believed that "chickens" meant (or included) stewing chickens; the buyer, honestly and reasonably, had believed that "chickens" meant only broilers. With the *Raffles* analogy evidently in mind, Judge Friendly commented that "the case neatly illustrates Holmes' remark 'that the making of a contract depends not on the agreement of two minds in one intention, but on the agreement of two sets of external signs — not on the parties' having *meant* the same thing but on their having *said* the same thing.'" (The passage quoted was taken from a paper by Holmes called The Path of the Law, in Collected Legal Papers 167, 178 (1920); Holmes was paraphrasing his earlier discussion of *Raffles* in The Common Law (see Note 4 *supra*). After having canvassed the various "objective" meanings of "chicken," Judge Friendly concluded that, in the trade, the word was used both in a narrow sense ("only broilers") and in a broad sense (any kind of chicken, including stewing chicken). He gave judgment for the defendant on a burden of proof theory: "[P]laintiff has the burden of showing that 'chicken' was used in the narrower rather than the broader sense, and that it has not sustained."

A year after he had decided the *Frigaliment* case as a District Judge, Judge Friendly sat as a member of a three-judge panel in Dadourian Export Corp. v. United States, 291 F.2d 178 (2d Cir. 1961). The case involved a sale by the United States of surplus army property which had been advertised as Cargo Nets made of Manila rope. Dadourian, without having inspected the nets but relying on the advertisement plus an oral statement by a Property Disposal Officer at the base where the nets were stored, bid $30,893 and, when its bid was accepted, made a down payment of $7,000. A clause in the standard government contract form provided that the United States disclaimed any "guaranty, warranty, or representation, express or implied, as to quantity, kind, character, quality, weight, size or description." The nets were not "cargo nets" (they were "saveall nets," which are not as strong as cargo nets) and not all of them were made of Manila rope. On discovering these facts, Dadourian refused to accept them or to pay the balance due under the bid and sued the United States to recover its $7,000 down payment. The United States resold the nets for $7,830.30 (at the resale the nets were not described as being made of Manila rope) and counterclaimed for damages measured by the contract price ($30,893) less the down payment and the resale price. The majority of the panel, in an opinion by Medina, J., held that, under the disclaimer of warranty clause and in the light of Dadourian's failure to inspect the nets before making its bid, Dadourian could not recover the down payment. With respect to the counterclaim for damages, the case was remanded for further hearings on the propriety of the resale. (No further proceedings in the case were reported.)

Judge Friendly dissented from the holding that Dadourian was not entitled to a rescission of the contract and a return of the down payment. He commented:

> Finally — and I pose this as a question rather than a conclusion — does not a buyer's right to reject goods not conforming to the description rest on a concept even more basic than breach of warranty? . . . [I]s there not a failure of the minds to meet bringing into play a principle akin to that of Raffles v. Wichelhaus? . . .

Id. at 187. To his citation of *Raffles*, Judge Friendly appended the following footnote: "It may be that [the *Frigaliment* case], decided by the writer, might better have been placed on that ground, with the loss still left on the plaintiff because of defendant's not unjustifiable change of position. . . ." Id. at 187 n.4.

6. In his *Dadourian* dissent Judge Friendly seems to suggest that he might better have decided *Frigaliment* on the "principle . . . of Raffles v. Wichelhaus" but that, if he had done so, he would have decided the case the same way (judgment for the defendant seller), because of the seller's "not unjustifiable change of position." But did not the seller in *Raffles* make a "not unjustifiable change of position" when he shipped the cotton on the December Peerless? Do you think that Judge Friendly meant that in cases of this type (whatever "this type" is) the loss always falls on the plaintiff in the ensuing litigation — i.e., on the seller if the buyer rejects the tender and the seller sues for the price (or for damages), but on the buyer if, after accepting and paying for the goods, he discovers his "mistake" and sues for rescission and restitution (or for damages)? At first

blush this interpretation of the *Dadourian* footnote may seem discreditable to Judge Friendly; on further consideration there may be more to it than initially meets the eye. Do you think that the buyer in *Raffles*, if he had accepted and paid for the cotton, would (or should) have succeeded in an action for restitution on the ground that he thought the cotton had been shipped on the October Peerless? It is, of course, in the highest degree unlikely that the confusion about the two Peerlesses was the real reason for the buyer's rejection of the seller's tender. What do you think the real reason was?

7. Assume that the seller in *Raffles* had not shipped any cotton on either Peerless and the buyer was suing seller for damages for breach of contract. What result? This hypothetical made its first appearance as a question on a Contracts examination. The students on whom it was inflicted split down the middle for and against liability. The hypothetical was then submitted to a jury of law professors who were all teaching Contracts. The law professors, like the first-year law students, split down the middle. How do you account for the diversity of views that the question inspired?

8. The centennial of *Raffles* was admirably celebrated in an article by Young, Equivocation in the Making of Agreements, 64 Colum. L. Rev. 619 (1964). Professor Young distinguished between vagueness or imprecision in the use of language and equivocation (or the use of words, frequently names or technical terms, that turn out to have multiple and inconsistent meanings). He concluded that the rule of Raffles v. Wichelhaus should apply only to cases of equivocation. Does Professor Young's analysis of *Raffles* seem to be in the same vein as Holmes' analysis of the case (Note 4 *supra*)?

9. In the 1960s Professor Corbin, possibly under the stimulus of Judge Friendly's opinion in *Frigaliment*, added a series of new sections to his chapter on Interpretation (these sections appear in the Supplement to 3 Corbin, ch. 24). In Section 543B, Process of Interpretation — Objective Meanings, he commented at length on *Frigaliment* as well as on Holmes' discussion of *Raffles* ("It should not be sacrilege to suggest that there is an 'ambiguity' in Holmes' use of the word 'said' . . ."). With respect to *Frigaliment*, he did not quarrel with Judge Friendly's disposition of the case but did deplore his attempt to find an "objective" meaning for "chicken." Referring to his own boyhood, Corbin wrote: "For ten years on a Kansas farm it had been a regular job to 'feed the chickens' with no suggestion that the old hens and roosters were to be excluded." Other new sections which Corbin added at this time included §543A, What is Ambiguity?; §543AA, Growth of the Law, in Spite of Long Repetition of Formalistic Rules; §543D, Semantic Stone Walls — What Are They Made Of? These sections must have been among the last things Corbin wrote before his hearing and eyesight failed; they are of extraordinary interest.

10. Restatement Second §20 "codifies" *Raffles* in Illustration 2. Further illustrations in §20 and Illustration 6 to §153 (When Mistake of One Party Makes a Contract Voidable) play games with the *Raffles* fact situation by making various assumptions about whether one party or both parties knew of the existence of the two Peerlesses and, if so, further knew which of the Peerlesses the other party had "intended."

MILLER v. STANICH
202 Wis. 539, 230 N.W. 47 (1930)

FRITZ, J. Plaintiff, engaged in the wholesale fruit and cold-storage business at Marshfield, Wisconsin, acquired property located in Milwaukee which was occupied by the defendant under a lease for a five-year term commencing on June 6, 1922, with provision for extension and renewal for a further five-year term, at the lessee's option, providing he gave thirty days' notice of such intention. On February 14, 1927, Joseph A. Fleckenstein, who collected the rents as agent for plaintiff, was notified by Joseph F. Schoendorf, defendant's attorney, that defendant desired a new lease for the further term of five years. On February 15, 1927, Schoendorf prepared and mailed to Fleckenstein two copies of a proposed lease for those five years, with a clause again giving the defendant an option for an extension for an additional five-year term. Fleckenstein, without consulting plaintiff, notified Schoendorf that he did not believe that plaintiff would give defendant another option for an additional five-year term. Thereupon Schoendorf prepared and mailed two copies of another lease for the five-year term, but without any option for a future renewal. Fleckenstein sent all of the copies to plaintiff during February, 1927. As plaintiff could not read the English language, his stenographer or one of his two adult sons, who were in business with him, read the leases to him, and he then discovered that one set contained the clause for another five-year renewal option, and that the other set did not contain such clause.

On March 15, 1927, defendant caused a notice of his intention to take advantage of the extension privilege to be served on the former owner and lessor and on Fleckenstein. On May 21, 1927, defendant also caused such a notice to be served on plaintiff. Thereupon plaintiff consulted his attorney at Wisconsin Rapids, and was advised that defendant was entitled to the first extension of five years. However, inadvertently, plaintiff's attorney inserted the date "May 24," in the blank spaces left for the date in the two copies which had the clause that granted defendant a new option for another five-year extension. Plaintiff returned to Marshfield, and there signed the two copies in which his attorney had inserted "May 24," and sent them to defendant, who signed them and returned one copy to plaintiff on June 1, 1927. There was no misrepresentation, concealment, or fraud in any respect on the part of either party or their respective agents or attorneys. The court found that the plaintiff intended to make a new lease for only the first extension of five years, without giving defendant any new option for a further extension; that plaintiff, on discovering his error, promptly demanded the cancellation of the provision for the second extension; and that upon defendant's refusal to consent to such cancellation, plaintiff promptly commenced this action. On the other hand, the court also found that the defendant intended to obtain an option for an additional term of five years, but, failing in that, he intended to secure a new lease for merely the five-year extension under the original lease. Upon those facts the court concluded that plaintiff was entitled to judgment "canceling and rescinding the provision contained in said lease purporting to grant an option for an additional five-year term"; and it was provided in the judgment that the lease dated May 24, 1927, "be and the same is hereby reformed by canceling and striking out" the provision for the second renewal.

Although plaintiff may have made a mistake in signing and sending to defendant the copies of the lease which contained the provision giving defendant an option for a further renewal, nothing had occurred because of which the defendant had reason to believe that plaintiff did not intend to agree to that provision, or that plaintiff had made a mistake. Defendant, in good faith, had submitted two forms. Without being misled by any trick or artifice on the part of any one, plaintiff signed and sent the two copies, containing the clause for another option, to defendant for his signature. When defendant also signed those copies he was entitled to assume that the minds of the parties had met as to all terms embodied in the signed instruments, and that the plaintiff, by signing, had evidenced his intention to agree to all of those terms. Nothing had been done by plaintiff, of which defendant had knowledge, that indicated an intention on plaintiff's part not to consent to the option for the additional extension. Nothing had occurred which can be said to evidence a meeting of the minds of the parties to another contract, which plaintiff is now entitled by reformation to have expressed in the lease which he voluntarily signed. There was no mutual mistake. At best it was merely a unilateral mistake, without any fraud on the part of the defendant. Under the circumstances there was no ground for reformation.

"In order to reform a contract on the ground of mistake the general rule is that the mistake must be mutual, or mistake on one side and fraud on the other." Chicago, St. P., M. & O. R. Co. v. Bystrom, 165 Wis. 125, 133, 161 N.W. 358; 1 Black on Rescission and Cancellation (2d ed.) pp. 396, 398, 399; Id. §131, pp. 402-405.

As was said in Grant Marble Co. v. Abbott, 142 Wis. 279, 287, 124 N.W. 264:

> The minds of the parties met upon this contract, hence there is no ground for reformation. There was no mutual mistake. The parties to the

contract made the contract they intended to make. Even if a mistake were made, it is established that it was the mistake of Mr. Grant, president of plaintiff; hence was not mutual. To allow reformation in this case would be to justify the court in making a contract for the parties which they themselves did not make. This the court cannot do. The plaintiff must show that the minds of the parties met upon the contract which it seeks to establish.

Likewise, in Jentzsch v. Roenfanz, 185 Wis. 189, 193, 195, 201 N.W. 504, this court said:

> The determination of this case must rest upon the question of whether or not there was a mutual mistake. A mistake, in order to be mutual, means one reciprocal and common to both parties, where each alike labors under the misconception in respect to the terms of the written instrument. Botsford v. McLean, 45 Barb. 478, 481.

(Page 193.)

> While a mistake of one of the parties in a proper case may be grounds for rescission or cancellation, in order that there may be a reformation the mistake must be mutual. In other words, the court cannot rewrite the contract which the parties have made so as to express an agreement which the parties had not entered into.

(Page 195.)

The mistake in the case at bar was in relation to but one clause or detail of the lease. It did not go to the entire contract as in the case of Chicago, St. P., M. & O. R. Co. v. Bystrom, *supra*. Consequently, in this case plaintiff could not have rescission of the entire contract. However, even if he sought such rescission, to entitle him to relief because of his mistake he would have to establish that there was fraud on defendant's part, or, at least, that he knew that plaintiff was laboring under a mistake. (Grant Marble Co. v. Abbott, *supra*, p. 289); or, in the case of a unilateral contract, such as a deed, that it was without consideration and that the mistake was excusable (Chicago, St. P., M. & O. R. Co. v. Bystrom, *supra*, p. 133).

Respondent also contends that the provision granting the new option for a further five-year term is subject to cancellation because there was no consideration for such grant, in excess of defendant's rights under the original lease. However, in so far as such grant constituted a modification of the original lease, no new consideration was necessary. Foley v. Marsch, 162 Wis. 25, 30, 154 N.W. 982; Schoblasky v. Rayworth, 139 Wis. 115, 117, 120 N.W. 822. The consideration for the original, executory contract is deemed imported into the modified contract, and such new contract becomes binding without any new consideration. Lynch v. Henry, 75 Wis. 631, 634, 44 N.W. 837.

For the reasons stated, the court erred in decreeing reformation of the lease dated May 24, 1927.

By the court. — Judgment reversed, with directions to dismiss the complaint.

FOWLER, J. I feel that I must record a dissent. The case is so simple that to my mind the mere statement of it proves the decision of the court wrong. The plaintiff executed to defendant a lease in writing containing an option to defendant for a five-year extension. The premises are in Milwaukee. The plaintiff resides at Marshfield and the defendant in Milwaukee. Near the end of the term the defendant submitted to plaintiff's agent in Milwaukee a new lease in the same terms as the original including an option for another five-year extension and asked him to procure plaintiff's signature to it. The plaintiff's agent answered that he did not think the plaintiff would execute a lease with the extension clause. The defendant thereupon submitted to the agent another lease like the original without the extension clause and asked that he get the plaintiff to execute and return one or the other of the leases. The plaintiff claims, and the court found, that he by mistake signed the lease containing the option for extension and sent it to the defendant instead of the one without such option which he intended to sign and deliver. On discovering the mistake plaintiff asked defendant to return the lease he had and accept the one without the option for extension. The defendant refused to do so. The plaintiff, promptly and before defendant had taken any steps whatever in reliance upon the provision for a five-year extension, comes into a court of equity and asks relief on the ground of his mistake.

The defendant gave timely and proper notice to entitle him to a five-year extension of his original lease. This he was entitled to. He was not entitled to anything more. No extra rental or other consideration for another five-year extension was agreed to or given. The defendant was not induced to accept the lease signed by the plaintiff and enter into his covenants therein contained because of the inclusion in the lease of the clause for the additional extension. He would have accepted the other lease had that lease been returned to him. It is true that when the defendant signed the lease returned by plaintiff he understood that the plaintiff had signed it advisedly and had thereby agreed to the additional extension. But the plaintiff had not so agreed. There was thus no meeting of the minds of the parties in respect to the extension. No such agreement was reached as the signed lease evidences.

No plainer case for relief from mistake was ever brought in a court of equity. It is true, as stated in the opinion of the court, that equity does not reform instruments for mistake unless the mistake is mutual, and that the mistake here involved is not mutual but unilateral. But equity rescinds written instruments for unilateral mistakes. The opinion of the court recognizes this rule. The complaint in terms erroneously asks for reformation of the lease by striking out the clause for extension. The plaintiff, strictly speaking, is not entitled to the particular form of relief he asks for, because the defendant did not by signing the lease returned to him agree to a lease without the extension. But the fact is proved and found by the court that entitles plaintiff to rescission of the lease signed by him. Striking from that lease the provision for extension and letting the lease stand as so changed, affords the plaintiff precisely the same relief that he would have were the lease declared canceled and the defendant adjudged to have the right to hold the premises for the extended term provided for by the original lease. Strictly speaking, that is the relief that should have been adjudged. But the error of decreeing reformation instead of rescission did not affect the substantial rights of the defendant, and under sec. 274.37, Stats., the judgment should be affirmed.

There would seem to be no more need to cite authorities in support of the above than to cite the multiplication table to support the statement that once one is one. However there is ample authority for the proposition that rescission or cancellation will be granted for a unilateral mistake. See 9 Corp. Jur. p. 1168, note 74; 21 Corp. Jur. p. 88, note 49. [Citations omitted.] The court may properly, as condition of granting the relief of rescission, require plaintiff to give to the defendant the option to take such a lease as the plaintiff intended to sign, as was in effect done in Brown v. Lamphear, 35 Vt. 252; Paget v. Marshall, L.R. 28 Ch. Div. 255; Keene v. Demelman, 172 Mass. 17, 51 N.E. 188. But here there is no need to do even that, as adjudication that the defendant has the right to hold under the original lease for the extended period would satisfy all requirements of equity.

The opinion of the court to support the lease signed by plaintiff invokes the rule that no consideration is necessary to uphold modification of a contract. It is true that the original consideration would support modification of the original lease as evidenced by the lease signed by plaintiff, if plaintiff had agreed to the modification so evidenced. But he did not agree to such modification. The trial court so found upon ample evidence. The rule invoked therefore has no application.

Mere inadvertence in signing the wrong lease is not such negligence as should bar plaintiff from relief. Almost every mistake involves some negligence. One using due care does not ordinarily make mistakes. Unless the mistake induces the other party to take some steps to his prejudice that he would not otherwise have taken, there is no good reason why relief should not be granted. Where no one is injured by a mistake except the party making it, and no one has changed his position in consequence of it, relief may be granted although a high degree of care was not exercised. See 21 Corp. Jur. p. 90. But in this case the plaintiff's mistake was excusable. The trial court found that the plaintiff cannot read English and on receipt of the two leases went to his lawyer for advice. The lawyer advised him that he was not bound to sign the lease with the extension but should sign the other, and by mistake inserted the date in the wrong lease and gave it to plaintiff to sign and send to defendant. A court of equity must, under the circumstances here involved, grant relief from a mistake so happening; else it is not a court of equity.

It does not at all detract from the force of the above to quote the maxim "Equity follows the law." Even the law gives adequate relief from mistakes less excusable than the one here involved; as where it refunds money paid to secure compliance with a bid for public work from which items are inadvertently omitted in making the estimate. Gavahan v. Shorewood, 200 Wis. 429, 228 N.W. 497.

I am authorized to state that Mr. Justice Stevens concurs in this dissent.

[A motion by the respondent for a rehearing was granted, and the cause was reargued. In an opinion by Fowler, J., with Fritz, J., dissenting, the Court changed its decision and ordered: judgment of cancellation entered upon condition that the plaintiff execute and file with the clerk of the court for the defendant a lease in form and terms of the lease he intended to sign and deliver. 202 Wis. 548, 233 N.W. 753 (1930).]

NOTE

1. The division within the Wisconsin court the first time the case was heard and the court's flip-flop after rehearing illustrate the process of breakdown of a once firmly established common law rule. The "mutuality" idea played a curious role in late nineteenth-century jurisprudence: consider, in addition to the distinction between mutual and unilateral mistake, the requirements of "mutuality of obligation" ("both parties must be bound or neither is bound," see Chapter 3, Section 11) and of "mutuality of remedy" ("A cannot have a decree of specific performance against B unless, if the case is reversed, B could have had such a decree against A," see Chapter 10, Section 2). It is no longer clear to the twentieth-century mind exactly what the "mutuality" rules meant to nineteenth-century judges or why the rules should have enjoyed, over so long a period, the vogue they evidently did. (Restatement Second §300, Illustration 3, approves the ultimate disposition of the principal case.)

2. Another nineteenth-century rule that has been in course of breakdown during this century distinguished between mistakes of fact and mistakes of law, with relief being granted only for mistakes of fact. The dividing line between "law" and "fact" is, of course, even more difficult to perceive than the dividing line between "unilateral" and "mutual." The two rules seem to have been prayed in aid mostly by courts that had decided to deny relief in a particular case (on the ground that the mistake was "merely unilateral" or was "a mistake of law"). An unsympathetic observer — such as Corbin — had no difficulty in collecting nineteenth-century cases in which relief was granted for mistakes which would seem

to have been "unilateral" or "of law"; in such cases the rules were not, of course, mentioned in the opinions.

3. A third way of denying relief for mistake was by invoking the parol evidence rule, which excluded any evidence whose effect would be to vary, contradict, or explain a writing found to be an "integration" of the agreement. On the vicissitudes of the parol evidence rule, see Chapter 7.

4. A factual situation which has accounted for a continuing stream of litigation involves errors in computation that result in contractors making bids or estimates lower than they would have been, but for the error. Strict application of the unilateral mistake rule requires that the contractor be held to his bargain even if, on discovering the error, he promptly notifies the other party before there has been any change of position or action in reliance. Such a case was Steinmeyer v. Schroeppel, 226 Ill. 9, 80 N.E. 564 (1907), in which the court commented: "If equity would relieve on account of such a mistake [a column of figures had been added to make the total $1,446; the correct total was $1,867], there would be no stability in contracts. . . ." The doctrine of contractual "stability" did not have a long run in Illinois. In Bromagin v. City of Bloomington, 234 Ill. 114, 84 N.E. 700 (1908), Bromagin's bid on a municipal contract was $25,500 but should have been $31,500; the next lowest bid was $29,000. Bromagin notified the City of his $6,000 error five hours after the bidding had closed; the City claimed the right to forfeit a $2,800 deposit which Bromagin had been required to make. In giving judgment for Bromagin the court distinguished the *Steinmeyer* case without overruling it. From then on in Illinois there was presumably a *Bromagin* line of "excusable mistake" cases and a *Steinmeyer* line of "inexcusable mistake" cases; an impartial observer would be hard put to find a reason why the *Bromagin* mistake was any more (or any less) excusable than the *Steinmeyer* mistake. A well-known case of a somewhat later vintage was Geremia v. Boyarski, 107 Conn. 387, 140 A. 749 (1928), in which the Connecticut court followed the *Bromagin* line (citing *Bromagin* but not *Steinmeyer* in its opinion). See also the contract bid cases in Chapter 3, Section 8. The cases of this type (including *Steinmeyer*, *Bromagin*, and *Geremia*) involve relatively small amounts of money. Errors of millions in high-level corporate finance seem never to have led to *Steinmeyer*-type litigation, although there is no reason to believe that people who deal in millions are any more careful or any less prone to error than people who deal in hundreds or in thousands.

5. The Restatement of Restitution (1937) treats the effect of unilateral mistake in §12, which states:

> A person who confers a benefit upon another, manifesting that he does so as an offer of a bargain which the other accepts or as the acceptance of an offer which the other has made, is not entitled to restitution because of a

mistake which the other does not share and the existence of which the
other does not know or suspect.

Comment *c* to §12 adds: "Where the transferee knows or suspects the
mistake of the transferor, restitution is granted if, and only if, the fact as
to which the mistake is made is one which is at the basis of the transaction
unless there is a special relation between the parties." Two illustrative
examples follow.

> A, looking at cheap jewelry in a store that sells both very cheap and expen-
> sive jewelry, discovers what he at once recognizes as being a valuable jewel
> worth not less than $100 which he correctly believes to have been placed
> there by mistake. He asks the clerk for the jewel and gives 10¢ for it. The
> clerk puts the 10¢ in the cash drawer and hands the jewel to A. The
> shopkeeper is entitled to restitution because the shopkeeper did not, as A
> knew, intend to bargain except with reference to cheap jewelry.
>
> B enters a second-hand bookstore where, among books offered for sale at
> one dollar each, he discovers a rare book having, as B knows, a market
> value of not less than $50. He hands this to the proprietor with one dollar.
> The proprietor, reading the name of the book and the price tag, keeps the
> dollar and hands the book to B. The bookdealer is not entitled to restitution
> since there was no mistake as to the identity of the book and both parties
> intended to bargain with reference to the ability of each to value the book.

Is the difference between these two cases clear?

6. The invention of the telegraph institutionalized the situation in
which an intermediary, for a small fee, transmitted messages from A to B,
the intermediary being in control of the message. Predictably, the employees of the telegraph companies garbled many of the messages. The
garbled messages led to a fifty-year spate of litigation. One class of cases
raised the question whether the party injured by the mistake was nevertheless bound by a contract that it had never meant to enter into. Cases
of this sort led the courts into curious speculations about whose "agent"
the telegraph company really was; under agency law a principal is bound
by the negligent acts of its agent. Another class of cases raised the question whether the telegraph companies could be held liable in substantial
damages for the losses caused (or the gains prevented) by their negligent
mistakes. In litigation of this type the telegraph companies fared remarkably well. See, e.g., the opinion of Cardozo, J., in Kerr S.S. Co., Inc. v.
Radio Corporation of America, *infra* p. 1152 (in which R.C.A., instead of
garbling, had failed to transmit a message). The telegraph company litigation disappeared shortly after World War I with the nonliability of the
companies being conceded.

7. Telegraph companies are not, of course, the only intermediaries
whose negligence or fraud may lead A and B into situations they had
never intended to be in and did not realize they were in until the interme-

diary's misconduct was revealed. If the truth is revealed early enough in the proceedings, the mess can be cleared up (if a court so desires) by reformation of the contract or by its rescission; neither remedy requires the presence of an intermediary but, in both types of cases (as in Miller v. Stanich), the intermediary is frequently present.

Reformation and rescission were remedies that were originally available only in equity but that gradually became available in actions at law; reformation continued to be thought of as essentially equitable long after rescission "at law" had become routine. The reformation idea is that A and B have reached agreement (their minds have met) but, because of what is disdainfully referred to as a "scrivener's error," the writing they have signed does not accurately memorialize their agreement; the writing is "reformed" to express that agreement. The rescission idea is that A and B never did reach agreement but, under some kind of misapprehension, signed a writing which purported to bind them; if the true state of facts can be shown, the only thing to do is to call off the deal by "rescinding" the purported contract. The principal case, Miller v. Stanich, illustrates how the two remedies blur at the edges.

An intermediary's misconduct may not be discovered until the damage has been done. In such a situation neither reformation nor rescission does any good and more heroic remedies are called for. For such a case, see Vickery v. Ritchie, *supra* p. 173.

RICKETTS v. PENNSYLVANIA R.R.
153 F.2d 757 (2d Cir. 1946)

L. HAND, Circuit Judge. The defendant appeals from a judgment awarding damages to the plaintiff — a waiter upon one of its dining cars — for injuries suffered while in its service on February 16, 1943. The action was brought under the Federal Employers' Liability Act, §§51-60, Title 45 U.S.C.A.; but the only question raised upon this appeal concerns the validity of two releases, dated August 23, 1943, by which the plaintiff released all claims against the defendant upon the payment of $600. The plaintiff had already executed a release for $150 in the same words on March 19, 1943, and one of the two releases of August 23, recited a payment of $750, the sum of the two payments; but, as that release plays no part in the result we shall ignore it and speak as though only the second release had been given in August. The plaintiff testified that he executed the first release after a talk with one Brown, the defendant's claim agent, who told him that the payment of $150 was only for the tips and wages which he had lost; and that, relying upon this representation, he did not read the release, but signed it as Brown told him to do. Between that time and July he made some efforts to work but still felt incapacitated; and towards the end of that month, or early in August, he

went again to Brown asking for more money. They could not agree, and
he left, saying to Brown: "Well, I will have to get somebody to get all my
tips and everything, my salary, because that is what I am getting." He
then went to an attorney named Reich, who, after talking to Brown on
the telephone, later brought to the plaintiff the release drawn on the
defendant's form and told him: "I was just to sign a receipt for the amount
of money that I got for the time I was off, my tips also included, to go
back to work and they won't have anything against you . . . he had the
word from the Pennsylvania that I will be taken care of." On his redirect
he somewhat amplified this. Reich had told him:

> [T]he $600 is just for my earnings and my tips, because that would be better
> such and such. He said he did not want to sue. He said that would be
> better, and the company wants you to sign. That is big money. If you do,
> they won't have anything against you. Since you stay in the company, you
> have eligibility to be retired. You will have full retirement pay.

Relying upon this, and again not reading the release, he signed it and the
defendant paid him $600. The plaintiff's wife also testified that Reich had
said that "the money was for his back pay and tips."

This version of the transaction the defendant denied. It called Reich,
who said that Brown, when Reich consulted him, agreed to pay $600 for a
complete release; and that all this Reich explained to the plaintiff when
the release was executed. The judge charged the jury that, if the plaintiff
executed the release "without fraud or misrepresentation, and understanding what he was doing," it bound him, but that if he "signed these
papers as receipts for wages, if it was as his understanding that that was all
he was signing, that he did not sign any general release, then, of course
you take up the question of damages." Again: "Was it represented to the
plaintiff by his lawyer that the papers he signed on August 23, 1943, were
releases of all claims or only for lost wages?" The defendant made several
requests to charge, but in none of them did it suggest that the jury should
find whether the plaintiff retained Reich to settle all claims he had against
the railroad, or whether — as the plaintiff testified — Reich's retainer
was limited to collecting wages and tips.

The right of action here in suit was created by act of Congress, and it is
abundantly settled that its interpretation is a matter of federal law and not
governed by state decisions, even when it speaks in the words of the
common-law. Chesapeake & Ohio R. Co. v. Kuhn, 284 U.S. 44, 52 S. Ct.
45, 76 L. Ed. 157. It would not inevitably follow that, after such a right
had come into existence, the legal effect upon it of a transaction within a
state — as here, of a release — was also to be treated as matter of federal
law; conceivably, its fate might be left to the law of the state. However, as
we read Garrett v. Moore-McCormack Co., 317 U.S. 239, 63 S. Ct. 246,
87 L. Ed. 239, this is not so. The right of action was there under the Jones
Act, but the action had been brought in a state court, which had held that
the burden of proof of establishing a release was governed by the law of

Pennsylvania. This the Supreme Court denied, holding that the admiralty rule controlled; and it would seem to follow that the validity of the release at bar is to be decided by the common-law, to be gathered from the same sources which, before Erie Railroad Co. v. Tompkins, 304 U.S. 64, 58 S. Ct. 817, 82 L. Ed. 1188, 114 A.L.R. 1487, we used to employ in cases depending on diversity of citizenship.

Although the law was at one time otherwise, at least in this country (Friedlander v. Texas & Pacific R. Co., 130 U.S. 416, 9 S. Ct. 570, 32 L. Ed. 991), it is now settled both in the federal system (Gleason v. Seaboard Airline R. Co., 278 U.S. 349, 49 S. Ct. 161, 73 L. Ed. 415), and in England (Lloyd v. Grace, Smith & Co., [1912] A.C. 716), that an agent does not cease to be acting within the scope of his authority when he is engaged in a fraud upon a third person. That has probably always been the more generally accepted doctrine. Fifth Avenue Bank v. Forty-Second Street & G. St. Ferry R. Co., 137 N.Y. 231, 33 N.E. 378, 19 L.R.A. 331, 33 Am. St. Rep. 712; Ripon Knitting Works v. Railway Express Agency, 207 Wis. 452, 240 N.W. 840; Tollett v. Montgomery Real Estate & Insurance Co., 238 Ala. 617, 622, 193 So. 127; Restatement of Agency, §262. We can see no distinction in principle between that situation and one in which the agent deceives, not the third person, but his principal. The reason in each case for holding the principal is that the third person has no means of knowing that the agent is acting beyond his authority, and it is a matter of entire indifference whether the agent adds deception of his principal to deception of the third person; for it is obviously true that for the agent consciously to exceed his powers is to deceive the third person. Hence we may assume in the case at bar that, if the plaintiff had retained Reich to settle any claim he might have against the defendant, the plaintiff would have been bound, if Reich had procured the execution of the release by deceiving him as to its contents.

On the other hand, if the plaintiff retained Reich merely to collect his wages and tips, as to which he had failed to come to a satisfactory agreement with Brown in July or early August, the release was invalid; for, whatever may be the law in England, it is well settled in this country that an attorney has no implied authority to compromise a claim. Holker v. Parker, 7 Cranch 436, 452, 453, 3 L. Ed. 396; United States v. Beebe, 180 U.S. 343, 351, 352, 21 S. Ct. 371, 45 L. Ed. 563; Glover v. Bradley, 4 Cir., 233 F. 721, Ann. Cas. 1917A, 921; McFarland v. Curtin, 4 Cir., 233 F. 728; Barber-Colman Co. v. Magnano Corp., 1 Cir., 299 F. 401; Jacob v. City of New York, 2 Cir., 199 F.2d 800 (reversed as to a different cause of action in Jacob v. City of New York, 315 U.S. 752, 62 S. Ct. 854, 86 L. Ed. 1166); Countryman v. Breen, 241 App. Div. 392, 394, 271 N.Y.S. 744, *affirmed* 268 N.Y. 643, 198 N.E. 536. The release would still be invalid even though the plaintiff signed it without reading it, for he would have been justified in relying upon what his lawyer told him of the contents. The theory upon which a document binds one who signs it, but who does not read it, is that either he accepts it whatever may be its contents, or

886   8. Mistake, Impossibility, and Frustration

that he has been careless in choosing his informant. Foster v. Mackinnon, L.R. 4 C.P. 704; Pimpinello v. Swift & Co., 253 N.Y. 159, 170 N.E. 530; Chapman v. Rose, 56 N.Y. 137, 15 Am. Rep 401; Williston, §95A. In the case at bar, whatever we may think about the correctness of the verdict on the facts, the jury could have interpreted the plaintiff's testimony to mean that he only told Reich to collect his wages and tips; which incidentally was consistent with his parting words to Brown. Indeed, it was not really possible to believe the words which he put in Reich's mouth, unless he had retained him for that limited purpose. At any rate, if the defendant had meant to raise the question whether Reich had been broadly commissioned, it should have done so by a proper request. This it did not do; and the result is that upon this, the turning point in the case — the extent of Reich's authority — the only question that remains upon this appeal is of the sufficiency of the evidence to support a verdict. It is true that the plaintiff did not offer to return the money received in March and in August, 1943; since however the defendant did not raise this point either in its answer, at the trial, or in this court, we have not considered it.

Judgment affirmed.

[The opinions of Frank, J., concurring and of Swan, J., dissenting, have been omitted.]

NOTE

Excerpts from the elaborate concurring opinion of Frank, J., are reprinted *supra* p. 867. Evidently, both Judge Hand and Judge Frank had concluded that Ricketts' action against the railroad was not barred by the release that he had signed. However, they preferred to reach (or rationalize) that conclusion by different conceptual routes. On the whole, do you prefer the Hand approach or the Frank approach? Or the view of Judge Swan, who dissented? And what is the connection between the *Ricketts* case and the struggle between the proponents of a subjective, as opposed to an objective, theory of contracts?

Section 3.   "The Value of a Thing Is Just Exactly What 'Twill Bring."

Samuel Butler, Hudibras.

WOOD v. BOYNTON

64 Wis. 265, 25 N.W. 42 (1885)

For a report of the case, see *supra* p. 84.

For a report of the case, see *supra* p. 84.

SHERWOOD v. WALKER

66 Mich. 568, 33 N.W. 919 (1887)

[Replevin for possession of a cow.

In the spring of 1886 the plaintiff, learning that the defendants had some "polled Angus cattle" for sale, was desirous of purchasing some of that breed, and, meeting the defendants, or some of them, at Walkerville, inquired about them, and was informed that they had none at Walkerville, "but had a few head left on their farm in Greenfield, and asked the plaintiff to go and see them, stating that in all probability they were sterile and would not 'breed.'" In accordance with said request, the plaintiff, on the fifth day of May, went out and looked at the defendants' cattle at Greenfield, and found one called "Rose 2d," which he wished to purchase, and the terms were finally agreed upon at five and one-half cents per pound, live weight, 50 pounds to be deducted for shrinkage. The sale was in writing, and the defendants gave an order to the plaintiff directing the man in charge of the Greenfield farm to [weigh it and] deliver the cow to plaintiff. This was done on the fifteenth of May. On the twenty-first of May plaintiff went to get his cow, and the defendants refused to let him have her; claiming at the time that the man in charge at the farm thought the cow was with calf, and, if such was the case, they would not sell her for the price agreed upon.[2]

Plaintiff tendered $80 to defendant for the cow, which weighed 1420 lbs., demanded possession, and upon refusal instituted this action. At the trial the defendants offered evidence to show that at the time of the alleged sale it was believed by both plaintiff and themselves that the cow was barren and would not breed; that she cost $850, and if not barren would be worth from $750 to $1000. The trial court charged the jury that it was immaterial whether the cow was with calf or not. Verdict for plaintiff and defendant appeals.]

MORSE, J. . . . It appears from the record that both parties supposed this cow was barren and would not breed, and she was sold by the pound for an insignificant sum as compared with her real value if a breeder. She was evidently sold and purchased on the relation of her value for beef, unless the plaintiff had learned of her true condition, and concealed such knowledge from the defendants. Before the plaintiff secured possession of the animal, the defendants learned that she was with calf, and therefore of great value, and undertook to rescind the sale by refusing to deliver her. The question arises whether they had a right to do so.

The circuit judge ruled that this fact did not avoid the sale, and it made no difference whether she was barren or not. I am of the opinion that the court erred in this holding. I know that this is a close question, and the dividing line between the adjudicated cases is not easily discerned. But it

---

2. The statement of facts is taken from the dissenting opinion of Sherwood, J. — EDS.

must be considered as well settled that a party who has given an apparent consent to a contract of sale may refuse to execute it, or he may avoid it after it has been completed, if the assent was founded, or the contract made, upon the mistake of a material fact, — such as the subject-matter of the sale, the price, or some collateral fact materially inducing the agreement; and this can be done when the mistake is mutual. 1 Benj. Sales, §§605, 606; Leake, Cont. 339; Story, Sales (4th ed.), §§148, 377. See also, Cutts v. Guild, 57 N.Y. 229; Harvey v. Harris, 112 Mass. 32; Gardner v. Lane, 9 Allen, 492; S.C. 12 Allen, 44; Hutchmacher v. Harris' Adm'rs, 38 Penn. St. 491; Byers v. Chapin, 28 Ohio St. 300; Gibson v. Pelkie, 37 Mich. 380, and cases cited; Allen v. Hammond, 11 Pet. 63, 71.

If there is a difference or misapprehension as to the substance of the thing bargained for, if the thing actually delivered or received is different in substance from the thing bargained for and intended to be sold, then there is no contract; but if it be only a difference in some quality or accident, even though the mistake may have been the actuating motive to the purchaser or seller, or both of them, yet the contract remains binding.

> The difficulty in every case is to determine whether the mistake or misapprehension is as to the substance of the whole contract, going, as it were, to the root of the matter, or only to some point, even though a material point, an error as to which does not affect the substance of the whole consideration.

Kennedy v. Panama, etc., Mail Co., L.R. 2 Q.B. 580, 588.

It has been held, in accordance with the principles above stated, that where a horse is bought under the belief that he is sound, and both vendor and vendee honestly believe him to be sound, the purchaser must stand by his bargain, and pay the full price, unless there was a warranty.

It seems to me, however, in the case made by this record, that the mistake or misapprehension of the parties went to the whole substance of the agreement. If the cow was a breeder, she was worth at least $750; if barren, she was worth not over $80. The parties would not have made the contract of sale except upon the understanding and belief that she was incapable of breeding, and of no use as a cow. It is true she is now the identical animal that they thought her to be when the contract was made; there is no mistake as to the identity of the creature. Yet the mistake was not of the mere quality of the animal, but went to the very nature of the thing. A barren cow is substantially a different creature than a breeding one. There is as much difference between them for all purposes of use as there is between an ox and a cow that is capable of breeding and giving milk. If the mutual mistake had simply related to the fact whether she was with calf or not for one season, then it might have been a good sale; but the mistake affected the character of the animal for all time, and for her present and ultimate use. She was not in fact the animal, or the kind of animal, the defendants intended to sell or the plaintiff to buy. She was not a barren cow, and, if this fact had been known, there would have been no contract. The mistake affected the substance of the whole consideration, and it must be considered that there was no contract to sell or sale of the cow as she actually was. The thing sold and bought had in fact no existence. She was sold as a beef creature would be sold; she is in fact a breeding cow, and a valuable one.

The court should have instructed the jury that if they found that the cow was sold, or contracted to be sold, upon the understanding of both parties that she was barren, and useless for the purposes of breeding, then the defendants had a right to rescind, and to refuse to deliver, and the verdict should be in their favor.

The judgment of the court below must be reversed, and a new trial granted, with costs of this Court to defendants.

Campbell, C.J., and Champlin, J., concurred.

SHERWOOD, J. (dissenting). I do not concur in the opinion given by my brethren in this case. I think the judgments before the justice and at the circuit were right.

I agree with my Brother Morse that the contract made was not within the statute of frauds, and that payment for the property was not a condition precedent to the passing of title from the defendants to the plaintiff. And I further agree with him that the plaintiff was entitled to a delivery of the property to him when the suit was brought, unless there was a mistake made which would invalidate the contract; and I can find no such mistake.

There is no pretense that there was any fraud or concealment in the case, and an intimation or insinuation that such a thing might have existed on the part of either of the parties would undoubtedly be a greater surprise to them than anything else that has occurred in their dealings or in the case. . . .

The record further shows that the defendants, when they sold the cow, believed the cow was not with calf, and barren; that from what the plaintiff had been told by defendants (for it does not appear he had any other knowledge or facts from which he could form an opinion) he believed the cow was farrow, but still thought she could be made to breed.

The foregoing shows the entire interview and treaty between the parties as to the sterility and qualities of the cow sold to the plaintiff. The cow had a calf in the month of October.

There is no question but that the defendants sold the cow representing her of the breed and quality they believed the cow to be, and that the purchaser so understood it. And the buyer purchased her believing her to be of the breed represented by the sellers, and possessing all the qualities stated, and even more. He believed she would breed. There is no pretense that the plaintiff bought the cow for beef, and there is nothing in the record indicating that he would have bought her at all only that he thought she might be made to breed. Under the foregoing facts, — and these are all that are contained in the record material to the contract, — it is held that because it turned out that the plaintiff was more correct in his judgment as to one quality of the cow than the defendants, and a quality, too, which could not by any possibility be positively known at the time by either party to exist, the contract may be annulled by the defendants at their pleasure. I know of no law, and have not been referred to any, which will justify any such holding, and I think the circuit judge was right in his construction of the contract between the parties.

It is claimed that a mutual mistake of a material fact was made by the parties when the contract of sale was made. There was no warranty in the case of the quality of the animal. When a mistaken fact is relied upon as ground for rescinding, such fact must not only exist at the time the contract is made, but must have been known to one or both of the parties. Where there is no warranty, there can be no mistake of fact when no such fact exists, or, if in existence, neither party knew of it, or could know of it; and that is precisely this case. If the owner of a Hambletonian horse had speeded him, and was only able to make him go a mile in three minutes, and should sell him to another, believing that was his greatest speed, for $300, when the purchaser believed he could go much faster, and made the purchase for that sum, and a few days thereafter, under more favorable circumstances, the horse was driven a mile in 2 min. 16 sec., and was found to be worth $20,000, I hardly think it would be held, either at law or in equity, by any one, that the seller in such case could rescind the contract. The same legal principles apply in each case.

In this case neither party knew the actual quality and condition of this cow at the time of the sale. The defendants say, or rather said, to the plaintiff, "they had a few head left on their farm in Greenfield, and asked plaintiff to go and see them, stating to plaintiff that in all probability they were sterile and would not breed." Plaintiff did go as requested, and found there three cows, including the one purchased, with a bull. The cow had been exposed, but neither knew she was with calf or whether she would breed. The defendants thought she would not, but plaintiff says that he thought she could be made to breed, but believed she was not with calf. The defendants sold the cow for what they believed her to be, and the plaintiff bought her as he believed she was, after the statements made by the defendants. No conditions whatever were attached to the terms of sale by either party. It was in fact as absolute as it could well be made, and I know of no precedent as authority by which this Court can alter the contract thus made by these parties in writing, and interpolate in it a condition by which, if the *defendants should be mistaken in their belief that the cow was barren,* she should be returned to them, and their contract should be annulled.

It is not the duty of the courts to destroy contracts when called upon to enforce them, after they have been legally made. There was no mistake of any such material fact by either of the parties in the case as would license the vendors to rescind. There was no difference between the parties, nor misapprehension, as to the substance of the thing bargained for, which was a cow supposed to be barren by one party, and believed not to be by the other. As to the quality of the animal, subsequently developed, both parties were equally ignorant, and as to this each party took his chances. If this were not the law, there would be no safety in purchasing this kind of stock.

I entirely agree with my brethren that the right to rescind occurs whenever "the thing actually delivered or received is different in substance from the thing bargained for, and intended to be sold; but if it be only a difference in some quality or accident, even though the misapprehension may have been the actuating motive" of the parties in making the contract, yet it will remain binding. In this case the cow sold was the one delivered. What might or might not happen to her after the sale formed no element in the contract.

The case of Kennedy v. Panama, etc., Mail Co., L.R. 2 Q.B. 588, and the extract cited therefrom in the opinion of my brethren, clearly sustain the views I have taken. See, also, Smith v. Hughes, L.R. 6 Q.B. 597; Carter v. Crick, 4 Hurl. & N. 416.

According to this record, whatever the mistake was, if any, in this case, it was upon the part of the defendants, and while acting upon their own judgment. It is, however, elementary law, and very elementary, too, "that the mistaken party, acting entirely upon his own judgment, without any common understanding with the other party in the premises as to the quality of an animal, is remediless if he is injured through his own mistake." Leake, Cont. 338; Torrance v. Bolton, L.R. 8 Ch. App. 118; Smith v. Hughes, L.R. 6 Q.B. 597. . . .

NOTE

1. The leading English case of Kennedy v. Panama, etc., Mail Co., L.R. 2 Q.B. 580 (1867), was relied on in both the majority and dissenting opinions in Sherwood v. Walker as well as in the opinion of the court in Wood v. Boynton. In the *Kennedy* case the Mail Company had issued shares to raise capital for building a fleet of ships to be used in the Pacific. In their prospectus the directors had in good faith represented that they had a contract with the government of New Zealand for carrying the European mails between New Zealand and Panama (in Panama the mails were transported across the Isthmus and reshipped for the Atlantic and Pacific legs of the journey). Relying on that representation, Kennedy subscribed for 1,600 shares at £7 per share. It turned out that the London

agent of the New Zealand government had exceeded his authority in negotiating the contract, which was subsequently repudiated by the government. A second contract was negotiated on terms less favorable to the Mail Company. Kennedy, who had paid down £2 per share, sued the Mail Company to get his money back; the Mail Company counterclaimed to recover the balance of £5 due on each share. At the time the actions were brought the shares were selling for £5 per share. Judgment was for the Mail Company on both the claim and counterclaim. (Mellish, whom we have met before as winning counsel in Raffles v. Wichelhaus, *supra* p. 869, was the losing counsel, appearing for Kennedy. The opinion in Queens Bench was by Blackburn, J., whom we shall meet again in Taylor v. Caldwell, *infra* p. 920). On the facts as stated, do you think the *Kennedy* case is "like" either Wood v. Boynton or Sherwood v. Walker? If you do, is it an authority in support of the *Wood* decision? Does it support the majority opinion or the dissent in *Sherwood*?

2. According to Professor (now Judge) Posner, Sherwood v. Walker can best be approached "by asking how the parties would have allocated the risk [of the cow's pregnancy] between them had they foreseen it." Economic Analysis of Law 73 (2d ed. 1977). He elaborates as follows:

> This approach decomposes the contract into two distinct agreements: an agreement respecting the basic performance (the transfer of the cow) and an agreement respecting a risk associated with the transfer (that the cow will turn out to be different from what the parties believed). In fact there was some evidence that Rose's sale price included her value if pregnant, discounted (very drastically of course) by the probability of that happy eventuality. This evidence, if believed, would have justified the court in concluding that the parties had intended to transfer the risk of the cow's turning out to be pregnant to the buyer, in which event delivery should have been enforced. Even in the absence of any such evidence, there would be an argument for placing on the seller the risk that the cow is not what it seems. In general, if not in every particular case, the owner will have superior access to information concerning the actual or probable characteristics of his property. This is the theory on which the seller of a house is liable to the buyer for any latent (as distinct from obvious) defects; a similar principle could be used to decide cases of mutual mistake. [footnotes omitted]

Do you agree with Posner's assessment of the case? The plaintiff in *Sherwood* was a banker; would it have made a difference if he had been a butcher?

3. In both *Wood* and *Sherwood* the thing being sold turned out to be immensely more valuable than the parties had, in good faith, assumed when they made their deal. In *Kennedy* the shares turned out to be less valuable than they presumably would have been if the representation in the prospectus had been true. Another case of the *Kennedy* type was

Smith v. Zimbalist, 2 Cal. App. 2d 324, 38 P.2d 170 (1934) (*hearing denied by Supreme Court of California*). Smith was an elderly and evidently wealthy collector of rare violins (that is, he was not a dealer). Zimbalist was a leading concert violinist. Having been invited to inspect Smith's collection, Zimbalist identified two violins as being a Stradivarius and a Guarnerius and offered to buy them. Smith agreed to sell the two violins for $8,000; Zimbalist paid $2,000 down and agreed to pay the balance in six equal monthly installments. A "bill of sale" signed by Smith described the violins as being a Stradivarius and a Guarnerius, stated the price and the terms of payment, acknowledged receipt of the $2,000 down payment and further provided: "I agree that Mr. Zimbalist shall have the right to exchange these for any others in my collection should he so desire." Zimbalist signed a comparable "memorandum." Before Zimbalist had made any further payments, it was discovered that the violins were copies that were not worth more than $300. Smith sued Zimbalist to recover the unpaid balance of $6,000. Judgment was for Zimbalist on two grounds. The first was that in a contract for the sale of goods "the parties to the proposed contract are not bound where it appears that in its essence each of them is honestly mistaken or in error with reference to the identity of the subject matter of such contract." The second was that, by the description in the bill of sale, Smith had warranted that the violins were genuine. (Note that it was Zimbalist who had initially identified the violins.) The trial court concluded that Smith had not given a warranty, but it gave judgment for Zimbalist, presumably on the first ground. It is curious that the appellate court, in affirming the judgment, should have gone to the trouble of reversing the trial judge on his handling of the warranty issue. Possibly that may be taken to suggest that the appellate court was not altogether satisfied with the first ground of decision. There is no further reference in the opinion to the provision of the bill of sale under which Zimbalist was to have the right to exchange the two violins for any others in Smith's collection. It does not appear that Zimbalist attempted to recover the $2,000 down payment. If he had, how do you think the court would (or should) have disposed of the claim?

4. Houser, J., in the course of his opinion in Smith v. Zimbalist, digested Sherwood v. Walker at some length, adding the following comment: "But to the contrary of such ruling on practically similar facts, see Wood v. Boynton. . . ." Evidently Judge Houser regarded the two cases as irreconcilable (same fact situations, opposite holdings). Do you agree? See further the Note on Bell v. Lever Brothers, Ltd., *infra* p. 896.

5. In Amalgamated Investment and Property Co. Ltd. v. John Walker & Sons, Ltd., [1976] 3 All. E.R. 509 (C.A.), Walker in 1973 advertised for the sale of land it owned in London. The land was occupied by a large warehouse that had originally been built for the use of Walker, a whiskey manufacturer, as a bonded warehouse and bottling factory but was no longer used for that or any other purpose. The land was described as

being suitable for "occupation or redevelopment." Amalgamated, making clear that it was interested in acquiring the property for redevelopment, offered £1,710,000. On July 19, 1973, Walker accepted the offer "subject to contract." On August 14 Walker, in response to an inquiry from Amalgamated, stated that it was not aware of any proposal to have its warehouse designated as a "building of special architectural or historic interest." On September 25 Amalgamated and Walker signed a contract for sale of the land for £1,710,000. On September 26 the Department of the Environment notified Walker that the warehouse had been listed as a "building of special architectural or historic interest." The listing made the land unavailable for redevelopment unless an exemption (a "listed building consent") could be obtained from the Department. Until receipt of the September 26 communication, neither Walker nor Amalgamated had known that the Department was considering the listing of the warehouse. The effect of the listing was to reduce the value of the property from £1,710,000 (the contract price) to £200,000.

Amalgamated sought rescission of the contract on the alternative grounds of "common mistake" and "frustration." The trial judge denied relief on either ground. A three-judge panel in the Court of Appeal unanimously affirmed. As to "common mistake," there was no ground for relief since the contract was signed on September 25 and the warehouse was not officially "listed" until the following day when the notification was signed and dispatched. As to "frustration," the possibility that a building might be "listed" and thus made unavailable for redevelopment was, as Buckley, L.J., put it, "a risk which inheres in all ownership of buildings . . . a risk that every owner and every purchaser of property must recognize that he is subject to." All the judges expressed their horror and disgust at the procedures that the Department of the Environment had followed in deciding to list the Walker warehouse as a "building of special architectural or historic interest" and wished Amalgamated the best of luck in its attempt to secure an exemption.

6. In City of Everett v. Estate of Sumstad, 26 Wash. App. 742, 614 P.2d 1294 (1980) the facts were that the Estate had commissioned an auctioneer to sell certain property belonging to the Estate, including a safe. The safe contained an inner compartment with a combination lock; the compartment was locked; the combination had been lost; neither the Estate nor the auctioneer had had the compartment opened by a locksmith, or knew what, if anything, was inside the compartment. At the auction, the auctioneer stated these facts to the bidders. A sign behind the auctioneer's block read: All Sales are Final. The Mitchells, who operated a second-hand store and were regular customers at the auction, bid on the safe for $50. They engaged a locksmith who, on opening the locked compartment, found $32,207. The locksmith turned the money over to the police. Both the Estate and the Mitchells claimed the money; the City commenced an interpleader action. Apparently no one knew

how long the money had been in the safe or who had originally owned it. The trial court awarded the fund to the Estate and was affirmed on appeal by the majority of a three-judge panel. The majority opinion concluded that resolution of the case "depends on an analysis of the objective theory of contract" and that "the parties did not objectively enter into a contract for the sale of the safe and its *contents*, but only a sale of the safe." [Emphasis in original] The dissenting opinion collects cases, old and new, involving property found in locked or sealed containers (see Annotation, 4 A.L.R.2d 318 (1949)). One of the cases is Durfee v. Jones, 11 R.I. 588, 23 Am. Rep. 528 (1877). Plaintiff was the owner of a safe, which he entrusted to the defendant for sale, but also with permission to use the safe until it was sold. The defendant found some bank notes in a crevice of the safe. The plaintiff (who did not claim to be the "original" or "true" owner of the bank notes) naturally claimed them. The Rhode Island court awarded the fund to the defendant, as a "finder." Holmes discussed the Rhode Island case in his lecture on Possession, in The Common Law 177 (M. Howe ed. 1963), commenting: "I venture to think this decision wrong." Young, Half Measures, 81 Colum. L. Rev. 19, 24 (1981), comments that in the *City of Everett* case the Washington court "if [it] had characterized the problem as one of mistake [instead of contract formation] . . . might have been willing to consider the argument that treasure troves ought to be divided between the parties to a sale." However the issue in the case is "characterized," how do you think the case should be decided? All the money to the Estate? All the money to the Mitchells? Half to each? Do any of the other materials in this section seem to you to throw any light on this problem?

7. Assume that A contracts to sell his Blackacre to B for $50,000 (which both A and B consider to be a fair price). Subsequently it is discovered that the land is oil-bearing and worth millions. "Subsequently" in the preceding sentence can be taken to mean: 50 years after the conveyance; immediately after the conveyance; immediately before the conveyance. Would you be in favor of taking the time scheduled for performance under the contract as an absolute cut-off? Or would you prefer a rule under which the seller could recover the land if he discovered its true value within a reasonable time after conveyance and sued to get it back before the buyer had substantially changed his position or third parties had acquired rights in the land? Or a rule under which, in cases of this type, seller and buyer would divide the unanticipated profits? Cady v. Gale, 5 W. Va. 547 (1871), is an oil-bearing land case in which the discovery of oil was made after the buyer of the land had paid the agreed consideration and at a time when the seller ought to have (but had not) conveyed to him. In the buyer's action for specific performance, the Supreme Court of Appeals reversed the lower court and ordered that the seller convey his interest in the land and account to the buyer for interim rents and profits.

Suppose the buyer in *Cady* had been a professional geologist who, after conducting a survey of the property in question, concluded it was oil-bearing but said nothing about this to the seller. Compare Laidlaw v. Organ, *supra* p. 89. Would you consider the buyer's position to be stronger or weaker under these circumstances? A case of this sort would probably be classified as one of unilateral mistake (since only the seller is mistaken as to the property's true value). Do you think it should be treated in the same fashion as the mistaken bid cases, *supra* pp. 323-348, which have also traditionally been classified under the heading of unilateral mistake? See Kronman, Mistake, Disclosure, Information and the Law of Contracts, 7 J. Legal Stud. 1 (1978).

8. In Bell v. Lever Brothers, Ltd., L.R. 1932 A.C. 161 (1931), the facts were these: Lever Brothers had entered into employment contracts with Bell and Snelling, under which the two men were to render various services for the company in connection with its West African cocoa business. Several years later, Lever Brothers decided to cancel the contracts for purely financial reasons, and paid Bell and Snelling £50,000 in return for their agreement to accept the cancellations. The company subsequently discovered that during the period of their employment, the two men had exploited their positions of trust in the company for their own personal gain. Bell and Snelling had apparently made no misrepresentations to the contrary, but neither had they disclosed their own wrongdoing. If the fact of their misconduct had been known at the time of the cancellation agreement, Lever Brothers could have simply dismissed Bell and Snelling with no compensation whatsoever. The company brought an action to recover the money it had already paid them, claiming that it had done so on the basis of an invalidating mistake, namely, its ignorance of the fact that it could "have got rid of them for nothing." The trial court gave judgment for Lever Brothers and was unanimously affirmed by a Court of Appeal that included Scrutton, L.J. However, a divided House of Lords reversed the judgment. In the course of his opinion (or speech) for the majority view, Lord Atkin remarked:

> [O]n the whole, I have come to the conclusion that it would be wrong to decide that an agreement to terminate a definite specified contract is void if it turns out that the agreement had already been broken and could have been terminated otherwise. The contract released is the identical contract in both cases, and the party paying for release gets exactly what he bargains for. It seems immaterial that he could have got the same result in another way, or that if he had known the true facts he would not have entered into the bargain. A. buys B.'s horse; he thinks the horse is sound and he pays the price of a sound horse; he would certainly not have bought the horse if he had known as the fact is that the horse is unsound. If B. has made no representation as to soundness and has not contracted that the horse is sound, A. is bound and cannot recover back the price. A. buys a picture from B.; both A. and B. believe it to be the work of an old master, and a

high price is paid. It turns out to be a modern copy. A. has no remedy in the absence of representation or warranty. A. agrees to take on lease or to buy from B. an unfurnished dwelling-house. The house is in fact uninhabitable. A. would never have entered into the bargain if he had known the fact. A. has no remedy, and the position is the same whether B. knew the facts or not, so long as he made no representation or gave no warranty. A. buys a roadside garage business from B. abutting on a public thoroughfare: unknown to A., but known to B., it has already been decided to construct a byepass road which will divert substantially the whole of the traffic from passing A's garage. Again A. has no remedy. All these cases involve hardship on A. and benefit B., as most people would say, unjustly. They can be supported on the ground that it is of paramount importance that contracts should be observed, and that if parties honestly comply with the essentials of the formation of contracts — i.e., agree in the same terms on the same subject-matter — they are bound, and must rely on the stipulations of the contract for protection from the effect of facts unknown to them.

The case was evidently not one of easy or obvious solution. Nine judges voted on the case. Six felt that Lever Brothers should recover the settlements it had paid over to Bell and Snelling. However, the three who felt that Bell and Snelling could keep the money were a bare majority of the House of Lords. It may not be altogether implausible to take this diversity of judicial views as illustrative of the transition from the nineteenth-century rules on excuse from contractual liability under mistake or impossibility theory to the much broader twentieth-century excuse rules. Arguably, if the case had been decided in the 1890s, all the judges would have held that Bell and Snelling could keep the money. Perhaps, if the case had been decided in the 1970s, all the judges would have held that Lever Brothers could get the money back.

9. Lever Brothers entered into the settlement agreements with Bell and Snelling in March of 1929, paid the money over on May 1, discovered the facts about their misconduct in July and sued to get the money back. Assume that Lever Brothers had discovered the facts in April, refused to make any payments, and been sued by Bell and Snelling. What result? Reconsider in this connection the time sequence in Wood v. Boynton, *supra* p. 84, Sherwood v. Walker, *supra* p. 887, and the cases digested in the Note following Sherwood. See also the Note following Raffles v. Wichelhaus, *supra* p. 869. It should be noted that none of the opinions in any of these cases (or in any other cases of the same type known to the editors) contains the slightest hint or suggestion that the time at which the true state of facts was discovered (that is, before or after performance) was relevant to the decision.

10.   Under a rational system of law, do you think the plaintiff in Wood v. Boynton should get the diamond back? If, in Smith v. Zimbalist, Zimbalist had paid the full price before finding out that the violins were copies, do you think he should get the money back? Do you think that

Bell and Snelling, despite their misconduct, should have been allowed to
keep the money Lever Brothers had paid them? And how would you
distribute the money found in the safe in the *City of Everett* case? Do you
think that your answers to the questions just put are consistent with one
another?

McRAE v. COMMONWEALTH
DISPOSALS COMMISSION

84 C.L.R. 377 (High Court of Australia, 1951)

The following written judgments were delivered: —

DIXON and FULLAGAR JJ. This is an appeal from a judgment of Webb J. in
an action in which the plaintiffs claimed damages on three causes of
action alleged alternatively — breach of contract, deceit and negligence.
The judgment, as passed and entered, was in favour of the plaintiffs
against the Commonwealth Disposals Commission for £756 10s. 0d. as
damages for deceit, and his Honour awarded the plaintiffs one-half of the
costs of the action. The plaintiffs appeal, asserting that they are entitled
to damages far in excess of £756 10s. 0d. The defendants cross-appeal,
asserting that the maximum amount recoverable by the plaintiffs on any
view of the case was £285. The amounts actually claimed by the statement of claim were, on the basis of one set of allegations, some £250,000,
and, on the basis of another set of allegations, some £10,000.

The case presents serious difficulties, the facts being in some respects
of an extraordinary character. Some aspects of them are probably not
fully explained by anything that appears in the evidence. They are summarized chronologically in the judgment of Webb J., and that summary
need not be repeated here. Though it may be necessary for some purposes to go back in point of time, we think that, for the purposes of this
appeal, the proper starting-point is the acceptance by the Commission of
a tender by the plaintiffs for the purchase from the Commission of a
wrecked or stranded oil tanker. It would be premature to speak of that
acceptance as creating a contract, because the defendants have contended throughout that the "contract" was "void," or, in other words,
that no contract was ever made. Only one thing need be said before
proceeding to the starting point. In the assumed background of the case
lay the facts that during the war a considerable number of ships, including "oil tankers," became wrecked or stranded in the waters adjacent to
New Guinea, that after the war the Commission had the function of
disposing of these as it thought fit, and that a purchaser from the Commission of any of these wrecked or stranded vessels might, but not necessarily would, make a very large profit by salving and selling the vessel, or
the materials of her hull and equipment, or her cargo. The realization of
a profit in this way (and the evidence suggests that a purchaser would not

contemplate a realization of profit by an immediate resale of what he had bought as such) could, of course, only be achieved after the expenditure of large sums of money. Such a purchaser would naturally regard himself as acquiring, at best, a chance of making a profit. But he would not regard himself as acquiring a certainty of making a loss.

In the Melbourne newspapers, Age and Argus, of 29th March 1947, appeared an advertisement inserted by the Commission. The advertisement read: —

Tenders are invited for the purchase of an OIL TANKER lying on JOUR-MAUND REEF, which is approximately 100 miles NORTH OF SAMARAI. THE VESSEL IS SAID TO CONTAIN OIL. OFFERS TO PURCHASE THE VESSEL AND ITS CONTENTS should be submitted to the COMMONWEALTH DISPOSALS COMMISSION, Nicholas Building, 37 Swanston Street, Melbourne, indorsed "OFFER FOR VESSEL ON JOURMAUND REEF," and should be lodged not later than 2 p.m., March 31, 1947.

In response to this advertisement, the plaintiffs, who are brothers trading in partnership, submitted a tender dated 31st March 1947. The tender was on a printed form. It was headed "Offer for vessel on Journmaund Reef." The form was divided into columns. In a column headed "Description of Goods" the words "1 oil tanker lying on Journmaund Reef as advertised Age, Argus, 29/3/47" were inserted. In the next column, which was headed "Location of Goods" the words "On Journmaund Reef, off Samarai" were inserted. The price quoted was £285, and a cheque for £28 10s. 0d. being the required deposit of ten per cent, was forwarded with the tender. Indorsed on the printed form of tender were a number of conditions. On 11th April 1947 the Commission wrote to the plaintiffs a letter saying: — "With reference to your tender of 31st March 1947, I desire to advise that your offer of £285 net has been accepted. A sales advice note to cover this transaction will be forwarded in the course of the next few days." This letter was followed by another letter of 15th April 1947, which says: — "I wish to inform you that your offer to purchase dated 31.3.47 is accepted for the quantities, the items, and at the price set out hereunder and/or in the attachment hereto bearing the same sales advice number as this acceptance." Below appear the words "One (1) Oil Tanker including Contents wrecked on Journmaund Reef approximately 100 miles north of Samarai. Price £285." Then come some provisions as to payment and delivery, followed by the signature on behalf of the Commission. After the signature come the words "Your offer to purchase, the general conditions contained in Form O, and this acceptance, shall constitute the contract. Kindly acknowledge receipt of this communication by return post." Finally, certain further "terms" are set out. The plaintiffs apparently did not, by return post or otherwise, acknowledge in writing the receipt of this remarkable "communication." Form O is a printed form which contains a number of "conditions of sale," most of which are entirely inappropriate to the particular case.

The contention of the Commission that no contract ever came into existence between itself and the plaintiffs was based on extrinsic facts which will have to be considered in a moment. It was not denied that, apart from those facts, a contract would have been made, and, on the assumption that a contract was made, a good deal of argument took place as to what were the terms of that contract. It will be convenient to deal with this matter at this stage. No less than five documents are involved — the advertisement, the tender, the letter of 11th April, the letter of 15th April, and "Form O." Mr. Gillard, for the plaintiffs, contended that the terms of the contract made were to be found in the first three documents only. He said that the letter of 11th April was an unequivocal acceptance of the offer contained in the tender, that the reference to "sales advice note" was not to be understood as contemplating the addition of further terms so as to make the letter in effect a counter-offer, and that the letter of 15th April was merely an ineffective attempt to add further terms to a contract which was concluded on the receipt of the plaintiffs' letter of 11th April. He referred to a well-known line of cases of which Bellamy v. Debenham[3] and Lennon v. Scarlett & Co.[4] are good examples. Mr. Tait, for the Commission, contended that the plaintiffs must be taken to have accepted the terms set out and referred to in the second letter, and that the terms of the contract were to be found in all five of the documents. He admitted that in the terms so found there was overlapping and inconsistency, and that some of those terms were entirely inappropriate to the subject matter of the contract, but he said that these facts merely meant that difficult problems of construction might arise. We are disposed to accept the view put by Mr. Gillard, but the question does not seem to us to matter, and for this reason. The only condition on which Mr. Tait affirmatively relied was a condition which is contained in clause 8 of the terms indorsed on the tender form. That clause provides that the goods "are sold as and where they lie with all faults" and that no warranty is given as to "condition description quality or otherwise." This clause cannot, in our opinion, help the Commission in this case. What the Commission sold was an "oil tanker." It was, therefore, a *condition* of the contract that what was supplied should conform to the description of an oil tanker, and it is settled that such a clause as clause 8 has no application to such a condition: see, e.g., Wallis, Son & Wells v. Pratt & Haynes[5] and Robert A. Munro & Co. Ltd. v. Meyer[6]; and cf. Shepherd v. Kain.[7]

There was, however, another communication from the Commission

3. (1890) 45 Ch. D. 481.
4. (1921) 29 C.L.R. 499.
5. (1911) A.C. 394.
6. (1930) 2 K.B. 312.
7. (1821) 5 B. & Ald. 240 [106 E.R. 1180].

to the plaintiffs, which is of considerable importance. The accepted tender described the subject matter as an "oil tanker lying on Jourmaund Reef as advertised Age, Argus, 29/3/47." The advertisement described her as "lying on Jourmaund Reef, which is approximately 100 miles North of Samarai." Now there appears to be no reef anywhere in the locality which is chartered or officially known as "Jourmaund Reef." There is a channel between two islands or reefs charted as "Jomard Entrance," and a few miles to the east of that channel is an island or reef charted as "Jomard Island." Jomard Island, however, is not approximately 100 miles from Samarai, but approximately 170 miles from Samarai, and its bearing from Samarai is not North but a little South of East. The plaintiffs, having bought as they thought, their tanker, looked for "Jourmaund Reef" on a map. They, of course, failed to find it, but they found Jomard Island, and thereupon, not unnaturally, asked the Commission to give them the precise latitude and longitude of the tanker. The Commission gave a latitude and longitude by telephone on 18th April, and confirmed this by a letter written on the same day. The letter read: — "Confirming our telephone conversation of this morning, in connection with the location of the Oil Tanker on Jourmond" (sic) "Reef, I wish to advise it is located as follows: — Latitude 11 degrees 16½ minutes South: Longitude 151 degrees 58 minutes East." The result of this letter was to resolve any ambiguity in the description of the locality of the tanker and to identify with precision, as against the defendant Commission, the place referred to in the relevant documents as the place where the thing which they were purporting to sell was lying.

Now, the simple fact is that there was not at any material time any oil tanker lying at or anywhere near the location specified in the letter of 18th April. There was, at a point about eleven miles east of the location specified, a wrecked vessel described as an "oil barge." Some years before 1947 strenuous but unavailing efforts to salve this vessel had been made by a fully equipped expedition sent out by the Commonwealth Salvage Board. It was contended before Webb J., and also, though faintly, before us, that this vessel was a tanker and that delivery of her to the plaintiffs would constitute performance of the contract by the Commission. Webb J. rejected this contention, and the evidence clearly establishes that a "tanker," according to common understanding, is a self-propelled, ocean-going vessel, fully equipped both for navigation and for the carriage of oil in bulk. A barge is merely a floating repository for oil, adapted to be towed, but not otherwise capable of movement under control. The existence of the wrecked barge in question here is not, we think, a directly relevant factor in the case, though it may serve to explain to some extent how a rumour that there was a wrecked tanker somewhere began to circulate in the offices of the Commission.

We say advisedly that such a rumour began to circulate, because there was indeed no better foundation for any supposition on the part of the officers of the Commission that they had a tanker to sell. They had no more definite information than was derived from an offer by a man named Jarrett to buy for £50 the contents of a wrecked vessel, which he said was within a radius of 200 miles from Samarai, and from what can be quite fairly described as mere gossip. The reckless and irresponsible attitude of the Commission's officers is clearly indicated by the description in the advertisement of the locality of the tanker. In an even worse light appears an attempt which was made later, without any foundation whatever, to suggest that at the time of the making of the contract there had been a tanker in the place specified but that she had since been washed off the reef in a storm. Unfortunately the plaintiffs, for their part, took the matter seriously. They believed, and there is evidence that they had some reason for believing, that an oil tanker wrecked at the place indicated was likely to prove a profitable proposition, and accordingly they paid on 23rd April the balance of their purchase money, and then proceeded to fit up a small ship, which they owned, with diving and salvage equipment, and they engaged personnel, and proceeded from Melbourne to New Guinea. It is sufficient at this stage to say that they expended a large sum of money in discovering that they had bought a non-existent tanker.

The plaintiffs, as has been said, based their claim for damages on three alternative grounds. They claimed, in the first place, for damages for breach of a contract to sell a tanker lying at a particular place. Alternatively they claimed damages for a fraudulent representation that there was a tanker lying at the place specified. In the further alternative, they claimed damages for a negligent failure to disclose that there was no tanker at the place specified after that fact became known to the Commission. The second and third of these alleged causes of action depend wholly or partly on certain further facts which have not so far been mentioned. On 19th April 1947 a telegram was sent from the District Officer at Misima to the Port Moresby office of the Commission, which read:

> Your S4382 stop Large approx. 100 ft. barge type tanker carrying oil machinery etc. apparently drifted on reef, Jomard Entrance high water during 1944 stop When inspected by Lieut. Middleton 1945 large hole stern admitted sea Machinery ruined stop Understand oil still in hold but quantity unknown Vessel exposed low tide only partly submerged high tide Can inspect when district vessel available.

This unquestionably refers to the wrecked barge. How and why this telegram came to be sent is one of the minor mysteries of this case: no Port Moresby message numbered S4382 was produced. It seems reasonable to infer that the plaintiff's request for a precise "fix" for their tanker prompted the making of inquiries which ought to have been made much earlier, and that the missing "S4382" was a belated attempt to find out whether the Commission had really had anything to sell to the plaintiffs. On 14th April the Port Moresby office of the Commission had telegraphed the District Officer at Samarai, saying: — "S4392 Would appreciate urgent reply details oil tanker Jourmaund Reef stop Understand vessel now moved under water and contents nil stop Can this be confirmed?" It seems quite possible that one of the quoted numbers is a mistake for the other, and that the telegram of 17th April is really in response to that of 14th April, which had been passed on from Samarai to Misima. Anyhow, the telegram of 17th April was set out in a letter of 19th April from the Port Moresby office to the Melbourne office of the Commission. The letter was minuted by Bowser, one of the officers of the Commission who were mainly responsible for the "selling" of the "tanker," as follows: — "Received 21/4/47. McRae (successful tenderer) already advised and confirmed by letter location of vessel." In the meantime Port Moresby had replied to Misima, saying: — "Appreciate report stop Vessel sold Melbourne syndicate Inspection not required."

The plaintiffs put their claim in deceit in this way. They said, first, that there was a false and fraudulent representation in the original advertisement. They said, secondly, that, even if the original representation as to the existence of a tanker was innocent, the representation was a continuing representation and the Commission knew, on 21st April at the latest, that it was false. By thereafter allowing the plaintiffs, on the faith of the truth of the representation, to pay the balance of purchase money and incur expenditure, they rendered themselves liable in deceit. The plaintiffs put their final alternative claim in this way. They said that, when the Commission was asked for the precise location of the vessel, they owed to the plaintiffs a duty to exercise reasonable care in obtaining the information required. The duty arose from the position of the parties. They at least believed that they were contractually bound. It must have been obvious to the Commission that the plaintiffs were likely to spend real money in reliance on the information supplied. So far from exercising any sort of care in the matter, they merely obtained a rough estimate of the latitude and longitude of Jomard Entrance and gave the result to the plaintiffs. The grossness of the negligence is emphasised by the fact that, on the very day (17th April) on which the latitude and longitude were telegraphed from Port Moresby to Melbourne, the Port Moresby office of the Commission received the telegram from Misima which should, the plaintiffs say, have made it plain to them that there was no tanker at Jomard Entrance.

Webb J. held that the contract for the sale of a tanker was void — in other words, that no contract for the sale of a tanker was ever made. He considered that the well-known case of Couturier v. Hastie[8] compelled

8. (1852) 8 Ex. 40 [155 E.R. 1250]; (1853) 9 Ex. 102 [156 E.R. 43]; (1856) 5 H.L.C. 673 [10 E.R. 1065].

him to this conclusion. His Honour held, however, as we read his judgment, that the plaintiffs had made out their case on the second aspect of their claim in deceit. He assessed damages on the basis that the plaintiffs were entitled to the return of the price paid plus an amount (necessarily, of course, approximate only) representing what it would have cost (without any preparations for salvage operations) to inspect the locality and ascertain that there was no tanker there. His Honour has not expressly stated the basis of his assessment, but it was common ground before us that this was the basis on which he proceeded.

The first question to be determined is whether a contract was made between the plaintiffs and the Commission. The argument that the contract was void, or, in other words, that there was no contract, was based, as has been observed, on Couturier v. Hastie. . . . The facts of the case were simple enough. A question of *del credere* agency was involved, which has no relevance to the present case, and the facts may be stated without reference to that question. A sold to B "1,180 quarters of Salonica Indian corn of fair average quality when shipped at 27/- per quarter f.o.b., and including freight and insurance, to a safe port in the United Kingdom, payment at two months from date upon handing over shipping documents." At the date of the contract the vessel containing the corn had sailed from Salonica, but, having encountered very heavy weather, had put in at Tunis. Here the cargo had been found to have become so heated and fermented that it could not be safely carried further. It had accordingly been landed at Tunis and sold there. These facts were unknown to either party at the date of the contract. On discovering them, B repudiated the contract. After the expiration of the two months mentioned in the contract, A, being able and willing to hand over the shipping documents, sued B for the price. The case came on for trial before Martin B. and a jury. Martin B. directed the jury that "the contract imported that, at the time of the sale, the corn was in existence as such, and capable of delivery."[9] The jury found a verdict for the defendant, and the plaintiff had leave to move. The Court of Exchequer (Parke B. and Alderson B., Pollock C.B. dissenting) made absolute a rule to enter a verdict for the plaintiff. This decision was reversed in the court of Exchequer Chamber, and the House of Lords, after consulting the Judges, affirmed the decision of the Exchequer Chamber, so that the defendant ultimately had judgment.

[In an omitted passage the court discussed at considerable length the true meaning of Couturier v. Hastie, concluding:

In that case (i.e., Couturier v. Hastie) there was a failure of consideration, and the purchaser was not bound to pay the price: if he had paid it before the truth was discovered, he could have recovered it back as money had

---

9. (1852) 8 Ex., at p. 47 [155 E.R., at pp. 1253, 1254].

and received. The construction of the contract was the vital thing in the case because, and only because, on the construction of the contract depended the question whether the consideration had really failed, the vendor maintaining that, since he was able to hand over the shipping documents, it had not failed. The truth is that the question whether the contract was void, or the vendor excused from performance by reason of the nonexistence of the supposed subject matter, did not arise in Couturier v. Hastie. It would have arisen if the purchaser had suffered loss through non-delivery of the corn and had sued the vendor for damages. If it had so arisen, we think that the real question would have been whether the contract was subject to an implied condition precedent that the goods were in existence. Prima facie, one would think, there would be no such implied condition precedent, the position being simply that the vendor promised that the goods were in existence.]

The position so far, then, may be summed up as follows. It was not decided in Couturier v. Hastie that the contract in that case was void. The question whether it was void or not did not arise. If it had arisen, as in an action by the purchaser for damages, it would have turned on the ulterior question whether the contract was subject to an implied condition precedent. Whatever might then have been held on the facts of Couturier v. Hastie, it is impossible in this case to imply any such term. The terms of the contract and the surrounding circumstances clearly exclude any such implication. The buyers relied upon, and acted upon, the assertion of the seller that there was a tanker in existence. It is not a case in which the parties can be seen to have proceeded on the basis of a common assumption of fact so as to justify the conclusion that the correctness of the assumption was intended by both parties to be a condition precedent to the creation of contractual obligations. The officers of the commission made an assumption, but the plaintiffs did not make an assumption in the same sense. They knew nothing except what the Commission had told them. If they had been asked they would certainly not have said: "Of course, if there is no tanker, there is no contract." They would have said: "We shall have to go and take possession of the tanker. We simply accept the Commission's assurance that there is a tanker and the Commission's promise to give us that tanker." The only proper construction of the contract is that it included a promise by the Commission that there was a tanker in the position specified. The Commission contracted that there was a tanker there. "The sale in this case of a ship implies a contract that the subject of the transfer did exist in the character of a ship" (Barr v. Gibson[10]). If, on the other hand, the case of Couturier v. Hastie and this case ought to be treated as cases raising a question of "mistake," then the Commission cannot in this case rely on any mistake as avoiding the contract, because any mistake was induced by the serious

10. (1833) 3 M. & W., at pp. 399, 400 [150 E.R., at pp. 1200, 1201].

fault of their own servants, who asserted the existence of a tanker reck-
lessly and without any reasonable ground. There *was* a contract, and the
Commission contracted that a tanker existed in the position specified.
Since there was no such tanker, there has been a breach of contract, and
the plaintiffs are entitled to damages for that breach.

Before proceeding to consider the measure of damages, one other
matter should be briefly mentioned. The contract was made in Melbourne, and it would seem that its proper law is Victorian law. Section 11
of the Victorian Goods Act 1928 corresponds to s. 6 of the English Sale of
Goods Act 1893, and provides that "where there is a contract for the sale
of specific goods, and the goods without the knowledge of the seller have
perished at the time when the contract is made is void."[11] This has been
generally supposed to represent the legislature's view of the effect of
Couturier v. Hastie. Whether it correctly represents the effect of the
decision in that case or not, it seems clear that the section has no application to the facts of the present case. Here the goods never existed, and the
seller ought to have known that they did not exist.

The conclusion that there was an enforceable contract makes it unnecessary to consider the other two causes of action raised by the plaintiffs. As to each of these, the plaintiffs would have been, to say the least,
faced with serious obstacles. We have already referred to the evidence
bearing on the issue of fraud. And the claim based on negligence would
have encountered the difficulties which were held by a majority of the
Court of Appeal to be fatal to the plaintiff in Candler v. Crane Christmas
& Co.[12]

The question of damages, which is the remaining question, again
presents serious difficulties. It is necessary first to arrive at the appropriate
measure of damages. The contract was a contract for the sale of goods,
and the measure of damages for non-delivery of goods by a seller is
defined in very general terms by s. 55(2) of the Goods Act 1928 as being
"the estimated loss directly and naturally resulting in the ordinary course
of events from the seller's breach of contract." This states, in substance,
the general prima-facie rule of the common law as to the measure of
damages for breach of contract. But, if we approach this case as an
ordinary case of wrongful non-delivery of goods sold, and attempt to
apply the ordinary rules for arriving at the sum to be awarded as damages,
we seem to find ourselves at once in insuperable difficulties. There was
obviously no market into which the buyers could go to mitigate their loss,
and the rule normally applied would require us to arrive at the value of
the goods to the buyer at the place where they ought to have been
delivered and at the time when they ought to have been delivered. But it

---

11. American sales legislation is to the same effect. See Uniform Sales Act, §7(1); Uniform Commercial Code, §2-613, p. 966 *infra*. — EDS.
12. (1951) 1 All E.R. 426.

is quite impossible to place any value on what the Commission purported to sell. . . .

There is, however, more in this case than that, and the truth is that to regard this case as a simple case of breach of contract by non-delivery of goods would be to take an unreal and misleading view of it. The practical substance of the case lies in these three factors — (1) the Commission promised that there was a tanker at or near to the specified place; (2) in reliance on that promise the plaintiffs expended considerable sums of money; (3) there was in fact no tanker at or anywhere near to the specified place. In the waste of their considerable expenditure seems to lie the real and understandable grievance of the plaintiffs, and the ultimate question in the case (apart from any question or quantum) is whether the plaintiffs can recover the amount of this wasted expenditure or any part of it as damages for breach of the Commission's contract that there was a tanker in existence. In the opinion of Webb J. it would have been reasonable, and within the proper contemplation of the Commission, that the plaintiffs should take steps, but should do no more than take steps, to see whether there was a tanker in the locality given, and, if so, whether any and what things should be done to turn her to account. And his Honour estimated the reasonable cost of taking such steps at the sum of £500. This view, however, seems to assume that the plaintiffs would be, or ought to be, in doubt as to whether they really had succeeded in buying a tanker. But they were clearly entitled to assume that there was a tanker in the locality given. The Commission had not, of course, contracted that she or her cargo was capable of being salved, but it does not follow that the plaintiff's conduct in making preparations for salvage operations was unreasonable, or that the Commission ought not to have contemplated that the course in fact adopted would be adopted in reliance on their promise. It would be wrong, we think, to say that the course which the plaintiffs took was unreasonable, and it seems to us to be the very course which the Commission would naturally expect them to take. There was evidence that salvage operations at the locality given would not have presented formidable difficulties in fair weather. The plaintiffs were, of course, taking a risk, but it might very naturally seem to them, as business men, that the probability of successful salvage was such as to make the substantial expense of a preliminary inspection unwarranted. It was a matter of business, of weighing one consideration with another, a matter of which businessmen are likely to be the best judges. So far as the purpose of the expenditure is concerned, the case seems to fall within what is known as the second rule in Hadley v. Baxendale.[13] A fairly close analogy may be found in a case in which there is a contract for the sale of sheep, and the buyer sends a drover to take delivery. There are no sheep at the point of delivery. Sheep have not risen in price, and the buyer has

---

13. (1854) 9 Ex. 341 [156 E.R. 145].

suffered no loss through non-delivery as such. But he will be entitled to recover the expense which he has incurred in sending the drover to take delivery: cf. Pollock v. Mackenzie,[14] and see also Foaminol Laboratories Ltd. v. British Ortid Plastics Ltd.[15]

There is, however, still another question. Mr. Tait not only strongly opposed the view so far expressed, but he also contended that, even if that view were accepted, it still could not be held that the alleged damage flowed from the alleged breach. Let it be supposed, he said in effect, that the plaintiffs acted reasonably in what they did, and let it be supposed that the Commission ought reasonably to have contemplated that they would so act. Still, he said, the plaintiffs are faced with precisely the same difficulty with which they are faced if the case is regarded as a simple and normal case of breach by non-delivery. Suppose there had been a tanker at the place indicated. *Non constat* that the expenditure incurred by the plaintiffs would not have been equally wasted. If the promise that there was a tanker in situ had been performed, she might still have been found worthless or not susceptible of profitable salvage operations or of any salvage operations at all. How, then, he asked, can the plaintiffs say that their expenditure was *wasted because* there was no tanker in existence?

The argument is far from being negligible. But it is really, we think, fallacious. If we regard the case as a simple and normal case of breach by non-delivery, the plaintiffs have no starting-point. The burden of proof is on them, and they cannot establish that they have suffered any damage unless they can show that a tanker delivered in performance of the contract would have had some value, and this they cannot show. but when the contract alleged is a contract that there was a tanker in a particular place, and the breach assigned is that there was no tanker there, and the damages claimed are measured by expenditure incurred on the faith of the promise that there was a tanker in that place, the plaintiffs are in a very different position. They have now a starting-point. They can say: (1) this expense was incurred; (2) it was incurred because you promised us that there was a tanker; (3) the fact that there was no tanker made it certain that this expense would be wasted. The plaintiffs have in this way a starting-point. They make a prima-facie case. The fact that the expense was wasted flowed prima facie from the fact that there was no tanker; and the first fact is damage, and the second fact is breach of contract. The burden is now thrown on the Commission of establishing that, if there had been a tanker, the expense incurred would equally have been wasted. This, of course, the Commission cannot establish. The fact that the impossibility of assessing damages on the basis of a comparison between what was promised and what was delivered arises not because what was promised was valueless but because it is impossible to value a nonexistent

14. (1866) 1 Q.S.C.R. 156.
15. (1941) 2 All E.R. 393, esp. at p. 397.

thing. It is the breach of contract itself which makes it impossible even to undertake an assessment on that basis. It is not impossible, however, to undertake an assessment on another basis, and, in so far as the Commission's breach of contract itself reduces the possibility of an accurate assessment, it is not for the Commission to complain.

For these reasons we are of opinion that the plaintiffs were entitled to recover damages in this case for breach of contract, and that their damages are to be measured by reference to expenditure incurred and wasted in reliance on the Commission's promise that a tanker existed at the place specified. The only problem now remaining is to quantify those damages, but this is itself a most serious problem, because the evidence is left by the plaintiffs in a highly unsatisfactory state.

[The court's "quantification" of the damages is omitted. It concluded that McRae and his associates had reasonably expended £3,000 in their attempt to salvage the nonexistent tanker. Reversing the judgment of Webb, J., the court ordered that plaintiffs recover £3,285 (i.e., £3,000 expended plus £285 paid on the purchase price.)]

NOTE

1. McRae pleaded three counts or "causes of action" — one in contract and two in tort (for deceit and negligence). Webb, J., in the trial court, concluded that there could be no recovery on either the contract count (because of the rule of Couturier v. Hastie, codified in the English Sale of Goods Act and its counterpart in Victoria) or the negligence count (because of the long-established rule of nonliability for negligent but nonfraudulent misrepresentation exemplified by the 1951 case of Candler v. Crane Christmas & Co., cited in the opinion). He gave judgment for McRae on the deceit count, as to which he was overruled by the High Court for the reasons stated in the opinion. The High Court agreed with him on the negligence count but managed to save the day for McRae by figuring out a theory under which he could recover on the contract count. It is fair to say that all English and American authorities on sales law (including the draftsmen of the codifying statutes) had always thought that Couturier v. Hastie meant what Webb, J., thought it meant. The High Court's analysis of Couturier v. Hastie, a dazzling piece of judicial footwork, was thus something new under the sun and repays careful study. According to the High Court, what did Couturier v. Hastie hold and why was the holding not fatal to McRae's recovery on the contract count? And just how did the High Court manage to avoid the statutory formulation of what had always been thought of as "the rule in Couturier v. Hastie"?

2. As to the negligence count: At the time *McRae* was decided, the rule that there was no liability for negligent but nonfraudulent misrepre-

sentations was well established in both American and English law. The
leading American case was Ultramares Corp. v. Touche, Niven Corp.,
discussed *infra* p. 1377. That rule of nonliability has come under increasing attack in this country and been abandoned in England (in Hedley
Byrne & Co. Ltd. v. Heller & Partners Ltd., [1964] A.C. 465, the House
of Lords overruled Candler v. Crane Christmas & Co.). On these matters
see Chapter 11, Section 4. For present purposes the point is that the
McRae case, if it had come up a few years later, would have been routinely decided for McRae on the negligence count and there would have
been no reason for the High Court to engage in its extraordinary exegesis
of Couturier v. Hastie.

3. *McRae* illustrates the type of case in which the pleading can be
framed either in contract or in tort (or, as in *McRae*, in both). It is a
truism — which, like most truisms, is frequently although not always
true — that the damages recoverable under tort theory are typically
greater than the damages recoverable under contract theory. See Chapter 10, Section 4. In *McRae*, Webb, J., grounding his judgment on the
tort count in deceit, limited the damages to £500 (the limit would presumably have been the same under the tort count in negligence). The High
Court, grounding its judgment on the contract count, increased the damages to £3,285. Thus *McRae* is a classic example of the sort of case in
which the truism was not true. Why were the tort damages, in this situation, so much less than the contract damages?

4. It is instructive to consider the *McRae* situation in the light of the
American doctrine of promissory estoppel (a doctrine that has made little
headway in England and its former dominions). Consider how the
McRae case should be decided under §90 of the Restatement First; under
§§87 and 90 of the Restatement Second. For the language of §90 in both
versions, see p. 281 *supra*. If you were litigating *McRae* in an American
court, would you include a count on promissory estoppel theory in addition to (or in lieu of) the contract and tort counts? And what would the
damages be if the court awarded judgment on the promissory estoppel
count?

Section 4. The Vanishing Synthesis (England)

For the past hundred years, English case law on the problem of discharge
from contractual liability by reason of changed circumstances has been
unusually rich. Generation by generation, the English judges have struggled, with no great success, to formulate their rules of discharge and
rationalize them. In this country, on the other hand, the problem has not
been much discussed in either the judicial or the scholarly literature until

relatively recent times. A possible reason why the subject got off to a head start in England is that in various types of international transactions (such as maritime charter parties and sales of goods) it has long been customary to provide for arbitration of disputes in London under English law even though the underlying transaction has no contact whatever with England. (Under English arbitration practice, unlike our own, appeals from arbitrators' awards may be taken to the courts on points of law.) In this century the disruption of commercial transactions because of war, revolution, or other causes has been even more common on the international than on the domestic scene. Thus the English courts have not lacked for cases of this type.

The materials collected in this section rehearse changing attitudes in the English case law, old and new, toward the discharge problem. In the following section we shall turn to related developments in our own law. American courts, forced to confront the problem, have, reasonably enough, taken the English precedents seriously — which does not mean that the English solutions have always won favor on this side of the Atlantic.

PARADINE v. JANE
Aleyn 26, 82 Eng. Rep. 897 (K.B. 1647)

In debt the plaintiff declares upon a lease for years rendering rent at the four usual feasts; and for rent behind for three years, ending at the Feast of the Annunciation, 21 Car. brings his action; the defendant pleads, that a certain German prince, by name Prince Rupert, an alien born, enemy to the King and kingdom, had invaded the realm with an hostile army of men; and with the same force did enter upon the defendant's possession, and him expelled, and held out of possession from the 19 of July 18 Car. till the Feast of the Annunciation, 21 Car. whereby he could not take the profits; whereupon the plaintiff demurred, and the pleas was resolved insufficient.

1. Because the defendant hath not answered to one quarters rent.

2. He hath not averred that the army were all aliens, which shall not be intended, and then he hath his remedy against them; and Bacon cited 33 H. 6.1. e. where the gaoler in bar of an escape pleaded, that alien enemies broke the prison, &c. and exception taken to it, for that he ought to shew of what countrey they were, viz. Scots, &c.

3. It was resolved, that the matter of the plea was insufficient; for though the whole army had been alien enemies, yet he ought to pay his rent. And this difference was taken, that where the law creates a duty or charge, and the party is disabled to perform it without any default in him, and hath no remedy over, there the law will excuse him. As in the case of waste, if a house be destroyed by tempest, or by enemies, the lessee is

excused. Dyer, 33 a. Inst. 53. d. 283, a. 12 H. 4.6. so of an escape. Co. 4. 84. b. 33 H. 6. 1. So in 9 E. 3.16 a supersedeas was awarded to the justices, that they should not proceed in a cessavit upon a cesser during the war, but when the party by his own contract creates a duty or charge upon himself, he is bound to make it good, if he may, notwithstanding any accident by inevitable necessity, because he might have provided against it by his contract. And therefore if the lessee covenant to repair a house, though it be burnt by lightening, or thrown down by enemies, yet he ought to repair it. Dyer 33. a. 40 E. Ill. 6. h. Now the rent is a duty created by the parties upon the reservation, and had there been a covenant to pay it, there had been no question but the lessee must have made it good, notwithstanding the interruption by enemies, for the law would not protect him beyond his own agreement, no more than in the case of the reparations; this reservation then being a covenant in law, and whereupon an action of covenant hath been maintained (as Roll said) it is all one as if there had been an actual covenant. Another reason was added, that as the lessee is to have the advantage of casual profits, so he must run the hazard of casual losses, and not lay the whole burthen of them upon his lessor; and Dyer 56.6 was cited for this purpose, that though the land be surrounded, or gained by the sea, or made barren by wildfire, yet the lessor shall have his whole rent; and judgment was given for the plaintiff.

NOTE

1. The case is also reported in Style 47, 82 Eng. Rep. 519. The version in Style is substantially to the same effect as the better known version in Aleyn. The Style version, however, has no analogue to the passage which begins: "[W]hen the party by his own contract creates a duty or charge upon himself, he is bound to make it good. . . ." According to Style the decision was placed principally on this ground; "[I]f the tenant for years covenant to pay rent, though the lands let him be surrounded with water, yet he is chargeable with the rent, much more here."

2. Rolle, J., who appears to have decided the case, was the author of the once-celebrated Abridgment des Plusieurs Cases et Resolutions del Commun Ley (London, 1668). In the Abridgment (450, Condition (G), pl. 10) Rolle states the following case:

> Si home covenant de edifier un maison devant tiel jour, et puis le plague est la devant le jour, et continue la tanque apres le jour, ceo excusera luy del breach del convenant pur non fesans de ceo devant le jour, car la ley ne voilt luy compell a venture son vie pur ceo, mes il doit ceo faire apres. . . .

In Hall v. Wright, El. Bl. & El. 746, 120 Engl. Rep. 688 (Q.B. 1858), Lord Campbell, C.J., rendered Rolle's law French into English as follows:

If a man covenant to build a house before such a day, and afterwards the plague is there before the day, and continues there till after the day, this shall excuse him from the breach of the covenant for not doing thereof before the day; for the law will not compel him to venture his life for it, but he may do it after.

For more on Hall v. Wright, see p. 916 *infra*.

3. Paradine v. Jane is regularly cited as the leading case for the proposition that, from the seventeenth century on, English law "did not recognize impossibility as an excuse for the promisor's nonperformance of his duty," Simpson, Handbook of the Law of Contract 359 (2d ed. 1965). Berman, Excuse for Nonperformance in the Light of Contract Practices in International Trade, 63 Colum. L. Rev. 1413, 1417 (1963) refers to "the strict seventeenth century English rule . . . that the parties to a contract undertake an 'absolute obligation', which is not discharged by force majeure or by supervening impossibility. . . ."

4. On the meaning of Paradine v. Jane in its own day, Monk v. Cooper, 2 Strange 763, 93 Eng. Rep. 833 (K.B. 1723), is instructive. The action was for nonpayment of rent. The lessee pleaded that the premises had been destroyed by fire, that the lessor, by an express covenant in the lease, was under a duty to rebuild them and that he had not done so. To this plea the lessor demurred. Counsel for the lessee argued that he should be excused from paying the rent because of the lessor's breach of his covenant to rebuild. However, the court disagreed: "The case in Allen 27 [Paradine v. Jane] is express to the contrary: if the defendant has any injury, he will have his remedy; but he cannot set it off against the demand for rent. The plaintiff must have judgment." Does this mean that the lessee in Paradine v. Jane could have brought a separate action against the lessor to recover whatever loss he might have suffered? On the early theories of "independent covenants," see Chapter 9, Section 2, particularly Nichols v. Raynbred (1615), reprinted *infra* p. 976.

5. 6 Corbin §1322:

In Paradine v. Jane there was no promised performance that was made impossible by Prince Rupert's army of invasion. The plaintiff had fully conveyed the leasehold interest in the land; and we are told of no covenant of quiet enjoyment. . . . [T]he agreed equivalent for the defendant's promise to pay rent was the conveyance of the leasehold property interest and delivery of possession. There was merely a frustration of the tenant's purpose of enjoying the profits of use and occupation.

6. Paradine v. Jane does not appear to have been a particularly famous case in its own day or for a hundred and fifty years thereafter. The modern vogue of the case may date from Serjeant Williams' note to Walton v. Waterhouse, 2 Wms. Saund. 420, 85 Eng. Rep. 1233 (K.B. 1684). According to the Dictionary of National Biography, Williams pre-

pared his edition of Saunders between 1799 and 1802. The note to Walton v. Waterhouse, without indicating what the facts in Paradine v. Jane had been, quoted the dictum: "if a lessee covenant to repair a house, though it be burnt by lightening or thrown down by enemies, yet he is bound [sic] to repair it." A good deal of the nineteenth-century discussion of Paradine v. Jane assumed, following the apparent meaning of Williams' note, that the case involved a covenant by the tenant to rebuild. See, e.g., 1 J. Story, Equity Jurisprudence §101 (1836). For another example, see the opinion of Whelpley, J., in School Trustees of Trenton v. Bennett, 27 N.J.L. 513 (1859), reprinted *supra* p. 99.

7. Those who are not English Civil War buffs may find themselves puzzled by the appearance of Prince Rupert's "army of invasion" in the 1640s. Rupert was the nephew of Charles I, whose sister had married a German prince. Rupert had acquired a considerable military reputation on the Continent during the Thirty Years' War and came to England, after the Civil War broke out, to command the royal cavalry. He was thus "an enemy to the King and kingdom" only in the sense that he fought on the King's side against Parliament. At the time Paradine v. Jane was decided, the first stage of the war had ended in victory for the Parliamentary forces.

SAVILE v. SAVILE

1 P. Wms. 745, 24 Eng. Rep. 596 (Chancery 1721)

In this cause there was a decree (inter al.) for the sale of Halifax-house in St. James's Square, to the best purchaser before the Master, and Thomas Frederick esq. was reported the best bidder at £10,500 having made £1,000 deposit.

On the days of petitions after Hilary term it was prayed, that Mr. Frederick might compleat his purchase, and pay the remainder of the purchase-money; upon which Mr. Frederick by his counsel declared that he elected to lose his deposit.

But the Lord Nottingham grandfather and guardian to the young ladies the plaintiffs (who were the daughters and co-heirs of William late Lord Marquis of Halifax by Lady Mary Finch) insisted, that Mr. Frederick being the best bidder ought to pay the residue of the purchase-money, and being present himself, urged, that his contract, since it was made with the court in trust for the plaintiffs, could not (as he thought) be discharged upon any other terms, than payment of the residue of the purchase money: that had it been the case of a private contract between party and party, and so much money paid as earnest, there could be no reason to imagine, that because the intended purchaser paid so much by way of earnest, therefore he should be at liberty to get off from the bargain by losing his earnest; and surely the contract made with the *court* was at least as strong as if made with the *party*; that if there had been no deposit, it would hardly have been a question but that the party should have been compelled to pay the whole purchase-money, and could it be imagined that the contract was the weaker because there was a deposit? This would be inverting the very sense and meaning of the parties, and to construe that a deposit should weaken instead of strengthening the contract: that forfeiting the deposit was surely the most unequal way that could be: for it made no alteration, whatever the deposit was, whether greater or smaller; and therefore in the case of Morrett v. Bennett, where the deposit was ten thousand pounds, the whole deposit was forfeited, and if in that case it had been but *one* thousand pounds, yet only so much as had been deposited could be forfeited; from whence it seemed, that as the deposit might bear a very great disproportion to the value of the estate, it could consequently be no proper measure of satisfaction to the seller, for the buyer's receding from his contract; that as the seller was bound to sell, so ought the tie to be mutual upon the buyer also.

Lord Chancellor took notice that more had been urged by the Lord Nottingham than he had ever heard on this subject, but that he had taken good advice and well considered before he made the like order in the other cases: that according to his apprehension, a court of equity ought to take notice under what a general delusion the nation was at the time when this contract was made by Mr. Frederick, when there was thought to be more money in the nation than there really was, which induced people to put imaginary values on estates: that as upon a contract betwixt party and party, the contractor would not be decreed to pay an unreasonable price (see Day v. Newman, 2 Cox, 77) for an estate, so neither ought the court to be partial to itself, and do more upon a contract made with itself, or carry that farther, than it would a contract betwixt party and party. On the other hand the court might be said to have rather a greater power over a contract made with *itself* than with any *other*.

That the deposit was supposed to be a proper pledge for securing the seller in case the intended purchaser should afterwards go off; and had it not been sufficient, the other side might have moved to have such deposit increased; but being thought a sufficient pledge, it was punishment enough if the party that made it was to lose it, and satisfaction enough to the seller, if he was to have the benefit of keeping the deposit: that in this case the deposit was near a tithe of the purchase-money; so that if the seller could get as much within £1000 of any other purchaser, he would be no loser; and if he could not get so much within £1000 then it would appear to be dear sold; and consequently a bargain not fit to be executed by this court: that the court had made several orders in cases of this nature, attended with stronger circumstances; as where the estates were greatly incumbered, and the creditors would lose their debts if the bargains did not proceed; but an hardship ought not to be decreed against one, in order to prevent its falling upon another: and if those orders should be discharged, whereby others got off from contracts by losing their deposits, it would make great confusion; and their money must be brought again into court. The best way certainly was, for the court to be uniform in its resolutions.

Wherefore it was ordered that Mr. Frederick should lose his deposit of £1000 and be discharged of his contract.

NOTE

The eighteenth-century reporter of the case (Peere Williams) comments: "[T]his is not the general law of the Court, and the decision was probably founded on the general delusion of the times, as taken notice of by Lord Macclesfield."

The "delusion" referred to by the Lord Chancellor was the fantastic speculative inflation in both stock and land values during the spring and summer of 1720, followed by their even more sudden collapse in the fall of the same year, occasioned by the operations of the South Sea Company. For a lively account of the episode see J. Carswell, The South Sea Bubble (1960). The Lord Chancellor (Thomas Parker, 1st Earl of Macclesfield), apparently sharing the general delusion, had himself invested heavily in South Sea shares shortly before the market broke (id. at 161, 223).

HALL v. WRIGHT

El. Bl. & El. 765, 120 Eng. Rep. 695 (Exchequer Chamber 1859)

[Isabella Hall brought an action against George Wright for breach of a contract to marry. The defendant pleaded 1) Non assumpsit and 2) Rescission before breach. On the issues raised by those pleas the jury found for the plaintiff. The defendant's third plea was after the agreement to marry he had been

> afflicted with dangerous bodily disease, which has occasioned frequent and severe bleeding from his lungs, and by reason of which disease defendant then became and was, and from thenceforth hitherto has been, and still is, incapable of marriage without great danger of his life, and therefore unfit for the married state. . . .

The jury, having assessed the damages at £100, found for the defendant on the third plea. The trial judge entered the verdict for defendant with leave to move to enter the verdict for plaintiff with £100 damages.

Plaintiff having so moved, the case was heard in Queen's Bench. The four judges were equally divided, whereupon the junior judge (who had held for the plaintiff) withdrew his opinion. Thus the plaintiff's rule to show cause was discharged and the verdict for the defendant allowed to stand. El. Bl. & El. 746, 120 Eng. Rep. 688 (Q.B. 1858).

The case was further appealed to the Exchequer Chamber. Mellish, as counsel for plaintiff, argued, citing Paradine v. Jane, that "a contractor may, by the common law, break his contract; but he must pay damages for doing so" and further that "the impossibility of performing a contract does not relieve the contractor from paying damages for the breach, though illegality would do so." With respect to Rolle's hypothetical case about the outbreak of the plague relieving a contractor from his duty to build a house, Mellish "doubted whether that is good law." For Rolle's case, see the note following Paradine v. Jane, *supra* p. 911.

In the Exchequer Chamber four of the judges (or barons) held for the plaintiff and three for the defendant. Thus Miss Hall apparently collected her £100 damages. Excerpts from the opinions of Williams, J. (who voted with the majority) and Pollock, C.B. (dissenting) follow.]

WILLIAMS J. I am of opinion that the plea is bad, and that the plaintiff is therefore entitled to judgment.

It appears to me to be a plea in confession and avoidance; that is to say, the defendant alleges that he is justified in not keeping his promise, because, after making it, he became incapable of marriage without great danger of his life. I am of opinion that, though this is a reason why he should not be compelled to a specific performance of the contract, and a very good reason why he should in prudence prefer paying damages for the breach of his contract to the performance of it, it is no ground for resisting the payment of such damages.

According to the general law applicable to contracts, the plea is insufficient by reason of the rule (cited in Lord Campbell's judgment) as laid down in Paradine v. Jane, and which is established by the authorities collected in Serjt. William's note (2) to the case of Walton v. Waterhouse.

But it is alleged that a contract to marry stands on a peculiar footing, and is subject to implied conditions peculiar to itself. And the authorities certainly afford ground for contending that, if the parties in this case had been reversed, and the present defendant were suing the present plaintiff on the contract, she might have set up his bodily inaptitude as a ground for refusing to perform her contract, just as he might have pleaded her corporal inaptitude, or want of chastity, which had supervened or had been discovered since the making of the contract. But there is no authority, that I am aware of, or any good reason, for allowing the one party to set up his or her corporal infirmity or unfitness for marriage, or his or her impurity, in answer to the requisition of the other, who may nevertheless wish for and insist upon the performance. A woman would not be allowed to plead her own want of chastity if she were sued for a breach of promise of marriage, notwithstanding the man might well set it up as an answer if she were to seek to enforce the contract. . . .

POLLOCK, C.B. After the discussion which this case has undergone, I do not think it necessary to say any thing upon the formal or technical parts of the case: but I shall proceed at once to the question as to which a difference of opinion prevails among the members of this Court, and of the Court below: and that is, What is the real meaning of a contract to marry within a reasonable time, which is the contract stated in the declaration?

Some learned Judges think it is of the same character as any other contract, and that no terms or conditions can be implied by the law: and that, if it be not performed in the terms expressed, the party failing to perform it may pay damages for the breach of it. Other learned Judges think that there are implied conditions or exceptions, and that the matter stated in the plea is one of them; and therefore that the defendant cannot be called upon to pay damages for the non-performance of the contract alleged in the declaration under the circumstances which appear on the whole record.

Now it must be conceded on all hands that there are contracts to which the law implies exceptions and conditions which are not expressed. All contracts for personal services which can be performed only during the lifetime of the party contracting are subject to the implied condition that he shall be alive to perform them: and, should he die, his executor is not liable to an action for the breach of contract occasioned by his death. So a contract by an author to write a book within a reasonable time, or by a painter to paint a picture within a reasonable time, would in my judgment be deemed subject to the condition that, if the author became insane or the painter paralytic, and so incapable of performing the contract by the act of God, he would not be liable personally in damages any more than his executors would be if he had been prevented by death. In truth, the reasonable time has not arrived, if the party contracting to perform the act has been deprived by illness of the means of performing it: but I should decline to put my judgment on that ground; though in this case, and on this record, I think it would be quite sufficient. I prefer putting it on the ground that there is an implied exception, including the state of facts alleged in the plea, and found by the jury to be true. . . .

. . . I think that a view of the law which puts a contract of marriage on the same footing as a bargain for a horse, or a bale of goods, is not in accordance with the general feelings of mankind, and is supported by no authority.

And I think the judgment of the Court below ought to be affirmed.

NOTE

1. By the time the principal case was decided the idea that contractual liability was absolute had evidently made great strides in England and the

process of reinterpreting Paradine v. Jane to fit with that theory had been completed. Of course the division among the judges also shows that absolute liability had not won a universal following, at least with respect to a case as extraordinary as Hall v. Wright. Mellish, who was counsel for plaintiff in Hall v. Wright, appeared a few years later as counsel for the defendant in Raffles v. Wichelhaus, *supra* p. 869. Do you think that his arguments in the two cases are intellectually consistent with each other?

2. Hall v. Wright can be taken as representing the high-water mark for absolute liability theory in England (or anywhere else for that matter). But the case does show that there was a moment in time when a leading barrister like Mellish could seriously, and, as it turned out, successfully, put forward the argument which is summarized in the report. For the turning of the tide in England, see the following principal case. The Restatement First rejected the holding in Hall v. Wright in an illustration to §459, although the restaters in their hypotheticals carefully distinguished between the case in which A contracts "tuberculosis" (A is discharged) and the case in which A "owing to overindulgence in alcoholic liquors . . . becomes a dipsomaniac" (A must pay damages).

In Restatement Second §262, Death or Incapacity of Person Necessary for Performance, the Hall v. Wright hypotheticals in former §459 (on which §262 is "based") have disappeared. However, the text of §262, indeed the caption alone, leaves no doubt that the holding in Hall v. Wright is still sternly disapproved.

3. Pollock, C.B., in his Hall v. Wright dissent, suggested a theory of "implied conditions" as an escape from the rule of absolute liability. For the further development of the "implied condition" idea, see Lord Blackburn's opinion in the following principal case; see also Note 7 following that case.

4. Assuming that a promisor is discharged by illness from a contract to perform personal services, what about the promisee? This aspect of the problem was much discussed in two cases which happened to come almost simultaneously before the Court of Queen's Bench; Blackburn, J., wrote the opinions in both cases.

In Poussard v. Spiers & Pond, L.R. 1 Q.B.D. 410 (1876), Mme. Poussard had been engaged to play a leading role in a new opera which was originally scheduled to open November 14, 1874, at the Criterion Theatre in London. The engagement was to continue for three months (if the opera ran that long) with an option on the part of the management to reengage Mme. Poussard for another three months. The opening was delayed until November 28. On November 23 Mme. Poussard became ill and did not recover until December 4. Meanwhile the management had engaged Miss Lewis to play Mme. Poussard's role. The arrangement with Miss Lewis was that, if she played the role at the November 28 opening (as she did), her engagement was to continue until December 25. Consequently the management refused to let Mme. Poussard resume the role after December 4 (as she offered to do) or to pay her any salary. Mme. Poussard's husband brought an action against the management to recover the agreed salary. Blackburn, J., commented:

> This inability having been occasioned by illness was not any breach of contract by plaintiff, and no action can lie against him for the failure thus occasioned. But the damage to the defendants and the consequent failure of consideration is just as great as if it had been occasioned by the plaintiff's fault, instead of by his wife's misfortune.

After reviewing the various alternatives that the defendant might have followed, Blackburn concluded that, under the circumstances, "in our opinion it follows, as a matter of law, that the failure on the plaintiff's part went to the root of the matter and discharged the defendants."

In Bettini v. Gye, L.R. 1 Q.B.D. 183 (1876), Bettini had been engaged to sing in operas and concerts in Great Britain and Ireland from March 30 until July 13, 1875. Under the agreement Bettini was "to be in London without fail at least 6 days before the commencement of his engagement for the purpose of rehearsals." Bettini was prevented by illness from arriving in London until March 28. At that point Gye apparently refused to go through with the agreement. In an action by Bettini against Gye, the court (per Blackburn, J.) concluded that Bettini's failure to appear on March 24 "does not go to the root of the matter so as to require us to consider it a condition precedent. The defendant must therefore, we think, seek redress by a cross-action for damages."

On the distinction between "conditions precedent" and "independent covenants," see Chapter 9, Section 1.

TAYLOR v. CALDWELL
3 Best & S. 826, 122 Eng. Rep. 310 (Q.B. 1863)

BLACKBURN, J. In this case the plaintiffs and defendants had, on May 27th, 1861, entered into a contract by which the defendants agreed to let the plaintiffs have the use of The Surrey Gardens and Music Hall on four days to come, viz., June 17, July 15th, August 5th, and August 19th, for the purpose of giving a series of four grand concerts, and day and night fêtes, at the Gardens and Hall on those days respectively; and the plaintiffs agreed to take the Gardens and Hall on those days, and pay £100 for each day.

The parties inaccurately call this a "letting" and the money to be paid a "rent"; but the whole agreement is such as to show that the defendants were to retain the possession of the Hall and Gardens so that there was to be no demise of them, and that the contract was merely to give the plaintiffs the use of them on those days. Nothing, however, in our opinion, depends on this. The agreement then proceeds to set out various stipulations between the parties as to what each was to supply for these concerts and entertainments and as to the manner in which they should be carried on. The effect of the whole is to show that the existence of the Music Hall in the Surrey Gardens in a state fit for a concert was essential for the fulfillment of the contract, — such entertainments as the parties contemplated in their agreement could not be given without it.

After the making of the agreement, and before the first day on which a concert was to be given, the Hall was destroyed by fire. This destruction, we must take it on the evidence, was without the fault of either party, and was so complete that in consequence the concerts could not be given as intended. And the question we have to decide is whether, under these circumstances, the loss which the plaintiffs have sustained is to fall upon the defendants. The parties when framing their agreement evidently had not present to their minds the possibility of such a disaster, and have made no express stipulation with reference to it, so that the answer to the question must depend upon the general rules of law applicable to such a contract.

There seems no doubt that where there is a positive contract to do a thing, not in itself unlawful, the contractor must perform it or pay damages for not doing it, although in consequence of unforeseen accidents the performance of his contract has become unexpectedly burdensome or even impossible. The law is so laid down in 1 Roll. Abr. 450, Condition (G), and in the note (2) to Walton v. Waterhouse (2 Wms. Saund. 421 a, 6th Ed.) and is recognized as the general rule by all the judges in the much discussed case of Hall v. Wright (E.B. & E. 746). But this rule is only applicable when the contract is positive and absolute, and not subject to any condition either express or implied; and there are authorities which, as we think establish the principle that where, from the nature of the contract, it appears that the parties must from the beginning have known that it could not be fulfilled unless when the time for the fulfilment of the contract arrived some particular specified thing continued to exist, so that, when entering into the contract, they must have contemplated such continuing existence as the foundation of what was to be done; there, in the absence of any express or implied warranty that the thing shall exist, the contract is not to be construed as a positive contract, but as subject to an implied condition that the parties shall be excused in case, before breach, performance becomes impossible from the perishing of the thing without default of the contractor.

There seems little doubt that this implication tends to further the great object of making the legal construction as to fulfill the intention of those who entered into the contract. For in the course of affairs men in making

such contracts in general would, if it were brought to their minds, say
that there should be such a condition. . . .[16]

There is a class of contracts in which a person binds himself to do
something which requires to be performed by him in person; and such
promises, e.g. promises to marry, or promises to serve for a certain time,
are never in practice qualified by an express exception of the death of the
party; and therefore in such cases the contract is in terms broken if the
promisor dies before fulfilment. Yet it was very early determined that, if
the performance is personal, the executors are not liable; Hyde v. The
Dean of Windsor (Cro. Eliz. 552, 553). See 2 Wms. Exors. 1560 (5th Ed.),
where a very apt illustration is given. "Thus," says the learned author, "if
an author undertakes to compose a work, and dies before completing it,
his executors are discharged from this contract; for the undertaking is
merely personal in its nature, and, by the intervention of the contractor's
death, has become impossible to be performed." For this he cites a dictum of Lord Lyndhurst in Marshall v. Broadhurst (1 Tyr. 348, 349) and a
case mentioned by Patteson, J., in Wentworth v. Cock (10 A. & E. 42,
45-46). In Hall v. Wright (E.B. & E. 746, 749), Crompton, J., in his
judgment, puts another case. "Where a contract depends upon personal
skill, and the act of God renders it impossible, as, for instance, in the case
of a painter employed to paint a picture who is struck blind, it may be that
the performance might be excused."

It seems that in those cases the only ground on which the parties or
their executors can be excused from the consequences of the breach of
the contract is, that from the nature of the contract there is an implied
condition of the continued existence of the life of the contractor, and
perhaps in the case of the painter of his eyesight. In the instances just
given, the person, the continued existence of whose life is necessary to
the fulfilment of the contract, is himself the contractor, but that does not
seem in itself to be necessary to the application of the principle, as is
illustrated by the following example. In the ordinary form of an apprentice deed the apprentice binds himself in unqualified terms to "serve until
the full end and term of seven years to be fully complete and ended,"
during which term it is covenanted that the apprentice his master "faithfully shall serve," and the father of the apprentice in equally unqualified
terms binds himself for the performance by the apprentice of all and
every covenant on his part. (See the form, 2 Chitty on Pleading, 370, 7th
Ed. by Greening.) It is undeniable that if the apprentice dies within seven
years, the covenant of the father that he shall perform his covenant to

16. The editors have omitted here Lord Blackburn's discussion of the Roman and civil
law, which although "not of itself authority in an English Court, . . . affords great assis-
tance in investigating the principles on which the law is grounded." For a criticism of Lord
Blackburn's interpretation of Pothier and the Roman law sources, see Buckland, Casus and
Frustration in Roman and Common Law, 46 Harv. L. Rev. 1281, 1287 et seq. (1933). —
EDS.

serve for seven years is not fulfilled, yet surely it cannot be that an action would lie against the father? Yet the only reason why it would not is that he is excused because of the apprentice's death.

These are instances where the implied condition is of the life of a human being, but there are others in which the same implication is made as to the continued existence of a thing. For example, where a contract of sale is made amounting to a bargain and sale, transferring presently the property in specific chattels, which are to be delivered by the vendor at a future day; there, if the chattels, without the fault of the vendor, perish in the interval, the purchaser must pay the price, and the vendor is excused from performing his contract to deliver, which has thus become impossible.

That this is the rule of the English law is established by the case of Rugg v. Minett (11 East, 210), where the article that perished before delivery was turpentine, and it was decided that the vendor was bound to refund the price of all those lots in which the property had not passed; but was entitled to retain without reduction the price of those lots in which the property had passed, though they were not delivered, and though in the conditions of sale, which are set out in the report, there was no express qualification of the promise to deliver on payment. It seems in that case rather to have been taken for granted than decided that the destruction of the thing sold before delivery excused the vendor from fulfilling his contract to deliver on payment.

This also is the rule of the civil law, and it is worth noticing that Pothier in his celebrated Traité du Contrat de Vente (see part 4, §301, etc.; and part 2, ch. 1, sec. 1 art. 4, §1), treats this as merely an example of the more general rule that every obligation de certo corpore is extinguished when the thing ceases to exist. See Blackburn on the Contract of Sale, p. 173. . . .

It may, we think, be safely asserted to be now English law, that in all contracts of loan of chattels or bailments if the performance of the promise of the borrower or bailee to return the things lent or bailed, becomes impossible because it has perished, this impossibility (if not arising from the fault of the borrower or bailee from some risk which he has taken upon himself) excuses the borrower or bailee from the performance of his promise to redeliver the chattel.

The great case of Coggs v. Bernard (1 Smith's L.C. 171, 5th Ed.; 2 L. Raym. 909) is now the leading case on the law of bailments, and Lord Holt, in that case, referred so much to the civil law that it might perhaps be thought that this principle was there derived direct from the civilians, and was not generally applicable in English law except in the case of bailments; but the case of Williams v. Lloyd (W. Jones, 179), above cited, shows that the same law had been already adopted by the English law as early as the Book of Assizes. The principle seems to us to be that, in contracts in which the performance depends on the continued existence of a given person or thing, a condition is implied that the impossibility of performance arising from the perishing of the person or thing shall excuse the performance.

In none of these cases is the promise in words other than positive, nor is there any express stipulation that the destruction of the person or thing shall excuse the performance; but that excuse is by law implied, because from the nature of the contract it is apparent that the parties contracted on the basis of the continued existence of the particular person or chattel. In the present case, looking at the whole contract, we find that the parties contracted on the basis of the continued existence of the Music Hall at the time when the concerts were to be given, that being essential to their performance.

We think therefore, that the Music Hall having ceased to exist, without fault of either party, both parties are excused, the plaintiffs from taking the Gardens and paying the money, the defendants from performing their promise to give the use of the Hall and Gardens and other things. Consequently the rule must be absolute to enter the verdict for the defendants.

Rule absolute.

NOTE

1. The plaintiffs were suing to recover money spent in advertising the concerts and in other unspecified preparations for them. They were not suing to recover the profits that might have been made if the concerts had been given. Would the advertising and other expenses have been recoverable even if the court had held that the defendants were not discharged by the destruction of the Music Hall? Consult the material collected in Chapter 10, Section 3. From another point of view, was the holding that the contract was discharged necessarily fatal to their claim? In this connection, read note 6, *infra* p. 943, on Albre Marble and Tile Co. v. John Bowen Co.

2. From the agreement between the parties, which is reproduced in the statement of facts of the report of the case, it appears that the arrangement for the concerts was, so to say, a cooperative one. Taylor was to provide, at his expense, all the necessary "artistes . . . including Mr. Sims Reeves, God's will permitting." On the other hand the owners of the Music Hall and Gardens were to provide, at their expense, for each of the four concerts,

> an efficient and organized military and quadrille band . . . ; colored minstrels, fireworks and full illuminations; a ballet or divertissement, if permitted; a wizard and Grecian statues; tightrope performances; rifle galleries; air gun shooting; Chinese and Parisian games; boats on the lake, and (weather permitting) aquatic sports. . . .

The Music Hall was destroyed on June 11; the first concert had been scheduled for June 17. It seems not unlikely, therefore, that the owners of the Music Hall had incurred expenses in preparation for the concerts, exactly as Taylor had. On the assumption that both parties had incurred expenses, which now represent a dead loss, how do you think that the case — and other cases like it — should, ideally, be decided? For some interesting suggestions, see Comment, Apportioning Loss after Discharge of a Burdensome Contract: A Statutory Solution, 69 Yale L.J. 1054 (1960) (the author proposes a draft statute of considerable interest).

3. Assume that Taylor had engaged Mr. Sims Reeves and other artistes to sing at the concerts. Does the destruction of the Music Hall dissolve the Taylor-Reeves contract as well as the Taylor-Caldwell contract? Would Taylor be under a duty toward the artistes to engage other facilities in which to put on the concerts?

4. To reverse the case, suppose that Mr. Sims Reeves and the other artistes had all been killed in a train wreck the day before the first concert. Assuming further that the Music Hall had not been destroyed by fire and was still available for the concerts, does it follow from the reasoning in Blackburn's opinion that Taylor would have been discharged from his duty to pay the "rent" (at least for the first concert)?

5. One of the classes of cases which Lord Blackburn used in developing his theory of the "implied condition" was that of cases relating to the sale of goods. Before going on the bench Blackburn had written a treatise on Sales, which he cites in the course of his opinion and which remained for a long time the leading English treatment of the subject. According to Blackburn, it was a rule both of the common law and of the civil law that a seller was discharged from liability if specific goods which he had contracted to sell were accidentally destroyed (or damaged) before the "property" in the goods had passed to the buyer. Under the sales rules the property (and the risk of loss) could pass to the buyer while the goods were still in the seller's possession, whether or not the buyer had paid for them. The early case of Rugg v. Minett, which Blackburn discusses in his Taylor v. Caldwell opinion, involved a sale of turpentine which the seller was required to put up in bottles before delivery to the buyer. Before delivery all the turpentine was destroyed in a fire; at the time of the fire some of the turpentine had been put up in bottles but the rest had not been. *Held*, that the buyer had to pay the full price for the bottled turpentine but could recover no damages for nondelivery of the turpentine which had not been bottled. These rules (including the holding in Rugg v. Minett) were subsequently codified in the Sale of Goods Act in England and in the Uniform Sales Act in this country; they are carried forward without substantial change in the Uniform Commercial Code (see, for the rule on seller's discharge, §2-613). See further the discussion in McRae v. Commonwealth Disposals Commission, *supra*, p. 898, regarding goods that had been destroyed, without the knowledge of the

parties, before the contract was entered into (or, as in the *McRae* case, goods that had never existed).

6. It follows from the discussion in the preceding paragraph that sellers of goods benefited from a liberal rule of discharge even during the nineteenth-century heyday of absolute liability theory. No comparable rule of discharge was constructed in favor of buyers, at least during the early sales law period. See Note 2 following the next principal case. It would, however, be unwise to conclude that commercial buyers fared quite as badly as all this suggests. Indeed such buyers, although denied any discharge under "impossibility" theory, came out quite well under the "perfect tender" rule that was adopted on both sides of the Atlantic during the 1880s. See the materials collected in Chapter 9, Section 6.

7. Blackburn's theory of an "implied condition" has come under attack in recent times. Thus in Ocean Tramp Tankers Corp. v. V/O Sovfracht (The Eugenia), [1964] 1 All E.R. 161 (C.A. 1963), Lord Denning, M. R., commented:

> It was originally said that the doctrine of frustration was based on an implied term. In short, that the parties, if they had foreseen the new situation, would have said to one another: "If that happens, of course, it is all over between us." But the theory of an implied term has now been discarded by everyone, or nearly everyone, for the simple reason that it does not represent the truth. The parties would not have said: "It is all over between us." They would have differed about what was to happen. Each would have sought to insert reservations or qualifications of one kind or another. Take this very case. The parties realised that the canal might become impassable. They tried to agree on a clause to provide for the contingency. But they failed to agree. So there is no room for an implied term.

Id. at 166. On the factual situation that Lord Denning was addressing in *The Eugenia*, see American Trading and Production Corp. v. Shell International Marine Ltd., *infra* p. 955, and the Note following that case.

In the same vein the Introductory Note to the Restatement Second, Chapter 11 (Impracticability of Performance and Frustration of Purpose), comments: "The rationale behind the doctrines of impracticability and frustration is sometimes said to be that there is an 'implied term' of the contract that such extraordinary circumstances will not occur. This Restatement rejects this analysis. . . ."

KRELL v. HENRY

L.R. 2 K.B. 740 (Ct. App. 1903)

[As a part of the coronation of Edward VII, coronation processions were planned for June 26 and 27, 1902. Induced by an announcement in the windows of the plaintiff's flat to the effect that windows to view the coronation processions were to be let, defendant by a contract in writing of June 20, 1902, agreed to hire the plaintiff's flat in Pall Mall for June 26 and 27. The contract, however, contained no express reference to the coronation processions. The defendant paid a deposit of £25 and promised to pay another £50 on June 24. Because of the illness of Edward VII the processions were cancelled on the morning of the 24th, and thereupon the defendant refused to pay the balance. In plaintiff's suit for the balance the defendant denied liability and counterclaimed for the return of his deposit. Judgment for defendant on both claim and counterclaim. The plaintiff appeals.]

VAUGHAN WILLIAMS, L.J. read the following written judgment: — The real question in this case is the extent of the application in English law of the principle of the Roman law which has been adopted and acted on in many English decisions, and notably in the case of Taylor v. Caldwell. That case at least makes it clear that

> where from the nature of the contract, it appears that the parties must from the beginning have known that it could not be fulfilled unless, when the time for the fulfillment of the contract arrived, some particular specified thing continued to exist, so that when entering into the contract they must have contemplated such continued existence as the foundation of what was to be done; there, in the absence of any express or implied warranty that the thing shall exist, the contract is not to be considered a positive contract, but as subject to an implied condition that the parties shall be excused in case, before breach, performance becomes impossible from the perishing of the thing without default of the contractor.

Thus far it is clear that the principle of the Roman law has been introduced into the English law. The doubt in the present case arises as to how far this principle extends. . . . It is said, on the one side, that the specified thing, state of things, or condition the continued existence of which is necessary for the fulfillment of the contract, so that the parties entering into the contract must have contemplated the continued existence of that thing, condition, or state of things as the foundation of what was to be done under the contract, is limited to things which are either the subject-matter of the contract or a condition or state of things, present or anticipated, which is expressly mentioned in the contract. But, on the other side, it is said that the condition or state of things need not be expressly specified, but that it is sufficient if that condition or state of things clearly appears by extrinsic evidence to have been assumed by the parties to be the foundation or basis of the contract, and the event which causes the impossibility is of such a character that it cannot reasonably be supposed to have been in the contemplation of the contracting parties when the contract was made. In such a case the contracting parties will not be held bound by the general words which, though large enough to include, were not used with reference to a possibility of a particular event rendering performance of the contract impossible. I do not think that the principle of the civil law as introduced into the English law is limited to cases in which the event causing the impossibility of performance is the destruction or non-existence of some thing which is the subject-matter of the contract or of some condition or state of things expressly specified as a condition of it. I think that you first have to ascertain, not necessarily from the terms of the contract, but, if required, from necessary inferences, drawn from surrounding circumstances recognised by both contracting parties, what is the substance of the contract, and then to ask the question whether that substantial contract needs for its foundation the assumption of the existence of a particular state of things. If it does, this will limit the operation of the general words, and in such case, if the contract becomes impossible of performance by reason of the non-existence of the state of things assumed by both contracting parties as the foundation of the contract, there will be no breach of the contract thus limited. . . .

In my judgment the use of the rooms was let and taken for the purpose of seeing the Royal procession. It was not a demise of the rooms, or even an agreement to let and take the rooms. It is a license to use rooms for a particular purpose and none other. And in my judgment the taking place of those processions on the days proclaimed along the proclaimed route, which passed 56A, Pall Mall, was regarded by both contracting parties as the foundation of the contract; and I think that it cannot reasonably be supposed to have been in the contemplation of the contracting parties, when the contract was made, that the coronation would not be held on the proclaimed days, or the processions not take place on those days along the proclaimed route; and I think that the words imposing on the defendant the obligation to accept and pay for the use of the rooms for the named days, although general and unconditional, were not used with reference to the possibility of the particular contingency which afterwards occurred. It was suggested in the course of the argument that if the occurence, on the proclaimed days, of the coronation and the procession in this case were the foundation of the contract, and if the general words are thereby limited or qualified, so that in the event of the non-occurrence of the coronation and procession along the proclaimed route they would discharge both parties from further performance of the contract, it would follow that if a cabman was engaged to take some one to Epsom on Derby Day at a suitable enhanced price for such a journey, say £10, both parties to the contract would be discharged in the contingency of the race at Epsom for some reason becoming impossible; but I do not think this follows, for I do not think that in the cab case the happening of the race would be the foundation of the contract. No doubt the purpose of the engager would be to go to see the Derby, and the price would be proportionately high; but the cab had no special qualifications for the purpose which led to the selection of the cab for this particular occasion. Any other cab would have done as well. Moreover, I think that, under the cab contract, the hirer, even if the race went off, could have said, "Drive me to Epsom; I will pay you the agreed sum; you have nothing to do with the purpose for which I hired the cab," and that if the cabman refused he would have been guilty of a breach of contract, there being nothing to qualify his promise to drive the hirer to Epsom on a particular day. Whereas in the case of the coronation, there is not merely the purpose of the hirer to see the coronation procession, but it is the coronation procession and the relative position of the rooms which is the basis of the contract as much for the lessor as the hirer; and I think that if the King, before the coronation day and after the contract, had died, the hirer could not have insisted on having the rooms on the days named. It could not in the cab case be reasonably said that seeing the Derby race was the foundation of the contract, as it was of the licence in this case. Whereas in the present case, where the rooms were offered and taken, by reason of their peculiar suitability from the position of the rooms for a view of the coronation procession, surely the view of the coronation procession was the foundation of the contract, which is a very different thing from the purpose of the man who engaged the cab — namely, to see the race — being held to be the foundation of the contract. Each case must be judged by its own circumstances. In each case one must ask oneself, first, what, having regard to all the circumstances, was the foundation of the contract? Secondly, was the performance of the contract prevented? Thirdly, was the event which prevented the performance of the contract of such a character that it cannot reasonably be said to have been in the contemplation of the parties at the date of the contract? If all these questions are answered in the affirmative (as I think they should be in this case), I think both parties are discharged from further performance of the contract. I think that the coronation procession was the foundation of this contract, and that the non-happening of it prevented the performance of the contract; and secondly, I think that the non-happening of the procession . . . was an event "of such a character that it cannot reasonably be supposed to have been in the contemplation of the contracting parties when the contract was made." . . . The test seems to be whether the event which causes impossibility was or might have been anticipated and guarded against. . . . I myself am clearly of opinion that in this case, where we have to ask ourselves whether the object of the contract was frustrated by the non-happening of the coronation and its procession on the days proclaimed, parol evidence is admissible to show that the subject of the contract was rooms to view the coronation procession, and was so to the knowledge of both parties. . . . This disposes of the plaintiff's claim for £50 unpaid balance of the price agreed to be paid for the use of the rooms. The defendant at one time set up a crossclaim for the return of the £25 he paid at the date of the contract. As that claim is now withdrawn it is unnecessary to say anything about it. . . . I think this appeal ought to be dismissed. . . . [The concurring opinions of Romer, L.J., and Stirling, L.J. are omitted.]

Appeal dismissed.

NOTE

1. The term "frustration" seems to have come into general use, both in England and in this country, following Krell v. Henry and the other so-called coronation cases, such as Chandler v. Webster digested below. Before 1900 courts had usually phrased the issue thus: Is the defendant discharged because performance of his contractual duty has become impossible (or, at the least, extremely burdensome)? After 1900 courts began to phrase what may have been the same issue thus: Is the defendant discharged because his purpose in entering into the contract has been frustrated? It is entirely unclear why this shift in terminology took place. We now speak of a "doctrine of frustration" instead of a "doctrine of impossibility" perhaps with no intended shift in meaning. In current usage, it is fair to say, "frustration" is often used as a loose synonym for what used to be called "impossibility." Neither term has ever acquired much clarity of outline or precision of meaning. In this connection, Lord Atkins' review of the English frustration cases in Bell v. Lever Brothers, Ltd., discussed *supra* p. 896, is instructive.

2. The suggestion has been made that the shift from "impossibility" to "frustration," as a way of describing what was going on, may have had unintended consequences:

> In most contractual situations one party is under a duty to manufacture or to build or to transfer property or to render services, while the other party is under a duty to pay money in exchange for the other party's performance. We shall speak of the performing party and the paying party. The common law rule has always been that impossibility of performance discharges the performing party and dissolves the contract. Two illustrations of the rule are that incapacity or death discharges a contract to perform personal services (that is, neither the party who has contracted to serve nor his estate is liable in damages for the nonperformance) and that destruction of goods contracted to be sold, before the property in the goods or their risk has passed to the buyer, discharges the seller. On the other hand, the general rule seems to have been that the paying party is never discharged merely because the performance he has promised to pay for has become, because of an unanticipated turn of events, useless, or even burdensome, to him. Since the performing party's discharge was put on the ground of "impossibility," the rule of no discharge for the paying party was sometimes sought to be explained by the observation that "it is never impossible to pay money."

The "frustration" cases which begin to appear in the English reports toward the end of the nineteenth century may be taken as representing an extension of the rule of discharge by reason of changed circumstances from performing parties to paying parties. Once that extension had been accomplished, it operated by a sort of backlash to expand the range of events which would discharge performing parties. Since "impossibility of performance" was no longer the key to the developing rule of discharge, performance, like payment, would evidently have to be excused by something less than absolute impossibility.

2 G. Gilmore, Security Interests in Personal Property 1100 (1965) (footnotes omitted).

CHANDLER v. WEBSTER, [1904] L.R., 1 K.B. 493, presents another facet of the problems which had to be solved in the coronation cases. Here the hirer of the room had made a down payment of 100 pounds, the balance being due before the time at which the coronation procession had to be cancelled. He brought suit for the return of the down payment and the owner counter-claimed for the balance. Judgment for the owner on both claims: Where a contract has been frustrated by a supervening event so as to release the parties from further performances, the loss will lie where it falls. In the course of his opinion Collins, M.R., gave the following exposition (499-500):

"[W]here, from causes outside the volition of the parties, something which was the basis of, or essential to the fulfilment of, the contract, has become impossible, so that, from the time when the fact of that impossibility has been ascertained, the contract can no further be performed by either party, it remains a perfectly good contract up to that point, and everything previously done in pursuance of it must be treated as rightly done, but the parties are both discharged from further performance of it. If the effect were that the contract were wiped out altogether, no doubt the result would be that money paid under it would have to be repaid as on a failure of consideration. But that is not the effect of the doctrine; it only releases the parties from further performance of the contract. Therefore the doctrine of failure of consideration does not apply. The rule adopted by the Courts in such cases is I think to some extent an arbitrary one, the reason for its adoption being that it is really impossible in such cases to work out with any certainty what the rights of the parties in the event which has happened should be. Time has elapsed, and the position of both parties may have been more or less altered, and it is impossible to adjust or ascertain the rights of the parties with exactitude. That being so, the law treats everything that has already been done in pursuance of the contract as validly done, but relieves the parties of further responsibility under it."

NOTE

This case has been severely criticized. Lord Shaw of Dunfermline, in Cantiare San Rocco v. Clyde Shipbuilding and Engineering Co., [1924] A.C. 226, 259, a Scottish case, had this to say:

> . . . Thus the rule, admitted to be arbitrary, is adopted because of the difficulty, nay the apparent impossibility, of reaching a solution of perfection. Therefore, leave things alone: *potior est conditio possidentis.* That maxim works well enough among tricksters, gamblers, and thieves; let it be applied to circumstances of supervenient mishap arising from causes outside the volition of parties: under this application innocent loss may and must be endured by the one party, and unearned aggrandisement may and must be secured at his expense to the other party. That is part of the law of England. I am not able to affirm that this is any part, or ever was any part, of the law of Scotland.
>
> No doubt the adjustment of rights after the occurrence of disturbances, interruptions, or calamities is in many cases a difficult task. But the law of Scotland does not throw up its hands in despair in consequence, and leave the task alone. The maxim just quoted found no place in the law of Scotland except in quite another connection — namely, where there is a *turpis causa.* Under that law restitution against calamity or mischance which produces a failure of consideration is one thing that the law must and will do its best to accomplish. But restitution *ob turpem causam,* that the law will not make. The mischief-makers appeal in vain, the answer to them is the maxim *potior est conditio possidentis.*

FIBROSA SPOLKA AKCYJNA v. FAIRBAIRN LAWSON COMBE BARBOUR, LTD., [1943] A.C. 32. By an agreement in writing dated July 12, 1939, the defendant, a manufacturer of textile machinery at Leeds, agreed to manufacture for, and supply to, the plaintiff, a Polish company, two sets of flax hackling machines for the price of £4,800, of which one third was to be paid with the order. The delivery was to be made three to four months from the settlement of final details, and the machinery was to be shipped c.i.f. Gdynia, Poland. Plaintiff made a down payment of £1,000 but never paid the remaining £600. At the end of August, 1939, Germany invaded Poland. In September, plaintiff asked for the return of the down payment, since, as a result of the outbreak of hostilities and the consequent operation of legal prohibitions against trading with the enemy, delivery of the hackling machines could not take place in Poland. The defendant refused to agree because considerable work had been done on the machines. Plaintiff brought suit, among other things, for return of the down payment. The substantial defense of the defendant was that the contract had been frustrated by the German occupation of Gdynia and plaintiff had no right to the return of the down payment under Chandler v. Webster. The lower courts held for the defendant on the basis of that case, the Court of Appeals implying the hope that the House of Lords would substitute for the rule of Chandler v. Webster "the more civilized rule of Roman and Scottish law." In that event MacKinnon, L.J., felt it would become necessary when fixing the amount of recovery to determine how much work was done under the contract and to what extent the £1,000 had been "a pure windfall" to defendant. On appeal to the House of Lords, Chandler v. Webster was overruled and judgment given for the plaintiff company. It was entitled to recover the down payment, not because of an implied term of the contract, but as a matter of quasi contract: as money paid for a consideration that had totally failed. Chandler v. Webster, the House of Lords felt, was wrongly decided because the court erroneously limited the application of the doctrine of failure of consideration to situations where the contract is wiped out altogether. The refutation of this position in the opinion of the Lord Chancellor pointing out that the word "consideration" has two meanings is particularly illuminating:

"In English law, an enforceable contract may be formed by an exchange of a promise for a promise, or by the exchange of a promise for an act — I am excluding contracts under seal — and thus, in the law relating to the formation of contract, the promise to do a thing may often be the consideration, but when one is considering the law of failure of consideration and of the quasi-contractual right to recover money on that ground, it is, generally speaking, not the promise which is referred to as the consideration, but the performance of the promise. The money was paid to secure performance and, if performance fails, the inducement which brought about the payment is not fulfilled.

"If this were not so, there could never be any recovery of money, for failure of consideration, by the payer of the money in return for a promise of future performance, yet there are endless examples which show that money can be recovered, as for a complete failure of consideration, in cases where the promise was given but could not be fulfilled. . . ."[17]

The argument that the defendant had partly completed the machines and that, therefore, it would be unjust to let plaintiff recover the down payment in full was regarded as immaterial.[18] The court granted that the principle laid down might work injustice in an individual case, but it took the position that the common law did not furnish the court with a yardstick as to the apportionment of losses. The question, therefore, had to be left to the legislature. The discussion of this point by the Lord Chancellor (at pp. 49-50) is worth quoting:

"While this result obviates the harshness with which the previous view in some instances treated the party who had made a prepayment, it

17. At p. 48; cf. opinions of Lord Russell, at p. 56, and of Lord Wright, at p. 65. For a criticism, see the opinion of Lord Atkin, at p. 53 — Eds.

18. Lord Roche mentioned incidentally (at p. 76) that according to the defendants themselves, the machines as far as completed were "realizable without loss." — Eds.

cannot be regarded as dealing fairly between the parties in all cases, and must sometimes have the result of leaving the recipient who has to return the money at a grave disadvantage. He may have incurred expenses in connexion with the partial carrying out of the contract which are equivalent, or more than equivalent, to the money which he prudently stipulated should be prepaid, but which he now has to return for reasons which are no fault of his. He may have to repay the money, though he has executed almost the whole of the contractual work, which will be left on his hands. These results follow from the fact that the English common law does not undertake to apportion a prepaid sum in such circumstances — contrast the provision, now contained in s. 40 of the Partnership Act, 1890, for apportioning a premium if a partnership is prematurely dissolved. It must be for the legislature to decide whether provision should be made for an equitable apportionment of prepaid moneys which have to be returned by the recipient in view of the frustration of the contract in respect of which they were paid. . . ."

LAW REFORM (FRUSTRATED CONTRACTS) ACT, 1943

6 & 7 Geo. 6, ch. 40

1. ADJUSTMENT OF RIGHTS AND LIABILITIES OF PARTIES TO FRUSTRATED CONTRACTS

(1)   Where a contract governed by English law has become impossible of performance or been otherwise frustrated, and the parties thereto have for that reason been discharged from the further performance of the contract, the following provisions of the section shall, subject to the provisions of section two of this Act, have effect in relation thereto.

(2)   All sums paid or payable to any party in pursuance of the contract before the time when the parties were so discharged (in this Act referred to as "the time of discharge") shall, in the case of sums so paid, be recoverable from him as money received by him for the use of the party by whom the sums were paid, and, in the case of sums so payable, cease to be so payable:

Provided that, if the party to whom the sums were so paid or payable incurred expenses before the time of discharge in, or for the purpose of, the performance of the contract, the court may, if it considers it just to do so having regard to all the circumstances of the case, allow him to retain or, as the case may be, recover the whole or any part of the sums so paid or payable, not being an amount in excess of the expenses so incurred.

(3)   Where any party to the contract has, by reason of anything done by any other party thereto in, or for the purpose of, the performance of the contract, obtained a valuable benefit (other than a payment of money

to which the last foregoing subsection applies) before the time of discharge, there shall be recoverable from him by the said other party such sum (if any), not exceeding the value of the said benefit to the party obtaining it, as the court considers just, having regard to all the circumstances of the case and, in particular, —

(a)   the amount of any expenses incurred before the time of discharge by the benefited party in, or for the purpose of, the performance of the contract, including any sums paid or payable by him to any other party in pursuance of the contract and retained or recoverable by that party under the last foregoing subsection, and

(b)   the effect, in relation to the said benefit, of the circumstances giving rise to the frustration of the contract.

(4)   In estimating, for the purposes of the foregoing provisions of this section, the amount of any expenses incurred by any party to the contract, the court may, without prejudice to the generality of the said provisions, include such sum as appears to be reasonable in respect of overhead expenses and in respect of any work or services performed personally by the said party.

(5)   In considering whether any sum ought to be recovered or retained under the foregoing provisions of this section by any party to the contract, the court shall not take into account any sums which have, by reason of the circumstances giving rise to the frustration of the contract, become payable to that party under any contract of insurance unless there was an obligation to insure imposed by an express term of the frustrated contract or by or under any enactment.

(6)   Where any person has assumed obligations under the contract in consideration of the conferring of a benefit by any other party to the contract upon any other person, whether a party to the contract or not, the court may, if in all the circumstances of the case it considers it just to do so, treat for the purposes of subsection (3) of this section any benefit so conferred as a benefit obtained by the person who has assumed the obligations as aforesaid.

NOTE

1. The "Frustrated Contracts" Act was passed in response to the Lord Chancellor's suggestion in the *Fibrosa* case that it was for the legislature to decide whether "provision should be made for an equitable apportionment" between the parties in cases like *Fibrosa*. At the time of the Act's passage it was widely heralded as a novel and significant departure. It seems to have played little or no part in subsequent English frustration litigation — of which there has been a great deal — perhaps because it was patterned too closely on the facts of *Fibrosa* and because there are very few cases exactly like *Fibrosa*. For a broader approach to the prob-

lem, see the draft statute proposed in Comment, Apportioning Loss after Discharge of a Burdensome Contract: A Statutory Solution, 69 Yale L.J. 1054 (1960). (The Yale Comment discusses the Frustrated Contracts Act at 1069-1074.)

2. Before the *Fibrosa* case, the English rule, illustrated by Chandler v. Webster, had been taken to be that in the event of discharge because of impossibility or frustration, the loss must lie where it falls. That is, the courts, although they might be willing to relieve the parties from further liability under a continuing contract, would do nothing about losses that had already accrued at the time the contract was held to have been discharged. American case law, at least in some states, seems to have followed a different course. See the Massachusetts case of Butterfield v. Byron, *infra* p. 937, and the cases discussed in the Note following that case. It is instructive to compare the English statutory solution in the Frustrated Contracts Act with the American case law solution in states that accepted the "Massachusetts rule." See further the discussion of the treatment of the loss problem in the Restatement (and its nontreatment in the Uniform Commercial Code) in the Note beginning *infra* p. 964.

3. Current English attitudes toward the problem of relief under mistake and frustration theory are illustrated by Amalgamated Investment and Property Co. Ltd. v. John Walker & Sons, Ltd., [1976] 3 All E.R. 509 (C.A.), digested in Note 5 following Sherwood v. Walker, *supra* p. 887. See further the trio of English cases that arose from the closing of the Suez Canal in 1956, digested and discussed in the Note following American Trading and Production Corp. v. Shell International Marine Ltd., 453 F.2d 939 (2d Cir. 1972), *infra* p. 955.

Section 5.   The Vanishing Synthesis (United States)

SCHOOL TRUSTEES OF
TRENTON v. BENNETT

27 N.J.L. 513 (1859)

For a report of the case, see p. 99 *supra*.

NOTE

1. For the court's use of Paradine v. Jane, see Note 6 following *Paradine, supra* p. 911.

2. The factual situation involved in the *Bennett* case came into litigation recurrently through most of the nineteenth century. See Adams v.

Nichols, 19 Pick. 275 (Mass. 1837); School District No. 1. v. Dauchy, 25 Conn. 530 (1857); Stees v. Leonard, 20 Minn. 494 (20 Gilfillan 448) (1874) (the two reported versions of the *Stees* case, it should be noted, are not identical). In all these cases the principle that commended itself to the New Jersey court in *Bennett* was stated and restated with varying degrees of emphasis and eloquence. The formulation by Young, J., in Stees v. Leonard enjoyed a considerable vogue:

> If a man bind himself, by a positive, express contract, to do an act in itself possible, he must perform his engagement, unless prevented by the act of God, the law, or the other party to the contract. No hardship, no unforeseen hindrance, no difficulty short of absolute impossibility, will excuse him from doing what he has expressly agreed to do. This doctrine may sometimes seem to bear heavily upon contractors, but in such cases, the hardship is attributable, not to the law, but to the contractor himself, who has improvidently assumed an absolute, when he might have undertaken only a qualified, liability. The law does no more than enforce the contract as the parties themselves have made it.

20 Minn. at 503.

3. In all the cases cited in Note 2, it appears that the recovery sought and awarded was the return of progress payments which the owner had made to the contractor in course of construction before the destruction of the building. (On the recovery in Stees v. Leonard, see L. Fuller & R. Braucher, Basic Contract Law 559 (1964)). What damages were awarded in the *Bennett* case? What damages are normally recoverable by an aggrieved party when the other party, without excuse, fails to complete work that it has undertaken? On the normal damage rule, see United States v. Behan, *infra* p. 1174, and the materials that follow it in Chapter 10, Section 3.

4. On the course of absolute liability theory in England during the nineteenth century, see Hall v. Wright, *supra* p. 916, and the Note following that case.

BUTTERFIELD v. BYRON
153 Mass. 517, 27 N.E. 667 (1891)

Contract, brought in the name of the plaintiff for the benefit of certain insurance companies, for breach of a building contract entered into between the plaintiff and the defendant. . . . The contract contained the following provisions:

> The said N. Byron covenants and agrees to and with the said A.M. Butterfield to make, erect, build, and finish in a good substantial, and workmanlike manner, a three and one half story frame hotel upon lot of

land situated in Montgomery, Mass., said hotel to be built agreeable to the
draught, plans, explanations, or specifications furnished, or to be furnished, to said A.M. Butterfield by Richmond and Seabury, of good and
substantial materials, and to be finished complete on or before the twentieth day of May, 1889.

And said A.M. Butterfield covenants and agrees to pay to said N. Byron
for the same eight thousand five hundred dollars, as follows: seventy-five
per cent of the amount of work done and materials furnished during the
preceding month to be paid for on the first of the following month, and the
remaining twenty-five percent to be paid thirty days after the entire completion of the building.

By the specifications referred to, the plaintiff was to do the grading,
excavating, stone-work, brick-work, painting, and plumbing.

The time for completing the contract was subsequently extended to
June 10, 1889, and a provision was made that the defendant should forfeit
$15 for every day's default after that date. Up to May 25, 1889, the defen-
dant had complied with the contract as far as he had gone, and had
almost finished the building. The plaintiff, who had insured his interest in
the building with the companies for whose benefit the action was
brought, had up to the same time made payments to the defendant
amounting to $5,652.30, for work done and materials furnished. On May
25, the building was struck by lightning and burned to the ground, by
which event it was rendered impossible for the defendant to complete the
building within the required time. The companies in which the plaintiff
had insured paid him the sum of $6,914.08, viz. $5,652.30 for advances
made to the defendant, and $1,261.78 for work done and materials fur-
nished by the plaintiff in laying the foundations; and the plaintiff assigned
to the companies whatever claims he might have against the defendant
for breach of the contract. The plaintiff never made any demand upon
the defendant to rebuild, nor offered to lay the necessary foundations for
a new building. The defendant never called upon the plaintiff to lay such
foundations, nor offered to rebuild.

At the trial, the plaintiff contended that he was entitled to recover in
his action (1) the whole of the sum of $6,914.08, (2) $38 for certain
shingles and window weights that had been saved from the fire and carried away by the defendant, and (3) the amount forfeited under the
contract at the rate of $15 a day from June 10, 1889, to the date of the
writ.

Upon these facts the judge directed a verdict for the defendant, and
reported the case for the determination of this court, such order to be
made as the court might direct. . . .

KNOWLTON, J. It is well established law, that, where one contracts to
furnish labor and materials, and construct a chattel or build a house on
land of another, he will not ordinarily be excused from performance of
his contract by the destruction of the chattel or building, without his

fault, before the time fixed for the delivery of it. Adams v. Nichols, 19 Pick. 275. Wells v. Calnan, 107 Mass. 514. Dermott v. Jones, 2 Wall. 1. School of Trustees of Trenton v. Bennett, 3 Dutcher, 513. Tomkins v. Dudley, 25 N.Y. 272. It is equally well settled, that when work is to be done under a contract on a chattel or building which is not wholly the property of the contractor, or for which he is not solely accountable, as where repairs are to be made on the property of another, the agreement on both sides is upon the implied condition that the chattel or building shall continue in existence, and the destruction of it without the fault of either of the parties will excuse performance of the contract, and leave no right of recovery of damages in favor of either against the other. Taylor v. Caldwell, 3 B. & S. 826. Lord v. Wheeler, 1 Gray, 282. Gilbert & Barker Manuf. Co. v. Butler, 146 Mass. 82. Eliot National Bank v. Beal, 141 Mass. 566, and cases there cited. Dexter v. Norton, 47 N.Y. 62. Walker v. Tucker, 70 Ill. 527. In such cases, from the very nature of the agreement as applied to the subject matter, it is manifest that, while nothing is expressly said about it, the parties contemplated the continued existence of that to which the contract relates. The implied condition is a part of the contract, as if it were written into it, and by its terms the contract is not to be performed if the subject matter of it is destroyed, without the fault of either of the parties, before the time for complete performance has arrived.

The fundamental question in the present case is, What is the true interpretation of the contract? Was the house while in the process of erection to be in the control and at the sole risk of the defendant, or was the plaintiff to have a like interest, as the builder of a part of it? Was the defendant's undertaking to go on and build and deliver such a house as the contract called for, even if he should be obliged again and again to begin anew on account of the repeated destruction of a partly completed building by inevitable accident, or did his contract relate to one building only, so that it would be at an end if the building, when nearly completed, should perish without his fault? It is to be noticed that his agreement was not to build a house, furnishing all the labor and materials therefor. His contract was of a very different kind. The specifications are incorporated into it, and it appears that it was an agreement to contribute certain labor and materials towards the erection of a house on land of the plaintiff, towards the erection of which the plaintiff himself was to contribute other labor and materials, which contributions would together make a completed house. The grading, excavating, stone-work, brick-work, painting, and plumbing were to be done by the plaintiff.

Immediately before the fire, when the house was nearly completed, the defendant's contract, so far as it remained unperformed, was to finish a house on the plaintiff's land, which had been constructed from materials and by labor furnished in part by the plaintiff and in part by himself. He was no more responsible that the house should continue in existence than the plaintiff was. Looking at the situation of the parties at that time, it was like a contract to make repairs on the house of another. His undertaking and duty to go on and finish the work was upon an implied condition that the house, the product of their joint contributions, should remain in existence. The destruction of it by fire discharged him from his contract. The fact that the house was not in existence when the contract was made is immaterial. Howell v. Coupland, 1 Q.B.D. 258.

It seems very clear that, after the building was burned, and just before the day fixed for the completion of the contract, the defendant could not have compelled the plaintiff to do the grading, excavating, stone-work, brick-work, painting, and plumbing for another house of the same kind. The plaintiff might have answered, "I do not desire to build another house which cannot be completed until long after the date at which I wished to use my house. My contract related to one house. Since that has been destroyed without my fault, I am under no further obligation." If the plaintiff could successfully have made this answer to a demand by the defendant that he should do his part towards the erection of a second building, then certainly the defendant can prevail on a similar answer in the present suit. In other words, looking at the contract from the plaintiff's position, it seems manifest that he did not agree to furnish the work and materials required of him by the specifications for more than one house, and if that was destroyed by inevitable accident, just before its completion, he was not bound to build another, or to do anything further under his contract. If the plaintiff was not obliged to make his contribution of work and materials towards the building of a second house, neither was the defendant. The agreement of each to complete the performance of the contract after a building, the product of their joint contributions, had been partly erected, was on an implied condition that the building should continue in existence. Neither can recover anything of the other under the contract, for neither has performed the contract so that its stipulations can be availed of. The case of Cook v. McCabe, 53 Wis. 250, was very similar in its facts to the one at bar, and identical with it in principle. There the court, in an elaborate opinion, after a full consideration of the authorities, held that the contractor could recover of the owner a pro rata share of the contract price for the work performed and the materials furnished before the fire. Clark v. Franklin, 7 Leigh, 1, is of similar purport.

What are the rights of the parties in regard to what has been done in part performance of a contract in which there is an implied condition that the subject to which the contract relates shall continue in existence, and where the contemplated work cannot be completed by reason of the destruction of the property without fault of either of the parties, is in dispute upon the authorities. The decisions in England differ from those of Massachusetts, and of most of the other States of this country. There the general rule, stated broadly, seems to be that the loss must remain where it first falls, and that neither of the parties can recover of the other for anything done under the contract. In England, on authority, and upon original grounds not very satisfactory to the judges of recent times, it is held that freight advanced for the transportation of goods subsequently lost by the perils of the sea cannot be recovered back. Allison v. Bristol Ins. Co. 1 App. Cas. 209, 226. Byrne v. Schiller, L.R. 6 Ex. 319. In the United States and in Continental Europe the rule is different. Griggs v. Austin, 3 Pick. 20, 22. Brown v. Harris, 2 Gray, 359. In England it is held that one who has partly performed a contract on property of another which is destroyed without the fault of either party, can recover nothing; and on the other hand, that one who has advanced payments on account of labor and materials furnished under such circumstances cannot recover back the money. Appleby v. Myers, L.R. 2 C.P. 651. Anglo-Egyptian Navigation Co. v. Rennie, L.R. 10 C.P. 271. One who has advanced money for the instruction of his son in a trade cannot recover it back if he who received it dies without giving the instruction. Whincup v. Hughes, L.R. 6 C.P. 78. But where one dies and leaves unperformed a contract which is entire, his administrator may recover any instalments which were due on it before his death. Stubbs v. Holywell Railway, L.R. 2 Ex. 311.

In this country, where one is to make repairs on a house of another under a special contract, or is to furnish a part of the work and materials used in the erection of a house, and his contract becomes impossible of performance on account of the destruction of the house, the rule is uniform, so far as the authorities have come to our attention, that he may recover for what he has done or furnished. . . .

The only question that remains in the present case is one of pleading. The defendant is entitled to be compensated at the contract price for all he did before the fire. The plaintiff is to be allowed for all his payments. If the payments are to be treated merely as advancements on account of a single entire consideration, namely, the completion of the whole work, the work not having been completed, they may be sued for in this action, and the defendant's only remedy available in this suit is by a declaration in set-off. If, on the other hand, each instalment due was a separate consideration for the payment made at the time, then as to those instalments and the payments of them the contract is completely executed, and the plaintiff can recover nothing, and the implied assumpsit in favor of the defendant can be only for the part which remains unpaid.

We are of opinion that the consideration which the defendant was to receive was an entire sum for the performance of the contract, and that the payments made were merely advances on account of it, and that, on his failure to perform the contract, there was a failure of consideration which gave the plaintiff a right to sue for money had and received, and that the like failure of consideration on the other side gave the defendant a right to sue on an implied assumpsit for work done and materials found.

The $38 due from the defendant to the plaintiff cannot be recovered in this action. The report and the pleadings show that the suit was brought under an assignment for the benefit of the insurers, to recover damages for a breach of the contract for the erection of the building, and not to recover the value of the shingles or weights carried away from the ruins.

According to the terms of the report, the ruling being wrong, such order may be made as this court shall direct. A majority of the court are of opinion that the verdict should be set aside, and the defendant be given leave to file a declaration in set-off, if he is so advised, on such terms as the Superior Court deems reasonable.

Verdict set aside.

NOTE

1. Justice Knowlton's statement of the general rule relies on the line of cases (including Adams v. Nichols, a Massachusetts case) referred to in Note 2, *supra* p. 936. How much of the "general rule" does the "exception" of Butterfield v. Byron seem to swallow up?

2. The plaintiff in Butterfield v. Byron was suing in the interest of the insurance companies to whom he had assigned his claims against the defendant. (On the nineteenth-century practice that required an assignee to sue in the name of the assignor, see the Introductory Note to Chapter 12.) The right of an insurer, after payment of loss, to sue as assignee or subrogee of its insured's contract rights, once generally conceded, has in recent years become increasingly doubtful. See Eastern Restaurant Equipment Co., Inc. v. Tecci, 347 Mass. 148, 196 N.E.2d 869 (1964); 2 G. Gilmore, Security Interests in Personal Property §42.7.1 (1965).

3. The principal case is a leading authority for what has been called the "American repair doctrine." Williston thus states the "general rule" (no discharge) and the "exception" under the doctrine of the principal case:

> Although one who contracts to build is not discharged from liability on his contract because of the destruction of his first or other attempts to perform the contract, the situation is different where the contract is to do work on a building and the building is destroyed. Here the parties assumed the continued existence of the building upon which the work was to be done, and if this assumption ceases to be true, the obligation is discharged.

18 Williston §1965 (Jaeger 3d ed. 1957). Williston goes on to say that "most decisions allow recovery on a quantum meruit for the value of the work which has been done prior to the destruction." (Id. §1975) It has been pointed out that the development of the "repair" doctrine, extended to include subcontracted work on initial construction as well as repairs on

completed buildings, "paralleled the development, in the construction industry, of intense specialization by means of subcontracts." E. Patterson, G. Goble & H. Jones, Cases and Materials on Contracts 1085 (4th ed. 1957). Thus the extended repair doctrine operated, in many cases, to protect the subcontractors. But what about the general contractor? Cases like School Trustees of Trenton v. Bennett, Stees v. Leonard, and Butterfield v. Byron disappear from the reports after 1900. How should their disappearance be accounted for?

4. In the early part of his opinion Knowlton, J., seems to analogize the principal case with the English case of Taylor v. Caldwell, *supra* p. 920, and to adopt the "implied condition" theory put forward by Blackburn, J., in that case. For recent criticism of this theory see Note 7 following Taylor v. Caldwell.

5. Toward the end of his opinion Knowlton, J., takes note of the divergence between English and American case law on the question whether a plaintiff can ever be compensated for loss suffered before discharge of a contract under impossibility (or frustration) theory. Knowlton, it may be observed, was writing thirteen years before Chandler v. Webster, *supra* p. 931. On the subsequent history of "the loss lies where it falls" proposition in England, see the *Fibrosa* case, *supra* p. 932, and the Frustrated Contracts Act (1943), *supra* p. 934.

6. The Massachusetts Supreme Judicial Court has continued to explore the quantum meruit or implied assumpsit recovery approved in the principal case, and the limitations on the recovery. In Albre Marble & Tile Co., Inc. v. John Bowen Co., 338 Mass. 394, 155 N.E.2d 437 (1959), Bowen was the general contractor on a hospital construction project for the Commonwealth of Massachusetts; Albre was one of the subcontractors. The general contract was invalidated, after construction had begun, because of irregularities in Bowen's original bid. At the time the general contract was invalidated Albre had incurred expenses (such as the making of shop drawings) in preparation for performance of its subcontracts. In Albre's quantum meruit action the court stopped short of approving the "principle that in every case recovery may be had for payments made or obligations reasonably incurred in preparation for performance of a contract where further performance is rendered impossible without fault of either party." Nevertheless the court felt that Albre should recover some of its expenses, particularly in view of the fact that it was Bowen's misconduct that had led to the invalidation of the general contract. On a second appeal, after retrial, 343 Mass. 777, 179 N.E.2d 321 (1962), the court approved a damage award for Albre to the extent that the award represented "work which the jury could say was undertaken by [Albre] in conformity with the specific request of [Bowen] as provided in the contract." In his opinion on the first *Albre* appeal, Spalding, J., noted that the court had held in Boston Plate & Window Glass Co. v. John Bowen Co., Inc., 335 Mass. 697, 141 N.E.2d 715 (1957) that Bowen's misconduct "was

not so culpable as to render it liable [to its subcontractors] for breach of contract." If the Court had held that the subcontractors could sue Bowen for "breach of contract," do you think they would have recovered greater damages than Albre finally received in quantum meruit?

7. In National Presto Industries, Inc. v. United States, 338 F.2d 99 (Ct. Cl. 1964), *cert. denied*, 380 U.S. 962 (1965), Presto during the Korean war had entered into a fixed price contract with the Army to produce artillery shells by a novel and untried process called the "hot cup-cold draw" method. Because of technological difficulties that had not been foreseen by either party, the cost of producing the shells by the new process was more than $700,000 over the contract price; the Army refused to reimburse Presto for any of the cost overrun. The majority of the Court of Claims held that Presto was entitled to some relief on a theory of "mutual mistake." Davis, J., after commenting that "though the particular result here may be unprecedented that is, of course, the way of the common law" (id. at 111), concluded that Presto should recover half the loss attributable to the unforeseen technological difficulties.

> In contract suits courts have generally seemed loath to divide damages, but in this class of case we see no objection other than tradition. Reformation, as the child of equity, can mold its relief to attain any fair result within the broadest perimeter of the charter the parties have established for themselves. . . . [A]n equal split would fit the basic postulate that the contract has assigned the risk to neither party.

Id. at 112.

It is fair to say that neither the Court of Claims nor any other court has, since the case was decided, shown any great enthusiasm for the "unprecedented" *Presto* approach to the problem of loss-splitting or dividing damages. On the other hand, what do you think the Massachusetts court was doing in cases like *Albre*, digested in Note 6, *supra*?

CANADIAN INDUSTRIAL ALCOHOL CO. v. DUNBAR MOLASSES CO.
258 N.Y. 194, 179 N.E. 383 (1932)

Appeal, by permission, from a judgment of the Appellate Division of the Supreme Court in the first judicial department, entered June 23, 1931, unanimously affirming a judgment in favor of plaintiff entered upon a verdict.

CARDOZO, Ch. J. A buyer sues a seller for breach of an executory contract of purchase and sale.

The subject-matter of the contract was "approximately 1,500,000 wine gallons Refined Blackstrap [molasses] of the usual run from the National Sugar Refinery, Yonkers, N.Y., to test around 60% sugars."

The order was given and accepted December 27, 1927, but shipments of the molasses were to begin after April 1, 1928, and were to be spread out during the warm weather.

After April 1, 1928, the defendant made delivery from time to time of 344,083 gallons. Upon its failure to deliver more, the plaintiff brought this action for the recovery of damages. The defendant takes the ground that, by an implied term of the contract, the duty to deliver was conditioned upon the production by the National Sugar Refinery at Yonkers of molasses sufficient in quantity to fill the plantiff's order. The fact is that the output of the refinery, while the contract was in force, was 485,848 gallons, much less than its capacity, of which amount 344,083 gallons were allotted to the defendant and shipped to the defendant's customer. The argument for the defendant is that its own duty to deliver was proportionate to the refinery's willingness to supply, and that the duty was discharged when the output was reduced.

The contract, read in the light of the circumstances existing at its making, or more accurately in the light of any such circumstances apparent from this record, does not keep the defendant's duty within boundaries so narrow. We may assume, in the defendant's favor, that there would have been a discharge of its duty to deliver if the refinery had been destroyed (Stewart v. Stone, 127 N.Y. 500; Dexter v. Norton, 47 N.Y. 62; Nitro Powder Co. v. Agency of C.C. & F. Co., 233 N.Y. 294, 297), or if the output had been curtailed by the failure of the sugar crop (Pearson v. McKinney, 160 Cal. 649; Howell v. Coupland, 1 Q.B.D. 258; 3 Williston on Contracts, §1949) or by the ravages of war (Matter of Badische Co., [1921] 2 Ch. 331; Horlock v. Beal, [1916] 1 A.C. 486) or conceivably in some circumstances by unavoidable strikes (American Union Line v. Oriental Navigation Corp., 239 N.Y. 207, 219; Normandie Shirt Co. v. Eagle, Inc., 238 N.Y. 218, 229; Delaware, L. & W. Co. v. Bowns, 58 N.Y. 573; and cf. Blackstock v. New York & Erie R.R. Co., 20 N.Y. 48; also 2 Williston on Contracts, §1099, pp. 2045, 2046). We may even assume that a like result would have followed if the plaintiff had bargained not merely for a quantity of molasses to be supplied from a particular refinery, but for molasses to be supplied in accordance with a particular contract between the defendant and the refiner, and if thereafter such contract had been broken without fault on the defendant's part (Scialli v. Correale, 97 N.J.L. 165; cf., however, Marsh v. Johnston, 125 App. Div. 597; 196 N.Y. 511). The inquiry is merely this, whether the continuance of a special group of circumstances appears from the terms of the contract, interpreted in the setting of the occasion, to have been a tacit or implied presupposition in the minds of the contracting parties, conditioning their belief in a continued obligation (Tamplin S.S. Co. v. Anglo-Mexican P.P. Co., [1916] 2 A.C. 397, 406, 407; Blackburn Bobbin Co. v. Allen & Sons, Ltd., L.R. [1918] 1 K.B. 540; Lorillard v. Clyde, 142 N.Y. 456; 3 Williston on Contracts, §1952).

Accepting that test, we ask ourselves the question what special group of circumstances does the defendant lay before us as one of the presuppositions immanent in its bargain with the plaintiff? The defendant asks us to assume that a manufacturer, having made a contract with a middleman for a stock of molasses to be procured from a particular refinery would expect the contract to lapse whenever the refiner chose to diminish his production, and this in the face of the middleman's omission to do anything to charge the refiner with a duty to continue. Business could not be transacted with security or smoothness if a presumption so unreasonable were at the root of its engagements. There is nothing to show that the defendant would have been unable by a timely contract with the refinery to have assured itself of a supply sufficient for its needs. There is nothing to show that the plaintiff in giving the order for the molasses, was informed by the defendant that such a contract had not been made, or that performance would be contingent upon obtaining one thereafter. If the plaintiff had been so informed, it would very likely have preferred to deal with the refinery directly, instead of dealing with a middleman. The defendant does not even show that it tried to get a contract from the refinery during the months that intervened between the acceptance of the plaintiff's order and the time when shipments were begun. It has wholly failed to relieve itself of the imputation of contributory fault (3 Williston on Contracts, §1959). So far as the record shows, it put its faith in the mere chance that the output of the refinery would be the same from year to year, and finding its faith vain, it tells us that its customer must have expected to take a chance as great. We see no reason for importing into the bargain this aleatory element. The defendant is in no better position than a factor who undertakes in his own name to sell for future delivery a special grade of merchandise to be manufactured by a special mill. The duty will be discharged if the mill is destroyed before delivery is due. The duty will subsist if the output is reduced because times turn out to be hard and labor charges high (cf. Day v. United States, 245 U.S. 159, 161; Northern Pac. Ry. Co. v. American Trading Co., 195 U.S. 439, 467).

[In an omitted passage Judge Cardozo concluded that there had been no error in the trial court's ruling in favor of plaintiff on a question of damages.]

The judgment should be affirmed with costs. (See 258 N.Y. 603.)

Pound, Crane, Lehman, Kellogg, O'Brien and Hubbs, JJ., concur.

Judgment affirmed.

NOTE

1. The fourth paragraph of Cardozo's opinion may be taken as an accurate summary of the situations in which, under sales law as it had been codified in England and the United States, sellers of goods would be

discharged from liability for nondelivery. For the origins of the rule in cases involving sales of specific goods, see Note 5 following Taylor v. Caldwell, *supra* p. 920. By Cardozo's time the beneficiaries of the discharge rule included both manufacturers (whose factories had been destroyed by fire, or according to Cardozo, shut down by "unavoidable" strikes) and farmers (whose crops had been blighted). Late nineteenth-century stalwarts of absolute liability theory occasionally objected to this liberalization of excuse. For an illustrative case see Anderson v. May, 50 Minn. 280, 52 N.W. 530 (1892), refusing to apply the discharge rule where a farmer's crop had been destroyed by an early and unusual frost. In holding the farmer liable in damages the court relied on the line of cases illustrated by School Trustees of Trenton v. Bennett, *supra* p. 99, and its own earlier case of Stees v. Leonard (see the quotation from the *Stees* opinion in the Note following the *Bennett* case, p. 937 *supra*). See also Globe Refining Co. v. Landa Cotton Oil Co., *infra* p. 1144, in which Justice Holmes, commenting on the hypothetical possibility of the destruction of a seller's mill by fire before delivery, wrote: "Such a misfortune would not have been an excuse, although probably it would have prevented performance of the contract." However, by the time Cardozo wrote his opinion in the principal case, the more "liberal" approach had clearly won the day. For the handling of the problem in the Sales Article of the Uniform Commercial Code, see *infra* p. 966.

2. Why was it that the defendant in the principal case did not benefit from the discharge rule rehearsed in the preceding paragraph?

3. Manufacturers and other sellers have, for a long time, included in their contracts so-called force majeure clauses (or, less elegantly, "strike and fire clauses"). Thus in New England Concrete Construction Co. v. Shepard & Morse Lumber Co., 220 Mass. 207, 107 N.E. 917 (1915), the contract included the provision: "All contracts are contingent upon strikes, fires, breakage of machinery, perils of navigation and all other causes beyond our control." (The reference to "perils of navigation" may suggest that the clause had been copied out of a form book; the case involved "maple flooring" to be manufactured at a mill in Burlington, Vermont, and shipped to the buyer in Salem, Massachusetts.) It is easy to understand why sellers, early in this century, should have felt they needed the protection of such clauses; there were courts like the Minnesota Supreme Court and judges like Holmes disinclined to rule favorably on the force majeure excuse unless it had been expressly contracted for. But once the law had developed to the state summarized by Cardozo in the principal case, the clauses had, evidently, become unnecessary: the manufacturing seller, for example, whose factory was destroyed by fire was discharged whether or not it had included a strike and fire clause in the contract. Nevertheless the clauses continued, and still continue, in use. Can you think of any reason, other than simple inertia, why sellers might be well advised to include such clauses in their contracts?

4. The clause quoted from the Massachusetts case in the preceding

paragraph was, in its vagueness, typical of many clauses of this type. Suppose only part of the seller's productive capacity was affected. Suppose the seller could supply some but not all of its buyers. Suppose the delay in delivery — because of, say, a strike — was only a week or a month. A moment's reflection will suggest other comparable problems — which could be, but never are, expressly dealt with in a force majeure clause. For the Code's attempt to solve some of these problems, see §2-615.

5. Force majeure clauses that operate to discharge buyers appear to be much less common than the clauses that operate to discharge sellers. For examples of a buyer's clause see The Western Alfalfa Milling Co. v. Worthington, 31 Wyo. 82, 223 P. 218 (1924), and Campbell Soup Co. v. Wentz, 172 F.2d 80 (3d Cir. 1948), reprinted *infra* p. 1097 (both agricultural cases); in neither case did the court seem particularly sympathetic to the buyer's attempt to provide an excuse by contract. A possible explanation for the failure of buyers' counsel to engage in force majeure drafting may be the ease with which commercial buyers could get out of unwelcome contractual obligations under the late nineteenth-century "perfect tender" rule; see Chapter 9, Section 3.

LLOYD v. MURPHY
25 Cal. 2d 48, 153 P.2d 47 (1944)

Appeal from a judgment of the Superior Court of Los Angeles County. John Beardsley, Judge. Affirmed.

Action by lessor against lessee for declaratory relief and for unpaid rent. Judgment for plaintiffs affirmed. . . .

TRAYNOR, J. — On August 4, 1941, plaintiffs leased to defendant for a five-year term beginning September 15, 1941, certain premises located at the corner of Almont Drive and Wilshire Boulevard in the city of Beverly Hills, Los Angeles County, "for the sole purpose of conducting thereon the business of displaying and selling new automobiles (including the servicing and repairing thereof and of selling the petroleum products of a major oil company) and for no other purpose whatsoever without the written consent of the lessor" except "to make an occasional sale of a used automobile." Defendant agreed not to sublease or assign without plaintiff's written consent. On January 1, 1942, the federal government ordered that the sale of new automobiles be discontinued. It modified this order on January 8, 1942, to permit sales to those engaged in military activities, and on January 20, 1942, it established a system of priorities restricting sales to persons having preferential ratings of A-1-j or higher. On March 10, 1942, defendant explained the effect of these restrictions on his business to one of the plaintiffs authorized to act for the others, who orally waived the restrictions in the lease as to use and subleasing and offered to reduce the rent if defendant should be unable to operate profitably. Nevertheless defendant vacated the premises on March 15, 1942, giving oral notice of repudiation of the lease to plaintiffs, which was followed by a written notice on March 24, 1942. Plaintiffs affirmed in writing on March 26th their oral waiver and, failing to persuade defendant to perform his obligations, they rented the property to other tenants pursuant to their powers under the lease in order to mitigate damages. On May 11, 1942, plaintiffs brought this action praying for declaratory relief to determine their rights under the lease, and for judgment for unpaid rent. Following a trial on the merits, the court found that the leased premises were located on one of the main traffic arteries of Los Angeles County; that they were equipped with gasoline pumps and in general adapted for maintenance of an automobile service station; that they contained a one-story storeroom adapted to many commercial purposes; that plaintiffs had waived the restrictions in the lease and granted defendant the right to use the premises for any legitimate purpose and to sublease to any responsible party; that defendant continues to carry on the business of selling and servicing automobiles at two other places. Defendant testified that at one of these locations he sold new automobiles exclusively and when asked if he were aware that many new automobile dealers were continuing in business replied: "Sure. It is just the location that I couldn't make a go, though, of automobiles." Although there was no finding to that effect, defendant estimated in response to inquiry by his counsel, that 90 per cent of his gross volume of business was new car sales and 10 per cent gasoline sales. The trial court held that war conditions had not terminated defendant's obligations under the lease and gave judgment for plaintiffs, declaring the lease as modified by plaintiffs' waiver to be in full force and effect, and ordered defendant to pay the unpaid rent with interest, less amounts received by plaintiffs from re-renting. Defendant brought this appeal, contending that the purpose for which the premises were leased was frustrated by the restrictions placed on the sale of new automobiles by the federal government, thereby terminating his duties under the lease.

Although commercial frustration was first recognized as an excuse for nonperformance of a contractual duty by the courts of England (Krell v. Henry [1903] 2 K.B. 740 [C.A.]; Blakely v. Muller, 19 T.L.R. 186 [K.B.]; see McElroy and Williams, The Coronation Cases, 4 Mod. L. Rev. 241) its soundness has been questioned by those courts (see Maritime National Fish, Ltd., v. Ocean Trawlers, Ltd. [1935] A.C. 524, 528-29, L.Q. Rev. 324, arguing that Krell v. Henry, *supra*, was a misapplication of Taylor v. Caldwell, 3 B. & S. 826 [1863], the leading case on impossibility as an excuse for nonperformance), and they have refused to apply the doctrine to leases on the ground that an estate is conveyed to the lessee, which carries with it all risks (Swift v. McBean, 166 L.T. Rep. 87 [1942] 1 K.B. 375; Whitehall Court v. Ettlinger, 122 L.T. Rep. 540, (1920) 1 K.B. 680, [1919] 89 L.J. [K.B.] N.S. 126; 137 A.L.R. 1199, 1224; see collection and discussion on English cases in Wood v. Bartolino, [48 N.M. 175, 146 P.2d 883, 886-87]. Many courts, therefore, in the United States have held that the tenant bears all risks as owner of the estate (Cusack Co. v. Pratt, 78 Colo. 28 [239 P. 22, 44 A.L.R. 55]; Yellow Cab Co. v. Stafford-Smith Co., 320 Ill. 294 [150 N.E. 670, 43 A.L.R. 1173]), but the modern cases have recognized that the defense may be available in a proper case, even in a lease. As the author declares in 6 Williston, Contracts (rev. ed. 1938), §1955, pp. 5485-87,

> The fact that a lease is a conveyance and not simply a continuing contract and the numerous authorities enforcing liability to pay rent in spite of destruction of leased premises, however, have made it difficult to give relief. That the tenant has been relieved, nevertheless, in several cases indicates the gravitation of the law toward a recognition of the principle that fortuitous destruction of the value of performance wholly outside the contemplation of the parties may excuse a promisor even in a lease. . . .
>
> Even more clearly with respect to leases than in regard to ordinary contracts the applicability of the doctrine of frustration depends on the total or nearly total destruction of the purposes for which, in the contemplation of both parties, the transaction was entered into.

The principles of frustration have been repeatedly applied to leases by the courts of this state . . . and the question is whether the excuse for nonperformance is applicable under the facts of the present case.

Although the doctrine of frustration is akin to the doctrine of impossibility of performance . . . since both have developed from the commercial necessity of excusing performance in cases of extreme hardship, frustration is not a form of impossibility even under the modern definition of that term, which includes not only cases of physical impossibility but also cases of extreme impracticability of performance (see Mineral Park Land Co. v. Howard, 172 Cal. 289, 293 [156 P. 458, L.R.A. 1916F 1]; Christian v. Superior Court, 9 Cal. 2d 526, 533 [71 P.2d 205, 112 A.L.R. 1153]; 6 Williston, op. cit. supra, §1935, p. 5419; Rest., Contracts, §454, comment a., and Cal. Ann. p. 254). Performance remains possible but the expected value of performance to the party seeking to be excused has been destroyed by a fortuitous event, which supervenes to cause an actual but not literal failure of consideration (Krell v. Henry, supra; Blakely v. Muller, supra; Marks Realty Co. v. Hotel Hermitage Co., 170 App. Div. 484 [156 N.Y.S. 179]; 6 Williston, (op. cit. supra, §§1935, 1954, pp. 5477, 5480; Restatement, Contracts, §288).

The question in cases involving frustration is whether the equities of the case, considered in the light of sound public policy, require placing the risk of a disruption or complete destruction of the contract equilibrium on defendant or plaintiff under the circumstances of a given case (Fibrosa Spolka Akcyjna v. Fairbairn Lawson Combe Barbour, Ltd.

[1942], 167 L.T.R. [H.L.] 101, 112-113; see Smith, Some Practical Aspects of the Doctrine of Impossibility, 32 Ill. L. Rev. 672, 675; Patterson, Constructive Conditions in Contracts, 42 Columb. L. Rev. 903, 949; 27 Cal. L. Rev. 461), and the answer depends on whether an unanticipated circumstance, the risk of which should not be fairly thrown on the promisor, has made performance vitally different from what was reasonably to be expected (6 Williston, *op. cit. supra*, §1963, p. 5511; Restatement, Contracts, §454). The purpose of a contract is to place the risks of performance upon the promisor, and the relation of the parties, terms of the contract, and circumstances surrounding its formation must be examined to determine whether it can be fairly inferred that the risk of the event that has supervened to cause the alleged frustration was not reasonably foreseeable. If it was foreseeable there should have been provision for it in the contract, and the absence of such a provision gives rise to the inference that the risk was assumed.

The doctrine of frustration has been limited to cases of extreme hardship so that businessmen, who must make their arrangements in advance, can rely with certainty on their contracts (Anglo-Northern Trading Co. v. Emlyn Jones and Williams, 2 K.B. 78; 137 A.L.R. 1199, 1216-1221). The courts have required a promisor seeking to excuse himself from performance of his obligations to prove that the risk of the frustrating event was not reasonably foreseeable and that the value of counterperformance is totally or nearly totally destroyed, for frustration is no defense if it was foreseeable or controllable by the promisor, or if counterperformance remains valuable. . . . Grace v. Croninger, 12 Cal. App. 2d 603, 606-607 [55 P.2d 940]; Industrial Development & Land Co. v. Goldschmidt, 56 Cal. App. 507, 511 [206 P. 134]. . . .

Thus laws or other governmental acts that make performance unprofitable or more difficult or expensive do not excuse the duty to perform a contractual obligation. . . . It is settled that if parties have contracted with reference to a state of war or have contemplated the risks arising from it, they may not invoke the doctrine of frustration to escape their obligations. . . .

At the time the lease in the present case was executed the National Defense Act (Public Act No. 671 of the 76th Congress [54 Stats. 601], §2A), approved June 28, 1940, authorizing the President to allocate materials and mobilize industry for national defense, had been law for more than a year. The automotive industry was in the process of conversion to supply the needs of our growing mechanized army and to meet lend-lease commitments. Iceland and Greenland had been occupied by the army. Automobile sales were soaring because the public anticipated that production would soon be restricted. These facts were commonly known and it cannot be said that the risk of war and its consequences necessitating restrictions of the production and sale of automobiles was so remote a contingency that its risk could not be foreseen by defendant, an experi-

enced automobile dealer. Indeed, the conditions prevailing at the time
the lease was executed, and the absence of any provision in the lease
contacting against the effect of war, gives rise to the inference that the
risk was assumed. Defendant has therefore failed to prove that the possibility of war and its consequences on the production and sale of new
automobiles was an unanticipated circumstance wholly outside the contemplation of the parties.

Nor has defendant sustained the burden of proving that the value of
the lease has been destroyed. The sale of automobiles was not made
impossible or illegal but merely restricted and if governmental regulation
does not entirely prohibit the business to be carried on in the leased
premises but only limits or restricts it, thereby making it less profitable
and more difficult to continue, the lease is not terminated or the lessee
excused from further performance. . . . Defendant may use the premises for the purpose for which they were leased. New automobiles and
gasoline continue to be sold. Indeed, defendant testified that he continued to sell new automobiles exclusively at another location in the same
county.

Defendant contends that the lease is restrictive and that the government orders therefore destroyed its value and frustrated its purpose. Provisions that prohibit subleasing or other uses than those specified affect
the value of a lease and are to be considered in determining whether its
purpose has been frustrated or its value destroyed (see Owens, The Effect
of the War Upon the Rights and Liabilities of Parties to a Contract, 19
California State Bar Journal 132, 143). It must not be forgotten, however,
that

> The landlord has not covenanted that the tenant shall have the right to
> carry on the contemplated business or that the business to which the prem-
> ises are by their nature or by the terms of the lease restricted shall be
> profitable enough to enable the tenant to pay the rent but has imposed a
> condition for his own benefit; and, certainly, unless and until he chooses to
> take advantage of it, the tenant is not deprived, of the use of the premises.

(6 Williston, Contracts, *op. cit. supra*, §1955, p. 5485; see also, People v.
Klopstock, 24 Cal. 2d 897, 901 [151 P.2d 641].) In the present lease plaintiffs reserved the rights that defendant should not use the premises for
other purposes than those specified in the lease or sublease without plaintiffs' written consent. Far from preventing other uses or subleasing they
waived these rights, enabling defendant to use the premises for any legitimate purpose and to sublease them to any responsible tenant. This
waiver is significant in view of the location of the premises on a main
traffic artery in Los Angeles County and their adaptability for many commercial purposes. The value of these rights is attested by the fact that the
premises were rented soon after defendants vacated them. It is therefore

clear that the governmental restrictions on the sale of new cars have not destroyed the value of the lease. Furthermore, plaintiffs offered to lower the rent if defendant should be unable to operate profitably, and their conduct was at all times fair and cooperative.

The consequences of applying the doctrine of frustration to a lease-hold involving less than a total or nearly total destruction of the value of the leased premises would be undesirable. Confusion would result from different decisions purporting to define "substantial" frustration. Litigation would be encouraged by the repudiation of leases when lessees found their business less profitable because of the regulations attendant upon a national emergency. Many leases have been affected in varying degrees by the widespread governmental regulations necessitated by war conditions.

The cases that defendant relies upon are consistent with the conclusion reached herein. In Industrial Development & Land Co. v. Goldschmidt, *supra*, the lease provided that the premises should not be used other than as a saloon. When national prohibition made the sale of alcoholic beverages illegal, the court excused the tenant from further performance on the theory of illegality or impossibility by a change in domestic law. The doctrine of frustration might have been applied, since the purpose for which the property was leased was totally destroyed and there was nothing to show that the value of the lease was not thereby totally destroyed. In the present case the purpose was not destroyed but only restricted, and plaintiffs proved that the lease was valuable to defendant. In Grace v. Croninger, *supra*, the lease was for the purpose of conducting a "saloon and cigar store and for no other purpose" with provision for subleasing a portion of the premises for bootblack purposes. The monthly rental was $650. It was clear that prohibition destroyed the main purpose of the lease, but since the premises could be used for bootblack and cigar store purposes, the lessee was not excused from his duty to pay the rent. In the present case new automobiles and gasoline may be sold under the lease as executed and any legitimate business may be conducted or the premises may be subleased under the lease as modified by plaintiff's waiver. Colonial Operating Corp. v. Hannon Sales & Service, Inc., 34 N.Y.S.2d 116, was reversed in 265 App. Div. 411 [39 N.Y.S.2d 217], and Signal Land Corp. v. Loecher, 35 N.Y.S.2d 25; Schantz v. American Auto Supply Co., Inc., 178 Misc. 909 [36 N.Y.S.2d 747]; and Canrock Realty Corp. v. Vim Electric Co., Inc., 37 N.Y.S.2d 139, involved government orders that totally destroyed the possibility of selling the products for which the premises were leased. No case has been cited by defendant or disclosed by research in which an appellate court has excused a lessee from performance of his duty to pay rent when the purpose of the lease has not been totally destroyed or its accomplishment rendered extremely impracticable or where it has been shown that the lease remains valuable to the lessee.

Gibson, C.J., Shenk, J., Curtis, J., Edmonds, J., Carter, J., and Schauer, J., concurred.

Appellant's petition for a rehearing was denied November 28, 1944.

NOTE

1. At the time Justice Traynor prepared his elaborate opinion in the principal case, judicial discussion of "frustration" was a rarity in American case law. American courts, dealing, of course, with the same types of cases that in England had come to be thought of as frustration cases, had been arriving at results comparable with the English results. There were, for example, a number of cases on whether buyers could get out of requirements contracts during the depression of the 1930s by going out of business (and thus ceasing to have any requirements at all). These cases obviously could have been (but were not) argued and decided as frustration cases. The question presented, according to the courts, was whether there should be implied in a requirements contract a condition (or covenant) that the buyer should remain in business for the term of the contract. The courts as a general rule refused to imply the condition (or covenant), so that the buyers escaped liability. Obviously, counsel for the lessee in Lloyd v. Murphy could not have argued discharge by impossibility (neither paying the rent nor carrying on some sort of business in the leased premises had become impossible) and seems to have elected to gamble on a frustration defense. Granted that requirements contracts and leases are not in all respects the same, counsel might have been well advised to stress the analogy of the "going out of business" cases instead of directing the court's attention to the vexed problem of whether English frustration theory was recognized in this country.

2. Justice Traynor, although concluding that the defense was unavailable on the facts of Lloyd v. Murphy, seems, in a remarkably open-ended discussion, to endorse the idea that frustration (even as applied to leases) is an entirely acceptable doctrine. On current American attitudes toward the use of the term, see the opinion in the following principal case. According to Justice Traynor, English courts had refused to apply frustration theory to leases "on the ground that an estate is conveyed to the lessee, which carries with it all risks. . . ." See Paradine v. Jane, *supra* p. 911, and the Note following that case. The question raised by Justice Traynor was much discussed, with a great diversity of views, in the several opinions read in the House of Lords in Cricklewood Property and Investment Trust, Ltd. v. Leighton's Investment Trust, Ltd., [1945] A.C. 221. The holding was that a 99-year lease had not been frustrated during World War II.

3. In Lloyd v. Murphy the California Court approved without discussion an award of damages, made in 1942, for the unexpired term of a lease

which ran until 1946. Other courts have had more difficulty with the question whether damages under long-term contracts (including leases) can properly be calculated before the term has run. See Hermitage Co. v. Levine, 248 N.Y. 333, 162 N.E. 97 (1928), digested in Note 2 appearing on p. 1300 *infra*.

AMERICAN TRADING AND PRODUCTION CORP. v. SHELL INTERNATIONAL MARINE LTD.
453 F.2d 939 (2d Cir. 1972)

MULLIGAN, Circuit Judge:

This is an appeal by American Trading and Production Corporation (hereinafter "owner") from a judgment entered on July 29th, 1971, in the United States District Court for the Southern District of New York, dismissing its claim against Shell International Marine Ltd. (hereinafter "charterer") for additional compensation in the sum of $131,978.44 for the transportation of cargo from Texas to India via the Cape of Good Hope as a result of the closing of the Suez Canal in June, 1967. The charterer had asserted a counterclaim which was withdrawn and is not in issue. The action was tried on stipulated facts and without a jury before Hon. Harold R. Tyler, Jr. who dismissed the claim on the merits in an opinion dated July 22, 1971.

We affirm.

The owner is a Maryland corporation doing business in New York and the charterer is a United Kingdom corporation. On March 23, 1967 the parties entered into a contract of voyage charter in New York City which provided that the charterer would hire the owner's tank vessel, WASHINGTON TRADER, for a voyage with a full cargo of lube oil from Beaumont/Smiths Bluff, Texas to Bombay, India. The charter party provided that the freight rate would be in accordance with the then prevailing American Tanker Rate Schedule (ATRS), $14.25 per long ton of cargo, plus seventy-five percent (75%), and in addition there was a charge of $.85 per long ton for passage through the Suez Canal. On May 15, 1967 the WASHINGTON TRADER departed from Beaumont with a cargo of 16,183.32 long tons of lube oil. The charterer paid the freight at the invoiced sum of $417,327.36 on May 26, 1967. On May 29th, 1967 the owner advised the WASHINGTON TRADER by radio to take additional bunkers at Ceuta due to possible diversion because of the Suez Canal crisis. The vessel arrived at Ceuta, Spanish Morocco on May 30, bunkered and sailed on May 31st, 1967. On June 5th the owner cabled the ship's master advising him of various reports of trouble in the Canal and suggested delay in entering it pending clarification. On that very day, the Suez Canal was closed due to the state of war which had developed in the

Middle East. The owner then communicated with the charterer on June 5th through the broker who had negotiated the charter party, requesting approval for the diversion of the WASHINGTON TRADER which then had proceeded to a point about 84 miles northwest of Port Said, the entrance to the Canal. On June 6th the charterer responded that under the circumstances it was "for owner to decide whether to continue to wait or make the alternative passage via the Cape since Charter Party Obliges them to deliver cargo without qualification." In response the owner replied on the same day that in view of the closing of the Suez, the WASHINGTON TRADER would proceed to Bombay via the Cape of Good Hope and "[w]e [are] reserving all rights for extra compensation." The vessel proceeded westward, back through the Straits of Gibraltar and around the Cape and eventually arrived in Bombay on July 15th (some 30 days later than initially expected), traveling a total of 18,055 miles instead of the 9,709 miles which it would have sailed had the Canal been open. The owner billed $131,978.44 as extra compensation which the charterer has refused to pay.

On appeal and below the owner argues that transit of the Suez Canal was the agreed specific means of performance of the voyage charter and that the supervening destruction of this means rendered the contract legally impossible to perform and therefore discharged the owner's unperformed obligation (Restatement of Contracts §460 (1932)). Consequently, when the WASHINGTON TRADER eventually delivered the oil after journeying around the Cape of Good Hope, a benefit was conferred upon the charterer for which it should respond in *quantum meruit*. The validity of this proposition depends upon a finding that the parties contemplated or agreed that the Suez passage was to be the exclusive method of performance, and indeed it was so argued on appeal. We cannot construe the agreement in such a fashion. The parties contracted for the shipment of the cargo from Texas to India at an agreed rate and the charter party makes absolutely no reference to any fixed route. It is urged that the Suez passage was a condition of performance because the ATRS rate was based on a Suez Canal passage, the invoice contained a specific Suez Canal toll charge and the vessel actually did proceed to a point 84 miles northwest of Port Said. In our view all that this establishes is that both parties contemplated that the Canal would be the probable route. It was the cheapest and shortest, and therefore it was in the interest of both that it be utilized. However, this is not at all equivalent to an agreement that it be the exclusive method of performance. The charter party does not so provide and it seems to have been well understood in the shipping industry that the Cape route is an acceptable alternative in voyages of this character.

The District of Columbia Circuit decided a closely analogous case, Transatlantic Financing Corp. v. United States, 124 U.S. App. D.C. 183, 363 F.2d 312 (1966). There the plaintiff had entered into a voyage charter with defendant in which it agreed to transport a full cargo of wheat on the CHRISTOS from a United States port to Iran. The parties clearly contemplated a Suez passage, but on November 2, 1956 the vessel reduced speed when war blocked the Suez Canal. The vessel changed its course in the Atlantic and eventually delivered its cargo in Iran after proceeding by way of the Cape of Good Hope. In an exhaustive opinion Judge Skelly Wright reviewed the English cases which had considered the same problem and concluded that "the Cape route is generally regarded as an alternative means of performance. So the implied expectation that the route would be via Suez is hardly adequate proof of an allocation to the promisee of the risk of closure. In some cases, even an express expectation may not amount to a condition of performance." Transatlantic Financing Corp. v. United States, *supra*, 363 F.2d at 317 (footnote omitted).

Appellant argues that *Transatlantic* is distinguishable since there was an agreed upon flat rate in that case unlike the instant case where the rate was based on Suez passage. This does not distinguish the case in our view. It is stipulated by the parties here that the only ATRS rate published at the time of the agreement from Beaumont to Bombay was the one utilized as a basis for the negotiated rate ultimately agreed upon. This rate was escalated by 75% to reflect whatever existing market conditions the parties contemplated. These conditions are not stipulated. Had a Cape route rate been requested, which was not the case, it is agreed that the point from which the parties would have bargained would be $17.35 per long ton of cargo as against $14.25 per long ton.

Actually, in *Transatlantic* it was argued that certain provisions in the P. & I. Bunker Deviation Clause referring to the direct and/or customary route required, by implication, a voyage through the Suez Canal. The court responded "[a]ctually they prove only what we are willing to accept — that the parties expected the usual and customary route would be used. The provisions in no way condition performance upon non-occurrence of this contingency." Transatlantic Financing Corp. v. United States, *supra*, 363 F.2d at 317 n.8. We hold that all that the ATRS rate establishes is that the parties obviously expected a Suez passage but there is no indication at all in the instrument or *dehors* that it was a condition of performance.

This leaves us with the question as to whether the owner was excused from performance on the theory of commercial impracticability (Restatement of Contracts §454 (1932)). Even though the owner is not excused because of strict impossibility, it is urged that American law recognizes that performance is rendered impossible if it can only be accomplished with extreme and unreasonable difficulty, expense, injury or loss.[19] There is no extreme or unreasonable difficulty apparent here. The alternate route taken was well recognized, and there is no claim that the vessel or the crew or the nature of the cargo made the route actually taken unreasonably difficult, dangerous or onerous. The owner's case here essentially rests upon the element of the additional expense involved —

19. This is the formula utilized in the Restatement of Contracts §454 (1932).

$131,978.44. This represents an increase of less than one third over the agreed upon $417,327.36. We find that this increase in expense is not sufficient to constitute commercial impracticability under either American or English authority.

Mere increase in cost alone is not a sufficient excuse for non-performance (Restatement of Contracts §467 (1932)). It must be an "extreme and unreasonable"[20] expense (Restatement of Contracts §454 (1932)).[21] While in the *Transatlantic* case *supra*, the increased cost amounted to an increase of about 14% over the contract price, the court did cite with approval[22] the two leading English cases Ocean Tramp Tankers Corp. v. V/O Sovfracht (*The Eugenia*), [1964] 2 Q.B. 226, 233 (C.A.1963) (which expressly overruled Société Franco Tunisienne D'Armement v. Sidermar S.P.A. (*The Messalia*), [1961] 2 Q.B. 278 (1960), where the court had found frustration because the Cape route was highly circuitous and involved an increase in cost of approximately 50%), and Tsakiroglou & Co. Lt. v. Noblee Thorl G.m.b.H., [1960] 2 Q.B. 318, 348, *aff'd*, [1962] A.C., 93 (1961) where the House of Lords found no frustration though the freight costs were exactly doubled due to the Canal closure.[23]

Appellant further seeks to distinguish *Transatlantic* because in that case the change in course was in the mid-Atlantic and added some 300 miles to the voyage while in this case the WASHINGTON TRADER had traversed most of the Mediterranean and thus had added some 9000 miles to the contemplated voyage. It should be noted that although both the time and the length of the altered passage here exceeded those in the *Transatlantic*, the additional compensation sought here is just under one third of the contract price. Aside from this however, it is a fact that the master of the WASHINGTON TRADER was alerted by radio on May

20. The Restatement gives some examples of what is "extreme and unreasonable" — Restatement of Contracts §460, Illus. 2 (tenfold increase in costs) and Illus. 3 (costs multiplied fifty times) (1932); compare §467, Illus. 3. See generally G. Grismore, Principles of the Law of Contracts §179 (rev. ed. J. E. Murray 1965).

21. Both parties take solace in the Uniform Commercial Code which in comment 4 to Section 2-615 states that the rise in cost must "alter the essential nature of the performance. . . ." This is clearly not the case here. The owner relies on a further sentence in the comment which refers to a severe shortage of raw materials or of supplies due to "war, embargo, local crop failure, unforeseen shutdown of major sources of supply or the like, which either causes a marked increase in cost. . . ." Since this is not a case involving the sale of goods but transportation of a cargo where there was an alternative which was a commercially reasonable substitute (see Uniform Commercial Code §2-614 (1)) the owner's reliance is misplaced.

22. Transatlantic Financing Corp. v. United States, *supra*, 363 F.2d at 319 n.14.

23. While these are English cases and refer to the doctrine of "frustration" rather than "impossibility" as Judge Skelly Wright pointed out in *Transatlantic*, *supra*, 363 F.2d at 320 n.16 the two are considered substantially identical, 6 A. Corbin, Contracts §1322, at 327 n.9 (rev. ed. 1962). While *Tsakiroglou* and *The Eugenia* are criticized in Schlegel, Of Nuts, and Ships and Sealing Wax, Suez, and Frustrating Things — The Doctrine of Impossibility of Performance, 23 Rutgers L. Rev. 419, 448 (1969), apparently on the theory that the charterer is a better loss bearer, the overruled *Sidermar* case was previously condemned in Berman, Excuse for Nonperformance in the Light of Contract Practices in International Trade, 63 Colum. L. Rev. 1413, 1424-27 (1963).

29th, 1967 of a "possible diversion because of Suez Canal crisis," but nevertheless two days later he had left Cueta (opposite Gibraltar) and proceeded across the Mediterranean. While we may not speculate about the foreseeability of a Suez crisis at the time the contract was entered, there does not seem to be any question but that the master here had been actually put on notice before traversing the Mediterranean that diversion was possible. Had the WASHINGTON TRADER then changed course, the time and cost of the Mediterranean trip could reasonably have been avoided, thereby reducing the amount now claimed. (Restatement of Contracts §336, Comment *d* to subsection (1) (1932)).

In a case closely in point, Palmco Shipping Inc. v. Continental Ore Corp. (*The "Captain George K"*), [1970] 2 Lloyd's L. Rep. 21 (Q.B.1969), *The Eugenia, supra,* was followed, and no frustration was found where the vessel had sailed to a point three miles northwest of Port Said only to find the Canal blocked. The vessel then sailed back through the Mediterranean and around the Cape of Good Hope to its point of destination, Kandla. The distances involved, 9700 miles via the initially contemplated Canal route and 18,400 miles actually covered by way of the Cape of Good Hope, coincide almost exactly with those in this case. Moreover, in *The "Captain George K"* there was no indication that the master had at anytime after entering the Mediterranean been advised of the possibility of the Canal's closure.

Finally, owners urge that the language of the "Liberties Clause," Para. 28(a) of Part II of the charter party[24] provides explicit authority for extra

---

24. "28. Liberty Clauses. (a) In any situation whatsoever and wheresoever occurring and whether existing or anticipated before commencement of or during the voyage, which in the judgment of the Owner or Master is likely to give rise to risk of capture, seizure, detention, damage, delay or disadvantage to or loss of the Vessel or any part of her cargo, or to make it unsafe, imprudent, or unlawful for any reason to commence or proceed on or continue the voyage or to enter or discharge the cargo at the port of discharge, or to give rise to delay or difficulty in arriving, discharging at or leaving the port of discharge or the usual place of discharge in such port, the Owner may before loading or before the commencement of the voyage, require the shipper or other person entitled thereto to take delivery of the Cargo at port of shipment and upon their failure to do so, may warehouse the cargo at the risk and expense of the cargo; or the owner or Master, whether or not proceeding toward or entering or attempting to enter the port of discharge or reaching or attempting to reach the usual place of discharge therein or attempting to discharge the cargo there, may discharge the cargo into depot, lazaretto, craft or other place; or the Vessel may proceed or return, directly or indirectly, to or stop at any such port or place whatsoever as the Master or the Owner may consider safe or advisable under the circumstances, and discharge the cargo, or any part thereof, at any such port or place; or the Owner or the Master may retain the cargo on board until the return trip or until such time as the Owner or the Master thinks advisable and discharge the cargo at any place whatsoever as herein provided or the Owner or the Master may discharge and forward the cargo by any means at the risk and expense of the cargo. The Owner may, when practicable, have the Vessel call and discharge the cargo at another or substitute port declared or requested by the Charterer. The Owner or the Master is not required to give notice of discharge of the cargo, or the forwarding thereof as herein provided. When the cargo is discharged from the Vessel, as herein provided, it shall be at its own risk and expense; such discharge shall constitute complete delivery and performance under this contract and the Owner shall be freed from any further responsibility. For any service rendered to the cargo as herein provided the Owner shall be entitled to a reasonable extra compensation."

compensation in the circumstances of this case. We do not so interpret the clause. We construe it to apply only where the master, by reason of dangerous conditions, deposits the cargo at some port or haven other than the designated place of discharge. Here the cargo did reach the designated port albeit by another route, and hence the clause is not applicable. No intermediate or other disposition of the oil was appropriate under the circumstances.

Appellant relies on C. H. Leavell & Co. v. Hellenic Lines, Ltd., 13 F.M.C., 76, 1969 A.M.C. 2177 (1969) for a contrary conclusion. That case involved a determination as to whether surcharges to compensate for extra expenses incurred when the Suez Canal was closed after the commencement of a voyage, were available to a carrier. The Federal Maritime Commission authorized the assessment since the applicable tariffs were on file as provided by section 18(b) of the Shipping Act (46 U.S.C. §817(b)) and also on the basis of Clause 5 of the bill of lading which is comparable to the Liberties Clause in issue here, except for the language which authorized the carrier to "proceed by any route. . . ." (Leavell, supra, 13 F.M.C. at 81, 1969 A.M.C. at 2182). This is the very language relied upon by the Commission in finding the surcharge appropriate (Leavell, supra, 13 F.M.C. at 89, 1969 A.M.C. at 2191) where the carrier proceeded to the initially designated port of destination via the Cape of Good Hope. Utilization of an alternate route contemplates berthing at the contracted port of destination. There is no such language in the clause at issue. Its absence fortifies the contention that the Liberties Clause was not intended to be applicable to the facts in litigation here.

Matters involving impossibility or impracticability of performance of contract are concededly vexing and difficult. One is even urged on the allocation of such risks to pray for the "wisdom of Solomon." 6 A. Corbin, Contracts §1333, at 372 (1962). On the basis of all of the facts, the pertinent authority and a further belief in the efficacy of prayer, we affirm.

NOTE

1. In the paragraph of his opinion beginning "Mere increase in cost alone is not a sufficient excuse," Judge Mulligan refers to a trio of English cases that arose out of the closing of the Suez Canal from November, 1956 to April, 1957. These cases, which were widely commented on in both the English and the American law reviews, were, chronologically, Sidermar (Q.B. 1960), Tsakiroglou (H.L. 1961), and The Eugenia (C.A. 1963).

2. Sidermar, like the principal case, involved a voyage charter, the charter rate (134s. per long ton) having been calculated on the assumption that the voyage (from India to Italy) would be made via Suez. By the

time the ship was ready to sail from India, the Canal had been closed to shipping for an indefinite period. The owners elected to make the longer voyage around the Cape of Good Hope and notified the charterers that they would be held liable for the increased costs; the charterers took the position that the owners were bound by the Suez rate specified in the charter. Pearson, J., held that the charter had been frustrated and that the owners were entitled to be compensated for their reasonable costs in going around Africa; he awarded them 195s. per long ton (the shipment amounted to approximately 5000 tons of iron ore).

3. *Tsakiroglou*, which reached the House of Lords, was a different type of case: an action by a buyer against a seller for nondelivery of 300 tons of groundnuts to be shipped from Port Sudan, on the east coast of Africa, to Hamburg, Germany. The contract of sale, executed about a month before the Canal was closed, was on c.i.f. (cost, insurance, freight) terms. In a c.i.f. contract the quoted price includes the freight to destination; the freight component in the price quotation in *Tsakiroglou* was based on the rate via Suez. The seller had booked space in vessels scheduled to sail from Port Sudan via Suez in November and December of 1956; those bookings were canceled when the Canal was closed on November 2. The seller, who had the groundnuts in a warehouse at Port Sudan, took the position that the c.i.f. contract had been discharged and made no shipment. The House of Lords, affirming the lower courts, held that the c.i.f. contract had not been frustrated and approved a damage award of £5,625, based on the differential between the contract price and the market price for shipments from Port Sudan c.i.f Hamburg in January, 1957. Both Pearson, J., in *Sidermar* and the judges who read opinions in the House of Lords in *Tsakiroglou* suggested that the question whether a voyage charter party had been frustrated (as in *Sidermar*) was quite different from the question whether a c.i.f. contract had been frustrated (as in *Tsakiroglou*). Thus *Tsakiroglou* did not overrule, or even express disapproval of, *Sidermar*.

4. *The Eugenia* was another charter party case (like *Sidermar*) but both the charter party arrangement and the facts of the case were quite different from those in *Sidermar*. *The Eugenia* involved a time (not a voyage) charter; under a time charter, the charterer pays charter hire (usually monthly) for as long as it is entitled to use the ship and during the term of the charter, the ship is subject to the charterer's orders. (Under a voyage charter the freight payable is stated as a lump sum and the ship remains subject to the owner's orders.) The Eugenia sailed from the Black Sea port of Odessa on October 25, bound for India via Suez, and arrived at Port Said on October 30. It was then widely known that English, French, and Israeli forces were about to attack the Canal (which had been nationalized by Egypt a few months earlier). Over the owner's objections, the charterers (a Russian trading corporation) nevertheless ordered the ship into the Canal, which it entered on October 31. By the next day the

Canal had been blocked and the Eugenia remained trapped until the
following January when a northward passage back to Port Said was
cleared. The Russian charterers claimed that the charter had been frustrated when the Eugenia was trapped in the Canal, and refused to pay the
charter hire for November, December, and January. The owners claimed
that the charter had not been frustrated and, further, that the charterer's
order that the Eugenia should enter the Canal on October 31 was a
breach of the "war clause" of the charter party, which gave the owners
the right to cancel the charter. The upshot was that a new charter, at
much higher rates, was negotiated and the Eugenia completed the original voyage to India by way of the Cape of Good Hope. The owners then
sued to recover the charter hire for the three months the ship had spent
trapped in the Canal. In the Court of Appeal a three-judge panel, reversing the trial court, held for the owners. Lord Denning, M.R., delivered
the principal opinion. The charterers, he said, could not claim frustration
in the light of what had actually happened, since they had been responsible for sending the ship into the Canal and "self induced frustration" is
unknown to the law. He also concluded that the order to enter the Canal
was a violation of the "war clause," so that the owners had properly
canceled the charter. He then went on to consider what the legal situation would have been if The Eugenia had not entered the Canal. Relying
on *Tsakiroglou*, he concluded that the charter would not have been frustrated and, his colleagues concurring, overruled the decision of Pearson,
J., in *Sidermar*. He could not, Denning wrote, see any difference between a
c.i.f. contract of sale and a charter party or, for that matter, between a
voyage charter and a time charter.

5. It can be argued that the three English cases digested above are
entirely consistent with each other and that Lord Denning and his colleagues in *The Eugenia* need not have (and should not have) overruled
Sidermar. See Schlegel, Of Nuts, and Ships and Sealing Wax, Suez and
Frustrating Things — The Doctrine of Impossibility of Performance, 23
Rutgers L. Rev. 419, 448 (1969), cited by Judge Mulligan, *supra* note 23.
The argument for consistency rests on the observation that, in all three
cases, the loss was cast on the charterer-shipper, who, it can be further
argued, was the best candidate to saddle with the risk. The argument,
evidently, did not prevail in the principal case or in the *Transatlantic* case
(which arose from the 1956 closing of the Canal) discussed by Judge
Mulligan in the first part of his opinion. In the last sentence of his opinion
Judge Mulligan seems to suggest that, in the deep recesses of his mind, he
was not altogether sure how the principal case should have been decided.
On the whole, do you prefer the decision in *Sidermar* or the decision in
the principal case?

6. Hellenic Lines, Ltd. v. United States, 512 F.2d 1196 (2d Cir. 1975)
may have been the last of the 1967 Suez cases litigated in this country.
Eighty percent of the capacity of the Italia, owned by Hellenic Lines, had

been booked by the Agency for International Development to carry a cargo of flour from United States Gulf Coast ports via Suez to the Red Sea port of Aqaba. The flour was intended for distribution to Palestinian refugees. Having loaded the flour and cleared the last of the Gulf Coast ports, the Italia, instead of proceeding directly to Aqaba, made stops at Norfolk and Brooklyn for the purpose of picking up additional cargo (which had nothing to do with the AID shipment). These stops added six days' sailing time to the voyage. The Italia's transatlantic crossing was further delayed by mechanical and navigational difficulties. If the Italia had sailed direct from the Gulf Coast to Aqaba, it might have arrived in time to go through the Canal and unload the flour at Aqaba. By the time it actually arrived the Canal had been closed. The owners of the Italia had the flour unloaded at the Greek port of Piraeus, where the Italia was docked for repairs. AID, which had not consented to the Piraeus unloading, eventually had the flour transported to the Mediterranean port of Ashdod where it was presumably distributed to Palestinian refugees. The freight to Aqaba, which had been prepaid by AID, was $114,301.51. The established "conference" rate for the shorter voyage to Piraeus was $215,403.54. Port expenses at Piraeus were $27,499.56. The freight charge for shipping the flour from Piraeus to Ashdod on an American-flag vessel was $140,178.81 (although the flour could have been shipped on a foreign-flag vessel for slightly more than half that sum). Hellenic started the litigation by suing the United States to recover the "conference" freight rate to Piraeus. The United States counterclaimed to recover the Piraeus expenses and the extra freight to Ashdod. A panel of the Second Circuit concluded that Hellenic could not recover the Piraeus freight rate (Hellenic's claim for the extra freight was described as "rather shocking") and that the United States could recover from Hellenic either (1) the prepaid Aqaba freight or (2) the Piraeus expenses plus what it would have cost to ship the flour to Ashdod in a foreign-flag vessel. (The district judge, for reasons that the panel found inexplicable, had awarded the United States both the prepaid freight and the extra expenses of getting the flour to Ashdod in a foreign-flag vessel.) Friendly, J., devoted the bulk of an elaborate opinion to disposing of Hellenic's contention that it was protected by exculpatory clauses in the bill of lading, including the "liberties clause" (see note 24, *supra*). His conclusion on that branch of the case was that the calls that the Italia had made at Norfolk and Brooklyn constituted an unjustifiable "deviation" from the Aqaba voyage; the consequence of the deviation, under maritime law, was to "oust" the exculpatory clauses. He then briefly discussed the question whether Hellenic could claim discharge "on general principles of maritime contract law," specifically the defense of "impossibility of performance." Citing the principal case, the earlier *Transatlantic* case, and "the leading English cases," he concluded that "the doctrine of impossibility has no application to the level of added expense here entailed." In a footnote Judge

Friendly commented that evidence had been introduced at the trial (and apparently not refuted) to the effect that "no vessels which left port before the 1967 crisis were permitted to recover any surcharge for making the longer voyage around the Cape of Good Hope." As if all that was not enough, Judge Friendly added the further thought that "the doctrine of impossibility . . . applies . . . only when the promisor is not 'in contributing fault' [citing Restatement First §457]" and that Hellenic had "made a considered decision to maximize its profits by stopping to take on additional cargo at Norfolk and Brooklyn" — a decision that led to the Italia's not being able to complete the Aqaba voyage.

Note on the Restatements of Contracts and the Uniform Commercial Code

On three occasions in this century, American draftsmen have attempted to formulate the rules of discharge from contractual liability by reason of impossibility or frustration — first, in the Restatement of Contracts (1932); second, in the Sales Article of the Uniform Commercial Code (drafted in the 1940s); third, in the Restatement of Contracts Second (drafted in the 1970s). The draftsmen of the English Frustrated Contracts Act (1943), reprinted *supra* p. 934, had the excuse of working under conditions of wartime emergency. The several sets of American draftsmen had the opportunity to carry out their labors in contemplative leisure. Even so, it cannot fairly be said that any of the American efforts was crowned with anything like success. The truth may be that a field of law that has been in course of rapid change, as this one has been for fifty years past, is not an apt subject for the draftsman's art.

Restatement First

Restatement First devoted Chapter 14 (§§454-469) to the topic of Impossibility. The term was defined (§454) to include "not only strict impossibility but impracticability because of extreme and unreasonable difficulty, expense, injury or loss involved." A distinction was then taken (§455) between subjective ("due to the inability of the individual promisor") and objective ("due to the nature of the performance") impossibility: only the latter "prevents the formation of a contract" or "discharges a duty created by a contract." "Objective impossibility," if existing at the time the contract was entered into, prevented the formation of a contract (§456) and, if thereafter supervening, discharged contractual duty (§457), provided the promisor was not chargeable with knowledge or fault; both sections provided that a promisor may assume the risk of impossibility. The distinction between subjective and objective impossibility was echoed, or perhaps reinforced, in §467, Unanticipated Difficulty: "Except to the extent required by the rules stated in §§455-466, facts existing when a bargain is made or occurring thereafter making performance of a promise more difficult or expensive than the parties anticipate, do not prevent a duty from arising or discharge a duty that has arisen." Sections 458-461 took up various "events" sufficient to discharge a duty (or prevent one from arising) under the objective theory: governmental action, death or illness of promisors who had agreed to render personal services, the destruction of "things" or the absence of facts "necessary for the performance of the promise." Succeeding sections dealt with "temporary impossibility," "partial impossibility," "apprehension of impossibility," and so on. Section 468, Rights of Restitution, merits special mention. Under §468 a party who had rendered part performance and had then been discharged from completing his performance (subsection (1)) or a party who had rendered performance after which the other party was discharged from "rendering the agreed exchange" (subsection (2)) could in either case recover judgment for the "value" of his performance; "value" was defined (subsection (3)) as "the benefit derived from the performance in advancing the object of the contract, not exceeding, however, a ratable portion of the contract price."

The Restatement First chapter on Impossibility was evidently designed to reflect late nineteenth-century and early twentieth-century ideas that had confined the impossibility defense within narrow limits. There were, it is true, a few soft spots in the drafting — notably, the definition of "impossibility" to include "impracticability." But, on the whole, it was clear that no amount of "unanticipated difficulty" (§467) was to discharge a performing party and that, under the basic distinction between subjective and objective impossibility, a paying party would never be discharged.

All of that would have been reasonably coherent (which is not the same as reasonably satisfactory), had it not been for the appearance in the chapter on Conditions of a section (§288) captioned "Frustration of the Object or Effect of the Contract." There had not been in the text or commentary of the Impossibility chapter a single reference to the doctrine of "frustration" — nor was there a cross-reference to §288. The Frustration section provided a two-way rule of discharge "[w]here the assumed possibility of a desired object or effect to be attained by either party to a contract forms the basis on which both parties enter into it, and this object or effect is or surely will be frustrated. . . ." The party claiming the discharge must have been "without fault in causing the frustration" and the whole section was subject to the cautionary statement "unless a contrary intention appears." The Illustrations to §288 "codified" the English Coronation cases, including Krell v. Henry, *supra* p. 926. The §288 commentary did not so much as mention the Impossibility chapter.

No plausible explanation has been — or could be — advanced for the Restatement's schizophrenic treatment of Impossibility and Frustration.

It sometimes happens in a drafting project that takes a number of years to complete that the draftsmen simply forget in the later stages what had been done years earlier. When the Restatement was published (1932), most scholars and judges seem to have assumed that the Impossibility chapter contained the whole truth. The very existence of §288 remained, for a long time, a well-kept secret; indeed, one of the first references to §288 occurs in the course of Justice Traynor's scholarly opinion in Lloyd v. Murphy (1944), *supra* p. 948. The general, albeit mistaken, belief that the authoritative Restatement had rejected the English doctrine of "frustration" was, no doubt, a contributing factor to the late development of frustration theory in American case law.

Corbin's discussion of the Restatement's treatment of Impossibility and Frustration is uncharacteristically hesitant (6 Corbin §1322). He suggests that the result reached in the Impossibility chapter "is, in most of its aspects, directly contra to the once much repeated rule that supervening impossibility is no defense" (which sounds like an overstatement). He then notes that the Impossibility chapter said nothing about Frustration, quotes the Frustration section (§288), and adds the comment that, "[f]urther consideration of this section (§288) since its publication has led the present writer to disapprove the quoted wording." Corbin's language seems to mean that he had originally "approved" §288 (perhaps he had drafted it) but had subsequently come to "disapprove" its wording. His disapproval focused on the assumption in §288 that it is possible to discover a "basis" on which both parties enter into a contract: "The court's attention should be directed, not to the discovery of a non-existent 'basis' or intention of a party, but to the allocation of risks in accordance with the business practices and mores of men in similar cases."

The Code

The Code's treatment of impossibility and frustration is localized in Article 2 on Sales. Though the Code provisions thus apply directly only to contracts for the sale of goods, a court that thought well of the Code's approach could of course apply its provisions more generally, on the theory that the statutory formulation merely reflects the underlying common law principle. See the following discussion of Restatement Second.

Section 2-613 carries forward the rule previously codified in the Uniform Sales Act under which the contract is avoided (i.e., the seller is discharged) if the goods are accidentally destroyed before the risk of loss (under pre-Code law the "property") has passed to the buyer. (For the common law origins of the rule, see Note 5 following Taylor v. Caldwell, *supra* p. 920; for its later development, see Note 1 following Canadian Industrial Alcohol Co. v. Dunbar Molasses Co., *supra* p. 944). The Code rules on risk of loss are set out in §§2-509 and 2-510. The §2-613 formulation is restricted to "goods identified when the contract is made." There seems to have been no intention to narrow the rule of discharge as stated by Cardozo in the *Canadian Industrial Alcohol* case but the language of §2-613 would not comfortably fit the case of crops not planted or goods not manufactured when the contract is made. Under the Code such cases are dealt with under §2-615, discussed below.

Section 2-614(1) provides in substance that when an agreed method of delivery becomes "commercially impracticable" (for example, loading or unloading facilities fail or a carrier whose use had been contemplated becomes unavailable) but "a commercially reasonable substitute is available," then "such substitute performance must be tendered and accepted." Section 2-614(2) deals in a roughly analogous fashion with the situation where the agreed method of payment fails "because of domestic or foreign governmental regulation."

Section 2-615, which is the heart of the matter, is captioned "Excuse by Failure of Presupposed Conditions." It provides in substance that a seller is excused or discharged from performance of his contract "if performance as agreed has been made impracticable by the occurrence of a contingency the non-occurrence of which was a basic assumption on which the contract was made. . . ." The preamble to §2-615 makes the point that a seller may assume "a greater obligation" than that specified. The section goes on to deal with the case where "only a part of the seller's capacity to perform" is affected and requires him to allocate deliveries to his customers "in any manner which is fair and reasonable."

Section 2-616 rounds out the treatment by giving the buyer the option to accept or reject any proposal for partial fulfillment of the contract proposed by the seller under the allocation requirement of §2-615. Under §2-616(3), "[t]he provisions of this section may not be negated by agreement except in so far as the seller has assumed a greater obligation under the preceding section."

The Code sections here digested require careful study — particularly §2-615, and its Official Comment, whose ambiguities outdo even the ambiguities of the statutory text. You will note, inter alia, that the text refers only to the discharge of sellers but that the Comment suggests, as through a glass darkly, that there may be situations in which "the reason of the present section may well . . . entitle the buyer to the exemption."

The Code does not deal with the question of recovery for expenses (either in performance of or in reliance on the contract) incurred before discharge. The Code need not have dealt with frustration at all; the Uniform Sales Act had left it to the general principles of contract law. Since the Code draftsmen did, however, decide to include a fairly detailed treatment of the subject in §§2-614, 2-615, and 2-616, it is inexplicable that they ignored this aspect of the problem — particularly in light of its treatment in Restatement §468 and the English Frustrated Contracts Act (1943). It is fairly arguable that an incomplete or partial codification does more harm than good.

Commentary on how the Code provisions have fared in the courts will be deferred until the approach taken in Restatement Second has been summarized.

Restatement Second

Chapter 11 is captioned "Impracticability of Performance and Frustration of Purpose": thus the schizophrenia which afflicted Restatement First has been cured and "Impossibility" has become "Impracticability," not hidden away in the definition of the term (see Restatement First §454), but open for all to see in the chapter title. A more important change may be the effective disappearance of Restatement First §467, which had sternly provided that "facts" making performance "more difficult or expensive" than anticipated do not discharge contractual duties or prevent them from arising.

The Restatement Second draftsmen elected to generalize the Code section on frustration (§2-615). The principal rules are stated in §261, Discharge by Supervening Impracticability, and §266, Existing Impracticability or Frustration. In all three sections the key to discharge is that a "basic assumption" on which the contract was entered into has proved to be untrue. The elaborate accompanying commentary may be read to suggest that the draftsmen were uneasily aware that, in their three sections, they were not dealing with three discrete concepts but with a single concept that might better have been dealt with as a whole (as the Code draftsmen had done in §2-615).

Following the lead of Restatement First §468, the Restatement Second draftsmen dealt (as the Code draftsmen had not) with what is to happen after discharge with respect to expenses and losses incurred before discharge. The relevant section, §272, went through an interesting evolution in the course of drafting. The section, as it originally appeared (Tentative Draft No. 9, 1974), read:

> §292. Relief Including Restitution; Supplying a Term
> (1) In any case governed by the rules stated in this Chapter, either party may have a claim for relief including restitution under the rules stated in §265 and prospective Chapter 16.
> (2) In any case governed by the rules stated in this Chapter, if those rules together with the rules stated in prospective Chapter 16 will not avoid injustice, the court may, under the rule stated in §230, supply a term which is reasonable in the circumstances.

(The "prospective Chapter 16" referred to in the text is the chapter on Remedies, which includes, but is not limited to, restitution.)

The original version of §272 would seem to have been open-ended to a fault. However, as the ideas of the draftsmen evolved, they evidently concluded that it was not open-ended enough. In Tentative Draft No. 14,

1979, §292 was revised by deletion of the final clause of subsection (2) (beginning with the cross-reference to §230) and substitution of new language so that the final clause now reads: ". . . the court may grant relief on such terms as justice requires including protection of the parties' reliance interests." Thus, the courts are being told that, with respect to granting "relief" after discharge, they are to do whatever "justice requires," no matter what Restatement Second says. (In the Restatement Second chapter on Mistake, §158 is a twin or clone of §272, using identical language.

In the Restatement Second chapter on Remedies, §377 provides:

> A party whose duty of performance does not arise or is discharged as a result of impracticability of performance, frustration of purpose, non-occurrence of a condition or disclaimer by a beneficiary is entitled to restitution for any benefit that he has conferred on the other party by way of part performance or reliance.

Note that under §377 the restitutionary remedy is available both for "performance" expenses and for "reliance" expenses but that in either case the recovery is limited to the "benefit . . . conferred on the other party." This seems to mean that there is to be no recovery for reliance expenses reasonably incurred that do not, on some theory, confer a benefit on the other party. Indeed the §377 commentary makes that point expressly. On the other hand in §349, Damages Based on Reliance Interest, there is no "benefit conferred" limitation, and both the §349 text and the commentary make clear that recovery may be had for "non-beneficial" reliance expenses. No cross-references between §363 and §377 are provided in the text or commentary of either section. Nor does the §377 commentary attempt to explain the relationship between that section and revised §272, discussed above. Note finally that the "cases" covered by §377 do not include cases of mistake.

To focus the discussion, consider the factual situation in L. Albert & Son v. Armstrong Rubber Co., *infra* p. 1197. Assume (contrary to the actual case) that the contract in *Albert* had been discharged by reason of impossibility, frustration or, for that matter, mistake. Would the cost of installing the concrete flooring be recoverable under the provisions of Restatement Second just discussed? Under the Code provisions? Under Restatement First? Under the English Frustrated Contracts Act, *supra* p. 934? Do you think they should be recoverable?

The Code in the Courts

During the inflationary period of the 1970s the Code provisions summarized above (particularly the discharge provision of §2-615) became a focus of litigation as well as the subject of a vast commentary in the law reviews. The Code draftsmen had lived during a period of stable or declining prices. As every draftsman knows, however, whatever formula he comes up with will run the gauntlet of litigation on states of facts he never dreamed of.

The bulk of the recent Code frustration litigation has involved attempts by sellers to get out of long-term requirements contracts, particularly in commodities like oil, coal, and uranium in which extraordinary increases in the seller's costs (frequently dictated by the operations of international cartels which had not been in existence when the contracts were entered into) have far outpaced the agreed price, even when the price has been tied to one of the available price indexes. The buyer naturally insists that the seller continue deliveries, no matter how many hundreds of millions the seller may lose. The seller naturally claims that he should be discharged under Code §2-615 on the ground that performance has become "impracticable."

The best-known litigation of this type involved the Westinghouse Electric Company. In the 1960s Westinghouse, which had gone into the business of manufacturing nuclear power plants, offered to supply the buyers of its plants with uranium at fixed prices over long terms of years. Many such contracts were entered into with various utilities. Westinghouse did not attempt to protect itself by stockpiling uranium. During the late 1960s the market price of uranium increased five-fold, principally as the result of the operations of an international cartel. In the early 1970s Westinghouse, faced with staggering losses, repudiated the uranium contracts on the ground that performance was excused under §2-615. The utilities brought suit against Westinghouse. The actions were consolidated for trial in the Federal District Court for the Eastern District of Virginia. The trial judge indicated in a bench opinion that he was prepared to hold against Westinghouse on the §2-615 discharge issue but refused to issue either his findings of fact or his conclusions of law. Instead, he urged the parties to arrive at out-of-court settlements and pursued his settlement policy with extraordinary diligence. Eventually the utilities agreed to settlements on terms relatively favorable to Westinghouse. The background of the Westinghouse litigation is discussed in Joskow, Commercial Impossibility, the Uranium Market and the Westinghouse Case, 6 J. Legal Stud. 119 (1977), and the litigation itself is reviewed in Speidel, Court-Imposed Adjustments under Long-Term Supply Contracts, 76 Nw. L. Rev. 369 (1981).

Legal scholars who go in for economic analysis have naturally had a field day with the §2-615 litigation. Those associated with the Chicago School, while disagreeing among themselves on details, have generally supported the conclusion that sellers should be denied any relief (either discharge or a price adjustment) and ordered either to perform their contracts or pay full compensatory damages for breach. They argue that the seller is the superior risk bearer, that the allocation of the risk of price increase to the seller is "efficient," and that the adoption by the courts of such a rule of liability would lead to more rational bargaining between the parties at the outset. See, e.g., Posner and Rosenfield, Impossibility and Related Doctrines in Contract Law: An Economic Analysis, 6 J. Legal Stud. 83 (1977).

Professor Speidel, after carefully reviewing the literature, dissociates himself from the Chicago position. He suggests that the parties be urged or even pressured (as the trial judge in the Westinghouse litigation may have done) to bargain in good faith about readjustments of their deal in the light of changed circumstances. Failure to bargain in good faith could lead to penalties, to be devised by the courts. Judicial intervention to reform the contract on equitable principles by granting a price adjustment (as was done in Aluminum Co. of America v. Essex Group, Inc., 499 F. Supp. 53 (W.D. Pa. 1980)) should be looked on as a last resort. In his discussion of the *Aluminum Co.* case, Professor Speidel concludes that the court did not pay sufficient attention to the bargaining behavior of the parties and, in imposing its own price adjustment, may have "gone too far too fast" (Speidel, *supra* page 970, at 421, n.204). (The contract involved in that case included an elaborate price index, but it did not cover the rise in the cost of electricity that was specifically at issue in that litigation.) Professor Speidel also suggests that decrees of specific performance could be conditioned on the buyer's agreeing to price adjustments in the seller's favor (citing as an example of such a decree Willard v. Tayloe, 75 U.S. (8 Wall.) 557 (1869). Recent examples of such "conditional decrees" have been, as he notes, "infrequent" (Speidel, *supra* page 970, at 417, n.193).

The requirements contracts litigation of the 1970s, which has focused on §2-615, should be compared with the 1930s litigation in which buyers sought, with great success, to get out of their long-term contracts by going out of business and thus ceasing to have requirements. See the materials in Chapter 3, Section 11. The issue is now covered in Code §2-306, which arguably codifies the 1930s "going-out of business" cases (per the Official Comment: "A shut down by a requirements buyer for lack of orders might be permissible . . ."). Do you think that §2-306 and §2-615 are consistent with each other? Do you think that the two sections should have been combined and rewritten (at least with respect to discharge or excuse)? What would you think of a rule under which buyers can get out of their long-term contracts when prices fall during a depression but sellers continue to be bound by their long-term contracts when prices rise during a period of inflation?

CHAPTER 9

Protection of the Exchange Relationship (Herein of the Theory of Conditions)

Section 1. Introductory Note

The preceding chapter dealt with the problem of excuse from performance of apparently binding contracts because of mistake or because of such change of circumstance as to bring into play the so-called doctrines of impossibility and frustration. It is clear enough that, under our system of law, contractual liability is not absolute. The courts have discovered and maintained various routes of escape from the conclusion that, given the formal requisites of offer, acceptance and consideration (plus a writing in cases falling within the Statute of Frauds), A is always entitled to collect the agreed pound of flesh from B in the event of B's nonperformance. Indeed the doctrine of consideration itself has often been manipulated in such a way as to protect the victims of fraud, duress, coercion and the like. We accept, then, a broad theory of what might be called invalidating cause and it is fairly arguable that the past seventy-five years or so have seen a notable expansion of such theories of excuse from liability.

Nevertheless, the institution of contract is essentially a device for allocating risks and losses among the contracting parties. As Holmes put it:

> In the case of a binding promise that it shall rain tomorrow, the immediate legal effect of what the promisor does is, that he takes the risk of the event, within certain defined limits, as between himself and the promisee. He does no more when he promises to deliver a bale of cotton.

The Common Law 235 (M. Howe ed. 1963). The party who loses the contractual gamble must pay up.

In this chapter we turn to a consideration of what happens when, without excuse, the promised performance or event does not come to pass. As Holmes' examples suggest, fault is not necessarily involved. I may promise that something over which I have no control either will or will not happen — as that it will rain tomorrow. Or my promise may involve a performance that is (or ought to be) entirely within my control: I have no business promising to deliver a bale of cotton unless I can count on having the cotton available for delivery at the agreed time. If, when the time comes, I do not have the cotton and have no excuse for not having it, I may well be considered to be at fault. But, at least according to Holmes, it should make no difference whether the promisor is at fault or not: within the limits of his risk-taking, the consequences should be the same for the defaulting promisor without regard to whether, from a moral point of view, he is innocent or guilty. If he is innocent, he must still pay up; if he is guilty, he should pay no more. In this sense, promissory liability in contract may be fundamentally different from liability in tort. In the materials which follow, we shall have occasion to consider to what extent Holmes' views on the moral indifference or neutrality of contract theory have prevailed.

In a bilateral executory contract, both parties are, by hypothesis, bound before performance by either. The contract may contemplate simultaneous performance on both sides — as in a sale of goods for cash — or may contemplate that one party is to perform his side of the bargain first, the other party coming under his duty of return performance (which is usually to pay for what he has received) only after the first performance has been rendered. It seems obvious to us that if A does not perform, B need not pay; there has been, we would say, a failure of consideration. (The point has not always seemed as obvious as it does to us: see the materials in the following section.) Furthermore, it seems equally obvious that if A fails to perform, B must, at some point, be released from any continuing obligation under the contract. If A has promised to deliver his bale of cotton this year and does not, few of us would assume that he can force B to take the cotton next year. A's breach or default has freed B from the contractual bond; if B chooses to avail himself of his freedom, the A-B contract survives only as the vehicle (or the explanation) for B's bringing a claim for damages against A.

But suppose that A's default, although conceded, goes merely to some trivial aspect of his total performance. He has contracted to deliver 1000 bales of cotton and tenders 999 (or, for that matter, 1001) bales. Or he has contracted to deliver cotton on September 15 and tenders delivery on September 16. In the illustrations just given, it should be noted that the buyer, if he is held privileged to reject the imperfect tender, retains no benefit from the seller's performance. The problem becomes more difficult when, from the nature of the performance, the party in default has conferred some benefit that the "innocent" party can no longer return. Thus, in a case which came before the court of King's Bench in 1626 it appeared that the plaintiff (a shipowner) had chartered his ship to the defendant for a voyage from England to Cadiz and return, "covenant-ing" that the ship would "sail with the next wind." For his part the defen-dant "covenanted" to pay a certain sum as freight if the ship completed the voyage. In an action to recover the freight money the plaintiff alleged that the ship had in fact made the voyage to Cadiz and returned to England. The defendant's plea, to which the plaintiff demurred, was that the ship had not "sailed with the next wind." On joinder in demurrer, the court held the plea bad. Thus the plaintiff apparently collected the freight money despite the conceded violation of his "covenant." Constable v. Clobery, K.B. 1626, Latch, 49. The seventeenth-century report of the case does not indicate whether the defendant would have been entitled to an offset against the plaintiff's recovery for any damages he might have suffered (for example, loss of a favorable market in Cadiz) as the result of the failure to sail with the next wind. On this point, consider the cases of Nichols v. Raynbred and Pordage v. Cole set out in the following section; for a more recent case, similar in many respects to Constable v. Clobery, see The Heron II, *infra* p. 1157.

The courts, for several centuries, have wrestled with the distinction between failures of performance which operate to release the "innocent" party from any further contractual obligation and failures which leave him still bound to the contract (although he may have a right to recover damages caused by the failure). The distinction has been, at various times, described as one between "total" and "partial" breach, between "material" and "immaterial" breach, between "dependent" and "indepen-dent" promises, between "conditions" and "covenants." See the opinion of Cardozo, J., in Jacob & Youngs v. Kent, reprinted *infra* p. 1042. In technical legal usage the term "condition" has gradually taken on the meaning of something so fundamental to the object of the contract that its failure to occur effects a release from contractual obligation or a discharge of the contract. See in this connection Pym v. Campbell, di-gested *supra* p. 83, in which Abernethie's approval of the invention was a "condition" of the contract's coming into force. The term "covenant" or "independent covenant" has come to mean something less fundamental, whose failure to occur does not effect a release or discharge. (Note, however, that in the report of Constable v. Clobery "covenant" was used to describe both the shipowner's "independent" promise to sail with the next wind and the charterer's fundamental promise to pay the freight money.) In current usage, furthermore, "covenant" usually refers to some act which the covenanting party has promised to perform. "Condi-tion" may refer to some event over which neither of the contracting parties has any control — such as the promise that it will rain tomorrow or the condition in Pym v. Campbell that Abernethie should approve the invention. For helpful discussion of the elusive difference between cove-nants and conditions, see E. A. Farnsworth, Contracts, §8.3, at 547, 548 (1982).

In this chapter we shall review the historical development of our theory of conditions and consider a few modern instances of its importance.

Section 2.   The Basic Themes: Some History by Way of Background

NICHOLS v. RAYNBRED
Hobart 88, 80 Eng. Rep. 238 (K.B. 1615)

Nichols brought an assumpsit against Raynbred, declaring that in consideration that Nichols promised to deliver the defendant to his own use a cow, the defendant promised to deliver him 50 shillings: adjudged for the plaintiff in both Courts, that the plaintiff need not to aver the delivery of the cow, because it is promise for promise. Note here the promises must be at one instant, for else they will be both nuda pacta.

PORDAGE v. COLE
1 Wms. Saunders 319h, 85 Eng. Rep. 449 (K.B. 1669)

Debt upon a specialty for £774 15s. The plaintiff declares that the defendant, by his certain writing of agreement made at, &c. by the plaintiff by the name, &c. and the defendant by the name, &c. and brings the deed into Court, &c., it was agreed between the plaintiff and defendant in manner and form following, (viz.) that the defendant should give to the plaintiff the sum of £775 for all his lands, with a house called Ashmole-House thereunto belonging, with the brewing vessels remaining in the said house, and with the malt-mill and wheel-barrow; and that in pursuance of the said agreement, the defendant had given to the plaintiff 5s. as an earnest; and it was by the said writing further agreed between the plaintiff and defendant, that the defendant should pay to the plaintiff the residue of the said sum of £775 a week after the Feast of St. John the Baptist the next following (all other moveables, with the corn upon the ground, excepted). And although the defendant has paid five shillings, parcel, &c. yet the said defendant, although often requested, has not paid the residue to the damage, &c. The defendant prays oyer of the specialty, which is entered in haec verba to wit:

11 May, 1668. It is agreed between Doctor John Pordage and Bassett Cole, Esquire, that the said Bassett Cole shall give unto the said doctor £775 for all his lands, with Ashmole-House, thereunto belonging, with the brewing-vessels as they are now remaining in the said house, and with the malt-mill and wheel-barrow. In witness whereof we do put our hands and seals:

mutually given as earnest in performance of this 5s.; the money to be paid before Midsummer 1668; all other moveables, with the corn upon the ground, excepted.

And upon oyer thereof the defendant demurs. And Withins, of counsel with the defendant, took several exceptions to the declaration: . . . 3. The great exception was, that the plaintiff in his declaration has not averred that he had conveyed the lands, or at least tendered a conveyance of them; for the defendant has no remedy to obtain the lands, and therefore the plaintiff ought to have conveyed them, or tendered a conveyance of them, before he brought his action for the money. And it was argued by Withins, that if by one single deed two things are to be performed, namely, one by the plaintiff and the other by the defendant, if there be no mutual remedy, the plaintiff ought to aver performance by his part: Trin. 12 Jac. 1, between Holder v. Tayloe, 1 Rol. Abr. 518 (C) pl. 2, 3; Ughtred's case, and Sir Richard Pool's case, there cited, and Gray's case: and that the word "pro" made a condition in things executory. And here in this case it is a condition precedent which ought to be performed before the action brought; wherefore he prayed judgment for the defendant.

But it was adjudged by the Court, that the action was well brought without an averment of the conveyance of the land; because it shall be intended that both parties have sealed the specialty. And if the plaintiff has not conveyed the land to the defendant, he has also an action of covenant against the plaintiff upon the agreement contained in the deed, which amounts to a covenant on the part of the plaintiff to convey the land; and so each party has mutual remedy against the other. But it might be otherwise if the specialty had been the words of the defendant only, and not the words of both parties by way of agreement as it is here. And by the conclusion of the deed it is said, that both parties had sealed it; and therefore judgment was given for the plaintiff, which was afterwards affirmed in the Exchequer-Chamber, Trin. 22 of King Charles the Second.

NOTE

1. In Pordage v. Cole the action was brought in debt on the specialty (or bond) which the vendee had given for the purchase price and which both parties had executed under seal. In holding that the vendor could recover on the bond without alleging conveyance of the land (or a tender of conveyance), the court seems to have assumed (see the last paragraph of the report) that the vendee could have compelled a conveyance in an action of covenant, "so each party has mutual remedy against the other." Both "debt" and "covenant" were traditional actions at law, not in equity, that were already passing out of use at the time Pordage v. Cole was decided. (On debt and covenant, see Chapter 1.) We have long since

come to believe that, with respect to land contracts, both the vendor's action to recover the price and the vendee's action to compel conveyance are to be described as actions for specific performance, a remedy available only in equity. (See Chapter 10, Section 2.) A possible reading of Pordage v. Cole is that remedies equivalent to specific performance were available in actions at law during the seventeenth century.

2. Nichols v. Raynbred, decided a half-century earlier than Pordage v. Cole, was in assumpsit (see Chapter 1), which was destined to replace the older actions of debt and covenant. The brief, enigmatic report of the case does not address the question whether Raynbred, having been held liable to pay the price, could, in a separate action, compel Nichols to deliver the cow. However unclear the parameters of assumpsit may have been in 1615, it does seem unlikely that the Court of Common Pleas, or any court in any legal system at any time, would have forced a buyer to pay for undelivered goods without somehow affording him an action to recover the goods, and it is almost certain that Raynbred could in fact have brought such an action in detinue. See Milsom, Sale of Goods in the Fifteenth Century, 77 L.Q. Rev. 257 (1961). On the whole we know much less about what such seventeenth-century cases may have meant in their own time than we like to think we do. For another example, see the Note following Paradine v. Jane, *supra* p. 911.

3. Pordage v. Cole has a modern echo in cases involving "installment land contracts" under which the vendee must pay the contract price before he is entitled to receive a deed. If the vendee defaults, should the vendor be entitled to recover the balance of the contract price without tendering a deed? If the vendor is so entitled, the vendee is left in a precarious situation; he must pay the judgment but may never get the land, either because the vendor has sold it to some third party or because the vendor has become insolvent and may no longer be able to make an effective conveyance. One answer to this problem, found in the older cases, was that the vendor could sue for all installments except the last. See, e.g., Gray v. Meek, 199 Ill. 136, 64 N.E. 1020 (1902). Other courts gave the vendee more realistic protection by making the judgment for the price conditional on delivery of the deed or by staying execution of the judgment until a deed was deposited with the court. See Noyes v. Brown, 142 Minn. 211, 171 N.W. 803 (1919). Giving the vendee such protection in an action at law raised the conceptual objection that the court was in effect converting the law judgment into an equity decree for specific performance. The problem is discussed and cases are collected in Comment, 34 Mich. L. Rev. 545 (1936).

4. By the end of the eighteenth century the original meaning, whatever it may have been, of cases like Nichols v. Raynbred and Pordage v. Cole had disappeared from sight. In Goodisson v. Nunn, 4 T.R. 761, 764, 100 Eng. Rep. 1288 (1792), Pordage v. Cole was said, by Kenyon, C.J., to "outrage common sense" — which would be true only if it is assumed

that the vendee was being required to pay without having a remedy to get the land. During the second half of the eighteenth century the English judges, having cut themselves loose from the older precedents, proceeded to construct a novel theory as to when breaches or defaults by one party do (or do not) discharge the other party from continuing obligations under the contract. The two following principal cases, both attributed to Lord Mansfield, illustrate the process.

KINGSTON v. PRESTON
2 Douglas 689, 99 Eng. Rep. 437 (K.B. 1773)

"It was an action of debt, for non-performance of covenants contained in certain articles of agreement between the plaintiff and the defendant. The declaration stated: — That, by articles made the 24th of March, 1770, the plaintiff, for the considerations thereinafter mentioned, covenanted, with the defendant, to serve him for one year and a quarter next ensuing, as a covenant-servant, in his trade of a silk-mercer, at £200 a year, and in consideration of the premises, the defendant covenanted, that at the end of the year and a quarter, he would give up his business of a mercer to the plaintiff, and a nephew of the defendant, or some other person to be nominated by the defendant, and give up to them his stock in trade, at a fair valuation; and that, between the young traders, deeds of partnership should be executed for 14 years, and from and immediately after the execution of the said deeds, the defendant would permit the said young traders to carry on the said business in the defendant's house. — Then the declaration stated a covenant by the plaintiff, that he would accept the business and stock in trade, at a fair valuation, with the defendant's nephew, or such other person, &c., and execute such deeds of partnership, and, further, that the plaintiff should, and would, at, and before the sealing and delivery of the deeds, cause and procure good and sufficient security to be given to the defendant, to be approved of by the defendant, for the payment of £250 monthly, to the defendant, in lieu of a moiety of the monthly produce of the stock in trade, until the value of the stock should be reduced to £4,000. — Then the plaintiff averred, that he had performed, and been ready to perform, his covenants, and assigned for breach on the part of the defendant, that he had refused to surrender and give up his business, at the end of the said year and quarter. — The defendant pleaded, 1. That the plaintiff did not offer sufficient security; and, 2. That he did not give sufficient security for the payment of the £250, &c. — And the plaintiff demurred generally to both pleas. — On the part of the plaintiff, the case was argued by Mr. Buller, who contended, that the covenants were mutual and independent, and, therefore, a plea of the breach of one of the covenants to be performed by the plaintiff was no bar to an action for a breach by the defendant of one

of which he had bound himself to perform, but that the defendant might
have his remedy for the breach by the plaintiff, in a separate action. On
the other side, Mr. Grose insisted, that the covenants were dependent in
their nature, and, therefore, performance must be alleged: the security to
be given for the money, was manifestly the chief object of the transaction, and it would be highly unreasonable to construe the agreement, so
as to oblige the defendant to give up a beneficial business, and valuable
stock in trade, and trust to the plaintiff's personal security, (who might,
and, indeed, was admitted to be worth nothing,) for the performance of
his part. — In delivering the judgment of the Court, Lord Mansfield
expressed himself to the following effect: There are three kinds of covenants: 1. Such as are called mutual and independent, where either party
may recover damages from the other, for the injury he may have received
by a breach of the covenants in his favour, and where it is no excuse for
the defendant, to allege a breach of the covenants on the part of the
plaintiff. 2. There are covenants, which are conditions and dependent, in
which the performance of one depends on the prior performance of
another, and therefore, till this prior condition is performed, the other
party is not liable to an action on his covenant. 3. There is also a third sort
of covenants, which are mutual conditions to be performed at the same
time; and, in these, if one party was ready, and offered, to perform his
part, and the other neglected, or refused, to perform his, he who was
ready, and offered, has fulfilled his engagement, and may maintain an
action for the default of the other; though it is not certain that either is
obliged to do the first act. — His Lordship then proceeded to say, that the
dependence, or independence, of covenants, was to be collected from the
evident sense and meaning of the parties, and, that, however transposed
they might be in the deed, their precedency must depend on the order of
time in which the intent of the transaction requires their performance.
That, in the case before the Court, it would be the greatest injustice if the
plaintiff should prevail: the essence of the agreement was, that the defendant should not trust to the personal security of the plaintiff, but before
he delivered up his stock and business, should have good security for the
payment of the money. The giving such security, therefore, must necessarily be a condition precedent. — Judgment was accordingly given for
the defendant because the part to be performed by the plaintiff was
clearly a condition precedent."

NOTE

The case is not reported under its title, but is stated in the course of an
argument by counsel in Jones v. Barkley, 2 Douglas 684, 99 Eng. Rep. 434
(1781). For a more colorful but rougher version, see Lofft 194, 98 Eng.
Rep. 606. Lord Mansfield is reported to have said:

It would be the most monstrous case in the world, if the argument on the side of Mr. Buller's client was to prevail. It's of the very essence of the agreement, that the defendant will not trust the personal security of the plaintiff. A Court of Justice is to say, that by operation of law he shall, against his teeth. He is to let him into his house to squander every thing there, without any thing to rely on but what he has absolutely refused to trust. This payment, therefore, was a precedent condition before the covenant of putting into possession was to be performed on the part of the defendant.

BOONE v. EYRE
1 H. Bl. 273, note, 126 Eng. Rep. 160(a) (K.B. 1777)

Covenant on a deed, whereby the plaintiff conveyed to the defendant the equity of redemption of a plantation in the West Indies, together with the stock of the negroes upon it, in consideration of £500 and an annuity of £160 per annum for his life; and covenanted that he had a good title to the plantation, was lawfully possessed of the negroes, and that the defendant should quietly enjoy. The defendant covenanted, that the plaintiff well and truly performing all and everything therein contained on his part to be performed, he the defendant would pay the annuity. The breach assigned was the non-payment of the annuity. Plea, that the plaintiff was not, at the time of making deed, legally possessed of the negroes on the plantation and so had not a good title to convey.

To which there was a general demurrer.

LORD MANSFIELD. The distinction is very clear, where mutual covenants go to the whole of the consideration on both sides, they are mutual conditions the one precedent to the other. But where they go only to a part, where a breach may be paid for in damages, there the defendant has a remedy on his covenant, and shall not plead it as a condition precedent. If this plea were to be allowed, any one negro not being the property of the plaintiff would bar the action.

Judgment for the plaintiff.

NOTE

1. Whatever the earlier situation may have been, the English courts, under Lord Mansfield's leadership, had, by the end of the eighteenth century, worked out a flexible theory of conditions that has indeed served us ever since. The theory, it should be noted, gives us everything but predictability. Who, except a majority of the judges of the court of last resort, can tell us when "mutual covenants go to the whole of the consideration," in which case they are true "conditions," and when they "go only to a part," in which case they are merely "independent covenants"?

Of course, as litigation goes on, it might be expected that, at least in recurrent situations, the line would come to be drawn clearly so that, for a time, everyone would know where he stood. For an example of this process, see the cases on the sale of goods collected in the following section.

Both Kingston v. Preston and Boone v. Eyre were, it may be thought, easy cases of obvious solution. In Kingston the plaintiff, who was "admitted to be worth nothing," was insisting that a valuable business be transferred to him without his posting the agreed security for payment of the price in installments. Had the defendant been forced to make the transfer under such circumstances, he would have been merely an unsecured creditor for the price, with no right to get the business back in case of default and condemned to share equally with other creditors in the event of insolvency proceedings instituted against the "young traders." And in Boone v. Eyre the defendant, who was apparently in possession of the plantation, was attempting to resist payment of the annuity on a pleading which (as Mansfield construed it) would have allowed him to keep the plantation without paying for it in the event of the slightest and most trivial defect in the seller's title. Whatever theory of conditions a court might adopt, it could hardly support such "monstrous" claims. It is, however, not without interest that Mansfield dealt with the cases as he did instead of relying on ideas of fraud (Kingston v. Preston) or unjust enrichment (Boone v. Eyre).

Note that Mansfield assumes, in Boone v. Eyre, that the defendant "has a remedy on his covenant" and may claim damages for the breach, if proved. Whatever the procedural situation may have been in Mansfield's time, it eventually became clear that the damages for breach of the covenant could be claimed in the main action on the principal obligation and allowed by way of offset or counterclaim.

2. Serjeant Williams, in his edition of Saunders (1801) (see the Note following Paradine v. Jane, *supra* p. 911), attempted in a note to Pordage v. Cole to weave together the developing case law on when mutual promises were to be treated as "dependent" ("conditions") and when they were to be treated as "independent" ("covenants"). Williams built in effect on the foundations laid by Lord Mansfield in such cases as Kingston v. Preston and Boone v. Eyre. Serjeant Williams' rules seem to have exercised a considerable influence during the nineteenth century. See C.C. Langdell, Summary of the Law of Contracts 187 et seq. (1880); Patterson, Constructive Conditions in Contracts, 42 Colum. L. Rev. 903, 907 (1942).

Note on the Historical Development of the Law of Conditions

Even after the main outlines of the new theory of conditions had been worked out, there was still a good deal of conceptual underbrush that had to be cleared away. Some examples of this process are summarized in this Note.

Concurrent Conditions

In Kingston v. Preston, Lord Mansfield had thrown out the suggestion that there is a class of "mutual conditions" in which both parties are required to perform at the same time (as, e.g., in a sale for cash where the seller is required to tender delivery and the buyer is required to tender payment). According to Mansfield, neither party to such a transaction could recover without alleging tender (or readiness to perform) and failure to perform on the other side. See Morton v. Lamb, 7 T.R. 125, 101 Eng. Rep. 890 (K.B. 1797) in which (per Lord Kenyon) a buyer's action against a seller for nondelivery of corn was dismissed because "as the plaintiff has not averred that he was ready to pay for the corn, he cannot maintain this action against the defendant for not delivering it." But what if, on the day scheduled for performance, neither party did anything? In land contracts the rule emerged that either party could put the other party in default by making a tender of performance within a reasonable time after the original day: thus the contract continued in force for an indefinite period. In commercial contracts for the sale of goods a quite different rule emerged, symbolized by the slogan that in contracts between merchants "time is always of the essence": if the seller did not tender delivery on the day stipulated in the contract, the buyer was discharged. See the materials in the following section. If both parties are, at the relevant time, able and willing to perform, who must act first? The problem has no logical solution. On a practical level, whichever party is in more urgent need of the return performance will perform first. Since in the typical commercial contract of sale, the seller was usually required to ship goods to the buyer, the seller had to perform first by arranging for the shipment, with the result that the buyer's duty to pay could not arise until tender of the goods (or shipping documents).

The Distinction between Conditions Precedent and Conditions Subsequent

For reasons that will forever remain obscure the courts began to distinguish between conditions that must have been fulfilled before a right of action accrued (conditions precedent) and conditions whose occurrence or non-occurrence defeated a right of action that was thought of as having accrued at some earlier point (conditions subsequent). It was universally held that the plaintiff (or moving party) bore the burden of proof as to the fulfillment (or performance) of conditions precedent; contrariwise, the defendant bore the burden of proof as to conditions subsequent. What this meant is illustrated by Gray v. Gardner, 17 Mass. 188 (1821). The case takes us back to the great days of whaling. The plaintiff was selling sperm oil to the defendants. The defendants agreed to pay sixty cents per gallon for the oil in any event and to pay an additional eighty-five cents per gallon if less sperm oil arrived in whaling vessels in the ports of Nantucket and New Bedford before midnight on October 1 of the current year (1819) than had arrived the previous year. The liability to pay the additional amount was evidenced by a promissory note executed by the defendants which stated "this obligation to be void" if more sperm oil arrived before the deadline in 1819 than had arrived in 1818. As things worked out, the question whether more oil had arrived in 1819 than in 1818 depended on whether the Lady Adams had "arrived" in Nantucket harbor before midnight, October 1. On that point there was no satisfactory evidence. Plaintiff sued on the note. If the condition was "precedent," plaintiff had to prove (but could not) that the Lady Adams had not "arrived" before midnight; if "subsequent," the defendants had to prove (but could not) that the Lady Adams had indeed "arrived" before midnight. Per Parker, C.J.:

> The defendants, in this case, promise to pay a certain sum of money, on condition that the promise shall be void on the happening of an event. It is plain that the burden of proof is upon them; and if they fail to show that the event has happened, the promise remains good.

Id. at 189. Wherefore, judgment for plaintiff.

The allocation of the burden of proof is, obviously, a matter of considerable importance in litigation; thus it is evidently essential for students to learn how to distinguish between conditions precedent and conditions subsequent. Holmes seems to have been the first to suggest that the distinction does not in fact exist, that any conceivable condition can be described as either precedent or subsequent, depending on the point in time which is used as a reference (The Common Law 247 (M. Howe ed. 1963)). The allocation of the burden of proof, Holmes suggested, is a matter of "convenience"; in the ordinary course of events the moving party is in possession of the facts and might as well be required to assume the burden of proof (call the conditions "precedent"); exceptionally, the other party is the only one who can prove what happened and should be required to do so (call the conditions "subsequent"). (Gray v. Gardner, digested above, was a freakish case in which the party to whom the burden was allocated necessarily lost. The Massachusetts court seems to have looked on the case as a gambling transaction.) A traditional example of a "true condition subsequent" was, Holmes suggested, "a policy of insurance conditioned to be void if not sued upon within one year from a failure to pay as agreed." But even here, Holmes went on, the bringing of suit within the year could just as easily be described as a condition precedent to the plaintiff's cause of action. Which, of course, did not mean that casting the burden of proof on the insurance company (by calling the condition "subsequent") did not make sense; insurance companies are after all in the business of record-keeping and can reasonably be required to make the proof. Thus Holmes was quarreling not with the results of the cases but with the unnecessary confusion introduced by the artificial, indeed idiotic, concept of "condition subsequent."

In this century, on the level of respectable jurisprudence, Holmes' skeptical approach has carried the day. See the discussions by Williston and Corbin in their treatises; 9 Wigmore on Evidence §§2483-2489 (3d ed. 1940); 3A Corbin §628. On less rarified levels the distinction is still taken seriously or at least treated respectfully (see e.g., G. Schaber & C. Rohwer, Contracts in a Nutshell §178 (1975) (West Nutshell Series)). And it may well be that a great many lawyers, judges, and, perhaps, bar examiners still believe that it is possible to distinguish "true conditions precedent" from "true conditions subsequent" and that they know how to do it. The editors of this casebook must confess their own inability to do so and, like Holmes, prefer to explain the burden of proof cases on grounds of "convenience."

Express Conditions vs. Implied Conditions

To the extent that A's contractual obligations toward B constitute true conditions of the contract (as distinguished from mere covenants), B is entitled to insist on a full, strict, and literal performance on A's part — failing which B is discharged from performance of his own obligations. Any aspect of the contractual construct that "goes to the whole of the consideration" (as Lord Mansfield had put it in Boone v. Eyre) is a condition; the courts stand ready to decide, by construction of the contract terms, which of the reciprocal obligations are conditions and which are not.

Our modern theory of conditions had been fully articulated by 1800 or thereabouts. It was not long before lawyers hit on the idea that the theory could be manipulated. Surely the principal function of the institution of contract is to provide a private law for the parties which the public authorities will respect. Why leave to the courts the decision of such important matters? Let the contract itself specify, in express terms, which aspects of performance are to be regarded as conditions. Thus, to put one party in a position where it can demand full performance from the other becomes merely a drafting problem for his lawyer — assuming of course that the first party is in a position to force the other party to accept the proposition as drafted.

To many, if not most, practicing lawyers the idea that the draftsman's art is paramount, that the contract itself can settle the condition problem once and for all, seems to commend itself as an article of faith. Express conditions, according to a popular slogan, must, under any and all circumstances, be literally performed; judge-made rules of substantial performance, materiality and the like apply only to implied (or, as they are sometimes called, constructive) conditions. In most respectable academic literature, however, the idea that express conditions are sacrosanct is introduced only to be dismissed as false and misleading. The academic consensus is that the courts will continue to decide condition questions according to their own ideas of materiality and will not be overborne by a nice choice of words in the contract.

Counsel for insurance companies are, and always have been, ardent believers in the sanctity of express conditions. By the terms of the policy every statement made by the insured in his application and every obligation imposed on the insured during the term (such as keeping records and giving notice) are erected into conditions (or warranties); on discovery, after loss, of the slightest irregularity the insurance company will be discharged from liability. Or so counsel for the companies profess to believe. There has always been a huge volume of litigation of this type. All that can be said about the case law results is that the companies win some and lose some. The only generalization that can be ventured is that judgment for the insurer on a conceded violation by the insured of something that the policy called a condition or warranty is by no means automatic. In the cases which go against the insurers the courts have resorted to a variety of techniques: disingenuous exercises in semantic interpretation (the policy did not clearly make the condition "express"), the rule (*contra proferentem*) that ambiguities in the policy will be construed against the insurer who drafted it, the discovery of facts amounting to a waiver or constituting an estoppel, and so on. There is even authority that flatly denies the effectiveness of conditions conceded to be express and unambiguous in the absence of either waiver or estoppel. Despite its relatively ancient vintage, Southern Surety Co. v. MacMillan Co., 58 F.2d 541 (10th Cir. 1932), continues to be instructive. Over a dissent, the court held that despite MacMillan's failure to make timely reports required by the policy, the Surety Company could claim a discharge only to the extent that it could prove it had been harmed or prejudiced by the delay. The two opinions delivered in the case collect multitudinous authorities on both sides of the issue. The majority opinion canvasses at length the various techniques which courts have used in holding against insurers. For fuller discussion of these and related issues in the field of insurance contracts, see Chapter 4, Section 3, *supra*.

A relatively recent development in insurance law has been a series of cases holding that insurance companies that have "in bad faith" refused to make prompt settlement of losses can be held liable, on tort-like damage theories, in amounts exceeding the face of the policy. See Holmes, Is There Life after Gilmore's *Death of Contract?* — Inductions from a Study of Commercial Good Faith in First-party Insurance Contracts, 65 Cornell L. Rev. 330 (1980). The added risk these cases pose for insurance company defendants may conceivably lead in time to a decrease in the volume of litigation. Some jurisdictions have enacted statutes on this problem; see, e.g., Mass. Gen. Laws chs. 93A, 176D.

Conditions of Personal Satisfaction

In Brown v. Foster, 113 Mass. 136 (1873), a tailor had agreed to make a suit of clothes "to the satisfaction" of a customer. When the suit was made, the customer, declaring himself dissatisfied, refused to accept (or pay) for it and also refused to give the tailor the chance to make whatever alterations might be necessary to make the suit fit properly. In the tailor's action to recover the price, the jury was permitted to hear "expert testimony" (from other tailors) that the suit (which the defendant consented to try on in the jury's presence) needed only a few alterations to be "a good fit" and that it was the custom of the trade for necessary alterations to be made after the clothes were finished. The testimony, said the Supreme Judicial Court, reversing the jury's verdict for the tailor, was irrelevant and should not have been admitted. The tailor had agreed to abide by the customer's "caprice" and should not be allowed to recover on a showing that the latter's refusal to accept the suit was unreasonable. In Gibson v. Cranage, 39 Mich. 49 (1878), the Michigan court reached the same result (agreement by an "artist" to make an "enlarged picture" of a girl which would be "perfectly satisfactory . . . in every particular" to the girl's father).

In Hawkins v. Graham, 149 Mass. 284, 21 N.E. 312 (1889), the plaintiff had agreed to install a heating system in the defendant's factory according to detailed specifications, which had evidently been drawn up by the plaintiff. Under the written agreement the system was to heat the factory to 70° F "in the coldest weather that may be experienced." If the system proved "satisfactory," the defendant was to pay $1,575 "after . . . acknowledgment has been made by the owner or the work demonstrated"; otherwise the plaintiff was to remove the system and get nothing, "it being distinctly understood that the providing of the entire system is to be done at my own risk absolutely." After installation of the system, the owner refused to acknowledge that it worked satisfactorily or to pay for it. The plaintiff sued to recover the agreed price (presumably the heating system was left in place pending the outcome of the litigation). At the trial there was contradictory evidence on whether the system heated the factory to 70° F in cold weather. The jury gave a verdict for the plaintiff which was affirmed on appeal. Holmes, J., after referring to Brown v. Foster, Gibson v. Cranage, and other cases of the type, went on to say:

> [A] just hesitation must be felt, and clear language required, before deciding that payment is left to the will, or even to the idiosyncrasies, of the interested party. In doubtful cases, courts have been inclined to construe agreements of this class as agreements to do the thing in such a way as

reasonably ought to satisfy the defendant. [Citing cases, including a pre-Brown v. Foster Massachusetts case.] . . . [W]e are of opinion that the satisfactoriness of the system and the risk taken by the plaintiff were to be determined by the mind of a reasonable man, and by the external measures set forth in the contract, not by the private taste or liking of the defendant.

Id. at 287-289, 21 N.E. at 313.

The progression from Brown v. Foster (1873) to Hawkins v. Graham (1889) can plausibly be related to the late nineteenth-century shift from a subjective ("meeting of the minds") to an objective ("reasonable man") theory of contract formation. See the materials in Chapter 8, Section 2. For a celebrated instance of the acceptance of the subjective approach by the Massachusetts court in the 1870s, see Boston Ice Co. v. Potter (1877), *infra* p. 1504. For Holmes' role in championing the objective approach, see the Note following Raffles v. Wichelhaus, *supra* p. 869.

The defendants in Brown v. Foster and Gibson v. Cranage did not accept or retain the clothes or the picture, any more than the defendant in Hawkins v. Graham wanted to keep the heating system. In Doll v. Noble, 116 N.Y. 230, 22 N.E. 401 (1889), the New York Court of Appeals dealt with a "personal satisfaction" contract under which services (staining and polishing woodwork in two houses) had been rendered and, in the nature of things, could not be returned; the defendant refused to pay on the ground that he was dissatisfied with the work. Held that, even though dissatisfied, he must pay. In Gerisch v. Herold, 82 N.J.L. 605, 83 A. 892 (1911), the New Jersey court took a dim view of Doll v. Noble. "The case," wrote Swayze, J., "is entitled to less weight for the reason that the learned judge failed to distinguish between a case where the owner withheld satisfaction unreasonably and one where he withheld it in bad faith." Held, in Gerisch v. Herold, that the dissatisfied owner of a house which was to have been completed "to [his] satisfaction" need not make the final payment ($3,000) on the house even though the architect had certified that the plaintiff was entitled to the payment. In Handy v. Bliss, 204 Mass. 513, 90 N.E. 864 (1910), the contract provided for building a house "to the entire satisfaction and approval" of the owner. In the builder's suit to recover the balance due on the contract ($1,250), the court elected to follow Hawkins v. Graham. Chief Justice Knowlton commented: "The erection of a building upon real estate ordinarily confers a benefit upon the owner, and he should not be permitted to escape payment for it on account of a personal idiosyncrasy."

The approval of a third party is frequently made a condition of acceptance of or payment for work. In building contracts a requirement that the architect certify that the work has been properly done before any payment is made is all but universal. The contracts in the New Jersey and Massachusetts cases referred to in the preceding paragraph were unusual in that the owner, as well as the architect, had to be personally satisfied with the work. The "architect's certificate" provision has been a prolific source of litigation; see Note 5 following Jacob & Youngs v. Kent, *infra* p. 1042.

Government Contracts and the "Disputes" Clause

Contracts executed by agencies of the United States have long contained a standard "disputes" clause which provides:

> Except as otherwise specifically provided in this contract, all disputes concerning questions of fact arising under this contract shall be decided by the contracting officer subject to written appeal by the contractor within 30 days to the head of the department concerned or his duly authorized representative, whose decision shall be final and conclusive upon the parties thereto.

(Standard government contract forms are set out in the Appendix to 41 U.S.C.)

By the "disputes" clause the United States purports to make itself the final judge — at least as to "questions of fact" — of all matters of contractual performance. Thus, on a formal and conceptual level, the United States under the "disputes" clause is in a position not unlike that of parties in private contracts who have stipulated that work must be done to their "personal satisfaction." It need hardly be argued that the formal resemblance is delusive. Tailors and artists who agree to make clothes or portraits to the satisfaction of their clients are, no doubt, engaging in a calculated gamble. Contractors who build airports or office buildings or produce military hardware for the United States are, to say the least, somewhat differently situated. And in the modern era the process of appeal from the contracting officer's decision has become formalized in reviewing agencies instituted by the various departments (e.g. the Armed Services Board of Contract Appeals) which, it may be, afford in fact if not in theory the equivalent of judicial review of administrative decisions. The aggrieved contractor who has lost his administrative appeal naturally seeks a further review in the courts. The opinions in the resulting litigation not infrequently read like rewrites of the old "personal satisfaction" cases, translated into a strange, new world.

In United States v. Wunderlich, 342 U.S. 98, 72 S. Ct. 154, 96 L. Ed. 113 (1951) the Supreme Court reversed the Court of Claims which had set aside a departmental decision on the ground that the decision was "arbitrary," "capricious" and "grossly erroneous." Under the "disputes" clause, said Justice Minton, the only ground for judicial intervention was fraud:

> By fraud we mean conscious wrongdoing, an intention to cheat or be dishonest. . . . [Respondents] have contracted for the settlement of dis-

putes in an arbitral manner. . . . The limitation on this arbitral process is fraud, placed there by this Court. If the standard of fraud that we adhere to is too limited, that is a matter for Congress.

342 U.S. at 100.

The Court's standard was, evidently, too limited to satisfy the Congress which in 1954 enacted a statute popularly known as the "Wunderlich Act" (41 U.S.C. §321). Under the Wunderlich Act, any departmental decision made pursuant to the "disputes" clause "shall be final and conclusive unless the same is fraudulent or capricious or arbitrary or so grossly erroneous as necessarily to imply bad faith, or is not supported by substantial evidence."

The volume of "Wunderlich" litigation, much of it localized in the Court of Claims, has long since reached flood proportions. In the current edition of 41 U.S.C.A., annotations to §321 in the bound volume (1954-1965) total 13 pages; annotations to §321 in the pocket part (1966-1985) total 72 pages. Following its misadventure in the original *Wunderlich* case, the Supreme Court has left most of the litigation to the lower courts. In United States v. Carlo Bianchi & Co., 373 U.S. 709 (1963) the Court held that, except for appeals on the ground of fraud, the courts must decide *Wunderlich* cases on the record established by the relevant agency; in S & E Contractors v. United States, 406 U.S. 1 (1972), the Court held (Brennan, White, and Marshall dissenting) that neither the General Accounting Office nor the Justice Department has the power to question (or to take an appeal from) a final determination of a dispute by an agency. The Court of Claims, which tends to take an expansive view of its own jurisdiction, has continued to exploit various routes of escape from the finality of administrative decision, thus encouraging aggrieved contractors who have lost at the agency level to file appeals.

Section 3. The Sale of Goods: A Case Study in the Implication of Conditions

NORRINGTON v. WRIGHT
115 U.S. 188 (1885)

This was an action of assumpsit, brought by Arthur Norrington, a citizen of Great Britain, trading under the name of A. Norrington & Co., against James A. Wright and others, citizens of Pennsylvania, trading under the name of Peter Wright & Sons, upon the following contract:

Philadelphia, January 19, 1880. Sold to Messrs. Peter Wright & Sons, for account of A. Norrington & Co., London: Five thousand (5,000) tons old T iron rails, for shipment from a European port or ports, at the rate of about one thousand (1,000) tons per month, beginning February, 1880, but whole contract to be shipped before August 1st, 1880, at forty-five dollars ($45.00) per ton of 2,240 lbs. custom-house weight, ex ship Philadelphia. Settlement cash on presentation of bills accompanied by custom-house certificate of weight. Sellers to notify buyers of shipments with vessels' names as soon as known by them. Sellers not to be compelled to replace any parcel lost after shipment. Sellers, when possible, to secure to buyers right to name discharging berth of vessels at Philadelphia.

EDWARD J. ETTING, Metal Broker

The declaration contained three counts. The first count alleged the contract to have been for the sale of about 5,000 tons of T iron rails, to be shipped at the rate of about 1,000 tons a month, beginning in February, and ending in July, 1880. The second count set forth the contract verbatim. Each of these two counts alleged that the plaintiffs in February, March, April, May, June and July shipped the goods at the rate of about 1,000 tons a month, and notified the shipments to the defendants; and further alleged the due arrival of the goods at Philadelphia, the plaintiff's readiness to deliver the goods and bills thereof, with custom-house certificates of weight, according to the contract, and the defendants' refusal to accept them. The third count differed from the second only in averring that 400 tons were shipped by the plaintiff in February and accepted by the defendants, and that the rest was shipped by the plaintiffs at the rate of about 1,000 tons a month in March, April, May, June and July. The defendants pleaded non assumpsit. The material facts proved at the trial were as follows:

The plaintiff shipped from various European ports 400 tons by one vessel in the last part of February, 885 tons by two vessels in March, 1,571 tons by five vessels in April, 850 tons by three vessels in May, 1,000 tons by two vessels in June, and 300 tons by one vessel in July, and notified to the defendants each shipment.

The defendants received and paid for the February shipment upon its arrival in March, and in April gave directions at what wharves the March shipments should be discharged on their arrival; but on May 14, about the time of the arrival of the March shipments, and having been then for the first time informed of the amounts shipped in February, March and April, gave Etting written notice that they should decline to accept the shipments made in March and April, because none of them were in accordance with the contract; and, in answer to a letter from him of May 16, wrote him on May 17 as follows:

> We are advised that what has occurred does not amount to an acceptance of the iron under the circumstances and the terms of the contract. You had a right to deliver in parcels, and we had a right to expect the stipulated quantity would be delivered until the time was up in which that

was possible. Both delivering and receiving were thus far conditional on there being thereafter a complete delivery in due time and of the stipulated article. On the assumption that this time had arrived, and that you had ascertained that you did not intend to, or could not, make any further deliveries for the February and March shipments, we gave you the notice that we declined accepting those deliveries. As to April, it is too plain, we suppose, to require any remark. If we are mistaken as to our obligation for the February and March shipments, of course we must abide the consequences; but if we are right, you have not performed your contract, as you certainly have not for the April shipments. There is then the very serious and much debated question, as we are advised, whether the failure to make the stipulated shipments in February or March has absolved us from the contract. If it does, we of course will avail ourselves of this advantage.

On May 18, Etting wrote to the defendants, insisting on their liability for both past and future shipments, and saying, among other things: "In respect to the objection that

there had not been a complete delivery in due time of the stipulated article, I beg to call your attention to the fact that while the contract is for five thousand tons, it expressly stipulates that deliveries may be made during six months, and that they are only to be at the rate of about one thousand tons per month.

As to April, while it seems to me "too plain to require any remark," I do not see how it can seem so to you, unless you intend to accept the rails. If you object to taking all three shipments made in that month, I shall feel authorized to deliver only two of the cargoes, or, for that matter, to make the delivery of precisely one thousand tons. But I think I am entitled to know definitely from you whether you intend to reject the April shipments, and, if so, upon what ground, and also whether you are decided to reject the remaining shipments under the contract. You say in your last paragraph that you shall avail yourselves of the advantage, if you are absolved from the contract; but as you seem to be in doubt whether you can set up that claim or not, I should like to know definitely what is your intention.

On May 19, the defendants replied:

We do not read the contract as you do. We read it as stipulating for monthly shipments of about one thousand tons, beginning in February, and that the six months clause is to secure the completion of whatever had fallen short in the five months. As to the meeting of "about," it is settled as well as such a thing can be; and certainly neither the February, March, nor April shipments are within the limits.

As to the proposal to vary the notices for April shipments, we do not think you can do this. The notice of the shipments, as soon as known, you were bound to give, and cannot afterwards vary it if they do not conform to the contract. Our right to be notified immediately that the shipments were known is as material a provision as any other, nor can it be changed now in order to make that a performance which was no performance within the time required.

You ask us to determine whether we will or will not object to receive further shipments because of past defaults. We tell you we will if we are entitled to do so, and will not if we are not entitled to do so. We do not think you have the right to compel us to decide a disputed question of law to relieve you from the risk of deciding it yourself. You know quite as well as we do what is the rule and its uncertainty of application.

On June 10, Etting offered to the defendants the alternative of delivering to them 1,000 tons strict measure on account of the shipments in April. This offer they immediately declined.

On June 15, Etting wrote to the defendants that two cargoes, amounting to 221 tons, of the April shipments, and two cargoes, amounting to 650 tons, of the May shipments (designated by the names of the vessels), had been erroneously notified to them, and that about 900 tons had been shipped by a certain other vessel on account of the May shipments. On the same day, the defendants replied that the notification as to April shipments could not be corrected at this late date, and after the terms of the contract had long since been broken.

From the date of the contract to the time of its rescission by the defendants, the market price of such iron was lower than that stipulated in the contract, and was constantly falling. After the arrival of the cargoes, and their tender and refusal, they were sold by Etting, with the consent of the defendants, for the benefit of whom it might concern.

At the trial, the plaintiff contended, 1st. That under the contract he had six months in which to ship the 5,000 tons, and any deficiency in the earlier months could be made up subsequently, provided that the defendants could not be required to take more than 1,000 tons in any one month. 2d. That, if this was not so, the contract was a divisible contract, and the remedy of the defendants for a default in any month was not by rescission of the whole contract, but only by deduction of the damages caused by the delays in the shipments on the part of the plaintiff.

But the court instructed the jury that if the defendants, at the time of accepting the delivery of the cargo paid for, had no notice of the failure of the plaintiff to ship about 1,000 tons in the month of February, and immediately upon learning that fact gave notice of their intention to rescind, the verdict should be for them.

The plaintiff excepted to this instruction, and, after verdict and judgment for the defendants, sued out this writ of error.

[A summary of the arguments of counsel is omitted. See Note 1 following the opinion.]

Mr. Justice GRAY delivered the opinion of the court. After stating the facts in the language reported above, he continued:

In the contracts of merchants, time is of the essence. The time of shipment is the usual and convenient means of fixing the probable time of arrival, with a view of providing funds to pay for the goods, or of fulfilling contracts with third persons. A statement descriptive of the subject-matter, or of some material incident, such as the time or place of shipment, is ordinarily to be regarded as a warranty, in the sense in which that term is used in insurance and maritime law, that is to say, a condition precedent, upon the failure or nonperformance of which the party aggrieved may repudiate the whole contract. Behn v. Burness, 3 B. & S. 751; Bowes v. Shand, 2 App. Cas. 455; Lowber v. Bangs, 2 Wall. 728; Davison v. Von Lingen, 113 U.S. 40.

The contract sued on is a single contract for the sale and purchase of 5,000 tons of iron rails, shipped from a European port or ports for Philadelphia. The subsidiary provisions as to shipping in different months, and as to paying for each shipment upon its delivery, do not split up the contract into as many contracts as there shall be shipments or deliveries of so many distinct quantities or iron. Mersey Co. v. Naylor, 9 App. Cas. 434, 439. The further provision, that the sellers shall not be compelled to replace any parcel lost after shipment, simply reduces, in the event of such a loss, the quantity to be delivered and paid for.

The times of shipment, as designated in the contract, are "at the rate of about 1,000 tons per month, beginning February, 1880, but whole contract to be shipped before August 1, 1880." These words are not satisfied by shipping one sixth part of the 5,000 tons, or about 833 tons, in each of the six months which begin with February and end with July. But they require about 1,000 tons to be shipped in each of the five months from February to June inclusive, and allow no more than slight and unimportant deficiencies in the shipments during those months to be made up in the month of July. The contract is not one for the sale of a specific lot of goods, identified by independent circumstances, such as all those deposited in a certain warehouse, or to be shipped in a particular vessel, or that may be manufactured by the seller, or may be required for use by the buyer, in a certain mill — in which case the mention of the quantity, accompanied by the qualification of "about," or "more or less," is regarded as a mere estimate of the probable amount, as to which good faith is all that is required of the party making it. But the contract before us comes within the general rule:

> When no such independent circumstances are referred to, and the engagement is to furnish goods of a certain quality or character to a certain amount, the quantity specified is material, and governs the contract. The addition of the qualifying words "about," " more or less," and the like, in such cases, is only for the purpose of providing against accidental variations, arising from slight and unimportant excesses or deficiencies in number, measure or weight.

Brawley v. United States, 96 U.S. 168, 171, 172.

The seller is bound to deliver the quantity stipulated, and has no right either to compel the buyer to accept a less quantity, or to require him to select part out of a greater quantity; and when the goods are to be shipped in certain proportions monthly, the seller's failure to ship the required quantity in the first month gives the buyer the same right to rescind the whole contract, that he would have had if it had been agreed that all the goods should be delivered at once.

The plaintiff, instead of shipping about 1,000 tons in February and about 1,000 tons in March, as stipulated in the contract, shipped only 400 tons in February, and 855 tons in March. His failure to fulfil the contract on his part in respect to these first two instalments justified the defendants in rescinding the whole contract, provided they distinctly and seasonably asserted the right of rescission.

The defendants, immediately after the arrival of the March shipments, and as soon as they knew that the quantities which had been shipped in February and in March were less than the contract called for, clearly and positively asserted the right to rescind, if the law entitled them to do so. Their previous acceptance of the single cargo of 400 tons shipped in February was no waiver of this right, because it took place without notice, or means of knowledge, that the stipulated quantity had not been shipped in February. The price paid by them for that cargo being above the market value, the plaintiff suffered no injury by the omission of the defendants to return the iron; and no reliance was placed on that omission in the correspondence between the parties.

The case wholly differs from that of Lyon v. Bertram, 20 How. 149, in which the buyer of a specific lot of goods accepted and used part of them with full means of previously ascertaining whether they conformed to the contract.

The plaintiff, denying the defendants' right to rescind, and asserting that the contract was still in force, was bound to show such performance on his part as entitled him to demand performance on their part, and, having failed to do so, cannot maintain this action.

For these reasons, we are of opinion that the judgment below should be affirmed. But as much of the argument at the bar was devoted to a discussion of the recent English cases, and as a diversity in the law, as administered on the two sides of the Atlantic, concerning the interpretation and effect of commercial contracts of this kind, is greatly to be deprecated, it is proper to add that upon a careful examination of the cases referred to they do not appear to us to establish any rule inconsistent with our conclusion.

In the leading case of Hoare v. Rennie, 5 H. & N. 19, which was an action upon a contract of sale of 667 tons of bar iron, to be shipped from Sweden in June, July, August and September, and in about equal portions each month, at a certain price payable on delivery, the declaration alleged that the plaintiffs performed all things necessary to entitle them to have the contract performed by the defendants, and were ready and willing to perform the contract on their part, and in June shipped a certain portion of the iron, and within a reasonable time afterwards offered to deliver to the defendants the portion so shipped, but the defendants refused to receive it, and gave notice to the plaintiffs that they would not accept the rest. The defendants pleaded that the shipment in June was of about 20 tons only, and that the plaintiffs failed to complete the shipment for that month according to the contract. Upon demurrer to the pleas, it was argued for the plaintiffs that the shipment of about one fourth of the iron in each month was not a condition precedent, and that the defendants' only remedy for a failure to ship that quantity was by a cross action. But judgment was given for the defendants, Chief Baron Pollock saying:

> The defendants refused to accept the first shipment, because, as they say, it was not a performance, but a breach of the contract. Where parties have made an agreement for themselves, the courts ought not to make another for them. Here they say that in the events that have happened one fourth shall be shipped in each month, and we cannot say that they meant to accept any other quantity. At the outset, the plaintiffs failed to tender the quantity according to the contract; they tendered a much less quantity. The defendants had a right to say that this was no performance of the contract, and they were no more bound to accept the short quantity than if a single delivery had been contracted for. Therefore the pleas are an answer to the action.

5 H. & N. 28. So in Coddington v. Paleologo, L.R. 2 Ex. 193, while there was a division of opinion upon the question whether a contract to supply goods "delivering on April 17, complete 8th May," bound the seller to begin delivering on April 17, all the judges agreed that if it did, and the seller made no delivery on that day, the buyer might rescind the contract.

On the other hand, in Simpson v. Crippin, L.R. 8 Q.B. 14, under a contract to supply from 6,000 to 8,000 tons of coal, to be taken by the buyer's wagons from the seller's colliery in equal monthly quantities for twelve months, the buyer sent wagons for only 150 tons during the first month; and it was held that this did not entitle the seller to annul the contract and decline to deliver any more coal, but that his only remedy was by an action for damages. And in Brandt v. Lawrence, 1 Q.B.D. 344, in which the contract was for the purchase of 4,500 quarters, ten per cent. more or less, of Russian oats, "shipment by steamer or steamers during February," or, in case of ice preventing shipment, then immediately upon the opening of navigation, and 1,139 quarters were shipped by one steamer in time, and 3,361 quarters were shipped too late, it was held that the buyer was bound to accept the 1,139 quarters, and was liable to an action by the seller for refusing to accept them.

Such being the condition of the law of England as declared in the lower courts, the case of Bowes v. Shand, after conflicting decisions in the Queen's Bench Division and the Court of Appeal, was finally determined by the House of Lords. 1 Q.B.D. 470; 2 Q.B.D. 112; 2 App. Cas. 455.

In that case, two contracts were made in London, each for the sale of 300 tons of "Madras rice, to be shipped at Madras or coast, for this port, during the months of March and/or April, 1874, per Rajah of Cochin." The 600 tons filled 8,200 bags, of which 7,120 bags were put on board and bills of lading signed in February; and for the rest, consisting of 1,030 bags put on board in February, and 50 in March, the bill of lading was signed in March. At the trial of an action by the seller against the buyer for refusing to accept the cargo, evidence was given that rice shipped in February would be the spring crop, and quite as good as rice shipped in March or April. Yet the House of Lords held that the action could not be maintained, because the meaning of the contract, as apparent upon its face, was that all the rice must be put on board in March and April, or in one of those months.

In the opinions there delivered the general principles underlying this class of cases are most clearly and satisfactorily stated. It will be sufficient to quote a few passages from two of those opinions.

Lord Chancellor Cairns said:

> It does not appear to me to be a question for your Lordships, or for any court, to consider whether that is a contract which bears upon the face of it some reason, some explanation, why it was made in that form, and why the stipulation is made that the shipment should be during these particular months. It is a mercantile contract, and merchants are not in the habit of placing upon their contracts stipulations to which they do not attach some value and importance. [2 App. Cas. 463.]
>
> If it be admitted that the literal meaning would imply that the whole quantity must be put on board during a specified time, it is no answer to that literal meaning, it is no observation which can dispose of, or get rid of, or displace, that literal meaning, to say that it puts an additional burden on the seller, without a corresponding benefit to the purchaser; that is a matter of which the seller and the purchaser are the best judges. Nor is it any reason for saying that it would be a means by which purchasers, without any real cause, would frequently obtain an excuse for rejecting contracts when prices had dropped. The nonfulfilment of any term in any contract is a means by which a purchaser is able to get rid of the contract when prices have dropped; but that is no reason why a term which is found in a contract should not be fulfilled. [pp. 465, 466.]
>
> It was suggested that even if the construction of the contract be as I have stated, still if the rice was not put on board in the particular months, that would not be a reason which would justify the appellants in having rejected the rice altogether, but that it might afford a ground for a cross action by them if they could show that any particular damage resulted to them from the rice not having been put on board in the months in question. My Lords, I cannot think that there is any foundation whatever for that argument. If the construction of the contract be as I have said, that it bears that

the rice is to be put on board in the months in question, that is part of the description of the subject-matter of what is sold. What is sold is not 300 tons of rice in gross or in general. It is 300 tons of Madras rice to be put on board at Madras during the particular months.

The plaintiff, who sues upon that contract, has not launched his case until he has shown that he has tendered that thing which has been contracted for, and if he is unable to show that, he cannot claim any damages for the nonfulfillment of the contract. [pp. 467, 468.]

Lord Blackburn said:

If the description of the article tendered is different in any respect, it is not the article bargained for, and the other party is not bound to take it. I think in this case what the parties bargained for was rice, shipped at Madras or the coast of Madras. Equally good rice might have been shipped a little to the north or a little to the south of the coast of Madras. I do not quite know what the boundary is, and probably equally good rice might have been shipped in February as was shipped in March, or equally good rice might have been shipped in May as was shipped in April, and I dare say equally good rice might have been put on board another ship as that which was put on board the Rajah of Cochin. But the parties have chosen, for reasons best known to themselves, to say: We bargain to take rice, shipped in this particular region, at that particular time, on board that particular ship; and before the defendants can be compelled to take anything in fulfilment of that contract it must be shown not merely that it is equally good, but that it is the same article as they have bargained for — otherwise they are not bound to take it. [2 App. Cas. 480, 481.]

Soon after that decision of the House of Lords, two cases were determined in the Court of Appeal. In Reuter v. Sala, 4 C.P.D. 239, under a contract for the sale of "about twenty-five tons (more or less) black pepper, October and/or November shipment, from Penang to London, the name of the vessel or vessels, marks and full particulars to be declared to the buyer in writing within sixty days from date of bill of lading," the seller, within the sixty days, declared twenty-five tons by a particular vessel, of which only twenty tons were shipped in November, and five tons in December; and it was held that the buyer had the right to refuse to receive any part of the pepper. In Honck v. Muller, 7 Q.B.D. 92, under a contract for the sale of 2,000 tons of pig iron, to be delivered to the buyer free on board at the maker's wharf "in November, or equally over November, December and January next," the buyer failed to take any iron in November, but demanded delivery of one third in December and one third in January; and it was held that the seller was justified in refusing to deliver, and in giving notice to the buyer that he considered the contract as cancelled by the buyer's not taking any iron in November.

The plaintiff in the case at bar greatly relied on the very recent decision of the House of Lords in Mersey Co. v. Naylor, 9 App. Cas. 434, affirming the judgment of the Court of Appeal in 9 Q.B.D. 648, and following the decision of the Court of Common Pleas in Freeth v. Burr, L.R. 9 C.P. 208.

But the point there decided was that the failure of the buyer to pay for the first instalment of the goods upon delivery does not, unless the circumstances evince an intention on his part to be no longer bound by the contract, entitle the seller to rescind the contract and to decline to make further deliveries under it. And the grounds of the decision, as stated by Lord Chancellor Selborne in moving judgment in the House of Lords, are applicable only to the case of a failure of the buyer to pay for, and not to that of a failure of the seller to deliver, the first instalment.

The Lord Chancellor said:

> The contract is for the purchase of 5,000 tons of steel blooms of the company's manufacture; therefore it is one contract for the purchase of that quantity of steel blooms. No doubt there are subsidiary terms in the contract, as to the time of delivery, "Delivery 1,000 tons monthly commencing January next"; and as to the time of payment, "Payment nett cash within three days after receipt of shipping documents"; but that does not split up the contract into as many contracts as there shall be deliveries for the purpose, of so many distinct quantities of iron. It is quite consistent with the natural meaning of the contract, that it is to be one contract for the purchase of that quantity of iron to be delivered at those times and in that manner, and for which payment is so to be made. It is perfectly clear that no particular payment can be a condition precedent of the entire contract, because the delivery under the contract was most certainly to precede payment; and that being so, I do not see how, without express words, it can possibly be made a condition precedent to the subsequent fulfilment of the unfulfilled part of the contract, by the delivery of the undelivered steel. [9 App. Cas. 439.]

Moreover, although in the Court of Appeal dicta were uttered tending to approve the decision in Simpson v. Crippin, and to disparage the decisions in Hoare v. Rennie and Honck v. Muller, above cited, yet in the House of Lords Simpson v. Crippin was not even referred to, and Lord Blackburn, who had given the leading opinion in that case, as well as Lord Bramwell, who had delivered the leading opinion in Honck v. Muller, distinguished Hoare v. Rennie and Honck v. Muller from the case in judgment. 9 App. Cas. 444, 446.

Upon a review of the English decisions, the rule laid down in the earlier cases of Hoare v. Rennie and Coddington v. Paleologo, as well as in the later cases of Reuter v. Sala and Honck v. Muller, appears to us to be supported by a greater weight of authority than the rule stated in the intermediate cases of Simpson v. Crippin and Brandt v. Lawrence, and to accord better with the general principles affirmed by the House of Lords in Bowes v. Shand, while it in nowise contravenes the decision of that tribunal in Mersey Co. v. Naylor.

In this country, there is less judicial authority upon the question. The two cases most nearly in point, that have come to our notice, are Hill v. Blake, 97 N.Y. 216, which accords with Bowes v. Shand, and King Philip Mills v. Slater, 12 R.I. 82, which approves and follows Hoare v. Rennie. The recent cases in the Supreme Court of Pennsylvania, cited at the bar, support no other conclusion. In Shinn v. Bodine, 60 Penn. St. 182, the point decided was that a contract for the purchase of 800 tons of coal at a certain price per ton, "coal to be delivered on board vessels as sent for during months of August and September," was an entire contract, under which nothing was payable until delivery of the whole, and therefore the seller had no right to rescind the contract upon a refusal to pay for one cargo before that time. In Morgan v. McKee, 77 Penn. St. 288, and in Scott v. Kittanning Coal Co., 89 Penn. St. 231, the buyer's right to rescind the whole contract upon the failure of the seller to deliver one instalment was denied, only because that right had been waived, in the one case by unreasonable delay in asserting it, and in the other by having accepted, paid for and used a previous instalment of the goods. The decision of the Supreme Judicial Court of Massachusetts in Winchester v. Newton, 2 Allen, 492, resembles that of the House of Lords in Mersey Co. v. Naylor.

Being of opinion that the plaintiff's failure to make such shipments in February and March as the contract required prevents his maintaining this action, it is needless to dwell upon the further objection that the shipments in April did not comply with the contract, because the defendants could not be compelled to take about 1,000 tons out of the larger quantity shipped in that month, and the plaintiff, after once designating the names of vessels, as the contract bound him to do, could not substitute other vessels. See Busk v. Spence, 4 Camp. 329; Graves v. Legg, 9 Exch. 709; Reuter v. Sala, above cited.

Judgment affirmed.

The Chief Justice was not present at the argument, and took no part in the decision of this case.

NOTE

1. The argument of counsel for Norrington, the seller, which is set out at length in the report, is of considerable interest. Counsel first went into the factual background of the case:

> Under this contract the plaintiff was at liberty to tender rails shipped by sailing vessels from any European port. It is apparent, therefore, that regularity of delivery was not deemed of importance, as the cargoes might have been sent from any port from the Baltic to the Black Sea, and the time of crossing might have varied from three weeks to four or five months. The

rate of shipment was to be "about 1,000 tons per month," but the whole contract was to be shipped within six months; and the entirety of the delivery was of so little consequence, that the sellers were not to be compelled to replace any parcel lost after shipment. The reasonable explanation of this latitude in performance is found in the condition of things in January, 1880, when the whole world was scoured for old iron to supply the extraordinary demand which had sprung up in this country, and in the fact, perfectly well known to the defendants, that the rails to be shipped under this contract would have to be picked up in odd lots, wherever they could be found, from one end of Europe to the other, and shipped from ports where promptness and dispatch could not be counted on. The natural meaning of the contract, therefore, is that the plaintiffs were to ship the iron as early as possible, "at the rate of about 1,000 tons per month"; but if the peculiar circumstances of the times rendered it impossible to comply exactly with this stipulation, an extra month should be allowed in which to complete the shipments. [115 U.S. at 193.]

In his principal argument on the law counsel remarked:

The question here raised is of the first importance, and, singularly enough, it has only been finally set at rest in England within the last few months [the reference is apparently to Mersey Co. v. Naylor, discussed toward the end of Justice Gray's opinion], while no authoritative decision has yet been made in the United States. It involves the whole law of dependent and independent covenants, and of entire and severable or divisible contracts; and it cannot well be discussed without some reference to the great cases [inter alia, Boone v. Eyre and Pordage v. Cole, both reprinted *supra* in Section 2 of this chapter].

Counsel went on to argue that the contract was clearly "severable or divisible" into five (or six) contracts for monthly shipments; buyer's remedy for deficiency (or excess) in any monthly shipment was to reject that shipment; he could not repudiate the balance of the contract. Counsel conceded that Hoare v. Rennie was an authority in favor of the buyer's contention but argued that Simpson v. Crippen had overruled Hoare v. Rennie. (See the discussion of the two cases in Justice Gray's opinion.) Principal reliance was placed on the Mersey case, in the absence of any "authoritative decision in the United States." So far as the summary of the argument goes, counsel made no attempt to deal with, or distinguish, the decision of the House of Lords in Bowes v. Shand. Do you think that Bowes v. Shand could have been distinguished from Norrington? How should it be distinguished from Mersey? Do you think that Justice Gray dealt adequately with counsel's argument that Simpson v. Crippen had overruled Hoare v. Rennie?

2. Norrington v. Wright is followed immediately in the reports by Filley v. Pope, 115 U.S. 213 (1885). Both cases were, indeed, decided on the same day, October 26, 1885; *Norrington* had been argued in January

of that year, *Filley* in April. The transaction litigated in *Filley* involved
the same apparently dramatic collapse of the market price of iron in 1880
that accounted for Norrington v. Wright. The facts in *Filley* may be
summarized as follows: There was a contract of sale between Pope (seller)
and Filley (buyer) covering "500 tons No. 1 Shott's (Scotch) pig iron, at
$26 per ton cash in bond at New Orleans. Shipment from Glasgow as
soon as possible. Delivery and sale subject to ocean risks." Shott's Iron
Factory, in Scotland, from which the pig iron was to come, was "equidis-
tant and equally accessible by railway from the ports of Glasgow on the
west coast and of Leith on the east coast." Shott's shipped sometimes
from Glasgow and sometimes from Leith. At the time the Filley order was
received, no shipping space was available at Glasgow or would be "for
weeks afterwards." A vessel was immediately available at Leith. The vessel at Leith was chartered, the iron was sent to Leith where it was loaded
with all possible dispatch, and the vessel made a direct voyage from Leith
to New Orleans. The Leigh-New Orleans voyage is longer than the
Glasgow-New Orleans voyage. The alternative to the direct voyage from
Leith to New Orleans would have been to send the vessel in ballast
around Scotland to Glasgow, there unload the ballast, load the iron, and
proceed to New Orleans. It seems to have been conceded that shipping
direct from Leith was, under the circumstances, the fastest way of getting
the iron to New Orleans. In a brief opinion Justice Gray remarked: "The
contract between these parties belongs to the same class as that sued on
in the case, just decided, of Norrington v. Wright. . . . The provision in
question in that case related to the time; in this it relates to the place of
shipment." 115 U.S. at 219-220. Thus the buyer in *Filley*, like the buyer
in *Norrington*, was privileged to reject the imperfect tender. There appeared to be some confusion about the meaning of the contract term:
"Sale and delivery subject to ocean risks." Counsel for the seller, whose
argument is set out in the report, suggested that it meant that seller bore
the risk of loss or delay in transit (so that it made no difference to the
buyer where the goods were shipped from). Justice Gray seemed to think
that the term put the risk on buyer if the goods were shipped from Glasgow (but not if they were shipped from Leith). The buyer, he suggested,
had, under the contract, an "insurable interest" in goods shipped from
Glasgow but not in goods shipped from any other port. There is no other
reference in the report to whether either seller or buyer did or did not
take out insurance on the shipment.

3. Counsel for the seller in Filley did, unlike counsel for the seller in
Norrington, try to distinguish his case from Bowes v. Shand. For the facts
of Bowes v. Shand, see Justice Gray's opinion in Norrington. How would
you go about making the distinction?

4. Bowes v. Shand, Norrington v. Wright and Filley v. Pope are often
cited to the proposition that, in contracts for the sale of goods, there
obtains a rule of "perfect tender" by the seller; given the slightest devia-

tion, the buyer is privileged to reject the goods. The first American treatise on sales law suggests that, half a century earlier, the tender rule had been quite different: except for serious defects in the goods, the buyer had to accept the tender and sue in damages for the breach; he did not have the privilege of rejection. See Story on Sales §448 (1847). Thus, aspects of the sales contract which had been "independent covenants" in the first half of the century had become true "conditions precedent" by 1890.

5. Both in England and the United States the law of sales was codified shortly after these decisions. In Mitsubishi Goshi Kaisha v. J. Aron, 16 F.2d 185 (2d Cir. 1926), Judge Learned Hand could find nothing in the Uniform Sales Act that changed the rule of perfect tender. The contract called for shipment of soy bean oil "f.o.b. seller's tank car, Pacific Coast," "net cash against shipping documents." The contract covered six tank cars of oil, five of which were shipped, accepted and paid for. The buyer should have given shipping instructions with respect to the sixth car on July 1 but gave no instruction until July 19 when he directed that the car be shipped from Seattle to East Rochester, N.Y. Under the contract, shipment was to be completed before the end of July. The seller tendered a car which had left Seattle on July 3 and had been "diverted" at Dallas to East Rochester; the bill of lading issued after the diversion showed Dallas as the point of shipment. Buyer rejected the tender and seller brought an action for damages. *Held:* for buyer. Judge Hand's opinion, after citing Filley v. Pope, goes on to say: "There is no room in commercial contracts for the doctrine of substantial performance. Bowes v. Shand, L.R. 2 App. Cas. 455. All the seller ever tendered was a bill of lading, Dallas to East Rochester, which was clearly not 'f.o.b. . . . Pacific Coast.' "

For a comparable English case, concluding that nothing in the Sale of Goods Act had changed the rule of Bowes v. Shand, see Arcos, Ltd. v. E.A. Ronaasen & Son, [1933] A.C. 470. In the *Arcos* case an arbitrator had held that a buyer was not privileged to reject goods for trivial defects but must take them with an allowance for damages. On appeal his award was set aside by the trial court which was affirmed by a unanimous Court of Appeal and finally by a unanimous House of Lords. In the House of Lords, Lord Atkin wrote: "It was contended that in all commercial contracts the question was whether there was a 'substantial' compliance with the contract. . . . I cannot agree. . . . [T]he right view is that the condition of the contract must be strictly performed. If a condition is not performed, the buyer has a right to reject." Id. at 479-480.

6. For the decline (and perhaps the fall) of the perfect tender rule in this country since the 1940s, see the Note on The Uniform Commercial Code and the Perfect Tender Rule, *infra* p. 1005. In Reardon Smith Line Ltd. v. Hansen-Tangen, [1976] 3 All E.R. 570 [H.L.], the continuing validity of the perfect tender rule in England was questioned by all the members of a five-judge panel. In 1973, Reardon Smith agreed to sub-

charter from Hansen-Tangen a tanker then in construction in Japan, referred to in the subcharter as "the good Japanese flag . . . Newbuilding motor tank vessel called Yard 354 at Osaka Zozen [shipbuilding]." The vessel was to have a deadweight of approximately 88,000 tons, which was larger than the Osaka company could build in its own shipyard. Osaka in a joint venture with the "Sumitomo group" set up a new shipbuilding company (Oshima) on the island of Kyushu, about 300 miles from Osaka. Oshima built the vessel in its new shipyard, giving it the number 004. In 1974, when the vessel was ready for delivery, the tanker market had collapsed. Reardon Smith attempted to get out of its subcharter with Hansen-Tangen (which was also attempting to get out of its head charter with a Japanese firm) on the ground that "004 Oshima" was not "354 Osaka." All the Law Lords conceded that if "354 Osaka" was to be taken as a "description" of the vessel, then under the older case law relating to both sales of goods and charter parties, Reardon Smith and Hansen-Tangen were entitled to reject the tender. They concluded, in a prodigy of intellection, that "354 Osaka" was not a "description" but merely an "identification." However, Lord Wilberforce, who delivered the principal speech, commented that some of the older sale of goods cases were "excessively technical and due for fresh examination in this House." Id. at 576. Lord Simon of Glaisdale, concurring, added: "It would be odd were the law to elevate a matter obviously immaterial to the parties at the time of contracting into a matter of fundamental obligation. I agree that the cases on the sale of goods may call for reconsideration on this basis." Id. at 579. The *Reardon Smith* case is particularly interesting in view of the fact that the House of Lords announced its intention to reexamine the sales case, including those decided under the nineteenth-century Sale of Goods Act, without benefit of a new statutory formulation like Article 2 of the Uniform Commercial Code.

7. Though seemingly inflexible in its application and clearly biased in the buyer's favor, the perfect tender rule was qualified by a number of counterrules and caveats, all of which helped to restore a measure of equality in the relation between buyer and seller. One of the most important of these counterrules was first announced in New York in 1899 in a case called Littlejohn v. Shaw, 159 N.Y. 188, 53 N.E. 810. The holding in *Littlejohn* was quite straightforward: if the buyer invoked the perfect tender rule, the court said, he could not rely, at trial, on any reason for rejection other than the reason he had actually given and would be conclusively presumed to have waived all objections save this one. This of course gave buyers an incentive to provide a careful statement of defects at the time of rejection and made it risky to rely on blanket claims like, "the goods aren't what I ordered." But just for this reason, the *Littlejohn* rule also put buyers in something of a predicament. A careful statement of defects requires an examination of the goods, and this takes time. But the longer a buyer holds the goods, the more likely it is he will be deemed

to have accepted them and by doing so, to have lost his right to avoid the contract. To this extent, the unstated objection rule functioned as a kind of antidote or counterweight to the perfect tender rule. In a remarkable law journal article, a student of Karl Llewellyn's named Lawrence Eno demonstrated that the unstated objection rule was most often invoked in cases where rejection came against the background of a falling market that made the contract disadvantageous from the buyer's point of view. Eno, Price Movement and Unstated Objections to the Defective Performance of Sales Contracts, 44 Yale L.J. 782 (1935). Eno hypothesized that where courts believed the real reason for rejecting was the desire to avoid a burdensome contract, they would find a way to apply the counterrule and enforce the contract (giving the buyer any damages he might be entitled to recover). Eno's article is one of the monuments of legal realism and is still worth reading today.

Note on the Uniform Commercial Code and the Perfect Tender Rule

During the 1940s, while the Code was being drafted, there was a good deal of discussion in the law reviews of the desirability of scrapping the late nineteenth-century rules that had given the buyer an almost unlimited right to reject. Something like the rule of substantial performance which §45(2) of the Uniform Sales Act had applied to installment contracts should, it was said, be made applicable to all contracts of sale. It was argued that such a rule would be more in line with actual business practice. In commercial arbitration, and under the rules of various trade associations, buyers were regularly required to accept defective tenders with an allowance on the price. A particularly dramatic example of this approach was to be found in regulations issued by the Secretary of Agriculture under the Perishable Agricultural Commodities Act of 1930, 7 U.S.C. §499 (1952). Under these regulations a buyer may be required to accept any goods, no matter how rotten or unfit for human consumption, and sue in damages for the breach. In general, perhaps with some reluctance, the courts agreed that the regulations were validly issued, whatever damage they may have done to the traditional concepts of sales law. See, e.g., Gillarde Co. v. Martinelli, 169 F.2d 60 (1st Cir. 1948); but cf. J. R. Simplot Co. v. L. Yukon & Son Produce Co., 227 F.2d 67 (8th Cir. 1955). For an excellent discussion, arguing that a generalized rule of substantial performance should be applied to all contracts of sale, see Honnold, Buyer's Right of Rejection, 97 U. Pa. L. Rev. 457 (1949).

Article 2 of the Code (Sales) seems at first blush to have rejected the arguments put forward by Professor Honnold and others and to have reproduced, with some modifications of detail, the state of things under the Uniform Sales Act. The further the matter is pursued, however, the

more difficult it becomes to make out what the draftsman was aiming at
(or at least managed to hit).

Article 2 reproduces the distinction between single delivery contracts
and installment contracts first introduced in the English Sale of Goods
Act and copied, with modifications, in the Uniform Sales Act. Section
2-601 reads like the perfect tender rule *in excelsis:* The buyer may reject
if the seller's tender fails "in any respect" to conform to the contract. Indeed the Article 2 buyer is given the option, unheard of in pre-Code law,
of accepting some of the goods and rejecting the rest. However, the
statutory text expressly makes §2-601 subject to §2-612 on installment
contracts. Section 2-612 appears to go much further than §45(2) of the
Uniform Sales Act, both in requiring the buyer to accept nonconforming
tenders and in limiting the buyer's right to get out of the balance of the
contract. The section introduces a novel distinction between a non-con-
formity that "substantially impairs the value of that installment" (subsection 2) and a nonconformity that "substantially impairs the value of the
whole contract" (subsection 3). However great the nonconformity in any
particular installment, if it does not substantially impair the value of the
whole contract, the seller can compel the buyer to accept it by giving him
what subsection 2 describes as "adequate assurance of its cure" (on cure,
see below). The permutations that can be worked by combining subsections 2 and 3 in different ways are almost endless, leading Professor (now
Judge) Ellen Peters to describe the Code's treatment of installment contracts as "a law professor's delight."

No one has ever offered a plausible explanation of why the draftsman
went to such extremes, both in the perfect tender rule of §2-601 and in
the substantial performance rule of §2-612. Indeed the draftsman, Professor Llewellyn, when queried on the issue, was accustomed to dismiss the
discrepancy with a joke: One of his advisors, now deceased, had once
convincingly explained why §2-601 and §2-612 had to be as they were but
unfortunately he (Llewellyn), although still convinced, could no longer
remember the explanation. However, the fog enveloping the Code in this
respect becomes truly impenetrable when (or if) the student runs across
other sections of Article 2 (not cross-referenced in the text or commentary to either §2-601 or §2-612) that arguably undercut both the sections
mentioned. Consult in this connection §2-504 (shipment by seller) which,
in some but not in all situations, cuts back the buyer's right to reject
under §2-601; §2-508 (Cure by Seller of Improper Tender or Delivery)
which gives the Code seller the right, previously unheard of, to make a
second try at a good tender after his first try has failed; §2-605 (Waiver of
Buyer's Objections by Failure to Particularize) which, in a large range of
situations, requires the buyer to state his reasons for rejection at the time
he rejects and precludes him from thereafter relying on unstated reasons.

The buyer's apparent right under §2-601 to reject the goods for any
defect, no matter how trivial, evaporates once he has accepted (or is

deemed to have accepted) them; in certain circumstances, a buyer may subsequently revoke his acceptance (under §2-608: Revocation of Acceptance in Whole or in Part), but only for defects that substantially impair the value of the goods "to him." Naturally, when a buyer invokes the Code's version of the perfect tender rule, his seller is likely to respond by arguing that the buyer has accepted the goods and must therefore satisfy the more stringent requirements of §2-608. Thus, depending upon how one construes the Code's definition of acceptance (§2-606: What Constitutes Acceptance of Goods), the reach of the perfect tender rule may be considerably less than it seems.

MIRON v. YONKERS RACEWAY, INC.
400 F.2d 112 (2d Cir. 1968)

J. JOSEPH SMITH, Circuit Judge:

. . . In September 1965, plaintiffs entered the horse "Red Carpet" in an auction called the "Old Glory Horse Sale," sponsored by Raceway. The contract by which Red Carpet was consigned to Raceway for sale provided that Raceway would act as plaintiffs' exclusive agent for the sale of the horse and would receive a commission of 10% on the accepted bid, and incorporated by reference the "Terms and Conditions of Sale." The Terms and Conditions of Sale provided, *inter alia:* that the horses were offered for sale according to the laws of New York, that title and "all risk and responsibility for the horse" pass to the buyer at the fall of the auctioneer's hammer, that "No delivery will be made until final settlement," and that

> unless otherwise expressly announced at time of sale, there is no guarantee of any kind as to the soundness or condition or other quality of any horse sold in this Sale except that horses which are unsound in eyes or wind, or are "cribbers," must be announced at time of sale. . . . Any horse whose condition is as aforesaid and is not so announced at time of sale, or where sex is incorrectly represented at time of sale, will be subject to return to Consignor . . . [provided that the buyer gives notice in writing] within seven days of sale. Any other representation, warranty or guarantee of the Consignor which is announced or otherwise given shall not extend beyond 24 hours after the fall of the Auctioneer's hammer or until final payment has been made, whichever is sooner.

Plaintiffs delivered Red Carpet to Raceway on October 17, 1965; the auction of the horse took place early in the afternoon of October 19. At $17,000 there was a lull in the bidding, whereupon Murray Brown, plaintiffs' employee, took the microphone and said:

> This horse has won 2 of his last 3 starts. On September 24, he raced on a muddy track, big stake race in Montreal . . . beating Mr. Sea Song. Now,

you know what Mr. Sea Song has done this year . . . he's a top free-for-all
horse and this horse beat him racing a good trip, and this is just recently.
He's as sound — as, as gutty a horse as you want to find anywhere. He'll
race a good mile for you every time. He's got loads of heart and you're way
off on the price of this horse.

The bidding then resumed, and defendant Finkelstein submitted the
highest bid, which was $32,000.

By about 3:00 p.m. that day, Raceway delivered possession of Red
Carpet to Finkelstein without obtaining any part of the purchase price,
and Finkelstein immediately had the horse transported to his barn at
Roosevelt Raceway, Westbury, Long Island. The next morning, Cruise,
the trainer for Finkelstein's horses, took Red Carpet out of his stall and
hitched him to a jog cart. He observed some swelling of the horse's left
hind leg at that time, and when the horse was caused to walk and trot, it
limped and favored its left hind leg. Cruise returned Red Carpet to the
stall, and summoned Dr. Bernard F. Brennan, a veterinarian, who found
that Red Crapet's left hind leg was swollen, warm and sensitive.

Finkelstein notified Raceway, at about 11:30 a.m. that day, October
20, that Red Carpet was lame and not sound, and that afternoon an
official of Raceway notified Brown, at plaintiffs' stables, of Finkelstein's
complaint. Finkelstein subsequently demanded, as we have said, that
plaintiffs take back the horse because it was not sound, as warranted, but
they have continued to refuse to accept its return. Neither Raceway nor
Finkelstein has paid plaintiffs any part of the purchase price for Red
Carpet.

The basic factual issue tried below was whether Red Carpet was sound,
as warranted, at the time when the auctioneer's hammer fell and all risks
passed to Finkelstein as the buyer. The defendants' evidence on this issue
consisted of X-rays of the horse's left hind leg.

Dr. Brennan testified that he took X-rays of Red Carpet's leg on the
afternoon of October 20, and prints were introduced as the defendants'
Exhibits B, C, D1 and E1. The X-rays revealed a broken splint bone,
which, it was agreed by witnesses for all of the parties, is enough to render
a racehorse unsound. Both of the defendants' expert witnesses, Dr. Brennan and Dr. Charles F. Reid, testified that Exhibits B and D1 revealed
calcification around the site of the fracture indicating that the fracture
was two or three weeks old. The plaintiffs' experts testified, however, that
Exhibit D1, unlike Exhibit B, did not show calcification, and concluded
that the X-rays must have been taken on different days. The defendants
countered by offering testimony that a difference in intensity between the
exhibits explained the fact that callus growth was less visible on D1 than
on B, but the court found that Exhibit D1 showed no calcification and
that it therefore was not taken on the same day as Exhibit B. The court
also found that Exhibits D1 and E1 were undated, that Exhibits B and C

were admittedly incorrectly dated, and that no business records sufficient to prove the date on which the X-rays were taken had been produced, and concluded that the exhibits lacked sufficient probative force to establish the date on which the fracture occurred. We see no reason why this conclusion should not stand.

The expert witnesses were in substantial agreement that the symptoms of a broken splint bone are swelling, heat which is perceptible to the touch, and sensitivity and lameness, and that these symptoms become apparent immediately or very soon after the occurrence of the fracture. Thus if Red Carpet's splint bone was broken at the time of sale, an examination of the horse after the sale would have disclosed that fact. Finkelstein testified that he was not an experienced horse buyer, and ordinarily has a trainer or veterinarian examine the legs of horses he buys, but he went to the auction on October 19, 1965 intending to buy two brood mares, and for that reason did not have his trainer or a veterinarian with him. Although he observed the horse when it was led into the ring at the auction, he did not examine it or look at its legs at the time of the sale. The court found that neither Finkelstein nor his agents inspected or examined the horse prior to the time when Cruise observed a swelling of its left hind leg on the day after the sale.

The plaintiffs offered, on the basic issue of the time of the fracture, testimony of persons who had observed and examined Red Carpet on the day of the sale. Roger White, a competitor of the Mirons, testified that he inspected the horse with the intention of buying it if the price was right, and that he couldn't see anything wrong with it. Dr. Rene Rosaire Gauthier, who accompanied White to the auction and examined Red Carpet for him, testified that when he examined Red Carpet's legs he observed no heat or swelling, and that he saw the horse trotting and walking without limping or manifesting any lameness. The court found, on the basis of this and other testimony, that "On October 19, 1965, prior to sale, the horse's left hind leg was neither swollen, hot, nor lame."

The District Court's finding on the basic factual issue was expressed in terms of failure to carry the burden of proof. Concluding that under New York law Finkelstein had accepted Red Carpet and therefore had the burden of proving a breach of warranty, the court found: "Defendant Finkelstein has failed to prove by a fair preponderance of the credible evidence that the horse was not 'sound' at the time of its sale to him on October 19, 1965. . . ."

We affirm the judgment below on the breach of warranty issue, because we agree with the District Court that under New York law Finkelstein had the burden of proving a breach of warranty and we find ample support in the record for the finding that Finkelstein did not carry that burden successfully. . . .

The District Court based its determination that Finkelstein had the burden on New York Uniform Commercial Code ("U.C.C.") §2-607(4), which provides: "The burden is on the buyer to establish any breach with respect to the goods accepted." The question thus is whether Finkelstein accepted the horse, and we turn for guidance to U.C.C. §2-606(1), which states:

> Acceptance of goods occurs when the buyer
> (a) after a reasonable opportunity to inspect the goods signifies to the seller that the goods are conforming or that he will take or retain them in spite of their nonconformity; or
> (b) fails to make an effective rejection (subsection (1) of Section 2-602), but such acceptance does not occur until the buyer has had a reasonable opportunity to inspect them; or
> (c) does any act inconsistent with the seller's ownership; but if such act is wrongful as against the seller it is an acceptance only if ratified by him.

It has not been argued that Finkelstein accepted the horse under subsection (a). We doubt he could be said to have done any act inconsistent with the plaintiffs' ownership of the horse, within the meaning of subsection (c), but we need not decide the applicability of that subsection, for we think the trial judge was right in finding that Finkelstein failed to make an effective rejection of the horse under U.C.C. §2-602(1), thereby accepting it under subsection (b). U.C.C. §2-602(1) provides: "Rejection of goods must be within a reasonable time after their delivery or tender. It is ineffective unless the buyer seasonably notifies the seller."

Finkelstein accepted the horse, then, if having had a reasonable opportunity to inspect it, he did not reject it within a reasonable time.[1] What is reasonable depends upon an evaluation of all of the circumstances, and we would therefore be reluctant to overturn the findings and conclusions of the trial judge on these issues. He has a feel for the circumstances of the case which we could not possibly have. Moreover, the finding that Finkelstein did not reject the horse within a reasonable time seems to us to be clearly correct.

As the trial judge rightly pointed out, "The fact that the subject matter of the sale in this case was a live animal . . . bears on what is a reasonable time to inspect and reject." Finkelstein's own testimony showed that it is customary, when buying a racehorse, to have a veterinarian or trainer examine the horse's legs, and we agree that the existence of this custom is

1. A "reasonable opportunity to inspect," U.C.C. §2-606(1)(b), may of course encompass more than merely a reasonable time to inspect; here, there is no question that Finkelstein had the facilities for inspection available, and the only question on appeal was whether he waited too long.

A reasonable period for rejection overlaps a reasonable opportunity to inspect under U.C.C. §2-606(1)(b). Thus if inspection discloses a defect, there remains the obligation to reject within a reasonable time. But in many cases where the buyer passes up a reasonable opportunity to inspect, he thus fails to reject within a reasonable time, and we think that this is one of those cases, for reasons stated in the text.

very important in determining whether there was a reasonable opportunity to inspect the horse. See Official Comment to U.C.C. §1-204, para. 2. We gather from the record that the reason it is customary to examine a racehorse's legs at the time of sale is that a splint bone is rather easily fractured (there was testimony that a fracture could result from the horse kicking itself), and although the judge made no specific findings as to this, we assume that is generally what he had in mind when he pointed out that "a live animal is more prone to rapid change in condition and to injury than is an inanimate object." As we have said, Finkelstein did not have the horse examined either at the place of sale or at his barn later the day of the sale. He thus passed up a reasonable opportunity to inspect Red Carpet.

Finkelstein having had a reasonable opportunity to inspect Red Carpet on the day of the sale, we have no problem with the finding that the attempted rejection on the next day did not come within a reasonable time. In addition to our reluctance to question the trial judge's finding as to what is a reasonable time, we take into account that what is a reasonable time for rejection depends on the purpose of rejection. See U.C.C. §1-204(2). Where goods are effectively rejected for breach of warranty, the burden of proving that they conform presumably remains on the seller,[2] whereas upon acceptance the buyer has the burden to establish any breach. U.C.C. §2-607(4). In this case, the subject of the sale is a racehorse warranted to be sound, and the record clearly shows that an injury such as occurred here, rendering a horse unsound, may be a matter of chance, proof of the exact time of injury being very difficult to make. In these circumstances, the burden of proof on the issue of soundness at the time of sale cannot fairly rest on the seller where the buyer has taken possession of the horse, transported it to his barn, and kept it overnight before discovering the injury and informing the seller of it. We conclude that rejection did not take place within a reasonable time after delivery, and Finkelstein thus accepted the horse. In short, since one of the consequences of acceptance is that the buyer bears the burden of proving any breach, the fairness of allocating the burden one way or the other is relevant in determining whether acceptance has occurred — here, whether rejection took place within a reasonable time.

The defendants have argued strenuously that inspection and rejection on the day after the sale is certainly soon enough, and the argument

---

2. The official comment to U.C.C. §2-602 (para. 3) states that the section applies only to rightful rejection by the buyer. Yet acceptance may depend upon whether there has been a rejection under that section, and the allocation of the burden of proving whether there was a defect, and thus whether or not there was "rightful rejection," depends upon whether there has been acceptance. See U.C.C. §§2-606(1)(b) and 2-607(4). The only sensible construction of these sections would seem to be that non-acceptance, consisting of attempted rejection within a reasonable time after delivery or tender, amounts to rightful rejection if the seller fails to prove that the goods conform, but is a breach if the seller proves conformity.

would gain substantial strength if another sort of defect were involved
and we took into account that the customary type of inspection at the
time of sale might not disclose aspects of a horse's soundness other than
the condition of its legs, and that these aspects, unlike the condition of
the legs, would be very unlikely to change overnight. There is nothing
in the record as to how much the customary inspection at the time of sale
would show; Finkelstein testified only that he has a trainer or veterinarian
examine the legs of horses he buys. In any case, if there are defects which
are not discoverable by the inspection which the District Court found
Finkelstein had a reasonable opportunity to make, the problem is taken
care of by U.C.C. §2-608(1), which provides in relevant part:

> The buyer may revoke his acceptance of a lot or commercial unit whose
> non-conformity substantially impairs its value to him if he has accepted
> it . . .
> (b) without discovery of such nonconformity if his acceptance was rea-
> sonably induced either by the difficulty of discovery before acceptance or
> by the seller's assurances.

The answer to the argument is that inspection is not necessarily final;
where there are defects discoverable by a customary inspection at the
time of sale, a buyer in Finkelstein's position will not be excused from
making that inspection and rejecting the goods within a reasonable time,
if a defect is disclosed, on the ground that there are possible critical
defects which only a more thorough inspection would disclose. There are
no conceptual problems involved in this approach, for there is nothing
ultimate about any of the conceptions we are using. Since a finding of
acceptance depends upon a finding that there was a reasonable opportunity to inspect, the question whether acceptance may be revoked as reasonably induced by the difficulty of discovery before acceptance, within
the meaning of U.C.C. §2-608(1), must be answered by reference to the
scope of the inspection which there was a reasonable opportunity to
make. Thus if Finkelstein had carried out the customary inspection and
accepted the horse, and the defect allegedly rendering Red Carpet unsound at the time of sale were a defect not discoverable by inspection on
the day of sale, rather than a broken splint bone, we may presume the
District Court would not have placed the burden of proof on Finkelstein,
and would have said that he had "revoked his acceptance."

The defendants argue that the provision in the Terms and Conditions
of Sale that any warranty of the consignor "shall not extend beyond 24
hours after the fall of the Auctioneer's hammer or until final payment has
been made, whichever is sooner," fixes by agreement, a reasonable time
for rejection, U.C.C. §1-204(1), and that since Finkelstein rejected within
24 hours of the fall of the hammer he did not accept Red Carpet under
U.C.C. §2-206(1)(b). There was considerable confusion over the meaning of this provision at the trial; Finkelstein submitted a memorandum in

which it was argued that under the provision any defect violating the warranty appearing within 24 hours is presumed to be a defect existing at the time of sale, so that the seller must show that "some external, intervening cause occurred after the horse passed from its possession." The trial judge interpreted this as an argument that the provision converted any warranty into a 24-hour insurance policy and, not surprisingly, rejected that notion. He concluded that "At most, the clause means that if any futuristic warranty is stated, it could extend no longer than the period mentioned."

We think this provision must be construed simply as setting a time within which defects must be reported in order for the warranty to be valid. The setting of such deadline does not necessarily mean that any unreasonable delay in inspection or rejection is acceptable so long as it does not extend past the deadline. Had Red Carpet been obviously lame, hobbling badly at the time he was delivered to Finkelstein, and had Finkelstein nonetheless taken the horse away to his barn without comment, it would be unreasonable to say that Finkelstein nontheless had twenty-four hours to report the defect, because of this provision. On our view of the case, whether rejection was within a reasonable time must be answered with reference to what inspection for defects is customary, and it appears that Finkelstein had no more excuse for taking the horse away without giving its legs the customary inspection than he would have had for taking it away without comment if it had been hobbling. We will not construe a provision which by its terms sets a maximum time for reporting defects to set a minimum time as well, for some defects may be more readily discoverable than others.

We conclude, then, that Finkelstein accepted the horse by failing to reject it within a reasonable time, and thus had the burden of proving any breach of warranty. As we have already said, we find ample support for the finding that he failed to prove a breach by a fair preponderance of the credible evidence. The only evidence submitted by the defendants to establish the time of the fracture was the X-rays discussed above, and we have explained why the trial judge found that these lacked sufficient probative force to establish the date of the fracture. . . .

NOTE

1. According to the "Terms and Conditions of Sale" set out at the beginning of the *Miron* case, any representation of soundness made by the consignor (Raceway) at the time of sale was not to "extend beyond 24 hours after the fall of the Auctioneer's hammer or until final payment has been made, whichever is sooner." Do you think the court's treatment of this provision adequate? How should the provision be interpreted? Is it arguable that the warranty is meant to protect the buyer against defects

caused by events occurring within 24 hours after the time of the sale? The least generous reading of the provision (from the buyer's point of view) would be: the seller only warrants his horse against defects existing at the time of the sale, and to recover damages even for a defect of this sort the buyer must discover and report the defect to the seller within 24 hours. Assuming the buyer in *Miron* did not lose his warranty claim by waiting too long to assert it, he would still have the burden of proving that the horse's leg was broken at the time of the sale, and as the discussion of his X-ray evidence suggests, that may be an almost impossible burden to carry. As a practical matter, then, allocation of the burden of proof on the warranty issue (which itself depends on whether the buyer is deemed to have accepted the horse) is likely to be decisive in determining whether the buyer can recover anything at all.

2. Section 2-606(1)(c) provides that a buyer accepts the goods (whether or not he says he is accepting them) when he "does any act inconsistent with the seller's ownership." Clearly, inspection within a reasonable time cannot constitute such an act, for if it did, subsections (1)(c) and (1)(a) would be in hopeless conflict. Beyond this, however, the meaning of "act inconsistent" remains obscure and, not surprisingly, has produced a considerable volume of litigation. For the discussion of the cases and an attempted rationalization, see Priest, Breach and Remedy for the Tender of Nonconforming Goods Under the Uniform Commercial Code: An Economic Approach, 91 Harv. L. Rev. 960, 989-91 (1978).

3. An attentive study of the sequence of Article 2 sections dealing with the perfect tender rule and its exceptions introduces another element of confusion. At several points (see §§2-504(b), 2-612(2)) a distinction is taken between contracts under which the seller is required to tender "goods" and contracts under which the seller is required to tender "documents." (The "documents" are principally bills of lading issued by carriers.) Arguably, the perfect tender rule remains in full force (even in installment contracts) with respect to documentary tenders (which are in common use in most overseas shipments) and the "cure" provisions of §2-508 do not apply.

As the next case and the Note following it suggest, there may be good reasons for preserving the rigors of the perfect tender rule in certain types of documentary commercial transactions, especially those employing a letter of credit.

MAURICE O'MEARA CO. v. NATIONAL PARK BANK OF NEW YORK

239 N.Y. 386, 146 N.E. 639 (1925)

McLaughlin, J. This action was brought to recover damages alleged to have been sustained by the plaintiff's assignor, Ronconi & Millar, by defendant's refusal to pay three sight drafts against a confirmed irrevocable letter of credit. The letter of credit was in the following form:

The National Park Bank of New York

Our Credit No. 14956   October 28, 1920

Messrs. Ronconi & Millar, 49 Chambers Street, New York City, N.Y. — Dear Sirs: In accordance with instructions received from the Sun-Herald Corporation of this city, we open a confirmed or irrevocable credit in your favor for account of themselves, in amount of $224,853.30 covering the shipment of 1,332⅔ tons of newsprint paper in 72½" and 36½" rolls to test 11-12, 32 lbs. at 8½¢ per pound net weight — delivery to be made in December 1920, and January 1921.

Drafts under this credit are to be drawn at sight on this bank, and are to be accompanied by the following documents of a character which must meet with our approval:

Commercial invoice in triplicate.

Weight returns.

Negotiable dock delivery order actually carrying with it control of the goods.

This is a confirmed or irrevocable credit, and will remain in force to and including February 15, 1921, subject to the conditions mentioned herein.

When drawing drafts under this credit, or referring to it, please quote our number as above.

Very truly yours,

R. STUART, Assistant Cashier (R.C.)

The complaint alleged the issuance of the letter of credit; the tender of three drafts the first on the 17th of December, 1920, for $46,301.71, the second on January 7, 1921, for $41,416.34, and the third on January 13, 1921 for $32,968.35. Accompanying the first draft were the following documents: . . . [The documents tendered were those required under the letter of credit.] The complaint also alleged defendant's refusal to pay; a statement of the amount of loss upon the resale of the paper due to a fall in the market price; expenses for lighterage, cartage, storage, and insurance amounting to $3,045.20; an assignment of the cause of action by Ronconi & Millar to the plaintiff; and a demand for judgment. . . .

The [plaintiff's] motion for summary judgment was denied and the defendant [sic; no doubt "plaintiff" is meant] appealed to the Appellate Division, where the order denying the same was unanimously affirmed, leave to appeal to this count granted, and the following question certified:

"Should the motion of the plaintiff for summary judgment herein have been granted?". . .

I am of the opinion that the order of the Appellate Division and the Special Term should be reversed and the motion granted. The facts set out in defendant's answer and in the affidavits used by it in opposition to the motion are not a defense to the action.

The bank issued to plaintiff's assignor an irrevocable letter of credit, a contract solely between the bank and plaintiff's assignor, in and by which the bank agreed to pay sight drafts to a certain amount on presentation to it of the documents specified in the letter of credit. This contract was in no way involved in or connected with, other than the presentation of the documents, the contract for the purchase and sale of the paper mentioned. That was a contract between buyer and seller, which in no way concerned the bank. The bank's obligation was to pay sight drafts when presented if accompanied by genuine documents specified in the letter of credit. If the paper when delivered did not correspond to what had been purchased, either in weight, kind or quality, then the purchaser had his remedy against the seller for damages. Whether the paper was what the purchaser contracted to purchase did not concern the bank and in no way affected its liability. It was under no obligation to ascertain, either by a personal examination or otherwise, whether the paper conformed to the contract between the buyer and seller. The bank was concerned only in the drafts and the documents accompanying them. This was the extent of its interest. If the drafts, when presented, were accompanied by the proper documents, then it was absolutely bound to make the payment under the letter of credit, irrespective of whether it knew, or had reason to believe, that the paper was not of the tensile strength contracted for. This view, I think, is the one generally entertained with reference to a bank's liability under consideration. . . . International Banking Corporation v. Irving Nat. Bank (D.C.) 274 F. 122, 125, affirmed (C.C.A) 283 F. 103. . . .

The defendant had no right to insist that a test of the tensile strength of the paper be made before paying the drafts. Nor did it even have a right to inspect the paper before payment, to determine whether it in fact corresponded to the description contained in the documents. The letter of credit did not so provide. All that the letter of credit provided was that documents be presented which described the paper shipped as of a certain size, weight, and tensile strength. To hold otherwise is to read into the letter of credit something which is not there, and this the court ought not to do, since it would impose upon a bank a duty which in many cases would defeat the primary purpose of such letters of credit. This primary purpose is an assurance to the seller of merchandise of prompt payment against documents.

It has never been held, so far as I am able to discover, that a bank has the right or is under an obligation to see the description of the merchandise contained in the documents presented is correct. A provision giving it such right, or imposing such obligation, might, of course, be provided for in the letter of credit. The letter under consideration contains no such provision. If the bank had the right to determine whether the paper was of the tensile strength stated, then it might be pertinent to inquire how much of the paper must it subject to the test? If it had to make a test as to tensile strength, then it was equally obligated to measure and weigh the paper. No such thing was intended by the parties and there was no such obligation upon the bank. The documents presented were sufficient. The only reason stated by defendant in its letter of December 18, 1920, for refusing to pay the draft, was that —

"There has arisen a reasonable doubt regarding the quality of the newsprint paper. . . . Until such time as we can have a test made by an impartial and unprejudiced expert we shall be obliged to defer payment."

This being the sole objection, the only inference to be drawn therefrom is that otherwise the documents presented conformed to the requirements of the letter of credit. All other objections were thereby waived. International Banking Corporation v. Irving Nat. Bank. *supra*. . . .

Finally, it is claimed that the plaintiff was not entitled to a summary judgment since there was an issue raised as to the amount of damages. It appears from the affidavits in support of the motion that after the defendant had refused to pay the drafts, due notice was given to it by the plaintiff of its intention to sell the paper for the best price possible, although no notice of such resale was necessary. Personal Property Law (Cons. Laws, c. 41), sec. 141 subd. 4. No attention was paid to the notice and the paper was sold as soon as practicable thereafter and for the best price obtainable, which represented the fair market value at the time of the sale. The plaintiff's damages, were primarily, the face amount of the drafts. Plaintiff, of course, was bound to minimize such damage so far as it reasonably could. This it undertook to do by reselling the paper, and for the amount received, less expenses connected with the sale, it was bound to give the defendant credit. There was absolutely no statement in defendant's affidavits to the effect that the plaintiff did not act in the utmost good faith or with reasonable care and diligence in making the resale. . . .

There was a loss on the resale of the paper called for under the first draft of $5,447.26, and under the second draft of $14,617.53, making a total loss of $20,064.79, for which amount judgment should be directed in favor of the plaintiff.

The orders appealed from should therefore be reversed and the motion granted, with costs in all courts. The question certified is answered in the affirmative.

CARDOZO, J. (dissenting). I am unable to concur in the opinion of the court. I assume that no duty is owing from the bank to its depositor which requires it to investigate the quality of the merchandise. Laudisi v. American Exchange Nat. Bank, 239 N.Y. 234, 146 N.E. 347. I dissent from the view that, if it chooses to investigate and discovers thereby that the merchandise tendered is not in truth the merchandise which the documents describe, it may be forced by the delinquent seller to make payment of the price irrespective of its knowledge. We are to bear in mind that this controversy is not one between the bank on the one side and on the other a holder of the drafts who has taken them without notice and for value. The controversy arises between the bank and a seller who has misrepresented the security upon which advances are demanded. Between parties so situated payment may be resisted if the documents are false.

I think we lose sight of the true nature of the transaction when we view the bank as acting upon the credit of its customer to the exclusion of all else. It acts not merely upon the credit of its customer, but upon the credit also of the merchandise which is to be tendered as security. The letter of credit is explicit in its provision that documents sufficient to give control of the goods shall be lodged with the bank when drafts are presented. I cannot accept the statement of the majority opinion that the bank was not concerned with any question as to the character of the paper. If that is so, the bales tendered might have been rags instead of paper, and still the bank would have been helpless, though it had knowledge of the truth, if the documents tendered by the seller were sufficient on their face. A different question would be here if the defects had no relation to the description in the documents. In such circumstances it would be proper to say that a departure from the terms of the contract between the vendor and the vendee was of no moment to the bank. That is not the case before us. If the paper was of the quality stated in the defendant's answer the documents were false.

I think the conclusion is inevitable that a bank which pays a draft upon a bill of lading misrepresenting the character of the merchandise may recover the payment when the misrepresentation is discovered, or at the very least, the difference between the value of the thing described and the value of the thing received. If payment might have been recovered the moment after it was made, the seller cannot coerce payment if the truth is earlier revealed.

We may find persuasive analogies in connection with the law of sales. One who promises to make payment in advance of delivery and inspection may be technically in default if he refuses the promised payment before inspection has been made. None the less, if the result of the inspection is to prove that the merchandise is defective, the seller must fail in an action for the recovery of the price. The reason is that "the buyer would have been entitled to recover back the price if he had paid it without inspection of the goods." 2 Williston on Sales (2d Ed.) §§479, 576.

I think the defendant's answer and the affidavits submitted in support of it are sufficient to permit a finding that the plaintiff's assignors misrepresented the nature of the shipment. The misrepresentation does not cease to be defense, partial if not complete, though it was innocently made. Bloomquist v. Farson, 222 N.Y. 375, 118 N.E. 855; 2 Williston on Sales (2d Ed.) §632.

The order should be affirmed and the question answered "No."

Hiscock, C.J. and Pound and Andrews, JJ., concur with Mc-Laughlin, J.

Cardozo, J., reads dissenting opinion, in which Crane, J., concurs. Lehman, J., not sitting.

Orders reversed, etc.

NOTE

1. Under the rule in the *O'Meara* case, as codified in Code §5-114(1), a seller who is in a position to require that a buyer provide for payment by having his bank issue a letter of credit can avoid the rigors and uncertainties of the perfect tender rule. Until recently, however, the letter of credit device has been used primarily in international trade and banks have typically issued letters only for buyers of unquestionable credit standing. (The bank's obligation to honor drafts is absolute, provided only that the documents specified in the letter are properly presented. In such a case the bank must pay even though its customer, the buyer, is insolvent and unable to reimburse the bank. Having paid, the bank holds the goods as security for its advance but, in the real world, a distress sale of the goods is unlikely to make the bank whole.) Short of having the buyer provide a bank letter of credit, a seller can to some extent protect himself against the perfect tender rule by requiring that the buyer pay, not against a tender of the goods, but against a tender of shipping documents (typically a negotiable bill of lading). Under a "documentary" term a buyer has no right to inspect the goods before payment (U.C.C. §2-513); he must pay "blind" and then, if the goods turn out to be defective, bring an action for breach of warranty against the seller, presumably in the seller's jurisdiction. On the other hand, if the buyer refuses to pay against a good documentary tender, the seller's only recourse is to bring an action for the price (or damages) on the contract of sale and in that action the buyer may interpose his contract defenses (e.g., nonconformity of the goods or of the manner of their tender). The bank letter of credit remains the only device under which a seller, by getting the bank's absolute obligation, can successfully insulate himself from the buyer's right to reject under the perfect tender rule. For an excellent treatment of the entire subject, see H. Harfield, Letters of Credit (1981).

2. In Sztejn v. Schroder Banking Corporation, 177 Misc. 719, 31 N.Y.S.2d 631 (Sup. Ct. 1941), a letter of credit had been issued by a New York bank in favor of a seller in Pakistan. The buyer petitioned for an order restraining the bank from honoring drafts drawn under the letter, alleging that the goods shipped were worthless junk. The court concluded that the rule in the *O'Meara* case did not preclude the issuance of the restraining order. The alleged nonconformity of the goods in *O'Meara*

amounted to a mere breach of warranty; the buyer's allegations in *Sztejn* went beyond breach of warranty to claim fraud on the part of the seller. U.C.C. §5-114(2)(b) apparently codifies the *Sztejn* limitation on (or explanation of) the rule in the *O'Meara* case. For a controversial extension of *Sztejn*, see NMC Enterprises, Inc. v. Columbia Broadcasting System, 14 U.C.C. Rep. 1427 (1974).

3. The letter of credit device was invented to reduce the risks associated with long-distance (especially international) sales transactions. In recent years, however, it has been put to a variety of new uses, one of which — the so-called standby or guaranty letter of credit — serves altogether different ends and has occasioned a great deal of litigation as courts have struggled to accommodate it to the well-defined principles of traditional letter of credit law. A standby letter of credit represents the issuing bank's commitment to pay the beneficiary (or reimburse him for his losses) if the customer fails to pay or breaches some other contractual obligation. To make a claim against the bank, the beneficiary must notify it, in writing, of the customer's default; typically, the written notice given by the beneficiary will be the "document" called for by the terms of the credit. A transaction of this sort is, in effect, a disguised form of suretyship. Ordinarily, a bank issuing a standby letter of credit does not expect to pay the customer anything at all since it will be called on to do so only if the bank's customer (the party whose performance the bank is guaranteeing) fails to meet its own responsibilities. And since the documents the bank receives when and if it *does* pay are pieces of paper that have no intrinsic worth (unlike the documents of title involved in a more traditional letter of credit transaction), a standby credit creates greater risks for the issuing bank and should be viewed as an unsecured loan (unless, of course, the bank's customer provides it with collateral of some other sort). Standby credits seem to have been adopted with special enthusiasm in the construction business, although they are used in other contexts as well. See Verkuil, Bank Solvency and Guaranty Letters of Credit, 25 Stan. L. Rev. 716 (1973). One recurrent issue raised by the standby credit concerns the effect of a "bad faith call" by the beneficiary, asserting a breach by the customer where no breach has occurred or is contemplated. For an examination of this rather technical issue in an extremely non-technical setting, see Comment, "Fraud in the Transaction": Enjoining Letters of Credit During the Iranian Revolution, 93 Harv. L. Rev. 992 (1980).

O.W. HOLMES, THE PATH OF THE LAW (1897) (in Collected Legal Papers (1920)) 181: "You can always imply a condition in a contract. But why do you imply it? It is because of some belief as to the practice of the community or of a class, or because of some opinion as to policy, or, in short, because of some attitude of yours upon a matter not capable of exact quantitative measurement, and therefore not capable of founding exact logical conclusions. Such matters really are battle grounds where the means do not exist for determinations that shall be good for all time, and where the decision can do no more than embody the preference of a given body at a given time and place. We do not realize how large a part of our law is open to reconsideration upon a slight change in the habit of the public mind."

Section 4.   The Problem of Forfeiture

BRITTON v. TURNER
6 N.H. 481 (1834)

Assumpsit for work and labour, performed by the plaintiff, in the service of the defendant, from March 9th 1831, to December 27, 1831.

The declaration contained the common counts, and among them a count in quantum meruit, for the labor, averring it to be worth one hundred dollars.

At the trial in the C.C. Pleas, the plaintiff proved the performance of the labor as set forth in the declaration.

The defence was that it was performed under a special contract — that the plaintiff agreed to work one year, from some time in March, 1831, to March 1832, and that the defendant was to pay him for said year's labor the sum of one hundred and twenty dollars; and the defendant offered evidence tending to show that such was the contract under which the work was done.

Evidence was also offered to show that the plaintiff left the defendant's service without his consent, and it was contended by the defendant that the plaintiff had no good cause for not continuing in his employment.

There was no evidence offered of any damage arising from the plaintiff's departure, farther than was to be inferred from his non fulfilment of the entire contract.

The court instructed the jury, that if they were satisfied from the evidence that the labor was performed, under a contract to labor a year, for the sum of one hundred and twenty dollars, and if they were satisfied that the plaintiff labored only the time specified in the declaration, and then left the defendant's service, against his consent, and without any good cause, yet the plaintiff was entitled to recover, under his quantum meruit count, as much as the labor he performed was reasonably worth, and under this direction the jury gave a verdict for the plaintiff for the sum of $95.

The defendant excepted to the instructions thus given to the jury.

[A summary of the argument of the counsel for defendant is omitted. See Note 1 following the opinion.]

PARKER, J. delivered the opinion of the court. It may be assumed, that the labor performed by the plaintiff, and for which he seeks to recover a compensation in this action, was commenced under a special contract to labor for the defendant the term of one year, for the sum of one hundred and twenty dollars, and that the plaintiff has labored but a portion of that time, and has voluntarily failed to complete the entire contract.

It is clear, then, that he is not entitled to recover upon the contract itself, because the service, which was to entitle him to the sum agreed upon, has never been performed.

But the question arises, can the plaintiff, under these circumstances, recover a reasonable sum for the service he has actually performed, under the count in quantum meruit.

Upon this, and questions of a similar nature, the decisions to be found in the books are not easily reconciled.

It has been held, upon contracts of this kind for labor to be performed at a specified price, that the party who voluntarily fails to fulfil the contract by performing the whole labor contracted for, is not entitled to recover anything for the labor actually performed, however much he may have done towards the performance, and this has been considered the settled rule of law upon this subject. . . .

That such rule in its operation may be very unequal, not to say unjust, is apparent.

A party who contracts to perform certain specified labor, and who breaks his contract in the first instance, without any attempt to perform it, can only be made liable to pay the damages which the other party has sustained by reason of such non performance, which in many instances may be trifling — whereas a party who in good faith has entered upon the performance of his contract, and nearly completed it, and then abandoned the further performance — although the other party has had the full benefit of all that has been done, and has perhaps sustained no actual damage — is in fact subjected to a loss of all which has been performed, in the nature of damages for the non fulfilment of the remainder, upon the technical rule, that the contract must be fully performed in order to a recovery of any part of the compensation.

By the operation of this rule, then, the party who attempts performance may be placed in a much worse situation than he who wholly disregards his contract, and the other party may receive much more, by the breach of the contract, than the injury which he has sustained by such breach, and more than he could be entitled to were he seeking to recover damages by an action.

The case before us presents an illustration. Had the plaintiff in this case never entered upon the performance of his contract, the damage could not probably have been greater than some small expense and trouble incurred in procuring another to do the labor which he had contracted to perform. But having entered upon the performance, and labored nine and a half months, the value of which labor to the defendant as found by the jury is $95, if the defendant can succeed in this defence, he in fact receives nearly five sixths of the value of a whole year's labor, by reason of the breach of contract by the plaintiff a sum not only utterly disproportionate to any probable, not to say possible damage which could have resulted from the neglect of the plaintiff to continue the remaining two and a half months, but altogether beyond any damage which could have been recovered by the defendant, had the plaintiff done nothing towards the fulfilment of his contract.

Another illustration is furnished in Lantry v. Parks, 8 Cowen, 83. There the defendant hired the plaintiff for a year, at ten dollars per month. The plaintiff worked ten and a half months, and then left saying he would work no more for him. This was on Saturday — on Monday the plaintiff returned, and offered to resume his work, but the defendant said he would employ him no longer. The court held that the refusal of the defendant on Saturday was a violation of his contract, and that he could recover nothing for the labor performed.

There are other cases, however, in which principles have been adopted leading to a different result.

It is said, that where a party contracts to perform certain work, and to furnish materials, as, for instance, to build a house, and the work is done, but with some variations from the mode prescribed by the contract, yet if the other party has the benefit of the labor and materials he should be bound to pay so much as they are reasonably worth. . . .

A different doctrine seems to have been holden in Ellis v. Hamlen, 3 Taunt. 52, and it is apparent, in such cases, that if the house has not been built in the manner specified in the contract, the work has not been done. The party has no more performed what he contracted to perform, than he who has contracted to labor for a certain period, and failed to complete the time.

It is in truth virtually conceded in such cases that the work has not been done, for if it had been, the party performing it would be entitled to recover upon the contract itself, which it is held he cannot do.

Those cases are not to be distinguished, in principle, from the present, unless it be in the circumstance, that where the party has contracted to furnish materials, and do certain labor, as to build a house in a specified manner, if it is not done according to the contract, the party for whom it is built may refuse to receive it — elect to take no benefit from what has been performed — and therefore if he does receive, he shall be bound to pay the value — whereas in a contract for labor, merely, from day to day, the party is continually receiving the benefit of the contract under an expectation that it will be fulfilled, and cannot, upon the breach of it, have an election to refuse to receive what has been done, and thus discharge himself from payment.

But we think this difference in the nature of the contracts does not justify the application of a different rule in relation to them.

The party who contracts for labor merely, for a certain period, does so with full knowledge that he must, from the nature of the case, be accepting part performance from day to day, if the other party commences the performance, and with knowledge also that the other may eventually fail of completing the entire term.

If under such circumstances he actually receives a benefit from the labor performed, over and above the damage occasioned by the failure to complete, there is as much reason why he should pay the reasonable worth of what has thus been done for his benefit, as there is when he enters and occupies the house which has been built for him, but not according to the stipulations of the contract, and which he perhaps enters, not because he is satisfied with what has been done, but because circumstances compel him to accept it such as it is, that he should pay for the value of the house.

Where goods are sold upon a special contract as to their nature, quality, and price, and have been used before their inferiority has been discovered, or other circumstances have occured which have rendered it impracticable or inconvenient for the vendee to rescind the contract in toto, it seems to have been the practice formerly to allow the vendor to recover the stipulated price, and the vendee recovered by a cross action damages for the breach of the contract.

> But according to the later and more convenient practice, the vendee in such case is allowed, in an action for the price, to give evidence of the inferiority of the goods in reduction of damages, and the plaintiff who has broken his contract is not entitled to recover more than the value of the benefits which the defendant has actually derived from the goods; and where the latter has derived no benefit, the plaintiff cannot recover at all.

2 Stark. Ev. 640, 642; 1 Starkie's Rep. 107, Okell v. Smith.

So where a person contracts for the purchase of a quantity of merchandize, at a certain price, and receives a delivery of part only, and he keeps that part, without any offer of a return, it has been held that he must pay the value of it. 5 Barn. & Cres. Shipton v. Casson; Com. Dig. Action F. Baker v. Sutton; 1 Camp. 55 note.

A different opinion seems to have been entertained, 5 Bos. & Pul. 61, Waddington v. Oliver, and a different decision was had, 2 Stark. Rep. 281, Walker v. Dixon.

There is a close analogy between all these classes of cases, in which such diverse decisions have been made.

If the party who has contracted to receive merchandise, takes a part and uses it, in expectation that the whole will be delivered, which is never done, there seems to be no greater reason that he should pay for what he has received, than there is that the party who has received labor in part, under similar circumstances, should pay the value of what has been done for his benefit.

It is said, that in those cases where the plaintiff has been permitted to recover there was an acceptance of what has been done. The answer is, that where the contract is to labor from day to day, for a certain period, the party for whom the labor is done in truth stipulates to receive it from day to day, as it is performed, and although the other may not eventually do all he has contracted to do, there has been, necessarily, an acceptance of what has been done in pursuance of the contract, and the party must have understood when he made the contract that there was to be such acceptance.

If then the party stipulates in the outset to receive part performance from time to time, with a knowledge that the whole may not be completed, we see no reason why he should not equally be holden to pay for the amount of value received, as where he afterwards takes the benefit of what has been done, with a knowledge that the whole which was contracted for has not been performed.

In neither case has the contract been performed. In neither can an action be sustained on the original contract.

In both the party has assented to receive what is done. The only difference is, that in the one case the assent is prior, with a knowledge that all may not be performed, in the other is it subsequent, with a knowledge that the whole has not been accomplished.

We have no hesitation in holding that the same rule should be applied to both classes of cases, especially, as the operation of the rule will be to make the party who has failed to fulfil his contract, liable to such amount of damages as the other party has sustained, instead of subjecting him to an entire loss for partial failure, and thus making the amount received in many cases wholly disproportionate to the injury. 1 Saund. 320, c; 2 Stark. Evid. 643.

It is as "hard upon the plaintiff to preclude him from recovering at all, because he has failed as to part of his entire undertaking," where his contract is to labor for a certain period, as it can be in any other description of contract, provided the defendant has received a benefit and value from the labor actually performed.

We hold then, that where a party undertakes to pay upon a special contract for the performance of labor, or the furnishing of materials, he is not to be charged upon such special agreement until the money is earned according to the terms of it, and where the parties have made an express contract the law will not imply and raise a contract different from that which the parties have entered into, except upon some farther transaction between the parties.

In case of a failure to perform such special contract, by the default of the party contracting to do the service, if the money is not due by the terms of the special agreement he is not entitled to recover for his labor, or for the materials furnished, unless the other party receives what has been done, or furnished, and upon the whole case derives a benefit from it. 14 Mass. 282, Taft v. Montague; 2 Stark. Ev. 644.

But if, where a contract is made of such a character, a party actually receives labor, or materials, and thereby derives a benefit and advantage, over and above the damage which has resulted from the breach of the contract by the other party, the labor actually done, and the value received, furnish a new consideration, and the law thereupon raises a promise to pay to the extent of the reasonable worth of such excess. This may be considered as making a new case, one not within the original agreement, and the party is entitled to "recover on his new case, for the work done, not as agreed, but yet accepted by the defendant." 1 Dane's Abr. 224.

If on such failure to perform the whole, the nature of the contract be such that the employer can reject what has been done, and refuse to receive any benefit from the part performance, he is entitled so to do, and in such case is not liable to be charged, unless he has before assented to and accepted of what has been done, however much the other party may have done towards the performance. He has in such case received nothing, and having contracted to receive nothing but the entire matter contracted for, he is not bound to pay, because his express promise was only to pay on receiving the whole, and having actually received nothing the law cannot and ought not to raise an implied promise to pay. But where the party receives value — takes and uses the materials, or has advantage from the labor, he is liable to pay the reasonable worth of what he has received. 1 Camp. 38, Farnsworth v. Garrard. And the rule is the same whether it was received and accepted by the assent of the party prior to the breach, under a contract by which, from its nature, he was to receive labor, from time to time until the completion of the whole contract; or whether it was received and accepted by an assent subsequent to the performance of all which was in fact done. If he received it under such circumstances as precluded him from rejecting it afterwards, that does not alter the case — it has still been received by his assent.

In fact we think the technical reasoning, that the performance of the whole labor is a condition precedent, and the right to recover any thing dependent upon it — that the contract being entire there can be no apportionment — and that there being an express contract no other can be implied, even upon the subsequent performance of service — is not properly applicable to this species of contract, where a beneficial service has been actually performed; for we have abundant reason to believe, that the general understanding of the community is, that the hired laborer shall be entitled to compensation for the service actually performed, though he do not continue the entire term contracted for, and such contracts must be presumed to be made with reference to that understanding, unless an express stipulation shows the contrary.

Where a beneficial service has been performed and received, therefore, under contracts of this kind, the mutual agreements cannot be considered as going to the whole of the consideration, so as to make them mutual conditions, the one precedent to the other, without a specific proviso to that effect. . . .

It is easy, if parties so choose, to provide by an express agreement that nothing shall be earned, if the laborer leaves his employer without having performed the whole service contemplated, and then there can be no pretense for a recovery if he voluntarily deserts the service before the expiration of the time.

The amount, however, for which the employer ought to be charged, where the laborer abandons his contract, is only the reasonable worth, or the amount of advantage he receives upon the whole transaction (ante 15, Wadleigh v. Sutton,) and, in estimating the value of the labor, the contract price for the service cannot be exceeded. . . .

If a person makes a contract fairly he is entitled to have it fully performed, and if this is not done he is entitled to damages. He may maintain a suit to recover the amount of damage sustained by the non performance.

The benefit and advantage which the party takes by the labor, therefore, is the amount of value he receives, if any, after deducting the amount of damage; and if he elects to put this in defence he is entitled so to do, and the implied promise which the law will raise, in such case, is to pay such amount of the stipulated price for the whole labor, as remains after deducting what it would cost to procure a completion of the residue of the service, and also any damage which has been sustained by reason of the non fulfilment of the contract.

If in such case it be found that the damages are equal to, or greater than the amount of the labor performed, so that the employer, having a right to the full performance of the contract, has not upon the whole case received a beneficial service, the plaintiff cannot recover.

This rule, by binding the employer to pay the value of the service he actually receives, and the laborer to answer in damages where he does not complete the entire contract, will leave no temptation to the former to drive the laborer from his service, near the close of his term, by ill treatment, in order to escape from payment; nor to the latter to desert his service before the stipulated time, without a sufficient reason; and it will in most instances settle the whole controversy in one action, and prevent a multiplicity of suits and cross actions.

There may be instances, however, where the damage occasioned is much greater than the value of the labor performed, and if the party elects to permit himself to be charged for the value of the labor, without interposing the damages in defense, he is entitled to do so, and may have an action to recover his damages for the nonperformance, whatever, they may be. 1 Mason's Rep. Crowninshield v. Robinson.

And he may commence such action at any time after the contract is broken, notwithstanding no suit has been instituted against him; but if he elects to have the damages considered in the action against him, he must be understood as conceding that they are not to be extended beyond the amount of what he has received, and he cannot afterwards sustain an action for farther damages.

Applying the principles thus laid down, to this case, the plaintiff is entitled to judgment on the verdict.

The defendant sets up a mere breach of the contract in defence of the action, but this cannot avail him. He does not appear to have offered evidence to show that he was damnified by such breach, or to have asked that a deduction should be made upon that account. The direction to the jury was therefore correct, that the plaintiff was entitled to recover as much as the labor performed was reasonably worth, and the jury appear to have allowed a pro rata compensation, for the time which the plaintiff labored in the defendant's service.

As the defendant has not claimed or had any adjustment of damages, for the breach of the contract, in this action, if he has actually sustained damage he is still entitled to a suit to recover the amount.

Whether it is not necessary, in cases of this kind, that notice should be given to the employer that the contract is abandoned, with an offer of adjustment and demand of payment; and whether the laborer must not wait until the time when the money would have been due according to the contract, before commencing an action, (5 B. & P. 61) are questions not necessary to be settled in this case, no objections of that nature having been taken here.

Judgment on the verdict.

NOTE

1. Handerson, arguing for the defendant, conceded that "in modern times courts have, to a certain extent, relaxed from the strict rules formerly adopted, and have sustained a count in quantum meruit in cases where the plaintiff had not fully performed his contract." The "relaxation" had taken place, he went on, both in construction contracts — "contracts to build a house, a bridge, or a highway" — and in contracts for the sale of goods where the seller delivers only a part of what he has agreed to deliver and the buyer keeps the part that has been delivered. The reason for allowing the quantum meruit recovery, he suggested, was the same in both types of cases: in the construction contract, the party for whom the work was being done allowed the defective work to continue when he could have stopped it; in the contract of sale, the buyer could have returned the goods. The employment contract in the case at bar differed from these other types of contract in that the employer could not refuse the labor as it was performed day by day and of course could not return it after the laborer quit. Handerson concluded with a rhetorical flourish: "To hold out inducements to men to violate their contracts, when fairly entered into, is of immoral tendency. . . ."

2. Parker, J., rejected the argument that different rules could apply to different types of contracts in favor of what might be called a unitary approach. In the following principal case, Smith v. Brady, Comstock, J., for the New York court, also adopted a unitary approach, with somewhat different results. The Massachusetts court seems to have been less concerned with logical consistency. In Stark v. Parker, 2 Pick. 149 (Mass. 1824), an employment case quite like Britton v. Turner on its facts, no recovery was allowed; in Hayward v. Leonard, 8 Pick. 178 (Mass. 1828), the quantum meruit recovery was allowed in the setting of a defectively performed construction contract. Hayward v. Leonard is discussed at some length in Comstock's opinion in Smith v. Brady, see p. 1032 *infra*. See further the Note on Massachusetts cases, p. 1050 *infra*.

3. A Note to a reprint of Britton v. Turner in 26 American Decisions (1881) commented at 722:

> [T]he doctrines of Britton v. Turner are . . . opposed to the general current of authority. . . . The case is, however, . . . the law in New Hampshire. Its masterly argument in support of its rulings have commended it to other courts, which, while recognizing the equity of the conclusions reached, deem it an unmistakable innovation upon the rules of the common law.

4. Even in New Hampshire in 1831, a year's labor was worth more than $120. The case evidently involved the familiar figure of the "hired man," who received his board and lodging and, perhaps, clothing, along with a small cash payment which was customarily paid at the end of the year. (The New York and Massachusetts cases — Lantry v. Parks and Stark v. Parker — which denied recovery involved the same situation.)

5. A large law firm has for many years distributed to its associates a "Christmas bonus" equivalent to a month's salary. Do you think that an associate who worked from January until the end of October and then quit should be entitled to claim $\frac{10}{12}$ of the Christmas bonus?

6. Do you think this is a fair statement of Parker's position in Britton v. Turner: "In any contractual situation, the value of any benefit received must be paid for even though the person conferring the benefit was in gross and willful violation of his contractual obligations." If it is a fair statement, do you agree with it?

SMITH v. BRADY
17 N.Y. 173 (1858)

[The contract was for the construction of several buildings, apparently residential. Progress payments were provided for and made. The final payment was to be made when the work was "completed and certified by the architect to that effect." Without having procured the architect's

certificate, the builder brought an action to recover the final payment.
The case was heard by a referee who concluded that the defendant had
waived the production of the architect's certificate by taking possession of
the buildings. In the hearing before the referee it appeared that the
plaintiff had not in all respects complied with the contract specifications.
Over objection the referee admitted testimony offered by the plaintiff to
show that the buildings, as constructed, were "sufficiently strong" for the
purpose they were designed to serve. The referee excluded testimony
offered by the defendant to show what it would cost to make the buildings
conform to the specifications. On the referee's report judgment was entered for plaintiff. The judgment was for the amount of the final payment, less $212.57, which was, the referee found, the "value" of the
defects in the construction.

The report of the case is extremely curious. After a brief procedural
statement there is printed an opinion by Harris, J., in which four other
judges (making up a majority of the court) "concurred." The opinion by
Harris, J., seems to have been, as we would say, "the opinion of the
court." There is then printed what would seem to be a concurring opinion by Comstock, J. (who is not listed as having "concurred" in the Harris
opinion). Finally, we are told that "all the judges concurred" in the Comstock opinion. Except that both Harris and Comstock were for reversing
the judgment for plaintiff, the two opinions are hopelessly inconsistent.
In the subsequent history of the case, "the rule of Smith v. Brady" always
meant the Comstock opinion, the Harris opinion being ignored. Harris
took the position that the plaintiff had "substantially executed" the contract but could not recover because of his failure to produce the architect's certificate. He also said that the referee was in error both in admitting the plaintiff's testimony (that the buildings were "sufficiently strong")
and in excluding the defendant's testimony on the cost of repair. It is
impossible to make out from the opinion whether Harris thought that the
plaintiff should recover nothing (because of the missing certificate) or
should recover the balance of the contract price less the cost of repairs
(which, at one point, he described as "the true rule of damages"). Comstock, in the concurring opinion, hardly referred to the architect's certificate and certainly did not make the plaintiff's failure to produce it a
ground of decision. In the first part of his opinion Comstock dealt with
the difficulty that defendant's counsel had not, by appropriate objections,
laid the foundation for "a review in this court of the decisions made
against him." Having by some nimble footwork got round that roadblock,
he went on:]

COMSTOCK, J. . . . . It was one of the specifications of the contract that
the "nailing joists" in the frames of the cottages were to be twelve inches
apart, measuring from centre to centre. The defendant's evidence tended
to show that these joists were in fact placed sixteen inches apart; that, in
consequence of this departure from the specification, the number of

joists used in all the buildings was less by about two hundred than the contract called for; that this defect in the work affected the value, strength and substantial character of the buildings. It appeared, also, that there was a similar breach of contract in respect to the distances between the beams in the third floor of the houses, being in fact twenty-four inches apart, while the contract allowed only sixteen. To meet the defence so far as it depended on these particular departures from the contract, the plaintiff was allowed to call other mechanics and ask them as follows: "Are the houses without these deficient joists and beams, sufficiently strong for the character of the buildings? The evidence was objected to on the part of the defendant, but the objection was overruled, the plaintiff's counsel stating that the object of the inquiry was to ascertain what damages, if any, should be allowed by reason of this deficiency in the work. This ruling of the referee was duly excepted to; and the evidence being given tended to show that the houses were sufficiently strong, that the joists and beams were placed at distances customary in that neighborhood, and that the defendant really was not injured at all by this violation of the contract. The question now to be determined is whether this evidence was proper; and this will, I think, involve the inquiry whether the plaintiff, having failed in substantially performing the contract, was entitled to recover for his work and materials, making to the defendant an allowance for the breaches, to be adjusted according to some principle of equity. The violation of the contract in several particulars had already appeared when this ruling was made. Indeed, the evidence itself, so offered, objected to and received, assumed that the contract had been departed from in respect to a specification about which it was impossible to err innocently. In avowing the object for which it was offered, the plaintiff necessarily assumed that a breach of the contract, instead of being fatal to a recovery, was the subject of equitable compensation merely; and in receiving such evidence the referee must have sustained that assumption. The defendant having chosen to require, in the plain letter of the contract, that there should be in each building a certain number of joists and beams placed at certain distances from each other, the plaintiff had no right to substitute another plan for this part of the work; nor could he justify his willful departure from the contract by the opinion of other builders, or by any custom whether local or general. All this is extremely evident; yet, if the only consequence of so violating a contract of this kind is, that the injured party shall be compensated in damages, there was no error in receiving the evidence. Upon the mere question of compensation that evidence bore with entire directness and force. We are therefore obliged to consider this question of law in a building contract, where performance is to precede payment and becomes a condition thereof, can the builder, having failed to perform on his part, recover for his work or materials, making to the other party a compensatory allowance for the wrong done to him, it being also a further condition of the question that the employer chooses to occupy and enjoy the erection rather than to remove or require the builder to remove it from his premises?

The right to recover in such a case has never been referred to any doctrine peculiar to such contracts. On the contrary, if we look at the adjudged cases, we shall find that the right, whenever asserted by judicial tribunals, has been supposed to result from a general doctrine applicable as well to other contracts. In Hayward v. Leonard (7 Pick., 181), the action was on a conditional note, to be void if the plaintiff failed to perform an agreement of the same date, by which he undertook to build a house for the defendant of a certain size and in a specified manner. The defence was that the house, although built within the time agreed on, was not in workmanship and materials according to the contract. Chief Justice Parker said:

> The point in controversy seems to be this: whether, where a party has entered into a special contract to perform work for another and to furnish materials, and the work is done and the materials furnished, but not in the manner stipulated for in the contract, so that he cannot recover the price agreed by action on that contract, yet, nevertheless, the work and materials are of some value and benefit to the other contracting party, he may recover on a quantum meruit for the labor, and on a quantum valebant for the materials.

He adds:

> We think the weight of modern authority is in favor of the action, and that, upon the whole, it is conformable to justice that the party who has the possession and enjoyment of the labor and materials of another shall be held to pay for them, so as in all events he shall lose nothing by the breach of the contract.

In that case, there were some special facts, but the decision seemed to turn essentially on the general principle suggested in the remarks quoted, and the principle was more emphatically approved by the same court in the subsequent case of Smith v. The First Congregational Meeting House in Lowell (8 Pick., 178), which was also upon a building contract.

It will be convenient next to cite a case directly opposed which arose in the English Common Pleas, and was tried before Sir James Mansfield. (Ellis v. Hamlin, 3 Taunt., 52.) The action was by a builder against his employer. The defence was, and the evidence supported it, that the plaintiff had omitted to put into the building certain joists and other materials. The plaintiff failing to prove performance of the special agreement resorted to a general count for work, labor and materials, claiming that the defendant having the benefit of the houses, was bound at least to pay for them according to their value. But Chief Justice Mansfield repudiated that doctrine. He said:

> The defendant agreed to have a building of such and such dimensions. Is he to have his ground covered with buildings of no use, which he would be glad to see removed, and is he to be forced to pay for them besides? It is said he has the benefit of the houses, and therefore the plaintiff is entitled to recover on a quantum valebant. To be sure it is hard that he should build houses and not be paid for them but the difficulty is to know where to draw the line, for if the defendant is obliged to pay for one deviation from his contract he may equally be obliged to pay for anything how far soever distant from what the contract stipulated for.

The plaintiff was accordingly nonsuited; and as the reporter states, the case was never moved again.

The two cases in Massachusetts above cited, and the one before Sir James Mansfield, were referred to in Britton v. Turner (6 N.H., 481). That was a very elaborately considered case. The plaintiff had agreed to work for the defendant for one year, and the defendant was to pay for that labor one hundred and twenty dollars. The plaintiff abandoned his contract without cause before the year was out. It was nevertheless held that he could recover as much as the labor was reasonably worth, there being no evidence of any special damages sustained by the defendant in consequence of the non-performance of the contract. The two cases in Massachusetts were cited with approbation by the court, while that before Chief Justice Mansfield was necessarily disapproved. In referring to that class of cases arising on building contracts, it was observed that such cases could not be distinguished from the one then under consideration.

> unless it be in the circumstance that when a party has contracted to furnish materials and do certain labor as to build a house in a specified manner, if it is not done according to the contract the party for whom it is built may refuse to receive it, elect to take no benefit from what has been performed, and therefore if he does receive it he shall be bound to pay the value, whereas in a contract for labor merely, from day to day, the party is continually receiving the benefit of the contract under an expectation that it will be fulfilled, and cannot upon the breach of it have an election to refuse to receive what has been done, and thus discharge himself from payment.

"But we think," the court proceeded to say, "this difference in the nature of the contracts does not justify the application of a different rule in relation to them." "There was just as much reason," it was added,

> why the employer should pay the reasonable worth of what has been done for his benefit as there is when he enters and occupies the house which has been built for him but not according to the stipulations of the contract, and

which he perhaps enters, not because he is satisfied with what has been
done, but because circumstances compel him to accept it such as it is, that
he should pay for the value of the house.

There are few cases to be found in the books more consistently reasoned
than this one in the Supreme Court of New Hampshire, although the
decision stands directly opposed to the settled law of this state. I have
referred to it, as well as the Massachusetts cases, somewhat at large, in
order to show that the supposed liability of a person who enters and
occupies a building erected on his ground to pay the builder, although
the latter failed in performing his contract, has always been referred to
the general doctrine that benefits received and retained under a contract
must be paid for without regard to the conditions of the contract itself. I
am confident that no case can be found in which the building contractor's right to recover has been maintained on the ground that the owner
by the mere possession and occupancy of the building has waived the
condition of performance.

The true inquiry then is, whether there is in the law of contracts in
general any such doctrine as that upon which the cases referred to in
New Hampshire and Massachusetts were determined. To those cases
others might be added proceeding essentially on the same ground; yet the
rule, I think, is quite well settled the other way. It is certainly so in this
state. (McMillan v. Vanderlip, 12 John., 165; Thorpe v. White, 13 id., 53;
Jennings v. Camp, id., 94, Champlin v. Rowley, 13 Wend., 258; S. C. in
error, 18 id., 187; Paige v. Ott, 5 Denio, 406; Pike v. Butler, 4 Comst. 360;
Pullman v. Corning, 5 Seld., 93.) Among these cases Champlin v. Rowley
may be referred to as a decisive determination of the question. The action
was to recover the price of hay sold and delivered. The plaintiff had
agreed to deliver the defendant one hundred tons of pressed hay between
the date of the contract and the close of navigation of the Hudson river,
$100 to be paid in advance and the residue when the whole should be
delivered. About fifty tons were delivered before the navigation closed,
when the further delivery was interrupted. The defendant sold or used
the quantity which he received under contract. The $100 due in advance
having been paid, it was held by the Supreme Court that entire performance was the condition of any further payment, and therefore that the
plaintiff could not recover. The case was very carefully considered, on
error, in the court of last resort, where the judgment was affirmed. The
case cited in the Supreme Court of New Hampshire was referred to, and
that, as well as the class of cases to which it belongs, were expressly
overruled. Indeed, in this state the sanctity of contracts in this respect at
least, has been steadily maintained, and no encouragement has ever been
given to that loose and dangerous doctrine which allows a person to
violate his most solemn engagements and then to draw the injured into a
controversy concerning the amount and value of the benefits received.

I think the principles which have with us been so uniformly asserted should have a peculiar application in contracts like the one under consideration. I suppose it will be conceded that every one has a right to build his house, his cottage or his store after such a model and in such style as shall best accord with his notions of utility or be most agreeable to his fancy. The specifications of the contract become the law between the parties until voluntarily changed. If the owner prefers a plain and simple Doric column, and has so provided in the agreement, the contractor has no right to put in its place the more costly and elegant Corinthian. If the owner, having regard to strength and durability, has contracted for walls of specified materials to be laid in a particular manner, or for a given number of joists and beams, the builder has no right to substitute his own judgment or that of others. Having departed from the agreement, if performance has not been waived by the other party, the law will not allow him to allege that he has made as good a building as the one he engaged to erect. He can demand payment only upon and according to the terms of his contract, and if the conditions on which payment is due have not been performed, then the right to demand it does not exist. To hold a different doctrine would be simply to make another contract, and would be giving to parties an encouragement to violate their engagements, which the just policy of the law does not permit.

Cases of this kind must not be confounded with others having, perhaps, a slight resemblance but no real analogy. No doubt a person may voluntarily accept a benefit under a contract of which the conditions precedent have not been performed by the other party, and he may do this in such circumstances that a new obligation to pay for the benefit will arise. Thus, if A. should agree to manufacture and deliver to B. a carriage of a particular kind and should make a different one, B. may elect whether he will take it or not. Until he so elects, he has no property in the fabric. If he voluntarily accepts the article, he thereby either waives the objections which he might make to it and is liable to pay for it according to his contract, or a new assumpsit arises from the act of acceptance as though no previous agreement had existed. The case cited on the argument of Vanderbilt v. The Eagle Iron Works (25 Wend., 665) was determined very distinctly upon these principles.

But the rule, as it is well settled with us, allows a party to retain without compensation the benefits of a partial performance, where from the nature of the contract he must receive such benefits in advance of a full performance, and by its terms or just construction he is under no obligation to pay until the performance is complete. Thus, if a person engages to perform a year's labor for another, and payment is to be made when the labor is done, in such a case the employer necessarily receives the benefit of each day's service when it is done, yet if the laborer without just cause abandons the service at any time, however short, before the year has expired he can recover no part of his wages. (Cases, *supra.*) So the contract may be to sell and deliver goods at different times, to be paid for when the whole are received. If the vendor refuses to perform entirely, without good cause, the purchaser is neither bound to pay for nor to return the goods received in part performance. (Champlin v. Rowley, *supra*.) If A. should agree to plow the field of B., consisting of twenty acres, at a given price for the whole service, or at so much per acre to be paid when the service is done, and after plowing nineteen acres should abandon the contract, he can recover nothing for his work. The owner of the field may enter, sow it with his grain and reap the harvest, thus enjoying fully the benefits of the part performance. In so doing he waives nothing; because he cannot reasonably do otherwise. He is not obliged to abandon his field in order to be enabled to insist upon the condition of the contract. Closely analogous is the case of a building contract. The owner of the soil is always in possession. The builder has a right to enter only for the special purpose of performing his contract. Each material as it is placed in the work becomes annexed to the soil, and thereby the property of the owner. The builder would have no right to remove the brick or stone or lumber after annexation, even if the employer should unjustifiably refuse to allow him to proceed with the work. The owner, from the nature and necessity of the case, takes the benefit of part performance, and therefore by merely so doing does not necessarily waive anything contained in the contract. To impute him a voluntary waiver of conditions precedent from the mere use and occupation of the building erected, unattended by other circumstances, is unreasonable and illogical because he is not in a situation to elect whether he will or will not accept the benefit of an imperfect performance. To be enabled to stand upon the contract he cannot reasonably be required to tear down and destroy the edifice if he prefers it to remain. As the erection is his by annexation to the soil he may suffer it to stand, and there is no rule of law against his using it without prejudice to his rights.

The present case was evidently tried upon an erroneous theory of the law. Although partial payments were to be made as the work proceeded under the contracts, yet the consideration and condition of those payments was the performance of the work according to plans and specifications, and in the best and most workmanlike manner, and the final payments were not to be made until after all the work was completed and certified by the architects. Although the contracts were not performed, the plaintiff has recovered all the installments, less the sum which the referee allowed as damages for the non-performance. In receiving the evidence as to the value and strength of the buildings, notwithstanding non-performance of the contracts, evidence which could have no bearing except upon the question of damages, it is manifest that he proceeded upon views on the law in such cases which I have endeavored to show are unsound.

It is not necessary to give any opinion upon the question whether the referee might properly find upon the evidence that the defendant waived the conditions of the contract by any express approval of the work, or by any other interference or conduct on his part. We only say that, according to the settled law in this state, the plaintiff cannot recover the payments which by the terms or true construction of the contract are due only on condition of performance by him, unless he can show such performance or prove that it has been waived. And the law does not adjudge that a mere silent occupation of the building by the owner amounts to a waiver, nor does it deny to him the right so to occupy and still insist upon the contract. The question of waiver of the condition precedent will always be one of intention to be arrived at from all the circumstances, including the occupancy.

To conclude, there is, in a just view of the question, no hardship in requiring builders, like all other men, to perform their contracts in order to entitle themselves to payment, where the employer has agreed to pay only on that condition. It is true that such contracts embrace a variety of particulars, and that slight omissions and inadvertences sometimes very innocently occur. These should be indulgently regarded, and they will be so regarded by courts and juries. But there can be no injustice in imputing to the contractor a knowledge of what his contract requires, nor in holding him to a substantial performance. If he has stipulated for walls of a given material and with a hard inside finish, he knows what he is to do and must perform it. If he has engaged for a given number and size of windows, joists, beams and sills, he cannot, with the specifications before him, innocently depart from his contract. If he fails to perform when the requirement is plain, and when he can perform if he will, he has no right to call upon the courts to make a new contract for him; nor ought he to complain if the law leaves him without remedy.

The judgment should be reversed and a new trial granted.

All the judges concurred in this opinion.

Judgment reversed, and new trial ordered.

NOTE

1. Harris, J., and the referee were in disagreement whether the "true rule of damages" (assuming that plaintiff was entitled to recover anything) was the "difference in value" or "the cost to repair." On this point, see Note 6 following Jacob & Youngs v. Kent, *infra* p. 1042. Under the Comstock opinion, plaintiff, of course, recovers nothing.

2. In the principal case it appears that various progress payments had been made in course of construction, so that only the final payment was involved in the litigation. Does it seem to follow, at least from the logic of Comstock's opinion, that plaintiff would still recover nothing even if no progress payments had been made (so that the entire contract price was

in dispute)? Does it seem to follow, further, that the defendant, if he were so advised, could have counter-claimed for the recovery of the progress payments made? What do you think of Comstock's hypothetical about A quitting after plowing 19 of the 20 acres?

3. We are not told what the contract price was, what the progress payments amounted to or what the amount of the final payment was. Assume that the final payment represented 10 per cent of the contract price. Assume further that plaintiff's breach had been not only intentional or wilful but also substantial. Whatever you may think about Comstock's rhetoric or moral philosophy, do you feel that the result in the case, on the assumptions stated, is bad? If you think it is bad, what result would you prefer, still on the same assumptions?

AVERY v. WILSON, 81 N.Y. 341 (1880). Contract for the sale of 699 boxes of glass, to be delivered all at one time. The seller delivered and the buyer accepted 365 boxes, the partial delivery having been made at the buyer's request. Subsequently the parties fell into dispute on the true meaning of the contract. Eventually the seller offered to complete the contract but the buyer refused to accept the remainder of the boxes on the ground that the time for performance had long since expired. Seller brought an action to recover for the 365 boxes delivered. Buyer, without making any counterclaim for damages, defended on the ground that seller, having only partially performed, could recover nothing. Miller, J., commented that: "The general rule in this State is that no action lies upon a special contract for the price agreed upon, until performance of such contract." He then rehearsed Comstock's opinion in Smith v. Brady at some length. The conclusion, however, was that: "While the defendants were not bound to accept a delivery of a portion of the boxes of glass, and had a right to reject or retain the same as they saw fit, yet if they elected to receive the part delivered, appropriated the same to their own use, and by their acts evinced that they waived this condition [of full performance], they became liable to pay for what was actually delivered." 81 N.Y. at 345. On the facts of the case, the court concluded, there had been a waiver.

In subsequent sales cases the New York courts obediently went through the two-way stretch required by what came to be known as "the rule in Avery v. Wilson": first reciting the "rule" (from Comstock's Smith v. Brady opinion) that "a party may retain, without compensation, the benefits of a partial performance, where, from the nature of the contract, he must receive such benefits in advance of a full performance, and by its terms or just construction is under no obligation to pay until the performance is complete," and then finding, as in Avery v. Wilson, that the defendant had waived his rights. The defendants, of course, protested strenuously, but to no avail, that the idea of waiver had never crossed their minds and would have immediately been rejected if it had. The only case in which the "rule of Avery v. Wilson" was applied, without a waiver being found, seems to be Kelso & Co. v. Ellis, 224 N.Y. 528, 121 N.E. 364 (1918), in which the facts were, to say the least, unusual. As part of an advertising promotion scheme, the defendant storeowner was to receive various prizes to be given away to winners of a "contest." The principal prize was a piano. Some of the lesser prizes (gift certificates, silver flat-ware) were delivered but the piano never was. Judge Pound commented that "the contest without a piano was like the play of Hamlet with the part of Hamlet left out." Consequently, under the rule of Avery v. Wilson, the defendant need not pay for the silverware. The defendant had, however, given its negotiable promissory notes to the originator of the advertising scheme. The Avery v. Wilson defense was held not to be available against a holder in due course of the notes, and the case remanded for further proceedings to determine whether the plaintiff was a holder in due course.

Avery v. Wilson employed the doctrine of waiver to avoid applying the rule in Smith v. Brady. Another escape, in sales cases, was to hold that contracts under which partial deliveries were either provided for or per-mitted were not "entire" contracts but were "separable" or "divisible" contracts. It is fair to say that, in the law of sales, the "rule of Smith v. Brady," translated to "the rule of Avery v. Wilson," has enjoyed at most a literary existence. See further, however, Amtorg Trading Corp. v. Miehle Printing Press & Mfg. Co., digested *infra* p. 1055, and the Note following that case.

The escape from Smith v. Brady by holding a contract to be "divisible" was, of course, equally available (and equally availed of) in employment contract cases. As soon as it came to be felt that an employee's wages were meant to be paid by the month or by the week or by the day the problem in cases like Britton v. Turner disappeared. Except of course for the shorter periods: if you agree to work from Monday to Friday, to be paid at the end of the week, and quit on Wednesday, are you entitled to three days' wages? At all events, Britton v. Turner and its analogues disap-peared from litigation after 1850 or so — which is not to say that the underlying problem disappeared.

CLARK v. WEST, 193 N.Y. 349, 86 N.E. 1 (1908). Clark was under contract to West to write a series of law books. If the manuscript was satisfactory, West was to pay Clark two dollars a page; furthermore, after publication of each book, he was to pay Clark additional royalties up to four dollars a page. Clark was to get one-sixth of the "net receipts" of sales of the books until the maximum of six dollars a page had been reached. The contract further provided that:

> [Clark] agrees to totally abstain from the use of intoxicating liquors during the continuance of this contract, and that the payment to him in accor-

dance with the terms of this contract of any money in excess of $2 per page is dependent on the faithful performance of this as well as the other conditions of this contract.

Clark completed a book (of 3,469 pages) known as "Clark and Marshall on Corporations" which West published, paying Clark only the two dollars a page. Clark brought an action for an accounting in which he alleged that West had received "large net receipts" from the sale of the book. Clark alleged full performance of his agreement with West, except that he "did not totally abstain from the use of intoxicating liquors during the continuance of the contract; but such use by the plaintiff was not excessive and did not prevent or interfere with the due and full performance by the plaintiff of all the other stipulations in said contract." Clark further alleged that West, knowing of Clark's use of liquor, had expressly waived the condition of total abstinence. West demurred to the complaint and its demurrer was sustained by the Appellate Division. The Court of Appeals held that the demurrer should have been overruled and remanded the case for further proceedings. The opinion by Werner, J., contains the following discussion of waiver (193 N.Y. at 359-361):

"This whole discussion is predicated, of course, upon the theory of an express waiver. We assume that no waiver could be implied from the defendant's mere acceptance of the books and his payment of the sum of $2 per page without objection. It was the defendant's duty to pay that amount in any event after acceptance of the work. The plaintiff must stand upon his allegation of an express waiver, and if he fails to establish that he cannot maintain his action.

"The theory upon which the defendant's attitude seems to be based is that, even if he has represented to the plaintiff that he would not insist upon the condition that the latter should observe total abstinence from intoxicants, he can still refuse to pay the full contract price for his work. The inequity of this position becomes apparent when we consider that this contract was to run for a period of years, during a large portion of which the plaintiff was to be entitled only to the advance payment of $2 per page; the balance being contingent, among other things, upon publication of the books and returns from sales. Upon this theory the defendant might have waived the condition while the first book was in process of production, and yet, when the whole work was completed, he would still be in a position to insist upon the forfeiture because there had not been strict performance. Such a situation is possible in a case where the subject of the waiver is the very consideration of a contract (Organ v. Stewart, 60 N.Y. 413, 420), but not where the waiver relates to something that can be waived. In the case at bar, as we have seen, the waiver is not of the consideration or subject-matter, but of an incident to the method of performance. The consideration remains the same. The defendant has had the work he bargained for, and it is alleged that he has waived one of the conditions as to the manner in which it was to have been done. He might have insisted upon literal performance, and then he could have stood upon the letter of his contract. If, however, he has waived that incidental condition, he has created a situation to which the doctrine of waiver very precisely applies.

"The cases which present the most familiar phases of the doctrine of waiver are those which have arisen out of litigation over insurance policies where the defendants have claimed a forfeiture because of the breach of some condition in the contract (Insurance Co. v. Norton, 96 U.S. 234, 24 L. Ed. 689; Titus v. Glens Falls Ins. Co., 81 N.Y. 410; Kiernan v. Dutchess Co. Mut. Insurance Co., 150 N.Y. 190, 44 N.E. 698), but it is a doctrine of general application which is confined to no particular class of cases. A "waiver" has been defined to be the intentional relinquishment of a known right. It is voluntary and implies an election to dispense with something of value, or forego some advantage which the party waiving it might at its option have demanded or insisted upon (Herman on Estoppel & Res Adjudicata, vol. 2, p. 954; Cowenhoven v. Ball, 118 N.Y. 234, 23 N.E. 470), and this definition is supported by many cases in this and other states. In the recent case of Draper v. Oswego Co. Fire R. Ass'n, 190 N.Y. 12, 16, 82 N.E. 755, Chief Judge Cullen, in speaking for the court upon this subject, said:

> While that doctrine and the doctrine of equitable estoppel are often confused in insurance litigation, there is a clear distinction between the two. A "waiver" is the voluntary abandonment or relinquishment by a party of some right or advantage. As said by my Brother Vann in the *Kiernan Case*, 150 N.Y. 190, 44 N.E. 698:
>
>> The law of waiver seems to be a technical doctrine, introduced and applied by the court for the purpose of defeating forfeitures. . . . While the principle may not be easily classified, it is well established that, if the words and acts of the insurer reasonably justify the conclusion that with full knowledge of all the facts it intended to abandon or not to insist upon the particular defense afterwards relied upon, a verdict of finding to that effect establishes a waiver, which, if it once exists, can never be revoked.
>
> The doctrine of equitable estoppel, or estoppel in pais, is that a party may be precluded by his acts and conduct from asserting a right to the detriment of another party who, entitled to rely on such conduct, has acted upon it. . . . As already said, the doctrine of waiver is to relieve against forfeiture. It requires no consideration for a waiver, nor any prejudice or injury to the other party.

To the same effect, see Knarston v. Manhattan Life Ins. Co., 140 Cal. 57, 73 Pac. 740."

NOTE

How do you think the case should be decided if it were to appear that West had never known about Clark's drinking and had never waived the condition of total abstinence but that the treatise on Corporations had been an immense success, with West receiving profits on the sales far in excess of what would be required to entitle Clark to his $6 a page? On the same assumptions, what result in Clark v. West under the doctrine of such cases as Smith v. Brady?

JACOB & YOUNGS, INC. v. KENT
230 N.Y. 239, 129 N.E. 889 (1921)

Appeal from an order of the Appellate Division of the Supreme Court in the first judicial department, entered May 13, 1919, reversing a judgment in favor of defendant entered upon a verdict directed by the court and granting a new trial.

Henry W. Hardon for appellant. The plaintiff made out no case of substantial performance. (Smith v. Brady, 17 N.Y. 190; North American Co. v. Jackson Co., 167 App. Div. 779; Spence v. Ham, 27 App. Div. 379; Steel S. & E. Co. v. Stock, 225 N.Y. 173.) There was no error in rulings on evidence. (Spence v. Ham, 27 App. Div. 379; Smith v. Brady, 17 N.Y. 173.)

Frederick Hulse and Cornelius J. Sullivan, Jr., for respondent. The case was disposed of by the trial court on a wholly erroneous theory, and it was error for that court to exclude the testimony offered by the plaintiff and to direct a verdict for the defendant. (Oberlies v. Bullinger, 132 N.Y. 598; Heckmann v. Pinkney, 81 N.Y. 210.)

CARDOZO, J. The plaintiff built a country residence for the defendant at a cost of upwards of $77,000, and now sues to recover a balance of $3,483.46, remaining unpaid. The work of construction ceased in June, 1914, and the defendant then began to occupy the dwelling. There was no complaint of defective performance until March, 1915. One of the specifications for the plumbing work provides that "all wrought iron pipe must be well galvanized, lap welded pipe of the grade known as 'standard pipe' of Reading manufacture." The defendant learned in March, 1915, that some of the pipe, instead of being made in Reading, was the product of other factories. The plaintiff was accordingly directed by the architect to do the work anew. The plumbing was then encased within the walls except in a few places where it had to be exposed. Obedience to the order meant more than the substitution of other pipe. It meant the demolition at great expense of substantial parts of the completed structure. The plaintiff left the work untouched, and asked for a certificate that the final payment was due. Refusal of the certificate was followed by this suit.

The evidence sustains a finding that the omission of the prescribed brand of pipe was neither fraudulent nor wilful. It was the result of the oversight and inattention of the plaintiff's subcontractor. Reading pipe is distinguished from Cohoes pipe and other brands only by the name of the manufacturer stamped upon it at intervals of between six and seven feet. Even the defendant's architect, though he inspected the pipe upon arrival, failed to notice the discrepancy. The plaintiff tried to show that the brands installed, though made by other manufacturers, were the same in quality, in appearance, in market value and in cost as the brand stated in the contract — that they were, indeed, the same thing, though manufactured in another place. The evidence was excluded, and a verdict directed for the defendant. The Appellate Division reversed, and granted a new trial.

We think the evidence, if admitted, would have supplied some basis for the inference that the defect was insignificant in its relation to the project. The courts never say that one who makes a contract fills the measure of his duty by less than full performance. They do say, however, that an omission, both trivial and innocent, will sometimes be atoned for by allowance of the resulting damage, and will not always be the breach of a condition to be followed by a forfeiture (Spence v. Ham, 163 N.Y. 220; Woodward v. Fuller, 80 N.Y. 312; Glacius v. Black, 67 N.Y. 563, 566; Bowen v. Kimbell, 203 Mass. 364, 370). The distinction is akin to that between dependent and independent promises, or between promises and conditions (Anson on Contracts [Corbin's ed.], sec. 367; 2 Williston on Contracts, sec. 842). Some promises are so plainly independent that they can never by fair construction be conditions of one another. (Rosenthal Paper Co. v. Nat. Folding Box & Paper Co., 226 N.Y. 313; Bogardus v. N.Y. Life Ins. Co., 101 N.Y. 328). Others are so plainly dependent that they must always be conditions. Others, though dependent and thus conditions when there is departure in point of substance, will be viewed as independent and collateral when the departure is insignificant (2 Williston on Contracts, secs. 841, 842; Eastern Forge Co. v. Corbin, 182 Mass. 590, 592; Robinson v. Mollett, L.R., 7 Eng. & Ir. App. 802, 814; Miller v. Benjamin, 142 N.Y. 613). Considerations partly of justice and partly of presumable intention are to tell us whether this or that promise shall be placed in one class or in another. The simple and the uniform will call for different remedies from the multifarious and the intricate. The margin of departure within the range of normal expectation upon a sale of common chattels will vary from the margin to be expected upon a contract for the construction of a mansion or a "skyscraper." There will be harshness sometimes and oppression in the implication of a condition when the thing upon which labor has been expended is incapable of surrender because united to the land, and equity and reason in the implication of a like condition when the subject-matter, if defective, is in shape to be returned. From the conclusion that promises may not be treated as dependent to the extent of their uttermost minutiae without a sacrifice of justice, the progress is a short one to the conclusion that they may not be so treated without a perversion of intention. Intention not otherwise revealed may be presumed to hold in contemplation the reasonable and probable. If something else is in view, it must not be left to implication. There will be no assumption of a purpose to visit venial faults with oppressive retribution.

Those who think more of symmetry and logic in the development of legal rules than of practical adaptation to the attainment of a just result will be troubled by a classification where the lines of division are so wavering and blurred. Something, doubtless, may be said on the score of consistency and certainty in favor of a stricter standard. The courts have balanced such considerations against those of equity and fairness, and found the latter to be the weightier. The decisions in this state commit us to the liberal view, which is making its way, nowadays, in jurisdictions slow to welcome it (Dakin & Co. v. Lee, 1916, 1 K.B. 566, 579). Where the line is to be drawn between the important and the trivial cannot be settled by a formula. "In the nature of the case precise boundaries are impossible" (2 Williston on Contracts, sec. 841). The same omission may take on one aspect or another according to its setting. Substitution of equivalents may not have the same significance in fields of art on the one side and in those of mere utility on the other. Nowhere will change be tolerated, however, if it is so dominant or pervasive as in any real or substantial measure to frustrate the purpose of the contract (Crouch v. Gutmann, 134 N.Y. 45, 51). There is no general license to install whatever, in the builder's judgment, may be regarded as "just as good" (Easthampton L. & C. Co., Ltd., v. Worthington, 186 N.Y. 407, 412). The question is one of degree, to be answered, if there is doubt, by the triers of the facts (Crouch v. Gutmann; Woodward v. Fuller, *supra*), and, if the inferences are certain, by the judges of the law (Easthampton L. & Co., Ltd., v. Worthington, *supra*). We must weight the purpose to be served, the desire to be gratified, the excuse for deviation from the letter, the cruelty of enforced adherence. Then only can we tell whether literal fulfilment is to be implied by law as a condition. This is not to say that the parties are not free by apt and certain words to effectuate a purpose that performance of every term shall be a condition of recovery. That question is not here. This is merely to say that the law will be slow to impute the purpose, in the silence of the parties, where the significance of the default is grievously out of proportion to the oppression of the forfeiture. The willful transgressor must accept the penalty of his transgression (Schultze v. Goodstein, 180 N.Y. 248, 251; Desmond-Dunne Co. v. Friedman-Doscher Co., 162 N.Y. 486, 490). For him there is no occasion to mitigate the rigor of implied conditions. The transgressor whose default is unintentional and trivial may hope for mercy if he will offer atonement for his wrong (Spence v. Ham, *supra*).

In the circumstances of this case, we think the measure of the allowance is not the cost of replacement, which would be great, but the difference in value, which would be either nominal or nothing. Some of the exposed sections might perhaps have been replaced at moderate expense. The defendant did not limit his demand to them, but treated the plumbing as a unit to be corrected from cellar to roof. In point of fact, the plaintiff never reached the stage at which evidence of the extent of the allowance became necessary. The trial court had excluded evidence that the defect was unsubstantial, and in view of that ruling there was no occasion for the plaintiff to go farther with an offer of proof. We think, however, that the offer, if it had been made, would not of necessity have been defective because directed to difference in value. It is true that in most cases the cost of replacement is the measure (Spence v. Ham, *supra*). The owner is entitled to the money which will permit him to complete, unless the cost of completion is grossly and unfairly out of proportion to the good to be attained. When that is true, the measure is the difference in value. Specifications call, let us say, for a foundation built of granite quarried in Vermont. On the completion of the building, the owner learns that through the blunder of a subcontractor part of the foundation has been built of granite of the same quality quarried in New Hampshire. The measure of allowance is not the cost of reconstruction.

> There may be omissions of that which could not afterwards be supplied exactly as called for by the contract without taking down the building to its foundations, and at the same time the omission may not effect the value of the building for use or otherwise, except so slightly as to be hardly appreciable.

(Handy v. Bliss, 204 Mass. 513, 519. Cf. Foeller v. Heintz, 137 Wis. 169, 178; Oberlies v. Bullinger, 132 N.Y. 598, 601; 2 Williston on Contracts, sec. 805, p. 1541). The rule that gives a remedy in cases of substantial performance with compensation for defects of trivial or inappreciable importance, has been developed by the courts as an instrument of justice. The measure of the allowance must be shaped to the same end.

The order should be affirmed, and judgment absolute directed in favor of the plaintiff upon the stipulation, with costs in all courts.

McLaughlin, J. (dissenting). I dissent. The plaintiff did not perform its contract. Its failure to do so was either intentional or due to gross neglect which, under the uncontradicted facts, amounted to the same thing, nor did it make any proof of the cost of compliance, where compliance was possible.

Under its contract it obligated itself to use in the plumbing only pipe (between 2,000 and 2,500 feet) made by the Reading Manufacturing Company. The first pipe delivered was about 1,000 feet and the plaintiff's superintendent then called the attention of the foreman of the sub-contractor, who was doing the plumbing, to the fact that the specifications annexed to the contract required all pipe used in the plumbing to be of the Reading Manufacturing Company. They then examined it for the purpose of ascertaining whether this delivery was of that manufacture and found it was. Thereafter, as pipe was required in the progress of the work, the foreman of the subcontractor would leave word at its shop that he wanted a specified number of feet of pipe, without in any way indicating of what manufacture. Pipe would thereafter be delivered and installed in the building, without any examination whatever. Indeed, no examination, so far as appears, was made by the plaintiff, the subcontractor, defendant's architect, or any one else, of any of the pipe except the first delivery, until after the building had been completed. Plaintiff's architect then refused to give the certificate of completion, upon which the final payment depended, because all of the pipe used in the plumbing was not of the kind called for by the contract. After such refusal, the subcontractor removed the covering or insulation from about 900 feet of pipe which was exposed in the basement, cellar and attic, and all but 70 feet was found to have been manufactured, not by the Reading Company, but by other manufacturers, some by the Cohoes Rolling Mill Company, some by the National Steel Works, some by the South Chester Tubing Company, and some which bore no manufacturer's mark at all. The balance of the pipe had been so installed in the building that an inspection of it could not be had without demolishing, in part at least, the building itself.

I am of the opinion the trial court was right in directing a verdict for the defendant. The plaintiff agreed that all the pipe used should be of the Reading Manufacturing Company. Only about two-fifths of it, so far as appears, was of that kind. If more were used, then the burden of proving that fact was upon the plaintiff, which it could easily have done, since it knew where the pipe was obtained. The question of substantial performance of a contract of the character of the one under consideration depends in no small degree upon the good faith of the contractor. If the plaintiff had intended to, and had complied with the terms of the contract except as to minor omissions, due to inadvertence, then he might be allowed to recover the contract price, less the amount necessary to fully compensate the defendant for damages caused by such omissions. (Woodward v. Fuller, 80 N.Y. 312; Nolan v. Whitney, 88 N.Y. 648.) But that is not this case. It installed between 2,000 and 2,500 feet of pipe, of which only 1,000 feet at most complied with the contract. No explanation was given why pipe called for by the contract was not used, nor was any effort made to show what it would cost to remove the pipe of other manufacturers and install that of the Reading Manufacturing Company. The defendant had a right to contract for what he wanted. He had a right before making payment to get what the contract called for. It is no answer to this suggestion to say that the pipe put in was just as good as that made by the Reading Manufacturing Company, or that the difference in value between such pipe and the pipe made by the Reading Manufacturing Company would be either "nominal or nothing." Defendant contracted for pipe made by the Reading Manufacturing Company. What his reason was for requiring this kind of pipe is of no importance. He wanted that and was entitled to it. It may have been a mere whim on his part, but even so, he had a right to this kind of pipe, regardless of whether some other kind, according to the opinion of the contractor or experts, would have been "just as good, better, or done just as well." He agreed to pay only upon condition that the pipe installed were made by that company and he ought not to be compelled to pay unless that condition be performed. (Schultze v. Goodstein, 180 N.Y. 248; Spence v. Ham, *supra*; Steel S. & E. C. Co. v. Stock, 225 N.Y. 173; Van Clief v. Van Vechten, 130 N.Y. 571; Glacius v. Black, 50 N.Y. 145; Smith v. Brady, 17 N.Y. 173, and authorities cited on p. 185.) The rule, therefore, of substantial performance, with damages for unsubstantial omissions, has no application. (Crouch v. Gutmann, 134 N.Y. 45; Spence v. Ham, 163 N.Y. 220.)

What was said by this court in Smith v. Brady (*supra*) is quite applicable here:

> I suppose it will be conceded that everyone has a right to build his house, his cottage or his store after such a model and in such style as shall best accord with his notions of utility or be most agreeable to his fancy. The specifications of the contract became the law between the parties until voluntarily changed. If the owner prefers a plain and simple Doric column, and has so provided in the agreement, the contractor has no right to put in its place the more costly and elegant Corinthian. If the owner, having regard to strength and durability, has contracted for walls of specified materials to be laid in a particular manner, or for a given number of joists and beams, the builder has no right to substitute his own judgment or that of others. Having departed from the agreement, if performance has not been waived by the other party, the law will not allow him to allege that he has made a good building as the one he engaged to erect. He can demand payment only upon and according to the terms of his contract, and if the conditions on which payment is due have not been performed, then the right to demand it does not exist. To hold a different doctrine would be simply to make another contract, and would be giving to parties an encouragement to violate their engagements, which the just policy of the law does not permit. (p. 186.)

I am of the opinion the trial court did not err in ruling on the admission of evidence or in directing a verdict for the defendant.

For the foregoing reasons I think the judgment of the Appellate Division should be reversed and the judgment of the Trial Term affirmed.

Hiscock, Ch. J., Hogan and Crane, JJ., concur with Cardozo, J.; Pound and Andrews, JJ., concur with McLaughlin, J.

Order affirmed, etc.

NOTE

1. Do you conclude that Smith v. Brady has now been overruled? Does the holding in the case, as distinguished from Cardozo's rhetoric, seem to commit the New York courts to a broad or to a narrow doctrine of "substantial performance"? What on earth could Cardozo have meant by the statement that "the omission of the prescribed brand of pipe was neither fraudulent nor willful"?

2. Cardozo said that his opinion was not meant "to say that the parties are not free by apt and certain words to effectuate a purpose that performance of every term shall be a condition of recovery." J. Dawson, W. Harvey, & S. Henderson, Cases and Comment on Contracts (4th ed. 1982), point out (at 816-817) that the record in the case (R. 108) shows that the contract contained the following clause:

> Any work furnished by the Contractor, the material or workmanship of which is defective or which is not fully in accordance with the drawings and specifications, in every respect, will be rejected and is to be immediately torn down, removed and remade or replaced in accordance with the drawings and specifications, whenever discovered.

3. The following excerpt from Richard Danzig's marvelous discussion of the facts in *Jacob & Youngs* helps to put the legal issues raised by that case in perspective:

> The Reading Company was by its account the largest manufacturer of wrought iron pipe in the country, having provided it for such famous New York buildings as the Metropolitan Life Insurance Building and the Chrysler Building.[3] Indeed, its 1911 brochure asserted that "the majority of the modern and most prominent buildings in New York City are equipped with READING wrought iron pipe" and that "many leading architects and engineers have drawn their specifications in favor of wrought iron pipe, in instances prohibiting steel pipe entirely."[4]
>
> Interestingly, as this last comment suggests, these trade publications made their comparative claims not so much with reference to their competitors who made wrought iron pipe, as to those who made steel pipe. According to a pipe wholesaler interviewed in New York City in 1975, genuine wrought iron pipe was manufactured in the pre-war period by four largely non-competing companies: Reading, Cohoes, Byers and Southchester. According to this informant, all of these brands "were of the same quality and price. The manufacturer's name would make absolutely no difference in pipe or in price."
>
> The testimony prepared for the Kent trial was to the same effect. If one reads between and around objections and exclusions of evidence it is appar-

---

3. Reading Iron Co., Court of Actual Experience: Wrought Iron Pipe vs. Steel Pipe 37 (9th ed., 1911).
4. Id., p. 2.

ent that Jacob and Youngs were prepared to show equality of price, weight, size, appearance, composition, and durability for all four major brands of wrought iron pipe. Indeed, in addition to other witnesses, an employee of the Reading Company was prepared to testify to this effect. Probably because of this evidence, Kent's briefs on appeal conceded that "experts could have testified that the substitute pipe was the same in quality in all respects. . . ."[5] It appears that this concession crystallized into a "stipulation" before argument in the Court of Appeals, and that Cardozo's reference was to this when he directed a judgment for Jacob and Youngs.

Why then was Reading Pipe specified? Apparently because it was the normal trade practice to assure wrought iron pipe quality by naming a manufacturer. In contemporary trade bulletins put out by Byers and Reading, prospective buyers were cautioned that some steel pipe manufacturers used iron pipe and often sold under misleading names like "wrought pipe." To avoid such inferior products, Byers warned: "When wrought iron pipe is desired, the specifications often read 'genuine wrought iron pipe' but as this does not always exclude wrought iron containing steel scrap, it is safer to mention the name of a manufacturer known not to use scrap." Reading's brochure said: "If you want the best pipe, specify 'Genuine wrought iron pipe made from Puddled Pig Iron' and have the Pipe-Fitter furnish you with the name of the manufacturer."[6]

The contract makes it especially clear that the use of Reading was primarily as a standard. Specification twenty-two says: "Where any particular brand of manufactured article is specified, it is to be considered as a standard. Contractors desiring to use another shall first make application in writing to the Architect stating the difference in cost and obtain their written approval of change." (Jacob and Youngs stressed the implications of this first sentence in their court of appeals brief.[7])

Why, given a realistic indifference to the maker of the pipe, did Kent refuse to pay for anything but Reading Pipe through three levels of litigation? Mr. Kent, according to some who knew him, carried cost conscious-

---

5. Appellant's Brief, New York Court of Appeals, p. 13.

6. This area of plumbing metallurgy had apparently been productive of conflict between builders and owners. The Reading pamphlet cited above, at p. 2, notes: "In some cases, where wrought iron was specified and steel pipe was substituted, it resulted after discovery in heavy fines to the contractor, and in some instances the steel pipe was ordered torn out and replaced with wrought iron pipe at a large expense." The Appellants' Brief in *Jacob and Youngs*, p. 13-14, quoted from Shultze v. Goodstein, 180 N.Y. 248, 73 N.E. 21, a case in which some type of pipe, probably steel, was substituted for the specified iron pipe. In that case, complete performance as to iron pipe was deemed a condition to the buyer's duty to pay. (The case is cited by McLaughlin in dissent, but Cardozo passed it off as a case relevant only to wilful breaches.)

7. The imprecision of the specifications is underscored by the fact that apparently it was not possible to make *lap welded* wrought iron in all of the sizes ($\frac{3}{4}$"-2" in diameter) necessary for such a house. (Trial testimony of Parke H. Holton, a pipe marketing expert from Nason Mfg. Co. And see *Byers Pipe*, a magazine put out by Byers Co. in July 1921, bulletin no. 34 which shows that lap welding is only done on pipes of $1\frac{1}{4}$, $1\frac{1}{2}$ and 2". A different kind of welding is used on smaller pipe.) Thus it is apparent that the specifications could NOT have been met. See also testimony by Henry S. Carland, a sales representative for Reading, showing that the specifications called for a non-existent pipe.) This evidence was ruled inadmissible on the ground both sides had accepted the specifications in the contract.

ness "to an extreme point." As one put it: "The old man would go all over town to save a buck." Perhaps having paid the extra cost of wrought iron pipe, he felt cheated when not indisputably assured of the highest quality and purity with which Reading's name was associated. However, a Reading representative's willingness to testify for the plaintiff, and the apparent ability of Jacob and Youngs to show the equality of Byers, Cohoes, Southchester and Reading pipes (an equality probably realized by Kent's architect) suggest that Kent may have seized upon the pipe substitution as an expression of other dissatisfactions in his relationship with Jacob and Youngs. . . .

Danzig, The Capability Problem in Contract Law 121-123 (1978).

4. Both opinions in the principal case refer to Spence v. Ham, 163 N.Y. 220, 57 N.E. 412 (1900). That was a construction case in which the contractor sought to recover the balance (about 40 percent) of the contract price on an allegation of substantial performance. Initially, judgment in favor of the contractor was entered on a report submitted by a referee. The referee, after concluding that the contractor had substantially performed the contract, held that it was up to the defendant to show the cost of making the building conform to the contract specifications; in the absence of such proof the contractor recovered in full. On appeal the judgment was reversed. In his opinion in the Court of Appeals Vann, J., commented that the referee had "inadvertently committed an error of law": the true rule was that in substantial performance cases the plaintiff must plead and prove not only what he had done but also the value (or cost of replacement) of what he had not done. (The court also disagreed with the referee on whether the contract had in any case been substantially performed.) In the principal case Cardozo clearly accepted the pleading (or burden of proof) rule of Spence v. Ham, which, equally clearly, the plaintiff had not complied with. To understand how Cardozo succeeded in both accepting and avoiding the Spence v. Ham rule requires a close reading (or rereading) of the opinion.

In Massachusetts a different pleading rule developed. In that state substantial performance cases were not looked on as being actions on the contract (as in New York) but as actions in quantum meruit or quasi-contract. Thus the Massachusetts plaintiff had merely to prove the value of what he had done. In Bowen v. Kimbell, 203 Mass. 364, 89 N.E. 542 (1909), Knowlton, C.J., went at length into the difference between the practice in Massachusetts and that elsewhere, concluding that the "anomalous form of proceeding in this Commonwealth does not give the plaintiff any larger rights than . . . under the rule which generally prevails in actions upon a building contract in other states." Id. at 371, 89 N.E. at 544. Note that Cardozo in his opinion in the principal case cites Massachusetts cases (including Bowen v. Kimbell) in double harness with New York cases. Thus it may be that the cases come out the same way no matter which rule is followed. However, in drafting pleadings and presenting proof, one of the things a practitioner has to keep in mind is whether the New York rule or the Massachusetts rule is in force in his jurisdiction.

5. Neither Cardozo for the majority nor McLaughlin for the dissenters made anything of the fact that the architect had refused to give the required certificate of completion. It may be that New York has always taken a relaxed view of such a condition. See Smith v. Brady, *supra* p. 1029. In Nolan v. Whitney, 88 N.Y. 648, 649 (1822), Earl, J., finding that a builder had substantially performed his contract, said:

> [W]hen he had substantially performed his contract, the architect was bound to give him the certificate, and his refusal to give it was unreasonable, and it is held that an unreasonable refusal on the part of an architect in such a case to give the certificate dispenses with its necessity.

Nolan v. Whitney was distinguished in Van Iderstine Co., Inc. v. Barnet Leather Co., Inc., 242 N.Y. 425, 152 N.E. 250 (1932), in which the contract covered the sale of "vealskins," subject to the "approval" of a broker. In an action by seller against buyer, following the broker's refusal to approve some of the skins, the trial court charged, in the light of Nolan v. Whitney, that the plaintiff could recover if "approval was unreasonably withheld." That was held to be error. On the facts of the *Van Iderstine* case plaintiff could recover only if "the certificate has been withheld dishonestly and in bad faith, and the defendant is a party to that bad faith through control of the expert or collusion with him." Nolan v. Whitney was said to apply only to "building contracts." Why the distinction between "building contracts" and other kinds of contracts?

In Hebert v. Dewey, 191 Mass. 403, 77 N.E. 822 (1906), the Massachusetts court took a different view of the requirement of an architect's certificate in a building contract. The trial judge had charged the jury that if the architect had "capriciously" withheld the certificate of completion, the plaintiff (builder) could recover on proof that "the work was done and the contract substantially performed." That was held to be error. The builder, said Knowlton, C.J., can recover in the absence of the certificate if the architect "wilfully, and without excuse, refuses to act at all, or if he acts dishonestly and in bad faith. . . ." Id. at 413, 77 N.E. at 826. However, he went on,

> [i]f the architect, acting in good faith, thought that the work was not properly done and the contract was not substantially performed, and refused the certificate for that reason, the mere fact that the certificate ought to have been given and that the work was done and the contract was performed would not entitle the plaintiff to recover without the certificate. The parties were bound by the decision of the architect made in good faith. . . ."

Id. at 414, 77 N.E. at 826.

In this context, do you prefer the approach of Nolan v. Whitney or that of Hebert v. Dewey? For adverse criticism of Nolan v. Whitney, see 3A Corbin §651; 5 Williston §797.

6. There are two aspects to the holding in the principal case. One is that the plaintiff could recover something. The other is that, on the facts of the case, the proper rule of damages was that the amount to be deducted from the plaintiff's recovery was not the "cost of replacement" (as suggested in Spence v. Ham) but the "difference in value," which would be "nominal or nothing." Thus the plaintiff recovered the full amount of the final payment. It will be remembered that the referee in Smith v. Brady had applied the "difference in value" rule which, according to Harris, J., was erroneous, the "true rule of damages" being the "cost of repair (or replacement)." Assuming that the plaintiff in Smith v. Brady was entitled to recover something, would Cardozo's approach in the principal case lead to the application of the "difference in value" rule or the "cost of replacement" rule on the Smith v. Brady facts?

The Court of Appeals returned to this problem in Bellizi v. Huntley Estates, Inc., 3 N.Y.2d 112, 143 N.E.2d 802 (1957). The defendant, a real estate developer, sold the plaintiff a lot and constructed a house with an attached garage for him. When construction was begun, it was discovered that there was rock close to the surface; instead of excavating, the defendant built the house on the rock. As a result the driveway to the garage was at a grade of $22\frac{1}{2}$ percent. Such a grade made the driveway both inconvenient and unsafe — the maximum permissible grade is 12 percent. There was nothing in the contract about the grade of the driveway; however, when the plaintiff protested while the house was being built, the president of the defendant assured him that the grade would not exceed 10 percent and that he (the plaintiff) would be "happy." Initially the rock could have been excavated "without too much trouble"; after completion of the house and garage, the excavation would be much more expensive. On those facts the Appellate Division, relying on Jacob & Youngs v. Kent, applied the "difference in value" rule. The Court of Appeals reversed. Dye, J., said:

> "The difference in value" rule in defective performance of construction contracts seems to be applied only when it would be unfair to apply the general rule (cf. Jacob & Youngs v. Kent, supra). In a case such as the present when the variance is so substantial as to render the finished building partially unusable and unsafe, the measure of damage is "the market price of completing or correcting the performance" [citing, among other authorities, 5 Williston on Contracts §1363 (rev. ed.)]. . . . This rule we have long applied [citing a string of New York cases which begins, oddly enough, with Smith v. Brady].

3 N.Y.2d at 115-116.

7. Restatement First §346 deals with the problem discussed in the preceding paragraph in terms of "economic waste." Plaintiff can get judgment for the "cost of replacement" unless "economic waste" would result; if cost of replacement would lead to economic waste, he is remitted to the "difference in value." Among the illustrations to §346 are the following:

> 3. A contracts with B to sink an oil well on A's own land adjacent to the land of B, for development and exploration purposes. Other exploration wells prove that there is no oil in that region; and A breaks his promise to sink the well. B can get judgment for only nominal damages, not the cost of sinking the well.
>
> 4. A contracts to construct a monumental fountain in B's yard for $5,000, but abandons the work after the foundation has been laid and $2,800 has been paid by B. The contemplated fountain is so ugly that it would decrease the number of possible buyers of the place. The cost of completing the fountain would be $4,000. B can get judgment for $1,800, the cost of completion less the part of price unpaid.

Do you find the illustrations helpful? Why should B be entitled to his "ugly fountain" (or its value) but not to his dry well?

There is much discussion of Restatement §346, as well as of the underlying problem, in Groves v. John Wunder Co., 205 Minn. 163, 286 N.W. 235 (1939). The case involved a lease of a sand and gravel quarry running from 1927 to 1934. The defendant, who was entitled to remove sand and gravel from the quarry during the term of the lease, had covenanted that, at the end of the term, it would leave the quarry "at a uniform grade." This it did not do. At trial it was proved that the cost of complying with the "uniform grade" covenant would have been $60,000; if that had been done, the land, so improved, would have had a 1934 market value of $12,000. (The explanation for these unlikely figures evidently lies in the facts that between 1927 and 1934 not only had land values collapsed but ongoing construction had come virtually to a halt, so that much less sand and gravel had been removed from the quarry than had been originally contemplated.) At trial the plaintiff recovered judgment for the value of the land plus interest ($15,000). Over a strong dissent, the Minnesota Supreme Court reversed and remanded the case for a new trial (in which it was to be determined whether the plaintiff was entitled to recover the full cost of putting the quarry at a uniform grade). According to J. Dawson & W. Harvey, Cases and Comment on Contracts 12 (3d ed. 1977), the case was settled for $55,000. Twenty years later three-fifths of the tract, which had still not been graded, was sold for $45,000. The Groves case was itself discussed (and distinguished) by the Oklahoma Supreme Court in Peevyhouse v. Garland Coal & Mining Co., 382 P.2d 109 (1963), reprinted infra p. 1119.

The idea of §346(1)(a) of Restatement First is expressed, in somewhat different language, in §348(2) of Restatement Second. Section 348(2)

provides that "if a breach results in defective or unfinished construction
. . . the loss in value to the injured party" may be based either on "diminution in the market price of the property" or on "the reasonable cost of
completing performance or of remedying the defects if that cost is not
clearly disproportionate to the probable loss in value to him." For an
explanation as to why the draftsmen of Restatement Second omitted the
phrase "economic waste," see Note 3 following the *Peevyhouse* case, *infra*
p. 1119.

LAWRENCE v. MILLER, 86 N.Y. 131 (1881). Under a contract for the
sale of land the vendee made a down payment of $2,000. The vendee was
to make a "further considerable payment of money, and to give a bond
with a mortgage on the lands." (The report of the case does not give the
amount of the contract price.) No time for performance was stated in
the contract. The parties met on April 1 "with a view to perform." The
vendor produced a deed and told the vendee that he was "ready." The
vendee was not "ready" and asked for more time. The parties agreed to
meet again on May 1 and this agreement was endorsed in writing on the
contract. (The original contract was under seal; the endorsement setting
May 1 as the closing date was not under seal.) On May 1 the vendor, as
before, was ready to perform, having the deed with him. The vendee said
he did not have the money and asked for more time. The vendor refused
any further extension of time. No further attempt to perform the contract
was ever made. The vendor kept the $2,000 down payment and subse-
quently sold the land to other parties. The vendee assigned his claim to
the plaintiff who, suing in the name of the vendee, brought an action to
recover the $2,000 down payment. (The circumstances of the assignment
to the plaintiff are not explained in the report. The court dealt with the
case as if the vendee himself were bringing the action.) It was argued for
the vendee that it was the vendor who was in breach for the reasons that
1) the vendor had merely "produced" the deed without making a technical "tender" and 2) the written endorsement setting May 1 for closing was
not binding because it was not under seal, so that the vendee was entitled
to a further reasonable time for performance. The greater part of the
opinion by Folger, J., is devoted to refuting these arguments. Counsel for
the vendee argued finally that, even if the vendee was in breach and the
vendor was not, the vendee should still recover the down payment less
whatever damages the vendor had sustained by reason of the breach. (In
fact, according to the summary of the argument of counsel, the vendor
had "sold the premises immediately to other persons at a better price," so
that he had sustained no loss; he had indeed made a greater profit than he
would have made if the vendee had performed the contract. The opinion
of the court does not refer to this point except to say that "[t]he matter of
the vendor's damage was not entered into at the trial. We cannot say that

it was nothing, nor how great it was.") On this branch of the case Folger said:

> [I]t is never permitted either at law or in equity, for one to recover back money paid on an executory contract that he had refused or neglected to perform. . . . To allow a recovery of this money would be to sustain an action by a party on his own breach of his own contract, which the law does not allow. When we once declare in this case that the vendor has done all that the law asked of him, we also declare that the vendee has not done so on his part. And then to maintain this action would be to declare that a party may violate his agreement, and make an infraction of it by himself a cause of action. That would be ill doctrine.

86 N.Y. at 140. (Smith v. Brady is not cited in the report of Lawrence v. Miller, either in the opinion or in the arguments of counsel.)

We may assume that the total contract price in Lawrence v. Miller was $10,000. Or $20,000. Or $50,000. Or $100,000. Assuming that the vendee was in breach and the vendor was not, do you think that the vendor's right to retain the down payment should be affected by the size of the contract?

Assume that the vendee, instead of (or in addition to) making a down payment, had, between April 1 and May 1 in the expectation of being able to perform the contract on May 1, made improvements to the lands to the value of $2,000. Can the vendor also keep the improvements without paying for them? On whether there is any difference between down payments and reliance expenses, see the opinion of L. Hand, J., in L. Albert & Son v. Armstrong Rubber Co., *infra* p. 1197.

AMTORG TRADING CORP. v. MIEHLE PRINTING PRESS & MANUFACTURING CO., 206 F.2d 103 (2d Cir. 1953). The plaintiff was a New York corporation acting as a purchasing agent for the Soviet Union. Under a contract entered into on August 1, 1947, the defendant's predecessor agreed to sell the plaintiff 30 printing presses for exportation to Russia, to be used in the printing of currency. The plaintiff made a 25% down payment on the total purchase price of $352,035.90. The first ten presses were delivered in February, 1948 and the plaintiff paid the balance of their purchase price over the portion of the down payment credited to them. The remainder of the original down payment, which amounted to $59,946.47, constituted, in effect, a prepayment on the 20 presses still to be delivered. As things turned out these presses were never delivered to the plaintiff, for on March 1, 1948, a new federal regulation became effective that prohibited the further exportation of such goods to the Soviet Union unless an export license was first obtained; the plaintiff's effort to obtain a license proved unavailing.

After Amtorg refused to pay the balance of the purchase price on the remaining 20 presses, the defendant brought an action in New York state court, and Amtorg naturally counterclaimed for the return of its prepayment. This action was discontinued by the defendant, however, after the 20 presses were purchased by the United States Bureau of Engraving and Printing at a profit, to the defendant, of $18,765. Subsequently, the plaintiff brought an action of its own in federal court, demanding return of its prepayment together with Miehle's profit from the resale. The trial court granted the defendant's motion for summary judgment, but the Second Circuit reversed.

Judge Clark began his opinion by noting that Amtorg could not avoid the contract on grounds of impossibility or frustration since delivery of the presses was to have been made in the United States, something that was clearly still possible even after the denial of an export license. In connection with what he considered the more interesting problem of unjust enrichment resulting from the forfeiture of plaintiff's down payment, Judge Clark discussed the New York precedents, including Britton v. Turner and Lawrence v. Miller, and also took note of §357 of the Restatement First, which states that a nonperforming party may recover his downpayment if his nonperformance was not "wilful and deliberate," unless the contract provides that the money may be retained and the amount involved "is not so greatly in excess of defendant's harm" as to constitute a penalty. Judge Clark also observed that New York had recently adopted a new statute, N.Y. Personal Property Law §145-a (not in effect at the time the contract was entered into) which provided that a nonperforming buyer could recover any prepayments made by him up to the amount by which such payments exceeded "either an agreed-upon sum in the contract which constitutes a reasonable liquidation in advance of the seller's anticipated damages or, in the absence of such a clause, 20 per cent of the value of the total performance for which the buyer is obligated under the contract." Under the doctrine of Erie v. Tompkins, Judge Clark declared, it might be more hazardous to interpret New York law in terms of the older cases than in terms of what seemed to be a rather clearly evolving policy against forfeitures. Luckily, Judge Clark concluded, it was not necessary for him "to try to look into the womb of time" with regard to New York law. The action of the United States government in purchasing the presses, and the legislation pursuant to which this purchase had apparently been made, evidenced, according to Judge Clark, a national policy to protect both producers *and* exporters of goods; to allow the defendant to keep the money made on the resale and also to retain the plaintiff's down payment would be to allow it a double recovery inconsistent with this policy. On this basis, the Second Circuit reversed the District Court's grant of summary judgment in the defendant's favor and remanded the case for further proceedings.

NOTE

1. Compare Judge Clark's treatment of the frustration issue in the *Amtorg* case with the English *Fibrosa* case, digested *supra* p. 932. How should the *Amtorg* case be decided, assuming that the contract was held to have been frustrated, under the English Frustrated Contracts Act, *supra* p. 934? In deciding whether Amtorg should recover the down payment, does it make any difference how the frustration issue is handled?

2. The substance of §145-a of the New York Personal Property Law to which Judge Clark refers is carried forward in §2-718(2) of the Uniform Commercial Code. In Procter & Gamble Distributing Co. v. Lawrence American Field Warehousing Corp., 16 N.Y.2d 344, 213 N.E. 873 (1965), Van Voorhis, J., commented as follows on the effect of this statutory provision (citations have been omitted):

> It was firmly settled in New York . . . that one who has failed to perform his part of an executory contract of sale may not recover the purchase money he has paid thereon. It was so held also in most of the rest of the United States. . . . This has been changed by the Uniform Commercial Code [§2-718(2)].

Id. at 354, 213 N.E. at 878. Assuming Amtorg to have been in breach, how much of the down payment would it be entitled to recover under §2-718(2)(b)? Do you have any explanation for the $500 limitation in that section's recovery formula?

3. In his discussion of changing attitudes toward "forfeitures," Judge Clark cited New York legislation (which was the New York version of the Uniform Conditional Sales Act) pursuant to which a defaulting buyer under a conditional sale contract was entitled to any "surplus" on a resale of the goods after repossession by the seller. The common law conditional sale rule had been that, on default by the buyer, the seller could retake the goods and forfeit all payments made by the buyer, although, if he did that, he had no right to sue the buyer for the unpaid balance of the price. That rule was abrogated by statute in most states long before the enactment of the Uniform Commercial Code; Article 9 of the Code also rejects the common law conditional sale rule.

4. Under the "famous §357" of Restatement First, as Judge Clark paraphrased it, how would you decide Lawrence v. Miller? For that matter, how would you decide Britton v. Turner? (Section 357 is not restricted to down payment cases but covers all situations in which the plaintiff, although himself in default, "has rendered a part performance under the contract that is a net benefit to the defendant.") In American Surety Co. of New York v. United States, 368 F.2d 475 (9th Cir. 1966), Pope, J., commented that the principle of §357 has been "universally approved" and proceeded to give it an expansive reading.

5. J. Calamari & J. Perillo, The Law of Contracts 428 (2d ed. 1977), comment:

> The modern trend is toward recognizing that a party in substantial default should not be treated as an outlaw. . . . [However] despite the inroads of statutes and fairly wide acceptance of the doctrine of Britton v. Turner, the majority of jurisdictions continue to adhere to the general principle that a defaulting party has no remedy notwithstanding the degree of hardship and forfeiture he may suffer.

In a footnote reference to Judge Clark's "able discussion" in the *Amtorg* case, they remark that his "prophesy" of a change in New York law "has not been fulfilled."

Gilmore, in The Death of Contract 88 (1974), speculates:

> We are fast approaching the point where, to prevent unjust enrichment, any benefit received by a defendant must be paid for unless it was clearly meant as a gift; where any detriment reasonably incurred by a plaintiff in reliance on a defendant's assurances must be recompensed. When that point is reached, there is really no longer any viable distinction between liability in contract and liability in tort.

The passage quoted was written in 1970. It may be that the learned author was overoptimistic in his speculations.

6. The Reporter's Note to Restatement Second §388 comments: "This Section is based on former §357, but it is more liberal in allowing recovery in accord with the policy behind Uniform Commercial Code §2-718(2)." Under §388(1) if one party "justifiably" refuses to perform because of the other party's breach, "the party in breach is entitled to restitution for any benefit he has conferred on the injured party by way of part performance or reliance." However, under §388(2) the party in breach has no right to restitution

> [t]o the extent that, under the manifested assent of the parties, a party's performance is to be retained in the case of breach . . . if the value of the performance as liquidated damages is reasonable in the light of the anticipated or actual loss caused by the breach and the difficulties of proof of loss.

The present state of the "plaintiff in default" problem is reviewed in a magisterial opinion by Peters, J., in Vines v. Orchard Hills, Inc., 181 Conn. 501, 435 A.2d 1022 (1980). (Before going on the Connecticut Court, Justice Peters had taught Contracts and Commercial Law at the Yale Law School for many years and was an Adviser in the drafting of Restatement Second.) *Vines* was an action to recover a down payment on a contract to buy a condominium; the buyer defaulted after making the down payment because he had been transferred by his employer to another state. Justice Peters, citing many authorities, wrote:

> Although earlier cases often refused to permit a party to bring an action that could be said to be based on his own breach . . . many of the more recent cases support restitution in order to prevent unjust enrichment and to avoid forfeiture [citing, inter alia, the *Amtorg* case and Restatement Second §388].

Id. at 505, 435 A.2d at 1026. In fine:

> We therefore conclude that a purchaser whose breach is not willful has a restitutionary claim to recover moneys paid that unjustly enrich his seller. In this case, no one has alleged that the purchasers' breach, arising out of a transfer to a more distant place of employment, should be deemed to have been willful.

Id. at 509, 435 A.2d at 1027. But suppose that Vines had breached "willfully", that he had found a condominium he liked better and had therefore decided to renege on the Orchard Hills contract. Should that make any difference? Under Restatement Second §388 as summarized above? See Freedman v. The Rector, Wardens & Vestrymen, 37 Cal. 2d 16, 230 P.2d 629 (1981) (willfully defaulting vendee under a land contract allowed to recover his down payment).

CHAPTER 10

Remedies

Section 1. Introduction

ACME MILLS & ELEVATOR CO. v. JOHNSON

141 Ky. 718, 133 S.W. 784 (1911)

On April 26th, 1909, appellee J.C. Johnson executed and delivered to appellant Acme Mills & Elevator Company the following contract:

April 26th, 1909

> I have this day sold to Ernest W. Steger, for Acme Mills & Elevator Company, 2,000 bushels No. 2 merchantable wheat, mill scale to apply, sacks to be furnished, to be paid for on delivery at Hopkinsville, Kentucky, at $1.03 per bushel, to be delivered from thresher 1909.

Appellee failed to deliver the wheat at the time agreed upon, and appellant brought this action to recover damages in the sum of $240 and for the further sum of $80, being the value of 1,000 sacks which appellant had furnished to appellee for his use in delivering the wheat. Appellee admitted the execution and breach of the contract, but denied that appellant was damaged. He further pleaded that he threshed his wheat after the 25th of July; that this was the time fixed for delivery, and wheat was then worth only about 97½ cents per bushel. He also pleaded that, at the time fixed for the delivery of the wheat, appellant had suspended business, was unable to comply with its contract, and had no money to pay for the wheat. In another paragraph he admitted his indebtedness for the item of $80 covering the sacks furnished him by appellant, and offered to confess judgment for that amount. The allegations of the answer were denied by reply. Subsequently appellant tendered and offered to file an amended reply, wherein it pleaded that on the 13th day of July, 1909, appellee, of his own wrong and without right or legal authority or the consent of appellant, sold his wheat to the Liberty Mills at Nashville, Tennessee, at the price of $1.16 per bushel, and that by reason of this fact he was estopped to plead in his answer that his wheat was not threshed until after the 25th of July, 1909, or that the market price for said wheat at the date

1061

of said threshing did not exceed $1 per bushel. The court declined to permit this amended reply to be filed, but entered an order making it a part of the record. The trial resulted in a verdict for appellant in the sum of $80 for the sacks, whereupon judgment was entered against appellee for $80 and costs. From that judgment this appeal is prosecuted.

The evidence for appellee is to the effect that he did not begin threshing his wheat until after the 25th of July, 1909; he completed his threshing about the 29th of the same month. This fact is established by appellee and his brother and the testimony of two or three other witnesses who passed appellee's field while he was engaged in the work of threshing. There is no evidence to the contrary. At the time he finished threshing, wheat of the kind which he had contracted to sell appellant was not worth over $1 per bushel. This fact is established by the evidence of several witnesses, and there is practically no evidence to the contrary. Appellee attempted to justify his conduct in breaching the contract by certain rumors to the effect that appellant had suspended business and was unable to pay for the wheat. While there may have been rumors to this effect, the evidence fails to establish the fact that appellant had suspended business. About the 14th or 15th of July, appellee sold his wheat to the Liberty Mills at Nashville for $1.16 per bushel. On the 24th of July the price of wheat began to fall, until it reached about $1 per bushel on the 29th.

The evidence of appellant and its witnesses is devoted, chiefly, to establishing the fact that appellant did not suspend business and was fully able to pay for the wheat contracted for. While their evidence tends to show that the price of wheat, from the 14th or 15th of July to the 24th, was far in excess of the contract price, they practically admit that wheat was not worth more than a dollar per bushel at the time appellee claims he finished threshing.

One of the errors relied upon is the failure of the court to permit appellant's amended reply to be filed, wherein it attempted to plead that appellee was estopped by his conduct, in selling the wheat, from claiming that he threshed it at a later date or that appellant was not damaged by reason of the breach of the contract. In this connection it is insisted that appellee had no right to violate his contract by selling the wheat to another at a price far in excess of the contract price, using for that purpose the sacks appellant had furnished, and then claim that as a matter of fact he had not threshed the wheat until a later date, and at that time the market price of wheat was below the contract price.

In contracts for the delivery of personal property at a fixed time and at a designated place, the vendee is entitled to damages against the vendor for a failure to comply, and the measure of damages is the difference between the contract price and the market price of the property at the place and time of delivery. (Miles v. Miller, 12 Bush, 134). This principle of law is so well settled, not only in this State, but in all the courts of this country, that it is no longer open to discussion. There is no reason why this rule should not apply to the facts of this case. The evidence clearly established the fact that the threshing was not completed until about the 29th of July. There is nothing in the evidence tending to show that appellee fraudulently delayed the threshing of the wheat for the purpose of permitting the market price of the wheat to go down. Indeed, all the circumstances pointed to an advance rather than a decline in the price, and appellee had no reason to anticipate that the market would decline. As he finished threshing on the 29th of July, and the wheat was to be delivered from the thresher, and appellant was not to accept and pay for the wheat until the time fixed for the delivery, that is the time which determines whether or not appellant was damaged. If appellee had sold his wheat on July 14th or 15th, at $1.16, and the price on July 29th was $1.50 per bushel, appellant would not be contending that the measure of his damages was the difference between the contract price and the price appellee received for it on July 14th or 15th, but would insist that he was entitled to the difference between the contract price and $1.50 per bushel. Besides, appellee was not required by his contract, to deliver to appellant any particular wheat. Had he delivered other wheat of like quantity and quality, he would have complied with the contract. When he sold his wheat on July 14th or 15th, for a price in excess of the contract price, and, therefore, failed to deliver to appellant wheat of the quantity and quality contracted for, he took the chances of being mulcted in damages for the breach of the contract. Estoppel can only be invoked where a party by his conduct has led another to act to his prejudice. There is nothing in the facts of this case to justify the application of that doctrine.

But it is insisted that the court improperly placed the burden of proof upon the appellee, and thereby gave him the closing argument, and improperly admitted and rejected certain evidence. The ruling of the court with reference to the burden of proof was improper, for, notwithstanding the fact that appellee admitted the execution and breach of the contract, yet it was still incumbent upon appellant to prove that it had been damaged. But the question still remains: Was the action of the court prejudicial? As stated before, the evidence overwhelmingly established the fact — indeed, it is practically admitted — that the market price of wheat of the kind and quality contracted to be delivered at the time and place designated in the contract did not exceed $1 per bushel. That being true, appellant, instead of being damaged by the breach of the contract, was actually benefited to the extent of about three cents per bushel. Had the jury upon this state of facts found anything for the appellant, it would have been the duty of this court to reverse the judgment because the verdict was flagrantly against the evidence.

The evidence which it is claimed was improperly admitted and rejected concerned only certain immaterial issues; it had no bearing upon the market price of wheat at the time and place fixed for delivery. We deem it unnecessary to pass upon the propriety of the court's action in regard to such evidence, for the reason that if he erred in the respects complained of, such error could not have prejudiced the substantial rights of appellant.

Judgment affirmed.

O. W. HOLMES, THE COMMON LAW 234-236 (M. Howe ed. 1963) [footnotes omitted]: "An assurance that it shall rain to-morrow, or that a third person shall paint a picture, may as well be a promise as one that the promisee shall receive from some source one hundred bales of cotton, or that the promisor will pay the promisee one hundred dollars. What is the difference in the cases? It is only in the degree of power possessed by the promisor over the event. He has none in the first case. He has equally little legal authority to make a man paint a picture, although he may have larger means of persuasion. He probably will be able to make sure that the promisee has the cotton. Being a rich man, he is certain to be able to pay the one hundred dollars, except in the event of some most improbable accident.

"But the law does not inquire, as a general thing, how far the accomplishment of an assurance touching the future is within the power of the promisor. In the moral world it may be that the obligation of a promise is confined to what lies within reach of the will of the promisor (except so far as the limit is unknown on one side, and misrepresented on the other). But unless some consideration of public policy intervenes, I take it that a man may bind himself at law that any future event shall happen. He can therefore promise it in a legal sense. It may be said that when a man covenants that it shall rain to-morrow, or that A shall paint a picture, he only says, in a short form, I will pay if it does not rain, or if A does not paint a picture. But that is not necessarily so. A promise could easily be framed which would be broken by the happening of fair weather, or by A not painting. A promise, then, is simply an accepted assurance that a certain event or state of things shall come to pass.

"But if this be true, it has more important bearings than simply to enlarge the definition of the word *promise*. It concerns the theory of contract. The consequences of a binding promise at common law are not affected by the degree of power which the promisor possesses over the promised event. If the promised event does not come to pass, the plaintiff's property is sold to satisfy the damages, within certain limits, which the promisee has suffered by the failure. The consequences are the same in kind whether the promise is that it shall rain, or that another man shall paint a picture, or that the promisor will deliver a bale of cotton.

"If the legal consequence is the same in all cases, it seems proper that all contracts should be considered from the same legal point of view. In the case of a binding promise that it shall rain to-morrow, the immediate legal effect of what the promisor does is, that he takes the risk of the event, within certain defined limits, as between himself and the promisee. He does no more when he promises to deliver a bale of cotton. . . . The only universal consequence of a legally binding promise is, that the law makes the promisor pay damages if the promised event does not come to pass. In every case it leaves him free from interference until the time for fulfilment has gone by, and therefore free to break his contract if he chooses."

E. A. HARRIMAN, THE LAW OF CONTRACTS §§551-552 (2d ed. 1901): [§551.] A man may incur contractural obligation with reference to a past, present, or future event. If he contracts that something is, or has been, what is the nature of his obligation? Clearly, in such a case, he simply assumes a risk and binds himself to pay to the other party a sum of money sufficient to compensate the latter for the non-fulfilment of the assurance. In such a case the contract is broken, if at all, as soon as it is made, and the primary obligation necessarily coincides with the second-ary or sanctioning obligation to pay damages. If the contract provides that something shall happen in the future, the promised event may or may not be within the control of the promisor. If the event is not within his control, his promise can amount only to the assumption of a risk as in the preceding case. In this case, also, the primary obligation to compensate the other party for the non-occurrence of the promised event is necessar-ily coincident with the secondary or sanctioning obligation to pay dam-ages for breach of contract. If, however, the promised event is one which in its nature is within the control of the promisor, a different situation arises. Here the primary obligation of the promisor is to perform his promise; and his failure to perform gives rise to a secondary obligation to pay damages. In every contract, therefore, there is the assumption of a risk; and every breach of contract gives rise to a secondary obligation to pay damages; but in contracts where the thing promised is within the control of the promisor, there is, in addition, a distinct primary obligation to perform the contract; while in other contracts the primary obligation is necessarily coincident with the secondary obligation.

[§552.] Chief Justice Holmes maintains[1] that the true view of contract is that a man who makes a contract incurs an obligation to respond in damages for the non-fulfilment of the contract, which obligation is defea-sible by performance. That this is true in all cases where the thing prom-ised is not within the control of the promisor is clear. That there is no primary obligation to perform a contract when performance is within the control of the promisor is a doctrine open to the following objections. First, the doctrine seems to rest only on the limitations of procedure in

1. Common Law, 298-303.

the king's courts, and not on any true historical theory of contract.[2] Second, the doctrine is entirely opposed to all equitable ideas; and the whole tendency of our modern law is in the direction of equitable theories.[3] Third, the doctrine involves an unreasonable departure by the law from fundamental ethical principles.

We all believe that people have an obligation to keep their promises. Sometimes, of course, the failure to keep a promise may be excused: If I agree to accompany you on a walk but break our date when my grandmother becomes ill and has to be rushed to the hospital, no blame attaches to my actions. Here, we are inclined to say, my general duty of promise-keeping is overridden by a conflicting and superior obligation and it is not wrong of me to stand you up (although I certainly owe you an explanation). But when a person's failure to keep his promise is unexcused (suppose that I break our date, without warning, because I prefer to stay home and read the newspaper instead), the person to whom the promise was made is justified in feeling that his trust has been abused, and may have any one of a number of reactions ranging from mild disappointment to moral disgust. He may also feel that the promisor's faithlessness has hurt him in a material sense — perhaps, in reliance on my promise to meet you for a walk, you have turned down an offer to see a film with someone else or left work early and lost an hour's pay.

In general, however serious its consequences, a broken promise gives the promisee a "right" to appeal to the promisor's own conscience (which presumably reflects the moral sentiment of the community) and to insist upon fair "compensation" — typically, an apology or some equivalent gesture of contrition. The right to make such an appeal is a form of moral coercion, and ordinary experience suggests that its power is far from insignificant. If a promise happens also to be a contract, however, its breach creates a legal as well as a moral claim; this is, in fact, the very thing that marks contracts out as a distinctive class of promises. The unexcused breach of a contractual obligation gives the promisee the right to enlist the aid of the state and its coercive apparatus in the protection or vindication of his interests, and where this right is missing there is no contractual liability on the part of the promisor (however compelling his moral responsibilities may be).

The relationship between a person's contract rights and his moral entitlements has been a subject of much controversy, as the passages

---

2. "The oldest actions of the common law aim for the most part not at 'damages,' but at what we call 'specific relief.' . . . . Even when the cause of action is in our eyes a contractual obligation, the law tries its best to give specific relief. . . . The common law has excellent intentions; what impedes it is an old-fashioned dislike to extreme measures." Pollock & Maitland, History of English Law, II. 593, 594.

3. Lingenfelder v. Wainwright Brewing Co., 103 Mo. 578; 15 S.W. 844; H. & W. 181; King v. Duluth, M. & N. Ry. Co., 61 Minn. 482; 63 N.W. 1105.

from Holmes and Harriman suggest. Suppose that A makes a legally enforceable promise to B which he then fails to keep for no other reason than that he would prefer to spend his time or resources in some other way. If, for purely fortuitous reasons, B suffers no financial loss (or is even placed in a better position than he would have been had A kept his promise), no legal action for damages will lie against the faithless promisor. Many will say, however, that A's breach ought still to be condemned from an ethical point of view, and that the lucky fact no one was hurt does not excuse A from moral responsibility for his misbehavior.

The inclination to blame A will be even stronger if he has benefitted from his breach, although B has not been harmed. To this one may reply (in the spirit of Holmes) that every contract is a promise in the alternative — to do a certain thing or else compensate the promisee for any harm he suffers if the thing remains undone — and that compliance with either requirement constitutes performance of the contract and satisfies the promisor's moral obligations. The Holmesian view has always had its adherents, but it seems never to have fully overcome the resistance of common sense, which stubbornly insists that moral blame (unlike legal liability) is not entirely a function of the consequences of an action but depends, as well, upon the motives and intentions of the actor.

If a breach of contract can be morally blameworthy even though the promisee has no legal claim for damages, the reverse also seems true (indeed, if anything, more obviously so). Imagine that a promisor is prevented from performing through no fault of his own; if he has assumed the risk of his own nonperformance, he must make compensation to the promisee, however blameless he appears from a moral point of view. But though we may be tempted to conclude that in cases of this sort there is legal liability unaccompanied by moral blame, closer reflection suggests that this is not actually the case; a promisor who without fault is unable to perform breaches his legal duty to the promisee only if he refuses to make the appropriate compensatory payment, and it is just at the point of refusal that he may be said to violate a moral duty as well. If we assume, with Holmes, that a contract is a promise cast in the alternative, it follows that every legally actionable claim for damages will be premised upon behavior that is also subject to moral blame, since a claim for damages can arise only if the promisor fails to keep one or the other of his two commitments. It may be morally wrong to break a contract even though no damages result; but where the promisee does in fact have a legal claim for damages he will always have a moral claim as well.

Economists, who tend to associate themselves with the Holmesian view of contractual obligation, are fond of saying that contract law is "amoral,"[4] by which they mean that even a promisor who deliberately

4. For an example of an implicitly amoral treatment of contract law, see R. Posner, Economic Analysis of Law (1972) §3.8.

violates his agreement for purely self-interested reasons will not be subject to legal sanctions so long as the other party is compensated for any harm he suffers as a result. This is true, of course, but it does not follow that a promisor who violates his legal duty — either to perform or to pay damages — is free of moral blame. Nor, more importantly, does it follow that a promisor who escapes legal liability (either through good fortune, like the seller in the *Acme Mills* case, or by paying compensation to the promisee) also, for that reason alone, avoids moral criticism. There are, perhaps, good reasons for opposing a rule that would have required the seller in *Acme Mills* to share his profit with the buyer (a rule of this sort might impede the movement of goods to their highest-valuing users, increase transaction costs, and reduce the overall wealth of society — though it should be stressed that each of these claims is controversial); but was it morally defensible for the seller to take risks with the buyer's welfare and then retain the full benefits of the resale for himself, rather than offering to divide his profits with the buyer in some fashion? Contract law is "amoral" because it does not reach this question, not because it answers the question affirmatively.

In the sections that follow, we will survey the wide range of remedial devices to be found in our law of contracts, consider the limitations that restrict their availability and condition their use, and reflect on the reasons for the often chilly reception accorded private efforts to supplement or replace existing legal remedies with different ones. We begin with specific performance, often described as an extraordinary remedy, and yet the one most likely, it would seem, to fully protect the promisee's expectations. The doctrine of specific performance immediately prompts two questions: Why is this remedy *ever* available? And supposing it should be available in some cases, why not in *all*? The materials collected in the following section explore these two related issues.

In Section 3 we turn to the broad topic of money damages, or what one writer has called "substitutional" relief.[5] Where there is an existing market for the goods or services that are the subject of the contract, how are money damages to be measured? How far is the promisor required to go in compensating for the harm caused by his breach? And what happens when a contract we would normally expect to be mutually advantageous turns out not to be so, and the party on the "winning" side inexplicably breaches? In the upside-down world of the "losing" contract, how should we apply our standard rules for measuring damages, rules which have been constructed upon entirely different assumptions? These and a number of related issues are treated in Section 3.

Section 4 deals with the general problem of private remedies and the power of the parties to create for themselves an enforceable remedial scheme. We begin with arbitration agreements, and then examine, in

---

5. Farnsworth, Legal Remedies for Breach of Contract, 70 Colum. L. Rev. 1145 (1970).

some detail, the time-honored distinction between legitimate liquidated damage provisions and illicit penalties. The section ends with a brief look at a related topic — the (increasingly restricted) freedom of sellers and lessors to reduce their warranty liability by means of contractual disclaimers, especially in consumer transactions. This is one of the many points in the chapter where the familiar boundary between tort and contract blurs into a hazy continuum.

The final section of the chapter deals with two related subjects — anticipatory repudiation and mitigation of damages. When a promise is repudiated well in advance of the time set for its performance, special problems may arise in measuring the promisee's damages, and the promisor will almost certainly want his innocent partner to make alternative arrangements so that the losses caused by the breach can be kept to a minimum. It may seem unfair to require the victim of a wrongful act to take affirmative steps for the benefit of the wrongdoer, but the mitigation rules that limit the recovery of even the most blameless promisee are perhaps more consistent with moral principle than they first appear. As you reflect on this issue, you may find it useful to return to the *Acme Mills* case and to reconsider the subject of contract remedies from the point of our departure.

Section 2.   Specific Performance and the Right to Break a Contract

No legal system can get very far without providing an answer to the question of what is to happen when A, without legal excuse, fails to perform his contractual obligation. Shall A, in situations in which this is factually possible, be forced to live up to his bond, to carry out his promised engagement? Or shall A, even when performance is not only possible but desired by the aggrieved party, be allowed to refuse to do whatever it is he has promised to do and be quit of his obligation on paying B a sum of money to compensate him for whatever loss he may have suffered by reason of A's breach? The answers that have been provided to this question are strikingly diverse, not only from one legal system to another, but, through time, within the same system. Thus, for example, it has often been said that, by way of contrast to the common law system, "in general in civil-law countries today what we call specific performance is the rule." R. Pound, An Introduction to the Philosophy of Law 240 (1922). There is undoubtedly some truth to Dean Pound's observation, at least at the level of black-letter principle. But its truth must be taken well-salted. In a well-known article, Professor Dawson has convincingly demonstrated that there is no single "rule" common to the "civil-law countries," and that the "rule" in each country is hedged about with various exceptions and procedural requirements that tend to minimize the differences, in practical application, between the civil-law rule and its common law antithesis. Dawson, Specific Performance in France and Germany, 57 Mich. L. Rev. 495 (1959). (Professor Dawson's article, whose range is broader than its title suggests, traces the development of the specific performance idea in Roman Law, classical, post-classical and medieval, and discusses the implications of the great variety of civil law theories for American law.)

It is true, or at any rate a truism, that in Anglo-American law, from at least the seventeenth century, specific performance has been regarded as an exceptional remedy in equity, available only when a judgment at law for money damages is, on some theory, "inadequate." Why the English courts should initially have adopted this posture is obscure; like so much else in our history it may have been one of the accidental by-products of the long struggle for jurisdiction between the common law courts and their rivals. In Bromage v. Genning, 1 Rolle 368 (K.B. 1616), it appeared that proceedings had been instituted in a court in Wales to compel the defendant, Genning, to execute a lease, as he had covenanted to do. A prohibition against the proceedings in Wales was sought in King's Bench. In the King's Bench proceeding, Lord Coke is reported to have said that

> this would subvert the intention of the covenantor when he intends it to be at his election either to lose the damages or to make the lease, and they wish to compel him to make the lease against his will; and so it is if a man binds himself in an obligation to enfeoff another, he cannot be compelled to make the feoffment.

For the historical background of Bromage v. Genning, see J. Dawson & W. Harvey, Contracts and Contract Remedies 102-103 (2d ed. 1969).

Quite different approaches have been suggested. Thus in 2 J. Story, Equity Jurisprudence 25 (1836), the learned Justice, after having explained the generally accepted limitations on the specific performance remedy, went on to comment:

> The truth is that, upon the principles of natural justice, Courts of Equity might proceed much farther, and insist upon decreeing a specific performance of all bona fide contracts; since that is a remedy, to which Courts of Law are inadequate. There is no pretense for the complaints sometimes made by the common lawyers, that such relief in Equity would wholly subvert the remedies by action on the case and actions of covenant; for it is against conscience, that a party should have a right of election, whether he would perform his covenant, or only pay damages for the breach of it. But, on the other hand, there is no reasonable objection to allowing the party injured by the breach to have an election, either to take damages at law, or to have a specific performance in Equity; the remedies being concurrent, but not coextensive with each other.

The Story approach has recently been defended on economic grounds in an article by Professor Alan Schwartz, The Case for Specific Performance, 89 Yale L.J. 271 (1979). After a lengthy and informative discussion of the problem, Professor Schwartz concludes:

> The compensation goal of contract law can be achieved by requiring the promisor to pay damages or by requiring the promisor to render the promised performance. Under current law, a promisee is entitled to a damage award as of right but the court retains discretion to decide whether specific performance should be granted. Because specific performance is a superior method for achieving the compensation goal, promisees should be able to obtain specific performance on request. An expanded specific performance remedy would not generate greater transaction costs than the damage remedy involves, nor would its increased use interfere unduly with the liberty interests of promisors. . . . If the law is committed to putting disappointed promisees in as good a position as they would have been had their promisors performed, specific performance should be available as a matter of course to those promisees who request it.

Id. at 305-306.

A half century after Story, we seem, with Holmes, to be back in Coke's seventeenth-century universe. In his lecture on the "Elements of Contract" in The Common Law 235-236 (M. Howe ed. 1963), Holmes, after making the point that the legal effect of a binding promise is that the promisor "takes the risk of the event, within certain defined limits, as between himself and the promisee," goes on to say:

> If it be proper to state the common-law meaning of promise and contract in this way, it has the advantage of freeing the subject from the superfluous theory that contract is a qualified subjection of one will to another, a kind of limited slavery. It might be so regarded if the law compelled men to perform their contracts, or if it allowed promisees to exercise such compulsion. If, when a man promised to labor for another, the law made him do it, his relation to his promisee might be called a servitude ad hoc with some truth. But that is what the law never does. It never interferes until a promise has been broken, and therefore cannot possibly be performed according to its tenor. It is true that in some instances equity does what is called compelling specific performance. But, in the first place, I am speaking of the common law, and in the next, this only means that equity compels the performance of certain elements of the total promise which are still capable of performance. For instance, take a promise to convey land within a certain time, a court of equity is not in the habit of interfering until the time has gone by, so that the promise cannot be performed as made. But if the conveyance is more important than the time, and the promisee prefers to have it late rather than never, the law may compel the performance of that. Not literally compel even in that case, however, but put the promisor in prison unless he will convey. This remedy is an exceptional one. The only universal consequence of a legally binding promise is,

that the law makes the promisor pay damages if the promised event does
not come to pass. In every case it leaves him free from interference until
the time for fulfillment has gone by, and therefore free to break his contract
if he chooses.

Holmes' point that "the law . . . never interferes until a promise has
been broken" would need some revision in the light of subsequent developments. The idea of declaratory relief was, of course, unknown at the
time he wrote. Nor does Holmes seem to consider in this context the
effect of the doctrine of anticipatory breach. Perhaps, as a Massachusetts
lawyer, he was influenced by the fact that the Massachusetts court had
recently rejected anticipatory breach doctrine in Daniels v. Newton, *infra*
p. 1270.

Holmes' observation that the law will put a recalcitrant promisor in
prison if he refuses to obey an order of specific performance also stands in
need of qualification. Since Holmes wrote, the harsh common law remedy of imprisonment for debt has been abolished in all jurisdictions,
generally by statute or constitutional provision, and most of the abolishing statutes are "broad enough to prevent imprisonment as a remedy to
compel performance of an equitable decree for payment of the price," 5A
Corbin §1145, n.76. However, where the performance ordered is something other than the payment of a money debt, a failure to comply may
still be treated as a contempt, and where it is, the promisor can be impris-
oned (in theory at least) until he agrees to perform. This marks an important difference between specific performance and money damages: unlike
a decree of specific performance, an award of damages is in form a judgment of law, a declaration of the rights of the litigants, and not a direct
order to the losing party. If the judgment is not paid, the plaintiff must
obtain the help of the state (typically, the local sheriff) in order to collect,
and in attempting to satisfy his claim, may seize the defendant's property
but not his person.

It is not surprising that Holmes should have approved of the remarks
attributed to Lord Coke in Bromage v. Genning. In his address, The Path
of the Law, delivered in 1897, after restating what was basically the position he had taken in the passage from The Common Law just quoted,
Holmes commented that

> such a mode of looking at the matter stinks in the nostrils of those who
> think it advantageous to get as much ethics into the law as they can. It was
> good enough for Lord Coke, however, and here as in many other cases, I
> am content to abide with him.

After stating Bromage v. Genning, Holmes went on: "This goes further
than we should go now, but it shows what I venture to say has been the
common law point of view from the beginning. . . ." Collected Legal
Papers 175 (1920). In this, as in other instances, Holmes, the scholar, and
Holmes, the judge, were not always on the same wavelength. In Jones v.

Parker, 163 Mass. 564, 40 N.E. 1044 (1895), which acquired a modest
vogue as a leading case, the action was to compel specific performance of
a covenant to complete a building by installing an adequate heating and
lighting system and then to lease it to the plaintiff. Per Holmes, J.:

> It does not need argument to show that the covenant is valid. Whether it
> should be enforced specifically admits of more doubt, the question being
> whether it is certain enough for that purpose (Fry, Spec. Perf. §§380-386)
> and whether a decree for specific performance would not call on the court
> to do more than it is in the habit of undertaking. [Citations omitted.] We
> are of the opinion that specific performance should be decreed. . . .
> There is no universal rule that courts of equity never will enforce a contract
> which requires some building to be done. They have enforced such con-
> tracts from the earliest days to the present time [citing inter alia, a case
> from the Yearbooks and 2 J. Story, Equity Jurisprudence §§725-728].

163 Mass. at 566-567. Bromage v. Genning is not cited in the Jones v.
Parker opinion.

One of the first things that the first-year student of Contracts learns is
that the "exceptional" remedy of specific performance is routinely available for the enforcement of land contracts, both in the vendee's suit to
compel conveyance and in the vendor's action to recover the price. The
traditional explanation of this result is that damages at law would never be
an adequate remedy since each Blackacre is unique; thus land can never
be valued as goods are. Professor Dawson, in the article referred to earlier, comments skeptically that: "The adequacy test . . . as framed and
usually applied . . . is arbitrary and irrational. It fades out completely in
contracts for the sale of land, through the artificial but useful 'presumption' that it is impossible to value interests in land." 57 Mich. L. Rev. at
532. How much sense the "uniqueness of Blackacre" idea[6] ever made is
questionable. It certainly makes less sense when translated into the brave
new world of Levittown in which land seems to have become fungible as
wheat or corn or oil.

Recognizing that some parcels are more unique than others, courts
have in recent years shown a marginally greater willingness to deny specific performance of contracts for the sale of real property, on the ground
that the plaintiff has an adequate remedy at law. See Watkins v. Paul, 95
Idaho 499, 511 P.2d 781 (1974); Suchan v. Rutherford, 90 Idaho 288, 410

6. The uniqueness of Blackacre may not have had as much to do with the traditional
availability of specific performance for land contracts as we are accustomed to think. Professor David Cohen has speculated that before the nineteenth century, many purchasers
bought land in order to obtain the voting rights and other political privileges that went with
it — an objective that could be guaranteed only if contracts for the sale of land were
specifically enforceable. If Professor Cohen is right, we should look for the origins of the
rule in the system of feudal tenures, not in the principle *de gustibus non est disputandum*,
which belongs to a later and more individualistic age. See Cohen, The Relationship of
Contractual Remedies to Political and Social Status: A Preliminary Inquiry, 32 U. Toronto
L.J. 31 (1982).

P.2d 434 (1966); Duckworth v. Michel, 172 Wash. 234, 19 P.2d 914 (1933).
It is interesting to note that in the two Idaho cases emphasis was placed
on the fact that the purchaser intended to resell the property rather than
to use it himself. The rule that land contracts are specifically enforceable
still holds true in the main, but seems to be giving way, here and there,
out of a recognition, perhaps, that the purchase even of a residence is
today in large part a speculative investment.

However, if the doctrine of specific performance has lost some of the
rigor it once had in the case of land contracts, it appears to be gaining
ground in other areas where the doctrine traditionally was thought un-
workable. For example, courts have in the past expressed great reluctance to compel the specific performance of an action that by its nature
would take a long time or require skill in its execution. The courts, it was
said, have neither the time nor the expert judgment to supervise such an
undertaking and can therefore do no more, in cases of this kind, than
award the plaintiff his damages. For a classic statement of this view, see
Edelen v. Samuels, 103 S.W. 360, 126 Ky. 295 (1907). How far we have
come from this view of the matter can be seen by a glance at Eastern
Rolling Mill Co. v. Michlovitz, digested *infra* p. 1094 (ordering the specific
performance of a long-term output contract), or City Stores Co. v. Ammerman, digested *infra* p. 1089 (specifically enforcing a contract to grant
the plaintiff a lease in the defendant's newly constructed shopping center
on terms "at least equal" to those offered the defendant's other major
lessees). Twenty years ago Professor Corbin noted that the cases "have
been numerous in which a decree has been refused on the ground that
the performance required is one of long duration and its enforcement
would involve long continued supervision by the court." Acknowledging
that "at times this may still be a sufficient reason for refusal," Professor
Corbin went on to argue that

> in many such cases the decree may be so constructed as to put an effective
> economic and moral pressure on the defendant, and the character of the
> performance rendered by the defendant can be determined by means of
> periodical reports to the court, with the aid and advice of expert advisers
> and masters in chancery. The court can count on the production of the
> necessary evidence by the parties in whose behalf the decree is rendered.

5A Corbin §1171. This is the modern view, and its growing acceptance
has certainly lowered the threshold to specific performance in areas
where the doctrine previously had little application.[7]

7. See Comment 1 to §2-716 of the Uniform Commercial Code and the Introductory
Note preceding the discussion of specific performance in the Second Restatement of Contracts, both of which endorse a "more liberal attitude" toward the application of the doctrine. For a review of this development, see Van Hecke, Changing Emphasis in Specific
Performance, 40 N.C.L. Rev. 1 (1961).

Expanding in certain respects, contracting in others, the doctrine of specific performance continues to lead an unsettled life, and in recent years scholars have redoubled their efforts to identify its rationale and explain its limits. In the materials that follow, we shall begin with a nostalgic look at one of the great moments of nineteenth-century jurisprudence, and then consider a few modern instances of the ebb and flow of doctrine in this traditionally confused area of the law.

LUMLEY v. WAGNER

1 DeG., M. & G. 604, 42 Eng. Rep. 687 (Ch. 1852)

The bill in this suit was filed on the 22nd April 1852, by Benjamin Lumley, the lessee of Her Majesty's Theatre, against Johanna Wagner, Albert Wagner, her father, and Frederick Gye, the lessee of Covent Garden Theatre: it stated that in November 1851, Joseph Bacher, as the agent of the defendants Albert Wagner and Johanna Wagner came to and concluded at Berlin an agreement in writing in the French language, bearing date the 9th November 1851, and which agreement being translated into English was as follows:

> The undersigned Mr. Benjamin Lumley, possessor of her Majesty's Theatre at London, and of the Italian Opera at Paris, of the one part, and Mademoiselle Johanna Wagner, cantatrice of the Court of his Majesty the King of Prussia, with the consent of her father, Mr. A. Wagner, residing at Berlin, of the other part, have concerted and concluded the following contract. — First, Mademoiselle Johanna Wagner binds herself to sing three months at the theatre of Mr. Lumley, her Majesty's at London, to date from the 1st of April 1852 (the time necessary for the journey comprised therein) and to give the parts following, 1st. Romeo, Montecchi; 2nd. Fides, Prophete; 3rd. Valentine, Huguenots; 4th. Anna, Don Juan; 5th. Alice, Robert le Diable; 6th. An opera chosen by common accord. — Second, The three first parts must necessarily be, 1st, Romeo, 2nd, Fides, 3rd, Valentine; these parts once sung, and then only she will appear, if Mr. Lumley desires it, in the three other operas mentioned aforesaid. — Third, These six parts belong exclusively to Mademoiselle Wagner, and any other cantatrice shall not presume to sing them during the three months of her engagement. If Mr. Lumley happens to be prevented, by any cause soever, from giving these operas, he is nevertheless held to pay Mademoiselle Johanna Wagner the salary stipulated lower down for the number of her parts as if she had sung them. — Fourth, In the case where Mademoiselle Wagner should be prevented by reason of illness from singing in the course of a month as often as it has been stipulated, Mr. Lumley is bound to pay the salary only for the parts sung. — Fifth, Mademoiselle Johanna Wagner binds herself to sing twice a week during the run of the three months; however, if she herself was hindered from singing twice in any week whatever, she will have the right to give at a later period the omitted

representation. — Sixth, If Mademoiselle Wagner, fulfilling the wishes of
the Direction, consent to sing more than twice a week in the course of
three months, this last will give to Mademoiselle Wagner £50 sterling for
each representation extra. — Seventh, Mr. Lumley engages to pay Mademoiselle Wagner a salary of £400 sterling per month, and payment will take
place in such manner that she will receive £100 sterling each week. —
Eighth, Mr. Lumley will pay by letters of exchange to Mademoiselle
Wagner at Berlin, the 15th of March 1852, the sum of £300 sterling, a sum
which will be deducted from her engagement in his retaining £100 each
month. — Ninth, In all cases except that where a verified illness would
place upon her a hindrance, if Mademoiselle Wagner shall not arrive in
London eight days after that from whence dates her engagement, Mr.
Lumley will have the right to regard the nonappearance as a rupture of
the contract, and will be able to demand an indemnification. — Tenth,
In the case where Mr. Lumley should cede his enterprise to another, he has
the right to transfer this contract to his successor, and in that case Mademoiselle Wagner has the same obligations and the same rights towards the
last as towards Mr. Lumley.

JOHANNA WAGNER,
ALBERT WAGNER.

[An additional clause was later added, under which Mlle. Wagner
agreed not to appear in any other theatre, concert, etc., without the
written permission of Lumley. Codefendant Gye subsequently persuaded
Mlle. Wagner to break the Lumley contract by singing at his Royal Italian
Opera in London. Lumley asked an injunction restraining Mlle. Wagner
from appearing at the proposed concert, or at any other concert, and also
another injunction restraining Gye from permitting Mlle. Wagner to appear at his Opera. The injunctions were granted in the court below, and
defendants appealed.]

The Lord Chancellor (LORD ST. LEONARDS). The question which I
have to decide in the present case arises out of a very simple contract, the
effect of which is, that the Defendant Johanna Wagner should sing at her
Majesty's Theatre for a certain number of nights, and that she should not
sing elsewhere (for that is the true construction) during that period. As I
understand the points taken by the Defendants' counsel in support of this
appeal they in effect come to this, namely, that a Court of equity ought
not to grant an injunction except in cases connected with specific performance, or where the injunction being to compel a party to forbear from
committing an act (and not to perform an act), that injunction will complete the whole of the agreement remaining unexecuted. . . .

The present is a mixed case, consisting not of two correlative acts to be
done, one by the Plaintiff and the other by the Defendants, which state of
facts may have and in some cases has introduced a very important difference, — but of an act to be done by J. Wagner alone, to which is super-
added a negative stipulation on her part to abstain from the commission

of any act which will break in upon her affirmative covenant — the one being ancillary to, concurrent and operating together with the other. The agreement to sing for the Plaintiff during three months at his theatre, and during that time not to sing for anybody else, is not a correlative contract, it is in effect one contract; and though beyond all doubt this Court could not interfere to enforce the specific performance of the whole of this contract, yet in all sound construction, and according to the true spirit of the agreement, the engagement to perform for three months at one theatre must necessarily exclude the right to perform at the same time at another theatre. It was clearly intended that J. Wagner was to exert her vocal abilities to the utmost to aid the theatre to which she agreed to attach herself. I am of the opinion, that if she had attempted, even in the absence of any negative stipulation, to perform at another theatre, she would have broken the spirit and true meaning of the contract as much as she would now do with reference to the contract into which she has actually entered.

Wherever this Court has not proper jurisdiction to enforce specific performance, it operates to bind men's consciences, as far as they can be bound, to a true and literal performance of their agreements; and it will not suffer them to depart from their contracts at their pleasure, leaving the party with whom they have contracted to the mere chance of any damages which a jury may give. The exercise of this jurisdiction has, I believe, had a wholesome tendency towards the maintenance of that good faith which exists in this country to a much greater degree perhaps than in any other; and although the jurisdiction is not to be extended, yet a Judge would desert his duty who did not act up to what his predecessors have handed down as the rule for his guidance in the administration of such an equity.

It was objected that the operation of the injunction in the present case was mischievous, excluding the Defendant J. Wagner from performing at any other theatre while this Court had no power to compel her to perform at her Majesty's Theatre. It is true, that I have not the means of compelling her to sing, but she has no cause of complaint, if I compel her to abstain from the commission of an act which she has bound herself not to do, and thus possibly cause her to fulfil her engagement. The jurisdiction which I now exercise is wholly within the power of the Court, and being of opinion that it is a proper case for interfering, I shall leave nothing unsatisfied by the judgment I pronounce. The effect too of the injunction, in restraining J. Wagner from singing elsewhere may, in the event of an action being brought against her by the Plaintiff, prevent any such amount of vindictive damages being given against her as a jury might probably be inclined to give if she had carried her talents and exercised them at the rival theatre: the injunction may also, as I have said, tend to the fulfilment of her engagement; though, in continuing the injunction, I disclaim doing indirectly what I cannot do directly.

Referring again to the authorities, I am well aware that they have not been uniform, and that there undoubtedly has been a difference of decision on the question now revived before me; but, after the consideration which I have been enabled to give to the subject, the conclusion at which I have arrived is, I conceive, supported by the greatest weight of authority. . . .

His Lordship concluded by saying that, looking at the merits and circumstances of the case, as well as at the point of law raised, he must refuse this motion with costs.

NOTE

1. For the subsequent history of the litigation, culminating in Lumley v. Gye, 2 E. & B. 216, 118 Eng. Rep. 749 (1853), see Z. Chafee & E. Re, Cases and Materials on Equity 233 (5th ed. 1967). For the development of the Lumley v. Gye doctrine which held a stranger to a contract liable in tort for "maliciously inducing" its breach, see Prosser on Torts 929 et seq. (4th ed. 1971). The monopolistic effects of the widespread use of rigid personal-service contracts in professional baseball are discussed in Topkis, Monopoly in Professional Sports, 58 Yale L.J. 691 (1949). See also Flood v. Kuhn, 407 U.S. 258 (1972) (upholding the exemption of baseball from the antitrust laws as an "established aberration").

2. The Lord Chancellor evidently believed that, as a matter of morals, men should so far as possible, be bound "to a true and literal performance of their agreements" and should not be permitted "to depart from their contracts at their pleasure," leaving the other party "to the mere chance of any damages which a jury may give." In this respect, his view of the promisor's moral duties seems to have been close to that expressed by Justice Story, supra p. 1070. The opposite point of view, championed by Holmes, rests on the assumption that a man does no wrong by breaking his promise as long as he is prepared to compensate the other party for the damages he suffers. When a person makes a contract, should we think of him as promising in the alternative ("I promise either to perform or pay damages")? What moral significance should we assign to the fact that some of the harms caused by a breach may be noncompensable (for example, the disappointment and loss of trust a promisee experiences even if he is fully reimbursed for his pecuniary loss)? For a recent discussion of the morality of promise-keeping and its implications for contract law, see C. Fried, Contract as Promise (1981). Professor Fried argues vigorously for the idea that contractual obligation is rooted in the duty to keep one's promises but assumes, without argument, the propriety of requiring the breaching party in most cases to pay only money damages (even where the breach is willful).

As to what the Lord Chancellor calls "the mere chance of damages," it should be noted that Lumley v. Wagner antedated by two years Baron Alderson's celebrated attempt to provide a rational basis for damage theory in Hadley v. Baxendale. See *supra* p. 106.

3. Suppose the shoe in Lumley v. Wagner had been on the other foot. If Benjamin Lumley had refused to allow Mademoiselle Wagner to sing and had hired someone else to perform her parts instead, could she have obtained an injunction forbidding Lumley from staging the operas without her? It has often been said that a court will not compel specific performance of a promise to perform personal services, on the theory that to do so would be to impose a kind of involuntary servitude on the promisor. But where it is the performing party who seeks specific performance, does the same argument apply? Consider the case of Staklinski v. Pyramid Electric Co., 6 N.Y.2d 159, 160 N.E.2d 78 (1959). Mr. Staklinski had entered into an eleven-year contract with Pyramid Electric. The contract contained a provision stating that any dispute arising under it was to be settled by arbitration in accordance with the rules of the American Arbitration Association. Two years after the contract was concluded, the company made a determination (as it was permitted to do under another provision of the contract) that Mr. Staklinski was permanently disabled and that his services should be terminated. Mr. Staklinksi challenged the company's finding and the parties submitted their dispute to arbitration. The arbitrators held in Mr. Staklinski's favor and ordered his reinstatement. On appeal, the company sought to invalidate the arbitrators' award on the grounds "that it is against public policy to compel a corporation to continue the services of an officer whose services are unsatisfactory to the directors." Six members of the Court of Appeals construed the arbitrators' award as requiring the specific performance of a long-term contract under which the Pyramid Company had retained Staklinski's services "at a large salary plus a percentage of net profits." Of the six judges who so read the award, three voted to confirm it and three to overturn it. The seventh judge, Froessel, J., voted to confirm on the ground that he read the award as merely providing for damages in case Pyramid refused to reinstate Staklinski.

STOKES v. MOORE
262 Ala. 59, 77 So. 2d 331 (1955)

Per Curiam.

This is an appeal by the respondent from a decree overruling his demurrer to a bill in equity authorized by section 755, Title 7, Code, and a decree ordering the issuance of a temporary injunction after a hearing as authorized by section 1057, Title 7, Code.

The complainants are partners and conduct a small loan business under the firm name of Reliance Finance Company in Mobile.

The bill alleges that on March 20, 1950 complainants entered into a contract with the respondent, H. E. Stokes, which provided for his employment by them as manager of their business. The purpose of the bill is to enjoin Stokes from violating the covenant of said agreement to the effect that in the event his employment is terminated for any reason he would not engage in the same or a similar line of business in Mobile either for himself or for another for a period of one year immediately following the termination of his employment. A copy of the contract is attached to the bill and made an exhibit. It provides for the employment of respondent by complainants without specification as to the length of time such employment shall continue, and provides for a monthly salary payable semimonthly. It authorizes the respondent, in the event he desired to terminate the contract of employment, to tender his written resignation effective not earlier than two weeks from the date of said resignation.

Another provision in the contract is to the effect that on account of the special nature of respondent's employment, in the event of a violation of any of its terms or pledges stated in the paragraph, a restraining order or injunction may be issued against him in any court of equity and that said court may assess and enter judgment against him in favor of complainants in the sum of $500 as liquidated damages for each such violation unless upon investigation it is proven that the loss resulting from each such violation is in excess of that amount, in which case such judgment may be assessed and entered against him for the full loss of same. Among the pledges stated in said paragraph is the covenant not to engage in a similar line of business in Mobile for one year immediately following the termination of his employment with the complainants.

The bill also alleges that the respondent began his employment under such contract with complainants on March 20, 1950, which is the date of its execution, as the manager of said finance company and served in that capacity until the 24th day of August 1954, at which time he voluntarily quit said employment; and that on the next day thereafter he took a job managing the Globe Finance Company, which was then set up by him and another as partners, and proceeded to engage in the same line of business in Mobile and was located only a short distance from the place of business of the Reliance Finance Company; and, further, that he breached said contract of employment by soliciting business from the former customers of complainants and communicated with them by mail, a sample copy of such communication being attached as an exhibit to the bill.

The prayer of the bill was that a temporary injunction issue enjoining the respondent from working for or engaging in the loan business in the city of Mobile for a period of one year in competition with the complainants; and further that a decree be rendered against the respondent in favor of the complainants in the sum of $500 as liquidated damages for a breach of said contract according to its stipulations.

The demurrer to the bill raised several questions with respect to its sufficiency, and on the hearing of the application for a temporary injunction an answer to the bill and affidavits were submitted for both complainants and respondent. These affidavits were principally devoted to the questions of whether such covenants are usual in contracts of that kind in Mobile, and whether it is customary to enforce them when they are set up in the contract and are violated; whether any actual damage has been sustained by the complainants on account of the breach of such covenants by the respondent, and whether the equities of the respective parties to the contract demand the issuance of a temporary injunction as prayed for. . . .

Section 23, Title 9, Code, has withdrawn from consideration some matters otherwise important. Rush v. Newsom Exterminators, Inc., Ala., 75 So. 2d 112. To enjoin one from breaching a covenant not to be employed in competition with another, and therefore in effect for a specific performance of his contract was, without the statute, encumbered with important principles not applicable since the enactment of the statute. 43 C.J.S., Injunctions, §84, page 571 et seq. The statute has fixed the public policy of this State in respect to employment contracts. To be enforceable under it there must be an employment contract mutually binding or executed by the employer in such manner as to provide valuable and reasonably adequate consideration for the contract of the employee, Hill v. Rice, [259 Ala. 587, 67 So. 2d 793], whereby the employee agrees "'to refrain from carrying on or engaging in a similar business and from soliciting old customers of such employer within a specified county, city, or part thereof, so long as . . . such employer carries on like business therein.'"

The contract here involved complies with those requirements when considered in connection with the facts alleged in the bill and affidavits. The contract does not in terms bind the employer for any definite time, but it is shown that the parties acted upon it from March 20, 1950 to August 24, 1954 when the employee voluntarily terminated the employment without alleging any fault on the part of the employer inducing it, and immediately began to operate a competitive business in the city of Mobile in direct conflict with his covenant. The compliance with the contract by the employer by giving respondent employment from March 20, 1950 to August 24, 1954 with apparent willingness to continue to do so for an indefinite period in the future provided a valuable and adequate consideration for the covenant of the employee to continue as expressed in the contract, although it was unilateral at its inception. It results that we find a valid contract supported by a sufficient consideration with covenants to be operative only in the city of Mobile and to extend for only one year. But a contract of that sort does not always justify the issuance of an injunction against its breach. In our case of Shelton v. Shelton, 238 Ala. 489, 192 So. 55, this Court carefully considered and declared the circumstances which would give rise to an injunction. It was held that an injunction is largely a discretionary remedy to prevent substantial injury where no adequate remedy at law obtains. It must not only be violative of the contract, but must be carried on in competition with the former employer, and inadequacy of legal remedy may arise from inability to prove with certainty the extent of the injury required for a recovery of damages at law, or from the insolvency of the employee violating his contract. Ordinarily an injunction will not be granted where the contract is inequitable and unfair so as not to appeal to the conscience of a court of equity. It was further emphasized that an injunction should issue when the contract is not per se illegal or oppressive; between persons dealing at arms' length; with the presence of freedom in making it, and not arbitrarily enforced by the employer so as to work an unnecessary hardship on the employee. It was held that the injunction was properly issued in that case. See, also, Slay v. Hess, 252 Ala. 455, 41 So. 2d 582.

There is no allegation of insolvency by the employee. The contract contained a provision for liquidated damages in the sum of $500 for each violation. There was only one breach of that covenant in the contract, which breach was continuous in its nature. Damages could not be recovered, though liquidated by the contract, and at the same time an injunction issue. The amount stipulated for liquidated damages covers the period of its breach for one year if there is an injunction effective during the year or any part of it, liquidated damages would not be recoverable. But that status is not a defect in the bill subjecting it to demurrer on that ground. While the prayer is not in the alternative for an injunction or liquidated damages, that is not a defect.

Complainants have seen fit to press for an injunction. Their claim for liquidated damages is not a matter for present determination except as it may affect the right to a temporary injunction. The provision in the contract for liquidated damages will not operate to prevent an injunction even though the employee is not insolvent, unless it appears from the contract that the provision for liquidated damages was intended to be the exclusive remedy for its breach. 43 C.J.S., Injunctions, §§80(6), 84, pages 556, 574. Here it is apparent from the contract that liquidated damages were not intended to be the exclusive remedy for a breach of that covenant, for the contract provides that if this covenant is breached

a restraining order or injunction may be issued and entered against me (employee) in any court of equity jurisdiction, and that such court may assess and enter judgment against me in favor of your company for the sum of five hundred dollars ($500.00) as liquidated damages for each such violation.

We do not wish to express the view that an agreement for the issuance of an injunction, if and when a stipulated state of facts arises in the future, is binding on the court to that extent. Such an agreement would serve to oust the inherent jurisdiction of the court to determine whether an injunction is appropriate when applied for and to require its issuance even though to do so would be contrary to the opinion of the court. The following authorities are pertinent in that respect: Sections 16 and 17, Title 20, Code; 17 C.J.S., Contracts, §229, page 603; Headley v. Aetna Ins. Co., 202 Ala. 384, 80 So. 466; Merchants' Grocery Co. v. Talledega Grocery Co., 217 Ala. 334, 116 So. 356; John Hancock Mutual Life Ins. Co. v. Large, 230 Ala. 621, 162 So. 277.

But the provision in the contract for the issuance of an injunction is expressive of the intention of the parties that the provision for liquidated damages was not to be the exclusive remedy. The result is that the right to an injunction is not foreclosed by the provision for liquidated damages. We also think the provision for an injunction is important in its influence upon an exercise of the discretionary power of the court to grant a temporary injunction.

The evidence shows that respondent set up a competitive business in close proximity to that of complainants. We infer from the evidence that the amount of business done by a small loan enterprise is largely the result of the activity of the manager and affected by personal influences which are not measurable in their effect. It was shown that as a manager of a rival business respondent did contact former customers of complainants. His stationery and communications show that he has been making personal appeals contrary to the terms of his covenant, although there was no fault on complainants' part, but because he was able to obtain a better contract. He stipulated against such contingency, with full knowledge of its possible effect. The terms of his covenant and attendant circumstances do not show an unusual hardship resulting from an injunction of its breach. There is a reasonable limitation on the area and time in which the covenant is to extend.

We find no defect in the bill pointed out in the demurrer and insisted on by appellant. There was therefore no reversible error in overruling it. The order for a temporary injunction should be here modified to be effective from its date, December 1, 1954, until the further orders of the court, but not extending beyond August 24, 1955, upon complainants entering into bond payable and conditioned and with surety to be approved, all as provided in section 1043, Title 7, Code, and in the penal sum of $2,000 as prescribed by the trial judge. As thus modified, the order for a temporary injunction and decree overruling the demurrer to the bill should be affirmed.

The foregoing opinion was prepared by FOSTER, Supernumerary Justice of this Court, while serving on it at the request of the Chief Justice under authority of Title 13, section 32, Code, and was adopted by the Court as its opinion.

Affirmed as modified.

Livingston, C.J., and Lawson, Stakely and Merrill, JJ., concur.

NOTE

1. The contract involved in Stokes v. Moore contained a provision empowering the employer to obtain an injunction against his employee in the event the latter breached his promise not to compete. In substance, if not in form, this provision represented an attempt by the parties to create a right of specific enforcement by contractual agreement. Should it have been enforced according to its terms, rather than treated merely as an important "influence" on the court's exercise of its discretionary power to grant or deny the injunction requested by the employer? MacNeil, Power of Contract and Agreed Remedies, 47 Cornell L.Q. 495, 521-522 (1962) comments:

> The question of "agreed specific performance clauses" apparently has arisen in court rarely. One can speculate on the reasons for this paucity, but the most likely one is historical. Since specific performance was an equitable remedy, its prerequisites were jurisdictional. And one scarcely went around attempting to confer jurisdiction on the Chancellor so blatantly. Consequently, the thought of putting such a provision in a contract would hardly have crossed the common-law mind, but such provisions are probably becoming more common.

Professor MacNeil reports that, apart from the special situation of cooperative marketing agreements, he was able to find only six cases that raised the question of "agreed specific performance." Typically, the opinions make no more than passing reference to the contract clause but, in cases where the court has decided to give judgment for plaintiff, go on to demonstrate at length that on the facts specific performance (or a restraining order) is an appropriate remedy.

2. Kronman, Specific Performance, 45 U. Chi. L. Rev. 351, 371-373 (1978):

> A private agreement that purports to give one party the right to specifically enforce the promise of another will be given some weight by courts in deciding whether to grant injunctive relief. But no court will consider itself foreclosed by the parties' contract from refusing specific relief. A contractual provision accompanied by a lengthy description of those aspects of the transaction that make specific performance desirable is likely to carry more weight than a provision unadorned by supporting explanation.[8] But in no

8. See Peters, Remedies for Breach of Contracts Relating to the Sale of Goods Under the Uniform Commercial Code: A Roadmap for Article Two, 73 Yale L.J. 199, 252 (1963).

event will the contract provision prevent a court from independently determining the appropriateness of injunctive relief.[9]

Perhaps judicial unwillingness to honor provisions such as the one in *Stokes* reflects a desire to avoid private abuse of a powerful and intrusive remedy. This is a legitimate concern. But if the purpose in scrutinizing a private agreement of the *Stokes* variety is to prevent abuse by an overreaching promisee, this end could be served as adequately and more directly by other legal tools — for example, by traditional common law doctrines of fraud, duress, and good faith.[10] If the concern is abuse of the contracting process, courts should focus on the voluntariness of the parties' agreement.

It may be, however, that courts prohibit the private creation of injunctive remedies not because specific performance provisions evidence some procedural unfairness in the parties' dealings, but rather because they are perceived to be substantively unacceptable limitations on personal freedom. A provision of the kind involved in *Stokes* might be viewed as a modified contract of self-enslavement, an attempt to transfer an entitlement whose transfer is prohibited by law (an "inalienable" right or entitlement in the scheme proposed by Calabresi and Melamed).[11] This idea is echoed in some of the older specific performance cases involving construction and employment contracts.[12]

Such an argument carries little weight in a case like *Stokes*, where the promise to be enforced is a negative one — a promise to refrain from doing something. More importantly, the argument is overdrawn. It is true that certain forms of domination (for example, slavery and peonage) are regarded as inherently bad. Our legal system prohibits these forms of domination, whether they are created by consensual act or by force. On the other hand, there are many relations of domination recognized and protected by law so long as they are voluntarily established and maintained. The relation created by a contract of employment is an important example of legally protected domination.

The nature, completeness, and duration of self-imposed limitations on personal freedom determine their legal and moral acceptability. Slavery is objectionable largely because it involves near-total control. By contrast the domination an employer exercises is partial and limited — the employer only controls certain aspects of his employee's life. Nevertheless, employ-

---

9. This is more frequently expressed by saying that specific performance is a discretionary remedy, and "the right to specific performance is not absolute, like the right to recover the legal judgment." [J. Pomeroy, A Treatise on the Specific Performance of Contracts §35 (J. Mann 3d ed. 1926).] It is well established that "[n]either party to a contract can insist, as a matter of right, upon a decree for its specific performance." Snell v. Mitchell, 65 Me. 48, 50 (1876). Only if a promise would be specifically enforced in the absence of a contractual provision purporting to give the promisee the power to enjoin its performance, will a court compel the promisor to do what he initially agreed to do and not permit him to substitute money damages: "If one who contracts to render personal service agrees that in case of breach the remedies of specific performance and imprisonment shall be available to the employer, the agreement would not be effective." [Corbin §1432]

10. See Epstein, Unconscionability: A Critical Reappraisal, 18 J. Law & Econ. 293 (1976).

11. See Calabresi & Melamed, [Property Rules, Liability Rules and Inalienability: One View of the Cathedral, 85 Harv. L. Rev. 1089, 1111-1115 (1972).]

12. See [11 Williston §1423.]

ees are not generally required by judicial order to submit to employer control. The judicial order, it may be argued, makes a crucial difference: if the employment relation is created or maintained by the threat of judicial sanctions, it is almost certain to be plagued by acrimony and ill-will. But although the unpleasantness of a forced employment relation should certainly be taken into account by an employer contemplating a suit for specific performance, it should not be a basis for refusing to impose such a relation upon parties who have agreed to an injunctive provision in their contract. Moreover, if the party in breach anticipates that the relation will be unbearable, he can buy his release from the contract.

Judicial insistence that the specific enforcement of certain contracts would create an objectionable form of personal servitude is made yet more puzzling by the numerous cases in which courts have been perfectly willing to negatively enjoin the party in breach from employing his time or talents save in performance of the contract.[13] This sort of decree will often have the same effect as a positive injunction to perform.

3. In Stokes v. Moore, the contract also provided for the payment of liquidated damages in the amount of $500 in the event of the employee's breach. Provisions of this sort are subject to judicial review and may be invalidated if they are construed to be "penalties" rather than the product of a good-faith effort to estimate the expected loss from a possible future breach. For more on this distinction, see the cases on liquidated damages collected in Section 4 of this chapter. Suppose that liquidated damage provisions were not subject to any requirement of "non-penalty." In that case, could not the employer in *Stokes* have achieved his aim simply by setting the penalty for breach at a sufficiently high level (say, $10,000 per violation)? Practically speaking, there is no significant difference, from the employee's point of view, between a penalty provision of this sort and an injunction ordering him to perform. It would seem, therefore, that the bar against penalty clauses and the invalidity of contractual provisions purporting to confer a right of specific enforcement on one of the parties have a similar justification (supposing, of course, that they are justifiable).

4. Think back, for a moment, to Lumley v. Wagner. What is the practical effect of the injunction Mr. Lumley obtained? Suppose that you are in Mademoiselle Wagner's position and have been offered a very lucrative contract with Mr. Gye, Lumley's competitor. Will you simply disregard the injunction and perform in Gye's theatre anyway? Will you resign yourself to the Lord Chancellor's decree and return to work for Lumley? There is, of course, a third alternative: you may approach Lumley and attempt to buy your way of your contract with him (by offering him, in effect, a share of the extra money you will make by singing for Gye). Since Lumley has already obtained an injunction, he can set the price for releasing you from your contractual obligation to him, and if he

13. See, e.g., Philadelphia Ball Club v. Lajoie, 202 Pa. 210, 51 A. 973 (1902).

refuses every offer you make, you must choose between singing for Lumley or not singing at all. Put more abstractly, a right of specific performance gives the promisee sole power to determine the price at which he will sell or transfer an asset he presently holds (the promisor's contractual obligation). In this respect, an injunction ordering specific performance differs fundamentally from an award of money damages, for in the latter case it is a court (and not the promisee himself) that fixes the value of the promisee's contractual entitlements — entitlements that the promisor may be said to appropriate by breaching. Does this way of looking at things help us to decide, in a more rational manner, when specific performance should be granted and when it should not? For conflicting answers, see Kronman, Specific Performance, *supra* p. 1084, at p. 351-369, and Schwartz, The Case for Specific Performance, *supra* p. 1071, at 278-296. The article by Calabresi and Melamed, cited in Note 2, *supra*, provides the foundation for this way of looking at the distinction between damages and specific performance. Every contracts student should read the Calabresi and Melamed article (even though it is not directly concerned with problems of contract law); it remains one of the most fertile and suggestive law review essays written in recent years.

5. Kronman, Paternalism and the Law of Contracts, 92 Yale L.J. 763, 778-779 (1983):

> . . . Every executory contract limits the freedom of the parties by creating an enforceable obligation, on both sides, to perform or pay damages: Once an individual has made a contractually binding commitment, his alternatives are limited to these two (assuming the other party is not himself in breach). The distinguishing mark of a contract of self-enslavement is that it purports to take away the latter alternative. From a legal point of view, it is not the length of service that makes a contract of employment self-enslaving, nor is it the nature of the services to be performed; even a contract of short duration that calls for the performance of routine and unobjectionable tasks is a contract of self-enslavement and therefore legally unenforceable if it bars the employee from substituting money damages for his promised performance.[14] The law will not permit an employee to contract away his right to "depersonalize" a relationship by paying damages in the event he chooses to breach. Whatever its other terms, an employment contract is enslaving if it gives the employer a right to compel specific performance of the agreement.[15]

14. This precise characteristic has been held to be the distinctive mark of the peonage system and other forms of involuntary servitude. [See Peonage Cases, 136 F. 707, 708 (E.D. Ark. 1905); Pollock v. Williams, 322 U.S. 4, 7-13 (1944); 18 U.S.C. §§1581-1588 (1976).] The peonage relationship — which often has a contractual origin — was distinguished from other legitimate employment contracts on the grounds that the peon only agreed to work for his master for a fixed or indefinite period of time, but also gave up his right to quit whenever he wished and avoid the contract by making a compensatory payment of money damages.

15. This theme links the Peonage Cases . . . to the well-established doctrine of contract law that an employee's obligations will not be specifically enforced, even if the parties have

Do you agree with this way of characterizing the difference between an ordinary labor contract and a contract of self-enslavement? Can the refusal to permit contracts of the latter sort be explained on economic grounds? If we assume that no third parties are harmed by a contract of self-enslavement, and that its prohibition cannot be convincingly explained on economic grounds alone, what moral principles might account for the abhorrence it immediately stimulates? John Stuart Mill suggested that the liberty to sell oneself into slavery would be self-defeating — a liberty that would mean the end of liberty. But doesn't the prohibition against such contracts also limit a person's liberty, by making it impossible for him to pursue whatever personal goals (wealth, security, etc.) such a contract might be intended to secure? Which of these liberties should be sacrificed for the other? For one approach to this problem, see Kronman, *supra*, at p. 775.

6. Shortly after the enactment of the Uniform Commercial Code in Pennsylvania, one of the lower courts in that state had occasion to consider a contract that provided "In the event of default by purchaser, seller shall have . . . in addition to any and all other rights under the Uniform Commercial Code and/or any other applicable law" the right to enter a judgment in replevin as well as the right to enter judgment for the full amount of the unpaid purchase price, with interest and costs, plus 15 percent for attorney's fees. (The goods involved were refrigerator cases and equipment for a food market and the contract price was $35,500; this was evidently a "commercial," as distinguished from a "consumer," transaction.) Counsel for the seller argued that this was a permissible "modification" of remedy under §2-719(1) [§2-719 is reprinted *infra* p. 1240]. The court, commenting that it was difficult to understand why anyone should sign such "a biased and one-sided agreement," concluded that the clause in question was "unconscionable and void." The court may have been influenced by the fact that another clause in the contract, not involved in the litigation, purported to give the seller the right to cancel the contract "at any time" before delivery, no comparable right being provided for the

---

provided that they shall be. [11 Williston §1423.] The well-known case of Lumley v. Wagner . . . is not to the contrary. Although the injunction awarded in that case prohibited the defendant from singing in other theaters, it did not subject her to the personal authority of the plaintiff; like money damages, the injunction in *Lumley* caused the defendant only economic loss (albeit a substantial one.)

An employee may specifically enforce an employment contract against a corporate employer. Staklinski v. Pyramid Elec. Co., 6 N.Y.2d 159, 160 N.E.2d 78, 188 N.Y.S.2d 541 (1959). This is consistent with the view that the right to depersonalize a contractual relationship is inalienable, since a corporation, though a legal person, lacks the elements of personal integrity this right protects. Note, Constitutional Rights of the Corporate Person, 91 Yale L.J. 1641, 1652-1655 (1982). . . .

In Canada, labor contracts are specifically enforceable against unions, which, like corporations, are deemed to lack the elements of personal integrity necessary to support the right to depersonalize contractual relationships. International Bhd. of Elec. Workers v. Winnipeg Builders Exch., 65 D.L.R.2d 242 (1967).

buyer. Denkin v. Sterner, 10 D. & C.2d 203 (C.P. of York County, 1956). Looking at §2-719 from a contract draftsman's point of view, what do you make of it?

CITY STORES CO. v. AMMERMAN, 266 F. Supp. 766 (D.D.C. 1967). The defendants (Ammerman and others) were interested in constructing a shopping center at Tyson's Corner in Fairfax County, Virginia. To help persuade the local zoning authorities to approve their plans, the defendants solicited a letter from the plaintiff expressing its interest in the project and its desire to become a major tenant if the center should in fact be built. In return, the defendants wrote a letter to the plaintiff promising to give it the opportunity to become one of the "contemplated center's major tenants with rental and terms at least equal to that of any other major department store in the center." The zoning application was granted and the center built, but the defendants refused to give the plaintiff a lease. City Stores sued for specific performance of the promise contained in the letter written by the defendants. After characterizing the letter as "a binding unilateral contract, which gave plaintiff an option to accept a lease" on the occurrence of certain "express and implied conditions precedent," Judge Gasch went on to consider whether the contract was sufficiently definite to be the subject of a decree for specific performance:

"It is not contested by the plaintiff that if it were to accept a lease tendered by defendants in accordance with the contract, there would be numerous complex details left to be worked out. The crucial elements of rate of rental and the amount of space can readily be determined from the Hecht and Woodward & Lothrop leases. But some details of design, construction and price of the building to be occupied by plaintiff at Tyson's Corner would have to be agreed to by the parties, subject to further negotiation and tempered only by the promise of equal terms with other tenants. The question is whether a court of equity will grant specific performance of a contract which has left such substantial terms open for future negotiation.

"The defendants have cited a number of cases in support of their argument that a court of equity will not grant specific performance of a contract in which some terms are left for further negotiations by the parties, or which would require a great deal of supervision by the court. I have examined those cases cited which were decided in this jurisdiction, because unless the precedents here establish a clear policy one way or the other, this court may exercise its discretion in fashioning an equitable decree. Moreover, this is an area of law in which not all jurisdictions are in agreement, and whichever way this court were to decide the case, there would be cases holding to the contrary in other parts of the country." A discussion of the cases followed.

After concluding that "the mere fact that a contract, definite in mate-

rial respects, contains some terms which are subject to further negotiation between plaintiff and defendant will not bar a decree for specific
performance, if in the court's discretion specific performance should be
granted," Judge Gasch continued:

"The question whether a contract which also calls for construction of a
building can or should be specifically enforced apparently never has been
decided before in this jurisdiction. The parties have cited no cases on this
point.

"At the outset, it should be noted that where specific performance of
such contracts has been granted the essential criterion has not been the
nature or subject of the contract, but rather the inadequacy or impracticability of legal remedies. See 5 Williston on Contracts §1423 (Rev. Ed.
1937); 4 Pomeroy's Equity Jurisprudence §§1401-1403 (5th Ed. 1941).
Contracts involving interests in land or unique chattels generally are
specifically enforced because of the clear inadequacy of damages at law
for breach of contract. As Pomeroy says:

> The foundation and measure of the jurisdiction is the desire to do jus-
> tice, which the legal remedy would fail to give. . . .
>   . . . The jurisdiction depending upon this broad principle is exercised in
> two classes of cases: 1. Where the subject-matter of the contract is of such a
> special nature, or of such a peculiar value, that the damages, when ascer-
> tained according to legal rules, would not be a just and reasonable substi-
> tute for or representative of that subject-matter in the hands of the party
> who is entitled to its benefit; or in other words, where the damages are
> *inadequate*; 2. Where, from some special and practical features or incidents
> of the contract inhering either in its subject matter, in its terms, or in the
> relations of the parties, it is impossible to arrive at a legal measure of
> damages at all, or at least with any sufficient degree of certainty, so that *no*
> real compensation can be obtained by means of an action at law; or in other
> words, where damages are *impracticable*.

"It is apparent from the nature of the contract involved in this case
that even were it possible to arrive at a precise measure of damages for
breach of a contract to lease a store in a shopping center for a period of
years — which it is not — money damages would in no way compensate
the plaintiff for loss of the right to participate in the shopping center
enterprise and for the almost incalculable future advantages that might
accrue to it as a result of extending its operations into the suburbs. Therefore, I hold that the appropriate remedy in this case is specific performance.

"Some jurisdictions in the United States have opposed granting specific performance of contracts for construction of buildings and other
contracts requiring extensive supervision of the court, but the better
view, and the one which increasingly is being followed in this country, is
that such contracts should be specifically enforced unless the difficulties

of supervision outweigh the importance of specific performance to the plaintiff. 5 Williston on Contracts §1423 (Rev. Ed. 1937). This is particularly true where the construction is to be done on land controlled by the defendant, because in that circumstance the plaintiff cannot employ another contractor to do the construction for him at defendant's expense. In the case at bar, the fact that more than mere construction of a building is involved reinforces the need for specific enforcement of the defendants' duty to perform their entire contractual obligation to the plaintiff. . . .

"The defendants contend that the granting of specific performance in this case will confront the court with insuperable difficulties of supervision, but after reviewing the evidence, I am satisfied that the standards to be observed in construction of the plaintiff's store are set out in the Hecht and Woodward & Lothrop leases with sufficient particularity (Plaintiff's Ex. F) as to make design and approval of plaintiff's store a fairly simple matter, if the parties deal with each other in good faith and expeditiously, as I shall hereafter order.

"For example, Article VIII, Sec. 8.1, Paragraph (G) of the Hecht lease (the Woodward & Lothrop lease contains a similar provision) says:

> The quality of (i) the construction, (ii) the construction components, (iii) the decorative elements (including landscaping irrigation systems for the landscaping) and (iv) the furnishings; and the general architectural character and general design, the materials selection, the decor and the treatment values, approach and standards of the Enclosed Mall shall be comparable, at minimum, to the qualities, values, approaches and standards as of the date hereof of the enclosed mall at Topanga Plaza Shopping Center, Los Angeles, California. . . .

"The existing leases contain further detailed specifications which will be identical to those in the lease granted to plaintiff. The site for plaintiff's store has already been settled by the design of the center. Although the exact design of plaintiff's store will not be identical to the design of any other store, it must be remembered that all of the stores are to be part of the same center and subject to its overall design requirements. If the parties are not in good faith able to reach an agreement on certain details, the court will appoint a special master to help settle their differences, unless they prefer voluntarily to submit their disagreements to arbitration. . . ." [footnotes omitted.]

NOTE

1. The situation involved in the *City Stores* case has, in recent years, accounted for a considerable amount of litigation with results surprisingly (in the light of traditional doctrine) favorable to plaintiffs seeking specific

performance decrees. There are collections of cases in various sections of
11 Williston, ch. 43; the principal case is cited in §1422A and analyzed at
length in §1425A. For a case taking the other side of the argument, see
Besinger v. National Tea Company, 75 Ill. App. 2d 395, 221 N.E.2d 156
(1966).

2. In a footnote to his opinion in the *City Stores* case, Judge Gasch
digested the 1960 New York case of Grayson-Robinson Stores, Inc. v. Iris
Construction Co., 8 N.Y.2d 133, 202 N.Y.S.2d 377, as follows:

> [T]he Court granted specific performance of an arbitration award to con-
> struct a store in a shopping center. This contract was in the form of a
> written agreement between Grayson and Iris whereby Iris undertook to
> build on its shopping center tract a building to be rented to Grayson for use
> as a retail department store for a term of 25 years. The contract contained a
> clause providing for arbitration of disputes and, when Iris refused to con-
> struct the building, Grayson submitted the matter to arbitration. The arbi-
> trators ordered Iris to proceed with construction. Iris refused to obey the
> award and Grayson took the matter to court. Iris argued that specific en-
> forcement of the award would be contrary to public policy because it would
> amount to the granting of specific performance of a building contract re-
> quiring long-continued supervision of the court. In affirming the decree
> awarding specific performance, the Court said: "Clearly there is no binding
> rule that deprives equity of jurisdiction to order specific performance of a
> building contract. At most there is discretion in the court to refuse such a
> decree."

266 F. Supp. at 777 n.5.

The *Grayson-Robinson* case followed Staklinski v. Pyramid Electric
Co., discussed *supra* p. 1079, in Note 3 following Lumley v. Wagner. Like
Staklinski, the *Grayson-Robinson* case concerned the validity of an arbitrator's award of specific performance. And, again like *Staklinski*, *Grayson-Robinson* also confirmed the award by a bare majority of the court
over a vigorous dissent. In *Grayson-Robinson*, however, all seven judges
agreed that the award ordered Iris to go out and construct the building;
the dissenting opinion pointed out that Iris, whose duty to go forward was
apparently contingent on its being able to obtain the necessary financing,
had applied to 27 lending institutions and been turned down by all of them.

In both *Staklinski* and *Grayson-Robinson* the prevailing faction of the
court emphasized that the parties, by agreeing to arbitration under the
rules of the American Arbitration Association, in effect agreed to specific
enforcement of their contracts. It is, of course, unlikely in the highest
degree that any court would, on its own, have ordered specific performance of the employment contract in *Staklinski*. Burke, J., dissenting in
Staklinski, wrote: "We conclude that the confirmation of an award compelling reinstatement of a non-resident official in a foreign corporation in
the form of specific performance of a contract for personal services

should not be made by this court even though the parties may have provided for it." 6 N.Y.S.2d at 167.

Can the majority view in *Staklinski* and *Grayson-Robinson* be reconciled with Stokes v. Moore and the authorities cited in the Note following that case, all of which state that the parties to a contract cannot create a right of specific performance by mutual agreement? See also Garrity v. Lyle Stuart, Inc., reprinted *infra* p. 1212.

3. In Northern Delaware Industrial Development Corp. v. E. W. Bliss Co., 245 A.2d 431 (Del. Ch. 1968), the plaintiffs sought specific enforcement of a provision in a construction contract under which the defendant had agreed to supply the labor and materials needed to modernize the plaintiffs' steel processing plant. Though its meaning was disputed, the provision in question apparently required the defendant to put extra workers on the job during the period that one of the plaintiffs' processing mills would have to be closed down to allow for its modernization. The defendant refused to hire the additional workers called for by the contract, and the plaintiffs sought an injunction compelling defendant to do so. The court refused to grant the injunction on the grounds that it should not "become committed to supervising the carrying out of a massive, complex, and unfinished construction contract," a result it feared "would necessarily follow as a consequence of ordering defendant to requisition laborers as prayed for." Id. at 432. City Stores v. Ammerman was noted, but distinguished: the plans for the shopping center involved in the *City Stores* cases "were quite definite" and the court in that case "was obviously impressed by the fact that unless the relief sought were to be granted, plaintiff would lose out on a promised opportunity to share in the expected profits of a shopping center in a burgeoning North Virginia suburb." Id. at 433. The court in the *Northern Delaware* case concluded by stating that

> to grant specific performance, as prayed for by plaintiffs, would be inappropriate in view of the imprecision of the contract provision relied upon and the impracticability if not impossibility of effective enforcement by the Court of a mandatory order designed to keep a specific number of men on the job at the site of a steel mill which is undergoing extensive modernization and expansion. If plaintiffs have sustained loss as a result of actionable building delays on defendant's part at the Phoenix plant at Claymont, they may, at an appropriate time, resort to law for a fixing of their claimed damages.

Id. at 433.

On reargument, the court reaffirmed its position and added an additional reason in support of its refusal to issue the requested injunction.

> Plaintiffs, in seeking specific performance of what they now term defendant's ministerial duty to hire a substantial number of additional laborers,

run afoul of the well-established principle that performance of a contract
for personal services, even of a unique nature, will not be affirmatively and
directly enforced, Lumley v. Wagner, 1 De G.M. & G. 404. See also Vol. 4,
Pomeroy's Equity Jurisprudence §1343. This is so, because, as in the closely
analogous case of a construction contract, the difficulties involved in compelling performance are such as to make an order for specific performance
impractical.

Id. at 434.

Do you find the reasons offered for denying the plaintiffs' request for
specific performance convincing? Which reason seems to you the strongest? Should the court in the *Northern Delaware* case have followed City
Stores v. Ammerman, instead of distinguishing it? If the plaintiffs in
Northern Delaware had subsequently sued the defendant for damages due
to the delayed reopening of the steel mill, their damages would probably
have been determined by applying the famous "rule" of Hadley v. Baxendale, reprinted *supra* p. 106. Under this rule, which governs the recovery
of lost profits, the plaintiffs would be awarded damages only for those
losses that were foreseeable by the defendant, given the defendant's general knowledge of the world and its more particularized knowledge of the
plaintiffs' affairs. Does this help to explain why the plaintiffs in the *Northern Delaware* case sought to compel the other party's performance, rather
than relying upon their remedy at law?

4. As the *City Stores* case suggests, the problem of accurately measuring the damages caused by breach becomes acute when the parties' relationship is intended to be a long-lasting one, continuing for a period of
months or even years. Generally speaking, the longer the term of the
contract, the more speculative any judicial effort to estimate the extent of
the promisee's damages is likely to be, and hence the greater the risk that
the promisee will not be fully compensated by whatever damages he receives. In cases of this sort, therefore, the pressures to grant a request for
specific performance will be strong, despite the administrative difficulties
that may be involved in the court's supervision of the parties' ongoing
relationship. One situation in which this problem has arisen with great
frequency is the long-term output or requirements contract, where the
difficulties caused by the duration of the contract are made even more
severe by the indefiniteness of the volume of goods to be bought or sold.
Not surprisingly, in such cases courts have for some time been willing to
compel specific performance of the contract despite the length of its term
and the indefiniteness of the promisor's obligations.

The case of Eastern Rolling Mill Co. v. Michlovitz, 157 Md. 51, 145 A.
378 (1929) is illustrative. Michlovitz and his partners were wholesale dealers in scrap iron. Eastern was a manufacturer of sheet steel. Its manufacturing process left large quantities of scrap. Since 1920, Eastern had been
in the habit of selling this scrap exclusively to Michlovitz. The contracts

involved in the litigation became effective in October 1927. They were output contracts for a five-year period, prices to be fixed at the beginning of each quarter. In November 1927, Eastern's president died. His successor attempted to obtain a rescission of the contracts, which he wanted replaced with similar ones for shorter time periods. Michlovitz refused. Deliveries continued until June, 1928, and then ceased. Michlovitz brought suit for specific performance, which was granted in the court below. Eastern appealed. The Maryland Court of Appeals found Eastern in breach and went on to consider the proper remedy.

Under the cases, the right to specific performance turns upon whether the plaintiffs can be properly compensated at law. The plaintiffs are entitled to compensatory damages, and, if an action at law cannot afford them adequate redress, equity will specifically enforce the contracts, which would not impose upon the court any difficulties in enforcement, as the subject-matter of the contracts is the accumulated scrap at the plant of the defendant. The defendant relied upon the case of Fothergill v. Rowland, L.R. 17 Eq. 132, but there the contract was one whose performance involved the working of a coal mine, which required personal skill, and this with its different facts distinguishes that case from the one at bar. The goods which the parties here had bargained for were not procurable in the neighborhood, and moreover, they possessed a quality and concentrated weight which could not be secured anywhere within the extensive region covered by the "Philadelphia Market." In addition, the delivery of the scrap at Baltimore was one of the valuable incidents of the purchase. It follows that the right to these specific goods is a consideration of great importance, and this and the difficulty of securing scrap of the same commercial utility are factors making for the inadequacy of damages.

The scrap is not to be delivered according to specified tonnage, but as it accumulates, which in the past has been at the rate of one and two, and occasionally three, carloads of scrap a day, so the quantities vary from quarter to quarter. If the plant should cease to operate or suffer an interruption, there would be no scrap accumulating for delivery under the contracts, and its deliveries would end or be lessened. Neither are the prices for the scrap constant during the period of the contracts, but change from quarter to quarter according to the quotations of two specified materials on the Philadelphia market whose quarterly prices are accepted as the standards upon which the contract prices are quarterly computed. The contracts run to September 30, 1932. By what method would a jury determine the future quarterly tonnage, the quarterly contract price, and quarterly market price during these coming years? How could it possibly arrive at any fair ascertainment of damages? Any estimate would be speculative and conjectural, and not, therefore, compensatory. It follows that the defendant's breach of its contracts is not susceptible of fair and proper compensation by damages; and that to refuse to compel the defendant to do merely what it bound itself to do, and to remit the plaintiffs to their action at law, is to permit the defendant to relieve itself of the contracts and to force the plaintiffs to sell their profits at a conjectural price. To substitute damages by guess for due performance of contract could only be because "there's no equity stirring."

Id. at 66-67, 145 A. at 384. Other output and requirements cases are collected and discussed in 5A Corbin §1142, and 11 Williston §1419B.

5. A widely cited recent case dealing with the same problem is Laclede Gas Co. v. Amoco Oil Co., 522 F.2d 33 (8th Cir. 1975). The parties in the *Laclede* case had entered into an agreement which provided that Amoco would supply Laclede with "propane gas distribution systems to various residential developments in Jefferson County, Missouri, until such time as natural gas mains were extended into these areas" (a period estimated to be between 10 and 15 years). The contract stated that "[i]f Laclede determined that such a [propane] system was appropriate in any given development, it could request Amoco to supply the propane to that specific development." The price Laclede was to pay for the propane was fixed at four cents a gallon above the price posted at Amoco's Wood River refinery. Two and a half years after the contract was entered into, Amoco notified Laclede that it intended to terminate their agreement. Laclede sued for specific enforcement. The District Court denied relief, on the grounds that the contract was void "for lack of mutuality" since Laclede had certain cancellation privileges that Amoco did not also enjoy. On appeal, the Eighth Circuit reversed, holding the contract to be enforceable, and granted Laclede's request for specific performance. In the course of its opinion, the court had this to say:

It is axiomatic that specific performance will not be ordered when the party claiming breach of contract has an adequate remedy at law. Jamison Coal & Coke Co. v. Goltra, 143 F.2d 889, 894 (8th Cir.), *cert. denied*, 323 U.S. 769, 65 S. Ct. 122, 89 L. Ed. 615 (1944). This is especially true when the contract involves personal property as distinguished from real estate.

However, in Missouri, as elsewhere, specific performance may be ordered even though personalty is involved in the "proper circumstances." Mo. Rev. Stat. §400.2-716(1); Restatement, Contracts, *supra*, §361. And a remedy at law adequate to defeat the grant of specific performance "must be as certain, prompt, complete, and efficient to attain the ends of justice as a decree of specific performance." National Marking Mach. Co. v. Triumph Mfg. Co., 13 F.2d 6,9 (8th Cir. 1926). *Accord*, Snip v. City of Lamar, 239 Mo. App. 824, 201 S.W.2d 790, 798 (1947).

One of the leading Missouri cases allowing specific performance of a contract relating to personalty because the remedy at law was inadequate is Boeving v. Vandover, 240 Mo. App. 117, 218 S.W.2d 175, 178 (1949). In that case the plaintiff sought specific performance of a contract in which the defendant had promised to sell him an automobile. At that time (near the end of and shortly after World War II) new cars were hard to come by, and the court held that specific performance was a proper remedy since a new car "could not be obtained elsewhere except at considerable expense, trouble or loss, which cannot be estimated in advance."

We are satisfied that Laclede has brought itself within this practical approach taken by the Missouri courts. As Amoco points out, Laclede has propane immediately available to it under other contracts with other suppliers. And the evidence indicates that at the present time propane is readily available on the open market. However, this analysis ignores the fact that the contract involved in this lawsuit is for a long-term supply of propane to these subdivisions. The other two contracts under which Laclede obtains the gas will remain in force only until March 31, 1977, and April 1, 1981, respectively; and there is no assurance that Laclede will be able to receive any propane under them after that time. Also it is unclear as to whether or not Laclede can use the propane obtained under these contracts to supply the Jefferson County subdivisions, since they were originally entered into to provide Laclede with propane with which to "shave" its natural gas supply during peak demand periods.[16] Additionally, there was uncontradicted expert testimony that Laclede probably could not find another supplier of propane willing to enter into a long-term contract such as the Amoco agreement, given the uncertain future of worldwide energy supplies. And, even if Laclede could obtain supplies of propane for the affected developments through its present contracts or newly negotiated ones, it would still face considerable expense and trouble which cannot be estimated in advance in making arrangements for its distribution to the subdivisions.

Specific performance is the proper remedy in this situation, and it should be granted by the district court.[17]

Id. at 39-40

CAMPBELL SOUP CO. v. WENTZ
172 F.2d 80 (3d Cir. 1948)

GOODRICH, Circuit Judge.

These are appeals from judgments of the District Court denying equitable relief to the buyer under a contract for the sale of carrots. The defendants in No. 9648 are the contract sellers. The defendant in No. 9649 is the second purchaser of part of the carrots which are the subject matter of the contract.

The transactions which raise the issues may be briefly summarized. On June 21, 1947, Campbell Soup Company (Campbell), a New Jersey corporation, entered into a written contract with George B. Wentz and Harry T. Wentz, who are Pennsylvania farmers, for delivery by the Wentzes to Campbell of all the Chantenay red cored carrots to be grown

16. During periods of cold weather, when demand is high, Laclede does not receive enough natural gas to meet all this demand. It, therefore, adds propane to the natural gas it places in its distribution system. This practice is called "peak shaving."
17. In fashioning its decree the district court must take into account any relevant rules and regulations promulgated under the Federal Mandatory Allocation Program.

on fifteen acres of the Wentz farm during the 1947 season. Where the contract was entered into does not appear. The contract provides, however, for delivery of the carrots at the Campbell plant in Camden, New Jersey. The prices specified in the contract ranged from $23 to $30 per ton according to the time of delivery. The contract price for January, 1948 was $30 a ton.

The Wentzes harvested approximately 100 tons of carrots from the fifteen acres covered by the contract. Early in January, 1948, they told a Campbell representative that they would not deliver their carrots at the contract price. The market price at that time was at least $90 per ton, and Chantenay red cored carrots were virtually unobtainable. The Wentzes then sold approximately 62 tons of their carrots to the defendant Lojeski, a neighboring farmer. Lojeski resold about 58 tons on the open market, approximately half to Campbell and the balance to other purchasers.

On January 9, 1948, Campbell, suspecting that Lojeski was selling it "contract carrots," refused to purchase any more, and instituted these suits against the Wentz brothers and Lojeski to enjoin further sale of the contract carrots to others, and to compel specific performance of the contract. The trial court denied equitable relief.[18] We agree with the result reached, but on a different ground from that relied upon by the District Court.

The case has been presented by both sides as though Erie Railroad v. Tompkins, 1938, 304 U.S. 64, 58 S. Ct. 817, 82 L. Ed. 1188, 114 A.L.R. 1487, and Klaxon Company v. Stentor Electric Manufacturing Co., Inc., 1941, 313 U.S. 487, 61 S. Ct. 1020, 85 L. Ed. 1477, had never been decided. We are not advised as to the place of the contract, although as we have pointed out in other cases, the Pennsylvania conflict of laws rule, which binds us here, refers matters concerning the validity and extent of obligation of the contract to the place of making. In this instance, however, the absence of data on which to base a rule of reference does not preclude the decision of the case. We have said several times in this Circuit that the question of the form of relief is a matter for a federal court to decide. But neither federal decisions nor the law of New Jersey or Pennsylvania as expressed in the Uniform Sales Act[19] differ upon this point. A party may have specific performance of a contract for the sale of chattels if the legal remedy is inadequate. Inadequacy of the legal remedy is necessarily a matter to be determined by an examination of the facts in each particular instance.

We think that on the question of adequacy of the legal remedy the case is one appropriate for specific performance. It was expressly found that at

---

18. The issue is preserved on appeal by an arrangement under which Campbell received all the carrots held by the Wentzes and Lojeski, paying a stipulated market price of $90 per ton, $30 to the defendants, and the balance into the registry of the District Court pending the outcome of these appeals.

19. Uniform Sales Act, §68, N.J.S.A. 46:30-74; 69 P.S. §313.

the time of the trial it was "virtually impossible to obtain Chantenay carrots in the open market." This Chantenay carrot is one which the plaintiff uses in large quantities, furnishing the seed to the growers with whom it makes contracts. It was not claimed that in nutritive value it is any better than other types of carrots. Its blunt shape makes it easier to handle in processing. And its color and texture differ from other varieties. The color is brighter than other carrots. The trial court found that the plaintiff failed to establish what proportion of its carrots is used for the production of soup stock and what proportion is used as identifiable physical ingredients in its soups. We do not think lack of proof on that point is material. It did appear that the plaintiff uses carrots in fifteen of its twenty-one soups. It also appeared that it uses these Chantenay carrots diced in some of them and that the appearance is uniform. The preservation of uniformity in appearance in a food article marketed throughout the country and sold under the manufacturer's name is a matter of considerable commercial significance and one which is properly considered in determining whether a substitute ingredient is just as good as the original.

The trial court concluded that the plaintiff had failed to establish that the carrots "judged by objective standards," are unique goods. This we think is not a pure fact conclusion like a finding that Chantenay carrots are of uniform color. It is either a conclusion of law or of mixed fact and law and we are bound to exercise our independent judgment upon it. That the test for specific performance is not necessarily "objective" is shown by the many cases in which equity has given it to enforce contracts for articles — family heirlooms and the like — the value of which was personal to the plaintiff.

Judged by the general standards applicable to determining the adequacy of the legal remedy we think that on this point the case is a proper one for equitable relief. There is considerable authority, old and new, showing liberality in the granting of an equitable remedy. We see no reason why a court should be reluctant to grant specific relief when it can be given without supervision of the court or other time-consuming processes against one who has deliberately broken his agreement. Here the goods of the special type contracted for were unavailable on the open market, the plaintiff had contracted for them long ahead in anticipation of its needs, and had built up a general reputation for its products as part of which reputation uniform appearance was important. We think if this were all that was involved in the case specific performance should have been granted.

The reason that we shall affirm instead of reversing with an order for specific performance is found in the contract itself. We think it is too hard a bargain and too one-sided an agreement to entitle the plaintiff to relief in a court of conscience. For each individual grower the agreement is made by filling in names and quantity and price on a printed form furnished by the buyer. The form has quite obviously been drawn by skillful draftsmen with the buyer's interests in mind.

Paragraph 2 provides for the manner of delivery. Carrots are to have their stalks cut off and be in clean sanitary bags or other containers approved by Campbell. This paragraph concludes with a statement that Campbell's determination of conformance with specifications shall be conclusive.

The defendants attack this provision as unconscionable. We do not think that it is, standing by itself. We think that the provision is comparable to the promise to perform to the satisfaction of another and that Campbell would be held liable if it refused carrots which did in fact conform to the specifications.

The next paragraph allows Campbell to refuse carrots in excess of twelve tons to the acre. The next contains a covenant by the grower that he will not sell carrots to anyone else except the carrots rejected by Campbell nor will he permit anyone else to grow carrots on his land. Paragraph 10 provides liquidated damages to the extent of $50 per acre for any breach by the grower. There is no provision for liquidated or any other damages for breach of contract by Campbell.

The provision of the contract which we think is the hardest is paragraph 9, set out in the margin.[20] It will be noted that Campbell is excused from accepting carrots under certain circumstances. But even under such circumstances the grower, while he cannot say Campbell is liable for failure to take the carrots, is not permitted to sell them elsewhere unless Campbell agrees. This is the kind of provision which the late Francis H. Bohlen would call "carrying a good joke too far." What the grower may do with his product under the circumstances set out is not clear. He has covenanted not to store it anywhere except on his own farm and also not to sell to anybody else.

We are not suggesting that the contract is illegal. Nor are we suggesting any excuse for the grower in this case who has deliberately broken an agreement entered into with Campbell. We do think, however, that a party who has offered and succeeded in getting an agreement as tough as this one is, should not come to a chancellor and ask court help in the enforcement of its terms. That equity does not enforce unconscionable bargains is too well established to require elaborate citation.

---

20. "Grower shall not be obligated to deliver any Carrots which he is unable to harvest or deliver, nor shall Campbell be obligated to receive or pay for any Carrots which it is unable to inspect, grade, receive, handle, use or pack at or ship in processed form from its plants in Camden (1) because of any circumstance beyond the control of Grower or Campbell, as the case may be, or (2) because of any labor disturbance, work stoppage, slow-down, or strike involving any of Campbell's employees. Campbell shall not be liable for any delay in receiving Carrots due to any of the above contingencies. During periods when Campbell is unable to receive Grower's Carrots, Grower may with Campbell's written consent, dispose of his Carrots elsewhere. Grower may not, however, sell or otherwise dispose of any Carrots which he is unable to deliver to Campbell."

The plaintiff argues that the provisions of the contract are separable. We agree that they are, but do not think that decisions separating out certain provisions from illegal contracts are in point here. As already said, we do not suggest that this contract is illegal. All we say is that the sum total of its provisions drives too hard a bargain for a court of conscience to assist.

This disposition of the problem makes unnecessary further discussion of the separate liability of Lojeski, who was not a party to the contract, but who purchased some of the carrots from the Wentzes.

The judgments will be affirmed.

UNIFORM COMMERCIAL CODE

§2-716.   BUYER'S RIGHT TO SPECIFIC PERFORMANCE OR REPLEVIN

(1)   Specific performance may be decreed where the goods are unique or in other proper circumstances.

(2)   The decree for specific performance may include such terms and conditions as to payment of the price, damages, or other relief as the court may deem just.

(3)   The buyer has a right of replevin for goods identified to the contract if after reasonable effort he is unable to effect cover for such goods or the circumstances reasonably indicate that such effort will be unavailing or if the goods have been shipped under reservation and satisfaction of the security interest in them has been made or tendered.

NOTE

1. Kronman, Specific Performance, 45 U. Chi. L. Rev. 351, 358-362 (1978) (footnotes omitted):

> In common discourse "unique" means without a substitute or equivalent. In the framework of conventional economic analysis, however, the concept of uniqueness is troublesome. Although it might seem reasonable to define the economic uniqueness of a good in terms of its attributes or properties, this is not the definition economists employ. Economists recognize this sort of uniqueness — they call it "technological" uniqueness — but they do not define the substitutability of goods in these terms. For the purposes of economics theory, the substitutability of a particular good is determined by observing consumer behavior, not by cataloguing the various properties of the good. If an alteration in the relative price of one good affects the demand for another, then these two goods are said to be eco-

nomic substitutes. The degree of their substitutability is called the "cross-elasticity of demand."

On this view, every good has substitutes, even if only very poor ones. Because all goods compete for consumer attention, a substantial change in the relative price of any good always affects the consumption of other goods. Economists are interested in determining how great a change in the price of one good is required to effect a change of given magnitude in the consumption of certain other goods. But these are really questions of degree, resting on the underlying assumption — fundamental to economic theory — that all goods are ultimately commensurable. If this assumption is accepted, the idea of a unique good loses meaning.

This point may be illustrated by a case that under present law would almost certainly be held to involve a unique good. Suppose that A contracts with Sotheby's to purchase the handwritten manuscript of Hobbes's *Leviathan*. If Sotheby's refuses to perform — perhaps because it has a more attractive offer from someone else — A will undoubtedly be disappointed. Yet no matter how strong his affection for Hobbes, it is likely there are other things that would make A just as happy as getting the manuscript for the contract price. For example, A may be indifferent between purchasing the manuscript at the specified price and having twenty-five hours of violin lessons for the same amount. If so, then A will be fully compensated for the loss he suffers by Sotheby's breach upon receiving the difference between the cost of twenty-five hours worth of violin lessons and the contract price. However, despite the fact that the manuscript has an economic substitute, a court would be likely to order specific performance of the contract (assuming Sotheby's still had the manuscript in its possession) on the ground that the subject matter of the contract is unique.

Pursing the matter further, it is not difficult to see why A's money damages remedy is likely to be inadequate and on the basis of this insight to develop an economic justification for the uniqueness test. Under a money damages rule, a court must calculate the amount Sotheby's is required to pay A to give A the benefit of his bargain. The amount necessary to fully compensate A is equal to the amount he requires to obtain an appropriate substitute. So in fixing the amount Sotheby's must pay A, the court must first determine what things A would regard as substitutes and then how much of any particular substitute would be required to compensate him for his loss.

In the hypothetical case, however, it would be very difficult and expensive for a court to acquire the information necessary to make these determinations. Perhaps some information of this sort would be produced by the parties. For example, A could introduce evidence to establish a past pattern of consumption from which the court might draw an inference as to what would be a satisfactory substitute for the manuscript. Sotheby's could then attempt to rebut the evidence and establish some alternative theory of preferences and substitutes. But of course it would be time-consuming to produce information this way, and any inference a court might draw on the basis of such information would be most uncertain.

Moreover, this uncertainty cannot be avoided by simply looking to the selling price of other manuscripts or even the expected resale price of the

Hobbes manuscript itself (unless, of course, A is a professional dealer). It would be risky to infer the value A places on the Hobbes manuscript from the value placed on it by others, and riskier still to infer it from the value others place on the manuscripts of, for example, Harrington's *Oceana* or Locke's *Second Treatise*. If a court attempts to calculate A's money damages on the basis of such information, there is a substantial probability that the award will miss the mark and be either under- or over-compensatory.

Of course, if a court could accurately identify a substitute for the manuscript, it could disregard the fact that A may value the manuscript in excess of the price that he, or anyone else, has agreed to pay for it. But where it is difficult to identify a satisfactory substitute (as I assume it is here), the goal of compensation requires that an effort be made to determine the value the promisee places on the promisor's performance, as distinct from what the promisee, or anyone else, has offered to pay for it.

Although it is true in a certain sense that all goods compete in the market — that every good has substitutes — this is an empty truth. What matters, in measuring money damages, is the volume, refinement, and reliability of the available information about substitutes for the subject matter of the breached contract. When the relevant information is thin and unreliable, there is a substantial risk that an award of money damages will either exceed or fall short of the promisee's actual loss. Of course this risk can always be reduced — but only at great cost when reliable information is difficult to obtain. Conversely, when there is a great deal of consumer behavior generating abundant and highly dependable information about substitutes, the risk of error in measuring the promisee's loss may be reduced at much smaller cost. In asserting that the subject matter of a particular contract is unique and has no established market value, a court is really saying that it cannot obtain, at reasonable cost, enough information about substitutes to permit it to calculate an award of money damages without imposing an unacceptably high risk of undercompensation on the injured promisee. Conceived in this way, the uniqueness test seems economically sound.

2. Why did the Campbell Soup Company insist on a contractual provision requiring the Wentzes to obtain the company's permission before selling "contract carrots" to a third party, even in situations where Campbell itself was excused from taking the carrots? Was the aim of this provision an illegitimate one? Do you think the Wentzes were compensated for the potential risks this clause involved?

3. The first footnote to Judge Goodrich's opinion indicates that Campbell Soup had already received the carrots, having bought them from Lojeski and the Wentzes for $90 a ton. If this is so, what is the dispute about? Normally, if Campbell sued for damages, it would be entitled to the difference between the contract price of the carrots ($30 a ton) and their market or "cover" price ($90 a ton). Under this formula, Campbell Soup would be entitled to the full amount paid into the registry of the District Court. Can it hope to gain more by suing for specific perfor-

mance? What do you suppose will be the effect, in Campbell's subsequent suit for damages, of Paragraph 10 of its contract with the Wentzes? Isn't Campbell Soup's request for specific performance an effort to evade the unexpectedly disadvantageous effects of a liquidated damages provision that was originally drafted for the soup company's benefit?

4. Schwartz, The Case for Specific Performance, 89 Yale L.J. 271, 274-277 (1979) (footnotes omitted):

[C]urrent doctrine authorizes specific performance when courts cannot calculate compensatory damages with even a rough degree of accuracy. If the class of cases in which there are difficulties in computing damages corresponds closely to the class of cases in which specific performance is now granted, expanding the availability of specific performance is obviously unnecessary. Further, such an expansion would create opportunities for promisees to exploit promisors. The class of cases in which damage awards fail to compensate promisees adequately is, however, broader than the class of cases in which specific performance is now granted. Thus the compensation goal supports removing rather than retaining present restrictions on the availability of specific performance.

It is useful to begin by examining the paradigm case for granting specific performance under current law, the case of unique goods. When a promisor breaches and the promisee can make a transaction that substitutes for the performance the promisor failed to render, the promisee will be fully compensated if he receives the additional amount necessary to purchase the substitute plus the costs of making a second transaction. In some cases, however, such as those involving works of art, courts cannot identify which transactions the promisee would regard as substitutes because that information often is in the exclusive possession of the promisee. Moreover, it is difficult for a court to assess the accuracy of a promisee's claim. For example, if the promisor breaches a contract to sell a rare emerald, the promisee may claim that only the Hope Diamond will give him equal satisfaction, and thus may sue for the price difference between the emerald and the diamond. It would be difficult for a court to know whether this claim is true. If the court seeks to award money damages, it has three choices: granting the price differential, which may overcompensate the promisee; granting the dollar value of the promisee's foregone satisfaction as estimated by the court, which may overcompensate or undercompensate; or granting restitution of any sums paid, which undercompensates the promisee. The promisee is fully compensated without risk of overcompensation or undercompensation if the remedy of specific performance is available to him and its use encouraged by the doctrine that damages must be foreseeable and certain.

If specific performance is the appropriate remedy in such case, there are three reasons why it should be routinely available. The first reason is that in many cases damages actually are undercompensatory. Although promisees are entitled to incidental damages, such damages are difficult to monetize. They consist primarily of the costs of finding and making a second deal, which generally involve the expenditure of time rather than cash; attaching a dollar value to such opportunity costs is quite difficult. Breach can also cause frustration and anger, especially in a consumer context, but these costs also are not recoverable.

Substitution damages, the court's estimate of the amount the promisee needs to purchase an adequate substitute, also may be inaccurate in many cases less dramatic than the emerald hypothetical discussed above. This is largely because of product differentiation and early obsolescence. As product differentiation becomes more common, the supply of products that will substitute precisely for the promisor's performance is reduced. For example, even during the period when there is an abundant supply of new Datsuns for sale, two-door, two-tone Datsuns with mag wheels, stereo, and air conditioning may be scarce in some local markets. Moreover, early obsolescence gives the promisee a short time in which to make a substitute purchase. If the promisor breaches late in a model year, for example, it may be difficult for the promisee to buy the exact model he wanted. For these reasons, a damage award meant to enable a promisee to purchase "another car" could be undercompensatory.

In addition, problems of prediction often make it difficult to put a promisee in the position where he would have been had his promisor performed. If a breach by a contractor would significantly delay or prevent completion of a construction project and the project differs in important respects from other projects — for example, a department store in a different location than previous stores — courts may be reluctant to award "speculative" lost profits attributable to the breach.

Second, promisees have economic incentives to sue for damages when damages are likely to be fully compensatory. A breaching promisor is reluctant to perform and may be hostile. This makes specific performance an unattractive remedy in cases in which the promisor's performance is complex, because the promisor is more likely to render a defective performance when that performance is coerced, and the defectiveness of complex performances is sometimes difficult to establish in court. Further, when the promisor's performance must be rendered over time, as in construction or requirements contracts, it is costly for the promisee to monitor a reluctant promisor's conduct. If the damage remedy is compensatory, the promisee would prefer it to incurring these monitoring costs. Finally, given the time necessary to resolve lawsuits, promisees would commonly prefer to make substitute transactions promptly and sue later for damages rather than hold their affairs in suspension while awaiting equitable relief. The very fact that a promisee requests specific performance thus implies that damages are an inadequate remedy.

The third reason why courts should permit promisees to elect routinely the remedy of specific performance is that promisees possess better information than courts as to both the adequacy of damages and the difficulties of coercing performance. Promisees know better than courts whether the damages a court is likely to award would be adequate because promisees are more familiar with the costs that breach imposes on them. In addition, promisees generally know more about their promisors than do courts; thus they are in a better position to predict whether specific performance decrees would induce their promisors to render satisfactory performances.

In sum, restrictions on the availability of specific performance cannot be justified on the basis that damage awards are usually compensatory. On the contrary, the compensation goal implies that specific performance should be routinely available. . . .

For a wide-ranging review from an economic perspective of the whole subject of specific performance, and a critical analysis of its relation to other remedies for breach, see Ulen, The Efficiency of Specific Performance: Toward a Unified Theory of Contract Remedies, 83 Mich. L. Rev. 341 (1984).

5. Under certain circumstances, a seller of goods may sue a breaching buyer for the full contract price, a remedy that is analogous to the buyer's right of specific performance. The seller's price action does not merely compensate him for the damages he has suffered — it gives him exactly what he bargained for. Since money is not a unique good, and since its payment (in contrast, say, to singing) is an uncomplicated task that does not require the exercise of skills that are difficult to monitor or evaluate, the seller's action for the price ought not to be (and in fact is not) subject to the same limitations as the buyer's right of specific performance. Nevertheless, the seller's price action *is* subject to some significant restrictions. Why should this be? Consult Uniform Commercial Code §2-709 and the accompanying Comment.

GROSSFELD, MONEY SANCTIONS FOR BREACH OF CONTRACT IN A COMMUNIST ECONOMY, 72 Yale L.J. 1326, 1330-1332 (1963): "In a communist economic system the payment of damages can by no means compensate completely the damage incurred. The damage to the society as a whole, for example, cannot be compensated, for every breach of contract disturbs a certain established pattern and demands an increased effort to overcome its consequences and to re-create order. The liquidation of the damages absorbs additional energy and time which could have been better used — if the damage had not occurred — for constructive activity. Moreover, the goods which could not be produced as a result of the breach of contract are missing in the final balance of the plan, or can be produced only at the expense of other goods. The fact that these arguments might equally be given in a western legal system throws some doubt on the contention that the most important goal of the money sanctions for breach of contract is compensation; the relevance of these arguments is at least not restricted to the law of a planned communistic economy. But there is another — I am inclined to say 'unique' — feature in a communist economy that makes compensation itself virtually impossible — the existence of a comprehensive plan by which the economy is ruled. In a free, competitive economy, with free access and exchange of goods, nearly every good can be evaluated and replaced by a certain amount of money. Consequently, in such an economic system a purchaser whose supplier breaches a contract can generally purchase the same goods from another supplier, provided the damages he sustained are compensated. Thus in our western legal systems a purchaser very often does not have a vital interest in the specific performance of the contract; whether he receives from the seller the goods he wanted or their money value may make little difference to him. This is not the case in a completely planned economy where there does not exist a free flow of goods available on the open market. If one particular producer or supplier fails to perform his contractual duties there are no others to whom the buyer can turn. Money, therefore, is no equivalent for the product itself. Thus the tasks imposed upon the enterprise by the plan cannot be accomplished when the enterprise receives money instead of the goods it needs for production, and from this it follows that in such an economy actual performance of every contract is of greatest importance. This 'principle of specific performance' is the basic principle of the communist system of contracts. It represents the categorical demand of the law that the goods which are to be delivered must not be replaced by money damages. Thus even an express agreement between the parties to a contract concluded under the plan that specific performance will be waived in favor of an equivalent in money is void. The money compensation is conceived exclusively as an 'emergency measure,' a 'last resort' when specific performance is virtually impossible.

"These unique features of the economic system demonstrate that the main purpose of the money sanctions for breach of contract cannot be compensation for losses. Rather, the emphasis shifts to prevention of losses or 'education.' The main task of money sanctions becomes the enforcement of contractual discipline, for the understanding is that the more difficult it is to compensate damage the more must be done to prevent it. The money sanctions serve their purpose best, therefore, when they prevent occurrence of a breach of contract. When a party does fail to perform the contract and has to pay damages, they function as a 'form of social criticism,' as a means of 'education through the Mark.' Simultaneously, of course, there is a compensatory effect, but, in direct contrast with the Western systems, compensation is warranted *only* if it can serve an educational purpose. Moreover, the effects of the money sanction go far beyond the particular contract in question, because the contract and the plan stand in very close nexus. Through the contracts the necessary combination between the central direction of the economy by the state and the economic independence of the enterprises is realized. When concluding contracts within the framework of the plan, each enterprise determines the precise content of its share in the implementation of the plan. The contract is thus a means of economic planning, an instrument by which the purposes of the state can be realized. Compensation for damages, then, is not paid for the benefit of the injured party, but constitutes an attempt by the state to use the individual interest as a tool to achieve social control, to secure the fulfillment of the plan. The party to the contract who sues for damages fulfills a 'public' task; his own interest is satisfied only where it serves the greater goals of the society."

Section 3.   Money Damages: The Limits of Compensation

SEDGWICK, ON THE MEASURE OF DAMAGES 6 (1847): "The common law, as it exists in England, and in the United States, is generally remedial in its character, and its remedies are of a pecuniary description. It has few preventive powers, it can rarely compel the performance of contracts specifically; its relief consists in the award of pecuniary damages. Whether it punishes wrongs, or remunerates for breach of contract, in either case its judgment simply makes compensation, by awarding damages to the sufferer."

It has frequently been said that the modern law of damages dates back no farther than the middle of the last century. To be sure, long before that time the legal profession had come to recognize the function of damages, namely, to give "compensation and satisfaction for some injury sustained." 2 Blackstone, Commentaries *438. And yet, the middle of the last century has rightly been hailed as the turning point in the evolution of the law of damages, for only then were decisive steps taken by judges and text writers to bring rationality and predictability into the substantive law of compensation and to develop efficient procedural techniques for translating theory into practice.

To enable the reader to appreciate the full meaning of this new phase in the development of damage law, a short survey of the preceding period may be helpful. From the beginning of trial by jury, the amount of damages was a "fact" to be found by the "petit" jury selected from the neighborhood where the transaction in litigation had occurred. The trial judge, "usually a stranger sent out from London, with no knowledge of the affair in controversy except from the pleadings, could seldom feel justified in correcting or overturning the findings of the neighbor witnesses." C. T. McCormick, Law of Damages 25 (1935). See also Tooley and Preston's Case, 3 Leon. 150, 74 Eng. Rep. 599 (1587).

But "outrageous and excessive" verdicts occurred so frequently that the development of techniques for controlling this grave judicial risk became a matter of necessity. Expectations created by promises were often vitiated completely by an inadequate award of damages or magnified unreasonably by an excessive award. Contracting parties began to attempt to bring this element of uncertainty under private control by incorporating into their agreements clauses providing for the payment of a specific sum of money in case of default. These clauses were honored, at first even where they provided for onerously high payments; only gradually, under the influence of equity, did there emerge the modern distinction between valid provisions for liquidated damages and unenforceable penalties. McCormick, *supra*, at 599 et seq. See further Section 4. But private control was not enough. A system of judicial control emerged slowly through a laborious process of trial and error. The first step taken was not very successful. As far back as 1300, a proceeding appeared that enabled the party aggrieved by the petit jury's verdict, particularly if it was excessive, to petition a jury of 24 knights for a retrial. If the retrial was granted, a writ of attaint issued. But this system had a rather serious shortcoming: if the aggrieved party was successful in the trial, not only was the "false" verdict replaced by a new verdict, but the members of the first jury were punished severely for having violated their oath to find a correct award based on their knowledge of the facts. Small wonder that the attaint came to be replaced by other methods of controlling the juridical risk, such as the granting of a new trial before a second petit jury, a step that was forced upon the common law courts by the intervention of equity.

The widening of the power of courts to set aside "false" verdicts was accompanied and put on a firmer basis by the gradual evolution of rules designed to standardize the *quantum* of recovery. These rules, at first, were used only in advising the jury; eventually they took the form of binding instructions, and slowly the doctrine emerged that a misdirection by the court was grounds for a new trial. Attempts to control the juridical risk by standardizing the *quantum* of damages made their first appearance in cases dealing with transactions as commercially significant as loans and sales, and it is striking that these early efforts at rationalization sought, almost without exception, to introduce order and predictability into the law of damages by limiting the amount a disappointed promisee could recover. Thus, for example, in a line of cases dating back to Lord Mansfield's decision in Robinson v. Bland, 2 Burr. 1077 at 1086, 97 Eng. Rep. 717 at 722 (1760),[21] the damages for nonpayment of a debt were limited to interest, no matter how great the real loss suffered by the creditor. Similarly, under the famous rule of Flureau v. Thornhill, 2 W. Blackstone 1078, 96 Eng. Rep. 635 (1766), the liability of the vendor of real estate who, without being guilty of bad faith, failed to make title to his purchaser was restricted to the return of the down payment and sometimes other expenses, i.e., to the reliance interest. Loss of profits (the expectation interest) remained unprotected. In the law of sales, it is true, early cases like Gainsford v. Carroll, 2 B. & C. 624, 107 Eng. Rep. 516 K.B.

---

21. For the further development of the rule, see Washington, Damages in Contract at Common Law (Pt. 2), 48 L.Q. Rev. 91 (1932); C.T. McCormick, Law of Damages 205 et seq. (1935).

(1828), *infra* p. 1129, recognized the promisee's right to his expectancy and thus helped to safeguard the profit motive in an area of economic activity where this seemed especially important. But even here, the promisee's damages were limited by the standardized rule restricting his recovery, in the event of nondelivery or nonacceptance, to the difference between the contract price and the market price prevailing at the time and place of delivery appointed in the contract.

Apart from these rather specialized rules dealing with the types of contracts just enumerated, we find in the case law before 1850 little more than occasional statements that damages must be the "natural" or "necessary" result of the promisor's breach. The development of an overall principle "by which the judges could justify keeping a firm hand upon amounts awarded for breach of contract, so as to confine such awards within the risks which the judges would believe to be in accord with the expectation of business men" (McCormick, *supra,* at 563) was slow in coming indeed. Not until Hadley v. Baxendale, 9 Ex. 341, 156 Eng. Rep. 145 (1854), *supra* p. 106, did a court succeed in devising persuasive and highly generalized formulae for determining the quantum of recovery for breach of contract, formulae that have served as models for the instruction of juries in countless cases ever since. In the language of the court:

> Where two parties have made a contract which one of them has broken, the damages which the other party ought to receive in respect of such breach of contract should be such as may fairly and reasonably be considered either arising naturally, i.e., according to the usual course of things, from such breach of contract itself, or such as may reasonably be supposed to have been in the contemplation of both parties, at the time they made the contract, as the probable result of the breach of it.

9 Ex. at 354, 156 Eng. Rep. at 151.[22]

In keeping, perhaps, with the spirit of the earlier damages rules described above, the great generalizations of Hadley v. Baxendale were also understood, by contemporary lawyers, to be aimed essentially at limiting, rather than expanding, the promisee's recovery. This restrictive view of the great case, which prevailed for some time both in the case law and the treatises, is strikingly illustrated by the following passage from J.D. Mayne, Treatise on the Law of Damages 8 (2d ed. 1872):

> . . . In the case of contract the measure of damages is much more strictly confined than in cases of tort. As a general rule, the primary and

---

22. In their attempt to reduce the juridical risk of uncertain jury awards by devising an overall formula for measuring contract damages, the courts were greatly aided by the work of a number of able text writers, both American and English, who, in turn, were strongly influenced by the development of the French law. Some of the great cases contain express references to Pothier (translated in 1806) and the French Civil Code (with which the legal profession had become familiar through Sedgwick's classic treatise on damages first published in 1847).

immediate result of the breach of contract can alone be looked to. Hence, in the case of non-payment of money, no matter what the amount of inconvenience sustained by the plaintiff, the measure of damages is the interest of the money only. So where the contract is to deliver goods, replace stock, or convey an estate, the profit which the plaintiff might have made by the resale of the matter in question cannot in general be taken into account; nor the loss which he has suffered from the fact of his ulterior arrangements, made in expectation of the fulfilment of the bargain, being frustrated. The principle of all these cases seems to be, that, in matters of contract, the damages to which a party is liable for its breach ought to be in proportion to the benefit he is to receive from its performance. Now this benefit, the consideration for his promise, is always measured by the primary and intrinsic worth of the thing to be given for it, not by the ultimate profit which the party receiving it hopes to make when he has got it. A bottle of laudanum may save a man his life, or a seat in a railway carriage may enable him to make his fortune; but neither is paid for on this footing. The price is based on the market value of the thing sold. It operates as a liquidated estimate of the worth of the contract to both parties. It is obviously unfair, then, that either party should be paid for carrying out his bargain on one estimate of its value, and forced to pay for failing in it on quite a different estimate. This would be making him an insurer of the other party's profits, without any premium for undertaking the risk.

In the preceding section on Specific Performance the suggestion was made that a restrictive or negative approach to the availability of the remedy has, in certain areas at least, gradually been replaced by an expansive and, perhaps, more liberal approach. In much the same way, the restrictive interpretation of the true meaning of the rule of Hadley v. Baxendale, current in the nineteenth century, has in this century gradually been replaced by a more expansive one. See *The Heron II, infra* p. 1157. This enlargement in our conception of compensable harm has done its part to help dissolve the idea of a narrow but strict liability that lay at the heart of the classical (that is to say, late nineteenth-century) view of contractual obligation. The broader the scope of his responsibility for remote or "consequential" damages, the more deeply the promisor will be drawn into the affairs of his contractual partner and the more likely he is to become, in effect, a guarantor of their success. To this extent, the liberalization of the rule in Hadley v. Baxendale belongs to the same general movement of ideas as our growing acceptance of the so-called duty to negotiate in good faith — a duty that the law imposes even before there is a contract, let along a breach by one of the parties. These two rules, operating, so to speak, at opposite ends of the life or career of a contractual relationship, both tend to transform the parties from self-interested entrepreneurs with only limited responsibilities for one another's welfare into joint-venturers engaged in a common undertaking premised upon reciprocal duties of support. How far this transformation has been (or should be) carried, and the way it affects our conception of the shifting boundary between tort and contract, are questions to which we shall return.

On this last issue — the relation of contract to tort — a further word is perhaps in order. In 1847, when he published his treatise on damages, Sedgwick already assumed, without discussion, that contract damages are meant to provide "simply . . . compensation," being in that respect unlike tort damages, which may include a punitive element. That twin proposition has been repeated so many thousands of times that one begins to wonder whether anything more than a sort of ritual incantation is involved.

The exact location of the dividing line between contract and tort is of course a mystery that the high priests of the legal profession have always been concerned to preserve and protect from public view. The cat was let out of the bag, however, in a moment of unusual candor, by Lord James of Hereford in Addis v. Gramophone Co., Ltd., [1909] A.C. 488 (H.L.). The manager of the defendant's Calcutta office had been wrongfully dismissed. Because of the "harsh and humiliating" manner of the dismissal, the jury had included in its verdict a substantial sum in addition to the salary and commissions to the end of the term to which plaintiff was concededly entitled. This was reversed in the Court of Appeal, which was in turn upheld in the House of Lords (although Lord Collins felt that the jury verdict should have been allowed to stand). Lord James of Hereford, concurring with the majority on the proposition that punitive damages are never recoverable in a contract action, said:

> . . . My Lords, I must say if I had arrived at a different conclusion I should have been subject to some feeling of remorse, because during many years when I was a junior at the Bar, when I was drawing pleadings, I often strove to convert a breach of contract into a tort in order to recover a higher scale of damages, it having been then as it is now, I believe, the general impression of the profession that such damages cannot be recovered in an action of contract as distinguished from tort, and therefore it was useless to attempt to recover them in such a case. That view, which I was taught early to understand was the law in olden days, remains true to this day.

[1909] A.C. at 492.

The proposition that exemplary or punitive damages are never recoverable in a contract action has suffered some erosion since the *Addis* case. The erosion, it may be, has gone further in this country than in England.[23] At all events, a considerable number of American cases can be found in which the courts, without going through the ritual of "converting a breach of contract into a tort" (which is, of course, another way of doing it), have allowed such damages in "contract" actions. Most of the cases involve situations in which the defendant's behavior could be, and

---

23. Note, The Expanding Availability of Punitive Damages in Contract Actions, 8 Ind. L. Rev. 668 (1975); Note, Punitive Damages in Contract Actions — Are the Exceptions Swallowing the Rule?, 20 Washburn L.J. 86 (1980).

was, characterized as "wanton," "willful," "reckless" and so on. Collections of such cases can be found in 11 Williston §§1340, 1341.

The other, and equally questionable, side of the "simply . . . compensation" coin is the implicit claim that a monetary award, calculated according to standard damage formulae, will in fact adequately compensate an injured promisee for the loss he has incurred. We have seen that the rules for measuring contract damages were, to begin with, undercompensatory (and may very well have been designed to be so). Perhaps a good deal of the difficulty that the courts have had with damage theory over the past hundred and thirty years is attributable to the fact that less-than-compensatory formulae have, somehow, had to be squared with the "compensation" idea, without, at least overtly, abandoning either the formulae or the idea.

FREUND v. WASHINGTON SQUARE PRESS
34 N.Y.2d 379, 314 N.E.2d 419 (1974)

SAMUEL RABIN, Judge.

In this action for breach of a publishing contract, we must decide what damages are recoverable for defendant's failure to publish plaintiff's manuscript. In 1965, plaintiff, an author and a college teacher, and defendant, Washington Square Press, Inc., entered into a written agreement which, in relevant part, provided as follows. Plaintiff ("author") granted defendant ("publisher") exclusive rights to publish and sell in book form plaintiff's work on modern drama. Upon plaintiff's delivery of the manuscript, defendant agreed to complete payment of a nonreturnable $2,000 "advance." Thereafter, if defendant deemed the manuscript not "suitable for publication," it had the right to terminate the agreement by written notice within 60 days of delivery. Unless so terminated, defendant agreed to publish the work in hardbound edition within 18 months and afterwards in paperbound edition. The contract further provided that defendant would pay royalties to plaintiff, based upon specified percentages of sales. (For example, plaintiff was to receive 10% of the retail price of the first 10,000 copies sold in the continental United States.) If defendant failed to publish within 18 months, the contract provided that "this agreement shall terminate and the rights herein granted to the Publisher shall revert to the Author. In such event all payments theretofore made to the Author shall belong to the Author without prejudice to any other remedies which the Author may have." The contract also provided that controversies were to be determined pursuant to the New York simplified procedure for court determination of disputes (CPLR 3031-3037, Consol. Laws, c. 8).

Plaintiff performed by delivering his manuscript to defendant and was paid his $2,000 advance. Defendant thereafter merged with another publisher and ceased publishing in hardbound. Although defendant did not

exercise its 60-day right to terminate, it has refused to publish the manuscript in any form.

Plaintiff commenced the instant action pursuant to the simplified procedure practice and initially sought specific performance of the contract.
The Trial Term Justice denied specific performance but, finding a valid
contract and a breach by defendant, set the matter down for trial on the
issue of monetary damages, if any, sustained by the plaintiff. At trial,
plaintiff sought to prove: (1) delay of his academic promotion; (2) loss of
royalties which would have been earned; and (3) the cost of publication if
plaintiff had made his own arrangements to publish. The trial court
found that plaintiff had been promoted despite defendant's failure to
publish, and that there was no evidence that the breach had caused any
delay. Recovery of lost royalties was denied without discussion. The court
found, however, that the cost of hardcover publication to plaintiff was
the natural and probable consequence of the breach and, based upon
expert testimony, awarded $10,000 to cover this cost. It denied recovery
of the expenses of paperbound publication on the ground that plaintiff's
proof was conjectural.

The Appellate Division, (3 to 2) affirmed, finding that the cost of
publication was the proper measure of damages. In support of its conclusion, the majority analogized to the construction contract situation
where the cost of completion may be the proper measure of damages for a
builder's failure to complete a house or for use of wrong materials. The
dissent concluded that the cost of publication is not an appropriate measure of damages and consequently, that plaintiff may recover nominal
damages only.[24] We agree with the dissent. In so concluding, we took to
the basic purpose of damage recovery and the nature and effect of the
parties' contract.

It is axiomatic that, except where punitive damages are allowable, the
law awards damages for breach of contract to compensate for injury
caused by the breach — injury which was foreseeable, i.e., reasonably
within the contemplation of the parties, at the time the contract was
entered into. (Swain v. Schieffelin, 134 N.Y. 471, 473, 31 N.E. 1025,
1026.) Money damages are substitutional relief designed in theory "to put
the injured party in as good a position as he would have been put by full
performance of the contract, at the least cost to the defendant and without charging him with harms that he had no sufficient reason to foresee
when he made the contract." (5 Corbin, Contracts, §1002, pp. 31-32; 11
Williston, Contracts [3d ed.], §1338, p. 198.) In other words, so far as
possible, the law attempts to secure to the injured party the benefit of his
bargain, subject to the limitations that the injury — whether it be losses
suffered or gains prevented — was foreseeable, and that the amount of
damages claimed be measurable with a reasonable degree of certainty

---

24. Plaintiff does not challenge the trial court's denial of damages for delay in promotion
or for anticipated royalties.

and, of course, adequately proven. (See, generally, Dobbs, Law of Remedies, p. 148; see, also, Farnsworth, Legal Remedies for Breach of Contract, 70 Col. L. Rev. 1145, 1159.) But it is equally fundamental that the injured party should not recover more from the breach than he would have gained had the contract been fully performed. (Baker v. Drake, 53 N.Y. 211, 217; see, generally, Dobbs, Law of Remedies, p. 810.)

Measurement of damages in this case according to the cost of publication to the plaintiff would confer greater advantage than performance of the contract would have entailed to plaintiff and would place him in a far better position than he would have occupied had the defendant fully performed. Such measurement bears no relation to compensation for plaintiff's actual loss or anticipated profit. Far beyond compensating plaintiff for the interests he had in the defendant's performance of the contract — whether restitution, reliance or expectation (see Fuller & Perdue, Reliance Interest in Contract Damages, 46 Yale L.J. 52, 53-56) an award of the cost of publication would enrich plaintiff at defendant's expense.

Pursuant to the contract, plaintiff delivered his manuscript to the defendant. In doing so, he conferred a value on the defendant which, upon defendant's breach, was required to be restored to him. Special Term, in addition to ordering a trial on the issue of damages, ordered defendant to return the manuscript to plaintiff and plaintiff's restitution interest in the contract was thereby protected. (Cf. 5 Corbin, Contracts, §996, p. 15.)

At the trial on the issue of damages, plaintiff alleged no reliance losses suffered in performing the contract or in making necessary preparations to perform. Had such losses, if foreseeable and ascertainable, been incurred, plaintiff would have been entitled to compensation for them. (Cf. Bernstein v. Meech, 130 N.Y. 354, 359, 29 N.E. 255, 257.)

As for plaintiff's expectation interest in the contract, it was basically two-fold — the "advance" and the royalties. (To be sure, plaintiff may have expected to enjoy whatever notoriety, prestige or other benefits that might have attended publication, but even if these expectations were compensable, plaintiff did not attempt at trial to place a monetary value on them.) There is no dispute that plaintiff's expectancy in the "advance" was fulfilled — he has received his $2,000. His expectancy interest in the royalties — the profit he stood to gain from sale of the published book — while theoretically compensable, was speculative. Although this work is not plaintiff's first, at trial he provided no stable foundation for a reasonable estimate of royalties he would have earned had defendant not breached its promise to publish. In these circumstances, his claim for royalties falls for uncertainty. (Cf. Broadway Photoplay Co. v. World Film Corp., 225 N.Y. 104, 121 N.E. 756; Hewlett v. Caplin, 275 App. Div. 797, 88 N.Y.S.2d 428.)

Since the damages which would have compensated plaintiff for anticipated royalties were not proved with the required certainty, we agree with the dissent in the Appellate Division that nominal damages alone are recoverable. (Cf. Manhattan Sav. Inst. v. Gottfried Baking Co., 286 N.Y. 398, 36 N.E.2d 637.) Though these are damages in name only and not at all compensatory, they are nevertheless awarded as a formal vindication of plaintiff's legal right to compensation which has not been given a sufficiently certain monetary valuation. (Cf. Baker v. Hart, 123 N.Y. 470, 474, 25 N.E. 948, 949; see, generally, Dobbs, Law of Remedies, p. 191; 11 Williston, Contracts [3d ed.], §1339A, pp. 206-208.)

In our view, the analogy by the majority in the Appellate Division to the construction contract situation was inapposite. In the typical construction contract, the owner agrees to pay money or other consideration to a builder and expects, under the contract, to receive a completed building in return. The value of the promised performance to the owner is the properly constructed building. In this case, unlike the typical construction contract, the value to plaintiff of the promised performance — publication — was a percentage of sales of the books published and not the books themselves. Had the plaintiff contracted for the printing, binding and delivery of a number of hardbound copies of his manuscript, to be sold or disposed of as he wished, then perhaps the construction analogy, and measurement of damages by the cost of replacement or completion, would have some application.

Here, however, the specific value to plaintiff of the promised publication was the royalties he stood to receive from defendant's sales of the published book. Essentially, publication represented what it would have cost the defendant to confer that value upon the plaintiff, and, by its breach, defendant saved that cost. The error by the courts below was in measuring damages not by the value to plaintiff of the promised performance but by the cost of that performance to defendant. Damages are not measured, however, by what the defaulting party saved by the breach, but by the natural and probable consequences of the breach *to the plaintiff*. In this case, the consequence to plaintiff of defendant's failure to publish is that he is prevented from realizing the gains promised by the contract — the royalties. But, as we have stated, the amount of royalties plaintiff would have realized was not ascertained with adequate certainty and, as a consequence, plaintiff may recover nominal damages only.

Accordingly, the order of the Appellate Division should be modified to the extent of reducing the damage award of $10,000 for the cost of publication to six cents, but with costs and disbursements to the plaintiff.

NOTE

1. An extract from the celebrated Fuller & Perdue article cited by Judge Rabin is reproduced *infra* p. 1172. The tripartite distinction drawn in that article between the promisee's restitution, reliance and expecta-

tion interests has become an established part of our legal vocabulary and its repeated invocation has tended to give our law of contract damages an appearance of reassuring orderliness. Whether the appearance is an illusion and the distinction a source of more mischief than illumination are questions to be kept in mind as you work through the materials collected in this section.

2. The basic aim of contract damages (to "secure to the injured party the benefit of his bargain" and thus to place him in the position he would have been in if the contract had been performed) is often contrasted with the purpose of compensation in tort (to restore to the victim whatever he has lost as a result of his injury, thereby returning him to the *status quo ante*). The famous case of Hawkins v. McGee, 84 N.H. 114, 146 A. 641 (1929), illustrates the difference between these two approaches. Hawkins had a badly scarred hand and Dr. McGee promised to make it "perfect." McGee also said that only a few days of hospitalization would be required, after which Hawkins could return to work. The doctor botched the job and Hawkins was left with a hand even more unsightly than the one he had had before the operation. Hawkins sued, asserting both negligence (a tort claim) and breach of warranty (a contract claim). The negligence count was nonsuited, but Hawkins was held entitled to recover on his contract claim. On the question of damages, the trial judge instructed the jury as follows: "If you find the plaintiff entitled to anything, he is entitled to recover for what pain and suffering he has been made to endure and what injury he has sustained over and above the injury he had before." On appeal, this instruction, which would have been perfectly appropriate in a tort action, was held to be in error. According to the New Hampshire Supreme Court, Hawkins' damages for breach of contract ought to have been measured by "the difference between the value to him of a perfect hand or a good hand, such as the jury found the defendant promised him, and the value of his hand in its present condition. . . ." Moreover, the court asserted,

> The extent of the plaintiff's suffering does not measure this difference in value. The pain necessarily incident to a serious surgical operation was a part of the contribution which the plaintiff was willing to make to his joint undertaking with the defendant to produce a good hand. It was a legal detriment suffered by him which constituted a part of the consideration given by him for the contract. It represented a part of the price which he was willing to pay for a good hand, but it furnished no test of the value of a good hand or the difference between the value of the hand which the defendant promised and the one which resulted from the operation.

Id. at 118, 146 A. at 644.

The difference between compensation for a tortious injury and for breach of contract is sometimes expressed by saying that while the former is backward-looking or restitutionary, the latter is essentially forward-looking since it aims to give the promisee the anticipated (but as yet unrealized) benefit of his bargain. But is the line between tort and contract as clear as this traditional way of viewing the matter suggests? A tort victim may, after all, sue for the loss of future income — something he merely "expected" at the time of his accident; and while it could be said that this expectancy is a species of property that already belonged to the victim's estate when the accident occurred (so that compensation for its loss or destruction is restitutionary), the same could be said, without stretching things too far, of the contractual expectancy that "belonged" to young Hawkins and that was destroyed by the doctor's breach. To be sure, the *source* of the property destroyed differs in the two cases, since in one (but not the other) the doctor's promise is needed to create it. But is this a difference that matters, or matters as much, as the traditional view suggests?

3. What is the justification, if any, for protecting the promisee's expectancy rather than merely compensating him for his out-of-pocket losses? Consider Professor (now Judge) Posner's explanation of the expectation rule. If two people make a contract, Posner argues, each has an incentive to breach whenever

> [h]is profit from breach would exceed his expected profit from completion of the contract. If his profit from breach would also exceed the expected profit to the other party from completion of the contract, and if damages are limited to loss of expected profit, there will be an incentive to commit a breach. There should be. The opportunity cost of completion to the breaching party is the profit that he would make from a breach, and if it is greater than his profit from completion, then completion will involve a loss to him. If that loss is greater than the gain to the other party from completion, breach would be value-maximizing and should be encouraged. And because the victim of the breach is made whole for his loss, he is indifferent; hence encouraging breaches in these circumstances will not deter people from entering into contracts in the future.
>
> An arithmetical illustration may be helpful here. I sign a contract to deliver 100,000 custom-ground widgets at $.10 apiece to A, for use in his boiler factory. After I delivered 10,000, B comes to me, explains that he desperately needs 25,000 custom-ground widgets at once since otherwise he will be forced to close his pianola factory at great cost, and offers me $.15 apiece for 25,000 widgets. I sell him the widgets and as a result do not complete timely delivery to A, who sustains $1000 in lost profits from my breach. Having obtained an additional profit of $1250 on the sale to B, I am better off even after reimbursing A for his loss. Society is also better off. Since B was willing to pay me $.15 per widget, it must mean that each widget was worth at least $.15 to him. But it was worth only $.14 to A — the $.10 that he paid plus his expected profit of $.04 ($1000 divided by 25,000). Thus the breach resulted in a transfer of the 25,000 widgets from a less to a more valuable use. To be sure, had I refused to sell to B, he could have gone to A and negotiated an assignment of part of A's contract with me to

him. But this would have introduced an additional step and so imposed additional transaction costs.

Thus far the emphasis has been on the economic importance of not awarding damages in *excess* of the lost expectation. It is equally important, however, not to award less than the expectation loss. Suppose A contracts to sell B for $100,000 a machine that is worth $110,000 to B, i.e., that would yield him a profit of $10,000. Before delivery C comes to A and offers him $109,000 for the machine promised B. A would be tempted to breach were he not liable to B for B's loss of expected profit. Given that measure of damages, C will not be able to induce a breach of A's contract with B unless he offers B more than $110,000, thereby indicating that the machine really is worth more to him than to B. The expectation rule thus assures that the machine ends up where it is most valuable.

R. Posner, Economic Analysis of Law 89-90 (2d ed. 1977).

4. Suppose that Professor Freund had been denied tenure on the grounds that his scholarly publications were insufficient, and had had to take another (lower paying) teaching job as a result. Would he have been entitled to compensation for his loss of income (supposing this could be measured with precision)? Could he have refused to seek alternative employment and simply sued for the full amount of his lost salary? Consult Jameson v. Board of Education, *infra* p. 1317.

JACOB & YOUNGS, INC. v. KENT

230 N.Y. 239, 129 N.E. 889 (1921).

For a report of the case, see p. 1042 *supra*.

PEEVYHOUSE v. GARLAND COAL & MINING CO.

382 P.2d 109 (Okla. 1962).

JACKSON, Justice.

In the trial court, plaintiffs Willie and Lucille Peevyhouse sued the defendant, Garland Coal and Mining Company, for damages for breach of contract. Judgment was for plaintiffs in an amount considerably less than was sued for. Plaintiffs appeal and defendant cross-appeals.

In the briefs on appeal, the parties present their argument and contentions under several propositions; however, they all stem from the basic question of whether the trial court properly instructed the jury on the measure of damages.

Briefly stated, the facts are as follows: plaintiffs owned a farm containing coal deposits, and in November, 1954, leased the premises to defendant for a period of five years for coal mining purposes. A "strip-mining" operation was contemplated in which the coal would be taken from pits on the surface of the ground, instead of from underground mine shafts. In addition to the usual covenants found in a coal mining lease, defendant specifically agreed to perform certain restorative and remedial work at the end of the lease period. It is unnecessary to set out the details of the work to be done, other than to say that it would involve the moving of many thousands of cubic yards of dirt, at a cost estimated by expert witnesses at about $29,000.00. However, plaintiffs, sued for only $25,000.00.

During the trial it was stipulated that all covenants and agreements in the lease contract had been fully carried out by both parties, except the remedial work mentioned above; defendant conceded that this work had not been done.

Plaintiffs introduced expert testimony as to the amount and nature of the work to be done, and its estimated cost. Over plaintiffs' objections, defendant thereafter introduced expert testimony as to the "diminution in value" of plaintiffs' farm resulting from the failure of defendant to render performance as agreed in the contract — that is, the difference between the present value of the farm, and what its value would have been if defendant had done what it agreed to do.

At the conclusion of the trial, the court instructed the jury that it must return a verdict for plaintiffs, and left the amount of damages for jury determination. On the measure of damages, the court instructed the jury that it might consider the cost of performance of the work defendant agreed to do, "together with all of the evidence offered on behalf of either party."

It thus appears that the jury was at liberty to consider the "diminution in value" of plaintiffs' farm as well as the cost of "repair work" in determining the amount of damages.

It returned a verdict for plaintiffs for $5000.00 — only a fraction of the "cost of performance," *but more than the total value of the farm even after the remedial work is done.*

On appeal, the issue is sharply drawn. Plaintiffs contend that the true measure of damages in this case is what it will cost plaintiffs to obtain performance of the work that was not done because of defendant's default. Defendant argues that the measure of damages is the cost of performance "limited, however, to the total difference in the market value before and after the work was performed."

It appears that this precise question has not heretofore been presented to this court. In Ardizonne v. Archer, 72 Okl. 70, 178 P. 263, this court held that the measure of damages for breach of a contract to drill an oil well was the reasonable cost of drilling the well, but here a slightly different factual situation exists. The drilling of an oil well will yield valuable geological information, even if no oil or gas is found, and of course if the well is a producer, the value of the premises increases. In the case before us, it is argued by defendant with some force that the performance of the remedial work defendant agreed to do will add at the most only a few hundred dollars to the value of plaintiffs' farm, and that the damages should be limited to that amount because that is all plaintiffs have lost.

Plaintiffs rely on Groves v. John Wunder Co., 205 Minn. 163, 286 N.W. 235, 123 A.L.R. 502. In that case, the Minnesota court, in a substantially similar situation, adopted the "cost of performance" rule as opposed to the "value" rule. The result was to authorize a jury to give plaintiff damages in the amount of $60,000, where the real estate concerned would have been worth only $12,160, even if the work contracted for had been done.

It may be observed that Groves v. John Wunder Co., *supra*, is the only case which has come to our attention in which the cost of performance rule has been followed under circumstances where the cost of performance greatly exceeded the diminution in value resulting from the breach of contract. Incidentally, it appears that this case was decided by a plurality rather than a majority of the members of the court.

Defendant relies principally upon Sandy Valley & E.R. Co. v. Hughes, 175 Ky. 320, 194 S.W. 344; Bigham v. Wabash-Pittsburg Terminal Ry. Co., 223 Pa. 106, 72 A. 318; and Sweeney v. Lewis Const. Co., 66 Wash. 490, 119 P. 1108. These were all cases in which, under similar circumstances, the appellate courts followed the "value" rule instead of the "cost of performance" rule. Plaintiff points out that in the earliest of these cases (Bigham) the court cites as authority on the measure of damages an earlier Pennsylvania *tort* case, and that the other two cases follow the first, with no explanation as to why a measure of damages ordinarily followed in cases sounding in tort should be used in contract cases. Nevertheless, it is of some significance that three out of four appellate courts have followed the diminution in value rule under circumstances where, as here, the cost of performance greatly exceeds the diminution in value.

The explanation may be found in the fact that the situations presented are artificial ones. It is highly unlikely that the ordinary property owner would agree to pay $29,000 (or its equivalent) for the construction of "improvements" upon his property that would increase its value only about ($300) three hundred dollars. The result is that we are called upon to apply principles of law theoretically based upon reason and reality to a situation which is basically unreasonable and unrealistic.

In Groves v. John Wunder Co., *supra*, in arriving at its conclusions, the Minnesota court apparently considered the contract involved to be analogous to a building and construction contract, and cited authority for the proposition that the cost of performance or completion of the building as contracted is ordinarily the measure of damages in actions for damages for the breach of such a contract.

In an annotation following the Minnesota case beginning at 123 A.L.R. 515, the annotator places the three cases relied on by defendant

(*Sandy Valley, Bigham* and *Sweeney*) under the classification of cases involving "grading and excavation contracts."

We do not think either analogy is strictly applicable to the case now before us. The primary purpose of the lease contract between plaintiffs and defendant was neither "building and construction" nor "grading and excavation." It was merely to accomplish the economical recovery and marketing of coal from the premises, to the profit of all parties. The special provisions of the lease contract pertaining to remedial work were incidental to the main object involved.

Even in the case of contracts that are unquestionably building and construction contracts, the authorities are not in agreement as to the factors to be considered in determining whether the cost of performance rule or the value rule should be applied. The American Law Institute's Restatement of the Law, Contracts, Volume 1, Sections 346(1)(a)(i) and (ii) submits the proposition that the cost of performance is the proper measure of damages "if this is possible and does not involve *unreasonable economic waste*"; and that the diminution in value caused by the breach is the proper measure "if construction and completion in accordance with the contract would involve *"unreasonable economic waste."* (Emphasis supplied.) In an explanatory comment immediately following the text, the Restatement makes it clear that the "economic waste" referred to consists of the destruction of a substantially completed building or other structure. Of course no such destruction is involved in the case now before us.

On the other hand, in McCormick, Damages, Section 168, it is said with regard to building and construction contracts that ". . . in cases where the defect is one that can be repaired or cured without *undue expense*" the cost of performance is the proper measure of damages, but where ". . . the defect in material or construction is one that cannot be remedied without *an expenditure for reconstruction disproportionate to the end to be attained*" (emphasis supplied) the value rule should be followed. The same idea was expressed in Jacob & Youngs, Inc. v. Kent, 230 N.Y. 239, 129 N.E. 889, 23 A.L.R. 1429, as follows:

> The owner is entitled to the money which will permit him to complete, unless the cost of completion is grossly and unfairly out of proportion to the good to be attained. When that is true, the measure is the difference in value.

It thus appears that the prime consideration in the Restatement was "economic waste"; and that the prime consideration in McCormick, Damages, and in Jacob & Youngs, Inc. v. Kent, *supra*, was the relationship between the expense involved and the "end to be attained" — in other words, the "relative economic benefit."

In view of the unrealistic fact situation in the instant case, and certain Oklahoma statutes to be hereinafter noted, we are of the opinion that the "relative economic benefit" is a proper consideration here. This is in accord with the recent case of Mann v. Clowser, 190 Va. 887, 59 S.E.2d 78, where, in applying the cost rule, the Virginia court specifically noted that ". . . the defects are remediable from a practical standpoint and the costs *are not grossly disproportionate to the results to be obtained*" (Emphasis supplied).

23 O.S.1961 §§96 and 97 provide as follows:

> §96. . . . Notwithstanding the provisions of this chapter, no person can recover a greater amount in damages for the breach of an obligation, than he would have gained by the full performance thereof on both sides. . . .
>
> §97. . . . Damages must, in all cases, be reasonable, and where an obligation of any kind appears to create a right to unconscionable and grossly oppressive damages, contrary to substantial justice no more than reasonable damages can be recovered.

Although it is true that the above sections of the statute are applied most often in tort cases, they are by their own terms, and the decisions of this court, also applicable in actions for damages for breach of contract. It would seem that they are peculiarly applicable here where, under the "cost of performance" rule, plaintiffs might recover an amount about nine times the total value of their farm. Such would seem to be "unconscionable and grossly oppressive damages, contrary to substantial justice" within the meaning of the statute. Also, it can hardly be denied that if plaintiffs here are permitted to recover under the "cost of performance" rule, they will receive a greater benefit from the breach than could be gained from full performance, contrary to the provisions of Sec. 96.

An analogy may be drawn between the cited sections, and the provisions of 15 O.S. 1961 §§214 and 215. These sections tend to render void any provisions of a contract which attempt to fix the amount of stipulated damages to be paid in case of a breach, except where it is impracticable or extremely difficult to determine the actual damages. This results in spite of the agreement of the parties, and the obvious and well know rationale is that insofar as they exceed the actual damages suffered, the stipulated damages amount to a penalty or forfeiture which the law does not favor.

23 O.S. 1961 §§96 and 97 have the same effect in the case now before us. *In spite of the agreement of the parties*, these sections limit the damages recoverable to a reasonable amount not "contrary to substantial justice"; they prevent plaintiffs from recovering a "greater amount in damages for the breach of an obligation" than they would have "gained by the full performance thereof."

We therefore hold that where, in a coal mining lease, lessee agrees to perform certain remedial work on the premises concerned at the end of the lease period, and thereafter the contract is fully performed by both parties except that the remedial work is not done, the measure of damages in an action by lessor against lessee for damages for breach of contract is ordinarily the reasonable cost of performance of the work; however, where the contract provision breached was merely incidental to the main purpose in view, and where the economic benefit which would result to lessor by full performance of the work is grossly disproportionate to the cost of performance, the damages which lessor may recover are limited to the diminution in value resulting to the premises because of the non-performance.

We believe the above holding is in conformity with the intention of the Legislature as expressed in the statutes mentioned, and in harmony with the better-reasoned cases from the other jurisdictions where analogous fact situations have been considered. It should be noted that the rule as stated does not interfere with the property owner's right to "do what he will with his own" (Chamberlain v. Parker, 45 N.Y. 569), or his right, if he chooses, to contract for "improvements" which will actually have the effect of reducing his property's value. Where such result is in fact contemplated by the parties, and is a main or principal purpose of those contracting, it would seem that the measure of damages for breach would ordinarily be the cost of performance.

The above holding disposes of all of the arguments raised by the parties on appeal.

Under the most liberal view of the evidence herein, the diminution in value resulting to the premises because of non-performance of the remedial work was $300.00. After a careful search of the record, we have found no evidence of a higher figure, and plaintiffs do not argue in their briefs that a greater diminution in value was sustained. It thus appears that the judgment was clearly excessive, and that the amount for which judgment should have been rendered is definitely and satisfactorily shown by the record.

We are asked by each party to modify the judgment in accordance with the respective theories advanced, and it is conceded that we have authority to do so. 12 O.S. 1961 §952; Busboom v. Smith, 199 Okl. 688, 191 P.2d 198; Stumpf v. Stumpf, 173 Okl. 1, 46 P.2d 315.

We are of the opinion that the judgment of the trial court for the plaintiffs should be, and it is hereby, modified and reduced to the sum of $300.00, and as so modified it is affirmed.

Welch, Davison, Halley, and Johnson, JJ., concur.

Williams, C.J., Blackbird, V.C.J., and Irwin and Berry, JJ., dissent.

IRWIN, Justice (dissenting).

By the specific provisions in the coal mining lease under consideration, the defendant agreed as follows:

> . . . 7b Lessee agrees to make fills in the pits dug on said premises on the property line in such manner that fences can be placed thereon and access had to opposite sides of the pits.

7c Lessee agrees to smooth off the top of the spoil banks on the above premises.

7d Lessee agrees to leave the creek crossing the above premises in such a condition that it will not interfere with the crossings to be made in pits as set out in 7b.

7f Lessee further agrees to leave no shale or dirt on the high wall of said pits. . . .

Following the expiration of the lease, plaintiffs made demand upon defendant that it carry out the provisions of the contract and to perform those covenants contained therein.

Defendant admits that it failed to perform its obligations that it agreed and contracted to perform under the lease contract and there is nothing in the record which indicates that defendant could not perform its obligations. Therefore, in my opinion defendant's breach of the contract was wilful and not in good faith.

Although the contract speaks for itself, there were several negotiations between the plaintiffs and defendant before the contract was executed. Defendant admitted in the trial of the action, that plaintiffs insisted that the above provisions be included in the contract and that they would not agree to coal mining lease unless the above provisions were included.

In consideration for the lease contract, plaintiffs were to receive a certain amount as royalty for the coal produced and marketed and in addition thereto their land was to be restored as provided in the contract.

Defendant received as consideration for the contract, its proportionate share of the coal produced and marketed and in addition thereto, the *right to use* plaintiffs' land in the furtherance of its mining operations.

The cost for performing the contract in question could have been reasonably approximated when the contract was negotiated and executed and there are no conditions now existing which could not have been reasonably anticipated by the parties. Therefore, defendant had knowledge, when it prevailed upon the plaintiffs to execute the lease, that the cost of performance might be disproportionate to the value or benefits received by plaintiff for the performance.

Defendant has received its benefits under the contract and now urges, in substance, that plaintiffs' measure of damages for its failure to perform should be the economic value of performance to the plaintiffs and not the cost of performance.

If a peculiar set of facts should exist where the above rule should be applied as the proper measure of damages, (and in my judgment those facts do not exist in the instant case) before such rule should be applied, consideration should be given to the benefits received or contracted for by the party who asserts the application of the rule.

Defendant did not have the right to mine plaintiffs' coal or to use plaintiffs' property for its mining operations without the consent of plaintiffs. Defendant had knowledge of the benefits that it would receive under the contract and the approximate cost of performing the contract. With this knowledge, it must be presumed that defendant thought that it would be to its economic advantage to enter into the contract with plaintiffs and that it would reap benefits from the contract, or it would have not entered into the contract.

Therefore, if the value of the performance of a contract should be considered in determining the measure of damages for breach of a contract, the value of the benefits received under the contract by a party who breaches a contract should also be considered. However, in my judgment, to give consideration to either in the instant action, completely rescinds and holds for naught the solemnity of the contract before us and makes an entirely new contract for the parties.

In Goble v. Bell Oil & Gas Co., 97 Okl. 261, 223 P. 371, we held:

> Even though the contract contains harsh and burdensome terms which the court does not in all respects approve, it is the province of the parties in relation to lawful subject matter to fix their rights and obligations, and the court will give the contract effect according to its expressed provisions, unless it be shown by competent evidence proof that the written agreement as executed is the result of fraud, mistake, or accident.

In Cities Service Oil Co. v. Geolograph Co. Inc., 208 Okl. 179, 254 P.2d 775, we said:

> While we do not agree that the contract as presently written is an onerous one, we think the short answer is that the folly or wisdom of a contract is not for the court to pass on.

In Great Western Oil & Gas Company v. Mitchell, Okl., 326 P.2d 794, we held:

> The law will not make a better contract for parties than they themselves have seen fit to enter into, or alter it for the benefit of one party and to the detriment of the others; the judicial function of a court of law is to enforce a contract as it is written.

I am mindful of Title 23 O.S. 1961 §96, which provides that no person can recover a greater amount in damages for the breach of an obligation than he could have gained by the full performance thereof on both sides, except in cases not applicable herein. However, in my judgment, the above statutory provision is not applicable here.

In my judgment, we should follow the case of Groves v. John Wunder Company, 205 Minn. 163, 286 N.W. 235, 123 A.L.R. 502, which defendant agrees "that the fact situation is apparently similar to the one in the case at bar," and where the Supreme Court of Minnesota held:

The owner's or employer's damages for such a breach (i.e. breach hypothesized in 2d syllabus) are to be measured, not in respect to the value of the land to be improved, but by the reasonable cost of doing that which the contractor promised to do and which he left undone.

The hypothesized breach referred to states that where the contractor's breach of a contract is wilful, that is, in bad faith, he is not entitled to any benefit of the equitable doctrine of substantial performance.

In the instant action defendant has made no attempt to even substantially perform. The contract in question is not immoral, is not tainted with fraud, and was not entered into through mistake or accident and is not contrary to public policy. It is clear and unambiguous and the parties understood the terms thereof, and the approximate cost of fulfilling the obligations could have been approximately ascertained. There are no conditions existing now which could not have been reasonably anticipated when the contract was negotiated and executed. The defendant could have performed the contract if it desired. It has accepted and reaped the benefits of its contract and now urges that plaintiffs' benefits under the contract be denied. If plaintiffs' benefits are denied, such benefits would inure to the direct benefit of the defendant.

Therefore, in my opinion, the plaintiffs were entitled to specific performance of the contract and since defendant has failed to perform, the proper measure of damages should be the cost of performance. Any other measure of damage would be holding for naught the express provisions of the contract; would be taking from the plaintiffs the benefits of the contract and placing those benefits in defendant which has failed to perform its obligations; would be granting benefits to defendant without a resulting obligation; and would be completely rescinding the solemn obligation of the contract for the benefit of the defendant to the detriment of the plaintiffs by making an entirely new contract for the parties.

I therefore respectfully dissent to the opinion promulgated by a majority of my associates.

NOTE

1. Suppose the court had upheld the Peevyhouses' right to recover the full cost of restoring their farm. From the coal company's point of view, wouldn't an award of this sort be equivalent to an order of specific performance? If the company were ordered to carry out the restorative work (or, what is the same thing, to pay the Peevyhouses an amount equal to the cost of doing so), what would be the likely result? Assume that the Peevyhouses would prefer $15,000 in cash to the restoration of their farm: isn't it likely that the parties will negotiate a mutually advantageous settle-

ment if the company is ordered to perform or to pay the full cost of restoration? (What will happen if the Peevyhouses care more about the restoration of their farm than anything else in the world?) Will there be a similar negotiation if the coal company is ordered to compensate the Peevyhouses only for the diminution in the market value of their farm? At the conclusion of the trial below, the jury awarded the Peevyhouses $5,000, an amount that cannot be rationalized on either of the damage theories at issue in the case. Might the jury's verdict nevertheless be explained, and perhaps even justified, as an effort to approximate the outcome of a settlement negotiated by the parties themselves? But if this is so, wouldn't the results of an actual negotiation have been preferable to the jury's speculative assessment of the parties' interests and expectations?

2. In both *Jacob & Youngs* and *Peevyhouse*, the plaintiffs recovered damages equal to the diminution in the market value of their property (a formula that yielded a small sum in the latter case and nothing in the former). Is this rule equally appropriate in both cases? To be sure, it seems more likely that the farmers in *Peevyhouse* attached a sentimental or aesthetic value to the appearance of their property — a value not reflected in its market price — than that the owner in *Jacob & Youngs* assigned a similarly unique or idiosyncratic value to one particular brand of otherwise indistinguishable pipe. But this is, after all, a judgment of taste; more exactly, it is a judgment about the frequency or distribution of certain tastes and hence a judgment about the credibility of the claim that a particular person has a certain taste and therefore values something more highly than the market does. (What, by the way, is the evidence for assuming the existence of such a discrepancy between the market and "personal" or "subjective" value of a thing?) Should the law make judgments of this sort? Can it avoid them? One might say, "No harm is done in making such a judgment, so long as the parties remain free to reverse its effect by placing an appropriately worded provision in their contract." Before you accept this sanguine proposal, recall Judge Cardozo's treatment of the contract in *Jacob & Youngs*.

3. Do you find the concept of "economic waste," emphasized by the majority in *Peevyhouse*, helpful? Suppose, to take a celebrated example, that I make a contract to have a monumental birdbath constructed on my front lawn; once the birdbath is built, let us assume, my home will be worth less than it presently is. Is this contract "economically wasteful"? Is it, from my point of view, a "losing" contract like the one in L. Albert & Son v. Armstrong Rubber Co., *infra* p. 1197? Suppose the contractor who has promised to build my birdbath subsequently refuses to do so. Can he argue that no compensation is owed me because the contract is economically wasteful? If this argument is disallowed, how should my damages be calculated? It is interesting to note that the expression "economic waste," which appeared in §346 of Restatement First, has been

dropped from the corresponding section (§348) of Restatement Second. Section 348(2) provides:

> If a breach results in defective or unfinished construction and the loss in value to the injured party is not proved with sufficient certainty, he may recover damages based on
> (a)   the diminution in the market price of the property caused by the breach, or
> (b)   the reasonable cost of completing performance or of remedying the defects if that cost is not clearly disproportionate to the probable loss in value to him.

In Comment C to §348 the restaters observe that the phrase "economic waste" is misleading, "since an injured party will not, even if awarded an excessive amount of damages, usually pay to have the defects remedied if to do so will cost him more than the resulting increase in value to him."

4.   Groves v. John Wunder Co., 205 Minn. 163, 286 N.W. 235 (1939), discussed and distinguished by the majority in *Peevyhouse*, held that the plaintiff's damages were properly measured by the cost to complete certain levelling and grading work promised by the defendant even though the resulting increase in the market value of the plaintiff's land would be substantially less. The property involved in the *Groves* case was devoted entirely to commercial use. Do you think *Groves* was rightly decided? Is the *Groves* case, on its facts, more like *Peevyhouse* or *Jacob & Youngs*?

GAINSFORD v. CARROLL
2 B. & C. 624, 107 Eng. Rep. 516 (K.B. 1828)

Assumpsit for the non-performance of three contracts entered into by the defendants with the plaintiff for the sale of fifty bales of bacon, to be shipped by them from Waterford, in the months of January, February, and March 1823 respectively. The defendant suffered judgment by default, and upon the execution of the writ of enquiry in London, the secondary told the jury that they were at liberty to calculate the damages according to the price of bacon on the day when the enquiry was executed, and the the difference between that and the contract price ought to be the measure of damages. Parke had obtained a rule nisi for setting aside the enquiry on the ground that the plaintiff was only entitled to recover the difference between the contract price and price which the article bore at or about the time when, by the terms of the contract, it ought to have been delivered. He cited Leigh v. Patterson (8 Taunt. 540), in which the Court of C.P. intimated an opinion that the damages should be calculated according to the price of the day on which the contract ought to have been performed. This is different from the case of a loan of stock; there the lender, by the transfer deprives himself of the means of replacing the stock, he has not the money to go to market with, but in the case of a purchase of goods, the vendee is in possession of his money, and he has it in his power, as soon as the vendor has failed in the performance of the contract, to purchase other goods of the like quality and description, and it is his own fault if he does not do so.

Wilde contra contended that the rule which had been laid down, as to the measure of damages, for not replacing stock, applied to the present, and he cited Stevens v. Johnson (2 East, 211), and Mc'Arthur v. Lord Seaforth (2 Taunt. 257).

PER CURIAM. Those cases do not apply to the present. In the case of a loan of stock the borrower holds in his hands the money of the lender, and thereby prevents him from using it altogether. Here the plaintiff had his money in his possession and he might have purchased other bacon of the like quality the very day after the contract was broken, and if he has sustained any loss, by neglecting to do so, it is his own fault. We think that the under sheriff ought to have told the jury that damages should be calculated according to the price of the bacon at or about the day when the goods ought to have been delivered.

Rule absolute.

NOTE

1. As Gainsford v. Carroll suggests, the contract and market rule had its origins in a series of late eighteenth-century cases that involved speculative transactions in shares (or "stock") on the London stock exchange. It would be helpful to know more about the operation of the exchange than we do, but it goes without saying that a "stock exchange," in the eighteenth century or today, is a market phenomenon of a most unusual kind. This is institutionalized gambling in a high velocity market where, it is assumed, every offer to sell is matched by a corresponding offer to buy and where prices fluctuate rapidly, unpredictably and over a wide range. In such a market (and only there) it is true that the disappointed seller (or buyer) can — and, perhaps should — immediately enter into a substitute contract "at the market." Any sort of "lost profits" formula in such a context would be idle folly; not even the devil has ever been able to predict what the "market" was going to do next. Reliance expenses in the customary transaction were, nor doubt, minimal or nothing and could be disregarded. In the peculiar situation that gave rise to the rule, contract and market, like most rules of law, made very good sense.

2. The process of generalizing the contract and market formula from a rule applicable to transactions on the stock exchange to a rule applicable to all contracts for the sale of all sorts of goods, whether for immediate or future delivery, whether for cash or on credit, seems to have been almost

mindless. Gainsford v. Carroll is typical of the absence of thought the problem received. Putting aside the special situation of the stock (or commodity) exchange, it is simply not true that the disappointed seller (or buyer) invariably has a "market" available in which he can immediately enter into a substitute contract that will liquidate damages "at the market." Nor do the prices of most goods fluctuate, day by day, in a wild and erratic course; absent such fluctuation, the contract and market formula will produce no damages at all. Of course the fact that no sanction for breach is provided by way of damages may be taken to mean that no interest worthy of protection has been invaded. On the other hand, there has long been evident in the literature, both judicial and academic, an uneasy feeling that there is something wrong with a damage rule that, over a wide range of factual situations, produces no damages and thus, so far as legal sanctions go, allows contracts to be breached with impunity. In general there is an inarticulate feeling that, Holmes to the contrary notwithstanding, there is something immoral about breaking a contract and that the wrongdoer should be, somehow, punished.

If, freed from the burden of history, we could take a fresh approach to the problem of providing a workable damage rule for breach of contracts for the sale of goods, it is by no means certain that anyone would come up with the contract and market rule as the (or even a) solution. Nevertheless, having once established itself in sales law, the contract and market rule has held on with astonishing tenacity. It should be pointed out, however, that even in sales law, contract and market has never been the whole truth. In addition to his damages remedy, the buyer of goods has (in certain circumstances at least) always had the right to compel specific performance of the contract or to replevy the goods from the seller (the buyer's so-called property remedies); the seller, likewise has under certain conditions always been entitled to sue for the full contract price. Furthermore, the contract and market rule was never applied to a buyer's action for breach of warranty with respect to goods accepted and kept. In that situation the basic damage rule was that buyer was entitled to the difference between the value of the goods as they were and the value they would have had if they had been as warranted. The warranty rule also opened automatically to allow the buyer to recover "special" or "consequential" damages for injury to person or property — as in the case of the exploding furnace, the mouse in the Coca-Cola bottle and so on. The domain of the contract and market formula, except as it was trenched upon by the "property" rules, which themselves tended to atrophy, was the seller's action with respect to goods which the buyer wrongfully refused to accept and the buyer's action with respect to goods which the seller wrongfully refused to deliver.

3. Contract and market was always stated as a two-way rule, as applicable to sellers on buyer's breach as to buyers on seller's breach. A moment's reflection suffices to make it clear that sellers and buyers are quite

differently situated with respect to the losses that breach by the other party may cause. It is hard, if not impossible, to imagine a case in which a seller could, on any theory, claim to have been damaged in an amount exceeding his costs of acquisition or manufacture (which, in the case of a losing contract, might exceed the contract price) plus his anticipated profit (if the contract would have been a winning gamble). On the other hand, a buyer's possible claim, if he is allowed to escape from contract and market into the happy hunting ground of special or consequential damages, is limited only by the imagination of counsel. For want of a nail, we are told, the shoe was lost, for want of a shoe the horse was lost, and so on through the loss of the battle, the war, and the kingdom. Shall we, then, cast the seller, who ought to have supplied the nail, in civil damages for the loss of the kingdom?

UNIFORM COMMERCIAL CODE

§2-706. SELLER'S RESALE INCLUDING CONTRACT FOR RESALE

(1) Under the conditions stated in Section 2-703 on seller's remedies, the seller may resell the goods concerned or the undelivered balance thereof. Where the resale is made in good faith and in a commercially reasonable manner the seller may recover the difference between the resale price and the contract price together with any incidental damages allowed under the provisions of this Article (Section 2-710), but less expenses saved in consequence of the buyer's breach. . . .

§2-708. SELLER'S DAMAGES FOR NON-ACCEPTANCE OR REPUDIATION

(1) Subject to subsection (2) and to the provisions of this Article with respect to proof of market price (Section 2-723), the measure of damages for non-acceptance or repudiation by the buyer is the difference between the market price at the time and place for tender and the unpaid contract price together with any incidental damages provided in this Article (Section 2-710), but less expenses saved in consequence of the buyer's breach.

(2) If the measure of damages provided in subsection (1) is inadequate to put the seller in as good a position as performance would have done then the measure of damages is the profit (including reasonable overhead) which the seller would have made from full performance by the buyer, together with any incidental damages provided in this Article (Section 2-710), due allowance for costs reasonably incurred and due credit for payments or proceeds of resale.

§2-710.   SELLER'S INCIDENTAL DAMAGES

Incidental damages to an aggrieved seller include any commercially reasonable charges, expenses or commissions incurred in stopping delivery, in the transportation, care and custody of goods after the buyer's breach, in connection with return or resale of the goods or otherwise resulting from the breach.

§2-712.   "COVER"; BUYER'S PROCUREMENT OF SUBSTITUTE
          GOODS

(1)   After a breach within the preceding section the buyer may "cover" by making in good faith and without unreasonable delay any reasonable purchase of or contract to purchase goods in substitution for those due from the seller.

(2)   The buyer may recover from the seller as damages the difference between the cost of cover and the contract price together with any incidental or consequential damages as hereinafter defined (Section 2-715), but less expenses saved in consequence of the seller's breach.

(3)   Failure of the buyer to effect cover within this section does not bar him from any other remedy.

§2-713.   BUYER'S DAMAGES FOR NON-DELIVERY OR
          REPUDIATION

(1)   Subject to the provisions of this Article with respect to proof of market price (Section 2-723), the measure of damages for non-delivery or repudiation by the seller is the difference between the market price at the time when the buyer learned of the breach and the contract price together with any incidental and consequential damages provided in this Article (Section 2-715), but less expenses saved in consequence of the seller's breach.

(2)   Market price is to be determined as of the place for tender or, in cases of rejection after arrival or revocation of acceptances, as of the place of arrival.

§2-715.   BUYER'S INCIDENTAL AND CONSEQUENTIAL DAMAGES

(1)   Incidental damages resulting from the seller's breach include expenses reasonably incurred in inspection, receipt, transportation and care and custody of goods rightfully rejected, any commercially reason-

able charges, expenses or commissions in connection with effecting cover
and any other reasonable expense incident to the delay or other breach.

(2)   Consequential damages resulting from the seller's breach include

(a)   any loss resulting from general or particular requirements and
      needs of which the seller at the time of contracting had reason to
      know and which could not reasonably be prevented by cover or
      otherwise; and

(b)   injury to person or property proximately resulting from any
      breach of warranty.

PANHANDLE AGRI-SERVICE INC. v. BECKER
231 Kan. 291, 644 P.2d 413 (1982).

[Becker made a contract to sell Panhandle 10,000 tons of hay. The hay
was to be delivered at the Becker farm near Garden City, Kansas, during
the 1978 season. The agreed-upon price for the hay was $45 a ton. By the
end of 1978, Becker had still not delivered the full 10,000 tons required by
the contract. Accordingly, he and the president of Panhandle agreed that
the amount still due — a little more than 912 tons — would be supplied
from Becker's 1979 hay crop. Sometime in 1979 Becker notified Panhandle that he would not deliver the additional hay, and Panhandle brought
an action for breach of contract, in which it was held entitled to recover.
At the time of Becker's breach, the market price for hay in Garden City
was $62 a ton. During the trial, the president of Panhandle testified that
he had contracted to resell the hay in Texas for $67 a ton, and that the
total cost of transporting the hay from Kansas to Texas was $7,371. The
trial court awarded Panhandle $12,698.63 in damages. It arrived at this
figure by multiplying the difference between the resale price ($67) and the
original contract price ($45) by the number of tons of hay still due and
then subtracting the cost of hauling the hay to Texas. On appeal, the
Kansas Supreme Court affirmed that Becker had indeed breached his
contract with Panhandle and then considered the issue of damages.]

We now turn to the question of what was the proper method of arriving at the amount of damages. As previously stated Panhandle argues on
appeal it should be entitled to loss of profits of $20,069.63. Becker argues
the entire judgment should be set aside but, if not, the judgment should
be reduced to $4,560.64, which would show a deduction from the loss of
profits claimed by plaintiff of the costs of trucking from Kansas to Texas.
McCoy [a professional trucker] was going to charge $17.00 per ton.

Under the facts of this case we believe both contentions are in error.
The Uniform Commercial Code concerning sales provides:

(1) Subject to the provisions of this article with respect to proof of
market price (section 84-2-723), the measure of damages for nondelivery or

repudiation by the seller is the difference between the market price at the time when the buyer learned of the breach and the contract price together with any incidental and consequential damages provided in this article (section 84-2-715), but less expenses saved in consequence of the seller's breach.

(2) Market price is to be determined as of the place for tender or, in cases of rejection after arrival or revocation of acceptance, as of the place of arrival.

K.S.A. 84-2-713.

The trial court determined that the market price of alfalfa hay at Garden City, Kansas, in 1979, was $62.00 per ton. The contract price agreed on by the parties was $45.00. So the measure of damages for nondelivery or repudiation by the seller would be $62.00 less $45.00 or $17.00 per ton, provided no incidental or consequential damages are recoverable in this case, and provided there was no evidence that "cover" was not possible.

The meaning of the word "cover" as used in the Uniform Commercial Code relating to sales is explained in K.S.A. 84-2-712 and refers roughly to the buyer's procurement of substitute goods when the seller nondelivers or repudiates. The philosophy underlying this "cover option" appears to be that an aggrieved buyer can obtain substituted goods without having to suffer any great loss. See the Official UCC Comment following K.S.A. 84-2-712.

Trucking or transportation expense was not deductible from the above figure. Under the Code it is assumed the buyer will attempt to "cover" the merchandise lost by seller's nondelivery at the seller's shipping point. If the buyer seeks a replacement of the merchandise at the shipping point, he would incur replacement shipping costs roughly equivalent to those on the original contract. Thus, by comparison with such a replacement contract there would be no expenses saved in consequence of the seller's breach because we assume the buyer must pay the expenses for shipment under the new contract as well. White & Summers, Uniform Commercial Code §6-4, pp. 231-232 (2nd ed. 1980).

The Official UCC Comment, appearing after the text of K.S.A. 84-2-713, at paragraphs one and two states:

1. The general baseline adopted in this section uses as a yardstick the market in which the buyer would have obtained cover had he sought that relief. So the place for measuring damages is the place of tender (or the place of arrival if the goods are rejected or their acceptance is revoked after reaching their destination) and the crucial time is the time at which the buyer learns of the breach.

2. The market or current price to be used in comparison with the contract price under this section is the price for goods of the same kind and in the same branch of trade.

As to incidental damages resulting from the seller's breach there was no evidence to support any of the items listed in K.S.A. 84-2-715(1). Incidental damages concern expenses when goods are tendered and rejected or have to be transported and cared for, or which concern charges in connection with effecting cover.

As to consequential damages K.S.A. 84-2-715(2)(a) provides:

> (2) Consequential damages resulting from the seller's breach include
> (a) any loss resulting from general or particular requirements and needs of which the seller at the time of contracting had reason to know and which could not reasonably be prevented by cover or otherwise.

Failure of the buyer to utilize the remedy of cover when such is reasonably available will preclude recovery of consequential damages, such as loss of profits. White & Summers §6-6, 234 fn.103, §6-7, 250, §10-4, 396. However, K.S.A. 84-2-712, which provides for cover, *i.e.*, the buyer's procurement of substitute goods, states:

> (3) Failure of the buyer to effect cover within this section does not bar him from any other remedy.

Therefore, cover is not a mandatory remedy for the buyer. The buyer is free to choose between cover and damages for nondelivery. In the present record we find no evidence which would support a finding that cover was attempted but found unavailable. We find nothing which would justify the trial court in arriving at damages using loss of business profits which are consequential damages. Consequential damages are limited under K.S.A. 84-2-715(2)(a) to those instances where it is established that the loss could not reasonably be prevented by cover or otherwise. A buyer does not have to cover under K.S.A. 84-2-712(3); however, on failure to attempt cover, consequential damages, including loss of profits, cannot be recovered. K.S.A. 84-2-715(2)(a). International Petroleum Services Inc. v. S & N Well Service, Inc., 230 Kan. 452, Syl. ¶ 7, 639 P.2d 29.

In view of our ultimate decision that loss of profits are not a proper basis for damages in this case it will not be necessary to address appellant's claim that it was error to disallow the testimony of Jake Holster [Panhandle's president] as to the amount of profit ordinarily realized on a ton of hay bought and sold by Panhandle.

The proper measure of damages under K.S.A. 84-2-713 based on the evidence before the trial court in this case is the difference between the contract price of $45.00 per ton and the market price of $62.00 at the place of delivery and at the time the buyer learned of nondelivery and repudiation. There was no evidence to indicate the buyer attempted and was unable to obtain cover. The proper award in this case is to be arrived at by subtracting $45.00 from $62.00 to make $17.00 per ton, the basis for arriving at damages. Multiplying 912 tons 256 pounds by $17.00 equals $15,506.18, which is the correct amount of the judgment to be entered in favor of plaintiff, plus interest and costs. Accordingly, the judgment of the district court is affirmed as modified herein.

NOTE

1. Under the Uniform Commercial Code, an aggrieved buyer may either "cover," that is, make an actual substitute contract for the goods his original seller had promised to deliver (in which case he is entitled to the difference between cover and contract price), or he may simply sue for the difference between the contract price and the market price at the time he learns of the breach. The latter formula is designed to compensate the buyer for the loss he *would* have suffered *if* he had re-entered the market and made a substitute purchase following the seller's breach, whether he has in fact done so or not. Put differently, the buyer's cover remedy contemplates an actual substitute transaction, while his market damages are based upon the assumption of a hypothetical one. The seller has a mirror-image pair of remedies; see U.C.C. §§2-706(1) and 2-708(1). If a buyer actually makes a substitute purchase, is he still free to measure his damages according to the hypothetical transaction yardstick of §2-713? Should he be? More generally, why should the buyer ever be allowed to claim damages under §2-713 if it is possible for him to cover? Is the buyer's right to choose between cover and market damages intended to protect the buyer or the seller? Or both? For a lucid discussion of these and related questions, see Peters, Remedies for Breach of Contracts Relating to the Sale of Goods Under the Uniform Commercial Code: A Roadmap for Article Two, 73 Yale L.J. 199 (1963).

2. Suppose that after Becker's breach, Panhandle had arranged to purchase hay from an Oklahoma farmer, the hay to be delivered to Panhandle's warehouse in Garden City, Kansas. Assume the price of the hay under the second contract is $65 a ton, that the contract calls for delivery of the hay "F.O.B. buyer's warehouse, Garden City, Kansas" and that the expected cost of transporting the hay from Oklahoma to Garden City is $5 a ton. How should Panhandle's damages be measured under §2-712(2)? For the meaning of the F.O.B. term, see §2-319. Suppose Panhandle arranges to have the hay it purchases in Oklahoma shipped directly to Texas for resale. If the cost of transporting the hay from Oklahoma to Texas is less than the cost of shipping it to the same destination from Garden City, Kansas, should Panhandle's damages be reduced by an amount equal to the difference in transportation costs?

3. Compare the damage rules of §§2-708(1) and 2-713(1). You will notice that for purposes of measuring the seller's damages, the relevant

market price is the one existing at the time of "tender," whereas the buyer's market damages are measured against the price prevailing at the time he "learned of the breach." These two moments often coincide but where one of the parties has repudiated his obligation before the time of tender, they may not. In cases of anticipatory repudiation, therefore, it will make a difference which formula is used to measure the contract-market differential. For more on the problem of anticipatory repudiation, see the cases collected in Section 5 of this chapter. Does one formula seem to you, on the whole, preferable? What explains this discrepancy in the treatment of buyer's and seller's damages? Consult J. White & R. Summers, Uniform Commercial Code §7.7 (2d ed. 1980).

4. As the principal case points out, a buyer's failure to cover will not deprive him of his right to compensation under the contract-market rule. It may, however, bar his recovery of consequential damages under §2-715(2). Why should the buyer's failure to cover have this effect? All things considered, would a rule that measured damages by the aggrieved party's loss of profits be preferable to the contract-market differential? Under what circumstances will these two approaches yield identical results? Different results? Which, in the majority of cases, better accomplishes the basic aim of compensation — to place the injured party in the position he would have been in if the contract had been performed?

HADLEY v. BAXENDALE
9 Ex. 341, 156 Eng. Rep. 145 (1854).

For a report of the case, see p. 106 *supra*.

NOTE

1. Alderson refers to certain types of cases as being governed by a "conventional rule." His reference to "breaches . . . in the nonpayment of money" is to the line of cases going back to Robinson v. Bland (see the Introductory Note to this section); the reference to "not making a good title to land" is, of course, to Flureau v. Thornhill. A third "conventional rule" that Alderson might have referred to was the contract and market rule of Gainsford v. Carroll, *supra* p. 1129. So far as protection of the expectation interest is concerned, do these several rules, which had become established by the time Alderson wrote, seem more or less restrictive than the formula that Alderson proposed in *Hadley*?

2. It appears to have been Alderson's view that cases involving the application of a "conventional" rule like those just mentioned fall under the second branch of the formula announced in Hadley v. Baxendale, since the parties in such cases "must be supposed to be cognizant" of the

special rule governing their transaction. This implies that the "special circumstances" to which the second branch of the rule refers include juridical as well as natural facts. If so, it would seem, the rule in Hadley v. Baxendale can have no more than a residual application, covering only whatever ground is left uncovered by existing (and subsequently established) rules of a more specialized sort.

3. R. Posner, Economic Analysis of Law §4.11 (2d ed. 1977) [footnotes omitted]:

> The economic rationale of contract damages is nicely illustrated by the famous rule of *Hadley v. Baxendale* that the breaching party is liable only for the foreseeable consequences of the breach. Consider the following variant of the facts in that case. A commercial photographer purchases a roll of film to take pictures of the Himalayas for a magazine. The cost of development of the film by the manufacturer is included in the purchase price. The photographer incurs heavy expenses (including the hire of an airplane) to complete the assignment. He mails the film to the manufacturer but it is mislaid in the developing room and never found.
>
> Compare the incentive effects of allowing the photographer to recover his full losses and of limiting him to recovery of the price of the film. The first alternative creates little incentive to avoid similar losses in the future. The photographer will take no precautions, being indifferent as to successful completion of his assignment or receipt of adequate compensation for its failure. The manufacturer of the film will probably not take additional precautions either; the aggregate costs of such freak losses are probably too small to justify substantial efforts to prevent them. The second alternative, in contrast, should induce the photographer to take precautions that turn out to be at once inexpensive and effective: using two rolls of film or requesting special handling when he sends in the roll to be developed.
>
> The general principle illustrated by this example is that where a risk of loss is known to only one party to the contract, the other party is not liable for the loss if it occurs. This principle induces the party with knowledge of the risk either to take any appropriate precautions himself or, if he believes that the other party might be the more efficient loss avoider, to disclose the risk to that party and pay him to assume it. In this way incentives are generated to deal with the risk in the most efficient fashion.
>
> This principle is not applied, however, where what is unforeseeable is the other party's lost profit. Suppose I offer you $40,000 for a house that has a market value of $50,000, you accept the offer but later breach, and I sue you for $10,000, my lost profit. You would not be permitted to defend on the ground that you had no reason to think that the transaction was such a profitable one for me. Any other rule would make it difficult for a good bargainer to collect damages unless he made disclosures that would reduce the advantage of being a good bargainer — disclosures that would prevent the buyer from appropriating the gains from his efforts to identify a resource that was seriously undervalued in its present use. The *Hadley* principle is thus confined, and rightly so, to "consequential" damages, i.e., damages unrelated to the profit from the contract.

The one case where application of the *Hadley* principle could produce
an inefficient result in a setting of consequential damages is that of monopoly. If the film manufacturer in our variant of the facts of *Hadley* had a
monopoly of film, he could use the information the photographer would
have to disclose in order to shift the risk of loss to him to discriminate
against the photographer in the price charged for the film more effectively
than he otherwise could; the information would indicate that the photographer's demand for the film was far less elastic than that of the amateur
photographers who comprise the great bulk of the manufacturer's customers (why would it indicate this?). This use of the information would
discourage risk shifting in some cases where the manufacturer was in fact
the superior risk bearer.

Is Posner right to define consequential damages as "damages unrelated to
the profit from the contract"? How is Posner's hypothetical case involving
the sale of a house different from Hadley v. Baxendale?

DANZIG, HADLEY v. BAXENDALE: A STUDY IN THE INDUSTRIALIZATION OF THE LAW
4 J. Legal Stud. 249, 267-274 (1975)

[T]he rule in Hadley v. Baxendale may have had its most significant
contemporary effects not for the entrepreneurs powering a modernizing
economy, but rather for the judges caught up in their own problems of
modernization.

By the middle of the nineteenth century Parliament had acted to modernize the judicial system in a number of important ways. Successive law
revision commissions and ensuing enactments had effected changes in
the substantive laws of tort, debt, criminal law and . . . contractual
liability. Antiquated aspects of pleading and procedure were similarly re-
modeled. But the size and case disposition capacity of the common law
courts remained remarkably stagnant.

In 1854 the entire national judiciary of Britain and Wales sitting in
courts of general jurisdiction numbered fifteen. These judges, distributed
equally between three benches — the Court of Common Pleas, the
Queen's Bench and the Exchequer — sat individually to hear all cases in
London and at Assize (court held in major provincial towns) for two
terms of about four weeks each year. They convened as panels of three or
four to hear appeals in London at other times. They sat in panels usually
numbering seven (confusingly denominated as the Exchequer Chamber)
to hear appeals from the panels of three or four. Only appeals from the
panels of seven would be heard by another body of men: The House of
Lords.

A quarter of a century earlier, in a famous speech in the House of
Commons, Lord Brougham had asked:

How can it be expected that twelve judges can go through the increased and increasing business now, when the affairs of men are so extended and multiplied in every direction, the same twelve, and at one time fifteen, having not been much more than sufficient for the comparatively trifling number of causes tried two or three centuries ago?

Brougham's call for more judges was answered in 1830 by the addition of one judge to each court. But even with this improvement, it was apparent that there was a severe limitation on the number and intricacy of the trials and appeals that these judges could process. Indeed over the fifty years surrounding the decision in Hadley v. Baxendale the number of cases brought to trial in the common law courts each year remained remarkably stable and low (around 2400 cases) despite the extraordinary increase in commercial transactions over the period. Although the modern observer is likely to approach this situation with his view colored by images of the endless, enervating litigation described in Dickens' Bleak House (published in 1853), this stability in case processing apparently was not achieved by allowing a case backlog to accumulate. Extant docket sheets show that at any given Assize no more than half a dozen cases would typically be held for later sittings. The Hadley v. Baxendale litigation is suggestive of this speed in disposition. The Hadleys suffered their injury in May; they brought their suit and received prompt jury trial and judgment in August. Baxendale appealed on the fifth of November, had the appeal argued on the first of February, and received a favorable decision by the end of the month.

Probably the most critical factor in enabling the Courts at Common Law to operate on so intimate a basis was the reconstruction, by act of Parliament in 1846, of the haphazardly functioning local "Courts of Requests" into an extensive and competent court system capable of handling a large volume of cases. This system of "county courts" was rendered inferior to the Common Law Courts (which began being called "Superior Courts") by permitting appeal from County Court judgments to a Common Law Court and by limiting county court claims to sums less than £20. Further, the intent of the legislature to effect a transfer of minor cases away from the Superior Courts was manifested by the enactment of a statute assessing costs against even a victorious plaintiff in Superior Court if his recovery in a contract case amounted to no more than £20, or in a tort case to £5.

After their creation in 1846, the County Courts immediately became the journeyman carriers of the judicial workload. Within their first year of operation they reported receiving 429,215 cases. In 1857 they dealt with 744,652 "plaints." We are properly cautioned to discriminate between substantial judicial business and routine administrative debt collection cases in assessing the significance of case loads over this period. This advice is particularly apt because the County Courts were initially conceived as debtor-creditor courts and always drew the bulk of their business from this context. But it seems clear that the County Courts also quickly began handling a substantial number of more substantial lawsuits, and this development was strongly reinforced by an Act of Parliament in 1850 which expanded County Court jurisdiction to encompass claims of up to £50. By the time of Hadley v. Baxendale the County Courts were very probably handling many times the number of tort, contract, and other nondebt cases then being processed by the Superior Court judges at Assizes.

Against this backdrop the rule in Hadley v. Baxendale can be seen to have had significant contemporary implications which are normally invisible to the modern observer. The bifurcation of the County and Superior Court systems effected a specialization of labor insofar as it tended to discriminate between unimportant and important cases at least on the basis of the amount of recovery they involved. This division of labor was perfectly sensible so long as County Court work was almost exclusively concerned with debts, because in that form of litigation the amount likely to be awarded can be ascertained with great certainty. But by 1854 the events I have sketched probably prompted an increase in contract litigation in the County Courts. If brought in Superior Courts these cases were pressed at the peril of securing only minor recovery and then having that success washed out by the burden of costs. Under such conditions it is not surprising that previously ignored questions of the calculation of damages in contracts cases began to receive attention, not so much because these rules were considered important as matters of substantive law as because they were important as rules of jurisdiction. By identifying the criteria by which damages were to be assessed, the Hadley v. Baxendale court enhanced the predictability of damages and therefore the correct allocation of cases between the systems. Moreover, since the rule of the case coupled this enhanced predictability with an assertion of limitations on recovery, it tended to shunt cases from the Superior Courts toward the County Courts and thus to protect the smaller systems from at least a portion of the workload that if untrammelled would overwhelm it.

Some standardization of court decisions was implicit in these developments. But this standardization afforded more advantages than simply those associated with caseload allocation and (because of enhanced predictability of outcome) caseload reduction through settlement. Standardization was a means by which the Superior Courts could enhance their authority over County Courts at the very moment they were yielding primary jurisdiction to them.

In 1854 it must have been apparent to the fifteen judges who composed the national judicial system that they had no hope of reviewing half a million cases or even that fraction of them which dealt with genuinely contested issues. Moreover the relatively small stakes involved in County Court cases left all but a minuscule proportion of litigants disinclined to incur the costs of appeal. Under these conditions it is not surprising that *ad hoc* review gave way to attempts at crystallized delineation of instructions for dispute resolution which more closely resembled legislation then they did prior common law adjudication.

In its centralization of control, the judicial invention here examined paralleled the industrial developments of the age. The importance of the centralization of control is particularly evident when the rule is put back into the context in which it was promulgated: in terms of judges' control over juries. Told at its simplest level, Hadley v. Baxendale is the tale of a litigation contest between two local merchants and a London-based entrepreneur in which the local jury decided for the local merchants and the London judges asserted the priority of their judgment for the national entrepreneur. The tension inherent in the conflict of perspectives between the two decision-making centers — local juries and appellate judges — is underscored when one focuses on the particular decision-makers in this case. It was a *special* jury that rendered a verdict for the Hadleys. Special juries were drawn, at the request of a party (probably on assertion of unusual complication in the litigation) from a limited list of property owners. At the Baxendale trial nine of the twelve jurors were designated "merchants." Three were labelled simply "Esquire." If life in the mid-nineteenth century was anything like life in our times, the jury members, themselves local merchants who must have suffered frustration or injury from the then frequent occurrence of carrier error, probably sympathized much more readily with the Hadleys than with Baxendale. In contrast, the panel which heard the case on appeal was "special" in a way quite different from the jury. Two of the panel's members had experienced the difficulties and adopted the perspective of Pickford's at one time or another. [Baron Martin, one of the three judges who decided the appeal, had previously represented the Pickford Company in the case of Black v. Baxendale, 1 Ex. 410, 154 Eng. Rep. 174 (1847), and Baron Parke's brother had at one time been the company's managing director.] Under these conditions the invention of the case must have seemed particularly appealing to its promulgators. It led not simply to a resolution of this case for Baxendale, but also, more generally, to a rule of procedure and review which shifted power from more parochial to more cosmopolitan decision-makers. As Baron Alderson put the matter, "we deem it to be expedient and necessary to state explicitly the rule which . . . the jury [ought] to be governed by . . . for if the jury are left without any definite rule to guide them, it will, in such cases as these, manifestly lead to the greatest injustice."

From a less personal perspective the invention also affected a modernization by enhancing efficiency as a result of taking matters out of the hands of the jurors. Whatever its other characteristics, jury justice is hand-crafted justice. Each case is mulled on an *ad hoc* basis with reference to little more than, as Chitty put it, "the circumstances of the case."

In an age of rapidly increasing numbers of transactions and amounts of
litigation, a hand-crafted system of justice had as little durability as the
hand-crafted system of tool production on which the Hadleys relied for
their mill parts. By moving matters from a special jury — which cost £24,
untold time to assemble, and a half hour to decide — to a judge, the rule
in Hadley v. Baxendale facilitated the production of the judicial product.
And by standardizing the rule which the judge employed, the decision
compounded the gain — a point of particular importance in relation to
the County Courts where juries were rarely called.

Thus, the judicial advantages of Hadley v. Baxendale can be summarized: after the opinion the outcome of a claim for damages for breach of
contract could be more readily predicted (and would therefore be less
often litigated) than before; when litigated the more appropriate court
could more often be chosen; the costs and biases of a jury could more
often be avoided; and County Court judges and juries alike could be more
readily confined in the exercise of their discretion. Clearly the rule invented in the case offered substantial rewards to the judges who promulgated it and in later years reaffirmed it [footnotes omitted].

GLOBE REFINING CO. v. LANDA COTTON OIL CO.
190 U.S. 540 (1903)

In error to the Circuit Court of the United States for the Western
District of Texas to review a judgment sustaining a plea that the damages
had been unduly magnified for the purpose of conferring jurisdiction,
and dismissing the cause. Affirmed.

Mr. Justice HOLMES delivered the opinion of the court: This is an
action of contract brought by the plaintiff in error, a Kentucky corporation, against the defendant in error, a Texas corporation, for breach of a
contract to sell and deliver crude oil. The defendant excepted to certain
allegations of damages, and pleaded that the damages had been claimed
and magnified fraudulently for the purpose of giving the United States
Circuit Court jurisdiction, when in truth they were less than $2,000. The
judge sustained the exceptions. He also tried the question of jurisdiction
before hearing the merits, refused the plaintiff a jury, found that the plea
was sustained, and dismissed the cause. The plaintiff excepted to all the
rulings and action of the court, and brings the case here by writ of error.
If the rulings and findings were right, there is no question that the judge
was right in dismissing the suit (North American Transp. & Trading Co.
v. Morrison, 178 U.S. 262, 267, 44 L. Ed. 1061, 1064, 20 S. Ct. Rep. 869);
but the grounds upon which he went are re-examinable here. Wetmore v.
Rymer, 169 U.S. 115, 42 L. Ed. 682, 18 S. Ct. Rep. 293.

The contract was made through a broker, it would seem by writing, and, at all events, was admitted to be correctly stated in the following letter:

Dallas, Texas, 7/30/97

Landa Oil Company
New Braunfels, Texas

Gentlemen:

Referring to the exchange of our telegrams today, we have sold for your account to the Globe Refining Company, Louisville, Kentucky, ten (10) tanks prime crude C/S oil at the price of 15¾ cents per gallon of 7½ pounds, f.o.b. buyers' tank at your mill. Weights and quality guaranteed.

Terms: Sight draft without exchange b/ldg. attached. Sellers paying commission.

Shipment: Part last half August and balance first half September. Shipping instructions to be furnished by the Globe Refining Company.

Yours truly,
THOMAS & GREEN, as Broker.

Having this contract before us, we proceed to consider the allegations of special damage over and above the difference between the contract price of the oil and the price at the time of the breach, which was the measure adopted by the judge. These allegations must be read with care, for it is obvious that the pleader has gone as far as he dared to go, and to the verge of anything that could be justified under the contract, if not beyond.

It is alleged that it was agreed and understood that the plaintiff would send its tank cars to the defendant's mills, and that the defendant promptly would fill them with oil (so far, simply following the contract), and that the plaintiff sent tanks. "In order to do this, the plaintiff was under the necessity of obligating itself unconditionally to the railroad company (and of which the defendant had notice) to pay to it for the transportation of the cars from said Louisville to said New Braunfels in the sum of $900," which sum plaintiff had to pay, "and was incurred as an advancement on said oil contract." This is the first item. The last words quoted mean only that the sum paid would have been allowed by the railroad as part payment of the return charges had the tanks been filled and sent back over the same road.

Next it is alleged that the defendant, contemplating a breach of the contract, caused the plaintiff to send its cars a thousand miles, at a cost of $1,000; that defendant canceled its contract on the 2d of September, but did not notify the plaintiff until the 14th, when, if the plaintiff had known of the cancelation, it would have been supplying itself from other sources; that plaintiff (no doubt defendant is meant) did so wilfully and maliciously, causing an unnecessary loss of $2,000.

Next it is alleged that, by reason of the breach of contract and want of notice, plaintiff lost the use of its tanks for thirty days — a loss estimated at $700 more. Next it is alleged that the plaintiff had arranged with its own customers to furnish the oil in question within a certain time, which contemplated sharp compliance with the contract by the defendant; "all of which facts, as above stated, were well known to the defendant, and defendant had contracted to that end with the plaintiff." This item is put at $740, with $1,000 more for loss of customers, credit, and reputation. Finally, at the end of the petition, it is alleged generally that it was known to defendant, and in contemplation of the contract, that plaintiff would have to send tanks at great expense from distant points, and that plaintiff "was required to pay additional freight in order to rearrange the destination of the various tanks and other points." Then it is alleged that by reason of the defendant's breach, the plaintiff had to pay $350 additional freight.

Whatever may be the scope of the allegations which we have quoted, it will be seen that none of the items was contemplated expressly by the words of the bargain. Those words are before us in writing, and go no further than to contemplate that when the deliveries were to take place the buyer's tanks should be at the defendant's mill. Under such circumstances the question is suggested how far the express terms of a writing, admitted to be complete, can be enlarged by averment and oral evidence; and, if they can be enlarged in that way, what averments are sufficient. When a man commits a tort, he incurs, by force of the law, a liability to damages, measured by certain rules. When a man makes a contract, he incurs, by force of the law, a liability to damages, unless a certain promised event comes to pass. But, unlike the case of torts, as the contract is by mutual consent, the parties themselves, expressly or by implication, fix the rule by which the damages are to be measured. The old law seems to have regarded it as technically in the election of the promisor to pay damages. Bromage v. Genning, 1 Roll. R. 368; Hulbert v. Hart, 1 Vern. 133. It is true that as people when contracting contemplate performance, not breach, they commonly say little or nothing as to what shall happen in the latter event, and the common rules have been worked out by common sense, which has established what the parties probably would have said if they had spoken about the matter. But a man never can be absolutely certain of performing any contract when the time of performance arrives, and, in many cases, he obviously is taking the risk of an event which is wholly or to an appreciable extent beyond his control. The extent of liability in such cases is likely to be within his contemplation, and whether it is or not, should be worked out on terms which it fairly may be presumed he would have assented to if they had been presented to his mind. For instance, in the present case the defendant's mill and all its oil might have burned before the time came for delivery. Such a misfortune would not have been an excuse, although probably it would have prevented performance of the contract. If a contract is broken, the measure of damages generally is the same, whatever the cause of the breach. We have to consider, therefore, what the plaintiff would have been entitled to recover in that case, and that depends on what liability the defendant fairly may be supposed to have assumed consciously, or to have warranted the plaintiff reasonably to suppose that it assumed, when the contract was made.

This point of view is taken by implication in the rule that "a person can only be held to be responsible for such consequences as may be reasonably supposed to be in the contemplation of the parties at the time of making the contract." Grebert-Borgnis v. Nugent, L.R. 15 Q.B. Div. 85, 92; Horne v. Midland R. Co. L.R. 7 C.P. 583, 591; Hadley v. Baxendale, 9 Exch. 341, 354; Western U. Teleg. Co. v. Hall, 124 U.S. 444, 456, 31 L. Ed. 479, 483, 8 S. Ct. Rep. 577; Howard v. Stillwell & B. Mfg. Co., 139 U.S. 199, 206, 35 L. Ed. 147, 150, 11 S. Ct. Rep. 500; Primrose v. Western U. Teleg. Co., 154 U.S. 1, 32, 38 L. Ed. 883, 895, 14 S. Ct. Rep. 1098. The suggestion thrown out by Bramwell, B., in Gee v. Lancashire & Y.R. Co., 6 Hurlst. & N. 211, 218, that perhaps notice after the contract was made and before breach would be enough, is not accepted by the later decisions. See further, Hydraulic Engineering Co. v. McHaffie, L.R. 4 Q.B. Div. 670, 674, 676. The consequences must be contemplated at the time of the making of the contract.

The question arises, then, what is sufficient to show that the consequences were in contemplation of the parties, in the sense of the vendor taking the risk? It has been held that it may be proved by oral evidence when the contract is in writing. Messmore v. New York Shot & Lead Co., 40 N.Y. 422. See Sawdon v. Andrew, 39 L.T.N.S.23. But, in the language quoted, with seeming approbation, by Blackburn, J., from Mayne on Damages, 2d Ed. 10, in Elbinger Actien-Gesellschaft v. Armstrong, L.R. 9 Q.B. 473, 478, "it may be asked, with great deference, whether the mere fact of such consequences being communicated to the other party will be sufficient, without going on to show that he was told that he would be answerable for them, and consented to undertake such a liability." Mr. Justice Willes answered this question, so far as it was in his power, in British Columbia & V.I. Spar, Lumber, & Saw-Mill Co. v. Nettleship, L.R. 3 C.P. 499, 500:

> I am disposed to take the narrow view that one of two contracting parties ought not to be allowed to obtain an advantage which he has not paid for. . . . If that [a liability, for the full profits that might be made by machinery which the defendant was transporting, if the plaintiff's trade should prove successful and without a rival] had been presented to the mind of the ship owner at the time of making the contract, as the basis upon which he was contracting, he would at once have rejected it. And though he knew, from the shippers, the use they intended to make of the articles, it could not be contended that the mere fact of knowledge, without more, would be a

reason for imposing upon him a greater degree of liability than would otherwise have been cast upon him. To my mind, that leads to the inevitable conclusion that the mere fact of knowledge cannot increase the liability. The knowledge must be brought home to the party sought to be charged, under such circumstances that he must know that the person he contracts with reasonably believes that he accepts the contract with the special condition attached to it.

The last words are quoted and reaffirmed by the same judge in Horne v. Midland R. Co., L.R. 7 C.P. 583, 591; S.C., L.R. 8 C.P. 131. See also Benjamin, Sales, 6th Am. Ed. §872.

It may be said with safety that mere notice to a seller of some interest or probable action of the buyer is not enough necessarily and as matter of law to charge the seller with special damage on that account if he fails to deliver the goods. With that established, we recur to the allegations. With regard to the first, it is obvious that the plaintiff was free to bring its tanks from where it liked, — a thousand miles away or an adjoining yard, — so far as the contract was concerned. The allegation hardly amounts to saying that the defendant had notice that the plaintiff was likely to send its cars from a distance. It is not alleged that the defendant had notice that the plaintiff had to bind itself to pay $900, at the time when the contract was made, and it nowhere is alleged that the defendant assumed any liability in respect of this uncertain element of charge. The same observation may be made with regard to the claim for loss of use of the tanks and to the final allegations as to sending the tanks from distant points. It is true that this last was alleged to have been in contemplation of the contract, if we give the plaintiff the benefit of the doubt in construing a somewhat confused sentence. But, having the contract before us, we can see that this ambiguous expression cannot be taken to mean more than notice, and notice of a fact which would depend upon the accidents of the future.

It is to be said further, with regard to the foregoing items, that they were the expenses which the plaintiff was willing to incur for performance. If it had received the oil, they were deductions from any profit which the plaintiff would have made. But if it gets the difference between the contract price and the market price, it gets what represents the value of the oil in its hands, and to allow these items in addition would be making the defendant pay twice for the same thing.

It must not be forgotten that we are dealing with pleadings, not evidence, and with pleadings which, as we have said, evidently put the plaintiff's case as high as it possibly can be put. There are no inferences to be drawn, and therefore cases like Hammond v. Bussey, L.R. 20 Q.B. Div. 79, do not apply. It is a simple question of allegations which, by declining to amend, the plaintiff has admitted that it cannot reinforce. This consideration applies with special force to the attempt to hold the defendant liable for the breach of the plaintiff's contract with third persons. The allegation is that the fact that the plaintiff had contracts over was well known to the defendant, and that "defendant had contracted to that end with the plaintiff." Whether, if we were sitting as a jury, this would warrant an inference that the defendant assumed an additional liability, we need not consider. It is enough to say that it does not allege the conclusion of fact so definitely that it must be assumed to be true. With the contract before us it is in a high degree improbable that any such conclusion could have been made good.

The only other allegation needing to be dealt with is that the defendant maliciously caused the plaintiff to send the tanks a thousand miles, contemplating a breach of its contract. So far as this item has not been answered by what has been said, it is necessary only to add a few words. The fact alleged has no relation to the time of the contract. Therefore it cannot affect the damages, the measure of which was fixed at that time. The motive for the breach commonly is immaterial in an action on the contract. Grand Tower Min. Mfg. & Transp. Co. v. Phillips, 23 Wall. 471, 480, 23 L. Ed. 71, 75; Wood's Mayne on Damages, §45, 2 Sedg. Damages, 8th Ed. §603. It is in this case. Whether, under any circumstances, it might give rise to an action of tort, is not material here. See Emmons v. Alvord, 177 Mass. 466, 470, 59 N.E. 126. . . .

Judgment affirmed.

NOTE

1. In Hooks Smelting Co. v. Planters' Compress Co., 72 Ark. 275, 79 S.W. 1052 (1904), the defendant on its counterclaim was awarded $5,450 damages for suspension of the operation of its plant caused by plaintiff's delay in repairing defendant's machinery. The cost of the repairs was $712, plaintiff's profits between $100 and $210. In reversing the judgment of the trial court the court said:

> Now, where the damages arise from special circumstances, and are so large as to be out of proportion to the consideration agreed to be paid for the services to be rendered under the contract, it raises a doubt at once as to whether the party would have assented to such a liability, had it been called to his attention at the making of the contract, unless the consideration to be paid was also raised so as to correspond in some respect to the liability assumed.

Id. at 286-287, 79 S.W. at 1056. Read also Horne v. Midland Railway Co., cited in the opinion in the principal case.

On the "large verdict" problem, see Comment, Lost Profits as Contract Damages: Problems of Proof and Limitations on Recovery, 65 Yale L.J. 992, 1020 et seq. (1956).

2. As to Bromage v. Genning, cited in the opinion, and Holmes' somewhat inconsistent attitudes toward the idea for which the case is said to stand, see the Introductory Note to Section 2 of this chapter.

3. The *British Columbia Saw-Mill* case, cited approvingly in the opinion, was also discussed by Holmes in The Common Law:

> [A]ccording to the opinion of a very able judge, which seems to be generally followed, notice, even at the time of making the contract, of special circumstances out of which special damages would arise in case of breach, is not sufficient unless the assumption of that risk is to be taken as having fairly entered into the contract. If a carrier should undertake to carry the machinery of a saw-mill from Liverpool to Vancouver's Island, and should fail to do so, he probably would not be held liable for the rate of hire of such machinery during the necessary delay, although he might know that it could not be replaced without sending to England, unless he was fairly understood to accept "the contract with the special condition attached to it."

The Common Law 236-237 (M. Howe ed. 1963).

4. The *Hadley* formula requires only that a harm be foreseeable to be compensable in damages; consequently, once the promisee has notified the promisor of the existence of certain special facts that will result in larger-than-usual losses if the promisor breaches, the losses in question become compensable unless the promisor disclaims responsibility for them. Under *Hadley*, liability results from the communication of special facts plus silence on the part of the promisor. Does the same result follow under the test that Holmes proposes in the principal case? ("[T]he mere fact of knowledge cannot increase the liability. The knowledge must be brought home to the party sought to be charged, under such circumstances that he must know that the person he contracts with reasonably believes that he accepts the contract with the special condition attached to it.") If we interpret the Holmes test as requiring explicit consent on the part of the promisor before he can be held responsible for any extraordinary losses, even when he is able to anticipate their occurrence, it seems to follow that the promisor can avoid liability simply by remaining silent (in contrast to the *Hadley* rule, which requires him to speak up and disclaim liability if he wishes not to be bound). Which approach seems to you the better one? Remember that silence can be ambiguous; by remaining silent, a promisor may encourage the belief that his assumption of liability for certain extraordinary losses is something that goes "without saying."

5. Mr. Justice Willes, author of the opinion in the *British Columbia Saw-Mill* case, had been one of England's leading commercial lawyers before his appointment to the Bench, and had participated in many famous lawsuits, including Hadley v. Baxendale, where he represented the

defendant shipping company. According to Richard Danzig, Willes' "academic orientation and . . . cosmopolitan outlook caused [him] to be thoroughly familiar with the French Civil Code's provision on damages and with the similar views of Sedgwick, then the outstanding American commentator on the subject," a fact that helps to explain the significant influence these foreign authorities appear to have had on the outcome of the case and that is illustrative, more generally, of the growing influence civilian treatise writers exercised over the common law of contracts in the second half of the nineteenth century, especially in the area of damages. See Danzig, Hadley v. Baxendale: A Study in the Industrialization of the Law, *supra* p. 1140, at 257-259.

6. Do you agree with Holmes that a recovery by plaintiff of the difference between contract price and market price plus the several items of "special damage" alleged "would be making the defendant pay twice for the same thing?" Does it indeed appear that plaintiff was asking for recovery of the contract and market differential? Should Holmes have distinguished between plaintiff's expenses in preparation to perform the contract before having learned of the breach and post-breach expenses which would not have been incurred except for the breach?

7. Uniform Commercial Code §2-715(2)(a) provides that an aggrieved buyer may recover for "any loss resulting from general or particular requirements and needs of which the seller at the time of contracting had reason to know and which could not reasonably be prevented by cover or otherwise. . . ." The official comment to §2-715 states that the Code's formula for measuring consequential damages rejects the "tacit agreement" test in favor of "the older rule at common law which made the seller liable for all consequential damages of which he had 'reason to know' in advance. . . ." Do you infer from this that Globe Refining v. Landa Cotton Oil is no longer good law in sale of goods cases governed by the U.C.C.? See R.I. Lampus Co. v. Neville Cement Products Corp., 474 Pa. 199, 378 A.2d 288 (1977).

How would *Globe Refining* be decided under the Code? Was the buyer attempting to recover "incidental damages" under §2-715(1) or "consequential damages" under §2-715(2)? As counsel for the buyer, would you prefer to argue the case under §2-715(1) or §2-715(2)? Would the buyer's §2-715 recovery be in addition to, or in substitution for, his contract-market damages under §2-713? What do you make of the phrase "together with" in §2-713?

8. Official Comment 6 to U.C.C. §2-715 states that "[i]n the case of sale of wares to one in the business of reselling them, resale is one of the requirements of which the seller has reason to know within the meaning of subsection (2)(a)." This brings the loss of resale profits under the second branch of the rule in Hadley v. Baxendale. To recover for the loss of such profits, however, a buyer must show that the loss "could not reasonably [have been] prevented by cover or otherwise." Under the Uniform

Sales Act, the recovery of lost resale profits was subject to a similar limitation; see Murarka v. Bachrack Bros., Inc., 215 F.2d 547 (2d Cir. 1954).

The Hadleys, of course, had no intention of reselling their crankshaft once it was repaired: they planned to use it in their business and suffered a loss of profits when they were forced to keep their mill shut for several extra days. Should a loss of profits that comes about in this more indirect way be treated differently from the loss that results when a buyer is unable to resell, to his own customers, the goods for which he has contracted (as was apparently the case in *Globe Refining*)? Are these two types of losses treated differently under the Uniform Commercial Code? Suppose that a buyer contracts for goods, some of which he plans to use, and some to resell. Assuming he could not have prevented the loss "by cover or otherwise," can the buyer measure his consequential damages by the profit he would have made if he had resold *all* the goods contracted for (on the theory that even those he planned to keep must have been worth at least this much to him — or else he would have sold them to someone else)? See Everett Plywood Corp. v. United States, 512 F.2d 1082 (Ct. Cl. 1975).

KERR S.S. CO., INC. v. RADIO CORPORATION OF AMERICA
245 N.Y. 284, 157 N.E. 140 (1927)

CARDOZO, C.J., On May 15, 1922, the plaintiff, Kerr Steamship Company, Inc., delivered to defendant, the Radio Corporation of America, a telegram consisting of 29 words in cipher to be transmitted to Manila, Philippine Islands. The telegram was written on one of the defendant's blanks, and is prefaced by the printed words:

"Send the following radiogram via R.C.A., subject to terms on back hereof which are hereby agreed to."

The defendant had no direct circuit for the transmission of radiograms to the Philippine Islands. A radiogram could have been sent to London, where by transfer to other companies it might have reached its destination. This was expensive for the customer. To reduce the expense and follow a more direct route, the defendant forwarded its Philippine messages over the line of the Commercial Cable Company, which transmitted them by cable. When messages were thus forwarded, the practice was to send them upstairs to be copied. One copy was then handed to the cable company and one kept for the defendant's files. That practice was followed in this instance, except that the copy intended for the cable company was mislaid and not delivered. As a consequence the telegram was never sent.

The telegram on its face is an unintelligible cipher. It is written in Scott's code. Translated into English, it remains at best obscure, though some inkling of the transaction may be conveyed to an ingenious mind. Untranslated, it is jargon. The fact is that one Macondray, to whom the telegram was addressed, had cabled the plaintiff for instructions as to the loading of a ship, the Blossom. The instructions were contained in the undelivered message. As a result of the failure to transmit them, the cargo was not laden and the freight was lost. The trial judge directed a verdict for $6,675.29, the freight that would have been earned if the message had been carried. He held that the cipher, though the defendant could not read it, must have been understood as having relation to some transaction of a business nature, and that from this understanding without more there ensued a liability for the damages that would have been recognized as natural if the transaction had been known. The defendant insists that the tolls which the plaintiff was to pay, $26.78, must be the limit of recovery.

The settled doctrine of this court confines the liability of a telegraph company for failure to transmit a message within the limits of the rule in Hadley v. Baxendale (9 Exch. 341). Where the terms of the telegram disclose the general nature of the transaction which is the subject of the message, the company is answerable for the natural consequences of its neglect in relation to the transaction thus known or foreseen. Leonard v. New York A. & B. Electro Magnetic Tel. Co., 41 N.Y. 544, 1 Am. Rep. 446; Rittenhouse v. Independent Line of Telegraph, 44 N.Y. 263, 4 Am. Rep. 673. On the other hand, where the terms of the message give no hint of the nature of the transaction, the liability is for nominal damages or for the cost of carriage if the tolls have been prepaid. Baldwin v. United States Tel. Co., 45 N.Y. 744, 6 Am. Rep. 165. This is in accord with authority elsewhere. Primrose v. Western Union Tel. Co., 154 U.S. 1, 29, 13 S. Ct. 1098, 38 L. Ed. 883; Wheelock v. Postal Tel. Cable Co. of Massachusetts, 197 Mass. 119, 83 N.E. 313, 14 Ann. Cas. 188; Sanders v. Stuart, L.R. 1 C.P. Div. 326; 3 Sutherland on Damages, §959.

We are now asked to hold that the transaction has been revealed within the meaning of the rule if the length and cost of the telegram or the names of the parties would fairly suggest to a reasonable man that business of moment is the subject of the message. This is very nearly to annihilate the rule in the guise of an exception. The defendant upon receiving from a steamship company a long telegram in cipher to be transmitted to Manila would naturally infer that the message had relation to business of some sort. Beyond that it could infer nothing. The message might relate to the employment of an agent or to any one of myriad transactions as divergent as the poles. Notice of the business, if it is to lay the basis for special damages, must be sufficiently informing to be notice of the risk. Primrose v. Western Union Tel. Co., *supra*; Western Union Tel. Co. v. Sullivan, 82 Ohio St. 14, 91 N.E. 867, 137 Am. St. Rep. 754; 3 Sutherland on Damages, §§959, 970.

At the root of the problem is the distinction between general and special damage as it has been developed in our law. There is need to keep in mind that the distinction is not absolute, but relative. To put it in other words, damage which is general in relation to a contract of one kind may be classified as special in relation to another. If A and B contract for the sale of staple goods, the general damage upon a breach is the difference between the market value and the price. But if A delivers to X a telegram to B in cipher with reference to the same sale, or a letter in a sealed envelope, the general damage upon the default of X is the cost of carriage and no more. As to him the difference between price and value is damage to be ranked as special, and therefore not recoverable unless the damage is disclosed. The argument for a larger liability loses sight of this distinction. It misses a sure foothold in that it shifts from general damage in one relation to general damage in another. The bearer of a message who infers from the surrounding circumstances that what he bears has relation to business of some kind is liable, we are told, for any damages that are natural with reference to the character of the business as to which knowledge is imputed. When we ask, however, to what extent the character of the business will be the subject of imputed knowledge, we are told that it is so much of the business only as will make the damage natural (cf. Western Union Tel. Co. v. Way, 83 Ala. 542, 557, 558, 4 So. 844; Daughtery v. American Union Tel. Co., 75 Ala. 168, 51 Am. Rep. 435). Thus we travel in a circle, what is natural or general being adapted to so much of a putative business as is constructively known, and what is constructively known being adapted to what is general and natural. One cannot build conclusions upon foundations so unstable. The loss of a cipher message to load a vessel in the Philippines may mean to one the loss of freight, to another an idle factory, to another a frustrated bargain for the sale or leasing of the cargo. We cannot say what ventures are collateral till we know the ventures that are primary. Not till we learn the profits that are direct can we know which one are secondary. There is a *contradictio in adjecto* when we speak of the general damages appropriate to an indeterminate transaction.

The key to Hadley v. Baxendale is lost if we fail to keep in mind the relativity of causation as a concept of the law. McLaughlin, "Proximate Cause," 39 Harv. L.R. 149; Edgerton, "Legal Cause," 72 U. of Pa. L.R. 211, 343; Bohlen, Studies in the Law of Torts, p. 503; Haldane, The Reign of Relativity, pp. 125, 126. The argument for the plaintiff mistakenly assumes that the test of what is general damage in a controversy between the sender of a message and the receiver is also the test between the sender and the carrier. To unify the two relations is to abandon Hadley v. Baxendale in its application to contracts for the transmission of a message. If knowledge that a message is concerned with business of some kind is by imputation knowledge of those forms of business, and those only, that are typical or normal, there must be search for a definition of the normal and typical. The quest is obviously futile. Every effect is natural when there is complete knowledge of the cause. Haldane, *supra*. Every damage becomes natural when the transaction out of which it arises has been fully comprehended. Imputed knowledge cannot stop with imputed notice of transactions that are standardized by usage. In the complexities of modern life, one does not know where the ordinary ends and the extraordinary begins. Imputed knowledge, if it exists, must rest upon an assumption less timid and uncertain. The assumption cannot be less than this, that whatever a carrier could ascertain by diligent inquiry as to the nature of the undisclosed transaction, this he should be deemed to have ascertained, and charged with damages accordingly. We do not need to consider whether such a rule might wisely have been applied in the beginning, when the law as to carriers of messages was yet in its infancy. Most certainly it is not the rule announced in our decisions. We cannot accept it now without throwing overboard the doctrine that notice is essential. Notice may indeed be adequate though the transaction is indicated in outline only. . . . The carrier must draw such reasonable inferences in respect of the character of the business as would be drawn by men of affairs from condensed or abbreviated dispatches. Something, however, there must be to give warning that the subject of the message is not merely business in general, but business of a known order. Sutherland on Damages, §959.

We are not unmindful of the force of the plaintiff's assault upon the rule in Hadley v. Baxendale in its application to the relation between telegraph carrier and customer. The truth seems to be that neither the clerk who receives the message over the counter nor the operator who transmits it nor any other employee gives or is expected to give any thought to the sense of what he is receiving or transmitting. This imparts to the whole doctrine as to the need for notice an air of unreality. The doctrine, however, has prevailed for years, so many that it is tantamount to a rule of property. The companies have regulated their rates upon the basis of its continuance. They have omitted precautions that they might have thought it necessary to adopt if the hazard of the business was to be indefinitely increased. Nor is the doctrine without other foundation in utility and justice. Much may be said in favor of the social policy of a rule whereby the companies have been relieved of liabilities that might otherwise be crushing. The sender can protect himself by insurance in one form or another if the risk of nondelivery or error appears to be too great. The total burden is not heavy since it is distributed among many, and can be proportioned in any instance to the loss likely to ensue. The company, if it takes out insurance for itself, can do no more than guess at the loss to be avoided. To pay for this unknown risk, it will be driven to increase rates payable by all, though the increase is likely to result in the protection of a few. We are not concerned to balance the considerations of policy that give support to the existing rule against others that weigh against it. Enough for present purposes that there are weights in either scale. Telegraph companies in interstate and foreign commerce are subject to the power of Congress. 36 Stat. 539, 544. If the rule of damages long recognized by state and federal decision is to give way to another, the change should come through legislation.

The plaintiff makes the point that the action is one in tort for the breach of a duty owing from a public service corporation, and that the rule of Hadley v. Baxendale does not protect the carrier unless sued upon the contract. There is much authority the other way. . . . Though the duty to serve may be antecedent to the contract, yet the contract when made defines and circumscribes the duty. . . . Possibly the existing rule of damage would have been rejected at the beginning if the carrier's default had been dissociated from the law of contracts and considered as a tort. . . . As it is, there is little trace of a disposition to make the measure of the liability dependent on the form of action. A different question would be here if the plaintiff were seeking reparation for a wrong unrelated to the contract, as, e.g., for a refusal to accept a message or for an insistence upon the payment of discriminatory rates. The plaintiff alleges in the complaint that the defendant did accept the message and "promised and agreed" to transmit it, and that the plaintiff has "duly performed each and every condition of the agreement" on its part to be performed and is willing to pay the charges. We do not stop to inquire whether such a complaint is turned into one in tort by the later allegation that the defendant was negligent in the performance of its promise. . . . Upon the acceptance of the message the defendant's duty was to deliver it in accordance with the contract, and the damages recoverable for nonperformance of the contract are the damages recoverable for nonperformance of the duty. . . .

The conclusion thus reached makes it unnecessary to consider whether a limitation of liability has been effected by agreement. . . . [The court's discussion of this point is omitted.]

NOTE

1. With respect to Cardozo's remarks that "[m]uch may be said in favor of the social policy of a rule whereby [telegraph] companies have been relieved of liabilities that might otherwise be crushing," compare his opinion in H. R. Moch Co., Inc. v. Rensselaer Water Co., *infra* p. 1386, with his opinion in Ultramares Corp. v. Touche, Niven & Co., digested in the Note *infra* p. 1377. The *Moch* opinion was written in 1928, a year after the opinion in the principal case; the *Ultramares* opinion was written in 1931.

2. Do you take Cardozo's approach to the true meaning of the *Hadley* rule (or to the theory of "special damages") to be the same as Holmes' approach in the preceding principal case? If not, how does it differ? How

would you expect Cardozo to have decided the *Globe* case, bearing in mind that "the relativity of causation" is the "key" to Hadley v. Baxendale and that *Globe Refining* was buyer vs. seller, not message-sender vs. telegraph company (as in *Kerr*) or shipper vs. carrier (as in *Hadley* itself)?

3. To protect themselves against liability for large consequential damages, telegraph companies long ago began inserting explicit disclaimers in their message forms; typically, such disclaimers state that the telegraph company's liability to the sender is limited to the cost of the transmission, unless the message in question is "repeated" (for which, of course, the sender has to pay an additional charge). In the absence of gross negligence on the company's part, the validity of such disclaimers has almost always been upheld.

The Mann-Elkins Amendment, 36 Stat. 539, 49 U.S.C. §§1 et seq. (1910), made telegraph companies subject to the Interstate Commerce Act. Section 1 of the Act (as amended) authorized telegraph companies, subject to the approval of the ICC, to classify messages into repeated and unrepeated "and such other classes as are just and reasonable" and to charge different rates for different kinds of messages. In Western Union Telegraph Co. v. Priester, 276 U.S. 252 (1928), the Supreme Court held that the rates established by telegraph companies for unrepeated messages pursuant to §1 of the Act

> became the lawful rates and the attendant limitation of liability became the lawful condition upon which messages might be sent. . . . What had previously been a matter of common-law liability, with such contractual restrictions as the states might permit, . . . became [with the enactment of the Mann-Elkins Amendment] the subject of federal legislation to secure reasonable and just rates for all without undue preference or advantage to any.

276 U.S. at 259.

Telegraph message cases like *Kerr v. RCA* appear to have largely disappeared from the reports (as a result, perhaps, of the widespread use of disclaimers and the codification of this whole area of law). Their place has been taken, appropriately enough, by the telephone cases — a line of cases in which the plaintiff typically is suing for consequential damages allegedly caused by the telephone company's failure to publish his advertisement as promised. See, for example, Mendel v. Mountain State Telephone & Telegraph Co., 117 Ariz. 491, 573 P.2d 891 (1977).

THE HERON II
(KAUFOS v. C. CZARNIKOW, LTD.)
[1967] 3 All E.R. 686 (H.L.)

LORD REID: . . . [B]y charterparty of Oct. 15, 1960, the respondents chartered the appellant's vessel, Heron II, to proceed to Constanza, there to load a cargo of three thousand tons of sugar; and to carry it to Basrah, or, in the charterers' option, to Jeddah. The vessel left Constanza on Nov. 1. The option was not exercised and the vessel arrived at Basrah on Dec. 2. The umpire has found that "a reasonably accurate prediction of the length of the voyage was twenty days." But the vessel had in breach of contract made deviations which caused a delay of nine days.

It was the intention of the respondent charterers to sell the sugar "promptly after arrival at Basrah and after inspection by merchants." The appellant shipowner did not know this, but he was aware of the fact that there was a market for sugar at Basrah. The sugar was in fact sold at Basrah in lots between Dec. 12 and 22 but shortly before that time the market price had fallen partly by reason of the arrival of another cargo of sugar. It was found by the umpire that if there had not been this delay of nine days the sugar would have fetched £32 10s. per ton. The actual price realised was only £31 2s. 9d. per ton. The charterers claim that they are entitled to recover the difference as damage for breach of contract. The shipowner admits that he is liable to pay interest for nine days on the value of the sugar and certain minor expenses but denies that fall in market value can be taken into account in assessing damages in this case.

McNair, J., following the decision in *The Parana*,[25] decided this question in favour of the appellant. He said:

"In those circumstances it seems to me almost impossible to say that the shipowner must have known that the delay in prosecuting the voyage would probably result, or be likely to result, in this kind of loss."

The Court of Appeal[26] by a majority (Diplock and Salmon, L.JJ., Sellers, L.J., dissenting) reversed the decision of the trial judge. The majority held that *The Parana* laid down no general rule, and, applying the rule (or rules) in Hadley v. Baxendale[27] as explained in Victoria Laundry (Windsor), Ltd. v. Newman Industries, Ltd.,[28] they held that the loss due to fall in market prices was not too remote to be recoverable as damages.

[Lord Reid then proceeded to give his own view of how the case should be decided.]

It may be well first to set out the knowledge and intention of the parties at the time of making the contract so far as relevant or argued to be relevant. The charterers intended to sell the sugar in the market at Basrah on arrival of the vessel. They could have changed their mind and exercised their option to have the sugar delivered at Jeddah, but they did not do so. There is no finding that they had in mind any particular date as the likely date of arrival at Basrah or that they had any knowledge or expectation that in late November or December there would be a rising or a

25. (1877), 2 P.D. 118.
26. [1966] 2 All E.R. 593; [1966] 2 Q.B. 695.
27. [1843-60] All E.R. Rep. 461; (1854), 9 Exch. 341.
28. [1949] 1 All E.R. 997; [1949] 2 K.B. 528.

falling market. The shipowner was given no information about these matters by the charterers. He did not know what the charterers intended to do with the sugar. But he knew there was a market in sugar at Basrah, and it appears to me that, if he had thought about the matter, he must have realised that at least it was not unlikely that the sugar would be sold in the market at market price on arrival. He must also be held to have known that in any ordinary market prices are apt to fluctuate from day to day: but he had no reason to suppose it more probable that during the relevant period such fluctuation would be downwards rather than upwards — it was an even chance that the fluctuation would be downwards.

So the question for decision is whether a plaintiff can recover as damages for breach of contract a loss of a kind which the defendant, when he made the contract, ought to have realised was not unlikely to result from a breach of contract causing delay in delivery. I use the words "not unlikely" as denoting a degree of probability considerably less than as even chance but nevertheless not very unusual and easily foreseeable. . . .

In cases like Hadley v. Baxendale or the present case it is not enough that in fact the plaintiff's loss was directly caused by the defendant's breach of contract. It clearly was so caused in both. The crucial question is whether, on the information available to the defendant when the contract was made, he should, or the reasonable man in his position would, have realised that such loss was sufficiently likely to result from the breach of contract to make it proper to hold that the loss flowed naturally from the breach or that loss of that kind should have been within his contemplation.

The modern rule in tort is quite different and it imposes a much wider liability. The defendant will be liable for any type of damage which is reasonably foreseeable as liable to happen in the most unusual case, unless the risk is so small that a reasonable man would in the whole circumstances feel justified in neglecting it; and there is good reason for the difference. In contract, if one party wishes to protect himself against a risk which to the other party would appear unusual, he can direct the other party's attention to it before the contract is made, and I need not stop to consider in what circumstances the other party will then be held to have accepted responsibility in that event. In tort, however, there is no opportunity for the injured party to protect himself in that way, and the tortfeasor cannot reasonably complain if he has to pay for some very unusual but nevertheless foreseeable damage which results from his wrongdoing. I have no doubt that today a tortfeasor would be held liable for a type of damage as unlikely as was the stoppage of Hadley's Mill for lack of a crank shaft: to any one with the knowledge the carrier had that may have seemed unlikely, but the chance of it happening would have been seen to be far from negligible. But it does not at all follow that Hadley v. Baxendale would today be differently decided.

As long ago as 1872 Willes, J., said in Horne v. Midland Ry. Co.:[29] "The cases as to the measure of damages for a tort do not apply to a case of contract. That was suggested in a case in Bulstrode but the notion was corrected in Hadley v. Baxendale. The damages are to be limited to those that are the natural and ordinary consequences which may be supposed to have been in the contemplation of the parties at the time of making the contract."

In Cory v. Thames Ironworks Co.,[30] Blackburn, J., said:

> I think it all comes to this. The measure of damages when a party has not fulfilled his contract is what might be reasonably expected in the ordinary course of things to flow from the non-fulfilment of the contract, not more than that, but what might be reasonably expected to flow from the non-fulfilment of the contract in the ordinary state of things, and to be the natural consequences of it. The reason why the damages are confined to that is, I think, pretty obvious, viz., that if the damage were exceptional and unnatural damage, to be made liable for that would be hard upon the seller, because if he had known what the consequences would be he would probably have stipulated for more time or, at all events, have used greater exertions if he knew that extreme mischief would follow from the nonfulfilment of his contract.

It is true that in some later cases opinions were expressed that the measure of damages is the same in tort as it is in contract, but those were generally cases where it was sought to limit damages due for a tort and not cases where it was sought to extend damages due for breach of contract, and I do not recollect any case in which such opinions were based on a full consideration of the matter. In my view these opinions must now be regarded as erroneous.

For a considerable time there was a tendency to set narrow limits to awards of damages. Such phrases were used as that the damage was not "the immediate and necessary effect of the breach of contract" (per Sir Alexander Cockburn, C.J., in Hobbs v. London & South Western Ry. Co.[31]). *The Parana* was decided during that period; but later a more liberal tendency can be seen. I do not think it useful to review the authorities in detail, but I do attach importance to what was said in this House in Re R. & H. Hall, Ltd. and W. H. Pim (Junior) & Co.'s Arbitration.[32] In that case Pim sold a cargo of wheat to Hall but failed to deliver it. Hall had resold the wheat but as a result of Pim's breach of contract lost the profit which they would have made on their sub-sale. Three of their lordships dealt with the case on the basis that the relevant question was whether it

29. (1873), L.R. 7 C.P. 583 at pp. 590, 591.
30. (1868), L.R. 3 Q.B. 181 at pp. 190, 191; [1861-73] All E.R. Rep. 597 at p. 599, letter C.
31. (1873), L.R. 10 Q.B. 111 at p. 118.
32. [1928] All E.R. Rep. 763.

ought to have been in the contemplation of the parties that a resale was probable. The finding of the arbitrators was:[33]

> The arbitrators are unable to find that it was in the contemplation of the parties or ought to have been in the contemplation of [the seller] at that time that the cargo would be resold or was likely to be resold before delivery; in fact, the chances of its being resold as a cargo and of its being taken delivery of by [the buyer] were about equal.

On that finding the Court of Appeal[34] had decided in favour of Pim, saying that, as the arbitrators had stated as a fact that the chances of the cargo being resold or not being resold were equal, it was therefore[35] "idle to speak of a likelihood or of a probability of a resale."

Viscount Dunedin pointed out that it was for the court to decide what was to be supposed to have been in the contemplation of the parties, and then said[36]:

> I do not think that "probability" . . . means that the chances are all in favour of the event happening. To make a thing probable, it is enough, in my view, that there is an even chance of its happening. That is the criterion I apply, and in view of the facts, as I have said above, I think there was here in the contemplation of parties the probability of a re-sale.

He did not have to consider how much less than a fifty per cent. chance would amount to a probability in this sense. Lord Shaw of Dunfermline went rather farther. He said:[37]

> To what extent in a contract of goods for future delivery the extent of damages is in contemplation of parties is always extremely doubtful. The main business fact is that they are thinking of the contract being performed, and not of its being not performed. But with regard to the latter, if their contract shows that there were instances or stages which made ensuing losses or damage a not unlikely result of the breach of the contract, then all such results must be reckoned to be within not only the scope of the contract, but the contemplation of parties as to its breach.

Lord Phillimore was less definite and perhaps went even farther. He said that the sellers of the wheat knew that the buyers[38] "might well sell it over again and make a profit on the re-sale"; and that being so they "must be taken to have consented to this state of things and thereby to have made themselves liable to pay" the profit on a re-sale.

33. [1928] All E.R. Rep. at p. 767, letter A.
34. (1927), 137 L.T. 585.
35. [1928] All E.R. Rep. at p. 767, letter E.
36. [1928] All E.R. Rep. at p. 767, letter F.
37. [1928] All E.R. Rep. at p. 769, letter A.
38. [1928] All E.R. Rep. at p. 771, letter B.

It may be that there was nothing very new in this, but I think that
Hall's case[39] must be taken to have established that damages are not to be
regarded as too remote merely because, on the knowledge available to the
defendant when the contract was made, the chance of the occurrence of
the event which caused the damage would have appeared to him to be
rather less than an even chance. I would agree with Lord Shaw[40] that it is
generally sufficient that that event would have appeared to the defendant
as not unlikely to occur. It is hardly ever possible in this matter to assess
probabilities with any degree of mathematical accuracy. But I do not find
in that case, or in cases which preceded it, any warrant for regarding as
within the contemplation of the parties any event which would not have
appeared to the defendant, had he thought about it, to have a very
substantial degree of probability.

Then it has been said that the liability of defendants has been further
extended by Victoria Laundry (Windsor), Ltd. v. Newman Industries,
Ltd. I do not think so. The plaintiffs bought a large boiler from the
defendants and the defendants were aware of the general nature of the
plaintiffs' business and the plaintiffs' intention to put the boiler into use as
soon as possible. Delivery of the boiler was delayed in breach of contract
and the plaintiffs claimed as damages loss of profit caused by the delay. A
large part of the profits claimed would have resulted from some specially
lucrative contracts which the plaintiffs could have completed if they had
had the boiler; that was rightly disallowed because the defendants had no
knowledge of these contracts. Asquith, L.J., said:[41] "It does not, however,
follow that the plaintiffs are precluded from recovering some general (and
perhaps conjectural) sum for loss of business in respect of dyeing contracts to be reasonably expected, any more than in respect of laundering
contracts to be reasonably expected." It appears to me that this was well
justified on the earlier authorities. It was certainly not unlikely on the
information which the defendants had when making the contract that
delay in delivering the boiler would result in loss of business: indeed it
would seem that that was more than an even chance. And there was
nothing new in holding that damages should be estimated on a conjectural basis. This House had approved of that as early as 1813 in Hall v.
Ross.[42]

What is said to create a "landmark," however, is the statement of
principles by Asquith, L.J.[43] This does to some extent go beyond the
older authorities and in so far as it does so, I do not agree with it. In para.
(2) it is said that the plaintiff is entitled to recover[44] "such part of the loss

39. [1928] All E.R. Rep. 763.
40. [1928] All E.R. Rep. at p. 769, letter F.
41. [1949] 1 All E.R. at p. 1005, letter B; [1949] 2 K.B. at p. 543.
42. (1813), 1 Dow. 201.
43. [1949] 1 All E.R. at pp. 1002, 1003; [1949] 2 K.B. at pp. 539, 540.
44. [1949] 1 All E.R. at p. 1002, letter G; [1949] 2 K.B. at p. 539.

actually resulting as was at the time of the contract reasonably foresee-able as liable to result from the breach." To bring in reasonable foresee-ability appears to me to be confusing measure of damages in contract with measure of damages in tort. A great many extremely unlikely results are reasonably foreseeable: it is true that Asquith, L.J., may have meant foreseeable as a likely result, and if that is all he meant I would not object farther than to say that I think that the phrase is liable to be misunder-stood. For the same reason I would take exception to the phrase[45] "liable to result" in para. (5). Liable is a very vague word, but I think that one would usually say that when a person foresees a very improbable result he foresees that it is liable to happen.

I agree with the first half of para. (6).[46] For the best part of a century it has not been required that the defendant could have foreseen that a breach of contract must necessarily result in the loss which has occurred; but I cannot agree with the second half of para. (6). It has never been held to be sufficient in contract that the loss was foreseeable as a "serious possibility" or "a real danger" or as being "on the cards." It is on the cards that one can win £100,000 or more for a stake of a few pence. — several people have done that; and anyone who backs a hundred to one chance regards a win as a serious possibility — many people have won on such a chance. Moreover The Wagon Mound (No. 2.) Overseas Tankship (U.K.), Ltd. v. Miller Steamship Co. Pty., Ltd.[47] could not have been decided as it was unless the extremely unlikely fire should have been foreseen by the ship's officer as a real danger. It appears to me that in the ordinary use of language there is a wide gulf between saying that some event is not unlikely or quite likely to happen and saying merely that it is a serious possibility, a real danger, or on the cards. Suppose one takes a well-shuffled pack of cards, it is quite likely or not unlikely that the top card will prove to be a diamond: The odds are only three to one against; but most people would not say that it is quite likely to be the nine of diamonds for the odds are then fifty-one to one against. On the other hand I think that most people would say that there is a serious possibility or a real danger of its being turned up first, and of course, it is on the cards. If the tests of "real danger" or "serious possibility" are in future to be authoritative, then the *Victoria Laundry* case would indeed be a land-mark because it would mean that Hadley v. Baxendale would be differ-ently decided today. I certainly could not understand any court deciding that, on the information available to the carrier in that case, the stoppage of the mill was neither a serious possibility nor a real danger. If those tests are to prevail in future, then let us cease to pay lip service to the rule in Hadley v. Baxendale. But in my judgment to adopt these tests would extend liability for breach of contract beyond what is reasonable or desir-

45. [1949] 1 All E.R. at p. 1003, letter A; [1949] 2 K.B. at p. 540.
46. [1949] 1 All E.R. at p. 1003, letter B; [1949] 2 K.B. at p. 540.
47. [1966] 2 All E.R. 709; [1967] 1 A.C. 617.

able. From the limited knowledge which I have of commercial affairs I
would not expect such an extension to be welcomed by the business
community, and from the legal point of view I can find little or nothing to
recommend it. . . .

It appears to me that, without relying in any way on the *Victoria
Laundry* case, and taking the principle that had already been established,
the loss of profit claimed in this case was not too remote to be recoverable
as damages. . . .

[Lord Morris of Borth-y-Gest, Lord Hodson, Lord Pearce, and Lord
Upjohn also delivered opinions or speeches, which are here omitted. All
agreed with Lord Reid that the damages were recoverable and that the
appeal should be dismissed. All the opinions wrestled mightily both with
Hadley v. Baxendale and the *Victoria Laundry* case. Lord Reid was,
perhaps, more critical of Asquith's opinion in *Victoria Laundry* than were
his colleagues, but all agreed that, if Asquith had said, or meant to say,
anything in *Victoria Laundry* that would in any way change the *Hadley*
rule, then and to that extent he should be disapproved.]

NOTE

1. The *Victoria Laundry* case involved events that took place in England shortly after the end of World War II. The Laundry wished to
expand its operation since there was, at the time, an "insatiable" demand
for laundry services. In order to expand, it had to acquire a boiler of
much greater capacity than the one it had. Boilers, like laundry services,
were in short supply in England in 1946. Newman Industries (which did
not manufacture boilers) advertised two second-hand boilers for sale.
The Laundry, on April 26, entered into a contract to buy one of them for
£2150. Under the contract Newman was responsible for having the boiler
dismantled at its then location and the Laundry was to take delivery on
June 5. In the course of negotiations for the contract the Laundry had
explained their intention to put the boiler into use "in the shortest possible space of time." Newman knew, obviously, that the Laundry was a
laundry, but had no other information about the Laundry's purpose in
buying the boiler. Newman employed a firm of contractors to dismantle
the boiler; in the course of that operation the boiler fell on its side and was
damaged. Consequently, delivery of the boiler to the Laundry was delayed from June 5 until November 8. The trial court held that, under
Hadley v. Baxendale, the Laundry was not entitled to recover anything
for its lost profits during the five months and three days delay. The Court
of Appeal reversed, in an opinion by Asquith, L.J.; the award of damages
the Court of Appeal thought proper is sufficiently stated in Lord Reid's
opinion in the principal case.

2. Do you think that Lord Reid and his colleagues in *The Heron II*

were disapproving the holding in *Victoria Laundry* or merely the exuberance of Asquith's rhetoric? Further on *Victoria Laundry*: do you think that Newman, having been required to reimburse the Laundry for its lost profits (or some of them), could then recover from the contractors, whose carelessness had caused the damage to the boiler in the first place? Would the criteria applicable in the action by the Laundry against Newman be the same as those that would be applicable in Newman's hypothetical action against the contractors?

3. In the last paragraph of his opinion, Lord Reid suggests, somewhat cryptically, that the damage rule applicable to contracts for the sale of goods is not necessarily the rule applicable to cases like *The Heron II* (charterer vs. shipowner). Do you think he meant that the sales rule is (or might be) more expansive than the general rule? Or more restrictive? Was not *Victoria Laundry* a "sale of goods" case?

4. Under the rule of Hadley v. Baxendale, as restated in *The Heron II*, what decision in Globe Refining Co. v. Landa Cotton Oil Co., *supra* p. 1144? In the *British Columbia Saw-Mill* case, discussed by Holmes in his opinion in *Globe Refining* as well as in The Common Law (see Note 3 following *Globe Refining*)? In the *Kerr Steamship Co.* case, *supra* p. 1152?

5. On the effect of "deviation" of a carrying ship under maritime law, see G. Gilmore & C. Black, The Law of Admiralty §§3-40 to 3-42 (2d ed. 1975). The learned authors pay great attention to the provisions of the Carriage of Goods by Sea Act (COGSA), which is the American version of an international convention that has been ratified by most of the carrying nations of the world, including both the United States and England. There is no reference to the English version of COGSA in any of the opinions delivered in *The Heron II*.

6. Suppose that instead of arriving nine days late, the ship had been five days early, reaching Basrah at a time when the market price of sugar was £1 per ton lower than it was on the scheduled delivery date. Could the plaintiff have sued the shipowner for the loss caused by premature delivery of the cargo? Is this loss any less foreseeable, or less likely, than the one that actually resulted from the ship's delay? In Hadley v. Baxendale, of course, an early delivery would have been all to the good so far as the Hadleys were concerned; only a late delivery could cause them harm. Does this suggest a basis for distinguishing the two cases?

NERI v. RETAIL MARINE CORP.

30 N.Y.2d 393, 285 N.E.2d 311 (1972)

GIBSON, Judge.

The appeal concerns the right of a retail dealer to recover loss of profits and incidental damages upon the buyer's repudiation of a contract governed by the Uniform Commercial Code. This is, indeed, the correct measure of damage in an appropriate case and to this extent the code (§2-708, subsection [2]) effected a substantial change from prior law, whereby damages were ordinarily limited to "the difference between the contract price and the market or current price."[48] Upon the record before us, the courts below erred in declining to give effect to the new statute and so the order appealed from must be reversed.

The plaintiffs contracted to purchase from defendant a new boat of a specified model for the price of $12,587.40, against which they made a deposit of $40. They shortly increased the deposit to $4,250 in consideration of the defendant dealer's agreement to arrange with the manufacturer for immediate delivery on the basis of "a firm sale," instead of the delivery within approximately four to six weeks originally specified. Some six days after the date of the contract plaintiffs' lawyer sent to defendant a letter rescinding the sales contract for the reason that plaintiff Neri was about to undergo hospitalization and surgery, in consequence of which, according to the letter, it would be "impossible for Mr. Neri to make any payments." The boat had already been ordered from the manufacturer and was delivered to defendant at or before the time the attorney's letter was received. Defendant declined to refund plaintiffs' deposit and this action to recover it was commenced. Defendant counterclaimed, alleging plaintiffs' breach of the contract and defendant's resultant damage in the amount of $4,250, for which sum defendant demanded judgment. Upon motion, defendant had summary judgment on the issue of liability tendered by its counterclaim; and Special Term directed an assessment of damages, upon which it would be determined whether plaintiffs were entitled to the return of any portion of their down payment.

Upon the trial so directed, it was shown that the boat ordered and received by defendant in accordance with plaintiffs' contract of purchase was sold some four months later to another buyer for the same price as that negotiated with plaintiffs. From this proof the plaintiffs argue that defendant's loss on its contract was recouped, while defendant argues that but for plaintiffs' default, it would have sold two boats and have earned two profits instead of one. Defendant proved, without contradiction, that its profit on the sale under the contract in suit would have been $2,579 and that during the period the boat remained unsold incidental expenses aggregating $674 for storage, upkeep, finance charges and insurance were incurred. Additionally, defendant proved and sought to recover attorneys' fees of $1,250.

The trial court found "untenable" defendant's claim for loss of profit, inasmuch as the boat was later sold for the same price that plaintiffs had contracted to pay; found, too, that defendant had failed to prove any incidental damages; further found "that the terms of section 2-718, subsection 2(b), of the Uniform Commercial Code are applicable and same make adequate and fair provision to place the sellers in as good a position as performance would have done" and, in accordance with paragraph (b) of subsection (2) thus relied upon, awarded defendant $500 upon its counterclaim and directed that plaintiffs recover the balance of their deposit, amounting to $3,750. The ensuing judgment was affirmed, without opinion, at the Appellate Division, 37 A.D.2d 917, 326 N.Y.S.2d 984, and defendant's appeal to this court was taken by our leave.

The issue is governed in the first instance by section 2-718 of the Uniform Commercial Code which provides, among other things, that the buyer, despite his breach, may have restitution of the amount by which his payment exceeds: (a) reasonable liquidated damages stipulated by the contract or (b) absent such stipulation, 20% of the value of the buyer's total performance or $500, whichever is smaller (§2-718, subsection [2], pars. [a], [b]). As above noted, the trial court awarded defendant an offset in the amount of $500 under paragraph (b) and directed restitution to plaintiffs of the balance. Section 2-718, however, establishes, in paragraph (a) of subsection (3), an alternative right of offset in favor of the seller, as follows:

(3) The buyer's right to restitution under subsection (2) is subject to offset to the extent that the seller establishes (a) a right to recover damages under the provisions of this Article other than subsection (1).

Among "the provisions of this Article other than subsection (1)" are those to be found in section 2-708, which the courts below did not apply. Subsection (1) of that section provides that

the measure of damages for non-acceptance or repudiation by the buyer is the difference between the market price at the time and place for tender and the unpaid contract price together with any incidental damages provided in this Article (Section 2-710), but less expenses saved in consequence of the buyer's breach.

However, this provision is made expressly subject to subsection (2), providing:

(2) If the measure of damages provided in subsection (1) is inadequate to put the seller in as good a position as performance would have done then the measure of damages is the profit (including reasonable overhead) which the seller would have made from full performance by the buyer, together with any incidental damages provided in this Article (Section 2-710), due allowance for costs reasonably incurred and due credit for payments or proceeds of resale.

The provision of the code upon which the decision at Trial Term rested (§2-718, subsection [2], par. [b]) does not differ greatly from the corresponding provisions of the prior statute (Personal Property Law, §145-a, subd. 1, par. [b]), except as the new act includes the alternative remedy of a lump sum award of $500. Neither does the present reference (in §2-718, subsection [3], par. [a]) to the recovery of damages pursuant to other provisions of the article differ from a like reference in the prior statute (Personal Property Law, §145-a, subd. 2, par. [a]) to an alternative measure of damages under section 145 of that act; but section 145 made no provision for recovery of lost profits as does section 2-708 (subsection [2]) of the code. The new statute is thus innovative and significant and its analysis is necessary to the determination of the issues here presented.

Prior to the code, the New York cases "applied the 'profit' test, contract price less cost of manufacture, only in cases where the seller [was] a manufacturer or an agent for a manufacturer" (1955 Report of N.Y. Law Rev. Comm., vol. 1, p. 693). Its extension to retail sales was "designed to eliminate the unfair and economically wasteful results arising under the older law when fixed price articles were involved. This section permits the recovery of lost profits in all appropriate cases, which would include all standard priced goods." (Official Comment 2, McKinney's Cons. Laws of N.Y., Book 62½, Part 1, p. 605, under Uniform Commercial Code, §2-708.) Additionally, and "[i]n all cases the seller may recover incidental damages" (*id.*, Comment 3). The buyer's right to restitution was established at Special Term upon the motion for summary judgment, as was the seller's right to proper offsets, in each case pursuant to section 2-718; and, as the parties concede, the only question before us, following the assessment of damages at Special Term, is that as to the proper measure of damage to be applied. The conclusion is clear from the record — indeed with mathematical certainty — that "the measure of damages provided in subsection (1) is inadequate to put the seller in as good a position as performance would have done" (Uniform Commercial Code, §2-708, subsection [2]) and hence — again under subsection (2) — that the seller is entitled to its "profit (including reasonable overhead) . . . together with any incidental damages . . . due allowance for costs reasonably incurred and due credit for payments or proceeds of resale."

It is evident, first, that this retail seller is entitled to its profit and, second, that the last sentence of subsection (2), as hereinbefore quoted, referring to "due credit for payments or proceeds of resale" is inapplicable to this retail sales contract.[49] Closely parallel to the factual situation now

49. The concluding clause, "due credit for payments or proceeds of resale," is intended to refer to "the privilege of the seller to realize junk value when it is manifestly useless to complete the operation of manufacture" (Supp. No. 1 to the 1952 Official Draft of Text and Comments of the Uniform Commercial Code, as Amended by the Action of the American Law Institute of the National Conference of Commissioners on Uniform Laws [1954], p. 14). The commentators who have considered the language have uniformly concluded that "the reference is to a resale as scrap under . . . Section 2-704" (1956 Report of N.Y. Law Rev. Comm., p. 397; 1955 Report of N.Y. Law Rev. Comm., vol. 1, p. 761; New York Annotations, McKinney's Cons. Laws of N.Y. Book 62½, Part 1, p. 606, under Uniform

before us is that hypothesized by Dean Hawkland as illustrative of the operation of the rules:

> Thus, if a private party agrees to sell his automobile to a buyer for $2,000, a breach by the buyer would cause the seller no loss (except incidental damages, i.e., expense of a new sale) if the seller was able to sell the automobile to another buyer for $2,000. But the situation is different with dealers having an unlimited supply of standard-priced goods. Thus, if an automobile dealer agrees to sell a car to a buyer at the standard price of $2,000, a breach by the buyer injures the dealer, even though he is able to sell the automobile to another for $2,000. If the dealer has an inexhaustible supply of cars, the resale to replace the breaching buyer costs the dealer a sale, because, had the breaching buyer performed, the dealer would have made two sales instead of one. The buyer's breach, in such a case, depletes the dealer's sales to the extent of one, and the measure of damages should be the dealer's profit on one sale. Section 2-708 recognizes this, and it rejects the rule developed under the Uniform Sales Act by many courts that the profit cannot be recovered in this case.

(Hawkland, Sales and Bulk Sales [1958 ed.], pp. 153-154; and see Comment, 31 Fordham L. Rev. 749, 755-756.)

The record which in this case establishes defendant's entitlement to damages in the amount of its prospective profit, at the same time confirms defendant's cognate right to "any incidental damages provided in this Article (Section 2-710)"[50] (Uniform Commercial Code, §2-708, subsection [2]). From the language employed it is too clear to require discussion that the seller's right to recover loss of profits is not exclusive and that he may recoup his "incidental" expenses as well (Procter & Gamble Distr. Co. v. Lawrence Amer. Field Warehousing Corp., 16 N.Y.2d 344, 354, 266 N.Y.S.2d 785, 792, 213 N.E.2d 873, 878). Although the trial court's denial of incidental damages in the uncontroverted amount of $674 was made in the context of its erroneous conclusion that paragraph (b) of subsection (2) of section 2-718 was applicable and was "adequate . . . to place the sellers in as good a position as performance would have done," the denial seems not to have rested entirely on the court's mistaken application of the law, as there was an explicit finding "that defendant completely failed to show that it suffered any incidental damages." We find no basis for the court's conclusion with respect to a deficiency of

---

Commercial Code, §2-708; 1 Willier and Hart, Bender's Uniform Commercial Code Service, §2-708, pp. 1-180 – 1-181). Another writer, reaching the same conclusion, after detailing the history of the clause, says that "'proceeds of resale' previously meant the resale value of the goods in finished form; now it means the resale value of the components on hand at the time plaintiff learns of breach" (Harris, Seller's Damages, 18 Stanf. L. Rev. 66, 104).

50. "Incidental damages to an aggrieved seller include any commercially reasonable charges, expenses or commissions incurred in stopping delivery, in the transportation, care and custody of goods after the buyer's breach, in connection with return or resale of the goods or otherwise resulting from the breach" (Uniform Commercial Code, §2-710).

proof inasmuch as the proper items of the $674 expenses (being for storage, upkeep, finance charges and insurance for the period between the date performance was due and the time of the resale) were proven without objection and were in no way controverted, impeached or otherwise challenged, at the trial or on appeal. Thus the court's finding of a failure of proof cannot be supported upon the record and, therefore, and contrary to plaintiffs' contention, the affirmance at the Appellate Division was ineffective to save it.

The trial court correctly denied defendant's claim for recovery of attorney's fees incurred by it in this action. Attorney's fees incurred in an action such as this are not in the nature of the protective expenses contemplated by the statute (Uniform Commercial Code, §1-106, subd. [1]; §2-710; §2-708, subsection [2]) and by our reference to "legal expense" in Procter & Gamble Distr. Co. v. Lawrence Amer. Field Warehousing Corp. (16 N.Y.2d 344, 354-355, 266 N.Y.S.2d 785, 792-793, 213 N.E. 2d 873, 878-879, *supra*), upon which defendant's reliance is in this respect misplaced.

It follows that plaintiffs are entitled to restitution of the sum of $4,250 paid by them on account of the contract price less an offset to defendant in the amount of $3,253 on account of its lost profit of $2,579 and its incidental damages of $674.

The order of the Appellate Division should be modified, with costs in all courts, in accordance with this opinion, and, as so modified, affirmed.

Fuld, C.J., and Burke, Scileppi, Bergan, Breitel and Jasen, JJ., concur.

NOTE

1. The principal case involved a so-called lost-volume seller (a term invented by Professor Harris, who wrote several articles on the subject, one of which is cited by the court in footnote 49.)[51] In one respect, the lost-volume seller is in the same predicament as the buyer of goods or services who claims to have suffered consequential damages; neither can be made whole — put in the position that performance would have put him in — if his recovery is limited to the contract-market differential. By hypothesis, a lost-volume seller has made one less sale than he might have, and to be fully compensated must receive the profit on the transaction of which he has been deprived by the buyer's breach; his action is necessarily an action for lost profits. (Though it is not always described in these same terms, the buyer's action for consequential damages also of-

51. The others are: A General Theory for Measuring Seller's Damages for Total Breach of Contract, 60 Mich. L. Rev. 577 (1962), and studies of the Michigan cases (61 Mich. L. Rev. 849 (1963)), the New York cases (34 Fordham L. Rev. 23 (1965)), and the California cases (18 Stan. L. Rev. 553 (1966)).

ten represents a disguised effort to recover lost profits, as *Kerr* and *Globe Refining* suggest.)

2. Would it have made a difference in the outcome of the case if the defendant had been a manufacturer of boats rather than a retail dealer? Dean Hawkland (in the passage from his treatise quoted in the opinion) focuses exclusively on the situation of the dealer. Is his argument restricted to dealers? Hawkland assumes that a dealer has, or can get, an unlimited supply of whatever it is he is selling. Is this true? Is it more true for dealers than for manufacturers?

3. What is the meaning of the concluding phrase in §2-708(2) (". . . due allowance for costs reasonably incurred and due credit for payments or proceeds of resale")? Reread footnote 49 to *Neri*. Does it seem that the interpretation of the clause offered there has anything to do with the lost-volume problem at issue in *Neri*? Suppose a seller of goods, after learning that his buyer has repudiated their agreement, decides to scrap the goods and sell them for their junk value. How should his damages be measured? To be fully compensated, it would seem, he should receive the profit he expected to make on the breached contract. Here, then, is another application for the lost profits formula of §2-708(2): one arising out of a situation, quite different from *Neri*, in which the otherwise puzzling clause at the end of that section makes perfect sense. See Harris, A Radical Restatement of the Law of Seller's Damages: Sales Act and Commercial Code Results Compared, 18 Stan. L. Rev. 66, 97-98 (1965). For more on this problem, and its relation to the seller's duty to mitigate damages, see Clark v. Marsiglia, *infra* p. 1313.

4. Consider the following argument: In a perfectly competitive market (one in which every seller must take the market price as given, *i.e.*, is unable to influence the quantity of goods he sells by varying their price), a seller interested in maximizing his profits will produce up to, but not beyond, the point where the marginal cost of his last sale just equals the marginal revenue he derives from it. A seller may have the technical capacity to increase his output beyond this point but he will not do so, since any such increase would diminish his overall profits. If we assume that he is already producing at his level of maximum profitability, then a breach by one of his buyers will of course give the seller an incentive to replace the lost transaction, but the second or replacement sale is by hypothesis *not* one he would have made in the absence of his buyer's breach. Thus, in a truly competitive market, a rational seller will never be in the position that the plaintiff in *Neri* claimed to be in and consequently should not be allowed to recover lost profits.

Do you agree? Does the same argument hold where the seller enjoys a degree of "market power" (*i.e.*, is able to raise his price and still sell at least some goods — a result that would be impossible in a perfectly competitive market)? See Goetz & Scott, Measuring Sellers' Damages: The Lost-Profits Puzzle, 31 Stan. L. Rev. 323 (1979).

FULLER & PERDUE, THE RELIANCE
INTEREST IN CONTRACT DAMAGES
(Pt. 1), 46 Yale L.J. 52, 53-57 (1936)

It is convenient to distinguish three principal purposes which may be pursued in awarding contract damages. These purposes, and the situations in which they become appropriate, may be stated briefly as follows:

First, the plaintiff has in reliance on the promise of the defendant conferred some value on the defendant. The defendant fails to perform his promise. The court may force the defendant to disgorge the value he received from the plaintiff. The object here may be termed the prevention of gain by the defaulting promisor at the expense of the promisee; more briefly, the prevention of unjust enrichment. The interest protected may be called the *restitution interest*. For our present purposes it is quite immaterial how the suit in such a case be classified, whether as contractual or quasi-contractual, whether as a suit to enforce the contract or as a suit based upon a rescission of the contract. These questions relate to the superstructure of the law, not to the basic policies with which we are concerned.

Secondly, the plaintiff has in reliance on the promise of the defendant changed his position. For example, the buyer under a contract for the sale of land has incurred expense in the investigation of the seller's title, or has neglected the opportunity to enter other contracts. We may award damages to the plaintiff for the purpose of undoing the harm which his reliance on the defendant's promise has caused him. Our object is to put him in as good a position as he was in before the promise was made. The interest protected in this case may be called the *reliance interest*.

Thirdly, without insisting on reliance by the promisee or enrichment of the promisor, we may seek to give the promisee the value of the expectancy which the promise created. We may in a suit for specific performance actually compel the defendant to render the promised performance to the plaintiff, or, in a suit for damages, we may make the defendant pay the money value of this performance. Here our object is to put the plaintiff in as good a position as he would have occupied had the defendant performed his promise. The interest protected in this case we may call the *expectation interest*.

It will be observed that what we have called the *restitution interest* unites two elements: (1) reliance by the promisee, (2) a resultant gain to the promisor. It may for some purposes be necessary to separate these elements. In some cases a defaulting promisor may after his breach be left with an unjust gain which was not taken from the promisee (a third party furnished the consideration), or which was not the result of reliance by the promisee (the promisor violated a promise not to appropriate the promisee's goods). Even in those cases where the promisor's gain results from the promisee's reliance it may happen that damages will be assessed somewhat differently, depending on whether we take the promisor's gain or the promisee's loss as the standard of measurement. Generally, however, in the cases we shall be discussing, gain by the promisor will be accompanied by a corresponding and, so far as its legal measurement is concerned, identical loss to the promisee, so that for our purposes the most workable classification is one which presupposes in the restitution interest a correlation of promisor's gain and promisee's loss. If, as we shall assume, the gain involved in the restitution interest results from and is identical with the plaintiff's loss through reliance, then the restitution interest is merely a special case of the reliance interest; all of the cases coming under the restitution interest will be covered by the reliance interest, and the reliance interest will be broader than the restitution interest only to the extent that it includes cases where the plaintiff has relied on the defendant's promise without enriching the defendant.

It should not be supposed that the distinction here taken between the reliance and expectation interests coincides with that sometimes taken between "losses caused" (*damnum emergens*) and "gains prevented" (*lucrum cessans*). In the first place, though reliance ordinarily results in "losses" of an affirmative nature (expenditures of labor and money) it is also true that opportunities for gain may be foregone in reliance on a promise. Hence the reliance interest must be interpreted as at least potentially covering "gains prevented" as well as "losses caused." (Whether "gains prevented" through reliance on a promise are properly compensable in damages is a question not here determined. Obviously, certain scruples concerning "causality" and "foreseeability" are suggested. It is enough for our present purpose to note that there is nothing in the definition of the reliance interest itself which would exclude items of this sort from consideration.) On the other hand, it is not possible to make the expectation interest entirely synonymous with "gains prevented." The disappointment of an expectancy often entails losses of a positive character.

It is obvious that the three "interests" we have distinguished do not present equal claims to judicial intervention. It may be assumed that ordinary standards of justice would regard the need for judicial intervention as decreasing in the order in which we have listed the three interests. The "restitution interest," involving a combination of unjust impoverishment with unjust gain, presents the strongest case for relief. If, following Aristotle, we regard the purpose of justice as the maintenance of an equilibrium of goods among members of society, the restitution interest presents twice as strong a claim to judicial intervention as the reliance interest, since if A not only causes B to lose one unit but appropriates that unit to himself, the resulting discrepancy between A and B is not one unit but two.[52]

52. Aristotle, Nicomachean Ethics, 1132a-1132b.

On the other hand, the promisee who has actually relied on the promise, even though he may not thereby have enriched the promisor, certainly presents a more pressing case for relief than the promisee who merely demands satisfaction for his disappointment in not getting what was promised him. In passing from compensation for change of position to compensation for loss of expectancy we pass, to use Aristotle's terms again, from the realm of corrective justice to that of distributive justice. The law no longer seeks merely to heal a disturbed status quo, but to bring into being a new situation. It ceases to act defensively or restoratively, and assumes a more active role.[53] With the transition, the justification for legal relief loses its self-evident quality. It is as a matter of fact no easy thing to explain why the normal rule of contract recovery should be that which measures damages by the value of the promised performance.

UNITED STATES v. BEHAN
110 U.S. 338 (1884)

[The plaintiff had a contract with the United States to furnish and lay down, under water, an artificial covering of cane mats over a portion of the bed of the Mississippi River at New Orleans, for the purpose of keeping the channel cleared for navigation. The price was fixed at so much per square yard. Plaintiff was ordered to stop work without cause. The plaintiff filed a petition in the Court of Claims for damages arising from the loss of profits, and also for outlay and expenses. Since this scheme was novel and experimental, plaintiff was unable to show he could have made a profit. The Court of Claims concluded that from the evidence it did not appear that he would have made a profit or incurred a loss and awarded plaintiff the actual cost of the work performed. The United States appealed.]

---

53. "No doubt, when, after having an object delivered, or profiting from a service, I refuse to furnish a suitable equivalent, I take from another what belongs to him, and we can say that society, by obliging me to keep my promise, is only preventing an injury, an indirect aggression. But if I have simply promised a service without having previously received remuneration, I am not less held to keep my engagement. [This is true in Anglo-American law in the case of the bilateral contract.] In this case, however, I do not enrich myself at the expense of another; I only refuse to be useful to him." Durkheim, On the Division of Labor in Society (Simpson's trans. 1933) 217. Where the defendant has not already received some remuneration, the enforcement of the contract is viewed by Durkheim as having "an eminently positive nature since it has for its purpose the determination of the way in which we ought to cooperate." Id. at 216.

". . . [T]he principle that promise or consent creates obligation is foreign to the idea of justice. . . . It is plain that if anyone promises a friend to give him something and does not do it, he does not commit an injustice, — at least, understand, if he does not wrong this friend indirectly." Tourtoulon, Philosophy in the Development of Law (Read's trans. 1922) 499-500.

BRADLEY, J. . . . The claimant has not received a dollar, either for what he did, or for what he expended, except the proceeds of the property which remained on his hands when the performance of the contract was stopped. Unless there is some artificial rule of law which has taken the place of natural justice in relation to the measure of damages, it would seem to be quite clear that the claimant ought at least to be made whole for his losses and expenditures. So far as appears, they were incurred in the fair endeavor to perform the contract which he assumed. If they were foolishly or unreasonably incurred, the government should have proven this fact. It will not be presumed. The court finds that his expenditures were reasonable. The claimant might also have recovered the profits of the contract if he had proven that any direct, as distinguished from speculative, profits would have been realized. But this he failed to do; and the court below very properly restricted its award of damages to his actual expenditures and losses.

The prima facie measure of damages for the breach of a contract is the amount of the loss which the injured party has sustained thereby. If the breach consists in preventing the performance of the contract, without the fault of the other party, who is willing to perform it, the loss of the latter will consist of two distinct items or grounds of damage, namely: first, what he has already expended towards performance (less the value of materials on hand); secondly, the profits that he would realize by performing the whole contract. The second item, profits, cannot always be recovered. They may be too remote and speculative in their character, and therefore incapable of that clear and direct proof which the law requires. But when, in the language of Chief Justice Nelson, in the case of Masterton v. Mayor of Brooklyn, 7 Hill, 69, they are "the direct and immediate fruits of the contract," they are free from this objection; they are then "part and parcel of the contract itself, entering into and constituting a portion of its very elements; something stipulated for, the right to the enjoyment of which is just as clear and plain as to the fulfilment of any other stipulation." Still, in order to furnish a ground of recovery in damages, they must be proved. If not proved, or if they are of such a remote and speculative character that they cannot be legally proved, the party is confined to his loss of actual outlay and expense. This loss, however, he is clearly entitled to recover in all cases, unless the other party, who has voluntarily stopped the performance of the contract, can show the contrary.

The rule as stated in *Speed's* case [8 Wall. 77 (U.S. 1869)] is only one aspect of the general rule. It is the rule as applicable to a particular case. As before stated, the primary measure of damage is the amount of the party's loss; and this loss, as we have seen, may consist of two heads or classes of damage — actual outlay and anticipated profits. But failure to prove profits will not prevent the party from recovering his losses for actual outlay and expenditure. If he goes also for profits, then the rule applies as laid down in Speed's case, and his profits will be measured by "the difference between the cost of doing the work and what he was to receive for it," &c. The claimant was not bound to go for profits, even though he counted for them in his petition. He might stop upon a showing of losses. The two heads of damage are distinct, though closely related. When profits are sought a recovery for outlay is included and something more. That something more is the profits. If the outlay equals or exceeds the amount to be received, of course there can be no profits.

When a party injured by the stoppage of a contract elects to rescind it, then, it is true, he cannot recover any damages for a breach of the contract, either for outlay or for loss of profits; he recovers the value of his services actually performed as upon a quantum meruit. There is then no question of losses or profits. But when he elects to go for the breach of the contract, the first and most obvious damage to be shown is, the amount which he has been induced to expend on the faith of the contract, including a fair allowance for his own time and services. If he chooses to go further, and claims for the loss of anticipated profits, he may do so, subject to the rules of law as to the character of profits which may be thus claimed. It does not lie, however, in the mouth of the party, who has voluntarily and wrongfully put an end to the contract, to say that the party injured has not been damaged at least to the amount of what he has been induced fairly and in good faith to lay out and expend (including his own services), after making allowance for the value of materials on hand; at least it does not lie in the mouth of the party in fault to say this, unless he can show that the expenses of the party injured have been extravagant, and unnecessary for the purpose of carrying out the contract.

It is unnecessary to review the authorities on this subject. Some of them are referred to in the extract made from the opinion of the court below; others may be found referred to in Sedgwick on the Measure of Damages, in Smith's Leading Cases, vol. 2, p. 36, &c. (notes to Cutter v. Powell); Addison on Contracts, §§881, 897. The cases usually referred to, and which, with many others, have been carefully examined, are Planche v. Colburn, 5 C. & P. 58; S.C. 8 Bing. 14; Masterton v. Mayor, &c., of Brooklyn, 7 Hill (N.Y.), 61; Goodman v. Pocock, 15 A. & E. 576; Hadley v. Baxendale, 9 Excheq. 341; Fletcher v. Tayleur, 17 C.B. 21; Smeed v. Ford, 1 El. & El. 602; Inchbald v. Western, &c., Coffee Company, 17 C.B.N.S. 733; Griffen v. Colver, 16 N.Y. 489; and the case of United States v. Speed, before referred to.

It is to be observed that when it is said in some of the books, that where one party puts an end to the contract, the other party cannot sue on the contract, but must sue for the work actually done under it, as upon a quantum meruit, this only means that he cannot sue the party in fault upon the stipulations contained in the contract, for he himself has been prevented from performing his own part of the contract upon which the stipulations depend. But surely, the willful and wrongful putting an end to a contract, and preventing the other party from carrying it out, is itself a breach of the contract for which an action will lie for the recovery of all damage which the injured party has sustained. The distinction between those claims under a contract which result from a performance of it on the part of the claimant, and those claims under it which result from being prevented by the other party from performing it, has not always been attended to. The party who voluntarily and wrongfully puts an end to a contract and prevents the other party from performing it, is estopped from denying that the injured party has not been damaged to the extent of his actual loss and outlay fairly incurred.

We think that the judgment of the Court of Claims was right, and it Is affirmed.

NOTE

1. The *Behan* case was followed in Holt v. United Security Life Ins. & Trust Co., 76 N.J.L. 585, 72 A. 301 (1909). The facts in the *Holt* case were these. One Chapman had requested a loan from the Insurance Company in order to buy a plot of land in Atlantic City and erect a new building on it. The Company agreed to loan the money if Chapman and Holt (Chapman's bookkeeper) would each secure the loan with an insurance policy on his own life. The policies in question were twenty-year endowment contracts. Under the terms of the loan agreement, premiums were to be paid on the insurance policies but the principal amount of the loans were not due until the death of Holt or Chapman or the expiration of the twenty-year endowment period, whichever came first. After Chapman and Holt had taken all of the necessary steps to obtain the loan, the Insurance Company reneged on its agreement (but not before Chapman had already allowed an existing structure on the property to be removed and made several contracts for the construction of a new building). In the course of his opinion Chancellor Pitney had this to say:

> The fundamental and cardinal principle that underlies all rules for the admeasurement of damages is that the injured party shall have compensation for that which he has directly lost by reason of the act of the other party, so far as such loss was or ought to have been in the contemplation of the parties. This includes the loss of anticipated profits where these are capable of legal ascertainment. But, where the profits are not capable of ascertainment, or are remote and speculative, and therefore not proper to be adopted as a legal measure of damage, it does not follow that the injured party is remediless.
>
> In the present case the plaintiff appears to have made no effort to prove the value of the contract nor the profits that he lost by reason of its repudiation. The reason is obvious. The contract was a very special one, not to say unusual. By its terms Chapman was not only to have from the defendant

the $32,500 to reimburse him for the cost of his new building, but was to be under no obligation to repay it saving from the proceeds of the endowment policies upon the lives of himself and Holt, which might mature shortly, and, at the latest, at the end of 20 years; Chapman in the meantime paying the stipulated premiums. No rule is suggested, nor are we aware of any, by which the value of such a contract may be estimated or the profits to arise from it be ascertained. And so, whether Chapman's property, when completed as proposed, would have been worth more or less than it would have cost him through performance of such an agreement, was, of course, unascertained, and probably unascertainable.

But the suggestion that he ought to have been limited to nominal damages because he might have elsewhere procured the money wherewith to complete the building, and presumably at no greater cost than under the agreement with the defendant, is, we think, entirely inadmissible, among other reasons, because there was nothing in the evidence to show, nor can we without evidence presume, the existence of a market in which money may be procured upon like terms at any rate of interest or premiums, and, besides, the existence of the mortgages in the hands of the defendant and undischarged upon record presumptively constituted a practical obstacle in the way of Chapman procuring the money elsewhere on any terms. Losses directly incurred, as well as gains prevented, may furnish a legitimate basis for compensation to the injured party. And, among such immediate losses, expenditures fairly incurred in preparation for performance or in part performance of the agreement, where such expenditures are not otherwise reimbursed, form a proper subject for consideration where the party injured, while relying upon his contract, makes such expenditures in anticipation of the advantage that will come to him from completed performance. Where the profits that have been lost are shown with such certainty as to entitle the plaintiff to damages under this head, we do not mean to say that he may have recovery for his preliminary outlay in addition; for this would seem to involve a double recovery. But where one party repudiates, and thus prevents the other from gaining the contemplated profit, it is not, we think, to be presumed in favor of the wrongdoer (in the absence of evidence) that complete performance of the agreement would not have resulted in at least reimbursing the injured party for his outlay fairly made in part performance of it. Ordinarily, the performance of agreements results in advantage to both parties over and above that with which they part in the course of its performance; otherwise there would soon be an end of contracting. And it seems to us, upon general principles of justice, that, if he who, by repudiation, has prevented performance, asserts that the other party would not even have regained his outlay, the wrongdoer ought at least to be put upon his proof.

76 N.J.L. at 595-597, 72 A. at 305-306.

2. In his opinion in *Behan*, Justice Bradley suggests that the normal rule for measuring the plaintiff's damages in cases of this sort is costs incurred ("what he has already expended towards performance"), less "the value of materials on hand," plus the profits that would have been

made if the contract had been completed. In New Era Homes Corporation v. Forster, 299 N.Y. 303, 86 N.E.2d 757 (1949), the court suggested that the proper rule in such a case is "the contract price, less payments made and less the cost of completion."

By way of testing the two formulae, assume the following situation (for simplicity's sake assume that the "value of materials on hand" under Justice Bradley's formula is zero and that no progress payments have been made, which would have to be deducted under the New York formula):

Contract Price:	10
Costs incurred to date of stoppage:	6
Estimated costs to complete the contract:	2
Anticipated profit if contract had been completed:	2

What answer do you come up with under the *Behan* formula? Under the formula of the *New Era* case? What do you make of Chancellor Pitney's remark in the *Holt* case that where lost profits "are shown with such certainty as to entitle the plaintiff to damages under this head, we do not mean to say that he may have recovery for his preliminary outlay in addition"? Is this the double-counting problem that Holmes was concerned about in *Globe Refining?* Does the problem arise under either the *Behan* or *New Era* formula?

KEHOE v. RUTHERFORD
56 N.J.L. 23, 27 A. 912 (1893)

The opinion of the Court was delivered by DIXON, J. On October 15, 1888, the plaintiff and defendant entered into a written contract under seal, by which the plaintiff became bound to grade, work, shape, level, smooth and roll Montrose Avenue, in the Borough of Rutherford, to its entire width, according to the established grade, commencing at Washington Avenue and ending at Pierpont Avenue, and the defendant became bound to pay him therefor sixty-five cents per lineal or running foot.

Soon afterwards the plaintiff began the work, and continued until it was discovered that some of the land to be graded under the contract was private property. Then, being forbidden by the owners to enter upon this property, the plaintiff stopped the work by direction of the borough authorities and concluded to abandon it. In the meantime he had been paid $1,850 of the contract price.

On this state of facts he brought suit against the defendant, relying, in one count of his declaration, upon the breach of the special contract, and in another on the quantum meruit for the work done.

At the trial in the Bergen Circuit, the plaintiff's evidence tended to prove that the length of the whole work required by the contract was four thousand two hundred and twenty feet, which, at the contract rate, sixty-five cents per lineal foot, made the aggregate price $2,743; that about three thousand five hundred feet in length had been substantially graded, but still needed trimming up and finishing; that in doing this work he had excavated about eight thousand cubic yards of earth, and had put in about one thousand three hundred cubic yards of filling; that, to complete the job, about fourteen thousand cubic yards of filling were still necessary, besides the trimming up and finishing of the entire length of the street. His evidence further indicated that the fair cost of the work done was —

8,000 cubic yards of excavation, at 35 cents	$2,800
900 cubic yards of filling, at 21 cents	189
400 cubic yards of filling, at 41 cents	164
Making a total of	$3,153

And that the fair cost of the work remaining to be done in completely performing the contract was —

14,000 cubic yards of filling, at 12 cents	$1,680
4,220 feet of finishing, at 5 cents	211
Making a total of	$1,891

Thus showing the fair cost of the whole work required by the contract to be $5,044.

These calculations are, in every instance, based upon the testimony most favorable to the plaintiff, allowing him the highest estimates for what he had done, and reckoning the residue at the lowest. If his own estimates or those of any single witness were taken throughout, the result would be more to his disadvantage.

Upon the evidence thus presented, the plaintiff was nonsuited and a rule allowed that the defendant show cause why a new trial should not be awarded.

The nonsuit was ordered upon the theory that the plaintiff could recover, for the work done, only such a proportion of the contract price as the fair cost of that work bore to the fair cost of the whole work required, and, in respect of the work not done, only such profit (if any) as he might have made by doing it, for the unpaid balance of the contract price. Under this theory, his recovery for the work done was to be limited to such a proportion of $2,743 as three thousand one hundred and fifty-three bears to five thousand forty-four, viz., $1,715; and as to the work not done, since it would cost him $1,891 to do it, while the unpaid balance of the price was only $893, no profit could be earned by doing it. Hence it was considered that he had been overpaid to the extent of the difference between $1,850 and $1,715.

But the contention of the plaintiff was and is that, as he was prevented from completing the contract without fault on his part, he is entitled to the reasonable value of the work done, without reference to the contract price; and if this be the correct rule, undoubtedly the case should have gone to the jury. But at the very threshold we are confronted with this possible result of the application of the rule contended for, that the plaintiff might recover $3,153 for doing about three-fifths of the work, while if he had done it all he could have recovered only $2,743. The absurdity of the result condemns the application of such a rule.

Circumstances may exist in which, for work done under a special contract, the plaintiff will recover its fair value. Thus, if the contract be within the prohibition of the statute of frauds (McElroy v. Ludlum, 5 Stew. Eq. 828), or if, the work being only partly done, that which is done or that which is left undone cannot be measured so as to ascertain its price at the rate specified in the contract (Derby v. Johnson, 21 Vt. 17), or, in the absence of evidence to the contrary, it may be assumed that the rate specified is a reasonable one. United States v. Behan, 110 U.S. 338.

But generally, when it can be determined what, according to the contract, the plaintiff would receive for that which he had done and what profit he would have realized by doing that which, without fault, he has been prevented from doing, then these sums become the legal, as they are the just, measure of his damages. He is to lose nothing, but, on the other hand, he is to gain nothing, by the breach of contract, except as the abrogation of a losing bargain may save him from additional loss.

This is the rule applied in the case of Masterson v. Mayor & c., of Brooklyn, 7 Hill N.Y. 61, where the plaintiff was to receive $271,600 for eighty-eight thousand eight hundred and nineteen feet of marble, and after he had delivered fourteen thousand seven hundred and seventy-nine feet, the defendant stopped him. He was awarded the contract price for the fourteen thousand seven hundred and seventy-nine feet, and the profit which he would have made by delivering the balance. The same principle was declared by this court in Boyd v. Meighan, 19 Vroom, N.J. 404, and accords with the fundamental doctrines laid down by Mr. Sedgwick (1 Sedgw. Dam. (200) 432) — first, that the plaintiff must show himself to have sustained damage, or, in other words, that actual compensation will only be given for actual loss; and, second, that the contract itself furnishes the measure of damages.

Sometimes it has been held that if the contract binds the defendant to pay otherwise than in money, and he refuses, then the plaintiff may recover the cash value of what he has done or delivered (Ankeny v. Clark, 148 U.S. 345); but in New Jersey the rule is that he shall recover the cash value of what he was to receive (Hinchman v. Rutan, 2 Vroom, N.J., 496), thus maintaining the standard fixed by the contract.

Some of the obscurity surrounding this subject springs, I think, from a failure to distinguish between the right to sue upon the quantum meruit when the contract remains uncompleted through the fault of the defendant and the measure of damages in such a state of facts. It is well settled that, if the plaintiff has fully performed his contract, so that nothing remains but the duty of the defendant to pay, the plaintiff may declare upon the quantum meruit, ignoring the special contract, and the plaintiff's readiness and offer to perform are to this extent — but to this extent only (Shannon v. Comstock, 21 Wend., N.Y., 457) — equivalent to actual performance. In both cases, however, the amount which the plaintiff deserves to recover is regulated by the contract. The refusal of the defendant to pay after all the work is done is no less a breach of the contract than is his refusal to permit the plaintiff to do all that the bargain entitled him to do; but neither breach does or ought to put the parties in the position they would have occupied if no contract had been made. In both cases, what is done was done under the contract and should be paid for accordingly.

If, on partial performance, the plaintiff confines himself to the common counts, he excludes, by his pleading, any claim for what he had not performed, but he does not thereby enhance his deserts for what he has performed, and therefore, in order to obtain complete justice on breach of a profitable bargain, he must resort to a special count.

Our conclusion is that, as the plaintiff had been paid up to the full measure of the contract for the work done, and could have made no profit by its further prosecution, the nonsuit was substantially right.

The rule to show cause is discharged.

PHILADELPHIA v. TRIPPLE
230 Pa. St. 480, 79 A. 703 (1911)

Appeal from Court of Common Pleas, Philadelphia County.

Action by the City of Philadelphia, to the use of John McMenamy, against William Y. Tripple, trustee in bankruptcy of George C. Dietrich, substituted defendant for George C. Dietrich and J. Hampton Moore, receiver of City Trust, Safe Deposit & Surety Company of Philadelphia, substituted defendant for such company. From an order dismissing exceptions to the referee's report, defendants appeal. Affirmed on the report of the referee.

Exceptions to report of George Wharton Pepper, Esq., referee.

[The findings of fact of the referee were substantially as follows: Dietrich was under contract with the City of Philadelphia to construct the foundations and superstructure of an engine and boilerhouse. Dietrich as principal and the City Trust, Safe Deposit and Surety Company of Philadelphia as surety executed and delivered to the city a bond in the sum of $56,500 conditioned as follows:

> That if the said George C. Dietrich shall and will promptly make payment to all persons, any and all sum or sums of money which may be due for supplying him with labor and materials, whether as a subcontractor or otherwise, in the prosecution of the work provided for in said contract, and shall and will comply with all the provisions of the ordinance of the Select and Common Councils of the city of Philadelphia entitled, "An ordinance for the protection of subcontractors," etc. . . .

Dietrich entered into a subcontract with McMenamy for excavating and laying certain conduits for the price of $35,000 to be paid monthly as the work progressed. In breach of his subcontract, Dietrich ordered Mc-Menamy to discontinue the work after the latter had spent $24,461.89 for labor and materials and had received $9,000 on account. Dietrich, in completing the work, spent a sum larger than the difference between the contract price and the subcontractor's expenditures. The opinion of the referee was as follows:]

The findings of fact heretofore made by the referee sufficiently indicate the view taken by him upon such conflicts of testimony as are disclosed by the record. Nor does it seem necessary to state more fully than in the findings of law the reasons which have led to the referee to conclude that the failure of McMenamy to finish his work within the time specified in the contract is not a material circumstance in the case.

The only question of law which seems to the referee to call for a more extended comment is the question of the right of McMenamy to recover his disbursements for labor and material in a case where it seems reasonable to infer that full performance by McMenamy would have involved an expenditure by him of sums in excess of the contract price. It may be remarked in passing that the large expenditures made by Dietrich when he undertook to complete the work begun by McMenamy do undoubtedly suggest the inference that McMenamy would have completed at a loss, although it is of course not a necessary conclusion of fact or of law that this would have been the case.

Even, however, if it be assumed that McMenamy, if allowed to complete his work, would have lost money in so doing, the referee is of opinion that the act of the defendant Dietrich, in discharging the plaintiff from further obligation to perform, gave rise to a right on the part of the plaintiff to recover for his disbursements. Let it be assumed that, in an extreme case, a builder has actually expended in the course of his work a sum in excess of the contract price and has not yet completed performance. If under such circumstances, the builder finishes his work, the owner, upon paying the contract price, will receive the benefit of a large expenditure actually made, in return for the payment of a smaller sum of money. This result, which may well involve a hardship upon the builder, is made necessary by a proper regard for the contractual rights of the owner. The owner has made a valid contract, and this contract must be protected and enforced even if the builder suffers.

Let it further be supposed, however, that the owner, who finds himself in this position of advantage, voluntarily puts an end to his contract rights in the premises. This in legal effect he does if he himself breaks the contract or discharges the builder from his obligation to perform it. The situation which then presents itself is one in which the builder has in good faith expended money in the course of work done for the benefit of the owner, and has, in the absence of contract, an equitable claim to be reimbursed. The owner, on the other hand, has deprived himself of the legal right which would have sufficed to defeat the equity. He accordingly stands defenseless in the presence of the builder's claim.

Such, it is submitted, is the legal analysis of the situation in which the parties to this action find themselves. It may, of course, be contended that Dietrich did not receive an actual benefit coextensive with McMenamy's expenditure. It is a sufficient answer to this contention to observe that (upon the facts as heretofore found) McMenamy expended the money in good faith and in the course of attempted performance. This is sufficient to give him an equitable claim for reimbursement.

The defendants do not dispute the general proposition that a plaintiff may, as if in the absence of contract, recover the cost of work and materials in case he is prevented by the owner from finishing his work. The defendants earnestly contend, however, that the rule meets with an exception in case the disbursements exceed the contract price. In other words, they regard the difference between the price specified in the contract and the sum of the disbursements as the measure of recovery, and they insist that if the aggregate of disbursements equals or exceeds the contract price there can be no recovery at all.

This view, as is indicated by the analysis made above, appears to the referee to involve a confusion of thought. How can the plaintiff's claim for disbursements actually made be met by the limitation contained in a contract, unless the defendant retains the right to enforce the contract? And how can it be contended that the defendant retains such a right when the contract has been discharged by his own act? It may well be that a plaintiff, upon defendant's breach may offer the discharged contract as evidence of the value of that for which he is seeking recovery. The plaintiff in such a case has not broken the contract; he may fairly contend that its terms are at least an admission by the defendant which the jury should take into consideration. But where the defendant undertakes to limit the plaintiff's recovery by treating the contract price as a limitation upon such recovery, he is asserting a right under the very contract which he himself has discharged. The defendants cite Brown v. Foster, 51 Pa. 165, as sustaining their contention. On examination, however, it is clear that the case does not help them. It was the case of a plaintiff not in default who was held to be entitled to offer the contract in evidence in an action upon the common counts. It was not the case of a defendant in default who attempted to enforce a right created by the broken contract. On the other hand, Mooney et al. v. York Iron Co., 82 Mich. 263 (46 N.W. Repr. 376), cited by the plaintiff, throws much light upon the question under consideration, for in that case the plaintiff was permitted to recover from defendant in default the fair value of labor and material which was said not to be correctly measured by their value to the defendant.

The case last referred to becomes particularly significant when we come to consider Doolittle v. McCullough, 12 Ohio St. 360, which is strongly relied upon by the defendants. If the opinion is read without attentive consideration of the facts, there are a number of statements by the court which support the defendant's view. That the case abounds in obiter dicta is recognized in the later decision of the same learned court in Wellston Coal Co. v. Franklin Paper Co., 57 Ohio St. 182 (48 N.E. Repr. 888). Even in the latter case, however, it is fair to the defendants to say that the court treats Doolittle v. McCullough as authority for the alleged general rule that a plaintiff cannot in indebitatus assumpsit recover more than the contract price. Curiously enough, the judge who criticises the looseness of the language in the earlier opinion fell into the same error himself. Doolittle v. McCullough is not an authority for any such general rule. What happened in that case was this: that contractor who had done excavation at the contract price of eleven cents per cubic yard and had received payment at the contract price for that which he had done, was permitted (after an alleged stoppage of the work by the defendant) to recover not only for subsequent disbursements, but additional compensation for work already paid for — on the ground that its fair value was in excess of the contract price. A verdict for the plaintiff involving such a recovery was set aside and the instruction which made it possible was held to be erroneous. An accurate statement of what was really decided in Doolittle v. McCullough will be found in Keener on Quasi Contracts, pp. 312 and 313. In the footnote on the latter page will be found a careful discrimination between those cases in which the plaintiff is in default and those in which the defendant is in default.

Doolittle v. McCullough is not, therefore, an authority in the present case. So far as the evidence shows, not a dollar of the sum now claimed by the plaintiff represents disbursements for work that has been paid for, nor is he seeking additional compensation for having done such work at a loss. He stands upon the proposition that a plaintiff not in default may recover in indebitatus assumpsit against a defendant in default the cost to the plaintiff of such labor and materials as have not yet been paid for, although such cost is in excess of the price fixed in the contract which the defendant's act has discharged. This proposition is of strength amply sufficient for the plaintiff's support. . . .

[The referee found that, on the pleadings, the plaintiff had abandoned his right to bring an action for loss of profits, but had elected to treat the contract as rescinded by Dietrich's action and, in the last analysis, had brought an action on the bond to recover the amount of his expenditures less a proper credit for the sums paid on account. He recommended judgment in favor of plaintiff for $15,461.89 with interest. Exceptions to the referee's report were dismissed by the trial court which entered judgment in accordance with the recommendations of the referee.]

Error assigned was in dismissing exceptions to referee's report.

PER CURIAM, February 27, 1911.

The judgment appealed from is affirmed for the reasons stated in the report of the learned referee.

NOTE

1. With respect to the referee's opinion in the *Tripple* case, Patterson, Builder's Measure of Recovery for Breach of Contract, 31 Colum. L. Rev. 1286, 1301 (1931), comments: "Several flaws in this analysis may be noted." Do you agree? Still, however flawed Referee Pepper's analysis may have been, all the commentators, including Professor Patterson, are in agreement that the *Tripple* case has carried the day and that Kehoe v. Rutherford may be dismissed as an eccentric aberration on the part of Judge Dixon. Professor Corbin, who does not dispute the almost universally accepted analysis of the problem, does suggest that Kehoe v. Rutherford on its facts may be distinguished from the general run of such cases in that in *Kehoe* it may well have been true that neither plaintiff nor defendant had committed a breach of their respective contractual duties (5 Corbin §1113, n.62 and parallel text). In such a case, Professor Corbin suggests, the plaintiff should not be entitled to a restitutionary remedy as distinguished from damages on the contract and the contract price or rate might well be allowed to control the award of damages against the guiltless defendant. On the nature of the "breaches" attributed to defendants in *Tripple* and cases like it, see Note 4 *infra*.

2. An often cited case of more recent vintage, following *Tripple*, is United States (for use of Susi Contracting Co.) v. Zara Contracting Co., 146 F.2d 606 (2d Cir. 1944). Clark, J., citing Williston, wrote:

> . . . the measure of recovery by way of restitution, though often compared with recovery on the contract, should not be measured or limited thereby; but . . . the contract may be important evidence of the value of the performance to the defendant, as may also the cost of the labor and materials. . . . It is to be noted that, since it is the defendant who is in default, the plaintiff's performance here is "part of the very performance"

for which the defendant had bargained, "it is to be valued, not by the extent to which the defendant's total wealth has been increased thereby, but by the amount for which such services and materials as constituted the part performance could have been purchased from one in the plaintiff's position at the time they were rendered" [quoting Restatement First §347, Comment *c*].

146 F.2d at 611.

The same rule is reformulated in Scaduto v. Orlando, 381 F.2d 587 (2d Cir. 1967). Anderson, J., commented that:

> The impact of the rule is to permit the promise to "rescind" even a contract upon which he would have lost money and base his recovery on the value of the services which he gave to the defendant irrespective of whether he would have been entitled to recovery in a suit on the contract.

381 F.2d at 595. The *Scaduto* case is instructive on the difficulty of determining which party is in fact in breach in any complicated construction job. The opinion cited was the second appeal to the Second Circuit in the case; the Circuit Court, for the second time, vacated the judgment of the District Court and remanded the case for still further proceedings.

3. In Acme Process Equipment Co. v. United States, 347 F.2d 509 (Ct. Cl. 1965), the Court of Claims applied what we may call the *Tripple* rule to a contract under which Acme was to manufacture recoilless rifles for the United States Army. The United States having wrongfully terminated the contract, Acme was held entitled to "restitution." It was vigorously argued by the government that Acme's recovery should be limited to "the reasonable value of the goods it actually delivered prior to cancellation." Judge Davis rejected this argument on the following grounds:

> It is clear . . . that restitution is permitted as an alternative remedy for breach of contract in an effort to restore the innocent party to its pre-contract *status quo*, and not to prevent the unjust enrichment of the breaching party. "Judgment will be given for the value of service . . . rendered, even though the product created thereby has been lost or destroyed by the defendant, and *even though there never was any product created by the service that added to the wealth of the defendant*." [First] Restatement, Contracts §348, Comment "a" (emphasis added). It is when the plaintiff is the party in default that his recovery may be limited by the amount of the benefit to the defendant. See Schwasnick v. Blandin, 65 F.2d 354, 357 (C.A. 2, 1933). But "if the promisee has performed so far as he has gone, and the promisor breaks his promise, the promisee may abandon the contract and sue for restitution, in which he can recover the reasonable value of his services, measured by what he could have got for them in the market, and not by their benefit to the promisor." Ibid. See, also, Restatement, Contracts §347, Comment "c". Acme's recovery is not limited to the

value of the goods received by the Government under the contract; rather, it can be based on the reasonable value of the entire performance.

Id. at 530.

4. As the earlier paragraphs of this Note suggest, there has long been, and continues to be, a considerable volume of litigation of the type illustrated by the principal case. The situation is that A has entered into a contract with B under which A, for a price of $10,000, has agreed to do work which, it becomes clear as the job progresses, will cost $20,000. Everyone agrees that, except for the remote possibility of reformation for mistake or something of the sort, A, if he completes the job, gets only $10,000. B merely has to sit tight, meanwhile punctiliously performing his own obligations under the contract, to get $20,000 worth of work for half its cost. Under such circumstances, is it plausible that B would ever lapse into a default which would allow A to get off the hook by "rescinding" the contract and bringing his quantum meruit action for restitution? Yet, in case after case of this type, we are solemnly assured by the court that B did in fact "default." One possible explanation is offered by cases like the *Scaduto* case (Note 2 *supra*): the actual situation is complicated and confused, there are mutual recriminations, each party accuses the other of bad faith, misconduct and faulty performance; until the judicial dice have been rolled, no one has the least idea which side is in breach and which is not. Most opinions in litigation of this sort, however, become extremely cryptic at the point of explaining exactly what B's mysterious default consisted in (the referee's opinion in *Tripple* is a good example). Apart from the explanation offered by cases like *Scaduto*, can you think of any reason why courts, in this type of situation, should, for the better part of a hundred years, have strained to discover, or invent, wholly mythical "defaults" on the part of B? Perhaps the materials in Chapter 8 on Impossibility and Mistake may suggest an answer.

SECURITY STOVE & MFG. CO. v. AMERICAN RY. EXPRESS CO.

227 Mo. App. 175, 51 S.W.2d 572 (1932)

BLAND, J.

This is an action for damages for the failure of defendant to transport, from Kansas City to Atlantic City, New Jersey, within a reasonable time, a furnace equipped with a combination oil and gas burner. The cause was tried before the court without the aid of a jury, resulting in a judgment in favor of plaintiff in the sum of $801.50 and interest, or in a total sum of $1,000. Defendant has appealed.

The facts show that plaintiff manufactured a furnace equipped with a special combination oil and gas burner it desired to exhibit at the American Gas Association Convention held in Atlantic City in October, 1926. The president of plaintiff testified that plaintiff engaged space for the exhibit for the reason "that the Henry L. Dougherty Company was very much interested in putting out a combination oil and gas burner; we had just developed one, after we got through, better than anything on the market and we thought this show would be the psychological time to get in contact with the Dougherty Company"; that "the thing wasn't sent there for sale but primarily to show"; that at the time the space was engaged it was too late to ship the furnace by freight so plaintiff decided to ship it by express, and, on September 18, 1926, wrote the office of the defendant in Kansas City, stating that it had engaged a booth for exhibition purposes at Atlantic City, New Jersey, from the American Gas Association, for the week beginning October 11th; that its exhibition consisted of an oil burning furnace, together with two oil burners which weighed at least 1500 pounds; that, "In order to get this exhibit in place on time it should be in Atlantic City not later than October the 8th. What we want you to do is to tell us how much time you will require to assure the delivery of the exhibit on time."

Mr. Bangs, chief clerk in charge of the local office of the defendant, upon receipt of the letter, sent Mr. Johnson, a commercial representative of the defendant, to see plaintiff. Johnson called upon plaintiff taking its letter with him. Johnson made a notation on the bottom of the letter giving October 4th, as the day that defendant was required to have the exhibit in order for it to reach Atlantic City on October 8th.

On October 1st, plaintiff wrote the defendant at Kansas City, referring to its letter of September 18th, concerning the fact that the furnace must be in Atlantic City not later than October 8th, and stating what Johnson had told it, saying:

> Now, Mr. Bangs, we want to make doubly sure that this shipment is in Atlantic City not later than October 8th and the purpose of this letter is to tell you that you can *have your truck call for the shipment between 12 and 1 o'clock on Saturday, October 2nd for this.*

(Italics plaintiff's.) On October 2nd, plaintiff called the office of the express company in Kansas City and told it that the shipment was ready. Defendant came for the shipment on the last mentioned day, received it and delivered the express receipt to plaintiff. The shipment contained twenty-one packages. Each package was marked with stickers backed with glue and covered with silica of soda, to prevent the stickers being torn off in shipping. Each package was given a number. They ran from 1 to 21.

Plaintiff's president made arrangements to go to Atlantic City to attend the convention and install the exhibit, arriving there about October 11th. When he reached Atlantic City he found the shipment had been placed in the booth that had been assigned to plaintiff. The exhibit was set up, but it was found that one of the packages shipped was not there. This missing package contained the gas manifold, or that part of the oil and gas burner that controlled the flow of gas in the burner. This was the most important part of the exhibit and a like burner could not be obtained in Atlantic City.

Wires were sent and it was found that the stray package was at the "over and short bureau" of defendant in St. Louis. Defendant reported that the package would be forwarded to Atlantic City and would be there by Wednesday, the 13th. Plaintiff's president waited until Thursday, the day the convention closed, but the package had not arrived at the time, so he closed up the exhibit and left. About a week after he arrived in Kansas City, the package was returned by the defendant.

Bangs testified that the reasonable time for a shipment of this kind to reach Atlantic City from Kansas City would be four days; that if the shipment was received on October 4th, it would reach Atlantic City by October 8th; that plaintiff did not ask defendant for any special rate; that the rate charged was the regular one; that plaintiff asked no special advantage in the shipment; that all defendant, under its agreement with plaintiff was required to do was to deliver the shipment at Atlantic City in the ordinary course of events; that the shipment was found in St. Louis about Monday afternoon or Tuesday morning; that it was delivered at Atlantic City at the Ritz Carlton Hotel, on the 16th of the month. There was evidence on plaintiff's part that the reasonable time for a shipment of this character to reach Atlantic City from Kansas City was not more than three or four days.

The petition upon which the case was tried alleges that plaintiff, on October 2d, 1926, delivered the shipment to the defendant; that defendant agreed, in consideration of the express charges received from plaintiff, to carry the shipment from Kansas City to Atlantic City, and

> to deliver the same to plaintiff at Atlantic City, New Jersey, on or before October 8th, 1926, *the same being the reasonable and proper time necessary to transport said shipment to Atlantic City,* in as good condition as when received of defendant (plaintiff) at Kansas City, Missouri; that previous to the delivery of said goods to defendant at Kansas City, Missouri, this plaintiff apprised defendant of the kind and nature of the goods and told defendant of the necessity of having the goods at Atlantic City by October 8th, 1926, and the reason therefor; that defendant knew that the goods were intended for an exhibit at the place and that they would have to be at Atlantic City by that date to be of any service to the defendant (plaintiff). [Emphasis added by the court.]
>
> That this defendant through its servants and agents, after being apprised of the nature of the shipment of goods and all of the necessity of having the goods at Atlantic City at the time specified, to-wit: October 8th, 1926, agreed with plaintiff and promised and assured plaintiff that if they would transport the goods through defendant, and deliver said goods to defendant

at Kansas City by October 4th, that they would be at Atlantic City by said date, to-wit: October 8th, 1926; that relying upon the promises and assurances of the defendant's agents and servants that the goods would be in Atlantic City by October 8th, 1926, this plaintiff delivered said goods to the defendant on October 2nd, 1926, at Kansas City, Missouri, and paid defendant the express charges on same, as above set out, in packages or parcels, numbered from 1 to 21 inclusive.

That relying upon defendant's promise and the promises of its agents and servants, that said parcels would be delivered at Atlantic City by October 8th, 1926, if delivered to defendant by October 4th, 1926, plaintiff herein hired space for an exhibit at the American Gas Association Convention at Atlantic City, and planned for an exhibit at said Convention and sent men in the employ of this plaintiff to Atlantic City to install, show and operate said exhibit, and that these men were in Atlantic City ready to set up this plaintiff's exhibit at the American Gas Association Convention on October 8th, 1926.

That defendant, in violation of its agreement, failed and neglected to deliver one of the packages to its destination on October 8th, 1926.

That the package not delivered by defendant contained the essential part of plaintiff's exhibit which plaintiff was to make at said convention on October 8th, was later discovered in St. Louis, Missouri, by the defendant herein, and that plaintiff, for this reason, could not show his exhibit.

Plaintiff asked damages, which the court in its judgment allowed as follows: $147.00 express charges (on the exhibit); $45.12 freight on the exhibit from Atlantic City to Kansas City; $101.39 railroad and pullman fares to and from Atlantic City, expended by plaintiff's president and a workman taken by him to Atlantic City; $48.00 hotel room for the two; $150.00 for the time of the president; $40.00 for wages of plaintiff's other employee and $270.00 for rental of the booth, making a total of $801.51.

Defendant contends that its instructions in the nature of demurrers to the evidence should have been given for the reason that the petition and plaintiff's evidence show that plaintiff has based its cause of action on defendant's breach of a promise to deliver the shipment at a specified time and that promise is non-enforceable and void under the Interstate Commerce Act; that the court erred in allowing plaintiff's expenses as damages; that the only damages, if any, that can be recovered in cases of this kind, are for loss of profits and that plaintiff's evidence is not sufficient to base any recovery on this ground.

No attack was made upon the petition at the trial and at this late day it must be adjudged to be sufficient if it states any cause of action whatever, however inartificially [sic] it may be drawn. Of course, the law applicable to the case is governed by the Statutes of the United States as construed by the Federal Courts. Bilby v. A., T.S.F. Ry. Co. (Mo. Sup.) 199 S.W.

1004. It is well established that a shipper cannot recover on a special contract to move a shipment within a specified time, for such would work an unjust discrimination among shippers. The only duty that the carrier is under is to carry the shipment safely and to deliver it at its destination within a reasonable time. . . .

While the petition alleges that defendant agreed to deliver the shipment at Atlantic City on or before October 8th, 1926, it also alleges that this was the reasonable and proper time necessary to transport said shipment to Atlantic City. Therefore, giving the petition a liberal construction, it would appear that all that plaintiff was contending therein was that defendant had agreed to transport the shipment within a reasonable time, and that delivery on or before October 8th was necessary to comply with the agreement. The petition refers several times to the agreement that if the goods were delivered to defendant by October 4th, they would be delivered at Atlantic City not later than October 8th, but it also alleges that the goods were not delivered to defendant until October 2nd. It is quite apparent from reading the petition, as a whole, that it was not upon a contract to deliver at Atlantic City on October 8th, goods delivered by plaintiff to defendant at Kansas City on October 4th. It would appear that the purpose of plaintiff, in pleading this agreement, was to allege sufficient facts to base its claim of special damages, that is that defendant was notified that it was necessary to have the shipment at Atlantic City by October 8th, and that the damages sustained accrued as a result of plaintiff's reliance on its being so delivered and that October 8th was plenty of time for defendant to have taken to transport the shipment. Much of the petition is surplusage but we cannot adjudge it wholly insufficient at this juncture.

There is nothing in the evidence tending to show any unjust discrimination between shippers in the agreement had between plaintiff and defendant. Boiled down to its last analysis, the agreement was nothing more than that the shipment would be transported within the ordinary time. Plaintiff sought no special advantage, was asking nothing that would be denied any other shipper, was asking no particular route, no particular train, nor for any expedited service. It was simply seeking the same rights any other shipper could have enjoyed on the same terms. No special instructions were given or involved in the case. Foster v. Cleveland, C. C. & St. L. Ry. Co. (C.C.) 56 F. 434; Copper River Packing Co. v. Alaska S.S. Co. (C.C.A.) 22 F.(2d) 12.

We think, under the circumstances in this case, that it was proper to allow plaintiff's expenses as its damages. Ordinarily the measure of damages where the carrier fails to deliver a shipment at destination within a reasonable time is the difference between the market value of the goods at the time of the delivery and the time when they should have been delivered. But where the carrier has notice of peculiar circumstances under which the shipment is made, which will result in an unusual loss by the shipper in case of delay in delivery, the carrier is responsible for the real damage sustained from such delay if the notice given is of such character, and goes to such extent, in informing the carrier of the shipper's situation, that the carrier will be presumed to have contracted with reference thereto. Central Trust Co. of New York v. Savannah & W. R. Co. (C.C.) 69 F. 683, 685.

In the case at bar defendant was advised of the necessity of prompt delivery of the shipment. Plaintiff explained to Johnson the "importance of getting the exhibit there on time." Defendant knew the purpose of the exhibit and ought to respond for its negligence in failing to get it there. As we view the record this negligence is practically conceded. The undisputed testimony shows that the shipment was sent to the over and short department of the defendant in St. Louis. As the packages were plainly numbered this, prima facie, shows mistake or negligence on the part of the defendant. No effort was made by it to show that it was not negligent in sending it there, or not negligent in not forwarding it within a reasonable time after it was found.

There is no evidence of claim in this case that plaintiff suffered any loss of profits by reason of the delay in the shipment. In fact defendant states in its brief:

> The plaintiff introduc' J not one whit of evidence showing or tending to show that he would have made any sales as a result of his exhibit but for the negligence of the defendant. On the contrary Blakesley testified that the main purpose of the exhibit was to try to interest the Henry L. Dougherty Company in plaintiff's combination oil and gas burner, yet that was all the evidence that there was as to the benefit plaintiff expected to get from the exhibit.
>
> As a matter of evidence, it is clear that the plaintiff would not have derived a great deal of benefit from the exhibit by any stretch of the imagination. . . .
>
> No where does plaintiff introduce evidence showing that the Henry L. Dougherty Company in all probability would have become interested in the combination oil and gas burner and made a profitable contract with the plaintiff.

There is evidence that the exhibit was not sent to make a sale.

In support of its contention that plaintiff can sue only for loss of profit, if anything, in a case of this kind, defendant, among other cases cites that of Adams Exp. Co. v. Egbert, 36 Pa. 360, 78 Am. Dec. 382. That case involved the shipment of a box containing architectural drawings or plans for a building to a building committee of the Touro Almshouse, in New Orleans. This committee had offered a premium of $500.00 to the successful competitor. These plans arrived after the various plans had been passed upon and the award made to another person. It was sought in that case to recover the value of the plans. The evidence, however, showed that the plans would not have won the prize had they arrived on time. The court held that the plans, under the circumstances, had no appreciable value and recovery could not be had for them and there was no basis for recovery for loss of the opportunity to compete for the prize. The opinion states that in denying recovery for the plans it is contrary to the English rule in such cases. Other cases cited by defendant involve loss of profits or the loss of opportunity to compete in such events as horse racing and the like. In one case, Delta Table & Chair Co. v. R.R., 105 Miss. 861, 63 So. 272, it was held that the plaintiff could recover for loss of profits that might have been made in the sale of its commodity, as a result of exhibiting a sample at an exhibition, where the shipment was delayed too late for the exhibit. Some of the cases cited by defendant hold that such profits in those classes of cases are not recoverable, and others to the contrary.

Defendant contends that plaintiff "is endeavoring to achieve a return of the status quo in a suit based on a breach of contract. Instead of seeking to recover what he would have had, had the contract not been broken, plaintiff is trying to recover what he would have had, had there never been any contract of shipment"; that the expenses sued for would have been incurred in any event. It is no doubt, the general rule that where there is a breach of contract the party suffering the loss can recover only that which he would have had, had the contract not been broken, and this is all the cases decided upon which defendant relies, including C., M. & St. P. Ry. v. McCaull-Dinsmore Co., 253 U.S. 97, 100, 40 S. Ct. 504, 64 L. Ed. 801. But this is merely a general statement of the rule and is not inconsistent with the holdings that, in some instances, the injured party may recover expenses incurred in relying upon the contract, although such expenses would have been incurred had the contract not been breached. . . .

In Sperry et al. v. O'Neill-Adams Co. (C.C.A.) 185 F. 231, the court held that the advantages resulting from the use of trading stamps as a means of increasing trade are so contingent that they cannot form a basis on which to rest a recovery for a breach of contract to supply them. In lieu of compensation based thereon the court directed a recovery in the sum expended in preparation for carrying on business in connection with the use of the stamps. The court said, loc. cit. 239:

> Plaintiff in its complaint had made a claim for lost profits, but, finding it impossible to marshal any evidence which would support a finding of exact figures, abandoned that claim. Any attempt to reach a precise sum would be mere blind guesswork. Nevertheless a contract, which both sides conceded would prove a valuable one, had been broken and the party who broke it was responsible for resultant damage. In order to carry out this contract, the plaintiff made expenditures which otherwise it would not have made. . . . The trial judge held, as we think rightly, that plaintiff was entitled at least to recover these expenses to which it had been put in

order to secure the benefits of a contract of which defendant's conduct deprived it.

In the case of Gilbert v. Kennedy, 22 Mich. 117, involved the question of the measure of plaintiff's damages, caused by the conduct of defendant in wrongfully feeding his cattle with plaintiff's in the latter's pasture, resulting in plaintiff's cattle suffering by the overfeeding of the pasture. The court said loc. cit. 135, 136:

> There being practically no market value for pasturage when there was none in the market, that element of certainty is wanting, even as to those cattle which were removed from the Pitcher farm to the home farm of the plaintiff for pasturage; and, as it could not apply to the others at all, and there being no other element of certainty by which the damages can be *accurately* measured, resort must be had to such principle or basis of calculation applicable to the circumstances of the case (if any be discoverable) as will be most likely to *approximate* certainty, and which may serve as a guide in making the most probable estimate of which the nature of the case will admit; and, though it may be less certain as a scale of measurement, yet if the principle be just in itself, and more likely to approximate the *actual damages*, it is better than any rule, however certain, which must certainly produce injustice, by excluding a large portion of the damages actually sustained.

In Hobbs v. Davis, 30 Ga. 423, a negro slave was hired to make a crop, but she was taken away by her owner in the middle of the year, the result of which the crop was entirely lost. The court said, loc. cit. 425:

> As it was, the true criterion of damages was, perhaps, the hire of the negro, the rent of the land and all the expense incurred, and actual loss sustained by the misconduct of the defendant, rather than the conjecture of the witness, as to what the crop would have been worth.

> Compensation is a fundamental principle of damages whether the action is in contract or in tort. Wicker v. Hoppock, 6 Wall. 94, 99, 18 L. Ed. 752. One who fails to perform his contract is justly bound to make good all damages that accrue naturally from the breach; and the other party is entitled to be put in as good a position pecuniarily as he would have been by performance of the contract.

Miller v. Robertson, 266 U.S. 243, 257, 258, 45 S. Ct. 73, 78, 69 L. Ed. 265.

The case at bar was to recover damages for loss of profits by reason of the failure of the defendant to transport the shipment within a reasonable time, so that it would arrive in Atlantic City for the exhibit. There were no profits contemplated. The furnace was to be shown and shipped back

to Kansas City. There was no money loss, except the expenses, that was
of such a nature as any court would allow as being sufficiently definite or
lacking in pure speculation. Therefore, unless plaintiff is permitted to
recover the expenses that it went to, which were a total loss to it by reason
of its inability to exhibit the furnace and equipment, it will be deprived of
any substantial compensation for its loss. The law does not contemplate
any such injustice. It ought to allow plaintiff, as damages, the loss in the
way of expenses that it sustained, and which it would not have been put
to if it had not been for its reliance upon the defendant to perform its
contract. There is no contention that the exhibit would have been entirely valueless and whatever it might have accomplished defendant knew
of the circumstances and ought to respond for whatever damages plaintiff
suffered. In cases of this kind the method of estimating the damages
should be adopted which is the most definite and certain and which best
achieves the fundamental purpose of compensation. 17 C. J. p. 846;
Miller v. Robertson, 266 U.S. 243, 257, 45 S. Ct. 73, 78, 69 L. Ed. 265.
Had the exhibit been shipped in order to realize a profit on sales and such
profits could have been realized, or to be entered in competition for a
prize, and plaintiff failed to show loss of profits with sufficient definiteness, or that he would have won the prize, defendant's cases might be in
point. But as before stated, no such situation exists here.

While, it is true that plaintiff already had incurred some of these expenses, in that it had rented space at the exhibit before entering into the
contract with defendant for the shipment of the exhibit and this part of
plaintiff's damages, in a sense, arose out of a circumstance which transpired before the contract was even entered into, yet, plaintiff arranged
for the exhibit knowing that it could call upon defendant to perform its
common law duty to accept and transport the shipment with reasonable
dispatch. The whole damage, therefore, was suffered in contemplation of
defendant performing its contract, which it failed to do, and would not
have been sustained except for the reliance by plaintiff upon defendant to
perform it. It can, therefore, be fairly said that the damages or loss suffered by plaintiff grew out of the breach of the contract, for had the
shipment arrived on time, plaintiff would have had the benefit of the
contract, which was contemplated by all parties, defendant being advised
of the purpose of the shipment.

The judgment is affirmed.

All concur.

NOTE

1. Suppose that Security Stove had agreed to deliver its stove parts to
the Railway Express office in Kansas City (rather than having them
picked up at its own factory). The expenses that the Stove Company

incurs in making this delivery will not directly benefit the shipper,[54] unlike the fee to be paid for transporting the goods to Atlantic City. However, until Security Stove has delivered its stove parts to the Express Company's Kansas City office, it has no right to insist that the shipper live up to its end of their agreement. Should the expenses incurred by the Stove Company in making this delivery be treated differently from the expenses incurred in preparation for the exhibition of the stove parts in Atlantic City, on the theory that the latter were less clearly foreseeable since they did not have to be incurred in order to put the Express Company in a position where its own failure to go forward would constitute a breach of contract?

2. Judge Bland dismisses as irrelevant the fact that Security Stove had incurred some of the expenses for which it sought reimbursement *before* making its contract with the shipping company. Is this, in general, a distinction that should be ignored or is Judge Bland's conclusion only justified where, as here, the defendant is legally obligated to contract with the plaintiff on terms available to the public at large, and this fact is known to the plaintiff in advance?

L. ALBERT & SON v.
ARMSTRONG RUBBER CO.
178 F.2d 182 (2d Cir. 1949)

L. HAND, Chief Judge. Both sides appeal from the judgment in an action brought by the Albert Company, which we shall speak of as the Seller, against the Armstrong Company, which we shall call the Buyer. The action was to recover the agreed price of four "Refiners," machines designed to recondition old rubber; the contract of sale was by an exchange of letters in December, 1942, and the Seller delivered two of the four "Refiners" in August, 1943, and the other two on either August 31st or September 8th, 1945. Because of the delay in delivery of the second two, the Buyer refused to accept all four in October, 1945 — the exact day not being fixed — and it counterclaimed for the Seller's breach. The judge dismissed both the complaint and the counterclaim; but he gave judgment to the Seller for the value without interest of a part of the equipment delivered — a 300 horsepower motor and accessories — which the Buyer put into use on February 20th, 1946. . . .

[In an omitted passage, Judge Hand concluded that the buyer had justifiably rejected the four Refiners.]

Coming next to the Buyer's appeal, it does not claim any loss of profit, but it does claim the expenses which it incurred in reliance upon the Seller's promise. These were of three kinds: its whole investment in its

54. Will they perhaps *indirectly* benefit the shipping company? On what theory?

"reclaim department," $118,474; the cost of its "rubber scrap," $27,555.63; the cost of the foundation which it laid for the "Refiners," $3,000. The judge in his opinion held that the Buyer had not proved that "the lack of production" of the reclaim department "was caused by the delay in delivery of plaintiffs' refiners"; but that that was "only one of several possible causes. Such a possibility is not sufficient proof of causation to impose liability on the plaintiffs for the cost of all machinery and supplies for the reclaim department." The record certainly would not warrant our holding that this holding was "clearly erroneous"; indeed, the evidence preponderates in its favor. The Buyer disposed of all its "scrap rubber" in April and May, 1945; and so far as appears, until it filed its counterclaim in May, 1947, it never suggested that the failure to deliver two of the four "Refiners" was the cause of the collapse of its "reclaim department." The counterclaim for these items has every apparance of being an afterthought, which can scarcely have been put forward with any hope of success.

The claim for the cost of the foundation which the Buyer built for the "Refiners," stands upon a different footing. Normally a promisee's damages for breach of contract are the value of the promised performance, less his outlay, which includes, not only what he must pay to the promisor, but any expenses necessary to prepare for the performance; and in the case at bar the cost of the foundation was such an expense. The sum which would restore the Buyer to the position it would have been in, had the Seller performed, would therefore be the prospective net earnings of the "Refiners" while they were used (together with any value they might have as scrap after they were discarded), less their price — $25,500 — together with $3,000, the cost of installing them. The Buyer did not indeed prove the net earnings of the "Refiners" or their scrap value; but it asserts that it is nonetheless entitled to recover the cost of the foundation upon the theory that what is expended in reliance upon the Seller's performance was a recoverable loss. In cases where the venture would have proved profitable to the promisee, there is no reason why he should not recover his expenses. On the other hand, on those occasions in which the performance would not have covered the promisee's outlay, such a result imposes the risk of the promisee's contract upon the promisor. We cannot agree that the promisor's default in performance should under this guise make him an insurer of the promisee's venture; yet it does not follow that the breach should not throw upon him the duty of showing that the value of the performance would in fact have been less than the promisee's outlay. It is often very hard to learn what the value of the performance would have been; and it is a common expedient, and a just one, in such situations to put the peril of the answer upon that party who by his wrong has made the issue relevant to the rights of the other.[55] On

55. Story Parchment Co. v. Paterson Parchment Paper Co., 282 U.S. 555, 563, 51 S. Ct. 248, 75 L. Ed. 544.

principle therefore the proper solution would seem to be that the promisee may recover his outlay in preparation for the performance, subject to the privilege of the promisor to reduce it by as much as he can show that the promisee would have lost, if the contract had been performed.

The decisions leave much to be desired. There is language in United States v. Behan[56] which, read literally, would allow the promisee to recover his outlay in all cases: the promisor is said to be "estopped" to deny that the value of the performance would not equal it. We doubt whether the Supreme Court would today accept the explanation, although the result was right under the rule which we propose. Moreover, in spite of the authority properly accorded to any decision of that court, we are here concerned only with Connecticut law; and the decisions in that state do not seem to be in entire accord. In the early case of Bush v. Canfield[57] the buyer sued to recover a payment of $5,000 made in advance for the purchase of 2,000 barrels of flour at $7.00 a barrel. Although at the time set for delivery the value of the flour had fallen to $5.50, the seller for some undisclosed reason failed to perform. The action was on the case for the breach, not in indebitatus assumpsit, and the court, Hosmer, J., dissenting, allowed the buyer to recover the full amount of his payment over the seller's objection that recovery should be reduced by the buyer's loss. The chief justice gave the following reason for his decision which we take to be that of the court, 2 Conn. page 488: "The defendant has violated his contract; and it is not for him to say that if he had fulfilled it, the plaintiffs would have sustained a great loss, and that this ought to be deducted from the money advanced." If there is no difference between the recovery of money received by a promisor who later defaults, and a promisee's outlay preparatory to performance, this decision is in the Buyer's favor. However, when the promisor has received any benefit, the promisee's recovery always depends upon whether the promisor has been "unjustly enriched"; and, judged by that nebulous standard, there may be a distinction between imposing the promisee's loss on the promisor by compelling him to disgorge what he has received and compelling him to pay what he never has received. It is quite true that the only difference is between allowing the promisee to recover what he has paid to the promisor and what he has paid to others; but many persons would probably think that difference vital.

In any event, unless this be a valid distinction, it appears to us that Santoro v. Mack[58] must be read as taking the opposite view. The plaintiff, the vendee under a contract for the sale of land, had paid an electrician and an architect whom he had employed in reliance upon the promised conveyance. These payments he sought to recover, and was unsuccessful on the ground that they had not benefited the vendor, and that they had

56. 110 U.S. 338, 345, 346, 4 S. Ct. 81, 28 L. Ed. 168.
57. 2 Conn. 485.
58. 108 Conn. 683, 145 A. 273.

been incurred without the vendor's knowledge or consent. Yet it would seem that such expenses were as much in reasonable preparation for the use of the land, as the cost of the foundation was for the use of the "Refiners." The point now before us was apparently not raised, but the decision, as it stands, seems to deny any recovery whatever. Three other Connecticut decisions — the only ones which at all approach the question — do not throw any light upon the point.[59]

The result is equally inconclusive if we consider the few decisions in other jurisdictions. The New Jersey Court of Errors and Appeals in Holt v. United Security Life Insurance & Trust Co.[60] recognized as the proper rule that, although the promisor had the burden of proving that the value of the performance was less than the promisee's outlay, if he succeeded in doing so, the recovery would be correspondingly limited. In Bernstein v. Meech[61] the promisee recovered his full outlay, and no limitation upon it appears to have been recognized, as may be inferred from the following sentence: "It cannot be assumed that any part of this loss would have been sustained by the plaintiff if he had been permitted to perform his contract." In Reynolds v. Levi[62] the promisee was a well digger, who had made three unsuccessful efforts to reach water, and the promisor — a farmer — stopped him before he had completed his fourth. The court limited the recovery to the amount earned on the fourth attempt, but for reasons that are not apparent. It appears to us therefore that the reported decisions leave it open to us to adopt the rule we have stated. Moreover, there is support for this result in the writings of scholars. The Restatement of Contracts[63] allows recovery of the promisee's outlay "in necessary preparation" for the performance, subject to several limitations, of which one is that the promisor may deduct whatever he can prove the promisee would have lost, if the contract had been fully performed. Professor McCormick thinks[64] that "the jury should be instructed not to go beyond the probable yield" of the performance to the promisee, but he does not consider the burden of proof. Much the fullest discussion of the whole subject is Professor Fuller's in the Yale Law Journal.[65] The situation at bar was among those which he calls cases of "essential reliance," and for which he favors the rule we are adopting. It is one instance of his "very simple formula: We will not in a suit for reimbursement of losses incurred in reliance on a contract knowingly put the plaintiff in a better

59. Edward DeV. Tompkins, Inc. v. City of Bridgeport, 94 Conn. 659, 110 A. 183, 191; Kastner v. Beacon Oil Co., 114 Conn. 190, 158 A. 214, 81 A.L.R. 97; Jordan v. Patterson, 67 Conn. 473, 35 A. 521.
60. 76 N.J.L. 585, 72 A. 301, 21 L.R.A., N.S., 691.
61. 130 N.Y. 354, 360, 29 N.E. 255, 257.
62. 122 Mich. 115, 80 N.W. 999.
63. §333(d).
64. McCormick on Damages, §142, p. 584.
65. 46 Yale Law Journal 52, pp. 75-80.

position than he would have occupied, had the contract been fully performed."

The judgment will therefore be affirmed with the following modifications. To the allowance for the motor and accessories will be added interest from February 20th, 1946. The Buyer will be allowed to set off $3,000 against the Seller's recovery with interest from October, 1945, subject to the Seller's privilege to deduct from that amount any sum which upon a further hearing it can prove would have been the Buyer's loss upon the contract, had the "Refiners" been delivered on or before May 1st, 1945.

Judgment modified as above, and affirmed as so modified.

NOTE

1. Do you agree with Judge Hand that there was no merit in the buyer's claim for the machinery and rubber which it had purchased for the "reclaim department," making allowance for their scrap or other disposal value? And should not some allowance be made, by way of deduction from the $3,000 recovery, for the increased value of the buyer's factory now that it has the new foundation?

2. If the seller can show what the losses would have been, then, according to Judge Hand, the losses are to be deducted from the $3,000 recovery. Do you assume that if the buyer could show that the reclaimed rubber operation would have been profitable, providing the Refiners had been delivered on time, then the profits should be added to the $3,000 for the foundation? Would there be at that point any problem of "double recovery" like the one that disturbed Justice Holmes in *Globe Refining*, *supra* p. 1144? Or was Holmes wrong in that case?

3. If the principle case came up under the Uniform Commercial Code, could the buyer recover the cost of the foundation under §2-715, set out *supra* p. 1133? Would the cost be "incidental damages" under §2-715(1) or "consequential damages" under §2-715(2)?

4. In his opinion, Judge Hand digests the early Connecticut case of Bush v. Canfield. Do you think the result in that case a sensible one? The amount recovered by the plaintiff in the *Bush* case appears to have placed him in a position better than the one he would have been in had he received the defendant's performance. What justifies an award that gives the injured party more than his expectancy? Can the result in Bush v. Canfield be reconciled with the *Acme Mills* case, *supra* p. 1061? With the general proposition that contract damages should be compensatory — no more, no less? With Judge Posner's account, *supra* p. 1118, of the economic rationale for protecting the promisee's expectancy? With Judge Hand's assertion, in the *L. Albert* case, that any losses avoided as a result of the defendant's breach should (in principle) be deducted from the plaintiff's recovery?

Section 4.   Freedom of Contract and the Judicial Prerogative: The Power of the Parties to Control Remedy and Risk

Broadly speaking, the law of contract remedies is addressed to two questions: when may a disappointed promisee compel the actual performance of his agreement and, once it has been determined that he is entitled to money damages only, how is his compensation to be measured? The materials collected in the preceding sections of this chapter indicate the range and complexity of the rules that have been devised to answer these two questions. In this section we take up what is, in some sense, a more fundamental question regarding the status of the law of remedies as a whole: to what extent are the legal rules that define the consequences of contractual breach subject to modification or displacement by the contracting parties themselves? Put differently, to what extent are the parties free to treat these legal rules as mere suggestions and to substitute for them a regime more to their own liking (which courts of law will then be bound to respect)?

On the one hand, it may be said that since contract law is merely an instrument for effectuating the wishes and intentions of the parties, they should be given maximum freedom to say what constitutes a breach and to define its consequences. On the other hand, it can be argued that courts properly take an interest in the preservation of their own authority and have an independent duty to look after the interests of the contracting parties — a duty that will require the invalidation of even the most voluntary agreement if it is judged too one-sided or burdensome or is considered prejudicial to the interests of third parties.

The tension between these two ideas — felt in every branch of the law of contracts — becomes especially acute at three points in the area of remedies. The first concerns the validity of arbitration agreements. Often, a contract will provide that disputes between the parties are to be resolved by an arbitrator, that is, someone other than a judge sitting in a state-created court of law. To what extent are such agreements, and the awards made under them, subject to judicial review? Although the mistrust that judges have traditionally felt toward arbitration agreements has largely dissipated, contractual provisions of this sort continue to be scrutinized for their compliance with elementary standards of fair dealing and the requirements of public policy, and are far from being treated as self-validating fiats; to this extent, their effectiveness between the parties still depends upon judicial approval.

A second point at which the tension between contractual freedom and judicial prerogative becomes acute concerns the enforcement of what are sometimes referred to as "liquidated damage" clauses. In the absence of such a clause, the compensatory damages that A must pay for breaking his promise to B will be determined by a judge applying one or another of the formulae surveyed in Section 3. Suppose, however, that the parties themselves include a provision in their own agreement specifying the amount of damages to be paid in the event of breach. Will such a provision always be honored, regardless of the amount set by the parties or the circumstances under which it is to be paid? The answer to this question has been, and continues to be, in the negative — but a negative that is today more muted and ambiguous, and less restrictive, perhaps, of the parties' contractual powers, than it once was.

A third point of conflict between the principles of contractual autonomy and judicial supervision concerns the validity of disclaimers of liability — agreements that purport to eliminate the liability of one of the parties to a contract for certain harmful consequences of his own failure to perform. Strictly speaking, it is not the purpose of such a disclaimer to modify the parties' legal remedies (in the way that a liquidated damage clause does). Its aim is a more fundamental one: to eliminate a certain branch of liability altogether and thereby deny the predicate for applying any remedial rule at all. But although disclaimers and liquidated damage provisions are distinguishable, they are also, in a rather obvious sense, substitutes for one another, and it is useful to treat them together.

The following materials, it is hoped, will throw some light on the uneven progress that the idea of contractual freedom has made in the three areas just described — advancing along some fronts, losing ground on others, and gradually coalescing into a recognizable body of law that is at once both more and less free than its nineteenth-century predecessor.

NUTE v. HAMILTON MUTUAL INSURANCE CO.

72 Mass. 174 (1856)

SHAW, C.J. The defence to this action, on a policy entered into by a mutual fire insurance company, is, that by the terms of the policy the contract was that the suit should be brought at a proper court in the county of Essex, within four months after the determination by the directors that nothing was due to the plaintiff upon the loss claimed. By a comparison of dates, it appears that this suit was brought within four months; but it was brought in the county of Suffolk, and not in the county of Essex; and on that ground the court of common pleas held that the action could not be maintained. The correctness of that ruling is the sole question now presented to this court.

In cases recently determined, it has been held that a stipulation in a policy of insurance, or in a by-law constituting in legal effect a part of such policy, by way of condition to their liability, that no recovery shall be had unless a suit is commenced within a certain time limited, was a valid condition, and that, unless complied with, the plaintiffs were not entitled to recover. Cray v. Hartford Fire Ins. Co., 1 Blatchf. C.C. 280. Wilson v. Ætna Ins. Co., 27 Verm. 99. In this case it is strenuously insisted that a stipulation, that an action shall be brought in a particular county, where by law it may be brought, is strictly analogous, and ought to be enforced as a condition precedent by a court which, without such stipulation and condition, would clearly have jurisdiction of the subject matter and of the parties.

[In an omitted passage, the Chief Justice concluded that the plaintiff was bound by the "by-laws" of the insurance company annexed to the policy.]

The provision on which this defence depends is found in art. 22d of the by-laws. After providing that notice of loss shall be given, and that thereupon the directors shall proceed to determine whether any loss has occurred for which the company are liable, and if so, ascertain the amount, it provides that, if the assured do not acquiesce in such determination, as to the liability or the extent of it, and both parties do not agree to refer, as they may, "the assured may, within four months after such determination, but not after that time, bring an action at law against the company for the loss claimed, *which action shall be brought at a proper court in the county of Essex.*"

Here are no negative words, and, strictly speaking, no stipulation that the action shall not be brought elsewhere, unless they are implied by the term "shall be brought" in Essex. These words were not necessary to give the assured a remedy, because without them it is conceded that they would have a remedy at common law, as in all cases of breach of contract, for which no stipulation is necessary. In this respect, the case differs essentially from that of Boynton v. Middlesex Mutual Fire Ins. Co., 4 Met. 212. There it was provided by the act of incorporation, which has all the force and effect of a general law, that in case the directors should find the company liable and award a certain sum, and the assured should not acquiesce, but be dissatisfied with the amount, the action should be brought in the county of Middlesex. In such case, the action to be brought was in the nature of an appeal from the decision of the directors, as in a case of allowance or disallowance of a debt by commissioners of insolvency on the estates of deceased persons, or, under the insolvent laws, in the case of a claim against a living insolvent debtor; and the legislature might rightfully regulate the time and mode of entering and prosecuting such appeal; and, as the law gave a new and specific right in such case of dissatisfaction with the amount awarded, and pointed out a specific remedy, by a well known rule of law, the specific remedy must be pursued. But it was also held, in that case, that as the directors had determined that the company were not liable and had awarded nothing, it was not the specific case of the statute, and that the assured were remitted to their remedy at law, by action in either of the counties where, by the general law, it might be brought.

Upon the particular question here presented, the court are of opinion that there is an obvious distinction between a stipulation by contract as to the time when a right of action shall accrue and when it shall cease, on the one hand; and as to the forum before which, and the proceedings by which an action shall be commenced and prosecuted. The one is a condition annexed to the acquisition and continuance of a legal right, and depends on contract and the acts of the parties; the other is a stipulation concerning the remedy, which is created and regulated by law. Perhaps it would not be easy or practicable to draw a line of distinction, precise and accurate enough to govern all these classes of cases, because the cases run so nearly into each other; but we think the general distinction is obvious.

The time within which money shall be paid, land conveyed, a debt released, and the like, are all matters of contract, and depend on the will and act of the parties; but, in case of breach, the tribunal before which a remedy is to be sought, the means and processes by which it is to be conducted, affect the remedy, and are created and regulated by law. The stipulation, that a contracting party shall not be liable to pay money, or perform any other collateral act, before a certain time, is a regulation of the right, too familiar to require illustration; a stipulation, that his obligation shall cease if payment or other performance is not demanded before a certain time, seems equally a matter affecting the right. A stipulation, that an action shall not be brought after a certain day or the happening of a certain event, although, in words, it may seem to be a contract respecting the remedy, yet it is so in words only; in legal effect, it is a stipulation that a right shall cease and determine if not pursued in a particular way within a limited time, and then it is a fit subject for contract, affecting the right created by it.

But the remedy does not depend on contract, but upon law, generally the lex fori, regardless of the lex loci contractus, which regulates the construction and legal effect of the contract.

Suppose it were stipulated in an ordinary contract, that in case of breach no action shall be brought; or that the party in default shall be liable in equity only and not at law, or the reverse; that in any suit to be commenced no property shall be attached on mesne process or seized on execution for the satisfaction of a judgment, or that the party shall never be liable to arrest; that, in any suit to be brought on such contract, the party sued will confess judgment, or will waive a trial by jury, or consent that the report of an auditor appointed under the statute shall be final, and judgment be rendered upon it, or that the parties may be witnesses, or, as the law now stands, that the plaintiff will not offer himself as a witness; that, when sued on the contract, the defendant will not plead the statute of limitations, or a discharge in insolvency; and many others might be enumerated; is it not obvious, that, although in a certain sense these are rights or privileges which the party, in the proper time and place, may give or waive, yet a compliance with them cannot be annexed to the contract, cannot be taken notice of and enforced by the court or tribunal before which the remedy is sought, and cannot therefore be relied on by way of defence to the suit brought on the breach of such contract?

We do not mean to say that many of these are stipulations which it would be unlawful to make, or void in their creation, if made on good consideration, or that they do not become executory contracts upon which an action would lie, and upon which damages, if any were sustained, might be recovered. Still they would not be conditions annexed to the contract, to defeat it if not complied with, and so to be used by way of defence to an action upon it.

This seems to have been the distinction taken in the latest English case cited at the bar. Livingston v. Ralli, 5 El. & Bl. 132. The point decided there was, that, though an agreement to submit a difference arising on a contract to arbitration is not a good plea in bar to an action on such contract, the breach of it may be a good ground of action.

It is true that a covenant never to sue after the breach of a contract, though a stipulation respecting the remedy to be pursued, may be allowed as a bar to an action upon it; but this is upon the ground that a covenant never to sue is, in legal effect, equivalent to a release, and, to avoid circuitry of action, may be pleaded by way of release.

The distinction between that which is matter of contract and may be a proper subject of consideration, to be applied in expounding it, making it what it is, and to be applied to the construction of it, whenever and wherever it is to be enforced; and that which is matter of remedy regulated by law, the law of the place where the remedy is sought, is recognized and stated in an early case of our own. Pearsall v. Dwight, 2 Mass. 84.

Supposing then the rule to be well settled by principle and authority, that a stipulation is valid which provides that no action shall be brought unless commenced within a specific time, which appears to us to be equivalent to a condition in the contract, that all liability shall cease and determine unless the claim upon it is made by an action within the time limited, and attaches to the contract itself, still, in our opinion, there is not such an analogy between that and the stipulation as to the forum in which a suit shall be commenced, that the one can be taken as an authority for the other. Upon the grounds stated, we think the two cases stand upon very different reasons.

Supposing the words in the by-law, "which action shall be brought at a proper court in the county of Essex," be deemed equivalent to a negative provision, that no action shall be brought in any other county — of which we give no opinion — we are not aware of any authority bearing upon the question that such stipulation or condition can be regarded as a condition of the contract, or that a noncompliance with it will be a defence to the action before a court having jurisdiction of the subject matter and of the parties.

In recurring to the full and elaborate written argument of the defendants' counsel, we find no authority upon this part of the case. In referring to the case of Boynton v. Middlesex Mutual Fire Ins. Co., 4 Met. 212, which we have already alluded to, it is urged, on the authority of Holden v. James, 11 Mass. 396, in which a special statute of limitations, (which was a strictly private act,) was held unconstitutional, that the ground on which the court decided must have been the contract of the parties, and not the law of the land. But the court, in 4 Met. 215, cite Rev. Sts. c. 2, §3, directing that all acts of incorporation shall be deemed public acts. If so, they are the law of the land, controlling, and, as far as they go, repealing other public acts. Whether this ground was correct or not, it was that on which the court decided, and the case therefore is not an authority for giving a like effect to matters of mere contract.

In a certain sense, all persons are said to be parties and assent to the laws of the government to which they owe allegiance; such laws are binding on them, and enter into and make part of every agreement which such persons make. But we are speaking of the known and familiar distinction between contracts between parties in pais, which are binding on them because they have so agreed; and duties created by law, which are binding on the parties because they are law, and do not derive their force from contract.

A party is barred by the statute of limitations, not because he has so agreed, but because such is the positive law, the lex fori, the aid of which he is seeking to obtain his rights. So of arrest of the person, sequestration of goods, levy on lands, and the like; the plaintiff does not derive his right to the use of these means from the agreement of the contractor, but from the positive law which gives him the remedy, and the means of obtaining satisfaction, incident thereto.

Most of the cases cited, both English and American, are conditions annexed to the contract; such as bringing the action within a certain time, procuring certificates of church-wardens, magistrates or others, practising no fraud, making seasonable and true representations of loss, and the like; as such, they are modifications of the contract, not of the remedy.

We place no great reliance upon considerations of public policy, though, as far as they go, we think they are opposed to the admission of such a defence. The rules to determine in what courts and counties actions may be brought are fixed, upon considerations of general convenience and expediency, by general law; to allow them to be changed by the agreement of parties would disturb the symmetry of the law, and interfere with such convenience. Such contracts might be induced by considerations tending to bring the administration of justice into disrepute; such as the greater or less intelligence and impartiality of judges, the greater or less integrity and capacity of juries, the influence, more or less, arising from the personal, social or political standing of parties in one or another county. It might happen that a mutual insurance company, in which every holder of a policy is a member, and of course interested, would embrace so large a part of the men of property and business in the county, that it would be difficult to find an impartial and intelligent jury. But as already remarked, these considerations are not of much weight. The greatest inconvenience would be in requiring courts and juries to apply different rules of law to different cases, in the conduct of suits, in matters relating merely to the remedy, according to the stipulations of parties in framing and diversifying their contracts in regard to remedies.

The law fixing the rate of interest is cited as an illustration of the point, that, though the law has fixed the rate of interest, yet parties may vary it by contract, and take a less interest. Undoubtedly they may. But take the whole statute together; what are its objects? Manifestly two; first, to fix a rate of interest where the parties have made no agreement as to the rate; secondly, to fix a rate beyond which a creditor cannot take or receive interest with impunity. The contract is not void, as formerly; but the creditor suffers a penalty for it. These objects are effectually accomplished by the provisions of the statute; and no more. Rev. Sts. c. 35, §2. St. 1846, c. 199. Of course it is not repugnant to these provisions, for parties to fix a rate of interest by agreement, within this limit. This has no analogy to the present question.

There being no authority upon which to determine the case, it must be decided upon principle. The question is not without difficulty, but, upon the best consideration the court have been able to give it, they are of opinion that it is not a good defence to this action, that it was brought in the county of Suffolk and not in the county of Essex; and therefore that the exceptions must be sustained, the verdict set aside, and a new trial granted.

NOTE

1. In the course of his discussion of the topic: To What Extent and in What Manner Can Parties by Private Agreement Affect Court Action, Professor Corbin wrote:

> At this point a distinction that is not at all unfamiliar will be suggested. It is the distinction between rights and remedies, between primary rights and remedial rights. Can it be that parties have full control over their primary

contractual rights and duties and no such control over their remedial (or secondary) rights and duties?

This distinction has played a part in the making of our law and it is of some importance in our present discussion. This is true, in spite of the fact that careful analysis will show that the distinction is in degree rather than in kind, and that no exact boundary line can be drawn. When one gets down out of the metaphysical clouds and stands on solid human earth, he must observe that the relation of right and duty has no juristic existence apart from a societal sanction that involves juristic remedy. The maxim that there is no right without a remedy is a truism, because it is the availability of some remedy, direct or indirect, that gives significance to the terms legal right and legal duty.

Even admitting all this, however, it is facts and events that will induce societal sanction and juristic remedy; and when we say that one party has a right and another owes a duty, we mean that the requisite facts exist and events have occurred. In very large measure, in the field of contract, individuals can control the existence of these facts and the occurrence of these events. This is what they are doing when they are "making a contract."

One can avoid making a promise; he can make a small promise rather than a large one; he can make a conditional promise instead of an absolute one. In making an arbitration agreement, are the parties merely exercising a control over the operative facts and events, or are they also trying to control the remedies — the juristic effect of those facts and events? In the field of free contract, it has often been judicially declared that parties may write their own contracts, and that it is the function of the courts to interpret those contracts and to enforce them as made. But it is not the declared law that parties may also limit and control judicial remedies, procedure, or modes of proof.

6A Corbin §1432 at 384-386.

2. Guaranty Trust and Safe Deposit Co. v. Green Cove Springs and Melrose R.R., 139 U.S. 137 (1891), involved proceedings for foreclosure of a railroad mortgage. In the course of his opinion, Justice Brown remarked:

It is true that there is a . . . provision in the deed of trust to the effect that neither the whole nor any part of the premises mortgaged shall be sold, under proceedings either at law or in equity, for the recovery of the principal or interest of the bonds, it being the intention and agreement of the parties that the mode of sale provided by the mortgage "shall be exclusive of all others." This clause, however, is open to the objection of attempting to provide against a remedy in the ordinary course of judicial proceedings, and oust the jurisdiction of the courts, which, as is settled by the uniform current of authority, cannot be done.

139 U.S. at 142-143.

The idea expressed by Justice Brown in the *Guaranty Trust* case that contractual stipulations as to remedy were invalid as attempts to "oust the jurisdiction of the courts" had a notable career in the context of agreements to arbitrate disputes. The history of judicial attitudes toward arbitration agreements was reviewed by Frank, J., in Kulukundis Shipping Co., S/A v. Amtorg Trading Corp., 126 F.2d 978, 982-985 (2d Cir. 1942) (elaborate footnotes by the court have been omitted):

> In considering these contentions in the light of the precedents, it is necessary to take into account the history of the judicial attitude towards arbitration: The English courts, while giving full effect to agreements to submit controversies to arbitration after they had ripened into arbitrators' awards, would — over a long period beginning at the end of the 17th century — do little or nothing to prevent or make irksome the breach of such agreements when they were still executory. Prior to 1687, such a breach could be made costly: a penal bond given to abide the result of an arbitration had a real bite, since a breach of the bond's condition led to a judgment for the amount of the penalty. It was so held in 1609 in Vynior's Case, 8 Coke Rep. 81b. To be sure, Coke there, in a dictum, citing precedents, dilated on the inherent revocability of the authority given to an arbitrator; such a revocation was not too important, however, if it resulted in a stiff judgment on a penal bond. But the Statute of Fines and Penalties (8 & 9 Wm. III c. 11, s. 8), enacted in 1687, provided that, in an action on any bond given for performance of agreements, while judgment would be entered for the penalty, execution should issue only for the damages actually sustained. Coke's dictum as to revocability, uttered seventy-eight years earlier, now took on a new significance, as it was now held that for breach of an undertaking to arbitrate the damages were only nominal. Recognizing the effect of the impact of this statute on executory arbitration agreements, Parliament, eleven years later, enacted a statute, 9 Wm. III c. 15 (1698), designed to remedy the situation by providing that, if an agreement to arbitrate so provided, it could be made a "rule of court" (i.e., a court order), in which event it became irrevocable, and one who revoked it would be subject to punishment for contempt of court; but the submission was revocable until such a rule of court had been obtained. This statute, limited in scope, was narrowly construed and was of little help. The ordinary executory arbitration agreement thus lost all real efficacy since it was not specifically enforceable in equity, and was held not to constitute the basis of a plea in bar in, or a stay of, a suit on the original cause of action. In admiralty, the rulings were much the same.
>
> It has been well said that "the legal mind must assign some reason in order to decide anything with spiritual quiet." And so, by way of rationalization, it became fashionable in the middle of the 18th century to say that such agreements were against public policy because they "oust the jurisdiction" of the courts. But that was a quaint explanation, inasmuch as an award, under an arbitration agreement, enforced both at law and in equity, was no less an ouster; and the same was true of releases and covenants not to sue, which were given full effect. Moreover, the agreement to arbitrate was not illegal, since suit could be maintained for its breach. Here was a clear instance of what Holmes called a "right" to break a contract and to

substitute payment of damages for non-performance; as, in this type of case, the damages were only nominal, the "right" was indeed meaningful.

An effort has been made to justify this judicial hostility to the executory arbitration agreement on the ground that arbitrations, if unsupervised by the courts, are undesirable, and that legislation was needed to make possible such supervision. But if that was the reason for unfriendliness to such executory agreements, then the courts should also have refused to aid arbitrations when they ripened into awards. And what the English courts, especially the equity courts, did in other contexts, shows that, if they had had the will, they could have devised means of protecting parties to arbitrations. Instead, they restrictively interpreted successive statutes intended to give effect to executory arbitrations. No similar hostility was displayed by the Scotch courts. Lord Campbell explained the English attitude as due to the desire of the judges, at a time when their salaries came largely from fees, to avoid loss of income. Indignation has been voiced at this suggestion; perhaps it is unjustified. Perhaps the true explanation is the hypnotic power of the phrase, "oust the jurisdiction." Give a bad dogma a good name and its bite may become as bad as its bark.

In 1855, in Scott v. Avery, 5 H.C.L. 811, the tide seemed to have turned. There it was held that if a policy made an award of damages by arbitrators a condition precedent to a suit on the policy, a failure to submit to arbitration would preclude such a suit, even if the policy left to the arbitrators the consideration of all the elements of liability. But, despite later legislation, the hostility of the English courts to executory arbitrations resumed somewhat after Scott v. Avery, and seems never to have been entirely dissipated.

That English attitude was largely taken over in the 19th century by most courts in this country. Indeed, in general, they would not go as far as Scott v. Avery, *supra*, and continued to use the "ouster of jurisdiction" concept: An executory agreement to arbitrate would not be given specific performance or furnish the basis of a stay of proceedings on the original cause of action. Nor would it be given effect as a plea in bar, except in limited instances, i.e., in the case of an agreement expressly or impliedly making it a condition precedent to litigation that there be an award determining some preliminary questions of subsidiary fact upon which any liability was to be contingent. Hamilton v. Liverpool, 1890, etc., Ins. Co., 136 U.S. 242, 255, 10 S. Ct. 945, 34 L. Ed. 419. In the case of broader executory agreements, no more than nominal damages would be given for a breach.

Generally speaking, then, the courts of this country were unfriendly to executory arbitration agreements. The lower federal courts, feeling bound to comply with the precedents, nevertheless became critical of this judicial hostility. There were intimations in the Supreme Court that perhaps the old view might be abandoned, but in the cases hinting at that newer attitude the issue was not raised. Effective state arbitration statutes were enacted beginning with the New York statute of 1920.

The United States Arbitration Act of 1925 was sustained as constitutional, in its application to cases arising in admiralty. Marine Transit Corp. v. Dreyfus, 1932, 284 U.S. 263, 52 S. Ct. 166, 76 L. Ed. 516. The purpose of that Act was deliberately to alter the judicial atmosphere previously existing. The report of the House Committee stated, in part:

> Arbitration agreements are purely matters of contract, and the effect of the bill is simply to make the contracting party live up to his agreement. He can no longer refuse to perform his contract when it becomes disadvantageous to him. An arbitration agreement is placed upon the same footing as other contracts, where it belongs. . . . The need for the law arises from an anachronism of our American law. Some centuries ago, because of the jealousy of the English courts for their own jurisdiction, they refused to enforce specific agreements to arbitrate upon the ground that the courts were thereby ousted from their jurisdiction. This jealousy survived for so long a period that the principle became firmly embedded in the English common law and was adopted with it by the American courts. The courts have felt that the precedent was too strongly fixed to be overturned without legislative enactment, although they have frequently criticized the rule and recognized its illogical nature and the injustice which results from it. The bill declares simply that such agreements for arbitration shall be enforced, and provides a procedure in the Federal courts for their enforcement. . . . It is particularly appropriate that the action should be taken at this time when there is so much agitation against the costliness and delays of litigation. These matters can be largely eliminated by agreements for arbitration, if arbitration agreements are made valid and enforceable.

In the light of the clear intention of Congress, it is our obligation to shake off the old judicial hostility to arbitration.

GARRITY v. LYLE STUART, INC.
40 N.Y.2d 354, 353 N.E.2d 793 (1976)

BREITEL, Chief Judge.

Plaintiff author brought this proceeding under CPLR 7510 to confirm an arbitration award granting her $45,000 in compensatory damages and $7,500 in punitive damages against defendant publishing company. Supreme Court confirmed the award. The Appellate Division affirmed, one Justice dissenting, and defendant appeals.

The issue is whether an arbitrator has the power to award punitive damages.

The order of the Appellate Division should be modified to vacate the award of punitive damages and otherwise affirmed. An arbitrator has no power to award punitive damages, even if agreed upon by the parties (Matter of Publishers' Ass'n of N.Y. City [Newspaper Union], 280 App. Div. 500, 504-506, 114 N.Y.S.2d 401, 404-406). Punitive damages is a sanction reserved to the State, a public policy of such magnitude as to call for judicial intrusion to prevent its contravention. Since enforcement of an award of punitive damages as a purely private remedy would violate strong public policy, an arbitrator's award which imposes punitive damages should be vacated.

Plaintiff is the author of two books published by defendant. While the publishing agreements between the parties contained broad arbitration clauses, neither of the agreements provided for the imposition of punitive damages in the event of breach.

A dispute arose between the parties and in December, 1971 plaintiff author brought an action for damages alleging fraudulent inducement, "gross" underpayment of royalties, and various "malicious" acts designed to harass her. That action is still pending.

In March, 1974, plaintiff brought a new action alleging that defendant had wrongfully withheld an additional $45,000 in royalties. Defendant moved for a stay pending arbitration, which was granted, and plaintiff demanded arbitration. The demand requested the $45,000 withheld royalties and punitive damages for defendant's alleged "malicious" withholding of royalties, which plaintiff contended was done to coerce her into withdrawing the 1971 action.

Defendant appeared at the arbitration hearing and raised objections concerning plaintiff's standing and the conduct of the arbitration hearing. Upon rejection of these objections by the arbitrators, defendant walked out.

After hearing testimony, and considering an "informal memorandum" on punitive damages submitted by plaintiff at their request, the arbitrators awarded plaintiff both compensatory and punitive damages. On plaintiff's motion to confirm the award, defendant objected upon the ground that the award of punitive damages was beyond the scope of the arbitrators' authority.

Arbitrators generally are not bound by principles of substantive law or rules of evidence, and thus error of law or fact will not justify vacatur of an award (see Matter of Associated Teachers of Huntington v. Board of Educ., 33 N.Y.2d 229, 235, 351 N.Y.S.2d 670, 674, 306 N.E.2d 791, 795, and cases cited). It is also true that arbitrators generally are free to fashion the remedy appropriate to the wrong, if they find one, but an authentic remedy is compensatory and measured by the harm caused and how it may be corrected (Matter of Staklinski [Pyramid Elec. Co.], 6 N.Y.2d 159, 163, 188 N.Y.S.2d 541, 542, 160 N.E.2d 78, 79; see Matter of Paver & Wildfoerster [Catholic High School Ass'n.], 38 N.Y.2d 669, 677, 382 N.Y.S.2d 22, 26, 345 N.E.2d 565, 569, and cases cited). These broad principles are tolerable so long as arbitrators are not thereby empowered to ride roughshod over strong policies in the law which control coercive private conduct and confine to the State and its courts the infliction of punitive sanctions on wrongdoers.

The court will vacate an award enforcing an illegal agreement or one violative of public policy. . . . Since enforcement of an award of punitive damages as a purely private remedy would violate public policy, an arbitrator's award which imposes punitive damages, even though agreed upon by the parties, should be vacated (Matter of Publishers' Ass'n of

N.Y. City [Newspaper Union], 280 App. Div. 500, 504-506, 114 N.Y.S.2d
401, 404-406, *supra*; Domke, Commercial Arbitration, §33.03; Fuchsberg,
9 N.Y. Damages Law, §81, p. 61, n. 9; 14 N.Y. Jur., Damages, §184, p. 46;
cf. Local 127, United Shoe Workers of Amer. v. Brooks Shoe Mfg. Co., 3
Cir., 298 F.2d 277, 278, 284).

Matter of Associated Gen. Contrs., N.Y. State Chapter (Savin Bros.),
36 N.Y.2d 957, 373 N.Y.S.2d 555, 335 N.E.2d 859, is inapposite. That
case did not involve an award of punitive damages. Instead, the court
permitted enforcement of an arbitration award of treble liquidated damages, amounting to a penalty, assessed however in accordance with the
express terms of a trade association membership agreement. The court
held that the public policy against permitting the awarding of penalties
was not of "such magnitude as to call for judicial intrusion" (p. 959). In
the instant case, however, there was no provision in the agreements
permitting arbitrators to award liquidated damages or penalties. Indeed,
the subject apparently had never even been considered.

The prohibition against an arbitrator awarding punitive damages is
based on strong public policy indeed. At law, on the civil side, in the
absence of statute, punitive damages are available only in a limited number of instances (see Walker v. Sheldon, 10 N.Y.2d 401, 404, 223
N.Y.S.2d 488, 490, 179 N.E.2d 497, 498). As was stated in Walker v.
Sheldon (*supra*):

> [p]unitive or exemplary damages have been allowed in cases where the
> wrong complained of is morally culpable, or is actuated by evil and repre-
> hensible motives, not only to punish the defendant but to deter him, as well
> as others who might otherwise be so prompted, from indulging in similar
> conduct in the future.

It is a social exemplary "remedy," not a private compensatory remedy.

It has always been held that punitive damages are not available for
mere breach of contract, for in such a case only a private wrong, and not
a public right, is involved (see, e.g., Trans-State Hay & Feed Corp. v.
Faberge, Inc., 35 N.Y.2d 669, 360 N.Y.S.2d 886, 319 N.E.2d 201, *affg. on
mem.* at App. Div., 42 A.D.2d 535, 344 N.Y.S.2d 730; Van Valkenburgh,
Nooger & Neville v. Hayden Pub. Co., 33 A.D.2d 766, 767, 306 N.Y.S.2d
599, 601 [breach of contract by book publisher, which failed deliberately
and in breach of good faith to use "best efforts" to promote plaintiff's
books; punitive damages denied], *affd.*, 30 N.Y.2d 34, 330 N.Y.S.2d 329,
281 N.E.2d 142 [discussing the facts and particularly the breach of fair
dealing in greater detail], *cert. den.*, 409 U.S. 875, 93 S. Ct. 125, 34 L. Ed.
2d 128; Restatement, Contracts, §342; 14 N.Y. Jur., Damages, §183, pp.
45-46).

Even if the so-called "malicious" breach here involved would permit of
the imposition of punitive damages by a court or jury, it was not the

province of arbitrators to do so. Punitive sanctions are reserved to the State, surely a public policy "of such magnitude as to call for judicial intrusion" (Matter of Associated Gen. Contrs., N.Y. State Chapter [Savin Bros.], 36 N.Y.2d 957, 959, 373 N.Y.S.2d 555, 556, 335 N.E.2d 859, 860, *supra*). The evil of permitting an arbitrator whose selection is often restricted or manipulatable by the party in a superior bargaining position, to award punitive damages is that it displaces the court and the jury, and therefore the State, as the engine for imposing a social sanction. As was so wisely observed by Judge, then Mr. Justice, Bergan in Matter of Publishers' Ass'n of N.Y. City (Newspaper Union), 280 App. Div. 500, 503, 114 N.Y.S.2d 401, 404, *supra*:

> The trouble with an arbitration admitting a power to grant unlimited damages by way of punishment is that if the court treated such an award in the way arbitration awards are usually treated, and followed the award to the letter, it would amount to an unlimited draft upon judicial power. In the usual case, the court stops only to inquire if the award is authorized by the contract; is complete and final on its face; and if the proceeding was fairly conducted.
>
> Actual damage is measurable against some objective standard — the number of pounds, or days, or gallons or yards; but punitive damages take their shape from the subjective criteria involved in attitudes toward correction and reform, and courts do not accept readily the delegation of that kind of power. Where punitive damages have been allowed for those torts which are still regarded somewhat as public penal wrongs as well as actionable private wrongs, they have had rather close judicial supervision. If the usual rules were followed there would be no effective judicial supervision over punitive awards in arbitration.

The dissent appears to have recognized the danger in permitting an arbitrator in his discretion to award unlimited punitive damages. Thus, it notes that the award made here was neither "irrational" nor "unjust" (40 N.Y.2d p. 365, 386 N.Y.S.2d p. 838, 353 N.E.2d p. 800). Standards such as these are subjective and afford no practical guidelines for the arbitrator and little protection against abuse, and would, on the other hand, contrary to the sound development of arbitration law, permit the courts to supervise awards for their justness (cf. Lentine v. Fundaro, 29 N.Y.2d 382, 386, 328 N.Y.S.2d 418, 422, 278 N.E.2d 633, 635).

Parties to arbitration agree to the substitution of a private tribunal for purposes of deciding their disputes without the expense, delay and rigidities of traditional courts. If arbitrators were allowed to impose punitive damages, the usefulness of arbitration would be destroyed. It would become a trap for the unwary given the eminently desirable freedom from judicial overview of law and facts. It would mean that the scope of determination by arbitrators, by the license to award punitive damages, would be both unpredictable and uncontrollable. It would lead to a Shylock principle of doing business without a Portia-like escape from the vise of a logic foreign to arbitration law.

In imposing penal sanctions in private arrangements, a tradition of the rule of law in organized society is violated. One purpose of the rule of law is to require that the use of coercion be controlled by the State (Kelsen, General Theory of Law and State, p. 21). In a highly developed commercial and economic society the use of private force is not the danger, but the uncontrolled use of coercive economic sanctions in private arrangements. For centuries the power to punish has been a monopoly of the State, and not that of any private individual (Kelsen, loc. cit., supra). The day is long past since barbaric man achieved redress by private punitive measures.

The parties never agreed or, for that matter, even considered punitive damages as a possible sanction for breach of the agreement (see dissenting opn. below by Mr. Justice Capozzoli, 48 A.D.2d 814, 370 N.Y.S.2d 6). Here there is no pretense of agreement, although plaintiff author argues feebly that the issue of punitive damages was "waived" by failure to object originally to the demands for punitive damages, but only later to the award. The law does not and should not permit private persons to submit themselves to punitive sanctions of the order reserved to the State. The freedom of contract does not embrace the freedom to punish, even by contract. On this view, there was no power to waive the limitations on privately assessed punitive damages and, of course, no power to agree to them by the failure to object to the demand for arbitration (cf. Brooklyn Sav. Bank v. O'Neil, 324 U.S. 697, 704, 65 S.Ct. 895, 900, 89 L.Ed. 1296, affg., 293 N.Y. 666, 56 N.E.2d 259 ["waiver" of right "charged or colored with the public interest" is ineffective]; see, generally, 6A Corbin, Contracts, §1515, pp. 728-732 [e.g., "waiver" of defenses to an usurious agreement is ineffective]).

Under common-law principles, there is eventual supervision of jury awards of punitive damages, in the singularly rare cases where it is permitted, by the trial court's power to change awards and by the Appellate Division's power to modify such awards (see Walker v. Sheldon, 10 N.Y.2d 401, 405, n.3, 223 N.Y.S.2d 488, 491, 179 N.E.2d 497, 499, supra). That the award of punitive damages in this case was quite modest is immaterial. Such a happenstance is not one on which to base a rule.

Accordingly, the order of the Appellate Division should be modified, without costs, to vacate so much of the award which imposes punitive damages, and otherwise affirmed.

GABRIELLI, Judge (dissenting).

Although espousing a desire to obviate a "trap for the unwary" and a "Shylock principle of doing business without a Portia-like escape" (40 N.Y.2d p. 359, 386 N.Y.S.2d p. 834, 353 N.E.2d p. 796) the majority reaches a result favoring a guileful defendant and voids a just and rational award of punitive damages to a wholly innocent and deserving plaintiff. Stripped to its essence the defendant, by willful and fraudulent guises, refused to pay plaintiff royalties known to be due and owing to her; forced her to commence actions claiming fraudulent acts and to enforce arbitration to redress the wrongs done to her and to collect the sums rightfully due; and, finally, defendant waived any objection to the claim for punitive damages, deliberately refused to participate in the arbitration hearing and abruptly left the hearing without moving against the claim for punitive damages or even so much as offering any countervailing evidence or argument on the merits of plaintiff's claims. I cannot, therefore, join with the majority and conclude, as they now do, that the ultimate limit of the damages awardable to plaintiff is that sum which was unquestionably due and owing to her in any event under the royalty agreement.

The basic issue presented for our determination is whether, in an arbitration proceeding brought pursuant to a contract containing a broad arbitration clause, an award of punitive damages is violative of public policy.

Plaintiff, the author of The Sensuous Woman and The Sensuous Man, entered into agreements with the defendant to publish the two books. The agreements contained identical, broad arbitration clauses which provide:

> Any controversy or claim arising out of this agreement or the breach or interpretation thereof shall be determined by arbitration in accordance with the rules then obtaining of the American Arbitration Association, and judgment upon the award may be entered in the highest court of the forum, State or Federal, having jurisdiction.

A dispute arose between the parties and in December, 1971 plaintiff commenced an action for damages against defendant alleging that defendant and its principal officer, Lyle Stuart, committed fraud in inducing her to enter into the agreements, substantially underpaid her royalties then due, and engaged in nefarious business activities calculated to harass and annoy her. Defendant moved for a stay of the action pending arbitration. The decision on the motion has been held in abeyance pending trial of the fraudulent inducement issue, which as yet has not been held due to protracted pretrial discovery proceedings.

In March, 1974 plaintiff commenced a new and separate action asserting that defendant had wrongfully withheld an additional $45,000 in royalties during the first half of 1973. Defendant obtained a stay of that action pending arbitration and plaintiff subsequently served a demand for arbitration. The demand restated the claim made in the March, 1974 complaint and also contained an additional claim for punitive damages allegedly resulting from defendant's maliciously withholding royalties due plaintiff who charged that it was done for the unjustifiable and vindictive purpose of coercing plaintiff to withdraw the pending 1971 action.

Defendant participated in the selection of the arbitrators and appeared at the hearing. Represented by counsel and two corporate officers, defendant promptly entered objections concerning the standing of plaintiff to bring the proceeding and certain administrative matters. No objection was addressed to the demand for punitive damages. The objections were overruled, and defendant's representatives walked out of the hearing and refused to participate any further in the arbitration proceeding. None of the objections raised at the hearing have ever been renewed.

Following the departure of defendant's officers and counsel, the arbitrators heard extensive and, of course, unchallenged evidence from plaintiff. As a result, the arbitrators awarded plaintiff $45,000 on her claim for royalties and $7,500 in punitive damages plus interest and fees. When plaintiff moved to confirm the award, defendant objected, for the first time, that an award of punitive damages is violative of public policy and beyond the scope of the authority of the arbitrators. Special Term confirmed the award and the Appellate Division upheld that determination. I would affirm.

In doing so, I would reject the notion that this award of punitive damages is violative of public policy. We have only recently treated with a somewhat similar argument in Matter of Associated Gen. Contrs., N.Y. State Chapter (Savin Bros.), 36 N.Y.2d 957, 373 N.Y.S.2d 555, 335 N.E.2d 859. There we considered the effect of a public policy argument against penalty awards with respect to an arbitration commenced by a national trade association in the construction industry against one of its employer-members pursuant to the provisions of a broad arbitration clause contained in the association agreement. Specifically at issue was whether an arbitration award of treble liquidated damages, assessed in accordance with the express terms of the agreement, was enforceable.[66] We held that since the arbitration was in consequence of a broad arbitration clause and concerned no third-party interests which could be said to transcend the concerns of the parties to the arbitration, there was present (p. 959, 373 N.Y.S.2d p. 556, 335 N.E.2d p. 860) "no question involving public policy of such magnitude as to call for judicial intrusion" (see also, Matter of Riccardi [Modern Silver Linen Supply Co.], 36 N.Y.2d 945, 373 N.Y.S.2d 551, 335 N.E.2d 856; cf. Hirsch v. Hirsch, 37 N.Y.2d 312, 372 N.Y.S.2d 71, 333 N.E.2d 371). The Associated Gen. Contrs. case may be

66. The agreement provided that where an arbitrator found that a member had violated the terms of the agreement, damages were to be awarded

"in an amount no less than three (3) times the daily liquidated damage amount provided for in each . . . heavy and highway construction contract to which the undersigned firm is a party within the geographic area of the applicable labor contract . . . for each . . . day the firm complained of is found by the arbitrator to have been in violation of its obligations."

(Matter of Associated Gen. Contrs., supra, 36 N.Y.2d 958, 373 N.Y.S.2d 555, 335 N.E.2d 859.)

contrasted with Matter of Aimcee Wholesale Corp. (Tomar Prods.), 21 N.Y.2d 621, 289 N.Y.S.2d 968, 237 N.E.2d 223, where the issue to be arbitrated concerned the enforcement of State antitrust law, a matter which was, as we said in Aetna Life & Cas. Co. v. Stekardis, 34 N.Y.2d 182, 186, n., 356 N.Y.S.2d 587, 589, 313 N.E.2d 53, 54, "of overriding public policy significance such as to call for judicial intervention dehors the provisions of CPLR 7503." Other policies, "especially those embodied in statutory form" (Matter of Aimcee, *supra*, 21 N.Y.2d at p. 629, 289 N.Y.S.2d at p. 974, 237 N.E.2d at p. 227), have also been accorded similar significance (see Matter of Knickerbocker Agency [Holz], 4 N.Y.2d 245, 173 N.Y.S.2d 602, 149 N.E.2d 885 [liquidation of defunct insurance companies]; Durst v. Abrash, 17 N.Y.2d 445, 266 N.Y.S.2d 806, 213 N.E.2d 887 [usury law]; Wilko v. Swan, 346 U.S. 427, 74 S. Ct. 182, 98 L. Ed. 168 [Securities Act of 1933 violation]; American Safety Equip. Corp. v. Maguire Co., 2 Cir., 391 F.2d 821 [Federal antitrust law]).

The case at bar falls within the rationale and rule of the *Associated Gen. Contrs.* case. Controlling here, as there, is the fact that the arbitration clause is broad indeed; there are no third-party interests involved; and the public policy against punitive damages is not so commanding that the Legislature has found it necessary to embody that policy into law, especially one that would apply to all cases involving such damages irrespective of the amount sought, the relative size of the award, or the punishable actions of the parties. Or, put another way, the public policy which "favors the peaceful resolutions of disputes through arbitration" (*Associated Gen. Contrs.*, *supra*, at p. 959, 373 N.Y.S.2d at p. 556, 335 N.E.2d at p. 859) outweighs the public policy disfavoring the assessment of punitive damages in this instance, where the unjustifiable conduct complained of is found to be with malice. I would conclude, therefore, that any public policy limiting punitive damage awards does not rise to that level of significance in this case as to require judicial intervention.

The majority would distinguish the *Associated Gen. Contrs.* case (*supra*) upon the thin ground that the enforcement of a treble liquidated damages clause which was applicable to numerous nationwide contracts that conceivably could have amounted to astronomical sums is not the equivalent of the enforcement of an award of penalty damages. However, as Mr. Justice Greenblott specifically stated for the majority below in that case, and in an opinion expressly approved by this court, the amount of damages therein computed in the arbitration bore "*no reasonable relationship to the amount of damages which may be sustained*" (emphasis added; 45 A.D.2d 136, 140, 356 N.Y.S.2d 374, 378); and a contract clause which is grossly disproportionate to the presumable damage or readily ascertainable loss is a penalty clause, irrespective of its label (Equitable Lbr. Corp. v. IPA Land Development Corp., 38 N.Y.2d 516, 521-522, 381 N.Y.S.2d 459, 462-463, 344 N.E.2d 391, 395-396; Ward v. Hudson Riv. Bldg. Co., 125 N.Y. 230, 235, 26 N.E. 256, 257; see Wirth & Hamid Fair

Booking v. Wirth, 265 N.Y. 214, 192 N.E. 297; Uniform Commercial
Code, §2-718, subd. [1]; Restatement, Contracts, §339; 3 Williston, Contracts [rev. ed.], §779). In short, Associated Gen. Contrs. is not only
apposite but is controlling. Conversely, Matter of Publishers' Assn. of
N.Y. City (Newspaper Union), 280 App. Div. 500, 504-506, 114 N.Y.S.2d
401, 404-406, decided in 1951, and a predicate for the majority holding,
has been seriously questioned and said to be of "doubtful validity" (8
Weinstein-Korn-Miller, N.Y. Civ. Prac., par. 7510.07) due to the subsequent enactment of CPLR 7501 which intentionally broadened the scope
of arbitration and made awards therein enforceable "without regard to
the justiciable character of the controversy." Even the court which authored *Publishers' Ass'n* now agrees that the issue there considered was
not properly framed (see Associated Gen. Contrs., 45 A.D.2d at p. 142,
356 N.Y.S.2d at p. 380, *supra*).

An affirmative here would do no violence to precedents in this court.
In at least two varied circumstances we have held that although public
policy would bar a civil suit for relief, that same public policy was not of
such overriding import as to preclude confirmation of an arbitration
award (Matter of Staklinski [Pyramid Elec. Co.], 6 N.Y.2d 159, 188
N.Y.S.2d 541, 160 N.E.2d 78; Matter of Ruppert [Egelhofer], 3 N.Y.2d
576, 170 N.Y.S.2d 785, 148 N.E.2d 129). In *Ruppert* was permitted the
enjoining of a work stoppage in a labor dispute by arbitration despite the
fact that the issuance of such relief by a court was prohibited by statute
(then Civil Practice Act, §876-a). Similarly, in *Staklinski*, citing *Ruppert*,
we upheld an arbitration award of specific performance of an employment contract in the face of the public policy against compelling a corporation to continue the services of an officer whose services were
unsatisfactory to the board of directors. The rule to be distilled from these
cases, therefore, is that only where the public interest clearly supersedes
the concerns of the parties should courts intervene and assert exclusive
dominion over disputes in arbitration (see Comment, Judicial Review of
Arbitration: Role of Public Policy, 58 Nw. U.L. Rev. 545, 554-555; see,
also, McLaughlin, Supplementary Practice Commentaries, McKinney's
Cons. Laws of N.Y., Book 7B, CPLR 7501, Supp., p. 164; Note, 52 Col.
L. Rev. 943, 945).

Nor can we hold, as defendant also urges, that the arbitrators exceeded
their authority in awarding punitive damages to plaintiff. Arbitrators are
entitled to "do justice. It has been said that, short of 'complete irrationality', 'they may fashion the law to fit the facts before them'" (Lentine v.
Fundaro, 29 N.Y.2d 382, 386, 328 N.Y.S.2d 418, 422, 278 N.E.2d 633,
636, quoting Matter of National Cash Register Co. [Wilson], 8 N.Y.2d
377, 383, 208 N.Y.S.2d 951, 955, 171 N.E.2d 302, 305, and Matter of
Exercycle Corp. [Maratta], 9 N.Y.2d 329, 336, 214 N.Y.S.2d 353, 357,
174 N.E.2d 463, 466; see, also, Matter of Spectrum Fabrics Corp. [Main
St. Fashions], 309 N.Y. 709, 128 N.E.2d 416, *affg.*, 285 App. Div. 710, 139

N.Y.S.2d 612). The award made here was neither irrational nor unjust. Indeed, defendant has not denied that its actions were designed to harass and intimidate plaintiff, as she claimed and the arbitrators obviously concluded. Hence, the award was within the power vested in the arbitrator.

As we have noted, plaintiff sought punitive damages as listed and set forth in the demand for arbitration, presenting of course a threshold question to which defendant failed to respond and, in fact, summarily refused to address himself. In effect, therefore, defendant's failure to act, respond or contest the claim is tantamount to a waiver of any objection thereto and, indeed, is equivalent to an agreement to arbitrate the allegation now complained of.

Accordingly, the order of the Appellate Division should be affirmed.

Jasen, Fuchsberg and Cooke, JJ., concur with Breitel, C.J.

Gabrielli, J., dissents and votes to affirm in a separate opinion in which Jones and Wachtler, JJ., concur.

Order modified, without costs, in accordance with the opinion herein and, as so modified, affirmed.

NOTE

1. The principal case is annotated at 83 A.L.R.3d 1024. Suppose the arbitration clause in the parties' contract had explicitly authorized an award of punitive damages in any amount the arbitrator thought fair and reasonable. Do you think Judge Breitel's analysis of the case would have been affected? Even if it had contained such a provision, couldn't one still distinguish the contract at issue here from the agreement involved in the *Associated General Contractors* case (discussed in both the majority and dissenting opinions)?

Judge Breitel's conclusion that the plaintiff's punitive damages should be disallowed appears to rest on considerations of public policy. Couldn't it have been based as easily, and perhaps less controversially, on familiar principles of contract interpretation? If the arbitrator thought the parties meant one thing, and Judge Breitel thought they meant another, whose interpretation should control (in the absence of any considerations of public policy)?

2. The facts in Matter of Aimcee Wholesale Corp., cited in the principal case, were these: Aimcee had purchased merchandise from Tomar Products, Inc. under a sales contract that contained a broad arbitration clause stating that "[a]ny controversy or claim arising out of or relating to" the contract was to be submitted to arbitration. Maintaining that the merchandise was defective, Aimcee sought arbitration of its claim for damages. Tomar responded by bringing a legal action against Aimcee for breach of contract. Aimcee then demanded that Tomar's counterclaim also be submitted to arbitration, and Tomar agreed. At this point, how-

ever, Tomar interposed a second counterclaim based on the allegation that Aimcee had violated certain federal and state antitrust laws by exacting a discriminatory reduction in the price of the goods it was purchasing. Aimcee moved to stay arbitration of Tomar's antitrust claims. Tomar consented to the stay with respect to its federal antitrust claim, but sought arbitration of its parallel state law claim. The trial court denied Aimcee's motion on the grounds that Tomar's state law antitrust claim was arbitrable. Following an affirmance by the Appellate Division, the Court of Appeals reversed. Writing for a unanimous court, Judge Keating had this to say:

> Arbitrators are not bound by rules of law and their decisions are essentially final. Certainly the awards may not be set aside for misapplication of the law (CPLR 7511). Even if our courts were to review the merits of the arbitrators' decision in antitrust cases, errors may not even appear in the record which need not be kept in any case. More important, arbitrators are not obliged to give reasons for their rulings or awards. Thus our courts may be called upon to enforce arbitration awards which are directly at variance with statutory law and judicial decision interpreting that law. Furthermore, there is no way to assure consistency of interpretation or application. The same conduct could be condemned or condoned by different arbitrators.
>
> If the arbitrators here should decide wrongly that the goods were or were not defective, the injustice done is essentially only to the parties concerned. If, however, they should proceed to decide erroneously that there was or was not a violation of the Donnelly Act [the New York antitrust statute at issue in the case], the injury extends to the people of the State as a whole. To illustrate, if Tomar is correct in its claim that the rebate here violates the Donnelly Act, and the arbitration panel should deny the claim, then in effect the arbitrators have permitted Aimcee to receive an unjustifiable price reduction which weakens the position of Aimcee's competitors. Conversely, if Tomar is incorrect in its contention, but the arbitrators should rule in its favor, then the award may be passed on to the consumer in the form of higher prices.
>
> Thus the issue which the arbitrators will be called upon to decide transcends the private interests of the parties. It is not simply that arbitrators can impose unnecessarily restrictive or lenient standards. The evil is that, if the enforcement of antitrust policies is left in the hands of arbitrators, erroneous decisions will have adverse consequences for the public in general, and the guardians of the public interest, the courts, will have no say in the results reached. To paraphrase the court's language in the Manhattan Stor. & Warehouse case, the parties will obtain a decision here on a matter of moment to the public at large, although the State is not a party to the proceedings, and no party to the proceedings is authorized to defend the interests of the public. . . .
>
> The realities of the commercial arbitration process bolster the conclusion that commercial arbitration is not a proper mechanism for a determination as to whether the price rebate here was discriminatory and violated the Donnelly Act. Arbitrators are often businessmen chosen usually for

their familiarity with the practices of a particular industry or for their expertise with the real issues in dispute, which are almost always unrelated to antitrust claims. This problem is aggravated by the fact that the enforcement of the State's antitrust policy has often been a by-product of Federal enforcement. Thus, even if we were to assume that we have knowledgeable arbitrators, who would willingly and earnestly seek to follow judicial precedent, we cannot ignore the fact that many of the most important issues in antitrust law, including specifically those in this case, have never been resolved definitely under New York law. This is shown by the fact that it has never been determined whether price discrimination would violate the Donnelly Act.

Moreover, we cannot overlook the fact that many undeserving litigants are awarded damages in antitrust cases. Arbitrators are more likely to give more consideration to equitable notions such as waiver, estoppel and *in pari delicto*. Every time this is done, however, the deterrent effect of the law on antitrust violations is severely diminished.

21 N.Y.2d 621, 626-629, 237 N.E.2d 223, 225-227 (1968).

KEMBLE v. FARREN

6 Bing. 141, 130 Eng. Rep. 1234 (C.P. 1829)

TINDAL, C.J. This is a rule which calls upon the Defendant to shew cause why the verdict, which has been entered for the Plaintiff for £750, should not be increased to £1000.

The action was brought upon an agreement made between the Plaintiff and the Defendant, whereby the Defendant agreed to act as a principal comedian at the Theatre Royal, Covent Garden, during the four then next seasons, commencing October 1828, and also to conform in all things to the usual regulations of the said Theatre Royal, Covent Garden; and the Plaintiff agreed to pay Defendant £3. 6s. 8d. every night on which the theatre should be open for theatrical performances, during the next four seasons, and that the Defendant should be allowed one benefit night during each season, on certain terms therein specified. And the agreement contained a clause, that if either of the parties should neglect or refuse to fulfill the said agreement, or any part thereof, or any stipulation therein contained, such party should pay to the other the sum of £1000, to which sum it was thereby agreed that the damages sustained by any such omission, neglect, or refusal, should amount; and which sum was thereby declared by the said parties to be liquidated and ascertained damages, and not a penalty or penal sum, or in the nature thereof.

The breach alleged in the declaration was, that the Defendant refused to act during the second season, for which breach, the jury, upon the trial, assessed the damages at £750; which damages the Plaintiff contends ought by the terms of the agreement to have been assessed at £1000.

It is, undoubtedly, difficult to suppose any words more precise or explicit than those used in the agreement; the same declaring not only affirmatively that the sum of £1000 should be taken as liquidated damages, but negatively also that it should not be considered as a penalty, or in the nature thereof. And if the clause had been limited to breaches which were of an uncertain nature and amount, we should have thought it would have had the effect of ascertaining the damages upon any such breach at £1000. For we see nothing illegal or unreasonable in the parties, by their mutual agreement, settling the amount of damages, uncertain in their nature, at any sum upon which they may agree. In many cases, such an agreement fixes that which is almost impossible to be accurately ascertained; and in all cases, it saves the expense and difficulty of bringing witnesses to that point. But in the present case, the clause is not so confined; it extends to the breach of any stipulation by either party. If, therefore, on the one hand, the Plaintiff had neglected to make a single payment of £3. 6s. 8d. per day, or on the other hand, the Defendant had refused to conform to any usual regulation of the theatre, however minute or unimportant, it must have been contended that the clause in question, in either case, would have given the stipulated damages of £1000. But that a very large sum should become immediately payable, in consequence of the nonpayment of a very small sum, and that the former should not be considered as a penalty, appears to be a contradiction in terms; the case being precisely that in which courts of equity have always relieved, and against which courts of law have, in modern times, endeavoured to relieve, by directing juries to assess the real damages sustained by the breach of the agreement. It has been argued at the bar, that the liquidated damages apply to those breaches of the agreement only which are in their nature uncertain, leaving those which are certain to a distinct remedy, by the verdict of a jury. But we can only say, if such is the intention of the parties they have not expressed it; but have made the clause relate, by express and positive terms, to all breaches of every kind. We cannot, therefore, distinguish this case, in principle, from that of Astley v. Weldon (2 B. & P. 346), in which it was stipulated, that either of the parties neglecting to perform the agreement should pay to the other of them the full sum of £200, to be recovered in his Majesty's courts at Westminster. Here there was a distinct agreement, that the sum stipulated should be liquidated and ascertained damages: there were clauses in the agreement, some sounding in uncertain damages, others relating to certain pecuniary payments; the action was brought for the breach of a clause of an uncertain nature; and yet it was held by the Court, that for this very reason it would be absurd to construe the sum inserted in the agreement as liquidated damages and it was held to be a penal sum only. As this case appears to us to be decided on a clear and intelligible principle, and to apply to that under consideration, we think it right to adhere to it, and this makes it unnecessary to consider the subsequent cases, which do not in any way break in upon it. The consequence is, we think the present verdict should stand, and the rule for increasing the damages be discharged.

Rule discharged.

McCARTHY v. TALLY

46 Cal. 2d 577, 297 P.2d 981 (In Bank, 1956)

CARTER, Justice. These two actions arose because of disputes concerning a ten-year lease of a summer resort known as Glenn Ranch owned by Tally and leased by him and his father to Mr. and Mrs. McCarthy.[67] In the first action Harold McCarthy sought declaratory relief and damages for fraud against Seymour Tally; Tally later brought an action against McCarthy in which he sought to establish certain rights under the lease in question and for the appointment of a receiver. The actions were consolidated for trial. The court made separate findings in each case and entered separate judgments. In the McCarthy case, the judgment was in favor of Tally; in the Tally case, judgment was rendered against McCarthy in the sum of $1,414.14 (unpaid rent and taxes), together with $2,000 as attorney's fees, $1,038.50 as costs and charges of the receiver appointed, $67.50 for certain other costs and disbursements, and it was concluded that plaintiff Tally was not entitled to recover any sum as liquidated damages. McCarthy was adjudged entitled to the sum of $821.32 for unearned premium of an insurance policy owned by him and retained by Tally. McCarthy appealed from the whole of the judgment in the McCarthy case except that portion denying Tally liquidated damages; Tally appealed only from that portion of the judgment in the Tally case denying him liquidated damages.

On July 17, 1944, T. L. Tally and Thomas Seymour Tally, as lessors, and Harold McCarthy and his wife, Barbara, as lessees, executed an agreement in writing by which the Tallys leased to the McCarthys certain real and personal property in the San Bernardino mountains, known as the "Glenn Ranch." The lease was for a term of ten years, at an annual rental of $10,000 and provided for the continuance of the operation of a hotel and summer resort then being operated by the Tallys.

The McCarthys entered into possession on August 1, 1944, operated the business and paid the rent until October 31, 1950. On or about November 28, 1950, Tally served McCarthy with a notice to pay rent or vacate the premises. On or about December 1, 1950, McCarthy served Tally with a notice that he had vacated and surrendered the property and that he was delivering possession to Tally. On January 4, 1951, a receiver was appointed to take charge of the business and the ranch.

---

67. McCarthy succeeded to the interest of his co-lessee wife upon her death; Tally succeeded to the interest of his co-lessor father upon his death.

In the McCarthy action, McCarthy sought damages on the theory that
certain false statements had been made by Tally to him to induce the
execution of the lease and that he had relied on such false representations. It was alleged that Tally had told him that the Glenn Ranch had
produced a net annual income of $27,000 in previous years, and that the
ranch was in "excellent," "very good," "wonderful" condition, and that
these representations were known by Tally to be untrue. Concerning
both allegations of fraudulent representations, the evidence was in sharp
conflict. With respect to the net income of the ranch, Tally testified that
he had not made the alleged statements, but that he had stated that
because of a decided increase in the business in the year in which the
McCarthys took over, it was expected that the net income would better
$27,000; that the maximum income he had ever made on the ranch was
$22,000 the previous year. The trial court found that the alleged fraudu-
lent misrepresentations as to income had not been made and the evidence is sufficient to support the finding.

In connection with the alleged representations concerning the condition of the ranch, the trial court found that Tally and his wife truthfully
represented to the McCarthys that the property and facilities referred to
in the lease were in "good operating condition." McCarthy testified that
at the time he took over the operation of the summer resort the place was
full of guests and reservations had been made for guests later in the year.
The record shows that McCarthy had inspected the ranch; that he had
been there as a guest of the Tallys on several occasions prior to leasing it;
that his wife had been there almost every week in 1943 and quite often in
1944. The record also shows that the ranch was one which had been
operated for many years as a summer resort and that McCarthy knew that
some of the buildings were very old. This evidence is sufficient to support
the finding of the trial court that the alleged fraudulent representations
were untrue and that it was true that the ranch was in good operating
condition. McCarthy's attempt to reargue the evidence and the weight
thereof in this court is unavailing. As we have frequently said, it is the
general rule on appeal that an appellate court will view the evidence in
the light most favorable to the respondent and will not weigh the evidence. An appellate court will indulge all intendments and reasonable
inferences which favor sustaining the finding of the trier of fact and will
not disturb that finding when there is substantial evidence in the record
in support thereof. Berniker v. Berniker, 30 Cal. 2d 439, 444, 182 P.2d
557.

A more troublesome point is that relating to the provision for liquidated damages. Paragraph (28) of the lease provides:

> That it is and will be impracticable and extremely difficult to fix the
> actual damages to said Parcel Four[68] in the event of termination of this

68. Parcel Four is described in the lease as "The said business and the goodwill thereof,
and the right to the use of the trade name of Glenn Ranch."

lease by the lessors for cause, or by reason of abandonment of the demised property by the lessees, and that the sum of $10,000.00 shall be and said sum is hereby fixed as the amount of the liquidated damages in the event of such termination or such abandonment; that said lessees have this day executed to the lessors a demand note for $10,000[69] secured by a deed of trust upon real property in Riverside County, California, to evidence and secure the payment of such liquidated damages; that said lessees may at any time deposit with the lessors the sum of $10,000.00 in lieu of said note and deed of trust;

That in the event said lessors successfully prosecute proceedings to terminate this lease for cause, the Court may, in addition to actual damages by reason of loss with respect to Parcels One, Two and Three, award to said lessors liquidated damages in the sum of $10,000.00 by reason of loss with respect to Parcel Four;

That in the event said lessees abandon and give up possession of said demised property to the lessors, said lessees shall be liable to the lessors for actual damages by reason of loss with respect to Parcels One, Two and Three, plus liquidated damages in the sum of $10,000.00 by reason of loss with respect to Parcel Four;

That in the event of such termination or such abandonment, the liquidated damages aforesaid shall be paid to the lessors from said deposit or from the proceeds derived from a sale under said Deed of Trust; that the payment of actual and liquidated damages, as aforesaid, shall fully satisfy all obligations of lessees under and by virtue of the provisions hereof.

Paragraph (29) provides

That default shall not be deemed to have occurred with respect to any of the terms, covenants and conditions herein set forth, other than the payment of the aforesaid installments of rental, unless the lessees, within ten days after written notice of the nature of the asserted breach, shall have failed to cure such breach.

Section 1670 of the Civil Code provides that "Every contract by which the amount of damage to be paid, or other compensation to be made, for a breach of an obligation, is determined in anticipation thereof, is to that extent void, except as expressly provided in the next section."

Section 1671 provides that "the parties to a contract may agree therein upon an amount which shall be presumed to be the amount of damage sustained by a breach thereof, when, from the nature of the case, it would be impracticable or extremely difficult to fix the actual damage."

Tally alleged, and the trial court found, that under the circumstances existing at the time the contract was entered into, it would have been impracticable or extremely difficult for actual damages to be fixed in the event of a breach of the conditions of the lease. In the McCarthy action, however, the trial court in amended findings found that in the event of a

---

69. Cash had been substituted therefor prior to trial.

breach the damages would *not* be difficult of ascertainment. It has been
held that whether or not damages would be impracticable or extremely
difficult to fix is a question of fact in each case for the trier of fact, Rice v.
Schmid, 18 Cal. 2d 382, 385, 115 P.2d 498, 138 A.L.R. 589; Better Food
Markets v. American District Telegraph Co., 40 Cal. 2d 179, 184, 253
P.2d 10, 42 A.L.R.2d 580; Atkinson v. Pacific Fire Extinguisher Co., 40
Cal. 2d 192, 195, 253 P.2d 18, unless the circumstances existing at the
time of making the stipulation are not in dispute and permit of but one
conclusion.

Ordinarily, provisions for liquidated damages will not lie for failure to
pay rent as provided in the lease. . . . This is so because in such a case
there is no presumption that the amount of damages which may result
from a tenant's breach of a covenant to pay rent is impossible or extremely difficult to fix. In the present case, however, while the breach was
failure to pay rent, the liquidated damage provision in the lease related to
a possible injury to the goodwill of the business of operating a summer
resort. Where a contract providing for the sale of the goodwill of a business was concerned, it has been held that an agreement for liquidated
damages was proper and that the plaintiff was required only to prove a
breach of the contract in order to recover such liquidated damages. . . .

We have here a breach of the contract occasioned by McCarthy's
failure to pay rent. The record shows that the breach occurred in November after the summer resort had been closed for the season. The court
found, specifically, that "there is no evidence establishing any damage to
or loss of said goodwill" and concluded that Tally was not entitled to
recover the agreed-upon sum of $10,000 as liquidated damages for the
possible injury to the goodwill of the business. The record bears out the
finding of the trial court that the goodwill of the business had not been
affected by McCarthy's failure to pay rent.

In Kelly v. McDonald, 98 Cal. App. 121, 125, 276 P. 404, 406, it was
held:

> While the term "liquidated damages" does imply that the parties have ascer-
> tained and agreed upon a sum which they assume will adequately compen-
> sate for a breach of the contract, this does not necessarily mean that the
> amount specified must be paid whether damages result from the breach or
> not. The very term of "damages" contemplates an injury sustained or detri-
> ment resulting from the breach of a contract or the non-performance of a
> duty. As the court said in Starr v. Lee, *supra* [88 Cal. App. 344, 348, 263 P.
> 376]: "We find authorities holding that recovery cannot be had when the
> evidence shows that no damage at all resulted from the breach." The ex-
> ception to the general rule to the effect that the predetermined amount of
> damages for the breach of an obligation is void, as that exception is ex-
> pressed in section 1671 of the Civil Code does not purport to declare that
> an amount of liquidated damages agreed upon shall be *conclusively* pre-
> sumed to be the exact figure which will adequately compensate for the

breach of contract. This section merely asserts that it is "presumed to be the amount of damages sustained." *This presumption may be rebutted by proof that no detriment whatever resulted from the breach.*

(Emphasis added.)

We held in Better Food Markets v. American District Telegraph Co., 40 Cal. 2d 179, 187, 253 P.2d 10, 15, 42 A.L.R.2d 580, that the amount agreed upon as liquidated damages "must represent the result of a reasonable endeavor by the parties to estimate a fair average compensation for any loss that may be sustained." Dyer Bros. Golden West Iron Works v. Central Iron Works, 182 Cal. 588, 189 P. 445; Rice v. Schmid, 18 Cal. 2d 382, 386, 115 P.2d 498, 138 A.L.R. 589; Rest. Contracts, §339, p. 554.[70] There is nothing in the record to show that the sum of $10,000 agreed upon as liquidated damages represented a "reasonable endeavor" to estimate the actual damage to be sustained in the event of a breach nor is there any finding on the subject by the trial court. As we have heretofore pointed out, the trial court in the Tally case found that damages would be difficult of ascertainment; in the McCarthy case; it was found that such damages would not be difficult of ascertainment. In the Tally case the trial court's conclusion that liquidated damages were not recoverable was obviously based on its finding that no actual damage had been sustained; in the McCarthy case, the conclusion was based on the finding that the provision for liquidated damages was void and ineffectual because damages were not difficult of ascertainment. Because of these inconsistent findings it is impossible for us to determine which of the two theories motivated the trial court's judgment in each case and we must, therefore, reverse the judgments.

The general rule in the United States with respect to provisions for liquidated damages appears to be that the plaintiff must plead and prove that at the time the contract was entered into damages in the event of a breach of the contract would be difficult of ascertainment; that the sum agreed upon represented a reasonable attempt to ascertain what such damages would be; and that a breach of the contract had occurred. A note in 34 A.L.R. 1336, 1341, points out that

> The majority of the cases hold that the amount stipulated in the contract as liquidated damages for a breach thereof, and which is regarded by the courts as liquidated damages, and not as a penalty, may be recovered in the event of a breach of the contract, even though no actual damages are suffered as a consequence of such breach

70. This reasonable endeavor to ascertain, in advance, the loss which may result from a possible breach distinguishes a provision for liquidated damages from one for a penalty since the characteristic feature of a penalty is its lack of any proportionate relation to the damage which may actually stem from the breach of a contract. Muldoon v. Lynch, 66 Cal. 536, 6 P. 417; People v. Central Pacific R. Co., 76 Cal. 29, 18 P. 90; Dyer Bros. Golden West Iron Works v. Central Iron Works, 182 Cal. 588, 189 P. 445.

(listing cases from Arkansas, Florida, Illinois, Indiana, Iowa, Kansas, Kentucky, Maryland, Michigan, Minnesota, New York, Oregon, Pennsylvania, Texas, Washington, West Virginia and Canada). The following statement from 15 Am. Jur., Damages, section 263, pages 696-697, is to the same effect:

> The majority of the cases hold that the amount stipulated in the contract as liquidated damages for a breach thereof, and which is regarded by the courts as liquidated damages, and not as a penalty, may be recovered in the event of a breach of the contract, even though no actual damages are suffered as a consequence of such breach. In many of the cases there are statements to the effect that actual damages need not be pleaded or proved in order to recover the stipulated amount. According to this view, the only evidence proper or necessary on this point is that the contract has been broken. In support of this rule it is said that the question of reasonableness is to be determined as of the time of the making of the contract — that is, in regard to any possible amount of damages which may be conceived to have been within the contemplation of the parties at that time — and that neither the intention of the parties nor the construction of the contract can depend upon occurrences happening afterward, which were not in their contemplation when the contract was made.
>
> Some courts, however, have held that where no damage has been sustained from the breach of the contract, the amount which the contract stipulates as liquidated damages cannot be recovered, even upon the assumption that the provision is to be regarded as one for liquidated damages, rather than a penalty, and that a mere technical breach resulting in nominal damages is not sufficient, although, in some of the cases apparently so holding at least, the real explanation of the result would seem to be that the court, in view of the lack of actual damages, regarded the provision in question as one for a penalty, although denominated by the contract itself as "liquidated damages."
>
> Under a provision construed to be a penalty nothing can be recovered for a breach of the contract where no actual damages appear.

We hold that in order to recover on a contract provision for liquidated damages the plaintiff must plead and prove that at the time the contract was entered into damages in the event of a breach would be impracticable or extremely difficult of ascertainment; that the sum agreed upon represented a reasonable endeavor to ascertain what such damages would be; and that a breach of the contract had occurred. In other words, no actual damage is necessary in order to recover under a liquidated damages provision provided that the case is, in other respects, a proper one under the conditions set forth in section 1671 of the Civil Code. As we have heretofore pointed out, there is, in the case under consideration, no finding that the sum of $10,000 represented a reasonable endeavor by the parties to ascertain what the damages would be in the event of a breach, and the findings as to whether, at the time the contract was entered into, the damages would be extremely difficult or impracticable of ascertainment in the event of a breach were fatally inconsistent.

The liquidated damages provision here involved related to the goodwill of a summer resort business. As we have heretofore pointed out, it has been held that a breach affecting the goodwill of a business may cause damages which, at the time the contract was entered into, may be impracticable or extremely difficult of ascertainment. Whether or not a breach such as occurred here in the non-operating months of the summer resort was within the contemplation of the parties is an issue to be pleaded and proved on a re-trial of the actions. It appears to us that if such a breach was within the contemplation of the parties, that the sum of $10,000 might not represent a reasonable endeavor to ascertain what the damages would be in the event of such a breach and that the provision might be invalid because of the time at which the breach occurred.

Any language in Kelly v. McDonald, 98 Cal. App. 121, 276 P. 404, and Starr v. Lee, 88 Cal. App. 344, 263 P. 376, contrary to the views herein expressed is disapproved.

McCarthy contends that the court erred in appointing a receiver and that the court wrongfully determined the costs and charges of such receiver. The clerk's transcript in the Tally case shows that the receiver was appointed on January 4, 1951, and that no appeal was taken from the order appointing the receiver. Such an order is appealable, Code Civ. Proc. §963(2), and will not be reviewed on appeal from the final judgment. 22 Cal. Jur., §61, p. 476; Weygandt v. Larson, 130 Cal. App. 304, 310, 19 P.2d 852.

Other contentions of the parties do not merit discussion.

The judgments are reversed.

NOTE

1. Do you take it that, in the century and a quarter that elapsed between Kemble v. Farren and McCarthy v. Tally, judicial attitudes toward liquidated damage clauses had become more receptive? Or more hostile? The provisions of the California Civil Code referred to in the opinion are from the so-called Field Code, originally drafted by David Dudley Field in the 1850s for enactment in New York.

2. Better Food Markets v. American District Telegraph Co., 40 Cal. 2d 179, 253 P.2d 10 (1953), referred to in the McCarthy opinion, is of interest. Shenk, J., in an opinion concurred in by five of the other Judges, stated the case as follows:

> This is an action brought on counts alleged in tort and in contract wherein the plaintiff seeks to recover damages resulting from the alleged failure of the defendants to properly transmit burglar alarm signals to their

own guards and to the headquarters of the municipal police department. Such failure is alleged to have permitted a burglar to escape with the sum of $35,930 taken from the plaintiff's food market.

On the first trial the court granted a motion for nonsuit in behalf of all the defendants except the American District Telegraph Company, and ordered judgment for those defendants. As against the defendant American District Telegraph Company the jury on the first trial found for the plaintiff, but a new trial was granted on the ground of insufficiency of the evidence. On the second trial the jury was unable to agree and was dismissed. Thereafter the defendant successfully moved for a directed verdict pursuant to section 630 of the Code of Civil Procedure (ordering judgment where motion for directed verdict should have been, but was not, granted), and the court ordered judgment for the defendant. On this appeal taken from that judgment the plaintiff contends that there is sufficient evidence of the defendant's negligence and breach of contract to sustain a verdict for the plaintiff, and that it was error to grant the motion for a directed verdict.

In June of 1947 the parties entered into a written agreement whereby the defendant was to install and maintain its standard "Central Station Burglar Alarm and Holdup System" in the plaintiff's food market. The contract provided that the defendant

> on receipt of a burglar alarm signal from the Subscriber's [plaintiff's] premises, agrees to send to said premises, its representatives to act as agent of and in the interest of the Subscriber. . . . The Subscriber hereby authorizes and directs the Contractor [defendant] to cause the arrest of any person or persons unauthorized to enter his premises and to hold him or them until released by the Subscriber. . . . The Contractor, on receipt of a holdup alarm signal from the Subscriber's premises, agrees to transmit the alarm promptly to headquarters of the public police department.

Viewing the evidence in the light most favorable to the plaintiff on this appeal from a judgment on a directed verdict for the defendant, Anthony v. Hobbie, 25 Cal. 2d 814, 155 P.2d 826, the following facts were established: On November 16, 1947, at approximately 7:30 p. m. the assistant manager of the plaintiff's market set the burglar alarm system and locked the building. As he entered his car in the parking lot he was accosted by an armed robber and at gun point forced to return and open the store, the inner office and the safe. The robber took the contents of the safe, taped the assistant manager, and left. Approximately 14 minutes elapsed between the time when the store was reopened and when the robber left the store with the loot. During this period signals were being received at the defendant's central station indicating the sequence of the opening and closing of the doors. The defendant's operators at the central station did not call a guard or inform the police until 7:51, 9 minutes after the signal indicating that the safe had been opened, was received. The assistant manager had succeeded in knocking a telephone off the hook and calling for help at approximately 7:50. The police arrived at the market at 7:52, within one minute after receiving a call. The defendant's guards arrived shortly thereafter. The assistant manager's watch was broken at the time he was taped and the hands had stopped at 7:50.

Under the circumstances of this case it would have been reasonable to conclude that the defendant had a duty to call the police as well as its own guards to the plaintiff's premises. Promptness being the essence of the defendant's obligation, its delay in acting could reasonably be found to be an omission to render the agreed service and a failure of performance of the contract.

There is evidence upon which it could have been found that the loss was the proximate result of the defendant's delay in responding to the alarms. There was but one individual committing the burglary. He acted deliberately and there is reason to believe that the agreement between the parties was entered into with the intention of providing for the apprehension of such a person before he left the premises. The time and distance factors indicate that this particular burglar may have been caught had the police and guards been called to the premises a few minutes earlier, and that the delay of nine minutes after the safe had been opened permitted the escape. Such probabilities are to be weighed in the light of common experience in such matters and present a triable issue of fact. There was substantial evidence from which a jury could have found that the plaintiff's loss was the proximate result of the defendant's breach of its contract. Therefore it was error for the trial court to order judgment for the defendant on its motion for a directed verdict.

There remains the question of the validity of the following provisions of the contract for liquidated damages:

> It is agreed by and between the parties that the Contractor is not an insurer, that the payments hereinbefore named are based solely on the value of the service in the maintenance of the system described, that it is impracticable and extremely difficult to fix the actual damages, if any, which may proximately result from a failure to perform such services and in case of failure to perform such services and a resulting loss its liability hereunder shall be limited to and fixed at the sum of fifty dollars as liquidated damages, and not as a penalty, and this liability shall be exclusive.

Id. at 182-184, 253 P.2d at 12-13.

The majority of the court held that, under the liquidated damage clause, the plaintiff's recovery was limited to $50. Carter, J., dissenting, wrote in part:

> This court holds the following provision a valid contract for liquidated damages:

> It is agreed by and between the parties that the Contractor [defendant] is not an insurer, that the payments hereinbefore named are *based solely on the value of the service in maintenance of the system described, that it is impracticable and extremely difficult to fix the actual damages, if any, which may proximately result from a failure to perform such services and in case of failure to perform such services and a resulting loss its liability hereunder shall be limited to and fixed at the sum of fifty dollars as liquidated damages,* and not as a penalty, and this liability shall be exclusive.

(Emphasis added.)

It is conceded that defendant failed to perform its duty; that plaintiff's loss resulted therefrom; that plaintiff's loss was the sum of $35,930 which was taken, by a burglar, from plaintiff's food market.

In order to uphold the so-called $50 liquidated damage provision, it was necessary for the majority to find that damages were "impracticable and extremely difficult" to fix at the time the contract was entered into, and further that the $50 provision bore a reasonable relation to any loss which the parties contemplated might be sustained as a result of a breach of the contract.

It is said in the majority opinion that "In determining this question [the losses which might be expected to occur] the court should place itself in the position of the parties at the time the contract was made and should consider the nature of the breaches that might occur and any consequences that were reasonably foreseeable." Placing myself in the position of the parties at the time the contract was entered into, I would say that one way of ascertaining the loss which might occur, was to take an average of the amount of cash left in the safe in the store overnight; an inventory of the average merchandise kept in the store. If the losses sustained did not approximate the damages provided for by the parties, the rule set forth in Kothe v. R. C. Taylor Trust, 280 U.S. 224, 50 S. Ct. 142, 74 L. Ed. 382, would be applicable. There the parties provided for excessive liquidated damages, and the Supreme Court held that the damages provided for in the contract bore no reasonable relation to the probable loss to be sustained and held the provision a penalty and therefore unenforceable. It is the rule that the validity of the provision must be proved by the one seeking to enforce it. And as is said in the majority opinion

> Where a trial court does find that such a situation did exist [impracticability or extreme difficulty in fixing damages] but it appears to a reviewing court that from the nature of the possible detriment the damages could have been fixed without difficulty, a judgment based on the finding will be reversed, Stark v. Shemada, *supra*, 187 Cal. 785, 204 P. 214.

It is also said in the majority opinion that "The question becomes one of law where the facts are not in dispute and admit of but a single conclusion." Even if the facts are not in dispute, they seldom admit of but one conclusion. In this case, one jury found for plaintiff and the second jury disagreed. Does this not prove that these facts admit of more than one conclusion? I think it does. It is also said here that whether damages are impracticable, or extremely difficult, to fix is "except on admitted facts . . . generally a question to be resolved by the trier of fact. . . ." In Rice v. Schmid, 18 Cal. 2d 382, 115 P.2d 498 (the latest pronouncement of this court on this subject), it was held that in "each instance" it was a question of fact. Further, even on admitted facts, more than one inference can be, and is often, drawn. See Black v. Black, 91 Cal. App. 2d 328, 204 P.2d 950 (stipulated facts; different inferences possible); Crisman v. Lanterman, 149 Cal. 647, 87 P. 89 (agreed statement of facts; different inferences possible); Anderson v. Thacher, 76 Cal. App. 2d 50, 172 P.2d 533 (evidence not conflicting; conflicting inferences therefrom possible); Rench v. McMullen, 82 Cal. App. 2d 872, 187 P.2d 111 (only documentary evidence offered was subject to conflicting inferences). Again, this court goes to great lengths to uphold the validity of a provision such as this. Note the "possibilities" which it considers might have happened from a failure of the burglar detection system. It is said that

> Entrances to the building after working hours might be made by persons having authority as well as by burglars or by persons bent on mischief. They might or might not cause damage. There might be the theft of a ham, or of a truckload of goods, or the contents of a safe. There might be a breaking in for the purpose of theft and no theft. If money was taken it might be a few dollars or many thousands. Books might be tampered with, or papers abstracted. Damage might be caused in many ways that were not foreseeable.

If persons having authority to enter did so, plaintiff would, in all probability, not have sued the defendant, or, if it had done so, that would have been a matter of defense at the trial. If a ham had been stolen, the provision for $50 in all probability, would have been held a penalty as disproportionate to the loss involved. These same arguments apply to the balance of the "reasoning" of the majority.

It is also necessary that the amount agreed upon by the parties "represent the result of a reasonable endeavor by the parties to estimate a fair average compensation for any loss that may be sustained. Dyer Bros. Golden West Iron Wks. v. Central Iron Wks., *supra*, 182 Cal. 588, 189 P. 445; Rice v. Schmid, *supra*, 18 Cal. 2d 382, 386, 115 P.2d 498, Restatement, Contracts, §339, p. 554." In other words, the amount agreed upon must bear some reasonable relation to the losses which might occur as a result of a breach. In my opinion, the $50 provision bears no reasonable relation to any amount which might have been lost by a failure of the system to operate.

Id. at 189-191, 253 P.2d at 16-17 (Carter, J., dissenting).

3. Fritz, "Underliquidated" Damages as Limitation of Liability, 33 Texas L. Rev. 196, 218-219 (1954) comments, with respect to the *Better Food Markets* case:

> However desirable the result may be under the circumstances, it seems fair to say that it was reached only by dint of a bold disregard for the realities of the situation if the court [i.e., the majority] can be taken to have meant what it said. . . . [T]he clause was intended not to liquidate damages but to limit the defendant's liability.

According to Professor Fritz, counsel for defendant in the *Better Food Markets* case did not argue the "limitation of liability" point, but counsel in a companion case, Atkinson v. Pacific Fire Extinguisher Co., 40 Cal. 2d 192, 253 P.2d 18 (1953), did. Shenk, J., who wrote the majority opinion (Carter, J., dissenting) in *Atkinson*, commented briefly with respect to the "limitation of liability" argument: "The language employed [in the contract clause] is clear and unambiguous and does not attempt to limit damages but rather to provide a fixed amount in the event of a breach,

whether the actual damages should be greater or less than that amount."
40 Cal. 2d at 198. If clauses like those in the *Better Food Markets* and
Atkinson cases are taken as attempts to limit liability rather than to liquidate damages, would the provisions of §§1670, 1671 of the Civil Code,
quoted in the opinion in the *McCarthy* case, be applicable? Do you think
the distinction Professor Fritz draws is a tenable one?

4. Priebe & Sons v. United States, 332 U.S. 407, 68 S. Ct. 123, 92 L.
Ed. 32 (1947), involved the following facts (as they are stated in the
majority opinion of Mr. Justice Douglas):

> Shortly after the enactment of the Lend-Lease Act of March 11, 1941, 55
> Stat. 31, 22 U.S.C. (Supp. V, 1946), §411 et seq., the United States acting
> through agencies of the Department of Agriculture embarked on a program
> of purchasing dried eggs for shipment to England and Russia. Petitioner
> [Priebe] agreed to furnish a quantity of dried eggs under that program to
> the Federal Surplus Commodities Corporation (FSCC). The contract
> called for "May 18 [1942] delivery" which date, according to the contract,
> "shall be the first day of a 10-day period within which the FSCC will accept
> delivery, the particular day within the period being at the FSCC's option."
> Petitioner was also required to have the eggs inspected, delivery to be
> accompanied by inspection and weight certificates.
>
> The contract contained two provisions respecting "liquidated damages."
> One, contained in paragraph 9, was applicable to delays in delivery. It has
> no application here, for as we shall see, deliveries were timely. The provi-
> sion for "liquidated damages" with which we are concerned is contained in
> paragraph 7 and is applicable to a totally different situation. It provides,
> with exceptions not material here, that "failure to have specified quantities
> of dried egg products inspected and ready for delivery by the date specified
> in the offer" will be cause for payment of "liquidated damages."
>
> On May 18, 1942, petitioner had not made delivery nor had the eggs
> been inspected. Inspection was, however, completed and certificates issued
> by May 22, which was prior to the time when FSCC asked for delivery. For
> it was not until May 26 that FSCC gave the first of several written notices
> for the shipment of eggs involved in this litigation. Petitioner made timely
> shipments pursuant to those instructions. Subsequently FSCC ascertained
> that petitioner's inspection certificates had been issued after May 18 and
> accordingly deducted from the price 10 cents per pound on the theory that
> the failure to have the eggs inspected and ready for delivery by May 18 was
> a default which put into operation the "liquidated damages" provision of
> the contract.

322 U.S. at 408-410.

After noting that "[t]oday the law does not look with disfavor upon
'liquidated damages' provisions in contracts" and approving the "useful
function" that such provisions perform "when damages are uncertain in
nature or amount or are unmeasurable" (id. at 411), Justice Douglas
concluded that the specific liquidated damages provision contained in
Paragraph 7 of the *Priebe* contract was nevertheless unenforceable.

[The provision in question] does not cover delays in deliveries. It can apply only where there was prompt performance when delivery was requested but where prompt delivery could not have been made, due to the absence of the certificates, had the request come on the first day when delivery could have been asked. A different situation might be presented had the contract provided for notice to the Government when the certificates were ready. Then we might possibly infer that promptness in obtaining them served an important function in the preparation of timetables for overseas shipments. But the contract contains no such provision; and it is shown that FSCC had no knowledge that the certificates were not ready on May 18 until long after deliveries had been made. So, it is apparent that the certificates were only an essential of proper delivery under this contract.

It likewise is apparent that the only thing which could possibly injure the government would be failure to get prompt performance when delivery was due. We have no doubt of the validity of the provision for "liquidated damages" when applied under those circumstances. . . . But under this procurement program delays of the contractors which did not interfere with prompt deliveries plainly would not occasion damage. That was as certain when the contract was made as it later proved to be. Yet that was the only situation to which the provision in question could ever apply. Under these circumstances this provision for "liquidated damages" could not possibly be a reasonable forecast of just compensation for the damage caused by a breach of contract. It might, as respondent suggests, have an in terrorem effect of encouraging prompt preparation for delivery. But the argument is a tacit admission that the provision was included not to make a fair estimate of damages to be suffered but to serve only as an added spur to performance. It is well-settled contract law that courts do not give their imprimatur to such arrangements. . . .

Id. at 412-413.

Is the *Priebe* case consistent with McCarthy v. Tally? With *Better Food Markets?* The report of the *Priebe* case contains dissenting opinions by Mr. Justice Black and Mr. Justice Frankfurter that are also worth reading.

KLAR v. H. & M. PARCEL ROOM, INC.

296 N.Y. 1044, 73 N.E.2d 912 (1947) (Memorandum Opinion)

Appeal, by permission of the Appellate Division of the Supreme Court in the first judicial department, from a judgment entered June 14, 1946, upon an order of said court which reversed, upon questions of fact and of law, a determination of the Appellate Term of the Supreme Court in the same judicial department (opinion 184 Misc. 477), entered in New York County, which modified a judgment of the Municipal Court of the City of New York, Borough of Manhattan (Katzenstein, J.), in favor of plaintiffs, by reducing plaintiff's recovery to the sum of $25 (the limit of loss appearing on the face of a parcel check) and affirming said judgment as so modified. The Appellate Division affirmed the judgment of the Municipal Court in favor of plaintiffs in the sum of $939.50 and in so doing reversed (1) a finding of the Appellate Term that it was adequately shown by the evidence that the limitation of defendant's liability to the sum of $25 was sufficiently brought to plaintiff's attention, and (2) a conclusion of law that defendant's liability under the contract was limited to $25. The action was brought to recover the alleged value of a paper-wrapped parcel of furs checked, for a fee of ten cents, by plaintiff's agent with defendant at its parcel room in the Hudson Terminal at 33d Street and Broadway in the city of New York. At the time of checking plaintiffs' agent received a parcel check of which the following is a facsimile:

> ### H. & M. PARCEL ROOM, INC.
> Broadway & 33rd St. Hudson Tunnels
> Open 7:00 A.M. — Close 1:00 A.M.
> (E. S. Time Except When Another Time is in Effect)
>
> —CONTRACT—
>
> This CONTRACT is made on the following conditions and in consideration of the low rate at which the service is performed. And its acceptance by the depositor. Expressly binds both parties to the CONTRACT.
>
> Charge — 10 cents for every 24 hours or fraction thereof. For each piece covered by this contract.
>
> Loss or damage — no claim shall be made in excess of $25 for loss or damage to any piece.
>
> Unclaimed articles remaining after 90 days may be sold at public or private sale to satisfy accrued charges.
>
> PHONE PEnnsylvania 6-2467   H. & M. PARCEL ROOM, INC.
> 34 — 971

The words were printed in black type on cream-colored cardboard, with the exception of the word "Contract" and the number "34 — 971" which were printed in red. Plaintiffs' agent testified that he did not read the parcel check when it was handed to him by the parcel room attendant; that he was not asked to read it and that he thought it were merely a receipt for the package. Two days later, when the check was presented at the parcel room, the package could not be found. It had, according to defendant, been delivered on another check. The Appellate Division stated, in substance, that parcel checking for nominal fee is generally deemed a bailment for hire and damages for a bailee's failure to exercise ordinary care measured by the reasonable value of the property checked and that, to limit its liability, the bailee must establish a special contract of which the bailor received reasonable notice and to which he assented.

In this case, the court ruled that it was a question of fact for the Trial Judge whether acceptance by the bailor of the receipt for the package constituted a contract between the parties limiting liability and that the Trial Judge's determination that there was no such agreement was amply supported by the evidence. . . .

Judgment affirmed, with costs; no opinion. . . .

NOTE

1. Does this case turn upon the same issue as the one involved in McCarthy v. Tally and Better Foods Markets v. American District Telegraph Co.? Suppose the plaintiff's agent testified that he had, in fact, read the parcel check. Would that affect your view of how the case should be decided?

2. A laundry and cleaning establishment unable to return a suit, when sued by the owner in damages, claims that its liability is limited by a clause in the contract which provides that "the maximum amount allowed for lost or damaged articles is twenty times the charge made for cleaning." Assuming it is to be established that the business is carried on in a negligent manner, will the clause limit liability effectively? See Alderslade v. Hendon Laundry, Ltd., 61 T.L.R. 216 (1945), noted in 61 L.Q. Rev. 115 (1945). Suppose the ticket contains the following additional clause: "Whilst every care is exercised in cleaning and dyeing garments, all orders are accepted at owner's risk entirely." Suppose, also, that this time the article of clothing is lost in some unknown way by a sub-contractor. See Davies v. Collins, 61 T.L.R. 218 (1945). When a customer has previous notice of a limitations clause because of earlier negotiations with the laundry owner regarding lost clothes, will the clause be enforced? Manhattan Co. v. Goldberg, D.C. Mun. App., 38 A.2d 172 (1944). When the customer's only notice of a limitation clause is its appearance on a blank receipt, the clause has been held ineffective. Palace Laundry Dry Cleaning Co. v. Cole, D.C. Mun. App., 41 A.2d 231 (1945). The American cases are collected in 175 A.L.R. 12.

UNIFORM COMMERCIAL CODE

§2-718.   LIQUIDATION OR LIMITATION OF DAMAGES; DEPOSITS

(1) Damages for breach by either party may be liquidated in the agreement but only at an amount which is reasonable in the light of the anticipated or actual harm caused by the breach, the difficulties of proof of loss, and the inconvenience or nonfeasibility of otherwise obtaining an adequate remedy. A term fixing unreasonably large liquidated damages is void as a penalty.

§2-719. CONTRACTUAL MODIFICATION OR LIMITATION OF
            REMEDY

(1)   Subject to the provisions of subsections (2) and (3) of this section
and of the preceding section on liquidation and limitation of damages,
    (a)   the agreement may provide for remedies in addition to or in sub-
          stitution for those provided in this Article and may limit or alter
          the measure of damages recoverable under this Article, as by
          limiting the buyer's remedies to return of the goods and repay-
          ment of the price or to repair and replacement of non-conform-
          ing goods or parts; and
    (b)   resort to a remedy as provided is optional unless the remedy is
          expressly agreed to be exclusive, in which case it is the sole rem-
          edy.
(2)   Where circumstances cause an exclusive or limited remedy to fail
of its essential purpose, remedy may be had as provided in this Act.
(3)   Consequential damages may be limited or excluded unless the
limitation or exclusion is unconscionable. Limitation of consequential
damages for injury to the person in the case of consumer goods is prima
facie unconscionable but limitation of damages where the loss is commercial is not.

NOTE

1.   Subsections (2), (3), and (4) of §2-718, which are not reprinted here,
deal with a defaulting buyer's right to recover down payments. Reconsider the Code provisions on damages reprinted *supra* p. 1132. Do you
take it that a liquidated damage clause, although "reasonable," would
nevertheless be unenforceable under §2-718(1) if one of the damage sections provided an "adequate remedy"? If that is so, can there ever be an
enforceable liquidated damage clause under the Code?

Under §§2-718(1) and 2-719, what result in Kemble v. Farren? Mc-
Carthy v. Tally? Better Food Markets v. American District Telegraph
Co.? Priebe & Sons v. United States? Klar v. H. & M. Parcel Room, Inc.?
Restatement Second §356(1) ("Liquidated Damages and Penalties") con-
tains language that is nearly identical to U.C.C. §2-718(1).

A liquidated damages provision requiring the payment of an amount
significantly larger than the harm actually suffered by the promisee may
or may not be enforced, depending upon whether the amount specified
in the provision represented (at the time of contracting) a reasonable
prediction of the damages likely to result from the promisor's breach. It

seems clear, however, that a provision will not be enforced if it deliberately sets liquidated damages at an amount greater than expected harm. A provision of this sort is a "penalty," and the distinction between penalties and legitimate liquidated damage provisions is the foundation on which this entire branch of contract doctrine rests. Recently, however, the soundness of the distinction has been questioned. Why *shouldn't* courts enforce penalty clauses, at least where they have been voluntarily agreed to by the parties? Consider the following argument:

[Penal clauses] have two important economic uses, and might be widely employed if they were permitted. First, . . . a penal clause may be useful to a buyer who has reason to believe that his normal money damages remedy will be inadequate and who wants to force his seller to buy his way out of the contract before breaching. Second, for a seller who has not yet developed a reputation for reliability, agreeing to a penal clause may be the cheapest way to persuade his buyers that he is willing and able to perform. . . .

The economic analysis of penal clauses makes clear that a clause of this sort cannot simply be condemned as nothing more than a side bet between the parties which serves no useful social purpose. A penal clause may often perform a role, either as a risk-allocating or an information-conveying device, which increases the economic value of an exchange. There is therefore no reason to think that every clause of this sort constitutes what earlier writers called an economically "sterile" agreement. And in any case, since many jurisdictions enforce wagering contracts but forbid the use of penal clauses, the nonenforcement of penal clauses cannot be explained by a generalized hostility to gambling. (Query: Is a wagering contract really economically sterile? How might it enhance the utility of the contracting parties?)

A second possible explanation for the hostility to penal clauses (although one which is rarely articulated) is that enforcement of such provisions would efface the fundamental distinction between punishment and compensation and give private parties the power to make breach of contract a crime. If private parties can create their own criminal law, one might argue, the power and authority of the state will be undermined.

This argument would have some force if, in addition to merely stipulating penalties for breach, the parties to a contract could also hire private protection agencies to enforce their bargains by any means necessary. Legal recognition of an arrangement of this sort would tend to weaken the state's monopoly on the means of violence and make it more difficult for the officers of the state to enforce even those agreements which fell within its jurisdiction. But legal recognition of penal clauses alone would not have this effect, so long as any private party wishing to enforce such a clause could do so only by invoking the power of the state through its judicial tribunals.

Furthermore, the economic utility of penal clauses makes it unreasonable to assume that almost all clauses of this sort are extracted under duress and that their flat prohibition is merely a convenient way of policing the bargaining process. Undoubtedly, some penal clauses ought to be invalidated because of duress, but an irrebuttable presumption is medicine which kills the patient. The important point is that even if courts were to continue to presume that every penal clause has been agreed to under duress, but to allow the introduction of evidence to rebut the presumption, it would be a doctrinal revolution.

A. Kronman & R. Posner, The Economics of Contract Law 260-261 (1978).

For a somewhat similar attack on the distinction between penalties and liquidated damages, see Goetz & Scott, Liquidated Damages, Penalties and the Just Compensation Principle: Some Notes on an Enforcement Model and a Theory of Efficient Breach, 77 Colum. L. Rev. 554 (1977). How might the distinction be defended? It has been suggested that penalty provisions give the promisee an incentive to make a (socially wasteful) investment in efforts to *induce* the promisor's breach and should therefore not be enforced. See Clarkson, Miller & Muris, Liquidated Damages v. Penalties: Sense or Nonsense?, 1978 Wis. L. Rev. 351. But doesn't the same problem exist where a liquidated damages clause, originally intended as a good faith estimate of the promisee's expected loss, sets damages at an amount well in excess of the parties' revised prediction of what the loss will be? Should a clause of this sort be enforced? *Would* it be enforced under the rule of McCarthy v. Tally? Under U.C.C. §2-718(1)?

As the passage quoted above suggests, a penal clause may be useful both to the promisee (since it gives him the power to compel the other party's performance if he wishes) and to the promisor (by providing him with the means to make his commitment more believable than it might otherwise be). Penal clauses are not, however, the only device the parties may employ to achieve these ends, and so long as such clauses remain unenforceable as a matter of law, alternative methods must be used. Consider the following case. A makes a long-term contract to supply B with parts B needs in his manufacturing process. B is worried that A may breach, after B (at great expense) has established a production line in reliance on A's contractual commitment. An enforceable penalty clause would increase B's confidence in A's promise. Alternatively, assuming that any clause of this kind would be unenforceable and therefore worthless, B may insist that A set up his own manufacturing process in such a way that, unless A makes expensive changes in his plant, he will only be able to produce parts for B's process. This is simply another way of raising the cost, to A, of breaking his promise, and A himself may benefit from such an arrangement since it gives him a way of increasing the credibility of his own promise. From the parties' point of view, the great advantage of an arrangement of this sort is that it is self-executing, that is to say, it is an arrangement whose effectiveness does not depend upon judicial approval (as a penalty clause does). For more on this fascinating subject, see Klein, Crawford & Alchian, Vertical Integration, Appropriable Rents, and the Competitive Contracting Process, 21 J. Law & Econ. 297 (1978); Klein & Leffler, The Role of Market Forces in Assuring Contractual Performance, 89 J. Pol. Econ. 615 (1981); Williamson, Credible Commitments: Using Hostages to Support Exchange, 73 Am. Econ. Rev. 519 (1983); Kronman, Contract Law and the State of Nature, 1 J. Law Econ. & Org. 5 (1985).

HENNINGSEN v. BLOOMFIELD MOTORS, INC.

32 N.J. 358, 161 A.2d 69 (1960)

[Plaintiff Claus Henningsen purchased a new Plymouth automobile from Bloomfield Motors and gave it to his wife, the co-plaintiff, as a present. The automobile was manufactured by the defendant, Chrysler Corporation, and sold by it to the other defendant, Bloomfield Motors, a retail dealer. When he purchased the car, Mr. Henningsen signed a purchase order without reading two paragraphs in fine print on its front[71] referring to the back of the purchase order, which contained $8\frac{1}{2}$ more inches of fine print. Included in this fine print was a clause providing that the manufacturer and the dealer gave no warranties, express or implied, except that they would make good at the factory any parts that became defective within 90 days of delivery of the car to the original purchaser, or before the car had been driven 4,000 miles, whichever event should occur first.

Mrs. Henningsen was badly injured while driving the car ten days after it had been delivered; the steering mechanism failed and the car turned into a wall. Mr. and Mrs. Henningsen sued Bloomfield Motors and Chrysler for negligence and for breach of an implied warranty of merchantability imposed by the Uniform Sales Act. The negligence count was dismissed by the trial court and the cause was submitted to the jury solely on the issues of implied warranty and merchantability. Verdicts were returned for plaintiffs against both defendants. Plaintiffs and defendants appealed and the appeal was certified directly to the Supreme Court.

---

71. The two paragraphs read as follows:

The front and back of this Order comprise the entire agreement affecting this purchase and no other agreement or understanding of any nature concerning same has been made or entered into, or will be recognized. I hereby certify that no credit has been extended to me for the purchase of this motor vehicle except as appears in writing on the face of this agreement.

I have read the matter printed on the back hereof and agree to it as a part of this order the same as if it were printed above my signature. I certify that I am 21 years of age, or older, and hereby acknowledge receipt of a copy of this order.

In Part I of its opinion, the Court held that an implied warranty of merchantability by Chrysler accompanied the sale of the automobile to Claus Henningsen, and that he and his wife could sue for breach of this warranty despite the fact that they and Chrysler were not in "privity" of contract. In Part II of the opinion, reprinted in part below, the court discussed the effect of the disclaimer or limitation of warranty on Chrysler's liability. In Part III of its opinion, the court reached a similar result regarding the effectiveness of the disclaimer with respect to Bloomfield Motors, the dealer.]

FRANCIS, J. . . .

II. THE EFFECT OF THE DISCLAIMER AND LIMITATION OF LIABILITY CLAUSES ON THE IMPLIED WARRANTY OF MERCHANTABILITY

Judicial notice may be taken of the fact that automobile manufacturers, including Chrysler Corporation, undertake large scale advertising programs over television, radio, in newspapers, magazines and all media of communication in order to persuade the public to buy their products. As has been observed above, a number of jurisdictions, conscious of modern marketing practices, have declared that when a manufacturer engages in advertising in order to bring his goods and their quality to the attention of the public and thus to create consumer demand, the representations made constitute an express warranty running directly to a buyer who purchases in reliance thereon. The fact that the sale is consummated with an independent dealer does not obviate that warranty. Mannsz v. Macwhyte Co., *supra*; Bahlman v. Hudson Motor Car Co., *supra*; Rogers v. Toni Home Permanent Co., *supra*; Meyer v. Packard Cleveland Motor Co., 106 Ohio St. 328, 140 N.E. 118, 28 A.L.R. 986 (1922); Baxter v. Ford Motor Co., *supra*; 1 Williston, Sales, *supra* §244a.

In view of the cases in various jurisdictions suggesting the conclusion which we have now reached with respect to the implied warranty of merchantability, it becomes apparent that manufacturers who enter into promotional activities to stimulate consumer buying may incur warranty obligations of either or both the express or implied character. These developments in the law inevitably suggest the inference that the form of express warranty made part of the Henningsen purchase contract was devised for general use in the automobile industry as a possible means of avoiding the consequences of the growing judicial acceptance of the thesis that the described express or implied warranties run directly to the consumer.

In the light of these matters, what effect should be given to the express warranty in question which seeks to limit the manufacturer's liability to replacement of defective parts, and which disclaims all other warranties, express or implied? In assessing its significance we must keep in mind the general principle that, in the absence of fraud, one who does not choose to read a contract before signing it, cannot later relieve himself of its burdens. Fivey v. Pennsylvania R.R. Co., 67 N.J.L. 627, 52 A. 472, (E. & A. 1902). And in applying that principle, the basic tenet of freedom of competent parties to contract is a factor of importance. But in the framework of modern commercial life and business practices, such rules cannot be applied on a strict, doctrinal basis. The conflicting interests of the buyer and seller must be evaluated realistically and justly, giving due weight to the social policy evinced by the Uniform Sales Act, the progressive decisions of the courts engaged in administering it, the mass production methods of manufacture and distribution to the public, and the bargaining position occupied by the ordinary consumer in such an economy. This history of the law shows that legal doctrines, as first expounded, often prove to be inadequate under the impact of later experience. In such case, the need for justice has stimulated the necessary qualifications or adjustments. Perkins v. Endicott Johnson Corporation, 128 F.2d 208, 217 (2 Cir. 1942), *affirmed* 317 U.S. 501, 63 S. Ct. 339, 87 L. Ed. 424 (1943); Greenberg v. Lorenz, *supra*.

In these times, an automobile is almost as much a servant of convenience for the ordinary person as a household utensil. For a multitude of other persons it is a necessity. Crowded highways and filled parking lots are a commonplace of our existence. There is no need to look any farther than the daily newspaper to be convinced that when an automobile is defective, it has great potentiality for harm.

No one spoke more graphically on this subject than Justice Cardozo in the landmark case of MacPherson v. Buick Motor Co., 217 N.Y. 382, 111 N.E. 1050, 1053, L.R.A. 1916F, 696 (Ct. App. 1916):

> Beyond all question, the nature of an automobile gives warning of probable danger if its construction is defective. This automobile was designed to go 50 miles per hour. Unless its wheels were sound and strong, injury was almost certain. It was as much a thing of danger as a defective engine for a railroad. . . . The dealer was indeed the one person of whom it might be said with some approach to certainty that by him the car would not be used. . . . Precedents drawn from the days of travel by stagecoach do not fit the conditions of travel to-day. The principle that the danger must be imminent does not change, but the things subject to the principle do change. They are whatever the needs of life in a developing civilization require them to be.

In the 44 years that have intervened since that utterance, the average car has been constructed for almost double the speed mentioned; 60 miles per hour is permitted on our parkways. The number of automobiles in use has multiplied many times and the hazard to the user and the public has increased proportionately. The Legislature has intervened in the public interest, not only to regulate the manner of operation on the highway but also to require periodic inspection of motor vehicles and to impose a duty on manufacturers to adopt certain safety devices and methods in their construction. R.S. 39:3-43 et seq., N.J.S.A. It is apparent that the public has an interest not only in the safe manufacture of automobiles, but also, as shown by the Sales Act, in protecting the rights and remedies of purchasers, so far as it can be accomplished consistently with our system of free enterprise. In a society such as ours, where the automobile is a common and necessary adjunct of daily life, and where its use is so fraught with danger to the driver, passengers and the public, the manufacturer is under a special obligation in connection with the construction, promotion and sale of his cars. Consequently, the courts must examine purchase agreements closely to see if consumer and public interests are treated fairly.

What influences should these circumstances have on the restrictive effect of Chrysler's express warranty in the framework of the purchase contract? As we have said, warranties originated in the law to safeguard the buyer and not to limit the liability of the seller or manufacturer. It seems obvious in this instance that the motive was to avoid the warranty obligations which are normally incidental to such sales. The language gave little and withdrew much. In return for the delusive remedy of replacement of defective parts at the factory, the buyer is said to have accepted the exclusion of the maker's liability for personal injuries arising from the breach of the warranty, and to have agreed to the elimination of any other express or implied warranty. An instinctively felt sense of justice cries out against such a sharp bargain. But does the doctrine that a person is bound by his signed agreement, in the absence of fraud, stand in the way of any relief?

In the modern consideration of problems such as this, Corbin suggests that practically all judges are "chancellors" and cannot fail to be influenced by any equitable doctrines that are available. And he opines that "there is sufficient flexibility in the concepts of fraud, duress, misrepresentation and undue influence, not to mention differences in economic bargaining power" to enable the courts to avoid enforcement of unconscionable provisions in long printed standardized contracts. 1 Corbin on Contracts (1950) §128, p. 188. Freedom of contract is not such an immutable doctrine as to admit of no qualification in the area in which we are concerned. As Chief Justice Hughes said in his dissent in Morehead v. People of State of New York ex rel. Tipaldo, 298 U.S. 587, 627, 56 S. Ct. 918, 930, 80 L. Ed. 1347, 1364 (1936):

> We have had frequent occasion to consider the limitations on liberty of contract. While it is highly important to preserve that liberty from arbitrary and capricious interference, it is also necessary to prevent its abuse, as otherwise it could be used to override all public interests and thus in the

end destroy the very freedom of opportunity which it is designed to safe-guard.

That sentiment was echoed by Justice Frankfurter in his dissent in United States v. Bethlehem Steel Corp., 315 U.S. 289, 326, 62 S. Ct. 581, 599, 86 L. Ed. 855, 876 (1942):

> It is said that familiar principles would be outraged if Bethlehem were denied recovery on these contracts. But is there any principle which is more familiar or more firmly embedded in the history of Anglo-American law than the basic doctrine that the courts will not permit themselves to be used as instruments of inequity and injustice? Does any principle in our law have more universal application than the doctrine that courts will not enforce transactions in which the relative positions of the parties are such that one has unconscionably taken advantage of the necessities of the other?
>
> These principles are not foreign to the law of contracts. Fraud and physical duress are not the only grounds upon which courts refuse to enforce contracts. The law is not so primitive that it sanctions every injustice except brute force and downright fraud. More specifically, the courts generally refuse to lend themselves to the enforcement of a "bargain" in which one party has unjustly taken advantage of the economic necessities of the other. . . .

The traditional contract is the result of free bargaining of parties who are brought together by the play of the market, and who meet each other on a footing of approximate economic equality. In such a society there is no danger that freedom of contract will be a threat to the social order as a whole. But in present-day commercial life the standardized mass contract has appeared. It is used primarily by enterprises with strong bargaining power and position.

> The weaker party, in need of the goods or services, is frequently not in a position to shop around for better terms, either because the author of the standard contract has a monopoly (natural or artificial) or because all competitors use the same clauses. His contractual intention is but a subjection more or less voluntary to terms dictated by the stronger party, terms whose consequences are often understood in a vague way, if at all.

Kessler, "Contracts of Adhesion — Some Thoughts About Freedom of Contract," 43 Colum. L. Rev. 629, 632 (1943); Ehrenzweig, "Adhesion Contracts in the Conflict of Laws," 53 Column L. Rev. 1072, 1075, 1089 (1953). Such standardized contracts have been described as those in which one predominant party will dictate its law to an undetermined multiple rather than to an individual. They are said to resemble a law rather than a meeting of the minds. Siegelman v. Cunard White Star, 221 F.2d 189, 206 (2 Cir. 1955).

Vold, in a recent revision of his Law of Sales (2d ed. 1959) at page 447, wrote of this type of contract and its effect upon the ordinary buyer:

> In recent times the marketing process has been getting more highly organized than ever before. Business units have been expanding on a scale never before known. The standardized contract with its broad disclaimer clauses is drawn by legal advisers of sellers widely organized in trade associations. It is encountered on every hand. Extreme inequality of bargaining between buyer and seller in this respect is now often conspicuous. Many buyers no longer have any real choice in the matter. They must often accept what they can get though accompanied by broad disclaimers. The terms of these disclaimers deprive them of all substantial protection with regard to the quality of the goods. In effect, this is by force of contract between very unequal parties. It throws the risk of defective articles on the most dependent party. He has the least individual power to avoid the presence of defects. He also has the least individual ability to bear their disastrous consequences.

The warranty before us is a standardized form designed for mass use. It is imposed upon the automobile consumer. He takes it or leaves it, and he must take it to buy an automobile. No bargaining is engaged in with respect to it. In fact, the dealer through whom it comes to the buyer is without authority to alter it; his function is ministerial — simply to deliver it. The form warranty is not only standard with Chrysler but, as mentioned above, it is the uniform warranty of the Automobile Manufacturers Association. Members of the Association are: General Motors, Inc., Ford, Chrysler, Studebaker-Packard, American Motors, (Rambler), Willys Motors, Checker Motors Corp., and International Harvester Company. Automobile Facts and Figures (1958 Ed., Automobile Manufacturers Association) 69. Of these companies, the "Big Three" (General Motors, Ford, and Chrysler) represented 93.5% of the passenger-car production for 1958 and the independents 6.5%. Standard & Poor (Industrial Surveys, Autos, Basic Analysis, June 25, 1959) 4109. And for the same year the "Big Three" had 86.72% of the total passenger vehicle registrations. Automotive News, 1959 Almanac (Slocum Publishing Co., Inc.) p. 25.

The gross inequality of bargaining position occupied by the consumer in the automobile industry is thus apparent. There is no competition among the car makers in the area of the express warranty. Where can the buyer go to negotiate for better protection? Such control and limitation of his remedies are inimical to the public welfare and, at the very least, call for great care by the courts to avoid injustice through application of strict common-law principles of freedom of contract. Because there is no competition among the motor vehicle manufacturers with respect to the scope of protection guaranteed to the buyer, there is no incentive on their part to stimulate good will in that field of public relations. Thus, there is lacking a factor existing in more competitive fields, one which tends to guarantee the safe construction of the article sold. Since all competitors operate in the same way, the urge to be careful is not so pressing. See "Warranties of Kind and Quality," 57 Yale L.J. 1389, 1400 (1948).

Although the courts, with few exceptions, have been most sensitive to problems presented by contracts resulting from gross disparity in buyer-seller bargaining positions, they have not articulated a general principle condemning, as opposed to public policy, the imposition on the buyer of a skeleton warranty as a means of limiting the responsibility of the manufacturer. They have endeavored thus far to avoid a drastic departure from age-old tenets of freedom of contract by adopting doctrines of strict construction, and notice and knowledgeable assent by the buyer to the attempted exculpation of the seller. 1 Corbin, *supra,* 337; 2 Harper & James, *supra,* 1590; Prosser, "Warranty of Merchantable Quality," 27 Minn. L. Rev. 117, 159 (1932). Accordingly to be found in the cases are statements that disclaimers and the consequent limitation of liability will not be given effect if "unfairly procured," Davis Motors, Dodge and Plymouth Co. v. Avett, 294 S.W.2d 882, 887 (Tex. Civ. App. 1956); International Harvester Co. of America v. Bean, 159 Ky. 842, 169 S.W. 549 (Ct. App. 1914); if not brought to the buyer's attention and he was not made understandingly aware of it, Vaughan's Seed Store v. Stringfellow, 56 Fla. 708, 48 So. 410 (Sup. Ct. 1908); Parsons Band Cutter & Self-Feeder Co. v. Haub, 83 Minn. 180, 86 N.W. 14 (Sup. Ct. 1901); Bell v. Mills, 78 App. Div. 42, 80 N.Y.S. 34 (1902); Landreth v. Wyckoff, 67 App. Div. 145, 73 N.Y.S. 388 (1901); St. Louis Cordage Mills v. Western Supply Co., 54 Okl. 757, 154 P. 646 (Sup. Ct. 1916); Reliance Varnish Co. v. Mullins Lumber Co., 213 S.C. 84, 48 S.E.2d 653 (Sup. Ct. 1948); Stevenson v. B.B. Kirkland Seed Co., 176 S.C. 345, 180 S.E. 197 (Sup. Ct. 1935); Black v. B.B. Kirkland Seed Co., 158 S.C. 112, 155 S.E. 268 (Sup. Ct. 1930); or if not clear and explicit, McPeak v. Boker, 236 Minn. 420, 53 N.W.2d 130 (Sup. Ct. 1952).

[In an omitted passage the court stated the facts of several of the cases just cited, quoting extensively from the opinions.]

It is undisputed that the president of the dealer with whom Henningsen dealt did not specifically call attention to the warranty on the back of the purchase order. The form and the arrangement of its face, as described above, certainly would cause the minds of reasonable men to differ as to whether notice of a yielding of basic rights stemming from the relationship with the manufacturer was adequately given. The words "warranty" or "limited warranty" did not even appear in the fine print above the place for signature, and a jury might well find that the type of print itself was such as to promote lack of attention rather than sharp scrutiny. The inference from the facts is that Chrysler placed the method of communicating its warranty to the purchaser in the hands of the dealer. If either one or both of them wished to make certain that Henningsen became aware of that agreement and its purported implications, neither the form of the document nor the method of expressing the precise nature of the obligation intended to be assumed would have presented any difficulty.

But there is more than this. Assuming that a jury might find that the fine print referred to reasonably served the objective of directing a buyer's attention to the warranty on the reverse side, and, therefore, that he should be charged with awareness of its language, can it be said that an ordinary layman would realize what he was relinquishing in return for what he was being granted? Under the law, breach of warranty against defective parts or workmanship which caused personal injuries would entitle a buyer to damages even if due care were used in the manufacturing process. Because of the great potential for harm if the vehicle was defective, that right is the most important and fundamental one arising from the relationship. Difficulties so frequently encountered in establishing negligence in manufacture in the ordinary case make this manifest. 2 Harper & James, *supra*, §§28.14, 28.15; Prosser, *supra*, 506. Any ordinary layman of reasonable intelligence, looking at the phraseology, might well conclude that Chrysler was agreeing to replace defective parts and perhaps replace anything that went wrong because of defective workmanship during the first 90 days or 4,000 miles of operation, but that he would not be entitled to a new car. It is not unreasonable to believe that the entire scheme being conveyed was a proposed remedy for physical deficiencies in the car. *In the context* of this warranty, only the abandonment of all sense of justice would permit us to hold that, as a matter of law, the phrase "its obligation under this warranty being limited to making good at its factory any part or parts thereof" signifies to an ordinary reasonable person that he is relinquishing any personal injury claim that might flow from the use of a defective automobile. Such claims are nowhere mentioned. The draftsmanship is reflective of the care and skill of the Automobile Manufacturers Association in undertaking to avoid warranty obligations without drawing too much attention to its effort in that regard. No one can doubt that if the will to do so were present, the ability to inform the buying public of the intention to disclaim liability for injury claims arising from breach of warranty would present no problem.

In this connection, attention is drawn to the Plymouth Owner Certificate mentioned earlier. Obviously, Chrysler is aware of it because the New Car Preparation Service Guide sent from the factory to the dealer directs that it be given to the purchaser. That certificate contains a paragraph called "Explanation of Warranty." Its entire tenor relates to replacement of defective parts. There is nothing about it to stimulate the idea that the intention of the warranty is to exclude personal injury claims.

[In an omitted passage the court approvingly discussed the case of Lachs v. Fidelity & Casualty Co. of New York, 306 N.Y. 357, 118 N.E.2d 555 (1954).]

The task of the judiciary is to administer the spirit as well as the letter of the law. On issues such as the present one, part of that burden is to protect the ordinary man against the loss of important rights through what, in effect, is the unilateral act of the manufacturer. The status of the automobile industry is unique. Manufacturers are few in number and strong in bargaining position. In the matter of warranties on the sale of their products, the Automotive Manufacturers Association has enabled them to present a united front. From the standpoint of the purchaser, there can be no arms length negotiating on the subject. Because his capacity for bargaining is so grossly unequal, the inexorable conclusion which follows is that he is not permitted to bargain at all. He must take or leave the automobile on the warranty terms dictated by the maker. He cannot turn to a competitor for better security.

Public policy is a term not easily defined. Its significance varies as the habits and needs of a people may vary. It is not static and the field of application is an ever increasing one. A contract, or a particular provision therein, valid in one era may be wholly opposed to the public policy of another. See Collopy v. Newark Eye & Ear Infirmary, 27 N.J. 29, 39, 141 A.2d 276 (1958). Courts keep in mind the principle that the best interests of society demand that persons should not be unnecessarily restricted in their freedom to contract. But they do not hesitate to declare void as against public policy contractual provisions which clearly tend to the injury of the public in some way. Hodnick v. Fidelity Trust Co., 96 Ind. App. 342, 183 N.E. 488 (App. Ct. 1932).

Public policy at a given time finds expression in the Constitution, the statutory law and in judicial decisions. In the area of sales of goods, the legislative will has imposed an implied warranty of merchantability as a general incident of sale of an automobile by description. The warranty does not depend upon the affirmative intention of the parties. It is a child of the law; it annexes itself to the contract because of the very nature of the transaction. Minneapolis Steel & Machinery Co. v. Casey Land Agency, 51 N.D. 832, 201 N.W. 172 (Sup. Ct. 1924). The judicial process has recognized a right to recover damages for personal injuries arising from a breach of that warranty. The disclaimer of the implied warranty and exclusion of all obligations except those specifically assumed by the express warranty signify a studied effort to frustrate that protection. True, the Sales Act authorizes agreements between buyer and seller qualifying the warranty obligations. But quite obviously the Legislature contemplated lawful stipulations (which are determined by the circumstances of a particular case) arrived at freely by parties of relatively equal bargaining strength. The lawmakers did not authorize the automobile manufacturer to use its grossly disproportionate bargaining power to relieve itself from liability and to impose on the ordinary buyer, who in effect has no real freedom of choice, the grave danger of injury to himself and others that attends the sale of such a dangerous instrumentality as a defectively made automobile. In the framework of this case, illuminated as it is by the facts and the many decisions noted, we are of the opinion that Chrysler's attempted disclaimer of an implied warranty of merchantability and of the obligations arising therefrom is so inimical to the public good as to compel an adjudication of its invalidity. See 57 Yale L.J., *supra*, at pp. 1400-1404; proposed Uniform Commercial Code, 1958 Official Text, §202.

The trial court sent the case to the jury against Chrysler on the theory that the evidence would support a finding of breach of an implied warranty of merchantability. In fact, at one point in his charge he seemed to say that as a matter of law such a warranty existed. He also told them that:

> A provision in a purchase order for an automobile that an express warranty shall exclude all implied warranties will not be given effect so as to defeat an implied warranty that the machine shall be fit for the purposes for which it was intended unless its inclusion in the contract was fairly procured or obtained.

Thereafter, the court charged that when the car was sold a warranty arose that it was reasonably suited for ordinary use, and that if they found that it was defective and "not reasonably suited for ordinary driving" liability would exist "provided . . . you find there was an implied warranty and a breach thereof." The reasonable inference to be drawn from the whole context is that a preliminary finding against the binding effect of the disclaimer would have to be made, i.e., that the disclaimer was not "fairly procured," before an implied warranty could be deemed to exist. Even assuming that the duty to make such a finding was not as explicit as it should have been, in view of our holding that the disclaimer is void as a matter of law, the charge was more favorable to the defendant than the law required it to be. The verdict in favor of the plaintiffs and against Chrysler Corporation establishes that the jury found that the disclaimer was not fairly obtained. Thus, this defendant cannot claim to have been prejudiced by a jury finding on an aspect of the case which the court should have disposed of as a matter of law.

Chrysler raises in this court for the first time the defense that plaintiffs' failure to give reasonable notice of the breach of warranty bars their recovery. The claim was not made in the answer, pretrial order, at the trial or as a ground of appeal in the brief filed on this review. It was added by letter filed after oral argument. It comes too late for consideration at this point in the proceedings.

The same situation arose in National Equipment Corporation v. Moore, 189 Minn. 632, 250 N.W. 677 (Sup. Ct. 1933). The contention was rejected, the court saying:

. . . It is enough to say that no such defense to the counterclaim was pleaded, litigated, or submitted to the jury. There was some testimony as to whether certain complaints were made . . . but nothing to indicate to the court or opposing counsel that such evidence was directed to prove non-compliance with said section 8423, and no such issue was submitted, or requested to be submitted, to the jury.

250 N.W. at page 679. . . .

NOTE

1. The principal case has become famous both for its treatment of the privity requirement and for its handling of the disclaimer clause contained in the contract of sale. The privity issue, which is discussed in a portion of the opinion not reprinted here, merits a word or two of commentary. Neither plaintiff had any direct contractual dealings with defendant Chrysler. And Mrs. Henningsen, not being the buyer of the car, was even further removed from the manufacturer than was her husband. The court nevertheless chose to extend the protection of the Uniform Sales Act to both plaintiffs by holding that Chrysler had made a promise — an implied warranty of merchantability — which the Henningsens were entitled to enforce, despite the lack of any immediate contractual connection between themselves and Chrysler (an approach that forced the court to consider the validity of the disclaimer clause in the contract of sale, since §71 of the Sales Act stated that implied warranties could be disclaimed by express agreement).

At the time the principal case was decided, however, an increasing number of courts had already indicated a willingness to protect remote consumers against the pitfalls of sales law (privity, disclaimer and the requirement of timely notice) by upholding their claims in tort, on a theory of strict liability. See Prosser, The Assault on the Citadel, 69 Yale L.J. 1099 (1960); Prosser, The Fall of the Citadel (Strict Liability to the Consumer), 50 Minn. L. Rev. 791 (1966); Shanker, Strict Tort Theory of Products Liability and the Uniform Commercial Code: a Commentary on Jurisprudential Eclipses, Pigeonholes and Communication Barriers, 17 W. Res. L. Rev. 5 (1965). This case law found its crystallization in §402A of the Restatement of Torts Second which reads as follows:

(1)   One who sells any product in a defective condition unreasonably dangerous to the user or consumer or to his property is subject to liability for physical harm thereby caused to the ultimate user or consumer, or to his property, if
(a)   the seller is engaged in the business of selling such a product, and
(b)   it is expected to and does reach the user or consumer without substantial change in the condition in which it is sold.

(2)   The rule stated in Subsection (1) applies although
(a)   the seller has exercised all possible care in the preparation and sale
      of his product, and
(b)   the user or consumer has not bought the product from or entered
      into any contractual relation with the seller.

Section 402A is remarkable not only for its attempt to make products liability independent of warranty law but also for its imposition of strict, as contrasted with negligence, liability. The protection of the consumer is rounded out by other sections. Section 402B imposes strict liability for physical harm caused by justifiable reliance upon a public misrepresentation (by advertising, label, or otherwise) of the character and quality of the chattel sold. For the parallel rule imposing strict liability for pecuniary loss, see §524A.

The public policy arguments in favor of strict liability as a risk distribution device are powerfully presented in Escola v. Coca Cola Bottling Co., 24 Cal. 2d 453, 462, 150 P.2d 436, 440-441 (1944) (Traynor, J., concurring).[72] See further, Vandermark v. Ford Motor Co., 61 Cal. 2d 256, 391 P.2d 168, 37 Cal. Rptr. 896 (1964); Goldberg v. Kollsman Instrument Corporation, 12 N.Y.2d 432, 240 N.Y.S.2d 592, 191 N.E.2d 81 (1963).

As to the desirability of dispensing with privity in the situation where the buyer's injury consists only in the diminished value of his bargain, see Santor v. A. & M. Karagheusian, 44 N.J. 52, 207 A.2d 305 (1965); Seely v. White Motor Co., 63 Cal. 2d 9, 403 P.2d 145, 45 Cal. Rptr. 17 (1965); Note, Economic Loss in Products Liability Jurisprudence, 66 Colum. L. Rev. 917 (1966); Note, Manufacturers' Liability to Remote Purchasers For Economic Loss Damages — Tort or Contract? 114 U. Pa. L. Rev. 539 (1966). For a thoughtful critique of strict enterprise liability, and a defense of the fault principle, see the dissenting opinion of Judge Burke in the *Goldberg* case *supra*; Plant, Strict Liability of Manufacturers for Injuries Caused by Defects in Products — An Opposing View, 24 Tenn. L. Rev. 938 (1957) and, generally, J. Blum & H. Kalven, Public Law Perspectives on a Private Law Problem (1965); Coase, The Problem of Social Cost, 3 J. Law & Econ. 1 (1960); O.W. Holmes, The Common Law 91-96 (1881).

It goes without saying that strict enterprise liability has not eliminated the existence of a defect as a prerequisite to liability. See, e.g., Keeton, Product Liability — Liability Without Fault and the Requirement of a Defect, 41 Texas L. Rev. 855 (1963); Traynor, The Ways and Meanings of Defective Products and Strict Liability, 32 Tenn. L. Rev. 363 (1965).

The Uniform Commercial Code deals with the problem of privity in §2-318. The original official version of §2-318 extended warranty protection "horizontally" to members of the buyer's family or household and to

---

72. Calabresi, Thoughts on Risk Distribution and the Law of Torts, 70 Yale L.J. 499 (1961); Kessler, Products Liability, 76 Yale L.J. 887, 924 (1967).

guests; however, unlike earlier unofficial drafts, it had no express provisions subjecting the manufacturer to vertical liability in favor of persons in the distribution chain beyond the immediate buyer. The Code is "neutral" with regard to their protection by developing case law (Comment 3).

Dissatisfaction with the initial version of §2-318 has led to two types of statutory modification. California, in adopting the Uniform Commercial Code, entirely omitted §2-318 as a "step backwards," the legislature preferring to rely upon California case law, which imposes strict liability in tort without contract or negligence. Report of the California State Bar Committee on Commercial Code, 37 S.B.J. 143 (1962). Virginia, by contrast, enacted an "anti-privity" statute replacing §2-318 but otherwise leaving the text of the Code intact. The substitute Section reads as follows:

> When Lack of Privity No Defense in Action Against Manufacturer
> or Seller of Goods
>
> Lack of privity between plaintiff and defendant shall be no defense in any action brought against the manufacturer or seller of goods to recover damages for breach of warranty, express or implied, or for negligence, although the plaintiff did not purchase the goods from the defendant, if the plaintiff was a person whom the manufacturer or seller might reasonably have expected to use, consume, or be affected by the goods; however, this section shall not be construed to affect any litigation pending at its effective date.[73]

Thus, while California chose the tort approach of the Restatement, Virginia elected to deal with the problem of products liability within the framework of the Uniform Commercial Code. See, in general, Speidel, The Virginia "Anti-Privity" Statute: Strict Products Liability under the Uniform Commercial Code, 51 Va. L. Rev. 804 (1965).

To meet the increasing criticism of §2-318, the Permanent Editorial Board for the Uniform Commercial Code in its Report No. 3 (1967) made §2-318 an optional alternative (A) and provided two other alternatives. Alternative B adopts an earlier version of the Code more favorable to the remote consumer. Alternative C is drawn to reflect the trend of modern decisions as indicated in §402A, limiting, however, the ineffectiveness of disclaimers to personal injuries.

For more on the demise of the privity requirement in modern contract law, see the Introductory Note to Chapter 11 on Third Party Beneficiaries.

2. Suppose the New Jersey court had elected to deal with the *Henningsen* case under the approach suggested by §402A of the Restatement of Torts Second, *supra* Note 1. What happens to the limitation of warranty under §402A? For the New Jersey court's subsequent adoption of

73. Va. Code Ann. §8-654.3 (Supp. 1964).

such a tort approach in a case involving a manufacturer's liability for a defective product, see Santor v. A. & M. Karagheusian, 44 N.J. 52, 207 A.2d 305 (1965). The *Santor* case did not purport to reject or abandon *Henningsen*, but the relationship between the two cases may not be entirely clear. As counsel for a plaintiff situated like Mrs. Henningsen, would you elect, if you had the choice, to bring your action in tort or in contract?

3. Did the court hold that the limitation of warranty was void as against public policy? If so, why did Francis J., discuss at such length the facts that (1) the warranty clause was not drawn to Mr. Henningsen's attention when he bought the car, (2) the warranty clause appeared in fine print, and (3) the warranty clause was so drafted that a layman unskilled in the niceties of warranty law would not realize that the clause was intended to disclaim all liability for physical injuries?

UNIFORM COMMERCIAL CODE

§2-316. EXCLUSION OR MODIFICATION OF WARRANTIES

(1) Words or conduct relevant to the creation of an express warranty and words or conduct tending to negate or limit warranty shall be construed wherever reasonable as consistent with each other; but subject to the provisions of this Article on parol or extrinsic evidence (Section 2-202) negation or limitation is inoperative to the extent that such construction is unreasonable.

(2) Subject to subsection (3), to exclude or modify the implied warranty of merchantability or any part of it the language must mention merchantability and in case of a writing must be conspicuous, and to exclude or modify any implied warranty of fitness the exclusion must be by a writing and conspicuous. Language to exclude all implied warranties of fitness is sufficient if it states, for example, that "There are no warranties which extend beyond the description on the face hereof."

(3) Notwithstanding subsection (2).

(a) unless the circumstances indicate otherwise, all implied warranties are excluded by expressions like "as is," "with all faults" or other language which in common understanding calls the buyer's attention to the exclusion of warranties and makes plain that there is no implied warranty; and

(b) when the buyer before entering into the contract has examined the goods or the sample or model as fully as he desired or has refused to examine the goods there is no implied warranty with regard to defects which an examination ought in the circumstances to have revealed to him; and

(c)   an implied warranty can also be excluded or modified by course of dealing or course of performance or usage of trade.

(4)   Remedies for breach of warranty can be limited in accordance with the provisions of this Article on liquidation or limitation of damages and on contractual modification of remedy (Sections 2-718 and 2-719). [These last sections are reprinted *supra* p. 1239.]

NOTE

1. The circumstances under which implied warranties of "merchantability" and "fitness" arise are dealt with in §§2-314 and 2-315. These sections make no great change from prior law.

2. What seems to be the relationship between §2-316 and §2-719?

3. Reread Code §2-302 (Unconscionable Contract or Clause), reprinted *supra* p. 561. As a matter of decent statutory construction, do you think that a clause which disclaimed a warranty under §2-316 or effectively limited the remedy under §2-719 could nevertheless be stricken for unconscionability under §2-302? The Comment to §2-302 cites eleven cases, nine of which involved attempted disclaimers of warranty that, on one theory or another, were held ineffective.

4. With respect to §2-719(3), Comment 3 observes:

Subsection (3) recognizes the validity of clauses limiting or excluding consequential damages but makes it clear that they may not operate in an unconscionable manner. Actually such terms are merely an allocation of unknown or undeterminable risk. The seller in all cases is free to disclaim warranties in the manner provided in Section 2-316.

5. New Jersey adopted the Code in 1963. After the enactment of the Code, do you think that the *Henningsen* case was still good law in New Jersey? Specifically, would the substance of the Chrysler Corporation's warranty, appropriately redrafted to fit Code requirements, be void as against public policy?

FAIR v. NEGLEY
257 Pa. Super. 478, 390 A.2d 240 (1978)

JACOBS, President Judge:

In the present action, Appellants Lewis and Grace Fair appeal the decision of the Court of Common Pleas of Butler County sustaining the demurrers of Appellee Alexander Negley to both counts of appellants' complaint. In asking us to reverse the trial court, appellants seek an extension of our recent decision to abolish the common law doctrine of *caveat emptor* as it applies to residential leases and to apply an implied warranty of habitability to all such leases. Pugh v. Holmes, 253 Pa. Super. 76, 384 A.2d 1234 (1978). The two major issues raised by appellants are whether the implied warranty may be used as a basis for a complaint and whether the warranty may be waived by agreement of the parties to the residential lease. We hold that the implied warranty is a valid basis for a complaint and that the warranty may not be waived. Furthermore, we reverse the trial court's decision sustaining appellee's demurrer to the second count of appellants' complaint which alleged intentional infliction of emotional distress.

On March 12, 1974, appellants entered into a written rental agreement with appellee for a six room house in Butler, Pennsylvania. Appellants made rental payments of eighty dollars ($80.) per month until they vacated the premises in September, 1975. The clause in the agreement most at issue in this case stated that "premises taken in 'as is' condition, tenant knows the roof has a leak in the same. . . ." Record at 10a and Appendix at 6.

Appellants filed a two count complaint against appellee. In the first court, they alleged that appellee breached the implied warranty of habitability on the rented premises; they sought reimbursement for all past rent paid ($1,560) and for excess water bills ($132) caused by appellee's failure to fix the defective water system. As examples of the alleged breach, appellants cited, *inter alia*, improper ventilation of a gas hot water heater and gas space heaters, lack of heat, falling plaster, defective electrical wiring, a malfunctioning water system, defective windows, broken porch steps and railings, and a leaking roof. Appellant's second count alleged that appellee had intentionally inflicted emotional distress upon them through his refusal to make the premises fit for human habitation; they sought $3,000 damages on the second count.

Appellee filed preliminary objections in the form of a demurrer to appellants' complaint. Argument was held on the demurrer and on January 12, 1977, Judge Dillon sustained appellee's demurrer and dismissed appellants' complaint with prejudice. This appeal followed.

We reverse the trial court's action in sustaining appellee's demurrer to the first count and reinstate appellants' complaint. In Pugh v. Holmes we held that the implied warranty of habitability may be used as the basis for a defense or for a counterclaim. Here, we hold that the warranty also may be used as the basis for a complaint. Just as with a counterclaim, standard contract remedies are available should appellants prove that appellee breached the implied warranty of habitability. For any time period during which the finder of fact determines that the premises were in an uninhabitable state, appellants may recover the difference between the amount of rent they paid and the reasonable rental value of the premises. Furthermore, they may recover any amount they spent on reasonable reparation and replacement in making the dwelling habitable. Finally, if the fact finder determines that their utility bills were excessive because of the uninhabitable condition of the premises, they may be reimbursed for the amount paid in excess of what their utility bills should have been had the premises been habitable. Of course, in order to succeed on their complaint, appellants must prove that they gave notice to appellee of the defective conditions, that appellee had a reasonable opportunity to correct the defects, and that he failed to do so. Pugh v. Holmes, 253 Pa. Super. at 88, 384 A.2d at 1241 and cases therein cited.

The major issue presented by this case is whether the implied warranty may be waived by agreement of the parties. In ruling on the "as is" clause in the lease the trial court adopted Section 2-316 of the Uniform Commercial Code and impliedly found that any warranty of habitability which may have existed had been waived. Act of April 6, 1953, P.L. 3, §2-316 *as reenacted by* the Act of October 2, 1959, P.L. 1023, §2, 12A P.S. §2-316. That section states

> [U]nless the circumstances indicate otherwise, all implied warranties are excluded by expressions like "as is," "with all faults" or other language which in common understanding calls the buyer's attention to the exclusion of warranties and makes plain that there is no implied warranty. . . .

12A P.S. §2-316(3)(a). While we recognize that our decision in Pugh v. Holmes declared that all leases are to be treated as contracts and while we recognize the necessity and value of the freedom to contract between parties, we do not find this language from the Uniform Commercial Code, designed to regulate dealings concerning the sale of goods, controlling in the area of landlord tenant law.[74]

Our initial decision to imply a warranty of habitability in residential leases was based primarily on four factors: the inability of tenants to adequately inspect or repair rental units, the disparity of bargaining power between landlord and tenant, the scarcity of housing in the Commonwealth, and the effect of uninhabitable dwellings on the public health and safety. We must now decide whether, despite the doctrine of freedom to contract, a waiver of the warranty would be so against public policy that it should not be permitted in residential leases.

---

74. If we were to find the language of §2-316 controlling here, we would find §2-302 of the Uniform Commercial Code to be controlling, as well. Section 2-302 states that

> If the court as a matter of law finds the contract or any clause of the contract to have been unconscionable at the time it was made the court may refuse to enforce the contract, or it may enforce the remainder of the contract without the unconscionable clause, or it may so limit the application of any unconscionable clause as to avoid any unconscionable result.

The Act of April 6, 1953, P.L. 3, §2-302, *as reenacted by* the Act of Oct. 2, 1959, P.L. 1023, §2, 12A P.S. §2-302(1). On the basis of §2-302, we would find the "as is" clause of the lease to be an unconscionable and ineffective waiver.

Although "public policy" is a term which escapes easy definition, we agree with Comment (e) to Section 5.6 of the Restatement (Second) of Property which states that "An agreement or provision may be against public policy if it will materially and unreasonably obstruct achievement of a well defined . . . common law policy." The Restatement lists several factors to be considered in determining whether an agreement violates public policy. Upon consideration of those factors applicable to residential leases like the one here at issue, we hold that a waiver of the implied warranty of habitability does violate the public policy sought to be achieved by the warranty and that, therefore, the warranty may not be waived.

One factor is whether the agreement will be counter to statutory and regulatory provisions concerning public health and safety. As we noted in Pugh v. Holmes,

> [A]t least one court has found that the continued letting of "tumbledown" houses is ". . . a contributing cause of such problems as urban blight, juvenile delinquency and high property taxes for conscientious land-owners." Pines v. Perssion, 14 Wis. 2d 590, 596, 111 N.W.2d 409, 413 (1961).

253 Pa. Super. at 84, 384 A.2d at 1239. Furthermore, appellants here attached as an exhibit to their complaint a "Notice of City Ordinance Violation" from the Housing Code Enforcement Office of Butler, Pennsylvania to appellee/landlord. The Notice listed seven (7) major defects in the rental premises found by the Code Enforcement Office and ordered to be remedied by appellee. Record at 12a. It is clear that if we were to enforce the alleged waiver of the implied warranty of habitability in this case, we would lend support not only to obvious violations of Butler ordinances but also to a situation hazardous to the public health and safety.

A second factor for consideration is the relative strength of the bargaining power held by the respective parties. The Courts of our Commonwealth have recognized that tenants in general have little or no bargaining power. In Reitmeyer v. Sprecher, the Supreme Court stated,

> [M]ost frequently today the average prospective tenant vis-a-vis the prospective landlord occupies a disadvantageous position. Stark necessity very often forces a tenant into occupancy of premises far from desirable and in a defective state of repair. The acute housing shortage mandates that the average prospective tenant accede to the demands of the prospective landlord as to conditions of rental, which, under ordinary conditions with housing available, the average tenant would not and should not accept.
>
> No longer does the average prospective tenant occupy a free bargaining status and no longer do the average landlord-to-be and tenant-to-be negotiate a lease on an "arm's length" basis. Premises which, under normal circumstances, would be completely unattractive for rental are now, by

necessity, at a premium. If our law is to keep in tune with our times we must recognize the present day inferior position of the average tenant vis-a-vis the landlord when it comes to negotiating a lease.

431 Pa. 284, 289-90, 243 A.2d 395, 398 (1968). In discussing a lease clause which would exculpate a landlord from liability for personal injury, a situation analogous to waiving the implied warranty of habitability, the Court said,

> The exculpatory clause is today contained in every form lease and, under-standably enough, landlords are unwilling to strike therefrom that provi-sion which strongly favors them. Thus it is fruitless for the prospective tenant of an apartment to seek a lease having no exculpatory clause. The result is that the tenant has no bargaining power and must accept his landlord's terms. There is no meeting of the minds, and the agreement is in effect a mere contract of adhesion, whereby the tenant simply adheres to a document which he is powerless to alter, having no alternative other than to reject the transaction entirely. It is obvious that analysis of the form lease in terms of traditional contract principles will not suffice, for those rules were developed for negotiated transactions, which embody the intention of both parties. [Citation omitted.]

Galligan v. Arovitch, 421 Pa. 301, 304, 219 A.2d 463, 465 (1966). *See also* Commonwealth v. Monumental Properties, Inc., 459 Pa. 450, 474-75, 329 A.2d 812, 824 (1974), and Klein v. Allegheny County Health Depart-ment, 441 Pa. 1, 7, 269 A.2d 647, 651 (1970) for discussions of the housing shortages in the Commonwealth.[75]

A review of the rental agreement in this case gives further support to these particular tenants' lack of bargaining power. Not only did the appel-lants agree to rent a house with a leaking roof, but also

> as a security for the payment of all rent falling due under this lease [appel-lants grant all right] to the lessor [in] *all the household and kitchen furni-*

---

75. Even assuming that some tenants may possess limited bargaining power, courts have determined that the public policy behind the implied warranty of habitability is more important than any negotiated waiver of the warranty. In at least one case, a court has found that knowledge of the defective conditions and reduced rent are inadequate bases for waiving the implied warranty:

> It can be argued, however, that the defendant should not be entitled to the protection of an implied warranty of habitability since he knew of a substantial number of defects when he rented the premises and the rent was reduced from $87 per month to $50 per month. We believe this type of bargaining by the landlord with the tenant is contrary to public policy and the purpose of the doctrine of implied warranty of habitability. A disadvantaged tenant should not be placed in a position of agreeing to live in an uninhabitable premises. Housing conditions, such as the record indicates exist in the instant case, are a health hazard, not only to the individual tenant, but to the community which is exposed to said individual.

Foisy v. Wyman, 83 Wash. 2d 22, 28, 515 P.2d 160, 164 (1973).

ture, and all property, good and merchandise of the lessee upon the premises, or to be brought thereon, without any exceptions. (Emphasis added.)

Record at 8a and Appendix at 6. Furthermore, the lease contained a clause granting appellee the right to enter a confessed judgment against appellants for any unpaid rent, or for breach of any of the covenants of the lease. Record at 9a-10a and Appendix at 6. In return for giving up substantially all of their rights as tenants, including the rights to sublet or assign without appellee's permission or to prevent appellee from entering onto the property without their permission, appellants received an uninhabitable dwelling place. A clearer case of disparity of bargaining power and disadvantage to the tenant would be difficult to imagine.

Were we to permit waiver of the implied warranty by an express provision in the lease, it would be a rare lease in which the waiver would not appear. As with the exculpatory clause, few, if any, tenants would be able to find housing on which the warranty had not been waived. To allow such wholesale, unbargained for waiver would make the implied warranty of habitability meaningless.

The third criterion is whether the provision is part of "an unduly harsh and unreasonable standard, 'boilerplate' lease document. . . ." A copy of the lease, as it appears in the reproduced record, is, in essence, boilerplate. The only provisions not in standard style and size of type in the lease are the names of the parties, the date, the address, the rental amount, and the "as is" clause. It is clear, then, that these are the only provisions upon which any negotiations *could* have taken place. In most cases, including this one, it would be unreasonable and unconscionable for a landlord and tenant to voluntarily negotiate for a tenant to live in uninhabitable housing. The "as is" clause, therefore, must be viewed simply as a part of the boilerplate lease agreement.

The final consideration applicable, here, is whether the agreement imposes unreasonable liabilities or burdens on persons financially ill equipped to assume the burdens or on persons without significant bargaining power. Such is certainly the case, here. There is no doubt that appellants were burdened by the attempted waiver of the habitability warranty. In addition, the printed lease form provided that appellants would pay for "[a]ny damage to building, fixtures, water or gas pipes, during the term of this lease. . . ." Not only, then, did appellee try to avoid having to rent a habitable house but also attempted to have appellants, without finances or bargaining power, maintain the premises after they rented them.

After considering the bases for our decision in Pugh v. Holmes, the public policy sought to be advanced by the implied warranty of habitability, and the factors to be employed in determining whether an agreement violates public policy, we can conclude only that an attempted waiver of the implied warranty of habitability in residential leases is unconscionable and must be held to be ineffective. Therefore, waiver is not a valid defense to a complaint based upon the warranty.

Finally, appellants allege that the trial court erred in sustaining appellee's demurrer to count two of their complaint which alleged intentional infliction of emotional distress. We agree and, therefore, reverse the court's ruling on the demurrer.

As defined by Section 46 of the Restatement (Second) of Torts,

> (1) One who by extreme and outrageous conduct intentionally and recklessly causes severe emotional distress to another is subject to liability for such emotional distress, and if bodily harm to the other results from it, for such bodily harm.

While we refuse to hold that a breach of the implied warranty of habitability constitutes intentional infliction of emotional distress as a matter of law, we do hold that appellants have the right to allege and to try to prove that appellee, by breaching the warranty, has intentionally inflicted emotional distress upon the appellants. At least one other court has reached a similar conclusion in the context of a landlord/tenant case. Aweeka v. Bonds, 20 Cal. App. 3d 278, 97 Cal. Rptr. 650 (1971). The Restatement (Second) of Torts also notes that landlords previously have been held liable for intentional infliction of emotional distress "for extreme abuse of their position." §46, comment (e).

"Preliminary objections in the nature of a demurrer should be sustained only where it appears with certainty that upon the facts averred the law will not permit the plaintiff to recover." Papieves v. Kelly, 437 Pa. 373, 381, 263 A.2d 118, 122 (1970). Upon reviewing the record in this case, we find that appellants alleged sufficient facts in both counts of their complaint to overcome a ruling against them as a matter of law. Accordingly, we reverse the ruling of the lower court, reinstate appellants' complaint, and remind this case for proceedings consistent with this opinion. . . .

SPAETH, Judge, concurring:

I join in the majority opinion. I do not understand it, however, to preclude a bona fide agreement whereby parties of equal bargaining power shift the obligation to render the leased premises habitable. For example, suppose a landlord has obtained residential zoning for the use of loft space. It should not, I think, be impossible for the landlord and a prospective tenant to agree that for a reduced amount of rent, the tenant, rather than the landlord, will make such agreed upon improvements as are necessary to make the premises fit for human habitation. The enforcibility of such an agreement would depend upon a showing of a bona fide understanding, between parties of equal bargaining power, that such improvements will in fact be made. In such circumstances the landlord's obligation to ensure compliance with the warranty would remain in full effect; the agreement would merely shift the obligation of performance of the agreed terms.

PRICE, Judge, dissenting.

Once again, the majority has elected to make a significant change in landlord-tenant law in this Commonwealth in order, in its opinion, to remedy inadequacies in today's residential housing. I dissent for the reasons stated in my dissenting opinion in Pugh v. Holmes, 253 Pa. Super. 76, 384 A.2d 1234 (1978).

The law in Pennsylvania has always been that while a landlord may expressly covenant premises as tenantable, there is no implied warranty to that effect, and the landlord has no ongoing duty of repair. Lopez v. Gukenback, 391 Pa. 359, 137 A.2d 771 (1958). The majority, however, has deemed it appropriate to adopt an implied warranty of habitability in residential leases. I adhere to my conviction that responsibility for such a change, if it is to be made, rests with the legislature, so that exact standards may be formulated and a rent-withholding mechanism may be established. I can foresee several problems which the *Pugh* majority did not intend, but which will inevitably flow from this court's adoption of an implied warranty of habitability in residential leases. The purpose of that decision was to reduce the shortage of decent dwellings available, particularly to low income tenants. Most assuredly, the cost of repairs will be passed on to the tenant through increased rent. But a more detrimental result of *Pugh* is that many owners of marginal housing may deem the cost of repairs too substantial and the return on investment too questionable, and they will opt to close dwellings, thereby compounding the housing problem.

Beyond that, I find the further extension of the *Pugh* case by the majority absolutely offensive to contract principles. *Pugh* maintained that a lease should be viewed as a contract, and that the covenants of the two parties thereto must be read as dependent. Yet in this case, the court ignores the contractual provisions of the agreement into which the two parties entered. One clause of the lease provides: "Premises taken in as is condition, tenants know the roof has a leak in the same."

The Uniform Commercial Code, Section 2-316(3)(a) provides:

[U]nless the circumstances indicate otherwise, all implied warranties are excluded by expressions like "as is," "with all faults" or other language which in common understanding calls the buyer's attention to the exclusion of warranties and makes plain that there is no implied warranty. . . .

The majority declares that "an attempted waiver of the implied warranty of habitability in residential leases is unconscionable and must be held to be ineffective." (Majority opn. at 245). Although Article 2 of the Uniform Commercial Code covers only the sale of goods, the freedom of contract which it recognizes in such transactions should likewise be acknowledged in the landlord-tenant relationship, which the majority has dubbed a contractual one. One should be free to bargain for premises of lesser quality to secure housing at a cheaper cost, if that is desired. At the very least, appellants in this case should not be entitled to any relief for alleged damages attributable to the leaking roof, a defect specified in the contract and accepted by appellants from the start of their tenancy. Instead, the majority is holding that as a matter of law, no waiver of the implied warranty of habitability will be upheld by our courts. . . .

NOTE

1. See generally, Moskowitz, The Implied Warranty of Habitability: A New Doctrine Raising New Issues, 62 Calif. L. Rev. 1444 (1974).

In footnote 75, Judge Jacobs quotes a passage from the Washington case of Foisy v. Wyman to support his contention that even a bargained-for disclaimer of the implied warranty of habitability should not be enforced. During the trial of the *Foisy* case, Wyman (the tenant-purchaser who was asserting the right to be protected by a nondisclaimable warranty of habitability) testified as follows in response to questions put by his own attorney:

Q. So, it was your understanding that you were purchasing the house and that is your only obligation to pay $50 a month?
A. That was the whole understanding at the conception of the deal because her mother told me [objection].
Q. So, the only time prior to March you were on the premises was to just look at it?
A. Right. I told them I would buy and they said fine. They put me in it for $50 a month.
Q. Had you done any work cleaning up the house or anything around the premises before you moved in on March?
A. Oh, yes, I had to.
Q. Before you moved in?
A. Right, I had to. In the basement there was termites and there was things.
Q. When were you doing those things?
A. In February. . . .
Q. At that time did you have any agreement with the Foisys as to whether or not you were going to purchase it?
A. I had the agreement before I walked in that house. That's when they told me you can have it for $50 a month. They wanted $87 a month. I said it isn't worth it because it's sitting still and the windows are out. [Interruption].
Q. That understanding was that you were going to pay $50 per month?

> A. Correct. That is the only way I would walk in that house because I wasn't in the proper position to bargain. They bargained to me because I saw a deal and I grabbed it. . . .

(This exchange is quoted in a dissenting opinion in the *Foisy* case, 515 P.2d 160 at 168-69.) If the plaintiff in Fair v. Negley had given similar testimony, do you think the majority's treatment of the "as is" clause at issue in that case would have been affected? Or does the majority's view of the clause rest upon considerations of public policy that no amount of voluntary bargaining can displace?

2. In his dissenting opinion in the principal case, Judge Price suggests that the implication of a nondisclaimable warranty of habitability in residential leases does the poor more harm than good by forcing the owners of marginal housing to withdraw their property from the market. For a detailed and critical assessment of this view, see Kennedy, Distributive and Paternalist Motives in Contract and Tort Law, with Special Reference to Compulsory Terms and Unequal Bargaining Power, 41 Md. L. Rev. 563, 604-609 (1982).

3. The majority in part rests its decision to disregard the "as is" clause in the parties' contract on what it takes to be the disparity in their relative bargaining power, viewing the agreement between them, in now-familiar terminology, as a "contract of adhesion."

There are, however, many contracts that fit this general description which we do not think objectionable for that reason alone. Suppose, for example, that A owns a painting B desperately wants and offers to sell it to B for a stated price, adding, "this is my final offer; take it or leave it." If B agrees, and then reneges, can he avoid A's claim for damages by arguing that their agreement was "adhesive"? How is this contract different from the one at issue in Fair v. Negley? Consult Kronman, Paternalism and the Law of Contracts, 92 Yale L.J. 763 (1983).

4. In O'Callaghan v. Waller & Beckwith Realty Co., 15 Ill. 2d 436, 155 N.E.2d 545 (1958), *as modified on denial of rehearing* (1959), the plaintiff sued to recover for personal injuries suffered while crossing the paved courtyard between her apartment and the garage in a large apartment complex maintained and operated by the defendant. The plaintiff was a tenant in defendant's building and her lease contained an "exculpatory" clause relieving the defendant of all liability to the plaintiff for personal injury or property damage caused by any act or neglect on the part of the defendant or its agents. Over a strong dissent, a majority of the Illinois Supreme Court affirmed a lower court decision holding that the plaintiff's action was barred by the exculpatory clause. In his opinion for the majority, Justice Schaefer wrote:

> A contract shifting the risk of liability for negligence may benefit a tenant as well as a landlord. (See Cerny-Pickas & Co. v. C. R. Jahn Co., 7 Ill. 2d 393.) Such an agreement transfers the risk of a possible financial burden and so lessens the impact of the sanctions that induce adherence to

the required standard of care. But this consideration is applicable as well to contracts for insurance that indemnify against liability for one's own negligence. Such contracts are accepted, and even encouraged. See Ill. Rev. Stat. 1957, chap. 95½, pars. 7-202(1) and 7-315.

The plaintiff contends that due to a shortage of housing there is a disparity of bargaining power between lessors of residential property and their lessees that gives landlords an unconscionable advantage over tenants. And upon this ground it is said that exculpatory clauses in residential leases must be held to be contrary to public policy. No attempt was made upon the trial to show that Mrs. O'Callaghan was at all concerned about the exculpatory clause, that she tried to negotiate with the defendant about its modification or elimination, or that she made any effort to rent an apartment elsewhere. To establish the existence of a widespread housing shortage the plaintiff points to numerous statutes designed to alleviate the shortage, (see Ill. Rev. Stat. 1957, chap. 67½, *passim*) and to the existence of rent control during the period of the lease. 65 Stat. 145 (1947), 50 append. U.S.C., sec. 1894.

Unquestionably there has been a housing shortage. That shortage has produced an active and varied legislative response. Since legislative attention has been so sharply focused upon housing problems in recent years, it might be assumed that the legislature has taken all of the remedial action that it thought necessary or desirable. One of the major legislative responses was the adoption of rent controls which placed ceilings upon the amount of rent that landlords could charge. But the very existence of that control made it impossible for a lessor to negotiate for an increased rental in exchange for the elimination of an exculpatory clause. We are asked to assume, however, that the legislative response to the housing shortage has been inadequate and incomplete, and to augment it judicially.

The relationship of landlord and tenant does not have the monopolistic characteristics that have characterized some other relations with respect to which exculpatory clauses have been held invalid. There are literally thousands of landlords who are in competition with one another. The rental market affords a variety of competing types of housing accommodations, from simple farm house to luxurious apartment. The use of a form contract does not of itself establish disparity of bargaining power. That there is a shortage of housing at one particular time or place does not indicate that such shortages have always and everywhere existed, or that there will be shortages in the future. Judicial determinations of public policy cannot readily take account of sporadic and transitory circumstances. They should rather, we think, rest upon a durable moral basis. Other jurisdictions have dealt with this problem by legislation. (McKinney's Consol. Laws of N.Y. Ann., Real Property Laws, sec. 234, Vol. 49, Part I; Ann. Laws of Mass., Vol. 6, c. 186, sec. 15.) In our opinion the subject is one that is appropriate for legislative rather than judicial action.

In 1959 the Illinois legislature enacted a statute that provided:

Every covenant, agreement or understanding in or in connection with or collateral to any lease of real property, except those business leases in which any municipal corporation, governmental unit, or corporation regulated by a State or Federal Commission or agency is lessor or lessee, exempting the lessor from liability for damages for injuries to person or property caused by or resulting from the negligence of the lessor, his agents, servants or employees, in the operation or maintenance of the demised premises or the real property containing the demised premises shall be deemed to be void as against public policy and wholly unenforceable.

Ill. Rev. Stat. 1967, ch. 80, par. 15a.

In Sweney Gasoline & Oil Co. v. Toledo, Peoria & Western R.R., 42 Ill. 2d 265, 247 N.E.2d 603 (1969), the Illinois Supreme Court held the 1959 statute unconstitutional on the ground that the exemption of municipal and regulated corporations constituted "a discriminatory classification without any reasonable basis." Therefore, a majority of the court concluded, the *O'Callaghan* case was still good law in Illinois, so that the exculpatory clause in the Railroad's lease to the Oil Company was effective. Schaefer, J., who had written the majority opinion in *O'Callaghan*, entered the following dissent in *Sweney:*

> In 1958, in O'Callaghan v. Waller & Beckwith Realty Co., 15 Ill. 2d 436, 155 N.E.2d 545, this court considered the validity, at common law, of exculpatory clauses in residential leases. The case was a very close one, and two members of the court joined in a strong dissent from the opinion which sustained their validity. The prevailing opinion concluded with a request for legislative action." Other jurisdictions have dealt with this problem by legislation. [Citations.] In our opinion the subject is one that is appropriate for legislative rather than judicial action." 15 Ill. 2d at 441, 155 N.E.2d at 547. The General Assembly responded promptly, and in 1959 adopted the statute which is now held unconstitutional.
>
> I agree that the statute as written violates the constitution, for the reasons stated in the opinion of the majority. But I regard the enactment of the statute as an expression of the public policy of the State which this court should respect, even though it cannot be given complete effect according to its terms. That statute declares "void as against public policy and wholly unenforceable" every exculpatory clause in any lease, business or residential, with the narrow and irrational exception in favor of particular lessors and lessees of business property which totally defeats its major purpose. I would hold that the statute, despite its invalidity, is an expression of public policy which fully justifies this court in now holding, as a matter of common law, that exculpatory clauses in leaseholds are void.

In 1971 the Illinois legislature reenacted the statute that had been declared unconstitutional in *Sweney*, with the invalid exception for municipal and regulated corporations deleted. Ill. Ann. Stat. ch. 80, §91 (Smith-Hurd Supp. 1980). The new statute has been strictly construed by the Illinois courts, but its constitutionality has not been seriously challenged.

Outside Illinois the general trend seems to be against the traditional view upholding exculpatory clauses. A few states, such as Maryland, Massachusetts, and New York, prohibit exculpatory clauses by statutes similar to the one adopted in Illinois. More importantly, the Uniform Residential Landlord and Tenant Act contains a section prohibiting exculpatory and indemnifying provisions, although it does permit some shifting of the landlord's duties to the tenant. U.R.L.T.A. §1.403 (1972). The courts have also contributed to the erosion of the traditional law on exculpatory clauses. Some courts have invalidated such clauses by finding inequality of bargaining power or unconscionability in the contract. Others have distinguished between active and passive negligence on the part of the landlord, and honored exculpatory clauses only where the latter was involved. For a discussion of the trend against exculpatory clauses in the general context of landlord-tenant relations, see Browder, The Taming of a Duty — The Tort Liability of Landlords, 81 Mich. L. Rev. 99 (1982). For a more detailed analysis of the validity of exculpatory clauses see Note, Country Club Apartments v. Scott: Exculpatory Clauses in Leases Declared Void, 32 Mercer L. Rev. 419 (1980).

Section 5.   The Burdens of Innocence: Anticipatory Repudiation and the Duty to Mitigate Damages

A (in return for a valuable consideration) promises B that on a specified date he will mow B's lawn, or deliver a truckload of coal to B's factory, or transfer to B the title to a particular parcel of land. If, on the appointed date, A fails without excuse to do what he has promised, he is in breach of contract and B is entitled to compensation for any loss he may have suffered as a result. (B may even have the right to compel A's performance, if the case is an appropriate one and it is still within A's power to comply.) But suppose that a week or a month or a year before the date set for his performance, A announces that he has no intention of keeping his promise and advises B to make alternative plans. An announcement of this sort is what has come to be known in the law of contracts as an "anticipatory repudiation," and a great deal of judicial energy has been spent, over the past century or so, in an effort to clarify its legal consequences.

Before the great case of Hochster v. De La Tour, 2 El. & Bl. 678 (1853), it appears to have been the rule that in circumstances of the sort just described, the promisee could not bring an action for damages before the time of performance agreed upon by the parties (which might, of course, be long after the promisor's repudiation of the contract). Whatever the reasons for the pre-*Hochster* view (whose most vigorous proponent was Samuel Williston, see *infra* p. 1287), it did not yield all at once, but gave way only by degrees and (in certain jurisdictions at least) only after considerable resistance. Nor did the eventual triumph of *Hochster* and the cases that canonized it (like Roehm v. Horst, *infra* p. 1279) mean the end of confusion and controversy in this area of law. In some contexts at least, as Phelps v. Herro, *infra* p. 1291, suggests, the old uncertainties linger on and a promisee may still find obstacles in the way of recovering the full value of his expectancy before the date on which the repudiating promisor had originally agreed to perform. And even where the existence of a right to recover immediately upon repudiation is a matter free of doubt, large problems can remain regarding the proper method for measuring the promisee's damages (which should, in theory, put him in the same position he would have been in had the promisor performed — no better and no worse).

The anticipatory repudiation cases collected in this section focus on the rights of the promisee; along with his rights, however, the promisee whose contract has been repudiated may also have certain responsibilities. Suppose A *does* announce that he no longer intends to deliver coal to B's factory on the appointed day. If B fails to obtain the coal he needs from someone else, may he sue A for the (easily foreseeable) damages that result when B is forced to close his factory for lack of fuel? This and related questions have traditionally been treated under the rubric of mitigation: When, and to what extent, must the innocent party in a contract dispute take steps to mitigate (i.e., reduce) the harm caused by the other party's breach? The scope of the duty to mitigate damages (which, strictly speaking, is not a duty at all but a condition or limit on the promisee's recovery) and its underlying rationale constitute the second set of problems addressed in the materials that follow. In fact, as the cases themselves make clear, the doctrinal distinction between mitigation and anticipatory repudiation is somewhat artificial and one should not expect the rules associated with these two ideas to be neatly separated. Functionally, they belong together, and in reflecting upon either, one is led by a natural progression to think about the other.

DANIELS v. NEWTON
114 Mass. 530 (1874)

WELLS, J. This action is for breach of an agreement in writing, under seal, for the purchase of certain land from the plaintiff by the defendants. The time for performance is indicated by two clauses; one that "said premises are to be conveyed within thirty days from this date"; the other that "in case the said parties of the second part should fail to sell their estate at the expiration of the thirty days, then we agree to extend this agreement for thirty days." The inference from the latter clause is that the defendants were to have the whole thirty days for performance on their part, and, in the contingency mentioned, thirty days more. Such was the effect given to the terms of the written instrument, by the ruling at the trial, and we think correctly.

The plaintiff relied upon a supposed breach of the agreement by the defendants within the thirty days; to wit, May 29, the writing being dated May 15, and thereupon had brought his action May 30. The ruling of the court upon this point was that if the defendants "fixed a day, within said thirty days, for the performance of said agreement by the respective parties, and the plaintiff was then ready to perform his part, and the defendants then refused absolutely to perform said agreement on their part, then or at any other time, that would be a breach of the agreement on their part for which the plaintiff can maintain this action."

We do not understand this ruling to have been based upon the supposition of an oral agreement in regard to the time of performance varying the terms of the written instrument as an executory contract. It would have been clearly erroneous in that aspect; first, because no such substituted agreement is set forth in the declaration; secondly, because such an oral agreement in regard to land would be within the statute of frauds, and could not be so enforced.

Subsequent oral agreements in regard to the mode and time of performance of written contracts relating to land, are doubtless admissible to affect the question whether the conduct of either party, as proved, constitutes a breach of his written agreement. In that aspect, the evidence adduced by the plaintiff in this case was competent, and might have warranted the jury in finding a breach of the contract by the defendants, if they did not revoke their refusal within the thirty days, even without any further offer to perform on the part of the plaintiff.

The action having been brought immediately upon the refusal, and within the time allowed for performance by the terms of the written contract sued upon, the effect of the ruling was that an absolute refusal of performance, purporting and intended to be a refusal to fulfil the contract at any time, would be of itself a breach of a contract for acts to be done within a time not yet expired, so that an action would lie forthwith. The proposition involved in this ruling, to wit, that there may be a breach of contract, giving a present right of action, before the performance is due by its terms, seems to have been adopted by recent English decisions. Frost v. Knight, L.R. 7 Ex. 111 (1872). Hochster v. De La Tour, 2 E. & B. 678 (1853).

It is said to be applicable, not only in cases where performance has been rendered impossible by the voluntary conduct of the party, as, in agreements for marriage or conveyance of land, by marriage or conveyance to another, and by way of exception to the general rule formerly maintained, but to the full extent of a general rule; so that an absolute and unqualified declaration of a purpose not to fulfil or be held by the contract, made by one party to the other, may be treated as of itself a present breach of the contract by repudiation, as well before as after the time stipulated for its fulfilment by such party. The point was elaborately discussed in Frost v. Knight, by Lord Chief Justice Cockburn; and the principle evolved is expressed in these propositions, on page 114:

> The promisee has an inchoate right to the performance of the bargain, which becomes complete when the time for performance has arrived. In the mean time he has a right to have the contract kept open as a subsisting and effective contract. Its unimpaired and unimpeached efficacy may be essential to his interests. His rights acquired under it may be dealt with by him in various ways for his benefit and advantage.
>
> The contract having been thus broken by the promisor and treated as broken by the promisee, performance at the appointed time becomes excluded, and the breach by reason of the future non-performance becomes virtually involved in the action as one of the consequences of the repudiation of the contract; and the eventual non-performance may therefore, by anticipation, be treated as a cause of action, and damages be assessed and recovered in respect of it, though the time for performance may yet be remote.

The first of these two propositions would apply with peculiar force to commercial paper, especially if its repudiation by the maker were made public. We see no reason for a distinction which should exclude it from the same rule that applies to other promises in writing, in respect to what will constitute a breach of the principal contract between the maker and payee. We are not aware, however, that any decision has carried out the rule by applying it to such contracts; and we doubt if the learned jurists who propounded it would have been willing to follow it to that extent.

The doctrine has never been adopted in this Commonwealth nor has it received any recognition, so far as we are able to learn, beyond that in Heard v. Bowers, 23 Pick. 455, 460. The court in that case, refer to Ford v. Tiley, 6 B. & C. 325, 327, and 5 Vin. Ab. 224; the doctrine announced in Ford v. Tiley, being, as it appears to us, an erroneous application of the maxims contained in Viner.

A renunciation of the agreement, by declarations or inconsistent conduct, before the time of performance, may give cause for treating it as rescinded, and excuse the other party from making ready for performance on his part, or relieve him from the necessity of offering performance in order to enforce his rights. It may destroy all capacity of the party, so disavowing its obligations, to assert rights under it afterwards, if the other party has acted upon such disavowal. But we are unable to see how it can, of itself, constitute a present violation of any legal rights of the other party, or confer upon him a present right of action. An executory contract ordinarily confers no title or interest in the subject matter of the agreement. Until the time arrives when, by the terms of the agreement, he is or might be entitled to its performance, he can suffer no injury or deprivation which can form a ground of damages. There is neither violation of right, nor loss upon which to found an action. The true rule seems to us to be that in order to charge one in damages for breach of an executory personal contract, the other party must show a refusal or neglect to perform, at a time when and under conditions such that he is or might be entitled to require performance. Frazier v. Cushman, 12 Mass. 277. Pomroy v. Gold, 2 Met. 500. Hapgood v. Shaw, 105 Mass. 276. Carpenter v. Holcomb, 105 Mass. 280. Such undoubtedly was the interpretation of the common law in all the earlier decisions. Phillpotts v. Evans, 5 M. & W. 475. Ripley v. M'Clure, 4 Exch. 345. Lovelock v. Franklyn, 8 Q.B. 371.

The case of Ford v. Tiley, 6 B. & C. 325, cited in Heard v. Bowers, was an action on an agreement of the defendant that he would, as soon as he should become possessed of a certain public house, execute a lease thereof to the plaintiff for a term of years from December 21, 1825. There was in fact an outstanding lease of the premises to another, to expire at midsummer, in 1827. Before that term expired, the defendant joined with the trustees, who held the legal title, in a lease to another party for 23 years. It was held to be a breach of his agreement with the plaintiff, for which an action would lie at once; because the defendant had given up his right to have the possession, and put it out of his power, so long as his own lease for twenty-three years should last. It does not appear that the suit was brought before December 21, 1825; nor that the time when the defendant would become possessed, was mentioned in the agreement. It was not the case of an agreement to make a lease at a named future day. The outstanding lease was an extrinsic fact, merely affecting the occurrence of the contingency upon which the performance of the agreement depended; it had no other force in the contract. When, therefore, the defendant made a lease to a stranger, he could no longer say that he was prevented from becoming possessed by the outstanding previous lease, because he had put it out of his power to come into possession, if that were surrendered or otherwise terminated. The plaintiffs' right to have a lease presently was subject only to a contingency, of which the defendant had no longer the ability to avail himself. The judgment accords with the rule we have indicated. But in giving judgment, Bayley, J., citing 1 Rol. Ab. 248; 5 Vin. Ab. 225; 21 Ed. IV. 55, and Co. Litt. 221 b, proceeds to say:

> Now if the feoffment of a stranger before the day be a breach of a condition to enfeoff J. S. at a given day, the granting of a lease to a stranger before the day will be a breach of a contract to grant a lease to J. S. at a given day, and a fortiori will it be a breach so long as the lease to such stranger remains in force.

It seems to us, however, that the reasoning from conditions of forfeiture or defeasance to executory contracts is illogical. If one, having an estate on condition, by his own act in dealing with the estate, puts it out of his power to perform or comply with the condition, he does what is inconsistent with the terms upon which alone he has the estate; and his grantor may reënter, even before the time of stipulated performance, not because of a new right acquired by the terms of the agreement, but because the right of the other party having become forfeited or extinguished by his breach of the condition, or violation of the terms of his tenancy, the grantor or feoffor is restored to his former estate and right. It is by virtue of that right or title that he enters, the other party being no longer able to avail himself of his conditional estate or right. The analogy holds good if the plaintiff's right to require performance of the agreement awaits only a contingency which the defendant removes by making it impossible, which was the real case in Ford v. Tiley. It gives no support to the very different proposition that, in a contract to be performed on a given day, the voluntary disability of one party will entitle the other to require performance, or to have an action for non-performance, before that day arrives.

The distinction is recognized by the authorities referred to by Mr. Justice Bayley. Lord Coke says: "And herein a diversity is to be observed between a disability for a time on the part of the feoffee, and a disability for a time on the part of the feoffor." In the one case, albeit "a certain day be limited, yet the feoffee being once disabled is ever disabled."

> And the reason of the diversity is, for that, as Littleton saith, maintenant by the disability of the feoffee, the condition is broken, and the feoffor may enter, but so it is not by the disability of the feoffor, or his heirs; for if they perform the condition within the time, it is sufficient, for that they may at any time perform the condition before the day.

Co. Litt. 221 b; 5 Vin. Ab. 224, Condition, B. c.

We have examined with care the opinions of Lord Chief Justice Cockburn in Frost v. Knight, and of Lord Campbell in Hochster v. De La Tour, and we are not convinced that the conclusions at which they arrive are founded in sound principles of jurisprudence, or sustained by the authorities cited in their support.

Frost v. Knight was an action upon a promise to marry the plaintiff on the death of the defendant's father. The defendant broke off the engagement by announcing his intention not to fulfil his promise. The action was brought without waiting for the death of the defendant's father. The plaintiff having recovered a verdict, judgment was arrested by the Court of Exchequer; but on error it was held, in the Exchequer Chamber, that she was entitled to retain the verdict. The lord chief justice cites Lovelock v. Franklin, 8 Q.B. 371, and Short v. Stone, 8 Q.B. 358, as having "established that where a party bound to the performance of a contract at a future time, puts it out of his own power to fulfil it, an action will at once lie." Neither decision cited establishes that proposition, where a definite time for performance is appointed by the terms of the contract; but only where the plaintiff was entitled to require performance upon some previous act or request which the conduct of the defendant has dispensed with.

Short v. Stone was upon a promise to marry the plaintiff "within a reasonable time after request." The defendant married another, and this was alleged as the breach. It was held that request was not necessary, and need not be alleged. It was rendered unavailing, and therefore unnecessary, by the act of the defendant, which was of itself a breach of the contract by rendering performance impossible. No question arose, or could arise, whether the action was premature, because there was no future time certain for performance. The defendant had made the only limit of time impossible.

Lovelock v. Franklyn was upon an agreement to assign a lease, at any time within seven years, upon payment of a sum named. The decision is explicitly upon the ground that the option as to the time, within the seven years, was with the plaintiff. "The defendant is to be ready throughout." Coleridge, J., p. 375. Denman, C.J., says:

> Here the party puts it out of his power to perform what he has agreed to perform; that is, to assign at any time at which he may be called upon. This distinction shows that the passage cited from Lord Coke is inapplicable; that proves no more, on the point now before us, than that if an act is to be performed at a future time specified, the contract is not broken by something which may merely prevent the performance in the mean time. We are introducing no novelty. In all the cases put for the defendants, the party had the means of rehabilitating himself before the time of performance arrived; here he has incapacitated himself at the very time when he may be called on and should be ready.

Patteson, J., says: "In this particular contract, the defendant has undertaken to keep himself ready for the whole time." So far from being sustained by this case, the proposition, to which it is cited by Lord Chief Justice Cockburn, is most carefully excluded, if not expressly disavowed.

The proposition, even if established, is not decisive of the case now before us. We have discussed it, however, because it has an important bearing upon the argument, and is essential to the result reached in Frost v. Knight. The lord chief justice, taking it as established by the cases cited, proceeds to the next step. He says, "The case of Hochster v. De La Tour, upheld in this court in the Danube & Black Sea Co. v. Xenos, [13 C.B.(N.S.) 825,] went further, and established that notice of an intended breach of a contract to be performed in futuro had a like effect."

Hochster v. De La Tour appears to us to be the only case which
sustains this position as an adjudication, although that decision has been
recognized in several subsequent cases. Avery v. Bowden, 5 E. & B. 714; 6
E. & B. 952. Wilkinson v. Verity, L.R. 6 C.P. 206. It was an action upon a
contract of hiring to go as courier for the plaintiff from June 1, 1852, at
monthly wages. There was notice of renunciation of the employment;
and the action brought May 22, 1852, was sustained. Lord Campbell says:

> But it cannot be laid down as a universal rule that, where by agreement an
> act is to be done on a future day, no action can be brought for a breach of
> the agreement till the day for doing the act has arrived. If a man promises to
> marry a woman on a future day, and before that day marries another
> woman, he is instantly liable to an action for breach of promise of marriage.
> Short v. Stone, 8 Q.B. 358.

The statement we have already made of Short v. Stone, will show how
the essential fact in that case is mistaken, and the reason of the decision
misapplied. He adds: "If a man contracts to execute a lease on and from a
future day for a certain term, and, before that day, executes a lease to
another for the same term, he may be immediately sued for breaking the
contract. Ford v. Tiley, 6 B. & C. 325." We have already shown in what
manner Ford v. Tiley fails to sustain the position for which it is cited.

[In an omitted passage, Wells, J., discussed several other English
cases.]

But the question, in what mode and at what time that remedy may be
sought, must depend upon the provisions of his contract, and the nature
of the rights to which it entitles him, and which are affected by the
conduct of the other party. Throughout the whole discussion both in
Hochster v. De La Tour, and Frost v. Knight, the question as to what
conduct of the defendant will relieve the plaintiff from the necessity of
showing readiness and an offer to perform at the day, in order to make
out a breach by the other, appears to us to be confounded with that of the
plaintiff's cause of action; or rather, the question, in what consists the
plaintiff's cause of action, is lost sight of; the court dealing only with
the conduct of the defendant in repudiating the obligations of his contract.

Much argument is expended in both cases upon the ground of convenience and mutual advantage to the parties from the rule sought to be
established. But before that argument can properly have weight, the
point to be reached must first be shown to be consistent with logical
deductions from the strictly legal aspects of the case. The legal remedy
must be founded on some present legal right, and must conform to the
nature of that right. Until the plaintiff has either suffered loss or wrong in
respect of that which has already vested in him in right, or has been
deprived of or prevented from acquiring that which he is entitled to have

or demand, he has no ground on which to seek a remedy by way of reparation. The conduct of the defendant is no wrong to the plaintiff until it actually invades some right of his. Actual injury and not anticipated injury is the ground of legal recovery. The plaintiff's rights are invaded by repudiation of the contract only when it produces the effect of non-performance, or prevents him from entering upon or completing performance on his part, at a time when and in the manner in which he is entitled to perform it or to have it performed.

That this is the natural and ordinary rule seems to be recognized by Lord Campbell, when he declares that "it cannot be laid down as a universal rule," and proceeds to point out exceptions. And Lord Chief Justice Cockburn concedes it to be true "that there can be no actual breach of a contract by reason of non-performance, so long as the time for performance has not yet arrived." L.R. 7 Ex. 114. But a preceding "inchoate right" is discovered, and a corresponding obligation implied, upon which there may be held to be "a breach of the contract when the promisor repudiates it and declares he will no longer be bound by it."

In Hochster v. De La Tour, Lord Campbell assigns, as one reason for the decision, that in case of employment as courier, and of promise to marry, a relation is established between the parties by the contract, even before the time of performance; "they impliedly promise that in the mean time neither will do anything to the prejudice of the other inconsistent with that relation"; and "it seems to be a breach of an implied contract if either of them renounces the engagement." In Frost v. Knight, the lord chief justice remarks of the promise to marry: "On such a contract being entered into, not only does a right to its completion arise with reference to domestic relations and possibly pecuniary advantages, as also to the social status accruing on marriage, but a new status, that of betrothment, at once arises between the parties." "Each becomes bound to the other; neither can, consistently with such a relation, enter into a similar engagement with another person; each has an implied right to have this relation continued till the contract is finally accomplished by marriage."

These, however, are considerations which touch the interpretation and effect of the particular kind of contract; and so far as they tend to sustain the decisions upon the ground of implied obligations arising and requiring observance at once upon entering into the relation by means of such a contract, they also tend to remove the decisions themselves out of the range of the question we are now discussing. If there be sound reason to deduce from a promise to marry, or to employ in a special capacity, at a future time, present obligations of implied contract, upon which an action may be founded, in which the breach of the entire agreement "by reason of the future non-performance" will be "virtually involved," "as one of the consequences of the repudiation of the contract," it surely is not sound reasoning by means of that process to arrive at the conclusion that all contracts, having a future day for their performance, include like rights and obligations, so as to enable one party to sue at once, as for a breach, whenever the other announces beforehand his purpose of future non-fulfilment. If this is the result, as it appears to be, of the English decisions referred to, or of the reasoning in those cases, we cannot accede to it. We have no occasion now to determine what may be the rule, where the contract may fairly be interpreted as establishing between the parties a present relation of mutual obligations, because we are of opinion that no such implied obligations can be engrafted upon the contract in the present case. It simply binds the defendants to receive a deed of real estate and pay or secure the purchase money; and its written provisions, by which alone their obligations are to be ascertained, allow them thirty days at least within which to fulfil their agreement. The plaintiff could require nothing of them until the expiration of that time; and no conduct on their part or declaration, whether of promise or denial, could give him any cause of action in respect of that agreement of sale. This action therefore cannot be maintained.

Exceptions sustained.

NOTE

1. The principal case was an action by a vendor of land against a repudiating vendee. Would the same considerations apply to an action by a vendee against a repudiating vendor? To the Massachusetts court the answer was yes. Daniels v. Newton is followed in the Massachusetts reports by Nason v. Holt, 114 Mass. 541 (1874). A contract for the sale of land was entered into on September 14, 1871, conveyance to be made within 14 days. On September 15 the vendor repudiated the agreement and on September 16 the vendee brought an action for breach of the contract. The vendor conveyed the land to one Smith by a deed dated September 16 which was acknowledged, delivered and recorded on September 23. *Held*, that the action did not lie. Wells, J., commented:

> The defendant was under no obligation to make the conveyance at that time [i.e., September 15], and was not called upon to do so. They [i.e., the "declarations" of repudiation made by the vendor] indicate a denial of his obligation, and a purpose to refuse compliance with the terms of the written agreement signed by his agents. But that would not prevent his subsequent conclusion to carry the agreement into effect. It is not, of itself, a present breach of the agreement. Daniels v. Newton, *supra*.

114 Mass. at 542.

Under the reasoning of the opinion in Daniels v. Newton, could the vendee in Nason v. Holt have properly brought his action on September 23 (when the deed to Smith was delivered) or would he have had to wait the full 14 days until September 28?

2. Hochster v. De La Tour, discussed in the opinion in Daniels v. Newton, became, on both sides of the Atlantic, the leading case in favor of the doctrine of anticipatory breach. For more on Hochster v. De La Tour see the opinion of Fuller, C.J., in the following principal case.

ROEHM v. HORST
178 U.S. 1 (1900)

Mr. Chief Justice FULLER, after stating the case, delivered the opinion of the court.

It is conceded that the contracts set out in the finding of facts were four of ten simultaneous contracts, for one hundred bales each, covering the furnishing of one thousand bales of hops during a period of five years, of which six hundred bales had been delivered and paid for. If the transaction could be treated as amounting to a single contract for one thousand bales, the breach alleged would have occurred while the contract was in the course of performance; but plaintiffs' declaration or statement of demand averred the execution of the four contracts, "two for the purchase and sale of Pacific Coast hops of the crop of 1896, and two for the purchase and sale of Pacific Coast hops of the crop of 1897," set them out in extenso, and claimed recovery for breach thereof, and in this view of the case, while as to the first of the four contracts, the time to commence performance had arrived, and the October shipment had been tendered and refused, the breach as to the other three contracts was the refusal to perform before the time for performance had arrived.

The first contract falls within the rule that a contract may be broken by the renunciation of liability under it in the course of performance and suit may be immediately instituted. But the other three contracts involve the question whether, where the contract is renounced before performance is due, and the renunciation goes to the whole contract, and is absolute and unequivocal, the injured party may treat the breach as complete and bring his action at once. Defendant repudiated all liability for hops of the crop of 1896 and of the crop of 1897, and notified plaintiffs that he should make (according to a letter of his attorney in the record that he had made) arrangements to purchase his stock of other parties, whereupon plaintiffs brought suit. The question is, therefore, presented, in respect of the three contracts, whether plaintiffs were entitled to sue at once or were obliged to wait until the time came for the first month's delivery under each of them.

It is not disputed that if one party to a contract has destroyed the subject-matter, or disabled himself so as to make performance impossible, his conduct is equivalent to a breach of the contract although the time for performance has not arrived; and also that if a contract provides for a series of acts, and actual default is made in the performance of one of them, accompanied by a refusal to perform the rest, the other party need not perform, but may treat the refusal as a breach of the entire contract, and recover accordingly.

And the doctrine that there may be an anticipatory breach of an executory contract by an absolute refusal to perform it, has become the settled law of England as applied to contracts for services, for marriage, and for the manufacture or sale of goods. The cases are extensively commented on in the notes to Cutter v. Powell, 2 Smith's Leading Cases, 1212, 1220, 9th edition by Richard Henn Collins and Arbuthnot. Some of these, though quite familiar, may well be referred to.

In Hochster v. De La Tour, 2 El. & Bl. 678, plaintiff, in April, 1852, had agreed to serve defendant, and defendant had undertaken to employ plaintiff, as courier, for three months from June first, on certain terms. On the eleventh of May, defendant wrote plaintiff that he had changed his mind, and declined to avail himself of plaintiff's services. Thereupon, and on May twenty-second, plaintiff brought an action at law for breach of contract in that defendant, before the said first of June, though plaintiff was always ready and willing to perform, refused to engage plaintiff or perform his promise, and then wrongfully exonerated plaintiff from the performance of the agreement, to his damage. And it was ruled that as there could be a breach of contract before the time fixed for performance, a positive and absolute refusal to carry out the contract prior to the date of actual default amounted to such a breach.

In the course of the argument, Mr. Justice Crompton observed:

> When a party announces his intention not to fulfill the contract, the other side may take him at his word and rescind the contract. The word "rescind" implies that both parties have agreed that the contract shall be at an end as if it had never been. But I am inclined to think that the party may also say:
>
>> Since you have announced that you will not go on with the contract, I will consent that it shall be at an end from this time; but I will hold you liable for the damage I have sustained; and I will proceed to make that damage as little as possible by making the best use I can of my liberty.

In delivering the opinion of the court (Campbell, C.J., Coleridge, Erle and Crompton, JJ.), Lord Campbell, after pointing out that at common law there were numerous cases in which an anticipatory act, such as an act rendering the contract impossible of performance, or disabling the party from performing it, would constitute a breach giving an immediate right of action, laid it down that a positive and unqualified refusal by one party to carry out the contract should be treated as belonging to the same category as such anticipatory acts, and said, p. 690:

> But it is surely much more rational, and more for the benefit of both parties, that, after the renunciation of the agreement by the defendant, the plaintiff should be at liberty to consider himself absolved from any future

performance of it, retaining his right to sue for any damage he has suffered from the breach of it. Thus, instead of remaining idle and laying out money in preparations which must be useless, he is at liberty to seek service under another employer, which would go in mitigation of the damages to which he would otherwise be entitled for a breach of the contract. It seems strange that the defendant, after renouncing the contract, and absolutely declaring that he will never act under it, should be permitted to object that faith is given to his assertion, and that an opportunity is not left to him of changing his mind. If the plaintiff is barred of any remedy by entering into an engagement inconsistent with starting as a courier with the defendant on the 1st of June, he is prejudiced by putting faith in the defendant's assertion; and it would be more consonant with principle, if the defendant were precluded from saying that he had not broken the contract when he declared that he entirely renounced it. Suppose that the defendant, at the time of his renunciation, had embarked on a voyage for Australia, so as to render it physically impossible for him to employ the plaintiff as a courier on the continent of Europe in the months of June, July and August, 1852; according to decided cases, the action might have been brought before the 1st of June; but the renunciation may have been founded on other facts, to be given in evidence, which would equally have rendered the defendant's performance of the contract impossible. The man who wrongfully renounces a contract into which he has deliberately entered cannot justly complain if he is immediately sued for a compensation in damages by the man whom he has injured; and it seems reasonable to allow an option to the injured party, either to sue immediately, or to wait till the time when the act was to be done, still holding it as prospectively binding for the exercise of this option, which may be advantageous to the innocent party, and cannot be prejudicial to the wrongdoer. An argument against the action before the 1st of June is urged from the difficulty of calculating the damages: but this argument is equally strong against an action before the 1st of September, when the three months would expire. In either case, the jury in assessing the damages would be justified in looking to all that had happened, or was likely to happen, to increase or mitigate the loss of the plaintiff down to the day of trial. We do not find any decision contrary to the view we are taking of this case.

In Frost v. Knight, L.R. 7 Ex. 111, defendant had promised to marry plaintiff so soon as his (defendant's) father should die. While his father was yet alive he absolutely refused to marry plaintiff, and it was held in the Exchequer Chamber, overruling the decision of the Court of Exchequer, L.R. 5 Ex. 322, that for this breach an action was well brought during the father's lifetime. Cockburn, C.J., said:

The law with reference to a contract to be performed at a future time, where the party bound to performance announces prior to the time his intention not to perform it, as established by the cases of Hochster v. De la Tour, 2 E. & B. 678, and the Danube & Black Sea Company v. Xenos, 13 C.B.(N.S.) 825, on the one hand, and Avery v. Bowden, 5 E. & B. 714,

Reid v. Hoskins, 6 E. & B. 953, and Barwick v. Buba, 2 C.B.(N.S.) 563, on the other, may be thus stated. The promisee, if he pleases, may treat the notice of intention as inoperative, and await the time when the contract is to be executed, and then hold the other party responsible for all the consequences of nonperformance; but in that case he keeps the contract alive for the benefit of the other party as well as his own; he remains subject to all his own obligations and liabilities under it, and enables the other party not only to complete the contract, if so advised, notwithstanding his previous repudiation of it, but also to take advantage of any supervening circumstance which would justify him in declining to complete it. On the other hand, the promisee may, if he thinks proper, treat the repudiation of the other party as a wrongful putting an end to the contract, and may at once bring his action as on a breach of it; and in such action he will be entitled to such damages as would have arisen from the nonperformance of the contract at the appointed time, subject, however, to abatement in respect of any circumstances which may have afforded him the means of mitigating his loss.

The case of Danube Company v. Xenos, 11 C.B.(N.S.) 152, is stated in the headnotes thus: On the 9th of July, A, by his agent, agreed to receive certain goods of B on board his ship to be carried to a foreign port, — the shipment to commence on the 1st of August. On the 21st of July A wrote to B, stating that he did not hold himself responsible for the contract, the agent having no authority to make it; and on the 23d he wrote again offering a substituted contract, but still repudiating the original contract. B by his attorneys gave A notice that he should hold him bound by the original contract, and that, if he persisted in refusing to perform it, he (B) should forthwith proceed to make other arrangements for forwarding the goods to their destination, and look to him for any loss. On the 1st of August, A again wrote to B, stating that he was then prepared to receive the goods on board his ship, making no allusion to the original contract. B had, however, in the meantime entered into a negotiation with one S for the conveyance of the goods by another ship, which negotiation ended in a contract for that purpose with S on the 2d of August. B thereupon sued A for refusing to receive the goods pursuant to his contract; and A brought a cross action against B for refusing to ship. Upon a special case stating these facts: Held, that it was competent to B to treat A's renunciation as a breach of the contract; and that the fact of such renunciation afforded a good answer to the cross action of A, and sustained B's plea that before breach A discharged him from the performance of the agreement.

Erle, C.J., said (p. 175):

In Cort v. Ambergate Railway Company, 17 Q.B. 127, it was held, that, upon the company giving notice to Mr. Cort that they would not receive any more of his chairs, he might abstain from manufacturing them, and sue the company for the breach of contract without tendering the goods for their acceptance. So, in Hochster v. De La Tour, 2 El. & Bl. 678, it was held that the courier whose services were engaged for a period to commence from a future day, being told before that day that they would not be accepted, was at liberty to treat that as a complete breach, and to hire himself to another party. And the boundary is equally well ascertained on the other side. Thus, in Avery v. Bowden, 5 El. & Bl. 714; 6 El. & Bl. 953, where the agent of the charterer intimated to the captain, that, in consequence of the breaking out of the war, he would be unable to furnish him with a cargo, and wished the captain to sail away, and the latter did not do so, it was held not to fall within the principle already adverted to, and not to amount to a breach or renunciation of the contract. But where there is an explicit declaration by the one party of his intention not to perform the contract on his part, which is accepted by the other as a breach of the contract, that beyond all doubt affords a cause of action.

The case was heard on error in the Exchequer Chamber before Cockburn, C.J., Pollock, C.B., Wightman, J., Crompton, J., Channel, B., and Wilde, B; and the judgment of the Common Pleas was unanimously affirmed. 13 C.B.(N.S.) 825.

[In an omitted passage, the Chief Justice reviewed other cases, English and American, in which the doctrine of Hochster v. De La Tour had been approved. He commented (178 U.S. at 13) that: "The doctrine which thus obtains in England has been almost universally accepted by the courts of this country, although the precise point has not been ruled by this court." He then continued:]

On the other hand, in Greenway v. Gaither, Taney, 227, Mr. Chief Justice Taney sitting on circuit in Maryland, declined to apply the rule in that particular case. The cause was tried in November, 1851, and more than two years after, at November term, 1853, application was made to the Chief Justice to seal a bill of exceptions. Hochster v. De La Tour was decided in June, 1853, and the decision of the Circuit Court had apparently been contrary to the rule laid down in that case. The Chief Justice refused to seal the bill, chiefly on the ground that under the circumstances the application came too late, but also on the ground that there was no error, as the rule was only applicable to contracts of the special character involved in that case, and the Chief Justice said as to the contract in hand, by which defendant engaged to pay certain sums of money on certain days:

It has never been supposed that notice to the holder of a bond, or a promissory note, or bill of exchange, that the party would not (from any cause) comply with the contract, would give to the holder an immediate cause of action, upon which he might sue before the time of payment arrived.

The rule is disapproved in Daniels v. Newton, 114 Mass. 530, and in Stanford v. McGill, 6 N. Dak. 536, on elaborate consideration. The opinion of Judge Wells in Daniels v. Newton is generally regarded as containing all that could be said in opposition to the decision of Hochster v. De La Tour, and one of the propositions on which the opinion rests is that the adoption of the rule in the instance of ordinary contracts would necessitate its adoption in the case of commercial paper. But we are unable to assent to that view. In the case of an ordinary money contract, such as a promissory note, or a bond, the consideration has passed; there are no mutual obligations; and cases of that sort do not fall within the reason of the rule.

In Nichols v. Scranton Steel Company, 137 N.Y. 471, 487, Mr. Justice Peckham, then a member of the Court of Appeals of New York, thus expresses the distinction:

> It is not intimated that in the bald case of a party bound to pay a promissory note which rests in the hands of the payee, but which is not yet due, such note can be made due by any notice of the maker that he does not intend to pay it when it matures. We decide simply this case where there are material provisions and obligations interdependent. In such case, and where one party is bound, from time to time, as expressed, to deliver part of an aggregate and specified amount of property to another, who is to pay for each parcel delivered at a certain time and in a certain way, a refusal to be further bound by the terms of the contract or to accept further deliveries, and a refusal to give the notes already demandable for a portion of the property that has been delivered, and a refusal to give any more notes at any time or for any purpose in the future, or to pay moneys at any time, which are eventually to be paid under the contract, all this constitutes a breach of the contract as a whole, and gives a present right of action against the party so refusing to recover damages which the other may sustain by reason of this refusal.

We think it obvious that both as to renunciation after commencement of performance and renunciation before the time for performance has arrived, money contracts, pure and simple, stand on a different footing from executory contracts for the purchase and sale of goods.

The other proposition on which the case of Daniels v. Newton was rested is that until the time for performance arrives, neither contracting party can suffer any injury which can form a ground of damages. Wells, J., said:

> An executory contract ordinarily affords no title or interest in the subject matter of the agreement. Until the time arrives when, by the terms of the agreement he is or might be entitled to its performance, he can suffer no injury or deprivation which can form a ground of damages. There is neither violation of right, nor loss upon which to found an action.

But there are many cases in which before the time fixed for performance, one of the contracting parties may do that which amounts to a breach and furnishes a ground of damages. It has always been the law that where a party deliberately incapacitates himself or renders performance of his contract impossible, his act amounts to an injury to the other party, which gives the other party a cause of action for breach of contract; yet this would seem to be inconsistent with the reasoning in Daniels v. Newton, though it is not there in terms decided "that an absolute refusal to perform a contract, after the time and under the conditions in which plaintiff is entitled to require performance, is not a breach of the contract, even although the contract is by its terms to continue in the future." Parker v. Russell, 133 Mass. 874.

In truth, the opinion goes upon a distinction between cases of renunciation before the arrival of the time of performance and those of renunciation of unmatured obligations of a contract while it is in course of performance, and it is said that before the argument on the ground of convenience and mutual advantage to the parties can properly have weight, "the point to be reached must first be shown to be consistent with logical deductions from the strictly legal aspects of the case."

We think that there can be no controlling distinction on this point between the two classes of cases, and that it is proper to consider the reasonableness of the conclusion that the absolute renunciation of particular contracts constitutes such a breach as to justify immediate action and recovery therefor. The parties to a contract which is wholly executory have a right to the maintenance of the contractual relations up to the time for performance, as well as to a performance of the contract when due. If it appear that the party who makes an absolute refusal intends thereby to put an end to the contract so far as performance is concerned, and that the other party must accept this position, why should there not be speedy action and settlement in regard to the rights of the parties? Why should a locus penitentiæ be awarded to the party whose wrongful action has placed the other at such disadvantage? What reasonable distinction per se is there between liability for a refusal to perform future acts to be done under a contract in course of performance and liability for a refusal to perform the whole contract made before the time for commencement of performance?

As Lord Chief Justice Cockburn observed, in Frost v. Knight, the promisee has the right to insist on the contract as subsisting and effective before the arrival of the time for its performance, and its unimpaired and unimpeached efficacy may be essential to his interests, dealing as he may with rights acquired under it in various ways for his benefit and advantage. And of all such advantage, the repudiation of the contract by the other party, and the announcement that it never will be fulfilled, must of course deprive him. While by acting on such repudiation and the taking of timely measures, the promisee may in many cases avert, or, at all events, materially lessen the injurious effects which would otherwise flow from the nonfulfillment of the contract.

During the argument of Cort v. Ambergate Railway Company, 17 Q.B. 127, Erle, J., made this suggestion: "Suppose the contract was that plaintiff should send a ship to a certain port for a cargo, and defendant should there load one on board; but defendant wrote word that he could not furnish a cargo; must the ship be sent to return empty?" And if it was not necessary for the ship owner to send his ship, it is not perceived why he should be compelled to wait until the time fixed for the loading of the ship at the remote port before bringing suit upon the contract.

If in this case these ten hop contracts had been written into one contract for the supply of hops for five years in instalments, then when the default happened in October, 1896, it cannot be denied that an immediate action could have been brought in which damages could have been recovered in advance for the breach of the agreement to deliver during the two remaining years. But treating the four outstanding contracts as separate contracts, why is it not equally reasonable that an unqualified and positive refusal to perform them constitutes such a breach that damages could be recovered in an immediate action? Why should plaintiff be compelled to bring four suits instead of one? For the reasons above stated, and having reference to the state of the authorities on the subject, our conclusion is that the rule laid down in Hochster v. De la Tour is a reasonable and proper rule to be applied in this case and in many others arising out of the transactions of commerce of the present day.

As to the question of damages, if the action is not premature, the rule is applicable that plaintiff is entitled to compensation based, as far as possible, on the ascertainment of what he would have suffered by the continued breach of the other party down to the time of complete performance, less any abatement by reason of circumstances of which he ought reasonably to have availed himself. If a vendor is to manufacture goods, and during the process of manufacture the contract is repudiated, he is not bound to complete the manufacture, and estimate his damages by the difference between the market price and the contract price, but the measure of damage is the difference between the contract price and the cost of performance. Hinckley v. Pittsburg Company, 121 U.S. 264. Even if in such cases the manufacturer actually obtains his profits before the time fixed for performance, and recovers on a basis of cost which might have been increased or diminished by subsequent events, the party who broke the contract before the time for complete performance cannot complain, for he took the risk involved in such anticipation. If the vendor has to buy instead of to manufacture, the same principle prevails, and he may show what was the value of the contract by showing for what price he could have made subcontracts, just as the cost of manufacture in the case of a manufacturer may be shown. Although he may receive his money earlier in this way, and may gain, or lose, by the estimation of his damage in advance of the time for performance, still, as we have seen, he has the right to accept the situation tendered him, and the other party cannot complain.

In this case plaintiffs showed at what prices they could have made subcontracts for forward deliveries according to the contracts in suit, and the difference between the prices fixed by the contracts sued on and those was correctly allowed.

Judgment affirmed.

[From the statement of the case in 178 U.S., it appears that the contracts were all entered into on August 25, 1893 between the partnership of Horst Brothers as sellers and Roehm as buyer. On June 23, 1896, the Horst Brothers partnership was "dissolved" and went into liquidation. On being notified of the "dissolution," Roehm, in a letter dated June 27, 1896, stated that, since Horst Brothers would not be able to carry out the hop contracts, he considered the contracts "annulled," would make other arrangements for the purchase of hops and released Horst Brothers from any liability under the contracts. Horst Brothers replied, in a subsequent letter, that Roehm had misconstrued the notice of dissolution; although the partnership would not enter into any new contracts, it intended to carry out all its existing contracts and did not ask to be released from them. To this letter Roehm made no reply. In October, 1896, Horst Brothers made the first of five scheduled monthly shipments under the first of the four contracts. Roehm refused to accept the hops on the grounds stated in his letter of June 27, although he offered to accept them, after inspection, if Horst Brothers would bill them "at the current market rate" under a new contract. No further tenders of delivery were made by Horst Brothers, which brought its action for damages in January, 1897. Deliveries under the second 1896 contract were scheduled to begin in March, 1897 and deliveries under the 1897 contracts were to be made in the fall of 1897 and the spring of 1898.]

NOTE

1. In a two-part article on Repudiation of Contracts, 14 Harv. L. Rev. 317, 421 (1901), Professor Samuel Williston mounted an all-out attack on the doctrine of Hochster v. De La Tour and Roehm v. Horst — that is, the doctrine that, following repudiation by one party, the other party can immediately bring an action without awaiting the time scheduled for performance. Williston wrote (14 Harv. L. Rev. at 438-439; footnotes have been omitted):

> The reason most strongly urged in support of the doctrine of anticipatory breach is, however, its practical convenience. It is said that it is certain that the plaintiff is going to have an action, it is better for both parties to

have it disposed of at once. It may be conceded that practical convenience is of more importance than logical exactness, but yet the considerations of practical convenience must be very weighty to justify infringing the underlying principles of the law of contracts. The law is not important solely or even chiefly for the just disposal of litigated cases. The settlement of the rights of a community without recourse to the courts can only be satisfactorily arranged when logic is respected. But it is not logic only which is injured. The defendant is injured. He is held liable on a promise he never made. He has only promised to do something at a future day. He is held to have broken his contract by doing something before that day. Enlarging the obligation of contracts is perhaps as bad as impairing it. This may be of great importance. Suppose the defendant, after saying that he will not perform, changes his mind and concludes to keep his promise. Unless the plaintiff relying on the repudiation, as he justly may, has so changed his position that he cannot go on with the contract without injury, the defendant ought surely to be allowed to do this. But if the plaintiff is allowed to bring an action at once this possibility is cut off. "Why," says Fuller, C.J., "should a locus pœnitentiæ be awarded to the party whose wrongful action has placed the other at such disadvantage?" Because such is the contract the parties made. A promise to perform in June does not preclude changing position in May.

With respect to Chief Justice Fuller's suggestion that "the doctrine of anticipatory breach only applies to contracts where there are mutual obligations," Williston commented: "This has not before been suggested, though in fact the cases where the doctrine has been applied have been cases of bilateral contracts. Lord Cockburn's line of reasoning [in Frost v. Knight] is certainly as applicable to unilateral as to bilateral contracts." 14 Harv. L. Rev. at 438 n.1.

2. In Hochster v. De La Tour, counsel for the defendant took the position, in his argument, that:

[A]n announcement of an intention to break the contract when the time comes is no more than an offer to rescind. It is evidence, till retracted, of a dispensation with the necessity of readiness and willingness on the other side; and, if not retracted, it is, when the time for performance comes, evidence of a continued refusal; but till then it may be retracted.

Crompton, J., put to counsel the question: "May not the plaintiff, on notice that the defendant will not employ him, look out for other employment, so as to diminish the loss?" Counsel replied: "If he adopts the defendant's notice, which is in legal effect an offer to rescind, he must adopt it altogether." Lord Campbell, C.J., remarked: "So that you say the plaintiff, to preserve any remedy at all, was bound to remain idle." Counsel conceded that that in effect was his position (118 Eng. Rep. at 925). Thus the argument was that plaintiff, on receiving defendant's notice of repudiation, had two permissible courses of action and only two: he could accept the "offer to rescind," thereby abandoning any claim for damages; alternatively, he must remain ready, willing and able to perform down to June 1, the defendant being at liberty at any point to "retract" his repudiation. What he could not do, according to counsel's argument, was to take the repudiation as final, accept other employment and still preserve a right to recover damages from the defendant for breach.

3. Professor Corbin was as thoroughgoing an advocate of the doctrine of anticipatory breach as Professor Williston (at least in 1901) had been its opponent. In Corbin's analysis of Hochster v. De La Tour he suggests that defendant's counsel may have lost his case by claiming too much in his all or nothing argument and thus have driven the court to an extreme position. It would have been entirely possible, Corbin points out, to handle the case by declaring that defendant's repudiation released the plaintiff from the contract and privileged him to accept other employment at once without thereby forfeiting his right to damages but that the damage action itself could not be brought before June 1 (or perhaps September 1) (4 Corbin §960). Williston, in the article referred to in Note 1 *supra*, had also made the point that Lord Campbell, who wrote the Hochster v. De La Tour opinion, was "apparently misled" by counsel's argument. 14 Harv. L. Rev. at 432.

4. What, exactly, did the Massachusetts court say in Daniels v. Newton, *supra* p. 1270? Do you feel that it was a good idea to allow the plaintiff in Hochster v. De La Tour to begin his action on May 22 instead of handling the case in the manner suggested by Professor Corbin? Do you feel the same way about allowing the action in Roehm v. Horst to be brought in January, 1897? It appears from the opinion in Roehm v. Horst that it was customary to make future or forward delivery contracts for hops. Suppose there had been no futures market. Should that make any difference?

5. In Pakas v. Hollingshead, 184 N.Y. 211, 77 N.E. 40 (1906), the contract was for the sale of 50,000 pairs of bicycle pedals, to be delivered and paid for in installments during 1898 and 1899. The seller defaulted after delivering 2,608 pairs of pedals. In March, 1899, the buyer brought an action in which he recovered damages for the pedals (19,000 pairs) which the seller ought to have delivered up to that point. In February, 1900, he brought a second action to recover damages for the balance. The second action was dismissed. O'Brien, J., commented that "the plaintiff cannot split up his demand and maintain successive actions, but must either recover all his damages in the first suit or wait until the contract matured or the time for the delivery of all the goods had arrived." Does this result seem to follow from Roehm v. Horst, which is cited approvingly in the course of Judge O'Brien's opinion?

6. In Equitable Trust Co. of New York v. Western Pacific Railway Co., 244 F. 485 (S.D.N.Y. 1917), it appeared that the Western Pacific was obligated to make periodic payments to Equitable, as trustee for its bond-

holders, to cover interest on the bonds and to establish a sinking fund.
The Denver & Rio Grande, at a time when it was about to take over
control of the Western Pacific, undertook that, to the extent the operating income of the Western Pacific was insufficient to allow it to make the
payments to Equitable, the Denver & Rio Grande would make up any
deficiencies by purchasing the Western Pacific's promissory notes. Subsequently, the Denver & Rio Grande publicly announced that it would
refuse to perform its obligation unless the Western Pacific bondholders
"consented to abate their legal demands [in a foreclosure proceeding] and
. . . deposit their bonds with the bankers so as to effect some compromise." 244 F. at 501. On March 1, 1915, the Denver & Rio Grande
defaulted on its undertaking. Equitable, as trustee, brought an action for
relief. Counsel for the defendant contended, inter alia, that

> the trustee might not elect to treat the default of the Denver Company of
> March 1, 1915, as a repudiation of all its liabilities under the contract in
> question and an anticipatory breach of the same, and therefore, even as-
> suming it might sue for a single breach and recover damages, it must be
> content to avail itself in some form of its successive rights as they become
> due semiannually.

244 F. at 494. Judge Learned Hand concluded that the conduct of the
Denver & Rio Grande amounted to "repudiation without even pretense
of justification," which gave the trustee "the right to treat the contract at
an end and to sue." He then went on:

> But it is said that such a result implied the possibility of the anticipatory
> breach of an obligation merely to pay money, and that the doctrine does
> not go so far. Washington Co. v. Williams, 111 Fed. 801, 49 C.C.A. 621;
> McCready v. Lindenborn, 172 N.Y. 400, 65 N.E. 208; Werner v. Werner,
> 169 App. Div. 9, 154 N.Y. Supp. 570. There are dicta to the same effect in
> Roehm v. Horst, 178 U.S. 1, 20 Sup. Ct. 780, 44 L. Ed. 953; Nicolls v.
> Scranton S. Co., 137 N.Y. 471, 33 N.E. 561; Kelly v. Security Mutual Life
> Ins. Co., 186 N.Y. 16, 78 N.E. 584, 9 Ann. Cas. 661; Moore v. Security
> Trust & Life Ins. Co., 168 Fed. 496, 93 C.C.A. 632. In these cases it is
> generally stated that the doctrine only applies to cases which are mutually
> executory, but that must be deemed authoritatively overruled by Central
> Trust Co. v. Chicago Auditorium, 240 U.S. 581, 36 Sup. Ct. 412, 60 L. Ed.
> 811, L.R.A. 1917B, 580, in which the promisee had wholly performed. In
> this court, at least the limitation of mutuality cannot therefore apply. Fur-
> thermore, if performance remains mutually executory, the doctrine still
> applies, even though the promise is only to pay money, because that is the
> situation in the ordinary contract of sale repudiated by the buyer, Roehm v.
> Horst, *supra*. Lovell v. St. Louis Mutual Ins. Co., 111 U.S. 264, 4 Sup. Ct.
> 390, 28 L. Ed. 423, is another case where the promise was only to pay
> money. If the doctrine has any limits, they only exclude, and that arbitrar-
> ily enough, cases in which at once the promisee has wholly performed, and
> the promise is only to pay money.

Assuming what I do not mean to admit, that it has such limits, they result because the eventual victory of the doctrine over vigorous attack (e.g., 14 Harv. Law Rev. 428; Daniels v. Newton, 114 Mass. 530, 19 Am. Rep. 384) has not left it scatheless. Its basis in principle is that a promise to perform in the future by implication includes an engagement not deliberately to compromise the probability of performance. A promise is a verbal act designed as a reliance to the promisee, and so as a means to the forecast of his own conduct. Abstention from any deliberate act before the time of performance which makes impossible that reliance and that forecast ought surely to be included by implication. Such intermediate uncertainties as arise from the vicissitudes of the promisor's affairs are, of course, a part of the risk, but it is hard to see how, except by mere verbalism, it can be supposed that the promisor may within the terms of his undertaking gratuitously add to those uncertainties by announcing his purpose to default. Even the opponents of the doctrine concede that, if there be such an implied promise, its breach may drag in the damages upon the main promise. 14 Harv. Law Rev. 434, 435.

Whatever the lack of logic in refusing to apply the doctrine to notes or bonds or the like, there can be no valid distinction between an ordinary contract of sale or of insurance, which the buyer or the insurer repudiates, and a contract like this, because this was not a contract unconditionally to pay fixed sums at fixed intervals. Rather, as the defendant is so fond of insisting, it was, at least in form, a contract of purchase, and no one has suggested that it makes any difference whether you buy hops or notes so far as this point goes. At least this consideration applies unconditionally to any repudiation of the new Denver Company to the Pacific Company. Not only in form was this a contract of purchase, but the Pacific Company had continuing obligations to perform while it continued. I agree that the same is not so true of the promises to the trustee which are here in suit, i.e., 4 (b) of article 2; yet I should, even if the trustee had no duties, be unwilling to make so arbitrary a cleavage in the doctrine at the expense of every consideration not only of principle, but of justice. For, if it were held that the doctrine applies as between the New Denver Company and the Pacific Company, but not between the New Denver Company and the trustee, this would be the result. Suppose that A. agrees with B. and C. to purchase a series of notes of B. and pay part of the proceeds serially to C., and he repudiates the whole enterprise midway in its performance. B. may sue at once, and recover damages for the future installments, but C. may not, because C. is bound to no further performance. It is safe to say that the law is not so whimsically capricious as that; yet that by hypothesis is precisely this case.

244 F. at 501-502.

PHELPS v. HERRO
215 Md. 223, 137 A.2d 159 (1957)

PRESCOTT, Judge. This appeal questions the validity of an order passed on April 3, 1957, that directed "the Plaintiffs' (appellees') motion for a

Summary Judgment be granted," and a judgment entered on April 8, 1957, in favor of the appellees against the appellants for the sum of $34,135.82; both in the Circuit Court for Anne Arundel County.

On October 21, 1955, the appellees and appellants entered into a written agreement whereby the appellees agreed to sell, and the appellants agreed to buy, fractional interests of the appellees in and to certain real property and corporate stock for the sum of $37,500. The agreement further provided that appellants should pay the purchase price as follows:

1. Five Thousand Dollars ($5,000.00) in cash on or before January 1, 1956.

2. A promissory note in the amount of Thirty-two Thousand Five Hundred Dollars ($32,500.00) calling for principal payments in the amount of Five Thousand Dollars ($5,000.00) plus interest at the rate of four per cent (4%) per annum on the first of each succeeding January and the entire balance to become due and payable January 1, 1961. However, Phelps and Sandsbury (appellants), may extend the maturity date until January 1, 1963, by giving notice of intention to so extend in writing to Herro (appellee) on or before July 1, 1960.

The appellants paid the first $5,000 as provided in the agreement. They and the appellees remained rather closely associated in several intricate and complicated business transactions until some time in September of 1956. At that time, the appellees transferred unto the appellants their fractional interests in the real estate and corporate stock named in the contract. Soon thereafter, negotiations were conducted by the parties, which had as their objective the sale to the appellants of all of the interests of the appellees in all business enterprises where there were mutual interests, or a purchase by the appellees of the appellants' interests therein. A meeting was held and attended by all of the parties on October 11, 1956, at the office of the appellees' counsel. At this meeting, the appellants contend the appellees made an oral proposal that was subsequently accepted unconditionally by the appellants in writing, thereby making a binding contract. While the appellants fully acknowledge the existence of the contract involved in the case at bar, this alleged contract, as set forth by them, materially changed their obligations thereunder. The appellees contend the appellants did not accept the proposal as made by them, and claim the purported acceptance contained a number of terms either in addition to or at variance with the oral offer made by them; consequently the purported acceptance was no more than a counter-proposal, which was not acceptable to them.

[An omitted passage dealt with summary judgments under Maryland law.]

It will be noted suit was filed December 7, 1956, and the next instalment of $5,000 was not due under the contract until January 1, 1957. It is well settled and familiar law that a cause of action must be ripe at the commencement of the suit and the non-existence of a cause of action at that time is fatal to the right to recover; therefore it would be superfluous to cite authorities in support of the proposition.

The appellees' theory of the case is that at the time of the hearing on the motion for a summary judgment, their allegations that the appellants had failed and refused, although requested and demanded, to execute and deliver a promissory note, and that the appellants had notified the appellees they would not pay the balance of the purchase price showed such a definite and specific repudiation of the contract that it entitled them to sue immediately for the *entire* sum due by the appellants under the contract. The appellants on the other hand, claim the suit was prematurely brought; that originally the contract was a bilateral one that became unilateral as soon as the appellees performed all of the matters and things required of them under the agreement (the fact that appellees had so performed being admitted in appellees' affidavit); that under the agreement of the parties, the appellants had not agreed to give a *negotiable* promissory note, or a note that was to be secured in any manner, but simply a promissory note payable to the appellees and signed by the appellants; that the consideration named was higher than the appellants would have agreed upon, unless the appellees had agreed to take an unsecured note payable over a long period of time; that when the contract became unilateral, the only obligation thereunder was that the appellants were required to pay several sums of money in instalments, which obligation, assuming a failure to give a note and a statement by their attorney that appellants would not pay the note, would not be accelerated so as to make the entire sum named in the contract, or any part thereof, due on December 7, 1956, when suit was instituted.

One of the leading cases on the question of the anticipatory breach of a contract is Hochster v. De la Tour, 2 El. and Bl. 678. There, the plaintiff in April, 1852, had agreed to serve the defendant, and the defendant had undertaken to employ the plaintiff, as courier, for three months from June 1, 1852, on certain terms. On May 11, 1852, the defendant wrote the plaintiff that he had changed his mind, and declined to avail himself of plaintiff's services. On May 22, 1852, the plaintiff brought an action at law for breach of the contract. It was held that there could be a breach before the time fixed for performance; that a positive and absolute refusal to carry out the contract prior to the date of actual default amounted to such a breach. Since the decision in this case, there have been numerous and varied rulings on the many and complex angles that have arisen in applying, or not applying, the doctrine of anticipatory breach of a contract, and it is entirely possible the law relating thereto is not, at the present, well settled in all of its aspects. Annotation, 105 A.L.R. 460, 462.

However, with reference to unilateral contracts, or bilateral contracts that have become unilateral by full performance on one side, for the payment of money in the future, without surety or other conditions involved (the situation in this case when suit was instituted), the text writers and decisions are in general accord that the doctrine of anticipatory breach has no application. 5 Williston, Contracts, sec. 1328; 4 Corbin, Contracts, sec. 963; Annotation, 105 A.L.R. 460, 465; Restatement, Contracts, sec. 318, comment e. In Roehm v. Horst, 178 U.S. 1, 20 S. Ct. 780, 44 L. Ed. 953, a leading case, the Supreme Court, on elaborate consideration by Chief Justice Fuller, recognized the principle. In Greenway v. Gaither, C.C., Fed. Cas. No. 5,788, Taney 227, 231, the facts were quite analogous to those in the case at bar. The plaintiff agreed to sell, and the defendant to buy, a house and lot for a sum of money to be paid in 18, 24, 30 and 36 months. The defendant repudiated the contract, and suit was instituted before the first instalment of the purchase-money was due. Chief Justice Taney decided the case had been prematurely brought. In ruling on an application to seal a bill of exceptions, he stated:

> It has never been supposed that notice to the holder of a bond, or a promissory note, or bill of exchange, that the party would not (from any cause) comply with the contract, would give to the holder an immediate cause of action, upon which he might sue before the time of payment arrived.

A similar ruling was made in General American Tank Car Corp. v. Goree, 4 Cir., 296 F. 32, 36, wherein the court stated flatly:

> No right of action arises from the repudiation before maturity of a unilateral contract, nor for repudiation of an independent promise in a bilateral contract. An action cannot be sustained on a promissory note before maturity on the ground that the maker had declared his intention not to pay it. A tenant's repudiation of his lease does not give his landlord an immediate right of action for future rent.

In a case decided by this Court, Appleman v. Michael, 43 Md. 269, the plaintiff agreed to sell, and the defendant to purchase, certain goods; payment therefor was to be made by the defendant by executing his note in the amount of the purchase price, payable in ninety days. The defendant refused to execute the note or to pay for the goods. Suit was instituted more than three years after the defendant's refusal to execute the note, but less than three years from the maturity of the note, which the defendant was alleged to have agreed to execute. The Statute of Limitations was pleaded. This Court held that this was not a sale upon condition that a note be given where no title would have passed unless the note were given; that it was a case where the sale and delivery of the goods were absolute, and where the title to them passed immediately, but they were to be paid for at a subsequent time; that the credit was not dependent upon the execution of the note, so that it could be terminated or treated at an end by the vendor upon the neglect or refusal of the purchaser to give the note; that the note would have given no additional security to the vendor and there was no stipulation in the contract for such security; that it was simply a case of a sale of goods upon an absolute credit of ninety days, and the Court was "clearly of (the) opinion (that) no action *for their value* could, under any circumstances, have been sustained if brought before the expiration of that time." In other words, the Court held that if the action had been brought after the neglect or refusal to give the note, but before its maturity date, the cause of action would not then have accrued and the suit would have been prematurely brought.[76]

We think the proper rule is that the doctrine of anticipatory breach of a contract has no application to money contracts, pure and simple, where one party has fully performed his undertaking, and all that remains for the opposite party to do is to pay a certain sum of money at a certain time or times, and, under the circumstances of this case, this is as far as we need to rule, although some of the cases cited hold that the doctrine of anticipatory breach has no application whatsoever in unilateral contracts, or bilateral contracts that have become unilateral by full performance on one side. . . .

[An omitted passage distinguished several cases relied on by the appellees.]

From what we have said above, we conclude this case was prematurely brought, so the judgments must be reversed.

This ruling renders it unnecessary to pass upon the other questions raised by the appellants and the appellees.

We have not overlooked the fact that suit possibly could have been entered on December 7, 1956, if the suit were regarded as an action for a breach of the contract by the appellants in refusing to give the note within a reasonable time, as distinguished from an action for the value of the interests sold. Appleman v. Michael, *supra*, 43 Md. at page 281. If it had been treated as such, the appellees would have been limited to nominal damages, or such as they could have proved resulted from the failure to give the note, alone; but they were not entitled to recover the instalments named in the contract, which were not then due.

---

76. For other cases holding that the doctrine of anticipatory breach of contract either has no application to unilateral contracts, or that it has no application to unilateral contracts for the pure and simple payment of money, see City of Hampton, Virginia v. United States, 4 Cir., 218 F.2d 401; Moore v. Security Trust and Life Ins. Co., 8 Cir., 168 F. 496; Brimmer v. Union Oil Co., 10 Cir., 81 F.2d 437; Sagamore Corp. v. Willcutt, 120 Conn. 315, 180 A. 464; Manufacturers' Furniture Co. v. Cantrell, 172 Ark. 642, 290 S.W. 353, 354; Huffman v. Martin, 226 Ky. 137, 10 S.W.2d 636, 638; Sheketoff v. Prevedine, 133 Conn. 389, 51 A.2d 922, 924, 171 A.L.R. 1009; Parks v. Maryland Casualty Co., D.C.W.D. Mo., 59 F.2d 736; Cf. Fidelity and Deposit Co. v. Brown, 230 Ky. 534, 20 S.W.2d 284; Better v. Williams, 203 Md. 613, 617, 102 A.2d 750; Weiss v. Sheet Metal Fabricators, 206 Md. 195, 203, 110 A.2d 671.

Judgments reversed without prejudice to the appellees' right to institute further proceedings to enforce whatever rights they may have under the contract, appellees to pay the costs.

[HAMMOND, J., although agreeing that the judgment below should be reversed, nevertheless dissented from the opinion of the court. He said, in part:]

The majority of the Court, instead of deciding that summary judgment should have been refused, unnecessarily decided an issue that might never have presented itself, by adopting for the first time as the law of Maryland a dubious exception to the rule of immediate allowance of damages for anticipatory breach of contract. That a right of action accrues on an anticipatory breach is firmly established. Williston opposes the idea and while forced to admit that it is the law, argues that it should not be. Perhaps because of his dislike of the doctrine, Williston urges that there should be no action for anticipatory breach of a unilateral contract or a bilateral contract that has been fully performed on one side. 5 Williston, Contracts (Rev. Ed.), Chap. XL. The cases, however, do not support this view, holding generally that there may be. Roehm v. Horst, 178 U.S. 1, 20 S. Ct. 780, 44 L. Ed. 953; Precision Development Co. v. Fast Bearing Co., 183 Md. 399, 37 A.2d 905. Williston, in endeavoring to limit the doctrine of anticipatory breach, is consistent when he declares that the violation of the bare promise to pay money in the future in a contract that always was, or has become, unilateral can never give rise to immediate action. He is apologetic for his view and, recognizing that it has been criticized, says in the work cited, Sec. 1328 at 3734, that since the whole doctrine of anticipatory breach "was founded on a confusion of a right of action with a defense, it seems undesirable to enlarge the boundaries of the doctrine." Corbin denies the validity of Williston's views and conclusions. 4 Corbin, Contracts, Chap. 54. In Sec. 963 at 866, Professor Corbin says that

> Although the author of this volume believes that the distinction should make no difference in the result reached, attention must be called to the fact that some courts have distinguished unconditional money debts from those in which the debtor's duty to pay is conditional on some performance yet to be rendered by his creditor, recognizing anticipatory breach in the latter cases and not in the former.

See also Sec. 965, where the learned author shows that the argument that recognition of anticipatory breach of money contracts involves "acceleration of date of maturity" is fallacious. To require immediate payment of sums that were to have been paid in the future does not give the promisee something he did not bargain for, if a discount that reflects the earlier date of payment is imposed.

Judge Learned Hand agrees with Corbin. See Equitable Trust Co. of New York v. Western Pac. Ry. Co., D.C., 244 F. 485, 501-502, where, speaking of the doctrine of anticipatory breach, he said:

> Furthermore, if performance remains mutually executory, the doctrine still applies, even though the promise is only to pay money. . . . If the doctrine has any limits, they only exclude, *and that arbitrarily enough,* cases in which at once the promisee has wholly performed, and the promise is only to pay money. Assuming what I do not mean to admit, that it has such limits, they result because the eventual victory of the doctrine over vigorous attack . . . has not left it scatheless.

(Emphasis supplied.)

In New York Life Ins. Co. v. Viglas, 297 U.S. 672, 56 S. Ct. 615, 618, 80 L. Ed. 971, 976-977, the Supreme Court denied an insured the immediate recovery of the total of monthly disability benefits measured by his life expectancy on a holding that the insurance company had not actually and completely repudiated the contract. Mr. Justice Cardozo pointed out that if one analyzes the cases one discovers the rationale of those

> which have stated at times, though with needless generality, that by reason of the subject-matter of the undertaking the rule applicable to contracts for the payment of money is not the same as that applicable for the performance of services or the delivery of merchandise. . . . *The root of any valid distinction is not in the difference between money and merchandise or between money and services.* What counts decisively is the relation between the maintenance of the contract and the frustration of the ends it was expected to subserve. *The ascertainment of this relation calls for something more than the mechanical application of a uniform formula.* To determine whether a breach avoids the contract as a whole one must consider what is necessary to work out reparation in varying conditions. . . . The law will be able to offer appropriate relief "where compensation is wilfully and contumaciously withheld."

(Emphasis supplied.)

Two of the three cases cited by the Court in the body of the opinion do not hold what the majority opinion holds; they merely repeat in discussion "in needless generality" what the majority opinion decides, and, on the facts before them, found a breach justifying full damages. Only three of the cases cited in the footnote actually hold what the majority opinion holds; in the others the contract was held to be bilateral, or there was no breach.

It is small wonder, then, that the author of the annotation in 105 A.L.R. 460, 461, on anticipatory breach of a bilateral contract which has been fully performed on one side, says:

From his own examination of the cases the writer is unable to state upon
what substantial reason the limitation in question may be said to rest. . . .
[O]ne would hesitate to say that the question under consideration in this
annotation has, with the *possible* exception of money contracts, become at
all settled. Yet the peculiar condition of the cases, as above outlined, the
numerous assumptions and dicta, the apparent rulings on matters of anticipatory breach where in fact the breaches if any were actual, not anticipatory, have created at least an appearance of generally settled law.

(Emphasis supplied.)

NOTE

1. The facts in New York Life Insurance Co. v. Viglas, quoted by
Judge Hammond in his dissent, were these: Viglas had taken out a life
insurance policy with the defendant. Under the terms of the policy, if the
insured became totally disabled before the age of 60, he was to received
monthly benefit payments from the defendant and be relieved of any
obligation to pay the semi-annual insurance premiums that would otherwise be due. The policy provided, however, that "[b]efore making any
income payment or waiving any premium the company might demand
due proof of the continuance of total disability. . . ." If the insured failed
to provide such proof or performed any work for profit, his disability
benefits were to be terminated and his obligation to make all subsequent
premium payments was revived. Thereafter, a failure on the part of the
insured to make such payments as they came due would constitute a
default of his obligations under the insurance contract. Even after default, however, the insured could collect the cash surrender value of his
policy or reinstate the policy itself (within five years after default) by
paying all past-due premiums.

The insured became totally disabled, within the meaning of the policy,
on September 11, 1931. According to the statement of facts in Justice
Cardozo's opinion,

> Upon proof of his condition the company paid [the insured] the monthly
> benefits called for by the policy from October 11, 1931, to July 11, 1933, and
> during the same period waived the payment of semi-annual premiums. It
> refused to make a monthly payment in August, 1933, and refused the same
> month to waive a semi-annual premium,
>
>> asserting to the plaintiff as its ground for such refusal that since it appeared to
>> the defendant that for some time past the plaintiff had not been continuously
>> totally disabled within the meaning of the disability benefit provision of the
>> policy, the defendant would make no further monthly disability payments,
>> and that the premiums due on and after August 7, 1933, would be payable in
>> conformity with the terms of the contract.

Later, upon the expiration of a term of grace, "the defendant, on or about September 19, 1933, declared the policy as lapsed upon its records."

297 U.S. at 675.

The insured sued to recover an amount equal to the total disability benefits he would receive under the policy if he lived for the full period of his present life expectancy. In rejecting the plaintiff's claim, Cardozo had this to say:

> Upon the showing made in the complaint there was neither a repudiation of the policy nor such a breach of its provisions as to make conditional and future benefits the measure of recovery.
>
> Repudiation there was none as the term is known to the law. Petitioner did not disclaim the intention or the duty to shape its conduct in accordance with the provisions of the contract. Far from repudiating those provisions, it appealed to their authority and endeavored to apply them. If the insured was still disabled, monthly benefits were payable, and there should have been a waiver of the premium. If he had recovered the use of hand or foot and was not otherwise disabled, his right to benefits had ceased, and the payment of the premium was again a contractual condition. There is nothing to show that the insurer was not acting in good faith in giving notice of its contention that the disability was over. . . . If it made a mistake, there was a breach of a provision of the policy with liability for any damages appropriate thereto. We do not pause at the moment to fix the proper measure. Enough in this connection that at that stage of the transaction there had been no renunciation or abandonment of the contract as a whole. . . .
>
> Renunciation or abandonment, if not effected at that stage, became consummate in the plaintiff's view at the end of the period of grace when the company declared the policy "lapsed upon its records." Throughout the plaintiff's argument the declaration of a lapse is treated as equivalent to a declaration that the contract is a nullity. But the two are widely different under such a policy as this. The policy survived for many purposes as an enforcible obligations, though default in the payment of premiums had brought about a change of rights and liabilities. The insurer was still subject to a duty to give the insured the benefit of the stipulated surrender privileges, cash or new insurance. It was still subject to a duty upon proof within six months that the disability continued to reinstate the policy as if no default had occurred. None of these duties was renounced. None of them was questioned. . . . Viewing the case before us independently, we hold that upon the facts declared in the complaint the insurer did not repudiate the obligation of the contract, but did commit a breach for which it is answerable in damages.

297 U.S. at 676, 677, 678.

Does Cardozo's distinction between breach and repudiation seem to you persuasive? Would you classify the plaintiff's insurance contract as unilateral or bilateral, in the sense in which these terms are used by the court in Phelps v. Herro?

2. In his opinion in *Phelps*, Judge Prescott quotes an earlier case that states that "[a] tenant's repudiation of his lease does not give his landlord an immediate right of action for future rent." In reality, the case law has been less consistent than this black-letter proposition might suggest. In Hermitage Co. v. Levine, 248 N.Y. 333, 162 N.E. 97 (1928) (another Cardozo opinion), the defendant, a tenant under a 21-year lease that ran from 1924 to 1945, was dispossessed for non-payment of rent at the end of 1924. After Levine's dispossession, the landlord made a "diligent effort" to relet the seven-story building covered by the lease. By August, 1925, it had relet 3½ floors for 15 years, 2½ floors for 10 years and 1 floor for 3 years. In March, 1926, the landlord brought his action to recover damages. The tenant was credited with a $30,000 "security deposit" which the landlord retained as well as with the rents under the new leases and profits that had been made by operating a garage in part of the building. The claimed deficiency was $25,529.39. Held, by a unanimous court, that no action could be brought, even for accrued rent, until 1945.

> To hold [the tenant] for monthly deficits is to charge him with the obliga-
> tions of a tenant without any of the privileges. He must pay in the lean
> months, without recouping in the fat ones. He must do this, though it may
> turn out in the end that there has been a gain and not a loss. A liability so
> heavy may not rest upon uncertain inference. We do not overlook the
> hardship to the landlord in postponing the cause of action until October,
> 1945.

Id. at 338, 162 N.E. at 98. Compare the result in the *Hermitage* case with Pakas v. Hollingshead, digested in Note 5 following Roehm v. Horst, *supra* p. 1279. Cardozo suggests in his *Hermitage* opinion that the tenant could have been made liable for "monthly deficits" by an aptly drawn damage clause, but no such clause appeared in the lease.

In Sagamore Corp. v. Willcutt, 120 Conn. 315, 180 A. 464 (1935), a tenant under a lease running from October, 1934, to October, 1935, quit the premises on February 1, 1935 and notified the landlord that he would pay no further rent. Banks, J., explained that the doctrine of anticipatory breach was not applicable, since the tenant's obligation was unilateral and anticipatory breach doctrine requires "dependency of performance." However, the tenant's failure to pay the February 1 rent followed by his statement that he would pay no further rent made the breach "a total one justifying an immediate action by the [landlord] to recover the damages which would naturally follow from such a breach." The landlord apparently recovered the rent reserved until the end of the term less the "rea-
sonable rental value" of the premises for that period.

Do you prefer the New York approach or the Connecticut approach? Of course, there is a considerable difference, when it comes to calculating damages, between a one-year lease broken after 5 months and a 21-
year lease broken before the end of the first year.

3. Judge Hammond in his dissent in Phelps v. Herro states that "[t]o require immediate payment of sums that were to have been paid in the future does not give the promisee something he did not bargain for, if a discount that reflects the earlier date of payment is imposed." But isn't it true that in addition to having the use of the money earlier than he expected, the plaintiff in *Phelps* would (if he had won his lawsuit) also have been spared the risk that the defendant might become insolvent or unavailable before the time originally set for payment? Can his recovery be "discounted" to reflect this latter benefit as well?

4. Suppose the contract at issue in Phelps v. Herro had contained an "acceleration" clause that by its terms made all of the defendant's outstanding obligations immediately "due and payable" upon his failure to make timely payment of any single installment. Sales contracts and leases routinely contain provisions of this sort and their validity is almost always upheld, suggesting that the parties to a contract have considerable power to alter the legal rules governing anticipatory repudiation, if they choose to do so. Can the result in Phelps v. Herro be explained on the grounds that the contract in that case (somewhat anomalously) did *not* contain an acceleration clause? See Jackson, "Anticipatory Repudiation" and the Temporal Element of Contract Law: An Economic Inquiry into Contract Damages in Cases of Prospective Nonperformance, 31 Stan. L. Rev. 69, 118 n.173 (1978).

5. Section 253 of the Restatement Second (Effect of a Repudiation as a Breach and on Other Party's Duties) provides:

> (1) Where an obligor repudiates a duty before he has committed a breach by non-performance and before he has received all of the agreed exchange for it, his repudiation alone gives rise to a claim for damages for total breach.
> (2) Where performances are to be exchanged under an exchange of promises, one party's repudiation of a duty to render performance discharges the other party's remaining duties to render performance.

Comment *c* to §253 states that "an obligor's repudiation alone . . . gives rise to no claim for damages at all if he has already received all of the agreed exchange for it." As the Reporter's Note to §253 makes clear, this proviso is meant to codify the rule in Phelps v. Herro and similar cases. Supposing it involved a contract for the sale of goods rather than real property, how would Phelps v. Herro be decided under §2-610 of the Uniform Commercial Code, reprinted *infra* p. 1307?

MISSOURI FURNACE CO. v. COCHRAN
8 F. 463 (C.C.W.D. Pa. 1881)

Acheson, D.J. This suit, brought February 26, 1880, was to recover damages for the breach by John M. Cochran of a contract for the sale and delivery by him to the plaintiff of 36,621 tons of standard Connellsville coke, at the price of $1.20 per ton, (subject to an advance in case of a rise in wages,) deliverable on cars at his works, at the rate of nine cars of 13 tons each per day on each working day during the year 1880. After 3,765 tons were delivered, Cochran, on February 13, 1880, notified the plaintiff that he had rescinded the contract, and thereafter delivered no coke. After Cochran's refusal further to deliver coke, the plaintiff made a substantially similar contract with one Hutchinson for the delivery during the balance of the year of 29,587 tons of Connellsville coke at four dollars per ton, which was the market rate for such a forward contract, and rather below the market price for present deliveries on February 27, 1880, the date of the Hutchinson contract. The plaintiff claimed to recover the difference between the price stipulated in the contract sued on, and the price which the plaintiff agreed to pay Hutchinson under the contract of February 27, 1880. But the court refused to adopt this standard of damages, and instructed the jury that the plaintiff was

> entitled to recover, upon the coke which John M. Cochran contracted to deliver and refused to deliver to the plaintiff, the sum of the difference between the contract price — that is, the price Cochran was to receive — and the market price of standard Connellsville coke, at the place of delivery, at the several dates when the several deliveries should have been made under the contract.

Under this instruction there was a verdict for the plaintiff for $22,171.49. As the plaintiff had in its hands $1,521.10 coming to the defendant for coke delivered, the damages as found by the jury amounted to the sum of $23,692.50.

The plaintiff moved the court for a new trial; and, in support of the motion, an earnest and certainly very able argument has been made by plaintiff's counsel. But we are not convinced that the instruction complained of was erroneous.

Undoubtedly it is well settled, as a general rule, that when contracts for the sale of chattels are broken by the vendor failing to deliver, the measure of damages is the difference between the contract price and the market value of the article at the time it should be delivered. Sedgwick on the Measure of Damages, (7th Ed.) 552. In *Shepherd* v. *Hampton*, 3 Wheat. 200, this rule was distinctly sanctioned. Chief Justice Marshall there says: "The unanimous opinion of the court is that the price of the article at the time it was to be delivered is the measure of damages." Id. 204. Nor does the case of *Hopkins* v. *Lee*, 6 Wheat. 118, promulgate a different doctrine; for, clearly, "the time of the breach" there spoken of is the time when delivery should have been made under the contract.

It is said in Sedgwick on the Measure of Damages, (7th Ed.) 558, note *b*: "Where delivery is required to be made by instalments, the measure of damages will be estimated by the value at the time each delivery should have been made." In accordance with this principle the damages were assessed in Brown v. Muller, Law Rep. 7 Ex. 319, and Roper v. Johnson, Law Rep. 8 C.P. 167, which were suits by vendee against vendor for damages for failure to deliver iron, in the one case, and coal, in the other, deliverable in monthly instalments. In one of these cases suit was brought after the contract period had expired; in the other case before its expiration; but in both cases the vendor had given notice to the plaintiff that he did not intend to fulfil his contract. To the argument, there urged on behalf of the *vendor*, that upon receiving such notice it is the duty of the vendee to go into the market and provide himself with a new forward contract, Kelly, C.B., in Brown v. Muller, said:

> He is not bound to enter into such a contract, which might be to his advantage or detriment, according as the market might fall or rise. If it fell, the defendant might fairly say that the plaintiff had no right to enter into a speculative contract, and insist that he was not called upon to pay a greater difference than would have existed had the plaintiff held his hand.

Where the breach is on the part of the *vendee*, it seems to be settled law that he cannot have the damages assessed as of the date of his notice that he will not accept the goods. Sedgwick on Measure of Damages, 601. The date at which the contract is considered to have been broken by the buyer is that at which the goods were to have been delivered, not that at which he may give notice that he *intends* to break the contract. Benjamin on Sales, §759. And, indeed, it is a most rational doctrine that a party, whether vendor or vendee, may stand upon his contract and disregard a notice from the other party of any intended repudiation of it. If this were not so, the party desiring to be off from a contract might choose his own time to discharge himself from further liability.

The law as to the effect of such notice is clearly and most satisfactorily stated by Cockburn, C.J., in Frost v. Knight, Law Rep. 7 Ex. 112.

> The promisee, if he pleases, may treat the notice of intention as inoperative, and wait the time when the contract is to be executed, and then hold the other party responsible for all the consequences of non-performance; but in that case he keeps the contract alive for the benefit of the other party as well as his own; he remains subject to all his own obligations and liabilities under it, and enables the other party not only to complete the contract, if so advised, notwithstanding his previous repudiation of it, but also to take advantage of any supervening circumstances which would justify him to decline to complete it. On the other hand, the promisee may, if he thinks proper, treat the repudiation of the other party as a wrongful putting an end to the contract, and may at once bring his action as on a breach of it; and in such action he will be entitled to such damages as would have arisen from the non-performance of the contract at the appointed time, subject, how-

ever, to abatement in respect of any circumstances which may have afforded him the means of mitigating his loss.

We do not think the force of the English cases referred to has been at all weakened by that of the Dunkirk Colliery v. Lever, 41 Law Times Rep. (U.S.) 632, so much relied on by the plaintiff's counsel. Nor are the facts of that case similar to those of the case in hand. There the controlling fact was that at the time the vendee definitively refused to accept, *there was no regular market for cannel coal,* and the vendors resold as soon as they found a purchaser according to the ordinary course of their business, and without unreasonable delay. Therefore, it was held that the plaintiffs were entitled to the full amount of the difference between the contract price and that which they obtained.

Our attention has been called to Masterton v. Brooklyn, 7 Hill, 61. Undoubtedly this is a leading case in this branch of the law, and especially upon the subject of the profits allowable as damages, and the principles upon which they are to be ascertained. The suit, however, was upon a contract to procure, manufacture, and deliver marble for a building, and involved an investigation into the constituent elements of the cost to which the contractor might have been subjected had the contract been carried out, such as the price of rough material in the quarry, expenses of dressing, etc. Upon the question as to the *time* at which the cost of labor and materials was to be estimated the court was divided, and I do not find that the views of the majority upon this precise point have been followed. The case, however, lacked the element of market value, (Id. 70;) and as Judge Nelson cited with approbation Boorman v. Nash, 9 Barn. & C. 145, and Leigh v. Paterson, 8 Taunt. 540, it cannot be supposed that the court intended, in a case of a marketable article having a market value, to sanction the principle contended for here.

I see nothing in the present case to distinguish it from the ordinary case of a breach by the vendor of a forward contract to supply a manufacturer with an article necessary to his business. For such breach what is the true measure of damages? Says Kelly, C.B., in Brown v. Muller: "The proper measure of damages is that sum which the purchaser requires to put himself in the same condition as if the contract had been performed." That result — which is compensation — is secured, it seems to me, by the rule given to the jury here, unless the case is exceptional. The vendee's real loss, whether delivery is to be made at one time or in instalments, ordinarily is the difference between the contract price and the market value at the times the goods should be delivered. If, however, the article is of limited production, and cannot, for that or other reason, be obtained in the market, and the vendee suffers damage beyond that difference, the measure of damages may be the actual loss he sustains. McHose v. Fulmer, 73 Pa. St. 367; Richardson v. Chynoweth, 26 Wis. 656; Sedgwick on Dam. 554. With this qualification to meet exceptional cases, the rule that the damages are to be assessed with reference to the times the contract should be performed, furnishes, I think, a safe and just standard from which it would be hazardous to depart.

In this case I fail to perceive anything to call for a departure from that standard. There was no evidence of any special damage to the plaintiff by the stoppage of its furnaces or otherwise. Furthermore, the contract with Hudson, February 27, 1880, was made at a time when the coke market was excited and in an extraordinary condition. Unexpectedly and suddenly coke had risen to the unprecedented price of four dollars per ton; but this rate was of brief duration. The market declined about May 1, 1880, and by the middle of that month the price had fallen to one dollar and thirty cents per ton. The good faith of the plaintiff in entering into the new contract cannot be questioned, but it proved a most unfortunate venture. By the last of May the plaintiff had in its hands more coke than was required in its business, and it procured — at what precise loss does not clearly appear — the cancellation of contracts with Hutchinson to the extent of 20,000 tons. As the plaintiff was not bound to enter into the new forward contract, it seems to me it did so at its own risk, and cannot fairly claim that the damages chargeable against the defendant shall be assessed on the basis of that contract.

The motion for a new trial is denied.

NOTE

1. At any given moment in the market for a particular commodity (coal, wheat, pork bellies, etc.) there are likely to be two different prices — one, the "spot" price, being the price for immediate delivery, and the other, the "future" price, the price for delivery at some later date. (Actually, there will be many future prices, depending on the date of delivery specified in the contract of sale.) The difference between the spot and future prices is explained by the fact that a promise to deliver in the future is subject to various contingencies (good or bad weather, fluctuations in supply from foreign sources, etc.), and immediate delivery is not. A promise to deliver in the future is always *riskier* than immediate delivery (which is not to say that the supply of goods will necessarily contract or the demand for them become more intense: the opposite may happen, in which case the *spot* price of the goods will decline). A contract for future delivery is therefore always more of a gamble than a spot sale, and the difference between the future and spot prices of a good will reflect the predictions (or "bets") of buyers concerning the various future events they expect to have some bearing on the market for the good in question.

With this in mind, do you think a buyer in the position of the Missouri Furnace Company generally would prefer to make a single substitute future contract or a series of contracts at the spot price? Would a breaching seller generally prefer that his buyer pursue one course of action rather than the other? Remember, this choice must be made at the time of breach and hence without the benefit of hindsight concerning subsequent developments in the relevant market. Do you think the court in the *Missouri Furnace* case was influenced by the fact that the price of coke fell precipitously after the buyer made its future contract? *Should* it have been influenced?

2. In an excellent law review article, "Anticipatory Repudiation" and the Temporal Element of Contract Law: An Economic Inquiry into Contract Damages in Cases of Prospective Nonperformance, 31 Stan. L. Rev. 69 (1978), Professor Jackson writes:

> If there were no contractual obligations affecting the rights and remedies of plaintiff and defendant which antedated the event of repudiation, there would be no compelling reason to require a transaction to be made either earlier, at a forward price, or later, at the spot price. Assuming that the forward cover price is the market's best guess of the future price — an assumption justified in the case of many commodities by an impressive body of data on rational market behavior — there is no *ex ante* reason to expect that a plaintiff or a defendant should prefer one to the other before the fact. Presumably the market's aggregate perception of risk (and that market's aggregate risk averseness) is a factor reflected in that forward market price. Put another way, the forward market price reflects a state of aggregate market indifference between buying and selling today, at the forward price, or waiting until later. Since there is no compelling reason to expect that either buyer or seller can outguess the market's perception of future price, there would likewise be no compelling reason to suspect, *ex ante*, that either of them would prefer that the transaction be made on the date of repudiation at the forward price for the date of performance, or on the date of performance at the spot price.
>
> An example may help to demonstrate this likely indifference in the absence of pre-existing contractual obligations. On April 1, a buyer decides it will need a delivery of coal on December 31. Assume that on April 1 the forward price of coal for delivery on December 31 is $500 (the spot price on April 1 being, at $550, slightly higher). Can we predict, on the basis of this information, whether this hypothetical buyer will enter into a contract on April 1 for delivery of the coal on December 31, or will wait and purchase on the spot market on December 31? The answer would seem to be no, at least if we also assume that the market for coal is efficient. This buyer knows that if it waits, any contract it would be able to make below $500 would leave it better off than if it entered the market immediately, whereas any contract it might make above $500 would have the opposite effect. But there is no reason to expect that this buyer should be able to outguess the market. While the buyer, of course, does not know what the actual December 31 spot price will be, it *does* know that the market's present estimate of that price, adjusted for the market's aggregate risk averseness, is $500, and that in an efficient market, the forward price is the best guess of the future spot price. Therefore, our hypothetical buyer should use that $500 figure as

the probable spot price on December 31. The actual figure used, of course, would vary with the buyer's perceptions of its own risk averseness, as well as with whatever individual views of the market or the future that it may have. But we have no reason in advance for concluding that this buyer's individual characteristics will be systematically biased on one side or the other of the market. We would be unable to conclude, on the basis of this information, which our buyer would prefer: to buy today, on a forward basis, or to wait to buy later, on a spot basis. There accordingly would be no compelling *ex ante* reason to prefer one to the other in the formulation of a legal rule.

This conclusion, however, no longer holds true if we assume a pre-existing contractual relationship between a buyer and a seller. . . .

31 Stan. L. Rev. at 83-86.

What does the last sentence in the passage from Professor Jackson's article mean? Consider this question in light of Oloffson v. Coomer, *infra* p. 1308.

UNIFORM COMMERCIAL CODE

§2-610.   ANTICIPATORY REPUDIATION

When either party repudiates the contract with respect to a performance not yet due the loss of which will substantially impair the value of the contract to the other, the aggrieved party may
- (a)   for a commercially reasonable time await performance by the repudiating party; or
- (b)   resort to any remedy for breach (Section 2-703 or Section 2-711), even though he has notified the repudiating party that he would await the latter's performance and has urged retraction; and
- (c)   in either case suspend his own performance or proceed in accordance with the provisions of this Article on the seller's right to identify goods to the contract notwithstanding breach or to salvage unfinished goods (Section 2-704).

§2-611.   RETRACTION OF ANTICIPATORY REPUDIATION

(1)   Until the repudiating party's next performance is due he can retract his repudiation unless the aggrieved party has since the repudiation cancelled or materially changed his position or otherwise indicated that he considers the repudiation final.

(2)   Retraction may be by any method which clearly indicates to the aggrieved party that the repudiating party intends to perform, but must

include any assurance justifiably demanded under the provisions of this Article (Section 2-609).

(3)   Retraction reinstates the repudiating party's rights under the contract with due excuse and allowance to the aggrieved party for any delay occasioned by the repudiation.

NOTE

1. Suppose a buyer notifies his repudiating seller that he intends to "await the latter's performance" and urges retraction. Without telling the seller, the buyer then makes a substitute "cover" purchase. The seller retracts but the buyer refuses to recognize the original contract and sues the seller for damages. What result under §§2-610 and 2-611? See Peters, Remedies for Breach of Contracts Relating to the Sale of Goods Under the Uniform Commercial Code: A Roadmap for Article Two, 73 Yale L.J. 199, 265-266 (1963).

2. Reread U.C.C. §§2-712 and 2-713 (buyer's cover and market remedies), *supra* p. 1133. Putting these sections together with those on anticipatory repudiation, how do you think Missouri Furnace Co. v. Cochran would be decided under the Code? If the buyer elects to sue for damages under §2-713, does §2-713(2) codify the holding in the *Missouri Furnace* case? What is the meaning of the phrase, "any reasonable purchase of or contract to purchase goods in substitution for those due from the seller," in §2-712(1)? Does the requirement in §2-712(1) that the buyer cover "without unreasonable delay" disallow the very thing which the court in *Missouri Furnace* thought mandatory (a series of purchases, over the term of the repudiated contract, at the then-prevailing spot price)?

OLOFFSON v. COOMER

11 Ill. App. 3d 918, 296 N.E.2d 871 (1973)

ALLOY, Presiding Justice:

Richard Oloffson, d/b/a Rich's Ag Service appeals from a judgment of the circuit court of Bureau County in favor of appellant against Clarence Coomer in the amount of $1,500 plus costs. The case was tried by the court without a jury.

Oloffson was a grain dealer. Coomer was a farmer. Oloffson was in the business of merchandising grain. Consequently, he was a "merchant" within the meaning of section 2-104 of the Uniform Commercial Code. (Ill. Rev. Stat. 1969, ch. 26 §2-104). Coomer, however, was simply in the business of growing rather than merchandising grain. He, therefore, was not a "merchant" with respect to the merchandising of grain.

On April 16, 1970, Coomer agreed to sell to Oloffson, for delivery in October and December of 1970, 40,000 bushels of corn. Oloffson testified at the trial that the entire agreement was embodied in two separate contracts, each covering 20,000 bushels and that the first 20,000 bushels were to be delivered on or before October 30 at a price of $1.12¾ per bushel and the second 20,000 bushels were to be delivered on or before December 15, at a price of $1.12¼ per bushel. Coomer, in his testimony, agreed that the 40,000 bushels were to be delivered but stated that he was to deliver all he could by October 30 and the balance by December 15.

On June 3, 1970, Coomer informed Oloffson that he was not going to plant corn because the season had been too wet. He told Oloffson to arrange elsewhere to obtain the corn if Oloffson had obligated himself to deliver to any third party. The price for a bushel of corn on June 3, 1970, for future delivery, was $1.16. In September of 1970, Oloffson asked Coomer about delivery of the corn and Coomer repeated that he would not be able to deliver. Oloffson, however, persisted. He mailed Coomer confirmations of the April 16 agreement. Coomer ignored these. Oloffson's attorney then requested that Coomer perform. Coomer ignored this request likewise. The scheduled delivery dates referred to passed with no corn delivered. Oloffson then covered his obligation to his own vendee by purchasing 20,000 bushels at $1.35 per bushel and 20,000 bushels at $1.49 per bushel. The judgment from which Oloffson appeals awarded Oloffson as damages, the difference between the contract and the market prices on June 3, 1970, the day upon which Coomer first advised Oloffson he would not deliver.

Oloffson argues on this appeal that the proper measure of his damages was the difference between the contract price and the market price on the dates the corn should have been delivered in accordance with the April 16 agreement. Plaintiff does not seek any other damages. The trial court prior to entry of judgment, in an opinion finding the facts and reviewing the law, found that plaintiff was entitled to recover judgment only for the sum of $1,500 plus costs as we have indicated which is equal to the amount of the difference between the minimum contract price and the price on June 3, 1970, of $1.16 per bushel (taking the greatest differential from $1.12¼ per bushel multiplied by 40,000 bushels). We believe the findings and the judgment of the trial court were proper and should be affirmed.

It is clear that on June 3, 1970, Coomer repudiated the contract "with respect to performance not yet due." Under the terms of the Uniform Commercial Code the loss would impair the value of the contract to the remaining party in the amount as indicated. (Ill. Rev. Stat. 1969, ch. 26, §2-610.) As a consequence, on June 3, 1970, Oloffson, as the "aggrieved party," could then:

(a) for a commercially reasonable time await performance by the repudiating party; or
(b) resort to any remedy for breach (Section 2-703 or Section 2-711), even though he has notified the repudiating party that he would await the latter's performance and has urged retraction. . . .

If Oloffson chose to proceed under subparagraph (a) referred to, he could have awaited Coomer's performance for a "commercially reasonable time." As we indicate in the course of this opinion, that "commercially reasonable time" expired on June 3, 1970. The Uniform Commercial Code made a change in existing Illinois law in this respect, in that, prior to the adoption of the Code, a buyer in a position as Oloffson was privileged to await a seller's performance until the date that, according to the agreement, such performance was scheduled. To the extent that a "commercially reasonable time" is less than such date of performance, the Code now conditions the buyer's right to await performance. (See Ill. Rev. Stat. Ann. 1969, ch. 26, §2-610, Illinois Code Comment, Paragraph (a)).

If, alternatively, Oloffson had proceeded under subparagraph (b) by treating the repudiation as a breach, the remedies to which he would have been entitled were set forth in section 2-711 (Ill. Rev. Stat. 1969, ch. 26, §2-711), which is the only applicable section to which section 2-610(b) refers according to the relevant portion of 2-711:

> (1)   Where the seller fails to make delivery or repudiates or the buyer rightfully rejects or justifiably revokes acceptance then with respect to any goods involved, and with respect to the whole if the breach goes to the whole contract (Section 2-612), the buyer may cancel and whether or not he has done so may in addition to recovering so much of the price as has been paid
>> (a)   "cover" and have damages under the next section as to all the goods affected whether or not they have been identified to the contract; or
>> (b)   recover damages for non-delivery as provided in this Article (Section 2-713).

Plaintiff, therefore, was privileged under Section 2-610 of the Uniform Commercial Code to proceed either under subparagraph (a) or under subparagraph (b). At the expiration of the "commercially reasonable time" specified in subparagraph (a), he in effect would have a duty to proceed under subparagraph (b) since subparagraph (b) directs reference to remedies generally available to a buyer upon a seller's breach.

Oloffson's right to await Coomer's performance under section 2-610(a) was conditioned upon his:

> (i)   waiting no longer than a "commercially reasonable time"; and
> (ii)   dealing with Coomer in good faith.

Since Coomer's statement to Oloffson on June 3, 1970, was unequivocal and since "cover" easily and immediately was available to Oloffson in the well-organized and easily accessible market for purchases of grain to be delivered in the future, it would be unreasonable for Oloffson on June 3,

1970, to have awaited Coomer's performance rather than to have proceeded under Section 2-610(b) and, thereunder, to elect then to treat the repudiation as a breach. Therefore, if Oloffson were relying on his right to effect cover under section 2-711(1)(a), June 3, 1970, might for the foregoing reason alone have been the day on which he acquired cover.

Additionally, however, the record and the finding of the trial court indicates that Oloffson adhered to a usage of trade that permitted his customers to cancel the contract for a future delivery of grain by making known to him a desire to cancel and paying to him the difference between the contract and market price on the day of cancellation. There is no indication whatever that Coomer was aware of this usage of trade. The trial court specifically found, as a fact, that, in the context in which Oloffson's failure to disclose this information occurred, Oloffson failed to act in good faith. According to Oloffson, he didn't ask for this information:

> I'm no information sender. If he had asked I would have told him exactly what to do. . . . I didn't feel my responsibility. I thought it his to ask, in which case I would tell him exactly what to do.

We feel that the words "for a commercially reasonable time" as set forth in Section 2-610(a) must be read relatively to the obligation of good faith that is defined in Section 2-103(1)(b) and imposed expressly in Section 1-203. (Ill. Rev. Stat. 1969, ch. 26, §2-103(1)(b) and §1-203.)

The Uniform Commercial Code imposes upon the parties the obligation to deal with each other in good faith regardless of whether they are merchants. The Sales Article of the Code specifically defines good faith, "in the case of a merchant . . . [as] honesty in fact and the observance of reasonable commercial standards of fair dealing in the trade." For the foregoing reasons and likewise because Oloffson's failure to disclose in good faith might itself have been responsible for Coomer's failure to comply with the usage of trade which we must assume was known only to Oloffson, we conclude that a commercially reasonable time under the facts before us expired on June 3, 1970.

Imputing to Oloffson the consequences of Coomer's having acted upon the information that Oloffson in good faith should have transmitted to him, Oloffson knew or should have known on June 3, 1970, the limit of damages he probably could recover. If he were obligated to deliver grain to a third party, he knew or should have known that unless he covered on June 3, 1970, his own capital would be at risk with respect to his obligation to his own vendee. Therefore, on June 3, 1970, Oloffson, in effect, had a duty to proceed under subparagraph (b) of Section 2-610 and under subparagraphs (a) and (b) of subparagraph 1 of Section 2-711. If Oloffson had so proceeded under subparagraph (a) of Section 2-711, he should have effected cover and would have been entitled to recover damages all as provided in section 2-712, which requires that he would have had to cover in good faith without unreasonable delay. Since he would have had to effect cover on June 3, 1970, according to section 2-712(2), he would have been entitled to exactly the damages which the trial court awarded him in this cause.

Assuming that Oloffson had proceeded under subparagraph (b) of Section 2-711, he would have been entitled to recover from Coomer under Section 2-713 and Section 2-723 of the Commercial Code, the difference between the contract price and the market price on June 3, 1970, which is the date upon which he learned of the breach. This would produce precisely the same amount of damages which the trial court awarded him. [See: Ill. Rev. Stat. 1969, ch. 26 §2-723(1)].

Since the trial court properly awarded the damages to which plaintiff was entitled in this cause, the judgment of the circuit court of Bureau County is, therefore, affirmed.

Affirmed.

NOTE

1. Suppose it were the buyer (Oloffson) who had repudiated the contract. If the seller elected to sue for his market damages under §2-708(1), he would be permitted to recover the "difference between the market price at the time and place for tender and the unpaid contract price." Is this consistent with the Code's definition of the buyer's market damages in cases of anticipatory repudiation? Which formula seems to you the better one? Consult the article by Jackson, quoted in Note 2, *supra* p. 1306, at 101-112.

2. U.C.C. §2-723 (Proof of Market Price: Time and Place) provides, in part:

> If an action based on anticipatory repudiation comes to trial before the time for performance with respect to some or all of the goods, any damages based on market price (Section 2-708 or Section 2-713) shall be determined according to the price of such goods prevailing at the time when the aggrieved party learned of the repudiation.

What is the rationale for this provision? Is the time a buyer learns of the seller's repudiation (§2-723) the same as the time he learns of the seller's breach (§2-713(1))? For a learned argument that in cases of anticipatory repudiation, a buyer may be said to learn of the seller's breach only at the time of performance, see J. White and R. Summers, Handbook of the Law Under the Uniform Commercial Code 197-202 (1972). For an equally learned criticism of this interpretation, see Professor Jackson's article, *supra* p. 1306, at 105.

CLARK v. MARSIGLIA
1 Denio 317 (N.Y. 1845)

Error from the New York common pleas. Marsiglia sued Clark in the court below in assumpsit, for work, labor and materials, in cleaning, repairing and improving sundry paintings belonging to the defendant. The defendant pleaded non assumpsit.

The plaintiff proved that a number of paintings were delivered to him by the defendant to clean and repair, at certain prices for each. They were delivered upon two occasions. As to the first parcel, for the repairing of which the price was seventy-five dollars, no defence was offered. In respect to the other, for which the plaintiff charged one hundred and fifty-six dollars, the defendant gave evidence tending to show that after the plaintiff had commenced work upon them, he desired him not to go on, as he had concluded not to have the work done. The plaintiff, notwithstanding, finished the cleaning and repairing of the pictures, and claimed to recover for doing the whole, and for the materials furnished, insisting that the defendant had no right to countermand the order which he had given. The defendant's counsel requested the court to charge that he had the right to countermand his instructions for the work, and that the plaintiff could not recover for any work done after such countermand.

The court declined to charge as requested, but, on the contrary, instructed the jury that inasmuch as the plaintiff had commenced the work before the order was revoked, he had a right to finish it, and to recover the whole value of his labor and for the materials furnished. The jury found their verdict accordingly, and the defendant's counsel excepted. Judgment was rendered upon the verdict.

PER CURIAM. The question does not arise as to the right of the defendant below to take away these pictures upon which the plaintiff had performed some labor, without payment for what he had done, and his damages for the violation of the contract, and upon that point we express no opinion. The plaintiff was allowed to recover as though there had been no countermand of the order; and in this the court erred. The defendant, by requiring the plaintiff to stop work upon the paintings violated his contract, and thereby incurred a liability to pay such damages as the plaintiff should sustain. Such damages would include a recompense for the labor done and materials used, and such further sum in damages as might, upon legal principles, be assessed for the breach of the contract: but the plaintiff had no right, by obstinately persisting in the work, to make the penalty upon the defendant greater than it would otherwise have been.

To hold that one who employs another to do a piece of work is bound to suffer it to be done at all events, would sometimes lead to great injustice. A man may hire another to labor for a year, and within the year his situation may be such as to render the work entirely useless to him. The party employed cannot persist in working though he is entitled to the damages consequent upon his disappointment. So if one hires another to build a house, and subsequent events put it out of his power to pay for it, it is commendable in him to stop the work, and pay for what has been done and the damages sustained by the contractor. He may be under a necessity to change his residence; but upon the rule contended for, he would be obliged to have a house which he did not need and could not use. In all such cases the just claims of the party employed are satisfied when he is fully recompensed for his part performance and indemnified for his loss in respect to the part left unexecuted; and to persist in accumulating a larger demand is not consistent with good faith towards the employer. The judgment must be reversed, and a venire de novo awarded.

Judgment reversed.

NOTE

1. In Rockingham County v. Luten Bridge Co., 35 F.2d 301 (4th Cir. 1929), the facts were that the Bridge Company was under contract to build a bridge for the county. The bridge was to be a connecting link in a new road which the county commissioners proposed to build through a forest. After the bridge had been partially constructed, the commissioners notified the Bridge Company to stop work. This action was taken because the commissioners had decided not to build the road. The Bridge Company disregarded the notification to stop, completed the bridge and brought suit for the contract price. Per Parker, J.:

> In the case at bar, the county decided not to build the road of which the bridge was to be a part, and did not build it. The bridge, built in the midst of the forest, is of no value to the county because of this change of circumstances. When, therefore, the county gave notice to the plaintiff that it would not proceed with the project, plaintiff should have desisted from further work. It had no right then to pile up damages by proceeding with the erection of a useless bridge.

35 F.2d at 307. The Bridge Company's action in completing the bridge may not have been as unreasonable as it sounds. The political situation within the county was confused. There was a pro-road (and bridge) faction as well as an anti-road (and bridge) faction. At the time the notice to stop work was given the antis were temporarily in control but it was far from clear which faction would ultimately prevail.

2. There can be no doubt that the rule of Clark v. Marsiglia, which is referred to as the "leading case on the subject" in Judge Parker's opinion

in the *Luten Bridge* case, is the prevailing rule in this country. White and Carter (Councils) Ltd. v. McGregor, [1961] 3 All E.R. 1178, may suggest a different approach in England. An advertising agency had a contract to prepare and display advertising signs for a three year period; the client attempted to cancel the contract before anything had been done under it. The agency nevertheless prepared the signs and displayed them for three years. In the House of Lords, by a 3 to 2 decision, the agency was granted recovery of the contract price.

Perhaps the English case is distinguishable on the ground that the defendant apparently allowed the signs to remain on display, thus accepting the benefit. Is it not also true, however, that the *plaintiff* in the *White and Carter* case also derived some benefit from the display of its signs (the signs being as much an advertisement of the plaintiff's skills as the defendant's product)? Could the loss of this benefit be compensated by money damages? If not, would it have been appropriate to require the advertising company to mitigate its damages by terminating performance upon learning of the defendant's breach? Might not the plaintiff in Clark v. Marsiglia have had a similar interest in enhancing, or at least preserving *his* reputation (which presumably he could have done only if he were allowed to finish cleaning the paintings)?

3. Suppose that Clark had in fact stopped work on the defendant's paintings when told to do so. Presumably, under the rule approved by the court, Clark could have recovered damages in an amount equal to his out-of-pocket expenses at the time of breach plus the profit he would have made on the contract if he had been allowed to complete it. Having been relieved of any duty to complete work on Marsiglia's paintings, however, Clark is now free to go to work for someone else and make a second profitable contract. Is it not true that Clark will therefore be better off if Marsiglia breaches and pays him damages than he would have been if everything had gone smoothly? Should Clark's damages be adjusted to insure that he is not *over*compensated by the party in breach? Would this problem arise if the contract had been one calling for the performance of services (e.g., housecleaning) for a specified period of time?

4. In a contract of sale, where the goods are unfinished at the time the buyer repudiates, U.C.C. §2-704(2) states that

> an aggrieved seller may in the exercise of reasonable commercial judgment for the purposes of avoiding loss and of effective realization either complete the manufacture and wholly identify the goods to the contract or cease manufacture and resell for scrap or salvage value or proceed in any other reasonable manner.

If Clark had agreed to paint pictures for Marsiglia, rather than clean them, how, according to §2-704(2), could (or should) he have responded to Marsiglia's repudiation?

MOUNT PLEASANT STABLE CO. v.
STEINBERG

238 Mass. 567, 131 N.E. 295 (1921)

CARROLL, J. The parties entered into a written contract dated June 25, 1914, by which the plaintiff was to furnish at an agreed price, single and double teams to do the defendants' trucking. There was evidence that after the parties had operated under the contract for a few months the defendants broke the contract. The auditor found that at the time of the breach the contract had four hundred and fifty days to run; that the defendants were using during the period on an average "four and one-half teams a day," and that the profit to the plaintiff would be $1 for each team, making the total profit $2,025. He also found that the plaintiff purchased for special use in the defendants' business, two "Cliest" horses for which it paid $625 and sold them for $485, sustaining a loss thereby of $140. The defendants contend that the plaintiff is entitled to damages only from the time the work under the contract was discontinued to the date of sale; that the rule of damages is the same as in a contract for personal services, and it is the duty of the party claiming damages for the breach of such contract, to make all reasonable efforts to secure another contract. In the superior court the case was heard on the auditor's report. The judge found for the plaintiff in the sum of $2,025 for damages, and interest from the date of the writ, and the case was reported to this court on the question of damages only, on the pleadings and the auditor's report.

The auditor found that eight days after the contract was broken, the plaintiff sold all its horses, caravans and other equipment at public auction; that at this time there was a demand for horses and caravans, and it could have found a ready market for their use at a price equal to that which it was to receive from the defendant; that the plaintiff could have found use for its horses and wagons, had it made any real effort to do so, at the contract price; and that if the plaintiff was entitled to damages only from the time of the breach to the time of the sale, it is entitled to recover $36.

The rule that when a contract calls for the personal services of a party, he is required in case the contract is broken by the other party, to use reasonable efforts to obtain other employment reasonably adapted to his abilities, thereby lessening the damages, Maynard v. Royal Worcester Corset Co., 200 Mass. 1, 6, 85 N.E. 877; Hussey v. Holloway, 217 Mass. 100, 104 N.E. 471, has no application to the case at bar. The auditor found that the contract did not require on the part of the plaintiff any special skill and could be performed by its employees. In Dixon v. Volunteer Cooperative Bank, 213 Mass. 345, 100 N.E. 655, the plaintiff was hired by the defendant to act as its attorney for one year. His work was to examine titles to land offered to the bank as security. Before he was discharged he had the right to do additional work without accounting to the defendant for the profits received. It was held that this was not lessened by the defendant's breach of the contract, that the plaintiff's time did not belong to the defendant under his contract, and he was not its servant and not bound to minimize the damages suffered by him, and that the rule of damages which is applicable when a contract for personal service is broken, did not apply. The same rule governs the case at bar. Wolf v. Studebaker, 65 Pa. 459; Allen v. Murray, 87 Wis. 41, 47, 48, 57 N.W. 979.

The contract did not preclude the plaintiff from carrying on as many other contracts as it saw fit. Its time did not belong to the defendants and the contract did not call for personal services on the part of the plaintiff. The defendants having broken the contract became liable to the plaintiff for all damages which would compensate it for its loss and such as the parties were supposed to have contemplated would result from its breach. The plaintiff was entitled to recover damages measured by the difference between the contract price and what it would have cost it to have performed the contract, or, as found by the auditor, a profit of $1 on each team from the time the contract was broken until its expiration according to its terms. [Citations.]

The auditor found that the plaintiff bought two "Cliest" horses specially for use in connection with the defendants' business, for which he paid $625 and sold them at a loss of $140. The plaintiff contends it is entitled to recover this amount in addition to the profits on the contract. If the plaintiff had completed the contract it could recover only the contract price. This expenditure for preliminary outlays could not be received in addition, and by recovering the profits on the contract, full compensation is given for its loss. See Holt v. United Security Life Insurance & Trust Co., 76 N.J.L. 585, 597, 599, 72 A. 301, 21 L.R.A., N.S., 691; Worthington v. Gwin, 119 Ala. 44, 51, 24 So. 739, 43 L.R.A. 382. It is not necessary to decide in this case, if a contract is broken what damages should be recovered for expenses in preparing for its performance, where the profits cannot be determined. See Pond v. Harris, 113 Mass. 114, 121, 122.

The plaintiff is entitled to interest from the date of the writ. Cormier v. Brock, 212 Mass. 292, 98 N.E. 1038; Jackson v. Brockton, 182 Mass. 26, 64 N.E. 418, 94 Am. St. Rep. 635; Speirs v. Union Drop Forge Co., 180 Mass. 87, 61 N.E. 825. According to the report, judgment is to be entered on the findings.

So ordered.

JAMESON v. BOARD OF EDUCATION
78 W. Va. 612, 89 S.E. 255 (1916)

Action by Hallie Janes Jameson against the Board of Education, etc. Judgment for plaintiff, and defendant brings error. . . .

WILLIAMS, President: Plaintiff recovered a judgment against defendant for $609.67, the amount of seven months wages, claimed to be due her on a contract of employment as teacher of music in the public schools of the cities of Benwood and McMechen, in the school district of Union, Marshall county, and by this writ of error defendant seeks a reversal.

Plaintiff declared upon the special contract, averring that she was employed by defendant for a period of nine months, beginning on the 11th of September, 1911, and continuing for nine school months, on an agreed salary of $75 per month, payable monthly; that, throughout the term of employment, she stood ready to perform her part of the contract; that she appeared at the schools on the morning of each school day and demanded of the respective superintendents thereof that her work be assigned her; and that she did actually perform her part of the contract. The declaration contains also the common counts in assumpsit. The only breach averred is the failure and refusal of defendant to pay the wages for the last seven months of the schools.

Defendant pleaded the general issue, and also tendered a special plea, which the court rejected on motion of plaintiff. It averred that plaintiff had theretofore sued defendant and recovered a judgment against it for $150, on account of salary claimed by plaintiff for the first two months of school, ending, respectively, on the 6th of October and the 3rd of November, 1911; that it was proven, on the trial of that action, that defendant had revoked or attempted to revoke plaintiff's appointment as music teacher, and had refused to permit her to teach; and that she had not, in fact, taught, though she held herself in readiness to do so; and that said judgment is still in force. Wherefore, defendant prayed judgment whether plaintiff ought to have or maintain her present action.

The case was tried by the court in lieu of jury, upon an agreed statement of facts, from which it appears that the plaintiff was not permitted by defendant to teach; that it sued out a writ of injunction to prevent her from continually appearing at the schools for the purpose of teaching, which writ was later dissolved on her motion. It thus appears that plaintiff actually performed no part of the contract, although she was at all times ready to do so, but that she was prevented from performing by defendant.

There was a total breach of the contract by defendant's refusal to permit plaintiff to perform her part of it. Her right of action for that breach was then complete, and it was not necessary for her to appear at the schools each day and demand opportunity to perform the contract. She could not thereby make her cause of action any more perfect than it was the moment she was informed that defendant had refused to be bound by the contract. Her suit is not for damages for a breach of the contract of employment, but is a suit for wages claimed to be due under the contract, for services which were never actually performed. She seeks to treat the contract as subsisting until the end of the term, and broken only in respect of the promise to pay her the agreed monthly wages. This she cannot do. Having performed no services whatever, she cannot recover upon the promise, as if wages were earned. Her only right of action is for a breach of the contract. It is insisted that she is entitled to recover on account of constructive service, that being always ready and willing to perform the contract she should be regarded in law as having actually performed it. That doctrine was first announced by Lord Ellenborough in Gandell v. Potigny, 4 Campbell 374, a nisi prius case decided in 1816, in which he held that a servant, employed for a quarter and wrongfully discharged before the end thereof, might recover upon an indebitatus assumpsit count for wages for the entire quarter. Although that doctrine was followed in a few later cases, it has, long since, been repudiated as unsound, both in England and in a majority of the states of the Union. . . .

The constructive service doctrine was followed for a while by the courts of New York, but was later repudiated. The court of appeals of that state, in Howard v. Daly, 61 N.Y. 362, 19 L.R.A. 285, expressly disapproves the doctrine of Gandell v. Potigny, *supra*, and overrules the earlier New York decisions. In that case plaintiff was employed to act at the Fifth Avenue Theatre, in such capacity and manner as defendant might direct, and was to be paid a salary of $10 a week during the season, beginning about September 15, 1870, and continuing until about July 1, 1871. There, as in this case, plaintiff was prevented by the defendant from entering upon the discharge of her engagement, and, in fact, never rendered any actual service. The court held that she could not maintain an action for wages, but could sue only for breach of the contract, and that it was not necessary to tender her services after the breach. Respecting the constructive service doctrine, Judge Dwight, at page 373, says:

> This doctrine is, however, so opposed to principle, so clearly hostile to the great mass of the authorities, and wholly irreconcilable to that great and beneficent rule of law, that a person discharged from service must not remain idle, but must accept employment elsewhere if offered, that we cannot accept it. If a person discharged from service may recover wages, or treat the contract as still subsisting, then he must remain idle in order to be always ready to perform the service. How absurd it would be that one rule of law should call upon him to accept other employment, while another rule required him to remain idle in order that he may recover full wages. The doctrine of "constructive service" is not only at war with principle, but with the rules of political economy, as it encourages idleness and gives compensation to men who fold their arms and decline service, equal to those who perform with willing hands their stipulated amount of labor. Though the master has committed a wrong, the servant is not for one moment released from the rule that he should labor; and no rule can be sound which gives him full wages while living in voluntary idleness. For these reasons, if the plaintiff was discharged after the time of service commenced, she had an immediate cause of action for damages, which were

prima facie a sum equal to the stipulated amount, unless the defendant should give evidence in mitigation of damages. . . .

The peculiar doctrine of successive liability for loss of wages, as if upon a contract of continuing indemnity, announced by the Minnesota court in McMullan v. Dickinson, 60 Minn. 156, 51 Am. St. Rep. 511, to be the proper rule, where a servant has been wrongfully discharged, we do not find to be followed by any other court. Such a rule produces a multiplicity of suits for one and the same wrong, and tends to encourage idleness in the discharged servant. Although wrongfully discharged, a servant still owes a duty, both to himself and to society, to be diligent in trying to secure other employment. A recovery once had, whether it be upon a count for damages for a breach of the contract or upon an indebitatus assumpsit count for services which could have been rendered, bars subsequent recovery. For the breach of an entire contract, the party aggrieved has a right to recover in the one action all damages, prospective as well as past. 2 Sedgwick, (9th ed.), Sec. 636g; Thomas v. Willoughby, 24 Grat. 521; Lamoreaux v. Rolfe, 36 N.H. 33; Wilkinson v. Dunbar, 149 N.C. 20; Sutherland v. Wyer, 67 Me. 64; Litchenstein v. Brooks, 75 Tex. 196; and Monarch Cycle M'f'g Co. v. Meuller, 83 Ill. App. 359.

That the contract, in this case, was entire needs no discussion. Plaintiff's declaration alleges that she was employed for a period of nine months — a school year.

Having declared on the special contract for wages which she claimed to be due thereunder, the performance of the services for which they were to be paid is put in issue by the general plea, and the agreed facts prove that plaintiff actually performed no services whatever, and, therefore, her suit must fail, unless her declaration may properly be regarded as a suit for damages for the breach of the contract for her employment. This question we need not determine, for the reason that, if it could be so regarded, her former recovery is a complete bar to the present action.

The judgment will be reversed; and, it being apparent from the agreed facts that plaintiff could not make out any better case, if a new trial should be awarded, judgment will be entered here for defendant.

On Re-hearing

After a careful reconsideration of this case and the authorities bearing thereon we are of opinion to adhere to our former conclusion. The authorities are not harmonious, but our decision harmonizes with the weight of the more modern and better reasoned cases from other states, and accords with what we regard as the better rule applicable to cases of this character. The contract was entire, the breach thereof also entire and plaintiff had but one right of action. She exhausted her remedy for her former suit and is barred of the present action by the judgment rendered therein. [The dissenting opinion of Poffenbarger, J., joined in by Miller, J., is omitted.]

NOTE

1. It appears that in the first action plaintiff recovered her full wages for the first two months of the school year. In the light of the Supreme Court's opinion on the appeal in the second action, that recovery was improper, was it not? If, as the New York court put it in Howard v. Daly, plaintiff is not allowed to collect full wages "while living in voluntary idleness," it must follow that the wrongfully discharged employee must look for other work. Does it also follow that the wages earned in the substituted employment are to be deducted from the recovery in the employee's action against the employer? And further, that if the employee could have found another job but did not take it, then the wages he (or she) could have made will likewise be deducted? To most American courts it has seemed obvious that these conclusions necessarily follow from the "no voluntary idleness" principle. The hypothetically innocent employee must thus labor for the benefit of the hypothetically wicked employer. The decisions show some sympathy for the employee. Work of a substantially different character need not be accepted: the discharged school teacher need not go to work in a factory. Nor is it necessary for the employee to accept work in a different place, which would require him to move his residence or to travel long distances to and from the job. And the employee has often been held privileged to reject the original employer's offer of re-employment at a lower wage. Assume, for example, that the School Board had offered to take Mrs. Jameson back at $50 per month. If she were required to accept this offer, or to have her damages reduced by an amount equal to the difference between her original salary and the one now proposed, the cost of suing her employer might well exceed her largest possible recovery, in which case the School Board could (up to a point) unilaterally "force" a wage cut on her.

Of course, the widely approved mitigation rule requiring a wrongfully dismissed employee to seek comparable work with another employer has similar consequences: so long as the damages recoverable under this rule are less than the expense of litigation, the employer who has breached his contract can be confident that his wrong will cost him nothing. Indeed, this is a general feature of all remedial systems (like our own) that do not fully compensate the winning party for the out-of-pocket expenses incurred in vindicating his legal rights. Judicial willingness to apply the standard mitigation rule to offers of re-employment must therefore rest on other grounds: Perhaps it simply reflects a desire not to force the employee into, or back into, a personal relationship that has grown sour and litigious. See Hubbard Broadcasting v. C. A. Loescher, 291 N.W.2d 216 (Minn. 1980). The cases on specific enforcement of personal service contracts express a similar idea; see *supra* p. 1079.

A related problem involves the question whether unemployment benefits and the like received by the discharged employee are to be credited to the employer and deducted from the recovery. In recent years, courts have expressed some diversity of opinion on this issue. In Billeter v. Posell, 94 Cal. App. 2d 858, 211 P.2d 621 (1949), the court concluded that such benefits are not deductible: "Benefits of this character are intended to alleviate the distress of unemployment and not to diminish the amount which an employer must pay as damages for the wrongful discharge of an employee." A different approach was suggested in United Protective Workers of America v. Ford Motor Co., 223 F.2d 49 (7th Cir. 1955). For multitudinous collections of cases on the points referred to in this Note, see 11 Williston §1358 et seq.

2. Under the rule discussed in the preceding Note, what happens to the aspect of anticipatory breach doctrine which says that one of the courses of action which the innocent party may elect to follow is to await performance by the repudiating party, who may meanwhile retract his repudiation?

3. We may assume that Mrs. Jameson could have waited until the end of the school year and then brought an action to recover damages, calculated in the manner described in Note 1. Alternatively could she bring her action immediately on being discharged? If she attempted to bring such an action, would it make any difference whether she had been discharged in July (before the beginning of the school year) or in October (after the first month of school)? And how should the damages be calculated if the action brought in July or October comes to trial before the end of the school year?

4. In Dixie Glass Co., Inc. v. Pollak, 341 S.W.2d 530 (Tex. Civ. App.), 91 A.L.R.2d 662 (1960), *error refused n.r.e.* 162 Tex. 440, 347 S.W.2d 596, 91 A.L.R.2d 681 (1961), Pollak had been employed in 1953 as comptroller of the Dixie corporation. The original contract was for five years but Pollak had the option to extend the contract for an additional fifteen years. He was discharged in 1955. Pollak brought an action against the corporation to recover 1) damages which had accrued at the time of trial and 2) damages for the balance of the twenty year term of the contract. His right to recover the accrued damages (assuming that the discharge was wrongful) was not contested. A jury verdict was taken on what his damages would be for the balance of the term. The jury calculated the damages at $78,000 (i.e., $156,000 which he would have received as salary, less $78,000 deducted on account of his expected future earnings for the remainder of the twenty years). The legal question whether the $78,000 recovery, plus interest, was proper under Texas law was referred to the Court of Civil Appeals. On this question the court observed:

We find there is a conflict in the authorities in the United States. The majority rule is that recovery of damages may be had for the full term, regardless of when the trial occurs. The minority view is that anticipatory damages may not be recovered but recovery is limited to damages suffered to the date of trial. . . .

341 S.W.2d at 537. Concluding that the issue had not been "authoritatively decided" in Texas, the court, ignoring contrary dicta in earlier Texas cases, decided to adopt the "majority rule." Remanding the case for a new trial on the issue of whether the discharge had been wrongful, the court cautioned that, if Pollak won on the wrongful discharge issue and a second jury came up with the same damage calculation, judgment should not be for the lump sum of $78,000 but for the $78,000 "discounted to its present worth, based on the unexpired term of the contract at the date of judgment, at the rate of 6% per annum." This disposition of the case was affirmed, per curiam, by the Supreme Court of Texas. An annotation beginning at 91 A.L.R.2d 682 collects authorities on the issue. The learned annotator concluded that Alabama, Arkansas, Georgia, Illinois, Minnesota, North Carolina, and Wisconsin adhered to the "minority view" (limiting recovery to damages accrued at the time of trial); in Kentucky the issue was "apparently unsettled."

5. Does the rule in the employment cases, illustrated by the *Jameson* case, seem consistent with the rule announced by the Massachusetts court in the *Steinberg* case? If the rules are consistent, how are cases like *Steinberg* to be distinguished from employment cases like *Jameson*? Further, in connection with *Steinberg*, do you agree with the court's refusal to allow recovery for the loss on the resale of the "Cliest" horses?

6. In Griswold v. Heat Incorporated, 108 N.H. 119, 229 A.2d 183 (1967), Griswold, a certified public accountant who was a member of a large firm of accountants in Portland, Maine, and Heat, a corporation doing business in Nashua, New Hampshire, entered into an agreement under which Heat was to pay Griswold "not less than two hundred dollars [per month] beginning January 1, 1964 for such services as he, in his sole discretion may render, the term of the contract to be not less than five years from January 1, 1964. . . ." The Board of Directors terminated Griswold's services at the end of 1964. The New Hampshire court, relying on Wood v. Lucy, Lady Duff-Gordon, *supra* p. 451, concluded that Griswold's promise was not "illusory," that the contract was binding and that Griswold had been wrongfully discharged. Nor did the court have any doubt (see Notes 3 and 4 *supra*) that Griswold could recover damages for the full five-year term. It is evident that Griswold was not required or expected to devote his full time to the affairs of the corporation. Assume, in addition, however, that any services Griswold *did* perform had to be rendered by Griswold himself and could not be delegated to anyone else (for example, an agent or a clerk in the Portland office of his accounting

firm). On that assumption, is Griswold's situation "like" that in the *Steinberg* case or "like" that in the employment cases? That is, must he deduct from his recovery whatever he could earn as an accountant in the time made available to him because he no longer has to perform services for the corporation or is he entitled to recover the full salary of $200 per month for the remaining four years of the contract without deduction?

7. In the principal case, which party bears the burden of showing that Mrs. Jameson did or did not have other comparable employment opportunities? See Levy v. Tharrington, 178 Okla. 276, 62 P.2d 641 (1936) ("the burden rests upon the employer to show by a preponderance of the evidence that the servant might, with reasonable diligence, have obtained other remunerative employment of a like character after his discharge").

LOUISE CAROLINE NURSING HOME, INC. v. DIX CONSTRUCTION CO.
362 Mass. 306, 285 N.E.2d 904 (1972)

QUIRICO, Justice.

This is an action of contract in which Louise Caroline Nursing Home, Inc. (Nursing Home) seeks damages from Dix Construction Corp. (Dix) for breach of a contract to build a nursing home, and from Reliance Insurance Company (Reliance), for its default on a surety bond guaranteeing performance by Dix. Dix filed no answer, was defaulted, and did not participate in the litigation. Reliance filed an answer and defended in its own behalf.

The case was referred to an auditor for hearing pursuant to a stipulation of the parties that his findings of fact would be final. After hearing the parties, the auditor filed a report in which he found generally: (1) that the Nursing Home had fulfilled all of its contractual obligations to Dix; (2) that Dix had committed a breach of its contractual obligations to the Nursing Home by failing, without justification, to complete the contract within the time agreed; and (3) that Reliance committed a breach of its obligations as surety by failing to take any action when Dix defaulted. However, he further found that the Nursing Home "suffered no compensable damages as a result of the breach by Dix . . . and the breach by Reliance . . . in that the cost to complete the nursing home . . . was within the contract price . . . less what had been paid to Dix. . . .

The Nursing Home filed a number of objections to the auditor's report and requested, pursuant to Rule 90 of the Superior Court (1954), that the auditor file a brief summary of the evidence relating to each such objection. After the auditor filed such a summary, the Nursing Home filed a motion to recommit the case to the auditor for correction of alleged errors. Reliance filed a cross motion asking (a) that the Nursing Home's objections to the report be overruled and (b) that judgment be entered in its favor on the report. The judge denied the motion of the Nursing Home and allowed that of Reliance. The case is before us on the Nursing Home's exceptions to those rulings which in turn involve its objections to the auditor's report.

1. The Nursing Home objected to the auditor's failure to grant four of its requests for findings. Although we could properly refuse to consider this objection because it was not argued in the Nursing Home's brief, it is sufficient to say that requests to an auditor to make findings of fact have no standing, without more, as the basis for objections, although they may be part of the foundation for a motion to recommit. . . .

2. The Nursing Home objects to the auditor's action in striking the testimony of one Goggin offered by it as an expert witness to establish (1) the value of the incomplete building when Dix ceased construction and (2) the projected value of the building when completed. With reference to Goggin's testimony the auditor stated in his report:

> I am disregarding this opinion evidence of Goggin and striking it out without regard to its relevancy. The principal reason for striking this testimony is that the witness never stated any valid basis in fact for his opinions. Further, I have doubts about the witness's qualifications to give such testimony.

A judge, or an auditor or master designated by a judge to hear a matter, has broad discretion to determine whether an expert witness has a proper basis, in terms of adequate information and preparation, to render an opinion on the matter in dispute. See State Tax Commn. v. Assessors of Springfield, 331 Mass. 677, 684-685, 122 N.E.2d 372; H. H. Hawkins & Sons Co. v. Robie, 338 Mass. 61, 65, 153 N.E.2d 768. The auditor's exclusion of Goggin's testimony for the reasons set forth in his report and in his summary of evidence under Superior Court Rule 90 was a proper exercise of his discretion and was not error.

The auditor's observation that he had doubts about Goggin's qualifications affords an additional ground for the exclusion of his testimony. We have often stated that

> [w]hether a witness who is called as an expert has the requisite qualifications and knowledge to enable him to testify, is a preliminary question for the court. The decision of this question is conclusive, unless it appears upon the evidence to have been erroneous, or to have been founded upon some error in law.

Perkins v. Stickney, 132 Mass. 217, 218, and cases cited. No such error appearing on the record, Goggin's testimony was also properly excluded on this ground.

3. Two of the Nursing Home's objections relate to the measure of the damages applied by the auditor in reaching his conclusion that it suffered

no "compensable damages." The rule of damages applied by the auditor was that if the cost of completing the contract by the use of a substitute contractor is within the contract price, less what had already been paid on the contract, no "compensable damages" have occurred. The Nursing Home argues that the proper rule of damages would entitle it to the difference between the value of the building as left by Dix and the value it would have had if the contract had been fully performed. Under this rule the Nursing Home contends that it was entitled to the "benefits of its bargain," meaning that if the fair market value of the completed building would have exceeded the contractual cost of construction, recovery should be allowed for this lost extra value. It bases this argument primarily upon our statement in Province Sec. Corp. v. Maryland Cas. Co., 269 Mass. 75, 94, 168 N.E. 252, 257, that

> [i]t is a settled rule that the measure of damages where a contractor has failed to perform a contract for the construction of a building for business uses is the difference between the value of the building as left by the contractor and its value had it been finished according to contract. In other words the question is how much less was the building worth than it would have been worth if the contract had been fully performed. . . .

This statement was probably not necessary to the court's decision in the *Province Sec. Corp.* case and, in any event, must be read in light of the cases cited by the court in support of it. All of these cases involved failure of performance in the sense of defective performance, as contrasted with abandonment of performance. In one of the cases, Pelatowski v. Black, 213 Mass. 428, 431, 100 N.E. 831, 832, the court expressly distinguished "cases where a contractor has abandoned his work while yet unfinished."

The fundamental rule of damages applied in all contract cases was stated by this court in Ficara v. Belleau, 331 Mass. 80, 82, 117 N.E.2d 287, 289, in the following language:

> It is not the policy of our law to award damages which would put a plaintiff in a better position than if the defendant had carried out his contract. . . .
> "The fundamental principle upon which the rule of damages is based is compensation. . . . Compensation is the value of the performance of the contract, that is, what the plaintiff would have made had the contract been performed." F. A. Bartlett Tree Expert Co. v. Hartney, 308 Mass. 407, 412, 32 N.E.2d 237, 240. . . . The plaintiff is entitled to be made whole and no more.

Consonant with this principle we have held that in assessing damages for failure to complete a construction contract,

> [t]he measure of the plaintiff's damages (at least in the absence of other elements of damage, as, for example, for delay in construction, which the

master has not found here) can be only in the amount of the reasonable cost of completing the contract and repairing the defendant's defective performance less such part of the contract price as has not been paid.

DiMare v. Capaldi, 336 Mass. 497, 502, 146 N.E.2d 517, 521. This principle was recently reiterated in Providence Washington Ins. Co. v. Beck, 356 Mass. 739, 255 N.E.2d 600.[77] In the face of this principle the Nursing Home's arguments attempting to demonstrate the amount of alleged "benefits of its bargain" lost are to no avail. In any event, it should be noted that any such "benefits of its bargain" as would derive from obtaining a building worth much more than the actual costs of construction are preserved if the building can be completed at a total cost which is still within the contract price, less any amount which has already been paid on the contract. The auditor was correct in applying the "cost of completion" measure of damages which excluded any separate recovery for lost "benefits of its bargain."

The Nursing Home additionally contends that even under the rule of damages applied by the auditor they were entitled, in the words of the DiMare case, supra, to recover "other elements of damage, as, for example, for delay in construction." 336 Mass. at 502, 146 N.E.2d at 521. The short answer to this contention is the auditor's express statement, in his summary of the evidence, that "[t]here was no specific evidence as to the costs of delay, if any."

The Nursing Home also argues that it is entitled to recover such additional interest as it was required to pay as a result of the default by Reliance and the breach of contract by Dix. This argument is based on the auditor's findings and summary of evidence that the interest rate on the $400,000 construction loan was to be one per cent per month "commencing with the date of maturity," and that the total interest paid, including all discounted interest, was $120,094.76. There was no evidence or finding, however, as to the rate of interest paid prior to maturity or as to the amount of alleged excess interest attributable to the defendants' defaults. The Nursing Home simply has not sustained its burden of proof on this point.

4. For the foregoing reasons the Nursing Home's exceptions to the denial of its motion to recommit the auditor's report and to the granting of Reliance's motion for entry of judgment in accordance with the auditor's report must be overruled.

Exceptions overruled.

77. In the earlier case of Pelatowski v. Black, 213 Mass. 428, 431, 100 N.E. 831, 832, the court had suggested that "[i]n such cases the measure of damages to be recovered or recouped well might be the reasonable cost of completing the work." However, this observation was subsequently disapproved in Ficara v. Belleau, 331 Mass. 80, 82, 117 N.E.2d 287, because it included no provision for the deduction of "such part of the contract price as has not been paid and is not still payable. . . ." 331 Mass. at 81, 117 N.E.2d at 289 (quoting from Restatement: Contracts, §346[1].

NOTE

1. If the court had adopted the Nursing Home's interpretation of the proper rule for measuring compensation, would the Home have been put (as Judge Quirico seems to imply) "in a better position than if the defendant had carried out his contract"? Do you think there is any basis for distinguishing, as the court does, between "defective" performance and "abandonment" of performance? Is the principal case consistent with Jacob & Youngs v. Kent, *supra* p. 1042, and Peevyhouse v. Garland Coal Co., *supra* p. 1119? (Remember that in the latter two cases the cost to complete performance of the contract exceeded any diminution in market value, whereas here, apparently, the reverse was true.)

2. Section 2-714 of the Uniform Commercial Code ("Buyer's Damages for Breach in Regard to Accepted Goods") reads as follows:

> (1) Where the buyer has accepted goods and given notification (subsection (3) of Section 2-607) he may recover as damages for any non-conformity of tender the loss resulting in the ordinary course of events from the seller's breach as determined in any manner which is reasonable.
>
> (2) The measure of damages for breach of warranty is the difference at the time and place of acceptance between the value of the goods accepted and the value they would have had if they had been as warranted, unless special circumstances show proximate damages of a different amount.
>
> (3) In a proper case any incidental and consequential damages under the next section may also be recovered.

How would the principal case be decided under §2-714? The buyer's cover and market remedies (§§2-712 and 2-713) give the buyer an incentive to mitigate his damages in the event of non-delivery or repudiation by the seller. Does §2-714 create a similar incentive where the buyer elects to accept the goods even though they fail to meet his legitimate contractual expectations?

CHAPTER 11

Third Party Beneficiaries

Section 1. Introductory Note

In preceding chapters the focus of attention has been on the two-party relationship. In this chapter on so-called Third Party Beneficiaries and in the following chapter on Assignment we shall consider the more complicated situation that results when C joins, or attempts to join, in the game along with those veteran warriors A and B.

The cast of characters need not, of course, remain frozen at three. Consider, for example, the contractual arrangements that cluster around the typical building contract. Landowner (A) enters into a contract with a construction company (B) under which B is to put a structure (house, factory, office building, airport) on A's land. The A-B contract requires B to furnish, for A's protection, a bond under which a surety company (C) guarantees that, if B defaults, C will complete the contract (performance bond) or pay all claims of laborers and materialmen against B (payment bond) or both. (If A is the United States, a federal statute known as the Miller Act[1] requires that all general contractors furnish both payment and performance bonds.) The general or prime contractor typically requires his subcontractors to furnish the same types of bonds running in the general contractor's favor — so that there may be several layers or levels of surety bonds arranged in hierarchical order below the prime contract. In form, the surety's payment bond may be described as a promise by C (surety company) to A (landowner) that the claims of D_1, D_2, D_3, etc. (laborers, materialmen, subcontractors) against B (construction company) will be paid. (If they were not paid, many of the claimants might be in a position, under applicable state law, to go against A directly and to acquire so-called mechanics' liens against his property.) In order to protect itself against possible liability on its bond, C (surety company) will require B (construction company) to assign to it moneys to be earned under the contract — the assignment to C to take effect on B's default under the A-B contract. If the construction project is a large one, B will

---

1. 40 U.S.C.A. §§270a-270e (West 1965 & Supp. 1985).

have to get outside financing. Usually it will borrow the money it needs from a bank (*E*). As security for the loan the bank will require that *B* assign to it all moneys to be earned in the course of performance of the *A-B* contract. (*B's* assignments to surety company and bank are of course in conflict with each other, since both assignments cover the same fund.)

The foregoing description of the relationships generated by the ordinary construction contract has been drastically oversimplified. Enough has been said, however, so that the student will not be surprised to learn that, for more than a hundred years past, state and federal courts have had to devote an inordinate amount of their time to disentangling the rights, duties and priorities of *A*, *B*, *C*, *D*, and *E*. Nor is there any present indication that the judges will ever produce a general agreement as to what those rights, duties, and priorities are. Business practice in the construction industry changes; the practices of banks and surety companies change; new statutes, state or federal, are passed that arguably may have, by accident or design, a bearing on some aspect of the complex. It is always possible to argue — it always is argued — that something has happened this year to cast doubt on last year's precedents. And so the dreary game drags on.[2]

For present purposes, we may restrict ourselves to the triangular or *A-B-C* relationship, which is already difficult enough without the additional presence of *D* and *E*.

The suggestion that *C* can acquire rights in a contract between *A* and *B* to which *C* is not a party is one that has always, when first put forward in some context, aroused judicial suspicion or hostility. The idea that a contract between *A* and *B* is a private link between them, and between them alone, is one that dies hard. *A* and *B*, we say, are in "privity" with each other; *C* is not in "privity" with them or with their contract; lacking "privity," *C* can acquire no rights (or duties) under the *A-B* contract. That, at all events, is a recurrent judicial reaction when a novel type of claim on behalf of *C* is put forward: what "privity" is or why the lack of it should be fatal is never inquired into. We may take the word "privity" as a sort of mystical absolute. To lack privity is to have failed to achieve the requisite state of contractual grace.

The history of the common law over the past several hundred years nevertheless reveals a succession of instances in which *C* has prevailed — however grudgingly his rights may have been recognized as an initial matter. Often, however, *C's* position has been vindicated by an appeal to the principles of agency or trust law, and his rights under the *A-B* agreement have therefore not appeared to be contractual at all. And even where *C's* rights have been upheld on contractual grounds, they have typically been explained not by general principles of promissory liability

---

2. For more on this problem, see p. 1364 *infra*, and the Note following that case.

but by the specialized rules belonging to one or another of the satellite systems thrown off by the common law of contracts in the course of its historical development.

The assumed unity of contract law has in fact always masked a centrifugal tendency. The law of sales and the law of labor agreements, to take two examples, both have (or once had) their roots in contract; sales law has long since become, and labor law is clearly in process of becoming, independent of the general law of contract. This centrifugal tendency has been particularly marked in what we may generically describe as the area of third party claims. Many types of triangular or A-B-C relationships have so completely won their independence that for generations or centuries no lawyer has thought of them as being a part of general contract law. This is true, for example, of the law of suretyship and the law of negotiable instruments. The fact that they split off from contract at an early date may reflect the deep-rooted difficulty that our contract theory has always had with third party claims. It seems to have been easier to establish a whole new body of law — and call it, say, suretyship — than to work out a general theory of contractual obligation under which A could transfer property to B for C's benefit.

The doctrine of third party beneficiaries starts from the idea that C can have rights under a contract to which he is not himself a party even though he has none of the special legal attributes that have long been recognized as a basis of third party claims. To this extent, the doctrine may be viewed as a generalization of what has been, until quite recently, an exceptional principle limited to certain specialized and largely independent branches of contract law. The recency of this development, and the resistance the doctrine has encountered in many jurisdictions — English courts still refuse to recognize any general principle establishing the rights of contract beneficiaries — attest to the influence that the idea of privity still exercises on our legal imagination. (It may be that recognition of the rights of beneficiaries as a matter of contract law was a belated acknowledgment of the fact that such rights had long been upheld under the noncontractual principles of trust or agency theory. A not uncommon theme in the opinions written in the early third party beneficiary cases was that C should be allowed to sue on the contract made between A and B because C's situation was essentially "like" that of the beneficiary of a trust. If C prevailed as a beneficiary when A and B had used language of trust, why should he not equally prevail when A and B had sought to achieve the same result but had used contract language instead? The contract beneficiary soon went on to argue, often successfully, that he should prevail even when the trust analogy failed — even when there was nothing remotely like a trust *res* anywhere in sight. And it may be that the success of the contract beneficiary's argument has contributed, in turn, to the expansion of the concept of fiduciary obligation that has been a notable feature of trust law in this century. A common law development not infrequently stimulates a process of reciprocal cross-fertilization.)

Established in our American law of contracts by the wonderfully obscure case of Lawrence v. Fox (1859), the doctrine of third party beneficiaries has followed a meandering course and been a subject of intense controversy (in Massachusetts, for example, the doctrine was not finally approved until 1979).[3] On the whole, however, the tendency of the third party beneficiary idea has been, in the words of a New York judge, "progressive, not retrograde,"[4] and in recent years the doctrine has been put to such expansive use that today one must wonder whether it has any limits at all. Efforts to impose limits on the doctrine have of course been made (by judges and restaters), but the third party beneficiary, loose in our law of contracts now for more than a century, appears to have gained an almost irresistible momentum.

The triumph of the third party beneficiary idea may be looked on as still another instance of the progressive liberalization or erosion of the rigid rules of the late nineteenth-century theory of contractual obligation. That such a process has been going on throughout this century is so clear as to be beyond argument. The movement on all fronts has been in the direction of expanding the range and the quantum of obligation and liability. We have seen the development of theories of quasi-contractual liability, of the doctrines of promissory estoppel and culpa in contrahendo, of the perhaps revolutionary idea that the law imposes on the parties to a contract an affirmative duty to act in good faith. During the same period the sanctions for breach of contract have been notably expanded. Recovery of "special" or "consequential" damages has become routinely available in situations in which the recovery would have been as routinely denied seventy-five years ago. The once "exceptional" remedy of specific performance is rapidly becoming the order of the day. On the other hand the party who has failed to perform his contractual duty but who, in the light of the circumstances, is nevertheless felt to be without fault has been protected by a notable expansion of theories of excuse, such as the overlapping ideas of mistake and frustration. To the nineteenth-century legal mind the propositions that no man was his brother's keeper, that the race was to the swift, and that the devil should take the hindmost seemed not only obvious but morally right. The most striking feature of nineteenth-century contract theory is the narrow scope of social duty it implicitly assumed. In our own century we have witnessed what it does not seem too fanciful to describe as a socialization of our theory of contract. The progressive expansion of the range of non-parties

3. Choate, Hall & Stewart v. SCA Serv., Inc., 378 Mass. 535, 392 N.E.2d 1045 (1979).

4. Kellogg, P.J., quoted in Seaver v. Ransom, 224 N.Y. 233, 120 N.E. 639 (1918), infra p. 1356.

allowed to sue as contract beneficiaries as well as of the situations in which they have been allowed to sue is one of the entries to be made in this ledger.

Section 2.   The Origins: Cross-Currents of Doctrine

LAWRENCE v. FOX
20 N.Y. 268 (1859)

Appeal from the Superior Court of the city of Buffalo. On the trial before Mr. Justice Masten, it appeared by the evidence of a bystander, that one Holly, in November, 1857, at the request of the defendant, loaned and advanced to him $300, stating at the time that he owed that sum to the plaintiff for money borrowed of him, and had agreed to pay it to him the then next day; that the defendant in consideration thereof, at the time of receiving the money, promised to pay it to the plaintiff the then next day. Upon this state of facts the defendant moved for a nonsuit, upon three several grounds; viz.: That there was no proof tending to show that Holly was indebted to the plaintiff; that the agreement by the defendant with Holly to pay the plaintiff was void for want of consideration, and that there was no privity between the plaintiff and defendant. The court overruled the motion, and the counsel for the defendant excepted. The cause was then submitted to the jury, and they found a verdict for the plaintiff for the amount of the loan and interest, $344.66, upon which judgment was entered; from which the defendant appealed to the Superior Court, at general term, where the judgment was affirmed, and the defendant appealed to this court. The cause was submitted on printed arguments.

H. GRAY, J. The first objection raised on the trial amounts to this: That the evidence of the person present, who heard the declarations of Holly giving directions as to the payment of the money he was then advancing to the defendant, was mere hearsay and therefore not competent. Had the plaintiff sued Holly for this sum of money no objection to the competency of this evidence would have been thought of; and if the defendant had performed his promise by paying the sum loaned to him to the plaintiff, and Holly had afterwards sued him for its recovery, and this evidence had been offered by the defendant, it would doubtless have been received without an objection from any source. All the defendant had the right to demand in this case was evidence which, as between Holly and the plaintiff, was competent to establish the relation between them of debtor and creditor. For that purpose the evidence was clearly competent; it covered the whole ground and warranted the verdict of the

jury. But it is claimed that notwithstanding this promise was established
by competent evidence, it was void for the want of consideration. It is
now more than a quarter of a century since it was settled by the Supreme
Court of this State — in an able and pains-taking opinion by the late
Chief Justice Savage, in which the authorities were fully examined and
carefully analysed — that a promise in all material respects like the one
under consideration was valid; and the judgment of that court was unanimously affirmed by the Court for the Correction of Errors. (Farley v.
Cleaveland, 4 Cow., 432, same case in error, 9 id., 639.) In that case one
Moon owed Farley and sold to Cleaveland a quantity of hay, in consideration of which Cleaveland promised to pay Moon's debt to Farley; and
the decision in favor of Farley's right to recover was placed upon the
ground that the hay received by Cleaveland from Moon was a valid
consideration for Cleaveland's promise to pay Farley, and that the subsisting liability of Moon to pay Farley was no objection to the recovery.
The fact that the money advanced by Holly to the defendant was a loan to
him for a day, and that it thereby became the property of the defendant,
seemed to impress the defendant's counsel with the idea that because the
defendant's promise was not a trust fund placed by the plaintiff in the
defendant's hands, out of which he was to realize money as from the sale
of a chattel or the collection of a debt, the promise although made for the
benefit of the plaintiff could not enure to his benefit. The hay which
[Moon] delivered to [Cleaveland] was not to be paid to Farley, but the
debt incurred by Cleaveland for the purchase of the hay, like the debt
incurred by the defendant for money borrowed, was what was to be paid.
That case has been often referred to by the courts of this State, and has
never been doubted as sound authority for the principle upheld by it.
(Barker v. Buklin, 3 Denio, 45; Hudson Canal Company v. The Westchester Bank, 4 id., 97.) It puts to rest the objection that the defendant's
promise was void for want of consideration. The report of that case shows
that the promise was not only made to Moon but to the plaintiff Farley.
In this case the promise was made to Holly and not expressly to the
plaintiff; and this difference between the two cases presents the question,
raised by the defendant's objection, as to the want of privity between the
plaintiff and defendant. As early as 1806 it was announced by the Supreme Court of this State, upon what was then regarded as the settled law
of England, "That where one person makes a promise to another for the
benefit of a third person, that third person may maintain an action upon
it." Schermerhorn v. Vanderheyden (1 John. R., 140), has often been re-
asserted by our courts and never departed from.

[In an omitted passage Judge Gray discussed other New York and
Massachusetts cases. He concluded his discussion by distinguishing from
the case at bar the recent Massachusetts decision, Mellen v. Whipple, 67
Mass. (1 Gray) 317 (1854). For more on Mellen v. Whipple, see the
dissenting opinion of Comstock, J.]

. . . But it is urged that because the defendant was not in any sense a trustee of the property of Holly for the benefit of the plaintiff, the law will not imply a promise. I agree that many of the cases where a promise was implied were cases of trusts, created for the benefit of the promiser. The case of Felton v. Dickinson (10 Mass., 189, 190), and others that might be cited are of that class; but concede them all to have been cases of trusts, and it proves nothing against the application of the rule to this case. The duty of the trustee to pay the cestuis que trust, according to the terms of the trust, implies his promise to the latter to do so. In this case the defendant, upon ample consideration received from Holly, promised Holly to pay his debt to the plaintiff; the consideration received and the promise to Holly made it as plainly his duty to pay the plaintiff as if the money had been remitted to him for that purpose, and as well implied a promise to do so as if he had been made a trustee of property to be converted into cash with which to pay. The fact that a breach of the duty imposed in the one case may be visited, and justly, with more serious consequences than in the other, by no means disproves the payment to be a duty in both. The principle illustrated by the example so frequently quoted (which concisely states the case in hand) "that a promise made to one for the benefit of another, he for whose benefit it is made may bring an action for its breach," has been applied to trust cases, not because it was exclusively applicable to those cases, but because it was a principle of law, and as such applicable to those cases. It was also insisted that Holly could have discharged the defendant from his promise, though it was intended by both parties for the benefit of the plaintiff, and therefore the plaintiff was not entitled to maintain this suit for the recovery of a demand over which he had no control. It is enough that the plaintiff did not release the defendant from his promise, and whether he could or not is a question not now necessarily involved; but if it was, I think it would be found difficult to maintain the right of Holly to discharge a judgment recovered by the plaintiff upon confession or otherwise, for the breach of the defendant's promise; and if he could not, how could he discharge the suit before judgment, or the promise before suit, made as it was for the plaintiff's benefit and in accordance with legal presumption accepted by him (Berley v. Taylor, 5 Hill, 577-584, et seq.), until his dissent was shown. The cases cited, and especially that of Farley v. Cleaveland, established the validity of a parol promise; it stands then upon the footing of a written one. Suppose the defendant had given his note in which, for value received of Holly, he had promised to pay the plaintiff and the plaintiff had accepted the promise, retaining Holly's liability. Very clearly Holly could not have discharged that promise, be the right to release the defendant as it may. No one can doubt that he owes the sum of money demanded of him, or that in accordance with his promise it was his duty to have paid it to the plaintiff; nor can it be doubted that whatever may be the diversity of opinion elsewhere, the adjudications in this State, from a very early period, approved by experience, have established the defendant's liability; if, therefore, it could be shown that a more strict and technically accurate application of the rules applied, would lead to a different result (which I by no means concede), the effort should not be made in the face of manifest justice.

The judgment should be affirmed.

Johnson, Ch. J., Denio, Selden, Allen and Strong, Js., concurred. Johnson, Ch. J., and Denio, J., were of opinion that the promise was to be regarded as made to the plaintiff through the medium of his agent, whose action he could ratify when it came to his knowledge, though taken without his being privy thereto.

COMSTOCK, J. (Dissenting.) The plaintiff had nothing to do with the promise on which he brought this action. It was not made to him, nor did the consideration proceed from him. If he can maintain the suit, it is because an anomaly has found its way into the law on this subject. In general, there must be privity of contract. The party who sues upon a promise must be the promisee, or he must have some legal interest in the undertaking. In this case, it is plain that Holly, who loaned the money to the defendent, and to whom the promise in question was made, could at any time have claimed that it should be performed to himself personally. He had lent the money to the defendant, and at the same time directed the latter to pay the sum to the plaintiff. This direction he could countermand, and if he had done so, manifestly the defendant's promise to pay according to the direction would have ceased to exist. The plaintiff would receive a benefit by a complete execution of the arrangement, but the arrangement itself was between other parties, and was under their exclusive control. If the defendant had paid the money to Holly, his debt would have been discharged thereby. So Holly might have released the demand or assigned it to another person, or the parties might have annulled the promise now in question, and designated some other creditor of Holly as the party to whom the money should be paid. It has never been claimed, that in a case thus situated, the right of a third person to sue upon the promise rested on any sound principle of law. We are to inquire whether the rule has been so established by positive authority.

The cases which have sometimes been supposed to have a bearing on this question, are quite numerous. In some of them, the dicta of judges, delivered upon very slight consideration, have been referred to as the decision of the courts. Thus, in Schermerhorn v. Vanderheyden (1 John., 140), the court is reported as saying, "We are of opinion, that where one person makes a promise to another, for the benefit of a third person, that third person may maintain an action on such promise." This remark was made on the authority of [Dutton] v. Poole (Vent., 318, 332), decided in England nearly two hundred years ago. It was, however, but a mere remark, as the case was determined against the plaintiff on another ground. Yet this decision has often been referred to as authority for similar observations in later cases.

In another class of cases, which have been sometimes supposed to favor the doctrine, the promise was made to the person who brought the suit, while the consideration proceeded from another; the question considered being, whether the promise was void by the statue of frauds. Thus, in Gold v. Phillips (10 Johns., 412), one Wood was indebted to the plaintiffs for services as attorneys and counsel, and he conveyed a farm to the defendants, who, as part of the consideration, were to pay that debt. Accordingly, the defendants wrote to the plaintiffs, informing them that an arrangement had been made by which they were to pay the demand. The defence was, that the promise was void within the statute, because although in writing, it did not express the consideration. But the action was sustained, on the ground that the undertaking was original and not collateral. So in the case of Farley v. Cleaveland (4 Cow., 432; 9 id., 639), the facts proved or offered to be proved were, that the plaintiff held a note against one Moon; that Moon sold hay to the defendant, who in consideration of that sale promised the plaintiff by parol to pay the note. The only question was, whether the statute of frauds applied to the case. It was held by the Supreme Court, and afterwards by the Court of Errors, that it did not. Such is also precisely the doctrine of Ellwood v. Monk (5 Wend., 235), where it was held, that a plea of the statute of frauds, to a count upon a promise of the defendant to the plaintiff, to pay the latter a debt owing to him by another person, the promise being founded on a sale of property to the defendant by the other person, was bad.

The cases mentioned, and others of a like character, were referred to by Mr. Justice Jewitt, in Barker v. Bucklin (2 Denio, 45). In that case, the learned justice considered at some length the question now before us. The authorities referred to were mainly those which I have cited, and others, upon the statute of frauds. The case decided nothing on the present subject, because it was determined against the plaintiff on a ground not involved in this discussion. The doctrine was certainly advanced which the plaintiff now contends for, but among all the decisions which were cited, I do not think there is one standing directly upon it. The case of Arnold v. Lyman (17 Mass., 400), might perhaps be regarded as an exception to this remark, if a different interpretation had not been given to that decision in the Supreme Court of the same State where it was pronounced. In the recent case of Mellen, Administratrix, v. Whipple (1 Gray, 317), that decision is understood as belonging to a class where the defendant has in his hands a trust fund, which was the foundation of the duty or promise in which the suit is brought.

The cases in which some trust was involved are also frequently referred to as authority for the doctrine now in question, but they do not sustain it. If A delivers money or property to B, which the latter accepts upon a trust for the benefit of C, the latter can enforce the trust by an

appropriate action for that purpose. (Berly v. Taylor, 5 Hill, 577.) If
the trust be of money, I think the beneficiary may assent to it and bring
the action for money had and received to his use. If it be of something
else than money, the trustee must account for it according to the terms of
the trust, and upon principles of equity. There is some authority even for
saying that an express promise founded on the possession of a trust fund
may be enforced by an action at law in the name of the beneficiary,
although it was made to the creator of the trust. Thus, in Comyn's Digest
(Action on the case upon Assumpsit, B. 15), it is laid down that if a man
promise a pig of lead to A, and his executor give lead to make a pig to B,
who assumes to deliver it to A, an assumpsit lies by A against him. The
case of The Delaware and Hudson Canal Company v. The Westchester
County Bank (4 Denio, 97), involved a trust because the defendants had
received from a third party a bill of exchange under an agreement that
they would endeavor to collect it, and would pay over the proceeds when
collected to the plaintiffs. A fund received under such an agreement does
not belong to the person who receives it. He must account for it specifically; and perhaps there is no gross violation of principle in permitting the
equitable owner of it to sue upon an express promise to pay it over.
Having a specific interest in the thing, the undertaking to account for it
may be regarded as in some sense made with him through the author of
the trust. But further than this we cannot go without violating plain rules
of law. In the case before us there was nothing in the nature of a trust or
agency. The defendant borrowed the money of Holly and received it as
his own. The plaintiff had no right in the fund, legal or equitable. The
promise to repay the money created an obligation in favor of the lender to
whom it was made and not in favor of any one else.

I have referred to the dictum in Schermerhorn v. Vanderheyden (1
Johns., 140), as favoring the doctrine contended for. It was the earliest in
this State, and was founded, as already observed, on the old English case
of Dutton v. Poole, in Ventris. That case has always been referred to as
the ultimate authority whenever the rule in question has been mentioned, and it deserves, therefore, some further notice. The father of the
plaintiff's wife being seized of certain lands, which afterwards on his
death descended to the defendant, and being about to cut £1,000 worth of
timber to raise a portion for his daughter, the defendant promised the
father, in consideration of his forbearing to cut the timber, that he would
pay the said daughter the £1,000. After verdict for the plaintiff, upon the
issue of non-assumpsit, it was urged in arrest of judgment, that the father
ought to have brought the action, and not the husband and wife. It was
held, after much discussion, that the action would lie. The court said,

> It might be another case if the money had been to have been paid to a
> stranger; but there is such a manner of relation between the father and the

child, and it is a kind of debt to the child to be provided for, that the
plaintiff is plainly concerned.

We need not criticise the reason given for this decision. It is enough for
the present purpose, that the case is no authority for the general doctrine,
to sustain which it has been so frequently cited. It belongs to a class of
cases somewhat peculiar and anomalous, in which promises have been
made to parent or person standing in a near relationship to the person for
whose benefit it was made, and in which, on account of that relationship,
the beneficiary has been allowed to maintain the action. Regarded as
standing on any other ground, they have long since ceased to be the law
in England. Thus, in Crow v. Rogers (1 Strange, 592), one Hardy was
indebted to the plaintiff in the sum of £70, and upon a discourse between
Hardy and the defendant, it was agreed that the defendant should pay
that debt in consideration of a house, to be conveyed by Hardy to him.
The plaintiff brought the action on that promise, and Dutton v. Poole
was cited in support of it. But it was held that the action would not lie,
because the plaintiff was a stranger to the transaction. Again, in Price v.
Easton (4 Barn. & Adolph., 433), one William Price was indebted to the
plaintiff in £13. The declaration averred a promise of the defendant to pay
the debt, in consideration that William Price would work for him, and
leave the wages in his hands; and that Price did work accordingly, and
earned a large sum of money, which he left in the defendant's hands.
After verdict for the plaintiff, a motion was made in arrest of judgment,
on the ground that the plaintiff was a stranger to the consideration.
Dutton v. Poole, and other cases of that class, were cited in opposition to
the motion, but the judgment was arrested. Lord Denman said, "I think
the declaration cannot be supported, as it does not show any consideration for the promise moving from the plaintiff to the defendant."
Littledale, J., said, "No privity is shown between the plaintiff and the
defendant. The case is precisely like Crow v. Rogers, and must be governed by it." Taunton, J., said, "It is consistent with all the matter alleged
in the declaration, that the plaintiff may have been entirely ignorant of
the arrangement between William Price and the defendant." Patterson,
J., observed, "It is clear that the allegations do not show a right of action
in the plaintiff. There is no promise to the plaintiff alleged." The same
doctrine is recognized in Lilly v. Hays (5 Ad. & Ellis, 548), and such is
now the settled rule in England, although at an early day there was some
obscurity arising out of the case of Dutton v. Poole, and others of that
peculiar class.

The question was also involved in some confusion by the earlier cases
in Massachusetts. Indeed, the Supreme Court of that State seem at one
time to have made a nearer approach to the doctrine on which this action
must rest, than the courts of this state have ever done. (10 Mass., 287; 17

id., 400.) But in the recent case of Mellen, Administratrix, v. Whipple (1 Gray, 317), the subject was carefully reviewed and the doctrine utterly overthrown. One Rollin was indebted to the plaintiff's testator, and had secured the debt by a mortgage on his land. He then conveyed the equity of redemption to the defendant, by a deed which contained a clause declaring that the defendant was to assume and pay the mortgage. It was conceded that the acceptance of the deed with such a clause in it was equivalent to an express promise to pay the mortgage debt; and the question was, whether the mortgagee or his representative could sue on that undertaking. It was held that the suit could not be maintained; and in the course of a very careful and discriminating opinion by Judge Metcalf, it was shown that the cases which had been supposed to favor the action belonged to exceptional classes, none of which embraced the pure and simple case of an attempt by one person to enforce a promise made to another, from whom the consideration wholly proceeded. I am of that opinion.

The judgment of the court below should therefore be reversed, and a new trial granted.

Grover, J., also dissented.

Judgment affirmed.

NOTE

1. In Mellen v. Whipple, 67 Mass. (1 Gray) 317 (1854), discussed in both the majority and dissenting opinions in Lawrence v. Fox, Metcalf, J., suggested that most of the cases in which third parties had been allowed to sue on contracts to which they were not parties fell into two classes:

> 1. . . . [C]ases . . . in which A has put money or property into B's hands as a fund from which A's creditors are to be paid, and B has promised, either expressly, or by implication from his acceptance of the money or property without objection to the terms on which it was delivered to him, to pay such creditors. In such cases, the creditors have maintained actions against the holder of the fund. . . .
>
> 2. Cases where promises have been made to a father or uncle, for the benefit of a child or nephew, form a second class, in which the person for whose benefit the promise was made has maintained an action for the breach of it. The nearness of the relation between the promisee and him for whose benefit the promise was made, has been sometimes assigned as a reason for these decisions. And though different opinions, both as to the correctness of the decisions, and as to this reason for them, have often been expressed by English judges, yet the decisions themselves have never been overruled, but are still regarded as settled law. Dutton v. Pool[e], 1 Vent. 318, is a familiarly known case of this kind, in which the defendant prom-

ised a father, who was about to fell timber for the purpose of raising a portion for his daughter, that if he would forbear to fell it, the defendant would pay the daughter £1,000. The daughter maintained an action on this promise. Several like decisions had been previously made. Rookwood's case, Cro. Eliz. 164. Oldham v. Bateman, 1 Rol. Ab. 31. Provender v. Wood, Hetl. 30. Thomas's case, Style, 461. Bell v. Chaplain, Hardr. 321. These cases support the decision of this court in Felton v. Dickinson, 10 Mass. 287.

67 Mass. (1 Gray) at 322-323.

Judge Metcalf also referred without disapproval to Brewer v. Dyer, 61 Mass. (7 Cush.) 337 (1851), in which a lessor had been allowed to sue a sublessee who had promised the original lessee to pay the rent and taxes. The cases in which third party suits had been allowed were, he said, exceptions to the general rule and the classes of third parties who should be allowed to bring them should not be expanded. Held, in Mellen v. Whipple, that a mortgagee could not sue the purchaser of the mortgagor's equity of redemption who had promised the mortgagor to pay the mortgage debt. (On "equities of redemption," see Note 1 following the next principal case, Vrooman v. Turner.)

The Supreme Judicial Court of Massachusetts finally rejected the rule of Mellen v. Whipple in Choate, Hall & Stewart v. SCA Services, Inc. 378 Mass. 535, 392 N.E.2d 1045 (1979). Choate, Hall & Stewart, a law firm, had done extensive legal work for its client, a former director of the defendant corporation. The law firm sued to recover legal fees which it claimed the defendant, in a contract with its former director, had agreed to pay. The trial court granted summary judgment for the defendant on the grounds that Massachusetts law did not give standing to third party beneficiaries. In reversing the trial court, Kaplan, J., noted that "this court has in fact frequently recognized the right of suit of creditor beneficiaries . . . but it has been in the form of 'exceptions' to . . . the supposed general prohibitory rule of the Mellen case." Judge Kaplan characterized the court's endorsement of the doctrine of third party beneficiaries in the *Choate, Hall* case as "a long anticipated but relatively minor change in the law of the Commonwealth."

The Massachusetts court's long resistance to third party beneficiaries may be some indication of its instinctive feeling for logical consistency, expressed elsewhere in the same court's rejection of the anticipatory breach idea (compare Daniels v. Newton, *supra* p. 1270).

2. Judge Metcalf might have confined the classes of third party beneficiaries even more narrowly than he did in Mellen v. Whipple if he had been as well up on English case law as Comstock, J., dissenting in Lawrence v. Fox. For the overruling in later cases of Dutton v. Poole, on which Metcalf relied, see Comstock's opinion. Price v. Easton, 4 B. & Ad. 433, 110 Eng. Rep. 518 (K.B. 1833), is sometimes taken as the defini-

tive rejection in English law of third party beneficiary doctrine. The rule that beneficiaries cannot sue on contracts to which they are not parties has come to be referred to in England as the rule of Tweddle v. Atkinson, 1 B. & S. 393, 121 Eng. Rep. 762, 30 L.J.Q.B. 265, 4 L.T. 468, [1861-1873] All E.R. 369 (Q.B. 1861). (According to the Chicago Note cited at the end of this Note, the case is reported with "considerable variation" in the several collections of reports.) It has, however, long been a commonplace (at least in American legal writing) to point out that English courts, while rejecting the beneficiary doctrine, have achieved results quite like those reached in this country by a somewhat tortured manipulation of trust theory. See 4 Corbin, ch. 46, which first appeared as an article in 46 L.Q. Rev. 12 (1930). It has been said that, after Professor Corbin's article appeared, the English courts were, at least for a while, somewhat more reluctant than they had been to protect contract beneficiaries by calling them trust beneficiaries.

The current state of English law on third party beneficiaries was inconclusively reexamined in Beswick v. Beswick, [1968] A.C. 58. The facts were that Peter Beswick had entered into an agreement with his nephew under which Peter turned his small trucking business over to the nephew who promised, among other things, that in the event of Peter's death he would pay Peter's widow an annuity. Peter having died, the nephew, after making one payment on the annuity, refused to make any more payments. Mrs. Beswick brought an action to compel payment of the annuity, claiming that she was entitled to a decree of specific performance either on the ground that she was the beneficiary of the contract between her late husband and the defendant or on the ground that, as executrix under her late husband's will, she could bring the action for the estate. The ultimate disposition of the case in the House of Lords was that she could bring the action in her capacity as executrix, so that it was unnecessary to decide whether, apart from that happy circumstance, she could have brought it in her individual capacity as a beneficiary. However, in the Court of Appeal, [1966] Ch. 538, [1966] 3 All E.R. 1, Lord Denning, M.R., had chosen to make the case a vehicle for reexamination of English third party beneficiary doctrine. Lord Denning, who had long been known as an advocate of the doctrine, wrote an elaborate opinion in which he argued that Dutton v. Poole had never in fact been overruled and that, both at common law and in equity, suits by beneficiaries were recognized in England. Even if that were not so, he went on, a provision in the Law of Property Act, 1925, had, perhaps by inadvertence, authorized suits by contract beneficiaries. On appeal to the House of Lords counsel for Mrs. Beswick abandoned the argument that English law recognized actions by beneficiaries, which seems rather hard on Lord Denning, and were duly congratulated for that wise decision in several of the opinions delivered in the House. Counsel did argue the point based on the Law of Property Act, 1925; all the opinions in the House of Lords were devoted, in large part, to demonstrating that the 1925 Act had had no such effect, intended or unintended. There was, thus, little discussion of the arguments advanced by Lord Denning, beyond rather casual statements that his historical reconstruction of English law had not so much as a leg to stand on. That is not to say that the members of the House of Lords considered the third party beneficiary idea noxious or evil. Lord Reid, for example, noted that in 1937 a "strong" Law Revision Committee had recommended the enactment of a statute providing that: "Where a contract by its express terms purports to confer a benefit directly on a third party it shall be enforceable by the third party in his own name. . . ." Nothing was ever done in Parliament about the Law Revision Committee's recommendation. In his *Beswick* opinion, Lord Reid commented: "If one had to contemplate a further long period of Parliamentary procrastination, this House might find it necessary to deal with this matter; but if legislation is probable at an early date, I would not deal with it in a case where that is not essential." His reference to the probability of an early legislative solution was to the work of the Law Commission which is currently engaged in the ambitious task of preparing a codification of the English law of obligations and had announced that the third party beneficiary problem was among the items which it proposed to consider (see the Editorial Note to the report of the *Beswick* case in the Court of Appeal, [1966] 3 All E.R. 1, 2).

In deciding to dispose of the case by holding that Mrs. Beswick could sue as executrix, the learned Lords had to hurdle the difficulty that it was far from apparent how the estate (as distinguished from Mrs. Beswick, personally) had been damaged by the nephew's failure to pay the annuity. The difficulty was hurdled in a manner that can only command an awed Transatlantic respect. It must be, however, a matter for jurisprudential regret that the faithless nephew had not been named executor of Peter Beswick's estate instead of Mrs. Beswick.

The history of the matter is traced and the *Beswick* case analyzed in an excellent Note, Third Party Beneficiary Contracts in England, 35 U. Chi. L. Rev. 544 (1968).

Continuing dissatisfaction with the English law on third party beneficiaries was again voiced in Woodar Investment Development Ltd. v. Wimpey Construction UK Ltd., [1980] 1 All E.R. 571. Lord Scarman, recalling Lord Reid's reference to "Parliamentary procrastination," commented: "the Committee reported in 1937; Beswick v. Beswick was decided in 1967. It is now 1979; but nothing has been done. If the opportunity arises, I hope the House will reconsider Tweddle v. Atkinson and the other cases which stand guard over this unjust rule."

3. In National Bank v. Grand Lodge, 98 U.S. 123 (1878), it appeared that the Masonic Hall Association had issued bonds. The Grand Lodge adopted a resolution that the Lodge would assume the payment of the bonds issued by the Association on condition that the Association issue its

stock to the Lodge in the amount of the bonds whose payment was assumed. The Bank, a bondholder, brought action against the Lodge to compel the payment of bond coupons. It did not appear that the Association had accepted the offer made by the Lodge or that stock of the Association had ever been issued to the Lodge. At trial the jury was directed to enter a verdict in favor of the Lodge. This disposition of the case was affirmed in the Supreme Court. Justice Strong commented on the third party beneficiary doctrine in the following passage:

> We do not propose to enter at large upon a consideration of the inquiry how far privity of contract between a plaintiff and defendant is necessary to the maintenance of an action of assumpsit. The subject has been much debated, and the decisions are not all reconcilable. No doubt the general rule is that such a privity must exist. But there are confessedly many exceptions to it. One of them, and by far the most frequent one, is the case where, under a contract between two persons, assets have come to the promisor's hands or under his control which in equity belong to a third person. In such a case it is held that the third person may sue in his own name. But then the suit is founded rather on the implied undertaking the law raises from the possession of the assets, than on the express promise. Another exception is where the plaintiff is the beneficiary solely interested in the promise, as where one person contracts with another to pay money or deliver some valuable thing to a third. But where a debt already exists from one person to another, a promise by a third person to pay such debt being primarily for the benefit of the original debtor, and to relieve him from liability to pay it (there being no novation), he has a right of action against the promisor for his own indemnity; and if the original creditor can also sue, the promisor would be liable to two separate actions, and therefore the rule is that the original creditor cannot sue. His case is not an exception from the general rule that privity of contract is required. There are some other exceptions recognized, but they are unimportant now. The plaintiff's case is within none of them.

Id. at 124-125.

4. In a brilliant article on the evolution of third party beneficiary doctrine, Professor Waters throws some additional light on the curious facts in Lawrence v. Fox (footnotes have been omitted):

> The mystery of Lawrence v. Fox is why Lawrence chose the tortuous route of suing Fox, with whom he had not dealt, rather than sue Holly, who was, it appears, his debtor. . . . From the records of the case, we learn that "Holly" was in fact one Hawley, referred to in the complaint as Samuel Hawley. The Buffalo census of 1855 lists no Samuel Hawley, but of the eighteen Hawleys who are listed, only one appears to have had sufficient means to have been involved in a three hundred dollar cash transaction. He was Merwin Spencer Hawley, a prominent merchant. In 1856, Hawley was President of the Buffalo Board of Trade, an organization with which Fox, at some point, was also connected. It is admittedly possible that the Hawley who dealt with Fox, and who was allegedly indebted to Lawrence,

was another Hawley from out of town, or out of state. That would explain his absence from the census and from the courtroom. But there are indications of other reasons why Lawrence may have avoided suing Hawley, even if he was affluent and available. Those reasons — which I shall deal with shortly — taken together with the fact that Merwin Hawley was a wealthy Buffalonian who moved in the same social circles as Arthur Fox, make it more likely that he is the Hawley of Lawrence v. Fox. The assumption that Hawley was affluent and available in Buffalo when Lawrence sued Fox does nothing, however, to solve the mystery of why Lawrence chose not to sue him. The solution to that mystery lies in the nature of Lawrence's transaction with Hawley, of which Hawley's dealings with Fox on the next day are highly suggestive.

In 1854, when the transaction took place, three hundred dollars was a very large amount of money. Even among successful entrepreneurs, a loan the size of Hawley's to Fox, to be repaid a day later, must have been out of the ordinary. At trial in the Superior Court in Buffalo, Fox's attorney, Jared Torrance, shed some light on the nature of that transaction. The only witness in the case was William Riley, by whom Lawrence's attorney, Edward Chapin, had proved that Hawley paid three hundred dollars to Fox; that Hawley told Fox that he, Hawley, owed that amount to Lawrence; and that Fox promised Hawley that he would repay that amount to Lawrence. On cross-examination, Torrance elicited four facts: that Lawrence was not present when Hawley made the loan to Fox; that the deal took place at Mr. Purdy Merritt's on Washington Street; that there were "two or three persons present . . . doing nothing but standing near them"; and that Hawley counted out the money as he handed it to Fox.

The first fact, that Lawrence was not present, formed the basis of Fox's privity defense. This defense makes sense only in an action based on contract, a point to which we shall return. For now, it is the other three facts — the location, the bystanders, and the cash being counted out — that are noteworthy, for they suggest the milieu in which the transaction took place, and help to explain its character.

William Riley, the witness, was a horse dealer. He did his business near the canal, the life line of Buffalo's then-thriving commerce. Not many steps away was Mr. Purdy Merritt's establishment, where the transaction took place; Merritt was also a horse dealer. Torrance's cross-examination presented a more complete picture: two well-to-do merchants in a horse dealer's establishment down by the canal; a large amount of cash changing hands; and several other people present, loitering. Of these facts, not the least significant was the location:

> Canal Street was more than a street. It was the name of a district, a small
> and sinful neighborhood. . . . As late as the 1800's, there were ninety-three
> saloons there, among which were sprinkled fifteen other dives known as con-
> cert halls plus sundry establishments designed to separate the sucker from his
> money as swiftly as possible, painlessly by preference, but painfully if neces-
> sary. . . . It must have been an eternal mystery to the clergy and the good
> people of the town why the Lord never wiped out this nineteenth century
> example of Sodom and Gamorrah with a storm or a great wave from Lake
> Erie.

In his cross-examination of Riley, Attorney Torrance had gone as far as he could go to set the scene for what he then sought to prove directly, also by William Riley: that Hawley lent the money to Fox for Fox to gamble with it, and that this unlawful purpose was known to Hawley.

Trial Judge Joseph Masten did not, however, permit Riley to testify to the alleged link with gambling. Attorney Chapin, for Lawrence, successfully objected on two grounds, neither of which bears upon the probable truth or untruth of the evidence that Riley was prepared to give. As to that question, the facts that Torrance had already elicited do suggest a setting in which gambling could have been taking place. But there is one more fact, this one uncontroverted, that is entirely consistent with the allegation of a connection with gambling and is difficult to explain otherwise. The fact — the central mystery of this case — is that Lawrence chose to sue not his debtor, Hawley, but his debtor's debtor, Fox. If, as seems to be the fact, Hawley was a person of considerable wealth in Buffalo, and if, as alleged, he owed three hundred dollars to Lawrence, then Lawrence must have had compelling reason to neglect the obvious action — suing Hawley — in favor of the much more difficult task of seeking recovery from Fox. A gambling debt would have presented just such a reason. If Hawley's debt to Lawrence from the day before, in the round sum of three hundred dollars, was itself the outcome of gambling and thus unenforceable at law, Lawrence was well advised to look for someone other than Hawley to sue. Furthermore, if we look to the law of gamblers rather than the law of commerce, it is clear that Fox, and not Hawley, was both the villain and the obvious person to pursue.

Commercial transactions were not then and are not now structured in such a way as to leave a creditor with no better means of recovery than to sue his debtor's debtor. The series of events described in Lawrence v. Fox makes no commercial sense. Had Hawley's dealings with Fox conformed to the norms of commercial behavior, Hawley would have requested a negotiable instrument either made out to Lawrence, or to be endorsed in his favor, in return for his loan to Fox. And had Lawrence's dealings with Hawley been of a kind condoned and upheld by the law of the land, then Lawrence would surely have sued Hawley, and not Fox. It is not surprising, therefore, that there was no theory of recovery in the law of contract by which Lawrence could collect from Fox.

Waters, The Property In the Promise: A Study of the Third Party Beneficiary Rule, 98 Harv. L. Rev. 1109, 1123-1127 (1985).

VROOMAN v. TURNER
69 N.Y. 280 (Ct. App. 1877)

Appeal from judgment of the General Term of the Supreme Court in the second judicial department, affirming a judgment in favor of plaintiff, entered upon the report of a referee. (Reported below, 8 Hun, 78.)

This was an action to foreclose a mortgage.

The mortgage was executed in August, 1873, by defendant Evans, who then owned the mortgaged premises. He conveyed the same to one Mitchell, and through various mesne conveyances the title came to one Sanborn. In none of these conveyances did the grantee assume to pay the mortgage. Sanborn conveyed the same to defendant Harriet B. Turner, by deed which contained a clause stating that the conveyance was subject to the mortgage, "which mortgage the party hereto of the second part hereby covenants and agrees to pay off and discharge, the same forming part of the consideration thereof."

The referee found that said grantee, by so assuming payment of the mortgage, became personally liable therefor, and directed judgment against her for any deficiency. Judgment was entered accordingly.

ALLEN, J. The precise question presented by the appeal in this action has been twice before the courts of this State, and received the same solution in each. It first arose in King v. Whitely, 10 Paige, 465, decided in 1843. There the grantor of an equity of redemption in mortgaged premises, neither legally nor equitably interested in the payment of the bond and mortgage except so far as the same were a charge upon his interest in the lands, conveyed the lands subject to the mortgage, and the conveyance recited that the grantees therein assumed the mortgage, and were to pay off the same as a part of the consideration of such conveyance, and it was held that as the grantor in that conveyance was not personally liable to the holder of the mortgage to pay the same, the grantees were not liable to the holder of such mortgage for the deficiency upon a foreclosure and sale of the mortgaged premises. It was conceded by the chancellor that if the grantor had been personally liable to the holder of the mortgage for the payment of the mortgage debt, the holder of such mortgage would have been entitled in equity to the benefit of the agreement recited in such conveyance, to pay off the mortgage and to a decree over against the grantees for the deficiency. This would have been in accordance with a well established rule in equity, which gives to the creditor the right of subrogation to and the benefit of any security held by a surety for the re-enforcement of the principal debt, and in the case supposed, and by force of the agreement recited in the conveyance, the grantee would have become the principal debtor, and the grantor would be a quasi surety for the payment of the mortgage debt. (Halsey v. Reed, 9 Paige, 446; Curtis v. Tyler, id., 432; Burr v. Beers, 24 N.Y., 178.)

King v. Whitely was followed, and the same rule applied by an undivided court in Trotter v. Hughes, 12 N.Y., 74, and the same case was cited with approval in Garnsey v. Rogers, 47 N.Y., 233.

The clause in the conveyance in Trotter v. Hughes was not in terms precisely like that in King v. Whitely, or in the grant under consideration. The undertaking by the grantees to pay the mortgage debt as recited, was not in express terms, or as explicit as in the other conveyances. But the recital was, I think, sufficient to justify the inference of a promise to pay the debt, and so it must have been regarded by the court. The case was not distinguished by the court in any of its circumstances from King v. Whitely, but was supposed to be on all fours with and governed by it. Had the grantor in that case been personally bound for the payment of the debt, I am of the opinion that an action would have been sustained against the grantee upon a promise implied from the terms of the grant accepted by him to pay it, and indemnify the grantor. It must have been so regarded by this court, otherwise no question would have been made upon it, and the court would not have so seriously and ably fortified and applied the doctrine of King v. Whitely. A single suggestion that there was no undertaking by the grantee and no personal liability for the payment of the debt assumed by him, would have disposed of the claim to charge him for the deficiency upon the sale of the mortgaged premises. The rule which exempts the grantee of mortgaged premises subject to a mortgage, the payment of which is assumed in consideration of the conveyance as between him and his grantor, from liability to the holder of the mortgage when the grantee [grantor?] is not bound in law or equity for the payment of the mortgage, is founded in reason and principle, and is not inconsistent with that class of cases in which it has been held that a promise to one for the benefit of a third party may avail to give an action directly to the latter against the promissor, of which Lawrence v. Fox (20 N.Y., 268), is a prominent example. To give a third party who may derive a benefit from the performance of the promise, an action, there must be first, an intent by the promissee to secure some benefit to the third party, and second, some privity between the two, the promissee and the party to be benefited, and some obligation or duty owing from the former to the latter which would give him a legal or equitable claim to the benefit of the promise, or an equivalent from him personally.

It is true there need be no privity between the promissor and the party claiming the benefit of the undertaking, neither is it necessary that the latter should be privy to the consideration of the promise, but it does not follow that a mere volunteer can avail himself of it. A legal obligation or duty of the promissee to him, will so connect him with the transaction as to be a substitute for any privity with the promissor, or the consideration of the promise, the obligation of the promissee furnishing an evidence of the intent of the latter to benefit him, and creating a privity by substitution with the promissor. A mere stranger cannot intervene, and claim by action the benefit of a contract between other parties. There must be either a new consideration or some prior right or claim against one of the contracting parties, by which he has a legal interest in the performance of the agreement.

It is said in Garnsey v. Rodgers (47 N.Y. 233), that it is not every promise made by one person to another from the performance of which a third person would derive a benefit that gives a right of action to such third person, he being privy neither to the contract nor the consideration. In the language of Judge Rapallo, "to entitle him to an action, the contract must have been made for his benefit. He must be the party intended to be benefited." See, also, Turk v. Ridge (41 N.Y., 201), and Merrill v. Green (55 id., 270), in which, under similar agreements third parties sought to maintain an action upon engagements by the performance of which they would be benefited, but to which they were not parties, and failed. The courts are not inclined to extend the doctrine of Lawrence v. Fox to cases not clearly within the principle of that decision. Judges have differed as to the principle upon which Lawrence v. Fox and kindred cases rest, but in every case in which an action has been sustained there has been a debt or duty owing by the promissee to the party claiming to sue upon the promise. Whether the decisions rest upon the doctrine of agency, the promissee being regarded as the agent for the third party, who, by bringing his action adopts his acts, or upon the doctrine of a trust, the promissor being regarded as having received money or other thing for the third party, is not material. In either case there must be a legal right, founded upon some obligation of the promissee, in the third party, to adopt and claim the promise as made for his benefit.

In Lawrence v. Fox a prominent question was made in limine, whether the debt from Halley to the plaintiff was sufficiently proved by the confession of Halley made at the time of the loan of the money to the defendant. It was assumed that if there was no debt proved the action would not lie, and the declaration of Halley the debtor was held sufficient evidence of the debt. Gray, J., said: "All the defendant had the right to demand in this case was evidence which as between Halley and the plaintiff was competent to establish the relation between them of debtor and creditor." In Burr v. Beers (24 N.Y., 178), and Thorp v. Keokuk Coal Co., (48 N.Y., 253), the grantor of the defendant was personally liable to pay the mortgage to the plaintiff, and the cases were therefore clearly within the principle of Lawrence v. Fox, Halsey v. Reed, and Curtis v. Tyler, *supra*. See also per Bosworth, J., Doolittle v. Naylor, (2 Bos., 225); and Ford v. David (1 Bos., 569). It is claimed that King v. Whitely and the cases following it were overruled by Lawrence v. Fox. But it is very clear that it was not the intention to overrule them, and that the cases are not inconsistent. The doctrine of Lawrence v. Fox, although questioned and criticised, was not first adopted in this state by the decision of the case. It was expressly adjudged as early as 1825, in Farley v. Cleveland, (4 Cow., 432), affirmed in the court for the correction of errors in 1827, per totam curiam, and reported in 9 Cow., 639. The chancellor was not ignorant of the decisions when he decided King v. Whitely, nor was Judge Denio and his associates unaware of them when Trotter v. Hughes was decided, and Judge Gray in Lawrence v. Fox says the case of Farley v. Cleveland had never been doubted.

The court below erred in giving judgment against the appellant for the deficiency after the sale of the mortgaged premises, and so much of the judgment as directs her to pay the same must be reversed with costs.

All concur, except Earl, J., dissenting.

Judgment accordingly.

NOTE

1. *Mortgagees, Mortgagors, Purchasers, and the Equity of Redemption.* In the mortgage transaction, property (real or personal) is transferred as security for a loan. If the loan is repaid according to the terms of the loan agreement, the security transfer may be said to lapse: the borrower-mortgagor, on repayment, regains whatever interest he had in the mortgaged property before he mortgaged it. If the borrower defaults on his payments, the mortgagee may look to the mortgaged property for satisfaction of the debt. In most states today the typical procedure is for the mortgagee to take possession of the property, sell it and apply the proceeds of sale, after deduction of his expenses, to the debt. If the property has been sold for more than enough to cover the debt and expenses, the surplus is remitted to the mortgagor (or to the holders of junior security interests in the property or to the mortgagor's trustee in bankruptcy or other representative of creditors in insolvency proceedings). If the proceeds of the sale do not cover the expenses and pay the debt in full, the mortgagor (or his insolvent estate) is liable for the deficiency. (For an account of the historical development of the mortgagee's rights against the security after default, see 2 G. Gilmore, Security Interests in Personal Property §43.2 (1965).)

During the period while the loan is outstanding, the mortgage transaction creates what may be called a divided interest in the mortgaged property. It is no longer fully the mortgagor's: he stands to lose it entirely if he does not make payments on the loan as they become due. It is not yet the mortgagee's: he cannot sell it until there has been a default under the loan agreement. The mortgagor's interest is called his "equity of redemption." That term, which came into use during the seventeenth century, reflects a great deal of history. The early land mortgage was, in form, a conveyance of the land to the mortgagee, to become absolute on the mortgagor's default. The seventeenth-century equity courts, however, allowed the mortgagor, on tender of the debt even long after default, to "redeem" the land from the mortgagee. Hence, equity of redemption.

Either the mortgagee or the mortgagor may elect to sell his interest in the mortgaged property before the loan has been repaid. In this discussion we shall not be concerned with the mortgagee's sale of his interest, although it may avoid confusion to point out that the mortgagee's sale of his security interest is always ancillary to an assignment of the debt secured and has nothing to do with a sale of the property after default. It should also be kept in mind that the borrower-mortgagor, by selling the property, does not escape liability on the debt. If he sells the property without authority from the mortgagee, the sale may be a default under the loan agreement; however, whether he sells with or without authority, he remains liable to pay the debt.

In this country there is a universal requirement that the mortgagee must file or record his mortgage with a public official as a condition of protection against third parties. If the mortgage has not been properly filed, a purchaser of the mortgaged property from the mortgagor, who is himself without notice of the mortgage, will take the property free of the mortgage. In such a case the mortgagee has lost his security interest in the property and is left with his money claim against the borrower-mortgagor under the loan agreement. However, if the mortgage has been properly filed and if the mortgagee has not authorized the mortgagor to sell the property free of the mortgage, the purchaser will take subject to the mortgage. That is to say, his purchase will not cut off the mortgagee's interest in the property; he acquires only the mortgagor's interest. Such a transaction is often referred to, as it was in the opinion in Vrooman v. Turner, as a purchase or sale of the mortgagor's equity of redemption. In the balance of our discussion we shall assume that the purchaser (or grantee) from the mortgagor acquires only the mortgagor's interest or equity. We shall also assume that the mortgage security is land. (Theoretically the Vrooman v. Turner situation could arise where the mortgage covered personal property, but it is in the highest degree unlikely that the situation would ever come up except in the context of a land mortgage).

Let us assume that A owns land which is subject to a mortgage securing a debt of $10,000. The debt has ten years to run before it is to be fully repaid. B wants to buy the land and A is willing to sell. They agree that the land is worth $20,000. How are they to carry out the transaction?

The simplest way is to pay off the mortgage debt before or at the time of the sale. A pays the mortgagee $10,000, discharges the mortgage and sells the land to B for $20,000. Or B pays $10,000 to the mortgagee and $10,000 to A and in that way acquires the land free of A's mortgage. B may now borrow $10,000 and mortgage the land as security, but the new B mortgage has nothing to do with the old A mortgage. No doubt today the overwhelming number of land transactions of this kind are carried out by paying off A's mortgage first and letting B find his own financing.

Another way is for B to buy A's interest (or equity) subject to the mortgage. This seems to have been more common in the past than it is today but this way of carrying out the transaction has by no means disappeared. If interest rates have risen since A executed his mortgage, it is obviously to B's interest to take over A's mortgage at the lower rate. If interest rates have fallen, the mortgagee would prefer to keep the mortgage alive and refuse to be paid off; whether or not he can rightfully refuse prepayment depends on the terms of the mortgage and loan agreement. For these reasons, or for no reason, transactions continue to appear in which B buys A's equity subject to the existing mortgage. We have already noted that A continues liable for the debt although he no longer owns the land. We may now turn to the relationship between B, the new owner of the land (or A's equity in it), and the mortgagee.

It was long ago accepted as a matter of legal doctrine that there was a difference between a transaction in which B, as part of his purchase of A's equity, assumed the mortgage debt (i.e., promised A that he would pay the debt) and one in which B did not assume the debt. In the latter case he was oddly described as a "non-assuming grantee." We shall presently return to the "assuming grantee" but it is first necessary to inquire into the situation of the grantee who did not assume.

What happens if, after equity has been sold to B (a non-assuming grantee), there is a default in the payment on the mortgage debt? Clearly (as we tend to say when dealing with obscure matters) the mortgagee can either sue A on the debt or he can foreclose the mortgage on the land in B's hands (i.e., have the land sold). Thus B stands to lose the land unless the mortgage payments are kept up (that is what we meant by saying that he bought the land, or A's equity, "subject to" the mortgage). But, as between B and A, which of them was supposed to pay? The answer to that question is that, in all probability, B was supposed to pay. It is theoretically possible to imagine an agreement between A and B under which A sold his equity to B and agreed to go on making the mortgage payments himself. In such a case, reverting to our hypothetical case of the land worth $20,000 subject to a mortgage debt of $10,000, B would presumably have paid A $20,000 for the land and trusted A to go on paying the mortgagee until the debt was discharged. In the real world B, whether or not he assumed the debt, did not pay A $20,000 and hope for the best; he paid him $10,000 and took over the mortgage payments himself. (From which, as the astute reader will have deduced, it must follow that, if the mortgagee on default collects the $10,000 from A instead of foreclosing the mortgage by having the land sold, then A will succeed to the mortgagee's interest and can himself foreclose the mortgage against B. The cases so hold. If they did not so hold, B would end up by acquiring land valued at $20,000 for which he had paid only $10,000.)

Thus the non-assuming grantee will lose the land if there is a default in paying down the mortgage debt and furthermore has, in connection with his purchase of the mortgagor's equity, almost certainly taken over payment of the debt himself. What then is the difference between a purchase of the equity by a grantee who assumes the debt and a purchase by a grantee who does not assume? The difference lies in the grantee's liability for a deficiency judgment if, on a foreclosure sale, the land sells for less than the amount of the debt. A, the original mortgagor, always remains liable for any deficiency. If he sells his equity to a grantee who assumes the debt, the grantee is also liable for the deficiency. If the mortgagee collects the deficiency from A in the first instance, A can recover over from the grantee on his assumption. If the grantee does not assume the debt, he will lose the land unless he keeps up the payments but he will not become liable for the deficiency. Thus, it might be said, the non-assuming grantee limits his liability to the amount of his investment in the land. If he concludes at any time that the land is not worth the additional amount he will have to pay to discharge the mortgage, he can stop paying and let the land go, thus cutting his loss.

In a period of rising land values, there is (factually) no difference between the situation of the assuming grantee and that of the non-assuming grantee. Presumably the land will always be worth more than the mortgage debt so that, if it is sold on foreclosure, there will be no resulting claim for a deficiency. It will always be to the grantee's interest to pay the mortgage debt, whether or not he has assumed it, and acquire the undivided ownership of the land. If land values fall during the term of the mortgage, the ultimate liability for a deficiency judgement shifts from the mortgagor to the grantee who assumes the debt; it remains with the mortgagor if the grantee does not assume.

It is a fair guess that mortgagors and grantees who engage in such transactions are frequently unaware of the difference between a sale of the equity with an assumption and a sale without an assumption. Whether the grantee assumes or does not assume may be the result of accident rather than a result consciously bargained for. Non-professionals who are not lawyers are in the highest degree unlikely to understand what is at stake. It would be comforting to think that all lawyers who have been admitted to practice have the distinction between asssuming grantees and non-assuming grantees at their fingertips. If that were true, however, there would not be nearly as many cases as there are, and always have been, in which both the sale contract and the deed leave shrouded in doubt the question whether the grantee did or did not assume the debt.

2. *Assuming Grantees, Mortgages, and Third Party Beneficiary Doctrine.* In the situation in which A mortgages his land and later conveys his equity of redemption to B who assumes the mortgage debt, most courts have allowed the mortgagee to proceed directly against B for a deficiency judgment. Mellen v. Whipple, 67 Mass. (1 Gray) 317 (1854), which is discussed in the Note following Lawrence v. Fox, *supra* p. 1333, as well as in the opinions delivered in that case, was exceptional in denying the mortgagee's direct action. Naturally, even the Massachusetts court would have concluded that if the mortgagee recovered a deficiency judgment against the original mortgagor, the mortgagor could recover the amount from the assuming grantee. Most courts saw no reason to require the successive suits and allowed the mortgagee to recover the deficiency from the assuming grantee in the course of his action to foreclose the mortgage.

It is not so clear that the courts which allowed the direct action
thought of it in terms of third party beneficiary doctrine. Thus, in a series
of New York cases that antedated Lawrence v. Fox, the mortgagee's right
to proceed directly against the assuming grantee was grounded on suretyship law, the third party beneficiary cases being dismissed as irrelevant. In
Halsey v. Reed, 9 Paige 446, 451 (N.Y. Ct. Chancery 1842), the Chancellor explained the result in this way:

> It is not necessary to inquire whether the holder of the bond and mort-
> gage could have maintained an action at law against Halsey upon this
> promise, within the principle of the decisions in the case of Starkey v. Mill,
> (Style's Rep. 296,) Dutton v. Poole, (2 Levintz, 210,) and of Schermerhorn
> v. Venderheyden, (1 John. Rep. 139.) For whatever may have been their
> right at law, there is no doubt that in equity the assignees of the bond and
> mortgage would have the right to a decree against Halsey or his personal
> representatives for the deficiency, upon a foreclosure and sale of the mort-
> gaged premises, if the proceeds of the sale should be found insufficient to
> pay the debt and costs. For it is a well settled principle of this court that the
> creditor is entitled to the benefit of the collateral obligations for the pay-
> ment of the debt which any person standing in the situation of surety for
> others has received for his indemnity and to discharge him from such
> payment.

Indeed in Lawrence v. Fox itself the New York cases on mortgagee vs.
assuming grantee were not mentioned in either the majority opinion or
the dissenting opinion, both of which not only dealt at length with the
New York precedents but also wrestled with Mellen v. Whipple in which
the Massachusetts court put its refusal to allow the mortgagee's action
squarely on the ground that the third party beneficiary doctrine was an
exceptional and, on the whole, doubtful novelty that should be confined
within narrow limits.

3. *The Situation in Vrooman v. Turner.* What distinguishes cases like
Vrooman v. Turner from the situation just discussed is that there have
been two or more conveyances of the equity of redemption, that an
intermediate grantee did not assume the mortgage debt and that the
purchaser from the non-assuming grantee did assume it. Since a non-
assuming grantee is not himself liable for a deficiency judgment, there is
no rational explanation for his requiring the purchaser of the equity from
him to assume the debt. However, as we have suggested earlier: (1) it is
frequently unclear, as a factual matter, whether a grantee has or has not
assumed the debt; (2) in any particular transaction neither the parties nor
their lawyers may understand the esoterics of assumption vs. non-as-
sumption. Thus one explanation is that the non-assuming grantee requires the purchaser from him to assume the debt simply in order to be
on the safe side; the alternative explanation is that nobody understood
what was going on so that the assumption following a break in the chain is
merely accidental.

In Vrooman v. Turner the court refers to two pre-Lawrence v. Fox cases in which a break in the chain of assumptions had been held fatal. In King v. Whiteley, 10 Paige 465 (N.Y. Ct. Chancery 1843), it was held that the mortgagee could not recover a deficiency from the grantee who assumed after the break. In Trotter v. Hughes, 12 N.Y. 74 (1854), it was held that the original mortgagor could not recover either. In those cases the decisions were based on suretyship law in the light of Halsey v. Reid, discussed in the preceding section of this Note. In Vrooman v. Turner the court, in the light of Lawrence v. Fox, dealt with the question as one of third party beneficiary law. Does the conceptual shift from suretyship language to contract beneficiary language seem to you to make any difference?

Cases like Vrooman v. Turner have reappeared in litigation during each period when land values have fallen and deficiency judgments have become important (most notably, of course, during the 1930s). No judicial consensus has ever emerged, but the tendency today seems to be in favor of allowing the mortgagee to sue. For example, in Somers v. Avant, 244 Ga. 460, 261 S.E.2d 334 (1979), the Supreme Court of Georgia held, on facts similar to those in Vrooman v. Turner, that a remote grantee who agreed to pay a mortgage not owed by his grantor was personally liable to the mortgagee. The Restatement Second, focusing on the intentions of the contracting parties, clearly rejects the rule of Vrooman v. Turner. See §304, Illustration 2 and §310, Illustration 2. In Schneider v. Ferrigno, 110 Conn. 86, 147 A. 303 (1929), Maltbie, J., put the case against Vrooman v. Turner as follows:

> . . . The basic question presented is, can the holder of a mortgage make liable one who, upon acquiring title to the premises, has assumed and agreed to pay that mortgage, despite the fact that in the chain of title from the original maker of the mortgage some owner of the equity of redemption has not assumed and agreed to pay it. Where such situations have come before the courts in the absence of statutory provision different conclusions have been reached. Those which deny a right of recovery advance various reasons. Wiltsie on Mortgage Foreclosure, Vol. 1 (4th Ed.) §246, states that such a conclusion is based upon the fact that there is no consideration for the assumption, but that can hardly be so; the agreement to assume is but one term in the contract by which the lands are acquired and if that contract as a whole is supported by a valuable consideration it cannot be said that any one term lacks such support. 2 Williston on Contracts, §386, suggests as the basis for the conclusion, that where the grantor of the equity of redemption was not himself liable by reason of an assumption of the mortgage and hence had no interest in the assumption of it by his grantee, the only intelligent object which can be attributed to him is to guard against a supposed or possible liability on his part, and he cannot be assumed to have intended to confer a benefit upon the holder of the mortgage; but it is difficult to see why, if his object is assumed to be to protect himself against a possible liability, his mental attitude is any different than it would be, had

he sought to protect himself against a definite liability fixed by his own
agreement to pay the mortgage. The cases which deny liability, such as the
leading case of Vrooman v. Turner, 69 N.Y. 280, 285, do not seem fully to
recognize the extent and force of the rule which permits a third party
beneficiary to sue upon a contract as it has now been developed. The
controlling test now is, was there any intent to confer a right of action upon
the third party. Amer. Law Inst. Restatement, Contracts, §§133, 135;
Byram Lumber & Supply Co. v. Page, 109 Conn. 256, 146 Atl. 293. If the
grantor of the equity of redemption who has not assumed the mortgage has
no object to protect himself, an intent to confer a right to sue upon the
holder of the mortgage would be the most natural motive to assign to him
in requiring his grantee to agree to pay it.

4. *The Suretyship Analogy.* In Vrooman v. Turner, Allen, J., remarks
that the relationship of a grantor to his assuming grantee is like that of a
"quasi surety" to a principal debtor. The same analogy is repeated in
hundreds of other opinions. The thought is that the grantor, if he is
forced to pay a deficiency claim, has a right to be reimbursed by the
grantee just as a surety who pays the creditor has a right to be reimbursed
by the principal debtor. Under suretyship law a surety is discharged if the
creditor, without the surety's consent, enters into an agreement with the
principal debtor to extend the time of payment. Another suretyship rule
discharges the surety, at least to the extent of his loss, if the creditor holds
collateral security which he could have applied to the debt and which has
depreciated in value during the period of the creditor's forbearance to
collect the debt. The theory of these, and other, suretyship defenses is
that the creditor should not deal with the principal debtor without the
surety's consent in any way that increases the risk assumed by the surety.
Does it seem to you that a mortgagor who has sold his equity of redemption should be discharged from his liability for a deficiency claim if the
mortgagee gives the present holder of the equity further time within
which to pay? Or at all events discharged in the amount by which the
value of the land has decreased during the period of forbearance? And
should it make any difference whether the mortgagor's grantee did or did
not assume the debt? See Kazunas v. Wright, 286 Ill. App. 554, 4 N.E.2d
118 (1936), in which the court concluded that the mortgagee's extension
of time to a non-assuming grantee discharged the original mortgagors.

SEAVER v. RANSOM
224 N.Y. 233, 120 N.E. 639 (1918)

Action by Marion E. Seaver against Matt C. Ransom and another, as
executors, etc., of Samuel A. Beman, deceased. From a judgment of the
Appellate Division (180 App. Div. 734, 168 N.Y.S. 454), affirming judgment for plaintiff, defendants appeal. Affirmed.

POUND, J. Judge Beman and his wife were advanced in years. Mrs. Beman was about to die. She had a small estate, consisting of a house and a lot in Malone and little else. Judge Beman drew his wife's will according to her instructions. It gave $1,000 to plaintiff, $500 to one sister, plaintiff's mother, and $100 each to another sister and her son, the use of the house to her husband for life, and remainder to the American Society for the Prevention of Cruelty to Animals. She named her husband as residuary legatee and executor. Plaintiff was her niece, 34 years old, in ill health, sometimes a member of the Beman household. When the will was read to Mrs. Beman, she said that it was not as she wanted it. She wanted to leave the house to plaintiff. She had no other objections to the will, but her strength was waning, and, although the judge offered to write another will for her, she said she was afraid she would not hold out long enough to enable her to sign it. So the judge said, if she would sign the will, he would leave plaintiff enough in his will to make up the difference. He avouched the promise by his uplifted hand with all solemnity and his wife then executed the will. When he came to die, it was found that his will made no provision for the plaintiff.

The action was brought, and plaintiff recovered judgment in the trial court, on the theory that Beman had obtained property from his wife and induced her to execute the will in the form prepared by him by his promise to give plaintiff $6,000, the value of the house, and that thereby equity impressed his property with a trust in favor of plaintiff. Where a legatee promises the testator that he will use property given him by the will for a particular purpose, a trust arises. O'Hara v. Dudley, 95 N.Y. 403, 47 Am. Rep. 53; Trustees of Amherst College v. Ritch, 151 N.Y. 282, 45 N.E. 876, 37 L.R.A. 305; Ahrens v. Jones, 169 N.Y. 555, 62 N.E. 666, 88 Am. St. Rep. 620. Beman received nothing under his wife's will but the use of the house in Malone for life. Equity compels the application of property thus obtained to the purpose of the testator, but equity cannot so impress a trust, except on property obtained by the promise. Beman was bound by his promise, but no property was bound by it; no trust in plaintiff's favor can be spelled out.

An action on the contract for damages, or to make the executors trustees for performance, stands on different grounds. Farmers' Loan & Trust Co. v. Mortimer, 219 N.Y. 290, 294, 295, 114 N.E. 389, Ann. Cas. 1918E, 1159. The Appellate Division properly passed to the consideration of the question whether the judgment could stand upon the promise made to the wife, upon a valid consideration, for the sole benefit of plaintiff. The judgment of the trial court was affirmed by a return to the general doctrine laid down in the great case of Lawrence v. Fox, 20 N.Y. 268, which has since been limited as herein indicated.

Contracts for the benefit of third persons have been the prolific source of judicial and academic discussion. Williston, Contracts for the Benefit of a Third Person, 15 Harvard Law Review, 767; Corbin, Contracts for the Benefit of Third Persons, 27 Yale Law Journal, 1008. The general rule, both in law and equity (Phalen v. United States Trust Co., 186 N.Y. 178, 186, 78 N.E. 943, 7 L.R.A., N.S. 734, 9 Ann. Cas. 595), was that privity between a plaintiff and a defendant is necessary to the maintenance of an action on the contract. The consideration must be furnished by the party to whom the promise was made. The contract cannot be enforced against the third party, and therefore it cannot be enforced by him. On the other hand, the right of the beneficiary to sue on a contract made expressly for his benefit has been fully recognized in many American jurisdictions, either by judicial decision or by legislation, and is said to be "the prevailing rule in this country." Hendrick v. Lindsay, 93 U.S. 143, 23 L. Ed. 855; Lehow v. Simonton, 3 Colo. 346. It has been said that "the establishment of this doctrine has been gradual and is a victory of practical utility over theory, of equity over technical subtlety." Brantly on Contracts (2d Ed.) p. 253. The reasons for this view are that it is just and practical to permit the person for whose benefit the contract is made to enforce it against one whose duty it is to pay. Other jurisdictions will adhere to the present English rule (7 Halsbury's Laws of England, 342, 343; Jenks' Digest of English Civil Law, §229) that a contract cannot be enforced by or against a person who is not a party (Exchange Bank v. Rice, 107 Mass. 37, 9 Am. Rep. 1). But see, also, Forbes v. Thorpe, 209 Mass. 570, 95 N.E. 955; Gardner v. Denison, 217 Mass. 492, 105 N.E. 359, 51 L.R.A., N.S., 1108.

In New York the right of the beneficiary to sue on contracts made for his benefit is not clearly or simply defined. It is at present confined: First, To cases where there is a pecuniary obligation running from the promisee to the beneficiary, "a legal right founded upon some obligation of the promisee, in the third party, to adopt and claim the promise as made for his benefit." Farley v. Cleveland, 4 Cow. 432, 15 Am. Dec. 387; Lawrence v. Fox, *supra*; Garnsey v. Rogers, 47 N.Y. 233, 7 Am. Rep. 440; Vrooman v. Turner, 69 N.Y. 280, 25 Am. Rep. 195; Lorillard v. Clyde, 122 N.Y. 498, 25 N.E. 917, 10 L.R.A. 113; Durnherr v. Rau, 135 N.Y. 219, 32 N.E. 49; Townsend v. Reckham, 143 N.Y. 516, 38 N.E. 731; Sullivan v. Sullivan, 161 N.Y. 554, 56 N.E. 116. Secondly. To cases where the contract is made for the benefit of the wife (Buchanan v. Tilden, 158 N.Y. 109, 52 N.E. 724, 44 L.R.A. 170, 70 Am. St. Rep. 454; Bouton v. Welch, 170 N.Y. 554, 63 N.E. 539), affianced wife (De Cicco v. Schweizer, 221 N.Y. 431, 117 N.E. 807, L.R.A. 1918E., 1004 Ann. Cas. 1918C, 816), or child (Todd v. Weber, 95 N.Y. 181, 193, 47 Am. Rep. 20; Matter of Kidd, 188 N.Y. 274, 80 N.E. 924) of a party to the contract. The close relationship cases go back to the early King's Bench Case (1677), long since repudiated in England, of Dutton v. Poole, 2 Lev. 211. See Schermerhorn v. Vanderheyden, 1 Johns. 139, 3 Am. Dec. 304. The natural and moral duty of the husband or parent to provide for the future of wife or child sustains the action on the contract made for their benefit. "This is the farthest the cases in this state have gone," says Cullen, J., in the marriage settlement case of Borland v. Welch, 162 N.Y. 104, 110, 56 N.E. 556.

The right of the third party is also upheld in, thirdly, the public contract cases [citations omitted], where the municipality seeks to protect its inhabitants by covenants for their benefit; and, fourthly, the cases where, at the request of a party to the contract, the promise runs directly to the beneficiary although he does not furnish the consideration [citations omitted]. It may be safely said that a general rule sustaining recovery at the suit of the third party would include but few classes of cases not included in these groups, either categorically or in principle.

The desire of the childless aunt to make provision for a beloved and favorite niece differs imperceptibly in law or in equity from the moral duty of the parent to make testamentary provision for a child. The contract was made for the plaintiff's benefit. She alone is substantially damaged by its breach. The representatives of the wife's estate have no interest in enforcing it specifically. It is said in Buchanan v. Tilden that the common law imposes moral and legal obligations upon the husband and the parent not measured by the necessaries of life. It was, however, the love and affection or the moral sense of the husband and the parent that imposed such obligations in the cases cited, rather than any common-law duty of husband and parent to wife and child. If plaintiff had been a child of Mrs. Beman, legal obligation would have required no testamentary provision for her, yet the child could have enforced a covenant in her favor identical with the covenant of Judge Beman in this case. De Cicco v. Schweizer, *supra*. The constraining power of conscience is not regulated by the degree of relationship alone. The dependent or faithful niece may have a stronger claim than the affluent or unworthy son. No sensible theory of moral obligation denies arbitrarily to the former what would be conceded to the latter. We might consistently either refuse or allow the claim of both, but I cannot reconcile a decision in favor of the wife in Buchanan v. Tilden, based on the moral obligations arising out of near relationship, with a decision against the niece here on the ground that the relationship is too remote for equity's ken. No controlling authority depends upon so absolute a rule. In Sullivan v. Sullivan, *supra*, the grandniece lost in a litigation with the aunt's estate, founded on a certificate of deposit payable to the aunt "or in case of her death to her niece"; but what was said in that case of the relations of plaintiff's intestate and defendant does not control here, any more than what was said in Durnherr v. Rau, *supra*, on the relation of husband and wife, and the inadequacy of mere moral duty, as distinguished from legal or equitable obligation, controlled the decision in Buchanan v. Tilden. Borland v. Welch, *supra*, deals only with the rights of volunteers under a marriage settlement not made for the benefit of collaterals.

Kellogg, P.J., writing for the court below well said: "The doctrine of Lawrence v. Fox is progressive, not retrograde. The course of the late decisions is to enlarge, not to limit, the effect of that case." The court in that leading case attempted to adopt the general doctrine that any third person, for whose direct benefit a contract was intended, could sue on it. The headnote thus states the rule. Finch, J., in Gifford v. Corrigan, 117 N.Y. 257, 262, 22 N.E. 756, 6 L.R.A. 610, 15 Am. St. Rep. 508, says that the case rests upon the broad proposition; Edward T. Bartlett, J., in Pond v. New Rochelle Water Co., 183 N.Y. 330, 337, 76 N.E. 211, 213, 1 L.R.A., N.S. 958, 5 Ann. Cas. 504, calls it "the general principle"; but Vrooman v. Turner, *supra,* confined its application to the facts on which it was decided. "In every case in which an action has been sustained," says Allen, J., "there has been a debt or duty owing by the promisee to the party claiming to sue upon the promise." 69 N.Y. 285, 25 Am. Rep. 195. As late as Townsend v. Rackham, 143 N.Y. 516, 523, 38 N.E. 731, 733, we find Peckham, J., saying that, "to maintain the action by the third person, there must be this liability to him on the part of the promisee." Buchanan v. Tilden went further than any case since Lawrence v. Fox in a desire to do justice rather than to apply with technical accuracy strict rules calling for a legal or equitable obligation. In Embler v. Hartford Steam Boiler Inspection & Ins. Co., 158 N.Y. 431, 53 N.E. 212, 44 L.R.A. 512, it may at least be said that a majority of the court did not avail themselves of the opportunity to concur with the views expressed by Gray, J., who wrote the dissenting opinion in Buchanan v. Tilden, to the effect that an employee could not maintain an action on an insurance policy issued to the employer which covered injuries to employees.

In Wright v. Glen Telephone Co., 48 Misc. 192, 195, 95 N.Y.S. 101, the learned presiding justice who wrote the opinion in this case said at Trial Term: "The right of a third person to recover upon a contract made by other parties for his benefit must rest upon the peculiar circumstances of each case rather than upon the law of some other case." "The case at bar is decided upon its peculiar facts." Edward T. Bartlett, J., in Buchanan v. Tilden.

But, on principle, a sound conclusion may be reached. If Mrs. Beman had left her husband the house on condition that he pay the plaintiff $6,000, and he had accepted the devise, he would have become personally liable to pay the legacy, and plaintiff could have recovered in an action at law against him, whatever the value of the house. Gridley v. Gridley, 24 N.Y. 130; Brown v. Knapp, 79 N.Y. 136, 143; Dinan v. Coneys, 143 N.Y. 544, 547, 38 N.E. 715; Blackmore v. White [1899] 1 Q.B. 293, 304. That would be because the testatrix had in substance bequeathed the promise to plaintiff, and not because close relationship or moral obligation sustained the contract. The distinction between an implied promise to a testator for the benefit of a third party to pay a legacy and an unqualified promise on a valuable consideration to make provision for the third party by will is discernible, but not obvious. The tendency of American authority is to sustain the gift in all such cases and to permit the donee beneficiary to recover on the contract. Matter of Edmundson's Estate (1918) 259 Pa. 429, 103 A. 277, 2 A.L.R. 1150. The equities are with the plaintiff, and they may be enforced in this action, whether it be regarded as an action for damages or an action for specific performance to convert the defendants into trustees for plaintiff's benefit under the agreement.

The judgment should be affirmed, with costs.

Hogan, Cardozo, and Crane, JJ., concur. Hiscock, C.J., and Collin and Andrews, JJ., dissent.

Judgment affirmed.

NOTE

1. In his Seaver v. Ransom opinion, Pound, J., suggests that De Cicco v. Schweizer, 221 N.Y. 431, 117 N.E. 807 (1917), had extended the range of New York third party beneficiary doctrine. The *De Cicco* case is reprinted *supra* p. 494. Do you read the opinion of Cardozo, J., in *De Cicco* as saying that Blanche Schweizer could have brought an action as third party beneficiary on the contract between her father and Count Gulinelli?

2. Does it seem to you that Seaver v. Ransom in effect overrules Vrooman v. Turner, *supra* p. 1346? If so, what test does *Seaver* establish for determining which classes of beneficiaries are entitled to sue?

Section 3.   The Search for Doctrinal Clarity

The erratic historical development of the third party beneficiary idea has left us with a considerable number of triangular groupings: trustor-trustee-beneficiary; principal-agent-third party; creditor-debtor-surety; promisor-promisee-third party. The relationship among these various categories has never been entirely clear; as a result, even after the "progressive" doctrine of Lawrence v. Fox had won wide acceptance, the exact nature and scope of the rights enjoyed by a third party beneficiary remained uncertain. One important, and unresolved, issue concerned the significance of the relationship between promisee and beneficiary: Judge Gray's opinion in Lawrence v. Fox seemed to imply that Lawrence's recovery was dependent upon his standing in a particular relationship to Holly — that of creditor to debtor — suggesting, perhaps, that if things had been otherwise Lawrence might have lost his lawsuit. Sixty years later, in Seaver v. Ransom, the same court emphasized the special relationship between niece (third party) and aunt (promisee),

carefully avoiding an explicit endorsement of what the headnote to Lawrence v. Fox had exuberantly declared to be the "general doctrine" of
that case — that "*any* third person, for whose direct benefit a contract
was intended, could sue on it" (emphasis added). All of this left the reach
of the doctrine in doubt; by 1918 no one could dispute that contract
beneficiaries had certain established legal rights, at least in New York and
a few other progressive jurisdictions, but the class of beneficiaries entitled
to protection remained almost as undefined as it had been in 1859.

The Restatement First of Contracts devoted an entire Chapter (Chapter 6, §§133-147) to the subject of third party rights. Chapter 6 was almost
certainly the handiwork of Arthur Corbin, a tireless proselytizer for the
rights of third party beneficiaries. (Corbin wrote six articles on the subject
and probably did more than any court to win acceptance for the doctrine.) See Waters, The Property In the Promise: A Study of the Third
Party Beneficiary Rule, 98 Harv. L. Rev. 1109, 1148-1172 (1985). The
nomenclature that the Restaters adopted to describe the rights of contract beneficiaries has been widely employed in subsequent opinions and,
on first appearance, seems a useful aid in reducing to a semblance of
order the doctrinal chaos reviewed in the preceding section.

The Restatement First's treatment of third party beneficiaries begins
with a distinction among what are termed "donee," "creditor," and "incidental" beneficiaries. Subsections (1) and (2) of §133 provide:

> (1) Where performance of a promise in a contract will benefit a person
> other than the promisee, that person is . . .
>
> (a) a donee beneficiary if it appears from the terms of the promise in
> view of the accompanying circumstances that the purpose of the
> promisee in obtaining the promise or all or part of the performance
> thereof is to make a gift to the beneficiary or to confer upon him a
> right against the promisor to some performance neither due nor
> supposed or asserted to be due from the promisee to the benefi-
> ciary;
>
> (b) a creditor beneficiary if no purpose to make a gift appears from the
> terms of the promise in view of the accompanying circumstances
> and performance of the promise will satisfy an actual or supposed
> or asserted duty of the promisee to the beneficiary, or a right of the
> beneficiary against the promisee which has been barred by the
> Statute of Limitations or by a discharge in bankruptcy, or which is
> unenforceable because of the Statute of Frauds;
>
> (c) an incidental beneficiary if neither the facts stated in Clause (a) nor
> those stated in Clause (b) exists.
>
> (2) Such a promise as is described in Subsection (1a) is a gift promise.
> Such a promise as is described in Subsection (1b) is a promise to discharge
> the promisee's duty.

Section 147 provides that: "An incidental beneficiary acquires by virtue
of the promise no right against the promisor or the promisee." Thus,

under the Restatement First's categorization, a beneficiary must be able to qualify either as a "donee beneficiary" or a "creditor beneficiary" in order to be entitled to bring an action. The term "incidental beneficiary" is used to described would-be beneficiaries who do not qualify. In the Comment to §133, the Restaters give the following illustrations of such would-be or non-qualifying beneficiaries:

> 9. B promises A for sufficient consideration to pay whatever debts A may incur in a certain undertaking. A incurs in the undertaking debts to C, D and E. If, on a fair interpretation of B's promise, the amount of the debts is to be paid by B to C, D and E, they are creditor beneficiaries; if the money is to be paid to A in order that he may be provided with money to pay C, D and E, they are at most incidental beneficiaries.
>
> 11. B contracts with A to erect an expensive building on A's land. C's adjoining land would be enhanced in value by the performance of the contract. C is an incidental beneficiary.
>
> 12. B contracts with A to buy A a new Gordon automobile. The Gordon Company is an incidental beneficiary. Though the contract cannot be performed without the payment of money to the Gordon Company, the payment is not intended as a gift nor is the payment a discharge of a real or supposed obligation of the promisee to the beneficiary.

The Comment to §147 adds a fourth illustration:

> A, an owner of land, enters into a contract with B, a contractor, by which B contracts to erect a building containing certain vats. C contracts with B to build the vats according to the specifications in the contract. The vats are installed in the building, but, owing to defective construction, leak and cause harm to A. C is under no duty to A who is only an incidental beneficiary of the contract between B and C, since C's performance is not given or received in discharge of B's duty to A.

In the Restatement Second, the topic of contract beneficiaries is addressed in Chapter 14 (§§302-315). The Introductory Note to Chapter 14 states that the terms "donee" and "creditor" beneficiary have been avoided because they "carry overtones of obsolete doctrinal difficulties." Instead, the Restaters have chosen to build their discussion of third party rights on a distinction between what are termed "intended" and "incidental" beneficiaries. Section 302 reads as follows:

> (1) Unless otherwise agreed between promisor and promisee, a beneficiary of a promise is an intended beneficiary if recognition of a right to performance in the beneficiary is appropriate to effectuate the intention of the parties and either
> > (a) the performance of the promise will satisfy an obligation of the promisee to pay money to the beneficiary; or
> > (b) the circumstances indicate that the promisee intends to give the beneficiary the benefit of the promised performance.

(2)   An incidental beneficiary is a beneficiary who is not an intended beneficiary.

As under the Restatement First "[a]n incidental beneficiary acquires by virtue of the promise no right against the promisor or the promisee" (§315).

Does this shift in terminology seem to you significant? Helpful? How would the cases in the preceding section have been decided under the two Restatements? It is clear enough that the plaintiff in Lawrence v. Fox was a "creditor" beneficiary and the niece in Seaver v. Ransom a "donee" beneficiary. But how about the mortgagee in the situation illustrated by Vrooman v. Turner? Can he even be described as an "intended" beneficiary? Under the approach adopted in the Restatement Second, C has rights under the A-B contract only if that is the intention of "the parties." Does this mean that A and B must *both* have such an intention, or is it sufficient that B (the promisee) intend to confer rights on C? Significantly, Comment *d* to §302 states that "if the beneficiary would be reasonable in relying on the promise as manifesting an intention to confer a right on him, he is an intended beneficiary." This is clearly meant to protect the reliance interest of the beneficiary and suggests that neither A *nor B* need have an *actual* intention to benefit C in order for C to have rights under their contract as a third party beneficiary. In a case of this sort, what would the extent of C's rights be? See Restatement Second §90(1) ("A promise which the promisor should reasonably expect to induce action or forbearance on the part of the promisee *or a third person* . . .") (emphasis added).

As you read the following materials, consider whether the Restatement First's emphasis on the promisee-beneficiary relationship or the Restatement Second's general requirement of intent seems more consistent with the case law, and whether either is desirable.

SOCONY-VACUUM OIL CO., INC. v. CONTINENTAL CASUALTY CO.
219 F.2d 645 (2d Cir. 1955)

HINCKS, Circuit Judge. The Bennett-Stewart Co., Inc. (hereinafter referred to as the prime contractor) was awarded a contract by the United States Government to construct a radar station at St. Albans, Vermont, and gave the "performance bond" and the "payment bond" required by the Miller Act, 40 U.S.C.A. §§270a, 270b.[5] The prime contractor entered

5. The Miller Act, 40 U.S.C.A. §270a provides:

(a) Before any contract, exceeding $2,000 in amount, for the construction, alteration, or repair of any public building or public work of the United States is awarded

into a subcontract with R. F. Carpenter, Inc. (hereinafter referred to as
the subcontractor) for road and parking area construction work around
the radar station. Obviously having in mind its liabilities under the Miller
Act to the subcontractor's materialmen, the prime contractor required
the subcontractor to furnish a surety bond. The subcontractor, accordingly, provided a surety bond whereby it, as principal, and the defendant
surety company, as surety, obligated themselves to the prime contractor
in the penal sum of $162,000. This bond, which was made a part of the
complaint, was conditioned as follows:

> Whereas, the above bounden Principal has entered into a certain writ-
> ten contract with the above named Obligee, dated the 8th day of May,
> 1950, for the construction of Roads, Parking Areas, etc., at St. Albans,
> Vermont.
> Which contract is hereby referred to and made a part hereof as fully and
> to the same extent as if copied at length herein.
> Now Therefore, The Condition of The Above Obligation Is Such, That
> if the above bounden Principal shall pay all labor and material obligations
> and shall well and truly keep, do and perform, each and every, all and
> singular, the matters and things in said contract set forth and specified to be
> by the said Principal kept, done and performed at the time and in the
> manner in said contract specified, and shall pay over, make good and
> reimburse to the above named Obligee, all loss and damage which said
> Obligee may sustain by reason of failure or default on the part of said

---

to any person, such person shall furnish to the United States the following bonds,
which shall become binding upon the award of the contract to such person, who is
hereinafter designated as "contractor":
  (1) A performance bond with a surety or sureties satisfactory to the officer award-
      ing such contract, and in such amount as he shall deem adequate, for the
      protection of the United States.
  (2) A payment bond with a surety or sureties satisfactory to such officer for the
      protection of all persons supplying labor and material in the prosecution of
      the work provided for in said contract for the use of each such person.

Section 270b provides:
  (a) Every person who has furnished labor or material in the prosecution of the
work provided for in such contract, in respect of which a payment bond is furnished
under section 270a of this title and who has not been paid in full therefor before the
expiration of a period of ninety days after the day on which the last of the labor was
done or performed by him or material was furnished or supplied by him for which
such claim is made, shall have the right to sue on such payment bond for the
amount, or the balance thereof, unpaid at the time of institution of such suit and to
prosecute said action to final execution and judgment for the sum or sums justly due
him: *Provided, however,* That any person having direct contractual relationship with
a subcontractor but no contractual relationship express or implied with the contractor furnishing said payment bond shall have a right of action upon the said payment
bond upon giving written notice to said contractor within ninety days from the date
on which such person did or performed the last of the labor or furnished or supplied
the last of the material for which such claim is made, stating with substantial accuracy the amount claimed and the name of the party to whom the material was
furnished or supplied or for whom the labor was done or performed.

Principal, then this obligation shall be void; otherwise to be and remain in full force and effect.

The plaintiff herein was a materialman of the subcontractor which, having failed within the time limitations of the proviso in Section 2 of the Miller Act, 40 U.S.C.A. §270b(a), to perfect its rights against the surety on the prime contractor's payment bond, brought this action in the United States District Court for the District of Vermont to recover for material furnished by it to the subcontractor for use in the performance of the subcontract and hence a part of the material provided in the prosecution of the main contract. The basis of jurisdiction is diversity of citizenship and no jurisdictional problem is presented.

In the court below the defendant moved to dismiss on the ground that the plaintiff had no right in the bond because the bond was for the benefit of the prime contractor only and not third parties, and that the plaintiff by failing to pursue its rights against the prime contractor under the Miller Act had injured the defendant. This motion was granted, 122 F. Supp. 621, on the ground that the bond was given only for the benefit of the prime contractor, and not for the protection of the plaintiff as a materialman. From the ensuing judgment this appeal is prosecuted.

The record shows that the defendant Casualty Company was an Illinois corporation, that its principal — the subcontractor — was a Vermont corporation, and that the prime contractor was a Massachusetts corporation, and that the subcontract was one to be performed in Vermont. There is nothing in the record to show that the parties to the bond contemplated or agreed that it was to be interpreted or governed by the law of any particular state. Accordingly, we think the problem presented should be determined by the law of Vermont. Erie R. Co. v. Tompkins, 304 U.S. 64, 58 S. Ct. 817, 82 L. Ed. 1188.

However, there seems to be neither statute nor judicial precedent in Vermont bearing on the problem. And the problem presented has been variously decided in various jurisdictions. Confronted with this dilemma our task is not to surmise which line of judicial precedent a Vermont court would follow if presented with the case, but rather, by looking to the same sources which a Vermont court would presumably consult and by weighing the comparative reasoning of learned authors and conflicting judicial decisions for their intrinsic soundness, to define the pertinent law which when thus ascertained is presumably the law of Vermont even though as yet unannounced by a Vermont Court. See Moore, Commentary on the United States Judicial Code, pp. 338-340.

Professor Corbin in his work on law of contracts, 4 Corbin on Contracts, Sections 798-804, has this to say:

 . . . the third party has an enforcible right if the surety promises in the bond, either in express words or by reasonable implication, to pay money to him. If there is such a promissory expression as this, there need be no discussion of "intention to benefit." We need not speculate for whose bene- fit the contract was made, or wonder whether the promisee was buying the promise for his own selfish interest or for philanthropic purposes. It is a much simpler question: Did the surety promise to pay money to the plaintiff?

See also Corbin, "Contractor's Surety Bonds," 38 Yale Law Journal 1. This doctrine, we think, has the support of the great weight of authority. A long line of cases cited to such doctrine in 77 A.L.R. 53 amplifies the cases which Professor Corbin particularly cites.

It is true that in the bond here sued on the only expressly promissory words are those whereby the surety acknowledges itself bound to the prime contractor, as obligee, in the penal sum of $162,000. But since the bond is stated to be on condition that the principal — here the subcon- tractor — "shall pay all labor and material obligations," the words of the condition are the full equivalent of words of direct promise.[6]

We are unable to recognize either the validity or the relevance of the conclusion of the trial judge that the bond was given only for the benefit of the prime contractor and not for the protection of materialmen. Doubtless the prime contractor in requiring a bond of its subcontractor sought protection against his own liability to materialmen of the subcon- tractor. But this he obtained through a bond requiring the payment of the materialmen. Obviously it was contemplated that performance under the bond would benefit not only the prime contractor who would thereby be exonerated from liability to the materialmen thus paid but also the mate- rialmen of the subcontractor who were thereby to be paid.

But this aside, we think it was wholly irrelevant for the trial judge to speculate as to the motives of the parties of the bond. The scope of the bond, like any written contract, must be determined not by the unex- pressed motive of the parties but rather by the ordinary meaning of the

---

6. 4 Corbin on Contracts, pages 177-178.

Words of "condition" are not words of "promise" in form; but in this class of cases it is sound policy to interpret the words liberally in favor of the third parties. In a majority of states, it is already done; and without question the surety's rate of com- pensation for carrying the risk is sufficiently adjusted to the law. The compensated surety has become an institution that is well suited to carry the risk of the principal contractor's default, whereas individual laborers and materialmen are frequently very ill prepared to carry the risk. The legislatures have recognized this fact, and in the case of public contracts have required surety bonds to protect the third parties. While this has not been done in the case of private construction, and while the courts should not on their own motion put such a provision into a private surety bond, they may well interpret a bond that is expressly conditioned on the payment of laborers and materialmen as being a promise to pay them and made for their benefit. The words reasonably permit it, and social policy approves it. The court need not strain the words of the bond, as has sometimes been done, to hold that the third persons were not intended as beneficiaries thereof, even though the promisee may have been thinking chiefly of himself when he paid for the bond.

words which they used. By this simple test, the defendant here was plainly obligated to pay "material obligations" such as that sued on here.

The situation is affected not at all by the fact that the plaintiff failed to perfect its rights under the Miller Act against the prime contractor and its surety. The bond now sought to reach was not one required under that Act and the rights to which it gave rise are not qualified by the Act or conditioned upon the timely pursuit of remedies under that Act. The rights under this bond must be determined by its language interpreted as of the date it was given. At that time, of course, it was not known whether all or some of the materialmen would fail or decline to press their rights under the Miller Act.

Moreover, the bond was conditioned not only on the *payment* of "material obligations" but also on reimbursement to the obligee of "all loss and damage which said obligee may sustain by reason or failure or default on the part of said Principal." This latter branch of the condition was broad enough to protect the prime contractor against claims of materialmen which through timely prosecution had actually caused loss to the prime contractor or *his* surety. The branch of the condition calling for *payment of material obligations* without limitation to those which might be timely prosecuted under the Miller Act imports an intent that all were to be included within the obligation of the bond.

The judge below relied on the case of Spokane Merchants' Ass'n v. Pacific Surety Co., 1915, 86 Wash. 489, 150 P. 1054, and in support of his ruling the plaintiff-appellee cites the recent case of McGrath v. American Surety Company of New York, 307 N.Y. 552, 122 N.E.2d 906. The *Mc-Grath* decision was predicated on prior decisions of that court, viz.: Eastern Steel Co. v. Globe Indemnity Co., 227 N.Y. 586, 125 N.E. 917; Buffalo Cement Co. v. McNaughton, 90 Hun 74, 35 N.Y.S. 453, *affirmed on opinion below*, 156 N.Y. 702, 51 N.E. 1089, and Fosmire v. National Surety Co., 229 N.Y. 44, 127 N.E. 472. But these three cases which the court cited in the *McGrath* opinion were all cases relating to bonds in which a prime contractor was the principal and the state or a municipality was the obligee: in each, the bond given was one required by statute or ordinance. Consequently none involved the rights of materialmen against the surety of a subcontractor under a private bond. Certainly these cases are not apposite to the case before us: considerations of public policy affecting the scope of statutory bonds are absent when it comes to determining the scope of a private bond. Notwithstanding, we find, at least in the *Fosmire* and *Buffalo Cement* cases, dicta which we think support our holding here as to the plaintiff's right under a private bond.

We do not blink at the fact that the *McGrath* case, as far as appears from the facts stated in the opinion, is legally indistinguishable from that now before us. True, in *McGrath* the subcontractor furnished both a payment bond and a performance bond whereas here a single bond is involved which is conditioned both for payment of "material obligations" and for performance of the subcontract. But this, we think, is a difference without legal significance. But both the *Spokane* and the *McGrath* cases and others of similar purport we think out of line with the great weight of authority referred to above. With deference, we suggest that it is unfortunate doctrine to modify the scope of a plainly stated written obligation in a private bond by the supposed motive of the obligee, as these cases seem to do. Such doctrine leads to unnecessary and undesirable uncertainty in business relationships. It means that one within the orbit of a private bond cannot rely upon a plainly stated obligation: instead he must search for the undisclosed motive of the parties and take that as the measure of his rights.

In cases such as these involving a private bond not required by statute, even if — contrary to our view — there be need to search for the motive which led to the taking of a bond, we find a lack of rational basis for an analysis which goes no further than to recognize intent to provide protection to the obligee against actually accrued liability under some statute such as the Miller Act. To say that the object of the bond was only to protect the obligee against liabilities imposed upon him by the Miller Act overlooks the fact that the bond was not required by that Act and calls for the payment of "*all* labor and material obligations" without express limitation to liabilities of the obligee under the Miller Act. In our view, the object of the bond was to accomplish the payment of these obligations and by such payment to provide protection to the obligee. If the obligee sought indemnity only or if it wished to exclude third parties from benefit under a surety bond, the natural presumption is that it would not have required a surety's payment bond. But here the prime contractor required a payment bond and paid the premium for a payment bond, at least indirectly under the terms of the subcontract whereby the subcontractor made the direct payment. And the defendant in return for the premium, furnished a payment bond. It follows that the surety should not be allowed to avoid the obligation which it was paid to assume by suggesting that as things turned out the obligee did not need all the protection which was bargained and paid for. Were we to hold otherwise, we should in effect, by substituting a mere contract for indemnity for the bond which was made, be presenting the defendant surety company with an unearned windfall.

Since we find it necessary to remand, it seems advisable to say that we find no merit in the defendant's assertion, by way of defense, that it was injured by the plaintiff's failure to pursue its right against the prime contractor under the Miller Act. If the plaintiff, when it furnished material, had a right against the prime contractor and his surety and also, as we hold, a right against the subcontractor and the defendant as its surety, we know of no principle of law which required the plaintiff first to exhaust its remedy against the prime contractor and its surety.

Reversed and remanded.

NOTE

1. In his opinion in the *Socony-Vacuum* case, Judge Hincks concluded that McGrath v. American Surety Co., 307 N.Y. 552, 122 N.E.2d 906 (1954), was "legally indistinguishable" from the case at bar, but evidently was not impressed by the reasoning of the New York court in *McGrath*.

Shortly after the Second Circuit's *Socony-Vacuum* decision had been handed down, the New York Court of Appeals decided Daniel-Morris Co., Inc. v. Glens Falls Indemnity Co., 308 N.Y. 464, 126 N.E.2d 750 (1955). The general contractor on a housing project, which was, apparently, privately financed, had required his subcontractors to furnish both performance and payment bonds. Plaintiff had furnished materials to a subcontractor and, remaining unpaid, brought an action against the surety company on the payment bond. Without overruling *McGrath*, the Court held for plaintiff. Dye, J., wrote:

> . . . The underlying contract, as we have pointed out, required the furnishing of work and materials "free of the lien of any third party" and indemnity for nonperformance. To meet this underlying obligation two separate and distinct bonds were given. Suit by this plaintiff to enforce the payment bond is an entirely different situation than that existing where the obligations of the surety are combined in a single payment-performance bond. In such a situation a materialman may not maintain a separate suit as a third-party beneficiary because the primary or dominant purpose of the combined bond is regarded as "performance" which should not be dissipated or defeated by the neglect of the subcontractor to meet his obligation (Fosmire v. National Sur. Co., 229 N.Y. 44).
>
> Here we are not confronted with the problem of ascertaining the dominant purpose of a bond having a twofold function, but simply whether the primary, paramount purpose of this bond — payment of materialmen — may be enforced by a materialman. On this record it is clear that he may. This introduces no new principle — a materialman is allowed to sue as a third-party beneficiary whenever "the primary purpose of [the] bond but . . . also [its] paramount purpose" is to benefit creditors (cf. McClare v. Massachusetts Bonding & Ins. Co., 266 N.Y. 371, 377). The language of the within bond specifically provides that the materials furnished are to be "free of the lien of any third party." When this is read in conjunction with the underlying contract, the inference is irresistible that the parties intended to benefit unpaid materialmen. The intention to benefit is pointed up by the fact that the separate performance bond given to the prime contractor afforded it protection for noncompletion of the work, which necessarily included the contingencies within the indemnification of the payment bond. The materialman, on the other hand, had no recourse against the performance bond.
>
> The intention to benefit the materialmen must not be confused with the motive of the parties in entering into the bond. Big-W's demand for indemnification, as pointed out in the opinion below, "supplies the motive in

securing the undertaking rather than the intent as to who shall be benefited." Once the right is created the law furnishes a remedy irrespective of
the motivation of the parties (Seaver v. Ransom, 224 N.Y. 233; Lawrence v.
Fox, 20 N.Y. 268; 2 Williston on Contracts, §§372-402; Corbin, Third Parties as Beneficiaries of Contractors' Surety Bonds, 38 Yale L.J. 1).

McGrath v. American Sur. Co. (283 App. Div. 693, 698, *revd.* 307 N.Y.
552) is not authority to the contrary. There it clearly appeared that the
bond sought to be enforced was not intended to supersede or supplement
the right of action given materialmen under the Miller Act (U.S. Code, tit.
40, §§270a, 270b; cf. Socony-Vacuum Oil Co. v. Continental Cas. Co., 219
F.2d 645 [U.S. Court of Appeals, 2d Cir.]).

Id. at 468-469, 126 N.E.2d at 752-753.

2. A Note in 41 Cornell L.Q. 482 (1956) reviews the New York cases
and concludes that the court reached a proper result in both the *McGrath*
and *Daniel-Morris* cases, albeit on faulty reasoning. The author remarks
that the "vexing problem" of the materialman's right to sue on the contractor's surety bond "has already caused an immense amount of unnecessary litigation, and court decisions, many hamstrung by outworn
dogma, leave the law in this area conflicting and uncertain." The author
proposes that the "intent-to-benefit" test be discarded and suggests that
"a test eliminating ambiguity and furnishing a sound basis would be: Was
it a distinct objective of the exact performance specified in the condition
of the bond that the surety assumes a direct obligation to materialmen."
This test, the author concludes, would result in payment to materialmen,
but without possible confusion with claims of incidental beneficiaries. Do
you agree?

3. In the principal case and the other cases referred to in this Note the
surety company writes its bond on account of its principal, the subcontractor, undertaking in favor of the general contractor (obligee of the
bond) that the subcontractor's debts for labor and materials will be paid.
In contract terminology, the surety company is the promisor and the
general contractor is the promisee. The plaintiff has furnished materials
(or labor) to the subcontractor. Under the definitions in Restatement
First §133, is the plaintiff (in states that allow him to recover) a creditor
beneficiary or a donee beneficiary? For contradictory answers to the question see 4 Corbin §802; 2 Williston §372.

LUCAS v. HAMM

56 Cal. 2d 583, 364 P.2d 685, 15 Cal. Rptr. 821 (1961), *cert. denied,*
368 U.S. 987 (1962)

GIBSON, Chief Justice. Plaintiffs, who are some of the beneficiaries
under the will of Eugene H. Emmick, deceased, brought this action for
damages against defendant L. S. Hamm, an attorney at law who had been

engaged by the testator to prepare the will. They have appealed from a judgment of dismissal entered after an order sustaining a general demurrer to the second amended complaint without leave to amend.

The allegations of the first and second causes of action are summarized as follows: Defendant agreed with the testator, for a consideration, to prepare a will and codicils thereto for him by which plaintiffs were to be designated as beneficiaries of a trust provided for by paragraph Eighth of the will and were to receive 15% of the residue as specified in that paragraph. Defendant, in violation of instructions and in breach of his contract, negligently prepared testamentary instruments containing phraseology that was invalid by virtue of section 715.2 and former sections 715.1 and 716 of the Civil Code relating to restraints on alienation and the rule against perpetuities. Paragraph Eighth of the instruments "transmitted" the residual estate in trust and provided that the "trust shall cease and terminate at 12 o'clock noon on a day five years after the date upon which the order distributing the trust property to the trustee is made by the Court having jurisdiction over the probation of this will." After the death of the testator the instruments were admitted to probate. Subsequently, defendant, as draftsman of the instruments and as counsel of record for the executors, advised plaintiffs in writing that the residual trust provision was invalid and that plaintiffs would be deprived of the entire amount to which they would have been entitled if the provision had been valid unless they made a settlement with the blood relatives of the testator under which plaintiffs would receive a lesser amount that that provided for them by the testator. As the direct and proximate result of the negligence of defendant and his breach of contract in preparing the testamentary instruments and the written advice referred to above, plaintiffs were compelled to enter into a settlement under which they received a share of the estate amounting to $75,000 less than the sum which they would have received pursuant to testamentary instruments drafted in accordance with the directions of the testator.

It was held in Buckley v. Gray, 110 Cal. 339, 42 P. 900, 31 L.R.A. 862, that an attorney who made a mistake in drafting a will was not liable for negligence or breach of contract to a person named in the will who was deprived of benefits as a result of the error. The court stated that an attorney is liable to his client alone with respect to actions based on negligence in the conduct of his professional duties, and it was reasoned that there could be no recovery for mere negligence where there was no privity by contract or otherwise between the defendant and the person injured. 110 Cal. at pages 342-343, 42 P. 900. The court further concluded that there could be no recovery on the theory of a contract for the benefit of a third person, because the contract with the attorney was not expressly for the plaintiff's benefit and the testatrix only remotely intended the plaintiff to be benefited as a result of the contract. 110 Cal. at pages

346-347, 42 P. 900. For the reasons hereinafter stated the case is over-ruled.

The reasoning underlying the denial of tort liability in the *Buckley* case, i.e., the stringent privity test, was rejected in Biakanja v. Irving, 49 Cal. 2d 647, 648-650, 320 P.2d 16, 65 A.L.R.2d 1358, where we held that a notary public who, although not authorized to practice law, prepared a will but negligently failed to direct proper attestation was liable in tort to an intended beneficiary who was damaged because of the invalidity of the instrument. It was pointed out that since 1895, when *Buckley* was decided, the rule that in the absence of privity there was no liability for negligence committed in the performance of a contract had been greatly liberalized. 49 Cal. 2d at page 649, 320 P.2d 16. In restating the rule it was said that the determination whether in a specific case the defendant will be held liable to a third person not in privity is a matter of policy and involves the balancing of various factors, among which are the extent to which the transaction was intended to affect the plaintiff, the foreseeability of harm to him, the degree of certainty that the plaintiff suffered injury, the closeness of the connection between the defendant's conduct and the injury, and the policy of preventing future harm. 49 Cal. 2d at page 650, 320 P.2d 16. The same general principle must be applied in determining whether a beneficiary is entitled to bring an action for negligence in the drafting of a will when the instrument is drafted by an attorney rather than by a person not authorized to practice law.

Many of the factors which led to the conclusion that the notary public involved in *Biakanja* was liable are equally applicable here. As in *Biakanja*, one of the main purposes which the transaction between defendant and the testator intended to accomplish was to provide for the transfer of property to plaintiffs; the damage to plaintiffs in the event of invalidity of the bequest was clearly foreseeable; it became certain, upon the death of the testator without change of the will, that plaintiffs would have received the intended benefits but for the asserted negligence of defendant; and if persons such as plaintiffs are not permitted to recover for the loss resulting from negligence of the draftsman, no one would be able to do so, and the policy of preventing future harm would be impaired.

Since defendant was authorized to practice the profession of an attorney, we must consider an additional factor not present in *Biakanja*, namely, whether the recognition of liability to beneficiaries of wills negligently drawn by attorneys would impose an undue burden on the profession. Although in some situations liability could be large and unpredictable in amount, this is also true of an attorney's liability to his client. We are of the view that the extension of his liability to beneficiaries injured by a negligently drawn will does not place an undue burden on the profession, particularly when we take into consideration that a con-

trary conclusion would cause the innocent beneficiary to bear the loss.
The fact that the notary public involved in *Biakanja* was guilty of unauthorized practice of the law was only a minor factor in determining that
he was liable, and the absence of the factor in the present case does not
justify reaching a different result.

It follows that the lack of privity between plaintiffs and defendant does
not preclude plaintiffs from maintaining an action in tort against defendant.

Neither do we agree with the holding in *Buckley* that beneficiaries
damaged by an error in the drafting of a will cannot recover from the
draftsman on the theory that they are third-party beneficiaries of the
contract between him and the testator.[7] Obviously the main purpose of a
contract for the drafting of a will is to accomplish the future transfer of
the estate of the testator to the beneficiaries named in the will, and
therefore it seems improper to hold, as was done in *Buckley*, that the
testator intended only "remotely" to benefit those persons. It is true that
under a contract for the benefit of a third person performance is usually
to be rendered directly to the beneficiary, but this is not necessarily the
case. (See Rest., Contracts, §133, com. *d*; 2 Williston on Contracts (3rd
ed. 1959) 829.) For example, where a life insurance policy lapsed because
a bank failed to perform its agreement to pay the premiums out of the
insured's bank account, it was held that after the insured's death the
beneficiaries could recover against the bank as third-party beneficiaries.
Walker Bank & Trust Co. v. First Security Corp., 9 Utah 2d 215, 341 P.2d
944, 945 et seq. Persons who had agreed to procure liability insurance for
the protection of the promisees but did not do so were also held liable to
injured persons who would have been covered by the insurance, the
courts stating that all persons who might be injured were third-party
beneficiaries of the contracts to procure insurance. Johnson v. Holmes
Tuttle Lincoln-Mercury, Inc., 160 Cal. App. 2d 290, 296 et seq., 325 P.2d
193; James Stewart & Co. v. Law, 149 Tex. 392, 233 S.W.2d 558, 561-562,
22 A.L.R.2d 639. Since, in a situation like those presented here and in the
Buckley case, the main purpose of the testator in making his agreement
with the attorney is to benefit the persons named in his will and this intent
can be effectuated, in the event of a breach by the attorney, only by
giving the beneficiaries a right of action, we should recognize, as a matter
of policy, that they are entitled to recover as third-party beneficiaries. See
2 Williston on Contracts (3rd ed. 1959) pp. 843-844; 4 Corbin on Contracts (1951) pp. 8, 20.

---

7. It has been recognized in other jurisdictions that the *client* may recover in a contract
action for failure of the attorney to carry out his agreement. (See 5 Am. Jur. 331; 49
A.L.R.2d 1216, 1219-1221; Prosser, Selected Topics on the Law of Torts (1954) pp. 438, 442.)
This is in accord with the general rule stated in Communale v. Traders & General Ins. Co.,
50 Cal. 2d 654, 663, 328 P.2d 198, 68 A.L.R.2d 883, that where a case sounds in both tort and
contract, the plaintiff will ordinarily have freedom of election between the two actions.

Section 1559 of the Civil Code, which provides for enforcement by a third person of a contract made "expressly" for his benefit, does not preclude this result. The effect of the section is to exclude enforcement by persons who are only incidentally or remotely benefited. See Hartman Ranch Co. v. Associated Oil Co., 10 Cal. 2d 232, 244, 73 P.2d 1163; cf. 4 Corbin on Contracts (1951) pp. 23-24. As we have seen, a contract for the drafting of a will unmistakably shows the intent of the testator to benefit the persons to be named in the will, and the attorney must necessarily understand this.

Defendant relies on language in Smith v. Anglo-California Trust Co., 205 Cal. 496, 502, 271 P. 898, and Fruitvale Canning Co. v. Cotton, 115 Cal. App. 2d 622, 625, 252 P.2d 953, that to permit a third person to bring an action on a contract there must be "an intent clearly manifested by the promisor" to secure some benefit to the third person. This language, which was not necessary to the decision in either of the cases, is unfortunate. Insofar as intent to benefit a third person is important in determining his right to bring an action under a contract, it is sufficient that the promisor must have understood that the promisee had such intent. (Cf. Rest., Contracts, §133, subds. 1(a) and 1(b); 4 Corbin on Contracts (1951) pp. 16-18; 2 Williston on Contracts (3rd ed. 1959) pp. 836-839). No specific manifestation by the promisor of an intent to benefit the third person is required. The language relied on by defendant is disapproved to the extent that it is inconsistent with these views.

We conclude that intended beneficiaries of a will who lose their testamentary rights because of failure of the attorney who drew the will to properly fulfill his obligations under his contract with the testator may recover as third-party beneficiaries.

However, an attorney is not liable either to his client or to a beneficiary under a will for errors of the kind alleged in the first and second causes of action.

[In an omitted passage the court concluded that, in view of the confused state of California law relating to perpetuities and restraints on alienation, "it would not be proper to hold that defendant failed to use such skill, prudence and diligence as lawyers of ordinary skill and capacity commonly exercise." There is also omitted the court's discussion of a third cause of action which alleged that the defendant had negligently procured improper or inadequate releases from a group of contestants of the will. The court concluded that "the third count does not state a cause of action for negligence." Judgment dismissing the complaint was affirmed by a unanimous court.]

NOTE

1. In Heyer v. Flaig, 70 Cal. 2d 223, 449 P.2d 161, 74 Cal. Rptr. 225 (1969), the California Supreme Court had an opportunity to reconsider

the rationale of the *Lucas* case. *Heyer*, like *Lucas*, was an action by the intended beneficiaries of a will against the attorney who had, it was alleged, negligently drafted the will with the result that the plaintiffs did not receive part of the bequest they had been meant to receive. Writing for the court *in bank*, Judge Tobriner had this to say:

> In the earlier case of Biakanja v. Irving (1958) 49 Cal. 2d 647, 320 P.2d 16, 65 A.L.R.2d 1358, we had held that a notary public who negligently failed to direct proper attestation of a will became liable in tort to an intended beneficiary who suffered damage because of the invalidity of the instrument. In that case, the defendant argued that the absence of privity deprives a plaintiff of a remedy for negligence committed in the performance of a contract. In rejecting this contention we pointed out that the inflexible privity requirement for such a tort recovery has been virtually abandoned in California. . . .
>
> Applying the *Biakanja* criteria to the facts of *Lucas*, the court found that attorneys incur a duty in favor of certain third persons, namely, intended testamentary beneficiaries. In proceeding to discuss the contractual remedy of such persons as the plaintiffs in *Lucas*, we concluded that "as a matter of policy, . . . they are entitled to recover as third-party beneficiaries." (56 Cal. 2d at p. 590, 15 Cal. Rptr. at p. 825, 364 P.2d at p. 689.) The presence of the *Biakanja* criteria in a contractual setting led us to sustain not only the availability of a tort remedy but of a third-party beneficiary contractual remedy as well. This latter theory of recovery, however, is conceptually superfluous since the crux of the action must lie in tort in any case; there can be no recovery without negligence. . . .
>
> When an attorney undertakes to fulfill the testamentary instructions of his client, he realistically and in fact assumes a relationship not only with the client but also with the client's intended beneficiaries. The attorney's actions and omissions will affect the success of the client's testamentary scheme; and thus the possibility of thwarting the testator's wishes immediately becomes foreseeable. Equally foreseeable is the possibility of injury to an intended beneficiary. In some ways, the beneficiary's interests loom greater than those of the client. After the latter's death, a failure in his testamentary scheme works no practical effect except to deprive his intended beneficiaries of the intended bequests. Indeed, the executor of an estate has no standing to bring an action for the amount of the bequest against an attorney who negligently prepared the estate plan, since in the normal case the estate is not injured by such negligence except to the extent of the fees paid; only the beneficiaries suffer the real loss. We recognize in *Lucas* that unless the beneficiary could recover against the attorney in such a case, no one could do so and the social policy of preventing future harm would be frustrated.
>
> The duty thus recognized in *Lucas* stems from the attorney's undertaking to perform legal services for the client but reaches out to protect the intended beneficiary. We impose this duty because of the relationship between the attorney and the intended beneficiary; public policy requires that the attorney exercise his position of trust and superior knowledge responsi-

bly so as not to affect adversely persons whose rights and interests are certain and foreseeable. . . .

Id. at 226-229, 449 P.2d at 163-165, 74 Cal. Rptr. at 227-229. Judge To-briner concluded that the plaintiff's complaint stated "a cause of action in tort under the doctrine of *Lucas.*" Would you view *Heyer* as an affirmation or repudiation of the contract beneficiary theory advanced in the *Lucas* case? Does it make any difference whether we treat the plaintiff's claim in *Lucas* as one that sounds in tort or contract?

2. In Lucas v. Hamm, the court held that the attorney was not liable because he had not been negligent. Thus its discussion of the attorney's theoretical liability if he had been negligent may be dismissed as dictum, albeit a peculiarly insistent kind of dictum. The court's approach suggests interesting possibilities in the case of lawyers who give opinions on, for example, the validity of municipal or corporate bond issues or the enforceability of security arrangements. In this connection, consider the case of Ultramares Corp. v. Touche, Niven & Co., 255 N.Y. 170, 174 N.E. 441, 74 A.L.R. 1139 (1931). In *Ultramares,* the New York Court of Appeals was asked to determine the liability of a public accountant to a third party who had made loans to an insolvent company in reliance on a balance sheet prepared and certified by the accountant which showed that the borrowing enterprise was solvent. The action in *Ultramares* was in tort, with one count that alleged merely negligent misrepresentation and a second count that alleged fraudulent misrepresentation. The Court of Appeals concluded that the accountant was not liable to the third party on the negligence count but remanded the case for further proceedings on the fraud count. In the course of his discussion of the negligence count Cardozo, C.J., compared the contract and tort cases on third party liability:

> The assault upon the citadel of privity is proceeding in these days apace. How far the inroads shall extend is now a favorite subject of juridical discussion (Williston, Liability for Honest Misrepresentation, 24 Harv. L. Rev. 415, 433; Bohlen, Studies in the Law of Torts, pp. 150, 151; Bohlen, Misrepresentation as Deceit, Negligence or Warranty, 42 Harv. L. Rev. 733; Smith, Liability for Negligent Language, 14 Harv. L. Rev. 184; Green, Judge and Jury, chapter Deceit, p. 280; 16 Va. Law Rev. 749). In the field of the law of contract there has been a gradual widening of the doctrine of Lawrence v. Fox (20 N.Y. 268), until today the beneficiary of a promise, clearly designated as such, is seldom left without a remedy (Seaver v. Ransom, 224 N.Y. 233, 238). Even in that field, however, the remedy is narrower where the beneficiaries of the promise are indeterminate or general. Something more must then appear than an intention that the promise shall redound to the benefit of the public or to that of a class of indefinite extension. The promise must be such as to "bespeak the assumption of a duty to make reparation directly to the individual members of the public if the benefit is lost" (Moch Co. v. Rensselaer Water Co., 247 N.Y. 160, 164;

American Law Institute, Restatement of the Law of Contracts, §145). In
the field of the law of torts a manufacturer who is negligent in the manufacture of a chattel in circumstances pointing to an unreasonable risk of
serious bodily harm to those using it thereafter may be liable for negligence
though privity is lacking between manufacturer and user (MacPherson v.
Buick Motor Co., 217 N.Y. 382; American Law Institute, Restatement of
the Law of Torts, §262). A force or instrument of harm having been
launched with potentialities of danger manifest to the eye of prudence, the
one who launches it is under a duty to keep it within bounds (Moch Co. v.
Rensselaer Water Co., *supra*, at p. 168). Even so, the question is still open
whether the potentialities of danger that will charge with liability are confined to harm to the person, or include injury to property (Pine Grove
Poultry Farm v. Newton B.-P. Mfg. Co., 248 N.Y. 293, 296; Robins Dry
Dock & Repair Co. v. Flint, 275 U.S. 303; American Law Institute, Restatement of the Law of Torts, *supra*). In either view, however, what is released
or set in motion is a physical force. We are now asked to say that a like
liability attaches to the circulation of a thought or a release of the explosive
power resident in words.

Three cases in this court are said by the plaintiff to have committed us to
the doctrine that words, written or oral, if negligently published with the
expectation that the reader or listener will transmit them to another, will
lay a basis for liability though privity be lacking. These are Glanzer v.
Shepard (233 N.Y. 236); International Products Co. v. Erie R.R. Co. (244
N.Y. 331), and Doyle v. Chatham & Phoenix Nat. Bank (253 N.Y. 369).

In Glanzer v. Shepard the seller of beans requested the defendants,
public weighers, to make return of the weight and furnish the buyer with a
copy. This the defendants did. Their return, which was made out in duplicate, one copy to the seller and the other to the buyer, recites that it was
made by order of the former for the use of the latter. The buyer paid the
seller on the faith of the certificate which turned out to be erroneous. We
held that the weighers were liable at the suit of the buyer for the moneys
overpaid. Here was something more than the rendition of a service in the
expectation that the one who ordered the certificate would use it thereafter
in the operations of his business as occasion might require. Here was a case
where the transmission of the certificate to another was not merely one
possibility among many, but the "end and aim of the transaction," as certain and immediate and deliberately willed as if a husband were to order a
gown to be delivered to his wife, or a telegraph company, contracting with
the sender of a message, were to telegraph it wrongly to the damage of the
person expected to receive it (Wolfskehl v. Western Union Tel. Co., 46
Hun, 542; DeRuth v. New York, etc., Tel. Co., 1 Daly, 547; Milliken v.
Western Union Tel. Co., 110 N.Y. 403, 410). The intimacy of the resulting
nexus is attested by the fact that after stating the case in terms of legal duty,
we went on to point out that viewing it as a phase or extension of Lawrence
v. Fox (*supra*), or Seaver v. Ransom (*supra*), we could reach the same
result by stating it in terms of contract (cf. Economy Building & Loan Assn.
v. West Jersey Title Co., 64 N.J.L. 27; Young v. Lohr, 118 Iowa, 624;
Murphy v. Fidelity, Abstract & Title Co., 114 Wash. 77). The bond was so
close as to approach that of privity, if not completely one with it. Not so in
the case at hand. No one would be likely to urge that there was a contrac-

tual relation, or even one approaching it, at the root of any duty that was
owing from the defendants now before us to the indeterminate class of
persons who, presently or in the future, might deal with the Stern company
in reliance on the audit. In a word, the service rendered by the defendant in
Glanzer v. Shepard was primarily for the information of a third person, in
effect, if not in name, a party to the contract, and only incidentally for that
of the formal promisee. In the case at hand, the service was primarily for
the benefit of the Stern company, a convenient instrumentality for use
in the development of the business, and only incidentally or collaterally for
the use of those to whom Stern and his associates might exhibit it thereafter. Foresight of these possibilities may charge with liability for fraud. The
conclusion does not follow that it will charge with liability for negligence.

Id. at 180-183, 174 N.E. at 445-446. Does Lucas v. Hamm reject the
approach adopted in *Ultramares* or are the two cases distinguishable and
reconcilable?

3. Cases like Lucas v. Hamm, Heyer v. Flaig, and *Ultramares* are
characterized by a recurrent interplay between contract and tort theory.
Another area in which the uneasy alliance between contract and tort
makes its appearance is that of a manufacturer's liability to remote consumers or users of a defective product. In recent years a great many
courts have adopted a rule, sometimes referred to as one of "strict liability," under which the manufacturer may be held liable even though it was
not in "privity" of contract with the injured plaintiff and even though it
was not chargeable with negligence in the manufacture of the goods. The
California Court announced such a rule in Greenman v. Yuba Power
Products, Inc., 59 Cal. 2d 57, 377 P.2d 897, 27 Cal. Rptr. 697 (1963), and
reaffirmed it in Seely v. White Motor Co., 63 Cal. 2d 9, 403 P.2d 145, 45
Cal. Rptr. 17 (1965). The New York Court of Appeals followed suit in
Goldberg v. Kollsman Instrument Corp., 12 N.Y.2d 432, 191 N.E.2d 81
(1963) (*held* that the administratrix of a passenger killed in an airplane
crash could recover on a theory of implied warranty from the manufac-
turer of the airplane). For excellent discussions of these developments,
see R. Epstein, Modern Products Liability Law 1-67 (1980); Priest, The
Invention of Enterprise Liability: A Critical History of the Intellectual
Foundations of Modern Tort Law, 14 J. Legal Stud. 461 (1985).

Could it plausibly be argued that the "strict liability" products cases,
which abolish the manufacturer's defenses based on theories of privity
and negligence, foreshadow a further expansion of the range of interests
protected by third party beneficiary doctrine? In the context of the New
York case law, is not the *Goldberg* case (1963) ultimately inconsistent with
the *Ultramares* case (1931)?

4. Section 2-318 of the Uniform Commercial Code reads as follows:

Third Party Beneficiaries. Warranties Express or Implied
A seller's warranty whether express or implied extends to any natural
person who is in the family or household of his buyer or who is a guest in

his home if it is reasonable to expect that such person may use, consume or
be affected by the goods and who is injured in person by breach of the
warranty. A seller may not exclude or limit the operation of this section.

In the California version of the Uniform Commercial Code, §2-318 was
deleted, apparently on the theory that the California case law (e.g., the
1963 *Greenman* case referred to above) had already gone beyond the
position taken in §2-318.

5. In his opinion in Lucas v. Hamm, Chief Justice Gibson refers to a
California statutory provision (Civil Code §1559) on third party beneficiaries. For the text of the statute, see Note 2, *infra* p. 1427.

ISBRANDTSEN CO., INC. v. LOCAL 1291 OF INTERNATIONAL LONGSHOREMEN'S ASSN.

204 F.2d 495 (3d Cir. 1953)

GOODRICH, Circuit Judge. This case involves a suit on a contract by
one not a party to it. Action was brought in the district court, and that
court, upon motion by the defendant, dismissed the case under rule
12(b), F.R.C.P. 28 U.S.C. We proceed, as did the district court, on the
assumption that all statements of fact alleged are true.

Here are the facts. Isbrandtsen Company, Inc., was the time charterer
of a ship called the "Nyco." Isbrandtsen in turn chartered the ship to the
Scott Paper Company for the purpose of transporting pulp from Nova
Scotia to Philadelphia. Under the terms of the charter Scott Paper Company was to load and unload the vessel. Scott in turn hired Lavino Shipping Company to do the unloading. When the vessel got to its destination
the employees of Lavino started to unload it, and during the unloading
stopped work contrary to the provisions of the contract which their union
had made with their employer. More needs to be said about that contract.
The parties to it were the Philadelphia Marine Trade Association, of
which Lavino Shipping Company was a member, "as collective bargaining agent for those of its members who employ longshoremen," and
Local 1291 of the International Longshoremen's Association. The contract provided among other things that there was to be no work stoppage
pending arbitration of disputes which might arise. Isbrandtsen, alleging
that the delay in unloading the ship caused it damage, sued under Section 301(a) of the Labor Management Relations Act of 1947. Alternatively
it claimed, there being diversity of citizenship and the requisite jurisdictional amount, to be able to recover as a matter of common law.

Local 1291 has made the point that the provision of the Labor Management Relations Act gives no right to sue to anyone except employer and
employee. The statute does not, however, so state. It says:

Suits for violation of contracts between an employer and a labor organization representing employees in an industry affecting commerce as defined
in this chapter, or between any such labor organizations, may be brought
in any district court of the United States having jurisdiction of the parties,
without respect to the amount in controversy or without regard to the
citizenship of the parties.

29 U.S.C.A. §185(a).

All the statute talks about is a suit for violation of the contract; it does
not say who may or who may not sue. The legislative history cited by the
appellee is certainly inconclusive with regard to the rights of those not
signatory to the contract, and a point of view contrary to appellee's argument seems to be indicated by the decision in Marranzano v. Riggs National Bank, 1950, 87 U.S. App. D.C. 195, 184 F.2d 439. We need not
decide this point, however.

We may assume that §301(a) does not impose any limitations upon the
persons who may sue. Our question then becomes, is Isbrandtsen to be
included as one who may sue for damages suffered by breach of this
contract?

It may aid in understanding the problem if it is kept in mind just how
far away Isbrandtsen stands from the actual parties to the contract. Signa-
tories were, as said above, Philadelphia Marine Trade Association and
Local 1291. Lavino Shipping Company is a member of that Association.
Scott made its contract for unloading the vessel with Lavino. Scott in
turn chartered this vessel from Isbrandtsen. Isbrandtsen is, then, three
steps away from the contracting party.

The question of determining what rights one who is not a party to a
contract has in its performance is one which is not free from difficulty. As
Professor Williston points out, the first recognition of such rights was in
the cases now called the donee beneficiary type. Here the courts protected the interest of the person for whose benefit the performance was
intended to prevent a failure of justice. The party to the contract would
have no action for its breach except for nominal damages since he was
not the one who suffered by the promisor's default. If the beneficiary
could not sue there could be no adequate recovery even though the
breach was established. The next extension was made, with hesitancy on
the part of some courts, to the creditor beneficiary situation. "[T]hrough
this travail," in Mr. Williston's words,

> the common law has given birth to a distinct, new principle of law which
> takes its own place in the family of legal principles, and gives not only to a
> donee beneficiary, but also to a creditor beneficiary, the right to enforce
> directly the promise from which he derives his interest.

So we have the classification of donee beneficiary, creditor beneficiary
and incidental beneficiary, a classification discussed in the works of both

Williston and Corbin and used in the Restatement. As Mr. Corbin says, the description of the term "incidental beneficiary" to describe one "whose relation to the contracting parties is such that the courts will not recognize any legal right in him" is not particularly helpful "for the problem of the courts is to determine what kinds of claimants asserting themselves to be beneficiaries have rights and what kinds have not."

Corbin goes on to describe what constitutes a creditor beneficiary and what constitutes a donee beneficiary. He says:

> If in buying the promise the promisee expresses an intent that some third party shall receive either the security of the executory promise or the benefit of performance as a gift, that party is a donee of either the contract right or of the promised performance or both. If, on the other hand, the promisee's expressed intent is that some third party shall receive the performance in satisfaction and discharge of some actual or supposed duty or liability of the promisee, the third party is a creditor beneficiary. All others who may in some way be benefited by performance have no rights and are called incidental beneficiaries.

We see no possibility that Isbrandtsen can be a creditor beneficiary of this labor union. The labor union was a complete stranger to Isbrandtsen so far as this transaction is concerned. Neither owed the other anything. And, therefore, there was no obligation on the part of either to do anything to or for the other. Nor do we see any possibility of making out of this situation a donee beneficiary relationship. This is not like a contract where a father buys an insurance policy to build up an estate for his son. It was a labor contract made between this association and a union. The contract recited that the association was acting on behalf of its members who employ longshoremen. Lavino is one of those members. But it does not appear that either Scott or Isbrandtsen was a member, and there is no allegation that either one employed longshoremen.

There is considerable language in the Restatement and in the cases and decisions about "intent" and "accompanying circumstances." From that the argument is made to us that the court should not have dismissed under Rule 12 but should have heard the plaintiff upon an attempt to make a showing of the supposed intention of the parties with regard to persons to benefit by this contract.

But we think that the whole setting of this fact situation as described in the complaint and exhibits is one which completely negatives a gift transaction under any possible interpretation of that term. The contract between the association and the labor union was a usual type of collective bargaining agreement. The contract between Isbrandtsen and Scott was a charter party in the ordinary form made upon stated money consideration. We do not have before us a copy of the contract between Scott and Lavino, but the complaint describes it as an agreement whereby Lavino promised Scott to discharge a cargo of wood pulp from the vessel. We cannot think that Lavino was making a gift to Scott or that Scott was making a gift to Isbrandtsen. In other words, all the transactions were usual business transactions in which parties were agreeing to do things for and pay money to each other.

We do not think, therefore, that in view of this business setting any statement by the marine association that it intended its agreement with the labor union to benefit all the world who might be helped by the faithful performance of the contract would give these remote parties rights against one who broke it. It may well be that Isbrandtsen suffered a loss of use of its boat because a strike stopped the unloading of the Nyco. It also may be that the people who had cargo to ship on the next voyage lost a market by the delay. And it may be that the people who did not get the goods on the next voyage, on time, lost a profitable bargain on that account. But neither in contract nor in tort have duties been extended very far beyond the immediate parties to the facts out of which a cause of action is said to arise. If one induces another to break a contract with a third person that third person has a tort claim against the one who procured the breach. But while Lumley could sue Gye for inducing Miss Wagner not to sing for Lumley as she had promised, no one would, we think, allow an action for breach of contract on the part of all the disappointed opera goers who did not hear Miss Wagner, even though the ultimate effect of performance by Miss Wagner would have been to send them home with the pleased feeling of having heard something beautiful.

The question was thoughtfully considered by the district judge. He concluded that Isbrandtsen was but "an incidental beneficiary" and in this conclusion he was right. Isbrandtsen is too far away from this contract to be included either as a donee or a creditor beneficiary and it must be one or the other in order to sue for breach of an agreement to which it was not a party.

It may be an arguable question whether the underlying law here will be found in federal decisions, assuming that plaintiff bases his claim upon a federal statute and comes within federal authority under the commerce power, or whether it is a question of Pennsylvania law by virtue of diversity of citizenship since the agreement and its breach took place in that state. That question need not be resolved. We think that Robins Dry Dock & Repair Company v. Flint, 1927, 275 U.S. 303, 48 S. Ct. 134, 72 L. Ed. 290, shows clearly that there could be no recovery under federal authority, and the same thing is true under the Pennsylvania decisions.

The judgment of the district court will be affirmed.

NOTE

1. Reconsider the Restatement First's definitions of "donee" and "creditor" beneficiaries, *supra* p. 1362. In the principal case Judge Good-

rich seems to have assumed that the crucial issue was the relationship
between Isbrandtsen and Local 1291. Should he not have focused, instead, on the relationship between Isbrandtsen and Lavino? Would that
make a difference? Suppose the action had been brought by Scott Paper
Co. instead of by Isbrandtsen?

2. Other courts have been more sympathetic to claims put forward by
third parties who allege that they have been injured by A's breach of his
contract with B. Thus in Visintine & Co. v. New York, Chicago & St.
Louis R.R., 169 Ohio St. 505, 160 N.E.2d 311 (1959), it appeared that
both Visintine and the Railroad had been awarded contracts with the
State of Ohio in connection with the elimination of a grade crossing. The
work to be done by Visintine apparently depended on the prior completion by the Railroad of its part of the project. Visintine brought an action
against the Railroad, with counts both in contract and in tort for negligence, to recover loss allegedly caused by the Railroad's improper performance of its contract with the State. The Railroad demurred to both the
contract count and the tort count. The court's conclusion, in a per curiam opinion, was as follows:

> Taken altogether, we believe the allegations of the petition are suffi-
> cient, as against demurrer, to qualify plaintiff as a beneficiary under the
> contracts between the defendants and the state of Ohio, particularly in
> view of the fact that the state is immune from suit for any alleged violations
> of the duties it assumed under its contract with plaintiff.
>
> We agree with the Court of Appeals in its affirmance of the sustaining of
> the demurrer to the tort cause of action. Tort is based on a duty owed by
> one party to another. The duty owed here by the defendants was to the
> state of Ohio, not to the plaintiff. The duty arising out of contract upon
> which plaintiff may rely in its first cause of action was that owed to it by the
> state. If defendants are liable to plaintiff it is due to a breach of the con-
> tracts they made with the state of Ohio and not to the violation of any duty
> owed directly to the plaintiff upon which a tort action may be based.

Section 4. Government Contracts and
Citizen Beneficiaries

Governments — local, state and federal — make an untold number of
contracts every day, most (if not all) of which are meant to benefit the
citizens for whose welfare governments are generally thought to be responsible. When a private landowner contracts to build a new hotel on
his property, the owner of the restaurant next door may be benefited; but
the benefit, no matter how large, is unintended — it is no part of the

landowner's purpose to confer a benefit on his neighbor — and we have little difficulty classifying the restaurant owner as an "incidental" beneficiary in the terminology of the Restatements. Government contracts are different: when it makes a contract to purchase sewage treatment services or to provide financing for a housing development, the government is exchanging its resources for something, or the promise of something, that is meant to benefit its citizens. The citizens who will use the sewage system and who will live in the housing development are, in the most obvious sense, "intended" beneficiaries of the government contracts made on their behalf. But if we permitted all of the intended beneficiaries of every such agreement to enforce its terms, the promisor would become contractually obligated to a limitless number of third parties. Courts have traditionally been reluctant to permit such a broadening of contractual responsibility unless, in Cardozo's words, the benefit conferred on the public by the contract is "primary and immediate in such a sense and to such a degree as to bespeak the assumption of a duty to make reparation directly to the individual members of the public if the benefit is lost."

The Restatement First reflected a similar uneasiness about government contracts. Section 145 provided that "a promisor bound to the United States or to a state or municipality" has no contractual obligations to the public unless "an intention is manifested in the contract, as interpreted in the light of the circumstances surrounding its formation, that the promisor shall compensate members of the public" for injuries resulting from the breach of his contract. Restatement Second §313(2) asserts, somewhat more cautiously, that a promisor who contracts with the government is not contractually liable to the public for consequential damages unless

(a) the terms of the promise provide for such liability; or
(b) the promisee is subject to liability to the member of the public for the damages and a direct action against the promisor is consistent with the terms of the contract and with the policy of the law authorizing the contract and prescribing remedies for its breach.

Despite such scholarly hesitation, the courts have in recent years shown an increased (though by no means universal) willingness to use the "progressive" third party beneficiary idea as a vehicle for expanding the legal rights of citizens in what Professor Charles Reich has called the "new property" — the diverse and all-embracing field of government benefits on which each of us increasingly depends. The following materials, which cover a period of more than fifty years, provide some milestones to measure our progress (or decline) in this regard, and illustrate the role that the third party beneficiary idea has played in the re-emergence of a status-based law of obligations.

H. R. MOCH CO., INC. v. RENSSELAER
WATER CO.

247 N.Y. 160, 159 N.E. 896 (1928)

Appeal from Supreme Court, Appellate Division, Third Department.

Action by the H. R. Moch Company, Inc., against the Rensselaer Water Company. From a judgment of the Appellate Division (219 App. Div. 673, 220 N.Y.S. 557), reversing an order of the Special Term, and granting defendant's motion for judgment dismissing the complaint for failure to state facts sufficient to constitute a cause of action, plaintiff appeals. Affirmed. . . .

CARDOZO, C.J. The defendant, a waterworks company under the laws of this state, made a contract with the city of Rensselaer for the supply of water during a term of years. Water was to be furnished to the city for sewer flushing and street sprinkling; for service to schools and public buildings; and for service at fire hydrants, the latter service at the rate of $42.50 a year for each hydrant. Water was to be furnished to private takers within the city at their homes and factories and other industries at reasonable rates, not exceeding a stated schedule. While this contract was in force, a building caught fire. The flames spreading to the plaintiff's warehouse near by, destroyed it and its contents. The defendant, according to the complaint, was promptly notified of the fire.

> but omitted and neglected after such notice, to supply or furnish sufficient or adequate quantity of water, with adequate pressure to stay, suppress, or extinguish the fire before it reached the warehouse of the plaintiff, although the pressure and supply which the defendant was equipped to supply and furnish, was adequate and sufficient to prevent the spread of the fire to and the destruction of the plaintiff's warehouse and its contents.

By reason of the failure of the defendant to "fulfill the provisions of the contract between it and the city of Rensselaer," the plaintiff is said to have suffered damage, for which judgment is demanded. A motion in the nature of a demurrer, to dismiss the complaint, was denied at Special Term. The Appellate Division reversed by a divided court.

Liability in the plaintiff's argument is placed on one or other of three grounds. The complaint, we are told, is to be viewed as stating: (1) A cause of action for breach of contract within Lawrence v. Fox, 20 N.Y. 268; (2) a cause of action for a common-law tort, within MacPherson v. Buick Motor Co., 217 N.Y. 382, 111 N.E. 1050, L.R.A. 1916F, 696, Ann. Cas. 1916C, 440; or (3) a cause of action for the breach of a statutory duty. These several grounds of liability will be considered in succession.

(1) We think the action is not maintainable as one for breach of contract.

No legal duty rests upon a city to supply its inhabitants with protection against fire. Springfield Fire & Marine Ins. Co. v. Village of Keesville, 148

N.Y. 46, 42 N.E. 405, 30 L.R.A. 660, 51 Am. St. Rep. 667. That being so, a member of the public may not maintain an action under Lawrence v. Fox against one contracting with the city to furnish water at the hydrants, unless an intention appears that the promisor is to be answerable to individual members of the public as well as to the city for any loss ensuing from the failure to fulfill the promise. No such intention is discernible here. On the contrary, the contract is significantly divided into two branches: One a promise to the city for the benefit of the city in its corporate capacity, in which branch is included the service at the hydrants; and the other a promise to the city for the benefit of private takers, in which branch is included the service at their homes and factories. In a broad sense it is true that every city contract, not improvident or wasteful, is for the benefit of the public. More than this, however, must be shown to give a right of action to a member of the public not formally a party. The benefit, as it is sometimes said, must be one that is not merely incidental and secondary. Cf. Fosmire v. National Surety Co., 229 N.Y. 44, 127 N.E. 472. It must be primary and immediate in such a sense and to such a degree as to bespeak the assumption of a duty to make reparation directly to the individual members of the public if the benefit is lost. The field of obligation would be expanded beyond reasonable limits if less than this were to be demanded as a condition of liability. A promisor undertakes to supply fuel for heating a public building. He is not liable for breach of contract to a visitor who finds the building without fuel, and thus contracts a cold. The list of illustrations can be indefinitely extended. The carrier of the mails under contract with the government is not answerable to the merchant who has lost the benefit of a bargain through negligent delay. The householder is without a remedy against manufacturers of hose and engines, though prompt performance of their contracts would have stayed the ravages of fire. "The law does not spread its protection so far." Robins Dry Dock & Repair Co. v. Flint, 275 U.S. 303, 48 S. Ct. 134.

So with the case at hand. By the vast preponderance of authority, a contract between a city and a water company to furnish water at the city hydrants has in view a benefit to the public that is incidental rather than immediate, an assumption of duty to the city and not to its inhabitants. Such is the ruling of the Supreme Court of the United States. German Alliance Ins. Co. v. Homewater Supply Co., 226 U.S. 220, 33 S. Ct. 32, 57 L. Ed. 195, 42 L.R.A. (N.S.) 1000. Such has been the ruling in this state . . . though the question is still open in this court. Such with few exceptions has been the ruling in other jurisdictions. Williston, Contracts, sec. 373, and cases there cited; Dillon, Municipal Corporations (5th Ed.) sec. 1340. The diligence of counsel has brought together decisions to that effect from 26 states. . . . Only a few states have held otherwise. Page, Contracts, sec. 2401. An intention to assume an obligation of indefinite extension to every member of the public is seen to be

the more improbable when we recall the crushing burden that the obligation would impose. Cf. Home v. Presque Isle Water Co., 104 Me. 217, at
p. 232, 71 A. 769, 21 L.R.A. (N.S.) 1021. The consequences invited would
bear no reasonable proportion to those attached by law to defaults not
greatly different. A wrongdoer who by negligence sets fire to a building is
liable in damages to the owner where the fire has its origin, but not to
other owners who are injured when it spreads. The rule in our state is
settled to that effect, whether wisely or unwisely. . . . If the plaintiff is to
prevail, one who negligently omits to supply sufficient pressure to extin-
guish a fire started by another assumes an obligation to pay the ensuing
damage, though the whole city is laid low. A promisor will not be deemed
to have had in mind the assumption of a risk so overwhelming for any
trivial reward.

The cases that have applied the rule of Lawrence v. Fox to contracts
made by a city for the benefit of the public are not at war with this
conclusion. Through them all there runs as a unifying principle the
presence of an intention to compensate the individual members of the
public in the event of a default. For example, in Pond v. New Rochelle
Water Co., 183 N.Y. 330, 76 N.E. 211, 1 L.R.A. (N.S.) 958, 5 Ann. Cas.
504, the contract with the city fixed a schedule of rates to be supplied, not
to public buildings, but to private takers at their homes. In Matter of
International R. Co. v. Rann, 224 N.Y. 83, 85, 120 N.E. 153, the contract
was by street railroads to carry passengers for a stated fare. In Smyth v.
City of New York, 203 N.Y. 106, 96 N.E. 409, and Rigney v. New York
Cent. & H.R.R. Co., 217 N.Y. 31, 111 N.E. 226, covenants were made by
contractors upon public works, not merely to indemnify the city, but to
assume its liabilities. These and like cases come within the third group
stated in the comprehensive opinion in Seaver v. Ransom, 224 N.Y. 233,
238, 120 N.E. 639, 2 L.R.A. 1187. The municipality was contracting in
behalf of its inhabitants by covenants intended to be enforced by any of
them severally as occasion should arise.

(2) We think the action is not maintainable as one for a common-law
tort.

"It is ancient learning that one who assumes to act, even though
gratuitously, may thereby become subject to the duty of acting carefully,
if he acts at all" (Glanzer v. Shepard, 233 N.Y. 236, 239; Marks v. Nambil
Realty Co., Inc., 245 N.Y. 256, 258). The plaintiff would bring its case
within the orbit of that principle. The hand once set to a task may not
always be withdrawn with impunity though liability would fail if it had
never been applied at all. A time-honored formula often phrases the
distinction as one between misfeasance and non-feasance. Incomplete
the formula is, and so at times misleading. Given a relation involving in
its existence a duty of care irrespective of a contract, a tort may result as
well from acts of omission as the commission in the fulfillment of the duty
thus recognized by law (Pollock, Torts [12th ed.], p. 555; Kelley v. Met.
Ry. Co., 1895, 1 Q.B. 944). What we need to know is not so much the

conduct to be avoided when the relation and its attendant duty are established as existing. What we need to know is the conduct that engenders the relation. It is here that the formula, however incomplete, has its value and significance. If conduct has gone forward to such a stage that inaction would commonly result, not negatively merely in withholding a benefit, but positively or actively in working an injury, there exists a relation out of which arises a duty to go forward (Bohlen, Studies in the Law of Torts, p. 87). So the surgeon who operates without pay, is liable though his negligence is in the omission to sterilize his instruments (cf. Glanzer v. Shepard, *supra*); the engineer, though his fault is in the failure to shut off steam (Kelley v. Met. Ry. Co., *supra*; cf. Pittsfield Cottonwear Mfg. Co. v. Shoe Co., 71 N.H. 522, 529, 533); the maker of automobiles, at the suit of some one other than the buyer, though his negligence is merely in inadequate inspection (MacPherson v. Buick Motor Co., 217 N.Y. 382). The query always is whether the putative wrongdoer has advanced to such a point as to have launched a force or instrument of harm, or has stopped where inaction is at most a refusal to become an instrument for good (cf. Fowler v. Athens Waterworks Co., 83 Ga. 219, 222).

The plaintiff would have us hold that the defendant, when once it entered upon the performance of its contract with the city, was brought into such a relation with every one who might potentially be benefited through the supply of water at the hydrants as to give a negligent performance, without reasonable notice of a refusal to continue, the quality of a tort. There is a suggestion of this thought in Guardian Trust Co. v. Fisher (200 U.S. 57), but the dictum was rejected in a later case decided by the same court (German Alliance Ins. Co. v. Home Water Supply Co., 226 U.S. 220) when an opportunity was at hand to turn it into law. We are satisfied that liability would be unduly and indeed indefinitely extended by this enlargement of the zone of duty. The dealer in coal who is to supply fuel for a shop must then answer to the customers if fuel is lacking. The manufacturer of goods, who enters upon the performance of his contract, must answer, in that view, not only to the buyer, but to those who to his knowledge are looking to the buyer for their own sources of supply. Every one making a promise having the quality of a contract will be under a duty to the promisee by virtue of the promise, but under another duty, apart from contract, to an indefinite number of potential beneficiaries when performance has begun. The assumption of one relation will mean the involuntary assumption of a series of new relations, inescapably hooked together. Again we may say in the words of the Supreme Court of the United States, "The law does not spread its protection so far" (Robins Dry Dock & Repair Co. v. Flint, *supra*; cf. Byrd v. English, 117 Ga. 191; Dale v. Grant, 34 N.J.L. 142; Conn. Ins. Co. v. N.Y. & N.H.R.R. Co., 25 Conn. 265; Anthony v. Slaid, 11 Metc. 290). We do not need to determine now what remedy, if any, there might be if the defendant had withheld the water or reduced the pressure with a malicious intent to do injury to the plaintiff or another. We put aside also the problem that would arise if there had been reckless and wanton indifferences to consequences measured and foreseen. Difficulties would be present even then, but they need not now perplex us. What we are dealing with at this time is a mere negligent omission, unaccompanied by malice or other aggravating elements. The failure in such circumstances to furnish an adequate supply of water is at most the denial of a benefit. It is not the commission of a wrong.

(3) We think the action is not maintainable as one for the breach of a statutory duty.

The defendant, a public service corporation, is subject to the provisions of the Transportation Corporations Act. The duty imposed upon it by that act is in substance to furnish water, upon demand by the inhabitants, at reasonable rates, through suitable connections at office, factory or dwelling, and to furnish water at like rates through hydrants or in public buildings upon demand by the city, all according to its capacity (Transportation Corporations Law [Cons. Laws, ch. 63], §81; Staten Island Water Supply Co. v. City of N.Y., 144 App. Div. 318; People ex rel. City of N.Y. v. Queens Co. Water Co., 232 N.Y. 277; People ex rel. Arthur v. Huntington Water Works Co., 208 App. Div. 807, 808). We find nothing in the requirements to enlarge the zone of liability where an inhabitant of the city suffers indirect or incidental damage through deficient pressure at the hydrants. The breach of duty in any case is to the one to whom service is denied at the time and at the place where service to such one is due. The denial, though wrongful, is unavailing without more to give a cause of action to another. We may find a helpful analogy in the law of common carriers. A railroad company is under a duty to supply reasonable facilities for carriage at reasonable rates. It is liable, generally speaking, for breach of a duty imposed by law if it refuses to accept merchandise tendered by a shipper. The fact that its duty is of this character does not make it liable to some one else who may be counting upon the prompt delivery of the merchandise to save him from loss in going forward with his work. If the defendant may not be held for a tort at common law, we find no adequate reason for a holding that it may be held under the statute.

The judgment should be affirmed with costs.

Pound, Crane, Andrews, Lehman and Kellogg, JJ., concur; O'Brien, J., not sitting.

Judgment affirmed, etc.

NOTE

1. As municipalities have increasingly taken over the business of supplying public services to their residents, cases like the principal case have of course gradually disappeared from the reports. See, however, Doyle v.

South Pittsburgh Water Co., 414 Pa. 199, 199 A.2d 875 (1964), a fire-loss case in which it was held that the complaint stated a good cause of action against the Water Company. With respect to Cardozo's opinion in the *Moch* case, Musmanno, J., commented that "at this point Homer nodded." (414 Pa. at 214.) For nearly a hundred years, however, there was a great deal of litigation of this type. In most situations the municipal residents were, more often than not, allowed to sue as third party beneficiaries of the contracts. In most states, however, the actions against privately owned water companies, typically for fire loss, were not allowed, either on contract or tort theory. Corbin suggests that the result in the water company cases may have been in part "accidental" in that "the earlier water cases were brought during a period of temporary reaction against the rule in Lawrence v. Fox," as illustrated by Vrooman v. Turner, *supra* p. 1346. (4 Corbin §§805, 806, 827.)

2. Another possible explanation of the judicial reluctance to allow actions against water companies for fire loss might be the universality of fire insurance covering residential and business property. However, the fact that the property owner is insured is not necessarily the end of the matter. It could be argued (though few courts have accepted this view) that the prudent property owner should be entitled to collect both his insurance and his damages. Or, alternatively, that the fire insurance company, after paying the loss, should be subrogated to the insured's right to collect damages from the water company. On the question of the insurer's subrogation to the insured's rights, in contract or in tort, against third parties, see 2 Harper & James, Torts §§25.19-25.23 (1974); 2 G. Gilmore, Security Interests in Personal Property §42.7.1 (1965).

MARTINEZ v. SOCOMA COMPANIES, INC.

11 Cal. 3d 394, 521 P.2d 841, 113 Cal. Rptr. 585 (1974)

WRIGHT, Chief Justice.

Plaintiffs brought this class action on behalf of themselves and other disadvantaged unemployed persons, alleging that defendants failed to perform contracts with the United States government under which defendants agreed to provide job training and at least one year of employment to certain numbers of such persons. Plaintiffs claim that they and the other such persons are third party beneficiaries of the contracts and as such are entitled to damages for defendants' nonperformance. General demurrers to the complaint were sustained without leave to amend, apparently on the ground that plaintiffs lacked standing to sue as third party beneficiaries. Dismissals were entered as to the demurring defendants, and plaintiffs appeal.

We affirm the judgments of dismissal. As will appear, the contracts nowhere state that either the government or defendants are to be liable to persons such as plaintiffs for damages resulting from the defendants' nonperformance. The benefits to be derived from defendants' performance were clearly intended not as gifts from the government to such persons but as a means of executing the public purposes stated in the contracts and in the underlying legislation. Accordingly, plaintiffs were only incidental beneficiaries and as such has no right of recovery.

The complaint names as defendants Socoma Companies, Inc. ("Socoma"), Lady Fair Kitchens, Incorporated ("Lady Fair"), Monarch Electronics International, Inc. ("Monarch"), and eleven individuals of whom three are alleged officers or directors of Socoma, four of Lady Fair, and four of Monarch. Lady Fair and the individual defendants associated with it, a Utah corporation and Utah residents respectively, did not appear in the trial court and are not parties to this appeal.

The complaint alleges that under 1967 amendments to the Economic Opportunity Act of 1964 (81 Stat. 688-690, 42 U.S.C. §§2763-2768, repealed by 86 Stat. 703 (1972)) "the United States Congress instituted Special Impact Programs with the intent to benefit the residents of certain neighborhoods having especially large concentrations of low income persons and suffering from dependency, chronic unemployment and rising tensions." Funds to administer these programs were appropriated to the United States Department of Labor. The department subsequently designated the East Los Angeles neighborhood as a "Special Impact area" and made federal funds available for contracts with local private industry for the benefit of the "hard-core unemployed residents" of East Los Angeles.

On January 17, 1969, the corporate defendants allegedly entered into contracts with the Secretary of Labor, acting on behalf of the Manpower Administration, United States Department of Labor (hereinafter referred to as the "Government"). Each such defendant entered into a separate contract and all three contracts are made a part of the complaint as exhibits. Under each contract the contracting defendant agreed to lease space in the then vacant Lincoln Heights jail building owned by the City of Los Angeles, to invest at least $5,000,000 in renovating the leasehold and establishing a facility for the manufacture of certain articles, to train and employ in such facility for at least 12 months, at minimum wage rates, a specified number of East Los Angeles residents certified as disadvantaged by the Government, and to provide such employees with opportunities for promotion into available supervisorial-managerial positions and with options to purchase stock in their employer corporation. Each contract provided for the lease of different space in the building and for the manufacture of a different kind of product. As consideration, the Government agreed to pay each defendant a stated amount in installments. Socoma was to hire 650 persons and receive $950,000; Lady Fair was to hire 550 persons and receive $999,000; and Monarch was to hire

400 persons and receive $800,000. The hiring of these persons was to be completed by January 17, 1970.

Plaintiffs were allegedly members of a class of no more than 2,017 East Los Angeles residents who were certified as disadvantaged and were qualified for employment under the contracts. Although the Government paid $712,500 of the contractual consideration to Socoma, $299,700 to Lady Fair, and $240,000 to Monarch, all of these defendants failed to perform under their respective contracts, except that Socoma provided 186 jobs of which 139 were wrongfully terminated, and Lady Fair provided 90 jobs, of which all were wrongfully terminated.

The complaint contains 11 causes of action. The second, fourth, and sixth causes of action seek damages of $3,607,500 against Socoma, $3,052,500 against Lady Fair, and $2,220,000 against Monarch, calculated on the basis of 12 months' wages at minimum rates and $1,000 for loss of training for each of the jobs the defendant contracted to provide. The third and fifth causes of action seek similar damages for the 139 persons whose jobs were terminated by Socoma and the 90 persons whose jobs were terminated by Lady Fair. The first, seventh, and eighth causes of action seek to impose joint liability on Socoma, Lady Fair, and Monarch as joint venturers, alleging that they negotiated the contracts through a common representative and entered into a joint lease of the Lincoln Heights jail building. The ninth, tenth, and eleventh causes of action seek to impose the liability of the corporate defendants upon their officers and directors named as individual defendants, alleging that the latter undercapitalized their respective corporations and used the same as their *alter egos*.

Each cause of action alleges that the "express purpose of the [Government] in entering into [each] contract was to benefit [the] certified disadvantaged hard-core unemployed residents of East Los Angeles [for whom defendants promised to provide training and jobs] and none other, and those residents are thus the express third party beneficiaries of [each] contract." . . .

Plaintiffs contend they are third party beneficiaries under Civil Code section 1559, which provides: "A contract, made expressly for the benefit of a third person, may be enforced by him at any time before the parties thereto rescind it." This section excludes enforcement of a contract by persons who are only incidentally or remotely benefited by it. (Lucas v. Hamm (1961) 56 Cal. 2d 583, 590, 15 Cal. Rptr. 821, 824, 364 P.2d 685, 688.) American law generally classifies persons having enforceable rights under contracts to which they are not parties as either creditor beneficiaries or donee beneficiaries. (Rest., Contracts, §§133, subds. (1), (2), 135, 136, 147; 2 Williston on Contracts (3d ed. 1959) §356; 4 Corbin on Contracts (1951) §774; see Rest. 2d Contracts (Tentative Drafts 1973) §133, coms. *b*, *c*.) California decisions follow this classification. (Southern Cal.

Gas Co. v. ABC Construction Co. (1962) 204 Cal. App. 2d 747, 752, 22 Cal. Rptr. 540; 1 Witkin, Summary of Cal. Law (8th ed. 1973) Contracts, §500.)

A person cannot be a creditor beneficiary unless the promisor's performance of the contract will discharge some form of legal duty owed to the beneficiary by the promisee. (Hartman Ranch Co. v. Associated Oil Co. (1937) 10 Cal. 2d 232, 244, 73 P.2d 1163; Rest., Contracts, §133, subd. (1)(b).) Clearly the Government (the promisee) at no time bore any legal duty toward plaintiffs to provide the benefits set forth in the contracts and plaintiffs do not claim to be creditor beneficiaries.

A person is a donee beneficiary only if the promisee's contractual intent is either to make a gift to him or to confer on him a right against the promisor. (Rest., Contracts, §133, subd. (1)(a).) If the promisee intends to make a gift, the donee beneficiary can recover if such donative intent must have been understood by the promisor from the nature of the contract and the circumstances accompanying its execution. (Lucas v. Hamm, *supra*, 56 Cal. 2d at pp. 590-591, 15 Cal. Rptr. 821, 364 P.2d 685.) This rule does not aid plaintiffs, however, because as will be seen, no intention to make a gift can be imputed to the Government as promisee.

Unquestionably plaintiffs were among those whom the Government intended to benefit through defendants' performance of the contracts which recite that they are executed pursuant to a statute and a presidential directive calling for programs to furnish disadvantaged persons with training and employment opportunities. However, the fact that a Government program for social betterment confers benefits upon individuals who are not required to render contractual consideration in return does not necessarily imply that the benefits are intended as gifts. Congress' power to spend money in aid of the general welfare (U.S. Const., art. I, §8) authorizes federal programs to alleviate national unemployment. (Helvering v. Davis (1937) 301 U.S. 619, 640-645, 57 S. Ct. 904, 81 L. Ed. 1307.) The benefits of such programs are provided not simply as gifts to the recipients but as a means of accomplishing a larger public purpose. The furtherance of the public purpose is in the nature of consideration to the Government, displacing any governmental intent to furnish the benefits as gifts. (See County of Alameda v. Janssen (1940) 16 Cal. 2d 276, 281, 106 P.2d 11; Allied Architects v. Payne (1923) 192 Cal. 431, 438-439, 221 P. 209.)

Even though a person is not the intended recipient of a gift, he may nevertheless be

> a donee beneficiary if it appears from the terms of the promise in view of the accompanying circumstances that the purpose of the promisee in obtaining the promise . . . is . . . to *confer upon him a right against the promisor* to some performance neither due nor supposed or asserted to be due from the promisee to the beneficiary.

(Rest., Contracts, §133, subd. (1)(a) (italics supplied); Gourmet Lane, Inc. v. Keller (1963) 222 Cal. App. 2d 701, 705, 35 Cal. Rptr. 398.) The Government may, of course, deliberately implement a public purpose by including provisions in its contracts which expressly confer on a specified class of third persons a direct right to benefits, or damages in lieu of benefits, against the private contractor. But a governmental intent to confer such a direct right cannot be inferred simply from the fact that the third persons were intended to enjoy the benefits. The Restatement of Contracts makes this clear in dealing specifically with contractual promises to the Government to render services to members of the public:

> A promisor bound to the United States or to a State or municipality by contract to do an act or render a service to some or all of the members of the public, *is subject to no duty* under the contract to such members to give compensation for the injurious consequences of performing or attempting to perform it, or of failing to do so, unless, . . . *an intention is manifested in the contract*, as interpreted in the light of the circumstances surrounding its formation, *that the promisor shall compensate members of the public for such injurious consequences.* . . .

(Rest., Contracts, §145 (italics supplied);[8] see City & County of San Francisco v. Western Air Lines, Inc. (1962) 204 Cal. App. 2d 105, 121, 22 Cal. Rptr. 216.)

The present contracts manifest no intent that the defendants pay damages to compensate plaintiffs or other members of the public for their nonperformance. To the contrary, the contracts' provisions for retaining the Government's control over determination of contractual disputes and for limiting defendants' financial risks indicate a governmental purpose to exclude the direct rights against defendants claimed here.

Each contract provides that any dispute of fact arising thereunder is to be determined by written decision of the Government's contracting officer, subject to an appeal to the Secretary of Labor, whose decision shall be final unless determined by a competent court to have been fraudulent, capricious, arbitrary, in bad faith, or not supported by substantial evidence. These administrative decisions may include determinations of related questions of law although such determinations are not made final.

---

8. The corresponding language in the Tentative Drafts of the Restatement Second of Contracts (1973), section 145, is:

> [A] promisor who contracts with a government or governmental agency to do an act for or render a service to the public *is not subject to contractual liability* to a member of the public for consequential damages resulting from performance or failure to perform unless . . . the terms of the promise provide for such liability. . . .

The language omitted in this quotation and the quotation in the accompanying text relates to the creditor beneficiary situation in which the government itself would be liable for non-performance of the contract. As noted earlier, plaintiffs do not claim to be creditor beneficiaries.

The efficiency and uniformity of interpretation fostered by these administrative procedures would tend to be undermined if litigation such as the
present action, to which the Government is a stranger, were permitted to
proceed on the merits.

In addition to the provisions on resolving disputes each contract contains a "liquidated damages" provision obligating the contractor to refund
all amounts received from the Government, with interest, in the event of
failure to acquire and equip the specified manufacturing facility, and, for
each employment opportunity it fails to provide, to refund a stated dollar
amount equivalent to the total contract compensation divided by the
number of jobs agreed to be provided. This liquidated damages provision
limits liability for the breaches alleged by plaintiffs to the refunding of
amounts received and indicates an absence of any contractual intent to
impose liability directly in favor of plaintiffs, or, as claimed in the complaint, to impose liability for the value of the promised performance. To
allow plaintiffs' claim would nullify the limited liability for which defendants bargained and which the Government may well have held out as an
inducement in negotiating the contracts.[9]

It is this absence of any manifestation of intent that defendants should
pay compensation for breach to persons in the position of plaintiffs that
distinguishes this case from Shell v. Schmidt (1954) 126 Cal. App. 2d 279,
272 P.2d 82, relied on by plaintiffs. The defendant in *Shell* was a building
contractor who had entered into an agreement with the federal government under which he received priorities for building materials and agreed
in return to use the materials to build homes with required specifications
for sale to war veterans at or below ceiling prices. Plaintiffs were 12
veterans, each of whom had purchased a home that failed to comply with
the agreed specifications. They were held entitled to recover directly
from the defendant contractor as third party beneficiaries of his agreement with the government. The legislation under which the agreement
was made included a provision empowering the government to obtain
payment of monetary compensation by the contractor to the veteran
purchasers for deficiencies resulting from failure to comply with speci-

---

9. Comment *a* of section 145 of the Tentative Drafts of the Restatement Second of
Contracts points out that these factors — retention of administrative control and limitation
of contractor's liability — make third party suits against the contractor inappropriate:

> Government contracts often benefit the public, but individual members of the public
> are treated as incidental beneficiaries unless a different intention is manifested. In
> case of doubt, a promise to do an act for or render a service to the public does not
> have the effect of a promise to pay consequential damages to individual members of
> the public unless the conditions of Subsection (2)(b) [including governmental liabil-
> ity to the claimant] are met. Among factors which may make inappropriate a direct
> action against the promisor are *arrangements for governmental control over the litiga-
> tion and settlement of claims, the likelihood of impairment of service or of excessive
> financial burden*, and the availability of alternatives such as insurance.

(Italics supplied.)

fications. Thus, there was "an intention . . . manifested in the contract . . . that the promisor shall compensate members of the public for such injurious consequences [of nonperformance]."[10]

Plaintiffs contend that section 145 of the Restatement of Contracts, previously quoted, does not preclude their recovery because it applies only to promises made to a governmental entity "to do an act or render a service to . . . the public," and, plaintiffs assert they and the class they represent are identified persons set apart from "the public." Even if this contention were correct it would not follow that plaintiffs have standing as third party beneficiaries under the Restatement. The quoted provision of section 145 "is a special application of the principles stated in §§133(1a), 135 [on donee beneficiaries]" (Rest., Contracts, §145, com. *a*), delineating certain circumstances which preclude government contractors' liability to third parties. Section 145 itself does not purport to confer standing to sue on persons who do not otherwise qualify under basic third party beneficiary principles.[11] As pointed out above, plaintiffs are not donee beneficiaries under those basic principles because it does not appear from the terms and circumstances of the contract that the Government intended to make a gift to plaintiffs or to confer on them a legal right against the defendants.

Moreover, contrary to plaintiffs' contention, section 145 of the Re-

---

10. In contrast to *Shell, supra*, is City & County of San Francisco v. Western Air Lines, Inc., *supra*, 204 Cal. App. 2d 105, 22 Cal. Rptr. 216. There, Western Air Lines claimed to be a third party beneficiary of agreements between the federal government and the City and County of San Francisco under which the city received federal funds for the development of its airport subject to a written condition that the airport "be available for public use on fair and reasonable terms and without unjust discrimination." Western Air Lines asserted that it had been charged for its use of the airport at a higher rate than some other air carriers in violation of the contractual condition, and therefore was entitled to recover the excess charges from the city. One of the reasons given by the court on appeal for rejecting this contention was the absence of any provision or indication of intent in the agreements between the government and the city to compensate third parties for noncompliance. The court said:

> The granting agreement in each instance entitles the [federal] administrator to recover all grant payments made where there has been any misrepresentation or omission of a material fact by the sponsor [i.e., the city]. We find no other provision for recovery of funds by the administrator and none whatsoever permitting recovery of money or excess rates by a private party. Indeed the language of the granting agreement itself appears to us to point up that it is simply and entirely a financial arrangement between two parties. As the agreement states, it constitutes "the obligations and rights of the United States and the Sponsor with respect to the accomplishment of the Project. . . ."

(204 Cal. App. 2d at p. 120, 22 Cal. Rptr. at p. 225.)

11. The same is true of the Tentative Draft of section 145 of the Restatement Second of Contracts which declares that the general rules on third party beneficiaries "apply to contracts with a government or governmental agency except to the extent that application would contravene the policy of the law authorizing the contract or prescribing remedies for its breach" and that "[i]n particular" the limitations of section 145, including those set forth in footnote 2, *supra*, apply to a government contractor's liability to a member of the public for nonperformance of a service to the public.

statement of Contracts does preclude their recovery because the services which the contracts required the defendants to perform *were* to be rendered to "members of the public" within the meaning of that section. Each contract recites it is made under the "Special Impact Programs" part of the Economic Opportunity Act of 1964 and pursuant to a presidential directive for a test program of cooperation between the federal government and private industry in an effort to provide training and jobs for thousands of the hard-core unemployed or under-employed. The congressional declaration of purpose of the Economic Opportunity Act as a whole points up the public nature of its benefits on a national scale. Congress declared that the purpose of the act was to "strengthen, supplement, and coordinate efforts in furtherance of [the] policy" of "opening to everyone the opportunity for education and training, the opportunity to work, and the opportunity to live in decency and dignity" so that the "United States can achieve its full economic and social potential as a nation." (42 U.S.C. §2701.)

In providing for special impact programs, Congress declared that such programs were directed to the solution of critical problems existing in particular neighborhoods having especially large concentration of low-income persons, and that the programs were intended to be of sufficient size and scope to have an appreciable impact in such neighborhoods in arresting tendencies toward dependency, chronic unemployment, and rising community tensions. (42 U.S.C. former §2763.) Thus the contracts here were designed not to benefit individuals as such but to utilize the training and employment of disadvantaged persons as a means of improving the East Los Angeles neighborhood. Moreover, the means by which the contracts were intended to accomplish this community improvement were not confined to provision of the particular benefits on which plaintiffs base their claim to damages — one year's employment at minimum wages plus $1,000 worth of training to be provided to each of 650 persons by one defendant, 400 by another, and 550 by another. Rather the objective was to be achieved by establishing permanent industries in which local residents would be permanently employed and would have opportunities to become supervisors, managers and part owners. The required minimum capital investment of $5,000,000 by each defendant and the defendants' 22-year lease of the former Lincoln Heights jail building for conversion into an industrial facility also indicates the broad, long-range objective of the program. Presumably, as the planned enterprises prospered, the quantity and quality of employment and economic opportunity that they provided would increase and would benefit not only employees but also their families, other local enterprises and the government itself through reduction of law enforcement and welfare costs.

The fact that plaintiffs were in a position to benefit more directly than certain other members of the public from performance of the contract does not alter their status as incidental beneficiaries. (See Rest., Contracts, §145, illus. 1: C, a member of the public cannot recover for injury from B's failure to perform a contract with the United States to carry mail over a certain route.)[12] For example, in City & County of San Francisco v. Western Air Lines, Inc., supra, 204 Cal. App. 2d 105, 22 Cal. Rptr. 216, the agreement between the federal government and the city for improvement of the airport could be considered to be of greater benefit to air carriers using the airport than to many other members of the public. Nevertheless, Western, as an air carrier, was but an incidental, not an express, beneficiary of the agreement and therefore had no standing to enforce the contractual prohibition against discrimination in the airport's availability for public use. The court explains the distinction as follows:

> None of the documents under consideration confers on Western the rights of a third-party beneficiary. The various contracts and assurances created benefits and detriments as between only two parties — the United States and the City. Nothing in them shows any intent of the contracting parties to confer any benefit directly and expressly upon air carriers such as the defendant. It is true that air carriers, including Western, may be *incidentally* benefited by City's assurances in respect to nondiscriminatory treatment at the airport. They may also be incidentally benefited by the fact that, through federal aid, a public airport is improved with longer runways, brighter beacons, or larger loading ramps, or by the fact a new public airport is provided for a community without one. The various documents and agreements were part of a federal aid program directed to the promoting of a national transportation system. Provisions in such agreements, including the nondiscrimination clauses, were intended to advance such federal aims and not for the benefit of those who might be affected by the sponsor's failure to perform.

(204 Cal. App. 2d at p. 120, 22 Cal. Rptr. at p. 225.)

For the reasons above stated we hold that plaintiffs and the class they represent have no standing as third party beneficiaries to recover the damages sought in the complaint under either California law or the general contract principles which federal law applies to government contracts.

The judgments of dismissal are affirmed.

McComb, Sullivan, and Clark, JJ., concur.

[In a strong dissenting opinion, joined by two other members of the court, Justice BURKE offered a different view of the California case law and the Restatement:]

In Lucas v. Hamm, 56 Cal. 2d 583, 590, 15 Cal. Rptr. 821, 364 P.2d 685, we noted that one of the usual characteristics of a third party benefi-

---

12. This illustration is repeated in Tentative Drafts, Restatement Second of Contracts, section 145, illustration 1.

ciary contract is that performance is to be rendered directly to the beneficiary. The direct benefits to accrue to the beneficiaries as enumerated above renders inescapable the conclusion that these are third party beneficiary contracts.

Although the contracts may also benefit particular communities and neighborhoods, this fact does not preclude the maintenance of the action by plaintiffs as intended beneficiaries of the contracts. It is not necessary under Civil Code section 1559, *supra*, that a contract be exclusively for the benefit of a third party to give him a right to enforce its provisions. (Hartman Ranch Co. v. Associated Oil Co., 10 Cal. 2d 232, 247, 73 P.2d 1163; Ralph C. Sutro Co. v. Paramount, 216 Cal. App. 2d 433, 437, 31 Cal. Rptr. 174). . . .

[N]or does the existence of a liquidated damages clause running in favor of the government defeat plaintiffs' right to recover under the contract; the fact that the government may also bring an action for the same breach does not bar the third party beneficiary from enforcing his rights. (Shell v. Schmidt, *supra*, 126 Cal. App. 2d 279, 290, 272 P.2d 82.) All that is necessary is that the third party show he is a member of a class for whose benefit the contract was made. (Shell v. Schmidt, *supra*; Ralph C. Sutro Co. v. Paramount, *supra*.) Thus, plaintiffs have standing to bring an action for the breach of defendants' contracts with the government.

The majority, relying on Restatement of Contracts section 145, and City and County of San Francisco v. Western Air Lines, Inc., 204 Cal. App. 2d 105, 22 Cal. Rptr. 216, contend that in the context of government contracts the intent to confer upon a third party a right of action against the promisor must be express; that intent "cannot be inferred simply from the fact that the third persons were intended to enjoy the benefits. . . ." (P. 589.) The majority insist that "The fact that plaintiffs were in a position to benefit more directly than certain other members of the public from performance of the contract does not alter their status as incidental beneficiaries." (P. 593.) The majority conclude (p. 592) that "section 145 of the Restatement of Contracts does preclude [plaintiffs'] recovery because the services which the contracts required the defendants to perform *were* to be rendered to 'members of the public' within the meaning of that section." (Italics added by majority.)

The majority's reliance on Restatement of Contracts section 145, and City and County of San Francisco v. Western Air Lines, Inc., *supra*, 204 Cal. App. 2d 105, 22 Cal. Rptr. 216, is misplaced. An analysis of section 145 of the Restatement (which also forms a part of the basis for the rule of *Western Air Lines*) indicates that its provisions are not applicable to the case at hand. Section 145 provides in pertinent part that

> A promisor bound to the United States or to a State or municipality by contract to do an act or render a service *to some or all of the members of the public*, is subject to no duty under the contract to *such members* to give

compensation for the injurious consequences of performing or attempting to perform it, or of failing to do so, unless,

> (a) an intention is manifested in the contract, as interpreted in the light of the circumstances surrounding its formation, that the promisor shall *compensate members of the public* for such injurious consequences. . . .

(Italics added.)

The express language of this provision indicates that it applies only to a promise to do an act or render a service to "some or all of the members of the public." The section deals solely with the promisor's duty to give compensation to "such" members of the public. The type of government contract to which section 145 applies is therefore distinguishable from the contracts in the instant case. Here, the contracts specify a particular class of persons who are to receive a direct benefit. The beneficiaries of these contracts are to receive the promised performance because of their membership in a particularly defined and limited class and not simply because they are members of the public in general. Defendants are not bound to "do an act or render a service to some or all of the members of the public"; thus, by its own terms, section 145 of the Restatement is not applicable.

In addition, as indicated by comment (*a*) to section 145 of the Restatement, that section is merely a special application of the principles stated in Restatement section 133 which provides in part that

> (1) Where performance of a promise in a contract will benefit a person other than the promisee, that person is, . . .
>
> (a) a donee beneficiary if it appears from the terms of the promise in view of the accompanying circumstances that the purpose of the promisee in obtaining the promise of all or part of the performance thereof is to make a gift to the beneficiary or to confer upon him a right against the promisor to some performance neither due nor supposed or asserted to be due from the promisee to the beneficiary. . . .

Section 135 of the Restatement makes such a contract enforceable by the donee beneficiary.

The language of section 133, standing alone, could reasonably suggest that members of the general public are "donee beneficiaries" under any contract whose purpose is to confer a "gift" upon them. Section 145 qualifies this broad language and treats the general public merely as incidental, not direct, beneficiaries under contracts made for the general public benefit, unless the contract manifests a clear intent to compensate such members of the public in the event of a breach. Section 145 does not, however, entirely preclude application of the "donee beneficiary" concept to every government contract. Whenever, as in the instant case, such a contract expresses an intent to benefit directly a particular person or ascertainable class of persons, section 145 is, by its terms, inapplicable and the contract may be enforced by the beneficiaries pursuant to the general provisions of section 133. Thus, I would conclude that section 145 is consistent with the holding of Shell v. Schmidt, *supra*, 126 Cal. App. 2d 279, 272 P.2d 82, and the City and County of San Francisco v. Western Air Lines, Inc., *supra*, 204 Cal. App. 2d 105, 22 Cal. Rptr. 216.[13]

In City and County of San Francisco v. Western Air Lines, Inc., *supra*, 204 Cal. App. 2d 105, 22 Cal. Rptr. 216, defendant airline was held to be merely an incidental beneficiary of contracts providing that an airport "'will operate . . . for the use and benefit *of the public,* on fair and reasonable terms and without unjust discrimination.'" (P. 118, 22 Cal. Rptr. p. 224, italics added.) Nothing in the various contracts and assurances involved in the case "shows any intent of the contracting parties to confer any benefit directly and expressly upon air carriers such as the defendant." (P. 120, 22 Cal. Rptr. p. 225.) The court stated that "To recover as a third party beneficiary, one must show that the contract in question was made expressly for his benefit. [Citations.]" (P. 120, 22 Cal. Rptr. p. 225.) . . .

Since in *Western Air Lines* the government contract at issue was not made expressly for the benefit of defendant but instead to benefit the general public, that case was correctly decided under Restatement of Contracts section 145. However, an interpretation to which the contracts

---

13. The tentative draft of section 145 in Restatement 2d, Contracts (The American Law Institute, Restatement of the Law Second, Contracts, Tentative Draft No. 3 [April 18, 1967], p. 76), also supports the conclusion that this provision of the Restatement does not bar plaintiff's action. The tentative draft states:

> In particular, a promisor who contracts with a government or governmental agency to *do an act for or render a service to the public* is not subject to contractual liability to a member of the public for consequential damages resulting from performance or failure to perform unless (a) the terms of the promise provide for such liability; or (b) the promisee is subject to liability to the member of the public for the damages and a direct action against the promisor is consistent with the terms of the contract and with the policy of the law authorizing the contract and prescribing remedies for its breach.

(Italics added.) Comment *a* to the draft of section 145 explains the rationale for the section in part as follows: "Subsection (2) applies to a particular class of contracts the classification of beneficiaries in §133. Government contracts often benefit the public, *but individual members of the public are treated as incidental beneficiaries unless a different intention is manifested.*" (Italics added.)

Comment *c* to the tentative draft of section 145 states further that "Government contractors sometimes make explicit promises to pay damages to third persons, and such promises are enforced. If there is no explicit promise, and no government liability, *the question whether a particular claimant is an intended beneficiary is one of interpretation, depending on all the circumstances of the contract.*" (Italics added.) Thus, under the tentative draft, section 145 is not an outright prohibition of the enforcement of government contracts by third parties absent the enumerated conditions. Comment *c* makes it clear that the question as to a particular claimant is one of interpretation, and that, where, as here, the contract manifests an intent to benefit a particular third party, liability is properly imposed upon the promisee in favor of such third party.

in the instant case "are reasonably susceptible and which is pleaded in the complaint or could be pleaded by proper amendment" (maj. opin. p. 588), in light of the legislative intent and the language of the contracts themselves, is that they were made expressly for the benefit of a particular class of persons, namely the class consisting of the certified hard-core unemployed of East Los Angeles. . . .

NOTE

1. The material covered by the Tentative Draft of §145 of the Restatement Second, discussed by the court in its opinion, is now contained in Restatement Second §§302 and 313.

2. In Zigas v. Superior Court of Calif., 120 Cal. App. 3d 827, 174 Cal. Rptr. 806 (1981), a group of tenants living in a building that had been financed with a federally insured mortgage brought an action against their landlords, seeking damages for an alleged breach of a provision in their landlord's financing agreement with the Department of Housing and Urban Development. Among other things, the agreement forbade the charging of rents in excess of those set out in a HUD-approved schedule. The plaintiffs claimed their landlords, in violation of this provision, had collected excessive rents of more than two million dollars. The trial court dismissed the action on the grounds that the plaintiffs had no right to enforce the provisions of a contract between their landlords and the federal government. On appeal, it was held that the tenants did indeed have a cause of action, under the law of California, as third party beneficiaries. After a lengthy examination of the relevant precedents (in particular, Martinez v. Socoma and Shell v. Schmidt), Justice Feinberg summarized the court's reasons for upholding the plaintiffs' right to sue:

> 1. In *Martinez*, the contract between the government and Socoma provided that if Socoma breached the agreement, Socoma would refund to the government that which the government had paid Socoma pursuant to the contract between them. Thus, it is clear in *Martinez* that it was the government that was out of pocket as a consequence of the breach and should be reimbursed therefor, not the people to be trained and given jobs. In the case at bench, as in *Shell*, the government suffered no loss as a consequence of the breach, it was the renter here and the veteran purchaser in *Shell* that suffered the direct pecuniary loss.
>
> 2. Unlike *Martinez*, too, in the case at bench, no governmental administrative procedure was provided for the resolution of disputes arising under the agreement. Thus, to permit this litigation would in no way affect the "efficiency and uniformity of interpretation fostered by these administrative procedures." (Martinez v. Socoma Companies, Inc., supra, 11 Cal. 3d at p. 402, 113 Cal. Rptr. 585, 521 P.2d 841.) On the contrary, as we earlier noted, lawsuits such as this promote the federal interest by inducing compliance with HUD agreements.

3. In *Martinez*, the court held that "To allow plaintiffs' claim would nullify the limited liability for which defendants bargained and which the Government may well have held out as an inducement in negotiating the contracts." (At p. 403, 113 Cal. Rptr. 585, 521 P.2d 841, fn. omitted.) Here, there is no "limited liability." As we shall point out, real parties are liable under the agreement, *without limitation*, for breach of the agreement.

4. Further, in *Martinez*, the contracts "were designed not to benefit individuals as such but to utilize the training and employment of disadvantaged persons as a means of improving the East Los Angeles neighborhood." (At p. 406, 113 Cal. Rptr. 585, 521 P.2d 841.) Moreover, the training and employment programs were but one aspect of a "broad, long-range objective" (*id.*) contemplated by the agreement and designed to benefit not only those to be trained and employed but also "other local enterprises and the government itself through reduction of law enforcement and welfare costs." (*Id.*)

Here, on the other hand, as in *Shell*, the purpose of the Legislature and of the contract between real parties and HUD is narrow and specific: to provide moderate rental housing for families with children; in *Shell*, to provide moderate priced homes for veterans.

5. Finally, we believe the agreement itself manifests an intent to make tenants direct beneficiaries, *not* incidental beneficiaries, of [the landlords'] promise to charge no more than the HUD approved rent schedule.

Section 4(a) and 4(c) of the agreement, providing that there can be no increase in rental fees, over the approved rent schedule, without the prior approval in writing of HUD, were obviously designed to protect the tenant against arbitrary increases in rents, precisely that which is alleged to have occurred here. Certainly, it was not intended to benefit the Government as a guarantor of the mortgage. . . .

Id. at 837-839, 174 Cal. Rptr. at 811-812.
Justice Feinberg noted in conclusion that

it would be unconscionable if a builder could secure the benefits of a government guaranteed loan upon his promise to charge no more than a schedule of rents he had agreed to and then find there is no remedy by which the builder can be forced to disgorge rents he had collected in excess of his agreement simply because the Government had failed to act.

Id. at 841, 174 Cal. Rptr. at 813.
Do you think the California cases are reconcilable, as Justice Feinberg suggests? In attempting to resolve the issues posed by cases like *Martinez* and *Zigas*, is the terminology proposed by the two Restatements an aid, or a source of mischief?

3. In the *Moch* case, the water company made a contract with the city to supply water at the city's hydrants. In *Zigas*, the landlord-mortgagors made a promise to the federal government to abide by the terms of HUD's rent schedule. In the latter case, however, there was also a contractual relation between promisor and beneficiary (though, apparently,

not one that by its own terms required the landlords to observe the rent restrictions imposed by HUD). Does this help to explain or justify the different outcome in the two cases? Was there a contractual relation between promisor and beneficiary in *Martinez*? Does the existence of such a relation necessarily mean that the beneficiary is a creditor beneficiary or even an intended beneficiary? Traditionally, third party beneficiary doctrine has evaluated the rights of the beneficiary on the basis of his relation to the promisee; *Moch* and *Zigas* suggest, however, that the beneficiary's relation to the promisor may be of equal importance.

4. The Supreme Court of Delaware put the doctrine of third party beneficiaries to unusual use in Blair v. Anderson, 325 A.2d 94 (Del. 1974). Plaintiff, a federal prisoner, was incarcerated in a Delaware state prison under a contract between the federal and state government according to which the federal government was to pay for the maintenance and support of federal offenders placed in the state's institutions. In return, the state agreed, among other things, to assume responsibility for the safety of the federal inmates. After being attacked by a fellow prisoner, plaintiff sued the state for damages in both contract and tort. The tort claim was barred by sovereign immunity, but the contract claim was permitted. The court, after finding that the state had waived sovereign immunity as to claims arising from the contract, argued: "while there may be semantic concerns about calling a prisoner a 'creditor' or 'beneficiary' (or both) of a Federal-State incarceration contract, the point is that plaintiff was the very subject of the agreement between the governments." Would you describe plaintiff as an intended beneficiary of the contracting parties? If so, what damages would you award for Delaware's violation of its contract with the federal government? In distinguishing *Zigas* from *Martinez*, Justice Feinberg partly relied on the fact that the federal job training program at issue in the latter case included "an administrative procedure . . . for the resolution of disputes." Blair presents a similar question: If the inmates have no standing to sue on the contract, will its policy be enforced?

HOLBROOK v. PITT

643 F.2d 1261 (7th Cir. 1981)

CUDAHY, Circuit Judge.

This is an appeal by tenants of certain housing projects in Wisconsin who are beneficiaries of housing assistance payments made by the United States Department of Housing and Urban Development ("HUD") under its housing assistance program for existing multifamily projects benefiting from HUD-insured or HUD-held mortgages. This program was established pursuant to Section 8 of the United States Housing Act of 1937 (as amended by §201(a) of the Housing and Community Development Act of

1974), 42 U.S.C. §1437f (1976) ("Section 8"). Under this program, HUD executes contracts with project owners to make rental payments on behalf of eligible low-income tenants (the "Contracts"). Appellants contend they are entitled to these rent subsidies within a reasonable time after the effective date of the Contracts between HUD and the various project owners. The tenants also argue that the rent subsidies should be made retroactive to the effective dates of the respective Contracts. Appellants further claim that HUD's procedures for making rental assistance payments violate the Due Process clause of the Fifth Amendment to the United States Constitution.

The district court granted summary judgment in favor of the Secretary of HUD (the "Secretary"), who was the third-party defendant, finding that the tenants had no claim under the Contracts since no provisions of the Contracts were breached. The district court also found that the tenants' interest in receiving housing assistance payments was only a "subjective expectancy" which was not entitled to due process protection. We hold that the Contracts were breached and that the tenants can recover retroactive benefits as third-party beneficiaries; we also find that tenants in existing HUD-insured projects assisted under Section 8 are generally entitled to housing assistance benefits within a reasonable time after the effective date of the applicable Section 8 Contract. We further determine that appellants have a legitimate claim of entitlement to housing assistance payments as of the effective dates of the Contracts. We therefore reverse and remand. . . .

Plaintiff Holbrook lived with her four minor children in Milwaukee, Wisconsin in Main Street Gardens, a housing development owned by Henry Pitt. On June 10, 1976, HUD and Pitt executed a Section 8 Contract under which housing assistance payments were to be paid to Pitt's eligible tenants, including Holbrook. Under the Contract, HUD committed funds to make housing assistance payments on behalf of eligible tenants as of June 1976. Funds were not disbursed under the Contract, however, until Pitt certified to HUD the names of the eligible tenants and the amount of subsidy to which each was entitled.

Despite prodding by Holbrook and HUD, a Section 8 application, and eligibility and certification forms were not mailed by Pitt to residents of Main Street Gardens until November 16, 1976. Holbrook and other eligible families at Main Street Gardens were then certified and received Section 8 payments beginning December 1976. But, at the time of certification, no retroactive payments were made, as were authorized and for which funds had been set aside. . . .

The regulations applicable to the making of housing assistance payments on behalf of tenants in projects subject to HUD-insured mortgages are found at 24 C.F.R. §886 (1980). These regulations, together with HUD's program instruction handbook, establish the policies and procedures pursuant to which HUD makes housing assistance payments for projects with HUD-insured mortgages. The heart of this Section 8 subprogram is the Contract between HUD and the owner, which governs the relationship between the contracting parties and defines the rights and duties of the owner with respect to the administration of the Section 8 subprogram.

Prior to execution of a Contract, the owner must submit information regarding the gross income, number of household members under age 18 and rent-to-income ratio for each resident household, present vacancies and any rental increases currently being processed by HUD. At the time a Contract is executed, HUD commits funds to that project. The dollar amount of HUD's maximum commitment of funds is set at 75 percent of the current HUD-approved rents for the units expected to receive Section 8 subsidies. These units include the units occupied by families whose gross incomes and rent payments would appear to make them eligible for Section 8 assistance as well as the units that were vacant when the owner applied for a Contract. This calculation of the maximum contract commitment can include a proposed rent increase if HUD anticipates its approval.

Pursuant to paragraph 1.9c of the model Contract, the owner is responsible for determining and verifying the eligibility of families, processing necessary application and verification forms, selecting families who will receive Section 8 assistance, and computing the amount of housing assistance payments to be made on their behalf, a process denominated as "certification." Upon the completion of certification of eligible families by the owner, HUD makes housing assistance payments to owners on behalf of tenants in accordance with the provisions of the Contract. . . .

Although HUD imposes no duty on owners to submit certifications at any specified time, HUD regulations allow housing assistance payments to be made as of the effective date of the Contract and funds are committed by HUD to provide for payments from that date. 24 C.F.R. §886.108 (1980). HUD, however, has refused to make housing assistance payments on behalf of tenants for the period between the effective date of the Contract and the month in which tenants are certified by the project owner, unless the owner provides for proper certification (termed "retroactive certification") for the intervening months.

After the effective date of a Contract, but before the initiation of housing assistance payments, HUD provides no administrative process for determining a tenant's eligibility to receive housing assistance payments. Nor does an administrative procedure exist whereby an eligible (whether certified or uncertified) family may, in appropriate circumstances, challenge either a project owner's initial delay in certifying eligible tenants for payments or an owner's unwillingness or refusal to certify tenants for payments retroactive to the Contract date.

1. TENANTS' THIRD-PARTY BENEFICIARY CLAIM

In Count II, the tenant class asserted their rights as third-party beneficiaries of the Contracts executed between HUD and the owners. The tenants sought prompt implementation of the Contracts as well as the receipt of retroactive benefits. The district court declined to rule on the third-party beneficiary issue but found that, in any event, the Contracts had not been breached since HUD had no contractual duty to pay benefits from the effective dates of the Contracts. Holbrook v. Pitt, 479 F. Supp. 990, 994 (E.D. Wis. 1979).

Plaintiffs' approach in this case seems to have made analysis of their claims for retroactive benefits unnecessarily difficult. They argue that HUD has improperly administered the Section 8 program by totally delegating certification responsibilities to the owners. While this argument may have merit in the context of a claim that HUD has failed to meet its Section 8 obligations, it is only obliquely related to plaintiffs' claim that HUD has breached the Contracts before us.

In her original action, Holbrook had named Pitt, the owner of her building, as defendant. Pitt was dismissed from this action when he certified Holbrook for retroactive benefits and those benefits were paid to Holbrook by HUD. The other Wisconsin project owners who had executed Contracts with HUD were not named as defendants, however, when plaintiff subsequently asserted her class claim. Yet, since the Contracts place the obligation to certify tenants on the owners, it is not HUD but the owners who have most clearly breached the duty to properly certify the tenants. Despite this discrepancy, however, we have concluded that tenants can recover retroactive benefits because HUD breached its obligation to properly administer the Contracts by accepting non-retroactive certifications from the owners.

Under settled principles of federal common law, a third party may have enforceable rights under a contract if the contract was made for his direct benefit. . . . If the agreement was not intended to benefit the third party, however, he is viewed as an "incidental" beneficiary, having no legally cognizable rights under the contract.[14] German Alliance Insurance Co. v. Home Water Supply Co., 226 U.S. 220, 33 S. Ct. 32, 57 L. Ed. 195 (1912); Williams v. Fenix & Scisson, Inc., 608 F.2d at 1208; 4 A. Corbin,

14. Consistent with the scheme set forth in the Restatement of Contracts §133 (1932), most court decisions have recognized three classes of third-party beneficiaries — donee, creditor and incidental — with different rules governing the rights of each class. It has been suggested, for example, that a contracting party's "intent to benefit" a third party is relevant if the third party is viewed as a donee beneficiary, but not if the third party is viewed as a creditor beneficiary. Isbrandtsen Co. v. Local 1291, Int'l Longshoremen's Ass'n, 204 F.2d 495, 497 n.11 (3d Cir. 1953).

We decline to follow this approach, since it fails to focus on the central interpretative question involved in third-party beneficiary problems: did the contracting parties intend that the third party benefit from the contract? We prefer the approach of the Restatement

Corbin on Contracts, §776 at 18-19 (1951); Restatement of Contracts, §133 at 151-52 (1932).

To determine whether plaintiffs have enforceable rights under the Contracts we must analyze the purposes underlying their formation. Plaintiffs maintain that HUD executed the Contracts in order to provide rental assistance to low income families. HUD, however, claims that plaintiffs are only incidental beneficiaries of the Contracts, since the primary purpose of the Section 8 program, and the Contracts entered into pursuant thereto, was to benefit financially troubled HUD-insured projects. We reject this argument, as it is contradicted by the language of Section 8, relevant legislative history, HUD's implementing regulations and interpretations and the terms of the Contracts.[15] HUD's position displays an astonishing lack of perspective about government social welfare programs. If the tenants are not the primary beneficiaries of a program designed to provide housing assistance payments to low income families, the legitimacy of the multi-billion dollar Section 8 program is placed in grave doubt.

Congress did not establish the Section 8 housing assistance program merely to limit claims on HUD's insurance fund that might be occasioned by assignments or foreclosures of HUD-insured mortgages. Congress authorized Section 8 payments "[f]or the purpose of aiding

---

(Second) of Contracts §133 (Tent. Draft No. 4, 1968), which divides beneficiaries into two classes — intended and incidental. Section 133 provides:

(1)   Unless otherwise agreed between promisor and promisee, a beneficiary of a promise is an intended beneficiary if recognition of a right to performance in the beneficiary is appropriate to effectuate the intention of the parties and either
   (a)   the performance of the promise will satisfy an obligation of the promisee to pay money to the beneficiary; or
   (b)   the promisee manifests an intention to give the beneficiary the benefit of the promised performance.
(2)   An incidental beneficiary is a beneficiary who is not an intended beneficiary.

We also decline to adopt the Restatement's position to the extent it may suggest that only the intentions of the "promisee" (the party through whom the beneficiary claims) and not the "promisor" (the party obligated to render performance that benefits the third party) are relevant to a determination of the third-party beneficiary's rights. Contracts are the product of shared intentions, and a promisor should be bound only by those objectively manifested intentions of the promisee to which the promisor has implicitly or explicitly assented. It is improper to neglect the reasonable expectations of the promisor, since the burden of the agreement to the promisor, and therefore the consideration he will require, may vary according to the number of parties who have enforceable rights under the contract. See generally Jones, Legal Protection of Third Party Beneficiaries: On Opening Courthouse Doors, 46 Cinn. L. Rev. 313 (1977).

15. We believe the legislative history and purpose of the Section 8 program may properly be used to interpret the parties' intentions. It is evident from the terms of the Contract that HUD, in executing the Contract, is acting to fulfill the objectives of the Section 8 program. The Contract itself is entitled "Section 8 Housing Assistance Payments Program" and Part I of the Contract expressly states that the "contract is entered into pursuant to the United States Housing Act of 1937." Cf. Inglewood v. Los Angeles, 451 F.2d 948, 955 (9th Cir. 1972); Feir v. Carabetta Enterprises, Inc., 459 F. Supp. 841, 848 n.3 (D. Conn. 1978).

lower-income families in obtaining a decent place to live and of promoting economically mixed housing." 42 U.S.C. §1437f(a) (1976).

Section 8 is designed to provide rent subsidies to needy families. If Congress had intended to design Section 8 primarily to assist financially troubled projects (rather than low-income families), it would have provided that Contracts would be awarded and funding structured in accordance with the financial condition of the housing projects. Instead, it provided that Section 8 funds should be allocated according to the financial needs of the tenants. The statue does not establish a preference for projects that may soon be in default on HUD-insured mortgages, but it does provide that 30 percent of the families assisted by Section 8 funds must be "very low-income families," 42 U.S.C. §1437f(c)(7) (1976), which are defined as "those families whose incomes do not exceed 50 per centum of the median income for the area." 42 U.S.C. §1437f(f)(2) (1976).

HUD has also recognized that the function of the Section 8 subprogram we are considering is to assist low income families in securing decent, safe and sanitary housing. Thus, HUD's introduction to the regulations that established this subprogram provides:

> The purpose of this program is to assist families presently in occupancy in a HUD-insured or HUD-assisted project to more easily carry their rental burden.

42 Fed.Reg. 5602 (Jan. 28, 1977).

HUD's regulations further demonstrate that the Section 8 program is designed primarily to benefit low-income families. Under the regulations, a Contract may be executed only after a project owner establishes that a significant number of existing or potential tenants are "eligible for and in need of Section 8 assistance." 24 C.F.R. §886.107(d) (1980). And, when a Contract is executed, HUD calculates and budgets funds not on the basis of the financial needs of the project's management but on the estimated rental assistance needs of eligible tenants.

The Contract terms also demonstrate that the tenants are intended beneficiaries of the Contracts. Paragraph 1.3(b)(1) provides, in part:

> The Government hereby agrees to make housing assistance payments on behalf of Families for the Contract Units, to enable such Families to lease Decent, Safe, and Sanitary housing pursuant to Section 8 of the Act.

Numerous other Contract provisions make it clear that the Contracts were executed primarily for the tenants' benefit. Paragraph 1.7, for example, requires the owners to "maintain and operate the Contract unit and related facilities so as to provide Decent, Safe and Sanitary housing." *See also* paragraph 1.9(a) (requiring affirmative action in owner's marketing of units and selection of families); paragraph 1.9(b) (restricting owner's discretion regarding the collection and refunding of utility and security deposits); paragraph 1.10 (restricting owner's right to evict tenants).

HUD, of course, perceives that the Section 8 program also serves to minimize claims on its insurance fund. The creation of a separate Section 8 subprogram exclusively for projects with HUD-insured mortgages is compelling evidence of this perception. It is also apparent from the introduction to HUD's Handbook, which reads:

> The Section 8 set-aside program for existing multifamily projects benefiting from HUD-insured or HUD-held mortgages . . . is designed to accomplish two goals: (1) reduce the claims on HUD's insurance funds by stabilizing the finances of projects intended for low and moderate income residents by avoiding project mortgage assignments or, in projects with assigned mortgages, by preventing foreclosure and (2) assure the continued availability of units in these existing multifamily projects to the lower income families for whom they were intended by reducing to affordable levels the rent obligation of assisted families.

We do not decide whether it is proper for HUD, in allocating Section 8 funds, to give priority to projects with serious financial problems. We believe, however, that this preference does not contradict the fact that the Contracts before us are intended primarily to benefit needy tenants. Plaintiffs have enforceable rights since the Contracts were intended to provide them with rental assistance. Subsidiary purposes, such as HUD's interest in minimizing claims on its insurance funds, do not defeat plaintiffs' status as protected beneficiaries. *See* King v. National Industries, Inc., 512 F.2d 29, 32 (6th Cir. 1975); Avco Delta Corp. v. United States, 484 F.2d 692, 702 (7th Cir. 1973), *cert. denied,* 415 U.S. 931, 94 S. Ct. 1444, 39 L. Ed. 2d 490 (1974); Beck v. Reynolds Metals Co., 163 F.2d 870, 871 (7th Cir. 1947).

Having concluded that plaintiffs have enforceable rights under the Contracts, we must determine whether the Contracts have been breached. The district court held that HUD did not violate any provision of the Contracts, since "it is the owner who is given the responsibility to effect certifications of eligibility, and there is no contract provision requiring HUD to make assistance payments until the necessary certifications [including retroactive certifications] are performed." *Holbrook v. Pitt,* 479 F. Supp. at 993. Because they are somewhat distinct, we will consider first the question whether HUD breached the Contracts because the tenants were not promptly certified, and second, the question whether HUD breached the Contracts because the tenants were not retroactively certified.

The district court refused to imply a Contract term that would require the owners to certify tenants within a reasonable time after execution of the Contract. We believe it is appropriate to imply such a term, since the purpose of the Contracts to provide housing assistance to lower income families would otherwise be frustrated. We agree with the district court, however, that *HUD* did not breach the Contracts with respect to the timing of certification.

The district court relied on paragraph 1.9(c) (Eligibility, Selection and Admission of Families) . . . and on paragraph 1.11(a) (Reduction of Number of Contract Units for Failure to Lease to Eligible Families) . . . of the Contracts in deciding that there was no contractual duty to certify tenants promptly. Paragraph 1.9(c), however, merely allocates the certification function to the owner. It does not address the form which certifications are to take, the date by which certifications are to be performed or the period of time certifications are intended to cover. Although paragraph 1.9(c) is silent on the question of time of performance, it is reasonably inferrable from the purpose of the Contract that the owner is obligated to perform his certification responsibilities within a reasonable time. . . .

Since all the tenants in the class designated in Count II have been certified, it is not necessary to determine what would be a reasonable time to perform certification under the circumstances of this case. *Cf.* A. M. R. Enterprises, Inc. v. United States Postal Savings Association, 567 F.2d 1277, 1281 (5th Cir. 1978). In any event, although we have implied a Contract term requiring prompt certification, we believe that the owners, and not HUD, breached this implied term, since HUD had no mechanism (in the Contracts before us) to force the owners promptly to certify tenants.

With respect to retroactive certification, the district court held that plaintiffs could not recover retroactive benefits because HUD was not "*required,* by the terms of the contract or otherwise, to pay retroactive benefits." Holbrook v. Pitt, 479 F. Supp. at 994. The court also refused to imply from the Contract that retroactive certification was required, finding again that paragraph 1.9(c) set "the terms and conditions of performance." *Id.* Yet we believe that paragraph 1.9(c) must be interpreted quite differently than the district court suggests. Paragraph 1.9(c) provides only that the owner is "responsible for . . . computation of the amount of housing assistance payments on behalf of each selected Family." It does not set forth the period for which housing assistance payments are to be requested or paid. It certainly does not suggest that the obligation to compute housing assistance payments includes the right to arbitrarily deny to tenants benefits from the date of Contract execution. The very use of the word "computation" connotes the application of a formula to numbers, not the exercise of discretion — either arbitrary or informed.

We believe it is necessary to interpret the language of paragraph 1.9(c) to mean that retroactive certification is required. First, "computation" is a mathematical process presumably involving, *inter alia*, the multiplication of the amount of rental subsidy to which a particular tenant is entitled by the number of months the subsidy is due; the Contract language in no way suggests that the number of months is a matter of discretion. Rather, that number must be the number of months the tenant has lived in the project since the Contract governing Section 8 payments was executed (and funds were set aside). Second, unless the language is construed to require retroactive payment, the primary purpose of the Contracts to provide housing assistance to low income families would be frustrated. HUD has not offered any justification for its policy of accepting certifications that do not provide for retroactive benefits covering all relevant months, and we can perceive no circumstances that would justify such a policy.

HUD's calculation of the dollar amount of financial assistance it sets aside in a project account is based on the estimated monthly rental assistance needs of specific tenants beginning with the month in which the Contract is executed. HUD, therefore, has committed funds to pay housing assistance payments from the first day of the Contract period.[16]

Although the owners may exercise limited discretion with regard to the selection of those families that are to receive benefits, the owners' obligation to "compute" the amount of housing assistance payments is entirely ministerial. No reason has been suggested for allowing the owners to determine whether tenants will or will not receive retroactive benefits. Therefore, by accepting deficient computations from the owners, we

16. By segregating funds exclusively to pay rent subsidies on behalf of particular tenants, HUD has created an identifiable res to which the tenants have a claim in the nature of the equitable lien imposed in Bennett Construction Co. v. Allen Gardens, Inc., 433 F. Supp. 825 (W.D. Mo. 1977).

Bennett Construction involved the rights of a general contractor — a third-party beneficiary — to enforce the terms of a construction loan agreement between HUD as assignee of a mortgage and a mortgagor project owner in default. The general contractor had completed construction and was owed certain undisbursed loan proceeds. *Bennett Construction* is like the instant case in that the mortgagor through whom the general contractor claimed was assertedly not entitled to performance in two respects: (1) it had not gone to final closing of the construction loan and (2) it was in default. These defects are analogous to the failure of the project owners in the instant case to certify tenants retroactively. *Bennett Construction* is, however, unlike the instant case in that the general contractor there was a *creditor* third-party beneficiary, and failure to impress the undisbursed loan proceeds with an equitable lien would have resulted in the unjust enrichment of HUD. "Unjust enrichment" is only at issue here to the extent that HUD might be said to be "enriched" by the opportunity to retain set-aside funds and to the extent that it is "unjust" to deny retroactive benefits to tenants who may have reasonably relied on receiving them.

In any case, *Bennett Construction* and the instant case are similar in that (1) there is an identifiable res (in *Bennett Construction* the undisbursed loan proceeds and here the set-aside funds) and (2) HUD in both cases is the "guiding spirit" and the dominant force. In *Bennett Construction*, the mortgagor owner was the "creature of HUD," 433 F. Supp. at 835. Here the project owners have (or should have) no meaningful discretion regarding the decision to pay retroactive benefits. Based on these similarities we think there are persuasive reasons for regarding the funds set aside by HUD as impressed with a lien dictated by the policy of the Section 8 program in favor of the tenants from the execution dates of the Contracts. It is unjust to deny tenants the funds set aside specifically for their benefit solely because of the capricious decisions of their project owners not to make their certifications retroactive.

believe HUD breached its obligation to properly administer the Contracts, *see* 24 C.F.R. §886.120(a) (1980), and its coordinate responsibility to third-party beneficiaries to fulfill the purposes of the Contracts, i.e., to provide full assistance benefits to certified families. Appellants can therefore recover retroactive benefits from HUD as third-party beneficiaries of the Contracts.

[In the remainder of its opinion, the court considered the plaintiffs' due process claim, concluding that they had a constitutional entitlement to be notified promptly of their right to receive retroactive payments as well as a right to "some sort of hearing" before such payments could be denied. In a footnote, the court observed that its decision "to provide appellants with due process protection" was "largely superfluous" given its conclusion that the tenants suing for relief had "enforceable rights to retroactive benefits as beneficiaries under the contracts."]

NOTE

1. Over twenty years ago, Professor Charles Reich wrote:

> One of the most important developments in the United States during the past decade has been the emergence of government as a major source of wealth. Government is a gigantic syphon. It draws in revenue and power, and pours forth wealth: money, benefits, services, contracts, franchises, and licenses. Government has always had this function. But while in early times it was minor, today's distribution of largess is on a vast, imperial scale.
>
> The valuables dispensed by government take many forms, but they all share one characteristic. They are steadily taking the place of traditional forms of wealth — forms which are held as private property. Social insurance substitutes for savings; a government contract replaces a businessman's customers and goodwill. The wealth of more and more Americans depends upon a relationship to government. Increasingly, Americans live on government largess — allocated by government on its own terms, and held by recipients subject to conditions which express "the public interest."

The New Property, 73 Yale L.J. 733, 733 (1964).
Professor Reich defined the main features of this emerging system of government largess, which he termed a "new feudalism," as follows:

> (1) Increasingly we turn over wealth and rights to government, which reallocates and redistributes them in the many forms of largess; (2) there is a merging of public and private, in which lines of private ownership are blurred; (3) the administration of the system has given rise to special laws and special tribunals, outside the ordinary structure of government; (4) the right to possess and use government largess is bound up with the recipient's

legal status; status is both the basis for receiving largess and a consequence of receiving it; hence the new wealth is not readily transferable; (5) individuals hold the wealth conditionally rather than absolutely; the conditions are usually obligations owed to the government or to the public, and may include the obligation of loyalty to the government; the obligations may be changed or increased at the will of the state; (6) for breach of condition the wealth may be forfeited or escheated back to the government; (7) the sovereign power is shared with large private interests; (8) the object of the whole system is to enforce "the public interest" — the interest of the state or society or the lord paramount — by means of the distribution and use of wealth in such a way as to create and maintain dependence. . . .

Id. at 770.

To protect individuals from an "all-pervasive system of regulation and control," Professor Reich urged that "those forms of largess which are closely linked to status . . . be deemed to be held as of right." Only in this way, he argued, would it be possible to create "a zone of privacy for each individual beyond which neither government nor private power can push. . . ." (Id. at 785.) In a memorable conclusion, he declared, "[j]ust as the Homestead Act was a deliberate effort to foster individual values at an earlier time, so we must try to build an economic basis for liberty today — a Homestead Act for rootless twentieth century man. We must create a new property." Id. at 787.

Does the expansive use of the third party beneficiary idea, in cases like *Holbrook*, belong to the general movement that Professor Reich describes? To what extent has the idea retained its contractual character in the process of its expansion?

3. Social contract theorists seek to explain the obligations of citizenship in contractual terms. Not all of them, however, view the relation between citizen and state as itself a contractual one. Hobbes, for example, vigorously denied this could ever be the case. According to Hobbes, the covenant that establishes the commonwealth is one made by each citizen with each other; the sovereign himself is not a party to the contract but is merely the agreed-upon agent or bystander to whom each of the citizens promises to relinquish his private right of self-protection (together, presumably, with whatever instruments of violence he happens to possess). The sovereign is, in other words, a third party beneficiary of the contract the citizens make with one another. One rather disturbing consequence of this view — which Hobbes did not flinch to draw — is that the sovereign, being a contract beneficiary, may enforce the contractual obligations of the citizens, but, since he is a non-party, owes them no such duties in return:

Because the Right of bearing the Person of them all, is given to him they make Soveraigne, by Covenant only of one to another, and not of him to any of them; there can happen no breach of covenant on the part of the

soveraigne; and consequently none of his subjects, by any pretense of forfeiture, can be freed from his subjection.

Leviathan, ch. 18 (M. Oakeshott ed. 1946).

WATERS, THE PROPERTY IN THE PROMISE: A STUDY OF THE
THIRD PARTY BENEFICIARY RULE, 98 Harv. L. Rev. 1109, 1192-
1199 (1985) (footnotes have been omitted): "During the past twenty years
or so, the federal courts have recognized and developed a theory of
constitutionally protected property that was first fully articulated by
Charles Reich in his influential 1964 article, 'The New Property.' This
'new property' consists of governmentally created rights, typically the
right to the tangible and intangible benefits of social welfare programs.
Reich argued that such new property rights should be afforded procedural safeguards. Soon thereafter, the Supreme Court embraced the new
property concept, according procedural due process protection to certain
statutory entitlements.

"In the twenty years since Reich's article was published, much ink has
been spilled in discussing the contours of the new property, but there
seems to be general agreement among commentators about one thing: it
has developed in an overtly teleological fashion. In this analysis, the first
question a court asks, in one way or another, is whether the claimed right
merits constitutional protection. If the court concludes that it does, it will
articulate the right, as a means to this end — for the sake of the remedy,
if you will — as a constitutionally protected property right.

"'New property' plainly has more to do with the broad set of values
thought to be pertinent to constitutional adjudication than with the common law definition of property, particularly where intangible benefits are
involved. This claim is borne out by the fact that when the Court has
limited its recognition of 'new property,' it has done so by moving away
from a broadly equitable property notion — a property right that is recognized because it ought to be — toward the more traditional common law
property idea.

"Constitutionally protected rights to intangible property, many of
which are not 'property rights' within the common law meaning of that
term, are by now well established. Those that concern us here are the
'new property' rights created by the government for the benefit of particular groups — specifically, what have come to be called statutory entitlements. Where such rights are protected as 'property,' it is the statute that
creates the property and the due process clause that protects it. Examples
of statutory entitlements that have passed muster in the Supreme Court
are welfare benefits, old-age benefits, federal civil service employment,
and social security benefits.

". . . The origin of the rule that enables third party beneficiaries to
secure compliance with federal statutes lies in quasi-contract, specifically, in the old common count for 'money had and received for and to

the use of the plaintiff.' Yet this action was not precisely a property claim. A plaintiff stating a claim for money had and received did not, for example, have to identify specific funds, but the defendant's right to act other than as trustee of the money would defeat the claim. The courts permitted all manner of 'tracing' when the money held had been mingled with other funds and identification of the specific property had become impossible. In holding that an action for money had and received is not defeated by 'incidental legal relationships' that arise when the money is passed from bank account to bank account, a modern English court described the claim as one 'of substance, founded in equity, which fastens upon the conscience of the recipient.' Professor Scott has explained the outcome in cases of this kind in terms of the plaintiff's having 'an equitable interest in the mingled fund.' On this analysis, what is involved is a kind of 'equitable property,' as distinct from the common law notion of property.

"The doctrinal innovation involved in Lawrence v. Fox was the substitution of the promise to pay money for the equitable property in the money itself. The rule of Lawrence v. Fox made the defendant a 'constructive trustee' of the benefit of the promise, extending the potential of the action considerably. So long as the promise remained a promise to pay money, this legal sleight of hand did not matter very much. But once courts developed a generalized right of 'intended beneficiaries' to enforce promises of all kinds, this type of 'equitable property' was enlarged enormously.

"This analysis of the role now being played by the third party beneficiary rule is supported not only by the history of the rule, but also by the nature of the rights it secures. Rights acquired by third party beneficiaries under contracts that are a part of statutory schemes of distribution and protection have a great deal in common with the kinds of rights the Supreme Court has held to be protected property under the due process clauses. This similarity is especially obvious with respect to intangible, 'new property' rights, which are not encompassed by traditional legal concepts of property.

"Setting aside for a moment the notion that the third party's right, thus created, is a 'contract right,' the right may be thought of in terms of its restitutionary, quasi-contractual origins. Quasi-contractual rights were dependent on the fiction of a promise 'implied by law' from the facts of the case — facts such as the receipt of money by the defendant for and to the use of the plaintiff. If a federal agency pays a subsidy to a provider of low-income housing to be credited toward the rent of an identified tenant, the tenant could maintain an action for money had and received, were it available, against the recipient of the funds if they were not so applied and could certainly recover as an intended beneficiary of the contract under which funds were paid. Thus, where money earmarked for the plaintiff's use or credit is the object of the claim, the grievance is virtually identical to that involved in Lawrence v. Fox.

"The same analysis applies where an apartment house owner charges rents in excess of the maximum permitted under its mortgage agreement with the federal government, and the tenants sue for a refund. The plaintiffs' claim is rather straightforward: 'We want our money back!' But the response of the law can be rather sophisticated, offering several formally distinct avenues to the same remedy. That which most accurately describes the grievance is the action for money had and received, which is as straightforward and as primitive as the claim itself. But this simple tool from yesteryear has been mislaid in the process of doctrinal development; an action 'on the promise' or another 'on the statute' must be made to do the job.

"Turning from the particular case of money paid to the credit of an identified beneficiary to cases of federal funding contracts generally, we move away from something very much like the 'old property' idea toward something that more closely resembles the 'new property.' Indeed, that so many modern third party beneficiary cases are class actions — status-based actions that straddle the divide between public and private law by making a nominally private law claim on behalf of a class created by statute — emphasizes the similarity between these cases and those involving statutory entitlements considered property for due process purposes. . . .

"The third party beneficiary's right, then, is better understood, and more precisely classified, as a restitutionary right to intangible property — the benefit of a promise — than as a contract action. This characterization is not limited to those cases in which the benefits being sought happen to resemble intangible benefits that have been constitutionally protected as property, but those cases do illustrate one point particularly well: there is sometimes a marked similarity between the kinds of rights constitutionally protected as property and those secured by the third party beneficiary rule that derives historically from a private law notion of equitable property. Given that both notions of property developed teleologically, one to protect due process values as they affect groups of citizens, the other for the more limited purpose of achieving 'justice as between man and man' in the form of restitution, it is not surprising that each should now address the same contemporary social concern over intangible property rights."

Section 5. The Problem of Defenses, Modifications, and Rescission

In the preceding sections we have considered principally the question whether the plaintiff is within one of the recognized classes of third party beneficiaries or whether he is, in Restatement terminology, merely an incidental beneficiary not entitled to sue on the A-B contract. The great bulk of third party beneficiary litigation has focused on this question of identification or categorization. Neither in the cases nor in the learned commentary has there been much discussion of the status of the plaintiff, once it has been conceded that he is entitled to sue as a contract beneficiary.

In Lawrence v. Fox, *supra* p. 1333, Fox promised Holly to pay Holly's debt to Lawrence. The consideration for Fox's promise was a loan made by Holly to Fox, which, under the Holly-Fox agreement, was to be discharged by Fox's payment to Lawrence. Assume that, in Lawrence's action against Fox, Fox pleads:

1. Failure of consideration between Holly and Lawrence — that is, Holly, the original debtor, had a defense which would have been good against Lawrence if Lawrence had sued Holly.

2. Failure of consideration between Holly and Fox — that is, Holly had not made the loan to Fox which was the consideration for Fox's promise to pay Lawrence.

3. Rescission of the Holly-Fox agreement — that is, Holly and Fox agreed that Fox should repay the money loaned directly to Holly and that he should not pay Lawrence (or that Fox should pay some other creditor of Holly instead of Lawrence).

It is a matter of interest that the opinions delivered in Lawrence v. Fox did in fact discuss two of the three hypothetical pleas which we have attributed to Fox. For the ensuing hundred years there was little or no discussion in the cases of either the freedom of promisor and promisee to modify or rescind their contract without the beneficiary's consent or of the availability to the promisor, when he is sued by the beneficiary, of defenses based on (a) the transaction between promisee and beneficiary or (b) the transaction between promisor and promisee. It is true that cases holding that the beneficiary could not sue at all, because he was not in privity of contract with the promisee, may have masked decisions based on the availability of defenses. (See, e.g., National Bank v. Grand Lodge, 98 U.S. 123 (1878), digested in the Note following Lawrence v. Fox, *supra* p. 1333, which could be analyzed as a case involving failure of consideration between promisor and promisee.)

It is a fair guess that the focus of beneficiary litigation will presently shift to questions of the type just discussed. There will, no doubt, continue to be fringe cases of the traditional type, as illustrated by the *Isbrandtsen* case, *supra* p. 1380. But the third party beneficiary doctrine is recognized almost everywhere in this country and there is today fairly widespread agreement on the classes of beneficiaries who are within the doctrine. That being so, it may be anticipated that in the future the courts will be less concerned with the metaphysics of privity and purpose and more concerned with the by no means simple problem of the effectiveness of defenses, modifications and rescissions against the beneficiary.

In this section we turn therefore to the bits and pieces of law that are available in cases and Restatement.

FORD v. MUTUAL LIFE INSURANCE COMPANY OF NEW YORK

283 Ill. App. 325 (1936)

Mr. Justice WOLFE delivered the opinion of the court. In an action of assumpsit the plaintiff secured a verdict and judgment against the defendant for $2,149.33 which the evidence shows was the cash surrender value of a policy of insurance issued by the defendant on the life of the plaintiff, in which the plaintiff's wife is named the beneficiary. The declaration of one count is based on the surrender clause of the policy. . . .

The application for the policy was signed by the plaintiff on August 24, 1896, at Galesburg, Illinois, where the plaintiff lived. The policy is dated September 2, 1896, and it was delivered by the defendant to the plaintiff at Galesburg. . . .

The policy on its face recites as follows:

Annual Premium for 20 years, $71.60. In consideration of the application for this policy, which is hereby made a part of this contract, The Mutual Life Insurance Company of New York promises to pay at its Home Office in the City of New York, unto Caroline Ford wife of Scott Ford of Galesburg in the County of Knox, State of Illinois, her executors, administrators or assigns, Two Thousand Dollars, upon acceptance of satisfactory proofs at its Home Office of the death of the said Scott Ford during the continuance of this policy, upon the following condition; and subject to the provisions, requirements and benefits stated on the back of this policy, which are hereby referred to and make a part thereof.

The condition mentioned is that,

The annual premium of Seventy-one Dollars and Sixty Cents, shall be paid in advance on the delivery of this policy, and thereafter to the company, at its Home office in the City of New York, on the Third Day of September in every year during the continuance of this contract, until premiums for Twenty full years shall have been duly paid to said Company.

The benefits referred to on the face of the policy and stated on the back thereof, which are material for consideration, are as follows: "Surrender — This policy may be surrendered to the Company at the end of the first period of twenty years, and the full reserve computed by the American Table of Mortality, and four per cent interest, and the surplus as defined above, will be paid therefor for cash." . . .

Premiums called for by the policy for 20 years after the date it was issued have been duly paid by the plaintiff to the defendant. The plaintiff has had possession of the policy from the time it was issued to him by the defendant. The contract of insurance does not contain any provisions either permitting or prohibiting the plaintiff from changing the beneficiary named in the policy, or surrendering the policy, either with or without the consent of the beneficiary. It is silent on those subjects. . . .

The evidence shows that on June 7, 1924, the beneficiary of the policy, Caroline Ford, assigned all her right, title and interest in the policy to "Caroline Ford, wife of insured, if living, if not, to Eloise Ford, birth November 12, 1897, and Pauline Ford, birth May 8, 1902, daughters of Caroline Ford, or the survivor, or the estate of the last survivor." The legality of the assignment is not involved in this case. The beneficiary and her two said daughters are living and none of them has consented to a change of beneficiary or surrender of the policy. They are not parties to this action, and do not reside in this State.

The beneficiary, the wife of the insured, had a vested right in the policy when the contract of insurance took effect. There are no terms or provisions of the policy inconsistent with this rule of law. . . . Since the beneficiary had a vested interest in the policy, the plaintiff did not have the right to surrender the policy and collect its surrender value, although the policy was in the possession of the plaintiff and he had paid the premiums thereon. . . .

The motion of the defendant for a directed verdict made at the close of all the evidence in the case should have been sustained by the trial court.

The judgment of the circuit court is reversed and judgment rendered to this court for the defendant.

Reversed and judgment entered here.

COPELAND v. BEARD

217 Ala. 216, 115 So. 389 (1928)

Suit by Mrs. B. V. Beard against Marvin Copeland. Judgment for plaintiff was affirmed by the Court of Appeals (22 Ala. App. 325, 115 So. 385), and defendant petitions for certiorari to review the judgment of the Court of Appeals. Writ granted. Judgment reversed, and case remanded.

BOULDIN, J. Taking the facts from the findings of the Court of Appeals, the essential question here for review on certiorari may be briefly stated thus: where the debtor sells and conveys real and personal property, upon consideration in part that the purchaser shall assume and pay specified debts of the vendor, and on the same day, before the creditors for whose benefit the promise is made have assented thereto, the purchaser resells and conveys the property upon consideration in part that the subpurchaser shall assume and pay the same indebtedness, and the original vendor debtor thereupon releases the original purchaser from his promise to pay, can such creditor thereafter maintain an action of assumpsit against the original purchaser?

In Clark v. Nelson, 216 Ala. 199, 112 So. 819, this court, after a review of the authorities, approved the general statement of the doctrine in cases of rescission by Mr. Williston:

"The creditor's right is purely derivative, and, if the debtor no longer has a right of action against the promisor, the creditor can have none." 1 Williston on Contracts, §397.

After quoting from our own cases, it was said:

> We think, therefore, this court is definitely committed to the doctrine that the promisor may interpose any defense that was permissible as between himself and the original debtor, including, of course, mutual rescission of the contract so long as the creditor had not acted in good faith upon the promise so as to alter his position.

Clark v. Nelson, 216 Ala. 199, 122 So. 821.

The Court of Appeals takes the view that the case at bar is to be differentiated from the *Nelson Case*, saying (22 Ala. App. 325, 115 So. 385):

> The recent case of Clark & Co. v. Nelson, 216 Ala. 199, 112 So. 819, is based upon the rescission of the contract, before acceptance by the debtor, thereby placing the parties in statu quo. There is a vast difference between a rescission, where the property transferred as the consideration for the agreement to pay a creditor is reconveyed to the contracting debtor and a subsequent agreement to release a purchaser of the debtor's property who had agreed to pay a creditor in consideration of property transferred to him without a reconveyance of the property.

Is the distinction thus declared sound in principle?

The transaction between the debtor, his vendee, and the subvendee, whereby the latter purchased the property, assumed the obligation to pay creditors, and the debtor released the original promisor, was as between them, a novation. It was supported by a valuable consideration, as in other cases of novation. All rights of action in the promisee, the debtor, as against his promisor, the vendee, was released. Whether such release may be aptly called a rescission of the promise to pay creditors seems unimportant. As between the immediate parties to the transaction it had the same effect.

When a debtor contracts with another, for a valuable consideration, to assume and pay his debt, the creditor has an election to accept or reject the new party as his debtor. He may ignore the offer and proceed to enforce all his remedies against the original debtor. Henry v. Murphy, 54 Ala. 246.

An election requires knowledge of the facts. So a suit against the original debtor without notice that another has assumed to pay it does not constitute an election to reject the agreement. Young v. Hawkins, 74 Ala. 370. An action against the promisor assuming to pay the debt is a sufficient acceptance — an election to affirm the contract made for the creditor's benefit. Carver v. Eads, 65 Ala. 191.

There is difference of view as to the status of the parties after acceptance of the agreement by the creditor. Some authorities hold that upon election to accept the benefits of the contract, he releases the original debtor. These cases proceed on the idea that the contract made between the debtor and the assuming party, while binding between themselves, is, as to the creditor, an offer of novation. Several of our earlier cases quite clearly proceed on this view. The *Nelson Case*, in course of discussion, recognizes these decisions.

The other view is that by the contract wherein the debtor sells property in consideration that the purchaser assumes the payment of debt, the latter becomes, as between the immediate parties, the principal and the debtor, a quasi surety, and the creditor, upon acceptance of the arrangement, may sue either or both. This latter view is distinctly held in People's Savings Bank v. Jordan, 200 Ala. 500, 76 So. 442; Tyson v. Austill, 168 Ala. 525, 53 So. 263; Moore v. First Nat. Bank of Florence, 139 Ala. 595, 606, 36 So. 777.

This is the prevailing doctrine in other jurisdictions. 1 Williston on Contracts, §393. While our cases involved directly conveyances by a mortgagor, the purchaser assuming the mortgage debt, no sound distinction exists between them and the instant case.

The question is here involved only incidentally in defining when the right of the creditor to sue the promisor becomes fixed, and not subject to rescission or release. It is said the promisor and promisee may rescind at any time before the creditor alters his position. If bringing suit against the promisor releases the original debtor, this would clearly alter the creditor's position for the worse, if a right of rescission still exists. If such action does not release the original debtor, then the inquiry is, When is the creditor's position so altered that his rights become fixed and beyond the power of the original parties to rescind or release?

We now adopt the doctrine that by acceptance of the promise made for his benefit and action thereon, the creditor does not release the original debtor, unless so stipulated in the contract and made known to the creditor.

Both parties invite the creditor to accept the contract. The debtor has the benefit of the promise for his protection in case he is still required to pay. The creditor being thus invited to avail himself of the contract, we think no fair intendment can be indulged that he shall thereby take the hazard of losing the debt, if the promise so recommended proves unavailing.

Coming then to the question of when the creditor's right of action against the promisor becomes fixed, we think it properly determinable on the basic law of contracts. So long as the contract to assume is between the debtor and his promisor only, the creditor is not a party thereto. He can become so only by his consent. At the same time, the contract, in the nature of it, is an open offer to the creditor. His assent while the offer is open is all that is required. When the minds of all parties consent to the same thing at the same time, and such consent is communicated between them, the contract is complete.

Consent in such case may be proven in the same manner as in other contracts. The consideration for the promise passing between promisor and promisee is also consideration for the completed contract between all parties. The tripartite contract being consummated, it cannot be rescinded without the consent of all. It follows that the creditor's assent to the contract, made known to the promisor, who is expected to pay, is the only change of position required. But the assent must be to a promise in force at the time. The right of contract is the right to rescind or modify . . . the principle in the *Nelson* case, *supra*, is applicable in the present case.

The Court of Appeals appears to hold the status quo as to ownership of the property must be restored. The ownership of the property is of no concern to the creditor except as it may affect his power to collect his debt. This turns upon an issue of fraud vel non in the transaction, as defined in the law of fraudulent conveyances. All participants in a fraud may be held to account in a proper form of action.

No such question is presented here. So far as appears, the original debtor and the subvendee, whose promise is still open to the plaintiff creditor, are solvent, able and ready to pay the demand. It is a case of election to sue the vendee, who, before any acceptance of his promise, conveyed the property to another, who assumed the payment of plaintiff's demand, and after the promise had released defendant from the obligation.

Writ of certiorari granted; reversed and remanded.

All the Justices concur.

Note on the Restatement of Contracts and the Problem of Rescission

Under the Restatement First, the power of A and B to rescind their contract, depriving C of his rights as a beneficiary, depended upon whether C was a "donee" or "creditor" of the promisee; this was, in fact, the most important consequence of the distinction between these two types of beneficiaries. Sections 142 and 143 read as follows:

§142.   Variation of the Duty to a Donee Beneficiary by Agreement
of Promisor and Promisee

Unless the power to do so is reserved, the duty of the promisor to the donee beneficiary cannot be released by the promisee or affected by any agreement between the promisee and the promisor, but if the promisee receives consideration for an attempted release or discharge of the promisor's duty, the donee beneficiary can assert a right to the consideration so received, and on doing so loses his right against the promisor.

§143.   Variation of the Promisor's Duty to a Creditor Beneficiary
by Agreement of Promisor and Promisee

A discharge of the promisor by the promisee in a contract or a variation thereof by them is effective against a creditor beneficiary if,

(a)   the creditor beneficiary does not bring suit upon the promise or otherwise materially change his position in reliance thereon before he knows of the discharge or variation, and

(b)   the promisee's action is not a fraud on creditors.

Under §142, it would seem, a donee beneficiary's rights "vest" immediately; unless the promisor and promisee have in their contract reserved the right to do so, they cannot, once the promise to the donee has been made, thereafter rescind or modify it without the donee's consent. On the other hand, as against a creditor beneficiary, promisor and promisee remain free to rescind or vary their agreement until the creditor has taken the type of action described in §143(a).

The Restatement's disparate treatment of creditor and donee beneficiaries was explained, and the distinction itself vigorously criticized, in Page, The Power of the Contracting Parties to Alter a Contract for Rendering Performance to a Third Person, 12 Wis. L. Rev. 141 (1937). After an elaborate review of the authorities, Professor Page concluded (at 183-184; footnotes have been omitted):

It seems that neither the rule of section 142 of the Restatement nor the rule of section 143 is taken from the common law as it exists in states which recognize the right of C as a contract right against A. While these states differ among themselves as to the stage of the transaction at which the right of A and B to terminate or to modify the contract by mutual agreement, without the consent of C, ends, they agree in the main that the stage of the transaction, wherever it may end, is the same whether C has a claim against B or whether he does not have a claim against B; and they agree that no advantage is to be given to C in the situation in which he does not have a claim against B, as compared to the situation in which he has a claim against B.

The rule of section 143, which applies where C has a claim against B, bears a strong resemblance to the rule which is laid down by the courts which deny that *C* has a contract right against *A* and which hold that *C's* right, if any, is by way of subrogation to *B's* right against *A*. Both under the holdings of these courts, and under section 143, *A* and *B* may terminate or modify the contract by mutual agreement up to the time that *C* brings suit against *A* or changes his position materially in reliance upon the contract, unless *B's* discharge of *A* would operate as a fraud against *C*.

The rule of section 142, which applies where *C* has no claim against B, bears a strong resemblance to the rule which the courts apply in cases of life insurance (not benefit certificates); a rule which originated in statute, and which is applied by courts, many of which say that *C's* right under the policy is either a gift or a trust, and not a contractual right against the insurance company.

Sections 142 and 143 of the Restatement, when taken together, are thus contrary to the common law rule as applied by the courts which treat the transactions in question as contracts; and they seem to be borrowed from cases in which the courts did not recognize as contracts the transactions with reference to which they laid down these rules.

The position of contracts to render performance to a third person would seem to be so clearly established in the United States (except in a few of the Eastern States) that the rights which arise should be determined by principles of contract law; and not by principles of gift, trust, and subrogation.

The Restatement Second adopts the position urged by Professor Page, asserting that "[t]he weight of authority is opposed to a distinction between donee beneficiaries and creditor beneficiaries with respect to the power of promisor and promisee to vary [their agreement]" (Reporter's Note to §311). Instead, the draftsmen of the Restatement Second have chosen to emphasize the elements of reliance and assent in formulating a rule that applies to all intended beneficiaries. Section 311 (Variation of a Duty to a Beneficiary) provides:

(1) Discharge or modification of a duty to an intended beneficiary by conduct of the promisee or by a subsequent agreement between promisor and promisee is ineffective if a term of the promise creating the duty so provides.

(2) In the absence of such a term, the promisor and promisee retain power to discharge or modify the duty by subsequent agreement.

(3) Such a power terminates when the beneficiary, before he receives notification of the discharge or modification, materially changes his position in justifiable reliance on the promise or brings suit on it or manifests assent to it at the request of the promisor or promisee.

(4) If the promisee receives consideration for an attempted discharge or modification of the promisor's duty which is ineffective against the beneficiary, the beneficiary can assert a right to the consideration so received. The promisor's duty is discharged to the extent of the amount received by the beneficiary.

NOTE

1. Does the Restatement Second's treatment of the rescission problem seem to you, on the whole, an improvement over the approach adopted in §§142 and 143 of the Restatement First? Does it seem to you to be, in all situations, sound policy to provide that promisor and promisee can no longer modify or rescind their agreement once the beneficiary has materially changed his position in reliance thereon? By the same token, are there cases in which it is appropriate that the beneficiary's rights vest even though he has neither given his assent to nor relied on the contract (which, let us assume, is silent on this issue)?

2. A legislative approach to the problem of rescission and modification, different from (and considerably simpler than) that of either Restatement, is illustrated by §1559 of the California Civil Code: "A contract made expressly for the benefit of a third person, may be enforced by him at any time before the parties thereto rescind it." Section 1559 was originally enacted in 1872.

3. In McCulloch v. Canadian Pacific Ry., 53 F. Supp. 534, (D. Minn., 1943), Nordbye, J., commented:

> While it must be recognized that [§142 of the] Restatement assumes to lay down the broad rule that a third party donee beneficiary contract cannot be rescinded without the donee's consent, this rule is not followed by the majority of the courts. 2 Williston on Contracts, Sec. 396; 13 C.J. 602; 17 C.J.S., Contracts, §390; note 53, A.L.R. 178. The only condition laid down by the majority of the courts with reference to the rescission of a donee beneficiary contract is that there must be an absence of reliance on the contract by the third party beneficiary. . . .
>
> The main arguments advanced in favor of the rule [set out in §142] are that a beneficiary in a life insurance policy cannot be changed without the consent of the existing beneficiary, and that, where there is a gift, it cannot be revoked without the donee's consent. But it will be seen that neither of these situations is analogous to the donee's rights under a third party beneficiary contract. First, it may be observed that insurance law is peculiar to itself. There has grown up in that field principles of law which are not applicable elsewhere. Public policy and the relationship between the parties largely have influenced the rule with reference to the change of beneficiaries in a life insurance contract. Therein, because of the peculiarity of the law, a beneficiary has a vested interest in absence of the right to change beneficiaries. Nor is the rule regarding revocation of gifts helpful or persuasive in determining the rule as to rescission of a third party beneficiary contract. Where the gift is executed, the donee accepts the gift from the donor and usually possession then rests in the donee. There is the element of delivery and the element of reliance by the donee on that which was done.

53 F. Supp. at 539.

ROUSE v. UNITED STATES

215 F.2d 872 (Ct. App. D.C. 1954)

Action by United States, which had taken assignment of F.H.A. note which was in default, to recover from purchaser who had bought house from maker to note. The United States District Court for the District of Columbia, Burnita Shelton Matthews, J., struck purchaser's defenses and granted summary judgment for plaintiff and purchaser appealed. The Court of Appeals, Edgerton, Circuit Judge, held that where vendor paid for heating plant in house with note, guaranteed by F.H.A., and sold house to purchaser, who promised to assume liability for heating plant cost, purchaser could set up defense of vendor's fraudulent misrepresentation of condition of heating plant.

Judgment reversed and cause remanded with instructions.

Before Edgerton, Bazelon, and Washington, Circuit Judges.

EDGERTON, Circuit Judge. Bessie Winston gave Associated Contractors, Inc., her promissory note for $1,008.37, payable in monthly installments of $28.01, for a heating plant in her house. The Federal Housing Administration guaranteed the note and the payee endorsed it for value to the lending bank, the Union Trust Company.

Winston sold the house to Rouse. In the contract of sale Rouse agreed to assume debts secured by deeds of trust and also "to assume payment of $850 for heating plant payable $28 per Mo." Nothing was said about the note.

Winston defaulted on her note. The United States paid the bank, took an assignment of the note, demanded payment from Rouse, and sued him for $850 and interest.

Rouse alleged as defenses (1) that Winston fraudulently misrepresented the condition of the heating plant and (2) that Associated Contractors did not install it satisfactorily. The District Court struck these defenses and granted summary judgment for the plaintiff. The defendant Rouse appeals.

Since Rouse did not sign the note he is not liable on it. D.C. Code 1951, §28-119; N.I.L. Sec. 18. He is not liable to the United States at all unless his contract with Winston makes him so. The contract says the parties to it are not "bound by any terms, conditions, statements, warranties or representations, oral or written" not contained in it. But this means only that the written contract contains the entire agreement. It does not mean that fraud cannot be set up as a defense to a suit on the contract. Rouse's promise to "assume payment of $850 for heating plant" made him liable to Associated Contractors, Inc., only if and so far as it made him liable to Winston; one who promises to make a payment to the promisee's creditor can assert against the creditor any defense that the promisor could assert against the promisee. Accordingly Rouse, if he had been sued by the corporation, would have been entitled to show fraud on the part of Winston. He is equally entitled to do so in this suit by an assignee of the corporation's claim. It follows that the court erred in striking the first defense. We do not consider whether Winston's alleged fraud, if shown, would be a complete or only a partial defense to this suit, since that question has not arisen and may not arise.

We think the court was right in striking the second defense.

> If the promisor's agreement is to be interpreted as a promise to discharge whatever liability the promisee is under, the promisor must certainly be allowed to show that the promisee was under no enforceable liability. . . . On the other hand, if the promise means that the promisor agrees to pay a sum of money to A, to whom the promisee says he is indebted, it is immaterial whether the promisee is actually indebted to that amount or at all. . . . Where the promise is to pay a specific debt . . . this interpretation will generally be the true one.[17]

The judgment is reversed and the cause remanded with instructions to reinstate the first defense.

Reversed and remanded.

NOTE

1. On the status of assuming grantees, and the distinction between assuming grantees and non-assuming grantees, see the Note following Vrooman v. Turner, *supra* p. 1346. It does not appear that the heating plant in the principal case was sold subject to a security interest (e.g., a conditional sale or chattel mortgage); the F.H.A. guaranty no doubt made such an arrangement unnecessary. In the absence of a security arrangement covering the heating plant, Rouse would not have been liable for the unpaid balance of the purchase price if he had not assumed the debt. Presumably he paid Winston less for the house than he would have done if he had not agreed to take over the monthly payments for the heating plant.

2. *Winston's Liability on the Note:* Disregard for the moment the sale to Rouse and assume that Winston still owned the house. When she bought the heating plant from Associated Contractors she executed a note for the purchase price. If the seller, having kept the note itself (or having been required to take the note up after default) sued Winston, she could interpose her defense of faulty installation. Such defenses as failure of consideration, breach of warranty, and the like are always available between the original parties to the underlying transaction. There is no way in which Associated Contractors can set up the transaction so that it can sue Winston free of such defenses.

17. 2 Williston, Contracts §399 (Rev. Ed. 1936).

Associated Contractors financed the sale by selling Winston's note to Union Trust Company. Let us assume that the note was negotiable and that Union Trust Company qualified as a holder in due course. (On negotiable instruments and the holder in due course concept, see the Note following Muller v. Pondir, *infra* p. 1444.) Normally, one who is the holder in due course of an instrument takes it free of all defenses of the sort involved in the *Rouse* case (failure of consideration and what is usually termed fraud "in the inducement"). If the Trust Company, as a holder in due course, held Winston's note free of her defenses against Associated Contractors, she would be liable for the full amount of the note; having paid the Trust Company, however, she could then sue Associated Contractors to recover damages for the faulty installation or breach of warranty. That is, the seller never escapes liability to the buyer for his default, even though the buyer may have become obligated to a financing institution to pay the full price without regard to the default.

Today, however, it is extremely unlikely that Winston could become obligated in this way. Some states flatly forbid the use of negotiable instruments in consumer transactions like the one between Winston and Associated Contractors (with the result that the Trust Company could not become a holder in due course of her note in the first place); other states have, by statute or judicial decision, made the defenses of a consumer-purchaser available against anyone who subsequently acquires a negotiable instrument issued in a consumer transaction (making the Trust Company's holder in due status worthless as a practical matter). For statutes illustrating these two approaches, see Wis. Stat. Ann. 422.406 (1974) and Mo. Ann. Stat. §408.405 (Vernon 1979). A leading case on the subject is Unico v. Owen, 50 N.J. 101, 232 A.2d 405 (1967).

When the note went into default, the United States, under the F.H.A. guaranty, was required to pay off Union Trust Company. As part of that transaction it acquired Winston's note from the Trust Company and succeeded to whatever rights the Trust Company had in the note. If the United States had sued Winston on the note, the situation would have been the same as that described in the preceding paragraph.

3. *Rouse's Liability:* Rouse was not liable on Winston's note because he was not a party to it (i.e., he had never signed it in any capacity). This, as the court says, is a standard rule of negotiable instruments law. Nor was he a party to the contract of sale between Winston and Associated Contractors. His liability thus is predicated on his assumption of the debt in his purchase of the house from Winston.

Rouse's first defense was that Winston had fraudulently misrepresented the condition of the heating plant and the court held that this defense, if established, was good against the United States. In third party beneficiary terminology, Rouse was the promisor and Winston was the promisee. Rouse's argument, with which the court agreed, was that the promisor, when sued by the beneficiary, could interpose the defense of fraud (or, presumably, failure of consideration) between himself and the promisee. It seems clear that if the United States had elected to collect from Winston, and Winston, having paid, had sued Rouse, the defense of Winston's fraud would have been available to Rouse. Does it necessarily follow that it should also be available against the United States? If it were held that the defense was not available to Rouse against the United States, what further remedies would Rouse have?

Rouse's second defense was faulty installation of the heating system by Associated Contractors — that is, failure of consideration or breach of warranty between the promisee (Winston) and the seller. The court held that this defense was not available to Rouse. Thus, if he fails to establish the fraudulent misrepresentation defense, he will have to pay the full amount of the unpaid purchase price even if the heating system had been improperly installed and was worthless. Did the court say that the United States, in its action against Rouse, was in the same position that Associated Contractors would have been in if they had sued Rouse after taking up the note from the United States? Or that the defense was not available against the United States but would have been available against Associated Contractors? If Rouse paid the United States, could he then bring an action for breach of warranty against the Contractors? Or could Winston bring such an action after Rouse had paid? It does seem necessary, does it not, to find a solution that will make Associated Contractors liable to *someone* if it has breached its contract with Winston.

4. In the last paragraph of his opinion, Judge Edgerton quoted from Williston on Contracts. Williston proposed a distinction between cases in which the promisor should, and cases in which he should not, be able to use the promisee's defenses against the beneficiary. Did the court in the *Rouse* case misapply Williston's distinction?

5. Reconsider the discussion of Lawrence v. Fox in the Introductory Note to this section. If Holly had a defense against Lawrence, should Fox be able to plead it? What would Williston say? If you conclude that Holly's defense would not be available to Fox, would it follow that Winston's defense would not be available to Rouse if he were sued by Associated Contractors?

LEWIS v. BENEDICT COAL CORP.
361 U.S. 459 (1960)

Mr. Justice BRENNAN delivered the opinion of the Court. The National Bituminous Coal Wage Agreement of 1950, a collective bargaining agreement between coal operators and the United Mine Workers of America, provides for a union welfare fund meeting the requirements of §302(c)(5) of the Taft-Hartley Act. The fund is the "United Mine Workers of America Welfare and Retirement Fund of 1950." Each signatory coal operator agreed to pay into the fund a royalty of 30¢, later increased to 40¢, for each ton of coal produced for use or for sale.

Benedict Coal Corporation, the respondent in both No. 18 and No. 19, is a signatory coal operator. From March 5, 1950, through July 1953, Benedict produced coal upon which the amount of royalty was calculated to be $177,762.92. Benedict paid $101,258.68 of this amount but withheld $76,504.24. The petitioners in No. 18, who are the trustees of the fund, brought this action to recover that balance in the District Court for the Eastern District of Tennessee. Benedict's main defense was that the performance of the duty to pay royalty to the trustees, regarding them as third-party beneficiaries of the collective bargaining agreement, was excused when the promisee contracting party, the union and its District 28 — who are the petitioners in No. 19 and who will be referred to as the union — violated the agreement by strikes and stoppages of work. Benedict also cross-claimed against the union for damages sustained from the strikes and stoppages. By its answer to the cross-claim, the union denied that its conduct violated the agreement.

The jury, using a verdict form provided by the trial judge, found that the trustees were entitled to recover the full amount of the unpaid royalty but that Benedict was entitled to a setoff of $81,017.68; the jury also gave a verdict to Benedict for that sum on its cross-claim against the union. In a single entry, two judgments were entered on this verdict. One was a judgment in favor of Benedict on its cross-claim on which immediate execution was ordered, but with direction that the sum collected from the union be paid into the registry of the court. The other was a judgment in favor of the trustees for the unpaid balance of the royalty. However, effect was given to Benedict's defense in the trustees' suit by refusing immediate execution, and interest, on the trustees' judgment and ordering instead that that judgment be satisfied out of the proceeds collected by Benedict on its judgment and paid into the registry of the court.

The union and the trustees prosecuted separate appeals to the Court of Appeals for the Sixth Circuit. The union alleged that the District Court erred in holding that the strikes and stoppages violated the collective bargaining agreement, contending that, properly construed, the agreement did not forbid the strikes and stoppages; in the alternative, the union urged that the damages awarded were excessive. The trustees alleged as error, primarily, the refusal of the trial court to allow them immediate and unconditional execution, and interest, on their judgment against Benedict.

The Court of Appeals affirmed the District Court except as to the amount of damages awarded to Benedict on its cross-claim, which the court adjudged was excessive. The court held that, under the evidence, Benedict's damages would not equal the amount of the trustees' judgment of $76,504.26. The case was remanded for a redetermination of Benedict's damages, with instructions that "[t]he judgment in favor of the

Trustees will then be amended by the district court to allow execution and interest on that part of the said judgment which is in excess of the set-off in favor of Benedict as so redetermined." 259 F.2d 346, 355. This left unaffected so much of the District Court's order as predicated the trustees' recovery, to the extent of the amount of Benedict's judgment as finally determined, upon Benedict's recovery of that judgment. The trustees and the union filed separate petitions for certiorari. We granted the trustees' petition, No. 18, and also the union's petition, No. 19, except that we limited the latter grant to the question whether the strikes and stoppages complained of by Benedict violated the collective bargaining agreement. 359 U.S. 905.

In No. 19, the Court is equally divided. The judgment of the Court of Appeals, so far as it sustains the holding of the District Court that the union violated the collective bargaining agreement, is therefore affirmed.

We turn to the question presented in No. 18, whether the lower courts were correct in holding in effect that Benedict might assert the union's breaches as a defense to the trustees' suit, for to the extent Benedict (the promisor) does not collect from the union (the promisee) the union's liability is set off against Benedict's liability to the third-party beneficiary. The answer to that question requires, we think, our consideration of the nature of interests of the union, the company, and the trustees in the fund under the collective bargaining agreement.

The provisions of the collective bargaining agreement creating the fund include the express provision that "this Fund is an irrevocable trust created pursuant to Section 302(c) of the "Labor-Management Relations Act, 1947.'" Another provision specifies that the purposes of the fund shall be all purposes "provided for or permitted in Section 302(c)." In this way the agreement plainly declares what the statute requires, namely, that the fund shall be used "for the sole and exclusive benefit" of the employees, their families and dependents. Thus, the fund is in no way an asset or property of the union.

Benedict does not, however, base its claim of setoff on any contention that the royalty was owing to the union and might because of this be applied to the payment of its damages. Benedict's position is that in an amount equal to the amount of the damages sustained from the union's breaches, no fund property came into existence under the terms of the collective bargaining agreement. This depends upon whether the agreement is to be construed as making performance by the union of its promises a condition precedent to Benedict's promise to pay royalty to the trustees. Benedict argues that the contracting parties expressed this meaning in an article at the close of the agreement — "This Agreement is an integrated instrument and its respective provisions are interdependent" — and in the provision in another article that the no-strike clauses are "part of the consideration of this contract." However, the specific provisions of the article creating the fund provide: (1) "During the life of this [collective bargaining] Agreement, there shall be paid into such Fund by each operator signatory . . . [a royalty] on each ton of coal *produced for use or for sale.*" (2) The operator is required to make payment "on the 10th day of each . . . calendar month covering *the production of all coal for use or sale* during the preceding month." (3) "This obligation of each Operator signatory hereto, which is several and not joint, to so pay such sums shall be a *direct and continuing obligation* of said Operator during the life of this Agreement. . . ." (4) "Title to all the moneys paid into and or *due and owing said* Fund shall be vested in and remain exclusively in the Trustees of the Fund. . . ." (Emphasis added.) These provisions, rather than the stipulations of general application, are controlling. Their clear import is that the parties meant that the duty to pay royalty should arise on the production of coal independent of the union's performance. Indeed, Benedict's conduct was not consistent with the interpretation which it is now urging. Benedict continued despite the breaches to perform all of its several promises under the contract, including the promise to pay royalty, paying over $100,000 on coal produced during the period in dispute and withholding only the portion in suit.

But our conclusion that the union's performance of its promises is not a condition precedent to Benedict's duty to pay royalty does not fully answer the question we are to decide. For it may reasonably be argued that the damages sustained by Benedict may nevertheless affect the *amount* of the trustees' recovery. Professor Corbin, while acknowledging that "No case of the sort has been discovered," states:

> It may perhaps, be regarded as just to make the right of the beneficiary not only subject to the conditions precedent but also subject (as in the case of an assignee) to counter-claims against the promisee — at least if they arise out of a breach by the promisee of his duties created by the very same contract on which the beneficiary sues.

Using terms like "counterclaim" or "setoff" in a third-party beneficiary context may be confusing. In a two-party contract situation, when a promisor's duty to perform is absolute, the promisee's breaches will not excuse performance of that duty; the promisor has an independent claim against the promisee in damages. Formerly the promisor was required to bring a separate action to recover his damages. Under modern practice, when the promises are to pay money, or are reducible to a money amount, the promisor, when sued by the promisee, offsets the damages which he has sustained against the amount he owes, and usually obtains a judgment for any excess.

However, a third-party beneficiary has made no promises and therefore has breached no duty to the promisor. Accordingly, to hold, as the lower courts in this case did, that a promisor may "set off" the damages caused by the promisee's breach is actually to read the contract, which is the measure of the third party's rights, as so providing. In other words, although the promisor's duty to perform has become fixed by the occurrence of applicable conditions precedent, the parties may be taken to have agreed that the *extent* of the promisor's duty to the third party will be affected by the promisee's breach of contract. When it is said that "it may be just" to make the third party subject to the counterclaim, what must be meant is that a court should infer an intention of the promisor and promisee that the third party's rights be so limited.

This may be a desirable rule of construction to apply to a third-party beneficiary contract where the promisor's interest in or connection with the third party, in contrast with the promisee's, begins with the promise and ends with its performance. Of course, in entering into such a contract, the promisor may be held to have given up some defense against the third party's claim to performance of the promise, for example, the right to defeat that claim by rescinding the contract at any time he and the promisee agree. Nevertheless it may be fair to assume that had the parties anticipated the possibility of a breach by the promisee they would have provided that the promisor might protect himself by such means as would be available against the promisee under a two-party contract. This suggestion has not been crystallized into a rule of construction. Our problem is whether we should infer such an intention in this contract because there may be reasons making it appropriate to do so in the generality of third-party beneficiary contracts.

This collective bargaining agreement, however, is not a typical third-party beneficiary contract. The promisor's interest in the third party here goes far beyond the mere performance of its promise to that third party, i.e., beyond the payment of royalty. It is a commonplace of modern industrial relations for employers to provide security for employees and their families to enable them to meet problems arising from unemployment, illness, old age and death. While employers in many other industries assume this burden directly, this welfare fund was jointly created by the coal industry and the union in this regard, but in compliance with §302(c)(5)(B) it has assumed equal responsibility with the union for the management of the fund. In a very real sense Benedict's interest in the soundness of the fund and its management is in no way less than that of the promisee union. This of itself cautions against reliance upon language which does not explicitly provide that the parties contracted to protect Benedict by allowing the company to set off its damages against its royalty obligation.

Moreover, unlike the usual third-party beneficiary contract, this is an industry-wide agreement involving many promisors. If Benedict and other coal operators having damage claims against the union for its breaches may curtail royalty payments, the burden will fall in the first instance upon the employees and their families across the country. Ultimately this might result in pressures upon the other coal operators to increase their royalty payments to maintain the planned schedule of benefits. The application of the suggested rule of construction to this contract would require us to assume that the other coal operators who are parties to the agreement were willing to risk the threat of diminution of the fund in order to protect those of their number who might have become involved in local labor difficulties.

Furthermore, Benedict promised in the collective bargaining agreement to pay a specified scale of wages to the employees. It would not be contended that Benedict might recoup its damages by decreasing these wages. This could be rationalized by saying that the covenant to pay wages is included in separate contracts to hire entered into with each employee. The royalty payments are really another form of compensation to the employees, and as such the obligation to pay royalty might be thought to be incorporated into the individual employment contracts. This is not to say that the treatment should necessarily be accorded to royalty payments as is accorded to wages, but the similarity militates against the inference that the parties intended that the trustees' claim be subject to offset.

Finally a consideration which is not present in the case of other third-party beneficiary contracts is the impact of the national labor policy. Section 301(b) of the Taft-Hartley Act provides that "[a]ny money judgment against a labor organization in a district court of the United States shall be enforceable only against the organization as an entity and against its assets, and shall not be enforceable against any individual member or his assets." At the least, this evidences a congressional intention that the union as an entity, like a corporation, should in the absence of an agreement be the sole source of recovery for injury inflicted by it. Although this policy was prompted by a solicitude for the union members, because they might have little opportunity to prevent the union from committing actionable wrongs, it seems to us to apply with even greater force to protecting the interests of beneficiaries of the welfare fund, many of whom may be retired, or may be dependents, and therefore without any direct voice in the conduct of union affairs. Thus the national labor policy becomes an important consideration in determining whether the same inferences which might be drawn as to other third-party agreements should be drawn here.

Section 301 authorizes federal courts to fashion a body of federal law for the enforcement of collective bargaining agreements. Textile Workers Union v. Lincoln Mills, 353 U.S. 448. In the discharge of this function, having appropriate regard for the several considerations we have discussed, including the national labor policy, we hold that the parties to a collective bargaining agreement must express their meaning in unequivocal words before they can be said to have agreed that the union's breaches of its promises should give rise to a defense against the duty assumed by an employer to contribute to a welfare fund meeting the requirements of

§302(c)(5). We are unable to find such words in the general provisions already mentioned — "This Agreement is an integrated instrument and its respective provisions are interdependent," and "The contracting parties agree that [the no-strike clauses are] . . . part of the consideration of this contract" — or elsewhere in the agreement. The judgment of the Court of Appeals is therefore modified to provide that the District Court shall amend the judgment in favor of the trustees to allow immediate and unconditional execution, and interest, on the full amount of the trustees' judgment for $76,504.26 against Benedict.

It is so ordered.

[The dissenting opinion of Justice Frankfurter has been omitted.]

NOTE

1. The decision in the *Lewis* case was, of course, based partly on provisions of the Taft-Hartley Act and partly on theories of public policy which the Court found persuasive with respect to collective bargaining agreements but which it might not have found equally persuasive with respect to the "typical" or "usual" third party beneficiary contract. However, if, for the sake of the argument, we take Justice Brennan's opinion as a contribution to private contract law, the decision is that the promisor (Benedict) when sued by the beneficiary (the trustees) may not interpose as a defense the promisee's (union's) breach of the promisor-promisee contract. The promisor must pay the beneficiary and bring a separate action against the promisee to recover damages for the breach. Do you think that is necessarily an unsound rule or do you prefer the approach suggested in the quotation from Corbin? Would what we may call the Brennan rule lead to a sensible result if applied (with respect to the fraudulent misrepresentation defense) in the *Rouse* case, *supra* p. 1428? Are there some types of cases in which the promisee's breach should be a defense to the promisor when sued by the beneficiary and other types in which Justice Brennan's solution might be preferable?

2. The applicability of general contract principles to collective bargaining agreements is admirably discussed in Summers, Collective Agreements and the Law of Contracts, 78 Yale L.J. 525 (1969). Professor Summers comments that "the legal rules governing everyday commercial contracts can contribute little but mischief when applied to collective agreements, but the basic principles of contract . . . can make valuable contributions to the law of collective agreements." 78 Yale L.J. at 527. Professor Summers discusses the contract third party beneficiary rules in the context of collective agreements at 538 et seq.

3. In Aetna Insurance Co. v. Eisenberg, 294 F.2d 301 (8th Cir. 1961), Aetna had issued a Furriers' Customers Basic Policy to Eisenberg, the owner of a fur store who stored furs for his customers. Under the policy

Eisenberg was authorized to issue "Storage Receipts" to his customers which stated that the furs in storage were insured up to a stated amount under the Aetna policy. Eisenberg was required to make monthly reports to Aetna of the stated value of the furs for which he had issued Storage Receipts and to pay monthly premiums based on that value. After a fire had destroyed furs covered by such Storage Receipts, it was discovered that Eisenberg in his monthly reports had consistently and grossly undervalued the furs in storage; by reason of the undervaluation he had, of course, paid lower premiums to Aetna than he would have had to pay if he had declared their actual value. The holders of Storage Receipts brought actions directly against Aetna. Aetna defended on the ground of Eisenberg's breach of his duty to Aetna in filing the false monthly reports. The court held that the holders of Storage Receipts were third party beneficiaries of Eisenberg's policy with Aetna and that Aetna was "estopped" to defend on the ground that Eisenberg (promisee) had breached his contract with Aetna (promisor). The court stressed the fact that Aetna had accepted Eisenberg's reports without making an independent check of whether the reports were true or false. Do you think the case would have been decided the same way if Eisenberg had failed to pay any premium for the month in which the fire took place?

In its discussion of the "estoppel" point the court, in a string citation, referred to the *Rouse* case, *supra* p. 1428, as one in which the plaintiff had not made the argument that the defendant (promisor) was estopped. Do you think that the United States, in the *Rouse* case, could have successfully argued that Rouse was estopped to raise the defense of Winston's fraudulent misrepresentation? Would the estoppel theory have been helpful to Justice Brennan as an alternative explanation of the Supreme Court's decision in the *Lewis* case? If you agree that Aetna should have been held liable to the holders of the Storage Receipts, can you suggest any theory, other than that of estoppel, to justify the result?

4. The Restatement Second deals with the question of availability of defenses against a beneficiary in §309:

Defenses Against the Beneficiary

(1) A promise creates no duty to a beneficiary unless a contract is formed between the promisor and the promisee; and if a contract is voidable or unenforceable at the time of its formation the right of any beneficiary is subject to the infirmity.

(2) If a contract ceases to be binding in whole or in part because of impracticability, public policy, nonoccurrence of a condition, or present or prospective failure of performance, the right of any beneficiary is to that extent discharged or modified.

(3) Except as stated in Subsections (1) and (2) and in §311 or as provided by the contract, the right of any beneficiary against the promisor is not subject to the promisor's claims or defenses against the promisee or to the promisee's claims or defenses against the beneficiary.

(4)   A beneficiary's right against the promisor is subject to any claim or defense arising from his own conduct or agreement.

Under the approach of the Restatement Second, how would you decide the *Rouse* case? The *Lewis* case? The *Eisenberg* case? The hypothetical variants on Lawrence v. Fox suggested in the Introductory Note to this section?

CHAPTER 12

Assignment: The Liquidity of Contractual Obligations

Section 1. Introductory Note

1 G. GILMORE, SECURITY INTERESTS IN PERSONAL PROP-
ERTY §7.3 (1965): "It is undoubtedly true that there was a time in the
development of English law when intangibles — choses in action —
could not be effectively assigned.[1] It is not clear from our imperfect
historical knowledge whether this had been true from the time of the
rebirth of a commercial society after the Dark Ages or whether the rule,
despite its appearance of antiquity, was a later invention. Several quite
different explanations are offered of why there should ever have been
such a rule at any time. One is that our simple-minded ancestors were
incapable of conceiving the transfer of rights in property that was not
visible and tangible.[2] Such an explanation does as little credit to ourselves
as it does to our ancestors, who appear to have been capable of conceiving quite difficult thoughts indeed. Another (which may be called the
Ames-Holdsworth approach) looks on the rule of non-assignability as a
deduction from, or an integral part of, an early phase of contract theory: a
contract created a 'personal' bond between the parties who were 'in
privity of contract,' and therefore (?) contractual rights could not be
assigned to one not in privity.[3] This explanation has the merit of linking

1. The statement in the text requires this qualification: some types of intangible claims
and rights which a present-day lawyer might instinctively assume to be (and always to have
been) "choses in action" were not so regarded by lawyers during the period when the rule of
non-assignability of "choses" prevailed. Rents, annuities and advowsons (the right to fill
certain church offices), for example, were not thought of as choses in action and were
assignable under certain conditions. See 7 Holdsworth, A History of English Law 264, 528
(1922); 2 Pollock and Maitland, History of English Law 138 (1905). An illustrative case is Sir
Anthony Sturlyn v. Albany, Cro. Eliz. 67, 78 Eng. Rep. 327 (Q.B. 1587) [*supra* p. 707 —
EDS.]
2. See Maitland, The Mystery of Seisin, 2 L.Q. Rev. 481 (1886). This theory has been
criticized by Bordwell, The Alienability of Non-Possessory Interests, 19 N.C.L. Rev. 279
(1941).
3. Ames, The Inalienability of Choses in Action, Lectures on Legal History 210 et seq.
(1913); Holdsworth, The Treatment of Choses in Action by the Common Law, 33 Harv. L.
Rev. 997 (1920); 8 Holdsworth, A History of English Law 115 (1922); the "personal bond"
theory was put forth earlier in 2 Spence, The Equitable Jurisdiction of the Court of Chancery 849 et seq. (1850).

the development of the law of choses in action to the general historical development of contract law but ultimately explains nothing, since it fails to tell us why the contractual bond should have been considered 'personal' in this sense and with this result. A third idea, ably put forward by Glenn, is that the rule had nothing to do with conceptual difficulties or deductions from premises but was a rule of public policy based on economic grounds.[4] Lord Coke remarked in Lampet's Case that if choses in action were assignable the result would be 'the occasion of multiplying contentions and suits, great oppression of the people, and chiefly terre-tenants, and the subversion of the due and equal execution of justice.'[5] The results which Coke feared were perhaps of the same order as those which have prompted modern legislation prohibiting or restricting the assignment of wage claims.[6] Consistently with this approach the transfer of choses in action — the buying up of claims — was long condemned under the law against champerty and maintenance.[7] The maintenance cases, as early as the sixteenth century, make the interesting distinction (apparently accepted both in chancery and in the law courts) that what was forbidden was buying up claims for a present consideration; assignment of claims for a past debt was recognized and protected.[8]

"It is familiar knowledge that the device used to escape the nonassignability rule was to allow the assignee to bring suit on the claim in the name of the assignor, on the theory that he held a 'power of attorney' by virtue of the assignment.[9] Proponents of the personal contract or tie-that-binds explanation of the origin of the rule have looked on this as proof of the soundness of their position; the conceptual difficulties of contract were overcome by a conceptual borrowing from another developing body of law, that of agency. Although a person to whom a contract right was owed could not transfer it to one whom the obligor was not bound in privity, he could appoint an agent or attorney to collect in his place or stead.[10] In time the fictitious agency became irrevocable and the nominal owner, after notice of the assignment to the obligor, lost any power to interfere with the assignee's rights. Thus by the typically muddle-headed process of thinking known as the genius of the common law, assignments

4. Glenn, The Assignment of Choses in Action: Rights of Bona Fide Purchaser, 20 Va. L. Rev. 621, 635 et seq. (1934).
5. 10 Co. Rep. 46b, 48a (publ. 1727), 77 Eng. Rep. 994.
6. See, e.g., Strasburger, The Wage Assignment Problem, 19 Minn. L. Rev. 536 (1935).
7. This was the traditional approach up to the early nineteenth century. See, e.g., 2 Story, Commentaries on Equity §§1048, 1049 (2d ed. 1839).
8. Glenn, The Assignment of Choses in Action: Rights of Bona Fide Purchaser, 20 Va. L. Rev. 621, 639 (1934), collects the authorities. See in particular two articles by Winfield, History of Maintenance, 35 L.Q. Rev. 50 (1919); Assignments in Relation to Maintenance, id. at 143.
9. See Holdsworth, The History of the Treatment of Choses in Action by the Common Law, 33 Harv. L. Rev. 997, 1018 et seq. (1920), for a detailed treatment.
10. See, e.g., Ames, The Inalienability of Choses in Action, Lectures on Legal History 210, 213 (1913).

of intangibles were made effective in fact while basic theory still proclaimed them to be legal impossibilities.

"A quite different and peculiarly fascinating theory has been put forward to explain the practice of the assignees' suing in the name of the
assignor. From the time of the Norman conquest until the end of the
twelfth century Jews were permitted to live in England and were to a
considerable extent under royal protection. Under Jewish law, assignments of claims were recognized. Disputes between Jews were settled in
Jewish courts but, by royal license, a Jew could sue a Christian in the
royal courts. It has been suggested that if a Christian took an assignment
from a Jew (for which a royal license was required) he would sue on the
debt in the name of the Jewish assignor because 'by this method, the
assignee obtained all the Jewish privileges of security, action and execution, which were not otherwise available to Christians.'[11] So attractive an
explanation ought to be true, even if it is not; the present author disclaims
sufficient learning to entitle him to an opinion. As Glenn points out, the
Jewish theory offers an explanation which does not require resort to the
assumed conceptual impossibility of transferring 'personal' contract
rights.[12]

"History is quite as much what has been believed about the past as what
happened in the past. In this sense what nineteenth century judges and
lawyers believed about English practices and rules in the sixteenth, seventeenth and eighteenth centuries is history even though modern research may prove that the supposed practices and rules never existed.
The treatises and judicial opinions of the first half of the nineteenth
century leave no doubt about the pattern into which the sense of history
had transmuted the past. It was believed that the English courts had at
one time refused to give effect to assignments of claims; that courts of
equity had rejected the legal rule and recognized assignments; that courts
of law, bowing to the injunctive powers of equity, had in turn recognized
the rights of assignees to sue on assigned claims, but only in the name of
the assignor and on the theory that the assignment constituted an irrevocable power of attorney; that although assignees could thus enforce their
claims in either the law courts or the equity courts, choses in action
remained, theoretically, assignable in equity but non-assignable at law;
that the interest of an assignee was therefore equitable and not legal."[13]

11. Bailey, Assignment of Debts in England from the Twelfth to the Twentieth Centuries, 47 L.Q. Rev. 516, 527 (1931).
12. Glenn, The Assignment of Choses in Action: Rights of Bona Fide Purchaser, 20 Va.
L. Rev. 621, 638 (1934).
13. In fact the law courts had become the normal forum for suits by assignees and were
becoming the exclusive forum:

> If the theory had actually been applied, that choses in action were not transferable,
> the assignee therefore needing the aid of equity, then two things would have fol-
> lowed. The assignee, in order to collect his debt, could have come into equity as of
> course; and we would not find earlier writers discussing any other reason why a

Section 2. Intangible Claims and their Transferability

MULLER v. PONDIR
55 N.Y. 325 (1873)

Appeal from order of General Term of the Supreme Court in the first judicial department, reversing a judgment in favor of the defendant Pondir, entered upon the decision of the court at Special Term, and granting a new trial. (Reported below, 6 Lans., 472)

This action was brought to recover possession of certain bills of exchange. Defendant Pondir only appeared and answered, claiming the bills as a bona fide purchaser.

On the 12th of May, 1869, Schepeler & Co., merchants in New York, sent to the plaintiff, a banker doing business in Havana, under the firm name of Muller & Co., an order, which the plaintiff received, directing him to draw bills of exchange, for £20,000, on J. Henry Schroder & Co., of London, to sell the bills so drawn in Havana, and invest the proceeds in bills of exchange on New York, payable in currency, and to send these last mentioned bills to Schepeler & Co. Upon receiving this order, the plaintiff proceeded to execute it by drawing bills of exchange, as therein directed, for Schepeler & Co., upon J. Henry Schroder & Co., London correspondents of Schepeler & Co., payable sixty days after sight, and

---

common law court would not enforce assignments. But at the very time when nineteenth century writers were urging this theory, neither of its logical consequences was in application.

In the first place, the common law courts were open to the assignee, and equity courts were not, save in exceptional cases. While Justice Story was writing his book on equity, he received a shock in the shape of an English decision where the Court of Chancery refused to entertain a bill by an assignee for the collection of the debt, because no special circumstances had been shown to justify equitable aid. This the learned writer treated as an innovation by no means to be commended: it was a rule "comparatively new," said he. But in this he was mistaken. The English Chancery had done the same thing on previous occasions; the first reported instance having occurred over a century before Story wrote. Further, the intervening period had been marked by similar decisions on both sides of the Atlantic. From these decisions, as well as those of the common law courts themselves, it appeared that the right of the assignee to sue at law, using the assignee's name for that purpose, was recognized not only in rules of court but in rules of law laid down by decisions.

Citations omitted. Glenn, *supra* note 12 at 32.

By the middle of the nineteenth century some writers were aware of the changing situation. See, e.g., 1 Parsons, Law of Contracts 192-197 (1855) (Parsons' most detailed statement appears in a footnote (f) at 193); 2 Spence, The Equitable Jurisdiction of the Court of Chancery 853-855 (1850).

[With the abolition of separate law and equity courts and the enactment of "real party in interest" statutes under which the assignee was required to sue in his own name, one would assume that the debate over whether an assignment creates a legal or equitable interest would have lost its significance. As the cases in this chapter suggest, however, this ancient distinction may have some life left in it still. — EDS.]

selling the same in the city of Havana; among these bills were bills amounting in the aggregate to £9,000, and the proceeds of these £9,000 constitute the fund in controversy in this action. The bills so purchased by the direction of Schepeler & Co. were all made payable to the order of Richard Smith, a clerk in the employment of Schepeler & Co. The bills were inclosed by the plaintiff with a letter of advice in an envelope addressed to Schepeler & Co., and on the 13th day of May, 1869, after the mailbag for the steamer Cleopatra, plying between the said city of Havana and the city of New York, had been closed and taken on board the vessel, was handed by a clerk of the plaintiff to the purser of the steamer.

On the said 13th day of May, 1869, after the purchase and shipment of the bills in question, the plaintiff at Havana sent to Schepeler & Co., at New York, the following telegram.

Havana, May thirteenth (13th), 1869.

Schepeler & Co.:

Drew nine (9) twelve (12) and eleven three-quarters (11¾), remit Cleopatra, sixty thousand (60,000) twenty-six half (26½).

MULLER.

This telegram was intended to and did give Schepeler & Co. to understand that the plaintiff had drawn £9,000 as directed, had sold a portion of the bills at 112 and a portion at 111¾, and against the bills so drawn would remit by the steamer Cleopatra, $60,000 in bills drawn on New York, which they had purchased at 26½ per cent discount. At the time the plaintiff sent this telegram he had no notice that Schepeler & Co. were in failing circumstances. This dispatch was received by Schepeler & Co. late in the afternoon on the same day it was sent, or the next morning.

For several years prior to the 15th day of May, 1869, Schepeler & Co. and the said Pondir had had transactions with each other, including borrowing and lending money. For a year prior to the 15th day of May, 1869, these transactions had been of almost daily occurrence; the loans of money made by Pondir to Schepeler & Co. were in large part made by him as a broker for account of other persons, and in part on his own account. These loans were sometimes made upon security, and sometimes without security, depending upon the state of accounts between the parties.

On the afternoon of the 13th of May, 1869, John F. Schepeler informed the defendant Pondir that he would want a good deal of currency the next day; Pondir inquired what securities he had to offer; Schepeler answered, that he did not know yet, but would see in the morning.

On the morning of the 14th of May, 1869, the defendant John F. Schepeler called upon the defendant Pondir, and exhibited to him the telegram of Muller & Co., and applied to him for a loan of $70,000. The defendant Pondir thereupon agreed to make a loan to Schepeler & Co. of $70,000 upon the security, and of the currency bills in question, with the understanding that Schepeler & Co. should surrender to him the dispatch, accompanied by a letter expressing their understanding.

Schepeler & Co. then addressed to Pondir a letter, of the following tenor:

New York, 14th May, 1869.

John Pondir, Esq.:

Dear Sir. — Being in want of some funds, and not having any available securities at hand, we inclose the cable telegram from Havana, advising remittances of about $60,000 currency, which, in case you can furnish us the money, we shall hand over to you upon their arrival.

Yours truly,
SCHEPELER & CO.

Upon the receipt of this letter, with the cable telegram in question, the defendant Pondir on the same day loaned to Schepeler & Co. the sum of $70,000, which money has not been repaid. This loan was made by Pondir in good faith, he relying upon the telegram of the plaintiff and the security of the bills in question. At the time of making this loan the defendant Pondir had no knowledge that Schepeler & Co. were in failing circumstances, and no reason to suppose that their pecuniary condition was not as good as at any time theretofore. In the afternoon of the 15th of May, 1869, the firm of Schepeler & Co. failed, owing the defendant Pondir the loan in question. The aforesaid sterling bills of exchange, drawn by Muller & Co. on J. Henry Schroder & Co., of London, were not accepted, but were protested for non-acceptance, and thereupon Muller & Co. provided J. Henry Schroder & Co. with funds with which to pay them at maturity, and they were so paid.

On the 17th of May, 1869, the day before the arrival of the steamer Cleopatra at the port of New York, the agent of the plaintiff applied to Schepeler & Co. to permit him to receive, on behalf of the plaintiff, the letter inclosing the currency bills in question, on the ground that Schepeler & Co. had failed, and the plaintiff would be obliged to provide for the sterling bills. This permission not being given, the present action was commenced.

The purser, after the arrival of the steamer at New York, handed said package to the postmaster at the city of New York; such delivery was not made until after the letters in the mail bag brought by said steamer had been delivered and distributed, and not until after bills inclosed in said letter had been demanded of the firm of Schepeler & Co. and of the postmaster, and not until after this action had been commenced, and an injunction obtained and served on Schepeler & Co. and Smith, restraining them from interfering with, or indorsing, said bills.

The court found as a conclusion of law that the plaintiff did not sustain such a relation to the currency bills of exchange purchased in Havana, the proceeds of which are in controversy in this action, as to entitle him to exercise the right of stoppage in transitu in respect thereof, and directed judgment awarding the bills to defendant Pondir.

ALLEN, J. Pondir, who claims title to the bills in controversy, under Schepeler & Co., alone defends this action. As between him and Schepeler & Co., it may be conceded that by the loan of money to the latter firm, under the circumstances established at the trial, and upon their promise to transfer the bills when they should arrive in New York, he acquired an equitable title, and could have enforced a specific performance of the promise, and an indorsement and delivery of the bills to him.

But this equitable right comes far short of conferring upon him the rights of a bona fide holder for value of negotiable paper when transferred in the usual method and in the ordinary course of business. A transferee of commercial paper for value, in the ordinary course of business, without notice of any defects in the title, is protected by the law-merchant against all latent equities, whether of third persons or of parties to the instrument. His title is perfect, and his right to enforce the obligation absolute. But if any of the circumstances are wanting which go to make up this perfect title, a purchaser or transferee of commercial paper takes it subject to the same rules which control in the case of a transfer or assignment of non-negotiable instruments.

The defendant Pondir never became the holder of the bills in dispute; they were not transferred to him by indorsement in the usual way or in any other manner, and were not at any time in his possession, either actual or constructive; they were never within his control or in the possession or within the control of Schepeler & Co., from and under whom he claims title. He only acquired such rights and equities as existed in Schepeler & Co., subject to all equities as against them. He occupies precisely the position of that firm; and whatever rights or remedies the plaintiffs or others had against them, in respect to the bills, can be asserted against Pondir as their equitable assignee. (Gilbert v. Sharp, 2 Lansing, 412; Hedges v. Sealy, 9 Barb., 214; Story on Prom. Notes, §120, note 1; id., §120, a; Savage v. King, 17 Maine, 301; Calder v. Billington, 15 id., 398; Southard v. Porter, 43 N.H.R., 379.)

Neither was there anything in the history of the transaction or the acts of the parties which will give Pondir a better or other title as against the plaintiff than the mere equitable title, valid as against Schepeler & Co. only. The plaintiff is not estopped from asserting the same equities and the same legal rights against Pondir which would have availed against Schepeler & Co. The only act of the plaintiff upon which stress is laid and upon which an estoppel is sought to be based, is his dispatch to Schepeler & Co.; elliptical and obscure in its terms, but which was understood by the parties to whom it was addressed, and which indicated that the sender had drawn and sold bills on London to the amount of £9,000, at the prices stated, and against the bills so drawn would remit, by the steamer Cleopatra, $60,000 in bills on New York, which had been purchased at the discount stated. The telegram was true in all its parts; and the plaintiff does not seek now to controvert the truth of any of the statements there made. There was nothing in it to indicate the relation of the plaintiff or his correspondents, Schepeler & Co., to the bills, or the title of either to them. There was no statement inconsistent with the absolute ownership, by the plaintiff, of the bills to arrive by the Cleopatra, or with any claim the plaintiff might make to or in respect of them as against Schepeler & Co., or any other person. The title of the bills was not the subject of or referred to in the dispatch; and if Pondir acted at all on the faith of Schepeler & Co.'s ownership or right to dispose of the bills, it was upon their statement of such ownership and right, and not upon any statement of the plaintiff; and the case shows, as the court has found, that Pondir did part with his money solely on the credit of Schepeler & Co., on the faith of their representations and promise to hand the bills over on their arrival. The only practical use of the telegram was to identify in a manner the bills which Schepeler & Co. claimed to own, and promised to transfer. The court below has found that the loan was made by Pondir in good faith; he relying upon the telegram of the plaintiff and the security of the bills in question. He could only rely on the telegram so far as it assumed to state facts; and the only security by means of or upon the bills he acquired was by the written promise of Schepeler & Co. to transfer them; and their representations de hors their dispatch.

But an insuperable difficulty in predicating an estoppel in pais against the plaintiff upon the dispatch is, that it was designed solely for the information of the persons to whom it was addressed, and not to influence the action of any other person; and the communication was not of a character calculated to or which could, in the usual course of business, influence the action of third persons; and least of all was it calculated to induce any one to part with money upon the credit of the bills referred to, and faith in the title of Schepeler & Co. to them. The plaintiff could not have foreseen that the dispatch would be used as the basis of a credit, or that money could be borrowed on the faith of it. Every element of an estoppel was wanting. A party is only concluded, that is, estopped from alleging the truth by a declaration or representation, inconsistent with the facts asserted and attempted to be proved, when it is made with intent, or is calculated, or may be reasonably expected to influence the conduct of another in a manner in which he will be prejudiced if the party making the statement is allowed to retract, and when it has influenced and induced action, from which injury and loss will accrue of a retraction as allowed. . . . There is no statement in the cable dispatch which is inconsistent with the rights now asserted by the plaintiff; and the assertion of such rights is not against good conscience in any view of the dispatch or the use designed or expected to be made of it, or which was actually made of it. The plaintiff is not therefore estopped from asserting any right he may have to the bills in controversy.

Neither does the rule invoked by Pondir, that when one of two innocent persons must suffer from the wrongful or fraudulent act of another, the loss should devolve upon him by whose act or omission the wrong-doer has been enabled to perpetrate the fraud, avail him. That applies only when the wrong-doer is invested by the party sought to be charged, with the ordinary indicia of ownership, and *jus disponendi* of property, or an apparent authority to do the act from which loss must accrue to one of two innocent parties. (Commercial Bank of Buffalo v. Kortright, 22 Wend., 348., Young v. Grote, 4 Bing., 253.) The evidence of ownership of negotiable bills is their possession, properly indorsed, so as to pass the title to the holder. There is no such thing as a symbolical delivery of negotiable instruments; and the law does not recognize, for commercial purposes, a right of possession as distinct from the actual possession. Had Schepeler & Co. had actual possession, themselves, of the bills, and then indorsed and transferred them to Pondir, the plaintiff would have been remediless. This is not only the legal evidence of ownership, but it is that required in dealing in commercial paper in the ordinary course of business; and he who acts with less evidence of title in one claiming to have the right of disposal, does so at his peril. As owners, Schepeler & Co. had no apparent title upon which the plaintiff could or did rely.

[In the balance of his opinion Allen, J., concluded that Schepeler & Co. had no real or apparent authority, as agents of Muller, to deal with the bills and that Muller had a right to recover the bills analogous to the right of a seller of goods to stop the goods in transit on discovery of the buyer's insolvency.]

NOTE

1. What seems to be meant by the statement at the beginning of the opinion that Pondir had acquired, as against Schepeler, "equitable title" to the bills?

2. If Schepeler had indorsed and delivered the bills to Pondir, Muller's equity of ownership would have been cut off, assuming that Pondir had taken the bills in good faith and without notice of Muller's claim. The transfer would then be referred to as a "negotiation" (see U.C.C. §3-202) and Pondir as a "holder in due course" (see U.C.C. §§3-302, 3-305). In the absence of indorsement and delivery Pondir did not even become a "holder" of the bills (which means that he could not have enforced payment of the bills against the obligors), let alone a "holder in due course" (i.e., a holder who holds free of equities of ownership, like those of Muller in the principal case, as well as of defenses such as failure of

consideration which may exist between the original parties to the instrument).

3. A basic rule of negotiable instruments law is that the only effective method of transferring a claim evidenced by an instrument negotiable in form is by the physical delivery of the instrument, together with any necessary indorsements. (On the formal requisites of negotiability see Britton on Negotiable Instruments (2d ed. 1961); Gilmore, The Commercial Doctrine of Good Faith Purchase, 63 Yale L.J. 1057 (1954).) This rule, as the principal case indicates, was firmly established at common law and has been carried forward by the codifying statutes (the Negotiable Instruments Law (N.I.L.), promulgated in 1896, was adopted in all American jurisdictions; it has now been superseded by Article 3 of the Uniform Commercial Code). The rule applies not only to short term instruments for the payment of money (bills, notes and checks) but to long-term investment securities as well (see Article 8 of the Code).

At the opposite pole from negotiable instruments and securities are what the common law called "choses in action." The original common law distinction was between "things" (choses) that could be transferred by delivery of possession (chattels, negotiable instruments and the like) and "things" that, having, in fact or in law, no physical or tangible existence, could not be so transferred but that were enforceable by action at law or in equity. Claims arising out of contract or other relationships, not evidenced by a negotiable instrument or other formal writing, were choses in action. The term continues in current use, although the term "contract rights" has gained popularity as a synonym for many types of claims which the older cases called choses in action. The term "assignment" has been used for centuries to describe the transfer, whether absolute or for security, of choses in action or contract rights.

We must thus distinguish between claims of the negotiable instrument type, evidenced by a writing whose physical possession is essential to ownership of the claim, and claims of the chose in action or contract right type, not evidenced by such a writing. The latter type is "assigned"; the former type is "negotiated" (i.e., by endorsement and delivery). As the principal case indicates, an attempted "assignment" of a negotiable instrument is ineffective, except possibly against the transferor himself. Consider, in the light of the subsequent case material, whether Pondir might not have been better off if the security for his loan to Schepeler had been non-negotiable choses in action bought up by Muller and by him assigned to Schepeler.

The student should be warned that the distinction between "assignable" claims (choses in action) and "negotiable" claims (choses in possession) is not, and never has been, as neat and tidy as the preceding discussion may have suggested. There have always been claims of an intermediate class that, although the delivery of the writing evidencing the claim is looked on as having some legal or jural significance, can nevertheless be transferred by a "mere assignment" (i.e., an agreement to transfer without delivery of the writing). Thus, under Article 9 of the Uniform Commercial Code, a security interest in "chattel paper" (the term is defined in §9-105) can be "perfected" (i.e., made effective against third parties) either by delivery of the chattel paper to the secured party or by the filing of a financing statement in the public records. By way of contrast, a security interest in a negotiable instrument can be perfected under Article 9 only by delivery of the negotiable instrument to the secured party and a security interest in pure intangibles of the chose in action type ("accounts" and "general intangibles" in the Article 9 terminology) can be perfected only by filing. (For the definitions of the "pure intangibles," see §9-106, discussed *infra* p. 1457; for the perfection provisions, see §§9-301, 9-304(1), 9-305.) See generally Clark, Abstract Rights Versus Paper Rights Under Article 9 of the Uniform Commercial Code, 84 Yale L.J. 445 (1975).

4. The consideration doctrine tells us that a promise to make a gift is usually unenforceable. If the donor revokes his promise (or dies) before making the gift, the disappointed donee, except to the extent that he may be helped by the doctrine of promissory estoppel, has no recourse against the promisor (or his estate). The point in time at which a promise to make a gift of an intangible claim is to be considered as having been executed poses obvious difficulties. One instructive line of cases has to do with attempts by dying persons to make gifts of bank accounts held in savings accounts or in checking accounts. A typical savings account case is Brooks v. Mitchell, 163 Md. 1, 161 A. 261, 84 A.L.R. 547 (1932) (delivery of passbook to donee held to effect valid gift causa mortis of the money in the account). Cf. Burrows v. Burrows, 240 Mass. 485, 134 N.E. 271 (1922) (delivery of check together with checking account passbook by dying mother to daughter held not to effect a valid gift causa mortis). Why the apparent distinction between savings accounts and checking accounts? See Whitney v. Canadian Bank of Commerce, 232 Ore. 1, 374 P.2d 441 (1962); 239 Ore. 472, 398 P.2d 183 (1965), which involved attempted gifts causa mortis by delivery of passbooks of both the decedent's savings account and his checking account. (On the rule that the delivery of a check does not of itself operate as an assignment to the checkholder of funds in the bank account, see Note 5. How can a gift of a pure intangible or chose in action be made? Reread the discussion in Gray v. Barton, 55 N.Y. 68 (1873), discussed *supra* p. 673; see further Adams v. Merced Stone Co., 176 Cal. 415, 178 P. 498, 3 A.L.R. 928 (1917). Chase National Bank v. Sayles, 11 F.2d 948 (1st Cir. 1926) contains an elaborate discussion of gift assignments that embalms much ancient learning.

5. There was some controversy at common law over the question whether a check drawn against a checking account was effective as an assignment to the checkholder of the money in the account up to the amount of the check. The majority common law position was that a

check was not an assignment but merely a revocable order (from which it followed that the drawer-depositor could stop payment of his check at any time until the bank had paid (or certified) it). That position was codified in N.I.L. §189 and recodified in U.C.C. §3-409(1). The Code formulation is as follows: "A check or other draft does not of itself operate as an assignment of any funds in the hands of the drawee available for its payment, and the drawee [i.e., the bank] is not liable on the instrument until he accepts it." Note that the provision is that the check or draft does not "of itself" operate as an assignment. N.I.L. §189 also contained the "of itself" language. Thus the codifying statutes left open the theoretical possibility that money held in a checking account could be "assigned," rather than merely drawn against by check in the normal manner. The leading pre-statutory case on when a check could operate as an assignment was Fourth Street Bank v. Yardley, 165 U.S. 634 (1897). However, the check that was held effective as an assignment in the Yardley case was not a check drawn by an individual on his checking account; it was a "check" drawn by one bank in favor of another bank from which it had borrowed money to meet its clearing-house balances. The consequence of holding the "check" to be an assignment was that the payee-bank was given a priority over general creditors in the drawer-bank's liquidation for insolvency. In recent years there seems to have been little litigation over attempted "assignments" of checking account balances.

SHIRO v. DREW
174 F. Supp. 495 (D. Me. 1959)

GIGNOUX, District Judge. This is an action brought pursuant to the provisions of Section 60 of the Bankruptcy Act, 11 U.S.C.A. §96, by plaintiff as trustee in bankruptcy of the American Fiberlast Company to recover as a voidable preference the sum of $2,056.87 paid by the bankrupt to defendant on February 11, 1957.

The facts necessary to a decision in the matter have been stipulated by the parties and, as stipulated, are so found by the Court as follows:

In August or September, 1956 the American Fiberlast Company obtained a contract from Hazeltine Electronics Corporation for the construction of a twenty-one foot Radome[14] for the price of $4,900. The purchase order for the Radome was delivered by Fiberlast to defendant and retained by him until February 11, 1957 for use in attempting to borrow money for the Corporation to perform the contract.

On November 1, 1956 Fiberlast, by Joseph L. Brewster, its president, executed under its corporate seal and delivered to J. Riker Proctor and

14. A Radome is a plastic cover for outdoor radar equipment.

defendant the following instrument, which was in letter form on the corporate stationery:

Nov. 1, 1956

To J. Riker Proctor and Gordon L. Drew

Gentlemen:

Whereas The American Fiberlast Co. has received a contract for a 21′ Radome from Hazeltine Electronics Corp. totaling $4900.00 but is unable to finance the purchase of the necessary materials and labor to construct the dome — the American Fiberlast Co. agrees that any money advanced by Mr. Proctor and Mr. Drew for the specific expense of manufacturing the Radome will be paid immediately to Mr. Proctor and Mr. Drew upon receipt of Hazeltine's remittance irrespective of any other demands from other creditors.

The American Fiberlast Co. (Corp. Seal)

/s/ J. L. BREWSTER

by JOSEPH L. BREWSTER, *President*

Subsequent to November 1, 1956 defendant loaned to Fiberlast the sum of $2,056.87 for the specific purpose of permitting it to perform its contract with Hazeltine. This amount was loaned by defendant in reliance upon the instrument of November 1, and the money so loaned was in fact used by Fiberlast for the performance of the Hazeltine contract. With the help of these funds Fiberlast completed the contract and received the $4,900 contract price from Hazeltine on February 11, 1957. On the same date Fiberlast repaid to defendant the $2,056.87 here in issue.

Fiberlast was adjudged a bankrupt on petition of J. Riker Proctor and two others filed on February 20, 1957. The stipulation recites that at all times material hereto Fiberlast was insolvent; defendant had reasonable cause to believe Fiberlast was insolvent; and there were in existence creditors of Fiberlast, other than defendant, who have not been repaid their debts.

Section 60 of the Bankruptcy Act provides in part as follows:

Sec. 60   *Preferred creditors*

a.   (1) A preference is a transfer . . . of any of the property of a debtor to or for the benefit of a creditor for or on account of an antecedent debt, made or suffered by such debtor while insolvent and within four months before the filing by or against him of the petition initiating a proceeding under this Act, the effect of which transfer will be to enable such creditor to obtain a greater percentage of his debt than some other creditor of the same class. . . .

b.   Any such preference may be avoided by the trustee if the creditor receiving it . . . has, at the time when the transfer is made, reasonable cause to believe that the debtor is insolvent. Where the preference is voidable, the trustee may recover the property. . . . For the purpose of any recovery or avoidance under this section, where plenary proceedings are necessary, any State court which would have had jurisdiction if bankruptcy had not intervened and any court of bankruptcy shall have concurrent jurisdiction.

On the stipulated facts, the disputed payment was concededly a transfer of property by a debtor, while insolvent, made within four months before the filing of a petition in bankruptcy, for the benefit of a creditor, who had reasonable cause to believe that the debtor was insolvent, the effect of which was to prefer that creditor. Thus the only question for determination by the Court is whether or not the sum of $2,056.87 was transferred to defendant "for or on account of an antecedent debt." On this issue defendant contends that the letter of November 1, 1956 was either a partial assignment or a declaration of trust by Fiberlast of a portion of the proceeds of the Hazeltine contract, and that the repayment of his loan was, in consequence not "for or on account of an antecedent debt." Plaintiff's position is that the letter was a mere promise to pay out of a particular fund, and that the subsequent payment was accordingly "for or on account of an antecedent debt," preferential and voidable.

With respect to defendant's first contention, it is clear that if the instrument of November 1, 1956 was a partial assignment[15] given as security for loans to be made to Fiberlast by defendant, no preference occurred when the corporation repaid the $2,056.87 subsequently loaned it by defendant. Doggett v. Chelsea Trust Co., 1 Cir., 1934, 73 F.2d 614. It is equally clear that if the instrument was no more than a promise to pay from a particular source, the repayment to defendant was in satisfaction of a pre-existing debt and preferential. See Lone Star Cement Corp. v. Swartwout, 4 Cir., 1938, 93 F.2d 767, 769. Decision of this aspect of this case consequently hinges upon the proper construction of the instrument of November 1, 1956 — a construction controlled by the law of Maine, where the instrument was executed. Manchester Nat. Bank v. Roche, 1 Cir., 1951, 186 F.2d 827, 829; Lone Star Cement Corp. v. Swartwout, *supra*, 93 F.2d 770; In re Dodge-Freedman Poultry Co., D.C.N.H. 1956, 148 F. Supp. 647, 650, *affirmed per curiam sub nom.* Dodge-Freedman Poultry Co. v. Delaware Mills, Inc., 1 Cir., 1957, 244 F.2d 314.

No Maine case succinctly sets forth the requisites of a valid assignment. However, it is hornbook law that an assignment is an act or manifestation by the owner of a right which indicates his intention to transfer, without further action, that right to another. See Restatement, Contracts §149(1) (1932). And the courts have uniformly recognized that an agreement to pay out of a particular fund, without more, is not an assignment, but that to constitute an assignment there must be a manifestation of an intention by the assignor to relinquish control of the right assigned and to

15. A partial assignment is valid in Maine. National Exchange Bank of Boston v. McLoon, 1882, 73 Me. 498.

appropriate that right to the assignee. Christmas v. Russell, 1871, 14 Wall. 69, 84, 81 U.S. 69, 84, 20 L. Ed. 762; Lone Star Cement Corp. v. Swartwout, *supra*; B. Kuppenheimer & Co. v. Mornin, 8 Cir., 1935, 78 F.2d 261, 101 A.L.R. 75, *certiorari denied* 1935, 296 U.S. 615, 56 S. Ct. 135, 80 L. Ed. 436; Farmers' Bank v. Hayes, 6 Cir., 1932, 58 F.2d 34, 37, *certiorari denied* 1932, 287 U.S. 602, 53 S. Ct. 8, 77 L. Ed. 524; East Side Packing Co. v. Fahy Market, 2 Cir., 1928, 24 F.2d 644, 645; In re Dodge-Freedman Poultry Co., *supra*, 148 F. Supp. 650; 2 Williston on Contracts §428 (Rev. ed. 1936). While no particular words are required for an assignment (See e.g. Wade v. Bessey, 1884, 76 Me. 413), the intent to transfer a present interest must be manifest, and the assignor must not retain any control over the right assigned or any power of revocation. In fact, it frequently has been said that the test is whether or not the debtor would be authorized to pay the amount directly to the person claiming to be the assignee, without further action or consent by the assignor. See Christmas v. Russell, *supra*, 14 Wall. 84, 81 U.S. 84; Farmers' Bank v. Hayes, *supra*, 58 F.2d 37; East Side Packing Co. v. Fahy Market, *supra*, 24 F.2d 645; 2 Williston on Contracts §428 (Rev. ed. 1936). As stated in Lone Star Cement Corp. v. Swartwout, *supra* (93 F.2d at pages 769-770):

> No particular phraseology is required to effect an assignment, and it may be either in oral or written form; *but the intent to vest in the asignee a present right in the thing assigned must be manifested by some oral or written word or by some conduct signifying a relinquishment of control by the assignor and an appropriation to the assignee.* . . . (Emphasis supplied.)

With these fundamental principles in mind, the Court turns to the interpretation and effect of the writing involved in this case. As with any written instrument, the intention of the parties controls in determining whether it constitutes an assignment. See Wolters Village Management Co. v. Merchants and Planters National Bank of Sherman, 5 Cir., 1955, 223 F.2d 793, 798. And the intention of the parties is to be gathered from the writing construed in light of the subject matter, the motive and purpose of making the agreement, and the object to be consummated, the words used being given their common and ordinary meaning. See Bar Harbor & Union River Power Co. v. Foundation Co., 1930, 129 Me. 81, 85, 149 A. 801; Salmon Lake Seed Co. v. Frontier Trust Co., 1931, 130 Me. 69, 71, 153 A. 671. So viewed, the instrument of November 1, 1956 is susceptible of only one reasonable interpretation. It provides that any money "advanced" by Mr. Proctor and defendant for the manufacture of the Radome "will be" repaid immediately "upon receipt of" Hazeltine's remittance, irrespective of any other demands from other creditors. There is nothing in its terms indicative of that manifestation of present surrender of control essential to an assignment. Language of present transfer is wholly lacking. Defendant asserts that the instrument was drawn by laymen, inartistically perhaps, solely with the intention of securing future advances this defendant and Mr. Proctor might make to attempt to save a sinking corporation. Mayhap such was the case. Unfortunately for this defendant, the Court has before it no evidence of what the parties intended save the instrument itself. Whether it was authored by laymen or lawyers, it speaks clearly in future terms and can rise to no higher legal status than a promise to pay out of a particular fund to come into existence in the future. Insofar as this record discloses, the debtor was not notified that the contract had been assigned, nor was any attempt made to limit the Corporation's control over the contract or its proceeds. Cf. Lone Star Cement Corp. v. Swartwout, supra, 93 F.2d 769. There being no evidence of an intent to transfer any immediate right to defendant, but rather evidence only of a promise to pay at a future date, the authorities which have been cited compel the conclusion that no assignment was intended or effected by the instrument of November 1, 1956.

[The court's discussion of several cases is omitted.]

Defendant's alternative suggestion that the November instrument constituted a declaration of trust must also fail. The Court's construction of the instrument as a promise to pay in the future requires rejection of this argument. See 1 Scott on Trusts §12 (2d ed. 1956). As stated in Northwestern Mutual Life Insurance Co. v. Collamore, 1905, 100 Me. 578, at pages 584, 62 A. 652, at page 655:

> A declaration of trust to be effectual, must be explicit, unconditional, and complete . . . the declaration must be of a present trust, vesting the equitable title in the beneficiary thereby and irrevocably.

On the analysis previously stated, the November instrument evidences no intent to vest equitable title to any of the proceeds of the Hazeltine contract irrevocably in defendant.

Since the November 1 instrument was neither a partial assignment nor a declaration of trust, it follows that the payment by Fiberlast to defendant on February 11, 1957 was a preference within the meaning of Section 60, sub. a of the Bankruptcy Act and may be avoided by the Trustee under Section 60, sub. b.

Judgment is accordingly ordered for plaintiff in the amount of $2,056.87, with costs.

NOTE

1. A trustee in bankruptcy is empowered to set aside or "avoid" certain transfers made by the bankrupt prior to the institution of bankruptcy proceedings and to draw the property transferred back into the estate for the benefit of all the bankrupt's unsecured creditors. Among the trustee's avoiding powers is his power to set aside certain entirely legitimate but preferential transfers to favored creditors. The two key

elements of a so-called voidable preference (there are several more) are that it be for an antecedent debt and be made shortly before the debtor's bankruptcy; the idea is to frustrate last-minute efforts by the debtor to insure better treatment for some of his creditors, even where (as in the principal case) the creditor receiving the preference has a perfectly valid claim against the estate. Contemporaneous exchanges (where the debtor receives something in return at the same time that he makes his transfer) are not treated as preferences on the theory that they do not deplete the debtor's estate and therefore do not disadvantage other creditors. See Jackson, Avoiding Powers in Bankruptcy, 36 Stan. L. Rev. 725 (1984).

The elements of a voidable preference are defined in §547 of the Bankruptcy Code of 1978, which replaced §60 of the Bankruptcy Act. There are some important differences between these two sections, but for purposes of understanding the principal case, they may be disregarded.

Since one of the elements of a preference is that it be for an *antecedent* debt, it must be determined when a transfer, alleged to be preferential, was made. There are two different moments at which Fiberlast might be said to have transferred the proceeds of its Radome contract to the defendant: on November 1, when it promised to do so, and on February 11, when the funds themselves were paid over. If, for voidable preference purposes, the transfer is deemed to have occurred on the earlier of these two dates, then it cannot have been for an antecedent debt since the defendant did not make his loan until some time after November 1; hence, Judge Gignoux's lengthy discussion of the distinction between an assignment (which constitutes the present transfer of a property right) and a promise (which is a commitment to make such a transfer in the future). Does this distinction — supported by a great deal of ancient legal learning — make much sense to you? Does not a promisee also acquire an immediate property right by virtue of the promise he receives, i.e., the right to sue for damages if the promisor fails to perform? This right, however, so long as it is unsecured, is only an inchoate or general right against the entirety of the debtor's estate, not a right to specific property. Is this what distinguishes an assignment from a promise?

2. Under Article 9 of the Uniform Commercial Code, the terms "account" and "general intangibles" are used to describe the types of intangible claims which the common law called "choses in action." These terms are defined in Code §9-106 as follows:

> "Account" means any right to payment for goods sold or leased or for services rendered which is not evidenced by an instrument or chattel paper, whether or not it has been earned by performance. "General intangibles" means any personal property (including things in action) other than goods, accounts, chattel paper, documents, instruments, and money. All rights to payment earned or unearned under a charter or other contract involving the use or hire of a vessel and all rights incident to the charter or contract are accounts.

§9-106 was amended in 1972; for a brief discussion of the pre-1972 version of §9-106, see the Note following Speelman v. Pascal, *infra* p. 1492.

3. U.C.C. §9-302 provides (by negative implication) that the transferee of an interest in accounts can "perfect" his interest (whether the transfer is an outright sale or merely for security) only by making a filing in the appropriate public office (§9-302). (Section 9-302(1)(e) excepts from this requirement "an assignment of accounts which does not alone or in conjunction with other assignments to the same assignee transfer a significant part of the outstanding accounts of the assignor.") So long as the transferee's interest remains unperfected, it is subordinate to the claims of competing lien creditors. Section 547(e)(1)(A) of the Bankruptcy Code provides that the transfer of an interest in personal property is made "at the time such transfer takes effect between the transferor and the transferee, if such transfer is perfected at, or within 10 days after, such time" and otherwise at the time the transfer is perfected. For the purposes of §547(e), the transfer of an interest in personal property is deemed to be perfected "when a creditor on a simple contract cannot acquire a judicial lien that is superior to the interest of the transferee." As to just when this happens the Bankruptcy Code is silent, leaving the question to be decided by state law (in this case, Article 9 of the Uniform Commercial Code). Does the enactment of the Code affect the outcome in Shiro v. Drew? Does it complicate or simplify Judge Gignoux's analysis? If the assignee in *Shiro* falls within the §9-302(1)(e) exception, how is his dispute with the trustee to be resolved? For a recent discussion of the scope of this exception, see In re B. Hollie Knight Co., 605 F.2d 397 (8th Cir. 1979).

4. Suppose that Proctor and Drew had sent a copy of the letter of November 1, 1956, to the Hazeltine Company, requesting that Hazeltine pay Proctor and Drew from the proceeds of the Radome contract the $2056.87 advanced by them to Fiberlast. Do you think that Hazeltine could safely disregard the request? Or should it make further inquiries? Or could it safely pay Proctor and Drew the amount requested?

5. Judge Gignoux assumed that the trustee in bankruptcy could not have recovered the money from Drew if Fiberlast had, on November 1, 1956, "assigned" the proceeds of the Radome contract. Note that, as of that date, Fiberlast had not even begun performance of the contract. The assumption is, then, that there can be a presently effective assignment of the unearned proceeds of an executory contract. On this point, see Rockmore v. Lehman, reprinted *infra* p. 1477.

In re DODGE-FREEDMAN POULTRY CO.
148 F. Supp. 647 (D.N.H. 1956)

CONNOR, District Judge. This is a petition for review of an order entered May 25, 1956, by the Referee in Bankruptcy. The petitioner, Dodge-

Freedman Poultry Company, the debtor in this proceeding, seeks to have set aside a dividend allowed one of the creditors.

On January 31, 1955, Dodge-Freedman Poultry Company, sometimes hereinafter referred to as Debtor, filed a petition for an arrangement under Chapter XI of the Act of Congress relating to Bankruptcy. Title 11 U.S.C.A. §§701-799. A *Plan of Arrangement* was subsequently adopted which provided that a total dividend of fifteen percent be paid to unsecured creditors as full satisfaction for their claims. Among the general creditors to file a proof of claim, together with a duly executed *Acceptance of the Agreement*, was Ann Freedman a/k/a Annette Freedman, who on April 15, 1955, set her claim at $51,000. On December 15, 1955, some time after the "acceptance" of the plan but before its "confirmation," she filed an affidavit under General Order 41 of the Bankruptcy Act, waiving any and all rights to share in the deposit made by the debtor to cover its obligations and to share in any dividend under the plan. She is the wife of Harry Freedman, who was and still is the president, clerk, director, and principal stockholder in the debtor corporation. For purposes of this proceeding, it has been agreed to consider the claim filed and waived by her as being a claim of Harry, and the amount of the debt has been reduced to $50,000. Since a dividend of fifteen percent was declared, this would have entitled Harry Freedman to receive a dividend of $7,500 had the claim not been waived.

Another unsecured creditor which accepted the *Plan of Arrangement* was Delaware Mills, Inc., sometimes hereinafter referred to as Delaware, a corporation duly chartered under the laws of the State of New York, which filed a proof of claim totaling $42,594.63 on April 25, 1955. This claim was allowed and a dividend of fifteen percent or $6,389.19 paid, leaving a balance of $36,205.44. On this unpaid balance, Delaware Mills, Inc. filed another proof of claim, asserting its right to an additional dividend of $7,500 by virtue of a subordination agreement duly executed on May 11, 1954, between itself and Harry Freedman.[16]

The debtor objected to allowance of this second dividend. It contended that the agreement was nothing more than a subordination contract which gave Delaware Mills, Inc. no property interest in the debt

---

16. The subordination agreement provides as follows:

  For and in consideration of the extension of credit by Delaware Mills, Inc. of Deposit, New York to the Dodge-Freedman Poultry Company of Concord, New Hampshire, I, the undersigned an officer and shareholder of the Dodge-Freedman Poultry Company do hereby subordinate all of my claims against the Poultry Company as reflected on their books in the amount of $50,000 to the account of Delaware Mills, Inc. and that no drawings of any kind as a reduction of the amounts due me from Dodge-Freedman Poultry Company will be made until all amounts due from them [to?] Delaware Mills, Inc. have been satisfied and paid.

  Dated at Concord New Hampshire, ———— this 11th day of May, 1954. Witness my hand and seal.

          s/ Harry Freedman, Pres.
          Officer and Shareholder of Dodge-Freedman Poultry Company

owed by Dodge-Freedman Poultry Company to Harry Freedman, at
least not until such debt was actually paid to him. It contended that by its
very language the contract was not an assignment or a subrogation agreement. Delaware, on the other hand, asserted that no matter what the
contract originally may have been, the intervention of bankruptcy, in
effect, caused it to become an equitable assignment. To support this
argument, Delaware relied upon Bird & Sons Sales Corporation v. Tobin, 8 Cir., 1935, 78 F.2d 371, 100 A.L.R. 654. In that case, a group of
creditors signed an agreement subordinating payment of the debtor's
then existing indebtedness to them to the prior payment and satisfaction
of all future indebtedness. Later the debtor went into bankruptcy, after
incurring indebtedness to the other creditors, and the signers, despite
their agreement, filed proofs of claim and demanded a dividend of the
same percentage due the subsequent creditors. They argued that Section
65, sub. a of the Bankruptcy Act, 11 U.S.C.A. §105, sub. a made all such
contractual agreements null and void since it requires equal distribution
of assets to all creditors.[17] The Court of Appeals for the Eighth Circuit
rejected this contention and held that there is nothing in the Bankruptcy
Act nullifying otherwise valid prior agreements between creditors. On the
strength of this opinion, Delaware Mills, Inc. suggested that the equity
power of a Bankruptcy Court automatically converts a subordination
agreement into an equitable assignment upon the filing of the petition in
bankruptcy.

This reasoning violates the basic principle that intervention of bankruptcy does not change the existing rights of the various parties, and the
Referee did not give it serious consideration. He did, however, refuse to
give "judicial sanction to an unconscionable, unjust, inequitable and
deliberate act of avoidance," ruling that Freedman was estopped from
voluntarily waiving the dividend due under the *Plan of Arrangement*. He
found that the subordination agreement is and always was an equitable
assignment of his claim by Freedman to Delaware Mills, Inc. Invoking
the equity powers of the Bankruptcy Court, he ordered that Debtor deposit $7,500 as an additional dividend for Delaware Mills, Inc.

In asking this court to overrule the referee's order, Debtor does not
question the soundness of the *Bird* case, admitting that it is a well-settled
practice in bankruptcy for courts to enforce agreements between creditors which provide for subordination in liquidation. See 3 Collier on
Bankruptcy (14th Ed.) page 2294 (Section 65.06) and cases cited therein.
It is Debtor's contention, however, that the *Bird* decision is not a precedent for the case at bar, since it was a liquidation proceeding and not one
under Chapter XI, and because the facts of that case are entirely different
from those here.

---

17. Section 65, sub. a provides: "Dividends of an equal per centum shall be declared and
paid on all allowed claims, except such as have priority or are secured."

The argument that the *Bird* principle cannot be applied to a Chapter XI proceeding is without merit. There is no language in that decision which shows any intention of the court to limit it, nor can any logical reason to do so be found. Speaking for a unanimous court, Woodrough, J., held that bankruptcy is not precluded from applying equitable principles and that it could order distribution of the assets "to accord with the rights of the parties, as such rights were fixed by their contract." 78 F.2d at page 373. This is just as true under a Chapter XI proceeding as under a liquidation proceeding, and a court may enforce all contracts which do not contravene public policy or the spirit of the Bankruptcy Act.

The second contention of Debtor, that the facts in the *Bird* case are substantially different from those here, raises a more troublesome question. There, the subordinating creditors actually filed for and attempted to collect dividends allowable on their claims. The court had little difficulty finding that this violated the agreement. In the case at bar, however, Freedman, the prior creditor, has made no attempt to personally collect the dividend due on his claim, but instead has waived all his rights to share in any distribution. Because of this difference in facts, Debtor correctly maintains that the *Bird* case is not authority here, since the principles which were determinative there cannot be applied to this situation.

The referee, however, did not rely upon the *Bird* case as direct precedent for his ruling, but rather he cited it as authority for finding prior agreements valid and for exercising equity powers in bankruptcy. He determined that the agreement created an equitable assignment on behalf of Delaware Mills and ordered that the money be paid to it. Although this court is sustaining this order, I do so for reasons different from those found by the referee.

While it is true that the rights of the parties under a contract claimed to constitute an equitable assignment are to be determined by the law of the state where the instrument was executed, there are no New Hampshire cases to guide us, see Pollard v. Pollard, 68 N.H. 356, 39 A.2d 329; Conway v. Cutting, 51 N.H. 407, and therefore we must look to federal principles. Measuring the facts of this case to those principles, it is clear that this was not an equitable assignment. All that Freedman agreed to do was forgo collection, but even if he had gone further and promised to collect and then turn the money over to Delaware Mills, Inc., it would not have been sufficient. "An agreement to pay out of a particular fund, however clear in its terms, is not an equitable assignment; a covenant in the most solemn form has no greater effect." Christmas v. Russell, 14 Wall. 69, at page 84, 81 U.S. 69, at page 84, 20 L. Ed. 762.

> The courts have recognized that an agreement to pay out of the particular fund, however clear in terms, is not an equitable assignment. To constitute an equitable assignment, the intent to do so and its execution are

indispensable. The assignor must not retain any control over the fund, any authority to collect, or any power of revocation. To do so is fatal to the claim. There must be a transfer of such a character that the fund holder can safely pay, and is compelled to do so, even though he be forbidden by the assignor.

East Side Packing Co. v. Fahy Market, 2 Cir., 1926, 24 F.2d 644, at page 645.

"No particular phraseology is required to effect an assignment. . . ." Lone Star Cement Corporation v. Swartwout, 4 Cir., 1938, 93 F.2d 767, at page 769. "The ultimate test is the intention of the assignor to give and the assignee to receive present ownership of the claim." 2 Williston on Contracts (Rev. Ed.) par. 428, page 1232.

In the case at bar, there was no manifestation of intention, either written, oral, or by conduct, on the part of Freedman to relinquish control, or to make any appropriation to Delaware Mills, Inc. Therefore, no equitable assignment was created, nor is there an equitable lien. Nevertheless, Delaware is entitled to receive the dividend.

When Freedman's claim was filed and allowed, he was faced by a dilemma for he apparently had two choices of disposition, either he could waive the claim or he could accept payment for himself. He was barred from doing either. The forbearance agreement prevented him from collecting and retaining any money on his own behalf so long as Delaware's claim had not been satisfied up to the agreed sum. As a result, it might seem that Freedman was actually fulfilling his contract when he waived all rights, because he was, in effect, forbearing. But equity will regard the substance rather than the form of every agreement and examine its purpose and intent. See 30 C.J.S., Equity, §107, pp. 513-514. Applying this principle to the contract, it is obvious from its language that its intent and purpose was that Delaware's claim would be "satisfied and paid." Therefore, by looking behind the mere formality of forbearance, equity can take cognizance of the fact that Freedman, to a limited extent, undertook to assure payment of Delaware's claim up to $50,000. Although it is true that Freedman had no duties to perform other than to forbear, he is, at the very least, barred by the spirit of the agreement from taking any action that might prevent the satisfaction of Delaware's claim. By waiving his right to a dividend, Freedman is doing just that. He is returning the money to the debtor against whom Delaware Mills has no further rights since it has already accepted its full, legal share under the *Plan of Arrangement*. Thus Freedman was estopped from waiving his claim, for to do so violates the intent and purpose behind the agreement.

This is Freedman's dilemma. On one hand he is barred at law from collecting and retaining the dividend, while on the other he is estopped by equitable principles from waiving his rights. The answer to this paradox is that he holds the right to collect the dividend on behalf of another. He is a constructive trustee for Delaware Mills, Inc.

> By the well-settled doctrines of equity, a constructive trust arises whenever one party has obtained money which does not equitably belong to him, and which he cannot in good conscience retain or withhold from another who is beneficially entitled to it; as, for example, when money has been paid by accident, mistake of fact, or fraud, or has been acquired through a breach of trust, or violation of fiduciary duty, and the like.

4 Pomeroy's Equity Jurisprudence, par. 1047; quoted and approved in In re Northrup, D.C., 152 F. 763, at page 771.

The theory behind constructive trusts as defined by the Restatement would seem appropriate here. "Where a person holding title to property is subject to an equitable duty to convey it to another on the ground that he would be unjustly enriched if he were permitted to retain it, a constructive trust arises." Restatement of the Law of Restitution, Section 160. Furthermore, to apply the doctrine of constructive trusts to the case at bar would be in accordance with the liberal scope given the basic principles by the New Hampshire Supreme Court in Morgan v. Morgan, 94 N.H. 116, 47 A.2d 569. And also by the Court of Appeals for this circuit which said:

> . . . It is only by looking at the intent, rather than at the form, that equity is able to treat that as done which in good conscience ought to be done. . . . Equity always attempts to get at the substance of things and to ascertain, uphold and enforce rights and duties which spring from the real relations of the parties. It will never suffer the mere appearance and external form to conceal the true purposes, objects and consequences of a transaction.

Peoples-Ticonic Nat. Bank v. Stewart, 86 F.2d 359, at page 361, quoting from Pomeroy's Equity Jurisprudence.

Unlike an equitable assignment, it is immaterial that the parties had no intention of creating a constructive trust. The law creates it for them out of their relationship toward each other.

> Constructive trusts include all those instances in which a trust is raised by the doctrines of equity for the purpose of working out justice in the most efficient manner, where there is no intention of the parties to create such a relation, and in most cases contrary to the intention of the one holding the legal title, and where there is no express or implied, written or verbal, declaration of the trust. They arise when the legal title to property is obtained by a person in violation, express or implied, of some duty owed to the one who is equitably entitled, and when the property thus obtained is held in hostility to his beneficial rights of ownership. As the trusts of this

class are imposed by equity, contrary to the trustee's intention and will, upon property in his hands, they are often termed trusts in invitum. . . .

4 Pomeroy's Equity Jurisprudence, par. 1044.

Professor Scott has pointed out that most attempts to define constructive trusts have been too narrow in scope. Nevertheless he offers a definition which seems to have met universal approval and is applicable to this case.

> A constructive trust arises where a person who holds title to property is subject to an equitable duty to convey it to another on the ground that he would be unjustly enriched if he were permitted to retain it. When a person holds the title to property which he is under an obligation to convey to another, and when that obligation does not arise merely because he has voluntarily assumed it, he is said to hold the property in constructive trust for the other and he is called a constructive trustee of the property. He is not compelled to convey the property because he is a constructive trustee; it is because he can be compelled to convey it that he is a constructive trustee.

4 Scott on Trusts (1956), par. 462, page 3103.

The petition for review is denied. The order of the Referee in Bankruptcy is sustained.

[Affirmed per curiam on the opinion of the District Court, Dodge-Freedman Poultry Co. v. Delaware Mills, Inc., 244 F.2d 314 (1st Cir. 1957).]

NOTE

1. Whether the subordination agreement in the principal case should be described as an equitable assignment, a constructive trust, or merely as a subordination agreement, in the common debtor's bankruptcy, the bankruptcy court will order dividends on the subordinated claim paid to the senior creditor (who thus receives double dividends — his own as well as the subordinator's). See Bankruptcy Code §510(a). From this point of view, the only unusual facet of the principal case was the subordinator's attempt to waive his dividend. Is the court's theory that Freedman was a "constructive trustee" for Delaware Mills the only way of preventing him from reneging on his agreement?

2. If Freedman is a "trustee" for Delaware, what happens if Freedman himself becomes bankrupt? Does Delaware still get the money or should the money now go to Freedman's trustee in bankruptcy? In re Wyse (Pioneer-Cafeteria Feeds, Ltd. v. Mack), 340 F.2d 719 (6th Cir. 1965) appears to be the first case to have considered the effectiveness of a

subordination agreement against the subordinator's trustee in bankruptcy. The majority and concurring opinions in the *Wyse* case, both notably obscure, suggest, as through a glass darkly, that the senior creditor does not prevail. For discussions of the *Wyse* case from somewhat different points of view, see 2 G. Gilmore, Security Interests in Personal Property §37.2 (1965); Coogan, Kripke & Weiss, The Outer Fringes of Article 9, 79 Harv. L. Rev. 229, 247-253 (1965). The similarities and dissimilarities between "assignment" of a claim and "subordination" of a claim are discussed in both the references just cited as well as in Calligar, Subordination Agreements, 70 Yale L.J. 376 (1961).

3. In Cherno v. Dutch American Mercantile Corp., 353 F.2d 147 (2d Cir. 1965) Blanmill had advanced money to Itemlab. The Blanmill loan was evidenced by Itemlab's promissory note and secured by a chattel mortgage that had been properly filed under New York Lien Law §230. Subsequently, in order to induce Dutch American to make a loan to Itemlab, Blanmill subordinated its claim against Itemlab to a note that Itemlab gave to Dutch American. The Dutch American loan was unsecured, except to the extent that, under the subordination agreement, it might be entitled to Blanmill's security. Blanmill, however, without Dutch American's knowledge, caused its mortgage to be released of record as satisfied. In fact the mortgage had not been satisfied; Blanmill released it in order to induce still a third lender (18th Avenue Land Corp.) to advance money to Itemlab, which it did, taking a mortgage on Itemlab's apparently unencumbered assets. Despite Blanmill's diligent efforts to shore it up, Itemlab finally collapsed into bankruptcy. In the bankruptcy proceeding, the mortgage given to 18th Avenue Land Corp. was declared invalid. Dutch American claimed that, by virtue of the subordination agreement, it was entitled to a first lien on the proceeds from the sale of the chattels which had been subject to Blanmill's mortgage. In this argument it was successful in the District Court on a theory of equitable assignment. The Second Circuit, however, reversed in an opinion by Judge Anderson which stated in part:

> The claims of Dutch American that it either has an equitable assignment, an equitable lien or a constructive trust all invoke the equity powers of the court. Even if there were substance to the claims, which we are satisfied there is not, Dutch American would be barred from equitable relief because of the basic principle that he who seeks equity must do equity. By its failure and neglect to file or record any instrument giving notice of its claim of an equitable interest in the chattels, Dutch American enabled Blanmill and Itemlab to mislead 18th Avenue Land Corp. As far as innocent third persons were concerned, Dutch American left it within its power of Blanmill to release the mortgage at any time without notice of any claim of interest on the part of Dutch American, which had an equitable duty to give notice to third persons, who might be dealing with Itemlab, that it asserted an equitable claim against the chattels either directly or via

Blanmill's mortgage. Having failed to do so, it cannot now assert in equity a
priority over 18th Avenue Land Corp., who, the Referee found, "made its
loan in reliance upon the fact that it had secured a release of the lien of
Blanmill and without knowledge of the subordination agreement held by
Dutch American Mercantile Corp.," nor can it gain a preference over
other unsecured creditors and over substantial wage claims which accrued
subsequent to the release of the Blanmill mortgage.

Id. at 155.

SILLMAN v. TWENTIETH CENTURY-FOX FILM CORP.

3 N.Y.2d 395, 144 N.E.2d 387 (1957)

FROESSEL, J. Defendant Berman Swarttz Productions, Inc., (hereinafter called Swarttz) entered into *separate* contracts, under date of June 30,
1953, with plaintiffs and various other persons interested in the Broadway
musical revue "New Faces of 1952," in order to produce a motion picture
version of the stage production. Plaintiffs' contracts may be summarized
as follows:

Swarttz agreed to pay each plaintiff a certain percentage of the net
profits of the picture. In exchange, The Intimate Revue Company (hereinafter called Revue), in the basic agreement, granted Swarttz the exclusive right to use the physical properties of the show; New Faces, Inc.,
(hereinafter called New Faces) granted Swarttz the exclusive right to use
its trade names; Julian K. Sprague (and others) invested moneys in the
picture by way of interest-bearing loans; and Leonard Sillman agreed to
act as the associated producer.

In addition, in the Revue and Sprague contracts, Swarttz agreed to
give the distributor of the picture a "Notice of Irrevocable Authority"
directing it to pay directly to Revue and Sprague their share of the profits.
Similarly, in the New Faces and Sillman contracts, Swarttz agreed to
deliver a "Notice of Irrevocable Assignment and Authority" directing
the distributor to pay directly to New Faces and Sillman their share of the
profits and also agreed that their share would be so paid. All of the
contracts permitted assignment.

It was originally contemplated that the picture was to be distributed by
the United Artists Corporation in third dimension and color. Shortly
thereafter, however, so as to obtain the benefits of the CinemaScope
process, it was decided to distribute the picture through defendant Twentieth Century-Fox Film Corporation (hereinafter called Twentieth Century).

In order to effect these new arrangement, Swarttz, on September 8,
1953, entered into a contract with defendant National Pictures Corpora-

tion (hereinafter called National), which had a CinemaScope license and a distribution agreement with Twentieth Century. Under this contract, Swarttz assigned National all of Swarttz's rights under the various agreements with persons, including plaintiffs, having an interest in the production. In consideration, National agreed to pay Swarttz a certain percentage of the net profits of the picture less the percentages to be paid to the persons, films and corporations, including plaintiffs, entitled thereto. National accepted such assignments and expressly assumed all of Swarttz's obligations thereunder. National also agreed to give Twentieth Century a "Notice of Irrevocable Authority" directing the latter to pay to Chemical Bank and Trust Company for the accounts of Swarttz and of plaintiffs their percentages of the profits and that the bank was to pay these sums directly to Swarttz and plaintiffs.

National's distribution agreement with Twentieth Century had been entered into on April 16, 1951, or more than two years prior to the making of any of the aforesaid agreements. Twentieth Century alleges that plaintiffs knew of this contract before Swarttz's contract with National, but plaintiffs deny that they had any knowledge of the contract until November, 1953. Under its terms, National is to furnish Twentieth Century with 7 to 10 pictures during the ensuing 7 years, each picture to cost a minimum of $400,000 and to be free from all incumbrances and from the claims of owners of any material used in the pictures.

At least 10 days prior to the delivery of each picture, National is to deliver to Twentieth Century: "Photostat copies of all contracts for the acquisition of literary or other material used in the Picture and with producers, directors, musicians, actors, actresses and any other persons who render services for or in connection with the production of the Picture." Twentieth Century is given the right (but not the obligation) to examine such contracts and if, in the opinion of Twentieth Century's attorneys, they are not sufficient to permit full exercise of Twentieth Century's rights or the picture fails to conform to the agreement, National shall, upon written notice within 60 days of receipt of the contracts, be deemed in default. Twentieth Century may terminate the contract upon any default of National. Acceptance of the picture by Twentieth Century shall not be construed to release or relieve National of any of its representations, warranties, indemnities or covenants in the agreement, one which was to "discharge (1) all claims."

After deduction of a distribution fee and expenses, the receipts of the picture are "payable to *or for the account* of" National (emphasis supplied). Except for assignments by National to two named corporations, or for the purpose of securing loans by a prescribed procedure, article Twenty-Fourth of the agreement provides, among other things:

   (a) . . . neither party hereto shall assign this agreement, in whole or in part, or any rights or monies payable hereunder, without the prior written

consent of the other party, nor shall any right hereunder or any property or
contract covered hereby devolve by operation of law or otherwise upon any
receiver, trustee, liquidator, successor or other person through or as representative of either party.

It was further provided that Twentieth Century shall not be required to
pay any sum payable to National to anyone except National or one desig-
nee only; that Twentieth Century shall not be required to recognize any
assignments; and that if Twentieth Century shall receive notice of the
existence of any assignment, *it shall have the right to withhold payments*
until the assignment is cancelled or withdrawn.

Under the provisions of this agreement, plaintiff's contracts with
Swarttz and Swarttz's contract with National were submitted for inspection to Twentieth Century, which evinced no objection to any part of
these contracts. The picture, although costing only $220,000 instead of
the required $400,000, was delivered to and accepted and distributed by
Twentieth Century under this agreement. Shortly after the first release
of the picture, plaintiffs' attorney gave notice to Twentieth Century's
attorney of the direct payment provisions in plaintiff's contracts and
was assured by him that Twentieth Century could and *would* "hold up
distribution of moneys to National" under its contract.

Chemical Bank and Trust Company has refused to accept such funds
as a distribution agent, and this contributed to the present controversy.
Twentieth Century now holds a portion of the receipts deposited with
defendant "Chase National Bank" and *threatens to distribute* such receipts *in disregard* of plaintiffs' claims. Both National and Swarttz have
refused to execute notices of irrevocable authority as required by their
contracts.

In this action, plaintiffs seek a declaration of their rights, the impression of a lien upon the receipts of the picture, a direction to pay to each of
them a stated percentage of such receipts, an injunction prohibiting
Twentieth Century from otherwise distributing them, an accounting and
a money judgment for such sums as they claim are now due them. In
addition, specific performance is sought of the agreements of National
and Swarttz to execute and deliver the irrevocable notices. At Special
Term, Twentieth Century's motion for summary judgment, or, in the
alternative, for joinder of indispensable parties, was denied. The Appellate Division reversed on the law, and granted summary judgment without passing on the motion for joinder.

Both National and Swarttz are California corporations doing no business and having no assets in New York. They were served only in California and neither has appeared in this action, although the corporate
defendant Swarttz has executed stipulations by Swarttz as president for
extensions of time to answer. Other persons, whose contracts with
Swarttz in regard to this picture entitle them to similar percentage pay-

ments as plaintiffs, have brought suit in California where their claims in some respects are said to conflict with those of plaintiffs.

In our opinion, Special Term was correct in denying defendants' alternative prayer for relief, viz., that assignees other than plaintiffs be brought into this action as *indispensable* parties. They are not such parties. Each of the plaintiffs in the case relies on a separate and distinct agreement. Even if we deemed them and other assignees as united in interest and conditionally necessary parties, they are all without the jurisdiction of this State, and therefore are not required to be brought into this action, for it can effectively be disposed of without them (Civ. Prac. Act, §194; Keene v. Chambers, 271 N.Y. 326; Howard v. Arthur Murray, Inc., 281 App. Div. 806; Silberfeld v. Swiss Bank Corp., 266 App. Div. 756; see China Sugar Refining Co. v. Anderson, Meyer & Co., 6 Misc 2d 184). And so with the defendants, National and Swarttz, plaintiffs' assignors (Bergman v. Liverpool & London & Globe Ins. Co., 269 App. Div. 103). Though also outside the jurisdiction of this State, they have nevertheless been named as parties defendant in this action, have been served outside the State under the provisions of sections 232-235 of the Civil Practice Act, and are subject to an in rem judgment.

Since plaintiffs have no direct contractual relationship with Twentieth Century, they can prevail in their claim for direct payments only on the theory of an assumption of such an obligation by Twentieth Century or on the theory of an assignment from Swarttz and National. We see no merit whatever as to the first theory, for, whatever the law may be elsewhere (see Restatement, Contracts, §164), it is well settled in this State that the assignee of rights under a bilateral contract does not become bound to perform the duties under that contract unless he expressly assumes to do so, . . . which is not this case.

As to the second ground pressed on us by plaintiffs, we conclude that Swarttz and National intended a present assignment to plaintiffs of a portion of the funds to become due to the former from Twentieth Century, and that such funds would ordinarily be assignable. (Matter of Gruner, 295 N.Y. 510, 517, 518.) All that was left for the future was the formality of a "Notice" to Twentieth Century of the assignment. Such notice to the obligor is not required for an effective assignment, except to defeat a subsequent bona fide payment by the obligor (Williams v. Ingersoll, 89 N.Y. 508, 522; State Factors Corp. v. Sales Factors Corp., 257 App. Div. 101, 103).

The funds accruing to National under its contract with Twentieth Century, however, may be made nonassignable if that agreement in appropriate language so provides. We all agree with the Appellate Division that said contract does so provide and that Allhusen v. Caristo Constr. Corp. (303 N.Y. 446) is controlling here.

A prohibition against assignment, however, may be waived (Devlin v. Mayor of City of N.Y., 63 N.Y. 8, 14; Brewster v. City of Hornellsville, 35

App. Div. 161, 166; Hackett v. Campbell, 10 App. Div. 523, 526, *affd.* 159 N.Y. 537; see, also, Woodlard v. Schaffer Stores Co., 272 N.Y. 304; Gillette Bros. v. Aristocrat Restaurant, 239 N.Y. 87, 89, 90; Murray v. Harway, 56 N.Y. 337, 342, 343; Ireland v. Nichols, 46 N.Y. 413, 416). The very wording of the clause that Twentieth Century "shall not be required to" recognize assignments made without consent and "shall have the right to withhold" payments indicates that the parties contemplated that Twentieth Century might recognize such assignments and thereby waive the anti-assignment clause. Waiver is "the intentional relinquishment of a known right" (Werking v. Amity Estates, 2 NY2d 43, 52). As we stated in Alsens Amer. Portland Cement Works v. Degnon Contr. Co. (222 N.Y. 34, 37):

> It is essentially a matter of intention. . . . Commonly, it is sought to be proved by various species of proofs and evidence, by declarations, by acts and by non-feasance, permitting differing inferences and which do not directly, unmistakably or unequivocally establish it. Then it is for the jury to determine from the facts as proved or found by them whether or not the intention existed.

(See Devlin v. Mayor of City of N.Y., *supra*; Brewster v. City of Hornellsville, *supra*.)

As to this issue of waiver, it appears from the papers that National's contract with Twentieth Century forbidding assignments was made in 1951, more than two years prior to the assignments in question; that Twentieth Century examined all the contracts here involved prior to accepting the picture from National in 1953, and consequently knew of the assignments to plaintiffs which it now alleges are a breach of its agreement with National; that, having examined these contracts, Twentieth Century was required by its agreement with National to notify National within 60 days if they were to be treated as a breach of the agreement; that Twentieth Century failed to so notify National; that Twentieth Century accepted the picture and exercised the rights created by the very contract which made the assignments to plaintiffs without notifying either plaintiffs or National of any intention to consider them void; that shortly after the picture was released, and after Chemical Bank refused to act as distributing agent, plaintiffs' attorney spoke about the assignments to Twentieth Century's attorney, who not only evinced no objection at the time, but stated that Twentieth Century would withhold distribution of moneys to National. While of course not decisive, these facts have an important bearing on the issue of waiver.

Rule 113 of the Rules of Civil Practice provides that when an answer is served with a defense, sufficient as a matter of law, founded upon facts established prima facie by documentary evidence, "the complaint *may* be dismissed on motion *unless* the plaintiff . . . shall show such facts *as may be deemed by the judge hearing the motion, sufficient to raise an issue with respect to the* verity *and conclusiveness* of such documentary evidence." The Judge who heard this motion at Special Term concluded that the question of waiver raised a triable issue; so did two Justices of the Appellate Division; and so do we. To hold that there is a triable issue as to waiver does not, as our dissenting brethren claim, frustrate the plain purpose of the anti-assignment clause, except as the waiver of any contractual provision, clearly recognized by law, frustrates such provision; indeed, to hold as a matter of law that there was no waiver here would sharply depart from our established summary judgment procedure.

To grant summary judgment it must clearly appear that no material and triable issue of fact is presented (Di Menna & Sons v. City of New York, 301 N.Y. 118). This drastic remedy should not be granted where there is any doubt as to the existence of such issues (Braun v. Carey, 280 App. Div. 1019), or where the issue is "arguable" (Barrett v. Jacobs, 255 N.Y. 520, 522); "issue-finding, rather than issue-determination, is the key to the procedure" (Esteve v. Avad, 271 App. Div. 725, 727). In Gravenhorst v. Zimmerman (236 N.Y. 22, 38-39) Chief Judge Hiscock, writing for this court, observed that one person may argue that as matter of law the assignor abandoned and lost the benefit of his rescission, whereas another might think that was a question of fact, and concluded:

> It never could have been, or in justice ought to have been, the intention of those who framed our Practice Act and rules thereunder that the decision of such a serious question as this should be flung off on a motion for summary judgment. Whatever the final judgment may be the defendants were entitled to have the issue deliberately tried and their right to be heard in the usual manner of a trial protected.

Inasmuch as it is our opinion, upon this record, that a triable issue is presented as to the alleged waiver of the anti-assignment clause, the judgment appealed from should be reversed and the order of Special Term reinstated, with costs.

FULD, J. (dissenting). Save for the issue of waiver, we are all agreed that defendant Twentieth Century-Fox would be entitled to summary judgment dismissing the complaint. On that question, too, I am persuaded, as was the Appellate Division, that no triable issue of fact is presented.

Plaintiffs are a few of a large number of artists and investors embroiled in a controversy with National Pictures Corporation and Berman Swarttz Productions over the distribution of profits from a motion picture released in 1954 and still being exhibited. The controversy is extensive and the disputants numerous. Some 17 other claimants, not parties to this action, have instituted suit in California and, according to the averment of the complaint in that California action, have assigned to the present plaintiffs different percentile shares of the profits than the latter now claim in the complaint before us. At any rate, in view of the inability of the parties to agree on their respective shares and in view of the consequent difficulty of distributing the profits as they are accumulated, at least one bank, the Chemical Bank and Trust Company, has refused to act as distributing agent. Plaintiffs now seek to foist this burden on Twentieth Century-Fox, the firm which distributed the film pursuant to a contract with National, on the theory that National assigned to the plaintiffs part of the payments due to it, in the proportions they claim.

I have no doubt, and, indeed, no one disputes, that it was to prevent entanglement in this very sort of controversy that Twentieth Century-Fox insisted, and explicitly provided in its contract with National, that it would not be "required to recognize or accept any assignments"; that payments would be made only to National and to "no other person"; that no right under the contract would "devolve . . . upon any . . . other person through or as representative of either party"; and that "*neither party*" *would assign* the agreement or any part of it "or any rights or monies payable" under it "*without the prior written consent of the other.*" Nevertheless, despite the admitted absence of such consent — though the plaintiffs had ample opportunity to obtain it — and, despite the fact that the plain and only purpose of the anti-assignment provisions would thereby be completely frustrated, plaintiffs urge that Twentieth Century-Fox must submit to the inconvenience, the expense and the uncertainty of a trial solely because it made no protest when it examined the contracts between plaintiffs and National or when it was told by plaintiffs' attorney of the assignments.

Allegations such as these, and they are the only ones made by plaintiffs, do not support the conclusion that a triable issue of fact is presented. That there was no "protest" from the attorneys for Twentieth Century-Fox means nothing. Inquiry, to be meaningful, must go deeper: did that failure reasonably reflect an "intentional relinquishment of a known right"? If it did not, then, there is no basis for either inference or finding of waiver. (Werking v. Amity Estates, 2 NY2d 43, 52; Alsens Amer. Portland Cement Works v. Degnon Contr. Co., 222 N.Y. 34, 37.)

Courts are properly hesitant about frustrating contract provisions which prohibit assignment and, accordingly, the rule is settled that "an estoppel or waiver must be established by the person claiming it by a preponderance of evidence, and neither an estoppel nor a waiver . . . can be inferred from mere silence or inaction." (Gibson Elec. Co. v. Liverpool & London & Globe Ins. Co., 159 N.Y. 418, 426-427; see, also, Truglio v. Zurich Gen. Acc. & Liability Ins. Co., 247 N.Y. 423, 427). And, more to the point, the affirmative acts required to defeat a nonassignment clause by a finding of waiver have invariably been such as are unquestionably inconsistent with anything but recognition of the assignment — as, for instance, making payment to the assignee (see Hacket v.

Campbell, 159 N.Y. 537, *affg.* 10 App. Div. 523, 526; Devlin v. Mayor of City of N.Y., 63 N.Y. 8, 14) allowing the assignee to complete the job (see Brewster v. City of Hornellsville, 35 App. Div. 161, 166) or, in the case of a lease, receiving rents knowing that the assignee is in possession. (See Woollard v. Schaffer Stores Co., 272 N.Y. 304, 312-313; Gillette Bros. v. Aristocrat Restaurant, 239 N.Y. 87, 89-90.)

Indeed, on facts far stronger than those asserted by plaintiffs, the courts have held, *as a matter of law*, that there was no waiver of the anti-assignment clause. (See, e.g., Allhusen v. Caristo Constr. Corp., 5 Misc 2d 749-750 [per Botein, J.], *affd.* 278 App. Div. 817, *affd.* 303 N.Y. 446; Concrete Form Co. v. Grange Constr. Co., 320 Pa. 205; Joint School Dist. v. Marathon County Bank, 187 Wis. 416.) In the *Allhusen* case (*supra*, 303 N.Y. 446), for instance, a contractor, the defendant, hired a subcontractor to do some painting work, their contract providing that there was to be no assignment without the contractor's written consent. The subcontractor, nevertheless, made an assignment of amounts due to it as security for a loan, the assignee, a bank, being unaware of the provision against assignment. When the subcontractor later sought to secure a further loan, the bank discussed the assignment with the contractor's general manager. No protest was voiced and no word uttered about the invalidity of an assignment, and, on the strength of that conversation, the bank declared, it made additional loans secured by further assignments. The subcontractor thereafter became insolvent and the contractor, relying on the anti-assignment clause, refused to honor the assignments made to the bank. In the suit thereafter brought by the bank's successor, Special Term granted the contractor's motion for summary judgment dismissing the complaint. The court stressed the fact that there had been no written consent to the assignment and ruled, as a matter of law, that no waiver could be inferred from the circumstance that the contractor had failed to object to the assignment when he had been advised of it. The Appellate Division affirmed (278 App. Div. 817) and so did we (303 N.Y. 446), although by the time the appeal reached us, the plaintiff, recognizing its weakness, had abandoned the argument of waiver.

The rightness of that result is reinforced and confirmed by cases decided in other jurisdictions. On facts even stronger than those in the Allhusen case, the highest courts of both Pennsylvania and Wisconsin have unanimously held, as a matter of law, that there was no waiver. (See Concrete Form Co. v. Grange Constr. Co., *supra*, 320 Pa. 205; Joint School Dist. v. Marathon County Bank, *supra*, 187 Wis. 416.) In the Pennsylvania case, which is particularly illuminating, an agreement between a contractor and a subcontractor provided that the latter would not "assign any payments thereunder except by and in accordance with the consent of [the] contractor." Without obtaining the requisite consent, the subcontractor executed an assignment of some of the moneys due it to a bank and the latter immediately notified the contractor by letter of the assignment, requesting an "acknowledgment." The contractor, acknowledging receipt of the letter "concerning an assignment" confirmed the existence of the account, but said nothing about the anti-assignment clause. In reversing the trial court, which had held that the contractor's acknowledgment of the assignment constituted a waiver of the nonassignment provision, the Supreme Court decided that "as a matter of law," there was no waiver (320 Pa. 208-209):

> This letter [acknowledging the assignment] did not constitute an unequivocal assent to the assignment. . . . There was no express consent; nor is there sufficient warrant for any implication of the necessary assent. The original contract expressly forbade assignment. By that provision defendant undoubtedly sought to provide against the introduction of one or more third parties. . . . Defendant wished to deal with its subcontractor and with it alone. *Any waiver of that provision or consent to its violation would have to be clear, distinct and unequivocal. Such is not the present case. The court below should have ruled as a matter of law that defendant did not consent to the assignment and could not, therefore, be held liable.*

(Emphasis supplied.)

Turning to the case before us, it is readily apparent that Twentieth Century-Fox also sought "to provide against the introduction of . . . third parties," that it wished, as it stated, to deal with National, and National alone, and that there is no "clear, distinct and unequivocal" evidence of waiver. The Appellate Division was, therefore, eminently correct in holding that there was no basis for any claim of waiver. Let us dwell for a moment on the facts relied upon to spell out waiver. The papers which Twentieth Century-Fox examined, far from making any reference to assignment, actually directed attention to the very agreement between National and Twentieth Century-Fox which, in explicit terms, prohibited assignments.[18] Moreover, that agreement, with all of its anti-assignment provisions, was actually attached to the contract which Berman Swartz negotiated with National upon plaintiffs' instructions. And, in addition to that, the Swartz-National agreement itself provided that it should not be construed as giving any right, legal or equitable, to third persons. In short, therefore, the papers examined, instead of informing Twentieth Century-Fox, as plaintiffs allege, that unless it protested it would be relinquishing the anti-assignment provisions, really reaffirmed the vitality of those provisions. Surely, then, Twentieth Century-Fox's "failure to protest" may not be regarded as evidence of an intention to waive. As earlier indicated, such an intent may only be predicated on action taken on the strength of known facts, and acts, to

---

18. Thus, plaintiffs had expressly authorized Berman Swartz to arrange for the production of the film "pursuant to" and "under" the contract containing the nonassignment clauses.

justify an inference of waiver, must be of an affirmative character, not mere silence or inaction. (See, e.g., Gibson Elec. Co. v. Liverpool & London & Globe Ins. Co., *supra*, 159 N.Y. 418, 427; Allhusen v. Caristo Constr. Corp., *supra*, 5 Misc 2d 749, *affd.* 278 App. Div. 817, *affd.* 303 N.Y. 446; Emerson Radio & Phonograph Corp. v. Standard Appliances, 201 Misc. 821, 827.)

Nor may any inference of waiver be said to flow from the fact that no objection was raised when, some time later, plaintiffs' attorney, in a conversation with counsel for Twentieth Century-Fox, advised him of the assignments. This is the same sort of inaction that has been held insufficient to establish waiver in precisely this type of case. (See Allhusen v. Caristo Constr. Co., *supra*, 5 Misc 2d 749, *affd.* 278 App. Div. 817, *affd.* 303 N.Y. 446; Concrete Form Co. v. Grange Constr. Co., *supra*, 320 Pa. 205; Joint School Dist. v. Marathon County Bank, *supra*, 187 Wis. 416.) It is nowhere alleged that Twentieth Century-Fox or anyone on its behalf expressly waived the non-assignment provisions and, if plaintiffs wanted them waived, their attorney should have requested the requisite consent in writing. Having failed to obtain such consent, plaintiffs should not be permitted to involve Twentieth Century-Fox in a troublesome and expensive trial by simply alleging a waiver, without support (as I have demonstrated) of any fact sufficient in law to substantiate the allegation. To hold otherwise not only frustrates the plain purpose of the anti-assignment provisions but amounts to a decided departure from our wise and established summary judgment procedure.

I would affirm the Appellate Division determination granting summary judgment.

Conway, Ch. J., Van Voorhis and Burke, JJ., concur with Froessel, J.; Fuld, J., dissents in an opinion in which Desmond and Dye, JJ., concur.

Judgment of the Appellate Division reversed and the order of special Term reinstated, with costs in this court and in the Appellate Division.

NOTE

1. Why did the Chemical Bank refuse to act as distribution agent? What reason could Twentieth Century have had for refusing to recognize the rights of the plaintiffs? In the *Allhusen* case, as the facts are stated in Judge Fuld's dissent, why should the contractor have refused to recognize the subcontractor's assignment of the proceeds of the subcontract?

2. Both the *Sillman* and the *Allhusen* cases were actions by an assignee against an obligor. Anti-assignment clauses have also been discussed in cases which involve contests for priority between an assignee, who has taken an assignment of proceeds in violation of the clause, and an adverse claimant who is not affected by the clause (e.g., a subsequent judgment creditor or a subsequent assignee who has obtained the obli-

gor's consent to his assignment). In Portuguese-American Bank of San
Francisco v. Welles, 242 U.S. 7 (1916) the Supreme Court gave priority to
an assignee over a subsequent lien creditor. With respect to the anti-
assignment clause, Justice Holmes remarked that a "covenantor" (the
obligor) may make his contractual undertaking as narrow as he pleases
but that

> . . . when he has incurred a debt, which is property in the hands of the
> creditor, it is a different thing to say that as between the creditor and a third
> person the debtor can restrain his alienation of that, although he could not
> forbid the sale or pledge of other chattels. When a man sells a horse, what
> he does, from the point of view of the law, is to transfer a right, and a right
> being regarded by the law as a thing, even though a res incorporalis, it is not
> illogical to apply the same rule to a debt that would be applied to a horse.

Does that seem to mean that, in Holmes' opinion, the anti-assignment
clause would have been invalid even between the assignee and the obligor? In Fortunato v. Patten, 147 N.Y. 277, 41 N.E. 572 (1895), the New
York Court of Appeals assumed that the anti-assignment clause would
have been effective between assignee and obligor ("for the reason that
they are parties to the contract") but nevertheless gave priority to the
assignee over adverse claimants.

3. Despite the assumption, in the *Fortunato* case and in many others,
of the validity of an anti-assignment clause between assignee and obligor,
the 1952 *Allhusen* case was the first in which the New York Court of
Appeals held that such a clause was fatal to the assignee's action against
an obligor. In earlier cases, which are reviewed in the *Allhusen* opinion,
the holdings had been either that the clause in question was not intended
to prohibit an assignment of proceeds or that, if the prohibition was clear,
the clause had been intended, not to defeat the assignee's action, but to
give the obligor a damage claim against the assignor for violation of the
clause. With respect to the latter type of holding (which was sometimes
referred to as the "personal covenant" doctrine), what damages do you
think an obligor could recover from the other party to the contract who
had breached it by assigning proceeds? Could the obligor, if he learned
that the other party was about to assign proceeds, secure a restraining
order forbidding the assignment? Would he want to?

4. The Uniform Commercial Code has two provisions that are relevant to the anti-assignment problem. Section 2-210(2) provides:

> Unless otherwise agreed all rights of either seller or buyer can be as-
> signed except where the assignment would materially change the duty of
> the other party, or increase materially the burden or risk imposed on him
> by his contract, or impair materially his chance of obtaining return perfor-
> mance. A right to damages for breach of the whole contract or a right
> arising out of the assignor's due performance of his entire obligation can be
> assigned despite agreement otherwise.

Section 9-318(4) provides:

> A term in any contract between an account debtor and an assignor is ineffective if it prohibits assignment of an account or prohibits creation of a security interest in a general intangible for money due or to become due or requires the account debtor's consent to such assignment or security interest.

Do you think these two provisions are consistent with each other?

5. New York has now adopted the Code. Article 2 of the Code applies to contracts for the sale of goods, and §2-210(2) applies to the assignment of rights arising under such contracts. Article 9 applies to security transfers of all kinds of personal property, tangible and intangible, and also to sales of "accounts." (There is no provision that makes Article 9 applicable to sales of the type of intangible property that the §9-106 definition, *supra* p. 1457, calls "general intangibles.")

Assume that the facts of the *Sillman* case are duplicated in a New York case to which the Code provisions are applicable, except that Twentieth Century succeeds in establishing that it has not waived its rights under the anti-assignment clause. What result?

6. There was at one time a considerable controversy over the effectiveness of "partial" assignments — that is, assignments of less than the entire claim. The *Sillman* case, which assumes without discussion that partial assignments are exactly as valid as total assignments, is typical of the modern approach. Restatement Second §326(1) provides that "an assignment of a part of a right, whether the part is specified as a fraction, as an amount, or otherwise, is operative as to that part to the same extent and in the same manner as if the part had been a separate right."

Subsection 2 states, however, that if the obligor has not contracted for separate performance of the assigned part of the right, "no legal proceeding can be maintained by the assignor or assignee against the obligor over his objection, unless all the persons entitled to the promised performance are joined in the proceeding, or unless joinder is not feasible and it is equitable to proceed without joinder." What is the point of this qualification? Did the courts in the *Sillman* case respect its spirit? (Section 156 of the Restatement First contained a nearly identical provision.)

Section 3.   The Present Assignability of Future Claims

ROCKMORE v. LEHMAN

128 F.2d 564 (2d Cir. 1942), *rev'd on rehearing*, 129 F.2d 892

AUGUSTUS N. HAND, Circuit Judge. On December 7, 1939, certain creditors of Surf Advertising Corporation filed a petition for a reorganization under Chapter X of the Bankruptcy Act, 11 U.S.C.A. §501 et seq. On December 26, Max Rockmore was appointed trustee. Surf had previously entered into three contracts with Calvert Distillers Corporation, whereby Surf was to furnish and maintain advertising signs for Calvert and the latter was to make instalment payments therefor. These contracts were dated May 28, 1937, July 28, 1937, and September 30, 1937, respectively. The contracts were assigned by Surf to the respondent Abrams in consideration of advances by the latter to enable Surf to erect and maintain the signs. Surf performed the contracts with Calvert from the time they were made until October 3, 1939, when Schub, the president of Surf, died. During the periods between the making of the contracts and the death of Schub, Abrams advanced to Surf $38,210.29. Subsequent to October 3, 1939, and prior to the appointment of the trustee, Abrams personally supervised the servicing of the signs under the contracts and expended $846.44 for that purpose. Checks aggregating $31,889.38, which Calvert issued as instalment payments under its contracts with Surf, were delivered by Schub to Abrams, leaving a difference between his total advances of $39,056.73 and his receipts from Surf of $31,889.38 amounting to $7,167.35.

On May 18, 1938, Calvert made a contract for the installation and servicing of an advertising sign with Fiegel Advertising Company Inc. whereby Calvert agreed to pay Fiegel $165 per month for three years, making a total for the period of $5,940. The latter performed all the obligations under the contract prior to the appointment of the trustee. On June 8, 1938, Fiegel made a contract with Mathilde Lehman reciting that it had made the agreement for installing and servicing the sign with Calvert and had acquired a lease of property on which the sign was to be erected. Fiegel promised to erect the sign at a cost of $1,000 and to service the same for three years. Lehman was to advance $1,000 to Fiegel and the latter was to repay the $1,000 in six instalments during the months of July, August, September, October, November and December, 1938, and also to pay $23 per month beginning with July 15, 1938, for the three succeeding years. The agreement between Fiegel and Lehman also provided that, "as security for the payment of the sums" provided to be paid to Lehman, Fiegel assigned all its rights and title both to the lease and to its contract with Calvert. The agreement also provided that Fiegel on receipt of payments from Calvert should forward them, or its own checks for like amounts, to Lehman, or, in the event of failure to do this, Lehman should have the right to receive the payments from Calvert direct. It was further provided that no written notice of the assignment should be given to Calvert, unless a default in the payments had taken place, and that after the repayment of the $1,000 to Lehman had been made Fiegel should be entitled to a re-assignment from Lehman of the lease and the contract upon Lehman's receiving from Fiegel satisfactory security covering the payments to be made for the balance of the term. After Fiegel had made the above assignment to Lehman it assigned its contract with Calvert to Surf. The payments received from Calvert by Fiegel were paid over to Lehman, but $964.52 still remained due under the terms of her agreement with Fiegel.

Calvert deposited $5,960 in the registry of the District Court which represented sums due after October 1, 1939, from Calvert under the various contracts of which Abrams and Lehman held assignments.

Out of the fund of $5,960 the District Court awarded $4,410.16 to Abrams and $964.52 to Lehman. The court awarded the balance amounting to $585.32 to the trustee as reimbursement to him for servicing the various signs. The trustee appealed from the order of distribution in so far as it directed the payments of $4,410.16 to Abrams and $964.52 to Lehman. In his petition he alleged that the assignments to Abrams were fraudulent because the debtor Surf was at the time insolvent and the consideration for the assignments was inadequate and contrary to the Bankruptcy Act and the laws of the State of New York applicable thereto. In respect to the assignment to Lehman of the indebtedness of Calvert to Fiegel it is claimed by the trustee that Fiegel agreed to repay its indebtedness out of a fund to be created in the future through services to be rendered by Fiegel under its contract. The trustee's contention seems to us sound in respect to both the Abrams and the Lehman assignments.

The court below did not determine whether the assignments to Abrams and Lehman were absolute or were only given as security for the advances and evidently thought it unimportant which view was adopted. The special master was of much the same mind as to lack of importance, though he seemed to regard the assignments given to Abrams as absolute rather than as security for the latter's advances. We think they were given both to Abrams and Lehman as security. Abrams filed his proof as one for a "Secured Claim" and therein reserved the right to collect moneys due and to become due under the contracts assigned. Moreover, he testified that the transactions with Surf consisted of "lending . . . money . . ." under assignments. A so-called master contract (Trustee's Exhibit 14) made in 1934 between Surf and Abrams provided in terms for securing advances out of all contracts assigned "and to be assigned."

The following assignment to Abrams of the rights of Surf in the contract between Surf and Calvert dated May 28, 1937, is typical of the other assignments covering the contracts of July 28 and September 30, 1937:

June 2, 1937.

Abrams & Company,
1140 Broadway,
New York, N. Y.

Gentlemen:

The undersigned, Surf Adv. Corp. by its President, Samuel Schub, does hereby acknowledge the receipt of the sum of One Thousand Dollars

($1000.00) as evidenced by your check of even date #12664 and in consider-
ation therefore, does hereby sell, assign, transfer and convey unto you
Abrams & Co., all right, title and interest in the account of Calvert Distillers Corp., 405 Lexington Ave., N.Y.C., in the total sum of Seventeen
Thousand Four Hundred Dollars ($17400.00) covering the service and
maintenance of one sign board at W. 8th St., & Boardwalk, Coney Island,
Bklyn., N.Y., for a period of three years.

This said One Thousand Dollars ($1000.00) will be used for immediate
requirements to bring this sign into working order on or about June 15,
1937.

There will be an additional advance of Twelve Hundred and Fifty Dollars ($1250.00) required to complete the work on this bulleting and we will
deliver to you invoices, statement and an accounting of all the money
disbursed on the One Thousand Dollars ($1000.00) together with the addi-
tional advance of Twelve Hundred and Fifty Dollars ($1250.00) which will
be required between now and the 15th of June, 1937.

Very truly yours,
SURF ADV. CORP.,
By SAMUEL L. SCHUB.

The contract between Calvert and Surf, dated May 28, 1937, contained a provision giving Calvert the right to cancel it on sixty days'
notice. The same right of cancellation is applicable to the supplementary
contract dated July 28, 1937. The third contract of September 30, 1937,
was made subject to cancellation by Calvert on thirty days' notice in
writing to Surf. In view of all the circumstances we cannot suppose that
Abrams would neglect to save for himself the right to require the repayment of his advances from Surf as the personal obligation of the latter.
Because of cancellations, the contracts, out of which the funds to repay
the advances by Abrams would normally be realized, might at any time
disappear from the picture and no recourse remain to Abrams other than
the enforcement of his claim against Surf. Moreover he not only filed his
claim as a secured creditor, but Sanders testified before the referee that
Abrams declared before the creditors that he "had a lien on the Calvert
contracts" and not that he owned them through the purchase and consequent elimination of all the rights of Surf.

For the foregoing reasons we hold that Abrams' rights were those of a
secured creditor and that Lehman had similar rights. Indeed the position
of Lehman as a secured creditor is even clearer than that of Abrams for
her assignment was given as security in express terms. The arrangement
in the case of both Abrams and Lehman was for the assignor to turn over
all checks received from Calvert in liquidation of the assignee's advances.

It is reasonably clear that under the New York law the assignments and
the actual dealings between the parties created no lien good at law against
the future instalments which might become payable by Calvert to Surf or
Fiegel but at best only created an equitable lien which would arise when
the payments became due from Calvert. Such a lien would disappear

against an execution creditor or a trustee in bankruptcy who under Section 70, sub. c, of the Act occupies the position of a judgment-creditor armed with an execution. [Citations] The decision of the New York Court of Appeals in Foreman v. Louis Jacques Construction Co., 261 N.Y. 429, 185 N.E. 690, is not contrary to the foregoing cases because no execution creditor or trustee in bankruptcy was involved. Likewise the rights of a trustee in bankruptcy were not involved in the case of Stephenson v. Go-Gas Co., 268 N.Y. 372, 378, 197 N.E. 317, or in Hinkle Iron Co. v. Kohn, 229 N.Y. 179, 128 N.E. 113.

We think that the assignments constituted no more than promises to pay the assignees out of funds to be created by the assignor's labor which could not withstand the attack of the trustee in bankruptcy. It is manifest that the distribution of the moneys in question to Abrams or Lehman would result in a preference.

The order of the District Court is reversed and the proceeding is remanded with directions that the sums of $4,410.16 awarded to Abrams and $964.52 awarded to Lehman be paid over by the Clerk to Max Rockmore as trustee in bankruptcy of Surf Advertising Corporation.

CLARK, Circuit Judge (dissenting). As is the case with so many problems of creditors' rights, New York law is none too clear on the point at issue. But if we take the matter irrespective of statute, I do not believe the decisions require so ancient a theory as that an assignment of definite contract rights, future only in the sense that they are conditioned upon the performance which the promisee has promised, is only a promise to pay out of future funds, and not a present transfer. The New York cases cited, to my mind, are all distinguishable. Some deal with after-acquired property; and some with future accounts receivable. Such cases emphasize the distinction between assignment of rights under an already existing contract and of rights to be created by promises in the future. See Restatement, Contracts, §§150, 154, 155, 161. The validity of an assignment of the former kind seems to me upheld by Niles v. Mathusa, 162 N.Y. 546, 57 N.E. 184, holding an assignment of a liquor license as security valid as against a judgment creditor; McNeeley v. Welz, 166 N.Y. 124, 59 N.E. 697, approving Niles v. Mathusa, *supra*, and distinguishing between assignment of a license and an agreement to assign a renewal; and Bloomer v. Offerman, 247 App. Div. 860, 287 N.Y.S. 133, holding an assignment of a lottery ticket valid against attachment after assignment, but before the lottery drawing. And before the amendment of 1896, requiring filing of assignments of money to become due upon performance of construction contracts, N.Y. Lien Law, Consol. Laws c. 33, §15, it was well settled that the assignee for security prevailed over subsequent mechanics' lienors. Bates v. Salt Springs Nat. Bank, 157 N.Y. 322, 51 N.E. 1033; Beardsley v. Cook, 143 N.Y. 143, 38 N.E. 109, 62 N.Y. St. Rep. 144; Stevens v. Ogden, 130 N.Y. 182, 29 N.E. 229, 41 N.Y. St. Rep. 331; Lauer v. Dunn, 115 N.Y. 405, 22 N.E. 270, 26 N.Y. St. Rep. 412. Judge Hincks, in a careful and persuasive opinion, also reached the conclusion that an assignment, similar to the one before us, was valid under New York law. In re New York, N.H. & H.R. Co., D.C. Conn., 25 F. Supp. 874. And the cases distinguished in the opinion herewith certainly tend to support validity for the assignments. See, also, Central Trust Co. v. West India Imp. Co., 169 N.Y. 314, 323, 324, 62 N.E. 387.

Furthermore, assignments of moneys to become due under a contract seem in reality more nearly comparable to an assignment of existing book accounts than to a mortgage of after-acquired property. Under Benedict v. Ratner, 268 U.S. 353, 45 S. Ct. 566, 69 L. Ed. 991, such assignments are valid unless the assignor exercises "dominion" over the accounts. See Lee v. State Bank & Trust Co., 2 Cir., 54 F.2d 518, 85 A.L.R. 216, *certiorari denied* 285 U.S. 547, 52 S. Ct. 395, 76 L. Ed. 938. Certainly there is no evidence before us indicating reservation of "dominion" by the assignor. It also seems to me that the transactions before us better fit the analogy of expectancies, upheld by us in In re Barnett, 2 Cir.,124 F.2d 1005, than the after-acquired property analogy relied on by the court here.

[In an omitted passage of his opinion Judge Clark discussed the possible applicability of the New York chattel mortgage act (Lien Law §230). The court, after thus disposing of the case, granted a petition for rehearing. On the rehearing a number of the principal New York City law firms appeared as "Amici Curiae for various banking institutions," urging reversal of the first opinion. The court then delivered the following opinion.]

AUGUSTUS N. HAND, Circuit Judge. The parties have had full opportunity to present their views upon all phases of this appeal in the briefs filed on the motion for a rehearing. We shall accordingly treat the petition for a rehearing as granted, a rehearing had and proceed to a final disposition of the appeal.

Upon a further examination of the authorities we have become convinced that the majority opinion did not correctly interpret the New York law as applied to loans upon bilateral contracts not completely performed on either side and the view of that law expressed in Judge Clark's dissenting opinion should in general be adopted.

In each of the cases before us, advances were made upon contracts whereby Surf in the first case and Fiegel Advertising Company in the second case were to furnish and maintain advertising signs for Calvert in return for which Calvert bound itself to pay fixed sums over a period of years for the furnishing and maintenance of the signs. The advances were not made upon a mere agreement to assign rights which might arise in the future and did not exist at the time contracts were made, but upon assignments of definite contractual obligations.

We are convinced that the New York Court of Appeals has differentiated assignments of existing contracts by way of pledge from agreements to assign rights that have not yet come into being, even as interests contingent upon counter-performance. The most recent decision is Kniffin v. State, 283 N.Y. 317, 28 N.E.2d 853, where a building contractor assigned his contract with the State of New York to a subcontractor as security for a preexisting indebtedness, and then became bankrupt. The State made payments under the contract to the assignor, but the assignee was allowed to recover the amount of its claim in spite of the fact that the assignment embraced moneys "to become due" under the contract. See 1 Restatement, Contracts, §154, sub. 1, Illustration 1; also Judge Hinck's opinion in In Re New York N.H. & H.R. Co., D.C. Conn., 25 F. Supp. 874, 877; Central Trust Co. v. West India Importing Co., 169 N.Y. 314, 62 N.E. 387; Arrow Iron Works, Inc., v. Greene, 260 N.Y. 330, 183 N.E. 515.

We cannot agree with appellant's contention that Section 60, sub. a, of the present Bankruptcy Act, 11 U.S.C.A. §96, sub. a, affects our decision, and that there would be an unlawful preference as to any sums paid or payable after knowledge of insolvency. On the contrary we hold that the date of the assignments governed the imposition of the liens on any sums due from Calvert. This is because the contracts, and not the moneys accruing under them, were the subjects of the assignments. Section 60, sub. a, provides that: "a transfer shall be deemed to have been made at the time when it became so far perfected that no bona-fide purchaser from the debtor and no creditor could thereafter have acquired any rights in the property so transferred superior to the rights of the transferee therein." It has long been the New York law that such an assignment is good against a bona fide purchaser, even though the bona fide purchaser is the first to give notice to the obligor. Fortunato v. Patten, 147 N.Y. 277, 283, 41 N.E. 572; Hooker v. Eagle Bank of Rochester, 30 N.Y. 83, 86 Am. Dec. 351. The same thing is true of an execution creditor or a trustee in bankruptcy. Harris v. Taylor, 35 App. Div. 462, 54 N.Y.S. 864; see for an interpretation of it Sullivan v. Rosson, 223 N.Y. 217, at page 226, 119 N.E. 405, 4 A.L.R. 1400; Conley v. Fine, 181 App. Div. 675, 679, 169 N.Y.S. 162; In re New York, N.H. & H.R. Co., D.C. Conn., 25 F. Supp. 874, 877; Williams v. Ingersoll, 89 N.Y. 508.

[In an omitted passage of his opinion, Judge Hand concluded that the assignments were not required to be filed under §230 of the Lien Law.]

It follows from the foregoing that our former decision in this matter was erroneous and that the decision of the court below in both cases should have been affirmed.

Order affirmed.

NOTE

1. Did Judge Hand's second opinion adopt the theory advocated by Judge Clark in his dissent from the first opinion?

2. In his first opinion Judge Hand relied on a series of New York cases which had held that, under a chattel mortgage that contained a clause covering after-acquired property, the mortgagee's claim to such property was defeated by a levy in aid of a judgment recovered by a creditor of the mortgagor. In dissent, Judge Clark suggested that the New York case law distinguished between a mortgagee's claim to after-acquired chattels and an assignee's claim to at least some types of intangibles not in existence when the assignment was made. That the New York case law did make such a distinction seems to have been first suggested in an article by Stone, The "Equitable Mortgage" in New York, 20 Colum. L. Rev. 519 (1920).

3. In Williams v. Ingersoll, 89 N.Y. 508 (1882), cited by Judge Hand in his second opinion, Heath assigned to his attorney, Williams, the proceeds, if any, of a pending action for malicious prosecution against Ingersoll. No doubt to everyone's surprise, Heath recovered a judgment for substantial damages. Held that the assignment gave Williams an "equitable" interest in the award which prevailed over the claim of a judgment creditor of Heath's who sought to attach the proceeds. Fairbanks v. Sargent, 117 N.Y. 320, 22 N.E. 1039 (1889) also involved an assignment to an attorney of the proceeds of pending litigation. Held that the "equitable" interest of the attorney under the assignment prevailed over the claim of a subsequent assignee to whom the proceeds were actually turned over.

Does "equitable" in the two cases just referred to seem to mean the same thing as the "equitable lien" that Judge Hand referred to in his first opinion? Or the "equitable title" referred to in Muller v. Pondir, *supra* p. 1444?

4. In Field v. The Mayor of New York, 6 N.Y. 179 (1852), Bell assigned to Garread (who made a further assignment to Field) money that might become due to him for printing work done for the City. Bell did such work for the City under contracts entered into after the date of the assignment. The City, despite notification of the assignment, paid the money to Bell (who was insolvent). In an action by Field against the City, Field recovered judgment. Welles, J., commented:

> It is contended by the counsel for the appellants, that the assignment of Bell to Garread did not pass any interest which was the subject of an assignment, for the reason that there was no contract, at the time, between Bell and the corporation of the city, by which the latter was under any binding obligation to furnish the former with job printing, or to purchase of him paper or stationery; and that therefore the interest was of too uncertain and fleeting a character to pass by assignment. There was indeed no present, actual, potential existence of the thing to which the assignment or grant related, and therefore it could not and did not operate eo instanti to pass the claim which was expected thereafter to accrue to Bell against the corporation; but it did nevertheless create an equity, which would seize

upon those claims as they should arise, and would continue so to operate until the object of the agreement was accomplished. On this principle an assignment of freight to be earned in future, will be upheld, and enforced against the party from whom it becomes due. . . . Whatever doubts may have existed heretofore on this subject, the better opinion, I think, now is, that courts of equity will support assignments, not only of choses in action, but of contingent interests and expectations, and of things which have no present actual existence, but rest in possibility only, provided the agreements are fairly entered into, and it would not be against public policy to uphold them. Authorities may be found which seem to incline the other way, but which upon examination will be found to have been overruled, or to have turned upon the question of public policy.

Id. at 186-187.

Does the *Field* case go further than Rockmore v. Lehman? than Williams v. Ingersoll or Fairbanks v. Sargent?

5. In his second opinion in Rockmore v. Lehman, Judge Hand considers, and rejects, the trustee's argument that the money paid to the assignee's of Surf's contracts with Calvert constituted voidable preferences under §60 of the Bankruptcy Act. According to Judge Hand, "the date of the assignments governed the imposition of the liens on any sums due from Calvert. This is because the contracts, and not the moneys accruing under them, were the subjects of the assignments." Is this consistent with Judge Gignoux's analysis in Shiro v. Drew, *supra* p. 1452? Judge Hand also points out that "[i]t has long been New York law" that assignments of future claims of the sort involved in Rockmore v. Lehman are "good against a bona fide purchaser, even though the bona fide purchaser is the first to give notice to the obligor." What is the relevance of this in evaluating the trustee's preference argument? Read, again, the material on voidable preferences in Note 1 following Shiro v. Drew, *supra* p. 1452. For more on the complicated issue of priority among successive assignees (to which Judge Hand's comment concerning the rights of bona fide purchasers is a dark allusion), see Section 6.

Has Judge Hand's treatment of the preference issue been invalidated by the enactment of the Uniform Commercial Code? Recall the definition of "account" in §9-106, and the exception in §9-302(1)(e) for what the comment to that section calls "casual or isolated assignments."

In re CITY OF NEW YORK v. BEDFORD BAR & GRILL, INC.

2 N.Y.2d 429, 141 N.E.2d 575 (1957)

DESMOND, J. On January 29, 1953 appellant bank made a loan to Bedford Bar & Grill, Inc., and took as security an assignment from Bedford of any refund that might become due to the latter should the liquor store license for which the latter was applying not be granted by the State, or if after grant that license should be surrendered or cancelled. The license was granted. In June, 1953 the bank called Bedford's note because of defaults in payment. A few days later the bank filed its assignment with the State Comptroller. A few days after that Bedford surrendered its license for cancellation by the State Liquor Authority. Then, about a month later appellant city docketed against Bedford (with the effect of docketing a judgment) a warrant for taxes due the city from Bedford. In September, 1953 the city served on the State Comptroller a third-party subpœna in supplementary proceedings (Civ. Prac. Act, §779, subd. 2) which service created for the city a judgment creditor's lien on Bedford's property in the Comptroller's hands resulting from Bedford's surrender of its license (see Matter of Strand v. Piser, 291 N.Y. 236). The question here is as to priority of lien between appellant and respondent.

On such a question of priority between creditors, we should follow the only previous decisions in this State precisely in point. Those decisions including this present case are nine in number (Alchar Realty Corp. v. Meredith Restaurant, 256 App. Div. 853; Palmer v. Tremaine, 259 App. Div. 951; Atlas Adv. Agency v. Casa Cubana, 259 App. Div. 951; Matter of Frank v. Lutton, 267 App. Div. 703, 707; Matter of Guarino, 285 App. Div. 1161; Schaefer Brewing Co. v. Amsterdam Tavern, 171 Misc. 352; Matter of O'Neill Co. v. Ward, 4 Misc. 2d 470; Matter of Mariano v. Cathay House Restaurant, 199 Misc. 410) and were rendered over a period of 16 years. Every one of them holds that an assignment of moneys due from a liquor license cancellation refund, executed before the fund came into existence, is subordinate to the lien of a judgment creditor who has served a third-party subpœna upon the State Comptroller after the surrender of the license. Especially as to such law merchant questions, adherence to the precedents on which businessmen and their lawyers rely is most desirable. Such adherence becomes imperative here when two more reasons for affirmance appear: first, that those decisions are in harmony with general rules, and, second, that several efforts to overrule those decisions by legislation have been unsuccessful.

The undoubted general rule (Zartman v. First Nat. Bank of Waterloo, 189 N.Y. 267; Titusville Iron Co. v. City of New York, 207 N.Y. 203) is that as between a judgment creditor's lien and the equitable lien of an assignee of property subsequently to be acquired, the latter, while his rights will be enforced in equity as against his assignor, has no right at all as against the former. The same rule was applied in Matter of Gruner (295 N.Y. 510) where it was carefully stated that an assignee of the prospective proceeds of the possible sale of a Stock Exchange seat had inchoate rights only until the net proceeds of an actual sale were actually at hand and available (pp. 518, 519), and the *Gruner* case in its final denouement is direct authority for affirmance here. On the *Gruner* appeal we held that New York State's income tax lien was subordinate to the equitable lien of the bank assignee but only because the State had never taken any steps at all to enforce its right (supra, pp. 523-525). But later, in response to a motion for reargument, we remanded the *Gruner* case to the Surrogate's Court to take proof as to what the State had in fact done by way of enforcement effort. In the Surrogate's Court it appeared that the State had filed its claim with the administratrix of the estate before the fund had been collected in by the estate. The Surrogate held, therefore, that the State had priority over the bank assignee (Matter of Gruner, 4 Misc 2d 471). The situations of the State in the *Gruner* case and of the city in the present case were therefore identical in law, each being equipped with the equivalent of a judgment creditor's lien. *Gruner* holds that such a judgment lienor has priority over an equitable assignee like the appellant bank here.

The same appellant bank was, in Matter of Capitol Distrs. Corp. v. 2131 Eighth Ave. (1 NY2d 842), given priority over a judgment creditor but the reason for its priority there shows why it should be denied priority in the fundamentally different situation in the present case. In the Capitol Distributors case the assignment was not one of a fund to come into existence in the future, but was of a present interest and for a present consideration; it was not, as here, a refund of a partly used-up license fee but a return to an unsuccessful license applicant of the deposit which he had made as against the issuance of a license applied for but never issued (see Alcoholic Beverage Control Law, §54, subd. 2; §63). Since this bank had in the Capitol Distributors case a legal assignment of an existing fund owned by its assignor, it got its priority over later creditors even when the latter were armed with judgment liens. But here appellant had only an inchoate or equitable claim on a yet to be created fund (see Matter of Strand v. Piser, 291 N.Y. 236, *supra*) and so it must yield priority to judgment lienors.

Finally, as a ground for affirmance we have the legislative history above mentioned. In 1953, 1954 and 1955, bills were introduced into the Legislature to give to bank assignees like appellant here priority over judgment creditors. The 1953 bill passed in one house only. The 1954 and 1955 bills passed both houses but each was vetoed by the Governor. Beyond all question those bills were intended to change the existing law as found by the courts in a series of cases. At the very least, their history shows that all concerned thought the law to be as the courts below have held in the present case (see Holmes Elec. Protective Co. v. City of New York, 304 N.Y. 202, 206, 207). When the bills failed of passage and signature, the law remained unchanged.

The order should be affirmed, with costs.

FROESSEL, J. (dissenting). The assignment here made to the bank embraced

> all monies due or which may become due [to the assignor] from the State
> Liquor Authority or the Comptroller of the State of New York . . . in the

event that a license is not granted . . . or in the event of surrender . . .
cancellation or other release, of the license fee granted to the

assignor. Notwithstanding the several decisions of the Appellate Division cited in the prevailing opinion, we upheld, in Matter of Capitol
Distrs. Corp. v. 2131 Eighth Ave. (1 NY2d 842), a determination that the
assignee, in a situation virtually identical with the one here involved
except that the refund arose out of the disapproval of the license application instead of by way of surrender, was entitled to priority as to such
refund where the judgment creditor served its third-party subpœna after
the filing of the assignment and after the State Liquor Authority had
forwarded a refund order to the Comptroller.

In our judgment, that determination compels the same result in the
case before us, and we should follow the decisions in our own court, to
which further reference will presently be made. After moneys have been
deposited, they are subject to return to the depositor in the event that the
license is not granted, or pro tanto in the event that the license is surrendered. If, therefore, after disapproval of the application on the one hand
or surrender of the license on the other, the whole or any part of the
moneys is payable to the depositor, there is no reason in law or logic why
an assignee who supplied the moneys should not in either case take
precedence over subsequent liens of a judgment creditor. In both cases,
assignments taken at the time of the loans were filed prior to the critical
date, and the subpœnas in supplementary proceedings were filed later.
We see no distinction whatever between the possibility of the return of a
deposit in case of disapproval and the return of a deposit in case of
surrender. Either eventuality may or may not happen. There is no more
certainty in the one case than in the other. To the extent to which the law
allows a licensee to surrender his license for cancellation, the fund to
which he is entitled belongs to him whenever he wants it (Alcoholic
Beverage Control Law, §127), just as if it were on deposit anywhere else.

The line of surrender cases in the lower courts, relied on in the prevailing opinion, sought to apply the rule enunciated by this court in Zartman
v. First Nat. Bank of Waterloo (189 N.Y. 267) and Titusville Iron Co. v.
City of New York (207 N.Y. 203). These two cases held that the equitable
lien created by the mortgage or pledge of chattels to be acquired in the
future was enforcible between the parties thereto but was void as to
creditors. The reason for such a holding was explained in the Zartman
case (p. 271) as a desire to protect "general creditors, who are presumed to
have dealt with the mortgagor in reliance upon its absolute ownership of
the stock on hand . . . who had little, if anything, to rely upon except the
shifting stock, which, directly or indirectly, they themselves had furnished," and (p. 273) as to whom the "agreement permitting the mortgagor to sell for his own benefit renders the mortgage fraudulent as matter
of law." (See, also, Rochester Distilling Co. v. Rasey, 142 N.Y. 570, as to
future crops.)

While this is the rule with regard to the *mortgage or pledge of future crops or afteracquired chattels*, it is not the general rule, and neither the rule (as to such crops and chattels) nor the reasons therefor have ever been applied by us to the *assignment of a fund* which is to come into existence out of a present property right, and which fund was advanced by the assignee. We have held, in a wide variety of circumstances, that where the fund is to arise out of an existing relationship between the assignor and the potential source of the fund, such an assignment is valid as against creditors of the assignor who acquire liens after the fund comes into existence (see, e.g., Matter of Gruner, 295 N.Y. 510 [proceeds from the sale of a seat on the Stock Exchange]; Niles v. Mathusa, 162 N.Y. 546 [refund on surrender of liquor tax certificate]; Bates v. Salt Springs Nat. Bank, 157 N.Y. 322 [payments under a building contract]; Fairbanks v. Sargent, 117 N.Y. 320 [proceeds of collection of debt]; Williams v. Ingersoll, 89 N.Y. 508 [recovery in personal injury litigation]; Stover v. Eycleshimer, 3 Keyes 620 [expectancy of an inheritance]; see, also, 2 Williston on Contracts, §413; 4 Pomeroy on Equity Jurisprudence, §§1283, 1291).

In Niles v. Mathusa (*supra*) we held that the assignee of a liquor tax certificate was entitled to the right to refund thereon over a creditor acquiring a lien by supplementary proceedings subsequent to the assignment. Under the law at that time, the licensing rights of such a certificate, as well as the refund rights, could be assigned; under the Alcoholic Beverage Control Law (§114, subds. 2, 3) the license rights cannot today be transferred. However, the assignor continued to use the license rights, keeping the certificate posted in his place of business, and the court treated the transaction as an assignment of a chose in action. The court rejected the argument, which was successfully used in the Zartman case (*supra*), that the assignor was clothed with apparent ownership and thus the assignee should be estopped from setting up the assignment against creditors. Citing Fairbanks v. Sargent (*supra*) and Williams v. Ingersoll (*supra*), the court decided that the creditor was in no different position than a subsequent assignee who would be subordinate to an assignee prior in time.

In Matter of Gruner (*supra*) we held that where the holder of a seat on the Stock Exchange assigned the proceeds of a future sale of such seat as security for a loan, the assignee was entitled to priority over the tax claims of the State, which had not issued a warrant prior to the time the seat was sold. Chief Judge (then Judge) Conway, writing the opinion for the court, stated the rule to be applied to such assignments (p. 525):

The assignee of a thing in action acquires at once "an equitable ownership therein, as far as it is possible to predicate *property* or ownership of such a species of right; . . ." (Pomeroy's Equity Jurisprudence [5th ed.], §168, p. 221). Where, as in this instance, the chose in action was turned into money and became available in the hands of the exchange for payment to the

assignor's administratrix, the equitable lien attached to it immediately and
equitable ownership of the fund passed to the trust company, needing but
the action of a court of equity to enforce its right to payment. At that
moment, the lien of the trust company, which was greater in amount than
the proceeds of the sale of the seat, and of all the assets of the estate,
became capable of perfection and so was perfected, and the trust company
became a secured creditor.

(Emphasis in original.) It is true that after our remand in that case, and
upon additional proofs, it developed that the lien of the State had attached on May 27, 1943, whereas the proceeds of the sale of the seat were
not available until March, 1944; hence it was properly held on those facts
that the lien of the trust company assignee was subordinate to that of the
State (Matter of Gruner, 4 Misc 2d 471).

In the case before us, in order to decide priority we must determine the
date on which the fund assigned came into existence so as to perfect the
bank's equitable interest. If the city acquired its lien after this date,
the bank is entitled to priority. The Appellate Division was of the opinion
that this was on October 5th, when the State Liquor Authority forwarded
the refund order to the Comptroller. In this they were in error.

In Matter of Strand v. Piser (291 N.Y. 236), this court was called upon
to determine (p. 238) "when, under section 127 of the Alcoholic Beverage
Control Law, a judgment debtor's right to a refund [as the result of
surrender] from the State Comptroller comes into existence" (bracketed
matter supplied). Rejecting the argument based on one of the surrender
cases (Palmer v. Tremaine, 259 App. Div. 951) that this occurred when
the State Liquor Authority delivered its certificate of approval to the
Comptroller, we held that a judgment creditor who served a third-party
subpoena, after the license had been surrendered but before the State
Liquor Authority certified its approval, was entitled to priority over creditors who served immediately after the approval of the Authority. In
reaching this conclusion, the court determined that, immediately upon
the surrender of the license (p. 239), "the Comptroller had in his custody
'property of the judgment debtor . . . or [was] indebted to him.'" We said
(pp. 240-241):

> We read in the excerpts from section 127, quoted above, an intention by
> the Legislature to declare a refund "due" on the date when the license is
> surrendered for cancellation. Accordingly in the present case the refund
> became due on . . . [the date of surrender], and created on that date in
> favor of the judgment debtor an obligation whereby the Comptroller, a
> third party, became "indebted" to the judgment debtor. . . . Although
> section 127 of the Alcoholic Beverage Control Law directs that payment of
> the refund be deferred for a period of thirty days, an obligation impressed
> upon the Comptroller by the statute remained and was sufficient to make
> the third party subpoena, served upon the Comptroller . . . , legally effec-

tive as a basis for determining the priority of the right asserted by the
appellant creditor to the refund.

The bank's equitable interest in the instant case, accordingly, was
perfected on July 8th when the license was surrendered and the refund
became "due" to Bedford, only one day intervening between that date
and the day the Comptroller acknowledged receipt of the assignment.
The tax claim of the city first became a judgment on August 13th when its
warrant was docketed. Its third-party subpoena based on that judgment
was served on the Comptroller on September 24th. Both of these events
were subsequent to the date of surrender as well as the 30-day period
thereafter, during which the State Liquor Authority might still cancel the
license because of a possible previous violation of the Alcoholic Beverage
Control Law and forfeit the refund (Alcoholic Beverage Control Law,
§127, subd. 1). Refund after the surrender date, and in any event after
this 30-day period, is a purely ministerial act. Of course the Comptroller
may make certain deductions for State taxes, but this does not delay the
date on which the fund comes into existence, for he can only do this on
the theory that the fund already belongs to the licensee and is no longer
part of the general license fee fund in his custody. Consequently, the
bank, by virtue of its assignment which was perfected prior to the date on
which the city perfected its lien, is entitled to priority in the satisfaction of
its claim out of the moneys held by the Comptroller to the credit of
Bedford.

The city also argues that the veto by the Governor (without memorandum) of two bills which were passed by the Legislature to amend section
127 of the Alcoholic Beverage Control Law in order to effect the result
recommended here (Assem. Int. No. 1905, Pr. No. 1976, 1954 Sess.; Sen.
Int. 1477, Pr. No. 1566, 1954 Sess.; Assem. Int. No. 1283, Pr. No. 1299,
1955 Sess.; Sen. Int. 892, Pr. No. 919, 1955 Sess.), is of significance "that
the law makers have rejected such a change." Aside from the fact that this
was not an example of the refusal by the Legislature to act, but quite the
contrary — it did so act — such refusal, if any there were, would only be
relevant where the interpretation of the legislation sought to be amended
is at issue, as in the cases cited by the city. Here we are concerned with
the effect of an assignment, a question with which section 127 of the
Alcoholic Beverage Control Law never attempted to deal. It may well be
argued that the reason why our lawmakers enacted the proposed legislation was because they wished to nullify the effect of the surrender decisions in the third department, none of which had been appealed to our
court, and thus conform to the law as laid down by us in kindred situations.

Accordingly, the orders of the Appellate Division and Special Term
should be reversed, the motion of the City of New York denied, the cross
motion of Manufacturers Trust Company granted, and the Comptroller

of the State of New York directed to pay to Manufacturers Trust Company the sum of $658 to the credit of the judgment debtor herein, with costs.

Dye, Fuld and Van Voorhis, JJ., concur with Desmond, J.; Froessel, J., dissents in an opinion in which Conway, Ch. J., concurs; Burke, J., taking no part.

Order affirmed.

NOTE

1. Does *Bedford* seem to overrule the *Williams, Fairbanks,* and *Field* cases discussed in the Note following Rockmore v. Lehman, *supra* p. 1477? Is it consistent with Judge Hand's second opinion in the *Rockmore* case?

2. Stathos v. Murphy, 20 A.D.2d 500, 276 N.Y.S.2d 727 (1966), involved an assignment of the proceeds of pending litigation. The trial court had held, on the authority of the *Bedford* and *Gruner* cases, that the assignee lost to a subsequent judgment creditor. The Appellate Division reversed in an opinion by Justice Breitel, who referred to Williams v. Ingersoll as "the leading case" and commented that the *Bedford* and *Gruner* cases "are easily reconciled with the prevailing rules." The Court of Appeals affirmed "upon the opinion at the Appellate Division," Stathos v. Murphy, 19 N.Y.2d 883, 227 N.E.2d 880 (1967).

SPEELMAN v. PASCAL

10 N.Y.2d 313, 178 N.E.2d 723 (1961), *motion for reargument denied,* 10 N.Y.2d 1011

Chief Judge DESMOND. Gabriel Pascal, defendant's intestate who died in 1954, had been for many years a theatrical producer. In 1952 an English corporation named Gabriel Pascal Enterprises, Ltd., of whose shares Gabriel Pascal owned 98, made an agreement with the English Public Trustee who represented the estate of George Bernard Shaw. This agreement granted to Gabriel Pascal Enterprises, Ltd., the exclusive world rights to prepare and produce a musical play to be based on Shaw's play "Pygmalion" and a motion picture version of the musical play. The agreement recited, as was the fact, that the licensee owned a film scenario written by Pascal and based on "Pygmalion." In fact Pascal had, some time previously, produced a nonmusical movie version of "Pygmalion" under rights obtained by Pascal from George Bernard Shaw during the latter's lifetime. The 1952 agreement required the licensee corporation to pay the Shaw estate an initial advance and thereafter to pay the Shaw estate 3% of the gross receipts of the musical play and musical movie with a provision that the license was to terminate if within certain fixed periods the licensee did not arrange with Lerner and Loewe or other similarly well-known composers to write the musical play and arrange to produce it. Before Pascal's death in July, 1954, he had made a number of unsuccessful efforts to get the musical written and produced and it was not until after his death that arrangements were made, through a New York bank as temporary administrator of his estate, for the writing and production of the highly successful "My Fair Lady." Meanwhile, on February 22, 1954, at a time when the license from the Shaw estate still had two years to run, Gabriel Pascal, who died four and a half months later, wrote, signed and delivered to plaintiff a document as follows:

Dear Miss Kingman

   This is to confirm to you our understanding that I give you from my shares of profits of the Pygmalion Musical stage version five per cent (5%) in England, and two per cent (2%) of my shares of profits in the United States. From the film version, five per cent (5%) from my profit shares all over the world.

   As soon as the contracts are signed, I will send a copy of this letter to my lawyer, Edwin Davies, in London, and he will confirm to you this arrangement in a legal form.

   This participation in my shares of profits is a present to you, in recognition for your loyal work for me as my Executive Secretary.

Very sincerely yours,
GABRIEL PASCAL.

The question in this lawsuit is: Did the delivery of this paper constitute a valid, complete, present gift to plaintiff by way of assignment of a share in future royalties when and if collected from the exhibition of the musical stage version and film version of "Pygmalion"? A consideration was, of course, unnecessary (Personal Property Law, §33, subd. 4).

   In pertinent parts the judgment appealed from declares that plaintiff is entitled to receive the percentages set out in the 1954 agreement, requires defendant to render plaintiff accountings from time to time of all moneys received from the musical play and the film version, and orders defendant to make the payments required by the agreement. The basic grant from the Shaw estate was to Gabriel Pascal Enterprises, Ltd., a corporation, whereas the document on which plaintiff sues is signed by Gabriel Pascal individually and defendant makes much of this, arguing that Gabriel Pascal, as distinguished from his corporation, owned no rights when he delivered the 1954 document to plaintiff. However, no such point was made in the courts below and no mention of it is made in the motion papers, affidavits, etc., on which plaintiff was granted summary judgment. It is apparent that all concerned in these transactions disregarded any distinction between Pascal's corporation in which he owned practically all the stock, and Pascal individually, as is demonstrated by the agreement between Lerner-Loewe-Levin, writers and producers of "My Fair Lady," and Gabriel Pascal's estate. Actually, all this makes little difference since what Pascal assigned to plaintiff was a percentage from Pascal's "shares of profits" and this would cover direct collections or collections through his corporation.

Defendant emphasizes also the use of the word "profits" in the February, 1954 letter from Pascal to plaintiff, and suggests that this means that plaintiff was not to get a percentage of Pascal's gross royalties but a percentage of some "profits" remaining after deduction of expenses. Again, the answer is that no such point was made in the proceedings below or in this record and everyone apparently assumed, at least until the case reached this court, that what the defendant Pascal estate will get from the musical play and movie is royalties collectible in full under the agreements pursuant to which "My Fair Lady" has been and will be produced. In this same connection defendant talks of possible creditors of the Pascal corporation and inquires as to what provision would be made for them if plaintiff were to get her percentages of the full royalties. This, too, is an afterthought and no such matter was litigated below.

The only real question is as to whether the 1954 letter above quoted operated to transfer to plaintiff an enforcible right to the described percentages of the royalties to accrue to Pascal on the production of a stage or film version of a musical play based on "Pygmalion." We see no reason why this letter does not have that effect. It is true that at the time of the delivery of the letter there was no musical stage or film play in existence but Pascal, who owned and was conducting negotiations to realize on the stage and film rights, could grant to another a share of the moneys to accrue from the use of those rights by others. There are many instances of courts enforcing assignments of rights to sums which were expected thereafter to become due to the assignor. A typical case is Field v. Mayor of New York (6 N.Y. 179). One Bell, who had done much printing and similar work for the City of New York but had no present contract to do any more such work, gave an assignment in the amount of $1,500 of any moneys that might thereafter become due to Bell for such work. Bell did obtain such contracts or orders from the city and money became due to him therefor. This court held that while there was not at the time of the assignment any presently enforcible or even existing chose in action but merely a possibility that there would be such a chose of action, nevertheless there was a possibility of such which the parties expected to ripen into reality and which did afterwards ripen into reality and that, therefore, the assignment created an equitable title which the courts would enforce. A case similar to the present one in general outline is Central Trust Co. v. West India Improvement Co. (169 N.Y. 314) where the assignor had a right or concession from the Colony of Jamaica to build a railroad on that island and the courts upheld a mortgage given by the concession owner on any property that would be acquired by the concession owner in consideration of building the railroad if and when the railroad should be built. The Court of Appeals pointed out in *Central Trust Co.*, at page 323, that the property as to which the mortgage was given had not yet come into existence at the time of the giving of the mortgage but that there was an expectation that such property, consisting of securities, would come into existence and accrue to the concession holder when and if the latter performed the underlying contract. This court held that the assignment would be recognized and enforced in equity. The cases cited by appellant (Young v. Young, 80 N.Y. 422; Vincent v. Rix, 248 N.Y. 76; Farmers' Loan & Trust Co. v. Winthrop, 207 App. Div. 356, *mod.* 238 N.Y. 477) are not to the contrary. In each of those instances the attempted gifts failed because there had not been such a completed and irrevocable delivery of the subject matter of the gift as to put the gift beyond cancellation by the donor. In every such case the question must be as to whether there was a completed delivery of a kind appropriate to the subject property. Ordinarily, if the property consists of existing stock certificates or corporate bonds, as in the *Young* and *Vincent* cases (*supra*), there must be a completed physical transfer of the stock certificates or bonds. In Farmers' Loan & Trust Co. v. Winthrop (*supra*) the dispute was as to the effect of a power of attorney but the maker of the power had used language which could not be construed as effectuating a present gift of the property which the donor expected to receive in the future from another estate. The *Farmers' Loan & Trust Co.* case does not hold that property to be the subject of a valid gift must be in present physical existence and in the possession of the donor but it does hold that the language used in the particular document was not sufficient to show an irrevocable present intention to turn over to the donee securities which would come to the donor on the settlement of another estate. At page 485 of 238 New York this court held that all that need be established is "an intention that the title of the donor shall be presently divested and presently transferred" but that in the particular document under scrutiny in the *Farmers' Loan & Trust Co.* case there was lacking any language to show an irrevocable intent of a gift to become operative at once. In our present case there was nothing left for Pascal to do in order to make an irrevocable transfer to plaintiff of part of Pascal's right to receive royalties from the productions.

The rules as to the requisites for completed gifts have recently been restated by us in Matter of Szabo (10 NY2d 94, 98).

The Beaver v. Beaver (117 N.Y. 421) and Matter of Van Alstyne (207 N.Y. 298) cases relied on by defendant deal with the transfer of tangible physical property and are not helpful here. In Young v. Young (80 N.Y. 422, *supra*) and Vincent v. Rix (248 N.Y. 76, *supra*), similarly cited by defendant, there was neither a physical delivery nor delivery of a writing.

The judgment should be affirmed, with costs.

Judges Dye, Fuld, Froessel, Van Voorhis, Burke and Foster concur.

Judgment affirmed.

NOTE

1. Does it follow from the *Bedford* case, *supra* p. 1485, that Miss Kingman's claim to the My Fair Lady royalties could have been defeated by a judgment creditor of Pascal? Or are the two cases distinguishable? Or does *Speelman* overrule *Bedford*?

2. In Miller v. Commissioner of Internal Revenue, 299 F.2d 706 (2d Cir. 1962), it appeared that in 1952 Mrs. Miller, widow of the bandleader Glenn Miller, granted to Universal Pictures Company "the exclusive right to produce, release, distribute and exhibit . . . one or more photo-plays based on the life and activities of Glenn Miller throughout the world." In 1954 Universal, which had produced "The Glenn Miller Story," paid Mrs. Miller approximately $400,000 under the 1952 agreement. The Commissioner of Internal Revenue claimed that the $400,000 was taxable as ordinary income. Mrs. Miller argued that it was taxable only as a capital gain. The difference between the two tax rates amounted to approximately $160,000. Mrs. Miller's case depended on proving that in 1952 she had sold "property" to Universal. Judge Kaufman commented:

> Undeterred by her failure to find case authority which would substantiate the existence of "property rights" petitioner invokes the authority of logic. With considerable ingenuity, she argues:
> (1)   Universal paid petitioner $409,336.34 in 1954, which is a great deal of money.
> (2)   Universal was a sophisticated corporate being to which donative intent would be difficult to ascribe.
> (3)   If there was no danger in free use of Glenn Miller material, why did Universal pay?
> Petitioner appears to find this question unanswerable unless it is conceded that there was a sale of a "property right." Petitioner is wrong.

Id. at 709. Thus Mrs. Miller had to pay the higher tax.

The *Speelman* case (1961) is not cited in the opinion in the *Miller* case (1962). If you had been counsel for Mrs. Miller would you have relied on *Speelman?* Under the assignment from Pascal, did Miss Kingman receive a "property right" in the future royalties of My Fair Lady, when and if the show was produced?

3. In the terminology of Article 9, Miss Kingman's claim to a share of the royalties from My Fair Lady would be classified as a "general intangible" (§9-106). Article 9 provides that a security interest in general intangi-

bles can be perfected only by filing; there is nothing in Article 9, however, that governs the assignment of such claims other than for security.

4. In 1972, Article 9 was substantially amended by the Code's Permanent Editorial Board. In its pre-1972 version, §9-106 had distinguished three different sorts of intangibles, rather than the two it now covers. The third category of intangibles, eliminated in 1972, consisted of what were termed "contract rights," defined as "any right to payment under a contract not yet earned by performance and not evidenced by an instrument or chattel paper." Prior to 1972, "accounts" covered only the right to payment under an executed contract; rights under executory contracts were covered by the separate category of contract rights. In the 1972 amendments to §9-106, the term "contract right" was dropped and "account" was redefined to include any right to payment "whether or not it has been earned by performance." Also eliminated in the 1972 revisions was §9-204(2), which had provided, in part, that a debtor has no rights "in a contract right until the contract has been made" or "in an account until it comes into existence." (It is important to determine when a debtor acquires rights in the property he is proposing to sell or use as collateral since this is one of the prerequisites for what, in the Article 9 scheme, is called "attachment," which in turn is one of the prerequisites for perfection. See §§9-203(1), 9-303(1).)

Do the revisions just described seem to you, on the whole, an improvement or would it be useful to preserve a distinction between what the Code originally called accounts and contract rights?

5. The Restatement Second deals with the assignment of future intangibles as follows:

§321.   Assignment of Future Rights

(1)   Except as otherwise provided by statute, an assignment of a right to payment expected to arise out of an existing employment or other continuing business relationship is effective in the same way as an assignment of an existing right.

(2)   Except as otherwise provided by statute and as stated in Subsection (1), a purported assignment of a right expected to arise under a contract not in existence operates only as a promise to assign the right when it arises and as a power to enforce it.

According to Restatement Second §330(2), the effect of a contract to assign "on the rights and duties of the obligor and third persons is determined by the rules relating to specific performance of contracts." Comment d to §330 adds:

In general a contract to give security is specifically enforceable as between the parties even as to rights arising after the contract is made. By statute or decision, however, an exception has been made for contracts to assign wages under future employments. See §321. And in some states, on the analogy of rules applied to mortgages of after-acquired tangible property, an "equitable assignment" of rights not in existence is subordinate to the claims of creditors of the assignor whose rights attach after the rights have arisen and before the assignor has made a present assignment. In the absence of statutory provision for public notice, the rights of the promisee are inferior to those of a subsequent good faith purchaser for value without notice of the prior contract.

The notice filing system of U.C.C. Article 9 constitutes one such "statutory provision."

6. This section has considered a sequence of New York cases, state and federal. New York, having long been an important commercial state, has a uniquely rich harvest of case law in this area. The rules that developed in other states as to the possibility of making an effective present assignment of future claims were exceedingly various. The pre-Code Massachusetts rule, for example, is said to have been that such an assignment was both a legal and a logical impossibility.

In Taylor v. Barton-Child Co., 228 Mass. 126, 117 N.E. 43 (1917), Rugg, C.J., wrote:

> The crucial question is whether the assignment of book accounts, which are to come into existence in the future in connection with an established business, will be enforced in equity against a trustee in bankruptcy.
>
> It is a well recognized principle of the common law that a man cannot sell or mortgage property which he does not possess and to which he has no title. The vendor must have a vested right in personal property in order to be able to make a sale of it. "A man cannot grant or charge that which he hath not." Jones v. Richardson, 10 Metc. 481, 488; Moody v. Wright, 13 Metc. 17, 46 Am. Dec. 706; Leverett v. Barnwell, 214 Mass. 105, 109, 101 N.E. 75.
>
> The ground of our decision may be stated shortly. There can be no present conveyance or transfer of property not in existence, or of property not in the possession of the seller to which he has no title. A sale of personal chattels is not good against creditors unless there has been a delivery. Manifestly there can be no delivery of chattels not in existence. In order that after-acquired chattels may be brought under the lien of a mortgage, or of hypothecation, there must be some act of the parties subsequent to the time when such chattels come into existence and into the ownership and possession of the mortgagor. The mortgage is held not to have the effect of changing the title to after-acquired chattels without some further act of the parties.
>
> There is an exception at the common law to the effect that one may sell that in which he has a potential title although not present actual possession. The present owner might sell the wool to be grown upon his flock, the crop to be harvested from his field or the young to be born of his herd, or assign the wages to be earned under existing employment. Kerr v. Crane, 212 Mass. 224, 229, 98 N.E. 783, 40 L.R.A., N.S., 692; St. Johns v. Charles, 105 Mass. 262; Farrar v. Smith, 64 Me. 74, 77; McCarty v. Blevins, 5 Yerg.

(Tenn.) 195, 26 Am. Dec. 262; Dugas v. Lawrence, 19 Ga. 557. But see now Sales Act, St. 1908, c. 237, §5(3). That principle of the common law has never been carried so far as to include the case at bar. The catch of fish expected to be made upon a voyage about to begin cannot be sold. Low v. Pew, 108 Mass. 347, 11 Am. Dec. 357. There can be no sale of the wool of sheep, the crop of a field or the increase of herd not owned but to be bought, and there can be no assignment of wages to be earned under a contract of employment to be made in the future. Eagen v. Luby, 133 Mass. 543; Citizens' Loan & Trust Co. v. Boston & Maine R.R., 196 Mass. 528, 531, 82 N.E. 696, 14 L.R.A., N.S., 1025, 124 Am. St. Rep. 584, 13 Ann. Cas. 365.

It is also the established doctrine in this commonwealth that a mortgage of future acquired property will not be enforced in equity before actual possession taken by the mortgagee as against persons subsequently acquiring an interest therein for value and having possession. That has long been settled although the contrary rule prevails more widely. Federal Trust Co. v. Bristol County St. Ry. Co., 222 Mass. 35, 45, 46, 109 N.E. 880, where cases are collected. It would be anomalous for a court governed by these principles as to sales and mortgages of future acquired goods and chattels to hold that there could be an assignment of future acquired book accounts valid and enforceable under circumstances where a like attempt to hypothecate future acquired chattels would be held unenforceable.

Note that Chief Justice Rugg in the passage quoted equates the problem of the after-acquired property interest in chattels with that of the assignability of future claims. Contrast the New York distinction between these two problems, discussed in Rockmore v. Lehman, *supra* p. 1477, and the Note following that case.

Pre-Code authorities on the "future intangible" problem are collected in 1 G. Gilmore, Security Interests in Personal Property §§7.10-7.12 (1965).

7. U.C.C. §9-204(1) states that except in certain consumer transactions, "a security agreement may provide that any or all obligations covered by the security agreement are to be secured by after-acquired collateral." According to the Official Comment, this means that

a security interest arising by virtue of an after-acquired property clause has equal status with a security interest in collateral in which the debtor has rights at the time value is given under the security agreement. That is to say: the security interest in after-acquired property is not merely an "equitable" interest; no further action by the secured party — such as the taking of a supplemental agreement covering the new collateral — is required.

The Comment continues:

This Article accepts the principle of a "continuing general lien." It rejects the doctrine — of which the judicial attitude toward after-acquired property interests was one expression — that there is reason to invalidate as a matter of law what has been variously called the floating charge, the free-handed mortgage and the lien on a shifting stock. This Article validates a security interest in the debtor's existing and future assets, even though (see Section 9-205) the debtor has liberty to use or dispose of collateral without being required to account for proceeds or substitute new collateral. (See further, however, Section 9-306 on Proceeds and Comment thereto.)

The widespread nineteenth century prejudice against the floating charge was based on a feeling, often inarticulate in the opinions, that a commercial borrower should not be allowed to encumber all his assets present and future, and that for the protection not only of the borrower but of his other creditors a cushion of free assets should be preserved. That inarticulate premise has much to recommend it. This Article decisively rejects it not on the ground that it was wrong in policy but on the ground that it was not effective. In pre-Code law there was a manipulation of security devices designed to avoid the policy: field warehousing, trust receipts, factor's lien acts and so on. The cushion of free assets was not preserved. In almost every state it was possible before the Code for the borrower to give a lien on everything he held or would have. There have no doubt been sufficient economic reasons for the change. This Article, in expressly validating the floating charge, merely recognizes an existing state of things. The substantive rules of law set forth in the balance of the Article are designed to achieve the protection of the debtor and the equitable resolution of the conflicting claims of creditors which the old rules no longer give.

Notice that the question of assignment of future accounts is treated like any other case or after-acquired property: no periodic list of accounts is required by this Act. Where less than all accounts are assigned such a list may of course be necessary to permit identification of the particular accounts assigned.

Section 4.   Assignment of Rights vs. Delegation of Duties

LANGEL v. BETZ
250 N.Y. 159, 164 N.E. 890 (Ct. App. 1928)

POUND, J. Plaintiff, on August 1, 1925, made a contract with Irving W. Hurwitz and Samuel Hollander for the sale of certain real property. This contract the vendees assigned to Benedict, who in turn assigned it to Isidor Betz, the defendant herein. The assignment contains no delegation to the assignee of the performance of the assignor's duties. The date for performance of the contract was originally set for October 2, 1925. This was extended to October 15, 1925, at the request of the defendant, the last assignee of the vendees. The ground upon which the adjournment was asked for by defendant was that the title company had not completed its search and report on the title to the property. Upon the adjourned date the defendant refused to perform. The vendor plaintiff was ready, able, and willing to do so, and was present at the place specified with a deed, ready to tender it to the defendant, who did not appear.

The plaintiff as vendor brought this action against the defendant assignee for specific performance of the contract. Upon the foregoing undisputed facts he has had judgment therefor.

The question is: "Can the vendor obtain specific performance of a contract for the sale of real estate against the assignee of the vendee, where the assignee merely requests and obtains an extension of time within which to close title?"

Here we have no novation, no express assumption of the obligations of the assignor in the assignment, and no demand for performance by the assignee.

The mere assignment of a bilateral executory contract may not be interpreted as a promise by the assignee to the assignor to assume the performance of the assignor's duties, so as to have the effect of creating a new liability on the part of the assignee to the other party to the contract assigned. The assignee of the vendee is under no personal engagement to the vendor where there is no privity between them. Champion v. Brown, 6 Johns. Ch. 398, 10 Am. Dec. 343; Anderson v. New York & H.R. Co., 132 App. Div. 183, 187, 188, 116 N.Y.S. 954; Hugel v. Habel, 132 App. Div. 327, 328, 117 N.Y.S. 78. The assignee may, however, expressly or impliedly, bind himself to perform the assignor's duties. This he may do by contract with the assignor or with the other party to the contract. It has been held (Epstein v. Gluckin, 233 N.Y. 490, 135 N.E. 861) that, where the assignee of the vendee invokes the aid of a court of equity in an action for specific performance, he impliedly binds himself to perform on his part and subjects himself to the conditions of the judgment appropriate thereto. "He who seeks equity must do equity." The converse of the proposition, that the assignee of the vendee would be bound when the vendor began the action, did not follow from the decision in that case. On the contrary, the question was wholly one of remedy rather than right, and it was held that mutuality of remedy is important only so far as its presence is essential to the attainment of the ends of justice. This holding was necessary to sustain the decision. No change was made in the law of contracts nor in the rule for the interpretation of an assignment of a contract.

A judgment requiring the assignee of the vendee to perform at the suit of the vendor would operate as the imposition of a new liability on the assignee which would be an act of oppression and injustice, unless the assignee had, expressly or by implication, entered into a personal and binding contract with the assignor or with the vendor to assume the obligations of the assignor.

It has been urged that the probable intention of the assignee is ordinarily to assume duties as well as rights, and that the contract should be so interpreted in the absence of circumstances showing a contrary intention. The American Law Institute's Restatement of the Law of Contracts (section 164) proposes a change in the rule of interpretation of assigned contracts to give as full effect to the assumed probable intention of the parties as the law permits. The following statement is proposed:

> Section 164.   Interpretation of Words Purporting to Assign a
> Bilateral Contract and Effect of Acceptance of the Assignment by
> the Assignee
>
> (1)   Where a party to a bilateral contract which is at the time wholly or partially executory on both sides, purports to assign the whole contract, his action is interpreted, in the absence of circumstances showing a contrary intention, as an assignment of the assignor's rights under the contract and a delegation of the performance of the assignor's duties.
>
> (2)   Acceptance by the assignee of such an assignment is interpreted, in the absence of circumstances showing a contrary intention, as both an assent to become an assignee of the assignor's rights and as a promise *to the assignor to assume the performance of the assignor's duties.*

This promise to the assignor would then be available to the other party to the contract. Lawrence v. Fox, 20 N.Y. 268; 1 Williston on Contracts, §412. The proposed change is a complete reversal of our present rule of interpretation as to the probable intention of the parties. It is, perhaps, more in harmony with modern ideas of contractual relations than is "the archaic view of a contract as creating a strictly personal obligation between the creditor and debtor" (Pollock on Contracts [9th Ed.] 232), which prohibited the assignee from suing at law in his own name and which denied a remedy to third party beneficiaries. "The fountains out of which these resolutions issue" have been broken up if not destroyed (Seaver v. Ransom, 224 N.Y. 233, 237, 120 N.E. 639, 2 A.L.R. 1187), but the law remains that no promise of the assignee to assume the assignor's duties is to be inferred from the acceptance of an assignment of a bilateral contract, in the absence of circumstances surrounding the assignment itself which indicate a contrary intention.

With this requirement of the interpretation of the intention of the parties controlling we must turn from the assignment to the dealings between the plaintiff and the defendant to discover whether the defendant entered into relations with the plaintiff whereby he assumed the duty of performance. The assignment did not bring the parties together, and the request for a postponement differs materially from the commencement of an action in a court of equity, whereby the plaintiff submits himself to the jurisdiction of the court or from a contractual assumption of the obligations of the assignor. If the substance of the transaction between the vendor and the assignee of the vendee could be regarded as a request on the part of the latter for a postponement of the closing day and a promise on his part to assume the obligations of the vendee if the request were granted, a contractual relation arising from an expression of mutual assent, based on the exchange of a promise for an act, might be spelled out of it; but the transaction is at least as consistent with a request for time for deliberation as to the course of conduct to be pursued as with an implied promise to assume the assignor's duties if the request were granted. The relation of promisor and promisee was not thereby expressly established, and such relation is not a necessary inference from the nature of the transaction. When we depart from the field of intention and enter the field of contract, we find no contractual liability; no assumption of duties based on a consideration.

Plaintiff contends that the request for an adjournment should be construed (time not being the essence of the contract) as an assertion of a right to such adjournment, and therefore as a binding act of enforcement, whereby defendant accepted the obligations of the assignee. Here again we have an equivocal act. There was no demand for an adjournment as a matter of right. The request may have been made without any intent to assert a right. It cannot be said that by that act alone the assignee assumed the duty of performance.

Furthermore, no controlling authority may be found which holds that a mere demand for performance by the vendee's assignee creates a right in the complaining vendor to enforce the contract against him. H. & H. Corporation v. Broad Holding Corporation, 204 App. Div. 569, 198 N.Y.S. 763. See 8 Cornell Law Quarterly, 374; 37 Harvard Law Review, 162. That question may be reserved until an answer is necessary.

The judgment of the Appellate Division and that of the Special Term should be reversed and the complaint dismissed, with costs in all courts.

Cardozo, C.J., and Crane, Andrews, Lehman, Kellogg, and O'Brien, JJ., concur.

Judgments reversed, etc.

NOTE

1. Is the situation of the assignee of the vendee in an executory land contract comparable with that of the purchaser of a mortgagor's equity of redemption? Consult the Note following Vrooman v. Turner, *supra* p. 1346, in which the distinction between assuming and non-assuming grantees of a mortgagor's equity of redemption is discussed.

2. As an alternative to suing Betz, could Langel have brought his action for specific performance against Hurwitz and Hollander (the original contract vendees)? If he recovered judgment against them, could they then require Benedict (to whom they had assigned) or Betz (to whom Benedict assigned) to take and pay for the land? Or could Betz, if he changed his mind, require Hurwitz and Hollander to transfer the land to him? Would it be relevant to inquire how much Benedict and Betz had paid for their assignments?

3. In Langel's action for specific performance against Hurwitz and Hollander, could they successfully plead that they were discharged by Langel's extension of time to Betz?

4. Restatement Second §328 provides:

> (1) Unless the language or the circumstances indicate the contrary, as in an assignment for security, an assignment of "the contract" or of "all my rights under the contract" or an assignment in similar general terms is an assignment of the assignor's rights and a delegation of his unperformed duties under the contract.
>
> (2) Unless the language or the circumstances indicate the contrary, the acceptance by an assignee of such an assignment operates as a promise to the assignor to perform the assignor's unperformed duties, and the obligor of the assigned rights is an intended beneficiary of the promise.
>
> *Caveat:* The Institute expresses no opinion as to whether the rule stated in Subsection (2) applies to an assignment by a purchaser of his rights under a contract for the sale of land.

The rather curious caveat was added, we are told, "in deference" to Langel v. Betz. Farnsworth, Contracts 806 (1982). Compare §328 with U.C.C. §2-210(4), reprinted *infra* p. 1519.

BOSTON ICE CO. v. POTTER
123 Mass. 28 (1877)

Contract on an account annexed, for ice sold and delivered between April 1, 1874, and April 1, 1875. Answer, a general denial.

At the trial in the Superior Court, before Wilkinson, J., without a jury, the plaintiff offered evidence tending to show the delivery of the ice and its acceptance and use by the defendant from April 1, 1874, to April 1, 1875, and that the price claimed in the declaration was the market price. It appeared that the ice was delivered and used at the defendant's residence in Boston, and the amount left daily was regulated by the orders received there from the defendant's servants; that the defendant, in 1873, was supplied with ice by the plaintiff, but, on account of some dissatisfaction with the manner of supply, terminated his contract with it; that the defendant then made a contract with the Citizens' Ice Company to furnish him with ice; that some time before April, 1874, the Citizens' Ice Company sold its business to the plaintiff, with the privilege of supplying ice to its customers. There was some evidence tending to show that the plaintiff gave notice of this change of business to the defendant, and informed him of its intended supply of ice to him; but this was contradicted on the part of defendant.

The judge found that the defendant received no notice from the plaintiff until after all the ice had been delivered by it, and that there was no contract of sale between the parties to this action except what was to be implied from the delivery of the ice by the plaintiff to the defendant and its use by him; and ruled that the defendant had a right to assume that the ice in question was delivered by the Citizens' Ice Company, and that the plaintiff could not maintain this action. The plaintiff alleged exceptions.

ENDICOTT, J. To entitle the plaintiff to recover, it must show some contract with the defendant. There was no express contract, and upon the facts stated no contract is to be implied. The defendant had taken ice from the plaintiff in 1873, but, on account of some dissatisfaction with the manner of supply, he terminated his contract, and made a contract for his supply with the Citizens' Ice Company. The plaintiff afterward delivered ice to the defendant for one year without notifying the defendant, as the presiding judge has found, that it had bought out the business of the Citizens' Ice Company, until after the delivery and consumption of the ice.

The presiding judge has decided that the defendant had a right to assume that the ice in question was delivered by the Citizens' Ice Company, and has thereby necessarily found that the defendant's contract with that company covered the time of the delivery of the ice.

There was no privity of contract established between the plaintiff and defendant, and without such privity the possession and use of the property will not support an implied assumpsit. Hills v. Snell, 104 Mass. 173, 177. And no presumption of assent can be implied from the reception and use of the ice, because the defendant had no knowledge that it was furnished by the plaintiff, but supposed that he received it under the contract made with the Citizens' Ice Company. Of this change he was entitled to be informed.

A party has a right to select and determine with whom he will contract, and cannot have another person thrust upon him without his consent. It may be of importance to him who performs the contract, as when he contracts with another to paint a picture or write a book, or furnish articles of a particular kind, or when he relies upon the character or qualities of an individual, or has, as in this case, reasons why he does not wish to deal with a particular party. In all these cases, as he may contract with whom he pleases, the sufficiency of his reasons for so doing cannot be inquired into. If the defendant, before receiving the ice, or during its delivery, had received notice of the change, and that the Citizens' Ice Company could no longer perform its contract with him, it would then have been his undoubted right to have rescinded the contract and to decline to have it executed by the plaintiff. But this he was unable to do, because the plaintiff failed to inform him of that which he had a right to know. Orcutt v. Nelson, 1 Gray, 536, 542. Winchester v. Howard, 97 Mass. 303. Hardman v. Booth, 1 H. & C. 803. Humble v. Hunter, 12 Q.B. 310. Robson v. Drummond, 2 B. & Ad. 303. If he had received notice and continued to take the ice as delivered, a contract would be implied. Mudge v. Oliver, 1 Allen, 74. Orcutt v. Nelson, *ubi supra.* Mitchell v. Lapage, Holt N.P. 253.

There are two English cases very similar to the case at bar. In Schmaling v. Thomlinson, 6 Taunt. 147, a firm was employed by the defendants to transport goods to a foreign market, and transferred the entire employment to the plaintiff, who performed it without the privity of the defendants, and was held that he could not recover compensation for his services from the defendants.

The case of Boulton v. Jones, 2 H. & N. 564, was cited by both parties at the argument. There the defendant, who had been in the habit of dealing with one Brocklehurst, sent a written order to him for goods. The plaintiff, who had on the same day bought out the business of Brocklehurst, executed the order without giving the defendant notice that the goods were supplied by him and not by Broklehurst. And it was held that the plaintiff could not maintain an action for the price of the goods against the defendant. It is said in that case that the defendant had a right of set-off against Brocklehurst, with whom he had a running account, and that is alluded to in the opinion of Baron Bramwell, though the other judges do not mention it.

The fact that a defendant in a particular case has a claim in set-off against the original contracting party shows clearly the injustice of forcing another person upon him to execute the contract without his consent, against whom his set-off would not be available. But the actual existence of the claim in set-off cannot be a test to determine that there is no implied assumpsit or privity between the parties. Nor can the non-existence of a set-off raise an implied assumpsit. If there is such a set-off, it is sufficient to state that as a reason why the defendant should prevail; but it by no means follows that because it does not exist the plaintiff can maintain his action. The right to maintain an action can never depend upon whether the defendant has or has not a defence to it.

The implied assumpsit arises upon the dealings between the parties to the action, and cannot arise upon the dealings between the defendant and the original contractor, to which the plaintiff was not a party. At the same time, the fact that the right of set-off against the original contractor could not, under any circumstances, be availed of in an action brought upon the contract by the person to whom it was transferred and who executed it, shows that there is no privity between the parties in regard to the subject matter of this action.

It is, therefore, immaterial that the defendant had no claim in set-off against the Citizens' Ice Company.

We are not called upon to determine what other remedy the plaintiff has, or what would be the rights of the parties if the ice were now in existence.

Exceptions overruled.

NOTE

1. W. A. Keener, Quasi Contracts 360-361 (1893):

This case differs from the case of Boulton v. Jones in that the plaintiff knew that the defendant did not desire to deal with him, and was, therefore, officious in supplying him with ice without notifying him of that fact; whereas in Boulton v. Jones, unless the fact that the order was addressed to Brocklehurst was a reason for the plaintiff's supposing that the defendant would not desire to deal with him, the plaintiff had no reason for supposing that the defendant would not be perfectly willing to have the order filled by him, the plaintiff. To have allowed a recovery by the plaintiff in the Boston Ice Company v. Potter would have been, to use the language of Lord Mansfield in Stokes v. Lewis, to have allowed a recovery against the defendant "in spite of his teeth," and would have been entirely destructive of the doctrine that a man has a right to select his creditor.

2. What does the statement in the last paragraph of the opinion mean? Costigan, The Doctrine of Boston Ice Company v. Potter, 7 Colum. L. Rev. 32 (1907); 4 Corbin §865 (1951). For a discussion of the *Boulton* case, see Goodhart, Mistake as to Identity in the Law of Contract, 57 L.Q. Rev. 228, 230 (1941); Cheshire, Mistake as Affecting Contractual Consent, 60 L.Q. Rev. 175, 185 (1944); Williston, Contracts §80 (Jaeger 3d ed. 1957); id. §1479 (Jaeger 3d ed. 1970).

3. Assuming that the plaintiff had merely bought a controlling interest in Citizens' Ice Co., could the latter still sue for the price of the ice delivered?

BRITISH WAGGON CO. v. LEA & CO.
5 Q.B.D. 149 (1880)

COCKBURN, C.J. This was an action brought by the plaintiffs to recover rent for the hire of certain railway waggons, alleged to be payable by the defendants to the plaintiffs, or one of them, under the following circumstances:

By an agreement in writing of the 10th of February, 1874, the Parkgate Waggon Company let to the defendants, who are coal merchants, fifty railway waggons for a term of seven years, at a yearly rent of 600*l.* a year, payable by equal quarterly payments. By a second agreement of the 13th of June, 1874, the company in like manner let to the defendants fifty other waggons, at a yearly rent of 625*l.*, payable quarterly like the former.

Each of these agreements contained the following clause:

The owners, their executors, or administrators, will at all times during the said term, except as herein provided, keep the said waggons in good and substantial repair and working order, and, on receiving notice from the tenant of any want of repairs, and the number or numbers of the waggons requiring to be repaired, and the place or places where it or they then is or are, will with all reasonable despatch, cause the same to be repaired and put into good working order.

On the 24th of October, 1874, the Parkgate Company passed a resolution, under the 129th section of the Companies Act, 1862, for the voluntary winding up of the company. Liquidators were appointed, and by an order of the Chancery Division of the High Court of Justice, it was ordered that the winding-up of the company should be continued under the supervision of the Court.

By an indenture of the 1st of April, 1878, the Parkgate Company assigned and transferred, and the liquidators confirmed to the British Company and their assigns, among other things, all sums of money, whether payable by way of rent, hire, interest, penalty, or damage, then due, or thereafter to become due, to the Parkgate Company, by virtue of the two contracts with the defendants, together with the benefit of the two contracts, all the interest of the Parkgate Company and the said liquidators therein; the British Company, on the other hand covenanting with the Parkgate Company "to observe and perform such of the stipulations, conditions, provisions, and agreements contained in the said contracts as, according to the terms thereof were stipulated to be observed and performed by the Parkgate Company." On the execution of this assignment the British Company took over from the Parkgate Company the repairing stations, which had previously been used by the Parkgate Company for the repair of the waggons let to the defendants, and also the staff of workmen employed by the latter company in executing such repairs. It is expressly found that the British Company have ever since been ready and willing to execute, and have, with all due diligence, executed all necessary repairs to the said waggons. This, however, they have done under a special agreement come to between the parties since the present dispute has arisen, without prejudice to their respective rights.

In this state of things the defendants asserted their right to treat the contract as at an end, on the ground that the Parkgate Company had incapacitated themselves from performing the contract, first, by going into voluntary liquidation, secondly, by assigning the contracts, and giving up the repairing stations to the British Company, between whom and the defendants there was no privity of contract, and whose services, in substitution for those to be performed by the Parkgate Company under the contract, they the defendants were not bound to accept. The Parkgate Company not acquiescing in this view, it was agreed that the facts should be stated in a special case for the opinion of this Court, the use of the waggons by the defendants being in the meanwhile continued at a rate agreed on between the parties, without prejudice to either, with reference to their respective rights.

The first ground taken by the defendants is in our opinion altogether untenable in the present state of things, whatever it may be when the affairs of the company shall have been wound up, and the company itself shall have been dissolved under the 111th section of the Act. Pending the winding-up, the company is by the effect of ss. 95 and 131 kept alive, the liquidator having power to carry on the business, "so far as may be necessary for the beneficial winding-up of the company," which the continued letting of these waggons, and the receipt of the rent payable in respect of them, would, we presume, be.

What would be the position of the parties on the dissolution of the company it is unnecessary for the present purpose to consider.

The main contention on the part of the defendants, however, was that, as the Parkgate Company had by assigning the contracts, and by making over their repairing stations to the British Company, incapacitated themselves to fulfil their obligation to keep the waggons in repair, that company had no right, as between themselves and the defendants, to substitute a third party to do the work they had engaged to perform, nor were the defendants bound to accept the party so substituted as the one to whom they were to look for performance of the contract; the contract was therefore at an end.

The authority principally relied on in support of this contention was the case of Robson v. Drummond, 2 B. & Ad. 303, approved of by this court in Humble v. Hunter, 12 Q.B. 310. In Robson v. Drummond a carriage having been hired by the defendant of one Sharp, a coachmaker, for five years, at a yearly rent, payable in advance each year, the carriage to be kept in repair and painted over once a year by the maker — Robson being then a partner in the business, but unknown to the defendant — on Sharp retiring from the business after three years had expired, and making over all interest in the business and property in the goods to Robson, it was held, that the defendant could not be sued on the contract — by Lord Tenterden on the ground that "the defendant might have been induced to enter into the contract by reason of the personal confidence which he reposed in Sharp, and therefore might have agreed to pay money in advance, for which reason the defendant had a right to object to its being performed by any other person"; and by Littledale and Parke, JJ., on the additional ground that the defendant had a right to the personal services of Sharp, and to the benefit of his judgment and taste, to the end of the contract.

In like manner, where goods are ordered of a particular manufacturer, another, who has succeeded to his business, cannot execute the order, so as to bind the customer, who has not been made aware of the transfer of the business, to accept the goods. The latter is entitled to refuse to deal with any other than the manufacturer whose goods he intended to buy. For this Boulton v. Jones, 2 H. & N. 564, is a sufficient authority. The case of Robson v. Drummond comes nearer to the present case, but is, we think, distinguishable from it. We entirely concur in the principle on which the decision in Robson v. Drummond rests, namely, that where a person contracts with another to do work or perform service, and it can be inferred that the person employed has been selected with reference to his individual skill, competency, or other personal qualification, the inability or unwillingness of the party so employed to execute the work or perform the service is a sufficient answer to any demand by a stranger to the original contract of the performance of it by the other party, and entitles the latter to treat the contract as at an end, notwithstanding that the person tendered to take the place of the contracting party may be equally well qualified to do the service. Personal performance is in such a case of the essence of the contract, which, consequently, cannot in its absence be enforced against an unwilling party. But this principle appears to us inapplicable in the present instance, inasmuch as we cannot suppose that in stipulating for the repair of these waggons by the company — a rough description of work which ordinary workmen conversant with the business would be perfectly able to execute — the defendants attached any importance to whether the repairs were done by the company, or by any one with whom the company might enter into a subsidiary contract to do the work. All that the hirers, the defendants, cared for in this stipulation was that the waggons should be kept in repair; it was indifferent to them by whom the repairs should be done. Thus if, without going into liquidation, or assigning these contracts, the company had entered into a contract with any competent party to do the repairs, and so had procured them to be done, we cannot think that this would have been a departure from the terms of the contract to keep the waggons in repair. While fully acquiescing in the general principle just referred to, we must take care not to push it beyond reasonable limits. And we cannot but think that, in applying the principle, the Court of Queen's Bench in Robson v. Drummond went to the utmost length to which it can be carried, as it is difficult to see how in repairing a carriage when necessary, or painting it once a year, preference would be given to one coachmaker over another. Much work is contracted for, which it is known can only be executed by means of subcontracts; much is contracted for as to which it is indifferent to the party for whom it is to be done, whether it is done by the immediate party to the contract, or by someone on his behalf. In all these cases the maximum *Qui facit per alium facit per se* applies.

In the view we take of the case, therefore, the repair of the waggons, undertaken and done by the British Company under their contract with the Parkgate Company, is a sufficient performance by the latter of their engagement to repair under their contract with the defendants. Consequently, so long as the Parkgate Company continues to exist, and, through the British Company, continues to fulfil its obligation to keep the waggons in repair, the defendants cannot, in our opinion, be heard to say that the former company is not entitled to the performance of the contract by them, on the ground that the company have incapacitated themselves from performing their obligations under it, or that, by transferring the performance thereof to others, they have absolved the defendants from further performance on their part.

That a debt accruing due under a contract can, since the passing of the Judicature Acts, be assigned at law as equity, cannot since the decision in Brice v. Bannister, 3 Q.B.D. 569, be disputed.

We are therefore of opinion that our judgment must be for the plaintiffs for the amount claimed.

ARKANSAS VALLEY SMELTING CO. v. BELDEN MINING CO.
127 U.S. 379 (1888)

This was an action brought by a smelting company, incorporated by the laws of Missouri, against a mining company, incorporated by the laws of Maine, and both doing business in Colorado by virtue of a compliance with its laws, to recover damages for the breach of a contract to deliver ore, made by the defendant with Billing and Eilers, and assigned to the plaintiff. The material allegations of the complaint were as follows:

On July 12, 1881, a contract in writing was made between the defendant of the first part and Billing and Eilers of the second part, by which it was agreed that the defendant should sell and deliver to Billing and Eilers at their smelting works in Leadville ten thousand tons of carbonate lead ore from its mines at Red Cliff, at the rate of at least fifty tons a day, beginning upon the completion of a railroad from Leadville to Red Cliff, and continuing until the whole should have been delivered, and that "all ore so delivered shall at once upon the delivery thereof become the property of the second party"; and it was further agreed as follows:

> The value of said ore and the price to be paid therefor shall be fixed in lots of about one hundred tons each; that is to say, as soon as such a lot of ore shall have been delivered to said party, it shall be sampled at the works of said second party, and the sample assayed by either or both of the parties hereto, and the value of such lots of ore shall be fixed by such assay; in cases the parties hereto cannot agree as to such assay, they shall agree upon some third disinterested and competent party, whose assay shall be final. The price to be paid by said second party for such lot of ore shall be fixed on the basis hereinafter agreed upon by the closing New York quotations for silver and common lead, on the day of the delivery of sample bottle, and so on until all of said ore shall have been delivered.
>
> Said second party shall pay said first party at said Leadville for such lot of ore at once, upon the determination of its assay value, at the following prices, specifying, by reference to the New York quotations, the price to be paid per pound for the lead contained in the ore, and the price to be paid

for the silver contained in each ton of ore, varying according to the proportions of silica and of iron in the ore.

The complaint further alleged that the railroad was completed on November 30, 1881, and thereupon the defendant, under and in compliance with the contract, began to deliver ore to Billing and Eilers at their smelting works, and delivered 167 tons between that date and January 1, 1882, when "the said firm of Billing and Eilers was dissolved, and the said contract and the business of said firm, and the smelting works at which said ores were to be delivered, were sold, assigned, and transferred to G. Billing, whereof the defendant had due notice"; that after such transfer and assignment the defendant continued to deliver ore under the contract, and between January 1 and April 21, 1882, delivered to Billing at said smelting works 894 tons; that on May 1, 1882, the contract, together with the smelting works, was sold and conveyed by Billing to the plaintiff, whereof the defendant had due notice; that the defendant then ceased to deliver ore under the contract, and afterwards refused to perform the contract, and gave notice to the plaintiff that it considered the contract cancelled and annulled; that all the ore so delivered under the contract was paid for according to its terms; that

the plaintiff and its said assignors were at all times during their respective ownerships ready, able, and willing to pay on the like terms for each lot as delivered, when and as the defendant should deliver the same, according to the terms of said contract, and the time of payment was fixed on the day of delivery of the "sample bottle," by which expression was, by the custom of the trade, intended the completion of the assay or test by which the value of the ore was definitely fixed;

and that

the said Billing and Eilers, and the said G. Billing, their successor and assignee, at all times since the delivery of said contract, and during the respective periods when it was held by them respectively, were able, ready and willing to and did comply with and perform all the terms of the same, so far as they were by said contract required; and the said plaintiff has been at all times able, ready and willing to perform and comply with the terms thereof, and has from time to time, since the said contract was assigned to it, so notified the defendant.

The defendant demurred to the complaint for various reasons, one of which was that the contract therein set forth could not be assigned, but was personal in its nature, and could not, by the pretended assignment thereof to the plaintiff, vest the plaintiff with any power to sue the defendant for the alleged breach of contract.

The Circuit Court sustained the demurrer, and gave judgment for the defendant; and the plaintiff sued out this writ of error. . . .

Mr. Justice GRAY, after stating the case as above reported, delivered the opinion of the court. If the assignment to the plaintiff of the contract sued on was valid, the plaintiff is the real party in interest, and as such entitled, under the practice of Colorado, to maintain this action in its own name. Rev. Stat. §914; Colorado Code of Civil Procedure, §3; Albany & Rensselaer Co. v. Lundberg, 121 U.S. 451. The vital question in the case, therefore, is whether the contract between the defendant and Billing and Eilers was assignable by the latter, under the circumstances stated in the complaint.

At the present day, no doubt, an agreement to pay money, or deliver goods, may be assigned by the person to whom the money is to be paid or the goods are to be delivered, if there is nothing in the terms of the contract, whether by requiring something to be afterwards done by him, or by some other stipulation, which manifests the intention of the parties that it shall not be assignable.

But every one has a right to select and determine with whom he will contract, and cannot have another person thrust upon him without his consent. In the familiar phrase of Lord Denman, "You have the right to the benefit you anticipate from the character, credit and substance of the party with whom you contract." Humble v. Hunter, 12 Q.B. 310, 317; Winchester v. Howard, 97 Mass. 303, 305; Boston Ice Co. v. Potter, 123 Mass. 28; King v. Batterson, 13 R.I. 117, 120; Lansden v. McCarthy, 45 Missouri, 106. The rule upon this subject, as applicable to the case at bar, is well expressed in a recent English treatise. "Rights arising out of contract cannot be transferred if they are coupled with liabilities, or if they involve a relation of personal confidence such that the party whose agreement conferred with those rights must have intended them to be exercised only by him in whom he actually confided." Pollock on Contracts (4th ed.) 425.

The contract here sued on was one by which the defendant agreed to deliver ten thousand tons of lead ore from its mines to Billing and Eilers at their smelting works. The ore was to be delivered at the rate of fifty tons a day, and it was expressly agreed that it should become the property of Billing and Eilers as soon as delivered. The price was not fixed by the contract, or payable upon the delivery of the ore. But, as soon as a hundred tons of ore had been delivered, the ore was to be assayed by the parties or one of them, and, if they could not agree, by an umpire; and it was only after all this had been done, and according to the result of the assay, and the proportions of lead, silver, silica and iron, thereby proved to be in the ore, that the price was to be ascertained and paid. During the time that must elapse between the delivery of the ore, and the ascertainment and payment of the price, the defendant had no security for its payment, except in the character and solvency of Billing and Eilers. The defendant, therefore, could not be compelled to accept the liability of any other person or corporation as a substitute for the liability of those with whom it had contracted.

The fact that upon the dissolution of the firm of Billing and Eilers, and the transfer by Eilers to Billing of this contract, together with the smelting works and business of the partnership, the defendant continued to deliver ore to Billing according to the contract, did not oblige the defendant to deliver ore to a stranger, to whom Billing had undertaken, without the defendant's consent, to assign the contract. The change in a partnership by the coming in or the withdrawal of a partner might perhaps be held to be within the contemplation of the parties originally contracting; but however that may be, an assent to such a change in the one party cannot estop the other to deny the validity of a subsequent assignment of the whole contract to a stranger. The technical rule of law, recognized in Murray v. Harway, 56 N.Y. 337, cited for the plaintiff, by which a lessee's express covenant not to assign has been held to be wholly determined by one assignment with the lessor's consent, has no application to this case.

The cause of action set forth in the complaint is not for any failure to deliver ore to Billing before his assignment to the plaintiff, (which might perhaps be an assignable chose in action,) but it is for a refusal to deliver ore to the plaintiff since this assignment. Performance and readiness to perform by the plaintiff and its assignors, during the periods for which they respectively held the contract, is all that is alleged; there is no allegation that Billing is ready to pay for any ore delivered to the plaintiff. In short, the plaintiff undertakes to step into the shoes of Billing, and to substitute its liability for his. The defendant had a perfect right to decline to assent to this, and to refuse to recognize a party, with whom it had never contracted, as entitled to demand further deliveries of ore.

The cases cited in the careful brief of the plaintiff's counsel, as tending to support this action, are distinguishable from the case at bar, and the principal ones maybe classified as follows:

First. Cases of agreements to sell and deliver goods for a fixed price, payable in cash on delivery, in which the owner would receive the price at the time of parting with his property, nothing further would remain to be done by the purchaser, and the rights of the seller could not be affected by the question whether the price was paid by the person with whom he originally contracted or by an assignee. Sears v. Conover, 3 Keyes, 113, and 4 Abbot (N.Y. App.) 179; Tyler v. Barrows, 6 Robertson (N.Y.) 104.

Second. Cases upon the question how far executors succeed to rights and liabilities under a contract of their testator. Hambly v. Trott, Cowper, 371, 375; Wentworth v. Cock, 10 Ad. & El. 42, and 2 Per & Dav. 251; Williams on Executors, (7th ed.) 1723-1725. Assignment by operation of law, as in the case of an executor, is quite different from assignment by act of the party; and the one might be held to have been in contemplation of the parties to this contract although the other was not. A lease, for instance, even if containing an express covenant against assignment by the lessee, passes to his executor. And it is by no means clear that an executor would be found to perform, or would be entitled to the benefit of, such a contract as that now in question. Dickinson v. Calahan, 19 Penn. St. 227.

Third. Cases of assignments by contractors for public works, in which the contracts, and the statutes under which they were made, were held to permit all persons to bid for the contracts, and to execute them through third persons. Taylor v. Palmer, 31 California, 240, 247; St. Louis v. Clemens, 42 Missouri, 69; Philadelphia v. Lockhardt, 73 Penn. St. 211; Devlin v. New York, 63 N.Y. 8.

Fourth. Other cases of contracts assigned by the party who was to do certain work, not by the party who was to pay for it, and in which the question was whether the work was of such nature that it was intended to be performed by the original contractor only. Robson v. Drummond, 2 B. & Ad. 303; British Waggon Co. v. Lea, 5 Q.B.D. 149; Parsons v. Woodward, 2 Zabriskie, 196.

Without considering whether all the cases cited were well decided, it is sufficient to say that none of them can control the decision of the present case.

Judgment affirmed.

NOTE

1. Are the three preceding principal cases consistent with each other? Would it make any sense to distinguish the assignment by a seller or other performing party from the assignment by a buyer or other party whose principal contractual duty is to pay for goods delivered or services rendered?

2. In the *British Waggon Co.* case, assume that the British Co. carries out the maintenance contract improperly. Should Lea and Co. bring its action for damages against the British Co. or against the Parkgate Co.? As between the British Co. and the Parkgate Co., which would be ultimately liable for breach of the maintenance contract? Will Lea and Co. still be bound to accept performance by the British Co. after the Parkgate Co. has been finally liquidated?

3. Assume that Lea and Co. are willing to accept performance by the British Co. Could the British Co. and the Parkgate Co. rescind their agreement without the consent of Lea and Co.? On this point consider the material collected in Section 5 of this chapter. Could Lea and Co. (at least under American doctrine) claim that the attempted rescission was ineffective because it was an intended beneficiary of the contract between the British Co. and the Parkgate Co.? Consider Restatement Second §311, reprinted *supra* p. 1426. Note Judge Pound's reference to Lawrence

v. Fox and third party beneficiary doctrine in his opinion in Langel v.
Betz, *supra* p. 1500.

4. In Tolhurst v. Associated Portland Cement Manufacturers Ltd.,
[1903] A.C. (H.L.) 414, Tolhurst sought a declaration that he was not
bound to carry out a contract which he had entered into with the Imperial Company and which Imperial had assigned to Associated. The principal opinion in the House of Lords was read by Lord Macnaghten who said
in part:

> Tolhurst was the owner of property at Northfleet, in Kent, containing
> extensive and valuable chalk quarries. He sold a piece of his land there
> known as the Little Dockyard to the Imperial Company, and that company
> bought another piece of land from the British White Lead Company, who
> also derived title from Tolhurst. The main object for which the Imperial
> Company was formed was to establish cement works at Northfleet and
> carry on there the business of Portland cement manufacturers. It was, of
> course, important for Tolhurst to secure a regular market for his chalk, and
> it was equally important for the Imperial Company to secure a regular
> supply of chalk for their works.
>
> The effect of the contract of January, 1898, may be stated shortly.
> Tolhurst had made a tramway to the boundary of the land bought by the
> Imperial Company from the White Lead Company, and the Imperial Com-
> pany was to make a tramway continuing Tolhurst's tramway to a conven-
> ient spot in its land in order to enable him to bring chalk to the company's
> works. On completion of this tramway the contract provides by clause 2
> that

>> the said Alfred Tolhurst will, for a term of fifty years, to be computed from the
>> 25th day of December, 1897, or for such shorter period (not being less than
>> thirty-five years) as he shall be possessed of chalk available and suitable for the
>> manufacture of Portland cement, and capable of being quarried and got in the
>> usual manner above water level, supply to the company, and the company will
>> take and buy of the said Alfred Tolhurst at least 750 tons per week, and so
>> much more, if any, as the company shall require for the whole of their manu-
>> facture of Portland cement upon their said land.

> Tolhurst was to provide rolling stock and traction power, carry the chalk
> over the company's tramway, and deliver it alongside the company's stores,
> but he was not to be precluded from supplying other persons. Delivery
> orders were to be sent in before 4 o'clock for the next day. The price was to
> be 1s. 3d. per ton, to be paid in cash monthly. The average monthly
> payment for any year after 1898 was to be not less than 188l. Then there
> was a clause providing for the case of strikes and unavoidable stoppages,
> and authorizing the company at its own expense to procure chalk else-
> where in the event of Tolhurst being thereby prevented from supplying the
> quantity required.
>
> In 1900 the Imperial Company sold its undertaking to the respondents,
> the Associated Company, and went into voluntary liquidation. Its affairs
> are fully wound up and all its assets have been distributed. Tollhurst

brought in no claim in the liquidation. He stood by while the Imperial Company was in process of dissolution.

Tolhurst's case now is that by parting with its undertaking and going into liquidation the Imperial Company rescinded or put an end to the contract of January, 1898, and that he is not bound under or in accordance with that contract to furnish supplies of chalk to the Associated Company for the purposes of the works at Northfleet which formerly belonged to the Imperial Company, whether the Associated Company requires delivery in its own name or in the name of the Imperial Company.

Now what is the meaning of the contract of January, 1898? I cannot think there is much difficulty about it. It is expressed to be made between Alfred Tolhurst and the Imperial Company. They, and they only, are named as the persons to perform the contract. From beginning to end of the instrument, if the contract be taken literally, there is not one word pointing to the continued existence of the contract in the hands of any other person, either by succession or substitution. The obligations and benefits of the contract on the one side begin and end with Alfred Tolhurst; on the other, they begin and end with the Imperial Company. And yet the contract is to endure for the period of fifty years, or if the supply of chalk in the quarries does not hold out so long, it is to last for thirty-five years at least. Now, when it is borne in mind that the Imperial Company must have been induced to establish its works at Northfleet by the prospect of the advantages flowing from immediate connection with Tolhurst's quarries, and that the contract in substance amounts to a contract for the sale of all the chalk in those quarries by periodical deliveries (less what Tolhurst might sell elsewhere), it is plain that it could not have been within the contemplation of the parties that the company would lose the benefit of the contract if anything happened to Tolhurst, or that Tolhurst would lose the benefit of the market which the contract provided for him at his very door in the event of the company parting with its undertaking, as it was authorized to do by its memorandum. . . .

. . . The contract is a contract for the mutual benefit and accommodation of the chalk quarries and the cement works, and of Tolhurst and the company as the owners and occupiers of those two properties. Construed fairly, the provision in clause 2, about which there was so much argument, means, I think, nothing more than this — that the Imperial Company was to take the whole of the supply of chalk required for the Northfleet works (the quantity to be ascertained by daily orders, but guaranteed not to be less than 750 tons per week), from Tolhurst's chalk quarries and from no other source whatever. As long as that is done, how can it matter who is carrying on the works? There is nothing in the contract to restrict the development of the works on the land which formerly belonged to the Imperial Company, or to check the expansion and improvement in the ordinary course of things of the process of manufacture there.

Id. at 417-420.

Lord Lindley concurred, remarking that "the British Waggon Co. v. Lea was, in my opinion, rightly decided, and is an authority very much in point for the Associated company." The Earl of Halsbury also concurred, albeit "with very great hesitation." Lord Robertson dissented. Judgment, therefore, went against Tolhurst.

5. Crane Ice Cream Co. v. Terminal Freezing and Heating Co., 147 Md. 588, 128 A. 280, 39 A.L.R. 1184 (1925), involved a contract between the Terminal Co. and Frederick, an ice cream manufacturer whose plant was located in Baltimore, Maryland. Terminal agreed to supply Frederick's requirements of ice, to the extent of 250 tons a week, at $3.25 a ton. Frederick was to pay each Tuesday for all ice delivered to his plant during the preceding week and was not privileged to buy ice from anyone but Terminal except ice in excess of the 250 ton weekly maximum.

Frederick sold his business (including all his contract rights) to the Crane Company, which was engaged in manufacturing ice cream both in Baltimore and Philadelphia. The Crane Company, which was apparently a larger enterprise than Frederick's had been, was willing to pay cash for all ice delivered. The Crane Company had taken over Frederick's Baltimore plant and seems to have demanded only that ice continue to be delivered there. The Terminal Company, however, refused to supply ice to the Crane Company under the Frederick contract. Crane brought an action for damages against Terminal. Terminal's demurrer to the action was sustained in the trial court and this disposition of the case was affirmed on appeal.

Parke, J., said in part:

> However, the analysis of the facts on this appeal leaves no room for doubt that the case at bar falls into the category of those assignments where an attempt is made both to transfer the rights and to delegate the duties of the assignor under an executory bilateral contract, whose terms and the circumstances make plain that the personal qualification and action of the assignor, with respect to both his benefits and burdens under the contract, were essential inducements in the formation of the contract; and further that the assignment was a repudiation of any future liability of the assignor. The attempted assignment before us altered the conditions and obligations of the undertaking. The appellee would here be obliged not only to perform the subsequent stipulations of the contract, for the benefit of a stranger and in conformity with his will, but also to accept the performance of the stranger in place of that of the assignor with whom it contracted, and upon whose personal integrity, capacity and management in the course of a particular business he must be assumed to have relied by reason of the very nature of the provisions of the contract and of the circumstances of the contracting parties. The nature and stipulations of the contract prevent it being implied that the non-assigning party had assented to such an assignment of rights and delegation of liabilities. The authorities are clear, on the facts at bar, that the appellant could not enforce the contract against the appellee.

Id. at 599, 128 A. at 284.

Parke, J., further commented that the *Tolhurst* case, digested in Note 4, "has never been accepted as wholly satisfactory." After stating the facts of *Tolhurst*, he continued:

> It is manifest that this case is to be distinguished from the one at bar, but, if not, this Court would not be prepared to follow the reasoning of the final decision, because the Imperial Company had renounced its obligation under the contract; had gone out of business, and had disposed of all its assets so as to be no longer able to pay the agreed price, and thereby the seller had lost the credit of the original contracting party, and the decision compelled Tolhurst to give credit to the assignee only. We take it to be sound doctrine that where one contracting party repudiates his obligations, the other party has the right of declining to be bound to a stranger by its terms.

Id. at 602, 128 A. at 285.

6. With respect to the *Crane* case, assume that Frederick had continued in business, but that the Terminal Company had sold its business to another ice manufacturer. Do you think the Maryland court would have held that Frederick was bound to continue taking ice from the Terminal Company's successor or would the court have held that Frederick was discharged?

UNIFORM COMMERCIAL CODE

§2–210.   DELEGATION OF PERFORMANCE; ASSIGNMENT OF RIGHTS

(1)   A party may perform his duty through a delegate unless otherwise agreed or unless the other party has a substantial interest in having his original promisor perform or control the acts required by the contract. No delegation of performance relieves the party delegating of any duty to perform or any liability for breach.

(2)   Unless otherwise agreed all rights of either seller or buyer can be assigned except where the assignment would materially change the duty of the other party, or increase materially the burden or risk imposed on him by his contract, or impair materially his chance of obtaining return performance. A right to damages for breach of the whole contract or a right arising out of the assignor's due performance of his entire obligation can be assigned despite agreement otherwise.

(3)   Unless the circumstances indicate the contrary a prohibition of assignment of "the contract" is to be construed as barring only the delegation to the assignee of the assignor's performance.

(4)   An assignment of "the contract" or of "all my rights under the contract" or an assignment in similar general terms is an assignment of rights and unless the language or the circumstances (as in an assignment

for security) indicate the contrary, it is a delegation of performance of the duties of the assignor and its acceptance by the assignee constitutes a promise by him to perform those duties. This promise is enforceable by either the assignor or the party to the original contract.

(5)   The other party may treat any assignment which delegates performance as creating reasonable grounds for insecurity and may without prejudice to his rights against the assignor demand assurances from the assignee (Section 2-609).

NOTE

1. Does the Code codify the position taken in such cases as *British Waggon Co.* and *Tolhurst* and reject the position taken in *Arkansas Valley Smelting Co.* and *Crane Ice Cream Co.?*

Under §2-210 would it make any difference if a corporate assignor had gone out of existence or if an individual assignor had died or become insolvent? On this point, is the second sentence of subsection (1) consistent with subsection (5)?

2. Langel v. Betz, *supra* p. 1500, involved a contract for the sale of land, to which §2-210 is not directly applicable. Assume, however, that *Langel* had involved a contract for the sale of, say, a valuable painting. Does §2-210(4) reject the rule of Langel v. Betz? What "language" or "circumstances" would, for the purpose of §2-210(4), indicate that an assignee had not assumed the assignor's contractual duties?

3. Does §2-210(4) suggest that the non-assigning party to the original contract is a third party beneficiary of the agreement between assignor and assignee, as §328(2) of the Restatement Second explicitly provides?

Section 5.   The Problem of Defenses, Modifications, and Rescission

CUBAN ATLANTIC SUGAR SALES CORP. v. THE MARINE MIDLAND TRUST CO. OF NEW YORK

207 F. Supp. 403 (S.D.N.Y. 1962)

WEINFELD, District Judge. The libelant seeks to recover $84,247.56 which it paid to the respondent The Marine Midland Trust Company as assignee of respondent Ocean Trading Corporation.

The payment represented prepaid freight charges for transportation of a cargo of sugar from Cuba to Japan under a voyage charter party between libelant and Ocean Trading Corporation as time chartered owner of s/s Aspromonte. Marine Midland concedes that the freight money was not due to Ocean Trading since Ocean failed to perform its obligations under the time charter; nonetheless it resists repayment to the libelant upon the ground that the money was paid voluntarily with knowledge that it was not due. I am satisfied that the libelant is entitled to the return of the payment, first upon the ground that it was made under a mistake of fact, and second because it was subject to a condition which was never satisfied.

The facts are these: On January 11, 1958 Ocean Trading Corporation time chartered the s/s Aspromonte for a period of twelve to fourteen months from the vessel's owners, hereinafter called "Garibaldi." Thereafter on January 22, 1958 Ocean Trading and libelant entered into a voyage charter party under which Ocean Trading was to transport from Cuba to Japan a cargo of sugar which libelant had purchased in Cuba and resold to a Japanese consignee. This charter party specified a rate per ton for the carriage of the sugar and further provided:

"All freight to be prepaid in New York in U.S. Currency on telegraphic advice of signing bills of lading on net bill of lading weight, ...

"Mate's receipts to be signed for each parcel of Sugar when on board, and Captain to sign Bills of Lading in accordance therewith, as requested by Shippers."

On January 29, 1958 Ocean Trading assigned to Marine Midland all freight moneys due or to become due under the voyage charter of the s/s Aspromonte as collateral for loans to finance Ocean's charter operations.

The cargo of sugar destined for delivery to libelant's purchaser at a port in Japan was to be loaded at Jucaro, Cuba. Libelant sold the goods by documents and was to receive payment from its Japanese customer upon presentation of the bills of lading to bankers in England.[19] Loading of the sugar aboard the s/s Aspromonte at Jucaro, Cuba commenced on March 7, 1958 and was complete at two o'clock on March 24th. Some time after the completion of the loading, a representative of Atlantic del Golfo (from whom libelant had purchased the sugar) telephoned from Cuba to Roger A. Coe, libelant's representative here in New York City, advising him to that effect and giving him data upon which to compute the freight charges payable under the charter. Libelant's practice was to check the freight charges upon receipt of such informal advice and on the basis thereof to make payment to the shipper's representative; it did not await formal telegraphic advice that the bills of lading had been signed by the ship's master as specified in the charter.

Under common practice and usage of the trade, the mate's receipts are tallied against cargo as it is delivered to the vessel and, as soon as the last of the cargo is received aboard, the bills of lading as prepared by the

---

19. Sale by shipping documents was usual in the sugar industry.

shipper are checked against the mate's receipts, following which the master signs the bills of lading as a matter of routine. This procedure usually took from two to three hours. Coe testified that in all his experience he knew of no instance where a master had refused to sign the bills of lading in accordance with mate's receipts showing delivery of cargo to a vessel by the shipper.

It was against this background that the payment here in question was made by libelant on the morning after it had been advised that the last of the cargo had been loaded. Libelant delivered to the respondent Marine Midland its check payable to "S/S Aspromonte and/or Owners and/or Agents and/or Operators," together with a letter as follows:

> We are enclosing our check in the amount of $84,247.56 covering ocean freight on shipment of raw sugar on S/S Aspromonte in accordance with the above Charter Party. Please instruct your Havana Agents to release the bills of lading to our affiliated company, Compania Azucarera Atlantica del Golfo, Havana, Cuba.

The check and letter were delivered at 12:40 P.M. on March 25th to William Gebhardt, then Marine Midland's Assistant Treasurer, who was in charge of the Ocean Trading account. Early that afternoon Coe, who had telephoned Atlantica del Golfo in Havana to inquire as to the departure time of the s/s Aspromonte from Jucaro, Cuba to Japan, learned for the first time that the ship's master, upon presentation of the bills of lading, had refused to sign them. The evidence establishes that when delivery of the cargo to the vessel was finally completed on March 24th, the bills of lading were presented to the master for his signature and, although he found them correct, he did not sign them under direct instructions of the shipowner, Garibaldi. The assigned reason for this was that Ocean Trading had been in default in the payment of charter hire.

When Coe learned of the master's refusal to sign the bills of lading, he promptly called Gebhardt. This was shortly after the latter had received libelant's check. Gebhardt than advised Coe that he was in touch with Ocean Trading and that matters would be worked out.

Gebhardt, who also testified upon the trial, was a less than frank witness. Many of his answers were either evasive or he failed of recollection on the material matters as to which Coe had testified specifically. His actions in connection with the transaction show a deliberate purpose to hold on to the freight payment. When Gebhardt received the check from libelant, he had already been put on notice on two separate occasions, March 20th and 21st, that the ship's owner had threatened to refuse to permit the master to sign the bills of lading unless Ocean's default in the payment of charter hire and port charges was cured.[20] In any event the

---

20. Ocean Trading had another vessel, the s/s Nazareno, also under a time charter with Garibaldi.

evidence is convincing that in the early afternoon of March 25th he was advised by Coe of the master's refusal to sign the bills of lading. Thereupon Gebhardt, then aware that the freight money was not due, caused libelant's check to be certified, notwithstanding that there was no question of libelant's financial responsibility. The certification was admittedly obtained after discussions among Marine Midland's officers regarding the possibility of libelant stopping payment on the check. And when Coe made a further effort to reach Gebhardt that afternoon, the latter made himself unavailable. Coe, obviously concerned about the payment, continued thereafter his attempts to reach Gebhardt, but without success.

On March 28th additional charter hire was due from Ocean to Garibaldi which was not paid. This default was suffered when Marine Midland refused to advance additional funds to Ocean. Thereupon Garibaldi, because of this default, withdrew the Aspromonte from the service of Ocean and demanded that libelant immediately discharge the sugar cargo from the vessel or make new arrangements directly with Garibaldi for its carriage to Japan. Since Ocean was in no position to perform its carriage contract, libelant was compelled to come to terms with Garibaldi.

Gebhardt was fully aware that his action on behalf of Marine Midland in refusing further to finance Ocean would cause it to default and in consequence that Ocean would not be in a position to carry out its obligation to libelant to transport the sugar cargo. As early as March 10th Gebhardt, following an examination of the books of Ocean Trading, knew its financial situation was so "shaky," as he phrased it, that it could not then meet its obligations on the time charter parties which it held. Yet, on March 13th, during the progress of the loading of libelant's sugar cargo, he advanced to Ocean an additional sum of $11,421.88 to cover charter hire due for the second half of the month; the loan was made to avoid possible withdrawal of the vessel from Ocean's service, which had been threatened by the vessel's owners. Obviously, had this occurred, libelant's cargo would not have been accepted and no moneys for freight would have been due Ocean.

It is unquestioned that since the bills of lading were never signed, the freight moneys were never due and payable to Ocean Trading, Marine Midland's assignor.[21] Marine Midland resists repayment on the ground that Coe, in prepaying the freight charges, was aware that the bills of lading had not been signed and hence there was no mistake of a present or pre-existing fact. However, it was a fact that Garibaldi had already issued an order to the vessel's master that the bills were not to be signed; it was a fact that the master had actually refused to sign them. Libelant had no knowledge or reason to know of either of these pre-existing facts; it is

21. Ocean S.S. Co. v. United States Steel Prods. Co., 239 F. 823 (2d Cir.), *cert. denied,* 244 U.S. 652, 37 S. Ct. 650, 61 L. Ed. 1373 (1917).

evident that libelant would not have paid the freight had it known of one or the other. Whether or not the bills had yet been signed, libelant paid the freight under an assumption that there was no existing impediment to completion of the usual procedure in the trade — that the bills of lading would be signed as a routine matter within hours after checking against the mate's receipts. It was unaware that the customary procedure already had been interrupted by the order of the vessel's owners and the refusal the day before by the master to sign the bills.

Respondent relies on Kaufman v. William Iselin & Co.,[22] and McMullen Leavens Co. v. L. I. Van Buskirk Co.,[23] the latter of which holds that, since an assignee does not assume duties imposed upon the assignor, [24] he will not be compelled to repay the purchase price of the goods when the purchaser rescinds because the goods are defective. However, in Langel v. Betz,[25] upon which the foregoing cases rest, the New York Court of Appeals acknowledged that its ruling was contrary to the Restatement of Contracts, section 164(2), which the Court conceded was "perhaps, more in harmony with modern ideas of contractual relations. . . ."[26] Accordingly, where, as here, recovery is not based upon contract, but rests upon equitable principles of restitution brought into play by a mistake of fact, there is no justification for extending the scope of Langel v. Betz and its progeny.[27]

Marine Midland, which had full knowledge that the freight payment was not due, if required to make restitution to libelant, will be in no worse position than that in which it would have been had libelant awaited the formality of telegraphic advice that the bills of lading had been signed. Upon all the facts here presented, on the ground of mistake of fact alone libelant is entitled to return of the money.

Libelant is also entitled to the return of the prepaid freight charges upon another theory — the failure to perform a condition subject to which the payment was made — the release of the bills of lading and their delivery to libelant or its representative.

When libelant paid the freight charges to Marine Midland its check was accompanied by a letter which contained the following statement: "Please instruct your Havana Agents to release the bills of lading to our affiliated company . . . Atlantica del Golfo, Havana, Cuba."

The respondent Marine Midland challenges that this attached any condition to the retention by it of the freight payment. True, it does not contain a precise legal definition of a condition, but it is clear under all

22. 272 App. Div. 578, 74 N.Y.S.2d 23 (1947).
23. 275 App. Div. 701, 87 N.Y.S.2d 355, *certified question affirmed*, 299 N.Y. 784, 87 N.E.2d 682 (1949).
24. Langel v. Betz, 250 N.Y. 159, 164 N.E. 890 (1928).
25. Ibid.
26. 250 N.Y. at 163, 164 N.E. at 892.
27. See Lawrence v. American Nat. Bank, 54 N.Y. 432 (1873). Cf. Restatement of Restitution §§6, 18 (1936).

the circumstances this was a businessman's expression that the payment was conditioned upon his receiving in return what he was supposed to get — the signed bills of lading. Otherwise there is no meaning or purpose to the letter. Gebhardt's statement that he assumed Ocean Trading's representative in Cuba had possession of properly executed bills of lading and that the letter only required him to notify Ocean to release the bills of lading is not only unpersuasive, but quite unbelievable. It flies in the face of the fact that payment of the freight charges was made by libelant to discharge its obligation under the voyage charter in return for which it was to receive the bills of lading, which it required in order to obtain payment from its buyer. As Judge Cardozo said:[28]

"They [letters from one merchant to another] are to be read as business men would read them, and only as a last resort are to be thrown out altogether as meaningless futilities. . . . In the transactions of business life, sanity of end and aim is at least a presumption. . . ."

The libelant, in addition to a decree in its favor against Marine Midland, is also entitled to a decree *pro confesso* against Ocean Trading.

The foregoing shall constitute the Court's Findings of Fact and Conclusions of Law. Either party may propose within five days from the date hereof additional findings upon three days' notice to the other side.

NOTE

1. Apart from the letter which, in Judge Weinfeld's opinion, conditioned the payment of the freight on release of the bills of lading, do you think that Marine Midland would have had to return the money even if it had had no knowledge of Ocean Trading's default under the charter party?

2. Firestone Tire & Rubber Co. v. Central National Bank of Cleveland, 159 Ohio St. 423, 112 N.E.2d 636 (1953), like the principal case, involved an assignee's liability to make restitution to an obligor. Firestone contracted to buy 30,000 sleds from Stan Wood Products. As security for a loan, Stan Wood assigned to the Bank invoices which purported to represent shipments of sleds to Firestone. The Bank notified Firestone of the assignment and Firestone sent its checks in payment of assigned invoices directly to the Bank. The Bank applied part of the proceeds of the checks to the reduction of the Stan Wood loan but credited the balance to Stan Wood's checking account, from which the money was in due course withdrawn. Firestone's payments to the Bank (in November, 1946) were made on receipt of invoices and without checking to see whether the sleds had been delivered. The court assumed that Firestone

28. Outlet Embroidery Co. v. Derwent Mills, Ltd., 254 N.Y. 179, 183, 172 N.E. 462, 463, 70 A.L.R. 1440 (1930).

made and the Bank received the payments in good faith and without notice of, or reason to suspect, fraud on Stan Wood's part. In February, 1947, Stan Wood was adjudicated bankrupt. In April, 1947, Firestone investigated the situation and learned, for the first time, that no sleds had ever been delivered or, for that matter, shipped. The invoices, against which Firestone had paid, were false and the accompanying bills of lading had been forged. Firestone brought an action against the Bank to recover the payments. *Held*, judgment for Firestone for the amount which the Bank had applied in reduction of the Stan Wood loan. As to the amount which the Bank had allowed Stan Wood to withdraw from its checking account, the majority of the court felt that the Bank had "changed its position" so that recovery by Firestone would be inequitable. A dissenting judge felt that Firestone should recover the full amount of its payment. (Before notification of the assignment, Firestone had made payment on another false invoice to Stan Wood, who had indorsed the check to the Bank which had applied the proceeds to reduce the loan. The Bank was allowed to keep that amount on the ground that it had been a "holder in due course" of the check which Firestone issued to Stan Wood.) In the opinion of the editors, the opinion delivered in the *Firestone* case is not particularly helpful, which is not to say that the court did not reach a sensible result. What do you think?

3. In his opinion in the principal case, Judge Weinfeld commented that "there is no justification for extending the scope of Langel v. Betz and its progeny." Langel v. Betz is reprinted *supra* p. 1500. What does it have to do with this situation? The two Appellate Division cases cited by Judge Weinfeld are instructive. In the *Kaufman* case a sales contract provided that disputes should be submitted to arbitration. A dispute over goods delivered arose after the buyer had paid the seller's assignee. *Held*, on the authority of Langel v. Betz, that the assignee could not be compelled to participate in the arbitration. In the *McMullen* case a buyer paid the seller's assignee and later brought an action for breach of warranty against both seller and assignee. *Held*, on the authority of *Kaufman* (which is the only case cited), the assignee's motion for summary judgment should be granted.

> The merchandise which was the subject matter of the sale has been properly returned to the seller, not to the factor [assignee], and it is the seller which is obligated to refund the purchase money to the buyer if the latter's contentions are well founded. . . . Any remedy on the part of the purchaser is exclusively against the seller.

275 A.D. 701, 87 N.Y.S.2d 356-357. This disposition of the case was affirmed without opinion by the Court of Appeals. Suppose the buyer in *McMullen* eventually recovered a judgment against the seller that turned

out to be uncollectible because of insolvency. Could he now recover from the assignee under the theory of money paid under a mistake of fact?

RESTATEMENT OF CONTRACTS SECOND

§336.   DEFENSES AGAINST AN ASSIGNEE

(1)   By an assignment the assignee acquires a right against the obligor only to the extent that the obligor is under a duty to the assignor; and if the right of the assignor would be voidable by the obligor or unenforceable against him if no assignment had been made, the right of the assignee is subject to the infirmity.

(2)   The right of an assignee is subject to any defense or claim of the obligor which accrues before the obligor receives notification of the assignment, but not to defenses or claims which accrue thereafter except as stated in this Section or as provided by statute.

(3)   Where the right of an assignor is subject to discharge or modification in whole or in part by impracticability, public policy, non-occurrence of a condition, or present or prospective failure of performance by an obligee, the right of the assignee is to that extent subject to discharge or modification even after the obligor receives notification of the assignment.

(4)   An assignee's right against the obligor is subject to any defense or claim arising from his conduct or to which he was subject as a party or a prior assignee because he had notice.

UNIFORM COMMERCIAL CODE

§9-318.   DEFENSES AGAINST ASSIGNEE; MODIFICATION OF
CONTRACT AFTER NOTIFICATION OF ASSIGNMENT;
TERM PROHIBITING ASSIGNMENT INEFFECTIVE;
IDENTIFICATION AND PROOF OF ASSIGNMENT

(1)   Unless an account debtor has made an enforceable agreement not to assert defenses or claims arising out of a sale as provided in Section 9-206 the rights of an assignee are subject to

(a)   all the terms of the contract between the account debtor and assignor and any defense or claim arising therefrom; and

(b)   any other defense or claim of the account debtor against the assignor which accrues before the account debtor receives notification of the assignment. . . .

NOTE

1. Section 167 of the Restatement First asserted that an assignee's rights are subject to all defenses, set-offs and counterclaims of the obligor "provided that such defenses and set-offs are based on facts existing at the time of the assignment, or are based on facts arising thereafter prior to knowledge of the assignment by the obligor." Under the Restatement Second, since set-offs and counterclaims arising out of independent transactions between the obligor and assignor are not among the defenses specifically enumerated in §336(3), they would appear to fall under the general or residual rule contained in subsection (2), a rule that is arguably more favorable from the assignee's point of view. Overall, however, the Restatement Second improves the position of the obligor by giving him the benefit of most contract defenses even when they accrue after he has been notified of the assignment. The Restatement Second's solution to the problem of defenses was apparently inspired by §9-318(1) of the Uniform Commercial Code. How would the *Cuban Atlantic Sugar* case be decided under §336 of the Restatement Second? Section 167 of the Restatement First? U.C.C. §9-318(1)?

2. In Sponge Divers' Association, Inc. v. Smith, Kline & French Co., 263 F. 70 (3d Cir. 1920), the Association assigned to Commercial Credit the "book account" arising from a contract to sell sponges to Smith, Kline & French. Commercial Credit notified Smith, Kline & French of the assignment. On delivery of the sponges, Smith, Kline & French rejected them on the ground that they were not of the quality specified in the contract. An action was then brought against Smith, Kline & French by the Association "to the use of Commercial Credit." There was a jury verdict that Smith, Kline & French had rightfully rejected the sponges and a judgment was rendered in their favor. Commercial Credit appealed, assigning as error the trial court's refusal to instruct the jury that:

> Where there has been an absolute assignment in good faith and for a valuable consideration of the whole interest of the assignor in a chose in action, the assignor's control over it ceases immediately after the assignment and notice, and he can do nothing thereafter to prejudice or defeat the rights of the assignee.

(The source of the requested instruction appears to have been the article on Assignment in Corpus Juris, 5 C.J. 959.)

The Circuit Court affirmed the judgment. Judge Buffington commented, with respect to Commercial Credit's claim, that

> Its right was to a book account, and if no sale was effected, if the goods ordered were never delivered, and those delivered were properly rejected, because they were not the goods of the contract of sale, then and in that

event there was no sale, there was no enforceable book account in existence to assign, the Sponge Company had nothing to assign, and the assignee of what there was no power to assign acquired no rights against the defendant, because the goods of the sale had never been delivered to it and a sale consummated.

Id. at 72.

Is there any difference, conceptually or practically, between Judge Buffington's approach in the *Sponge Divers* case and the approach of Restatement Second §336 or U.C.C. §9-318(1)?

3. For the provisions of §9-206, referred to in §9-318(1), see Note 2 following the next case.

COMMERCIAL CREDIT CORP. v. ORANGE COUNTY MACHINE WORKS
34 Cal. 2d 766, 214 P.2d 819 (1950)

EDMONDS, J. — Commercial Credit Corporation sued Orange County Machine Works, the maker of a promissory note representing the amount unpaid upon a conditional sales contract. The appeal from a judgment in favor of the maker presents for decision questions concerning the negotiability of the instrument and the respective rights of the parties in connection with the defense of failure of consideration.

The Machine Works was in the market for a Ferracute press. Ermac Company knew of one which could be purchased from General American Precooling Corporation for $5,000 and offered to sell it to the Machine Works for $5,500. Commercial Credit was consulted by Ermac and asked to finance the transaction. It agreed to do so by taking an assignment of the contract of sale between Ermac and the Machine Works.

During a period of about eight months before this time, Ermac had obtained similar financing from Commercial Credit and had some blank forms suppled to it by the latter. By a contract written upon one of these forms, which was entitled "Industrial Conditional Sales Contract," Ermac agreed to sell and Machine Works bound itself to purchase the press.

The terms of the contract relating to deferred payments were stated as follows:

The balance shown to be due hereunder (evidenced by my note of even date to your order) is payable in 12 equal consecutive installments of $355.09 each, the first installment payable one month from date hereof. Said note is a negotiable instrument, separate and apart from this contract, even though at the time of execution it may be temporarily attached hereto by perforation or otherwise.

The agreement also provided: "This contract may be assigned and/or said note may be negotiated without notice to me and when assigned and/or negotiated shall be free from any defense, counterclaim or cross complaint by me."

The note sued upon was originally the latter part of this printed form of contract but at a dotted or perforated line could be detached from it. At the time the president of Machine Works signed the contract and note, he raised a question about that portion of the document below the line. He was told it was just "a part of the contract."

Machine Works paid $1,512.50 to Ermac. That company, pursuant to the arrangements which it had made with Commercial Credit, assigned the contract and endorsed the note to the latter, which gave Ermac its check for $4,261. At the time the contract was delivered to the finance company the note had not been detached. Ermac deposited in its bank that check and the one received from the Machine Works, and sent to Precooling Corporation its check for $5,000. Upon presentation, this check was dishonored and because it was not paid, Precooling Corporation did not deliver the press.

By the present action, Commercial Credit is endeavoring to obtain a judgment against Machine Works and Ermac for the amount paid to Ermac, together with incidental fees and interest. Ermac defaulted. By cross-complaint, Machine Works demands $1,512.50 from Ermac and also seeks declaratory relief against Commercial Credit. Upon these pleadings and the evidence stated, which in all essential respects is uncontradicted, judgment was rendered in favor of Commercial Credit and Machine Works against Ermac, but in favor of Machine Works insofar as the demands of Commercial Credit against it are concerned. The court found that at the time Commercial Credit paid $4,261 to Ermac it knew that the mechanical press did not belong to that company, and had not been delivered to Machine Works. As a conclusion of law, the court determined that Commercial Credit is not a holder in due course of the note.

As grounds for a reversal of the judgment in favor of Machine Works, the finance company insists that the note, in form, is negotiable, and its status, as such, was not changed because of original physical attachment to, nor later detachment from, the sales contract. A note, otherwise negotiable, does not lose that status, says, the appellant, because it was given in connection with a conditional sales contract. Another point urged is that the character of an otherwise negotiable note is not destroyed by reason of the simultaneous assignment of a conditional sales contract, for security, to the endorsee of the note. Finally, the appellant argues, the note here sued upon is a separate and distinct instrument, negotiable in form; Machine Works knew its purpose and legal effect and is estopped to assert failure of consideration as a defense to an action upon it.

Machine Works directly challenges these contentions and asserts that Commercial Credit did not acquire the instrument in good faith and for value, and had notice of infirmities in the instrument and of the defect in the title of Ermac. As to the form of the instrument, the respondent takes the position that the conditional sales contract and the attached note must be construed as constituting a single document. As so construed it is a sales contract, assignable but not negotiable, and subject to all equities and defenses which the original parties to the contract may have had. Moreover, Machine Works asserts that the finance company was a party to the original transaction rather than a subsequent purchaser; it took title subject to all equities or defenses existing in its favor against Ermac, and any negotiability of the note was destroyed when it and the conditional sales contract were transferred together as one instrument.

Under section 3133 of the Civil Code, a holder in due course is one who has taken the instrument under the following conditions:

1. That it is complete and regular upon its face;
2. That he became the holder of it before it was overdue, and without notice that it had been previously dishonored, if such was the fact;
3. That he took it in good faith and for value;
4. That at the time it was negotiated to him he had no notice of any infirmity in the instrument or defect in the title of the person negotiating it.

In some states it has been held that in a suit upon a note executed concurrently with a conditional sales contract, a personal defense to the contract may be interposed (Von Nordheim v. Cornelius, 129 Neb. 719 [262 N.W. 832]; Federal Credit Bureau, Inc. v. Zelkor Dining Car Corp., 238 App. Div. 379 [264 N.Y.S. 723]; Todd v. State Bank, 182 Iowa 276 [165 N.W. 593, 3 A.L.R. 971]; State National Bank v. Contrell, 47 N.M. 389 [143 P.2d 592, 152 A.L.R. 1216]). Authorities in other jurisdictions are to the contrary (Thal v. Credit Alliance Corp., 64 App. D.C. 328 [78 F.2d 212, 100 A.L.R. 1354] (containing a review of the cases); Commercial Credit Co. v. McDonough Co., 238 Mass. 73 [130 N.E. 179]; Northwestern Finance Co. v. Crouch, 258 Mich. 411 [242 N.W. 771]; B.A.C. Corp v. Cirucci, 131 N.J.L. 93 [35 A.2d 36]; Motor Finance Corp. v. Huntsberger, 116 Ohio St. 317 [156 N.E. 111]; Shawano Finance Corp. v. Julius, 214 Wis. 637 [254 N.W. 355]. The latter view is more in keeping with the necessities of business, and also better serves the underlying spirit of the Negotiable Instruments Act. There is no good reason why the concurrent execution of a note and a conditional sales contract should deprive an otherwise negotiable instrument of the characteristics which give it commercial value. That factor alone should not defeat negotiability. Nor, in the absence of fraudulent misrepresentation, not here present, is there reason to hold that the physical attachment of a note and a conditional sales contract at the time of execution renders the note nonnegotiable where the contract clearly shows the facts in regard to it.

In Commercial Credit Co. v. Childs (1940), 199 Ark. 1073 [137 S.W.2d 260, 128 A.L.R. 726], the court said:

> . . . The note and contract are attached and constitute one instrument covering an agreement of the sale and purchase of the automobile in question. . . . The note, contract and assignment were all executed and signed the same day. The instrument was prepared and delivered to the Arkansas Motors, Inc., by appellant to be used by it in the sale and purchase of cars. Appellant financed the deal.
>
> We think appellant was so closely connected with the entire transaction or with the deal that it cannot be heard to say that it, in good faith, was an innocent purchaser of the instrument for value before maturity. . . . Rather than being a purchaser of the instrument after its execution it was to all intents and purposes a party to the agreement and instrument from the beginning. . . ."

The case is commented upon in 53 Harvard Law Review, page 1200, as follows:

> By abandoning the test of the "white heart and the empty head" in the case of a transferee who is more like a party to the original transaction than a subsequent purchaser, the decision increases the protection afforded the consumer who has not received what he was promised. . . . The holding is desirable in that it shifts the risk of the dealer's insolvency to the party better able to bear it, and since holders in due course from the finance company will be protected, the decision does not clog negotiability.

In the present case, Commercial Credit supplied Ermac with forms and was twice consulted by telephone as to the impending deal. It knew all of the details of the transaction. Indeed, financing was applied for because Ermac did not have the money to but the machinery which Machine Works desired to obtain. Throughout the entire transaction, Commercial Credit dealt chiefly with Ermac, the future payee, rather than with Machine Works, the future maker. Commercial Credit advanced money to Ermac with the understanding that the agreement and note would be assigned or endorsed to it immediately. In a very real sense, the finance company was a moving force in the transaction from its very inception, and acted as a party to it. Moreover, Commercial Credit knew the financial status of Ermac. As stated in the appellant's brief, Ermac was ". . . one of innumerable independent sellers of merchandise on conditional sales whose credit had been checked and financial integrity demonstrated."

When a finance company actively participates in a transaction of this type from its inception, counseling and aiding the future vendor-payee, it cannot be regarded as a holder in due course of the note given in the transaction and the defense of failure of consideration may properly be maintained. Machine Works never obtained the press for which it bargained and, as against Commercial, there is no more obligation upon it to pay the note than there is to pay the installments specified in the contract.

The judgment is affirmed.

Gibson, C.J., Shenk, J., Carter, J., Traynor, J., Schauer, J., and Spence, J., concurred.

Appellant's petition for a rehearing was denied March 23, 1950.

NOTE

1. In addition to the negotiable note executed by the Machine Works, there was a clause in the conditional sale contract that provided that the assignee should hold free of Machine Works' contract defenses. The court refers to the waiver of defense clause but does not discuss it. In American National Bank v. Sommerville, 191 Cal. 364, 216 P. 376 (1923), the court dealt with a waiver of defense clause in a conditional sale contract unaccompanied by a negotiable note. In the *Sommerville* case Tomlinson executed conditional sale contracts in favor of Sommerville, an automobile dealer. Each contract recited that Tomlinson had received delivery of the automobile and further provided that, if the contract should be "in good faith" assigned, Tomlinson should be

> precluded from in any manner attacking the validity of this contract on the ground of fraud, duress, mistake, want of consideration, or failure of consideration or upon any other ground, and all moneys payable under this contract by [Tomlinson] shall be paid to such assignee or holder without recoupment, setoff or counterclaim of any sort whatsoever.

The contracts were assigned to a finance company, which further assigned them to the Bank. The Bank brought an action on the contracts against both Sommerville and Tomlinson. Tomlinson offered to prove at the trial that Sommerville had never delivered any cars to him. The trial court excluded the offer of proof but was reversed by the Supreme Court, which held that Tomlinson was not precluded by the recital in the contracts that the cars had been delivered. As to the waiver of defense clause, the court concluded that it was an impermissible, and therefore ineffective, attempt to turn non-negotiable instruments (the conditional sale contracts) into negotiable instruments. The waiver clause by itself, said Waste, J., would not create an "estoppel by contract" although it would be open to the Bank on retrial to show an "estoppel in pais" against Tomlinson. What is the difference between "estoppel by contract" and "estoppel in pais"?

2. Uniform Commercial Code §9-206(1) provides:

> Subject to any statute or decision which establishes a different rule for
> buyers or lessees of consumer goods, an agreement by a buyer or lessee that
> he will not assert against an assignee any claim or defense which he may
> have against the seller or lessor is enforceable by an assignee who takes his
> assignment for value, in good faith and without notice of a claim or de-
> fense, except as to defenses of a type which may be asserted against a holder
> in due course of a negotiable instrument under the Article on Commercial
> Paper (Article 3). A buyer who as part of one transaction signs both a
> negotiable instrument and a security agreement makes such an agreement.

The term "consumer goods" is defined (§9-109) as goods "used or bought
for use primarily for personal, family or household purposes." The phrase
"defenses of a type which may be asserted against a holder in due course"
refers to the distinction between so-called real and personal defenses
under negotiable instruments law. Forgery, infancy, and extreme duress
are "real defenses" which are good even against a holder in due course.
Want of consideration and failure of consideration are "personal defenses" which are cut off by negotiation of an instrument to a holder in
due course.

Is the principal case still "good law" in California under U.C.C. §9-
206(1)? There appears to be nothing in Article 3 of the Code that would
preclude the court from adhering to its pre-Code holding that Commercial Credit, because of its close involvement in the underlying transaction, failed to qualify as a holder in due course of the negotiable note. But
how about the waiver clause in the contract?

3. The issues involved in the principal case and in the *Sommerville*
case have, since 1920 or thereabouts, accounted for a substantial amount
of litigation, particularly in the consumer field. It is fair to say that, since
1950, finance companies and banks have fared poorly in their attempts to
enforce consumer obligations free of contract defenses, either as holders
of negotiable notes or under waiver of defense clauses.

Fairfield Credit Corp. v. Donnelly, 158 Conn. 543, 264 A.2d 547 (1969)
is illustrative of the consumer litigation. The defendants in the *Fairfield
Credit* case, which was decided several years after Connecticut's enactment of the Uniform Commercial Code, agreed to purchase a television
set from D.W.M. Advertising following a home solicitation. Along with
the television, they received a service contract. Shortly after the set was
delivered, a representative of Fairfield Credit called the defendants and
was told the television was working properly; following this conversation,
D.W.M. assigned all its rights under the contract to Fairfield Credit.
Defendants subsequently experienced problems with the television and
eventually stopped using it. Repeated efforts to get D.W.M. to make the
necessary repairs proved unavailing, and D.W.M. itself went out of business about two months after the defendants had purchased their set. The

defendants refused to make any further payments under their contract, and Fairfield Credit brought suit. The Supreme Court of Connecticut held, among other things, that the defendants could assert all their contract defenses against Fairfield Credit despite the inclusion in their contract of a clause which read, "[t]he Buyer will settle all claims against the named Seller (the assignor) directly with such Seller and will not assert or use as a defense any such claim against the assignee." In discussing the effectiveness of the waiver clause, Judge King had this to say:

> Such a provision is generally referred to as a waiver of defense clause and is specifically dealt with in the Uniform Commercial Code in General Statutes §42a-9-206(1), which provides that,
>
>> [s]ubject to any statute or decision which establishes a different rule for buyers or lessees of consumers goods, an agreement by a buyer or lessee that he will not assert against an assignee any claim or defense which he may have against the seller or lessor is enforceable by an assignee who takes his assignment for value, in good faith and without notice of a claim or defense, except as to defenses of a type which may be asserted against a holder in due course of a negotiable instrument under article 3. . . .
>
> The statute quoted above has specifically made effective a waiver of defense clause in favor of an assignee of a contract not involving a sale or lease of "consumer goods," as defined in General Statutes §42a-9-109(1). But the statute takes no position on whether such a clause constitutes a valid waiver by the buyer in a transaction involving consumer goods. Connecticut General Statutes Annotated (West Ed.) §42a-9-206, comment 2, p. 434.
>
> We see no reason why the plaintiff, in taking an assignment of a contract under the circumstances here, should be able to recover against the buyer where the seller could not. If a seller carries out his contract obligations, either he or the assignee can recover against the buyer for any default in performance on his part. The only purpose of a waiver of defense clause such as was used in this case is to give the assignee the status of a holder in due course of a negotiable instrument. . . .
>
> While we have not heretofore had occasion to consider the validity of such a waiver of defense clause, it has been the subject of judicial consideration in a number of states. The decisions have not been entirely in accord. . . . We consider that the better rule is that set forth in cases such as Unico v. Owen, 50 N.J. 101, 124, 232, A.2d 405, which holds that such a clause in consumer-goods-conditional-sales contracts, chattel mortgages and other instruments of like character is void as against public policy.
>
> In the first place, the use of a waiver of defense clause is an attempt to impart the attributes of negotiability to an otherwise non-negotiable instrument. General Statutes §42a-3-104. An attempt to evade the clear prerequisites of negotiability by the use of such clauses (often, as here, in fine print and couched in technical language the significance of which is difficult for the ordinary consumer to appreciate) is opposed to the policy and spirit of General Statutes §42a-3-306, which provides that one not a holder in due

course of an instrument is subject to all claims and defenses which would have been available against the original holder. See cases such as Quality Finance Co. v. Hurley, 337 Mass. 150, 155, 148 N.E.2d 385; American National Bank v. A. G. Sommerville, Inc., 191 Cal. 364, 370, 216 P. 376.

In addition, since Connecticut's adoption of the Uniform Commercial Code in 1959, it has become increasingly clear that the policy of our state is to protect purchasers of consumer goods from the impositions of over-reaching sellers. For example, the General Assembly, in its February, 1965 session, passed Public Act No. 350 . . . entitled "An Act Concerning Consumer Frauds," which makes illegal certain deceptive trade practices and empowers the department of consumer protection to enforce the act. In 1967, the General Assembly authorized the creation of a "consumers advisory council" to assist the department of consumer protection in formulating standards for consumer goods. [Public Acts 1967, No. 73.] In that same session, an "Act Concerning Home Solicitation and Referral Sales," outlawing the referral system employed in this very case [Public Act No. 749] and an act concerning the disclosure of finance charges [Public Act No. 758] were passed, each of which was intended to provide extensive protection to the consumer. Finally, in the 1969 session of the General Assembly, no less than four acts were passed which were designed to afford protection to the consumer. Public Acts 1969, Nos. 13, 178, 325 and 454. There can be no question that there exists in Connecticut a very strong public policy in favor of protecting purchasers of consumer goods and that for a court to enforce a waiver of defense clause in a consumer-goods transaction would be contrary to that policy. See cases such as Unico v. Owen, 50 N.J. 101, 124, 232 A.2d 405. . . .

Id. at 548-551, 264 A.2d at 549-551.

4. The pro-consumer case law trend illustrated by cases like Fairfield Credit Corp. v. Donnelly and Unico v. Owen has been reinforced by statutory provisions, under so-called Retail Installment Sales Acts, which limit the effectiveness or forbid the use of waiver of defense clauses or, occasionally, of negotiable notes. For a general survey of legislation affecting holder in due course and related doctrines, see Hudak & Carter, The Erosion of the Holder in Due Course Doctrine: Historical Perspective and Development (pt. 2), 9 U.C.C. L.J. 235 (1977); see also the discussion in Chapter 4, Section 2. Earlier drafts of U.C.C. §9-206 contained comparable consumer protection provisions which were deleted from the final draft as the result of a decision to leave such matters to the Retail Installment Sales Acts. Section 9-203(2) is designed to make clear that the consumer-protective provisions of such Acts are not repealed by the enactment of Article 9 of the Code. The Uniform Consumer Credit Code (U.C.C.C.), promulgated in 1974 by the National Conference of Commissioners on Uniform State Laws, contains provisions (§§3.307, 3.404) designed to limit the use of negotiable notes and to invalidate waiver of defense clauses in consumer transactions. Section 3.404 reads, in part, as follows:

(1)   With respect to a consumer credit sale or consumer lease [, except one primarily for an agricultural purpose], an assignee of the rights of the seller or lessor is subject to all claims and defenses of the consumer against the seller or lessor arising from the sale or lease of property or services, notwithstanding that the assignee is a holder in due course of a negotiable instrument issued in violation of the provisions prohibiting certain negotiable instruments (Section 3.307).

(2)   A claim or defense of a consumer specified in subsection (1) may be asserted against the assignee under this section only if the consumer has made a good faith attempt to obtain satisfaction from the seller or lessor with respect to the claim or defense and then only to the extent of the amount owing to the assignee with respect to the sale or lease of the property or services as to which the claim or defense arose at the time the assignee has notice of the claim or defense. Notice of the claim or defense may be given before the attempt specified in this subsection. Oral notice is effective unless the assignee requests written confirmation when or promptly after oral notice is given and the consumer fails to give the assignee written confirmation within the period of time, not less than 14 days, stated to the consumer when written confirmation is requested.

(4)   An agreement may not limit or waive the claims or defenses of a consumer under this section.

What does the first sentence of subsection (2) mean?

5. Finally, as if all this weren't enough, the Federal Trade Commission promulgated a "trade regulation rule" in 1975 that made it a deceptive trade practice for a seller (or lessor) of consumer goods to "take or receive a consumer credit contract" that fails to contain, in bold type, the following provision:

NOTICE

ANY HOLDER OF THIS CONSUMER CREDIT CONTRACT IS SUBJECT TO ALL CLAIMS AND DEFENSES WHICH THE DEBTOR COULD ASSERT AGAINST THE SELLER OF GOODS OR SERVICES OBTAINED PURSUANT HERETO OR WITH THE PROCEEDS HEREOF. RECOVERY HEREUNDER BY THE DEBTOR SHALL NOT EXCEED AMOUNTS PAID BY THE DEBTOR HEREUNDER.

6. Comment, A Case Study of the Impact of Consumer Legislation: The Elimination of Negotiability and the Cooling-Off Period, 78 Yale L.J. 618 (1969), is an empirical study of the effect on the financing of home improvement transactions in Connecticut of anti-negotiability provisions in the Connecticut Home Solicitation Sales Act of 1967. The authors' conclusions (78 Yale L.J. at 655) are that:

First, while the elimination of negotiability per se places major additional costs on financers, these institutions are able to pass most of them on.

Second, dealers . . . bear many of the additional costs, and some are seriously injured by difficulty in obtaining financing. Third, although consumers directly benefit from the Act, they must ultimately bear much of the cost of the change.

The Yale Comment discusses various legislative approaches to the problem of restricting the use of negotiable notes in consumer transactions, or of eliminating their use altogether, at 630 et seq. For a discussion of this problem from an economic point of view, see the comments of John Prather Brown, Holder in Due Course: Does the Consumer Pay?, 32 Business Lawyer 591 (1977) at 614.

HOMER v. SHAW, 212 Mass. 113, 98 N.E. 697 (1912). One Lancaster made a contract with the defendant, a general contractor, to perform certain construction work on the Tremont Street subway in Boston. The plaintiff advanced funds to Lancaster to enable him to meet his labor and material expenses; to secure the loan he had received, Lancaster assigned to the plaintiff the amounts "due and coming due" under his contract with the defendant. Shortly afterwards, the plaintiff gave Lancaster a check with which to meet his weekly labor expenses but then stopped the check before Lancaster could cash it. Lancaster told the defendant that he would be unable to complete the work he had begun and the two of them agreed

> that Lancaster should go on with the work and that the defendant should pay his debts for labor and material already incurred in carrying out the contract, and should advance the money necessary in the future to pay for labor and material used in completing the work, and should pay the further sum of $25 per week to Lancaster personally.

The plaintiff subsequently brought an action against the defendant to recover the amounts paid and payable to Lancaster under his new arrangement with the defendant on the theory that these funds belonged to the plaintiff by virtue of his prior assignment. The trial judge held for the defendant, and his view of the matter was affirmed on appeal. Judge Braley, writing for the Massachusetts Supreme Judicial Court, had this to say: "After the assignor entered upon the performance of the contract he informed the defendant, that owing to the failure of the plaintiff to advance money, which apparently he had agreed to furnish, he would be unable to complete the work as his workmen had not been paid, and if their wages remained in arrears they would leave his employment. The evidence, if no further action had been taken by the parties, and performance of the work had ceased, would have warranted a finding, that, the assignor having repudiated or abandoned his contract before the first instalment of the contract price became payable, the defendant would not have been indebted to the plaintiff. Homer v. Shaw, 177 Mass. 1. Bowen v. Kimbell, 203 Mass. 364, 370, 371. Barrie v. Quinby, 206 Mass. 259, 267. But without any ostensible change the assignor remained in charge of the work until completion, and the plaintiff contends under the substituted declaration, that the money thereafter received should be considered as earned under the original contract. The assignor needed immediate financial assistance, and if the defendant might have advanced the money which the evidence shows he furnished to enable him to pay his employees, yet if he had done so the plaintiff's assignment would have been given priority over the loan. Buttrick Lumber Co. v. Collins, 202 Mass. 413. The parties while they could not modify to his prejudice the terms of the contract assigned without the plaintiff's consent, or by a secret fraudulent arrangement deprive him of the benefit of the assignment, were not precluded from entering into a new agreement if performance by the assignor had become impossible from unforeseen circumstances. Eaton v. Mellus, 7 Gray, 566, 572. Linnehan v. Matthews, 149 Mass. 29. It consequently was a question of fact upon all the evidence for the presiding judge before whom the case was tried without a jury, to decide, whether upon facing the exigencies of changed conditions the parties mutually agreed to a cancellation, and thereupon in good faith an independent contract was substituted, by the terms of which the defendant undertook to furnish sufficient funds to pay the workmen the wages then due, and their future wages as they accrued, while the assignor was to receive a weekly salary for his personal services of supervision. . . ."

NOTE

1. In Brice v. Bannister, 3 Q.B.D. 569 (1878), the English court, on facts quite similar to those in Homer v. Shaw, came to the opposite conclusion. Gough, who had contracted to build a ship for Bannister, assigned the proceeds from the contract to Brice, who notified Bannister of the assignment. Thereafter Gough fell into difficulties and Bannister made further advances to him which, under the assignment, should have gone to Brice. Brice sued Bannister and recovered judgment. Brett, L.J., dissenting, wrote:

> . . . I cannot bring my mind to think that this doctrine [of "equitable assignment"] should be extended so as to prevent the parties to an unfulfilled contract from either cancelling or modifying, or dealing with regard to it in the ordinary course of business. I quite agree that they ought not to be allowed to act mala fide for the purpose of defeating an equitable assignee: but if what they do is done bona fide and in the ordinary course of business, I cannot think their dealings ought to be impeded or imperilled by this doctrine. . . . If they cannot modify it [their contract], it seems to me

to denote a state of slavery in business that ought not to be suffered; but I apprehend the parties to the contract can modify it.

Id. at 579-580.

2. In Madison Industrial Corp. v. Elisberg, 152 Misc. 167, 271 N.Y.S. 891 (City Ct. 1934), Wendel, J., delivered the following opinion (reprinted in its entirety):

This action is brought to recover for work, labor, and services, consisting of dyeing and finishing of textiles, performed by plaintiff's assignor. The work done was concededly in the amount of $2,611.40, but the defendants are admittedly entitled to offset certain credits; these offsets reduce the balance now sought to be recovered to the sum of $1,055.06.

As against the latter sum, however, defendants seek to offset a further credit of $1,212.04, which was issued by plaintiff's assignor to defendants on March 23, 1933. This credit was given by plaintiff's assignor some time subsequent to the assignment and the consequent accrual of plaintiff's rights as assignee. The proof shows that the credit in question relates to and was intended to be applied against certain invoices dated from February 1 to February 10; that, although the credit is in excess of $1,200, these invoices aggregate in amount little more than $500; that the credit was issued on the same day plaintiff's assignor entered into an assignment for the benefit of its creditors; that it was obtained by defendants from plaintiff's assignor six days after plaintiff had written defendants a letter threatening suit; that the amount of this credit was far greater than of any other single credit disclosed by the documentary evidence. At the time of the issuance of the credit, plaintiff's assignor was no longer the owner of the cause of action against defendants for the work, labor, and services in question, since it had theretofore assigned it to plaintiff. The assignor then was no longer in a position to defeat plaintiff's rights merely by issuing a credit memorandum to the defendants.

In Superior Brassiere Co. v. Zimetbaum, 214 App. Div. 525, 528, 212 N.Y.S. 473, 476, the following is quoted with approval from 5 Corpus Juris, 966, 967:

As against the assignor the assignee becomes the owner of the chose from the time of the assignment, subject to the qualifications heretofore stated. After that time the assignor loses all right to control over the same and will not be allowed to defeat the rights of the assignee, whether the assignment is good at law or only in equity. He has no right to collect or compromise the chose, nor in any way to discharge the debtor therefrom, nor to modify the chose, as by an extension of time to the debtor.

Since the credit in question relates directly to the subject-matter of the assignment, the court is not precluded, notwithstanding what has been said, from considering whether the credit was bona fide; that is to say, whether it in fact represented actual damage in that or any amount to the merchandise dyed by plaintiff's assignor. The preponderance of the credible evidence establishes that the claim for damages upon the basis of which the credit was allowed has no foundation in fact.

Judgment is directed in favor of plaintiff and against the defendants in the sum of $1,055.06 and appropriate interest. Settle order.

Is the *Elisberg* case reconcilable with Homer v. Shaw? On the *Zimetbaum* case, from which the *Elisberg* opinion quotes, see the Note following State Factors Corp. v. Sales Factors Corp., *infra* p. 1550.

BABSON v. VILLAGE OF ULYSSES
155 Neb. 492, 52 N.W.2d 320 (1952)

YEAGER, Justice. Here are two actions instituted by Henry B. Babson, plaintiff and appellant, against the Village of Ulysses, a municipal corporation, defendant and appellee. The two were consolidated for the purposes of trial and tried as a single action. They will be regarded and treated as one action here.

By the actions plaintiff claims that there is due him from the defendant $100 a month from December 1930 to and including July 1936 with interest at seven percent per annum. The indebtedness is denied by the defendant.

A trial was had to the court at the conclusion of which it was adjudged and decreed that the defendant was not indebted to plaintiff and plaintiff's actions were dismissed. Motions for new trial were duly filed and overruled. From the judgments and the orders overruling the motions for new trial the plaintiff has appealed.

The basis of the litigation is substantially the following: The Village of Ulysses entered into an agreement with the Blue River Power Company to supply the village with electric current for all its needs for a period of 20 years commencing April 1, 1920, which energy was to be delivered at the village substation and by the village distributed to its customers. This contract was not actually entered into until September 20, 1921. As a part of the consideration the village agreed to pay to the company $100 a month for 200 months. This part of the consideration was by the parties denominated a "primary charge." It was a part of the rate structure and it appears that its design was to amortize the cost of a transmission line constructed by the company which was necessary to serve the village. The further consideration of the contract was the payment of a specific rate for each kilowatt hour for all electric current used. This was referred to as a "secondary charge." The validity of this contract was not brought into question on the trial.

There was full and complete performance by both parties under the contract until October 17, 1925. On October 17, 1925, all of the stock of the Blue River Power Company was sold to the United Light and Power Company. The stock had been owned by the plaintiff herein. By the terms of the agreement whereby the United Light and Power Company obtained this stock Babson became entitled by assignment to the payment of the $100 a month or "primary charge" from the defendant herein. He became entitled to other properties and interests theretofore belonging to the Blue River Power Company but we deem it unnecessary to describe these interests here since the village was not a party to the agreement and it is not made to appear that it ever prior to this action became informed as to its contents.

It is to be observed that this assignment represented an obligation of the United Light and Power Company to plaintiff and not one of the village to him, and that this was the method adopted by the power company and plaintiff for its liquidation.

The village was notified of assignment of the "primary charge" of $100 a month provided for in the contract. The body of the notification is the following:

> I have been instructed to inform you that at a recent meeting of the Board of Directors of the Blue River Power Company, resolutions were passed, assigning the $100.00 per month, identified as being a primary charge, in our contract with the Village, to H. B. Babson.
>
> In the future, commencing with the next payment, you will therefore please remit this $100.00 each month, as provided for in the contract, to H. B. Babson, 19th St. & California Avenue, Chicago, Illinois. Payments due for actual current consumed, and stipulated in the contract as being secondary charge, will be payable to the Blue River Power Company, here at Seward, as in the past.
>
> I kindly ask that you acknowledge receipt of this letter and make payments as per above instructions.

On May 31, 1926, the Nebraska Gas and Electric Company succeeded the United Light and Power Company and became the assignee of the Blue River Power Company contract, and on August 30, 1927, the Iowa-Nebraska Light and Power Company became the assignee thereof.

The village continued to make the monthly payments of $100 each to the plaintiff until December 1930.

On December 2, 1930, the village sold its distributing system to the Iowa-Nebraska Light and Power Company and granted this company a non-exclusive right and franchise for a term of 25 years to build, operate, and maintain an electric power system in the village. The village at this time ceased to be a distributor of electric current. It ceased also to be a purchaser except for a sufficient amount of current to operate its water system. It became such purchaser under the new contract.

Upon the completion of this arrangement the power company and the village regarded the relationship, which by agreement commenced on April 1, 1920, as ended and in consequence the defendant made no further payments to the plaintiff.

The actions here are by the plaintiff to recover from the defendant the monthly payments remaining after December 1930 under the contract between the Blue River Power Company and the village of Ulysses hereinbefore described which became effective as of April 1, 1920, and entered into on September 20, 1921, except the payments for four months which were not due at the time of the commencement of the second action.

Plaintiff by his actions contends that by virtue of his assignment he became entitled to these amounts as they would have come due had the contract and performance thereof not been abandoned by the parties thereto, and to a judgment therefor against the defendant. The judgment of the trial court was a denial of this contention and a dismissal of the actions.

The briefs of plaintiff contain numerous assignments of error and the assertion of many reasons why the judgment should be reversed. We think however that a proper decision herein depends upon the one question of whether or not the plaintiff was entitled to assert a claim against the village under his assignment after the village and the Iowa-Nebraska Light and Power Company ceased to operate under the Blue River Power Company contract.

In the determination of this question it becomes necessary to examine and apply certain facts as well as certain legal principles.

There is no substantial dispute as to controlling facts. The cases come here on the transcript which contains the pleadings and judgment, a stipulation of facts, and the testimony of a single witness. The testimony of this witness was contained in a deposition which was read at the trial.

It is not disclosed by the record that the village ever was notified or had authentic knowledge of the substance or effect of any of the agreements whereby the agreement of the Blue River Power Company or the obligations thereof were transferred to the United Light and Power Company, then to the Nebraska Gas and Electric Company, and then to the Iowa-Nebraska Light and Power Company. The only thing in that connection which came authentically to its knowledge was the information contained in the notification of assignment of the "primary charge." This notification has been previously quoted at large herein. It will be observed that by this the village was notified only that the "primary charge" of $100 a month was assigned to plaintiff and the village was directed to make payments as they became due to him.

Further the record does not disclose any contractual relationship or privity with reference to this subject matter between plaintiff and defendant. In this connection the record discloses only that the village became informed that through an undisclosed arrangement between plaintiff and the power company plaintiff became entitled to receive a part of the consideration which flowed to the company under the terms of a contract which it had with the village. Whatever right plaintiff had to receive the payments of $100 each flowed from and was the obligation of the agreement or agreements between him and the power companies successively and not from any agreement with the village.

Under this state of facts the defendant contends that it and the company had the right under law to discontinue operation and performance under the contract or in other words to rescind it without liability thereafter on the part of the defendant to the plaintiff on his assignment. It contends that no obligation to pay remained after the parties by mutual action discontinued operation under and performance of the agreement which became effective April 1, 1920.

The contentions of the defendant in this respect must be sustained.

The assignment here was of payments of money to become due under an executory contract which the parties thereto were privileged to rescind or discharge entirely or to modify by agreement thus relieving each from the further obligations thereof in case of rescission or discharge and substituting the new ones in case of modification. [Citations.]

An assignment of a contract or a right flowing therefrom does not create a contractual obligation between the assignee and the other party to the contract in the absence of assumption of the liabilities of the assignor by the assignee. [Citations.]

In the present instance there was no assumption by the plaintiff of liabilities of the assignor to the village.

An assignee of the obligation of a contract takes subject to its burdens in the hands of the assignor and in order to recover he must show that the conditions have been performed. He is bound by the terms of the contract to the same extent as the assignor. [Citations.]

Here there was an absence of performance by the power company covering the entire period contemplated by the actions.

An assignee of a non-negotiable chose in action ordinarily acquires no greater right than that possessed by his assignor. He stands in the shoes of the assignor. He cannot sue if the assignor could not have maintained an action. [Citations.]

After the agreement was mutually rescinded and performance abandoned no burden of payment remained upon the village. The assignor and its successors surrendered their right to receive or recover the monthly amounts. Consequently the right of the assignee to receive them from the village no longer existed.

It must be said therefore that the mutual rescission of the contract which is brought into question here destroyed the right of plaintiff to recover thereafter from the village on his assignment unless, as plaintiff contends, the pretended rescission was void and of no effect.

The basis of this contention is that the village trustees had no authority or power to alter the terms of or abandon the contract of September 20, 1921. The theory is that authority for the proceedings in this connection was not received through a vote of the electors of the village, which plaintiff insists was a condition precedent to the exercise of such power.

Our attention however has not been called to any statutory provision in existence at the time of the rescission imposing any such requirement. Attention is directed to section 70-604, C.S. 1931, erroneously referred to as section 70-605, which prohibits the sale, lease, or transfer of an electric light or power plant, distribution system, or transmission lines by a village without a vote of the qualified electors. This provision however did not come into being until one day following this rescission.

Reliance is had also on section 17-508, Comp. St. 1929, now sections 17-901 to 17-904, R.S. 1943. This section in nowise relates to existing contractual relationships. It relates to powers and restrictions thereon to enter into contracts.

It is concluded that the claim of the plaintiff as made that the rescission was void and of no effect is without merit.

The judgments of the district court are affirmed.

Affirmed.

NOTE

1. With respect to the freedom of the contracting parties to modify or rescind without the assignee's consent, does the Nebraska court in the principal case seem to take a more extreme position than the Massachusetts court took in Homer v. Shaw, *supra* p. 1538?

2. If you were counsel to a Nebraska bank, would you advise it, in the light of the *Babson* case, to rely on an assignment of rights under an executory contract? Suppose the proceeds of an executory contract represented the only available security for a proposed bank loan. In the terminology of Article 9, how would you classify such collateral, and what would the bank have to do, under Article 9, in order to perfect its security interest in the borrower's executory contract rights? Read, again, the discussion of the relevant Article 9 provisions in the Notes following Shiro v. Drew, *supra* p. 1452, and Speelman v. Pascal, *supra* p. 1492. Supposing that the bank had taken whatever steps were necessary (if, indeed, any were) to perfect its security interest in the contract rights assigned to it, would the bank be protected against the loss of its collateral as the result of a modification or rescission of the contract made without its consent? According to §9-318(2), the answer appears to be a qualified "yes." That subsection provides as follows:

> So far as the right to payment or a part thereof under an assigned contract has not been fully earned by performance, and notwithstanding notification of the assignment, any modification of or substitution for the contract made in good faith and in accordance with reasonable commercial

standards is effective against an assignee unless the account debtor has otherwise agreed but the assignee acquires corresponding rights under the modified or substituted contract. The assignment may provide that such modification or substitution is a breach by the assignor.

The official comment to §9-318(2) explains the policy of that section:

> Prior law was in confusion as to whether modification of an executory contract by account debtor and assignor without the assignee's consent was possible after notification of an assignment. Subsection (2) makes good faith modifications by assignor and account debtor without the assignee's consent effective against the assignee even after notification. This rule may do some violence to accepted doctrines of contract law. Nevertheless it is a sound and indeed a necessary rule in view of the realities of large scale procurement. When for example it becomes necessary for a government agency to cut back or modify existing contracts, comparable arrangements must be made promptly in hundreds and even thousands of subcontracts lying in many tiers below the prime contract. Typically the right to payments under these subcontracts will have been assigned. The government, as sovereign, might have the right to amend or terminate existing contracts apart from statute. This subsection gives the prime contractor (the account debtor) the right to make the required arrangements directly with his subcontractors without undertaking the task of procuring assents from the many banks to whom rights under the contracts may have been assigned. Assignees are protected by the provision which gives them automatically corresponding rights under the modified or substituted contract. Notice that subsection (2) applies only so far as the right to payment has not been earned by performance, and therefore its application ends entirely when the work is done or the goods furnished.

The Massachusetts annotation to U.C.C. §9-318(2) remarks: "The freedom of modification and substitution allowed by subsection (2) would change Massachusetts law. Under present [i.e., pre-Code] law the original parties could not modify the contract to the prejudice of the assignee without his consent. Homer v. Shaw, 212 Mass. 113, 117, 93 N.E. 697 (1912)."

The New York version of §9-318(2) amended the official Code version to make the modification provision read: "any modification of or substitution for the contract made in good faith, in accordance with reasonable commercial standards and without material adverse effect upon the assignee's rights is effective against an assignee. . . ." With respect to the New York amendment, the Permanent Editorial Board for the Uniform Commercial Code, in Report No. 2 (1964), commented:

> The New York limitation in subsection (2) is necessarily implied from the applicable requirements of good faith and observance of reasonable commercial standards. Material modifications adversely affecting the assignee's

rights or the assignor's ability to perform, without the assignee's consent, would not conform to these standards. Thus the proposed New York change is unnecessary.

3. The Restatement of Contracts First did not contain a provision dealing expressly with the power of assignor and obligor to modify or rescind their contract without the assignee's consent. Recall, however, that the Restatement First did address the closely related issue of the power of promisor and promisee to vary the promisor's duties without the consent of a third party beneficiary (in §§142 and 143, reprinted *supra* p. 1425). What explains the Restatement First's failure to provide for the similar problem of contractual modification by obligor and assignor?

This puzzling omission has been cured in the Restatement Second by the inclusion of a section (§338(2)) that is nearly identical in its wording to U.C.C. §9-318(2). Compare §9-318(2) of the Code with §311 of the Restatement Second, reprinted *supra* p. 1426, dealing with the contractual modification of duties owed to a third party beneficiary. Who fares better under these provisions, an assignee or a contract beneficiary? In light of these provisions, would a lender on the security of executory contract rights have greater protection against subsequent modifications or rescission as a third party beneficiary than he would as an assignee? For contradictory answers to the question, see Comment, Contract Rights as Commercial Security: Present and Future Intangibles, 67 Yale L.J. 847, 888-892 (1958); 2 G. Gilmore, Security Interests in Personal Property §41.3 (1965). Assuming that there is something in the third party beneficiary idea, how should the hypothetical Nebraska bank referred to in Note 2 go about turning itself into a "beneficiary"? Or should it claim to be both "beneficiary" and "assignee" of the underlying contract?

Section 6.   Priorities

A.   *The Common Law Rules*

DEARLE v. HALL

3 Russ. 1, 38 Eng. Rep. 475 (Ch. 1828)

LYNDHURST, Lord Chancellor: Zachariah Brown was entitled, during his life, to about £93 a-year, being the interest arising from a share of the residue of his father's estate, which, in pursuance to the directions in his father's will, had been converted into money, and invested in the names of the executors and trustees. Among those executors and trustees was a solicitor of the name of Unthank, who took the principal share in the management of the trust. Zachariah Brown, being in distress for money, in consideration of a sum of £204, granted to Dearle, one of the Plaintiffs in the suit, an annuity of £37 a-year, secured by a deed of covenant and a warrant of attorney of the grantor and a surety; and, by way of collateral security, Brown assigned to Dearle all his interest in the yearly sum of £93: but neither Dearle nor Brown gave any notice of this assignment to the trustees under the father's will.

Shortly afterwards, a similar transaction took place between Brown and the other Plaintiff, Sherring, to whom an annuity of £27 a-year was granted. The securities were of a similar description; and, on this occasion, as on the former, no notice was given to the trustees.

These transactions took place in 1808 and 1809. The annuities were regularly paid till June 1811; and then, for the first time, default was made in payment.

Notwithstanding this circumstance, Brown, in 1812, publicly advertised for sale his interest in the property under his father's will. Hall, attracted by the advertisement, entered, through his solicitor, Mr. Patten, into a treaty of purchase; and it appears from the correspondence between Mr. Patten and Mr. Unthank, that the former exercised due caution in the transaction, and made every proper inquiry concerning the nature of Brown's title, the extent of any incumbrances affecting the property, and all other circumstances of which it was fit that a purchaser should be apprised. No intimation was given to Hall of the existence of any previous assignment; and his solicitor being satisfied, he advanced his money for the purchase of Brown's interest, and that interest was regularly assigned to him. Mr. Patten requested Unthank to join in the deed: but Mr. Unthank said, "I do not choose to join in the deed; and it is unnecessary for me to do so, because Z. Brown has an absolute right to this property, and may deal with it as he pleases." The first half-year's interest, subject to some deductions, which the trustees were entitled to make, was duly paid to Hall; and, shortly afterwards, Hall for the first time ascertained, that the property had been regularly assigned, in 1808 and 1809, to Dearle and to Sherring.

Sir Thomas Plumer was of opinion, that the Plaintiffs had no right to the assistance of a court of equity to enforce their claim to the property as against the Defendant Hall, and that, having neglected to give the trustees notice of their assignments, and having enabled Z. Brown to commit this fraud, they could not come into this Court to avail themselves of the priority of their assignments in point of time, in order to defeat the right of a person who had acted as Hall had acted, and who, if the prior assignments were to prevail against him, would necessarily sustain a great loss. In that opinion I concur.

It was said, that there was no authority for the decision of the Master of the Rolls — no case in point to support it; and certainly it does not appear that the precise question has ever been determined, or that it has been even brought before the Court, except, perhaps, so far as it may have been discussed in an unreported case of Wright v. Lord Dorchester. But the case is not new in principle. Where personal property is assigned, delivery is necessary to complete the transaction, not as between the vendor and the vendee, but as to third persons, in order that they may not be deceived by apparent possession and ownership remaining in a person, who, in fact, is not the owner. This doctrine is not confined to chattels in possession, but extends to choses in action, bonds, &c.: in Ryall v. Rowles (1 Ves. Sen. 348; 1 Atk. 165) it is expressly applied to bonds, simple contract-debts, and other choses in action. It is true that Ryall v. Rowles was a case in bankruptcy; but the Lord Chancellor called to his assistance Lord Chief Justice Lee, Lord Chief Baron Parker, and Mr. Justice Barnett; so that the principle, on which the Court there acted, must be considered as having received most authoritative sanction. These eminent individuals, and particularly the Lord Chief Baron and Mr. Justice Burnett, did not, in the view which they took of the question before them, confine themselves to the case of bankruptcy, but stated grounds of judgment which are of general application. Lord Chief Baron Parker says, that, on the assignment of a bond debt, the bond should be delivered, and notice given to the debtor; and he adds, that, with respect to simple contract-debts, for which no securities are holden, such as book-debts for instance, notice of the assignment should be given to the debtor in order to take away from the debtor the right of making payment to the assignor, and to take away from the assignor the power and disposition over the thing assigned (1 Ves. Sen. 367; 2 Atk. 177). In cases like the present, the act of giving the trustee notice, is, in a certain degree, taking possession of the fund: it is going as far towards equitable possession as it is possible to go; for, after notice given, the trustee of the fund becomes a trustee for the assignee who has given him notice. It is upon these grounds that I am disposed to come to the same conclusion with the late Master of the Rolls.

I have alluded to a case of Wright v. Lord Dorchester, which was cited as an authority in support of the opinion of the Master of the Rolls. In that case, a person of the name of Charles Sturt, was entitled to the dividends of certain stock, which stood in the names of Lord Dorchester and another trustee. In 1793, Sturt applied to Messrs. Wright and Co., bankers at Norwich, for an advance of money, and, in consideration of the monies which they advanced to him, granted to them two annuities, and assigned his interest in the stock as a security for the payment. No notice was given by Messrs. Wright and Co. to the trustees. It would appear that Sturt afterwards applied to one of the defendants, Brown, to purchase his life-interest in the stock; Brown then made inquiry of the trustees, and they stated that they had no notice of any incumbrance on the fund: upon this B. completed the purchase, and received the dividends for upwards of six years. Messrs. Wright then filed a bill, and obtained an injunction, restraining the transfer of the fund or the payment of the dividends; but, on the answer of Brown, disclosing the facts with respect to his purchase, Lord Eldon dissolved that injunction. At the same time, however, that he dissolved the injunction, he dissolved it only on condition that Brown should give security to refund the money, if, at the hearing, the Court should give judgment in favour of any of the other parties. That case was attended also with this particular circumstance, that the party, who pledged the fund, stated by his answer, that, when he executed the security to Wright and Co., he considered that the pledge was meant to extend only to certain real estates. For these reasons, I do not rely on the case of Wright v. Lord Dorchester as an authority; I rest on the general principle to which I have referred; and, on that principle, I am of opinion that the Plaintiffs are not entitled to come into a court of equity for relief against the Defendant Hall. The decree must, therefore, be affirmed, and the deposit paid to Hall.

NOTE

1. Dearle v. Hall and a companion case, Loveridge v. Cooper, were heard and decided together. The report in Russell contains an elaborate statement of the facts of both cases, the opinion of Sir Thomas Plumer, Master of the Rolls, and a detailed summary of the arguments of counsel both at trial and on appeal. The two cases were evidently felt to involve an important principle.

2. In this country Dearle v. Hall came to be the customary reference for the so-called English rule as to priorities between successive assignees of the same chose in action. For the number of American jurisdictions which are thought to have followed the English rule, see Part B of this section.

STATE FACTORS CORP. v. SALES FACTORS CORP.

257 App. Div. 101, 12 N.Y.S.2d 12 (1939)

UNTERMYER, J. In 1937 Lerner Bros., a partnership engaged in the business of manufacturing fur coats, found it necessary to factor their accounts receivable. For that purpose, on April 30, 1937, they entered into a factoring contract with the defendant under which the defendant agreed to purchase "without recourse," and Lerner Bros. agreed to assign to the defendant, all accounts receivable, subject to the right of the defendant to approve the credit of any account. Upon such assignment the defendant agreed to pay eighty per cent of the face amount of the invoices. The agreement further required that all such invoices to cus-

tomers of Lerner Bros. bear a printed indorsement that the account had
been assigned and that the billing on such invoices, by whomever done,
should operate as an assignment to the defendant.

On September 8, 1937, Lerner Bros. also entered into a contract with
the plaintiff by which all such accounts receivable as might be approved
by the plaintiff were agreed to be assigned to the plaintiff "as the same are
created" against advances of seventy per cent of the face amount of the
assigned accounts. The plaintiff was accorded the right, presumably for
its own protection, but was not required, to give notice of the assignment
to customers of Lerner Bros., which right, however, the plaintiff did not
exercise. The contract provided that any remittance paid to Lerner Bros.
on an assigned account should be held in trust and immediately delivered
to the plaintiff in the identical form in which it was received.

On September 8, 11, 14, 16, 20 and 21, 1937, Lerner Bros. delivered
written assignments of certain accounts receivable to the plaintiff together with supporting documents and received payments in accordance
with the contract of September 8, 1937. Thereafter, and in each instance
subsequent to delivery of the assignments to the plaintiff, Lerner Bros.
executed assignments of the same accounts to the defendant and received payments from the defendant in accordance with the contract of
April 30, 1937. With these assignments were delivered to the defendant
and mailed to the respective purchasers, invoices bearing an indorsement
of the assignment of the account to the defendant. Payment of the accounts was, therefore, made to the defendant notwithstanding the plaintiff's assignments, of which the purchasers of merchandise from Lerner
Bros. do not appear to have been aware. The Special Term has found
upon sufficient evidence that neither plaintiff nor defendant was aware of
the transactions between Lerner Bros. and the other.

The present action is not concerned with the rights of purchasers of
merchandise from Lerner Bros., who no doubt were protected in making
payment to the defendant under the only assignment of which notice was
given. Failure of the plaintiff to give such notice, however, would not
affect its right to recover from the defendant if the accounts which were
collected were the plaintiff's property. (Salem Trust Co. v. Manufacturers' Finance Co., 264 U.S. 182.) It is upon this theory that the action is
maintained to require the defendant to account for payments received on
debts which, it is claimed, had previously been assigned to the plaintiff.

The question thus presented is which of these two innocent parties
shall suffer the loss occasioned by the fraud of Lerner Bros. We think
upon the conceded facts the plaintiff is entitled to prevail. If we assume,
notwithstanding the plaintiff's contention to the contrary, that the defendant's contract is supported by a sufficient consideration, it entitled the
defendant to an assignment of all accounts thereafter to be created. Legal
title did not thereby pass to the defendant until further action on the part
of Lerner Bros. manifesting such a purpose after accounts had been

created by the sale of merchandise. (Rochester Distilling Co. v. Rasey, 142 N.Y. 570.) The contract only created equitable rights (Stephenson v. Go-Gas Co., 268 N.Y. 372) enforcible against Lerner Bros. or any assignee of Lerner Bros. having notice thereof. (Hinkle Iron Co. v. Kohn, 229 N.Y. 179.) Those equities might also prevail if the plaintiff, though without notice, had acquired the accounts without payment of a new consideration. (Central Trust Co. v. West India Imp. Co., 169 N.Y. 314; Suchy v. Frankenberg, 251 App. Div. 349.) But where, as here occurred, the plaintiff acquired legal title to the accounts without knowledge of infirmity and upon payment of a new consideration, it occupied the position of a purchaser for value without notice, whose legal title is superior both to the defendant's earlier equitable rights under the contract of April 30, 1937 (Glass v. Springfield L.I. Cemetery Society, 252 App. Div. 319; *leave to appeal denied*, 276 N.Y. 687) and to subsequent assignments. (Fortunato v. Patten, 147 N.Y. 277; Fairbanks v. Sargent, 104 id. 108.)

The judgment should be reversed, with costs, and judgment directed in favor of the plaintiff for the relief demanded in the complaint, with costs.

NOTE

1. The "factoring" arrangement developed principally in the New York textile industry. The factor, who was originally a sales agent for the textile mill, subsequently became a banker in all but name and provided the mill's working capital. This financing was done originally on the security of the inventory but, after 1920 or thereabouts, on the security of the accounts receivable. See 1 G. Gilmore, Security Interests in Personal Property, ch. 5 (1965). With respect to the accounts receivable, the typical factoring arrangement was that the factor bought the accounts "without recourse" (i.e., the factor assumed the credit risk in the event the accounts proved to be uncollectible by reason of the account debtors' inability to pay) and collected the accounts directly from the account debtors who were notified of the assignment. The unusual aspect of the principal case is that State Factors had not notified the account debtors to make payment directly to it.

Factoring, with respect to receivables, was often referred to as "notification" or "direct collection" financing. A competing system of "non-notification" or "indirect collection" receivables financing also began to develop after 1920. Under this system the assignee, who did not notify the account debtors, trusted the assignor to collect and remit the proceeds of assigned accounts. Under non-notification financing, the assignee typically took assignments of accounts "with recourse" and thus did not assume the credit risk in the way the old-style textile factor had done. Both types of receivables financing are still widely used, although the distinctions between them have tended to become somewhat blurred. See 1 G. Gilmore, *supra*, §5.2.

2. The principal case and Superior Brassiere Co. v. Zimetbaum, 214 App. Div. 525, 212 N.Y.S. 472 (1925), are among the cases most frequently cited for the "New York rule" that, as between successive assignees, "first in time is first in right." The principal case illustrates the point that the determination of which of the two assignees is "first in time" can itself become a problem of some difficulty. Reread Rockmore v. Lehman, *supra* p. 1477. On the basis of *Rockmore* and the cases discussed in the Note following that case, do you think that an effective argument could have been made that Sales Factors was "first in time" under the agreement of April 30? Is Justice Untermyer's manipulation of the legal title vs. equitable title dichotomy an accurate rendering of such cases as Fairbanks v. Sargent? The principal case indicates that, whatever the theoretical possibilities may have been, it had become the practice for assignees of receivables to insist on periodic assignments as the accounts came into existence.

RESTATEMENT OF CONTRACTS SECOND

§342. SUCCESSIVE ASSIGNEES FROM THE SAME ASSIGNOR

Except as otherwise provided by statute, the right of an assignee is superior to that of a subsequent assignee of the same right from the same assignor, unless

(a) the first assignment is ineffective or revocable or is voidable by the assignor or by the subsequent assignee; or

(b) the subsequent assignee in good faith and without knowledge or reason to know of the prior assignment gives values and obtains

(i)   payment or satisfaction of the obligation,
(ii) judgment against the obligor,
(iii) a new contract with the obligor by novation, or
(iv) possession of a writing of a type customarily accepted as a symbol or as evidence of the right assigned.

NOTE

The Restatement rule, associated with Massachusetts, has been nicknamed the "four horsemen rule." The "horsemen," of course, make their appearance in §342(b). Note that the fourth and last of the horsemen deals with claims of the negotiable instrument type rather than of the chose in action or contract right type. See the Note following Muller v. Pondir, *supra* p. 1444. A leading Massachusetts common law case on the priority of successive assignees was Herman v. Connecticut Mutual Life Insurance Co., 218 Mass. 181, 105 N.E. 450 (1914).

B.   The Klauder *Case and the End of the Common Law Priority Rules*

2 G. GILMORE, SECURITY INTERESTS IN PERSONAL PROP-ERTY §25.7 (1965) (some footnotes have been omitted): ". . . The pressures generated by novel methods of receivables financing would sooner or later have collapsed the common law rules and led to a statutory reformulation. However, the common law phase came to an unexpectedly sudden end on March 8, 1943, or *Klauder* day. On that date the Supreme Court held, in Corn Exchange National·Bank & Trust Co. v. Klauder,[29] that a non-notification accounts receivable financing arrangement in an English-rule state (Pennsylvania) was invalid against the assignor's trustee in bankruptcy under the 1938 version §60 of the Bankruptcy Act on voidable preferences. We are not presently concerned with §60 or with the merits of Mr. Justice Jackson's *Klauder* opinion as an essay in statutory construction or an act of judicial statesmanship. The wreckage left in *Klauder's* immediate wake was that non-notification receivables financing was impossible in an unknowable number of states. The number of states was unknowable for two reasons. In the first place, it was far from clear how many English-rule states there were: authorities were ambiguous in some states and lacking in others.[30] In the second place, *Klauder* threw no clear light on the question whether its doctrine applied only to English-rule states or whether it might extend to Massachusetts, Restatement or four-horsemen states as well. (The status of the Massachusetts rule under *Klauder* was debated in the lower federal courts for several years, with varying results, until the problem was otherwise put to rest.)[31] It was, however, clear that non-notification receivables financing was safe in New York rule states — although once again there was no way of knowing how many such states (besides New York) there were. The New York rule stood up under *Klauder* for this reason: the *Klauder* construction of §60 (1938 version) was that any transfer of property, although made in fact for a present consideration, was to be treated as if it had been

29. 318 U.S. 434, 63 S. Ct. 679, 87 L. Ed. 884 (1943).
30. One estimate of the time found the states lined up as follows: fourteen states probably followed either the New York rule or the Massachusetts rule and three more states possibly followed one of these two rules; seven states probably followed the English rule and possibly seven more. The remaining states either had no relevant decisions or had completely confusing decisions. Kupfer and Livingston, Corn Exchange National Bank & Trust Co. v. Klauder Revisited: The Aftermath of Its Implications, 32 Va. L. Rev. 910, 914-915 (1946).
31. See, e.g., In re Rosen, 157 F.2d 997 (3d Cir. 1946), *cert. denied*, 330 U.S. 835 (1947) (assignment upheld); In re Vardaman Shoe Co., 52 F. Supp. 562 (E.D. Mo. 1943) (assignment invalid).

made for a past consideration and therefore vulnerable to attack as a voidable preference, if, under applicable state law, a subsequent good faith purchaser of the property could take priority over the transferee. In English-rule states a non-notifying assignee could be defeated by a later assignee who first notified; therefore (without notification) it was impossible for him ever to perfect his interest against a trustee in bankruptcy. In New York rule states a non-notifying assignee could not be defeated by any subsequently accruing claim; in such states, therefore, *Klauder* had no effect on non-notification financing.

"If non-notification financing was not to be given up altogether, there were, after *Klauder*, two possible routes to salvation. One was to procure the amendment of §60 by deleting from it the so-called 'good faith purchaser test' of the 1938 version. The other was to procure a statutory enactment of the New York rule in all states which had not clearly and unambiguously adopted the rule at common law. Both routes were followed and, in time, successfully. Congress, which had, to be sure, more important issues than non-notification accounts receivable financing to concern it, proceeded at a stately pace; §60 was finally amended in 1950, the 'good faith purchaser test' being replaced (as to personal property) by a 'lien creditor test.' But before that had happened, most of the doubtful states had already enacted statutes which, whatever else they did, thoroughly codified the New York rule on priorities between successive assignees of a chose in action.

"If the Bankruptcy Act amendment had come first and the state accounts receivable statutes later, the draftsmen of the state statutes would have been in a position to weigh the merits of the various priority rules and select whichever seemed best fitted to the occasion. It should be borne in mind that, drafting under the whip of *Klauder*, the draftsmen were in no position to consider what might be the best policy. They were engaged in an emergency operation and, with respect to priorities, they had only one choice: a rule of absolute priority, with no exception whatever. Nothing else was safe so long as the *Klauder* construction of §60 remained in force. All the statutes, whether they required filing as a condition of perfection or were of the so-called 'validation' (or automatic perfection) type, adopted in different verbal formulations such an absolute priority rule. The Texas statute, although wordier than most, may be quoted as typical of the result aimed at. Section 6 of the Texas statute provided that from the time an assignment became 'protected'

> . . . all subsequent assignees, purchasers and transferees of or from the assignor shall be conclusively deemed to have received notice of such assignment . . . no purchaser from the assignor, no creditor of any kind of the assignor, and no prior or subsequent assignee or transferee of the assignor . . . shall in any event have, or be deemed to have acquired, any right in the account or accounts so assigned or in proceeds thereof, or in any obligation substituted therefor, superior to the rights therein of the [first filing] assignee. . . .

"What the drafting may have lacked in felicity, it more than made up for in emphasis. It will be noted that the Texas statute quoted extended the assignee's priority to the 'proceeds' of assigned accounts; a comparable reference to 'proceeds' was found in almost all the statutes. Taken literally, the 'proceeds' provision could have been read to mean that a 'protected' assignee would have priority even over a creditor of the assignor to whom proceeds of assigned accounts had been paid over in ordinary course of business — a result which would go beyond need or reason. Such a contention seems never to have been made in litigation, and, if made, would be, it must be hoped, unsuccessful. The point is, however, worth making as an illustration of the thoroughness with which the draftsmen went about the business of fashioning their absolute priority rule.

"The somewhat erratic coverage of the accounts receivable statutes is discussed in another chapter. For present purposes it is enough to point out that the statutes by no means covered the entire range of intangibles which may become collateral in financing arrangements. Indeed some of the better drafted statutes were quite precisely limited to the trouble area revealed by *Klauder:* short-term receivables of the type which were customarily the subject of non-notification financing. Thus, even after most states had enacted accounts receivable statutes containing an absolute priority rule, the several common law rules continued to have a considerable area in which to operate."

NOTE

For the language of the "good faith purchaser" test of the 1938 version of §60 and the status of New York assignments under that test, see Rockmore v. Lehman (Judge Augustus Hand's second opinion), *supra* p. 1482. The "lien creditor test" adopted in the 1950 revision of §60 has been carried forward in the voidable preference section of the 1978 Bankruptcy Code; see §547(e)(1)(B), discussed in the Note following Shiro v. Drew, *supra* p. 1452. It should be kept in mind that the lien creditor test applies only to transfers of personal property; transfers of real property are still governed by the good faith purchaser test that created such problems for non-notification accounts receivable financers in the *Klauder* case. See Bankruptcy Code §547(e)(1)(A).

C. Priorities under Article 9 of the Uniform Commercial Code

Article 9, like the short-lived accounts receivable statutes it replaced, adopted (with minor qualifications that we need not go into) a rule of absolute priority for the first assignee of accounts, contract rights, or general intangibles to "perfect" his interest. To perfect an interest in such intangibles, the assignee (or "secured party") must file with the public records a "financing statement" signed by the debtor, which gives the names of both assignor and assignee and describes the "collateral" by type or item. The financing statement "may be filed before a security agreement is made or a security interest otherwise attaches" (§9-402(1)). "Attaches," in the provision just quoted, is Article 9 terminology for the time when a security interest becomes enforceable against the debtor. See §9-203(2). Section 9-203(1) deals with the time when a security interest attaches. The term "security interest" is defined in §1-201(37). The part of the definition relevant to our discussion is: "'Security interest' means an interest in personal property . . . which secures payment or performance of an obligation. . . . The term . . . includes any interest of a buyer of accounts . . . which is subject to Article 9."

The rule as to priorities between successive assignees of the same account is stated in §9-312(5). The two assignments, if both have been perfected, rank "according to priority in time of filing or perfection," whichever is earlier, "provided that there is no period thereafter when there is neither filing nor perfection" (§9-312(5)(a)). Section 9-312(5)(b) provides that "so long as conflicting security interests are unperfected, the first to attach has priority."

The complicated distinction between the "first to file" rule of (5)(a) and the "first to attach" rule of (5)(b) can be illustrated by putting a few questions with respect to the *State Factors Corp.* case, *supra* p. 1550.

1. If neither State Factors nor Sales Factors files, who wins? As to when the security interest "attaches," note particularly §9-203(1)(c).

2. If Sales Factors files on April 30, 1937, who wins?

3. If State Factors files on September 8, 1937 and Sales Factors files after that date (or does not file at all), who wins?

4. Suppose that on September 21, 1937, neither assignee has filed. Thereafter, having learned of the September assignments to State Factors and knowing that State has not filed, Sales Factors files a financing statement and takes assignments of the accounts already assigned to State. Under §9-312(5)(a), Sales Factors wins, does it not? Does that seem a proper result?

A few further questions may be put to illustrate the Article 9 treatment of assignments of intangibles.

1. Shiro v. Drew, *supra* p. 1452. If Proctor and Drew had filed a financing statement, describing the collateral as proceeds of the Radome contract, would they prevail? Under §9-402, the financing statement would have to be signed by the Fiberlast Company, as debtor. In order for a security interest to attach, there would also have to be a "security agreement" signed by Fiberlast (§9-203(1)(a)). "Security agreement" (§9-105(g)) "means an agreement which creates or provides for a security interest." Would the letter of November 1, 1956 suffice?

2. In re Dodge-Freedman Poultry Company, *supra* p. 1458. Does the "subordination agreement" create a security interest (a) against the Poultry Company (the common debtor)? (b) against Freedman (the subordinator)? Note that one consequence of calling the senior creditor's interest an Article 9 security interest is that, in order to protect his interest against third parties, he will be required to perfect by filing. These questions are much discussed in the references cited in Note 2 following the *Dodge-Freedman* case. (Section 1-209, added to the Code as an "optional provision" in 1966, provides that a subordination by a creditor "does not create a security interest as against either the common debtor or a subordinated creditor" and adds that "[t]his section shall be construed as declaring the law as it existed prior to the enactment of this section and not as modifying it." For a case construing the meaning of §1-209, see Chase Manhattan Bank v. First Marion Bank, 437 F.2d 1040 (5th Cir. 1971)).

3. Rockmore v. Lehman, *supra* p. 1477. Under §9-203 when did the assignee's interest "attach"?

4. *In re* City of New York v. Bedford Bar & Grill, Inc., *supra* p. 1485. Is the case still "good law" in New York following the enactment of Article 9?

TABLE OF CASES

Abbington v. Dayton Malleable, Inc., 63
A.B.C. Outdoor Advertisement, Inc. v. Dolhoun's Marine, Inc., 769
A.B.C. Packard, Inc. v. General Motors Corp., 96
Ablett v. Sencer, 795, 796
Abraham v. H.V. Middleton, Inc., 769
Acme Mills & Elevator Co. v. Johnson, 1061, 1201
Acme Process Equipment Co. v. United States, 1187
Adams v. Department of Motor Vehicles, 602
Adams v. Lindsell, 352
Adams v. Merced Stone Co., 1451
Adams v. Nichols, 942
Adams v. Southern California First National Bank, 602
Addis v. Gramophone Co., Ltd., 1112
Aetna Insurance Co. v. Eisenberg, 1437, 1439
Agnew, Matter of, 168
Ahmed Angullia Bin Hadjee Mohamed Salleh Angullia v. Estate and Trust Agencies, 105
Ahnapee & Western Ry. Co. v. Challoner, 303
Aimcee Wholesale Corp., Matter of, 1221
Air Products & Chem., Inc. v. Fairbanks Morse, Inc., 265
Alaska Airlines, Inc. v. Stephenson, 814, 818
Alaska Packers Assn. v. Domenico, 652, 657
Albert, L., & Son v. Armstrong Rubber Co., 969, 1055, 1128, 1197, 1201
Albre Marble & Tile Co. v. John Bowen Co., 924, 943, 944
Aldeslade v. Hendon Laundry, Ltd., 1239
Alexander v. Russo, 380
Allegheny College v. National Chautauqua County Bank of Jamestown, 501, 509, 510
Aller v. Aller, 731
Allhusen v. Caristo Constr. Corp., 1475, 1476
Amalgamated Investment & Property Co., Ltd. v. John Walker & Sons, Ltd., 893, 936

American Chain Co. v. Arrow Grip Mfg. Co., 323
American Home Improvement Co. v. MacIver, 589
American National Bank v. Sommerville, 1533, 1534
American Seating Co. v. Zell, 859
American Surety Co. of New York v. United States, 1057
American Trading & Production Corp. v. Shell International Marine Ltd., 926, 936, 955
Amsinck v. American Insurance Co., 781, 783
Amtorg Trading Corp. v. Miehle Printing Press & Manufacturing Co., 1055, 1057
Anderson v. Backlund, 129
Anderson v. May, 947
Approved Personnel, Inc. v. Tribune Co., 66
Arcos, Ltd. v. E.A. Ronaasen & Son, 1003
Arkansas Valley Smelting Co. v. Belden Mining Co., 1511, 1520
Armstrong v. M'Ghee, 128
Armstrong & Armstrong v. United States, 209
Asco Mining Co. v. Gross Mining Co., 667
Asinof v. Freudenthal, 257
Associated General Contractors, New York State Chapter (Savin Bros.), Matter of, 1221
Astley v. Reynolds, 655
Atkinson v. Pacific Fire Extinguisher Co., 1235
Atlantic Fish Co. v. Dollar S.S. Line, 665
Austin v. Burge, 242
Austin Instrument, Inc. v. Loral Corp., 657
Avery v. Wilson, 1038
Ayer v. Western Union Tel. Co., 252
Ayers, L.S., & Co. v. Hicks, 56

Babson v. Village of Ulysses, 1545
Backus v. Maclaury, 88
Baggs v. Anderson, 490
Bader v. Hiscox, 770

Bailee Lumber Co. v. Kincaid Carolina
  Corp., 685
Baily v. Austrian, 418
Baird, James, Co. v. Gimbel Bros., 323
Baker v. Hart, 1116
Baldridge v. Centgraf, 780, 793, 795
Balfour v. Balfour, 116, 119
Bard v. Kent, 319
Barile v. Wright, 288
Barnet's Estate, 152
Bartholomew v. Jackson, 173
Baumgartner v. Meek, 412, 417, 418
Bell v. Lever Bros., Ltd., 862, 893, 896,
  897, 898, 930
Bellizi v. Huntley, 1052
Bernstein v. W. B. Manufacturing Co.
  (235 Mass. 425), 467
Bernstein v. W. B. Manufacturing Co. (238
  Mass. 589), 465, 467
Besinger v. National Tea Company, 1092
Beswick v. Beswick, 1342, 1343
Better Food Markets v. American District
  Telegraph Co., 1231, 1235, 1237, 1239,
  1240
Bettini v. Gye, 920
Bickerstaff v. Gregston, 409
Billeter v. Posell, 1322
Bishop v. Eaton, 400
Blair v. Anderson, 1405
Blair v. National Security Insurance Co.,
  96
Blank v. Borden, 417
Block v. Tobin, 209
Blue Valley Creamery Co. v. Consolidated
  Products Co., 775
Boone v. Coe, 808, 814
Boone v. Eyre, 981, 982, 1001
Borg-Warner Corp. v. Anchor Coupling
  Co., 203, 226, 236
Boshart v. Gardner, 701
Boston & Maine R.R. v. Bartlett, 319
Boston Ice Co. v. Potter, 73, 988, 1507
Boston Plate & Window Glass Co. v. John
  Bowen Co., Inc., 943
Bowen v. Kimbell, 1050
Bowes v. Shand, 1002, 1001, 1003
Brauer v. Shaw, 352
Brewer v. Dyer, 1341
Brice v. Bannister, 1539
British Columbia & V.I. Spar, Lumber, &
  Saw-Mill Co. v. Nettleship, L.R., 1150,
  1165
British Columbia Saw-Mill Case, 1150,
  1165
British Waggon Co. v. Lea & Co., 1515,
  1517, 1520
Britton v. Turner, 1021, 1029, 1057
Broadcast Music, Inc. v. CBS, 61
Bromage v. Genning, 1072, 1073, 1150
Bromagin v. City of Bloomington, 881

Brooks v. Mitchell, 1451
Brown v. Foster, 987
Bucci, In re Estate of, 494
Burlington Industries v. Foil, 769
Bush v. Canfield, 1201
Butler v. Foley, 250, 882
Butterfield v. Byron, 104, 936, 937, 943

Cady v. Gale, 895
Cafritz v. Koslow, 517
Caldwell v. Cline, 368
Calhoun v. Downs, 792
Callen v. Pennsylvania Railroad Co., 680
Campbell Soup Co. v. Wentz, 562, 563,
  948, 1097, 1103
Canadian Industrial Alcohol Co. v. Dun-
  bar Molasses Co., 944, 966
C. & J. Fertilizer, Inc. v. Allied Mutual
  Insurance Co., 201
C. & K. Engineering Contractors v. Am-
  ber Steel Co., 225
Candler v. Crane Christmas & Co., 909,
  910
Capital Savings & Loan Assn. v. Przybylo-
  wicz, 299
Cargill Commn. Co. v. Swartwood, 823
Carlill v. Carbolic Smoke Ball Co., 373,
  380
Carlton v. Smith, 461
Casebolt, G.C., Co. v. United States, 368
Cash v. Clark, 797
Celanese Corp. of America v. John Clark
  Indus., Inc., 265
Central Hanover Bank and Trust Co. v.
  United Traction Co., 517
Central London Property Trust, Ltd. v.
  High Trees House, Ltd., 663, 664
Chandler v. Webster, 930, 931, 936
Channel Master Corp. v. Aluminum Ltd.
  Sales, 196, 200, 201
Chapman v. Bomann, 303
Chase Manhattan Bank v. First Marion
  Bank, 1558
Chase National Bank v. Sayles, 1451
Cherno v. Dutch American Mercantile
  Corp., 1465
Chicago Joint Board, Amalgamated Cloth-
  ing Workers v. Chicago Tribune, 67
Choate, Hall & Stewart v. S.C.A. Ser-
  vices, Inc., 1341
Chrysler Corp. v. Quimby, 211, 212, 225
C. Itoh & Co., Inc. v. Jordan Intl. Co.,
  264
City Mortgage & Discount Co. v. Palatine
  Insurance Co., 241
City Stores Co. v. Ammerman, 1074, 1089,
  1091, 1092, 1093, 1094
Clark v. Marsiglia, 1171, 1313, 1314, 1315
Clark v. West, 1039

Cochran v. Taylor, 739
Coggs v. Bernard, 923
Cohen v. Blessing, 95
Cohen & Sons, Inc. v. Lurie Woolen Co., 180
Cole-McIntyre-Norfleet Co. v. Holloway, 244
Coleman v. Garrison, 137
Collins Radio Co., 212
Colonial Savings Assn. v. Taylor, 287
Colpitts v. L.C. Fisher Co., 760, 765, 769
Columbia Nitrogen Corp. v. Royster Co., 144, 843
Combe v. Combe, 664
Comfort v. McCorkle, 288
Commercial Bank of Lake Erie v. Norton & Fox, 519
Commercial Credit Corp. v. Orange County Machine Works, 1533, 1534
Commercial Union Ins. Co. v. Padrick Chevrolet Co., 782
Commonwealth v. Scituate Savings Bank, 475
Conduit & Foundation Corporation v. Atlantic City, 326
Conn Organ Corp. v. Walt Whitman Music Studies, 836
Consolidated Edison Co. v. Arroll, 681
Constable v. Clobery, 975
Construction Aggregates Corp. v. Hewitt-Robins, Inc., 264
Continental Forest Products, Inc. v. Chandler Supply Co., 67
Continental T.V., Inc. v. G.T.E. Sylvania, Inc., 62
Cook v. Wright, 566
Copeland v. Beard, 1421
Coppage v. Kansas, 12
Corbett v. Cronkhite, 744
Corn Exchange National Bank & Trust Co. v. Klauder, 1554, 1556
Cotnam v. Wisdom, 57, 163, 173, 760
Countess of Rutland Case, 823
Couturier v. Hastie, 909, 910
Crabtree v. Elizabeth Arden Sales Corp., 783
Crane Ice Cream Co. v. Terminal Freezing & Heating Co., 1518, 1519, 1520
Crawford v. France, 832
Crisan Estate, In re, 168
Cronin v. National Shawmut Bank, 207
Crook v. Cowan, 391
Cropsey v. Sweeney, 153
Crosbie v. M'Doual, 476
Crowell-Collier Pub. Co. v. Josefowitz, 848
Cuban Atlantic Sugar Sales Corp. v. The Marine Midland Trust Co. of New York, 1525, 1528

Cushing v. Thompson, 349, 352
Custodio v. Bauer, 141
C———— v. W————, 527

Dadourian Export Corp. v. United States, 872, 873, 874
Danann Realty Corp. v. Harris, 843, 847, 848
Danby v. Osteopathic Hosp. Assn. of Delaware, 509
Daniel-Morris Co., Inc. v. Glens Falls Indemnity Co., 1370, 1371
Daniels v. Newton, 1072, 1270, 1278, 1289, 1341
Davies v. Collins, 1239
Davis v. General Foods Corp., 121
Davis v. Jacoby, 385
Davis & Co. v. Morgan, 77, 79
Dearle v. Hall, 1550
De Cicco v. Schweizer, 494, 501, 773, 1361
Deere, John, Co. v. Babcock, 404
Denkin v. Steiner, 1089
Department of Human Resources v. Williams, 121
Devecmon v. Shaw, 480, 501
Dick v. United States, 357, 367
Dickinson v. Dodds, 316, 319, 320, 871
Dixie Glass Co., Inc. v. Pollak, 1322
Dodge-Freeman Poultry Co. v. Delaware Mills, Inc., In re, 1464, 1558
Doe v. Bridgeton Hospital Assn., 58
Doll v. Noble, 988
Doyle v. Dixon, 773
Doyle v. South Pittsburgh Water Co., 1391
Drennan v. Star Paving Co., 326, 340
Dr. Miles Medical Co. v. John D. Park & Sons Co., 62
Duckworth v. Michel, 1074
Dufton v. Mechanicks National Bank, 288
Durfee v. Jones, 895
Dutton v. Poole, 1341, 1342

Eames Vacuum Brake Co. v. Prosser, 684
Earl v. Peck, 537
Eastern Restaurant Equipment Co., Inc. v. Tecci, 942
Eastern Rolling Mill Co. v. Michlovitz, 1074, 1094
Eastwood v. Kenyon, 519, 760, 761
Edelen v. Samuels, 1074
Edelman v. FHA, 208
Eisen v. Carlisle, 625
Elbinger v. Capitol & Teutonia Co., 537
Ellsworth Dobbs, Inc. v. Johnson, 417
Elsinore Union Elementary School District v. Kastorff, 341
Embola v. Tuppela, 574

Entores, Ltd. v. Miles Far East Corp., 349
Equitable Trust Company of New York v.
   Western Pacific Railway Co., 1289
Erwin & Williams v. Erwin, 473
Escola v. Coca Cola Bottling Co., 1254
Eugenia Case, The, 960
Eustis Mining Co. v. Beer, Sondheimer &
   Co., 827, 836
Everett, City of, v. Estate of Sumstad,
   894, 898
Everett Plywood Corp. v. United States,
   1152
Ever-Tite Roofing Corp. v. Green, 407

Fair v. Negley, 96, 1257, 1266
Fairbanks v. Sargent, 1484, 1485, 1492,
   1553
Fairbanks, Bank of, v. Kay, 703
Fairfield Credit Corp. v. Donnelly, 1534,
   1536
Fairmount Glass Works v. Crunden-Martin
   Woodenware Co., 193
Falconer v. Mazess, 370
Farabee-Treadville Co. v. Bank & Trust
   Co., 427
Farmland Service Coop., Inc. v. Klein,
   819
Federal Trade Commission. See FTC
Fedun v. Mike's Cafe, Inc., 674
Feinberg v. Pfeiffer Co., 308
Fibrosa Spolka Akcyjna v. Fairbairn Law-
   son Combe Barbour, 932, 935, 936, 943,
   1057
Field, Matter of, 510
Field v. The Mayor of New York, 1484,
   1485, 1492
Filley v. Pope, 1001, 1002, 1003
Firestone Tire & Rubber Co. v. Central
   National Bank of Cleveland, 1525, 1526
First National City Bank v. Valentia, 383
First National Maintenance Corporation
   v. NLRB, 63
Fischer v. Union Trust Co., 710
Fisher v. Jackson, 291
Fitts v. Panhandle & S.F. Ry., 679
Flood v. City National Bank of Clinton,
   380
Flood v. Kuhn, 1078
Flowers' Case, 694
Flureau v. Thornhill, 1109, 1138
Foakes v. Beer, 651, 664, 668, 672, 673,
   674
Foisy v. Wyman, 1265
Foley v. Classique Coaches, Ltd., 223
Ford v. Mutual Life Insurance Company
   of New York, 1420
Ford Motor Co., Ltd. v. Amalgamated
   Union of Engineering and Foundry
   Workers, 120

Forrer v. Sears Roebuck & Co., 294
Fortunato v. Patten, 1476
Forward v. Armstead, 475
Four Seasons Nursing Centers of Amer-
   ica, Inc., In re, 427
Fourth Street Bank v. Yardley, 1452
Fox's Estate, In re, 155
Freedman v. The Rector, 1059
Freund v. Washington Square Press, 1113
Fried v. Fisher, 299
Friedman & Co. v. Newman, 792
Frigaliment Importing Co., Ltd. v. B.N.S.
   International Sales Corp., 872, 873, 874
Frye v. Hubble, 673
FTC v. Texaco, 647
Fuller v. Kemp, 684

Gabrielson v. Hogan, 574
Gainsford v. Carroll, 1109, 1129, 1130,
   1131, 1138
Garrity v. Lyle Stuart, Inc., 1093, 1212
Gateway Co., Inc. v. Charlotte Theatres,
   668
G.C. Caseboly Co. v. United States,
   368
George v. Schuman, 718
Geremia v. Boyarski, 881
Gerisch v. Herold, 988
Gibbs v. Blanchard, 763
Gibson v. Cranage, 987
Gillarde Co. v. Martinelli, 1005
Gillingham v. Brown, 512
Globe Refining Co. v. Landa Cotton Oil
   Co., 109, 947, 1144, 1151, 1157, 1165,
   1171, 1179, 1201
Globe Rubber Mfg. Co. v. Conard, 735
Goebel v. Linn, 652, 655, 657, 678
Goldbard v. Empire State Mutual Life
   Insurance Co., 694
Goldberg v. Kollsman Instrument Corpo-
   ration, 1254, 1379
Goode v. Riley, 827
Goodman v. Dicker, 209, 211, 212, 225
Goodwin v. Gillingham, 478
Gordon, J.J., Inc. v. Worcester Telegram
   Publishing Co., 66
Gordon, Robert, Inc. v. Ingersoll-Rand
   Co., 340
Goulet v. Goulet, 730
Grand Isle v. McGowan, 77
Gray v. Barton, 673, 674, 1451
Gray v. Gardner, 983, 984
Gray v. Meek, 978
Grayson-Robinson Stores, Inc. v. Iris
   Construction Co., 1092
Great Atlantic & Pacific Tea Co. v. Cream
   of Wheat Co., 58, 59
Great Northern Ry. v. Witham, 420, 473
Green v. Superior Court, 95

Greenman v. Yuba Power Products, Inc., 1379
Griffin v. Louisville Trust Co., 511, 535
Griswold v. Heat Inc., 1323
Groves v. John Wunder Co., 1053, 1129
Gruner, Matter of, 1492
Guarantee Trust & Safe Deposit Co. v. Green Cove Springs & Melrose R.R., 1209
Guilbert v. Phillips Petroleum Co., 212
Gurfein v. Werbelovsky, 467

Hackley v. Headley (45 Mich. 569), 674, 678
Hackley v. Headley (50 Mich. 43), 678
Hadley v. Baxendale, 106, 1079, 1094, 1110, 1138, 1139, 1140, 1150, 1151, 1156, 1157, 1165
Haigh v. Brooks, 564
Hall v. Bean, 380
Hall v. Wright, 912, 916, 919, 921
Halsey v. Reed, 1354, 1355
Hamer v. Sidway (64 N.Y. Sup. Ct. (57 Hun.) 229), 490
Hamer v. Sidway (124 N.Y. 538), 483, 490
Hammond v. C.I.T. Financial Corp., 453
Handy v. Bliss, 988
Harper v. Baptist Medical Center-Princeton, 56
Harrington v. Taylor, 544
Harris v. Carter, 652
Harris v. Watson, 652
Harry Rubin & Sons, Inc. v. Consolidated Pipe Co. of America, Inc., 798
Hartford Mining Co. v. Cambria Mining Co., 851
Hartley v. Ponsonby, 652
Hartung v. Billmeier, 775
Harvey v. J.P. Morgan & Co. (166 Misc. 455), 775
Harvey v. J.P. Morgan & Co. (25 N.Y.S. 2d 636), 777
Hatten's Estate, In re, 537
Hawkes v. Saunders, 511
Hawkins v. Graham, 987
Hawkins v. McGee, 137, 1117
Hay v. Fortier, 383
Hayward v. Leonard, 1029
Hazlett v. First Federal Savings & Loan Assn., 287
Hebert v. Dewey, 1051
Hebrew University Assn. v. Nye, 491
Hedley Byrne & Co., Ltd. v. Heller & Partners, Ltd., 910
Heggblade-Marquleas-Tenneco, Inc. v. Sunshine Biscuit, Inc., 851
Helen Whiting, Inc. v. Trojan Textile Corp., 797
Hellenic Lines, Ltd. v. United States, 962

Henningsen v. Bloomfield Motors, Inc., 1243, 1255, 1257
Herbert v. Lankersheim, 550
Herman v. Connecticut Mutual Life Insurance Co., 1554
Hermitage Co. v. Levine, 955, 1300
Heron II, The (Kaufos v. Czarnikow, Ltd.), 109, 975, 1111, 1157, 1165
Hertzog v. Hertzog, 147
Hertzog v. Hertzog's Administrator, 152
Hetchler v. American Life Ins. Co., 302
Hewitt v. Hewitt, 121, 155, 162
Heyer v. Flaig, 1375, 1377, 1379
Heyer Products Co. v. United States (135 Ct. Cl. 63), 207
Heyer Products Co. v. United States (147 Ct. Cl. 256), 208, 209, 225
Hill v. Waxberg, 203
Hillas & Co. v. Arcos, Ltd., 180
Hirsch v. Hirsch, 510
H.K. Porter Co. v. N.L.R.B., 202
Hoare v. Rennie, 1001
Hochster v. De La Tour, 1269, 1270, 1279, 1287, 1288, 1289
Hoffman v. Red Owl Stores, Inc., 223, 224, 225
Hoffman v. S.V. Co., 788
Holbrook v. Pitt, 1405
Holman v. Johnson, 98
Holsomback v. Caldwell, 121
Holt v. United Security Life Ins. & Trust Co., 1177
Holtz v. Western Union Telegraph Co., 252
Home Building & Loan Assn. v. Blaisdell, 143
Homefinders v. Lawrence, 539
Homer v. Shaw, 1539, 1541, 1545
Hooks Smelting Co. v. Planters' Compress Co., 1149
Horne v. Midland Railway Co., 1149
Hotchkiss v. National City Bank of New York, 866
Household Fire & Carriage Accident Ins. Co. v. Grant, 364
Howard v. Daly, 1321
Hoyt v. Hoyt, 121
H.R. Moch Co., Inc. v. Rensselaer Water Co., 1156, 1386, 1391
Hubbard Broadcasting v. C.A. Loescher, 1322
Hudson v. Yonkers Fruit Co., Inc., 683, 685
Hughes v. Payne, 789, 792
Hughes v. Strusser, 95
Huhtala v. Travelers Ins. Co., 225
Humber v. Morton, 95
Hurley v. Eddingfield, 56, 167
Hurst v. Lake & Co., Inc., 849
Hyde v. The Dean of Windsor, 922

I. & I. Holding Corp. v. Gainsberg, 510
Imperator Realty Co., Inc. v. Tull, 801, 807
International Milling Co. v. Hochmeister, Inc., 848
Investment Trust, Ltd. v. Leighton's Investment Trust, Ltd., 954
Isbrandtsen Co., Inc. v. Local 1291 of International Longshoremen's Assn., 1380
Itek Corp. v. Chicago Aerial Industries, Inc. (248 A.2d 625), 236
Itek Corp. v. Chicago Aerial Industries, Inc. (274 A.2d 141), 238
Itoh, C., & Co., Inc. v. Jordan Intl. Co., 264

Jack, Sy, Realty Co. v. Pergament Syosset Corp., 364
Jackson v. New York Life Ins. Co., 354
Jackson v. Security Mutual Life Ins. Co., 679
Jackson v. Seymour, 96, 569
Jacobs v. J.C. Penney Co., 665
Jacobs & Youngs v. Kent, 975, 989, 1037, 1042, 1048, 1052, 1119, 1128, 1129, 1328
James Baird Co. v. Gimbel Bros., 323
Jameson v. Board of Education, 1119, 1317, 1323, 1324
Jefferson Parish Hosp. Dist. 2 v. Hyde, 61
Jenkins Towel Service, Inc. v. Fidelity-Philadelphia Trust Co., 186, 190
J.J. Gordon, Inc. v. Worcester Telegram Publishing Co., 66
John Deere Co. v. Babcock, 404
Johnson v. Boston & Maine R.R., 173
Jones v. Barkley, 980
Jones v. Parker, 1073
Jones v. Patavatton, 119
Jones v. Star Credit Corp., 607, 611
Jordan v. Dobbins, 320
J.R. Simplot Co. v. L. Yukon & Son Produce Co., 1005

Kahn v. Waldman, 768
Kaufman v. Miller, 478
Kaufman v. William Iselin & Co., 1526
Kaufos v. C. Czarnikow (The Heron II), 109, 975, 1111, *1157,* 1165
Kazunas v. Wright, 1356
Kearns v. Andre, 813
Keco Industries, Inc. v. United States, 209
Kehoe v. Rutherford, 1179, 1186
Keller v. Holderman, 129
Kelly Asphalt Block Co. v. Barber Asphalt Paving Co., 74
Kemble v. Farren, 1223, 1231, 1240
Kennedy v. Brown, 518

Kennedy v. Panama, etc. Mail Co., 891
Kerr S.S. Co., Inc. v. Radio Corp. of America, 882, *1152,* 1157, 1165, 1171
King v. Duluth, Massabe & Northern Ry., 663
King v. Whiteley, 1355
Kingston v. Preston, 979, 982, 983
Kirksey v. Kirksey, 473
Klar v. H. & M. Parcel Room, Inc., 1237, 1240
Klochner v. Green, 818
Knight, B. Hollie, Co., In re, 1458
Krell v. Codman, 705, 728
Krell v. Henry, 926, 930, 965
Kugler v. Romain, 611
Kukukundis Shipping Co., S/A v. Amtorg Trading Corp., 1210
Kurland v. United Pacific Insurance Co., 104
Kyle v. Kavanagh, 870

Laclede Gas Co. v. Amoco Oil Co., 1096
Laidlaw v. Organ, 89, 91, 93, 896
L. Albert & Son v. Armstrong Rubber Co., 969, 1055, 1128, *1197,* 1201
Lampet's Case, 1442
Lampleigh v. Brathwait, 518
Lampus, R.I., Co. v. Neville Cement Products Corp., 1151
Langel v. Betz, 1503, 1504, 1516, 1520, 1526
Langellier v. Schaefer, 247
Lantry v. Parks, 1029
Lawrence v. Anderson, 167, 757, 759
Lawrence v. Fox, 1332, *1333,* 1344, 1353, 1354, 1355, 1361, 1362, 1391, 1417, 1419, 1431, 1439, 1516
Lawrence v. Miller, 1054, 1057
Lawrence v. Oglesby, 547, 751
Lefkowitz v. Great Minneapolis Surplus Store, Inc., 183
Letch Gold Mines, Ltd. v. Texas Gulf Sulphur, 96
Levine v. Blumenthal, 665
Lewis v. Benedict Coal Corp., 1431, 1437, 1438, 1439
Lewis v. Browning, 353
Levy v. C. Young Construction Co., 95
Levy v. Tharrington, 1324
Liebreich v. State Bank & Trust Co., 665
Lima Locomotive & Machine Co. v. National Steel Castings Co., 427
Lingenfelder v. The Wainwright Brewing Co., 652, 655
Linn v. Employers Reinsurance Corp., 349
Liston v. S.S. Carpathian, 652
Littlejohn v. Shaw, 1004
Lloyd v. Murphy, 948, 954, 966

Local 1330, United Steel Workers of America v. United States, 63
Lochner v. New York, 13
Loeb v. Gendel, 807
Loranger Construction Corp. v. E.F. Hauserman Co., 331
Los Angeles Traction Co. v. Wilshire, 407
Louise Caroline Nursing Home, Inc. v. Dix Construction Co., 1324
Loveridge v. Cooper, 1550
L.S. Ayres & Co. v. Hicks, 56
Lucas v. Hamm, 1371, 1376, 1377, 1379, 1380
Lumley v. Wagner, 1075, 1086
Lusk-Harbison-Jones, Inc. v. Universal Credit Co., 288, 289
Lyons v. Grether, 56

Mabley & Carew Co., The v. Borden, 124
McCarthy v. Talley, 1225, 1231, 1236, 1237, 1239, 1240, 1242
McClary v. Michigan R.R., 173
McConnell's Estate, In re, 550
McCulloch v. Canadian Pacific Ry., 1427
McCulloch v. Eagle Insurance Co., 352
McCulloch v. Tapp, 770
McCurly Corp. v. United States, 209
McGee v. United States Fidelity Guaranty Co., 137
McGrath v. American Surety Co., 1370, 1371
McKenzie v. Harrison, 674
Mackie v. Dwyer, 770
McMullen Leavens Co. v. L.I. Van Buskirk Co., 1526
McRae v. Commonwealth Disposals Commission, 898, 909, 910
McTernan v. Le Tendre, 352
Madison Industrial Corp. v. Elisberg, 1540, 1541
Manhattan Co. v. Goldberg, 1239
Manhattan Sav. Inst. v. Gottfried Baking Co., 1116
Marks v. Gates, 571
Marsh v. Lott, 718
Marshall v. Broadhurst, 922
Martin v. Campanaro, 178
Martinez v. Socoma Companies, Inc., 1391, 1403, 1404
Marvin v. Marvin (18 Cal. 3d 660), 162
Marvin v. Marvin (122 Cal. App. 3d 871), 163
Massee v. Gibbs, 215
Masterson v. Sine, 842
Matlack Coal & Iron Corp. v. New York Quebracho Extract Co., 684
Maughs v. Porter, 319
Maurice O'Meara Co. v. National Park Bank of New York, 1014, 1019

Medberry v. Olcovich, 532, 544, 550
Megines v. McChesney, 535
Mellen v. Whipple, 1340, 1353, 1354
Meltzer v. Koenigsberg, 777
Mendel v. Mountain State Telephone & Telegraph Co., 1157
Mercy Medical Center of Oshkosh, Inc. v. Winnebago County, 58
Mersey Co. v. Naylor, 1001
Metropolitan Life Insurance Co. v. Richter, 684
Meyers v. Selznick Co., 831
Michigan Central R.R. v. State, 175
Miller v. Commissioner of Internal Revenue, 1496
Miller v. Miller, 120
Miller v. Stanich, 875, 883
Miller v. Walter, 404
Mills v. Wyman, 523
Millsap v. National Funding Corp., 294
Miron v. Yonkers Raceway, Inc., 1007, 1014
Missouri Furnace Co. v. Cochran, 1301, 1306, 1308
Mitchell v. C.C. Sanitation Co., 679
Mitchell v. Henry, 851
Mitchell v. Lath, 837
Mitchell v. W.T. Grant, 602
Mitsubishi Goshi Kaisha v. J. Aron, 1003
Moch, H.R., Co., Inc. v. Rensselaer Water Co., 1156, 1386, 1391
Monarcho v. Lo Greco, 817, 818
Monsanto Co. v. Spray-Rite Service Co., 62
Montuori v. Bailen, 777, 779
Morrison v. Tholke, 368
Morton v. Lamb, 983
Moulton v. Kershaw, 190
Mount Pleasant Stable Co. v. Steinberg, 1316, 1323
Mount Sinai Hospital, Inc. v. Jordan, 510
Muir v. Kane, 523, 593
Muller v. Pondir, 1430, 1449, 1553
Murarka v. Bachrack Bros., Inc., 1152
Murphy, Thompson & Co. v. Reed, 713

Nash v. Royster, 57
Nason v. Holt, 1278
Nassau Supply Company, Inc. v. Ice Service Co., 450
Nassoiy v. Tomlinson, 684
National Bank of Cleburne v. M.M. Potman Roller Mill, 427
National Bank v. Grand Lodge, 1343, 1419
National Historic Shrines Foundation v. Dali, 781
National Presto Industries, Inc. v. United States, 944

National Union Fire Insurance Co. v. Joseph Erlich, 241

Neer v. Lang, 252

Neri v. Retail Marine Corp., 1165, 1171

New England Concrete Construction Co. v. Shepard & Morse Lumber Co., 947

New Era Homes Corp. v. Forster, 1179

New York Casualty Co. v. Sinclair Refining Co., 142

New York, City of, v. Bedford Bar & Grill, Inc., In re, 1492, 1496, 1558

New York Life Insurance Co. v. Viglas, 1298

Nichols v. Raynbred, 913, 976, 978

NMC Enterprises, Inc. v. Columbia Broadcasting System, 1020

Noble v. Williams, 76, 144, 145, 171

Nolan v. Whitney, 1051

Norrington v. Wright, 990, 1001, 1002

Northern Delaware Industrial Development Corp. v. E.W. Bliss Co., 1093

Noyes v. Brown, 978

Nute v. Hamilton Mutual Insurance Co., 1203

Oakland-Alameda County Builders' Exchange v. F.P. Lathrop Constr. Co., 340

Obde v. Schlemeyer, 95

O'Callaghan v. Waller & Beckwith Realty Co., 1266, 1267

Ocean Tramp Tankers Corp. v. V/O Sovfracht (The Eugenia), 926

Odorizzi v. Bloomfield School District, 662

Ohio Co. v. Rosmeier, 87

Oloffson v. Coomer, 1307, 1308

O'Meara, Maurice, Co. v. National Park Bank of New York, 1014, 1019

Osborn v. Boeing Airplane Company, 123

Pacific Alaska Contractors, Inc. v. United States, 357

Padgham v. Wilson Music Co., 770

Pakas v. Hollingshead, 1289, 1300

Palace Dry Cleaning Co. v. Cole, 1239

Palo Alto Town & Country Village, Inc. v. BBTC Co., 357

Panhandle Agri-Service, Inc. v. Becker, 1134, 1137

Paradine v. Jane, 911, 913, 919, 978, 982

Paramount Famous Players Corp. v. United States, 260

Parev Products v. Rokeach, 145

Patterson v. Chapman, 752

Patterson v. Walker-Thomas Furniture, 603, 607

Paul v. Rosen, 463

Peevyhouse v. Garland Coal & Mining Co., 1053, 1119, 1127, 1128, 1129, 1328

Pennsylvania Co. v. Wilmington Trust Co., 182

Perreault v. Hall, 512, 532

Petterson v. Pattberg, 410, 689

Phelan v. Carey, 795

Phelps v. Herro, 1270, 1291, 1299, 1300, 1301

Philadelphia v. Tripple, 1182, 1186

Pillans & Rose v. Van Mierop & Hopkins, 744

Plowman v. Indian Refining Co., 314

Poel v. Brunswick-Balk-Collender Co., 259

Pordage v. Cole, 976, 978, 982, 1001

Porter, H.K., Co. v. N.L.R.B., 202

Portuguese-American Bank of San Francisco v. Welles, 1476

Postal Telegraph-Cable Co. v. Willis, 365

Poughkeepsie Buying Service, Inc. v. Poughkeepsie Newspapers, Inc., 64

Poussard v. Spiers & Pond, 919

Prescott v. Jones, 238

Price v. Easton, 1341

Priebe & Sons v. United States, 1236, 1237, 1240

Prince v. Miller Brewing Co., 211

Procter & Gamble Distributing Co. v. Lawrence American Field Warehousing Corp., 1057

Pym v. Campbell, 831, 836, 975

Raedeke v. Gibraltar Savings & Loan Assn., 298

Raffles v. Wichelhaus, 869, 870, 872, 873, 874, 875, 892, 897, 919, 988

Rankin v. New York, New Haven & Hartford R.R., 680

Rann v. Hughes, 750

Rasmussen v. New York Life Insurance Co., 851

Ratner v. Chemical Bank N.Y. Trust Co., 625

Real Estate Co. of Pittsburgh v. Rudolph, 716, 718

Reardon Smith Line Ltd. v. Hansen-Tangen, 1003

Refining Associates, Inc. v. United States, 326

Reinert v. Lawson, 463

Rennie & Laughlin, Inc. v. Chrysler Corp., 667

Republic Natl. Life Insurance Co. v. Merkley, 354

Rhode Island Tool Co. v. United States, 352, 354, 357, 368

Richard v. Bartlett, 558

Richards v. Richards, 474

Ricketts v. Pennsylvania R.R., 179, 681, 867, 868, 883, 886
Ricketts v. Scothorn, 491
R.I. Lampus Co. v. Neville Cement Products Corp., 1151
Robert F. Simmons & Associates v. United States, 208
Robert Gordon, Inc. v. Ingersoll-Rand, 340
Roberts-Horsfield v. Gedicks (94 N.J. Eq. 82), 478
Roberts-Horsfield v. Gedicks (96 N.J. Eq. 384), 480
Robinson v. Bland, 1109, 1138
Rockingham County v. Luten Bridge Co., 1314, 1315
Rockmore v. Lehman, 1458, 1483, 1484, 1485, 1492, 1499, 1553, 1556, 1558
Roehm v. Horst, 1270, 1279, 1289, 1300
Rose v. Spa Realty Assn., 673
Rose & Frank Co. v. J.R. Crompton & Bros., 120
Roto-Lith, Ltd. v. F.P. Bartlett & Co., 260, 264
Rouse v. United States, 1428, 1429, 1430, 1431, 1437, 1438, 1439
Rubin, Harry, & Sons, Inc. v. Consolidated Pipe Co. of America, Inc., 798
Rugg v. Minett, 923, 925
Ryan v. Schott, 215

Sagamore Corp. v. Willcutt, 1300
Salinen v. Frankson, 363
Salsbury v. Northwestern Bell Tel. Co., 509
S & E Contractors v. United States, 990
San Rocco v. Clyde Shipbuilding & Engineering Co., 932
Santor v. A. & M. Karagheusian, 1254, 1256
Savile v. Savile, 914
Scaduto v. Orlando, 1187
Sceva v. True, 141
Schlegel Manufacturing Co. v. Cooper's Glue Factory (189 A.D. 843), 450
Schlegel Manufacturing Co. v. Cooper's Glue Factory (231 N.Y. 459), 446
Schmoll Fils & Co. v. Wheeler, 788
Schneider v. Ferrigno, 1355
Schnell v. Nell, 710, 737
Schoenberg v. Rose, 167
Schoenkerman's Estate, In re, 535
School Trustees of Trenton v. Bennett, 99, 914, 936, 943, 947
Schwartz v. Greenberg, 215
Schwartzreich v. Bauman-Basch, Inc., 79, 657, 663
Seaver v. Ransom, 1356, 1361
Seavey v. Drake, 476, 794

Security Stove & Mfg. Co. v. American Ry. Express Co., 1188, 1197
Sedmak v. Charlie's Chevrolet, 797
Seeley v. White Motor Co., 1254, 1379
Setser v. Commonwealth, Inc., 417
Shaheen v. Knight, 137
Sharrington v. Strotten, 500
Shaw v. Shaw, 154
Sheldon v. Thornberg, 152
Shell v. Schmidt, 1403, 1404
Shepard v. Carpenter, 180
Sherwood v. Walker, 88, 887
Shiro v. Drew, 1458, 1485, 1545, 1557
Sidermar Case. *See* Societe Franco Tunisienne D'Armement v. Sidermar S.P.A. (The Messalia)
Siegel v. Spear & Co., 285
Sillman v. Twentieth Century-Fox Film Corp., 1475, 1477
Simkins v. Pays, 119
Simmons, Robert F., & Associates v. United States, 208
Simplot, J.R., Co. v. L. Yukon & Son Produce Co., 1005
Simpson v. Crippen, 1001
Sir Anthony Sturlyn v. Albany, 706, 707
Sistrom v. Anderson, 84
Skinner v. Tober Foreign Motors, Inc., 665
Slade's Case, 32, 754
Smith v. Brady, 1029, 1042, 1048, 1051, 1052, 1055
Smith v. Hughes, 91
Smith v. Zimbalist, 893
Societe Franco Tunisienne D'Armement v. Sidermar S.P.A. (The Messalia), 960
Socony-Vacuum Oil Co., Inc. v. Continental Casualty Co., 1364, 1370
Somers v. Avant, 1355
Sommers v. Putnam Board of Education, 77, 168, 173
Southern California Acoustics Co. v. C.V. Holder, Inc., 335
Southern Surety Co. v. MacMillan Co., 986
Southwest Engineering Co. v. Martin Tractor Co., 201
Speelman v. Pascal, 1458, 1496, 1545
Spence v. Ham, 1050, 1052
Spiegel v. Metropolitan Life Ins. Co., 288
Sponge Divers' Assn., Inc. v. Smith, Kline & French Co., 1528, 1529
Spooner v. Reserve Life Insurance Co., 127
Stack's Estate, In re, 509
Staklinski v. Pyramid Electric, 1079, 1092
Standard Oil Company of California v. United States, 419, 647
Standard Oil Company v. United States, 61

Stark v. Parker, 1029
State Factors Corp. v. Sales Factors
    Corp., 1541, 1552, 1553, 1557
Stathos v. Murphy, 1492
Steinmeyer v. Schroeppel, 881
Stees v. Leonard, 104, 943, 947
Sternaman v. Metropolitan Life Ins. Co.,
    96
Stilk v. Myrick, 651
Stipcich v. Metropolitan Life Insurance
    Co., 96
Stokes v. Moore, 1079, 1084, 1085, 1086,
    1093
Stonsz v. Equitable Life Assur. Soc., 250
Strong v. Sheffield, 381
Sturlyn, Sir Anthony v. Albany, 706, 707
Suchan v. Rutherford, 1073
Sullivan v. O'Connor, 131
Sun Printing & Publishing Assn., The v.
    Remington Paper & Power Co., Inc.,
    216
Superior Brassiere Co. v. Zimetbaum,
    1541, 1553
Sweney Gasoline & Oil Co. v. Toledo,
    Peoria & Western R.R., 1268
Swift v. Tyson, 751
Swindell & Co. v. First National Bank,
    424
Swinton v. Whitinsville Savings Bank, 93
Sy Jack Realty Co. v. Pergament Syosset
    Corp., 364
Sylvan Crest Sand & Gravel Co. v. United
    States, 457
Sztejn v. Schroder Banking Corp., 1019

Taft v. Hyatt, 377
Taylor v. Barton-Child Co., 1498
Taylor v. Caldwell, 892, 920, 925, 943,
    947, 960, 966
Taylor v. Lee, 761, 763
Thomas v. Caldwell, 87
Thomas v. Thomas, 707, 710
Thomason v. Besher, 744
Thompson v. Libby, 827
Thorne v. Deas, 288
Threlkeld v. Inglett, 320
Times-Picayune Publishing Co. v. United
    States, 66
Tolhurst v. Associated Portland Cement
    Manufacturers Ltd., 1516, 1519, 1520
Tooley & Preston's Case, 1108
Transatlantic Case, 962
Transbel Investment Co. v. Venetos, 737
Travelers Indemnity Co. v. Holman, 303
Troppi v. Scarf, 141
Trotter v. Hughes, 1355
Tsakiroglou & Co. Lt. v. Noblee Thorl
    G.m.b.H., 960
Tweddle v. Atkinson, 1342

Ultramares Corp. v. Touche, Niven &
    Co., 910, 1156, 1377, 1379
Underwood Typewriter Co. v. Century
    Realty Co., 294
Unico v. Owen, 593, 1536
United Protective Workers of America v.
    Ford Motor Co., 1322
United States (for use of Susi Contracting
    Co.) v. Zara Contracting Co., 1186
United States v. Behan, 1174, 1177, 1178,
    1179
United States v. Bethlehem Steel Corp.,
    576
United States v. Braunstein, 253
United States v. Carlo Bianchi & Co., 990
United States v. Colgate & Co., 59
United States v. Parke, Davis & Co., 61
United States v. Wunderlich, 989
Upton-On-Severn Rural District Council
    v. Powell, 171
Utah International Inc. v. Colorado-Ute
    Electric Assn., Inc., 437

Vandermark v. Ford Motor Co., 1254
Van Iderstine Co., Inc. v. Barnet Leather
    Co., Inc., 1051
Vargas, Estate of, 155
Vickery v. Ritchie (202 Mass. 247), 173,
    883
Vickery v. Ritchie (207 Mass. 318), 175
Victoria Laundry v. Newman Industries,
    109, 1164, 1165
Vines v. Orchard Hills, 1058
Visintine & Co. v. New York, Chicago &
    St. Louis R.R., 1384
Vrooman v. Turner, 1341, 1346, 1354,
    1355, 1356, 1361, 1391, 1429, 1503

Wall v. World Pub. Co., 186
Walton v. Waterhouse, 913, 921
Ward v. Goodrich, 385
Warder v. Lee Elevator, Inc. v. Britten,
    819
Warren v. Lynch, 725
Warren v. Whitney, 518
Watkins v. Paul, 1073
Watkins & Son v. Carrig, 662
Watteau v. Fenwick, 74
Webb v. McGowin (27 Ala. App. 82), 539,
    777
Webb v. McGowin (232 Ala. 374), 543, 777
Webbe v. Western Union Telegraph Co.,
    252
Wentworth v. Cock, 922
Western Alfalfa Milling Co. v.
    Worthington, 948
Western Union Telegraph Co. v. Cowin &
    Co., 252

Westesen v. Olathe State Bank (71 Colo. 102), 422

Westesen v. Olathe State Bank (75 Colo. 340), 424

Westesen v. Olathe State Bank (78 Colo. 217), 424

Wheat v. Morse, 720

Wheeler v. White, 225

Wheelock v. Clark, 354

White v. Corlies, 405

White & Carter (Councils) Ltd. v. McGregor, 1315

Whiting, Helen, Inc. v. Trojan Textile Corp., 797

Whitney v. Canadian Bank of Commerce, 1451

Whitney v. Stearns, 707

Wilhelm Lubricating Co. v. Battrud, 196

Wilkinson v. Coverdale, 288

Williams v. Favret, 326

Williams v. Ingersoll, 1484, 1492

Williams v. Lloyd, 923

Williams v. Walker-Thomas Furniture Co. (198 A.2d 914), 600

Williams v. Walker-Thomas Furniture Co. (350 F.2d 445), 596, 601, 602, 603, 611, 623

Wilmington Trust Co. v. Coulter, 183

Witschard v. A. Brody & Sons, Inc., 763, 765

Wood v. Boynton, 84, 886, 891, 892, 897

Wood v. Lucy, Lady Duff-Gordon, 223, 451

Woodall v. Prevatt, 744

Woodar Investment Development Ltd. v. Wimpey Construction U.K. Ltd., 1343

Woodburn v. Northwestern Bell Telephone Co., 276

Woodbury v. United States Casualty, 678

Woodhouse A.C. Israel Cocoa Ltd., S.A. v. Nigerian Produce Marketing Co., Ltd., 664

Wright v. Schutt, 417

Wyse, In re(Pioneer-Cafeteria Feeds, Ltd. v. Mack), 1464, 1465

Young & Ashburnham's Case, 146, 183

Young Men's Christian Assn. v. Estill, 491

Zell v. American Seating Co., 831, 852

Zigas v. Superior Court of California, 1403, 1404

INDEX

Absolute liability
  contract and, 99
  warranty liability as, 96
Acceptance
  after death of offeror, 320-323
  by performance, 391
  crossing offers, 257. *See also*
      Bargain
  mailbox rule, 348-350
  matching acceptance rule, 259-272
  silence as, 238-247
  variation of terms, 247-257
  withdrawal after dispatch, 354-370
Act of God, 101
Adhesion, contracts of
  battle of the forms, 257-278
  boiler-plate, 272
  generally, 2, 272
  Llewellyn solution for, 272-273
  unconscionability and, 275
Agency
  contract and, 35
Anticipatory repudiation, 1061-1328. *See*
      also Remedies
Antitrust laws, 11-13, 58-62
  common law, 60
  per se and rule of reason yardsticks, 61
  plant shutdowns and, 63
  refusal to deal and, 62
  resale price maintenance and, 62
Arm's length transactions, 201
Assent. *See* Bargain
Assignment, 1441-1558
  anti-assignment clauses, 1466-1475
  assignment of rights vs. delegation of
      duties, 1500-1558
    assignee of vendee in land contract,
      whether liable in vendor's specific
      performance action, 1500-1504
    delivery of ice without contract, 1504-
      1507
    duties under executory contract,
      when assignable (or delegable),
      1511-1519
    right to select contractee, 1504-1507
  defenses, modifications, and rescission,
      1520-1547
    can obligor recover from assignee,
      1520-1527

    clauses purporting to make obligor's
      defenses against assignor unavail-
      able against assignee, effect of,
      1529-1533
    consumer credit contracts, FTC rule
      as to, 1537-1538
    consumer goods litigation and, 1534-
      1539
    modification or rescission of underly-
      ing contract by assignor and
      obligor without assignee's con-
      sent, 1538-1547
  intangible claims and their transferabil-
      ity, 1444-1478
    anti-assignment clauses, 1466-1475
    assignable claims and negotiable
      claims, 1450
    assignee, status of, compared with
      holder in due course, 1444-1450
    assignment distinguished from prom-
      ise to pay out of a particular
      fund, 1452-1456
    assignment of accounts, 1457-1458
    check as an assignment, 1451-1452
    distinguished from "negotiation,"
      1444-1450
    gifts, unenforceable aspects of, 1451
    partial assignment clauses, 1477
    subordination agreements and assign-
      ments, 1458-1466
    voidable preference in bankruptcy,
      1456-1458
  introductory note, 1441-1443
    choses in action, assignability of,
      1441
    Gilmore on, 1441-1443
    suit by assignee in name of assignor,
      1443
  lease, 294-299
  partial assignment clauses, 1477
  present assignability of future claims,
      1477-1500
    money to be earned under existing
      contract, 1477-1485
    pre-Code Mass. rule, 1498-1499
    proceeds of liquor license, 1485-1492
    profits to be earned on musical com-
      edy not yet produced, 1492-1496
  priorities, 1547-1558

Assignment—(*continued*)
end of the common law priority
rules, 1554-1556
accounts receivable statutes, 1554-
1556
Gilmore on, 1554-1556
factoring arrangements, 1552-1553
good faith purchaser test, 1556
lien creditor test, 1556
priorities between successive assignees
common law rules, 1547-1554
New York Rule, 1553
priorities under Article 9 of UCC,
1556-1558
Restatement of Contracts
§167, 1528
Restatement of Contracts Second
§336(3), 1528
§338(2), 1547
§342, 1553
Uniform Commercial Code
Art. 9 and priorities, 1556-1558
§206(1), 1534
§318(1), 1528
§318(2), 1546, 1547
Assumpsit, action of, 28-35
and covenant, 30-32
and debt, 32-34
Slade's Case, 32-34
elaboration of: the common counts, 34-
35
indebitatus assumpsit, 34
special assumpsit, 34

Bankruptcy
debt discharged in bankruptcy, promise
to pay, 517
voidable preference, assignment, 1456-
1458
Bargain, 111-551
assent, 238-257
completion of agreement necessary,
247-250
delay in acceptance or rejection, 244-
247
promissory estoppel and estoppel in
pais, 241
renewal policy and, 241-242
Restatement of Contracts Second
§37, 250
§69, 247
silence and, 238
subscriptions received, conditions
making for contract, 242-243
telegram, use of in arranging terms,
250-257
bargain theory of contract and the
reliance principle, 279-314
assignment of lease, 294-299

benefit-detriment development, 280
consideration doctrine, 279 et seq.
defenders of doctrine, 283
movement to abolish, 282
employment contract, 291-294
English Law Revision Commission,
Sixth Interim Report, 282-283
exchange, bargain, and reciprocity,
279
gift promise and, 284
half-completed bargain, 284
inconsistent terms in mortgage, 299-
303
insurance contracts, 285-291, 625-634
equitable estoppel or estoppel in
pais in, 302-303
gratuitous promise to obtain policy, 285-289
misfeasance and nonfeasance, 288
promissory estoppel and, 282, 308-314
Statute of Frauds and, 303-308
reliance factor, 279
remedies under, 284
Restatement of Contracts
§75, 312
Restatement of Contracts Second
§90, 281, 287, 305
unconscionability and, 284
contract as a promissory transaction,
111-141
beauty, promise to enhance, 131-137
benefit and reliance theory of contracts, 115
cohabitation agreements, 121
collective bargaining agreements, 120
continental influence, 113-114
contraceptives and, 141
"contract" defined, 111
contract to sterilize, 137
general theory development, 113-114
gentlemen's agreement, 119
husband and wife transactions, 116-
119, 121
indefiniteness of contract, 121-123,
129-131
employee at will, 124
fairness and liberality doctrine, 121-
124
intent to contract and, 119-129
marriage contracts, 121
physician
promise to enhance beauty of
patient by plastic surgery, 131-137
promise to make patient sterile,
137-141
promise
debate over importance of, 115
role of, 112
promise-based liability
theory questioned, 115

Restatement of Contracts Second
§1, 111
§2, 111-112, 131
§3, 112
§17, 112
§18, 112
§21, 119, 120
§22, 112
§23, 113
§24, 113
Uniform Commercial Code
§1-201, 113
will theory and, 114-115
decline of, 115
correspondence
bids, withdrawal of, 354-357
consideration and the contract by,
348-370
delivery, 348
hypothetical problems, 349
irrevocable offer, 363
Langdell on, 364
life insurance policies, 353
Llewellyn on, 364, 365
mailbox rule, 349-353, 357
methods of making contract binding,
348
moment offeror informed of acceptance, 348
mutual letters, contract made by, 353
option, effective on mailing, 357-364
posting of acceptance, 348
relation back to moment acceptance
was dispatched, 348
Restatement of Contracts Second
§56
§63, Comment a, 357
§63, Comment b, 364
§63, Comment f, 357, 360, 363
§64, 353
telegraph company
liability for delay in delivery, 365-
368
time limits in offer and, 368-370
course of dealing
Uniform Commercial Code
§1-201(23), 467
§1-208, 467
§2-309, 460
§2-609, 467
§2-702, 467
Uniform Sales Act
§54,1(c), 467
§76(3), 467
Worth Street Rules, 467
express contracts. See subhead tripartite
distinction of contracts
fairness of the bargain and equality,
553-703. See also Fairness of the
bargain

firm offers, 315-348
agreement or offer to sell property,
316-320
bids
bid depositories, 340
clerical error and, 341-348
estimate or offer, 331-335
mistake and, 323-326
subcontractor and, 326-331
construction industry and, 326, 341
English Law Revision Commission,
320
listed subcontractors and, 335-341
naked offer and, 315
postscripts and, 319
promissory liability, 320
reliance on an offer and liability, 315
Restatement of Contracts
§90, 315, 337
§87(1), 315
revocation by death, 320-323
subcontractors, 341
Uniform Commercial Code
§2-205, 315
writing, in, 315, 319
good faith, duty to bargain in, 201-238
arm's length, dealing at, 201
bad faith, 225
bidding
generally, 457-460
wanton disregard of bid, 207-208
condition precedent, 463-464
contract to bargain, 203
discretion factor, 451
franchises, promises made with regard
to, 209-212
imperfection in a contract, 216-223
letter of intent, 236-238
payment for expenses incurred,
212-216
NLRB and, 202
promissory estoppel and, 223-225
Restatement of Contracts Second
§77, 470
§90, 212
§205, 202
§225, Illus. 8, 464
specific performance as an element
of, 226-236
Uniform Commercial Code
§1-203, 202
gratuitous noncommercial promise, 470-
510
abstinence, promise based on, 483-490
scholarship, 490
assurances of assistance, 473-476
charitable contribution in memory of
loved one, 501-510
consideration and, 472
executed gifts and gift promises, 472

Bargain—(*continued*)
  gifts, 470 et seq.
  hypotheticals, 490
  improvements on land and, 476-478
  intrafamilial gift promises, 509
  land, gift of, 478-480
  Llewellyn on, 482
  marriage considerations, 494-501
  promise to pay for trip to Europe,
      forseeable substantial reliance
      on, 480-482
  promise to quit work, 491-494
  reluctance to enforce, 471
  Restatement of Contracts Second
      §90, 472, 475, 480, 490
      §90(2), 501
  tramp hypothetical, 472-473
  Williston on, 472-473
implied contracts. *See subhead* tripartite
    distinction of contracts
indefinite contracts, 179-201
  advertisement
    as offer, 190-193
    binding offer originating in, 183-186
  bid as invitation or firm offer, 186-190
  business honor concept, 182
  innocent misrepresentations, 196-201
  meeting of minds and, 180-181
  mutual manifestation of assent, 180-
    181
  quotation of prices and, 193-196
  Restatement of Contracts Second
      §22, 180, 181
      §23, 180
      §24, 180
      §26, 180
      §33, 180, 181, 182
      §34, 181, 182
      §50, 180
      §202, 181
      §204, 181, 182
      §205, 181
      §221, 181
      §362, 181
  Uniform Commercial Code
      §1-201, 181
      §1-205, 181
      §2-204, 181, 182, 183
      §2-207, 181
      §2-208, 181
      §2-305, 181, 182
"instinct with an obligation," 450-470
moral consideration, 510-551
  automobile accident, agreement of
      driver to pay hospital bills, 544-
      547
  brokerage agreement, 537-539
  California Civil Code, 550
  charity payment or instalment, 512-
    517

child support agreement as to illegiti-
    mate child, 527-532
debt of another, promise to pay, 523-
    526
debts discharged in bankruptcy, 517-
    518
Georgia Code Annotated, 550
historical basis, 510 et seq.
inferring consideration, 511
marriage, agreement to refrain from,
    532-535
New York General Obligations Law,
    549-550
pardon, to obtain a, 518
Restatement of Contracts Second
    §86, 511, 512, 527, 537, 551
Restatement of Restitution
    §116, 526
saving of life, agreement based on,
    539-544
services rendered to decedent, 535-
    537
statutes of limitations, 517
third persons, promise made to en-
    rich, 547-549
quasi contract. *See subhead* tripartite
    distinction of contracts
requirement contracts and mutuality,
    418-450
  blanket orders, 420-422
  contract over a period of time, 427-
    450
  lines of credit and, 426-427
  maximum and minimum contracts,
    419
  output contracts, 419
  promise to loan money, 422-426
  Uniform Commercial Code
      §1-201(19), 434
      §2-103, 434
      §2-205, 422
      §2-208, 435
      §2-306(1), 433
      §2-326, 418
standard form contracts, 257-278
  adhesion, contracts of, 272-278
  battle of the forms and, 257-278
  boiler-plate and, 272
  Llewellyn solution for, 272-273
  presumptively unenforceable, argu-
      ment as to being, 275
  telephone directories, failure to list
      physician, 276-278
  unconscionability and, 275
  classical contract theory, battle of
      forms and, 258 et seq.
  consumer transactions and, 274
  fair and acceptable types of, 259
  freedom of contract and, 257
  insurance policies and, 258

irrational factor and, 258
last shot doctrine, 264
Restatement of Contracts Second
    §211, 272 et seq.
standardized mass contract, 257-
    258
take-it-or-leave-it nature of, 258
Uniform Commercial Code
    §1-201(10), 260
    §1-205, 260
    §2-204, 260
    §2-206, 260
    §2-207, 262, 264, 265, 268-270
    §2-209, 260
    §2-314, 268
    §2-315, 268
    §2-316, 260
    §2-714, 268, 271
    §2-715, 271, 272
warranties
    limitations as to in contract, 260-
        272
Worth Street Rules, 259
tripartite distinction of contracts, 141-
    179
benefit, effect of receiving, 145-146
Blackstone and the reason and justice
    position, 149
breach of contract and restitution,
    145
express contracts, 141
fire, obligation of home owner to
    volunteer brigade, 171-173
husband and wife
    action for compensation by wife,
        152-155
    cohabitation, 155-163
        critical legal studies view, 163
    marriage not consummated, 155-
        163
implied contracts, 141-179
implied-in-fact, 141
implied-in-law, 141
    officious intermeddlers, 144
indefinite contracts, 179-201. See
    subhead indefinite contracts
innocent mistake in amount of con-
    tract by both parties, 173-175
innocent mistake in delivery of coal,
    175-179
interpretation factor, 143
parent's right to collect from school
    board for transportation expenses
    not supplied by school, 168-171
physician's right to recover when
    summoned to scene of accident,
    163-168
Restatement of Restitution
    §107, 145
    §117, 173

Restatement of Contracts Second
    §202, 144
    §203, 144
    §214, 144
    §§219-223, 144
restitution and damages, difference
    between, 146
services rendered by son to father,
    147-152
    dead man's statute and, 152
Uniform Commercial Code
    §1-205, 144
    §2-202, 144
    statutory framework provided by,
        143
unilateral vs. bilateral contracts, 370-418
advertisement for cure, 373-377
consideration factor, 381, 382
contract to make a will, 385-391
countermand and, 405-407
English Law Revision Commission,
    370-371
forbearance to sue and, 383-385
great dichotomy of, 370 et seq.
Llewellyn on, 371-372
mutual assent, Whittier on, 410-411
performance vs. promise to perform,
    409
real estate brokerage agreements, 411-
    417
Restatement of Contracts
    §12, 372
    §31, 371, 372
    §45, 371, 409-410
    §56, 371, 404
    §63, 371, 400
    §90, 409
Restatement of Contracts Second
    §2, 382
    §32, 373, 391
    §54, 400
    §62, 400
    §75, 385
Restatement of Security
    §86, 404
reward, right to, 377-381
shipment, effect of, 391-400
time as a factor, 407-409
Uniform Commercial Code
    §2-206, 372, 400
    §2-206(1), 391
    §2-206, Comment 2, 407
    §3-303(b), 383
    §3-408, 383
Benefits conferred without contract, 41-
    43, 76
Bids
    bid depositories, 340
    clerical error and, 341-348
    estimate or offer, 331-335

Bids—(*continued*)
  instinct with an obligation, 450-470
  invitation or firm offer, 186-190
  mistake and, 323-326
  subcontractor and, 326-331
  wanton disregard of bid, 207-208
  withdrawal of, 354-357
Bilateral contract
  consideration in, 79-84
  evolution of, 28 et seq.
Blackstone, Sir William
  contribution to law of contract, 42-46
  express and implied contracts, on, 44-45
  obligations, 45
Bonds, exchange of, and debt, 28
Breach of contract, rule for damages, 106-110
Brokerage contracts
  exclusive agency arrangement, 451-453
  exclusive right to sell, 453-456

Canon law, consideration in, 30
Caveat emptor, 7, 9, 16, 558
Chancery, protection of contractual promise in, 27
Charitable contributions, promise and, 501-510
Choses in action, assignment of, 1441
Classical law of contract, 47-48
Codifications, 50-53
Collective bargaining, 16, 121
Common calling, 26
Common counts, 33, 34
Common law, antitrust laws and, 11-13
Competition, freedom of, and freedom of contract, 7
Compulsory contracts, 2, 10 et seq.
Concealment, 54-59
Conditions, 973-1059
  basic themes, 976-990
    17th and 18th century cases, 976-981
  condition and independent covenant, distinction between, 979-981
  covenants and conditions, 975
  express conditions, 985-987
  forfeiture, 1021-1059
    architect's certificate requirement, 1051
    breach of condition, for, 1021-1059
    breach of contract to work a full year, effect of, 1021-1029
    construction contracts, failure to comply with specifications, 1029-1048
    divisible contracts, 1039
    impossibility of delivery to another country because of law, 1055-1057

    partial performance and conditions, 1038-1039
    substantial performance cases, 1050-1051
      defaulter not an outlaw, 1058
    unitary approach, 1029
    use of different brand pipe, 1042-1050
    waiver of delivery stipulations, 1038-1039
  government contracts and the "disputes" clause, 989-990
  historical development, 982-990
    concurrent conditions, 983
    condition precedent and condition subsequent, distinguished, 983-985
    express and implied conditions, 985-987
      insurance companies and, 986
    personal satisfaction, conditions of, 987-989
  installment land contracts, predecessor to, in English law, 978
  introductory note, 973-976
  letter of credit, uses for, 1020
  liquor, refraining from, 1039
  perfect tender rule, 1002-1004
    Uniform Commercial Code and, 1005-1007
  precedent, 983-985
  Restatement of Contracts
    §346, 1053
    §357, 1057-1058
  Restatement of Contracts Second
    §348(2), 1053-1054
    §388, 1058
  risk, not fault, is governing factor, 973-974
  sale of goods, 990-1021
    collapse of market price and, 990-1002
    implication of conditions, a case study in, 990-1021
    letters of credit, perfect tender and, 1014-1019
    monthly shipping arrangement, 990-1002
    perfect tender in contracts for, 990 et seq.
    reasonable inspection, sale of horse and, 1007-1014
  subjective vs. objective approach, 988
  subsequent, 983-985
  Uniform Commercial Code
    §5-114(1), 1019
    Art. 2, 1005-1007
    perfect tender rule, 1005-1007
Consideration
  adequacy of, 84-87
  classical view of, 55 et seq.
  doctrine of, 279 et seq.

early development, 37-38
freedom of contract, 7, 37, 77
meritorious consideration, 710-713
moral consideration, 510-551
nominal consideration, 707
peppercorn theory of, 706-723
preexisting duty to the promisor, 77, 79
public policy, 76-78, 97
Construction contracts and forfeiture,
    1029-1048
Consumer protection, 583-625
add-on clauses, 596-603
class actions, 625
classical theory an ideal, 583-584
closed-end credit sales, 594
complex nature of contracts today, 584
Consumer Credit Protection Act, 594
consumer in modern world, 584
Consumer Warranty Act, 595
credit card usage in financing, 593, 594
disclosure statutes, effectiveness ques-
    tioned, 595
Equal Credit Opportunity Act, 603, 607
Fair Debt Collection Practices Act, 602
federal agencies protecting consumer,
    623-625
FTC regulations, 592-593
home improvement contract, 589-592
    financing factor, 589-592
home solicitation sales, 611
house to house sale of educational
    materials, 611-623
laesio enormis doctrine, 607
legislation, growth of, 585-586
licensing statutes, 593
Model Unfair Trade Practice Law, 624
need for protection, 585
overpricing of goods and, 603-611
Regulation Z, 594, 595
rescission within three days, 594
Restatement of Contracts Second
    §208, 601
retail installment sales acts, 593
state agencies protecting consumer,
    623-625
straight loans, 594
truth in lending statutes, 594, 595
Uniform Commercial Code
    §2-302, 586, 592, 598, 602, 607, 610
    §2-314, 603
    §2-315, 603
    §9-206, 593
    §9-503, 602
    §9-506, 602
Uniform Consumer Credit Code
    critique of, 595
    §5.103, 602
    §5.108, 587-589
    security interest limitation under,
        602

Uniform Consumer Sales Practices
    Act, 624
Uniform Deceptive Trade Practices
    Act, 624
usury statutes, 593
Contracts
absolute liability, 99
adhesion contracts, 2
agency, 35
background from status to contract, 22
bargain theory, 37
beauty, promise to enhance, 131-137
bilateral contracts, 370-418. See also
    Bargain
business activities, role in, 15
classical law of, 47-48
classical theory of contractual obliga-
    tion, 3
    overview of doctrines of, 55-110
    trend away from, 16
cohabitation agreements, 121
collective bargaining agreements, 121
commutative justice, 8
compulsory contracts, 2, 12
correspondence, by, 21
damages for breach of, rule for, 106-
    110. See also Damages
definition in Termes de la Ley, 21
distributive justice and, 8
economics and, 16
employment contracts, 291-294
equity, role of in, 9, 10
formalism and the law of, 705-752. See
    also Formalism
formative period of, 8, 9
freedom of, 36-38
free market system, 2-6
Holmes on, 105
home improvement contracts, 589-592
implied contracts 35-37, 141-179
indefinite contracts, 179-201
individual freedom and social control
    and, 2-4, 6, 7 et seq.
individualism and, 5, 6
individualist law of contracts, 55-110
industrial welfare and, 11
jury, role of, 40, 41
non-formalistic conception of, 50
principle of order, as, 1-17
rationality of conduct, and, 4
risk distribution, 65
socialist economy and, 1, 8
socialization of modern law and, 3
status to contract, 5, 19-53. See also
    History of contract law
substantive law of
    emancipation and evolution of, 38-
        50
    pleading, golden age of, 39
theories of, 15

Contracts—(*continued*)
  unilateral contracts, 370-418. *See also*
      Bargain
  unitary theory of
      erosion of, 16
      trend away from, 14
  unity of law and contracts, 2 et seq.
Covenant, assumpsit and, 30-32
Critical legal studies
  bibliography, 53, 64
  freedom of contract and, 64
Culpa in comprehendo, 201-238

Damages
  anticipatory repudiation, 1269-1328
  beginning of law of, 40
  breach of contract and, 106-110
  cover, 1134-1138
  foreseeable consequences, 1138-1165
  Hadley v. Baxendale, 1140-1144
  liquidated damages clause, 1223-1237
  lost-volume seller cases, 1165-1171
  market value of property as measure,
      1119-1129
  money damages, 1108-1201. *See also*
      Remedies
  Uniform Commercial Code and, 1132
Death, offer revoked by, 320-323
Debt
  action of debt, 25-28
  exchange of bonds, 28
  preexisting debt as consideration for a
      promise, 31-32
  wager of law, 27
Deceit, action of, 27-28
Defective goods, caveat emptor and, 93-95
Defenses. *See also* Remedies
  assignment of contracts, 1540-1547
Delegation, assignment compared, 1500-
      1558. *See also* Assignment
Detinue, action of, 22-23
Divisible contracts, 1039
Duress, use of, 657-663, 674-678
Duty to contract
  antitrust laws, 11, 41
  common calling, 26
  common carriers, 56
  innkeepers, 31, 56
  insurance companies, 11, 41
  newspapers, 40-41
  physicians, 56-57
  public utilities, 10
Duty to give public service, 10

Economic interpretation, use of to decide
      issues, 104
Emergency, duty to give aid in,
      56-57

Employment contracts, 291-294
  employee at will, 124
Equitable estoppel in insurance cases,
      302-303
Equity
  historical role of in contract law, 9-10
  rescission for gross inadequacy of price,
      53-54
Equity of redemption, 9, 10
Equality, fairness of the bargain and, 553-
      703. *See also* Fairness of the
      bargain and equality
Executory contracts, assignability of,
      1511-1519
Express contracts, 33

Fair Debt Collection Practices Act, 602
Fair exchange doctrines, 553
Fairness of the bargain and equality, 553-
      703
  creditor and debtor relationship, 650-703
  check
      deduction of commission from
          challenged, 685-689
      notation as to payment in full, 681-
          684
  consideration, unscrupulous debtor
      and, 650
  demand for additional compensation
      for same work, 652-655
  duress, use of, 657-663, 674-678
  executory accord, 700
      New York law on, 700
  impediment of preexisting legal duty,
      668-674
  insurance claims, 678-679
  liquidated and non-liquidated claims,
      685
  modification
      airplane seller reneges on change of
          installment terms, 665-667
      course of conduct and, 668
      oral modification to adjust terms, 665-
          667
  readjustment of a going business deal
      and discharge, 650-703
  release given on promise of job, 679-
      680
  Restatement of Contracts Second
      §45, 694
      §89, 663, 664, 667
      §90, 694
      §682, 684
  revocation of an offer, 689-694
  seaman's wages obtained under du-
      ress, 651-652
  settlement and compromise, 694-703
  unfair demand during shortage of
      goods, 655-657

I

Uniform Commercial Code
§1-207, 684, 685
§2-209, 667
wartime conditions and, 663-664
franchises, 634-649
antitrust policy and, 636
automobile franchising, 637-638
adequate performance requirement, 638
antitrust laws, 639-640
cancellation or termination threat,
638-641
economic power of manufacturer,
638
legislation to protect dealer, 641-644
protection of territory, 639
standardized contracts, 638
state legislation, 644-645
control by franchisor, 636
defined, 634, 635
gasoline dealer franchises, 645 et seq.
antitrust laws and, 646-648
federal legislation, 648-649
good faith test, 649
state legislation, 648
termination factor, 646
tie-ins, 647
nature of, 634 et seq.
retail price maintenance, 647
shortcomings of, 636-637
freedom of contract and economic
liberty, 553-583
capitalism, effect of, 556
caveat emptor, 558
clean-up principle, 574
Cohen on, 553
common law, freedom of contract
emphasized, 559
common sense approach, 553
Corpus Juris, 555
dual system of law, undue influence
developed under, 560-561
equivalence of exchange values,
bibliography, 554
exploitation as factor, 556, 557
fair exchange, doctrine of, 553
German law on, 556-557
government contracts, 576-583
Grotius and, 555
guarantee for the debt of another,
564-566
inadequacy and gross inadequacy, 554
just price theory, 555-558
laesio enormis principle, 555, 556
laissez-faire and, 554
Middle Ages and, 558
peppercorn theory of consideration,
553
Pothier on, 559
Pufendorf and, 555

Restatement of Contracts
§81, 558
§84(a), 558
Restatement of Contracts Second
§79(b), 558
§87(1), 558
sound price doctrine of common
law, 558
unconscionability doctrine
cases on, 564 et seq.
critique of, 562
equity and, 560
expansion of, 564
procedural and substantive, 564
Uniform Commercial Code
§2-302, 561
§2-313, 559
unconscionability, 561, 563
insurance
freedom of contract in private insurance, 625-634
judicial inroads, 632-634
mass industry, effect on consumer,
626
practices of insurance companies, 627
regulation of, 628-631
standardized mass contract, 626-627
technical language problem, 631
Federal Trade Commission consumer sales
regulations, 592-593
Feudal contract, 18, 19
Forbearance as consideration, 31
Forfeiture, conditions and, 1021-1059. See
also Conditions
Formal contracts, history of, 21-22
Formalism, 705-752
consideration as form, 705
Cohen on, 705-706
Fuller on, 706
meritorious consideration, 710-713
nominal consideration, 707
option to sell real estate, 720-722
one dollar, 713-719
peppercorn theory of consideration,
706-723
Restatement of Contracts
§83, 719
seal and the written obligation, 723-752
commercial cases, 744-751
consideration, as, 724-725
Holmes on, 728-729
history of, 723
legal equivalent of a seal, 752
legislation abolishing the seal, 736-737
L.S., use of, 725-728
New York law as to, 752
state requirements, 728
testamentary attempt, 737-739
Uniform Written Obligations Act,
751-752

Formalism—(*continued*)
    voluntary agreement under seal, 731-
        735
Forms of action
    history of, 23 et seq.
    pleading and, 39
Franchises
    automobile franchising, 637-638
    gasoline dealer franchises, 645 et seq.
    promises made with regard to, 209-212
Fraud, 84 et seq.
    silence as, 96
Freedom of contract. *See also* Contract
    consideration and, 12, 13
    distribution of property and, 11, 12
    ethical considerations, 2
    Fourteenth Amendment and, 12, 13
    limitations on
        credit market and, 58
        list of, 58
Free enterprise
    contract and, 4
Frustration, 861-971. *See also* Mistake,
        impossibility, and frustration

Gifts
    executed gifts and gift promises, 472
    intrafamilial gift promises, 509
    land, gift of, 478-480
    promise and, 284
Good faith
    duty to bargain in, 201-238
    in labor agreements, 16
Good samaritan laws, 57-58
Government contracts, 14
Gratuitous promises, 37, 47-51

History of contracts, 5, 18-53
    assumpsit, 28-30
        and covenant, 30-32
        and debt, 32-34
    background, 22-38
    codifications and restatements, 50-53
    common counts, 34
    consideration, 37-38
    covenant, 24-25
    debt, 25-28
    early definitions of contract, 21
    implied contracts, 35-37
    Maine, Sir Henry, Ancient Law, 19
    Smith, Adam, 20
Hohfeld's analysis, 106
Holder in due course, assignee status
        compared, 1444-1450
Holmes, O. W.
    breach of contract, on, 105
    Common Law, The, 50
    maximum hours, on, 12, 13

Hume, D., fundamental laws of nature, 1
Husband and wife, transactions between,
        116-119, 121

Identity of offeror or offeree, mistake as
        to, 41-48
Illegal bargains, 60-61, 97, 98
    restitution, 60-61
    restraint of trade, 12 et seq.
    wagering contracts, 36
Implied contract, 35-37, 141-179
    implied in fact, 35-37
    implied in law, 35-37
    quasi contract, or, 67-73
Implied warranties, 93-95
    habitability, of, 95-96
Impossibility, 861-971. *See also* Mistake,
        impossibility, and frustration
Improvident bargain, 84-96
Inadequacy of consideration as evidence
        of fraud, 51 et seq.
Increase of salary or compensation, con-
        sideration for promise of, 77-79
Indebtitatus assumpsit, action of, 34, 35
Indefiniteness
    bargain and, 179-201. *See also* Bargain
    generally, 121-123, 129-131
Innkeeper, duty to contract, 56-57
Insurance contracts, 625-634. *See also*
        Bargain
Intangible claims, assignability, 1444-1478
        See also Bargain
Interpretation as mechanism of social
        control, 14
Irrevocable offers, 363

Jury's role in development of contracts,
        40-41
Just price theory, 91

Labor relations
    contracts and, 14
    freedom of contract and, 12, 13
    plant shutdowns and, 63, 64
Laesio enormis, 54
Laissez-faire, 6-7, 10
Land
    gift of, 478-480
    installment land contracts, 978
    statute of frauds and, 770-774
Leases, assignment of, 294-299
Letters of credit
    conditions and, 1020
    sale of goods, 1014-1019
Liquidated damages, 1223-1237
Local courts, role in evolution of contract
        law, 21, 30

Mailbox rule, 349-353, 357
Maine, Sir Henry, "from status to contract," 4, 19
Mansfield, Lord
   changed role of jury, 41-42
   consideration, on, 41-42
   development in law of contracts and, 41
      et seq.
Marriage, contracts of, 121
Misfeasance
   liability for, 31
   nonfeasance distinction, 31
Misrepresentations, innocent, 196-201
Mistake, impossibility, and frustration,
      861-971
   bids, 323-326
   discharge problem, 936
   failure to meet quota due to supplier's
      problem, 944-948
   formulation of doctrines, 862-863
   Frustrated Contracts Act (England),
      934-936
   frustration
      commercial frustration due to war,
         vacating of lease for, 948-955
      exchange at some time in future, 862
      impossibility and, 930
      leases, whether doctrine applicable
         to, 948-954
      Paradine v. Jane
         impossibility not recognized, 913
         possible meanings of, 911-914
   identity of other contracting party,
      mistake as to, 41-48
   impossibility
      absolute liability in early case, 916-919
      allocation of losses after discharge,
         931-935
      concert hall, destruction of before
         performance date, and, 920-926
      construction contracts, whether dis-
         charged by, 937-942
      coronation cases, 926-932
         whether discharged by, 937-942
      death or incapacity of performing
         party, discharge and, 916-920
      destruction of building by fire
         American repair doctrine, 942
         impossibility of completing job,
            937-944
      exchange at some time in future, 862
      frustration and, 930
      performing parties contrasted with
         paying parties, discharge and,
         930-931
      Restatement of Contracts, 964 et seq.
      sellers of goods, 925-926
      Suez Canal crisis cases, 955-964
      war and, 932-934
   innocent mistake as to amount, 173-175

mistake
   computation mistakes, 881
   exchange of values at time of con-
      tract, 862
   formulation of doctrine, 862-863
   inflation (and deflation), effect of on
      existing contracts, 914-916
   mistaken assumptions, 862
   mistaken predictions, 862
   mistake of fact and mistake of law,
      880
   objective and subjective theories
      of contract in relation to,
      867-868
   release, signing of, and, 883-886
   sale of nonexistent goods, 898-909
   telegraph errors, 882
   unilateral mistake, reformation of
      contract for, 875-880
   use of words with more than one
      meaning, 869-875
mistake in value, 51-54, 886-910
   building undevelopable due to legisla-
      tion, 893-894
   employment contracts, 896
   fertile cow sold as barren cow, 887 et
      seq.
   imitation Stradivarius violin, 892-893
objectivist and subjectivist interpretations, 867-868
parol evidence rule and, 881
reformation and, 883
rescission and, 883
Restatement of Contracts, 964-966
   §71, 868
Restatement of Contracts Second, 968-
   969
   Chapter 11 (Impossibility, Impractica-
      bility, and Frustration), 864
   Chapter 12 (Mistake), 864
   flexible handing of, 865
   §21A, 868
   §87, 910
   §90, 910
Restatement of Restitution
   §12, 881-882
risk allocation and, 863-864
subject matter, as to, 84-87
terms intertwined, 865
tort law analogy, 864
Uniform Commercial Code, 964, 966-
   968, 969-971
   §2-322, 871
vanishing synthesis
   England, 910-936
   United States, 936-971
Modification, criteria for enforcement, 79-
   84
Moral consideration, 32-33, 510-551. See
   also Bargain

Mortgages, inconsistent terms in, 299-303
Mutual assent to changes, consideration
        requirement and, 76-79

Negotiation, assignment compared, 1444-
        1450
Newspaper, duty to publish, 40, 41
Nondisclosure, 89-93
    ordinary prudent man and, 91-92
Nonfeasance and misfeasance distin-
        guished, 31

Offers
    death, revocation by, 320-323
    firm offers, 315-348
    irrevocable offer, 363
    promissory liability, 320
    revocation of, 689-694
    time limits in, 368-370
Options, effective on mailing, 357-364
Output contracts, 419

Parol evidence rule, 821-859
    admissible for purposes of interpreta-
        tion, 826
    ambiguities and, 835-836
    collateral agreements, as applied to,
        837-841, 849-851
    fraud, accident, or mistake, 843-849
    Holmes on, 827
    implied warranties, 827-830
    introductory note, 821-827
    judicial response to gaps in agreement,
        822
    merger clauses, 843-849
    oral agreement, admissibility under,
        832-835
    proof of extrinsic condition, 831-832
    rationale for rule, 823
    Restatement of Contracts Second
        §215, 836
        §216, 836
    rule of procedure or of substantive law,
        852-859
    silence and, 831
    standardized agreements, 836
    Statute of Frauds compared, 825
    text of rule, 822
    Uniform Commercial Code
        §2-202, 836, 842
        §2-314, 831
        §2-316, 831
    usage of trade, 843, 849-851
Partial performance, conditions and, 1038-
        1039
Perfect tender rule, 1002-1004

Performance, preexisting duty as consider-
        ation, 76-79
Physician
    duty to contract, 56-57
    promise to enhance beauty, 131-137
    promise to sterilize, 137
    scene of accident, right to recover, 163-
        168
Pleading, golden age of, and forms of
        action, 39
Pledge of faith, 21
Preexisting duty
    consideration and, 76-79
    creditor and debtor, 668-674
Price, 84-90
Priorities and assignment. See Assignment
Privity of contract, 41-48
Promises
    gift promise, 284
    gratuitous promise, 285-299
    gratuitous noncommercial promise, 470-
        510
Promissory estoppel
    bargain theory of contracts, 282, 308-
        314
    good faith and, 223-225
    offers, 320
Public policy
    consideration and, 37, 76-78, 97
    contracts against, 95
    dynamic concept, 97
    emotive function of the notion of, 60
    enforcement denied by reason of, 97
    freedom of contract and, 7, 37
    illegal bargain and, 98
    illegal by legislation, 97
Public service, duty to give, 14, 56-58

Quantum meruit, 35-36
Quantum valebat, 35-36
Quasi contract
    contract and quasi contract distin-
        guished, 35-36
    history of, 35-36
    officious intermeddling, 76
    unjust enrichment and, 67-74
Quid pro quo, 23, 28, 31

Rationality
    common law and, 9
    freedom of contract and, 4
    need for met, 49-50
Readjustment of going business deal and
        mutual release of executory
        obligations, 76-79
Real contracts, 22
Reciprocity, 21
    consideration and, 37

Recognizance, 23-24
Refusal to deal
  freedom of contract and, 58-60
  newspapers, refusal to publish advertis-
    ing, 40-41
Reliance, bargain theory of contract and,
  279-314
Remedies, 1061-1328
  anticipatory repudiation
    acceptance of doctrine by United
      States Supreme Court, 1279-1287
    commodities and, 1305-1312
    completion of work though asked not
      to, 1313-1315
    contracts to pay money and, 1290-
      1291
    dismissed teacher and obligation to
      seek work, 1317-1321
    duty to mitigate damages, 1269-1328
    employment cases, 1321-1324
    executory contracts and, 1290
    Hochster v. De La Tour, 1287-1289
    measure of damages, 1324-1328
    mitigation of damages, 1269-1328
    rejection of doctrine, 1270-1278
    Williston against anticipatory breach,
      1287-1288, 1296
  damages. *See also subhead* money dam-
    ages
    anticipatory repudiation and duty to
      mitigate damages, 1269-1328
    vendor of land against repudiating
      vendee, 1270-1278
  introduction, 1061-1069
    Holmes on the promise, 1064-1065
    morals and promises, 1066-1068
  money damages, 1108-1201
    birdbath hypothetical, 1128
    communist economy, in, 1106-1107
    contract and market rule, 1129-1132
    cover and contract price formula,
      1134-1138
    foreseeable consequences, 1138-1165
      deviations in delivery, 1157-1166
      disclaimers, use of, 1157
      Holmes test, 1150
      nondelivery of telegraph, 1152-1157
      Posner on, 1139-1140
    history in Anglo-American law, 1108-
      1113
    lost-volume seller cases, 1165-1171
    market value of property as measure,
      1119-1129
    Posner on expectation rule, 1118-1119
    refusal to publish manuscript as con-
      tracted, 1113-1119
    reliance interest in contract damages,
      1172-1201
    Restatement of Contracts Second
      §348(2), 1129

Restitution instead of damages, 1186-
  1188
Uniform Commercial Code
  §2-706, 1132
  §2-708, 1132
  §2-710, 1133
  §2-712, 1133
  §2-713, 1133
  §2-715, 1133-1134, 1151, 1201
private remedies, 1202-1269
  arbitration of disputes
    antitrust and, 1222-1223
    judicial attitude toward, Judge
      Frank on, 1210-1212
    punitive damages and, 1212-1221
  contractual stipulations as to remedy,
    1209-1210
  freedom of contract and the judicial
    prerogative, 1202-1269
  implied warranty of habitability, 1257-
    1269
    exculpatory clauses and, 1269
  implied warranty of merchantability,
    1243-1253
    defect requirement, 1254
    disclaimer clause, 1253
  introduction, 1202-1203
  liquidated damages clauses, 1223-1237
    failure of burglar alarms, 1231-1235
    parcel checks, 1237-1239
    penalty provisions, 1240-1243
    refusal to act provision, 1223-1225
    termination of lease, 1225-1231
  penal clauses in contracts, 1241-1243
  policy stipulates court action to be
    brought in, 1203-1212
  power of parties to control remedy
    and risk, 1202-1269
  privity issue, 1253-1256
Restatement of Torts Second
  §402A, 1253 et seq.
specific performance, 1069-1108
  arbitration and, 1092
  civil law countries, 1069
  communist economy and, 1106-1108
  contract not to compete and, 1079-
    1086
  damages, problem of measuring,
    1094
  growing popularity in use of, 1074
  Holmes on, 1071-1072
  introduction, 1069-1075
  land contracts, remedy in, 1073-1074
  lease, refusal to give, 1089-1092
  output and requirement cases, 1094-
    1096
  personal service contracts, 1075-1079,
    1086, 1087
  self-enslavement, 1087-1088
  Story on, 1071

Remedies—(*continued*)
   unconscionable bargain and, 1097-
      1101
      farmer's carrot crop, 1097-1101
   uniqueness, 1101-1106
   Uniform Commercial Code
      §2-302, 1257
      §2-314, 1257
      §2-315, 1257
      §2-316, 1256, 1257
      §2-318, 1254, 1255
      §2-610, 1307
      §2-611, 1307
      §2-711, 1312
      §2-712, 1308, 1328
      §2-713, 1308, 1312, 1328
      §2-714, 1328
      §2-716, 1101
      §2-718, 1239
      §2-719, 1240, 1257
      §2-723, 1312
Requirement contracts, mutuality and,
      418-450. *See also* Bargain
Resale price maintenance, agreements as
      to, 58-59
Restatement of Contracts, background as
      to, 58-59
Restatement of Contracts Second
   assent, 247, 250
   background to, 51
   bargain theory of contracts, 281, 287,
      305
   correspondence as bargain, 357
   firm offers, 315, 337
   good faith, 202, 212
   gratuitous promises, 472, 475, 480, 490
   moral consideration, 511, 512, 527,
      537
   standard form contracts, 272 et seq.
   statute of frauds, 760, 761, 765
Restitution
   evolution of remedy, 33-34
   treatment of volunteer, 76-79
Restraint of trade. *See also* Antitrust
   freedom of contract and, 58-60
Revocation of offer, 689-694
Reward, right to, 377-381

Sale, enforcement of executory contract
      for, 24, 28
Sale of goods, conditions and, 990-1021
Scholarship, promise regarding, 490
Seal
   contract under, 21
   generally, 723-752. *See also* Formalism
Shutdowns, antitrust laws and plant, 63
Sidgwick, Henry, 5, 6
Smith, Adam, 20
Social Darwinism, 12

Specific performance
   generally, 1069-1108. *See also* Remedies
   Uniform Commercial Code, 1257
Statute of Frauds, 753-819
   An Act for the Prevention of Frauds and
      Perjuries, 753
   background, 753-754
      assumpsit and debt, role in develop-
         ment of, 754
      English statute, adoption of, 755
      jury verdicts and, 754
      problem of compliance, 755
      scope of coverage, 754
   compliance with statute, 783-801
      memorandum required, 781-788, 798-
         800
         not required, 798-801
      part performance, 793-797
      reformation of contract, 789-792
      sufficiency of several writings, 783-788
   contract for sale of interest in land, 770-
      774
   contract to support for life, 775-777
   contracts of guaranty, 757-768
   guaranty and suretyship and, 763
   estoppel and restitution, 801-819
      airline employment contract, 814-819
         promise to put contract in writing,
            814-819
      husband's misinformation to wife
         and, 807-808
      oral modification of written contract,
         801-807
      reliance damage and restitution, 808-
         813
   executors or administrators, 770
   interest in land, 777-780
   Llewellyn on, 756-757
   main purpose rule, 765-769
   marriage, contracts in consideration of,
      770-773
   narrowly construed by American
      courts, 755-756
   novation, 769
   one year, performance not within, 773-
      775, 814-819
   original or collateral promise, 764
   parol evidence rule compared, 825
   promissory estoppel and, 757
   rationale for, 756
   Restatement of Contracts Second
      §112, 760, 761, 765
      §116, 768
      §129, 794
      §131, 788
      §148, 807
      §150, 807
      §156, 792
   third party, effect of noncompliance
      on, 781-782

third party not bound, 763-768
transactions affected, 757-783. *See also*
    specific entries under this topic
medical emergency and third party
    promise to pay, 757-760
Uniform Commercial Code
    §1-206, 780, 781
    §2-201, 780
    §2-201(3)(b), 797
    §8-319, 780
    §9-203, 780
Strict liability
    contract liability, as, 99
    warranty liability, as, 95
Subcontractors, bids and, 326-331
Subordination agreements and assign-
    ments, 1458-1466
Substantial performance, 1050-1051

Telegrams
    assent to contract and, 250-257
    delay in delivery, 365-368
Termites, duty to disclose, 93
Third party beneficiaries, 1329-1439
    attorney's liability to intended beneficia-
        ries of invalid will, 1371-1377
    Cardozo on assault on citadel of priv-
        ity, 1377-1378
    categories recognized in New York,
        1358-1359
    collective labor agreements and, 1380-
        1384
    contract and tort theory, interplay
        between, 1379-1380
    defenses, modifications and rescission,
        1418-1439
    collective bargaining agreement,
        applicability of third party benefi-
        ciary doctrine to, 1431-1437
    defenses available to promisor when
        sued by beneficiary, 1428-1431
    negotiable instruments in consumer
        transactions, 1428-1431
    rescission, restatement and, 1424-1427
    right to surrender policy when benefi-
        ciary has vested interest, 1420-
        1421
    doctrinal clarity, search for, 1361-1384
    English law presently, 1342-1343
    government contracts and citizen benefi-
        ciaries, 1384-1418
    action by municipal residents for fire
        loss as beneficiaries of municipal
        contracts with water companies,
        1386-1391
    class action by job seekers for failure
        of company to create jobs under
        contract to governmental body,
        1391-1405

incidental benefits distinguished from
    government benefits, 1385
New Property, The, 1385, 1414-1418
right of prisoner to safety under fed-
    eral-state arrangement, 1405
tenant's third party beneficiary
    claims, 1405-1414, 1418
introductory note, 1329-1333
    advance from rigid rules of past, 1332
    beneficiary relationship compared
        with other three-party situations,
        1331, 1361
    parties to in typical building con-
        tract, 1329-1330
Lawrence v. Fox, 1333-1340, 1361, 1417,
    1419
    curious facts in, 1344-1346
    trust theory discussed, 1335, 1337-
        1338
mortgagees, mortgagors, purchasers,
    and the equity of redemption,
    1350-1356
    assuming and non-assuming grant-
        ees, 1352-1354, 1429
    privity requirement, 1346-1350
    rising land values and, 1353
    suretyship analogy, 1356
pre-third party cases, types of, 1340-1341
resistance to adopting rule as to, 1341
Restatement of Contracts
    Chapter 6, 1362
    §133, 1362
    §142, 1424-1427
    §143, 1424-1427
    §145, 1385
    §147, 1362
Restatement of Contracts Second
    Chapter 14, 1363
    §302, 1363, 1403
    §309, 1438-1439
    §311, 1426
    §313, 1403
    §313(2), 1385
    subcontractor's laborers or materialmen
        as beneficiaries of prime contrac-
        tor's payment bond, 1364-1371
Tort
    distinguished from contract, 24-28
    measure of damages, 69
    progress through, 24-28
Trespass, action of, 30, 37
Trespass on the case, action of, 30

Unconscionability
    adhesion contracts, 275
    bargain theory of contracts, 284
    cases on, 564 et seq.
    equity and, 564
    Uniform Commercial Code and, 561

Undisclosed principle doctrine, 44-46
Uniform Commercial Code, 52
    assignment. *See* Assignment
    indefinite contracts. *See* Bargain
    requirements contracts, 434, 435
    specific performance, 1257
    standard form contracts, 260
    Statute of Frauds, 780, 781
    unilateral vs. bilateral contracts, 372-400
Uniform Land Sales Practices Act, 95
Uniform Land Transactions Act, 95
Uniform Residential Landlord and Tenant
        Act, 95
Uniform Sales Act, 51
Unilateral contracts, bilateral compared,
        370-418. *See also* Bargain
Unjust enrichment
    criterion for, 88
    generally, 35-36
    quasi contract, 67-74

Usury, 29
    agreement as to, 96-97

Vertical integration, 61

Wager of law, 27
Warranties
    absolute liability, 96
    implied warranty of habitability, 1257-
        1269
    implied warranty of merchantability,
        1243-1253
    standard form contracts, 260-272
Welfare state, 15

Yellow dog contracts, 12